# Business Jets International 2010

# BUSINESS JETS INTERNATIONAL 2010

Steven Sowter and Barrie Towey

Twenty-Fifth Edition

Published by: Air-Britain (Historians) Limited

Sales Department: 41 Penshurst Road, Leigh, Tonbridge, Kent TN11 8HL, UK

Sales e-mail: sales@air-britain.co.uk

Membership Enquiries: 1 Rose Cottages, 179 Penn Road, Hazlemere, Bucks HP15 7NE, UK (email: membenquiry@air-britain.co.uk)

Web-site: http://www.air-britain.co.uk



ISBN: 978-0-85130-426-7

*Cover photographs:*

*Front cover:*

Beech 390 Premier 1A N452AS c/n RB-252 taxies past at the 62nd NBAA Convention at Orlando Executive Airport, Florida on 18th October 2009. (Rod Simpson)

*Back cover:*

*Top:* Boeing 737-7BC BBJ N800KS c/n 30782 of AEJ Services was parked at Sydney-Mascot on 6th March 2009. (Stuart Kedar)

*Centre:* Cessna 510 Mustang PH-ORJ c/n 510-0025 in Sky-Taxi titles at Rotterdam - Zestienhoven, Netherlands on 14th May 2009. (Henk Wadman)

*Bottom:* The Swedish Air Force operates a fleet of four Gulfstream IVs one of which, seriall 102004 c/n 1274, was visiting Rotterdam on 14th July 2009. (Henk Wadman)

Printed by Bell & Bain Ltd, Glasgow G46 7UQ

# CONTENTS

# INTRODUCTION

This is the twenty-fifth edition of Business Jets International and follows the title's long-established format.

The prime purpose of this book continues to be to record the registration history of all purpose-designed business jets, with supplements that detail airliner variants that have been designed specifically for corporate usage alongside the traditional Grumman G159 supplement and the listing of Experimental and Non-Production types.

It has always been our policy, unlike that of some other publications, to include and to distinguish marks that have not been fully allocated, for example those only reserved. To identify such marks we use the symbols * ^ + and also put unofficial marks within inverted commas. The full description of these symbols can be found within the Explanatory Notes.

In a work of this nature there are bound to be some errors and data omitted; the editorial team (whose address appears below) would welcome notification of any errors or omissions. While we still have particular problems in confirming the identities of aircraft that have been exported particularly to Mexico, a growing problem is recording the fates of early military aircraft which have been withdrawn from use with their increasing age. This has not been made any easier post-September 11th when the US authorities withdrew the data on the AMARC website. We would be delighted to hear from anyone who can assist us in this area.

Those interested in ownership data should refer to other publications such as Jet & Prop Jet, published by our friends Avdata Inc/Jetnet Inc. Those in the industry are recommended to contact them direct at 101 First Street, Utica, NY 13501, USA if they wish to commission Avdata to supply ownership and other detailed reports.

The data in this issue of Business Jets International is correct to mid March 2010 and contains some items that will appear in the April 2010 issue of Air-Britain News, a monthly publication that can be used throughout the year to keep this book up to date. Non-subscribers to News will find details of subscriptions and Air-Britain membership at the back of this book.

2009 will be recorded as the year in which the gathering gloom of late 2008 finally precipitated into a tumultuous storm for most aircraft manufacturers. Biz jet deliveries fell from 1200 to 700. Lines closed, but are gradually re-opening again. Yet more casualties came about as a result of the closure of Eclipse and Epic. Amongst aircraft operators the previously buoyant fractional businesses began to feel the pinch with many airframes being placed into storage rather than attempting to sell into an already depressed used market.

With many of the fledgling VLJ makers no longer in business, it has been Cessna's Mustang and Embraer's Phenom 100 which have notched up the largest percentage of new sales. Embraer also recently gained certification for its Phenom 300 with other notable highlights being the first flights of Gulfstream's newly launched 250 and 650. Many industry analysts are now stating that the worst is over and that business aviation will begin to see gains in activity over the coming year.

March 2010

Address for correspondence:
Steven Sowter
78 Laburnum Road
Hayes
Middlesex UB3 4JZ
United Kingdom

email address:StevenSowter@aol.com

## ACKNOWLEDGEMENTS

Business Jets International has been produced with the valued past and present assistance of, and from information provided by, the following companies and individuals:

Aerospatiale/EADS
Ascend Worldwide Ltd
Atlantic Aviation
Aviation Data Service of Wichita
British Aerospace plc
Beech Aircraft Co
Canadair Limited
Canadair Challenger Limited
Cessna Aircraft Co
Gulfstream Aerospace
Israeli Aircraft Industries
Jetnet LLC Utica NY
Lockheed Aircraft Co
Mitsubishi Aircraft Co
Raytheon Aircraft Co
Rockwell International
Sabreliner Corp

Barry Ambrose
Joseph Anckner
Steve Bailey
H W Barrett
Colin Berry
Bill Blanchard
Mike Brown
David C Buck
Peter Budden
B J Burt
Lyn Buttifant
Jim Cain
Russell Carter
Nick C Challoner
Chris Chatfield
Alan E Clark
Colin Clark
Dennis Clement
Paul Compton
Colin Darvill
John Davies
J F Elliott
Robert D Elliott
David England
Brian Gates
Wayne Gates
Ian Gibson
Jennifer Gradidge
S Graham
Nigel Green
Andrew Griffiths
Kay Hagby
Philip Hancock
Noam Hartoch
Richard Hill
Mike Holdstock
Gerry Hollands
Carolos Hopkins
Nigel Howarth
Heinz Kasmanhuber
John Kim
Bruce Leatherborrow
John MacMaster
Michael Magnusson
Stephen L Mart
J A Newton
Ole Nikolajsen
Justin Palmer
Pierre Parvaud
Nigel Prevett
Brian Print
Glyn Ramsden
Mark Reavey
Morian Reed
Doug Robinson
Terry Ross
Ian Sant
Don Schofield
Mike Schofield
Simon Scott-Kemball
D Sheldon
Peter Simmonds
Graham Slack
Terry Smith
Claude Soussi
Neville Spalding
David Thompson
Peter Thompson
Bob Underwood
Richard Urbeck
D F Walsh
Pete Watson

Plus the many regular contributors to the BIZ-JETS section of Air-Britain News. Due acknowledgement is also given to the monograph "Le Morane-Saulnier Paris MS760" by Pierre Parvaud and Pierre Gaillard published by Le Trait d'Union (the magazine of the French Branch of Air-Britain) and to the article in the Winter 1989 Air-Britain Digest by the same two authors on the HFB320 Hansa. We must also thank the Air-Britain Gulfstream specialist, Alain Jeneve, for his review of the Gulfstream I section. Thanks are also due to Brian Gates for supplying data on the Learjet AvCom fin conversions. Special thanks go to Pete Webber for the Airbus, BBJ's Canadair and Legacy lists.

## EXPLANATORY NOTES

The following abbreviations have been used in the text:

| | | | | | |
|---|---|---|---|---|---|
| A/c | Aircraft | cx/canx | cancelled | ntu | not taken up |
| A/P | Airport | dbr | damaged beyond repair | r/o | rolled out |
| AFB | Air Force Base | dest | destroyed | TL | total landings |
| Avn | Aviation | exp | expired | TT | total time |
| b/u | broken up | ff | first flight | wfs | withdrawn from service |
| c/s | colour scheme | Inds | Industries | wfu | withdrawn from use |
| cvtd | converted | Inst | Institute | w/o | written off |

\+ following a set of marks is to bring to the readers attention a note which follows, sometimes on the next line, sometimes at the end of the listing

* An asterisk following the last registration indicates that at the time of compilation these marks were only reserved.

^ Indicates marks which the owner/operator of the aircraft has requested. On many occasions such marks may never be taken up.

" " Quotation marks around a registration indicate that the marks were painted on the aircraft, either in error or for publicity purposes, but were not officially allocated.

( ) Brackets around a registration indicate that these marks were not taken up.

NOTE: when an aircraft has been sold to another country and the new marks are not known at the time of compilation, the country prefix only is shown. For Brazil and Mexico PT- and XA- are used even though they may eventually carry other prefixes for these countries.

# BEECH 390 PREMIER I

| C/n | Srs | Identities | | | | | |
|---|---|---|---|---|---|---|---|
| RB-1 | | N390RA | [rolled out 19Aug98; ff 23Dec98] | | | [wfu; cx 18Feb09] | |
| RB-2 | | N704T | [wfu; cx 23Feb09] | | | | |
| RB-3 | | N390TC | [wfu; cx 18Feb09] | | | | |
| RB-4 | | N842PM | N414TE | | | | |
| RB-5 | | N155GD | N808V | | | | |
| RB-6 | | N390R | N155RM | | | | |
| RB-7 | | N343PR | | | | | |
| RB-8 | | N460AS | | | | | |
| RB-9 | | N390EM | N60ME | XA-IAS | XA-ZUL | N21XP | |
| RB-10 | | N5010X | [w/o North Las Vegas, NV, 27May04; remains moved to Wichita/Mid-Continent, KS] | | | | |
| RB-11 | | N5121P | N50PM | N50PN | | | |
| RB-12 | | N390TA | N390P | XA-TSN | N390BW | OE-FRJ | |
| RB-13 | | N48TC | | | | | |
| RB-14 | | N969RE | | | | | |
| RB-15 | | N73WC | N335JB | N929SS | | | |
| RB-16 | | N151KD | N444SS | C-GYPV | | | |
| RB-17 | | N5017T | N88EL | N88ER | | | |
| RB-18 | | N88MM | N711AJ | LX-POO | N23WA | | |
| RB-19 | | N65TB | N16DK | | | | |
| RB-20 | | N777MG | N777MQ | (N390BP) | YL-KSC | | |
| RB-21 | | N390MB | PR-AMA | | | | |
| RB-22 | | N45NB | N45ND | N223F | N232F | N323CM* | |
| RB-23 | | N109PM | N488PC | N488RC | VT-RAL | [w/o 19Mar08 Udaipur, India] | |
| RB-24 | | N5024J | (ZS-PRF) | ZS-PRM | N124BR | N903MT | |
| RB-25 | | N390CL | N808W | N719L | (N713L) | | |
| RB-26 | | N390RB | (N390HR) | [w/o 07Jan03 Santo Domingo-Herrera Intl Airport, Dominican Republic] | | | |
| RB-27 | | N3216P | D-IFMC | (HB-...) | | | |
| RB-28 | | N128RM | N128JL | | | | |
| RB-29 | | N747BK | N110PR | | | | |
| RB-30 | | N390BL | N84ML | N84FM | | | |
| RB-31 | | N3231K | ZS-AVM | | | | |
| RB-32 | | N5132D | PR-CIM | | | | |
| RB-33 | | N50843 | N677AS | | | | |
| RB-34 | | N390DP | N7JT | N390DP | | | |
| RB-35 | | N435K | D-IAGG | | | | |
| RB-36 | | N1XT | | | | | |
| RB-37 | | N452A | N567T | | | | |
| RB-38 | | N972PF | | | | | |
| RB-39 | | N39KT | N390JK | | | | |
| RB-40 | | N51140 | PR-BER | N86RB | N390CE | | |
| RB-41 | | N142HH | (N111HH) | N43HJ | OE-FMC | | |
| RB-42 | | N390CK | N324AM | | | | |
| RB-43 | | N1EG | | | | | |
| RB-44 | | N5044X | N88MM | | | | |
| RB-45 | | N809RM | N100WE | | | | |
| RB-46 | | N460L | | | | | |
| RB-47 | | N5147Y | (N145SD) | N581SF | | | |
| RB-48 | | N51480 | D-IATT | | | | |
| RB-49 | | N5049U | N25MC | | | | |
| RB-50 | | N344W | N390NS | D-ISXT | N523DR | | |
| RB-51 | | N4251D | LX-LCG | N530PT | | | |
| RB-52 | | N605TC | | | | | |
| RB-53 | | N50453 | N351CB | N351CW | | | |
| RB-54 | | N61754 | ZS-MGK | N354RB | | | |
| RB-55 | | N390PL | N85PL | | | | |
| RB-56 | | N390RC | PK-TWL | PK-PRM | | | |
| RB-57 | | N457K | N488PC | VP-CRD | OE-FRC | | |
| RB-58 | | N5158B | N34GN | | | | |
| RB-59 | | N701DF | N622JK | | | | |
| RB-60 | | N6160D | LX-PRE | G-PREI | | | |
| RB-61 | | N61161 | EC-IOZ | | | | |
| RB-62 | | N6162Z | N800CS | | | | |
| RB-63 | | N6163T | ZS-DDM | ZS-SRU | | | |
| RB-64 | | N6164U | LX-PMR | | | | |
| RB-65 | | N4395D | PR-GCA | | | | |
| RB-66 | | N50586 | VP-BAE | N931BR | G-VONJ | | |
| RB-67 | | N6167D | ZS-MGK | N167DP | | | |
| RB-68 | | N447TF | N50648 | N133B | | | |
| RB-69 | | N205BC | | | | | |
| RB-70 | | N5070W | N731UG | (N391RB) | ZS-ABG | N70BR | N998PA |
| RB-71 | | N4471P | N71KV | | | | |
| RB-72 | | N5072X | N535BC | N535BR | ZS-SGS | ZS-MCO | |
| RB-73 | | N371CF | N371CE | N107WR | (N107YR) | F- | |
| RB-74 | | N61474 | N902RD | (N9011P) | VP-CWW | | |
| RB-75 | | N213PC | N213PQ | | | | |
| RB-76 | | N6076Y | N1XH | | | | |

# BEECH 390 PREMIER I/1A*

| C/n | Srs | Identities | | | | | |
|---|---|---|---|---|---|---|---|
| RB-77 | | N6177A | TC-MHS | N32BR | OE-FKW | | |
| RB-78 | | N390JW | | | | | |
| RB-79 | | N200PR | [w/o 07Apr04 Blackbushe, UK; remains 07Feb05 Air Salvage Intl. Alton, Hants, UK] | | | | |
| RB-80 | | N50280 | N50PM | | | | |
| RB-81 | | N50468 | N390P | N134SW | | | |
| RB-82 | | N61882 | D-IBBB | | | | |
| RB-83 | | N6183G | N88EL | N88EU | LY-HER | F-HBFA | G-HFAA |
| RB-84 | | N61784 | PR-JRR | | | | |
| RB-85 | | N4485B | N487DT | | | | |
| RB-86 | | N390TA | N96NC | | | | |
| RB-87 | | N6187Q | (B-8006) | N952GL | N952GM | | |
| RB-88 | | N4488F | G-OMJC | | | | |
| RB-89 | | N61589 | D-IWWW | | | | |
| RB-90 | | N32SG | | | | | |
| RB-91 | | N24YP | N24YD | N45NB | | | |
| RB-92 | | N62LW | N592HC | | | | |
| RB-93 | | N322BJ | | | | | |
| RB-94 | | N6194N | ZS-PFE | | | | |
| RB-95 | | N6195S | N24YP | | | | |
| RB-96 | | N535CD | | | | | |
| RB-97 | | N6197F | G-FRYL | | | | |
| RB-98 | | N61998 | N500CZ | | | | |
| RB-99 | | N24YP | N24YR | N199RM | | | |
| RB-100 | | N122DS | | | | | |
| RB-101 | | N6201A | N101PN | N73PJ | | | |
| RB-102 | * | N6182F | N3901A | N227FH | | | |
| RB-103 | | N61930 | N701KB | N781KB | N700KB | | |
| RB-104 | | N5104G | N855JB | | | | |
| RB-105 | | N5105A | N777JF | | | | |
| RB-106 | | N61706 | N20NL | | | | |
| RB-107 | | N61717 | N877W | | | | |
| RB-108 | | N61908 | | | | | |
| RB-109 | | N50078 | D-IFMG | | | | |
| RB-110 | | N701KB | N300SL | | | | |
| RB-111 | | N6111F | N713AZ | | | | |
| RB-112 | | N60322 | N76HL | | | | |
| RB-113 | | N11PM | N727KG | N113BR | N390PR | | |
| RB-114 | | N143CM | | | | | |
| RB-115 | | N6015Y | N72SJ | | | | |
| RB-116 | | N200LB | | | | | |
| RB-117 | | N6117G | | | | | |
| RB-118 | | N6118C | B-8018 | N390BR | | | |
| RB-119 | | N6119C | N1CR | N39DM | N84EA | N14EA | |
| RB-120 | | N6120U | N311SL | UN-P1001 | UP-P1001 | | |
| RB-121 | | N390GM | (N72DV) | N602DV | N520CH | N550CP | |
| RB-122 | | N3722Z | G-CJAG | PH-JCI | | | |
| RB-123 | | N3723A | N112CM | | | | |
| RB-124 | | N6124W | N23SP | | | | |
| RB-125 | | N3725F | N312SL | G-PHTO | VQ-BEP | | |
| RB-126 | | N3726G | G-OEWD | | | | |
| RB-127 | | N3727H | N18RF | | | | |
| RB-128 | | N6128Y | VT-ANF | | | | |
| RB-129 | | N6129U | N390JV | | | | |
| RB-130 | | N5030V | N401PP | | | | |
| RB-131 | | N36731 | G-CJAH | OE-FWW | | | |
| RB-132 | | N3332C | N9LV | (N48VC) | | | |
| RB-133 | | N3733J | (N545PT) | N575PT | N967F | | |
| RB-134 | | N3734C | N84VA | | | | |
| RB-135 | | N3735V | N390PT | | | | |
| RB-136 | * | N36636 | N462CB | | | | |
| RB-137 | * | N6137U | N451MM | VH-TMA | | | |
| RB-138 | * | N5118J | VP-BPO | M-VBPO | | | |
| RB-139 | * | N3039G | N239RT | N239RF | PR-PRE | | |
| RB-140 | * | N3540R | N22VK | | | | |
| RB-141 | * | N3481V | N484AT | N784MA | | | |
| RB-142 | * | N6142Y | (G-CJAI) | N646S | N767CS | | |
| RB-143 | * | N61948 | N727KG | | | | |
| RB-144 | * | N541RS | | | | | |
| RB-145 | * | N37245 | N42EL | | | | |
| RB-146 | * | N6146J | N1CR | M-YAIR | | | |
| RB-147 | * | N61678 | ZS-KBS | N61678 | N147FM | | |
| RB-148 | * | N6148Z | D-ISAR | | | | |
| RB-149 | * | N36979 | F-HAST | | | | |
| RB-150 | * | N6150Y | (N575PT) | C-FBPL | | | |
| RB-151 | * | N37071 | D-ICJA | N102SK | N103SK | | |
| RB-152 | * | N3732Y | HB-VOI | | | | |
| RB-153 | * | N36873 | N888MN | | | | |

## BEECH 390 PREMIER I/1A*

| C/n | Srs | Identities | | | | |
|---|---|---|---|---|---|---|
| RB-154 | * | N36964 | (G-CJAJ) | XA-RRG | | |
| RB-155 | * | N3725L | | | | |
| RB-156 | * | N3726T | N508RN | | | |
| RB-157 | * | N6178X | N88EL | | | |
| RB-158 | * | N36758 | N727MH | N727ML | | |
| RB-159 | * | N37059 | N146JF | N145JF | | |
| RB-160 | * | N36890 | EC-KHH | | | |
| RB-161 | * | N71761 | (N606JR) | N6JR | | |
| RB-162 | * | N608CW | | | | |
| RB-163 | * | N7163E | N72GD | (N59RK) | | |
| RB-164 | * | N36864 | D-IDBA | | | |
| RB-165 | * | N7165X | N800FR | M-FROG | | |
| RB-166 | * | N36866 | | | | |
| RB-167 | * | N71167 | N404JM | | | |
| RB-168 | * | N7268M | N64PM | | | |
| RB-169 | * | N7269Z | N837JM | (N237JM) | PR-PRA | |
| RB-170 | * | N7170Y | (N181JT) | | | |
| RB-171 | * | N17CJ | | | | |
| RB-172 | * | N7102U | G-EVRD | | | |
| RB-173 | * | N73736 | N213PC | | | |
| RB-174 | * | N71874 | N855RM | | | |
| RB-175 | * | N71865 | VH-VHP | | | |
| RB-176 | * | N7176J | N906FM | | | |
| RB-177 | * | N37019 | (A6-RZA) | A6-RZJ | N37019 | N527PM |
| RB-178 | * | N3378M | N102CL | | | |
| RB-179 | * | N7079N | N33PJ | | | |
| RB-180 | * | N133CM | N133CQ | N835ZT | | |
| RB-181 | * | N7081V | VP-BBQ | M-VBBQ | | |
| RB-182 | * | N7082V | N246DF | N999ZG | | |
| RB-183 | * | N994JR | N1J | | | |
| RB-184 | * | N368CS | N368CC | I-GSAL | | |
| RB-185 | * | N7085V | N502PM | | | |
| RB-186 | * | N37086 | N2HZ | | | |
| RB-187 | * | N7187J | HB-VOS | | | |
| RB-188 | * | N7088S | | | | |
| RB-189 | * | N7189J | VP-CFW | | | |
| RB-190 | * | N70890 | N537RB | | | |
| RB-191 | * | N7191K | N992SC | | | |
| RB-192 | * | N7192M | N91BB | | | |
| RB-193 | * | N7193W | N408J | | | |
| RB-194 | * | N7294E | N276RS | | | |
| RB-195 | * | N74065 | A9C-RJA | A6-RZA | G-RIZA | |
| RB-196 | * | N37346 | D-IIMC | OE-FIM | | |
| RB-197 | * | N7257U | (LX-VAZ) | N115WZ | | |
| RB-198 | * | N7198H | C-FDMM | | | |
| RB-199 | * | N133CM | N716GS | | | |
| RB-200 | * | N81HR | | | | |
| RB-201 | * | N801BP | I-DMSA | | | |
| RB-202 | * | N202BP | VP-CAZ | | | |
| RB-203 | * | N203BP | | | | |
| RB-204 | * | N204BP | RP-C390 | | | |
| RB-205 | * | N205GY | N801SA | | | |
| RB-206 | * | N306BP | N146JF | | | |
| RB-207 | * | N207AH | | | | |
| RB-208 | * | N208BP | N430GW | | | |
| RB-209 | * | N209BP | M-YSKY | | | |
| RB-210 | * | N210KP | PT-SBF | | | |
| RB-211 | * | N701KB | N701KD | (D-IWAJ) | OE-FKK | |
| RB-212 | * | N42SC | | | | |
| RB-213 | * | N213BP | N952GL | | | |
| RB-214 | * | N814BP | | | | |
| RB-215 | * | N215BR | OE-FAP | | | |
| RB-216 | * | N3216G | YL-MLV | | | |
| RB-217 | * | N3217P | C-GXMB | | | |
| RB-218 | * | N3K | | | | |
| RB-219 | * | N34859 | VT-VRL | | | |
| RB-220 | * | N34820 | VP-BFU | | | |
| RB-221 | * | N31921 | D-ISAG | | | |
| RB-222 | * | N32022 | PT-CBA | | | |
| RB-223 | * | N3203L | N427DB | | | |
| RB-224 | * | N3204P | (PP-LUG) | PR-VPP | | |
| RB-225 | * | N3205W | VT-BKG | N3205W | | |
| RB-226 | * | N97JP | N26DK | | | |
| RB-227 | * | N166AN | | | | |
| RB-228 | * | N3228M | F-HCJP | | | |
| RB-229 | * | N229RB | N50VM | | | |
| RB-230 | * | N3330S | F-HNCY | | | |

## BEECH 390 PREMIER I/1A*

| C/n | Srs | Identities | | | |
|---|---|---|---|---|---|
| RB-231 | * | N390GS | PR-PRC | | |
| RB-232 | * | N208HP | | | |
| RB-233 | * | N233WC | SP-RDW | | |
| RB-234 | * | N367CS | N368CS | | |
| RB-235 | * | N33805 | D-IIBE | | |
| RB-236 | * | N3186C | VT-UPN | | |
| RB-237 | * | N33837 | PR-RRN | | |
| RB-238 | * | N3198N | ZS-DDM | | |
| RB-239 | * | N3289H | VT-KBN | | |
| RB-240 | * | N3400Y | PR-RSN | | |
| RB-241 | * | N3241G | I-NGIR | | |
| RB-242 | * | N390EU | N69SB | | |
| RB-243 | * | N443BP | N111LP | N111LQ | |
| RB-244 | * | N3344T | N9CH | | |
| RB-245 | * | N3415A | I-AFOI | | |
| RB-246 | * | N3216L | PR-VMD | | |
| RB-247 | * | N3187G | N668Z | | |
| RB-248 | * | N3188V | N1899 | | |
| RB-249 | * | N3194R | D-IAYL | | |
| RB-250 | * | N3200X | N357PT | | |
| RB-251 | * | N3151W | | | |
| RB-252 | * | N3352W | N452AS | N111LP | |
| RB-253 | * | N3223G | | | |
| RB-254 | * | N3354S | I-DMSB | | |
| RB-255 | * | N3355D | C-GYMB | N255AG | N69YM |
| RB-256 | * | N3396P | OM-VPB | | |
| RB-257 | * | N3197P | N701KB | | |
| RB-258 | * | N3298W | N826TG | | |
| RB-259 | * | N3395H | N42LG | | |
| RB-260 | * | N3400X | N952SP | | |
| RB-261 | * | N3441A | | | |
| RB-262 | * | N42LG | N262RB | SX-FCA | |
| RB-263 | * | N42LG | N42LQ | D-ISAS* | |
| RB-264 | * | N264HB | N79CB | | |
| RB-265 | * | N6465W | ZS-AAM | | |
| RB-266 | * | N266AZ | N390MM | | |
| RB-267 | * | N64467 | C-FJTN | | |
| RB-268 | * | N63768 | N33EM | | |
| RB-269 | * | N60669 | F-GDRR | | |
| RB-270 | * | N6470P | N124EK | | |
| RB-271 | * | N6471N | | | |
| RB-272 | * | N64312 | N23HD | | |
| RB-273 | * | N64373 | N21FM | | |
| RB-274 | * | N6174Q | UP-P1002 | | |
| RB-275 | * | N390P | | | |
| RB-276 | * | N76EU | | | |
| RB-277 | * | | | | |
| RB-278 | * | | | | |
| RB-279 | * | | | | |
| RB-280 | * | | | | |
| RB-281 | * | | | | |
| RB-282 | * | | | | |
| RB-283 | * | | | | |
| RB-284 | * | | | | |
| RB-285 | * | | | | |
| RB-286 | * | | | | |
| RB-287 | * | | | | |
| RB-288 | * | | | | |
| RB-289 | * | | | | |
| RB-290 | * | | | | |
| RB-291 | * | | | | |
| RB-292 | * | | | | |
| RB-293 | * | | | | |
| RB-294 | * | | | | |
| RB-295 | * | | | | |
| RB-296 | * | | | | |
| RB-297 | * | | | | |
| RB-298 | * | | | | |
| RB-299 | * | | | | |
| RB-300 | * | | | | |
| RB-301 | * | | | | |
| RB-302 | * | | | | |
| RB-303 | * | | | | |
| RB-304 | * | | | | |
| RB-305 | * | N124EK | N305BP | | |
| RB-306 | * | | | | |
| RB-307 | * | | | | |

# BEECH 390-2 PREMIER II

| C/n | Identities |
|---|---|
| RD-1 | N392X |
| RD-2 | |
| RD-3 | |
| RD-4 | |
| RD-5 | |

# BEECHJET 400

* Denotes aircraft originally manufactured by Mitsubishi as MU300-2s and then converted to Beechjet 400 standard. The c/n shown in brackets in these cases is the old Mitsubishi c/n. C/n RJ-12 is the first pure Beechjet 400.

| C/n | Series | Identities |
|---|---|---|
| *RJ-1 (A1001SA) | 400 | N64VM |
| *RJ-2 (A1002SA) | 400 | N103AD N402FB N369EA |
| *RJ-3 (A1003SA) | 400 | N508DM N203BA N49JN |
| *RJ-4 (A1004SA) | 400 | N504DM N92RW (N401TJ) N8YM |
| *RJ-5 (A1005SA) | 400 | N77GA N54TK N933AC |
| *RJ-6 (A1006SA) | 400 | N106DM N18JN YV-737CP YV-738CP YV-838CP N406TS |
| *RJ-7 (A1007SA) | 400 | N507DM N207BA N106VC N25BN N85BN N403JP |
| A1008SA | 2 | N411BW [reportedly w/o at unknown location in Mar97; to Dodson Avn, Rantoul, KS Oct97, for spares use] |
| *RJ-9 (A1009SA) | 400 | N109DM N209BA (N248PA) N42SR N242SR N800FT N65RA |
| *RJ-10 (A1010SA) | 400 | N499DM N410BA I-ALSE N131AP |
| *RJ-11 (A1011SA) | 400 | N114DM N111BA N72HG |
| RJ-12 | 400 | N3112B N129DB N3112K N106CG [parted out by AvMATS, St Louis, MO] |
| RJ-13 | 400 | N3113B (N400TN) N428JD |
| RJ-14 | 400 | N3114B N208R N208D N58AU N672AT (N770TB) N599JL [parted out by White Inds, Bates City, MO] |
| RJ-15 | 400 | N3115B N25W N25WA N73BL N73BE N902P N415CT |
| RJ-16 | 400 | N165F N512WP N803E (N440MP) |
| RJ-17 | 400 | N417BJ N877S N400T N94BJ N84BJ N486MJ N1CG N455FD N655CM |
| RJ-18 | 400 | N3180T I-STAP N940GA ZS-NOD N595PT N824SS N418RM |
| RJ-19 | 400 | N3119W N800HM (N700HM) N880HM PJ-SOL N24BA N101CC N598JL [parted out by White Inds, Bates City, MO] |
| RJ-20 | 400 | N3120Y I-ONDO (N20CV) N901P N455DW |
| RJ-21 | 400 | N3121B N721FA |
| RJ-22 | 400 | N3122B 9M-ATM N992GA (VR-BLG) I-INCZ OY-JAT N724AA N48CK N913SF N913MC (N315SA) N567BA |
| RJ-23 | 400 | N3123T [rebuilt using parts of RK-11, following accident] (I-ALSU) N400GJ |
| RJ-24 | 400 | N3124M N510WS N512WS N800WW N800WV |
| RJ-25 | 400 | N3025T I-MPIZ N125RJ I-OTTY N425BJ ZS-OUU N425BJ |
| RJ-26 | 400 | N3026U N88WG N90SR N388DA N426MD N91MT N401GJ |
| RJ-27 | 400 | N3127R N484CC (N427CW) N611TG |
| RJ-28 | 400 | N31428 I-ACIF N48GA N700LP N51EB |
| RJ-29 | 400 | N3129E N503EB N193TR (N597N) XA-OAC N129BT |
| RJ-30 | 400 | N3130T (N815BS) N486MJ N777FE |
| RJ-31 | 400 | N545GM N5450M I-ALSI N5450M I-ALSI N114AP N499P |
| RJ-32 | 400 | N31432 XA-RAR |
| RJ-33 | 400 | N31733 (N233BJ) XA-JJA XA-BNG XA-JMM |
| RJ-34 | 400 | N3134N I-ALSO N96WW (N41TJ) N80TS (N800TS) (N1X) N1TY N7EY N80TS |
| RJ-35 | 400 | N3035T N85TT I-SAMI N71GA N737MM N137MM N1AG |
| RJ-36 | 400 | N3236Q G-RSRS N3236Q G-MARS I-RDSF VR-BNV N52GA XA-OAC |
| RJ-37 | 400 | N31437 LV-PAM LV-RCT N31437 ZS-ORW |
| RJ-38 | 400 | N3238K N147CC N447CC VT-OAM N438DA N52AL |
| RJ-39 | 400 | N3239K N48SR N393BB N398BB |
| RJ-40 | 400 | N3240M PK-ERA N3240M N400DW |
| RJ-41 | 400 | N3141G (N441EE) (N270BJ) N241BJ |
| RJ-42 | 400 | N3142E N31542 N400PL I-FTAL N735GA N444WB N442JC N40MA N418CT |
| RJ-43 | 400 | N3143T N401CG N500DG N416CT |
| RJ-44 | 400 | N3144A HB-VJE N3144A I-GCFA N22WJ I-TOPJ N110GA N922TR |
| RJ-45 | 400 | N3145F N58AU N218RG N241TR |
| RJ-46 | 400 | N1546T N146JB VT-TEL |
| RJ-47 | 400 | N1547B (N900EF) |
| RJ-48 | 400 | N1548D XB-JHE XC-LJS |
| RJ-49 | 400 | N1549J N88UA |
| RJ-50 | 400 | N1550Y G-OTMC N56GA N102MC N406GJ N8HQ |
| RJ-51 | 400 | N1551B [converted to RK-1 (qv)] |
| RJ-52 | 400 | N196KC (N196KQ) (N52EB) N196JH N930MG N324MM |
| RJ-53 | 400 | N195KC N195KA N711EC N53EB N520WS |
| RJ-54 | 400 | N1554R XB-FDH N418MG |
| RJ-55 | 400 | N1555P (VH-...) N711FG N711FC N780GT N724HB |
| RJ-56 | 400 | N1556W G-BSZP OK-UZI N70DE |
| RJ-57 | 400 | N1557D N25BR [w/o 11Dec91 Lavender Mt, NW of Rome Airport, GA; cx Jun92] |
| RJ-58 | 400 | N1558F XA-RNG XA-MII N258BJ N458HC (N750KP) |
| RJ-59 | 400 | N1559U ZS-MHN |
| RJ-60 | 400 | N1560T G-BRBZ N89GA N400FT XA-LEG N250KD N95RT N700WH |
| RJ-61 | 400 | N1561B XA-RNE N701LP N461EA |
| RJ-62 | 400 | N89KM N89KK N333RS N424BT |
| RJ-63 | 400 | N848C |
| RJ-64 | 400 | N1564B N195JH N215TP |
| RJ-65 | 400 | N1565B N16MF |

End of production from Japanese components; production continues with US-built components from c/n RK-1

# BEECHJET 400A/ HAWKER 400XP

| C/n | Series | Identities |
|---|---|---|
| RK-1 | 400A | N1551B [converted from c/n RJ-51] N294FA N294AW (N401CW) N481CW |
| RK-2 | 400A | N1902W N272BC N272BQ N402CW N827SB |
| RK-3 | 400A | N400A XA-CLA N640AC N400VG N400VK N519RW |
| RK-4 | 400A | N147CC N147CG N400BE N777FL N771EL N494CW N222JE |
| RK-5 | 400A | N501BG (N405CW) N495CW N30XL |
| RK-6 | 400A | N56576 I-IPFC N3119H N600CC (N401FF) N401EE N406CW (N406ML) N480M N408M PR-ALY* |
| RK-7 | 400A | VR-COG N416RP N631RP (N631RR) N401AB N9PW N848TC |
| RK-8 | 400A | N440DS |
| RK-9 | 400A | N8152H N315R (N150TF) |
| RK-10 | 400A | N2842B (D-CLSG) D-CEIS |
| RK-11 | 400A | N2843B N5680Z I-ALSU [w/o 27Nov91 Parma, Italy; remains to Dodson Avn, Ottawa, KS - parts used to rebuild RJ-23 (N3123T) q.v.] |
| RK-12 | T-1A | [built as Jayhawk c/n TT-1; for USAF] |
| RK-13 | 400A | N56BE N56BX N13GB N610EG |
| RK-14 | 400A | N28..B N81709 (F-GKCJ) F-GLYO (N414RK) N81TJ N916SB |
| RK-15 | T-1A | [built as Jayhawk c/n TT-2; for USAF] |
| RK-16 | 400A | N8163G N71FE N46FE N416CW XA-MGM N16HD |
| RK-17 | 400A | N505EB N877S N877Z N417CW (N401LX) N857C |
| RK-18 | 400A | N5598Q N717DD N717DW N418CW (N402LX) TC-ASE |
| RK-19 | 400A | N1901W N11GE (N8ME) N41ME N419CW (N403LX) N144AW ZP-BJB |
| RK-20 | 400A | N82628 I-UNSA N82628 N870P N703LP |
| RK-21 | 400A | (N401TC) N1904W N1881W N717VL N717VA N1920 |
| RK-22 | 400A | N56616 N51ML N85CR N422CW (N404LX) (N522KJ) N870BB |
| RK-23 | 400A | N107BJ N200BL (N960AJ) N250AJ |
| RK-24 | 400A | N8073R [wfu; canx 01Jul09] |
| RK-25 | 400A | N81918 (VR-CDA) D-CLBA |
| RK-26 | 400A | N8097V VH-BBJ VH-IMP N700GB N8097V N80DX (N80DE) HK-4446X HK-4446-W HK-4446-G |
| RK-27 | 400A | N10FL N10FQ N427CW (N405LX) N95GK |
| RK-28 | 400A | N42SK N411SK PT-WLM (N902PC) N400NS [retro-fitted with Williams FJ44 engines; rebranded as Beechjet 400NXT] N401NX |
| RK-29 | 400A | I-IPIZ N15693 I-IPIZ |
| RK-30 | 400A | N205R N430CW (N406LX) N494CC |
| RK-31 | 400A | N10J N10JX N431CW (N407LX) N850C |
| RK-32 | 400A | N999GP N998GP N553PF N432CW (N408LX) N932EA |
| RK-33 | 400A | N1878C N60B N197PF N197BE |
| RK-34 | 400A | N400A N700GM N74VF N232BJ N511JP N511JF N721SS N134FA N184AR |
| RK-35 | 400A | N81661 VH-BJD VH-LAW VH-BJD VH-LAW VH-BJD N435CW (N409LX) (N936EA) N492AM |
| RK-36 | 400A | XA-RZG N56327 N57B N156DH N155DH N568SD |
| RK-37 | 400A | (F-GLPD) N8014Q (F-GLOR) SE-DRS |
| RK-38 | 400A | N5685X N522EE N522EF N515MW YV363T |
| RK-39 | 400A | N400Q N34VP N70BJ (N97XP) N492P |
| RK-40 | 400A | N8252J N496EE N440CW (N410LX) |
| RK-41 | 400A | N8265Y I-FSJA N920SA N546BZ N101WR |
| RK-42 | 400A | N8253Y N442CW (N411LX) N443C |
| RK-43 | 400A | N56400 N45RK |
| RK-44 | 400A | N8249Y N404VP N908R N712GK |
| RK-45 | 400A | N56423 N490TN (N8051H) N445E (N600CC) N445CC N445CW (N412LX) N445PK |
| RK-46 | 400A | N8239E N515RY |
| RK-47 | 400A | N8053V N400FT N408PC N109CP |
| RK-48 | 400A | N8060V N94HT N48SE |
| RK-49 | 400A | N8060Y N54HP N54HD (N349HP) |
| RK-50 | 400A | N80KM N750AB N450CW (N413LX) |
| RK-51 | 400A | N8085T (N7113Z) |
| RK-52 | 400A | N709JB (N709EW) N709EL |
| RK-53 | 400A | N62KM N200GP N200GB N453CW (N414LX) N896C |
| RK-54 | 400A | N80938 PT-WHG |
| RK-55 | 400A | N400Q N404CC N42AJ |
| RK-56 | 400A | N89KM N456CW (N415LX) N56FF XA-JAM XA-KJM |
| RK-57 | 400A | N8157H ZS-NZO N762BG N457CW (N416LX) N368EA |
| RK-58 | 400A | N56356 PT-WHC |
| RK-59 | 400A | N80544 N50KH N5PF N27JJ |
| RK-60 | 400A | N8260L (N794SM) N61SM N55SQ |
| RK-61 | 400A | N82378 G-RAHL N461CW (N417LX) N478DR |
| RK-62 | 400A | N8083N N462CW (N418LX) N5895K |
| RK-63 | 400A | N2792B N82412 PT-JQM N163RK N304JR |
| RK-64 | 400A | N8164M N53MS |
| RK-65 | 400A | N39HF (N97TT) (N81TT) |
| RK-66 | 400A | N400A (N400DT) N400Y HB-VLM N6048F I-AVSS |
| RK-67 | 400A | N8167Y (N850RG) N467RG |
| RK-68 | 400A | N8280J N295FA (N419LX) XA-PYN N900EF YV2452 |
| RK-69 | 400A | N8169Q N877S N877J |
| RK-70 | 400A | C-FOPC N750T N73HM N79HM N826JH |

## BEECHJET 400A/ HAWKER 400XP

| C/n | Series | Identities | | | | | |
|---|---|---|---|---|---|---|---|
| RK-71 | 400A | N82497 | I-IFPC | N777ND | N73BL | N402GS | | |
| RK-72 | 400A | N8210W | N709JB | (N72BJ) | N910SH | N428WE | N82QD | |
| RK-73 | 400A | N8070Q | PT-WHB | | | | | |
| RK-74 | 400A | N8146J | N26JP | N93XP | | | | |
| RK-75 | 400A | (N275PC) | N82400 | N125JG | | | | |
| RK-76 | 400A | N8166A | N261JP | | | | | |
| RK-77 | 400A | N8277Y | PT-WHD | | | | | |
| RK-78 | 400A | N8278Z | N611PA | [dbr in hangar collapse at Boca Raton, FL, 24Oct05; to Dodson Av'n, Rantoul, KS, for spares] | | | | |
| RK-79 | 400A | N8279G | (N30SF) | OH-RIF | N8279G | | | |
| RK-80 | 400A | N8180Q | AP-BEX | [w/o in hangar collapse at Lahore 06Jun04] | | | | |
| RK-81 | 400A | N8167G | PT-WHE | | | | | |
| RK-82 | 400A | N8282E | PT-WHF | | | | | |
| RK-83 | 400A | N8283C | XA-SNP | XA-MII | N8283C | | | |
| RK-84 | 400A | N8138M | D-CHSW | OE-GFB | | | | |
| RK-85 | 400A | N8299Y | N419MS | N419MB | | | | |
| RK-86 | 400A | N1563V | N777GC | (N72PP) | N757CE | N20ZC | | |
| RK-87 | 400A | N1567L | N702LP | N87EB | | | | |
| RK-88 | 400A | N1549W | N654AT | N654AP | | | | |
| RK-89 | 400A | N1560G | N94HE | | | | | |
| RK-90 | 400A | N1570L | N165HB | N132WE | | | | |
| RK-91 | 400A | N1545N | N296FA | N491CW | (N420LX) | N511VB | | |
| RK-92 | 400A | N3240J | N555KK | N124PP | | | | |
| RK-93 | 400A | N3038V | N493CW | (N421LX) | | | | |
| RK-94 | 400A | N3051S | HB-VLN | N585G | N681WD | N661WD | | |
| RK-95 | 400A | N3114X | HS-UCM | N747RR | | | | |
| RK-96 | 400A | N3196N | N924JM | N824JM | N800GF | | | |
| RK-97 | 400A | N3197Q | VH-MGC | | | | | |
| RK-98 | 400A | N3210X | N400A | N866BB | N999JF | N999YB | | |
| RK-99 | 400A | N3199Q | N95FA | N575RB | | | | |
| RK-100 | 400A | N1570B | N400SH | | | | | |
| RK-101 | 400A | N3221T | ZS-JRO | N400FT | N490AM | | | |
| RK-102 | 400A | N3232U | N916GR | N111FW | | | | |
| RK-103 | 400A | D-CIGM | HB-VLW | N103LP | N403CW | (N422LX) | N12NV | YV0157 |
| RK-104 | 400A | N3224X | LV-PLT | LV-WPE | N704SC | PR-DOT | | |
| RK-105 | 400A | N3235U | (N8252J) | (N423LX) | N127BW | N124BV | N105AX | |
| RK-106 | 400A | N3246H | N1HS | N625W | | | | |
| RK-107 | 400A | N3227X | N733MK | N907JE | | | | |
| RK-108 | 400A | N3218L | N498CW | N408CW | (N424LX) | | | |
| RK-109 | 400A | N3269A | N121EZ | N491AM | B-3905 | | | |
| RK-110 | 400A | N1090X | N400VP | (N400A) | XA-FRO | | | |
| RK-111 | 400A | N42SK | N411SK | N412WP | N13SY | N116SS | | |
| RK-112 | 400A | N3272L | N94LH | N112BJ | | | | |
| RK-113 | 400A | N3263N | N400VG | [w/o 17Apr99 Beckley, WV, cx Dec02] | | | | |
| RK-114 | 400A | N1084D | N363K | N698PW | N855RA | | | |
| RK-115 | 400A | N3265A | (N369EA) | N52AW | N512F* | | | |
| RK-116 | 400A | N1116R | | | | | | |
| RK-117 | 400A | N1117S | N97FB | N97FF | N12MG | N12MQ | N496AS | |
| RK-118 | 400A | N1118Y | LV-PMH | LV-WTP | | | | |
| RK-119 | 400A | N1119C | N456JG | (N456NS) | (N7981M) | | | |
| RK-120 | 400A | N3261Y | TC-MDJ | N9146Z | N159AK | N702NV | | |
| RK-121 | 400A | N1121Z | N419MS | N473JE | | | | |
| RK-122 | 400A | N1102B | PT-WJS | | | | | |
| RK-123 | 400A | N1123Z | N110TG | N740TA | N203FL | | | |
| RK-124 | 400A | N1124Z | TC-MSA | N124BG | OE-GUK | YU-BVA | 4O-BVA | |
| RK-125 | 400A | N1105U | N400KP | N400KL | N939GP | | | |
| RK-126 | 400A | N3226B | N197SD | XB-INI | | | | |
| RK-127 | 400A | N1127U | N696TR | N686TR | | | | |
| RK-128 | 400A | N1108Y | N912SH | | | | | |
| RK-129 | 400A | N1129X | N129MC | N334SR | N129WH | | | |
| RK-130 | 400A | N1130B | TC-NEO | | | | | |
| RK-131 | 400A | N1083Z | N305MD | | | | | |
| RK-132 | 400A | N1087Z | N106KC | | | | | |
| RK-133 | 400A | N1133T | VP-BMR | N133BP | I-TOPB | | | |
| RK-134 | 400A | N1094D | N134BJ | N134WF | LV-CBJ | | | |
| RK-135 | 400A | N1135A | N135BJ | | | | | |
| RK-136 | 400A | N1136Q | N780TP | N397CA | N130WW | | | |
| RK-137 | 400A | N1117Z | N400AJ | | | | | |
| RK-138 | 400A | N40PL | N48PL | | | | | |
| RK-139 | 400A | N1099S | VH-PNL | VH-MZL | VH-BZL | | | |
| RK-140 | 400A | N1094N | ZS-OCG | A6-ELJ | ZS-OCG | A2-MCG | | |
| RK-141 | 400A | N1027S | N974JD | N874JD | N855FC | | | |
| RK-142 | 400A | N142BJ | (N223DK) | YV-943CP | N142BJ | N9WW | | |
| RK-143 | 400A | N191NC | N191NQ | N824HG | | | | |
| RK-144 | 400A | N134CM | PR-SKB* | | | | | |
| RK-145 | 400A | N745TA | (N425LX) | N144JS | | | | |

## BEECHJET 400A/ HAWKER 400XP

| C/n | Series | Identities | | | | | | |
|---|---|---|---|---|---|---|---|---|
| RK-146 | 400A | N146TA | N746TA | (N426LX) | N456FL | | | |
| RK-147 | 400A | N147BJ | | | | | | |
| RK-148 | 400A | N1108T | TC-SMB | N663AJ | OE-GHM | | | |
| RK-149 | 400A | N149TA | N749TA | (N427LX) | N499LX | | | |
| RK-150 | 400A | N1135U | N100AG | N100AW | | | | |
| RK-151 | 400A | N1126V | PT-MAC | N115CD | N586SF | N196CT | N198CT | N548KK |
| RK-152 | 400A | N2252Q | N97FB | YV-754CP | YV213T | | | |
| RK-153 | 400A | N153BJ | N500HY | | | | | |
| RK-154 | 400A | N2354B | VH-BJC | VH-EXB | | | | |
| RK-155 | 400A | N2355T | N627RP | N631RP | N631PP | N567DK | PR-JPK | |
| RK-156 | 400A | N2056E | N400PU | | | | | |
| RK-157 | 400A | N397AT | N897AT | ZS-ONP | N897AT | N157WH | | |
| RK-158 | 400A | N2358X | PT-MPL | | | | | |
| RK-159 | 400A | N2159P | N3337J | | | | | |
| RK-160 | 400A | N2360F | N54HP | | | | | |
| RK-161 | 400A | N761TA | N471CW | (N428LX) | N706RM | | | |
| RK-162 | 400A | N2362G | ZS-PDB | N2362G | OY-SIS | N520CH | OE-GMC | |
| RK-163 | 400A | N2363A | XA-JET | N163BJ | I-TOPD | | | |
| RK-164 | 400A | N2164Z | TC-MDB | N2164Z | (N69LS) | N280AJ | N717CH* | |
| RK-165 | 400A | N2225Y | N224MC | | | | | |
| RK-166 | 400A | N2299T | N975CM | N93FT | | | | |
| RK-167 | 400A | N2267B | N711EC | N501BW | | | | |
| RK-168 | 400A | N2168G | N768TA | (N429LX) | N679SJ | | | |
| RK-169 | 400A | N2329N | N757WS | | | | | |
| RK-170 | 400A | N2289B | TC-MCX | TC-MSB | | | | |
| RK-171 | 400A | N2201J | PT-WUF | N287CD | XA-LEG | | | |
| RK-172 | 400A | N2272K | N615HP | N200GP | | | | |
| RK-173 | 400A | N2273Z | | | | | | |
| RK-174 | 400A | N2204J | N174AB | HK-4645 | | | | |
| RK-175 | 400A | N175BJ | | | | | | |
| RK-176 | 400A | N476BJ | | | | | | |
| RK-177 | 400A | N2277G | N717CF | | | | | |
| RK-178 | 400A | N708TA | (N478CW) | (N430LX) | N406LX | | | |
| RK-179 | 400A | N2279K | N75GF | N75GK | N400CT | OD- | | |
| RK-180 | 400A | N709TA | (N480CW) | (N407LX) | | | | |
| RK-181 | 400A | N2235V | N314TL | | | | | |
| RK-182 | 400A | N2322B | N234DK | | | | | |
| RK-183 | 400A | N710TA | (N432LX) | N488LX | | | | |
| RK-184 | 400A | N2314F | N141DR | | | | | |
| RK-185 | 400A | N2298L | N140GB | N148GB | (N450AT) | (N185FN) | | |
| RK-186 | 400A | N712TA | (N433LX) | N12NV | | | | |
| RK-187 | 400A | N2298S | N400TE | | | | | |
| RK-188 | 400A | N2298W | TC-VIN | N2298W | VP-CPH | | | |
| RK-189 | 400A | N715TA | (N434LX) | | | | | |
| RK-190 | 400A | N2290F | TC-YRT | N2290F | N325JG | VT-RPG | | |
| RK-191 | 400A | N2291T | N960JJ | N960JA | N367EA | N400HD | | |
| RK-192 | 400A | N492BJ | N272BC | N272BQ | N116AD | N116AP | | |
| RK-193 | 400A | N13US | N914SH | N366EA | N193BJ | | | |
| RK-194 | 400A | N194BJ | N909ST | | | | | |
| RK-195 | 400A | N718TA | (N485CW) | (N435LX) | (N410LX) | | | |
| RK-196 | 400A | N2283T | XA-MEX | N619GA | N619G | | | |
| RK-197 | 400A | N3197A | N214WM | N940VA | | | | |
| RK-198 | 400A | N798TA | (N436LX) | N403WC | N168WC | | | |
| RK-199 | 400A | N739TA | N446M | | | | | |
| RK-200 | 400A | N200NA | VP-CKK | N399RA | | | | |
| RK-201 | 400A | N741TA | (N437LX) | N402FL | | | | |
| RK-202 | 400A | N742TA | N438LX | | | | | |
| RK-203 | 400A | N2359W | B-3989 | N2359W | VP-CHF | N203RK | N262PA | |
| RK-204 | 400A | N2357K | I-ASER | | | | | |
| RK-205 | 400A | N3030D | N143HM | (N17CM) | | | | |
| RK-206 | 400A | N3014R | N30046 | N982AR | | | | |
| RK-207 | 400A | N3015F | N717DD | N257CB | | | | |
| RK-208 | 400A | N3101B | N890BH | HI-766SP | HI766 | | | |
| RK-209 | 400A | N799TA | (N439LX) | N413LX | | | | |
| RK-210 | 400A | N111CX | | | | | | |
| RK-211 | 400A | N3028U | TC-NNK | N3028U | N686SC | | | |
| RK-212 | 400A | N3029F | N299AW | N11UB | | | | |
| RK-213 | 400A | N3033A | N175PS | N545TC | | | | |
| RK-214 | 400A | N79EL | | | | | | |
| RK-215 | 400A | N3038W | N515WA | | | | | |
| RK-216 | 400A | N3050P | N213BK | | | | | |
| RK-217 | 400A | N217MB | N385PB | | | | | |
| RK-218 | 400A | N3068M | N48MF | | | | | |
| RK-219 | 400A | N3059H | N511JP | N80BL | N219SJ | 4X-CPY | | |
| RK-220 | 400A | N220BJ | N799SM | N499AS | | | | |
| RK-221 | 400A | N221BJ | N18BR | N400KG | N400SF | | | |

## BEECHJET 400A/ HAWKER 400XP

| C/n | Series | Identities | | | | | |
|---|---|---|---|---|---|---|---|
| RK-222 | 400A | N748TA | N482CW | (N440LX) | N482RK | VH-YRC | VH-IPG |
| RK-223 | 400A | N3223R | N777FL | N877FL | | | |
| RK-224 | 400A | N3224N | N51NP | N642AC | | | |
| RK-225 | 400A | N751TA | N415LX | | | | |
| RK-226 | 400A | N3226Q | N59BR | N59BP | N750TA | (N416LX) | |
| RK-227 | 400A | N3197K | N362KM | N862KM | N497AS | | |
| RK-228 | 400A | N3228V | N12WF | | | | |
| RK-229 | 400A | N3129X | N515TJ | | | | |
| RK-230 | 400A | N753TA | (N441LX) | N417LX | N431FL* | | |
| RK-231 | 400A | N781TP | N615HP | | | | |
| RK-232 | 400A | N2355N | N674SF | N674DJ | | | |
| RK-233 | 400A | N2293V | N233MW | | | | |
| RK-234 | 400A | N783TA | (N442LX) | N418LX | | | |
| RK-235 | 400A | N695BK | | | | | |
| RK-236 | 400A | N2349V | N11WF | | | | |
| RK-237 | 400A | N784TA | N437CW | N443LX | | | |
| RK-238 | 400A | N23525 | XA-DOS | XA-VRO | N96GA | | |
| RK-239 | 400A | N785TA | (N421LX) | N485FL | | | |
| RK-240 | 400A | N3240J | N749SS | N150TF | N393GH | | |
| RK-241 | 400A | N3241Q | N993H | | | | |
| RK-242 | 400A | N2322B | N32AA | N32AJ | XA-... | | |
| RK-243 | 400A | N782TP | | | | | |
| RK-244 | 400A | N428HR | N793TA | (N445LX) | N493LX | | |
| RK-245 | 400A | N3199Z | N744TA | (N446LX) | N424LX | HS-CKI | |
| RK-246 | 400A | N500TH | | | | | |
| RK-247 | 400A | N40252 | N20FL | N25XP | | | |
| RK-248 | 400A | N786TA | N447LX | | | | |
| RK-249 | 400A | N4249K | N611WM | C9-CFM | | | |
| RK-250 | 400A | N2293V | N250HP | | | | |
| RK-251 | 400A | N3106Y | N705LP | N495AS | | | |
| RK-252 | 400A | N790TA | | | | | |
| RK-253 | 400A | N4053T | | | | | |
| RK-254 | 400A | N3254P | TC-BYD | N254RK | HA-YFJ | | |
| RK-255 | 400A | N988JG | N3255B | N960JJ | N400JJ | N960JJ | N402FB |
| RK-256 | 400A | N3079S | N397AT | N387AT | N26PA | | |
| RK-257 | 400A | N739TA | N449LX | | | | |
| RK-258 | 400A | N40215 | (PP-LUA) | PP-WRV | | | |
| RK-259 | 400A | N3259Z | XA-AFS | XA-UKU | | | |
| RK-260 | 400A | N787TA | (N450LX) | | | | |
| RK-261 | 400A | N3261A | N51B | | | | |
| RK-262 | 400A | N300GB | | | | | |
| RK-263 | 400A | N724MH | N724KW | | | | |
| RK-264 | 400A | N792TA | (N451LX) | N428LX | | | |
| RK-265 | 400A | N797TA | (N452LX) | N429LX | | | |
| RK-266 | 400A | N3166Q | N41283 | N10FL | N27XP | | |
| RK-267 | 400A | N4467X | OY-JJO | | | | |
| RK-268 | 400A | N789TA | (N453LX) | N489FL* | | | |
| RK-269 | 400A | N400MV | N400MR | N440RC | | | |
| RK-270 | 400A | N3231H | N800SD | | | | |
| RK-271 | 400A | N743TA | (N454LX) | (N431LX) | N800GV | | |
| RK-272 | 400A | N3237H | N701CP | | | | |
| RK-273 | 400A | N731TA | (N483CW) | (N455LX) | (N433LX) | N725T | |
| RK-274 | 400A | N735TA | (N456LX) | N434LX | | | |
| RK-275 | 400A | N4275K | N426EA | | | | |
| RK-276 | 400A | N775TA | (N457LX) | N435LX | N427DJ? | | |
| RK-277 | 400A | N4477X | (N566W) | N101CC | | | |
| RK-278 | 400A | N4378P | N823TT | N750AJ | | | |
| RK-279 | 400A | N773TA | (N458LX) | N436LX | N436FL | | |
| RK-280 | 400A | N4480W | N26XP | | | | |
| RK-281 | 400A | N4081L | XA-TDQ | N311JV | | | |
| RK-282 | 400A | N794TA | (N482LX) | (N459LX) | N88CA | | |
| RK-283 | 400A | N4083N | N600SB | N404MS | | | |
| RK-284 | 400A | N795TA | (N460LX) | N439LX | | | |
| RK-285 | 400A | N3185G | N149SB | N249SB | N249RM | | |
| RK-286 | 400A | N400MV | | | | | |
| RK-287 | 400A | N4467E | N361AS | | | | |
| RK-288 | 400A | N51VC | N848PF | | | | |
| RK-289 | 400A | N796TA | (N461LX) | N440LX | | | |
| RK-290 | 400A | N23263 | N400QW | N204DH | | | |
| RK-291 | 400A | N3191L | N816DK | | | | |
| RK-292 | 400A | N899TA | N441LX | | | | |
| RK-293 | 400A | N4293K | EC-HTR | | | | |
| RK-294 | 400A | N5094E | HS-TPD | | | | |
| RK-295 | 400A | N898TA | (N463LX) | N406FL* | | | |
| RK-296 | 400A | N311HS | N68JV | | | | |
| RK-297 | 400A | N699TA | N497CW | (N464LX) | N497RC | | |

## BEECHJET 400A/ HAWKER 400XP

| C/n | Series | Identities | | | | |
|---|---|---|---|---|---|---|
| RK-298 | 400A | N698TA | N445LX | | | |
| RK-299 | 400A | N697TA | N446LX | YV.... | | |
| RK-300 | 400A | N4001M | VP-CVP | | | |
| RK-301 | 400A | N696TA | (N465LX) | (N496LX) | XA-... | |
| RK-302 | 400A | N5002G | XA-TTS | | | |
| RK-303 | 400A | N695TA | N400HS | N400HD | SE-RBO | |
| RK-304 | 400A | N5004Y | N304SE | | | |
| RK-305 | 400A | N693TA | N405CW | (N466LX) | N448LX | |
| RK-306 | 400A | N4056V | YV-968CP | YV198T | | |
| RK-307 | 400A | N692TA | N407CW | (N467LX) | PT-TRA | |
| RK-308 | 400A | N51008 | N400KP | | | |
| RK-309 | 400A | N3239A | I-VITH | | | |
| RK-310 | 400A | N695TA | N410CW | (N468LX) | N451LX | |
| RK-311 | 400A | N755TA | N711GD | N711GL | N311GL | N40SC |
| RK-312 | 400A | N5012U | N75RL | | | |
| RK-313 | 400A | N4483W | (PH-BBC) | | | |
| RK-314 | 400A | N5014G | N400HS | | | |
| RK-315 | 400A | N3215J | N6MF | | | |
| RK-316 | 400A | N3216X | XA-AFA | | | |
| RK-317 | 400A | N691TA | (N469LX) | N452LX | N452SB | |
| RK-318 | 400A | N3185K | HB-VNE | | | |
| RK-319 | 400A | N689TA | N660CC | | | |
| RK-320 | 400A | N4469E | N717TG | | | |
| RK-321 | 400A | N688TA | N379DR | XA-TYD | | |
| RK-322 | 400A | N687TA | N800EL | N800EH | | |
| RK-323 | 400A | N5003G | N268PA | | | |
| RK-324 | 400A | N5024U | N755TA | (N470LX) | (N412FL) | N224FL | N224FD |
| RK-325 | 400A | N272BC | N275BC | N408PC | | |
| RK-326 | 400A | N749RH | N420DH | | | |
| RK-327 | 400A | N689TA | (N471LX) | N454LX | | |
| RK-328 | 400A | N5028J | N686TA | (N472LX) | N455LX | N423AK |
| RK-329 | 400A | N5129U | N580RJ | N580RK | | |
| RK-330 | 400A | N4330B | (N450CB) | N33NL | N330TS | |
| RK-331 | 400A | N5031D | N12MG | | | |
| RK-332 | 400A | N5032H | XA-TWW | | | |
| RK-333 | 400A | N72FL | N903CG | | | |
| RK-334 | 400A | N5034J | N684TA | N484CW | (N473LX) | N442FL |
| RK-335 | 400A | N5015B | N400GR | | | |
| RK-336 | 400A | N5136T | (N706PL) | N706LP | | |
| RK-337 | 400A | N5037L | N726PG | | | |
| RK-338 | 400A | N5038V | N116AD | | | |
| RK-339 | 400A | N4309N | N439CW | N400TL | | |
| RK-340 | 400A | N51540 | N500LJ | | | |
| RK-341 | 400A | N51241 | N61GB | | | |
| RK-342 | 400A | N50552 | N400A | N522EE | N522EL | |
| RK-343 | 400A | N4357H | N806GG | N106DD | OE-GTM | |
| RK-344 | 400A | N6144S | N99ZB | | | |
| RK-345 | 400A | N4445Y | N425CW | (N474LX) | (N457LX) | N445FL |
| RK-346 | 400A | N446CW | (N475LX) | N422FL | | |
| RK-347 | 400A | N447CW | N108PJ | N168PJ | N498AS | |
| RK-348 | 400A | N448CW | N309AK | | | |
| RK-349 | 400A | N449CW | N975RR | | | |
| RK-350 | 400A | N61850 | PR-MVB | | | |
| RK-351 | 400A | N6051C | N371CF | | | |
| RK-352 | 400A | N6052U | | | | |
| RK-353 | 400A | N400A | N353AE | XA-GAO | | |
| RK-354 | 400A | N5084U | N717EA | EC-KRS | | |
| RK-355 | 400A | N6055K | N767SB | N400RY | | |
| RK-356 | 400XP | N6056M | N400XP | N800GR | N800HT | N808HT | N217EC |
| RK-357 | 400XP | N5057Z | N317PC | | | |
| RK-358 | 400XP | N5158D | N865AM | | | |
| RK-359 | 400XP | N61959 | XA-UAW | | | |
| RK-360 | 400XP | N6200D | N823ET | | | |
| RK-361 | 400XP | N61661 | N25CU | | | |
| RK-362 | 400XP | N6162V | N362XP | Indonesia P-2034 | | Indonesia P-8001 |
| RK-363 | 400XP | N6193D | (N363XP) | N790SS | | |
| RK-364 | 400XP | N394BB | | | | |
| RK-365 | 400XP | N455CW | N459LX | | | |
| RK-366 | 400XP | N466CW | N460LX | N466CW | OD-STW | |
| RK-367 | 400XP | N404BL | | | | |
| RK-368 | 400XP | N448CW | N461LX | N427FL | | |
| RK-369 | 400XP | N369XP | N624B | | | |
| RK-370 | 400XP | N60270 | (N470CW) | N72GH | | |
| RK-371 | 400XP | N371CW | N401CW | N824GB | N72NE | |
| RK-372 | 400XP | N6172V | N375DT | | | |
| RK-373 | 400XP | N373XP | N490JC | | | |

## BEECHJET 400A/ HAWKER 400XP

| C/n | Series | Identities | | | |
|---|---|---|---|---|---|
| RK-374 | 400XP | N374XP | N109NT | | |
| RK-375 | 400XP | N375XP | XA-UCV | | |
| RK-376 | 400XP | N476CW | N476LX | | |
| RK-377 | 400XP | N477CW | N477LX | N477FL | |
| RK-378 | 400XP | N370FC | | | |
| RK-379 | 400XP | N979XP | PP-UQF | | |
| RK-380 | 400XP | N102QS | | | |
| RK-381 | 400XP | N106QS | | | |
| RK-382 | 400XP | N108QS | | | |
| RK-383 | 400XP | N115QS | | | |
| RK-384 | 400XP | N84XP | N302TB | | |
| RK-385 | 400XP | N116QS | | | |
| RK-386 | 400XP | N524LP | N502N | N300R | |
| RK-387 | 400XP | N478LX | | | |
| RK-388 | 400XP | N479LX | N45LX | (N45LN) | N997RS |
| RK-389 | 400XP | N50727 | N717DD | | |
| RK-390 | 400XP | N480LX | N975RD | | |
| RK-391 | 400XP | N117QS | | | |
| RK-392 | 400XP | N36792 | AP-BHQ | | |
| RK-393 | 400XP | N118QS | N835TB | | |
| RK-394 | 400XP | N119QS | | | |
| RK-395 | 400XP | N7600 | | | |
| RK-396 | 400XP | N31496 | XA-MEX | | |
| RK-397 | 400XP | N36997 | N479LX | N473FL | |
| RK-398 | 400XP | N483LX | N480LX | N480FL* | |
| RK-399 | 400XP | N700FA | N402CB | | |
| RK-400 | 400XP | N400XP | ZS-POT | | |
| RK-401 | 400XP | N36701 | CS-DMA | | |
| RK-402 | 400XP | N485LX | N61CP | OE-GSG | |
| RK-403 | 400XP | N36803 | CS-DMB | | |
| RK-404 | 400XP | N37204 | CS-DMC | | |
| RK-405 | 400XP | N481LX | N40ZH | N94LH | |
| RK-406 | 400XP | N140QS | | | |
| RK-407 | 400XP | N36607 | CS-DMD | | |
| RK-408 | 400XP | N37108 | CS-DME | | |
| RK-409 | 400XP | N120QS | | | |
| RK-410 | 400XP | N37310 | CS-DMF | | |
| RK-411 | 400XP | N611XP | N380JR | | |
| RK-412 | 400XP | N37312 | N412GJ | | |
| RK-413 | 400XP | N482LX | | | |
| RK-414 | 400XP | N136QS | | | |
| RK-415 | 400XP | N37115 | XA-UFS | | |
| RK-416 | 400XP | N116XP | N900ST | N900SQ | XA-LMG |
| RK-417 | 400XP | N36907 | CS-DMG | | |
| RK-418 | 400XP | N618XP | N418GJ | | |
| RK-419 | 400XP | N619XP | N279AK | | |
| RK-420 | 400XP | N620XP | N877S | N400VK | |
| RK-421 | 400XP | N145QS | N145WC | N145QS | |
| RK-422 | 400XP | N151QS | | | |
| RK-423 | 400XP | N223XP | N462LX | | |
| RK-424 | 400XP | N24XP | N1JB | N24XP | |
| RK-425 | 400XP | N37325 | CS-DMH | | |
| RK-426 | 400XP | N26XP | N463LX | | |
| RK-427 | 400XP | N132QS | | | |
| RK-428 | 400XP | N28XP | OE-GYR | EC-JPN | |
| RK-429 | 400XP | N29XP | N263PA | | |
| RK-430 | 400XP | N30XP | N990DF | PR-BED | |
| RK-431 | 400XP | N131QS | | | |
| RK-432 | 400XP | N142QS | | | |
| RK-433 | 400XP | N125QS | | | |
| RK-434 | 400XP | N34XP | (N464LX) | XA-UEV | |
| RK-435 | 400XP | N161QS | | | |
| RK-436 | 400XP | N147QS | | | |
| RK-437 | 400XP | N37337 | CS-DMI | | |
| RK-438 | 400XP | N162QS | N438BC | | |
| RK-439 | 400XP | N166QS | N159AK | | |
| RK-440 | 400XP | N152QS | N440WF | | |
| RK-441 | 400XP | N130QS | N610PR | N43BD | |
| RK-442 | 400XP | N124QS | N442GJ | | |
| RK-443 | 400XP | N36646 | CS-DMJ | | |
| RK-444 | 400XP | N465LX | N144XP | N702LP | |
| RK-445 | 400XP | N466LX | N45XP | N536V | |
| RK-446 | 400XP | N46XP | N188JF | | |
| RK-447 | 400XP | N467LX | N467FL* | | |
| RK-448 | 400XP | N146QS | N212FH | OE-GAG | |
| RK-449 | 400XP | N133QS | N127BW | | |

# BEECHJET 400A/ HAWKER 400XP

| C/n | Series | Identities | | | |
|---|---|---|---|---|---|
| RK-450 | 400XP | N650XP | N61VC | | |
| RK-451 | 400XP | N51XP | N964JD | | |
| RK-452 | 400XP | N36752 | XA-UFR | | |
| RK-453 | 400XP | N464LX | | | |
| RK-454 | 400XP | N465LX | | | |
| RK-455 | 400XP | N466LX | N800HT | | |
| RK-456 | 400XP | N61256 | LV-BEM | | |
| RK-457 | 400XP | N6137Y | PR-MMS | | |
| RK-458 | 400XP | N50858 | N339SM | | |
| RK-459 | 400XP | N459XP | N517MD | | |
| RK-460 | 400XP | N460XP | N460KG | N460JW* | |
| RK-461 | 400XP | N61XP | N101AR | | |
| RK-462 | 400XP | N462XP | N689AK | | |
| RK-463 | 400XP | N469LX | | | |
| RK-464 | 400XP | N36764 | CS-DMK | | |
| RK-465 | 400XP | N37165 | CS-DML | | |
| RK-466 | 400XP | N466XP | N610PR | PR-SCE | |
| RK-467 | 400XP | N122QS | | | |
| RK-468 | 400XP | N468LX | | | |
| RK-469 | 400XP | N37079 | (CS-DMM) | N114QS | |
| RK-470 | 400XP | N470XP | PR-IND | | |
| RK-471 | 400XP | N471LX | N471XP | | |
| RK-472 | 400XP | N36632 | CS-DMM | | |
| RK-473 | 400XP | N149QS | | | |
| RK-474 | 400XP | N474XP | N474ME | | |
| RK-475 | 400XP | N61675 | CS-DMN | | |
| RK-476 | 400XP | N36846 | TC-STA | | |
| RK-477 | 400XP | N477XP | (N2944M) | N477GJ | |
| RK-478 | 400XP | N470LX | | | |
| RK-479 | 400XP | N479XP | PP-JCF | | |
| RK-480 | 400XP | N36880 | SU-ZBB | | |
| RK-481 | 400XP | N472LX | | | |
| RK-482 | 400XP | N482XP | N482GS | | |
| RK-483 | 400XP | N139QS | | | |
| RK-484 | 400XP | N101QS | | | |
| RK-485 | 400XP | N485XP | | | |
| RK-486 | 400XP | N123QS | | | |
| RK-487 | 400XP | N487XP | G-EDCS | | |
| RK-488 | 400XP | N719EL | | | |
| RK-489 | 400XP | N489XP | N489B | | |
| RK-490 | 400XP | N153QS | | | |
| RK-491 | 400XP | N491XP | N491HR | | |
| RK-492 | 400XP | N138QS | | | |
| RK-493 | 400XP | N493XP | CC-CRT | | |
| RK-494 | 400XP | N72594 | CS-DMO | | |
| RK-495 | 400XP | N495XP | N410CT | N419TM | |
| RK-496 | 400XP | N496XP | N410KD | PR-VHB* | |
| RK-497 | 400XP | N497XP | | | |
| RK-498 | 400XP | N141QS | | | |
| RK-499 | 400XP | N499XP | I-GFVF | | |
| RK-500 | 400XP | N500XP | I-FDED | | |
| RK-501 | 400XP | N501XP | F-HITM | | |
| RK-502 | 400XP | N502XP | G-STOB | | |
| RK-503 | 400XP | N203XP | XA-FLX | N121GF | XA-FLX |
| RK-504 | 400XP | N204XP | (N45LN) | N202TT | |
| RK-505 | 400XP | N505XP | | | |
| RK-506 | 400XP | N471LX | | | |
| RK-507 | 400XP | N466LX | N507HB | N507WM* | |
| RK-508 | 400XP | N70158 | CS-DMP | | |
| RK-509 | 400XP | N154QS | | | |
| RK-510 | 400XP | N510XP | N225SB | | |
| RK-511 | 400XP | N511XP | VT-TVR | | |
| RK-512 | 400XP | N37339 | CS-DMQ | | |
| RK-513 | 400XP | N513XP | | | |
| RK-514 | 400XP | N514XP | N416RX | | |
| RK-515 | 400XP | N3735U | I-ALVC | | |
| RK-516 | 400XP | N74116 | CS-DMR | | |
| RK-517 | 400XP | N517XP | N420CT | | |
| RK-518 | 400XP | N518XP | N473LX | N219DC | |
| RK-519 | 400XP | N72539 | CS-DMS | | |
| RK-520 | 400XP | N157QS | | | |
| RK-521 | 400XP | N521XP | EI-ICE | N521XP | |
| RK-522 | 400XP | N522XP | (N385PB) | N522MB | |
| RK-523 | 400XP | N523XP | N425CT | | |
| RK-524 | 400XP | N524XP | PR-OEC | | |
| RK-525 | 400XP | N502CA | | | |

## BEECHJET 400A/ HAWKER 400XP

| C/n | Series | Identities | | |
|---|---|---|---|---|
| RK-526 | 400XP | N7226P | AP-PAL | |
| RK-527 | 400XP | N527XP | (N527DF) | |
| RK-528 | 400XP | N528XP | HA-YFH | |
| RK-529 | 400XP | N167QS | N918TT | |
| RK-530 | 400XP | N530XP | OY-CJN | |
| RK-531 | 400XP | N435CT | | |
| RK-532 | 400XP | N532XP | CS-DMT | |
| RK-533 | 400XP | N533HB | EC-KKD | |
| RK-534 | 400XP | N440CT | | |
| RK-535 | 400XP | N445CT | | |
| RK-536 | 400XP | N470CT | | |
| RK-537 | 400XP | N537XP | N537DF | |
| RK-538 | 400XP | N538XP | CS-DMU | |
| RK-539 | 400XP | N539XP | N300RC | |
| RK-540 | 400XP | N540RK | N777G | |
| RK-541 | 400XP | N32051 | N474LX | |
| RK-542 | 400XP | N542XP | N393BB | |
| RK-543 | 400XP | N731PS | | |
| RK-544 | 400XP | N480CT | | |
| RK-545 | 400XP | N485CT | | |
| RK-546 | 400XP | N490CT | | |
| RK-547 | 400XP | N495CT | | |
| RK-548 | 400XP | N548XP | TC-NEU | |
| RK-549 | 400XP | N34249 | CS-DMV | |
| RK-550 | 400XP | N3500R | CS-DMW | |
| RK-551 | 400XP | N551XP | (N551EU) | |
| RK-552 | 400XP | N552XP | N552EU | G-KLNR |
| RK-553 | 400XP | N553XP | N975BD | |
| RK-554 | 400XP | N475LX | N465TM | |
| RK-555 | 400XP | N31975 | CS-DMX | |
| RK-556 | 400XP | N3186B | CS-DMY | |
| RK-557 | 400XP | N557XP | YV.... | |
| RK-558 | 400XP | N558XP | | |
| RK-559 | 400XP | N3289R | CS-DMZ | |
| RK-560 | 400XP | N560XP | N475TM | |
| RK-561 | 400XP | N3501M | CS-DOB | |
| RK-562 | 400XP | N33062 | B-77701 | |
| RK-563 | 400XP | N63XP | (N475LX) | |
| RK-564 | 400XP | N564XP | N491TM | |
| RK-565 | 400XP | N565XP | N565EU | |
| RK-566 | 400XP | N3206K | VT-GRG | |
| RK-567 | 400XP | N567XP | | |
| RK-568 | 400XP | N3468D | | |
| RK-569 | 400XP | N180QS | | |
| RK-570 | 400XP | N570XP | N979CM | |
| RK-571 | 400XP | N979CM | N571TW | |
| RK-572 | 400XP | N3502T | | |
| RK-573 | 400XP | N573XP | N449TM | |
| RK-574 | 400XP | N175QS | | |
| RK-575 | 400XP | N575XP | N112WC | |
| RK-576 | 400XP | N576XP | N451TM | |
| RK-577 | 400XP | N577XP | N452TM | |
| RK-578 | 400XP | N179QS | | |
| RK-579 | 400XP | N579XP | CN-TJD | |
| RK-580 | 400XP | N580XP | N492TM | |
| RK-581 | 400XP | N481LX | N453TM | |
| RK-582 | 400XP | N582XP | N493TM | |
| RK-583 | 400XP | N176QS | N583XP | AP-RBA |
| RK-584 | 400XP | N3204Q | VH-NTX | |
| RK-585 | 400XP | N585XP | N456TM | |
| RK-586 | 400XP | N586XP | N480M | |
| RK-587 | 400XP | N587XP | HZ-SPAA | |
| RK-588 | 400XP | N588XP | HZ-SPAB | |
| RK-589 | 400XP | N589XP | HZ-SPAC | |
| RK-590 | 400XP | N3190C | N5031T | |
| RK-591 | 400XP | N591XP | HZ-SPAD | |
| RK-592 | 400XP | N492TM | N592XP | HZ- |
| RK-593 | 400XP | N493TM | N593XP | |
| RK-594 | 400XP | N594XP | | |
| RK-595 | 400XP | N595XP | | |
| RK-596 | 400XP | N596XP | | |
| RK-597 | 400XP | | | |
| RK-598 | 400XP | N598EU | | |
| RK-599 | 400XP | | | |
| RK-600 | 400XP | | | |
| RK-601 | 400XP | | | |

## BEECHJET 400A/ HAWKER 400XP

| C/n | Series | Identities |
|---|---|---|
| RK-602 | 400XP | |
| RK-603 | 400XP | |
| RK-604 | 400XP | |
| RK-605 | 400XP | |
| RK-606 | 400XP | |
| RK-607 | 400XP | |
| RK-608 | 400XP | |
| RK-609 | 400XP | |
| RK-610 | 400XP | |
| RK-611 | 400XP | |
| RK-612 | 400XP | |
| RK-613 | 400XP | |
| RK-614 | 400XP | |
| RK-615 | 400XP | |
| RK-616 | 400XP | |
| RK-617 | 400XP | |
| RK-618 | 400XP | |
| RK-619 | 400XP | |
| RK-620 | 400XP | |

## T-1A JAYHAWK

| C/n | Identities | | | |
|---|---|---|---|---|
| TT-1 | N2886B | 91-0077 | | |
| TT-2 | N2887B | 90-0412 | N2887B | 90-0412 |
| TT-3 | N2892B | 90-0400 | | |
| TT-4 | 90-0405 | | | |
| TT-5 | N2876B | 89-0284 | | |
| TT-6 | N2872B | 90-0404 | | |
| TT-7 | N2896B | 90-0401 | | |
| TT-8 | N2868B | 90-0402 | | |
| TT-9 | 90-0403 | | | |
| TT-10 | 90-0407 | | | |
| TT-11 | 90-0406 | | | |
| TT-12 | 90-0408 | | | |
| TT-13 | 90-0409 | | | |
| TT-14 | 90-0410 | | | |
| TT-15 | 90-0411 | | | |
| TT-16 | 90-0413 | | | |
| TT-17 | 91-0076 | | | |
| TT-18 | 91-0075 | | | |
| TT-19 | 91-0078 | | | |
| TT-20 | 91-0079 | | | |
| TT-21 | 91-0080 | | | |
| TT-22 | 91-0081 | | | |
| TT-23 | 91-0082 | | | |
| TT-24 | 91-0083 | | | |
| TT-25 | 91-0084 | | | |
| TT-26 | 91-0085 | | | |
| TT-27 | 91-0086 | | | |
| TT-28 | 91-0087 | | | |
| TT-29 | 91-0088 | | | |
| TT-30 | 91-0089 | | | |
| TT-31 | 91-0090 | | | |
| TT-32 | 91-0091 | | | |
| TT-33 | 91-0092 | | | |
| TT-34 | 91-0093 | [damaged 16Aug03 at Kessler AFB, MS; moved 10Mar05 to Aeronautical Systems Center, Wright Patterson AFB] | | |
| TT-35 | 91-0094 | | | |
| TT-36 | 91-0095 | | | |
| TT-37 | 91-0096 | | | |
| TT-38 | 91-0097 | | | |
| TT-39 | 91-0098 | | | |
| TT-40 | 91-0099 | | | |
| TT-41 | 91-0100 | | | |
| TT-42 | 91-0101 | | | |
| TT-43 | 91-0102 | | | |
| TT-44 | 92-0330 | | | |
| TT-45 | 92-0331 | | | |
| TT-46 | 92-0332 | | | |
| TT-47 | 92-0333 | | | |
| TT-48 | 92-0334 | | | |
| TT-49 | 92-0335 | | | |

## JAYHAWK

| C/n | Identities | |
|---|---|---|
| TT-50 | 92-0336 | |
| TT-51 | 92-0337 | |
| TT-52 | 92-0338 | |
| TT-53 | 92-0339 | |
| TT-54 | 92-0340 | |
| TT-55 | 92-0341 | |
| TT-56 | 92-0342 | |
| TT-57 | 92-0343 | |
| TT-58 | 92-0344 | |
| TT-59 | 92-0345 | |
| TT-60 | 92-0346 | |
| TT-61 | 92-0347 | |
| TT-62 | 92-0348 | |
| TT-63 | 92-0349 | |
| TT-64 | 92-0350 | |
| TT-65 | 92-0351 | |
| TT-66 | 92-0352 | |
| TT-67 | 92-0353 | |
| TT-68 | 92-0354 | |
| TT-69 | 92-0355 | |
| TT-70 | 92-0356 | |
| TT-71 | 92-0357 | |
| TT-72 | 92-0358 | |
| TT-73 | 92-0359 | |
| TT-74 | 92-0360 | |
| TT-75 | 92-0361 | |
| TT-76 | 92-0362 | |
| TT-77 | 92-0363 | |
| TT-78 | 93-0621 | |
| TT-79 | 93-0622 | |
| TT-80 | 93-0623 | |
| TT-81 | 93-0624 | |
| TT-82 | N2830B | 93-0625 |
| TT-83 | 93-0626 | |
| TT-84 | 93-0627 | |
| TT-85 | 93-0628 | |
| TT-86 | 93-0629 | |
| TT-87 | 93-0630 | |
| TT-88 | 93-0631 | |
| TT-89 | 93-0632 | |
| TT-90 | 93-0633 | |
| TT-91 | 93-0634 | |
| TT-92 | 93-0635 | |
| TT-93 | 93-0636 | |
| TT-94 | 93-0637 | |
| TT-95 | 93-0638 | |
| TT-96 | 93-0639 | |
| TT-97 | 93-0640 | |
| TT-98 | 93-0641 | |
| TT-99 | 93-0642 | |
| TT-100 | 93-0643 | |
| TT-101 | 93-0644 | |
| TT-102 | 93-0645 | |
| TT-103 | 93-0646 | |
| TT-104 | 93-0647 | |
| TT-105 | 93-0648 | |
| TT-106 | 93-0649 | |
| TT-107 | 93-0650 | |
| TT-108 | 93-0651 | |
| TT-109 | 93-0652 | |
| TT-110 | 93-0653 | |
| TT-111 | 93-0654 | |
| TT-112 | 93-0655 | |
| TT-113 | 93-0656 | |
| TT-114 | 94-0114 | |
| TT-115 | 94-0115 | |
| TT-116 | 94-0116 | |
| TT-117 | 94-0117 | |
| TT-118 | 94-0118 | |
| TT-119 | 94-0119 | |
| TT-120 | 94-0120 | |
| TT-121 | 94-0121 | |
| TT-122 | 94-0122 | |
| TT-123 | 94-0123 | |
| TT-124 | 94-0124 | |

## JAYHAWK

| C/n | Identities |
|---|---|
| TT-125 | 94-0125 |
| TT-126 | 94-0126 |
| TT-127 | 94-0127 |
| TT-128 | 94-0128 |
| TT-129 | 94-0129 |
| TT-130 | 94-0130 |
| TT-131 | 94-0131 |
| TT-132 | 94-0132 |
| TT-133 | 94-0133 |
| TT-134 | 94-0134 |
| TT-135 | 94-0135 |
| TT-136 | 94-0136 |
| TT-137 | 94-0137 |
| TT-138 | 94-0138 |
| TT-139 | 94-0139 |
| TT-140 | 94-0140 |
| TT-141 | 94-0141 |
| TT-142 | 94-0142 |
| TT-143 | 94-0143 |
| TT-144 | 94-0144 |
| TT-145 | 94-0145 |
| TT-146 | 94-0146 |
| TT-147 | 94-0147 |
| TT-148 | 94-0148 |
| TT-149 | 95-0040 |
| TT-150 | 95-0041 |
| TT-151 | 95-0042 |
| TT-152 | 95-0043 |
| TT-153 | 95-0044 |
| TT-154 | 95-0045 |
| TT-155 | 95-0046 |
| TT-156 | 95-0047 |
| TT-157 | 95-0048 |
| TT-158 | 95-0049 |
| TT-159 | 95-0050 |
| TT-160 | 95-0051 |
| TT-161 | 95-0052 |
| TT-162 | 95-0053 |
| TT-163 | 95-0054 |
| TT-164 | 95-0055 |
| TT-165 | 95-0056 |
| TT-166 | 95-0057 |
| TT-167 | 95-0058 |
| TT-168 | 95-0059 |
| TT-169 | 95-0060 |
| TT-170 | 95-0061 |
| TT-171 | 95-0062 |
| TT-172 | 95-0063 |
| TT-173 | 95-0064 |
| TT-174 | 95-0065 |
| TT-175 | 95-0066 |
| TT-176 | 95-0067 |
| TT-177 | 95-0068 |
| TT-178 | 95-0069 |
| TT-179 | 95-0070 |
| TT-180 | 95-0071 |

## T400 JAYHAWK

| C/n | Identities | | | |
|---|---|---|---|---|
| TX-1 | N82884 | Japan 41-5051 | [code 051] | |
| TX-2 | N82885 | Japan 41-5052 | [code 052] | |
| TX-3 | N82886 | Japan 41-5053 | [code 053] | |
| TX-4 | N3195K | Japan 41-5054 | [code 054] | |
| TX-5 | N3195Q | Japan 41-5055 | [code 055] | |
| TX-6 | N3195X | Japan 51-5056 | [code 056] | |
| TX-7 | N3228M | Japan 51-5057 | [code 057] | |
| TX-8 | N3228V | Japan 51-5058 | [code 058] | |
| TX-9 | N1069L | Japan 71-5059 | [code 059] | |
| TX-10 | "N3221Z" | N32212 | Japan 91-5060 | [code 060] |
| TX-11 | N50561 | Japan 21-5061 | [code 061] | |
| TX-12 | N50512 | Japan 21-5062 | [code 062] | |
| TX-13 | N50543 | Japan 41-5063 | [code 063] | |

# BRITISH AEROSPACE (RAYTHEON) 125 SERIES

The majority of the series 3, 400 and 700 aircraft which were exported to North America were allocated an additional number in the NA... range, and these numbers are quoted as the c/n. This practice was reintroduced on production 800 and 1000 series aircraft but has since ceased. The production list is in the normal c/n order, and a cross-reference of the two sets of numbers follows the production list.

Early-build aircraft were known as DH125s and then HS125s and subsequently BAe125s. 800 series aircraft above c/n 258208 and 1000 series aircraft above c/n 259024 are known by the nomenclature Corporate Jets BAe125. Following the sale of Corporate Jets by BAe to Raytheon, owner of Beechcraft, yet another nomenclature change took place to Hawker 800 (at c/n 258255) and Hawker 1000 (at c/n 259043).

Only the first use of the UK class B marks are given from G-5-501 onwards as these are only used (and re-used!) by one aircraft.

| C/n | Series | Identities |
|---|---|---|
| 25001 | 1 | G-ARYA [ff 13Aug62; CofA exp 01Oct65; wfu Kelsterton College, UK. Small remains (the cockpit section) to Mosquito Museum, London Colney UK Feb04] |
| 25002 | 1 | G-ARYB [CofA exp 22Jan68; wfu BAe Hatfield, UK; cx 04Mar69 - Midland Air Museum, Coventry, UK] |
| 25003 | 1 | G-ARYC [CofA exp 01Aug73; wfu Mosquito Museum, London Colney, UK] |
| 25004 | 1/521 | G-ASEC G-FIVE [wfu by Jun83; cx 14May85, used for spares - wings to c/n 25008] |
| 25005 | 1 | G-ASNU (D-CFKG) D-COMA G-ASNU [wfu by Dec82; impounded Lagos, Nigeria; cx 18Nov91] |
| 25006 | 1 | HB-VAG I-RACE [CofA exp Nov87; wfu] |
| 25007 | 1 | (G-ASSH) HB-VAH G-ASTY HB-VAH F-BKMF [w/o 05Jun66 Nice, France] |
| 25008 | 1 | G-ASSI 5N-AWD [wfu by Dec83, Luton, UK; to Staggenhoe Farm, Whitewell, Beds UK for use by emergency services in crash exercises 10Sep98] |
| 25009 | 1 | G-ATPC XW930 [wfu, scrapped Jordan's scrapyard, Portsmouth, UK by Jun97] |
| 25010 | 1/522 | G-ASSM 5N-AMK [wfu by Dec83; to Science Museum, Kensington, London, UK, painted as G-ASSM] |
| 25011 | T1 | G-37-65 XS709 [code M] |
| 25012 | T1 | XS710 [code O] 9259M [stored RAF Cosford, UK circa 1997] |
| 25013 | 1A | G-ASSJ N125J N2426 N7125J N4646S N88MR [wfu prior to Jun82; remains to White Industries, Bates City, MO] |
| 25014 | 1A/522 | G-ASSK N125G N734AK N621ST (N125WC) XA-JUZ N621ST [wfu by Dec82; b/u 1985] |
| 25015 | 3B | VH-CAO (9M-AYI) VH-CAO (N750D) [Australian marks cx May91 stripped of re-usable parts by Dodson Int'l Parts Inc during 1998. Fuselage to Australian Air Museum at Sydney-Bankstown, moved to The Oaks, South West of Sydney, NSW by Jun05 to join c/n 25062 reportedly to restore one of the two to flying condition] |
| 25016 | 1A | G-ASSL CF-RWA CF-OPC C-FOPC C6-BPC N4997E N222NG |
| 25017 | 1A/522 | G-ASSH N3060 N3060F N306MP N123JB N495G N333M XA-RSR [wfu at Fort Lauderdale Executive, FL] |
| 25018 | 731 | CF-DOM C-FDOM N125LM C-GXPT N125PT N118TS N218TJ (P4-ZAW) [cx Oct05, wfu at Toluca, Mexico] |
| 25019 | 1A | G-ASYX N1125G N1135K [w/o 25Feb66 Des Moines, IA] |
| 25020 | 731 | G-ASZM N167J N959KW N2KW N2KN N365DJ N711WM (N128TJ) N55RF [parted out following landing accident Seattle, WA Dec02; cx Aug 03] |
| 25021 | 1A/522 | G-ASZN N575DU N2504 N228G N228GL N125BT N125KC N711WJ N300HW [wfu; parted out by White Inds, Bates City, MO] |
| 25022 | 1A/522 | G-ASZO CF-SDA N505PA N100GB N50HH [w/o 02Aug86 Bedford, IN] |
| 25023 | 731 | G-ASZP N1125 N338 (N125BW) N125BM N58BT N284DB N584DB N62TJ (N89FF) ZS-PJE ZS-TBN |
| 25024 | T1 | XS711 [code L] |
| 25025 | 1B | D-COME HB-VAR F-BOHU (F-OCGK) 5N-AWB [wfu by early 87] |
| 25026 | 1A | G-5-11 G-ATAY N225KJ N225K N225LL N4400E (N40AD) [wfu by Apr86; used for spares early 86] |
| 25027 | 1A | CF-SEN C-FSEN N227DH N125BH N777RN |
| 25028 | 1B | Ghana G.511 (N48172) C-GLFI N48172 N50SS XA-ESQ N29977 [w/o 14Dec81 as XA-ESQ and parted out; last allocated US marks, N29977, were not worn; cx Apr91; remains to White Industries, Bates City, MO] |
| 25029 | 1A/522 | G-ATAZ N10122 N391DA N10D [wfu Mar04 Tulsa/Jones Field, OK; parted out by White Inds, Bates City, MO; cx 29Apr09] |
| 25030 | 1A | G-ATBA N413GH N123VM (N97VM) XB-MBM XA-MBM XA-RDD [preserved at Saltillo, Mexico] |
| 25031 | 1A | G-ATBB N1923M N43WJ N79AE N105HS [wfu circa Oct05 Oklahoma City, OK] |
| 25032 | 731 | G-ATBC N65MK (N657K) N90WP N692FC N98TJ N942DS (N16GG) |
| 25033 | 1A/522 | G-ATBD N125G N1125G N111AG N111AD (N111AX) (N700AB) N63BL (N32HE) N125LC N125AL N125LL RP-C125 |
| 25034 | 1A | CF-HLL C-FHLL [wfu Quebec City by Jun83; possibly following accident 18Apr83 at Gashe, PQ, Canada; fuselage noted at Montreal-St.Hubert Oct95; wings used on c/n 25027; cx Dec90] |
| 25035 | 1A | G-ATCO N1515P N1515E N151SG (N57TS) |
| 25036 | 1A | CF-PQG C-FPQG N136DH [cx Jul95 as destroyed/scrapped] |

# BAe 125

| C/n | Series | Identities |
|---|---|---|
| 25037 | 1A | G-ATFO D-CAFI N787X N26T N26TL (N26WJ) (N389DA) [b/u for spares; cx Jul92] |
| 25038 | 731 | G-ATCP N926G N125G (N900KC) N66KC (N15UB) N27RC N301CK (N417TF) (N28MM) N28M N42CK N806CB |
| 25039 | 1A | CF-SIM C-FSIM N125TB N911AS [wfu to Sanford, FL; b/u & cx Sep03] |
| 25040 | T1 | XS712 [code A] |
| 25041 | T1 | XS713 [code C] |
| 25042 | 731 | CF-ANL C-FANL N79TS (N42FD) N725WH [Jul04 to White Industries Bates City, MO for parts use; cx 25Oct07] |
| 25043 | 1A/522 | G-ATGA N125J N1230V N3007 N300R N70HB N522BW N522ME N65TS (N165AG) [to spares Rantoul, KS circa Jan01] |
| 25044 | T1 | XS726 [code T] 9273M [wfu RAF Cosford, UK circa 1997; to Everett Aero, Sproughton, UK, 2007] |
| 25045 | T1 | XS727 [code D] |
| 25046 | 1A/S-522 | G-ATGS N48UC N4886 N125P N666AE N812TT N125AD LV-YGC |
| 25047 | 1A/522 | G-ATGT N778SM N580WS N75CT N800DA (N717GF) |
| 25048 | T1 | XS728 [code E] |
| 25049 | T1 | XS729 [code G] 9275M [wfu 1996; stored RAF Cosford, UK; to Everett Aero, Sproughton, UK, 2007] |
| 25050 | T1 | XS730 [code H] |
| 25051 | 731 | G-ATGU N9300 N9300C N125HD C6-BEY N77VK [wfu 18Dec85; cx Jan87, used for spares] |
| 25052 | 1A/522 | G-ATIK N816M N816MC N812M N812N N388WM N125JR (N252MA) [impounded Jun01 Toluca, Mexico; still present Mar06] |
| 25053 | 1A/522 | CF-IPG CF-IPJ C-FIPJ N4465N N125TB N254JT N250JT N25JT [cx 30Sep04, wfu at Monterrey/del Norte, Mexico] |
| 25054 | TI | XS714 [code P] 9246M [wfu; to RAF Manston, UK for fire training use] |
| 25055 | T1 | XS731 [code J] |
| 25056 | T1 | XS732 [code B] [wfu Jan91 due to fuselage corrosion; fuselage to Research Establishment, Fort Halstead, Kent, UK 27Mar91; TT 11,955.20, TL 9,067] |
| 25057 | 1A/522 | G-ATIL N188K N125AW [cx 02Apr86; b/u for spares Pontiac, MI] |
| 25058 | 1A | D-COMI N9308Y N215G N470R N632PB N632PE (EC-...) [used for spares; canx Nov05 as b/u] |
| 25059 | T1 | XS733 [code Q] 9276M [wfu 1996; stored RAF Cosford, UK; to Everett Aero, Sproughton, UK, 2007] |
| 25060 | 1A/522 | G-ATIM N2601 N26011 N2728 N22DL N22DE XB-FIS XB-EAL XA-BOJ XA-HOU XB-CXZ N96SG [cx 25Aug09, parted out] |
| 25061 | T1 | XS734 [code N] 9260M [stored RAF Cosford, UK circa 1997; to Everett Aero Sproughton, UK, 2007] |
| 25062 | 3B | VH-ECE [wfu 21Jul81; to Camden Airport Museum, NSW; TT 13936, TL 53882; derelict at The Oaks, NSW by May97] |
| 25063 | 1B | HB-VAN G-BAXG G-ONPN 5N-ASZ [wfu 03Jun86 Southampton, UK; used for spares] |
| 25064 | 1A/522 | G-ATKK N230H N125JG N33BK N222G XA-RYW N222G XB-GGK XA-TAL [w/o 09Jul99 Toluca A/P, Mexico] |
| 25065 | 1A/522 | G-ATKL N631SC N631SQ N1YE XA-KOF |
| 25066 | 731 | G-ATKM N925CT N369JB (N374DH) N373DH (XA-...) N372RS XA-UEX |
| 25067 | 1B/522 | 9J-RAN ZS-MAN 9J-SAS 9J-EPK Z-TBX ZS-MAN |
| 25068 | 1A/522 | XB-BEA XA-BEM XB-VUI XA-MIR XB-SBC [reported Oct89 with dual marks XA-MIR/XB-SBC] N5274U [to Dodson Avn for spares use at Rantoul, KS] |
| 25069 | 3B | VH-ECF G-BAXL G-OBOB [w/o 31Jan90 Concordia, MO; remains to White Industries, Bates City, MO] |
| 25070 | 1A/522 | G-ATKN N520M N214JR N2148R N84W N51V N470TS N333GZ [parted out by White Inds, Bates City, MO; cx 29Apr09] |
| 25071 | T1 | XS735 [code R] [wfu; ground instructional airframe at RAF St Athan, UK May02] |
| 25072 | T1 | XS736 [code S] [parted out RAF Cranwell, UK; remains to Everett Aero, Sproughton, UK, 2007] |
| 25073 | 1A/522 | G-ATLI N372CM N372GM N36MK [w/o 28Dec70 Boise, ID] |
| 25074 | 1A/522 | G-ATOV N400NW N400UW N300GB N411FB |
| 25075 | 731 | G-ATLJ N666M CF-MDB C-FMDB N9124N N750GM N731BW N600EG XB-GAM |
| 25076 | T1 | XS737 [code K] |
| 25077 | T1 | XS738 [code U] 9274M [stored RAF Cosford, UK circa 1997; to RNAS Predannack fire training area by 2007] |
| 25078 | 1A/522 | G-ATLK N40DC N448DC N125NT (N770BC) (N16PJ) XA-DCS |
| 25079 | 731 | G-ATLL N440DC N448DC N40DC N425DC N425FD N79TJ N425FD N942Y N942WN P4-AOC N963YA |
| 25080 | 1A/522 | VQ-ZIL 3D-AAB G-BDYE EI-BGW C-GLEO N23KL EC-EGT [wfu Jan93 with Dodson Avn, Ottawa, KS] |
| 25081 | T1 | XS739 [code F] |
| 25082 | 1A/522 | G-ATNM N909B N2125 N125CA N1MY N17SL [wfu; cx Dec92; remains to White Industries, Bates City, MO] |
| 25083 | 1A/522 | G-ATOW N16777 N435T N437T N533 N538 N50AS [wfu for spares 1988 by OK Aircraft, Gilroy, CA; cx Sep92] |

# BAe 125

| C/n | Series | Identities |
|---|---|---|
| 25084 | 1A/522 | G-ATNN N1125G N453CM N154TR N30EF N784AE (N745HG) N71BL N890RC N888CJ |
| 25085 | 1B/522 | G-ATPD 5N-AGU G-ATPD [wfu circa Sep00 at Bournemouth A/P, UK, to fire training mid 2002; cx Dec03] |
| 25086 | 1A/522 | CF-DSC N3699T XA-COL [w/o 11Oct73 Acapulco, Mexico] |
| 25087 | 731/S | G-ATOX CF-ALC C-FALC N66AM N330G |
| 25088 | 1A/522 | G-ATNO N1230B 5B-... |
| 25089 | 1B/522 | G-ATPB OO-SKJ 5N-ALH |
| 25090 | 1B/S522 | HB-VAT G-AWYE N102TW N429DA |
| 25091 | 1A/522 | G-ATNP N1230G N20RG N90RG N65FC XA-RSP [wfu at Fort Lauderdale Executive, FL] |
| 25092 | 1B/522 | G-ATPE [CofA exp 01Apr87; to Southampton Airport Fire Svce 1989; canx 14Mar90] |
| 25093 | 1A/522 | G-ATSN N77D N306L N3MF [w/o 26Jan79 Taos NM] |
| 25094 | 1B/R522 | G-ATWH HZ-BO1 G-ATWH G-YUGO [cx 29Mar93 as wfu; remains to Biggin Hill, UK circa 2000 for fire training] |
| 25095 | 1A/522 | G-ATSO N125Y CF-SHZ N1923G N5001G (N5012P) N80CC N61BL N25AW N831LC [w/o 16Mar91 nr San Diego, CA] |
| 25096 | 1A/522 | G-ATNR N235KC [w/o 21Nov66 Grand Bahama, Bahamas] |
| 25097 | 1A/S522 | G-ATSP LN-NPE N125V N12KW N21MF N89HB N67TS [a/c broken up; cx Jan02] |
| 25098 | 731 | G-ATNS N10121 N666SC N57G N11AR N45SL N926LR N29CR YV-815CP (N77LJ) YV2416 |
| 25099 | 1B/522 | HB-VAU 5N-AER (N2246) (N121AC) [wfu; located at aircraft trades school Zaira, Nigeria] |
| 25100 | 1A/522 | G-ATNT N125J N952B N7SZ N104 N44TG N44TQ N6SS |
| 25101 | 731/S | G-5-11 G-ATXE N142B N124BM XA-RCH XA-RUX N251LA N78AG XA-MBM |
| 25102 | 1A/522 | G-ATUU N756 N756M XB-AKW N3274Q [to spares Houston, TX circa 1995 (cx Feb96) reported marks N3274Q were never carried] |
| 25103 | 1A/522 | G-ATUV N533 N210M (N700UU) N601UU N60HU N402AC |
| 25104 | 1A/522 | G-ATUW N257H N140AK C-FMTC [derelict Nov97 Vancouver, Canada; hulk removed to Lakeland, FL circa Mar00] |
| 25105 | 1B/522 | (D-CKOW) D-CKCF G-AYRY HZ-FMA [reported wfu] |
| 25106 | 1B/522 | HZ-BIN G-AWUF 5N-ALY G-AWUF G-DJMJ G-OMCA G-BOCB [wfu 1994 Luton, UK; cx 22Feb95; cockpit to Sth.Yorks Aircraft Museum, Doncaster, UK] |
| 25107 | 1A/522 | G-ATUX N7125J N2426 C-GFCL N107BW N694JC XA-GOC XA-HFM XA-UBK |
| 25108 | 731 | G-ATUY N1025C N901TC N901TG N31B C-FTAM N11QD N25LA C-GTTS N46190 [wfu circa Sep04 parted out by White Industries, Bates City, MO Jly05 still wearing C-GTTS] |
| 25109 | 1A/S522 | G-ATUZ N201H N4CR |
| 25110 | 1A/522 | G-5-11 G-ATZE N3125B N125E [w/o 30Jun83 Houston Hobby, TX] |
| 25111 | 3A | G-ATYH N1041B N125GC C-GKRL N31AS N177GP N900CD [w/o 30May94 Waukegan Regional A/P, Waukegan, IL; remains to White Industries, Bates City, MO] |
| 25112 | 3A | G-ATYI N2525 N252V XB-AXP XA-LFU XB-FFV XA-SLR |
| 25113 | 3B/RA | G-5-13 G-AVDX 5N-AVZ [noted semi-derelict Dec96 Lagos, Nigeria] |
| 25114 | 3A | G-ATYJ N425K N44K N44KG N78RZ N25PM XA-SGP N114WD |
| 25115 | 731 | G-ATYK N229P N333ME N333MF N317EM N111DT N180ML N21GN N429AC (N750WC) N249BW N249MW N420JC N48DD [w/o 09Mar01 Bridgeport, CT] |
| 25116 | 3A | G-ATZN N93TC N136LK N345DA (N90SR) N345CT N726CC SX-BSS [wfu at Thessalonkia, Greece circa Jul01] |
| 25117 | 3B | 5N-AET 5N-AKT G-BSAA G-DBAL [cx 16Apr93; wfu] |
| 25118 | 731 | G-ATYL N743UT N45PM N731KC N300KC N227HF N14HH N118DA |
| 25119 | 731 | G-5-11 G-AVAD N213H N500XY |
| 25120 | 3B | G-AVGW [w/o 23Dec67 Luton, UK] |
| 25121 | 731 | G-AVAE N795J N307G N807G N200PB N200PF XA-SKZ XB-GHC N125TJ N125LK N685FF [parted out Spirit of St Louis a/p, MO; cx 15Sep07] |
| 25122 | 3A | G-AVAF N12225 N555CB N255CB (N123AG) N123AC [parted out 1992 San Jose, CA; remains to OK Aircraft, Gilroy, CA; cx Nov01] |
| 25123 | 3A | G-AVAG N700M N706M N77C N77CD N46TG N44PW N125FD [parted out by Dodson Int'l, Rantoul, KS circa Oct01] |
| 25124 | 3A | G-AVAH N125J N552N N912AS [wfu to Titusville/Cocoa Beach, FL] |
| 25125 | F3B | G-AVAI LN-NPA G-AVAI F-GFMP 5N-AAN (EL-AMJ) (EL-ELS) [to instructional airframe at Newcastle Aviation Academy, Newcastle UK] |
| 25126 | 3B | G-5-11 G-AVDL N510X N66HA [w/o 13Aug89 Houston, TX - remains to Aviation Warehouse film prop company warehouse at El Mirage, CA] |
| 25127 | F3B | G-AVPE G-5-623 G-KASS N125GK [w/o at Barcelona, Venezuela, 26Jun06] |
| 25128 | 3B | G-AVOI F-GECR ZS-SMT [wfu at Lanseria, South Africa] |
| 25129 | 3A | G-5-12 G-AVDM N521M [w/o 12Dec72 Findlay, OH] |
| 25130 | 3B | G-5-14 G-AVRD HB-VAZ F-BSIM TR-LXO F-BSIM TR-LFB |
| 25131 | 3B | G-5-11 G-AVRE F-BPMC G-FOUR I-RASO F-GFDB 3A-MDB F-GJDE 3A-MDE 7T-VVL |
| 25132 | 3B | OY-DKP G-AZVS G-MRFB G-OCBA EI-WDC G-OCBA EI-WDC G-OCBA S9-PDH |

# BAe 125

| C/n | | Series | Identities |
|---|---|---|---|
| 25133 | | 3B | G-AVRF G-ILLS VT-EQZ |
| 25134 | NA700 | 3A/RA | G-5-11 G-AVHA N514V N514VA N338 N366MP N366BR N117TS N725DW N946FS N230TS [to Dodson International Parts May05] |
| 25135 | | 3B | G-5-14 HB-VAY G-AXPS [w/o 20Jul70 Edinburgh, UK] |
| 25136 | NA701 | 3A/RA | G-AVHB N501W N506N N505W N605W N700RG N700RD N700RG N125HS Brazil VU93-2113 |
| 25137 | NA702 | 3A/RA | G-5-11 G-AVJD CF-AAG CF-KCI C-FKCI N13MJ N813PR C-GMEA [parted out Arnoni Avn, Houston, TX circa Sep00; cx Aug99] |
| 25138 | | 3B | (G-5-12) G-5-16 G-AVVA HB-VBN I-BOGI 5N-AVV |
| 25139 | NA703 | 3A/RA | G-5-11 G-AVOJ N612G N2G N22GE N140JS XB-JLY |
| 25140 | | 3B/RA | (G-5-16) G-5-17 G-AVVB G-DJLW C6-MED N140LF [parted out by Dodson International Parts, Rantoul, KS] |
| 25141 | NA704 | 3A/RA | G-5-12 G-AVOK N75C N55G N208H N14GD N14GQ (N90WP) N888WK C-GSKV N132RL [parted out by White Inds, Bates City, MO; cx 29Apr09] |
| 25142 | NA705 | 731 | G-AVOL N7055 N9040 N688CC N9040 N744CC N7440C N822CC N770DA (N60AM) N25MJ N705EA [parted out by White Inds, Bates City, MO; cx 29Apr09] |
| 25143 | | 3B/RA | G-5-18 G-AVXK D-CHTH G-AVXK 5N-AOG [wfu before Jun93; b/u for spares Hurn, UK] |
| 25144 | | 3B/RA | G-5-12 G-AVRG G-OHEA [cx Jun94; wfu to Cranfield Inst of Technology, Cranfield, UK, as instructional airframe] |
| 25145 | | 3B | G-5-20 G-AVXL LN-NPC G-AVXL I-SNAF [CofA exp 1983; derelict 1989 Milan-Linate; cx 1990] |
| 25146 | NA706 | 3A/RA | G-AVRH N77617 N214JR N214TC N711SW N214TC N114PC N21AR N999SA (N899SA) N777GA XA-ADR XB-JKG |
| 25147 | | 3B/RA | G-5-14 PK-PJR PK-DJW [CofA expired 20Oct86; wfu derelict near Jakarta - Halim Airport, Indonesia circa 99] |
| 25148 | | 3A/R | G-5-13 G-AVRI N8125J N450JD (N100TT) XB-ERN N814P (N819P) XA-TTH |
| 25149 | | 3A/R | G-AVRJ N1125E N99SC N99GC N99KR [wfu 09Sep80; donated to Northrop University nr Los Angeles A/P, CA; cx Apr91; moved 1998 to Malaysian Institute of Aviation Technology, Dengkil nr Kuala Lumpur, painted as N1125E] |
| 25150 | | F3A | G-5-13 G-AWMS N511BX VR-BKY VP-BKY N42AS |
| 25151 | | 3A/RA | G-AVTY N125F [wfu at Lima, Peru, circa 1997; fuselage to Collique, Peru, by Feb07] |
| 25152 | | 3A/RA | G-AVTZ CF-QNS C-FQNS N45793 N123RZ XA-IIT N28686 N50MJ N23CJ |
| 25153 | | 731 | G-5-19 G-AVXM N30F N30FD N731G N336MB N676PC N88DJ N88DU |
| 25154 | | 3B/RA | G-5-11 EP-AHK G-AZCH [b/u Luton, UK Dec82 due to corrosion; TT 4261, TL 4695, CofA exp 16Aug81; rear fuselage/fin used on c/n 25270] |
| 25155 | | 3A/RA | G-AVXN N32F N466MP (N411MF) N999LF N333CJ N77BT N158AG [still painted as N77BT circa Dec00; wfu to Titusville/Cocoa Beach, FL; b/u, cx Sep03] |
| 25156 | | 3A/RA | G-AVZJ N522M N10LN [b/u 1993 Lakeland, FL; fuselage remains only] |
| 25157 | | 3B/RA | D-CAMB VR-BGD G-GGAE G-JSAX [wfu Dec82; cx 10Jan86 - at Eastleigh, UK minus outer wings] |
| 25158 | | 3A/RA | G-AVZK XB-PUE (N702GA) XA-DAN |
| 25159 | | 731 | G-5-19 G-AVZL CF-WOS C-FWOS N4767M N511WM N511WN N67TJ N600SV ZS-CNA |
| 25160 | NA707 | 3A/RA | G-5-15 G-AWKH N350NC N873D N873G N627CR SE-DHH N160AG |
| 25161 | NA708 | 3A/RA | G-AWKI N9149 N756N N75GN XA-RPT |
| 25162 | | 3B/RC | Brazil VC93-2120 Brazil VU93-2120 |
| 25163 | NA709 | 731 | G-5-16 G-AWMV N208H N55G (N2G) |
| 25164 | | 3B/RC | Brazil EC93-2125 Brazil EU93-2125 |
| 25165 | | 3B/RC | Brazil VC93-2121 Brazil EU93-2121 [wfu] |
| 25166 | | 3B/RC | Brazil VC93-2122 [w/o 19Jun79 Brasilia, Brazil] |
| 25167 | | 3B/RC | Brazil VC93-2123 Brazil VU93-2123 |
| 25168 | | 3B/RC | Brazil VC93-2124 Brazil VU93-2124 [wfu] |
| 25169 | | 3A/RA | G-5-17 G-AWWL VH-BBJ N3AL G-AWWL N84TF (N9300P) N9300C N99SC (N711SC) N122AW N163AG [cx 24Jul08, b/u] |
| 25170 | NA710 | 3A/RA | G-AWMW N1259K N226G N228G N223G C-GKCO N500YB C-FMKF N322TP N814ER N314ER (N767LC) |
| 25171 | | F3B/RA | G-5-19 HB-VBT G-AXPU G-IBIS G-AXPU G-BXPU (N171AV) G-OPOL G-IFTC (N171AV) D2-FEZ |
| 25172 | | F3B/RA | G-AXEG ZS-CAL G-AXEG ZS-CAL |
| 25173 | NA711 | 400A | G-AWMX N125J N3711L (N610HC) N711AQ N601JJ ZP-TDF ZP-TKO |
| 25174 | NA712 | 400A | G-AWMY N1199M N1199G N511WP N60JC N496G N7777B N712VS N713SS [parted out by White Inds, Bates City, MO circa Oct05] |
| 25175 | NA713 | 731 | G-AWPC N217F YV-825CP N272B N773AA XA-... |
| 25176 | NA714 | 731 | G-AWPD CF-NER C-FNER N176TS N311JA N811JA N31EP YV.... |
| 25177 | | 400B | G-AWXN S Africa 02 [w/o 26May71 Devils Peak, S Africa] |
| 25178 | | 400B | G-AWXO 5N-BUA G-OOSP 5N-WMA |
| 25179 | NA715 | 731 | G-AWPE N778S N200CC N400CC N800CB N800QB N22EH N629P N824TJ N284DB XA-... |

# BAe 125

| C/n | | Series | Identities |
|---|---|---|---|
| 25180 | NA716 | 400A | G-AWPF N196KC N196KQ N888CR N400PH [w/o 05Dec87 Blue Grass Field, Lexington, KY] |
| 25181 | | 400B | (G-5-13) G-AXLU S Africa 01 [w/o 26May71 Devils Peak, S Africa] |
| 25182 | | 400B | G-AXLV S Africa 03 [w/o 26May71 Devils Peak, S Africa] |
| 25183 | NA717 | 731 | G-5-18 G-AWXB N162A N162D N100HF N984HF [w/o 07Nov85 Sparta, TN] |
| 25184 | | 400B | G-AXLW S Africa 04 ZS-LPE [wfs - stored at Waterkloof AFB, South Africa] |
| 25185 | NA720 | 400A | G-AWXE N140C N4PN N7LG XA-GUB XB-DSQ XA-RMN XB-FRP XA-FRP XB-MSV |
| 25186 | NA721 | 731 | G-AWXF N125G N93BH N933 N40SK N666JT N668JT (N105EJ) N99CK HR-AMD N12YS (N999NM) N186NM N777GD N43TS |
| 25187 | NA718 | 731 | G-AWXC N600L N600LP N600JA N900DS (N7WG) N16WG N50SL N141JL XA-SSV N250DH |
| 25188 | NA719 | 731 | G-AWXD N545S XB-IPX |
| 25189 | | 400B | G-5-20 (G-AXFY) Malaysia FM1200 FM1801 M24-01 [wfu, to technical school at Alor Setar, Malaysia, wearing fake marks M24-02] |
| 25190 | NA722 | 400A | G-AXDO N1393 N75CS N75QS N75TJ N51MN N209NC N38TS (N280CH) XB-ILD [impounded at Portoviejo, Ecuador, Oct03 for drug-running] |
| 25191 | NA723 | 731 | G-AXDP N511YP N900KC N100T N723TS N401JR N444HH YV-1145CP YV1687 |
| 25192 | NA724 | 731 | CF-SDH C-FSDH N724TS |
| 25193 | NA725 | 400A | CF-CFL [w/o 11Nov69 Newfoundland, Canada] |
| 25194 | | 400B | G-AXDM [wfu & dismantled at Edinburgh, UK Sep03; to Farnborough, UK; cx as destroyed 13Nov03] |
| 25195 | NA726 | 731 | G-AXDR N111MB N949CW N949CV N60B N60BD N731G N31VT YV-141CP N922RR N922GK |
| 25196 | NA727 | 731 | G-AXDS N814M N114B N81RR N117RH N100RH XA-TNY |
| 25197 | | 400B | G-5-11 PP-EEM PT-LHK |
| 25198 | NA728 | 731 | G-AXJD N24CH N400KC N320JJ N410PA N32GM |
| 25199 | | 400B | G-AXLX HB-VBW G-AXLX (HB-VGU) HB-VBW N3118M (N905Y) [parted out 1994 by Dodson Avn, Ottawa, KS] |
| 25200 | NA729 | 400A | G-AXJE N702S N1C N702SS Brazil VU93-2118 |
| 25201 | NA730 | 731 | G-AXJF N220T N56BL N125MD N800JC N810MC N730TS N101HS N730TS N82CA |
| 25202 | NA731 | 400A | G-AXJG N65LT N700CC N300LD (N125DC) N31TJ (N700PG) (N600DP) XA-JRF N336AC XB-MAR XB-ASO^ |
| 25203 | NA732 | 400A | G-AXOA N500AG N73JH N44CN N21ES N100LR N109LR N2020 N70JC N732TS N400PR |
| 25204 | NA733 | 731 | G-AXOB N380X N31GT (N125RT) N243JB ZS-PLC |
| 25205 | NA734 | 731 | G-AXOC N125J N111RB N621L N621S N621B N99ST (N38TS) XA-GTC |
| 25206 | NA735 | 400A | G-AXPX VP-BDH N125AJ N400AG N11SQ XA-ROJ N165AG N800GE |
| 25207 | NA736 | 400A | G-AXOD N30PR N30PP N112M (N400HF) N800AF N736LE |
| 25208 | NA737 | 400A | G-AXOE N2500W N65EC N65DW (N165AG) N643JL N400KD XA-YSM [impounded for drug-running Valencia, Venezuela, Sep07] |
| 25209 | | 400B | Malaysia FM1201 FM1802 M24-02 [wfu, to Malaysian Institute of Aviation Technology, Dengkil nr Kuala Lumpur, Malaysia] |
| 25210 | NA738 | 400A | G-AXOF N702D Brazil VU93-2117 Brazil XU93-2117 [wfu at Guaratingueta, Brazil, by May05] |
| 25211 | NA739 | 731 | G-AXTR N125DH N820MC N820MG |
| 25212 | NA740 | 400A | G-AXTS N702P Brazil VU93-2114 [wfu 1998] |
| 25213 | NA741 | 400A | G-AXTT CF-CFL C-FCFL [w/o 09Dec77 Newfoundland, Canada] |
| 25214 | NA742 | 731 | G-AXTU N40PC N60PC N60QA G-AXTU G-5-20 N731HS N12BN N12AE N369CS N569CS (N87DC) N74RT N843B |
| 25215 | | 403B | HB-VBZ G-BHFT 9M-SSB G-BHFT Z-VEC ZS-NPV D2-EXR |
| 25216 | NA743 | 400A | G-AXTV N9138 XC-GOB Mexico TP0206 Mexico TP108/XC-UJH N125JW HP-125JW HP-1128P N400D HK-3653X HK-3653 N400LC XA-... |
| 25217 | | 403B | G-5-14 G-AXYJ 9Q-CGM 9Q-CHD G-5-651 G-BRXR G-OLFR 5N-EAS |
| 25218 | NA744 | 400A | G-AXTW N575DU N575 (N382DA) N711BP N440BC |
| 25219 | | F400A | G-5-14 G-AYEP 4W-ACA 9K-AEA G-5-12 N5594U N292GA (N292RC) N128DR N219EC RA-02805 N219EC (ZS-OZU) D2-FFH |
| 25220 | NA745 | 731 | G-AXYE N41BH N125AR N125AP N427DA N745TS N400XJ N700TR XA-... |
| 25221 | NA746 | 731 | N42BH CF-BNK C-FBNK N468LM N62CH N74WF N103RR ZS-OIF |
| 25222 | NA747 | 731 | G-AXYF N43BH N125EH N900EL N400FE N590CH N125NW P4-AOB N401AB |
| 25223 | | 403B | G-5-15 G-AYIZ PJ-SLB F-BSSL G-AYIZ G-TACE [cx 09Jan90; wfu] |
| 25224 | NA748 | 731 | G-AXYG N44BH N22DH N222RB N222RG N144PA N189B N199B N143CP N728KA N777SA YV-1111CP N748TS N601KK N748TS N62TW N77WD N748TS |
| 25225 | NA749 | 731 | G-AXYH N45BH N81T N119CC N583CM N100HF N100HE N45NC N45NQ (N45ND) SE-DVS N498R N498RS XB-KKS N498RS XB-KNH |
| 25226 | NA750 | 400A | G-AXYI N46BH N300P N304P XA-DIW XB-CCM N3933A N20RG N251AB XA-RWN N131LA |
| 25227 | | F403B | G-AYFM G-MKOA 5N-AMY N227MS N355AC XB-MYA |

# BAe 125

| C/n | | Series | Identities |
|---|---|---|---|
| 25228 | NA751 | 731 | N47BH N640M G-BCLR N640M G-BCLR N120GA N120GB N75RD N75RN N125GH N79B HC-BTT N400FR |
| 25229 | NA752 | 731 | N48BH N914BD N61MS N61MX N731HS N700PL N700FA N602JR N998PS* |
| 25230 | NA753 | 731 | N49BH N400BH N840H N345GL N145GL |
| 25231 | | 731 | D-CBVW G-BEME 5N-AQY G-BEME N125GC N707EZ N707SH (N125TJ) N832MR (N832MB) N831NW N831DF YV113T |
| 25232 | NA754 | 731 | CF-TEC C-FTEC C-GVQR N62TF N125VC N125EC N60RE N711HL N227LT |
| 25233 | NA755 | 400A | N50BH N711SD N755GW (N5MW) XB-AXP XB-LXP XB-AXP N755WJ (N871MA) ZS-MEG |
| 25234 | NA756 | 731 | N51BH N701Z N7NP N100MT C-GFCD N40Y N400JK N624PD |
| 25235 | | F403A | G-5-18 HB-VCE G-AYNR G-BKAJ G-5-19 N235AV N227LA N297JD N101UD N101UR N330AM |
| 25236 | NA757 | 731 | N52BH N125BH N10C N154 (N44BH) N999RW N499SC N50NE (N745WG) N900WG XA-AGL |
| 25237 | NA761 | 400A | N56BH N125BH N1924L N500MA N580MA XA-RIL N814D |
| 25238 | | F403B | G-AYER 9K-ACR G-AYER G-TOPF N125GC N808V VR-BKK VP-BKK G-36-1 VP-BKK |
| 25239 | NA758 | 731 | G-5-19 N53BH N6709 N731MS N800NP |
| 25240 | | 400B | G-5-11 G-AYLI I-GJBO VR-BKN VR-BMB [stripped of spares - to fire section at Stansted A/P, UK circa Apr99; b/u there Sep03 and remains removed] |
| 25241 | NA759 | 400A | G-5-20 N54BH N6702 N702M N702MA N810CR N127CM N125CF (N400MR) YV.... |
| 25242 | | 403B | G-5-20 VH-TOM G-BDKF 3D-ABZ ZS-LME [wfu stored at Waterkloof AFB, SA] |
| 25243 | | F400A | G-5-14 (G-AYOI) PT-DTY N243TS VP-CTS N4ES |
| 25244 | NA760 | 400A | G-5-12 N55BH N731X N70LY N456WH YV-.... |
| 25245 | NA762 | 731 | N57BH N523M N400GP N125DH |
| 25246 | | 403B | G-AYOJ 9Q-COH (G-5-16) G-AYOJ G-LORI [derelict Nigeria for many years; cx 21Apr93; wfu] |
| 25247 | | 403B | G-AYRR 9Q-CCF G-5-672 G-AYRR 9Q-CSN 9Q-CPR |
| 25248 | | F403B | D-CFCF G-5-707 G-BTUF G-SHOP (N792A) G-SHOP N792A G-TCDI N189RR YV-1122CP (N119GH) N189RR |
| 25249 | | 731 | G-5-16 G-AZAF N51993 N72HT N72HA N107AW N125KC N200KC N200VT N711VT N54JC N154JC (N303BX) N27UM |
| 25250 | | 731 | G-AYOK TR-LQU G-AYOK N20S N24S N300CC N300QC N125G N125HG (N125SJ) N7SJ N888TJ |
| 25251 | | 400B | Argentina 5-T-30/0653 LV-AXZ CX-BVD |
| 25252 | | 400B | G-5-17 XX505 G-BAZB N48US P4-AMB [parted out in 2003] |
| 25253 | | F400A | G-5-18 OY-APM G-BROD N731HS N3338 N50EB N50FC N610HC XA-SKE N253MT (N253CC) N911RD |
| 25254 | | F400B | G-AYLG 3D-AVL G-AYLG G-5-624 G-VJAY VT-UBG G-5-624 VT-UBG |
| 25255 | | CC1A/F400A | XW788 G-BVTP (N255TS) N4QB |
| 25256 | | 600B | G-AYBH RP-C111 G-5-13 G-AYBH Ireland IAC236 [w/o 27Nov79 Dublin, Ireland] |
| 25257 | | 403B | G-5-19 G-BATA 9M-HLG [wfu Jun93] |
| 25258 | | F600B | (G-AYRR) G-AZHS G-BFAN VR-CJP VP-CJP G-OJPB TL-ADK 9Q-CBC [wfu at Kinshasa/N'Djili, Democratic Republic of Congo] |
| 25259 | | 400B | G-AZEK S Africa 05 ZS-JBA [b/u for spares following accident at Lanseria, South Africa; cx Mar03] |
| 25260 | | 400B | G-AZEL S Africa 06 ZS-JIH D2-EFM |
| 25261 | NA763 | 731 | N58BH (N91BH) N246N N46B (N68BW) N246N N55B N125MT N62TC N19H N1QH |
| 25262 | NA764 | 400A | N59BH XB-CUX N55RZ |
| 25263 | NA765 | 731 | N62BH N125PA N700BW N708BW N61MS N68CB N765TS |
| 25264 | | CC1A/F400A | XW789 G-BVTR N264TS N7171 (N264WD) (N731WB) (N264TS) N93TS N178PC |
| 25265 | NA766 | 731 | N63BH N711YP N711YR N300LD N200CC N125MD VH-PAB N150SA N854SM |
| 25266 | | CC1A/F400A | XW790 G-BVTS (N266TS) N135CK N125CK |
| 25267 | NA767 | 400A | N64BH N92BH N28GP N28GE N125CM [used for spares Oct94 at Spirit of St Louis A/P, MO; canx Jun95 - remains to Av-Mats, Paynesville, MO] |
| 25268 | | CC1A/F400A | XW791 G-BVTT (N268TS) N41953 [w/o 07Apr95 Santo Domingo-Herrera Intl Apt, Dominican Republic; parted out by Arnoni Avn, Houston, TX circa Sep00] |
| 25269 | | 400B | G-AZEM S Africa 07 ZS-LPF EX-269 AP-BGI |
| 25270 | | F403B | G-5-13 G-BBGU G-BKBA N270AV N400GP N440RD |
| 25271 | | 400A | G-5-14 G-BABL XX506 G-BABL EC-CMU N37516 N103CJ N365DA N400DP N70AP N810HS [parted out by AvMats, St Louis, MO, Jan04; cx] |
| 25272 | | F400A | G-5-15 G-BAZA N4759D N121VA N121VF N800JT N63EM |
| 25273 | NA768 | 400A | G-5-20 N65BH N125BH N69KA XA-DIN N11FX N7WC XA-SFQ N2155P XA-SFQ |
| 25274 | | 403B | G-5-20 Brazil EU93-2119 [wfu] |
| 25275 | NA769 | 400A | N66BH N872D N972D N125PP N42BL N369JH N900AD |
| 25276 | NA770 | 731 | G-5-11 N67BH N88GA N300CF N74B N7170J N38LB N805WD |
| 25277 | | 403B | G-5-11? Brazil VU93-2126 |

# BAe 125

| C/n | | Series | Identities | | | | | | | |
|---|---|---|---|---|---|---|---|---|---|---|
| 25278 | NA771 | 731 | N68BH | CF-AOS | C-FAOS | N731H | VR-BVI | N298NM | N4WC | |
| 25279 | NA772 | 400A | G-5-12 | N69BH | XA-CUZ | [w/o 27Dec80 Cancun, Mexico] | | | | |
| 25280 | NA773 | 731 | N70BH | CF-PPN | C-FPPN | N32KB | | | | |
| 25281 | NA774 | 731 | N71BH | N1BG | N18GX | N125DB | EI-BRG | N70338 | N774EC | RA-02804 |
| | | | G-5-821 | RA-02804 | N774TS | | | | | |
| 25282 | NA775 | 731 | N72BH | N5V | N7HV | N17HV | N333DP | XA-EMA | N223RR | |
| 25283 | NA776 | 403A | N73BH | G-BACI | XA-LOV | XA-SGM | XB-GNF | XA-LOV | | |
| 25284 | NA777 | 731 | N74BH | N571CH | N571GH | N228GC | N125FM | N125MD | N101AD | (N425JF) |
| | | | [w/o 06May91 Shreveport, LA; cx Sep91 - fuselage remains at Tulsa, OK circa Oct99] | | | | | | | |
| 25285 | NA778 | 731 | N75BH | N555CB | N733K | C-GCEO | N2694C | N67EC | N89SR | N88AF |
| | | | N778JA | | | | | | | |
| 25286 | NA779 | 731 | N76BH | N88SJ | N33CP | N84CP | N400WT | N408WT | N808CC | N731JR |
| | | | N781JR | (N989AB) | | | | | | |
| 25287 | NA780 | 731 | N78BH | N72HC | N65DL | N265DL | N800TG | 9Q-CPF | | |
| 25288 | | 403B | Brazil VU93-2127 | | | | | | | |
| 25289 | | 403B | G-5-16 | Brazil VU93-2128 | | | | | | |
| 25290 | | 403B | Brazil VU93-2129 | | [w/o 08Sep87 Carajas, Brazil] | | | | | |

Production complete

# SERIES 600

| C/n | Series | Identities |
|---|---|---|
| 256001 | FA | G-AZUF N82BH N711AG G-BEWW N711AG N82RP N82PP N444PE N444PD N700R N709R N561RP N61TS N773JC N699TS |
| 256002 | A | G-5-15 N79BH (N925BH) N631SC N631SQ N915JT N61SB N602MM XA-SLP |
| 256003 | A | N80BH CF-HSS C-FHSS N256FC N42TS N91KH N91KP |
| 256004 | A | N81BH N94BD N94BB N19HH N19HE VR-BRS N4TS (N103RA) N399GA N5AH N600MK |
| 256005 | B | G-BART (G-BJXV) (G-BJUT) G-CYII EC-EAC N4253A [reported b/u for spares by Western A/C Parts; to White Inds, Bates City, MO; cx Jun95] |
| 256006 | FB | XX507 N606TS N21SA [w/o 21Feb05 Bromont, Canada; parted out Montgomery, AL; cx 17Jan08] |
| 256007 | A | N21BH N125BH N125KR N3007 N317TC [parted out Houston, TX; cx 14Jan08] |
| 256008 | FA | XX508 N256WJ |
| 256009 | A | N22BH N3PW N219ST (N210ST) N183RD "N183RM" N28TS |
| 256010 | A | N23BH N40PC [w/o 28Apr77 McLean, VA] |
| 256011 | A | N24BH N6001H N555CB N555GB VR-BGS N42622 N81D EC-EHF [used for spares Oct94 at Spirit of St Louis A/P, MO unmarked - remains to Dodson Int'l Parts, Ottawa, KS circa 1998] |
| 256012 | B | G-5-17 G-BAYT 5N-ALX G-BAYT G-BNDX G-BAYT EC-272 EC-EOQ N8000Z [to spares at Houston, TX circa 95; canx Feb96; reported never carried N8000Z] |
| 256013 | A | N25BH N25BE N505W (N65GB) N218AC N627HS N80TS VR-CDG 5N-YET |
| 256014 | A | N26BH N922CR N922GR N5SJ N47HW N47HV [parted out by Dodson Int'l Parts, Rantoul, KS] |
| 256015 | FA | G-5-19 G-BBCL G-BJCB G-BBCL 9K-ACZ G-BBCL Ireland 239 G-BBCL G-5-11 (D-CCEX) G-BBCL N600AV N917K N777SA (N74TJ) (N615TJ) N777TK N700XJ N957MB |
| 256016 | A | N27BH N99SC XA-SAI [parted out by White Inds, Bates City, MO] |
| 256017 | B | G-5-18 G-BBAS PK-PJD N600WJ (N415BA) N225HR [parted out by White Inds, Bates City, MO] |
| 256018 | A | N28BH N500GD (N780SC) N880SC N125E N600AW N93TS N288MW XA-JRF N16GA XA-TNX XB-ADZ |
| 256019 | B | G-BARR HZ-AA1 G-FANN [cx 29Mar93, wfu; fuselage on fire dump Dunsfold, UK, still marked as HZ-AA1] |
| 256020 | A | N29BH (N501H) N125CU N334JR C-GDUP N334JR N5NG XA-NTE N5NG [derelict Monterrey, Mexico and scrapped; cx Sep00] |
| 256021 | A | G-5-11 HB-VDL C-GSTT N125HS N125JJ (N128JJ) N125JA XA-SNH N37SG C-GKHR N111UN N220TS 3D-BOS S9-DBG S9-PDG |
| 256022 | A | N34BH N701Z N701A N1515P N757M N757P XA-XET N2114E [reported to spares; marks N2114E not carried] |
| 256023 | A | N35BH N514V EC-121 EC-EGL N523MA N702HC [parted out by White Inds, Bates City, MO] |
| 256024 | A | G-BBMD N50GD G-BBMD G-BSHL G-OMGA YR-DVA (N731TC) N669SC N411GA |
| 256025 | A | N36BH C-GTPC N721LH |
| 256026 | FA | N37BH G-5-16 N124GS N699SC N818TP XA-SWK N125NA N450TB XA-ATC |
| 256027 | FA | D-CJET G-5-585 D-CJET OE-GIA N693TJ N800NM N245RS |
| 256028 | A | G-5-12 VP-BDH C6-BDH C-GDHW XA-KUT [w/o 18Jan88 Houston-Hobby, TX; remains Jan93 to Dodson Av'n, Ottawa, KS] |
| 256029 | FB | G-BBRT PK-PJE PK-HMG N629TS N35WP |
| 256030 | B | G-BBEP G-BJOY G-BBEP 5N-ARD G-BBEP G-TOMI N217A [reported to spares by Arnoni Avn, Houston, TX still marked as G-TOMI] |
| 256031 | B | G-5-14 9Q-CFW "9Q-CFG" 9Q-CGF 9Q-CJF |
| 256032 | A | N38BH N4BR (N14BR) G-DBOW C-GLBD N332TA EC-EAV N921RD N801BC N334PS |
| 256033 | B | F-BUYP G-DMAN HZ-YA1 N330G G-PJWB G-HALK N6033 XB-FMF N303MW N600HS N514AJ N514MH* |
| 256034 | A | N39BH N90B N90BL N600FL N600SB EC-115 EC-EGS [used for spares Oct94 at Spirit of St Louis A/P, MO; fuselage to Elsberry, MO by Apr96] |
| 256035 | A | F-BKMC G-BETV G-SUFC VP-BCN "N635PA" N128YT [to White Inds, Bates City, MO 18Jan05 for spares] |
| 256036 | B | (G-BBRT) [used for paint-spraying trials Chester, UK; aircraft not completed] |
| 256037 | B | (VH-ARJ) AN-BPR YN-BPR VH-NJA RP-C1600 VP-BBW (N16VT) N63810 N228MD |
| 256038 | A | N40BH N77C N77CU SE-DKF N199SG XA-ACN |
| 256039 | B | G-BCCL G-BKBM N61TF N410AW G-BKBM EC-EAO EC-183 EC-EAO G-OMGB [wfu Oct94; TT 6,944 hrs; to spares at Houston, TX] |
| 256040 | A | N41BH C-GJCM N4224Y N125GS N601BA N621BA N16VT N287DL (N301JJ) N287DM TJ-... |
| 256041 | B | G-5-13 G-BCJU VR-CBD N450DA N888PM N273K N42TS N808RP N603TS |
| 256042 | B | G-BBRO G-BKBU G-5-505 5N-AWS [w/o 15Dec86 Casablanca, Morocco] |
| 256043 | B | G-BCUX [w/o 20Nov75 Dunsfold, UK] |
| 256044 | A | N42BH N600MB N46B (N46BE) C-GKCC N848W N992SF XA-CAH N9282Y N116DD N454DP N453DP |
| 256045 | FB | G-5-18 EC-CQT G-5-11 G-BGYR N508VM N803LL* |
| 256046 | FA | N43BH N91HR (N401HR) N402HR N117EM XA-AGL N299BW N299GA N299TJ (N299DG) N299GS |
| 256047 | A | G-5-16 "N44BH" (C-GBNS) "N4203S" N4203Y N400NW N400NE N600TT XA-JEQ N47EX N47WU XA-RYK N68GA 9Q-CYA 9Q-CAI |

# BAe 125-600

| C/n | Series | Identities |
|---|---|---|
| 256048 | A | G-5-15 HB-VDS G-BHIE YU-BME N6567G TC-COS N852GA [parted out by Arnoni Aviation, Houston, TX] |
| 256049 | B | G-BCXL ZS-JHL G-BCXL HZ-KA5 P4-VJR 5V-TTP |
| 256050 | B | G-5-12 5N-ANG G-BLOI 5N-AOL [wfu, believed scrapped in 1997] |
| 256051 | A | (N45BH) C-GBNS N22DL N5DL N35DL N601PS N601JJ N616PA N600AL N95TS N601JA 9Q-CFJ |
| 256052 | B | G-5-11 G-BDJE G-BKBH TR-LAU G-5-698 G-BKBH G-5-698 G-BKBH G-5-698 5N-NBC 5N-DNL G-5-698 5N-DNL G-BKBH [cx Jly99 wfu Southampton, UK] |
| 256053 | B | D-CFSK HC-BUR N125WJ N5NR N721RM |
| 256054 | B | G-5-17 G-BCXF 9K-AED "G-BKFS" G-BCXF 5N-YFS 5N-RNO [w/o May01, Lagos, Nigeria] |
| 256055 | A | G-5-19 G-BDOP N94B N94BF N777SA N100QR N100QP N125GS N20FM N111UN (N600GP) |
| 256056 | B | G-5-13 G-BDOA G-BKCD 5N-ARN G-BKCD G-OMGC [wfu Sep94; TT 6,404 hrs; to spares at Houston, TX circa 1995] |
| 256057 | B | G-5-17 HZ-KA2 G-FFLT VR-BNW VP-BNW N602CF N11AF [parted out by Arnoni Aviation, Houston, TX] |
| 256058 | FA | G-5-18 G-BGKN N9043U N701Z N129BA (N429BA) (N658TS) N200XR N658TS N658KA N20FM |
| 256059 | B | G-5-19 HZ-DAC HZ-SJP G-BLUW ZF130 [stored St. Athan, UK, March 2002; wings and tail removed 21Oct02; fuselage to Farnborough, UK, by 24Oct02 for spares, then to Hanningfield Metals scrapyard, Stock, Essex, UK, 07Jan03; to Elektrowerkz nightclub, London EC1, UK, 2006; removed and scrapped 2008] |
| 256060 | B | G-5-12 HZ-MF1 G-BFIC 5N-AYK N660TC N422TK N422TR N395EJ [parted out by MTW Aerospace, Montgomery, AL] |
| 256061 | FA | G-5-14 G-BDOB N125HS N5253A N8253A N707WB N169B N189B N169B N331DC N701MS |
| 256062 | B | G-5-15 G-MFEU G-TMAS EC-319 EC-ERX G-TMAS 5N-MAY 5N-DOT [parted out] |
| 256063 | A | G-5-13 A6-RAK G-BSPH N484W EC-349 EC-ERJ 5N-OPT N9AZ YV345T |
| 256064 | A | G-5-17 HZ-AMM N105AS N666LC N500MA N580MA N600SN N125HF XA-MKY |
| 256065 | A | G-5-16 G-BJCB XA-MAH N73JA N59JR VR-CSF V2-LSF N125SF N4SA N10SA |
| 256066 | FA | G-5-15 G-BDZH N32RP N800JP N600G (N700SM) XA-... |
| 256067 | A | G-BEIN N522X N522C N270MC N270MQ N1884 N67MR XA-SKH N822BL N822BD (N157RP) CX-CBS |
| 256068 | FA | G-5-20 G-BDZR N33RP N90WP G-5-16 N90WP N14GD N54GD N500R N501R N600AE |
| 256069 | A | G-BEIO N350MH N600AG N369TS 5N-EMA |
| 256070 | FA | G-5-11 G-BEDT N322CC G-5-15 N322CC N319MF (N411TC) N411TP N83TJ N365SB (N76TJ) N75GA |
| 256071 | A | G-5-14 G-BEES N91884 N571DU N571E N121SG N171TS [cx May04, parted out in Mexico] |

Production complete

## SERIES 700

| C/n | Series | Identities | | | | | | | |
|---|---|---|---|---|---|---|---|---|---|
| 257001 | A | G-BEFZ | VR-HIM | G-BEFZ | N4555E | N700SV | N101SK | N101XS | N80KA |
| | | N189GE | N97TS | VH-LYG | N257AJ | N193TA | N701CW | (N807CW) | N425KG |
| 257002 NA0201 | A | G-5-20 | N700HS | N40WB | N40GT | N700NY | N886GB | VR-BNB | G-IECL |
| | | N701TS | (N828SA) | N530BL | "N509SM"+ | [+mispainted at Fort Lauderdale Int'l, | | | |
| | | FL, Jan09] | | N529SM | | | | | |
| 257003 NA0202 | A | G-5-19 | G-BERP | N64688 | N333ME | N727TA | N403BG | XA-ULT | |
| 257004 NA0218 | A | G-5-15 | G-BGDM | G-5-15 | N37975 | N222RB | N700RJ | N546BC | N746BC |
| | | N648WW | N704CW | N804CW | N804FF | N903SC | M-JCPO | | |
| 257005 NA0203 | A | G-BERV | N620M | N104AE | N828PJ | | | | |
| 257006 NA0204 | A | G-5-18 | G-BERX | N724B | | | | | |
| 257007 | A | HB-VFA | D-CADA | G-5-721 | D-CADA | G-BUNL | RA-02800 | G-5-721 | RA-02800 |
| | | (N307TC) | N257TH | N257WJ | N54WJ | (N545SH) | N49RJ | | |
| 257008 NA0205 | A | G-5-11 | (G-BEWV) | C-GYYZ | N333PC | N807TC | N700FW | N618KR | |
| 257009 NA0206 | A | G-5-12 | G-BEYC | N813H | (N20GT) | N986H | XA-SNN | N701NW | N818KC |
| | | N828KC | N706AM | | | | | | |
| 257010 | A | HZ-MMM | LX-MJM | G-5-631 | N700WH | N700ER | N3399P | (N339BW) | (N41CC) |
| | | N977CC | N425RJ | N424RJ | N819WG | | | | |
| 257011 NA0207 | A | G-5-13 | G-BFAJ | N255CT | (N255QT) | N255TT | N500FC | N33RH | N70X |
| | | N7UV | N816JM | | | | | | |
| 257012 NA0208 | A | G-5-14 | G-BFBI | N125HS | N700HS | N162A | N700FS | N622AB | N622AD |
| | | N37PL | N38PA | N41HF | N449EB | RA-02810 | | | |
| 257013 | A | G-CBBI | N219JA | N75ST | N101HF | N96FT | N36FT | P4-AOH | P4-SKY |
| | | N813VC | | | | | | | |
| 257014 NA0209 | A | G-5-17 | G-BFDW | N46901 | N120GA | N60MS | N453EP | N586JR | N74B |
| | | N843CP | N209TS | | | | | | |
| 257015 NA0210 | A | G-5-18 | G-BFFL | N37P | SE-DPZ | (N725WH) | OY-JPJ | N418RD | P4-AOF |
| | | N418RD | | | | | | | |
| 257016 NA0216 | A | G-BFFH | N72505 | N800CB | N23SB | N23SK | (N23SN) | N999JF | "N197FT" |
| | | N98FT | | | | | | | |
| 257017 NA0211 | A | G-5-19 | G-BFFU | N62MS | N454EP | N757M | N757C | (I-DRVM) | I-DVMR |
| | | HB-VLH | RA-02806 | N211WZ | N411PA | (N602JJ) | | | |
| 257018 NA0212 | A | G-BFGU | N733H | N662JB | N125CS | (N125MJ) | N425SD | | |
| 257019 NA0213 | A | G-BFGV | N370M | N370RR | N339CA | | | | |
| 257020 | B | (G-BFTP) | (G-BFVN) | G-EFPT | VR-BHE | (N2634B) | N125HM | N818 | N311JD |
| | | N777EH | | | | | | | |
| 257021 NA0214 | A | N34CH | N900KC | N1868M | N1868S | (N526JC) | N926ZT | N926TC | N926MC |
| 257022 | A | (G-5-11) | F-GASL | G-5-17 | N34RE | N92RP | N109AF | N700WC | |
| 257023 NA0215 | A | G-BFLF | N54555 | N125GP | N6JB | N6UB | N35LM | N195XP | N215RS |
| 257024 NA0217 | A | G-BFLG | N94BD | N94BE | N7005 | N7006 | (N6960) | N700RR | |
| 257025 | B | G-5-12 | G-BFPI | VR-HIN | G-BFPI | N93TC | N7782 | N886S | N205TW |
| 257026 NA0219 | A | G-BFMO | N1230A | N372BC | N372BD | N685FM | N685EM | N788WG | N428AS |
| | | N428FS | N219TS | N45BP | [w/o 20Sep03 Beaumont, TX] | | | | |
| 257027 NA0220 | A | G-BFMP | C-GPPS | N705CC | N725CC | XA-SAU | | | |
| 257028 | A | G-BFSO | G-5-534 | N700TL | N603GY | N7728 | N899DM | VP-COK | N949EB |
| 257029 NA0221 | A | N465R | N700PD | (N248JH) | N705JH | C-GTOR | | | |
| 257030 NA0222 | A | G-BFSI | C-GSCL | C-FFAB | HB-VLJ | C-GNAZ | N18CC | | |
| 257031 | BA | G-BFSP | G-PRMC | G-BFSP | G-5-701 | D-CBAE | G-BFSP | G-5-701 | N89TJ |
| | | HB-VLA | N703TS | N703JN | | | | | |
| 257032 NA0223 | A | G-5-14 | G-BFUE | N700BA | N353WC | N853WC | N154JS | (N158JS) | N154JD |
| | | N720PT | | | | | | | |
| 257033 NA0224 | A | N50JM | N50TN | N200GX | N200GY | XA-MJI | N336AC | XB-JYS | |
| 257034 | A | G-5-14 | G-BFXT | N7007X | N510HS | G-PLGI | N402GJ | N34GG | |
| 257035 NA0225 | A | G-5-16 | N36NP | SE-DPY | N486MJ | N995SK | (N995SL) | N995SA | N137WR |
| | | (N137WK) | | | | | | | |
| 257036 NA0226 | A | G-5-17 | N60JM | N60TN | N600HC | N902RM | N902PM | N47TJ | N42SR |
| | | (N42SE) | N7WC | N1776E | N102BP | | | | |
| 257037 | B | G-5-18 | G-BFVI | G-IFTE | | | | | |
| 257038 NA0227 | A | G-5-19 | N10CZ | N81KA | | | | | |
| 257039 NA0228 | A | G-5-11 | N555CB | N555CR | N545GM | | | | |
| 257040 | B | HZ-RC1 | G-OWEB | EC-375 | EC-413 | EC-ETI | N47TJ | VR-BPE | VP-BPE |
| | | HB-VMD | G-BYFO | G-OWDB | P4-LVF | | | | |
| 257041 NA0229 | A | G-5-12 | N700BB | N400NW | N400NU | (N601UU) | N700LS | N825CT | N820CT |
| | | XA-BYP | | | | | | | |
| 257042 NA0230 | A | G-5-13 | N360X | (N360DE) | N881S | N899AB | | | |
| 257043 NA0232 | A | G-BFYV | (N300LD) | N900CC | N500ZB | N22EH | N22KH | N232TN | (N331CG) |
| | | [wfu at Fort Lauderdale Int'l, FL, after wheels-up landing 1Nov06] | | | | | | | |
| 257044 NA0231 | A | G-5-17 | G-BFYH | N35D | N5735 | N125G | (N125GB) | N225BJ | |
| 257045 NA0240 | A | G-BFZJ | N130BA | N700HH | N800E | | | | |
| 257046 | A | 4W-ACE | G-BKJV | VH-JCC | VH-LRH | N7465T | XA-LEG | N746TS | N55MT |
| | | "N55TS" | N746TS | LV-ZRS | N828AN | N587VV | N257AM | N770AZ | |
| 257047 NA0233 | A | G-BFZI | C-GABX | N79TS | N79EH | | | | |
| 257048 NA0234 | A | G-5-16 | N711YP | N205BS | N731DL | N323JK | | | |
| 257049 NA0239 | A | G-5-17 | G-BGBL | N33BK | C-GKPM | C-GNOW | C-GOHJ | | |
| 257050 NA0235 | A | G-5-18 | N700GB | N10C | | | | | |
| 257051 NA0236 | A | G-5-11 | N700UK | N14JA | N64HA | N236BN | [dbr 20Dec00 Jackson, WY; to | | |
| | | Arnoni Avn, TX for parting out Aug01] | | | | | | | |

# BAe 125-700

| C/n | | Series | Identities | | | | | | | |
|---|---|---|---|---|---|---|---|---|---|---|
| 257052 | NA0237 | A | G-5-19 | G-BGBJ | N737X | N697NP | N511GP | N511KA | | |
| 257053 | NA0238 | A | G-5-20 | N700AR | N33CP | N130MH | N120MH | N200JP | ZS-SDU | |
| 257054 | | B | C6-BET | G-BVJY | RA-02802 | G-BVJY | G-NCFR | G-OURB | OD-HHF | OD-BBF^ |
| 257055 | | A | G-5-16 | HZ-RC2 | N876JC | G-5-598 | G-BOXI | F-WZIG | F-GHHG | N46PL |
| | | | (N696JH) | (N755TS) | N47PB | N347TC | | | | |
| 257056 | NA0241 | A | G-5-13 | N700NT | N492CB | N6VC | N25MK | N300BS | (N388BS) | XA-UCU |
| | | | N84GA | XA-UCU | | | | | | |
| 257057 | NA0242 | A | G-5-14 | N700UR | N60HJ | (N60HU) | C-GPCC | N125BW | N701CF | (N988GA) |
| | | | N418BA | N241RT | | | | | | |
| 257058 | NA0245 | A | G-5-15 | N125HS | N700BA | N354WC | N854WC | N750GM | N8PL | N810V |
| | | | N81QV | VP-CLU | | | | | | |
| 257059 | NA0243 | A-II | G-5-17 | N130BH | N20S | N20SK | N702BA | XA-JRF | N104JG | N9395Y |
| | | | N717AF | | | | | | | |
| 257060 | NA0244 | A | G-5-18 | N130BG | N1103 | N1183 | N230DP | N414RF | | |
| 257061 | | A | G-5-19 | G-BGGS | G-OJOY | N700SS | N700SF | N810GS | XA-UEA | |
| 257062 | | B | G-5-16 | HB-VGF | G-5-708 | HB-VGF | G-5-708 | N7062B | G-5-708 | (G-BWJX) |
| | | | RA-02809 | N62EA | N416RD | EI-WJN | | | | |
| 257063 | NA0246 | A | G-5-20 | N130BB | N79HC | N700NW | | | | |
| 257064 | | B/A | HZ-NAD | HZ-OFC | G-BMOS | G-5-519 | VH-JFT | N395RD | N48LB | |
| 257065 | NA0247 | A | G-5-11 | N130BC | N30PR | N530TL | (N530TE) | N87AG | N120JC | |
| 257066 | NA0248 | A | G-5-13 | G-BGSR | C-GKCI | C-FBMG | N900CQ | N900CP | | |
| 257067 | | B | HZ-DA1 | N9113J | (N115RS) | N360N | N144DJ | HB-VKJ | N267TS | N42TS |
| 257068 | NA0249 | A | G-5-14 | N130BD | N31LG | N799SC | XB-FMK | XA-FMK | | |
| 257069 | NA0250 | A | G-5-15 | N130BE | N29GP | N29GD | N308DD | (N900JG) | (N54TJ) | N418DM |
| 257070 | | B | HB-VGG | G-5-604 | HB-VGG | G-5-604 | G-BWCR | "G-JETG" | G-BWCR | G-DEZC |
| | | | P4-AMH | | | | | | | |
| 257071 | NA0251 | A | G-5-17 | N130BF | N514B | N396U | N810CR | N571CH | CX-CIB | |
| 257072 | NA0252 | A | G-5-18 | N700HS | N900MR | N401GN | N513GP | N895CC | N237WR | N237RG* |
| 257073 | | B | G-5-12 | G-BGTD | N7788 | (N59TJ) | N701TA | N210RK | | |
| 257074 | NA0253 | A | G-5-19 | N422X | (N831CJ) | | | | | |
| 257075 | NA0254 | A | G-5-13 | (G-BHKF) | N125AM | N125TR | N124AR | N125XX | M-ALUN | |
| 257076 | | A | G-5-17 | 7Q-YJI | MAAW-J1 | G-5-524 | G-BMWW | G-5-571 | XA-LML | N111ZN |
| | | | N111ZS | N180CH | (N776TS) | N111ZS | | | | |
| 257077 | NA0255 | A | G-5-14 | N125AJ | N540B | XA-SEN | | | | |
| 257078 | NA0256 | A | G-5-15 | N125AK | N571CH | N455BK | (N830LR) | | | |
| 257079 | NA0268 | A | G-5-16 | XA-JIX | N74JA | (N74JE) | N501MM | XA-SON | | |
| 257080 | NA0257 | A | G-5-18 | N125HS | N611MC | (N611EL) | | | | |
| 257081 | NA0258 | A | G-5-19 | (N125AM) | N700CU | N711CU | N809M | N812M | N193RC | N227MM |
| 257082 | | A | Ireland 238 | | (N98AF) | XA-TCB | N70HF | N752CM | | |
| 257083 | NA0259 | A | G-5-12 | (N150RH) | N125AH | N100Y | N128CS | N941CE | | |
| 257084 | NA0260 | A | G-5-14 | N130BK | N202CH | N965JC | N184TB | XA-HXM | | |
| 257085 | | B | G-5-15 | G-BHIO | RP-C1714 | N10TN | | | | |
| 257086 | NA0261 | A | G-5-17 | N125AL | N277CT | N500EF | N983GT | N999CY | | |
| 257087 | NA0262 | A | G-5-16 | (N130BL) | C-GKRS | N3234S | N404CB | (N601JR) | N908JE | N988JE |
| | | | N350DH | N711WM | N3RC | (N313RC) | N396RC | N561PS | | |
| 257088 | | B | HZ-DA2 | G-5-531 | N29RP | N222HL | N224EA | | | |
| 257089 | NA0263 | A | G-5-18 | N130BL | N151AE | (N130AE) | N101FC | (N263TN) | N125RG | N125EK |
| 257090 | NA0264 | A | G-5-19 | N299CT | N88MX | N264WC | (N160WC) | N161WC | N724EA | |
| 257091 | | B | G-BHLF | G-OCAA | VP-CLX | | | | | |
| 257092 | NA0265 | A | G-5-20 | N733M | N783M | N91CM | N299WB | | | |
| 257093 | NA0266 | A | G-5-11 | G-BHMP | C-GBRM | N7UJ | N86MD | N497PT | N804CS | |
| 257094 | | B | G-OBAE | HB-VEK | G-5-16 | N49566 | N80KM | N713KM | N713K | D-CKIM |
| | | | (G-....) | 9M-STR | N415RD | N483FG | | | | |
| 257095 | NA0267 | A | G-5-12 | N125L | N215G | N352WC | N852WC | N427MD | N745TH | N36GS |
| | | | N267JE | | | | | | | |
| 257096 | NA0276 | A | G-5-14 | XA-KEW | [w/o 01May81 Monterrey, Mexico] | | | | | |
| 257097 | | B | (G-BHTJ) | G-HHOI | G-BRDI | G-BHTJ | RA-02801 | G-5-810 | RA-02801 | |
| 257098 | NA0269 | A | G-5-15 | N125Y | N89PP | N70SK | N50HS | XA-NTE | N702NW | N972LM |
| | | | N438PM | (N61GF) | XA-AMI | | | | | |
| 257099 | NA0270 | A | G-5-16 | G-BHSK | C-GDAO | N621JH | N621JA | PK-CTC | N52GA | |
| 257100 | | A | G-5-19 | D-CLVW | G-5-549 | G-BNFW | N858JR | N801RA | N925WC | |
| 257101 | NA0272 | A | G-5-17 | (N700E) | N89PP | (N700E) | N109JM | N14SY | N77D | N89GN |
| | | | N700XF | | | | | | | |
| 257102 | NA0280 | A | G-5-18 | XA-KIS | N700CN | N700K | N810M | XA-TCR | N280AJ | N280VC |
| | | | N500FM | | | | | | | |
| 257103 | | B | G-5-12 | G-BHSU | G-LTEC | VR-BOJ | VP-BOJ | YL-VIP | YL-VIR | G-GIRA |
| | | | OY-MFL | | | | | | | |
| 257104 | NA0273 | A | G-5-20 | N10PW | N411SS | N46TJ | N110EJ | (N4477X) | N815TR | |
| 257105 | NA0274 | A | G-5-11 | N125BA | N125TA | N44BB | N700DE | HB-VLL | N560SB | (OY-VIA) |
| | | | G-CFBP | | | | | | | |
| 257106 | NA0275 | A | G-5-13 | N125V | N661JB | N664JB | N404CE | N404CF | N125SJ | (N550JP) |
| | | | XB-JND | | | | | | | |
| 257107 | | A | G-BHSV | G-5-808 | N90AR | VR-CVD | N71MA | (N38HH) | N85HH | N900MD |
| | | | N880RG | | | | | | | |
| 257108 | NA0278 | A | G-5-14 | XA-KON | N45500 | N6GG | N6GQ | N86WC | N700FE | N77SA |
| | | | N130AP | N770CC | N518RR | | | | | |

## BAe 125-700

| C/n | Series | Identities | | | | | | | |
|---|---|---|---|---|---|---|---|---|---|
| 257109 | B | G-BHSW | VR-BPT | VR-BTZ | VP-BTZ | VP-BOY | OD-BOY | | |
| 257110 NA0271 | A | G-5-15 | XA-KAC | N277JW | N177JW | N154FJ | | | |
| 257111 NA0277 | A | G-5-16 | N125AF | N324K | N824K | N500 | N509 | (N799FL) | N509QC |
| | | N972W | | | | | | | |
| 257112 | B | D-CMVW | G-5-536 | G-BNBO | G-5-553 | 9M-SSL | (D-CLUB) | G-SVLB | RA-02850 |
| 257113 NA0279 | A | G-5-17 | N125AD | N204R | N204N | N5511A | N1VQ | N90FF | ZS-ICU |
| 257114 NA0281 | A | G-5-18 | N125AN | N533 | C-GXYN | N169TA | N403DP | N281BT | N101LT |
| 257115 | A | HZ-DA3 | G-5-502 | G-BMIH | 5N-AMX | G-5-502 | G-BMIH | N125YY | N333MS |
| | | OD-MAS | | | | | | | |
| 257116 NA0282 | A | G-5-19 | N125AP | N1982G | N120YB | | | | |
| 257117 NA0283 | A | G-5-20 | N125AS | N90B | (N90BN) | N220FL | N93CR | N93GR | N26SC |
| 257118 | A | (G-BIHZ) | 5N-AVJ | G-BWKL | VP-BBH | VP-CRA | C-GNND | N619TD | N810KB |
| 257119 NA0284 | A | G-5-11 | N125AE | N326K | N826K | N125AR | N125AP | N10UC | (N311MG) |
| 257120 NA0285 | A | G-5-13 | N125AT | N40CN | (N14WJ) | N130YB | | | |
| 257121 NA0286 | A | G-5-14 | N125AU | N20FX | N700SB | N301PH | (N156K) | N150CA | (N501MD) |
| | | N83MD | | | | | | | |
| 257122 NA0287 | A | G-5-15 | N125U | N77LP | N299FB | N3444H | (N731GA) | N564BR | |
| 257123 NA0288 | A | G-5-16 | N125AH | N700BW | N198GT | | | | |
| 257124 | B | HZ-DA4 | OD-FNF | OD-FAF | | | | | |
| 257125 NA0289 | A | G-5-17 | N125AJ | N125CG | N62WH | N62WL | N369G | N27KL | N302PC |
| | | N802RC | N70QB | | | | | | |
| 257126 NA0290 | A | G-5-18 | N700AC | N246VF | N7WG | N17WG | N710AF | | |
| 257127 | B | G-TJCB | OY-MPA | (F-GNDB) | F-GODB | HB-VLC | N795A | | |
| 257128 NA0291 | A | G-5-19 | N125BC | N126AR | XA-MSH | N45AF | N947CE | | |
| 257129 NA0292 | A | G-5-20 | N125AK | (N256MA) | N256EN | N805M | N728JW | N748FB | N48FB |
| | | N241FB | | | | | | | |
| 257130 | A | G-DBBI | G-CCAA | G-BNVU | N700FR | G-5-588 | N700FR | G-RJRI | RP-C235 |
| | | N130TS | N499GA | N405DP | N405TP | N405DW | | | |
| 257131 NA0293 | A | G-5-11 | N700BA | N80G | N520M | N52LC | N7CT | N7WG | N700NB |
| | | N996RP | N296RG | N406J | | | | | |
| 257132 NA0294 | A | G-BIMY | C-FIPG | N925WC | N925WG | N925DP | N188KA | | |
| 257133 | B | G-5-14 | LV-PMM | LV-ALW | [w/o 11Apr85 Salta, Argentina] | | | | |
| 257134 NA0295 | A | G-5-13 | N871D | N371D | N888SW | N89MD | N134NW | (N134RT) | |
| 257135 NA0296 | A | G-5-15 | N490MP | N31AS | N28GP | N28GG | N700DA | N100JF | N10QJ |
| | | N927LL | | | | | | | |
| 257136 | B | G-BIRU | G-5-545 | OH-JET | N136TN | N318CD | P4-AOE | P4-XZX | |
| 257137 NA0297 | A | G-5-16 | N125BD | N78CS | (N78QS) | N589UC | N945CE | | |
| 257138 NA0298 | A | G-5-17 | N125G | N80K | N298TS | N298BP | N917TF | | |
| 257139 | B | G-5-18 | (G-GAIL) | G-BKAA | G-MHIH | RA-02803 | G-5-875 | RA-02803 | |
| 257140 NA0299 | A | G-5-19 | N125BE | VR-BHH | N125BE | N555RB | N703JP | N700NY | N800LM |
| 257141 NA0300 | A | G-5-20 | N70PM | N80PM | N80PN | N700SA | N943CE | | |
| 257142 | B | G-5-12 | G-BJDJ | G-RCDI | G-BJDJ | P4-OBE | RA-02802 | | |
| 257143 NA0325 | A | G-5-20 | N700HA | N26H | C-GOGM | C-GQGM | C-FCSS | | |
| 257144 NA0326 | A | G-5-11 | N522M | N70AR | N94SA | (N702TJ) | N164WC | N194WC | N819DM |
| | | ZS-... | | | | | | | |
| 257145 NA0339 | A | G-5-18 | N70FC | N125BJ | PT-ORJ | N700SA | N83HF | | |
| 257146 NA0301 | A | G-5-13 | N700HB | N711RL | N713RL | N744DC | N421SZ | N107LT | |
| 257147 NA0303 | A | G-5-14 | N125P | N70PM | N70PN | N67PW | N678W | N900JT | |
| 257148 NA0304 | A | G-5-17 | N700BB | N707DS | C-GTDN | N99JD | N96PR | N700NH | N237DX |
| 257149 NA0302 | A | G-5-19 | N700AA | N700HA | N290PC | N795HE | (N795HL) | C-GEPF | C-GLIG |
| 257150 NA0305 | A | G-5-11 | N700HS | N73G | N730H | N305TH | 5N-BFC | | |
| 257151 | B | G-5-12 | N161MM | N161G | N613MC | (N613EL) | N825MS | | |
| 257152 NA0306 | A | G-5-17 | N700DD | N270MH | C-FEXB | N400WP | N800MP | N141AL | |
| 257153 NA0313 | A | G-BJOW | XB-CXK | N18G | PK-CTA | N419RD | P4-AOD | [w/o 02Jan06 | |
| | | Karkiv, Ukraine] | | | | | | | |
| 257154 NA0307 | A | G-5-18 | N700GG | N270MC | N270KA | | | | |
| 257155 NA0308 | A | G-5-19 | N700KK | N1620 | C-GYPH | N1843S | N10CN | N9999V | N314RC |
| 257156 NA0309 | A | G-5-17 | N15AG | N700MK | N529DM | N526DM | N309WM | N95CM | N57AY |
| 257157 NA0310 | A | G-5-20 | N700LL | N64GG | N2640 | N18SH | (N168WU) | N128WU | N109BG |
| 257158 | A | G-5-14 | G-BJWB | N45KK | XB-DZN | N700VT | XA-NEM | | |
| 257159 NA0311 | A | G-5-15 | N91Y | N50JR | (N620CC) | (N502R) | VR-CKP | N311NW | N425WN |
| | | N700LP | ZS-WJW | | | | | | |
| 257160 | B | G-5-19 | 5N-AVK | | | | | | |
| 257161 NA0323 | A | G-5-17 | N700RR | C-GZZX | N700RR | N2630 | N2830 | VT-AAA | [cx 2009 |
| | | instructional airframe] | | | | | | | |
| 257162 NA0312 | A | G-5-18 | N700NN | N1896T | N1896F | N176RS | N500GS | N412DP | C-GLBJ |
| 257163 | B | G-5-12 | 7T-VCW | | | | | | |
| 257164 NA0314 | A | G-5-11 | N152AE | (N106AE) | N53GH | | | | |
| 257165 NA0315 | A | G-5-14 | N869KM | N26ME | | | | | |
| 257166 | B | G-5-18 | F-BYFB | F-GRON | EC-HRQ | RP-C5998 | | | |
| 257167 NA0316 | A | G-5-15 | N700PP | N125BA | N2989 | N640PM | N63PM | N73PM | N333NR |
| | | (N501F) | N18BA | | | | | | |
| 257168 NA0317 | A | G-5-20 | N700SS | N612MC | (N612EL) | N789BA | | | |
| 257169 | B | G-5-21 | (VH-SOA) | VH-HSS | "B-HSS" | VR-HSS | B-HSS | 5N-MAZ | |
| 257170 NA0318 | A | G-5-14 | N819M | N80CL | EI-RRR | N114BA | N356SR | | |

# BAe 125-700

| C/n | Series | Identities |
|---|---|---|
| 257171 NA0319 | A | G-5-15 N710BP (N168H) N120MH N128MH N319NW XB-MLC N319NW XA-JAI |
| 257172 | B | 5H-SMZ G-BKFS 5H-SMZ G-5-568 5H-SMZ G-5-765 G-BKFS VT-MPA N355WJ ZS-CAG |
| 257173 NA0320 | A | G-5-17 N710BN N500LS N300LS N300HB N100LR (N100FF) N320GP N700HW N7490A |
| 257174 NA0321 | A | G-5-18 N710BL N469JR C-GTLG N165DL N65DL N65DU [parted out Houston, TX; cx 19Sep07] |
| 257175 | B | (C9-TTA) C9-TAC N770TJ VP-CEK VP-BEK G-MKSS RA-02804 |
| 257176 NA0322 | A | G-5-20 N109G C-FCHT N322BC |
| 257177 NA0324 | A | G-5-11 N710BJ N711TG N2000T N1996F (N1996E) N69SB (N880CR) N507F N2KZ (N944TB) |
| 257178 | A | G-5-14 4W-ACM G-5-530 G-BMYX G-5-570 VH-LMP G-5-747 N700CJ N621S EI-COV N178WB N803BF N175MC |
| 257179 NA0327 | A | G-5-15 N810SC C-GAAA |
| 257180 NA0328 | A | G-5-16 N710BG N2HP N192A C-FEAE |
| 257181 | CC3 | G-5-16 ZD620 |
| 257182 NA0329 | A | G-5-17 N710BF (N277CB) N1824T N18243 N756N N512GP N190WC 5N-DAO |
| 257183 NA0330 | CC3 | G-5-20 N710BD G-5-20 ZD703 |
| 257184 | B | G-5-12 9K-AGA YI-AKG 9K-AGA G-OMGD SU-PIX G-88-03 SU-PIX G-36-2 SU-PIX RA-02808 |
| 257185 NA0331 | A | G-5-12 N700BA N900BL XB-JTN |
| 257186 NA0332 | A | G-5-11 N710BC N400CH N400QH N16GS XA-STX N332WE 5N-MAO |
| 257187 | B | G-5-14 9K-AGB YI-AKH [dest 1991 during first Gulf War, Muthenna AFB, Iraq] |
| 257188 NA0333 | A | G-5-15 N523M N125DP (N301AS) (N301LX) N125AS N511LD |
| 257189 | B | G-BKHK (G-OBSM) G-OSAM N700BA N94B N81HH N8KG N45KG |
| 257190 | CC3 | ZD621 |
| 257191 NA0336 | A | G-5-17 N710BA N677RW (N477RW) N11TS VT-SRR N770HS (N778HS) XA-UKR |
| 257192 NA0337 | A | G-5-14 N125MT N2015M N201PM N300TW N300TK N818LD |
| 257193 NA0338 | A | G-5-15 N710BZ N710AG (N797EM) N797FA N350PL |
| 257194 | CC3 | ZD704 G-5-870 ZD704 |
| 257195 NA0334 | A | G-5-18 N710BY N702M N93GC N46WC N46WQ TY-SAM |
| 257196 | B | G-5-11 5N-AXO G-5-693 5N-AXO G-5-766 5N-AXO [w/o 17Jan96 Kano, Nigeria] |
| 257197 | A | G-5-12 N790Z N207PC N207RC N3GL (N2QL) 5N-BEX |
| 257198 NA0335 | A | G-5-18 N710BX N702E C-GJBJ |
| 257199 NA0340 | A | G-5-12 N710BW N702W VR-BKZ N921RD XA-SSY N23BJ N23EJ N804WJ N242AL XA-HOM |
| 257200 | B | G-5-14 G-MSFY VR-BMD VP-BMD |
| 257201 NA0341 | A | G-5-19 N710BV N2KW I-CIGH N700KG I-AZFB |
| 257202 NA0342 | A | G-5-17 N710BU N518S N65LC N8400E N93FR N230R (ZS-IPI) ZS-IPE |
| 257203 | B | G-5-14 5N-AXP [w/o 31Dec85 Kaduna, Nigeria] |
| 257204 NA0343 | A | G-5-15 N524M N949CE |
| 257205 | CC3 | G-5-19 ZE395 |
| 257206 NA0344 | A | G-5-16 N710BT N1C N502S C-FWCE C-GMBA N11YR XA-GIC N511RG N27BH |
| 257207 NA0345 | A | G-5-18 N710BS N774GF N686SG N686FG N21NY N21NT N913V "N313VR" N913V N700NP |
| 257208 NA0346 | A | N710BR G-5-19 (G-BLMJ) G-BLSM N501GF |
| 257209 | A | G-5-20 VR-BHW VP-BHW N127SR N805CD RP-C9808 |
| 257210 NA0347 | A | N710BQ G-5-18 (G-BLMK) G-BLTP N502GF |
| 257211 | CC3 | ZE396 |
| 257212 | B | G-5-12 G-RACL N81CH N81CN G-IJET G-5-659 OH-BAP G-5-659 OH-BAP LY-ASL LY-BSK VP-BMU |
| 257213 | A | G-5-16 G-BLEK N213C N700NP (N703MJ) N700CE |
| 257214 | B | G-5-17 HZ-SJP G-UKCA G-OMID VR-BCF VP-BCF P4-CMP VP-CMP |
| 257215 | B | G-5-20 VH-HSP VT-OBE |

Production complete

## SERIES 800 (HAWKER 800)

(1) * after the c/n indicates US assembled aircraft.
(2) 800SP/800XP2 aircraft are those which have been converted by the addition of Aviation Partners blended winglets and are noted in the series column

| C/n | Series | Identities | | | | | | | |
|---|---|---|---|---|---|---|---|---|---|
| 258001 | B | G-5-11 | [ff 26May83] | | "N800BA" | G-BKTF | G-5-522 | G-UWWB | G-5-557 |
| | | ZK-TCB | N785CA | OH-JOT | N801CR | N800RM | | | |
| 258002 | B | (G-5-16) | G-DCCC | (VH-CCC) | VH-III | G-DCCC | VH-NJM | G-DCCC | N800RY |
| | | (N1169D) | (N802CW) | N882CW | N15AX | | | | |
| 258003 | A | G-5-20 | G-BKUW | N800BA | N800N | N454JB | N803TJ | N803BA | N583VC |
| | | N803GE | N803RK | | | | | | |
| 258004 | A | G-5-15 | G-BLGZ | N800EE | N94BD | (N98DD) | N94SD | XA-SEH | XA-RET |
| | | XA-TVI | N84GA | XA-KTY | | | | | |
| 258005 | A | (G-5-12) | (G-5-19) | G-5-15 | G-BLJC | N800GG | (N219JA) | N601UU | N800FL |
| 258006 | A | G-5-17 | N800WW | N800S | N70SK | N861CE | N886CW | (N886GW) | N800FH |
| 258007 | B | G-5-20 | G-GAEL | G-5-554 | C-GKRL | C-GYPH | C-GWLL | C-GWLE | |
| 258008 | A | G-5-11 | N722CC | N850LA | | | | | |
| 258009 | A | G-5-15 | N400AL | N408AL | N45Y | N48Y | | | |
| 258010 | A | G-5-19 | (G-BLKS) | (G-OVIP) | N84A | N810BG | N810CW | (N800LX) | N810BA |
| 258011 | A | G-5-20 | N800VV | N1BG | N186G | N811CW | (N144AW) | N820GA | N801RM |
| 258012 | SP | G-5-18 | N800TT | N400NW | N80BF | N80BR | N106JL | N644JL | N801CW |
| | | (N801LX) | N804MR | | | | | | |
| 258013 | B | G-5-14 | G-OCCC | N334 | "N500RH" | N300RB | N802RM | | |
| 258014 | A | G-5-15 | N800MM | N294W | N800BS | N94WN | N298AG | | |
| 258015 | A | G-5-17 | G-BLPC | C-FTLA | C-GWFM | C-GWEM | N705BB | | |
| 258016 | SP | G-5-18 | F-GESL | N415PT | N904SB | N906SB | N816CW | N800VR | |
| 258017 | A | G-5-16 | N800LL | N801G | N801P | (N801R) | N217RM | N888ZZ | |
| 258018 | A | G-5-12 | N800PP | N818TG | N350WC | N350WG | N601RS | N36TJ | N525CF |
| | | N904JR | | | | | | | |
| 258019 | A | G-5-12 | VH-SGY | VH-LKV | N900MD | G-5-704 | N799SC | N799S | (N800NW) |
| | | N7996 | N880WW | N614AJ | | | | | |
| 258020 | SP | G-5-14 | N800ZZ | N270HC | (N251TJ) | | | | |
| 258021 | B | G-5-15 | G-GEIL | VR-CEJ | G-RCEJ | (N582CP) | G-IFTF | | |
| 258022 | B | G-5-16 | G-JJCB | G-5-569 | HZ-KSA | EC-193 | EC-ELK | G-5-874 | EC-ELK |
| | | N4257R | N822BL | | | | | | |
| 258023 | A | G-5-15 | N810AA | (N10AA) | N1910H | N1910J | N47HW | | |
| 258024 | A | G-5-18 | N811AA | N800DP | N802DC | N802D | N337RE | | |
| 258025 | B | G-5-14 | 3D-AVL | G-5-742 | G-BUIY | N7C | C-GMLR | C-GGYT | PR-LTA |
| 258026 | SP | G-5-18 | N800HS | N6TM | N6TU | N826CW | N82SR | | |
| 258027 | A | G-5-12 | N812AA | (N100PM) | N800PM | (N553US) | N553M | N558M | (N80CC) |
| | | N880M | | | | | | | |
| 258028 | B | G-5-12 | G-TSAM | N85KH | N277SS | | | | |
| 258029 | A | G-5-16 | (N600TH) | N813AA | N600HS | N77LA | | | |
| 258030 | A | G-5-14 | N600TH | N6GG | N10WF | N91CH | N616WG | | |
| 258031 | B | G-5-15 | PT-ZAA | PT-LHB | | | | | |
| 258032 | A | G-5-11 | N815AA | N526M | HZ-WBT5 | | | | |
| 258033 | A | G-5-19 | N157H | N57FF | I-CASG | N24RP | N673TM | N833CW | (N802LX) |
| | | N408MM | N621WP | | | | | | |
| 258034 | B | G-5-12 | G-HYGA | G-5-595 | G-HYGA | G-5-595 | N85DW | N125HH | |
| 258035 | SP | G-5-20 | N816AA | N30F | HB-VKM | PT-ORH | (N.....) | HB-VKM | PT-WIA |
| | | N835TS | N835CW | N85MG | | | | | |
| 258036 | A | G-5-18 | N817AA | N31F | HB-VKN | D-CFRC | N621MT | XA-ISH | [w/o |
| | | 27Oct03 near Tampico, Mexico] | | | | | | | |
| 258037 | B | G-5-15 | G-5-501 | 4W-ACN | 7O-ADC | M-HDAM | | | |
| 258038 | SP | G-5-20 | N800TR | N206PC | N206WC | N550RH | D-CHEF | C-GTNT | C-FDDD |
| 258039 | A | G-5-19 | N818AA | N400TB | N200KF | N193TR | N173TR | | |
| 258040 | B | G-5-15 | VH-IXL | G-5-697 | I-IGNO | N832MJ | N832MR | N713HC | N718HC |
| 258041 | A | G-5-18 | N819AA | N71NP | N626CG | | | | |
| 258042 | A | G-5-11 | N820AA | N20S | N112K | N804RM | N904BW | | |
| 258043 | SP | G-5-12 | (D-CAZH) | N319AT | N313CC | N313CQ | N937BC | M-ISSY | HA-YFI |
| | | N800SN | | | | | | | |
| 258044 | A | G-5-12 | N821AA | N72NP | N833JP | XA-UEH | | | |
| 258045 | SP | G-5-16 | N822AA | N800TF | N845CW | (N803LX) | N802SA | | |
| 258046 | A | G-5-20 | N823AA | N800BA | N125SB | | | | |
| 258047 | A | G-5-11 | N824AA | N84BA | N84FA | N324SA | XA-FGS | | |
| 258048 | A | G-5-16 | G-BMMO | (N125BA) | C-GCIB | N716DB | | | |
| 258049 | A | G-5-19 | N825AA | N800EX | N24SB | N24SP | N93CT | N796CH | |
| 258050 | B | G-5-503 | HZ-OFC | G-BUCR | I-OSLO | N9LR | G-ICFR | G-OURA | D-CLBC |
| | | N65GD | ZS-PAR | | | | | | |
| 258051 | A | G-5-18 | N826AA | N889DH | N888DH | N258SR | N851CW | (N804LX) | XA-ELM |
| 258052 | SP | G-5-20 | N360BA | N87EC | N68DA | N233KC | N221HB | C-FKGN | |
| 258053 | A | G-5-11 | N361BA | N5G | N484RA | N489SA | | | |
| 258054 | A | G-5-15 | N527M | | | | | | |
| 258055 | A | G-5-504 | N528M | N508MM | XA-UHI | | | | |
| 258056 | B | G-5-509 | G-JETI | M-JETI | | | | | |
| 258057 | A | G-5-508 | N362BA | N300GN | N800GN | N614AF | N614AP | | |

# BAe 125-800

| C/n | | Series | Identities | | | | | | | |
|---|---|---|---|---|---|---|---|---|---|---|
| 258058 | | B | G-5-510 | (ZK-EUR) | ZK-EUI | VH-NMR | N125JW | G-5-637 | N125JW | G-OMGG |
| | | | G-JJSI | | | | | | | |
| 258059 | | SP | G-5-506 | N363BA | N400GN | N355RB | N255RB | N355RB | N686CP | |
| 258060 | | A | G-5-511 | N364BA | N686CF | N330X | N330DE | N303SE | | |
| 258061 | | A | G-5-515 | N365BA | N161MM | N611MM | (N611CR) | N861CW | (N805LX) | N412DA |
| 258062 | | A | G-5-516 | N366BA | N961JC | N862CW | (N806LX) | | | |
| 258063 | | A | G-5-518 | N367BA | N684C | N74ND | N391TC | | | |
| 258064 | | B | G-5-514 | Malawi MAAW-J1 | | N803BG | PR-C8082 | | | |
| 258065 | | A | G-5-520 | N368BA | N77CS | N77CU | N65FA | N16GH | | |
| 258066 | | A | G-5-521 | N369BA | N75CS | N55RF | | | | |
| 258067 | | B | G-5-525 | D-CEVW | G-BUZX | G-5-807 | N801MM | N801MB | N801MM | N867CW |
| | | | N801MM | N867CW | (N807LX) | N469AL | | | | |
| 258068 | | B | G-5-539 | HZ-SJP | G-5-653 | HZ-SJP | G-5-738 | G-BUIM | N68GP | N68HR |
| | | | N167DD | | | | | | | |
| 258069 | | SP | G-5-526 | N519BA | (N743UP) | N746UP | N364WC | N160WC | | |
| 258070 | | A | G-5-527 | N520BA | N528AC | N255DV | N255DA | N998PA | N798PA | |
| 258071 | | A | G-5-528 | N521BA | N890A | N789LT | N94JT | | | |
| 258072 | | SP | G-5-529 | N522BA | (N745UP) | N747UP | N164WC | | | |
| 258073 | | SP | G-5-532 | D-CFVW | G-BVBH | N802MM | VR-BSI | VP-BSI | N2236 | N212RG |
| 258074 | | A | G-5-541 | ZK-MRM | N800MD | G-5-640 | N800MD | N800MN | N300BW | N850SM |
| | | | N103HT | N518S | | | | | | |
| 258075 | | A | G-5-533 | N518BA | N189B | N533P | XA-GFB | N3GU | XA-RYM | |
| 258076 | | B | G-5-535 | D-CGVW | G-BVAS | RA-02807 | [w/o near Minsk, Belarus, 26Oct09] | | | |
| 258077 | | A | G-5-538 | N523BA | N509GP | N877CW | N897CW | (N808LX) | | |
| 258078 | | B | G-5-544 | G-BNEH | G-5-713 | G-BNEH | ZS-FSI | OE-GHS | YL-VIP | G-88-01 |
| | | | YL-VIP | | | | | | | |
| 258079 | | B | G-5-542 | G-GJCB | G-BVHW | SE-DRV | 9M-DDW | N800LL | | |
| 258080 | | A | G-5-540 | N524BA | N800BP | N800WH | | | | |
| 258081 | | A | G-5-543 | N525BA | N650PM | N700PM | N196MC | N196MG | | |
| 258082 | | A | G-5-548 | ZK-RJI | N499SC | N90ME | N601BA | (N601BX) | N800S | |
| 258083 | | A | G-5-546 | N526BA | (N800HS) | N5C | N8UP | N852A | (N805AF) | |
| 258084 | | A | G-5-547 | N527BA | N780A | N877RP | N884CF | N24JG | N124JG | N323SL |
| 258085 | | A | G-5-551 | G-WBPR | N285AL | (N910VP) | N457J | | | |
| 258086 | | A | G-5-550 | N528BA | N125BA | N523WC | N523WG | (N523W) | | |
| 258087 | | A | G-5-552 | N529BA | N800TR | C-GAWH | C-FIGO | | | |
| 258088 | | SP | G-5-563 | (ZK-RHP) | G-BOOA | G-BTAB | N757BL | | | |
| 258089 | | A | G-5-555 | N530BA | N125JB | N862CE | N593HR | | | |
| 258090 | | SP | G-5-556 | N531BA | N2SG | N2YG | N410US | N8090 | N800FJ | N800FN |
| | | | N900RL | N901RL | N901RP | N414PE | | | | |
| 258091 | | A | G-5-560 | HB-VIK | N165BA | N1776H | | | | |
| 258092 | | A | G-5-558 | N532BA | N2MG | N3007 | N3008 | | | |
| 258093 | | A | G-5-559 | N533BA | N331SC | N800S | (A6-HMK) | N358LL | N317CC | N317CQ |
| | | | N2033 | | | | | | | |
| 258094 | | B | G-5-576 | D-CFAN | (LN-BEP) | LN-ESA | | | | |
| 258095 | | A | G-5-561 | N534BA | N200LS | (N500LL) | C-FPCP | C-GHXY | N40255 | ZS-OXY |
| | | | AP-BJL | ZS-OXY | | | | | | |
| 258096 | | SP | G-5-562 | N535BA | N800UP | N10TC | N596SW | N311JA | N311JX | N234GF |
| 258097 | | B | G-5-567 | HB-VIL | N170BA | N800BV | | | | |
| 258098 | | A | G-5-564 | N536BA | N300LS | N181FH | | | | |
| 258099 | | A | G-5-565 | (G-BNUB) | N537BA | C-FAAU | OY-MCL | N10YJ | | |
| 258100 | NA0401 | A | G-5-566 | N538BA | N108CF | N815CC | N180NE | | | |
| 258101 | NA0402 | A | G-5-572 | N539BA | N1125 | N757M | | | | |
| 258102 | NA0403 | A | G-5-573 | N540BA | N89K | (N89KT) | N89NC | N316EC | | |
| 258103 | NA0404 | A | G-5-574 | N541BA | N916PT | N494AT | VP-CCH | N801ST | N13SY | |
| 258104 | NA0405 | A | G-5-575 | N542BA | N527AC | N211JN | | | | |
| 258105 | NA0406 | A | G-5-577 | (N551BA) | G-BNZW | C-GKLB | C-FSCI | C-FSCY | C-FSCI | C-GCCU |
| 258106 | | B | G-5-580 | PK-WSJ | PK-RGM | (N107CF) | N888SS | G-OLDD | RA-02806 | |
| 258107 | NA0407 | A | G-5-578 | N552BA | N70NE | | | | | |
| 258108 | NA0408 | A | G-5-579 | N553BA | N61CT | N309G | N703VZ | N118GA | | |
| 258109 | | B | (N554BA) | G-5-581 | 5N-NPC | | | | | |
| 258110 | | B | (N555BA) | G-5-584 | D-CMIR | N710A | | | | |
| 258111 | NA0409 | SP | (N556BA) | G-5-582 | N554BA | N800TR | N375SC | N875SC | XA-TKQ | N870CA |
| | | | N801LM | | | | | | | |
| 258112 | | A | G-5-583 | Botswana OK-1/Z-1 | | G-5-664 | PT-OBT | N112NW | N331DC | N831DC |
| | | | N812GJ | | | | | | | |
| 258113 | NA0410 | A | G-5-587 | N555BA | N683E | N683F | | | | |
| 258114 | NA0411 | SP | G-5-586 | N556BA | N600LS | N800EC | (4X-COZ) | N807MC | | |
| 258115 | | B | G-5-599 | (G-BPGR) | Saudi Arabia 104 | | G-5-665 | Saudi Arabia 104 | | G-5-599 |
| | | | G-TCAP | P4-BOB | 9H-BOB | | | | | |
| 258116 | | B | G-5-592 | PT-LQP | | | | | | |
| 258117 | NA0412 | A | G-5-589 | N557BA | N825PS | N826CT | C-GBIS | | | |
| 258118 | | B | (G-5-590) | G-5-605 | (G-BPGS) | Saudi Arabia 105 | | HZ-105 | | |
| 258119 | NA0413 | SP | G-5-591 | N558BA | N203R | N221RE | N239R | N166WC | | |
| 258120 | | SP | G-5-606 | G-POSN | HB-VLI | VT-EAU | N120AP | G-POSN | N120AP | |
| 258121 | NA0414 | A | G-5-593 | (N559BA) | G-BOTX | C-FRPP | N4361Q | N800WA | | |
| 258122 | NA0415 | A | G-5-594 | N560BA | N800VC | N830BA | | | | |

## BAe 125-800

| C/n | | Series | Identities |
|---|---|---|---|
| 258123 | NA0416 | A | G-5-600 N561BA N353WC N353WG C-GCGS |
| 258124 | NA0417 | A | G-5-596 N562BA N800BA N376SC N876SC N801NW C-GCRP C-GRGE N824CW (N809LX) N67JF N620RM |
| 258125 | NA0418 | A | G-5-601 N563BA N802X (N99DA) N913SC |
| 258126 | NA0419 | SP | G-5-597 N564BA (N82BL) HZ-BL2 N196GA N818WM |
| 258127 | NA0420 | A | G-5-602 N565BA N803X N3QG |
| 258128 | NA0421 | SP | G-5-603 N566BA N804X N40GS |
| 258129 | | A | G-5-622 N269X USAF 88-0269 N94 N8029Z XA-IZA |
| 258130 | | B | G-5-620 G-FDSL G-TPHK G-BVFC G-ETOM D-CPAS G-OSPG G-DCTA G-GRGA |
| 258131 | | A | G-5-611 (N271X) N270X USAF 88-0270 N95 N8030F |
| 258132 | NA0422 | A | G-5-607 N567BA N125TR N222MS |
| 258133 | | B | G-5-616 G-GSAM G-5-642 N800FK G-JETK N800FK HP-1262 PT-WAU N800FK PR-SOL |
| 258134 | | A | G-5-634 (N270X) N271X USAF 88-0271 N96 N1061 N54ES* |
| 258135 | NA0423 | A | G-5-608 N568BA N801AB N801RJ (N241SM) N204SM N423SJ |
| 258136 | NA0424 | A | G-5-609 N569BA N452SM I-SDFG N80GJ |
| 258137 | NA0425 | A | G-5-610 N570BA N733K (N100MH) N110MH N800SE |
| 258138 | NA0428 | A | G-5-614 N582BA N244JM N384TC N800FJ |
| 258139 | NA0426 | A | G-5-612 N580BA N125BA (VR-BPA) VR-BLP N47VC N49VG (N47TJ) N795PH N726EP N797EP N218AD |
| 258140 | NA0427 | A | G-5-613 N581BA N45Y N856AF N858XL N326N |
| 258141 | NA0429 | A | G-5-615 N583BA N72K C-FGLF N106GC N73WF N141MR |
| 258142 | NA0430 | A | G-5-617 N584BA N1903P N850BM N149VB N149VP N50BN N45GD |
| 258143 | | B | G-5-656 5N-NPF 5N-AGZ |
| 258144 | NA0431 | A | G-5-618 N585BA N682B N682D |
| 258145 | NA0432 | SP | G-5-619 N586BA N540M N805CW N810LX N22NF |
| 258146 | | B | G-5-629 (G-BPYD) "HZ-109" G-5-703 HZ-109 |
| 258147 | NA0433 | A | G-5-621 N587BA N919P N9UP N812AM |
| 258148 | | B | G-5-630 (G-BPYE) HZ-110 Saudi Arabia 110 HZ-110 |
| 258149 | | SP | G-5-635 G-FASL N155T N577T YV2477 |
| 258150 | NA0434 | A | G-5-625 N588BA N77W N432AC N432AQ |
| 258151 | | 1000 | G-EXLR [prototype BAe125-1000; ff 16Jun90; last flight 10Jly92; wfu Nov93; shipped to Wichita, KS 27Sep95; remains located in scrapyard, Wichita, KS circa Mar96; to Raytheon Svs hangar, Wichita, KS circa Sep99 to train South Korean Hawker 800XP engineers] |
| 258152 | | B | G-5-626 HB-VHU (N42US) N800WG XA-UVH |
| 258153 | | B | G-5-627 HB-VHV |
| 258154 | | A | G-5-655 N272X USAF 88-0272 N97 N359CF |
| 258155 | | SP | G-5-628 N800BM D-CBMW N159RA N238AJ N300BL (N800LV) N711PE N702PE N723LK |
| 258156 | | A | G-5-661 N273X USAF 88-0273 N98 N355FA |
| 258157 | NA0435 | A | G-5-632 N589BA N800BA C-GMTR |
| 258158 | | SP | G-5-667 N274X USAF 88-0274 N99 N8064Q N158TN N800AF |
| 258159 | | 1000 | G-OPFC [second prototype BAe125-1000; ff 25Nov90] N10855 [used for ground tests; cx 05Sep03, parted out by APPH Houston Inc, Houston, TX] |
| 258160 | NA0436 | A | G-5-633 N590BA N354WC N354WG N369BG N389BG N160NW N803JL |
| 258161 | NA0437 | A | G-5-636 G-BPXW C-FFTM N17DD |
| 258162 | NA0438 | A | G-5-638 N591BA N753G N800PA |
| 258163 | NA0443 | A | G-5-639 G-BRCZ C-GMOL C-FWCE N360DE N717MT |
| 258164 | | B | G-5-654 Botswana OK1 [code Z2] Botswana OK2 G-OBLT (VR-BND) G-5-654 Saudi Arabia 130 HZ-130 |
| 258165 | | A | G-5-657 VR-BPG ZS-BPG VT-RAY N324BG |
| 258166 | NA0439 | A | G-5-641 N592BA N74PC N74PQ C-GKPP |
| 258167 | | A | G-5-662 N125AS VR-CAS VP-CAS (N802SJ) N825DA N48AL |
| 258168 | NA0440 | A | G-5-643 N593BA N74NP N295JR |
| 258169 | | A | G-5-644 N47CG N526AC N255DV C-FDKJ |
| 258170 | NA0441 | A | G-5-645 N594BA N75NP N79NP N24JG |
| 258171 | NA0442 | A | G-5-646 N595BA N754G N4444J N707PE N729HZ N729EZ |
| 258172 | NA0444 | SP | G-5-647 N596BA N290EC N811AM |
| 258173 | NA0447 | SP | G-5-648 N599BA N95AE N82XP C-FCRH C-FCRF C-GTAU |
| 258174 | NA0445 | A | G-5-649 N597BA N174A N174NW N800QC |
| 258175 | NA0446 | A | G-5-650 N598BA (VR-BPB) VR-BLQ N204JC HB-VMF N175U N2032 |
| 258176 | | B | (N610BA) G-5-652 HB-VJY N176WA XA-TPB N176TL XA-... |
| 258177 | | A | G-5-668 PT-OJC N411RA N217AL N5119 |
| 258178 | NA0449 | B | G-5-658 N611BA D-CWIN N800WT N868WC N178AX N430BB |
| 258179 | NA0448 | A | G-5-660 N610BA N125BA N60TC N60TG N904GP N904GR |
| 258180 | | B | G-5-675 G-XRMC G-BZNR VP-BMH |
| 258181 | NA0450 | SP | G-5-663 N612BA N355WC N355WG C-GAGU C-GAGQ N861CE |
| 258182 | | B | G-5-676 (VR-B..) G-PBWH G-5-676 N128RS N12F |
| 258183 | NA0451 | A | G-5-666 N613BA N50PM N90PM N63PM N599EC CS-DNI N883EJ N731JR XA-GIC |
| 258184 | | B | G-5-678 (PT-WAW) PT-OSW |
| 258185 | NA0452 | A | G-5-669 N614BA N207PC (N207RC) XA-SIV N801CF |

# BAe 125-800

| C/n | | Series | Identities |
|---|---|---|---|
| 258186 | | A | G-5-683 G-BSUL VR-BPM G-BSUL N8186 N818G N818MV [w/o 31Jul08 Owatonna, MN] |
| 258187 | NA0453 | SP | G-5-670 N615BA N60PM N750RV (N750PB) (N242JG) N4242 |
| 258188 | NA0454 | A | G-5-671 N616BA N1910A N191BA N180EG (N892BP) |
| 258189 | NA0455 | A | G-5-673 N617BA N6JB N6UB N195KC N25BB |
| 258190 | | B | G-5-684 G-BTAE PT-OHB PT-JAA |
| 258191 | NA0456 | A | G-5-674 N618BA N152NS N801P (N730BG) |
| 258192 | | A | TR-LDB G-5-691 TR-LDB N192SJ |
| 258193 | NA0457 | A | G-5-677 N619BA N300PM N699EC CS-DNH N893EJ C-GKGD C-GDBC |
| 258194 | | B | G-5-692 PT-OTC |
| 258195 | NA0458 | A | G-5-679 N630BA N800BA N800GX N100GX N940HC N941HC N28ZF |
| 258196 | NA0459 | A | G-5-680 N631BA N125TR N511WM N511WD N929WG N929WQ N189TM |
| 258197 | | A | G-5-696 G-BTMG G-OMGE N150SB |
| 258198 | | B | G-5-694 PT-WAL |
| 258199 | NA0460 | SP | G-5-681 N632BA N4402 |
| 258200 | NA0461 | A | G-5-682 N633BA N461W N722A |
| 258201 | | B | G-5-699 (D-C...) G-OCCI G-BWSY P4-AMF |
| 258202 | NA0462 | A | G-5-685 N634BA N200GX N800DR N800DN A6-MAA |
| 258203 | NA0463 | A | G-5-686 N635BA YV-735CP N228G N453TM N805JL |
| 258204 | NA0464 | A | G-5-687 N636BA N341AP N57LN N703SM |
| 258205 | NA0465 | A | G-5-689 N637BA N805X N939TT |
| 258206 | NA0466 | A | G-5-688 N638BA (N800BJ) PT-OMC N638BA N466CS N466AE N395HE |
| 258207 | NA0467 | A | G-5-690 N639BA N600KC (N48DD) N2BG N2QG (N103BG) |
| 258208 | | A | "G-5-670" G-5-700 (PT-...) G-BUID TC-ANC N208BG N123HK |
| 258209 | NA0468 | A | G-5-695 N670BA YV-800CP N168BA N693C N410BT N661JN N9990S |
| 258210 | | B | G-5-705 G-RAAR HB-VMI VP-CSP |
| 258211 | | A | G-5-724 PT-OSB N91DV N151TC N855GA |
| 258212 | | B | G-5-710 G-BUCP D-CSRI RP-C8008 (N323L) |
| 258213 | | B | G-5-709 D-CWBW G-BURV N10857 [cx 21Jly05; parted out Houston, TX] |
| 258214 | | B | G-5-706 VR-CCX PT-OOI |
| 258215 | | U-125 | G-5-727 G-JFCX Japan 29-3041 [code 041] |
| 258216 | NA0469 | A | G-5-714 N671BA N500J N50QJ |
| 258217 | NA0470 | SP | G-5-715 N672BA N600J N60QJ N125GB N800SV |
| 258218 | NA0471 | SP | G-5-725 N673BA N57PM N118K (N503RJ) N118KL |
| 258219 | | A | G-5-740 (9M-WCM) 9M-AZZ N8881J |
| 258220 | NA0472 | A | G-5-728 N674BA N58PM N125AW N999JF |
| 258221 | NA0473 | SP | G-5-731 N675BA N25W N25WN VP-BHB N919SS |
| 258222 | | B | G-5-745 G-VIPI |
| 258223 | NA0474 | A | G-5-733 N677BA N800BA N622AB N622AD N44HH |
| 258224 | | SP | G-5-763 ZS-NJH N827RH N847RH N618JL N478PM N810V N65DL |
| 258225 | NA0475 | A | G-5-739 N682BA N800BA N800CJ N935H |
| 258226 | | A | G-5-755 (9M-...) G-BVCU D-CSRB RP-C1926 N709EA N800MJ |
| 258227 | | U-125 | G-5-769 G-BUUW Japan 39-3042 [code 042] |
| 258228 | | A | G-5-758 HB-VKV N130LC |
| 258229 | | SP | G-5-744 N683BA PT-OTH N229RY TC-TEK N984HM |
| 258230 | | A | G-5-748 N678BA N71MT N800RG |
| 258231 | | A | G-5-750 N685BA N75MT ZS-PSE 5N-... |
| 258232 | | A | G-5-752 N686BA N900KC XA-NGS XA-AEN N723HH C-FBUR |
| 258233 | | B | G-5-770 D-CAVW F-WQCD (VR-BQH) VR-BTM VP-BTM G-BYHM M-AZAG |
| 258234 | | B | G-5-757 VR-CDE YV-814CP VR-CDE VP-CDE N65CE |
| 258235 | | B | G-5-774 D-CBVW G-BWVA OY-RAA N258SA D-CWOL (PH-WOL) OY-RAA |
| 258236 | | A | G-5-764 N162BA N80PM N800TJ (N39BL) N58BL |
| 258237 | | A | G-5-775 D-CCVW G-BWRN 9M-DRL VP-BAW N237RA N250JE N250MB |
| 258238 | | SP | G-5-767 N163BA N70PM N100AG |
| 258239 | | A | G-5-768 N164BA VR-BPN N904H N62TC (N262CT) N84CT C-GMLR |
| 258240 | | B | G-5-772 G-BUWC G-SHEA HB-VLT G-HCFR G-CJAA G-WYNE |
| 258241 | | SP | G-5-777 N165BA N125CJ N94NB N540BA XA-CHA |
| 258242 | | U-125 | G-5-793 G-BVFE Japan 49-3043 [code 043] |
| 258243 | | SP | G-5-778 (G-BUWD) G-SHEB VH-XMO C-GSCL C-FLPH C-FTVC |
| 258244 | | SP | G-5-780 N166BA N800CJ N95NB N530BA N252DH N252DT N252DH N252DT N862CE |
| 258245 | | U-125A | G-JHSX Japan 52-3001 [code 001] |
| 258246 | | A | G-5-782 N387H HB-VKW |
| 258247 | | U-125A | G-5-813 G-BVRF Japan 52-3002 [code 002] |
| 258248 | | A | G-5-784 N388H N789LB |
| 258249 | | A | G-5-786 N933H N326SU (N826SU) N500HF N249SR |
| 258250 | | U-125A | G-5-815 G-BVRG Japan 52-3003 [code 003] |
| 258251 | | A | G-5-787 N937H N194JS N192JS |
| 258252 | | A | G-5-788 N938H XB-GCC XA-GCC |
| 258253 | | A | G-5-790 N942H N801CE N3RC |
| 258254 | | A | G-5-791 N943H N2015M N800NY |
| 258255 | | SP | G-5-792 [first Hawker 800] N946H N127KC N575MR |
| 258256 | | | G-5-795 N947H N256BC (N256FS) |
| 258257 | | | G-5-796 N951H N802DC N415BJ N304AT |
| 258258 | | B | G-5-798 G-BVJI (N953H) G-BVJI N54SB N910JD N910JN N258SP N258MR |

## BAe 125-800

| C/n | Series | Identities | | | | | | | |
|---|---|---|---|---|---|---|---|---|---|
| 258259 | | G-5-799 | N954H | (N966L) | | | | | |
| 258260 | | G-5-800 | N957H | | | | | | |
| 258261 | | G-5-802 | N958H | PT-GAF | | | | | |
| 258262 | | G-5-803 | N959H | N521JK | | | | | |
| 258263 | | G-5-804 | N961H | N826GA | | | | | |
| 258264 | | G-5-806 | N805H | HB-VLF | 5N-BMR | | | | |
| 258265 | | G-5-809 | N806H | HB-VLG | | | | | |
| 258266 | XP | G-5-811 | (N293H) | G-BVRW | (N293H) | N800XP | (N800GT) | N414XP | N800CC |
| 258267 | | G-5-812 | N294H | N811CC | N980DC | N601VC | I-SIRF | VP-CAF | |
| 258268 | U-125A | G-5-829 | G-BVYV | Japan 62-3004 | | N809H | Japan 62-3004 [code 004] | | |
| 258269 | | G-5-814 | N295H | N380X | N380DE | N302SE | | | |
| 258270 | SP | G-5-816 | N297H | N802CE | N838JL | | | | |
| 258271 | | G-5-818 | N298H | N803CE | N787CM | | | | |
| 258272 | | G-5-819 | N299H | N2426 | N4426 | | | | |
| 258273 | | G-5-820 | N803H | N967L | N258RA | N337WR | | | |
| 258274 | | G-5-822 | N804H | N2428 | N4428 | N41HF | | | |
| 258275 | | G-5-823 | N905H | N77TC | N7775 | XA-RBV | | | |
| 258276 | SP | G-5-824 | N667H | N126KC | | | | | |
| 258277 | XP | G-BVYW | N97SH | N333PC | (N339PC) | N339CC | | | |
| 258278 | XP | G-BVZK | N872AT | | | | | | |
| 258279 | XP | G-BVZL | (N817H) | 4X-CZM | N817H | N877DM | | | |
| 258280 | XP | G-BWDC | N351SP | N351SB | N100LA | | | | |
| 258281 | XP | G-BWDD | N914H | VH-ELJ | N281XP | N781TA | N832LX | | |
| 258282 | XP | G-5-827 | G-BWDW | N916H | PT-WHH | N782TA | (N811LX) | (N800LX) | |
| 258283 | XP | G-5-828 | G-BWGB | N918H | (N283XP) | 4X-COV | N283BX | N82EA | C-FJHS |
| 258284 | XP | G-5-830 | G-BWGC | N919H | (PT-LTA) | PT-WNO | N919H | PR-DBB | |
| 258285 | XP2 | G-5-831 | G-BWGD | N808H | (N800XP) | N285XP | | | |
| 258286 | XP | G-5-832 | G-BWGE | N807H | N501F | N304RJ | | | |
| 258287 | XP2 | G-5-833 | N668H | (N287XP) | N801WB | XA-UFK | | | |
| 258288 | U-125A | G-5-848 | N816H | Japan 72-3005 | | [code 005] | | | |
| 258289 | XP2 | G-5-834 | N669H | N515GP | N863CE | | | | |
| 258290 | XP | G-5-835 | N670H | N348MC | | | | | |
| 258291 | XP | "G-5-837" | G-5-836 | N672H | N291XP | N291SJ | N791TA | N833LX | |
| 258292 | XP | G-5-838 | N673H | N33BC | | | | | |
| 258293 | XP | G-5-839 | N679H | N404CE | N150NC | | | | |
| 258294 | XP2 | G-5-840 | N682H | N404BS | N632FW | N35CC | | | |
| 258295 | XP | G-5-841 | N683H | VH-LAW | VH-LAT | VH-KEF | VH-EJL | | |
| 258296 | XP | G-5-842 | N685H | N801JT | N707TA | (N812LX) | N934RD | | |
| 258297* | XP | [first US-assembed aircraft] | | | N297XP | N725TA | N725JA | N725TA | N843LX |
| 258298 | XP | G-5-843 | N298XP | N880SP | | | | | |
| 258299 | XP | G-5-844 | N299XP | (N32BC) | N601DR | N87RB^ | | | |
| 258300 | XP | G-5-845 | N689H | N800VF | N950PC | (N800NE) | | | |
| 258301* | XP | N1105Z | PT-WMA | | | | | | |
| 258302 | XP | G-5-847 | N302XP | XA-RUY | XA-GIE | N302MT | XA-GIE | | |
| 258303 | XP2 | G-5-849 | N303XP | N876H | N621CH | N4SA | N303DT | | |
| 258304* | XP | N802JT | N5734 | | | | | | |
| 258305 | U-125A | G-5-864 | N305XP | Japan 72-3006 [code 006] | | | | | |
| 258306* | U-125A | N1103U | Japan 82-3007 [code 007] | | | | | | |
| 258307 | XP | G-5-850 | N307XP | N109TD | N802WM | N307AD | N85CC | | |
| 258308 | XP | G-5-851 | N308XP | (N11WC) | N345BR | N875LP | | | |
| 258309* | XP | N803JT | N5735 | N92UP | | | | | |
| 258310 | XP2 | G-5-852 | N310XP | PT-WMG | N33VC | | | | |
| 258311* | XP | N804JT | N800RD | N850J | | | | | |
| 258312 | XP2 | G-5-853 | N312XP | PT-WMD | N251X | B-3998 | N251X | N924JM | A6-ZZZ |
| 258313* | XP | N2159X | N313XP | N84BA | N908VZ | N411VZ | | | |
| 258314 | XP | G-5-854 | N314XP | OM-SKY | N800NJ | | | | |
| 258315* | XP | N2169X | N9292X | | | | | | |
| 258316 | XP | G-5-855 | N316XP | N516GP | C-GDII | | | | |
| 258317* | XP | N2173X | N9NB | N520BA | N520JF | | | | |
| 258318 | XP | G-5-856 | N318XP | N1910H | | | | | |
| 258319* | XP | N2291X | C-FIPE | OD-TSW | | | | | |
| 258320* | XP | N2322X | N720TA | (N813LX) | (N801LX) | XB-MCB | | | |
| 258321 | XP | G-5-857 | N691H | N32BC | | | | | |
| 258322* | XP2 | N722TA | (N814LX) | N307RM | | | | | |
| 258323 | XP | G-5-858 | N323XP | N877S | N877SL | N752CS | | | |
| 258324 | XP | G-5-860 | N324XP | N303BC | | | | | |
| 258325* | U-125A | N1112N | Japan 82-3008 [code 008] | | | | | | |
| 258326* | XP2 | N326XP | N1897A | N897A | | | | | |
| 258327 | XP2 | G-5-861 | N327XP | N111ZN | N801HB | (N219DC) | N22GA | | |
| 258328 | XP | G-5-866 | N328XP | VH-SGY | VH-SCY | A6-MAH | | | |
| 258329 | XP2 | G-5-862 | N329XP | N901K | N903K | N825CP | | | |
| 258330 | XP2 | G-5-869 | N330XP | N139M | N86MN | | | | |
| 258331* | XP2 | N10NB | N510BA | N160CT | N864CE | | | | |
| 258332 | XP2 | G-5-865 | N332XP | N36H | N53LB | | | | |
| 258333* | U-125A | N3261Y | Japan 82-3009 [code 009] | | | | | | |
| 258334* | XP2 | N334XP | N399JC | N80HD | N60HD | | | | |

# BAe 125-800

| C/n | Series | Identities |
|---|---|---|
| US Production | | |
| 258335 | XP | G-5-867 N335XP OY-RAC OE-GHU |
| 258336* | XP | N336XP N2286U N745UP |
| 258337 | XP | G-5-868 N337XP [last to be assembled at Chester, UK - rolled out 22Apr97, ff 29Apr97, del to USA 08May97] (9M-VVV) N337XP N733TA (N815LX) |
| 258338 | XP | N838QS N838WC |
| 258339 | XP2 | N23395 SE-DVD N14SA N294CV |
| 258340 | XP | N840QS N840WC N907MC |
| 258341 | U-125A | N3251M "N2351M" Japan 92-3010 [code 010] |
| 258342 | XP | N2320J South Korea 258-342 |
| 258343 | XP | N1102U South Korea 258-343 |
| 258344 | XP | N29GP |
| 258345 | XP | N1135A D-CBMV D-CBMW (G-VONI) OY-LKG |
| 258346 | XP | N23204 South Korea 258-346 |
| 258347 | XP | N1115G N40PL N409AV |
| 258348 | U-125A | N2175W Japan 92-3011 [code 011] |
| 258349 | XP2 | N723TA VP-BHL (N74WF) N349GA C-FEPC N377JC |
| 258350 | XP | N23207 South Korea 258-350 |
| 258351 | XP | N23208 South Korea 258-351 |
| 258352 | XP | N2321S South Korea 258-352 |
| 258353 | XP | N2321V South Korea 258-353 |
| 258354 | XP | N2G N262G |
| 258355 | XP | N855QS |
| 258356 | XP | N550H N55BA |
| 258357 | XP | N2321Z South Korea 258-357 |
| 258358 | XP | N240B D-CJET OY-JBJ |
| 258359 | XP | N25WX P4-ALE |
| 258360 | U-125A | N3189H Japan 92-3012 [code 012] |
| 258361 | XP | N861QS N861WC |
| 258362 | XP | N862QS N862WC (N862JA) N949JA |
| 258363 | XP | N726TA N816LX |
| 258364 | XP | N728TA (N817LX) (N804LX) |
| 258365 | XP2 | N865SM N243BA |
| 258366 | XP | N1133N (CS-MAI) N894CA VH-ZUH |
| 258367 | XP | N3263E N367DM OY-GIP N704JM |
| 258368 | XP | N804AC |
| 258369 | XP | N800PC |
| 258370 | U-125A | N23556 Japan 02-3013 [code 013] |
| 258371 | XP | N848N |
| 258372 | XP | N1251K N372XP LV-ZHY N800GN |
| 258373 | XP | N3270X N168BF |
| 258374 | XP | N729TA (N874CW) (N818LX) N805LX |
| 258375 | XP | N875QS N154RR |
| 258376 | XP | N1640 |
| 258377 | XP | N1251K N984GC [1,000th DH/HS/BAe/Raytheon 125 sale] N993SA |
| 258378 | XP | N494RG N442MA |
| 258379 | XP | N879QS [w/o 28Aug06 Carson City, NV] N879WC [parted out Atlanta/DeKalb-Peachtree, GA] |
| 258380 | XP2 | N8SP N999JF N101FC |
| 258381 | U-125A | N23566 Japan 02-3014 [code 014] |
| 258382 | XP | N23451 SE-DYE EI-WXP |
| 258383 | XP | N730TA (N819LX) N806LX |
| 258384 | XP | N23455 TC-MDC N23455 N955MC G-LAOR M-LAOR |
| 258385 | XP | N23466 SE-DYV G-0502 SE-DYV |
| 258386 | XP2 | N23479 N61DF N61DN N715WG N715WT XA-FYN |
| 258387 | XP | N887QS |
| 258388 | XP | N23488 TC-OKN N809TA (N809TP) N809BA |
| 258389 | XP | N23493 I-DDVA YR-VPA YL-MAR |
| 258390 | XP | N23509 (N800SG) N800FD |
| 258391 | XP | N391XP N771SV 4X-CPS N543LF |
| 258392 | XP | N23569 "LX-BYG" LX-GBY G-0504 LX-GBY F-HBOM |
| 258393 | XP | N893QS |
| 258394 | XP | N394XP N800DW N800ER N800TL |
| 258395 | XP | N23577 PT-WVG |
| 258396 | XP | N23585 N21EL |
| 258397 | XP | N752TA (N887CW) (N820LX) (N752LX) N852LX |
| 258398 | XP | N168HH TC-VSC LY-HCW |
| 258399 | XP | N899QS CS-DNJ N979JB |
| 258400 | XP | N404JC N314TC |
| 258401 | XP | N23592 Brazil EU93A-6050 |
| 258402 | XP | N729AT |
| 258403 | XP | N23550 ZS-DCK N25XP N601RS N111VG |
| 258404 | XP | N30289 VP-BCM N404DB N448JM |
| 258405 | XP | N405XP N866RR N866RB D-CLBD M-CLAA |
| 258406 | XP | N754TA (N821LX) N821LX |

## BAe 125-800

| C/n | Series | Identities | | | | | | |
|---|---|---|---|---|---|---|---|---|
| 258407 | U-125A | N30562 | Japan 02-3015 [code 015] | | | | | |
| 258408 | XP | N30319 | B-3990 | | | | | |
| 258409 | XP | N30337 | PT-WPF | N929AK | N929AL | (VP-LV.) | N929AL | VP-BSK | N827NS |
| | | XA-TPB | | | | | | |
| 258410 | XP2 | N755TA | N322LA | N315BK | N885M | OD-EAS | | |
| 258411 | XP2 | N617TM | | | | | | |
| 258412 | XP | N30682 | N990HC | | | | | |
| 258413 | XP | N760TA | N813CW | (N822LX) | N807LX | | | |
| 258414 | XP | N30742 | N800XP | N800XM | EI-RNJ | N800XM | | |
| 258415 | XP | N31016 | TC-BHD | TC-STR | N800LR | N444MG | | |
| 258416 | XP | N816QS | | | | | | |
| 258417 | XP | N747NG | N246V | N240V | | | | |
| 258418 | XP | N31046 | N806XM | (N516TM) | N516TH | | | |
| 258419 | XP | N419XP | N508BP | N559DM | | | | |
| 258420 | XP2 | N31340 | N910JD | | | | | |
| 258421 | XP | N31820 | Brazil EU93A-6051 | | | | | |
| 258422 | XP | N822QS | CS-DNM | VT-SRA | | | | |
| 258423 | XP | N925JF | N388BS | | | | | |
| 258424 | XP | N1899K | YL-NST | | | | | |
| 258425 | XP2 | N825XP | N800VA | N59BR | N89BR | N438PM | N802CF | |
| 258426 | XP | N426XP | N27FL | | | | | |
| 258427 | U-125A | N31833 | Japan 02-3016 [code 016] | | | | | |
| 258428 | XP | N772TA | N828CW | (N823LX) | (N808LX) | N842FL | | |
| 258429 | XP | N88HD | N68HD | ZS-PKY | | | | |
| 258430 | XP | N31590 | CS-DNK | N905MT | | | | |
| 258431 | XP | N144HM | XA-TEM | | | | | |
| 258432 | XP | N432XP | N1650 | N165L | N832CW | (N824LX) | N809LX | A6-SKA |
| 258433 | XP | N833QS | | | | | | |
| 258434 | XP | N40027 | Brazil EU93A-6052 | | | | | |
| 258435 | XP | N835QS | CS-DNN | | | | | |
| 258436 | XP | N836QS | | | | | | |
| 258437 | XP | N780TA | (N825LX) | N812LX | | | | |
| 258438 | XP | N40113 | VP-BHZ | N827SA | | | | |
| 258439 | XP | N31596 | CS-DNL | N497AG | | | | |
| 258440 | XP | N40488 | N801MB | N408RT | | | | |
| 258441 | XP | N800PE | N800PB | N370DE | | | | |
| 258442 | XP | N40202 | PT-XDY | N442XP | N80PK | | | |
| 258443 | XP | N310AS | N489VC | | | | | |
| 258444 | XP | N40489 | EC-HJL | LX-ARC | C-GBAP | | | |
| 258445 | U-125A | N40708 | Japan 12-3017 [code 017] | | | | | |
| 258446 | XP | N529M | (N983EC) | N983CE | | | | |
| 258447 | XP | N40310 | Brazil EU93A-6053 | | | | | |
| 258448 | XP | N41280 | N532PJ | N19DD | N19DU | | | |
| 258449 | XP | N41431 | N365AT | | | | | |
| 258450 | XP | N41441 | D-CTAN | I-DLOH | | | | |
| 258451 | XP | N41534 | N475HM | | | | | |
| 258452 | XP | N852QS | | | | | | |
| 258453 | XP | N802TA | N68CB | | | | | |
| 258454 | XP | N41093 | N802TA | (N826LX) | N813LX | N854FL | | |
| 258455 | XP | N803TA | (N827LX) | N803FL | | | | |
| 258456 | XP | N800EM | N41762 | G-JMAX | | | | |
| 258457 | XP | N41984 | CS-DNO | | | | | |
| 258458 | XP | N42685 | N228TM | | | | | |
| 258459 | XP | N43259 | N939LE | N800WW | N800WP | | | |
| 258460 | XP | N81SN | N810N | C-FHRD | N85PK | N460WF* | | |
| 258461 | XP | N804TA | N881CW | N828LX | N846FL* | | | |
| 258462 | XP | N43230 | LV-PIW | LV-ZTR | | | | |
| 258463 | XP | N863QS | | | | | | |
| 258464 | XP | N41964 | HZ-KSRA | N828NS | | | | |
| 258465 | XP | N43265 | ZS-DDT | VT-RPL | | | | |
| 258466 | XP | N805TA | N866CW | N829LX | N866CW | N829LX | | |
| 258467 | XP | N5732 | N43310 | N5732 | N42FB | | | |
| 258468 | XP | N43436 | CS-DNT | | | | | |
| 258469 | U-125A | N43079 | Japan 12-3018 [code 018] | | | | | |
| 258470 | XP | N42830 | B-3991 | | | | | |
| 258471 | XP2 | N43642 | N5736 | | | | | |
| 258472 | XP | N44722 | N872QS | | | | | |
| 258473 | XP | N73UP | | | | | | |
| 258474 | XP | N874QS | | | | | | |
| 258475 | XP | N43675 | HZ-KSRB | N829NS | | | | |
| 258476 | XP | N44676 | N192NC | N830NS | VT-HCB | N830NS | XA-... | |
| 258477 | XP | N44767 | OE-GEO | VP-BOO | | | | |
| 258478 | XP | N44648 | N806TA | N800DR | N989ST | | | |
| 258479 | XP | N44779 | CS-DNU | | | | | |
| 258480 | XP | N4403 | N73WW* | | | | | |
| 258481 | XP | N43926 | HZ-KSRC | | | | | |

# BAe 125-800

| C/n | Series | Identities | | | | | | |
|---|---|---|---|---|---|---|---|---|
| 258482 | XP | N43182 | N882QS | | | | | |
| 258483 | XP | N44883 | N807TA | N830LX | N830FL | | | |
| 258484 | XP | N84UP | | | | | | |
| 258485 | XP | N44515 | (HZ-KSRD) | A7-AAL | N485LT | N125XP | | |
| 258486 | XP | N886QS | | | | | | |
| 258487 | XP | N51387 | N3007 | | | | | |
| 258488 | XP | N50788 | N488HP | N719HG | | | | |
| 258489 | XP | N28GP | | | | | | |
| 258490 | XP | N50490 | N327LJ | | | | | |
| 258491 | XP | N51191 | VP-BKB | N51191 | XA-TYH | | | |
| 258492 | XP | N51192 | N800FJ | N800LF | C-GCIX | | | |
| 258493 | U-125A | N40933 | Japan 22-3019 [code 019] | | | | | |
| 258494 | XP | N808TA | VP-BXP | M-HAWK | | | | |
| 258495 | XP | N51495 | C-GGCH | 5B-CKL | SX-FAR | | | |
| 258496 | XP | N125TM | N175TM | G-RDMV | EI-ECE | | | |
| 258497 | XP | N51197 | N825CT | | | | | |
| 258498 | XP | N809TA | N11UL | | | | | |
| 258499 | XP | N51099 | CS-DNV | | | | | |
| 258500 | XP | N50600 | C-FPCP | C-FPCE | | | | |
| 258501 | XP | N5001S | B-3992 | | | | | |
| 258502 | XP2 | N4469B | XA-AET | N502HR | HK-4670 | | | |
| 258503 | XP | N802WM | N801WM | | | | | |
| 258504 | XP | N5004B | TC-AHS | | | | | |
| 258505 | XP | N50005 | N805QS | N835QS | | | | |
| 258506 | XP | N50166 | I-RONY | | | | | |
| 258507 | XP | N507BW | C-GIBU | | | | | |
| 258508 | XP | N5008S | N800PE | | | | | |
| 258509 | XP | N4109E | N509XP | N313CC | N983CE | N162JB | | |
| 258510 | XP | N810TA | N890CW | N831LX | | | | |
| 258511 | XP | N5011J | CS-DNX | | | | | |
| 258512 | XP | N501CT | | | | | | |
| 258513 | U-125A | N50513 | Japan 22-3020 [code 020] | | | | | |
| 258514 | XP | N4021Z | D-CHEF | (M-CHEF) | M-OOUN | | | |
| 258515 | XP | N321EJ | N321MS | | | | | |
| 258516 | XP | N811TA | N896CW | (N832LX) | N817LX | N415JA | | |
| 258517 | XP | N817QS | | | | | | |
| 258518 | XP | N29B | | | | | | |
| 258519 | XP | N443M | N72FC | | | | | |
| 258520 | XP | N4469U | VP-CRS | OE-GEA | VP-CEA | JY-AW4 | JY-AWD | JY-WJA |
| 258521 | XP | N50521 | HB-VNJ | N58521 | VT-RAN | | | |
| 258522 | XP | N812TA | N746UP | | | | | |
| 258523 | XP | N5023J | N824QS | | | | | |
| 258524 | XP | N4224H | N7374 | (N73741) | (N666BC) | N872BC | | |
| 258525 | XP | N4425R | B-3993 | | | | | |
| 258526 | XP | N50626 | B-3995 | N526XP | N837RE | | | |
| 258527 | XP | N813TA | N56BE | | | | | |
| 258528 | XP | N828QS | | | | | | |
| 258529 | XP | N814TA | N259RH | | | | | |
| 258530 | XP | N890SP | C-FBBF | N76LV | | | | |
| 258531 | XP | N4469F | N259SP | N622VL | VT-HBC | N259SP | | |
| 258532 | XP | N317CC | | | | | | |
| 258533 | U-125A | N50733 | JASDF 32-3021 [code 021] | | | | | |
| 258534 | XP | N815TA | (N833LX) | N818LX | | | | |
| 258535 | XP | N51335 | N853QS | N255DX | | | | |
| 258536 | XP | N51336 | B-3996 | N102PA | OE-GCE | | | |
| 258537 | XP2 | N100NG | N600NG | N650JS | | | | |
| 258538 | XP | N816TA | N25853 | 4X-CRY | N538LD | P4-SNT | | |
| 258539 | XP | N51239 | VP-BKB | JY-AW5 | JY-AWE | | | |
| 258540 | XP | N50440 | N700MG | N571CH | | | | |
| 258541 | XP2 | N50441 | N800XP | OY-FCG | N541XP | | | |
| 258542 | XP | N842QS | | | | | | |
| 258543 | XP | N806TA | N843CW | (N834LX) | N819LX | | | |
| 258544 | XP | N799JC | | | | | | |
| 258545 | XP | N50445 | N845QS | | | | | |
| 258546 | XP | N50461 | N108BP | N488VC | | | | |
| 258547 | XP | N4469N | PR-OPP | | | | | |
| 258548 | XP | N808TA | (N835LX) | N850JL | N860JL | | | |
| 258549 | XP | N51149 | N155NS | | | | | |
| 258550 | XP | N793RC | | | | | | |
| 258551 | XP | N44759 | N190NC | N777DB | N85594 | N800LQ | | |
| 258552 | XP | N817TA | (N836LX) | N834LX | | | | |
| 258553 | XP | N51453 | PR-LUG | | | | | |
| 258554 | XP | N50034 | (5B-CKG) | XA-GTE | | | | |
| 258555 | XP | N820TA | N300CQ | | | | | |
| 258556 | XP2 | N51556 | N800WY | | | | | |
| 258557 | XP | N51457 | N1630 | | | | | |

# BAe 125-800

| C/n | Series | Identities | | | | | |
|---|---|---|---|---|---|---|---|
| 258558 | XP | N51058 | N225PB | | | | |
| 258559 | XP | N50459 | N819AP | N819AB | PR-FAP | N223FA | |
| 258560 | XP | N50740 | N877S | N8778 | | | |
| 258561 | XP | N1630 | N16300 | I-ALHO | | | |
| 258562 | XP | N5062H | (N877S) | N802DC | | | |
| 258563 | XP | N4469M | N981CE | | | | |
| 258564 | XP | N864QS | | | | | |
| 258565 | XP | N4465M | N240Z | | | | |
| 258566 | XP | N4466Z | N664AC | | | | |
| 258567 | XP | N50667 | N74PC | N24SM | | | |
| 258568 | XP2 | N4468K | N96FT | | | | |
| 258569 | XP | N4469X | N244LS | N906AS | | | |
| 258570 | XP | N50670 | "N873QS" | N880QS | | | |
| 258571 | XP | N4471N | RP-C8576 | | | | |
| 258572 | XP | N5072L | N80FB | N293S | | | |
| 258573 | XP | N873QS | | | | | |
| 258574 | XP | N51274 | N915AM | (N915MT) | N915AP | | |
| 258575 | XP | N3215M | B-3997 | | | | |
| 258576 | XP | N867QS | | | | | |
| 258577 | XP | N51027 | N800UK | | | | |
| 258578 | XP | N50378 | N91HK | | | | |
| 258579 | XP | N50309 | PK-TVO | | | | |
| 258580 | XP | N880QS | N1989D | | | | |
| 258581 | XP | N50661 | XA-ICF | N581GE | XA-JCT | | |
| 258582 | XP | N50182 | (N170SK) | XA-JMS | VP-CFS | N48AM | |
| 258583 | XP | N50983 | XA-GLG | | | | |
| 258584 | XP2 | N51384 | N884VC | | | | |
| 258585 | XP2 | N50285 | (N885VC) | N585VC | | | |
| 258586 | XP | N876QS | | | | | |
| 258587 | XP | N50657 | N261PA | N703RK | (N778CC) | (N703RE) | N770CC |
| 258588 | XP | N44888 | N799S | | | | |
| 258589 | 850XP | N51289 | N974JD | N874JD | [converted to prototype 850XP] | ZS-PCY | |
| | | N810AF | | | | | |
| 258590 | XP | N50910 | (N890VC) | (N590VC) | N733H | | |
| 258591 | XP2 | N61791 | N380GG | N380GP | | | |
| 258592 | XP | N892QS | | | | | |
| 258593 | XP | N898QS | | | | | |
| 258594 | XP | N61904 | N140GB | N323MP | VH-RIO | | |
| 258595 | XP | N61495 | N76CS | | | | |
| 258596 | XP | N896QS | N596XP | N804BH | | | |
| 258597 | XP | N895QS | N597XP | XA-TYK | | | |
| 258598 | XP2 | N61198 | (N800JA) | N92FT | (N92FL) | N988RS | |
| 258599 | XP | N51169 | N59BR | | | | |
| 258600 | 850XP | N61500 | N250SP | | | | |
| 258601 | XP | N61101 | ZS-DDA | N68HB | XA-PBT | | |
| 258602 | XP2 | (N898QS) | N61702 | N899SC | N401TM | | |
| 258603 | XP | N803QS | (N803CW) | N893CW | N893FL | | |
| 258604 | XP | N60664 | N8186 | | | | |
| 258605 | XP | N61805 | C-GJKI | C-GJKK | | | |
| 258606 | XP | N60506 | N895QS | | | | |
| 258607 | XP | N60507 | N919RT | | | | |
| 258608 | XP2 | N61708 | N500BN | I-KREM | | | |
| 258609 | XP | N60159 | N80HD | | | | |
| 258610 | U-125A | N61320 | Japan 42-3022 [code 022] | | | | |
| 258611 | XP | N809QS | (N944PP) | N944BB | | | |
| 258612 | XP | (N896QS) | N50522 | N711GD | N612XP | OM-OIG | |
| 258613 | XP | N90FB | | | | | |
| 258614 | XP | N811QS | | | | | |
| 258615 | XP | N61515 | VP-CKN | | | | |
| 258616 | XP | N61216 | N88HD | | | | |
| 258617 | XP | N5117F | N617XP | N551VB | N557VB | P4-SEN | |
| 258618 | XP | (N895QS) | N896QS | N618XP | N82GK | G-IWDB | A6-MAB |
| 258619 | XP | N61719 | N676JB | | | | |
| 258620 | XP | N61920 | N620XP | N77CS | | | |
| 258621 | XP | N61681 | (N621XP) | N522EE | N522EF | | |
| 258622 | XP | N622XP | N800EL | | | | |
| 258623 | XP | N623XP | (N823CW) | N221PB | | | |
| 258624 | XP | N624XP | N866RR | N660HC | | | |
| 258625 | XP | N625XP | N305JA | VP-BNK | | | |
| 258626 | XP | N626XP | N25W | | | | |
| 258627 | 850XP | N627XP | N929AK | | | | |
| 258628 | XP | N628XP | XA-JET | | | | |
| 258629 | U-25A | N61729 | Japan 52-3023 [code 023] | | | | |
| 258630 | XP | N630XP | N125ZZ | N599AK | | | |
| 258631 | XP | N631XP | N74NP | | | | |
| 258632 | XP2 | N632XP | ZS-PZA | TY-VLT | | | |

# BAe 125-800

| C/n | Series | Identities | | | | | | |
|---|---|---|---|---|---|---|---|---|
| 258633 | XP | N633XP | N800NS | ZS-PTP | | | | |
| 258634 | XP | N808BL | | | | | | |
| 258635 | XP | N635XP | N919SF | | | | | |
| 258636 | XP | N636XP | N800CQ | (N775RB) | N438PM | | | |
| 258637 | XP | N637XP | PP-ANA | | | | | |
| 258638 | XP | N638XP | XA-NTE | | | | | |
| 258639 | XP | N639XP | N95UP | | | | | |
| 258640 | XP | N640XP | N896QS | | | | | |
| 258641 | XP | N641XP | N513ML | | | | | |
| 258642 | XP | N642XP | N12PA | | | | | |
| 258643 | XP | N883CW | (N843TS) | N33NL | | | | |
| 258644 | 850XP | N644XP | N484JC | | | | | |
| 258645 | XP | N645XP | N733K | (N645XP) | N733L | N618AR | OY-OAA | HB-VOT |
| 258646 | XP | N646XP | N528BP | | | | | |
| 258647 | XP | N847CW | (N837LX) | | | | | |
| 258648 | XP | N848CW | (N823LX) | N848FL* | | | | |
| 258649 | XP | N649XP | N800EM | | | | | |
| 258650 | XP | N650XP | N50AE | | | | | |
| 258651 | 850XP | N651XP | N470BC | N159FM | | | | |
| 258652 | XP | N652XP | N241JS | | | | | |
| 258653 | XP | N653XP | N203TM | (N203TR) | | | | |
| 258654 | XP | N654XP | N149SB | | | | | |
| 258655 | XP | N655XP | N535BC | N655XP | (N16SM) | N22SM | | |
| 258656 | XP | N656XP | CS-DFX | | | | | |
| 258657 | XP | N657XP | (N857CW) | N839LX | N417TM | | | |
| 258658 | 850XP | N658XP | (ZS-ARK) | 5N-JMA | | | | |
| 258659 | 850XP | N659XP | 5N-JMB | | | | | |
| 258660 | XP | N660XP | N800RC | | | | | |
| 258661 | XP | N661XP | N800WW | | | | | |
| 258662 | XP | N662XP | N305SC | | | | | |
| 258663 | XP | N663XP | CS-DFY | | | | | |
| 258664 | XP | N664XP | CS-DFW | | | | | |
| 258665 | XP | N665XP | N689AM | | | | | |
| 258666 | XP | N876CW | N840LX | N840FL | | | | |
| 258667 | XP | N667XP | N802DR | N405TM | | | | |
| 258668 | XP | N668XP | N156NS | | | | | |
| 258669 | XP | N669XP | N520SP | N333PC | | | | |
| 258670 | 850XP | N670XP | N1776N | ZS-PZX | | | | |
| 258671 | XP | N671XP | N184TB | N184TR | | | | |
| 258672 | XP | N672XP | N1CA | | | | | |
| 258673 | XP | N673XP | CS-DFZ | | | | | |
| 258674 | XP | N674XP | N841WS | G-OJWB | | | | |
| 258675 | XP | N675XP | N351TC | | | | | |
| 258676 | XP | N676XP | N676GH | | | | | |
| 258677 | XP | N677XP | N850CT | | | | | |
| 258678 | XP | N678XP | N9867 | | | | | |
| 258679 | XP2 | N679XP | N800AH | N800LA | [damaged in hangar collapse at Washington/Dulles | | | |
| | | VA 06Feb10, probable w/o] | | | | | | |
| 258680 | XP | N680XP | N80E | N80EH | | | | |
| 258681 | XP | N681XP | N80J | N80JE | | | | |
| 258682 | XP | N682XP | 4X-CRU | D-CLBG | N682DK | P4-PRT | | |
| 258683 | XP | N61343 | N832QS | | | | | |
| 258684 | 850XP | N684DK | | | | | | |
| 258685 | U-125A | N36685 | Japan 62-3024 | | [code 024] | | | |
| 258686 | XP | N61746 | CS-DRA | | | | | |
| 258687 | XP | N61987 | N733A | | | | | |
| 258688 | 850XP | N688G | C-FMRI | | | | | |
| 258689 | XP | N36689 | F-HBFP | | | | | |
| 258690 | XP | N36690 | CS-DRB | | | | | |
| 258691 | XP | N858QS | | | | | | |
| 258692 | XP | N37092 | N700R | | | | | |
| 258693 | XP | N693XP | N302PE | N322PE | | | | |
| 258694 | XP | N36894 | N800R | | | | | |
| 258695 | XP | N695XP | N39H | | | | | |
| 258696 | XP | N36896 | N800PL | | | | | |
| 258697 | XP | N697XP | N530SM | N137LA | | | | |
| 258698 | XP | N860QS | | | | | | |
| 258699 | 850XP | N699XP | | | | | | |
| 258700 | XP2 | N108DD | | | | | | |
| 258701 | XP | N501XP | N6NR | | | | | |
| 258702 | XP | N841LX | N96SK | N966K | VP-BAS | | | |
| 258703 | XP | N50553 | N707JC | | | | | |
| 258704 | XP | N614BG | | | | | | |
| 258705 | XP | N815QS | | | | | | |
| 258706 | XP | N706XP | N74GW | | | | | |
| 258707 | XP | N707XP | LV-PJL | LV-BBG | | | | |

# BAe 125-800/850

| C/n | Series | Identities | | | |
|---|---|---|---|---|---|
| 258708 | XP | N799RM | | | |
| 258709 | XP | N709XP+ | [+marks worn but not registered as such] | | N821QS |
| 258710 | XP | N37010 | G-CDLT | | |
| 258711 | XP | N37211 | N1910A | | |
| 258712 | XP | N36672 | N18AQ | VH-MBP | |
| 258713 | 850XP | N713XP | N199DF | XA-SJM | |
| 258714 | XP | N61944 | CS-DRC | | |
| 258715 | 850XP | N715XP | N715PH | XA-JBT | |
| 258716 | XP | N716XP | VT-RBK | | |
| 258717 | 850XP | N717XP | ZS-PPH | | |
| 258718 | XP | N718XP | N718SJ | | |
| 258719 | XP | N19XP | VP-BCW | | |
| 258720 | XP | N36820 | OM-USS | | |
| 258721 | XP | N36621 | CS-DRD | | |
| 258722 | XP | N37322 | I-PZZR | | |
| 258723 | 850XP | N723XP | N627AK | | |
| 258724 | 850XP | N724XP | ZS-AFG | | |
| 258725 | XPi | N30355 | CS-DRE | | |
| 258726 | XP2 | N726XP | N405LA | | |
| 258727 | XPi | N787JC | | | |
| 258728 | XPi | N728XP | N110DD | VP-CXP | |
| 258729 | 850XP | N729XP | N729AG | | |
| 258730 | XPi | N37060 | CS-DRF | | |
| 258731 | 850XP | N37061 | XA-UGO | XA-CHG | |
| 258732 | XPi | N870QS | | | |
| 258733 | XPi | N333XP | HB-VOB | | |
| 258734 | XPi | N884QS | | | |
| 258735 | U-125A | N6135H | Japan 72-3025 | | |
| 258736 | XPi | N136XP | TC-TAV | | |
| 258737 | XPi | N518M | | | |
| 258738 | XPi | N138XP | TC-ADO | | |
| 258739 | XPi | N739XP | N499PA | | |
| 258740 | XPi | N740XP | N824LX | | |
| 258741 | XPi | N36841 | CS-DRG | | |
| 258742 | 850XP | N742XP | TC-FIN | | |
| 258743 | XPi | N885QS | | | |
| 258744 | 850XP | N744XP | | | |
| 258745 | 850XP | N745XP | VT-FAF | | |
| 258746 | XPi | N6046J | CS-DRH | | |
| 258747 | 850XP | N519M | | | |
| 258748 | 850XP | N748XP | EC-JNY | | |
| 258749 | 850XP | N36669 | N50UG | | |
| 258750 | 850XP | N950XP | N1776A | | |
| 258751 | 850XP | N751MT | | | |
| 258752 | 850XP | N752MT | | | |
| 258753 | 850XP | N805M | N546MG | | |
| 258754 | 850XP | N37054 | N754AE | | |
| 258755 | 850XP | N575JR | | | |
| 258756 | XPi | N37056 | CS-DRI | | |
| 258757 | 850XP | N757XP | N345MP | N437JD | N437JR |
| 258758 | 850XP | N37158 | N725CS | | |
| 258759 | 850XP | N801RR | N426MJ | | |
| 258760 | XPi | N37160 | CS-DRJ | | |
| 258761 | 850XP | N761XP | | | |
| 258762 | 850XP | N762XP | N901SG | N801SG | |
| 258763 | XPi | N871QS | | | |
| 258764 | 850XP | N764XP | N522EE | | |
| 258765 | XPi | N61285 | CS-DRK | | |
| 258766 | 850XP | N542M | | | |
| 258767 | XPi | N767XP | (N143RL) | N825LX | |
| 258768 | 850XP | N768XP | N850VP | | |
| 258769 | 850XP | N769XP | CC-CAB | | |
| 258770 | XPi | N36970 | CS-DRL | | |
| 258771 | XPi | N6171U | CS-DRM | | |
| 258772 | XPi | N672XP | CS-DRN | | |
| 258773 | XPi | N883QS | | | |
| 258774 | 850XP | N774XP | N143RL | N820M | |
| 258775 | XPi | N37105 | CS-DRO | | |
| 258776 | 850XP | N36726 | N535BC | N776RS | |
| 258777 | 850XP | N877XP | N900ST | | |
| 258778 | 850XP | N36578 | OE-IPH | N36578 | |
| 258779 | XPi | N37179 | CS-DRP | | |
| 258780 | 850XP | N37070 | VH-SGY | | |
| 258781 | 850XP | N37261 | A6-ELC | | |
| 258782 | 850XP | N782XP | (N706CW) | (N260G) | N126HY |
| 258783 | XPi | N37146 | CS-DRQ | | |

# BAe 125-800/850

| C/n | Series | Identities | | | |
|---|---|---|---|---|---|
| 258784 | 850XP | N784XP | N76FC | | |
| 258785 | 850XP | N785XP | N785VC | | |
| 258786 | XPi | N36986 | CS-DRR | | |
| 258787 | 850XP | N72617 | N851CC | | |
| 258788 | 850XP | N891QS | | | |
| 258789 | 850XP | N789XP | N850NS | | |
| 258790 | 850XP | N790XP | TC-TKC | | |
| 258791 | 850XP | N70791 | N255RB | | |
| 258792 | 850XP | N792XP | A6-TBF | | |
| 258793 | 850XP | N793XP | TC-STB | | |
| 258794 | 850XP | N71794 | VT-JHP | | |
| 258795 | XPi | N37295 | CS-DRS | | |
| 258796 | 850XP | N796XP | N850KE | N858KE | |
| 258797 | U-125A | N71907 | Japan 82-3026 | | Japan 92-3026 |
| 258798 | 850XP | N798XP | N850ZH | | |
| 258799 | 850XP | N37009 | HB-VOJ | | |
| 258800 | 850XP | N880XP | N865JT | | |
| 258801 | 850XP | N7101Z | (N906BL) | TC-DOY | |
| 258802 | XPi | N7102Z | CS-DRT | | |
| 258803 | 850XP | N853CC | | | |
| 258804 | 850XP | N71904 | OE-GRS | | |
| 258805 | 850XP | N71025 | EI-KJC | | |
| 258806 | 850XP | N36826 | N906BL | | |
| 258807 | 850XP | N36878 | VH-MQY | | |
| 258808 | 850XP | N70708 | TC-CLK | N220PK | N228PK |
| 258809 | 850XP | N70409 | I-TOPH | | |
| 258810 | 850XP | N71010 | OE-GJA | G-CERX | |
| 258811 | 850XP | N71881 | LY-DSK | | |
| 258812 | 850XP | N812XP | D-CLBH | | |
| 258813 | 850XP | N73793 | OE-GRF | | |
| 258814 | 850XP | N70214 | N189TA | VH-TNX | |
| 258815 | 850XP | N74155 | VT-KNB | | |
| 258816 | 850XP | N74166 | (N850ZH) | VP-COD | M-FRZN |
| 258817 | 850XP | N37170 | N85HH | | |
| 258818 | 850XP | N403CT | | | |
| 258819 | 850XP | N405CT | VT-ARR | | |
| 258820 | | [Hawker 900XP c/n HA-0001] | | | |
| 258821 | XPi | N73721 | CS-DRU | | |
| 258822 | 850XP | N822XP | N103AL | | |
| 258823 | 850XP | N823XP | N150GF | | |
| 258824 | U-125A | N60724 | Japan 02-3027 | | |
| 258825 | XPi | N3725Z | CS-DRV | | |
| 258826 | 850XP | N826LX | | | |
| 258827 | 850XP | N7077S | G-HSXP | | |
| 258828 | 850XP | N7128T | C-GCGT | | |
| 258829 | XPi | N73729 | CS-DRW | | |
| 258830 | 850XP | N72520 | N111ZN | | |
| 258831 | 850XP | N676AH | | | |
| 258832 | 850XP | N74142 | SU-MAN | | |
| 258833 | 850XP | N72233 | HS-CPG | | |
| 258834 | XPi | N71934 | CS-DRX | | |
| 258835 | 850XP | N7235R | VP-CMA | VT-AGP | |
| 258836 | 850XP | N7236L | N773HR | | |
| 258837 | 850XP | N662JN | | | |
| 258838 | 850XP | N71938 | VT-OBR | | |
| 258839 | | [Hawker 900XP c/n HA-0002] | | | |
| 258840 | XPi | N70040 | CS-DRY | | |
| 258841 | 850XP | N70431 | VP-BMM | | |
| 258842 | | [Hawker 900XP c/n HA-0003] | | | |
| 258843 | U-125A | N63600 | [for JASDF] | | |
| 258844 | 850XP | N71944 | VH-RAM | | |
| 258845 | 850XP | N72645 | TC-STD | | |
| 258846 | | [Hawker 900XP c/n HA-0004] | | | |
| 258847 | XPi | N74476 | CS-DRZ | | |
| 258848 | 850XP | N827LX | | | |

Production continues as a mix of special-order Hawker 850XPs using the old-style BAe 6-digit c/n sequence, Hawker 900XPs with c/ns beginning HA- and Hawker 750s with c/ns beginning HB-. The latter two models are shown in their own separate production lists.

| | | | | |
|---|---|---|---|---|
| 258849 to 258851 | | [c/ns not used] | | |
| 258852 | 850XP | N7302P | C-GROG | |
| 258853 to 258854 | | [c/ns not used] | | |
| 258855 | 850XP | N7255U | LX-OKR | F-GVIA |
| 258856 | 850XP | N7256C | B-3901 | |
| 258857 | | [c/n not used] | | |

## BAe 125-800/850

| C/n | Series | Identities | | |
|---|---|---|---|---|
| 258858 | 850XP | N71958 | N71958 | B-3902 |
| 258859 | 850XP | N859XP | OE-GNY | |
| 258860 | | [c/n not used] | | |
| 258861 | 850XP | N861ME | N850ME | |
| 258862 to 258871 | | [c/ns not used] | | |
| 258872 | 850XP | N872XP | TC-SHE | |
| 258873 | | [c/n not used] | | |
| 258874 | 850XP | N874XP | TC-NUB | |
| 258875 | | [c/n not used] | | |
| 258876 | 850XP | N349AK | N349AS | N850EM |
| 258877 to 258890 | | [c/ns not used] | | |
| 258891 | 850XP | N31991 | (N315ML) | N315JL |
| 258892 | | [c/n not used] | | |
| 258893 | 850XP | N1620 | | |
| 258894 | | [c/n not used] | | |
| 258895 | 850XP | N3195F | HB-VOY | |
| 258896 to 258899 | | [c/ns not used] | | |
| 258900 | 850XP | N850HB | | |
| 258901 | 850XP | N3201T | EI-GEM | |
| 258902 to 258903 | | [c/ns not used] | | |
| 258904 | 850XP | N3204T | VT-BTA | |
| 258905 to 258906 | | [c/ns not used] | | |
| 258907 | 850XP | N3207T | N448H | |
| 258908 | | [c/n not used] | | |
| 258909 | 850XP | N3289N | VT-BTB | |
| 258910 to 258911 | | [c/ns not used] | | |
| 258912 | 850XP | N32012 | VT-BTC | |
| 258913 to 258914 | | [c/ns not used] | | |
| 258915 | 850XP | N3115Y | N383MR | |
| 258916 to 258920 | | [c/ns not used] | | |
| 258921 | 850XP | N32061 | N888WY | |
| 258922 to 258958 | | [c/ns not used] | | |
| 258959 | 850XP | N3400S | | |
| 258960 | | [c/n not used] | | |
| 258961 | 850XP | N3201P | N850KE | |
| 258962 | | [c/n not used] | | |
| 258963 | 850XP | N3193B | N437WR | |
| 258964 to 258976 | | [c/ns not used] | | |
| 258977 | 850XP | N977LC | | |
| 258978 to 258979 | | [c/ns not used] | | |
| 258980 | 850XP | N3188X | | |
| 258981 | | [c/n not used] | | |
| 258982 | 850XP | N3482Y | P4-NUR | N982XP |
| 258983 | 850XP | N62783 | N438WR | |
| 258984 | 850XP | N63984 | XA-KBA | |

# HAWKER 900XP

The Hawker 900XP is a re-engined development of the Hawker 850XP

| C/n | fuselage | Identities | | | |
|---|---|---|---|---|---|
| HA-0001 | 258820 | N90XP | N170DC | | |
| HA-0002 | 258839 | N1776C | | | |
| HA-0003 | 258842 | N903XP | A6-PJB | | |
| HA-0004 | 258846 | N904XP | N351SP | | |
| HA-0005 | 258849 | N894QS | | | |
| HA-0006 | 258851 | N71956 | N96SK | | |
| HA-0007 | 258853 | N807HB | N77TC | | |
| HA-0008 | 258854 | N900LD | | | |
| HA-0009 | 258857 | N809HB | N901K | | |
| HA-0010 | 258860 | N890QS | | | |
| HA-0011 | 258862 | N211XP | C-GGMP | | |
| HA-0012 | 258863 | N852CC | | | |
| HA-0013 | 258864 | N113XP | N900R | | |
| HA-0014 | 258865 | N897QS | | | |
| HA-0015 | 258866 | N915XP | C-GVMP | | |
| HA-0016 | 258867 | N575MA | | | |
| HA-0017 | 258868 | N917XP | ZS-KBS | | |
| HA-0018 | 258869 | N901RD | | | |
| HA-0019 | 258870 | N889QS | N899QS | | |
| HA-0020 | 258871 | N920XP | P4-ALA | | |
| HA-0021 | 258873 | N899QS | N889QS | | |
| HA-0022 | 258875 | N922XP | N900PF | | |
| HA-0023 | 258877 | N923XP | HZ-BIN | | |
| HA-0024 | 258879 | N924XP | N108PJ | | |
| HA-0025 | 258880 | N33055 | P4-ANG | | |
| HA-0026 | 258881 | N32926 | ZS-SAH | | |
| HA-0027 | 258882 | N33527 | N799AG | | |
| HA-0028 | 258883 | N31958 | B-MBD | | |
| HA-0029 | 258884 | N700WY | | | |
| HA-0030 | 258885 | N930XP | N630JS | | |
| HA-0031 | 258886 | N848QS | | | |
| HA-0032 | 258887 | N932BC | ZS-SGJ | ZS-BOT | |
| HA-0033 | 258888 | N933XP | EC-KMT | | |
| HA-0034 | 258889 | N31624 | OK-KAZ | | |
| HA-0035 | 258890 | N33235 | P4-PET | | |
| HA-0036 | 258892 | N34956 | B-MBE | | |
| HA-0037 | 258894 | N865LS | N918JL | | |
| HA-0038 | 258896 | N34838 | HB-VPJ | | |
| HA-0039 | 258897 | N580RJ | | | |
| HA-0040 | 258898 | N16SM | | | |
| HA-0041 | 258899 | N34441 | G-ODUR | | |
| HA-0042 | 258902 | N888QS | | | |
| HA-0043 | 258903 | N87PK | | | |
| HA-0044 | 258906 | N944XP | VH-EVF | | |
| HA-0045 | 258908 | N3285N | XA-AET | | |
| HA-0046 | 258910 | N31946 | TC-KHA | | |
| HA-0047 | 258911 | N22VS | | | |
| HA-0048 | 258914 | N34548 | A6-RZB | A7-RZB | |
| HA-0049 | 258916 | N31959 | VH-ACE | | |
| HA-0050 | 258918 | N881QS | | | |
| HA-0051 | 258920 | N951XP | CS-DGZ | | |
| HA-0052 | 258922 | N104AG | (N952XP) | XA-KBL | |
| HA-0053 | 258924 | N3193L | B-3903 | | |
| HA-0054 | 258926 | N878QS | | | |
| HA-0055 | 258928 | N32185 | N816SE | | |
| HA-0056 | 258927 | N3386A | (D-BGRL) | I-BBGR | |
| HA-0057 | 258931 | N900PE | | | |
| HA-0058 | 258933 | N3088A | M-AJOR | | |
| HA-0059 | 258935 | N3400D | M-INOR | | |
| HA-0060 | 258937 | N3260J | LY-FSK | | |
| HA-0061 | 258939 | N34451 | VT-ICA | | |
| HA-0062 | 258940 | N32862 | | | |
| HA-0063 | 258942 | N3363U | N288MB | | |
| HA-0064 | 258943 | N31964 | VH-NKD | | |
| HA-0065 | tbc | N365JR | N819JR | | |
| HA-0066 | tbc | N877QS | | | |
| HA-0067 | tbc | N3217H | ZS-SGV | | |
| HA-0068 | tbc | N3198C | XA-ESP | | |
| HA-0069 | tbc | N3198V | CS-DPA | | |
| HA-0070 | 258955 | N3207Y | N902BE | N131JR | |
| HA-0071 | 258957 | N3371D | (D-CAJA) | (M-ABCE) | PK-JBH |
| HA-0072 | 258959 | N33612 | M-LCJP | | |
| HA-0073 | 258961 | N3283V | M-ONAV | | |

## HAWKER 900XP

| C/n | fuselage | Identities | | | |
|---|---|---|---|---|---|
| HA-0074 | 258962 | N3204W | I-MFAB | | |
| HA-0075 | 258966 | N869QS | (N975XP) | N979TM | N979TB |
| HA-0076 | 258968 | N300R | N330R | N100R | |
| HA-0077 | 258970 | N710HM | | | |
| HA-0078 | 258972 | N3378M | PP-ARG | | |
| HA-0079 | 258975 | N190SW | | | |
| HA-0080 | 258980 | N31842 | A6-HWK | | |
| HA-0081 | 258978 | N3217G | (N902BE) | | |
| HA-0082 | 258979 | N3222W | (N979TM) | N159M | |
| HA-0083 | 258981 | N83XP | "M-HARP"+ | [+marks worn but ntu] | M-NICO |
| HA-0084 | 258984 | N984XP | VP-CIS | | |
| HA-0085 | 258986 | N985RM | EI-JJJ | | |
| HA-0086 | 258988 | N986XP | TC-ENK | | |
| HA-0087 | 258973 | N87XP | N865JM | | |
| HA-0088 | 258989 | N988AG | | | |
| HA-0089 | 258990 | N60089 | PR-DBD | | |
| HA-0090 | 258985 | N63890 | F-HGBY | | |
| HA-0091 | 259101 | N61391 | CN-RBS | | |
| HA-0092 | 259103 | N64292 | CS-DPJ | | |
| HA-0093 | 259106 | N30VP | | | |
| HA-0094 | 258982 | N301ML | | | |
| HA-0095 | 259113 | N62895 | (A6-HBC) | A7-RZD | |
| HA-0096 | 259107 | N996XP | LX-KSD* | | |
| HA-0097 | 259111 | N62297 | | | |
| HA-0098 | 259112 | N6198P | TC-CLG | | |
| HA-0099 | 259115 | N60099 | M-LION | | |
| HA-0100 | 259104 | N125ML | VT-UPM | | |
| HA-0101 | 259116 | N15QB | | | |
| HA-0102 | 259109 | N6452L | (ZS-HWK) | N955SE | |
| HA-0103 | 259120 | N6403N | VT-BKL | | |
| HA-0104 | 259124 | N6434R | ZS-SME | | |
| HA-0105 | 259125 | N900FG | N900FU | N105XP | N21FX |
| HA-0106 | 259118 | N803D | | | |
| HA-0107 | | N107XP | | | |
| HA-0108 | 259121 | N6408F | VQ-BPH | | |
| HA-0109 | | [not yet built, cancelled/deferred order] | | | |
| HA-0110 | | N804D | | | |
| HA-0111 | | [not yet built, cancelled/deferred order] | | | |
| HA-0112 | | N63812 | G-OTAZ | | |
| HA-0113 | | N805D | | | |
| HA-0114 | | [not yet built, cancelled/deferred order] | | | |
| HA-0115 | | [not yet built, cancelled/deferred order] | | | |
| HA-0116 | | [not yet built, cancelled/deferred order] | | | |
| HA-0117 | | N117XP | N437JD | | |
| HA-0118 | | [not yet built, cancelled/deferred order] | | | |
| HA-0119 | | [not yet built, cancelled/deferred order] | | | |
| HA-0120 | | N60820 | N239RT | | |
| HA-0121 | | N6151C | M-JOLY | | |
| HA-0122 | | N859QS | (N869QS) | N122XP | |
| HA-0123 | | [not yet built, cancelled/deferred order] | | | |
| HA-0124 | | [not yet built, cancelled/deferred order] | | | |
| HA-0125 | | [not yet built, cancelled/deferred order] | | | |
| HA-0126 | | [not yet built, cancelled/deferred order] | | | |
| HA-0127 | | [not yet built, cancelled/deferred order] | | | |
| HA-0128 | | [not yet built, cancelled/deferred order] | | | |
| HA-0129 | | [not yet built, cancelled/deferred order] | | | |
| HA-0130 | | [not yet built, cancelled/deferred order] | | | |
| HA-0131 | | [not yet built, cancelled/deferred order] | | | |
| HA-0132 | | N857QS | N132XP | | |
| HA-0133 | | [not yet built, cancelled/deferred order] | | | |
| HA-0134 | | [not yet built, cancelled/deferred order] | | | |
| HA-0135 | | [not yet built, cancelled/deferred order] | | | |
| HA-0136 | | [not yet built, cancelled/deferred order] | | | |
| HA-0137 | | [not yet built, cancelled/deferred order] | | | |
| HA-0138 | | [not yet built, cancelled/deferred order] | | | |
| HA-0139 | | [not yet built, cancelled/deferred order] | | | |
| HA-0140 | | N6340T | LX-KAT | | |
| HA-0141 | | [not yet built, cancelled/deferred order] | | | |
| HA-0142 | | [not yet built, cancelled/deferred order] | | | |
| HA-0143 | | N6273X | G-OZAT | | |
| HA-0144 | | [not yet built, cancelled/deferred order] | | | |
| HA-0145 | | [not yet built, cancelled/deferred order] | | | |
| HA-0146 | | N146XP | N702A | | |
| HA-0147 | | N147XP | N703A | | |
| HA-0148 | | N148XP | OD-MIG | | |
| HA-0149 | | N149XP | XA-... | | |

# HAWKER 900XP

| C/n | fuselage | Identities | |
|---|---|---|---|
| HA-0150 | | N950XP | N916JB* |
| HA-0151 | | N6351Y | |
| HA-0152 | | N6452S | |
| HA-0153 | | N153XP | |
| HA-0154 | | N154XP | |
| HA-0155 | | N155XP | N80E |
| HA-0156 | | N156XP | N80J |
| HA-0157 | | N157XP | |
| HA-0158 | | N158XP | |
| HA-0159 | | N6409A | |
| HA-0160 | | N160XP | |
| HA-0161 | | N161XP | |
| HA-0162 | | N362XP | |
| HA-0163 | | N163XP | |
| HA-0164 | | N964XP | |
| HA-0165 | | N165XP | |
| HA-0166 | | | |
| HA-0167 | | | |
| HA-0168 | | N6368D | |
| HA-0169 | | | |
| HA-0170 | | | |
| HA-0171 | | | |
| HA-0172 | | | |
| HA-0173 | | | |
| HA-0174 | | | |
| HA-0175 | | | |
| HA-0176 | | | |
| HA-0177 | | | |
| HA-0178 | | | |
| HA-0179 | | | |
| HA-0180 | | | |
| HA-0181 | | | |
| HA-0182 | | | |
| HA-0183 | | | |
| HA-0184 | | | |
| HA-0185 | | | |
| HA-0186 | | | |
| HA-0187 | | | |
| HA-0188 | | | |
| HA-0189 | | | |
| HA-0190 | | | |
| HA-0191 | | | |
| HA-0192 | | | |
| HA-0193 | | | |
| HA-0194 | | | |
| HA-0195 | | | |
| HA-0196 | | | |
| HA-0197 | | | |
| HA-0198 | | | |
| HA-0199 | | | |
| HA-0200 | | | |

## HAWKER 750

The Hawker 750 is a re-engined development of the Hawker 800XPi.

| C/n | fuselage | Identities | | | |
|---|---|---|---|---|---|
| HB-1 | 258850 | N750HB | (N751NS) | B-MBF | |
| HB-2 | 258878 | N752HB | (N752NS) | (N751NS) | N787FF |
| HB-3 | 258905 | N752NS | N770GS | | |
| HB-4 | 258913 | N804HB | CS-DUA | | |
| HB-5 | 258917 | N31685 | CS-DUB | | |
| HB-6 | 258919 | N3206V | (CS-DUA) | CS-DUC | |
| HB-7 | 258923 | N3207V | (CS-DUB) | (N753NS) | VT-RSR |
| HB-8 | 258925 | N3198Z | CS-DUD | | |
| HB-9 | 258929 | N3501Q | B-MBG | | |
| HB-10 | 258930 | N3210N | (N232AV) | | |
| HB-11 | 258932 | N3211G | CS-DUE | | |
| HB-12 | 258934 | N3212H | N750KH | | |
| HB-13 | 258936 | N3093T | B-MBH | | |
| HB-14 | 258938 | N3194Q | (M-OANH) | N555RU | G-NLPA |
| HB-15 | 258941 | N3215J | PR-NCJ | | |
| HB-16 | tbc | N3216R | | | |
| HB-17 | tbc | N3217D | HZ-KSRD | | |
| HB-18 | tbc | N3418C | N750EL | | |
| HB-19 | tbc | N3491F | CS-DUF | | |
| HB-20 | 258960 | N3220K | CS-DUG | | |
| HB-21 | 258964 | N3201K | CS-DUH | | |
| HB-22 | 258967 | N3222S | XA-AEM | | |
| HB-23 | 258969 | N3433D | N751NS | | |
| HB-24 | 258971 | N3417F | EC-KXS | | |
| HB-25 | 258974 | N3285Q | B-MBI | | |
| HB-26 | 258977 | N3276L | N209HP | | |
| HB-27 | 258976 | N3497J | N666NF | | |
| HB-28 | 258983 | N3488P | N752NS | | |
| HB-29 | 258987 | N3197K | N753NS | | |
| HB-30 | 259110 | N730HB | (C-GXMP) | VT-CMO | |
| HB-31 | 259102 | N731TH | (C-GYMP) | N200RG | |
| HB-32 | 259105 | N732HB | I-EPAM | | |
| HB-33 | 259100 | N63633 | ES-PHR | | |
| HB-34 | 259119 | N760NS | N434HB | | |
| HB-35 | | N735XP | | | |
| HB-36 | | [not yet built, cancelled/deferred order] | | | |
| HB-37 | | [not yet built, cancelled/deferred order] | | | |
| HB-38 | | [not yet built, cancelled/deferred order] | | | |
| HB-39 | | [not yet built, cancelled/deferred order] | | | |
| HB-40 | | [not yet built, cancelled/deferred order] | | | |
| HB-41 | | N62991 | N219TF | | |
| HB-42 | | [not yet built, cancelled/deferred order] | | | |
| HB-43 | | N761NS | N743HB | | |
| HB-44 | | [not yet built, cancelled/deferred order] | | | |
| HB-45 | | [not yet built, cancelled/deferred order] | | | |
| HB-46 | | [not yet built, cancelled/deferred order] | | | |
| HB-47 | | [not yet built, cancelled/deferred order] | | | |
| HB-48 | | [not yet built, cancelled/deferred order] | | | |
| HB-49 | | [not yet built, cancelled/deferred order] | | | |
| HB-50 | | [not yet built, cancelled/deferred order] | | | |
| HB-51 | | [not yet built, cancelled/deferred order] | | | |
| HB-52 | | [not yet built, cancelled/deferred order] | | | |
| HB-53 | | [not yet built, cancelled/deferred order] | | | |
| HB-54 | | [not yet built, cancelled/deferred order] | | | |
| HB-55 | | [not yet built, cancelled/deferred order] | | | |
| HB-56 | | [not yet built, cancelled/deferred order] | | | |
| HB-57 | | [not yet built, cancelled/deferred order] | | | |
| HB-58 | | [not yet built, cancelled/deferred order] | | | |
| HB-59 | | [not yet built, cancelled/deferred order] | | | |
| HB-60 | | [not yet built, cancelled/deferred order] | | | |
| HB-61 | | [not yet built, cancelled/deferred order] | | | |
| HB-62 | | N762XP | | | |
| HB-63 | | N6173K | | | |
| HB-64 | | | | | |
| HB-65 | | N6405K | | | |
| HB-66 | | | | | |
| HB-67 | | N767HB | | | |
| HB-68 | | N768HB | | | |
| HB-69 | | N769HB | | | |
| HB-70 | | N770HB | | | |
| HB-71 | | | | | |
| HB-72 | | | | | |
| HB-73 | | | | | |
| HB-74 | | | | | |

## SERIES 1000 (BAe 1000) (HAWKER 1000)

| C/n | | Series | Identities | | | | | | | |
|---|---|---|---|---|---|---|---|---|---|---|
| 259001 | | B | [built as c/n 258151] | | G-EXLR | [ff 16Jun90; reported wfu Nov93; see c/n 258151] | | | | |
| 259002 | | B | [built as c/n 258159] | | G-OPFC | N10855 | [see c/n 258159; canx 05Sep03 as b/u] | | | |
| 259003 | | B | G-5-702 | G-ELRA | [built between c/ns 258195-6] | | | N503QS | (N503LR) | N261PA |
| 259004 | | B | G-LRBJ | G-5-779 | VR-CPT | VP-CPT | M-ACPT | | | |
| 259005 | NA1000 | A | G-BTTX | G-5-735 | N1AB | N81AB | N410US | N505QS | N505LR | |
| 259006 | NA1001 | A | G-BTTG | N1000U | N100U | (N108U) | N850JA | | | |
| 259007 | | B/A | G-BTSI | N84WA | N119PW | N119U | | | | |
| 259008 | | B/A | G-5-720 | HZ-OFC | HZ-OFC2 | N195L | D-CADA | N207TT | | |
| 259009 | NA1002 | A | G-5-716 | G-BTYN | N229U | N168WU | | | | |
| 259010 | NA1009 | A | G-5-722 | (HZ-...) | N125CJ | N52SM | | | | |
| 259011 | NA1003 | A | G-5-717 | G-BTYO | N14GD | N208R | N208L | | | |
| 259012 | | B/A | G-5-726 | HZ-SJP2 | N512QS | (N512HR) | N512LR | I-SRAF | VP-BMX | |
| 259013 | NA1004 | A | G-5-711 | G-BTYP | N125BA | N513QS | (N513RA) | N513LR | | |
| 259014 | NA1005 | A | G-5-712 | G-BTYR | N680BA | N125CJ | N514QS | N514LR | | |
| 259015 | NA1006 | A | G-5-718 | G-BTYS | N1000E | N515QS | N515LR | | | |
| 259016 | | B/A | (D-BJET) | G-5-732 | G-BULI | (5N-...) | G-5-732 | N291H | N678SB | N707HD |
| 259017 | | B | G-5-719 | ZS-NEW | ZS-AVL | N963H | N204R | N517QS | N517LR | A6-ELA |
| | | | N517LR | | | | | | | |
| 259018 | | B | G-5-741 | 5N-FGR | 5N-DGN | | | | | |
| 259019 | NA1007 | A | G-5-730 | N125CA | N792H | N2SG | N600LS | N448CC | | |
| 259020 | NA1008 | A | G-5-723 | N676BA | N520QS | N520LR | (N405FF) | | | |
| 259021 | | B/A | G-5-736 | G-BUKW | XA-GRB | N5794J | VR-CMZ | VP-CMZ | N137RP | N401FF |
| | | | HB-VOQ | | | | | | | |
| 259022 | | B | G-5-734 | VH-LMP | | | | | | |
| 259023 | NA1010 | A | G-5-729 | (VH-...) | N679BA | N523QS | N523LR | | | |
| 259024 | | B | G-5-737 | G-BUIX | N5ES | N263R | N524QS | N524LR | A6-ELB | N524LR |
| | | | (G-WWDB) | ZS-ABG | | | | | | |
| 259025 | | B | G-5-759 | (5N-...) | G-BVDL | N292H | N525QS | N501LR | | |
| 259026 | | B | G-5-743 | ZS-CCT | ZS-ACT | N9026 | G-GDEZ | P4-MAF | | |
| 259027 | | B | G-5-746 | 5H-BLM | G-BVLO | N333RL | N333RU | N333RL | | |
| 259028 | | B | G-5-749 | D-CBWW | N46WC | | | | | |
| 259029 | | B | G-5-751 | G-BUNW | EK-B021+ | EZ-B021 | | | | |
| 259030 | | B/A | G-5-753 | G-BUPL | G-DCCI | N530QS | N430LR | LN-SUU | HB-VOO | |
| 259031 | | B/A | G-5-754 | G-BUUY | G-HJCB | N301PH | N301PE | N301PB | | |
| 259032 | | B/A | G-5-760 | ZS-NHL | F-WQAU | G-BWCB | VR-CXX | VP-CXX | N401LS | N300LS |
| | | | N850TC | | | | | | | |
| 259033 | | A | G-5-756 | N684BA | N850BL | N533QS | N533LR | | | |
| 259034 | | B | G-5-761 | G-BUWX | N290H | N81HH | G-GMAB | | | |
| 259035 | | A | G-5-773 | N160BA | N535QS | N525LR | | | | |
| 259036 | | A | G-5-762 | N161BA | N1AB | N127RP | (N402FF) | N600MV | | |
| 259037 | | B | G-5-771 | G-SCCC | G-SHEC | XA-TGK | XA-RGG | G-FINK | M-FINK | |
| 259038 | | A | G-5-776 | N167BA | N125GM | N107RP | N403FF* | | | |
| 259039 | | A | G-5-781 | N169BA | N539QS | N539LR | | | | |
| 259040 | | A | G-5-783 | N22UP | N540QS | N540LR | | | | |
| 259041 | | A | G-5-785 | (N937H) | N936H | N541QS | N541LR | | | |
| 259042 | | A | G-5-789 | N941H | N542QS | N542LR | | | | |
| 259043 | | | G-5-794 | N948H | [first Hawker 1000] | | (N543QS) | TC-AKH | (N881JT) | XA-RYB |
| | | | N698DC | (N117CP) | N8888H | | | | | |
| 259044 | | | G-5-797 | N956H | N544QS | N544LR | | | | |
| 259045 | | | G-5-801 | (N296H) | N545QS | (N545LR) | N207R | | | |
| 259046 | | | G-5-805 | N962H | N546QS | N546LR | | | | |
| 259047 | | | G-5-817 | N296H | N547QS | N547LR | | | | |
| 259048 | | | G-5-826 | N802H | N548QS | N548LR | | | | |
| 259049 | | | G-5-837 | N679H | N549QS | N549LR | | | | |
| 259050 | | | G-5-846 | N550QS | N150LR | | | | | |
| 259051 | | | G-5-859 | N551QS | N551LR | N880LT | | | | |
| 259052 | | | G-5-863 | N552QS | N552LR | N800WD | | | | |

Production complete

## 125 NA NUMBER DECODE

| NA | C/n |
|---|---|
| NA700 | 25134 |
| NA701 | 25136 |
| NA702 | 25137 |
| NA703 | 25139 |
| NA704 | 25141 |
| NA705 | 25142 |
| NA706 | 25146 |
| NA707 | 25160 |
| NA708 | 25161 |
| NA709 | 25163 |
| NA710 | 25170 |
| NA711 | 25173 |
| NA712 | 25174 |
| NA713 | 25175 |
| NA714 | 25176 |
| NA715 | 25179 |
| NA716 | 25180 |
| NA717 | 25183 |
| NA718 | 25187 |
| NA719 | 25188 |
| NA720 | 25185 |
| NA721 | 25186 |
| NA722 | 25190 |
| NA723 | 25191 |
| NA724 | 25192 |
| NA725 | 25193 |
| NA726 | 25195 |
| NA727 | 25196 |
| NA728 | 25198 |
| NA729 | 25200 |
| NA730 | 25201 |
| NA731 | 25202 |
| NA732 | 25203 |
| NA733 | 25204 |
| NA734 | 25205 |
| NA735 | 25206 |
| NA736 | 25207 |
| NA737 | 25208 |
| NA738 | 25210 |
| NA739 | 25211 |
| NA740 | 25212 |
| NA741 | 25213 |
| NA742 | 25214 |
| NA743 | 25216 |
| NA744 | 25218 |
| NA745 | 25220 |
| NA746 | 25221 |
| NA747 | 25222 |
| NA748 | 25224 |
| NA749 | 25225 |
| NA750 | 25226 |
| NA751 | 25228 |
| NA752 | 25229 |
| NA753 | 25230 |
| NA754 | 25232 |
| NA755 | 25233 |
| NA756 | 25234 |
| NA757 | 25236 |
| NA758 | 25239 |
| NA759 | 25241 |
| NA760 | 25244 |
| NA761 | 25237 |
| NA762 | 25245 |
| NA763 | 25261 |
| NA764 | 25262 |
| NA765 | 25263 |
| NA766 | 25265 |
| NA767 | 25267 |
| NA768 | 25273 |
| NA769 | 25275 |
| NA770 | 25276 |
| NA771 | 25278 |
| NA772 | 25279 |
| NA773 | 25280 |
| NA774 | 25281 |
| NA775 | 25282 |
| NA776 | 25283 |
| NA777 | 25284 |
| NA778 | 25285 |
| NA779 | 25286 |
| NA780 | 25287 |
| NA0201 | 257002 |
| NA0202 | 257003 |
| NA0203 | 257005 |
| NA0204 | 257006 |
| NA0205 | 257008 |
| NA0206 | 257009 |
| NA0207 | 257011 |
| NA0208 | 257012 |
| NA0209 | 257014 |
| NA0210 | 257015 |
| NA0211 | 257017 |
| NA0212 | 257018 |
| NA0213 | 257019 |
| NA0214 | 257021 |
| NA0215 | 257023 |
| NA0216 | 257016 |
| NA0217 | 257024 |
| NA0218 | 257004 |
| NA0219 | 257026 |
| NA0220 | 257027 |
| NA0221 | 257029 |
| NA0222 | 257030 |
| NA0223 | 257032 |
| NA0224 | 257033 |
| NA0225 | 257035 |
| NA0226 | 257036 |
| NA0227 | 257038 |
| NA0228 | 257039 |
| NA0229 | 257041 |
| NA0230 | 257042 |
| NA0231 | 257044 |
| NA0232 | 257043 |
| NA0233 | 257047 |
| NA0234 | 257048 |
| NA0235 | 257050 |
| NA0236 | 257051 |
| NA0237 | 257052 |
| NA0238 | 257053 |
| NA0239 | 257049 |
| NA0240 | 257045 |
| NA0241 | 257056 |
| NA0242 | 257057 |
| NA0243 | 257059 |
| NA0244 | 257060 |
| NA0245 | 257058 |
| NA0246 | 257063 |
| NA0247 | 257065 |
| NA0248 | 257066 |
| NA0249 | 257068 |
| NA0250 | 257069 |
| NA0251 | 257071 |
| NA0252 | 257072 |
| NA0253 | 257074 |
| NA0254 | 257075 |
| NA0255 | 257077 |
| NA0256 | 257078 |
| NA0257 | 257080 |
| NA0258 | 257081 |
| NA0259 | 257083 |
| NA0260 | 257084 |
| NA0261 | 257086 |
| NA0262 | 257087 |
| NA0263 | 257089 |
| NA0264 | 257090 |
| NA0265 | 257092 |
| NA0266 | 257093 |
| NA0267 | 257095 |
| NA0268 | 257079 |
| NA0269 | 257098 |
| NA0270 | 257099 |
| NA0271 | 257110 |
| NA0272 | 257101 |
| NA0273 | 257104 |
| NA0274 | 257105 |
| NA0275 | 257106 |
| NA0276 | 257096 |
| NA0277 | 257111 |
| NA0278 | 257108 |
| NA0279 | 257113 |
| NA0280 | 257102 |
| NA0281 | 257114 |
| NA0282 | 257116 |
| NA0283 | 257117 |
| NA0284 | 257119 |
| NA0285 | 257120 |
| NA0286 | 257121 |
| NA0287 | 257122 |
| NA0288 | 257123 |
| NA0289 | 257125 |
| NA0290 | 257126 |
| NA0291 | 257128 |
| NA0292 | 257129 |
| NA0293 | 257131 |
| NA0294 | 257132 |
| NA0295 | 257134 |
| NA0296 | 257135 |
| NA0297 | 257137 |
| NA0298 | 257138 |
| NA0299 | 257140 |
| NA0300 | 257141 |
| NA0301 | 257146 |
| NA0302 | 257149 |
| NA0303 | 257147 |
| NA0304 | 257148 |
| NA0305 | 257150 |
| NA0306 | 257152 |
| NA0307 | 257154 |
| NA0308 | 257155 |
| NA0309 | 257156 |
| NA0310 | 257157 |
| NA0311 | 257159 |
| NA0312 | 257162 |
| NA0313 | 257153 |
| NA0314 | 257164 |
| NA0315 | 257165 |
| NA0316 | 257167 |
| NA0317 | 257168 |
| NA0318 | 257170 |
| NA0319 | 257171 |
| NA0320 | 257173 |
| NA0321 | 257174 |
| NA0322 | 257176 |
| NA0323 | 257161 |
| NA0324 | 257177 |
| NA0325 | 257143 |
| NA0326 | 257144 |
| NA0327 | 257179 |
| NA0328 | 257180 |
| NA0329 | 257182 |
| NA0330 | 257183 |
| NA0331 | 257185 |
| NA0332 | 257186 |
| NA0333 | 257188 |
| NA0334 | 257195 |
| NA0335 | 257198 |
| NA0336 | 257191 |
| NA0337 | 257192 |
| NA0338 | 257193 |
| NA0339 | 257145 |
| NA0340 | 257199 |
| NA0341 | 257201 |
| NA0342 | 257202 |
| NA0343 | 257204 |
| NA0344 | 257206 |
| NA0345 | 257207 |
| NA0346 | 257208 |
| NA0347 | 257210 |
| NA0401 | 258100 |
| NA0402 | 258101 |
| NA0403 | 258102 |
| NA0404 | 258103 |
| NA0405 | 258104 |
| NA0406 | 258105 |
| NA0407 | 258107 |
| NA0408 | 258108 |
| NA0409 | 258111 |
| NA0410 | 258113 |
| NA0411 | 258114 |
| NA0412 | 258117 |
| NA0413 | 258119 |
| NA0414 | 258121 |
| NA0415 | 258122 |
| NA0416 | 258123 |
| NA0417 | 258124 |
| NA0418 | 258125 |
| NA0419 | 258126 |
| NA0420 | 258127 |
| NA0421 | 258128 |
| NA0422 | 258132 |
| NA0423 | 258135 |
| NA0424 | 258136 |
| NA0425 | 258137 |
| NA0426 | 258139 |
| NA0427 | 258140 |
| NA0428 | 258138 |
| NA0429 | 258141 |
| NA0430 | 258142 |
| NA0431 | 258144 |
| NA0432 | 258145 |
| NA0433 | 258147 |
| NA0434 | 258150 |
| NA0435 | 258157 |
| NA0436 | 258160 |
| NA0437 | 258161 |
| NA0438 | 258162 |
| NA0439 | 258166 |
| NA0440 | 258168 |
| NA0441 | 258170 |
| NA0442 | 258171 |
| NA0443 | 258163 |
| NA0444 | 258172 |
| NA0445 | 258174 |
| NA0446 | 258175 |
| NA0447 | 258173 |
| NA0448 | 258179 |
| NA0449 | 258178 |
| NA0450 | 258181 |
| NA0451 | 258183 |
| NA0452 | 258185 |
| NA0453 | 258187 |
| NA0454 | 258188 |
| NA0455 | 258189 |
| NA0456 | 258191 |
| NA0457 | 258193 |
| NA0458 | 258195 |
| NA0459 | 258196 |
| NA0460 | 258199 |
| NA0461 | 258200 |
| NA0462 | 258202 |
| NA0463 | 258203 |
| NA0464 | 258204 |
| NA0465 | 258205 |
| NA0466 | 258206 |
| NA0467 | 258207 |
| NA0468 | 258209 |
| NA0469 | 258216 |
| NA0470 | 258217 |
| NA0471 | 258218 |
| NA0472 | 258220 |
| NA0473 | 258221 |
| NA0474 | 258223 |
| NA0475 | 258225 |
| NA1000 | 259005 |
| NA1001 | 259006 |
| NA1002 | 259009 |
| NA1003 | 259011 |
| NA1004 | 259013 |
| NA1005 | 259014 |
| NA1006 | 259015 |
| NA1007 | 259019 |
| NA1008 | 259020 |
| NA1009 | 259010 |
| NA1010 | 259023 |

## HAWKER 750/900XP FUSELAGE NUMBER DECODE

Airbus UK at Chester, in its capacity as Hawker Beechcraft's fuselage contractor, continues to use the old HS/BAe 6-digit numbering system for the fuselages it builds for the Hawker 750, 900XP and special-order 850XP. These are then given new aircraft c/ns by Hawker Beechcraft after arrival at Wichita/Beech Field. Tie-ups known to us are as follows:

| Fuselage | C/n | Fuselage | C/n | Fuselage | C/n | Fuselage | C/n |
|---|---|---|---|---|---|---|---|
| 258849 | HA-0005 | 258892 | HA-0036 | 258935 | HA-0059 | 258978 | HA-0081 |
| 258850 | HB-1 | 258893 | 258893 | 258936 | HB-13 | 258979 | HA-0082 |
| 258851 | HA-0006 | 258894 | HA-0037 | 258937 | HA-0060 | 258980 | HA-0080 |
| 258852 | 258852 | 258895 | 258895 | 258938 | HB-14 | 258981 | HA-0083 |
| 258853 | HA-0007 | 258896 | HA-0038 | 258939 | HA-0061 | 258982 | HA-0094 |
| 258854 | HA-0008 | 258897 | HA-0039 | 258940 | HA-0062 | 258983 | HB-28 |
| 258855 | 258855 | 258898 | HA-0040 | 258941 | HB-15 | 258984 | HA-0084 |
| 258856 | 258856 | 258899 | HA-0041 | 258942 | HA-0063 | 258985 | HA-0090 |
| 258857 | HA-0009 | 258900 | 258900 | 258943 | HA-0064 | 258986 | HA-0085 |
| 258858 | 258858 | 258901 | 258901 | 258944 | tba | 258987 | HB-29 |
| 258859 | 258859 | 258902 | HA-0042 | 258945 | tba | 258988 | HA-0086 |
| 258860 | HA-0010 | 258903 | HA-0043 | 258946 | tba | 258989 | HA-0088 |
| 258861 | 258861 | 258904 | 258904 | 258947 | tba | 258990 | HA-0089 |
| 258862 | HA-0011 | 258905 | HB-3 | 258948 | tba | 259100 | HB-33 |
| 258863 | HA-0012 | 258906 | HA-0044 | 258949 | tba | 259101 | HA-0091 |
| 258864 | HA-0013 | 258907 | 258907 | 258950 | tba | 259102 | HB-31 |
| 258865 | HA-0014 | 258908 | HA-0045 | 258951 | tba | 259103 | HA-0092 |
| 258866 | HA-0015 | 258909 | 258909 | 258952 | tba | 259104 | HA-0100 |
| 258867 | HA-0016 | 258910 | HA-0046 | 258953 | tba | 259105 | HB-32 |
| 258868 | HA-0017 | 258911 | HA-0047 | 258954 | tba | 259106 | HA-0093 |
| 258869 | HA-0018 | 258912 | 258912 | 258955 | HA-0070 | 259107 | HA-0096 |
| 258870 | HA-0019 | 258913 | HB-4 | 258956 | tba | 259108 | |
| 258871 | HA-0020 | 258914 | HA-0048 | 258957 | HA-0071 | 259109 | HA-0102 |
| 258872 | 258872 | 258915 | 258915 | 258958 | 258977 | 259110 | HB-30 |
| 258873 | HA-0021 | 258916 | HA-0049 | 258959 | HA-0072 | 259111 | HA-0097 |
| 258874 | 258874 | 258917 | HB-5 | 258960 | HB-20 | 259112 | HA-0098 |
| 258875 | HA-0022 | 258918 | HA-0050 | 258961 | HA-0073 | 259113 | HA-0095 |
| 258876 | 258876 | 258919 | HB-6 | 258962 | HA-0074 | 259114 | |
| 258877 | HA-0023 | 258920 | HA-0051 | 258963 | 258980 | 259115 | HA-0099 |
| 258878 | HB-2 | 258921 | 258921 | 258964 | HB-21 | 259116 | HA-0101 |
| 258879 | HA-0024 | 258922 | HA-0052 | 258965 | 258982 | 259117 | |
| 258880 | HA-0025 | 258923 | HB-7 | 258966 | HA-0075 | 259118 | HA-0106 |
| 258881 | HA-0026 | 258924 | HA-0053 | 258967 | HB-22 | 259119 | HB-34 |
| 258882 | HA-0027 | 258925 | HB-8 | 258968 | HA-0076 | 259120 | HA-0103 |
| 258883 | HA-0028 | 258926 | HA-0054 | 258969 | HB-23 | 259121 | HA-0108 |
| 258884 | HA-0029 | 258927 | HA-0056 | 258970 | HA-0077 | 259122 | |
| 258885 | HA-0030 | 258928 | HA-0055 | 258971 | HB-24 | 259123 | |
| 258886 | HA-0031 | 258929 | HB-9 | 258972 | HA-0078 | 259124 | HA-0104 |
| 258887 | HA-0032 | 258930 | HB-10 | 258973 | HA-0087 | 259125 | HA-0105 |
| 258888 | HA-0033 | 258931 | HA-0057 | 258974 | HB-25 | 259126 | |
| 258889 | HA-0034 | 258932 | HB-11 | 258975 | HA-0079 | 259127 | |
| 258890 | HA-0035 | 258933 | HA-0058 | 258976 | HB-27 | 259128 | |
| 258891 | 258891 | 258934 | HB-12 | 258977 | HB-26 | 259129 | |

The fuselages numbered 258944 to 258954 inclusive and 258956 were used in the construction of Hawker 900XPs c/n HA-0065 to HA-0069 inclusive, Hawker 750s c/n HB-16 to HB-19 inclusive and Hawker 850XPs c/n 258959, 258961 and 258963 - but their tie-ups remain unknown at present.

Numbers 258991 to 259099 were not used to avoid any clash with the old BAe.125-1000 construction numbers.

# HAWKER 4000

The Hawker 4000 was originally known as the Hawker Horizon.

| C/n | Identities | | |
|---|---|---|---|
| RC-1 | N4000R | [ff 11Aug01] | |
| RC-2 | N802HH | [ff 10May02] | |
| RC-3 | N803HH | [wfu, cx 29Jun09] | |
| RC-4 | N804HH | [ff 29Apr04] | |
| RC-5 | N805HH | (N974JD) | |
| RC-6 | (N806HH) | N15QS | N607HB |
| RC-7 | (N807HH) | N7007Q | N711GD |
| RC-8 | (N808HH) | N803SA | |
| RC-9 | (N809HH) | N119AK | |
| RC-10 | (N810HH) | N126ZZ | |
| RC-11 | N974JD | | |
| RC-12 | N400MR | ZS-DTD | |
| RC-13 | N413HB | (ZS-PPR) | N440HB |
| RC-14 | N514HB | VP-BCM | |
| RC-15 | N515HB | ZS-DDT | |
| RC-16 | N455BP | (N988DT) | N699AK |
| RC-17 | N61407 | N408U | |
| RC-18 | N163DK | N163DE | N86LF |
| RC-19 | N419HB | N163DK | |
| RC-20 | N50QS | N420HB | N899AK |
| RC-21 | N621HB | (ZK-ABC) | A6-SHH |
| RC-22 | N10QS | (N422HB) | N339RA |
| RC-23 | N423HB | ZS-ZOT | |
| RC-24 | N35004 | N995BE | |
| RC-25 | N3185G | (VT-VIP) | N143RL |
| RC-26 | N3186N | VT-HJA | |
| RC-27 | N3187N | (N36QS) | M-KENF |
| RC-28 | N25QS | N979TM | |
| RC-29 | N14QS | | |
| RC-30 | N830TS | | |
| RC-31 | N12QS | N78KN | |
| RC-32 | N3502N | N984JC | |
| RC-33 | N3433T | N440MB | |
| RC-34 | N3194F | M-PAUL | |
| RC-35 | N986JC | | |
| RC-36 | N616EA | | |
| RC-37 | N3197H | | |
| RC-38 | N438HB | | |
| RC-39 | N439HB | | |
| RC-40 | N40VK | | |
| RC-41 | N41HV | | |
| RC-42 | N40QS | N542HB | N349AK* |
| RC-43 | N60143 | | |
| RC-44 | N63744 | | |
| RC-45 | N6005V | | |
| RC-46 | N446HB | | |
| RC-47 | N447HB | | |
| RC-48 | N448HB | | |
| RC-49 | | | |
| RC-50 | | | |
| RC-51 | | | |
| RC-52 | | | |
| RC-53 | | | |
| RC-54 | | | |
| RC-55 | N6455T | B-3906 | |
| RC-56 | N984JC | N560RC | |
| RC-57 | | | |
| RC-58 | | | |
| RC-59 | | | |
| RC-60 | | | |
| RC-61 | | | |
| RC-62 | | | |
| RC-63 | | | |
| RC-64 | | | |
| RC-65 | | | |
| RC-66 | | | |
| RC-67 | | | |
| RC-68 | | | |
| RC-69 | | | |
| RC-70 | | | |
| RC-71 | | | |
| RC-72 | | | |
| RC-73 | | | |
| RC-74 | | | |
| RC-75 | | | |

# BOMBARDIER BD-100 CHALLENGER 300

The Challenger 300 was originally called the Continental.

| C/n | Identities | | | | | |
|---|---|---|---|---|---|---|
| 20001 | C-GJCJ | [ff 14Aug01] | | | | |
| 20002 | C-GJCF | [cx 22Aug06, wfu] | | | | |
| 20003 | C-GIPX | N303CZ | | | | |
| 20004 | C-GJCV | OE-HPK | | | | |
| 20005 | C-GIPZ | N850EJ | C-GIPZ | | | |
| 20006 | N5014F | N505FX | N505BX* | | | |
| 20007 | N506FX | XA-JGT | | | | |
| 20008 | C-GZDV | N507FX | N507BX | | | |
| 20009 | C-GZDY | N508FX | N306MF | | | |
| 20010 | C-GZEB | N41DP | | | | |
| 20011 | C-GZED | N300LJ | (N311DB) | N17UC | | |
| 20012 | C-GZEH | N509FX | PR-WSC | | | |
| 20013 | C-GZEI | N315LJ | I-SDFC | | | |
| 20014 | C-GZEJ | N27MX | XA-JCP | | | |
| 20015 | C-GZEM | N115LJ | A6-SMS | N300SM | (N309SM) | A6-SAM |
| 20016 | C-GZEO | N316LJ | N777VC | C-GFHR | | |
| 20017 | C-GZEP | N510FX | M-EANS | | | |
| 20018 | C-GZER | N84ZC | N74ZC | | | |
| 20019 | C-GZES | N319RG | N60SB | | | |
| 20020 | C-GZET | N789MB | | | | |
| 20021 | C-GZDQ | N511FX | N31CA | | | |
| 20022 | C-GZDS | N512FX | | | | |
| 20023 | C-GZDV | N513FX | N514FX | M-YFLY | | |
| 20024 | C-GZDY | C-FAUZ | (N515FX) | N184R | | |
| 20025 | C-GZEB | N125LJ | EC-JEG | N375WB | N375RF | N497EC |
| 20026 | C-GZED | C-FDHV | N26FA | N604RF | | |
| 20027 | C-GZEH | N448AS | | | | |
| 20028 | C-GZEI | (N328RC) | C-FDIA | N328CC | | |
| 20029 | C-GZEJ | N129LJ | HB-JEC | | | |
| 20030 | C-GZEM | C-FDIH | N300BZ | | | |
| 20031 | C-GZEO | N131LJ | N411ST | N411SF | | |
| 20032 | C-GZEP | C-FDIJ | N515FX | | | |
| 20033 | C-GZER | C-FCMG | OE-HRR | | | |
| 20034 | C-GZES | C-FCXJ | ZS-ACT | | | |
| 20035 | C-GZET | N900WY | | | | |
| 20036 | C-GZDQ | N516FX | | | | |
| 20037 | C-GZDS | N885TW | | | | |
| 20038 | C-GZDV | (ZS-SCT) | (ZS-ACT) | N517FX | | |
| 20039 | C-GZDY | N139LJ | HB-JEU | OE-HNL | | |
| 20040 | C-GZEB | N1967M | N234DP | | | |
| 20041 | C-GZED | N141LJ | VP-CLV | | | |
| 20042 | C-GZEH | C-FDSR | A7-AAN | A7-CEC | | |
| 20043 | C-FCZS | N143LJ | N818KC | | | |
| 20044 | C-FDSZ | ZS-YES | N74WL | SP-ZSZ | | |
| 20045 | N145LJ | N618R | | | | |
| 20046 | N518FX | | | | | |
| 20047 | C-FEUQ | OE-HPZ | | | | |
| 20048 | C-FDXU | A6-RJM | N348TS | N70CR | | |
| 20049 | C-FFZI | N1980Z | | | | |
| 20050 | C-FEPU | N350TG | A6-KNH | | | |
| 20051 | C-FCZN | C-FFLJ | N424TM | | | |
| 20052 | C-FCZV | N606XT | | | | |
| 20053 | C-GZDY | C-FGBP | N353PC | | | |
| 20054 | N302EM | | | | | |
| 20055 | C-GZEI | C-FFZE | N519FX | | | |
| 20056 | C-GZES | C-FGMR | N520FX | | | |
| 20057 | C-GDZQ | C-FGGF | N521FX | | | |
| 20058 | C-GZDV | C-FGJI | N300DG | N380DG* | | |
| 20059 | C-FDAH | C-FGNO | N620JF | | | |
| 20060 | C-GZEB | C-FGUT | N228N | (N372N) | | |
| 20061 | C-GZEO | C-FGUD | N422CP | | | |
| 20062 | C-GZER | N888CN | N300MY | | | |
| 20063 | C-GZET | N363CL | | | | |
| 20064 | C-GZDS | C-FGXW | N522FX | | | |
| 20065 | C-FFNT | 4X-CPV | OE-HDD | | | |
| 20066 | C-FCZM | C-FGXK | N866TM | | | |
| 20067 | C-FCZS | C-FGZI | N304BC | N300BC | | |
| 20068 | C-GZEM | C-FGZE | N303EM | | | |
| 20069 | C-GZEP | C-FGZD | N987HP | | | |
| 20070 | C-FGYU | N78TC | | | | |
| 20071 | C-FGFB | D-BTIM | N371TS | D-BSMI | | |
| 20072 | N724SC | | | | | |
| 20073 | C-FHDN | N731DC | (N731BF) | | | |
| 20074 | C-FHDE | N523FX | | | | |
| 20075 | C-FHCY | N575WB | | | | |

# BD-100 CHALLENGER 300

| C/n | Identities | | | | | |
|---|---|---|---|---|---|---|
| 20076 | C-FGBY | N54HA | | | | |
| 20077 | C-FGCD | N304EM | | | | |
| 20078 | C-FGCE | "XA-FRO" | [painted in error at completion centre] | | | XA-FRD |
| 20079 | C-FGCJ | D-BETA | | | | |
| 20080 | C-FGCL | N960CR | | | | |
| 20081 | C-FGCN | N845UP | | | | |
| 20082 | C-FGCV | N594CA | | | | |
| 20083 | C-FGCW | N555DH | N31112 | N1DH | N906TC | N903TC |
| 20084 | C-FGCX | XA-GPR | | | | |
| 20085 | C-FGCZ | N42GJ | | | | |
| 20086 | C-FGVJ | N846UP | | | | |
| 20087 | C-FGVK | N387PC | | | | |
| 20088 | C-FGVM | N130CH | | | | |
| 20089 | C-FGVS | N71FA | N605RF | | | |
| 20090 | C-FGWB | N55HA | | | | |
| 20091 | C-FGWF | N391W | | | | |
| 20092 | C-FGWL | N500AL | | | | |
| 20093 | C-FGWR | C-FDOL | | | | |
| 20094 | C-FGWW | I-CCCH | | | | |
| 20095 | C-FGWZ | N524FX | | | | |
| 20096 | C-FHMI | C-GPCZ | | | | |
| 20097 | C-FHMM | LX-PMA | | | | |
| 20098 | C-FHMQ | N305EM | | | | |
| 20099 | C-FHMS | N991GS | | | | |
| 20100 | C-FHMZ | (N928MC) | VP-CAO | | | |
| 20101 | C-FHNC | N306EM | | | | |
| 20102 | C-FHND | N555TF | N926AG | | | |
| 20103 | C-FHNF | N926JR | | | | |
| 20104 | C-FHNH | N125TM | | | | |
| 20105 | C-FHNJ | N56HA | N788MM | | | |
| 20106 | C-FIDX | G-KALS | | | | |
| 20107 | C-FIDZ | C-FGIL | | | | |
| 20108 | C-FIDU | N388WS | | | | |
| 20109 | C-FIDV | N955H | | | | |
| 20110 | C-FIEA | C-GESO | | | | |
| 20111 | C-FIED | OE-HII | | | | |
| 20112 | C-FIEE | N525FX | | | | |
| 20113 | C-FIEM | N985FM | | | | |
| 20114 | C-FIEP | C-FCSI | | | | |
| 20115 | C-FIOB | N57HA | | | | |
| 20116 | C-FIOC | D-BADO | | | | |
| 20117 | C-FIOE | N211TB | N202DH | | | |
| 20118 | C-FIOG | N526FX | | | | |
| 20119 | C-FIOH | N214RW | | | | |
| 20120 | C-FIOJ | N15GT | | | | |
| 20121 | C-FIOK | N963RS | N963RB | N104FT | | |
| 20122 | C-FION | N5262 | | | | |
| 20123 | C-FIOO | N592SP | D-BFLY | M-BFLY | | |
| 20124 | C-FIOP | N527FX | | | | |
| 20125 | C-FJQD | N528FX | | | | |
| 20126 | C-FJQH | 3B-SSD | | | | |
| 20127 | C-FJQP | N297MC | | | | |
| 20128 | C-FJQR | N529FX | | | | |
| 20129 | C-FJQT | N660AL | | | | |
| 20130 | C-FJQX | N300KH | | | | |
| 20131 | C-FJQZ | N390DB | | | | |
| 20132 | C-FJRE | N518GS | | | | |
| 20133 | C-FJRG | 3B-NGT | | | | |
| 20134 | C-FLCY | N600LS | | | | |
| 20135 | C-FLDD | 9M-TAN | 9M-TST | | | |
| 20136 | C-FLDK | TC-SCR | | | | |
| 20137 | C-FLDO | N301TG | HB-JFO | | | |
| 20138 | C-FLDW | N247SS | N12SS | (N812SS) | TC-ISR | |
| 20139 | C-FLDX | N610LS | | | | |
| 20140 | C-FLEC | VP-CDV | | | | |
| 20141 | C-FLEJ | N341TS | LN-AIR | HB-JTB | | |
| 20142 | C-FLEK | (N888UD) | N605UK | N228KT | | |
| 20143 | C-FLEN | N300FS | | | | |
| 20144 | C-FLQF | N629GB | N302PE | | | |
| 20145 | C-FLQG | D-BUBI | | | | |
| 20146 | C-FLQH | N58HA | | | | |
| 20147 | C-FLQM | (N600LS) | N480CB | | | |
| 20148 | C-FLQO | N530FX | | | | |
| 20149 | C-FLQP | TC-KAR | | | | |
| 20150 | C-FLQR | N531FX | | | | |
| 20151 | C-FLQX | M-NEWT | | | | |
| 20152 | C-FLQY | N487F | | | | |
| 20153 | C-FLQZ | N772JS | | | | |

## BD-100 CHALLENGER 300

| C/n | Identities | | | |
|---|---|---|---|---|
| 20154 | C-FMYA | N532FX | | |
| 20155 | C-FMYB | OH-FLM | | |
| 20156 | C-FMXX | N895BB | | |
| 20157 | C-FMXW | N296SB | | |
| 20158 | C-FMXU | N797CB | | |
| 20159 | C-FMXQ | LX-TQJ | | |
| 20160 | C-FMXK | N533FX | | |
| 20161 | C-FMXH | N534FX | | |
| 20162 | C-FMWX | N888RT | | |
| 20163 | C-FMWG | N58LC | | |
| 20164 | C-FNUH | N782BJ | | |
| 20165 | C-FOAE | N120GS | N818RC | |
| 20166 | C-FOAI | N166CL | N225AR | |
| 20167 | C-FOAJ | N535FX | | |
| 20168 | C-FOAQ | (PR-MDB) | PR-IDB | |
| 20169 | C-FOAT | G-UYGB | A9C-DAR | |
| 20170 | C-FOMU | C-FOAU | N3975A | |
| 20171 | C-FPMQ | N536FX | | |
| 20172 | C-FPMU | M-TAGB | D-BAVA | RA-67223 |
| 20173 | C-FOBJ | RA-67217 | | |
| 20174 | C-FOQR | VT-RAK | | |
| 20175 | C-FOQW | 5A-UAA | | |
| 20176 | C-FORB | VP-BEK | | |
| 20177 | C-FOSB | N896BB | | |
| 20178 | C-FOSG | PP-BIR | | |
| 20179 | C-FOSM | D-BSKY | M-BSKY | OE-HEO |
| 20180 | C-FOSQ | N269MJ | | |
| 20181 | C-FOSW | TC-ARB | | |
| 20182 | C-FOSX | C-GRCY | | |
| 20183 | C-FOTF | N313DS | | |
| 20184 | C-FPZZ | N384RV | | |
| 20185 | C-FQCF | N329CH | | |
| 20186 | C-FQEI | N725CF | N300GM | |
| 20187 | C-FQOA | N537FX | | |
| 20188 | C-FQOF | N414DH | | |
| 20189 | C-FQOI | G-KSFR | | |
| 20190 | C-FQOK | (TC-THY) | N235AF | N335AF |
| 20191 | C-FQOL | XA-LLA | | |
| 20192 | C-FQOM | C-FJCB | | |
| 20193 | C-FQOQ | N794RC | | |
| 20194 | C-FRQA | N194LE | | |
| 20195 | C-FRQC | N300AH | N632FW | |
| 20196 | C-FRQH | VT-JSE | | |
| 20197 | C-FRQK | N480BA | | |
| 20198 | C-FRQM | N202XT | | |
| 20199 | C-FRQN | N703VZ | | |
| 20200 | C-FRQP | OE-HVJ | | |
| 20201 | C-FROY | N538FX | | |
| 20202 | C-FSMO | N539FX | | |
| 20203 | C-FSMW | LN-SOL | XA-DLA | |
| 20204 | C-FSNB | N552KF | N302R | |
| 20205 | C-FSNP | N540FX | | |
| 20206 | C-FSNQ | M-NOEL | | |
| 20207 | C-FSNU | N746E | | |
| 20208 | C-FSLL | N729SB | | |
| 20209 | C-FSLR | N184BK | OH-ZIP* | |
| 20210 | C-FSLU | N752M | | |
| 20211 | C-FTKA | N541FX | | |
| 20212 | C-FTKC | D-BAVB | | |
| 20213 | C-FTKH | N300LJ | N537XJ | |
| 20214 | C-FTKG | OE-HVV | C-GDIK | N214BL |
| 20215 | C-FTKK | N215BL | RP-C8215 | |
| 20216 | C-FUBE | N97DK | | |
| 20217 | C-FUBK | N542FX | | |
| 20218 | C-FUBM | LX-VPG | | |
| 20219 | C-FUBO | LV-BSS | | |
| 20220 | C-FUBP | N101UD | | |
| 20221 | C-FUBQ | D-BANN | | |
| 20222 | C-FUBT | OE-HRM | | |
| 20223 | C-FUJA | N229BP | | |
| 20224 | C-FUJE | N538XJ | | |
| 20225 | C-FUJM | N7000C | | |
| 20226 | C-FUJR | OE-HAP | | |
| 20227 | C-FUJT | OE-HAB | | |
| 20228 | C-FUJX | N30XC | | |
| 20229 | C-FURA | N147AG | | |
| 20230 | C-FURB | N539XJ | | |
| 20231 | C-FURC | N742E | | |

# BD-100 CHALLENGER 300

| C/n | Identities | | | |
|---|---|---|---|---|
| 20232 | C-FURD | OE-HAA | | |
| 20233 | C-FURF | TC-CMK | C-FURF | M-HSNT |
| 20234 | C-FURH | N825TB | | |
| 20235 | C-FVNB | RA-67221 | | |
| 20236 | C-FVNC | (I-STEF) | | |
| 20237 | C-FVND | HB-JGQ | | |
| 20238 | C-FVNF | N540XJ | C-FLDD | |
| 20239 | C-FVNI | N541XJ | N584D | |
| 20240 | C-FVNL | N544FX | N347K | |
| 20241 | C-FVNS | N801EL | | |
| 20242 | C-FVNT | N542XJ | C-FKCI | |
| 20243 | C-FVLX | EC-LES | | |
| 20244 | C-FVLZ | N300BY | N301PE | |
| 20245 | C-FWUZ | N543XJ | C-FYUQ | C-GJEI |
| 20246 | C-FWUT | | | |
| 20247 | C-FWUO | N402EF | | |
| 20248 | C-FWUL | N544XJ | N217GH | |
| 20249 | C-FWUK | N138CH | | |
| 20250 | C-FWUI | N999ND | | |
| 20251 | C-FWUC | OY-EKS | | |
| 20252 | C-FWRE | CS-TFV* | | |
| 20253 | C-FWRG | N545XJ | N300GP | |
| 20254 | C-FWRX | N7100C | | |
| 20255 | C-FWTK | VP-BJT | | |
| 20256 | C-FWTQ | VP-CPF | | |
| 20257 | C-FWTY | C-FFBC | | |
| 20258 | C-FWVH | N672BP | | |
| 20259 | C-FXPB | N83JJ | | |
| 20260 | C-FXPI | (N546XJ) | C-GFCB | |
| 20261 | C-FXPL | OE-HDV | | |
| 20262 | C-FXPQ | N254DV | | |
| 20263 | C-FXPR | N526AC | | |
| 20264 | C-FXPT | N40QG | | |
| 20265 | C-FXPW | N265K | | |
| 20266 | C-FYBG | N411ST | | |
| 20267 | C-FYBJ | N302K | | |
| 20268 | C-FLDD | C-FYBZ | N1967M | |
| 20269 | C-FYBM | N295SG | | |
| 20270 | C-FYBN | N800BD | | |
| 20271 | C-FYBO | M-CLAB | | |
| 20272 | C-FYBS | (D-BPWR) | D-BCLA | |
| 20273 | C-FYBU | VT-JUA | | |
| 20274 | C-FYBV | OE-HCA | | |
| 20275 | C-FZLX | D-BEKP* | | |
| 20276 | C-FZLY | | | |
| 20277 | C-FZLZ | M-ABCM | | |
| 20278 | C-GAKE | | | |
| 20279 | C-GAKF | N541XJ | | |
| 20280 | C-GAKL | | | |
| 20281 | C-GAKN | | | |
| 20282 | C-GAKO | | | |
| 20283 | C-GAKZ | | | |
| 20284 | C-GBZE | | | |
| 20285 | C-GBZI | | | |
| 20286 | C-GBZL | | | |
| 20287 | C-GBZV | | | |
| 20288 | C-GBXZ | | | |
| 20289 | C-GDTF | OE-HIX* | | |
| 20290 | C-GDTQ | | | |
| 20291 | C-GDUH | | | |
| 20292 | C-GDUJ | | | |
| 20293 | | | | |
| 20294 | | | | |
| 20295 | | | | |
| 20296 | | | | |
| 20297 | | | | |
| 20298 | | | | |
| 20299 | | | | |
| 20300 | | | | |
| 20301 | | | | |
| 20302 | | | | |
| 20303 | | | | |
| 20304 | | | | |
| 20305 | | | | |
| 20306 | | | | |
| 20307 | | | | |
| 20308 | | | | |
| 20309 | | | | |

# BOMBARDIER BD-700 GLOBAL EXPRESS/GLOBAL 5000

| C/n | Identities |
|---|---|
| 9001 | C-FBGX [rolled out 26Aug96; ff 13Oct96; converted to RAF ASTOR (Airborne Stand-Off Radar) test aircraft in 2001; later converted to BACN (Battlefield Airborne Communications Node) platform for USAF] N901GX |
| 9002 | C-FHGX N711MC N711MN N881WT |
| 9003 | C-FJGX C-FBDR |
| 9004 | C-FKGX N1TK C-FKGX N1TK (N11TK) N115HK HB-JGO N617JN |
| 9005 | C-GEGX (VP-CPC) N700HX N613WF (N938WF) N618WF F-GOVV* |
| 9006 | C-GCGY N1TM N906GX N161WC |
| 9007 | C-GCRW Malaysia M48-01 C-GCRW Malaysia M48-01 C-GCRW N907GX (C-....) EC-IUQ |
| 9008 | C-GDBG N9008 (N90005) N917R |
| 9009 | C-GDGO N816SR N816SQ N813SQ N998AM N980GG |
| 9010 | C-GDGQ N701WH M-ABAK |
| 9011 | C-GDGW N700KJ VP-BJJ HB-IHQ |
| 9012 | C-GDGY N70PS |
| 9013 | C-GDXU HB-IUR C-GZSM LX-GEX |
| 9014 | C-GDXV N700GX C-FGGX N700GX (D-AFLW) C-FRGX XA-NGS |
| 9015 | C-GDXX N700KS N708KS HB-JEN N900LF |
| 9016 | C-GEIM N700AH N16GX N300ES N309ES EC-KVU |
| 9017 | C-GEIR VP-BDD HB-JER |
| 9018 | C-GEVO VP-BGG N84SD N818TS C-FOXA PR-VDR |
| 9019 | C-GEVU N600CC HL7576 N203JE |
| 9020 | C-GEVV N700GK VP-BEN N81ZZ |
| 9021 | C-GEYY N8VB |
| 9022 | C-GEYZ N700HG N622AB N226HD N393BZ |
| 9023 | C-GEZD N324SM |
| 9024 | C-GEZF N700BH N288Z N287Z N9253V |
| 9025 | C-GEZJ N700AQ N616DC N816DC |
| 9026 | C-GEWV N70EW |
| 9027 | C-GEZX N305CC |
| 9028 | C-GEZY N117TF N717TF VP-BSE |
| 9029 | C-GEZZ HZ-AFA N929TS N5UU |
| 9030 | C-GFAD VP-BYY |
| 9031 | C-GFAE N700VN N724AF |
| 9032 | C-GFAK N700HE (N2T) G-52-26 G-CBNP OY-MSI |
| 9033 | C-GFAN N600AK |
| 9034 | C-GFAP N700HF JA005G |
| 9035 | C-GFAQ (D-AFLW) N817LS N711LS N818LS N838SC |
| 9036 | C-GFAT N777GX HB-ITG VP-BEM |
| 9037 | C-GFJQ N777SW N777VU N400GX [damaged in hangar collapse at Washington/Dulles 06Feb10, possible w/o] |
| 9038 | C-GFJR G-52-24 G-LOBL N738TS N20EG C-GSAP |
| 9039 | C-GFJS N700GT N90EW |
| 9040 | C-GFJT N22BH N228H |
| 9041 | C-GFKT N195WM N887WM N387WM |
| 9042 | C-GFKV N700WL N170SW |
| 9043 | C-GFKW N700BU N700ML N416BD |
| 9044 | C-GFKX N700BP I-MOVE OE-IGS |
| 9045 | C-GFKY N17GX |
| 9046 | C-GFLS N700BV N1TS N517TT |
| 9047 | C-GFLU N410WW N373SB |
| 9048 | C-GFLW N700BY N4GX |
| 9049 | C-GFLX N471DG N949GP N471DG N949GP |
| 9050 | C-GFLZ N700FJ VP-COP N502JL |
| 9051 | C-GFWI N700DZ N421AL |
| 9052 | C-GFWP N700DQ N752DS N620K [damaged in hangar collapse at Washington/Dulles 06Feb10, possible w/o] |
| 9053 | C-GFWX N700LJ N53GX |
| 9054 | C-GFWY N700LA HB-IKZ N550LF |
| 9055 | C-GFWZ N449ML N540CH |
| 9056 | C-GCGY N700DU N421SZ N928SZ |
| 9057 | C-GGIR (TC-DHG) N700EX N18WF N18WY VP-BDU |
| 9058 | C-GGJA N700AD N79AD |
| 9059 | C-GGJF (VP-BXX) N700EG N18WF N18WZ N3PC |
| 9060 | C-GGJH "EC-FPI" [painted in error at completion centre] EC-IBD |
| 9061 | C-GGJJ N16FX ZS-ESA |
| 9062 | C-GGJR N700CJ N801PN |
| 9063 | C-GGJS N700BD B-HMA (N733EY) N933EY |
| 9064 | C-GGJU N700PL N264A |
| 9065 | C-GGKA N700CV N789TP N711SW (N711SQ) N704MF |
| 9066 | C-GGKC N898SC N708SC N823DF |
| 9067 | C-GGPZ N700BK N67RX |
| 9068 | C-GGQC N700BX (N889JC) |
| 9069 | C-GGQF N700LD N1868M N568M* |
| 9070 | C-GGQG N700XR N34U |

# BD-700 GLOBAL EXPRESS/GLOBAL 5000

| C/n | Srs | Identities | | | | | | | | |
|---|---|---|---|---|---|---|---|---|---|---|
| 9071 | | C-GHDQ | D-ADNB | | | | | | | |
| 9072 | | C-GHDV | N700LN | N983J | | | | | | |
| 9073 | | C-GHDW | N700XN | N338TP | | | | | | |
| 9074 | | C-GHEA | N399GS | | | | | | | |
| 9075 | | C-GHEI | N316GS | | | | | | | |
| 9076 | | C-GHER | N700XT | LX-VIP | | | | | | |
| 9077 | | C-GHET | N700XY | N100A | N200A | N520E | | | | |
| 9078 | | C-GHEZ | N700AH | N85D | | | | | | |
| 9079 | | C-GHFB | N700AP | (N217JC) | VH-VGX | | | | | |
| 9080 | | C-GHFH | N283S | N125CH | | | | | | |
| 9081 | | C-GHGC | G-52-25 | G-CBNR | G-52-25 | C-GZTZ | F-GVML | | | |
| 9082 | | C-GHYQ | N700AY | JA006G | | | | | | |
| 9083 | | C-GHYT | N700AU | C-GKLF | VP-CEB | | | | | |
| 9084 | | C-GHYX | N700GU | N2T | (N4LZ) | N908BX | N984TS | VP-COU | EC-KKN | |
| 9085 | | C-GHZB | N700GQ | N404VL | | | | | | |
| 9086 | | C-GHZC | HB-INJ | | | | | | | |
| 9087 | | C-GHZD | N700BQ | N360LA | | | | | | |
| 9088 | | C-GHZF | N15FX | C-FDLR | C-GNCB | | | | | |
| 9089 | | C-GHZH | EC-IFS | | | | | | | |
| 9090 | | C-GIOD | N18TM | | | | | | | |
| 9091 | | C-GIOJ | N700XM | N1FE | | | | | | |
| 9092 | | C-GIOK | N15FX | N799WW | | | | | | |
| 9093 | | C-GIOW | N17FX | C-GZVZ | VP-CDF | | | | | |
| 9094 | | C-GIOX | (ZS-DAJ) | ZS-DLJ | OY-GLA | A6-EJB | EC-KJH | | | |
| 9095 | | C-GIPA | HB-IUJ | N97DQ | | | | | | |
| 9096 | | C-GIPC | Malaysia M52-01 | | C-GIPC | Malaysia M48-02 | | | | |
| 9097 | | C-GIPD | N903TF | N908TE | N902MM | | | | | |
| 9098 | | C-GIPF | N700CE | N149VB | N100VR | | | | | |
| 9099 | | C-GIPJ | N700CU | C-GZKL | (ZS-DFN) | OE-IEL | | | | |
| 9100 | | C-GIXI | N700CX | N1SA | XA-PIL | | | | | |
| 9101 | | C-GIXJ | VP-BOK | | | | | | | |
| 9102 | | C-GIXM | N700CY | HB-IGS | VP-CGS | | | | | |
| 9103 | | C-GIXO | N700CZ | N122BN | | | | | | |
| 9104 | | C-GJIU | N190WP | N889CP | | | | | | |
| 9105 | | C-GJIW | N700EC | N100A | N500E | | | | | |
| 9106 | | C-GJIY | N816SG | N816SQ | N10E | OE-IRP | | | | |
| 9107 | R-1 | C-GJRG | United Kingdom ZJ690 | | | | | | | |
| 9108 | | C-GJRK | N700EK | N100ES | | | | | | |
| 9109 | | C-GJRL | N700DU | N700KS | | | | | | |
| 9110 | | C-GJTH | N700EL | N14R | N906JW | | | | | |
| 9111 | | C-GJTK | VT-DHA | | | | | | | |
| 9112 | | C-GJTP | C-GBLX | OE-IKM | | | | | | |
| 9113 | | C-GKCG | N920DS | N8762M | | | | | | |
| 9114 | | C-GKCM | N11EA | N1SL | N999YY | N999YA | VT-JSB | | | |
| 9115 | | C-GKCN | (F-GOAK) | LX-PAK | N915AV | C-FNDF | VP-BEB | N915AV | | |
| 9116 | | C-GKGZ | N700EW | N320GX | | | | | | |
| 9117 | | C-GKHC | N700EY | N917GL | | | | | | |
| 9118 | | C-GKHE | N700EZ | N904DS | | | | | | |
| 9119 | | C-GKHF | N700FE | C-GZOW | XA-OVR | | | | | |
| 9120 | | C-GKHG | N700FG | N887WS | N910TS* | (D-AGTH) | (OE-IFH) | | | |
| 9121 | | C-GKHH | N700FN | N711MC | | | | | | |
| 9122 | | C-GKHI | N700FQ | ZS-GJB | | | | | | |
| 9123 | R-1 | C-FZVM | United Kingdom ZJ691 | | | | | | | |
| 9124 | | C-FZVN | N700GB | | | | | | | |
| 9125 | | C-FZVS | N700FR | N711SX | | | | | | |
| 9126 | | C-FZVV | N60GX | C-GZPT | A7-AAM | | | | | |
| 9127 | 5000 | C-GERS | [prototype Global 5000 ff 07Mar03] | | | | | | | |
| 9128 | | C-FZWB | N700FY | N18WF | (N38WF) | N613WF | | | | |
| 9129 | | C-FZWF | N700FZ | N725LB | | | | | | |
| 9130 | 5000 | C-GLRM | 4X-COI | | | | | | | |
| 9131 | R-1 | C-FZWW | United Kingdom ZJ692 | | | | | | | |
| 9132 | R-1 | C-FZXC | United Kingdom ZJ693 | | | | | | | |
| 9133 | | C-FZXE | G-XPRS | LX-AAA | | | | | | |
| 9134 | | C-FZXZ | A7-GEX | N452CS | N451CS | | | | | |
| 9135 | R-1 | C-FZYL | United Kingdom ZJ694 | | | | | | | |
| 9136 | | C-GZPV | P4-AAA | M-YAAA | | | | | | |
| 9137 | | C-GZPW | C-GCDS | | | | | | | |
| 9138 | | C-GZRA | N51SE | | | | | | | |
| 9139 | | C-FYZP | OY-CVS | VQ-BAM | | | | | | |
| 9140 | 5000 | C-GAGQ | N140AE | N50DS | | | | | | |
| 9141 | | C-GAGS | VP-BOW | | | | | | | |
| 9142 | | C-GAGT | N700EW | VP-BSC | N442LF | N44GX | | | | |
| 9143 | | C-FAGU | VH-TGG | | | | | | | |
| 9144 | | C-FAGV | N6VB | | | | | | | |
| 9145 | | C-FAHN | N914DT | HB-JEX | | | | | | |
| 9146 | | C-FAHQ | EC-JIL | | | | | | | |

## BD-700 GLOBAL EXPRESS/GLOBAL 5000

| C/n | Srs | Identities | | | | |
|---|---|---|---|---|---|---|
| 9147 | | C-FAHX | P4-VVF | | | |
| 9148 | | C-FAIO | N889JA | | | |
| 9149 | 5000 | C-FAIY | N356MS | N456MS | VT-BAJ | |
| 9150 | | C-FAIV | N488CH | | | |
| 9151 | | C-FBOC | | | | |
| 9152 | 5000 | C-FBPK | N605VF | | | |
| 9153 | | C-FBPJ | N454AJ | N120AK | | |
| 9154 | 5000 | C-FBPL | N555EF | N388RF | | |
| 9155 | 5000 | C-FBPT | N711LS | | | |
| 9156 | 5000 | C-FBPZ | N156DG | N1DG | | |
| 9157 | 5000 | C-FBQD | VP-BAM | | | |
| 9158 | | C-FCOG | N375G | (N858TS) | C-GPPI | |
| 9159 | XRS | C-FCOI | D-ATNR | OH-TNR | | |
| 9160 | 5000 | C-FCOJ | N47 | | | |
| 9161 | 5000 | C-FCOK | N944AM | VP-BWB | | |
| 9162 | | C-FCOZ | N2T | | | |
| 9163 | | C-FCPH | OY-ILG | | | |
| 9164 | 5000 | C-FCSF | N376G | | | |
| 9165 | XRS | C-FCSH | VP-BOS | M-ASRI | | |
| 9166 | 5000 | C-FCSI | N166J | N1990C | | |
| 9167 | XRS | C-FCSL | N167GX | (OE-LNX) | HB-JGY | 9H-AFP |
| 9168 | 5000 | C-FCSP | OE-INC | | | |
| 9169 | XRS | C-FCSR | G-XXRS | | | |
| 9170 | 5000 | C-FCSY | D-AAAZ | | | |
| 9171 | XRS | C-FCTE | VP-CGO | | | |
| 9172 | 5000 | C-FCTK | N729KF | | | |
| 9173 | XRS | C-FCUA | HB-JEY | | | |
| 9174 | 5000 | C-FCUF | HB-JRS | | | |
| 9175 | XRS | C-FCUG | N771TF | N117TF | | |
| 9176 | 5000 | C-FCUK | N720WS | | | |
| 9177 | XRS | C-FCUS | N528J | N528JR | [damaged in hangar collapse at Washington/Dulles 06Feb10, possible w/o] | |
| 9178 | 5000 | C-FCUX | C-GDPG | | | |
| 9179 | XRS | C-FCVC | HL7748 | N905T | | |
| 9180 | 5000 | C-FCVD | N818FH | N939AP | | |
| 9181 | XRS | C-FEAB | N302AK | | | |
| 9182 | 5000 | C-FECA | N182GX | OE-IFG | | |
| 9183 | XRS | C-FEAD | N821AM | | | |
| 9184 | XRS | C-FEAE | HL7749 | | | |
| 9185 | XRS | C-FEAG | N1955M | | | |
| 9186 | 5000 | C-FECI | P4-HER | OY-FIT | | |
| 9187 | XRS | C-FEAK | N540WY | N54SL | | |
| 9188 | 5000 | C-FECN | F-HFBY | | | |
| 9189 | XRS | C-FEAQ | LX-GJM | M-GYQM | | |
| 9190 | 5000 | C-FECX | N99XN | PR-XDN | | |
| 9191 | XRS | C-FEAZ | N91NG | N6D | | |
| 9192 | 5000 | C-FECY | N700LK | | | |
| 9193 | XRS | C-FEBG | VP-BVG | | | |
| 9194 | XRS | C-FEBH | N313RF | | | |
| 9195 | XRS | C-FEBL | N195GX | N4T | | |
| 9196 | XRS | C-FEBQ | VP-CRC | G-CEYL | | |
| 9197 | XRS | C-FEBS | LX-PAK | | | |
| 9198 | 5000 | C-FECZ | HB-JRR | | | |
| 9199 | XRS | C-FEBU | (N799TS) | N379G | | |
| 9200 | XRS | C-FEBX | G-LXRS | | | |
| 9201 | 5000 | C-FHPQ | N95ZZ | N205EL | | |
| 9202 | XRS | C-FHPB | F-GVMV | | | |
| 9203 | XRS | C-FHPG | N203XX | N200A | | |
| 9204 | 5000 | C-FIHP | OE-IAK | LX-ZAK | | |
| 9205 | XRS | C-FIHL | N205EX | N100A | | |
| 9206 | 5000 | C-FIIB | N92ZZ | N343DF | | |
| 9207 | 5000 | C-FIIC | N723AB | | | |
| 9208 | XRS | C-FIHN | EC-KFS | | | |
| 9209 | 5000 | C-FIIG | N171JJ | "M-BIJJ"+ | [+ fake marks worn at Luton Jul08] | N171JJ |
| 9210 | XRS | C-FIOT | N190H | M-GBAL | | |
| 9211 | 5000 | C-FIPH | C-GXPR | [w/o Fox Harbour, Newfoundland, Canada 11Nov07; cx Mar08; parted out] | | |
| 9212 | 5000 | C-FIPJ | N13JS | | | |
| 9213 | XRS | C-FIOZ | (VP-CAH) | D-AEKT | (VH-ZXH) | VQ-BIS M-VQBI |
| 9214 | 5000 | C-FIPM | N93ZZ | VT-JSK | | |
| 9215 | 5000 | C-FIPC | N94ZZ | N18WF | | |
| 9216 | 5000 | C-FIPN | N900LS | | | |
| 9217 | 5000 | C-FIPP | N700LS | | | |
| 9218 | XRS | C-FIPF | N96ZZ | N86TW | | |
| 9219 | 5000 | C-FIPQ | N80ZZ | N611VT | SP-ZAK | |
| 9220 | XRS | C-FIPG | P4-CBA | | | |
| 9221 | 5000 | C-FIPT | N10SL | | | |

## BD-700 GLOBAL EXPRESS/GLOBAL 5000

| C/n | Srs | Identities | | | | |
|---|---|---|---|---|---|---|
| 9222 | 5000 | C-FJNJ | N81ZZ | N45JE | | |
| 9223 | XRS | C-FJML | N83ZZ | VP-BAH | | |
| 9224 | 5000 | C-FJNQ | N224GX | N989RJ | | |
| 9225 | XRS | C-FJMP | N36LG | | | |
| 9226 | 5000 | C-FJNX | A6-DHG | | | |
| 9227 | 5000 | C-FJNZ | (N200LS) | M-LLGC | M-SKSM | |
| 9228 | XRS | C-FJMQ | N87ZZ | N289Z | N288Z | |
| 9229 | 5000 | C-FJOA | N84ZZ | YR-TIK | | |
| 9230 | XRS | C-FJMV | A7-GEY | N57LE | | |
| 9231 | 5000 | C-FJOK | VP-CAU | G-TSLS | | |
| 9232 | XRS | C-FJMX | D2-ANG | | | |
| 9233 | 5000 | C-FJOU | (A6-OWC) | N233FJ | C-GGLO | |
| 9234 | XRS | C-FLKZ | N234GX | (D-AANA) | OE-LAF | |
| 9235 | XRS | C-FLLA | OE-LXR | | | |
| 9236 | XRS | C-FLLF | N624BP | | | |
| 9237 | XRS | C-FLLH | (OE-LNY) | OH-PPS | | |
| 9238 | XRS | C-FLLN | HB-JGP | | | |
| 9239 | XRS | C-FLLO | N71ZZ | N421SZ | | |
| 9240 | XRS | C-FLLV | N999YX | N999YY | | |
| 9241 | 5000 | C-FLKY | (G-LLGC) | N941TS | G-OCSA | G-CGFA |
| 9242 | XRS | C-FLTB | N942TS | (OH-PPS) | N942TS | N375G |
| 9243 | 5000 | C-FLTH | OE-IMA | VP-CMA | | |
| 9244 | XRS | C-FLTI | C-FCNN | VP-CZK | | |
| 9245 | 5000 | C-FLTJ | N200ES | | | |
| 9246 | XRS | C-FMFK | VP-BNX | | | |
| 9247 | XRS | C-FMFN | N881TS | | | |
| 9248 | XRS | C-FMFO | N888GX | | | |
| 9249 | 5000 | C-FMGE | HB-JGN | 9H-AFR | | |
| 9250 | XRS | C-FMGK | D-AKAZ | | | |
| 9251 | XRS | C-FMKW | N73ZZ | OE-IGG | | |
| 9252 | XRS | C-FMKZ | LX-FLY | | | |
| 9253 | XRS | C-FMLB | ZS-ZBB | | | |
| 9254 | XRS | C-FMLE | N754TS | VQ-BGS | | |
| 9255 | 5000 | C-FMLI | N193LA | | | |
| 9256 | XRS | C-FMLQ | OE-ICN | | | |
| 9257 | 5000 | C-FMLT | VP-CVU | 5A-UAC | | |
| 9258 | XRS | C-FMLV | N700ML | PR-MLJ | | |
| 9259 | XRS | C-FMMH | N89ZZ | Botswana OK1 | | |
| 9260 | XRS | C-FMND | N74ZZ | ZS-XRS | | |
| 9261 | 5000 | C-FMUI | N878HL | | | |
| 9262 | XRS | C-FMUN | N962TS | VT-STV | | |
| 9263 | 5000 | C-FMUO | VP-CSB | | | |
| 9264 | XRS | C-FNDN | C-GLUL | | | |
| 9265 | 5000 | C-FNDK | N265DE | N501JT | | |
| 9266 | XRS | C-FNDO | N76ZZ | N104DA | | |
| 9267 | XRS | C-FNDQ | N78ZZ | M-MMAS | | |
| 9268 | XRS | C-FNDT | VQ-BJA | | | |
| 9269 | 5000 | C-FNRP | OE-IBC | | | |
| 9270 | XRS | C-FNRR | VP-CNY | | | |
| 9271 | 5000 | C-FNSN | VP-CJC | N898WS | | |
| 9272 | XRS | C-FNSV | VP-CVV | N15SD | | |
| 9273 | 5000 | C-FNZZ | VP-BJN | | | |
| 9274 | XRS | C-FOAB | N974TS | G-EXRS | | |
| 9275 | 5000 | C-FOAD | N87ZZ | VH-KTG | | |
| 9276 | XRS | C-FOKD | VP-BJI | | | |
| 9277 | XRS | C-FOKF | N194WM | | | |
| 9278 | XRS | C-FOKH | N709DS | | | |
| 9279 | 5000 | C-FOKJ | N79ZZ | N468KL | | |
| 9280 | XRS | C-FOVD | (D-AVIA) | OY-WIN | | |
| 9281 | XRS | C-FOVE | N981TS | | | |
| 9282 | 5000 | C-FOVG | N216PA | A6-FBQ | | |
| 9283 | XRS | C-FOVH | VQ-BEB | | | |
| 9284 | XRS | C-FOVK | N77UF | | | |
| 9285 | 5000 | C-FPFF | 5A-UAB | | | |
| 9286 | XRS | C-FPGB | C-FHYL | OE-IPA | | |
| 9287 | XRS | C-FPGD | N169DT | HB-JGE | | |
| 9288 | 5000 | C-FPGI | N375WB | | | |
| 9289 | 5000 | C-FPQE | N26ZZ | VT-DBA | | |
| 9290 | XRS | C-FPQF | N774KK | N797KK* | | |
| 9291 | XRS | C-FPQG | OH-PPT | | | |
| 9292 | XRS | C-FPQH | N837WM | N887WM | | |
| 9293 | 5000 | C-FPQI | HZ-SJP | "HZ-BJP" | M-JANP | |
| 9294 | XRS | C-FQXW | M-CRVS | | | |
| 9295 | 5000 | C-FQXX | B-LIM | | | |
| 9296 | XRS | C-FQXY | N96ZZ | N616DC | | |
| 9297 | XRS | C-FQYB | VQ-BSC | | | |

## BD-700 GLOBAL EXPRESS/GLOBAL 5000

| C/n | Srs | Identities | | |
|---|---|---|---|---|
| 9298 | 5000 | C-FQYD | N900GX | |
| 9299 | XLS | C-FQYE | N37ZZ | VH-LAW |
| 9300 | XRS | C-FRJV | N709FG | |
| 9301 | 5000 | C-FRJY | (D-AMOS) | OE-IOO |
| 9302 | 5000 | C-FRKL | N95ZZ | N352AF |
| 9303 | XRS | C-FRKO | EC-LEB | |
| 9304 | XRS | C-FRKQ | N89MX | [damaged in hangar collapse at Washington/Dulles 06Feb10, possible w/o] |
| 9305 | 5000 | C-FRMW | N815PA | |
| 9306 | XRS | C-FRNG | G-SHEF | |
| 9307 | XRS | C-FRNJ | N528MP | |
| 9308 | 5000 | C-FSRX | N103ZZ | |
| 9309 | XRS | C-FSRY | G-CJME | |
| 9310 | XRS | C-FSRZ | | |
| 9311 | 5000 | C-FSSE | M-SALE | VH-DNK |
| 9312 | XRS | C-FTIK | PP-VDR | |
| 9313 | XRS | C-FTIO | [Global Vision Flight Deck test aircraft] | |
| 9314 | XRS | C-FTIQ | N807DC | |
| 9315 | 5000 | C-FTIR | B-LRW | |
| 9316 | XRS | C-FTIS | | |
| 9317 | XRS | C-FTUX | VT-HMA* | |
| 9318 | 5000 | C-FTUY | TC-KRM | |
| 9319 | XRS | C-FTVF | | |
| 9320 | XRS | C-FTVK | HB-JGH | |
| 9321 | 5000 | C-FTVN | VP-CWN | |
| 9322 | XRS | C-FTVO | XA-BUA | |
| 9323 | XRS | C-FUCV | | |
| 9324 | 5000 | C-FUCY | | |
| 9325 | 5000 | C-FUCZ | N723HH | |
| 9326 | XRS | C-FUDH | VH-OCV | |
| 9327 | XRS | C-FUDN | N105ZZ | |
| 9328 | 5000 | C-FUOJ | N555HD | |
| 9329 | XRS | C-FUOK | 9H-XRS | |
| 9330 | 5000 | C-FUOL | N939ML | |
| 9331 | XRS | C-FUOM | G-KANL^ | |
| 9332 | XRS | C-FURP | LX-GXR* | |
| 9333 | XRS | C-FUSI | G-SANL | |
| 9334 | 5000 | C-FUSR | G-PVEL | |
| 9335 | XRS | C-FUTF | | |
| 9336 | XRS | C-FUTL | S5-ADE | |
| 9337 | 5000 | C-FUTT | N109ZZ | M-ATAK |
| 9338 | XRS | C-FVFW | | |
| 9339 | XRS | C-FVGP | N112ZZ | |
| 9340 | 5000 | C-FVGX | N340GF | |
| 9341 | XRS | C-FVHE | | |
| 9342 | XRS | C-FVUI | N39ZZ | |
| 9343 | 5000 | C-FVUK | OY-SGC | |
| 9344 | XRS | C-FVUP | | |
| 9345 | XRS | C-FVUZ | N113ZZ | |
| 9346 | 5000 | C-FVVE | VH-LEP | |
| 9347 | XRS | C-FWGB | N115ZZ | |
| 9348 | XRS | C-FWGH | | |
| 9349 | XRS | C-FWGP | | |
| 9350 | 5000 | C-FWGV | | |
| 9351 | XRS | C-FWHF | | |
| 9352 | XRS | C-FWIK | N868SC | |
| 9353 | 5000 | C-FWZR | CS-EAM | |
| 9354 | XRS | C-FWZX | N92ZZ | |
| 9355 | XRS | C-FXAQ | N770AG | |
| 9356 | 5000 | C-FXAY | | |
| 9357 | XRS | C-FXBF | N40ZZ | |
| 9358 | XRS | C-FXIY | N760AG | |
| 9359 | 5000 | C-FXJD | HB-JIH* | |
| 9360 | XRS | C-FXJM | | |
| 9361 | XRS | C-FXKE | N65ZZ | |
| 9362 | XRS | C-FXKK | | |
| 9363 | 5000 | C-FXYK | | |
| 9364 | XRS | C-FXYS | | |
| 9365 | XRS | C-FXYY | N75ZZ | |
| 9366 | 5000 | C-FYGJ | N59ZZ | |
| 9367 | XRS | C-FYGP | | |
| 9368 | XRS | C-FYGX | | |
| 9369 | XRS | C-FYHT | | |
| 9370 | 5000 | C-FYIG | | |
| 9371 | XRS | C-FYIH | | |
| 9372 | 5000 | C-FYIZ | | |
| 9373 | 5000 | C-FYJC | | |

# BD-700 GLOBAL EXPRESS/GLOBAL 5000

| C/n | Srs | Identities | |
|---|---|---|---|
| 9374 | XRS | C-FYJD | |
| 9375 | XRS | C-FYMT | N121ZZ |
| 9376 | 5000 | C-FYMU | |
| 9377 | XRS | C-FYNI | |
| 9378 | XRS | C-FYNQ | |
| 9379 | 5000 | C-FYNV | |
| 9380 | XRS | C-FYOC | |
| 9381 | XRS | C-GBTY | |
| 9382 | 5000 | C-GBUA | N15PX |
| 9383 | 5000 | C-GBUI | |
| 9384 | XRS | C-GCKR | |
| 9385 | XRS | C-GCLI | |
| 9386 | 5000 | C-GCMJ | |
| 9387 | XRS | C-GCOX | |
| 9388 | XRS | C-GCPI | |
| 9389 | 5000 | C-GCPV | |
| 9390 | XRS | C-GCWQ | |
| 9391 | XRS | C-GCWU | |
| 9392 | 5000 | C-GCWV | |
| 9393 | XRS | C-GCWX | |
| 9394 | XRS | C-GCXE | |
| 9395 | | | |
| 9396 | | | |
| 9397 | | | |
| 9398 | | | |
| 9399 | | | |
| 9400 | | | |
| 9401 | | | |
| 9402 | | | |
| 9403 | | | |
| 9404 | | | |
| 9405 | | | |
| 9406 | | | |
| 9407 | | | |
| 9408 | | | |
| 9409 | | | |
| 9410 | | | |
| 9411 | | | |
| 9412 | | | |
| 9413 | | | |
| 9414 | | | |
| 9415 | | | |
| 9416 | | | |
| 9417 | | | |
| 9418 | | | |
| 9419 | | | |
| 9420 | | | |

# CANADAIR CL600 CHALLENGER

| C/n | Srs | Identities |
|---|---|---|
| 1001 | | C-GCGR-X [ff 08Nov78; w/o 03Apr80 Mojave, CA, while flight testing] |
| 1002 | S | C-GCGS-X Canada 144612 code "X" [displayed Heritage Park, Air Command HQ, Winnipeg, Canada] |
| 1003/3991 | S | C-GCGT-X C-GCGT [wfu circa Feb06 to Canadian Aviation Museum, Rockcliffe, Canada for display] |
| 1004 | S | C-GXKQ N2677S N227CC N600BP N640TS N50PA [parted out] |
| 1005 | S | C-GBDH N600CL C-GBCC N444WA D-BJET N600CL N605TS N180CH N244AL |
| 1006 | S | C-GCSN N110KS HZ-A04 C-GCSN Canada 144603 N296V N515BP (N6972Z) |
| 1007 | S | C-GBKC HZ-TAG C-GBKC Canada 144604 N600WJ (N799HF) (N607BH) |
| 1008 | S | C-GBEY (D-BBAD) Canada 144605 N380V N604SH |
| 1009 | S | C-GBFY N606CL C-GCVQ Canada 144606 N396V |
| 1010 | S | C-GCIB N909MG N802Q N7JM N2105 |
| 1011 | S | C-GBHS N42137 N510PC N510PS N601JR N678ML N116RA N3RP |
| 1012 | S | C-GBKE N600KC (N78499) N750PM N750BM N121VA N8KG N167SC N310PE N604AC |
| 1013 | S | C-GBHZ N2428 N601SA N129BA N72SR N16RW |
| 1014 | S | C-GBLL-X N97941 HZ-TAG C-GBLL Canada 144607 N370V [w/o 02Feb05 Teterboro Airport, NJ] |
| 1015 | S | C-GBLN N37LB N604CL C-GBLN Canada 144608 N25V |
| 1016 | S | C-GWRT EI-GPA VR-BKJ N757MC N16TS N920RV (N812XL) |
| 1017 | S | C-GBPX N4247C N777XX C-GBPX Canada 144609 N270V |
| 1018 | S | C-GLWR N1812C N198CC N375PK N875PK N771WW N618AJ N618RL |
| 1019 | S | C-GLWT N9071M N603CL N600FF ZS-NER 3B-GFI N619TS |
| 1020 | S | C-GLWV N36LB N602CL N600MG N600PD N808TM N600BD N602AJ |
| 1021 | S | C-GLWX N914X N914XA N63HJ [canx 14Oct04 and parted out] |
| 1022 | S | C-GLWZ C-GOGO Canada 144610 N260V |
| 1023 | S | C-GLXB N630M N680M N90UC (N610TS) N920DS (N333TS) N777GD |
| 1024 | S | C-GLXD N637ML N567ML N326MM N810MT N811MT |
| 1025 | S | C-GLXF N2636N N111G N111J HB-ILH N888LW N620SB (OY-VIA) (OY-CKO) N711GA N399WB |
| 1026 | S | C-GLXH N507CC N507HC (N507WY) N694JC N694PG |
| 1027 | S | C-GLXK N420L N420TX (N456CG) N678CG N111FK N112FK N93BA N111JL |
| 1028 | S | C-GLXM HB-VHC N600ST 5B-CHX N600BZ YV-1111CP N858PJ |
| 1029 | S | C-GLXO HB-VGA D-BMTM (N205A) OH-WIH N600TN N722DJ |
| 1030 | S | C-GLXQ N1622 N604CL C-GCZU Canada 144611 (N196V) N60S N630BB N721ST |
| 1031 | S | C-GLXS N620S |
| 1032 | S | C-GLXU N455SR N200CN N11AZ (N31DC) N1884 N70X |
| 1033 | S | C-GLXW N2642F VR-CKK N600YY N101SK N101ST N357RT N304TT (N518FS) |
| 1034 | | C-GLXY N2634Y N153SR (N151SR) N209WF (N209WE) N481JT LV-YLB N134VS |
| 1035 | S | C-GLYA N122TY N122WF N64FC C-FEAQ (EI-BYD) VR-BLD N700CL N187AP N163EG |
| 1036 | S | C-GLYC C-GBOQ N80AT N88AT N66MF N900DP N900LG |
| 1037 | | C-GLYE N805C [w/o 03Jan83 Sun Valley Friedman Memorial, ID] |
| 1038 | S | C-GLYH N8010X N1045X N65HJ N616DF N903DD |
| 1039 | S | C-GLYK N26640 N1868M N1868S N722HP N895CC N905MP |
| 1040 | S | C-GLYM Canada 144601 |
| 1041 | S | C-GLYO N733K N733CF N193DQ (N95DQ) N141TS N141RD |
| 1042 | S | C-GLWV N770CA N999SR N999TF (N939CG) N604MH N604SJ |
| 1043 | S | C-GLWX N229GC C-GJPG C-FSXG N43NW N100QR |
| 1044 | S | C-GLWZ N541MM N205MM N55AR N800BT |
| 1045 | S | C-GLXB N55PG N900FC C-GBKB N247CK |
| 1046 | S | C-GLXD C-GTXV N46SR N246JL |
| 1047 | S | C-GLXH C-GBSZ N2741Q N601WW N818LS N555WD N556WD (N500EX) N315MK N249AJ |
| 1048 | S | C-GLXK N29687 N600TT N500LS N600LS N601LS (EI-BXN) C-FSIP C-GDDR |
| 1049 | S | C-GLXM N2720B HB-VFW N491DB N491TS N39RE N600CF N601CT |
| 1050 | S | C-GLXO N600MK N82CW N82CN N710HL |
| 1051 | S | C-GLXQ N27341 N20CX (N601CR) N601SR N91UC N27BH N505PM |
| 1052 | S | C-GLXS N3330M N3330L N110M N110TD N409KC N600LG N620AC "N168TS" N620AC N152TS N222LH N222LM |
| 1053 | S | C-GLYA HB-VHO N4424P N32BC N32BQ N397BE N415PT N54SK N54SU LV-BAS |
| 1054 | S | C-GLYC N80TF N7008 N9008 VR-CLI N602AS N660RM N217RM |
| 1055 | | C-GLYE N2707T N1FE N55SR N271MB N643CR |
| 1056 | S | C-GLYH N26895 N600CC N600TE N712HL N1HZ N2HZ N777GA |
| 1057 | S | C-GLXU C-GBTK N605CL (VH-OZZ) N508CC N508HC XA-RAP XA-TIV XA-ISR N78SR N6MW |
| 1058 | S | C-GLXW N4000X N60HJ N658CF |
| 1059 | S | C-GLXY N227G N227GL (C-FRST) (C-GFCD) N3HB N103HB N403WY N396KM |
| 1060 | S | C-GLYK N29984 N22AZ N74JA |
| 1061 | S | C-GLYO N600JW VH-MXX VH-MCG N770JC N661TS N601KK (N661TS) |
| 1062 | S | C-GLWV C-GBTT Malaysia M31-01 N4FE N62BL N68SD N95EB N444ET |
| 1063 | S | C-GLWX N31240+ N102ML PT-LXW N102ML XA-SOA N8260D (N74TJ) (N711AJ) (N88TJ) (N98TW) N409CC N457HL [+recorded for a while in error on FAA files as N32140] |

# CL600 CHALLENGER

| C/n | Srs | Identities | | | | | | | | | |
|---|---|---|---|---|---|---|---|---|---|---|---|
| 1064 | S | C-GLWZ | C-GBUB | Malaysia M31-02 | | N14FE | N64GL | N75B | N100LR | | |
| 1065 | S | C-GLXB | C-GBVE | Canada 144602 | | N601WJ | N287DL | | | | |
| 1066 | S | C-GLXD | N67B | N721SW | N701QS | N701GA | N51TJ | D-BSNA | | | |
| 1067 | S | C-GLXH | "VR-CBP" | C-GLXH | C-GBZE | N50928 | N800AB | N205EL | N240AK | M-IFES | |
| 1068 | S | C-GLXK | N215RL | N938WH | N160LC | N604EF | | | | | |
| 1069 | S | C-GLXM | N203G | N816PD | I-LPHZ | N74LM | (N100LR) | N500RH | N788WG | N818TH | |
| | | (N818E) | N455BE | N817CK | N80CK | | | | | | |
| 1070 | S | C-GLXO | N3237S | HZ-MF1 | N70DJ | N24JK | N670CL | D-BUSY | | | |
| 1071 | S | C-GLXQ | N607CL | N523B | N588UC | N121DF | N127DF | N671SR | N711DB | N220LC | |
| | | N600HA | | | | | | | | | |
| 1072 | S | C-GLXW | N82A | (N137FP) | N331FP | N125AC | N10PN | N302PC | | | |
| 1073 | S | C-GLXY | N234RG | N234MW | N31WT | (N331WT) | N661JB | N888KS | VH-NKS | N600BP | |
| | | (VR-BBP) | (N512AC) | N125AN | (N600EC) | N673TS | N673YS | (N673BH) | | | |
| 1074 | | C-GLYK | N317FE | N1FE | N10FE | HZ-SAA | HZ-WT2 | HZ-WBT1 | HZ-RFM | N800HH | N674CW |
| 1075 | S | C-GLXO | N600CP | N2FE | N25SR | N751DB | N450AJ | | | | |
| 1076 | S | C-GLXK | N8000 | N7SP | I-BLSM | N601WW | N87TR | | | | |
| 1077 | S | C-GLXM | N994TA | (N778XX) | C-GBZK | N152SM | N71M | N500R | N507R | (N940DH) | |
| | | N300TK | | | | | | | | | |
| 1078 | S | C-GLYO | N600DL | N600CF | I-MRDV | N53SR | N1500 | (N1504) | VH-ZSU | | |
| 1079 | S | C-GLWV | N46ES | N125N | N601Z | N888FW | N600RE | N601SA | N601CM | | |
| 1080 | S | C-GLWX | N800CC | N3JL | N300TW | N677LM | | | | | |
| 1081 | S | C-GLWZ | N19HF | (N54PA) | (N681TS) | N456DK | N19DD | N199D | N19DD | N199D | ZS-ISA |
| 1082 | S | C-GLXB | N3854B | N600ST | I-PTCT | N700KK | N777KK | N777KZ | N333KK | N388DD | |
| 1083 | S | C-GLXD | N47ES | N471SP | N471SB | N399FL | | | | | |
| 1084 | S | C-GLXH | N730TL | (N10MZ) | N175ST | N550CW | | | | | |
| 1085 | S | C-GLXQ | N20G | N20GX | N600ST | OE-HET | LZ-YUM | | | | |
| 1086 | | C-GLXS | [marks reserved 29Mar83 but aircraft not completed - fuselage to Canadian Forces Fire Fighting Academy, CFB Borden] | | | | | | | | |
| 1087 | | [aircraft not completed - fuselage to Canadian Forces Fire Fighting Academy, CFB Borden] | | | | | | | | | |
| 1088 | | [aircraft not completed - fuselage to Canadian Forces Fire Fighting Academy, CFB Borden] | | | | | | | | | |

Production complete

# CANADAIR CL601 CHALLENGER

| C/n | Identities |
|---|---|
| 3001 | C-GBUU-X [ff 17Sep82] N601CL N601AG N789DR N74GR |
| 3002 | C-GBXH (N509PC) N4449F N273G N601SR N750GT N602CW N227PE N600NP |
| 3003 | C-GLXU N500PC N500TB N500TD C-GESR N601CL (N680FA) VH-MXK |
| 3004 | C-GLXK N509PC N967L N501PC N45PH |
| 3005 | C-FAAL N601TX |
| 3006 | C-GLXY N372G (N3728) HB-IKX N372G (EI-TAM) P4-TAM N606BA ZS-ONL N256SD N601JG |
| 3007 | C-GLYE N711SR N711SX N711SZ N910KB N275MT |
| 3008 | C-GLYK N733A N783A N61AF (N999SW) N38SW N608CW N698CW (N600LX) N710GA |
| 3009 | C-GLYO N373G N873G (N651AC) [w/o 28Nov04 Montrose, CO] |
| 3010 | C-GLWV C-GBLX N80CS N601UT N601SQ N601BD N411TJ |
| 3011 | C-GLWX C-GBYC N601AG N399WW N899WW N700MK N7788 N205EL N205EE N202PH N453GS |
| 3012 | C-GLXB N226GL N226G C-GMII VR-BMA N6165C XA-SHZ N603GJ N23BJ N23BN N878RM C-FKJM |
| 3013 | C-GLXD N601TG VR-BLA VP-BLA N124BC N633CW (N602LX) N213TS (N32WR) |
| 3014 | C-GLXH N14PN N292GA N698RS N698RT C-GDBF |
| 3015 | C-GLXM N374G XA-KIM |
| 3016 | C-GLWV N4562Q N1107Z N601CL VP-BIE N388DB |
| 3017 | C-GLWX N778XX (HZ-AMA) HZ-SFS N778YY VR-CAR C-GJPG C-FBYJ A6-EJD JY-RY1 JY-RYA |
| 3018 | C-GLWZ C-GBXW N779XX [w/o 07Feb85 Milan, Italy; cx May91; cockpit section conv to flight simulator and used by Flight Safety Intl at Montreal-Dorval, Canada] |
| 3019 | C-GLXB N375G N875G XA-SMS |
| 3020 | C-GLXO C-GCFI [stored Mesa/Falcon Field, AZ] |
| 3021 | C-GLXQ N5069P (N711SP) N711SJ N967L N503PC N966L N150MH |
| 3022 | C-GLXS C-GCFG |
| 3023 | C-GLXY N778YY N100WC N967L N501PC N524PC N601KF N601KE N601FJ AP-MIR |
| 3024 | C-GLYA N711ST HB-ILM N98CR N93CR N888AZ |
| 3025 | C-GLWV N1620 N529DM N529D N363CR N997GC |
| 3026 | C-GLWX N5373U N927A N601GL N300S N80RP N716HP N810MT (N810MB) N307SC |
| 3027 | C-GLWZ N5402X N17CN (N401NK) N627CW (N603LX) C-GPSI |
| 3028 | C-GLXB C-FBEL C-FBEI |
| 3029 | C-GLXD N5491V N1824T N629TS N773JC N629TS |
| 3030 | C-GLXH N611CL N34CD N39CD |
| 3031 | C-GLXK C-GCTB N607CL C-GCTB Germany 1201 VP-CCF N303BX (N631CF) N54JC (N181SM) G-LWDC |
| 3032 | C-GLXM N779YY HZ-AK1 N7011H N111G N111GX N392FV |
| 3033 | C-GLXQ N601TJ HB-ILK VP-BBF |
| 3034 | C-GLXU N374BC N372BC N372BG N372PG N120MP C-GSAP C-GLOJ |
| 3035 | C-GLXW C-GCUN Canada 144613 [w/o 24Apr95 Shearwater AFB, Nova Scotia, Canada; to be rebuilt for museum display at CFB Greenwood, Canada] |
| 3036 | C-GLXY C-GCUP Canada 144614 |
| 3037 | C-GLXB C-GCUR Canada 144615 |
| 3038 | C-GLYA C-GCUT Canada 144616 |
| 3039 | C-GLYH C-GPGD C-GPCC N639CL N500PG |
| 3040 | C-GLYK N608CL Germany 1202 |
| 3041 | C-GLWV C-GRBC N610MS N600MS N169TA N169TD |
| 3042 | C-GLWX N613CL N900CC N333GJ N951RM |
| 3043 | C-GLWZ N609CL Germany 1203 |
| 3044 | C-GLXD N921K N125N N955DB N601GB (N801PA) LV-BPV |
| 3045 | C-GLXH N914BD N914BB N601RP OE-HCL N3045 N998JR N601PR |
| 3046 | C-GLXK C-GDBX B-4005 N601HJ N601TJ LX-AEN N46SR N228PK N600GA |
| 3047 | C-GLXM C-GBZQ B-4006 N602HJ N602TJ OE-HLE N824DH |
| 3048 | C-GLXO N35FP N601JM (N628WC) |
| 3049 | C-GLXQ N610CL C-FQYT Germany 1204 |
| 3050 | C-GLXS (N9680N) N9680Z N62MS N62MU N95SR N601AE N802PA (N626JP) |
| 3051 | C-GLWR N445AC N60MS N60MU N4415D N95SR N651CW (N604LX) N97SG |
| 3052 | C-GLWT C-GDCQ B-4007 N603HJ (N601GF) N801GC VP-CRX N425WN |
| 3053 | C-GLWV N604CL Germany 1205 |
| 3054 | C-GLWX N605CL VH-MZL N54PR N601PR N601TP N601ZT N375PK N315SL N50TG N722HP N57MH |
| 3055 | C-GLWZ N100HG N608RP N601RC |
| 3056 | C-GLXB N612CL Germany 1206 |
| 3057 | C-GLXD N19J 9J-RON (N602TS) N747TS N163WG |
| 3058 | C-GLXU N125PS |
| 3059 | C-GLXW N614CL Germany 1207 |
| 3060 | C-GLXY (N601SN) N601S |
| 3061 | C-GLYO N9708N N999JR N597FJ N601AA |
| 3062 | C-GLYK N601HP N601GT N2183N N628CM |
| 3063 | C-GLYH C-FURG |

## CL601 CHALLENGER

| C/n | Identities |
|---|---|
| 3064 | C-GLYC N566N N356N N224N N224F (N224HF) N224U (N424JM) N664CW (N606LX) N425SU |
| 3065 | C-GLYA N602CC N1623 (N128PE) N500PE N601JP "N603TS" N601JP (N54PA) LX-GDC G-IMAC |
| 3066 | C-GLXQ N609CL N144SX VR-CLE VP-CLE N105UP |

Production complete

# MODEL 601-3A

| C/n | Identities |
|---|---|
| 5001 | C-GDDP [ff 28Sep86] N245TT N245TL (N59FJ) N604FJ |
| 5002 | C-GDEQ N611CL C-GDEQ N611CL N585UC N43PR N602TS |
| 5003 | C-GDHP N778XX HB-IKT N601FR |
| 5004 | C-GDKO N100KT N180KT N618DC N504TS XA-VDG |
| 5005 | C-GLWR N613CL N101PK HB-IKU N14GD N64FE N902BW |
| 5006 | C-GLWT C-FLPC C-GENA N506TS |
| 5007 | C-GLWV N60GG N607CL (N607CZ) N17TE N17TZ N666CT |
| 5008 | C-GLWX N601CC N601EG N1M N42EE |
| 5009 | C-GLWZ N399SW N699CW (N610LX) N654CM |
| 5010 | C-GLXB N57HA (N57HK) N1812C N181AP N429WG |
| 5011 | C-GLXD N603CC JA8283 N611MH N602UK VR-CIC VP-CIC |
| 5012 | C-GLXU N107TB N1868M N500LR |
| 5013 | C-GLXW N711PD I-CTPT N604MC N301MF N950FB N116LS |
| 5014 | C-GLXY N21CX N31WH N311G N311GX N888DH (N714TS) N514TS |
| 5015 | C-GLXH N601KR N200DE N514RB N204JK |
| 5016 | C-GLXQ N604CC N49UR N622AB (N622AD) N868CE C-GQWI N325DA N551SD |
| 5017 | C-GLWX N700KC N202HG N77058 N404HG |
| 5018 | C-GLWV N606CC C-FBHX 9Q-CBS C-FBHX N601HH N618DB (D-AMTM) N601GS (N601DR) (N601GR) N893AC N828SK N908DG |
| 5019 | C-GLWT N915BD N915BB (N247GA) N237GA N602BD C-GJFQ N575CF C-GHGC |
| 5020 | C-GLYA C-FBKR I-BEWW C-GZHZ N604CF N39RE |
| 5021 | C-GLYC N64F N122WF N48FU (N305M) N621CF N620HF N989BC |
| 5022 | C-GLYK N449ML N449MC VP-CJP G-SAJP VP-CJP N655TH N618RR |
| 5023 | C-GLYO N608CC EI-LJG N601CJ N175ST N623CW (OE-...) D-AAMA |
| 5024 | C-GLYH C-FCDF B-4010 N604HJ N601NB N601DT |
| 5025 | C-GLWR C-FCGS B-4011 N605HJ N1TK N11TK N93DW N1DW N931DW |
| 5026 | C-GLWT N601WM |
| 5027 | C-GLWV N244BH N64BH N421SZ N420SZ N420ST N7PS |
| 5028 | C-GLWX N601TL N601RL (N601EA) |
| 5029 | C-GLWZ C-FDAT N602CC VR-BMK N67MR N83LC N594RJ |
| 5030 | C-GLXB N312CT N816SQ N816SP N1HZ |
| 5031 | C-GLXD N900CL N908CL N721MC N721MD N64LE |
| 5032 | C-GLXF N604CC N667LC N667CC 4X-COT N601ER N950SW N684SW LV-BYG |
| 5033 | C-GLXH VH-ASM N32GG N397J (N397JQ) N397Q N144BS |
| 5034 | C-GLXK C-GIOH |
| 5035 | C-GLXU N606CC N333MG N202W HB-JRV |
| 5036 | C-GLXW N225N N468KL N468KE |
| 5037 | C-GLXY N608CC (JA8360) N707GG N353TC N212LM N710LM |
| 5038 | C-GLXQ C-GBJA (N602CN) N1271A N78RP (N220LC) N78PP N91KH |
| 5039 | C-GLWX N811BB N811BP N811BR N765WT |
| 5040 | C-GLWV N652CN N807Z N898AK |
| 5041 | C-GLWT C-FETZ G-FBMB C-FTIE N641CL N352AF N352AE "N541TS" N953FA |
| 5042 | C-GLYA C-FEUV HB-IKS N28UA HB-IKS |
| 5043 | C-GLYC N779YY VR-COJ N601BH N601VH |
| 5044 | C-GLYK C-FFBY I-NNUS N901BM VR-CMC VP-CMC VP-CBS |
| 5045 | C-GLXS C-FFSO N616CC N500GS N601AF |
| 5046 | C-GLXW N6SG N818TH N818TY N426PF N426PE |
| 5047 | C-GLXD N140CH N547FP N900SS N384MP |
| 5048 | C-GLXY N2004G N716RD N907WS |
| 5049 | C-GLXF N721EW N721SW N721BW D-AGKG N628VK VR-CVK VP-CVK N888JA B-MAI |
| 5050 | C-GLXK N826JP N831CJ N881CJ (N25GG) N710VF |
| 5051 | C-GLXM N1903G N190GG N300KC N190SB C-GQBQ |
| 5052 | C-GLXO N4PG N652CW N125ST (N615SA) |
| 5053 | C-GLXU N5PG (N553CW) N653CW (N611LX) N440KM |
| 5054 | C-GLXB N619FE N3FE |
| 5055 | C-GLXH N601HC N46F N460F |
| 5056 | C-GLXQ N614CC N153NS N525SD |
| 5057 | [Was to have been first CL601S with c/n 6001 but built as 601-3A] C-GLWR N900NM N830CB N830CD N733CF |
| 5058 | C-GLWZ N404SK N101SK N527JA |
| 5059 | C-GLWV XA-GEO XA-JFE XA-TTD C-GZNC N627KR C-FJNS |
| 5060 | C-GLYO N5060H N630M ZS-NKD N506BA N573AC EC-JKT (D-ADLA) D-ARTE |
| 5061 | C-GLYH C-FHHD 9Q-CBS N661CL (N575MA) VP-BEJ |

## CL601 CHALLENGER

| C/n | Identities |
|---|---|
| 5062 | C-GLWX N60FC N540W N548W N142B N727S N316BG N601ER |
| 5063 | [Was to have been the second CL601S with c/n 6002 but built as 601-3A, last Cartierville-built airframe] C-GLXS N612CC N79AD N78AD N611JW N811JW N801FL (N315FX) N304FX N304BX N50DS N563TS XA-UEW |
| 5064 | [First Dorval-built airframe] C-GLXW C-FIOB VH-BRG N564TS N601EC |
| 5065 | C-GLXD N601BF N882C |
| 5066 | C-GLXY N506TN N100KT N3PC N566TS N221LC N16KB |
| 5067 | C-GLXF N603CC 9A-CRO 9A-CRT N220TW HB-IUF VP-CFT |
| 5068 | C-GLXK N609CC N88WG JA8361 N602WA D-AOHP N113WA C-FNNT N66NT C-FNNS C-FLRP |
| 5069 | C-GLXM C-FIGR I-FIPP VR-BNF N655CN N324B |
| 5070 | C-GLXO N980HC N780HC N305FX (D-AAFX) OY-CLD ZS-SGC |
| 5071 | C-GLWT+ N500PC (N5032H) TR-AAG [+shown in Canadian DoT files as C-FLWT in error] |
| 5072 | C-GLYC N609K N88HA [w/o 20Mar94 Bassett, NE; cx Apr95; remains to Executive Aircraft Corp, Wichita, KS; fuselage to Addison, TX, 2008] |
| 5073 | C-GLYK N60KR PK-HMK N5073 (VR-CKC) (N400KC) N803RR |
| 5074 | C-GLXH N23SB |
| 5075 | C-GLXU N65357 N810D VR-CCV PT-OSA N601Z N409KC N607AX |
| 5076 | C-GLXB N5TM XA-GUA |
| 5077 | C-GLXQ N1622 N64YP N118MT |
| 5078 | C-GLWR N601MG N601MD N53DF N553DF N578FP N702RV |
| 5079 | C-GLWV C-FJDF VR-CCR VP-CCR |
| 5080 | C-GLYO C-FJGR N601DB N135BC N135BD N903TA N900H |
| 5081 | C-GLYH [also reported as C-GLXH] N619CC HL7202 N601ST |
| 5082 | C-GLWX C-GBJA N611NT N611GS N6BB N82FJ N794SB |
| 5083 | C-GLYA N189K N683UF |
| 5084 | C-GLWT [also reported as C-GLWZ] N399CF N622WM |
| 5085 | C-GLXD C-FJPI N618CC D-ACTU D-ACTE I-DAGS PH-ABO M-YONE |
| 5086 | C-GLXS N353K N343K N343KA N601JE C-GIXI |
| 5087 | C-GLXW N601CC C-FLUT XA-RZD N587CC XA-ULQ XA-OHS |
| 5088 | C-GLXH N601CD N601HC C-GPOT C-GPCS N613SB |
| 5089 | C-GLXY N968L N516SM N360SL |
| 5090 | C-GLXF N601CB N404CB N818LS N818TH N400KC VP-CAM HB-ITK N621CF N226EC |
| 5091 | C-GLXM N915BD (N715BD) C-FTFC |
| 5092 | C-GLXQ [also reported as C-GLXO] C-FKIY HB-IKV N300CR N308CR |
| 5093 | C-GLYA N302EC N601CH N875H N375H N331DC N331DQ C-GGMP C-GMGB |
| 5094 | C-GLWT C-FKNN TC-OVA TC-DHB N675CF VP-BZT 5B-CKK N774PC |
| 5095 | C-GLYC N95FE N2FE |
| 5096 | C-GLYK C-FKTD HB-IKW C-GSQI N66NT N66NS C-FNNS C-FJJC |
| 5097 | C-GLXK C-FKVW XA-JJS XA-TLM N120PA N227CP |
| 5098 | C-GLXH N812GS N808G |
| 5099 | C-GLXU N509W N504M N801P N801R N601DW N203JE N203JD (N121GG) |
| 5100 | C-GLXB N510 N505M N225N N241N |
| 5101 | C-GLXQ N604CC N105BN (N108BN) N213GS |
| 5102 | C-GLWR C-FLYJ (HS-TDL) HS-TVA VR-CHK VP-CHK N604AC (N983CE) N494LC N241FB N241FR |
| 5103 | C-GLWV N76CS N601BE |
| 5104 | C-GLYO N777XX VR-COJ VR-CEG N145ST (N233SG) 9M-SWG N233SG (N604TS) N212CT N720LM N111FK |
| 5105 | C-GLYH C-FMVQ OK-BYA Czech Republic 5105 |
| 5106 | C-GLWX (N601PR) N106PR N523JM |
| 5107 | C-GLWZ N417CL N729HZ |
| 5108 | C-GLXD N428CL N224N N236N |
| 5109 | C-GLXS N439CL N721S N721G |
| 5110 | C-GLXU N392PT N308FX N308BX TC-MDG |
| 5111 | C-GLXH C-GBJA N46SG N4SG N502F N502HE |
| 5112 | C-GLXF N112NC N109NC N404AB N604ME N605CK |
| 5113 | C-GLXM N605CC N163M N163MR N733EY N733EX N128GB |
| 5114 | C-GLYA C-FOSK VR-BOA VP-BOA |
| 5115 | C-GLYC N25SB |
| 5116 | C-GLXW N841PC N1904P |
| 5117 | C-GLXY N606CC N80BF C-FBCR C-GAOB |
| 5118 | C-GLXK N824JK N24JK N900FN |
| 5119 | C-GLXO VR-BNG VP-BNG N519DB C-GJDG N519DB N601FS C-FNEU |
| 5120 | C-GLWT N400TB (N500TB) N408TB |
| 5121 | C-GLYK N502PC N702PC XA-GCD |
| 5122 | C-GLXS N908CL N7046J N900CL N65FF |
| 5123 | C-GLWR N601UP N147HH |
| 5124 | C-GLXD C-FBOM C-GFCB C-GFCD |
| 5125 | C-GLWZ C-FPIY HB-IKY N512BC N604WB (N14DP) P4-EPI VP-CEI |
| 5126 | C-GLXU N21CL N21NY N99UG N650LG |
| 5127 | C-GLXB N718P N718R N555LG |
| 5128 | C-GLWX C-FPOX XA-GME |
| 5129 | C-GLXH N129RH (N603AF) N129TF VP-CRR |
| 5130 | C-GLXQ N603KS N601GB VR-BQA N601SR N349JR |

## CL601 CHALLENGER

| C/n | Identities | | | | | | | | |
|---|---|---|---|---|---|---|---|---|---|
| 5131 | C-GLWV | N602JB | N6JB | (N405DP) | | | | | |
| 5132 | C-GLYO | N610DB | N289K | | | | | | |
| 5133 | C-GLYH | N53DF | N121DF | N121FF | N486BG | | | | |
| 5134 | C-GLXS | N43R | N43RK | N511WM | N511WN | N898EW | | | |

# MODEL 601-3R

| C/n | Identities | | | | | | | | |
|---|---|---|---|---|---|---|---|---|---|
| 5135 | C-GLWR | N1902J | N1902P | N144MH | | | | | |
| 5136 | C-GLXW | N51GY | N20G | | | | | | |
| 5137 | C-GLWZ | N137CL | N90AR | OY-GSE* | | | | | |
| 5138 | C-GLXF | N138CC | N85 | | | | | | |
| 5139 | C-GLXK | N139CD | N34CD | (N348D) | N902TA | (N612LX) | N639TS | | |
| 5140 | C-GLXM | N1061D | N79AD | N79AN | N630AR | | | | |
| 5141 | C-GLXO | N312AT | N601ER | N601TM | N901TA | (N613LX) | N601JP | | |
| 5142 | C-GLWT | C-FRGV | VR-CJJ | N330TP | (XA-...) | N22AQ | XA-MYN | | |
| 5143 | C-GLYA | [built as CL604 prototype with c/n 5991 (qv)] | | | | | | | |
| 5144 | C-GLYC | N616CC | N347BA | N601CV | | | | | |
| 5145 | C-GLYK | C-GPGD | C-GDPF | N145LJ | N1DH | | | | |
| 5146 | C-GLXW | C-FRQA | LX-MMB | N137MB | C-GWUG | N137MB | N96DS | | |
| 5147 | C-GLWR | C-FRJX | XA-SOR | | | | | | |
| 5148 | C-GLXD | N793CT | N792CT | N601DS | | | | | |
| 5149 | C-GLXY | N601GR | XA-GRB | N63ST | VP-BFS | VP-BZI | | | |
| 5150 | C-GLXU | N602CC | N601BW | N710AN* | | | | | |
| 5151 | C-GLXB | C-GBJA | VR-BWB | VP-BWB | N333MX | C-GMMI | | | |
| 5152 | C-GLWX | N777XX | VR-COJ | VP-COJ | N605BA | N18RF | (N933PG) | N388PG | G-FBFI |
| | N601FB | (HB-JRX) | G-FBFI | G-CHAI | | | | | |
| 5153 | C-GLXH | N601EB | VR-CHA | N604BA | OY-APM | N653AC | N115WF | | |
| 5154 | C-GLXQ | N602DP | 9M-TAN | N154BA | 4X-COY | N601VF | C-FJLA | N601HW | |
| 5155 | C-GLWV | N342TC | N401RJ | | | | | | |
| 5156 | C-GLYO | C-FSXH | VR-BAA | N255CC | N601TP | | | | |
| 5157 | C-GLYH | N512DG | N471SP | N800KC | N808HG | | | | |
| 5158 | C-GLXS | C-FSYK | XA-ZTA | XA-MKY | XA-MKI | XA-JZL | | | |
| 5159 | C-GLWR | C-FTNN | EI-SXT | N159TS | C-GICI | N814PS | N659TS | N623BM | |
| 5160 | C-GLXW | N710HM | N94BA | N813VZ | N601MU | | | | |
| 5161 | C-GLWZ | N994CT | (N997CT) | N190MP | N805DB | | | | |
| 5162 | C-GLXF | C-FTNE | VR-BCC | VP-BCC | N850FL | N850FB | N117RY | | |
| 5163 | C-GLXK | N709JM | N980HC | N224F | | | | | |
| 5164 | C-GLXM | N715BG | N7008 | N164CC | N431CB | | | | |
| 5165 | C-GLXO | C-FTOH | VR-CPO | VP-CPO | C-GHCD | N165SC | N723HA | N723HH | XA-PTR |
| 5166 | C-GLWT | N618CC | 9M-NSK | N601A | HB-IVS | | | | |
| 5167 | C-GLYA | N151CC | N86 | | | | | | |
| 5168 | C-GLYC | C-GRPF | | | | | | | |
| 5169 | C-GLYK | N773A | N154NS | | | | | | |
| 5170 | C-GL.. | N166A | N888WS | | | | | | |
| 5171 | C-GLXW | N213MC | N614AF | | | | | | |
| 5172 | C-GLXD | N601FS | C-FUND | N777YG | | | | | |
| 5173 | C-GLXY | N181JC | D-AKUE | | | | | | |
| 5174 | C-GLXU | N605CC | N477DM | N877DM | N47HR | N47HF | C-GHBV | 4X-CMH | N28KA |
| | (N386K) | | | | | | | | |
| 5175 | C-GLXB | N601FR | N306FX | N306BX | N601KF | N800YB | | | |
| 5176 | C-GLWX | N142LL | ZS-CCT | N600DR | N600DH | N779AZ | | | |
| 5177 | C-GLXH | N602MC | N757MC | N601UC | N227RH | N227RE | N895CC | | |
| 5178 | C-GLXQ | (N602AN) | C-FWGE | CS-MAC | B-MAC | | | | |
| 5179 | C-GLWV | (N604CC) | N608CC | N307FX | N307BX | N179TS | N168TS | N168LA | C-GDLI |
| 5180 | C-GLYO | N518CL | | | | | | | |
| 5181 | C-GLYH | N602D | C-FCIB | | | | | | |
| 5182 | C-FVZC | HL7577 | | | | | | | |
| 5183 | C-GLWR | N601HF | N55HF | | | | | | |
| 5184 | C-GLXW | N605RP | N607RP | | | | | | |
| 5185 | C-GLWZ | N611CC | N914X | | | | | | |
| 5186 | C-GLXF | N612CC | N9700X | N601AD | | | | | |
| 5187 | C-GLXK | N601KJ | N511DD | | | | | | |
| 5188 | C-GLXM | N614CC | HS-JJA | N575CF | N10FE | | | | |
| 5189 | C-FXCK | PT-WLZ | C-GZWY | N203G | XA-IMY | N54VS | | | |
| 5190 | C-GLWT | N190EK | N87 | | | | | | |
| 5191 | C-GLYA | N191BE | N605T | | | | | | |
| 5192 | C-GLYC | N354TC | N750LG | | | | | | |
| 5193 | C-GLYK | N604D | VR-BCI | VP-BCI | (N601HJ) | VP-BIH | N11LK | VP-CLZ | |
| 5194 | C-FXIP | EI-MAS | N601R | A9C-BXD | | | | | |

CL601 production complete, continues as CL604

Note: C/ns beginning 6001 were earmarked for the abortive CL601S programme

# CANADAIR CL604 CHALLENGER

C/n Identities

5991 C-GLYA [ff 18Sep94] C-FTBZ N604CC+ [+unofficial marks applied during 1994 NBAA Show at New Orleans, LA] C-FTBZ [w/o 10Oct00 Wichita/Mid-Continent A/P, KS]

5301 C-FVUC N604CC N608CC N123KH N604BL
5302 C-GLXD C-GBJA N355CC N255CC
5303 C-GLXY C-FXKE HL7522 N604BD (OY-CLE) N609BD OY-TNF OE-INF (D-ARWE) (D-AKAT) N360PL
5304 C-GLXU C-FXHE I-MILK N604VM C-GITG N604VM (N604TS) N604CA
5305 C-GLXB N604B N747 N747Y N888DH
5306 C-GLWX N309FX N309BX N604AB N604WB
5307 C-GLXH C-FXUQ VR-BHA VP-BHA (N604BA) C-GIDG LX-FAZ G-UYAD
5308 C-GLYO N604KS N604TS N982J N713HC (N713HG)
5309 C-GLYH C-FXZS VR-BAC VP-BAC C-GHRK (N604LM) N666TR N666TF (N509TS) N814PS N609TS
5310 C-GLXS C-FCCP C-GPGD C-GPFC
5311 C-GLWR N225LY N604JS (N989DH)
5312 C-GLXW N604KC N312AM (N905SB)
5313 C-GLXD N605KC N312AT N906SB N3HB N712PR
5314 C-GLWZ N604CT VT-NGS
5315 C-GLXF N604LS N818LS N818TH
5316 C-GLXK N604BB N411BB N1848U N200UL N203TA N208R
5317 C-FYXC D-AMIM C-GGPK C-FNNT C-GYMM C-GKGN
5318 C-GLXO C-FYYH (TC-DHE) HB-IKQ HB-IVR ZS-LEO
5319 C-GLWT N604KR N14R N14RU N100SA N2SA N5319 N27X
5320 C-GLXQ N605CC HZ-AFA2
5321 C-GLYA C-FZDY PT-WXL C-FZPG N604CP
5322 C-GLXY N604CL 9A-CRO
5323 C-GLXU N604DS N623TS N604TC N604TS*
5324 C-GLXB N601CC N667LC N667LQ N55LB
5325 C-GLWX N60CT N331TH N604JW
5326 C-GLYC N908G N1903G
5327 C-GLYK N609CC HB-IKJ D-AJAB N146BA
5328 C-GLXH N712DG ZS-AVL (A6-EJB) N328BX LN-BWG N604AZ
5329 C-GLWV N8MC N1GC N1QF N222MC (N222MZ)
5330 C-GLYO N812G
5331 C-GLYH N810D
5332 C-GLXS C-FZRR VP-BNF N606JL C-FNYU N606JL
5333 C-GLWR N603CC N811BB N600MS N991TW
5334 C-GLXU N604RC N43R
5335 C-GLXB C-FZVN VP-CAN N8206S N801P N604B
5336 C-GLXW N310FX N310BX N212RR
5337 C-GLXD N270RA N990AK
5338 C-GLWZ N604PL N913JB N78RP N426CF
5339 C-GLXF C-GBJA N604CU C-GCNR
5340 C-GLXK N606CC N194WM N134WM
5341 C-GLXM C-GBJA N604SA
5342 C-GLXO N311FX N311BX N371JC N604AX VT-DBG
5343 C-GLWT C-GAUK C-GHKY
5344 C-GLXQ N344BA N604DH
5345 C-GLYA N345BA N600AM
5346 C-GLXS N604JP HZ-SJP3 M-KARN
5347 C-GLXW C-GBDK PT-MKO N747TS N205EL N205EE (N154JC) N54JC
5348 C-GLWR N881TW
5349 C-GLXY N312FX N312BX N5349 N359V
5350 C-GLXU N331TP
5351 C-GLXB N374G N372G
5352 C-GLWX C-GBKE 4X-COE N5352J N770BC
5353 C-GLXH C-GRIO VH-LAM N758CC
5354 C-GLYC N604PM (N604AG) N604BM N11A
5355 C-GLWV N555WD
5356 C-GLYO N605PM (N605AG) N880CR
5357 C-GLYH N604FS XA-AST XA-EVG
5358 C-GLXS C-GBRQ TC-DHE N127SB N127SR C-GJQN N127SR
5359 C-GLWR N497DM N597DA
5360 C-GLXW N606PM (N606AG) N14SR C-GZEK C-GHML
5361 C-GLXD N346BA N254AM
5362 C-GLWZ N607PM N995MA JY-AW3 A6-AAH
5363 C-GLXF N964H
5364 C-GLXK C-FBNS
5365 C-GLXM N604DC N618DC N280K
5366 C-GLXO N604DD Denmark C-066 N604DD RP-C1937 N604DD C-GJFC N906TF
5367 C-GCCZ EI-TAM VP-COJ N145DL C-FZOP N145DL N848CC N898CC N16YD
5368 C-GLXQ N368G N374G
5369 C-GCQB (D-AZPP) HB-IVP N247WF N247WE
5370 C-GLXS (N370CL) N320CL N755RV VT-KAV N370TS

## CL604 CHALLENGER

| C/n | Identities | | | | | | | | |
|---|---|---|---|---|---|---|---|---|---|
| 5371 | C-GLYK | N371CL | C-GGWH | | | | | | |
| 5372 | C-GLWR | N314FX | (N413LV) | G-LVLV | | | | | |
| 5373 | C-GCVZ | HB-ILL | N604LC | | | | | | |
| 5374 | C-GLXU | N98FJ | N97FJ | N203 | | | | | |
| 5375 | C-GLXB | N604HP | (D-ASTS) | XA-GRB | | | | | |
| 5376 | C-GLXW | N604CR | N604CC | N604CD | N604ZH | | | | |
| 5377 | C-GLXH | N315FX | N315BX | N604RB | | | | | |
| 5378 | C-GLYC | C-GDBZ | D-ASTS | | | | | | |
| 5379 | C-GLWV | N604CA | C-GQPA | | | | | | |
| 5380 | C-GLYO | C-GDFA | N604DE | C-GEGM | Denmark C-080 | | | | |
| 5381 | C-GLYH | N900ES | (N909ES) | PR-TUB | N604MM | | | | |
| 5382 | C-GLXS | N604HJ | | | | | | | |
| 5383 | C-GLYK | N383DT | G-EMLI | M-EMLI | | | | | |
| 5384 | C-GLXW | C-GDLH | HB-IVV | VP-BNS | N684TS | | | | |
| 5385 | C-GLXD | N72NP | | | | | | | |
| 5386 | C-GLWZ | N315DG | N1DG | N37DG | N119GA | N203R | | | |
| 5387 | C-GLXF | N316FX | N387CL | N999PX | | | | | |
| 5388 | C-GLXK | C-GDVM | 4X-CMY | | | | | | |
| 5389 | C-GLXM | N604JE | D-AUKE | | | | | | |
| 5390 | C-GLXO | N604KG | ZS-DGB | (N200DE) | N541DE | N200DE | | | |
| 5391 | C-GLWT | N604PA | VP-BCA | N2409W | (N818SL) | N708SC | N788SC | N267BW | N267DW |
| 5392 | C-GLXQ | C-GDZE | C-FLPC | C-FCDE | | | | | |
| 5393 | C-GLYA | N355CC | N615TL | | | | | | |
| 5394 | C-GLXS | N604CH | HB-IVT | N141DL | N72WY | | | | |
| 5395 | C-GLYK | N606CC | N82CW | N82CN | | | | | |
| 5396 | C-GLWR | N604SH | N273S | N604SH | N273S | C-GKTO | | | |
| 5397 | C-GLXY | N605PA | VP-BCB | HB-IIV | VP-BJH | A6-PJA | | | |
| 5398 | C-GLXU | N597DM | N477DM | N577DA | | | | | |
| 5399 | C-GLXB | N604GM | | | | | | | |
| 5400 | C-GLWX | N604S | (N237G) | N237GA | N266GA | N60055 | | | |
| 5401 | C-GLXH | N98FJ | N528GP | (N604GJ) | VT-MGF | | | | |
| 5402 | C-GLYC | N603JM | RP-C5610 | N15SP | N98AG | VP-BDX | | | |
| 5403 | C-GLWV | N604DC | D-ADND | G-JMCW | G-MPJM | G-MPTP | | | |
| 5404 | C-GLYO | VP-BGO | M-SKZL | | | | | | |
| 5405 | C-GLYH | N311BP | N811BP | N340AK | | | | | |
| 5406 | C-GLXS | N604MU | | | | | | | |
| 5407 | C-GLWR | N317FX | N317BX | N604GG | LV-BNO | N548LF* | | | |
| 5408 | C-GLXW | N898R | N898AN | | | | | | |
| 5409 | G-GLXD | C-GETU | N401NK | | | | | | |
| 5410 | C-GLWZ | N191BA | N199BA | N805VZ | | | | | |
| 5411 | C-GLXF | N604JJ | PP-OSA | N604TS | N3PC | N66ZC | | | |
| 5412 | C-GLXK | N99FJ | N529GP | TS-IAM | | | | | |
| 5413 | C-GLXM | C-FSJR | | | | | | | |
| 5414 | C-GLXO | N604AG | N90AG | [w/o 04Jan02 Birmingham A/P, UK] | | | | | |
| 5415 | C-GLWT | N318FX | VP-CAP | | | | | | |
| 5416 | C-GLXQ | N604MG | N161MM | N161MN | N161MD | G-FTSL | | | |
| 5417 | C-GLYA | N605MP | D-AETV | | | | | | |
| 5418 | C-GLXS | N319FX | (N609CR) | N604CR | | | | | |
| 5419 | C-GLYK | N500 | N252DH | | | | | | |
| 5420 | C-GLWR | N603CC | VP-BCO | N604TS | C-GBKB | | | | |
| 5421 | C-GLXY | N200JP | N604JP | N604W | | | | | |
| 5422 | C-GLXU | N605DC | D-ADNE | G-JMMD | G-MPCW | G-MPSP | | | |
| 5423 | C-GLXB | N238SW | N38SW | N38SV | N91MG | | | | |
| 5424 | C-GLWX | N604CR | G-DAAC | N604GW | | | | | |
| 5425 | C-GLXH | N320FX | N604PC | VT-IBR | | | | | |
| 5426 | C-GLYC | N604JA | JY-ONE | N51VR | G-XONE | | | | |
| 5427 | C-GLWV | N321FX | N902CG | USCG 02 | [designation C-143A] | | | | |
| 5428 | C-GLYO | N640CH | N300TW | | | | | | |
| 5429 | C-GLYH | N604KM | Korea 701 | | | | | | |
| 5430 | C-GLXS | (N604MA) | C-GFOE | OY-MMM | | | | | |
| 5431 | C-GLWR | N276GC | | | | | | | |
| 5432 | C-GLXM | C-FDRS | C-GPGD | | | | | | |
| 5433 | C-GLXD | N433FS | N181J | | | | | | |
| 5434 | C-GLXY | N322FX | N322BX | N604AU | | | | | |
| 5435 | C-GLWZ | N604PN | OE-IYA | OE-INJ | | | | | |
| 5436 | C-GLXF | N604LA | (N955CE) | N926SS | | | | | |
| 5437 | C-GLXK | N437FT | N17TE | N17TZ | N604AV | | | | |
| 5438 | C-GLXM | N609CC | AP-GAK | | | | | | |
| 5439 | C-GLXQ | N600ES | N300ES | | | | | | |
| 5440 | C-GLXU | N500PE | N208LT | | | | | | |
| 5441 | C-GLXB | N641CA | N1CA | N441CL | N33PA | N36HA | | | |
| 5442 | C-GLWR | N604PS | G-POAJ | YL-WBD | HB-JRT | | | | |
| 5443 | C-GLWT | N605JA | JY-TWO | JY-IMK | | | | | |
| 5444 | C-GLWV | N604VF | N604AF | | | | | | |
| 5445 | C-GLWX | N604HD | N877H | | | | | | |
| 5446 | C-GLWZ | N604CE | | | | | | | |

## CL604 CHALLENGER

| C/n | Identities | | | | | | |
|---|---|---|---|---|---|---|---|
| 5447 | C-GLYC | N323FX | N323BX | N1NA | | | |
| 5448 | C-GLXD | N604CB | TC-DHH | VP-BHH | | | |
| 5449 | C-GLXF | N604GT | N604JR | VP-CCP | LX-SPK | | |
| 5450 | C-GLXH | N450DK | 4X-CMZ | | | | |
| 5451 | C-GLXK | N816CC | (N120MT) | N831ET | | | |
| 5452 | C-GLXM | N452WU | OH-WIC | | | | |
| 5453 | C-GLXO | N453AD | C-FHGC | | | | |
| 5454 | C-GLXQ | N324FX | D-ARWE | [w/o Almaty, Kazakstan, 25Dec07] | | | |
| 5455 | C-GLXS | C-GCDS | C-GCDF | N604CW | | | |
| 5456 | C-GLXU | N456MS | VP-BNG | N604LE | VH-MXK | VH-ZZH | |
| 5457 | C-GLXW | N325FX | D-AKBH | | | | |
| 5458 | C-GLXY | N458MS | C-GZPX | | | | |
| 5459 | C-GLYA | N459MT | TC-TAN | | | | |
| 5460 | C-GLYH | N460WJ | VP-BMG | N698RS | | | |
| 5461 | C-GLYK | N832SC | | | | | |
| 5462 | C-GLYO | N462PG | D-AHLE | | | | |
| 5463 | C-GLXB | N463AG | D-AHEI | | | | |
| 5464 | C-GLWR | N326FX | (N326BX) | (OE-IRJ) | I-IRCS | | |
| 5465 | C-GLWT | C-GHIH | C-GLBB | N465AV | N604FS | | |
| 5466 | C-GLWV | N327FX | | | | | |
| 5467 | C-GLWX | N467RD | G-REYS | | | | |
| 5468 | C-GLWZ | C-GHRJ | Denmark C-168 | | | | |
| 5469 | C-GLYC | N469RC | N78SD | (N32FF) | | | |
| 5470 | C-GLXD | N604DW | N604AC | N150BB | | | |
| 5471 | C-GLXF | N471MK | N604WS | N604DE | | | |
| 5472 | C-GLXH | C-GHRZ | Denmark C-172 | | | | |
| 5473 | C-GLXK | N604RP | | | | | |
| 5474 | C-GLXM | N328FX | C-FXPB | C-FXCN | | | |
| 5475 | C-GLXO | N475AD | D-ASIE | YR-DIP | | | |
| 5476 | C-GLXQ | N329FX | N343K | A9C-BXH | | | |
| 5477 | C-GLXS | N477AT | A9C-BXB | | | | |
| 5478 | C-GLXU | N478BA | N604GR | | | | |
| 5479 | C-GLXW | N479KA | ZS-CMB | N604ST | | | |
| 5480 | C-GLXY | N480LB | N121DF | N500M | | | |
| 5481 | C-GLYA | N481KW | N198DC | JY-AAD | | | |
| 5482 | C-GLYH | N482BB | N322LA | N581TS | | | |
| 5483 | C-GLYK | N483BA | N483CC | N956PP | | | |
| 5484 | C-GLYO | N484GC | PT-XYW | N684TS | C-GWLL | | |
| 5485 | C-GLXB | N485CL | "LX-RFBY" | LX-FBY | A9C-BXG | | |
| 5486 | C-GLWR | N486EJ | ZS-OSG | 9J-ONE | | | |
| 5487 | C-GLWT | N330FX | | | | | |
| 5488 | C-GLWV | N604D | N604CC | N870CM | N670CM | (N8570) | |
| 5489 | C-GLWX | N489BA | N604BD | C-GGBL | C-FVSL | N490AJ | N230LC |
| 5490 | C-GLWZ | N604GD | N14GD | | | | |
| 5491 | C-GLYC | N331FX | N331PS | | | | |
| 5492 | C-GLXD | N604SX | N711SX | N604SX | | | |
| 5493 | C-GLXF | N604VK | LV-BHP | | | | |
| 5494 | C-GLXH | N494JC | D-ANKE | HB-JRN | | | |
| 5495 | C-GLXK | N495BA | N495BC | N495CE | | | |
| 5496 | C-GLXM | N496DB | N604UP | N604TH | N604Z | | |
| 5497 | C-GLXO | N604RT | | | | | |
| 5498 | C-GLXQ | N598DA | N599DA | | | | |
| 5499 | C-GLXS | N499KR | N999VK | | | | |
| 5500 | C-GLXU | N225AR | N606GG | | | | |
| 5501 | C-GLXW | N501AJ | XA-SOL | | | | |
| 5502 | C-GLXY | N502TF | D-ACTO | D-ACTU | HB-JRY | N598MT | N777DB |
| 5503 | C-GLYA | N298DC | N503PC | | | | |
| 5504 | C-GLYH | N71NP | | | | | |
| 5505 | C-GLYK | N505JD | VP-BHS | N655TS | (D-ARTE) | G-OCSC | N664D |
| 5506 | C-GLYO | C-GJFI | C-FHYL | C-FLCY | | | |
| 5507 | C-GLXB | N53DF | | | | | |
| 5508 | C-GLWR | N528DK | P4-FAY | LZ-YUN | | | |
| 5509 | C-GLWT | N604BG | N112CF | | | | |
| 5510 | C-GLWV | N511SC | B-7696 | N610SA | VP-CHU | HB-JFZ | |
| 5511 | C-GLWX | N815PA | N815RA | N598WC | | | |
| 5512 | C-GLWZ | (N626JW) | N512SH | N902AG | | | |
| 5513 | C-GLYC | N604NG | N729KF | N729KP | | | |
| 5514 | C-GLXD | C-GJOE | N880ET | | | | |
| 5515 | C-GLXF | N515DM | EI-IRE | | | | |
| 5516 | C-GLXH | N516DG | N1DG | N516DG | N118RH | | |
| 5517 | C-GLXK | C-GJSO | N517RH | LN-SUN | | | |
| 5518 | C-GLXM | N8SP | | | | | |
| 5519 | C-GLXO | N519MZ | P4-AVJ | | | | |
| 5520 | C-GLXQ | C-GJTR | N520JR | XA-TVG | N116BJ | VP-CBR | A6-MBH |
| 5521 | C-GLXS | N521RF | Australia A37-001 | | | | |
| 5522 | C-GLXU | N522FP | C-GKCB | (N.....) | 4X-CMF | | |

# CL604 CHALLENGER

| C/n | Identities | | | | |
|---|---|---|---|---|---|
| 5523 | C-GLXW | N552SC | B-7697 | N523CL | LX-ZAV |
| 5524 | C-GLXY | N251VG | N251CP | N601GT | |
| 5525 | C-GLYA | N525E | XA-JFE | | |
| 5526 | C-GLYH | N804CB | N604CB | I-WISH | |
| 5527 | C-GLYK | N554SC | (B-....) | XA-TZF | |
| 5528 | C-GLYO | N528DT | D-AJAG | G-JMMP | G-MPMP |
| 5529 | C-GLXB | C-GJZB | HB-JRA | | |
| 5530 | C-GLWR | C-GJZD | HB-JRB | | |
| 5531 | C-GLWT | N168NQ | | | |
| 5532 | C-GLWV | N532DM | N432MC | YL-SKY | |
| 5533 | C-GLWX | N533DK | C-GKGR | Canada 144617 | |
| 5534 | C-GLWZ | N534RF | Australia A37-002 | | |
| 5535 | C-GLYC | C-GKGS | Canada 144618 | | |
| 5536 | C-GLXD | N536MP | N25GG | N25ZG | |
| 5537 | C-GLXF | N537DR | N437MC | | |
| 5538 | C-GLXH | N538RF | Australia A37-003 | | |
| 5539 | C-GLXK | N539AB | PP-BIA | VP-BDY | VP-CEO |
| 5540 | C-GLXM | C-GKMU | HB-JRC | | |
| 5541 | C-GLXO | N329FX | | | |
| 5542 | C-GLXQ | N876H | | | |
| 5543 | C-GLXS | N332FX | (N605BA) | | |
| 5544 | C-GLXU | N333FX | N604TS | N50DS | N544TS N814PS |
| 5545 | C-GLXW | N334FX | N6757M | | |
| 5546 | C-GLXY | N335FX | N604BA | N459CS | |
| 5547 | C-GLYA | N350ZE | N426PF | | |
| 5548 | C-GLYH | N548LP | N416BD | N410BD | N604LL |
| 5549 | C-GLYK | N540JW | N2JW | N26WK* | |
| 5550 | C-GLYO | N250CC | N1987 | | |
| 5551 | C-GLXB+ | C-GLXF+ | [+shown as C-GLXB in Transport Canada records but reported as C-GLXF while on production line] | N551BT N604RS | N501PC |
| 5552 | C-GLWR | N552CC | ZS-ALT | N552TS | VP-COP |
| 5553 | C-GLWT | C-GZTU | HB-JRZ | P4-SAI | |
| 5554 | C-GLWV | N604KJ | | | |
| 5555 | C-GLWX | N555VV | N604HC | | |
| 5556 | C-GLWZ | N373G | | | |
| 5557 | C-GLYC | C-FZSO | C-GAWH | | |
| 5558 | C-GLXD | N604SR | N604KS | N508PC | |
| 5559 | C-GLXF | N559JA | N902MP | | |
| 5560 | C-GLXH | N604CC | (N560TS) | N604BS | |
| 5561 | C-GLXK | N561CC | N604WF | VH-MZL | VH-VRE |
| 5562 | C-GLXM | N562BA | N562ME | M-EIRE | |
| 5563 | C-GLXO | N563BA | N300BC | N604BC | |
| 5564 | C-GLXQ | N564BA | N99KW | | |
| 5565 | C-GLXS | N604KB | D-ABCD | | |
| 5566 | C-GLXU | N604PA | | | |
| 5567 | C-GLXW | N567NT | C-FAOL | P4-TAT | RA-67216 |
| 5568 | C-GLXY | N604JC | N383MB | | |
| 5569 | C-GLYA | C-GZVZ | N604SB | | |
| 5570 | C-GLYH | N604CL | | | |
| 5571 | C-GLYK | N604BA | N571BA | | |
| 5572 | C-GLYO | N572MS | N400 | (N472TS) | D-AIND |
| 5573 | C-GLXB | N573BA | N573BC | N509GE | |
| 5574 | C-GLWR | N574F | N46F | | |
| 5575 | C-GLWT | N529DM | N604HF | N950PG | |
| 5576 | C-GLWV | N1090X | | | |
| 5577 | C-GLWX | N577CJ | C-FEUR | OO-KRC | |
| 5578 | C-GLWZ | N606RP | | | |
| 5579 | C-GLYC | N110BP | C-FBCR | | |
| 5580 | C-GLXD | C-FADG | XA-IGE | P4-CHV | |
| 5581 | C-GLXF | N604MC | | | |
| 5582 | C-GLXH | N604BB | | | |
| 5583 | C-GLXK | N121ET | A6-ASQ | | |
| 5584 | C-GLXM | C-FAWU | N828KD | | |
| 5585 | C-GLXO | N585BD | (D-ARTN) | OE-IMB | D-AAOK |
| 5586 | C-GLXQ | N334FX | | | |
| 5587 | C-GLXS | N826JS | (N604UC) | N64UC | |
| 5588 | C-GLXU | N88 | | | |
| 5589 | C-GLXW | N604SF | N22SF | | |
| 5590 | C-GLXY | N721J | | | |
| 5591 | C-GLYA | N604CD | G-OCSD | G-CGFD | CN-IAM |
| 5592 | C-GLYH | N385CT | | | |
| 5593 | C-GLYK | N604SC | VP-BJM | | |
| 5594 | C-GLYO | N594SF | N43SF | | |
| 5595 | C-GLXB | C-FCOE | (D-AINI) | OE-INI | |
| 5596 | C-GLWR | C-FCSD | OY-SGM | RA-67222 | |
| 5597 | C-GLWT | N597JA | VP-CKR | VP-CHL | C-GMRL |

# CL604 CHALLENGER

| C/n | Identities | | | | |
|---|---|---|---|---|---|
| 5598 | C-GLWV | C-FDJN | OE-IGJ | | |
| 5599 | C-GLWX | OE-IKP | | | |
| 5600 | C-GLWZ | N800BN | N810GT | | |
| 5601 | C-GLXB | N44SF | | | |
| 5602 | C-GLXD | C-FDBJ | HB-JRW | LZ-YUP | |
| 5603 | C-GLXF | N76SF | | | |
| 5604 | C-GLXH | N78RP | (N78RX) | B-LBL | |
| 5605 | C-GLXK | C-FDUY | EC-JNV | N605CL | VP-BJE |
| 5606 | C-GLXM | N606CC | N310TK | | |
| 5607 | C-GLXO | N607LC | N954L | | |
| 5608 | C-GLXQ | C-FDWU | G-DGET | M-TRIX | |
| 5609 | C-GLXS | C-FEFU | N604JC | D-ATTT | |
| 5610 | C-GLXU | C-FEFW | G-LGKO | | |
| 5611 | C-GLXW | C-FEIH | TC-ARD | | |
| 5612 | C-GLXY | C-FEPN | OE-IPK | G-VVPA | |
| 5613 | C-GLYA | C-FEPR | HB-JEM | | |
| 5614 | C-GLYH | N614JA | N614BA | | |
| 5615 | C-GLYK | N604SG | N904JK | | |
| 5616 | C-GLYO | C-FEXH | VP-CFD | | |
| 5617 | C-GLXB | C-FEYU | G-PRKR | | |
| 5618 | C-GLXF | C-FEYZ | VP-CMB | | |
| 5619 | C-GLWT | N335FX | | | |
| 5620 | C-GLWV | C-FFGE | OE-IVE | VP-BST | M-YBST |
| 5621 | C-GLWX | C-FFHX | VP-CNK | | |
| 5622 | C-GLWZ | C-FFLA | B-LLL | VP-CCE | |
| 5623 | C-GLYC | C-FFMQ | VP-CJB | N623HA | G-STCC | G-OCSH |
| 5624 | C-GLXD | C-FFMS | N604GD | OY-MKS | HB-JGR |
| 5625 | C-GLXF | C-FFQQ | VH-OCV | LZ-YUR | |
| 5626 | C-GLXH | N807RH | VP-BSS | VP-BZM | OH-BZM | G-CGGU |
| 5627 | C-GLXK | N604DT | | | |
| 5628 | C-GLXM | C-FFZP | P4-ABC | TS-IBT | |
| 5629 | C-GLXO | C-FGBE | (D-AINX) | OE-INX | |
| 5630 | C-GLXQ | C-FGBD | XA-SAD | | |
| 5631 | C-GLXS | N724MF | | | |
| 5632 | C-GLXU | N604CG | D-AEUK | | |
| 5633 | C-GLXW | N604CC | | | |
| 5634 | C-GLXY | N336FX | | | |
| 5635 | C-GLYC | N604SL | N604EG | | |
| 5636 | C-GLYH | N636HC | (N636TS) | OE-ITH | |
| 5637 | C-GLYK | N637TF | | | |
| 5638 | C-GLYO | N604MG | N604HT | | |
| 5639 | C-GLXB | C-FGYI | VP-BJA | M-JSTA | |
| 5640 | C-GLXD | N640PN | N910J | | |
| 5641 | C-GLWT | N641DA | A6-IFA | | |
| 5642 | C-GLWV | N642JA | OH-WII | | |
| 5643 | C-GLWX | N643CT | N793CT | | |
| 5644 | C-GLWZ | C-FHCM | (D-AINY) | OE-INY | |
| 5645 | C-GLYC | C-FHCL | 4X-CUR | | |
| 5646 | C-GLXD | N646JC | G-HARK | | |
| 5647 | C-GLXF | N337FX | | | |
| 5648 | C-GLXH | C-FHDV | EC-JYT | | |
| 5649 | C-GLXK | N649JA | P4-BTA | | |
| 5650 | C-GLXM | C-FIEX | C-FRCI | | |
| 5651 | C-GLXO | N651JC | HB-JRQ | | |
| 5652 | C-GLXQ | N604CM | N225N | | |
| 5653 | C-GLXS | C-FIMF | N720AS | | |
| 5654 | C-GLXU | N604MG | OE-IDG | | |
| 5655 | C-GLXW | N604TF | | | |
| 5656 | C-GLXY | C-FIXN | N338FX | | |
| 5657 | C-GLYA | C-FIYA | VP-BNP | | |
| 5658 | C-GLYH | N658JC | (OH-WIA) | (OH-NEM) | OH-MOL |
| 5659 | C-GLYK | C-FJCB | G-TAGA | | |
| 5660 | C-GLYO | N650KS | N848CC | | |
| 5661 | C-GLXB | N224NS | N224N | | |
| 5662 | C-GLWR | N652MC | N868CC | | |
| 5663 | C-GLWT | N664JC | N604TB | | |
| 5664 | C-GLWV | C-FKDV | OE-IMK | | |
| 5665 | C-GLWX | N665CT | N657CT | | |

Production complete

# CANADAIR CL605 CHALLENGER

| C/n | Identities | | | | |
|---|---|---|---|---|---|
| 5701 | C-FGYM | [ff 23Jan06] | N605KS | N980SK | N2MG |
| 5702 | C-FIFK | N605CC | (N225AR) | A6-DNH | |
| 5703 | C-FLGN | VP-BML | | | |
| 5704 | C-FLKC | (D-AIFB) | OE-IFB | | |
| 5705 | C-GLXD | C-FLNZ | N933ML | | |
| 5706 | C-GLXF | C-FLSF | ZS-SDZ | | |
| 5707 | C-GLXH | C-FLSJ | N605BA | OE-INS | |
| 5708 | C-GLXK | N605CB | | | |
| 5709 | C-GLXM | C-GCSB | HB-JRP | 9H-AFQ | |
| 5710 | C-GLXO | C-FMNL | C-GSAP | N710TS | G-OCSE |
| 5711 | C-GLXQ | C-FMNR | N529D | N529DM | |
| 5712 | C-GLXS | C-FMNW | (OE-IPR) | S5-ADA | N541LF |
| 5713 | C-GLXU | C-FMVQ | N604D | 9H-AFC | |
| 5714 | C-GLXW | C-FMVN | PP-SCB | | |
| 5715 | C-GLXY | C-FNIJ | (OE-IVB) | S5-ADB | |
| 5716 | C-GLYA | C-FNIN | N605JM | VP-CHH | |
| 5717 | C-GLYH | C-FSCI | | | |
| 5718 | C-GLYK | C-FNTM | N723HA | N571TS | N555NN |
| 5719 | C-FOBK | N339FX | | | |
| 5720 | C-FNUF | N720HG | N605HC | | |
| 5721 | C-FNTP | N605HG | N4AS | | |
| 5722 | C-FOGE | M-BIGG | | | |
| 5723 | C-FOGI | N340FX | | | |
| 5724 | C-GLWX | C-FOMS | N17TE | | |
| 5725 | C-FOMU | D-ACUA | | | |
| 5726 | C-FOXU | N605JP | HB-JRE | | |
| 5727 | C-FOXV | N400ES | | | |
| 5728 | C-FOYE | N605GG | | | |
| 5729 | C-FOBF | N540BA | | | |
| 5730 | C-FPWI | N605LD | TC-SAB | | |
| 5731 | C-FPQT | M-RLIV | | | |
| 5732 | C-FPQV | (OE-III) | OY-GBB | | |
| 5733 | C-FPQW | N533TS | G-OCSF | G-CGFF | |
| 5734 | C-FPQY | G-NCCC | | | |
| 5735 | C-FPQZ | N605DX | EZ-B022 | | |
| 5736 | C-FPSJ | HB-JGT | | | |
| 5737 | C-FPSQ | N542BA | | | |
| 5738 | C-FPSV | N538TS | | | |
| 5739 | C-FQQE | N605AG | VP-CRS | A6-AAG | |
| 5740 | C-FQQG | N667LC | | | |
| 5741 | C-FQQH | N741TS | | | |
| 5742 | C-FQQK | N341FX | N950RJ | | |
| 5743 | C-FQQO | OE-INN | | | |
| 5744 | C-FQQS | N744JC | G-CFSC | M-NHOI | |
| 5745 | C-FQQW | OE-INP | | | |
| 5746 | C-FQVE | C-GGBL | | | |
| 5747 | C-FSIP | N605GL | TC-FIB | | |
| 5748 | C-FSIQ | VP-BGM | | | |
| 5749 | C-FSIU | N749BA | OE-INU* | | |
| 5750 | C-FSJH | VT-STV | N605AT | EZ-B023 | |
| 5751 | C-FSJT | N605JA | P4-UNI | | |
| 5752 | C-FSJV | N342FX | | | |
| 5753 | C-FSJY | HB-JRN | N65HD | N605PA | |
| 5754 | C-FSKT | S5-ADD | | | |
| 5755 | C-FSKX | N605GB | | | |
| 5756 | C-FTLB | D-ATYA | | | |
| 5757 | C-FTLH | S5-ADF | | | |
| 5758 | C-FTRY | OE-INT | | | |
| 5759 | C-FTRO | N605CJ | A7-RZC | | |
| 5760 | C-FTRQ | G-SJSS | | | |
| 5761 | C-FTRM | N343FX | | | |
| 5762 | C-FTRF | 9H-AFG | P4-SAT | | |
| 5763 | C-FTQY | N605RJ | VQ-BZB | TC-CLH | |
| 5764 | C-FTQZ | OE-ISU | | | |
| 5765 | C-FUAU | N605FH | C-FYTZ | VQ-BDG | |
| 5766 | C-FUAS | N605TX | N605GF | | |
| 5767 | C-FUAK | N605FH | N605H | TC-CMK | |
| 5768 | C-FUIT | LZ-BVD | | | |
| 5769 | C-FUIU | N769CC | | | |
| 5770 | C-FUIV | VP-BES | D2-EBR* | | |
| 5771 | C-FUVA | N548BA | | | |
| 5772 | C-FUVC | C-FKMC | | | |
| 5773 | C-FUVF | N344FX | N8888G | | |
| 5774 | C-FUVG | (LZ-BVF) | N68888 | | |
| 5775 | C-FUVH | N549BA | | | |

## CL605 CHALLENGER

| C/n | Identities | | |
|---|---|---|---|
| 5776 | C-FUUF | (N75NP) | VP-CLJ |
| 5777 | C-FUUI | N878CC | |
| 5778 | C-FUUM | | |
| 5779 | C-FUUQ | | |
| 5780 | C-FUUW | M-TOPI | |
| 5781 | C-FVOC | N605BL | M-VSSK |
| 5782 | C-FVON | OE-INA | |
| 5783 | C-FVOQ | A7-CEA | |
| 5784 | C-FVOZ | A7-CEB | |
| 5785 | C-FWQH | OH-ANS | |
| 5786 | C-FWQL | C-FLMK | |
| 5787 | C-FWQM | VT-APL | |
| 5788 | C-FWQO | N605S | |
| 5789 | C-FWQV | N605BT | |
| 5790 | C-FWQY | N605TA | N169TA |
| 5791 | C-FVMI | N899ST | |
| 5792 | C-FVMW | N605AB | |
| 5793 | C-FXQG | N880HK | |
| 5794 | C-FXQH | M-ARIE | |
| 5795 | C-FXQJ | N605PS | |
| 5796 | C-FXQM | C-GHMW | |
| 5797 | C-FXQR | | |
| 5798 | C-FXQX | N605RZ | A7-RZA |
| 5799 | C-FYAY | | |
| 5800 | C-FYAW | N605RC | |
| 5801 | C-FYAV | N605RP | |
| 5802 | C-FYAP | C-FBEL | |
| 5803 | C-FYAI | | |
| 5804 | C-FYAB | N65PX | |
| 5805 | C-FXRD | | |
| 5806 | C-FYBK | | |
| 5807 | C-FYUD | | |
| 5808 | C-FYUH | OE-IPZ | |
| 5809 | C-FYUK | | |
| 5810 | C-FYUP | | |
| 5811 | C-FYUR | | |
| 5812 | C-FYUS | | |
| 5813 | C-FYUY | | |
| 5814 | C-FYTY | | |
| 5815 | C-FZLA | N605BX | |
| 5816 | C-FZLB | | |
| 5817 | C-FZLM | N605JK | |
| 5818 | C-FZLR | N880CM^ | |
| 5819 | C-FZLS | | |
| 5820 | C-FZLU | | |
| 5821 | C-FZKY | N605MS | |
| 5822 | C-GAIP | N605KR | |
| 5823 | C-GAJG | | |
| 5824 | C-GALP | | |
| 5825 | C-GANU | | |
| 5826 | C-GBYG | | |
| 5827 | C-GBYH | N605AZ | |
| 5828 | C-GBYK | | |
| 5829 | C-GBYM | | |
| 5830 | C-GBYS | N1500 | |
| 5831 | C-GDRJ | | |
| 5832 | C-GDRU | | |
| 5833 | C-GDRY | | |
| 5834 | C-GDSG | | |
| 5835 | C-GDSO | | |
| 5836 | C-GDSQ | | |
| 5837 | | | |
| 5838 | | | |
| 5839 | | | |
| 5840 | | | |
| 5841 | | | |
| 5842 | | | |
| 5843 | | | |
| 5844 | | | |
| 5845 | | | |
| 5846 | | | |
| 5847 | | | |
| 5848 | | | |
| 5849 | | | |
| 5850 | | | |

# CESSNA CITATION AND CITATION I

This production list is presented in order of the Unit Number which was used and allocated by Cessna, rather than by the normally used c/n. A c/n-Unit Number cross-reference follows the production list.

Citation Eagle conversions are marked with an asterisk (*) alongside the unit number. Eagle II conversions are aircraft re-engined with Williams FJ44 engines and are shown in the text as such.

| Unit No | C/n | Identities |
|---|---|---|
| | 669 | N500CC [ff 15Sep69; cx Jan78; scrapped] |
| | 701 | N501CC [a model 501 converted from c/n 670, a model 500; ff 23Jan70; cx 03Nov09] |
| 001 | 500-0001 | (N510CC) N502CC N20SM N38SM N501RM N501KG N715JS |
| 002* | 500-0002 | N8202Q CF-CPW C-FCPW ZS-ONE |
| 003 | 500-0003 | N503CC |
| 004 | 500-0004 | N504CC N500GS N500GE N5005 N505K (N22CA) [w/o 05Nov05 Houston-Hobby, TX] |
| 005 | 500-0005 | N505CC N501PC N981EE N815HC PT-OIG |
| 006 | 500-0006 | N506CC OE-FGP N506CC N506TF N500MX N506MX N506SR N500AD (N500AH) [cx May91; scrapped for spares] |
| 007 | 500-0007 | N507CC N500LF N555AJ [w/o 19Nov79 Denver, CO] |
| 008 | 500-0008 | N508CC HB-VCX N502CC N11TC N11QC ZP-TYO ZP-TYP PT-WBY |
| 009 | 500-0009 | N509CC N500JD N700JD N147DA N147DB (N147DA) N147WS N55FT |
| 010 | 500-0010 | N510CC XC-FIT XC-SCT XC-DGA XB-IKS N501SE |
| 011* | 500-0011 | N511CC N227H N13UR N18UR N20FM C-GJEM N700VC |
| 012 | 500-0012 | N6563C N512CC XC-FIU N512CC |
| 013 | 500-0013 | N513CC XC-FIV |
| 014 | 500-0014 | N514CC N6563C N766FT N900W N800W N18FM |
| 015 | 500-0015 | N515CC N5867 N58CC N979EE (N332GJ) N14JL PT-LPZ |
| 016* | 500-0016 | N516CC N3JJ N15FS N711CR N7110K N9AX C-GPLN |
| 017 | 500-0017 | N517CC (N317AB) N500PB N508PB N49E N49EA N565SS [24Jan05 to Griffin, GA for parting out by Atlanta Air Salvage] |
| 018 | 500-0018 | N518CC N5Q N5QZ (N58AN) N978EE N222MS C-FDJQ N70841 C-FSKC [w/o 25Jly98 at Rawlings, WY, and scrapped] |
| 019* | 500-0019 | N519CC USCG 519 N519CC N11DH N11DQ N256WN N111QP OB-S-1280 OB-1280 N397SC |
| 020 | 500-0020 | N520CC CF-BAX C-FBAX N556AT [scrapped for spares Jun87; canx Feb93] |
| 021 | 500-0021 | N521CC JA8421 N5B N550CC N208N (N133N) XA-JLV N7GJ |
| 022 | 500-0022 | N522CC N522JD N800JD C-GESZ [parted out Montreal/Saint Hubert, Canada; canx Mar97] |
| 023 | 500-0023 | N523CC N523JD N900JD I-ALBS N523CC N50FT N200QC [parted out 2008 Punta Gorda, FL] |
| 024 | 500-0024 | N524CC N524CA N33TH VH-ICN N94AJ |
| 025 | 500-0025 | N525CC D-IMAN N70703 N745US N976EE N220W N57LL |
| 026 | 500-0026 | N526CC N501GP [w/o 21Jan81 Bluefield, WV] |
| 027 | 500-0027 | N527CC N502GP N51B N777AN PT-OVK |
| 028 | 500-0028 | N528CC N10DG N103WV N284AM N133JM |
| 029 | 500-0029 | N529CC N31ST C-GDWN N424DA |
| 030 | 500-0030 | N530CC N52AN [reported wfu for spares] |
| 031 | 500-0031 | N531CC YU-BIA N81883 N666SA YV-646CP YV-939CP |
| 032 | 500-0032 | N532CC N536V C-GXFZ (N5364U) [w/o 26Sep84 Orillia A/P, Ontario, Canada] |
| 033 | 500-0033 | N533CC N533BF N65MA N58PL N20RT N20RF N990AL (N130AL) |
| 034 | 500-0034 | N534CC N25HC N980EE N500DN (N111FS) N11HJ N716LT |
| 035 | 500-0035 | N535CC N10108 YV-2479P N35SE XA-JOV XC-MMM |
| 036 | 500-0036 | N536CC OY-DVL SE-DEU D-IEXC N18HJ OO-LCM N50812 [parted out at Brussels, Belgium, still marked as OO-LCM] |
| 037 | 500-0037 | N537CC N109AL SE-DPL N109AL N407SC EC-GTS |
| 038 | 500-0038 | N538CC HB-VCU N2EL N81BA N777FC (N207L) N27L |
| 039 | 500-0039 | N539CC N555CC PT-OOK N118LA [to White Inds, Bates City, MO for parts Jly03] |
| 040 | 500-0040 | N540CC JA8422 N714US D-IKAN OY-ARP N2170J N600WM N98Q |
| 041 | 500-0041 | N541CC N541AG N50AS N50AM |
| 042 | 500-0042 | N542CC CF-BCL C-FBCL N [scrapped circa 1997] |
| 043 | 500-0043 | N543CC N104UA N34UT N5072L N5072E PT-KXZ N5072E N32DD N502RL N502RD (N96EJ) N502RD YV1152 |
| 044 | 500-0044 | N544CC N942B N712US N892CA VR-CWW N501WW OO-ATS PH-CTY N501WW N501VH ZS-DSA N28AR |
| 045 | 500-0045 | N545CC N4VF N6VF N7KH N11AQ N31MW N666ES N666BS N628BS (N628FS) |
| 046 | 500-0046 | N546CC N50SK N50SL N109AP N109BL N929CA N929RW PT-OTQ |
| 047 | 500-0047 | N547CC N180PF PT-WAB N7281Z (N60181) YV- |
| 048 | 500-0048 | N548CC N727LE N727EE N11DH N5500S N44BW N67JR N911GM |
| 049 | 500-0049 | N549CC PP-FXB PT-FXB PT-LDH N25UT [parted out at Montgomery, AL] |
| 050* | 500-0050 | N550CC N471MM N471MH N471HH N333PP VH-HKX (N565GW) |
| 051 | 500-0051 | N551CC N51BP (N51BR) (N61BP) N61BR N4646S VH-ICX VH-EMM VH-EGK |
| 052 | 500-0052 | N552CC N52MA N52FP YV-2267P YV-2477P YV-2628P YV-881CP YV1316 |
| 053 | 500-0053 | N553CC I-CITY N90WJ I-KUNA HB-VGO I-AEAL |
| 054 | 500-0054 | N554CC N54SK N98MB (N28U) (N54FT) XB-PBT |

## CITATION I

| Unit No | C/n | Identities |
|---|---|---|
| 055 | 500-0055 | N900KC N900MP N999SF N716CB [parted out at Muskegon, MI, 2007] |
| 056* | 500-0056 | N556CC N777JM N500DB C-GCTD N360DA N956S N52FT N52ET N777JJ |
| 057 | 500-0057 | N557CC PT-ILJ [w/o 03Jly97 Guanabara Bay/Rio-Santos Dumont A/p, Brazil - to Dodson Av'n, Rantoul, KS, for spares] |
| 058 | 500-0058 | N558CC N11WC N11WQ N46RB C-GJLQ N6145Q YV-901CP YV1713 |
| 059 | 500-0059 | N559CC N559BC N40RD N40PD N913RC N117TW N501DZ |
| 060 | 500-0060 | N560CC N712J N712G XA-SEN XA-PAZ N712G PT-OOL |
| 061 | 500-0061 | N561CC XC-GAD XC-ASA N490EA N52AJ N916RC [US Navy Squadron VT-8 colours, code 01 with legend "T-27A serial 061" where the Bu number would normally appear] ZS-DBS |
| 062 | 500-0062 | N562CC N4CH N4KH N334RC XA- |
| 063 | 500-0063 | N563CC SE-DDE N70451 OO-RST N70MG |
| 064 | 500-0064 | N564CC N27SF |
| 065 | 500-0065 | N565CC (N565TW) |
| 066 | 500-0066 | N566CC N66CC C-GQCC [cx to USA 22Apr05, no N-number allocated - parted out?] |
| 067 | 500-0067 | N567CC N3PC XB-DBA N5301J C-FADL N567EA (F-GIHT) (N949SA) |
| 068 | 500-0068 | N568CC N568CM PT-LAY N53MJ N92FA XB-FDN XA-RYE XB-VGT |
| 069 | 500-0069 | N569CC PT-IQL N969SE N255RD C-FTMI |
| 070 | 500-0070 | N570CC N500TD N600MT YV-707CP VR-CMO VP-CMO N227MK |
| 071 | 500-0071 | N571CC CF-BCM C-FBCM ZS-AMB D2-EDC D2-AJL D2-EDC V5-LOW |
| 072 | 500-0072 | N572CC N49R N491 XC-BEZ N590EA N103AJ PT-OYA N114LA N72DJ YV238T |
| 073 | 500-0073 | N573CC N720C (N881M) C-FKMC [parted out by White Inds, Bates City, MO; cx 22Dec06] |
| 074 | 500-0074 | N574CC N574W N8JG PT-OOF N500ML |
| 075 | 500-0075 | N575CC (N600TT) N575RD [parted out by White Inds, Bates City, MO; cx 29Apr10] |
| 076 | 500-0076 | N576CC N801SC N801SG C-GIAC N90CC N500CV N65WS ZS-PWT |
| 077 | 500-0077 | N577CC N342AP N869K ZS-OAM N147SC N28WL |
| 078 | 500-0078 | N578CC N2HD ZS-IYY TL-AAW N54531 N21TV N429RC N110CK N269RC |
| 079 | 500-0079 | N579CC D-INHH N31088 N40JF PT-LBN |
| 080 | 500-0080 | N580CC N50CC N419K C-GJAP N59019 N222KW N767PC N10JP N10UP ZS-NGR V5-OGL |
| 081 | 500-0081 | N581CC N5B HB-VDA I-PEGA D-IEGA* |
| 082 | 500-0082 | N582CC EC-CCY HB-VGD N4434W N103JA N911JD N500CV N178HH N173HH N482RJ N428RJ C-GREK |
| 083 | 500-0083 | N583CC N10UC N10UQ N800KC CP-2131 N50602 CP-2131 N50602 [painted as "50602"] VR-CCP VR-BMT N50602 VR-BMO VR-CHH VP-CHH "VP-CRH" [painted in error] VP-CHH N31LW |
| 084 | 500-0084 | N584CC N10 N2 N25 N4 N7 N935GA XB-FPK XA-SMH [w/o 25Mar95 Vera Cruz, Mexico] |
| 085 | 500-0085 | N585CC N51MW N515AA (N64AJ) 5N-BCI ZS-PTT |
| 086 | 500-0086 | N586CC N503GP C-FMAN LX-YKH D-ICIA (PH-TEU)+ [+ntu marks worn at Rotterdam, Netherlands, Jun09] PH-TEV |
| 087 | 500-0087 | N587CC N85AT (N64792) N700RY N500CP (N911A) (N911CJ) N633AT |
| 088 | 500-0088 | N588CC PH-CTA (OO-FAY) G-HOLL PH-CTA N170MD N251DD |
| 089 | 500-0089 | N589CC EC-EBR N39LH [parted out by Int'l Turbine Services, TX; cx May05] |
| 090 | 500-0090 | N590CC N590RB XB-EFR Mexico ETE-1329 |
| 091 | 500-0091 | N591CC N76RE (PT-LAW) N50PR C-FCHJ (N1899) N500AD |
| 092 | 500-0092 | N592CC Venezuela 0222 |
| 093 | 500-0093 | N593CC PH-CTB OO-FBY N611SW G-OXEC G-OCPI N62BR YV-317T [conv to Citation Long Wing] |
| 094 | 500-0094 | N594CC N94DE VR-CEB N80GB N96FB |
| 095 | 500-0095 | N595CC N2200R (N578WB) YV-15CP N4294A N500KP I-AMAW N950AM I-ARON |
| 096 | 500-0096 | N596CC N222SL N202VS N202VV C-GXPT N202VV N837MA (N187AP) |
| 097 | 501-0446 | N597CC N14CF N63CF N888MJ A7-ASA |
| 098 | 500-0098 | N598CC PH-CTC G-BNVY PH-CTC N500GR N500GB [parted out by White Inds, Bates City, MO] |
| 099 | 500-0099 | N599CC N21CC [to spares circa 1999] |
| 100 | 500-0100 | N69566 HB-VDC D-ICPW OE-FNL HB-VDC OE-FNP D-IFAI N80AJ (N58BT) |
| 101 | 500-0101 | N601CC N12MB N101CD N1HM N6JL N6JU N15CC N15CQ C-GKCZ N666AG N370LN |
| 102 | 500-0102 | (N602CC) N800PL N400K N491BT N491PT |
| 103 | 500-0103 | (N603CC) N103CC PT-KIR C-GJVK |
| 104 | 500-0104 | (N604CC) N200KC N200KQ C-GPJW N40HP N3030C (N3330) N353PJ |
| 105 | 500-0105 | N105CC N105JJ N32W N234UM [w/o 26Feb01 Sault Ste Marie, MI; scrapped] |
| 106 | 500-0106 | N606CC ZS-RCC |
| 107 | 500-0107 | (N607CC) N107CC N107SC C-GWVC N230JS N40RW N79RS |
| 108 | 500-0108 | N108CC EC-CGG [w/o 22Nov74 Barcelona, Spain] |
| 109 | 500-0109 | N44SA G-RAVY I-AMCU N221AM YV1677 |
| 110 | 500-0110 | (N610CC) N500AB N154G (N52WS) N500Y N363K N368K N172MA XB-JDG |

# CITATION I

| Unit No | C/n | Identities |
|---|---|---|
| 111 | 500-0111 | N111CC N11A XA-SHO XA-SLQ [w/o 06Feb96 Ensenada A/P, Mexico] |
| 112* | 500-0112 | N512CC VH-DRM N3LG C-GRJC N29858 N515DC N500TM |
| 113 | 500-0113 | (N613CC) N113CC N684HA N684H N500NJ [parted out by Alliance Air Parts Oklahoma City, OK] |
| 114 | 500-0114 | (N614CC) N999JB N899N (G-BNZP) N899N I-AMCT N65SA |
| 115 | 500-0115 | YV-T-AFA YV-21CP [w/o 08Mar05 Charallave, Venezuela] |
| 116 | 500-0116 | N116CC EC-CJH D-IATC EC-HRH [instructional airframe at Berufskolleg fur Technik & Medien, Monchengladbach, Germany, Oct09] |
| 117 | 500-0117 | N617CC N90BA N161WC N442JB |
| 118 | 500-0118 | (N618CC) N220CC N221CC N972JD (N10BF) N972GW N50MM [to spares circa 1999, fuselage to Aviation Fabrications Inc, MO who use it to demonstrate their range of Citation modifications] |
| 119 | 500-0119 | N619CC N111SU N11KA N95Q N501EJ |
| 120 | 500-0120 | (N620CC) N120CC N10DG N141DR N141DP N999TC (N500NX) N127BJ N712MB |
| 121 | 500-0121 | D-IANE N9871R N939SR OY-SUJ N3QE N661AC |
| 122* | 500-0122 | N122CC CF-ENJ C-FENJ N122LM N122AP ZS-PFG |
| 123* | 500-0123 | N123CC (PI-C7777) N523CC RP-C7777 RP-C102 N123CX N947CC VH-LJL ZK-LJL VH-ECD ZS-PMA |
| 124 | 500-0124 | N124CC N300HC N300HQ N303PC N8FC N92SM |
| 125 | 500-0125 | CF-CFP C-FCFP XA-SFE N108RL YV.... |
| 126 | 500-0126 | (N626CC) HB-VDM D-IDWH N404MA N902DD |
| 127 | 500-0127 | N701AS N701AT N22DN N500R N580R |
| 128 | 500-0128 | D-INCC N53584 N40HL N501AR N3490L [parted out Montgomery, AL, 2007] |
| 129 | 500-0129 | D-IMLN N8114G N500SK |
| 130* | 500-0130 | VH-CRM N4LG OY-ARW N4LG N130G ZS-MCP N800AB N130CE |
| 131 | 500-0131 | D-IDAU N1045T N745DM (N725DM) N457CA PT-OJF [wfu Mojave, CA] |
| 132 | 500-0132 | (N632CC) N35LT N80CC (N10GR) N888JD N888GA N881CA N132BP N501RB N713SA (N992HG) |
| 133 | 500-0133 | N133CC F-BUYL OO-SEL N2070K N1270K PT-LXH |
| 134 | 500-0134 | N134CC PT-JMJ |
| 135 | 500-0135 | N135CC N135BC N900T N902T N975EE N111AM N220MT (N500EN) YV-717CP [modified with winglets] HK-3885 [reportedly crashed 07Mar97 into mountains in NW Colombia] |
| 136 | 500-0136 | (N136CC) F-BUUL N136SA XA-JRV |
| 137 | 500-0137 | N137CC N12MB N12ME ZS-MCU (N922BA) |
| 138 | 500-0138 | N3056R N138SA |
| 139 | 500-0139 | (N5353J) OE-FDP N3771U N15AW YV2498 |
| 140 | 500-0140 | N140CC N300PX N111AT (N777SC) N977EE XA-EKO N135JW N2FA N4LK N4ZK N441TC N972AB |
| 141 | 500-0141 | N141CC XA-PIC XB-EWQ N727TK |
| 142 | 500-0142 | N142CC VH-UCC N650TF N200GM N69XW |
| 143 | 500-0143 | N143CC XC-GUQ XB-CXF N3W N14JZ N14T N787BA SE-DUZ |
| 144 | 500-0144 | (N644CC) N332H OH-CAR [w/o 19Nov87 Tuusula, Helsinki, Finland] |
| 145 | 500-0145 | N145CC N145FC N145TA (N415FC) |
| 146 | 500-0146 | N194AT N111ME |
| 147 | 500-0147 | N404G N494G N688CF YV.... |
| 148 | 500-0148 | (N100JC) N718VA N748VA N410GB N225DC LV-PMP LV-WXJ N989SC N500DB |
| 149 | 500-0149 | N4TL N4TE (N43TC) N100RG (N100FF) N149PJ ZS-TMG |
| 150 | 500-0150 | N150CC N5B VH-WRM N5LG OE-FAU N501JG (N78MC) N9V N914CD |
| 151 | 500-0151 | N151CC N6CD [cx Nov91; parted out by White Inds, Bates City, MO] |
| 152 | 500-0152 | N152CC (N194AT) I-FERN N53J N152CC XB-AMO N2782D XB-AMO |
| 153 | 500-0153 | 9J-ADU N153WB N153JP N2RM |
| 154 | 500-0154 | C-GOCM N54MC PT-WFT C-GRFT |
| 155 | 500-0155 | (N655CC) N920W N5ZZ N88GJ (N188DR) N155MK |
| 156 | 500-0156 | PT-KBR |
| 157 | 500-0157 | PH-CTD N190AB CS-DCA EC-HFY EC-HPQ |
| 158 | 500-0158 | N999CM N910Y N910N (N158TJ) OY-TAM N233DB |
| 159 | 500-0159 | N36MC N165BA N50AC N831CW N881JT N97DD N159KC |
| 160 | 500-0160 | N146BF (N146BE) N146JC N1951E N59TS C-GNSA [parted out by White Inds, Bates City, MO; cx 20Jul06] |
| 161 | 500-0161 | (C-GTEL) C-GHEC N161CC ZS-BTC A2-JDJ ZS-BTC |
| 162 | 500-0162 | PT-JXS [w/o 16Mar75 Belem, Brazil] |
| 163 | 500-0163 | N192G (N94ZG) N8KH N54JV |
| 164 | 500-0164 | N164CC D-IHSV N4209K F-GEPL N382JP N334PS (N164GJ) N73MP |
| 165 | 500-0165 | N19M N19MQ G-PNNY VR-CSP VP-CSP N501LB (N501FF) OD-SAS |
| 166 | 500-0166 | N500WR N313JL (N29MW) N8DE N511AT [dbr Beverly, CA, 17Mar07; parted out at Punta Gorda, FL] |
| 167 | 500-0167 | PH-CTE N191AB N246RR N801KT YV-2821P YV1432 |
| 168 | 500-0168 | N91BA N918A N135BK N135MA N891CA (N46JA) |
| 169 | 500-0169 | N20FL N19CM XC-CON XC-BOC XA-SJW N676CW (N676WE) N75GM C-GTNG |
| 170* | 500-0170 | N60MS N90237 N818R N66LE |
| 171 | 500-0171 | N171CC YV-370CP N728US PT-LIX (PP-LEM) |
| 172 | 500-0172 | N172CC PT-KIU [w/o 12Nov76 Aracatuba, Brazil] |
| 173 | 500-0173 | N77CP N59CL N500EL [parted out by White Inds Inc, Bates City, MO] |

## CITATION I

| Unit No | C/n | Identities |
|---|---|---|
| 174* | 500-0174 | N26HC N21NA N211DB N14MH N931CA N19AJ N16LG N15JH |
| 175 | 500-0175 | N175CC XA-HOO XB-CCO XA-SIG N175CC N1DK [w/o 06Jan98 Pittsburgh-Allegheny County A/P, PA] |
| 176 | 500-0176 | G-BCII G-TEFH N150TT |
| 177 | 500-0177 | PH-CTF N192AB N888XL N883XL N431LC |
| 178 | 500-0178 | D-IKFJ I-FBCK (HB-VJP) HB-VKK EC-IBA |
| 179 | 500-0179 | N444J N111KR N427DM (N997S) EI-BYM N179EA PT-OMT |
| 180 | 500-0180 | N180CC I-AMBR N31079 SE-DDO HB-VFH N31079 PT-LAZ N61MJ N772C N500ET |
| 181 | 500-0181 | N181CC PT-KPA [cx by 2000 last permit 1996; reported wfu] |
| 182 | 500-0182 | D-IABC N525GA C-FNOC N590EA N13HJ OO-DCM N23W N900TA |
| 183 | 500-0183 | N183CC (VH-FRM) N1VC (N721CC) N1880S N112CP N151AS [parted out Montgomery, AL; cx 24Aug07] |
| 184 | 500-0184 | N77RC N71RC N67SF N67BE N67BF N184NA N550LT |
| 185 | 500-0185 | N22EH N22FH N500JB N500WP N500AZ C-GIAD N500AZ ZP-TZH N141SA |
| 186 | 500-0186 | N186MW N186SC (N501WL) N186CP |
| 187 | 500-0187 | (HB-VDR) (TI-ACB) N187MW N20VP (N75KC) N99MC N345KC N99BC (N95TJ) N5FW N130DW |
| 188 | 500-0188 | N5223J PT-KPB N505AZ |
| 189 | 500-0189 | XC-GOV XA-SJV N189CC N500HH [b/u; cx Jan01] |
| 190 | 500-0190 | N190CC (N424RD) N99BC N99MC N500HK N602BC N434UM [parted out; cx 29May09] |
| 191 | 500-0191 | N5600M N448EC N23WK N155CA N701BR LV-YRB |
| 192 | 500-0192 | N4TK N508S N220S N100JJ I-AMCY (N70WA) |
| 193 | 500-0193 | XC-GOW XA-SQZ N293S OY-JAI |
| 194 | 500-0194 | D-IMSM OY-ASR N310U PT-LAX N991SA (N728RX) N194TS N501DG+ N225RD [+ flew as N501DG between Oct02 and Apr04 without officially being taken up] |
| 195 | 500-0195 | N14JA N100AC N100AQ N440EZ N500LJ N502BE [parted out by White Inds, Bates City, MO] |
| 196 | 500-0196 | N74FC C-GENJ N499BA (N969ZS) (N711FW) N270PM |
| 197 | 500-0197 | XC-GOX XA-SRB N297S N95VE |
| 198 | 500-0198 | G-BCKM G-JETE N9UJ N700MP N997CA XB-IJW XB-IUW |
| 199 | 500-0199 | N199SP C-FGAT XA-ASR XB-JVK |
| 200 | 500-0200 | N520CC N200MW N250AA N96G N96EA CS-DBM N102VP (YV-1071CP) |
| 201 | 500-0201 | XC-GUO N690EA (F-GIHU) N690EA F-GRCH C-GLAA N221DA |
| 202 | 500-0202 | N202MW N240AA N500JK N500VK N500WJ N550RS |
| 203 | 500-0203 | N95DR (N724CC) N101HF N101HB CC-PZM (N51099) [parted out] |
| 204 | 500-0204 | C-GBCK N204Y TG-OZO N204Y N928RD |
| 205 | 500-0205 | N520N (N541NC) N700CW [w/o 01Apr83 Eagle Pass, TX] |
| 206 | 500-0206 | N33NH N946CC VH-LGL N771HR [w/o 30Jun07 Conway, AR] |
| 207 | 500-0207 | N92BA N929A N39J N107SF N501TL |
| 208 | 500-0208 | N82JT N22JG (N520SC) N501AT (N508CC) N515WE N770AF |
| 209 | 500-0209 | N209MW (N919AT) N800AV EC-HFA [to parts use circa Feb05 by Atlanta Air Salvage, Griffin, GA] |
| 210 | 500-0210 | TR-LTI N9011R N210MT N716GA YV-625CP [modified with winglets, removed on resale in USA] N501TK XB-TRY |
| 211 | 500-0211 | N990CB N999CB N999CV [parted out by White Inds, Bates City, MO, 2000] |
| 212* | 500-0212 | N1LB N222LB N223LB N223AS N223MC N92B N74LL |
| 213 | 500-0213 | N62HB N355H N741JB N73WC N100UF N100UH N101HG (N213CE) XA-AEI |
| 214 | 500-0214 | N214CC N371HH (N371W) N214CA N709TB N601GN |
| 215 | 500-0215 | N215CC YV-T-000 YV-55CP YV2030 |
| 216 | 500-0216 | (N216CC) N314TC N99CK N199CK (N612CA) YV1686 |
| 217 | 500-0217 | N217CC N500GA N560GA N625GA XA-ODC N2201U XA-SOX N217S N55GR YV.... |
| 218 | 500-0218 | (N218CC) N4AC N271AC (N271MF) |
| 219 | 500-0219 | N219CC N25CS N101KK (N161KK) N408CA PT-LIY [w/o 01Dec02 Marilia, Brazil] |
| 220 | 500-0220 | N5220J N93WD N932HA G-BOGA G-OBEL N619EA G-ORHE [cx 24Jul08, CofA expired] |
| 221 | 500-0221 | N221CC XC-GUH N24AJ |
| 222 | 500-0222 | N222CC N636SC N52PM |
| 223 | 500-0223 | N223CC N444LP N444KV N400SA OH-COC N223P I-CLAD |
| 224 | 500-0224 | (N224CC) N77RE N3ZD N5FG N145CM N697MB ZS-ISA ZS-SGT |
| 225 | 500-0225 | N5225J N5B PH-SAW OO-GPN D-IDFD VH-FSQ VH-OIL RP-C1500 [w/o 01Feb97 Mount Balakukan, Mindanao Island, Philippines] |
| 226 | 500-0226 | N5226J JA8418 N100AD PT-LTI |
| 227 | 500-0227 | (N227CC) G-BCRM N423RD C-GMMO N227HP (N776JS) N227GM TI-AZX |
| 228 | 500-0228 | (N228CC) N6365C N769K [parted out by White Inds, Bates City, MO] |
| 229 | 500-0229 | N22FM [w/o 26Apr83 Wichita, KS] |
| 230 | 500-0230 | N5230J N230CC HB-VEH I-PLLL N92AJ N24S (N300TB) N299TB N200CG |
| 231 | 500-0231 | (N5231J) N99TD N2TN C-GMAT N500SJ N501GB |
| 232 | 500-0232 | N5232J N500PB N126R N999AM (N971AB) |
| 233 | 500-0233 | N5233J N233CC N233VM N223S N228S N233JJ |
| 234 | 500-0234 | (N5234J) PH-CTG N70CA |

# CITATION I

| Unit No | C/n | Identities |
|---|---|---|
| 235 | 500-0235 | N5235J N235CC N12AM (SE-RKZ) [to Sweden as instructional airframe; cx 17Dec09] |
| 236 | 500-0236 | N5236J N236CC N24PA N2801L N801L N801K N600SR N337TV N236TS N1X N742K N320RG N70SW |
| 237 | 500-0237 | (N5237J) N14TT VH-FSA [w/o 20Feb84 Proserpine, Queensland, Australia] |
| 238 | 500-0238 | (N5238J) N3Q N3QZ OO-IBI N68AG N53FT VP-CON N409S |
| 239 | 500-0239 | (N5239J) N239CC N6034F PT-LOS [parted out by Dodson Av'n, Rantoul, KS] |
| 240 | 500-0240 | N5240J N240CC N234AT |
| 241 | 500-0241 | (N9AT) N5241J XA-DAJ N9060Y XB-EPN N288SP N610ED |
| 242 | 500-0242 | N5242J RP-C1964 N888JL (N884DR) N888PA* |
| 243 | 500-0243 | N5243J XC-GOY XC-BEN XA-SQY N53AJ N243SH |
| 244 | 500-0244 | (N5244J) (SE-DMM) SE-DDM N244WJ N400BH N91LS (N91BS) N46RD N516AB PT-OQD |
| 245 | 500-0245 | N5245J (TI-AHE) TI-AHH XC-BUR N2019V 9M-FAZ (N245MG) (N245BC) D-IAJJ [wfu Monchengladbach, Germany] |
| 246 | 500-0246 | (N5246J) N50WM N227VG PT-LQR |
| 247 | 500-0247 | (N5247J) N4110S N9065J XA-JUA C-GMAJ [arrived Addison, TX, 27Dec04 and parted out] |
| 248 | 500-0248 | (N5248J) N75PX (N70PB) N111BB |
| 249 | 500-0249 | N5249J N27PA N411DR PT-LPF (N789DD) N501SE N1GG HA-JET |
| 250 | 500-0250 | (N5250J) N250CC N25PA N25CK XA-JEL N444RP C-GRJQ N160JS (N413KA) (N200BA) N251P N251MG |
| 251 | 500-0251 | N5251J I-COKE (HB-VGI) N500LP XC-QEO XC-ASB N790EA PT-OMS |
| 252 | 500-0252 | N5252J N10PS N200WN C-GZXA N244WJ N501JC N622AT |
| 253 | 500-0253 | N5253J YV-T-MMM YV-19P YV-07P N722US N8TG N592WP |
| 254 | 500-0254 | N5254J N26PA C-GJTX N29991 N79DD [w/o 24Sep90 San Luis Obispo, CA] |
| 255 | 500-0255 | N5255J D-INCI N37643 N877BP N885CA XA-SAM XB-HND N907RT N752CK |
| 256 | 500-0256 | N256CC SE-DDN N83TF N73TF N456GB N73HB PT-OZT N131SB N676DG |
| 257 | 500-0257 | N5257J N75MN N75FN N75GW ZS-PXD |
| 258 | 500-0258 | (N5258J) TI-AFB N80639 (N76AM) N66GE N886CA N125DS |
| 259 | 500-0259 | N5259J N410ND JA8247 RP-C1299 N259DH |
| 260 | 500-0260 | (N5260J) N260CC OK-FKA N50RD ZS-OGS N260RD ZS-OGS A6-ESJ N202HM |
| 261 | 500-0261 | N5261J N261CC N55HF N55LF N711SE N711SF (N124DH) N58TC XA- |
| 262 | 500-0262 | N5262J N44JF N111MU N110AF N110AB (N642CT) ZS-BFS |
| 263 | 500-0263 | N126KR (N126KP) N819H (N90WA) I-DUMA N263AL VH-AQR VH-AQS VH-ZMD |
| 264 | 500-0264 | N5264J N205FM F-GLJA G-BWFL G-OEJA G-JTNC |
| 265 | 500-0265 | N5265J N504GP XA-VYF N38MH LV-ZPU N501SC N595DC |
| 266 | 500-0266 | N5266J N5TK N751CC N424AD N7543H (N40RF) N11MN |
| 267 | 500-0267 | N5267J N28PA N1UT N626P OY-CPK N70704 N41SH (N4090P) N401RD [parted out by Dodson Av'n, Rantoul, KS, circa 2000] |
| 268 | 500-0268 | N5268J ZS-JKR 3D-ACR VH-NEW A6-RKH N900G |
| 269 | 500-0269 | N5269J (D-IKUC) D-ICCC (PH-CTW) SP-KBM |
| 270 | 500-0270 | N5270J N712J N712N N72BC N68CB N4238X G-SWET G-OSCA N501DR N915RP N970RP |
| 271 | 500-0271 | N5271J N168RL N4403 N53FB PT-LQG [cx Dec97, fate not known] |
| 272 | 500-0272 | N5272J N505GP N30SB N30JN N89AJ [parted out by White Inds, MO; cx 29Apr09] |
| 273 | 500-0273 | N5273J N273RC XA-LEO XB-OBE XA-RUR XB-GBF |
| 274 | 500-0274 | (N5274J) N111TH N140H XA-IIX N111TH XB-ETE N225BC N70TF N5LK |
| 275 | 500-0275 | (N5275J) N600SR N40MM (N38MM) N352WC N352WG N102HF N71HB ZP-TZY N275GK (N275MB) (N275BH) N411TN |
| 276 | 500-0276 | (N5276J) N276CC N100CM N473LP N473LR SE-DEG (N340TB) N29EB SE-DEG YU-SEG |
| 277 | 500-0277 | (N5277J) N277CC N67MP N67MA N652ND N662CC N662CG |
| 278 | 500-0278 | (N5278J) N278CC N278SP (N278SR) ZS-LYB N278SP XB-FQO XB-UAG N103PL VP-BBE (SE-RDA) N103PL OY-PCW EC-JXC |
| 279 | 500-0279 | (N5279J) D-IMEN OY-AJV SE-DEX N70454 VH-NMW N120S N501KG N700LW |
| 280 | 500-0280 | (N5280J) N280CC N100HP N102AD N814ER [w/o 01Feb06 Greensboro, NC] |
| 281 | 500-0281 | N5281J N49R N72WC N144JP (N721TB) N62TW N70TS |
| 282 | 500-0282 | (N5282J) N282CC N26WD N520RB N501SS N501CW N510RC HB-VNU [wfu Zurich, Switzerland; cx Dec09] |
| 283 | 500-0283 | N5283J N10UC N18AF VH-ANQ [w/o 11May90 Mt Emerald, Cairns, QLD, Australia] |
| 284 | 500-0284 | (N5284J) N284CC YV-43CP N8508Z N37DW PT-LOG |
| 285 | 500-0285 | N5285J (N285CC) N2U N86SS N113SH [w/o 04Mar08 nr Oklahoma City/Wiley Post, OK] |
| 286 | 500-0286 | N5286J N286CC 5N-APN |
| 287 | 500-0287 | (N5287J) N287CC N73LL N57MB OY-CGO N31LH PT-WHZ N287AB VP-BGE [crashed on approach to Biggin Hill, England, 30Mar08; w/o] |
| 288 | 500-0288 | (N5288J) N288CC D-IDWN OY-ASD N9013S N5TR (N502BA) N1DA |

## CITATION I

| Unit No | C/n | Identities |
|---|---|---|
| 289 | 500-0289 | N5289J YV-50CP N5591A XA-KAH N939KS OE-FAN [w/o 24Feb04 Cagliari, Italy] |
| 290 | 500-0290 | (N5290J) N290CC D-ICFA N4246Y N826RD N88AF (N390S) N896MA N896MB N400RM |
| 291 | 500-0291 | N5291J ZS-JOO N291DS OE-FGN |
| 292* | 500-0292 | N5292J N10FM N255LJ C-FSUN N18BG SE-DDX N501RL N501HK N333JH XB-ESG |
| 293 | 501-0643 | (N5293J) N8RF N54CM N54TS [Sierra Stallion conversion with Williams FJ44-2A engines, ff 14Jun06] C-GQPJ |
| 294 | 500-0294 | N5294J HL7226 (N501LG) N924AS SE-DVB OY-VIP OE-FCM |
| 295 | 500-0295 | N5295J EP-PAO EP-KIA N2274B N44HC N10FG |
| 296 | 500-0296 | (N5296J) N98DM N882CA ZS-NHF (N245BC) N296BF XA-BET |
| 297 | 500-0297 | N5297J (N818CD) YV-62CP N48DA N38SA |
| 298 | 500-0298 | N5298J N900GC |
| 299 | 500-0299 | N5299J HB-VEO N3JJ N66TR N55AK ZS-MGH N5133K YV-940CP PT-OZX N80364 (OY-EBD) OY-TKI N80364 |
| 300 | 500-0300 | (N5300J) OE-FAP (N500CX) [parted out by Dodson Av'n, Ottawa, KS, following accident 06Oct84 in Greece; cx Jun90] |
| 301 | 500-0301 | N5301J EP-PAP N81MJ N747WA OE-FNG N305S |
| 302 | 500-0302 | N5302J N302CE N469PW (N777QE) N710VL |
| 303 | 500-0303 | (N5303J) N19M N19U C-GDWS N8DX |
| 304 | 500-0304 | N5304J N304CC N5253A N5253E N70U N10UH [cx Jun05, parted out then used for fire training at San Antonio, TX] |
| 305 | 500-0305 | (N5305J) N305BB N805BB C-GMLC N137WC N100AM |
| 306 | 500-0306 | N5306J N36CJ N36SJ N606KK N606KR |
| 307 | 500-0307 | N5307J N2607 N2613 N777SL |
| 308 | 500-0308 | (N5308J) N308CC N38CJ N70TG N6525J (F-GIRS) F-GMLH F-GSMC F-HDMB |
| 309 | 500-0309 | N5309J (N1GB) N1JN N1UG N1382C N57LC SE-DKM N791MA N88NW N83NW |
| 310 | 500-0310 | (N5310J) N510CC N1851T N1851N N820FJ N820 XA-STT N998AA N222VV N941JC N900CC YV.... |
| 311 | 500-0311 | N5311J N818CD OH-COL N501RL N39RE SE-DRT (OY-VIP) LN-AAF I-RAGW |
| 312 | F500-0312 | N5312J N33ME (N233ME) N33MQ N82AT F-GJDG EC-KGE F-HBMS |
| 313 | 500-0313 | (N5313J) N76GT XA-KUJ XB-DYF XA-SDS N313BA HB-VLE D-ISKM |
| 314 | 500-0314 | N5314J (N314CC) N501SC N100UF N180UF N66ES N668S |
| 315 | 500-0315 | N5315J N55SK N55SH SE-DRZ |
| 316 | 500-0316 | N5316J N398RP N97SK N711MT (N127CJ) |
| 317 | 500-0317 | N53MJ D-ICCA N37489 C-GPCO N317VP YV-1133CP YV233T |
| 318 | 500-0318 | N5318J N518CC N944B VR-COM VP-COM |
| 319 | 500-0319 | N5319J HZ-NC1 N5319J N22LH D-ICUW N94MA "F-GKIL" F-GKID |
| 320 | 500-0320 | (N5320J) N320CC N341CC N299WV N341CC I-NORT N74WA N70WA I-.... |
| 321 | 500-0321 | N5321J JA8438 [cx Sep96 as WFU; To Japan Newspaper Museum, Yokohama, Japan] |
| 322 | 500-0322 | N5322J N1AP N108MC |
| 323 | 500-0323 | N5323J N300PB N474L N523CC N307EW (N268GM) N388GM N386SC LV-CDI |
| 324 | 500-0324 | (N5324J) N324C N52TC N324JC (N721HW) |
| 325 | 500-0325 | (N5325J) N25CJ N50TR N60MP PT-OSD |
| 326 | 500-0326 | N5326J N45LC G-UESS [w/o 08Dec83 Stornoway, Scotland] |
| 327 | 500-0327 | N5327J HL7277 S Korea 5327 S Korea 70327 N399PA RP-C3958 |
| 328 | 500-0328 | (N5328J) N328CC (N571K) PT-LSF N168AS XB-IXE |
| 329 | 500-0329 | N5329J ZS-JOK N5329J XC-IPP XC-PPM N4999H OY-CEV |
| 330 | 500-0330 | (N5330J) N330CC (N82CF) I-JESE N270BH (N237JP) N141SG N800CJ |
| 331 | 500-0331 | (N5331J) N331CC N86RE N96RE N40AC LN-NAT EC-500 EC-FUM LN-NAT G-LOFT |
| 332 | 500-0332 | N5332J LV-PUY LV-LZR N332SE |
| 333 | 500-0333 | (N5333J) N275AL VH-SOU |
| 334 | 500-0334 | N5334J N500DD N44RD (N527TA) ZS-MPI N334JC [canx Apr98 as scrapped] |
| 335 | 500-0335 | N5335J ZP-PNB ZP-PUP N2937L PT-LDI |
| 336 | 500-0336 | (N5336J) N336CC YV-O-MAC-1 [w/o Jun79 Caracas, Venezuela] |
| 337 | 500-0337 | N5337J N873D N22MB (F-GNAB) N17KD |
| 338 | 500-0338 | N5338J (N868D) HB-VEX N8499B N3300M N92LA N97LA N73WC (N404JW) N41HL |
| 339 | 500-0339 | (N5339J) G-JEAN N707US N300EC G-JEAN G-DJAE |
| 340 | 500-0340 | (N5340J) N2630 (N2610) N505AM HB-VIV VR-BTQ ZS-MBS N340DN PT-WOD (N340RL) N26NS N344RJ |
| 341 | 500-0341 | (N5341J) N2650 N505JC C-GVKL C-FDMB N383SC LV-BPW |
| 342 | 500-0342 | (N5342J) N530TL N711TE N501DR N501LH |
| 343 | 500-0343 | (N5343J) N525AC C-FRHL N91D HB-VJR N91DZ C-FOSM N501JF |
| 344 | 500-0344 | (N5344J) N632SC HB-VHI VR-BLV VP-BLV CX-CCT |
| 345 | 500-0345 | (N5345J) N23ND N410NA N410N VR-BUB N345TL N747RL (N747KL) XA-TOF XB-CSI |
| 346 | 500-0346 | N5346J D-IJON N4234K (N99WB) N82SE N56DV PT-LUA |
| 347 | 500-0347 | (N5347J) N500XY N876WB |
| 348 | 500-0348 | (N5348J) N300HC N301HC C-GCLQ N712KM |

# CITATION I

| Unit No | C/n | Identities |
|---|---|---|
| 349 | 500-0349 | (N5349J) N888AC (N988AC) N888GZ VH-HVM VH-HVH N501DA |
| 350 | 501-0027 | N5350J N350CC N10EH N54DS JA8380 |
| 351 | 501-0001 | N5351J N51CJ N506TF [converted to Sierra Stallion] |
| 352 | 501-0261 | N5352J N52CC N7NE N501VP YV.... |
| 353 | 501-0002 | N5353J OE-FPO N165CB XA-LUN N39301 N501WJ (N501WK) N88TB |
| 354 | 501-0263 | N5354J N948N N501BE (N501BF) |
| 355 | 501-0003 | N5355J N55CJ N781L N81EB |
| 356 | 501-0004 | N5356J N88JJ N86JJ N142DA |
| 357 | 501-0005 | N5357J N661AA N665JB N143EP N284RJ N455FD |
| 358 | 501-0006 | (N5358J) N358CC N121JW N121UW (N1236P) N5016P N93TJ I-ERJA N501GR |
| 359 | 501-0264 | (N5359J) 9J-AEJ N353WB N27WW |
| 360 | 501-0007 | N5360J N222WA |
| 361 | 500-0361 | N5361J D-IKPW N5361J C-GOIL N5361J N90EB F-GKIR |
| 362 | 501-0008 | N5362J N362CC N6HT (N501DB) N900PS N909PS |
| 363 | 500-0354 | (N5363J) G-BEIZ N51GA G-CCCL G-TJHI N354RC N694LM |
| 364 | 501-0011 | N36842 (N1UB) N36JG N770MH N650AC N1UM |
| 365 | 501-0267 | N36846 G-DJBB D-IAEV N944TG N565VV N565V |
| 366 | 500-0356 | N5366J N36848 Argentina AE-185 |
| 367 | 501-0009 | N36850 N67CC N715EK (N715JM) N505BC N505RJ |
| 368 | 501-0269 | N5368J N36854 YV-120CP N120RD N545GA (N545G) XB-GVY N501JJ |
| 369 | 501-0012 | N36858 N190K N999RB N99XY N99GC N8P N8PJ HI-527 HI-527SP N4196T N501GS N15FJ N449DT [Eagle II conversion] |
| 370 | 501-0010 | N36859 N7WF EP-PBC N7WF (N500MD) VH-POZ EC-EDN |
| 371 | 501-0014 | N36860 N22TP N888FL |
| 372 | 501-0013 | N36861 (N622SS) VR-BJK N501TJ |
| 373 | 501-0015 | N36862 N1823B N18328 XA-MAL N4446P N454AC |
| 374 | 501-0270 | N36863 N300WK N893CA N105JM N501ST |
| 375 | 501-0016 | N36864 N517A C-GHOS N501DL N38DA (N58DT) N58BT N38DA (N38DL) N255TS N17TJ N45TL |
| 376 | 501-0017 | N36869 N877C N100WJ N501AT |
| 377 | 500-0358 | N36870 (EP-PAQ) N82MJ SE-DEP I-UUNY |
| 378 | 501-0018 | N36871 N378CC N18BG N550TG N501GR N228AK N228AJ N228FS N228ES XB-JXG |
| 379 | 501-0272 | N36872 N5072L N700JR N700JA N44MK |
| 380 | 501-0020 | N36873 N32JJ N123EB N60GG* |
| 381 | 501-0041 | N36880 N50MC N173SK N120ES [w/o 24Apr95 San Salvador Intl A/P, remains to Dodson Av'n, Ottawa, KS for spares] |
| 382 | 501-0273 | N36881 (I-CCCB) XA-HEV N46106 D-IDPD N333PD N333PE N501MD (N273DA) N501JF (N501EM) N302TS N302AJ N110JA N301DR |
| 383 | 501-0019 | N36882 (N301MC) N501SP (N5EM) [dbr Mexicali, Mexico, 03Dec06] |
| 384 | 501-0021 | N36883 (YV-135CP) YV-166CP XA-IEM N121SJ N203LH ZS-MGL N151SP |
| 385 | 501-0022 | N36884 N385CC N11DH N110H (N995AU) N10GE [w/o 21May85 Harrison Airport, AR] |
| 386 | 501-0023 | N36885 N56MC N56MT (N501FB) N56MK |
| 387 | 501-0024 | N36886 (N10CA) N1CA N711NR Z-WSY N724EA N70BG |
| 388 | 501-0032 | N36887 N388CJ N33AA N377KC N690MC N550T N550L N85WP N642BJ (N501SK) N307D |
| 389 | 501-0025 | N36888 N389CC N21BS N20RM |
| 390* | 501-0030 | N36890 N301MC N301MG N100CJ C-GSLL N96BA N911MM (N911MU) |
| 391 | 501-0026 | N36891 N92C N92CC N92BL |
| 392 | 500-0364 | N36892 HB-VFF N221AC (N221JB) N20WP N40DA G-OKSP G-ORJB N501E SE-RGN SX-FDB |
| 393 | 501-0275 | N36893 YV-159CP N31AJ ZS-MPN (N41AJ) N40AJ |
| 394 | 501-0028 | N36895 N1234X N501PV |
| 395 | 501-0031 | N36896 N395SC XA-SDI N510AJ LV-BFM |
| 396 | 500-0370 | N36897 SE-DEY |
| 397 | 501-0262 | N36898 YV-O-SID-3 YV-79CP N9712T LN-AFC N50WJ N794EZ (N58T) N20CC N20CZ |
| 398 | 501-0050 | N36901 N20SP N880CM N750LA N59MA |
| 399 | 500-0367 | N36906 YV-52CP YV1541 |
| 400 | 501-0033 | N36908 N400GB N300PB (N715DG) N517BA (N101HC) N411DS N411ME N700LW C-GQJK N91PE |
| 401 | 501-0034 | N36911 N444MW N444MV N501CP |
| 402 | 501-0278 | N36912 G-BFAR ZS-LPH G-BFAR A6-SMH G-BFAR A6-SMH G-BFAR G-DANI N104AB N53RG N129AP N124NB N124NS N322ST |
| 403 | 501-0039 | N36914 N403CC N800DC N800BH N432DG N808BC N507DS N141M |
| 404 | 501-0035 | N36915 (N800M) N500WN N112MC N25MH (N35K) N35JF N501DD |
| 405 | 501-0046 | N36916 N405CC N5VP |
| 406 | 501-0036 | N36918 N406CJ N36CC HI-493 N360MC N2904 |
| 407 | 501-0279 | N36919 SE-DEZ (N371GP) (N371GA) N371GP N43BG SE-DEZ N66HD SE-DEZ PH-DEZ |
| 408 | 501-0037 | N36922 N10J N19J N234JW N501U |
| 409 | 501-0038 | N36923 N315S (N315P) N501JG |
| 410 | 501-0042 | N87185 N773FR I-TOSC (N120DP) N420AM I-AROM [w/o Rome-Ciampino, Italy, 09Sep05] |

## CITATION I

| Unit No | C/n | Identities |
|---|---|---|
| 411 | 501-0029 | N87253 (N411CJ) N411WC (N411RJ) N816LL N31JM (N45AQ) XA-TKY |
| 412 | 501-0040 | N87258 N85FS I-KWYJ N501E N21EP LV-BPZ |
| 413 | 501-0047 | N87496 HB-VFI N1021T N550T N550U |
| 414 | 501-0048 | N87510 N414CC (I-DAEP) I-OTEL |
| 415 | 501-0280 | N98449 YU-BKZ T9-BKA N212M |
| 416 | 501-0045 | N98468 N833 N833JL N22EL |
| 417 | 501-0043 | N98510 N10NL N16NL |
| 418 | 501-0053 | N98528 N59PC YV-253P YV-253CP N14EA N52TL |
| 419 | 501-0054 | N98563 N2BT N501EA |
| 420 | 501-0049 | N98586 N2ZC (N36WS) (N347DA) OY-SVL ZS-CWD |
| 421 | 501-0062 | N98599 D-IBWB N208W N900DM N980DM |
| 422 | 501-0051 | N98601 N422CC N150TJ N303CB N422DA |
| 423 | 501-0281 | N36943 LV-PZI LV-MGB N501SJ N501CB |
| 424 | 501-0044 | N98675 N5TC N944JD (N122LG) N131SY N50US N600RM |
| 425 | 501-0055 | N98682 N552MD N400PC N400PG N145DF N145AJ N223LC [w/o 18Aug08, crashed into Caribbean Sea] |
| 426 | 501-0056 | N98688 (N426CC) (N501SF) N55WH CC-CTE N56WE |
| 427 | 501-0052 | N98715 N900MC N677JM |
| 428 | 501-0282 | (N98718) N36949 XC-PMX XA-SQX N82AJ [Eagle II conversion] |
| 429 | 501-0283 | N98749 C-GPTC N204CA |
| 430 | 501-0057 | N98751 N500JC N505BG N577VM N577JT |
| 431 | 501-0059 | N2079A N431CC N13RC ZS-EHL N16HL |
| 432 | 501-0066 | N2098A D-IHEY N501BG N501CX C-GHRX N945AA VR-CTB VP-CTB N501CD |
| 433 | 501-0284 | N2131A N115K N409AC VR-BBY N788SS N284PC N729PX N45AF [Eagle II conversion] |
| 434 | 501-0058 | N2627A N44MC N444AG N36GC N32MJ N65RA (N400PG) N501FT N211EF N211X N501EZ [w/o 02Dec98 Grannis, AR] |
| 435 | 501-0060 | N2741A N435CC N500ZC N5737 N573L N11TM |
| 436 | 501-0061 | N2757A N436CC N34DL N1401L N202CF SE-RBZ EC-KGX |
| 437 | 501-0064 | N2768A (N33KW) N9TK N96DS N12WH |
| 438 | 501-0068 | N2841A N438CC N9GT N50GT N68EA N363TD |
| 439 | 501-0285 | N2887A N100BX N13ST |
| 440 | 501-0065 | N2888A N33WW |
| 441 | 501-0069 | N2906A N501EF N636N |
| 442 | 501-0067 | N2959A SE-DEO D-IGMB HB-VJB VR-BLW HB-VJB |
| 443 | 501-0063 | N2991A N305M N408MM N408MW F-GESZ N501BA N555KW |
| 444 | 501-0070 | N3062A (N444CW) N78AB N21HJ N96G N96GT N70VP HC-BTQ (N277RW) N628ZG N45MM |
| 445 | 501-0286 | N3104M N445CC I-ROST (N789AA) N381BJ |
| 446 | 501-0071 | N3105M N501SR N501KR N501KB N509P YV-697CP YV232T N666TS |
| 447 | 501-0072 | N3110M N1HA N17HA |
| 448* | 501-0073 | N3117M N100SV N299RP (N840MC) N70FJ [w/o Hailey, ID 15Mar03; cx Jul03] |
| 449 | 501-0074 | N3118M YV-232CP N888DS N717RB N28GC N552AJ |
| 450 | 501-0075 | N3120M N773LP N773LR N325BC (N325PM) N51ET N713JD |
| 451 | 501-0076 | N3122M N451CJ N315MR N315MP N150RM |
| 452 | 501-0077 | (N3124M) N15PR N42HM N678JD (N678JG) I-FRAI |
| 453 | 501-0078 | (N3127M) N13BT ZS-MZO N13BT N501EK N25MB |
| 454 | 500-0369 | N3132M C-GVER N46253 [parted out circa 06Jly05 Bates City, MO as C-GVER] |
| 455 | 500-0374 | N3141M C-GRQA N501SS (N501BB) (N505BB) |
| 456 | 501-0079 | N3144M N555EW N33CX VP-CFF D-ICAM N250GM N79FT |
| 457 | 501-0080 | N3145M N51CC N51CG N347DA N37LA N800BF |
| 458 | 501-0081 | N3146M N12DE N12CQ N12CV |
| 459 | 501-0289 | N3147M LV-PAT LV-MMR N501NA N1KC (N501SK) N501NZ N82DT |
| 460 | 501-0082 | N3150M N460CC N84CF C-GEVF N6RF (N386DA) XB-ERX N5WF |
| 461 | 500-0378 | N3156M C-GBNE [to instructional airframe Stephenson Technical College, Winnipeg, Canada] |
| 462 | 501-0083 | N3158M N462CC N5YP N420PC N420RC (N83TJ) N101LD N910G |
| 463 | 501-0084 | N3160M (N463CJ) (N11JC) G-CITI VR-CDM VP-CDM G-CITI EC-ISP |
| 464 | 501-0098 | N3161M N44RD N144AR (N144AB) HB-VIC N92BE |
| 465 | 501-0093 | N3163M N88CF N31RC N623LB N501RM N501AD |
| 466 | 501-0090 | N3165M XC-CIR N41JP N3GN |
| 467 | 501-0099 | N3170A I-FLYA |
| 468 | 501-0101 | N3170M C-GDDM N100TW N106EA (N501GS) (N323JB) N501KM |
| 469 | 501-0095 | N3172M N612DS XA-AGA |
| 470 | 500-0386 | N3173M LV-PAX LQ-MRM |
| 471 | 501-0089 | (N3175M) N471H N106WV N588CA VH-LJG VH-CCJ VH-MMC |
| 472 | 501-0292 | N3180M YV-O-MTC-2 YV-2295P N456R N339HP |
| 473 | 501-0088 | (N3181A) N473CC N31MT N22TS N22TY N86MT N23YZ (N23TZ) N3WT |
| 474 | 501-0087 | (N3183M) N501SE C-GVVT (N22508) N501SJ N501BB |
| 475 | 501-0085 | N3189M N575CC N475CC N34AA N25DD N707W |
| 476 | 501-0091 | N3194M (N887DM) (N55BE) N33BE N39BE (JA8361) I-OMEP N2158U HB-VKY N2158U |
| 477 | 501-0086 | N3195M N8LG N88CF (N711AE) N583MP N32SX N501CW N501JP N11SQ (N864TT) N554T N11SQ (N554T) EC-INJ |

## CITATION I

| Unit No | C/n | Identities |
|---|---|---|
| 478 | 501-0092 | N3197M (HB-VGD) N112WC (N78BT) LV-PLM LV-WOI N501X N303A |
| 479 | 501-0097 | N3198M N479CC N479JS N501RS N251CF N251CB |
| 480 | 501-0096 | N3202A N660AA (N480CC) N660KC N501HS |
| 481 | 501-0293 | N3202M Ecuador ANE-201 HC-BVP N850MA N597CS |
| 482 | 501-0107 | N3204M (N333BG) (N33VV) N1UL N107CC N501LS N54TB 3A-MTB (N75471) EC-GJF |
| 483 | 501-0294 | N3205M N2LN N38TM N8CH N80SL |
| 484 | 500-0387 | N3206M N484KA N504D |
| 485 | 501-0100 | (N3207M) N485CC N41ST (N26MW) C-GSUN C-GSUM N54FT |
| 486 | 501-0102 | (N2646X) N486CC (N223RE) I-AIRV N501CG N45FS [Eagle II conversion] VH-FCS |
| 487 | 501-0120 | N2646Y N487HR N487LS OY-CPW N71LP |
| 488 | 501-0094 | (N2646Z) N488CC N103PC N59CC N159LC C-FBDS |
| 489 | 500-0392 | N26461 I-FLYB D-ISSS 3D-IER 40-000 |
| 490 | 501-0103 | (N2647U) N49WC N611AT (N906EA) ZS-PHP |
| 491 | 501-0109 | (N2647Y) N30RL N30RE N567WB LV-BXH |
| 492 | 501-0104 | (N2647Z) N312GK N81CC N29CA N33HC N998EA |
| 493 | 501-0105 | N2648X (N231LC) |
| 494 | 501-0297 | (N2648Y) VH-SWC N32DA N35LD N41GT |
| 495 | 501-0108 | (N2648Z) (N56CJ) N777AJ N777GG N707GG |
| 496 | 501-0110 | (N26481) N15NY [w/o 02Aug79 Akron, OH] |
| 497 | 501-0119 | (N26486) N35AA N35TM N53RC N77GJ N53EZ N13KD |
| 498 | 501-0111 | N2649D N140WC (N333RB) N777FE I-FOMN N94SL N59WP N79BK |
| 499 | 501-0112 | N2649E (N900LL) N350M N14TV (N84TV) N74PM (N74PN) N112EB N224GP |
| 500 | 501-0127 | N2649H N500K N88BM N96SK N86SK N117DJ |
| 501 | 501-0106 | (N2649J) (N1234F) OE-FYF D-IANE N793AA (D-ISKY) |
| 502 | 501-0113 | (N2649S) (N515CC) N502CC N200ES N502CC |
| 503 | 501-0114 | N2649Y N673LP N673LR N485RP N711HL (N725RH) N811HL [to White Inds, MO 17Feb05 for spares] |
| 504 | 501-0118 | N2649Z I-DECI N61572 N311ME XB-TMG |
| 505 | 501-0126 | N26492 N505SP N505JH |
| 506 | 501-0117 | N26493 LV-PDW LV-MZG N91AP |
| 507 | 501-0115 | N26494 N501GF (N26540) N501GK N95RE N728MC N5ZN |
| 508 | 501-0122 | (N26495) N275CC N275CQ N400DB N501HC (N501MD) N501MB |
| 509 | 501-0116 | (N26496) N500XX N7CJ N7QJ (N90MT) N7TK |
| 510 | 501-0239 | N26497 LV-PDZ LV-MYN N164CB OE-FMS |
| 511 | 501-0298 | N26498 (PH-JOB) I-GERA OE-FIW N65M VR-CMS N501D |
| 512 | 501-0129 | (N26499) (N50WP) N70WP PT-LQQ N501JD |
| 513 | 501-0123 | N2650C N513CC N627L N627E |
| 514 | 501-0249 | N2650M RP-C237 N4263X ZS-LOW N133DM G-OHLA I-DIDY N249AS N851BC XA-OAC N40MA (N82MP) N117MA |
| 515 | 501-0124 | N2650N N95RE OE-FFK [w/o 26Oct88 nr Salzburg, Austria] |
| 516 | 501-0134 | N2650S N501LW N501EM N841CW |
| 517 | 501-0130 | (N2650V) N148JB N148JS (N726BB) (N300RN) N102HS N505CF |
| 518 | 501-0131 | N2650X N490WC YV-301P N301PP YV-2605P N133SC (N501NP) |
| 519 | 501-0135 | N2650Y N77TW N711GL N49MP N63CG N501WL |
| 520 | 501-0136 | (N26502) N66AT N66AG N800TW N511HC |
| 521 | 501-0137 | N26503 N46SC N14VA |
| 522 | 501-0128 | (N26504) N522CC N900MM N501CF |
| 523 | 501-0121 | N26506 D-IANO HB-VID D-IANO OE-FHW |
| 524 | 501-0142 | N26507 HB-VHA N310AF N880M I-SATV YV-688CP N197FS (N123PL) N15FJ N67BE N142FJ |
| 525* | 501-0138 | (N26509) 8P-BAR 8P-BAB C-GBTB N501CE N74FH |
| 526 | 501-0139 | N2651B N526CC N1LQ (N3UG) N108JL N888BH N501AF |
| 527 | 501-0132 | N2651G N50US N91WZ N717JL N39HH |
| 528 | 501-0133 | N2651J (N955WP) N51WP N700SP |
| 529 | 501-0140 | (N2651R) (N99TD) N96TD N96CF OE-FDM 9A-CHC |
| 530 | 500-0395 | N2651S XA-JEX XB-JFV |
| 531 | 501-0125 | (N2651Y) (N2DP) (N501DP) N45MC N96TC N69EP N125EA |
| 532 | 501-0141 | N26510 N166CB VR-BJN N841MA N501GG N501DR |
| 533 | 500-0396 | N26514 (XA-JEW) XC-GTO |
| 534 | 501-0156 | N26517 N123FG N44FM |
| 535 | 501-0143 | N26523 D-IGGK OY-ONE N501MG 4X-CMG N520BH N501WJ |
| 536 | 501-0144 | N2652U N270SF N270NF OE-FMK |
| 537 | 501-0159 | N2652Y D-IGLU N666JJ N308AT N1AT N8189J N80CJ |
| 538 | 501-0145 | N2652Z (ZS-KGF) VH-LCL N2652Z [w/o 22Apr90 Norfolk Island while regd VH-LCL; hulk to Dodson Avn, Ottawa, KS still marked as VH-LCL; US marks cx Jly94] |
| 539 | 501-0163 | N1354G (I-AGIK) I-CIGB |
| 540 | 500-0403 | N1710E G-BPCP [w/o 01Oct80 Jersey, Channel Is, UK] |
| 541 | 501-0147 | N1728E N254TW CP-2105 N392DA N27TS N551MS |
| 542 | 501-0148 | N1758E (OO-ECT) N167CB N700ER N500DL I-GJMA N148EA N148ED XB-KHL |
| 543 | 501-0149 | (N1772E) N104CF N97FD (N721CG) N96FP N72VJ |
| 544* | 501-0302 | (N1779E) (G-BHIW) XA-JFE XB-ELU XA-RLE XA-JCE N301EL N801EL N7EN |

# CITATION I

| Unit No | C/n | Identities | | | | | | | |
|---|---|---|---|---|---|---|---|---|---|
| 545* | 501-0146 | (N1782E) | N545CC | N54MH | N61CD | N1VU | N194RC | N53BB | N804ST |
| 546 | 501-0151 | (N1820E) | N269MD | N269CM | N2690M | N797SF | N797SE | | |
| 547 | 501-0152 | (N1874E) | N547CC | N501FM | N501ED | N40FJ | N48FJ | N15CV | (N15UJ) |
| | | VP-CMA | VP-CCD | N15CY | | | | | |
| 548 | 501-0153 | (N1930E) | N105CF | (N118AT) | N99CK | (N484CS) | | | |
| 549 | 501-0160 | N1951E | (N58BD) | N60PR | C-GAAA | N999PW | | | |
| 550 | 501-0161 | N1955E | OY-CYD | N5UM | XB-FXO | XB-GRE | N501FP | N96MB | |
| 551 | 501-0303 | (N1958E) | N6563C | OH-CIT | OY-FFC | SE-DVA | N301JJ | N610GD | N370TP |
| | | N303RH | | | | | | | |
| 552 | 501-0162 | N1959E | N455H | N55H | N44SW | N446V | N501DP | | |
| 553 | 501-0157 | N2052A | (N88BR) | N16VG | | | | | |
| 554 | 500-0399 | N2069A | YU-BML | T9-SBA | E7-SBA | | | | |
| 555 | 501-0175 | N2072A | EI-BJN | VR-BKP | VP-BKP | VP-BVK | N23VK | | |
| 556 | 501-0158 | N2611Y | N1MX | N501WB | | | | | |
| 557 | 501-0165 | N2612N | (N20KW) | N557CC | N165NA | N501RC | | | |
| 558 | 501-0154 | N2613C | N80MF | CC-CWW | N154SC | | | | |
| 559 | 501-0166 | N2614C | N476X | I-CIPA | (N30AF) | OY-INI | N166FA | | |
| 560 | 500-0404 | N2614H | G-BHTT | G-ZAPI | N789DD | N789DK | LV-BID | | |
| 561 | 501-0185 | N2614K | N653DR | N72787 | N111RB | N1CR | N501LL | N505BG | |
| 562 | 501-0150 | N2616G | N95MJ | N73FW | N405PC | [w/o 02Apr01 Depere, WI] | | | |
| 563 | 501-0167 | (N2616L) | N563CC | N323CB | N38RT | N900TW | N723JM | N501FJ | |
| 564 | 501-0155 | N2617B | (N108CT) | N110TV | N110TP | N800DW | VR-CJB | VP-CJB | N299D |
| | | N321TS | N347MH | | | | | | |
| 565 | 500-0401 | N2617K | N2651 | I-FARN | | | | | |
| 566 | 501-0169 | N2617U | D-IBWG | C-GFEE | | | | | |
| 567 | 501-0183 | N6777V | ZS-KPA | CS-AYY | (N8NC) | | | | |
| 568 | 501-0168 | (N6777X) | N39LL | PT-LNV | N168EA | N601WT | N328NA | | |
| 569 | 501-0188 | N6778C | N1JB | N93JM | N61DT | N251CT | N525PV | | |
| 570 | 501-0164 | (N6778L) | N570CC | N223GC | N750LA | N50DS | N170JS | N286PC | |
| 571 | 501-0193 | N6778T | N164CB | XA-LIM | N39300 | N45MK | N89MF | N199DJ | |
| 572 | 501-0173 | (N6778V) | OE-FPH | N25GT | N91MS | N91TE | | | |
| 573 | 501-0170 | (N6778Y) | N501HP | G-GENE | G-MTLE | N170EA | N610TT | N610GG | |
| 574 | 501-0171 | N67780 | VH-BNK | N171WJ | | | | | |
| 575 | 501-0184 | N67786 | N90CF | N433MM | N501VC | N318DN | | | |
| 576 | 501-0187 | N6779D | N576CC | (N414CB) | N21EH | N23EH | (N576CC) | N137GK | (N600DH) |
| | | N900DH | N900DL | N713AL | N7MC | N70CG | (N614DD) | | |
| 577 | 501-0176 | N6779L | N44LC | N49LC | (VR-CIA) | VR-CFG | VP-CFG | N96DA | |
| 578 | 501-0177 | N6779P | (N999RB) | N22SD | N501DG | N501NC | N501GW | N457CS | N98AV |
| 579 | 501-0174 | N6779Y | N20GT | N721US | N702NC | N702NY | (N174CF) | N50JG | N454DQ |
| | | N1AG | N921BE | | | | | | |
| 580 | 501-0178 | N67799 | LV-PML | N4246A | N83ND | G-FLVU | G-VUEM | | |
| 581 | 501-0186 | (N6780A) | N95EW | N37HW | N999WS | | | | |
| 582 | 501-0189 | N6780C | N80SF | VH-FUM | | | | | |
| 583 | 501-0182 | N6780J | N360DJ | I-PALP | N535GA | (N125CA) | D-ISIS | VP-CAP | N220HM |
| 584 | 501-0190 | (N6780M) | N584CC | N333MS | N393DA | N40AW | N723JR | | |
| 585 | 501-0191 | N6780Y | N98ME | N64RT | | | | | |
| 586 | 500-0410 | N6780Z | XC-GAW | | | | | | |
| 587 | 500-0408 | N67805 | XA-LUD | XB-DVF | | | | | |
| 588 | 501-0181 | N6781C | N250SP | N250SR | N501KK | | | | |
| 589 | 501-0179 | (N6781D) | N589CJ | N414CB | HB-VLD | N718SA | (N406RH) | | |
| 590 | 501-0192 | (N6781G) | N190K | | | | | | |
| 591 | 501-0194 | N6781L | N28JG | N65WW | | | | | |
| 592 | 501-0222 | N6781R | N25HS | N690DM | N690WY | | | | |
| 593 | 501-0180 | (N6781T) | (N593CC) | N695CC | N593DS | N9NE | N180VP | N650MW | N510NJ |
| | | LV-BHJ | | | | | | | |
| 594 | 501-0197 | N6781Z | N100SN | N324L | | | | | |
| 595 | 501-0195 | N67814 | N161CB | N7111H | N109DC | (N123KD) | N109DC | N123KD | |
| 596 | 500-0409 | N67815 | XC-FEZ | | | | | | |
| 597 | 501-0196 | N6782B | (N597JV) | N575SR | N311TP | (N311TT) | | | |
| 598 | 500-0412 | N6782F | XA-LUV | XB-GDJ | | | | | |
| 599 | 501-0172 | (N6782P) | N907KH | HI-581SP | N110JB | | | | |
| 600 | 501-0311 | (N6782T) | SE-DES | OY-JEY | N311VP | | | | |
| 601 | 501-0199 | N6782X | N501MM | N441JT | N62RG | N7SV | N91HG | | |
| 602 | 501-0198 | N67822 | (N602CC) | N105TW | N500LE | N500LH | N198VP | N800DT | |
| 603 | 500-0406 | N67829 | SE-DET | OY-FFB | | | | | |
| 604 | 501-0231 | N6783C | N55WG | N29HE | N501BP | D-IAWU | | | |
| 605 | 501-0200 | N6783L | 7Q-YTL | N47TL | | | | | |
| 606 | 501-0201 | N6783U | N801L | N130JS | N123SF | N55BM | N417RC | N417RQ | N78CN |
| | | N953SL | N953HC | | | | | | |
| 607 | 501-0202 | N6783V | N520RP | N607CJ | (XA-PEV) | XA-BOA | N202VP | N477KM | N501G |
| 608 | 500-0413 | N6783X | (PT-LBZ) | PT-LCC | | | | | |
| 609 | 501-0203 | N67830 | D-IAEC | [w/o 31May87 Blankensee A/P, Lubeck, Germany] | | | | | |
| 610 | 501-0207 | N67839 | N968DM | (N207CF) | OE-FYC | VP-BHO | | | |
| 611 | 501-0204 | N6784L | (N123HP) | N345N | (N345HB) | N367HB | | | |
| 612 | 501-0208 | N6784P | N54MJ | I-LAWN | N208EA | N82P | | | |
| 613 | 501-0205 | N6784T | PT-LVB | N6784T | (N501DA) | N528RM | (N501DL) | | |

## CITATION I

| Unit No | C/n | Identities | | | | | | | |
|---|---|---|---|---|---|---|---|---|---|
| 614 | 501-0209 | N6784X | N56MJ | N501CR | N111DT | N36FD | N98RG | N70NB | |
| 615 | 501-0206 | N6784Y | N501HM | N795MA | OE-FBA | N314EB | N943LL | N943RC | N528DS |
| 616 | 501-0210 | N6784B | N32FM | YU-MDV | | | | | |
| 617 | 501-0211 | N6785C | N617CC | [cx Jun96, parted out] | | | | | |
| 618 | 501-0213 | N6785D | I-AUNY | | | | | | |
| 619 | 501-0212 | N6785L | N67GM | N70AA | N2243 | | | | |
| 620 | 501-0314 | N6887M | N56MC | N56LW | | | | | |
| 621 | 501-0214 | N6887R | N567L | I-JUST | (N794WB) | N3312T | N2296S | N2298S | (N340AC) |
| | | N241MH | N241BF | | | | | | |
| 622 | 501-0215 | N1354G | N50MM | ZS-LXT | N215NA | | | | |
| 623 | 501-0217 | N1710E | N623RM | N600SS | N500TW | N7MZ | | | |
| 624 | 501-0216 | N1758E | N57MJ | (N65T) | N57TW | TG-RIF | TG-RIE | | |
| 625 | 501-0219 | N1772E | N25CJ | N678DG | N625CH | N625J | N58BT | N501BW | N12RN |
| | | N18RN | N510GA | N56PB | | | | | |
| 626 | 501-0218 | N1958E | I-KODE | N218AM | N218JG | | | | |
| 627 | 501-0223 | N1959E | N18HC | (N26HA) | | | | | |
| 628 | 501-0220 | N2052A | N628CH | N100CH | N100QH | N100LX | | | |
| 629 | 500-0415 | N2072A | JA8474 | N50KR | N53RD | | | | |
| 630 | 501-0224 | N2611Y | N630CE | N456CE | N825PS | | | | |
| 631 | 501-0228 | N2612N | (N999CB) | N501CM | JA8284 | N228EA | XA-SEY | N665MM | |
| 632 | 501-0260 | N2613C | N224RP | N500GA | N7UF | N41LE | N501RG | | |
| 633 | 501-0225 | N2614C | N49BL | TG-MIL | TG-KIT | N412SE | N5411 | | |
| 634 | 501-0227 | (N2614Y) | N2614H | N374GS | N47CF | N83DM | | | |
| 635 | 501-0226 | (N2615D) | N29AC | N226VP | N501JM | | | | |
| 636 | 501-0229 | (N2615L) | N636CC | N57MC | N57FC | | | | |
| 637 | 501-0232 | (N2616G) | N2616C | N853KB | N35TL | VR-CHF | VR-CAT | VP-CAT | |
| 638 | 501-0230 | (N2617B) | N2616G | N653F | N5RL | G-ICED | N505CC | HB-VLB | 9A-DVR |
| | | N999MS | | | | | | | |
| 639 | 501-0234 | N2617B | N61PR | N711RP | PT-LIZ | N643RT | N77PA | N77PX | N123PL |
| | | N125PL | N123PL | | | | | | |
| 640 | 501-0237 | (N2617K) | N640BS | N237SC | N831CB | N29UF | N420PC | N712VF | (N712VE) |
| | | N420PC | | | | | | | |
| 641 | 501-0235 | N2617U | (N31CF) | (N13BN) | | | | | |
| 642 | 501-0236 | N26227 | N711VF | C-GQJJ | | | | | |
| 643 | 501-0221 | (N26228) | N643MC | N217RR | N389JP | HB-VKD | N555HR | N221EB | N107GM |
| | | N106GM | (N643VP) | N501HG | | | | | |
| 644 | 501-0240 | N26232 | N13BK | N711BT | OY-JET | N62864 | N77UB | N501DY | N238BG |
| 645 | 500-0411 | N6784Y | G-BIZZ | G-NCMT | SE-DLZ | | | | |
| 646 | 501-0242 | N2623B | N40PL | N500BK | N71L | | | | |
| 647 | 501-0241 | (N2624L) | N174CB | N207G | C-GSTR | N101RR | | | |
| 648 | 501-0243 | N2624Z | N43SP | | | | | | |
| 649 | 501-0238 | N2626A | N238JS | I-DVAL | (N501EZ) | N995PA | N737RJ | | |
| 650 | 501-0244 | N2626J | N650CJ | (N711VF) | N701VF | N418R | N244SL | N176FB | N501T |
| | | N501HD* | | | | | | | |
| 651 | 501-0317 | N2626Z | 5N-AVL | (N317JQ) | N706DC | N51FT | | | |
| 652 | 501-0245 | N26263 | (N678DG) | ZS-LDO | A2-AGM | ZS-ACE | | | |
| 653 | 501-0233 | N26264 | 5N-AVM | N18860 | N501Q | | | | |
| 654 | 501-0246 | N2627N | N85RS | N26LC | OE-FHH | | | | |
| 655 | 501-0247 | N2627U | (N24CH) | [w/o 12Nov82 Wichita, KS] | | | | | |
| 656 | 500-0418 | N2628B | ZS-LDV | | | | | | |
| 657 | 501-0252 | N2628Z | N825HL | N574CC | I-TOIO | | | | |
| 658 | 501-0254 | N2629Z | N84CF | N66BK | (N84GF) | | | | |
| 659 | 501-0256 | N2631N | D-ILLL | I-PAPE | N256P | | | | |
| 660 | 501-0257 | N2631V | (N992NW) | N500NW | OE-FLY | N12NM | N570D | N501WX | |
| 661 | 501-0255 | N661TV | N661TW | N501MR | N707WF | G-SBEC | N400LX | N901NB | N501X |
| 662 | 501-0248 | N2633N | N7700T | (N711EG) | | | | | |
| 663 | 501-0250 | N77FD | | | | | | | |
| 664 | 501-0258 | N664CC | N900RB | N900RD | N87FL | VR-BHI | VP-BHI | N16KW | N599BR |
| 665 | 501-0319 | N124KC | N60EW | | | | | | |
| 666 | 501-0251 | N30BK | N945BC | N400LX | N501RG | N501WD | | | |
| 667 | 501-0320 | N2649D | ZS-LHP | 3D-ADH | N70467 | N401G | C-GPTI | C-GTOL | |
| 668 | 501-0321 | OE-FHP | N321VP | N550MH | N170MK | N510SJ | N986DS | | |
| 669 | 501-0322 | N2663J | N374GS | N314GS | (N669DM) | (N769EW) | N527EW | | |
| 670 | 501-0253 | N2650Y | N501JE | N1SH* | | | | | |
| 671 | 501-0323 | N2651B | N55HL | N501RF | N501LE | (N142AL) | N505BB | | |
| 672 | 501-0324 | N2651J | JA8493 | | | | | | |
| 673 | 501-0325 | N1710E | (D-IFGP) | N501LM | N64BH | | | | |
| 674 | 501-0259 | N1758E | (N77111) | (N261WB) | N261WR | N261WD | VR-BJW | N501MS | D-IEIR |
| | | (N225WT) | | | | | | | |
| 675 | 501-0675 | N8900M | N501MT | N593BW | | | | | |
| 676 | 501-0676 | N1958E | N676CC | (N76JY) | | | | | |
| 677 | 501-0677 | (N1958E) | N727MC | (N184SC) | C-GAAA | N54CG | N74HR | | |
| 678 | 501-0678 | N2052A | N3FE | N678CF | PT-ODC | (N26AA) | | | |
| 679 | 501-0679 | N2611Y | N200GF | N679CC | N2611Y | VR-BLF | VP-BLF | N73SK | (N501HH) |
| 680 | 501-0680 | N2614C | PT-LFR | PP-EIF | | | | | |
| 681 | 501-0681 | N2616G | N82LS | N427SS | | | | | |

## CITATION I

| Unit No | C/n | Identities | | | | | | | |
|---|---|---|---|---|---|---|---|---|---|
| 682 | 501-0682 | N2617B | N3951 | N19GB | N55TK | N682DC | N682HC | N682BF | |
| 683 | 501-0683 | N501BK | N501FR | N170HL | (N49TA) | N96LC | N702RT | | |
| 684 | 501-0684 | N3683G | N501TP | | | | | | |
| 685 | 501-0685 | N5346C | N400SR | N501TB | (N243AB) | N501EG | XB-IXT | | |
| 686 | 501-0686 | N6763M | N750PP | | | | | | |
| 687 | 501-0687 | N321FM | N154CC | N361DB | N361DE | | | | |
| 688 | 501-0688 | D-IMRX | [w/o 16Feb06 Northern Iraq] | | | | | | |
| 689 | 501-0689 | N46MT | N689CC | (N88MT) | N88MM | N75TJ | N88MM | N288MM | C-FNHZ |

Production complete

## CITATION 500 UNIT NUMBER CROSS-REFERENCE

Note: From c/n 500-0001 to 500-0349 unit numbers match the last three digits of the c/n, then the tie-ups are as follows:

| C/n | Unit | C/n | Unit | C/n | Unit | C/n | Unit | C/n | Unit | C/n | Unit |
|---|---|---|---|---|---|---|---|---|---|---|---|
| 500-0354 | 363 | 500-0369 | 454 | 500-0387 | 484 | 500-0401 | 565 | 500-0408 | 587 | 500-0412 | 598 |
| 500-0356 | 366 | 500-0370 | 396 | 500-0392 | 489 | 500-0403 | 540 | 500-0409 | 596 | 500-0413 | 608 |
| 500-0358 | 377 | 500-0374 | 455 | 500-0395 | 530 | 500-0404 | 560 | 500-0410 | 586 | 500-0415 | 629 |
| 500-0361 | 361 | 500-0378 | 461 | 500-0396 | 533 | 500-0406 | 603 | 500-0411 | 645 | 500-0418 | 656 |
| 500-0364 | 392 | 500-0386 | 470 | 500-0399 | 554 | | | | | | |

## CITATION 1 CONVERSIONS

The following a/c have been converted from Model 500s to Model 501s (and, in one example, back again):

500-0097 to 501-0446
500-0293 to 501-0643
500-0350 to 501-0027
500-0351 to 501-0261
500-0352 to 501-0263
500-0353 to 501-0264
500-0355 to 501-0267
500-0357 to 501-0269
500-0359 to 501-0270
500-0360 to 501-0272
500-0361 to 501-0265 to 500-0361
500-0362 to 501-0275
500-0363 to 501-0273

500-0365 to 501-0262
500-0366 to 501-0285
500-0368 to 501-0278
500-0371 to 501-0279
500-0372 to 501-0281
500-0373 to 501-0280
500-0375 to 501-0289
500-0376 to 501-0282
500-0377 to 501-0283
500-0379 to 501-0284
500-0381 to 501-0286
500-0383 to 501-0292
500-0389 to 501-0293

500-0391 to 501-0294
500-0393 to 501-0239
500-0394 to 501-0297
500-0397 to 501-0303
500-0398 to 501-0298
500-0400 to 501-0249
500-0402 to 501-0302
500-0405 to 501-0311
500-0414 to 501-0314
500-0416 to 501-0260
500-0417 to 501-0317
500-0476 to 501-0063
500-0667 to 501-0320

# CITATION 501 UNIT NUMBER CROSS-REFERENCE

| C/n | Unit | C/n | Unit | C/n | Unit | C/n | Unit |
|---|---|---|---|---|---|---|---|
| 501-0001 | 351 | 501-0080 | 457 | 501-0159 | 537 | 501-0238 | 649 |
| 501-0002 | 353 | 501-0081 | 458 | 501-0160 | 549 | 501-0239 | 510 |
| 501-0003 | 355 | 501-0082 | 460 | 501-0161 | 550 | 501-0240 | 644 |
| 501-0004 | 356 | 501-0083 | 462 | 501-0162 | 552 | 501-0241 | 647 |
| 501-0005 | 357 | 501-0084 | 463 | 501-0163 | 539 | 501-0242 | 646 |
| 501-0006 | 358 | 501-0085 | 475 | 501-0164 | 570 | 501-0243 | 648 |
| 501-0007 | 360 | 501-0086 | 477 | 501-0165 | 557 | 501-0244 | 650 |
| 501-0008 | 362 | 501-0087 | 474 | 501-0166 | 559 | 501-0245 | 652 |
| 501-0009 | 367 | 501-0088 | 473 | 501-0167 | 563 | 501-0246 | 654 |
| 501-0010 | 370 | 501-0089 | 471 | 501-0168 | 568 | 501-0247 | 655 |
| 501-0011 | 364 | 501-0090 | 466 | 501-0169 | 566 | 501-0248 | 662 |
| 501-0012 | 369 | 501-0091 | 476 | 501-0170 | 573 | 501-0249 | 514 |
| 501-0013 | 372 | 501-0092 | 478 | 501-0171 | 574 | 501-0250 | 663 |
| 501-0014 | 371 | 501-0093 | 465 | 501-0172 | 599 | 501-0251 | 666 |
| 501-0015 | 373 | 501-0094 | 488 | 501-0173 | 572 | 501-0252 | 657 |
| 501-0016 | 375 | 501-0095 | 469 | 501-0174 | 579 | 501-0253 | 670 |
| 501-0017 | 376 | 501-0096 | 480 | 501-0175 | 555 | 501-0254 | 658 |
| 501-0018 | 378 | 501-0097 | 479 | 501-0176 | 577 | 501-0255 | 661 |
| 501-0019 | 383 | 501-0098 | 464 | 501-0177 | 578 | 501-0256 | 659 |
| 501-0020 | 380 | 501-0099 | 467 | 501-0178 | 580 | 501-0257 | 660 |
| 501-0021 | 384 | 501-0100 | 485 | 501-0179 | 589 | 501-0258 | 664 |
| 501-0022 | 385 | 501-0101 | 468 | 501-0180 | 593 | 501-0259 | 674 |
| 501-0023 | 386 | 501-0102 | 486 | 501-0181 | 588 | 501-0260 | 632 |
| 501-0024 | 387 | 501-0103 | 490 | 501-0182 | 583 | 501-0261 | 352 |
| 501-0025 | 389 | 501-0104 | 492 | 501-0183 | 567 | 501-0262 | 397 |
| 501-0026 | 391 | 501-0105 | 493 | 501-0184 | 575 | 501-0263 | 354 |
| 501-0027 | 350 | 501-0106 | 501 | 501-0185 | 561 | 501-0264 | 359 |
| 501-0028 | 394 | 501-0107 | 482 | 501-0186 | 581 | 501-0267 | 365 |
| 501-0029 | 411 | 501-0108 | 495 | 501-0187 | 576 | 501-0269 | 368 |
| 501-0030 | 390 | 501-0109 | 491 | 501-0188 | 569 | 501-0270 | 374 |
| 501-0031 | 395 | 501-0110 | 496 | 501-0189 | 582 | 501-0272 | 379 |
| 501-0032 | 388 | 501-0111 | 498 | 501-0190 | 584 | 501-0273 | 382 |
| 501-0033 | 400 | 501-0112 | 499 | 501-0191 | 585 | 501-0275 | 393 |
| 501-0034 | 401 | 501-0113 | 502 | 501-0192 | 590 | 501-0278 | 402 |
| 501-0035 | 404 | 501-0114 | 503 | 501-0193 | 571 | 501-0279 | 407 |
| 501-0036 | 406 | 501-0115 | 507 | 501-0194 | 591 | 501-0280 | 415 |
| 501-0037 | 408 | 501-0116 | 509 | 501-0195 | 595 | 501-0281 | 423 |
| 501-0038 | 409 | 501-0117 | 506 | 501-0196 | 597 | 501-0282 | 428 |
| 501-0039 | 403 | 501-0118 | 504 | 501-0197 | 594 | 501-0283 | 429 |
| 501-0040 | 412 | 501-0119 | 497 | 501-0198 | 602 | 501-0284 | 433 |
| 501-0041 | 381 | 501-0120 | 487 | 501-0199 | 601 | 501-0285 | 439 |
| 501-0042 | 410 | 501-0121 | 523 | 501-0200 | 605 | 501-0286 | 445 |
| 501-0043 | 417 | 501-0122 | 508 | 501-0201 | 606 | 501-0289 | 459 |
| 501-0044 | 424 | 501-0123 | 513 | 501-0202 | 607 | 501-0292 | 472 |
| 501-0045 | 416 | 501-0124 | 515 | 501-0203 | 609 | 501-0293 | 481 |
| 501-0046 | 405 | 501-0125 | 531 | 501-0204 | 611 | 501-0294 | 483 |
| 501-0047 | 413 | 501-0126 | 505 | 501-0205 | 613 | 501-0297 | 494 |
| 501-0048 | 414 | 501-0127 | 500 | 501-0206 | 615 | 501-0298 | 511 |
| 501-0049 | 420 | 501-0128 | 522 | 501-0207 | 610 | 501-0302 | 544 |
| 501-0050 | 398 | 501-0129 | 512 | 501-0208 | 612 | 501-0303 | 551 |
| 501-0051 | 422 | 501-0130 | 517 | 501-0209 | 614 | 501-0311 | 600 |
| 501-0052 | 427 | 501-0131 | 518 | 501-0210 | 616 | 501-0314 | 620 |
| 501-0053 | 418 | 501-0132 | 527 | 501-0211 | 617 | 501-0317 | 651 |
| 501-0054 | 419 | 501-0133 | 528 | 501-0212 | 619 | 501-0319 | 665 |
| 501-0055 | 425 | 501-0134 | 516 | 501-0213 | 618 | 501-0320 | 667 |
| 501-0056 | 426 | 501-0135 | 519 | 501-0214 | 621 | 501-0321 | 668 |
| 501-0057 | 430 | 501-0136 | 520 | 501-0215 | 622 | 501-0322 | 669 |
| 501-0058 | 434 | 501-0137 | 521 | 501-0216 | 624 | 501-0323 | 671 |
| 501-0059 | 431 | 501-0138 | 525 | 501-0217 | 623 | 501-0324 | 672 |
| 501-0060 | 435 | 501-0139 | 526 | 501-0218 | 626 | 501-0325 | 673 |
| 501-0061 | 436 | 501-0140 | 529 | 501-0219 | 625 | 501-0446 | 097 |
| 501-0062 | 421 | 501-0141 | 532 | 501-0220 | 628 | 501-0643 | 293 |
| 501-0063 | 443 | 501-0142 | 524 | 501-0221 | 643 | 501-0675 | 675 |
| 501-0064 | 437 | 501-0143 | 535 | 501-0222 | 592 | 501-0676 | 676 |
| 501-0065 | 440 | 501-0144 | 536 | 501-0223 | 627 | 501-0677 | 677 |
| 501-0066 | 432 | 501-0145 | 538 | 501-0224 | 630 | 501-0678 | 678 |
| 501-0067 | 442 | 501-0146 | 545 | 501-0225 | 633 | 501-0679 | 679 |
| 501-0068 | 438 | 501-0147 | 541 | 501-0226 | 635 | 501-0680 | 680 |
| 501-0069 | 441 | 501-0148 | 542 | 501-0227 | 634 | 501-0681 | 681 |
| 501-0070 | 444 | 501-0149 | 543 | 501-0228 | 631 | 501-0682 | 682 |
| 501-0071 | 446 | 501-0150 | 562 | 501-0229 | 636 | 501-0683 | 683 |
| 501-0072 | 447 | 501-0151 | 546 | 501-0230 | 638 | 501-0684 | 684 |
| 501-0073 | 448 | 501-0152 | 547 | 501-0231 | 604 | 501-0685 | 685 |
| 501-0074 | 449 | 501-0153 | 548 | 501-0232 | 637 | 501-0686 | 686 |
| 501-0075 | 450 | 501-0154 | 558 | 501-0233 | 653 | 501-0687 | 687 |
| 501-0076 | 451 | 501-0155 | 564 | 501-0234 | 639 | 501-0688 | 688 |
| 501-0077 | 452 | 501-0156 | 534 | 501-0235 | 641 | 501-0689 | 689 |
| 501-0078 | 453 | 501-0157 | 553 | 501-0236 | 642 | | |
| 501-0079 | 456 | 501-0158 | 556 | 501-0237 | 640 | | |

# CESSNA 510 CITATION MUSTANG

A new entry-level very light twinjet that Cessna unveiled at the 2002 NBAA convention. The aircraft can accommodate four passengers and a crew of two.

| C/n | Identities | | | | |
|---|---|---|---|---|---|
| 712 | N27369 | [ff 23Apr05; c/n originally quoted as E510-712001] | | | |
| 0001 | N510CE | [ff 29Aug05] | | N510ND | N91FP |
| 0002 | N510KS | [ff 27Jan06] | | N199ML | |
| 0003 | N403CM | [ff 15Jun06] | | | |
| 0004 | N404CM | | | | |
| 0005 | N600DE | | | | |
| 0006 | N245MU | | | | |
| 0007 | N510FF | N4FF | | | |
| 0008 | N396DM | | | | |
| 0009 | N910SY | | | | |
| 0010 | N654EA | N24YY | N49MW | | |
| 0011 | N2243W | (VH-SJP) | ZK-LCA | | |
| 0012 | N443HC | | | | |
| 0013 | N50HS | (N565VV) | N1VV | | |
| 0014 | N510VV | N307TC* | | | |
| 0015 | N406CM | | | | |
| 0016 | N416CM | | | | |
| 0017 | N17MU | N510WC | | | |
| 0018 | N827DK | | | | |
| 0019 | N2427N | OK-PPC | | | |
| 0020 | N24329 | | | | |
| 0021 | N80HQ | | | | |
| 0022 | N4089Y | OY-LPU | | | |
| 0023 | N888TF | | | | |
| 0024 | N75ES | | | | |
| 0025 | N325RR | PH-ORJ | | | |
| 0026 | N1693L | N83EM | | | |
| 0027 | N327CM | G-FBLK | | | |
| 0028 | N54PV | | | | |
| 0029 | N4059H | N45SP | VH-NEQ | | |
| 0030 | N725JB | | | | |
| 0031 | N528DM | | | | |
| 0032 | N4107D | N814WS | | | |
| 0033 | N4110T | VH-CCJ | VH-SJP | ZK-PGA | |
| 0034 | N4155B | XA-JRT | | | |
| 0035 | N4202M | D-ISRM | | | |
| 0036 | N510GH | N999JD | | | |
| 0037 | N33NP | | | | |
| 0038 | N4115W | N821ND | | | |
| 0039 | N4159Z | XB-RYE | XA-RYE | | |
| 0040 | N4009F | OE-FID | | | |
| 0041 | N4021E | PP-NNN | | | |
| 0042 | N591ES | C-GMMU | | | |
| 0043 | N4030W | PP-MIS | | | |
| 0044 | XA-BAT | N366FW | OE-FCB | | |
| 0045 | N761JP | (D-IJKP) | | | |
| 0046 | N946CM | PP-MTG | | | |
| 0047 | N22EM | | | | |
| 0048 | D-IEGO | | | | |
| 0049 | N13616 | 9A-CSG | YU-SPM | | |
| 0050 | PH-TXI | G-OAMB | | | |
| 0051 | N510JH | | | | |
| 0052 | G-LEAI | | | | |
| 0053 | EC-KNL | OE-FTR | OK-FTR | | |
| 0054 | N1749L | ZK-MUS | ZK-MOT | | |
| 0055 | N551WH | | | | |
| 0056 | PT-FLO | | | | |
| 0057 | PR-MCL | | | | |
| 0058 | PR-XSX | | | | |
| 0059 | XA-VMX | | | | |
| 0060 | N212C | ZS-CTF | | | |
| 0061 | N1EL | | | | |
| 0062 | N6183Q | PR-BSA | | | |
| 0063 | PR-DRI | | | | |
| 0064 | N13ZM | N60CP | | | |
| 0065 | N61706 | OE-FFB | | | |
| 0066 | N902LG | | | | |
| 0067 | N967CM | G-FBNK | | | |
| 0068 | N968CM | G-FLBK | | | |
| 0069 | N6193S | T7-VIG | | | |
| 0070 | N235SS | VH-YDZ | | | |
| 0071 | N921TX | | | | |

# CESSNA 510 CITATION MUSTANG

| C/n | Identities | | |
|---|---|---|---|
| 0072 | G-LEAA | | |
| 0073 | G-LEAB | | |
| 0074 | N510LL | | |
| 0075 | N4084A | G-LEAC | |
| 0076 | N4085A | G-NGEL | |
| 0077 | N774AR | | |
| 0078 | N724DL | | |
| 0079 | ZS-JDM | N816CW | |
| 0080 | N4086L | PR-MPM | |
| 0081 | OE-FHA | | |
| 0082 | OE-FLR | | |
| 0083 | N510GJ | | |
| 0084 | PR-RDM | | |
| 0085 | PR-VDL | | |
| 0086 | N808RD | | |
| 0087 | N6200C | (PP-PMR) | PR-FMP* |
| 0088 | N6197D | (PH-TXA) | |
| 0089 | N63223 | M-USTG | |
| 0090 | N6324L | ZS-LKG | 4X-DFZ |
| 0091 | N6196M | ZS-KPM | |
| 0092 | N6325U | ZS-DIY | |
| 0093 | N6332K | ZS-DFI | |
| 0094 | N510SA | | |
| 0095 | N6203C | N102DS | |
| 0096 | N996CM | G-FBKA | |
| 0097 | N97HT | N214HT | |
| 0098 | N510BW | | |
| 0099 | PP-WGS | | |
| 0100 | N6202W | HS-IOO | |
| 0101 | PP-EVG | | |
| 0102 | N903JP | | |
| 0103 | N923JP | | |
| 0104 | OE-FWH | | |
| 0105 | N245DR | N61EP* | |
| 0106 | (OE-FWW) | OE-FMY | |
| 0107 | N710EB | | |
| 0108 | N939JC | | |
| 0109 | N510MW | | |
| 0110 | N66ES | | |
| 0111 | (PH-TXB) | PH-TXA | |
| 0112 | N801GE | | |
| 0113 | N853JL | C-GDJG | |
| 0114 | N510PT | | |
| 0115 | N69AY | | |
| 0116 | OE-FMZ | | |
| 0117 | N62076 | HS-VIP | |
| 0118 | N510MB | | |
| 0119 | PR-NRN | | |
| 0120 | N4041T | N1RD | |
| 0121 | N60CP | N510K | |
| 0122 | N230BF | CS-DPV | |
| 0123 | PT-TOP | | |
| 0124 | N510AZ | | |
| 0125 | OO-PRM | | |
| 0126 | N826CM | G-FBKB | |
| 0127 | N627CM | G-FBKC | |
| 0128 | N178SF | | |
| 0129 | PR-FAC | | |
| 0130 | G-FBLI | | |
| 0131 | (PH-TXC) | N510TX | |
| 0132 | LX-FGL | | |
| 0133 | (PH-TXB) | N6206W | N17RP |
| 0134 | ZS-AFD | | |
| 0135 | N5223F | JA510M | |
| 0136 | C-FDSH | | |
| 0137 | ZS-MUS | | |
| 0138 | N309MT | | |
| 0139 | N921PP | | |
| 0140 | N987CM | | |
| 0141 | N141BG | LZ-AMA | |
| 0142 | N609TC | | |
| 0143 | N510BA | | |
| 0144 | N5044V | EI-SFA | |
| 0145 | N6207Z | EI-SFB | |
| 0146 | N4082U | N914GW | |
| 0147 | PT-FLC | | |

# CESSNA 510 CITATION MUSTANG

| C/n | Identities | | |
|---|---|---|---|
| 0148 | N700YY | | |
| 0149 | F-HDPY | | |
| 0150 | N220DK | | |
| 0151 | N738DC | | |
| 0152 | N4085D | EC-LAF | EC-LDK |
| 0153 | N4085S | N442LV | |
| 0154 | N510SV | | |
| 0155 | N4085Z | N510KB | |
| 0156 | G-MICE | | |
| 0157 | G-KLNW | | |
| 0158 | N271CS | | |
| 0159 | N510LF | | |
| 0160 | I-FITO | | |
| 0161 | G-ZJET | | |
| 0162 | (N4RH) | N620WB | |
| 0163 | CS-DPN | | |
| 0164 | N251MC | | |
| 0165 | N81WL | | |
| 0166 | N870HY | XA-UMS | |
| 0167 | N638AH | | |
| 0168 | N510GG | | |
| 0169 | HB-VWL | | |
| 0170 | N426LF | C-GXOP | |
| 0171 | N510PS | | |
| 0172 | N510K | N510WP | |
| 0173 | N510CJ | | |
| 0174 | N40049 | XA-ULO | |
| 0175 | N42WZ | | |
| 0176 | N417GR | | |
| 0177 | N247DR | | |
| 0178 | N5020J | N662CC | |
| 0179 | N520JM | | |
| 0180 | N884TM | | |
| 0181 | N59VM | | |
| 0182 | M-USTG | F-GISH | |
| 0183 | N3QE | | |
| 0184 | N123AD | | |
| 0185 | I-MCAS | | |
| 0186 | N4076J | S5-CMT | |
| 0187 | N453DW | | |
| 0188 | N878SP | N878MM | |
| 0189 | SP-KHK | | |
| 0190 | T7-HOT | | |
| 0191 | N509DM | N123TF | |
| 0192 | N4107D | | |
| 0193 | N530AG | | |
| 0194 | LX-RSQ | | |
| 0195 | N41227 | N52338 | PR-HOT* |
| 0196 | N41297 | EI-SFC | |
| 0197 | PP-PRV | | |
| 0198 | N995AU | | |
| 0199 | N4202M | N978PC | |
| 0200 | N15GJ | | |
| 0201 | N352AS | N91CH* | |
| 0202 | N510MD | | |
| 0203 | N76GP | | |
| 0204 | N1245 | | |
| 0205 | N4047W | C-GBPL | |
| 0206 | N620CM | | |
| 0207 | N101FU | | |
| 0208 | N510DH | | |
| 0209 | N209CJ | N888GS | |
| 0210 | N54NG | | |
| 0211 | N369PA | C-FBCI | |
| 0212 | N32FM | | |
| 0213 | N59LW | | |
| 0214 | VH-EJT | | |
| 0215 | N603WS | | |
| 0216 | EI-SFD | | |
| 0217 | EI-SFE | | |
| 0218 | N949JB | | |
| 0219 | N625TX | | |
| 0220 | N510DP | | |
| 0221 | C-GDLL | | |
| 0222 | F-GMTJ | | |
| 0223 | N520KC | | |

## CESSNA 510 CITATION MUSTANG

| C/n | Identities | | |
|---|---|---|---|
| 0224 | C-GROP | | |
| 0225 | N52733 | SU-BQF | |
| 0226 | N73AH | | |
| 0227 | N377RV | | |
| 0228 | N823M | | |
| 0229 | N7876C | | |
| 0230 | N230BF | | |
| 0231 | PR-MDE | | |
| 0232 | N4082Y | C-GRRD | |
| 0233 | N301AJ | | |
| 0234 | N530AJ | | |
| 0235 | EC-LCX | | |
| 0236 | N778JE | | |
| 0237 | N918WA | | |
| 0238 | N960PT | | |
| 0239 | N4085C | N914G | |
| 0240 | N510TW | | |
| 0241 | N270MK | | |
| 0242 | N530RM | | |
| 0243 | N520BE | N243MS | |
| 0244 | N700GD | | |
| 0245 | N774ST | | |
| 0246 | N510EG | | |
| 0247 | N60GS | | |
| 0248 | N369GC | | |
| 0249 | N510BD | | |
| 0250 | N85VR | (D-IGEL) | N510JL |
| 0251 | N510KZ | | |
| 0252 | N40864 | OK-LEO | |
| 0253 | N54CF | | |
| 0254 | N30NF | | |
| 0255 | N5274G | SU-BQG | |
| 0256 | N991BB | | |
| 0257 | N257CM | | |
| 0258 | N5274K | SU-BQH | |
| 0259 | N4021E | (D-IMMH) | M-MHDH |
| 0260 | N4030W | OO-ACO | |
| 0261 | N52498 | | |
| 0262 | (D-ICMH) | M-MHBW | |
| 0263 | N362B | | |
| 0264 | N4058A | OE-FAJ | |
| 0265 | | | |
| 0266 | YR-DAD | | |
| 0267 | N5274M | SU-BQI | |
| 0268 | OK-MYS | | |
| 0269 | | | |
| 0270 | OM-AES | | |
| 0271 | N324DR | | |
| 0272 | OK-AJA | | |
| 0273 | N786AF | | |
| 0274 | N713MD | D-IEMG | |
| 0275 | N510EE | | |
| 0276 | N76BF | | |
| 0277 | N105J | | |
| 0278 | N278MS | | |
| 0279 | N127FJ | | |
| 0280 | | | |
| 0281 | YR-DAE* | | |
| 0282 | N876AM | | |
| 0283 | G-XAVB | | |
| 0284 | N520BE | | |
| 0285 | M-COOL* | | |
| 0286 | N4059H | | |
| 0287 | | | |
| 0288 | N4074M | | |
| 0289 | N40742 | | |
| 0290 | N510HW | | |
| 0291 | N39EG | | |
| 0292 | N578CM | | |
| 0293 | N293MM | | |
| 0294 | N4077P | N5251F | |
| 0295 | | | |
| 0296 | D-ISIO | | |
| 0297 | N4078L | D-IWHA* | |
| 0298 | N4078M | | |
| 0299 | N510DT | N61LF* | |

## CESSNA 510 CITATION MUSTANG

| C/n | Identities | |
|---|---|---|
| 0300 | N40780 | ZK-MUS* |
| 0301 | N301DN | |
| 0302 | N4079S | |
| 0303 | ZS-YES* | |
| 0304 | N919MB | |
| 0305 | N1956A* | |
| 0306 | N146EP | |
| 0307 | N307SH | |
| 0308 | | |
| 0309 | | |
| 0310 | | |
| 0311 | | |
| 0312 | | |
| 0313 | | |
| 0314 | N1618L | |
| 0315 | | |
| 0316 | | |
| 0317 | | |
| 0318 | | |
| 0319 | | |
| 0320 | | |
| 0321 | (D-ISIO) | N136MC |
| 0322 | | |
| 0323 | N510KM* | |
| 0324 | | |
| 0325 | | |
| 0326 | | |
| 0327 | | |
| 0328 | | |
| 0329 | | |
| 0330 | | |
| 0331 | | |
| 0332 | N229JR | |
| 0333 | | |
| 0334 | | |
| 0335 | | |
| 0336 | | |
| 0337 | | |
| 0338 | | |
| 0339 | | |
| 0340 | | |
| 0341 | | |
| 0342 | | |
| 0343 | | |
| 0344 | | |
| 0345 | | |
| 0346 | | |
| 0347 | | |
| 0348 | | |
| 0349 | | |
| 0350 | | |
| 0351 | | |
| 0352 | | |
| 0353 | | |
| 0354 | | |
| 0355 | | |
| 0356 | | |
| 0357 | | |
| 0358 | | |
| 0359 | | |
| 0360 | | |
| 0361 | | |
| 0362 | | |
| 0363 | | |
| 0364 | | |
| 0365 | | |
| 0366 | | |
| 0367 | | |
| 0368 | | |
| 0369 | | |
| 0370 | | |
| 0371 | | |
| 0372 | | |
| 0373 | | |
| 0374 | | |
| 0375 | | |

# CESSNA 525 CITATIONJET

| C/n | Identities | | | | | | | |
|---|---|---|---|---|---|---|---|---|
| 702 | N525CJ [prototype; ff 29Apr91 - cx Mar99 re-engineered to serve as the Cessna 525A Citation Jet CJ-2 prototype with c/n 708 q.v.] | | | | | | | |
| 0001 | N525CC [ff 20Nov91; pre-production prototype] | N444RH | "N444RF" | N444RH | N800VT | N800VL | N525VP | N525GV |
| 0002 | N1326B | N25CJ | N137AL | N46JW | N54BP | (VH-VCJ) | | |
| 0003 | N1326D | N44FJ | N45FJ | | | | | |
| 0004 | N1326G | N4YA | N24CJ | N7CC | N7CQ | | | |
| 0005 | N1326H | (N1326D) | N56K | N58KJ | N521PF | | | |
| 0006 | N1326P | N106CJ | | | | | | |
| 0007 | (N1327E) | N525KN | | | | | | |
| 0008 | N1327G | C-GDKI | N525FD | | | | | |
| 0009 | N1327J | (N529CC) | | | | | | |
| 0010 | (N1327K) | N210CJ | ZS-MVX | N525JV | | | | |
| 0011 | (N1327N) | N525AL | | | | | | |
| 0012 | (N1327Z) | N12PA | N86LA | | | | | |
| 0013 | N1328A | N550T | N550TF | | | | | |
| 0014 | N1328D | N70TR | N620TC | | | | | |
| 0015 | (N1328K) | N115CJ | PT-MPE | | | | | |
| 0016 | N1328M | N216CJ | D-IKOP | | | | | |
| 0017 | (N1328Q) | N525AE | N28PT | | | | | |
| 0018 | (N1328X) | N525MC | | | | | | |
| 0019 | (N1328Y) | N19CJ | N63HB | (N525SP) | N525KA | | | |
| 0020 | N1329D | "OO-LFU" | N1329D | OE-FGD | | | | |
| 0021 | (N1329G) | N793CJ | | | | | | |
| 0022 | N1329N | G-BVCM | G-THNX | | | | | |
| 0023 | (N1329T) | N525RF | N525RP | | | | | |
| 0024 | N13291 | F-GNCJ | N525DJ | F-HAOA | D-IAOA | F-HEQA | | |
| 0025 | (N1330D) | N9LR | D-IOBO | D-IBBA | | | | |
| 0026 | (N1330G) | N525FS | N286CW | (N214LX) | N602CA | | | |
| 0027 | N1330N | N825GA | N861PD | N861RD | N700CJ | | | |
| 0028 | N1330S | G-OICE | (N25EA) | G-OHAT | G-GRGG | N665DP | N7RL | N525WH |
| 0029 | N13308 | D-IWHL | (N525KT) | | | | | |
| 0030 | N1331X | "PT-MPE" | N177RE | (N93KV) | N53KV | | | |
| 0031 | (N13312) | (N131CJ) | N31CJ | N831S | | | | |
| 0032 | (N13313) | N532CJ | N95DJ | N32VP | N900DS | | | |
| 0033 | N1354G | ZS-NHE | N526CA | N472SW | N116AP | N501KR | | |
| 0034 | N1772E | N96G | N9GU | N333VS | | | | |
| 0035 | N1779E | N525HS | | | | | | |
| 0036 | N1782E | N525MB | | | | | | |
| 0037 | N1820E | HB-VKB | EC-IAB | HB-VKB | OO-IDE | | | |
| 0038 | N1874E | N135MM | N600HR | | | | | |
| 0039 | N1958E | N39CJ | | | | | | |
| 0040 | N1959E | D-ISCH | VP-CCC | N525AJ | OE-FMU | | | |
| 0041 | N2098A | N525GG | HB-VJQ | D-IAMM | F-HADA | N565JP | N565JF | |
| 0042 | N26105 | N96GD | PH-MGT | D-IBWA | | | | |
| 0043 | N2616L | N525PL | | | | | | |
| 0044 | N2617K | XA-SKW | N55DG | D-IDBW | EC-KKE | | | |
| 0045 | N2617P | N525AP | LV-AMB | | | | | |
| 0046 | N26174 | N123JN | N127SG | | | | | |
| 0047 | N2621U | N47TH | (N47VP) | N47FH | | | | |
| 0048 | N2621Z | N500HC | N525NA | N484J | | | | |
| 0049 | N2633Y | N49CJ | N349SF | | | | | |
| 0050 | N2634E | N70KW | N205BN | | | | | |
| 0051 | N2637R | N800HS | N808HS | N726SC | | | | |
| 0052 | N26379 | N252CJ | N52PK | | | | | |
| 0053 | N2638A | N53CJ | N66ES | N60ES | (N603JC) | N3WB | N654WW | |
| 0054 | N2638U | N54CJ | N851DB | | | | | |
| 0055 | N2639Y | N923AR | N570DM | | | | | |
| 0056 | N2646X | N56NZ | JA8420 | N525KK | | | | |
| 0057 | N525DG | N585DG | N525FM^ | | | | | |
| 0058 | N2647Y | N525CK | N526CK | N525F | | | | |
| 0059 | N2647Z | N71GW | N816FC | | | | | |
| 0060 | N2648Y | XA-SOU | XA-TRI | N525WW | | | | |
| 0061 | N26481 | N61CJ | N525PS | | | | | |
| 0062 | N26486 | C-FRVE | C-GINT | C-FPWB | | | | |
| 0063 | N2649J | N55SK | | | | | | |
| 0064 | N2649S | D-IHEB | | | | | | |
| 0065 | N2649Y | N5259Y | EC-704 | EC-FZP | N525GC | | | |
| 0066 | N26495 | N420CH | N545ES | N823ES | N545ES | N824ES | | |
| 0067 | N26499 | N594JB | N525TF | | | | | |
| 0068 | N2650V | N68CJ | N303LC | N888KU | | | | |
| 0069 | N26502 | N169CJ | N20FL | N20VL | | | | |
| 0070 | N26504 | (N70HW) | D-ISGW | | | | | |
| 0071 | N26509 | N940SW | | | | | | |
| 0072 | N2651R | (TG-FIL) | TG-RIF | | | | | |
| 0073 | N2656G | (D-IHEB) | N77794 | | | | | |

# CITATIONJET

| C/n | Identities | | | | | | | | |
|---|---|---|---|---|---|---|---|---|---|
| 0074 | N26581 | N511TC | | | | | | | |
| 0075 | N5076K | N719L | N719D | N775TB | | | | | |
| 0076 | N5079V | N80TF | N4TF | N805VC | | | | | |
| 0077 | N50820 | N1000E | | | | | | | |
| 0078 | N5085E | N525CH | | | | | | | |
| 0079 | N5086W | N179CJ | N525WB | | | | | | |
| 0080 | N5090A | N80CJ | N33DT | | | | | | |
| 0081 | N5090V | N181JT | N525HA | | | | | | |
| 0082 | N5090Y | D-IHHS | N525LW | | | | | | |
| 0083 | N5091J | N34TC | (N121CP) | (N421CP) | (N50PL) | | | | |
| 0084 | (N5092D) | D-ITSV | G-CITJ | | | | | | |
| 0085 | N5093D | VR-CDN | PT-MJC | | | | | | |
| 0086 | (N5093L) | PT-MIL | | | | | | | |
| 0087 | (N5093Y) | N175PS | (N717DA) | N926CH | N100CH | N100CQ | N606HC | | |
| 0088 | (N50938) | N188CJ | N722SG | | | | | | |
| 0089 | N5135K | N189CJ | N920MS | N202BG | EC-KSB | | | | |
| 0090 | N5136J | N8288R | (N525KF) | LZ-DIN | | | | | |
| 0091 | N5138F | N295DS | | | | | | | |
| 0092 | N51396 | N525AS | N523AS | N534TX | (N534LL) | N801PJ | | | |
| 0093 | N5151S | I-IDAG | N525CM | | | | | | |
| 0094 | (N51522) | N94MZ | | | | | | | |
| 0095 | N5153K | N61SH | | | | | | | |
| 0096 | N5153X | (EC-...) | D-ICEE | | | | | | |
| 0097 | (N5153Z) | N234WS | N130MR | [w/o 26Mar00 nr Buda, TX; to White Inds, Bates City, MO for spares] | | | | | |
| 0098 | N5156D | N511AC | | | | | | | |
| 0099 | N5156V | N525SC | N525CP | N526CP | | | | | |
| 0100 | N51564 | N525CC | (N808HS) | N800HS | VH-CIT | VH-KXL | | | |
| 0101 | (N5157E) | F-GPFC | OM-OPR | | | | | | |
| 0102 | N52038 | N202CJ | TC-CRO | LX-LOV | HB-VWP* | | | | |
| 0103 | N5204D | (N203CJ) | D-IVHA | OE-FLG | | | | | |
| 0104 | N5207A | N606MM | N608MM | | | | | | |
| 0105 | N52081 | N305CJ | (D-IAFD) | G-EDCJ | | | | | |
| 0106 | N5211A | N21VC | (N444H) | | | | | | |
| 0107 | N5211F | N525WC | | | | | | | |
| 0108 | N5211Q | N108CJ | | | | | | | |
| 0109 | N52113 | N37DG | N393N | C-GDWS | | | | | |
| 0110 | N5213S | N195ME | | | | | | | |
| 0111 | N52136 | N776DF | | | | | | | |
| 0112 | N5214J | N1006F | VT-OPJ | | | | | | |
| 0113 | N5214K | N111AM | G-SEAJ | | | | | | |
| 0114 | N5214L | N96GM | N294CW | (N215LX) | | | | | |
| 0115 | N52141 | OO-PHI | | | | | | | |
| 0116 | N5201M | N41EB | N216CW | (N202LX) | N323JA | | | | |
| 0117 | N5203J | N217CJ | (N349CB) | N26CB | N26QB | | | | |
| 0118 | N5203S | N52178 | (N61TF) | N118AZ | D-IRWR | | | | |
| 0119 | (N5264E) | N47TH | N466F | PT-FBM | | | | | |
| 0120 | N5264M | PT-WGD | (N665AJ) | N525CZ | PR-VGD | | | | |
| 0121 | N5264S | TC-EMA | D-ICSS | | | | | | |
| 0122 | N5264U | N102AF | N41YP | | | | | | |
| 0123 | (N52642) | N5223P | D-IRKE | | | | | | |
| 0124 | N5090A | N525JH | VP-CWW | (ZS-BSS) | OE-FRR | | | | |
| 0125 | N5090V | N525PE | N525PT | | | | | | |
| 0126 | N5090Y | N1264V | N14TV | D-IFUP | VP-CFP | D-IHGW | D-IMPC | D-IAHG | |
| 0127 | N5091J | N127CJ | N63LB | N63LF | | | | | |
| 0128 | N5092D | N535LR | | | | | | | |
| 0129 | N5093D | N52642 | N229CJ | C-GPOS | | | | | |
| 0130 | N5093L | N416KC | N418KC | | | | | | |
| 0131 | N5093Y | (N577SD) | N577SV | N281CW | (N203LX) | N800AJ | N41EA | | |
| 0132 | N50938 | N132AH | (N132RP) | | | | | | |
| 0133 | N52038 | EC-261 | EC-GIE | | | | | | |
| 0134 | N5204B | N234CJ | N525JM | (N525TL) | | | | | |
| 0135 | N5207A | N888RA | | | | | | | |
| 0136 | N52081 | N525KL | [w/o 09Dec99 Branson-Point Lookout, MO] | | | | | | |
| 0137 | N5211A | N810SS | (N525SE) | | | | | | |
| 0138 | N5211F | VH-MOJ | VH-DAA | | | | | | |
| 0139 | N52457 | N76AE | N36RG | | | | | | |
| 0140 | N5246Z | N725L | N111BF | | | | | | |
| 0141 | N5250E | N774CA | N237DG | N525TA | N525JJ | N725CF | N545RW | | |
| 0142 | N5068R | N815MC | N5068R | N815MC | | | | | |
| 0143 | N51993 | D-IOMP | D-IALL | EC-KJV | | | | | |
| 0144 | N5200R | D-IDAG | | | | | | | |
| 0145 | N52141 | N145CJ | N424TV | | | | | | |
| 0146 | N5100J | N1329G | (OE-FGG) | | | | | | |
| 0147 | N52178 | N996JR | [w/o 22Jul03 Penn Cove, WA] | | | | | | |
| 0148 | N52144 | N148CJ | XB-ATH | N300DL | | | | | |
| 0149 | N5218R | N67GH | (N57GH) | (N67GU) | N77215 | [w/o 12 Jan07 Van Nuys, CA] | | | |
| 0150 | N5090V | ZS-NUW | N8341C | | | | | | |
| 0151 | N5086W | N1015B | 9A-CGH | (9A-CAD) | (N151TT) | N7EN | N400RL | N28DM | N242GB |

## CITATIONJET

| C/n | Identities | | | | | | | |
|---|---|---|---|---|---|---|---|---|
| 0152 | N5112K | N152KC | N152KV | | | | | |
| 0153 | N5090V | N551G | N551Q | (N525EF) | VP-CNF | G-PWNS | | |
| 0154 | N51246 | N401LG | N401EG | N254CW | (N204LX) | N520DF | | |
| 0155 | N5132T | N155CJ | I-EDEM | | | | | |
| 0156 | N156ML | | | | | | | |
| 0157 | N51817 | N1115V | N57HC | N54HC | | | | |
| 0158 | N5093D | N749CP | N800RL | N800RK | | | | |
| 0159 | N51872 | N131RG | N351BC | | | | | |
| 0160 | N5076J | N66AM | | | | | | |
| 0161 | N5076K | N525BT | (N39GA) | | | | | |
| 0162 | N5122X | N1XT | N525JW | (N39GA) | | | | |
| 0163 | N5138F | N51CD | VH-CDG | | | | | |
| 0164 | N51444 | D-ICGT | N204J | | | | | |
| 0165 | N5148B | D-IJYP | (OY-FCE) | D-IHCW | N525P | | | |
| 0166 | N5148N | N343PJ | F-GRRM | N252JK | | | | |
| 0167 | N5151S | (N4EF) | N1EF | N525RA | | | | |
| 0168 | N51522 | D-IRON | | | | | | |
| 0169 | N5153K | N68CJ | N230LL | | | | | |
| 0170 | N5153X | N170BG | N170MU | | | | | |
| 0171 | N5153Z | N97VF | | | | | | |
| 0172 | N5156B | N172CJ | D-IAVB | N350GM | VP-CTA | D-IFUP | OO-CEJ | |
| 0173 | N51564 | N970SU | N129RP | | | | | |
| 0174 | N5157E | N817CJ | N417C | (N417Q) | N66BE | | | |
| 0175 | N175CP | N41PG | | | | | | |
| 0176 | N5161J | PT-WLX | [w/o 16Sep05 Rio de Janeiro-Santos Dumont, Brazil] | | | | | |
| 0177 | N5163C | N1280A | (RP-C717) | G-OCSB | G-OWRC | F-HASC | OE-FWM | |
| 0178 | N525RC | | | | | | | |
| 0179 | N5166U | N377GS | N877GS | N608DB | | | | |
| 0180 | N5168F | N123AV | (N133AV) | VP-BDS | | | | |
| 0181 | N5180K | N181CJ | N88LD | SE-RIO | | | | |
| 0182 | N5183U | (N740JB) | N177JB | N177JF | | | | |
| 0183 | N5185J | (N97CJ) | N399G | | | | | |
| 0184 | N5185V | N525J | | | | | | |
| 0185 | N5187B | N51176 | N1241N | (RP-C8288) | | N83TR | N13FH | PR-HAP |
| 0186 | N51246 | N186CJ | N92ND | | | | | |
| 0187 | N5130J | N696ST | | | | | | |
| 0188 | N51342 | (D-IVID) | D-IVIN | OE-FMA | | | | |
| 0189 | N189CM | | | | | | | |
| 0190 | N51396 | N41NK | N701TF | N708TF | N701TP | N79MX | | |
| 0191 | N5145P | N525BF | (N525BL) | C-FIMA | N15LV | PR-CLB* | | |
| 0192 | N51444 | N84FG | | | | | | |
| 0193 | N5132T | N193CJ | D-ILCB | HB-VOX | D-IPOD | | | |
| 0194 | N5148B | N81RA | (N194VP) | I-DEAC | | | | |
| 0195 | N5138F | N525DC | (N525ST) | | | | | |
| 0196 | N5135A | D-IURH | N250GM | N525LP | | | | |
| 0197 | N5151S | N525KH | EC-HIN | | | | | |
| 0198 | N51522 | N315MR | N198RG* | | | | | |
| 0199 | N5153K | N1216K | 9A-CAD | N524AF | N525DY | N299CW | (N205LX) | |
| 0200 | N5153Z | N1276J | N226B | | | | | |
| 0201 | N5156D | N525HV | | | | | | |
| 0202 | N5120U | N202CJ | N747AC | | | | | |
| 0203 | N5122X | N525GP | N33FW | | | | | |
| 0204 | N5133E | N1293G | (N323LM) | B-4108 | B-7027 | | | |
| 0205 | N5156V | N550MC | N275CW | N206LX | (N205NP) | N525DU | | |
| 0206 | N5136J | N17VB | (N45PF) | | | | | |
| 0207 | N51872 | N31SG | N26RL | | | | | |
| 0208 | N5153X | N208JV | N211GM | | | | | |
| 0209 | N5162W | D-ILAT | | | | | | |
| 0210 | N5157E | N210CJ | N999EB | XA-CAH | N28CK | | | |
| 0211 | D-IMMD | | | | | | | |
| 0212 | N51176 | N67VW | N800NB | | | | | |
| 0213 | N5168F | N525WM | N486TT | | | | | |
| 0214 | N51743 | D-IFAN | N130NM | N130LM | | | | |
| 0215 | N5166U | N28GA | N28QA | | | | | |
| 0216 | N5183V | N18GA | N18QA | | | | | |
| 0217 | N5202D | (5Y-TCI) | D-IEWS | OE-FMT | | | | |
| 0218 | N51881 | N64LF | N288CW | (N207LX) | N713SD | | | |
| 0219 | N5197A | N219CJ | | | | | | |
| 0220 | N220CJ | C-GHPP | N25MX | PR-HIP | | | | |
| 0221 | N5203S | D-IWIL | | | | | | |
| 0222 | N52038 | N111LR | [w/o 04Apr98 Roswell, GA] | | | | | |
| 0223 | N5211Q | D-IGAS | OY-INV | OM-HLZ | | | | |
| 0224 | N52038 | N224CJ | | | | | | |
| 0225 | N5211F | N525RM | | | | | | |
| 0226 | N5214J | N1216N | TC-LIM | OE-FSS | | | | |
| 0227 | N5214K | N741CC | | | | | | |
| 0228 | N5216A | N668VP | N668VB | N669DB | N525CP | | | |
| 0229 | N5218R | D-IHOL | LX-TRA | LX-FOX | F-GXRK | | | |

## CITATIONJET

| C/n | Identities | | | | | | |
|---|---|---|---|---|---|---|---|
| 0230 | N5218T | N323LM | N934AM | (N904AM) | | | |
| 0231 | N5223D | N606JR | N606MG | [also wears fake USAF serial 97-0231] | | | |
| 0232 | N5223Y | N525PF | N525PB | N525GB | C-GABE | | |
| 0233 | N5235G | N233CJ | N53CG | PR-CAN | | | |
| 0234 | N900P | N950P | (N91GH) | | | | |
| 0235 | N5246Z | VP-BZZ | I-ESAI | LX-GCA | F-HIVA | | |
| 0236 | D-ISWA | | | | | | |
| 0237 | N237CJ | N61YP | | | | | |
| 0238 | N5203S | PT-WQI | | | | | |
| 0239 | N5188N | (PT-WQJ) | PT-XJS | N525VG | | | |
| 0240 | N525GM | N524SF | | | | | |
| 0241 | N52081 | N241WS | N207BS | N209BS | N110FD | N307BS | |
| 0242 | N242LJ | (N27FB) | | | | | |
| 0243 | CC-PVJ | CC-CVO | CC-PVJ | CC-CVO | | | |
| 0244 | N66ES | N68BS | N525ET | | | | |
| 0245 | N5214J | N33CJ | G-SFCJ | | | | |
| 0246 | N525EC | N525WF | | | | | |
| 0247 | N533JF | (N538JF) | N247CW | (N208LX) | N241EP | N609SM | |
| 0248 | N248CJ | | | | | | |
| 0249 | N5214L | N909M | (N909F) | | | | |
| 0250 | N250CJ | HB-VMT | F-HMJC | OO-JDK | | | |
| 0251 | N50ET | N1JB | N86JB | N616BM | PR-DCE | | |
| 0252 | (N5223P) | N740JV | VP-CIS | N252RV | | | |
| 0253 | N5223P | N8940 | N894Q | N253CW | (N209LX) | | |
| 0254 | N5183V | OE-FGI | | | | | |
| 0255 | N514DS | | | | | | |
| 0256 | (N196DR) | N196HA | | | | | |
| 0257 | N9003 | N116DK | N26DK | N561BC | | | |
| 0258 | N5203J | N108CR | OY-SML | | | | |
| 0259 | N5235G | PT-MSP | | | | | |
| 0260 | N5197A | D-IGZA | N260AM | | | | |
| 0261 | N31HD | (N61CV) | | | | | |
| 0262 | N52457 | N262BK | | | | | |
| 0263 | N263CT | | | | | | |
| 0264 | (D-IKHV) | VP-CHV | EC-HBC | D-IPCS | | | |
| 0265 | N198JH | | | | | | |
| 0266 | N52081 | N266CJ | | | | | |
| 0267 | N5201J | PT-XMM | | | | | |
| 0268 | N850DG | | | | | | |
| 0269 | N5219T | N607DB | | | | | |
| 0270 | N5194J | N525HC | | | | | |
| 0271 | N860DD | N860DB | HB-VNK | G-OSOH | | | |
| 0272 | N4GA | N4QP | | | | | |
| 0273 | (N525HC) | N911NP | | | | | |
| 0274 | PT-XDB | | | | | | |
| 0275 | N700GW | N42AA | | | | | |
| 0276 | N800GW | N187MC | | | | | |
| 0277 | N277CJ | OY-JMC | | | | | |
| 0278 | N5145V | N1127K | N100SM | N901CJ | | | |
| 0279 | D-IGME | | | | | | |
| 0280 | N5151D | PT-XAC | | | | | |
| 0281 | N5154J | N1280S | N41NK | N500TL | N508TL | VH-APJ | |
| 0282 | N625PG | | | | | | |
| 0283 | N95BS | | | | | | |
| 0284 | N256JB | | | | | | |
| 0285 | N55PZ | N55PX | PR-SMJ | | | | |
| 0286 | N51666 | D-ICEY | D-INFS | | | | |
| 0287 | N73PM | C-GBPM | | | | | |
| 0288 | N288AG | RP-C525 | | | | | |
| 0289 | D-ISHW | | | | | | |
| 0290 | N808WA | | | | | | |
| 0291 | N51744 | F-GPLF | OE-FEM | | | | |
| 0292 | N117W | N171W | N525CU | OE-FCW | | | |
| 0293 | N1127K | [crash-landed in Romania 31Jan01 - status?] | | | | | |
| 0294 | N294AT | | | | | | |
| 0295 | N5209E | N295CM | (PT-MTU) | OE-FJU | YU-MTU | | |
| 0296 | N296DC | | | | | | |
| 0297 | N316MJ | VP-CAD | | | | | |
| 0298 | G-RSCJ | N55CJ | | | | | |
| 0299 | N525BE | N711BE | N711BX | | | | |
| 0300 | N300CQ | N881KS | | | | | |
| 0301 | N27CJ | N270J | N291CW | N915ST | | | |
| 0302 | N302CJ | N326B | | | | | |
| 0303 | N51612 | D-IMMI | | | | | |
| 0304 | N1128G | EC-HBX | N154RA | N525TX | (N444L) | N605HP | N525TX |
| 0305 | N826HS | | | | | | |
| 0306 | (N525BE) | N4RH | N525DY | | | | |
| 0307 | N114FW | (N114FG) | | | | | |

## CITATIONJET/CJ1

| C/n | Identities | | | | | |
|---|---|---|---|---|---|---|
| 0308 | N72SG | N525DR | N373AF | | | |
| 0309 | D-IBMS | EC-LCM | | | | |
| 0310 | D-IVBG | D-IIJS | OK-SLA | | | |
| 0311 | N523BT | N270J | N27CJ | | | |
| 0312 | F-GTMD | CN-TLB | | | | |
| 0313 | N525MP | N525MR | N525MF | | | |
| 0314 | N5154J | N428PC | N525DM | | | |
| 0315 | (D-IIRR) | D-IAME | S5-BAY | OE-FMI | | |
| 0316 | N5136J | N187DL | N316EJ | N458MT | | |
| 0317 | N51444 | N317CJ | N51GS | | | |
| 0318 | N5145P | N525DP | | | | |
| 0319 | N5148N | PT-FNP | | | | |
| 0320 | N150BV | | | | | |
| 0321 | D-IAAS | PH-ECI | | | | |
| 0322 | N52LT | LX-YSL | F-HCPB | | | |
| 0323 | N900GW | | | | | |
| 0324 | (N428PC) | N5163C | G-IUAN | | | |
| 0325 | N464C | N764C | N115BB | | | |
| 0326 | N5183U | N23KG | N226CW | (N211LX) | N188TW | |
| 0327 | N398EP | LV-AXN | | | | |
| 0328 | N328CJ | | | | | |
| 0329 | XA-DGP | XB-DGA | | | | |
| 0330 | N5153K | N330CJ | N331MS | N38SC | | |
| 0331 | N888RK | N9UG | PH-KOM | OE-FGK | | |
| 0332 | N5161J | OO-FNL | (N332VP) | N511BP | | |
| 0333 | N5185J | N99CJ | | | | |
| 0334 | N51872 | N44FE | N525M | | | |
| 0335 | N5156D | N335CJ | N335CT | N467F | | |
| 0336 | N51564 | N105P | | | | |
| 0337 | N5241Z | PT-FJA | | | | |
| 0338 | N51575 | N525RL | N977DM | N907DK | | |
| 0339 | N5225K | N339B | N239CW | (N212LX) | N841TC | |
| 0340 | N5165T | N392RG | | | | |
| 0341 | N341AR | | | | | |
| 0342 | N5216A | N342AC | N918OK | N918CW | N49TH | |
| 0343 | N5244F | D-IURS | | | | |
| 0344 | N77VR | N77VZ | | | | |
| 0345 | N5185V | G-ZIZI | | | | |
| 0346 | N5153J | N5136J | PP-CRS | | | |
| 0347 | N5145P | N1133G | I-DAGF | | | |
| 0348 | N348KH | N248CW | (N213LX) | N8288R | | |
| 0349 | D-ICWB | | | | | |
| 0350 | N51444 | HP-1410HT | HP-1410 | N1348T | N1848T | N720GM |
| 0351 | N5246Z | VP-BRJ | LX-SUP | F-HGOL | OK-DSJ | |
| 0352 | N5185V | N99JB | N31JB | N573CM | | |
| 0353 | N5211Q | D-ICOL | LN-FDB* | | | |
| 0354 | N5225K | N821P | (D-IMMP) | OE-FCA | I-CABD | |
| 0355 | N51396 | N205FH | N312SB | N312SE | N525TK | |
| 0356 | N5213S | PP-YOF | | | | |
| 0357 | N5214J | N357JV | N194MG | | | |
| 0358 | N51564 | G-HMMV | M-PARK | | | |
| 0359 | F-GTRY | | | | | |

## CJ1

| C/n | Identities | | | | |
|---|---|---|---|---|---|
| 0360 | N5156D | N31CJ | N525CD | | |
| 0361 | N5183U | N361RB | N128CS | | |
| 0362 | N5214L | N362CJ | N362PE | N362FL | |
| 0363 | N5161J | N525AS | N523TS | | |
| 0364 | N5211F | N525DL | N525DE | C-FTKX | VP-CHE |
| 0365 | N5130J | N651CJ | | | |
| 0366 | N5223Y | D-IRMA | N850GM | D-IRMA | |
| 0367 | N51872 | N525MD | N525FT | (N525CY) | |
| 0368 | N5185J | N820CE | N525FN | | |
| 0369 | N5200U | N629DM | N161SM | | |
| 0370 | N5145P | N525MW | | | |
| 0371 | N5165T | N175SB | HZ-BL1 | | |
| 0372 | N372CP | N345MG | | | |
| 0374 | N12GS | N12GY | | | |
| 0373 | N415CS | | | | |
| 0375 | N5225K | N375KH | HB-VNL | | |
| 0376 | N52352 | N802JH | C-GTRG | N814DM | |
| 0377 | N5241Z | N15C | N900BT | | |
| 0378 | N5135K | N525CP | N203BG | | |
| 0379 | N5188A | I-IMMI | | | |
| 0380 | N5228Z | N381CJ | N525GB | N83DC | B-3669 |
| 0381 | N5185J | N856BB | (N476JD) | | |
| 0382 | N5124F | N525LF | | | |

## CJ1

| C/n | Identities | | | | | | |
|---|---|---|---|---|---|---|---|
| 0383 | N5231S | N600AL | | | | | |
| 0384 | N5148B | PP-JET | | | | | |
| 0385 | N5136J | N1326P | N417C | N417Q | | | |
| 0386 | N51993 | N45MH | N386RF | | | | |
| 0387 | N51564 | N7715X | N7715Y | N724FS | N33SW | | |
| 0388 | N5162W | N525MH | N525LB | N520GB | | | |
| 0389 | N5156D | N389CJ | D-IDAS | D-IDAZ | | | |
| 0390 | N51396 | N100PF | | | | | |
| 0391 | N5130J | LX-IIH | | | | | |
| 0392 | N5165T | N392SM | | | | | |
| 0393 | D-IBIT | OM-HLY | | | | | |
| 0394 | N5132T | N64PM | N64PZ | S5-BAJ | | | |
| 0395 | N5183U | (N525AJ) | N525AR | N507HP | | | |
| 0396 | N51575 | D-IMAC | | | | | |
| 0397 | N5163C | I-RVRP | | | | | |
| 0398 | N5183V | N398CJ | C-GMTI | | | | |
| 0399 | N5135A | (VP-CTN) | D-ITAN | | | | |
| 0400 | N5120U | (C-GPWM) | N525EZ | N526EZ | (N88798) | F-GMDL | |
| 0401 | N51246 | D-IFFI | N142EA | N44CK | | | |
| 0402 | N525ML | | | | | | |
| 0403 | N51817 | PT-PRR | | | | | |
| 0404 | N5145P | N88AD | (N746JB) | | | | |
| 0405 | N5125J | N121EB | N7895Q | | | | |
| 0406 | N5124F | N72JW | | | | | |
| 0407 | N51872 | N525JL | | | | | |
| 0408 | N5156D | N408GR | PP-JBS | | | | |
| 0409 | N5212M | N657RB | (N334DB) | N530AG | N530AQ | N525BW | |
| 0410 | N52144 | N4108E | | | | | |
| 0411 | N51575 | N525RF | N535RF | D-ILIF | | | |
| 0412 | N5161J | N82AE | | | | | |
| 0413 | N5185J | N525RK | | | | | |
| 0414 | N5223P | N726TM | N26DV* | | | | |
| 0415 | N5250E | N26SW | EC-ISS | D-IUWE | HB-VOD | | |
| 0416 | N80C | N8UC | N186TW | | | | |
| 0417 | N5203B | D-IEAI | PH-SOL | | | | |
| 0418 | N51444 | N300BV | | | | | |
| 0419 | N7NE | N7XE | | | | | |
| 0420 | N5183U | N96SK | N86SK | N726CL | | | |
| 0421 | D-ILME | OE-FET | | | | | |
| 0422 | N51881 | N125DJ | N927CC | | | | |
| 0423 | N5201J | N62SH | N292SG | G-OEBJ | G-ORAN | F-HFMA | |
| 0424 | N5231S | N28SW | N711WG | | | | |
| 0425 | N5188A | N335J | C-FWBK | | | | |
| 0426 | N5197A | N426ED | | | | | |
| 0427 | N5202D | N128GW | N525LM | | | | |
| 0428 | N5203J | PR-ABV | | | | | |
| 0429 | N429PK | EC-IVJ | | | | | |
| 0430 | N52081 | N430GR | | | | | |
| 0431 | N51993 | N431YD | ZS-PWU | | | | |
| 0432 | N51342 | N94AL | | | | | |
| 0433 | N5223D | N102PT | [w/o 01Feb08 nr Augusta, ME] | | | | |
| 0434 | N5226B | N860DD | N860DB | | | | |
| 0435 | N5244F | N525AD | G-CJAD | | | | |
| 0436 | N5141F | EC-HVQ | | | | | |
| 0437 | N5185V | N717NA | G-HEBJ | | | | |
| 0438 | N51942 | N103CS | N325DM | N525RY | | | |
| 0439 | N5200Z | N395SD | N54CG | | | | |
| 0440 | N5233J | C-GPWM | N440CJ | N525NT | (N525JT) | | |
| 0441 | N5200R | PR-ARA | | | | | |
| 0442 | N5187Z | D-IFIS | D-ILLY | | | | |
| 0443 | N5136J | N443CJ | N77DB | | | | |
| 0444 | N52136 | N525BR | (N525WS) | | | | |
| 0445 | N445CJ | N207BS | | | | | |
| 0446 | N5211A | N246GS | | | | | |
| 0447 | N5120U | N116CS | N952SP | N525LE | | | |
| 0448 | N448JC | EC-JFD | N448EA | F-GMMC | | | |
| 0449 | N5153K | N1259Y | (JA-001T) | JA525A | | | |
| 0450 | N5156D | I-BOAT | | | | | |
| 0451 | N5135A | N165CA | | | | | |
| 0452 | N52178 | N107GM | (N107PK) | N585PK | N585MC | | |
| 0453 | N5211Q | N103CS | N80VP | N902RD | N929VC | N928VC | N869CB |
| 0454 | N5225K | N541CJ | N101U | | | | |
| 0455 | N5183V | N75FC | (N15SS) | N900TW* | | | |
| 0456 | N5185J | PR-LJM | | | | | |
| 0457 | N118CS | N774GE | | | | | |
| 0458 | N5188A | LX-MSP | N525NP | PR-BJM | | | |
| 0459 | N459NA | | | | | | |
| 0460 | N5185V | D-IMMM | [rebuilt after accident 12Mar04 Florence, Italy] | | | | N57EC |

## CJ1

| C/n | Identities | | | | | |
|---|---|---|---|---|---|---|
| 0461 | N5207A | N200SL | | | | |
| 0462 | N5197A | N965LC | | | | |
| 0463 | N5200U | N1284D | Chile 361 | | | |
| 0464 | N1284P | Chile 362 | | | | |
| 0465 | N1285P | Chile 363 | | | | |
| 0466 | N5200Z | N119CS | D-INCS | | | |
| 0467 | N5157E | N620BB | | | | |
| 0468 | N468RW | | | | | |
| 0469 | N52038 | N122CS | N520RM | | | |
| 0470 | N901GW | | | | | |
| 0471 | N768R | N471CJ | B-3668 | | | |
| 0472 | N124CS | N525KM | | | | |
| 0473 | N5201M | LX-MRC | HB-VOR | F-HJAV | | |
| 0474 | N31CJ | | | | | |
| 0475 | N52113 | N475CJ | XA-TTG | | | |
| 0476 | N476CJ | N50ET | N74PG | D-IRSB | | |
| 0477 | N5216A | D-INOC | D-IDIG | OE-FOI | | |
| 0478 | N5233J | N869GR | | | | |
| 0479 | N5200R | N525BP | | | | |
| 0480 | N5223Y | N888SF | (N66FH) | OE-FIX | N103SK | OE-FIX |
| 0481 | N5204D | N4DF | N795BM | | | |
| 0482 | N5211Q | PR-EXP | | | | |
| 0483 | N5250E | PR-EOB | | | | |
| 0484 | N5211F | N484CJ | F-HALO | | | |
| 0485 | N52136 | N674JM | N672JM | | | |
| 0486 | N5211A | N334BD | EC-JIU | | | |
| 0487 | N5200U | N243LS | CC-CMS | N191PP | PP-LJR | |
| 0488 | N5218R | N525WH | N488SR | | | |
| 0489 | N5218T | N489ED | N489CB | | | |
| 0490 | N52141 | N130CS | (N130MH) | N120CS | | |
| 0491 | N5244F | N491CJ | N491LT | N926CC | | |
| 0492 | N5226B | N492CJ | N888PS | N888PY | | |
| 0493 | N5203J | N65CK | N95CK | (N220JM) | (N315N) | |
| 0494 | N71HR | D-ITIP | | | | |
| 0495 | N5246Z | OY-RGG | OO-STE | | | |
| 0496 | N5223P | N382EM | | | | |
| 0497 | N5235G | N132CS | N525JJ | | | |
| 0498 | N5223K | N498YY | N5201J | N498YY | | |
| 0499 | N5200Z | HB-VNP | | | | |
| 0500 | N525CJ | N111GJ | | | | |
| 0501 | (N501CJ) | N41LF | | | | |
| 0502 | N51881 | N133CS | SE-RGX | | | |
| 0503 | N904DP | N909DP | N818ER* | | | |
| 0504 | N52081 | N665CH | | | | |
| 0505 | N502TN | (F-HBSC) | | | | |
| 0506 | N242ML | | | | | |
| 0507 | N5263U | Chile 364 | | | | |
| 0508 | N5225K | N508CJ | EC-JSH | F-HBSC | | |
| 0509 | N993GL | | | | | |
| 0510 | N5058J | N1DM | N971DM | (N278CA) | G-EDCK | |
| 0511 | N5212M | ZK-TBM | N326JK | | | |
| 0512 | N411MY | LN-FDC* | | | | |
| 0513 | N52591 | N513RV | (N439PW) | | | |
| 0514 | N52136 | N514RV | PH-FIS | | | |
| 0515 | N52141 | N132CS | N551FP | | | |
| 0516 | N5060K | EC-IRB | N525CF | D-INER | | |
| 0517 | N52626 | D-IFDH | | | | |
| 0518 | D-ILLL | D-IETZ | F-HAGH | | | |
| 0519 | N926TF | D-IAMF | | | | |
| 0520 | N135CS | N520CJ | | | | |
| 0521 | N5066U | N521CJ | VH-ANE | VH-YNE | | |
| 0522 | N138CS | N125CS | (N525BA) | | | |
| 0523 | N51246 | F-HAJD | | | | |
| 0524 | N5202D | N524CJ | N759R | N770BX | N3WB | |
| 0525 | N123S | | | | | |
| 0526 | N5163C | (SP-KCL) | N526LC | SP-KCL | VP-CJI | |
| 0527 | N5211Q | N527CJ | N15BV | N358K | | |
| 0528 | N50612 | N528CJ | G-GEBJ | M-DINO | | |
| 0529 | N50820 | N151CS | N151EW | | | |
| 0530 | N5244F | N430JH | | | | |
| 0531 | N5211A | N333J | N525FC | | | |
| 0532 | N32BG | N323G | | | | |
| 0533 | N5180K | (D-IPMM) | D-IPMI | | | |
| 0534 | N52113 | N1269B | JA100C | N534NA | | |
| 0535 | N5090A | N535CJ | JA525Y | | | |
| 0536 | N52369 | [re-serialled 525-0600 q.v] | | | | |
| 0537 | N5261R | N837AC | N839AC | N678RF | | |
| 0538 | N51564 | N525AM | | | | |

# CJ1/CJ1+

| C/n | Identities | | | | |
|---|---|---|---|---|---|
| 0539 | N152CS | OE-FRF | | | |
| 0540 | N5172M | N40CJ | | | |
| 0541 | N458SM | N739LN | | | |
| 0542 | N5125J | N500CW | PR-MFJ | | |
| 0543 | N5200U | N43NW | | | |
| 0544 | OE-FUJ | HB-VOG | | | |
| 0545 | N545TG | | | | |
| 0546 | N5188N | N981LB | | | |
| 0547 | N5211Q | N547ST | N547TW | | |
| 0548 | N5216A | N153CS | N257MV | | |
| 0549 | N51995 | N549CJ | JA525J | | |
| 0550 | N5112K | N1288P | SP-KKA | | |
| 0551 | N5105F | N1279A | B-3644 | | |
| 0552 | N51564 | N1279V | B-3645 | | |
| 0553 | N51612 | N902GW | | | |
| 0554 | N5157E | N1290N | B-3647 | | |
| 0555 | N5214L | N1287B | B-3648 | | |
| 0556 | N93LS | | | | |
| 0557 | N5250E | N1287F | B-3649 | | |
| 0558 | N51993 | N1288N | B-3650 | | |

## CJ1+

| | | | | | |
|---|---|---|---|---|---|
| 0600 | N525AD | (N55KT) | N919MC | [built from 525-0536; ff 08Oct04; received FAA type certificate 20Jun05] | |
| 0601 | N52626 | N601CJ | N29ET | | |
| 0602 | N5248V | N602CJ | N46JV | N74UK | D-ISJM |
| 0603 | N51143 | N805CJ | | | |
| 0604 | N5183U | N122LM | | | |
| 0605 | N5188A | N800PF | | | |
| 0606 | N51896 | N713WH | | | |
| 0607 | N5218T | N59JN | N58JN | | |
| 0608 | N52229 | N970RP | N4017L | N915RP | |
| 0609 | N5161J | N50VC | M-TEAM | | |
| 0610 | N51817 | N35TK | | | |
| 0611 | N52645 | D-ICEY | | | |
| 0612 | N5155G | N525RZ | | | |
| 0613 | N5112K | N1309V | PH-CMW | | |
| 0614 | N51564 | (OE-FMU) | D-IMMG | OE-FMD | |
| 0615 | N5095N | N65EM | | | |
| 0616 | N999EB | | | | |
| 0617 | N18TG | N1TG | N116LJ | D-IWPS | |
| 0618 | N618KA | | | | |
| 0619 | N1317Y | VT-NAB | | | |
| 0620 | N620CJ | N5UD | | | |
| 0621 | N52475 | N621AD | | | |
| 0622 | N5270K | N622SL | | | |
| 0623 | N5124F | HB-VOF | | | |
| 0624 | N5141F | D-IOWA | | | |
| 0625 | N5236L | N625CJ | (VH-ODJ) | D-IEPR | |
| 0626 | N5117U | N626CV | | | |
| 0627 | N5264N | N627MW | | | |
| 0628 | N52433 | T7-FRA | | | |
| 0629 | N56KP | | | | |
| 0630 | N50054 | N711C | | | |
| 0631 | N5206T | YV2331 | | | |
| 0632 | N50715 | N1314H | CC-PGK | CC-CSA | JY-AWF |
| 0633 | N5163K | (N28FM) | N43BH | | |
| 0634 | N5196U | N634CJ | OE-FSR | | |
| 0635 | N5241R | (N525JN) | N817BT | | |
| 0636 | N5066U | C-GTRG | N636VP | LN-FDA* | |
| 0637 | N51993 | N637CJ | N779RB | C-GWGZ | |
| 0638 | N51342 | VH-MYE | | | |
| 0639 | N5201M | (D-ICPO) | D-IMPC | | |
| 0640 | N5076L | N34DZ | | | |
| 0641 | N5214K | C-GIRL | | | |
| 0642 | N5151D | N466AE | | | |
| 0643 | N5228Z | N380CR | | | |
| 0644 | N50321 | N902DP | EC-LDE | | |
| 0645 | OE-FPO | | | | |
| 0646 | N5154J | A7-CJI | N646VP | | |
| 0647 | N1895C | | | | |
| 0648 | N5152X | G-CJDB | | | |
| 0649 | N51806 | N794PF | | | |
| 0650 | N51511 | HB-VWF | | | |
| 0651 | N5267D | N24BC | | | |
| 0652 | N5148B | N41159 | RA-67705 | | |
| 0653 | N52526 | N7715X | | | |

# CJ1+

| C/n | Identities | | | | |
|---|---|---|---|---|---|
| 0654 | N52691 | N94HL | | | |
| 0655 | N51612 | N1367D | B-7777 | | |
| 0656 | N5069E | N388FW | | | |
| 0657 | "N52594"+ | [+test marks as quoted, but already in use on a Cessna 182] | | | N65BK |
| 0658 | N907WL | | | | |
| 0659 | N5266F | N659CJ | OE-FNA | LZ-FNA | |
| 0660 | N5057F | N197RJ | PR-OUD | | |
| 0661 | N5244F | N613AL | LN-RYG | | |
| 0662 | N5267G | N607TN | | | |
| 0663 | N5244W | N297RJ | PR-GFS | | |
| 0664 | N664CJ | N88QC | | | |
| 0665 | N5037F | N665CJ | HB-VOV | | |
| 0666 | N5076K | N7277 | T9-SMS | E7-SMS | |
| 0667 | N5061P | N629DR | | | |
| 0668 | N52613 | N557HP | | | |
| 0669 | N5200R | N224BA | | | |
| 0670 | N5161J | VH-LDH | | | |
| 0671 | N5053R | N525AJ | SE-RIX | | |
| 0672 | N52071 | N858SD | | | |
| 0673 | N5241Z | N525AJ | | | |
| 0674 | N5061F | N4123S | N324BD | | |
| 0675 | N5270E | N41196 | (D-ILHA) | D-ILHB | |
| 0676 | N5120U | N903GW | | | |
| 0677 | N413CQ | | | | |
| 0678 | N5250E | N528CB | | | |
| 0679 | N5076K | N525GE | | | |
| 0680 | N5061P | N680KH | | | |
| 0681 | N5266F | N904GW | | | |
| 0682 | N5245U | N905GW | | | |
| 0683 | N5053R | N397RJ | | | |
| 0684 | N5207A | D-IAMS | | | |
| 0685 | N994JG | | | | |
| 0686 | N50549 | N980MB | HL8201 | | |
| 0687 | N687CJ | N535WT | | | |
| 0688 | N5270E | N2259D | HL8283 | | |
| 0689 | N5263D | N101LD | | | |
| 0690 | N52627 | HB-VWM | | | |
| 0691 | N4RH | N691CJ | HL8202 | | |
| 0692 | N929MM | | | | |
| 0693 | N5214K | CN-TJE | | | |
| 0694 | N52609 | (D-ILHB) | D-ILHD | | |
| 0695 | N5201M | D-ILHC | | | |
| 0696 | N51684 | (D-ILHD) | D-ILHA | | |
| 0697 | N5057F | N595DM | | | |
| 0698 | | | | | |
| 0699 | | | | | |
| 0700 | | | | | |
| 0701 | | | | | |
| 0702 | | | | | |
| 0703 | | | | | |
| 0704 | | | | | |
| 0705 | | | | | |
| 0706 | | | | | |
| 0707 | | | | | |
| 0708 | | | | | |
| 0709 | | | | | |
| 0710 | | | | | |
| 0711 | | | | | |
| 0712 | | | | | |
| 0713 | | | | | |
| 0714 | | | | | |
| 0715 | | | | | |
| 0716 | | | | | |
| 0717 | | | | | |
| 0718 | | | | | |
| 0719 | | | | | |
| 0720 | D-IBTI* | | | | |
| 0721 | | | | | |
| 0722 | | | | | |
| 0723 | | | | | |
| 0724 | | | | | |
| 0725 | | | | | |

Note: *In 1993-94, Cessna developed a military jet trainer from the Model 525 for the US JPATS contract evaluation. It was given the model number 526 and used many 525 parts, although the complete aircraft bore no actual resemblance to the CitationJet. For the record, two prototypes were built, N526JT c/n 704, ff 20Dec93, and N526JP c/n 705, ff 02Mar94.*

# CESSNA 525A CITATIONJET CJ2

| C/n | Identities | | | | | | |
|---|---|---|---|---|---|---|---|
| 708 | N2CJ | [ff 27Apr99 McConnell AFB, Wichita, KS - converted from original 525 prototype c/n 702 q.v.] | N244CJ | [test-bed for Williams FJ44-4A engine that will power the CJ4, ff 02Apr07] | | | |
| 0001 | N525AZ | N529PC | | | | | |
| 0002 | N5252 | N765CT | N400WD | | | | |
| 0003 | N5148N | N132CJ | N525DT | | | | |
| 0004 | N52136 | N142CJ | N200KP | N692JM | (N699JM) | N308GT | N7773A |
| 0005 | N5235G | N552CJ | N372CT | OY-LLA | I-LALL | | |
| 0006 | N5204D | (N411PB) | N411GC | N800WC | N256SP | | |
| 0007 | N5213S | N7CC | (N8CQ) | N525CC | | | |
| 0008 | N52141 | N900EB | N901EB | | | | |
| 0009 | N5235G | N525LC | F-HAPP | M-AJDM | | | |
| 0010 | N5194J | N121CP | | | | | |
| 0011 | N51881 | N567JP | OE-FLP | | | | |
| 0012 | N525MP | N525MA | | | | | |
| 0013 | N5201M | N4115Q | N8940 | N894C | (N177RE) | | |
| 0014 | N110MG | N110MQ | N18TF | | | | |
| 0015 | N125DG | N606XG | N629PA | F-HASF | | | |
| 0016 | N5207A | N306CJ | (N547AC) | | | | |
| 0017 | N5162W | N172CJ | HB-VOE | | | | |
| 0018 | N5148N | N96G | N96NJ | | | | |
| 0019 | N51942 | N57GH | N67GH | S5-BBB | F-GXRL | | |
| 0020 | N52141 | N904AM | N323LM | N823L | | | |
| 0021 | N525TG | [cx 16Sep09, status?] | | | | | |
| 0022 | N5165T | N217W | (N117W) | N630TF | | | |
| 0023 | N5135K | N525PF | | | | | |
| 0024 | N5216A | N525TJ | N915MP | | | | |
| 0025 | N51396 | N550T | N550TB | | | | |
| 0026 | N5203S | N126CJ | D-IMYA | D-IHAP | EK-52526 | | |
| 0027 | N5194J | N420CH | N420EH | | | | |
| 0028 | N5218T | (N592DR) | D-IBBB | N592DR | | | |
| 0029 | N5132T | N92CJ | D-IKJS | | | | |
| 0030 | N5223Y | N302DM | D-ISJP | | | | |
| 0031 | N5204D | N312CJ | VP-BFC | M-XONE | G-SONE | | |
| 0032 | N5250E | D-IOBU | D-IOBO | D-IGIT | | | |
| 0033 | N163PB | HB-VNO | (D-IETZ) | EC-JJU | | | |
| 0034 | N5211F | D-IJOA | | | | | |
| 0035 | N51564 | N288G | | | | | |
| 0036 | N5246Z | (D-IJOA) | D-IEVX | [w/o 08Oct01 Milan-Linate A/P, Italy] | | | |
| 0037 | N5221Y | N401LG | | | | | |
| 0038 | N5235G | I-IMMG | | | | | |
| 0039 | N5223P | N842HS | (N525L) | N900HA | | | |
| 0040 | N525HB | | | | | | |
| 0041 | N43ND | D-IHHN | | | | | |
| 0042 | N52352 | PR-JET | | | | | |
| 0043 | N52002 | N432CJ | D-IEKU | | | | |
| 0044 | N5241Z | PR-JST | | | | | |
| 0045 | N5214L | N3ST | | | | | |
| 0046 | N51246 | N40RL | N46JW | N46NT | | | |
| 0047 | N5148N | N2250G | | | | | |
| 0048 | N5183U | PT-FTC | | | | | |
| 0049 | N51575 | D-IEFD | OE-FHB | | | | |
| 0050 | N525DL | | | | | | |
| 0051 | N6M | (N606MM) | N6JR | N415SL | G-OCJZ | | |
| 0052 | N51881 | D-ISCH | | | | | |
| 0053 | N5194J | PT-FTE | | | | | |
| 0054 | N5161J | (EI-OPM) | D-IAAS | PH-ECL | OO-SKA | | |
| 0055 | N5163C | N207BS | N525ZZ | | | | |
| 0056 | N5202D | N743JG | | | | | |
| 0057 | N57EJ | [w/o 07Oct02 Plainville, CT; canx 08Mar05] | | | | | |
| 0058 | N52035 | N811RC | N525KT | | | | |
| 0059 | N59CJ | | | | | | |
| 0060 | N6877L | N57HC | N525RW | | | | |
| 0061 | N5214J | PR-TOP | | | | | |
| 0062 | N5125J | N30HD | | | | | |
| 0063 | N5135A | N263CJ | N5208F | VH-MOR | | | |
| 0064 | N513SK | EC-IEB | I-OMRA | | | | |
| 0065 | N5136J | N225EL | N225WW | N55KT | | | |
| 0066 | N51396 | N741PC | | | | | |
| 0067 | N5141F | N525PM | | | | | |
| 0068 | N51444 | N69FH | N69AH | N315MC | | | |
| 0069 | N51564 | N757CP | | | | | |
| 0070 | N5157E | D-ILAM | | | | | |
| 0071 | N51575 | N34RL | N701SF | | | | |
| 0072 | N5120U | N65PZ | (N65PX) | | | | |

# CJ2

| C/n | Identities | | | | |
|---|---|---|---|---|---|
| 0073 | N5165T | I-LVNB | | | |
| 0074 | N5125J | N222NF | | | |
| 0075 | N51246 | HP-1461 | N52AG | | |
| 0076 | N5156D | N1277E | | | |
| 0077 | N5148N | N377GS | | | |
| 0078 | N5162W | N113BG | | | |
| 0079 | N51872 | N117W | N717HA | | |
| 0080 | N5135K | N525EZ | N525TK | F-HEKO | |
| 0081 | N51342 | N414FW | | | |
| 0082 | N5183V | N282CJ | OE-FGL | | |
| 0083 | N975DM | N975DN | G-EDCL | | |
| 0084 | N525DG | N523DG | N512TB | | |
| 0085 | N5185J | N85JV | | | |
| 0086 | N5132T | N520JM | N759R | | |
| 0087 | N474PC | | | | |
| 0088 | N569DM | | | | |
| 0089 | OY-JET | [crashed into sea 15May05 off Atlantic City-Bader Field, NJ; repaired] | N525SA | | |
| | PR-WOB | | | | |
| 0090 | N475DH | | | | |
| 0091 | N8940 | N431MC | | | |
| 0092 | N21RA | | | | |
| 0093 | N5216A | N96SK | N93PE | N98PE | N954RM |
| 0094 | N942CJ | VH-RJB | | | |
| 0095 | N5221Y | I-DEUM | | | |
| 0096 | N5223D | N96CJ | JA525G | N96NA | |
| 0097 | N97CJ | | | | |
| 0098 | N5223Y | N57HG | N57HC | | |
| 0099 | N5223P | N444RH | N777HN | | |
| 0100 | N170TM | | | | |
| 0101 | N1255J | (N533JF) | N125BJ | | |
| 0102 | N888KL | D-IWIR | | | |
| 0103 | N5218R | N800VT | | | |
| 0104 | N80C | | | | |
| 0105 | N13M | N91A | | | |
| 0106 | N5148B | D-IUAC | OE-FUX | | |
| 0107 | N525WD | | | | |
| 0108 | N5136J | D-ICMS | | | |
| 0109 | N692JM | N301EL | N22LX | | |
| 0110 | N451AJ | | | | |
| 0111 | N219FL | N971TB | [w/o in hangar fire 12Sep07 Danbury, CT] | | |
| 0112 | N51575 | N525U | N701TF | N620GB | |
| 0113 | N525VV | G-OCJT | M-WMWM | | |
| 0114 | N726RP | | | | |
| 0115 | N115CJ | | | | |
| 0116 | N5233J | N711BE | N411BE | N46BE | |
| 0117 | N5214K | PT-FTG | | | |
| 0118 | N5163C | N464C | N971TB | | |
| 0119 | N525DV | | | | |
| 0120 | N5130J | N144EM | N220JD | N35CT | |
| 0121 | N121YD | N5YD | YV.... | | |
| 0122 | N5135A | N224WD | | | |
| 0123 | N5203S | N37BG | | | |
| 0124 | N27CJ | N523BT | | | |
| 0125 | N52038 | N125CE | N525CC | N525CG | D-IBJJ |
| 0126 | N534CJ | N999WE | VT-MON | | |
| 0127 | N5211A | N12GS | N112GS | | |
| 0128 | N5204D | N525CK | | | |
| 0129 | N129SG | | | | |
| 0130 | N51396 | N525JD | N550KR | | |
| 0131 | N51564 | N20GP | | | |
| 0132 | N5211F | N75PP | D-ITOP | | |
| 0133 | N251KD | | | | |
| 0134 | N323SK | | | | |
| 0135 | N5211Q | N4RP | (N114RP) | N70KW | |
| 0136 | N5141F | N345CJ | | | |
| 0137 | N717VB | | | | |
| 0138 | N722TS | | | | |
| 0139 | N5228Z | N526HV | | | |
| 0140 | N140DA | | | | |
| 0141 | N51872 | PT-FTR | N141JV | N6ZE | |
| 0142 | N5207A | OE-FPS | | | |
| 0143 | D-ISUN | | | | |
| 0144 | N144YD | | | | |
| 0145 | N7GZ | | | | |
| 0146 | N1220W | | | | |
| 0147 | N5188W | VP-BJR | D-IVVA | | |

# CJ2

| C/n | Identities | | | | |
|---|---|---|---|---|---|
| 0148 | N5132T | N148FB | | | |
| 0149 | N90CJ | | | | |
| 0150 | N525GM | OE-FRA | | | |
| 0151 | N122SM | D-ISCO | | | |
| 0152 | N123JW | N128JW | | | |
| 0153 | N5233P | N500SV | | | |
| 0154 | N5091J | N708GP | | | |
| 0155 | N5180C | N105PT | EC-KES | | |
| 0156 | N522KN | N256CJ | JA525B | | |
| 0157 | N5270E | N88KC | N913DC | | |
| 0158 | N158CJ | SP-KCK | | | |
| 0159 | N5026 | | | | |
| 0160 | N525KR | | | | |
| 0161 | N5100J | N28MH | N28NH | N525FF | |
| 0162 | N335JJ | | | | |
| 0163 | N5151D | ZS-CJT | VT-NJB | | |
| 0164 | N164CJ | OO-DDA | | | |
| 0165 | N5243K | N30AD | | | |
| 0166 | N5218R | D-IAMO | | | |
| 0167 | N51806 | D-ILDL | | | |
| 0168 | N767W | D-IHRA | JY-FMK | | |
| 0169 | N5262W | F-GPUJ | | | |
| 0170 | N915RJ | C6-LVU | N170VP | C6-EVU | VT-BJA |
| 0171 | N271CJ | (F-GPSS) | CC-CHE | | |
| 0172 | N179DV | N706TF | N525PB | | |
| 0173 | N525MR | | | | |
| 0174 | N5076K | D-IDMH | | | |
| 0175 | N525SM | | | | |
| 0176 | N100JS | N319R | OE-FYH | | |
| 0177 | N55KT | N25LZ | | | |
| 0178 | N52655 | N7715X | N80AX | N44FJ | |
| 0179 | N179FZ | OO-FLN | | | |
| 0180 | N604LJ | | | | |
| 0181 | N5218T | N93AK | N93AQ | N525CE | |
| 0182 | N777CJ | | | | |
| 0183 | N283CJ | N183TX | | | |
| 0184 | N357J | | | | |
| 0185 | N5257V | N65CK | N65CR | PR-TAP | |
| 0186 | N5247U | N350BV | | | |
| 0187 | N187MG | | | | |
| 0188 | N5138J | N188JR | N837AC | | |
| 0189 | N5124F | N777DY | | | |
| 0190 | N5141F | N680JB | G-OODM | | |
| 0191 | N776LB | G-TBEA | | | |
| 0192 | N688DB | (N688DP) | N193PP | | |
| 0193 | N5183U | D-IKAL | F-HAMG | | |
| 0194 | N806MN | N194SJ | | | |
| 0195 | N51942 | D-IMAX | | | |
| 0196 | N5166T | D-INOB | | | |
| 0197 | N197CJ | OO-SKY | | | |
| 0198 | N5162W | N57FL | | | |
| 0199 | N5152X | I-GOSF | LN-AVA | N248RF | |
| 0200 | N5203S | F-GZUJ | CS-DGQ | | |
| 0201 | N888GL | | | | |
| 0202 | N202CJ | N719WP | G-EEBJ | G-MROO | |
| 0203 | N736LB | OE-FSG | | | |
| 0204 | "N5188W"+ | [+ marks as quoted, already current at the time on a homebuilt] OE-FCY | | | |
| 0205 | N5241Z | N205YY | | | |
| 0206 | N29MR | OO-CIV | | | |
| 0207 | N5117U | N1267B | VT-JSP | | |
| 0208 | N400HT | | | | |
| 0209 | N5085E | OY-UCA | | | |
| 0210 | N5214K | N280DM | N28DM | OE-FCU | |
| 0211 | N515EV | | | | |
| 0212 | N5226B | N104PC | | | |
| 0213 | N5244W | N213CJ | (OE-FJR) | ES-LUX | G-EDCM |
| 0214 | N51511 | N1DM | N7QM | | |
| 0215 | N748RE | N748RF | | | |
| 0216 | N51246 | OY-GGR | EC-JMS | | |
| 0217 | N5211F | N67GH | | | |
| 0218 | D-IPVD | | | | |
| 0219 | N5247U | F-HEOL | | | |
| 0220 | N800RL | | | | |
| 0221 | N5153K | N27VQ | YV305T | | |
| 0222 | N778MA | VT-DOV | | | |
| 0223 | D-IWAN | | | | |

## CJ2/CJ2+

| C/n | Identities | | | | |
|---|---|---|---|---|---|
| 0224 | N5264N | N424CJ | N576SC | | |
| 0225 | N67BC | N67CC | | | |
| 0226 | N5266F | N526DV | PR-CNP | | |
| 0227 | N5174W | N761KG | | | |
| 0228 | N5154J | PR-NTX | | | |
| 0229 | N5223P | SX-SMH | OE-FVB | | |
| 0230 | N5136J | D-IGRO | | | |
| 0231 | N5211A | D-IWIN | | | |
| 0232 | N5245D | [re-serialled 525A0300 q.v.] | | | |
| 0233 | N5236L | D-IBBE | D-IOHL | | |
| 0234 | N313CR | | | | |
| 0235 | N235KS | C-FTRM | | | |
| 0236 | N5259Y | TC-VYN | | | |
| 0237 | N5263U | N333BD | | | |
| 0238 | N5117U | N1290Y | N228FS | N227FS | N777AG |
| 0239 | N5120U | (OE-FEB) | OE-FIN | OM-OPE | |
| 0240 | N5194B | N77VR | N109TW* | | |
| 0241 | N52081 | N777QP | | | |
| 0242 | N5073G | PH-JNE | | | |
| 0243 | N5165T | N551WM | | | |
| 0244 | N52086 | N13087 | JA525C | | |

## CJ2+

| C/n | Identities | | | |
|---|---|---|---|---|
| 0300 | N5245D | [converted from 525A0232 ff 3.4.05, received type certificate 03Oct05] N432MA | | |
| 0301 | N52609 | N301PG | N525HD | |
| 0302 | N52690 | N302CJ | N6M | N302CJ |
| 0303 | N5260M | N85JE | OY-GLO | |
| 0304 | N52699 | N912GW | | |
| 0305 | N5213S | N660S | | |
| 0306 | N5180K | N306JR | | |
| 0307 | N5239J | N674AS | | |
| 0308 | N5188N | N308CJ | N110FD | |
| 0309 | N309CJ | M-TSGP | | |
| 0310 | N5267G | N926JJ | | |
| 0311 | N5211A | N1317X | JA001T | |
| 0312 | N5000R | N786AC | | |
| 0313 | N5157E | D-IBBS | | |
| 0314 | N5096S | N1DM | N791DM | N747JJ |
| 0315 | N5094D | N1414P | | |
| 0316 | N5165T | PR-NNP | | |
| 0317 | N9UD | | | |
| 0318 | N5268V | N525TA | YV289T | |
| 0319 | N967TC | | | |
| 0320 | N5188A | F-ONYY | | |
| 0321 | N13195 | OE-FII | | |
| 0322 | N51575 | (LX-WGR) | F-GMIR | |
| 0323 | N5132T | N65CK | | |
| 0324 | N5228Z | N586ED | | |
| 0325 | N437JD | N487JD | PP-BBS | |
| 0326 | N5223P | OE-FXX | N207BG | |
| 0327 | N5226B | N525RF | | |
| 0328 | N52352 | D-IBCT | | |
| 0329 | N5147B | N525PH | | |
| 0330 | N5231S | D-IFLY | | |
| 0331 | N5148B | OY-REN | HB-VPC | |
| 0332 | N50282 | D-IOBU | D-IOBO | |
| 0333 | N929BC | N939BC | | |
| 0334 | N52699 | G-HCSA | | |
| 0335 | N525LD | | | |
| 0336 | N336CJ | N15YD | | |
| 0337 | N5063P | N525XD | | |
| 0338 | N722SM | | | |
| 0339 | N500NB | | | |
| 0340 | N5086W | D-IFIS | | |
| 0341 | N5064Q | N241CJ | HB-VOL | |
| 0342 | N18TD | N178WG | | |
| 0343 | N5108G | D-IFDN | D-IHTM* | |
| 0344 | N5200Z | N45MH | | |
| 0345 | N5153K | N9180K | | |
| 0346 | N525EP | | | |
| 0347 | N5262X | M-ICRO | | |
| 0348 | N5076J | S5-BAS | | |
| 0349 | N52609 | N535TV | N535JF | |
| 0350 | N5260Y | N117W | | |
| 0351 | N909MN | | | |

## CJ2+

| C/n | Identities | | | |
|---|---|---|---|---|
| 0352 | N51896 | N525HG | | |
| 0353 | N929VC | | | |
| 0354 | N5101J | OE-FOA | | |
| 0355 | N5079V | D-IWBL | | |
| 0356 | N5197A | N617CB | PR-FSA | |
| 0357 | N50820 | N624PL | | |
| 0358 | N5061F | D-IEFA | | |
| 0359 | N52682 | N12742 | JA359C | |
| 0360 | N52655 | N13474 | G-HGRC | G-SYGC |
| 0361 | N5157E | N361JR | | |
| 0362 | N51564 | OE-FGB | | |
| 0363 | N5197M | D-IETZ | | |
| 0364 | N5090V | D-ITOR | | |
| 0365 | N50736 | OE-FLA | | |
| 0366 | N366CJ | N999QE | | |
| 0367 | N367CJ | D-IAKN | | |
| 0368 | N5032K | N93AK | | |
| 0369 | N5181U | OE-FLB | | |
| 0370 | N51993 | N370JJ | | |
| 0371 | N51160 | N574BB | | |
| 0372 | N5103J | OY-NDP | | |
| 0373 | N5270E | N41174 | VT-BRT | |
| 0374 | N5108G | N245RA | | |
| 0375 | N51055 | OE-FOE | | |
| 0376 | N51444 | PR-JVF | | |
| 0377 | N5211F | N950DB | | |
| 0378 | N5214J | N41184 | VT-VID | |
| 0379 | N5270J | N896P | | |
| 0380 | N5168Y | N5192U | JA021R | |
| 0381 | N52627 | EC-KOI | | |
| 0382 | N5241Z | N129CK | D-IPAD* | |
| 0383 | N5120U | HB-VWA | | |
| 0384 | N5218R | N118CJ | | |
| 0385 | N50820 | HB-VOP | | |
| 0386 | N5270P | N2040E | JA516J | |
| 0387 | N5268M | N111JW | N525RG | |
| 0388 | N5267T | G-CROO | | |
| 0389 | N5153K | M-PSAC | D-ITMA | |
| 0390 | N52639 | OE-FKO | | |
| 0391 | N2151Q | JA391C | | |
| 0392 | N52081 | PR-ARS | | |
| 0393 | N51896 | N775TF | | |
| 0394 | N5152X | C-FITC | | |
| 0395 | N5154J | XA-UJY | | |
| 0396 | N5162W | N400CV | | |
| 0397 | N5148B | G-ODAG | | |
| 0398 | N5270K | OE-FNB | LZ-FNB | |
| 0399 | N5048U | N810PF | | |
| 0400 | N5235G | D-IMMM | | |
| 0401 | N5094D | YU-VER | | |
| 0402 | N5263U | N2224G | VT-PSB | |
| 0403 | N5103J | N250BL | | |
| 0404 | N5103J | N85ER | | |
| 0405 | N5180C | N405CJ | N413FC | |
| 0406 | N5072X | PR-WAT | | |
| 0407 | N5225K | N407CJ | N59JN | |
| 0408 | N5248V | G-NMRM | | |
| 0409 | N5270J | D-IPCC | | |
| 0410 | N5165P | N2297X | VT-BPS | |
| 0411 | N5211F | YU-BUU | | |
| 0412 | N5141F | 9A-DWA | | |
| 0413 | N52086 | N19KT | | |
| 0414 | N5165T | N208BG | | |
| 0415 | N5225K | OE-FHC | | |
| 0416 | N108KJ | | | |
| 0417 | N5090A | PR-RJN | | |
| 0418 | N5265N | N677SL | N642WW* | |
| 0419 | N52655 | N785MT | | |
| 0420 | N5130J | N10AU | | |
| 0421 | N5265B | N379R | | |
| 0422 | N757EM | HB-VPB | | |
| 0423 | N806CJ | S5-BAR | | |
| 0424 | N5136J | N41212 | N285JE | |
| 0425 | N5155G | N2044S | N96SW | |
| 0426 | N426CJ | N476JD | | |
| 0427 | N5066U | I-CALZ | | |

## CJ2+

| C/n | Identities | | | |
|---|---|---|---|---|
| 0428 | N51396 | SP-DLB | | |
| 0429 | N5048U | D-ISCV | | |
| 0430 | N5076L | N2046D | (VT-BJC) | N501KE |
| 0431 | N5163C | OO-ACC | | |
| 0432 | N5093D | N10WZ | | |
| 0433 | N5183V | N433CJ | D-IJKP | |
| 0434 | N5200R | 9A-CLN | | |
| 0435 | N52081 | VP-BRL | SE-RKM* | |
| 0436 | N5257V | N2051A | (VT-BJD) | 7T-VNF |
| 0437 | N5165T | OE-FPK | | |
| 0438 | N5026Q | N438TA | EI-ECR | |
| 0439 | N52141 | N125WT | | |
| 0440 | N52086 | PR-KYK | | |
| 0441 | N50522 | N440CJ | | |
| 0442 | N52655 | N2064M | N494TB | |
| 0443 | N52645 | D-IDAS | | |
| 0444 | N5235G | N20669 | D-IWWP | |
| 0445 | N50282 | N145SF | | |
| 0446 | N5068F | N2067E | N446CJ | |
| 0447 | N5265B | N447CJ | N312SB | |
| 0448 | N52446 | N360PK | | |
| 0449 | N525EG | | | |
| 0450 | N5180K | N926PY | | |
| 0451 | N5245L | N451FP | | |
| 0452 | N721ES | | | |
| 0453 | N5161J | N484CW | N238RM | |
| 0454 | N234CJ | | | |
| 0455 | N50054 | YR-TOY | | |
| 0456 | N5136J | C-GTRG | | |
| 0457 | N5268V | ZS-PAJ | | |
| 0458 | N52235 | N6245J | N674JM | |
| 0459 | N5180C | D-IEVB | | |
| 0460 | N525AP | | | |
| 0461 | N5267G | N461CJ | | |
| 0462 | | | | |
| 0463 | (N234CJ) | | | |
| 0464 | | | | |
| 0465 | | | | |
| 0466 | | | | |
| 0467 | | | | |
| 0468 | | | | |
| 0469 | | | | |
| 0470 | (D-IWWP) | | | |
| 0471 | | | | |
| 0472 | | | | |
| 0473 | | | | |
| 0474 | | | | |
| 0475 | | | | |
| 0476 | | | | |
| 0477 | | | | |
| 0478 | | | | |
| 0479 | | | | |
| 0480 | | | | |
| 0481 | | | | |
| 0482 | | | | |
| 0483 | | | | |
| 0484 | | | | |
| 0485 | | | | |
| 0486 | | | | |
| 0487 | | | | |
| 0488 | | | | |
| 0489 | | | | |
| 0490 | | | | |
| 0491 | | | | |
| 0492 | | | | |
| 0493 | | | | |
| 0494 | | | | |
| 0495 | | | | |
| 0496 | | | | |
| 0497 | | | | |
| 0498 | | | | |
| 0499 | | | | |
| 0500 | | | | |

# CESSNA 525B CITATIONJET CJ3

| C/n | Identities | | | | | |
|---|---|---|---|---|---|---|
| 711 | N3CJ | [ff 17Apr03] | | | | |
| 0001 | N753CJ | [ff 08Aug03] | | (N929SF) | N53SF | |
| 0002 | N763CJ | N62SH | | | | |
| 0003 | N52059 | N103CJ | N432LW | (N627BB) | | |
| 0004 | N5207A | N1308L | N6525B | | | |
| 0005 | N5270E | N105CJ | | | | |
| 0006 | N5227G | N1278D | N417C | | | |
| 0007 | N5239J | N7CC | | | | |
| 0008 | N52627 | N51HF | N946RM | | | |
| 0009 | N51806 | N777NJ | N5GU | | | |
| 0010 | N5097H | N917RG | | | | |
| 0011 | N110MG | N585PK | D-CELE | | | |
| 0012 | N5093D | N172DH | M-UPCO | | | |
| 0013 | N5228Z | N831V | F-HBPP | | | |
| 0014 | N114CJ | N300ET | | | | |
| 0015 | N5163K | N4RH | N747KR | | | |
| 0016 | N50820 | N200GM | (D-CORA) | S5-BAW | | |
| 0017 | N614B | | | | | |
| 0018 | N51896 | N52ET | | | | |
| 0019 | N79LB | N11LB | | | | |
| 0020 | N52038 | N899RR | N33UM | | | |
| 0021 | N5073G | N325RC | | | | |
| 0022 | N5109W | N528CE | | | | |
| 0023 | N51055 | N77M | N15C | | | |
| 0024 | N5221Y | N525GM | | | | |
| 0025 | N5201J | N7NE | | | | |
| 0026 | N162EC | | | | | |
| 0027 | "N5188W"+ | [+marks as quoted, already current on a homebuilt] | | | N1287D | ZK-TBM |
| 0028 | N5085E | PR-SPO | | | | |
| 0029 | N726AG | | | | | |
| 0030 | N5145P | N401CS | | | | |
| 0031 | N303CJ | | | | | |
| 0032 | N52433 | N137BG | | | | |
| 0033 | N5243K | N404CS | | | | |
| 0034 | N52446 | N65VM | | | | |
| 0035 | N51511 | N93JW | | | | |
| 0036 | N5244F | N405CS | | | | |
| 0037 | N52653 | C-FXTC | | | | |
| 0038 | N51942 | N100RC | | | | |
| 0039 | N526DG | N525DG | | | | |
| 0040 | N52369 | N550T | | | | |
| 0041 | N525PC | N3CT | | | | |
| 0042 | N5163K | N69FH | | | | |
| 0043 | N5183V | N406CS | | | | |
| 0044 | N144AL | | | | | |
| 0045 | N5221Y | N408CS | | | | |
| 0046 | N5124F | N860DD | | | | |
| 0047 | N50820 | PR-EBD | | | | |
| 0048 | N853JL | N92MA | | | | |
| 0049 | N628CB | | | | | |
| 0050 | N409CS | | | | | |
| 0051 | N5148N | N525L | | | | |
| 0052 | N999SM | | | | | |
| 0053 | N53NW | | | | | |
| 0054 | N5200U | N535GH | | | | |
| 0055 | N5151D | N4GA | | | | |
| 0056 | N5093L | N156TW | N748RM | | | |
| 0057 | N5239J | N999LB | | | | |
| 0058 | N5066U | N885BT | | | | |
| 0059 | N412CS | | | | | |
| 0060 | N5250P | N125DG | | | | |
| 0061 | N361TL | | | | | |
| 0062 | N5269A | XC-GDC | | | | |
| 0063 | N5226B | N123CJ | N128CJ | N611CS | | |
| 0064 | N5263S | N1CH | | | | |
| 0065 | N5269J | N105CQ | LN-HOT | | | |
| 0066 | N362JM | N6243M | N602MJ | | | |
| 0067 | N51160 | N96MR | OM-LBG | | | |
| 0068 | N5269Z | N51JJ | | | | |
| 0069 | N5231S | N3UD | N535DT | | | |
| 0070 | N51055 | N279DV | | | | |
| 0071 | N51511 | N531CM | | | | |
| 0072 | N5214L | N107CQ | N8106V | | | |
| 0073 | N51995 | N899MA | N550RB* | | | |
| 0074 | N5221Y | N742AR | | | | |

## CJ3

| C/n | Identities | | | | |
|---|---|---|---|---|---|
| 0075 | N528JC | D-CJAK | | | |
| 0076 | N5207A | N1KA | | | |
| 0077 | N52433 | N7877T | | | |
| 0078 | N525DR | VH-MIF | | | |
| 0079 | N52081 | N835DM | | | |
| 0080 | N52352 | N380CJ | N451GP | | |
| 0081 | N52457 | N868EM | | | |
| 0082 | N413CS | | | | |
| 0083 | N5166T | N13001 | HS-MCL | | |
| 0084 | N51744 | N841AM | | | |
| 0085 | N51881 | D-CLAT | | | |
| 0086 | N51993 | D-CKJS | (D-CDIG) | D-CVHM | |
| 0087 | N687DS | | | | |
| 0088 | N5264U | N525MP | | | |
| 0089 | N5076J | N525EZ | [w/o in hangar fire 12Sep07 Danbury, CT] | | |
| 0090 | N5197A | N417CS | | | |
| 0091 | N5214J | N219L | | | |
| 0092 | N52653 | N852SP | | | |
| 0093 | N5259Y | N93PE | | | |
| 0094 | N83TF | | | | |
| 0095 | N5214K | N100JS | | | |
| 0096 | N5270J | LX-GAP | 3A-MRG | | |
| 0097 | N5216A | N888RK | | | |
| 0098 | N5270E | N87VM | | | |
| 0099 | N777NJ | | | | |
| 0100 | N50820 | N77M | | | |
| 0101 | N52113 | D-CTEC | PP-AVX | | |
| 0102 | N5213S | N812JM | N3JM | | |
| 0103 | N5188N | (N103CJ) | N417KM | N221LC | N443PW |
| 0104 | N5192E | N5216A | N560PJ | N590PJ | N525GT |
| 0105 | N5135K | N247MV | | | |
| 0106 | N5218T | N106JT | | | |
| 0107 | N709PG | D-COBO | | | |
| 0108 | N5218T | N418CS | | | |
| 0109 | N5145J | N1255J | | | |
| 0110 | N51246 | N28MH | | | |
| 0111 | N5101J | N96PD | | | |
| 0112 | N731WH | | | | |
| 0113 | N5263U | N55GP | | | |
| 0114 | N52234 | N114CJ | N901MV | (D-CELE) | N96G |
| 0115 | N5207A | N420CS | | | |
| 0116 | N5244W | ZS-CJT | | | |
| 0117 | N5212M | F-GRUJ | | | |
| 0118 | N51143 | C-GSSC | | | |
| 0119 | N5257V | D-CNOB | | | |
| 0120 | N5211A | D-CEFD | | | |
| 0121 | N52229 | N423CS | | | |
| 0122 | N12GS | | | | |
| 0123 | N73EM | | | | |
| 0124 | N5203S | PR-ALC | | | |
| 0125 | N5194J | OE-GPO | | | |
| 0126 | N5030U | N621GA | | | |
| 0127 | N5268A | N107PT | | | |
| 0128 | N17CN | | | | |
| 0129 | N629EE | PR-ALV | | | |
| 0130 | (N910BH) | N329CJ | | | |
| 0131 | N5057E | N331CJ | N30UD | AP-PFL | |
| 0132 | N5058J | N425CS | | | |
| 0133 | N5031E | N233MM | | | |
| 0134 | N52691 | N41ND | | | |
| 0135 | N5059X | OE-GRA | | | |
| 0136 | N5073G | PT-TJS | | | |
| 0137 | N51042 | N550MX | | | |
| 0138 | N51942 | N356MR | | | |
| 0139 | N52059 | N93CW | | | |
| 0140 | N51612 | N42AA | N15PG | | |
| 0141 | N50756 | N238SW | | | |
| 0142 | N28DM | | | | |
| 0143 | N5185V | N320BP | | | |
| 0144 | N51055 | (C-FXFJ) | N847NG | | |
| 0145 | N332SB | | | | |
| 0146 | CS-DIY | D-CCCG* | | | |
| 0147 | N5168Y | OO-FPC | | | |
| 0148 | N52397 | N148CJ | M-ELON | | |
| 0149 | N5261R | N123CJ | | | |
| 0150 | N52626 | N317BR | OE-GHG | | |

## CJ3

| C/n | Identities | | | | |
|---|---|---|---|---|---|
| 0151 | N52086 | N420CH | | | |
| 0152 | N5262B | N427CS | | | |
| 0153 | N5145P | N28FR | G-ODCM | | |
| 0154 | D-CRAH | | | | |
| 0155 | N831FC | | | | |
| 0156 | N5145V | F-GVUJ | | | |
| 0157 | N5096S | N157JL | | | |
| 0158 | N5180K | (OO-FPD) | OO-FPE | | |
| 0159 | N50275 | N565JP | | | |
| 0160 | N5201J | VP-BUG | M-ASRY | | |
| 0161 | N5268M | D-CMHS | | | |
| 0162 | N503LC | | | | |
| 0163 | N5267K | N80HB | | | |
| 0164 | N5125J | N1314V | N500AS | | |
| 0165 | N5267T | N428CS | | | |
| 0166 | N5061W | N7814 | | | |
| 0167 | N450BV | | | | |
| 0168 | N970DM | | | | |
| 0169 | N5250P | D-CUBA | | | |
| 0170 | N50543 | N996PE | | | |
| 0171 | N5172M | N727YB | | | |
| 0172 | N51780 | N535DL | | | |
| 0173 | N5228J | OO-LIE | | | |
| 0174 | N174SJ | | | | |
| 0175 | N149WW | | | | |
| 0176 | N5188N | (F-HAFC) | F-GYFC | | |
| 0177 | N5037F | N429CS | | | |
| 0178 | N5203S | F-GSGL | | | |
| 0179 | N5211A | N179CJ | G-OMBI | | |
| 0180 | N5185J | N360CK | | | |
| 0181 | N5239J | N143JT | | | |
| 0182 | N5243K | N535CM | | | |
| 0183 | N5062S | N4115H | A6-SAB | F-HBER | |
| 0184 | N52639 | N914FF | | | |
| 0185 | N5076K | N430CS | | | |
| 0186 | N186CJ | N111JW | | | |
| 0187 | N5076P | PR-MRG | | | |
| 0188 | N541WG | | | | |
| 0189 | N5197A | N525CF | | | |
| 0190 | N5036Q | N81ER | | | |
| 0191 | N52626 | N379DB | | | |
| 0192 | N5214L | XA-AVX | | | |
| 0193 | N5262B | N1382N | (SX-EDP) | SX-PAP | YU-BTN |
| 0194 | N52645 | OY-WWW | | | |
| 0195 | N5202D | N400GG | | | |
| 0196 | N396CJ | VH-ANE | | | |
| 0197 | N5262X | D-CUUU | OO-FYS | | |
| 0198 | N52069 | "VP-BJR"+ | [+marks worn at factory] | | VP-BRJ |
| 0199 | N51817 | PR-CVC | | | |
| 0200 | N5073G | OO-EDV | | | |
| 0201 | N5260Y | C-FANJ | | | |
| 0202 | N51896 | N7CH | | | |
| 0203 | N50776 | N328RC | | | |
| 0204 | N5066F | N5WN | | | |
| 0205 | N52682 | N428BR | | | |
| 0206 | N52086 | C-GPMW | | | |
| 0207 | N5262W | N856BB | | | |
| 0208 | N5180K | N414KD | | | |
| 0209 | N5228Z | HB-VOW | | | |
| 0210 | N52114 | N1DM | | | |
| 0211 | N51396 | ZS-DPP | | | |
| 0212 | N52235 | N711BE | | | |
| 0213 | N5188A | N527HV | | | |
| 0214 | N52433 | N92MS | | | |
| 0215 | N5201J | D-CTEC | | | |
| 0216 | N5250E | HB-VWB | | | |
| 0217 | N52690 | D-CASH | OM-VPT | | |
| 0218 | N5201M | N7725D | | | |
| 0219 | N5243K | OE-GRZ | | | |
| 0220 | N52136 | (D-CJVC) | D-COWB | | |
| 0221 | N15ZZ | | | | |
| 0222 | N5061W | OE-GRU | | | |
| 0223 | N5117U | N229CN | N7773J* | | |
| 0224 | N5250P | F-HCIC | | | |
| 0225 | N5296X | N27UB | | | |
| 0226 | N50543 | N880MR | | | |

# CJ3

| C/n | Identities | | | |
|---|---|---|---|---|
| 0227 | N5211A | LX-DCA | | |
| 0228 | N5000R | N431CS | | |
| 0229 | N5185J | N826CS | | |
| 0230 | N5068F | F-GSMG | | |
| 0231 | N5247U | OE-GJF | G-TSJF | |
| 0232 | N52682 | D-CPAO | | |
| 0233 | N5194J | N956GA | | |
| 0234 | N5214K | EC-KQO | | |
| 0235 | N5174W | CS-DGW | | |
| 0236 | N5151D | N308GT | | |
| 0237 | N50736 | N525WL | | |
| 0238 | N5062S | N525EZ | M-OODY | |
| 0239 | N5076P | PR-SCF | | |
| 0240 | N51160 | N240CJ | N75JK | |
| 0241 | N5226B | N241KA | N241CJ | |
| 0242 | N5227G | N899NH | | |
| 0243 | N5101J | C6-LUV | | |
| 0244 | N432CS | | | |
| 0245 | N50776 | PR-TBL | | |
| 0246 | N5266F | N246CZ | | |
| 0247 | N5244F | N377GA | J8-JET | |
| 0248 | N5109W | N839DM | | |
| 0249 | N5163C | N608SG | | |
| 0250 | N5245U | N403CH | N403ND | |
| 0251 | N5026Q | N220LC | (N37JK) | N716MB |
| 0252 | N5093L | N941AM | | |
| 0253 | N38M | | | |
| 0254 | N5214J | N307PE | | |
| 0255 | N5181U | M-BIRD | | |
| 0256 | N52627 | N6M | | |
| 0257 | N433CS | | | |
| 0258 | N5262W | F-HAGA | D-CFRA* | |
| 0259 | N5180K | N724CV | UP-CS301 | |
| 0260 | N5096S | N23BV | | |
| 0261 | N5223Y | N100DW | | |
| 0262 | N812HF | | | |
| 0263 | N5270M | N888PS | | |
| 0264 | N5244W | F-GSCR | | |
| 0265 | N5262B | N227JP | | |
| 0266 | N5218R | N41203 | EI-MJC | |
| 0267 | N5163K | N500WD | | |
| 0268 | N434CS | N151KD | | |
| 0269 | N5194B | OM-OPA | | |
| 0270 | N5091J | N58JV | | |
| 0271 | N52144 | N39GG | | |
| 0272 | N52352 | HB-VWC | | |
| 0273 | N5228Z | N79JS | | |
| 0274 | N5201J | N436CS | | |
| 0275 | N52690 | OE-GNA | | |
| 0276 | N5214K | N70NF | | |
| 0277 | N5213K | N2074H | OE-GET | |
| 0278 | N50736 | N2111W | PR-ADL | |
| 0279 | N51160 | N279CJ | | |
| 0280 | N5197A | N150MJ | M-MIKE | |
| 0281 | N5174W | LX-JET | | |
| 0282 | N437CS | N578CJ | | |
| 0283 | N283RA | | | |
| 0284 | N5076K | N835CB | | |
| 0285 | N11UD | | | |
| 0286 | N5066F | D-CPMI | | |
| 0287 | N5062S | D-CURA | | |
| 0288 | N5076P | D-CWIR | | |
| 0289 | N5226B | N4RP | | |
| 0290 | N5101J | N125PL | | |
| 0291 | N50776 | PH-FJK | | |
| 0292 | N5241Z | N329BH | | |
| 0293 | N28GA | | | |
| 0294 | N52229 | N108WQ | N106WQ | N294CC |
| 0295 | N5207V | N525EZ | | |
| 0296 | N5216A | N296CJ | N296PM | |
| 0297 | N196MR | PP-MPP | | |
| 0298 | N567HB | | | |
| 0299 | N299CS | | | |
| 0300 | N52059 | F-GVVB | | |
| 0301 | N110JC | N256DV* | | |
| 0302 | N51881 | N302CZ | (N88QC) | N18GA |

## CJ3

| C/n | Identities | | | | |
|---|---|---|---|---|---|
| 0303 | N5112K | N724BP | N724PB | | |
| 0304 | N5061F | N20AU | | | |
| 0305 | N5120U | N800FM | | | |
| 0306 | N525H | N949LL | | | |
| 0307 | N815LP | XA-ALT | | | |
| 0308 | N5260Y | N27EW | | | |
| 0309 | N5218R | N41226 | TC-GUR | N627V | TC-GUR |
| 0310 | N5163K | PR-RBO | | | |
| 0311 | N5194B | M-MHMH | | | |
| 0312 | N5091J | N312CJ | OE-GPK | | |
| 0313 | N123CZ | | | | |
| 0314 | N52352 | OE-GPD | | | |
| 0315 | N315CJ | | | | |
| 0316 | N52690 | N316BD | | | |
| 0317 | N52613 | CS-EAA* | | | |
| 0318 | N5226B | OE-GMZ | | | |
| 0319 | N50736 | N52WC | | | |
| 0320 | N5124F | UR-PME | | | |
| 0321 | N438CS | N5GQ | | | |
| 0322 | N5108G | UR-DWH | | | |
| 0323 | N5030U | N6132U | UP-CS302 | | |
| 0324 | N5267T | PR-MON | | | |
| 0325 | N510RC | | | | |
| 0326 | N439CS | N480CC | | | |
| 0327 | N5185V | N527DV | | | |
| 0328 | N51038 | N994MP | N421MP | | |
| 0329 | N5270P | N528DV | | | |
| 0330 | N5066F | D-CAST | | | |
| 0331 | (D-CIOL) | N819CW | | | |
| 0332 | N434CS | N91GT | | | |
| 0333 | N525CJ | | | | |
| 0334 | N5206T | D-CCBH | | | |
| 0335 | N335CJ | N929BC | | | |
| 0336 | N336CJ | N466F* | | | |
| 0337 | | | | | |
| 0338 | N338CZ | | | | |
| 0339 | (D-CAVB) | D-CBVB* | | | |
| 0340 | | | | | |
| 0341 | | | | | |
| 0342 | | | | | |
| 0343 | (N91GT) | | | | |
| 0344 | | | | | |
| 0345 | | | | | |
| 0346 | | | | | |
| 0347 | | | | | |
| 0348 | | | | | |
| 0349 | | | | | |
| 0350 | | | | | |
| 0351 | | | | | |
| 0352 | | | | | |
| 0353 | | | | | |
| 0354 | | | | | |
| 0355 | | | | | |
| 0356 | | | | | |
| 0357 | | | | | |
| 0358 | | | | | |
| 0359 | | | | | |
| 0360 | | | | | |
| 0361 | | | | | |
| 0362 | | | | | |
| 0363 | | | | | |
| 0364 | | | | | |
| 0365 | | | | | |
| 0366 | | | | | |
| 0367 | | | | | |
| 0368 | | | | | |
| 0369 | | | | | |
| 0370 | | | | | |
| 0371 | | | | | |
| 0372 | | | | | |
| 0373 | | | | | |
| 0374 | | | | | |
| 0375 | | | | | |
| 0376 | | | | | |
| 0377 | | | | | |
| 0378 | | | | | |

# CESSNA 525C CITATIONJET CJ4

| C/n | Identities | | |
|---|---|---|---|
| 714001 | N4CJ | [ff 05May08] | |
| 0001 | N525NG | [ff 19Aug08] | |
| 0002 | N525KS | [ff 02Dec08] | N747HS |
| 0003 | N52141 | N525NB | |
| 0004 | N525CZ | | |
| 0005 | N5211Q | | |
| 0006 | N615PL | | |
| 0007 | | | |
| 0008 | | | |
| 0009 | | | |
| 0010 | | | |
| 0011 | | | |
| 0012 | N4M | | |
| 0013 | N105AD* | | |
| 0014 | | | |
| 0015 | | | |
| 0016 | | | |
| 0017 | | | |
| 0018 | | | |
| 0019 | | | |
| 0020 | | | |
| 0021 | | | |
| 0022 | | | |
| 0023 | | | |
| 0024 | | | |
| 0025 | | | |
| 0026 | | | |
| 0027 | | | |
| 0028 | | | |
| 0029 | | | |
| 0030 | | | |

# CESSNA CITATION II/BRAVO

This production list is presented in order of the Unit Number which was used and allocated by Cessna, rather than by the normally-used c/n. A c/n-Unit Number cross-reference follows the production list.

| Unit No | C/n | Identities |
|---|---|---|
| | 686 | N550CC [ff 31Jan77; cvtd to S550 standards;cx Apr91 presumed wfu] |
| 001 | 550-0001 | (N98751) (N551CC) N5050J N560CC [converted to Model 560; canx 11Apr05; wfu] |
| 002 | 551-0027 | N98753 N552CC N44GT N552CC N522CC N46PJ |
| 003 | 550-0003 | N98784 N553CJ YV-19CP N19CP N199Q N19CP |
| 004 | F550-0004 | N98786 C-GPAW N312GA F-GNCP |
| 005 | 550-0005 | N98817 OE-GKP N77ND [w/o 30Sep05 70 miles North of Fairbanks, AK; to White Inds, Bates City, MO, for spares] |
| 006 | 550-0006 | N98820 N2 N6 N152GA N725RH N550LA |
| 007 | 550-0007 | N98830 N300PB (N447FM) N650WC N650WG (N550TY) N127JJ |
| 008 | 550-0008 | N98840 N575W OE-GIW (N108AJ) N550JF N70X N70XA G-VUEZ |
| 009 | 550-0009 | N98853 N744SW N744DC N656PS |
| 010 | 550-0010 | N98858 OE-GEP N550PL N806C PT-LPK |
| 011 | 550-0021 | N98871 N296AB (N171CB) N900LJ N52RF |
| 012 | 550-0011 | (N99876) Venezuela 0002 |
| 013 | 550-0012 | N3208M N513CC C-GHOL N11FH N586CP |
| 014 | 551-0002 | N3210M YV-140CP N20FM N700AS XA-SLD N39ML N502CL |
| 015 | 550-0014 | N3212M N702R N780GT (N94FS) N780CF |
| 016 | 550-0013 | N3216M YV-151CP N3952B N21SW N21SV PT-LML [w/o 15Aug87 Criciuma, Brazil: remains to Dodson Avn, for parts, cx Aug97] |
| 017 | 550-0016 | N3221M N276AL (N216VP) HC-BTJ N204MC N116LA |
| 018 | 551-0007 | N3223M YV-169CP (N169CP) YV-169CP YV-05CP N60FJ N42MJ* |
| 019 | 550-0018 | (N3225M) N752CC |
| 020 | 551-0006 | N3227A YV-06CP YV-O-CVG-2 Venezuela 1967 |
| 021 | 550-0017 | N3230M VH-MAY P2-RDZ N771ST N744AT |
| 022 | 550-0019 | N3232M N1851T N1851D (HI-530) HI-534 HI-534CA N1851D (N200GP) N900AF N7RC [w/o 26Apr95 Walkers Cay, Bahamas; cx Oct95 - remains to Dodson Avn, KS] |
| 023 | 551-0071 | N3236M PH-HES OO-RJT PH-HES N4578F N79CD N790D N551DS N551HH |
| 024 | 551-0003 | N3237M YV-205CP N4445N N72RC I-MESK |
| 025 | 550-0025 | N3239M (EP-KID) EP-KIC N9014S N664JB N664J N78PH N78PR 9H-ACR OY-GMC N551DA |
| 026 | 550-0026 | N3240M N256W (N2231B) N30AV |
| 027 | 550-0027 | N3245M N527CC G-BFRM N222DE N222D N127PM |
| 028 | 550-0028 | (N3246M) (G-BFLY) OE-GAU N501BL N888MW N100CX (F-GHUA) 5Y-HAB N310AV N551CZ (N370CD) [retro-fitted with Williams FJ44 engines] |
| 029 | 550-0029 | (N3247M) G-JEEN N502AL N718VA N202PB N7CC N550TJ N524MA |
| 030 | 550-0030 | (N3249M) G-DJBI G-FERY G-MSLY N64CA VR-CSS N507AB N501KC (N200G) N601KK N4TS N16TS |
| 031 | 550-0031 | N3250M RP-C550 RP-C296 N22GA N9DC |
| 032 | 550-0032 | N3251M N810SC N810SG N55BP N66ES N50US N905EM N112JS N232CW |
| 033 | 550-0033 | (N3252M) TR-LYE N59MJ N755CM N46DA F-GPLT F-WPLT LX-GDL LX-JET LX-GDL G-CEUO |
| 034 | 550-0034 | N3258M N771A N697A N60CC N922SL |
| 035 | 550-0219 | (N3261M) N108WG HB-VGK N4457A N108WG VH-ORE N12AC YV-606CP N550RP N550PM N10JA |
| 036 | 550-0036 | (N3262M) N58AN N5Q (N54DA) N36CE N711BP (N789RR) N789BR N336MA |
| 037 | 550-0037 | (N3268M) N37HG N361DJ XA-SDV (N551NA) N535MA N829NL N237CW (N37GA) N622PG |
| 038 | 550-0038 | (N3271M) N526AC N526AG C-FLDO N642CC (N842CC) N550JC |
| 039 | 550-0039 | (N3273M) G-BJHH EI-BJL N78FA ZP-TYO N848D |
| 040 | 550-0040 | (N3274M) N220CC N277CJ N900LC HK-3607X N554BA N550SC (N551GA) N545GA N554MB |
| 041 | 550-0024 | N3276M N533M N85MG N313CK XA-SJZ N313CK N413CK N404RP |
| 042 | 550-0035 | N3278M N8417B N50XX N333X N74G (N50GG) N15JA |
| 043 | 550-0041 | N3279M N8418B N341AG N985BA N177HH OE-GCI |
| 044 | 550-0042 | N3283M N666RC N57MB N66AT C-FPEL C-FLBC N41GA |
| 045 | 550-0045 | N3284M N4CH N4CR 5N-AMR [w/o 21May91 private airstrip Bauchi, Nigeria] |
| 046 | 550-0043 | N3285M N6Q VR-CCI N801JP N112SH |
| 047 | 550-0044 | N3286M N3526 N550HM N300TW N308TW (N452AJ) |
| 048 | 550-0048 | N3288M N534M N161BH N384DA N10BF N19ER |
| 049 | 551-0010 | N3291M YV-137CP N55AL D-ICAC |
| 050 | 550-0046 | (N3292M) C-GRHC |
| 051 | 551-0095 | N3296M N1AP N66LB G-HOTL N999WA N49TJ N314CK N200TJ (N127TA) C-GAMW N627TA N400PC N402TJ N48DK |
| 052 | F550-0050 | (N3298M) N102FC N362DJ D-CJJJ N250CF F-ODUT F-GMCI N342AJ |
| 053 | 550-0053 | (N3300M) N4VF N53VP N53KB TC-NKB N550EC N519AA |
| 054 | 550-0054 | (N3301M) N501AA VH-WGJ VH-OYW VH-PSM |
| 055 | 550-0055 | (N3308M) N55CC N2JZ (N1466K) N10EG |
| 056 | 550-0047 | N3313M (N66VM) OB-M-1171 N66VM N44AS |
| 057 | 550-0075 | N3314M N55BH N58BH C-GSFA N710MT N910MT |
| 058 | 550-0068 | N3319M N558CC N558CB N402ST N1WB N91VB N406CJ* |
| 059 | 550-0242 | N1955E N551BC |
| 060 | 550-0051 | N1958E C-GJAP C-GBCB N678CA ZS-RKV |

# CITATION II

| Unit No | C/n | Identities |
|---|---|---|
| 061 | 550-0263 | N1959E D-IMTM (N458N) N13VP [w/o 20May02 Oklahoma-Wiley Post,OK: b/u for spares by Dodson Int'l Parts circa Oct02; but cx to Italy 20Dec04] |
| 062 | 551-0017 | N2052A N1UH (N33FW) N53WF N811VC N811VG |
| 063 | 550-0069 | N2069A F-GBPL 3A-MWA HZ-AAA HZ-ALJ N550CE OE-GIN (N269AJ) N551JF N550AB C-FFCL N712PD |
| 064 | 550-0070 | N2072A N564CC N108DB N777FL N550KA N892PB |
| 065 | 550-0065 | N4191G N55SX ZS-RCS N144GA |
| 066 | 550-0071 | N4308G C-GDPD N404BF (N404BV) CS-DCI (OY-GMB) OY-GMK (D-CIRR) OE-GAD |
| 067 | 550-0052 | N4620G (OO-LFX) OY-ASV N90MJ N534MW N67TM PH-CTZ N550DR N302SJ |
| 068 | F550-0073 | N4621G F-GBTL VP-CTJ G-JBIZ |
| 069 | 550-0074 | N4754G N48ND (N86JM) LN-AAI N386MA (N551GN) (N10GN) D-CIFA LX-THS N174DR |
| 070 | 550-0056 | N5342J N752RT N444FJ N89D |
| 071 | 550-0058 | N5348J N71CJ N100HB |
| 072 | 550-0072 | (N2661H) N360N N36QN (N700EA) N969MT N551SR N770JM N778JM N905CW |
| 073 | 550-0057 | (N2661N) VH-WNZ |
| 074 | 550-0338 | (N2661P) (D-ICWB) (N71RL) N22RJ HB-VGE N28968 N550DW N500GM N500QM N900SE N900MF N992AS |
| 075 | 550-0060 | N26610 (N550KR) N75KR N98BE N315CK OE-GIL |
| 076 | 551-0015 | N26613 YV-213CP YV-2671P YV2073 |
| 077 | 550-0061 | (N26614) N456N N458N |
| 078 | 550-0062 | (N26615) (N77SF) C-GDLR |
| 079 | 551-0117 | (N26616) C-GHYD N11AB OO-SKS N551AD 4X-CZD |
| 080 | 550-0064 | N26617 YV-36CP N64TF (N550TJ) |
| 081 | 550-0066 | N26619 (N3031) N3032 N733H N783H N10JP (N410JP) N19HU N360RP |
| 082 | 550-0077 | (N2662A) N582CC N578W XA-PIJ XA-AGN |
| 083 | 550-0078 | (N2662B) N31KW N71FM N78GA C-GPTR (N277A) N533MA N432NM |
| 084 | 551-0122 | (N2662F) N10LR |
| 085 | 550-0090 | N2662Z N4110S N4110C N410NA N290VP |
| 086 | 550-0371 | (N26621) N551MC C-GCJN N585DM N550LS |
| 087 | 550-0079 | (N26622) N930BS (N26DA) N789SS N33RH N232DM |
| 088 | 550-0089 | (N26623) N88MJ (N44JX) (N444WJ) N43RW N81CC N800RR (N111DT) |
| 089 | 550-0080 | (N26624) G-BFLY HB-VGR N22511 N45ME |
| 090 | 550-0081 | N26626 I-FBCT N254AM I-AROO N..... |
| 091 | 550-0082 | N26627 G-BMCL N21DA N49U |
| 092 | 551-0024 | N26628 N2CA [w/o 18Dec82 Mountain View, MO] |
| 093 | 550-0084 | N26229 N222LB N808DM N156N N226N N226L N521WM (N467MW) N391AN N84NP N550SS |
| 094 | 550-0067 | N2663B N81TC N74TC N867CW N267CW N267BB |
| 095 | 551-0018 | N2663F N455DM N666AJ N556CC LN-AAD N387MA D-IEAR |
| 096 | 550-0086 | N2663G N414GC (N93CW) N43SA XC-HGZ N43SA |
| 097 | 551-0132 | N2663J (C-FCFP) C-GTBR N78GA SE-DYR |
| 098 | 551-0133 | N2663N G-JRCT N222TG I-JESA HB-VDO |
| 099 | 550-0076 | (N2663X) LN-HOT VH-LSW VH-TFY VH-XDD P2-MBD VH-QQZ |
| 100 | 550-0085 | (N2663Y) OY-GKC N57AJ OE-GBA |
| 101 | 550-0094 | (N26630) G-JETA G-RDBS G-JETA |
| 102 | 550-0095 | N26631 N400DT N100UF N550CG |
| 103 | 550-0096 | N26632 N550EW N30UC N87SF |
| 104 | 550-0097 | N26634 N404G N404E N202CE N999GR C- |
| 105 | 550-0098 | (N26635) N17S N212H N211JS |
| 106 | 550-0374 | N26638 YV-147CP YV-1478P (N772AC) YV-678CP N477A (N999LL) |
| 107 | 551-0021 | N26639 N107BB N307AJ N551CF N55LS N1HA |
| 108 | 551-0141 | N2664F (N108CT) N95CC N210MJ N888RF N888HW N100SC N388MA CC-CWZ N451DA (N636MA) N311TT |
| 109 | 550-0099 | N2664L N109JC |
| 110 | 550-0100 | N2664T (N801L) N801G N2S C-FKHD N140DA C-GLMK |
| 111 | 550-0101 | (N2664U) N91MJ (N42BM) [w/o 31Dec95 Marco Island Airport, FL] |
| 112 | 550-0102 | N2664Y VH-WNP VH-JCG VH-JPG VH-OYC VH-INT |
| 113 | 550-0376 | N26640 N313BT N30FJ N30EJ N73ST |
| 114 | F550-0092 | (N26643) N89B N89Q F-GFPO N89Q F-GNLF N567CA |
| 115 | 551-0026 | (N26648) N551R N12TV N25NH N32PB N612VR |
| 116 | 550-0105 | N26649 N116CC D-CNCP I-MTNT N105BA N550LH |
| 117 | 550-0106 | N2665A Argentina AE-129 LQ-TFM AE-129 (N83MA) N37CR N308CK N820MC (N820MQ) |
| 118 | 551-0149 | N2665D N550CB N225AD N225FM N550JS (N715PS) N5WT |
| 119 | 550-0108 | (N2665F) N4TL N4EK (N65SA) VP-CBE N36NA N690EW |
| 120 | 550-0109 | N2665N N753CC |
| 121 | 550-0091 | (N2665S) N527AC N527AG N601BC |
| 122 | 550-0110 | (N2665Y) N222SG N122G N550SF |
| 123 | 550-0111 | N26652 N3R N34WP (N3184Z) N123VP |
| 124 | 550-0112 | (N26656) (C-GDPE) C-GDPF N550PS N3FA N213CF YV2317 |
| 125 | 550-0113 | N2666A N227PC C-GDMF C-FIMP N90DA N550KD |
| 126 | 550-0114 | N2745G (N89B) N55HF N88HF N83HF (N900BM) N991BM N819KR |
| 127 | 550-0115 | N2745L N127SC SE-DDY OY-CCU SE-DDY |
| 128 | 550-0116 | N2745M HZ-AAA HZ-AAI PT-LGM N413CA N669MA N575BW |
| 129 | 550-0117 | N2745R N575FM N150HR N150HE N550RB N490DC |

## CITATION II

| Unit No | C/n | Identities |
|---|---|---|
| 130 | 550-0162 | N2745T VH-UOH N550KP N1UA N85HD |
| 131 | 550-0118 | N2745X LV-PHH N131ET N999BL N162DW EC-743 EC-FIL N118EA N138J N650BP |
| 132 | 551-0163 | N27457 N80BS D-IGRC ZS-ARG |
| 133 | 550-0378 | N2746B YV-299CP N3999H OH-CAT D-CIFA SE-RIK |
| 134 | 550-0121 | N2746C N655PC OB-M-1195 OB-1195 N850BA N51FT N896MA N899MA N121HL |
| 135 | 550-0122 | N2746E N135CC N70GM C-FCEL G-OSMC HB-VKH N221GA C-GCUL N89GA |
| 136 | 550-0123 | N2746F (CC-CGX) N36CJ N81TF SE-DEV LN-NEA SE-DEV LN-NLA N748DC N948DC |
| 137 | 550-0124 | N2746U LN-VIP N4557W N57MK N57MF N124CR N109GA (N789DD) |
| 138 | 550-0125 | N2746Z N5500F N320S N125RR 5N-NPF |
| 139 | 551-0169 | (N2747R) OE-GHP N26863 N82RP N82RZ N50HW N700YM N14RM |
| 140 | 550-0103 | N2747U XA-JEZ N90MA |
| 141 | 551-0171 | N26178 (9V-PUW) ZS-PMC 5R-MHF |
| 142 | 550-0184 | N2619M N80DR N813DH N200NC (N20TV) |
| 143 | 550-0127 | N2631N N29TC (N29TG) N550TJ G-GAUL G-ESTA |
| 144 | 551-0174 | N2631V N536M N220LA YU-BPU RC-BPU 9A-BPU F-WLEF EI-CIR N60AR EI-CIR |
| 145 | 550-0129 | N2632Y N537M N129TC N122MM N122HM (N550RD) N237WC |
| 146 | 550-0104 | N2633N CC-ECN Chile E-301 CC-CLC |
| 147 | 550-0132 | N2633Y G-CJHH N13627 N500VB (N330MG) PT-LLU |
| 148 | 550-0133 | N2634Y G-BHBH C-GRIO N228CC N198NS |
| 149 | 551-0179 | N2635D HZ-AAI HZ-ZTC N203BE N127BU |
| 150 | 551-0029 | N26369 (G-BHGH) N168CB N551PL N500ER D-ICUR N450GM N35403 [w/o 01Jan05 Ainsworth, TX; parted out] |
| 151 | 551-0180 | N8520J (D-CACS) N852WR D-ICAB N166MA (N729MJ) N222VV D-IHAG |
| 152 | 551-0181 | N2638A N56GT N137CF N29B N565VV (N61442) N551GE |
| 153 | 550-0138 | N2646X XC-SCT |
| 154 | 550-0139 | N2646Y ZS-KOO N222MJ PT-LJA N39FA PT-ORD (PT-WQG) OY-ELY |
| 155 | 550-0140 | N2646Z N55WL (N45WL) |
| 156 | 550-0141 | N26461 VH-ING VH-INX VH-EJY |
| 157 | 550-0142 | N2648Z PT-LCR N387SC |
| 158 | 550-0143 | N2649D N100VV N550TT PT-LQW (N660AC) N150RD N50JP N507EC* |
| 159 | 550-0144 | N2649E RP-C689 N418MA [w/o 18Nov03 Mineral Wells, TX] N97315 |
| 160 | 550-0145 | N2653R N444JJ VH-TFQ P2-MBN P2-TAA |
| 161 | 550-0146 | N26610 N580AV (N611RR) N501LC |
| 162 | 551-0036 | N2661P N162CC N160D N317SM N3170B N889FA VH-JMM |
| 163 | 551-0191 | N222AG N550CP (N771R) N107SB D-IVOB N127KR N386AM |
| 164 | 550-0149 | N116K |
| 165 | 550-0150 | N2668A N1SV |
| 166 | 550-0279 | (N88838) N566CC N886AT N566CC N550KA |
| 167 | 550-0152 | N88840 (N107) RP-C581 N88840 N550CA |
| 168 | 550-0153 | (N88842) N27BA N278A N50HS N50HE N27MH N37MH |
| 169 | 550-0130 | (N88845) N77RC N778C N630CC |
| 170 | 550-0381 | (N88848) N170CC N155PT N155BT (N49VP) N391BC N391KC N381VP |
| 171 | 550-0154 | (N8777N) G-DJBE G-EJET G-JETJ |
| 172 | 550-0382 | (N98715) YV-300CP N551TT N852SP N852SB |
| 173 | 550-0383 | (N98718) N551AB N561AS |
| 174 | 551-0031 | (N98749) N6565C YV-301CP N75TG N5T N5TQ EC-JTH |
| 175 | 550-0155 | N6566C (YV-209CP) YV-298CP N65TF N31RC N155TJ N168AM N215CW (N155FF) C-FNCT |
| 176 | 550-0156 | N98784 N6567C (N31F) N205SG N205SC (EC-IAX) N205SC |
| 177 | 551-0201 | N177CJ C-GGSP N550JB N550GB D-ISEC |
| 178 | 550-0175 | N10JK C-FWWW C-GHWW N550CU |
| 179 | 550-0165 | N98871 3D-ACQ ZS-LHU N976GA |
| 180 | 550-0166 | N88731 PH-MBX N166CF N166VP N367JC N867JC |
| 181 | 551-0205 | N88732 N999AU XA-KIQ N3951Z N342DA HB-VIO N828SS |
| 182 | 550-0167 | N88737 N100CJ N717DT |
| 183 | 550-0158 | N88738 (N662AA) N423D N550AJ N2JW N49HS N258CW N769H |
| 184 | 550-0168 | N88740 (VH-ICT) VH-TNP VH-LJK N785CA VH-LJK N68GA ZS-NII |
| 185 | 550-0169 | (N88743) N185CC N6001L XC-HHA N6001L |
| 186 | 550-0170 | N88791 N550TP N550TR N37BM N500CV N508CV N550DA |
| 187 | 550-0172 | N88795 (N28MM) N72MM N88JJ N78CS N412P N800TV SE-RCZ M-LEFB |
| 188 | 550-0171 | (N88797) (C-GDPE) N43D N934H (N984H) N333CG EI-BYN (N171VP) N19AJ N1TY |
| 189 | 550-0234 | N88798 N511WC C-FLPD N65DA N173AA |
| 190 | 551-0214 | N8881N N107T N163DA N178HH N9SS |
| 191 | 551-0215 | N88822 (N36NW) N286G N169JM (N169DA) N550HP (N151PR) N500PX N551CL |
| 192 | 550-0179 | N88824 N60MM N673LP N673LR |
| 193 | 550-0180 | N88825 N320V N77WD N77WU N3030C (N303GC) (N89TA) N3030T N219MS |
| 194 | 550-0181 | N88826 RP-C653 N550GP N50US |
| 195 | 550-0182 | N88830 (F-BKFB) F-GCSZ N78TF F-GEFB N30XX N165MC (F-....) N107CF F-HACA |
| 196 | 551-0050 | N98403 N1823B N196HA N196HR N228AK N228MH |
| 197 | 550-0186 | N98418 N80AW YV-187CP N80AW |
| 198 | 550-0187 | N98432 N303X N143DA N6WU N57CE N57CK C-GHOM N598CA |

## CITATION II

| Unit No | C/n | Identities | | | | | | | | |
|---|---|---|---|---|---|---|---|---|---|---|
| 199 | 550-0218 | N98436 | N45EP | PT-LPP | (N250DR) | | | | | |
| 200 | 551-0223 | N98468 | (N200MR) | N550LP | LN-AFG | 5B-CIS | LN-AAC | N754AA | YV-2567P | (N28GZ) |
| | | YV1776 | | | | | | | | |
| 201 | 550-0174 | (N98510) | N201CC | N666WW | N87PT | | | | | |
| 202 | 550-0151 | (N98528) | N35HC | N495CM | | | | | | |
| 203 | 550-0176 | N98563 | N552TF | N900TF | (N900TE) | N900TJ | N83SF | N83SE | (N24TR) | N61MA |
| 204 | 551-0023 | N98599 | N155TA | N34DL | PT-LME | [w/o 23Jly03 Sorocaba, Brazil] | | | | |
| 205 | 550-0189 | N98601 | D-CAAT | HB-VGP | D-CCCF | | | | | |
| 206 | 550-0183 | N98630 | (XC-DUF) | HB-VGS | G-JMDW | | | | | |
| 207 | 550-0188 | N98675 | VH-SWL | HB-VIZ | N38NA | N280PM | | | | |
| 208 | 550-0147 | N98682 | N155JK | N80GM | | | | | | |
| 209 | 550-0190 | N98715 | F-BTEL | F-GZLC | F-BTEL | F-GZLC | EC-JON | | | |
| 210 | 550-0083 | N98718 | N54CC | N200VT | | | | | | |
| 211 | 550-0164 | N164CC | N7YP | (N24PT) | N916RC | N721DR | | | | |
| 212 | 551-0033 | N88692 | D-IJHM | [w/o 19May82 Kassel, Germany] | | | | | | |
| 213 | 550-0191 | N88707 | C-GWCR | C-GWCJ | N550PA | | | | | |
| 214 | 550-0192 | N88716 | N44ZP | YV-900CP | N192DW | | | | | |
| 215 | 550-0249 | N88718 | N829JM | (N401U) | N201U | PT-LZO | (N48NA) | N39GA | N456AB | N456TX |
| 216 | 550-0159 | (N88721) | N45ZP | N188SF | C-GAPT | N444GB | N550PW | | | |
| 217 | 550-0194 | N88723 | N91B | | | | | | | |
| 218 | 550-0205 | (N88727) | N30JD | | | | | | | |
| 219 | 550-0196 | N6798Y | N68DS | N1212H | N800EC | N88ML | N400DK | HB-VLS | N196JS | |
| 220 | 550-0197 | N6798Z | (N30F) | N44FC | HB-VIT | N510JC | | | | |
| 221 | 550-0198 | (N67980) | XC-DOK | XA-SQV | | | | | | |
| 222 | 550-0199 | N67983 | N586RE | | | | | | | |
| 223 | 550-0260 | N67986 | N32JJ | N82JJ | N8CF | N6HF | | | | |
| 224 | 551-0245 | N67988 | N224CC | LN-AAE | [w/o 15Nov89 Mt Langfjelltind, nr Bardufoss, Norway] | | | | | |
| 225 | 550-0200 | N67989 | (G-BHVA) | N34SS | N28S | N287 | N28S | N284 | N810MC | (N810MG) |
| | | N797SF | N606KK | | | | | | | |
| 226 | 550-0206 | N6799C | XC-DUF | XA-SQW | N280TA | | | | | |
| 227 | 550-0201 | N6799E | N334AM | N566TX | N1GH | | | | | |
| 228 | 550-0185 | N6799L | N815GK | N600EZ | N370AC | N511DR | N511DL | N317HC | | |
| 229 | 550-0157 | N6799T | N550K | N101BX | N257CW | N535PC | N61HT | | | |
| 230 | 550-0202 | N6799Y | N590RB | N10CF | (N5GA) | N175VB | N550NE | N704DA | | |
| 231 | 550-0203 | N67990 | N12JA | N62HA | N766AE | (N766AF) | (N857BT) | YV252T | | |
| 232 | 550-0209 | N67997 | N121C | N101KK | (N877GB) | N444G | | | | |
| 233 | 550-0238 | N67999 | N97S | N204CF | | | | | | |
| 234 | 550-0207 | N6800C | (N95CC) | N163CB | N60BB | N1823C | HB-VJH | N207BA | N196RJ | |
| 235 | 550-0135 | N6800J | VH-KDI | N39142 | ZS-LLO | N555BC | TF-JET | N555BC | N550BP | |
| | | YV-888CP | YV2103 | | | | | | | |
| 236 | 550-0214 | N6800S | N13BJ | N44WF | N75Z | N75ZA | YV205T | YV2443 | | |
| 237 | 550-0222 | N6800Z | N17RG | PT-LNC | | | | | | |
| 238 | 550-0215 | N68003 | N500WP | (N400MT) | N40MT | N550MJ | | | | |
| 239 | 550-0204 | (N6801H) | N820 | N200JR | (N300PR) | N815CE | | | | |
| 240 | 550-0216 | N6801L | N240AR | (N911NJ) | N550PG | N304TH* | | | | |
| 241 | 550-0208 | N6801P | N54RC | N222WL | [scrapped for spares, cx Mar91] | | | | | |
| 242 | 550-0223 | N6801Q | N900BA | N901RM | N701RM | N400PC | N81TJ | N239CD | N550WL | |
| 243 | 550-0284 | N6801R | I-ARIB | OY-JEV | | | | | | |
| 244 | 550-0211 | N6801T | XA-LOT | N611CF | N77PH | N77PR | | | | |
| 245 | 550-0212 | (N6801V) | N245CC | | | | | | | |
| 246 | 551-0038 | N6801Z | D-IBPF | N550DA | N103M | N551BB | YU-BTT | | | |
| 247 | 550-0210 | N68018 | N762PF | (N177CM) | N3PC | N37WP | (N3184V) | N19VP | XA-SDN | XA-KMX |
| | | N850PM | | | | | | | | |
| 248 | 550-0220 | N6802S | N95CC | N275CC | N288CC | HI-500 | HI-500SP | HI-500CT | N80513 | |
| | | (N962HA) | N4CS | N4ZS | N123RF | N614SJ | | | | |
| 249 | 550-0193 | N6802T | (N47RP) | XC-FOO | XC-ROO | N2160N | N492ST | N72FL | N260J | N485AK |
| 250 | 550-0213 | N6802X | N420P | N421TX | N550HB | N213CC | | | | |
| 251 | 550-0224 | N6802Y | YV-O-MTC | YV-O-MTC-20 | | Venezuela 2222 | | | | |
| 252 | 550-0228 | N6802Z | (N702BC) | 5N-AWJ | N96CS | VH-EXM | N334ED | N334RJ | | |
| 253 | 550-0221 | N68026 | N253W | N95AX | N31GA | | | | | |
| 254 | 550-0227 | N68027 | N254CC | (N71CG) | PT-LND | N227DR | XA-GMP | | | |
| 255 | 550-0229 | N6803E | N550JM | OY-GRC | N50FC | C-FGAT | N229MC | | | |
| 256 | 550-0239 | N6803L | 8P-BAR | N4720T | N66MC | | | | | |
| 257 | 550-0235 | (N6803T) | N67SG | I-PNCA | | | | | | |
| 258 | 550-0225 | (N6803Y) | (N34SS) | N258CC | PT-LTJ | | | | | |
| 259 | 550-0195 | N68032 | N60JD | (N41CK) | N61CK | N343CM | | | | |
| 260 | 550-0236 | N68033 | N611ER | N611CR | N711VR | LN-AAD | N823NA | | | |
| 261 | 550-0248 | N6804C | N550SA | N233ST* | | | | | | |
| 262 | 550-0226 | N6804F | N29WS | N300JK | N550RG | N772HP | N872RT | N872RD | | |
| 263 | 550-0217 | N6804L | N88DD | N66DD | N66DN | N340DA | I-CIGA | N217SA | | |
| 264 | 550-0237 | N6804M | 3D-ACT | ZS-NHO | N41WJ | | | | | |
| 265 | 550-0230 | (N6804N) | (G-OTKI) | N3254G | N270RA | N141DA | N550EK | N550WB | | |
| 266 | 551-0285 | N6804S | (N550RL) | N551SR | ZS-MLN | N551HK | Venda VDF-030 | | ZS-MLN | |
| 267 | 551-0046 | N6804Y | C-GDDC | N34YL | N81GD | N518MV | | | | |
| 268 | 550-0241 | N6804Z | N10FN | N268J | (N32TJ) | XC-BCS | N241FT | XA-TQL | N241FT | |
| 269 | 550-0390 | N6805T | N58GG | (N500EE) | N500AE | N135BC | N136BC | VT-VPS | N14RZ | N717LC |

# CITATION II

| Unit No | C/n | Identities |
|---|---|---|
| 270 | 550-0250 | N68599 N9LR N33GK N250VP |
| 271 | 550-0231 | N6860A N28RF (N221BW) N671B N88TB N140DR N148DR N41SM |
| 272 | 551-0289 | N6860C N98GC N666JT N551BW PT-LJF |
| 273 | 550-0243 | N6860L TI-APZ VR-BHG N1333Z XA-POR XA-REN N214MD N67SF |
| 274 | 550-0307 | N6860R N37BM N550VW |
| 275 | 550-0254 | N6860S N171CB XA-TEL (N828SH) N112SA N888RT N888RL |
| 276 | 550-0247 | N6860T (N18DD) N928DS PT-LJJ (N85NA) |
| 277 | 551-0035 | N6860U N277HM N277JM |
| 278 | 551-0039 | N6860Y ECT-023 EC-DOH N71LP N550TA N551GF |
| 279 | 550-0245 | N68607 N505GP N388SB |
| 280 | 550-0257 | N68609 XC-HEQ XA-SQQ N187TA N53RG F-HCRT |
| 281 | 550-0303 | N6861D (N281AM) N160VE N40FJ N4JS N450CC XB-GLZ |
| 282 | 550-0246 | N6861E N72TC N78TC N69ME (N396DA) N68ME N35BP N551TK N550BP [w/o 04Jun07 Lake Michigan nr Milwaukee, MI] |
| 283 | 550-0255 | N6861L I-DEAF N28GA I-JESO D-CIAO |
| 284 | 550-0232 | N6861P N929DS N797CW |
| 285 | 550-0258 | N6861S N172CB (N550DD) N550CM N463C N550FB N258JS N550PR N424TG N752GS |
| 286 | 550-0256 | N6861X N3300L N550SM N550BM N75HS N75TP N55TP N111AF |
| 287 | 550-0251 | N68615 PK-WSO PK-TRV N550HF N20FB XA-GYA |
| 288 | 550-0261 | N68616 N40GS C-FLDM N41JP C-FLDM (N261VP) N261SS N50AZ N551WL |
| 289 | 550-0259 | N68617 VH-KDP N810JT OY-BZT |
| 290 | 551-0304 | N6862C G-DJHH G-TIFF N7028U N702KH N304KT N999MK N551NH |
| 291 | 550-0393 | N6862D N12GK I-FLYD |
| 292 | 550-0264 | N6862L N550KC N777WY N771WY N610JC |
| 293 | 550-0265 | N6862Q (N314MC) (N265QS) CN-TKK N16PL |
| 294 | 550-0252 | N6862R N507GP N6JL N6JU N525JA |
| 295 | 550-0253 | N68621 N23ND N18ND N31DA N75EC N202TS N953FT N157DW |
| 296 | 550-0266 | N68622 N296CC N296PH N296CF OE-GEC N15NA N825JW N825JV N550TT N550TP N330DK |
| 297 | 550-0267 | N68624 N932LM N15Y (N194JM) N502BG XA-OAC N910RB |
| 298 | 551-0311 | N68625 N298CJ N500EX N500FX N38TT |
| 299 | 550-0289 | N68629 D-CBAT OE-GST N550MD N820FJ N820SA N22HP C-FTIL C-FTMS VH-JMK |
| 300 | 551-0313 | N6863B OE-GLS N270CF YV-2426P |
| 301 | 551-0051 | N6863C (D-IHAT) D-ICTA |
| 302 | 550-0269 | N6863G N74MG N760 N28RC N1MM N28RC N1MM N550HJ |
| 303 | 550-0271 | N6863J (N303EC) N555EW N655EW N550CA N303J PT-ORO N167MA N729MJ N1NL |
| 304 | 550-0290 | N6863L VH-JBH OE-GCH N290BA N217LG N312NC |
| 305 | 550-0285 | N6863T N20CN N20CF (N17PL) N40PL N989TW N989TV C-GQCC |
| 306 | 550-0286 | N68631 N306SC SE-DLY N78BA N2GG |
| 307 | 550-0272 | N68633 9M-WAN VH-JPK HB-VKX VR-BVV VP-BVV SE-DVV Sweden 103001 [code 031] SE-DVV YU-BVV |
| 308 | 550-0273 | N68637 N217FS N121KM* |
| 309 | 550-0277 | N6864B N44LF (N550MT) N550WJ N550BJ |
| 310 | 550-0274 | N6864C ZS-LDK N14GA HB-VKT VP-CCM EC-HJD N75GA XB-JLJ N2057H |
| 311 | 551-0323 | N6864L (N990Y) N819Y N555RT |
| 312 | 551-0056 | N6864X (N312CC) I-GAMB N214AM I-NIAR N36WJ N826RT |
| 313 | 550-0280 | N6864Y N280MH N864D N300TC N7SN C-GKAU |
| 314 | 550-0281 | N6864Z N31RK N33EK |
| 315 | 550-0282 | N68644 G-JETC G-JCFR G-JETC |
| 316 | 550-0283 | (N68646) N316CC N316H N316CF N316CC TC-BAY N124GA N225J N257DW |
| 317 | 550-0287 | N68648 N444MM N65LC N67LC N920E YV-909CP N550RL N771AA (N221JS) N527DS YV.... |
| 318 | 550-0276 | N68649 C-GGFW N53FT |
| 319 | 550-0288 | N6865C G-JETB N4564P G-JETB G-MAMA G-JETB (G-OXEH) [w/o 26May93 Eastleigh, Southampton, UK] |
| 320 | 550-0291 | N6887T ZP-PNB ZP-TNB N550CD N41C N1AF N40MA N262Y |
| 321 | 550-0292 | N6887X N114EL (N63FS) C-FTOM C-FTOC C-GTDK |
| 322 | 550-0293 | N6887Y [w/o 19Dec92 Billings, MT; cx May93] |
| 323 | 550-0294 | N68872 PH-HET N323CJ PT-LPN |
| 324 | 550-0298 | N68873 N74KV N431DS D-ILCC N888FG |
| 325 | 550-0295 | N68876 N483G N800LA N345JR (N295EA) N339MC N48KH |
| 326 | 550-0296 | N6888C G-BJIR G-DWJM |
| 327 | 550-0304 | N6888D N208TC N369DA (N70PH) N42PH |
| 328 | 550-0299 | N6888L N538M HB-VIR N511AB |
| 329 | 550-0302 | N6888T N329CC N441T N133BC N33BC N792MA (SE-RCX) SE-RCY |
| 330 | 550-0306 | N6888X N303EC N550MT N341CW N296CW N206AG VH-NSB |
| 331 | 550-0396 | N6888Z N8AD N99DE N99CN |
| 332 | 550-0300 | N68881 YV-162CP YV2246 |
| 333 | 550-0310 | N68887 N130TC (N779DD) (N730TC) N779DD N7798D N530P |
| 334 | 551-0059 | N68888 N114DS N59FA N59FY N59DY |
| 335 | 550-0312 | N6889E N58H N61HA N61CF YV-1055CP YV255T |
| 336 | 550-0313 | N6889K (N393HC) N393RC N246NW N960CP N32TM N32TK |
| 337 | 550-0311 | N6889L N43TC N43TE N44TC N121CP N2RC N211SP N300GC |

## CITATION II

| Unit No | C/n | Identities | | | | | | | | |
|---|---|---|---|---|---|---|---|---|---|---|
| 338 | 550-0398 | N6889T | VH-BRX | N101DD | I-KESO | (N550SC) | N398S | PH-CTX | N610ED | N707LM |
| 339 | 550-0318 | N6889Y | N642BB | PT-LJT | PT-WJZ | | | | | |
| 340 | 550-0315 | N6889Z | N90JD | N618DB | N59GU | SE-RBK | | | | |
| 341 | 550-0308 | N68891 | 3D-AVH | N30SA | (F-GIRS) | N15XM | | | | |
| 342 | 550-0399 | (N6890C) | N66MS | N165RD | | | | | | |
| 343 | 550-0320 | (N6890D) | N343CC | N300GM | N800SB | N800EL | N800VJ | N3MB | N57MB | N204PM |
| 344 | 551-0351 | (N6890E) | N7FD | N612CC | N27U | N322CS | N5TR | | | |
| 345 | 550-0319 | N6890G | N8BX | N26SC | N26CT | N76CK | N78CK | | | |
| 346 | 550-0316 | N5428G | N828B | N143RW | N42KC | N129TS | N741JC | N26HH | | |
| 347 | 550-0321 | N5430G | N321SE | TC-COY | N321GN | VP-CCO | YU-FCS | | | |
| 348 | 551-0355 | N5451G | N551AS | I-ALPG | | | | | | |
| 349 | 550-0327 | N5474G | N74JA | N74JN | PT-LLT | | | | | |
| 350 | 550-0400 | N5492G | N350CC | N888EB | N53CC | [w/o 02Oct89 Roxboro, NC; cx Jul90] | | | | |
| 351 | 550-0323 | (N5703C) | OE-GCP | TC-FAL | TC-FMB | TC-YZB | (N323AM) | VP-CLD | N550LD | |
| 352 | 550-0324 | N5873C | N171LE | I-JESJ | N23W | HB-VLQ | F-HBMB | | | |
| 353 | 551-0359 | N67983 | (N551SE) | N142TJ | N740JB | | | | | |
| 354 | 551-0360 | N67988 | G-BJIL | N550MD | C-GSCR | N24CJ | N551EA | | | |
| 355 | 551-0361 | N6799C | LV-PNB | LV-APL | | | | | | |
| 356 | 550-0275 | N6799L | N550JR | N550CP | N555DS | | | | | |
| 357 | 550-0301 | N6799T | China 091 | B-4103 | B-7024 | | | | | |
| 358 | 550-0333 | N67990 | PT-LCW | N313CE | N123GM | N365WA | | | | |
| 359 | 550-0305 | N67999 | China 090 | B-4105 | B-7026 | | | | | |
| 360 | 550-0329 | N6800C | (N49N) | N491N | N949SA | | | | | |
| 361 | 550-0334 | N6800S | N92LT | N404KS | N755BP | N44FR | | | | |
| 362 | 550-0297 | N68003 | China 092 | B-4104 | B-7025 | | | | | |
| 363 | 551-0369 | N696A | N999GP | N998GP | N68BK | N778JC | | | | |
| 364 | 550-0401 | N6825X | N242WT | (N551GC) | N550KT | | | | | |
| 365 | 550-0335 | N6829Y | N1847B | N1847P | N51PS | N667CG | N204AB | N235TS | N187JN | |
| 366 | 550-0402 | N6830X | N700LB | N717PC | N57SF | | | | | |
| 367 | 550-0336 | N6830Z | N90Z | | | | | | | |
| 368 | 550-0337 | N6802S | N727C | N75F | (N78BA) | N54HJ | (N54HC) | N406SS | N3FW | N93AJ |
| 369 | 550-0326 | N6802T | N12FC | PT-OAF | (N983AJ) | N390AJ | (N390JP) | | | |
| 370 | 550-0339 | N6802Y | VH-KTK | VH-SCD | | | | | | |
| 371 | 550-0403 | N68027 | N101RL | N637EH | N362CP | N404BS | | | | |
| 372 | 550-0332 | N6803L | N372CC | N1880F | N12CQ | N120Q | | | | |
| 373 | 550-0341 | N68032 | C-GJAP | N182U | C-FDYL | N141JC | (N367EA) | | | |
| 374 | 550-0340 | N6804F | N374FC | N219SC | N219CS | N219SC | N235DB | ZP-TWN | N38DD | |
| 375 | 551-0378 | N6804L | G-BJVP | N4581Y | (N43D) | N115VH | N6EL | (F-OGUO) | (F-OGVA) | N322MA |
| 376 | 550-0345 | N6804Y | N312DC | N3GT | N30CZ | N267TG | N267TC | (N782NA) | (N50NA) | N982NA |
| 377 | 551-0060 | N6805T | N465D | N46SD | N458HW | (N458H) | (N60HW) | N59GB | | |
| 378 | 550-0344 | (N6806Y) | N6806X | N532M | PT-LKR | N550GM | C-GVGM | | | |
| 379 | 550-0357 | N6808C | N632SC | N29G | HB-VJA | N29FA | PT-OAG | | | |
| 380 | 550-0347 | N6826U | ZS-LEE | VH-ZLE | | | | | | |
| 381 | 550-0348 | N381CC | I-VIKI | N550CA | C-GSCX | XA-... | | | | |
| 382 | 550-0346 | N550CF | N106SP | N106SR | | | | | | |
| 383 | 550-0349 | N8FD | N870PT | (N221LC) | N600ST | N600SZ | N525LC | | | |
| 384 | 550-0350 | N86SG | | | | | | | | |
| 385 | 550-0405 | YV-276CP | YV-604P | YV-778CP | YV1813 | | | | | |
| 386 | 550-0351 | N99KW | I-ALKA | (N167WE) | | | | | | |
| 387 | 551-0388 | N711WM | [w/o 06Nov86; no details known; cx Nov87] | | | | | | | |
| 388 | 550-0354 | N121CG | N121C | VR-CJR | VP-CJR | SE-RBD | | | | |
| 389 | 550-0358 | N6801Q | Myanmar 4400 | | | | | | | |
| 390 | 550-0356 | N6801Z | PT-OER | N133WA | | | | | | |
| 391 | 550-0343 | (N1214D) | G-MINE | N721US | N20GT | N56FB | A6-SMS | G-ORCE | N789TT | |
| 392 | 551-0393 | N1214H | (N18CC) | N122SP | | | | | | |
| 393 | 550-0352 | (N1214J) | (N140DV) | N140V | (N72B) | I-ALKB | N352AM | VT-EUN | N352DA | |
| 394 | 550-0363 | N1214S | (N777NJ) | N444CC | HK-3400X | N363SP | N741T | (N46NR) | | |
| 395 | 551-0396 | (N1214Z) | N395CC | N39K | N39KY | N45GA | LV-WXD | | | |
| 396 | 550-0362 | N12142 | N396M | (N440PJ) | | | | | | |
| 397 | 550-0353 | (N12149) | G-GAIL | N3251H | N922RA | N922RT | LN-AAB | N922RT | N477KM | N353FT |
| 398 | 550-0406 | (N1215A) | N398CC | C-GHKY | N551CE | C-FTAM | N781SC | LV-ZPD | N815MA | |
| 399 | 550-0366 | N1215G | N200E | N2008 | N773LP | N55FM | (N614GA) | N110LD | | |
| 400 | 551-0400 | (N67983) | N550WR | N95CT | N280JS | D-IMME | | | | |
| 401 | 550-0407 | (N1215S) | N600CR | (N767TR) | N758S | (N950FC) | N55MV | | | |
| 402 | 550-0368 | (N12155) | N94ME | N94MF | N718CK | | | | | |
| 403 | 550-0364 | N12157 | N100AC | N550AV | C-GLTG | N180FW | N10VT | | | |
| 404 | 550-0365 | (N12159) | N712J | N100AG | N100AY | N129DV | N122WW | | | |
| 405 | 550-0367 | (N1216A) | N95CC | N17LK | N17LV | N3MB | N45ML | | | |
| 406 | 550-0408 | N1216H | N400TX | N110WA | | | | | | |
| 407 | 550-0409 | N1216J | N22T | HI-496 | (N22TZ) | HI-496SP | N7153X | VR-CIT | N102HB | |
| 408 | 550-0410 | N1216K | (N258P) | N46MK | N46MF | C-GNWM | | | | |
| 409 | 550-0411 | N1216N | N200YM | C-FMPP | N550KW | | | | | |
| 410 | 550-0412 | N1216Q | N410CC | N830VL | N223J | N450KD | | | | |
| 411 | 550-0355 | (N1216Z) | N122CG | N125CJ | N440TX | N500BR | N355DF | N52LT | | |
| 412 | 551-0412 | N12160 | G-OMCL | N413VP | OY-PDN | EC-KJR | | | | |
| 413 | 550-0414 | N12162 | N342CC | (N414VP) | N814AM | | | | | |

## CITATION II

| Unit No | C/n | Identities | | | | | | | | |
|---|---|---|---|---|---|---|---|---|---|---|
| 414 | 550-0415 | N12164 | D-CNCI | OH-CUT | N1949B | N1949M | F-GJYD | EC-KJJ | | |
| 415 | 550-0416 | N12167 | N416CC | | | | | | | |
| 416 | 550-0417 | N1217D | ZS-LHW | N17DM | | | | | | |
| 417 | 550-0418 | N1217H | N550J | N418CG | N214JT | | | | | |
| 418 | 550-0419 | N1217N | G-JETD | VH-JVS | G-WYLX | G-DCFR | G-FJET | | | |
| 419 | 550-0420 | N1217P | N200RT | N200RN | (N10PX) | I-AGSM | N555KT | | | |
| 420 | 550-0421 | N1217S | N67HW | N510GP | | | | | | |
| 421 | 551-0421 | N1217V | N421CJ | OO-RJE | SE-DEF | OE-GES | N550RD | D-IAWA | 3A-MRB | G-LUXY |
| 422 | 550-0423 | N12171 | N45MC | C-GUUU | C-FCCC | N248HA | | | | |
| 423 | 550-0424 | (N12173) | N18CC | N46A | (N469) | N24AJ | N555DH | N271CG | N551BP | N435UM |
| 424 | 550-0425 | N1218A | (LN-FOX) | Spain U.20-1/01-405 | | | | | | |
| 425 | 550-0426 | N1218F | N404SB | N434SB | (N426SP) | | | | | |
| 426 | 550-0427 | N1218K | N923RL | PT-LHY | N527EA | N840MC | N840MQ | N711CC | | |
| 427 | 550-0428 | (N1218P) | N7004 | N7864J | N107WV | N97BG | N550PF | | | |
| 428 | 551-0428 | N1218S | (N70HC) | (N147RP) | [w/o 22Dec99 Crisp County-Cordele, GA; cx Jun00] | | | | | |
| 429 | 550-0430 | N1218T | N264A | N1278 | HB-VLY | N567S | N56FT | XB-AGV | | |
| 430 | 551-0431 | N1218V | N21EH | N218H | N900TN | N59CC | (N431JC) | N4MM | N4NM | N551GS |
| 431 | 550-0369 | N1218Y | (N342CC) | N324CC | N431CB | N55MT | N725BA | N725BF | N725FL | |
| 432 | 550-0433 | N1219D | I-KIWI | N131GA | N7ZU | | | | | |
| 433 | 550-0434 | (N1219G) | N1109 | N1178 | (N515M) | N152JC | (N152JQ) | (D-CVAU) | N53FP | |
| 434 | 550-0435 | (N1219N) | N434CC | N20CL | N390DA | N674G | | | | |
| 435 | 550-0436 | N1219P | N711Z | N717DM | | | | | | |
| 436 | 551-0436 | N1219Z | N235KK | N437CF | N11SS | N102DR | | | | |
| 437 | 550-0438 | N12190 | (N555TD) | N437CC | N643TD | N100CH | | | | |
| 438 | 550-0432 | (N12191) | N432CC | I-ASAZ | N76AS | | | | | |
| 439 | 550-0439 | N1220A | ZS-LHT | N550RS | HK-3191X | N550RS | N511WS | N1250V | | |
| 440 | 550-0440 | (N1220D) | N31F | N31FT | N120TC | OY-CYV | | | | |
| 441 | 550-0441 | N1220J | N50LM | N56PC | VR-CCE | HB-VKS | N221GA | G-RVHT | N80LA | G-JETO |
| 442 | 550-0442 | (N1220N) | N32F | N53M | N943LL | N442MR | N442ME | N668AJ | | |
| 443 | 550-0443 | N1220S | N777FE | N777FB | OY-CYT | D-CGAS | EC-IMF | | | |
| 444 | 550-0444 | (N1248G) | N67MP | (N67ME) | N47SW | N71GA | C-FMJM | | | |
| 445 | 550-0445 | N1248K | (N666WW) | N453S | | | | | | |
| 446 | 550-0446 | N1248N | Spain U.20-2/01-406 | | | | | | | |
| 447 | 550-0447 | "N1248K" | N12482 | (N447CJ) | HB-VIS | G-JBIS | | | | |
| 448 | 550-0448 | N1249B | N964JC | N964J | N309AT | N82GA | N93DW | (N39HD) | N938W | N994CF |
| 449 | 550-0449 | N1249H | (YV-1107) | YV-2338P | Venezuela 1107 | | YV-2338P | | | |
| 450 | 550-0450 | N1249K | N15EA | N505RP | | | | | | |
| 451 | 550-0451 | N1249P | | | | | | | | |
| 452 | 550-0452 | (N1249T) | N452CJ | N150DM | N707WF | N707PE | N707PF | | | |
| 453 | 550-0453 | N1249V | N962JC | N962J | | | | | | |
| 454 | 550-0454 | N1216K | (N258P) | N12490 | N93BD | N938D | (N250KD) | | | |
| 455 | 550-0455 | N1250B | (YV-04CP) | N90SF | PT-MMO | | | | | |
| 456 | 550-0456 | N1250C | (N456CM) | N549CC | N24RF | N20RF | C-GMPQ | N283DF | | |
| 457 | 550-0457 | N1250L | N220CC | N457CF | N63TM | OY-TMA | | | | |
| 458 | 550-0458 | N1250P | N458CC | (N458DS) | XA-SET | N25MK | N664SS | LV-BCO | | |
| 459 | 550-0459 | N12500 | N15TW | N15TV | N315ES | N604PJ | | | | |
| 460 | 550-0460 | N12505 | N818TP | N818TB | (PT-...) | N6523A | PT-OKP | | | |
| 461 | 550-0461 | N12507 | N22FM | | | | | | | |
| 462 | 550-0462 | N12508 | N509TC | N67JW | XA-LTH | XB-LTH | N501DK | N550AL | N62TL | |
| 463 | 551-0463 | N1251B | N121JW | (N131EL) | YV-05C | YV-713CP | YV1563 | | | |
| 464 | 550-0464 | N1251D | XC-HEP | XA-SQR | N117TA | N822HA | | | | |
| 465 | 550-0465 | N1251H | N206TC | N68JW | HB-VIU | N784A | N387HA | N551WJ | N90PT | |
| 466 | 550-0466 | N1251K | HI-420 | (N1251K) | HI-420 | N1251K | I-TNTR | N412MA | N10LY | |
| 467 | 550-0467 | N1251N | N1883 | N64PM | N64CM | YV-810CP | YV2166 | | | |
| 468 | 550-0468 | (N1251P) | N468CJ | D-CBEL | N123FH | N120JP | | | | |
| 469 | 550-0469 | N1251V | G-BKSR | VR-BIZ | HB-VIP | N123SR | N50N | [crashed 18Oct01 Bolzano A/P | | |
| | | Italy; cx Nov01] | | (OY-ERY) | N50N | (I-....) | (OY-...) | N420SS | N550GT | |
| 470 | 550-0470 | N1251Z | N10RU | F-GFJL | N10RU | N202SW | N60FT | | | |
| 471 | 550-0471 | N12510 | N797WC | N787WC | N92B | (N623KC) | N271AG | N770TB | | |
| 472 | 550-0472 | N12511 | HZ-AFP | N12511 | N492MA | N492AT | [w/o 24Jan07 Butler, PA; parted out] | | | |
| 473 | 550-0473 | N12513 | HZ-AFQ | N12513 | N484MA | XB-HZF | N70224 | XB-IZK | | |
| 474 | 550-0474 | N12514 | ZS-LIG | | | | | | | |
| 475 | 550-0475 | N1252B | N870MH | N475WA | N475HC | | | | | |
| 476 | 550-0476 | N1252D | | | | | | | | |
| 477 | 550-0477 | N1252J | N1515P | N151JC | N648WW | N649WW | N47TW | (N477JR) | N269JR | N269JD |
| | | N344KK | (N846L) | | | | | | | |
| 478 | 550-0478 | N1252N | N4FE | N57BC | N214RW | N17WC | N32SM | | | |
| 479 | 550-0479 | N1252P | N999RC | PT-OOM | N45NS | N68TS | | | | |
| 480 | 550-0480 | (N12522) | N72K | N72U | YU-BPL | SL-BAC | S5-BAC | N335CC | N380MS | ZS-OIE |
| 481 | 550-0481 | N1253D | N550MW | D-IADD | N531A | CC-LLM | N481VP | N97EM | | |
| 482 | 550-0482 | N1253G | N62GC | N62WG | N594G | N99DY | | | | |
| 483 | 550-0483 | (N1253K) | N141AB | N483AS | N83AG | N147PS | N483SC | N412PE | N17FS | N17VP |
| | | N729TA | | | | | | | | |
| 484 | 550-0484 | N1253N | N84EA | N501GG | | | | | | |
| 485 | 550-0485 | N1253P | N474SP | N74SP | N485A | PT-WBV | N727C | | | |
| 486 | 550-0486 | N1253Y | A40-SC | N410CS | (N35PN) | XA-AAK | | | | |

# CITATION II

| Unit No | C/n | Identities |
|---|---|---|
| 487 | 550-0487 | N12532 (N487CC) N444BL N550DW |
| 488 | 550-0488 | N12536 N84EB C-FCSS N990MM N990MR |
| 489 | 550-0489 | N12539 N63CC N15RL (N801TA) N489SS |
| 490 | 550-0490 | N1254C N490CC (N490CD) |
| 491 | 550-0491 | (N1254D) I-AVRM |
| 492 | 550-0492 | (N1254G) I-AVGM |
| 493 | 550-0493 | N1254P (N258P) N84AW N84GC |
| 494 | 550-0494 | N1254X (XC-JBR?) N1254X |
| 495 | 550-0495 | (N1254Y) N495CC JA8495 N505GL PT-LLQ (N400MC) N10TC |
| 496 | 551-0496 | (N12543) N232CC N8008F N999GH LX-PRS LN-ACX OE-FAD 9A-DOF |
| 497 | 550-0497 | (N12549) N1257B (XC-JBQ?) N1257B |
| 498 | 550-0498 | (N1255D) N550CJ N1823B N78FK N772SB |
| 499 | 550-0499 | (N1255G) N550PT PT-LIV |
| 500 | 551-0500 | N1255J N90RC N501MC N9CR |
| 501 | 550-0501 | N12549 |
| 502 | 550-0502 | N1255D Turkey 12-001 Turkey 84-007 Turkey 007 |
| 503 | 550-0503 | N1255G Turkey 12-002 Turkey 84-008 Turkey 008 |
| 504 | 550-0504 | (N1255J) N979C N979G N72SL XA-TQA |
| 505 | 550-0505 | N1255K (XC-JAY?) N1255K |

Unit numbers 506 to 549 not used (506 to 531 built as S550s c/n 0001 to 0026 - qv)

| Unit No | C/n | Identities |
|---|---|---|
| 550 | 550-0550 | N1299N PT-LOC N550FM HK-4128W N550FM N177RJ |
| 551 | 550-0551 | N487LD N600AT |
| 552 | 551-0552 | OE-FPA D-IADV |
| 553 | 550-0553 | N553CC N46MT XA-ODC (N555SL) N5XR N553MJ |
| 554 | 550-0554 | N1297Y ZS-NAT N2140L N40FC (N40WE) N40YC N700JR (N705JT) N750SL |
| 555 | 550-0555 | N1297Z (EI-BUN) EI-BUY D-IRKE N93BA N560CB N104HW |
| 556 | 551-0556 | (N12979) N200GF |
| 557 | 551-0557 | N1298C N711NV |
| 558 | 550-0558 | (N1298G) N209G N558VP N558AG LV-WJN |
| 559 | 550-0559 | (N1298H) G-BNSC VR-CHB D-ICHE OO-MMP N409ST |
| 560 | 550-0560 | N1298J ZS-LNP N560AJ D-IMMF N550GX |
| 561 | 550-0561 | N1298K I-SALV N916WJ PT-OYP (N234RA) C-GYCJ [canx 14Oct03 as sold in USA; to Dodsons Intl Parts following accident 12Nov02 Sandspit, BC, Canada] |
| 562 | 550-0562 | (N1298N) D-CBAT N562CD PT-OJT N813A N54RM |
| 563 | 550-0563 | N1298P G-THCL N518N |
| 564 | 550-0564 | N1298X PH-MCX (N87683) N564VP C-GBCF N674CA D-CASH [w/o 19Feb96 nr Freilassing, Salzburg, Austria] |
| 565 | 550-0565 | N1298Y N565CJ N88BM N565JS N565NC |
| 566 | 550-0566 | (N1299B) N15SP N15SN N900PB |
| 567 | 550-0567 | (N1299H) N321F N41BH N926RM |
| 568 | 550-0568 | N1299K N988RS N83KE N47SM |
| 569 | 550-0569 | N1299P G-JFRS G-OSNB 5Y-TWE ZS-SCX C-GQYL |
| 570 | 550-0570 | (N1299T) N2KH N570VP N570WD N270CW (N189WW) |
| 571 | 550-0571 | N12990 N90JJ (N278S) |
| 572 | 551-0572 | N12992 N193SS N719EH D-IRUP |
| 573 | 550-0573 | (N12993) C-FJOE N944AF PT-OKM N155AC |
| 574 | 551-0574 | N12998 N60GL N60GF OE-FBS |
| 575 | 550-0575 | N12999 N910G N46BA N337RE N387RE |
| 576 | 550-0576 | (N1300G) N576CC N438SP N675SS |
| 577 | 550-0577 | (N1300J) N557CC N100CX N120HC N827JB N8344M |
| 578 | 550-0578 | N1300N PT-LQJ N54NS N203PM |
| 579 | 550-0579 | (N13001) N579L N750TB |
| 580 | 550-0580 | (N13006) N912BD N18NA |
| 581 | 550-0581 | (N13007) N905LC N805LC |
| 582 | 550-0582 | (N1301A) Colombia FAC1211 |
| 583 | 550-0583 | N1301B N62WA (N583VP) N12L N12LW N22PC (N22PQ) (N228G) |
| 584 | 550-0584 | N1301D N550WW N550WV N25QT N25QF N979WC |
| 585 | 550-0585 | N1301K C-GTCI N94AF N79SE N89SE N65AR N585PS VP-CRA |
| 586 | 550-0586 | N1301N F-GGGA |
| 587 | 550-0587 | N1301S ZS-MBX N550SM N1301S N18HJ |
| 588 | 550-0588 | N1301V N255CC N92BD (N747RT) N633RT |
| 589 | 550-0589 | N1301Z N679BC N787JD N589SJ |
| 590 | 550-0590 | C-GBCA N673CA N88NM XA-UGG |
| 591 | 551-0591 | C-GBCE N672CA N1AT N608JR |
| 592 | 550-0592 | N1302N Spain U.20-3/01-407 |
| 593 | 550-0593 | N1302V N26621 (XC-JBT?) N26621 |
| 594 | 550-0594 | N1302X N2531K |
| 595 | 550-0595 | N2734K |
| 596 | 550-0596 | N96TD D-CAWA EC-HGI |
| 597 | 550-0597 | N13027 G-SSOZ G-MRTC N24EP N400LX N400EX N213JS |
| 598 | 550-0598 | N13028 (PT-...) XC-ROO N7WY N888XL |
| 599 | 550-0599 | G-SYKS N599FW VR-BPF VR-BYE N571BC |
| 600 | 550-0600 | N1303H PT-LSR N415AJ |
| 601 | 550-0601 | (N1303M) G-ELOT G-OCDB G-CBTU N42NA N501RL |

## CITATION II

| Unit No | C/n | Identities | | | | | | | | |
|---|---|---|---|---|---|---|---|---|---|---|
| 602 | 550-0602 | N2663Y | (XC-JAZ?) | N2663Y | | | | | | |
| 603 | 550-0603 | N603CJ | C-GMSM | N560AB | N550TW | | | | | |
| 604 | 550-0604 | N821G | N30WE | LV-WIT | N64VP | N827JB | N887SA | N904SJ | | |
| 605 | 550-0605 | N26494 | | | | | | | | |
| 606 | 550-0606 | N770BB | N602AT | | | | | | | |
| 607 | 550-0607 | N26496 | | | | | | | | |
| 608 | 550-0608 | N12419 | PT-LTL | (N675DM) | N608VP | N608AM | N990M | | | |
| 609 | 550-0609 | (N1242A) | N609TC | D-CHOP | N344A | F-GLTK | | | | |
| 610 | 550-0610 | N1242B | "M-JMF" | 9M-JMF | (9M-UEM) | 9M-NSA | N610BL | N610JB | | |
| 611 | 550-0611 | (N1242K) | F-GGGT | | | | | | | |
| 612 | 550-0612 | N1244V | N300AK | N380AK | (N534M) | N578M | | | | |
| 613 | 550-0613 | N1250P | PT-OAC | N664AJ | | | | | | |
| 614 | 551-0614 | (N1251P or N1251V) | | D-ILAN | N26HG | | | | | |
| 615 | 550-0615 | N12522 | N88HF | N87CF | CS-AYS | N615EA | N577VM | N577VN | N803SC | |
| 616 | 550-0616 | (N1253K) | N55LS | (D-IAFA) | PT-OVV | | | | | |
| 617 | 551-0617 | (N1253Y) | N617CM | D-ILTC | N450GM | N747JB | N881SA | N40EP | | |
| 618 | 550-0618 | N1254C | PT-LXG | PP-ESC | | | | | | |
| 619 | 550-0619 | (N1254D) | N170TC | (N619BA) | N550BD | XA-LRL | N15FJ | N522FJ | N552FJ | N67BE |
| 620 | 550-0620 | N1254G | PT-LYA | N250GM | N508DW | (N508AJ) | N477JE | (N391DH) | N391DT | |
| 621 | 550-0621 | N12543 | ZS-MLS | N502SU | OY-RDD | N102PA | N99TK | | | |
| 622 | 550-0622 | (N1255J) | N326EW | N826EW | HB-VKP | LX-VAZ | F-HAJV | | | |
| 623 | 550-0623 | (N1255L) | N89LS | | | | | | | |
| 624 | 550-0624 | N1255Y | PT-LYS | N662AJ | N65DV | | | | | |
| 625 | 550-0625 | (N12554) | PT-LYN | N625EA | N6846T | (F-HCCN) | F-HBFK | | | |
| 626 | 550-0626 | (N1256G) | N117GS | N626VP | LV-PLR | LV-WOZ | N466SS | | | |
| 627 | 550-0627 | (N1256N) | N17FL | N650WC | N804BC | | | | | |
| 628 | 550-0628 | (N1256P) | N183AJ | N183AB | Ecuador IGM-628 | | | | | |
| 629 | 550-0629 | N1256T | D-CHVB | [w/o 25Jan95 Allendorf, Germany; cx Mar95] | | | | | | |
| 630 | 550-0630 | N1257K | PH-CSA | N220AB | N198DF | N198ND | | | | |
| 631 | 550-0631 | (N1257M) | N631CC | XA-RUD | XA-ICP | N631EA | N631TS | | | |
| 632 | 550-0632 | N12570 | 5N-AYA | | | | | | | |
| 633 | 550-0633 | N12576 | PT-OSK | N388FA | N7AB | N550AB | | | | |
| 634 | 550-0634 | (N1258B) | PH-MDX | N550SB | SE-DVT | F-HDGT | | | | |
| 635 | 550-0635 | N1258H | PT-OAA | N550NS | (N622EX) | N622VH | (N214CP) | N277JE | N550HW | |
| 636 | 550-0636 | N1258M | N4EW | N50NF | | | | | | |
| 637 | 550-0637 | (N1258U) | YV-376CP | YV2286 | | | | | | |
| 638 | 550-0638 | (N12582) | N500RR | N1717L | N255TC | | | | | |
| 639 | 550-0639 | (N1259B) | N22RG | N62RG | N100DS | | | | | |
| 640 | 550-0640 | (N1259K) | N1308V | PT-ODL | | | | | | |
| 641 | 550-0641 | (N1259N) | N1309A | PT-OOA | N1309A | PT-WON | N395HE | (N391DT) | N895HE | |
| 642 | 550-0642 | (N1259R) | N1309K | XA-JRF | XA-SEX | XB-IKY | | | | |
| 643 | 550-0643 | (N1259S) | N13091 | PT-ODW | N643MC | N747CR | G-EJEL | | | |
| 644 | 550-0644 | (N1259Y) | (N13092 or N1310B) | | XC-PGM | | | | | |
| 645 | 550-0645 | (N1259Z) | N1310C | PT-ODZ | | | | | | |
| 646 | 550-0646 | (N12593) | (N1310G) | N9VF | N562RM | | | | | |
| 647 | 550-0647 | (N12596) | N647CC | N205BE | N140MD | N800MT | N604DS | | | |
| 648 | 550-0648 | N1260G | (N1310Q) | XC-PGP | | | | | | |
| 649 | 550-0649 | (N1310Z) | I-ATSE | N4320P | N44LC | N44LQ | HB-VMH | N649DA | G-SOVA | |
| 650 | 550-0650 | (N1311A) | PK-WSG+ | [+ marks worn but not officially reg'd] | | | | N28RC | N824CT | N823CT |
| | | C-GBBX | | | | | | | | |
| 651 | 550-0651 | (N1131K) | N24E | | | | | | | |
| 652 | 550-0652 | (N1311P) | N3262M | [uses marks XC-HJF when flying missions on behalf of Mexican Customs] | | | | | | |
| 653 | 550-0653 | N36854 | N30RL | | | | | | | |
| 654 | 550-0654 | N36886 | XA-RZB | XB-BON | | | | | | |
| 655 | 550-0655 | N37201 | [uses marks XC-HJH when flying missions on behalf of Mexican Customs] | | | | | | | |
| 656 | 550-0656 | N30GR | | | | | | | | |
| 657 | 550-0657 | N3986G | CC-DGA | | | | | | | |
| 658 | 550-0658 | N550MZ | RP-C1180 | N137PA | | | | | | |
| 659 | 550-0659 | N4614N | (XC-HGZ?) | N4614N | | | | | | |
| 660 | 550-0660 | N5233J | D-CMJS | 5B-CIQ | N550JF | D-CILL | N160SP | N827DP | | |
| 661 | 550-0661 | N5252C | N550RA | N847HS | N3444B | N3444P | XA-AFU | N550AR | VT-CLB | |
| 662 | 550-0662 | N5294C | N911CB | N911QB | N623DS | N623JL | | | | |
| 663 | 550-0663 | N5314J | | | | | | | | |
| 664 | 550-0664 | N5315J | N67LH | XA-RYR | N70PC | N45BE | | | | |
| 665 | 550-0665 | N5348J | N665MC | N998BC | | | | | | |
| 666 | 550-0666 | (N5703C) | N5408G | [uses marks XC-JBS when flying missions on behalf of Mexican Customs] | | | | | | |
| 667 | 550-0667 | EC-621 | EC-FDL | N668EA | VR-CWM | VP-CWM | N167EA | N107EE | | |
| 668 | 550-0668 | N668CM | N1879W | (N866VP) | XA-TVH | | | | | |
| 669 | 550-0669 | N6170C | N98TJ | N6170C | N846HS | N677GS | VH-CFO | | | |
| 670 | 550-0670 | N6637G | [uses marks XC-JEG when flying missions on behalf of Mexican Customs] | | | | | | | |
| 671 | 550-0671 | (N6761L) | 9M-TAA | N671EA | G-BWOM | G-VUEA | | | | |
| 672 | 550-0672 | N6763C | PT-OMB | N550PF | G-OTIS | (N394MA) | OY-VIS | SE-RHP | | |
| 673 | 550-0673 | N6763L | (XC-HHA?) | N6763L | XC-HHA | N6763L | | | | |
| 674 | 550-0674 | (N6770S) | (N550FB) | N1883M | N1888M | N45TP | N65TP | N910HM | N918HM | N690AN |
| 675 | 550-0675 | N6773P | PT-OJK | N275BD | PT-WKQ | | | | | |
| 676 | 550-0676 | N67741 | PT-OJG | | | | | | | |

## CITATION II/BRAVO

| Unit No | C/n | Identities | | | | | | | |
|---|---|---|---|---|---|---|---|---|---|
| 677 | 550-0677 | N6775C | [uses marks XC-HJC when flying missions on behalf of Mexican Customs] | | | | | | |
| 678 | 550-0678 | N6775U | EC-777 | EC-FES | SE-RCI | EC-KBZ | | | |
| 679 | 550-0679 | (N6776P) | I-FJTO | N250GM | N622EX | N782ST | | | |
| 680 | 550-0680 | N6776T | [uses marks XC-HJE when flying missions on behalf of Mexican Customs] | | | | | | |
| 681 | 550-0681 | (N6776Y) | N1200N | [uses marks XC-LHA when flying missions on behalf of Mexican Customs] | | | | | |
| 682 | 550-0682 | N682CM | YV-662CP | N682CJ | N90BL | N90BY | N73HH | | |
| 683 | 550-0683 | YV-701CP | YV1192 | | | | | | |
| 684 | 550-0684 | N6778L | C-FJXN | | | | | | |
| 685 | 550-0685 | C-FJWZ | | | | | | | |
| 686 | 550-0686 | C-FKCE | | | | | | | |
| 687 | 550-0687 | N6778Y | C-FKDX | | | | | | |
| 688 | 550-0688 | C-FKEB | | | | | | | |
| 689 | 550-0689 | N12001 | XA-JPA | XA-JYO | N689VP | | | | |
| 690 | 550-0690 | N6780C | OE-GLZ | VH-VLZ | | | | | |
| 691 | 550-0691 | N910H | C-GAPD | C-GAPV | N600JB | | | | |
| 692 | 550-0692 | N692TT | N75RJ | | | | | | |
| 693 | 550-0693 | VR-BTR | VP-BTR | N594WP | | | | | |
| 694 | 550-0694 | N694CM | N550KE | N807MB | | | | | |
| 695 | 550-0695 | N6782T | N695VP | N870WC | N7851M | N77DD | N153TH | | |
| 696 | 550-0696 | N29PF | N67PC | N67NC | N696VP | (N74EH) | | | |
| 697 | 550-0697 | N6851C | ZS-NFL | N697EA | HB-VMP | D-CHEP | N697BA | LV-BRE | |
| 698 | 550-0698 | N12003 | YV-911CP | N550RM | VT-CLC | | | | |
| 699 | 550-0699 | C-FKLB | | | | | | | |
| 700 | 550-0700 | C-FJCZ | | | | | | | |
| 701 | 550-0701 | C-FLZA | | | | | | | |
| 702 | 550-0702 | C-FMFM | | | | | | | |
| 703 | 550-0703 | N308A | | | | | | | |
| 704 | 550-0704 | N704CD | (N197GH) | N197HF | (N187HF) | N197PR | | | |
| 705 | 550-0705 | N521TM | | | | | | | |
| 706 | 550-0706 | 7Q-YLF | N706NA | | | | | | |
| 707 | 550-0707 | N1202T | RP-C4654 | (SE-DYY) | N707EA | OE-GDM | HS-RBL | OE-GRD | |
| 708 | 550-0708 | N12022 | N720WC | N923JH | | | | | |
| 709 | 550-0709 | N1203D | N709CC | N12RN | N18RN | N85KC | N709VP | N709RS | VT-SGT |
| 710 | 550-0710 | N1203N | ZP-TCA | N510VP | N90BJ | | | | |
| 711 | 550-0711 | N1203S | N711CN | N58LC | XB-ZZZ | | | | |
| 712 | 550-0712 | (N12030) | PH-LAB | | | | | | |
| 713 | 550-0713 | N12033 | N293PC | N95HE | N283CW | N400EC | | | |
| 714 | 550-0714 | N12035 | N593EM | G-SPUR | | | | | |
| 715 | 550-0715 | N1204A | PT-OTN | N715AB | LV-PNL | LV-YHC | | | |
| 716 | 550-0716 | N1205A | N4VR | (N800KC) | VR-CTE | VP-CTE | VP-CTF | N550TL | |
| 717 | 550-0717 | (N1205M) | XA-TCM | N600GH | TC-SES | Sweden 103002 | | SE-RBM | OE-GBC F-HBMR |
| 718 | 550-0718 | N12060 | XA-FIR | N142GA | N129ED | | | | |
| 719 | 550-0719 | N12068 | (N550BG) | | | | | | |
| 720 | 550-0720 | (N1207A) | N720CC | XA-SMV | N72WE | N848HS | N260TB | N550MW | |
| 721 | 550-0721 | N1207B | N721CC | | | | | | |
| 722 | 550-0722 | N1207C | XA-SMT | N1886G | N220LE | | | | |
| 723 | 550-0723 | N1207D | N5NE | (N888NA) | N777JE | | | | |
| 724 | 550-0724 | N1207F | LV-PGU | LV-WEJ | | | | | |
| 725 | 550-0725 | N1207Z | N222FA | N725CC | | | | | |
| 726 | 550-0726 | N1209T | XT-AOK | N918GA | VP-CMD | N726BM | N726AM | | |
| 727 | 550-0727 | (N1209X) | N727CM | N521BH | LV-ZNR | N232JS | N550DG | N550KR | VT-CLD |
| 728 | 550-0728 | (N1210N) | N728CC | LV-PHN | LV-WJO | | | | |
| 729 | 550-0729 | N1210V | VR-CBM | VP-CBM | N38NA | | | | |
| 730 | 550-0730 | N1211M | N730BR | (N730VP) | N2NT | N773VP | (N650JP) | N501JP | XA-... |
| 731 | 550-0731 | N12117 | N550BP | XC-SST | | | | | |
| 732 | 550-0732 | N1213S | N101AF | N902DK | | | | | |
| 733 | 550-0733 | N1213Z | C-GFCI | N4347F | N550VR | N550TR | N44SW | | |
| 734 | 550-0734 | [first Bravo model] | (N1214J) | N550BB | | | | | |

Production continues as Citation Bravo

## CITATION BRAVO

| C/n | Identities | | | |
|---|---|---|---|---|
| 550-0801 | N5135K | N801BB | | |
| 550-0802 | N5135R | N802CB | N550HH | |
| 550-0803 | N52113 | N550FB | N141HL | N251CF |
| 550-0804 | N5214J | N804CB | N550BC | (N41VY) |
| 550-0805 | N5214K | N108RF | N4AT | |
| 550-0806 | N52141 | N300PY | | |
| 550-0807 | N52144 | C-FANS | C-GPGA | |
| 550-0808 | N5216A | N1299B | SE-DVZ | YU-BSM |
| 550-0809 | N800AK | N300AK | N380AK | |
| 550-0810 | N5218T | VH-MGC | VH-XCJ | VH-XBP |

## CITATION BRAVO

| C/n | Identities | | | | |
|---|---|---|---|---|---|
| 550-0811 | N5221Y | PT-MMV | | | |
| 550-0812 | N5223P | C-FJBO | | | |
| 550-0813 | N5096S | N813CB | N100KU | | |
| 550-0814 | N5093L | PT-WNH | N303CS | | |
| 550-0815 | N51038 | N126TF | | | |
| 550-0816 | N5225K | C-FMCI | | | |
| 550-0817 | N5076J | N817CB | (YV-....) | N123GF | |
| 550-0818 | N5097H | LV-PMV | LV-WYH | N818AJ | N300CS |
| 550-0819 | N5092D | N1259B | N15CV | N15CN | N324JT |
| 550-0820 | N5117U | N820CB | N302CS | | |
| 550-0821 | N5093Y | N77797 | N225WT | | |
| 550-0822 | N5214L | N550TG | N822CB | N52MW | N2029E | N725DS |
| 550-0823 | N50715 | (N823CB) | N25FS | | |
| 550-0824 | N5121N | N824CB | | | |
| 550-0825 | N5060P | N25HV | (N45HV) | N305CS | |
| 550-0826 | N51072 | N595PC | | | |
| 550-0827 | N51042 | D-CCAB | | | |
| 550-0828 | N5058J | N6FR | | | |
| 550-0829 | N5096S | N829CB | | | |
| 550-0830 | N5076J | (N550KE) | N830KE | N717CB | |
| 550-0831 | N5145P | N331PR | | | |
| 550-0832 | N5148B | PT-WSO | N832UJ | | |
| 550-0833 | N5145P | PT-WVC | N833PA | PR-FEP | |
| 550-0834 | N834CB | D-CALL | | | |
| 550-0835 | N835CB | N198SL | (N835VP) | (N10PZ) | N226PC |
| 550-0836 | N51872 | N122NC | | | |
| 550-0837 | N5185J | OE-GPS | | | |
| 550-0838 | N49FW | N49KW | N813JD | | |
| 550-0839 | N839DW | N101FG | | | |
| 550-0840 | N5086W | N442SW | N773CA | | |
| 550-0841 | N5086W | N841WS | N841W | N999CX | |
| 550-0842 | N86AJ | N842CB | N621KR* | | |
| 550-0843 | N5079V | N627L | AP-BHE | | |
| 550-0844 | N550KL | | | | |
| 550-0845 | N51817 | N550WS | | | |
| 550-0846 | N5101J | N517AF | | | |
| 550-0847 | N5076K | N133AV | N304CS | | |
| 550-0848 | N997HT | N550J | | | |
| 550-0849 | (N849CB) | N51143 | N541JG | N246CB | N315N | N623N |
| 550-0850 | N5073G | N551G | N551V | | |
| 550-0851 | N7NN | | | | |
| 550-0852 | N5076J | VH-FGK | | | |
| 550-0853 | N5086W | N398LS | | | |
| 550-0854 | N5188A | N550KH | N550KJ | | |
| 550-0855 | N132LF | N232JR | | | |
| 550-0856 | N820JM | N300GF | N300GP | N426JK | N103CX |
| 550-0857 | N51246 | VP-CNM | VP-CCP | N984BK | |
| 550-0858 | N1273Q | N100WT | | | |
| 550-0859 | N551KH | (N550KH) | I-BENN | | |
| 550-0860 | N860JH | (N860J) | N844DR | | |
| 550-0861 | N861BB | N26CB | N26CV | | |
| 550-0862 | N442SW | N1962J | N888HS | N1976J | |
| 550-0863 | N704JW | N709JW | N577VM | | |
| 550-0864 | N864CB | OE-GTZ | D-CCWD | HB-VOH | |
| 550-0865 | N505X | D-CPPP | | | |
| 550-0866 | N866CB | D-CHZF | | | |
| 550-0867 | N161TM | | | | |
| 550-0868 | N5117U | N627BC | | | |
| 550-0869 | N98RX | N499WM | | | |
| 550-0870 | N50612 | VP-CED | | | |
| 550-0871 | N5108G | N871CB | I-GIWW | | |
| 550-0872 | N5093L | OE-GKK | | | |
| 550-0873 | N5109R | PT-XSX | | | |
| 550-0874 | N5194B | D-CHAN | LX-EJH | D-CHMC | |
| 550-0875 | N51055 | TG-BAC | N800AB | N877SD | |
| 550-0876 | N5135A | N876CB | 5Y-MNG | | |
| 550-0877 | N5085J | N21SL | | | |
| 550-0878 | N5135K | VH-ZLT | | | |
| 550-0879 | N5000R | N4M | N35ET | | |
| 550-0880 | N5112K | N7YA | | | |
| 550-0881 | N5105F | N546MT | (N312RD) | N306CS | N546MT | N306CS |
| 550-0882 | N5068R | N488A | N12MA | N438SP | VH-VFP | N882WF |
| 550-0883 | N469DE | | | | |
| 550-0884 | N5090Y | N602BW | N1318Y | N361DB | VP-CGL | D-CSWM |
| 550-0885 | N5109W | N820JM | N88AJ | | |
| 550-0886 | N550KH | N500TS | | | |

# CITATION BRAVO

| C/n | Identities | | | | | |
|---|---|---|---|---|---|---|
| 550-0887 | N887BB | XA-ABE | | | | |
| 550-0888 | N550BF | N162TJ | (N218G) | | | |
| 550-0889 | N619JM | N360HS | N368HS | | | |
| 550-0890 | N1961S | | | | | |
| 550-0891 | N5093L | N82MA | N86PC | | | |
| 550-0892 | N22GR | (N84CF) | | | | |
| 550-0893 | N5073G | N333EB | | | | |
| 550-0894 | N51160 | N550TE | N107EG | | | |
| 550-0895 | N199BB | N87GS | | | | |
| 550-0896 | N121L | N58WV | | | | |
| 550-0897 | N5079V | EI-GHP | G-GHPG | | | |
| 550-0898 | N550GH | | | | | |
| 550-0899 | N5076K | N899DC | N535SW | | | |
| 550-0900 | N327LJ | N327LN | N214TJ | N138CA | | |
| 550-0901 | N5058J | N857AA | | | | |
| 550-0902 | N5095N | N770JM | N770UM | N688JD | | |
| 550-0903 | N51055 | N14HB | N903VP | PR-ERP | | |
| 550-0904 | N5093Y | N904BB | | | | |
| 550-0905 | N5101J | N505AG | | | | |
| 550-0906 | N5166T | C-GLCE | N850GM | D-CSSS | HB-VNZ | |
| 550-0907 | N5155G | N316MA | HB-VMM | SX-BMK | | |
| 550-0908 | N5264M | N242SW | | | | |
| 550-0909 | N5076J | N706CP | (N909CA) | C-GDSH | N40KW | N44KW | N391BC |
| 550-0910 | N5207V | N574M | | | | |
| 550-0911 | N52655 | N575M | | | | |
| 550-0912 | N5117U | N588AC | | | | |
| 550-0913 | N5096S | N232BC | N66MT | | | |
| 550-0914 | N5105F | N897MC | N499GS | | | |
| 550-0915 | N51143 | N915BB | N346CM | N348CM | | |
| 550-0916 | N5265N | N555BK | | | | |
| 550-0917 | N5100J | EI-DAB | (SE-RBY) | G-IDAB | | |
| 550-0918 | N5109R | N45VM | | | | |
| 550-0919 | N52601 | N100Y | | | | |
| 550-0920 | N5109W | N63LB | N854JA | | | |
| 550-0921 | N5073G | N40MF | | | | |
| 550-0922 | N51896 | I-FJTB | OE-GAH | | | |
| 550-0923 | N51160 | N676BB | N676PB | N23YC | | |
| 550-0924 | N5090Y | XT-COK | N550VC | YU-BZZ | | |
| 550-0925 | N5090V | N1305C | 5N-DUK | N550PF | N10UH | |
| 550-0926 | N5154J | N72PB | N100Z | N144Z | | |
| 550-0927 | N5061P | PH-DYE | | | | |
| 550-0928 | N5000R | PH-DYN | (N928DA) | | | |
| 550-0929 | N5086W | N552SM | | | | |
| 550-0930 | N5066U | PP-ORM | | | | |
| 550-0931 | N233DW | C-FAMJ | | | | |
| 550-0932 | N5103J | G-MIRO | I-MTVB | | | |
| 550-0933 | N5262X | N417KW | N325WP | | | |
| 550-0934 | N5260Y | N200AS | | | | |
| 550-0935 | N5264A | EI-PAL | G-IPAL | G-IPAC | G-YPRS | |
| 550-0936 | N5101J | N550TM | | | | |
| 550-0937 | N51666 | N440CE | | | | |
| 550-0938 | N51038 | N5VN | EC-HRO | | | |
| 550-0939 | N5076K | (N939BB) | VP-BNS | N48NS | | |
| 550-0940 | N5263S | G-FIRM | | | | |
| 550-0941 | N5093Y | N900SS | N878AG | 4X-CPW | | |
| 550-0942 | N5095N | N72SG | N265TS | | | |
| 550-0943 | N5117U | N706CP | YV-2711P | YV266T | | |
| 550-0944 | N5267J | N723RE | | | | |
| 550-0945 | N5109R | N585KS | | | | |
| 550-0946 | N52229 | HB-VMX | | | | |
| 550-0947 | N947CB | N514BC | | | | |
| 550-0948 | N5264E | N49FW | N48FW | | | |
| 550-0949 | N550KG | N45NS | | | | |
| 550-0950 | N555HM | | | | | |
| 550-0951 | N5076J | TC-TPE | N51KR | LN-SUV | | |
| 550-0952 | N5268V | N952CH | | | | |
| 550-0953 | N50612 | N953GM | C-GZEK | N550WG | VH-CCJ | |
| 550-0954 | N5079V | PP-OAA | | | | |
| 550-0955 | N50715 | HB-VMW | EC-KHP | | | |
| 550-0956 | N51666 | N572PB | N800VA | | | |
| 550-0957 | N51780 | N957PH | G-IKOS | | | |
| 550-0958 | N5168Y | N333BD | N833BD | N404RK | D2-... | |
| 550-0959 | N5172M | N418KW | N511JP | N418KW | | |
| 550-0960 | N52229 | N960CB | TC-MKA | | | |
| 550-0961 | N5181U | N961BB | HK-4250X | HK-4250 | N641L | HK-.... |
| 550-0962 | N5212M | N797TE | | | | |

# CITATION BRAVO

| C/n | Identities | | | | |
|---|---|---|---|---|---|
| 550-0963 | N52114 | N24QT | N24QF | N990TC | |
| 550-0964 | N52234 | HB-VMY | | | |
| 550-0965 | N52086 | N741PP | N965BB | N741PP | N256CC |
| 550-0966 | N51806 | N36PT | | | |
| 550-0967 | N52397 | N967CB | N432RJ | | |
| 550-0968 | N51612 | N551G | | | |
| 550-0969 | N5228J | N401KC | N119LC | | |
| 550-0970 | N5243K | N367BP | N78MD | | |
| 550-0971 | N5239J | N717KQ | N717GK | | |
| 550-0972 | N52462 | PH-HMA | | | |
| 550-0973 | N5245U | N129PB | | | |
| 550-0974 | N307CS | N307MS | OE-GAL | | |
| 550-0975 | N975HM | 5Y-MSR | | | |
| 550-0976 | N5168Y | N308CS | N308MS | OE-GML | |
| 550-0977 | N5172M | N309CS | (OE-GLM) | OE-GLG | |
| 550-0978 | N52475 | N696CM | N95AN | | |
| 550-0979 | N5147B | N311CS | | | |
| 550-0980 | N51666 | N312CS | N146CT | N67JB | |
| 550-0981 | N5093L | N313CS | N800MT | | |
| 550-0982 | N5260U | C-GDSH | C-GVIJ | C-FMOS | |
| 550-0983 | N51055 | XA-SDI | | | |
| 550-0984 | N5227G | VH-HVM | (N984VP) | | |
| 550-0985 | N5269J | G-FCDB | | | |
| 550-0986 | N52690 | N986PA | N45NF | N458F | |
| 550-0987 | N51780 | N987GR | N471WR | N500VA | N500VT |
| 550-0988 | N5174W | N32FJ | I-FJTC | (D-CFTC) | OE-GVR |
| 550-0989 | N5270E | XA-LOF | | | |
| 550-0990 | N5154J | N990JM | N448RL | | |
| 550-0991 | N5270J | N4190A | N628CB | N628GB | |
| 550-0992 | N52086 | N777NG | G-EKWS | D-COFY | EC-KKO |
| 550-0993 | N5244W | N721T | | | |
| 550-0994 | N580SH | C-GLGB | | | |
| 550-0995 | N550PD | 5Y-SIR | | | |
| 550-0996 | N5270P | CC-LLM | | | |
| 550-0997 | N5192E | N67BK | | | |
| 550-0998 | N5165P | OE-GHP | D-CGHP* | | |
| 550-0999 | N5270E | XA-UVA | XB-UVA | XA-GEN | |
| 550-1000 | N5194B | N121CN | | | |
| 550-1001 | N26CB | | | | |
| 550-1002 | N52397 | N101JL | | | |
| 550-1003 | N51743 | N777UU | Pakistan 1003 | | |
| 550-1004 | N314CS | N114VP | | | |
| 550-1005 | N5247U | CS-DHA | | | |
| 550-1006 | N5212M | N106BB | N992HE | | |
| 550-1007 | N51995 | N717CB | N67PC | N67PV | XA- |
| 550-1008 | N5181U | N40435 | D2-ECE | | |
| 550-1009 | N5155G | CS-DHB | | | |
| 550-1010 | N5228J | N316CS | N116VP | N544PS | |
| 550-1011 | N51780 | C-FRST | | | |
| 550-1012 | N20AU | N20RU | | | |
| 550-1013 | N5166U | CS-DHC | | | |
| 550-1014 | N52475 | N610CB | | | |
| 550-1015 | N5253S | N81ER | N81LR | N140TF | |
| 550-1016 | N926ED | N926EC | N958GC | | |
| 550-1017 | N51666 | CS-DHD | | | |
| 550-1018 | N5259Y | SU-HEC | (D-CEFM) | OO-IIG | |
| 550-1019 | N5231S | N317CS | N117VP | | |
| 550-1020 | N5166T | N212BH | N219LC | N495MH | |
| 550-1021 | N5174W | N49KW | | | |
| 550-1022 | N5168Y | CS-DHE | | | |
| 550-1023 | N4405 | C-FEVC | | | |
| 550-1024 | N5254Y | N550FP | | | |
| 550-1025 | N5172M | CS-DHF | | | |
| 550-1026 | N5180K | N552CB | N438SP | | |
| 550-1027 | N52691 | OO-FYG | | | |
| 550-1028 | N442LW | N442LV | C-FYUL | C-GWUL | |
| 550-1029 | N5270J | N318CS | N118VP | | |
| 550-1030 | N52397 | N322GT | | | |
| 550-1031 | N525PE | | | | |
| 550-1032 | N5223X | N880CM | N910N | | |
| 550-1033 | N52114 | N933BB | N701VV | | |
| 550-1034 | N52086 | CS-DHG | | | |
| 550-1035 | N585TH | | | | |
| 550-1036 | N319CS | N119VP | | | |
| 550-1037 | N5180C | N1258B | YU-BTB | | |
| 550-1038 | N551VB | (N551VP) | SE-RBY | | |

# CITATION BRAVO

| C/n | Identities | | | | |
|---|---|---|---|---|---|
| 550-1039 | N320CS | N711HA | N511HA | OE-GRB | |
| 550-1040 | N52446 | N12378 | OK-VSZ | | |
| 550-1041 | N5206T | N412ET | N7725D | N7765D | N31JB |
| 550-1042 | N51869 | G-ORDB | G-OJMW | M-WOOD | |
| 550-1043 | N52235 | CS-DHH | | | |
| 550-1044 | N52369 | N141AB | | | |
| 550-1045 | N52690 | PP-BMG | | | |
| 550-1046 | N300GF | | | | |
| 550-1047 | N5231S | N889B | | | |
| 550-1048 | N5253S | CS-DHI | | | |
| 550-1049 | N5267G | N249CB | N299HS | YU-BSG | |
| 550-1050 | N5268E | N105BX | A9C-BXC | D-CMIX | OY-EVO |
| 550-1051 | N5155G | N251CB | N745CC | | |
| 550-1052 | N322CS | | | | |
| 550-1053 | N57MC | | | | |
| 550-1054 | N5239J | N254CB | N600ST | 5R-... | |
| 550-1055 | N896CG | | | | |
| 550-1056 | N52601 | N45678 | | | |
| 550-1057 | N5245U | N714RM | | | |
| 550-1058 | N52691 | VH-SCC | | | |
| 550-1059 | N324CS | N159VP* | | | |
| 550-1060 | N669B | | | | |
| 550-1061 | N5267K | N325CS | | | |
| 550-1062 | N662CB | | | | |
| 550-1063 | N5268V | N96TM | N151TM | | |
| 550-1064 | N823PM | | | | |
| 550-1065 | N326CS | N175CW | N896MA | | |
| 550-1066 | N573M | | | | |
| 550-1067 | N5085E | N6TM | | | |
| 550-1068 | N668CB | | | | |
| 550-1069 | N5093Y | OE-GLL | | | |
| 550-1070 | N5296X | N327CS | XA-CAP | | |
| 550-1071 | N5090A | N104FL | | | |
| 550-1072 | N5148B | N143BP | | | |
| 550-1073 | N899B | | | | |
| 550-1074 | N328CS | | | | |
| 550-1075 | N5162W | N275BB | N8701L | N87011 | N26T |
| 550-1076 | N51872 | N359GW | N550TT | VT-IBS | |
| 550-1077 | N329CS | | | | |
| 550-1078 | N442NR | | | | |
| 550-1079 | N5268E | C-FRNG | N1271B | N444EA | |
| 550-1080 | N132MT | | | | |
| 550-1081 | N332CS | | | | |
| 550-1082 | N5180C | CS-DHJ | | | |
| 550-1083 | N5201M | I-PABL | | | |
| 550-1084 | N52141 | N338CS | | | |
| 550-1085 | N5068R | N339CS | | | |
| 550-1086 | N52446 | N58HK | G-OMRH | | |
| 550-1087 | N5265B | [not fully confirmed] | | N151FD | N876BB |
| 550-1088 | N153SG | N158SG | N188VP* | | |
| 550-1089 | N334CS | | | | |
| 550-1090 | N51038 | CS-DHK | | | |
| 550-1091 | N335CS | | | | |
| 550-1092 | N52645 | CS-DHL | | | |
| 550-1093 | N5263D | CS-DHM | | | |
| 550-1094 | N5109W | N308DT | | | |
| 550-1095 | N336CS | | | | |
| 550-1096 | N52626 | N877B | N707HP | VT-... | |
| 550-1097 | N5148B | N337CS | | | |
| 550-1098 | N5132T | CS-DHN | | | |
| 550-1099 | N5180C | CS-DHO | | | |
| 550-1100 | N5203S | N110BR | G-WAIN | | |
| 550-1101 | N5264U | N342CS | | | |
| 550-1102 | N5214L | N1276A | AP-BHD | | |
| 550-1103 | N50612 | LZ-ABV | N1276Z | LZ-ABV | |
| 550-1104 | N52144 | CS-DHP | | | |
| 550-1105 | N5117U | N332MT | | | |
| 550-1106 | N341CS | | | | |
| 550-1107 | N51744 | TC-AHE | | | |
| 550-1108 | N5181U | N717VL | | | |
| 550-1109 | N5212M | N1281A | CS-DHQ | | |
| 550-1110 | N877B | | | | |
| 550-1111 | N5165P | OK-ACH | | | |
| 550-1112 | N5202D | N47NM | | | |
| 550-1113 | N5218R | N724EH | N724EB | | |
| 550-1114 | N5223Y | N1298Y | CS-DHR | | |

# CITATION BRAVO

| C/n | Identities | | | |
|---|---|---|---|---|
| 550-1115 | N5223X | N4002Y | HZ-133 | |
| 550-1116 | N52457 | N4060Y | HZ-134 | |
| 550-1117 | N52591 | OO-FPB | | |
| 550-1118 | N550CY | PR-SCP | | |
| 550-1119 | N51072 | N630JS | N230JS | N63NW |
| 550-1120 | N5109W | N112BR | LV-BEU | |
| 550-1121 | N5061W | N1309B | 9M-ZAB* | |
| 550-1122 | N5211Q | N984GB | OE-GEN | LZ-GEN |
| 550-1123 | N5212M | N106FT | | |
| 550-1124 | N5076K | N417JD | | |
| 550-1125 | N5262X | VH-YXY | | |
| 550-1126 | N5233J | N12993 | HZ-135 | |
| 550-1127 | N52623 | N1298P | HZ-136 | |
| 550-1128 | N5296X | N23AJ | | |
| 550-1129 | N52059 | N60LW | | |
| 550-1130 | N5125J | D-CSMB | | |
| 550-1131 | N5227G | N110TP | | |
| 550-1132 | N5165P | N338B | | |
| 550-1133 | N5201M | N579M | | |
| 550-1134 | N5068R | N412ET | N412BT | |
| 550-1135 | N5180C | D2-GES | | |
| 550-1136 | N51743 | N998SR | OE-GMV | LZ-GMV |

Production complete

# CITATION 550 UNIT NUMBER CROSS-REFERENCE

| C/n | Unit | C/n | Unit | C/n | Unit | C/n | Unit | C/n | Unit | C/n | Unit |
|---|---|---|---|---|---|---|---|---|---|---|---|
| 550-0001 | 001 | 550-0081 | 090 | 550-0169 | 185 | 550-0247 | 276 | 550-0326 | 369 | 550-0426 | 425 |
| 550-0003 | 003 | 550-0082 | 091 | 550-0170 | 186 | 550-0248 | 261 | 550-0327 | 349 | 550-0427 | 426 |
| 550-0004 | 004 | 550-0083 | 210 | 550-0171 | 188 | 550-0249 | 215 | 550-0329 | 360 | 550-0428 | 427 |
| 550-0005 | 005 | 550-0084 | 093 | 550-0172 | 187 | 550-0250 | 270 | 550-0332 | 372 | 550-0430 | 429 |
| 550-0006 | 006 | 550-0085 | 100 | 550-0174 | 201 | 550-0251 | 287 | 550-0333 | 358 | 550-0432 | 438 |
| 550-0007 | 007 | 550-0086 | 096 | 550-0175 | 178 | 550-0252 | 294 | 550-0334 | 361 | 550-0433 | 432 |
| 550-0008 | 008 | 550-0089 | 088 | 550-0176 | 203 | 550-0253 | 295 | 550-0335 | 365 | 550-0434 | 433 |
| 550-0009 | 009 | 550-0090 | 085 | 550-0179 | 192 | 550-0254 | 275 | 550-0336 | 367 | 550-0435 | 434 |
| 550-0010 | 010 | 550-0091 | 121 | 550-0180 | 193 | 550-0255 | 283 | 550-0337 | 368 | 550-0436 | 435 |
| 550-0011 | 012 | 550-0092 | 114 | 550-0181 | 194 | 550-0256 | 286 | 550-0338 | 074 | 550-0438 | 437 |
| 550-0012 | 013 | 550-0094 | 101 | 550-0182 | 195 | 550-0257 | 280 | 550-0339 | 370 | 550-0439 | 439 |
| 550-0013 | 016 | 550-0095 | 102 | 550-0183 | 206 | 550-0258 | 285 | 550-0340 | 374 | 550-0440 | 440 |
| 550-0014 | 015 | 550-0096 | 103 | 550-0184 | 142 | 550-0259 | 289 | 550-0341 | 373 | 550-0441 | 441 |
| 550-0016 | 017 | 550-0097 | 104 | 550-0185 | 228 | 550-0260 | 223 | 550-0343 | 391 | 550-0442 | 442 |
| 550-0017 | 021 | 550-0098 | 105 | 550-0186 | 197 | 550-0261 | 288 | 550-0344 | 378 | 550-0443 | 443 |
| 550-0018 | 019 | 550-0099 | 109 | 550-0187 | 198 | 550-0262 | 282 | 550-0345 | 376 | 550-0444 | 444 |
| 550-0019 | 022 | 550-0100 | 110 | 550-0188 | 207 | 550-0263 | 061 | 550-0346 | 382 | 550-0445 | 445 |
| 550-0021 | 011 | 550-0101 | 111 | 550-0189 | 205 | 550-0264 | 292 | 550-0347 | 380 | 550-0446 | 446 |
| 550-0024 | 041 | 550-0102 | 112 | 550-0190 | 209 | 550-0265 | 293 | 550-0348 | 381 | 550-0447 | 447 |
| 550-0025 | 025 | 550-0103 | 140 | 550-0191 | 213 | 550-0266 | 296 | 550-0349 | 383 | 550-0448 | 448 |
| 550-0026 | 026 | 550-0104 | 146 | 550-0192 | 214 | 550-0267 | 297 | 550-0350 | 384 | 550-0449 | 449 |
| 550-0027 | 027 | 550-0105 | 116 | 550-0193 | 249 | 550-0268 | 298 | 550-0351 | 386 | 550-0450 | 450 |
| 550-0028 | 028 | 550-0106 | 117 | 550-0194 | 217 | 550-0269 | 302 | 550-0352 | 393 | 550-0451 | 451 |
| 550-0029 | 029 | 550-0108 | 119 | 550-0195 | 259 | 550-0271 | 303 | 550-0353 | 397 | 550-0452 | 452 |
| 550-0030 | 030 | 550-0109 | 120 | 550-0196 | 219 | 550-0272 | 307 | 550-0354 | 388 | 550-0453 | 453 |
| 550-0031 | 031 | 550-0110 | 122 | 550-0197 | 220 | 550-0273 | 308 | 550-0355 | 411 | 550-0454 | 454 |
| 550-0032 | 032 | 550-0111 | 123 | 550-0198 | 221 | 550-0274 | 310 | 550-0356 | 390 | 550-0455 | 455 |
| 550-0033 | 033 | 550-0112 | 124 | 550-0199 | 222 | 550-0275 | 356 | 550-0357 | 379 | 550-0456 | 456 |
| 550-0034 | 034 | 550-0113 | 125 | 550-0200 | 225 | 550-0276 | 318 | 550-0358 | 389 | 550-0457 | 457 |
| 550-0035 | 042 | 550-0114 | 126 | 550-0201 | 227 | 550-0277 | 309 | 550-0362 | 396 | 550-0458 | 458 |
| 550-0036 | 036 | 550-0115 | 127 | 550-0202 | 230 | 550-0279 | 166 | 550-0363 | 394 | 550-0459 | 459 |
| 550-0037 | 037 | 550-0116 | 128 | 550-0203 | 231 | 550-0280 | 313 | 550-0364 | 403 | 550-0460 | 460 |
| 550-0038 | 038 | 550-0117 | 129 | 550-0204 | 239 | 550-0281 | 314 | 550-0365 | 404 | 550-0461 | 461 |
| 550-0039 | 039 | 550-0118 | 131 | 550-0205 | 218 | 550-0282 | 315 | 550-0366 | 399 | 550-0462 | 462 |
| 550-0040 | 040 | 550-0121 | 134 | 550-0206 | 226 | 550-0283 | 316 | 550-0367 | 405 | 550-0464 | 464 |
| 550-0041 | 043 | 550-0122 | 135 | 550-0207 | 234 | 550-0284 | 243 | 550-0368 | 402 | 550-0465 | 465 |
| 550-0042 | 044 | 550-0123 | 136 | 550-0208 | 241 | 550-0285 | 305 | 550-0369 | 431 | 550-0466 | 466 |
| 550-0043 | 046 | 550-0124 | 137 | 550-0209 | 232 | 550-0286 | 306 | 550-0370 | 076 | 550-0467 | 467 |
| 550-0044 | 047 | 550-0125 | 138 | 550-0210 | 247 | 550-0287 | 317 | 550-0371 | 086 | 550-0468 | 468 |
| 550-0045 | 045 | 550-0127 | 143 | 550-0211 | 244 | 550-0288 | 319 | 550-0374 | 106 | 550-0469 | 469 |
| 550-0046 | 050 | 550-0129 | 145 | 550-0212 | 245 | 550-0289 | 299 | 550-0376 | 113 | 550-0470 | 470 |
| 550-0047 | 056 | 550-0130 | 169 | 550-0213 | 250 | 550-0290 | 304 | 550-0378 | 133 | 550-0471 | 471 |
| 550-0048 | 048 | 550-0132 | 147 | 550-0214 | 236 | 550-0291 | 320 | 550-0381 | 170 | 550-0472 | 472 |
| 550-0050 | 052 | 550-0133 | 148 | 550-0215 | 238 | 550-0292 | 321 | 550-0382 | 172 | 550-0473 | 473 |
| 550-0051 | 060 | 550-0135 | 235 | 550-0216 | 240 | 550-0293 | 322 | 550-0383 | 173 | 550-0474 | 474 |
| 550-0052 | 067 | 550-0138 | 153 | 550-0217 | 263 | 550-0294 | 323 | 550-0390 | 269 | 550-0475 | 475 |
| 550-0053 | 053 | 550-0139 | 154 | 550-0218 | 199 | 550-0295 | 325 | 550-0393 | 291 | 550-0476 | 476 |
| 550-0054 | 054 | 550-0140 | 155 | 550-0219 | 035 | 550-0296 | 326 | 550-0396 | 331 | 550-0477 | 477 |
| 550-0055 | 055 | 550-0141 | 156 | 550-0220 | 248 | 550-0297 | 362 | 550-0398 | 338 | 550-0478 | 478 |
| 550-0056 | 070 | 550-0142 | 157 | 550-0221 | 253 | 550-0298 | 324 | 550-0399 | 342 | 550-0479 | 479 |
| 550-0057 | 073 | 550-0143 | 158 | 550-0222 | 237 | 550-0299 | 328 | 550-0400 | 350 | 550-0480 | 480 |
| 550-0058 | 071 | 550-0144 | 159 | 550-0223 | 242 | 550-0300 | 332 | 550-0401 | 364 | 550-0482 | 482 |
| 550-0060 | 075 | 550-0145 | 160 | 550-0224 | 251 | 550-0301 | 357 | 550-0402 | 366 | 550-0483 | 483 |
| 550-0061 | 077 | 550-0146 | 161 | 550-0225 | 258 | 550-0302 | 329 | 550-0403 | 371 | 550-0484 | 484 |
| 550-0062 | 078 | 550-0147 | 208 | 550-0226 | 262 | 550-0303 | 281 | 550-0405 | 385 | 550-0485 | 485 |
| 550-0064 | 080 | 550-0149 | 164 | 550-0227 | 254 | 550-0304 | 327 | 550-0406 | 398 | 550-0486 | 486 |
| 550-0065 | 065 | 550-0150 | 165 | 550-0228 | 252 | 550-0305 | 359 | 550-0407 | 401 | 550-0487 | 487 |
| 550-0066 | 081 | 550-0151 | 202 | 550-0229 | 255 | 550-0306 | 330 | 550-0408 | 406 | 550-0488 | 488 |
| 550-0067 | 094 | 550-0152 | 167 | 550-0230 | 265 | 550-0307 | 274 | 550-0409 | 407 | 550-0489 | 489 |
| 550-0068 | 058 | 550-0153 | 168 | 550-0231 | 271 | 550-0308 | 341 | 550-0410 | 408 | 550-0490 | 490 |
| 550-0069 | 063 | 550-0154 | 171 | 550-0232 | 284 | 550-0310 | 333 | 550-0411 | 409 | 550-0491 | 491 |
| 550-0070 | 064 | 550-0155 | 175 | 550-0234 | 189 | 550-0311 | 337 | 550-0412 | 410 | 550-0492 | 492 |
| 550-0071 | 066 | 550-0156 | 176 | 550-0235 | 257 | 550-0312 | 335 | 550-0414 | 413 | 550-0493 | 493 |
| 550-0072 | 072 | 550-0157 | 229 | 550-0236 | 260 | 550-0313 | 336 | 550-0415 | 414 | 550-0494 | 494 |
| 550-0073 | 068 | 550-0158 | 183 | 550-0237 | 264 | 550-0315 | 340 | 550-0416 | 415 | 550-0495 | 495 |
| 550-0074 | 069 | 550-0159 | 216 | 550-0238 | 233 | 550-0316 | 346 | 550-0417 | 416 | 550-0497 | 497 |
| 550-0075 | 057 | 550-0162 | 130 | 550-0239 | 256 | 550-0318 | 339 | 550-0418 | 417 | 550-0498 | 498 |
| 550-0076 | 099 | 550-0164 | 211 | 550-0241 | 268 | 550-0319 | 345 | 550-0419 | 418 | 550-0499 | 499 |
| 550-0077 | 082 | 550-0165 | 179 | 550-0242 | 059 | 550-0320 | 343 | 550-0420 | 419 | 550-0501 | 501 |
| 550-0078 | 083 | 550-0166 | 180 | 550-0243 | 273 | 550-0321 | 347 | 550-0421 | 420 | 550-0502 | 502 |
| 550-0079 | 087 | 550-0167 | 182 | 550-0245 | 279 | 550-0323 | 351 | 550-0423 | 422 | 550-0503 | 503 |
| 550-0080 | 089 | 550-0168 | 184 | 550-0246 | 282 | 550-0324 | 352 | 550-0424 | 423 | 550-0504 | 504 |
| | | | | | | | | 550-0425 | 424 | 550-0505 | 505 |

Note: From c/n 550-0550 onwards, unit number and c/n correspond

## CITATION 551 UNIT NUMBER CROSS-REFERENCE

| C/n | Unit | C/n | Unit | C/n | Unit | C/n | Unit |
|---|---|---|---|---|---|---|---|
| 551-0001 | - | 551-0038 | 246 | 551-0171 | 141 | 551-0355 | 348 |
| 551-0002 | 014 | 551-0039 | 278 | 551-0174 | 144 | 551-0359 | 353 |
| 551-0003 | 024 | 551-0046 | 267 | 551-0179 | 149 | 551-0360 | 354 |
| 551-0006 | 020 | 551-0050 | 196 | 551-0180 | 151 | 551-0361 | 355 |
| 551-0007 | 018 | 551-0051 | 301 | 551-0181 | 152 | 551-0369 | 363 |
| 551-0010 | 049 | 551-0056 | 312 | 551-0191 | 163 | 551-0378 | 375 |
| 551-0017 | 062 | 551-0059 | 334 | 551-0201 | 177 | 551-0388 | 387 |
| 551-0018 | 095 | 551-0060 | 377 | 551-0205 | 181 | 551-0393 | 392 |
| 551-0021 | 107 | 551-0071 | 023 | 551-0214 | 190 | 551-0496 | 495 |
| 551-0023 | 204 | 551-0095 | 051 | 551-0215 | 191 | 551-0400 | 400 |
| 551-0024 | 092 | 551-0117 | 079 | 551-0223 | 200 | 551-0412 | 412 |
| 551-0026 | 115 | 551-0122 | 084 | 551-0245 | 224 | 551-0421 | 421 |
| 551-0027 | 002 | 551-0132 | 097 | 551-0285 | 266 | 551-0428 | 428 |
| 551-0029 | 150 | 551-0133 | 098 | 551-0289 | 272 | 551-0431 | 430 |
| 551-0031 | 174 | 551-0141 | 108 | 551-0304 | 290 | 551-0436 | 436 |
| 551-0033 | 212 | 551-0149 | 118 | 551-0313 | 300 | 551-0463 | 463 |
| 551-0035 | 277 | 551-0163 | 132 | 551-0323 | 311 | 551-0481 | 481 |
| 551-0036 | 162 | 551-0169 | 139 | 551-0351 | 344 | 551-0496 | 496 |

Note: From c/n 551-0550 onwards, unit number and c/n are the same.

## CITATION CONVERSIONS

The following Citations have been converted from 550 to 551 or 551 to 550:

550-0002 to 551-0027
550-0020 to 551-0071
550-0030 to 551-0077
550-0040 to 551-0085 to 550-0040
550-0044 to 551-0092 to 550-0044
550-0049 to 551-0095
550-0059 to 551-0122
550-0063 to 551-0117
550-0074 to 551-0109 to 550-0074
550-0084 to 551-0129 to 550-0084
550-0087 to 551-0132
550-0088 to 551-0133
550-0092 to 551-0146
550-0093 to 551-0141
550-0098 to 551-0140 to 550-0098
550-0100 to 551-0143 to 550-0100
550-0107 to 551-0149
550-0118 to 551-0162 to 550-0118
550-0126 to 551-0169
550-0128 to 551-0174
550-0131 to 551-0201
550-0134 to 551-0179
550-0136 to 551-0180
550-0137 to 551-0181
550-0139 to 551-0184
550-0148 to 551-0191
550-0160 to 551-0171
550-0161 to 551-0205
550-0163 to 551-0214
550-0177 to 551-0223 to 550-0177 to 551-0223
550-0178 to 551-0245
550-0240 to 551-0285
550-0244 to 551-0289
550-0246 to 551-0296
550-0249 to 551-0236 to 550-0249
550-0253 to 551-0308 to 550-0253
550-0262 to 551-0304
550-0266 to 551-0309 to 550-0266
550-0268 to 551-0311
550-0270 to 551-0313
550-0278 to 551-0323
550-0298 to 551-0335
550-0299 to 551-0339 to 550-0299
550-0306 to 551-0341
550-0313 to 551-0345 to 550-0313
550-0314 to 551-0396
550-0317 to 551-0355
550-0322 to 551-0351
550-0328 to 551-0360
550-0331 to 551-0369
550-0342 to 551-0378
550-0353 to 551-0398 to 550-0353
550-0359 to 551-0400
550-0373 to 551-0018
550-0397 to 551-0059
550-0413 to 551-0413
550-0420 to 551-0419
550-0422 to 551-0422
550-0429 to 551-0428
550-0435 to 551-0434
550-0437 to 551-0436
550-0450 to 551-0450
550-0452 to 551-0452
550-0459 to 551-0459
550-0460 to 551-0460 to 550-0460
550-0463 to 551-0463
550-0475 to 551-0475 to 550-0475
550-0476 to 551-0476 to 550-0476
550-0481 to 551-0481 to 550-0481
550-0485 to 551-0485 to 550-0485
550-0487 to 551-0487 to 550-0487
550-0490 to 551-0491 to 550-0490
550-0496 to 551-0496
550-0559 to 551-0559
550-0572 to 551-0572
550-0574 to 551-0575
550-0584 to 551-0584
550-0591 to 551-0591
550-0604 to 551-0604 to 550-0604
550-0617 to 551-0617
551-0004 to 550-00031
551-0005 to 550-0013
551-0008 to 550-0219
551-0009 to 550-0263 to 551-0009 to 550-0263
551-0014 to 550-0068
551-0012 to 550-0242
551-0016 to 550-0338 to 551-0016 to 550-0338
551-0018 to 550-0373
551-0019 to 550-0371
551-0020 to 550-0374
551-0022 to 550-0376
551-0025 to 550-0378
551-0026 to 550-0377 to 551-0026
551-0029 to 550-0379 to 551-0029
551-0030 to 550-0383
551-0032 to 550-0382
551-0047 to 550-0390
551-0048 to 550-0307
551-0049 to 550-0381
551-0050 to 550-0385 to 551-0050
551-0052 to 550-0228
551-0053 to 550-0399
551-0055 to 550-0400
551-0057 to 550-0402
551-0058 to 550-0403
551-0059 to 550-0397 to 551-0059
551-0062 to 550-0406
551-0065 to 550-0396
551-0066 to 550-0401
551-0077 to 550-0030
551-0084 to 550-0039
551-0109 to 550-0074
551-0296 to 550-0246
551-0311 to 550-0268
551-0335 to 550-0298
551-0341 to 550-0306
551-0345 to 550-0313
551-0351 to 550-0322
551-0419 to 550-0420
551-0445 to 550-0445
551-0496 to 550-0496 to 551-0496
551-0551 to 550-0551
551-0555 to 550-0555
551-0559 to 550-0559
551-0560 to 550-0560
551-0567 to 550-0567
551-0584 to 550-0584

# CESSNA S550 CITATION II

| C/n | Unit No | Identities | | | | | | | | |
|---|---|---|---|---|---|---|---|---|---|---|
| 0001 | (0506) | (N1255L) | N95CC | (N969MC) | (N36H) | N969MC | N969MQ | N151DD | N86BA | (N550VS) |
| 0002 | (0507) | (N1255Y) | (N507CC) | N507CJ | N111VP | N211VP | CC-CWW | | | |
| 0003 | (0508) | (N12554) | (N21AG) | N847G | N847C | N847G | | | | |
| 0004 | (0509) | N1256B | N830CB | N554CA | N72AM | N178DA | | | | |
| 0005 | (0510) | (N1256G) | N666LN | N123FF | | | | | | |
| 0006 | (0511) | (N1256N) | N101EC | N71FM | N71EM | N27MH | (N66EA) | N29EA | N65DT | N181G |
| 0007 | (0512) | (N1256P) | N51JH | N573CC | TC-SAM | N30CX | CS-DCE | OO-MMJ | CS-DCE | OO-SKP |
| 0008 | (0513) | (N1256T) | N40PL | SE-DKI | N204A | (N40KM) | N600KM | | | |
| 0009 | (0514) | N1256Z | N550A | N165JB | | | | | | |
| 0010 | (0515) | (N1257K) | N651CC | N49MJ | N47MJ | XA-INF | XA-INK | N747RL | N747KL | N422MJ |
| | | N550F | | | | | | | | |
| 0011 | (0516) | (N1257M) | N68SK | N211QS | N25GZ | | | | | |
| 0012 | (0517) | (N12570) | N550TB | N550RV | N777GG | | | | | |
| 0013 | (0518) | (N12576) | (N518AS) | N277AL | N389L | N561PS | N551PS | N84LG | | |
| 0014 | (0519) | (N12583) | N32JJ | N32TJ | N214QS | N777AM | N84EC | | | |
| 0015 | (0520) | (N1258U) | C-GMTV | N600EA | | | | | | |
| 0016 | (0521) | (N1259B) | (N99VC) | N85MP | N557CS | | | | | |
| 0017 | (0522) | (N1259G) | (N47LP) | N1259G | N88G | (N1259G) | (N188G) | N88GD | N86PC | N413CT |
| 0018 | (0523) | (N1259K) | N501NB | N814CC | N1AF | N145DF | N627X | | | |
| 0019 | (0524) | (N1259M) | N15TT | N519CJ | N29AU | N119EA | (N600VE) | N550TB | N670JD | |
| 0020 | (0525) | (N1259R) | N550AS | | | | | | | |
| 0021 | (0526) | (N1259S) | N593M | N693M | N320DG | N945ER | | | | |
| 0022 | (0527) | (N1259Y) | N258P | N360M | N460M | | | | | |
| 0023 | (0528) | (N1259Z) | N420CC | N94RT | N293RT | N500ZB | | | | |
| 0024 | (0529) | (N12593) | PT-LGI | N34NS | N790AL | | | | | |
| 0025 | (0530) | (N12596) | PT-LGJ | [w/o 06Sep88 Rio-Santos Dumont, Brazil] | | | | | | |
| 0026 | (0531) | (N1260G) | N19AF | (N126LP) | N24PH | N24PF | N32TX | | | |
| 0027 | | N1260K | D-CBUS | N27EA | N27FP | N5WC | C-GSSK | | | |
| 0028 | | (N1260L) | HB-VHH | S5-BAX | | | | | | |
| 0029 | | (N1260N) | N185SF | N608LB | HB-VMJ | | | | | |
| 0030 | | (N1260V) | N7007V | N7007Q | (N999GL) | N999HC | | | | |
| 0031 | | (N12605) | N531CC | N50DS | N54WJ | N50BK | [w/o 13Aug02 Big Bear, CA] | | | |
| 0032 | | (N1261A) | N532CC | N532CF | N232QS | CS-DNA | N232WC | N48BV | | |
| 0033 | | (N1261K) | (G-BLSG) | G-BLXN | N550ST | N531CM | N581CM | | | |
| 0034 | | (N1261M) | OE-GAP | N34CJ | N59EC | N610GD | N220BP | | | |
| 0035 | | (N1261P) | N712S | N711JG | N711JN | XA-THO | N834DC | | | |
| 0036 | | (N12615) | N95CC | N36H | N36HR | N27B | N63JG | N63JU | N63CR | C-FRGY |
| | | C-FOBQ | | | | | | | | |
| 0037 | | (N12616) | C-GERC | N72WC | N573BB | N578BB | | | | |
| 0038 | | N3D | N1982U | N100KP | (N801CC) | N214PN | N406CT | | | |
| 0039 | | N22UL | | | | | | | | |
| 0040 | | (N1269D) | C-FEMA | | | | | | | |
| 0041 | | (N1269E) | N772M | N592M | N692M | N74BJ | N74LM | [retro-fitted with Williams | | |
| | | FJ44 engines] | | ZS-BEN | | | | | | |
| 0042 | | (N1269J) | N250AL | N250AF | N241DS | | | | | |
| 0043 | | (N1269N) | N101EG | (N727NA) | (N727AL) | N727NA | N727EF | | | |
| 0044 | | (N1269P) | N92ME | | | | | | | |
| 0045 | | N1269Y | YU-BOE | BH-BIH | T9-BIH | N97CC | | | | |
| 0046 | | (N12690) | N553CC | N760NB | N103VF | | | | | |
| 0047 | | N12695 | I-CEFI | N16RP | | | | | | |
| 0048 | | N1270D | N797TJ | N999TJ | N705SP | | | | | |
| 0049 | | N1270K | B-4101 | | | | | | | |
| 0050 | | N1270S | B-4102 | | | | | | | |
| 0051 | | N1270Y | N251QS | CS-DNB | N132WC | N77PA | N311AF | | | |
| 0052 | | N12703 | N4TL | N4TU | (N552CF) | N27SD | N27GD | N57BJ | | |
| 0053 | | N12705 | N75BL | N253QS | N1223N | N393E | | | | |
| 0054 | | N12709 | N717LS | N57MB | N999CB | N599CB | N812HA | | | |
| 0055 | | N1271A | N374GS | N374GC | N87FL | N417RC | N408CT | | | |
| 0056 | | (N1271B) | C-GERL | N550F | N52FT | | | | | |
| 0057 | | N1271D | N1UL | N1UH | N1UL | N57CJ | | | | |
| 0058 | | N1271E | N633EE | | | | | | | |
| 0059 | | (N1271N) | PT-LHD | N36NS | N829JC | N329JC | (N904VA) | N531PM | N329JC | |
| 0060 | | (N1271T) | N85AB | N588CT | N314G | N260QS | N442KM | | | |
| 0061 | | (N12712) | N540JB | N46A | (N464) | N53JM | N200LX | N811RG | | |
| 0062 | | N12715 | I-AVVM | | | | | | | |
| 0063 | | (N12717) | VH-EMO | | | | | | | |
| 0064 | | (N1272G) | N2000X | N200CX | (N990HP) | N45H | N200CX | N200CV | N575SG | (N557MG) |
| 0065 | | (N1272N) | N7118A | N612ST | (N900RG) | (N909RG) | N995DC | N90FJ | XA-... | |
| 0066 | | N1272P | N711MD | | | | | | | |
| 0067 | | (N1272V) | N550FS | C-GMAV | N70AF | N789MA | (N67VP) | "EW94228" | HC-BTY | N550HA |
| | | N900DM | N828AF | | | | | | | |
| 0068 | | N1272Z | N404G | N4049 | N7070A | | | | | |
| 0069 | | (N12720) | N43VS | | | | | | | |
| 0070 | | (N12722) | N570CC | N570RC | XB-EEP | | | | | |
| 0071 | | (N12727) | N571CC | N1865M | | | | | | |

## S550 CITATION II

| C/n | Identities |
|---|---|
| 0072 | (N1273A) (N572CC) N1273A N186MT N686MC TC-NMC N62NS N627HS |
| 0073 | (N1273E) N1958N |
| 0074 | N1273J N550LC N22EH N274QS N274PG N74JE N74GZ |
| 0075 | (N1273N) N554CC N882KB N882RB (N275VP) |
| 0076 | (N1273Q) N95CC C-GQMH N89TD N52CK N25DY |
| 0077 | (N1273R) N747CP (N747GP) N277QS CS-DNC N202WC N999EA N999QH |
| 0078 | N1273X ZS-CAR |
| 0079 | (N1273Z) N1000W N100QW N97AJ N97LB (N27TB) 5N-BEL N578GG* |
| 0080 | N12730 C-GTDO N581EA (N269MT) XA-TMI N260BS XA-VGF |
| 0081 | (N1274B) N168HC N550KM PR-MCN N404KK |
| 0082 | N1274D N97TJ N9KH N282QS N27TB |
| 0083 | N1274K N511BB N511BR OE-GNS N511BR N883PF N683PF |
| 0084 | N1274N PT-LJL |
| 0085 | N1274P N683MB N683CF N54AM (N285CF) N220CA N8BG N143BP N550BT |
| 0086 | (N1274X) N586CC N900RB N86QS 4X-COO OB-1792-T OB-1792 N11SU D-CJJJ |
| 0087 | N1274Z N21EG ZS-DES |
| 0088 | (N12744) N825HL N288QS N127RC (N557TC) |
| 0089 | N12745 (N289CC) N134GB VT-RHM VT-ETG |
| 0090 | N12746 N777GF N320S N76FC (N4BP) N97BP (N50BM) N113VP XA-AEZ N113VP N499RC |
| 0091 | (N12747) N595CC N595CM N241LA N477LC+ [+ marks reserved in error] N476LC |
| 0092 | (N1275A) N92QS N923S N489GM |
| 0093 | N1275B N593CC N33DS N93QS N400RE N629RA |
| 0094 | (N1275D) N594CC (N347CP) N594CC F-OHAH N560AJ N6LL N1H N19ZA |
| 0095 | N1275H N200NK N200NV N345CC N409CT |
| 0096 | (N1275N) N95CC N29X N29XA [w/o 05Mar89 Poughskeepsie, NY] |
| 0097 | N1290B N97QS N828WB N551BE N551RF N302MB |
| 0098 | N1290E N98QS CS-DDA N598WC N598KW |
| 0099 | N1290G N44GT N299QS N777FD YV.... |
| 0100 | (N1290N) N3000W (N616GB) N300QW N550SJ |
| 0101 | (N1290Y) N101QS C-FABF |
| 0102 | N1290Z N287MC N285MC |
| 0103 | N12900 N103QS N22HP [w/o 03May07 Dillon, MT] |
| 0104 | N12903 N224KC [retro-fitted with Williams FJ44 engines] |
| 0105 | (N12907) N105BG |
| 0106 | (N12909) N106QS N666TR N9072U |
| 0107 | N1291E N474L N713DH N550HT C-GBGC N553SD |
| 0108 | (N1291K) N108QS N316MH |
| 0109 | N1291P N509CC N1GC N7QC N38EC N61TL N75MC (N50SL) |
| 0110 | N1291V N45GP (N116LD) |
| 0111 | (N1291Y) N111QS (N777HN) |
| 0112 | (N12910) N112QS A2-MCB ZS-PSG |
| 0113 | (N12911) N553CC PT-LJQ |
| 0114 | N1292A PT-LKS |
| 0115 | (N1292B) N505CC N520RP C-FDDD C-GWBF N92JT N92JC |
| 0116 | N1292K N125CG N550HC |
| 0117 | N1292N PT-LKT [w/o 01Dec92 Sao Paulo-Congonhas, Brazil] |
| 0118 | N12920 N600TF N820FJ N820F VH-IWU N118AJ N110LH N721LR 4X-... |
| 0119 | (N12922) N261WR N261WD N700SW N700SV (N500LH) N11TS N11TR N11TS N63HA |
| 0120 | N12924 N1283M N716DB N716DD |
| 0121 | (N12925) D-CLOU N23NM (N20NM) N711XR |
| 0122 | N12929 I-TALG N122WS |
| 0123 | N1293A N121CG |
| 0124 | (N1293E) N1867W N52CK N550JC N554T N555WV |
| 0125 | N1293G N122CG N97CT (N552SM) N125QA |
| 0126 | N1293K N126QS (N127RC) ZS-EDA |
| 0127 | N1293N N14UM (N127CF) PT-OSL N14UM N674JM N874JM N97SK N431MS |
| 0128 | N1293V N911BB N370M N550CZ |
| 0129 | N1293X N87TH N480CC N488CC N323JR* |
| 0130 | (N1293Z) N130CC N302PC N550PL N552SD |
| 0131 | N12934 D-CHJH N87BA |
| 0132 | (N1294D) N533CC N91ME N91ML N394HA |
| 0133 | (N1294K) G-VKRS N7047K I-ZAMP N133VP N431WM N133VP |
| 0134 | N1294M N134QS D-CFAI SE-DYO OY-GMJ N66HD SE-DYO |
| 0135 | (N1294N) OE-GPD D-CIAO N2235 VT-KMB |
| 0136 | (N1294P) [converted on line to prototype Citation V c/n 560-0001] |
| 0137 | (N12945) D-CNCA HB-VKA N100TB PT-WIB |
| 0138 | (N1295A) N538CC N305PC N138QS N713HH (N501BE) N552BE N20CS ZS-CWG |
| 0139 | (N1295B) N906SB N706SB N39TF N881A |
| 0140 | (N1295G) C-GLCR N575EW |
| 0141 | (N1295J) N907SB N707SB N26JJ N550AJ |
| 0142 | (N1295M) N542CC C-FALI C-GCRG N701BG |
| 0143 | (N1295N) N143QS N1VA N458PE CC-CWZ |
| 0144 | (N1295P) D-CNCB N6516V N543SC |
| 0145 | (N1295Y) (PH-HMC) (PH-HMA) PH-RMA N145VP 4X-CPT N900LM |

## S550 CITATION II

| C/n | Identities | | | | | | | |
|---|---|---|---|---|---|---|---|---|
| 0146 | (N1296B) | (G-JBCA) | N1296B | N81SH | N815H | YV.... | | |
| 0147 | N1296N | OO-OSA | CS-DDV | | | | | |
| 0148 | N1296Z | ZS-IDC | N170RD | D-CSFD | N550BG | (SE-RCY) | SE-RCX* | |
| 0149 | N149QS | C-GMGB | N816V | N810V | N43RC | N777AX | | |
| 0150 | (N1297B) | N150CJ | N107RC | | | | | |
| 0151 | (N2634E) | N151QS | N151Q | N550SP | N88NW | | | |
| 0152 | N26369 | N848G | N843G | N987CJ | | | | |
| 0153 | (N2637R) | N153QS | N242LA | N476LC+ | [+ marks reserved in error] | | | N477LC |
| 0154 | N26379 | PT-LQI | N910DS | N660AJ | N550DS | | | |
| 0155 | (N2638A) | N155QS | N155GB | N550DL | [retro-fiited with winglets and Williams FJ44 engines] | | | |
| 0156 | (N2638U) | N156QS | N766NB | (N400AJ) | N901PV | N63JT | | |
| 0157 | N2639N | N157QS | N157BM | N802Q | | | | |
| 0158 | (N2639Y) | N158QS | N301QS | N158QS | N66EH | N886RP | N889RP | N550EZ |
| 0159 | (N2646X) | N50GT | N289CC | N9GT | N9GY | | | |
| 0160 | N2642Z | N550GT | PT-OSM | | | | | |

Production complete

# CESSNA 552 CITATION (T-47A)

| C/n | Identities | | | |
|---|---|---|---|---|
| 0001 | N552CC | N12855 | 162755 | [w/o 20Jly93 in hangar fire Forbes Field, Topeka, KS] |
| 0002 | N12756 | 162756 | [w/o 20Jly93 in hangar fire Forbes Field, Topeka, KS] | |
| 0003 | N12557 | 162757 | [w/o 20Jly93 in hangar fire Forbes Field, Topeka, KS] | |
| 0004 | N12058 | 162758 | [w/o 20Jly93 in hangar fire Forbes Field, Topeka, KS; cx Sep93] | |
| 0005 | N12859 | 162759 | [w/o 20Jly93 in hangar fire Forbes Field, Topeka, KS; cx Sep93] | |
| 0006 | N12660 | 162760 | [w/o 20Jly93 in hangar fire Forbes Field, Topeka, KS; cx Sep93] | |
| 0007 | N12761 | 162761 | [w/o 20Jly93 in hangar fire Forbes Field, Topeka, KS; cx Sep93] | |
| 0008 | N12762 | 162762 | [w/o 20Jly93 in hangar fire Forbes Field, Topeka, KS; cx Sep93] | |
| 0009 | N12763 | 162763 | [w/o 20Jly93 in hangar fire Forbes Field, Topeka, KS; cx Sep93] | |
| 0010 | N12564 | 162764 | [w/o 20Jly93 in hangar fire Forbes Field, Topeka, KS; cx Sep93] | |
| 0011 | N12065 | 162765 | [w/o 20Jly93 in hangar fire Forbes Field, Topeka, KS; cx Sep93] | |
| 0012 | N12566 | 162766 | [in compound outside Columbus State Community College hangar at Columbus Bolton Field, OH as N12566] | |
| 0013 | N12967 | 162767 | [w/o 20Jly93 in hangar fire Forbes Field, Topeka, KS; cx Sep93] | |
| 0014 | N12568 | 162768 | [cx 03Nov09, scrapped] | |
| 0015 | N12269 | 162769 | [w/o 20Jly93 in hangar fire Forbes Field, Topeka, KS; cx Sep93] | |

Production complete

# CESSNA 560 CITATION V/ULTRA/ENCORE

| C/n | Identities | | | | | | | | | |
|---|---|---|---|---|---|---|---|---|---|---|
| 707 | N5079V | N560VU | [cvtd to Citation Ultra Encore prototype, c/n 0424 reworked qv] | | | | | | | |
| 550-0001 | N560CC | [Model 550 aircraft cvtd to 560 standard] | | | | | | | | |
| 560-0001 | (N1294P) | N560CV | N1217V | N561VP | [cvtd on production line from c/n S550-0136] | | | | | |
| 0002 | N1209T | N562CV | N90PG | N101HB | N560VP | N560CZ | | | | |
| 0003 | (N1209X or N1216A) | | N563CV | SY-AAP | Seychelles SY-001 | | S7-AAP | | | |
| | Seychelles SY-001 | | N560BA | N560ER | N413LC | | | | | |
| 0004 | (N1210N or N1216J) | | N189H | | | | | | | |
| 0005 | (N1210V or N1216K) | | N953F | | | | | | | |
| 0006 | (N1211M or N1216N) | | N962JC | N566VP | N570MH | N269TA | N569TA | | | |
| 0007 | (N12117 or N1216Q) | | N964JC | (N57VP) | N717MB | N763D | | | | |
| 0008 | (N1213S or N1216Z) | | N561B | | | | | | | |
| 0009 | (N1213Z or N12160) | | N456FB | VH-HEY | N77HN | N77HU | N77NR | N37NR | N91CV | |
| 0010 | (N1214J or N12162) | | N205PC | N205BC | N643RT | N560JM | | | | |
| 0011 | (N1214Z or N1217H) | | N700TF | N913BJ | | | | | | |
| 0012 | N1217N | N560ME | N560RR | | | | | | | |
| 0013 | (N1217P) | N560WH | | | | | | | | |
| 0014 | N1217S | N1MC | N88TJ | N12ST | (N650ST) | N900SM | | | | |
| 0015 | N12171 | N800DL | N560MR | N580MR | N480DG | | | | | |
| 0016 | N12173 | N68HC | N68HQ | N462B | | | | | | |
| 0017 | (N1218P or N1223A) | | N89BM | N560H | C-FPJT | | | | | |
| 0018 | (N1218Y or N12249) | | N164DW | N114CP | N500FZ | | | | | |
| 0019 | (N1219D or N1226X) | | N99WR | OE-GRW | N61TW | N643RT | | | | |
| 0020 | (N1219G or N1228N) | | N520CV | N560HC | N560HG | | | | | |
| 0021 | N1228V | N682D | C-FDLT | N560DC | N669AJ | N410DW | N83EP | | | |
| 0022 | (N1228Y) | N211MA | N574BB | N574BP | | | | | | |
| 0023 | (N12283) | OE-GDP | VR-CTL | N560JM | N31RC | N345MB | N3FA | | | |
| 0024 | (N12284) | N501QS | N4CS | N560FN | N140U | | | | | |
| 0025 | (N12285) | CNA-NV | | | | | | | | |
| 0026 | (N12286) | N560LC | N49MJ | N350RD | N380RD | | | | | |
| 0027 | (N12289) | N560JR | N20CC | (N20YC) | N560JR | N531MB | N531MF | N625WA | | |
| 0028 | (N1229A) | N6FE | N6FZ | N757CK | | | | | | |
| 0029 | (N1229C) | N590A | | | | | | | | |
| 0030 | (N1229D) | N560W | XB-MTS | N570BJ | N40HT | | | | | |
| 0031 | N1229F | D-CHDE | | | | | | | | |
| 0032 | N1229M | G-DBII | N96MT | N96MY | N560BC | | | | | |
| 0033 | N1229N | I-ATSB | N4333W | C-GAPC | | | | | | |
| 0034 | (N1229Q) | N895LD | N401MC | N560PY | | | | | | |
| 0035 | N1229Z | N36H | N561EJ | | | | | | | |
| 0036 | (N12295 or N2663B) | | (N107CF) | (N107CR) | HZ-ZTC | N532MA | (N560EJ) | N200MM | N50EL | |
| 0037 | (N12297 or N2663X) | | N17LK | N416HF | | | | | | |
| 0038 | (N12298 or N2663Y) | | N301QS | N2296S | N212BW | | | | | |
| 0039 | (N1230A or N26630) | | CNA-NW | | | | | | | |
| 0040 | (N1230G or N2664U) | | N12403 | N71NK | N91NK | N91NL | N560CF | | | |
| 0041 | N26643 | VH-NTH | N400KS | | | | | | | |
| 0042 | (N26648) | N42CV | D-CAWU | N142GA | | | | | | |
| 0043 | (N2665F) | N991PC | [w/o 30Dec95 Eagle River Airport, WI; cx May96; to White Inds, Bates City, MO for spares] | | | | | | | |
| 0044 | N2665S | N111VP | N331CC | N560JL | | | | | | |
| 0045 | N2665Y | PT-LZQ | | | | | | | | |
| 0046 | (N26656) | G-CZAR | G-CJAE | N846MA | | | | | | |
| 0047 | N2666A | N500FK | N560WW | | | | | | | |
| 0048 | N2667X | N4TL | N74TL | N57CE | N57CN | N870AJ | N220CM | N240CM | | |
| 0049 | (N2672X) | N560EL | | | | | | | | |
| 0050 | (N26771) | (N208BC) | N208PC | N208BC | N501CW | | | | | |
| 0051 | N2680A | N599SC | N599SG | N314RW | | | | | | |
| 0052 | N2680D | N500LE | N500UB | | | | | | | |
| 0053 | (N2680X) | N53CV | I-NYCE | N111CF | C-GCUW | C-FACO | C-FACC | C-GNGV | | |
| 0054 | (N26804) | N531F | N100SC | N100SY | (N748DC) | | | | | |
| 0055 | N2681F | HB-VJZ | N282RH | (N21JJ) | (N560CP) | N200CP | (N201CP) | N209CP | N715PS | N55EA |
| 0056 | N2682F | N78AM | (N56EP) | N560AE | N406VJ | | | | | |
| 0057 | (N2683L) | N560BL | N561BC | N561TS | N553SC | | | | | |
| 0058 | (N2686Y) | F-GKGL | N62GA | N710LC | | | | | | |
| 0059 | (N2687L) | F-GKHL | G-PPLC | | | | | | | |
| 0060 | (N2689B) | N2697Y | N90MF | PT-FTB | | | | | | |
| 0061 | (N2697X) | N2701J | D-CNCI | N46GA | | | | | | |
| 0062 | N2716G | ZS-MVV | N560EA | EC-411 | EC-GLM | N500UJ | (N405RH) | | | |
| 0063 | (N2701J) | N7FE | (N7FZ) | N68CK | N63FF | | | | | |
| 0064 | N2717X | (ZS-MYN) | ZS-MVZ | N45GA | OE-GPC | OY-NUD | | | | |
| 0065 | N2721F | N77711 | N560JV | N608CT | | | | | | |
| 0066 | (N27216) | N60S | N501JS | | | | | | | |
| 0067 | N2722F | N45BA | JA119N | | | | | | | |
| 0068 | N2722H | (N40PL) | N711GF | N712GF | N246NW | N560LM | | | | |
| 0069 | (N2724R) | D-CNCP | N65229 | N70TG | N357WC | N857WC | N367JC | | | |

## CITATION V

| C/n | Identities | | | | | | | |
|---|---|---|---|---|---|---|---|---|
| 0070 | (N2725A) | F-GJXX | N570VP | | | | | |
| 0071 | (N2725X) | N271CA | | | | | | |
| 0071A | N2728N | N45RC | | | | | | |
| 0072 | N2726J | (N72FE) | (N91FA) | N572CV | N72CT | (N772KC) | JA120N | |
| 0073 | (N2726X) | N100WP | | | | | | |
| 0074 | N2727F | N27WW | N174JS | N593MD | C-GBNX | | | |
| 0075 | (N2745L) | N75CV | N617PD | (N619PD) | N817PD | | | |
| 0076 | (N2745M) | N777FE | N777FH | N777FN | N94NB | N623KC | N217GL | |
| 0077 | N2745R | G-BSVL | C-GNND | N42NA | HB-VLV | [w/o 20Dec01 Zurich A/P, Switzerland] | | |
| 0078 | N2748B | SE-DLI | OY-CKT | D-CSUN | PH-ILA | OY-CKT | | |
| 0079 | (N2746C) | N560GL | | | | | | |
| 0080 | N2746E | JA8576 | (N803EA) | N5JU | N300CH | | | |
| 0081 | (N2746F) | OE-GID | N560HP | N318CT | | | | |
| 0082 | (N2746U) | N950WA | C-FETJ | N247DG | | | | |
| 0083 | (N2747R) | N22LP | N568WC | N577XW | | | | |
| 0084 | (N2747U) | N16NM | C-GHEC | N51C | | | | |
| 0085 | (N2748F) | N591M | N891M | N85VP | N599LP | | | |
| 0086 | (N2748V) | SE-DPG | N560CX | N560CJ | N218SE | N560CJ | | |
| 0087 | N2749B | 5N-IMR | N167WE | N600BW | N60QB | | | |
| 0088 | (N6783X) | OE-GSW | D-CMCM | OK-SLS | | | | |
| 0089 | N67830 | ZS-MPT | N54DD | | | | | |
| 0090 | (N67839) | N30PC | N30PQ | LV-AHX | | | | |
| 0091 | N6784P | (N18SK) | N56GT | N3GT | (N8GY) | N32PB | N103BG | |
| 0092 | N6784X | XA-RTT | XB-RTT | N719RM | | | | |
| 0092A | N6784Y | N906SB | N592VP | (N713HH) | | | | |
| 0093 | (N6785C) | F-GKJL | N93EA | | | | | |
| 0094 | N6785D | N1823S | (N594VP) | N340DR | N1827S | N94VP | | |
| 0095 | N6788P | N707CV | N404G | | | | | |
| 0096 | N67890 | (N96JJ) | N10TD | | | | | |
| 0097 | (N6790L) | N898CB | | | | | | |
| 0098 | (N6790P) | (N18SK) | N59DF | | | | | |
| 0099 | (N67905) | OE-GPA | D-CDUW | N560GM | N565EJ | | | |
| 0100 | (N6792A) | PH-PBM | N560WE | N560AF | | | | |
| 0101 | (N67980) | N101CV | N560EC | N560DM | N560EP | | | |
| 0102 | (N67988) | VR-BUL | VP-BUL | N560BA | N555PG | | | |
| 0103 | (N67989) | N98E | | | | | | |
| 0104 | (N6799L) | (N560CT) | N400CT | (N416H) | N815CM | (N907EA) | | |
| 0105 | (N6800C) | N105CV | LN-AAA | N147VC | N149VG | N560MH | | |
| 0106 | N6801H | (HB-V..) | (N560PT) | N60SH | N525RD | | | |
| 0107 | (N6801L) | N78NP | N560RJ | N365EA | | | | |
| 0108 | (N6801P) | N8HJ | VH-NHJ | N777KY | N73ME | N73MN | N573BB | (N573BP) |
| 0109 | (N6801Q) | N6801V | N2 | N27 | N109VP | N480RL | | |
| 0109A | (N68018) | N907SB | N560RS | (N22YP) | N4MM | N387MM | | |
| 0110 | (N6802S) | N560LC | N832CB | N832QB | N26DY | N95TD | | |
| 0111 | (N6802T) | (N91AN) | OE-GAA | | | | | |
| 0112 | (N68027) | N4110S | N145MK | N560G | | | | |
| 0113 | N6803L | N26 | N4 | N113VP | N555FD | | | |
| 0114 | (N6803T) | OE-GPS | D-CZAR | PH-ILI | OY-CKJ | | | |
| 0115 | N6803Y | I-NEWY | N91YC | N87JK | | | | |
| 0116 | N68032 | N901RM | N49NS | N561PA | | | | |
| 0117 | (N6804F) | D-CMEI | | | | | | |
| 0118 | N6804L | XA-RXO | XA-SKX | N118DF | N626SL | N900PS | | |
| 0119 | (N6804N) | F-GLIM | N119CV | N450MM | | | | |
| 0120 | (N6804Y or N6806X) | N120CV | N1824S | N560PS | (N994CF) | N129MC | | |
| 0121 | N6808C | PT-MTG | N898GF | N821VP | N960CD | | | |
| 0122 | (N6808Z) | N261WR | N510MT | N561MT | | | | |
| 0123 | (N6809G) | N611ST | (N321VP) | N583CW | N92TE | | | |
| 0124 | (N6809T) | D-CBIG | N124VP | OB-1626 | N7513D | N823WB | | |
| 0125 | N6809V | OE-GCC | | | | | | |
| 0126 | N68097 | LV-PFN | LV-RED | | | | | |
| 0127 | (N6810L) | N64HA | N127VP | (C-....) | N127VP | XB-JHD | | |
| 0128 | (N6810N) | N19MK | N19ME | N85KC | N504BW | N154JK | | |
| 0129 | (N6811F) | N22AF | | | | | | |
| 0130 | (N6811T) | N130CV | N14VF | (N19VF) | PR-CCV | | | |
| 0131 | (N6811X) | N131CV | PT-ORE | N223JV | | | | |
| 0132 | N6811Z | HZ-SFA | N226JV | N521LF | | | | |
| 0133 | (N68118) | N77HF | N88HF | N93DW | N560PK | | | |
| 0134 | N6812D | YV-811CP | YV1022 | | | | | |
| 0135 | (N6812L or N6871L) | N560BB | N560RL | N19HU | | | | |
| 0136 | (N6812Z or N6872T) | (N136CV) | N501T | N772AA | N999AD | N560PA | | |
| 0137 | (N560RB) | N6874Z | N7338 | N733H | N193G | N137JC | | |
| 0138 | (N68746) | (OY-JET) | OY-FFV | N511WV | | | | |
| 0139 | (N68753) | N561A | N75F | (N75FV) | N59NH | | | |
| 0140 | (N6876Q) | N562E | N75G | (N75GV) | N24JD | | | |
| 0141 | N6876S | N141AQ | | | | | | |
| 0142 | N6876Z | PT-OLV | N722OL | PT-WPC | N560FA | N560GT | N64FT | |

# CITATION V

| C/n | Identities | | | | | | | | |
|---|---|---|---|---|---|---|---|---|---|
| 0143 | N6877C | N65HA | (N543VP) | N744WW | N10TB | N734DB | | | |
| 0144 | N6877G | N2000X | N500VC | | | | | | |
| 0145 | (N6877L) | N57MK | N57ML | D-CFLY | PH-ILZ | | | | |
| 0146 | (N6877Q) | N2000M | N500AT | [w/o 16Feb05 Pueblo, CO; cx] | | | | | |
| 0147 | (N6877R) | N27SD | XA-RKX | N125RH | N410J | N147RJ | (N880EF) | N508KD | |
| 0148 | N68770 | N92HW | N560FB | N115K | | | | | |
| 0149 | (N68786) | N565JW | | | | | | | |
| 0150 | (N6879L) | D-CTAN | (N560ED) | N191VF | N191VE | | | | |
| 0151 | N6881Q | ZS-NDU | V5-CDM | | | | | | |
| 0152 | N6882R | ZS-NDX | | | | | | | |
| 0153 | N6804Y | N502T | N502F | (N153VP) | N1SN | SE-DYZ | OO-SKV | EC-LEP | |
| 0154 | N6805T | N503T | (N503F) | (N154SV) | N154VP | | | | |
| 0155 | N6872T | N40WP | N155VP | | | | | | |
| 0156 | (F-GLIM) | N6885L | XA-RKH | N560L | N75B | | | | |
| 0157 | N6885V | N5734 | N5704 | N502TS | N88WC | N157TF | | | |
| 0158 | (N6885Y) | N601AB | N801AB | N560RP | | | | | |
| 0159 | (N68854) | N68MA | D-CLEO | G-JOPT | | | | | |
| 0160 | N6886X | ZS-NDT | N458CK | | | | | | |
| 0161 | N68860 | Spain TR.20-01/403-11 | | | | | | | |
| 0162 | N68864 | [painted as N6864 for a short while end 1991] | | | | | XA-SDT | N388RD | |
| 0163 | N68869 | N529X | N953C | (N163L) | N97JL | N104LR | | | |
| 0164 | (N6887T) | N164CV | N392BS | N570EJ | | | | | |
| 0165 | (N6887X) | N910V | C-GAPD | N24HX | | | | | |
| 0166 | N68872 | ZS-NDW | N166JV | HB-VMV | | | | | |
| 0167 | (N68873) | N20CN | (N167WE) | N211DG | N311DG | N560JT | N580JT | | |
| 0168 | (N68876) | N168CV | N168EA | | | | | | |
| 0169 | N6888C | N80AB | | | | | | | |
| 0170 | N6888L | N170CV | N814CM | (N417H) | LV-CAK | | | | |
| 0171 | (N6888T) | N5735 | N573F | N567F | | | | | |
| 0172 | (N6888X) | N172CV | N560BP | (N560BD) | | | | | |
| 0173 | N68881 | N918BD | N247CN | | | | | | |
| 0174 | N6889E | N563C | N164TC | N560JD | | | | | |
| 0175 | (N564D) | N1279Z | N49LD | N43LD | | | | | |
| 0176 | N12798 | PT-OOR | N176VP | PT-WOM | N661AJ | N83ZA | | | |
| 0177 | N12799 | VR-CNS | D-CHHS | N242AC | N650CM | | | | |
| 0178 | N1280A | N531CC | N500PX | N997EA | | | | | |
| 0179 | (N179CJ) | N1280D | N865M | N885M | N65RL | | | | |
| 0180 | N1280K | N550WW | | | | | | | |
| 0181 | N1280R | N181SG | | | | | | | |
| 0182 | (N1280S) | N560RA | N920PM | C-FCRH | C-FEPG | | | | |
| 0183 | N12807 | N83RR | N83RE | EC-... | | | | | |
| 0184 | N1281A | N873DB | N410DM | | | | | | |
| 0185 | N1281K | N29WE | N29WF | N989TW | N939TW | | | | |
| 0186 | N1281N | N583M | (N586CC) | N583N | N586CC | N47PW | | | |
| 0187 | N12812 | N60GL | N80GE | N922AC | | | | | |
| 0188 | N12813 | (N188CJ) | N64PM | N395R | N62CR | | | | |
| 0189 | N12815 | N189CV | N62HA | N63JG | | | | | |
| 0190 | N12816 | LV-PGC | LV-VFY | N555WF | N303CB | (N214LS) | N404LN | N650JS | N200NG |
| 0191 | N12817 | PT-ORT | N2JW | N45KB | | | | | |
| 0192 | (N1282D) | D-CEWR | N713HH | N238JC | N3444B | | | | |
| 0193 | N1282K | Spain TR.20-02/403-12 | | | | | | | |
| 0194 | (N1282M) | N194CV | N352WC | (N352WQ) | N852WC | N413CK | N413GK | N628CK | |
| 0195 | N1282N | PT-ORC | | | | | | | |
| 0196 | N12824 | N196CV | XA-SEJ | N560JS | N4JS | (N560JS) | N357AZ | N560RW | |
| 0197 | N12826 | N197CV | (EI-DUN) | XA-SJC | N21LG | | | | |
| 0198 | N1283F | N135BC | N560RG | N560BG | (N198VP) | N598CW | N198CV | N550DC | |
| 0199 | (N1283K) | N63HA | N7895Q | N4895Q | N500DW | | | | |
| 0200 | N1283M | OE-GDA | YR-TIC | | | | | | |
| 0201 | N1283N | ZS-NGM | N98GA | SU-EWA | N255RM | | | | |
| 0202 | N1283V | (N202CV) | ZS-NGL | | | | | | |
| 0203 | N1283X | (N203CV) | ZS-NHC | N770OL | N970OT | | | | |
| 0204 | N1283Y | N1000W | | | | | | | |
| 0205 | N12838 | F-GLYC | N205VP | N1AK | | | | | |
| 0206 | N1284A | N560TX | N900E | | | | | | |
| 0207 | (N1284B) | N207CV | N52SN | N780BF | N560CK | | | | |
| 0208 | (N1284D) | N208CV | N892SB | N88G | N208VP | (N758PM) | | | |
| 0209 | (N1284F) | N209CV | | | | | | | |
| 0210 | N1284N | N20MK | N420DM | N277RC | | | | | |
| 0211 | (N1284P) | N250SP | N250SR | | | | | | |
| 0212 | N1284X | TC-LAA | | | | | | | |
| 0213 | N12845 | PT-OTS | | | | | | | |
| 0214 | (N1285D) | OE-GCP | | | | | | | |
| 0215 | (N1285G) | PT-OTT | N23NS | N315EJ | | | | | |
| 0216 | N1285N | TC-LAB | | | | | | | |
| 0217 | N1285P | N602AB | N802AB | | | | | | |
| 0218 | N1285V | XA-SIT | N218BR | N218DF | N5T | N5GE | N561AC | | |

## CITATION V

| C/n | Identities | | | | | | | |
|---|---|---|---|---|---|---|---|---|
| 0219 | N12850 | N318MM | N318MN | N229VP | N515RW | | | |
| 0220 | N12852 | N23UD | N23UB | N73KH | | | | |
| 0221 | (N1286A) | N24UD | N24UB | N701DK | N626RB | | | |
| 0222 | N1286C | N456SW | | | | | | |
| 0223 | N1286N | N575PC | N93AG | N500MG | N223VP | N593CW | N223CV | N560MG |
| 0224 | N1287B | N224CV | N523KW | N528KW | (N47TW) | | | |
| 0225 | N1287C | (N1865S) | N1823S | N525CW | N225CV | N545PL | N969GB | |
| 0226 | N1287D | N893CM | N226CV | | | | | |
| 0227 | N1287F | (N227CV) | LV-PGR | LV-WDR | | | | |
| 0228 | N1287G | N228CV | XA-SLA | N87GA | N560MM | | | |
| 0229 | N1287K | XA-SNX | N98GA | N193SB | N193SE | | | |
| 0230 | N1287N | YV-169CP | N169CP | N394AJ | N384AJ* | | | |
| 0231 | N1287Y | N501E | N12CQ | | | | | |
| 0232 | (N12879) | N502E | | | | | | |
| 0233 | N1288A | Pakistan 0233 | | | | | | |
| 0234 | N1288B | N234AQ | | | | | | |
| 0235 | N1288D | N22RG | N52RG | N129PJ | N560MM | N335EJ | N92BF | N633SA |
| 0236 | N1288N | N506E | N840CT | | | | | |
| 0237 | N1288P | N593M | N893M | N237VP | | | | |
| 0238 | N238CV | N1288T | N46WB | (N95HW) | N194SA | | | |
| 0239 | N1288Y | N239CV | N1GC | N93CV | (N560RB) | | | |
| 0240 | N1289G | N91ME | N966JM | N55CH | | | | |
| 0241 | N1289N | N241CV | ZS-NGS | | | | | |
| 0242 | N1289Y | N242CV | N605AT | N826AC | | | | |
| 0243 | N12890 | N39N | D-CAMS | | | | | |
| 0244 | (N12895) | (N244CV) | N60RD | N701NB | C-GBNE | | | |
| 0245 | N12896 | N615AT | (N508DW) | N508KD | N43RC | | | |
| 0246 | N1290N | N5060P | LV-PHD | LV-WGY | | | | |
| 0247 | N12907 | N94TX | | | | | | |
| 0248 | N12909 | N248CV | N226N | (N229N) | (N123NW) | (N226U) | N50DR | N749TT |
| 0249 | N1291K | N10CN | N733M | N2000X | | | | |
| 0250 | (N1291K) | (N250CV) | N1291Y | N205CM | | | | |
| 0251 | N12910 | LV-PGZ | LV-WGO | N625AC | (N621AC) | | | |
| 0252 | N12911 | N252CV | N44GT | | | | | |
| 0253 | N1292B | N253CV | N46MT | N20LT | N553CW | N858ME | | |
| 0254 | N12921 | N560GB | (N561GB) | N568GB | N710MT | N710ML | | |
| 0255 | N12922 | N255CV | ZS-NHD | N255WA | N355EJ | N61KM | | |
| 0256 | N12929 | N22KW | N52KW | N356EJ | N356SA | | | |
| 0257 | N1293E | N155PT | | | | | | |
| 0258 | N1293Y | PT-OZB | N60NS | PP-ISJ | | | | |
| 0259 | N1293Z | N37WP | N56GA | | | | | |

## CITATION ULTRA

| C/n | Identities | | | | | | | |
|---|---|---|---|---|---|---|---|---|
| 0260 | N1294B | N260CV | C-GPAW | N888RE | N888RT | N883RT | N180FW | N69VT* |
| 0261 | N1294K | N261CV | XB-PYC | N261UH | N305QS | N135WC | | |
| 0262 | N1294N | N262CV | N444GG | | | | | |
| 0263 | N12945 | N979C | N560GS | | | | | |
| 0264 | N1295A | N5250K | N264CV | N264U | N294RT | | | |
| 0265 | N1295P | N5270K | LV-PHJ | LV-WIJ | N86CE | [w/o 24Jan06 Carlsbad, CA] | | |
| 0266 | N1295G | N456JW | N458JW | N269JR | N288JR | N306QS | N350WC | |
| 0267 | N1295J | N96NB | N197JH | N267VP | N267WG | | | |
| 0268 | N1295M | "N5270M" | (XA-...) | N12012 | N269CM | N750FL | | |
| 0269 | N1295N | N331EC | N357EC | C-GRCC | | | | |
| 0270 | N1295Y | N68HC | N68HQ | N159JH | (N259JH) | N4FC | N394CK | |
| 0271 | N1296N | PH-VLG | N49TT | HB-VNB | CS-DTA | | | |
| 0272 | N5094B | N220JT | N372EJ | N672SA | N790PS | N15SL | | |
| 0273 | N5095N | N910PC | N61JB | N861CE | (N861CF) | N521LL | | |
| 0274 | N5096S | N751CF | N511DR | (N511DP) | N137LA | (N137LX) | N560HD | |
| 0275 | (N5097H)+ | N1297V | D-CVHA | (N560LW) | N560LT | N717D | | |
| 0276 | N5100J | N183AJ | N376QS | N376WC | N145KK | | | |
| 0277 | (N5101J)+ | D-CFOX | N804WA | N308QS | N130WC | N560BG | | |
| 0278 | N5103J | N2HJ | VH-FHJ | N560EM | | | | |
| 0279 | (N5103B)+ | (N331EC) | N361EC | N594M | | | | |
| 0280 | (N51042)+ | PH-MDC | HB-VNA | | | | | |
| 0281 | (N5105F)+ | N511ST | N281VP | N716SX | N560HW | | | |
| 0282 | N51055 | D-CBEN | | | | | | |
| 0283 | (N51072)+ | N560JC | N1CH | N560JC | N568JC | | | |
| 0284 | N5108G | N966SW | (N369TC) | | | | | |
| 0285 | (N5109R)+ | N285CV | N147VC | N285CC | | | | |
| 0286 | (N5109W)+ | N286CV | N57MB | N31NS | | | | |
| 0287 | (N5112K)+ | N287CV | N117CC | N117MR | N863RD | | | |
| 0288 | N5141F | N522JA | | | | | | |
| 0289 | N51444 | LV-PHY | LV-WLS | | | | | |
| 0290 | N5145P | N97BH | | | | | | |
| 0291 | N5148B | N744R | N470DP | | | | | |

## CITATION ULTRA

| C/n | Identities | | | | | | | |
|---|---|---|---|---|---|---|---|---|
| 0292 | N5148N | N1295N | HL7501 | | | | | |
| 0293 | N51575 | N293QS | N131WC | N50CV | N136JD | | | |
| 0294 | N5161J | N1295Y | HL7502 | | | | | |
| 0295 | (N5162W)+ | N295CV | N61HA | N80LP | N80EP | N295BM | N903BH | |
| 0296 | (N5163C)+ | N560LC | | | | | | |
| 0297 | N5165T | N1296N | HL7503 | | | | | |
| 0298 | N5166U | N200CK | N25CV | N112CW | N656JG | | | |
| 0299 | N5168F | (N550TM) | VT-EUX | | | | | |
| 0300 | N51743 | N1297V | HL7504 | | | | | |
| 0301 | N5180K | (HB-V..) | VR-BQB | N560AG | HB-VOC | | | |
| 0302 | (N5223Y) | N560CE | I-NYSE | N560CE | N580CE | N302EJ | (N602SA) | N901AB |
| 0303 | N5225K | (N560BD) | (D-CAFB) | N560BJ | N190JH | N190JK | | |
| 0304 | N5226B | N47VC | N401KH | C-GWWU | | | | |
| 0305 | N5228Z | LV-PLE | LV-WMT | | | | | |
| 0306 | N5231S | N49MJ | N306TR | N753BD | (N753BB) | (N753GL) | N753GJ | |
| 0307 | N5233J | N307QS | N139WC | N51FK | | | | |
| 0308 | N5235G | PT-WFD | | | | | | |
| 0309 | N52352 | N212BD | N560RN | N615HR | | | | |
| 0310 | N5241Z | N410CV | N868JT | N228PC | N228PG* | | | |
| 0311 | (N5244F) | N311QS | (N211WC) | N531VP | N421LT | | | |
| 0312 | (N52457) | N312QS | N521VP | | | | | |
| 0313 | N5246Z | N313CV | | | | | | |
| 0314 | N5250E | N314CV | C-FYMM | C-FYMT | N561DA | | | |
| 0315 | (N5250K) | N315QS | (N215WC) | N515VP | | | | |
| 0316 | (N5251Y) | N12RN | | | | | | |
| 0317 | (N52526) | N317QS | N217WC | | | | | |
| 0318 | N5261R | N1273R | N877RF | N877RB | N910HM | | | |
| 0319 | N52613 | N1319D | N52613 | LV-WOE | N2RC | | | |
| 0320 | N5262B | N46WB | (N28ET) | VR-CCV | VP-CCV | N320VP | VH-SMF | VH-MXJ |
| 0321 | N5262W | N320QS | N220WC | N560AV | | | | |
| 0322 | N5262X | "ZS-NNV" | ZS-NVV | N850BA | N300QS | N300WC | N607HM | |
| 0323 | (N5097H) | N323QS | N808AC | | | | | |
| 0324 | N5100J | N55LC | N55LQ | N342QS | N152WC | N853CR | | |
| 0325 | (N5101J) | N96AT | N313QS | N140WC | N566KB | | | |
| 0326 | N5103J | N583M | (N711Z) | N200SC | N220SC | N902AV* | | |
| 0327 | (N51038) | N327QS | | | | | | |
| 0328 | (N5104Z) | N554R | N554EJ | (N554UJ) | N984GA | N926NC | | |
| 0329 | N5105F | N330QS | N302WC | | | | | |
| 0330 | (N51055) | N351WC | N851WC | N330VP | | | | |
| 0331 | N51072 | N331QS | N231WC | | | | | |
| 0332 | (N5108G) | N332LC | N332AE | | | | | |
| 0333 | (N5109R) | N333QS | N397WC* | | | | | |
| 0334 | N5109W | N4TL | N905LC | | | | | |
| 0335 | N335QS | N301WC | VH-WFE | | | | | |
| 0336 | N5265B | N336QS | N128WC* | | | | | |
| 0337 | N5265N | N108LJ | | | | | | |
| 0338 | N52645 | N592M | N338R | | | | | |
| 0339 | N339QS | N539VP | | | | | | |
| 0340 | N5267T | N21CV | | | | | | |
| 0341 | N341QS | N541VP | | | | | | |
| 0342 | N5267T | (N14VF) | XA-RDM | N86CW | (N82CW) | N86CV | | |
| 0343 | N5268A | N343CV | N60AE | N303QS | N325WC | | | |
| 0344 | N5268M | N344QS | N126WC | | | | | |
| 0345 | N5268E | N345CV | N75Z | (N560NS) | N64LV | | | |
| 0346 | N5269A | N346CC | C-GFCL | C-FNTM | | | | |
| 0347 | N5268V | N72FC | N72FE | N106SP | | | | |
| 0348 | N52682 | N348QS | N399WC* | | | | | |
| 0349 | N5151S | N1127P | JA001A | | | | | |
| 0350 | N51522 | N645M | N250JH | N991L | N2500N | Colombia FAC5760 | | |
| 0351 | N5153K | N699CC | N560DM | C-GAWR | C-GAWU | | | |
| 0352 | N5153X | N352QS | N133WC* | | | | | |
| 0353 | N51564 | N353CV | N1873 | N187S | N353Z | N20SM | | |
| 0354 | N5157E | N4200K | | | | | | |
| 0355 | N51575 | N355CV | N67GW | N67GU | HK-4304 | | | |
| 0356 | N5153Z | N354QS | N130WC* | | | | | |
| 0357 | N5148N | N81SH | N347QS | N110WC | ZP-BZH | | | |
| 0358 | N5163C | N358CV | N12TV | (N12TU) | N30TV | N284CP | | |
| 0359 | N5166U | ZS-SMB | N416BA | | | | | |
| 0360 | N5168F | N6780A | N62WA | N62WD | | | | |
| 0361 | N5156B | N361QS | N560VP | | | | | |
| 0362 | N5183U | OE-GMI | PH-ILO | N831MM | N998TW | | | |
| 0363 | N5180K | N59KG | N59KC | | | | | |
| 0364 | N5260Y | N991PC | N560A | N51ND | | | | |
| 0365 | N5235G | N7547P | N375CM | N712L | N2500D | Peru 721 | N2500D | Colombia FAC5763 |
| 0366 | N52352 | SX-DCI | | | | | | |
| 0367 | N5161J | N367QS | N395WC | | | | | |

## CITATION ULTRA

| C/n | Identities |
|---|---|
| 0368 | N5194J N343CC N348CC |
| 0369 | N52113 N5200 N520G N5200 N680GW N210CM |
| 0370 | N5262B N607RJ N749DC |
| 0371 | N5262X N371CV N315CS |
| 0372 | N52601 N372CV N76CK N372QS N372WC N592MA* |
| 0373 | N373QS |
| 0374 | N5214L N7728T N166KB N163L Colombia FAC5761 N1066W Colombia FAC5761 |
| 0375 | N375QS N575VP |
| 0376 | N5097H VR-BCY N1217H N713DH N600LF N600EF N554T |
| 0377 | N5264A N377RA N450RA N377QS N377WC N537VP |
| 0378 | N5090A N350WC N850WC (N378VP) N808TH |
| 0379 | N5101J C-GWCR N560RF |
| 0380 | N5103J N380CV N190KL N147SB |
| 0381 | N2762J N857BL N214L N5373D Columbia FAC5764 |
| 0382 | N382QS N582VP N560TX |
| 0383 | N51038 N57ST N63TM N631M N579BJ (N241KP) |
| 0384 | N5231S N196SA (N86DD) N950TC N331MW |
| 0385 | N5109R N333WM (N833WM) |
| 0386 | N7274A N720SJ N615L N2500B Columbia FAC5762 |
| 0387 | N5108G US Army 95-0123 [UC-35A] |
| 0388 | N5269A N92SS |
| 0389 | N5092B PT-WRR N389JV N118RK |
| 0390 | N5093L N390CV C-GMGB N390VP N560SE C-GNLQ N217TH |
| 0391 | N5092D N391CV N92DE |
| 0392 | N5124F US Army 95-0124 [UC-35A] |
| 0393 | N5156V N393QS N116WC* |
| 0394 | N5093Y N394QS |
| 0395 | N5093Y (N395QS) N19MK (N19MU) N15SK |
| 0396 | N50938 N396QS N596VP ZK-AWK N3937E ZK-AWK |
| 0397 | N50715 PT-WKS N397AF N560RC N44LV |
| 0398 | N5061W ZS-NUZ |
| 0399 | N51881 N97NB N560WD (N560DW) N969DW |
| 0400 | N51942 N916CS N916CG N42ND |
| 0401 | N5197A N401CV VP-CSN OY-KLG |
| 0402 | N5200U N302QS N122WC* |
| 0403 | N5201J N1202D JA01TM |
| 0404 | N5201M US Army 96-0107 [UC-35A] |
| 0405 | N5202D PT-WMQ N137FA N45TP N45TE |
| 0406 | N5203S PT-WMZ |
| 0407 | N5204D N1218Y F-OHRU N560RK |
| 0408 | N5207A PT-WOA N560NS N304QS N408JT YV.... |
| 0409 | N52081 PT-WVH (N409VP) N390BA C-FKBC |
| 0410 | N5211A US Army 96-0108 [UC-35A] |
| 0411 | N5226B PT-WNE N38NS |
| 0412 | N5228Z PT-WNF (N412EA) N412CW N513EF N17PL |
| 0413 | N5233J N413CV VP-CKM N8041R N561JS |
| 0414 | N5235G ZS-CDS SE-RGY |
| 0415 | N52457 US Army 96-0109 [UC-35A] |
| 0416 | N5109R N19PV N713DH N713DA N416VP N561CC |
| 0417 | N5090A N1248B RP-C8818 N560TJ VH-XTT N525BA N560RV |
| 0418 | N5112K N318QS |
| 0419 | N5233J EC-GOV |
| 0420 | N51942 US Army 96-0110 [UC-35A] |
| 0421 | N322QS |
| 0422 | N20SB N5XP N58RG N59TF |
| 0423 | N5073G N324QS N523VP N528VM |
| 0424 | (N324QS) N424CV [cx Sep97 cvtd to prototype Citation Ultra Encore with c/n 707 in the Cessna prototype series] |
| 0425 | N325QS |
| 0426 | N5101J US Army 96-0111 [UC-35A] |
| 0427 | N5105F N11LC N11LQ N573AB N891FV |
| 0428 | N328QS |
| 0429 | N392QS |
| 0430 | N433CV C-GLIM N560TA |
| 0431 | N5076K PT-WZW N431JV N560JP N76TF |
| 0432 | N51143 N356WC N856CW N564TJ |
| 0433 | N5231S N33LX N88EX XA-CDF N660SB |
| 0434 | N334QS |
| 0435 | N52352 N410NA N5263 |
| 0436 | N5086W N36LX N86EX N96FC N560BJ N97TE |
| 0437 | N337QS |
| 0438 | N5207A (PT-WQE) N438MC |
| 0439 | N50612 (N39LX) VP-CSC N6NY |
| 0440 | N5076K PT-WSN N400MC |
| 0441 | N314QS |
| 0442 | N5226B N23UD N152JH N752JH N888SV N778FW N323NE |

## CITATION ULTRA

| C/n | Identities | | | | | |
|---|---|---|---|---|---|---|
| 0443 | N5228Z | N24UD | N568RL | N561CM | | |
| 0444 | N343QS | | | | | |
| 0445 | N5000R | N345QS | | | | |
| 0446 | N51038 | HB-VLZ | | | | |
| 0447 | N5108G | N51246 | N261WR | | | |
| 0448 | N5100J | C-GSUN | C-GSUM | N4ZL | | |
| 0449 | N5120U | N560BP | N555WF | N555WK | N75WP | |
| 0450 | N51246 | PT-XCF | | | | |
| 0451 | N5124F | N351QS | | | | |
| 0452 | N5130J | US Army 97-0101 | | [UC-35A] | | |
| 0453 | N5132T | N453CV | N400LX | N60KM | | |
| 0454 | N5135K | TC-ROT | N1216Z | TC-ROT | N454RT | N63GB | C-GOOB |
| 0455 | N51396 | N358QS | | | | |
| 0456 | N51444 | US Army 97-0102 | | [UC-35A] | | |
| 0457 | N51564 | N59HA | VP-CMS | G-GRGS | HB-VNW | |
| 0458 | N5161J | LV-PNR | LV-YMA | N458DA | | |
| 0459 | N5162W | N79PM | N76WR | | | |
| 0460 | N5157E | N360QS | | | | |
| 0461 | N5185V | XA-ICO | N461VP | N61TL | | |
| 0462 | N5183U | US Army 97-0103 | | [UC-35A] | | |
| 0463 | N50612 | N56K | N58KJ | N48LC | N48LQ | D-CEMG |
| 0464 | N420DM | N53PE | | | | |
| 0465 | N5086W | N465CV | N848G | | | |
| 0466 | N366QS | N224WC* | | | | |
| 0467 | N5096S | ZS-OFM | N98NA | N20CC | | |
| 0468 | N51042 | US Army 97-0104 | | [UC-35A] | | |
| 0469 | N5183V | N701CR | N7010R | N469DN | | |
| 0470 | N44FG | | | | | |
| 0471 | N5188A | N371QS | | | | |
| 0472 | N5097H | US Army 97-0105 | | [UC-35A] | | |
| 0473 | N5093D | N9LR | N473SB | N1CF | | |
| 0474 | N51160 | N474CV | XA-TKZ | N474VP | N321GG | |
| 0475 | N374QS | N374WC | | | | |
| 0476 | N150S | N941RM | | | | |
| 0477 | N5085E | N50GP | | | | |
| 0478 | N5095N | N70BR | N111JW | N458NC | | |
| 0479 | N5125J | N379QS | N743DB | | | |
| 0480 | N51246 | N71JJ | N560VR | N566VR | | |
| 0481 | N5153K | C-GXCO | C-GXCG | | | |
| 0482 | N5156D | N44LC | N44LQ | | | |
| 0483 | N383QS | | | | | |
| 0484 | N5125J | C-GYMM | C-FWHH | | | |
| 0485 | N998SA | | | | | |
| 0486 | N386QS | | | | | |
| 0487 | N50820 | N46MW | N43KW | N51EF | | |
| 0488 | N12688 | N555WF | N555WL | | | |
| 0489 | N66U | | | | | |
| 0490 | N390QS | N390WC | N565NC | | | |
| 0491 | N51564 | N404MM | N484MM | | | |
| 0492 | N5152X | N492CV | C-GDSH | N41VP | N41VR | N85EB |
| 0493 | N391QS | | | | | |
| 0494 | N5166T | N80GR | N86GR | N452AJ | | |
| 0495 | US Army 98-0006 | | [UC-35A] | | | |
| 0496 | N395QS | | | | | |
| 0497 | N5161J | TC-MET | N497EA | OE-GCD | G-OBCC | |
| 0498 | (N24QT) | N26QT | N26QL | | | |
| 0499 | N556BG | | | | | |
| 0500 | N500CU | N35TF | N960CR | N860CR | | |
| 0501 | N51896 | US Army 98-0007 | | [UC-35A] | | |
| 0502 | N1298X | D2-EBA | | | | |
| 0503 | N52059 | (ZS-FCB) | VP-BDB | N204BG | | |
| 0504 | N504CC | | | | | |
| 0505 | N52229 | US Army 98-0008 | | [UC-35A] | [crashed Elmendorf, AK, 06Oct09] | |
| 0506 | N50820 | G-RIBV | G-OGRG | EC-JFT | | |
| 0507 | N5095N | N1129L | (N994HP) | | | |
| 0508 | N5085E | US Army 98-0009 | | [UC-35A] | | |
| 0509 | N309QS | | | | | |
| 0510 | N399QS | | | | | |
| 0511 | N200NK | YV2110 | | | | |
| 0512 | N29WE | N10AU | N10RU | | | |
| 0513 | N5061W | US Army 98-0010 | | [UC-35A] | | |
| 0514 | N340QS | | | | | |
| 0515 | N51042 | VH-PSU | | | | |
| 0516 | N316QS | | | | | |
| 0517 | N5145V | G-OTGT | N424HH | OE-GCB | | |
| 0518 | N51817 | N1295B | JA02AA | | | |

# CITATION ULTRA/ENCORE

| C/n | Identities | | | | | | |
|---|---|---|---|---|---|---|---|
| 0519 | N319QS | | | | | | |
| 0520 | N51072 | N620AT | N101KP | | | | |
| 0521 | N5086W | N521CV | N22LC | N22LQ | N560AT | | |
| 0522 | N398QS | | | | | | |
| 0523 | N332QS | | | | | | |
| 0524 | N5091J | US Marines 165740 | | [UC-35C] | | | |
| 0525 | N5093Y | N593M | N777WY | | | | |
| 0526 | N326QS | | | | | | |
| 0527 | N51396 | N627AT | N102KP | | | | |
| 0528 | N52WF | | | | | | |
| 0529 | N5097H | US Marines 165741 | | [UC-35C] | | | |
| 0530 | N353QS | | | | | | |
| 0531 | N397QS | [w/o 02May02 Leaky, TX; by Jan05 remains at Lancaster TX] | | | | | |
| 0532 | N5268V | N5209E | US Army 99-0100 | | [UC-35A] | | |
| 0533 | N591M | XA-GSS | | | | | |
| 0534 | N5112K | US Army 99-0101 | | [UC-35A] | | | |
| 0535 | N5267D | N1247V | N57MK | (N57ML) | N403ET | | |
| 0536 | N363QS | | | | | | |
| 0537 | N5181U | G-TTFN | OO-CLX | | | | |
| 0538 | N51143 | US Army 99-0102 | | [UC-35A] | | | |

# CITATION ENCORE

| C/n | Identities | | | | | | |
|---|---|---|---|---|---|---|---|
| 0539 | N5108G | N539CE | N303CP | | | | |
| 0540 | N540CV | N154JS | N158JS | | | | |
| 0541 | N51780 | N541CV | (N486BG) | N812DC | | | |
| 0542 | N5093L | N542CE | (N120SB) | N12MW | N12MY | I-CMCC | |
| 0543 | N51995 | N543LE | | | | | |
| 0544 | N901DK | N701DK | D-CASA | | | | |
| 0545 | N5091J | US Army 99-0103 | | [UC-35B] | | | |
| 0546 | N5151D | N368BE | | | | | |
| 0547 | N51995 | N68MA | N906AS | N908AS | N610GD | | |
| 0548 | N5097H | US Army 99-0104 | | [UC-35B] | | | |
| 0549 | N5090A | N713DH | N486BG | N11TS | N33TS | | |
| 0550 | N51072 | N865M | N3865M | | | | |
| 0551 | N52670 | N560RG | N86SK | | | | |
| 0552 | N5154J | N55HV | N552HV | | | | |
| 0553 | N5145V | G-KDMA | | | | | |
| 0554 | N5154J | N747RL | N749RL | N8486 | | | |
| 0555 | N5155G | N154JH | | | | | |
| 0556 | N5165P | N539WA | | | | | |
| 0557 | N221CE | N557PG | | | | | |
| 0558 | N5174W | N560RV | N558V | N558CG | (D-CEBM) | N558GG | N558AK |
| 0559 | N5192E | N359EJ | (N659SA) | N359EC | N444RF | | |
| 0560 | N5180C | N560JW | | | | | |
| 0561 | N5197M | N120SB | N511TH | N60AE* | | | |
| 0562 | N5180K | N60NF | N911UM | | | | |
| 0563 | N51995 | N59KG | | | | | |
| 0564 | N5241R | N7895Q | N660LT | N5601T | | | |
| 0565 | N5211A | US Army 00-1051 | | [UC-35A] | | | |
| 0566 | N5000R | N560BL | C-FAMI | N560FP | | | |
| 0567 | N5268A | US Marines 165938 | | [UC-35C] | [w/o 10Mar04 NAS Miramar, CA] | | |
| 0568 | N52639 | N155JH | | | | | |
| 0569 | N52433 | (N600LF) | N1315C | N600LF | D-CEBM | | |
| 0570 | N5262W | US Marines 165939 | | [UC-35C] | | | |
| 0571 | N5244W | N3616 | | | | | |
| 0572 | N174JS | | | | | | |
| 0573 | N162TF | C-FALI | C-FRKI | C-FRKL | | | |
| 0574 | N52526 | US Army 00-1052 | | [UC-35A] | | | |
| 0575 | N5257C | N156JH | | | | | |
| 0576 | N51072 | N200JR | N280JR | C-GTGO | | | |
| 0577 | N5207V | US Army 00-1053 | | [UC-35A] | | | |
| 0578 | N5264N | D-CAUW | | | | | |
| 0579 | N5259Y | N579CE | | | | | |
| 0580 | N5267G | N580CE | N1871R | N486SB | [w/o Upland, CA, 24Jun06] | | |
| 0581 | N5269Z | N157JH | | | | | |
| 0582 | N52229 | N843HS | N560CX | | | | |
| 0583 | N52591 | N583CE | | | | | |
| 0584 | N5296X | N7HB | N90HB | N428SJ | | | |
| 0585 | N5254Y | N221VP | (N585VP) | N832R | | | |
| 0586 | N52691 | N201SU | | | | | |
| 0587 | N5270K | N120SB | (N587K) | N4TL | | | |
| 0588 | N5243K | C-GJEI | C-FQYB | N560GT | | | |
| 0589 | N5151D | US Army 01-0301 | | [UC-35A] | | | |
| 0590 | N5166T | OE-GPH | | | | | |
| 0591 | N591DK | | | | | | |

# CITATION ENCORE

| C/n | Identities | | | | | |
|---|---|---|---|---|---|---|
| 0592 | N5180C | US Marines 166374 | | [UC-35D] | | |
| 0593 | N5260M | N121LS | N300AK | | | |
| 0594 | N52446 | N560MR | | | | |
| 0595 | N560TE | | | | | |
| 0596 | N52235 | N844HS | N507PD | | | |
| 0597 | N51869 | N597KC | JA002A | | | |
| 0598 | N5250P | N800QS | N806WC | N757TR | | |
| 0599 | N52690 | N288HL | | | | |
| 0600 | N52369 | PR-LAM | | | | |
| 0601 | N5239J | N801QS | | | | |
| 0602 | N5206T | N9CN | | | | |
| 0603 | (N66W) | N5236L | N603CV | N313HC | | |
| 0604 | N911CB | | | | | |
| 0605 | N5257C | N605CE | N250AL | | | |
| 0606 | N5245U | N802QS | N606CE | N91AG | N166ST | |
| 0607 | N5270K | ZS-UCH | SE-RGZ | | | |
| 0608 | N52059 | N608CE | | | | |
| 0609 | N5269Z | N847HS | N242AC | | | |
| 0610 | N52699 | N804QS | | | | |
| 0611 | N98AC | N98AQ | N560CH | N568CH | N611MR | |
| 0612 | N5260U | N89MD | | | | |
| 0613 | N44SH | N448H | N25QT | | | |
| 0614 | N5296X | N806QS | | | | |
| 0615 | N510BG | N152JH | | | | |
| 0616 | N52114 | N616CE | N80GR | | | |
| 0617 | N5207A | N807QS | | | | |
| 0618 | N51995 | N933PB | | | | |
| 0619 | N52135 | N808QS | | | | |
| 0620 | N101WY | | | | | |
| 0621 | N102WY | | | | | |
| 0622 | N5197A | N560KL | | | | |
| 0623 | N51993 | N977MR | | | | |
| 0624 | N5257V | N1242K | N500MG | | | |
| 0625 | N810QS | | | | | |
| 0626 | N41VP | | | | | |
| 0627 | N5260M | N191VB | N191VF | | | |
| 0628 | N812QS | | | | | |
| 0629 | N844QS | | | | | |
| 0630 | N5180K | US Marines 166474 [UC-35C] | | | | |
| 0631 | N813QS | N813QS | N560HC | | | |
| 0632 | N5228J | N6521F | N109WS | | | |
| 0633 | N866QS | (N860Q) | N427CD | C-FTOM | | |
| 0634 | (N911CB) | N5254Y | N90NB | | | |
| 0635 | N5257C | N535CE | | | | |
| 0636 | N83TF | N83TK | N636SE | [w/o Cresco, IA, 19Jul06] | | |
| 0637 | N5073G | CS-DIG | (PR-ALL) | LN-IDB | | |
| 0638 | N5263S | (N814QS) | N1269P | N23YZ | | |
| 0639 | N5214L | N639CV | N24GF | | | |
| 0640 | N640CE | N800BW | | | | |
| 0641 | N5270J | N67GW | | | | |
| 0642 | N642LF | | | | | |
| 0643 | N5264N | N960JH | (N990JH) | (N960BM) | C-FTJF | |
| 0644 | N5270K | N814QS | N95NB | N93NB | N644VP* | |
| 0645 | N5269A | N299DH | | | | |
| 0646 | N5260U | N846QS | N535BP | | | |
| 0647 | N647CE | C-GDSH | C-FYUL | | | |
| 0648 | N5248V | N820QS | C-GTOG | C-FVEJ | N648VP | C-FAMI |
| 0649 | N5267T | US Army 03-0016 | | [UC-35B] | | |
| 0650 | N5260Y | N820QS | | | | |
| 0651 | US Marines 166500 | | N5156D | US Marines 166500 | | [UC-35D] |
| 0652 | N652NR | YR-ELV | | | | |
| 0653 | N5265N | PR-SCR | | | | |
| 0654 | N52653 | N654CE | | | | |
| 0655 | N825QS | | | | | |
| 0656 | N656Z | | | | | |
| 0657 | N5214L | N778BC | N450MQ | | | |
| 0658 | N52234 | N560RM | | | | |
| 0659 | N191KL | N721NB | | | | |
| 0660 | N5264M | N844TM | | | | |
| 0661 | N5162W | N591CF | | | | |
| 0662 | N5212M | N560CR | N338MC | | | |
| 0663 | N5266F | N357BE | | | | |
| 0664 | N5151D | N664CE | | | | |
| 0665 | N5200R | OE-GEJ | YR-RPG | M-FRED | | |
| 0666 | N51160 | N700JR | | | | |
| 0667 | N52462 | US Army 03-0726 | | [UC-35B] | | |

## CITATION ENCORE/ENCORE+

| C/n | Identities | | | | |
|---|---|---|---|---|---|
| 0668 | N5214L | N560TG | (N560TP) | N45TP | |
| 0669 | N5216A | N834QS | | | |
| 0670 | N5243K | N670CE | N611CS | N560JT | |
| 0671 | N52457 | N600BW | | | |
| 0672 | N5253G | US Navy 166712 | | [UC-35D] | |
| 0673 | N5245U | N96NB | | | |
| 0674 | N52601 | N552TC | N552CN | | |
| 0675 | N29QC | | | | |
| 0676 | N227WS | C-FSNC | | | |
| 0677 | N5079V | US Navy 166713 | | [UC-35D] | |
| 0678 | N5203J | N399HS | N177JE | | |
| 0679 | US Marines 166714 | | [UC-35D] | | |
| 0680 | N5245L | N595MA | N595JJ | | |
| 0681 | N5265B | N681CE | | | |
| 0682 | N5204D | US Navy 166715* | | [UC-35D] | |
| 0683 | N51042 | F-HLIM | | | |
| 0684 | N5161J | N684CE | N684BM | (N827TV) | N370TC |
| 0685 | N5086W | N837QS | | | |
| 0686 | N5188A | [c.f. c/n 0751 below] | | | |
| 0687 | N5207V | XA-UEF | | | |
| 0688 | N5248B | N254AD | | | |
| 0689 | N52059 | XC-GDT | | | |
| 0690 | N5218T | N839QS | | | |
| 0691 | N5241Z | N300PX | N500PX | N560PX | N960M |
| 0692 | N5166T | N40166 | N999CB | | |
| 0693 | N5076K | US Navy 166766 | | [UC-35D] | |
| 0694 | N5079V | N4018S | JA560Y | | |
| 0695 | N5172M | N695V | | | |
| 0696 | N50715 | US Navy 166767 | | [UC-35D] | |
| 0697 | N5093D | N697CE | LV- | | |
| 0698 | N5216A | N809QS | | | |
| 0699 | N52462 | N560HM | | | |
| 0700 | N5268E | N700NK | | | |
| 0701 | N113US | | | | |
| 0702 | N702AM | | | | |
| 0703 | N52144 | VH-VPL | VH-VRL | | |
| 0704 | N5248V | PR-GQG | | | |
| 0705 | N52639 | C-FYMM | | | |
| 0706 | N802QS | | | | |
| 0707 | N13092 | HL7778* | | | |

## CITATION ENCORE+

| C/n | Identities | | | | |
|---|---|---|---|---|---|
| 0751 | N560CC | [Encore+ prototype, believed to originally be c/n 560-0686, ff 22Mar06 Cedar Rapids, IA] | | | |
| | N560KW | | | | |
| 0752 | N5112K | N752CE | | | |
| 0753 | N5095N | N753CE | N120SB | C-FACC | C-FACO |
| 0754 | N5100J | (N960JH) | N990JH | | |
| 0755 | N5218R | N56TE | | | |
| 0756 | N52645 | N545BP | | | |
| 0757 | N52141 | YV2389 | | | |
| 0758 | N62WA | | | | |
| 0759 | N387SV | | | | |
| 0760 | N5245L | PR-CTB | | | |
| 0761 | N5036Q | N560DL | | | |
| 0762 | N68HC | N68NC | N24QT | | |
| 0763 | N50612 | N926CE | | | |
| 0764 | N5174W | N764CE | LN-AKA | | |
| 0765 | N5245U | N713WD | | | |
| 0766 | N766CE | N15CV | | | |
| 0767 | N5247U | I-ZACK | | | |
| 0768 | N5085E | N179RP | EC-KKB | EC-KOV | |
| 0769 | N5241Z | N769CS | | | |
| 0770 | N5093Y | EC-KKK | | | |
| 0771 | N237BG | | | | |
| 0772 | N5244F | N772CS | | | |
| 0773 | N5207A | M-ANSL | SE-RIT | N560RH | |
| 0774 | N774CC | N422JT | | | |
| 0775 | N5211Q | N803QS | | | |
| 0776 | N5223D | N814QS | | | |
| 0777 | N5216A | N777EN | | | |
| 0778 | N5223X | N818QS | | | |
| 0779 | N5185V | N787CW | | | |
| 0780 | N780CE | N560CL | | | |
| 0781 | N781CE | C-GDSH | | | |
| 0782 | N826QS | | | | |

## CITATION ENCORE+

| C/n | Identities | | | | |
|---|---|---|---|---|---|
| 0783 | N5091J | N560CH | | | |
| 0784 | N830QS | | | | |
| 0785 | N5257C | N203WS | | | |
| 0786 | N819QS | | | | |
| 0787 | N887CS | | | | |
| 0788 | N5259Y | N788CE | N468CE | | |
| 0789 | N822QS | | | | |
| 0790 | N843QS | | | | |
| 0791 | N5079V | N507CR | | | |
| 0792 | N831QS | | | | |
| 0793 | N793CS | | | | |
| 0794 | N823QS | | | | |
| 0795 | N51942 | N114EB | | | |
| 0796 | N829QS | | | | |
| 0797 | N846QS | | | | |
| 0798 | N5214L | N808PL | | | |
| 0799 | N841QS | | | | |
| 0800 | N800CV | N101CP* | | | |
| 0801 | N827QS | | | | |
| 0802 | N52136 | N866TC | | | |
| 0803 | N5247U | N865M | N803CJ | (N69LD) | N49LD |
| 0804 | N804CV | | | | |
| 0805 | N5188A | | | | |
| 0806 | N5196U | D-CAPB | | | |
| 0807 | N5064M | | | | |
| 0808 | N360HS | | | | |
| 0809 | N5097H | N610BK | | | |
| 0810 | N5204D | N810CV | N337CC | | |
| 0811 | N50736 | | | | |
| 0812 | N5268A | N812CV | | | |
| 0813 | N51942 | N100U | N813CJ | | |
| 0814 | N5200Z | D-CIFM | | | |
| 0815 | N488JD | N815CJ | N2426 | | |
| 0816 | | | | | |
| 0817 | | | | | |
| 0818 | | | | | |
| 0819 | | | | | |
| 0820 | D-CNSC* | | | | |
| 0821 | | | | | |
| 0822 | | | | | |
| 0823 | N823CE | | | | |
| 0824 | | | | | |
| 0825 | | | | | |
| 0826 | | | | | |
| 0827 | | | | | |
| 0828 | | | | | |
| 0829 | | | | | |
| 0830 | | | | | |
| 0831 | | | | | |
| 0832 | | | | | |
| 0833 | | | | | |
| 0834 | | | | | |
| 0835 | | | | | |
| 0836 | | | | | |
| 0837 | | | | | |
| 0838 | | | | | |
| 0839 | | | | | |
| 0840 | | | | | |
| 0841 | | | | | |
| 0842 | | | | | |
| 0843 | | | | | |
| 0844 | | | | | |
| 0845 | | | | | |
| 0846 | | | | | |
| 0847 | | | | | |
| 0848 | | | | | |
| 0849 | | | | | |
| 0850 | | | | | |
| 0851 | | | | | |
| 0852 | | | | | |

+ after a registration indicates test marks not fully confirmed

# CESSNA 560XL CITATION EXCEL/XLS/XLS+

| C/n | Identities | | | | | | | | |
|---|---|---|---|---|---|---|---|---|---|
| 706 | N560XL | [ff 29Feb96] | | | | | | | |
| 5001 | N561XL | | | | | | | | |
| 5002 | N5060K | N562XL | N12L | D-CAWM* | | | | | |
| 5003 | N5165T | N563XL | (PT-WZO) | PT-FPP | | | | | |
| 5004 | N5148N | OE-GAP | N504VP | N504BM | Pakistan J-754 | | | | |
| 5005 | N51575 | N208PC | SE-RBB | N166MB | N77UW | | | | |
| 5006 | N5141F | N8005 | | | | | | | |
| 5007 | N5200R | N83RR | N97VN | OE-GTK | | | | | |
| 5008 | N5204D | N207PC | SE-RBC | N944AH | | | | | |
| 5009 | N52113 | N398RS | | | | | | | |
| 5010 | N52178 | N27XL | VT-CLA | | | | | | |
| 5011 | N52141 | N560L | | | | | | | |
| 5012 | N52144 | N561DA | I-JETS | N560CE | | | | | |
| 5013 | N5216A | N1243C | N1PB | | | | | | |
| 5014 | N5221Y | N60GL | (N58KJ) | N56K | N1SN | N10SN | (N16SN) | N989TW | N531MB |
| 5015 | N5223D | N523KW | | | | | | | |
| 5016 | N615RG | | | | | | | | |
| 5017 | N517XL | N157AE | N600BJ | N500PX | (N300PX) | N865CE | N580AW | | |
| 5018 | N5250E | ZS-FCB | N223AM | N410MT | | | | | |
| 5019 | N980DK | N990DK | | | | | | | |
| 5020 | N5246Z | PT-XCL | (N61850) | | | | | | |
| 5021 | N5244F | D-CMIC | N560GM | N862CE | N862CF | N909LA | | | |
| 5022 | N522XL | HZ-FYZ | D-CSFD | | | | | | |
| 5023 | N51933 | N822MJ | N236LD | N236LB | | | | | |
| 5024 | N654EL | N622PC | | | | | | | |
| 5025 | N534CC | N584CC | LV-BMH | | | | | | |
| 5026 | N5201M | N17UC | (N17UG) | C-GJRB | | | | | |
| 5027 | N5202D | N560GB | N560GP | N560ML* | | | | | |
| 5028 | N5203J | N528XL | CS-DDB | OO-MLG | | | | | |
| 5029 | N5203S | (PT-...) | SE-DYX | | | | | | |
| 5030 | N52038 | N1228N | N899BC | N17AN | | | | | |
| 5031 | N531BJ | N560BT | | | | | | | |
| 5032 | N165JB | N108EK | | | | | | | |
| 5033 | N5211Q | N456JW | XA-UVA | | | | | | |
| 5034 | N52113 | PP-RAA | | | | | | | |
| 5035 | N5213S | N35XL | N4JS | | | | | | |
| 5036 | N52136 | N884BB | N36XL | N884BB | N910CS | N317ML | | | |
| 5037 | N5214J | D-CIII | OE-GTI | (D-CGTI) | D-CADY | | | | |
| 5038 | N5214K | N404BT | N590AK | | | | | | |
| 5039 | N39JV | N88WU | N87WU | | | | | | |
| 5040 | N5214L | N54HA | N840CC | | | | | | |
| 5041 | N52141 | N1XL | N39RC | | | | | | |
| 5042 | N52178 | N42XL | SU-EWC | N418CK | N413CK | N418CK | | | |
| 5043 | N5218R | PT-XIB | | | | | | | |
| 5044 | N5218T | N544XL | | | | | | | |
| 5045 | N5221Y | PP-JFM | | | | | | | |
| 5046 | N5223D | N966MT | A9C-BXA | N83GG | | | | | |
| 5047 | N5223P | C-FCEL | N838RT | N888RT | N838RT | | | | |
| 5048 | N868JB | N548XL | VP-CAI | | | | | | |
| 5049 | N5223Y | N24PH | N24PY | N680VR | N560VR | | | | |
| 5050 | N5225K | N184G | N88HP | | | | | | |
| 5051 | N5226B | N1324B | SX-DCM | TC-TMO | | | | | |
| 5052 | N5228Z | N990MF | | | | | | | |
| 5053 | N5231S | I-BENT | | | | | | | |
| 5054 | N5233J | N1306V | N80X | | | | | | |
| 5055 | N488CP | (N560KN) | | | | | | | |
| 5056 | N51993 | D-CVHB | EC-IRU | N688AG | SE-RBX | OH-RBX | | | |
| 5057 | N52457 | N350RD | N240B | N53WF | | | | | |
| 5058 | N5235G | N555WF | N555WE | HB-VNC | S5-BBD | | | | |
| 5059 | N55HA | N55HX | N580BC | | | | | | |
| 5060 | N5201J | PT-WYU | | | | | | | |
| 5061 | N5200R | HB-VMO | | | | | | | |
| 5062 | N5197A | N22KW | N23LM | | | | | | |
| 5063 | N5200U | N56HA | N56HX | | | | | | |
| 5064 | N5194J | N2JW | N555WF | N586SF | N386SF | N227MC | | | |
| 5065 | N5204D | N100SC | N112CW | | | | | | |
| 5066 | N134SW | HB-VMU | | | | | | | |
| 5067 | N42PA | HB-VMZ | OE-GPZ | N864CC | N309BT | | | | |
| 5068 | N52081 | N57HA | N57HX | N56LP | | | | | |
| 5069 | N5201M | N404SB | N189WW | | | | | | |
| 5070 | N5207A | VP-CNM | N507VP | N789CN | HB-VOU | | | | |
| 5071 | N51881 | N671QS | | | | | | | |
| 5072 | N52178 | N565AB | N565BA | | | | | | |
| 5073 | N5214K | D-CDBW | N79EA | N121TL | N121TE | N560DR | | | |

## CITATION EXCEL

| C/n | Identities | | | | | |
|---|---|---|---|---|---|---|
| 5074 | N636GS | N466LM | 4X-CPU | N574AV | N66LM | |
| 5075 | N558R | | | | | |
| 5076 | N521RA | | | | | |
| 5077 | N51575 | N221LC | N46VE | N76VE | | |
| 5078 | N5203J | C-FPWC | N560HJ | | | |
| 5079 | N5218T | ZS-OHZ | | | | |
| 5080 | N52141 | N90CF | | | | |
| 5081 | N4000K | | | | | |
| 5082 | N145SM | N469RS | | | | |
| 5083 | N52144 | N520G | N520Q | | | |
| 5084 | N5211A | N684QS | N384WC | | | |
| 5085 | N52113 | N85XL | N883PF | | | |
| 5086 | N51817 | N62GB | N269JR | N394WJ | N957BJ | |
| 5087 | N5165T | PT-MSK | | | | |
| 5088 | N52081 | VP-BSD | G-WCIN | EC-KOL | | |
| 5089 | N51942 | N868JB | N868J | N21MA | N560GC | |
| 5090 | N51246 | N690QS | N590VP | | | |
| 5091 | N5183V | N560CH | N83SD | N170SD | | |
| 5092 | N5125J | N692QS | | | | |
| 5093 | N5203S | N19MK | N19MZ | N903DK | N210VS* | |
| 5094 | N1094L | | | | | |
| 5095 | N5135A | N95XL | | | | |
| 5096 | N5202D | C-GCXL | | | | |
| 5097 | N5226B | C-GLMI | | | | |
| 5098 | N5244F | N200PF | N502BC | | | |
| 5099 | N58XL | N58HA | N58HX | | | |
| 5100 | N51444 | N510XL | N49MJ | N49MU | N100CJ | |
| 5101 | N5216A | N88845 | N81SH | | | |
| 5102 | N5153K | N997CB | | | | |
| 5103 | N5218R | N68HC | N68HG | | | |
| 5104 | N5223D | (F-HACD) | LX-JCD | (F-GXXX) | | |
| 5105 | N5185V | PR-RAA | PP-JGV | | | |
| 5106 | N5221Y | N506AM | HB-VND | G-ELOA | | |
| 5107 | N51342 | N560DA | I-NYNY | N300SJ | | |
| 5108 | N562DB | N562DD | | | | |
| 5109 | N324LX | (N324LE) | N561GR | N58LC | N458LC | N58LQ |
| 5110 | N5200Z | PH-RSA | | | | |
| 5111 | N5141F | N532CC | (N530CC) | N522CC | N380M | |
| 5112 | N52457 | N1129E | | | | |
| 5113 | N52178 | OE-GME | | | | |
| 5114 | N5223P | N20SB | N717MB | N38HG* | | |
| 5115 | N5157E | N20WE | VT-ARA | | | |
| 5116 | N5246Z | N498AB | | | | |
| 5117 | N5233J | N202RL | | | | |
| 5118 | N5214L | N1241K | B-7019 | | | |
| 5119 | N5197A | N357WC | N75HU | | | |
| 5120 | N5211Q | PR-AAA | | | | |
| 5121 | N5223Y | N560CG | | | | |
| 5122 | N5211F | N67TW | | | | |
| 5123 | N5201J | N699BC | N59EC | | | |
| 5124 | N5207A | N24NG | | | | |
| 5125 | N5214K | N4JB | | | | |
| 5126 | N626QS | | | | | |
| 5127 | N560KT | | | | | |
| 5128 | N5228Z | PH-CJI | | | | |
| 5129 | N5214J | N359WC | N94LA | | | |
| 5130 | N52113 | N630QS | | | | |
| 5131 | N52136 | N631QS | N131VP | | | |
| 5132 | N5225K | N632QS | N513VP | LV-... | | |
| 5133 | N23NG | | | | | |
| 5134 | (N5250E) | N52352 | N561BP | LV-BRX | | |
| 5135 | N5200U | N135ET | LV-ZXW | N885BB | | |
| 5136 | N52639 | N4005G | VP-CWM | N560JP | N522RA | N100YB |
| 5137 | N637QS | N300WC | LV- | | | |
| 5138 | N5265N | N704JW | N924JE | | | |
| 5139 | N639QS | N239WC | N560HX | | | |
| 5140 | N52655 | N884B | | | | |
| 5141 | N52235 | N17AN | N701CR | N901CR | | |
| 5142 | N5093D | N705SG | | | | |
| 5143 | N5096S | N1836S | N966JM | | | |
| 5144 | N5108G | C-GOEL | N713DF | N713DH | N52MW | N560TS | N552SC |
| 5145 | N52645 | N645QS | | | | |
| 5146 | N291DV | | | | | |
| 5147 | N52059 | N24UD | | | | |
| 5148 | N52234 | N777FH | N200SC | | | |
| 5149 | N627XL | | | | | |

# CITATION EXCEL

| C/n | Identities | | | | |
|---|---|---|---|---|---|
| 5150 | N5100J | N650QS | N150WC | LV- | |
| 5151 | N5147B | N79PF | C-GHCB | | |
| 5152 | N5101J | N652QS | N650RJ* | | |
| 5153 | N5105F | N916CS | N816CS | | |
| 5154 | N51160 | N154XL | HB-VNI | | |
| 5155 | N5095N | N1837S | | | |
| 5156 | N5155G | N2ZC | | | |
| 5157 | N5163G | N40577 | OH-ONE | OE-GCA | |
| 5158 | N5151D | N917EE | N615EC | | |
| 5159 | N5163K | C-GMNC | N336MA | N326MA | |
| 5160 | N51869 | N595A | N903FH | N901FH | |
| 5161 | N404MM | N405MM | G-VECT | | |
| 5162 | N51511 | N168BG | | | |
| 5163 | N5166T | N63LX | N68LX | N591MA | |
| 5164 | N5166U | N64LX | N84LX | | |
| 5165 | N5109W | N665QS | | | |
| 5166 | N52059 | N5068R | N580RC | | |
| 5167 | N5188N | N250SM | G-REDS | | |
| 5168 | N565DR | N780CS | VT-SWC | | |
| 5169 | N923PC | OE-GPN | | | |
| 5170 | N670QS | | | | |
| 5171 | N5236L | SU-EWB | N632BL | | |
| 5172 | N5086W | HB-VNH | N105RJ | I-BEDT | |
| 5173 | N51743 | N5173F | N560JF | | |
| 5174 | N5223X | N624AT | | | |
| 5175 | N52114 | N625AT | | | |
| 5176 | N676QS | | | | |
| 5177 | N5061P | N841DW | | | |
| 5178 | N562TS | | | | |
| 5179 | N51984 | N512DR | N86TW | N188WS | (N186WS) |
| 5180 | N52235 | N868JB | N868J | | |
| 5181 | N681QS | | | | |
| 5182 | N5058J | N98RX | N563CH | | |
| 5183 | N5090V | G-CFRA | G-IAMS | OK-CAA | |
| 5184 | N5061W | N184XL | N531RC | N531RQ | |
| 5185 | N51042 | G-SIRS | | | |
| 5186 | N186XL | | | | |
| 5187 | N687QS | | | | |
| 5188 | N688QS | | | | |
| 5189 | N5073G | OY-GKC | OO-SAV | | |
| 5190 | N51038 | N560S | G-XLSB | N104LV | |
| 5191 | N5090A | N767BS | | | |
| 5192 | N50820 | N119LP | N192XL | N164AS | |
| 5193 | N811ST | | | | |
| 5194 | N694QS | | | | |
| 5195 | N51143 | D-CVHI | D-CINI | D-CJOY* | |
| 5196 | N51038 | XA-ICO | | | |
| 5197 | N697QS | | | | |
| 5198 | N552MA | N560NY | | | |
| 5199 | N699QS | | | | |
| 5200 | N5109R | C-GXCO | N950BA | | |
| 5201 | N5096S | N533CC | N523CC | N828CK | |
| 5202 | N5095N | N50XL | N82KW | | |
| 5203 | N603QS | | | | |
| 5204 | N604QS | | | | |
| 5205 | N5100J | N503CS | N525VP | N503CS | |
| 5206 | N5101J | N821DG | N921DG | N206CX | N561CE |
| 5207 | N5076J | N62GB | N62GR | N592CF | |
| 5208 | N5109W | XA-TKZ | | | |
| 5209 | N5093Y | N501XL | (PH-DYX) | HB-VNS | |
| 5210 | N610QS | | | | |
| 5211 | N5076K | PR-VRD | | | |
| 5212 | N5090Y | N560DP | | | |
| 5213 | N5108G | N1130G | (D-CASH) | N24EP | |
| 5214 | N57KW | | | | |
| 5215 | N50612 | N560TH | N5091J | VP-CPC | N560TH |
| 5216 | N5103J | CS-DNY | | | |
| 5217 | N5079V | (OY-LEG) | OY-EKC | SE-RCL | HB-VWJ |
| 5218 | N218AM | P4-ALM | VP-CFM | | |
| 5219 | N5079H | N877RF | | | |
| 5220 | N5112K | N318MM | | | |
| 5221 | N5094D | CS-DNW | | | |
| 5222 | N2HB | N560JP | N426CH | | |
| 5223 | N5068R | PR-EMS | | | |
| 5224 | N5093L | N146EP | N595G | | |
| 5225 | N5117U | N351WC | N351CG | | |

# CITATION EXCEL

| C/n | Identities | | | | |
|---|---|---|---|---|---|
| 5226 | N5196U | N350WC | N562WD | N411KQ | |
| 5227 | N5197M | N627QS | | | |
| 5228 | N5000R | EI-PAX | G-IPAX | | |
| 5229 | N5105F | N504CS | N529VP | | |
| 5230 | N5085E | G-NETA | OO-PGG | | |
| 5231 | N231XL | N417JD | N511DN | N153SG | |
| 5232 | N451W | N34WP | | | |
| 5233 | N233XL | | | | |
| 5234 | N5076J | C-FCXL | | | |
| 5235 | N5086W | CS-DNZ | | | |
| 5236 | N51072 | N236LD | S5-BAZ | | |
| 5237 | N5061W | N751PL | | | |
| 5238 | N5061P | N238SM | | | |
| 5239 | N239XL | N626AT | | | |
| 5240 | N51055 | N640QS | | | |
| 5241 | N5090V | N100AR | | | |
| 5242 | N51042 | TC-LMA | G-LDFM | | |
| 5243 | N5093D | N567CH | N243CH | (D-CSLX) | OK-SLX |
| 5244 | N51743 | N5090A | N244XL | N898MC | |
| 5245 | N50820 | N245J | | | |
| 5246 | N646QS | | | | |
| 5247 | N51038 | N7RL | N57RL | G-CIEL | |
| 5248 | N5109R | HB-VNR | OO-FPA | | |
| 5249 | N5096S | N80LP | | | |
| 5250 | N5095N | N25NG | N56FE | | |
| 5251 | N651QS | | | | |
| 5252 | N5145V | N505CS | N552VP^ | | |
| 5253 | N5154J | N72SG | (N62SG) | N73SG | C-FTIL |
| 5254 | N631RP | N681RP | N626TN | | |
| 5255 | N52081 | N60AG | N15TF | | |
| 5256 | N5194B | N4107V | PR-GAM | | |
| 5257 | N5196U | CS-DFM | | | |
| 5258 | N52334 | C-GWII | PH-DRK | | |
| 5259 | N52526 | G-XLMB | G-XLGB | | |
| 5260 | N527SC | N711HA | N711VH | | |
| 5261 | N5091J | N75TP | N57TP | | |
| 5262 | N662QS | | | | |
| 5263 | N663QS | | | | |
| 5264 | N5066U | N664QS | | | |
| 5265 | N5100J | OE-GPA | N5535 | | |
| 5266 | N5245D | G-CBRG | | | |
| 5267 | N5246Z | N506CS | | | |
| 5268 | N668QS | | | | |
| 5269 | N51160 | HB-VAA | Switzerland T-784 | | |
| 5270 | N5058J | N356WC | N300DA | | |
| 5271 | N5103J | LN-SUX | G-CGMF | | |
| 5272 | N5079V | N1326A | | | |
| 5273 | N5073G | N1268D | N617PD | | |
| 5274 | N5060K | PR-ACC | | | |
| 5275 | N675QS | | | | |
| 5276 | N276A | | | | |
| 5277 | N5076K | N560CM | | | |
| 5278 | N16GS | N176GS | N95CC | | |
| 5279 | N679QS | | | | |
| 5280 | N621QS | | | | |
| 5281 | N68AA | N142AA | | | |
| 5282 | N5094D | N507CS | N528VP | | |
| 5283 | N5097H | CS-DFN | | | |
| 5284 | N5109W | N560DE | (OO-VIZ) | N560JP | C-GUPC |
| 5285 | N5112K | N285XL | N422AB | N58FE | |
| 5286 | N51143 | N622QS | | | |
| 5287 | N118ST | | | | |
| 5288 | N5117U | SX-DCE | | | |
| 5289 | N5105F | PR-NBR | | | |
| 5290 | N691QS | | | | |
| 5291 | N5086W | N829JC | N829JQ | N397BC | |
| 5292 | N5101J | N666MX | | | |
| 5293 | N695QS | | | | |
| 5294 | N5068R | N508CS | | | |
| 5295 | N50820 | N641QS | | | |
| 5296 | N696QS | | | | |
| 5297 | N51612 | N821DG | (N721DG) | N1871R | |
| 5298 | N5061P | C-GSEC | C-FBXL | | |
| 5299 | N623QS | | | | |
| 5300 | N5085E | N613GY | N613KS | N618KS* | |
| 5301 | N601QS | | | | |

## CITATION EXCEL

| C/n | Identities | | | | |
|---|---|---|---|---|---|
| 5302 | (N118ST) | N624QS | | | |
| 5303 | N1867M | | | | |
| 5304 | N636QS | N636EJ | | | |
| 5305 | N628QS | | | | |
| 5306 | N629QS | | | | |
| 5307 | N51072 | XA-DRM | | | |
| 5308 | N608QS | | | | |
| 5309 | N5093D | N309XL | C-GMKZ | | |
| 5310 | N509CS | | | | |
| 5311 | N5090A | N712KC | N560JP | N560PD | |
| 5312 | N612QS | | | | |
| 5313 | N562XL | [first Citation XLS; re-serialled 560-5501 q.v.] | | | |
| 5314 | N5000R | CS-DFO | | | |
| 5315 | N5095N | CS-DFP | | | |
| 5316 | N5096S | D-CWWW | OE-GCG | | |
| 5317 | N5269J | N57WP | | | |
| 5318 | N51743 | N102FS | OO-FTS | | |
| 5319 | N625QS | | | | |
| 5320 | N5194J | N66W | N151KV | | |
| 5321 | N605QS | | | | |
| 5322 | N5196U | N1838S | N183JS | | |
| 5323 | N606QS | N606Q | N560RS | N561RW | |
| 5324 | N511CS | | | | |
| 5325 | N52397 | N568DM | | | |
| 5326 | N512CS | | | | |
| 5327 | N175WS | | | | |
| 5328 | N514CS | | | | |
| 5329 | N848DM | | | | |
| 5330 | N638QS | (N638Q) | N395WJ | | |
| 5331 | N643QS | N6430S | N946TC | N510HF | |
| 5332 | N727YB | N710MT | | | |
| 5333 | N533XL | N2 | | | |
| 5334 | N5093L | CS-DFQ | | | |
| 5335 | N515CS | | | | |
| 5336 | N5165P | N336XL | (N404PK) | (N336BC) | |
| 5337 | N51942 | N198DF | N560JP | N79BC | YR-RPR |
| 5338 | N5094D | N606QS | | | |
| 5339 | N51143 | OE-GNW | | | |
| 5340 | N50820 | N607QS | | | |
| 5341 | N5061W | N3 | | | |
| 5342 | N5223P | N7337F | N777JV | N228Y | |
| 5343 | N5145V | G-WINA | | | |
| 5344 | N51055 | I-CMAL | | | |
| 5345 | N616QS | | | | |
| 5346 | N517CS | N346XL | | | |
| 5347 | N47HF | | | | |
| 5348 | N470SK | | | | |
| 5349 | N676BB | | | | |
| 5350 | N5270M | N325FN | LV-AIW | | |
| 5351 | N5101J | N53XL | N1HS | N71HS | N560AW |
| 5352 | N5245D | ZS-IDC | ZS-FOS | | |
| 5353 | N678QS | N5250E | EC-ISQ | | |
| 5354 | N518CS | (N71RL) | N178BR | | |
| 5355 | N659QS | N5200Z | CS-DFR | | |
| 5356 | N5101J | N519CS | XA-UAF | | |
| 5357 | N5161J | N567MC | | | |
| 5358 | N5235G | N635QS | | | |
| 5359 | N659QS | | | | |
| 5360 | N5079V | N615QS | | | |
| 5361 | N52397 | N361XL | VP-CGG | G-CFGL | N112AB |
| 5362 | N521CS | | | | |
| 5363 | N638QS | | | | |
| 5364 | N522CS | | | | |
| 5365 | N667QS | | | | |
| 5366 | N5216A | N585PC | N555WF | N555WZ | (N560WF) |
| 5367 | N677QS | | | | |
| 5368 | N5094D | N12686 | VT-CSP | | |
| 5369 | N5197A | N678QS | N504PK | N504LV | |
| 5370 | N5270P | N770JM | | | |
| 5371 | N371P | PR-OUR | | | |
| 5372 | N5091J | CS-DFS | | | |

# CITATION XLS

| C/n | Identities | | | | | |
|---|---|---|---|---|---|---|
| 5501 | N562XL | [conv from c/n 560-5313] | N633RP | N683RP | N883RP | |
| 5502 | N52144 | N502XL | N502EG | | | |
| 5503 | N503XS | N732JR | | | | |
| 5504 | N5223Y | N111GU | | | | |
| 5505 | N901DK | | | | | |
| 5506 | N618QS | | | | | |
| 5507 | N523CS | | | | | |
| 5508 | N72SG | | | | | |
| 5509 | N617QS | | | | | |
| 5510 | N52352 | N41118 | N357EC | | | |
| 5511 | N52609 | N670MW | | | | |
| 5512 | N52433 | CS-DFT | | | | |
| 5513 | N196SB | | | | | |
| 5514 | N5086W | N143DH | | | | |
| 5515 | N5157E | N4118K | N361EC | | | |
| 5516 | N540CS | | | | | |
| 5517 | N52639 | PR-RAV | N778BC | N475JC | | |
| 5518 | N52699 | N602QS | | | | |
| 5519 | N52655 | N43HF | | | | |
| 5520 | N5269A | CS-DFU | | | | |
| 5521 | N541CS | | | | | |
| 5522 | N51872 | N609QS | | | | |
| 5523 | N542CS | | | | | |
| 5524 | N5267G | N546CS | | | | |
| 5525 | N5264A | N370BA | | | | |
| 5526 | N5194B | N633QS | | | | |
| 5527 | N5254Y | N713DH | (N712DH) | N321CL | | |
| 5528 | N5296X | N579BJ | N456SL | HB-VON | | |
| 5529 | N5262X | OE-GEG | | | | |
| 5530 | N5270J | N4107W | N491N | | | |
| 5531 | N52229 | N560JG | | | | |
| 5532 | N5270E | N562DB | N562LD | | | |
| 5533 | N711NK | N711NR | | | | |
| 5534 | N5165P | N424HH | | | | |
| 5535 | N5141F | PT-ORM | | | | |
| 5536 | N25XL | D-CHSP | | | | |
| 5537 | N5152X | I-TAKA | | | | |
| 5538 | N5163C | N538XL | OE-GCM | D-CMMI | | |
| 5539 | N52178 | N4007J | B-3642 | | | |
| 5540 | N5090Y | N4008S | B-3643 | | | |
| 5541 | N5201J | N560JC | LV-BCS | N63FT | | |
| 5542 | N5267K | N547CS | | | | |
| 5543 | N5165T | CS-DFV | | | | |
| 5544 | N5268M | PP-BRS | N754V | PP-SBR | | |
| 5545 | N5269J | N45XL | N560TV | | | |
| 5546 | N51881 | N549CS | | | | |
| 5547 | N5156D | N647QS | | | | |
| 5548 | N5168Y | N611QS | | | | |
| 5549 | N51780 | CS-DXA | N39GA | N727MH | | |
| 5550 | N200JR | | | | | |
| 5551 | N550CS | | | | | |
| 5552 | N5231S | PP-MDB | | | | |
| 5553 | N5103J | N12778 | CS-DXB | | | |
| 5554 | N5166U | JY-AW1 | EC-JZK | | | |
| 5555 | N51869 | (D-CLDI) | D-CAAA | | | |
| 5556 | N385MG | C-GSLC | | | | |
| 5557 | N5197M | N551CS | N5NR | | | |
| 5558 | N52609 | N634QS | | | | |
| 5559 | N5093L | N1281N | CS-DXC | | | |
| 5560 | N51984 | N553CS | N264SC | N560CR | | |
| 5561 | N5296X | N642QS | | | | |
| 5562 | N5109R | N619QS | | | | |
| 5563 | N5226B | N45NF | | | | |
| 5564 | N560TM | EC-JVF | | | | |
| 5565 | N5196U | N370M | | | | |
| 5566 | N52113 | N70XL | | | | |
| 5567 | N5213S | (D-CKLI) | D-CBBB | | | |
| 5568 | N5197A | N6779D | CS-DXD | | | |
| 5569 | D-CTLX | | | | | |
| 5570 | N10VQ | N155RW | | | | |
| 5571 | N5211F | N24PH | | | | |
| 5572 | N5194B | N554CS | | | | |
| 5573 | N51881 | (OE-GAL) | D-CTTT | | | |
| 5574 | N5090A | N648QS | | | | |
| 5575 | N5267J | N75XL | | | | |
| 5576 | N5245U | HB-VNY | CS-DPZ | | | |

# CITATION XLS

| C/n | Identities | | | | |
|---|---|---|---|---|---|
| 5577 | N5267K | N556CS | | | |
| 5578 | N5261R | N1299H | CS-DXE | | |
| 5579 | N5253S | N2HB | PP-RST | | |
| 5580 | N614QS | | | | |
| 5581 | N5153K | N577PS | | | |
| 5582 | N644QS | | | | |
| 5583 | N5076J | PR-CON | | | |
| 5584 | N51342 | G-CDOL | I-CDOL | | |
| 5585 | N51396 | (D-CTLX) | N558CS | N560BA | |
| 5586 | N5145V | N1299K | CS-DXF | | |
| 5587 | N5135A | N806MN | N808MN | | |
| 5588 | N643QS | | | | |
| 5589 | N5262W | N842DW | N500PX | | |
| 5590 | N5197M | N590XL | N103PG | | |
| 5591 | N771DE | | | | |
| 5592 | N52639 | N586SF | | | |
| 5593 | N5152X | N559CS | N593XL | EC-JXI | D-CCEA |
| 5594 | N5180C | N4017R | (VT-XLS) | VT-JSS | |
| 5595 | N5135K | CS-DXG | | | |
| 5596 | N5181U | N82GM | N1HS | | |
| 5597 | N5228J | N562CS | N780CC | | |
| 5598 | N5264A | N12990 | PK-ILA | | |
| 5599 | N613QS | | | | |
| 5600 | N51780 | N560PL | | | |
| 5601 | N5268M | N563CS | N563XL | N867W | |
| 5602 | N52235 | N499HS | | | |
| 5603 | N5244W | N868XL | | | |
| 5604 | N562DB | N562DL | | | |
| 5605 | N5101J | OB-1824 | | | |
| 5606 | N566F | | | | |
| 5607 | N52038 | N7HB | (N560HB) | N301HB | |
| 5608 | N5103J | LN-XLS | SX-ADK | | |
| 5609 | N5162W | N442LW | N442LU | N90BL | |
| 5610 | N52613 | LX-GDX | G-OMEA | | |
| 5611 | N654QS | | | | |
| 5612 | N5141F | N564CS | N926DR | N441BP | |
| 5613 | N5265B | N613XL | G-PKRG | G-CXLS | |
| 5614 | N5206T | N45PK | | | |
| 5615 | N5266F | CS-DXH | | | |
| 5616 | N5267T | N678QS | | | |
| 5617 | N5201J | N563XP | [XLS+ prototype] | | |
| 5618 | N52136 | N618XL | C-GRPB | | |
| 5619 | N5246Z | PR-LFT | | | |
| 5620 | N5264E | D-CAIR | | | |
| 5621 | N52682 | N1300J | CS-DXI | | |
| 5622 | N52691 | N561MK | | | |
| 5623 | N5244F | D-CDDD | | | |
| 5624 | N5267K | N1312K | SE-RCM | | |
| 5625 | N5245D | N916CS | | | |
| 5626 | N5197M | N68GW | | | |
| 5627 | N51396 | CS-DXJ | | | |
| 5628 | N51038 | N890LE | | | |
| 5629 | N5261R | N560VH | N1897A | | |
| 5630 | N51612 | D-CEEE | | | |
| 5631 | N51042 | SX-SMR | | | |
| 5632 | N5262W | N632XL | | | |
| 5633 | N5185J | N13218 | CS-DXK | | |
| 5634 | N51612 | D-CFFF | | | |
| 5635 | N51806 | N1312T | N573AB | | |
| 5636 | N657QS | | | | |
| 5637 | N5225K | N568CS | | | |
| 5638 | N4086L | N64LX | | | |
| 5639 | N5152X | XA-MMX | | | |
| 5640 | "N5188W"+ | [+Marks current on a homebuilt] | | N1319X | CS-DXL |
| 5641 | N51342 | PH-JNX | | | |
| 5642 | N5181U | N642XL | D-CRUW | HB-VOM | OE-GKE |
| 5643 | N683QS | | | | |
| 5644 | N52626 | PR-TRJ | | | |
| 5645 | N5223X | N88SF | | | |
| 5646 | N5223P | N921MW | | | |
| 5647 | N660QS | | | | |
| 5648 | N5109W | N1320P | N711HA | | |
| 5649 | N5155G | SP-KCS | | | |
| 5650 | N685QS | | | | |
| 5651 | N5228J | N673QS | | | |
| 5652 | N5183V | N226JT | | | |

# CITATION XLS

| C/n | Identities | | | | |
|---|---|---|---|---|---|
| 5653 | N5257C | N698QS | | | |
| 5654 | N5264S | N682QS | | | |
| 5655 | N5161J | N655QS | | | |
| 5656 | N52369 | N35SE | | | |
| 5657 | N693QS | | | | |
| 5658 | N5135A | A9C-BXI | HZ-BSA | | |
| 5659 | N689QS | | | | |
| 5660 | N5247U | N602MA | S5-BAV | | |
| 5661 | N686QS | | | | |
| 5662 | N5211Q | SX-DCD | | | |
| 5663 | N5268E | N672QS | | | |
| 5664 | N5241R | N600QS | | | |
| 5665 | N52601 | N658QS | | | |
| 5666 | N51780 | LN-EXL | EI-XLS | | |
| 5667 | N5192E | XA-UGQ | N128AW | D-CKHG | |
| 5668 | N5183U | (I-LAST) | (I-AGLS) | OE-GZK | |
| 5669 | N5202D | N633RP | N637RP | N357TW | |
| 5670 | N52655 | N670XL | (D-CCWD) | D-CAJK | |
| 5671 | N5269Z | N55NG | | | |
| 5672 | (N656QS) | N5207V | C-FTXL | | |
| 5673 | N5269J | VH-XCJ | VH-XCU | | |
| 5674 | N51160 | D-CHHH | | | |
| 5675 | N5266F | G-OXLS | | | |
| 5676 | N5265N | A9C-BXJ | N560RB | N612AC | |
| 5677 | N5180K | N661QS | | | |
| 5678 | N52613 | N702AC | N513SK | | |
| 5679 | N5263S | N1230F | A6-GJB | | |
| 5680 | N52690 | N571CS | | | |
| 5681 | N5221Y | C-GPAW | | | |
| 5682 | N50549 | F-GVYC | | | |
| 5683 | N5256Z | N1130X | CS-DXM | | |
| 5684 | N5061P | N669TT | | | |
| 5685 | N5259Y | N11963 | CS-DXN | | |
| 5686 | N5061W | N86XL | C-FNXL | | |
| 5687 | N5068F | N533CC | | | |
| 5688 | N50639 | D-CVHB | | | |
| 5689 | N50275 | N669QS | | | |
| 5690 | N5130J | (VP-BWC) | N560FC | M-BWFC | |
| 5691 | N5264E | C-FWXL | | | |
| 5692 | N5026Q | N1198V | CS-DXO | | |
| 5693 | N5069E | TC-LNS | | | |
| 5694 | N5072X | N717NB | | | |
| 5695 | N5166T | OE-GSR | | | |
| 5696 | N5105F | LV-BIB | | | |
| 5697 | N5136J | N594QS | | | |
| 5698 | N5091J | G-XBEL | | | |
| 5699 | N5148N | G-RSXL | | | |
| 5700 | N52235 | ES-SKY | N813DH | N713DH | |
| 5701 | N5264U | N414AA | A6-GJC | | |
| 5702 | N1275T | CS-DXP | | | |
| 5703 | N5250E | N560MF | 5N-BJS | | |
| 5704 | N1281R | CS-DXQ | | | |
| 5705 | N50736 | N574CS | | | |
| 5706 | N592QS | | | | |
| 5707 | N5253S | N534CC | | | |
| 5708 | N576QS | | | | |
| 5709 | N5227G | XA-UHQ | | | |
| 5710 | N5254Y | N1312T | 5A-DRK | | |
| 5711 | N51744 | N51744 | N1315D | (VT-...) | N560TD |
| 5712 | N595QS | G-LEAX | | | |
| 5713 | N51881 | N614EP | | | |
| 5714 | N599QS | | | | |
| 5715 | N32KM | | | | |
| 5716 | N38KW | | | | |
| 5717 | N52369 | C-GAWR | | | |
| 5718 | N399SF | | | | |
| 5719 | N5236L | N12UD | D-CMMP | | |
| 5720 | N52397 | N121KL | | | |
| 5721 | N588QS | | | | |
| 5722 | N5165T | D-CLLL | | | |
| 5723 | N5260M | D-CVVV | | | |
| 5724 | N5263U | G-OROO | | | |
| 5725 | N5260U | N725XL | | | |
| 5726 | N50054 | N577CS | | | |
| 5727 | N5192E | VH-NGH | LX-INS | | |
| 5728 | N5264A | N946PC | | | |

## CITATION XLS

| C/n | Identities | | | |
|---|---|---|---|---|
| 5729 | N5264N | C-GKEG | C-GTOG | |
| 5730 | N575QS | | | |
| 5731 | N51995 | I-CMAB | | |
| 5732 | N656QS | | | |
| 5733 | N51143 | OO-AIE | | |
| 5734 | N411EC | | | |
| 5735 | N577QS | | | |
| 5736 | N52229 | N777LX | | |
| 5737 | N404MM | | | |
| 5738 | N590QS | | | |
| 5739 | N52623 | "PR-FJU"+ | [+marks worn at factory] | PR-FJA |
| 5740 | N166RD | | | |
| 5741 | N580QS | | | |
| 5742 | N5221Y | N911EK | | |
| 5743 | N52613 | N806AD | | |
| 5744 | N5063P | N2003J | PR-MMV | |
| 5745 | N5067U | PH-ANO | | |
| 5746 | N50715 | N8000U | | |
| 5747 | N47XL | C-FSXL | | |
| 5748 | N5246Z | N585QS | CS-DXR | |
| 5749 | N5076L | N169SM | OE-GBR | |
| 5750 | N5095N | PR-ANP | | |
| 5751 | N8701L | | | |
| 5752 | N412AB | | | |
| 5753 | N52653 | EC-KPB | | |
| 5754 | N51042 | N578QS | CS-DXS | |
| 5755 | N51038 | OE-GEH | | |
| 5756 | N5265B | OE-GSP | | |
| 5757 | N51246 | OY-CKK | | |
| 5758 | N5241R | N758XL | | |
| 5759 | N575NR | | | |
| 5760 | N50756 | YU-SPA | | |
| 5761 | N5156D | N2060V | B-3666 | |
| 5762 | N51780 | D-CRON | | |
| 5763 | N51869 | OE-GSZ | | |
| 5764 | N51666 | EC-KPE | | |
| 5765 | N5233J | CS-DXT | | |
| 5766 | N5155G | N2065X | B-3667 | |
| 5767 | N5059X | CC-CDE | | |
| 5768 | N5064Q | N75TP | | |
| 5769 | N5066U | N1387E | TC-DAG | |
| 5770 | N5030U | "G-SOVM"+ | [+marks worn at factory] | G-OSVM |
| 5771 | N5068R | XA-UJP | | |
| 5772 | N5076J | OE-GVL | | |
| 5773 | N5109R | N579QS | | |
| 5774 | N5263S | N357MP | | |
| 5775 | N50522 | CS-DXU | | |
| 5776 | N51342 | XA-VGR | | |
| 5777 | N5069E | SE-RIL | | |
| 5778 | N52141 | PR-TEN | | |
| 5779 | N5085E | N579CL | TC-LAC | |
| 5780 | N5204D | C-GFCL | | |
| 5781 | N51984 | PH-MHM | OO-SLM | |
| 5782 | N5145P | CS-DXV | | |
| 5783 | N52113 | N783XL | VT-VDD | |
| 5784 | N5264M | D-CCVD | | |
| 5785 | N5260U | G-KPEI | | |
| 5786 | N5267D | D-CNNN | | |
| 5787 | N5145V | CS-DXW | | |
| 5788 | N5259Y | D-CWWW | D-CLIC | D-CFLO* |
| 5789 | N5211Q | CS-DXX | | |
| 5790 | N5223D | D-CZZZ | | |
| 5791 | N5268A | CS-DXY | | |
| 5792 | N5200Z | PH-DRS | | |
| 5793 | N5264A | G-FCAP | YR-DPH | |
| 5794 | N576CS | | | |
| 5795 | N52229 | N595CL | TC-LAD | |
| 5796 | N5268E | CS-DXZ | | |
| 5797 | N52061 | D-CAWU | | |
| 5798 | N5157E | CS-DQA | | |
| 5799 | N50321 | N771PM | | |
| 5800 | N578CS | N560ES | | |
| 5801 | N5267J | I-CMAD | | |
| 5802 | N731BP | | | |
| 5803 | N50715 | CS-DQB | | |
| 5804 | N52626 | N41233 | PK-BKS | |

## CITATION XLS/XLS+

| C/n | Identities | | | |
|---|---|---|---|---|
| 5805 | N587QS | | | |
| 5806 | N51612 | N67PK | N67PC* | |
| 5807 | N579CS | SE-RGS | | |
| 5808 | N5060K | N2067V | 5A-DRL | |
| 5809 | N5203J | N145PK | | |
| 5810 | N589QS | | | |
| 5811 | N5086W | (D-CSYB) | OE-GKM | |
| 5812 | N583QS | | | |
| 5813 | N52591 | XA-UKQ | | |
| 5814 | N5161J | (D-CMIC) | D-CNOC | |
| 5815 | N580CS | N728EC | | |
| 5816 | N5108G | N41237 | VT-BSL | |
| 5817 | N581CS | | | |
| 5818 | N565QS | | | |
| 5819 | N5267G | XA-DST | | |
| 5820 | N574QS | | | |
| 5821 | N51038 | N2116N | N673MG | |
| 5822 | N5228J | (G-XMAR) | (OE-GEM) | PP-ADD |
| 5823 | N5264N | PP-PRR | | |
| 5824 | N5090V | N2087K | TC-DLZ | |
| 5825 | N566QS | | | |
| 5826 | N5000R | OE-GWV | | |
| 5827 | N573QS | | | |
| 5828 | N52235 | N21076 | B-9330 | |
| 5829 | N568QS | | | |
| 5830 | N51995 | N2112X | 5N-BMM | |

## CITATION XLS+

| C/n | Identities | | | |
|---|---|---|---|---|
| 6001 | | | | |
| 6002 | N502XL | (D-CRUW) | D-CAWM | |
| 6003 | N563XL | | | |
| 6004 | N5253S | N343CC | | |
| 6005 | N52609 | N575JC | N562DB | |
| 6006 | N5200U | N508MV | | |
| 6007 | N892Z | | | |
| 6008 | N748RE | | | |
| 6009 | N560DG | | | |
| 6010 | N33LX | | | |
| 6011 | N68HC | | | |
| 6012 | N595S | | | |
| 6013 | N5061W | N2011Z | OE-GGG | |
| 6014 | N868JB | D-CFLY | | |
| 6015 | N5211A | N488JD | | |
| 6016 | N51666 | N906DK | | |
| 6017 | N52653 | N7877D | | |
| 6018 | N51780 | N881VP | | |
| 6019 | N5233J | N193SB | | |
| 6020 | N5103J | N310BN | | |
| 6021 | N5223X | (HB-VWE) | HB-VWD | |
| 6022 | N52691 | (HB-VWG) | HB-VWE | |
| 6023 | N5085E | N623CL | 7T-... | |
| 6024 | N50321 | | | |
| 6025 | N5153K | OO-EBE | | |
| 6026 | N52639 | LX-FGB | | |
| 6027 | N5076J | (D-CHAM) | D-CXLS | |
| 6028 | N5059X | N712DH | N7TM | |
| 6029 | N826AG | OE-GWH | | |
| 6030 | N5241R | N560GB | | |
| 6031 | N51342 | N853JA | N95NB | |
| 6032 | N5250P | N932XL | N743JA | |
| 6033 | N5223Y | YR-GCI | | |
| 6034 | N5218T | PR-RMC | | |
| 6035 | N949LL | N635CJ | PK-DPD | |
| 6036 | N5105F | OE-GES | | |
| 6037 | N50275 | YU-BZM | | |
| 6038 | N5202D | N563WD | | |
| 6039 | N50756 | D-CCWD | | |
| 6040 | N5100J | TC-TSY | | |
| 6041 | N5147B | (D-CDCC) | N100U | |
| 6042 | N5261R | N2370S | CN-AMJ | [or CN-AMK] |
| 6043 | N51806 | | | |
| 6044 | N221AM | I-GGLA | | |
| 6045 | N5072X | I-CNDG | | |
| 6046 | N5248V | PR-RTS | | |
| 6047 | N5096S | N2384K | CN-AMK | [or CN-AMJ] |

## CITATION XLS+

| C/n | Identities | | |
|---|---|---|---|
| 6048 | N5192E | N61442 | TC-DAK |
| 6049 | N5270M | D-CDCD* | |
| 6050 | N50612 | N565AP | N565AB* |
| 6051 | N5157E | N912EL | |
| 6052 | N52626 | N332BN | |
| 6053 | N52433 | N2401X | N53XL |
| 6054 | N50715 | N54XL | |
| 6055 | N5264U | | |
| 6056 | N51896 | | |
| 6057 | N5037F | | |
| 6058 | N58XL | | |
| 6059 | N5262Z | | |
| 6060 | N51160 | | |
| 6061 | N5269A | | |
| 6062 | N5254Y | D-CDCE* | |
| 6063 | D-CDCF* | | |
| 6064 | (N583CS) | | |
| 6065 | | | |
| 6066 | | | |
| 6067 | | | |
| 6068 | | | |
| 6069 | | | |
| 6070 | | | |
| 6071 | | | |
| 6072 | | | |
| 6073 | | | |
| 6074 | | | |
| 6075 | | | |
| 6076 | | | |
| 6077 | | | |
| 6078 | | | |
| 6079 | | | |
| 6080 | | | |
| 6081 | | | |
| 6082 | | | |
| 6083 | | | |
| 6084 | | | |
| 6085 | | | |
| 6086 | | | |
| 6087 | | | |
| 6088 | | | |
| 6089 | | | |
| 6090 | | | |
| 6091 | | | |
| 6092 | | | |
| 6093 | | | |
| 6094 | | | |
| 6095 | | | |
| 6096 | | | |
| 6097 | | | |
| 6098 | | | |
| 6099 | | | |
| 6100 | | | |
| 6101 | | | |
| 6102 | | | |
| 6103 | | | |
| 6104 | | | |
| 6105 | | | |
| 6106 | | | |
| 6107 | | | |
| 6108 | | | |
| 6109 | | | |
| 6110 | | | |
| 6111 | | | |
| 6112 | | | |
| 6113 | | | |
| 6114 | | | |
| 6115 | | | |
| 6116 | | | |
| 6117 | | | |
| 6118 | | | |
| 6119 | | | |
| 6120 | | | |
| 6121 | | | |
| 6122 | | | |
| 6123 | | | |

# CESSNA 650 CITATION III

| C/n | Identities |
|---|---|
| 696 | N650CC [ff 30May79 cx Nov89; wfu] |
| 697 | N650 [converted to Citation VII standards 1991; fitted with GMA3007 turbofan in connection with Citation X programme 1992; b/u circa 2001; front section used for training purposes - rear to scrapyard at Wichita Mid-Continent, KS] |
| 0001 | N651CC N1AP (N651AP) N654CC N651CC N651CG N345SK |
| 0002 | N652CC N5000C (N650BG) N650AS |
| 0003 | N653CC HZ-AAA N187CP N92LA OY-CCG N166MC N411SL |
| 0004 | (N654AR) N654GC N650GT N650LA |
| 0005 | N137S N439H N693BA N700RY |
| 0006 | N656CC N44HS (N306QS) N58RW N1TS N650TS N39RE N27TS N128GB N129GB |
| 0007 | (N13047) (N3Q) N657CC N929DS C-FLTL (N20EA) N52SY N719HG N650MG XA... |
| 0008 | (N13049) N618CC N10TC N84TJ N84WU N926CB N926CR N777XS |
| 0009 | (N1305C) N933DB N933SH |
| 0010 | (N1305N) N2UP N2EP (N610VP) OK-NKN N650LW |
| 0011 | N1305U (C-GWPA) (N90LA) N91LA N17TE N17TN N311CW N362TW |
| 0012 | N1305V N15VF OE-GCO |
| 0013 | (N13052) N119EL (N13QS) N313QS N377JE N770GF |
| 0014 | (N1306B) (N664RB) N650CJ C-GHOO OE-GCN (N855DH) OY-EDP |
| 0015 | (N1306F) N83CT N369G N15QS N766MH |
| 0016 | N1306V N720ML N720ME N555DH (N45US) N32MG N316CW N21LL |
| 0017 | N1307A C-GHLM N900CM N900QM (N650BP) N651BP |
| 0018 | (N1307C) N715BC N275WN N650SB |
| 0019 | (N1307D) (N44BH) N30CJ N333RL N833RL XA-TBA N650JL N650MS N707MS N71LU N970GW |
| 0020 | N1307G XA-VIT N488JT N10PN N650WB N420GT |
| 0021 | N2624M N2604 N650SS N460CP |
| 0022 | N650J |
| 0023 | N889G C-GHKY N658MA VR-CCC N38DD N650CG |
| 0024 | N1UP N1UH N624VP N643CR N95SR N650SL N422BC |
| 0025 | N10PX N200RT (N376HW) (N277HG) N700RR N650VP N625VP N16FE (N522GS) N16SU |
| 0026 | (N656CC) [damaged on production line early 1984 and not completed; fuselage used as test frame] |
| 0027 | N375SC N875SC N650NY N433LF N993LC |
| 0028 | N148C N328QS LN-NLC N38ED N650BW |
| 0029 | (N30CJ) N600GH N70TT (N81TT) N89AC N409SF |
| 0030 | N650SC SE-DHL N650SC N380CW N51EM |
| 0031 | N631CC N1ZC N7ZG |
| 0032 | N54WC N38WP N3184Z N332FW XA-HVP N632VP* |
| 0033 | (N1309A) CC-ECE Chile E-302 [w/o 09Jly92 4km from runway 20 Concepcion, Chile] |
| 0034 | N80CC N34QS N777LF (N45US) N650GH |
| 0035 | N650MD N400JD N408JD XA-GJC |
| 0036 | N700CS (N700RD) N20RD N36CD N43TC (N143RC) XA-TGA N650BS N651CV |
| 0037 | N411BB N37CD VH-OZI N37VP I-GASD (D-CLDF) D-CVAI |
| 0038 | N366G N366GE N373DJ |
| 0039 | N81TC N39WP N171L XA-KMX |
| 0040 | N82TC VR-BJY HB-VIY N650WE |
| 0041 | N55BH |
| 0042 | N142AB N342QS N342AS C-GPOP |
| 0043 | (N1310B) OY-GKL N643CC N953JF |
| 0044 | (N234HM) N650M (D-CRRR) N129PJ N126MT |
| 0045 | N84G N67SF N67SE N669W N689W |
| 0046 | N658CC N57TT N650TT C-FBNA |
| 0047 | N1102 (N1109) N650CN N33BC N33BQ N711VH N711VZ N706HB |
| 0048 | N98BD N98DD N986M N650MM (A6-GAN) VP-CGK A6-CGK A7-CGK |
| 0049 | (N1311A) C-FJOE PJ-MAR PT-LSN N30AF (N650AN) |
| 0050 | (N1311K) N44M N44MU N51JV |
| 0051 | (N1311P) N910F N651BH N777MX |
| 0052 | N20MW XA-SDU |
| 0053 | N367G N306PA |
| 0054 | (N1312D) N1103 N1183 (N26RG) N17AN N47AN |
| 0055 | N173LP N173LR N515VC N16AS N652CV |
| 0056 | N273LP (N273LB) N760EW N397CS N56JV N78AP |
| 0057 | N368G N101YC (N101PC) N400PC N31TJ N400PC N955HG |
| 0058 | N88DD N70DJ (N282PC) (N292PC) (N650JS) N143PL N72EP |
| 0059 | N1313G PT-LHA N660AA N370TP |
| 0060 | (N1313J) HB-VHW N848US TC-CAO N660TJ N220TW N220TV OY-JPJ |
| 0061 | (N1313T) N137M (N129TC) N137X N650TP N650TC N450RS N440PC |
| 0062 | N626CC C-GHGK N388DA N19FR N342HM N650CN N475M N84PH |
| 0063 | N13138 N41ST N72LE N650AT N651AT |
| 0064 | (N1314H) N801CC N650TC N444CW |
| 0065 | (N1314T) N500E C-FIMO |
| 0066 | (N1314V) N138M N138V N650CD |
| 0067 | (N1314X) N210F N9AX N232CF N232CE |

# CITATION III

C/n Identities

0068 (N1314X) N273W N985M N9KL N650AJ XA-TMZ
0069 (N13142) N910M XB-GRN N455JD
0070 (N1315A) N149C N370QS N370TG LN-NLD OY-NLA N38ED OY-NLA
0071 (N1315B) N334H N297DD N97DD
0072 (N1315C) N277W N651CN N72ST N139MY
0073 (N1315D) N650JA N673JS N85DA XA-LEY
0074 (N1315G) (N555EW) N234YP N194DC N93CL N81SF
0075 N1315T N16AJ N85MS
0076 N1315V N376SC N876SC HB-VJT N731GA XA-SEP N424LB XA-PVR
0077 (N1315Y) N677CC N701AG VR-BGB (N42NA) TC-EES TC-SIS (N701AG) N800GM
0078 (N13150) N652CC PK-TRJ PK-WSE N650WJ N50DS (XA-...) N650WL N650KB
0079 (N1316A) N66ME N290SC N288CC N59CD N217RR N211RR N69VC N217RJ
N650RB
0080 N1316E N69LD C-FDJC
0081 (N1316N) PT-LGT (N881BA) N910DP N910DF
0082 (N13162) N651AP N1AP N81AP N82VP N4VF N4VY N825JW
0083 N13166 N944H N944CA TC-TOP N2NR N5NR N677LM N650HG
0084 (N13168) N85AW N431CB (N431CQ) N650CB
0085 N1317G JA8249 N650DA I-CIST [w/o 04Nov00 Rome-Ciampino A/P, Italy parted out by
White Inds, Bates City MO circa Oct01]
0086 (N1317X) PT-LHC
0087 (N1317Y) N988H N988HL N687VP C-FQCY N680BC N37VP PP-AIO
0088 (N13170) PT-LGZ N290AS N590AS N650TA
0089 (N13175) N653CC N650JC N86WP N86VP (N229J)
0090 (N1318A) N694CC N1823S N651TC N850MC N1DH N555DH N651PW
0091 N1318E N68HC N58HC PT-LUE
0092 (N1318L) N692CC N692BE
0093 (N1318M) (N693CC) N773M N93VP N222GT CS-DND N196SG N196SD
0094 (N1318P) N5114 N6114 N94VP N94TJ 5B-CSM N650SP N651RS N650SP
N926HC N699MG
0095 (N1318Q) N5115 N6115 (N95VP) N882KB N883KB N941KA
0096 (N1318X) N5116 N96VP N700SW N702SW N629RM N629MD
0097 (N1318Y) N697MC N725WH N697MC [w/o 27Oct07 Atlantic City, NJ; parted out by White Inds
Bates City, MO]
0098 (N13189) N399W N389W N54HC N398CW N398DL
0099 N1319B (N555EW) N26SD N403CB XA-PYN N994U XA-AEB
0100 (N1319D) N200LH N200LL N202JK
0101 N1319M N847G C-GPEA N330TJ N650HR XB-GXV XA-LTH N9NL VH-SPJ
0102 (N1319X) (N406M) N406MM N406LM N24237
0103 (N13194) (N407M) N407MM N407LM N2411A (N907RM)
0104 N13195 I-BETV N650CF C-FLMJ C-GOXB C-FORJ
0105 (N1320B) N655CC N15TT N48TT N67BG I-FEEV [w/o nr Rome/Ciampino, Italy,
07Feb09]
0106 (N1320K) N106CC N650CE N725RH N404LN*
0107 (N1320P) N8000U N650MP N650JG N397CW N397DR
0108 (N1320U) N650Z
0109 (N1320V) (N650AT) N20AT N134M (N134MJ) (N649AF) N109ST N106ST VH-SBU
0110 (N1320X) N76D N303PC
0111 (N13204) N500CM N381CW (N381EM) (N650RJ)
0112 N1321A N60BE N93DK N598C N598AW
0113 N1321C N10ST N872EC (N650AF) N652JM N393CW N393JC
0114 (N1321J) N7000G N651AF N650DA
0115 N1321K PT-LJC N1419J N541S
0116 (N1321L) N78D (N78DL) N788BA C-FJJC C-FJJG N928PS
0117 N1321N F-GGAL
0118 (N13210) N6000J N118CD N770MP N770MR N79KF
0119 (N13217) VR-BJS HB-VIN N100WH EC-EQX N96AF 8P-KAM N770AF N147PS
N147TA N650HM N888KG
0120 N13218 N143AB (N818TP) (N650AF) I-SALG N650AF N1223N N30NM N907DF
0121 (N1322D) D-CATP N1322D N121AG N24VB N818DE
0122 (N1322K) EC-EAS N650TT (N650MT) N65WL N122EJ
0123 (N1322X) N624CC N434H N59FT (N491SS)
0124 (N1322Y) N95CC N7HV N650HC N776GM
0125 (N13222) EC-EAP N650AF N170HL N178HL
0126 (N1323A) N55HF N65HF XA-RZQ N65HF N311MA N101PG
0127 N1323D N723BH N92TX (N18PV) N95TJ N95UJ+ [+ marks worn at 2002 NBAA but not
officially registered] N700MH
0128 (N1323K) N628CC N125Q LV-CAE
0129 (N1323N) N61BE (N309TA) PT-LUO N125N N330MB
0130 (N1323Q) N227LA N227BA N543SC N159M N159MR N130TS (N130RK) N603HC
N603HP N918BH N901RH
0131 (N1323R) CC-ECL Chile E-303 Chile 303
0132 N1323V N24KT N49SM N727AW
0133 N1323X N633CC N133LE N133LH ZK-NLJ N133LE N250CM N213HP
0134 (N1323Y) N75RD N75RN N27SD N123SL N1239L D-CARE (PH-EVY) PH-MSX
0135 (N1324B) N5109 N135AF VP-CAR

# CITATION III

| C/n | Identities | | | | | | | | |
|---|---|---|---|---|---|---|---|---|---|
| 0136 | (N1324D) | N841G | N60AF | N779AZ | N779AF | N650DF | N3170B | | |
| 0137 | (N1324G) | N874G | N4Y | | | | | | |
| 0138 | (N1324R) | N828G | N650JV | N35PN | N717JM | | | | |
| 0139 | (N13242) | N4EG | N96CP | | | | | | |
| 0140 | (N1325D) | N95CC | N290SC | N220CC | N90CN | (N650SS) | N4FC | N1400M | |
| 0141 | N1325E | N110TM | TC-CMY | N21WJ | N140TS | | | | |
| 0142 | (N1325L) | N142CC | N20RD | D-CRHR | (N492BA) | | | | |
| 0143 | N1325X | N143WR | N11NZ | N28S | N312CF | N40FC | | | |
| 0144 | N1325Y | N644CC | VH-KTI | N644CC | N650KM | N2605 | PK-TSM | N2605 | N384CW |
| | N384EM | | | | | | | | |
| 0145 | N1325Z | C-GCFP | N650AF | N29AU | N385CW | N385EM | [w/o in Venezuela 18Feb08] | | |
| 0146 | N13256 | N646CC | XA-PIP | N650FC | | | | | |
| 0147 | N13259 | OE-GNK | N148N | N141M | N456AF | N94BJ | N151DR | | |
| 0148 | N1326A | N55SC | N55SQ | N50PH | N50EJ | N7HF | N92RP | | |
| 0149 | N1326B | N649CC | N139M | N139N | (CS-DNE) | D-CBPL | | | |
| 0150 | N1326D | N150F | N61CK | | | | | | |
| 0151 | N1326G | G-MLEE | N91D | PK-KIG | N660AF | N321AR | | | |
| 0152 | (N1326H) | (N4EG) | N650AE | (N152VP) | N627R | N327R | N260VP | N255VP | (N260VP) |
| | N605SA | | | | | | | | |
| 0153 | N1326K | N95CC | N653CC | N47CM | N777ZC | N1DH | N2DH | N845FW | |
| 0154 | (N1326P) | N154CC | N696HC | N650CH | | | | | |
| 0155 | N13264 | N788NB | N97AL | | | | | | |
| 0156 | N13267 | N68SK | N38SK | XA-ARS | N209A | N74VF | N650CC | | |
| 0157 | N1327A | N657CC | N516SM | N10JP | N650RP | | | | |
| 0158 | N1327B | N658CJ | N121AT | N135HC | N735HC | (N745EA) | N721ST | VH-SSZ | |
| 0159 | N13113 | N683MB | N267TG | N359CW | | | | | |
| 0160 | N1312D | N95CC | N24UM | N831CB | N830CB | (N830GB) | N33UL | N650PT | N220CM |
| 0161 | (N1312K) | N161CC | I-ATSA | N500AE | N510SD | | | | |
| 0162 | N1312Q | N202RB | N275GC | N660Q | | | | | |
| 0163 | N1312T | N137M | (N137MR) | N163AF | N749CP | N163JM | | | |
| 0164 | N1312V | N138M | N138MR | N164AF | N364CW | N162DS | | | |
| 0165 | N1312X | XA-FCP | XC-PGN | (N650GJ) | | | | | |
| 0166 | N1313J | PT-LTB | | | | | | | |
| 0167 | N667CC | N532CC | (N532C) | N832CC | N88DJ | | | | |
| 0168 | N1314H | N175J | | | | | | | |
| 0169 | N169CC | N88JJ | N749DC | N73HM | | | | | |
| 0170 | N1314V | N95CC | N170CC | N32JJ | XA-RIE | | | | |
| 0171 | N1354G | PT-LVF | PR-ITN | | | | | | |
| 0172 | (N1772E) | N672CC | N934H | | | | | | |
| 0173 | (N1779E) | N843G | N173VP | | | | | | |
| 0174 | (N1782E) | N674CC | D-CLUE | | | | | | |
| 0175 | (N175J) | N1820E | N235KK | N835KK | N175SR | | | | |
| 0176 | N176L | N1874E | N1526L | N2TF | N48TF | N176AF | N504RP | | |
| 0177 | N1930E | JA8367 | N707HJ | N834H | | | | | |
| 0178 | N1958E | N95CC | N178CC | JA8378 | N178CC | N603AT | TC-RAM | N650BA | N57CE |
| | N605DS | N896RJ | | | | | | | |
| 0179 | N1959E | N679CC | XA-RMY | N35FC | N63GC | N287CD | | | |
| 0180 | N2098A | N768NB | N498CS | | | | | | |
| 0181 | N2131A | (N181CC) | PT-OBX | N743CC | N650DR | N857DN | | | |
| 0182 | N26105 | N682CC | N491JB | | | | | | |
| 0183 | N2614Y | EI-SNN | N820FJ | (N820F) | | | | | |
| 0184 | N2615D | N95CC | N1128B | N11288 | | | | | |
| 0185 | N2615L | N708CT | N708CF | N185VP | VR-BMG | N650HS | N533CC | N538CC | (N650MG) |
| | 4X-CMR | N521BH | N468ES | | | | | | |
| 0186 | N2616L | PT-OAK | N186VP | N386CW | XA-UIS | | | | |
| 0187 | N2617K | N187CM | N500RP | (N55PC) | N70PT | (N78PT) | D-CAYK | N39VP | LN-AAA |
| | D-CRRR | N226EM | 4X-CZA | | | | | | |
| 0188 | N2617P | N587S | N650FP | | | | | | |
| 0189 | N26174 | XA-RGS | | | | | | | |
| 0190 | (N2621U) | N142B | N190JJ | N350CD | N260VP | D-CCEU | | | |
| 0191 | (N2621Z) | N191CM | N59B | TC-KLS | N650TJ | N650SG | | | |
| 0192 | N2622C | N15TT | N15TZ | LN-AAU | N78EM | D-CREY | | | |
| 0193 | N2622Z | N95CC | N95CM | N55HF | N55HD | N650CC | N2DH | N91KK | |
| 0194 | N26228 | N111VW | N2606 | N831GA | | | | | |
| 0195 | N26233 | N411BB | N411BP | C-GAPT | N800MC | N140WH | | | |
| 0196 | (N2625C) | N196CM | N896EC | N534H | | | | | |
| 0197 | N2625Y | N95CC | N197CC | (N197VP) | N797T | N800R | N840R | N100R | N50QN |
| 0198 | N2624L | (N650GA) | N198CM | N553AC | (N650BW) | XA-INF | N650BC | XA-XGX | |
| 0199 | (N2626X) | (N900JD) | N65KB | N890MC | N527CP | N400RE | | | |
| 0200 | [Built as Citation VI (qv)] | | | | | | | | |
| 0201 | [Built as Citation VI (qv)] | | | | | | | | |
| 0202 | [Built as Citation VI (qv)] | | | | | | | | |
| 0203 | N26271 | N95CC | (N203CD) | N4612 | (N4612S) | N4612Z | N350M | N350MQ | VT-IPA |
| 0204 | N2630B | XA-RZK | (N691DE) | N811JT | N108WV | | | | |
| 0205 | N2630N | PT-OMU | | | | | | | |
| 0206 | N2630U | PT-OKV | N39H | N826RP | N610RP | N119ES | | | |

Production complete

# CESSNA 650 CITATION VI

Note: The Citation VI was to have used model number 660 but in the end used 650 in common with the Citation III and VII

| C/n | Identities | | | | | |
|---|---|---|---|---|---|---|
| 0200 | (N2626Z) | N650CM | PT-OMV | [w/o 23Mar94 25 miles NW Bogota, Colombia] | | |
| 0201 | (N26264) | N40PH | N347BG | N1419J | XA-... | |
| 0202 | N2627A | (N202CV) | PT-OJO | N202TJ | N65BP | UP-CS401 |
| 0203 | [Built as Citation III (qv)] | | | | | |
| 0204 | [Built as Citation III (qv)] | | | | | |
| 0205 | [Built as Citation III (qv)] | | | | | |
| 0206 | [Built as Citation III (qv)] | | | | | |
| 0207 | (N2632Y or N6812D) | N207CC | N334WC | N107CG | N818SE | |
| 0208 | N6812L | N91TG | I-TALW | N500FR | | |
| 0209 | (N6812Z) | N650L | N198DF | N198D | N902VP | N930MG | N830MG |
| 0210 | (N6868P) | N610CM | VR-CVP | N7059U | N733H | N783H |
| 0211 | N6820T | N335WC | N333WC | (N59CC) | N211CC | N211CQ |
| 0212 | (N6820Y) | N805GT | N972VZ | N651AR | D-CCSD | |
| 0213 | (N6823L) | N900JD | N900UD | PR-KKA | | |
| 0214 | N68231 | N95CC | N95CM | TC-CEY | N771JB | N7777B |
| 0215 | (N900JD) | (N6824G) | N215CM | N650KC | N650GC | |
| 0216 | N68269 | I-BLUB | | | | |
| 0217 | (N6828S) | N217CM | PH-MEX | | | |
| 0218 | N6829X | XA-GAN | N218CC | XA-MTZ | XA-ACH | |
| 0219 | N6829Z | N219CC | G-HNRY | (N211MA) | N650TS | |
| 0220 | N6830T | B-4106 | B-7022 | | | |
| 0221 | N1301A | B-4107 | B-7023 | [w/o 02Sep02 Xichang, China] | | |
| 0222 | N222CD | N733K | N738K | N780GT | | |
| 0223 | N1301D | N111Y | N111YW | | | |
| 0224 | N224CD | N1UP | (N7UL) | | | |
| 0225 | N1301Z | (N225CV) | N606AT | | | |
| 0226 | N1302A | N400JH | XA-GPS | | | |
| 0227 | N1302C | (N227CV) | N2UP | (N2UX) | | |
| 0228 | N1302V | N228CM | XA-SLB | | | |
| 0229 | N1302X | TC-ANT | | | | |
| 0230 | N1305N | N616AT | N660PA | | | |
| 0231 | N13052 | LV-WHY | N67SF | N400WK | (N650FA) | |
| 0232 | N1303A | F-GKJS | N517MT | (N512MT) | N711LV | |
| 0233 | N1303H | CC-DAC | | | | |
| 0234 | N1306V+ | N334CM | TC-SBH | N733AU | N733A | (N735A) | XA-GBM |
| 0235 | (N1307A) | N1303V | N235CM | N235SV | | |
| 0236 | (N1307C) | N1303M | N600JD | N600UD | N184GP | |
| 0237 | (N1307D) | N1306B | N650MC | (N656LE) | N650W | |
| 0238 | N1304B | (N9UC) | N19UC | N19QC | | |
| 0239 | N1304G | N17UC | N17QC | N68ED | | |
| 0240 | N51143 | PH-MFX | D-CAKE | PH-MFX | | |
| 0241 | N5202D | (N651JM) | N666JM | N651JM | N651EJ | |

Production complete

# CESSNA 650 CITATION VII

Note: The Citation VII was to have used model number 670 but in the end used 650 in common with the Citation III and VI

| C/n | Identities | | | | | | | |
|---|---|---|---|---|---|---|---|---|
| 7001 | N1259B | N701CD | N111RF | N404JF | N701HA | | | |
| 7002 | N1259K | N702CM | N95CC | N19SV | | | | |
| 7003 | N1259N | N1AP | N17AP | N888TX | (N650RJ) | | | |
| 7004 | N1259R | N708CT | N913SQ | N174VP | | | | |
| 7005 | N1259S | N200LH | | | | | | |
| 7006 | (N1259Y) | N966H | N966K | (N706VP) | TC-KOC | OE-GCH | | |
| 7007 | N1259Z | N944H | N944L | N28TX | | | | |
| 7008 | N12593 | (N708CM) | N95CC | N901SB | N902SB | N909SB | N16KB | N678EQ |
| 7009 | N12596 | (N709CM) | N93TX | N709VP | N711NB | | | |
| 7010 | N1260G | N1S | (N1902) | N317MZ | N150JP | (N403BL) | | |
| 7011 | N1260N | N5111 | (N6111) | N700VP | SE-DVY | VH-DHN | | |
| 7012 | N1260V | N712CM | N5112 | N5144 | N317MB | N817MB | | |
| 7013 | N12605 | N5113 | N5118 | (N713VP) | N2NT | N15LN | | |
| 7014 | N1261A | N864EC | (N865EC) | (N714VP) | N375E | | | |
| 7015 | N1261K | N5115 | N5119 | (N715VP) | (N317MX) | N317MQ | N817MQ | N750CK |
| 7016 | N1261M | N18SK | N68SK | N650RP | N650CP | | | |
| 7017 | (N1261M) | N775M | | | | | | |
| 7018 | (N1261P) | N5114 | N5174 | N718VP | N119RM | N623PM | | |
| 7019 | N12616 | XA-TCZ | XA-TRE | | | | | |
| 7020 | N1262A | N95CC | N700RR | N832CB | | | | |
| 7021 | N1262B | PT-MGS | | | | | | |
| 7022 | N1262E | N722CM | N902RM | N902F | [2000th Citation] | | | |
| 7023 | N1262G | N6110 | | | | | | |
| 7024 | N1262Z | Turkey 93-7024 | | [code ETI-024] | | Turkey 004 | | |
| 7025 | N1263B | N442WT | N442WJ | N68BC | XA-RTS | XA-UHO | XA-RRQ | |
| 7026 | N1263G | Turkey 93-7026 | | [code ETI-026] | | Turkey 005 | | |
| 7027 | N1263P | N500 | N657ER | N900MN | N622PM | | | |
| 7028 | (N1263V) | N728CM | XA-SPQ | | | | | |
| 7029 | (N1263Y) | N95CM | XA-SOK | N650RL | N444KE | JY-RYN | | |
| 7030 | N12632 | N1263Z | N8JC | (N703VP) | N95CC | N782CC | | |
| 7031 | N12636 | N40N | N4QN | | | | | |
| 7032 | N12637 | XA-XIS | N32FJ | | | | | |
| 7033 | N1264B | PT-OVU | | | | | | |
| 7034 | N1264E | XA-SWM | N4360S | VP-CDW | N650K | | | |
| 7035 | N1264M | VR-CIM | N3273H | PT-WLC | N95RX | N757MB | | |
| 7036 | N1264P | N95CC | N95HF | N77HF | | | | |
| 7037 | (N1264V) | N737CC | N95TX | | | | | |
| 7038 | N12642 | N399W | N398W | PR-PTL | N156BA | N398W | PR-JAP | |
| 7039 | N12643 | D-CACM | OY-GGG | D-CBIZ | | | | |
| 7040 | N1265B | N504T | | | | | | |
| 7041 | N1265C | N430SA | (N449SA) | | | | | |
| 7042 | N1265K | N657T | | | | | | |
| 7043 | N1265P | N78D | N78DL | TC-ATC | N650DH | N44M | N44MQ | |
| 7044 | N1265U | N7005 | N650CJ | | | | | |
| 7045 | N12652 | N95CM | CC-PGL | CC-CPS | N745VP | CS-DGR | | |
| 7046 | N51160 | N746CM | N746BR | N747TX | N703RB | N328BT* | | |
| 7047 | N5117U+ | N647CM | N1828S | N198TX | N650DD | N650KD | | |
| 7048 | N51176 | N18GB | | | | | | |
| 7049 | N5120U | N749CM | N900FL | N750FB | N182PA | N73UC | | |
| 7050 | N5121N | N6150B | N33GK | N83GK | N650CZ | | | |
| 7051 | N51817 | (N95CC) | N965JC | N77LX | | | | |
| 7052 | N5183U | N752CM | N24NB | N24KT | | | | |
| 7053 | (N5183V) | N344AS | N650AS | N650AB | N123SL | N128SL | N650AT | |
| 7054 | N5185J | (N754CM) | PT-WFC | N7243U | LV-WTN | | | |
| 7055 | N5185V | N755CM | N317M | N317MZ | N817MZ | D-CMPI | | |
| 7056 | N52144 | N6781C | N60PL | N444EX | | | | |
| 7057 | N5216A | N157CM | N653EJ | N361EE | N808VA | | | |
| 7058 | N52178 | N625CC | N98XS | | | | | |
| 7059 | N5218R | (N95CC) | N4EG | N76PR | N144MH | N14DG | | |
| 7060 | N5218T | N55SC | | | | | | |
| 7061 | N5221Y | N903SB | N908SB | N202CW | N102CE | | | |
| 7062 | N5262Z | N876G | | | | | | |
| 7063 | N52623 | N95CC | N877G | | | | | |
| 7064 | N52626 | HB-VLP | N5117 | N5112 | N82GM | | | |
| 7065 | N52627 | (N765W) | N650W | N96MT | | | | |
| 7066 | N5263D | N766CG | N669W | | | | | |
| 7067 | (N5263S) | N51143 | N502T | C-FTOR | | | | |
| 7068 | N51160 | N111HZ | N111BZ | N7AB | | | | |
| 7069 | N5117U | (N769CM) | XA-TMX | N191JT | XA-CTK | | | |
| 7070 | N51176 | N95CM | N22RG | N322RG | (N770VP) | N654EJ | OY-CKE | N556RA |
| 7071 | N5120U | HS-DCG | N1130N | HS-DCG | | | | |
| 7072 | N5141F | (N8494C) | N35HS | | | | | |
| 7073 | N51444 | N1867M | N1887M | XA-UAM | PK-YRL | PK-RJB | | |

# CITATION VII

| C/n | Identities | | | | | |
|---|---|---|---|---|---|---|
| 7074 | N5183V | PT-WLY | | | | |
| 7075 | N52613 | N12295 | N711GF | | | |
| 7076 | N5213S | N286MC | | | | |
| 7077 | N5203J | N877CM | N532JF | (N582JF) | VP-CGE | N603HD | N603HC |
| 7078 | N5079V | N78BR | N84NG | | | |
| 7079 | N779QS | (N132WC) | N779VP | Spain U.21-01 | | [code 01-408] |
| 7080 | N780QS | CS-DNF | S5-BBA | YU-BTM | | |
| 7081 | N781QS | CS-DNG | N8VX | XA-FRI | | |
| 7082 | N5086W | N782QS | (N133WC) | N782VP | N2RF | N91KC |
| 7083 | N50820 | PT-WQH | | | | |
| 7084 | N5094D | TC-KON | N1127G | TC-KON | | |
| 7085 | N5112K | N785QS | (N136WC) | N785CC | D-CLDF | |
| 7086 | N51342 | N860W | | | | |
| 7087 | N5163C | N787QS | (N139WC) | N149WC | N43FC | |
| 7088 | N5073G | N449SA | N440SA | XA-UGX | XA-PYN | |
| 7089 | N5117U | N789QS | N789VP | VH-VRC | N789VP | |
| 7090 | N790QS | N790VP | (D-CVII) | T7-VII | | |
| 7091 | N791QS | N791VP | TC-STO | | | |
| 7092 | N792QS | (N792VP) | N792CC | C-GCIX | C-FSBC | |
| 7093 | N793QS | CS-DNE | OY-CLP | | | |
| 7094 | N794QS | N794VP | D-CVII | | | |
| 7095 | N795QS | N795VP | VH-LYM | | | |
| 7096 | N5162W | N796QS | N287MC | | | |
| 7097 | N797QS | N797CC | | | | |
| 7098 | N5212M | N798QS | N601AB | (N612AB) | N621AB | N1254C |
| 7099 | N5141F | PT-XFG | | | | |
| 7100 | N710QS | N710VP | | | | |
| 7101 | N5157E | N602AB | (N621AB) | N612AB | N650JL | |
| 7102 | N5223X | D-CNCJ | | | | |
| 7103 | N713QS | N713VP | | | | |
| 7104 | N5148B | VH-ING | | | | |
| 7105 | N715QS | N118MM | | | | |
| 7106 | N5188A | N716QS | N71NK | N33RL | | |
| 7107 | N559AM | N652CC | | | | |
| 7108 | N202AV | | | | | |
| 7109 | N5269A | N709QS | [reported w/o Dec99 in ground accident Wichita A/P, KS] | | | |
| 7110 | N52235 | (N12909) | RP-C650 | N657JW | OE-GLS | |
| 7111 | N5172M | N256W | N226W | PR-AJG | | |
| 7112 | N5174W | N257W | (N267W) | N269TA | | |
| 7113 | N5192E | PP-JRA | N650JB | N737MM | | |
| 7114 | N5194B | N68BR | N926CB | | | |
| 7115 | N5267K | N314SL | | | | |
| 7116 | N5268M | N175DP | | | | |
| 7117 | N5263D | N33D | N135HC | PH-MYX | | |
| 7118 | N5264U | N33L | | | | |
| 7119 | N5152X | N651CC | | | | |

Production complete

+ indicates test marks not fully confirmed

# CESSNA 680 CITATION SOVEREIGN

The Sovereign gained its type certificate from the FAA on 02Jun04

| C/n | Identities | | | | |
|---|---|---|---|---|---|
| 709 | N680CS | [ff 27Feb02] | | | |
| 0001 | N681CS | N605CS | [ff 27Jun02] | | |
| 0002 | N682CS | N747RL | N747RC | | |
| 0003 | N52114 | N103SV | N602CS | | |
| 0004 | N5233J | XA-GMO | | | |
| 0005 | N52229 | N105SV | OE-GMM | | |
| 0006 | N5264U | N409GB | | | |
| 0007 | N52081 | N604CS | | | |
| 0008 | N900EB | | | | |
| 0009 | N682DB | | | | |
| 0010 | N5135A | N301QS | | | |
| 0011 | N5135K | N338QS | | | |
| 0012 | N970RC | N61DF | | | |
| 0013 | N5136J | N346QS | | | |
| 0014 | N5270K | XA-HIT | | | |
| 0015 | N272MH | | | | |
| 0016 | N616CS | (D-CNIC) | (N21FR) | XA-RTS | |
| 0017 | N5248V | N757EG | (N121LS) | N446RT | |
| 0018 | N79PG | | | | |
| 0019 | N5188N | N63TM | | | |
| 0020 | N5245U | N914SP | | | |
| 0021 | N5200Z | N1276L | N621SV | N174TM | N988TM |
| 0022 | N1901 | | | | |
| 0023 | N52235 | N44SH | | | |
| 0024 | N5241R | N565A | | | |
| 0025 | N52475 | N680AR | | | |
| 0026 | N5260Y | SU-EWD | | | |
| 0027 | N5264S | N532CC | N522CC | VH-EXA | N827DC |
| 0028 | N5264E | N865EC | | | |
| 0029 | N5183V | N349QS | | | |
| 0030 | N680PH | N86LF | N808WC | N200Y | |
| 0031 | N5223P | N156PH | | | |
| 0032 | N51575 | N52433 | N132SV | C-FDHD | |
| 0033 | N52114 | ZS-JDL | D-CAFE | OE-GEM | |
| 0034 | N5260U | N2426 | N211CC | | |
| 0035 | N5155G | N157PH | | | |
| 0036 | N5108G | N350QS | | | |
| 0037 | N5130J | N631RP | N681RP | | |
| 0038 | N456SM | | | | |
| 0039 | N39SV | N680SB | VP-CFP | | |
| 0040 | N5241R | N785RC | | | |
| 0041 | N5200U | N789H | | | |
| 0042 | N5090V | N29WE | | | |
| 0043 | N5233J | N718MN | XA-GAN | | |
| 0044 | N52623 | N680SW | N680CG | | |
| 0045 | N5203S | N145BL | | | |
| 0046 | N5260M | N2428 | | | |
| 0047 | N5267G | N737KB | N544KB | | |
| 0048 | N52601 | N777UT | | | |
| 0049 | N5058J | N158PH | | | |
| 0050 | N5257V | D-CVHA | | | |
| 0051 | N362QS | | | | |
| 0052 | N5203J | N12925 | N19MK | | |
| 0053 | N5076K | N53HS | XA-FUD | | |
| 0054 | N5168Y | N2425 | | | |
| 0055 | N5147B | OE-GNB | | | |
| 0056 | N747CC | (N5YH) | N680SV | VT-VED | |
| 0057 | N51872 | N365QS | | | |
| 0058 | N5060K | N121TL | ZK-JTH | | |
| 0059 | N5214J | N4017X | SE-RFH | | |
| 0060 | N5207A | N51246 | PR-SUN | (N68GA) | |
| 0061 | N51575 | N606CS | | | |
| 0062 | N364QS | | | | |
| 0063 | N5148B | N608CS | | | |
| 0064 | N5214L | C-GNEQ | N413CK | | |
| 0065 | N901G | | | | |
| 0066 | N5223D | OE-GUP | D-CUPI | OE-GBY | |
| 0067 | N5203S | (OY-JET) | OY-WET | | |
| 0068 | N68HC | (N68HQ) | C-GSUN | | |
| 0069 | N5166U | N1315Y | PR-SOV | | |
| 0070 | N51869 | N927LT | | | |
| 0071 | N5061P | C-GJKI | | | |
| 0072 | N5254Y | VH-EXG | | | |

## CESSNA 680 CITATION SOVEREIGN

| C/n | Identities | | | |
|---|---|---|---|---|
| 0073 | N5264S | N368QS | | |
| 0074 | N5105F | N391KK | | |
| 0075 | N5163C | N1312V | A6-GJA | |
| 0076 | N5270M | N121LS | | |
| 0077 | N961TC | | | |
| 0078 | N51872 | N678SV | (OO-SIN) | N680SE |
| 0079 | N5172M | N680HC | | |
| 0080 | N5090V | OE-GLP | N345PF | |
| 0081 | N369QS | | | |
| 0082 | N7402 | | | |
| 0083 | N50612 | N44M | | |
| 0084 | N5250E | N4087B | N63LX | N137WH |
| 0085 | N5202D | N1ZC | | |
| 0086 | N5090Y | N227DH | | |
| 0087 | N5093Y | (N666BK) | EC-JYG | |
| 0088 | N305QS | | | |
| 0089 | N380QS | | | |
| 0090 | N868GM | (N84LF) | PR-RCB | |
| 0091 | N5200R | N595SY | | |
| 0092 | N51444 | N610CS | | |
| 0093 | N5245U | N204RP | (N4RP) | N497KK |
| 0094 | N5263D | G-SVSB | | |
| 0095 | N5136J | N711NK | (N711NL) | |
| 0096 | N5200Z | N16GS | | |
| 0097 | N381QS | | | |
| 0098 | N52178 | N202DF | | |
| 0099 | N370QS | | | |
| 0100 | N5120U | C-GAGU | | |
| 0101 | N51072 | N696HC | N686HC | |
| 0102 | N617CS | | | |
| 0103 | N378QS | | | |
| 0104 | N51872 | N680GG | (G-GALI) | N928JK |
| 0105 | N389QS | N305EJ | | |
| 0106 | N51869 | N83SD | | |
| 0107 | N5235G | N531RC | | |
| 0108 | N680VR | | | |
| 0109 | N900JD | | | |
| 0110 | N384QS | | | |
| 0111 | N282DR | | | |
| 0112 | N52446 | N829JC | | |
| 0113 | N388QS | | | |
| 0114 | N5223D | N11084 | SE-RFI | D-CCFF |
| 0115 | N5250P | N385QS | | |
| 0116 | N5225K | N308QS | | |
| 0117 | N5094D | N681SV | EC-KKC | |
| 0118 | N52653 | (N2UJ) | SU-SMA | |
| 0119 | N5260M | N387QS | | |
| 0120 | N52038 | N621CS | | |
| 0121 | N5188N | N822DS | | |
| 0122 | N52526 | N122SV | N468SA | N63CR |
| 0123 | N52582 | N396BB | | |
| 0124 | N5233J | N622CS | | |
| 0125 | N5053R | N666FH | D-CBAY | |
| 0126 | N5270M | N359QS | | |
| 0127 | N51038 | N111Y | | |
| 0128 | N5062S | N228RH | | |
| 0129 | N50522 | VH-EXQ | N1314T | VH-EXQ |
| 0130 | N52178 | N307QS | | |
| 0131 | N5000R | N624CS | | |
| 0132 | N5090A | PR-SPR | | |
| 0133 | N5060K | (LN-TIH) | LN-SSS | |
| 0134 | N5076K | N323QS | | |
| 0135 | N5172M | N229LC | N138BG | |
| 0136 | N5093D | N320TM | | |
| 0137 | N5093L | N192CN | | |
| 0138 | N51984 | M-AGIC | | |
| 0139 | N52081 | OK-UNI | | |
| 0140 | N313QS | | | |
| 0141 | N230LC | N905WS | | |
| 0142 | N51817 | N685CS | | |
| 0143 | N5257C | N1318X | G-XBLU | |
| 0144 | N397QS | | | |
| 0145 | N5117U | OE-GVO | G-GEVO | |
| 0146 | N599GB | | | |
| 0147 | N52462 | N1TG | | |
| 0148 | N51072 | N515TB | N112MV | |
| 0149 | N5030U | N389QS | | |

## CESSNA 680 CITATION SOVEREIGN

| C/n | Identities | | | |
|---|---|---|---|---|
| 0150 | D-CHDC | | | |
| 0151 | N5204D | N681LF | | |
| 0152 | N52113 | N152SV | N930MG | |
| 0153 | N5223P | OE-GTT | D-CGTT | D-CATE |
| 0154 | N52234 | N888SF | | |
| 0155 | N5040E | N357QS | | |
| 0156 | N5235G | D-CHIP | D-CHIL | D-CYOU* |
| 0157 | N5226B | C-FCPR | | |
| 0158 | N158SV | C-GKEG | | |
| 0159 | N51872 | TC-IST | | |
| 0160 | N51869 | N317QS | | |
| 0161 | N5268V | G-NSJS | | |
| 0162 | N5218T | D-CMES | N710MS | |
| 0163 | N5267J | N1RF | | |
| 0164 | N52627 | N300QS | | |
| 0165 | N5268A | N629CS | | |
| 0166 | N5086W | N1FJ | N75SJ | |
| 0167 | N5180C | SU-SMB | | |
| 0168 | N5094D | N442LW | | |
| 0169 | N5263D | N320QS | | |
| 0170 | N5268E | N630CS | | |
| 0171 | N5093D | (D-CLLS) | VP-CMH | |
| 0172 | N5045W | N633RP | | |
| 0173 | N52475 | N1315G | JA680C | |
| 0174 | N5212M | TC-TKN | | |
| 0175 | N52144 | D-CCJS | | |
| 0176 | N5072X | N701CR | | |
| 0177 | N52446 | N338TM | | |
| 0178 | N5163K | EC-KMK | | |
| 0179 | N5200Z | N2UJ | A6-DPD* | |
| 0180 | N5124F | N376QS | | |
| 0181 | N5174W | N751BG | | |
| 0182 | N5194B | PR-HLW | | |
| 0183 | N5130J | LN-SOV | | |
| 0184 | N5231S | PP-BST | | |
| 0185 | N50275 | PH-CIJ | | |
| 0186 | N5135K | "OE-GAC"+ | [+marks worn at factory] | OE-GAK |
| 0187 | N5135A | N377QS | | |
| 0188 | N51881 | N626CS | | |
| 0189 | N5245D | G-CJCC | | |
| 0190 | N52352 | ZS-SAP | | |
| 0191 | N5136J | N339QS | | |
| 0192 | N680RC | | | |
| 0193 | N5257V | ZS-JDL | | |
| 0194 | N52526 | N680CM | | |
| 0195 | N5207V | N973AC | | |
| 0196 | N5203S | N311QS | | |
| 0197 | N5061F | N631CS | | |
| 0198 | N51072 | G-SVGN | M-SVGN | |
| 0199 | N50655 | N806MN | | |
| 0200 | N51564 | N100KZ | OE-GKZ | |
| 0201 | N5223P | N372QS | | |
| 0202 | N5197M | VP-CAV | | |
| 0203 | N50282 | N203DN | | |
| 0204 | N51511 | SX-BMI | | |
| 0205 | N5112K | N1406S | SE-RFJ | |
| 0206 | N5269Z | N606SV | N120SB | XA-... |
| 0207 | N50612 | N306QS | | |
| 0208 | N50549 | N68EU | | |
| 0209 | N5090Y | N1388J | | |
| 0210 | N52059 | N680GR | | |
| 0211 | N5058J | N2208L | | |
| 0212 | N52369 | PH-RID | | |
| 0213 | N52397 | G-TLFK | | |
| 0214 | N5188W | N342QS | | |
| 0215 | N5093Y | OH-WIA | | |
| 0216 | N5100J | G-SIRJ | | |
| 0217 | N52446 | PR-BNP | | |
| 0218 | N51881 | N444A | | |
| 0219 | N5061F | N843DW | | |
| 0220 | N5109R | N315QS | | |
| 0221 | N5096S | N401PG | | |
| 0222 | N632CS | N7403 | | |
| 0223 | N223SV | C-GSOE | | |
| 0224 | N5166T | ZS-IDC | | |
| 0225 | N5135K | N341QS | | |
| 0226 | N5135A | VP-CRH | D-CAHH | |

# CESSNA 680 CITATION SOVEREIGN

| C/n | Identities | | | |
|---|---|---|---|---|
| 0227 | N5105F | N631CB | | |
| 0228 | N5264U | N41199 | SE-RFK | N221LC |
| 0229 | N5147B | N61KT | | |
| 0230 | N375QS | | | |
| 0231 | N5264S | N570RZ | | |
| 0232 | N51444 | TC-ATP | | |
| 0233 | N5036Q | N208MF | | |
| 0234 | N5057F | G-CFGB | | |
| 0235 | N50054 | N361QS | | |
| 0236 | N633CS | N680LN | | |
| 0237 | N51042 | N21NR | | |
| 0238 | N28WE | | | |
| 0239 | N680RP | | | |
| 0240 | N52623 | N396QS | | |
| 0241 | N5246Z | N2157D | PR-BRS | |
| 0242 | N52178 | N324QS | | |
| 0243 | N51896 | N520G | | |
| 0244 | N634CS | N955KC | | |
| 0245 | N5221Y | N382QS | | |
| 0246 | N5162W | SU-SMC | | |
| 0247 | N5185J | N9661S | | |
| 0248 | N5269Z | N312QS | N95SJ | |
| 0249 | N456CJ | N219LC | | |
| 0250 | N5231S | N680JG | VH-VPL | |
| 0251 | N5201M | C-GDCP | | |
| 0252 | N5296X | PR-SMK | | |
| 0253 | N51869 | LX-DEC | | |
| 0254 | N5194J | ZS-AKG | | |
| 0255 | N5206T | (N681MR) | N680PA | |
| 0256 | N5068R | N631RP | | |
| 0257 | N188TL | | | |
| 0258 | N51744 | N21654 | N702AB | |
| 0259 | N5212M | N310QS | PR-AGP | |
| 0260 | N5031E | PP-AAD | | |
| 0261 | N5227G | N261SV | N261AH | |
| 0262 | N5257C | N262SV | N84EE | |
| 0263 | N51072 | N263SV | N41225 | TC-TVA |
| 0264 | N5065S | N68SL | | |
| 0265 | N5203S | M-ISLE | | |
| 0266 | N5154J | N696HC | | |
| 0267 | N51564 | PR-RTJ | | |
| 0268 | N5197M | N6GU | | |
| 0269 | N51511 | | | |
| 0270 | N52699 | N41221 | SU-SMD | |
| 0271 | N5132T | OO-ALX | | |
| 0272 | N5063P | N2465N | TC-RED | |
| 0273 | N5145P | N6242R | | |
| 0274 | N5267D | N41222 | SU-SME | |
| 0275 | N635CS | | | |
| 0276 | N5223D | G-CPRR | | |
| 0277 | N5094D | N88JJ | | |
| 0278 | N5201J | N278SV | | |
| 0279 | N5264A | OK-EMA | | |
| 0280 | N5064Q | HB-JIG | | |
| 0281 | N5145V | N149JS | | |
| 0282 | N5203J | OE-GJM | | |
| 0283 | N52369 | (SU-SMF) | N680AK | |
| 0284 | N5109R | N284RP | | |
| 0285 | N5264S | N61855 | JY-AWH | |
| 0286 | N5036Q | N715WE | | |
| 0287 | N681HS | | | |
| 0288 | N5267J | N288JA | | |
| 0289 | N5247U | N680FD | | |
| 0290 | | | | |
| 0291 | N5268E | N682HS | | |
| 0292 | N292CS | | | |
| 0293 | | | | |
| 0294 | | | | |
| 0295 | | | | |
| 0296 | | | | |
| 0297 | | | | |
| 0298 | | | | |
| 0299 | | | | |
| 0300 | | | | |
| 0301 | | | | |
| 0302 | | | | |
| 0303 | | | | |

# CESSNA 750 CITATION X

| C/n | Identities | | | | | | | |
|---|---|---|---|---|---|---|---|---|
| 703 | N750CX | [ff 21Dec93; ff with winglets 25Sep07] | | | | | | |
| 0001 | N751CX | [ff 27Sep94] | | TC-ATV | N754SE | HB-JGU | | |
| 0002 | N752CX | N902QS | (N752VP) | C-FPUI | N902VP | | | |
| 0003 | N5223D | N1AP | N200AP | (N300AT) | (N300VP) | | | |
| 0004 | N5223P | N754CX | (N96UD) | N597U | N62VE | PR-LUZ | | |
| 0005 | N5263S | N99BB | | | | | | |
| 0006 | N5263U | N76D | N484T | N484H | N706VP | | | |
| 0007 | N52655 | N750EC | | | | | | |
| 0008 | N5266F | N1014X | N353WC | N853WC | N708VP | N750CW | | |
| 0009 | N5223Y | N96TX | N909QS | (N109VP) | N978DB | | | |
| 0010 | N5225K | N5112 | N5112S | N808CZ | PR-CTA | | | |
| 0011 | N5122X | N944H | N944D | N960KC | | | | |
| 0012 | N52136 | N966H | N912QS | N712VP | VH-RCA | | | |
| 0013 | N5241Z | N5113 | N5113S | LV-BRJ | | | | |
| 0014 | N5244F | N757T | (N14VP) | N478PM | | | | |
| 0015 | N5085E | N715CX | N326SU | N915QS | N715VP | VH-XCJ | | |
| 0016 | N5263U | N206PC | N521FP | | | | | |
| 0017 | N51072 | N5114 | N5144 | | | | | |
| 0018 | N5091J | N95CC | N5115 | N199WT | | | | |
| 0019 | N5109W | N5116 | N199XP | | | | | |
| 0020 | N5125J | N95CM | N8JC | N8JQ | | | | |
| 0021 | N5131M | (N164M) | N138A | N630M | N61KB | N49FW | | |
| 0022 | N51313 | (N5116) | N52639 | (N722CX) | N10JM | OH-CXO | (N750AG) | N750VP |
| 0023 | N5000R | N923QS | N923VP | | | | | |
| 0024 | N52682 | N164M | N5125J | N924EJ | N504SU | N942QS | | |
| 0025 | N50612 | N750RL | [2500th Citation built] | | | | | |
| 0026 | N5066U | N926QS | N926VP | | | | | |
| 0027 | N5068R | N354WC | N854WC | N27VP | | | | |
| 0028 | N5058J | N728CX | N100FF | PR-FNP | | | | |
| 0029 | N5090V | N500RP | N500FP | (N992QS) | N929EJ | N945QS | | |
| 0030 | N5095N | N355WC | N369B | | | | | |
| 0031 | N5061W | N22RG | | | | | | |
| 0032 | N932QS | | | | | | | |
| 0033 | N5093D | N710AW | | | | | | |
| 0034 | N934QS | N34VP | | | | | | |
| 0035 | N5071M | N97DK | N96DK | | | | | |
| 0036 | N5085E | N936QS | | | | | | |
| 0037 | N51160 | N75HS | | | | | | |
| 0038 | N51176 | (N938QS) | N739CX | N938EJ | N938CC | (N788CW) | N700LX | N710FL* |
| 0039 | N51055 | N98TX | N750LM | N22NG | N32NG | | | |
| 0040 | N52136 | N68LP | N68LF | N740VP | N40KW | N110PK | | |
| 0041 | N5066U | (N95CC) | (N22NG) | N98TX | C-GIWD | C-GIWZ | | |
| 0042 | N5090A | N95CM | N915RB | | | | | |
| 0043 | N5090Y | N943QS | | | | | | |
| 0044 | N5103J | N96RX | | | | | | |
| 0045 | N5109R | N45BR | N621FP | | | | | |
| 0046 | N5109W | N746CX | N946EJ | N749DX | N749P | | | |
| 0047 | N5091J | N947QS | | | | | | |
| 0048 | N5135A | N84PJ | | | | | | |
| 0049 | N5153K | N949QS | | | | | | |
| 0050 | N5156D | N950QS | | | | | | |
| 0051 | N5058J | N750J | (N1419J) | N119RM | (N119PM) | | | |
| 0052 | N5000R | N712JC | N681WD | PR-LAT | | | | |
| 0053 | N5061P | N795HG | (N795HC) | | | | | |
| 0054 | N45ST | N450T | N610HC | | | | | |
| 0055 | N5068R | N955QS | | | | | | |
| 0056 | N5105F | PP-JQM | | | | | | |
| 0057 | N505MA | N74VF | | | | | | |
| 0058 | N5120U | N758CX | N87N | | | | | |
| 0059 | N5108G | N751BH | | | | | | |
| 0060 | N5090Y | N95CM | N98CX | PR-JAQ | | | | |
| 0061 | N5109R | N961QS | | | | | | |
| 0062 | N724CC | | | | | | | |
| 0063 | N51038 | N750JB | | | | | | |
| 0064 | N964QS | N964EJ | N931QS | | | | | |
| 0065 | N5163C | (N965QS) | N750JJ | | | | | |
| 0066 | N750GM | | | | | | | |
| 0067 | N967QS | | | | | | | |
| 0068 | N5100J | N377SF | | | | | | |
| 0069 | N51055 | N100FR | N96TX | | | | | |
| 0070 | N970QS | | | | | | | |
| 0071 | N971QS | | | | | | | |
| 0072 | XA-VER | N72FD | | | | | | |
| 0073 | (N532JF) | N999CX | N269JR | N706LX | | | | |

# CITATION X

| C/n | Identities | | | | | | |
|---|---|---|---|---|---|---|---|
| 0074 | N774CZ | N2418Y | N2418N | N2418F | N7418F | N703LX | N713FL |
| 0075 | N5196U | G-HERS | (SE-DZX) | N21HE | N21HQ | P4-AND | |
| 0076 | N5197M | N400RB | N702LX | N702FL | | | |
| 0077 | N977QS | | | | | | |
| 0078 | N51160 | N199NP | (N711HE) | N121HE | N711HE | N711HQ | N707LX |
| 0079 | N979QS | | | | | | |
| 0080 | N5165T | ZS-SAB | (N178AT) | PT-PTL | | | |
| 0081 | N810X | N1BS | | | | | |
| 0082 | N82BG | (N242LT) | N705LX | | | | |
| 0083 | N983QS | | | | | | |
| 0084 | N984QS | | | | | | |
| 0085 | (N985QS) | N5103J | D-BTEN | | | | |
| 0086 | N5124F | N888CN | N986QS | | | | |
| 0087 | N987QS | | | | | | |
| 0088 | N5130J | N88EJ | | | | | |
| 0089 | N989QS | | | | | | |
| 0090 | N5132T | N1932P | N193ZP | C-GCUL | | | |
| 0091 | N5061P | N991EJ | N991CX | (N791CW) | N704LX | | |
| 0092 | N5066U | PT-WUM | | | | | |
| 0093 | N993QS | N71RP | N114VW | | | | |
| 0094 | N51038 | N750XX | N84EA | | | | |
| 0095 | N415FW | N19DD | | | | | |
| 0096 | N585M | | | | | | |
| 0097 | N5060K | (N81SN) | VP-CYK | C-FTEL | C-GIGT | C-GMNC | |
| 0098 | N5090V | N998EJ | N998CX | (N798CW) | | | |
| 0099 | N5090A | N442WT | N442WJ | N93TX | | | |
| 0100 | N5100J | N104CT | (N104UT) | N170HL | | | |
| 0101 | N901QS | N881G | N711VT | N711VJ | | | |
| 0102 | N51995 | N901QS | | | | | |
| 0103 | N5260Y | N96TX | N750HS | | | | |
| 0104 | N5147B | N5T | | | | | |
| 0105 | N905QS | | | | | | |
| 0106 | N52642 | N106CX | | | | | |
| 0107 | N5086W | N107CX | (N332CM) | N520CM | N307RX | | |
| 0108 | N51744 | N908QS | | | | | |
| 0109 | N900EJ | N750PT | N708LX | | | | |
| 0110 | N910QS | | | | | | |
| 0111 | N5264A | N750BP | | | | | |
| 0112 | N51072 | N1107Z | N173WF | (N910RL) | PR-GRD | | |
| 0113 | N913QS | | | | | | |
| 0114 | N50820 | N114CX | N701LX | | | | |
| 0115 | N5085E | OH-PPI | | | | | |
| 0116 | N916QS | | | | | | |
| 0117 | N50612 | N426CM | | | | | |
| 0118 | N5266F | N753BD | PR-XDY | | | | |
| 0119 | N5223X | XA-FMX | | | | | |
| 0120 | N920QS | | | | | | |
| 0121 | N51042 | N358WC | N93LA | | | | |
| 0122 | N800W | N577JC | | | | | |
| 0123 | N51038 | N900QS | | | | | |
| 0124 | N924QS | | | | | | |
| 0125 | N5061W | N444CX | N977AE | | | | |
| 0126 | N5076K | N962QS | | | | | |
| 0127 | N52639 | N15TT | | | | | |
| 0128 | N5145V | N67CX | N1873 | | | | |
| 0129 | N929QS | | | | | | |
| 0130 | N930QS | | | | | | |
| 0131 | N5155G | N131CX | C-GAPT | | | | |
| 0132 | N51055 | N627R | | | | | |
| 0133 | N933QS | | | | | | |
| 0134 | N51780 | CS-DCT | [impounded at Caracas-La Carlotta, Venezuela, 24Oct04] (YV1969) Venezuela 1060 | YV2470 | Venezuela 1060 | | |
| 0135 | N935QS | | | | | | |
| 0136 | N5058J | N799TG | N1DH | N8TU | XA-BAE | | |
| 0137 | N937QS | | | | | | |
| 0138 | N5241Z | N138SP | | | | | |
| 0139 | N5196U | N26MJ | | | | | |
| 0140 | N5112K | D-BLUE | CS-DGO | | | | |
| 0141 | N5068R | N941QS | | | | | |
| 0142 | N5172M | N700SW | | | | | |
| 0143 | N51744 | N825GA | | | | | |
| 0144 | N944QS | | | | | | |
| 0145 | N5174W | N145CX | (N745CW) | N709LX | | | |
| 0146 | N5152X | N750DM | | | | | |
| 0147 | N5085E | N147CX | (N787CW) | | | | |
| 0148 | N700LH | | | | | | |

# CITATION X

| C/n | Identities | | | | | | |
|---|---|---|---|---|---|---|---|
| 0149 | N52601 | N948QS | | | | | |
| 0150 | N51896 | TC-VZR | N750MD | N750TX | | | |
| 0151 | N951QS | | | | | | |
| 0152 | N51744 | OH-PPJ | N934BD | N750GS | | | |
| 0153 | N953QS | | | | | | |
| 0154 | N5206T | N8JC | | | | | |
| 0155 | N551AM | N73ME | | | | | |
| 0156 | N956QS | | | | | | |
| 0157 | N52081 | B-7021 | | | | | |
| 0158 | N958QS | | | | | | |
| 0159 | N5245D | N1128V | N7600G | | | | |
| 0160 | N960QS | | | | | | |
| 0161 | N5245L | I-KETO | N280DM | N232CF | | | |
| 0162 | N903QS | | | | | | |
| 0163 | N5253S | N610GR | | | | | |
| 0164 | N964QS | | | | | | |
| 0165 | N5257V | N15RL | | | | | |
| 0166 | N966QS | | | | | | |
| 0167 | N5117U | N802W | N4165Y | N721VT | | | |
| 0168 | N52653 | N1288B | N123SL | | | | |
| 0169 | N5248V | N68LP | N563BA | | | | |
| 0170 | N5060K | N90NF | | | | | |
| 0171 | N51160 | (B-....) | N399W | | | | |
| 0172 | N5066U | N750NS | | | | | |
| 0173 | N5093D | N173CX | N749DX | D2-EZR | | | |
| 0174 | N5270M | N174CX | N87SL | | | | |
| 0175 | N975QS | | | | | | |
| 0176 | N51806 | N1AP | | | | | |
| 0177 | N177EL | | | | | | |
| 0178 | N5152X | N275NM | N750BL | | | | |
| 0179 | N5147B | OE-HFE | HB-JEZ | | | | |
| 0180 | N51511 | N353WC | | | | | |
| 0181 | N181BR | N600AW | | | | | |
| 0182 | N982QS | | | | | | |
| 0183 | N938QS | | | | | | |
| 0184 | N51896 | I-JETX | HS-CDY | | | | |
| 0185 | N5223X | N7SB | N185CX | N45ST | N185CX | N370EK | N750DD |
| 0186 | N5188N | N970SK | | | | | |
| 0187 | N978QS | | | | | | |
| 0188 | N5163K | C-FTEN | | | | | |
| 0189 | N51984 | N93S | | | | | |
| 0190 | N990QS | | | | | | |
| 0191 | N5267G | N354WC | | | | | |
| 0192 | N51817 | N5FF | | | | | |
| 0193 | N939QS | | | | | | |
| 0194 | N5192E | N194CX | G-CDCX | | | | |
| 0195 | N5241R | N946QS | | | | | |
| 0196 | N996QS | | | | | | |
| 0197 | N585T | | | | | | |
| 0198 | N998QS | | | | | | |
| 0199 | N5245L | N484T | | | | | |
| 0200 | N952QS | | | | | | |
| 0201 | N907QS | | | | | | |
| 0202 | N300JD | | | | | | |
| 0203 | N999QS | | | | | | |
| 0204 | N5197M | N22NG | | | | | |
| 0205 | N5181U | N4005T | C-GSUX | | | | |
| 0206 | N906QS | | | | | | |
| 0207 | N5152X | N751GM | | | | | |
| 0208 | N997QS | | | | | | |
| 0209 | N52229 | N7SB | | | | | |
| 0210 | N51666 | N904QS | | | | | |
| 0211 | N5247U | N954QS | N954Q | N65ST | | | |
| 0212 | N51744 | N4101Z | N69SB | OY-LKS | | | |
| 0213 | N50715 | N9NG | | | | | |
| 0214 | N5154J | OE-HGG | | | | | |
| 0215 | N215CX | VH-TEN | | | | | |
| 0216 | N51817 | N1268F | N882KB | | | | |
| 0217 | N5166T | N217CX | (N221AL) | N217AL | | | |
| 0218 | N5223X | D-BLDI | | | | | |
| 0219 | N5192E | D-BKLI | N288CX | | | | |
| 0220 | N52613 | N48HF | | | | | |
| 0221 | N51042 | N256W | | | | | |
| 0222 | N5166U | N222CX | (N850PT) | N750PT | N722XJ | | |
| 0223 | N52526 | N918QS | | | | | |
| 0224 | N919QS | | | | | | |

## CITATION X

| C/n | Identities | | | | | | | |
|---|---|---|---|---|---|---|---|---|
| 0225 | N52526 | N5223D | N921QS | N5223D | N215RX | | | |
| 0226 | N5262X | N226CX | N257AL | | | | | |
| 0227 | N5267J | P4-LJG | M-DKDI | | | | | |
| 0228 | N5269Z | N228BD | N228DB | | | | | |
| 0229 | N5268A | N229CE | | | | | | |
| 0230 | N750WM | | | | | | | |
| 0231 | N5109R | N432AC | | | | | | |
| 0232 | N5120U | N232CX | OE-HAC | | | | | |
| 0233 | N51612 | N442WT | N442WP | | | | | |
| 0234 | N52526 | PP-AAA | | | | | | |
| 0235 | N400JD | | | | | | | |
| 0236 | N5246Z | N53HF | N349RR | | | | | |
| 0237 | N5228J | N5197M | PR-MJC | | | | | |
| 0238 | N5183U | N238CX | N78SL | | | | | |
| 0239 | N5268V | N500N | N50QN | N910DP | | | | |
| 0240 | N51666 | N40CX | N1962J | | | | | |
| 0241 | N5197M | N921QS | | | | | | |
| 0242 | N5194J | N1289G | 9M-ATM | | | | | |
| 0243 | N5214J | N373AB | | | | | | |
| 0244 | N52655 | N750GF | | | | | | |
| 0245 | N5269A | N200CQ | | | | | | |
| 0246 | N5214K | C-GSEC | C-GSEO | N812KD | N15SD | N490CC | | |
| 0247 | N5257C | N751PT | N747XJ | | | | | |
| 0248 | N5268A | N1298G | N48VE | (N750CR) | | | | |
| 0249 | N5109R | N49VE | N265RX | | | | | |
| 0250 | N52526 | N752PT | N750XJ | | | | | |
| 0251 | N5096S | N251CX | VP-CFZ | | | | | |
| 0252 | N5000R | N252CX | G-CEDK | | | | | |
| 0253 | N5268V | N253CX | | | | | | |
| 0254 | N52627 | N254CX | | | | | | |
| 0255 | N51666 | N712KC | | | | | | |
| 0256 | N5268A | N753PT | N756XJ | | | | | |
| 0257 | N5090A | N754PT | N757XJ | | | | | |
| 0258 | N5264N | N755PT | N758XJ | | | | | |
| 0259 | N52114 | OE-HAL | | | | | | |
| 0260 | N5260Y | N260CX | N760PT | N760XJ | | | | |
| 0261 | N5079V | OE-HJA | | | | | | |
| 0262 | N5093D | N262CX | SX-ECI | | | | | |
| 0263 | N52609 | N750DX | | | | | | |
| 0264 | N52462 | N764PT | N764XJ | | | | | |
| 0265 | N5262Z | N765PT | N765XJ | | | | | |
| 0266 | N5201M | N355WC | | | | | | |
| 0267 | N5267G | N17CX | | | | | | |
| 0268 | N5262W | CC-CPS | | | | | | |
| 0269 | N5066F | N769PT | N769XJ | | | | | |
| 0270 | N5165P | N270CX | N570PT | N770XJ | | | | |
| 0271 | N271CX | (M-KAZZ) | P4-BUS | | | | | |
| 0272 | N5200R | N772PT | N772XJ | | | | | |
| 0273 | N5132T | OE-HUB | | | | | | |
| 0274 | N5109W | N874PT | N774XJ | | | | | |
| 0275 | N5141F | N4119S | N104CT | | | | | |
| 0276 | N51743 | N776PT | N776XJ | | | | | |
| 0277 | N52178 | (OE-HEC) | [ntu marks worn at completion centre] | | | | UP-CS501 | VP-CEG |
| 0278 | N5203J | N778PT | N778XJ | | | | | |
| 0279 | N5031E | N879PT | N779XJ | | | | | |
| 0280 | N5163C | N780PT | N780XJ | | | | | |
| 0281 | N50639 | G-CTEN | | | | | | |
| 0282 | N5064M | N282CX | N782PT | N782XJ | | | | |
| 0283 | N5221Y | N711VT | | | | | | |
| 0284 | N52178 | N784PT | N784XJ | N750HH | | | | |
| 0285 | N5060K | N940QS | | | | | | |
| 0286 | N5245L | N786XJ | | | | | | |
| 0287 | N5183V | N787XJ | | | | | | |
| 0288 | N928QS | | | | | | | |
| 0289 | N52457 | N789XJ | | | | | | |
| 0290 | N5032K | N927QS | | | | | | |
| 0291 | N5125J | N2068G | M-PRVT | | | | | |
| 0292 | N51743 | N792XJ | | | | | | |
| 0293 | N5090A | N922QS | | | | | | |
| 0294 | N5168Y | N794XJ | | | | | | |
| 0295 | N5264E | N795XJ | | | | | | |
| 0296 | N914QS | | | | | | | |
| 0297 | N5268M | N797XJ | N797CX | | | | | |
| 0298 | N52114 | N20768 | HS-KCS | | | | | |
| 0299 | N925QS | N299CX | | | | | | |
| 0300 | N50639 | (N800XJ) | OE-HAK | | | | | |

# CITATION X

| C/n | Identities | |
|---|---|---|
| 0301 | N5156D | N92CX |
| 0302 | N750JT | |
| 0303 | N5244F | N442WT |
| 0304 | N5109W | |
| 0305 | N305CX | C-FNRG |
| 0306 | | |
| 0307 | | |
| 0308 | | |
| 0309 | | |
| 0310 | | |
| 0311 | | |
| 0312 | | |
| 0313 | | |
| 0314 | | |
| 0315 | | |
| 0316 | | |
| 0317 | | |
| 0318 | | |
| 0319 | | |
| 0320 | | |
| 0321 | | |
| 0322 | | |
| 0323 | | |
| 0324 | | |
| 0325 | | |
| 0326 | | |
| 0327 | | |
| 0328 | | |
| 0329 | | |
| 0330 | | |

# DASSAULT FALCON 10/100

| C/n | Series | Identities |
|---|---|---|
| 01 | 10 | F-WFAL [ff 01Dec70] [w/o 31Oct72 Romorantin, France] |
| 02 | 10 | F-WTAL [ff 15Oct71] F-ZJTA France 02/F-ZACB [wfu preserved at Ailes Anciennes Museum, Toulouse-Blagnac, France] |
| 03 | 10 | F-WSQN [ff 14Oct72] F-BSQN [CofA expired Apr81, wfu, cx 1988] |
| 1 | 10 | F-WSQU [ff 30Apr73] F-BSQU PH-ILT F-WJLH F-BJLH N333FJ |
| 2 | 10 | F-WJMM N10FJ N103JM C-GRIS |
| 3 | 10 | F-WJMJ N100FJ N731FJ N661GL (N10PN) N52TJ (N149DG) [wfu, cx 06Aug08] |
| 4 | 10 | F-WJMK N101FJ XB-SII EC-353 EC-FTV XA-SYY N888FJ [Parted out by White Inds, Bates City, MO] |
| 5 | 100 | F-WLCT F-BVPR F-V10F F-WVPR F-BVPR |
| 6 | 10 | F-WJML N102FJ N600BT (N110FJ) N10AG N139DD C-GRDT N54H N999MH N32BL N32VC N59CC N77JW |
| 7 | 10 | F-WJMN VR-BFF F-BXAG HB-VDE I-LUBE HB-VKE D-CASH HB-VKE N769SC [Parted out by White Inds, Bates City, MO] |
| 8 | 10 | F-WJMN N104FJ N21ES N21ET N21EK N88ME N108KC |
| 9 | 10 | F-WJMM N103FJ N10TX N149TJ N510CL |
| 10 | 10 | F-WJMJ N105FJ N253K [w/o 30Jan80 Chicago, IL; remains to White Inds, Bates City, MO, for spares] |
| 11 | 10 | F-WJMK N106FJ N23ES N23ET (N23ED) N942C N452DP (N190DB) N211TJ (N11WC) N419WC N858SP |
| 12 | 10 | F-WJML N107FJ N3100X N10F (N76TJ) |
| 13 | 10 | F-WLCS N108FJ N734S N210FJ N72EU N10JZ N777SN N15TX [b/u for spares 1992; cx Feb93] |
| 14 | 10 | F-WJMK SE-DEL N59TJ (N50B) N333KE |
| 15 | 10 | F-WJMM N109FJ N60MB [w/o 03Apr77 Denver, CO] |
| 16 | 10 | F-WLCT N110FJ N48TT F-GELA N416AS N416HC N127WL |
| 17 | 10 | F-WLCS OH-FFB VH-FFB N29966 N27DA N33HL F-GHDZ EC-949 F-GNDZ |
| 18 | 10 | F-WJMJ N111FJ N78MD N48MS (N74TJ) N1TJ N80CC N1TJ N241RS [parted out by Dodson Int'l Parts; canx Feb06] |
| 19 | 10 | F-WLCU N112FJ N30JM (N30JH) (N36KA) N36JM N937J F-GJFZ 3A-MGT [while regd and painted as 3A-MGT used call sign C-GORI at 1995 NBAA] LX-TRG N600HL |
| 20 | 10 | F-WLCV N113FJ N42G |
| 21 | 10 | F-WJMK (HB-VDT) 3D-ACB N40WJ N60ND N40ND |
| 22 | 10 | F-WLCX N114FJ N44JC N48JC F-GJLL VP-BBV |
| 23 | 10 | F-WLCY N115FJ N73B N310FJ N91MH N20WP N90LC XA-GPA |
| 24 | 10 | F-WJML N116FJ N1924V F-GBTI N301JJ N991RV N230RS N69GB |
| 25 | 10 | F-WJMJ N117FJ N40N N83RG N22EH N83RG N60FC N600GM N719AL N177BC C-GJET |
| 26 | 10 | F-WJMK N118FJ N592DC N707AM N720DF |
| 27 | 10 | F-WLCX SE-DDF OK-EEH N38DA XA-AAY |
| 28 | 10 | F-WJML N119FJ N130B N813AV N500DS N42EH (N655DB) |
| 29 | 10 | F-WJMM N120FJ N234U N66MF N332J N999F N404JW |
| 30 | 10 | F-WLCT N121FJ N294W N30FJ N156X N3WZ N191MC N171MC [w/o 24Jan96 Romulus, MI, as N191MC; to White Inds, Bates City, MO, for spares] |
| 31 | 10 | F-WLCU N122FJ N2MP N27C N50TC N81P (N952TC) (N29AA) N27AJ |
| 32 | MER | France 32 |
| 33 | 10 | F-WJMJ N123FJ N881P (N246N) N900UC F-GHFO N54WJ (N18BG) TC-ORM N20373 C-FBVF N33BV (N933TS) |
| 34 | 10 | F-WLCS N124FJ N110M N220M N18SK |
| 35 | 10 | F-WLCV N125FJ N54V N777JJ N83TJ N726MR N17WG N73LR |
| 36 | 10 | F-WJMJ HB-VDD N10UN N224CC N894CA N676PC N76AF XA-MMM |
| 37 | 10 | F-WJML C-GFCS N39515 N123VV N123TG N347K N48JC N72GW N945MC [b/u for spares by Air Salvage, Griffin, GA cx Feb04] |
| 38 | 10 | F-WJMM N127FJ N20ES N20ET N20EE F-GBRF |
| 39 | MER | F-WPUX France 39 [w/o 30Jan80 Toul-Rosieres, France] |
| 40 | 10 | F-WJMN N128FJ N10XX N15SJ XA-LIO N11697 [parted out by Dodson Int'l Parts, Rantoul, KS] |
| 41 | 10 | F-WLCS N129FJ N1HM N50DM N53DB F-GKLV N61TJ N116DD N34TJ |
| 42 | 10 | F-WLCU N126FJ N18X (N9147F) N100UB N282T |
| 43 | 10 | F-WJMN N135FJ N1515P N510CP (F-GHFI) F-GIQP N17TJ |
| 44 | 10 | F-WJMJ N130FJ N205X N62TJ N277SF N244TJ (N90AB) C-FZOP |
| 45 | 10 | F-WJML N131FJ N120HC N110CG C-FTEN N444CR PR-EGB |
| 46 | 10 | F-WLCT N134FJ N911RF N815LC (N908SB) N908RF N401JW |
| 47 | 10 | F-WLCY N132FJ YV-07CP PJ-AYA YV-221CP YV-101CP N3914L N101GZ N91LA N90LA N79PB (N190MD) F-GJGB [w/o 30Sep93 Besancon, France] |
| 48 | 10 | F-WJMM N133FJ N720ML N720ME N333SR F-WGTF F-GHRV LX-EPA N20LW |
| 49 | 10 | F-WLCV N136FJ (N490A) N49AS N449A N26EN N700TT PT-LMO N67LC |
| 50 | 10 | F-WLCS VH-MEI (ZK-WNL) N133FJ PT-OHM N411SC N299DB |
| 51 | 10 | F-WJML N137FJ N51BP N909TF |
| 52 | 10 | F-WLCX N138FJ N342G N52TJ N8100E N860E N711TF (N117RR) |
| 53 | 10 | F-WLCS N139FJ N8100E N810US N125EM (N890E) N891CQ I-LCJG N53WA HI-836SP N824LA |
| 54 | 10 | F-WPUU N140FJ (XA-SAR) N464AC N4875 N53SN N54FJ VR-BFW VP-BFW N561D N110LA N791CP |
| 55 | 10 | F-WPUV N141FJ N55FJ N702NC N702NG N700AL (N700PD) |

# FALCON 10/100

| C/n | Series | Identities |
|---|---|---|
| 56 | 10 | F-WPUY HB-VDX OY-FRM N56WJ N16DD N56WJ N297PF |
| 57 | 10 | F-WJMJ N142FJ N142V N50TB (N50YJ) N10YJ (N6366W) [w/o 30Jun97 White Plains, NY; parted out by White Inds, Bates City, MO] |
| 58 | 10 | F-WJMM N143FJ N76FJ N58AS N458A N500FF (F-GHJL) N170CS [cx 29Oct07 after cracks found in fuselage] |
| 59 | 10 | F-WJMN N144FJ N300GN N300A N302A N633WW N52JA |
| 60 | 10 | F-WJML N145FJ N77GT N810E SE-DKD N69WJ N769BH |
| 61 | 10 | F-WPUV D-CBMB F-WZGD (F-BIPF) F-BFDG 3D-ART [w/o 03Oct86 Magoebaskloof, Transvaal, S Africa] |
| 62 | 10 | F-WJMM N146FJ N12LB N6VG |
| 63 | 10 | F-WLCX N147FJ PT-KTO N70TS N876MA |
| 64 | 10 | F-WLCT N148FJ N100BG N721DP N500DE N718CA N444WJ [parted out by White Inds, Bates City, MO] |
| 65 | 10 | F-WJMJ N149FJ XB-BAK N21DB (F-GJMA) N66CF |
| 66 | 10 | F-WJMN N150FJ N50RL YV-70CP N63TS [parted out by AvMATS, St Louis, MO] |
| 67 | 10 | F-WLCU N151FJ D-COME N427CJ YV2474 |
| 68 | 10 | F-WLCV N152FJ N7NP (N7NL) N11DH N91DH N80MP F-GFPF |
| 69 | 10 | F-WJML N153FJ N43CC N3RC F-GELE N7TJ N711JC N530TC |
| 70 | 10 | F-WJMM HB-VEG F-WQCO VR-BCH VP-BCH N349JC |
| 71 | 10 | F-WJMM D-CMAN N229JB (N728SA) (N203PV) N190H (N202PV) N341DB N220KS |
| 72 | 10 | F-WLCX N154FJ N10TB N31SJ N50TY ZS-FOX |
| 73 | 10 | F-WNGL N155FJ N88AT C-GDCO N130FJ YV-601CP N130FJ VR-BNT N378C N362PT |
| 74 | 10 | F-WJMJ N156FJ N30TH N34TH N518S N108MR N5JY N55FJ [displayed at Aerospace Museum of California, Sacramento/McClellan, CA] |
| 75 | 10 | F-WNGM N157FJ N12U N937D (N75MH) N97TJ N796SF N97DD N97DX N71TS [cx Mar06, b/u] |
| 76 | 10 | F-WPUU F-BYCC N727TS N528JD |
| 77 | 10 | F-WNGN N158FJ N82MD N301HC N53TS N107TB N607TC |
| 78 | 10 | F-WLCT N159FJ N83MD (N83MF) N784CE N178TJ N199SA C-FEXD |
| 79 | 10 | F-WPXB F-BPXB N160FJ N73B N692US |
| 80 | 10 | F-WPXD N161FJ N48R F-GMJS N1080Q N39RE (N320GP) N577RT N4RT (N803RA) N567RA |
| 81 | 10 | F-WPXF N162FJ N700BD N81TX |
| 82 | 10 | F-WPXE N168FJ N97MC N602NC N101HS |
| 83 | 10 | F-WPXG N163FJ N5GD XA-FIU N83EA N67TJ N76MB N724AS |
| 84 | 10 | F-WPXH N164FJ N8447A JA8447 N8447A N526D N6PA N192MC (N100TW) N106TW |
| 85 | 10 | F-WPXI N165FJ N85JM (N95DW) (OE-...) [w/o 17Feb93 Aurillac, France; to White Inds, Bates City, MO, for spares 1993] |
| 86 | 10 | F-WPXJ N166FJ N410WW N411WW N50TE [w/o at McCall, ID, 18Dec1992; to White Inds, Bates City, MO, for spares] |
| 87 | 10 | F-WPXK N167FJ (N200AF) N662D N682D C-FBSS N80TS N99BL N549AS C-FNND N156BF N156BE N515LP |
| 88 | 10 | F-WPXL N169FJ N3600X (F-GKCD) F-GHER N71M |
| 89 | 10 | F-WPXM D-CADB F-WZGF I-CAIC 3X-GCI HB-VIG I-EJIC HB-VKF D-CENT TC-AND (N888WJ) N23TJ |
| 90 | 10 | F-WNGD N170FJ N14U N12TX [parted out by White Inds, Bates City, MO, Jun06] |
| 91 | 10 | F-WJMJ D-CBAG N790US N23VP |
| 92 | 10 | F-WNGM N172FJ (N61BP) N1PB (N58B) F-GHLT N95TJ N724DS N824DS |
| 93 | 10 | F-WNGN F-BYCV N40180 (N98TW) [to White Inds, Bates City, MO, for spares] |
| 94 | 10 | F-WNGO N171FJ N54RS N13BK |
| 95 | 10 | F-WPXD N173FJ PT-ASJ [w/o 17Feb89 nr Rio-Santos Dumont, Brazil] |
| 96 | 10 | F-WNGD N174FJ XA-SAR OE-GLG I-LCJT N174FJ N96TJ N115TD |
| 97 | 10 | F-WPXF N175FJ |
| 98 | 10 | F-WPXG D-CBUR [w/o 08Aug96 near Offenburg, Germany] |
| 99 | 10 | F-WPXH N176FJ N10TJ (N65HS) N656PC N500GM N67JW F-GKBC N63BA N923HB (N923HE) N715JC |
| 100 | 10 | F-WPXI N177FJ N10FJ YV-17CP (N217CP) N100FJ XA-MGM [cx 2008; stored Spirit of St Louis, MO, pending resale] |
| 101 | MER | F-WPXJ France 101 |
| 102 | 10 | F-WPXK N178FJ N61BP N908TF |
| 103 | 10 | F-WPXL F-GBMH N103TJ N339TG N103TJ N9TE N26TJ N63XG |
| 104 | 10 | F-WPUU N179FJ N90DM VR-BHJ N4557P N913V N913VL N800SB N100CU |
| 105 | 10 | F-WPUV N180FJ N942B N71TJ N711MT N16DD N16WJ N804JJ |
| 106 | 10 | F-WPUX N181FJ N1JN N10FJ N730PV (N918PC) N902PC N913VS N103MM N20CF |
| 107 | 10 | F-WPUY N182FJ XB-ZRB XB-CAM XB-FWX XC-ZRB N160TJ N100T N91BP N907TF |
| 108 | 10 | F-WPUZ (HZ-KAI) HZ-AKI F-WZGF F-BIPC N246FJ N11DH N91DH N88LD (F-GFJK) F-GJHK [w/o 26Mar92 Brest, France; scrapped Mar93] |
| 109 | 10 | F-WNGD N183FJ N77NR C6-BEN N69EC N89EC N840GL |
| 110 | 10 | F-WNGO N184FJ N90MH N901MH I-SHIP N712US N104DD N43US N653FJ |
| 111 | 10 | F-WNGO N185FJ N8200E N820CE N10HE N289CA |
| 112 | 10 | F-WPXD N186FJ N12XX N12MB N598JC [parted out by White Inds, Bates City, MO; cx 29Apr09] |

# FALCON 10/100

| C/n | Series | Identities |
|---|---|---|
| 113 | 10 | F-WPXE (I-SHOP) I-CHOC HB-VIW (F-GFHG) F-GFHH LX-DPA VP-BGD N220PA (N716JC) |
| 114 | 10 | F-WPXF N187FJ N200YM N100YM N807F N15TM N555DH N108TG N982MC [cx 03Feb10, scrapped] |
| 115 | 10 | F-WPXH N188FJ N511S N211SR N420JD F-GGAR I-ITPR N115WA N636SC N169LS |
| 116 | 10 | F-WNGL N189FJ N4DS (N927DS) N925DS N525RC F-GJMA [w/o 27Sep96 Madrid-Barajas, Spain, but still current with no C of A] |
| 117 | 10 | F-WPXG N190FJ N23DS N923DS N18MX |
| 118 | 10 | F-WPXI HZ-AMA HZ-NOT HZ-A02 N848MP I-DNOR F-GJJL HB-VJN F-GIJG N41TJ (N97RJ) N118AD |
| 119 | 10 | F-WPXK N191FJ N257W N257V N119SJ |
| 120 | 10 | F-WPXM N192FJ N20ES N359V N369V N100WG N402JW N710JC N631KA* |
| 121 | 10 | F-WPUU (HB-VFS) HB-VFT F-GDLR N381MF |
| 122 | 10 | F-WPUV N193FJ N22ES N312A N312AT OE-GSC N911UN (N104KW) |
| 123 | 10 | F-WPUX N194FJ N23ES N312AT N312AM N312AN N50TK N25FF SE-DKC N23WJ N110TP N689WC |
| 124 | 10 | F-WPUY F-GBTC [w/o 15Jan86 nr Chalon-Vatry, France] |
| 125 | 10 | F-WNGD N195FJ N400SP N100CK XA-SAR N269SW |
| 126 | 10 | F-WNGM (N196FJ) I-CHIC F-WZGS I-CHIC HB-VIX (F-GFHH) F-GFHG N26WJ N36WJ PR-CDF |
| 127 | 10 | F-WZGG F-GCTT I-CALC N8GA (N7RZ) ZS-SEB |
| 128 | 10 | F-WNGO N197FJ N1871R N79HA N79PB N99MC N99BC N175BC N228SJ P4-AVN CN-TKN |
| 129 | MER | F-WZGA France 129 |
| 130 | 10 | F-WZGB I-SFRA (N777ND) N921GS N432EZ N454DP |
| 131 | 10 | F-WZGC N196FJ N654PC (D-CAJC) HB-VME N133EP |
| 132 | 10 | F-WZGD N198FJ N500GS N580GS SE-DKB N250MA TC-ATI [dbr Nov94 Le Bourget A/P, Paris, France; cx Mar95] N9258U [fuselage with White Inds, Bates City, MO by Apr96; cx 29Oct07] |
| 133 | MER | F-WZGE F-ZGTI France 133 |
| 134 | 10 | F-WZGF N202FJ N900T N509TC VH-MCX VH-WJW |
| 135 | 10 | F-WZGG N199FJ N835F N969F N707CX N245SP N707CX N272DN |
| 136 | 10 | F-WZGH I-MUDE F-WZGS F-GFMD |
| 137 | 10 | F-WZGI N200FJ N837F C-GTVO [cx to USA 24May05, no N-number allocated - parted out?] |
| 138 | 10 | F-WZGJ N203FJ N30TH N100BG (N942M) F-GGVR N236DJ C-GNVT [w/o 14Jan01 Kuujuaq, Quebec] |
| 139 | 10 | F-WZGK N204FJ N10AH (N810J) (N610J) (N110J) (N803SR) N110J N518RJ* [wfu Fort Lauderdale Executive, FL] |
| 140 | 10 | F-WZGL N205FJ N70WC N88WL F-GHDX |
| 141 | 10 | F-WZGM N206FJ (N10AH) N900D N77SF |
| 142 | 10 | F-WZGN N207FJ N10HK N11DH N5LP N174B |
| 143 | MER | F-WZGO France 143 |
| 144 | 10 | F-WZGP N208FJ N1TC (N79FJ) N101TF (N144HE) N502BG N502PG |
| 145 | 10 | F-WZGQ N209FJ N244A |
| 146 | 10 | F-WZGR N211FJ F-GHVK (N17ZU) N461AS XA-CEG N110GF XA-CEG XA-UJG |
| 147 | 10 | F-WZGS N212FJ N12TX F-GHPL N125GA N212FJ |
| 148 | 10 | F-WZGT N213FJ N103PJ N79TJ |
| 149 | 10 | F-WZGU N214FJ N711FJ (N830SR) N711EJ |
| 150 | 10 | F-WZGV N215FJ N212N N212NC (HB-V..) N99WA 9Q-CCA |
| 151 | 10 | F-WZGX N217FJ N26CP OE-GAG N4581R N27AC N256W N256V RP-C9999 |
| 152 | 10 | F-WZGY N216FJ N8463 JA8463 N8463 F-GDRN SE-DPK N152WJ N999LL (N999AH) |
| 153 | 10 | F-WZGZ N218FJ N344A N81P N81PX N600TW |
| 154 | 10 | F-WZGA N219FJ PT-LCO N777FJ N149HP [to White Inds, Bates City, MO, Oct97 for spares] |
| 155 | 10 | F-WZGC (N220FJ) D-CIEL N725PA F-GTOD |
| 156 | 10 | F-WZGE N221FJ N618S SE-DEK ZS-SEA |
| 157 | 10 | F-WZGF N222FJ (N900AR) N101EF N80GP F-GFBG N157EA N64AM N703JS (N157JA) (N814AA) (N450CT) N76AM |
| 158 | 10 | F-WZGI N223FJ N81LB N220SC N790FH N700FH |
| 159 | 10 | F-WZGJ N224FJ N224RP N224BP (N88TB) N10WE N707DC N707AM |
| 160 | 10 | F-WZGK N225FJ N223HS N31TM F-GFFP LX-JCG (ZS-SEB) N160FJ |
| 161 | 10 | F-WZGM N230FJ N30CN N50SL I-CREM F-WWZK I-CREM G-ECJI F-GOJI* |
| 162 | 10 | F-WZGN N226FJ N664JB N796MA N47RK (N162TJ) (N713G) N170MK N602DM N425JR |
| 163 | 10 | F-WZGP N227FJ N151WC N163F F-GJRN (N2CH) N163CH N163AV (N73TJ) N983CC N83JJ N50HT |
| 164 | 10 | F-WZGQ N228FJ N222MU |
| 165 | 10 | F-WZGR N229FJ N111WW N56LP N707CG [cx Oct05; parted out by Dodson Int'l Parts, Rantoul, KS] |
| 166 | 10 | F-WZGS N232FJ N94MC (F-GIPH) F-GJFB N94MG N747AC N21CL (N166SS) N211EC |
| 167 | 10 | F-WZGT N233FJ N39K 5V-TAE 5V-MBG 5V-TAE N167AC N516SM N82CG N111WW |

# FALCON 10/100

| C/n | Series | Identities | | | | | | | | |
|---|---|---|---|---|---|---|---|---|---|---|
| 168 | 10 | F-WZGU | N234FJ | N175BL | N43EC | | | | | |
| 169 | 10 | F-WZGV | N235FJ | VH-DJT | N725P | F-GHFB | (N107AF) | PT-WSF | | |
| 170 | 10 | F-WZGX | N236FJ | N821LG | [w/o 22Feb86 Westchester, PA] | | | | | |
| 171 | 10 | F-WZGY | N237FJ | N30TB | N26ES | PT-OIC | N42US | | | |
| 172 | 10 | F-WZGZ | N238FJ | YV-99CP | N172CP | N10NC | | | | |
| 173 | 10 | F-WZGA | N239FJ | N72BB | N441DM | N211CN | N555SR | N554SR | 9A-CRL | N8LT |
| 174 | 10 | F-WZGE | N240FJ | N5ES | N402ES | RP-C1911 | | | | |
| 175 | 10 | F-WZGF | N241FJ | XA-LOK | N12EP | | | | | |
| 176 | 10 | F-WZGI | N242FJ | HK-2968X | HK-2968 | N179AG | N66HH | N231JH | | |
| 177 | 10 | F-WZGJ | N243FJ | N533CS | F-GFGB | N101VJ | | | | |
| 178 | 10 | F-WZGK | N244FJ | N10QD | N79BP | N87TH | | | | |
| 179 | 10 | F-WZGL | I-DJMA | (F-GGRA) | F-GERO | N100RR | N3PW | N777RF | | |
| 180 | 10 | F-WZGM | N245FJ | N593DC | N398DC | N25MC | N211JL | | | |
| 181 | 10 | F-WZGC | N247FJ | N87GT | N151GS | (N151DC) | F-GJHG | N138DM | | |
| 182 | 10 | F-WZGN | N248FJ | N111MU | N809F | C-GOJC | | | | |
| 183 | 100 | F-WZGO | N249FJ | N82CR | N183SR | SE-DLB | | | | |
| 184 | 10 | F-WZGP | N250FJ | N346P | N4AC | (C-....) | N725DM | | | |
| 185 | MER | F-WZGQ | France 185 | F-WQBJ | France 185 | | | | | |
| 186 | 10 | F-WZGB | N251FJ | N2426 | N2426G | N63TJ | N420PC | N186TJ | N555DH | N555DZ |
| 187 | 10 | F-WZGR | N252FJ | N2427F | "N2427N" | N81TJ | N303PL | N555DH | N1DH | (N600AP) |
| | | N5CA | | | | | | | | |
| 188 | 10 | F-WZGS | N253FJ | N188DH | N64F | D-CLLL | HB-VJM | I-TFLY | N84TJ | |
| 189 | 10 | F-WZGT | N254FJ | N605T | N60SL | N600PB | N812KC | N189JM | N155PX | |
| 190 | 10 | F-WZGU | N255FJ | N1887S | N36BG | N190L | C-FBNW | | | |
| 191 | 10 | F-WZGV | N256FJ | N700DK | [w/o 23Sep85 Palwaukee, IL] | | | | | |
| 192 | 100 | F-WZGX | N258FJ | N100FJ | N121FJ | [w/o 15Oct87 Sacramento, CA] | | | | |
| 193 | 100 | F-WZGY | N259FJ | N3BY | OH-AMB | (N30TN) | EC-HVV | | | |
| 194 | 100 | F-WZGZ | N260FJ | N100FJ | N61FC | F-GIPH | | | | |
| 195 | 100 | F-WZGA | N261FJ | N561NC | N5736 | N10NL | (N10NV) | N95WJ | TS-IAM | F-WWZL |
| | | TS-IAM | N1993 | | | | | | | |
| 196 | 100 | F-WZGB | N262FJ | N581NC | N5734 | N573J | N125CA | C-FICA | | |
| 197 | 100 | F-WZGC | F-GEDB | F-WEDB | F-GEDB | N888G | N52N | | | |
| 198 | 100 | F-WZGF | N263FJ | N551NC | N5738 | N100RB | N1PB | N91PB | N25ST | |
| 199 | 100 | F-WZGG | N264FJ | N330MC | (N1CN) | N39TH | PT-OXB | N886MJ | N486MJ | N96VR |
| | | N60HM | N655PE | | | | | | | |
| 200 | 100 | F-WZGG | N265FJ | N662D | (N682D) | N80BL | N808L | N1JW | | |
| 201 | 100 | F-WZGH | N266FJ | N8494 | JA8494 | N30TH | (F-GKPZ) | F-GKCC | N100NW | N844F |
| 202 | 100 | F-WZGD | F-GDSA | 3D-ADR | N80WJ | N202DN | [w/o 09Dec01 Lawrence A/P, KS. To White Inds, Bates City, MO, for spares] | | | |
| 203 | 100 | F-WZGJ | N267FJ | VR-CLA | N100CT | XA-TBL | N45JB | N54FH | F-WQBM | I-FJDC |
| | | F-GPGL | | | | | | | | |
| 204 | 100 | F-WZGK | N268FJ | N101EU | F-WGTG | XA-TAB | XA-UDP | C-FFEV | | |
| 205 | 100 | F-WZGL | N269FJ | N700DW | N606AM | | | | | |
| 206 | 100 | F-WZGM | N270FJ | N100FJ | N367F | N46MK | | | | |
| 207 | 100 | F-WZGN | N271FJ | N711MT | F-GKPB | (N107US) | N207US | N456CM | N55DG | N456CM |
| | | N55DG | ZS-JLK | | | | | | | |
| 208 | 100 | F-WZGO | F-GELS | I-OANN | N71M | F-WQBJ | F-GSLZ | | | |
| 209 | 100 | F-WZGP | N272FJ | N312AT | (N312AR) | HB-VKR | OY-PHN | EC-KPP | | |
| 210 | 100 | F-WZGR | N273FJ | N312AM | N812AM | N85WN | N35WN | N110PP | N210EM | VP-BAF |
| | | [w/o Samedan, Switzerland, 12Feb09] | | | | | | | | |
| 211 | 100 | F-WZGT | F-GELT | | | | | | | |
| 212 | 100 | F-WZGU | CN-TNA | F-WWZM | CN-TNA | CN-ANZ | | | | |
| 213 | 100 | F-WZGV | N274FJ | ZK-MAZ | F-GKAE | F-WKAE | N711HF | | | |
| 214 | 100 | F-WZGX | N275FJ | N147G | N147GX | | | | | |
| 215 | 100 | F-WZGY | F-GHPB | | | | | | | |
| 216 | 100 | F-WZGZ | N276FJ | N100H | VH-JDW | 9M-ATM | N999WJ | SE-DYB | | |
| 217 | 100 | F-WZGA | N277FJ | N100FJ | N100WG | F-GIFL | N68GT | N214RV | | |
| 218 | 100 | F-WZGB | F-GHSK | TC-ARK | N218BA | N130DS | N303FZ | | | |
| 219 | 100 | F-WZGC | N123FJ | N2649 | PT-ORS | N219JW | N485AS | | | |
| 220 | 100 | F-WZGD | N124FJ | N368F | N326EW | N326LW | N702NC | N569DW | | |
| 221 | 100 | F-WZGH | OE-GHA | F-GPFD | | | | | | |
| 222 | 100 | F-WZGF | N125FJ | N100CK | N98VR | N100YP | | | | |
| 223 | 100 | F-WZGG | N126FJ | PT-LVD | | | | | | |
| 224 | 100 | F-WZGH | N128FJ | (PT-...) | C-FREE | N135FJ | SE-DVP | F-WWZN | SE-DVP | |
| 225 | 100 | F-WZGI | N127FJ | PT-LXJ | N225CC | (N814PJ) | | | | |
| 226 | 100 | F-WZGJ | N130FJ | XA-RLX | N121AT | | | | | |

Production complete

# DASSAULT FALCON 20/200

Notes: "European Line Numbers" are quoted alongside the c/n where appropriate. These were numbers allocated by Dassault for administrative purposes but do from time to time get quoted as the c/n on its own, or jointly with the actual c/n.

Aircraft converted as part of the TFE-731 re-engining programme are known as 20-5s; known conversions are shown in the series column. Aircraft with TFE-731-5A engines (the earlier conversion) retain the series number in the designation, eg 20C-5 (c/n 24), while later conversions which use the TFE-731-5B engines (as also used in the Falcon 900B) do not retain the series letter; we have however retained this so that readers can be aware of the original model type.

Was known as the CC117 while in Canadian military service

| C/n | Series | Identities |
|---|---|---|
| 01 | 20 | F-WLKB [ff 04May63] F-BLKB F-WLKB [last flt 06Feb76; used as mock-up for Guardian trials: donated to Musee de L'Air, Le Bourget, Paris, France] |
| 1/401 | 20C | F-WMSH [ff 01Jan65] F-BMSH F-WMSH France 1/F-ZACV [wfu 31Dec81; TT 6,248 hrs, with 13,329 landings; to Bordeaux-Merignac Museum as F-WMSH] |
| 2/402 | 20C | F-WMSS F-BMSS [canx Jan04 as wfu; to Musee de l'Air et de l'Espace site at Le Bourget, France on 02Mar05] |
| 3/403 | 20C | F-WMKG F-BMSX VR-BCG HB-VAV N92MH N301R [wfu Oscoda, MI] |
| 4 | 20C | F-WMKF N801F N116JD N121GW [w/o 18May78 Memphis, TN] |
| 5 | 20C | F-WMKI N804F N747W F-GJPR N295TW |
| 6 | 20C | F-WMKH F-BMKH N805F N20JM N21JM (N21DT) C-GOQG N65311 N497 N750SS EC-EDC |
| 7 | 20C | F-WMKK N807F N607S N740L CF-GWI N777FA N20GH N12GH N110CE N93CP N600JC XA-ACI N666BT [canx 28Jly05; b/u] |
| 8 | 20C | F-WMKJ N806F N1500 N150CG N1500 N190BD N612GA N277RA |
| 9 | 20C | F-WMKI N809F N366G N3668 C-GSKA LV-PLC LV-WMF N611GA [wfu; cx 24Dec08] |
| 10 | 20C | F-WMKK N810F N111M [b/u for spares; cx Aug87, remains at Av-Mats' facility at Paynesville, MO] |
| 11 | 20C | F-WMKH N808F CF-SRZ N2200M N220CM N30CC N30CQ N4351M N4351N N409PC OO-DDD N983AJ N216CA [wfu at Addison, TX] |
| 12 | 20C | F-WMKI N803F N221B N51SF LN-AAB [cx Mar89; to USA, no marks allocated; b/u for spares Jul89 Memphis, TN] |
| 13 | 20C | F-WMKH F-BOEF TR-LOL F-BOEF D-CILL F-BTCY N977TW |
| 14 | 20C | F-WMKJ N804F CF-DML N22DL N22HC N91JF N41MH |
| 15 | 20C | F-WMKK N806F N622R N1502 N151CG N1501 [wfu at Detroit-Willow Run by Nov03] |
| 16 | 20DC | F-WNGL N807F N354H N10FE N122CA N120AF N216TW N216SA [parted out by Dodson Av'n, Rantoul, KS] |
| 17 | 20C | F-WMKF N802F N545C N5450 N5C N5CE N55TH N234CA [wfu at Addison, TX] |
| 18 | 20C | F-WNGM N840F N803LC D-COLO N777JF N9DM N210RS [wfu 1996 for spares] |
| 19 | 20C | F-WNGN N841F N500PC N500PX N41PC (N41PD) C-GKHA [b/u for spares Mar04 at Ottawa-Rockcliffe, Canada] |
| 20 | 20DC | F-WMKJ N842F N367G N367GA N5FE (N146FE) (N25FR) N903FR G-FRAJ |
| 21 | 20C | F-WMKI N843F N3444G N370 (N500NU) N500EW N91TS XA-SWC N20LT C-FTUT N50446 [wfu at Addison, TX] |
| 22/404 | 20C | F-WMKK F-BMKK France 22/F-ZACS [wfu Bonneuil-en-France, nr Le Bourget, France] |
| 23 | 20C | F-WNGL F-BNKX N844F N424JX N15CC N256EN N256MA (N582G) Venezuela 5761 [stored El Libertador, Venezuela] |
| 24 | 20C-5 | F-WNGM N845F N297AR N30JM (N13FE) N2255Q N738RH N60SM N60SN N703SC N20YA N25TX N204JP N1M N240TJ (N794SB) N240CK |
| 25/405 | 20C | F-WNGN F-BOON HB-VCO F-BSYF N813AA TG-GGA N813AA [wfu at Detroit-Willow Run, MI; to spares use] |
| 26 | 20C | F-WNGO N846F N802F N11827 N819AA [wfu at Detroit-Willow Run, MI] |
| 27 | 20C-5 | F-WMKJ N847F N677SW N33TP N174GA N326VW N481FL |
| 28 | 20C | F-WMKG N848F N367EJ N10WA N573EJ YV-78CP N50CA (N280RC) (N126JM) N50CA C-GEAQ N333AV [at Montreal - Saint Hubert Aeronautical College] |
| 29 | 20C | F-WMKI N849F N368G N368L C-GSKC LV-PLD? LV-WMM [parted out Buenos Aires/San Fernando] |
| 30 | 20CF | F-WMKF N804F N368EJ YV-126CP N368EJ N407PC CS-ATD F-GPIM N514SA N123RA |
| 31 | 20C | F-WNGM N806F N34C N814AA N828AA N131MV |
| 32 | 20C | F-WNGL N805F N418S N218S 5B-CGB TL-AJK F-GIVT N232TW |
| 33 | 20C | F-WNGO N807F N369EJ N888AR [w/o 07Aug76 Acapulco, Mexico] |
| 34 | 20C | F-WMKJ N808F N369G N3690 C-GSKS LV-PHV LV-WLH [w/o 07Feb97 into mountains near Salta, Argentina] |
| 35 | 20C | F-WMKG N809F (N1777R) N809P 9M-BCR [wfu by 2005; for sale in stripped down state for static use] |
| 36 | 20C | F-WMKI N810F N900P N711BC N644X N85N OE-GUS N818AA [wfu at Detroit-Willow Run, MI] |
| 37/406 | 20C | F-WMKF (HB-VWW) HB-VAP (N7922) (N11WA) [w/o 01Oct77 Goose Bay, Canada; parts used in rebuild of c/n 28] |
| 38 | 20C | F-WMKF N842F N1107M N957TH [wfu 1987; cx Jan93; remains to Elberry, MO] |
| 39 | 20C | F-WNGM N843F N5555U N6565A N50MM N910U XA-LOB XB-EDU XA-RMA [wfu Toluca, Mexico] |

# FALCON 20/200

| C/n | Series | Identities |
|---|---|---|
| 40 | 20C | F-WNGL N870F CF-BFM N19BC N354H N354WC N854WC N65LC N65LE C-GSKQ N240TW |
| 41/407 | 20F-5B | F-WNGL (S Africa 431) F-BOED LN-FOI Norway 041 [ECM Aircraft] |
| 42 | 20C | F-WNGO N871F N1503 N7824M [w/o 16Jan74 Fort Worth, TX] |
| 43 | 20C | F-WMKJ N872F N990L [w/o 03Mar75 Dallas, TX] |
| 44 | 20C | F-WNGN N873F N355WB N355WC N355WG N692G N76TS N377BT (N773HS) N800PP N120EN* |
| 45 | 20C | F-WMKI N876F N147X N159FC N90JF N202KH N175GA N589DC |
| 46 | 20DC | F-WMKG CF-ESO N23555 N7FE (N144FE) N46VG EC-EHC |
| 47 | 20C | F-WNGM N875F N1846 [w/o 13Mar68 Parkersburg, WV] |
| 48 | 20C-5 | F-WMKG N878F N910Y N91CV (N23NQ) N23ND N541FL |
| 49/408 | 20C | F-WNGN France 49/F-RAFJ F-TEOA France 49/F-RHFA [code 120-FA] [preserved Villacoublay, France] |
| 50 | 20DC | F-WMGO N879F N804F N565A N6FE (N145FE) N56VG EC-EDO N699TW |
| 51 | 20C | F-WMKJ N880F N880P N218US N425JF N425JA [scrapped for spares Aug91; cx Oct94] |
| 52 | 20C | F-WNGN N881F N72ET N85DB N825TC D-CLBR UR-CLG |
| 53/417 | 20C | F-WNGO F-BNRE LN-FOD Norway 053 [ECM Aircraft] |
| 54 | 20C-5 | F-WMKI N886F N200P N2005 N10726 N54SN N100HG (N205TS) (N103RA) N380RA N405JW D2-JMM |
| 55/410 | 20C | F-WNGO VR-BCJ HB-VBS EC-EHD N550AL CCCP-01100 UR-EFA N520FD N830AA [wfu at Detroit-Willow Run, MI] |
| 56 | 20C | F-WNGM N882F N671SR N100SR N185S N932S (OO-PPP) OO-OOO N388AJ N560RA [b/u for parts at Detroit-Willow Run, MI circa May05] |
| 57 | 20C | F-WNGO N883F N499MJ N678BM N677BM N3JJ N76RY N711KG N812AA [cx 24Apr09; to Saudi Arabia as instructional airframe] |
| 58 | 20C | F-WNGL N884F N600KC F-BTQZ HB-VDG N2954T [scrapped for spares spring 1987 Van Nuys, CA] |
| 59 | 20DC | F-WNGO N971F N263MW N710MW N710MR N710MT N227GC N227CC N202TA N72BB N771LD N159MV N900RA |
| 60 | 20C | F-WMKJ N885F N805F [w/o 05Jly71 Boca Raton, FL] |
| 61 | 20C | F-WMKI N887F N299NW N20NY |
| 62/409 | 20C | F-WMKJ F-BOLX LN-FOE (N17401) [w/o 12Dec73 Norwich, UK and used by Federal Express for spares, marks N17401 were reserved after the w/o] |
| 63/411 | 20C | F-WMKI PH-LPS D-CBNA [w/o 04Aug01 Narssarssuaq, Greenland] |
| 64 | 20C | F-WMKG N889F N806F N200JW N916AN N513AN N513AG N425JF |
| 65 | 20C | F-WNGN N890F N383RF (N393RF) N393F N777WJ N777WL N1U N5052U C-GSKN N165TW [w/o Jamestown, NY, 21Dec08] |
| 66 | 20C | F-WNGL N891F N401AB N581SS N109RK N181RB N766NW N830RA N814ER |
| 67/414 | 20C | F-WJMN F-BOOA F-BTML N821AA N826AA |
| 68 | 20C-5 | F-WMKJ N892F N577S N458SW N521FL |
| 69 | 20C | F-WMKF N893F N176NP N176BN N31LT [Parted out by March Aviation, Naples, FL, 2006] |
| 70 | 20C | F-WMKH N966F N647JP (N647SA) N78JR (N400NL) [wfu 20Mar89; b/u for spares Mojave, CA (TT 4,326 hrs) remains to Aviation Warehouse film prop yard at El Mirage, CA] |
| 71 | 20C | F-WNGM N967F N807F N807PA N33SC N818SH N818CP (N293GT) N195AS N209CA [wfu at Addison, TX] |
| 72/413 | 20C | F-WNGO HB-VAW N1270F N99KT VH-DWA N725P F-GJCC (N172MV) [wfu by Sep04 Middletown, OH] |
| 73/419 | 20C | F-WJML VH-BIZ (F-BRHB) F-WMKG 9Q-CKZ (OO-RJX) (OO-ADA) LX-AAA LN-AAA [cx Dec89; scrapped for spares May89 Memphis, TN] |
| 74 | 20C-5 | F-WMKG N968F N1851T N1MB N57HH N800MC N800PA N800DC N702DM N702DD N522DD N8TP N221BR |
| 75 | 20C | F-WNGL N969F N100V N256MA N2568 N800DC N77QM UR-EFB N217CA [wfu at Addison, TX] |
| 76 | 20C | F-WMKF N970F N937GC N776DS F-GGFO F-GJDB |
| 77/429 | 20C | F-WNGO I-RIED (F-GJBR) F-GHDN F-WGTF F-GHSG N613GA N844SL [wfu by Sep04 Toledo, OH still wearing N613GA; fuselage to Pontiac, MI by Oct05 for parts; cx 03Oct07] |
| 78/412 | 20C | F-WNGM Australia A11-078 VH-JSX N6555C [canx 10Nov04 for parts; b/u] |
| 79/415 | 20C | F-WMKH F-BNRH France 79/F-ZACT |
| 80 | 20C | F-WMKI N972F N115K N356WB N356WC N356JB N76MB N24TW N925BE [fuselage only noted 28Aug05 on trailer Pontiac, MI] |
| 81 | 20C | F-WNGN N973F N799G N661JB N661J N747T N93RS N810RA [wfu Oscoda, MI] |
| 82/418 | 20C | F-WJMM Canada 20501 Canada 117501 G-FRAS |
| 83 | 20C | F-WJMJ N974F N805CC N80506 N22JW N12WP N1TC N55ME N68JK N20PL (N82SR) N283SA |
| 84 | 20C | F-WJMK N975F N530L N1FE (N150FE) N9FE [exhibited within Federal Express HQ, Memphis, TN] |
| 85/425 | 20C | F-WMKH Australia A11-085 VH-JSY N6555L |
| 86 | 20C | F-WMKI N976F N808F N622R (G-BBEK) F-BUYI G-BBEK (HB-VDW) F-WRGQ France 86/F-ZACG |
| 87/424 | 20C | F-WJMJ Canada 20502 Canada 117502 G-FRAT |
| 88 | 20C | F-WNGN N977F N130B N665P N665B N41CD N617GA [b/u Apr04 for spares by White Industries at Bates City, MO] |
| 89 | 20C | F-WMKG N978F N345BM N71CP N505AJ |

# FALCON 20/200

| C/n | Series | Identities |
|---|---|---|
| 90/426 | 20C | F-WNGL Australia A11-090 VH-JSZ VH-CIR PK-CIR [wfu by Dec04 Jakarta-Soekarno, Indonesia] |
| 91 | 20C-5 | F-WMKJ N979F N115TW N25DB N8WN (N91MH) N777DC N20UA (N200SS) |
| 92/421 | 20C | F-WJMM Canada 20503 Canada 117503 C-GWPB [in use as instructional airframe at BC Institute of Technology, Vancouver, Canada; wore marks "N9747I" in 2000 for film "Josie & The Pussycats"] |
| 93/435 | 20C | F-WMKF F-RAFN F-RBQA France 93/F-RAFN France 93/F-RAEC France 93/F-RAED [code 65-ED] France 93/F-RAEE |
| 94/428 | 20C | F-WNGO I-ATMO F-ODSK CS-ATE F-GLNL N614GA N566YT N461FL |
| 95 | 20C | F-WNGO N980F N802F N664P (OO-EEF) N664B N950RA N995CK |
| 96 | 20C | F-WNGM N981F N511S N5RT N89SC F-GERT France 96/F-ZACB |
| 97/422 | 20C | F-WJMJ Canada 20504 Canada 117504 G-FRAU |
| 98/434 | 20C | F-WNGN TU-VAD OY-AZT N408PC OO-RRR N781AJ N980R N998CK |
| 99 | 20C | F-WJMK N982F N921ML |
| 100 | 20C | F-WJMN N983F N605RP N200FT I-VEPA N179GA [w/o 08Apr03 Mississippi River landing at St Louis-Lambert, MO; remains to Dodson Intl Parts] |
| 101 | 20C | F-WMKJ N984F N342K N342F N97WJ |
| 102 | 20C | F-WMKI N985F N223B N53SF N710EC (N710EG) N710WB N403JW N204AN |
| 103/423 | 20C | F-WMKH Canada 20505 Canada 117505 [ECM Aircraft] G-FRAV F-GPAA N103FJ |
| 104/454 | 20C | F-WJMK (OT-JFA) F-BOXV France 104/F-ZACW |
| 105 | 20C | F-WNGL N986F N243K N77GR N97FJ N460MC [wfu & b/u for spares Jly87 Memphis, TN; cx Mar89; remains to Spirit of St.Louis A/P, MO circa Jan02] |
| 106 | 20C | F-WJMM N987F F-GBPG N9300M N31V EC-EKK |
| 107 | 20C | F-WMKJ N988F N965BC N155NK N330PC N213LS N107J |
| 108/430 | 20DC | F-WNGO (D-CDAS) D-CBAT N5CA N4FE (N147FE) N26VG N101ZE N108R [wfu Oscoda, MI] |
| 109/427 | 20C | F-WNGM Canada 20506 Canada 117506 [ECM Aircraft] C-FIGD |
| 110 | 20C | F-WMKG N989F CF-WRA C-FWRA VH-FWO [wfu and b/u for spares Oct88 Memphis, TN; cx Feb89] |
| 111 | 20C | F-WMKI N990F N111AC N990F N111AM N111BP (XC-HIX) |
| 112 | 20C | F-WJMJ N991F N2989 N830MF N200CX (HB-V..) CS-ATF UR-CCD UR-NIK [parted out by Atlanta Air Salvage, Griffin, GA] |
| 113 | 20C-5 | F-WNGL N993F PP-FOH PT-FOH (N713PE) N100WK N333WF N315PA N500HK (N731RG) F-WTFF N731F N129JE N129JF N400PC N400PG N22WJ N531FL |
| 114/420 | 20C | F-WJMM Canada 20507 Canada 117507 [ECM Aircraft] G-FRAW |
| 115/432 | 20 | F-WJML France 115/F-UGWL France F-UKJG [code 339-JG] [SNA model] [stored Chateaudun, France by Jun02] |
| 116 | 20C-5 | F-WMKJ N994F HB-VJD OO-JBB F-WGTH (F-GPNG) F-GLMM F-WLMM F-GLMM N770FG |
| 117 | 20C-5 | F-WMKH N995F N171PF N421ZC TS-IRS HB-VKC EC-855 EC-FJP F-GLMD N207JS |
| 118 | 20C | F-WMKG N996F N512T F-GGKE N820AA [wfu at Detroit-Willow Run, MI] |
| 119/431 | 20C | F-WJMK I-SNAV F-GHFP N20FJ |
| 120 | 20C-5 | F-WMKI N4340F N410US N205FJ (F-GKAF) F-GICF N20AF N647JP |
| 121 | 20C | F-WJMJ N4341F N242LB N813PA N813P N1199M N25CP N500BG N121DJ [to be parted out Oct04 at Rantoul, KS] |
| 122 | 20C-5 | F-WNGL N4342F N779P N335WR N335WJ N32PB N900LC N33QS N302TT N511FL |
| 123 | 20C | F-WNGM N4343F N513T N45MR N223TW |
| 124/433 | 20C | F-WJMJ France 124/F-ZACC [to Air France technical school, Massy, France] |
| 125 | 20C-5B | F-WJMN N4344F N6810J N812PA LN-FOE Norway 0125 [ECM Aircraft] |
| 126/438 | 20C | F-WMKH HB-VBL PH-BAG N1047T N10VG N102ZE N126R [wfu Detroit-Willow Run, MI circa Oct01] |
| 127 | 20C | F-WNGN N4345F N50AD XB-EPB XA-REY XB-GCR XB-HRA |
| 128/436 | 20C | F-WMKJ 5A-DAF YN-BZH C-GNAA EC-551 EC-FAM N228CK N70CK |
| 129 | 20C | F-WJMM N4346F N1823F N1823A N666DA N68TS PT-WUV N119LA PR-SUL |
| 130 | 20C | F-WMKJ N4347F N514T XA-SCL (N130MV) (N130TJ) N722KS [canx 21Apr04; b/u; by Oct04 fuselage dumped at Ontario CA] |
| 131/437 | 20C | F-WJMK France 131/F-ZACD |
| 132 | 20DC | F-WMKG N4348F N560L N2FE (N149FE) (N23FR) N902FR G-FFRA |
| 133 | 20C | F-WNGO N4349F N894F VR-BKR F-GJLA N133FJ N200JE [dbr 21Jan04 Pueblo, CO; to Dodson Intl Parts for parts] |
| 134 | 20C | F-WMKH N4350F N895F N897DM N897D I-NLAE [w/o 25Sep91 Kiel-Holtenau, Germany] |
| 135 | 20C-5 | F-WMKI N4351F N6820J N40XY N9999E N194MC N800DW N4MB |
| 136/439 | 20C | F-WJMJ HB-VBM 9K-ACQ F-GCGU HB-VBM SP-FCP LX-IAL N20MY RA-09007 [w/o 20May05 Moscow-Sheremetyevo, Russia] |
| 137 | 20C | F-WLLK F-BLLK F-WLLK N4352F N8999A N777PV N200GT [parted out by AvMATS, St Louis, MO] |
| 138/440 | 20C | F-WLCS D-CALL D-CGJH (G-BAOA) F-BUIC France 138/F-ZACR |
| 139 | 20C | F-WNGM N4353F N334JR N926LR N1868M N1868N N23PL N900WB N235CA [wfu at Addison, TX] |
| 140 | 20C | F-WNGN N4354F N4350M N3350M N160WC N314AE N165WC [Volpar PW305 conversion; ff 05Feb91] [wfu 1994 at Detroit-Willow Run, MI; b/u for spares by Active Aero cx Aug03] |
| 141/441 | 20C-5 | F-WMKF F-BPIO F-BIHY (UR-BCA) UR-CCB |

# FALCON 20/200

| C/n | Series | Identities |
|---|---|---|
| 142 | 20C-5 | F-WJMM N4355F N100S N1BF N298W N777WJ N511T N511TA N43SM N220RT (N205FJ) XA-RNB N300BA |
| 143/442 | 20C | F-WMKH 5A-DAG |
| 144 | 20C | F-WJMJ N4356F N888L N888JR N800LS (N200WF) N800KR N911RG N385AC N960AA |
| 145/443 | 20C | F-WNGN F-BPJB OO-PJB F-GCGY France 145/F-ZACU |
| 146 | 20CF | F-WJMN N4357F N964M N777EG N11TC C-FCDS N182GA N345FH N299RA |
| 147/444 | 20CF | F-WLCH PH-ILF (D-CORT) (D-CCNA) N41154 N183GA [w/o 08Apr03 Toledo, OH] |
| 148 | 20C | F-WMKG N4358F N120HC N126HC N657MC N888WS N148WC N148TW |
| 149 | 20C | F-WNGO N4359F N1818S (N4359F) N568Q EC-263 EC-EQP |
| 150/445 | 20C | F-WMKH HB-VBO (N95591) N8227V N777XX N679RE N123RE (VR-C..) TG-RBW HC-BSS |
| 151 | 20DC | F-WMKI N4360F N810F N810PA N3FE (N148FE) (N24FR) N904FR G-FRAL |
| 152/446 | 20DC | F-WJMJ CN-MBG CN-ANN |
| 153 | 20C | F-WLCT N4361F N70MD N207CA |
| 154/447 | 20C | F-WLCV France 154/F-RAFK [w/o 22Jan76 nr Villacoublay, France] |
| 155 | 20C | F-WJMK N4362F N500Y N205SC N212C (N205SE) N404R N68BC N68BP |
| 156/448 | 20C | F-WMKI 7T-VRE [w/o 30May81 Bamako, Mali] |
| 157 | 20C | F-WJMM N4363F N166RS Canada 117508 C-GRSD-X C-GRSD N5096F |
| 158/449 | 20C | F-WMKJ D-CMAX N450MA N158TW |
| 159 | 20C | F-WMKJ N4364F N5RC N411CC N96WC N96RT XA-ICG XA-PCC N67AX XA-PCC |
| 160/450 | 20C | F-WMKG I-DKET F-GHBT N48BT N100UF N301TT |
| 161 | 20C | F-WMKF N4365F N93CD N19BD N93FH N21NC N10PP N10RZ N503RV N620RB |
| 162/451 | 20C | F-WNGO OO-WTB D-CBBT HB-VED F-ODOK OO-DOK (F-GFLL) F-GFUN N162CT N911DG (N389AC) |
| 163 | 20D | F-WNGM N4366F (N500HD) N500FE N500LD N178GA N258PE N471FL |
| 164 | 20C | F-WJMN N4367F N654E N164NW |
| 165/452 | 20C | F-WJMJ CN-MBH CNA-NM [ECM Aircraft] |
| 166 | 20C-5 | F-WLCS N4368F N33D N33DY N71TJ N201BR |
| 167/453 | 20C | F-WMKG France 167/F-RAFL France 167/F-RAEB [code 65-EB] [wears full "regn" on tail] |
| 168 | 20C-5 | F-WLCX N4369F N100KW N108NC N300FJ N731RG N112CT N514JJ N168DJ |
| 169 | 20C | F-WNGN N4370F XC-SEY XC-MIC |
| 170/455 | 20C | F-WPUV I-EKET F-GHPA RA-09004 [cx; to scrapyard, Geneva, Switzerland, 14Mar06] |
| 171 | 20D-5 | F-WMKG N4371F N570L N900JL (F-GHRE) F-GICB N217AJ LV-BRZ |
| 172/456 | 20C | F-WNGM F-BRHB I-LIAB [cx, C of A expired] |
| 173 | 20D | F-WLCU F-BLCU N70PA N729S PK-TRI |
| 174/457 | 20C | F-WNGL TL-AAY TL-KAZ (HB-VER) F-WSHT HZ-KA3 HZ-NES (D-CFAI) N174BD [wfu parted out at Fayetteville, AR circa Oct05] |
| 175 | 20D-5 | F-WMKF N4373F N866MM F-BUFG D-COFG F-ODHA F-GBMS I-CAIB N4246R N688MC N116BK HB-VJW SU-OAE 5A-DKQ [parted out by Atlanta Air Salvage, Griffin, GA Sep08] |
| 176/458 | 20C-5 | F-WMKG I-SNAM F-WGTM F-GHDT F-WQBM EC-JJH |
| 177 | 20D | F-WMKI N4374F N6701 N14FG N41BP N82PJ |
| 178/459 | 20C | F-WPXF OH-FFA G-FRBA |
| 179 | 20D | F-WNGO N4375F N10LB N12LB N12MF N17JT XA-ACA N341PF XA-PVM |
| 180/460 | 20C-5 | F-WMKF OY-BDS I-GOBJ F-GVJR F-OVJR [w/o 15Mar06 Kiel, Germany] |
| 181 | 20D | F-WNGL N4376F N836UC N966L N200GH N200GL N817JS N5225G |
| 182/461 | 20C | F-WNGN HB-VCB F-WTDJ I-ROBM F-WVFV F-BVFV France 182/F-ZJTA France 182/F-UKJA |
| 183 | 20D | F-WLCY N4377F N2979 EC-EFR RA-09003 [wfu at Moscow/Domodedovo by Aug07] |
| 184/462 | 20D | F-WRQQ F-BTMF D-COMF F-GAPC OE-GCJ EC-HCX |
| 185/467 | 20D-5 | F-WMKF I-IRIF N3WN N147X N813LS N818LS N653MF |
| 186/463 | 20 | F-WPXL France 463/F-UGWM [code 339-WM] [then code 339-JE] France 463/F-UKJE [code 339-JE] [SNA Model] [stored at Chateaudun, France by Jun02] |
| 187 | 20D | F-WLCV N4379F N40AC N750R N811AA [wfu at Detroit-Willow Run, MI] |
| 188/464 | 20C | F-WJMK F-BRPK France 188/F-ZACX |
| 189 | 20D | F-WPUU N4380F N950L N47JF N47JE N444BF EC-EFI [w/o 11Oct87 off Keflavik, Iceland] |
| 190/465 | SNA | F-WNGN Libya 002 5A-DCO |
| 191 | 20D-5 | F-WPUX N4381F N910L N200DE N200CG N800CF OE-GCR N20HF |
| 192 | 20DF | F-WPUY N4382F N920L N57JF N910W N192R N192CK |
| 193 | 20D | F-WMKG N4383F N930L N37JF N400DB 9Q-CTT N219CA [wfu at Addison, TX] |
| 194 | 20DF | F-WPUZ N4384F N100M N555RA N297W N287W [w/o 11Feb88 Akron, OH; b/u Jun89; cx Jun92; remains at Av-Mats' facility at Paynesville, MO] |
| 195 | 20D | F-WPXD N4385F N200SR N186S N191C N500GM N43JK N195MP N822AA |
| 196 | 20D | F-WPXE N4386F N811PA N701MG N369WR N216BG N79AE N255RK N196TS (N141JF) (N142JF) |
| 197 | 20D | F-WPXF N4387F N399SW C-GTAK N5098F |
| 198/466 | 20D | F-WNGO VR-BDK (N14FE) N74196 (XC-GAM) XC-BIN XA-SQS N520TJ N339TG N724DS |
| 199 | 20DC | F-WMKH N4388F N8FE [wfu Aug83; displayed National Air & Space (Smithsonian) Museum, Steven F. Udvar-Hazy Center, Washington-Dulles, VA] |
| 200 | 20D | F-WMKJ N4389F N550MC N44MC N44CC N48CC N38CC YV-200C HC-BUP YV-876C N12AR [b/u May03 still marked as YV-876C cx Jun03] |

# FALCON 20/200

| C/n | Series | Identities |
|---|---|---|
| 201/469 | 20D | F-WLCY D-CELL "D-CEUU" D-CELL I-DRIB [wfu by 2004 Rome-Ciampino, Italy] |
| 202 | 20D-5 | F-WNGM N4391F N814PA N33L N33LV N48TJ N9TE N29TE N9TE |
| 203 | 20D | F-WPXH N4378F N1857B N20BE N911WT OE-GDR N36P N821AA [parted out by Dodson Av'n, Rantoul, KS] |
| 204 | 20DC | F-WMKI N4392F N26FE N120FS EC-113 EC-EGM N204TW |
| 205 | 20D | F-WPXF N4393F N21W N82A N4LH (N426CC) N815AA N915SA N585AC N961AA |
| 206 | 20D | F-WLCS N4394F N815AC N632PB N801SC N28RK (N410FJ) [crashed into sea off Bahamas 17Dec09, w/o] |
| 207 | 20DC | F-WMKF N4395F N27FE N908FR G-FRAP |
| 208/468 | 20D | F-WPXD HB-VCA VH-BRR N300JJ N125CA [w/o 29Jun89 Cartersville, GA] |
| 209 | 20DC | F-WLCX N4396F N28FE N909FR G-FRAR |
| 210 | 20DC | F-WNGL N4397F N29FE N66VG EC-ECB [w/o 30Sep87 Las Palmas, Canary Islands, Spain] |
| 211 | 20DC | F-WJMK N4398F N30FE Portugal 8101 Portugal 17101 N618GA N764LA N120RA |
| 212 | 20DC | F-WPXG N4399F N31FE N212R [wfu Oscoda, MI] |
| 213 | 20DC | F-WJMM N4390F N32FE N905FR G-FRAK (N213FC) |
| 214 | 20DC | F-WNGO N4400F N33FE N906FR G-FRAO |
| 215 | 20DC | F-WLCS N4401F N34FE Portugal 8102 Portugal 17102 N619GA N510BM [wfu for parts use; fuselage at Pontiac, MI by Oct05; canx Jan06 as b/u] |
| 216 | 20DC | F-WLCT N4402F N9FE Venezuela 5840 [stored El Libertador, Venezuela] |
| 217 | 20DC | F-WLCY N4403F N35FE Portugal 8103 Portugal 17103 [wfu] |
| 218 | 20DC | F-WMKJ N4372F N36FE N86VG OO-STE N86VG EC-EEU N218CA |
| 219/470 | 20D | F-WPXH EC-BVV Spain TM.11-3/401-04 Spain TM.11-3/45-04 Spain TM.11-3/408-11 Spain TM.11-3/47-23 |
| 220 | 20DC | F-WPUU N4404F N24FE N36VG OO-STF EC-EDL EC-EDC+ N220CA [+ reported painted as EC-EDC for at least one flight (to Luton, UK) during 1987] |
| 221 | 20DC | F-WPUV N4406F N25FE N300NL EC-165 EC-EIV N221TW |
| 222/471 | 20D | F-WNGL EC-BXV Spain TM.11-2/401-03 Spain TM.11-2/45-03 Spain TM.11-2/47-22 |
| 223 | 20DC | F-WPUX N4407F N22FE (N904FR) N900FR G-60-01 G-FRAH |
| 224 | 20DC | F-WPUY N4408F N23FE N907FR G-FRAM 9M-FRA |
| 225/472 | 20D | F-WPXD TR-KHA TR-LRU F-BOFH OH-FFJ N125MJ N37WT N332FE N338DB (N30AD) N102AD C-FONX N5098H [parted out Milwaukee, WI] |
| 226 | 20DC | F-WPXI F-WSQK N4409F N21FE N226R N226CK |
| 227 | 20DC | F-WMKG N4410F N14FE N24EV N227R N227CK |
| 228/473 | 20D | F-WNGL ZS-LAL ZS-LLG 3D-LLG C-GWSA HB-VEZ 5N-AYM OE-GRU N823AA |
| 229 | 20DC | F-WJMJ N4411F N15FE N25EV N229R N229CK |
| 230 | 20DC | F-WJML N4412F N16FE N26EV N230RA [wfu Oscoda, MI] |
| 231/474 | 20D | F-WPXE HB-VCG [w/o 20Feb72 nr St Moritz, Switzerland] |
| 232 | 20DC | F-WJMN N4413F N17FE N27EV N232RA [w/o 15Feb89 Bingham, NY; cx Mar91] |
| 233 | 20DC | F-WLCV N4414F N18FE N76VG I-TIAG N817AA [parted out by Dodson Av'n, Rantoul, KS] |
| 234/475 | 20D | F-WLCU (D-CIBM) D-COLL I-LIAC [cx, C of A expired] |
| 235 | 20DC | F-WPXJ N4415F N20FE Venezuela 0442 [stored El Libertador, Venezuela] |
| 236 | 20D | F-WPXK (N4416F) CF-JES C-FJES N375PK N375BK YR-DSA N128AP N618GH N936NW N236TW |
| 237/476 | 20D-5 | F-WPXF (D-CHCH) (D-CALM) D-CITY N4227Y VR-CBT VR-BKH HB-VJV EC-JDV UR-MOA |
| 238/477 | 20C | F-WRQP France 238/F-RAFM France 238/F-RAED France 238/F-RAEE France 238/F-RAFM France 238/F-RAEE [code 65-EE] [to Air France technical school, Massy, France] |
| 239 | 20F | F-WPXM N4417F N10MT C-GBFL N134CJ I-AGEC PH-OMC N39WJ N697BH N239CD N239BD N300BP |
| 240/478 | 20E-5 | F-WLCX I-SNAG N240AT HB-VMN F-GYCA |
| 241/479 | 20E | F-WRQP SE-DCO N48AD HZ-HE4 HZ-PL7 I-FLYK N241JC [cx 25Jun07, wfu] |
| 242 | 20F | F-WPUZ N4418F N800CF (N320FJ) N2622M N911TR N66WB YR-DSB N129AP (N711RT) "N4RT" (N242RJ) N513AC (N242MA) |
| 243/480 | 20F | F-WMKH OH-FFW [w/o 01Mar72 nr Montreal, Canada; remains to Sunstream Avn, Chicago-DuPage County A/P, MI, gone by Jun95] |
| 244 | 20F | F-WMKI N4420F N20FJ N11LB N226G N61LL VR-BJB [w/o 15Jan88 Lugano, Switzerland; remains to Dodson Avn, Ottawa, KS] |
| 245/481 | 20E | F-WLCS SX-ABA F-BUIX HB-VDP HB-VDY EL-VDY [to spares by Dodson Int'l Parts, Rantoul, KS circa Oct98] |
| 246/482 | 20F | F-WJMK F-BSTR (F-GLMT) N970GA [b/u for spares at White Inds. Bates City, MO] |
| 247 | 20E | F-WPXE N4419F N730S VH-FAX N730S N67JR N95JR N70PL N247PL |
| 248/483 | 20F | F-WRQV OH-FFV N37JJ XB-AQU XB-OEM XB-VRM XC-HIX |
| 249 | 20F | F-WJMM N4421F N11AK N777JF N451DP |
| 250 | 20F | F-WMKF N4422F N111AM XA-HEW N223BG |
| 251/484 | 20E | F-WRQR EP-VAP EP-FIE EP-IPA |
| 252/485 | 20E | F-WRQP I-GIAZ France 252/F-ZACA |
| 253/486 | 20E | F-WRQS EC-BZV Spain T.11-1/401-02 Spain T.11-1/45-02 Spain T.11-1/47-21 |
| 254 | 20F | F-WNGO N4423F CF-YPB C-FYPB G-FRAC F-GPAB |
| 255/487 | 20E | F-WRQP Jordan 122 HB-VDZ N2724K VH-HIF VH-MIQ N721J F-GHLN [w/o 20Jan95 Paris-Le Bourget A/P, France] |
| 256 | 20F | F-WNGL N4416F N3RC C-GNTZ F-GKME UR-CCA N368DS N868DS N15SL N651SD |
| 257 | 20F-5 | F-WMKH N4425F N781W N300CC C-GNTL (F-GJPI) F-GKDD HB-VKO N18HN |
| 258 | 20F | F-WNGM N4426F N20JM N544X N20AE N300SF N380SF N68UP |

# FALCON 20/200

| C/n | Series | Identities |
|---|---|---|
| 259 | 20F | F-WLCT N4418F N212H N45WH N45WN SE-DHK F-GIFP N569BW N569DW N569D |
| 260/488 | 20E | F-WMKJ France 260/F-RAEA [code 65-EA] |
| 261 | 20F-5 | F-WLCU N4368F N200WK |
| 262 | 20F-5 | F-WJMK N4427F N720ML N750ME VH-WLH N501AS C-GTLU F-GHVR (N.....) D2-ESV (OO-MDN) (OO-RYB) N795AB N189RB |
| 263/489 | 20E | F-WMKJ HB-VCR (PH-LEN) F-BSBU France 263/F-ZACY |
| 264 | 20F | F-WJMN N4428F N373KC N777V N773V (N86BL) F-GJJS CS-ATG N264TN XA-III XA-NCC |
| 265 | 20F | F-WLCX N4429F N606RP N265MP |
| 266/490 | 20EF | F-WRQR PH-ILX N4115B N184GA [w/o 13Jun00 Peterborough, Canada; to White Inds, Bates City, MO for parts use circa Jan01] |
| 267/491 | 20E | F-WRQZ I-REAL N731G N627JG N267H N129JE |
| 268/492 | 20E | F-WNGN France 268/F-RAEB France 268/F-RAFK France 268/F-RAEF [code 65-EF] |
| 269 | 20F | F-WPUX N4430F N1902W N501F XA-NAY XA-DUC |
| 270 | 20DC | F-WPUZ N4435F N37FE (N907FR) N901FR G-FRAI |
| 271/493 | 20E | F-WNGN 7T-VRP (F-GHPO) F-GKDB [cx to Switzerland 08Mar05 but no Swiss marks allocated; b/u, fueslage used as cabin trainer] |
| 272 | 20E | F-WMKF N4431F N20FJ N732S N888RF N913MK N813MK (N803MM) XA-TAN (N272FA) N272JP N885BH N20FE N770RR N224WE |
| 273 | 20F-5 | F-WPUU N4432F N212T N212TC N212TG 5N-EPN F-WQBK N596DA N720JC N632KA* |
| 274 | 20F-5 | F-WJMM N4433F N370WT N121WT N256M N26LA (D-CHEF) N260MB N100AS |
| 275 | 20E | F-WMKH N4434F N661JB N9FB VR-BRJ SX-DKI N999EQ (N999BG) N200CP |
| 276/494 | 20E | F-WNGL Belgium CM-01 |
| 277/501 | 20E | F-WPXD Pakistan J-753 |
| 278/495 | 20E-5 | F-WNGM Belgium CM-02 F-WQBN Belgium CM-02 |
| 279/502 | 20E | F-WMKJ I-FKET F-GHFQ N279AL F-GROC N854GA D-CLBE UR-CLE |
| 280/503 | 20E | F-WPXK I-EDIS N910FR G-FRAE F-GPAD |
| 281/496 | 20F | F-WRQR D-CORF N20CG LN-AAC N70830 N347K N281JJ N341K N341KA N116GB |
| 282 | 20E | F-WMKG N4436F N131JA N282JJ N282C XC-DIP XB-1YK XC-HID [code PF-203] |
| 283/497 | 20E | F-WRQX EP-AGX [w/o 21Nov74 Kermanshah, Iran] |
| 284 | 20E | F-WPXM N4437F N132JA N284JJ N98RH N444FJ N441FA XA-BCC N441FA N284CE N501MD (N801MD) N201GF |
| 285/504 | 20EF | F-WRQT A40-AA A40-GA PH-WMS VR-CCF PH-WMS N285AP N285TW |
| 286/498 | 20E | F-WRQU EP-AGY |
| 287 | 20E | F-WMKF N4438F YV-T-AVA YV-38CP XB-ALO XA-SAG XC-PFJ/PF-239 XC-QER |
| 288/499 | 20E | F-WRQZ F-BUYE France 288/F-ZACV |
| 289 | 20F | F-WMKG N4439F N20FJ N54J N54JJ N1HF N40994 N211HF N105TW N75TJ N450CP |
| 290 | 20E | F-WMKH N4440F N133JA I-TIAL N816AA [instructional airframe, Doha, Qatar] |
| 291/505 | 20E | F-WRQT France 291/F-RAEC France 291/F-RCAP France 291/F-RAEG [code 65-EG] [wfu Mar07, stored at Chateaudun, France] |
| 292 | 20F-5B | F-WMKI N4441F N733S N510WS 9M-LLJ |
| 293 | 20E-5 | F-WMKJ N4442F N2615 N2613 HZ-PL1 HB-VJX OY-CKY F-WQBN F-GOBZ I-GOBZ F-WQVA RA-09005 UR-CLF |
| 294/506 | 20E-5B | F-WRQT F-BVPM SU-AXN |
| 295/500 | 20E | F-WRQQ I-EDIM N911FR G-FRAF |
| 296/507 | 20F-5 | F-WRQP HB-VDB D2-EBB J5-GAS N4960S N214JP N297CK N19TX N20TX N220LA |
| 297 | 20E | F-WMKF N4443F (N370EU) N121EU PK-TIR "N297AG" CS-DCK |
| 298 | 20E | F-WMKG N4444F N86W N98LB OE-GNN N827AA |
| 299 | 20F | F-WMKI (N734S) N21FJ N456SR N90CN N585UC F-GJSF TC-EZE (N669AC) N299JC |
| 300/508 | 20E | F-WRQP I-EDIF (F-GIBT) (F-GEJX) F-GGMM N300FJ (N953DC) N600WD |
| 301/509 | 20E | F-WNGL EP-AKC |
| 302/510 | 20E | F-WRQP D-COMM OE-GDP N84V F-WQBM F-GOPM |
| 303 | 20F | F-WMKH N4445F N27R [w/o 12Nov76 Naples, FL] |
| 304/511 | 20E | F-WRQP G-BCYF G-FRAD 9M-BDK G-FRAD |
| 305 | 20F-5 | F-WMKJ N4446F N16R N56SL VR-CDB N282U N34CW N715WS |
| 306/512 | 20E | F-WRQS (HB-VDY) (HB-VDO) D-CGSO VH-HFJ (N725P) N76662 N205WM N205WP |
| 307/513 | 20E-5 | F-WRQT HB-VDV I-GCAL OE-GLL F-GKIS F-GYPB F-GYMC CS-DPW |
| 308 | 20F | F-WMKF N4447F N668P N668S N37RM SE-DKA N81AJ N453SB N458SB |
| 309/514 | 20SNA | F-WRQT TR-LUW France 309/F-RAFU France 309/F-UGWP [code 339-WP] [named L'Etoile du Berger] [w/o 02Dec91 Villacoublay, France] |
| 310 | 20F | F-WMKH N4450F (N370ME) N121AM N831HG N31FJ N724JC |
| 311/515 | 20F-5 | F-WRQS F-BVPN |
| 312 | 20F | F-WMKH N4448F N2605 N619MW N1971R N132AP N741MR |
| 313 | 20F-5B | F-WMKJ N4449F N220FJ N744CC N56CC N560R I-PERF F-GHCR N212PB N183TS N184TS N339RK |
| 314/516 | 20E | F-WNGL D-COTT F-GDLU N314TW |
| 315/517 | 20E-5 | F-WRQP F-BVPQ OO-VPQ F-GDLO F-SEBI F-GSXF D-CLBB UR-CLD |
| 316 | 20F-5 | F-WMKF N4451F N734S N242CT N424XT |
| 317 | 20F | F-WMKG N4452F N31CM N99E N92K N88FE HB-VEV N939CK |
| 318/518 | 20E | F-WRQT (EP-VAS) EP-VSP EP-FIG Iran 15-2235 |
| 319 | 20F-5 | F-WMKF N4453F N730V N44NT C-GNTM N70LG N77LA N205K N724CP |

# FALCON 20/200

| C/n | Series | Identities |
|---|---|---|
| 320/519 | 20E | F-WRQS EP-AHV EP-FIF |
| 321 | 20F-5 | F-WJMJ N4454F N2525 N702SC N244CA N20FM (PH-BPS) N104SB PH-BPS |
| 322 | 20F | F-WMKH N4455F N1971R N999DC N94GW N464M N300CV |
| 323/520 | 20E | F-WRQS HB-VEB I-FCIM OE-GLF XU-008 [instructional airframe, Singapore/ Seletar] |
| 324 | 20F | F-WMKF N4456F N444SC N324TC N312K N373DN |
| 325 | 20F | F-WMKG N4457F N100GN N400GN (N400GX) (N700GN) VH-RRC N7WG N599RR N555TF (N325MC) N877JG |
| 326/521 | 20E | F-WRQQ PH-ILY TC-CEN TC-GGG |
| 327 | 20F | F-WMKI N4458F N3H N2H N96L VH-NMN N900DB N25WG XA-HHF XA-ABF N327BC XA-MSA |
| 328/522 | 20F | F-WMKJ (N4459F) YK-ASA [crashed Damascus, Syria, 19Oct08; on rebuild at Le Bourget, France, 2010] |
| 329/523 | 20E | F-WRQV D-CMET |
| 330 | 20F | F-WNGM N4460F N300AL C-GNTY N770MC (N227LA) |
| 331/524 | 20F | F-WRQS YK-ASB |
| 332/525 | 20E | F-WRQP EC-CTV Spain TM.11-4/401-05 Spain TM.11-4/45-01 Spain TM.11-4/408-12 Spain TM.11-4/47-24 |
| 333/526 | 20E | F-WNGL Iran 5-2801 Iran 15-2233 [w/o 09Jan06 Aidinlou, NW Iran] |
| 334/527 | 20E | F-WRQU EP-FIC |
| 335 | 20F | F-WMKF N4459F N901TC N903SB D-CFAI N335AJ N707JC (N707JZ) (N301FC) N335TW |
| 336/528 | 20E | F-WRQP Iran 5-2802 [wfu Tehran, Iran] |
| 337/529 | 20F | F-WRQR YI-AHH Iran 5-9014 |
| 338/530 | 20E | F-WMKG EP-FID |
| 339 | 20F-5 | F-WMKH N4461F N200GN N100GN N200GN (N200GX) N131DB (N402NC) N22FS N19MX SE-DSA N38TJ N239CD |
| 340/531 | 20E | F-WRQX Iran 5-2803 [wfu Tehran, Iran] |
| 341 | 20F-5B | F-WMKF N4462F N20FJ N66GA N511WP N511WR N78BC N311JS VR-CDT F-OHCJ F-GYSL |
| 342/532 | 20F | F-WRQP YI-AHI J2-KAC France 342/F-RAEC France 342/F-RAEG France 342/F-RAEC [code 65-EC] |
| 343/533 | 20F | F-WRQR YI-AHJ Iran 5-9015 |
| 344/534 | 20F-5 | F-WRQP A6-HEM A6-EXA N344FJ (N731F) N731AS (N731AE) N227WE N227WL |
| 345 | 20F | F-WMKI N4463F N678BM F-GHMD N133AP OH-FPC UR-NOA N345FJ UR-NOA |
| 346/535 | 20E | F-WRQP Iran 5-2804 [wfu Tehran, Iran] |
| 347 | 20F | F-WMKF N4464F N744CC N298CK N347HS N20VF N711FJ |
| 348/536 | 20E | F-WRQR Iran 5-4039 Iran 5-3020 [w/o 03Mar97 Ardabil, Iran] |
| 349 | 20F | F-WMKG N4465F N273K N66NT N767AC N767AG N287SA N220WE |
| 350/537 | 20E | F-WRQS Iran 5-4040 Iran 5-3021 |
| 351/538 | 20F | F-WMKJ Iran 5-9001 [reportedly destroyed Feb91, no other details known] |
| 352 | 20F-5 | F-WMKF N4466F N920G N184WW |
| 353/539 | 20F | F-WRQP Iran 5-9002 [reportedly destroyed Jan91, no other details known] |
| 354/540 | 20F | F-WRQR Iran 5-9003 |
| 355 | 20F-5 | F-WMKF N4467F N20FJ N27AC N344G N550M N63PM N61PM N200MK N712ME N803WC N335MC N632PB |
| 356 | 20F | F-WMKG N4468F N27R N27RX G-FRAB F-GPAE N111F N11UF N69SW N621JS |
| 357 | 20F-5 | F-WMKI N4469F N435T N435TP N342K N342KF N357PS M-ABCD |
| 358/541 | 20F-5B | F-WRQS SU-AZJ F-WRQY SU-AZJ |
| 359/542 | 20F | F-WRQR (N64769) HZ-TAG HZ-A01 N64769 N647JP N35RZ N50SL (N508L) N369CA N369CE OH-WIP |
| 360 | 20F | F-WMKJ N1010F N901YP N905SB N911SB F-GJEA N165PA N865VP N390AG N349MR |
| 361/543 | 20F-5 | F-WMKF SU-AYD |
| 362 | 20G | (F-WZAS) F-WATF F-WDFJ F-GDFJ F-WDFJ [wfu Istres, France circa Sep00] |
| 363/544 | 20F-5 | F-WRQV HZ-DC2 N363FJ N3VF |
| 364 | 20F | F-WMKI N1013F N235U N285U OE-GCS N285U XA-FLM N134PA XB-KBW |
| 365 | 20F | F-WMKJ N1018F N777TX N50BH N50BV |
| 366 | 20F | F-WMKG N1020F N83V N300CT N100AC |
| 367/545 | 20F | F-WRQR EP-SEA |
| 368 | 20F-5 | F-WMKI N1036F N800CF N200DE N800CF VH-NCF N83D I-FIPE N110TJ F-GHTK N110TJ N65TS N107LW N23A N15H |
| 369 | 20F | F-WRQP N1037F N20SR (N414JC) N415JW N509WP N420J N138FJ |
| 370 | 20F | F-WMKG N1038F HL7234 N370HF N269SR N20WN |
| 371 | HU25C | F-WMKJ N1039F USCG 2141 |
| 372/546 | 20F | F-WRQV ST-PRS |
| 373 | 20F-5 | F-WMKI N1041F N53DS N922DS N91Y (N620CC) N610CC N620CC N399FG C-FSJI |
| 374 | HU25A | F-WRQP N1045F USCG 2101 |
| 375/547 | 20F | F-WRQR F-GBMD France 375/F-ZACZ |
| 376 | 20F-5B | F-WRQS N103F N2624M N2614 N2616H N1892S N1897S |
| 377/548 | 20F-5 | F-WRQP D-CCMB N30FT N5VJ N377RP N600CD |
| 378 | 20F-5 | F-WRQT N107F (N662PP) N662P (N6621) N305AR N500JD N97SJ |
| 379 | 20F-5 | F-WMKF N130F (N37AH) (N33AJ) N33AH F-GGBL N62570 N892SB N892S (N724JS) XA-RHA |
| 380 | 20F | F-WMKI N136F N8BX N1BX N9654N N922ML (N288MM) N289MM N3848U I-ULJA |

# FALCON 20/200

| C/n | Series | Identities |
|---|---|---|
| 381/548 | 20F-5 | F-WRQS (I-LAFA) D-CCDB N20TZ N20T N85TZ N602LP N840DP |
| 382 | 20F | F-WMKG N138F HP-1A N138F N138E N382E N10AZ N453SB |
| 383/550 | 20F-5 | F-WRQR D-CONU 5N-AYO HB-VJS N900CH N908CH |
| 384/551 | 20F-5 | F-WRQU OO-PSD N384JK N120CG N120TF N120DE N82TN N384PS |
| 385 | 20F-5 | F-WJMJ N139F N118R G-FRAA N120WH N87TN N385FJ ZS-KGS |
| 386 | HU25A | F-WJMK N149F USCG 2102 |
| 387 | 20F | F-WJML N162F N56CC N676DW N387CE N676DW N384K |
| 388 | 20F-5 | F-WJMM N169F N90GS N920CF F-WTFE N731RG N756 N502BG |
| 389/552 | 20F | F-WRQV I-CMUT UR-KKA |
| 390 | HU25C | F-WJMN N173F USCG 2104 |
| 391 | 20F | F-WLCS N175F N376SC N876SC VH-HPF N503F N995PT N990PT N550PT N420DP N420CL N420GL TR-LGZ |
| 392/553 | 20F | F-WRQT D-CALL N328EW N326EW N326LW (N392FJ) N713MC |
| 393 | 20F | F-WLCT N176F N21NL N76TA N809F XA-REY XA-PUE XB-FVH XC-FVH XC-SON |
| 394 | HU25A | F-WMKF N178F USCG 2103 |
| 395/554 | 20F | F-WRQX (HZ-AKI) OD-PAL (N395BB) [unmarked at the White Inds facility at Bates City, MO circa Oct98] |
| 396 | 20F-5 | F-WMKG N179F N881J N711GL N711WV |
| 397/555 | 20F | F-WRQP F-GBTM F-WBTM F-GBTM |
| 398 | HU25A | F-WMKF N183F USCG 2105 |
| 399 | 20F-5 | F-WMKI N184F N881G N70NE N70NF N70U N21FE N728JC N633KA* |
| 400/556 | 20F | F-WRQR RP-C1980 [w/o 24Apr96 at Davao City, Philippines; spares use by White Inds, Bates City, MO] |
| 401 | 200 | F-WZAH F-GATF (F-WDHA) N200FJ N207FJ F-GATF VR-BJJ F-GATF VR-BJJ F-GEXF Chile 301 code VP-1 N699GA N501KC |
| 402 | HU25A | F-WJMJ N187F USCG 2106 [wfu AMARC Davis-Monthan, AZ 04Jul95; park code AC410007] |
| 403 | 20F | F-WJMK N189F N15AT N108BG N960TX (N175BC) |
| 404 | 20F | F-WJMK N404F N28C N313K |
| 405 | HU25A | F-WMKI N405F USCG 2108 [wfu AMARC Davis-Monthan, AZ 10Aug01; park code AC410016] |
| 406/557 | 20F | F-WMKF G-BGOP N800FF |
| 407 | HU25A | F-WJMJ N406F USCG 2109 |
| 408 | 20F-5 | F-WRQS (PK-CAJ) PK-CAG (N508TC) N408PA N757CX |
| 409 | HU25A | F-WMKJ N407F USCG 2107 [wfu AMARC Davis-Monthan, AZ 04Sep01; park code AC410018] |
| 410 | 20F-5B | F-WRQT N200CP N200J N410SB N410AZ |
| 411 | HU25A | F-WMKG N408F USCG 2110 |
| 412 | 20F-5 | F-WMKI N409F N85V N85VE N2FU N12FU N620A |
| 413 | HU25A | F-WJMK N410F USCG 2111 [wfu; placed into Atlantic Ocean 6 miles off N.Carolina coast to create new reef 04May05] |
| 414 | 20F-5B | F-WJML N412F N1881Q |
| 415 | HU25A | F-WLCV N413F USCG 2112 |
| 416 | 20F | F-WLCT N415F N416F N88NT N9VG N416F N725JG |
| 417 | HU25A | F-WJMM N416F N416FJ USCG 2113 |
| 418 | HU25A | F-WJMN N417F USCG 2114 |
| 419 | HU25A | F-WMKJ N419F USCG 2115 [wfu AMARC Davis-Monthan, AZ 04Sep01; park code AC410017] |
| 420 | HU25A | F-WMKG N420F USCG 2116 [wfu AMARC Davis-Monthan, AZ 25Apr94; park code AC410005] |
| 421 | HU25A | F-WMKI N422F USCG 2117 |
| 422 | 20F | F-WRQU (N422F) F-ZJTJ France 422/F-RCAL France 422/F-RAEH [code 65-EH] |
| 423 | HU25B | F-WJMJ N423F USCG 2118 |
| 424 | HU25A | F-WMKF N424F USCG 2119 [damaged in storms Nov93 Mobile, AL; wfu AMARC Davis-Monthan AZ circa Jan94; park code AC410002] |
| 425 | HU25A | F-WMKG N425F USCG 2120 |
| 426 | 20F-5B | F-WJMK N427F N123WH N555PT N416RM I-BAEL HB-VNM N426ST |
| 427 | 20F | F-WRQV 5N-AYN I-ACTL N42WJ |
| 428 | 20F-5B | F-WMKI N426F N98R I-FLYF N98R N148MC N93MC |
| 429 | 20F-5B | F-WMKF VR-BHL HB-VHY N4286A N149MC N702CA N331DM |
| 430 | 20F-5 | F-WMKG N428F N660P N243FJ |
| 431 | HU25A | F-WMKJ N429F USCG 2121 |
| 432 | 20F-5B | F-WJMK N430F N667P N237PT N855DG N355DG N4TB |
| 433 | HU25B | F-WJML N432F USCG 2122 [wfu AMARC Davis-Monthan, AZ 07Sep01; park code AC410020] |
| 434 | 20F | F-WRQP Peru 300/OB-1433 |
| 435 | HU25A | F-WJMM N433F USCG 2123 [damaged in storms Nov93 Mobile, AL; wfu AMARC Davis-Monthan AZ circa Jan94; park code AC410003] |
| 436 | 20F-5 | F-WJMN N434F N181CB N436MP N8000U N436RB N70PL |
| 437 | HU25A | F-WMKG N435F USCG 2124 [wfu AMARC Davis-Monthan, AZ; park code AC410022] |
| 438 | 20F-5 | F-WMKI N442F N263K N256A N258A |
| 439 | HU25B | F-WMKJ N443F USCG 2125 [AMARC Davis-Monthan, AZ; park code AC410023] N523NA N448TB N523NA N448TB |
| 440 | 20F | F-WRQQ N452F N5152 N768J (N768V) VR-CAR N32TC N32TE N7000G N205JC |
| 441 | HU25A | F-WJMK N445F USCG 2126 [wfu AMARC, Davis-Monthan, AZ; park code AC410021] |
| 442 | 20F-5 | F-WJML N446F VH-FJZ N203TA I-SREG N747CX |
| 443 | HU25A | F-WMKG N447F USCG 2127 [wfu AMARC Davis-Monthan, AZ, circa Jul91; park code AC410001] USCG 2127 [returned to USCG service by Jan08] |
| 444 | 20F-5B | F-WJMJ N453F N665P N244FJ LV-BIY |
| 445 | HU25A | F-WJMM N449F USCG 2128 |
| 446 | 20F | F-WJMN N454F N31WT N901SB N904SB N270RA N446D N81P |
| 447 | HU25A | F-WLCS N455F USCG 2129 |

# FALCON 20/200

| C/n | Series | Identities |
|---|---|---|
| 448 | 20G | F-WJMK France 48/F-ZWVF |
| 449 | 20F | F-WLCT N457F N39TT N73MR |
| 450 | HU25A | F-WMKG N458F USCG 2130 [wfu AMARC Davis-Monthan, AZ, 25Apr94; park code AC410004] |
| 451 | 20F | F-WRQR F-ZJTS France 339/F-UGWN [code 339-WN] France 339/F-UKJC [code 339-JC] |
| 452 | HU25A | F-WMKI N459F USCG 2131 |
| 453 | 20F | F-WJMK N460F N25S N189MM N520AW |
| 454 | HU25A | F-WJML N461F USCG 2132 [wfu AMARC Davis-Monthan, AZ 06Sep01; park code AC410019] |
| 455 | 20F-5 | F-WRQS F-GKAL N555SR N404HR |
| 456 | HU25A | F-WJMJ N462F USCG 2133 |
| 457 | 20F-5 | F-WJMM N463F N4351M N4362M N47LP |
| 458 | HU25B | F-WJMN N465F USCG 2134 |
| 459 | HU25A | F-WMKJ N466F USCG 2135 |
| 460 | HU25B | F-WJML N467F USCG 2136 [preserved Elizabeth City USCGAS, NC] |
| 461 | 20F | F-WMKG N469F N747V N353CP OH-WIF N221H |
| 462 | HU25A | F-WMKI N470F USCG 2137 [wfu AMARC Davis-Monthan, AZ 10Apr95; park code AC410008] |
| 463 | 20F | F-WJMJ N471F N134JA N132EP |
| 464 | HU25A | F-WJMK N472F USCG 2138 [wfu AMARC Davis-Monthan, AZ 13Apr95; park code AC410009] |
| 465 | 20G | France 65/F-ZJTS |
| 466 | HU25C | F-WJML N473F USCG 2139 |
| 467 | HU25A | F-WJMM N474F USCG 2140 |
| 468 | 20F | F-WMKG Pakistan J-468 |
| 469 | 20F | F-WMKI Pakistan J-469 |
| 470 | 20F-5 | F-WJMJ N477F N607RP N470G N500NH |
| 471 | 20F-5 | F-WJMK N478F N44JC N44JQ N911DT (N611DT) |
| 472 | 20G | France 72 |
| 473 | 20F | F-WRQT F-GEJR 3A-MGR 3A-MJV N473SH 3A-MJV N473SH N393S N404FZ |
| 474 | 20F-5 | F-WMKF F-GFFS I-ACCG F-WGTG N211HF N1HF |
| 475 | 20F | F-WJML Spain T.11-5/45-05 N475EZ XA-YUR |
| 476 | 20F | F-WJMM France 76/F-ZJTD Venezuela 1650 |
| 477 | 20G | France 77 |
| 478 | 20F-5 | F-WJMN N161WT N181WT N300RT N39RP C-GBCI |
| 479 | 200 | F-WPUU N200FJ (N200FX) N200WD (N200FJ) N200LS N400WT (N60DD) (N200SA) N349MG N240RS N7KC N767AG |
| 480 | 20G | France 80/F-ZJSA |
| 481 | 20F-5B | F-WLCS N502F N250RA OH-WIN N599ZM |
| 482 | 200 | F-WPUZ F-WDSB F-GDSB SE-DDZ F-WGDZ VR-CCL VP-CCL (N94TJ) |
| 483 | 20F | F-WRQQ France 483/F-UKJI [code 339-JI] |
| 484 | 200 | F-WPUV N202FJ N28U N357CL N422MU N24JG N425RJ |
| 485 | 20F-5 | F-WLCT N161EU N997TT (N23SJ) N22FW |
| 486 | 20F-5 | F-WLCV F-GEFS N6VF |
| 487 | 200 | F-WZZB (N206FJ) F-GDSD "I-WDSD" I-SOBE N137TA (N387FJ) |
| 488 | 200 | F-WZZF HB-VHS N682JB N123CC N2HW C-GTNT N146CF N200NP N488KF |
| 489 | 200 | F-WPUX N203FJ (N109FC) N109NC N109NQ N200RT (TC-...) N7654F TC-DEM N489TK N489BB N613BS |
| 490 | 200 | F-WPUY N204FJ N14EN N806F N2TF N95JT N200RT (N208RT) HC-BVH N917JC N917JG PH-APV N490SJ M-JETT |
| 491 | 200 | F-WZZA N205FJ N200FJ N120FJ VH-PDJ VH-HPJ N491MB N343MG N843MG N500RR |
| 492 | 200 | F-WPUV VR-BHZ N805C N803F N412AB N492CC |
| 493 | 200 | F-WZZC N208FJ N901SB N1847B VH-ECG ZS-SOS ZS-JVS |
| 494 | 200 | F-WZZD N209FJ N85LB LV-PFM LV-BAI N49US N204DD EC-HEG N200FJ |
| 495 | 200 | F-WZZE N210FJ (N290BC) VH-BGL N522C N48FU N48HU N800HM C-GSCL C-GSCR N800EG N1D |
| 496 | 200 | F-WZZC VR-BHY F-GFAY I-LXOT (F-GGAR) F-OGSR F-WGSR Chile 302 CC-PES N496RT N227TA N256JC N202AR |
| 497 | 200 | F-WZZA N212FJ N720HC N20CL |
| 498 | 200 | F-WPUV N215FJ N200ET N422D N422L N69EC |
| 499 | 200 | F-WZZJ N213FJ N565A N14CJ N200CU |
| 500 | 200 | F-WPUU N214FJ N595DC C-GMPO C-GRPM N734DB N777TE |
| 501 | 200 | F-WZZD I-MAFU F-WWGP F-GOJT N200TJ N57TT N214AS |
| 502 | 200 | F-WPUU N216FJ N5732 N573E N232F N64YP N64YR HB-VNG |
| 503 | 200 | F-WPUY N218FJ N300HA N50MW (N50MX) |
| 504 | 200 | F-WPUX N217FJ N902SB N702SB VH-CPE (N504CL) N504FJ |
| 505 | 200 | F-WZZA N221FJ ZK-MAY VH-NGF XA-SKO N221FJ N45JB |
| 506 | 200 | F-WPUZ I-CNEF N147TA XA-MAM |
| 507 | 200 | F-WPUV N220FJ N200FJ (N122FJ) C-FCEH N79MB N50MG N50LG N22HS |
| 508 | 200 | F-WPUU N219FJ N1851T XA-RKE N777FC |
| 509 | 200 | F-WPUX N222FJ (N8495B) JA8270 N70TH N200WY (N277AT) PR-SMT N202AT |
| 510 | 200 | F-WPUY N223FJ N79PM N515DB N510LF N36DA N84MJ |
| 511 | 200 | F-WWGR F-OGSI F-WGTF F-OLET (F-GNMF) VT-TTA F-WQBK EC-JBH |
| 512 | 200 | F-WPUU N224FJ N45WH N999TH |
| 513 | 200 | F-WPUV N225FJ XB-ECR XA-ECR N881JT (N200UP) (N10UU) N5UU N5UQ N618GH |
| 514 | 200 | F-WWGP (F-GJIS) F-OHES PT-OQG N531WB (N81AG) N87AG N322RR |
| 515 | 200 | F-WWGO VR-CCQ VR-CHC F-GOBE XA-PFM N181RK |

Production complete

# DASSAULT FALCON 50

* Denotes Falcon 50EX

| C/n | Identities |
|---|---|
| 1 | F-WAMD [ff 07Nov76] "F-BAMD"+ [+ marks worn at 1977 Paris Air Show]F-WNDB F-BNDB F-WNDB F-BNDB F-WNDB [wfu fuselage to Conservatoire de l'Air et de l'Espace d'Aquitaine, Merignac circa Oct99] |
| 2 | F-WINR F-BINR France 2/F-RAFJ F-BINR F-GSER N50BL |
| 3 | F-WFJC F-GBIZ N50FJ N50EJ N880F N8805 N728LW |
| 4 | F-WZHA N110FJ N50FJ YV-452CP YV-O-SATA-12 YV-462CP YV2165 |
| 5 | (F-WZHB) (F-GBRF) France 5/F-RAFI |
| 6 | F-WZHB N50FB N1871R N815CA 9XR-NN [w/o 06Apr94 Kigali, Rwanda] |
| 7 | F-WZHA HZ-AKI HZ-AO3 N8516Z N26LB N5DL N50HE F-WQBN France 7 |
| 8 | F-WZHC N50FE N50PG N409ER (N408ER) (N119HB) (N119HT) N119PH N508EJ N550CL |
| 9 | F-WZHD I-SAFP XA-LOH (HB-IED) VR-CBR "N100WJ" F-GGCP TR-LGY |
| 10 | F-WZHD N50FG N65B N420CL |
| 11 | F-WZHE N50FH N501NC N5739 F-GGVB |
| 12 | F-WZHC CN-ANO |
| 13 | F-WZHF N50FK N150BG (N150NW) N150TX |
| 14 | F-WZHG N50FL N233U N283U N9X N955E N917SB N880TD* |
| 15 | F-WZHM PH-ILR N350JS (N595CW) |
| 16 | F-WZHH (N50FM) D-BIRD D-BFAR F-WQBL (F-GYBM) F-HBBM F-WQBL F-HBBM |
| 17 | F-WZHI 5A-DGI TY-BBM HB-IEB N4679T N3456F N349K N349KS N727S N517CW (N550LX) N9TE N114TD |
| 18 | F-WZHJ N50FN N187S N720M N1102A N82RP N82LP N518EJ (N525MA) (N10UG) N963JF |
| 19 | F-WZHB N50FM N63A N253L N519CW (N551LX) N519EM |
| 20 | F-WZHK N50FR C6-BER N63537 N590CW (N552LX) N590RA |
| 21 | F-WZHN (9K-ACQ) 9K-AEE N299W (F-GJKT) F-GHGT N70AF N77CE N770E N56LT |
| 22 | F-WZHF N50FS N203BT N866FP XA-SFP XA-AVE XA-TUH N220JP N50FL Venezuela 0018 YV1083 |
| 23 | F-WZHG (D-BBAD) D-BBWK PH-ILD N725PA N821BS N523CW (N553LX) N523PB |
| 24 | F-WZHL N51FJ N817M N200RT N280RT N929T |
| 25 | F-WZHI Yugoslavia 72101/YU-BPZ [carried both marks] YU-BPZ "N34S"+ [+marks worn but ntu] N502EZ N753JC N877DF* |
| 26 | F-WZHA N52FJ N190MC N190MQ |
| 27 | F-WZHN HB-IEU F-WGTG France 27/F-RAFK |
| 28 | F-WZHE N53FJ N131WT PH-LEM N47UF N800FM N752JC |
| 29 | F-WZHB I-SAFR F-WGTH CS-TMF N534MA N290TJ N529CW N529MM C-GRGE |
| 30 | F-WZHD I-SNAC (YV-553CP) I-SNAC F-WQFZ France 30 |
| 31 | F-WZHC (N54FJ) I-KIDO N211CN N145W N145WF N105EJ XA-AAS N931CC (N931EJ) N890FH N292FH N987RC N250RJ N468AM |
| 32 | F-WZHJ VR-BTT N80TR N717LA |
| 33 | F-WZHA N56FJ N8100E N8300E |
| 34 | F-WZHH HB-IEV F-WEFS France 34/F-RAFL |
| 35 | F-WZHF N57FJ N800BD N907M N350AF XA-FVK |
| 36 | F-WZHJ N54FJ N345PA N450AF N59GS F-WWHZ F-ZWTA F-ZJTL France 36 |
| 37 | F-WZHM (I-CAIK) I-SAME F-GMCU F-HAIR |
| 38 | F-WZHK N58FJ N993 N505CL |
| 39 | F-WZHL N59FJ N754S N326FB N850EP |
| 40 | F-WZHG 9K-AEF N90005 N50GF N1PR N695ST N150JT N156DB |
| 41 | F-WZHI N60FJ N546EX (N760DL) N76FD (N76FB) N352JS (N541FJ) (N841FJ) N888MF N888ME |
| 42 | F-WZHE N61FJ N82MP D-BDWO OE-HCS OO-LFT (N250UC) N442AM ZS-LBB N185BA N405DC |
| 43 | F-WZHO Yugoslavia 72102 YU-BNA |
| 44 | F-WZHA N62FJ N150JP N50LT N44MK N285CP YV2346 |
| 45 | F-WZHF N63FJ N731F N9BX N569BW |
| 46 | F-WZHK N64FJ N908EF N911RF N725LB N728LB N347K N547K N777ZL |
| 47 | F-WZHP N65FJ N150WC N23AC N23AQ N1BX (N81CH) (N601CH) N37ER |
| 48 | F-WZHK HB-IET I-ERDN N134AP N247EM (N2478) N247BC C-FBVF |
| 49 | F-WZHL N66FJ N43ES N43BE N978W N650AL N800DW |
| 50 | F-WZHQ N67FJ N747 N747Y XA-GCH |
| 51 | F-WZHR N70FJ N52DC N52DQ F-GMGA N113WA N551CW (N554LX) (N551S) N524S |
| 52 | F-WZHV F-BMER F-WZHV JY-HAH N18G N86AK N163WW N900KE |
| 53 | F-WZHS N150JT (N77SW) N45SJ (N50SJ) N22T N22TZ N90AM N53FJ N22YP N53FJ YV1128 |
| 54 | F-WZHT N71FJ N450X (N50EF) N204DD N202DD N392U N130A (OY-GDA) LX-GED N589KM N100DV N51MJ N400KE |
| 55 | F-WZHU N73FJ N839F (N30N) N1CN N332MC N332MQ N625CR N300CR N96UH N200UP |
| 56 | F-WZHR F-WDFE F-GDFE N112FJ N84HP (N844J) C-FCRH |
| 57 | F-WZHC HB-IER N57B N138F N138E N505TC |
| 58 | F-WZHA N72FJ N744X N50KR |
| 59 | F-WZHB N75FJ N31DM N31V N900JB N910CN |
| 60 | F-WZHD JY-HZH N900W (N50RG) N560EJ CS-DFJ N105WC |
| 61 | F-WZHI HB-IES VP-CRF |

# FALCON 50

| C/n | Identities |
|---|---|
| 62 | F-WZHE N77FJ N292BC N50FH N562EJ (CS-DFK) N230BT |
| 63 | F-WZHF N78FJ N841F HB-IAL VR-CGP N48GP C-FKCI N63FJ YV1129 |
| 64 | F-WZHH N79FJ N418S N300A N731DD |
| 65 | F-WZHT N50FJ N90FJ N65HS D-BFFB N50LV N1EV F-GPPF |
| 66 | F-WZHP (PH-SDL) F-WZHP N500BL N50BL N4413N (VR-B..) 9U-BTB N789JC |
| 67 | F-WZHG N76FJ HB-IEP Switzerland T-783 |
| 68 | F-WZHQ 5A-DCM |
| 69 | F-WZHJ N80FJ N650X (N69VJ) N909VJ |
| 70 | F-WZHL N81FJ N230S N130K (N651SB) N699SC N300ES N306ES N700MP |
| 71 | F-WZHF YI-ALB J2-KBA N352WB |
| 72 | F-WZHM N82FJ N1181G [w/o 12May85 Lake Geneva, WI; remains to Clarkesville, MO] |
| 73 | F-WPXE HZ-SAB F-WGTG VR-CCQ N48TW N15TW (N15TA) N573CW (N556LX) N67JF |
| 74 | F-WZHA N83FJ |
| 75 | F-WZHH N95FJ N45ES N45BE N850CA N78LT |
| 76 | F-WZHB N84FJ N85MD N410WW N411WW N450CL |
| 77 | F-WZHC N85FJ N366F N992 N77NT N78LF |
| 78 | F-WPXF F-ODEO TR-LAI F-GEOY France 78/F-RAFJ |
| 79 | F-WZHE N86FJ N60CN (N881K) (N79FJ) N56LN |
| 80 | F-WZHN N87FJ XB-OEM XA-FTC N4154G XA-GFC N80WE N50SJ N50BZ N50XJ |
| 81 | F-WZHA N89FJ N718DW N504CX [converted to Falcon 50-4] |
| 82 | F-WZHG N88FJ N293BC RP-C754 (N767W) (N40F) N511GG N450KP N150BP N582EJ |
| 83 | F-WZHJ N88U N881M N50HD N50XY |
| 84 | F-WZHK N2711B F-WZHK Spain T.16-1/401-09 Spain T.16-1/45-20 N503EZ N500JD |
| 85 | F-WZHO N90FJ N50FJ N40TH N254DV N82ST |
| 86 | F-WPXD N94FJ N238U F-GKDR HB-IAT N150UC N86JC N960S |
| 87 | F-WZHS N91FJ N283K N55NT C-GLRP C-GOIL |
| 88 | F-WZHU N92FJ XA-OVR N188FJ F-WQCP VR-CRT VP-CRT N588FJ F-WQBK F-GYOL LZ-OIO F-GYOL (D-CHIC) N943RL |
| 89 | F-WZHV N93FJ N212K N212KM N890GA N400PC (N400LC) N120TJ N97BZ N589EJ CS-DFI N156WC TR-LGV |
| 90 | F-WZHX N290W N298W N600AS (N650AS) N4351M N925GS |
| 91 | F-WZHY (ZS-BFB) ZS-BMB ZS-CAS |
| 92 | F-WZHZ N97FJ N85A N40CN (N881J) N929ML |
| 93 | F-WZHB N98FJ N844X N868BT |
| 94 | F-WZHC N99FJ N82NC N212JP XA-MVR (XA-AFG) XA-TVQ N504PA [converted to Falcon 50-4] N946TC |
| 95 | F-WPXD VR-CBL N3950N N331MC C-GSSS TC-KAM F-WQBJ N29YY N70FL N95FJ N101ET |
| 96 | F-WPXE N4AC C-FMFL |
| 97 | F-WZHL (N101FJ) C-FSCL N33GG N33GQ LZ-OII N597FJ C-FPDO N850MC N412PG |
| 98 | F-WPXF VR-CBO N39461 N50MK (N50ML) N600WG |
| 99 | F-WZHM (N96FJ) C-FMYB N816M N292PC |
| 100 | F-WZHN N102FJ N14CG N450AK |
| 101 | F-WPXH YI-ALC Iran 5-9012 EP-TFA |
| 102 | F-WZHO N103FJ N50BX (N50WB) N350WB |
| 103 | F-WZHQ N104FJ N83MP N370KP |
| 104 | F-WZHR N105FJ N90AE F-GFGQ F-WWHK N50VG SE-DVG N351JS LX-UAE F-GUAE HB-IGR N725PA N49KR |
| 105 | F-WZHS N106FJ N80CN (N881L) N100EG (N214GA) N990MM |
| 106 | F-WZHT N96FJ N50BF N9300C N74TS |
| 107 | F-WPXK (ZS-LJM) LX-RVR VR-BUC VP-BUC F-WQBM F-GIQZ VP-BCZ F-GTCD F-WQBM N253SJ F-GLSJ |
| 108 | F-WZHM N101FJ N350X N150K N399GG |
| 109 | F-WZHV N109FJ N280BC N280BG N5107 |
| 110 | F-WPXG 5N-ARE VR-BJA N77TE N84TN |
| 111 | F-WZHZ N297W F-GKTV VR-CDF N50AH F-GMOT |
| 112 | F-WZHA N107FJ N144AD N193TR N652AL N216WD |
| 113 | F-WZHB N108FJ N186S N394U N35RZ N75RZ N450DR N900JB |
| 114 | F-WPXM ST-PSR |
| 115 | F-WZHC N111FJ N777MJ N50TC N522GS (N369CA) N569CA N569CC N502JB N950S N850BA |
| 116 | F-WZHD N112FJ N781B N69R F-GIDC N70AF XA-SOL XB-SOL N678MA |
| 117 | F-WPXI HB-ITH N50TG N124HM N50J N896DA |
| 118 | F-WZHF N113FJ N784B (N183B) N784B [w/o 10Nov85 on approach to Teterboro A/P, NJ] |
| 119 | F-WZHN N114FJ N83FC N57DC XA-SSS N168JC TS-JBT N929WT |
| 120 | F-WPXJ YI-ALD Iran 5-9011 EP-TFI |
| 121 | F-WZHO N115FJ N9311 N824R N121FJ N51FE |
| 122 | F-WZHG YI-ALE Iran 5-9013 |
| 123 | F-WZHH (F-GDSC) VH-SFJ N211EF F-GPSA |
| 124 | F-WZHA N116FJ N711TU N6666R N500RE N600JM N25JM VP-BFM N50MV N987F |
| 125 | F-WZHB N118FJ N711KT I-DENR HB-IBQ TS-JAM N102TF |
| 126 | F-WZHI N119FJ (YV-269CP) N9312 N931G N52DC N52DQ N200RT (N986PA) |
| 127 | F-WZHD N121FJ N1896T N1896F N129JE N48KR |
| 128 | F-WZHF N122FJ N9313 N733E N223DD N42NA |
| 129 | F-WZHQ N123FJ N1903W N4903W N99JD N751JC N634KA* |
| 130 | F-WZHR N124FJ N9314 N630L N988T C-GSRS P4-BAK |

# FALCON 50

| C/n | Identities | | | | | | | | | |
|---|---|---|---|---|---|---|---|---|---|---|
| 131 | F-WPXD | HZ-BB2 | I-ADAG | (F-GPLH) | F-WGTF | F-GOAL | N750BR | | | |
| 132 | F-WPXF | I-EDIK | France 132 | | | | | | | |
| 133 | F-WPXH | HB-IEA | HZ-AKI | HB-IEA | ZS-CAQ | | | | | |
| 134 | F-WPXK | HB-IEC | VR-CLD | VP-CLD | F-GOGL | VP-BCD | F-GUDP | F-WQBN | N134FJ | F-GOCT |
| | (OY-CKH) | F-HALM | | | | | | | | |
| 135 | F-WZHA | N125FJ | N293BC | | | | | | | |
| 136 | F-WZHB | N126FJ | N204HC | (N500HC) | N50HC | VR-BLL | N6550W | YV-455CP | YV1495 | |
| 137 | F-WZHC | N127FJ | N50FJ | (N119FJ) | C-GTPL | N119FJ | N117SF | C-FJUH | N137FA | |
| 138 | F-WPXD | N75G | N941CC | I-CAFB | N138NW | VR-CEZ | VP-CEZ | N380TJ | N138AV | N903CS |
| 139 | F-WZHD | N128FJ | N96CE | N1S | N7GX | | | | | |
| 140 | F-WPXH | VR-BHX | (F-GJTR) | F-WGTF | I-MMEA | N303JW | N750DF | | | |
| 141 | F-WZHE | N129FJ | N16R | (N222MC) | N86MC | N96NX | N924WJ | | | |
| 142 | F-WZHK | N132FJ | N4350M | N860BA | | | | | | |
| 143 | F-WZHI | N130FJ | N77CP | N444PE | | | | | | |
| 144 | F-WZHL | N133FJ | N70FL | VR-BZE | VP-BZE | N544RA | (LX-FTJ) | N7011 | | |
| 145 | F-WPXE | F-GEXE | A6-ZKM | I-CAFC | N50KD | | | | | |
| 146 | F-WZHA | N131FJ | N747 | N7228K | XA-DUQ | | | | | |
| 147 | F-WPXG | HB-IED | F-WPXG | VR-BKG | VP-BKG | N526CC | N844NX | N1CG | | |
| 148 | F-WZHB | N134FJ | N81R | N81U | YR-FNA | N28KB | N254NA | N50LQ | N770JD | |
| 149 | F-WZHJ | N135FJ | N1904W | F-GHAQ | N149MD | N1971R | N198M | N198MR | | |
| 150 | F-WZHC | N136FJ | HB-IAE | N8200E | N8400E | | | | | |
| 151 | F-WPXD | Italy (MM151) | | Italy MM62020 | | F-WQBM | I-DARK | F-GPGS | | |
| 152 | F-WZHD | N137FJ | N1841F | N75W | N75WE | N152FJ | | | | |
| 153 | F-WZHE | N138FJ | N50FJ | N16CP | N50HM | | | | | |
| 154 | F-WZHA | N139FJ | N320K | N920K | N404R | N404E | N154PA | N117AJ | | |
| 155 | F-WPXH | Italy MM62021 | | F-WQBM | I-RODJ | F-GTHS | F-GKGO | | | |
| 156 | F-WZHF | N140FJ | N5733 | N4MB | N4MR | N377HW | N500RE | | | |
| 157 | F-WPXG | N141FJ | N312A | N341M | N911HB | N901MK | N15FX | N19FX* | | |
| 158 | F-WZHH | N142FJ | N54YR | | | | | | | |
| 159 | F-WZHC | LX-NUR | I-LXAG | VR-CWI | VP-CWI | HB-ISD | N839RM | N343PM | | |
| 160 | F-WZHI | N143FJ | N48R | N487F | N4VF | | | | | |
| 161 | F-WZHA | N144FJ | N863BD | N800BD | TC-EYE | N301JJ | N770MP | N766HK | | |
| 162 | F-WZHB | N145FJ | N90R | C-GYPJ | N244AD | N750JC | | | | |
| 163 | F-WZHA | N146FJ | N50FJ | (N165FJ) | N185FJ | N5VF | N5VH | N85HP | (N854W) | N521DC |
| 164 | F-WZHD | N164FJ | HB-IAM | N164MA | N164GB | | | | | |
| 165 | F-WZHF | HZ-SM3 | LX-FMR | HB-JSR | | | | | | |
| 166 | F-WZHE | N165FJ | N500AF | (N3115U) | N500AE | N316PA | N5VF | | | |
| 167 | F-WZHG | N166FJ | N186HG | N2T | N2FQ | | | | | |
| 168 | F-WZHH | N167FJ | N711SC | N48GL | XA-RXZ | N48GL | VR-CQZ | N48GL | (N420JP) | N514MB |
| 169 | F-WPXD | I-SNAB | F-GUAJ | | | | | | | |
| 170 | F-WZHI | N169FJ | N293K | N500AF | N508AF | N504YP | [converted to Falcon 50-4] | | | |
| 171 | F-WZHJ | N170FJ | N171FJ | N40AS | (N650AS) | N750H | | | | |
| 172 | F-WZHK | N170FJ | N98R | N9000F | N256A | | | | | |
| 173 | F-WZHL | N172FJ | (JA....) | PT-LJI | N544CM | | | | | |
| 174 | F-WPXE | HB-IAG | N79PF | N565A | N8KG | N988SB | | | | |
| 175 | F-WZHM | N177FJ | N50FJ | N334MC | N330MC | N200RT | VR-B.. | N530AR | N50FX | M-AGER* |
| 176 | F-WZHN | N178FJ | VH-PDJ | N157SP | N95GC | I-DEGF | VR-CFI | C-FNNC | N568VA | N711T |
| | N777XY | | | | | | | | | |
| 177 | F-WPXF | 9Q-CGK | 9Q-CPK | (N68BA) | ZS-PFB | N14NE | XA-UCN | XA-TAB | | |
| 178 | F-WZHO | N179FJ | N239R | N59PM | N634H | | | | | |
| 179 | F-WZHP | N180FJ | HL7386 | N222MC | N212Q | N232PR | N500TS | | | |
| 180 | F-WWHC | I-POLE | N45FG | N2254S | N50SF | | | | | |
| 181 | F-WWHA | N181FJ | N345AP | N367TP | N93AX | N600CH | N26WJ | | | |
| 182 | F-WWHB | N182FJ | N250AS | N713SN | | | | | | |
| 183 | F-WWHF | I-CAFD | | | | | | | | |
| 184 | F-WWHD | N183FJ | N50FJ | N89FC | N25MB | N25ME | N633W | | | |
| 185 | F-WWHE | N184FJ | C-GDCO | N23SY | N238Y | F-GKBZ | LX-THS | | | |
| 186 | F-WWHH | N278FJ | N450K | N25SJ | | | | | | |
| 187 | F-WWHG | N279FJ | N4CP | N4QP | VH-PPF | N187PN | | | | |
| 188 | F-WWHA | N280FJ | N50FJ | PT-WAN | LV-WXV | N160AF | XA-ALA | N188FJ | | |
| 189 | F-WWHB | N281FJ | N50WG | N55SN | N51V | N51VT | N51V | | | |
| 190 | F-WWHG | I-CAFE | CS-TMJ | F-GXMC | | | | | | |
| 191 | F-WWHD | N282FJ | N950F | | | | | | | |
| 192 | F-WWHE | N283FJ | N212T | N96LT | N96UT | | | | | |
| 193 | F-WWHH | Italy MM62026 | | | | | | | | |
| 194 | F-WWHM | N284FJ | N10AT | N10LT | N95PH | N194K | | | | |
| 195 | F-WWHK | Portugal 7401 | | Portugal 17401 | | | | | | |
| 196 | F-WWHD | N285FJ | N8575J | JA8575 | N71TH | D-BNTH | VP-BSA | N388TC | N196FJ | |
| 197 | F-WWHA | N286FJ | N50FJ | N500KJ | N404JF | N57MK | | | | |
| 198 | F-WWHC | Portugal 7402 | | Portugal 17402 | | | | | | |
| 199 | F-WWHB | N287FJ | N291BC | N290MX | | | | | | |
| 200 | F-WWHE | N288FJ | N664P | N664B | N595JS | N749CP | N769CP | | | |
| 201 | F-WWHA | N289FJ | N41TH | N54DA | N553M | | | | | |
| 202 | F-WWHB | N290FJ | N212N | N97LT | N97UT | N202CP | N750MC | N512JB | | |
| 203 | F-WWHA | I-CSGA | C-GNCA | N203NC | | | | | | |
| 204 | F-WWHD | F-GKAR | VR-CGP | VP-CGP | EC-GPN | EC-HHS | (F-HDCB) | N725PA | F-HDCB | |

# FALCON 50

| C/n | Identities | | | | | | | | | |
|---|---|---|---|---|---|---|---|---|---|---|
| 205 | F-WWHD | N291FJ | N57EL | N59EL | N52JJ | N348K | (N848K) | N504MK | | |
| 206 | F-WWHB | VR-BMF | VP-BMF | N801DL | | | | | | |
| 207 | F-WWHC | N292FJ | N55BP | N50CS | N396EG | N275HH | | | | |
| 208 | F-WWHP | I-CSGB | VR-CCQ | C-GWEI | N50AE | N50HC | | | | |
| 209 | F-WWHE | N293FJ | N59CF | N59CH | EC-168 | EC-FPG | N1902W | N96DS | VP-BSL | N358MH |
| 210 | F-WWHL | F-GICN | XA-TXB | N411GC | | | | | | |
| 211 | F-WWHR | Italy MM62029 | | | | | | | | |
| 212 | F-WWHH | N294FJ | N50FJ | N30TH | N40TH | N85WN | LX-APG | UR-CCF | | |
| 213 | F-WWHW | N295FJ | XA-RVV | | | | | | | |
| 214 | F-WWHX | N296FJ | N55AS | (N214FJ) | N265G | | | | | |
| 215 | F-WWHT | N297FJ | XA-SIM | D-BOOK | (D-BOOI) | HB-JSV | F-GOLV | | | |
| 216 | F-WWHZ | N298FJ | N180AR | N56SN | N84NW | N722FS | | | | |
| 217 | F-WWHV | N122FJ | N5732 | N573AC | N573TR | | | | | |
| 218 | F-WWHA | N50NK | N218WA | D-BERT | N750FJ | N703TM | | | | |
| 219 | F-WWHS | N129FJ | YV-450CP | YV1496 | | | | | | |
| 220 | F-WWHG | N131FJ | N75RD | N100RR | N528JR | N50FF | | | | |
| 221 | F-WWHL | Portugal 7403 | | Portugal 17403 | | | | | | |
| 222 | F-WWHM | D-BELL | OE-HIT | | | | | | | |
| 223 | F-WWHN | N132FJ | N633L | N840FJ | N451CL | | | | | |
| 224 | F-WWHO | N133FJ | VR-CNV | XA-SDK | XA-BEG | N800BD | N87TN | | | |
| 225 | F-WWHP | N134FJ | N50FJ | N32TC | N428CC | | | | | |
| 226 | F-WWHC | N119AM | F-WQBN | VP-BBD | CS-DPO | | | | | |
| 227 | F-WWHE | N226FJ | N50FJ | (N227FJ) | N1848U | N630SR | N37LC | (N37LQ) | C-GGFP | |
| 228 | F-WWHR | (F-GNFS) | F-GNFF | VR-BJJ | F-GJEK | F-WWHR | N313GH | VR-CAE | C-GAZU | N228FJ |
| 229 | F-WWHH | N114FJ | C-GMII | C-GMID | N550WM | | | | | |
| 230 | F-WWHD | F-GNGL | HB-IAV | 3B-NSY | OY-LIN | F-OMON | N506BA | N930JG | | |
| 231 | F-WWHA | N228FJ | (VR-B..) | XA-SIF | N10PQ | N10PP | N199FG | | | |
| 232 | F-WWHT | F-WNLR | F-GNLR | N244FJ | N45NC | N45NQ | N100KP | N108KP | ZS-MGS | |
| 233 | F-WWHB | (N233FJ) | N232FJ | N48HB | N318GA | (N919GA) | | | | |
| 234 | F-WWHC | N233FJ | PT-AAF | PR-WYW | | | | | | |
| 235 | F-WWHM | F-GKRU | (UR-ACA) | UR-CCC | | | | | | |
| 236 | F-WWHD | N234FJ | N50FJ | N70FJ | XA-HGF | N195SV | N196SV | XA-HHF | N725PA | N347K |
| | N50FJ | | | | | | | | | |
| 237 | F-WWHE | N237FJ | N2425 | (N5425) | N94BJ | N74BJ | N89BM | N85TN | | |
| 238 | F-WWHF | N238FJ | N50FJ | XA-LRA | N796A | N238DL | SE-DVL | N970S | | |
| 239 | F-WWHG | N239FJ | N200SG | | | | | | | |
| 240 | F-WWHH | F-GNMO | (N40SK) | N780F | N33TY | N34TY | (N200BN) | N398AC | | |
| 241 | F-WWHF | F-OKSI | N233BC | N86TN | | | | | | |
| 242 | F-WWHA | N241FJ | XA-SPM | N599SC | N9000F | N733M | N733N | N733K | | |
| 243 | F-WWHM | N243FJ | N742R | N62HM | | | | | | |
| 244 | F-WWHK | N243FJ | N50FJ | N95HC | | | | | | |
| 245 | F-WWHL | N240FJ | N720ML | N720ME | N530DG | N827CT | | | | |
| 246 | F-WWHF | N246FJ | TC-YSR | F-GTJF | 3C-LGE | | | | | |
| 247 | F-WWHP | N247FJ | N740R | N520AF | | | | | | |
| 248 | F-WWHB | N249FJ | N25UD | N25UB | N67PW | | | | | |
| 249 | F-WWHN | N248FJ | (XA-DMS) | N663MN | SE-DVK | N247CJ | N980S | | | |
| 250 | F-WWHR | N250FJ | N696HC | N696HQ | N277JW | N917JC | | | | |
| 251* | F-WOND | [ff 10Apr96] | | (F-GOND) | VR-CLN | VP-CLN | (F-GIVD) | N870 | N565 | N171TG |
| 252 | F-WWHE | (N313GH) | N93GH | N50FJ | XA-TDD | N52FJ | XA-RUY | | | |
| 253* | F-WWHA | N253EX | PT-WSC | N85F | | | | | | |
| 254* | F-WWHB | N50FJ | N50AE | N345AP | N94PC | | | | | |
| 255* | F-WWHC | N255CM | N50MG | | | | | | | |
| 256* | F-WWHD | VP-CBT | N600N | | | | | | | |
| 257* | F-WWHE | F-OKSY | N925BC | | | | | | | |
| 258* | F-WWHF | F-WQHU | VP-BST | N48G | N726JG | | | | | |
| 259* | F-WWHG | VP-CHG | N373RS | | | | | | | |
| 260* | F-WWHK | N586CS | | | | | | | | |
| 261* | F-WWHL | N140RT | (N97FJ) | N73GH | | | | | | |
| 262* | F-WWHM | N262EX | N1896T | C-GOFJ | | | | | | |
| 263* | F-WWHN | N8550A | N503PC | N503PQ | | | | | | |
| 264* | F-WWHO | F-GVDN | C6-BHD | N900CH | C-GWFM | | | | | |
| 265* | F-WWHP | N9550A | N501PC | N838DB | | | | | | |
| 266* | F-WWHQ | VP-BPA | N50NM | | | | | | | |
| 267* | F-WWHR | (D-BETI) | F-OHFO | D-BETI | | | | | | |
| 268* | F-WWHS | EC-GTR | CS-TMS | PH-JNL | F-WQBL | N268FJ | F-WQBL | G-ITIH | G-DASO | M-DASO |
| 269* | F-WWHT | F-GPBG | F-GJBZ | | | | | | | |
| 270* | F-WWHU | N270EX | N148M | C-GJLB | | | | | | |
| 271* | F-WWHV | TC-BHO | N30FE | N30FT | N865PC | | | | | |
| 272* | F-WWHW | N272EX | N50FJ | C-GMII | N272F | C-GKCI | C-FZYB | | | |
| 273* | F-WWHX | N158M | N198M | | | | | | | |
| 274* | F-WWHY | N138M | N80GP | | | | | | | |
| 275* | F-WWHA | F-GODP | N56LC | N44LC | N44EQ | N75FJ | | | | |
| 276* | F-WWHB | N159M | N128M | N789ME | | | | | | |
| 277* | F-WWHC | N368M | N198M | N192F | N818KF | | | | | |
| 278* | F-WWHD | VP-CFI | N623QW | C-GXBB | | | | | | |
| 279* | F-WWHE | N181MC | N928WK | | | | | | | |

# FALCON 50

| C/n | Identities | | | | | |
|---|---|---|---|---|---|---|
| 280* | F-WWHF | N50FJ | N1829S | | | |
| 281* | F-WWHG | N17AN | C-GNET | | | |
| 282* | F-WWHH | N191MC | | | | |
| 283* | F-WWHK | VP-CEF | VP-BEF | N283FJ | N223HD | |
| 284* | F-WWHL | N904SB | N703AW* | | | |
| 285* | F-WWHM | N901TF | | | | |
| 286* | F-WWHN | (F-GKIN) | VP-BMI | N286ZT | VP-BEA | |
| 287* | F-WWHO | ZS-ONG | | | | |
| 288* | F-WWHP | N288EX | N33TY | N83TY | | |
| 289* | F-WWHQ | N214DV | N315DV | (N589FJ) | M-GPIK | |
| 290* | F-WWHR | N44SK | N42SK | (N660AH) | (N302WY) | |
| 291* | F-WWHS | N294EX | XA-GMD | XA-UDW | | |
| 292* | F-WWHT | N292EX | N38WP | | | |
| 293* | F-WWHU | N293EX | N195SV | | | |
| 294* | F-WWHV | N39WP | | | | |
| 295* | F-WWHW | I-FJDN | P4-JET | | | |
| 296* | F-WWHX | N296EX | N50FJ | N23FM | | |
| 297* | F-WWHY | N119AG | F-WQBJ | OE-HHH | F-HCDD | |
| 298* | F-WWHZ | N615SR | | | | |
| 299* | F-WWHA | N299EX | PP-PMV | | | |
| 300* | F-WWHB | N344CM | N749CP | | | |
| 301* | F-WWHC | N301EX | N476MK | N504MS | | |
| 302* | F-WWHD | N302FJ | N45NC | | | |
| 303* | F-WWHE | N902TF | | | | |
| 304* | F-WWHF | N918JM | N909JM | | | |
| 305* | F-WWHG | TC-BNT | F-WQBK | N302BG | N102BG | N102BQ | N710BG |
| 306* | F-WWHH | LX-AKI | F-HCEF | | | |
| 307* | F-WWHK | N950H | | | | |
| 308* | F-WWHL | N902SB | N719DW | | | |
| 309* | F-WWHM | N903SB | N37WX | | | |
| 310* | F-WWHN | N310EX | N50FJ | N310EX | N50FQ | N50SN |
| 311* | F-WWHO | N507AS | VP-CBF | | | |
| 312* | F-WWHP | N26WP | | | | |
| 313* | F-WWHR | G-JPSI | F-WQBM | N921EC | N225HD | |
| 314* | F-WWHT | N314EX | N55LC | N55LQ | N311BP | |
| 315* | F-WWHU | N668P | PH-LSV | | | |
| 316* | F-WWHV | N316EX | N696HC | N696HQ | N1838S | |
| 317* | F-WWHW | N1839S | N607SG | | | |
| 318* | F-WWHX | N416KC | N410KC | N771HM | | |
| 319* | F-WWHY | N319EX | N50FJ | (N319EX) | N85CL | N85DN | XA-PRR |
| 320* | F-WWHZ | N662P | N500AF | | | |
| 321* | F-WWHA | N321EX | N900CM | | | |
| 322* | F-WWHB | N5322 | | | | |
| 323* | F-WWHC | N323EX | N500N | N50QN | N500R | |
| 324* | F-WWHD | N324EX | F-WWHD | LX-IRE | N150RJ | |
| 325* | F-WWHE | N325EX | N146AS | | | |
| 326* | F-WWHF | N37LC | N33LC | N33EQ | N850EN | |
| 327* | F-WWHG | N327EX | N188DM | | | |
| 328* | F-WWHH | N328EX | N308DM | N223F | | |
| 329* | F-WWHK | N329EX | (N50FJ) | N98AC | | |
| 330* | F-WWHL | N330EX | N115SK | | | |
| 331* | F-WWHM | N331EX | (N331SE) | | | |
| 332* | F-WWHN | N332EX | N280BC | | | |
| 333* | F-WWHO | N334EX | N701WC | | | |
| 334* | F-WWHP | N335EX | OE-HPS | F-HDPB | | |
| 335* | F-WWHQ | N535EX | C-GMII | | | |
| 336* | F-WWHR | N224HD | | | | |
| 337* | F-WWHS | N50FJ | N89NC | N988GC | | |
| 338* | F-WWHT | N338FJ | N883RA | N883RW | N137LR* | |
| 339* | F-WWHU | 5B-CKN | I-PBRA | | | |
| 340* | F-WWHV | N340EX | N109CQ | | | |
| 341* | F-WWHW | I-ZUGR | G-KPTN | | | |
| 342* | F-WWHX | N342EX | N649TT | | | |
| 343* | F-WWHY | N343EX | N733M | | | |
| 344* | F-WWHZ | N344EX | N50YP | | | |
| 345* | F-WWHA | VP-BMP | | | | |
| 346* | F-WWHB | N346EX | F-HAPM | | | |
| 347* | F-WWHC | F-HAPN | | | | |
| 348* | F-WWHD | N905SB | P4-SNS | | | |
| 349* | F-WWHE | N906SB | N30JC | N575JC | | |
| 350* | F-WWHF | N350DV | N214DV | | | |
| 351* | F-WWHH | N158M | | | | |
| 352* | F-WWHK | N1836S | | | | |

Production complete

# DASSAULT FALCON 7X

The Falcon 7X was originally known as the Falcon FNX.

| C/n | Identities | | | | |
|---|---|---|---|---|---|
| 1 | F-WFBW | [rolled out 15Feb05; ff 05May05] | | | |
| 2 | F-WTDA | [ff 05Jly05] | | (F-HNFG) | HB-JSS |
| 3 | F-WSKY | [ff 20Sep05] | | VP-BIL | |
| 4 | F-WWUA | [ff 08Jun06] | | HB-JSZ | |
| 5 | F-WWUB | VP-BGG | | | |
| 6 | F-WWUC | (N200L) | N607X | PR-WRM | |
| 7 | F-WWUD | N70FL | | | |
| 8 | F-WWUE | N999BE | | | |
| 9 | F-WWUF | (N9707X)+ | [+ ntu marks worn at completion centre] | | VP-BVY |
| 10 | F-WWUG | XA-MAR | | | |
| 11 | F-WWUH | VP-BAR | | | |
| 12 | F-WWUI | HB-JSO | | | |
| 13 | F-WWUJ | N907SB | | | |
| 14 | F-WWUK | VP-BZE | | | |
| 15 | F-WWUL | CS-TLY | | | |
| 16 | F-WWUM | (HB-JSS)+ | [+ ntu marks worn at completion centre] | | N7707X |
| 17 | F-WWUN | HB-JST | | | |
| 18 | F-WWUO | N273JC | | | |
| 19 | F-WWUP | F-GYDA | F-WWUP | F-HAKA | |
| 20 | F-WWUQ | M-SVNX | OH-FFD | | |
| 21 | F-WWUR | VP-BEH | | | |
| 22 | F-WWUS | PR-DNZ | | | |
| 23 | F-WWZK | N188SW | | | |
| 24 | F-WWZL | N171EX | | | |
| 25 | F-WWZM | N8000E | | | |
| 26 | F-WWZN | N7MR | | | |
| 27 | F-WWZO | VQ-BFN | | | |
| 28 | F-WWZP | | | | |
| 29 | F-WWZQ | N671WB | | | |
| 30 | F-WWZR | CS-DSA | | | |
| 31 | F-WWZS | N786CS | | | |
| 32 | F-WWZT | XA-CXW | | | |
| 33 | F-WWZU | N7X | | | |
| 34 | F-WWZV | (F-GVRB) | I-AFIT | | |
| 35 | F-WWZW | (N100HC)+ | [+ ntu marks worn at completion centre] | | N207TR |
| 36 | F-WWZX | G-SRDG | | | |
| 37 | F-WWZY | HB-JSI | | | |
| 38 | F-WWZZ | N55LC | | | |
| 39 | F-WWVK | N900DW | | | |
| 40 | F-WWVL | M-ROLL | | | |
| 41 | F-WWVM | N741FJ | OO-NAD | | |
| 42 | F-WWVN | F-HCCX | F-WHLV | OE-IVA | |
| 43 | F-WWVO | CS-DSB | | | |
| 44 | F-WWVP | HB-JLK | | | |
| 45 | F-WWVQ | | | | |
| 46 | F-WWVR | VQ-BAA | | | |
| 47 | F-WWVS | | | | |
| 48 | F-WWVT | N748FJ | | | |
| 49 | F-WWUA | VT-RGX* | | | |
| 50 | F-WWUB | C-GMGX | | | |
| 51 | F-WWUC | N817X | | | |
| 52 | F-WWUD | G-CNUK | | | |
| 53 | F-WWVU | N12U | | | |
| 54 | F-WWVV | OY-JDE | | | |
| 55 | F-WWVX | OE-LLL | | | |
| 56 | F-WWVY | LX-ZXP | | | |
| 57 | F-WWVZ | OO-AAA | | | |
| 58 | F-WWHA | VQ-BSN | | | |
| 59 | F-WWHB | G-PVHT | | | |
| 60 | F-WWHC | CS-DTD | | | |
| 61 | F-WWHD | | | | |
| 62 | F-WWHE | N62FJ | N11HD | | |
| 63 | F-WWHF | N763FJ | | | |
| 64 | F-WWHH | VQ-BSO | | | |
| 65 | F-WWHK | | | | |
| 66 | F-WWHL | (D-AJAB) | OH-FFF | | |
| 67 | F-WWUE | | | | |
| 68 | F-WWUG | F-GJLQ | France 68/F-RAFA | | |
| 69 | F-WWUH | G-CGGN | | | |
| 70 | F-WWUJ | C-GRGM | | | |
| 71 | F-WWHM | | | | |
| 72 | F-WWHN | N312P | | | |
| 73 | F-WWHO | | | | |
| 74 | F-WWHP | | | | |

## FALCON 7X

| C/n | Series | Identities | |
|---|---|---|---|
| 75 | F-WWHQ | | |
| 76 | F-WWHR | HB-JSN | |
| 77 | F-WWHS | D-ACGN | D-APLC |
| 78 | F-WWHT | SE-DJC | |
| 79 | F-WWHU | | |
| 80 | F-WWUF | | |
| 81 | F-WWUI | | |
| 82 | F-WWUK | | |
| 83 | F-WWUL | VQ-BSP | |
| 84 | F-WWUM | | |
| 85 | F-WWUN | | |
| 86 | F-WWUS | | |
| 87 | F-WWUO | | |
| 88 | F-WWUP | | |
| 89 | F-WWUQ | | |
| 90 | F-WWUR | | |
| 91 | F-WWZL | | |
| 92 | F-WWZM | | |
| 93 | F-WWZN | | |
| 94 | F-WWZQ | | |
| 95 | F-WWZT | | |
| 96 | F-WWZU | | |
| 97 | F-WWZX | | |
| 98 | F-WWNA | | |
| 99 | F-WWNB | | |
| 100 | F-WWNC | | |
| 101 | F-WWND | | |
| 102 | F-WWNE | | |
| 103 | F-WWNF | | |
| 104 | F-WWVO | | |
| 105 | F-WWVR | | |
| 106 | F-WWZK | | |
| 107 | F-WWZR | | |
| 108 | F-WWZS | | |
| 109 | F-WWVL | | |
| 110 | F-WWVM | | |
| 111 | F-WWVN | | |
| 112 | F-WWVK | | |
| 113 | F-WWVP | | |
| 114 | F-WWZO | | |
| 115 | F-WWZW | | |
| 116 | F-WWZY | | |
| 117 | F-WWZV | | |
| 118 | F-WWZZ | | |
| 119 | F-WWHA | | |
| 120 | F-WWHB | | |
| 121 | F-WWHC | | |
| 122 | | | |
| 123 | | | |
| 124 | | | |
| 125 | | | |
| 126 | | | |
| 127 | | | |
| 128 | | | |
| 129 | | | |
| 130 | | | |
| 131 | | | |
| 132 | | | |
| 133 | | | |
| 134 | | | |
| 135 | | | |
| 136 | | | |
| 137 | | | |
| 138 | | | |
| 139 | | | |
| 140 | | | |
| 141 | | | |
| 142 | | | |
| 143 | | | |
| 144 | | | |
| 145 | | | |
| 146 | | | |
| 147 | | | |
| 148 | | | |
| 149 | | | |
| 150 | | | |

# DASSAULT FALCON 900

| C/n | Series | Identities |
|---|---|---|
| 1 | B | F-WIDE [ff 21Sep84] F-GIDE [converted to prototype 900B] F-HOCI G-HMEI F-GOEI* |
| 2 | | F-WFJC F-GFJC France 2/F-RAFP |
| 3 | | F-WWFA N403FJ N327K N991RF N728GH |
| 4 | | F-WWFC (HB-...) VR-BJX F-WWFA France 4/F-RAFQ |
| 5 | B | F-WWFB N404FJ VH-BGF F-GGRH N905TS PT-WQM N905FJ (D-ACDC) G-HMEV F-GOEV* |
| 6 | B | F-WWFD N405FJ N80F N885 |
| 7 | B | F-WWFG TR-LCJ 3B-XLA F-GMOH |
| 8 | B | F-WWFE N406FJ N5731 N316SS |
| 9 | | F-WWFJ (PH-ILC) HB-IAB C6-BHN N900TR N193TR N232CL |
| 10 | B | F-WWFF N407FJ N900FJ (N910FJ) N26LB N96LB N5MC N349K N349H |
| 11 | | F-WWFK LX-AER F-WEFX UN-09002 F-GLGY N251SJ F-GKHJ |
| 12 | B | F-WWFH N408FJ N991AS N77CE N8VF |
| 13 | B | F-WWFI N409FJ N328K (N75V) (N75W) N75V N61TS N297AP |
| 14 | | F-WWFL N410FJ N900SB N906SB N324SR VP-BLP N44EG (N47EG) |
| 15 | | F-WWFM HB-IAK XA-RGB (N115FJ) N999EH |
| 16 | B | F-WWFN N412FJ (N187HG) N187H VR-CTA N619BD VP-CBD N64BD N900SF |
| 17 | B | F-WWFO N411FJ N944AD N790JC |
| 18 | | F-WWFA N413FJ N72PS N72PX |
| 19 | | F-WWFB N414FJ N900SJ N45SJ N1L* |
| 20 | | F-WWFC N415FJ (N711T) N999PM N70FJ N911RF N256DV N920DB |
| 21 | B | F-WWFJ (HZ-R4A) HZ-AFT |
| 22 | B | F-WWFD N416FJ N54DC OE-ICF |
| 23 | | F-WWFK I-BEAU |
| 24 | | F-WWFE N417FJ N901B N67WB N93GR N93CR N93GR N202WR |
| 25 | B | F-WWFF N418FJ N70EW N75EW N660BD N615MS |
| 26 | B | F-WWFM HB-IAC SX-ECH N900RN VP-CJF YR-CJF |
| 27 | B | F-WWFH N419FJ N90EW N91EW N5VJ |
| 28 | | F-WWFK N420FJ N85D N86MC N1S |
| 29 | | F-WWFA N421FJ C-GTCP N19VF |
| 30 | | F-WWFL HB-IAF F-WGTH (F-GIRZ) I-DIES |
| 31 | B | F-WWFB N422FJ N900FJ N910JW |
| 32 | B | F-WWFG N423FJ VH-BGV F-GJBT N800BL N500BL N10MZ N18MZ |
| 33 | B | F-WWFC N424FJ N298W F-GHEA N9138Y N901SB N931SB N203CW TY-AOM |
| 34 | B | F-WWFD N425FJ N8100E N8200E |
| 35 | | F-WWFC HB-IAD F-GLMU PP-PPA F-GNDK PH-OLI N139AL |
| 36 | B | F-WWFE N426FJ N96PM N91MK N922JW |
| 37 | B | F-WWFN N427FJ N45SJ N41SJ VH-FCP VH-ACE N394WJ |
| 38 | | F-WWFE Spain T.18-1/45-40 |
| 39 | B | F-WWFF N428FJ (N900BF) N1818S N181BS N5733 N573J N239AX |
| 40 | B | F-WWFH N429FJ N904M N145W N369BG (N389BG) (N940SJ) N924S N839RM |
| 41 | | F-WWFI N430FJ N404F N404FF N76FD |
| 42 | B | F-WWFJ N431FJ N900FJ N42FJ N117TF N901BB N990BB |
| 43 | B | F-WWFC I-MTDE N288Z N388Z (N692SH) N693SH N410KA* |
| 44 | B | F-WWFA N432FJ N914J N914JL HB-IBY N100UP |
| 45 | B | F-WWFB N433FJ N64BE N298W |
| 46 | | F-WWFD N434FJ N329K N779SG N46FJ TR-AFJ |
| 47 | | F-WWFA A6-ZKM F-WQBJ (F-GOFC) F-GNMF F-WQBK N678CH |
| 48 | B | F-WWFM N435FJ N900MJ N233KC |
| 49 | | F-WWFD VR-BLB VP-BLB |
| 50 | B | F-WWFH N436FJ N330K N900TA (N711WK) N950SF |
| 51 | B | F-WWFG N437FJ N59LB N26LB (N50RG) N9RG N528JR N328JR VP-BMB |
| 52 | | F-WWFC 5N-FGO |
| 53 | | F-WWFN N438FJ JA8570 |
| 54 | | F-WWFC (LX-IMN) I-FICV F-GKAY N954FJ |
| 55 | B | F-WWFO N439FJ C-FJES N495GA N404R N704R (N955FJ) C-GSMR N117SF |
| 56 | | F-WWFB N440FJ JA8571 |
| 57 | B | F-WWFK N441FJ N900WK |
| 58 | B | F-WWFE OE-ILS HB-IGL |
| 59 | B | F-WWFD N442FJ N32B TR-AFR |
| 60 | | F-WWFG N443FJ N900FJ N91TH N900VL |
| 61 | B | F-WWFB VR-CSA HZ-AB2 HZ-AFZ |
| 62 | B | F-WWFJ F-GIVR N62FJ F-WQBL F-GSCN F-WQBJ LX-LFB OO-LFQ LX-LFB VP-CAX |
| 63 | | F-WWFF N445FJ N90TH N127EM N75W N311JA |
| 64 | | F-WWFH N446FJ Malaysia M37-01 |
| 65 | | F-WWFM N447FJ N216FP N216FB N990MC (N990MQ) N988T |
| 66 | | F-WWFE F-GJPM CS-TMK CS-TFN |
| 67 | B | F-WWFD N448FJ N900MA N900MG |
| 68 | B | F-WWFL N449FJ N900HC N900HE |
| 69 | | F-WWFD I-SNAX F-WQBM HB-JSP F-GPGK |
| 70 | | F-WWFN N450FJ Australia A26-070 VH-VIW N105BK |
| 71 | B | F-WWFB N451FJ (N900BF) PK-TRP N280BC N280BQ N642JC |
| 72 | | F-WWFF VR-BLM VP-BLM |

# FALCON 900

| C/n | Series | Identities | | | | | | | | |
|---|---|---|---|---|---|---|---|---|---|---|
| 73 | | F-WWFA | N452FJ | Australia A26-073 | VH-WII | N109BK | Spain T.18-5/45-44 | | | |
| 74 | | F-WWFF | N453FJ | Australia A26-074 | VH-WIZ | N108BK | Spain T.18-4/45-43 | | | |
| 75 | | F-WWFC | N458FJ | C-FWSC | HB-IAI | N60RE | N60TL | | | |
| 76 | | F-WWFE | N454FJ | Australia A26-076 | VH-WIZ | N106BK | N54SK | HZ-DME | | |
| 77 | | F-WWFG | N455FJ | Australia A26-077 | VH-WIM | N107BK | Spain T.18-3/45-42 | | | |
| 78 | B | F-WWFH | N456FJ | N332MC | C-GSSS | N522KM | LX-GES | F-GVMO | | |
| 79 | B | F-WWFM | N457FJ | N900FJ | N901FJ | N6BX | N6PX | N952GD | | |
| 80 | B | F-WWFA | N459FJ | N914BD | N914DD | | | | | |
| 81 | | F-WWFL | 7T-VPA | N81GN | I-TLCM | | | | | |
| 82 | | F-WWFM | 7T-VPB | N82GP | (N561CM) | N649TT | N699BG | | | |
| 83 | B | F-WWFG | N460FJ | N900WG | N900NE | N361K | | | | |
| 84 | | F-WWFD | A6-AUH | F-WQBM | ST-PSA | | | | | |
| 85 | | F-WWFC | N461FJ | N74FS | | | | | | |
| 86 | | F-WWFE | A6-UAE | F-GVAE | HB-JEI | | | | | |
| 87 | B | F-WWFA | N462FJ | N33GG | N402FG | | | | | |
| 88 | B | F-WWFH | VR-BLT | F-GNDA | N987QK | N987GK | | | | |
| 89 | | F-WWFB | I-NUMI | | | | | | | |
| 90 | | F-WWFG | Spain T.18-2/45-41 | | | | | | | |
| 91 | | F-WWFH | A7-AAD | N91WF | CS-DFA | N991EJ | CS-DFH | | | |
| 92 | | F-WWFL | N463FJ | PT-OEX | | | | | | |
| 93 | B | F-WWFM | EC-617 | EC-FEN | N900Q | N780SP | | | | |
| 94 | | F-WWFC | A7-AAE | N94WA | CS-DFB | N889TD | | | | |
| 95 | B | F-WWFO | N464FJ | N478A | N343MG | N898TS | | | | |
| 96 | | F-WWFF | F-GHTD | F-WWFF | 5N-OIL | 5N-FGE | | | | |
| 97 | B | F-WWFA | EC-765 | EC-FFO | XA-SJX | (N900DU) | N902NC | | | |
| 98 | B | F-WWFM | N465FJ | N900FJ | (N903FJ) | N59CF | N590F | | | |
| 99 | | F-WWFE | ZS-NAN | | | | | | | |
| 100 | | F-WWFN | YK-ASC | | | | | | | |
| 101 | B | F-WWFO | N466FJ | D-ALME | VP-CAB | | | | | |
| 102 | | F-WWFK | N467FJ | N906WK | | | | | | |
| 103 | B | F-WWFL | F-GHYB | F-WWFJ | V5-NAM | | | | | |
| 104 | B | F-WWFA | N468FJ | N104FJ | N881G | N900CS | N945TM | | | |
| 105 | B | F-WWFD | N469FJ | N8572 | JA8572 | N71TH | F-GTGJ | F-WQBJ | F-GTGJ | CN-TFU |
| | | N767CF | N405EJ | N225KS | N974BK | | | | | |
| 106 | B | F-WWFL | F-GKDI | 9M-BAN | F-GJRH | N332EC | N333EC | EC-JVR | | |
| 107 | B | F-WWFJ | N470FJ | XA-GTR | N823BJ | N23BJ | N71GK | | | |
| 108 | B | F-WWFN | N471FJ | N334MC | N511WM | N229HD | (N108FJ) | YV2039 | N108FJ | |
| 109 | B | F-WWFB | G-BTIB | Belgium CD-01 | | | | | | |
| 110 | B | F-WWFH | OY-CKK | F-GHGO | N110FJ | C-GJPG | | | | |
| 111 | B | F-WWFH | N472FJ | N8BX | TS-JSM | | | | | |
| 112 | B | F-WWFM | N473FJ | N246AG | N248AG | N908JB | | | | |
| 113 | B | F-WWFB | HZ-SAB2 | N612NL | N525MH | | | | | |
| 114 | B | F-WWFC | N474FJ | XA-SIM | | | | | | |
| 115 | B | F-WWFL | EC-235 | EC-FPI | LX-TAG | HB-IBG | LX-MEL | I-FLYS | F-GSNK | |
| 116 | B | F-WWFO | N475FJ | N900FJ | N5VF | N5VN | N82RP | | | |
| 117 | B | F-WWFA | N476FJ | N70TH | N900WF | | | | | |
| 118 | B | F-WWFB | F-GNFI | RA-09000 | | | | | | |
| 119 | B | F-WWFD | N477FJ | N22T | | | | | | |
| 120 | B | F-WWFN | VR-BNJ | VP-BNJ | F-GRAX | F-WQBM | CS-DLA | F-GXDZ | | |
| 121 | B | F-WWFE | N478FJ | 9M-BAB | HB-IFQ | | | | | |
| 122 | B | F-WWFF | N479FJ | XA-SGW | N612BH | N247CJ | | | | |
| 123 | B | F-WWFL | RA-09001 | | | | | | | |
| 124 | B | F-WWFG | N480FJ | VR-BWS | VP-BWS | N14NA | | | | |
| 125 | B | F-WWFL | F-GPAX | F-WWFL | VR-BSK | VP-BSK | RP-C7808 | N978PW | | |
| 126 | B | F-WWFM | N481FJ | N900FJ | N733A | N733HL | N910CS | N94NA | N3HB | |
| 127 | B | F-WWFC | N482FJ | N654CN | N390F | N909AS | N963RS | N964RS | XA-... | |
| 128 | B | F-WWFM | N128FJ | N999PM | (N999PN) | N11LK | N98NX | | | |
| 129 | B | F-WWFD | N483FJ | XA-VTO | | | | | | |
| 130 | B | F-WWFC | F-GOAB | F-WWFB | VR-CID | VP-CID | F-WQBN | F-GKBQ | G-HAAM | A6-SAC |
| 131 | B | F-WWFH | N131FJ | N900FJ | N158JA | XA-TJG | N900VT | N900KD | N900D | |
| 132 | B | F-WWFI | N132FJ | N707WB | N767WB | | | | | |
| 133 | B | F-WWFH | F-GODE | HZ-OFC3 | N395L | N5UU | N813TS | YV2040 | | |
| 134 | B | F-WWFA | N134FJ | N88YF | N322CP | | | | | |
| 135 | B | F-WWFJ | VR-BPW | VP-BPW | F-GYCP | | | | | |
| 136 | B | F-WWFE | N137FJ | N1818S | N187S | (N1836S) | N609SG | | | |
| 137 | B | F-WWFF | N139FJ | XA-GAE | N99DQ | (N98DQ) | N35RZ | | | |
| 138 | B | F-WWF. | VR-BHJ | VP-BHJ | VH-FHR | C-FGFI | | | | |
| 139 | B | F-WWFG | N140FJ | N523AC | (N523AG) | N900SX | | | | |
| 140 | B | F-WWFL | VR-CES | N70HS | N900UT | M-RURU | | | | |
| 141 | B | F-WWFK | N141FJ | XA-OVR | XA-OVA | C-GHML | M-SAIR | | | |
| 142 | B | F-WWFN | N142FJ | N10AT | F-WSMF | F-GSMF | TC-CAG | F-HAAP | N103DT | VP-BPC |
| | | N100FF | F-GXRM | | | | | | | |
| 143 | B | F-WWFH | F-GNMR | ZS-ZBB | VP-BZB | CS-DDI | PH-LCG | | | |
| 144 | B | F-WWFO | N144FJ | N453JS | N512JY | N111 | | | | |
| 145 | B | F-WWFK | VR-CGB | VP-CGB | | | | | | |
| 146 | B | F-WWFF | N146FJ | N216FP | N881P | N4MB | N81SV | N900KR | | |

# FALCON 900

| C/n | Series | Identities | | | | | | | | |
|---|---|---|---|---|---|---|---|---|---|---|
| 147 | B | F-WWFG | N147FJ | N900FJ | (N901FJ) | OE-IMI | N147FJ | XA-ISR | | |
| 148 | B | F-WWFD | N148FJ | N522AC | N900DV | N900VG | (N900VH) | N148FJ | | |
| 149 | B | F-WWFH | VR-BPI | VP-BPI | ZS-DAV | N88879 | N924S | | | |
| 150 | B | F-WWFC | N150FJ | N335MC | HB-IUW | | | | | |
| 151 | B | F-WWFK | G-OPWH | EC-HHK | N908CA | | | | | |
| 152 | B | F-WWFJ | N337MC | N660EG | N902M | N902MK | N18FX | | | |
| 153 | B | F-WWFK | N153FJ | N57EL | N67EL | | | | | |
| 154 | B | F-WWFL | VR-BJA | VP-BJA | F-WQBJ | VP-BGF | F-WQBK | F-GVBF | LX-LFA | I-TCGR |
| 155 | B | F-WWFM | N2056 | N730SA | N814M | N155FJ | N900TG | | | |
| 156 | B | F-WWFA | N202FJ | HL7301 | N910Q | | | | | |
| 157 | B | F-WWFB | N157FJ | N1868M | N1868S | N626EK | N62NW | | | |
| 158 | B | F-WWFC | N158FJ | N900FJ | N404VL | N404VC | N721HM | | | |
| 159 | B | F-WWFD | P4-NAN | N263PW | LX-NAN | F-WQBL | LX-NAN | LX-COS | CS-DPE | M-JMMM |
| 160 | B | F-WWFE | N176CF | N506BA | | | | | | |
| 161 | B | F-WWFF | F-GSAB | VP-CTT | G-GSEB | PH-ILC | | | | |
| 162 | B | F-WWFJ | N162FJ | N611JW | | | | | | |
| 163 | B | F-WWFM | N163FJ | F-WWFM | (PH-EFA) | (F-GSAD) | VP-BEH | VP-CGP | N25MB | N82SV |
| 164 | B | F-WWFC | G-MLTI | F-WQBM | VP-CFL | | | | | |
| 165 | B | F-WWFD | G-EVES | VP-BEC | N183WW | | | | | |
| 166 | B | F-WWFG | N166FJ | N900FJ | F-GLHI | N995SK | | | | |
| 167 | B | F-WWFO | F-GUEQ | 3C-ONM | | | | | | |
| 168 | B | F-WWFA | N167FJ | XA-TEL | | | | | | |
| 169 | C | F-WWFP | F-GRDP | VP-BGC | EC-KFA | | | | | |
| 170 | B | F-WWFR | VP-BKA | N900DA | N900TR | N901TX | | | | |
| 171 | B | F-WWFW | TC-AKK | | | | | | | |
| 172 | B | F-WWFD | N177FJ | N352AF | N352AE | | | | | |
| 173 | B | F-WWFI | PH-LBA | VP-BFH | | | | | | |
| 174 | B | F-WWFK | N138FA | N138F | | | | | | |
| 175 | B | F-WWFN | CS-TMQ | PH-NDK | | | | | | |
| 176 | B | F-WWFW | N900SM | N909PM | | | | | | |
| 177 | B | F-WWFY | N886DC | | | | | | | |
| 178 | B | F-WWFF | N179FJ | XA-APE | | | | | | |
| 179 | C | F-WWFQ | N900FJ | N900DW | N902DW | | | | | |
| 180 | C | F-WWFX | N90TH | | | | | | | |
| 181 | C | F-WWFZ | HB-IUY | N833AV | EC-JNZ | | | | | |
| 182 | C | F-WWFB | N168HT | EC-JBB | | | | | | |
| 183 | C | F-WWFK | N900CC | (N900WP) | N900RX | | | | | |
| 184 | C | F-WWFP | N129KJ | N184FJ | | | | | | |
| 185 | C | F-WWFF | HB-IGT | VH-PPD | | | | | | |
| 186 | C | F-WWFJ | N900LC | | | | | | | |
| 187 | C | F-WWFO | N181FJ | N901SS | | | | | | |
| 188 | C | F-WWFZ | PH-EDM | | | | | | | |
| 189 | C | F-WWFD | N189FJ | C-GMND | N144FH | | | | | |
| 190 | C | F-WWFI | N900NB | N906NB | N468GH | | | | | |
| 191 | C | F-WWFM | N31D | | | | | | | |
| 192 | C | F-WWFQ | N192FJ | PR-SEA | N192LW | VH-LAW | VH-LAL | VH-LUL | | |
| 193 | C | F-WWFV | N193FJ | (VP-CGR) | F-WQBL | VP-BCX | | | | |
| 194 | C | F-WWFZ | OO-ACT | | | | | | | |
| 195 | C | F-WWFB | N195FJ | N100ED | (N100EQ) | N666TR | | | | |
| 196 | C | F-WWFH | N196FJ | N501DB | | | | | | |
| 197 | C | F-WWFQ | N197FJ | F-WWFQ | (LX-MAM) | LX-GJL | | | | |
| 198 | C | F-WWFR | N198FJ | C-GAZU | | | | | | |
| 199 | C | F-WWFA | N199FJ | N900KJ | | | | | | |
| 200 | C | F-WWFG | N207FJ | N404ST | N404TR | | | | | |
| 201 | C | F-WWFA | N210FJ | LX-FTA | | | | | | |
| 202 | C | F-WWFF | VP-BMV | UR-CRD | | | | | | |

Production complete

# DASSAULT FALCON 900DX

| C/n | Identities | | | |
|---|---|---|---|---|
| 601 | F-WWFA | [ff 13.5.05] | HB-JSW | A6-RTS |
| 602 | F-WWFB | N950JB | | |
| 603 | F-WWFC | OO-VMI | | |
| 604 | F-WWFD | OE-IDX | | |
| 605 | F-WWFE | N605FJ | N453JS | |
| 606 | F-WWFF | D-AUCR | | |
| 607 | F-WWFI | (N607DX) | N907DX | C-GPOT |
| 608 | F-WWFN | N50LB | | |
| 609 | F-WWFO | VP-BNS | | |
| 610 | F-WWFI | VP-CIT | | |
| 611 | F-WWFP | N886BB | N890BB | |
| 612 | F-WWFJ | HB-JSU | | |
| 613 | F-WWFQ | B-8021 | | |
| 614 | F-WWFS | VP-CHA | | |
| 615 | F-WWFX | LX-AFD | | |
| 616 | F-WWFM | A6-SMS | | |
| 617 | F-WWFH | OE-ISM | | |
| 618 | F-WWFO | N416KC | | |
| 619 | F-WWVB | LX-SVW | | |
| 620 | F-WWFI | N620DX | | |
| 621 | F-WWFA | N16FX | | |
| 622 | F-WWFO | | | |
| 623 | F-WWFA | D-AMIG | | |
| 624 | F-WWFY | N14FX | | |
| 625 | F-WWFS | | | |
| 626 | | | | |
| 627 | | | | |
| 628 | | | | |
| 629 | | | | |
| 630 | | | | |
| 631 | | | | |
| 632 | | | | |
| 633 | | | | |
| 634 | | | | |
| 635 | | | | |
| 636 | | | | |
| 637 | | | | |
| 638 | | | | |
| 639 | | | | |
| 640 | | | | |
| 641 | | | | |
| 642 | | | | |
| 643 | | | | |
| 644 | | | | |
| 645 | | | | |
| 646 | | | | |
| 647 | | | | |
| 648 | | | | |
| 649 | | | | |
| 650 | | | | |

# DASSAULT FALCON 900EX/900LX

* after the c/n indicates 900EX EASy cockpit-configured aircraft
\+ after the c/n indicates a 900LX model

| C/n | Identities | | | | | | |
|---|---|---|---|---|---|---|---|
| 1 | F-WREX | [ff 01Jun95] | | F-GREX | PH-ERP | N900HG | |
| 2 | F-WWFA | N200L | N209FJ | | | | |
| 3 | F-WWFG | N903FJ | JA50TH | N760 | | | |
| 4 | F-WWJC | N204FJ | N8100E | | | | |
| 5 | F-WWFJ | N205FJ | 9M-JJS | N905EX | N500VM | N600JM | |
| 6 | F-WWFK | F-OIBL | EC-GMO | N143DL | N900FH | N711T | |
| 7 | F-WWFN | N907FJ | N45SJ | N374MV | N900SJ | | |
| 8 | F-WWFB | N30LB | | | | | |
| 9 | F-WWFE | N909FJ | N70LF | | | | |
| 10 | F-WWFG | N910FJ | N22CS | N900Q | N910EX | | |
| 11 | F-WWFI | F-GOYA | CS-DTB | | | | |
| 12 | F-WWFJ | N913FJ | N900EX | (N900SB) | N912EX | F-WQBL | F-HAXA |
| 13 | F-WWFK | VP-BRO | N127SF | | | | |
| 14 | F-WWFN | N72WS | N7KC | | | | |
| 15 | F-WWFO | N915EX | N914J | N914JL | C-GOAG | | |
| 16 | F-WWFA | N916EX | N67WB | | | | |
| 17 | F-WWFB | N600AS | N990H | VP-BEG | | | |
| 18 | F-WWFE | N918EX | N18RF | N166FB | | | |
| 19 | F-WWFJ | N919EX | N7301 | N96DS | N900CX | N88ND | |
| 20 | F-WWFN | N920EX | N158JA | (F-OIBE) | D-AWKG | | |
| 21 | F-WWFH | N330MC | N901MM | | | | |
| 22 | F-WWFQ | N331MC | (N332MC) | (N21HJ) | | | |
| 23 | F-WWFS | SE-DVE | OH-FFC | | | | |
| 24 | F-WWFU | TR-LEX | | | | | |
| 25 | F-WWFV | N925EX | N55TY | N607CV | N602CV* | | |
| 26 | F-WWFX | N900SB | | | | | |
| 27 | F-WWFY | N927EX | N900EX | N626CC | I-FLYW | | |
| 28 | F-WWFZ | HB-IAH | | | | | |
| 29 | F-WWFA | N25UD | N900MK | N17FX | | | |
| 30 | F-WWFB | N662P | N860FJ | N100NG | | | |
| 31 | F-WWFC | F-GSAI | HZ-OFC4 | M-FALC | | | |
| 32 | F-WWFE | N2425 | N4425 | N97NX | | | |
| 33 | F-WWFF | N933EX | (N810M) | XA-TMH | XA-BEG | | |
| 34 | F-WWFI | VP-CLB | | | | | |
| 35 | F-WWFJ | N2BD | HB-IAQ | N96NX | N913SN | | |
| 36 | F-WWFM | N326K | N826K | | | | |
| 37 | F-WWFV | N327K | N900BZ | | | | |
| 38 | F-WWFX | N328K | N68CG | N901MD | 70- | | |
| 39 | F-WWFA | N939EX | VP-BID | N39NP | | | |
| 40 | F-WWFB | N940EX | N900EX | N606DR | N990WM | | |
| 41 | F-WWFC | N5737 | N81SN | | | | |
| 42 | F-WWFD | N942EX | VP-BMS | | | | |
| 43 | F-WWFE | F-GSDP | F-WQBK | EC-HOB | | | |
| 44 | F-WWFG | G-JCBG | N900PL | N947LF | PR-WRI | | |
| 45 | F-WWFJ | Italy MM62171 | | | | | |
| 46 | F-WWFM | N946EX | XA-FEX | | | | |
| 47 | F-WWFO | N58CG | | | | | |
| 48 | F-WWFP | G-GPWH | G-CBHT | | | | |
| 49 | F-WWFR | N949EX | N404F | | | | |
| 50 | F-WWFS | F-GPNJ | | | | | |
| 51 | F-WWFU | F-GVDP | OE-IDM | | | | |
| 52 | F-WWFV | Italy MM62172 | | | | | |
| 53 | F-WWFW | N953EX | PT-WQS | VP-BDZ | N53FJ | | |
| 54 | F-WWFY | HB-IUX | | | | | |
| 55 | F-WWFA | N498A | (N399CG) | N388GS | | | |
| 56 | F-WWFC | N956EX | N404A | N909SB | | | |
| 57 | F-WWFD | N900MT | N900MJ | N10HZ | | | |
| 58 | F-WWFF | N958EX | N11WM | | | | |
| 59 | F-WWFH | N959EX | N694JP | (N6940P) | | | |
| 60 | F-WWFI | N960EX | PT-XSC | N60EX | YV2053 | | |
| 61 | F-WWFL | N961EX | N240LG | | | | |
| 62 | F-WWFM | EC-HNU | N960SF | | | | |
| 63 | F-WWFO | N963EX | N900EX | N435T | | | |
| 64 | F-WWFR | N900VM | D-AJAD | C-GBBX | | | |
| 65 | F-WWFW | N965EX | N965M | VP-CGD | | | |
| 66 | F-WWFA | N377SC | (N677SC) | N66FJ | | | |
| 67 | F-WWFB | N967EX | N312P | N312PV | | | |
| 68 | F-WWFC | N390DE | N271DV | | | | |
| 69 | F-WWFD | N969EX | C-FJOI | | | | |
| 70 | F-WWFE | N970EX | N999PM | | | | |
| 71 | F-WWFG | N111NG | (N971EX) | N110EX | | | |
| 72 | F-WWFH | N2BD | | | | | |

## FALCON 900EX/900EX EASy

| C/n | Identities |
|---|---|
| 73 | F-WWFI N973M VP-CGE |
| 74 | F-WWFK N315KP N811AV N600LF G-HNJC VP-CNZ N740LM |
| 75 | F-WWFL (F-GYDP) VP-BEH F-WQBK F-GXBV |
| 76 | F-WWFN F-GLJV F-WLJV N80F C-GMLH |
| 77 | F-WWFQ N977LP N83SV |
| 78 | F-WWFR G-DAEX D-AGSI F-GXHG |
| 79 | F-WWFS N788CG |
| 80 | F-WWFV N881Q |
| 81 | F-WWFW N404N N404R N908SB |
| 82 | F-WWFX N982EX PR-GPA |
| 83 | F-WWFY HB-IGI |
| 84 | F-WWFA N984EX N900EX N984EX N326K (N82KK) N420KK N420PD |
| 85 | F-WWFB N985EX (N410MW) N910MW |
| 86 | F-WWFC N986EX HB-IGX VP-BEZ M-ODKZ |
| 87 | F-WWFE OE-IMA N487MA C-GGMI OE-IMI |
| 88 | F-WWFF N909MM C-GLBB |
| 89 | F-WWFH N990EX N871MM (N802CB) N802CJ VT-SBK |
| 90 | F-WWFG VP-CLO |
| 91 | F-WWFJ N989EX F-WWFJ (F-OINA) F-WQBJ I-CAEX |
| 92 | F-WWFK HB-IFJ |
| 93 | F-WWFL N993EX N993GT |
| 94 | F-WWFN N994EX N663MK |
| 95 | F-WWFO HB-IGY |
| 96 | F-WWFP N93CR N900ZA HB-JSY |
| 97* | F-WNCO (F-GNCO) (F-GOEA) [both sets of ntu marks reserved simultaneously] CS-DFL N970RJ N963RS |
| 98 | F-WWFR N998EX N900KX N209CQ |
| 99 | F-WWFS N996EX N890FH XA-GMD |
| 100 | F-WWFU N997EX JA55TH N550TH |
| 101 | F-WWFW N966H (N875F) N730LM |
| 102 | F-WWFX N6666P N6666R |
| 103 | F-WWFY N103EX N900EX N327K F-GYCM N103FJ N900HD |
| 104 | F-WWFA N588GS |
| 105 | F-WWFC G-LCYA |
| 106 | F-WWFD F-GSDA LX-ZAK SE-DJM |
| 107 | F-WWFE F-HBOL |
| 108 | F-WWFF G-JCBX N9WV N501MK |
| 109 | F-WWFG VP-BEE |
| 110 | F-WWFI N176CL |
| 111 | F-WWFJ N101EX N57EL N508PC VP-BFV OE-IEX |
| 112 | F-WWFK G-JJMX N900MF |
| 113 | F-WWFL G-RBSG F-GYRB N121DF |
| 114 | F-WWFM N114EX N900EX (N114EX) N900YP |
| 115 | F-WWFN N720ML N720ME |
| 116 | F-WWFO Italy MM62210 |
| 117 | F-WWFP N117EX (N900EX) N900SN |
| 118 | F-WWFS OH-PPR |
| 119 | F-WWFU N119EX N958DM |
| 120* | F-WWFV (N120EZ) N900EX F-WWFV N900EX N106RW [damaged in hangar collapse at Washington/Dulles, VA, 06Feb10, possible w/o] |
| 121* | F-WWFW F-GSEF F-WWFW F-GSEF OO-FOI |
| 122* | F-WWFX N901SB |
| 123* | F-WWFY N990ML N990MC |
| 124* | F-WWFZ N919SA |
| 125* | F-WWFB N988H |
| 126* | F-WWFC N966H N966E* |
| 127* | F-WWFD N900HC |
| 128* | F-WWFE OY-OKK |
| 129* | F-WWFF N129EX XA-RGB |
| 130* | F-WWFH VP-BEF |
| 131* | F-WWFI VP-BFM N900MV |
| 132* | F-WWFJ G-JPSX |
| 133* | F-WWFK F-WQBJ D-AZEM |
| 134* | F-WWFL VP-CEZ VP-CFR |
| 135* | F-WWFM N246AG |
| 136* | F-WWFN N22LC |
| 137* | F-WWFO N88LC |
| 138* | F-WWFP OE-IVK (OY-VIK) OY-IVK |
| 139* | F-WWFQ N139EX N265H |
| 140* | F-WWFR N940EX (N900EX) N54HG |
| 141* | F-WWFS N141EX HB-JSX |
| 142* | F-WWFU N142EX RA-09008 |
| 143* | F-WWFV HA-LKN |
| 144* | F-WWFW N144EX VP-BSO |
| 145* | F-WWFX F-GSNA (LN-SEH) |
| 146* | F-WWFZ N146EX |

# FALCON 900EX EASy

| C/n | Identities |
|---|---|
| 147* | F-WWFE N193F |
| 148* | F-WWFG 5A-DCN |
| 149* | F-WWFH Italy MM62244 |
| 150* | F-WWFI N900NS G-SABI |
| 151* | F-WWFJ VP-BSP G-EGVO |
| 152* | F-WWFK P4-SCM |
| 153* | F-WWFL N7818S N1818S |
| 154* | F-WWFM N47EG |
| 155* | F-WWFN (F-GSMT) N955EX F-WQBN F-GSMT (LN-SEH) LN-AOC N852CA G-FFFG |
| 156* | F-WWFO MM62245 |
| 157* | F-WWFP N227HD |
| 158* | F-WWFQ N15FF N18DF |
| 159* | F-WWFR N959EX N900EX N900SG G-FNES |
| 160* | F-WWFS I-DAKO |
| 161* | F-WWFU TC-MMG |
| 162* | F-WWFW N962EX PR-CCC N876C |
| 163* | F-WWFX G-GALX |
| 164* | F-WWFY RA-09006 |
| 165* | F-WWFZ N165FJ (N777SA) (F-GUDA) OE-IMC F-HDLJ |
| 166* | F-WWFM VT-ISH |
| 167* | F-WWFP N167EX N85CL |
| 168* | F-WWFQ N900JG (N900JF) |
| 169* | F-WWFH N900NF N900NB N906NB* |
| 170* | F-WWFJ N585BP |
| 171* | F-WWFK SE-DJA |
| 172* | F-WWFL G-SIRO |
| 173* | F-WWFE N7600S |
| 174* | F-WWFR F-HCBM F-WQBN VP-BOZ N789ZZ |
| 175* | F-WWFV N513HS |
| 176* | F-WWFW N176EX (LX-GDX) D-AMBI OE-IBN |
| 177* | F-WWFZ N900KM F-WQBM VT-AKU |
| 178* | F-WWFA N178EX N900EX N178EX N900VG |
| 179* | F-WWFC SE-DJB |
| 180* | F-WWFD HZ-OFC5 |
| 181* | F-WWFH N181EX PR-FRU |
| 182* | F-WWFU N93KD |
| 183* | F-WWFG A6-MAF |
| 184* | F-WWFN G-JMMX |
| 185* | F-WWFV LN-AKR |
| 186* | F-WWFY N186EX (XA-SCO) XA-TEI |
| 187* | F-WWFA N904JY |
| 188* | F-WWFW N460D |
| 189* | F-WWFZ OE-INB |
| 190* | F-WWFF N190FJ C-GLXC |
| 191* | F-WWFP N191AE |
| 192* | F-WWFR I-SEAS |
| 193* | F-WWFU G-REYG N843MG N343MG |
| 194* | F-WWFK N987AL |
| 195* | F-WWFL C6-SZN 3A-MGA |
| 196* | F-WWVA N196EX YV2485 |
| 197* | F-WWFC N197EX YV2486 |
| 198* | F-WWFF CS-DPF |
| 199* | F-WWFJ N199FJ N918JM |
| 200* | F-WWFW F-HBDA |
| 201* | F-WWFY N900EX C-GIPX |
| 202* | F-WWVC N606SG |
| 203* | F-WWVD N203FJ XA-RET |
| 204* | F-WWVE I-FLYI |
| 205* | F-WWFB (M-TECH) VT-CAP |
| 206* | F-WWFD N206EX N33LC |
| 207* | F-WWFE N907EX PR-PMV |
| 208* | F-WWFG N286MJ |
| 209* | F-WWFK N209EX (N900RF)+ [+ntu marks worn at completion centre] |
| 210* | F-WWFM N210FJ (N600US) N984H* |
| 211* | F-WWFN G-WTOR |
| 212* | F-WWFC N212EX N48CG |
| 213* | F-WWFI N213EX N28VL |
| 214* | F-WWFH OE-IOE |
| 215* | F-WWFJ N375SC |
| 216* | F-WWFQ N44LC |
| 217* | F-WWFS LX-GET |
| 218* | (F-WWFV) F-WWFL N606US P2-ANW |
| 219* | (F-WWFX) F-WWFR |
| 220* | (F-WWFZ) F-WWFD OH-FFE |
| 221* | (F-WWVA) F-WWFE N221EX N5MV |
| 222* | (F-WWVF) F-WWFF N399EX |

# FALCON 900EX EASy/900LX

| C/n | Identities | | | |
|---|---|---|---|---|
| 223* | (F-WWVG) | F-WWFG | N223EX | B-MBL* |
| 224* | (F-WWVH) | F-WWFC | G-JPSZ | |
| 225* | (F-WWVI) | F-WWFK | VP-BPW | |
| 226* | F-WWVJ | N7600P | | |
| 227* | F-WWFI | (D-ASIE) | D-ALMS | |
| 228* | F-WWFJ | N228EX | N18CG | |
| 229* | F-WWFP | N229DK | | |
| 230* | F-WWFL | F-GMDS | LN-BRG* | |
| 231* | F-WWFQ | N231FJ | N720ML | |
| 232* | F-WWFU | | | |
| 233* | F-WWFE | N900FJ | | |
| 234* | F-WWFV | N432FJ | | |
| 235* | F-WWFF | N235FJ | (PR-RJZ) | |
| 236* | F-WWFW | | | |
| 237* | F-WWFX | | | |
| 238* | F-WWFG | | | |
| 239* | F-WWFZ | | | |
| 240* | F-WWFH | | | |
| 241* | F-WWFM | | | |
| 242* | F-WWFN | | | |
| 243* | F-WWVA | | | |
| 244* | F-WWFJ | | | |
| 245* | F-WWFQ | | | |
| 246* | F-WWFA | | | |
| 247* | F-WWFD | | | |
| 248+ | F-WWFE | | | |
| 249* | F-WWFB | | | |
| 250* | F-WWFC | | | |
| 251* | F-WWFF | | | |
| 252* | F-WWFI | | | |
| 253* | F-WWFY | | | |
| 254* | F-WWVB | | | |
| 255* | F-WWVC | | | |
| 256* | F-WWVD | | | |
| 257* | F-WWVE | | | |
| 258* | | | | |
| 259* | | | | |
| 260* | | | | |
| 261* | | | | |
| 262* | | | | |
| 263* | | | | |
| 264* | | | | |
| 265* | | | | |
| 266* | | | | |
| 267* | | | | |
| 268* | | | | |
| 269* | | | | |
| 270* | | | | |

# DASSAULT FALCON 2000

| C/n | Identities | | | | | | | | | |
|---|---|---|---|---|---|---|---|---|---|---|
| 1 | (F-WNEW) | F-WNAV | [rolled out 10Feb93; ff 04Mar93] | | | | (F-GMIR) | F-GMOE | VP-CAS | |
| 2 | F-WNEW | [rolled out Dec93; ff 11Jly94] | | | ZS-NNF | F-GJHJ | N201CR | | | |
| 3 | F-WWFA | N2000A | N15AS | | | | | | | |
| 4 | F-WWMA | N925AJ | | | | | | | | |
| 5 | F-WWMB | N27R | | | | | | | | |
| 6 | F-WWMD | F-GPAM | F-WQBL | N93GH | N93GT | PR-WSM | | | | |
| 7 | F-WWME | N28R | | | | | | | | |
| 8 | F-WWMF | N610AS | F-WQBK | VT-VLM | | | | | | |
| 9 | F-WWMG | N435T | N435TM | N209FJ | N783FS | | | | | |
| 10 | F-WWMH | N652PC | N131EP | | | | | | | |
| 11 | F-WWMK | N101NS | (N787RA) | N721BS | N248JF | N48FB | | | | |
| 12 | F-WWMM | I-SNAW | (F-GLHJ) | | | | | | | |
| 13 | F-WWML | N2004 | N722JB | | | | | | | |
| 14 | F-WWMN | N2034 | N70KS | N51MN | | | | | | |
| 15 | F-WWMO | N790L | | | | | | | | |
| 16 | F-WWMB | HB-IAW | | | | | | | | |
| 17 | F-WWMA | N2035 | N77A | N88TY | N89TY | N659FM | | | | |
| 18 | F-WWMG | F-GMPR | EI-LJR | VP-CJA | | | | | | |
| 19 | F-WWMC | N790M | | | | | | | | |
| 20 | F-WWME | N389GS | N822TP | N405ST | N427GW | | | | | |
| 21 | F-WWMA | N390GS | N11BV | | | | | | | |
| 22 | F-WWMF | N200NE | N609CH | N202CE | | | | | | |
| 23 | F-WWMH | N2036 | N375SC | N575SC | N23FJ | N10JP | | | | |
| 24 | F-WWMK | N2039 | N376SC | N876SC | N18MV | | | | | |
| 25 | F-WWML | N2042 | N96FG | N122SC | (N406ST) | N25FJ | | | | |
| 26 | F-WWMN | N2046 | N2000A | F-WQFL | TC-CIN | VP-BHC | TC-CIN | F-WQBN | N112CD | HB-ISF |
| | OY-ICE | (F-GSAE) | LX-SAM | | | | | | | |
| 27 | F-WWMM | G-JCBI | F-GJSK | D-BSIK | F-WQBL | LX-SIK | F-WQBK | F-GSYC | B-8020 | |
| 28 | F-WWMO | N596A | N160WS | N8888 | | | | | | |
| 29 | F-WWMA | N2028 | XA-TDU | N700FL | | | | | | |
| 30 | F-WWMB | HB-IAZ | | | | | | | | |
| 31 | F-WWMC | N2032 | N790Z | | | | | | | |
| 32 | F-WWMD | N65SD | N324CL | N175BC | | | | | | |
| 33 | F-WWME | HB-IAX | | | | | | | | |
| 34 | F-WWMF | HB-IAY | N234FJ | | | | | | | |
| 35 | F-WWMG | N27WP | N1927G | | | | | | | |
| 36 | F-WWMA | F-GSAA | (PH-WOL) | PH-INJ | F-GNBL | VT-COT | N480LP | N602LP | | |
| 37 | F-WWMH | EC-GNK | | | | | | | | |
| 38 | F-WWMI | N3BM | N8QM | (N800BG) | N710ET | | | | | |
| 39 | F-WWMJ | N2061 | N151AE | N42ST | | | | | | |
| 40 | F-WWMK | N1C | | | | | | | | |
| 41 | F-WWMD | N2073 | N48CG | N148CG | N214LD | | | | | |
| 42 | F-WWMG | HB-IBH | | | | | | | | |
| 43 | F-WWMK | (N2077) | PT-MML | N101BE | N43FJ | N86TW | (N86TY) | N775ST | | |
| 44 | F-WWML | N2074 | N2000A | N49MW | N37TH | N623QW | | | | |
| 45 | F-WWMM | N45SC | N190MC | | | | | | | |
| 46 | F-WWMN | N2080 | (N220JM) | F-WWMN | F-GMCK | CS-DCM | N505RR | | | |
| 47 | F-WWMB | N220JM | N800BL | N435JF | | | | | | |
| 48 | F-WWMC | N2089 | N701WC | N701WG | N48WK | | | | | |
| 49 | F-WWMD | (PH-EFB) | VP-BEF | G-GEDI | F-GHGO | F-WQBK | VT-TBT | | | |
| 50 | F-WWME | D-BEST | | | | | | | | |
| 51 | F-WWMF | N82AT | N2AT | N797CM | | | | | | |
| 52 | F-WWMI | N212T | N749GP | | | | | | | |
| 53 | F-WWMJ | N981 | N149VB | N149V | N149VB | | | | | |
| 54 | F-WWML | D-BIRD | D-BOND | I-JAMY | | | | | | |
| 55 | F-WWMM | HB-IVM | F-WQBK | F-GJTG | EC-JXR | | | | | |
| 56 | F-WWMO | TC-CYL | N784BX | | | | | | | |
| 57 | F-WWMA | N2132 | N18CG | N918CG | | | | | | |
| 58 | F-WWMB | N2133 | N326EW | N826EW | | | | | | |
| 59 | F-WWMC | N2146 | PT-WYC | | | | | | | |
| 60 | F-WWMD | N2147 | XA-GNI | (N260FJ) | XA-TYT | N524SA | N898CT | | | |
| 61 | F-WWME | HB-IVN | F-WQBJ | F-GJTH | EC-JVI | | | | | |
| 62 | F-WWMF | HB-IVO | | | | | | | | |
| 63 | F-WWMG | N2155 | N2000A | N804JH | N800JH | N806JH | N302JC | (N863TS) | | |
| 64 | F-WWMH | N996AG | | | | | | | | |
| 65 | F-WWMI | F-GODO | (F-OIBA) | VT-TAT | | | | | | |
| 66 | F-WWMJ | N30TH | N429SJ | | | | | | | |
| 67 | F-WWMK | N150BC | | | | | | | | |
| 68 | F-WWMN | N200GN | | | | | | | | |
| 69 | F-WWMA | N220JN | (N220JM) | N220EJ | (N220MR) | N220DF | (N346SR) | | | |
| 70 | F-WWMB | N2168 | N207QS | P4-IKR | D-BAMA | F-WQBK | VT-HDL | | | |
| 71 | F-WWMC | N92LT | N811AV | N811AG | N811TY | N811AG | | | | |
| 72 | F-WWMD | N2169 | N96LT | N769JW | N768JW | | | | | |
| 73 | F-WWMG | N2176 | (N97LT) | N273JC | N273JE | N73FJ | | | | |
| 74 | F-WWMH | HB-IUZ | F-GJSC | OO-VMB | N988DV | N986DV | | | | |
| 75 | F-WWMK | N275QS | | | | | | | | |
| 76 | F-WWML | OY-CKN | F-WQBN | OY-CKN | | | | | | |

# FALCON 2000

| C/n | Identities | | | | | |
|---|---|---|---|---|---|---|
| 77 | F-WWMM | N278QS | | | | |
| 78 | F-WWMJ | G-PYCO | N262PC | N78FJ | [retrofitted with winglets 2010] | |
| 79 | F-WWMN | N929HG | N772MC | N774MC | N79FJ | |
| 80 | F-WWMO | N2CW | N60TC | | | |
| 81 | F-WWVA | N281QS | | | | |
| 82 | F-WWVB | N752S | | | | |
| 83 | F-WWVC | N1128B | | | | |
| 84 | F-WWVD | N1929Y | | | | |
| 85 | F-WWVE | N220JM | N221EJ | N344GC | XA-HHF | |
| 86 | F-WWVF | N111HZ | | | | |
| 87 | F-WWVG | N287QS | N4200 | N910CS | | |
| 88 | F-WWVH | N753S | C-FJPV | C-GSCL | C-GSMR | |
| 89 | F-WWVI | N2189 | N2000A | N800GH | | |
| 90 | F-WWVJ | F-GKIP | F-WQBM | N930SD | N5200 | |
| 91 | F-WWVK | N46HA | | | | |
| 92 | F-WWVL | N2191 | N2000L | | | |
| 93 | F-WWVM | N292QS | | | | |
| 94 | F-WWVN | N48HA | N517PJ | N286MG | (N94FJ) | M-IIII |
| 95 | F-WWVO | N628CC | [retrofitted with winglets 2010] | | | |
| 96 | F-WWVP | N88DD | N50TG | N53TG | N755FL | |
| 97 | F-WWVQ | N620AS | N922H | N922J | N12MW | |
| 98 | F-WWVR | N298QS | | | | |
| 99 | F-WWVS | (N2099) | N111VU | N111VW | N770MP | |
| 100 | F-WWVT | VP-CGA | | | | |
| 101 | F-WWVU | N2093 | N399FA | OO-GFD | F-WHLX | VT-RVL |
| 102 | F-WWVV | N515TK | N440AS | N410AS | N286CX | |
| 103 | F-WWVX | I-FLYP | | | | |
| 104 | F-WWVY | N204QS | | | | |
| 105 | F-WWVZ | N220EJ | N105LF | N711PE | | |
| 106 | F-WWVA | N635E | | | | |
| 107 | F-WWVB | VP-CGC | | | | |
| 108 | F-WWVC | I-FLYV | | | | |
| 109 | F-WWVD | CS-DNP | N2218 | F-WWVD | CS-DNP | |
| 110 | F-WWVE | N2194 | PP-CFF | | | |
| 111 | F-WWVF | VP-BDL | | | | |
| 112 | F-WWVG | N2197 | N2000A | N2112L | N410GS | |
| 113 | F-WWVH | N213QS | | | | |
| 114 | F-WWVI | ZS-PKR | | | | |
| 115 | F-WWVK | CS-DNQ | | | | |
| 116 | F-WWVL | N2216 | N52DC | | | |
| 117 | F-WWVM | N2217 | N54DC | | | |
| 118 | F-WWVN | N218QS | | | | |
| 119 | F-WWVO | F-GXDP | F-WQBN | D-BDNL | F-GESP | |
| 120 | F-WWVP | CS-DNR | | | | |
| 121 | F-WWVQ | HZ-KSDA | F-ORAX | (F-GVDA) | VP-BNT | N78NT |
| 122 | F-WWVR | N222QS | | | | |
| 123 | F-WWVS | LZ-OOI | | | | |
| 124 | F-WWVU | N224QS | | | | |
| 125 | F-WWVV | N313GH | N813GH | N911SH | | |
| 126 | F-WWVW | N226QS | | | | |
| 127 | F-WWVY | N227QS | | | | |
| 128 | F-WWVZ | N228EJ | N628SA | N350M | | |
| 129 | F-WWVD | N229QS | | | | |
| 130 | F-WWVE | N99TY | N202TH | N902MC | | |
| 131 | F-WWVG | N707MM | | | | |
| 132 | F-WWVH | N97NX | N905B | | | |
| 133 | F-WWVI | HZ-KSDB | F-WQBK | LX-SVW | F-WQBJ | B-MBK |
| 134 | F-WWVF | SX-DCF | N493S | (N493SV) | N622QW | |
| 135 | F-WWVJ | N222BN | N196RG | | | |
| 136 | F-WWVL | N236QS | | | | |
| 137 | F-WWVM | N61KW | N510RR | | | |
| 138 | F-WWVN | N799BC | N856F | | | |
| 139 | F-WWVR | CS-DNS | | | | |
| 140 | F-WWVT | N797SM | N797WC | | | |
| 141 | F-WWVU | N2227 | N2000A | N54J | | |
| 142 | F-WWVV | HZ-KSDC | | | | |
| 143 | F-WWVW | N2230 | N872EC | | | |
| 144 | F-WWVX | F-GUJP | N317ML | N317MR | N203WB | |
| 145 | F-WWVZ | N245QS | | | | |
| 146 | F-WWVA | N844AV | N866AV | N317MN | N455DX | |
| 147 | F-WWVB | N999BE | N777MN | N700CH | | |
| 148 | F-WWVC | CS-DFC | | | | |
| 149 | F-WWVG | N2235 | XA-MAV | | | |
| 150 | F-WWVH | EC-HYI | | | | |
| 151 | F-WWVI | G-IBSF | N151GR | | | |
| 152 | F-WWVJ | N98NX | N70XC | N317MQ | N246V | N243V |
| 153 | F-WWVK | N253QS | | | | |
| 154 | F-WWVL | OY-CKI | | | | |

# FALCON 2000

| C/n | Identities | | | | | |
|---|---|---|---|---|---|---|
| 155 | F-WWVM | N255QS | | | | |
| 156 | F-WWVN | N844UP | | | | |
| 157 | F-WWVO | TC-RMK | | | | |
| 158 | F-WWVP | N258QS | | | | |
| 159 | F-WWVQ | N259QS | | | | |
| 160 | F-WWVZ | VP-CGM | TC-PLM | F-WQBL | VP-BBP | |
| 161 | F-WWVA | I-DDVF | | | | |
| 162 | F-WWVU | N262QS | | | | |
| 163 | F-WWVW | N163J | OY-CKF | G-CGHI | | |
| 164 | F-WWVY | N44JC | | | | |
| 165 | F-WWVE | N265QS | | | | |
| 166 | F-WWVD | (N2259) | TC-DGC | OY-CKW | F-WQBL | F-GVTC |
| 167 | F-WWVG | 3A-MGR | 3A-MGA | 3A-MMA | VP-BHD | |
| 168 | F-WWVV | N268QS | | | | |
| 169 | F-WWVJ | N269QS | | | | |
| 170 | F-WWVC | N220AB | | | | |
| 171 | F-WWVK | (HZ-KSDD) | F-ORAV | N797HT | | |
| 172 | F-WWVN | N272EJ | N36EP | | | |
| 173 | F-WWVR | N673BA | OY-SIR | | | |
| 174 | F-WWMA | CS-DFD | | | | |
| 175 | F-WWMB | N2258 | XA-AVE | | | |
| 176 | F-WWMC | N676BA | | | | |
| 177 | F-WWMD | N277QS | | | | |
| 178 | F-WWME | N279QS | N884WY | N100WY | N101NY | |
| 179 | F-WWMF | OH-FIX | | | | |
| 180 | F-WWMG | N2260 | (N203DD) | N680DF | | |
| 181 | F-WWMH | N280QS | | | | |
| 182 | F-WWMI | N2264 | N2000A | N329K | N826KR | |
| 183 | F-WWMJ | N2265 | N88MX | N903GS | | |
| 184 | F-WWMK | N2261 | XA-RET | N71AX | G-MDBA | |
| 185 | F-WWML | N284QS | | | | |
| 186 | F-WWMM | N2270 | N551SS | N98RP | | |
| 187 | F-WWMN | (F-GZAK) | LX-ZAK | F-GNDO | N87FJ | VP-BCV |
| 188 | F-WWMD | N2288 | N317MZ | N317M | | |
| 189 | F-WWMB | N2267 | N2000A | N330K | | |
| 190 | F-WWVA | N290QS | | | | |
| 191 | F-WWVB | F-GUYM | TC-PRK | F-WQBJ | I-BNTN | |
| 192 | F-WWVC | N2289 | N2000A | N515PV | | |
| 193 | F-WWVE | N239QS | N278GS | | | |
| 194 | F-WWVF | N671WM | | | | |
| 195 | F-WWVH | N297QS | N196KC | | | |
| 196 | F-WWVI | N296QS | | | | |
| 197 | F-WWVJ | N2290 | N215KH | I-KERE | | |
| 198 | F-WWVL | N203QS | | | | |
| 199 | F-WWVM | N2295 | N899U | | | |
| 200 | F-WWVN | I-SEAE | | | | |
| 201 | F-WWVO | N201WR | | | | |
| 202 | F-WWVP | N251QS | | | | |
| 203 | F-WWVQ | I-ARIF | | | | |
| 204 | F-WWVR | N240QS | N2317 | N88DD | | |
| 205 | F-WWVS | CS-DFE | | | | |
| 206 | F-WWVT | N208QS | N2319 | N414CC | N331DC | N831DC | N900NH |
| 207 | F-WWVU | N207EM | OE-HEM | | | |
| 208 | F-WWVV | G-GEDY | LX-MBE | | | |
| 209 | F-WWVW | N209FS | N209TM | OE-HPH | | |
| 210 | F-WWVX | N270QS | N2325 | N850K | | |
| 211 | F-WWVY | N210QS | | | | |
| 212 | F-WWVZ | N2322 | N523W | N523WC | | |
| 213 | F-WWVA | N212QS | N684KF | | | |
| 214 | F-WWVB | N214FJ | N215QS | | | |
| 215 | F-WWVC | N215RE | N203CK* | | | |
| 216 | F-WWVD | N718KS | OE-HFA | | | |
| 217 | F-WWVE | N863TM | OE-HVA | | | |
| 218 | F-WWVF | N218PH | | | | |
| 219 | F-WWVG | N219FJ | N1999 | | | |
| 220 | F-WWVH | N620BA | | | | |
| 221 | F-WWVI | N102MG | N1MG | N950RL | | |
| 222 | F-WWVJ | N297RG | N296RG | | | |
| 223 | F-WWVK | OE-HAF | | | | |
| 224 | F-WWVL | N33FJ | N33D | | | |
| 225 | F-WWVM | VT-AAT | | | | |
| 226 | F-WWVN | OE-HKY | | | | |
| 227 | F-WWVO | P4-IKF | | | | |
| 228 | F-WWVP | N900MC | | | | |
| 229 | F-WWVQ | F-GXDA | TC-SNK | | | |
| 230 | F-WWVR | (F-HDFS) | N230FJ | N532CC | | |
| 231 | F-WWVS | VT-HGL | | | | |

Production complete, replaced by the Falcon 2000DX

# DASSAULT FALCON 2000DX

| C/n | Identities | | |
|---|---|---|---|
| 601 | F-WWGY | [ff 19Jun07] | N331DC |
| 602 | F-WWMC | N30LF | |
| 603 | F-WWGD | LX-ATD | |
| 604 | F-WWGV | VT-VKR | |
| 605 | | | |
| 606 | | | |
| 607 | | | |
| 608 | | | |
| 609 | | | |
| 610 | | | |
| 611 | | | |
| 612 | | | |
| 613 | | | |
| 614 | | | |
| 615 | | | |
| 616 | | | |
| 617 | | | |
| 618 | | | |
| 619 | | | |
| 620 | | | |

# DASSAULT FALCON 2000EX/2000EX EASy/2000LX

* alongside the c/n indicates a 2000EX EASy cockpit-configured aircraft
\+ alongside the c/n indicates a 2000LX aircraft

| C/n | | Identities | | | | | |
|---|---|---|---|---|---|---|---|
| 1 | | F-WMEX | [r/o 19Jly01; ff 25Oct01] | | (F-GMEX) | VP-BMJ | N900CH |
| 2 | | F-WWGA | N202EX | | | | |
| 3 | | F-WWGC | HB-IAJ | | | | |
| 4 | | F-WWGD | N200CH | N909CF | | | |
| 5 | | F-WWGE | LX-DKC | F-GUDN | PH-VBG | | |
| 6 | * | F-WXEY | [fitted with 2000LX winglets 2008] | | | | |
| 7 | | F-WWGF | D-BIRD | N40TH | | | |
| 8 | | F-WWGG | G-JOLI | F-GUTD | OO-IAR | OE-HRA | LX-AAM | OE-HNM |
| 9 | | F-WWGH | (N209EX) | HB-IGQ | | | |
| 10 | | F-WWGI | (SE-RBV) | VP-BER | OE-HKK | | |
| 11 | | F-WWGJ | I-NATS | | | | |
| 12 | | F-WWGK | N313CC | | | | |
| 13 | | F-WWGL | N500R | N500FE | N71FE | | |
| 14 | | F-WWGM | HB-IAU | | | | |
| 15 | | F-WWGN | N215EX | N97GM | S5-ABR | | |
| 16 | | F-WWGO | PP-AAF | | | | |
| 17 | | F-WWGP | N217EX | F-WWGP | N977CP | | |
| 18 | | F-WWGQ | F-GUHB | N943JB | | | |
| 19 | | F-WWGR | N528BD | N855TJ | | | |
| 20 | | F-WWGS | N219EX | XA-GNI | | | |
| 21 | | F-WWGT | N221EX | N521CD | N801WW | | |
| 22 | | F-WWGU | N218EX | PR-WQT | N218EX | VP-BDV | |
| 23 | | F-WWGV | N223EX | N101PV | | | |
| 24 | | F-WWGW | N224EX | N341AP | | | |
| 25 | | F-WWGX | N225EX | N699MC | | | |
| 26 | | F-WWGY | N226EX | N6453 | | | |
| 27 | | F-WWGZ | OH-FEX | | | | |
| 28 | * | F-WWGC | F-GUFM | N2CC | N4QG | (N28EX) | |
| 29 | * | F-WWGD | SX-DCA | | | | |
| 30 | * | F-WWGG | D-BERT | | | | |
| 31 | * | F-WWGJ | N31EX | N620MS | | | |
| 32 | * | F-WWGK | N666BE | N999BE | N377GM | | |
| 33 | * | F-WWGL | D-BILL | D-BOSS | N924BC | | |
| 34 | * | F-WWGM | HB-JEG | C-FJAJ | | | |
| 35 | * | F-WWGQ | OY-CLN | | | | |
| 36 | * | F-WWGR | N185G | N163EB | | | |
| 37 | * | F-WWGS | N308U | | | | |
| 38 | * | F-WWGT | N3BM | N8QM | N909MM | | |
| 39 | * | F-WWGU | CS-TLP | | | | |
| 40 | * | F-WWGV | N240EX | PR-PPN | N888NX | PH-CHT | |
| 41 | * | F-WWGW | CS-DFF | | | | |
| 42 | * | F-WWGX | F-GUTC | D-BMVV | | | |
| 43 | * | F-WWGY | N9871R | | | | |
| 44 | * | F-WWGA | CS-DFG | | | | |
| 45 | * | F-WWGE | VP-BVP | N205CW | | | |
| 46 | * | F-WWGF | N21HE | N10EU | | | |
| 47 | * | F-WWGH | N711HE | N404UK | N365FJ | G-LSMB | |
| 48 | * | F-WWGI | N48NC | N1NC | | | |
| 49 | * | F-WWGN | F-GUDC | N50TG | | | |
| 50 | * | F-WWGO | N57MN | N133RL | | | |
| 51 | * | F-WWGP | ZS-MGD | | | | |
| 52 | * | F-WWMA | G-KWIN | | | | |
| 53 | * | F-WWMB | N36TH | | | | |
| 54 | * | F-WWMC | N221QS | | | | |
| 55 | * | F-WWMD | N226EW | N326EW | | | |
| 56 | * | F-WWME | N56EX | N954SP | | | |
| 57 | * | F-WWMF | N376SC | | | | |
| 58 | * | F-WWMG | N158EX | VH-CRQ | VH-CRW | | |
| 59 | * | F-WWMH | N230QS | | | | |
| 60 | * | F-WWMI | N100MB | | | | |
| 61 | * | F-WWMJ | LX-NLK | VP-CBC | | | |
| 62 | * | F-WWMK | N346PC | | | | |
| 63 | * | F-WWML | OY-EJD | | | | |
| 64 | * | F-WWMM | N493SF | N493S | | | |
| 65 | * | F-WWMN | CS-DFK | | | | |
| 66 | * | F-WWMO | N822ST | | | | |
| 67 | * | F-WWGA | OH-FOX | | | | |
| 68 | * | F-WWGC | N934ST | N360M | | | |
| 69 | * | F-WWGD | N56EL | N57EL | | | |
| 70 | * | F-WWGE | D-BOOK | | | | |
| 71 | * | F-WWGG | N71EL | N56EL | | | |
| 72 | * | F-WWGH | N613GH | (N431GH) | N995GH | | |
| 73 | * | F-WWGJ | N85MQ | N85M | | | |
| 74 | * | F-WWGK | D-BAMM | | | | |
| 75 | * | F-WWGL | F-GUPH | OO-GML | | | |

# FALCON 2000EX EASy/2000LX

| C/n | | Identities | | | | |
|---|---|---|---|---|---|---|
| 76 | * | F-WWGM | A6-SMS | F-WQBL | (D-BBED) | D-BIKA |
| 77 | * | F-WWGN | N377EX | XA-LFA | | |
| 78 | * | F-WWGO | (F-GOTF) | I-JETF | G-JETF | |
| 79 | * | F-WWGP | N88HE | | | |
| 80 | * | F-WWGQ | CS-DLB | | | |
| 81 | * | F-WWGR | N81EX | N89CE | | |
| 82 | * | F-WWGS | VP-CMD | C-GSEC | | |
| 83 | + | F-WWGT | N83EX | F-WWGT | N83EX | N283SL |
| 84 | * | F-WWGU | N522BD | | | |
| 85 | * | F-WWGV | N993GH | | | |
| 86 | * | F-WWGW | N223QS | | | |
| 87 | * | F-WWGX | N287F | C-GTPL | | |
| 88 | * | F-WWGY | OE-HOT | M-ILES | G-LATE | |
| 89 | * | F-WWGZ | VP-CAM | | | |
| 90 | * | F-WWGC | N190EX | C-GOHB | | |
| 91 | * | F-WWGD | N91EX | [trialled with temporary winglets Jun06-Aug06] | N233QS | |
| 92 | + | F-WWGG | N176CG | | | |
| 93 | * | F-WWGH | D-BFFB | | | |
| 94 | * | F-WWGI | N912MT | | | |
| 95 | * | F-WWGJ | N168CE | N887CE | M-ROWL | |
| 96 | * | F-WWGN | 5B-CKO | | | |
| 97 | * | F-WWGA | N12AR | N855DG | | |
| 98 | * | F-WWGP | CS-DLC | | | |
| 99 | * | F-WWMA | PP-MJC | | | |
| 100 | * | F-WWMB | N310U | | | |
| 101 | * | F-WWMC | N204CW | | | |
| 102 | * | F-WWMD | G-ITIG | | | |
| 103 | * | F-WWME | (OY-FPN) | OY-PNO | | |
| 104 | * | F-WWGE | TC-DGN | | | |
| 105 | * | F-WWGR | N994GP | | | |
| 106 | + | F-WWGU | N771DV | | | |
| 107 | * | F-WWGV | N367BW | N267BW | | |
| 108 | * | F-WWGW | I-JAMJ | | | |
| 109 | * | F-WWGX | CS-DLD | | | |
| 110 | * | F-WWMG | VP-BAK | M-STCO | | |
| 111 | * | F-WWMH | D-BASE | | | |
| 112 | * | F-WWMI | N619SM | | | |
| 113 | * | F-WWMJ | VP-CMI | | | |
| 114 | * | F-WWMK | F-GVNG | [fitted with mock-up Falcon 2000LX winglets 2007] | M-AMND | |
| 115 | * | F-WWML | N232QS | | | |
| 116 | * | F-WWMM | N116EX | N72PS | | |
| 117 | * | F-WWMO | VT-VLN | | | |
| 118 | * | F-WWGC | D-BONN | | | |
| 119 | * | F-WWGD | N2000A | N62YC | [damaged in hangar collapse at Washington/Dulles, VA, 06Feb10, possible w/o] | |
| 120 | * | F-WWGG | N333MX | | | |
| 121 | * | F-WWGI | N121EX | XA-CMM | | |
| 122 | * | F-WWGF | N147G | | | |
| 123 | * | F-WWGJ | OO-PAP | N925AK | | |
| 124 | + | F-WWGK | N124EX | N888CE | | |
| 125 | * | F-WWGM | (D-BONN) | VP-BVV | | |
| 126 | * | F-WWGO | N669PG | VP-BGI | | |
| 127 | * | F-WWGQ | CS-DLE | | | |
| 128 | * | F-WWGS | (VP-BOE) | M-CHEM | | |
| 129 | * | F-WWGU | N129EX | C-GENW | | |
| 130 | * | F-WWGA | N1JK | | | |
| 131 | * | F-WWGH | N131AG | | | |
| 132 | * | F-WWGN | G-OJAJ | | | |
| 133 | + | F-WWGP | "VP-BAH" | [painted in error at completion centre] | VP-BRA | |
| 134 | * | F-WWGV | CS-DLF | | | |
| 135 | * | F-WWGE | N414TR | | | |
| 136 | * | F-WWGF | TC-ATC | | | |
| 137 | * | F-WWGG | N137EM | N119EM | | |
| 138 | * | F-WWGI | N168AM | | | |
| 139 | * | F-WWGZ | N470D | VP-CTT | | |
| 140 | + | F-WWMA | OO-DFG | | | |
| 141 | + | F-WWGK | G-WLVS | | | |
| 142 | * | F-WWGO | N100KP | | | |
| 143 | + | F-WWGR | (P4-LGM) | M-LJGI | | |
| 144 | * | F-WWGW | CS-DLG | | | |
| 145 | * | F-WWMB | N345EX | N47WS | C-FDBJ | |
| 146 | + | F-WWGH | N268DM | N785AD | | |
| 147 | + | F-WWGU | N278DM | N786AD | | |
| 148 | + | F-WWGE | M-YJET | | | |
| 149 | * | F-WWGJ | CS-DLH | | | |
| 150 | + | F-WWGL | N150FJ | N772MC | | |
| 151 | * | F-WWMD | N151EX | N2000A | N151EX | |
| 152 | + | F-WWGA | OE-HMR | | | |
| 153 | + | F-WWGC | | | | |

# FALCON 2000EX EASy/2000LX

| C/n | | Identities | | | | |
|---|---|---|---|---|---|---|
| 154 | + | F-WWGG | HB-JET | | | |
| 155 | * | F-WWGZ | (CS-DLH) | N155EX | CS-DLI | N606TJ |
| 156 | + | F-WWME | OY-MHA | | | |
| 157 | + | F-WWGQ | N157EX | (PT-FLX) | PR-NXG | |
| 158 | + | F-WWGS | N234QS | N60FK | | |
| 159 | + | F-WWGT | VT-TDT | | | |
| 160 | + | F-WWGH | (G-CNGM) | OY-CKH | | |
| 161 | + | F-WWGX | (G-LSMB) | OY-MGO | | |
| 162 | + | F-WWMB | (N162NS) | | | |
| 163 | + | F-WWMC | N480D | N209SU | | |
| 164 | + | F-WWMF | N64EX | PP-PPN* | | |
| 165 | + | F-WWGL | N204CE | | | |
| 166 | + | F-WWGN | | | | |
| 167 | + | F-WWGP | N167EX | C-GSLU | | |
| 168 | + | F-WWGU | (N168NS) | | | |
| 169 | + | F-WWGY | VT-BRK | | | |
| 170 | + | F-WWMG | N404UK | (N170LX) | N2000A | |
| 171 | * | F-WWMH | N449SA | | | |
| 172 | + | F-WWMI | | | | |
| 173 | * | (F-WWMJ) | F-WWGI | M-ALRV | | |
| 174 | + | (F-WWMK) | F-WWGK | N250QS | | |
| 175 | * | (F-WWML) | F-WWGO | N175EX | N747RL | |
| 176 | + | (F-WWMM) | F-WWGF | | | |
| 177 | + | (F-WWMN) | F-WWGQ | (N177NS) | | |
| 178 | + | (F-WWMO) | F-WWGS | N429SA | | |
| 179 | + | F-WWMA | N179EX | PR-OBE | | |
| 180 | + | F-WWMJ | TC-SGO | | | |
| 181 | + | F-WWMK | (N928GC)+ | [+ntu marks worn at completion centre] | | LX-EVM |
| 182 | + | F-WWML | G-EDHY | | | |
| 183 | + | F-WWGW | | | | |
| 184 | * | F-WWMC | N9895 | | | |
| 185 | + | F-WWMM | HB-JGF | | | |
| 186 | + | F-WWMN | | | | |
| 187 | + | F-WWMO | N781EX | | | |
| 188 | + | F-WWGE | HB-JGG | | | |
| 189 | + | F-WWGL | N720WY | | | |
| 190 | + | F-WWGP | EI-TDV | | | |
| 191 | + | F-WWMD | N257QS | | | |
| 192 | + | F-WWGA | N192LX^ | | | |
| 193 | + | F-WWGD | TC-MRK | | | |
| 194 | + | F-WWGG | | | | |
| 195 | + | F-WWGK | F-GVFX | | | |
| 196 | + | F-WWGO | | | | |
| 197 | + | F-WWMF | | | | |
| 198 | + | F-WWGR | | | | |
| 199 | + | F-WWGS | OE-HTO | | | |
| 200 | + | F-WWME | | | | |
| 201 | + | F-WWMG | D-BEKY | | | |
| 202 | + | F-WWMA | | | | |
| 203 | + | F-WWMH | N203LX | | | |
| 204 | + | F-WWJN | I-FEDN | | | |
| 205 | + | F-WWJO | N205LX | N769JW* | | |
| 206 | + | F-WWJP | N696SB | | | |
| 207 | + | F-WWJQ | | | | |
| 208 | + | F-WWJR | N1903W | | | |
| 209 | + | F-WWJS | N209LX^ | | | |
| 210 | + | F-WWJT | (D-BEKY) | N410SG | | |
| 211 | + | F-WWJU | N988DV | | | |
| 212 | + | F-WWJV | | | | |
| 213 | + | F-WWJX | | | | |
| 214 | + | F-WWJY | | | | |
| 215 | + | F-WWJZ | | | | |
| 216 | + | F-WWGB | | | | |
| 217 | + | F-WWGJ | | | | |
| 218 | + | F-WWGL | | | | |
| 219 | + | F-WWGM | | | | |
| 220 | + | F-WWGT | | | | |
| 221 | + | F-WWGD | | | | |
| 222 | + | F-WWGE | | | | |
| 223 | + | F-WWGH | | | | |
| 224 | + | F-WWGI | | | | |
| 225 | + | F-WWGS | | | | |
| 226 | + | F-WWGV | | | | |
| 227 | + | F-WWGY | | | | |
| 228 | + | F-WWGZ | | | | |
| 229 | | | | | | |
| 230 | | | | | | |
| 231 | | | | | | |
| 232 | | | | | | |

# ECLIPSE AVIATION ECLIPSE 500

| C/n | Identities |
|---|---|
| EX500-100 | N500EA [rolled out Albuquerque-Double Eagle II 13Jly02; ff 26Aug02; retired Oct03, tt 55hrs] |
| EX500-101 | (N502EA) "N500EA" [Not completed following decision to change from Williams EJ22 to P&W PWF610F engines; used as display exhibit] |
| EX500-102 | [Not built following decision to change from Williams EJ22 to P&W PWF610F engines] |
| EX500-103 | N502EA [ff 14Apr05] |
| EX500-104 | [static test airframe completed 11May05] |
| EX500-105 | [fatigue test airframe completed 20Dec05] |
| EX500-106 | N505EA [Beta test aircraft 1; ff 09Jly05] |
| EX500-107 | N506EA [Beta test aircraft 2; ff 24Aug05] |
| EX500-108 | N503EA [ff 31Dec04] |
| EX500-109 | N504EA [ff 21Apr05] |
| 000001 | N508JA |
| 000002 | N126DJ |
| 000003 | N816KD |
| 000004 | N229BW |
| 000005 | N504RS |
| 000006 | N109DJ |
| 000007 | N110DJ |
| 000008 | N941NC |
| 000009 | N513EA |
| 000010 | N500VK |
| 000011 | N777VE |
| 000012 | N651FC |
| 000013 | N317BH |
| 000014 | N705PT |
| 000015 | N515MP |
| 000016 | N15ND N320LA |
| 000017 | N17AE |
| 000018 | N875NA |
| 000019 | N519EJ |
| 000020 | N115DJ |
| 000021 | N116DJ |
| 000022 | N119DJ |
| 000023 | N130DJ |
| 000024 | N561EA |
| 000025 | N546BW |
| 000026 | N612KB |
| 000027 | N502LT |
| 000028 | N963JG |
| 000029 | N55BX |
| 000030 | N768JF |
| 000031 | N531EA |
| 000032 | N80TF |
| 000033 | N131DJ |
| 000034 | N132DJ |
| 000035 | N134DJ |
| 000036 | N135DJ |
| 000037 | N136DJ |
| 000038 | N112EA |
| 000039 | N858GS |
| 000040 | N444RL |
| 000041 | N541LB |
| 000042 | N168TT |
| 000043 | N62RC |
| 000044 | N489JC |
| 000045 | N500CD |
| 000046 | N6100 |
| 000047 | N218JT |
| 000048 | N570RG |
| 000049 | N549AF |
| 000050 | N456MF |
| 000051 | N500UK |
| 000052 | N502ET |
| 000053 | N514EA |
| 000054 | N139DJ |
| 000055 | N141DJ |
| 000056 | N142DJ |
| 000057 | N145DJ |
| 000058 | N146DJ |
| 000059 | N147DJ |
| 000060 | N429CC |
| 000061 | N148DJ |
| 000062 | N150DJ |
| 000063 | N778VW |

## ECLIPSE 500

| C/n | Identities | | |
|---|---|---|---|
| 000064 | N717LK | | |
| 000065 | N23PJ | | |
| 000066 | N370P | | |
| 000067 | N568PB | | |
| 000068 | (N370P) | N615RH | |
| 000069 | N71MT | | |
| 000070 | N570EA | | |
| 000071 | N152DJ | | |
| 000072 | N153DJ | N94GA* | |
| 000073 | N156DJ | | |
| 000074 | N158DJ | | |
| 000075 | N575CC | | |
| 000076 | N576EA | | |
| 000077 | N160DJ | | |
| 000078 | N161DJ | | |
| 000079 | N162DJ | | |
| 000080 | N580WC | | |
| 000081 | N163DJ | | |
| 000082 | N382EA | | |
| 000083 | N38DA | | |
| 000084 | N509JA | | |
| 000085 | N778TC | | |
| 000086 | N990NA | | |
| 000087 | N50EJ | | |
| 000088 | N457TB | | |
| 000089 | N44EJ | N316CP | |
| 000090 | N2486B | | |
| 000091 | N54KJ | | |
| 000092 | N355BM | | |
| 000093 | (N457TB) | N233MT | |
| 000094 | N417CG | | |
| 000095 | N317DJ | | |
| 000096 | N464PG | | |
| 000097 | N502TS | | |
| 000098 | N598EA | | |
| 000099 | N911MX | | |
| 000100 | N9922F | | |
| 000101 | N539RM | | |
| 000102 | N277G | | |
| 000103 | N333MY | | [w/o 30Jul08 West Chester/Brandywine, PA; parted out by White Inds, Bates City, MO] |
| 000104 | N117EA | | |
| 000105 | N522DK | | |
| 000106 | N516EA | | |
| 000107 | N706PT | | |
| 000108 | N812MJ | | |
| 000109 | N777ZY | | |
| 000110 | N501DX | | |
| 000111 | N175JE | | |
| 000112 | N112EJ | | |
| 000113 | N717HD | | |
| 000114 | N197AR | | |
| 000115 | N727HD | | |
| 000116 | N75EA | | |
| 000117 | N117UH | | |
| 000118 | N105LB | | |
| 000119 | N815WT | | |
| 000120 | N27052 | | |
| 000121 | N855MS | | |
| 000122 | N164MW | | |
| 000123 | N696NA | | |
| 000124 | N227G | | |
| 000125 | N370EA | | |
| 000126 | N953JB | | |
| 000127 | N261DC | | |
| 000128 | N528EA | | |
| 000129 | N500DG | | |
| 000130 | N322JG | | |
| 000131 | N67NV | | |
| 000132 | N964S | | |
| 000133 | N21EK | | |
| 000134 | N800EJ | | |
| 000135 | N3MT | | |
| 000136 | N136EA | (N326LA) | |
| 000137 | N36FD | | |
| 000138 | N100VA | | |
| 000139 | N500MM | | |

# ECLIPSE 500

| C/n | Identities | | |
|---|---|---|---|
| 000140 | N100MZ | | |
| 000141 | N504TC | | |
| 000142 | N2711H | | |
| 000143 | N533DK | | |
| 000144 | N545MA | | |
| 000145 | N145EA | | |
| 000146 | N146EA | | |
| 000147 | N414TW | | |
| 000148 | N148LG | | |
| 000149 | N149EA | | |
| 000150 | N920GB | | |
| 000151 | N85SM | | |
| 000152 | N113EA | | |
| 000153 | N800AZ | | |
| 000154 | N66BX | | |
| 000155 | N114EA | | |
| 000156 | N234EA | | |
| 000157 | N500CE | | |
| 000158 | N500ZH | | |
| 000159 | N727CW | | |
| 000160 | N2YU | | |
| 000161 | N448HC | | |
| 000162 | N224ZQ | | |
| 000163 | N63AD | | |
| 000164 | N884AM | | |
| 000165 | N669CM | | |
| 000166 | N23FK | | |
| 000167 | N800JR | | |
| 000168 | N568EA | (N335LA) | |
| 000169 | N166EA | | |
| 000170 | N170EA | | |
| 000171 | N58EH | | |
| 000172 | N964JG | | |
| 000173 | N173PD | | |
| 000174 | N21YP | N21YR* | |
| 000175 | N512MB | | |
| 000176 | N9900R | | |
| 000177 | N177EA | D-ILAC* | |
| 000178 | N721MA | N721NA | |
| 000179 | N220BW | | |
| 000180 | N712WG | | |
| 000181 | N99KP | | |
| 000182 | N177CK | | |
| 000183 | N555EJ | | |
| 000184 | N118EA | | |
| 000185 | N500FB | | |
| 000186 | N204ZQ | | |
| 000187 | N187EA | | |
| 000188 | N652FC | | |
| 000189 | N435NF | | |
| 000190 | N190CK | | |
| 000191 | N678PS | | |
| 000192 | N61DT | | |
| 000193 | N193EA | | |
| 000194 | N70EJ | | |
| 000195 | N227LS | | |
| 000196 | N508CP | | |
| 000197 | N218G | | |
| 000198 | N888DZ | | |
| 000199 | N165DJ | N120EA | (N477JN) |
| 000200 | N166DJ | N119EA | |
| 000201 | N167DJ | N201EA | |
| 000202 | N169DJ | N202EA | |
| 000203 | N883LC | | |
| 000204 | N607LM | | |
| 000205 | N653FC | | |
| 000206 | N977VH | | |
| 000207 | N207EA | | |
| 000208 | N55TJ | | |
| 000209 | N209EA | | |
| 000210 | N140EA | N160FF | |
| 000211 | N500VH | | |
| 000212 | N212EA | | |
| 000213 | N888ZY | | |
| 000214 | N301MK | | |
| 000215 | N762DL | (N792DL) | |

# ECLIPSE 500

| C/n | Identities | | |
|---|---|---|---|
| 000216 | N375ET | | |
| 000217 | N7FY | | |
| 000218 | N142EA | N165DL | |
| 000219 | N219EA | | |
| 000220 | N724ML | N18BM | |
| 000221 | N666TM | | |
| 000222 | N161BB | | |
| 000223 | N141EA | | |
| 000224 | N722TD | | |
| 000225 | N5005 | | |
| 000226 | N226BR | | |
| 000227 | N654FC | (N227UH) | |
| 000228 | N478F | | |
| 000229 | N229EA | | |
| 000230 | N265DP | | |
| 000231 | N619RJ | | |
| 000232 | N707ES | | |
| 000233 | N869AW | | |
| 000234 | N461N | | |
| 000235 | N747LG | | |
| 000236 | N67LP | | |
| 000237 | N828PA | | |
| 000238 | N989RF | | |
| 000239 | N867K | | |
| 000240 | N929KD | | |
| 000241 | N279E | | |
| 000242 | N23VA | | |
| 000243 | N121G | | |
| 000244 | N20KS | | |
| 000245 | N853TC | | |
| 000246 | N144EA | | |
| 000247 | N207WM | | |
| 000248 | N889BW | | |
| 000249 | N29MR | | |
| 000250 | N163BB | | |
| 000251 | N147EA | | |
| 000252 | N214MS | | |
| 000253 | N427X | | |
| 000254 | N618SR | | |
| 000255 | N49PL | | |
| 000256 | N375SH | | |
| 000257 | N257K | | |
| 000258 | N257AK | | |
| 000259 | N84UR | | |
| 000260 | N877PM | | |
| 000261 | N159EA | | |
| 000262 | N511ED | | |
| 000263 | N522EA | | |

Production complete following the liquidation of Eclipse Aviation in February 2009. The following aircraft also had marks assigned in anticipation of being built:

| C/n | Identities | |
|---|---|---|
| 000264 | (N29SS) | |
| 000265 | (N767PW) | |
| 000266 | N143EA | [marks still current on USCAR, status?] |
| 000267 | N533GT | [marks still current on USCAR, status?] |
| 000268 | (N106WH) | |
| 000269 | (N500YD) | |
| 000270 | (N202JG) | |
| 000272 | (N444EJ) | |
| 000274 | (N610PW) | |
| 000275 | (N89RF) | |
| 000277 | (N510JA) | |
| 000278 | (N278JC) | |
| 000279 | (N10HH) | |
| 000280 | (N502BH) | |
| 000297 | (N79EA) | |

# EMBRAER EMB-500 PHENOM 100

| C/n | Identities | | |
|---|---|---|---|
| 50099801 | PP-XPH | [rolled out 16Jun07; ff 26Jul07] | |
| 50000001 | PP-XOM | [ff 26Sep07] | |
| 50000002 | PP-XOJ | [ff 21Dec07] | |
| 50000003 | PP-XOH | [ff 26Mar08] | |
| 50000004 | PP-XOG | | |
| 50000005 | PP-XON | | |
| 50000006 | PP-XOO | N131ML | |
| 50000007 | PP-XOQ | | |
| 50000008 | PP-XOR | N82DU | |
| 50000009 | PP-XPD | N26SH | |
| 50000010 | PP-XPE | N673DC | |
| 50000011 | PP-XPF | N68ER | |
| 50000012 | PP-XPG | N168FG | N6DQ |
| 50000013 | PT-ZYA | N76EM | |
| 50000014 | PT-ZYB | (N777SG) | Pakistan V-4102 |
| 50000015 | PT-ZYC | N100PZ | |
| 50000016 | PT-ZYD | N484JH | |
| 50000017 | PT-ZYE | Pakistan V-4101 | |
| 50000018 | PT-ZYF | N600AS | |
| 50000019 | PT-ZYG | N458LM | |
| 50000020 | PT-ZYH | N73DB | |
| 50000021 | PT-ZYI | N300LJ | |
| 50000022 | PT-ZYT | N389MW | |
| 50000023 | PT-ZYX | N108JA | |
| 50000024 | PT-ZYL | M-INXY | |
| 50000025 | PT-TFA | N605AS | |
| 50000026 | PT-TFB | PT-MAH | |
| 50000027 | PT-TFC | PR-DCJ | |
| 50000028 | PT-TFD | N190BW | |
| 50000029 | PT-TFE | N200XT | |
| 50000030 | PT-TFF | N102PA | |
| 50000031 | PT-TFG | PP-LGT | |
| 50000032 | PT-TFH | PR-IVI | |
| 50000033 | PT-TFI | | |
| 50000034 | PT-TFJ | PR-DHC | |
| 50000035 | PT-TFK | SX-NSS | |
| 50000036 | PT-TFL | N600HT | |
| 50000037 | PT-TFM | N100WX | |
| 50000038 | PT-TFN | N353SB | |
| 50000039 | PT-TFO | N514AF | |
| 50000040 | PT-TFP | D-IPHE | M-KELY |
| 50000041 | PT-TFQ | N777BF | |
| 50000042 | PT-TFR | PR-FBS | |
| 50000043 | PT-TFS | (EI-JBA) | PR-NPP* |
| 50000044 | PT-TFT | N610AS | |
| 50000045 | PT-TFU | N620AS | |
| 50000046 | PT-TFV | N574JS | |
| 50000047 | PT-TFW | Pakistan V-4103 | |
| 50000048 | PT-TFX | PR-CSW | |
| 50000049 | PT-TFY | PP-AFM | [w/o 12Oct09 Angra dos Reis, Brazil] |
| 50000050 | PT-TFZ | HB-VWQ | |
| 50000051 | PT-TGA | N575JS | |
| 50000052 | PT-TGB | N430TB | |
| 50000053 | PT-TGC | N999RN | |
| 50000054 | PT-TGD | | |
| 50000055 | PT-TGE | G-DRBN | |
| 50000056 | PT-TGF | G-SRBN | |
| 50000057 | PT-TGG | N576JS | N224MD |
| 50000058 | PT-TGH | N27WP | |
| 50000059 | PT-TGI | | |
| 50000060 | PT-TGJ | (EI-EHN) | |
| 50000061 | PT-TGK | N644RM | |
| 50000062 | PT-TGL | (EI-EHO) | HB-JFK |
| 50000063 | PT-TGM | N32KC | |
| 50000064 | PT-TGN | N579JS | |
| 50000065 | PT-TGO | PR-DAY | |
| 50000066 | PT-TGP | (PR-SKD) | PP-SKD |
| 50000067 | PT-TGQ | N629AS | |
| 50000068 | PT-TGR | PR-VEL | |
| 50000069 | PT-TGS | ZS-STS | |
| 50000070 | PT-TGT | N241DE | |
| 50000071 | PT-TGU | N226CP | |
| 50000072 | PT-TGV | N777JQ | |
| 50000073 | PT-TGW | (EI-EHS) | PP-IME |
| 50000074 | PT-TGX | N784JP | |

# EMBRAER EMB-500 PHENOM 100

| C/n | Identities | | |
|---|---|---|---|
| 50000075 | PT-TGY | N639AS | N876JC |
| 50000076 | PT-TGZ | (EI-EHT) | PR-SPJ |
| 50000077 | PT-THA | PR-PTA | |
| 50000078 | PT-THB | | |
| 50000079 | PT-THC | N580JS | |
| 50000080 | PT-THD | YV2609 | |
| 50000081 | PT-THE | N59PW | |
| 50000082 | PT-THF | N100EQ | |
| 50000083 | PT-THG | PR-JAJ | |
| 50000084 | PT-THH | N725MW | N600CS |
| 50000085 | PT-THI | PR-IEI | |
| 50000086 | PT-THJ | | |
| 50000087 | PT-THK | N149GK | |
| 50000088 | PT-THL | N210FF | |
| 50000089 | PT-THM | N354RX | |
| 50000090 | PT-THN | N91TQ | |
| 50000091 | PT-THO | N6745 | |
| 50000092 | PT-THP | M-PHNM | OE-FOM |
| 50000093 | PT-THQ | PR-UUT | |
| 50000094 | PT-THR | PR-LMP | |
| 50000095 | PT-THS | OO-NOA | PT-THS |
| 50000096 | PT-THT | PR-MJD | |
| 50000097 | PT-THU | | |
| 50000098 | PT-THV | PR-DLM* | |
| 50000099 | PT-THW | | |
| 50000100 | PT-THX | OE-FAM | |
| 50000101 | PT-THY | PR-ADQ | |
| 50000102 | PT-THZ | N102EP | |
| 50000103 | PT-TIH | N511WK | |
| 50000104 | PT-TII | | |
| 50000105 | PT-TIJ | N67WG | |
| 50000106 | PT-TIK | N175EM | |
| 50000107 | PT-TIL | N926JK | |
| 50000108 | PT-TIM | PR-OFP | |
| 50000109 | PT-TIN | PP-VDP* | |
| 50000110 | PT-TIO | N581JS | |
| 50000111 | PT-TIP | N723GB | |
| 50000112 | PT-TIQ | M-YTOY | |
| 50000113 | PT-TIR | Pakistan V-4104 | |
| 50000114 | PT-TIS | N645AS | |
| 50000115 | PT-TIT | CS-DTC | |
| 50000116 | PT-TIU | N917LJ | |
| 50000117 | PT-TIV | N777ZA | |
| 50000118 | PT-TIW | | |
| 50000119 | PT-TIX | | |
| 50000120 | PT-TIY | | |
| 50000121 | PT-TIZ | | |
| 50000122 | PT-TYA | HB-VWS* | |
| 50000123 | PT-TYB | N661EP | |
| 50000124 | PT-TYC | N190HL | |
| 50000125 | PR-CPC | | |
| 50000126 | PP-KKA* | | |
| 50000127 | PT-TYD | PT-FQA* | PR-OVD* |
| 50000128 | PT-FQB | | |
| 50000129 | PT-FQC | | |
| 50000130 | PT-FQD | N600PB | |
| 50000131 | PT-FQE | | |
| 50000132 | PT-FQF | PH-PST* | |
| 50000133 | PT-FQG | N80EJ | |
| 50000134 | PT-FQH | | |
| 50000135 | PT-FQI | | |
| 50000136 | PT-FQJ | N937DM | |
| 50000137 | PT-FQK | N100FZ | |
| 50000138 | PT-FQL | | |
| 50000139 | PT-FQM | | |
| 50000140 | PT-FQN | | |
| 50000141 | PT-FQO | N100FF | |
| 50000142 | PT-FQP | | |
| 50000143 | PT-FQQ | | |
| 50000144 | PT-FQR | | |
| 50000145 | PT-FQS | | |
| 50000146 | PT-FQT | | |
| 50000147 | PT-FQU | | |
| 50000148 | PT-FQV | | |
| 50000149 | PT-FQW | | |

# EMBRAER EMB-500 PHENOM 100

| C/n | Identities |
|---|---|
| 50000150 | PT-FQX |
| 50000151 | PT-FQY |
| 50000152 | PT-FQZ |
| 50000153 | PT-FUA |
| 50000154 | PT-FUB |
| 50000155 | PT-FUC |
| 50000156 | PT-FUD |
| 50000157 | PT-FUE |
| 50000158 | PT-FUF |
| 50000159 | PT-FUG |
| 50000160 | PT-FUH |
| 50000161 | PT-FUI |
| 50000162 | PT-FUJ |
| 50000163 | PT-FUK |
| 50000164 | PT-FUL |
| 50000165 | PT-FUM |
| 50000166 | PT-FUN |
| 50000167 | PT-FUO |
| 50000168 | PT-FUP |
| 50000169 | PT-FUQ |
| 50000170 | PT-FUR |
| 50000171 | PT-FUS |
| 50000172 | PT-FUT |
| 50000173 | PT-FUU |
| 50000174 | PT-FUV |
| 50000175 | PT-FUW |
| 50000176 | PT-FUX |
| 50000177 | PT-FUY |
| 50000178 | PT-FUZ |
| 50000179 | PT-FYA |
| 50000180 | PT-FYB |
| 50000181 | PT-FYC |
| 50000182 | PT-FYD |
| 50000183 | PT-FYE |
| 50000184 | PT-FYF |
| 50000185 | PT-FYG |
| 50000186 | PT-FYH |
| 50000187 | PT-FYI |
| 50000188 | PT-FYJ |
| 50000189 | PT-FYK |
| 50000190 | PT-FYL |
| 50000191 | PT-FYM |
| 50000192 | PT-FYN |
| 50000193 | PT-FYO |
| 50000194 | PT-FYP |
| 50000195 | |
| 50000196 | |
| 50000197 | |
| 50000198 | |
| 50000199 | |
| 50000200 | |
| 50000201 | |
| 50000202 | |
| 50000203 | |
| 50000204 | |
| 50000205 | |
| 50000206 | |
| 50000207 | |
| 50000208 | |
| 50000209 | |
| 50000210 | |
| 50000211 | |
| 50000212 | |
| 50000213 | |
| 50000214 | |
| 50000215 | |
| 50000216 | |
| 50000217 | |
| 50000218 | |
| 50000219 | |
| 50000220 | |
| 50000221 | |
| 50000222 | |
| 50000223 | |
| 50000224 | |

# EMBRAER EMB-500 PHENOM 100

| C/n | Identities |
|---|---|
| 50000225 | |
| 50000226 | |
| 50000227 | |
| 50000228 | |
| 50000229 | |
| 50000230 | |
| 50000231 | |
| 50000232 | |
| 50000233 | |
| 50000234 | |
| 50000235 | |
| 50000236 | |
| 50000237 | |
| 50000238 | |
| 50000239 | |
| 50000240 | |
| 50000241 | |
| 50000242 | |
| 50000243 | |
| 50000244 | |
| 50000245 | |
| 50000246 | |
| 50000247 | |
| 50000248 | |
| 50000249 | |
| 50000250 | |
| 50000251 | |
| 50000252 | |
| 50000253 | |
| 50000254 | |
| 50000255 | |
| 50000256 | |
| 50000257 | |
| 50000258 | |
| 50000259 | |
| 50000260 | |
| 50000261 | |
| 50000262 | |
| 50000263 | |
| 50000264 | |
| 50000265 | |
| 50000266 | |
| 50000267 | |
| 50000268 | |
| 50000269 | |
| 50000270 | |
| 50000271 | |
| 50000272 | |
| 50000273 | |
| 50000274 | |
| 50000275 | |
| 50000276 | |
| 50000277 | |
| 50000278 | |
| 50000279 | |
| 50000280 | |
| 50000281 | |
| 50000282 | |
| 50000283 | |
| 50000284 | |
| 50000285 | |
| 50000286 | |
| 50000287 | |
| 50000288 | |
| 50000289 | |
| 50000290 | |
| 50000291 | |
| 50000292 | |
| 50000293 | |
| 50000294 | |
| 50000295 | |
| 50000296 | |
| 50000297 | |
| 50000298 | |
| 50000299 | |

# EMBRAER EMB-505 PHENOM 300

| C/n | Identities | | |
|---|---|---|---|
| 50599801 | PP-XVI | [rolled out 12Apr08; ff 29Apr08] | |
| 50500001 | PP-XVJ | | |
| 50500002 | PP-XVK | | |
| 50500003 | PP-XVL | | |
| 50500004 | PP-XVM | [ff 08Aug09] | |
| 50500005 | PT-ZXS | N454DR | |
| 50500006 | PT-ZXT | N585TV | |
| 50500007 | PT-ZXW | | |
| 50500008 | PT-ZXX | | |
| 50500009 | PT-ZXY | | |
| 50500010 | PT-ZXZ | | |
| 50500011 | PP-ZZC | | |
| 50500012 | PP-ZZD | | |
| 50500013 | PP-ZZE | | |
| 50500014 | PP-PVB | | |
| 50500015 | PP-PVC | | |
| 50500016 | PP-PVD | | |
| 50500017 | PP-PVE | | |
| 50500018 | PP-PVF | | |
| 50500019 | PP-PVG | | |
| 50500020 | PP-PVH | | |
| 50500021 | PP-PVI | | |
| 50500022 | PP-PVJ | | |
| 50500023 | PP-PVL | | |
| 50500024 | PP-PVM | PP-MCL* | |
| 50500025 | PP-PVN | | |
| 50500026 | PP-PVO | | |
| 50500027 | PP-PVP | | |
| 50500028 | PP-PVQ | | |
| 50500029 | PP-PVK | | |
| 50500030 | | | |
| 50500031 | | | |
| 50500032 | | | |
| 50500033 | | | |
| 50500034 | | | |
| 50500035 | | | |
| 50500036 | | | |
| 50500037 | | | |
| 50500038 | | | |
| 50500039 | | | |
| 50500040 | | | |
| 50500041 | | | |
| 50500042 | | | |
| 50500043 | | | |
| 50500044 | | | |
| 50500045 | | | |
| 50500046 | | | |
| 50500047 | | | |
| 50500048 | | | |
| 50500049 | | | |
| 50500050 | | | |
| 50500051 | | | |
| 50500052 | | | |
| 50500053 | | | |
| 50500054 | | | |
| 50500055 | | | |
| 50500056 | | | |
| 50500057 | | | |
| 50500058 | | | |
| 50500059 | | | |
| 50500060 | | | |
| 50500061 | | | |
| 50500062 | | | |
| 50500063 | | | |
| 50500064 | | | |
| 50500065 | | | |
| 50500066 | | | |
| 50500067 | | | |
| 50500068 | | | |
| 50500069 | | | |
| 50500070 | | | |
| 50500071 | | | |
| 50500072 | | | |
| 50500073 | | | |

# EMIVEST (WAS SINO-SWEARINGEN) SJ30-2

| C/n | Identities | | |
|---|---|---|---|
| 001 | N30SJ | [ff 13Feb91 Stinson Field, TX. Stretched to become SJ30-2 prototype and ff 8Nov96; cx Oct99, wfu. To Lone Star Flight Museum, Galveston, TX, Dec06] | |
| 002 | N138BF | [rolled out 17Jly00; ff 30Nov00; crashed near Del Rio, TX, 26Apr03 during high-speed test-flight, killing Sino-Swearingen's chief test pilot; w/o] | |
| 003 | N30SJ | N110SJ | |
| 004 | N709JB | N404SJ | |
| 005 | N50SJ | [ff Jan05] | |
| 006 | N60SJ | N901HB | N30SJ |
| 007 | N70SJ | N7SJ | |
| 008 | (N80SJ) | N200DV | |
| 009 | | | |
| 010 | N30GZ | | |
| 011 | | | |
| 012 | | | |
| 013 | | | |
| 014 | | | |
| 015 | | | |
| 016 | | | |
| 017 | | | |
| 018 | | | |
| 019 | | | |
| 020 | | | |
| | | | |
| TF-2 | | [static test frame] | |
| TF-3 | | [static test frame] | |

Notes: Originally to be known as the SA-30 Fanjet, the SJ30-2 received its FAA type certification 27Oct05

# G1159 GULFSTREAM II

Notes: G1159B Gulfstream 2B conversion programme numbers have been included alongside the c/n (see also at the end of the production list)

TT indicates aircraft with tip tanks (some 2Bs were built as "TT" models)
SP indicates a specialist conversion by Aviation Partners with winglets, known as Gulfstream 2SPs; these are not 2B aircraft, the prototype was c/n 12
* in the series column indicates that engine hush kits have been fitted

| C/n | Series | Identities |
|---|---|---|
| 1 | SP | N801GA [ff 02Oct66] N55RG |
| 2 | SP | N802GA N801GA N369CS N869CS N721SW N434JW N902GT [cx Jly03; to Air Classics Museum, IL] |
| 3 | | N831GA N214GP N311JJ N555RS N300GP (N417RD) N300RD |
| 4/8 | 2B | N832GA N680RW N680RZ 9K-ACY VR-CAS HZ-MPM N849OP N36RR |
| 5 | | N100P N100PJ N65ST N655TJ N34S N3LH |
| 6 | | N834GA N430R N122DJ N122DU [broken up Geneva, Switzerland, 2006; remains to Air Salvage Int'l, Alton, Hants, UK, for parts; removed from site by Aug08] |
| 7 | SP | CF-HOG N9300 N93QQ N118NP N701JA [parted out by Int'l Turbine Service circa Nov 03; cx Nov03] |
| 8 | SP | N833GA N18N N400SJ N400SA HB-IMV N400SA N777GG PJ-ARI N504TF N5UD N225CC N11UF N22CX S9-CRH S9-GOT ZS-TGG N267PS N225MS |
| 9/33 | 2B | CF-SBR N320FE (N115RS) N209GA N343K N48EC N129WA |
| 10 | SP | N343K N343N N888CF XA-ROI N555LG N51TJ N667CX XB-JPL HR-AUJ N900CE [wfu; cx 15Sep08] |
| 11 | | N835GA N902 N902GA N611TJ N463HK |
| 12 | SP | N500R N11UM N154X N115MR N121EA N160WC+ N212TJ N794SB N622RR +[while regd N160WC was tested with spiroid winglets for about 50 hours] |
| 13 | | N678RW N678RZ N98AM 5N-AMN N2GP N373LP N373LB VR-BOS N269MH N269HM N169HM |
| 14 | SP | N663P N663B N217JD N369AP N500JW XA-RBS XA-RBP |
| 15 | | N375PK N77SW N416SH N125JJ N571BJ [parted out at Islip, NY, 2004 onwards] |
| 16/13 | 2B | N890A N697A N711MT N38GL N24YS |
| 17 | SP | N119K N819GA N456AS N91AE N305AF N917R N217GA N1PR (N121PR) N422DV N143G N143V N202PX (N217DA) |
| 18 | | N838GA N205M N43R (N48RA) XA-SDE XA-LZZ XC-AA70 |
| 19 | SP | N839GA N1929Y N19NW N590CH (N213DC) ZS-LOG |
| 20 | | N2PG N755S N4SP N331P N747NB N88LN |
| 21 | | N4PG N3PG N7ZX N8PG N8PQ [cx Jan93; to CIS; but unable to obtain CofA] N8PQ N244DM HP-... |
| 22 | SP | N862GA N5152 N145ST N22FS N683FM N206MD (N800TE) (N655JH) N217RR N216RR |
| 23 | | N863GA USCG 01 [VC-11A] N7TJ N890TJ |
| 24 | | N536CS N4S (N98G) N26WP (N224TS) N800XL (N800XC) XA-... |
| 25 | | N327K N527K N711RL N711RZ YV1681 |
| 26 | SP | N328K N202GA PK-PJZ N975GA (N711RT) N4RT ZS-PYY |
| 27 | SP | N1807Z N121JJ N430BC N227TS (N227TJ) N227BA |
| 28 | | N695ST N700ST N7004T C-GCFB N120EA N85EQ N68DM N17KW |
| 29 | SP | N869GA N930BS N919G N41RC N71TJ N941CW N188JS |
| 30/4 | 2B | N870GA N788S N2601 N2607 N333AX N338AX N47HR XA-FHR XA-TRG N30438 XA-EHR XA-STT XB-KBO XB-KCX XC-LKN |
| 31 | | N1621 N685TA N789FF N200CC N105TB [test a/c with nose probe and underwing pods] |
| 32/2 | 2B | N7602 (N7601) N976B N971EC N971EQ N200AQ |
| 33 | SP | N1624 N1324 N217TL (N217TE) N327TL N327TC N926NY N747NB |
| 34 | | N230E N130A N11SX VR-CBM N500JR N204RC [w/o 17Jun91 Caracas-Oscar Machada, Venezuela; cx Oct91] |
| 35 | | N1004T N830TL N30PR |
| 36/3 | 2B | N26L N26LA N5400G (N211GA) N901K N901KB N74A |
| 37 | | N179AR N179AP N994JD N397RD [cx Nov02; b/u, remains to Aviation Warehouse film prop facility at El Mirage, CA and then restored Feb03] |
| 38 | | N80A N880A [Quiet Spey development a/c with BAC1-11 thrust reverser on starboard engine] [cx Jun95; wfu for spares] |
| 39 | SP | N80Q N8000 N401HR (N124BN) N425A (N12BN) N1TJ N87HB N87TD [wfu at Chino, CA, 2006] |
| 40 | | N1040 (N5040) N1039 VR-BLJ [w/o 20Jun96 Jos, 465m NE of Lagos, Nigeria] |
| 41 | SP | N38N (N417GA) N401GA N416K N365TC N311MG |
| 42/12 | 2B | N8000J N937M N880GM VR-BMQ N1164A N36PN |
| 43 | | N17583 F-BRUY N84X N33ME N691RC (N243TS) N270TS N899GA (N247LG) XA-... [impounded at Toluca Aug07 still wearing N899GA] |
| 44 | | N814GA N830G N585A N830G [b/u Fort Lauderdale Executive, FL circa Jan02; cx Feb02] |
| 45 | SP | N815GA N711R PK-PJG N152RG N215RL VR-BHA N115GA N40CE US Army 89-0266 N51741 US Army 89-0266 N245GA N250MS |
| 46 | TT | N806CC N40CC N111RF C-GSLK N9272K N721CP N9BF N505JT N565KC [canx 19Jly05 aircraft b/u at, then removed from, Islip, NY] |
| 47 | SP | N803GA N35JM N553MD N809GA N809LS N800FL N800RT |

# GULFSTREAM II

| C/n | Series | Identities |
|---|---|---|
| 48/29 | 2B | N109G N4411 N711MC N61WH N61WE N865AA |
| 49 | | N871GA N747G N74JK N830TL N830TE N830TL (N830TE) N830BH N511PA |
| | | N511BA (N33EN) |
| 50 | | N39N N39NX N767FL N800FL N220FL N220JR N650KA |
| 51 | SP* | N2013M VR-BNE N7C N20H N20HE N20H |
| 52 | | CF-FNM C-FFNM N69SF N38KM N5SJ (N52NE) "N52TJ" N711MT N211MT |
| | | N52NW [canx 28Oct05 parted out] |
| 53 | SP | N107A N167A N102AB N104CD N104VV |
| 54/36 | 2B | N123H CF-NOR C-FNOR N955CC N148V |
| 55 | | N875GA N225SF N225SE N125DC |
| 56 | SP | N10XY N20XY N105Y N805Y N610CC N690PC N2000 |
| 57 | SP | N876GA N770AC N300DK N300DL (N333ST) N33PJ N466JB |
| 58 | | N878GA N720Q [w/o 24Jun74 Kline, SC] |
| 59 | SP | N879GA N1823D [b/u; cx 19Nov08] |
| 60 | | N892GA N500J [w/o 26Sep76 Hot Springs, VA] |
| 61 | SP | N18N N711MM N497TJ N800MC N57BG N61LH N41AV |
| 62 | | N834GA N372CM N372GM N1PG N3ZQ N7PG N7PQ |
| | | Russia 62 [Black or Dark Blue] (N777TX) N20LW N262PA N128KG |
| 63 | | N835GA N238U N239P N149JW N17ND (N20GP) N12GP |
| 64/27 | 2B | N836GA N940BS N950BS N341NS N95SV N620K N82CK N43RJ N95SJ |
| | | N351SE |
| 65 | | N837GA N720E N1JG N500PC N58JF (N300FN) |
| 66 | | N838GA N720F N165W N165U N718JS N718JA |
| 67 | SP | N839GA N711S EL-WRT N10HR N400JD N67PR N568TN ZS-WHG |
| 68 | | N308EL N308EE [cx to Panama 22Jun06, shot down over Colombia 12Aug06] |
| 69 | SP | N69NG N25JM N33CR N45JM N45Y N45YP VH-HKR N21066 N123CC |
| | | N440DR N701S XA-MEM XC-LKA |
| 70/1 | 2B | N711SC N711SB VR-BML N165A N451CS N451GS N908EJ N908CE N510SR |
| | | N510SE N660AF [wfu at Mojave, CA; cx 25Feb2010] |
| 71 | | N4CP N4CQ N711SW N907SW N48JK N47A N200AB |
| 72 | | N397F [w/o 22Feb76 Burlington, VT] |
| 73/9 | 2B | N116K N555CS N920DS N436JW 3D-TCB 7P-TCB N436JW |
| 74 | SP | N845GA N111AC N311AC (3X-GBD) N204GA N92SV N74TJ N74HH |
| 75/7 | 2B | N823GA N1000 N100AC N100CC N600CS N760U N94TJ N211SJ |
| | | Venezuela 0010 |
| 76 | SP | N711LS N227G N227GL N227GX N227G N227GA [canx 25May04; b/u] |
| 77 | | N824GA N100WK N40CH N140CH N34MZ N84MZ N777JS N385M N7TJ |
| | | N707SH N7TJ N700JP N125WM N994GC N994GG |
| 78 | SP* | N17585 PH-FJP CF-IOT C-FIOT N90HH HP-1A [wfu Jan10; cx] |
| 79 | SP | N826GA N719GA N204A XA-SFB XA-STO XA-ARA |
| 80 | SP | N827GA N85V N85VT N500RH N510RH N82CR [structurally modified for US |
| | | Navy BAMS system development] |
| 81 | SP | N828GA? N777SW N44MD N281GA N283MM N688MC N681AR XB-PGR+ N681AR |
| | | (N281NW) N151SD N419MS [+ was not canx from USCAR at this time] |
| 82 | SP | N711DP N10LB N9040 N600B N600BT N728T N492JT |
| 83 | | N404M N409M N409MA (N48MS) [w/o 03May95 Quito, Ecuador] |
| 84 | | N5101 N5101T N27SL |
| 85 | SP | N5102 Denmark F-085 N5102 N510G N86SK N931CW N93AT N524MM |
| | | N598GS ZS-MMG |
| 86/16 | 2B | N880GA N179T (N179DE) |
| 87/775/6 | 2B | N804GA N13GW N723J N6PC N692EB N165PA |
| 88/21 | 2B | N881GA N2600 N2637M HB-IMZ N901AS N80WD N779LC |
| 89 | SP* | N882GA N100A N203A N36MW [conv to prototype "Paragon" before SP] N98WJ |
| 90 | | N883GA N7789 N20GP N671LW |
| 91 | SP | N17586 G-AYMI VH-ASM N219GA G-OVIP VR-BRM N291GA N99ST N183SC |
| | | N81FC N914MH XB-KIV XC-LKS |
| 92 | SP | N884GA N300L N300U N114HC N994JD N430SA N722TP N589HM N691HM |
| | | (N584DM) N629TD N374PS (N883KF) N888YZ |
| 93 | SP | N885GA N8785R TJ-AAK N215GA N62K N484TL N396BC N922MR |
| 94 | SP | N886GA N200A N202A N623MW N420JM N420JT N18AQ N685SF N665SF |
| 95/39 | 2B | N887GA VH-ASG N427AC N836MF N836ME N113CS N118GS N889DF N2DF |
| 96 | SP | N888GA N100KS N100WC N75WC N75SR XC-MEX XB-EBI N3005P XA-EYA |
| | | N396CF |
| 97 | SP | N889GA I-SMEG N66TF N11AL N930SD N397J (N397L) N55HY N25GJ |
| | | XA-... |
| 98/38 | 2B | N850GA N93M N955H N988H N988DS N925DS N17MX XA-CHR XA-PSD |
| | | N198AV N812RS N888CS N888ES N883ES N982B N44YS |
| 99 | SP | N851GA N99GA N822CA N900VL N900MP N1218C |
| 100 | SP | N852GA N4000X N400CX N234DB N911DB XB-FVL N400D |
| 101 | SP | N853GA N1159K (N237LM) N240CX N623CX N512JT N412JT |
| 102/32 | 2B | N854GA N88AE N210GA N119CC N400CC N102CX |
| 103 | SP | N855GA N801GA G-BDMF N833GA P2-PNF P2-PNG N833GA HZ-MS4 |
| | | (N103WJ) N89TJ [b/u for spares circa Feb05 by Dodson Intl Parts, Rantoul, KS] |
| 104/10 | 2B/2 | N856GA N856W N858W [cvtd back to G2 standards 1989; wings to G3 c/n 303] |
| | * | C-FHPM N712MQ |
| 105 | SP | N807GA N23M N5997K N405GA N6060 N711TE N754JB |

# GULFSTREAM II

| C/n | Series | Identities |
|---|---|---|
| 106 | | N808GA N33M (N519TW) N397LE N226GA (N106TJ) N141JF (N473JF) |
| 107 | * | N809GA N5113H N10123 [modified for aerial survey use] |
| 108 | SP | N810GA N11UC N60GG N600MB N700FS N801GA N200GH (N200GL) N900AK N183PA |
| 109 | SP | N811GA N679RW N882W N86CE N862CE N73AW N581MB |
| 110 | SP | N814GA N5000G N200GN N200PB N21AM N21AX N92AG N417EK |
| 111 | | N815GA N10LB N13LB N765A N900BR N900DH |
| 112 | SP | N816GA N102ML N102HS VR-BJG N36JK N909L N108DB N87AG N168VA |
| 113 | SP | N817GA N30RP N34RP N60CT N203GA N2S N32HC N2S N216HE (N216MF) N1BL N211BL N217JS N74RT N74RQ [dbr 19Jan05 Logan, UT; to White Inds, Bates City, MO for spares; cx 22Jan09] |
| 114 | | N818GA N100PM N25BF XA-TDK (N114WJ) XB-KBE XB-KCW XC-LKL |
| 115 | SP | N819GA N677S N457SW N47JK N200BP N700BH N40AG N42PP N424GC [wfu at Mojave, CA; cx 02Jul09] |
| 116 | | N821GA 9M-ARR N20XY N23W (N410LR) N716TE N218SE |
| 117 | SP | N822GA N580RA N888SW N75CC N7500 N750RA |
| 118 | | N823GA N399CB (N301FP) N399FP N650PF/NASA650 [for Prop Fan Experiments] (N651NA) N945NA |
| 119/22 | 2B | N824GA TU-VAF N825GA C-FHBX N2991Q N60HJ (N875E) N720G N73LP N928GF (N103EL) N305SJ N500MA XB-KKU [w/o in Venezuela 07Oct07] |
| 120 | SP | N825GA N901BM N777V N677V N20FX N393BD N392BD C-GTEW N711VL |
| 121 | SP | N200P N90EA N507JC N721RL N721PL N892TM |
| 122 | | N832GA N429JX N4290X N61SM N84A N500RL N500RQ |
| 123/25 | 2B | N805CC N345CP N345AA N344AA N344AB N368DS N868DS |
| 124 | | N834GA HB-IEW VR-BGL VR-BGO N203GA Venezuela 0004 (N980EF) N124TV [wfu Mojave, CA circa Sep03; cx 15Jun05 as b/u; fuselage to Long Beach, CA, Nov07 for training use] |
| 125/26 | 2B | N870GA N367G N364G N3643 N92LA N92NA N178B |
| 126 | | N43M N581WD (HB-I..) N578DF N416K N901WG [wfu; cx 13Jan10] |
| 127 | TT | N17581 TR-KHB [w/o 06Feb80 Ngaoundere, Cameroun] |
| 128 | | N73M N367EG N128TS N829NL |
| 129 | SP | N871GA N1H N711DS N83TE N626TC N711EV [b/u cx Nov03] |
| 130 | SP | N872GA N127V N518GS N512SD A6-PHY N666SA |
| 131/23 | 2B | N17582 9M-ATT N759A N2JR |
| 132 | SP | N873GA N400M |
| 133 | TT | N88906 N17583 5X-UPF N44UP N444QG N442QG N930LS [wfu Mojave, CA; cx 31Mar09] |
| 134 | | N806CC C-FROC N555HD N555KH N628HC (N810MY) |
| 135 | SP* | N83M N113EV (N518FE) N518JT N515JT N552JT N525XL |
| 136 | SP | N874GA N65M ZS-JIS 3D-AAC N207GA 6V-AFL 6V-AGQ N26WB XA-ABA XA-AFP XA-FCP N95RT N190RP |
| 137 | SP | N875GA N1875P N2711M VR-BJT N23AH N115MC N485GM N435GM [dbr by Hurricane Rita at Beaumont, TX, Sep05] |
| 138 | | N6JW |
| 139/11 | 2B | N880GA N18N HZ-PET HB-ITV N2UJ (N763PD) N663PD N339GA N139CF N113AR N139CF |
| 140/40 | 2B* | N881GA C-GTWO N2667M (N101AR) N104AR N212GA VR-BJQ N189TC N730TK N159NB |
| 141 | | N17584 JA8431 [Mitsubishi special test aircraft] |
| 142 | | N882GA N60CC N5RD N742TS N588SS |
| 143 | | N883GA N334 N204C [w/o 04Sep91 Kota Kinabalu, Borneo; cx Nov93] |
| 144 | | N17585 HB-ITR N944NA |
| 145 | SP | N894GA N871D N871E N339H N226RM |
| 146 | | N897GA N946NA |
| 147 | | N898GA N947NA |
| 148/5 | 2B | N710MR N710MP N2615 N2815 N180AR |
| 149 | | N896GA N17586 5V-TAA [w/o 26Dec74 Lome, Togo] |
| 150 | SP | N803GA N966H N988H N636MF N638MF (N631CK) N613CK N319GP N60GU ZS-TPG |
| 151/24 | 2B | N804GA N979RA N979GA N908JE (N988JE) N909JE |
| 152 | | N17587 XA-FOU N202GA N62WB N559LC |
| 153 | SP | N881GA N23A (N602CM) N111VW N110VW N132FP |
| 154/28 | 2B | N1625 N1JN N18JN N836MF N110GD N719SA N719SQ HI871 |
| 155/14 | 2B | N308A XA-GAC N477GG |
| 156/31 | 2B | N806GA N400SJ N7000G N16NK N18NK N525JT N83TE N864YD (N159DJ) ZS-DJA |
| 157 | | N805GA N914BS N940BS N74JK N658PC N683EC N468HW |
| 158 | SP | N76CS N76QS N401M N2S N889JC |
| 159 | SP | N345UP N800DM N800DJ N880RJ |
| 160 | | N80J N801 N214GA N900TP N919TG N1123G N241MH |
| 161 | * | N17589 XA-ABC XC-FEZ XC-CFE Mexico TP-04/XC-UJK XB-GSN XA-RUS XA-AHM |
| 162 | | (C-GANE) N530SW N74RV C-GTCB N74RV N666JT N668JT |
| 163 | SP | N17581 (YV-60CP) PJ-ABA N117JJ N117JA N117JJ |
| 164 | SP | N17582 9K-ACX A6-HHZ N93LA N80AG XA-ESC XA-BBO |
| 165/37 | 2B* | N810GA N7000C N788C VR-BHR N26L N965CC N183V N696MJ |
| 166/15 | 2B | N811GA N515KA N66AL (N84AL) N826GA N826AG XA-SWP N776MA ZS-DGW |

# GULFSTREAM II

| C/n | Series | Identities |
|---|---|---|
| 167 | SP | N17583 5V-TAC VR-CBC N204GA N900SF N430DP N681FM N82204 N682FM N683FM N120GS N368AG N868AG XA-UEC XA-CVS |
| 168 | SP | N812GA N10LB N26LB N193CK N635AV N168JW N317AF (N370SP) N318SP N501JV |
| 169 | SP | N17584 HB-IEX N39JK N31SY N710JL N7155P N169P N169EA N467AM |
| 170 | | N991GA N14PC N502PC (N318GD) N111GD N202XT N111GD |
| 171 | | N17585 HZ-AFH SX-BTX [b/u Geneva, Switzerland, Nov09] |
| 172 | SP | N804GA N903G N903GA N903AG N987SA [shot down while drug-running in Mexico 24Sep07, w/o] |
| 173 | TT | N801GA XC-PET XA-SQU N98FT N173EL (N444ML) [parted out Van Nuys, CA] |
| 174 | SP | N805GA N401M N144ST N7766Z N900ES N540EA |
| 175 | SP | N17586 HZ-AFG 5T-UPR N770PA XA-FNY XC-PFT [code PF-210] |
| 176 | SP | N806GA N176P N176SB N15UC N15UG N794SB N794SC N550WP |
| 177 | | N17587 5N-AGV "5N-BLV" 5N-BGV |
| 178 | SP | N819GA N390F N104ME (N128AD) N42LC N720JW N502RG |
| 179 | | N17588 HZ-CAD HZ-PCA |
| 180 | SP* | N859GA N329K N359K N37WH (N47WH) N702JA N416CG XA-... |
| 181 | | N860GA N24DS N924DS N48CC N48CQ [wfu Tulsa, OK circa Nov02; canx 02Dec05 believed b/u] |
| 182 | TT* | N17589 CN-ANL |
| 183 | SP | N17581 A40-AA N23AZ (N10NW) N801WC N806WC N400PJ N821PA |
| 184 | | N861GA N80E N220GA N254CR N777RW |
| 185 | SP | N862GA N372CM N3E N3EU N511WP XA-BRE N297GB N950NA [modified for use as USAF YAL-1A (Airborne Laser) target aircraft] |
| 186 | SP | N17582 (D-ACVG) D-AFKG 5N-AML (D-AAMD) VR-BJV VP-BJV VP-BFF |
| 187 | | N17583 N804GA HZ-ADC N202GA N802CC |
| 188 | | N823GA N862G N662G N555MW N555MU N188DC |
| 189/42 | 2B | N333AR N512VB (N515JT) N555XL N404AC N711MQ |
| 190 | SP | N130K N159B N169B N900WJ N1WP N7WQ N59CD N59JR N914DZ N914CF N190CS |
| 191 | SP | N810GA N680RW N679RW N677RW N675RW N951RK |
| 192 | SP | N811GA N678RW N677RW HB-ITW N273LP N192FG N192WF |
| 193 | * | N808GA N26L N26LT N54J N54JJ N227LA |
| 194 | | N17584 HB-IMW C6-BEJ C6-BFE VR-BRM N194WA N57HJ N57HE |
| 195 | | N212K N71TP XA-ILV N195AR [parted out San Antonio, TX, 2006] |
| 196 | | N400J N200BE N610MC N619MC |
| 197 | | N800GA N5117H (N217AH) N608MD |
| 198/35 | 2B | N825GA N365G N3652 N91LA N91NA |
| 199/19 | 2B* | N829GA N75WC N75RP N74RP N71RP VR-BND VP-BND N900TJ N338CL |
| 200 | SP | N826GA N1806P N135CP N99VA XA-AVR N17GG N281RB N17KJ (N200UJ) |
| 201 | TT | N17585 HZ-AFI N105AJ |
| 202 | TT | N17586 A9C-BG |
| 203 | TT | N17587 HZ-AFJ [wfu circa Dec05 Geneva, Switzerland; b/u Oct07] |
| 204 | SP | N17588 G-CXMF N806CC N937US N659PC N659WL VR-CPA VP-CPA N659WL |
| 205 | SP* | N25UG N1000 N205BL N623BM N345GL |
| 206 | SP | N2PK N900BF N721CN |
| 207/34 | 2B | N700PM (N780PM) N111UB VR-CUB VP-CUB N4UB |
| 208 | SP | N808GA N62CB C-FNCG N818DA N247AD N247AB |
| 209 | SP* | N806GA N277T N720DR |
| 210 | SP | HB-IEY G-IIRR (HK-....) 8P-LAD N30FW N826GW |
| 211 | SP | N17581 VR-BGT VP-BGT N7079N XA-FNY |
| 212 | TT | N807GA N551MD N807CC N706TJ |
| 213 | SP | N1707Z N96JA (N96BK) N213X |
| 214 | SP | N17585 G-BSAL A40-HA Oman 601 N11NZ N214NW N914KA N914KB N707KD |
| 215 | SP | N816GA N748MN |
| 216 | TT | HB-IEZ N63SD N200RG HZ-ND1 HZ-HA1 |
| 217 | | N88GA N81728 N880WD N880WE |
| 218 | | TU-VAC N218GA N187PH (N187PA) N188MR ZS-CTL |
| 219/20 | 2B | N84V VR-BJD N307AF N923ML N505RX N575E N74RT |
| 220 | | N805GA N404M N307M N405MM N315TS N117GL |
| 221 | SP | N575SF N575SE N2HF N600CD N827K N949NA |
| 222 | | N817GA N5253A N948NA [to Pima Air & Space Museum, Tucson, AZ, for display Jul07] |
| 223 | SP | N510US N257H N510US [wfu Mojave, CA, 23Jun09] |
| 224 | TT | N17584 N810GA N631SC N90CP N800PM N860PM |
| 225 | SP | N17585 G-BGLT N55922 N289K N225TR N450MH |
| 226 | SP | N1902P N1902L N5DL N448PC |
| 227 | SP | N818GA N1841D N1841L N1BX N18XX N200LS N264CL |
| 228 | SP | N819GA (N700CQ) (N30B) N157LH N189WS |
| 229 | | N821GA N702H N117FJ |
| 230 | | N17586 7T-VHB [w/o 03May82 over NW Iranian border] |
| 231 | | N808GA N1102 VR-CAG VR-BHD N18RN N205K N47EC N416KD |
| 232 | | N806GA C-GDPB N71WS N508T N10RQ |
| 233 | TT | N807GA N320TR N233RS N720LH |
| 234 | TT | N808GA N910S N910R N480GA N222PV (N220GA) N500JW (N956MJ) |
| 235 | TT | N17581 G-HADI N5519C N16FG N256M N430RG N840RG |
| 236 | TT | N812GA N2998 N630PM N50PM N54BM N211DH N311DH N311BD |

## GULFSTREAM II

| C/n | Series | Identities | | | | | | | | |
|---|---|---|---|---|---|---|---|---|---|---|
| 237/43 | 2B | N816GA | N25BH | XA-MIX | XA-BAL | XA-SDM | EC-363 | EC-FRV | N237RF | N302DP |
| 238 | TT | N831GA | N335H | N72BP | | | | | | |
| 239 | TT | N17582 | HZ-AFK | (N239WJ) | | | | | | |
| 240 | | 5A-DDR | TT-AAI | (N240EA) | | | | | | |
| 241 | SP | N830GA | (N60TA) | (N801GA) | N90MD | N902MP | (N902MK) | N909MK | N909FK | N380AC |
| 242 | | 5A-DDS | | | | | | | | |
| 243 | | N119R | N119RC | N46TE | [w/o 19Jan90 Little Rock, AR] | | | | | |
| 244 | SP | N17584 | 9K-AEB | N500T | N509T | N509TT | N811DF | N811DE | | |
| 245/30 | 2B | N829GA | N141GS | N871D | N99WJ | N222NB | N222NP | YV.... | | |
| 246 | TT | N17587 | HB-IEZ | N14LT | N81RR | | | | | |
| 247 | SP* | N828GA | N888MC | C-GTEP | N73MG | N75MG | N530GA | | | |
| 248 | SP | N17589 | 9K-AEC | N501T | N510T | N510TL | N248TH | N7WG | (N70WG) | N71WJ |
| 249 | | [Gulfstream 3 airframe] | | | | | | | | |
| 250 | TT | N821GA | N309EL | (N94SF) | N985BB | | | | | |
| 251 | | N944H | N9PG | N9PY | N567A | N36GS | N251JS | N933RD | | |
| 252 | | [Gulfstream 3 airframe] | | | | | | | | |
| 253 | SP | N15TG | N154C | N915C | XB-LHW | XA-GEG | | | | |
| 254/41 | 2B | N254AR | N706TS | N868SM | | | | | | |
| 255/18 | 2B | N442A | N4NR | | | | | | | |
| 256 | | N17581 | HZ-MSD | (N135WJ) | N61TJ | [parted out Nov04 by Dodson Av'n, Rantoul, KS] | | | | |
| 257/17 | 2B | N822GA | N872E | N411WW | N911WW | N56D | N1CC | | | |
| 258 | SP | N823GA | N301EC | N929GV | N437H | N87GS | N689JE | | | |
| 775 | | see c/n 87 | | | | | | | | |

## GULFSTREAM G1159B CONVERSION PROGRAMME

| No | C/n | Completion date | No | C/n | Completion date |
|---|---|---|---|---|---|
| 1 | 70 | 17Sep81 | 19 | 199 | 04Jan84 |
| 2 | 32 | 02Apr82 | 20 | 219 | 17Feb84 |
| 3 | 36 | 13Aug82 | 21 | 88 | 18Feb84 |
| 4 | 30 | 06Aug82 | 22 | 119 | 27Mar84 |
| 5 | 148 | 18Aug82 | 23 | 131 | 25Apr84 |
| 6 | 775 | 19Sep82 | 24 | 151 | 04Jun84 |
| 7 | 75 | 16Nov82 | 25 | 123 | 11Jun84 |
| 8 | 4 | 29Nov82 | 26 | 125 | 11Jly84 |
| 9 | 73 | 15Dec82 | 27 | 64 | 28Sep84 |
| 10 | 104 | 09Feb83 | 28 | 154 | 15Oct84 |
| 11 | 139 | 15Mar83 | 29 | 48 | 02Nov84 |
| 12 | 42 | 05May83 | 30 | 245 | 10Jan85 |
| 13 | 16 | 09May83 | 31 | 156 | 19Feb85 |
| 14 | 155 | 22Jun83 | 32 | 102 | 07Mar85 |
| 15 | 166 | 14Jly83 | 33 | 9 | 30Apr85 |
| 16 | 86 | 09Aug83 | 34 | 207 | 02May85 |
| 17 | 257 | 17Oct83 | 35 | 198 | 07May85 |
| 18 | 255 | 09Nov83 | 36 | 54 | 05Jly85 |

PLUS

| No | C/n | Completion date | |
|---|---|---|---|
| 37 | 165 | Dec85 | |
| 38 | 98 | Jan86 | |
| 39 | 95 | Mar86 | |
| 40 | 140 | Jun86 | |
| 41 | 254 | Sep86 | (rolled out as G1159B 06Oct86) |
| 42 | 189 | Jly87 | |
| 43 | 237 | Oct87 | |

The following aircraft were built as Gulfstream 2TT aircraft. Those marked * have since been converted to 2SP standards:
46, 127, 133, 173, 182, 183*, 201, 202, 203, 212, 216, 228*, 234, 235, 236, 238, 239, 246, 250

# G1159A GULFSTREAM III

* alongside the c/n indicates fitted with engine hush kits

| C/n | Identities |
|---|---|
| 249 | N300GA [ff 02Dec79] N901GA Denmark F-249 N163PA |
| 252 | (N777SL) N17582 (N301GA) XA-MEY N247RG N516TR |
| 300* | N300GA N700VA N71TJ N918BG |
| 301 | N100P N21NY (N100P) N110BR N444GA N973MW |
| 302 | N302GA N62GG N2610 N56L N56LA (XA-TOT) (N561ST) VP-BCT N49US N109ST N302ST |
| 303 | N300GA N303GA TU-VAF [rebuilt with wings from G2B c/n 104/10] N1761W N303GA [w/o 29Mar01 Aspen, CO] |
| 304 | N17583 HZ-NR2 N600YY N768J N763J (N18SL) VR-BSL N304TS |
| 305* | N305GA N235U N305MD N682FM PK-OCN N552JT N553JT N106KM |
| 306 | N306GA N777SW N72RK N72PK N862CE N863CE (N868CE) N104BK N360MB |
| 307 | N17584 C-GSBR C-GGPM N111FA |
| 308 | N717A N606PT VR-BNO N308GA N308HG |
| 309 | N18LB N1NA N2NA N803NA N992NA* |
| 310 | N719A C-FYAG N6513X (N373LP) (N173LP) N982RK |
| 311 | N17585 HZ-AFL N311GA N721RB N711SW (N311BK) N127BK N127GK |
| 312* | N304GA N100GN N200GN N200JJ N800JH N312NW XA-RCM N116AR ZS-JGC |
| 313 | Denmark F-313 N173PA |
| 314 | N1040 N1540 N1640 N93CX N99PD (N99YD) |
| 315 | N315GA N2600 N2600Z N315GS N710EC N718EC N21PJ (N901JF) N90ML |
| 316 | N316GA N2601 N26018 PK-CAP PK-BND N316FA N691AC (N69EH) N300UJ |
| 317* | C-GKRL N344GA A6-CKZ N83D HZ-DG2 N90EP N186PA |
| 318 | N308GA N300L (N300LF) (XA-...) N70050 N150GX N150QX N150RK N500WW N17NC N184PA |
| 319 | N319Z N200SK |
| 320* | N873E N69FF VR-BNX N320WE N624BP N624PP N410UJ |
| 321 | N30RP N94GC N321GA N100GX N100QX N313RG N310RG N9KL (N91KL) N830SU |
| 322 | N130A N110LE (N110EE) N322GA N555NT N600ES N606ES N706JA |
| 323 | XA-MIC N323G XA-ERH |
| 324 | N17587 HZ-AFM N44200 N67JR N96MR N450CB |
| 325 | N890A N89QA N393U N155MM |
| 326 | N17582 TR-KHC N333GA (N326DD) N420JC |
| 327 | N70PS (N72PS) N57BJ N777RY N711LT N829MG N259SK |
| 328 | N309GA N75RP N78RP N98RP N97AG N36WL ZS-LAH |
| 329 | N301GA N862G N1JN (N329N) N327JJ N1LW A6-ZAB N15ZA |
| 330 | Denmark F-330 [w/o 03Aug96 nr Vagar, Faroe Islands] |
| 331 | N307GA N17LB HZ-RC3 (N231WJ) |
| 332 | N310GA N77TG N300BE N65BE N121JM (N121JN) N921AS N909RR |
| 333 | N600PM N50PM N901FH N901EH |
| 334 | N1PG (N1PU) N41PG N700SB N3DP |
| 335 | HB-IMX N117MS N717MS N456BE |
| 336 | N3PG N3PY (N523TX) (N523PT) (N102PT) N147X N378MB |
| 337 | N456SW N330WR |
| 338 | N862GA N372CM N372GM N87HP (N338RJ) N750SW |
| 339 | N302GA N522SB N339A N684AT N774AK |
| 340 | F-WDHK F-GDHK N99WJ N90WJ N340GA N4PC N2LY N57NP N557JK |
| 341 | N263C N1PR |
| 342 | N441A N91LJ N82A N82AE N1AQ N1JK N818SS N555XS |
| 343 | N305GA N664P N664S N400AL N221CM |
| 344 | N306GA N7000C 5N-IMR N344DD N344GW |
| 345 | N17585 G-BSAN VR-CCN G-GIII 5X-UOI N76TJ N454JB N550PP |
| 346* | N17581 HZ-RH2 HZ-HR2 (N126AH) VP-BHR |
| 347 | N17583 VR-BJE N545JT N888LV |
| 348 | N756S N357PR |
| 349* | N89AE N89AB N1KE N6453 N6458 N711EG |
| 350 | N317GA N1454H N1454 |
| 351 | N888MC N308AF N836MF N18TM N623MS |
| 352 | N17586 HB-ITM Mexico TP-06/XC-UJN |
| 353 | N26619 HZ-BSA HZ-108 N212BA |
| 354* | 3D-AAC 3D-AAI N16NK N420RC N429DD N913PD |
| 355 | N318GA N676RW (N103HS) N876RW 8P-GAC (N105HS) N355TS ZS-TEX |
| 356* | N17608 A6-HEH N356TJ N356BR |
| 357 | N303GA N340 N802GA N891MG N723MM N623NP |
| 358* | N1761B HZ-DA1 N9711N N200DE (N1149E) N475DJ (N475CY) N358CY |
| 359 | N800J N305TC N25MT N50BH |
| 360 | N341GA N90LC (N405LM) N705JA N425SV |
| 361 | (N875E) N874RA (N361RA) (N863A) (N874RR) |
| 362 | N408M N800AR |
| 363 | N83AL N77FK N77EK N855SA |
| 364 | N1761D HZ-AFN |
| 365* | N1761J HZ-AFO CN-ANU |
| 366 | N2SP N90SF N222KC N333KC (N333KD) N555KC N333LX N366JA |

## GULFSTREAM III

| C/n | Identities |
|---|---|
| 367 | (N910A) N17588 HB-ITN (N6164Z) N367GA N700FS N300FS N933PA |
| 368 | N17589 7T-VRB N368GA (N368TJ) C-GBBB (N112GS) |
| 369* | N910A N740SS N17ND N15HE 4X-CMM* |
| 370 | N319GA N100A N200A N400K N697BJ N463LM N105VS |
| 371 | HZ-NR3 N680FM N8220F N681FM N353VA |
| 372 | N320GA N200A N500E N500EX N724DB N724DD N523AM |
| 373 | N340GA N232HC VR-BAB VP-BAB N162JC N373GS N373RR N550RM |
| 374 | N339GA N122DJ VR-CMF N24GA N270MC |
| 375 | N955CP VR-BOB N375GA N375NM N375NW (N75GJ) N375LT |
| 376 | N17582 A6-HHS N70AG (N5HG) N60AG N376EJ N376PJ |
| 377* | N342GA N40CH N707RX N760AC N377RX |
| 378 | N343GA N955H N378HC N803CC N960DC N141MH N444KM N378SE |
| 379 | N17586 HZ-MAL N379RH N282Q N28QQ N900LA N96757 |
| 380 | N345GA N159B N30WR |
| 381 | N304GA N277NS (N46ES) N747G N1871R N621S N221WR |
| 382 | N305GA 83-0500 US Navy 830500 [C20A] |
| 383 | N308GA 83-0501 [C20A] N65CE N30501 |
| 384 | N1982C N399WW N399BH N369CS N112GS N818TJ |
| 385 | N1761K HZ-MS3 |
| 386 | N316GA N902K N902KB Mexico TP-07/XC-UJO |
| 387 | N26L N621JH N621JA N620JH N620JA N485GM |
| 388 | N309GA N902C N1C N748T N561ST N8JL N797BD |
| 389 | N310GA 83-0502 [C20A - transferred to NASA] |
| 390* | N200SF VR-BKS VR-BLO VR-BOK VP-BOK N67TJ N1M N102AK N102AQ N124DT |
| 391 | N349GA N29S N1S N194 (N222AP) N94BN N14SY N288KA |
| 392 | N30AH N6BX N6BZ N60GN N1GN N9WN N800WC N805WC N801WC N391SH N734TJ |
| 393 | N17587 A9C-BB HZ-MWD N33GZ XA-ABD N33GZ N519AF N200EL |
| 394 | N1761P N311GA N379XX N99WJ |
| 395 | N1761Q PK-PJA N5NW N395EJ N422TK |
| 396 | N1761S 7T-VRC N437GA N800MK N175BG |
| 397 | N351GA N59HA N978FL N692TV N767CB N888WZ* |
| 398 | N315GA N88AE N827GA N827G N777RZ N610AB |
| 399* | N17581 7T-VRD N188TJ N528AP N399AP |
| 400 | N17585 Venezuela 0005 N990ML N500EF |
| 401 | N352GA N717 N400LH (N80AG) Denmark F-400 N97AG N370JL |
| 402 | N301GA N303HB N3338 VR-BLN VP-BLN [w/o 06Feb98 Lac du Bourget, Chambery, France] |
| 403 | N347GA N39NA N39N XA-TCO (N333KC) N403NW XB-HIZ N403WJ N555GL |
| 404 | N355GA N404M N404MM N403LM (N402LM) N8115N (N24TJ) N560SH |
| 405 | N348GA N40NB N40N N91CH N91CR N990WC N991WC (N9718P) N789TP N789TR N456AL |
| 406 | N356GA N80L N406FA XA-STT |
| 407 | N17603 G-XMAF N407GA N913MK N813MK |
| 408 | N17608 9K-AEG YI-AKI [w/o 1991 Baghdad Airport, Iraq during Operation Desert Storm] |
| 409 | (N353GA) N300BK N320GA N1526M N1526R N457ST N457SF N828MG N555RE |
| 410 | N350GA HZ-AFR |
| 411 | N314GA N966H N461GT |
| 412 | N354GA N20XY N50XY N610CC N105Y N527CC N450BD |
| 413 | N357GA N77SW N778W N1 N8226M Ireland 249 N166WC N766WC N59AJ N762GS |
| 414 | N358GA N165ST N165G |
| 415 | N17582 (HZ-SOG) HZ-HR4 HZ-NR2 N21NR N109DD |
| 416 | N312GA N500AL N883A N4500X (N500XB) N19H |
| 417 | N317GA N111AC N1119C N300M N431JT |
| 418* | N17583 JY-ABL JY-AMN N717TR PT-ALK N103CD |
| 419 | 9K-AEH YI-AKJ [w/o 1991 Baghdad Airport, Iraq during Operation Desert Storm] |
| 420 | N333GA "40420" N47449 India K-2960/VT-ENR [but marks K-2960 not actually worn] |
| 421 | N318GA N99GA N421GM N721FF N921FF N711UF |
| 422 | N319GA N750AC (N128AG) N407CA N903G (N903GL) N820BA N171TV |
| 423* | N1761D HZ-MIC (VR-CMC) N7134E N225SF N399RV N712AS |
| 424 | N320GA N60AC N228G N94FL |
| 425 | N344GA N425SP N492A |
| 426 | N321GA N151MZ N751MZ VR-CNJ VP-CNJ N703JA XA-ABA |
| 427* | N327GA N44MD N42MD N87AC N300WY |
| 428 | N322GA N760A N760G N702DM |
| 429 | N323GA N429SA N423SA N100HG N100HZ N77BT |
| 430 | N324GA N760C N23A N600BG N608BG |
| 431* | N25SB (N259B) PK-CTP N99WJ P4-AEA N17LK |
| 432 | N333GA N713KM N995BC N997CM (N997HM) N704JA N469BT |
| 433 | N325GA N399CB N579TG N45KR |
| 434 | N326GA N811JK N311JK N226G N226GC XA-SNG XB-FXD N23ET (N23SK) (N73ET) N323JH N18ZL |
| 435 | N17581 HB-ITS N435U N888PM N32KA N357KM |
| 436 | N346GA V8-HB3 V8-A11 V8-007 V8-009 N436GA N10EH |
| 437* | N380TT N100AK N171AM |
| 438 | N302GA N1841D N911KT N473KT N30LX [modified as Airborne Multi-INT Laboratory] |

# GULFSTREAM III

| C/n | Identities | | | | | | | | | |
|---|---|---|---|---|---|---|---|---|---|---|
| 439 | N17586 | SU-BGU | | | | | | | | |
| 440* | N304GA | N5103 | (N3PY) | N222BW | N265A | N71RP | N458BE | N124EP | | |
| 441 | N306GA | N80J | N214WY | | | | | | | |
| 442 | N17587 | SU-BGV | | | | | | | | |
| 443 | N315GA | N5104 | N21AM | N813LS | | | | | | |
| 444 | N328GA | N110MT | N555HD | N554HD | ZS-VIP | | | | | |
| 445* | N316GA | (N5103) | N5105 | N599DA | N590DA | N606DH | N850PG | | | |
| 446 | N309GA | N446U | N58AJ | | | | | | | |
| 447 | N186DS | N186DC | N144PK | N707JA | N776MA | | | | | |
| 448 | N339GA | N117JJ | N255SB | I-MADU | N123AP | N178HH | N710CF | | | |
| 449 | N310GA | XA-FOU | N7C | N85V | N85VT | [w/o 22Nov04 Houston-Hobby Airport, TX] | | | | |
| 450 | N329GA | HZ-AFS | N329GA | PT-AAC | VR-CTG | N888VS | N801MJ | N36DA | | |
| 451 | (N370GA) | N330GA | Italy MM62022 | | N351FJ | N500RH | N5159Y | N600RH | N693PB | N951XF |
| 452 | N331GA | N27R | N633P | VR-BNZ | VP-BNZ | N123TL | N800TD | | | |
| 453 | N332GA | HZ-109 | Saudi Arabia 103 | | HZ-103 | N213BA | | | | |
| 454 | N334GA | N60CT | N1GT | N273G | N111G | N111GX | N903TC | N740VC | | |
| 455 | N335GA | N1SF | (N103GA) | N103GC | N123CC | N123MR | N147MR | N28YC | N818DD | |
| 456 | N336GA | US Army 85-0049 | | [C20C] | | | | | | |
| 457 | N337GA | N457H | N972G | N457JC | | | | | | |
| 458 | N338GA | US Army 85-0050 | | [C20C] | | | | | | |
| 459 | N321GA | N600B | N586C | N566C | N54HF | N555DW | | | | |
| 460* | N322GA | N500LS | N500VS | N500MM | N500MN | I-FCHI | N2TQ | N2TF | N317ML | N460PG |
| | N32MJ | | | | | | | | | |
| 461 | N323GA | N104AR | N108AR | | | | | | | |
| 462 | N324GA | N303GA | TU-VAF | | | | | | | |
| 463 | N327GA | N80AT | N808T | VR-BMY | VP-BMY | N463GE | N886DT | N196CC | | |
| 464 | N340GA | N535CS | N83AG | N83PP | | | | | | |
| 465* | N17586 | 86-0200 | [C20B] | N465GA | Chile 911 | N35GZ | (N33GZ) | N33NT | N35GZ | |
| 466* | N17583 | N325GA | N37HE | N102AK | N817MF | | | | | |
| 467 | N341GA | JY-HAH | N551AC | N400WY | | | | | | |
| 468 | N342GA | 86-0202 | [C20B] | | | | | | | |
| 469 | N343GA | JY-HZH | N1956M | N469TB | N598GS* | | | | | |
| 470 | N344GA | 86-0201 | [C20B] | N770GA | | | | | | |
| 471 | N347GA | N888WL | N583D | N57TT | N975RG | | | | | |
| 472 | N348GA | N800CC | N806CC | N800CC | N806CC | N357H | N780RH | N780RA | (N454BE) | N353MA |
| 473 | N326GA | US Army 86-0403 | | [C20C] | | | | | | |
| 474 | N311GA | D2-ECB | | | | | | | | |
| 475 | N312GA | 86-0203 | [C20B] | | | | | | | |
| 476 | N314GA | 86-0204 | [C20B] | | | | | | | |
| 477 | N317GA | 86-0205 | US Coast Guard 01 | | [VC20B] | N477SJ | N477WG | | | |
| 478 | N318GA | 86-0206 | [C20B] | | | | | | | |
| 479 | N319GA | Italy MM62025 | | N50RL | N556AF | | | | | |
| 480 | N302GA | USN 163691 [C20D] | | | | | | | | |
| 481 | N304GA | USN 163692 [C20D] | | | | | | | | |
| 482 | N306GA | N333HK | N600BL | N164RJ | N268RJ | N111HC | | | | |
| 483* | N309GA | N66DD | N766DD | N19H | (N483H) | N343DF | N343DP | N794ME | | |
| 484 | N310GA | N4UP | N856W | N506T | VP-BOR | N62MW | | | | |
| 485 | N315GA | N721CW | N777MW | | | | | | | |
| 486 | N316GA | TJ-AAW | | | | | | | | |
| 487* | N324GA | (TJ-...) | TC-GAP | N377GA | N90005 | N488SB | N618KM | N416WM | | |
| 488 | N325GA | N700CN | (N100BG) | N800BG | N446GA | N401RJ | N401PJ | N399SC | (N45PG) | N500GF |
| 489* | N328GA | N272JS | N888CW | N388CW | XA-LCA | | | | | |
| 490 | N332GA | N28R | N388MM | | | | | | | |
| 491 | N337GA | N73RP | N998JB | N531JF | (N531JC) | N101PT | N51MF | N51FF | A6-INF | HZ-HHT |
| 492 | N339GA | N212AT | N212AD | PT-WRC | N492DD | N188TC | N848RJ | N939KM | | |
| 493 | N322GA | N400J | N40QJ | Ghana G540 | N7513H | | | | | |
| 494 | N370GA | India K-2961 | | | | | | | | |
| 495 | N371GA | India K-2962 | | | | | | | | |
| 496 | N372GA | N310SL | N21NY | N89AE | N89AB | N99SC | (N99SU) | N843HS | VP-CNP | N384BB |
| 497 | N373GA | US Army 87-0139 | | N7096G | US Army 87-0139 | | [C20E] | | | |
| 498 | N374GA | US Army 87-0140 | | N7096E | US Army 87-0140 | | [C20E] | | | |
| 875 | N333GA | N333GU | N210GK | N290GA | N728CP | N845FW | N298TB | N416NP | N300JZ | |

Production complete

# GULFSTREAM IV/GULFSTREAM 300/350/400/450

We have been advised by Gulfstream Aerospace that the Gulfstream IV does not have the model number G1159C as has been quoted elsewhere.

| C/n | Series | Identities | | | | | | | | |
|---|---|---|---|---|---|---|---|---|---|---|
| 1000 | | N404GA | [ff 19Sep85] | | N234DB | N404DB | N971EC | N552WF | | |
| 1001 | | N17581 | N441GA | N400GA | VR-BSS | VP-BSS | N31001 | N981SW | N181CW | N181CR |
| 1002 | | N440GA | N168WC | N168WM | | | | | | |
| 1003 | | N403GA | N986AH | N685TA | N885TA | N864YC | N250RG | | | |
| 1004 | | N424GA | N184CW | (N199LX) | N124TF | | | | | |
| 1005 | | N17582 | VR-BJZ | N823GA | | | | | | |
| 1006 | | N99GM | N3338 | N614RD | | | | | | |
| 1007 | | N420GA | N100GN | N100GJ | N59JR | N575E | N710WJ | | | |
| 1008 | | N26LB | N10LQ | N10LB | VR-BLH | N412GA | N119R | N85WD | | |
| 1009 | | N423GA | N500LS | N500VS | N700LS | N780LS | VR-BOY | Netherlands V-11 | | |
| 1010 | | N426GA | N444TJ | N824CA | N950DM | XA-AVZ | | | | |
| 1011 | | N17581 | A6-HHH | | | | | | | |
| 1012 | | N445GA | N636MF | N838MF | N713VT | (N713VL) | N636GD | N836MF | | |
| 1013 | | N446GA | N130B | N321PT | N321RT | N1625 | (N16251) | N97FT | N64AL | XA-BVG |
| 1014 | | N447GA | N777SW | N779SW | Sweden 102001 [code 021] | | | | | |
| 1015 | | N17583 | VR-BRF | VP-BRF | N450BF | | | | | |
| 1016 | | N427GA | N95AE | N29GY | N880GC | | | | | |
| 1017 | | N405GA | N678RW | (C-FNCG) | VR-BHG | VP-BHG | N402KC | N818BA | | |
| 1018 | | N407GA | N300L | N43KS | N418QA | N113AR | | | | |
| 1019 | | N17584 | TU-VAD | | | | | | | |
| 1020 | | N408GA | N600CS | N9300 | N93AT | | | | | |
| 1021 | | N412GA | N3M | N3NU | EC-HGH | N310EL | | | | |
| 1022 | | "N63M" [painted on a/c but not officially reg'd] | | | | | N23M | N23MU | N663PD | |
| 1023 | | N415GA | N77SW | N778W | N85M | N85MG | N830EF | N300JA | | |
| 1024 | | (N130B) | N412GA | N96AE | "N16JM" | N116HM | N820HB | | | |
| 1025 | | N419GA | N5BK | N420SZ | N420SL | N421SZ | N928SZ | N928ST | N900GB | N595E |
| 1026 | | N17584 | N151A | N277RP | (N277AG) | N100HG | | | | |
| 1027 | | N416GA | TC-GAP | Turkey 001 [wears dual marks TC-GAP/001] | | | | | | |
| 1028 | | N428GA | N712CW | N712CC | | | | | | |
| 1029 | | N429GA | VR-BKI | VP-BKI | VP-BKH | N44ZF | | | | |
| 1030 | | N430GA | N811JK | N1WP | | | | | | |
| 1031 | | N434GA | HZ-AFU | | | | | | | |
| 1032 | | N17585 | C-FSBR | N315MA | N315MC | N888UE | N432QS | N254GA | | |
| 1033 | | (HB-IMY) | N69GP | N173LP | N1KE | N6453 | N6458 | N711SW | N711FW | N76EJ |
| 1034 | | N413GA | N800BG | N800BQ | N841PA | N388CA | | | | |
| 1035 | | N435GA | HZ-AFV | | | | | | | |
| 1036 | | N152A | N45AC | | | | | | | |
| 1037 | | N17588 | VR-BKE | HZ-ADC | HZ-103 | | | | | |
| 1038 | | N17603 | N438GA | HZ-AFW | | | | | | |
| 1039 | | (N431GA) | N1901M | N726RW | | | | | | |
| 1040 | | N432GA | N74RP | N620DS | N908DH | | | | | |
| 1041 | | N433GA | N366F | N888FR | | | | | | |
| 1042 | | N17608 | N400GA | N22 | N220GA | N71TJ | N68SL | N217RR | N889TC | |
| 1043 | | N1761B | TC-ANA | TC-ATA | | | | | | |
| 1044 | | N423GA | N1040 | N1540 | N154G | | | | | |
| 1045 | | N420GA | N227G | N227GH | N247EM | | | | | |
| 1046 | | N1761D | (HB-ITT) | VR-BKU | (HB-ITE) | VR-BKU | HB-ITP | N119K | N400CC | 3B-PGF |
| 1047 | | N1761J | N461GA | N23AC | [w/o 30Oct96 Palwaukee, IL; cx Apr97] | | | | | |
| 1048 | | N1761K | N448GA | (VR-BKL) | SU-BGM | | | | | |
| 1049 | | N402GA | N372CM | N372GM | N113CS | | | | | |
| 1050 | | N153RA | N195WS | | | | | | | |
| 1051 | | N403GA | N399CC | N919CT | (N903JF) | (N903KP) | N515UJ* | | | |
| 1052 | | N419GA | N800CC | N940DC | N152TS | N722MM | N48GL | | | |
| 1053 | | N47SL | N26SL | N91AE | N165ST | N17ND | N168PK | | | |
| 1054 | | N426GA | N400UP | N480UP | N745UP | N745UR | N789DK | (N1DC) | N860JB | N220LH |
| 1055 | | N1761P | VR-BKV | XB-EXJ | XB-OEM | N255GA | | | | |
| 1056 | | N436GA | N33M | N33MX | N770SC | N685SF* | | | | |
| 1057 | | N437GA | N43M | N43MU | N222AD | N226AL | N842PA | | | |
| 1058 | | N458GA | N70PS | VP-BSF | VP-BME | G-GMAC | [w/o 01Dec04 Teterboro, NJ; cx 17Aug05] | | | |
| 1059 | | N17581 | V8-RB1 | V8-ALI | V8-SR1 | V8-007 | N415GA | N701QS | N799WW | N199WW |
| | | N612AC | N271PS | | | | | | | |
| 1060 | | N427GA | N1SF | VT-AMA | | | | | | |
| 1061 | | N17582 | N457GA | F-GPAK | N161AK | N429AL | HB-IWZ | N999GP | | |
| 1062 | | N17583 | N462GA | N688H | VR-CMF | VP-CMF | N104JG | N619KK | | |
| 1063 | | N17584 | N54SB | N333AX | N720LH | N745RS | | | | |
| 1064 | | N439GA | HB-ITT | N7RP | N797CM | XA-AEX | | | | |
| 1065 | | N442GA | N584D | N511C | N599CN | C-FCNR | | | | |
| 1066 | | N443GA | N118R | N466TS | N773JC | | | | | |
| 1067 | | N446GA | N145ST | N200LC | | | | | | |
| 1068 | | N17585 | N95AE | N90AE | N82A | N189J | | | | |
| 1069 | | N459GA | N765A | N450AR | N1AR | | | | | |
| 1070 | | N407GA | N107A | N40KJ | | | | | | |
| 1071 | | N410GA | N1 | | | | | | | |

## GULFSTREAM IV

| C/n | Series | Identities | | | | | | | | |
|---|---|---|---|---|---|---|---|---|---|---|
| 1072 | | N17586 | N100A | N500E | N260CH | N472MM | | | | |
| 1073 | | N75RP | N75PP | N177BB | | | | | | |
| 1074 | | N17587 | (HB-I..) | VR-BKT | VP-BKT | N740JA | N995GG | | | |
| 1075 | | N412GA | N901K | N121JJ | N121JV | N61WH | | | | |
| 1076 | | N17586 | HZ-MNC | N338MM | | | | | | |
| 1077 | | N445GA | N119R | N119RC | PK-NSP | N477TS | N457DS | | | |
| 1078 | | N17589 | (G-BPJM) | G-DNVT | N211DK | | | | | |
| 1079 | | N17603 | XA-PUV | (N100WJ) | (N15WJ) | N479TS | N691RC | N794MH | | |
| 1080 | | N447GA | N20XY | N205X | M-YGIV | | | | | |
| 1081 | | N955H | (N955HC) | N777SA | N797SA | XA-RCM | | | | |
| 1082 | | N1082A | (N82BR) | M-GULF | | | | | | |
| 1083 | | N1761Q | HB-ITZ | VH-CCC | VH-CGF | | | | | |
| 1084 | | (N448GA) | N1761S | HB-IMY | | | | | | |
| 1085 | | N449GA | N88GA | N864CE | N677RP | N423TT | | | | |
| 1086 | | N460GA | N888MC | N23SY | N1086 | | | | | |
| 1087 | | N463GA | (N94SL) | N310SL | N1TM | N110TM | N368AG | | | |
| 1088 | | N464GA | N4UP | N2600 | N2600J | N1JN | N71JN | N93MK | N385PD | |
| 1089 | | N465GA | N53M | N53MU | Chile 911 | | | | | |
| 1090 | | N466GA | VR-CYM | VP-CYM | N9999M | VP-CYM | N9999M | N8989N* | | |
| 1091 | | N467GA | N364G | N984JW | | | | | | |
| 1092 | | N468GA | N937US | N3H | N3HX | N661R | N18RF | N515PL | N515PE | N786JB |
| 1093 | | VR-BLC | HB-ITX | N399PA | N624BP | N100JF | | | | |
| 1094 | | N2610 | N740K | (N628NP) | | | | | | |
| 1095 | | N469GA | N311EL | | | | | | | |
| 1096 | | N17582 | (G-....) | VR-CBW | VP-CBW | N167AA | | | | |
| 1097 | | N402GA | N900AL | N900AP | | | | | | |
| 1098 | | N403GA | N404CC | XA-AIS | N282CD | N7800 | VP-BSF | N198GS | | |
| 1099 | | N489H | N299FB | (N499QS) | N199QS | N999LX | | | | |
| 1100 | | N100AR | N100GX | B-8080 | | | | | | |
| 1101 | | N404GA | N365G | N900EG | | | | | | |
| 1102 | | N405GA | N910B | XA-RBS | | | | | | |
| 1103 | | N433GA | N90005 | N103BC | VP-BIV | N3KN | C-FHPM | | | |
| 1104 | | N600ML | N700GD | N2SA | | | | | | |
| 1105 | | N408GA | N312EL | | | | | | | |
| 1106 | | N17608 | 9M-ISJ | | | | | | | |
| 1107 | | N17581 | (JA8366) | N101MU | N11FX | VH-CCO | N74TJ | N844GS | N844GF | N848GF |
| 1108 | | N17584 | N410GA | N114AN | (N11AN) | N522AC | VH-NCP | N778MT | N463MA | |
| 1109 | | N1761D | V8-ALI | V8-SR1 | V8-007 | N101GA | EC-IKP | G-MATF | | |
| 1110 | | N415GA | N404M | N404MY | N88MX | N526EE | N888MX | N721MC | | |
| 1111 | | N416GA | N111JL | N111ZT | N511PA | | | | | |
| 1112 | | N417GA | N12UT | N12U | N12UM | | | | | |
| 1113 | | N423GA | N902K | N168TR | N169TT | XA-JJS | | | | |
| 1114 | | N428GA | N444LT | N555WL | XA-BAL | XA-TOO | N314GA | N44LX | N763DB | |
| 1115 | | N430GA | N410M | N410MY | N440TC | | | | | |
| 1116 | | N431GA | N971L | N305TC | | | | | | |
| 1117 | | N1761J | G-HARF | N105BH | VP-CMR | | | | | |
| 1118 | | N439GA | N1526M | N2WL | N440CP | N418TT | N720CH | N269HM | | |
| 1119 | | N407GA | N614HF | N768J | N524AN | | | | | |
| 1120 | | N410GA | VR-BOB | N400SA | N70AG | N20H | N888ES | | | |
| 1121 | | N412GA | N7776 | N411WW | N811WW | N214TS | N962SS | N178MH | N962SS | |
| 1122 | | N40N | N226G | N317M | N317MJ | | | | | |
| 1123 | | N457GA | I-LUBI | N529AL | N619A | | | | | |
| 1124 | | N420GA | N1900W | | | | | | | |
| 1125 | | N432GA | N415SH | N700WB | N888LK | N888LG | N56AG | N49PP | N44CE | |
| 1126 | | N426GA | 5N-FGP | | | | | | | |
| 1127 | | N427GA | VR-BLR | VR-BUS | VP-BUS | | | | | |
| 1128 | | N429GA | HZ-MFL | | | | | | | |
| 1129 | | N17585 | EI-CAH | ZS-NMO | N1129X | N8MC | | | | |
| 1130 | | N436GA | N401MM | N404LM | N711GL | | | | | |
| 1131 | | N437GA | N679RW | N55TD | | | | | | |
| 1132 | | N442GA | A6-ALI | N60NY | N604M | N80BR | N4T | N71NR | N7JM | |
| 1133 | | N443GA | N700CN | | | | | | | |
| 1134 | | N445GA | VR-BJD | VP-BJD | N334JC | N8796J | N990PT | (N990PJ) | N990PM | |
| 1135 | | N435GA | N500MM | N100ES | N190ES | N456BE | N85KV | | | |
| 1136 | | N401GA | N27CD | | | | | | | |
| 1137 | | N402GA | N299DB | N21CZ | N7RX | N37RX | N777TC | | | |
| 1138 | | N403GA | N200A | (N501E) | N520E | N520EP | N777SA | | | |
| 1139 | | N404GA | N99WJ | N21KR | N21KP | N325RC | N331P | N134BR | N572EC | |
| 1140 | | N405GA | N811JK | (N827JK) | N827JM | N77WL | | | | |
| 1141 | | N407GA | N767FL | N767EL | N115FL | N729TY | | | | |
| 1142 | | N408GA | I-LADA | N142NW | N222 | N222GY | | | | |
| 1143 | | N410GA | HZ-AFX | | | | | | | |
| 1144 | | N415GA | N100PM | N250J | B-HWA | N114GA | B-3999 | N233GA | B-8091 | |
| 1145 | | N416GA | N102MU | N797CD | N569CW | LV-BYC | | | | |
| 1146 | | N417GA | N77SW | (N778W) | N777UE | N776US | N970SJ | | | |
| 1147 | | N419GA | N200PM | N820MS | | | | | | |

# GULFSTREAM IV/IVSP

| C/n | Series | Identities | | | | | | | | |
|---|---|---|---|---|---|---|---|---|---|---|
| 1148 | | N427GA | (JA8380) | N427GA | HB-IEJ | N306TT | | | | |
| 1149 | | N430GA | N777SW | N149GU | N152KB | N108DB | N108DU | | | |
| 1150 | | N433GA | V8-ALI | V8-009 | V8-SR1 | N151G | VP-BIS | N386AG | N900RL | |
| 1151 | | N375GA | N80AT | N109ST | N151ST | N109ST | | | | |
| 1152 | | N446GA | N63M | N63MU | | | | | | |
| 1153 | | N448GA | N110LE | N589HM | N590HM | N589HM | | | | |
| 1154 | | N1761D | N150PG | N150GX | N151GX | N186DS | | | | |
| 1155 | | N1761B | N910S | N719SA | | | | | | |
| 1156 | | N1761K | N987AC | N987AR | VH-TGG | VH-XGG | N156TS | N5RD | | |
| 1157 | | N17581 | 9K-AJA | N457GA | OE-IJA | N157FQ | B-8082 | | | |
| 1158 | | N17582 | N917W | | | | | | | |
| 1159 | | N17583 | 9K-AJB | N458FA | HB-IKR | D-AAGF* | | | | |
| 1160 | | N17584 | Ireland 251 | | | | | | | |
| 1161 | | N17585 | 9K-AJC | N459FA | N20EG | N461TS | N495RS | | | |
| 1162 | C20F | N457GA | US Army 91-0108 | | N7096B | US Army 91-0108 | | | | |
| 1163 | | N458GA | Turkey 12-003 | | | | | | | |
| 1164 | | N459GA | N300GX | N420CC | | | | | | |
| 1165 | | N460GA | N780E | N780N | | | | | | |
| 1166 | | N461GA | HZ-SAR | HZ-AFY | | | | | | |
| 1167 | | N17586 | N1SL | N49SL | N1SL | | | | | |
| 1168 | | N462GA | A40-AB | | | | | | | |
| 1169 | | N463GA | N500DG | N600DW | N600CK | | | | | |
| 1170 | | N464GA | N711SW | (N811SW) | N997BC | N880WD | | | | |
| 1171 | | N465GA | N72RK | N686CG | N3SA | | | | | |
| 1172 | | N466GA | XA-SEC | N472TS | N85V | N85VM | N227SV | | | |
| 1173 | | N17587 | Botswana OK1 | | Botswana OK2 | | | | | |
| 1174 | | N467GA | N174LM | HB-IEQ | N174SJ | N4PC | N6VB | N41VB | N10ZK | N914EG |
| 1175 | | N17588 | HB-ITJ | (N1175B) | VH-CCA | N18WF | G-EVLN | | | |
| 1176 | | N468GA | V8-008 | N176G | VP-CRY | N9253V | HB-IWY | | | |
| 1177 | | N469GA | N677RW | N236MJ | | | | | | |
| 1178 | | N470GA | N900LS | N909LS | N611JM | | | | | |
| 1179 | | N471GA | N41CP | N41QR | N265ST | N527JC | | | | |
| 1180 | | N472GA | N700LS | N709LS | N827K | XA-ASI | | | | |
| 1181 | C20H | N473GA | USAF 90-0300 | | | | | | | |
| 1182 | | N475GA | N200LS | N202LS | N75CC | | | | | |
| 1183 | SP | N476GA | [ff as Gulfstream IV 23Dec91; cvtd to SP prototype and ff as such 24Jun92] | | | | | | | |
| | | VR-BDC | HB-IBX | N510ST | N510SR | | | | | |
| 1184 | | N477GA | N111NL | (N508JM) | (N805JM) | N583AJ | | | | |
| 1185 | SP | N478GA | N485GA | N635AV | N570DC | | | | | |
| 1186 | | N479GA | 8P-MAK | N345AA | | | | | | |
| 1187 | C20G | N481GA | US Navy 165093 [cargo door] | | | | | | | |
| 1188 | | N482GA | HL7222 | | | | | | | |
| 1189 | C20G | N402GA | US Navy 165094 [code JR] [cargo door] | | | | | | | |
| 1190 | | N403GA | JA001G | | | | | | | |
| 1191 | SP | N404GA | N979RA | N317M | N317MR | N317MB | N403TB | | | |
| 1192 | SP | N407GA | N212K | N180CH | | | | | | |
| 1193 | SP | N412GA | (N980ML) | N163M | N620K | N620KA | N608CL | | | |
| 1194 | SP | N415GA | N77CP | N77QR | N473CW | | | | | |
| 1195 | SP | N419GA | XA-CHR | N47HR | N867CE | N888PM | | | | |
| 1196 | | N420GA | A40-AC | | | | | | | |
| 1197 | | N423GA | N150GX | XA-CAG | N969SG | N4753 | N771AV* | | | |
| 1198 | | N425GA | N99GA | | | | | | | |
| 1199 | C20G | N428GA | US Navy 165151 [code RG] | | | | | | | |
| 1200 | C20G | N430GA | US Marines 165153 | | | | | | | |
| 1201 | C20G | N431GA | US Navy 165152 | | | | | | | |
| 1202 | | N432GA | V8-MSB | V8-009 | JY-RAY | N369XL | HB-ITF | G-CFOH | | |
| 1203 | SP | N434GA | N410WW | N411WW | N412WW | (N199PZ) | | | | |
| 1204 | | N435GA | N212AT | N252CH | | | | | | |
| 1205 | SP | N439GA | VH-ASQ | N8203K | N393BD | N671AF | | | | |
| 1206 | | N437GA | N1040 | N1620 | N162G | N315MK | | | | |
| 1207 | | N441GA | C-FDCS | C-FJES | N77SW | (N77VU) | N344AA | | | |
| 1208 | SP | N443GA | VR-BNY | VP-BNY | N297GB | | | | | |
| 1209 | | N445GA | N157H | N724DB | | | | | | |
| 1210 | | N448GA | (N909SP) | N9PC | N410QS | N144PK | | | | |
| 1211 | | N447GA | N2107Z | | | | | | | |
| 1212 | SP | N413GA | VR-BOT | VP-BOT | N88HP | N884L | (N38NZ) | (N777NZ) | N502JT | |
| 1213 | | N416GA | N56L | | | | | | | |
| 1214 | | N405GA | N414BM | N2615 | N2615B | N477JB | | | | |
| 1215 | SP | N426GA | Sweden 102002 | | | | | | | |
| 1216 | SP | N440GA | Sweden 102003 | | | | | | | |
| 1217 | SP | N417GA | N981HC | N711MC | N711HE | (N711PE) | N979CB | | | |
| 1218 | SP | N418SP | N5MC | | | | | | | |
| 1219 | SP | N446GA | PK-NZK | N50HE | N87HP | N874C | | | | |
| 1220 | SP | N449GA | N79RP | N688TT | | | | | | |
| 1221 | SP | N451GA | | | | | | | | |
| 1222 | SP | N452GA | N71RP | N171JC | | | | | | |

# GULFSTREAM IVSP

| C/n | Series | Identities | | | | | | | | |
|---|---|---|---|---|---|---|---|---|---|---|
| 1223 | SP | N453GA | N935SH | N257H | | | | | | |
| 1224 | SP | N454GA | N18TM | N18TD | N124TS | C-GEIV | | | | |
| 1225 | SP | N459GA | N316GS | N816GS | N773MJ | N773AJ | | | | |
| 1226 | SP | N460GA | N41PR | N41PL | N50MG | N415WW | N96JA | | | |
| 1227 | SP | N463GA | (XA-VAD) | XA-DPS | N626TG | N626TC | N600VC | | | |
| 1228 | SP | N464GA | N18AN | | | | | | | |
| 1229 | SP | N465GA | N830EC | N270SC | | | | | | |
| 1230 | SP | N467GA | 9M-TRI | N101CV | | | | | | |
| 1231 | SP | N470GA | N250VC | N250VZ | N255TS | VT-DLF | VT-ONE | | | |
| 1232 | SP | N471GA | N232K | | | | | | | |
| 1233 | SP | N472GA | N575SF | VP-BFW | A6-OME | N450JE | | | | |
| 1234 | SP | N475GA | N924ML | I-LXGR | VP-BNB | N999NB | | | | |
| 1235 | SP | N477GA | N100A | N500E | N500EP | N17JK | | | | |
| 1236 | SP | N478GA | N100GN | N99SC | | | | | | |
| 1237 | SP | N480GA | N1904W | | | | | | | |
| 1238 | SP | N483GA | N499SC | (N71LA) | N92LA | (N92LU) | N415PG | C-GCPM | | |
| 1239 | SP | N484GA | N1JN | N909RX | (N105TR) | N699HH | | | | |
| 1240 | SP | N486GA | N333PV | N212AW | N705PC | | | | | |
| 1241 | SP | N487GA | N169CA | N343DF | N843DF | N117MS | | | | |
| 1242 | SP | N490GA | N982HC | N407GC | | | | | | |
| 1243 | SP | N491GA | N404SP | VR-CBL | N39WH | N37WH | (N39WH) | | | |
| 1244 | SP | N404GA | JA002G | | | | | | | |
| 1245 | SP | N405GA | N101HC | (N7602) | N7601 | N459BE | N588LS | | | |
| 1246 | SP | N407GA | N49RF | | | | | | | |
| 1247 | SP | N408GA | (N990UH) | N14UH | N477RP | N211MA | | | | |
| 1248 | SP | N422GA | N62MS | N6VN | N244DS | N72RK | N700PP | | | |
| 1249 | SP | N423GA | N63HS | N634S | N151SD | | | | | |
| 1250 | SP | N425GA | VR-CBB | VP-CBB | N47HR | XA-CHR | N169JC | XA-JPS | | |
| 1251 | SP | N429GA | (N321PT) | N60PT | N60PE | N165JF | | | | |
| 1252 | SP | N433GA | N252C | N394TR | | | | | | |
| 1253 | SP | N435GA | N676RW | N225DC | | | | | | |
| 1254 | SP | N436GA | N801CC | N930DC | N920DS | N920TB | VT-PLL | | | |
| 1255 | SP | N437GA | N600PM | VP-BNN | N934DF | VP-BKI | | | | |
| 1256 | C20H | N438GA | USAF 92-0375 | | | | | | | |
| 1257 | SP | N448GA | N4CP | N4QP | (N99PD) | N603CS | | | | |
| 1258 | SP | N416GA | N400UP | N585D | | | | | | |
| 1259 | SP | N495GA | N1PG | N4PG | N4UG | | | | | |
| 1260 | SP | N461GA | N3PG | N810LP | N415P* | | | | | |
| 1261 | SP | N469GA | N399CB | N57HJ | | | | | | |
| 1262 | SP | N496GA | N462QS | N326AZ* | | | | | | |
| 1263 | SP | N497GA | N830CB | N263S | N128TS | | | | | |
| 1264 | SP | N499GA | N464QS | N120JJ | | | | | | |
| 1265 | SP | N465GA | N540W | VP-CFF | N165GD | | | | | |
| 1266 | SP | N412GA | N300K | N61LA | N91LA | (N91LU) | N77DY | N77D | VP-BOL | |
| 1267 | SP | N417GA | N301K | N624GJ | | | | | | |
| 1268 | SP | N427GA | N990WC | N600BG | N888MF | | | | | |
| 1269 | SP | N434GA | N677SW | N677VU | N250LB | N925JS | | | | |
| 1270 | U4 | N442GA | Japan 75-3251 | | | | | | | |
| 1271 | U4 | N452GA | Japan 75-3252 | | | | | | | |
| 1272 | SP | N454GA | N621JH | N621JA | N620JH | | | | | |
| 1273 | SP | N457GA | N372BC | N372BG | N102BG | N102BQ | | | | |
| 1274 | SP | N458GA | "LV-WOW" | [painted in error at completion centre] | | | LV-WOM | Sweden 102004 | | |
| 1275 | SP | N459GA | N475QS | N505GF | | | | | | |
| 1276 | SP | N460GA | N1955M | N1990C | N515XL | N856AF | N557WY | | | |
| 1277 | SP | N462GA | N5GF | | | | | | | |
| 1278 | SP | N464GA | VR-CTA | N98LT | | | | | | |
| 1279 | SP | N466GA | N2002P | (N451C) | N925DC | | | | | |
| 1280 | SP | N468GA | N531MD | N688LS | | | | | | |
| 1281 | SP | N470GA | N481QS | N129NS | | | | | | |
| 1282 | SP | N471GA | (N96FL) | VR-CFL | VP-CFL | N9KN | N1925M | | | |
| 1283 | SP | N472GA | N401JL | N402JP | N898AW | | | | | |
| 1284 | SP | N475GA | N1GN | N21GN | N150CM | (N577SW) | N90AM | N575CT | N707EA | |
| 1285 | SP | N477GA | N874A | N972MS | | | | | | |
| 1286 | SP | N480GA | (N486GA) | N286GA | N464SP | N4SP | N464SP | N880G | N192NC | N192N |
| | | N7LA | | | | | | | | |
| 1287 | SP | N484GA | N487QS | | | | | | | |
| 1288 | SP | N403GA | 7T-VPR | | | | | | | |
| 1289 | SP | N405GA | N844HS | N802WC | N804WC | N800WC | N334MC | N202VZ | N289MU | N677FR* |
| 1290 | SP | N408GA | N6NB | N730BA | N71VR | N988LS | | | | |
| 1291 | SP | N412GA | 7T-VPS | | | | | | | |
| 1292 | SP | N413GA | N1GT | N917VZ | | | | | | |
| 1293 | SP | N415GA | N493QS | N429DD | | | | | | |
| 1294 | SP | N416GA | HZ-MAL | N416GA | HZ-KAA | N718GM | N131SW | | | |
| 1295 | SP | N417GA | N495QS | | | | | | | |
| 1296 | SP | N419GA | N725LB | N728LB | | | | | | |
| 1297 | SP | N420GA | LV-WSS | N728JP | N710LX | | | | | |

# GULFSTREAM IVSP

| C/n | Series | Identities | | | | | |
|---|---|---|---|---|---|---|---|
| 1298 | SP | N422GA | N501PC | N961V | | | |
| 1299 | SP | N423GA | N499QS | | | | |
| 1300 | SP | N432GA | N1BN | N321BN | (N500BL) | N226MP | |
| 1301 | SP | N433GA | N92AE | | | | |
| 1302 | SP | N434GA | (N98AE) | N93AE | N818SS | | |
| 1303 | U4 | N435GA | Japan 85-3253 | | | | |
| 1304 | SP | N436GA | N404QS | | | | |
| 1305 | SP | N439GA | (N913SC) | N888SQ | N305GA | M-FMHG | |
| 1306 | SP | N441GA | N540CH | N811DF | | | |
| 1307 | SP | N443GA | N94AE | N94AN | | | |
| 1308 | SP | N446GA | N408QS | | | | |
| 1309 | SP | N447GA | N309GA | N824CA | N56D | | |
| 1310 | SP | N448GA | (N2425) | N902 | | | |
| 1311 | SP | N449GA | N411QS | | | | |
| 1312 | SP | N453GA | 9M-ABC | | | | |
| 1313 | SP | N455GA | N94LT | N100DF | | | |
| 1314 | SP | N461GA | N429SA | N427SA | | | |
| 1315 | SP | N413GA | N315GA | N950CM | | | |
| 1316 | SP | N427GA | N416QS | | | | |
| 1317 | SP | N417GA | N929WT | N333PY | | | |
| 1318 | SP | N418GA | N1624 | N15Y | | | |
| 1319 | SP | N429GA | N878SM | | | | |
| 1320 | SP | N437GA | N420QS | | | | |
| 1321 | SP | N444GA | (N600CC) | N500CD | N905LP | | |
| 1322 | SP | N445GA | N422QS | | | | |
| 1323 | SP | N454GA | N503PC | N565RV | | | |
| 1324 | SP | N457GA | N424QS | | | | |
| 1325 | SP | N459GA | N102FM | (N24EE) | Pakistan J-755 | | |
| 1326 | U4 | N325GA | Japan 95-3254 | | | | |
| 1327 | SP | N327GA | TR-KHD | TR-KSP | | | |
| 1328 | SP | N328GA | N428QS | | | | |
| 1329 | SP | N329GA | SU-BNC | | | | |
| 1330 | SP | N324GA | N400J | | | | |
| 1331 | SP | N331GA | N878G | EC-KEY | N74GG | | |
| 1332 | SP | N332GA | SU-BND | | | | |
| 1333 | SP | N333GA | N800J | | | | |
| 1334 | SP | N334GA | N434QS | N626JS | N626LJ | | |
| 1335 | SP | N335GA | N720BA | N918CC | | | |
| 1336 | SP | N636GA | N41CP | N235LP | | | |
| 1337 | SP | N637GA | N52MK | | | | |
| 1338 | SP | N638GA | N401WT | N100HF | | | |
| 1339 | SP | N339GA | N327TL | | | | |
| 1340 | SP | N340GA | N1TF | N800AL | N77D | | |
| 1341 | SP | N341GA | N441QS | | | | |
| 1342 | SP | N342GA | N555KC | N808T | | | |
| 1343 | SP | N343GA | N99SC | N2CC | | | |
| 1344 | SP | N344GA | N18AC | N411LL | | | |
| 1345 | SP | N345GA | (JY-ONE) | N457ST | N857ST | (N121PP) | |
| 1346 | SP | N346GA | N104AR | | | | |
| 1347 | SP | N347GA | N988H | N933JJ | N155RJ | | |
| 1348 | SP | N348GA | N80A | | | | |
| 1349 | SP | N349GA | HZ-KS1 | N349GA | N616DC | N616DG | N510MG |
| 1350 | SP | N330GA | N396U | | | | |
| 1351 | SP | N351GA | N451QS | N265SJ | | | |
| 1352 | SP | N352GA | N452QS | | | | |
| 1353 | SP | N353GA | A9C-BAH | | | | |
| 1354 | SP | N354GA | N397J | N397JJ | | | |
| 1355 | SP | N355GA | N66DD | | | | |
| 1356 | SP | N319GA | (JY-TWO) | N600DR | | | |
| 1357 | SP | N357GA | N77FK | | | | |
| 1358 | SP | N358GA | N1625 | | | | |
| 1359 | SP | N359GA | Japan 05-3255 | | | | |
| 1360 | SP | N360GA | N460QS | | | | |
| 1361 | SP | N361GA | N545CS | | | | |
| 1362 | SP | N362GA | N888LK | (N888LF) | ZK-KFB | | |
| 1363 | SP | N363GA | N463QS | N463G | N48CC | VH-DBT | |
| 1364 | SP | N364GA | N143KS | | | | |
| 1365 | SP | N365GA | HZ-MS04 | HZ-MS4 | | | |
| 1366 | SP | N320GA | N404M | N404XT | | | |
| 1367 | SP | N367GA | HZ-KS2 | N367GA | N422ML | N1EB | N618SA N335LL |
| 1368 | SP | N322GA | N1967M | N610MC | N411AL | N125SJ | |
| 1369 | SP | N323GA | N469QS | N469G | N400MP | | |
| 1370 | SP | N370GA | N240CX | | | | |
| 1371 | SP | N371GA | VP-CIP | N371FP | | | |
| 1372 | SP | N372GA | N472QS | | | | |
| 1373 | SP | N373GA | N373KM | N106KA | N595PE | | |

## GULFSTREAM IVSP

| C/n | Series | Identities | | | | | |
|---|---|---|---|---|---|---|---|
| 1374 | SP | N374GA | N7PG | N1PG | | | |
| 1375 | SP | N375GA | N247KB | B-8088 | | | |
| 1376 | SP | N376GA | N12NZ | | | | |
| 1377 | SP | N377GA | N477QS | | | | |
| 1378 | SP | N378GA | N2PG | | | | |
| 1379 | SP | N379GA | N60PT | VT-MST | | | |
| 1380 | SP | N380GA | N480QS | | | | |
| 1381 | SP | N381GA | VP-BZA | VP-BIV | VP-BYS | A6-NMA | |
| 1382 | SP | N382GA | N1TF | (N222MC) | N1GC | N428M | |
| 1383 | SP | N383GA | N955H | N955E | (N507TE) | N707TE | |
| 1384 | SP | N384GA | (HZ-KS3) | N404AC | | | |
| 1385 | SP | N485GA | N577SW | N577VU | N1818C | N4818C | |
| 1386 | SP | N486GA | N486QS | | | | |
| 1387 | SP | N487GA | N254SD | N854SD | N4387 | | |
| 1388 | SP | N477GA | N38BG | N4SP | XA-EYA | | |
| 1389 | SP | N389GA | N489QS | | | | |
| 1390 | SP | N490GA | N1874M | VP-CSF | | | |
| 1391 | SP | N391GA | N827GA | | | | |
| 1392 | SP | N392GA | N492QS | | | | |
| 1393 | SP | N393GA | N297MC | N352BH | | | |
| 1394 | SP | N394GA | N721RL | | | | |
| 1395 | SP | N395GA | N961SV | N396NS | | | |
| 1396 | SP | N396GA | N890A | N664JN | | | |
| 1397 | SP | N397GA | N669BJ | | | | |
| 1398 | SP | N398GA | N498QS | | | | |
| 1399 | SP | N499GA | N121JM | | | | |
| 1400 | SP | N478GA | N215TM | N700FS | | | |
| 1401 | SP | N401GA | N900LS | N300CR | | | |
| 1402 | SP | N479GA | N602PM | (N602AG) | (N602KF) | N602PL | VP-CLA |
| 1403 | SP | N403GA | N403QS | | | | |
| 1404 | SP | N404GA | N404HS | XA-FCP | | | |
| 1405 | SP | N310GA | N45ET | | | | |
| 1406 | SP | N311GA | VP-BNZ | N404GA | N526EE | N104AD | |
| 1407 | SP | N312GA | N407QS | N40HB | N407NS | | |
| 1408 | SP | N316GA | (N448QS) | N401QS | | | |
| 1409 | SP | N317GA | N67TM | | | | |
| 1410 | SP | N318GA | N80AT | | | | |
| 1411 | SP | N411GA | N56MD | N56D | N303TP | | |
| 1412 | SP | N412GA | N700LS | N709LS | A6-DWD | | |
| 1413 | SP | N413GA | 5X-UEF | N92SA | | | |
| 1414 | SP | N323GA | "N819JF" | N5VS | N505VS | N333EC | N787AF* |
| 1415 | SP | N415GA | N71BD | | | | |
| 1416 | SP | N416GA | N900WR | | | | |
| 1417 | SP | N417GA | (N417QS) | N122RS | XA-RYR | | |
| 1418 | SP | N418GA | 7T-VPC | | | | |
| 1419 | SP | N419GA | EI-CVT | VP-BVT | (N419GA) | N600AR | |
| 1420 | SP | N420GA | N72BD | | | | |
| 1421 | SP | N324GA | 7T-VPM | | | | |
| 1422 | SP | N422GA | N999GP | N7UF | | | |
| 1423 | SP | N423GA | N621JH | | | | |
| 1424 | SP | N328GA | SU-BNO | | | | |
| 1425 | SP | N425GA | XA-ABA | P4-TAK | | | |
| 1426 | SP | N426GA | N426QS | | | | |
| 1427 | SP | N427GA | SU-BNP | | | | |
| 1428 | SP | N330GA | N512C | N990NB | | | |
| 1429 | SP | N429GA | N777KK | | | | |
| 1430 | SP | N331GA | N530JD | N14456 | N913SQ | N71TV | |
| 1431 | SP | N334GA | N818ME | | | | |
| 1432 | SP | N335GA | N211DH | | | | |
| 1433 | SP | N433GA | N1SN | | | | |
| 1434 | SP | N434GA | N663P | | | | |
| 1435 | SP | N435GA | N144KK | N435GA | N994GC | N502PC | |
| 1436 | SP | N436GA | N436QS | | | | |
| 1437 | SP | N437GA | | | | | |
| 1438 | SP | N388GA | N228RE | | | | |
| 1439 | SP | N439GA | N586D | | | | |
| 1440 | SP | N391GA | N997AG | N76RP | N84HD | | |
| 1441 | SP | N341GA | N1289M | N123LC | VH-OSW | | |
| 1442 | SP | N442GA | N481FB | N345LC | N718DW | | |
| 1443 | SP | N443GA | N305LM | | | | |
| 1444 | SP | N344GA | (N444GV) | N400HF | N904TC | | |
| 1445 | SP | N445GA | N445QS | N474D | | | |
| 1446 | SP | N446GA | N317M | N317ML | N817ME | | |
| 1447 | SP | N447GA | N667P | N822A | | | |
| 1448 | SP | N448GA | N1LB | N300LB | N808MF | | |
| 1449 | SP | N449GA | N200LS | N209LS | (N4SP) | N309SG | |

# GULFSTREAM IVSP/300/400

| C/n | Series | Identities | | | | |
|---|---|---|---|---|---|---|
| 1450 | SP | N370GA | N809C | N435HC | | |
| 1451 | SP | N351GA | N372CM | N522BP | N522BR | N244J |
| 1452 | SP | N452GA | N603PM | (N603AG) | N603KF | N603KE |
| 1453 | SP | N453GA | N444QG | | | |
| 1454 | SP | N454GA | N454QS | | | |
| 1455 | SP | N455GA | N616CC | | | |
| 1456 | SP | N396GA | N507SA | | | |
| 1457 | SP | N357GA | N234DB | N234DN | N305CF | |
| 1458 | SP | N358GA | N235KK | | | |
| 1459 | SP | N399GA | (D-AJJJ) | D-AJGK | | |
| 1460 | SP | N460GA | (N825LM) | HB-ILV | N331LV | (N326LM) N326JD |
| 1461 | SP | N461GA | N877A | | | |
| 1462 | SP | N462GA | N462CS | N462CK | N457H | |
| 1463 | SP | N463GA | N465QS | | | |
| 1464 | SP | N464GA | N950AV | N950HB | N119FM | |
| 1465 | SP | N465GA | RA-10201 | | | |
| 1466 | SP | N266GA | VP-BSH | N888ZF | | |
| 1467 | SP | N467GA | (N225BK) | N225CX | N226CX | XA- |
| 1468 | SP | N468GA | N700NY | | | |
| 1469 | SP | N269GA | N5956B | | | |
| 1470 | SP | N470GA | N34UH | N394AK | | |
| 1471 | SP | N471GA | N471CR | N923CL | | |
| 1472 | SP | N372GA | N4DA | N475LC | | |
| 1473 | SP | N373GA | XA-EOF | N620M | | |
| 1474 | SP | N374GA | (N948AV) | N248AB | N7799T | |
| 1475 | SP | N475GA | N24TH | N67TH | N324FP | |
| 1476 | SP | N476GA | N59AP | [damaged in hangar collapse at Washington/Dulles 06Feb10, possible w/o] | | |
| 1477 | SP | N477GA | (N949AV) | N244DS | N284DS | N468AB |
| 1478 | SP | N378GA | N478GS | | | |
| 1479 | SP | N479GA | N1479G | N226RS | | |
| 1480 | SP | N480GA | N482QS | CS-DKA | N36MW* | |
| 1481 | SP | N281GA | N621SC | N691SC | 4X-CPX | |
| 1482 | SP | N482GA | N13J | N121JJ | | |
| 1483 | SP | N483GA | N810TM | | | |
| 1484 | SP | N484GA | N721FF | | | |
| 1485 | SP | N485GA | N5NG | | | |
| 1486 | SP | N486GA | N608PM | (N608AG) | (N608KF) | |
| 1487 | SP | N487GA | N428AS | N428AZ | XA-SKY | |
| 1488 | SP | N488GA | N490QS | | | |
| 1489 | SP | N389GA | N142HC | N142HQ | N212WZ | N119AF |
| 1490 | SP | N490GA | (N490QS) | N1TM | | |
| 1491 | SP | N491GA | N491EC | | | |
| 1492 | SP | N392GA | N123MR | N500PC | | |
| 1493 | SP | N493GA | N235DX | N717DX | N104DX | N154C |
| 1494 | SP | N494GA | N400FJ | | | |
| 1495 | SP | N495GA | N250VC | N251MM | | |
| 1496 | SP | N496GA | N308AB | | | |
| 1497 | SP | N397GA | (N497QS) | N702GH | | |
| 1498 | SP | N398GA | N780RH | N757MC | | |
| 1499 | SP | N499GA | N941AM | N918TB | [last a/c to bear the Gulfstream IV name] | |
| 1500 | 400 | N520GA | N400GA | (N55GJ) | N50EE | |
| 1501 | 400 | N401GA | (N402QS) | N128AB | | |
| 1502 | 400 | N202GA | N710EC | | | |
| 1503 | 300 | N403GA | A6-RJA | | | |
| 1504 | 400 | N374GA | (N402QS) | N902L | | |
| 1505 | 300 | N405GA | A6-RJB | | | |
| 1506 | 400 | N306GA | SU-BPE | | | |
| 1507 | 300 | N307GA | N91KL | N826RP | | |
| 1508 | 300 | N508GA | N820TM | | | |
| 1509 | 300 | N509GA | N607PM | N607KF | N789RR | |
| 1510 | 300 | N510GA | N609PM | (N609KF) | (N609RM) | N349K |
| 1511 | 400 | N201GA | N161MM | | | |
| 1512 | 300 | N512GA | N606PM | (N606KF) | | |
| 1513 | 400 | N113GA | N4UC | N928GC | N500RL | |
| 1514 | 400 | N314GA | N1932P | (N1931P) | LV-CAZ | |
| 1515 | 400 | N415GA | N851EL | N342AP | | |
| 1516 | 400 | N516GA | N400GA | N721BS | | |
| 1517 | 300 | N517GA | N129MH | | | |
| 1518 | 400 | N218GA | SU-BPF | | | |
| 1519 | 400 | N519GA | N527JG | | | |
| 1520 | 300 | N520GA | HZ-MF3 | | | |
| 1521 | 400 | N221GA | N413QS | | | |
| 1522 | 400 | N522GA | N251DV | | | |
| 1523 | 400 | N423GA | N401FT | | | |

## GULFSTREAM 300/400/350/450

| C/n | Series | Identities | | | | | | |
|---|---|---|---|---|---|---|---|---|
| 1524 | 400 | N524GA | N522AC | | | | | |
| 1525 | 300 | N425GA | HZ-MF4 | | | | | |
| 1526 | 300 | N526GA | N160TM | | | | | |
| 1527 | 400 | N327GA | N402FT | | | | | |
| 1528 | 400 | N528GA | N523AC | N706VA | | | | |
| 1529 | 400 | N529GA | N477SA | | | | | |
| 1530 | 400 | N330GA | N650PW | | | | | |
| 1531 | 400 | N531GA | N212VZ | | | | | |
| 1532 | 300 | N532GA | HZ-MF5 | | | | | |
| 1533 | 400 | N533GA | N467QS | | | | | |
| 1534 | 400 | N434GA | (N650PW) | (N616KF) | N616KG | | | |
| 1535 | 300 | N435GA | N825T | | | | | |

# GULFSTREAM 350/450

The Gulfstream 450 was originally dubbed the GIV-X and was awarded its FAA Type certificate 13Aug04
The Gulfstream 350 is essentially a shorter-range Gulfstream 450

| | | | | | | | | |
|---|---|---|---|---|---|---|---|---|
| 4001 | 450 | N401SR | | | | | | |
| 4002 | 450 | N442SR | N820AV | | | | | |
| 4003 | 450 | N403SR | N821AV | N704JW | | | | |
| 4004 | 450 | N404SR | N450GA | N428TT | (N8875) | D-ARKK | N156WC | N4500X |
| 4005 | 450 | N165GA | N512JT | | | | | |
| 4006 | 450 | N166GA | N111CQ | | | | | |
| 4007 | 450 | N185GA | N142HC | | | | | |
| 4008 | 450 | N608GA | N97FT | | | | | |
| 4009 | 450 | N909GA | N885AR | N885RR* | | | | |
| 4010 | 450 | N910GA | N425QS | | | | | |
| 4011 | 350 | N121GA | N502GM | | | | | |
| 4012 | 450 | N812GA | N80Q | N80QL | N450Z | | | |
| 4013 | 350 | N913GA | N5113 | | | | | |
| 4014 | 450 | N314GA | N415QS | | | | | |
| 4015 | 350 | N915GA | N117WR | | | | | |
| 4016 | 350 | N816GA | N5114 | | | | | |
| 4017 | 450 | N917GA | N7RX | | | | | |
| 4018 | 450 | N618GA | B-KHK | | | | | |
| 4019 | 350 | N989GA<br>N5115 | "N350GA"+ | [+ fake marks worn in NBAA Static park Nov05 Orlando Executive, FL] | | | | |
| 4020 | 450 | N990GA<br>N588AT | (N450GA)+ | [+ ntu marks worn in NBAA Static park Nov05 Orlando Executive, FL] | | | | |
| 4021 | 450 | N621GA | N430QS | | | | | |
| 4022 | 450 | N622GA | N464ST | | | | | |
| 4023 | 350 | N623GA | N5116 | | | | | |
| 4024 | 450 | N624GA | N451CM | (N927EM) | | | | |
| 4025 | 450 | N998GA | N440QS | | | | | |
| 4026 | 350 | N626GA | N5117 | XA-LAA | | | | |
| 4027 | 450 | N627GA | HB-JEQ | S5-ADC | G-SADC | | | |
| 4028 | 450 | N628GA | N915BD | N881E | | | | |
| 4029 | 450 | N629GA | N888HH | | | | | |
| 4030 | 450 | N630GA | N235CG | N285CG | | | | |
| 4031 | 450 | N631GA | (N450JK) | N1JK | VP-CAE | | | |
| 4032 | 450 | N632GA | N24XC | N82A | | | | |
| 4033 | 450 | N633GA | N989WS | N404PX | | | | |
| 4034 | 450 | N634GA | N122GV | N442HM | | | | |
| 4035 | 450 | N635GA | N409CC | N119AD | | | | |
| 4036 | 450 | N936GA | N922H | | | | | |
| 4037 | 450 | N537GA | N445QS | | | | | |
| 4038 | 350 | N538GA | N450RG | | | | | |
| 4039 | 450 | N439GA | N450GA | N760G | N539VE | | | |
| 4040 | 350 | N440GA | N350FK | | | | | |
| 4041 | 450 | N401GA | N451DC | | | | | |
| 4042 | 450 | N442GA | N776JB | | | | | |
| 4043 | 450 | N443GA | N450AB | | | | | |
| 4044 | 450 | N644GA | N663CP | N450KR | | | | |
| 4045 | 450 | N445GA | 4K-AZ888 | | | | | |
| 4046 | 450 | N446GA | N450QS | | | | | |
| 4047 | 450 | N447GA | N664CP | | | | | |
| 4048 | 450 | N448GA | N900AL | | | | | |
| 4049 | 450 | N449GA | N665CP | | | | | |
| 4050 | 450 | N850GA | N244DS | | | | | |
| 4051 | 450 | N351GA | N908VZ | | | | | |
| 4052 | 450 | N452GA | N500J | | | | | |
| 4053 | 450 | N453GA | N845G | | | | | |
| 4054 | 450 | N454GA | N405QS | | | | | |
| 4055 | 450 | N455GA | N237GA | | | | | |

# GULFSTREAM 350/450

| C/n | Series | Identities | | | |
|---|---|---|---|---|---|
| 4056 | 450 | N556GA | (N450PG) | N500N | |
| 4057 | 450 | N457GA | N500RP | | |
| 4058 | 450 | N458GA | N218WW | | |
| 4059 | 450 | N459GA | N222NB | | |
| 4060 | 450 | N460GA | G-TAYC | | |
| 4061 | 450 | N461GA | N450LV | | |
| 4062 | 450 | N462GA | N450XX | | |
| 4063 | 450 | N463GA | N930DC | | |
| 4064 | 450 | N464GA | N768JJ | N763JJ | N338TZ |
| 4065 | 450 | N465GA | N450GD | (N555LR) | N767DX | N767DT |
| 4066 | 450 | N466GA | OY-GVG | | |
| 4067 | 450 | N467GA | N475M | | |
| 4068 | 450 | N468GA | N435QS | | |
| 4069 | 450 | N469GA | N612AF | | |
| 4070 | 450 | N470GA | N818G | | |
| 4071 | 450 | N471GA | N24TH | | |
| 4072 | 450 | N372GA | N450PG | | |
| 4073 | 450 | N373GA | N474M | | |
| 4074 | 450 | N374GA | N455QS | | |
| 4075 | 450 | N375GA | N440AS | N913MK | |
| 4076 | 450 | N376GA | N779CS | N796MA | B-8098 |
| 4077 | 350 | N377GA | N723MM | | |
| 4078 | 450 | N378GA | N310GJ | | |
| 4079 | 450 | N379GA | N450NS | HZ-KSGA | |
| 4080 | 450 | N380GA | N555TF | | |
| 4081 | 450 | N381GA | N926RR | | |
| 4082 | 450 | N382GA | N451NS | | |
| 4083 | 450 | N383GA | N251VP | | |
| 4084 | 450 | N384GA | N470QS | | |
| 4085 | 450 | N385GA | N711SW | N711SZ* | |
| 4086 | 350 | N486GA | N722MM | | |
| 4087 | 450 | N387GA | N800AL | | |
| 4088 | 450 | N388GA | N450EJ | VP-CKD | |
| 4089 | 450 | N389GA | N606CH | | |
| 4090 | 450 | N490GA | Pakistan J-756 | | |
| 4091 | 450 | N391GA | N450GA | (N450GQ) | D-AABB |
| 4092 | 450 | N392GA | VP-BIV | VQ-BGA | |
| 4093 | 450 | N393GA | VP-CMG | | |
| 4094 | 450 | N494GA | N452NS | | |
| 4095 | 450 | N495GA | N450PU | | |
| 4096 | 450 | N496GA | VP-BMY | | |
| 4097 | 450 | N397GA | N59CF | | |
| 4098 | 450 | N398GA | N608CH | | |
| 4099 | 450 | N199GA | N841WS | | |
| 4100 | 450 | N120GA | N448QS | | |
| 4101 | 450 | N401GA | N424PX | | |
| 4102 | 450 | N702GA | XA-GMX | | |
| 4103 | 450 | N603GA | VP-BTB | | |
| 4104 | 450 | N704GA | OE-ICH | | |
| 4105 | 450 | N405GA | N450T | | |
| 4106 | 450 | N606GA | A6-FLG | | |
| 4107 | 450 | N607GA | N717DX | | |
| 4108 | 450 | N608GA | N227RH | | |
| 4109 | 450 | N609GA | N950SW | | |
| 4110 | 450 | N610GA | N450WB | | |
| 4111 | 450 | N131GA | N178SD | | |
| 4112 | 450 | N612GA | N703LH | | |
| 4113 | 450 | N913GA | D-AGVS | | |
| 4114 | 450 | N614GA | N421QS | | |
| 4115 | 450 | N815GA | SX-SEE | VP-BSA | |
| 4116 | 450 | N216GA | N990PT | N516VE | |
| 4117 | 450 | N417GA | N450GD | N770XB | |
| 4118 | 450 | N418GA | N7GU | | |
| 4119 | 450 | N819GA | VP-BAE | | |
| 4120 | 450 | N420GA | N851GG | | |
| 4121 | 450 | N821GA | | | |
| 4122 | 450 | N422GA | HB-JGJ | | |
| 4123 | 450 | N423GA | A6-DJL | | |
| 4124 | 450 | N424GA | N944AL | N512RJ | |
| 4125 | 450 | N425GA | N461QS | | |
| 4126 | 450 | N426GA | N192NC | | |
| 4127 | 450 | N427GA | N450LC | | |
| 4128 | 450 | N528GA | N988AL | Mexico AMT-205 | |
| 4129 | 450 | N429GA | N596DC | | |
| 4130 | 450 | N130GA | OE-IAG | | |
| 4131 | 450 | N531GA | N667HS | | |

## GULFSTREAM 350/450

| C/n | Series | Identities | | | |
|---|---|---|---|---|---|
| 4132 | 450 | N532GA | N851CB | | |
| 4133 | 450 | N433GA | N478QS | (N478WC) | A6-ORX |
| 4134 | 450 | N434GA | N9939T | | |
| 4135 | 450 | N535GA | N499SC | | |
| 4136 | 450 | N436GA | N65QT | A6-AZH | |
| 4137 | 450 | N337GA | VP-CFB | M-YGKL | |
| 4138 | 450 | N138GA | N458X | | |
| 4139 | 450 | N439GA | N212LF | | |
| 4140 | 450 | N740GA | N1BX | | |
| 4141 | 450 | N541GA | N451QS | N18CJ | |
| 4142 | 450 | N742GA | N432AS | | |
| 4143 | 450 | N843GA | N884WT | | |
| 4144 | 450 | N444GA | N450GA | N72LN | |
| 4145 | 450 | N545GA | N9BX | | |
| 4146 | 450 | N146GA | N468QS | | |
| 4147 | 450 | N447GA | N10SN | | |
| 4148 | 450 | N448GA | VQ-BCE | | |
| 4149 | 450 | N449GA | N246V | | |
| 4150 | 450 | N950GA | VP-BMV | | |
| 4151 | 450 | N651GA | N459X* | | |
| 4152 | 450 | N152GA | N451JC | | |
| 4153 | 450 | N453GA | N27YA | | |
| 4154 | 450 | N454GA | N92HL | N975GR | |
| 4155 | 450 | N455GA | A6-FLH | | |
| 4156 | 450 | N656GA | A9C-BHR | | |
| 4157 | 450 | N657GA | N451BH | | |
| 4158 | 450 | N458GA | N202VZ | | |
| 4159 | 450 | N459GA | N451C | | |
| 4160 | 450 | N360GA | N844GF | | |
| 4161 | 450 | N461GA | VP-BSR | | |
| 4162 | 450 | N462GA | N37JL | | |
| 4163 | 450 | N463GA | N450GD | | |
| 4164 | 450 | N464GA | N718JS | | |
| 4165 | 450 | N565GA | | | |
| 4166 | 450 | N126GA | VP-CET | | |
| 4167 | 450 | N467GA | N597DC | | |
| 4168 | 450 | N468GA | B-8099 | | |
| 4169 | 450 | N569GA | N922CB | | |
| 4170 | 450 | N570GA | | | |
| 4171 | 450 | N571GA | N225CX | | |
| 4172 | 450 | N572GA | SX-GAB | | |
| 4173 | 450 | N175GA | N936MP | | |
| 4174 | 450 | N574GA | N9SC | | |
| 4175 | 450 | N475GA | TC-KHB | | |
| 4176 | 450 | N178GA | N1DW | | |
| 4177 | 450 | N577GA | N918LL | | |
| 4178 | 450 | N478GA | | | |
| 4179 | 450 | N479GA | N915AM | | |
| 4180 | 450 | N418GA | | | |
| 4181 | 450 | N181GA | N123LV | | |
| 4182 | 450 | N482GA | B-LCK | | |
| 4183 | 450 | N483GA | N903G | | |
| 4184 | 450 | N984GA | N333SZ | | |
| 4185 | 450 | N985GA | | | |
| 4186 | 450 | N986GA | N510AK* | | |
| 4187 | 450 | N187GA | | | |
| 4188 | 450 | N188GA | | | |
| 4189 | 450 | N989GA | N450GA | | |
| 4190 | 450 | N790GA | | | |
| 4191 | 450 | N491GA | | | |
| 4192 | 450 | N492GA | | | |
| 4193 | 450 | N693GA | | | |
| 4194 | 450 | N494GA | | | |
| 4195 | 450 | N495GA | | | |
| 4196 | 450 | N996GA | | | |
| 4197 | 450 | N397GA | | | |
| 4198 | 450 | N398GA | | | |
| 4199 | 450 | N499GA | | | |
| 4200 | 450 | N820GA | | | |
| 4201 | 450 | N401GA | | | |
| 4202 | 450 | N202GA | | | |
| 4203 | 450 | N403GA | | | |
| 4204 | 450 | N904GA | | | |
| 4205 | 450 | N452GA | | | |
| 4206 | 450 | N906GA | | | |
| 4207 | 450 | N907GA | | | |

# GULFSTREAM 350/450

| C/n | Series | Identities |
|---|---|---|
| 4208 | 450 | N608GA |
| 4209 | 450 | N909GA |
| 4210 | 450 | N120GA |
| 4211 | 450 | N711GA |
| 4212 | 450 | N922GA |
| 4213 | 450 | N413GA |
| 4214 | 450 | N214GA |
| 4215 | 450 | N425GA |
| 4216 | 450 | N216GA |
| 4217 | 450 | N427GA |
| 4218 | 450 | N218GA |
| 4220 | 450 | N920GA |
| 4221 | 450 | N712GA |
| 4222 | 450 | N422GA |
| 4223 | 450 | N423GA |
| 4224 | | |
| 4225 | | |
| 4226 | | |
| 4227 | | |
| 4228 | | |
| 4229 | | |
| 4230 | | |
| 4231 | | |
| 4232 | | |
| 4233 | | |
| 4234 | | |
| 4235 | | |
| 4236 | | |
| 4237 | | |
| 4238 | | |
| 4239 | | |
| 4240 | | |
| 4241 | | |
| 4242 | | |
| 4243 | | |
| 4244 | | |
| 4245 | | |
| 4246 | | |
| 4247 | | |
| 4248 | | |
| 4249 | | |
| 4250 | | |

# GULFSTREAM V/GULFSTREAM 500/550

We have been advised by Gulfstream Aerospace that the Gulfstream V does not have the model number G1159D as has been quoted elsewhere.

| C/n | Series | Identities | | | | | | | | |
|---|---|---|---|---|---|---|---|---|---|---|
| 501 | | N501GV | [rolled out 22Sep95; ff 28Nov95] | | | | N22 | | | |
| 502 | | N502GV | N502KA | N5GV | N502KA | | | | | |
| 503 | | N503GV | N767FL | | | | | | | |
| 504 | | N504GV | N313RG | | | | | | | |
| F5 | | [Static test airframe] | | | | | | | | |
| 505 | | N505GV | EI-WGV | N505AX | N371JC | | | | | |
| 506 | | N506GV | N158AF | N500GV | N33XE | | | | | |
| 507 | | N507GA | N300L | | | | | | | |
| 508 | | N508GA | N777GV | N899GM | N777TY | N777PY | [canx 10Aug04; b/u West Palm Beach FL, | | | |
| | | remains to Savannah, GA by Oct04] | | | | | | | | |
| 509 | | N509GA | V8-009 | V8-001 | V8-009 | N509GA | "N61GV" | N5GA | VP-BNZ | N509GV |
| | | N855RB | | | | | | | | |
| 510 | | N598GA | N513MW | B-8092 | | | | | | |
| 511 | | N511GA | VP-CBX | | | | | | | |
| 512 | | N512GV | N636MF | N838MF | | | | | | |
| 513 | | N513GA | HB-IVL | | | | | | | |
| 514 | | N514GA | N777SW | N304K | N320K | N256LK | | | | |
| 515 | | N599GA | V8-007 | V8-001 | N55GV | | | | | |
| 516 | | N516GA | N555CS | N740BA | | | | | | |
| 517 | | N517GA | HB-IMJ | | | | | | | |
| 518 | | N518GA | HZ-MIC | N555GN | (N36GA) | N1GN | N555GN | N555GV | N5GV | (N55GV) |
| | | N885G | (N917ND) | N17ND | | | | | | |
| 519 | | N597GA | VP-CMG | N526EE | | | | | | |
| 520 | | N596GA | N17GV | N450AR | N818DA | (N786CW) | N767CW | | | |
| 521 | C-37A | N521GA | USAF 97-0400 | | | | | | | |
| 522 | | N595GA | (N158RA) | N39PY | N20H | N20HN | N70AG | | | |
| 523 | | N523GA | N711SW | N790MC | N54TG | | | | | |
| 524 | | N524GA | N400JD | N674RW | N1892 | | | | | |
| 525 | | N594GA | N252JS | N40SR | VT-SMI | | | | | |
| 526 | | N526GA | N675RW | N125GH | | | | | | |
| 527 | | N527GA | N5SA | | | | | | | |
| 528 | | N528GA | N80RP | N75RP | | | | | | |
| 529 | | N529GA | N73RP | | | | | | | |
| 530 | | N530GA | N780F | N780W* | | | | | | |
| 531 | | N531GA | (N8CA) | N531AF | | | | | | |
| 532 | | N532GA | N282Q | (N282QT) | N282QA | N740SS | | | | |
| 533 | | N533GA | XA-CPQ | | | | | | | |
| 534 | | N534GA | (N158JJ) | N920DC | N127GG | | | | | |
| 535 | | N593GA | N775US | (N535GV) | N535V | | | | | |
| 536 | | N536GA | N5UH | N688TY | | | | | | |
| 537 | | N537GA | 8P-MAK | N132SD | | | | | | |
| 538 | | N538GA | N601MD | N1JN | | | | | | |
| 539 | | N539GA | N1GC | N162JC | | | | | | |
| 540 | | N640GA | XA-OEM | | | | | | | |
| 541 | | N641GA | N405LM | | | | | | | |
| 542 | C-37A | N642GA | USAF 97-0401 | | | | | | | |
| 543 | | N643GA | N91CW | | | | | | | |
| 544 | | N644GA | N910DC | N383LS | | | | | | |
| 545 | | N645GA | N1HC | N55GV | N5GV | N888CW | N545CC | | | |
| 546 | | N646GA | XA-BAL | | | | | | | |
| 547 | | N647GA | N73M | | | | | | | |
| 548 | | N648GA | N245TT | N245TJ | N32BD | | | | | |
| 549 | | N649GA | N317JD | N718MC | N718MD | N123FT | | | | |
| 550 | | N650GA | N5101 | | | | | | | |
| 551 | | N651GA | N5102 | | | | | | | |
| 552 | | N652GA | N9SC | N189SC | | | | | | |
| 553 | | N653GA | N516GH | | | | | | | |
| 554 | | N654GA | N589HM | N450BE | HB-JKA | N38NZ | XA-AZT | | | |
| 555 | | N655GA | VP-BSM | VP-BSJ | | | | | | |
| 556 | | N656GA | N556AR | HB-JES | | | | | | |
| 557 | | N657GA | N83M | | | | | | | |
| 558 | | N658GA | N750BA | N600RH | N500RH | | | | | |
| 559 | | N659GA | N559GV | N144KK | | | | | | |
| 560 | | N660GA | 9K-AJD | | | | | | | |
| 561 | | N661GA | | | | | | | | |
| 562 | | N662GA | N95AE | | | | | | | |
| 563 | | N463GA | N8CA | N169CA | (N169PG) | (N180CH) | N225EE | | | |
| 564 | | N664GA | (JY-...) | "N18VS" | N664GA | N54PR | A6-DEJ | | | |
| 565 | | N460GA | N77CP | | | | | | | |
| 566 | C-37A | N466GA | US Army 97-0049 | | N8VQ | US Army 97-1944 | | | | |
| 567 | | N467GA | N93M | | | | | | | |
| 568 | | N461GA | N845HS | N568JC | HB-INQ | N5HN | N89HE | | | |
| 569 | | N469GA | 9K-AJE | | | | | | | |

# GULFSTREAM 500/550

| C/n | Series | Identities | | | | | |
|---|---|---|---|---|---|---|---|
| 570 | | N470GA | N451CS | N521HN | | | |
| 571 | C-37A | N671GA | USAF 99-0402 | | | | |
| 572 | | N472GA | (N223SS) | P4-FAZ | HB-IIS | OE-IIS | |
| 573 | | N673GA | 9K-AJF | | | | |
| 574 | | N674GA | N1KE | | | | |
| 575 | | N475GA | N410M | | | | |
| 576 | | N476GA | N991LF | | | | |
| 577 | | N577GA | HB-IVZ | | | | |
| 578 | | N578GA | N1GN | N21GN | N410LM | | |
| 579 | | N579GA | N23M | | | | |
| 580 | | N580GA | N1540 | | | | |
| 581 | | N581GA | N379P | N8068V | N44982 | N126CH | VH-CCC |
| 582 | | N582GA | N271JG | EC-IRZ | | | |
| 583 | | N583GA | HZ-MS05 | HZ-MS5 | HZ-MS5B | | |
| 584 | | N584GA | N84GV | | | | |
| 585 | | N585GA | N18NK | N16NK | | | |
| 586 | | N586GA | N2N | | | | |
| 587 | | N587GA | N300K | | | | |
| 588 | | N588GA | VP-BAC | | | | |
| 589 | | N589GA | N15UC | N15UQ* | | | |
| 590 | C-37A | N590GA | USAF 99-0404 | | | | |
| 591 | | N591GA | N301K | | | | |
| 592 | | N592GA | N90AM | | | | |
| 593 | | N593GA | (I-MPUT) | I-DEAS | | | |
| 594 | | N594GA | N33M | | | | |
| 595 | | N595GA | N85V | (N595GV) | | | |
| 596 | | N596GA | (USAF 99-0405) | | N383JA | | |
| 597 | | N495GA | N302K | N540M | | | |
| 598 | | N598GA | N1SF | N598F | | | |
| 599 | | N496GA | N401WJ | N428WT | N800PM | | |
| 600 | | N650GA | N100GV | | | | |
| 601 | | N536GA | N502QS | | | | |
| 602 | | N538GA | N602GV | VP-BKZ | | | |
| 603 | | N539GA | N35CD | | | | |
| 604 | | N551GA | LV-ZXI | N551GA | XA-EAJ | | |
| 605 | | N554GA | N62MS | N62ML | N691RC | | |
| 606 | | N558GA | N63HS | N53HS | N551GA | | |
| 607 | | N559GA | N303K | VP-BNL | | | |
| 608 | | N561GA | N111LX | N608WB | | | |
| 609 | | N566GA | N5733 | N418SG | N418SM | N101MH | |
| 610 | | N567GA | (N610CM) | N253CM | | | |
| 611 | | N568GA | N5000X | | | | |
| 612 | | N569GA | N350C | N88D | N88DZ | | |
| 613 | | N570GA | N504QS | N721MM | B-8097 | | |
| 614 | | N571GA | N614CM | | | | |
| 615 | | N572GA | N914J | | | | |
| 616 | | N574GA | (N457ST) | N1HC | N141HC | N5616 | |
| 617 | | N575GA | 7T-VPG | | | | |
| 618 | | N585GA | N585JC | (N123H) | [damaged in hangar collapse at Washington/Dulles, VA, 6Feb10 possible w/o] | | |
| 619 | | N608GA | N1454H | | | | |
| 620 | C-37A | N535GA | USAF 01-0028 | | | | |
| 621 | | N621GA | (N605M) | N605CH | N702TY | | |
| 622 | | N622GA | N304K | N806AC | VP-BBX | | |
| 623 | | N623GA | N506QS | | | | |
| 624 | C-37A | N624GA | USAF 01-0029 | | | | |
| 625 | | N625GA | N507QS | | | | |
| 626 | | N626GA | N5JR | N846QM | | | |
| 627 | | N627GA | N54KB | | | | |
| 628 | | N628GA | N18RF | N42GX | N628BD | | |
| 629 | | N629GA | N711RL | N711RQ | N707GW | | |
| 630 | | N630GA | N130GV | | | | |
| 631 | | N631GA | N508QS | | | | |
| 632 | V-SP | N632GA | N5SP | N532SP | [first GV-SP; ff 31Aug01] | | |
| 633 | | N633GA | N222LX | | | | |
| 634 | | N534GA | ZS-AOL | | | | |
| 635 | | N522GA | N83CP | | | | |
| 636 | | N556GA | N910V | VP-BEP | N886DT | | |
| 637 | | N637GA | N509QS | | | | |
| 638 | | N638GA | HB-IIY | N888HE | (N888HK) | | |
| 639 | | N639GA | N501CV | | | | |
| 640 | | N580GA | N752BA | N600JD | | | |
| 641 | | N641GA | HB-IIZ | OE-IIA | | | |
| 642 | | N562GA | N510QS | CS-DKB | N626JS | | |
| 643 | | N523GA | 5N-FGS | | | | |
| 644 | | N644GA | HZ-MS5A | | | | |
| 645 | C-37A | N645GA | USAF 01-0076 | | | | |

## GULFSTREAM V/500/550

| C/n | Series | Identities | | | | | |
|---|---|---|---|---|---|---|---|
| 646 | | N524GA | N51FL | | | | |
| 647 | | N647GA | N511QS | | | | |
| 648 | | N648GA | N85M | N85ML | VP-BSN | | |
| 649 | | N649GA | N83CW | | | | |
| 650 | | N520GA | N1040 | | | | |
| 651 | | N581GA | N651GV | N1DC | | | |
| 652 | C-37A | N582GA | USAF 01-0065 | | | | |
| 653 | VC-37A | N527GA | US Coast Guard 01 | | | | |
| 654 | | N584GA | (N654GV) | N960AV | VP-BLA | N404M | XA-MPS |
| 655 | | N529GA | N825LM | | | | |
| 656 | | N256GA | (N218CP) | N218EC | | | |
| 657 | C-37B | N587GA | USN 166375 | | | | |
| 658 | | N532GA | N516QS | | | | |
| 659 | | N589GA | N50KC | | | | |
| 660 | | N533GA | N130TM | | | | |
| 661 | | N561GA | N405HG | | | | |
| 662 | | N662GA | N697A | | | | |
| 663 | C-37A | N663GA | USAF 01-0030 | | | | |
| 664 | | N664GA | N564QS+ [+marks were applied but ntu] | | | N664GA | XA-MKI |
| 665 | | N565GA | N845HS | N223MD | N128GV | | |
| 666 | | N566GA | (N958AV) | N699GA | [c/n changed to 699 on rereg'n to N699GA qv] | | |
| 667 | | N567GA | N1BN | N121BN | N123M | N168NJ | |
| 668 | | N568GA | N721S | | | | |
| 669 | | N569GA | N144KK | N544KK | N1UB | VP-CES | |
| 670 | C-37A | N670GA | USAF 02-1863 | | | | |
| 671 | | N571GA | N671LE | N671LB | N703RK | | |
| 672 | | N672GA | VP-BJD | N225GV | N3546 | | |
| 673 | | N873GA | N282QT | N673P | | | |
| 674 | | N674GA | N25GV | (N26GV) | N36GV | | |
| 675 | | N675GA | N505RX | N1956M | | | |
| 676 | | N676GA | Israel 676 ["Nachshon Shavit" ELINT platform] | | | | |
| 677 | | N677GA | N677F | | | | |
| 678 | | N678GA | Greece 678 | | | | |
| 679 | | N679GA | Israel 679 ["Nachshon Shavit" ELINT platform] | | | | |
| 680 | | N680GA | (OK-ONE) | | | | |
| 681 | | N981GA | (N519QS) | N624N | | | |
| 682 | | N682GA | (VP-BFD) | G-JCBV | N551M | N38BA | N919YC |
| 683 | | N683GA | JA500A | [code LAJ500] | | | |
| 684 | | N684GA | Israel 684 ["Nachshon Shavit" ELINT platform] | | | | |
| 685 | | N585GA | N685TA | | | | |
| 686 | | N686GA | N524AC | | | | |
| 687 | | N687GA | OE-IVY | | | | |
| 688 | | N688GA | (N254W) | N543H | | | |
| 689 | | N689GA | JA501A | [code LAJ501] | | | |
| 690 | | N690GA | N914BD | | | | |
| 691 | | N691GA | N250DV | N525AC | | | |
| 692 | | N692GA | N100TM | | | | |
| 693 | | N693GA | N508P | | | | |
| 694 | | c/n not used | | | | | |
| 695 | | c/n not used | | | | | |
| 696 | | c/n not used | | | | | |
| 697 | | c/n not used | | | | | |
| 698 | | c/n not used | | | | | |
| 699 | | N566GA | (N958AV) | N699GA | N885KT | [orginally built as c/n 666] | |

## GULFSTREAM 500/550

| C/n | Series | Identities | | | | | |
|---|---|---|---|---|---|---|---|
| 5001 | 500 | N901GA | [rolled out 19Jun02 ff 18Jly02] N5SP | | | N621KD | N501ZK |
| 5002 | 550 | N702GA | N550GA | N92LA | | | |
| 5003 | 550 | N703GA | N245TT | | | | |
| 5004 | 550 | N904GA | HB-IGM | | | | |
| 5005 | 550 | N805GA | N4CP | | | | |
| 5006 | 550 | N906GA | N550GW | | | | |
| 5007 | 550 | N907GA | N754BA | | | | |
| 5008 | 550 | N908GA | XA-EOF | N378L | | | |
| 5009 | 550 | N909GA | N1HC | | | | |
| 5010 | 550 | N910GA | N711RL | | | | |
| 5011 | 550 | N991GA | (N522QS) | VP-BGN | N811GA | | |
| 5012 | 550 | N812GA | N888LK | | | | |
| 5013 | 550 | N913GA | N63HS | | | | |
| 5014 | 550 | N914GA | Israel 514 ["Nachshon Eitam" AEW platform] | | | | |
| 5015 | 550 | N915GA | N565ST | | | | |
| 5016 | 550 | N916GA | N944H | | | | |
| 5017 | 550 | N917GA | N62MS | | | | |
| 5018 | 550 | N518GA | N818RF | | | | |

# GULFSTREAM 500/550

| C/n | Series | Identities | | | | |
|---|---|---|---|---|---|---|
| 5019 | 550 | N919GA | SE-RDX | G-GSSO | | |
| 5020 | 550 | N920GA | N221DG | | | |
| 5021 | 550 | N921GA | N5DA | | | |
| 5022 | 550 | N922GA | N550GV | OE-ISS | | |
| 5023 | 550 | N923GA | N1GN | | | |
| 5024 | 550 | N924GA | VP-BLA | N424GA | B-8100 | |
| 5025 | 550 | N925GA | HB-JEE | | | |
| 5026 | 550 | N926GA | N550MT | | | |
| 5027 | 550 | N927GA | N91LA | | | |
| 5028 | 550 | N928GA | N55UH | HL7799 | | |
| 5029 | 550 | N929GA | (N550RN) | N155AN | | |
| 5030 | 550 | N830GA | 5H-ONE | | | |
| 5031 | 550 | N931GA | N795BA | | | |
| 5032 | 550 | N932GA | G-HRDS | | | |
| 5033 | 550 | N933GA | VP-BNR | | | |
| 5034 | 550 | N934GA | US Army 04-1778 | | [C37A] | |
| 5035 | 550 | N935GA | N1TF | | | |
| 5036 | 550 | N936GA | N1BN | | | |
| 5037 | 550 | N637GA | Israel 537 ["Nachshon Eitam" AEW platform] | | | |
| 5038 | 550 | N938GA | N372BG | N102BG | | |
| 5039 | 550 | N939GA | N401HF | | | |
| 5040 | 550 | N940GA | N418SG | (N13J) | HB-JEV | |
| 5041 | 550 | N841GA | US Navy 166376 | | [C37A] | |
| 5042 | 550 | N942GA | N528QS | | | |
| 5043 | 550 | N943GA | N550GA | N83TE | VP-BGL | N107VS |
| 5044 | 550 | N944GA | Israel 544 Singapore 016 | | | [AEW platform] |
| 5045 | 550 | N945GA | N789RR | N560DM | | |
| 5046 | 550 | N946GA | N5PG | | | |
| 5047 | 550 | N947GA | (N550YM) | | | |
| 5048 | 550 | N948GA | VP-CIF | VP-CIP | | |
| 5049 | 550 | N949GA | N109ST | N89NC | | |
| 5050 | 550 | N950GA | VP-BNO | | | |
| 5051 | 550 | N851GA | VP-BNE | | | |
| 5052 | 550 | N952GA | XA-ATL | | | |
| 5053 | 550 | N953GA | N2929 | | | |
| 5054 | 550 | N954GA | OE-IVV | | | |
| 5055 | 550 | N955GA | N144KK | N755VE | | |
| 5056 | 550 | N956GA | N45ST | N556TT | | |
| 5057 | 550 | N957GA | CS-DKC | | | |
| 5058 | 550 | N958GA | N74RP | | | |
| 5059 | 550 | N959GA | VP-BLR | N659GA | B-8095 | |
| 5060 | 550 | N960GA | G-JCBC | N143G | | |
| 5061 | 550 | N961GA | N718MC | | | |
| 5062 | 550 | N962GA | N159JA | | | |
| 5063 | 550 | N963GA | N759WR | N411WW | | |
| 5064 | 550 | N964GA | VP-BJD | | | |
| 5065 | 550 | N965GA | N747AE | | | |
| 5066 | 550 | N966GA | N250DV | | | |
| 5067 | 500 | N967GA | N50HA | | | |
| 5068 | 550 | N968GA | EI-GDL | | | |
| 5069 | 550 | N969GA | Israel 569 ["Nachshon Eitam" AEW platform] | | | |
| 5070 | 550 | N870GA | HB-JEP | | | |
| 5071 | 550 | N571GA | (N550GA)+ | [+ ntu marks worn in NBAA Static display, Orlando Executive, FL, Nov05] | | |
| | | I-LUXO | | | | |
| 5072 | 550 | N572GA | (N25GV) | N572EC | N528M | |
| 5073 | 550 | N673GA | N800JH | | | |
| 5074 | 550 | N574GA | HZ-ARK | | | |
| 5075 | 550 | N575GA | N518QS | | | |
| 5076 | 550 | N576GA | N870CM | | | |
| 5077 | 550 | N577GA | N933H | | | |
| 5078 | 550 | N578GA | EC-JPK | | | |
| 5079 | 550 | N579GA | N860AA | | | |
| 5080 | 550 | N580GA | SE-RDY | | | |
| 5081 | 550 | N581GA | CS-DKD | | | |
| 5082 | 550 | N582GA | N550FG | N709DW | | |
| 5083 | 550 | N583GA | N985JC | | | |
| 5084 | 550 | N584GA | VP-BSI | | | |
| 5085 | 550 | N585GA | N235DX | | | |
| 5086 | 550 | N586GA | N609PM | | | |
| 5087 | 550 | N587GA | US Navy 166377 | | | |
| 5088 | 550 | N588GA | N5VS | | | |
| 5089 | 550 | N589GA | N771JT | | | |
| 5090 | 550 | N590GA | N282Q | | | |
| 5091 | 550 | N591GA | N3PG | | | |
| 5092 | 550 | N592GA | VP-CVI | | | |
| 5093 | 550 | N593GA | D-ADLR | [High Altitude Long-Range research aircraft] | | |
| 5095 | 550 | N595GA | N550KF | | | |

## GULFSTREAM 500/550

| C/n | Series | Identities | | | | |
|---|---|---|---|---|---|---|
| 5096 | 550 | N696GA | N3050 | | | |
| 5097 | 550 | N597GA | N550GA | N806AC | | |
| 5098 | 550 | N598GA | US Navy 166378 | | | |
| 5099 | 550 | N699GA | CS-DKF | | | |
| 5100 | 500 | N820GA | N51MF | N760CC | | |
| 5101 | 550 | N821GA | N550M | | | |
| 5102 | 550 | N822GA | VP-CVT | B-HVT* | | |
| 5103 | 550 | N923GA | N534QS | | | |
| 5104 | 550 | N824GA | N661CP | | | |
| 5105 | 500 | N935GA | N500RD | | | |
| 5106 | 550 | N986GA | N234DB | | | |
| 5107 | 550 | N937GA | N662CP | | | |
| 5108 | 550 | N828GA | N311CG | | | |
| 5109 | 550 | N829GA | VP-BIP | N818HK | | |
| 5110 | 550 | N940GA | N585A | | | |
| 5111 | 550 | N981GA | B-KGV | VP-CKC | | |
| 5112 | 550 | N832GA | N636MF | | | |
| 5113 | 550 | N833GA | VP-CNR | | | |
| 5114 | 550 | N834GA | D-ADCA | | | |
| 5115 | 550 | N835GA | B-KID | | | |
| 5116 | 550 | N836GA | EC-JYR | | | |
| 5117 | 550 | N967GA | N595A | | | |
| 5118 | 550 | N838GA | N855G | | | |
| 5119 | 550 | N519GA | RA-10202 | | | |
| 5120 | 550 | N920GA | N254SD | N284SD | B-8108 | |
| 5121 | 550 | N921GA | N550PR | | | |
| 5122 | 550 | N522GA | N837BA | | | |
| 5123 | 550 | N523GA | VP-BBO | | | |
| 5124 | 550 | N524GA | EC-KBR | | | |
| 5125 | 550 | N295GA | N550GD | N388AC | | |
| 5126 | 550 | N526GA | N676RW | | | |
| 5127 | 550 | N527GA | CS-DKG | | | |
| 5128 | 550 | N928GA | N940DC | (N1759) | N1759C | |
| 5129 | 550 | N529GA | VP-BLW | | | |
| 5130 | 550 | N130GA | N671LE | | | |
| 5131 | 550 | N531GA | N671RW | | | |
| 5132 | 550 | N432GA | Israel 532 | Singapore 017 | | [AEW platform] |
| 5133 | 550 | N533GA | N531QS | | | |
| 5134 | 550 | N534GA | N712KT | | | |
| 5135 | 550 | N535GA | N522BP | | | |
| 5136 | 500 | N536GA | N110ED | | | |
| 5137 | 550 | N287GA | 8P-MSD | | | |
| 5138 | 550 | N638GA | N600J | | | |
| 5139 | 550 | N539GA | OE-IRG | | | |
| 5140 | 550 | N740GA | N838BA | | | |
| 5141 | 550 | N541GA | N10MZ | | | |
| 5142 | 550 | N42GA | D-ADCB | | | |
| 5143 | 550 | N643GA | Singapore 018 | | [AEW platform] | |
| 5144 | 500 | N644GA | N515PL | | | |
| 5145 | 550 | N545GA | N345LC | | | |
| 5146 | 550 | N646GA | N607PM | | | |
| 5147 | 550 | N647GA | B-LUE | | | |
| 5148 | 500 | N648GA | N551KF | N650PL | | |
| 5149 | 550 | N649GA | VP-CGN | | | |
| 5150 | 550 | N43GA | CS-DKH | | | |
| 5151 | 550 | N921GA | EC-KJS | | | |
| 5152 | 550 | N652GA | 06-0500 | | | |
| 5153 | 550 | N923GA | SE-RDZ | | | |
| 5154 | 550 | N654GA | N557GA | | | |
| 5155 | 550 | N935GA | N550GA | EC-KUM | | |
| 5156 | 550 | N936GA | N529QS | | | |
| 5157 | 550 | N657GA | N785QS | | | |
| 5158 | 500 | N998GA | N56UH | | | |
| 5159 | 550 | N659GA | N607CH | | | |
| 5160 | 550 | N660GA | N813QS | | | |
| 5161 | 550 | N261GA | N725MM | | | |
| 5162 | 550 | N662GA | EC-KLS | | | |
| 5163 | 550 | N663GA | N57UH | | | |
| 5164 | 550 | N764GA | N372BG | | | |
| 5165 | 550 | N965GA | N245BD | | | |
| 5166 | 550 | N966GA | CS-DKI | | | |
| 5167 | 550 | N967GA | G-EGNS | | | |
| 5168 | 550 | N668GA | N528AP | | | |
| 5169 | 550 | N569GA | N203A | | | |
| 5170 | 550 | N770GA | N105ST | | | |
| 5171 | 550 | N971GA | N550BM | | | |

## GULFSTREAM 500/550

| C/n | Series | Identities | | | |
|---|---|---|---|---|---|
| 5172 | 550 | N972GA | HB-JGX | G-LGKD | |
| 5173 | 550 | N673GA | N401HB | | |
| 5174 | 550 | N974GA | CS-DKJ | | |
| 5175 | 550 | N975GA | HB-JGC | N887AG | |
| 5176 | 550 | N476GA | VP-BTC | G-CGUL | |
| 5177 | 550 | N977GA | VP-BCO | | |
| 5178 | 550 | N978GA | HB-JKB | | |
| 5179 | 550 | N979GA | VP-BZC | | |
| 5180 | 550 | N980GA | N108DB | | |
| 5181 | 550 | N181GA | N550AN | VP-CEA | VP-CJM |
| 5182 | 550 | N782GA | XA-CHR | | |
| 5183 | 550 | N983GA | N88D | | |
| 5184 | 550 | N284GA | N550GD | N550RP | |
| 5185 | 550 | N185GA | | | |
| 5186 | 550 | N286GA | G-JCBB | | |
| 5187 | 550 | N187GA | N816MG | | |
| 5188 | 550 | N188GA | N554CE | | |
| 5189 | 550 | N189GA | D-AAAM | | |
| 5190 | 550 | N290GA | N546QS | | |
| 5191 | 550 | N291GA | D-AJJK | | |
| 5192 | 550 | N492GA | N323BD | | |
| 5193 | 550 | N293GA | P4-TPS | | |
| 5194 | 550 | N394GA | N1EB | | |
| 5195 | 550 | N295GA | N1LB | N550SN | |
| 5196 | 550 | N196GA | N45ST | | |
| 5197 | 550 | N597GA | SX-MFA | | |
| 5198 | 550 | N298GA | LZ-FIA | | |
| 5199 | 550 | N399GA | N443M | | |
| 5200 | 550 | N990GA | VP-BJK | | |
| 5201 | 550 | N991GA | CS-DKK | | |
| 5202 | 550 | N992GA | N1SF | | |
| 5203 | 550 | N203GA | EC-KXF | | |
| 5204 | 550 | N104GA | 4K-MEK8 | | |
| 5205 | 500 | N405GA | | | |
| 5206 | 550 | N806GA | N211HS | (N721V) | N169SD |
| 5207 | 550 | N607GA | N101CP | N418SG | |
| 5208 | 550 | N908GA | 5X-UGF | | |
| 5209 | 550 | N609GA | N517QS | | |
| 5210 | 550 | N610GA | M-ONEM | | |
| 5211 | 550 | N711GA | N550GA | (N550JE) | N653MK |
| 5212 | 550 | N512GA | TC-DAP | | |
| 5213 | 550 | N413GA | N888HK | | |
| 5214 | 550 | N314GA | N4PG | | |
| 5215 | 550 | N615GA | VQ-BLA | | |
| 5216 | 550 | N516GA | VP-CJL | | |
| 5217 | 550 | N517GA | N768JJ | | |
| 5218 | 550 | N518GA | VQ-BGN | | |
| 5219 | 550 | N419GA | (N885AR) | B-KVC | |
| 5220 | 550 | N520GA | G-TFKR | | |
| 5221 | 550 | N221GA | VQ-BLV | | |
| 5222 | 550 | N622GA | N801TM | | |
| 5223 | 550 | N623GA | N550SG | | |
| 5224 | 550 | N624GA | N678SC | | |
| 5225 | 550 | N325GA | M-VRNY | | |
| 5226 | 550 | N526GA | N803TM | | |
| 5227 | 550 | N217GA | M-FPIA | M-FUAD | |
| 5228 | 550 | N828GA | B-KCK | | |
| 5229 | 550 | N509GA | N535QS | N55AL | |
| 5230 | 550 | N330GA | C-GNDN | | |
| 5231 | 550 | N131GA | N899SR | | |
| 5232 | 550 | N932GA | N773MJ | | |
| 5233 | 550 | N733GA | HL8200 | | |
| 5234 | 550 | N934GA | N674RW | | |
| 5235 | 550 | N435GA | N589K | | |
| 5236 | 550 | N563GA | PR-WRO | | |
| 5237 | 550 | N937GA | N885WT | | |
| 5238 | 550 | N838GA | B-KGP | | |
| 5239 | 550 | N339GA | N928GC | | |
| 5240 | 550 | N840GA | HB-JKC | | |
| 5241 | 550 | N841GA | Turkey 09-001 | | |
| 5242 | 550 | N842GA | A9C-BRN | | |
| 5243 | 550 | N924GA | (N803TG) | B-99888 | |
| 5244 | 550 | N744GA | N800DL | | |
| 5245 | 550 | N845GA | N802AG | | |
| 5246 | 550 | N846GA | M-IPHS | | |
| 5247 | 550 | N847GA | USAF 09-0501 | | |
| 5248 | 550 | N748GA | 9K-GFA | | |

# GULFSTREAM 500/550

| C/n | Series | Identities | | |
|---|---|---|---|---|
| 5249 | 500 | N849GA | N757PL | |
| 5250 | 550 | N952GA | "N592GA"+ | [+incorrect marks worn for test-flight at Long Beach 18Nov09] |
| | | N952GA | B-LSM | |
| 5251 | 550 | N351GA | HZ-ALFA | |
| 5252 | 550 | N552GA | N550PM | |
| 5253 | 550 | N523GA | PR-OGX | |
| 5254 | 550 | N554GA | Turkey 10-002 | |
| 5255 | 550 | N955GA | N94924 | |
| 5256 | 550 | N856GA | N1932P | |
| 5257 | 550 | N957GA | N253DV* | |
| 5258 | 550 | N558GA | | |
| 5259 | 550 | N959GA | VH-LAL* | |
| 5260 | 550 | N960GA | ZK-KFB* | |
| 5261 | 550 | N561GA | | |
| 5262 | 550 | N562GA | | |
| 5263 | 550 | N263GA | | |
| 5264 | 550 | N564GA | | |
| 5265 | 550 | N965GA | | |
| 5266 | 550 | N926GA | | |
| 5267 | 550 | N867GA | | |
| 5268 | 550 | N568GA | | |
| 5269 | 550 | N369GA | | |
| 5270 | 550 | N370GA | | |
| 5271 | 550 | N971GA | | |
| 5272 | 550 | N772GA | | |
| 5273 | 550 | N927GA | | |
| 5274 | 550 | N174GA | | |
| 5275 | 550 | N575GA | | |
| 5276 | 550 | N276GA | | |
| 5277 | 550 | N527GA | | |
| 5278 | 550 | N528GA | | |
| 5279 | 550 | N579GA | | |
| 5280 | 550 | N508GA | | |
| 5281 | 550 | N581GA | | |
| 5282 | 550 | N282GA | | |
| 5283 | 550 | N283GA | | |
| 5284 | 550 | N584GA | | |
| 5285 | 550 | N285GA | | |
| 5286 | 550 | N526GA | | |
| 5287 | 550 | N587GA | | |
| 5288 | 550 | N588GA | | |
| 5289 | 550 | N589GA | | |
| 5290 | 550 | N290GA | | |
| 5291 | 550 | N591GA | | |
| 5292 | 550 | N592GA | | |
| 5293 | 550 | N829GA | | |
| 5294 | 550 | N594GA | | |
| 5295 | 550 | N295GA | | |
| 5296 | 550 | N896GA | | |
| 5297 | 550 | N792GA | | |
| 5298 | 550 | N598GA | | |
| 5299 | 550 | N529GA | | |
| 5300 | 550 | N300GA | | |
| 5301 | | | | |
| 5302 | | | | |
| 5303 | | | | |
| 5304 | | | | |
| 5305 | | | | |
| 5306 | | | | |
| 5307 | | | | |
| 5308 | | | | |
| 5309 | | | | |
| 5310 | | | | |
| 5311 | | | | |
| 5312 | | | | |
| 5313 | | | | |
| 5314 | | | | |
| 5315 | | | | |
| 5316 | | | | |
| 5317 | | | | |
| 5318 | | | | |
| 5319 | | | | |
| 5320 | | | | |
| 5321 | | | | |
| 5322 | | | | |
| 5323 | | | | |
| 5324 | | | | |

# GULFSTREAM VI/650

Gulfstream's new wide-bodied aircraft, officially the Gulfstream VI but marketed as the Gulfstream 650

| C/n | Identities | | |
|---|---|---|---|
| 6001 | N601GD | N650GA | [r/o 29Sep09, ff 25Nov09] |
| 6002 | N602GD | N652GD | [ff 25Feb10] |
| 6003 | N603GD | N653GD | |
| 6004 | N604GD | N650GD | |
| 6005 | N606GD | | |
| 6006 | N607GD | | |
| 6007 | N607GD | | |
| 6008 | N608GD | | |
| 6009 | N609GD | | |
| 6010 | N110GA | | |
| 6011 | N611GD | | |
| 6012 | N612GD | | |
| 6013 | N613GD | | |
| 6014 | N614GD | | |
| 6015 | N615GD | | |
| 6016 | | | |
| 6017 | | | |
| 6018 | | | |
| 6019 | | | |
| 6020 | | | |
| 6021 | | | |
| 6022 | | | |
| 6023 | | | |
| 6024 | | | |
| 6025 | | | |
| 6026 | | | |
| 6027 | | | |
| 6028 | | | |
| 6029 | | | |
| 6030 | | | |
| 6031 | | | |
| 6032 | | | |
| 6033 | | | |
| 6034 | | | |
| 6035 | | | |
| 6036 | | | |
| 6037 | | | |
| 6038 | | | |
| 6039 | | | |
| 6040 | | | |
| 6041 | | | |
| 6042 | | | |
| 6043 | | | |
| 6044 | | | |
| 6045 | | | |
| 6046 | | | |
| 6047 | | | |
| 6048 | | | |
| 6049 | | | |
| 6050 | | | |

# IAI 1125 ASTRA/GULFSTREAM 100

Note: The SPX has model number 1125A

| C/n | Series | Identities | | | | | | | | |
|---|---|---|---|---|---|---|---|---|---|---|
| 001 | | 4X-WIN | [ff 19Mar84; wfu Aug86] | | | | | | | |
| 002 | | 4X-WIA | | | | | | | | |
| 003 | | [non-flying test airframe] | | | | | | | | |
| 004 | | 4X-CUA | N96PC | "N425TS" | N96PC | N425TS | OB-1703 | | | |
| 005 | | ) | | | | | | | | |
| 006 | | ) | | | | | | | | |
| 007 | | ) [Aircraft not built as the owner of the first aircraft to be delivered specified that he did | | | | | | | | |
| 008 | | ) not want one of the first ten aircraft being built!] | | | | | | | | |
| 009 | | ) | | | | | | | | |
| 010 | | ) | | | | | | | | |
| 011 | | 4X-CUK | N450PM | N450BM | N705MA | N991RV | N500FA | | | |
| 012 | | 4X-CUL | N1125A | N25AG | N312W | N27BH | N610HC | N618HC | N939MC | |
| 013 | | 4X-CUM | (N413SC) | N713SC | N112PR | | | | | |
| 014 | | 4X-CUN | N400J | N400JF | N8484P | N116JC | | | | |
| 015 | | 4X-CUP | N887PC | N46UF | N46UP | N14SR | N755PA | N157GA | | |
| 016 | | 4X-CUK | N716W | N36FD | N221DT | N221PA | | | | |
| 017 | | 4X-CUD | N717WW | VR-BES | N996JP | N711JG | N711JQ | N455SH | (N800JS) | |
| 018 | | 4X-CUR | N1188A | N500M | N500MQ | N72FL | N72EL | | | |
| 019 | | 4X-CUE | N30AJ | N49MW | (N499MW) | N49MN | | | | |
| 020 | | 4X-CUS | N279DP | N212LD | N917SC | N15BA | | | | |
| 021 | | 4X-CUR | N1125A | N1125S | N1125 | N200CK | | | | |
| 022 | | 4X-CUT | PT-MBZ | | | | | | | |
| 023 | | 4X-CUG | N125GB | N23TJ | N345GC | | | | | |
| 024 | | 4X-CUT | N300JJ | N999BL | | | | | | |
| 025 | | 4X-CUH | N387PA | N887PA | N902AU | | | | | |
| 026 | | 4X-CUI | N120BJ | N120WH | N120WS | N9VL | N24PR | | | |
| 027 | | 4X-CUJ | N199GH | N199HF | N199HE | | | | | |
| 028 | | N10MZ | N11MZ | N816HB | N800ZZ | | | | | |
| 029 | | N79AD | N15TW | N94TW | N154DD | N131DA | N956PP | N959PP | | |
| 030 | | 4X-CUI | N50AJ | N90U | N90UG | N902G | N900DL | | | |
| 031 | | N40AJ | N125AJ | N987GK | N987G | N962A | | | | |
| 032 | | 4X-CUN | N1125A | N232S | N125MG | N116PB | | | | |
| 033 | | 4X-CUP | N980ML | N922RA | N52KS | N441BC | | | | |
| 034 | | 4X-CUJ | N53SF | VR-CMG | N511WA | N541RL | | | | |
| 035 | | N1125K | | | | | | | | |
| 036 | | I-FLYL | N82RT | N195FC | N230AJ | N757BD | | | | |
| 037 | | N3PC | N589TB | N100SR | | | | | | |
| 038 | | N803JW | N930SC | N930UC | N777AM | | | | | |
| 039 | | N359V | N359VP | N359VS | N402TS | N885CA | XA-JRM | N636BC | | |
| 040 | | N279DS | N666K | N666KL* | | | | | | |
| 041 | SP | N96AR | VR-BME | N45MS | N41AU | (N29UC) | | | | |
| 042 | SP | N60AJ | N575ET | N575EW | EC-339 | EC-GIA | N588R | N528RR | | |
| 043 | SP | N56AG | (N34CE) | N90CE | N1M | N43MH | | | | |
| 044 | SP | N50AJ | N676TC | N844GA | N1UA | | | | | |
| 045 | SP | N91FD | VH-FIS | D-CFIS | VH-FIS | N880CH | N916BG | N916CG | | |
| 046 | SP | N140DR | N630S | | | | | | | |
| 047 | SP | N30AJ | (N134RV) | N166RM | | | | | | |
| 048 | SP | N1125V | N88MF | | | | | | | |
| 049 | SP | N1125Y | JA8379 | N4420E | N145AS | N323P | (N1M) | N293P | | |
| 050 | SP | N4EM | XA-TJF | N501JT | N45H | | | | | |
| 051 | SP | N1125A | | | | | | | | |
| 052 | SP | N90AJ | | | | | | | | |
| 053 | SP | N227N | N227NL | (N315S) | N853SP | N121SG | N717CP | N419WC | | |
| 054 | SP | N70AJ | N198HF | N187HF | N770FF | | | | | |
| 055 | SP | 4X-CUI | N1125Z | N1MC | N828C | N880CA | VP-CDR | N120GA | ZS-MDA | N111EL |
| 056 | SP | 4X-CUG | N3175T | N790FH | | | | | | |
| 057 | SP | 4X-CUH | N3175S | YV-2199P | YV-785CP | YV-2564P | YV-785CP | N157SP | YV.... | |
| 058 | SP | N1125E | C-FDAX | | | | | | | |
| 059 | SP/100 | N4341S | D-CCAT | HB-VNF | LX-GOL | D-CABB | [rebranded as Gulfstream 100 - but has no winglets!] | | | |
| 060 | SP | N227AN | YV-757CP | VR-BON | VP-BON | | | | | |
| 061 | SP | 4X-CUG | N60AJ | N550M | N200ST | | | | | |
| 062 | SP | 4X-CUJ | N1125 | N999GP | N9990P | N100AK | N262SP | N866G | N866Q | N874WD |
| 063 | SP | 4X-CUI | Eritrea 901 | | N74TJ | N331SK | (N60RV) | | | |
| 064 | SP | 4X-CUG | N650GE | N650GF | | | | | | |
| 065 | SP | 4X-CUJ | N75TT | N50TG | N50TQ | | | | | |
| 066 | SP | N101NS | N419MK | C-FMHL | | | | | | |
| 067 | SP | N20FE | N28NP | (N28NR) | N28NF | N267SP | N467MW | N46386 | N730DF | |
| 068 | SP | N1125Z | N401WT | | | | | | | |
| 069 | SP | N804JW | N247PS | | | | | | | |
| 070 | SP/100 | N300AJ | N805JW | N100GA | (N100GQ) | N448GR | (N149LP) | [rebranded as Gulfstream 100 - but has no winglets!] | | |
| 071 | SP | 4X-CUW | N60AJ | N71FS | | | | | | |
| 072 | SP | N1125L | N314AD | N32TM | N365GA | | | | | |

# ASTRA/GULFSTREAM 100

| C/n | Series | Identities | | | | | | | |
|---|---|---|---|---|---|---|---|---|---|
| 073 | SPX | 4X-WIX | [first model SPX] | N173W | N918MJ | N24ZD | | | |
| 074 | SP | N500AJ | N789CA | | | | | | |
| 075 | SP | 4X-CUW | ZS-BCT | N75GZ | (N175SP) | N225AL | N928JA | | |
| 076 | SP | 4X-CUV | N1125 | 4X-CUV | N1125 | N1125G | N699MC | N699MQ | N20YL |
| 077 | SP | N220AJ | N771CP | YV-771CP | YV1771 | | | | |
| 078 | SP | N1125J | | | | | | | |
| 079 | SPX | 4X-CUX | C-FCFP | N800PW | | | | | |
| 080 | SPX | 4X-CUY | (D-CCBT) | N333AJ | N333CZ | VP-CUT | C-GSSS | N411MM | |
| 081 | SPX | N800AJ | N801G | | | | | | |
| 082 | SPX | N121GV | N882GA | | | | | | |
| 083 | SPX | N383SF | | | | | | | |
| 084 | SPX | N795HP | N795HB | N801RS | | | | | |
| 085 | SPX | N796HP | N796HR | | | | | | |
| 086 | SPX | N793A | PT-WBC | | | | | | |
| 087 | SPX | 4X-CUU | C-FRJZ | | | | | | |
| 088 | C-38A | N398AG | USAF 94-1569 | | | | | | |
| 089 | SPX | N918MK | N89HS | | | | | | |
| 090 | C-38A | N399AG | USAF 94-1570 | | | | | | |
| 091 | SPX | N297GA | N500MZ | N500M | N91GX | N818WF | | | |
| 092 | SPX | N789A | VP-BMA | N92UJ | N8MC | N8MN | N100G | [crash-landed 14Sep07 Atlanta/ DeKalb-Peachtree, GA; parted out] | |
| 093 | SPX | N65TD | N149TD | N707BC | N207BC | | | | |
| 094 | SPX | N294S | | | | | | | |
| 095 | SPX | N98AD | C6-JET | N98AD | N608DC | | | | |
| 096 | SPX | N66KG | VP-CKG | N96AL | N323P | | | | |
| 097 | SPX | N273RA | N363NH | | | | | | |
| 098 | SPX | N275RA | N98FJ | N919CH | | | | | |
| 099 | SPX | N987A | 5B-CJG | N830DB | N838DB | N115BR | | | |
| 100 | SPX | N807JW | N907DP | | | | | | |
| 101 | SPX | N202GA | N297GA | N711WK | (N291WK) | N610SM | | | |
| 102 | SPX | N525M | N359V | N359D | N877D | | | | |
| 103 | SPX | N755A | | | | | | | |
| 104 | SPX | N957P | (N104GA) | N957F | | | | | |
| 105 | SPX | N217PT | HB-VMG | N105FN | | | | | |
| 106 | SPX | N122GV | N876GA | N800MK | N800WS | | | | |
| 107 | SPX | N997GA | D-CRIS | | | | | | |
| 108 | SPX | N998GA | N999GP | N998GP | N302TS | N108CG | | | |
| 109 | SPX | N96FL | N377AC | | | | | | |
| 110 | SPX | N97FL | N212T | | | | | | |
| 111 | SPX | N848GA | N297GA | OE-GAM | HB-VOA | OY-YAM | | | |
| 112 | SPX | N633GA | N1MC | N61JE | | | | | |
| 113 | SPX | N113GA | HB-VMK | N35GX | (N297GA) | N82BE | | | |
| 114 | SPX | N114GA | N114SN | | | | | | |
| 115 | SPX | N526GA | HB-VMR | C-GRGE | OE-GPG | N514MM | | | |
| 116 | SPX | N527GA | N456PR | N12ND | N125GR | | | | |
| 117 | SPX | N528GA | C-FTDB | C-GGHZ | | | | | |
| 118 | SPX | N529GA | N28NP | | | | | | |
| 119 | SPX | 4X-CUZ | B-20001 | | | | | | |
| 120 | SPX | N635GA | N770UP | C-GPDA | N100GY | | | | |
| 121 | SPX | N843GA | N100AK | N188AK | | | | | |
| 122 | SPX | N69GX | (N297GA) | N419TK | N110MG | | | | |
| 123 | SPX | 4X-CVJ | N36GX | "C-GWST" | VH-WSM | N36GX | N307JW | | |
| 124 | SPX | 4X-CVE | N42GX | N777FL | N777FZ | | | | |
| 125 | SPX | 4X-CVG | N44GX | N248SL | N248BL | N625MM | N625BE | | |
| 126 | SPX | 4X-CVJ | India L3458 | | | | | | |
| 127 | SPX | 4X-CVG | N621KD | N327GA | N247PS | N919DS | | | |
| 128 | SPX | 4X-CVF | N45GX | N179DC | N676TC | N314AD | | | |
| 129 | SPX | 4X-CVG | N52GX | N424MP | | | | | |
| 130 | SPX | 4X-CVI | N55GX | N297GA | N100GA | C-GBSW | | | |
| 131 | SPX | 4X-CVG | N57GX | N400CP | | | | | |
| 132 | SPX | 4X-CVI | N1125V | N775DF | N722AZ | | | | |
| 133 | SPX | 4X-CVG | N65GX | VP-CAR | D-CGMA | OE-GBD | | | |
| 134 | SPX | 4X-CVG | N64GX | N1125S | | | | | |
| 135 | SPX | 4X-CVI | N58GX | N809JW | | | | | |
| 136 | SPX | 4X-CVG | N68GX | N43RJ | (N32UC) | | | | |
| 137 | SPX | 4X-CVI | N75GX | N620KE | | | | | |
| 138 | SPX | 4X-CVG | N80GX | N810JW | | | | | |
| 139 | 100 | 4X-CVI | N99GX | N100GA | N420CE | | | | |
| 140 | SPX | 4X-CVK | N104GX | N811JW | | | | | |
| 141 | SPX | 4X-CVI | N106GX | CC-CWK | N223GA | M-YEDT | | | |
| 142 | 100 | 4X-CVK | N109GX | | | | | | |
| 143 | SPX | 4X-CVH | N261GA | VT-BAV | | | | | |
| 144 | SPX | 4X-CVK | N262GA | VP-BMT | | | | | |
| 145 | SPX | 4X-CVK | N264GA | N387PA | N3FD | | | | |
| 146 | 100 | 4X-CVI | N646GA | VP-BMW | N853M | C-GTLG | | | |
| 147 | 100 | 4X-CVF | N647GA | N147SW | | | | | |

# ASTRA/GULFSTREAM 100

| C/n | Series | Identities | | | | | |
|---|---|---|---|---|---|---|---|
| 148 | 100 | 4X-CVI | N648GA | 4X-CVI | India L3467 | | |
| 149 | 100 | N749GA | | | | | |
| 150 | 100 | 4X-CVK | N750GA | C-FHRL | | | |
| 151 | 100 | 4X-CVG | N751GA | C-GTDO | | | |
| 152 | 100 | 4X-CVE | N352GA | N150CT | N160CT | | |
| 153 | 100 | 4X-CVJ | N353GA | OE-GBE | N133SN | N100AK | |
| 154 | 100 | N354GA | N221AL | XA-MEG | | | |
| 155 | 100 | 4X-CVJ | N445AK | | | | |
| 156 | 100 | N996GA | C-FHNS | | | | |
| 157 | 100 | 4X-CVK | N327GA | | | | |
| 158 | 100 | 4X-CVJ | N995GA | EC-JXE | ZS-SFY | EC-JXE | EC-LDS |

Production complete

Note: Most, if not all, aircraft were first test flown with 4X- marks - only those known are shown above.
The Astra his been replaced by the Gulfstream 150 which has the same wingset, engines and tail unit of the old model, but has a larger cabin and re-designed nose. Type given FAA type certificate 07Nov05

# IAI GULFSTREAM 150

| C/n | Identities | | | | |
|---|---|---|---|---|---|
| 201 | 4X-TRA | [rolled out at Tel Aviv 18Jan05; ff 05May05] | | | N150RT |
| 202 | 4X-WID | [ff 2.9.05] | N150GA | N703HA | |
| 203 | 4X-CVK | N528GA | N530GP | | |
| 204 | 4X-WID | N373ML | | | |
| 205 | 4X-CVK | N405GA | N715WG | N301SG | |
| 206 | 4X-WID | N806GA | N830DB | | |
| 207 | N807GA | N531GP | | | |
| 208 | N208GA | N150CT | | | |
| 209 | 4X-CVK | N409GA | N501RP | | |
| 210 | 4X-WID | N510GA | N650GE | | |
| 211 | 4X-CVK | N757GA | N248SL | | |
| 212 | 4X-WID | N412GA | N502RP | | |
| 213 | 4X-CVK | N613GA | N595OC | | |
| 214 | 4X-WID | N314GA | N777FL | | |
| 215 | 4X-CVK | N615GA | N503RP | | |
| 216 | 4X-WID | N216GA | N192SW | | |
| 217 | 4X-CVK | N217GA | N150GD | N217MS | |
| 218 | 4X-WID | N218GA | N969WR | | |
| 219 | 4X-CVL | N219GA | CC-CWK | | |
| 220 | 4X-CVM | N220GA | N197HF | | |
| 221 | 4X-WID | N532GP | | | |
| 222 | 4X-CVL | N422GA | N717EP | | |
| 223 | 4X-CVK | N350BN | | | |
| 224 | 4X-CVM | N424GA | N590FA | | |
| 225 | 4X-WID | N399GA | N150PU | | |
| 226 | N8821C | | | | |
| 227 | 4X-CVK | N451R | | | |
| 228 | 4X-CVM | N628GA | VP-BMA | | |
| 229 | 4X-WID | N8841C | | | |
| 230 | 4X-CVK | N630GA | N722SW | | |
| 231 | 4X-CVL | N9611Z | N787BN | | |
| 232 | 4X-CVM | N928ST | | | |
| 233 | 4X-WID | N633GA | EC-KMF | | |
| 234 | 4X-CVK | N511CT | | | |
| 235 | 4X-CVL | N635GA | D-CKDM | | |
| 236 | 4X-TRA | N77709 | | | |
| 237 | 4X-CVM | N537GA | EC-KMS | | |
| 238 | 4X-WID | N150GA | N222LR | | |
| 239 | 4X-CVK | N639GA | AP-MMM | | |
| 240 | 4X-TRA | N360AV | | | |
| 241 | 4X-CVL | N631GA | N480JJ | | |
| 242 | 4X-CVM | N442GA | UR-KAS | OE-GAS | |
| 243 | 4X-WID | N443GA | EC-KPJ | | |
| 244 | 4X-CVK | N744GA | N950N | N302SG | |
| 245 | 4X-TRA | N745GA | OE-GSK | | |
| 246 | 4X-CVL | N96AD | | | |
| 247 | 4X-CVM | N110FS | | | |
| 248 | 4X-WID | N637SF | | | |
| 249 | 4X-CVK | N191CP | N67KP | | |
| 250 | 4X-TRA | N850GA | N918MJ | | |
| 251 | 4X-CVL | N351GA | N22ST | | |
| 252 | 4X-CVK | N352GA | N769MS | | |
| 253 | 4X-WID | N353GA | EC-KTV | | |
| 254 | 4X-CVM | N354GA | EC-KTK | | |
| 255 | 4X-TRA | N556GA | XA-PAZ | | |
| 256 | 4X-CVL | N262GA | N150GD | | |
| 257 | 4X-WID | N457GA | XA-ADR | | |
| 258 | 4X-CVK | N458GA | N10RZ | | |
| 259 | 4X-CVM | N746GA | RP-C5168 | | |
| 260 | 4X-TRA | N260GA | N802RR | N150GV | |
| 261 | 4X-CVL | N261GA | OE-GLF | | |
| 262 | 4X-WID | N272CB | | | |
| 263 | 4X-CVK | N263GA | (N150GV) | N802RR | |
| 264 | 4X-CVM | N264GA | C-GXNW | | |
| 265 | 4X-CVL | N465GA | N993AC | | |
| 266 | 4X-WID | N888YC | | | |
| 267 | 4X-TRA | N367GA | N119KW | | |
| 268 | 4X-CVK | N268GA | (D-CKDN) | N365SC | |
| 269 | 4X-CVM | N469GA | (D-CKDO) | N520CH | |
| 270 | 4X-CVL | N470GA | (D-CKDP) | N110JJ | |
| 271 | N471GA | C-FTRP | | | |
| 272 | N372GA | N399SC | | | |
| 273 | 4X-CVK | N373GA | C-GZCZ | | |
| 274 | 4X-CVM | N374GA | N1FC | | |
| 275 | 4X-WID | N375GA | N116HW | | |
| 276 | 4X-CVL | N46WY | | | |

# GULFSTREAM 150

| C/n | Identities | | |
|---|---|---|---|
| 277 | 4X-CVK | N7FF | N1FS |
| 278 | 4X-TRA | N700FA | |
| 279 | 4X-CVM | N489GA | N935SS |
| 280 | 4X-WID | N980GA | VP-CEP |
| 281 | 4X-CVK | N631GA | N372AS |
| 282 | N382GA | | |
| 283 | 4X-CVL | N683GA | |
| 284 | 4X-WID | N484GA | |
| 285 | 4X-CVM | N485GA | |
| 286 | 4X-CVK | N486GA | |
| 287 | N487GA | | |
| 288 | N208GA | | |
| 289 | | | |
| 290 | | | |
| 291 | | | |
| 292 | | | |
| 293 | | | |
| 294 | | | |
| 295 | | | |
| 296 | | | |
| 297 | | | |
| 298 | | | |
| 299 | | | |
| 300 | | | |

# IAI 1126 GALAXY/GULFSTREAM 200

Note: Some Galaxys have been re-branded as Gulfstream 200s, as shown

| C/n | Series | Identities | | | | | | | | |
|---|---|---|---|---|---|---|---|---|---|---|
| 001 | | [reportedly non-flying test airframe] | | | | | | | | |
| 002 | | [reportedly non-flying test airframe] | | | | | | | | |
| 003 | | 4X-IGA | [rolled out 04Sep97; ff 25Dec97] | | | | | | | |
| 004 | 200 | 4X-IGO | 4X-CVF [not confirmed] | (N7AU) | N844GA | N711JG | (N711JU) | (N711JQ) | | |
| | | VP-CHW | N789AT | PR-WTR | | | | | | |
| 005 | 200 | 4X-IGB | N505GA | | | | | | | |
| 006 | | N7AU | N81TT | N8MF | | | | | | |
| 007 | | N847GA | (C-GRJZ) | HB-IUT | | | | | | |
| 008 | | N998G | (N288GA) | VP-CRS | N479PR | | | | | |
| 009 | 200 | N849GA | N83EJ | N200AX | | | | | | |
| 010 | | N808JW | N121LS | N672PS | | | | | | |
| 011 | | N634GA | HB-IUU | N634GA | "HB-IGA" | HB-IUU | N56AG | (N223AM) | LZ-FIB | |
| 012 | | 4X-CVE | "N1TA" | N845GA | (HB-IGK) | YR-TIG | | | | |
| 013 | 200 | 4X-CVG | N13GX | N200GA | "XA-MAK" | N200GA | (N13GX) | XA-MAK | N160HA | HB-IGP |
| | | N200BH | | | | | | | | |
| 014 | 200 | N37GX | N121GV | N121GX | N467MW | | | | | |
| 015 | | 4X-CVI | N38GX | N622SV | | | | | | |
| 016 | | 4X-CVK | N40GX | N35BP | N135BP | N35BP | | | | |
| 017 | | 4X-CVF | N48GX | (N406LM)+ | [+marks worn but ntu] | | | | | |
| 018 | 200 | 4X-CVH | N47GX | N18GZ | 4X-COG | | | | | |
| 019 | | 4X-CVK | N39GX | N407LM | N219GA | N219AX | | | | |
| 020 | | 4X-CVI | N46GX | N516CC | | | | | | |
| 021 | | 4X-CVF | N321SF | (N41GX) | N321SF | | | | | |
| 022 | 200 | 4X-CVE | N43GX | N414KD | N414KB | N200AX | N322AD | | | |
| 023 | 200 | 4X-CVH | N50GX | N414DH | N414DK | N32TM | (N32JN) | | | |
| 024 | | 4X-CVI | N101L | N101LD | N188ML | N818CR | | | | |
| 025 | | 4X-CVK | N54GX | N2HL | N263GA | N302MC | N866G | | | |
| 026 | | 4X-CVE | N56GX | N800PJ | | | | | | |
| 027 | | 4X-CVF | N878CS | PR-OFT | | | | | | |
| 028 | 200 | 4X-CVH | N60GX | N199HF | | | | | | |
| 029 | | 4X-CVK | N61GX | VP-BLH | VP-CAS | D-BAIR | N929GA | | | |
| 030 | 200 | 4X-CVF | N303MC | B-HWB | N133BA | B-8086 | | | | |
| 031 | | 4X-CVH | N62GX | | | | | | | |
| 032 | 200 | 4X-CVE | N66GX | N406LM | HB-JEB | | | | | |
| 033 | | 4X-CVK | N31SJ | N212MP | | | | | | |
| 034 | 200 | 4X-CVF | N34GX | (N200GA) | N134AX | N274JC | | | | |
| 035 | 200 | 4X-CVH | N59GX | N110HA | | | | | | |
| 036 | | 4X-CVK | N67GX | N144KK | N408LM | N408LN | B-KSJ | | | |
| 037 | 200 | 4X-CVH | N337JD | N204AB | B-8083 | | | | | |
| 038 | | 4X-CVE | N168EC | N602VC | N858DN | | | | | |
| 039 | | 4X-CVE | N72RK | N132JC | (N302HM) | | | | | |
| 040 | | 4X-CVH | N90GX | 4X-CLL | | | | | | |
| 041 | | 4X-CVE | N101GX | YV-772CP | YV1401 | | | | | |
| 042 | | 4X-CVF | N102GX | N701HB | N755PA | | | | | |
| 043 | | 4X-CVH | N103GX | N122GV | N123GV | | | | | |
| 044 | | 4X-CVE | N105GX | N621KD | N621KB | N882LT | | | | |
| 045 | | 4X-CVF | N107GX | N70TT | | | | | | |
| 046 | | 4X-CVH | N108GX | PR-MEN | N889G | | | | | |
| 047 | 200 | 4X-CVF | N110GX | N601AB | N721CJ | | | | | |
| 048 | 200 | 4X-CVE | N112GX | N602AB | | | | | | |
| 049 | 200 | 4X-CVH | N290GA | N751BC | N753BC | B-8090 | B-LUX | | | |
| 050 | 200 | 4X-CVE | N291GA | N789RR | N789PR | OE-HFC | | | | |
| 051 | | 4X-CVF | N293GA | OY-RAK | LN-SUS | N140KR | B-8089 | | | |
| 052 | | 4X-CVG | N294GA | N700QS | | | | | | |
| 053 | 200 | 4X-CVE | N295GA | (N601AV) | N815JW | | | | | |
| 054 | 200 | 4X-CVI | N296GA | N200GA | N54AX | N272JC | | | | |
| 055 | | 4X-CVF | N255JT | N885AR | N885RR | N212SL | | | | |
| 056 | | 4X-CVE | N298GA | N929WG | | | | | | |
| 057 | 200 | 4X-CVG | N299GA | N886G | | | | | | |
| 058 | 200 | 4X-CVI | N360GA | (N702QS)+ | [+marks worn but ntu] | N272MW | N726DC | | | |
| 059 | 200 | 4X-CVE | N361GA | (N602AV) | N409LM | | | | | |
| 060 | 200 | N270GA | N703QS | | | | | | | |
| 061 | 200 | N271GA | N705QS | | | | | | | |
| 062 | 200 | N362GA | N957P | | | | | | | |
| 063 | 200 | N363GA | N20PL | N363GA | N20PL | N363GA | SX-IFB | | | |
| 064 | 200 | N364GA | (N706QS) | N2BG | | | | | | |
| 065 | 200 | N275GA | (N628RC) | N118KA | (SX-MAD) | SX-ONE | OE-HSG | | | |
| 066 | 200 | N276GA | N707QS | | | | | | | |
| 067 | 200 | 4X-CVK | N367GA | N916GR | N916GB | | | | | |
| 068 | 200 | 4X-CVE | N368GA | N179AE | | | | | | |
| 069 | 200 | 4X-CVF | N279GA | N708QS | | | | | | |
| 070 | 200 | 4X-CVG | N268GA | N702QS | | | | | | |
| 071 | 200 | 4X-CVH | N371GA | (N706QS) | N459BN | N458BN | | | | |

# GALAXY/GULFSTREAM 200

| C/n | Series | Identities | | | | | |
|---|---|---|---|---|---|---|---|
| 072 | 200 | 4X-CVK | N272GA | N65R | N679RW | N892SB | |
| 073 | 200 | 4X-CVF | N673GA | N712QS | | | |
| 074 | 200 | 4X-CVJ | N274GA | N80R | N889MR | | |
| 075 | 200 | 4X-CVG | N875GA | N200YB | N365CX | | |
| 076 | 200 | 4X-CVK | N376GA | N200BA | | | |
| 077 | 200 | 4X-CVH | N277GA | VT-PLA | | | |
| 078 | 200 | 4X-CVJ | N278GA | (HB-IUS) | | | |
| 079 | 200 | 4X-CVE | N379GA | N382G | | | |
| 080 | 200 | 4X-CVK | N380GA | XA-MDK | | | |
| 081 | 200 | 4X-CVG | N881GA | N414DH | N86CW | | |
| 082 | 200 | 4X-CVJ | N282GA | N402LM | | | |
| 083 | 200 | N283GA | N403LM | | | | |
| 084 | 200 | N284GA | N414KD | N1Z | | | |
| 085 | 200 | 4X-CVJ | N285GA | N720QS | | | |
| 086 | 200 | 4X-CVH | N286GA | XA-JHE | | | |
| 087 | 200 | 4X-CVE | N287GA | (N747SG) | N707SG | | |
| 088 | 200 | 4X-CVJ | N388GA | (N721QS) | N200GA | N704JW | N179JA |
| 089 | 200 | 4X-CVH | N289GA | OE-HTI | YR-TII | | |
| 090 | 200 | 4X-CVK | N790GA | B-KMJ | | | |
| 091 | 200 | 4X-CVJ | N391GA | N2HL | (N19HL) | | |
| 092 | 200 | 4X-CVH | N492GA | N721QS | | | |
| 093 | 200 | 4X-CVK | N393GA | N722QS | | | |
| 094 | 200 | 4X-CVI | N394GA | N121GV | | | |
| 095 | 200 | 4X-CVF | N595GA | N331BN | N311MK | | |
| 096 | 200 | 4X-CVG | N196GA | N600YB | | | |
| 097 | 200 | 4X-CVI | N397GA | N816JW | | | |
| 098 | 200 | 4X-CVK | N398GA | ZS-PKD | VT-ARV | | |
| 099 | 200 | 4X-CVF | N499GA | N723QS | | | |
| 100 | 200 | 4X-CVI | N500GA | N724QS | | | |
| 101 | 200 | 4X-CVJ | N201GA | | | | |
| 102 | 200 | 4X-CVK | N702GA | N601DV | OE-HAZ | | |
| 103 | 200 | 4X-CVH | N203GA | EC-JGN | | | |
| 104 | 200 | 4X-CVI | N104GA | N271RA | | | |
| 105 | 200 | 4X-CVJ | N305GA | N725QS | | | |
| 106 | 200 | 4X-CVG | N606GA | "N200GA"+ | [+ marks worn in NBAA static display at Orlando Executive, FL, Nov05] | N851LE | N2G |
| 107 | 200 | 4X-CVF | N107GA | N707BC | | | |
| 108 | 200 | 4X-CVI | N508GA | N726QS | | | |
| 109 | 200 | 4X-CVE | N409GA | N819AP | N819VE | | |
| 110 | 200 | 4X-CVG | N510GA | N721BS | N221BS | N967PC | |
| 111 | 200 | 4X-CVH | N995GA | N88WU | | | |
| 112 | 200 | 4X-CVI | N112GA | C-GTRL | | | |
| 113 | 200 | 4X-CVK | N413GA | N727QS | | | |
| 114 | 200 | 4X-CVE | N214GA | B-LSJ | N833BA | B-8085 | |
| 115 | 200 | 4X-CVF | N615GA | N200LV | | | |
| 116 | 200 | 4X-CVH | N216GA | N728QS | | | |
| 117 | 200 | N217GA | N62GB | N162GB | | | |
| 118 | 200 | 4X-CVJ | N118GA | N729QS | | | |
| 119 | 200 | 4X-CVI | N419GA | C-GWPB | | | |
| 120 | 200 | 4X-CVE | N220GA | N730QS | | | |
| 121 | 200 | 4X-CVH | N818JW | | | | |
| 122 | 200 | 4X-CVG | N422GA | N200GA | N173JM | | |
| 123 | 200 | 4X-CVJ | N223GA | N731QS | | | |
| 124 | 200 | 4X-CVF | N765M | | | | |
| 125 | 200 | 4X-CVI | N221GA | EC-JQE | | | |
| 126 | 200 | 4X-CVG | N126GA | N916GR | | | |
| 127 | 200 | 4X-CVH | N424GA | N737QS | | | |
| 128 | 200 | 4X-CVE | N102FD | | | | |
| 129 | 200 | 4X-CVF | N229GA | N711QS | | | |
| 130 | 200 | 4X-CVG | N330GA | N565GB | | | |
| 131 | 200 | 4X-CVH | N771GA | N706QS | | | |
| 132 | 200 | 4X-CVI | N732GA | N751BC | | | |
| 133 | 200 | 4X-CVE | N433GA | N200GX | (N202GJ) | N200VR | |
| 134 | 200 | 4X-CVJ | N434GA | N88AY | | | |
| 135 | 200 | 4X-CVG | N435GA | B-8081 | | | |
| 136 | 200 | 4X-CVF | N436GA | N718QS | | | |
| 137 | 200 | 4X-CVH | N137WB | | | | |
| 138 | 200 | N787PR | | | | | |
| 139 | 200 | 4X-CVJ | N139GA | N204DD | | | |
| 140 | 200 | N640GA | PR-AUR | | | | |
| 141 | 200 | 4X-CVG | N641GA | N701QS | | | |
| 142 | 200 | N842GA | N235LC | SX-IRP | | | |
| 143 | 200 | 4X-CVH | N143GA | (N81TT) | | | |
| 144 | 200 | 4X-CVI | N217BA | | | | |
| 145 | 200 | 4X-CVJ | N645GA | EC-KBC | | | |
| 146 | 200 | 4X-CVE | N138GA | N602RF | | | |

## GALAXY/GULFSTREAM 200

| C/n | Series | Identities | | | | |
|---|---|---|---|---|---|---|
| 147 | 200 | 4X-CVF | N603RF | | | |
| 148 | 200 | 4X-CVG | N844GA | N716QS | | |
| 149 | 200 | 4X-CVH | N404GA | (SX-IFB) | SX-IDA | |
| 150 | 200 | 4X-CVI | N698GA | EC-KCA | | |
| 151 | 200 | 4X-CVJ | N651GA | N200GA | N619KS | |
| 152 | 200 | 4X-CVE | N152GA | N752QS | | |
| 153 | 200 | 4X-CVF | N653GA | B-LMJ | | |
| 154 | 200 | 4X-CVG | N236LC | | | |
| 155 | 200 | 4X-CVH | N136FT | N135FT | | |
| 156 | 200 | 4X-CVI | N656GA | N101L | | |
| 157 | 200 | 4X-CVJ | N557GA | N748QS | | |
| 158 | 200 | 4X-CVE | N658GA | ZK-RGB | | |
| 159 | 200 | 4X-CVF | N559GA | (VP-CSG) | SX-SMG | M-MSGG |
| 160 | 200 | 4X-CVG | N670RW | | | |
| 161 | 200 | 4X-CVH | (N361GA) | N49VC | N80GK | |
| 162 | 200 | 4X-CVI | N562GA | N719QS | | |
| 163 | 200 | 4X-CVJ | N360GA | N35BP | SX-SEA | |
| 164 | 200 | N164GA | N200JB | | | |
| 165 | 200 | 4X-CVE | N565GA | N749QS | | |
| 166 | 200 | 4X-CVG | N566GA | N631DV | | |
| 167 | 200 | 4X-CVH | N367GA | N200GV | N178TM | |
| 168 | 200 | 4X-CVI | N368GA | N755QS | | |
| 169 | 200 | 4X-CVF | N10XQ | | | |
| 170 | 200 | 4X-CVJ | N370GA | N745QS | | |
| 171 | 200 | 4X-CVE | N671GA | EC-KLL | | |
| 172 | 200 | 4X-CVG | N672GA | N172EX | | |
| 173 | 200 | 4X-CVI | N403GA | N200GA | | |
| 174 | 200 | 4X-CVH | N674GA | B-8087 | | |
| 175 | 200 | 4X-CVF | N675GA | N62GB | N148MC | |
| 176 | 200 | 4X-CVJ | N276GA | N761QS | | |
| 177 | 200 | 4X-CVE | N677GA | EC-KOR | | |
| 178 | 200 | 4X-CVG | N678GA | N758QS | | |
| 179 | 200 | 4X-CVM | N479GA | N797M | | |
| 180 | 200 | 4X-CVF | N480GA | EC-KPF | | |
| 181 | 200 | 4X-CVJ | N461GA | N929WC | | |
| 182 | 200 | 4X-CVE | N482GA | N282CM | | |
| 183 | 200 | 4X-CVG | N636GA | EC-KPL | | |
| 184 | 200 | 4X-CVF | N384GA | HB-JKG | | |
| 185 | 200 | 4X-CVH | N285GA | N750QS | | |
| 186 | 200 | 4X-CVJ | N486GA | N715WG | | |
| 187 | 200 | N387GA | VP-BPH | | | |
| 188 | 200 | 4X-CVG | N388GA | EC-KRN | | |
| 189 | 200 | 4X-CVF | N289GA | 4K-AZ88 | | |
| 190 | 200 | 4X-CVH | N590GA | N369JK | | |
| 191 | 200 | 4X-CVJ | N391GA | N819AP | | |
| 192 | 200 | 4X-CVE | N692GA | N501DV | | |
| 193 | 200 | 4X-CVG | N493GA | HB-JGL | | |
| 194 | 200 | 4X-CVI | N494GA | N740QS | | |
| 195 | 200 | 4X-CVF | N595GA | N459BN | | |
| 196 | 200 | 4X-CVH | N696GA | N988KD | | |
| 197 | 200 | 4X-CVJ | N116FE | | | |
| 198 | 200 | [4X-CVE or 4X-CVI] | | N398GA | N739QS | |
| 199 | 200 | 4X-CVG | N139GA | LX-LAI | | |
| 200 | 200 | 4X-CVI | N910GA | P4-ADD | | |
| 201 | 200 | 4X-CVF | N901GA | N332TM | | |
| 202 | 200 | 4X-CVH | N682GA | | | |
| 203 | 200 | 4X-CVE | N683GA | N98SP | | |
| 204 | 200 | 4X-CVG | N804GA | N738QS | | |
| 205 | 200 | 4X-CVJ | N805GA | M-OSPB | | |
| 206 | 200 | 4X-CVI | N306GA | OE-HAS | | |
| 207 | 200 | 4X-CVE | N307GA | SX-MAJ | | |
| 208 | 200 | 4X-CVF | N94FT | | | |
| 209 | 200 | 4X-CVH | N809GA | N90FT | | |
| 210 | 200 | 4X-CVG | N510GA | N333SZ | B-LSS | |
| 211 | 200 | N378GA | N184TB | | | |
| 212 | 200 | 4X-CVJ | N612GA | N741QS | N612GA | N104SG |
| 213 | 200 | 4X-CVE | N379GA | VT-JUM | | |
| 214 | 200 | 4X-CVF | N614GA | | | |
| 215 | 200 | 4X-CVH | N715GA | SX-TAJ | | |
| 216 | 200 | 4X-CVG | N616GA | N743QS | | |
| 217 | 200 | 4X-CVI | N417GA | N168RR | | |
| 218 | 200 | 4X-CVJ | N618GA | PR-BBD | | |
| 219 | 200 | 4X-CVE | N619GA | EC-LAE | | |
| 220 | 200 | 4X-CVF | N420GA | VQ-BDS | | |
| 221 | 200 | 4X-CVH | N381GA | N200BN | | |
| 222 | 200 | 4X-CVG | N722GA | EC-LBB | | |

## GALAXY/GULFSTREAM 200

| C/n | Series | Identities | | | |
|---|---|---|---|---|---|
| 223 | 200 | 4X-CVJ | N383GA | OE-HSB | |
| 224 | 200 | 4X-CVI | N824GA | M-GZOO | |
| 225 | 200 | 4X-CVE | N385GA | OE-HSN | |
| 226 | 200 | 4X-CVF | N626GA | (N525GF) | N525AG |
| 227 | 200 | 4X-CVG | N627GA | N742QS | N367GA |
| 228 | 200 | 4X-CVH | N928GA | N488RC | |
| 229 | 200 | 4X-CVI | N629GA | B-8120 | |
| 230 | 200 | 4X-CVJ | N630GA | N331BN* | |
| 231 | 200 | 4X-CVG | N631GA | | |
| 232 | 200 | 4X-CVE | N632GA | N262GA | |
| 233 | 200 | N533GA | | | |
| 234 | 200 | N534GA | | | |
| 235 | 200 | N935GA | | | |
| 236 | 200 | N536GA | | | |
| 237 | 200 | N417GA | | | |
| 238 | | | | | |
| 239 | | | | | |
| 240 | | | | | |
| 241 | | | | | |
| 242 | | | | | |
| 243 | | | | | |
| 244 | | | | | |
| 245 | | | | | |
| 246 | | | | | |
| 247 | | | | | |
| 248 | | | | | |
| 249 | | | | | |
| 250 | | | | | |

Note: It is almost certain that all aircraft were first test flown with 4X- marks, but only those known are shown above.

# IAI GULFSTREAM 250

| C/n | Identities | | |
|---|---|---|---|
| 2001 | 4X-WSJ | [rolled out as "N250GA" 06Oct09; ff 11.12.09] | N250GA^ |
| 2002 | 4X-WSM | | |
| 2003 | 4X-WBJ | | |
| 2004 | | | |
| 2005 | | | |

# JET COMMANDER/WESTWIND

| C/n | Series | Identities |
|---|---|---|
| 1 | 1121 | N610JC [ff 27Jan63] N112AC N172AC [dismantled 1975] |
| 2 | 1121 | N611JC [test aircraft for static fatigue] |
| 3 | 1121 | N612J N316 N316E N400WT N409WT |
| 4 | 1121 | N77F N77TC N72TC N72TQ |
| 5 | 1121 | N364G N334RK N18CA C-GKFT N18CA [cx Oct86; b/u Miami, FL mid 1986; remains to Dodson Avn, Ottawa, KS] |
| 6 | 1121 | N5418 CF-ULG N420P N42QB [wfu; cx Dec91; b/u 1982 by White Inds, Bates City, MO] |
| 7 | 1121 | N112JC N1173Z N22CH N30RJ (N711VK) N77KT N77NT [b/u for spares 1989; cx Nov91] |
| 8 | 1121 | N157JF N31CF N749MC N749MP N101LB [wfu 1998 Tucson, AZ; b/u circa Nov00 at Tucson, AZ] |
| 9 | 1121 | N450JD N459JD CF-WUL N9BY N66EW N89MR (N98KK) [wfu cx Jan94 remains to Aviation Warehouse prop facility at El Mirage, CA] |
| 10 | 1121 | N31S N31SB N600CD N5BP N9023W [wfu Jly87 to Bardufoss Videregarude Skole, Norway; TT 5322 hrs as technical airframe - circa 2002 reported b/u] |
| 11 | 1121 | N1172Z N1172L N111TD [parted out at St. Simons Island, GA circa late 03] |
| 12 | 1121 | N8300 N613J N777V N37BB N711GW N302AT N344DA LV-RDD [w/o (details unknown); wreckage noted 14May92 Moron, Argentina] |
| 13 | 1121 | N450RA N50VF N12CJ N1JU (N404PC) XA-SFS [wfu; b/u 1983 by White Inds, Bates City, MO] |
| 14 | 1121 | N350M N121BN N87DC N87DG [b/u remains with White Inds, Bates City, MO; cx Jly94] |
| 15 | 1121 | N365G HB-VAX N125K N320W [wfu; b/u 1983 by White Inds, Bates City, MO; cx Apr91] |
| 16 | 1121 | N96B N217PM N177A YV-123CP [wfu Mar93 Caracas, Venezuela; derelict Feb97] |
| 17 | 1121 | (HB-VAL) CF-SUA C-FSUA N91669 [wfu - still current remains to Aviation Warehouse prop facility at El Mirage CA] |
| 18 | 1121 | N1166Z N121HM [wfu Dec79, to Skolen for Luftfahrtsuddannel, Copenhagen-Kastrup, Denmark; scrapped 2008] |
| 19 | 1121 | N95B [sold May88 in Norway as technical airframe - circa 2002 reported b/u] |
| 20 | 1121 | N334LP N1121E |
| 21 | 1121 | N252R CF-WOA N2579E [wfu; b/u 1983 by White Inds, Bates City, MO; last allocated US marks not worn; cx Mar91] |
| 22 | 1121 | N148E [w/o 13Sep68 Burbank, CA] |
| 23 | 1121 | N2100X N349M [b/u 1983 by White Inds, Bates City, MO] |
| 24 | 1121 | N94B N360M N360MC N7GW N360MC N560MC [wfu 1993] |
| 25 | 1121 | N555DM [to spares 1992 with Dodson Avn, Ottawa, KS; cx Aug92] |
| 26 | 1121 | N614J N614JC N10MC N77FV [cx Oct88; to spares Aug88 Wiley Post, OK] |
| 27 | 1121 | N93B N93BE [b/u for spares 1989 by White Inds, Bates City, MO; cx Apr91] |
| 28 | 1121 | N1190Z N77NR N234G |
| 29 | 1121 | N615J 4X-COJ [w/o 21Jan70 Tel Aviv, Israel] |
| 30 | 1121 | N401V N400CP [w/o 21Jan71 Burlington, VT] |
| 31 | 1121 | N399D N99GS [wfu 1994] |
| 32 | 1121B | N92B N92BT N32JC N101BU N98SC [wfu Washington County A/P, PA circa 2001; canx 09Dec05 presumed b/u] |
| 33 | 1121 | N1180Z N151CR N104CJ VT-ERO [wfu and b/u in India, rear fuselage and some other parts to Hollister, CA] |
| 34 | 1121 | N1210 N1210G N102SV N102SY N329HN N777MH N130RC N111XL N500MF TG-OMF N500MF [wfu; remains with White Inds, Bates City, MO] |
| 35 | 1121 | N6504V N22AC N100TH N101GS N189G N7HL N710JW [cx Nov92 as "destroyed/scrapped"] |
| 36 | 1121 | N1121M N730PV N780PV [sold May88 to Norway as technical airframe; scrap late 1990] |
| 37 | 1121 | N967L N123JB N723JB N445 [noted derelict 11May88 Wiley Post, OK; still regd] |
| 38 | 1121 | N901JL N217PM N217AL N1776F (N200WN) N106CJ N37SJ |
| 39 | 1121 | N6505V N550NM N666JD N66TS N80TF N1BC N16FP N10EA [wfu May82 to Skolen for Luftfahrtsuddannel, Copenhagen-Kastrup, Denmark; cx Apr91; to Teknisk Erhvervsskole Centre, Hvidovre, Copenhagen, 2008] |
| 40 | 1121 | N913HB N40JC N40AJ N40UA [wfu; remains with White Inds, Bates City, MO] |
| 41 | 1121 | N6510V N187G N41FL ZP- N40593 N499TR [canx 02Mar06; b/u by Dodson Aviation for parts] |
| 42 | 1121 | N6511V N599KC N3DL N6361C N111Y (N359C) N111YL [noted derelict 12Mar86 Wiley Post, OK; cx Jly94 wfu] |
| 43 | 1121 | N6518V N271E N186G N121CS (N385G) N386G [wfu; b/u for parts 1989; cx Oct90] |
| 44 | 1121 | N200M N700C N700CB N273LP N273LF N69GT N60CD [b/u for parts Rantoul, KS circa Jan01] |
| 45 | 1121 | N920R N340DR N340ER N121PG N910MH [wfu; at aeronautical college, nr.La Guardia A/P, NY] |
| 46 | 1121 | N1500C N200BP N200RM N200GT N220ST N99W [wfu for spares at Tamiami, FL] |
| 47 | 1121 | N6513V HB-VBX N33GL N222GL N222HM N200LF [cx Sep87; b/u for parts by White Inds, Bates City, MO] |
| 48 | 1121 | N541SG N541M N400LR N444WL N8LC N486G N85MA N929GV N502U N301AJ [w/o 13Aug90 Cozumel, Mexico; cx Oct92] |
| 49 | 1121 | N430C N5JR [wfu; remains with White Inds, Bates City, MO] |
| 50 | 1121 | N612JC N133ME [in scrapyard 12Oct88 Wiley Post, OK; still regd] |

# JET COMMANDER/WESTWIND

| C/n | Series | Identities |
|---|---|---|
| 51 | 1121 | N618JC SE-DCK N303LA N69WW N21BC N93JR N18JL N1EC [b/u Dodson Avn, Ottawa, KS; cx Sep94] |
| 52 | 1121 | N701AP N1121G N696GW N159YC N159MP N159DP [wfu; displayed Darwin Aviation Museum, Australia; some parts to Dodson Avn, Ottawa, KS] |
| 53 | 1121 | N1230 N1230D N10MF N103F N925HB N27BD [wfu; remains with White Inds, Bates City, MO] |
| 54 | 1121 | N6534V N848C [cx Aug88; b/u for spares 1989] |
| 55 | 1121B | (D-CHAS) D-CEAS 4X-CON N11MC N747LB [b/u; cx Jan04] |
| 56 | 1121 | N6550V (N53AA) N382AA XA-... N382AA |
| 57 | 1121 | N6544V N770WL N121AJ [wfu May82; b/u for spares] |
| 58 | 1121 | N90B N721AS N120GH N660W N957RC CP-2263 N580NJ [to spares; cx Dec00] |
| 59 | 1121 | N6538V N59JC N21AK [b/u for spares; still regd] |
| 60 | 1121 | N6545V N100RC [w/o 14Nov70 Lexington, KY] |
| 61 | 1121 | N1196Z N666DC N51CH N100NR N999FB N29LP N29LB [w/o 19Dec80 Many Airport, LA] |
| 62 | 1121 | N5415 N1777T C-GKFS N1777T [wfu circa 1995 at Tucson, AZ & b/u 9-10Dec00] |
| 63 | 1121 | N6546V N7784 N15G N9DM N8GA N8GE [wfu to spares White Inds, Bates City, MO] |
| 64 | 1121 | N6512V N500GJ N124JB N124VS [wfu Manila, Philippines circa 1999] |
| 65 | 1121 | N500JR [w/o 26Sep66 North Platte, SD] |
| 66 | 1121 | N1966J [wfu; remains with White Inds, Bates City, MO] |
| 67 | 1121 | N650M N1121G [wfu; used for spares by Dodson Avn, Ottawa, KS] |
| 68 | 1121 | N196KC [w/o 01Jly68 Fayetteville, AR] |
| 69 | 1121 | N6527V N89B N10SN N50JP [wfu; remains with Dodson Avn, Ottawa, KS] |
| 70 | 1121 | N1194Z N129K [wfu; remains with White Inds, Bates City, MO] |
| 71 | 1121 | N1500M N150CM N150CT N150HR N721GB 4X-COA [preserved Israeli Air Force Museum at Hatzerim with Mig-21 nose] |
| 72 | 1121 | N757AL N777WJ N7KR I-LECO N2WU VR-CAU N2WU [w/o 02Dec90 Laguna del Saule, Uruguay] |
| 73 | 1121 | N98SA N98S N100W N100WM [parted out at Sarasota, FL] |
| 74 | 1121 | N6610V N535D N47DM N300DH N93RM N74GM N274MA (N149SF) |
| 75 | 1121 | N6611V N1121R N212CW [wfu with White Inds, Bates City, MO] |
| 76 | 1121 | N6612V N1121C CF-VVX N100DG N100DR N100TR [wfu with OK Aircraft, Gilroy, CA; still regd - fuselage reported at Hollister, CA, Sep95] |
| 77 | 1121 | N1121X N523AC N442WT N11BK N21JW N121JC N177JC |
| 78 | 1121 | N6613V N1121E N866DH N102CJ [used as spares at Opa-Locka, FL, circa Dec95] |
| 79 | 1121 | N454SR N100LL N36PT [reportedly scrapped; cx Jan97] |
| 80 | 1121 | N87B N900JL N173A N173AR N925R [wfu 1994] |
| 81 | 1121 | N6617V CF-KBI C-FEYG [w/o 26May78 Winnipeg, Canada] |
| 82 | 1121 | N9932 N4NK N82JC N927S C-GPDH N103BW N240AA [parted out & b/u Sep03] |
| 83 | 1121A | N4550E N23FF N83AL C-GHPR N503U [w/o 19Dec95 Guatemala City, Guatemala] |
| 84 | 1121 | N312S N600TD N600TP N600ER N16MK [wfu Dallas-Redbird, TX circa Dec05] |
| 85 | 1121 | N4554E N201S XC-HAD [b/u 1990 Mexico City, Mexico] |
| 86 | 1121 | N1100M N2JW N13TV N116MC XA-RIW XA-SHA [wfu Houston-Hobby, TX, to Dodson Int'l Parts, KS] |
| 87 | 1121 | N920G N920GP N400PC N430PC N430DC N116KX [wfu to spares at Hollister, CA] |
| 88 | 1121 | N963WM N70CS N751CR [b/u May87; still regd; remains to Aviation Warehouse prop facility at El Mirage, CA] |
| 89 | 1121 | N6B N1195N N10BK N163DC [wfu New Orleans-Lakefront A/P, LA] |
| 90 | 1121 | N188WP N1121E N93SC [with Dodson Int'l Parts, Rantoul, KS circa May00] |
| 91 | 1121 | N365RJ N1972W N73535 N711JT [w/o 13Mar75 Tullahoma, TN] |
| 92 | 1121 | N5420 N524X N33PS N401DE [b/u; remains at Wiley Post, OK 12May88; cx Mar89] |
| 93 | 1121 | N619JC N221CF N50LB (N999RA) N1PT [wfu; cx Oct94 "destroyed/scrapped" - used for spares] |
| 94 | 1121 | N1424 N1424Z (N144JC) N1424 N94WA N64AH |
| 95 | 1121B | N5412 N6412 N7090 N709Q N210FE N100CA N200MP (N3031) N200MZ N95JK N614MH CP-2259 N85JW N55HL |
| 96 | 1121 | N56S N56WH N59CT N7EC N1QL N1QH N10JP N10JV (N2ES) YV-2454P [wfu by Jun05 at Caracas-Charallave, Venezuela] |
| 97 | 1121 | N4644E N96B N3032 N3082B N34SW [parted out at Hollister, CA; cx 28Apr06] |
| 98 | 1121 | N1121N C-FWRN N6DB N101DE N482G N301L N333BG [parted out & b/u] |
| 99 | 1121B | N4661E N922CR N922CP N22RT N22RD N63357 |
| 100 | 1121 | N4663E N605V N16GR N11WP N305AJ [wfu; still regd; remains to Aviation Warehouse prop facility at El Mirage, CA] |
| 101 | 1121 | N899S N100KY N45JF N5JC N16A N16MA N16SK [sold May88 in Norway as technical airframe; later to Bodo Aviation Museum, Bodo, Norway] |
| 102 | 1121 | N27MD [wfu 1986 for spares; remains with White Inds, Bates City, MO; still regd] |
| 103 | 1121 | N1121S N136K N487G N10HV N13AD N77HH N998RD [parted out by Dodson Int'l Parts at Rantoul, KS] |
| 104 | 1121 | N4674E N87B N8RA |
| 105 | 1121 | N618JC F-BPIB N230RC C-GWPV N5094B [wfu with White Inds, Bates City, MO & b/u; cx Dec03] |
| 106 | 1121B | N4690E N3711H N40AB N88AD N114HH (N114HE) N180TJ N814K N814T |
| 107 | 1123 | N4691E 4X-COL (4X-COK) Israel 4X-JYG/064 N2120Q Ciskei CA-01 N2120Q [b/u at Oklahoma City, OK; cx Dec90] |

## JET COMMANDER/WESTWIND

| C/n | Series | Identities |
|---|---|---|
| 108 | 1121B | N1121Z N1WP N12JA N12JX N77ST LV-WHZ |
| 109 | 1121 | N350X N9DC N379TH N1MW TG-VWA XA-THF |
| 110 | 1121B | N4716E 4X-CPA N101SV N181SV N16GH N1121N [wfu to spares at Hollister, CA] |
| 111 | 1121 | N344PS N999CA C-GDJW N1121M [cx Aug92; wfu for spares by OK Aircraft, Gilroy, CA; remains to scrapyard Long Beach, CA] |
| 112 | 1121B | N4730E N91B N91WG N4WG N44WG N773WB N372Q N710DC (C-....) N710DC |
| 113 | 1121 | N4732E 4X-CPB N8534 [b/u circa early 2003, remains at Deland, FL] |
| 114 | 1121 | N4734E 4X-CPC N442WT N448WT N111ST N10GR N85MR N333SV [to spares at Hollister, CA, circa 1995; fuselage used as static testbed for overhauled engines] |
| 115 | 1121 | CF-WEC C-FWEC N3252J N500VF XB-FJI [b/u Monterrey, Mexico] |
| 116 | 1121 | N4743E N236JP [w/o 31Oct69 Marion, VA] |
| 117 | 1121 | N237JF N200BP N400HC N220KP N54WC N34NW [being parted out Sep97 White Inds, Bates City, MO] |
| 118 | 1121 | N312S N438 N117GM (N712GM) N716BB N381DA N696RV |
| 119 | 1121 | C-FFBC N119AC (LV-...) [reported parted out in Argentina as N119AC, after cancellation] |
| 120 | 1121 | N200M N203M [scrapped during 1984; cx Jan85] |
| 121 | 1121A | N1121X N840AR N250JP N1121R N250UA (N121JC) [w/o 27Apr78 Flatwood, LA] |
| 122 | 1121B | N4940E N801NM N122JC N666BP N122HL N122ST (XA-SCV) |
| 123 | 1121A | N5410 N155VW N1121A N580WE [parted out by Dodson Int'l Parts at Rantoul, KS] |
| 124 | 1121B | N1300M N300M XA-REO XA-RQT N8070U [for spares; cx Jan99] |
| 125 | 1121A | N1121N N30LS N1121R |
| 126 | 1121B | 4X-COM N4983E N315SA N113MR N87DC N87DL LV-WEN [w/o 28Sep94 Cordoba, Argentina] |
| 127 | 1121A | N6B N27X N34HD N209RR N20GB N100SR N550K N277MG [to Dodson International Parts 01Apr05 for parting out] |
| 128 | 1121A | N660RW N74XL N74XE N1121U N386MC (N386JM) N404WC |
| 129 | 1121A | N5032E N525AW N110ST (N1121B) N102CE N121PA [to Dodson International Parts Oct05 for parts use] |
| 130 | 1121A | N5038E 4X-CPD N84 N44 [w/o 02Nov88 en route Westmoreland County A/P, Latrobe, LA] |
| 131 | 1121A | N5039E 4X-CPE N83 N43 N7028F [at Fairmont State College, WV; canx as "possibly scrapped" Aug96] |
| 132 | 1121 | N200M N403M [w/o 16Dec79 Salt Lake City, UT] |
| 133 | 1121B | N5041E N1172Z N56AG N56AZ N133JC N666JM N22976 N161X N122JB XA-LYM XB-GBZ N132LA |
| 134 | 1121B | N111E 4X-FVN UAF1 5X-AAB 4X-COP N7638S N134N |
| 135 | 1121B | N5043E N700HB N2DB N1KT N721GB N1121N XC-COL N900PJ |
| 136 | 1121 | N5044E SE-DCY [w/o 04Dec69 Stockholm, Sweden] |
| 137 | 1121B | N5045E SE-DCZ N50VF N3VF N873 N500LS N300LS N5BP N700BF (N700GA) N707TE XB-FKV N47CE |
| 138 | 1121B | N5046E 4X-COB N5BA N972TF |
| 139 | 1121B | N5047E 4X-CPF N8535 I-ARNT N188G N481DH |
| 140 | 1121 | N9040N 4X-CPG N200RC [w/o 25Sep73 Tampa, FL] |
| 141 | 1121B | N9041N 4X-CPH N100CJ N160WC N177PC N177HB N163WC N163WS 5N-EZE N163WS [wfu Columbia Metropolitan, SC; cx Dec03] |
| 142 | 1121C | N9042N 4X-CPI N82 N42 N50138 N51038 N1944P [at Pittsburgh Inst of Aeronautics] |
| 143 | 1121C | N9043N 4X-CPJ N81 N41 N30AD [scrapped at Boeing Field, WA circa May98] |
| 144 | 1121C | N9044N 4X-CPK N80 N45 N20K (N920KP) [wfu with White Industries, KS] |
| 145 | 1121B | N9045N HB-VCC (N17DW) F-BTDA N349DA N145BW N145AJ (N805SA) N805SM |
| 146 | 1121B | N9046N N99CV N99CK N923JA N926JM N444TJ [b/u for spares at Atlanta Air Salvage, Griffin, GA circa 1999] |
| 147 | 1121B | N9047N N720ML N728MC N147JK N912DA (N888MP) |
| 148 | 1121B | N9048N 4X-CPL N8536 N200DE N200DF N101NK N600K (N22LL) [cx Jun99 - being parted out at Hollister, CA mid 99] |
| 149 | 1121B | N9049N 4X-CPM N100MC N100PC N45SL N489G N78MN N700R N1121E (N9LP) (N149BP) N606JM N666JM (N129ME) N343DA N303AJ (N308AJ) (N803AU) N149SF [wfu Kingston, Jamaica; cx Nov03] |
| 150 | 1121B | N9050N 4X-CPN N1884Z N173MC N121FM N1121F [w/o 20May97 San Louis Potosi, Mexico] |
| 151 | 1123 | 4X-CJD N1123E N88WP ZP-AGD [stored Fort Lauderdale Executive, FL] |
| 152 | 1124N | 4X-CJC Israel 4X-JYF/029 4X-CJC Israel 4X-JYR/035 Israel 4X-JYR/929 |
| 153 | 1123 | 4X-CJB N773EJ N200WC N223WW XA-PUF |
| 154 | 1124 | 4X-CJA (D-CBBE) N919JH D-CBBE N722AW N176AK N176DT |
| 155 | 1123 | 4X-CJE N23Y N707TE N707TF |
| 156 | 1123 | 4X-CJF N1123H N40AS N40BG (N666MP) N566MP N35D |
| 157 | 1123 | 4X-CJG N1123Q N10MB (N820RT) [wfu; b/u c 1989-90; cx Aug92; remains with OK Aircraft, Gilroy, CA] |
| 158 | 1123 | 4X-CJH N1123G N123DR |
| 159 | 1123 | 4X-CJI N1123E N722W N1123Z (N12FH) N344CK N96TS [wfu to spares at Hollister, CA; canx 25Mar05] |
| 160 | 1123 | 4X-CJJ N1123R USCG 160 4X-CJJ N1123W N221MJ N221RJ XA-AVE XA-MUI XA-RIZ |
| 161 | 1123 | 4X-CJK D-CGLS (N653J) N185G N33WD XA-POJ [wfu after accident (no details known); remains to Dodson Av'n, Ottawa, KS, for spares] |

# JET COMMANDER/WESTWIND

| C/n | Series | Identities |
|---|---|---|
| 162 | 1123 | 4X-CJL N1123S N78LB N234RC N9VC N9VQ XA-SDW (N163W) N13GW HK-.... [cx from USCAR early 1995 but still marked N13GW circa Feb97 at Bogota-El Dorado, Colombia] |
| 163 | 1123 | 4X-CJM N1123T N4444U N47DC N163DL [canx Oct97, status?] |
| 164 | 1123 | 4X-CJN D-CAAS N9114S N32WE [b/u by White Inds, Bates City, MO; still regd] |
| 165 | 1123 | 4X-CJO N1123R C-GWSH N102BW N22RD N30156 |
| 166 | 1123 | 4X-CJP C-GDOC N360HK [b/u during 1989; still regd] |
| 167 | 1123 | 4X-CJQ N873EJ N1123H [being parted out by White Industries 1998] |
| 168 | 1123 | 4X-CJR N973EJ N66SM N111NF [b/u Dallas-Love Field, TX circa 1998] |
| 169 | 1123 | 4X-CJS N1123U N1500C N1100D N44PR [wfu; cx 18Feb09] |
| 170 | 1123 | 4X-CJT N1123W N112RC N150HR N90HM [wfu; cx May94] |
| 171 | 1123 | 4X-CJU C-GJLL N223PA N89XL (ZS-ODP) [stored at Lanseria, South Africa] |
| 172 | 1123 | 4X-CJV N1123H XB-AER N19EE YV-58CP YV-2482P |
| 173 | 1123 | 4X-CJW N1123Q N680K N30JM N30AN [prop at Aviation Warehouse, El Mirage CA] |
| 174 | 1124 | 4X-CJX N1123X N112MR N124VF N74TS N760C XA-PVR XA-UHJ N92RB |
| 175 | 1123 | 4X-CJY N1123R N500M N500ML N51TV N523RB (N571MC) N384AT [parted out by Dodson Int'l Parts, Rantoul, KS] |
| 176 | 1123 | 4X-CJZ N1123T C-GJCD N661MP C-FNRW N661MP N27AT N35CR |
| 177 | 1123 | 4X-CKA N1123U N11WC N777CJ N118AF (N114ED) [cx 1991 wfu] |
| 178 | 1123 | 4X-CKB N1123Z N999U N123CV [wfu Columbia Metropolitan, SC; cx 01Oct04] |
| 179 | 1123 | 4X-CKC N1123Y LV-WJU N114RA |
| 180 | 1123 | 4X-CKD HP-1A N1019K (N180JS) N72LT N72ET (N190LH) N192LH N3VL [cx May01, aircraft was b/u] |
| 181 | 1124 | 4X-CKE HK-2150X HK-2150 N107CF N325AJ N325LJ N345BS |
| 182 | 1123 | 4X-CKF N1123Q N200HR N700EC N13KH N18BL N78BL N10122 LV-WYL [wfu Buenos Aires/San Fernando, Argentina] |
| 183 | 1123 | 4X-CKG Honduras 318 HR-001 XB-DNY N51990 LV-WLR |
| 184 | 1123 | 4X-CKH N1123T N666JM N866JM YV-119P CC-CRK N481MC [instructional airframe Midland College, Midland, TX] |
| 185 | 1124N | 4X-CKI N1123U Israel 4X-JYJ/027 Israel 4X-JYJ/927 |
| 186 | 1123N | 4X-CKJ N1123R Israel 4X-JYO/031 Israel 4X-JYO/931 |
| 187 | 1124 | 4X-CKK N1124N N18GW (N943CL) (N715GW) (N416NL) N516AC (N789DD) N1M N280DB (N1TS) (N187TS) N241RH N187TJ |
| 188 | 1124 | 4X-CKL N1124G C-GRDP N118RJ [parted out by Dodson Int'l Parts, Rantoul, KS] |
| 189 | 1124 | 4X-CKM N26DS N926DS N200DL N42CM |
| 190 | 1124 | 4X-CKN N50AL N890WW N190WW N313TW N510GT |
| 191 | 1124 | 4X-CKO N3VF N13VF N711MR YV-777CP (N771AC) N326AJ N900FS N900JF |
| 192 | 1124 | 4X-CKP N71M (N736US) N319BG N819RC |
| 193 | 1124 | 4X-CKQ N60AL (YV-37CP) N101HS N420J N420JM N428JM N515LG N98BM |
| 194 | 1124 | 4X-CKR N222SR N343AP N124FM N40TA N807BF |
| 195 | 1124 | 4X-CKS N887PL N880WW (N24TE) TC-ASF (N195ML) N951DB N920AD* |
| 196 | 1124 | 4X-CKT N1124E N250JP N505U N500WK (N615DM) N863AB N606MA |
| 197 | 1124 | 4X-CKU N214CC N29GH N29CL SE-DLK [w/o 21Sep92 Umea, Sweden; cx Jan93] |
| 198 | 1124 | 4X-CKV N800Y N744JR N600TJ N98TS N51MN N71PT N750SP (N750SB) |
| 199 | 1124 | 4X-CKW N1124P N111AG N999MS D-CHDL N199WW C-FTWO |
| 200 | 1124 | 4X-CKX N1124X N4WG |
| 201 | 1124 | 4X-CKY N1124Q N1124N N56AG N58WW N85EQ (N85EA) N95CP N300TE (N29UF) C-FOIL N124WW |
| 202 | 1124 | 4X-CKZ D-CBAY N49968 N54MC (N254MC) N202DD (N37WC) N141LB N168DB YV-297CP N274HM N59PT N469WC |
| 203 | 1124 | 4X-CLA N1124G N124WW N880Z N22RD |
| 204 | 1124 | 4X-CLB N221MJ N156CW N26TJ N10UJ (N100XJ) [b/u; cx Jly03] |
| 205 | 1124 | 4X-CLC N96BA N967A N124NY N125AC SE-DLL N205AJ (N775JC) N331AP YV.... |
| 206 | 1124 | 4X-CLD N215G N215C N215M N943LL N943JL N100ME N148H |
| 207 | 1124 | 4X-CLE N1124P N6053C N330PC N519ME N666K D-CHAL N207WW C-FTWR |
| 208 | 1124 | 4X-CLF N961JC (N961JD) N961JE N208MD N208ST N324AJ N311DB N57PT |
| 209 | 1124 | 4X-CLG N661JB N663JB N662JB N938WH N988WH N222LH N705AC |
| 210 | 1124 | 4X-CLH N662JB N69HM N661CP N662JB N23AC N38WW N444MM N59KC N337RE N425JF N428JF N2150H |
| 211 | 1124 | 4X-CLI YV-160CP [w/o 19Feb97 near Guatemala City/La Aurora, Guatemala] |
| 212 | 1124 | 4X-CLJ N212WW N900CS N700MD |
| 213 | 1124 | 4X-CLK N213WW N555J N530GV N580GV N30YM (4X-NOY) 4X-CLK N27TZ |
| 214 | 1124 | 4X-CLL N1124N N214WW N24RH (N248H) N46BK N21SF |
| 215 | 1124 | 4X-CLM N215DH N500WH N946GM N238DB |
| 216 | 1124 | 4X-CLN N216SC N1124G (N65BK) N290CA C-FAPK |
| 217 | 1124 | 4X-CLO N8QP N8QR N217SC N217SQ N217WC N163WC |
| 218 | 1124 | 4X-CLP N218WW N100AK C-GFAN N218DJ N74GR N218PM N425RJ N426RJ |
| 219 | 1124 | 4X-CLQ YV-190CP N290CP |
| 220 | 1124 | 4X-CLR N1124G C-GHBQ N9134Q N106BC N9RD |
| 221 | 1124 | 4X-CLS N108GM N969PW N969KC (N969EG) VH-AJS [w/o 27Apr95 Alice Springs, Australia] |
| 222 | 1124 | 4X-CLT N294W N294B N36EF N86EF N700R N3RC N598JM |
| 223 | 1124 | 4X-CLU N1124P N124TY N303PC N20KH N518WA |
| 224 | 1124 | 4X-CLV N898SR XA-KUG N2756T N349MC |
| 225 | 1124 | 4X-CLW N1124U N30MR |
| 226 | 1124 | 4X-CLX N500LS N300LS N100BC (N10BY) N124MB N120S D-CHBL N226WW C-FTWV |

# JET COMMANDER/WESTWIND

| C/n | Series | Identities |
|---|---|---|
| 227 | 1124 | 4X-CLY N250PM N64FG N624KM |
| 228 | 1124 | 4X-CLZ N305BB N795FM |
| 229 | 1124 | 4X-CMA N1212G N1625 N162E N40GG |
| 230 | 1124 | 4X-CMB N4995N XC-HCP XC-HDA N102U N1KT |
| 231 | 1124 | 4X-CMC HB-VFP N8514Y N777CF N70CA (N27TA) N331CW N331GW N600NY |
| 232 | 1124 | 4X-CMD N1124Q N19UC N190M N773AW N4MH |
| 233 | 1124 | 4X-CME N1124X N650GE N650G N67DF N36SF |
| 234 | 1124 | 4X-CMF (N1124Z) HC-BGL N1124Z N161X |
| 235 | 1124 | 4X-CMG N1124E (N24PP) N65A N30AB N903MM |
| 236 | 1124 | 4X-CMH N35LH N236W N22LZ N618WA |
| 237 | 1124 | 4X-CMI N39GW N723M N28TJ N24KL |
| 238 | 1124 | 4X-CMJ VH-AJP |
| 239 | 1124A | 4X-CMK [conv to 1124A prototype] HK-2485 HK-2485W HK-2485G |
| 240 | 1124 | 4X-CML N240WW (N400Q) N400SJ N400NE N72787 N298HM |
| 241 | 1124 | 4X-CMM N789TE N300TC |
| 242 | 1124 | 4X-CMN N340DR N140DR N500BJ |
| 243 | 1124 | 4X-CMO N1124G N59WK N215SC 4X-AIP [w/o 23Jly96 Rosh-Pina/ Mahanaim-I-Ben-Yaakov, Israel] |
| 244 | 1124 | 4X-CMP N124PA N911SP N124PA N911SP |
| 245 | 1124 | 4X-CMQ N1124P N404CB N270LC |
| 246 | 1124 | 4X-CMR N101SV N911CU |
| 247 | 1124 | 4X-CMS N1125G N280LM N280AZ N280AT [w/o 02Jly04 Panama City-Tocumen; dbf] |
| 248 | 1124 | 4X-CMT N25RE VH-AJJ |
| 249 | 1124 | 4X-CMU N1JS [reported stolen/crashed 1985 in Mexico] |
| 250 | 1124 | 4X-CMV N250WW C-GFAO N29995 N60RV (N250KD) N914MM N418WA |
| 251 | 1124 | 4X-CMW N6MJ CX-CMJ PT-LDY |
| 252 | 1124 | 4X-CMX N1WS (N9WW) N553MC |
| 253 | 1124 | 4X-CMY N511CC N511CQ N800WW N800WS N253MD VH-LLW [b/u Perth-Jandakot, Australia by 06Apr98] |
| 254 | 1124 | 4X-CMZ N600TD N888R N112AB N72HB N60AV RP-C59 RP-C5988 |
| 255 | 1124 | 4X-CNA N222MW N202MW N424CS |
| 256 | 1124 | 4X-CNB VH-AJK |
| 257 | 1124 | 4X-CNC N573P N317M N317MB N755CM N942FA N124UF N79LC N576LC |
| 258 | 1124 | 4X-CND N10MR N1857W N29AP N24DS YV-770CP N258AV (N258CF) N572M N58FB N771B |
| 259 | 1124 | 4X-CNE N1124N C-GSWS N19AP N315JM VH-LLX [b/u Perth-Jandakot, Australia by 06Apr98] |
| 260 | 1124 | 4X-CNF N401BP N525ML C-GAGP N49TA (N503RH) N80FD N525AK |
| 261 | 1124 | 4X-CNG N167C N249E N87GS N39JN N11LN |
| 262 | 1124 | 4X-CNH N262WW N40DG YV-393CP N262WC N79KP N150EX |
| 263 | 1124 | 4X-CNI N29PC N918SS |
| 264 | 1124 | 4X-CNJ N351C XA-MAR N351C (N125NY) N88PV N351C N809VC N810CC |
| 265 | 1124 | 4X-CNK N167J N7DJ |
| 266 | 1124 | 4X-CNL N24KT N24KE N50DR N7HM N5HQ |
| 267 | 1124 | 4X-CNM N297W N297A N100SR N241CT N55FG |
| 268 | 1124 | 4X-CNN (N13HH) N821H N606AB N21CX N200HR N41WH N56BP |
| 269 | 1124 | 4X-CNO N3031 N50SL N21DX |
| 270 | 1124 | 4X-CNP (N270WW) N270A (N27SJ) (N270DT) N501DT N475AT [w/o May06 Exuma Island, Bahamas] |
| 271 | 1124 | 4X-CNQ N368S N102KJ N218SC C-GWKF C-FREE C-FJOJ |
| 272 | 1124 | 4X-CNR N26GW N723R VH-LLY [b/u Perth-Jandakot, Australia by 06Apr98] |
| 273 | 1124 | 4X-CNS N104RS (N566PG) |
| 274 | 1124 | 4X-CNT N701Z N701W N274K |
| 275 | 1124 | 4X-CNU N1141G N1621 N36PT N6TM N96TM |
| 276 | 1124 | 4X-CNV VR-CAD XA-BQA N269AJ N800XL N300XL |
| 277 | 1124 | 4X-CNW N288WW (N2AJ) N504JC D-CHCL N277WW C-GAWJ |
| 278 | 1124 | 4X-CNX N505BC C-GJLK N10S C-GHYD |
| 279 | 1124 | 4X-CNY N1126G N885DR N230TL N230JK N952HF N400TF XC-COL [w/o 24Feb05 Sapotita, Mexico] |
| 280 | 1124 | 4X-CNZ N290W (N5BP) (N5S) N29LP N250RA N500R N508R N949CC |
| 281 | 1124 | 4X-CQA VH-AJQ N4251H N1124F (N200XJ) VH-AJG |
| 282 | 1124 | 4X-CQB N711MB N186G VH-AJV |
| 283 | 1124 | 4X-CQC N483A N666JM (N70WW) N17UC N95JK |
| 284 | 1124 | 4X-CQD N99WH N296NW N217BL N727AT |
| 285 | 1124 | 4X-CQE VR-CAC XA-LIJ VR-CBK XA-LIJ N85PT |
| 286 | 1124 | 4X-CQF N1124U C-GMBH N4447T N92FE N111LP N110LP N113GH |
| 287 | 1124 | 4X-CQG N146BF N530DL |
| 288 | 1124 | 4X-CQH N1124Q C-GMTT N116AT N94AT N48AH N711KE |
| 289 | 1124 | 4X-CQI N711CJ N45SJ N23SJ VR-CIL N900VP |
| 290 | 1124 | 4X-CQJ N800JJ N719CC |
| 291 | 1124 | 4X-CQK N124WK N917BE |
| 292 | 1124 | 4X-CQL N292JC N741C |
| 293 | 1124 | 4X-CQM N26TV N26T N26TZ |
| 294 | 1124 | 4X-CQN D-CBBA N24DB (N73GB) HK-3884X N147A |
| 295 | 1124A | 4X-CQO N295WW N100AK N100AQ N555CW N730CA |
| 296 | 1124 | 4X-CQP D-CBBB N64KT N770JJ N92WW N89TJ N710SA |
| 297 | 1124 | 4X-CQQ D-CBBC N76TG N51PD N801SM N335VB |
| 298 | 1124 | 4X-CQR N610JA C-GESO C-GRGE N298CM N809JC |

## JET COMMANDER/WESTWIND

| C/n | Series | Identities |
|---|---|---|
| 299 | 1124A | 4X-CQS N922CR N922CK N74JM N600TC (N288SJ) N67TJ |
| 300 | 1124A | 4X-CQT N500M N500MD (N20NW) N10MV PR-STJ |
| 301 | 1124A | 4X-CQU N500GK N815RC N815BC XB-GRN N230JS N301KF N890BA |
| 302 | 1124A | 4X-CQV N600J N60QJ N100AK N422BC [w/o 26Dec99 Milwaukee, WI] |
| 303 | 1124A | 4X-CQW N500J N50QJ N211ST |
| 304 | 1124A | 4X-CQX N304WW N369BG N389BG N10NL N13NL N78PT |
| 305 | 1124A | 4X-CQY N464EC N717LA N717EA N629WH N804CC |
| 306 | 1124A | 4X-CQZ YV-387CP N555BY (N9WW) (N722W) HK-3971X HK-4204X HK-4204 N306PT |
| 307 | 1124A | 4X-CRA YV-388CP N1124K N300HC (N301HC) N825JL N925Z N97SM N494BP N4SQ |
| 308 | 1124A | 4X-CRB YV-210CP YV-0-CVG-1 N308JS N308TS N628KM N639AT |
| 309 | 1124A | 4X-CRC (N200LH) N240S N50SK [w/o 04Apr86 nr Rosewater, TX] |
| 310 | 1124 | 4X-CRD D-CBBD N78GJ |
| 311 | 1124 | 4X-CRE N700MM N50XX N700MM N788MA N53LM |
| 312 | 1124 | 4X-CRF N200LH N300LH N97HW N24FJ N316TD |
| 313 | 1124 | 4X-CRG N146J C-FAWW N711WU N711WV N611WV C-GDSR |
| 314 | 1124 | 4X-CRH VH-IWW N2454M N84PH N2HZ N49CT |
| 315 | 1124A | 4X-CRI N371H N400YM VH-BCL VH-NJW N315TR (N89TJ) N124GR YV.... |
| 316 | 1124 | 4X-CRJ VH-ASR N93KE N33TW |
| 317 | 1124 | 4X-CRK VH-AYI P2-BCM VH-JPW (VH-NIJ) VH-UUZ VH-KNU |
| 318 | 1124 | 4X-CRL N298W N298A N10FG N38AE |
| 319 | 1124A | 4X-CRM XA-LOR N560SH N700WM (N50XX) N200KC N225N N783FS N788FS |
| 320 | 1124 | 4X-CRN N60JP N204TM |
| 321 | 1124 | 4X-CRO N900WW N1124N N83CT N93WW N666K N666KL N217F N810VC |
| 322 | 1124A | 4X-CRP N2AV N990S |
| 323 | 1124 | 4X-CRQ N816H VH-KNS |
| 324 | 1124A | 4X-CRR N3VF N90CL C-FCEJ N91MK N404HR N323MR |
| 325 | 1124 | 4X-CRS VH-WWY N504U N124HL SE-DPT N525AJ N467MW N68PT |
| 326 | 1124 | 4X-CRT (N88JE) N66JE [w/o 21Feb95 Denver-Stapleton Airport, CO] |
| 327 | 1124 | 4X-CRU N50M |
| 328 | 1124A | 4X-CRV N816JA N819JA C-GPFC N328PC |
| 329 | 1124 | 4X-CRW N30NS N711SE N7HM N124HS |
| 330 | 1124A | 4X-CRX N52GW N723K YV-332CP YV1685 |
| 331 | 1124 | 4X-CRY N556N N228N N228L LV-WOV N228L N811VC |
| 332 | 1124A | 4X-CRZ N24SR N332DF N43RP |
| 333 | 1124 | 4X-CTA HR-002 HR-CEF HR-PHO |
| 334 | 1124A | 4X-CTB (N45MP) N40MP N325LW N42NF |
| 335 | 1124A | 4X-CTC N300HR N359JS N501BW EC-254 EC-GIB N21HR |
| 336 | 1124 | 4X-CTD N245S C-FOIL N336SV N255RB N525XX |
| 337 | 1124A | 4X-CTE N14BN N639J N900NW 4X-CTE N2518M VP-BLT N127PT |
| 338 | 1124A | 4X-CTF N338W N350PM N850WW N114WL N50PL [w/o 12Dec99, Gouldsboro, PA; cx Sep03] |
| 339 | 1124A | 4X-CTG (XC-HDA) N333CG N782PC N74AG N90KC ZK-RML |
| 340 | 1124A | 4X-CTH 4X-CUA (XC-BDA) N1124L N212CP PT-OLN N340PM N118MP N3RC N118MP VH-KNR |
| 341 | 1124A | 4X-CTI 4X-CUB N1124P N23AC N23AQ N80RE N555HD N556HD N728LW N728LM N868CP N52KS N818JH |
| 342 | 1124A | 4X-CTJ XA-MAK N342AJ N39RE N342TS N204AB N274HM |
| 343 | 1124A | 4X-CTK YV-451CP YV-0-CVG-3 YV-0-FMO-6 N343RD N999AZ N911GU |
| 344 | 1124A | 4X-CTL N334 N311BR N849HS N379AV N769MS N769M |
| 345 | 1124A | 4X-CTM N1424 (N533) N534 N534R N345TR |
| 346 | 1124A | 4X-CTN N100AG N1124N N610HC N610SE |
| 347 | 1124 | 4X-CTO N347WW N30PD N21GG YV-666CP N666CP N178HH N347GA |
| 348 | 1124A | 4X-CTP N348WW N348SJ N960FA |
| 349 | 1124A | 4X-CTQ N78WW N65GW N723L N728L N123RC |
| 350 | 1124A | 4X-CTR VR-CBB XA-MAK N3838J N777LU N309CK [w/o 15Dec93 Orange County A/P, CA; cx Oct95] |
| 351 | 1124A | 4X-CTS N106WT N351TC N722AZ N728AZ N111EL N124BC |
| 352 | 1124A | 4X-CTT N15BN N117JW N117AH |
| 353 | 1124A | 4X-CTU N379JR N90CH N86UR N89UH C-GRGE EC-GSL RP-C5880 |
| 354 | 1124 | 4X-CTV N443A N512CC N506U N124LS N894TW |
| 355 | 1124A | 4X-CUI N355WW N355JK N241CT |
| 356 | 1124A | 4X-CUJ N356WW N8GA N533 N530GV N929GV N43ZZ N861GS N767AC N38TJ N993DS |
| 357 | 1124 | 4X-CUK (N357W) C-GDUC N357EA N66FG N357BC N914DM |
| 358 | 1124A | 4X-CUL N358CT N13UR N800MA N830MA N787RP N720MC N404PG |
| 359 | 1124A | 4X-CUM N8JL N86RR N500RR N500AX C-GRGE N14CN |
| 360 | 1124 | 4X-CUN N816S N816ST N816S N500KE |
| 361 | 1124A | 4X-CUO N6053C N610HC N3AV |
| 362 | 1124 | 4X-CUP N445A YV251T |
| 363 | 1124 | 4X-CUQ N3320G N1629 N54PT (N723JM) N420JM |
| 364 | 1124A | 4X-CUR N60DG N199GH N198GH N198HF N198HE RP-C2480 N944M N67DT |
| 365 | 1124A | 4X-CUS N793JR (N185BR) N185MB N2BG N73CL |
| 366 | 1124 | 4X-CUT VH-SQH VH-LOF N388GA N707BC N65TD N320MD |
| 367 | 1124 | 4X-CUD N446A N511CC N455S N367WW |
| 368 | 1124A | 4X-CUE N28WW N368MD N83SG |
| 369 | 1124A | 4X-CUF N24SB (N54BC) N300JK N85WC N76ER |
| 370 | 1124 | 4X-CUG N641FG N471TM N875HS N875P |

# JET COMMANDER/WESTWIND

| C/n | Series | Identities |
|---|---|---|
| 371 | 1124 | 4X-CUH VH-IWJ [w/o 10Oct85 nr Sydney, Australia] |
| 372 | 1124 | 4X-CUB N372WW N988NA N810MT (N800MT) N810ME (N5TH) N921DT N502BG N444MW N404MW N406CH N224GP N942EB |
| 373 | 1124A | 4X-CUK N373CM N900LM N555DH N794TK |
| 374 | 1124A | 4X-CUL N18SF N56AG N248H N33MK N43W N30TK |
| 375 | 1124 | 4X-CUF N79AD N79AP N66LX N66VA |
| 376 | 1124A | 4X-CUH 4X-CJP N1124P N110SF N376WA N376BE VH-ZYH |
| 377 | 1124A | 4X-CUJ N301PC |
| 378 | 1124 | 4X-CUI N84LA N481NS C-GXKF N481NS |
| 379 | 1124 | 4X-CUJ N52FC N62ND N302SG N851E |
| 380 | 1124A | 4X-CUM N50DW N380DA C-FMWW [w/o 27Jan94 Meadow Lake, Saskatchewan, Canada; cx Jly94] |
| 381 | 1124 | 4X-CUO VH-KNJ N501U N929GV N928GV N928G N92EB N381W N50FD |
| 382 | 1124A | 4X-CUP N900BF N410NA (N445BL) N999BL N445BL [w/o 01May92 Waterbury, Oxford, CT; cx Mar93] |
| 383 | 1124 | 4X-CUQ (N301PC) N82HH N20DH N84WU N84VV N942WC |
| 384 | 1124A | 4X-CUB N48WW N61RS (N50MF) [w/o 08Nov02, Taos, NM; cx Mar03] |
| 385 | 1124A | 4X-CUC N96AL YV-962CP N962MV N317JS |
| 386 | 1124 | 4X-CUE N68WW (VH-JPL) N348DH N386RL |
| 387 | 1124A | 4X-CUJ N97AL VH-NGA [w/o 18Nov09 off Norfolk Island, Australia] |
| 388 | 1124 | 4X-CUH N1124K N900H N388WW |
| 389 | 1124A | 4X-CUF N49WW N812M (N612M) N812G N100WP N812G N89AM |
| 390 | 1124A | 4X-CUB N57WW N3RL (N303E) N290RA ZS-MZM (HB-...) N59SM N122MP |
| 391 | 1124 | 4X-CUG N24WW N24VH C-GMPF N155ME N303SG N59PT |
| 392 | 1124A | 4X-CUA N92WW N95WC N793BG |
| 393 | 1124 | 4X-CUK N53WW N491AN |
| 394 | 1124A | 4X-CUM N94WW N314AD N352TC N516CC N21RA N63PP N98HG |
| 395 | 1124A | 4X-CUC N95WW VH-SGY VH-APU N395SR N395TJ |
| 396 | 1124 | 4X-CUR 8P-BAR N1124N N37BE |
| 397 | 1124A | 4X-CUN N52SM N11CS N777HD |
| 398 | 1124 | 4X-CUO N98WW N59AP N41C |
| 399 | 1124A | 4X-CUF N78WW N48SD |
| 400 | 1124A | 4X-CUP N200LS N300LS N900PA N900TN N917LH |
| 401 | 1124 | 4X-CUQ N84WW N980S N30GF |
| 402 | 1124A | 4X-CUS N87WW N999LC N51TV |
| 403 | 1124 | 4X-CUH N403W (N825EC) |
| 404 | 1124A | 4X-CUG 4X-CJR N404W N29CL |
| 405 | 1124A | 4X-CUJ N1124L N211DB N420TJ N420CE N424JR |
| 406 | 1124 | 4X-CUA N406W N651E (N651ES) N100CH N830 |
| 407 | 1124A | 4X-CUK N407W |
| 408 | 1124 | 4X-CUB N408W N408MJ N125HF |
| 409 | 1124A | 4X-CUM VH-JJA 4X-CUM? 4X-CUO Chile 130 N7051J N409WW XA-RET N4426Z N217RM N217BM N26KL N629WH |
| 410 | 1124A | 4X-CUO N1124Z (N410EL) N22BG N26VF N26VB N777DC |
| 411 | 1124 | 4X-CUC N96WW N47LP N47LR HC-BVX N224PA |
| 412 | 1124A | 4X-CUP N412W N412SC N50XX N50HS N999MC N870BA |
| 413 | 1124 | 4X-CJS 4X-CUD N413WW N35LH |
| 414 | 1124A | 4X-CPO 4X-CUC N86MF (N66MF) N980AW N24MN N524RH N550HB |
| 415 | 1124A | 4X-CUS N415EL N105BE N415EL N415TH |
| 416 | 1124 | 4X-CUD N416W N303TS N815RK N600KE |
| 417 | 1124A | 4X-CUE N417EL (N417GW) N700WE N115BP (N99WF) N34FS |
| 418 | 1124 | 4X-CUB PT-LIP N124PA N662K N317MX (N317MV) N420MP N26T N26TN |
| 419 | 1124A | 4X-CUF N419W N551TP N51MN N411HB N728MB |
| 420 | 1124A | 4X-CUH N420W N91SA N728TG |
| 421 | 1124 | 4X-CUJ N111HN N801MS N317MQ N520MP |
| 422 | 1124A | 4X-COC 4X-CUI N422AW N251SP N87GS N87GJ |
| 423 | 1124 | 4X-CUC N223WA N680ME |
| 424 | 1124A | 4X-CUJ N424W N790JR |
| 425 | 1124A | 4X-CUK N425WA N600LE N365CX (N365QX) N328SA |
| 426 | 1124 | 4X-CUF N426WW N75BC |
| 427 | 1124A | 4X-CUN N427WW N256N N229N N229D |
| 428 | 1124A | 4X-CUO N428W (N92BE) N327SA N57BE |
| 429 | 1124 | 4X-CUK (N429W) C-FROY N42FL |
| 430 | 1124 | 4X-CUM N430W N821LG N430A N430BJ N430PT |
| 431 | 1124 | 4X-CUN N431AM C-FGGH N431WA |
| 432 | 1124 | 4X-CUH N87NS N317M N62276 N317MB (N317MT) N320MP N432HS N282SM N60BT |
| 433 | 1124A | 4X-CUH N433WW N433WR N433GM |
| 434 | 1124A | 4X-CUC N330MG (N346CP) N222KC N601DR N187EC N919BT (N102AK) N564RM |
| 435 | 1124 | 4X-CUG (N435W) N501CB (N501CP) (N669SB) N297JS N140VJ N500MA |
| 436 | 1124A | 4X-CUE N436WW N50XX N436WW N110AF N1904G N100AK N444EP |
| 437 | 1124A | 4X-CUF N437WW N437SJ |
| 438 | 1124 | 4X-CUJ (N438W) N438AM N100BC (N438FS) |
| 439 | 1124A | 4X-CUG N439WW |
| 440 | 1124A | 4X-CUJ N440WW N127SA N220DH |
| 441 | 1124 | 4X-CUP PT-LPV HK-3893X C-FZEI C-FPEP |
| 442 | 1124A | 4X-CUO N406W N830 N71WF N830C |

Production complete

# LEARJET MODELS 23 & 24

| C/n | Model | Identities |
|---|---|---|
| 001 | 23 | N801L [ff 07Oct63; w/o 04Jun64 Wichita, KS] |
| 002 | 23 | N802L [ff 05May64; last flight 17Jun66; displayed at Smithsonian National Air & Space Museum's Steven F. Udvar-Hazy Center, Washington-Dulles, VA] |
| 003 | 23 | N803L N200Y N2008 (N10MC) N3BL |
| 004 | 23 | N804LJ [became c/n 23-015A] |
| 005 | 23 | N232R N570FT N994SA N721HW N721GB N15BE N500JW [b/u for spares around Mar87; cx Aug87 - remains to Bounty Avn Scrapyard, Detroit-Willow Run, MI] |
| 006 | 23 | N505PF N578LJ N23CH N111JD N505PF [donated Oct93 to Kansas Aviation Museum] |
| 007 | 23 | N826L D-IHAQ [w/o 12Dec65 Zurich] |
| 008 | 23 | N825LJ N1203 N20S N20BD N20EP [wfu circa Mar93; exhibited outside White Inds, Bates City, MO] |
| 009 | 23 | N425EJ N5BL N13SN N49CK N23BY [to Arkansas Air Museum, Fayetteville, AR 2008] |
| 010 | 23 | N805LJ N292BC N2920C N333BF N29BF N400BF N500BF [b/u for spares Oct88 Detroit-Willow Run, MI - remains to Bounty Avn Scrapyard, Detroit-Willow Run, MI] |
| 011 | 24A | N806LJ N233VW N1966K N150WL N50JF N711PJ N711TJ N225LJ N24LG (N40TV) |
| 012 | 24 | N1965L N1967L N1969L N1965L |
| 013 | 23 | N613W N201BA N888DS N37BL N28ST [w/o 31Jul87 10km east of Guatemala City/La Aurora A/P, Guatemala; cx Dec89] |
| 014 | 23 | N814L N426EJ JY-AEG (HB-VEL) F-BXPT [wfu by Jun05 Limoges, France] |
| 015 | 24 | N88B [donated 28Feb92 to Pima County Air Museum, AZ; cx Mar92] |
| 015A | 23 | N804LJ [w/o 21Oct65 nr Jackson, MI] |
| 016 | 23 | N500K N7CF N7GF N96CK [fuselage and detached wing set at compound near Davis-Monthan, AZ by Feb02; remains to Aviation Warehouse, El Mirage, CA by Oct04] |
| 017 | 23 | N233R N658L N32SD N30BP F-GBTA F-GDAV [w/o 30Jan89 Lisbon, Portugal; wreckage to Troyes, France, by Jun90; cx Nov92] |
| 018 | 23 | N807LJ N661FS D-IKAA N652J N866DB N866JS [w/o 06May80 Richmond, VA; remains with White Inds, Bates City, MO] |
| 019 | 24 | N4641J HB-VAI N889JF N654DN N100EA N747SC (N954SC) |
| 020 | 23 | N388R N338KK N2GP N210GP N310KR (N144WC) N388R N820L |
| 021 | 23 | N427EJ N427NJ N133W [w/o Burbank, CA; cx Jul81, parted out] |
| 022 | 23 | N428EJ N400CS N103TC N88TC N456SC N114GB [b/u; cx Feb93; remains to White Inds, Bates City, MO] |
| 023 | 23 | N429EJ JY-AEH HB-VEL F-GAMA [w/o after on-board fire 05Jun81 Le Bourget, France; cx 10Feb92 - to technical college at Perigueux, France] |
| 024 | 23 | N202Y N21U N488J N803JA (N702RK) N3ZA [b/u for spares 1982; cx Apr91; remains to White Inds, Bates City, MO] |
| 025 | 23 | N600G N60QG N5DM N3JL N37DM N50DM N508M N24SA [b/u for spares after accident 21Jun85; cx May89] |
| 026 | 23 | N706L HB-VBA F-BSTP N26008 N404AJ N222GH N404DB N540CL [parted out at Hollister, CA circa early 2000; cx 28Apr06 as b/u] |
| 027 | 23 | N430EJ JY-AEI HB-VES F-GAPY (N108TW) [b/u for spares 1983 Kansas City, KS; remains to White Inds, Bates City, MO; rear fuselage & tail unit used as engineering testbed for Avcom Intl ventral fin retrofit programme] |
| 028 | 23 | N818LJ N5DM (N56PR) (N500YY) N5QY N37CP [b/u for spares 1994 Kansas City, KS; remains to White Inds, Bates City, MO] |
| 028A | 23 | N803LJ N432EJ [w/o 25Oct67 Muskegon, MI] |
| 029 | 23 | N7000K N715BC N1BU N66AS N61TS [wfu Sep88; b/u for spares Detroit-Willow Run, MI; cx Jan96] |
| 030 | 23 | N431EJ N431CA ZS-JWC N431CA ZS-JWC [sold in USA circa May02, to be used for spares for c/n 23-081; remains to Aviation Warehouse, El Mirage, CA] |
| 031 | 24A | N175FS N477BL N777TF N777TE N202BA N175FS |
| 032 | 23 | N235R [w/o 23Apr66 Clarendon, TX] |
| 033 | 23 | N158MJ N453LJ N453JT XA-LGM XA-GAM N60DH N23TJ [wfu Sep87; cx Feb93 remains to scrapyard at Hastings-Earls Air Park, FL by Mar01] |
| 034 | 23 | N242WT N241BN N24FF N154AG [to Museum of Flight, Seattle WA. Displayed at Everett/Paine Field, WA] "N407V" |
| 035 | 23 | N100X (N10QX) N992TD [wfu; cx23Jul08] |
| 036 | 23 | N477K N210PC N111WM N38DM YV-278CP N123MJ |
| 037 | 23 | N266JP N988SA N51AJ N65LJ N41AJ N13LJ N10LJ N50AJ XA-ESS XC-UJP XC-AA28 XC-LGD [w/o 07Dec08 Lake Atlangatepec, Mexico] |
| 038 | 23 | N812LJ VR-BCF LN-NPE N1002B 9Q-CGM 9Q-CHB N433J N433JB N100TA N100JZ N300TA N175BA PT-LKQ [wfu Detroit-Willow Run, MI; to Detroit technical school as instructional airframe - then reportedly b/u circa 2000] |
| 039 | 23 | N43B N800JA N15SC N30SC N9JJ (N43CT) N121CK XA-... N121CK |
| 040 | 23 | N433EJ N673WM YV-01CP N98386 N12HJ [b/u for spares 1989] |
| 041 | 23 | N205RJ N666MP C-GDDB N77VJ [b/u for spares circa 2001] |
| 042 | 23 | N293BC N2932C N1ZA N701RZ N69KB [b/u for spares 1982 by White Inds, Bates City, MO; cx Dec91; remains still present Nov94] |
| 043 | 24 | N368MJ N39T N24MW N50BA (N43AC) [sold for spares during 1987; cx Sep89] |
| 044 | 23 | N22B HB-VAM [w/o 28Aug72 Innsbruck, Austria] |
| 045 | 23 | N242F N711MR N100TA [w/o 06May82 Savannah, GA] |
| 045A | 23 | N803LJ HB-VBB F-BSUX N959SC [w/o 23Jly91 Detroit City, MI] |
| 046 | 23 | N434EJ [w/o 09May70 Pellston, MI] |

## LEARJET 23/24

| C/n | Model | Identities |
|---|---|---|
| 047 | 23 | N2503L N347J YV-E-GPA YV-15CP N9260A N444WC N2503L [parted out at Rantoul, KS, circa early 2000] |
| 048 | 23 | N805LJ N1GW N48MW N140RC [wfu at Montgomery, AL by Jul04] |
| 049 | 23 | NASA701 N701NA N933NA (N933N) N605NA |
| 050 | 24 | N828MW N828M N823M N650CA N24ET N24NJ [instructional airframe Mumbai/ Juhu, India] |
| 050A | 23 | N808LJ N808JA [w/o 23May(?) 1982 in ground fire; probably at Sarasota-Bradenton, FL, where burnt fuselage was noted 25Jun82; remains to Taylorville, IL] |
| 051 | 24 | N1500B N1500G N100MJ (N69LL) N990TM N70JC N24VM [parted out by White Inds, Bates City, MO, 1987] |
| 052 | 23 | N360EJ HB-VBD N360EJ N856JB |
| 053 | 23 | N361EJ HB-VBC F-BTQK N23AJ [parted out by Dodson Av'n, Rantoul, KS, 1988; cx Sep92] |
| 054 | 23 | CF-TEL N351WB N351WC N351NR N351N [parted out by Dodson Av'n, Rantoul, KS] |
| 055 | 24 | N809LJ N2366Y N511WH N711CW |
| 056 | 23 | N362EJ N332PC [w/o 06Jan77 Flint, MI; parted out by White Inds, Bates City, MO] |
| 057 | 23 | N448GC N448GG [parted out by Dodson Av'n, Ottawa, KS] |
| 058 | 23 | N363EJ N66MP N7FJ N153AG |
| 059 | 23 | N364EJ N31DP N331DP [b/u for spares Jun87 Detroit-Willow Run, MI - remains to Bounty Avn Scrapyard] |
| 060 | 24 | N889WF N90J XA-ADJ |
| 061 | 23 | N316M [w/o 19Mar66 Lake Michigan, MI] |
| 062 | 23 | N670MF N20TA |
| 063 | 23 | N243F [w/o 14Nov65 Palm Springs, CA] |
| 064 | 23 | N365EJ N200G N400RB N401RB N73JT N66AM ZS-MBR 3D-AFJ ZS-MBR [wfu Oct93 Lanseria, S Africa; to Atlanta Air Salvage, Griffin, GA, Jan95 for spares for possible re-build] N259DB |
| 065 | 24 | N2000M N200DM N7500K (N750QK) N750WJ N957SC N707SC (XA-...) N707SC |
| 065A | 23 | N388Q N28BP (N28BR) N1GZ N122M (N156AG) [fuselage and detached wing set at compound near Davis-Monthan AFB, AZ by Feb02; remains to Aviation Warehouse, El Mirage, CA by Oct04] |
| 066 | 23 | N216RG N72MK N66MW XA-RVB XA-SDP N211TS XB-MYE |
| 067 | 23 | N815LJ N2ZA N703DC N720UA N331DP [w/o 18Jan90 nr Dayton, OH; cx Oct90] |
| 068 | 23 | N460F N902AR N902AB N575HW N9RA N400PG N152AG XA-ARG XB-GRR N73CE [to Yanks Air Museum, Chino, CA] |
| 069 | 23 | N814LJ N9AJ N6GJ N37BL (N34TR) [converted at some time to Model 24 standards; w/o 04Mar98 Oakland, CA, remains to White Ind's, Bates City, MO circa Oct98] |
| 070 | 23 | CF-ARE N1976L N197GL N111CT N101DB XA-RZM XA-TII XC-AA104 XC-JDX [wfu Mexico City] |
| 071 | 23 | N1001A N71LJ XA-RZC N6262T [with Dodson Avn, Rantoul, KS, for parts Jly95, still marked as XA-RZC] |
| 072 | 23 | N331WR N331JR N4VS N31S N2SN RP-C848 |
| 073 | 23 | N806LJ |
| 074 | 23 | 5A-DAC D-IATD N23TC N74MW N23AN N68WM N150AG XA-LAR XB-GRQ N83CE [sold to Maricopa County Community College, AZ] |
| 075 | 23 | 5A-DAD [w/o 05Jun67 Damascus, Syria] |
| 076 | 23 | N1966W N801JA N12GP N50PJ N83LJ |
| 077 | 23 | N812LJ N740J N868J N500P N90658 N88EA (N611CA) N745F [w/o 30Jul88 March AFB, Riverside, CA; cx Mar90] |
| 078 | 23 | N690LJ [w/o 30Nov67 Orlando, FL] |
| 079 | 23 | N240AG N240AQ N31CK [fuselage and detached wing set at compound near Davis-Monthan, AZ by Feb02; remains to Aviation Warehouse, El Mirage, CA by Oct04] |
| 080 | 23 | N822LJ [w/o 09Dec67 Detroit, MI] |
| 081 | 23 | N369EJ N437LJ XC-JOA N418LJ (N81LJ) ZS-MDN N265DC [cx 18Apr07, wfu] |
| 082 | 23 | N280C N805JA N7GP (N700NP) (N216SA) [wfu Hampton - Tara Field, Atlanta GA] |
| 082A | 23 | N823LJ N255ES N744CF N100TA N613BR N618BR (N118LS) |
| 083 | 23 | N824LJ [donated to the Kalamazoo Air Zoo, MI for public static display] |
| 084 | 23 | N788DR N101JR N119BA |
| 085 | 23 | N825LJ N385J N101PP [w/o 04Jun84 Windsor Locks, CT] |
| 086 | 23 | N1021B [w/o 06Nov69 Racine, WI] |
| 087 | 24 | N407V CF-UYT N7VS D-IKAB C-GEEN N998RL N24YA N24YE [parted out by Dodson Intl Parts, Rantoul, KS cx Feb03] |
| 088 | 23 | N816LJ N616PS N11JK N804JA N48AS N500FM (N500LH) [w/o 02Jul91 Columbia, TN; noted dumped Oct91 Bounty Avn Scrapyard, Detroit-Willow Run, MI; cx Jun99] |
| 089 | 23 | N869B N969B N1968W [cx Apr01; b/u for spares by Dodson Int'l Parts, Rantoul, KS circa 2002] |
| 090 | 23 | PP-FMX [w/o 30Aug69 Rio de Janeiro, Brazil] |
| 091 | 23 | N430JA N430J N110M N11QM [cx Dec89; b/u for spares 1989] |
| 092 | 23 | N415LJ N422JR N105BJ N344WC N415LJ |
| 093 | 23 | N416LJ N3350 N416LJ N12TA N38JD N486G N101AR N101AD N97MJ XA-SHN N80775 N7GF XA-... |
| 094 | 23 | N417LJ N20M [w/o 15Dec72 Detroit, MI] |
| 095 | 23 | N366EJ N974D N5D N9RA N46452 [to India as instructional airframe; cx 27Oct09] |
| 096 | 24A | N1967W N421L N527ER N33BK N1972L N1973L N1972L N464CL |

# LEARJET 23/24

| C/n | Model | Identities |
|---|---|---|
| 097 | 23 | N425SC N79LS N1968A N1963A [to spares 1995 remains at Hampton - Tara Field, Atlanta, GA] |
| 098 | 23 | N112T N11111 N2DD N711 N711AE N99TC [b/u for spares May87 Cincinnati-Lunken Field, OH but still regd; remains to Brandis Avn, Taylorville, IL] |
| 099 | 23 | N7200K |
| 100 | 24A | N427LJ CF-BCJ N144X N989SA N424NJ N361AA N24BA N616SC N427LJ N224SC [w/o 26Sep99 Gainsville, GA; remains to Atlanta Air Salvage, Griffin, GA] |
| 101 | 24 | N316M N316MF N15PL N473EJ N473 N68DM (N68FN) N24GJ XA-SGU N24WX [noted wfu at Corona Municipal apt, CA 1997; moved to Mesa/Falcon Field, AZ, by Feb08 for rebuild] |
| 102 | 24A | N436LJ N365EJ N705NA N805NA [w/o 07Jun01 Victorville, CA; cx Sep01] |
| 103 | 24 | N430LJ N714X ZS-LTK N72442 ZS-LTK N90532 ZS-LTK N90532 ZS-LTK N90532 ZS-LTK N105EC XB-ADR |
| 104 | 24 | N433LJ N924ED N45ED |
| 105 | 24 | N425NJ N111EK N111EJ TR-LYB F-GDAE [cx Aug96 as wfu; reported w/o in 1989, no details] |
| 106 | 24 | N888NS N969J N100GP N70RL N103RB N888MC C-FNMC N888MC |
| 107 | 24A | N48L |
| 108 | 24 | N1966L N745W N661CP N661BS N661SS C-GSIV N45811 N29LA N900JA N315AJ [b/u circa Apr04 for spares by White Industries, Bates City, MO] |
| 109 | 24 | HB-VAS OY-RYA SE-DCW (F-GBBV(2)) N900DL XA-NLK |
| 110 | 24A | N388R N1969H N362AA N35JF N88JF [b/u Oct86 possibly following accident at Detroit, MI in Oct86; cx Jul89; remains with Brandis Avn, Taylorville, IL] |
| 111 | 24A | N900Y N500FM N44WD N900NA |
| 112 | 24 | N447LJ CF-ECB N2200T N10CP (OB-....) N112DJ N104GA XA-TRQ |
| 113 | 24 | N438LJ (N402Y) N204Y N100SQ [to spares 1989 by Brandis Avn, Taylorville, IL] |
| 114 | 24 | N443LJ N999M N99DM PT-LNE [wfu at Belo Horizonte, Brazil by 2005] |
| 115 | 24 | N449LJ N458LJ N591D N591DL N86CC [b/u for spares during 1989 Denver, CO; remains with Brandis Avn, Taylorville, IL] |
| 116 | 24A | N461F N52EN N77GH N8FM N400EP N40BP N51B N105GA (N12MB) (N1420) |
| 117 | 24XR | N288VW F-BRAL N16MJ HZ-SMB N90DH N92DF N140EX N24SA |
| 118 | 24 | N452LJ N100GS N1008S N1919W N31SK [w/o 27Mar87 Eagle County A/P, Vail, CO] |
| 119 | 24 | N453LJ N453SA N605GA N994SA N110W N500PP N500P (N500PJ) N61CK N63CK [b/u for spares by Dodson Int'l Parts, Rantoul, KS circa Oct02] |
| 120 | 24 | N457LJ N633J N633NJ N44AJ N44NJ PT-LMF N244RD [b/u for spares by Dodson Int'l Parts, Rantoul, KS, circa Oct02] |
| 121 | 24 | N454LJ N454GL N454RN [w/o 26Feb73 Atlanta, GA] |
| 122 | 24 | N461LJ PT-CXK [w/o 04May73 Rio Galeon, Brazil] |
| 123 | 24 | N262HA N700C (N700ET) XA-JSC XA-JSO N35EC N25LJ N3137 |
| 124 | 24 | N462LJ OY-EGE SE-DCU (N252DL) XA-RTV N991TD |
| 125 | 24A | N651LJ |
| 126 | 24 | N653LJ N352WR N332FP (N345SF) N16HC [parted out by Dodson Av'n, Rantoul, KS] |
| 127 | 24 | N654LJ N654JC N654LD N111LJ N127LJ N37CB (N6462) N124JL |
| 128 | 24 | N655LJ HB-VBK N914BA N333X N383X N4CR HB-VBK N37594 N802W (D-CJAD) N128BJ N911KB XA-TDP (N128WD) [to spares by Dodson Int'l Parts, Rantoul, KS circa 1999] |
| 129 | 24 | N656LJ D-IFUM N44GA C-GSAX N44GA [w/o 30Jan84 Santa Catalina, CA; cx Nov86] |
| 130 | 24 | N657LJ N420WR N1871R N1871P N130J N33CJ N330J N234MR [b/u for spares Dec87] |
| 131 | 24 | N659LJ N232R N282R N11FH N241JA [Wings Over the Rockies Museum, Denver, CO] |
| 132 | 24 | N658LJ N233R N238R N32CA [cx Sep01; aircraft was b/u] |
| 133 | 24 | N660LJ N40JF N40JE N555PV N46WB N16WJ N133DF N133BL [b/u; cx Feb04] |
| 134 | 24 | N231R N281R N282R N215J N200GP (N202GP) N200TC N270TC N7GN N911TR N26BA [parted out at Rantoul, KS circa early 2000] |
| 135 | 24 | N85W N77LB LV-WMR [w/o 28Aug95 Pasadas, Argentina; fuselage at Buenos Aires-Aeroparque, for spares] |
| 136 | 24 | N664LJ N222RB N954S N24LW XA-JLV [wfu following flood damage; to spares Oct94 Spirit of St Louis A/P, MO] |
| 137 | 24 | N907CS N73HG N77RY N72FP N151AG |
| 138 | 24 | N37P N808DP N808D N575G N106CA N45JF (N106CA) N400RS N94JJ N130RS [being converted to a 4-seat 'suborbital spaceplane' fitted with a Rocketdyne RS-88 rocket, new wings and a new tail assembly. First flight was planned for July 2006, to be followed by 25 flights beginning in January 2007, current project status unknown] |
| 139 | 24 | N590GA N52JH N42AJ N481EZ N96AA [b/u for spares by Dodson Int'l, Rantoul, KS circa Oct02] |
| 140 | 24 | N663LJ N663L N663LJ N593KR N252M N100VC N100VQ [to instructional airframe at National Aviation Academy, St Petersburg-Clearwater, FL by Oct02] |
| 141 | 24 | N348VL N348BJ N43AJ N141PJ XB-FJW XB-GHO |
| 142 | 24 | N591GA N200NR N777MR N723JW |
| 143 | 24 | N592GA N145JN N778GA N49AJ N900BD N2YY (N727LG) N724LG N24WF [wfu still painted as N724LG, to compound near Davis-Monthan, AZ by Nov02; cx 19Jul04; remains to Aviation Warehouse, El Mirage, CA by Oct04] |

# LEARJET 23/24

| C/n | Model | Identities |
|---|---|---|
| 144 | 24 | N593GA N397L N397BC N9KC N700C N303AF [parted out by White Inds, Bates City, MO, 1986; cx 11Mar05] |
| 145 | 24 | N690J N57ND (N57NB) N282AC (ZS-PBI) [cx 30Mar09; wfu in South Africa] |
| 146 | 24 | N672LJ N235Z N44CJ [w/o 02Oct81 Felt, OK] |
| 147 | 24 | N673LJ N595GA N16CP N444KW N33NJ N825AA (N67CK) N147KH N147CK [instructional airframe JRN Institute of Aviation Technology, India; cx 21Jan09] |
| 148 | 24 | N406L N80CB N133TW HB-VDH N8482B N426PS (N47NR) N41MP N24ET |
| 149 | 24 | N294BC N2945C N300HH N300LB N64HB N995TD [cx 09Mar06; aircraft used as an instructional airframe] |
| 150 | 24XR | N3807G N596GA N596HF N211HJ N211BL N24XR XA-RQB [parted out by Dodson Av'n, Rantoul, KS Oct04] |
| 151 | 24 | N153H N111HJ N664CL N664GL N50JF N24AJ N53GH N6177Y |
| 152 | 24 | N3807G N597GA N21U N98DK N9LM N48BA [wfu 1993 Kissimmee, FL; cx Aug93; parted out by Dodson Av'n, Rantoul, KS] |
| 153 | 24 | N524SC N1TK N159J (N53DE) N878DE (N555DH) N153BR N120RA [wfu; cx 13Jan09] |
| 154 | 24 | N123VW N12315 N424RD N7HA N11AK N123RE [w/o 17Oct78 Lancaster, CA] |
| 155 | 24 | N598GA N422U N462B N462BA N833GA N210FP N660A [b/u for spares during 1987; remains to Aviation Film Prop Warehouse, at El Mirage, CA, wearing marks N464CL] |
| 156 | 24 | N599GA N468DM N111RF N111RP N712R LZ-VTS |
| 157 | 24 | N640GA N1919W N1919G N191DA N94HC N124WL N43ZP N659AT (N157BP) XA-SNZ (N650AT) N659AT N157TW |
| 158 | 24 | N642GA N392T N855GA N500MH PT-LPX N500MH N220PM PT-WEW |
| 159 | 24 | N647GA N855W N661JB N66MR N710TV (N269AL) |
| 160 | 24 | N645G N111WJ C-GTJT N4791C N989TL |
| 161 | 24 | N649G N224KT N24KT N24KF N222TW |
| 162 | 24 | N841G N338DS N91MK N919K N835AC N835AG N55NJ [w/o 07May86 Hollywood, FL; remains to Dodson Av'n, Ottawa, KS; rear fuselage & tail to Guthrie, OK] |
| 163 | 24 | N701AP N1AP N65339 N77AE (N777JA) N65WM N68LU [wfu and donated to mechanics school, Lewis Univ, IL Jul86] |
| 164 | 24 | N711L N464J N924BW N831RA XA-RYN N831RA XA-TKC+ N831RA [+ remained current on USCAR, while also on the Mexican register] |
| 165 | 24 | N844GA N469J ZS-KJY V5-KJY ZS-KJY V5-KJY ZS-KJY |
| 166 | 24 | N993KL N500SB N124PJ N124HF N993TD |
| 167 | 24 | N847GA N841LC N888B N664CL |
| 168 | 24 | N109JR N109JB N51CH C-GBWB N155BT N333TW |
| 169 | 24 | D-ICAR N9033X (N127DN) N127DM N927AA N93BP [parted out by Dodson Int'l Parts, Rantoul, KS circa Oct02] |
| 170 | 24 | N200DH N151WW [wfu Addison, TX] |
| 171 | 24 | N737FN N417WW |
| 172 | 24 | N234WR N48AJ [parted out by White Inds, Bates City, MO] |
| 173 | 24 | N852GA N872JR N110SQ N33ST N102GP N3GL N623RC YV-824CP YV1079 |
| 174 | 24 | N854GA N661CP N661JG N999JR N321GL N77WD N77GJ XA-LNK |
| 175 | 24 | N859GM N859L N288K N28BK N881FC [w/o 02Feb92 New Tamiami, FL; cx Mar93] |
| 176 | 24 | PT-CXJ N3034B [cx 31Jan05; b/u] |
| 177 | 24 | N321Q N104MB N555LB N555LA N555LB (N524DW) [fuselage and detached wing set at compound near Davis-Monthan, AZ by Feb02; remains to Aviation Warehouse, El Mirage, CA by Oct04] |
| 178 | 24 | N674LJ N55KS N55KX N56LB N56LS N24AJ N41BJ N723JW N11AQ [parted out at Addison, TX, circa 2005] |
| 179 | 24 | N920FF N300CC N111RA N111RE N410PD N410PB N412PD N717DB XC-GII XA-RQP N994TD |
| 180 | 24 | N566RB N802JA N100RA XA-SBR XA-NLA |
| 181 | 24B | N234Q N1QC N651J N44PA (N144PA) N87CF N254JT N426TA |
| 182 | 24B | N945GA N171L N500ZA N500ZH N155J RP-C2324 |
| 183 | 24B | N676LJ OY-AGZ F-BRNL [w/o 18Dec85 Toulouse, France] |
| 184 | 24B | N950GA D-IMWZ N84J N36RS N78BH N28DL N58DM N58FN |
| 185 | 24B | N754M N44CP N144CP [parted out at Rantoul, KS circa early 2000] |
| 186 | 24B | N266P N100AJ N1SS N18G (N7300G) N7300K N73PS N196CF [b/u for parts; cx Feb06] |
| 187 | 24B | ZS-SGH F-GAJD N5WJ N129DM [b/u for spares Feb90] |
| 188 | 24B | N230R N280R [cx 14Jan08, wfu Guthrie, OK] |
| 189 | 24B | D-CJET D-IKAF D-CONA N14MJ N711DS N711DX N915US [cx 21Feb06 as b/u for parts] |
| 190 | 24B | N4291G N9HM N50TC HZ-GP4 F-GBLA N190SC (N190DB) N190BP N600XJ [w/o 23Dec03 Helendale, CA] |
| 191 | 24B | N855W N44LJ (N44TL) N80DH [b/u 1984 after accident; cx Mar89; remains to Dodson Av'n, Ottawa, KS] |
| 192 | 24B | N1919W N12MK [w/o 06Jan77 Palm Springs, CA] |
| 193 | 24B | D-IOGI N31TC N500RP N500RE N33RE N140CA N83H N83HC (N488BL) N193JF N193DB |
| 194 | 24B | N952GA N77LS N851BA N62DM (N62FN) N2093A |
| 195 | 24B | N202BT N272GL F-BUUV N803L N555LJ (N721MD) (N46LM) |
| 196 | 24B | N99SC N1125E N99ES N99E N173LP N573LP N573LR N88RD N196AF N196TB |

# LEARJET 23/24

| C/n | Model | Identities |
|---|---|---|
| 197 | 24B | N953GA CF-CSS C-FCSS N52GH N87AC C-FCSS N711CN N711 N711UR N710TJ XB-SUD XA-RXA N84CT XA- N24FU N89ES |
| 198 | 24B | N66RP N111GW N21XL N21XB N39KM [to India as instructional airframe; cx 12Nov08] |
| 199 | 24B | N333CR N855W N444HC N70TJ XA-TTT |
| 200 | 24B | (N24NP) N721J N721JA N246CM N119MA [being parted out at Bates City, MO circa early 2000] |
| 201 | 24B | N3871J N273GL D-IDDD D-CDDD C-GTFA N100DL [w/o 23May98, Orlando Executive FL; parted out at Bates City, MO, circa early 2000] |
| 202 | 24B | N3816G N77JN F-BUFN N26MJ N999MF N123SV N814HH N814JR N333RY [reported parted out at San Antonio, TX circa 2001] |
| 203 | 24B | N515WC N3GW (N43TL) N55LJ N55MJ N203CK N203JL |
| 204 | 24B | N957GA N957E N176CP N510ND N510MS [fuselage only with OK Turbines at Hollister, CA by Feb05] |
| 205 | 24B | N974JD N64CF N64CE (N721J) [wfu; cx 16Sep08] |
| 206 | 24B | HB-VBY F-BTYV N116RM N24YA |
| 207 | 24XR | N851JH N878W N457JA ZS-MGJ |
| 208 | 24B | D-ILDE N72335 N42HC N444AG N32MJ N444AG N444AQ N14PT XA-AAA |
| 209 | 24B | N970GA N16MT N14BC ZS-LWU |
| 210 | 24B | ZS-LLG F-BSRL [w/o 10Jun85 over Provins nr Paris, France] |
| 211 | 24B | N388P N30EH N222AP N31LB N413WF N680CJ |
| 212 | 24B | N291BC N328TL N328JK YV.... |
| 213 | 24B | N555MH N986WC N886WC N999RA N43KC N103TC N95AB N895J N24JZ XA-... N24JZ |
| 214 | 24B | N192MH N192MB N666CC N668MC N214MJ N42NF N234CM [w/o 16Dec88 nr Monclova, Mexico; cx Apr91] |
| 215 | 24B | N971GA N201WL N10EC N29CA (N57JR) N29CA (N57JR) N400EP |
| 216 | 24B | N212LF N723LL N711DB N411SP (N821LL) N777LB N900GG |
| 217 | 24B | N777MC N777MQ C-GPDB N8536Y C-GDKS N45824 N217AT C-FZHT N876MC |
| 218 | 24B | N682LJ N101VS |
| 219 | 24B | N658AT N711CE N100KK F-GECI N977GA ZS-TOY |
| 220 | 24B | N292BC N248J N17FN [wfu for spares by Dodson Avn, Ottawa, KS] |
| 221 | 24B | N977GA N570P (N570JG) N59JG N233TW |
| 222 | 24B | N692LJ N740E N740F N740EJ [cx 19Jly05 as b/u] |
| 223 | 24B | D-IOGA D-COGA D-IFVG D-CFVG N7074X [wfu for spares by Feb94] |
| 224 | 24B | D-IOGE N99606 N30DH C-GPCL N102PA (N722DM) N61DM (N61FN) (N51GJ) XA-TCA |
| 225 | 24B | N618R D-IHLZ [w/o 18Jun73 Marlensel, W Germany] |
| 226 | 24B | N454LJ N335JW (N335JR) N335RY RP-C2424 |
| 227 | 24B | XA-TIP N90797 N10CB N43W N4576T N28AT N27BJ |
| 228 | 24B | N245GL N4292G N7DL (D-IIDD) D-IIPD N777SA N150AB PT-OBD [wfu at Belo Horizonte, Brazil by 2005] |
| 229 | 24B | N293BC N298H N551AS N864CL [w/o 08Oct84 San Francisco, CA] |
| 230 | 24D | N252GL N329HN N93C N93CB N433J N433JA N18SD N477JB N482CP N819GF N67JR N7121K XA-VVI N32287 XA-SSU |
| 231 | 24D | HB-VBU I-CART N693LJ N37DH N93BR [wfu; remains with Brandis Avn, Taylorville, IL; still regd] |
| 232 | 24D | N123CB [w/o 17Apr71 Butte, MT] |
| 233 | 24R | N253GL D-IGSO N78AF N23SG N23SQ N500RW N124TS (N56GH) N143GB N19LJ |
| 234 | 24D | LV-PRA LV-JTZ |
| 235 | 24XR | N51VL N701SC |
| 236 | 24D | N26VM N48JW N25ZW N55DD N3TJ N25LJ N236TS N236WJ N93DD N990PT N890PT N47TK N59AL |
| 237 | 24D | N902AR N111TT N25TA N112J N32AA N353J N889WF XA-... N25RJ N825DM N237TW |
| 238 | 24D | N262GL N472EJ N49DM N48FN [to Hampton University, Newport News, VA Mar04] |
| 239 | 24D | D-ILVW D-ILHM F-GBLZ N83MJ PT-LAU [w/o 10Sep94 Brasilia A/P, Brazil] |
| 240 | 24D | LV-PRB LV-JXA [possibly to spares with Dodson Int'l Parts, O'Lathe/New Century Air Center, KS circa Oct00] |
| 241 | 24D | HB-VCT N120J N363BC (N61TJ) N63GA |
| 242 | 24D | N1972G N45CP N1972G N999WA [to India as instructional airframe; cx 28Aug09] |
| 243 | 24XR | HB-VCI N2909W (N85DH) N83RG N56WS N57FL N37HT N929HF N929MC |
| 244 | 24D | PT-DZU [w/o 23Aug71 Sao Paulo, Brazil] |
| 245 | 24D | N275LE N275E JA8446 N275E (N44KB) |
| 246 | 24D | N215Z N21NA N5SJ N35SJ N50SJ (N69SF) N61BA N184AL N600JC N444SC (N444HE) N24TE N99JB N6JM N500MS N400MS |
| 247 | 24D | HB-VCN D-ICAP N23AM N42PG N247DB N997TD [w/o 10Dec01 on approach to El Paso, TX] |
| 248 | 24D | OO-LFA 9Q-CBC [w/o 18Jan94 Kinshasa, Zaire] |
| 249 | 24D | 9J-ADF N27MJ N999M N998M XA-POS XC-AA63 N249RA N440KT |
| 250 | 24D | N112C D-IMAR N122CG N2U N1U N85CA N85CD Venezuela 0006 |
| 251 | 24D | N333X N338X N251TJ N95DD XA-SBZ XA-RIC N46JA N69XW N39EL |
| 252 | 24D | N711L N711LD N972 N157AG (N252TJ) (C6-BGF) XA-... N157AG |
| 253 | 24D | N123VW N999U N30FL N711DB (N30FL) N97DM N417JD N97DM [collided with Learjet N39DM c/n 35-040 over Pacific Ocean nr San Clemente Islands 05Mar86, w/o] |

## LEARJET 23/24

| C/n | Model | Identities |
|---|---|---|
| 254 | 24D | D-ICAY D-CCAT N13606 PT-LCV |
| 255 | 24D | XC-SAG XA-BBE XA-SMU N255AR |
| 256 | 24D | HB-VCW N703J C-GWFG C-GWEG N256MJ N256WM [b/u Jan06 Mankato, MN; cx 04Apr06; fuselage to Guthrie, OK, by 01Oct06] |
| 257 | 24D | N427JX C-GHDP N888FA |
| 258 | 24D | N75KV N25VZ N25GW N19TJ N24CK (N24DZ) (N77RS) N424RS |
| 259 | 24D | N200JR N22MH (N24EA) (N22ML) I-EJIA N22MH XA-RRC [to White Inds, Bates City, MO, for spares] |
| 260 | 24D | N60GL C-GFJB XA-ROX XA-GBA XC-PFP XC-AGU |
| 261 | 24D | D-IDAT D-COOL C-GBWA [b/u for spares 1993 by Global Inds; cx Jun94; remains to Bounty Avn Scrapyard, Detroit-Willow Run, MI] |
| 262 | 24D | N2GR OH-GLB N38788 N110PS OH-GLB [wfu; cx Apr03 - to RAOL Technical Vocational School, Rovaniemi, Finland; in use as instructional airframe] |
| 263 | 24D | N3812G XB-JOY [w/o 29Jun76 Mexico City, Mexico] |
| 264 | 24XR | PI-C1747 RP-C1747 [wfu Manila, Philippines] |
| 265 | 24D | N2WL N32WL N456JA [w/o 24Oct85 Juneau, AK] |
| 266 | 24D | N266BS VH-BSJ N266BS N266TW |
| 267 | 24XR | HB-VCY N46032 N78AE N124GA VR-BHC HB-VCY N95DA VR-BMN N267MP ZS-OEA |
| 268 | 24D | N53GL N111WW N123CC N92TC (N66FN) N58BL N98WJ N24TK |
| 269 | 24D | XA-DIJ XA-MOV XA-DIJ |
| 270 | 24D | XB-NAG XA-BUY N3979P PT-LEM [w/o 07Apr99 Ribeirao Preto, Brazil] |
| 271 | 24D | N3818G HB-VDK F-BVEC N4305U XA-SCE |
| 272 | 24D | N51GL N117K |
| 273 | 24D | OH-GLA N118J 5Y-GEO N51AJ XC-DOP XB-DZR |
| 274 | 24D | N3871J N1U N48CT |
| 275 | 24D | XB-NUR N24TC N216HB PT-LPH |
| 276 | 24D | PT-JGU N25CV N56PT |
| 277 | 24D | N131CA N181CA (N163ME) (N181RW) N106MC N57BC N277TW |
| 278 | 24D | PT-JKR N5695H N202JS |
| 279 | 24D | VH-SBC N849GL N3DU N3DZ I-FREU N75CJ N101AR N955EA |
| 280 | 24XR | D-ICHS N79RS ZS-NGG [b/u for spares at Nelspruit, South Africa] |
| 281 | 24D | SE-DFB OY-BIZ N23MJ N281FP [to Frontiers of Flight Museum, Dallas-Love Field TX] |
| 282 | 24D | D-INKA N300JA [w/o 02Dec79 Dutch Harbor, AK] |
| 283 | 24D | SE-DFA D-IEGO N51JT N20GT N31WT N47WT (N711SC) N24XR XA-UHT |
| 284 | 24D | PT-JKQ |
| 285 | 24D | XC-AZU XA-REK XB-GBC N995DR (N995RD) N430JW N300TJ |
| 286 | 24XR | N59GL N86GC N56RD N57DB N77JL [w/o 12Nov03 St. Louis Downtown apt, IL] |
| 287 | 24D | HB-VDN EC-CJA HB-VDN I-MABU N92565 PT-LCN [w/o 04Apr84 Florianapolis, Brazil] |
| 288 | 24D | N288DF N7701L |
| 289 | 24D | (HB-VDO) F-BRGF N131MA XA-RUJ N131MA N289SA N289G N98CG |
| 290 | 24D | N462B N23JC N934H N87AP N627ER N24TK XA-RMF N24TK N88LJ N308SM |
| 291 | 24D | ZS-GLD N45862 N148J N24PJ PT-LYL N114WC (N919MA) N488DM N483DM |
| 292 | 24D | N426NA N600PC N426NA N800PC N888TW |
| 293 | 24D | XA-TIP N917BF N293MC |
| 294 | 24D | N4F PT-LNK PP-EIW PT-WKL |
| 295 | 24D | N717HB N717HE N49TJ (N160GC) N590CH N295NW |
| 296 | 24D | XA-FIW N222BN N500RK N500DJ PT-LMS |
| 297 | 24D | N297EJ XA-ACC N716US (N317MR) HK-3265 N8094U N24S |
| 298 | 24D | N298EJ XA-ADD N98AC N151AG N470TR N169US |
| 299 | 24D | N299EJ XA-ABB XC-JCN XB-GJS N299TW |
| 300 | 24D | N300EJ N455JA [w/o 20Aug85 Gulkana, AK] |
| 301 | 24D | N137JL N111TT (N87MJ) N31BG N249HP |
| 302 | 24D | N302EJ N39DM N302EJ [w/o 14Apr83 Puerta Vallarta, Mexico] |
| 303 | 24D | N303EJ PT-LOJ N303EJ [to White Inds, Bates City, MO 21Jun04 for spares; cx 26Oct07] |
| 304 | 24D | N304EJ N304LP N500CG N588CG [wfu at Detroit-Willow Run, MI] |
| 305 | 24D | N305EJ N98DK N305EJ (N725DM) N43DM (N43FN) N510PA N666MW N930PJ |
| 306 | 24D | N306EJ N55CD N98AA N132MA XA-SAV XA-SAA N306JA (N243RK) |
| 307 | 24D | N307EJ N307BJ XA-RRK [w/o 02Jan98 Tampico, Mexico; to spares by Dodson Int'l Parts, Rantoul, KS] |
| 308 | 24D | N308EJ N99AA N39TT (N308LJ) N89AA XB-IRH |
| 309 | 24D | N310LJ N45FC N45AJ (N4445J) N789AA N80CK N309TC |
| 310 | 24D | HB-VDU I-AMME [w/o 06Feb76 Bari, Italy] |
| 311 | 24D | N66LW N5TR N5TD N19HM N19FM N50DR N56DR N748GM N10WJ (N76PW) N311LJ |
| 312 | 24D | Ecuador IGM-401 N312NA N80AP |
| 313 | 24D | Mexico MTX-01 Mexico MTX-02 [reported w/o 20Nov98 Mexico City, Mexico - parted out at Bates City, MO circa early 2000] |
| 314 | 24D | N501MH N13MJ [w/o 06Nov82 Elizabeth City, NC; cx Sep92] |
| 315 | 24D | PT-KPE [wfu Sao Paulo/Congonhas, Brazil circa Sep99; fuselage to Jundiai, Brazil] |
| 316 | 24D | LV-LRC Argentina T-03 LV-LRC |
| 317 | 24D | N133GL ZS-JJO N45AJ XA-JIQ |
| 318 | 24D | N114JT N611DB |

# LEARJET 23/24

| C/n | Model | Identities | | | | | | |
|---|---|---|---|---|---|---|---|---|
| 319 | 24XR | XC-SUP | XA-SUP | XC-SUP | N174RD | | | |
| 320 | 24D | N3802G | YU-BIH | SL-BAB | S5-BAB | N996TD | 9V-... | |
| 321 | 24D | N10WF | N122RW | N224JB | C-FRNR | N33TP | N351MH | |
| 322 | 24D | XA-DAT | N105GL | N972H | N7RL | (N322TJ) | N322RS | |
| 323 | 24D | N61AW | N744JC | N104MC | N453 | N27AX | [cx Nov05, wfu] | |
| 324 | 24D | N107GL | (possibly XA-SUY) | XA-SCY | N324TW | | | |
| 325 | 24D | N76RV | N416G | N500SW | N500SQ | N721SF | | |
| 326 | 24D | N326EJ | (N400XB) | N326KE | N322AU | | | |
| 327 | 24D | N327EJ | F-GGPG | N327GJ | N711PC | [instructional airframe VARIA-Vantaa Vocational School, Helsinki, Finland Dec08; cx 10Mar09] | | |
| 328 | 24D | D-IMMM | D-CMMM | | | | | |
| 329 | 24E | N102GL | N21AG | N22MJ | XA-RAQ | XA-PFA | N329TJ | N24FW |
| 330 | 24E | N511AT | N330TW | | | | | |
| 331 | 24E | N12MJ | XA-REA | N32DD | | | | |
| 332 | 24F | N13KL | N56MM | | | | | |
| 333 | 24E | N76TR | N32WT | N75GP | N75GR | PT-LQK | | |
| 334 | 24E | N6KM | N66MJ | N944KM | | | | |
| 335 | 24E | N721GL | N87JL | N2DD | N8AE | N2DD | | |
| 336 | 24F | N3818G | I-DDAE | N162J | N9LD | N49GS | | |
| 337 | 24F | XA-GEO | XA-DET | | | | | |
| 338 | 24E | N729GL | N30LM | N30EM | [b/u for spares 1989; cx Dec89; remains with Brandis Avn, Taylorville, IL] | | | |
| 339 | 24E | N15MJ | N851CC | N690 | N60FN | N1TJ | N52DD | N207RG |
| 340 | 24E | N10FU | C-FHFP | N54JC | (N95CP) | N106TJ | N457GM | N825AM N627JJ |
| 341 | 24E | N22BM | N22NM | N3PW | (N103JW) | N14DM | | |
| 342 | 24F | N40144 | YV-178CP | N824GA | N123DG | | | |
| 343 | 24E | N102B | N102C | N1DK | N7EJ | (N602JF) | | |
| 344 | 24F | N81MC | [w/o 10Nov84 St Thomas, Virgin Islands] | | | | | |
| 345 | 24E | N500RP | N500RR | D-CFPD | N435AS | N217JS | (N99UP) | N217AJ |
| 346 | 24E | N61SF | N41TC | N117AJ | N117AE | N69AX | (HP-....) | XC-LJE XB-JXZ |
| 347 | 24E | N724GL | N124EZ | N500LL | N500TS | N500SR | N508SR | |
| 348 | 24F | N725GL | N4RT | N4RU | (N106M) | N8BG | N444TW | [w/o Guadalajara, Mexico, 09Jan07] |
| 349 | 24F | VH-FLJ | N349BS | XA-CAP | XB-DZD | XB-KJW | | |
| 350 | 24F | N741GL | N500ZA | | | | | |
| 351 | 24E | N19MJ | N31WT | N81WT | N77MR | (N94BD) | N75NE | |
| 352 | 24F | N101US | (N449JS) | N352MD | | | | |
| 353 | 24F | N740GL | N711PD | N411MM | N63BW | PT-LMA | [w/o 24Feb88 Macre, Brazil] | |
| 354 | 24F | N678SP | PT-LYE | ZS-FUN | [possibly w/o 14Jan06 Kinshasa, Republic of Congo] | | | |
| 355 | 24E | N7AB | N7ZB | N500NH | N165CM | | | |
| 356 | 24F | N3283M | N677SW | N113JS | PT-LKD | | | |
| 357 | 24F | N288J | N129ME | | | | | |

Production complete

# LEARJET MODEL 25

| C/n | Series | Identities |
|---|---|---|
| 001 | | N463LJ [used in construction of 25-002] |
| 002 | | N661LJ [wfu Jly72 and used for AiResearch engine tests] |
| 003 | | N594GA N11JC N4PN N97DM N97FN [to Hampton University, Newport News, VA May04] |
| 004 | | N641GA N1121 N1121C N7GJ N47MJ N251AF N225KA |
| 005 | | N646GA N1969W N777RA N707TR (N707TP) (N24FN) N28FN N711SQ XA-SDQ N39CK |
| 006 | | N6804L N256P N90MH N88CJ (N88GJ) N522SC N852SC N188FC (N25JX) (N857SC) N252SC N44CP XA-... |
| 007 | | N551MD N551MB N7TJ N25NM N500JA N52JA (N58JA) N726WR |
| 008 | | N648GA N744W VP-BDM N744W N1976S N645L N88NJ N800GG XA-MUU |
| 009 | | N843GA N670LJ 9Q-CHC N40LB [w/o 25Sep73 Omaha, NB] |
| 010 | | N846GA N846HC N671WM N102PS (N10BF) (N82UH) (N121GL) N121EL [cx May03 to Kingston University, UK as instructional airframe] |
| 011 | | N167J N49BA C-GHMH N108GA N525TW |
| 012 | | N853GA N853DS N191DA N846YT N846YC N102AR [parted out by White Inds, Bates City, MO; cx 29Apr09] |
| 013 | | N856G N515VW [w/o 17Apr69 Delemont, Switzerland] |
| 014 | | N857GA N914SB N204A N316M N127AJ N8CL N14LJ N754DB [canx 07Jun04; b/u by Clay Lacy Avn for parts] |
| 015 | | N858GM CF-HMV N713US N708TR N25FN N25GJ N125U XA-LLL |
| 016 | | N145JN CF-KAX N424RD N711EV N83TH N8FF N976BS (N35WE) [canx 12Sep05; b/u for parts by Jet Components Aircraft Parts, TX; hulk to Alliance Air Parts, Oklahoma City, OK] |
| 017 | | N720AS N101WR N16JP N666WL N55WJ N128DM N123JS N53FL |
| 018 | | N861GA N323WA N77SA N32PC N99ES N117CH N15MJ (N23FN) N29FN [wfu; with Brandis Avn, Taylorville, IL; still regd] |
| 019 | | N591KR N88EP N88FP N100MK [w/o 21Oct78 Sandusky, OH] |
| 020 | | N941GA N215Z N30TT (N90TC) N113AK N900JD N900CJ N500JS N76CK |
| 021 | | N942GA N111LL N1JR N1LL N40SW N40SN N6NF [wfu; cx Apr95; displayed Ozark Municipal A/P, AL] |
| 022 | XR | N943GA N925WP N1ZC N99CQ (N93JH) N131MS N24BS N111WB N111WR ZS-SSM |
| 023 | | N577LJ N72CD N13CR (N861L) N47AJ (N820RT) (N12RA) N850SC N767SC N147TW |
| 024 | | N425RD N125ST N137BC N20HJ N20RZ |
| 025 | | N920S N928S N920S N92V N49BB N242AG N225DS (N111LM) N110RA |
| 026 | | N4005S N7ZA C-GMAP N283R N281R N25EC |
| 027 | | N7000G N423RD N35WB N835WB (N835GM) EC-EBM N500DL N900AJ [b/u] |
| 028 | | N592KR N263GL N277LE N33PF N727LJ |
| 029 | XR | N280LC N28LA N107HF [parted out by White Inds, Bates City, MO; cx 29Apr09] |
| 030 | | N951GA N999M N999MK N745W N30PS N48HM N380LC N45DM N51CA [w/o 30Mar83 Newark, NJ] |
| 031 | | N294NW (N294M) |
| 032 | | N373W N711DB N712DC N357HC XA-ZYZ XA-RQI [was on display in terminal at Mexico City A/P, Mexico, in 1994 but has since been removed] |
| 033 | | HB-VBP N143J N786MS YV-88CP N77NJ [cx Aug03; parted out] |
| 034 | | N954GA N954FA N242WT N6GC N3UC N17AR N19FN N309AJ N309LJ [cx Oct03; in use at Staverton, UK as ground instructional frame] |
| 035 | | N683LJ N33GF N33TR N616NA |
| 036 | TF | N956GA N956J N741E N741ED N15CC N15M [also carried "N25TF"] N45BK |
| 037 | | N737EF N18JF N28AA N155AG [parted out circa Nov00; fuselage used as a cabin interior display exhibit by Best AeroNet Ltd TX; canx 18Sep03] |
| 038 | | HB-VBR EC-CKD HB-VBR N738GL N36MW N444WS N83GG N400AJ N813JW N130CK |
| 039 | | N959GA N959RE N17JF N66NJ N308AJ (N25VJ) N273CA [to India as instructional airframe; cx 12Nov09] |
| 040 | | N687LJ HB-VBI F-BSUR (N2273G) C-GOSL N41AJ N9CZ (N98RH) N23FN N238CA [to India as instructional airframe 2009] |
| 041 | | N960GA N205SC N205SA N31AA (N25RE) [wfu, stored Edgewater, FL] |
| 042 | | N958GA N958DM (N429TJ) N50DT N800JA N797SC (N25LG) (N125WD) [derelict at Deland, FL since 2002 with marks N125WD reserved at one time] |
| 043 | | N30LJ N808DP N300PP N234ND N473TC |
| 044 | | N962GA N658TC [w/o 18Jan72 Victoria, TX] |
| 045 | | N963GA CF-DWW N815J N33CJ N123EL N24FN N28CK [fuselage noted with MTW Aerospace's facility near Montgomery, AL in Apr02; canx 07Apr05] |
| 046 | | N964GA N55KC N55KQ N33PT N345MC |
| 047 | | N222B (N68CK) |
| 048 | | N965GA N200G XA-TCY N48GR |
| 049 | | N966GA N900P N900Q HP-1141P N900Q N70HJ N70SK [w/o 21Jul07 St Augustine, FL] |
| 050 | | N44EL N44EE D-CONE N27MJ N55FN N999MF |
| 051 | | N973GA N70MP PT-LPT N12WW N76UM (N760A) |
| 052 | | N232MD N8280 N828QA N250CC (N132MA) N133MA N692FC N692FG (N69LJ) |

# LEARJET 25

| C/n | Series | Identities |
|---|---|---|
| 053 | | N974GA N974M N37MB N37GB N153TW [w/o 24Aug01 Lansing, NY; cx Jan02] |
| 054 | | OY-AKL N12373 N500JW N509G N25MD |
| 055 | | N1500B N65RC N511AJ [parted out by White Inds, Bates City, MO] |
| 056 | XR | N780A PT-LBW |
| 057 | | CF-TXT C-FTXT N920EA (N225EA) N507HF [parted out by White Inds, Bates City, MO; cx 29Apr09] |
| 058 | | N2366Y N273LP N273LR [parted out by Alliance Air Parts, Oklahoma City, OK] |
| 059 | | N425JX N211MB [w/o 03Mar80 Port au Prince, Haiti] |
| 060 | | N695LJ N564CL |
| 061 | C | N251GL PT-DUO N9CN YV-203CP [wfu Fort Lauderdale Executive, FL] |
| 062 | | OY-AKZ N4981 N105BJ N303JJ HZ-GP4 N86MJ N27FN N25ME N21FN |
| 063 | | N919S C-GPDZ N184J N680J N68PJ N5DM N24LT N25FM |
| 064 | | N266GL [rebuilt to Model 28 standard to act as prototype; reverted to Model 25 standards] N566NA [wfu 1998; canx 07Apr03 - on display at the John C.Stennis Space Center, MS] |
| 065 | | [airframe not built] |
| 066 | | [airframe not built] |
| 067 | | [airframe not built] |
| 068 | | [airframe not built] |
| 069 | | [airframe not built] |
| 070 | C | N255GL CF-ROX C-FROX N32SM C-FZHU N911LM [parted out Griffin, GA] |
| 071 | C | N257GL YV-T-DTT YV-130P YV-132CP N97AM LV-ZTH |
| 072 | C | N256GL PT-IBR [w/o 26Sep76 Sao Paulo, Brazil] |
| 073 | XR | HB-VCM I-TAKY N3JL N3JX HZ-SMB N63SB N85FJ N888DB N45CP [w/o 30Aug02 Lexington, KY - remains with Atlanta Air Salvage, Griffin, GA] |
| 074 | B | N251GL SX-ASO [w/o 18Feb72 Antibes, France] |
| 075 | B | N241AG N241AQ N417PJ N138JB VR-CGD VR-CHT VP-CHT VP-CJF N82025 N307HF [parted out by White Inds Bates City, MO; cx 29Apr09] |
| 076 | B | HB-VCL D-CCWK N160J N711CA N831WM N222MC N222MQ N77KW XA-SJS |
| 077 | B | PT-DVL [w/o 12Nov76 Sao Paulo, Brazil] |
| 078 | B | N258GL N64MP N64MR N276LE N188BC N778JC N778GM |
| 079 | B | D-CCAT OE-GLA N50DH N36CC (N85HR) XA-SVG XA-AVV |
| 080 | B | N1976L N1978L (N90DH) N30AP XA-POG [wfu Toluca, Mexico] |
| 081 | B | N111GL N110GL HZ-MOA HZ-AZP HZ-BB1 N66TJ N524DW |
| 082 | B | HB-VCK N30P N427RD N15AK N11AK N654 N700FC N62DM |
| 083 | C | N31CS N200Y N200MH N54FN |
| 084 | C | N2000M (C-GWUZ) N200QM N200SF F-BYAL N777TX |
| 085 | B | N8MA N8MQ [b/u for spares - fuselage in compound near Lake City, FL] |
| 086 | B | N123DM N28BP N23DB N65WH [wfu Perris, CA, by Sep09] |
| 087 | C | N723LF N777LF N99XZ N25TE [dbr 09Feb03 Bethel, AK; parted out by White Inds, Bates City, MO; cx 29Apr09] |
| 088 | B | N88GC N88GQ N123SF N176G N42FE N125JL N5UJ [w/o 22Nov01 Pittsburgh, PA] |
| 089 | C | PT-IIQ (N890K) |
| 090 | B | N265GL N112CT N112CH N112ME C-GBOT N754CA C-FPUB |
| 091 | B | N500CA N500CD N500MJ D-CBPD N96MJ C-FDAC N2138T (N816JA) VR-CCH N91PN |
| 092 | B | N1ED N9671A N258G N18AK N113ES N60DK N80EL |
| 093 | B | N33HM N33NM PT-LEN |
| 094 | C | SX-CBM VR-BFV N97J N77RS [w/o 14Dec78 Anchorage, AK; remains to White Inds, Bates City, MO, for spares] |
| 095 | B | N200BC N303SC N303SQ C-GRCO N2094L |
| 096 | B | N742E N742Z N48FN N405RS C-GCJD N235JW N20NW XA-... |
| 097 | C | HB-VCS (OY-ASK) I-SFER N22NJ (N220AR) N79EV |
| 098 | C | N7JN VR-BEM N139J VR-BGF YV-26CP N96MJ N502MH ZS-NYG |
| 099 | C | PT-IKR PT-FAF PT-LHU [w/o 28Jly92 Icuape, Brazil] |
| 100 | B | N262JE N741E N741F "N59AC"+ [+marks worn at 1988 NBAA Convention, Dallas/Love Field, TX] N25TK N829AA |
| 101 | B | N268GL N575GD N269AS N30AP N156CB N600HT N600HD N74JL N821AW N47MR [to India as instructional airframe; cx 08Jul09] |
| 102 | B | N267GL N999M N999ML N311CC N52AJ N962 N52AJ N64WH N254SC N325SJ |
| 103 | B | N428JX [b/u for parts 1989 by Brandis Av'n, Taylorville, IL] |
| 104 | B | N1JR N101JR N392T XA-JAX XA-RIN N128TJ N35WJ N104WJ |
| 105 | B | N1BR N1RA N711WE N713Q N234RB N905WJ N7AT N55PD XA-SXD N55PD LY-AJB N25WJ |
| 106 | XR | N10NP N10FL N974JD N458JA N458J [w/o 01Jly91 Columbus, OH; cx Aug91] |
| 107 | B | N225CC N57DM N25NP N25NB N252BK [parted out Houston/Hobby, TX] |
| 108 | C | PT-CMY [w/o 06Apr90 Juiz de Fora, Brazil] |
| 109 | B | N888DH N333HP C-GSAS N860MX [parted out by Dodson Av'n, Rantoul, KS] |
| 110 | B | N50GL N63ET N75CA N110HA N52SD N343RK LV-... N198MA |
| 111 | B | N30TP N55ES PT-LXS N825A N45BS N25PJ |
| 112 | B | OY-BFC N173J N279LE |
| 113 | C | PT-ISN [w/o 04Nov89 Belo Horizonte-Pampulha, Brazil] |
| 114 | B | N47HC (C-GLRE) N45HB N77PK N25JD N114HC XA-VMC |
| 115 | C | PT-ISO |
| 116 | C | CF-CXY N600PC N819GY (N818GY) N666TW [w/o 19Sep03 Del Rio TX, cx Nov03] |

# LEARJET 25

| C/n | Series | Identities |
| --- | --- | --- |
| 117 | B | N40AS N170GT N170RL N4402 N4405 C-FMGM N731CW N7810W [parted out by White Inds, Bates City, MO] |
| 118 | B | OO-LFZ (D-CITO) N601J N118SE (N800JA) N124MA (N79AX) VP-CMB N118MB N818CK |
| 119 | B | N3810G PT-JBQ [w/o 04Sep82 Rio Branco, Brazil] |
| 120 | B | N111AF N744MC N278LE N10BD N10BU VH-OVS (N100FU) N101FU N120SL XA-AJL |
| 121 | B | N7GA HZ-MRP N39JJ N500PP N1036N [may have been XA-SAL] XA-SIO N8005Y (N821MS) [to India as instructional airframe; cx 12Nov09] |
| 122 | B | N23TA N332LS N122BS N122WC N751CA C-FSYO N751CA XB-KVX XB-LCI |
| 123 | B | N360AA N973JD (N914RA) N906SU N688GS |
| 124 | B | N44MJ N39JE N59BP N15CC N15CU N54H N54HU (N400DB) (N95TW) N33TW XA-ALV [to museum at Cajititlan, Mexico, Sep08] |
| 125 | B | N4MR N9AT (N85AT) N89AT N94AT N97AC (N11MC) N10VG N1VG |
| 126 | C | N12WK N114CC (N162AC) N14FN YV2465 |
| 127 | B | N93C N93CE N83JM (N42BJ) N450 N450SC N222AK N425JL N225LC |
| 128 | B | N67PC N1MX N40BC [w/o 06Jly79 Pueblo, CO; parted out by White Inds, Bates City, MO] |
| 129 | C | N551WC N71DM (N193DR) N25MR N25MT |
| 130 | B | N111BL N25PL N26AT |
| 131 | C | N3803G PT-JDX [w/o 26Dec78 Sao Paulo-Congonhas, Brazil; front of fuselage in use at Belo Horizonte-Pampulha, Brazil as a link trainer] |
| 132 | B | N202BT N132GL N54MC N54MQ N715JF N715MH [w/o 26Oct01 Ciudad Victoria, Mexico; cx Oct02; parted out by Dodson Av'n, Rantoul, KS] |
| 133 | B | N10RE N10RZ N51MJ N58CP XA-RZY N233CA |
| 134 | B | N52GL N15BH N712JA N26FN N65A |
| 135 | B | G-BBEE N3803G N1103R G-BBEE N7600K (N1RW) N50RW |
| 136 | B | N920CC N920US N180YA N221TC N71CE (N48WA) N753CA N48WA |
| 137 | B | N400 N37BJ N500WW N752CA N752EA |
| 138 | B | N11BU N100EP N36204 N777PD N711PD N811PD (N2HE) N73LJ N911RF [parted out by Atlanta Air Salvage, Griffin, GA] |
| 139 | XR | N618R N225AC N12MH (N14PT) N605NE N111MP |
| 140 | B | N42G N42GX N68TJ N401AC N403AC N140CA [wfu Addison, TX] |
| 141 | XR | N52L N424JR N424JP N94RS N25HA ZS-BXR |
| 142 | B | N515WH N42HC (N142HC) N70CE (N70WA) N49WA |
| 143 | B | N96VF (N33VF) N111RF N113RF N143CK |
| 144 | B | N10NT N44PA [w/o 23Dec91 Carlsbad, CA; b/u Jun92] |
| 145 | B | N131GL C-GRDR N2127E N145SH |
| 146 | C | N146LJ N9HM N9HN C-GRQX N9HN N6KJ I-BMFE |
| 147 | B | N55KC N25KC N150WW N911JG N147BP XA-GGG |
| 148 | XR | N58GL N336WR N98RS (N98JA) |
| 149 | B | HB-VDI EC-CIM N149J N239CA 9V-... |
| 150 | B | N714K N714KP N888RB (N25LP) N251JA N150CK |
| 151 | B | N366AA [w/o 31Aug74 Briggsdale, CO] |
| 152 | XR | N50L N515SC N452ET XA-POI XA-JSC N105BA N165AA |
| 153 | B | N501PS [w/o 26May77 Detroit, MI; parted out by Dodson Av'n, Ottawa, KS] |
| 154 | B | N100K N30DK N47DK N82TS N210NC N82TS [wfu Pontiac, MI] |
| 155 | B | N24TA PT-LEA |
| 156 | C | PT-KAP N613SZ N75BL N725JS |
| 157 | B | N2427F N157CA N57CK N50CK |
| 158 | B | N158GL HZ-GP3 N85MJ N334LS N71RB N924BW |
| 159 | B | Peru FAP 522/OB-1429 N24RZ [w/o 20Feb04 Fort Lauderdale Executive, FL; cx 03Feb05; parted out by Dodson Intl Parts, Rantoul, KS] |
| 160 | B | ZS-MTD VP-WKY Z-WKY ZS-MTD 3D-AEZ ZS-MTD |
| 161 | B | N4VC N61EW N236CA [wfu Addison, TX] |
| 162 | XR | N62ZS N661MP N663JB N97RS N97JJ N150RS |
| 163 | B | SE-DFC N70606 N173LP N173LR C-FBEA N333AW N59SG N25RE (N65RC) N911AJ |
| 164 | B | Peru FAP 523/OB-1430 N23RZ |
| 165 | C | PT-KBC [w/o 04Jun96 Ribeirao Preto, Brazil; cx Aug97] |
| 166 | B | PT-KBD N918TD N166PC |
| 167 | B | C-GBFP |
| 168 | B | N72TP N88BT N88BY [wfu Pontiac, MI] |
| 169 | B | N471MM N743E N743F N893WA N59FL XA-KKK |
| 170 | B | N131G N711DS N170EV (N170EP) N98796 N627WS [w/o 13Jan98 Houston Intercontinental, TX; cx Oct98] |
| 171 | B | I-ELEN N1DD OY-ASP N1DD N55MF N55PT N42DG N888LR N401AJ N171WW* |
| 172 | C | PT-KKV [w/o 11Jan91 nr Belo Horizonte, Brazil] |
| 173 | XR | N780AC N780AQ N777NJ N104BW XA-JSC |
| 174 | B | N74G N410SP N412SP N16KK |
| 175 | XR | N462B N462BA N96RS (N96JJ) N307AJ N75SJ N127GB |
| 176 | C | N55VL N50PE N25KV N28KV PT-LLN |
| 177 | B | N11PH N745W D-CDPD [w/o 18May83 in Atlantic approx 320 km S of Reykjavik, Iceland] |
| 178 | B | N75B N999M N999MV N999HG [w/o 08Sep77 Sanford, NC] |
| 179 | B | N659HX C-GBQC C-GSKL [parted out by White Inds, Bates City, MO; cx 02Jun08] |

# LEARJET 25

| C/n | Series | Identities |
|---|---|---|
| 180 | B | VH-BLJ N95BS C-FEWB N95BS VH-LJB N266BS N102VS |
| 181 | C | VH-TNN N94PK N73TW N73TA N100NB |
| 182 | B | C-GLBT N4300L F-GFMZ N225JL N99MC |
| 183 | B | N66JD N5LL N83CK |
| 184 | B | EC-CKR [w/o 13Aug96 RAF Northolt, UK; to spares by White Inds, Bates City, MO 1998] |
| 185 | B | N666LP N55V N988DB N988AA N988AC N606SM |
| 186 | B | YU-BJH [w/o 18Jan77 Sarajevo, Yugoslavia] |
| 187 | B | YU-BJG N187CA |
| 188 | B | G-BCSE A40-AJ N1JR [w/o 28Jly84 Waterville, ME and used for spares; remains to White Inds, Bates City, MO] |
| 189 | B | N111SF N111SZ N352SC N888DF N67HB [to Museum of Aeronautical Sciences, Tokyo/Narita, Japan 2008] |
| 190 | B | XA-DAK N190AR XA-... |
| 191 | B | N1DD N78BT N38DJ [w/o 12Jun92 Sheboygan, WI; cx Dec94; remains to Hampton/Tara Field, Atlanta, GA] |
| 192 | B | Bolivia 008 Bolivia 010 |
| 193 | B | HB-VEF I-KISS HB-VIE I-SIMD N80GR N350DH N125RM N125TN XA-WWW |
| 194 | B | XA-COC XB-EGP XA-SXG XC-NSP |
| 195 | B | OB-M-1004 N108PA [b/u for spares 1984; cx 05May06] |
| 196 | B | N711WD N25TA [w/o 11Apr80 New Mexico] |
| 197 | B | N104GL N240AG N197WC N197CF (N96DM) |
| 198 | B | N20DK N29TS N198JA |
| 199 | XR | HB-VEI HZ-RI1 HZ-GP5 [w/o 11Jan82 Narssarssuaq, Greenland] |
| 200 | B | N2022R N680BC N350JH [parted out by White Inds, Bates City, MO] |
| 201 | B | N227RW N777SA N111AD N11TK N713B N43TS N59BL N251TS |
| 202 | B | N3807G Yugoslavia 10401 Yugoslavia 70401 YU-BRA N343CA |
| 203 | B | N3811G Yugoslavia 10402 Yugoslavia 70402 YU-BRB N344CA N927FW |
| 204 | B | N376SC N373SC N472J PT-KZY [w/o 16May82 Uberaba, Brazil] |
| 205 | B | N1468B YU-BKJ Z3-BAA |
| 206 | D | N206EC N206EQ ZS-LXH |
| 207 | D | N3513F (I-GIAN) I-LEAR (N3513F) N207JC [parted out by White Industries, Bates City, MO circa 99] |
| 208 | D | N54YR N54YP C-GZIM "N500PP" N54YP N500PP N500MP N300SC N188CA |
| 209 | D | N36SC N770AC (N770PA) N770AQ N18NM N30LJ |
| 210 | D | N133MR XA-JIN XA-RPV N97FT N75TJ N764RH XA-... |
| 211 | D | N3514F Bolivia 010 |
| 212 | D | N1450B N911MG N212NE [b/u for spares during 1989] |
| 213 | D | N551DP HZ-SS2 VR-CDH N803PF N925DW N910JB |
| 214 | D | N30W N3UW N90BR I-AVJD N61826 N214ME N214LJ N245BS N70TF N56MD |
| 215 | D | N44FE N325JL N25UJ |
| 216 | D | N3556F N2426 (N345FJ) N80RE N80RP (N87MW) XA-PRO N216SA N767SA N68AX N724TN XA-... N724TN N77FN |
| 217 | D | N41H N217WM YV.... |
| 218 | D | N18MJ N155AU XA-RAX N14NA N251DS [parted out by Dodson Av'n, Rantoul, KS] |
| 219 | XR | N55SL XA-CCC XA-MCC |
| 220 | XR | N220HS (N419BL) (N25WL) N220NJ N99NJ N969AR |
| 221 | D | N3819G YU-BKR N147CA XA-UKH |
| 222 | XR | N1476B N726GL N4MR XA-KEY XA-MHA N4MR N225TJ N134WE XA-... |
| 223 | D | N23AM XC-DAD XA-BBA [w/o 18Jun94 Washington-Dulles A/P, VA] |
| 224 | D | N50B (N32TJ) N711NM N80AX XB-MGM XB-OZA XB-AZD |
| 225 | D | 9J-AED N222AP N808DS N140GC [parted out by Dodson Av'n, Rantoul, KS] |
| 226 | D | N333SG N234SV N90LJ |
| 227 | D | N44BB N444PB N882SB XA-ROO (N25RE) N227EW N25RE |
| 228 | D | N228SW [parted out by Dodson International Parts Inc, Rantoul, KS] |
| 229 | D | N39415 LV-MBP CX-ECO N229WJ N890BJ |
| 230 | D | N16GT N16LJ N161AC N7RL N207HF [parted out by White Inds, Bates City, MO; cx 29Apr09] |
| 231 | D | (OO-LFW) (OO-HFW) N999M N999ME N60DK N31MJ N225HW N531CW |
| 232 | D | N744LC N500EW N500LW N264TW |
| 233 | D | N55LJ N75LM N947TC |
| 234 | D | N3815G (N27GW) N234KK (N234EJ) (N28CC) XA-ESQ N234KK (N11SQ) N300JE N39BL N88DJ (N432AS) N18BL N764KF YV.... |
| 235 | XR | N400PC N400JS N400VC (N25XR) N221LV YV.... |
| 236 | D | N1466B XC-RPP |
| 237 | D | (N28BP) N137GL (N55MF) [w/o 19Jan79 Detroit, MI] |
| 238 | D | N39416 N40SW N45ZP N238MP N500TL N300TL N41NK |
| 239 | D | N192MH N45H N499EH N499BS |
| 240 | D | N78GL N83EA N33PT (N339BA) |
| 241 | D | N432SL N25TA N25TB N711WD N712BW N713RR N713LJ N213CA [wfu Addison, TX] |
| 242 | D | N749GL N363HA N102RA N242GM (N242AF) N242GS |
| 243 | D | N711JT PT-LSD [w/o 02Mar96 Serra de Cantareira, near Sao Paulo, Brazil] |
| 244 | D | N7LA XA-LET N24EP N831LH N125PT [w/o 12Aug07 Farmingdale, NY; parted out by MTW Aerospace, Montgomery, AL] |
| 245 | D | N39398 LV-PAF LV-MST N245DK N60DK N606GB (N531GC) |

# LEARJET 25

| C/n | Series | Identities |
|---|---|---|
| 246 | XR | N40162 N51DB [w/o 21Oct86 nr Jeddah, Saudi Arabia] |
| 247 | D | N300PL [parted out] |
| 248 | D | N80BT N80BE N500PP N900WA N95CK (N248LJ) N248CK |
| 249 | D | N20PY N249SC N211JB (N500EF) N249LJ XA-FMU N800L XA-FMU N34TN |
| 250 | D | N30LM N438DM (N60DK) N112JM N19JM N127BH |
| 251 | D | N752GL N78SD N290 N25FA TG-VOC N85TW |
| 252 | D | N1468B N44FH N444MK |
| 253 | D | N253EJ N97DK (N202DR) N253J N253M N253SC N8MF N321AU YV-1049CP YV129T N69PL YV1346 |
| 254 | D | N973 I-AVJE N76AX |
| 255 | D | N1433B N1ED N91ED N91MT N25GJ N717EP N219RB |
| 256 | D | N6LL N75CK |
| 257 | D | N700BJ N377C N377Q N988AS |
| 258 | D | N144FC (N54888) N54TA N888GC N333CD N258MD PT-LLL [w/o 18Mar91 Brasilia, Brazil] |
| 259 | D | LV-PAW LV-MMV [w/o 23Sep89 in Marana River, nr Posadas, Argentina - fuselage and detached wingset noted at Moron AFB Apr04, still present Apr07] |
| 260 | D | N39413 (D-CHBM) D-CHEF N43783 N74RD N80PJ |
| 261 | D | N3802G N180MC N24JK N261WC |
| 262 | D | N23HM N440F N333CG [w/o 12Jun01 Salina A/P, KS - regd to Pacific Aeromotive Jun03 assumed for parts use] |
| 263 | D | N40162 N14VC N20DL N825D XA-YYY |
| 264 | D | N716NC N133JF N502JC N547JG |
| 265 | D | N1462B N265EJ N279TG N265LJ N31WT (N61WT) N69GF N265TW |
| 266 | D | N3807G PT-KYR [reported w/o circa Aug89; no further details; cx during 1990] |
| 267 | D | N15ER (N400VC) |
| 268 | D | N268WC XA-SPL N268WC XA-... N268WC |
| 269 | D | N109SJ N269MD N51BL LV-PLL LV-WOC |
| 270 | D | N842GL (N123CG) N842GL N123CG (N45KB) N75AX XA-... |
| 271 | D | N183AP N125NE [w/o 21May80 Gulf of Mexico; cx Nov82] |
| 272 | D | N272EJ N272JM N747AN N717AN N520SR N25CY |
| 273 | D | N321AS N73DJ |
| 274 | D | N600CD D-CEPD N3131G N602NC N602N N110FP N274LJ XA-MAL XA-RZE XA-FMR |
| 275 | D | N211CD N254CL |
| 276 | D | N188TC N188TQ N188TA XA-UUU |
| 277 | D | N20MJ N34CW N283U N321GL N81MW N9RA |
| 278 | D | N70JF [parted out by White Inds, Bates City, MO; cx 29Apr09] |
| 279 | D | N41ZP N81AX |
| 280 | D | N280LA N18TA N18RA N225AC N95EC (N510L) N280C N901PM |
| 281 | D | (N245KK) N45KK N45KB N555PG N800RF |
| 282 | D | N711WD XA-SKA |
| 283 | D | N40144 XC-DAA N45826 N312GK N444WW |
| 284 | D | XC-CFM N284TJ |
| 285 | D | N6666R (N28RW) N6666K N666KK N422G I-COTO [w/o Feb86 Paris-Le Bourget, France] |
| 286 | D | N28MJ XA-ROZ N6596R XA-RVI XC-AA83+ XA-TAQ N850MX N9QM [cx 01Mar07, wfu][+ marks not confirmed] |
| 287 | D | N39416 RP-C4121 N63KH N287MF XA-ZYZ N20AD XA-ZZZ [parted out by White Inds, Bates City, MO, circa 2001] |
| 288 | D | N31WT N61WT N40BC N100WN (N40BC) |
| 289 | D | N1087T RP-C6610 RP-C400 N389GA N321GL N321GE XA-TWH |
| 290 | D | N221AP XA-ELR N221EL N321RB N600GM |
| 291 | D | N1088D N666RB N952 N600JT N530DC (N477MM) N453MA |
| 292 | D | N1088C N92MJ N92CS N711VT N711VK N604AS |
| 293 | D | N999TH N97JP XA-PIU |
| 294 | D | N27K N419GL N125TJ N161RB N88NJ N881J [parted out by Dodson Av'n, Rantoul, KS; cx 20Apr06] |
| 295 | D | N229AP N137K ZS-LUD OE-GHL N295DJ (N298GS) N45ES XC-AGR N25HF XB-MYG |
| 296 | D | N712RW N712SJ N55DD N55MJ PT-OHD |
| 297 | D | N297EJ N36NW N297EJ N24KW N389AT |
| 298 | D | N923GL N711TG N711TQ (N712CB) XA-ABH N298DR N242PF |
| 299 | D | N222LW I-KIOV (N8217W) N299MW (N5B) |
| 300 | D | (N46BA) N659HX N108FL |
| 301 | D | N416RM N610LM (N888JA) N25CZ N82AX |
| 302 | D | N521JP N28BP N740K N700DA N702DA N25CY N881P |
| 303 | D | XA-JOC |
| 304 | D | N25NY |
| 305 | D | N88JA N53TC N188R XA-AAS XA-TAK XA-TAQ |
| 306 | D | XA-DUB XC-GUB |
| 307 | D | LV-PEU LV-OEL |
| 308 | D | N23AM XA-RMF N2721U XB-GDR XA-SXY N102RR N727LM |
| 309 | D | XA-GRB XB-DKS XA-DAZ XA-PAZ XB-KWN |
| 310 | D | N1088C N211PD N211JC (N211JE) |
| 311 | D | N39391 N199BT ZS-NJF N199BT |

## LEARJET 25

| C/n | Series | Identities | | | | | | | | |
|---|---|---|---|---|---|---|---|---|---|---|
| 312 | D | N94MJ | XC-HIS | | | | | | | |
| 313 | D | N31MJ | N31GS | N37RR | N727AW | N727CS | N631CW | N727CS | N251AL | |
| 314 | D | N1466B | I-DEAN | HB-VHM | N38328 | N30AD | N40AD | XA-LUZ | XA-REE | N42825 |
| | | N95BP | N305AR | | | | | | | |
| 315 | D | N10873 | N3798A | N83TC | N273KH | N273M | XA-TSL | N315FW | XA-ASP | |
| 316 | D | N3793X | N1AH | (N782JR) | N17AH | [fitted with Williams-Rolls FJ44 engines ff 09Jan03 | | | | |
| | | at Guthrie, OK] | | | | | | | | |
| 317 | D | N821LM | N660TC | N969SS | (N96DC) | N317TS | N317VS | N25CY | N35DL | XA- |
| 318 | D | N522JP | N522TA | N999BH | [w/o 05Sep93 Rowe Mera, 30m from Santa Fe Municipal A/P, NM; | | | | | |
| | | cx May94] | | | | | | | | |
| 319 | D | N319EJ | N911EM | N680JC | N712DP | [instructional airframe at Savo Vocational College | | | | |
| | | Finland; cx 23Nov09] | | | | | | | | |
| 320 | D | N320EJ | OO-LFR | N690JC | | | | | | |
| 321 | D | N25AM | | | | | | | | |
| 322 | D | 5N-AOC | N19GE | | | | | | | |
| 323 | D | N323EJ | N70SE | N6YY | PT-LMM | | | | | |
| 324 | D | N711BF | XA-POP | N970WJ | | | | | | |
| 325 | D | N123NC | N523SA | N1411S | XA-RXB | N1411S | N2U | XA-TBV | N325JB | XB-HGE |
| | | XB-GCP | | | | | | | | |
| 326 | D | N771CB | N25NB | | | | | | | |
| 327 | D | N54GP | N52DA | (N54JC) | (N327BC) | N444TG | | | | |
| 328 | D | N7LC | (N12FS) | OB-R-1313 | OB-1313 | N58DJ | N200NR | N725DM | N328JW | N518JG |
| | | XB-JLU | | | | | | | | |
| 329 | D | N3799B | XC-GNL | XA-GNL | N613GL | N83TE | N401DP | | | |
| 330 | D | (N523JP) | N521JP | XA-RZT | XA-RCG | XC-AA84 | N330LJ | N330L | | |
| 331 | D | N462B | N422B | N462B | N482CP | N657BM | | | | |
| 332 | D | XC-FIF | XB-DZQ | XA-AFH | | | | | | |
| 333 | D | N34MJ | N555SD | | | | | | | |
| 334 | D | N20RD | N57DL | N334MD | XA-RYH | N23W | XB-JKK | XA-ULG | | |
| 335 | D | N27KG | PT-LUZ | | | | | | | |
| 336 | D | XA-LAP | N6354N | XA-VYA | XA-JYL | | | | | |
| 337 | G | N3810G | N937GL | N337GL | LV-P... | LV-WBP | N14CK | XA-UKK | | |
| 338 | D | XA-LOF | N4447P | | | | | | | |
| 339 | D | N3798D | HK-2624X | HK-2624P | N21HR | Mexico MTX-03 | | Mexico AMT-202 | | |
| 340 | D | N980A | N625AU | N891P | | | | | | |
| 341 | D | N341FW | N101DL | XA-TAM | (N.....) | XA-SAE | N58HC | | | |
| 342 | D | N820M | N984JD | (N187DY) | I-RJVA | N707CA | XA-RXQ | N342AA | N342GG | N25PW |
| 343 | D | N3797L | N456CG | (N458CG) | | | | | | |
| 344 | D | N3798L | N37943 | 5N-ASQ | [w/o 22Jly83 Lagos, Nigeria] | | | | | |
| 345 | D | N345EJ | N345KB | N711SC | LV-PHU | LV-WLG | | | | |
| 346 | D | N39412 | N3798V | N300WG | N41TC | N72AX | XA-ZZZ | | | |
| 347 | D | N39415 | N347EJ | D-CHIC | N25NM | N347MD | N347AC | N202JW | N347AC | (N347JW) |
| | | N347JV | N203VS | | | | | | | |
| 348 | D | N37949 | N440DM | N522GS | N522JS | N988AA | | | | |
| 349 | D | N40146 | N349EJ | N20GT | XA-NOG | [w/o 02Sep93 Tijuana, Mexico] | | | | |
| 350 | D | N350AG | (N428CH) | N648JW | LV-BZC | | | | | |
| 351 | D | N878ME | XA-POQ | N837CS | N302PC | N402DP | N425RH | N425RA | N21NW | |
| 352 | D | N3794P | RP-C1261 | N7035C | XA-MMO | (N352XR) | N25FN | N125JW | | |
| 353 | D | N353EJ | N800DR | (N50MT) | XA-RKP | XA-RLI | N510TP | N71AX | N43DR | |
| 354 | D | N3795U | N515TC | | | | | | | |
| 355 | D | (N830WM) | N202WM | N7801L | N713DJ | XA-SNO | XA-EAS | N355AM | LV-WRE | |
| 356 | D | N78DT | N100NR | N108NR | N25PT | N251MD | N62DK | | | |
| 357 | D | N40149 | N3797U | N148JW | N812MM | XA-ROC | N250LB | N27KG | LV-WXY | |
| 358 | D | N1461B | N37971 | | | | | | | |
| 359 | D | N6307H | N37973 | N359SK | N666RE | N666PE | N116JR | XA-LRJ | | |
| 360 | D | N6340T | N8563B | N618R | N618P | N360JG | | | | |
| 361 | D | N4291K | N218NB | N218NR | N804PH | N804RH | XA-TYW | | | |
| 362 | D | N39398 | N25GL | N52CT | N717CW | (N107MS) | N107RM | | | |
| 363 | D | N39416 | N85654 | N91MT | N2PW | XA-RSU | N197LS | YV.... | | |
| 364 | D | N10873 | N8565Y | N25TZ | XA-TIE | XB-LYG | | | | |
| 365 | D | N1473B | N7260C | N218R | N365CM | XA-SJN | XB-KDQ | | | |
| 366 | D | N1088D | N7261B | (ZS-LRI) | XA-SWX | N366LJ | ZS-CAT | N366LJ | XB-IFW | XA-SOH |
| 367 | D | N7262A | N51DT | VT-SWP | N4488W | N25HF | | | | |
| 368 | D | N1088A | N8567J | XA-PIM | N8567J | N368D | | | | |
| 369 | D | N10872 | N8566Z | N369MJ | N2213T | N369D | XB-JJS | | | |
| 370 | D | N39399 | N72600 | N610JR | N610JB | N220TG | N223TG | C-GSWS | XA-SJO | N370LJ |
| | | N252HS | N972H | N888DV | [parted out by Dodson Av'n, Rantoul, KS] | | | | | |
| 371 | D | N1468B | N72603 | N125DB | N44SK | N1WT | N1U | (N102U) | N4ZB | N72WC |
| | | N188PR | | | | | | | | |
| 372 | D | N40149 | N72606 | N5NC | N722EM | | | | | |
| 373 | D | N3819G | N29EW | EC-EGY | XA-ACX | | | | | |

Production complete

# LEARJET MODEL 28

| C/n | Identities | | | | | | | |
|---|---|---|---|---|---|---|---|---|
| 28-001 | N9RS | N9KH | N128MA | N3AS | N128LR | | | |
| 28-002 | N39404 | N511DB | XC-VSA | | | | | |
| 28-003 | N157CB | N42ZP | N555JK | N44QG | N14QG | N28LR | N25GW | N800GA |
| 28-004 | N39394 | N125NE | HB-VGB | XA-KAJ | N225MS | XA-KAJ | N28AY | N43PJ | N769CA |
| 28-005 | (N31WT) | N8LL | N500LG | | | | | |

Production complete

# LEARJET MODEL 29

| C/n | Identities | | | | |
|---|---|---|---|---|---|
| 29-001 | HB-VFY | N929GL | XC-IST | | |
| 29-002 | N723LL | N920GL | XC-DFS | XC-HIE/PF-201 | XB-JHV |
| 29-003 | N289CA | VT-EHS | | | |
| 29-004 | N39412 | N294CA | VT-EIH | | |

Production complete

# LEARJET MODEL 31

| C/n | Series | Identities | | | | | | | | |
|---|---|---|---|---|---|---|---|---|---|---|
| 001 | | N311DF | N984JD | [w/o 23Feb90 Taiyuan, China; cx Mar90; to spares by Dodson Avn, Ottawa, KS] | | | | | | |
| 002 | | N7262Y | PT-LVO | N102NW | N350DS | N322TS | | | | |
| 003 | | N10873 | N31CG | N331CC | N888CP | | | | | |
| 004 | | N1088D | XA-ZTH | | | | | | | |
| 005 | | N39415 | XA-GMD | XA-RFS | N942BY | (N963Y) | N431BC | PR-AVM | | |
| 006 | | N6331V | N26LC | C-GKMS | | | | | | |
| 007 | | N3819G | PT-LXX | | | | | | | |
| 008 | | N71JC | [w/o 02Sep97 Aberdeen, MS; to Atlanta Air Salvage, GA Nov97 for spares] | | | | | | | |
| 009 | | OO-JBA | N173PS | N727CP | N38MG | | | | | |
| 010 | | N31LJ | N446 | PT-LLK | N311TS | N89HB | | | | |
| 011 | | N3803G | HB-VJI | D-CTWO | M-LEAR | | | | | |
| 012 | | N917MC | XA-RUU | XA-TUL | XA-LMS | | | | | |
| 013 | | PT-LVR | N213PA | PT-XTA | | | | | | |
| 014 | | N1468B | N5VG | PT-OFJ | N5VG | | | | | |
| 015 | | N111TT | N260LF | | | | | | | |
| 016 | | N4291K | N666RE | N92LJ | N1DE | | | | | |
| 017 | | N4289U | N17VG | PT-OFK | [crashed 26Feb93 Rio de Janeiro-Santos Dumont, Brazil; rebuilt with new wingset] | N17VG | N600AW | N801CT | PR-LRR | |
| 018 | | N40144 | HB-VIM | N19TJ | (N20LL) | N90BA | | | | |
| 019 | | (N19LT) | PT-OFL | N19LT | N818LJ | | | | | |
| 020 | | N42905 | N31LJ | N337FP | XA-UJQ | | | | | |
| 021 | | N3802G | XA-RNK | XA-CYA | | | | | | |
| 022 | | N331N | | | | | | | | |
| 023 | | N111VV | PR-SFA | | | | | | | |
| 024 | | N30LJ | LV-PFK | LV-RBV | N90PB | N92EC | N912TB | XA-MRS | N731GA | |
| 025 | | N39399 | I-AIRW | | | | | | | |
| 026 | | N91164 | XA-HRM | XA-HGF | XA-DIN | N39TJ | N45HG | N706SA | (N184RM) | |
| 027 | | N91201 | N30LJ | N2FU | | | | | | |
| 028 | | N90WA | | | | | | | | |
| 029 | | N9173L | (XB-ZRB) | XB-FKT | | | | | | |
| 030 | | N525AC | N255DV | N255DY | XA-JYC | | | | | |
| 031 | | N5000E | N9132Z | N31HA | ZS-OFW | N878MA | ZS-OFW | N878MA | N93SK | |
| 032 | | N5010U | XA-AAP | XA-BRG | XB-KDK | | | | | |
| 033 | | N5012H | 9V-ATA | N603LJ | N632PB | (N638PB) | N407BS | | | |
| 033A | | N2603S | 9V-ATC | N311LJ | N156JS | N990GC | | | | |
| 033B | | N2600S | 9V-ATD | [w/o 21Jly97 30m S of Ranong, Thailand] | | | | | | |
| 033C | | N5013L | 9V-ATE | N310LJ | N158JS | N555VR | N55VR | | | |
| 033D | | N5023D | 9V-ATF | N312LJ | N157JS | N539BA | | | | |
| 034 | | N5015U | 9V-ATB | N604LJ | N45PK | N394SA | CS-DDZ | | | |
| 035 | A | N50111 | N618R | N618RF | N3VJ | | | | | |
| 036 | A | N31LJ | N88MM | D-CVGP | N316LJ | N127V | N127VL | (N127V) | | |
| 037 | A | N31TF | PT-OVZ | | | | | | | |
| 038 | A | N5016V | N4 | N131NA | N500WR | | | | | |
| 039 | A | N90LJ | N10ST | N16ST | N22AX | N23AX | N71AL | | | |
| 040 | A | VR-CHJ | N9HJ | VR-CHJ | VR-CGS | N340LJ | N314MK | N55VY | | |
| 041 | A | N131TA | N9CH | N319CH | RP-C8822 | | | | | |
| 042 | A | D-CGGG | D-CURT | | | | | | | |
| 043 | A | N5009V | C-GLRJ | N43LJ | N531SK | | | | | |
| 044 | A | N50163 | XA-MJG | XA-HRM | XA-OLE | | | | | |
| 045 | A | N50159 | N67SB | YU-BRZ | | | | | | |
| 046 | A | D-CCKV | N131PT | N352EF | | | | | | |
| 047 | A | N31UK | N39TW | | | | | | | |
| 048 | A | N43SF | N43SE | N314XS | N864KB | | | | | |
| 049 | A | D-CDEN | D-CADC | N107GM | N131TT | | | | | |
| 050 | A | N92UG | N38SK | | | | | | | |
| 051 | A | N9152R | N1905H | N351AC | | | | | | |
| 052 | A | N50LJ | N301AS | N75MC | N899CS | XA-TGM | | | | |
| 053 | A | N9173Q | N44QG | (N44ZG) | N31FF | N555JS* | | | | |
| 054 | A | N2603G | N92FD | N82KK | N82KL | N54TN | LV-BFG | | | |
| 055 | A | N9143F | N666RE | N425M | | | | | | |
| 056 | A | N25685 | N303WB | N56LF | | | | | | |
| 057 | A | N9147Q | D-CSAP | | | | | | | |
| 058 | A | N5017J | N26018 | N770CC | "ZS-OJO" | (N258SC) | N590MH | N298CH | N825AC | LV-BRC |
| 059 | A | N25999 | (N31LJ) | N31TK | (N67MP) | | | | | |
| 060 | A | N2600Z | N156SC | N156EC | N696PA | N699CP | | | | |
| 061 | A | N51057 | (N740E) | N9152X | N740E | N740F | N261SC | | | |
| 062 | A | N25997 | AP-BEK | | | | | | | |
| 063 | A | (N27) | N2 | N995AW | N707NV | (N31AX) | N131LJ | | | |
| 064 | A | N142GT | N444HC | | | | | | | |
| 065 | A | N50153 | N26005 | N44SF | N44SU | N64NB | | | | |
| 066 | A | N5009V | N26006 | PK-CAH | | | | | | |
| 067 | A | N9173M | TG-AIR | | | | | | | |
| 068 | A | N2603X | N743E | N743F | N500CG | (N500CQ) | N500EW | C-GWXK | N680AF | N131GR |
| 069 | A | N9173V | N744E | N744N | (N169SC) | | | | | |

# LEARJET 31

| C/n | Series | Identities | | | | | | |
|---|---|---|---|---|---|---|---|---|
| 070 | A | N2602Y | N741E | N741F | (N270SC) | N370SC | | |
| 071 | A | N9173N | N742E | N742F | N271SC | | | |
| 072 | A | N31LJ | N45UF | (N14WT) | N211RN | | | |
| 073 | A | N46UF | XA-ZYZ | | | | | |
| 074 | A | N999AU | (VP-B..) | N999AU | N128GB | N174TS | N131BR | |
| 075 | A | N418R | N418RT | N631SF | N636SF | | | |
| 076 | A | N40339 | XA-SPR | XA-PIC | N518SA | N215TT | | |
| 077 | A | N26002 | PK-CAJ | | | | | |
| 078 | A | N40280 | N31LJ | XA-SNM | N112CM | N539LB | | |
| 079 | A | N40349 | N41DP | N91DP | | | | |
| 080 | A | N2601K | N80LJ | N986MA | | | | |
| 081 | A | N31LJ | N81LJ | N83WM | N83WN | LV-YMB | | |
| 082 | A | N5014F | N4022X | PT-MVI | N727BT | | | |
| 083 | A | N5012Z | N40363 | N789SR | | | | |
| 084 | A | N4034H | N196HA | N840SW | | | | |
| 085 | A | N5013Y | N4005G | XA-PEN | N531AT | N321GL | N480ME | |
| 086 | A | N2603Q | N867JS | N105FX | OY-LJB | N166BA | N969 | N1BR |
| 087 | A | N9173T | N868JS | N106FX | OY-LJC | N167BA | N535PS | |
| 088 | A | N50088 | N31LJ | N500JE | N508J | N500JE | | |
| 089 | A | N5009L | N77PH | N77PY | | | | |
| 090 | A | N9173X | N78PH | N78PR | | | | |
| 091 | A | N5019Y | V5-NAG | | | | | |
| 092 | A | N50302 | N711FG | | | | | |
| 093 | A | N4031K | (N917BD) | N916BD | N716BD | | | |
| 094 | A | N4027K | N31AX | (N916BD) | N917BD | N817BD | N36BL | |
| 095 | A | N50459 | N163JD | OK-AJD | N395LJ | | | |
| 096 | A | N5009V | N4006G | N30LX | N30TK | (N31TK) | N37BM | |
| 097 | A | N50207 | N31LJ | | | | | |
| 098 | A | N5012H | N50378 | N148C | N721MJ | (N521MJ) | N797KB | N200KB |
| 099 | A | N5049J | N1932P | N1932K | | | | |
| 100 | A | N5001X | N31LR | PT-MCB | N31LK | PR-SCB | | |
| 101 | A | N5010J | N293SA | N900R | N79BJ | XA-MGM | | |
| 102 | A | N5002D | N107FX | N731RA | C-GWXP | N681AF | C-GHJJ | |
| 103 | A | N5003F | (N31AZ) | PT-TOF | N766AJ | N407RA | PT-BBB | |
| 104 | A | N4010N | N108FX | OY-LJI | N104BX | N631CC | | |
| 105 | A | N51054 | N5005K | N109FX | N109HV | N109FX | N109HV | |
| 106 | A | N29RE | N531RA | N581RA | N531TS | | | |
| 107 | A | N5012H | N31HY | C-GHCY | N107TS | N107LP | N213AR | N942RC |
| 108 | A | N110FX | (N110BX) | (N288BF) | N288FF | | | |
| 109 | A | N5029F | N261PC | N261PQ | N722JS | N882JD | N728CL | |
| 110 | A | N40130 | PT-WIV | | | | | |
| 111 | A | N50114 | C-GRVJ | N113AF | N111AF | N420LJ | LV-BTF | |
| 112 | A | N5082S | LX-PCT | | | | | |
| 113 | A | N31LJ | N331SJ | (N642GG) | N131GG | | | |
| 114 | A | N524HC | | | | | | |
| 115 | A | (N5005M) | N112FX | N31NR | ZS-NYV | | | |
| 116 | A | N113FX | N112FX | N112HV | N31UJ | | | |
| 117 | A | N317LJ | N517CC | | | | | |
| 118 | A | N318LJ | N815A | N815E | | | | |
| 119 | A | N114FX | N114HY | N996JS | | | | |
| 120 | A | N5020Y | I-TYKE | N200TJ | C-GHJU | | | |
| 121 | A | N121LJ | | | | | | |
| 122 | A | (N112FX) | N122LJ | PT-WLO | | | | |
| 123 | A | N323LJ | N48AM | N23NP | N23VG | N85KH | | |
| 124 | A | N124LJ | N931FD | | | | | |
| 125 | A | N125LJ | N527JG | N125FS | | | | |
| 126 | A | N8066P | N22SF | N22UF | N18BL | N100BL | | |
| 127 | A | N80727 | HB-VLR | N54HT | | | | |
| 128 | A | N8082J | N400 | (N469) | N365GL | | | |
| 129 | A | N8079Q | N115FX | N115BX | | | | |
| 130 | A | N5013N | N31PV | | | | | |
| 131 | A | N80631 | N31LR | N319SC | | | | |
| 132 | A | N116FX | N116BX | N929JH | | | | |
| 133 | A | N8073Y | N117FX | OY-LJL | N331ZX | N314SG | | |
| 134 | A | N5014E | N118FX | N118BX | N977AR | N134LJ | | |
| 135 | A | N80645 | PT-WSB | | | | | |
| 136 | A | N119FX | N119BX | N119FX | N131DA | N47TR | | |
| 137 | A | N120FX | N120RV | N459A | | | | |
| 138 | A | N138LJ | V5-NPC | | | | | |
| 139 | A | N139LJ | N131AR | N229KD | N29KD | | | |
| 140 | A | N140LJ | N96LF | VP-BML | N314AC | N45HG | N95HG | N997JP |
| 141 | A | N121FX | (N121HV) | N121PX | XA-ARQ | | | |
| 142 | A | N142LJ | ZS-EAG | N698MM | N382AL | | | |
| 143 | A | N122FX | N122BX | | | | | |
| 144 | A | N144LJ | JA01CP | | | | | |
| 145 | A | N124FX | N145LJ | N29RE | N89RF | (N696RB) | LV-BDM | |

## LEARJET 31

| C/n | Series | Identities | | | | | | |
|---|---|---|---|---|---|---|---|---|
| 146 | A | N30046 | N218NB | (ZS-DCT) | ZS-AGT | N218NB | | |
| 147 | A | N198KF | N202LC | N157EC | N45KK | N31GQ | | |
| 148 | A | N148LJ | (PT-XIT) | PT-XPP | | | | |
| 149 | A | N1904S | N685RC | PR-JJV | | | | |
| 150 | A | N31NR | N6666R | N6666A | N316RS | N316AS | N595PA | N381AL |
| 151 | A | N3019S | N583PS | N583LJ | N31NF | PR-ENE | | |
| 152 | A | N517GP | | | | | | |
| 153 | A | N6666R | N30111 | RP-C6153 | (N37RA) | N153NP | N349HP | |
| 154 | A | N337RB | N154RT | | | | | |
| 155 | A | N525GP | D-CPRO | | | | | |
| 156 | A | N124FX | (N29RE) | N181PA | | | | |
| 157 | A | N125FX | N800CK | | | | | |
| 158 | A | N126FX | N126BX | PR-LRJ | | | | |
| 159 | A | N127FX | N127BX | XA-AFX | | | | |
| 160 | A | N31LR | VP-BMX | LX-EAR | (D-CPRO) | N160CF | | |
| 161 | A | N3016X | N177JB | | | | | |
| 162 | A | N525GP | N162LJ | N125GP | ES-PVH | | | |
| 163 | A | N128FX | N431DA | | | | | |
| 164 | A | N131GM | N164SB | | | | | |
| 165 | A | N31TD | N885TW | N808W | | | | |
| 166 | A | N166DT | N811PS | N366TS | PR-GBN | | | |
| 167 | A | N167LJ | I-ERJB | N613SA | D-CGOM | LX-OMC | I-CFLY | |
| 168 | A | N168LJ | N811CP | N31CV | YV-952CP | N952VS | PP-CTA | |
| 169 | A | N197PH | | | | | | |
| 170 | A | N31NR | (ZS-DHL) | ZS-OML | OY-LJN* | | | |
| 171 | A | N50157 | N129FX | N31MW | | | | |
| 172 | A | N197PH | N130FX | N312CC | | | | |
| 173 | A | N173LC | N31KH | | | | | |
| 174 | A | N9VL | Mexico MTX-02 | | Mexico AMT-201 | | | |
| 175 | A | N131FX | N175FF | N27AL | N31WU | N240B | | |
| 176 | A | N176WS | XA-LRD | | | | | |
| 177 | A | N132FX | N569SC | | | | | |
| 178 | A | N50145 | RP-C6178 | N178NP | PR-MKB | | | |
| 179 | A | N133FX | N133BG | XA-RAN | | | | |
| 180 | A | N1926S | | | | | | |
| 181 | A | N134FX | N526GP | N418DL | | | | |
| 182 | A | N136FX | N527GP | N399RW | | | | |
| 183 | A | N183DT | N183ML | LV-BFE | | | | |
| 184 | A | N931RS | | | | | | |
| 185 | A | N31LR | N110SC | N31MJ | | | | |
| 186 | A | N137FX | N45PK | N45PD | RP-C1432 | | | |
| 187 | A | N932FD | | | | | | |
| 188 | A | N70AE | N70AY | | | | | |
| 189 | A | N138FX | N316RS | N158R | | | | |
| 190 | A | N316AC | N8TG | | | | | |
| 191 | A | N631AT | OE-GTA | Mexico AMT-206 | | | | |
| 192 | A | N50088 | N531RA | | | | | |
| 193 | A | N44SF | N44SZ | N129JD | | | | |
| 194 | A | N29SM | N29SN | | | | | |
| 195 | A | N134FX | N134CG | | | | | |
| 196 | A | N136FX | N136BX | N1JM | | | | |
| 197 | A | N20XP | | | | | | |
| 198 | A | N500MP | | | | | | |
| 199 | A | N900P | N901P | | | | | |
| 200 | A | N31NR | N797WB | N599CT | N900EL | | | |
| 201 | A | N4003K | N137FX | N776PH | N32HH | | | |
| 202 | A | N4003L | ZS-PNP | ZS-AJD | OO-ENZ | | | |
| 203 | A | N63SE | VP-BAW | OD-PWC | | | | |
| 204 | A | N204RT | | | | | | |
| 205 | A | N50153 | VP-CFB | N71FB | | | | |
| 206 | A | N5000E | N79SE | | | | | |
| 207 | A | N50126 | D-CSIE | | | | | |
| 208 | A | N138FX | N138FY | N751BP | N518JG | N518JC | N227KT | |
| 209 | A | N139FX | N139FY | N209HR | N428BB | XA-... | | |
| 210 | A | N927DJ | N928DJ* | | | | | |
| 211 | A | N5013Y | N574DA | N574BA | N5NC | N276PS | | |
| 212 | A | N31KJ | N480JJ | N481JJ | N128BG | | | |
| 213 | A | N5009V | D-CMRM | | | | | |
| 214 | A | N5000E | N124DF | PT-FZA | N125DF | PR-PJD | | |
| 215 | A | N40075 | N30051 | N786YA | (N784LB) | | | |
| 216 | A | N40077 | N999GH | N321GL | | | | |
| 217 | A | N40078 | N10SE | N110SE | | | | |
| 218 | A | N30050 | N1ED | | | | | |
| 219 | A | N214RW | N214PW | N518JG | | | | |
| 220 | A | N5009T | N220LJ | N521CH | N521WH | N54AP | | |
| 221 | A | N68ES | N278JM | | | | | |

# LEARJET 31

| C/n | Series | Identities | | | | | | | |
|---|---|---|---|---|---|---|---|---|---|
| 222 | A | N5013U | N200CH | N770CH | N14T | LV-BSO | | | |
| 223 | A | N40012 | N8064K | N800CH | N501RS | | | | |
| 224 | A | N3001H | (XA-VMX) | N224LJ | N411DJ | | | | |
| 225 | A | N3003S | N334AF | N834AF | | | | | |
| 226 | A | N138FX | N226LJ | N7SN | | | | | |
| 227 | A | N30054 | N40073 | D-CGGG | | | | | |
| 228 | A | N3018P | N955JS | | | | | | |
| 229 | A | N50005 | (N11TK) | N229LJ | | | | | |
| 230 | A | N5004Z | N295PS | N556HD | N558HD | | | | |
| 231 | A | N5005Q | XA-VTR | N712EJ | (N759FS) | N724FS | | | |
| 232 | A | N5008S | N668VP | N68VP | | | | | |
| 233 | A | N5005X | LX-PAT | N233BX | EI-MAX | | | | |
| 234 | A | N5028E | N376MB | XA-EFX | | | | | |
| 235 | A | N31NR | N317K | XA-UBI | | | | | |
| 236 | A | N314DT | N57TS | | | | | | |
| 237 | A | N23UP | N19UP | N84MJ | N44LG | N37LG | N962FM | | |
| 238 | A | N36UP | | | | | | | |
| 239 | A | N686AB | | | | | | | |
| 240 | A | N998AL | N990AE | N440SC | | | | | |
| 241 | A | N335AF | N633SF | | | | | | |
| 242 | A | N40043 | (PR-BOI)+ | +[ntu marks worn at Tucson completion centre Apr03] | | | | N40031 | N903LJ |
| | | N600AW | N600AN | N680SW | | | | | |

Production complete

# LEARJET MODEL 35

* after the series letter or in the series column indicates the aircraft has been fitted with Avcom delta fins.

| C/n | Series | Identities |
|---|---|---|
| 001 | | N731GA [ff 22Aug73] N351GL [on display at entrance to Learjet factory, Wichita, KS] |
| 002 | | N352GL N35SC C-GVVA N11382 [parted out by Alliance Air Parts, Oklahoma City, OK] |
| 003 | | N731GA N931BA N263GL N370EC N4RT N960AA N700WL N703MA N111WB |
| 004 | | N74MP N74MB N74MJ C-GIRE |
| 005 | | EC-CLS TR-LXP EC-CLS N175J N178CP |
| 006 | | N356P N39DM N39FN |
| 007 | | D-CONI N75DH N47JR (N65FN) N35UJ N357RM N110UN |
| 008 | | N673M PT-LFS PP-ERR |
| 009 | | N44EL N14EL N275J N263GL PT-LGR N335AT |
| 010 | | N888DH N888DE N35AJ |
| 011 | | N3816G N400RB N408RB N531AJ XA-RJT |
| 012 | | N711 N71LA C-GVCB N2242P N95SC N975AA N975AD N97TJ XA-SVX |
| 013 | * | N1DA N7TJ N304AF N35JN N35BN N535TA N913CK |
| 014 | | N71TP N73TP (N72TB) N98VA N69PS N77LJ N190GC N844L |
| 015 | | N291BC N57FF N58FF N58CW N335JL (N335SS) N354PM |
| 016 | | N136GL N5867 N9CN N1SC N18CV VP-CLT N31HK |
| 017 | | N119GS N551CC N456MS N600DT |
| 018 | | D-CORA F-GBMB N696SC N435JL N696SC N435JL (N435EC) [Parted out by White Inds, Bates City, MO; cx 29Apr09] |
| 019 | | N959AT PT-LGF N19NW N71LG N1AK N157AK N750RM YV1828 |
| 020 | | XA-BUX N95TC [w/o 20Dec84 Waco Airport, TX; remains to White Inds, Bates City, MO] |
| 021 | A | N101GP N91CH N33TS N442JT N4415S N53FN N220NJ |
| 022 | | OY-BLG N90WR |
| 023 | | N986WC N886WC N886CS N443RK |
| 024 | | N316 N24GA N528JD N528EA N241RT N411BA |
| 025 | | 9K-ACT N40TF N135TX N510LJ N185BA (N188JA) N435UJ [parted out by Dodson Int'l, Rantoul, KS] |
| 026 | | D-CDHS D-CBRK N54754 N89TC |
| 027 | | N31WS |
| 028 | | N135GL N20BG XC-IPP [carried dual marks XC-IPP/TP104] Mexico TP104 |
| 029 | | N711AF [w/o Katab, Egypt 11Aug79 en route Athens-Jeddah] |
| 030 | * | N816M N16FN N542PA [code "TX"] (N30TK) C-GKPE N542PA |
| 031 | | N77FC N77U N77TE N160AT N233CC |
| 032 | | N711CH (N711QH) N711MA N235JW N711MA N710GS |
| 033 | | N7KA HZ-KA1 N2297B N31FN N524PA |
| 034 | | N37TA |
| 035 | | N711R (N711RQ) N7125 N350TS N92TS |
| 036 | | N134GL N76GL N76GP N90AH |
| 037 | * | N1462B N100GL N58M N35GQ N600WT N520PA [code "OR"] N45TK N333KC |
| 038 | | (VH-UDC) VH-ELJ C-FBFP N10972 [parted out by Alliance Air Parts, Oklahoma City,OK] |
| 039 | | N1HP N382TC |
| 040 | | C-GGYV N39DM [w/o 05Mar86 over Pacific Ocean nr San Clemente Island; collided with Learjet 24D-253 N97DM qv] |
| 041 | | N202BT N202BD N711BH N41PJ (N433JW) N41NW (N694PG) |
| 042 | | N221UE N73TJ N270CS XA-FFF XB-RYT |
| 043 | | C-GVCA N575WW [parted out at Scottsdale, AZ] |
| 044 | | N38TA N44MW N44VW N130F |
| 045 | * | N1461B HB-VEN N35HB N99786 N999M XA-HOS N45MJ N117CH N304TZ N304AT N1140A (N40AN) |
| 046 | | VH-SLJ VH-FSX VH-LJL N58EM |
| 047 | A | XA-ALE N13MJ N701AS |
| 048 | * | N233R N64MH F-GHMP N8040A |
| 049 | | JY-AEV N3759C C-GBWL N235JL N899WA LV-ZZF |
| 050 | | CC-ECO Chile 351 |
| 051 | | SE-DEA N2BA (N123MJ) |
| 052 | | JY-AEW [w/o 28Apr77 Riyadh, Saudi Arabia] |
| 053 | | N1976L N53FN N541PA |
| 054 | | VR-BFX N53650 N54PR N109MC N435MS |
| 055 | | D-CONO N70WW I-NIKJ N255RG N255JH C-GCJD N354LQ |
| 056 | | (JY-AEX) N106GL N645G |
| 057 | | N551MD N57GL C-GHOO N57GL N35MR C-GTDE |
| 058 | | C-GPUN [w/o 11Jan95 Massett, Queen Charlotte Islands, BC, Canada] |
| 059 | | N221Z N51FN [w/o 02Apr90 Carlsbad, CA; remains to White Inds, Bates City, MO] |
| 060 | | N64MP N64MR N47BA (N590CH) [w/o 25Oct99 near Mina, SD] |
| 061 | | N424DN N4246N N238RC N235EA |
| 062 | | N217CS ZS-LII TL-ABD N701US N310BA N31DP |
| 063 | | N828M N663CA N80PG |
| 064 | | N290BC N291BC N100GP (N257DP) N257SD N622RB |
| 065 | | N425DN N4358N [parted out by Alliance Air Parts, Oklahoma City, OK] |
| 066 | | CC-ECP Chile 352 |
| 067 | A | N118K N888DJ (N66FN) N32FN (N52FL) N135FA |

# LEARJET 35

| C/n | Series | Identities |
|---|---|---|
| 068 | A | HB-VEM Switzerland T-781 N168TR |
| 069 | A | N103GL N591D N1CA N10AQ N35NW N48GP N51FN |
| 070 | A | D-CITA N3GL N503RP N50FN N543PA N50FN |
| 071 | A | JY-AFD F-WDCP F-GDCP N82GA N199CJ N99FN VH-ESW |
| 072 | A | N2015M N4415M PR-MLA |
| 073 | A | N108GL N163A (N64FN) N352TX N610GA N536KN |
| 074 | A | N5000B N530J N666JR N100T N198T N351PJ |
| 075 | A | N3503F HB-VEV JY-AFE N3503F (N117DA) N48RW N30FN SE-DHP |
| 076 | A | N959SA |
| 077 | A | N814M N819JE (N707BJ) N46TJ (XA-...) ZS-NRZ N98LC [parted out by Alliance Air Parts, Oklahoma City, OK] |
| 078 | A | N95BA N95BH N711SW N711SD N440JB N112EL N45AW N145AM |
| 079 | A | N6000J N660CJ N560KC N7777B N500DS N68QB |
| 080 | A | N109GL N23HB N10AZ N17AZ |
| 081 | A | N3523F JY-AFF N3523F N118DA N81FR |
| 082 | A | N235HR N285HR N700GB N700SJ [parted out by Alliance Air Parts, Oklahoma City,OK] |
| 083 | A | (N600CC) N400CC (N400MJ) (N45SL) N500CD N121CL YV-100CP N400LV N581CC N581PH |
| 084 | A | N111GL N56HF N135WB N184TS (N696JH) N903AL |
| 085 | A | N15WH |
| 086 | A | N435M N26DA N98MD N86CS N860S |
| 087 | A | N720GL N835GA N862PD (N862BD) N18AX N48ES |
| 088 | A | N3545F HB-VEW N35GE OE-GBR N72JF |
| 089 | A | N3547F D-CCHB |
| 090 | A | HB-VEY I-FIMI N88BG |
| 091 | A | VH-TLJ C-GBLF N8GA D-CIRS N37FA (N900JV) |
| 092 | A | N722GL N424JR C-GPFC N46931 N92NE N92EJ N39WA N73CK |
| 093 | A | N804CC C-GFRK N5474G N44PT PT-LOT |
| 094 | A | N506C N935BD N200EC N92EC N94GP (N65PF) (N35PF) N94AF |
| 095 | A* | N971H N971F N68UW N66KK |
| 096 | A | N214LS (N11JV) N87AT (D-CHRC) N96FA N94RL |
| 097 | A | N135J N108RB |
| 098 | A* | N20CR N21GL N44UC (N998DJ) (N998M) N72DA |
| 099 | A | N40146 HB-VFC I-MCSA [w/o 22Feb78 Palermo, Sicily] |
| 100 | A | N550E N558E C-GRFO |
| 101 | A | N40149 N109JR N109JU N721AS N751AC |
| 102 | A | N1451B N232R PT-OEF [w/o 02May92 Morelia, Mexico; remains to Dodson Int'l for spares] |
| 103 | A | N96RE N50MJ PT-LCD |
| 104 | A | N87W N873LP [w/o 22Sep85 Auburn, AL] |
| 105 | A | (N720GH) N102GH N102GP N612KC N18FN N444WB |
| 106 | A | N101BG N15TW [w/o 08Dec85 Minneapolis, MN; remains to Brandis Avn, Taylorville, IL] |
| 107 | A | N723GL [w/o 12Dec85 Esterwood, TX] |
| 108 | A* | D-COCO F-GCLE N86PC (N86PQ) D-CJPG |
| 109 | A | N506GP N911AE [parted out by White Inds, Bates City, MO] |
| 110 | A | (N12EP) N4J |
| 111 | A | N3815G (HB-VFE) (I-SIDU) OE-GMA I-LIAD D-CONE |
| 112 | A | N3810G D-CCAY N247TA N299LR N999ND N20HJ (N120WH) N354JC (N354DT) N354SS |
| 113 | A | N763GL N35CL N35RN N14M N684LA N684HA (N113AN) |
| 114 | A | N3807G D-CONA N18G N851L D-CATY [w/o 14Dec94 Moscow-Sheremetyevo A/P, Russia; to Dodson Av'n for spares use] N851L |
| 115 | A | Argentina T-21 [w/o 09Mar06 La Paz, Bolivia] |
| 116 | A | I-MMAE N116AM N58CW |
| 117 | A | N3155B N78MC |
| 118 | A | N39391 HB-VFK N115MA N50MT N88JA N118FN |
| 119 | A | HB-VFG D-CHER N93MJ OY-ASO N93MJ N36FN (N64DH) N549PA [code "GA"] |
| 120 | A* | N400JE (N400RV) |
| 121 | A | N43EL (D-CFVG) N43TJ N752AC |
| 122 | A | D-CCHS OE-GMP N27TT |
| 123 | A | N3802G N900JE N900BJ |
| 124 | A | N1500E N35WG N8LA C-GTJL |
| 125 | A | N3803G N777MC N777NQ N111MZ N125GA N351EF |
| 126 | A | N744GL N15EH |
| 127 | A | N727GL N351TX (N800VL) |
| 128 | A | N231R N257AL N39PJ [parted out by White Inds, Bates City, MO] |
| 129 | A | N22BX N229X XA-ZAP |
| 130 | A | N230R (N44KW) N757AL (N116PR) |
| 131 | A | N3812G N26GB N26GD N155AM |
| 132 | A | N431M N420PC N37TJ N135AG |
| 133 | A | N728GL N35NB N58RW I-ALPM N133GJ N133EJ |
| 134 | A | N1473B N88EP N235DH N238JA [parted out by White Inds, Bates City, MO; cx 29Apr10] |
| 135 | A* | (OO-LFX) N22MJ D-CDAX N719US N11AK I-ZOOM N135GJ D-CFAX |
| 136 | A | Argentina T-22 |
| 137 | A | N3819G HB-VFL EC-DEB N41FN N35TJ |

# LEARJET 35

| C/n | Series | Identities |
|---|---|---|
| 138 | A | N7735A N31FB N3RA N83TJ N35WH N100MS N138NA N124ZT |
| 139 | A* | N15SC D-CGFD |
| 140 | A | N742GL N888BL N72TP N40BD |
| 141 | A | N743GL N66WM N553M N553V |
| 142 | A | N815A N815L N241CA |
| 143 | A* | N3811G N301SC OE-GER N20DK LV-BPA |
| 144 | A | N39398 D-CCAP N705US N35KC OY-CCT N118MA N135JW (N118MA) N56HF N56EM |
| 145 | A | N39394 HB-VFB Switzerland T-782 N145GJ (N166AG) VH-SLD |
| 146 | A | N55AS N351AS |
| 147 | A | N717W HZ-KTC N499G N717W N55F [parted out by Alliance Air Parts, Oklahoma City, OK] |
| 148 | A | N103GH N103GP N333RP N500RW [w/o 24May88 Teterboro, NJ] |
| 149 | A | OO-KJG HB-VGN N85351 N273MC N273MG N600LE N600AE N600AW N800AW (N40AN) [w/o 19Mar04 Utica-Oneida County, NY; parted out by Dodson Int'l, KS, circa Dec05] |
| 150 | A | N100EP [w/o 12May87 West Mifflin, PA; cx 01May90] |
| 151 | A | N39399 N711L N813M [aircaft stolen 13Apr85; fate unknown] |
| 152 | A | N101HB N964CL [confiscated in Bolivia and donated post 12Jun90 to AF] Bolivia 009 N964CL XA-RIN XA-WIN |
| 153 | A | C-GZVV N573LP N573LR |
| 154 | A | N650NL N117RB N244RG |
| 155 | A | N760LP N760DL N110KG "N1001L" N110AE N70AX |
| 156 | A | N170L N190EB N190DA N35WE N720RA [crashed on approach to PalWaukee, IL, 05Jan10, w/o] |
| 157 | A | N746GL YV-01CP N57FF N57FP N157DJ ZS-MWW N26GP |
| 158 | A | N835AC N158MJ N158NE N800GP |
| 159 | A | N93C N93CK (N135CK) D-CAPO |
| 160 | A | D-CCCA |
| 161 | A | N39415 YV-65CP N433DD |
| 162 | A | N751GL (HB-VFO) N711HH N1978L N222SL XA-CZG |
| 163 | A | YV-173CP N27BL |
| 164 | A | N1473B N248HM N50MJ |
| 165 | A | N40144 A40-CA VH-HOF N16BJ N72CK |
| 166 | A | N831CJ N831J N719JB N10UF |
| 167 | A* | N725P N813AS |
| 168 | A | N22SF N22SY N36TJ N75RJ N68TJ C-GPDO C-FZQP |
| 169 | A | N135ST N48CN N500JS N707RG |
| 170 | A | N100K N354RZ C-GPDQ C-GFEH N335NA N335AS N88NJ |
| 171 | A* | N747GL C-GNSA N823J N1968A N1968T N196DT N455RM (N48DK) N40DK N171WH |
| 172 | A | N748GL SE-DDG N72TJ N32JA SX-BFJ (N32JA) N50AK ZS-ZZZ* |
| 173 | A | N750GL HZ-MIB N750GL (HZ-NCI) N100GU N116EL (N83DM) YU-BPY N326DD |
| 174 | A | TR-LYC N65DH D-CAVI (F-GGRG) N130TA D-CAMB N82283 N38AM N773DL |
| 175 | A | D-CDWN SE-RCA |
| 176 | A | N317MR XA-ACC N176JE (N67GA) XA-BUX |
| 177 | A | N1461B N77CP N77CQ N174CP D-CITY |
| 178 | A | N40146 N22CP N22CQ N35GG N900JC (N104AA) |
| 179 | A* | N39412 D-CCAR D-CAPD N718SW (N696SC) C-FHLO N801PF D-CGFA |
| 180 | A | N3819G N222BE N222BK N35CX N44HG N701DA |
| 181 | A | N35LJ N35PR N35PD N5114G PT-LSJ |
| 182 | A | N1450B N33HB N3HB N3HA N221SG |
| 183 | A | N3802G N720M N72JM N106XX N51TJ N137RS (N137TS) N183FD N717AJ |
| 184 | A | N1462B HB-VFO [w/o 06Dec82 Paris-Le Bourget, France] N7092C [for parts use] |
| 185 | A | N99ME N99VA N10BF N99VA N900EM TC-GEM OE-GAV ZS-SES RP-C5354 |
| 186 | A | N753GL N590 N96DM (N317JD) N96FN |
| 187 | A | N755GL N32HM (N888DT) N799TD |
| 188 | A | VH-AJS N39293 N20RT (N38FN) N3MJ N343MG N135AC N35TK N88TJ N999JF N924AM |
| 189 | A | N3811G VH-AJV N39292 (N189TC) N32TC N32FN N35KC N18NM N727JP I-AVJG [w/o 24Oct99 on approach to Genoa A/P, Italy] |
| 190 | A | N32BA N202VS N202WR (N208WR) N181EF |
| 191 | A | N3810G (YV-15CP) HB-VFX N75TF N35NP N35SE N535AF |
| 192 | A | N4995A N225CC N225QC N49PE N49BE VH-LRX |
| 193 | A | N1465B (YV-131CP) VH-SBJ N620J VH-SBJ N2743T N9EE N359EF |
| 194 | A | N91W N86BL N86BE [w/o 5Apr00 Marianna Municipal apt, FL] |
| 195 | A | N1471B D-CONY N555JE SE-DHO |
| 196 | A | HB-VFU EC-DFA [w/o 13Aug80 Palma, Spain] |
| 197 | A | N754GL N754WS |
| 198 | A | N25FS I-ALPT N198GJ |
| 199 | A | N40144 N9HM (N9HV) N30DH N34TC N444HC N235JS |
| 200 | A | N3818G D-CCAR OO-LFY N200LJ N606 N80UT |
| 201 | A | N39415 N79MJ N35RT N35RF XA-PIN N35AZ N136WE |
| 202 | A | VH-MIQ N499G D-CGPD N55FN |
| 203 | A | N744E N744P VR-CUC N203RW N97CE |
| 204 | A | N1466B D-COSY N87MJ N99ME N7PE (N277AM) D-CFTG |
| 205 | A | N39418 N80SM N59DM N59FN N568PA |

# LEARJET 35

| C/n | Series | Identities |
|---|---|---|
| 206 | A | N760GL (N66HM) HB-VGH N189TC N123CC N38PS (N46KB) |
| 207 | A | N40146 N711 N3PW N620JM [w/o 15Jul05 Vail/Eagle County, CO] |
| 208 | A | N40149 N40TA (N691NS) N39DK (N39DJ) N67PA |
| 209 | A | N399W N339W N711DS N22MS |
| 210 | A | N840GL (N35HM) N42HM N721CM XB-FNF N210WL N770JP |
| 211 | A | N1461B D-CATY N15MJ N600LC N500KK N500GM N998JP N44TT N621RB |
| 212 | A | N3803G N180MC N291A N989AL |
| 213 | A | N800RD (N935NA) XC-CUZ |
| 214 | A | N279DM [parted out by White Inds, Bates City, MO] |
| 215 | A | VH-UPB N2951P N80CD N80GD N35ED |
| 216 | A | N3819G D-CATE N24MJ N39MB N142LG N335RD N991AL |
| 217 | A* | N39412 N111RF N122JW |
| 218 | A | N256TW N481FM (N601WT) (N83TE) N781RS [w/o 28Dec05 Truckee-Tahoe, CA] |
| 219 | A | N39416 VH-BJQ N502G N350JF [shot down 29Aug99 Ethiopia/Eritrea Border] |
| 220 | A | N79BH N333RB N220GH N873LP N873LR (N373LP) N220GS |
| 221 | A | N1462B N845GL VH-WFE VH-FSY N221TR |
| 222 | A* | N1468B HB-VFZ I-EJID N90AL HB-VFZ N789KW D-CGFG |
| 223 | A | N215JW D-CGRC |
| 224 | A* | N96AC N56PB N40RW N28MJ |
| 225 | A | N225MC TG-JAY N34TJ N225CF |
| 226 | A | N1127M N30HJ [parted out by White Industries Inc, Bates City, MO; cx 29Apr09] |
| 227 | A | N211BY N25RF N88NE N85GW (N227MJ) N902JC N366TT |
| 228 | A | N101PG N4GB SX-BNT N100NW N72LG N921CH |
| 229 | A | N1476B N8MA N717JB N718EA N41WT N31WT (N214LS) N415LS N4415W |
| 230 | A | N39418 N714K PT-WAR N81458 N356AC N37HJ N595BA |
| 231 | A* | (N10AB) (N712DM) N911DB N62DK VH-JCR |
| 232 | A | N8281 N4415S |
| 233 | A | N35SL N35AW (N442HC) N23A |
| 234 | A | N35WR |
| 235 | A | N841GL N600CN N256MA (N256MB) N166HL N166HE LV-ZSZ |
| 236 | A | G-ZOOM N8537B N90LP N4XL N900EC N600GP (N415RD) EC-HLB N65RZ |
| 237 | A | N843GL N78MN I-KUSS (N37DJ) N72LE N237TJ (N36BP) N300TW N300TE N11UF |
| 238 | A | N844GL N80HK ZS-INS 3D-ACZ ZS-INS N248DA N500CG N500HG N500HZ N32RZ [dismantled at Boca Raton, FL while still painted as N500HZ circa Jan04; to White Inds, Bates City, MO for spares use] |
| 239 | A | N1473B N847GL (HB-VGC) VH-KTI VH-LEQ N239GJ N521PA [code "OR"] [w/o 14Dec94 Fresno, CA; cx Jun95] |
| 240 | A | N240B N249B N135WE |
| 241 | A | N42FE N500GP N500FD N240JS N500EX N500ED |
| 242 | A | N846GL VH-WFJ VH-FSZ N242DR |
| 243 | A | N3812G HZ-ABM N81863 I-AGEB N2217Q XA-HYS N152TJ XA-THD N747RY |
| 244 | A | N1451B RP-57 RP-C57 N244TS N244LJ (N116KV) |
| 245 | A | N2WL N1526L N30PA |
| 246 | A | N50PH N50PL N555GB N1DC N628DB |
| 247 | A | YV-265CP N110JD N38FN N523PA [code "NY"] N544PA |
| 248 | A | N3811G C-GBFA N128CA |
| 249 | A | N107JM I-KALI N249DJ N300DA C-FICU [parted out in USA; cx 16Feb09] N374LJ* |
| 250 | A | N3250 (N87RS) N63LE N63LF N947GS |
| 251 | A | N27NB N27HF N251CT N387HA |
| 252 | A | N28CR PT-KZR |
| 253 | A | N40144 N211DH N611CM N611SH N129TS |
| 254 | A | N666CC N34FN N522PA (N54TK) N254US N720WW |
| 255 | A | N44EL N44ET N610HC N616HC XB-LHS XB-FNW XB-USD XA-USD |
| 256 | A | N712L N6GG N50DD N911ML (N402FW) (N811ML) (N66PJ) N335RC |
| 257 | A | F-GCMS N257DJ N417BA |
| 258 | A | (N1700) N28BG N35MH N583PS N583BS (N218CR) N17UF |
| 259 | A | N39413 HB-VGC N9113F N259HA (N259JC) HK-3983X N25AN [parted out by Alliance Air Parts, Oklahoma City, OK] |
| 260 | A | N40PK |
| 261 | A | N900RD XA-ELU N35SJ N35FN N63DH N58MM |
| 262 | A | N237GA N237AF |
| 263 | A | D-CCAD N4577Q N37FN EC-GXX N8228P EC-GXX (N2422J) (ZS-PBA) [dbr Olbia, Italy, as EC-GXX 25Aug02; ntu reservations made later, for parts use] |
| 264 | A* | XA-ATA N35GX N40DK N3056R VR-CDI N64CP |
| 265 | A | N1462B (G-ZEST) G-LEAR United Arab Emirates 801 A6-RJI G-LEAR |
| 266 | A | N3904 SE-DDI N922GL N35GC |
| 267 | A | N39418 XA-LAN [w/o 08Jan93 nr Hermosillo, Mexico] |
| 268 | A* | N10870 YV-286CP N3857N (N286CP) N510SG N2U D-CGFB |
| 269 | A | N881W N225F N211WH N886R |
| 270 | A | N10871 (YV-15CP) YV-O-MRI-1 Venezuela FAV0013 N31MC [w/o 17Oct07, Goodland, KS; parted out by Alliance Air Parts, Oklahoma City, OK] |
| 271 | A* | N1088A LV-PET LV-OAS N40AN [w/o 10Jan07 Columbus, OH; parted out by Alliance Air Parts, Oklahoma City, OK] |
| 272 | A | N39398 N272HS N500EF N321AN |

# LEARJET 35

| C/n | Series | Identities |
|---|---|---|
| 273 | A | N1465B N35FH N103C N103CL N273LJ |
| 274 | A | N1087Y N274JS N274JH N83CP N711BE (N35WG) N274FD N274JS N53G |
| 275 | A | N10872 G-ZEAL (N43PE) N43FE (N65WH) N235SC N72LL ZS-SFV |
| 276 | A | N44LJ N613RR N69BH |
| 277 | A | N925GL N723LL N70CN N127HC XA-PUI N350MD (N9876S) N27TJ N42B (N6362D) (N489) N2WQ N999JS |
| 278 | A | N1476B HB-VGL ECT-028 EC-DJC N300ES N17GL N12RP |
| 279 | A | N19LH [w/o 15Jly97 Avon Park, FL] |
| 280 | A(C21A) | N80MJ HP-912 YN-BVO US Army 87-0026 N35AX N142LM |
| 281 | A | N80WG N425M N425AS |
| 282 | A | N504Y N80CD N80GD N9CH N444CM N62MB |
| 283 | A | N920C N205EL N205FL N386CM |
| 284 | A | (D-CEFL) D-CCAX OO-GBL N43MF |
| 285 | A | N777RA N75KV N34TB VH-MZL N818WS N42PJ (N528VP) N725ST |
| 286 | A | N333X (N333XX) N200SX PT-LSW N286WL N286SD |
| 287 | A | N17EM N71HS N929SR N929SL N156BA N170LD |
| 288 | A | N1476B HB-VGM N43DD N288NE N288JE N288JP |
| 289 | A | N3JL N802CC N289MJ N289NE N289LJ N36TJ N217TA |
| 290 | A | N2022L XA-RAV XA-ORO |
| 291 | A | N7US N535PC [w/o 14Feb91 2 miles N of Aspen Airport, CO; cx Jly91] |
| 292 | A | N634H N292ME |
| 293 | A | N182K [w/o Groton, CT, 02Jun06] |
| 294 | A | N745E N745F N35VP N440HM [w/o 27Feb97 Greenville, SC; remains to White Inds, Bates City, MO] |
| 295 | A | PT-LAA N94AA N474AN |
| 296 | A | N296BS XA-LML N51JA N66NJ |
| 297 | A | N746E N746F N38US N777DM |
| 298 | A | I-FLYC N298NW |
| 299 | A | N244FC PT-LGS N148X (PT-PMV) PT-XLI |
| 300 | A | N365N |
| 301 | A | N301TP N999RB N102ST N102BT N190VE N98AC N945W |
| 302 | A | N717DS N780A N78QA N41ST N631CW N51LC |
| 303 | A | N771A PT-LLS |
| 304 | A | N464HA N112PG N534H N534A N53GH N53GL (N97QA) N995CR ZS-BLE |
| 305 | A | N3VG N33NJ |
| 306 | A | N926GL N66LM N601MC N77LN N111US N1110S N71E (N63602) (N485) N9ZD |
| 307 | A | N120MB (N119HB) N677CT N623KM |
| 308 | A | N99MJ N747GM (N7LA) (N747RL) |
| 309 | A | (YV-328CP) HB-VGT OE-GAR N8216Z N100MN D-CHPD C-GUAC |
| 310 | A | N97JL N13HB (N13HQ) N8280 N310ME |
| 311 | A | D-CDHS N723US N35BG OE-GPN N311BP HC-BSZ N121JT N581AS N711EC |
| 312 | A | LV-PHX LV-OFV N369BA |
| 313 | A | N39413 (F-GCLT) TR-LZI N31WR |
| 314 | A | N35AK (N118GM) N777LD |
| 315 | A | N927GL N662AA D-CCAA (N121JT) |
| 316 | A | N39398 N1503 N1507 N35AH N18ST N99GK N89GK N384JW N884JW XA-UKF |
| 317 | A | N10871 SE-DEM N98TE N317TT |
| 318 | A | N444WB N103CF N318NW (N35WU) |
| 319 | A | Argentina T-23 |
| 320 | A | N905LC N905LD N35FS N320M N30GJ N393JP N32PJ N727MG N35RT |
| 321 | A | N14TX (N19LM) N77LP XA-RVB XC-AA60 (N321WJ) Mexico TP-106 Mexico 3909/XC-UJG |
| 322 | A | N305SC PT-WGF |
| 323 | A* | N735A N357EF |
| 324 | A | G-JJSG G-JETN G-JETG N8064A VH-LJJ |
| 325 | A | D-CARO I-FFLY N325NW |
| 326 | A | PT-LAS N155WL N255JC N612DG N35SA |
| 327 | A | N3797N N135UT N327F N32PF N32PE |
| 328 | A | N3807G N1502 N35NY N35NX N392JP N408MG |
| 329 | A | N39412 N53DM N261PC N261PG |
| 330 | A | N930GL [partially destroyed Dec89 during US invasion of Panama; b/u for spares; cx Jly91] |
| 331 | A* | N10870 HB-VGU I-EJIB N700NW N435JW D-CGFC |
| 332 | A | N600LN N332FG (N598WW) N543WW N827CR XA-... |
| 333 | A | Argentina T-24 [w/o 07Jun82 S Atlantic] |
| 334 | A | N2815 N350RB N334SP (N334AB) N235MC |
| 335 | A | N25MJ N155TD N8YY N15Y N335DJ N335NE N335EE N800CD N800CH N880CH N3MB |
| 336 | A | HB-VGW N590J N166RM N782JR XA-PYC (N336EA) XA-BNO XC-DGO |
| 337 | A | N80ED N337WC N710AT N39HJ |
| 338 | A | N1473B RP-C7272 N610GE RP-C610 |
| 339 | A | N24JK N24CK N15CC N1500 PT-LZP |
| 340 | A* | N11AM N11YM N504F XA-DAZ |
| 341 | A | N3802G D-CARE XA-HOS N259WJ ZS-CEW P4-KIS OE-GMS |

# LEARJET 35

| C/n | Series | Identities |
|---|---|---|
| 342 | A | N1088D N37931 VH-SDN VH-LGH N678S YV-15CP N56JA [parted out by Alliance Air Parts, Oklahoma City, OK] |
| 343 | A | N135MB N80BT N21NA N21NG N998GC LV-BPO |
| 344 | A | N40149 YV-327CP N344MC N630SJ (N111BJ) |
| 345 | A | N3818G N10RE VH-EMP N345LJ N30DK [w/o 24Oct04 San Diego-Brown Field, CA] |
| 346 | A | N3803G C-GMGA N35AJ I-DLON (N34LZ) EC-IIC D-CTRI |
| 347 | A | OE-GNP N85SV |
| 348 | A | (N17ND) N3798B N600BE N500MJ N35TL N35DL (N8JA) N7ZH |
| 349 | A | N272T XA-TCI N252WJ (N349TS) ZS-ARA |
| 350 | A | N88NE N35WB |
| 351 | A | N500RP N500DD N500ND [w/o 11Aug07 Melville Hall, Dominica; parted out by Alliance Air Parts, Oklahoma City, OK; cx 12Jan10] |
| 352 | A | YV-326CP N30GD N600G N71A (N999JA) N35CZ N800GJ |
| 353 | A | N3819G C-GDJH |
| 354 | A | N1450B D-CART N212GA N405GJ |
| 355 | A | N1468B LV-PJZ LV-ONN N64RV N345 N351WB N721EC |
| 356 | A | N54YR N54YP N800WJ (VR-C..) PT-LUG |
| 357 | A | N3797S N1001L (N289GA) ZS-MGK (N100L) N104SB N357LJ |
| 358 | A | N524HC N358PG N108JN |
| 359 | A | (N127RM) HB-VHB N136JP |
| 360 | A | N185FP N1129M (N360GL) N360LJ (N901MS) (N987DK) YV |
| 361 | A | N924GL PT-LBS PT-FAT PT-OCZ |
| 362 | A | N3794M N888MV N399KL N773LP N633DS N362FW |
| 363 | A | N52MJ N183JC N19RP PP-CRT* |
| 364 | A | N3794Z (N65TA) N981TH N950CS N490BC N353EF |
| 365 | A | G-ZONE (N4564S) G-ZIPS G-SEBE G-CJET G-GJET D-CFAI [w/o 12Jun08 Kinsangani, DR Congo] |
| 366 | A | N411LC N49AT (N94AA) N119CP N350DA HS-CFS |
| 367 | A | N714S (N67TJ) N97RJ N232CC N360AX |
| 368 | A | N35FM SE-DHE N368BG N99KW N450MC N351TV |
| 369 | A | Argentina VR-17 Argentina T-24 Argentina T-26 |
| 370 | A | HB-VGY N11MY N1MY (N56PR) VR-BKB N8216Q XA-RKY XA-OFA XA-CVD N87GA XA-... |
| 371 | A | LV-PLY LV-ALF N399BA |
| 372 | A | HB-VGX N372AS PT-LJK |
| 373 | A | SE-DER XA-BRE XA-RUY N97AN N971K LV-BNR |
| 374 | A | HZ-106 HZ-MS1A [parted out by Atlanta Air Salvage, Griffin, GA, 2009] |
| 375 | A | (YV-270CP) HZ-107 HZ-MS1B [parted out by Atlanta Air Salvage, Griffin, GA, 2009] |
| 376 | A | N458JA N77FK N33WB XA-SBF N979RF |
| 377 | A | (N711EV) N933GL N10WF N18WE N46MF |
| 378 | A | CX-BOI/FAU 500 (N900DG) N354ME N354EF |
| 379 | A | N23VG N18LH N217RT XB-IWL |
| 380 | A | N82JL N291BX N291BC N281BC XA-SBA N11SQ XA-SGK XA-MSH N903WJ C-GAJS |
| 381 | A | D-CORA N65DH (N40TM) N300CM N335K N35NA N131AJ |
| 382 | A | N382BL N382BP OE-GAF N60WL |
| 383 | A | N66FE N364CL |
| 384 | A | N37984 N811DF N811DD N384CF |
| 385 | A | N535MC N350EF |
| 386 | A | N13VG N999FA LV-BAW |
| 387 | A* | D-CARL |
| 388 | A | N1929S N388PD N388LS [w/o 24Dec96 Smarts Mountain on approach to Lebanon-Municipal, NH; cx May98] |
| 389 | A | N59MJ N377C N31WT N31WE VR-BLU N436DM N79AX N389KA |
| 390 | A | N500PP N508P N831CW C-FJEF C-FPRP |
| 391 | A | N3793D N444BF N813RR N89AT I-RYVA N888PT XA-SWF [w/o 23Jun95 Tepico, Mexico] |
| 392 | A | N931GL N1ED N18DY N1XL |
| 393 | A | N923GL N666RB N700WJ PT-LOE |
| 394 | A | N1466K N816JA N94MJ N60DK N626JS N232PR N238PR |
| 395 | A | HB-VHD N3261L N30GL N246CM N395MY |
| 396 | A | N2000M N938GL N5139W VR-CBU N5FF N74JL PT-OPJ |
| 397 | A | N33PT D-CLAN N200TW N335JD* |
| 398 | A | N3797A N1AH [w/o 16May97 Great Falls, MT; cx Nov97; to spares by White Inds, Bates City, MO, 1998] |
| 399 | A | N37965 N540HP (N399DJ) N399AZ PT-OVC (N399AZ) [w/o 04Nov07 Sao Paulo, Brazil] |
| 400 | A | VH-CPH (VH-CPQ) VH-TPR VH-JIG VH-RHQ VH-OVB |
| 401 | A | N66LJ (N177SB) N771SB N535JM |
| 402 | A | N3402 N610JR N7AB N35BG |
| 403 | A | N37966 N312CT N312CF N312CE N100NR N101HW N100HW N403FW [parted out by Alliance Air Parts, Oklahoma City, OK] |
| 404 | A | N500JS N404BB N404KA N404DP N804TF |
| 405 | A | N41MJ (N181GL) N35AS N35FS N442DM N135DA |
| 406 | A | N764G N35Q I-KELM ER-LGA HS-EMS |
| 407 | A | N3793P N234DT N221MC N407MR C-GIWD C-GIWO |

# LEARJET 35

| C/n | Series | Identities |
|---|---|---|
| 408 | A | (N33VG) N3798P LV-POG LV-AIT |
| 409 | A | N50PD N858TM N123LC N888BS N35FE N351AM |
| 410 | A | N12109 N1210M C-FHDM N441CW (N21WS) N820RP N89RP N352TV |
| 411 | A | PT-LBY N94GP |
| 412 | A | N37980 N6666R N412GL (N31LM) N314C XA-RGH |
| 413 | A | HB-VHE N2637Z F-GHAE N413MA N27KG D-CFCF |
| 414 | A | (N135AB) N39MW PT-SMO N414TJ N196SD N196SP N815DD |
| 415 | A | N125AX N19GL N415DJ D-COSY SE-DZZ |
| 416 | A | N306M N35MV N40GG N841TT N841TF |
| 417 | A | N934GL N117FJ (N117RJ) D-CONO N97D N90RK HC-BTN (N37HR) N281CD LX-ONE |
| 418 | A | XA-KCM XA-SCA N366AC LV-BPL |
| 419 | A | N935GL N25EL N53JM N35SM N72AX |
| 420 | A | N35RT N35PT N100KK N100KZ N181CA |
| 421 | A | N44MJ N85CA N85QA (N88AH) N3AH N413JP I-VULC D-CDSF |
| 422 | A | YV-434CP N86BL N45AE |
| 423 | A | N369XL N200TC (N335GA) D-CAVE |
| 424 | A | N2844 N508GP N52FN |
| 425 | A | N111KK N111KZ N425SA |
| 426 | A* | D-CARD N43W N43H ZS-NID N1128J RP-C1426 N143LG |
| 427 | A | N1087Z VH-FOX N42LL N358AC N36HJ [parted out by MTW Aerospace, AL] |
| 428 | A | N1465B VH-ELC N17LH VH-SLE |
| 429 | A | G-ZING G-GAYL G-ZENO United Arab Emirates 800 A6-RJH G-ZING D-CSOS* |
| 430 | A | N10870 Finland LJ-1 |
| 431 | A | N1088A YV-433CP N34FD N431CW N431AS N355PC |
| 432 | A | F-GDCN N4445Y N330BC VR-CAD G-HUGG VH-VLJ |
| 433 | A | N39416 D-CARG HB-VCZ N26583 N95AC (N93RC) PT-LIH [w/o 15Mar91 Uberlandia, Brazil] |
| 434 | A | N4401 N469BB |
| 435 | A | N435N XC-HHJ |
| 436 | A | N37988 PT-LDN N436BL N100AT |
| 437 | A | N3803G YV-432CP YV2044 |
| 438 | A | N17ND N600LL N12GJ N300R N308R N308BW |
| 439 | A | N439ME HK-3121X HK-3121 N55RZ N35LW (N35FT) N402DP N911WX N611TA |
| 440 | A | N101HK N101PK N903HC N908HC (N354EM) N917SC N300SC |
| 441 | A | N1471B N551WC TC-MEK N441PC N441PG N74SP N404JS RP-C1404 N699ST |
| 442 | A | N40149 N3799C N35BK N442NE [w/o 26Jul88 Morristown, NJ; remains to White Inds, Bates City, MO] |
| 443 | A | N135RJ N258G N335MR |
| 444 | A | N3818G D-CARH N44695 N444MJ N144WB N1U N44SK N615HP N615HB |
| 445 | A | N3802G HB-VHG I-MOCO [w/o 08Feb01 Nurnberg, Germany] |
| 446 | A | N37962 N80AS N96CP N96CR N794GC N403DP |
| 447 | A | N127K N300FN D-COKE |
| 448 | A | N48MJ N222BG N595PL |
| 449 | A | N37947 N777LF N449QS XA-GDO |
| 450 | A | N450KK N950SP |
| 451 | A | N1462B Finland LJ-2 |
| 452 | A | N25MJ N279SP N452DA |
| 453 | A | N124MC N802JW (N802EC) N453AM |
| 454 | A | N3794W (N379BW) N80AR (N80KR) |
| 455 | A | N3794U N455NE N988QC |
| 456 | A | N711CD N456CL |
| 457 | A | N1451B N900P N974JD (N113LB) N874JD N113LB N49WL |
| 458 | A | N276JS YV-997CP N86RX N4EA |
| 459 | A | VH-MIE N306SP N80BL N969MT N829CA [w/o 13Jul04 Charlestown, St. Kitts & Nevis; to Dodson Av'n, Rantoul, KS for spares] |
| 460 | A | XC-PGR XA-MPS XA-JJJ |
| 461 | A | N64CF |
| 462 | A | N3811G N8562W N147K N801K N7117 N135TP N394PA LV-BXU |
| 463 | A | N1088D VH-ULT VH-FSW VH-FSU N68LL N32HJ N699BA |
| 464 | A | (N75PK) N1DC PT-LHX N464WL VP-BJS N111KR |
| 465 | A | N465NW |
| 466 | A | VH-WFP N39SA (N700WJ) N600WJ D-COCO [w/o 08Jun93 Cologne-Bonn, Germany; remains to Dodson Av'n, Ottawa, KS] |
| 467 | A | N3796Q HZ-MS1 HZ-MS1C [parted out by Atlanta Air Salvage, Griffin, GA, 2009] |
| 468 | A* | VH-ANI N468LM OY-CCJ |
| 469 | A | N39416 N3202A N660SA N444TG N71MH N35JN |
| 470 | A | N3810G Finland LJ-3 |
| 471 | A | VH-BQR N95AP N110FT N529BC |
| 472 | A | N1468B N448GC N448WC N448WG PT-ONK (N472AS) N54HF N35TN N335MW N138WE N612SQ |
| 473 | A | N3796P PT-LFT N3UJ N44AB N35TH N777LB N35CY |
| 474 | A | N39413 N37975 PT-LEB [wfu Jundiai, Brazil] |
| 475 | A | N10873 N3797K 3D-ADC ZS-TOW (N42AJ) |
| 476 | A | N3818G N476VC N777LB N776JS |

# LEARJET 35

| C/n | Series | Identities |
|---|---|---|
| 477 | A | N40162 N3797B N82GL N80CD N95EC N477WB (N477MS) N24JG N235UJ N155RD N608GF N376HA |
| 478 | A | N3815G LV-TDF [w/o 15May84 Ushuaia, Argentina] |
| 479 | A | N3816G N8565J N31WT N30SA PT-LHT |
| 480 | A* | N3819G (VH-ALH) N8563A N35CK (N484) (N35FH) N39DK |
| 481 | A | N1466B N6666K N666KK N728MP N729HS HK-3122X HK-3122 N729HS N27NR OO-LFV N99NJ |
| 482 | A | N482U [w/o at 2130 13Feb83 en route Kuala Lumpur-Colombo; restored May94 N2286D; purpose unknown] |
| 483 | A | N40144 N8562Y N202BT (N203AL) N327CB N990LC |
| 484 | A | N4289U Argentina VR-18 Argentina T-25 |
| 485 | A | N4290C N485S XA-RZZ N710WL N485AC |
| 486 | A | N4291G N821PC N117EL N810CC N925DM |
| 487 | A* | N4289Y N206FC N206EC N400MC N391JP N391JR N487FW N890LR N890LJ |
| 488 | A | N8563G N848GL N30W N30WY N900R N907R XA-UGK N61SJ XC-OAH |
| 489 | A | N1473B N222BE |
| 490 | A | N1087Z N64MP N502JF |
| 491 | A | N1087Y N8563N N491HS N241AG N485 I-AGEN N135PG N394JP N35NK |
| 492 | A | N39399 N8566B N35NP N37SV N335UJ N492RM N994CR N492RM |
| 493 | A | N3811G N8564M N482SG I-FFRI N493NW N493CH N354CL |
| 494 | A | N1476B PT-LDM |
| 495 | A | N1088D N440MC |
| 496 | A | N3803G N8564K N856RR N496SW N39TH N496SW (N496LJ) N825LJ |
| 497 | A | N1450B N8565N N50PH N21DA N15RH N518PR |
| 498 | A | N3815G N8564P I-FLYH N498JR N400FF C-GTDM |
| 499 | A | N3818G N85645 N84AD PT-LII HK-3921 N38AL N499WJ N1TS N911DX |
| 500 | A | N1465B N8566X N66LN N101US N81CH N81QH N144LG |
| 501 | A* | N3816G HB-VHR N711PR N35HW N326HG N565GG |
| 502 | A | N1476B N8565X N747CP |
| 503 | A | N1087Z N8567A HB-VII HK-3646X N8567A N77NR N542SA |
| 504 | A | N10871 N8568B G-RAFF N505DH OE-GMJ |
| 505 | A | N1471B N7259J N505EE N494PA N60DK |
| 506 | A | N3819G N317BG N10BD [on display in the terminal at Denver Int'l by May03 having been the first aircraft to land at the new airport in 1993] |
| 507 | A | N3802G N35GJ N35HP N42HP N42HN |
| 508 | A | N40144 N741E N741F N7777B N881CA N508TF N452AC LV-BOX |
| 509 | C21A | N6317V N7263C 84-0063 N35AL N826RD N135PT [w/o 04Aug03 Poquonock River, Groton, CT] |
| 510 | C21A | N6331V N7263D 84-0064 |
| 511 | C21A | N4289X N7263E 84-0065 |
| 512 | C21A | N4290J N7263F 84-0066 [w/o Decatur, IL, 02Oct06] |
| 513 | C21A | N4291G N7263H 84-0067 N35AQ N117PK HK-4662 |
| 514 | C21A | N4289Z N7263K 84-0068 [wfu AMARC 26Jan07, park code AACJ0020] |
| 515 | C21A | N4290K N7263L 84-0069 [code KS] |
| 516 | C21A | N4291K N7263N 84-0070 [code KS] |
| 517 | C21A | N6340T N7263R 84-0071 [code KS] |
| 518 | C21A | N4289Y N7263X 84-0072 [code KS] |
| 519 | C21A | N6307H N400AD 84-0073 [wfu AMARC 16Jan07, park code AACJ0011] |
| 520 | C21A | N42905 N400AK 84-0074 [wfu AMARC 08Jan07, park code AACJ0005] |
| 521 | C21A | N4291N N400AN 84-0075 |
| 522 | C21A | N4290Y N400AP 84-0076 |
| 523 | C21A | N4289U N400AQ 84-0077 |
| 524 | C21A | N6317V N400AS 84-0078 [wfu AMARC 08Jan07, park code AACJ0006] |
| 525 | C21A | N6331V N400AT 84-0079 |
| 526 | C21A | N4289X N400AU 84-0080 [wfu AMARC 10Jan07, park code AACJ0007] |
| 527 | C21A | N4290J N400AX 84-0081 |
| 528 | C21A | N4289Z N400AY 84-0082 |
| 529 | C21A | N4291G N400AZ 84-0083 |
| 530 | C21A | N4290K N400BA 84-0084 |
| 531 | C21A | N4291K N400FY 84-0085 |
| 532 | C21A | N6340T N400BN 84-0086 [wfu AMARC 18Jan07, park code AACJ0013] |
| 533 | C21A | N4289Y N400BQ 84-0087 |
| 534 | C21A | N6307H N400BU 84-0088 [wfu AMARC 22Jan07, park code AACJ0015] |
| 535 | C21A | N4290C N400BY 84-0089 (N61905) [wfu AMARC 10Jan07 park code AACJ0008] |
| 536 | C21A | N42905 N400BZ 84-0090 [code OF] |
| 537 | C21A | N4290Y N400CD 84-0091 [code OF] |
| 538 | C21A | N400CG 84-0092 [code FF] |
| 539 | C21A | N400CJ 84-0093 [code OF] |
| 540 | C21A | N400CK 84-0094 [code OF] |
| 541 | C21A | N400CQ 84-0095 [code OF] |
| 542 | C21A | N400CR 84-0096 |
| 543 | C21A | N400CU 84-0097 [w/o 02Feb02 Ellsworth AFB, SD] |
| 544 | C21A | N400CV 84-0098 |
| 545 | C21A | N400CX 84-0099 |
| 546 | C21A | N400CY 84-0100 |
| 547 | C21A | N400CZ 84-0101 |

# LEARJET 35

| C/n | Series | Identities |
|---|---|---|
| 548 | C21A | N400DD 84-0102 |
| 549 | C21A | N400DJ 84-0103 [code CS] |
| 550 | C21A | N400DL 84-0104 [wfu AMARC 16Jan07, park code AACJ0012] |
| 551 | C21A | N400DN 84-0105 [wfu AMARC 08Jan07, park code AACJ0004] |
| 552 | C21A | N400DQ 84-0106 [code CS] |
| 553 | C21A | N400DR 84-0107 [code CS] |
| 554 | C21A | N400DU 84-0108 [wfu AMARC 12Jan07, park code AACJ0010] |
| 555 | C21A | N400DV 84-0109 |
| 556 | C21A | N400DX 84-0110 |
| 557 | C21A | N400DY 84-0111 |
| 558 | C21A | N400DZ 84-0112 |
| 559 | C21A | N400EC 84-0113 [wfu AMARC 24Jan07, park code AACJ0018] |
| 560 | C21A | N400EE 84-0114 [code FF] |
| 561 | C21A | N400EF 84-0115 [wfu AMARC 12Jan07, park code AACJ0009] |
| 562 | C21A | N400EG 84-0116 [wfu AMARC 24Jan07, park code AACJ0017] |
| 563 | C21A | N400EJ 84-0117 [wfu AMARC 22Jan07, park code AACJ0016] |
| 564 | C21A | N400EK 84-0118 |
| 565 | C21A | N400EL 84-0119 |
| 566 | C21A | N400EM 84-0120 |
| 567 | C21A | N400EN 84-0121 [w/o 15Jan87 Alabama, LA] |
| 568 | C21A | N400EQ 84-0122 [wfu AMARC 18Jan07, park code AACJ0014] |
| 569 | C21A | N400ER 84-0123 [code AU] |
| 570 | C21A | N400ES 84-0124 [code AU] |
| 571 | C21A | N400ET 84-0125 [code AU] |
| 572 | C21A | N400EU 84-0126 [code RA] |
| 573 | C21A | N400EV 84-0127 |
| 574 | C21A | N400EX 84-0138 [wfu AMARC, park code AACJ0001] |
| 575 | C21A | N400EY 84-0128 |
| 576 | C21A | N400EZ 84-0129 |
| 577 | C21A | N400FE 84-0130 |
| 578 | C21A | N400FG 84-0131 |
| 579 | C21A | N400FH 84-0132 [wfu AMARC 26Jan07, park code AACJ0019] |
| 580 | C21A | N400FK 84-0133 [wfu AMARC 08Jan07, park code AACJ0002] |
| 581 | C21A | N400FM 84-0134 [code RA] |
| 582 | C21A | N400FN 84-0135 [code RA] |
| 583 | C21A | N400FP 84-0136 [code RA] [w/o 17Apr95 Alexandra City, AL] |
| 584 | C21A | N400FQ 84-0141 [wfu AMARC 03Jan07, park code AACJ0003] |
| 585 | C21A | N400FR 84-0137 [code CS] |
| 586 | C21A | N400FT 84-0142 |
| 587 | C21A | N400FU 84-0139 |
| 588 | C21A | N400FV 84-0140 |
| 589 | A | N1087T N8567K PT-GAP N3215K* |
| 590 | A | N1451B N35GA N35KT N969MC N827CA (N822SF) N882SC |
| 591 | A | N3803G N8567Z N72626 N500EX N822CA N822CP N9ZM N9ZB N880Z |
| 592 | A | N3810G N952GL N45KK N93LE |
| 593 | A* | N40146 N32B I-FLYG N593LR N593PN VH-PPF VH-LPJ |
| 594 | A | N1088C N72596 N7007V (ZS-PTL) (ZS-EFD) OY-LJA N410BD N747BW |
| 595 | A | N3815G N85PM N414KL N95JN |
| 596 | A | N1473B N72612 N62WM YV-850CP N850MM N826CA N826CP N352HS |
| 597 | A | N39394 N8567R N54GL N597BL N597JT N355CA N604S |
| 598 | A | N39415 N8567T PT-LGW |
| 599 | A | N40144 N58GL N367DA |
| 600 | A | N823CA N823CP N995DP |
| 601 | A | N3818G China HY986 |
| 602 | A | N10873 China HY987 |
| 603 | A | N1471B China HY988 |
| 604 | A | N1462B N59GL N604BL N73LP N604GS |
| 605 | A | N1088D N185HA N35AS N825CA N925CA |
| 606 | A | N3803G N1735J N35PD N3WP N96GS |
| 607 | A | N39399 N72614 PT-LIJ N68MJ D-CGFH |
| 608 | A | N40162 N8567Z N111SF N14T N96AX ZS-IGP |
| 609 | A | N4290J N36NW N788QC XA-JRH N609TF N986SA |
| 610 | A | N1473B N101AR N161MA N610LJ (N354GG) (N354GE) |
| 611 | A* | N39413 N622WG N611TW VH-ESM |
| 612 | A | N3812G N8568D N2FU N501TW N551TW N551HM N36BP D-CGFI |
| 613 | A/R35A | N4289X Brazil 6000 |
| 614 | A | N3815G G-PJET HB-VJC G-SOVN G-VIPS G-OCFR N335EA N683EL N683EF |
| 615 | A/R35A | N1466B N7260E Brazil 6001 |
| 616 | A | N3807G N8568Q PT-LQF N616LJ N876CS N876C D-CEXP |
| 617 | A/R35A | N4289Z Brazil 6002 |
| 618 | A | N10871 YU-BOL SL-BAA S5-BAA N618DM N618CF |
| 619 | A | N4290K N8568V PT-POK |
| 620 | A* | N1451B I-KODM VR-BNI N232FX XA-COI N620EM |
| 621 | A | N1468B N999TH N999TN PT-OFW N242MT PR-ABP |
| 622 | A | N4290C N7260H N610R N81MR |
| 623 | A | N40149 N7260Q Thailand B.TL12-1/30 60504 Thailand B.TL12-1/30 40207 |

# LEARJET 35

C/n Series Identities

624 C21A N39404 86-0374
625 C21A N4289Y 86-0375 N625BL (N522AG)
626 A N39398 N7261R N35AJ N711NF C-GNPT N335MG (N385MG)
627 A N4289U N7260T PT-LMY
628 C21A N3810G 86-0376 N628BL N628WJ CX-VRH N628DC N628GZ LX-TWO
629 C21A N40144 86-0377
630 A N42905 N72630 N742E N742P N388PD
631 A/VU35A N3818G Brazil 2710
632 A/VU35A N1461B Brazil 2711
633 A/VU35A N39416 Brazil 2712
634 ZR N1462B I-EAMM N626BM [has Raisbeck modified wing set]
635 A N1471B Thailand B.TL12-2/31 60505 Thailand B.TL12-2/31 40208 [w/o 08Non06 Nakhon Sawan, Thailand]
636 A/VU35A N1476B Brazil 2713
637 [airframe not built]
638 A/VU35A N39412 Brazil 2714
639 A/VU35A N6317V Brazil 2715
640 A/VU35A N3816G N8568Y Brazil 2716
641 A/VU35A N1087Y N7261H Brazil 2717
642 A/VU35A N1465B N7262X Brazil 2718
643 A N39418 G-LJET (N35NK) N643MJ D-CGFJ
644 A N1088C N1043B PT-LLF (N54SB) C-GMMY
645 A* N43TR N645AM
646 A N3812G XA-UMA N646EA N717JB N712JB G-MURI [w/o 2May00 Lyon-Satolas A/P, France]
647 A N410RD N915RB N815RB (N647TJ) ZS-DJB N335PR
648 A N1045J N974JD XB-LHS N648JW RP-C648 N648J N97LE
649 A* N10870 HB-VJJ N35QB ZK-XVL
650 A* N1022G PT-LYF N135MW N650LR
651 A HB-VJK N405PC
652 A N6307H N99FN D-CURE N652SA N49AZ N2KZ N652KZ
653 A HB-VJL LX-LAR
654 A N4290K N633WW N600LF (N95EC) (B-98183) ZS-NSB B-98183 N8189 N770BM
655 A N1088A N16FG PT-MFR N785JM C-GMMA
656 A N3810G G-JETL N335SB N356JW
657 A N1473B N1CA N10AH
658 A* N39404 N573LP N162EM N77NJ
659 A N4290Y N873LP (N878LP) N413LC N776BG
660 A N1087Z C-GLJQ N660L C-GLJQ N421SV
661 A (N8888D) N1268G VH-PFA [operated by Singapore AF as a target towing aircraft]
662 A G-NEVL G-BUSX N35UK N27AX
663 A N91480 D-CCCB
664 A N9130F N117RJ C-GRMJ N640BA
665 A N5009T N291K N35UA LV-BRT
666 [airframe not built as this number is considered unlucky in the USA]
667 A N5018G N91566 N135DE
668 A N5011L N9168Q N441PC
669 A* N5014F N91452 OO-JBS N7XJ (N487LP) A6-FAJ N669LJ N393CF N893CF C-GWFG
670 A N5012K N35UK N599SC OY-CCO (HP-....) HK-3949X (N670WJ) OY-CCO N787LP N987LP N460SB
671 A N9141N (ZS-NEX) (ZS-NFS) ZS-NFK N671BA LV-PLV LV-WPZ N671BX N671TS G-JMED
672 A N9140Y N672DK N45KK XA-FMT
673 A N5014F N9173G C-FBDH C-GPDO N835MC
674 A N2601G N22SF N22SN N900JE N674LJ LV-BIE
675 A N2602M B-98181 [w/o 17Sep94, shot down in error while target-towing off coast of Taiwan]
676 A N5012Z N35LJ N235AC N620MJ

Production complete

# LEARJET MODEL 36

* after the series letter or in the series column indicates the aircraft has been fitted with Avcom delta fins.

| C/n | Series | Identities |
|---|---|---|
| 001 | | N26GL [ff 09Jan73 as a model 26 c/n 26-001; used as development airframe for both the model 35 and 36] C-GBRW [has winglets in place of tip tanks; cx Apr97 to Montreal - St Hubert Aeronautical College painted as C-XPWC to celebrate its active life as a flying test bed with Pratt & Whitney Canada] |
| 002 | | N362GL D-CMAR YV-T-ASG YV-161P YV-89CP N18AT D-CELA N3239A N84DM N84FN |
| 003 | * | N363GL N36TA N55CJ N361PJ |
| 004 | * | N1918W (D-CCAC) D-CCPD N50DT N180GC N54PA |
| 005 | * | LV-LOG N9108Z N905CK |
| 006 | | (I-CRYS) HB-VEA D-CAFO D-CDFA [w/o 25Mar80 Libya] |
| 007 | * | N138GL N173JA N226CC SX-AHF VR-BHB N83DM N83FN |
| 008 | * | N20JA VR-BJD VR-BJO N84MJ N101AR (N701AR) N101AJ (N43A) |
| 009 | | N2000M N704J N44GL N25CL N15CC N505RA N505HG |
| 010 | * | N50SF N45FG |
| 011 | | PT-KQT N26MJ N26FN |
| 012 | | N139GL N215RL VR-BFR N2267Z C-GBWD N666TB N36CW N222AW N55GH N712JE N547PA [code "AK"] |
| 013 | * | N352WC (N852WC) SE-DDH N3280E N3PC N13JE D-CBRD N71PG |
| 014 | | N900Y N200Y VH-SLJ |
| 015 | * | N14CF N10FN |
| 016 | * | HB-VEE JY-AET F-GBGD N616DJ N12FN |
| 017 | * | N1010A N17LJ (N32JA) (N361PJ) |
| 018 | A* | PT-KTU N418CA PT-ACC N418CA* |
| 019 | A | N300CC N89MJ C-GLMK N718US N300DK N300DL C-GLAL N719JE N540PA N527PA |
| 020 | A | JY-AFC [w/o 21Sep77 Amman, Jordan] |
| 021 | A | N3524F I-AIFA [w/o 10Dec79 Forli, Italy] |
| 022 | A* | N761A N38WC N36PD N44EV |
| 023 | A | N1871R N1871P N187MZ (N64FN) N767RA N6YY N56PA |
| 024 | A | N38D N978E C-FEMT |
| 025 | A | N774AB N730GL OE-GLP C-GVVB N500MJ (N98A) N800BL N32PA |
| 026 | A | (N762L) N762GL N23G C-GGPF N6617B N8U (N888TN) (N8UB) N1U N8UA N86BL |
| 027 | A* | N836GA N484HB N27MJ N16FN |
| 028 | A | N731GA N75TD N545PA [code "HI"] |
| 029 | A | (N79JS) HB-VFD N116MA |
| 030 | A | N71TP N74TP N360LS N36PJ (N36AX) N160GC |
| 031 | A | N20UC N20UG D-CFOX N20UG N62PG |
| 032 | A | N40146 N745GL N22BM N36BP HB-VLK N950G (N16AJ) VH-CMS |
| 033 | A | N762L N14TX [w/o 06Dec96 Stephenville, Newfoundland, Canada. Parted out by White Industries Inc, Bates City, MO] |
| 034 | A | N763R China HY985 B-4599 |
| 035 | A | N3807G VH-BIB N266BS VH-BIB N71CK |
| 036 | A* | N1462B N610GE N36MJ N136DH |
| 037 | A | RP-C5128 N555WH C-GRJL C-FCLJ |
| 038 | A | N304E N15FN N548PA N700GG N363PJ |
| 039 | A | N217CS C-GSRN N4998Z N25PK N99RS |
| 040 | A | HB-VFV N902WJ N110PA N70UT N70UP (N444SC) (N442SC) N500SV N72AV N82GG |
| 041 | A | N79SF [w/o 08Jan88 Monroe, LA] |
| 042 | A | N39391 HB-VFS [w/o 23Sep95 Zarzaitine, Algeria] |
| 043 | A | N1010G N43LJ N53JA (N143JW) N432JW (N521JW) XB-JPX |
| 044 | A | N1010H N44LJ N54JA (N77JW) N286AB N70LJ |
| 045 | A | (N700MD) N900MD N13FN N546PA [w/o 03Dec02, Astoria, WA; parted out; cx Jun03] |
| 046 | A* | F-BKFB N4448Y N146MJ N17A |
| 047 | A | G-ZEIZ N2972Q N14CN N36SK OE-GMD N36PJ |
| 048 | A* | HB-VHF N3999B (N14FU) N2FU N24PT N3NP PT-WGM N32AJ D-CFGG |
| 049 | A | N661AA N136ST VH-SLF |
| 050 | A | N3456L XA-RIA Mexico TP-105/XC-UJR [also carries XC-AA24] |
| 051 | A | N4290J Peru 524/OB-1431 |
| 052 | A | N1087T Peru 525/OB-1432 |
| 053 | A | N39418 China HY984 |
| 054 | A/U36A | (N54GL) N1087Z Japan 9201 |
| 055 | A | N10871 OE-GNL N365AS PP-JAA S9-CRH ZS-CRH |
| 056 | A/U36A | N3802G Japan 9202 [w/o 21May03 Iwakuni AFB, Japan] |
| 057 | A | N39394 HB-VIF VH-JCX |
| 058 | A/U36A | N4290J Japan 9203 [w/o 28Feb91 Shikoku Island, Japan] |
| 059 | A/U36A | N1087Z Japan 9204 |
| 060 | A/U36A | N1088A Japan 9205 |
| 061 | A/U36A | N50154 N2601B Japan 9206 |
| 062 | A* | N4291N D-CGFE |
| 063 | A* | N6340T N1048X D-CGFF |

Production complete

# LEARJET MODEL 40

| C/n | Identities | | | | | |
|---|---|---|---|---|---|---|
| 45-001 | N45XL | N40LX | [converted from model 45 circa 2002 and ff as such on 31Aug02] | | | |
| 45-2001 | N40LJ | [ff 05Sep02] | N401LJ | | | |
| 45-2002 | N40KJ | N789AH | | | | |
| 45-2003 | N404MK | LQ-BFS | | | | |
| 45-2004 | N40082 | N605FX | | | | |
| 45-2005 | N40083 | N606FX | | | | |
| 45-2006 | N50111 | D-CNIK | | | | |
| 45-2007 | N50126 | N40PX | G-MOOO | | | |
| 45-2008 | N5013U | N2408 | N99GK | | | |
| 45-2009 | N40LJ | CC-CMS | | | | |
| 45-2010 | N50163 | N46E | | | | |
| 45-2011 | N4001G | N51001 | N411AJ | | | |
| 45-2012 | N607FX | | | | | |
| 45-2013 | N5018G | XA-GRR | | | | |
| 45-2014 | N608FX | | | | | |
| 45-2015 | N40077 | I-ERJG | OE-GGC | | | |
| 45-2016 | N40078 | I-ELYS | | | | |
| 45-2017 | N5009T | N502JM | N700KG | | | |
| 45-2018 | N5018G | OE-GGB | D-CGGB | | | |
| 45-2019 | N50111 | G-FORN | I-FORR | | | |
| 45-2020 | N50153 | PR-ONE | | | | |
| 45-2021 | N5013U | N401EG | | | | |
| 45-2022 | N5013Y | N609FX | | | | |
| 45-2023 | N50163 | N521CH | | | | |
| 45-2024 | N424LF | N40ML | I-YLFC | | | |
| 45-2025 | N225LJ | N240RP | | | | |
| 45-2026 | N5014E | OE-GVI | EC-JYY | | | |
| 45-2027 | N50154 | N40LJ | N610FX | | | |
| 45-2028 | N40XR | | | | | |
| 45-2029 | N40073 | N996AL | N998AL | N998AQ* | | |
| 45-2030 | N40076 | XA-SNI | | | | |
| 45-2031 | N40085 | RP-C3110 | | | | |
| 45-2032 | N5015U | N10SE | | | | |
| 45-2033 | N404EL | | | | | |
| 45-2034 | N5018G | I-PARS | | | | |
| 45-2035 | N40050 | N1848T | | | | |
| 45-2036 | N100HW | | | | | |
| 45-2037 | N237LJ | N611FX | | | | |
| 45-2038 | N22GM | | | | | |
| 45-2039 | N612FX | | | | | |
| 45-2040 | N5009V | (XA-GPE) | XA-CGF | | | |
| 45-2041 | N614FX | | | | | |
| 45-2042 | N256AH | | | | | |
| 45-2043 | N4001G | C-FMHA | | | | |
| 45-2044 | N5016V | N140LJ | | | | |
| 45-2045 | N176CA | | | | | |
| 45-2046 | N4004Q | N40LJ | N773RS | XC-TJN | | |
| 45-2047 | N616FX | N473BD | XA-RAB | | | |
| 45-2048 | N40077 | N80169 | PR-JBS | | | |
| 45-2049 | N5012K | N140WW | | | | |
| 45-2050 | N5015U | VP-BHT | | | | |
| 45-2051 | N615FX | | | | | |
| 45-2052 | N784CC | | | | | |
| 45-2053 | N5018G | I-ERJJ | | | | |
| 45-2054 | N50111 | G-MEET | | | | |
| 45-2055 | N5010U | N55XR | N506KS | | | |
| 45-2056 | N411HC | | | | | |
| 45-2057 | N616FX | | | | | |
| 45-2058 | N71NF | | | | | |
| 45-2059 | N619FX | N695BD | I-GURU | | | |
| 45-2060 | N999EK | | | | | |
| 45-2061 | N5016Z | D-CLUX | | | | |
| 45-2062 | N4005Q | PT-XDN | | | | |
| 45-2063 | N240WG | N740KG | | | | |
| 45-2064 | N5000E | (OY-KVP) | "OY-KPV" | "N34AG" | N540LH | OY-KVP |
| 45-2065 | N617FX | | | | | |
| 45-2066 | N50154 | N2758W | | | | |
| 45-2067 | N618FX | XA-NJM | | | | |
| 45-2068 | N5012G | PP-FMW | | | | |
| 45-2069 | N24VP | N29RN | N29RE | | | |
| 45-2070 | N77HN | | | | | |
| 45-2071 | N40077 | OY-ZAN | | | | |
| 45-2072 | N4003K | N83JJ | N15UB | | | |
| 45-2073 | N40083 | N975DM | | | | |

# LEARJET 40

| C/n | Identities | | | |
|---|---|---|---|---|
| 45-2074 | N40012 | G-STUF | | |
| 45-2075 | N75XR | N484CH | | |
| 45-2076 | N618FX | | | |
| 45-2077 | N5015U | XA-VFV | | |
| 45-2078 | N40079 | I-GOCO | | |
| 45-2079 | N40082 | D-CVJP | OE-GVA | |
| 45-2080 | N40076 | D-CPDR | | |
| 45-2081 | N24VP | PR-DIB | | |
| 45-2082 | N619FX | | | |
| 45-2083 | N51054 | N419ET | N412ET | |
| 45-2084 | N40LJ | N65TP | | |
| 45-2085 | N620FX | | | |
| 45-2086 | N4003W | PR-PTR | | |
| 45-2087 | N40NB | | | |
| 45-2088 | N288AS | | | |
| 45-2089 | N621FX | | | |
| 45-2090 | N4003K | N90XR | | |
| 45-2091 | N5009T | D-CVJN | | |
| 45-2092 | N426JK | N173DS | | |
| 45-2093 | N5016Z | D-CAHB | | |
| 45-2094 | N40079 | CS-TFO | | |
| 45-2095 | N622FX | | | |
| 45-2096 | N40083 | OY-RED | | |
| 45-2097 | N40078 | (D-CVJT) | OE-GVX | |
| 45-2098 | N40043 | N346CN | N346CM | |
| 45-2099 | N623FX | | | |
| 45-2100 | N959RP | | | |
| 45-2101 | N152UT | VT-VSA | | |
| 45-2102 | N4003K | G-HPPY | | |
| 45-2103 | N140HM | | | |
| 45-2104 | N624FX | | | |
| 45-2105 | N40085 | N295SG | N296SG | |
| 45-2106 | N700MB | | | |
| 45-2107 | N50145 | D-CGGC | | |
| 45-2108 | N5009T | (G-RMPI) | N718EJ | N945EJ |
| 45-2109 | N625FX | N77NR | | |
| 45-2110 | N50157 | N556HD | | |
| 45-2111 | N40PD | | | |
| 45-2112 | N40050 | OE-GXX | | |
| 45-2113 | N40075 | N477XR | | |
| 45-2114 | N40083 | N663LB | | |
| 45-2115 | N5012Z | | | |
| 45-2116 | N625FX | | | |
| 45-2117 | N4004Q | (XA-LOA^) | | |
| 45-2118 | N4008G | N289JP | | |
| 45-2119 | N40082 | N119NJ | | |
| 45-2120 | (D-COIN) | N626FX | | |
| 45-2121 | N40081 | D-COIN* | | |
| 45-2122 | N40162 | N990WA | | |
| 45-2123 | N4003W | | | |
| 45-2124 | N50126 | (N627FX) | N403LS | |
| 45-2125 | N5016Z | N44LG | | |
| 45-2126 | N5017J | N46MW | | |
| 45-2127 | N5016V | | | |
| 45-2128 | | | | |
| 45-2129 | | | | |
| 45-2130 | | | | |
| 45-2131 | | | | |
| 45-2132 | | | | |
| 45-2133 | | | | |
| 45-2134 | | | | |
| 45-2135 | | | | |
| 45-2136 | | | | |
| 45-2137 | | | | |
| 45-2138 | | | | |
| 45-2139 | | | | |
| 45-2140 | | | | |
| 45-2141 | | | | |
| 45-2142 | | | | |
| 45-2143 | | | | |
| 45-2144 | | | | |
| 45-2145 | | | | |
| 45-2146 | | | | |
| 45-2147 | | | | |
| 45-2148 | | | | |
| 45-2149 | | | | |

# LEARJET MODEL 45

| C/n | Series | Identities | | | | | | | |
|---|---|---|---|---|---|---|---|---|---|
| 001 | | N45XL | [ff 07Oct95] | | N40LX | [converted to Model 40 circa 2002 qv] | | | |
| 002 | | N45LJ | N452LJ | | | | | | |
| 003 | | N453LJ | (N789H) | [to ground instruction airframe, Pima Community College, Tucson, AZ] | | | | | |
| 004 | | N454LJ | [w/o 27Oct98 Wallops Island, VA] | | | | | | |
| 005 | | N455LJ | G-ZXZX | | | | | | |
| 006 | | N456LJ | ZS-OIZ | N456LM | N721CP | YV351T | | | |
| 007 | | N457LJ | (ZS-JBR) | (ZS-BAR) | ZS-OPD | VH-EJK | (ZS-ITT) | TC-CMB | |
| 008 | | N745E | N80RP | | | | | | |
| 009 | | N984GC | N459LJ | N500CG | | | | | |
| 010 | | (D-CWER) | N41DP | N903HC | N311BP | N811BP | | | |
| 011 | | N741E | N741F | N89RP | | | | | |
| 012 | | N5009V | N412LJ | (OE-...) | D-COMM | D-CMLP | N450TJ | | |
| 013 | | N5010U | N413LJ | D-CEWR | D-CFWR | N45LR | | | |
| 014 | | N708SP | | | | | | | |
| 015 | | N31V | | | | | | | |
| 016 | | N743E | N743F | N74SG | | | | | |
| 017 | | (D-CWER) | N417LJ | D-CESH | D-CSMS | | | | |
| 018 | | N418LJ | OO-LFS | | | | | | |
| 019 | | N56WD | N45LJ | C-GCMP | (N.....) | C-GLRJ | N442LF | VT-CRA | |
| 020 | | N5000E | HB-VMA | N45NP | C-GVVZ | | | | |
| 021 | | N5009T | HB-VMB | CS-TFI | | | | | |
| 022 | | N5012G | PT-TJB | N453BL | N345RL | N845RL | C-GSWQ | | |
| 023 | | N740E | (N740SG) | | | | | | |
| 024 | | N145ST | C-FBCL | C-FVSL | D-CNMB | | | | |
| 025 | | N742E | N742F | | | | | | |
| 026 | | N405FX | N405BX | XC-HIE | | | | | |
| 027 | | N156PH | N156PB | N445SB | N838TH | | | | |
| 028 | | N5014E | HB-VMC | XC-VMC | [w/o 04Nov08 Mexico City, Mexico] | | | | |
| 029 | | N5013Y | 9V-ATG | N290LJ | N170LS | | | | |
| 030 | | N5012H | N157PH | N157PB | | | | | |
| 031 | | N5016V | 9V-ATH | N310LJ | | | | | |
| 032 | | N4FE | | | | | | | |
| 033 | | N50162 | 9V-ATI | VH-SQD | | | | | |
| 034 | | N45FE | N454LP | XA-VYC | | | | | |
| 035 | | N5013U | 9V-ATJ | VH-SQM | | | | | |
| 036 | | N345WB | I-FORU | | | | | | |
| 037 | | N50145 | OE-GDI | G-CPRI | | | | | |
| 038 | | N454AS | (N454RR) | N14FE | N14BX | XA-RIU | | | |
| 039 | | N456AS | N15FE | | | | | | |
| 040 | | (N145MC) | N68PC | N68PQ | N501CG | | | | |
| 041 | | N541LJ | C-GPDQ | | | | | | |
| 042 | | N10R | | | | | | | |
| 043 | | D-CRAN | N45VB | | | | | | |
| 044 | | D-CLUB | N888CX | | | | | | |
| 045 | | N4545 | | | | | | | |
| 046 | | ZS-PTL | ZS-OLJ | ZS-BAR | ZS-OXB | N136MA | N336UB | XB-RMT | XA-RMT |
| 047 | | N158PH | N158PD | N206CK | [2000th Learjet built] | | | | |
| 048 | | PT-XLR | | | | | | | |
| 049 | | N711R | | | | | | | |
| 050 | | N16PC | N16PQ | LV-BOU | | | | | |
| 051 | | N145KC | N927SK | | | | | | |
| 052 | | N5011L | ZS-DCT | N745SA | | | | | |
| 053 | | N685RC | N3211Q | N1904S | | | | | |
| 054 | | N345MA | | | | | | | |
| 055 | | N63MJ | N45LR | G-JRJR | G-OLDF | G-GOMO | | | |
| 056 | | N196PH | | | | | | | |
| 057 | | N75TE | N83TN | N83TZ | XA-SUK | | | | |
| 058 | | N50111 | RP-C1944 | N660HC | N237DM | N55DG | | | |
| 059 | | N50153 | VP-CVL | N590JC | ZS-PNP | | | | |
| 060 | | N1MG | N459LC | | | | | | |
| 061 | | N111KK | | | | | | | |
| 062 | | N512RB | N543CM | | | | | | |
| 063 | | N10J | N10JY | | | | | | |
| 064 | | N800MA | N800UA | EC-ILK | | | | | |
| 065 | | N100KK | | | | | | | |
| 066 | | N94CK | D2-FFX | | | | | | |
| 067 | | N5087B | XA-LRX | XA-QUE | | | | | |
| 068 | | I-ERJD | | | | | | | |
| 069 | | N50157 | SU-MSG | D2-EBN | | | | | |
| 070 | | N50163 | LX-IMS | N450JC | | | | | |
| 071 | | N145K | N145KL | N989PA | | | | | |
| 072 | | N5016Z | I-ERJC | N720CC | | | | | |
| 073 | | N65U | N66SG | | | | | | |
| 074 | | N815A | N740TF | | | | | | |
| 075 | | N450BC | | | | | | | |

## LEARJET 45

| C/n | Series | Identities | | | | |
|---|---|---|---|---|---|---|
| 076 | | N245K | N2451Y | N988PA | | |
| 077 | | N5018G | PT-XVA | N770DS | XA-AIM | |
| 078 | | N5016Z | N116AS | | | |
| 079 | | N5FE | | | | |
| 080 | | N42HP | N45UJ | N451DJ | (N451DZ) | N45EJ |
| 081 | | N76TE | N145GM | N30TL | | |
| 082 | | N40082 | N1HP | | | |
| 083 | | N5013Y | OY-LJG | ZS-TJS | | |
| 084 | | N5009V | HB-VML | OE-GVM | HB-VML | |
| 085 | | N454CG | C-FPBX | | | |
| 086 | | N4001G | N386K | C-GMRO | | |
| 087 | | N645HJ | N64HH | | | |
| 088 | | N454MK | C-FMGL | C-FLLH | | |
| 089 | | N406FX | N406BX | XA-EFM | | |
| 090 | | N407FX | N452CJ | | | |
| 091 | | N408FX | (N408BX) | N451WM | | |
| 092 | | N5016V | ZS-LOW | (ZS-PPR) | ZS-PDG | 3B-... |
| 093 | | N5014F | N450TR | (PT-XLF) | I-ERJC | [w/o 01Jun03 Milan-Linate, Italy] |
| 094 | | N300JE | N800WC | | | |
| 095 | | N409FX | N409F | N786CC | | |
| 096 | | N5009T | C-GDMI | N450JG | | |
| 097 | | N5017J | D-CMSC | | | |
| 098 | | N6FE | | | | |
| 099 | | (N545RS) | N7FE | | | |
| 100 | | N50145 | N45LJ | RP-C1958 | N345BH | |
| 101 | | N410FX | N410BX | N22AX | | |
| 102 | | N411FX | N411BX | N810YS | XA-EEA | |
| 103 | | N412FX | (N412F) | N720MC | | |
| 104 | | N40012 | OH-IPJ | N450BK | 3D-BIS | |
| 105 | | N105LJ | N397AT | | | |
| 106 | | N145XL | | | | |
| 107 | | N145CG | (N145CM) | N762EL | | |
| 108 | | N50154 | N313BW | N313BH | | |
| 109 | | N60PC | N451CF | N945HC | | |
| 110 | | N4002P | N222MW | | | |
| 111 | | N414FX | N414BX | XA-BFX | | |
| 112 | | N415FX | CN-TJB | | | |
| 113 | | N416FX | N124BP | | | |
| 114 | | N417FX | N318SA | | | |
| 115 | | N90UG | (N405MW) | N45MW | | |
| 116 | | N50111 | OY-LJJ | A6-MED | OY-LJJ | |
| 117 | | N40081 | ZS-DCA | | | |
| 118 | | N50163 | N5XP | N75XP | | |
| 119 | | N5016V | N316SR | N1RB | | |
| 120 | | N418FX | N418FA | N45TU | | |
| 121 | | N316SR | (N666BG) | N45HF | | |
| 122 | | N945FD | | | | |
| 123 | | N454LC | N484LC | N21AX | N750CR | |
| 124 | | N4003Q | G-OLDL | N124AV | G-JANV | |
| 125 | | N419FX | N145MW | N145MN | | |
| 126 | | N420FX | C-FXHN | | | |
| 127 | | N421FX | N421FY | XA-ALF | | |
| 128 | | N10NL | | | | |
| 129 | | N4003W | N9CH | N455DG | | |
| 130 | | N583FH | N4001G | (ZS-OSP) | N418MN | |
| 131 | | N444MW | | | | |
| 132 | | N132LJ | N889CA | | | |
| 133 | | N645KM | N183CM | | | |
| 134 | | N4004Q | N423FX | N423FA | | |
| 135 | | N4004Y | N422FX | N423DC | XA-UJR | |
| 136 | | N45BA | (N136LJ) | N583PS | N883BS | N654AT |
| 137 | | N45AJ | N800AB | | | |
| 138 | | N5018G | G-OLDJ | N138AX | G-SOVB | |
| 139 | | N45VL | XA-UAG | | | |
| 140 | | N40050 | XA-AED | N345SV | | |
| 141 | | N142HC | N142HQ | N858MK | | |
| 142 | | N145SB | (N450DS) | | | |
| 143 | | N4005Q | N145GS | N334AF | | |
| 144 | | N5011L | D-CEMM | CS-TLW | | |
| 145 | | N50145 | N421FX | N942FK | | |
| 146 | | N424FX | N460DC | | | |
| 147 | | N425FX | N425LW | | | |
| 148 | | N40075 | N8084R | D-CDEN | OE-GAR | |
| 149 | | N451CL | N451GL | N904HD | | |
| 150 | | N245KC | N348K | | | |
| 151 | | N345K | N345FM | | | |

# LEARJET 45

| C/n | Series | Identities | | | | | |
|---|---|---|---|---|---|---|---|
| 152 | | N3013Q | N5014E | VH-CXJ | | | |
| 153 | | N30137 | C-GCMP | | | | |
| 154 | | N3008P | N886CA | N918EG | | | |
| 155 | | N145MC | N882CA | | | | |
| 156 | | N3017F | G-OLDC | N156AV | C-FLRJ | | |
| 157 | | N545RA | N341K | | | | |
| 158 | | N3019T | LX-DSL | I-DFSL | | | |
| 159 | | N5001J | N828CA | | | | |
| 160 | | N455PM | N455DE | N863CA | | | |
| 161 | | N3000S | G-OLDR | N161AV | G-SOVC | SE-RKY | |
| 162 | | N426FX | N426LW | | | | |
| 163 | | N427FX | N427BX | 5N-BGR | C-FZAU | | |
| 164 | | N428FX | | | | | |
| 165 | | N429FX | | | | | |
| 166 | | N430FX | | | | | |
| 167 | | N5012V | G-GMAA | | | | |
| 168 | | N50088 | VH-PFS | | | | |
| 169 | | N5013D | N77HN | N332K | | | |
| 170 | | N5013E | (XA-SKY) | N50154 | N45UP | N45VS | |
| 171 | | N171DP | N342K | | | | |
| 172 | | N70PC | | | | | |
| 173 | | N900P | N906P | | | | |
| 174 | | N45HC | | | | | |
| 175 | | N328RR | N30SF | N41TF | | | |
| 176 | | N5016S | N45TK | N176TK | XA-IKE | | |
| 177 | | N431FX | | | | | |
| 178 | | N50207 | XA-JMF | | | | |
| 179 | | N5023U | N863CA | N541AL | N45MR | N179MR | |
| 180 | | N880LJ | N345RL | | | | |
| 181 | | N5024E | ZS-PTL | (ZS-FUL) | ZS-AJN* | | |
| 182 | | N50248 | N345AW | | | | |
| 183 | | N5025K | N511WP | C-GHMP | | | |
| 184 | | N45VP | N866CA | | | | |
| 185 | | N273LP | | | | | |
| 186 | | N158EC | | | | | |
| 187 | | N5030J | N146XL | | | | |
| 188 | | N5018G | N21BD | XA-UJZ | | | |
| 189 | | N5030N | N800MA | D-CSUL | | | |
| 190 | | N41PC | N41PQ | | | | |
| 191 | | N158EC | N191LJ | | | | |
| 192 | | N433FX | | | | | |
| 193 | | N434FX | N865CA | | | | |
| 194 | | N5040W | ZS-YES | ZS-ULT | | | |
| 195 | | N5040Y | VH-SQR | | | | |
| 196 | | N50353 | N473LP | N531AC | | | |
| 197 | | N432FX | | | | | |
| 198 | | N5048K | N45UG | | | | |
| 199 | | N545EC | N1925P | | | | |
| 200 | | N451ST | | | | | |
| 201 | | N473LP | N452ST | | | | |
| 202 | | N5048Q | N445N | | | | |
| 203 | | N145AR | | | | | |
| 204 | | N5010U | N204MK | VH-ZZH | N45NP | | |
| 205 | | N5011L | N5052K | N88AF | | | |
| 206 | | N45UG | N5042A | N45AX | N445AX | N445RM | |
| 207 | | N5000E | VH-SQV | | | | |
| 208 | | N5009V | N5050G | N715CG | | | |
| 209 | | N435FX | (N435FA) | N300JC | N209KM | XA-CFX | |
| 210 | | N5009V | N866RA | N29RE | N29ZE | XA-ALA | |
| 211 | | N50145 | N50490 | N300AA | N300AQ | (N299BB) | |
| 212 | | N50111 | N434FX | | | | |
| 213 | | N50126 | D-CEWR | G-MUTD | G-RWGW | | |
| 214 | | N214LF | N29SM | N555CK | | | |
| 215 | | N5018G | N822CA | N352K | | | |
| 216 | | N5016V | C-GHCY | N359K | | | |
| 217 | | N5016Z | N1RL | N400 | N401Q | N217MJ | N977AR* |
| 218 | | N50163 | N310ZM | N451JC | ZS-OPY | | |
| 219 | | N4003K | ZS-BAR | ZS-OPR | | | |
| 220 | | N40077 | N825CA | | | | |
| 221 | | N823CA | | | | | |
| 222 | | N673LP | N673LB | N826CA | | | |
| 223 | | N40081 | (D-CTAN) | C-FNRG | C-GPKS | | |
| 224 | | N822CA | N822GA | N77702 | C-GQPM | | |
| 225 | | N436FX | N518GS | N558GS | N90GS | | |
| 226 | | N40085 | I-ERJE | | | | |
| 227 | | N437FX | N721BS | N821BS | N903RL | N70AE | |

# LEARJET 45

| C/n | Series | Identities | | | | |
|---|---|---|---|---|---|---|
| 228 | | N5012Z | ZS-LOW | | | |
| 229 | | N40079 | N159EC | | | |
| 230 | | N4008G | N451N | | | |
| 231 | | N40073 | N30PC | N30PF | N145HC | |
| 232 | | N40076 | N45XR | LV-ARD | | |
| 233 | | N5000E | N45KX | | | |
| 234 | | N5009T | Ireland 258 | | | |
| 235 | | N50145 | N30PC | | | |
| 236 | | N5018G | N125GW | N66DN | G-LLOD | XA-SAA |
| 237 | | N5017J | N45QG | N44QG | N43QG | PP-HSI |
| 238 | | N570AM | N577CC* | | | |
| 239 | | N45LJ | C-GJCY | | | |
| 240 | | N5016Z | (D-CTAN) | N50579 | N9FE | |
| 241 | | N241LJ | | | | |
| 242 | | N4003W | N45SY | PR-OTA | | |
| 243 | | N4004Q | G-IOOX | OE-GFF | | |
| 244 | | N5009V | N545K | | | |
| 245 | | N5010U | N745K | | | |
| 246 | | N5012G | XA-HFM | N1019K | XA-SAP | |
| 247 | | N50154 | N3AS | | | |
| 248 | | N4004Y | N48TF | (N83TR) | N48TE | LV-CAR |
| 249 | | N40075 | C-GLRS | M-GLRS | | |
| 250 | | N40050 | OO-LFN | | | |
| 251 | | N40073 | N145XR | XA-MVG | N45VG | |
| 252 | | N40076 | N272BC | N876BC | | |
| 253 | | N4008G | N45NM | | | |
| 254 | | N729SB | N728SB | LV-BXD | | |
| 255 | | N40081 | C-FSDL | | | |
| 256 | | N5011L | B-3988 | N97XR | XA-GTP | |
| 257 | | N5012H | N555VR | | | |
| 258 | | N5015U | N45LJ | N395BC | | |
| 259 | | N40PC | | | | |
| 260 | | N745TC | | | | |
| 261 | | N5010U | N451BW | | | |
| 262 | | N50126 | VH-VVI | N45AU | VH-VVI | |
| 263 | | N50157 | N263RA | N263MR | | |
| 264 | | N5016V | N910BD | N916BD | | |
| 265 | | N5017J | G-OLDT | | | |
| 266 | | N40012 | "LX-IMS" | [wrongly painted at completion centre] LX-IMZ (D-CLHM) D-CHLM | | |
| 267 | | N4002P | N451HC | | | |
| 268 | | N5009V | N145K | | | |
| 269 | | N4003W | N245K | | | |
| 270 | | N4004Q | (ZS-FUL) | C-FBLJ | C-FXYN | |
| 271 | | N4004Y | N45XR | N435FX | | |
| 272 | | N40043 | N288CB | | | |
| 273 | | N4005Q | N183TS | | | |
| 274 | | N40075 | N274CZ | | | |
| 275 | | N40082 | C-FRYS | | | |
| 276 | | N40084 | N88WV | | | |
| 277 | | N40086 | N912BD | N918BD | | |
| 278 | | N63WR | | | | |
| 279 | | N4008G | N45LJ | N279AJ | [w/o 03Jan09 Telluride, CO; parted out by Alliance Air Parts Oklahoma City, OK] | |
| 280 | | N40079 | G-CDNK | | | |
| 281 | | N5012H | N617BD | N917BD | | |
| 282 | | N456Q | | | | |
| 283 | | N4DA | | | | |
| 284 | | N40078 | XA-ARB | | | |
| 285 | | N5012Z | N300AA | | | |
| 286 | | N50126 | G-CDSR | | | |
| 287 | | N5013Y | CS-TLT | F-HACP | | |
| 288 | | N5014F | C-FBCL | | | |
| 289 | | N5013U | N68PC | | | |
| 290 | | N45BZ | | | | |
| 291 | | N4002P | OO-EPU | | | |
| 292 | | N4003W | JA01GW | N98XR | | |
| 293 | | N45XR | (N694SC) | TG-ABY | | |
| 294 | | N5014E | G-OLDW | | | |
| 295 | | N4004Y | XA-UFB | | | |
| 296 | | N4003K | N454LC | | | |
| 297 | | N50154 | (N145CG) | N145CM | | |
| 298 | | N5000E | N191TD | | | |
| 299 | | N453ST | | | | |
| 300 | | N145AP | | | | |
| 301 | | N45KJ | N996BP | | | |
| 302 | | N4008G | JA02GW | N99XR | CS-TFQ | |

## LEARJET 45

| C/n | Series | Identities | | | | |
|---|---|---|---|---|---|---|
| 303 | | N40043 | C-FANS | | | |
| 304 | | N40086 | N400 | N4009 | | |
| 305 | | N40073 | N45XR | N808KS | ZS-KAA | |
| 306 | | N5009T | OY-OCV | M-EOCV | N306AV | |
| 307 | | N425G | | | | |
| 308 | | N436FX | N415CL | ZS-OPM | | |
| 309 | | N436FX | | | | |
| 310 | | N5014F | N345K | | | |
| 311 | | N40078 | G-OLDK | | | |
| 312 | | N575AG | | | | |
| 313 | | N45KH | | | | |
| 314 | | N74PT | | | | |
| 315 | | N437FX | | | | |
| 316 | | N50145 | AP-BHY | | | |
| 317 | | N438FX | N605SE | | | |
| 318 | | N45LJ | (N45XR) | N196CT | | |
| 319 | | N16PC | | | | |
| 320 | | N452A | PR-CAO | | | |
| 321 | | N4002P | ZS-OPN | | | |
| 322 | | N5011L | N313BW | | | |
| 323 | | N50157 | N125BW | | | |
| 324 | | N50126 | N12VU | | | |
| 325 | | N40085 | N390GG | | | |
| 326 | | N50126 | N507FG | | | |
| 327 | | N50153 | N726EL | N816LP | N526EL | |
| 328 | | N40081 | F-HCGD | G-HCGD | | |
| 329 | | N5012K | N454JF | PR-CSM | | |
| 330 | | N5009V | N45XT | N2HP | | |
| 331 | | N40084 | N583PS | | | |
| 332 | | N45XR | N445TG | | | |
| 333 | | N438FX | | | | |
| 334 | | N4003Q | N445SE | | | |
| 335 | | N435HH | | | | |
| 336 | | N40073 | N45YH | 4X-CYH | M-EANS | N55EP |
| 337 | | N10J | | | | |
| 338 | | N45TK | | | | |
| 339 | | N454N | | | | |
| 340 | | N5014F | N300JQ | N300JC | | |
| 341 | | N439FX | | | | |
| 342 | | N5011L | ZS-OPO | | | |
| 343 | | N45HG | | | | |
| 344 | | N607FG | | | | |
| 345 | | N5017J | N45MR | | | |
| 346 | | N440FX | | | | |
| 347 | | N40050 | D-CINS | | | |
| 348 | | N4005Q | N744E | | | |
| 349 | | N45HK | | | | |
| 350 | | N50153 | 5N-BLW | | | |
| 351 | | N60PC | | | | |
| 352 | | N988MC | | | | |
| 353 | | N903BT | | | | |
| 354 | | N40077 | N135CG | | | |
| 355 | | N4008G | N45XP | | | |
| 356 | | N745E | | | | |
| 357 | | N441FX | | | | |
| 358 | | N40081 | 5N-DAL | | | |
| 359 | | N710R | | | | |
| 360 | | N5012H | C-FMGL | | | |
| 361 | | N45LJ | N44QG | | | |
| 362 | | N40075 | C-GLYS | | | |
| 363 | | N453A | | | | |
| 364 | | N442FX | | | | |
| 365 | | N5XP^ | | | | |
| 366 | | N20FE | | | | |
| 367 | | N741E | | | | |
| 368 | | N4003W | EI-WFO | | | |
| 369 | | N40082 | ZS-AJD | | | |
| 370 | | N4005Q | N743E | | | |
| 371 | | N443FX | N21AX | | | |
| 372 | | N5009V | 40-BBB | | | |
| 373 | | N5013U | N984XR | | | |
| 374 | | N5014F | VP-BSF | | | |
| 375 | | N4003L | G-SNZY | | | |
| 376 | | N4002P | N145GR | N145GM | | |
| 377 | | N50163 | N54AX | N45AX | | |
| 378 | | N444FX | | | | |

# LEARJET 45

| C/n | Series | Identities | | | | |
|---|---|---|---|---|---|---|
| 379 | | N50154 | N379LJ | | | |
| 380 | | N45XR | N774CC | N729JM | | |
| 381 | | N5010U | N45XR | RP-C8338* | | |
| 382 | | N40073 | CS-TFR | | | |
| 383 | | N5016V | N176MG | | | |
| 384 | | N5012H | N694LP | N745KD | | |
| 385 | | N5015U | XA-HUR | | | |
| 386 | | N545CG | | | | |
| 387 | | N41PC | | | | |
| 388 | | N40078 | LV-BTO | | | |
| 389 | | N389CG | YV2565 | | | |
| 390 | | N390CG | YV2567 | | | |
| 391 | | N40086 | G-OSRL | | | |
| 392 | | N40144 | N45LJ | | | |
| 393 | | N40146 | N93XR | | | |
| 394 | | N40043 | (N45LJ) | N818CH | | |
| 395 | | N40149 | D-CLMS | | | |
| 396 | | N396GC | YV1118 | | | |
| 397 | | N40079 | (N445FX) | N458A | | |
| 398 | | N398CG | N818CH | N694SH | N5014E | LX-JAG |
| 399 | | N50145 | (N545K) | N545KS | N32AA | |
| 400 | | N40085 | N145MW | | | |
| 401 | | N50111 | N848CA | | | |
| 402 | | N10873 | (N745K) | N26QT | | |
| 403 | | N40012 | N245CM | | | |
| 404 | | N4001G | OO-KJD | | | |
| 405 | | N5015U | (N451K) | N474TC | | |
| 406 | | N40149 | (N452K) | | | |
| 407 | | N5011L | | | | |
| 408 | | N4005Q | C-FVSL^ | | | |
| 409 | | N40077 | (N453K) | | | |
| 410 | | | | | | |
| 411 | | | | | | |
| 412 | | | | | | |
| 413 | | | | | | |
| 414 | | | | | | |
| 415 | | | | | | |
| 416 | | | | | | |
| 417 | | | | | | |
| 418 | | | | | | |
| 419 | | | | | | |
| 420 | | | | | | |
| 421 | | | | | | |
| 422 | | | | | | |
| 423 | | | | | | |
| 424 | | | | | | |
| 425 | | | | | | |
| 426 | | | | | | |
| 427 | | | | | | |
| 428 | | | | | | |
| 429 | | | | | | |
| 430 | | | | | | |

# LEARJET MODEL 55

| C/n | Series | Identities |
|---|---|---|
| 001 | 60 | N551GL [model 55 prototype converted to 55C prototype] N551DF [converted to Model 60 prototype] N60XL [cx Sep96; wfu] |
| 002 | | N552GL [given new c/n 55-139A on conversion to 55C standards (qv); cx Apr91] |
| 003 | | N553GP N162GA N553DJ (N553GJ) N612EQ |
| 004 | | N90E N50L N24JK N24CK D-CLIP (N500FA) N155DD N155PJ N728MG |
| 005 | | N40ES N128VM N550CS (N94TJ) N440DM |
| 006 | | N113EL N212JP N126EL N355DB N228PK N427TL N655TR |
| 007 | | N41ES I-KILO [w/o 04Apr94 San Pablo Airport, Seville, Spain; remains to Atlanta Air Salvage, Griffin, GA] |
| 008 | | N551SC N322GC |
| 009 | | N42ES N55SJ HB-VIB N955FD N955MD N955LS N559BC N800LJ |
| 010 | | N57TA [w/o 13Nov81 Waterkloof AFB, S Africa] |
| 011 | | N37951 (N57TA) N411GL N574W D-CREW N200BA ES-PVV LY-LRJ SE-RCK D-CMAX |
| 012 | | N55GH N23G N104BS N48HC N85XL N666TV |
| 013 | | N10872 (D-CCHS) OE-GNK N3238K PT-LEL N82679 (N519AC) (N155AJ) (D-CEWR) D-CUTE N82679 D-CUTE N155SB |
| 014 | | N40144 N90BS N55KC XA-PIL N550RH N155MP (N554EM) N455EM N551CG N1CG N441CG N303PM |
| 015 | | (YV-41CP) N39413 HB-VGV N515DJ N550LJ D-CION N27DD N551MF |
| 016 | | N646G N717EP N717EB (N116GL) |
| 017 | | N760AC N760AQ D-CCGN |
| 018 | | N39E N599EC N797CS N822MC |
| 019 | | YV-41CP N141SM C-GSWP |
| 020 | | N720M N20DL N57B N8GT N123LC N35PF N55NY |
| 021 | | N3794B N700TG EI-BSA I-LOOK N619MJ (N721GS) |
| 022 | | N64WM VR-BOL VP-BOL N155GM |
| 023 | | N3796B N7784 N110ET (N236PJ) |
| 024 | | HB-VGZ N224DJ HB-VGZ N900FA (N54NW) N824CC |
| 025 | | N236R N57PM N57FM N92MG |
| 026 | | N8565H N55HD N21VB D-CILY (N96AF) N421QL (N321GL) N318JH N1324B N285DH |
| 027 | | N3796X OE-GKN N3796X N123LC B-3980 N227A B-3980 N59HJ |
| 028 | | N3794C PT-LDR N3794C PT-LOF N7244W (N53HJ) N556GA N556HJ |
| 029 | | N4CP D-CLIP N29DJ N10CP PT-OHU N10CP N82JA N100VA N29NW (N55PJ) |
| 030 | | N986WC N959WC N117WC N55LJ (N155CD) N122LX |
| 031 | | YV-12CP YV1794 |
| 032 | | N75TP (N72TP) N71TP N81CH N11TS N83SD N183SD N255UJ N125LR |
| 033 | | N96CE N960E N917S N414RF N155CS (VR-CJA) VR-CML PT-OOW N38JA (N377JW) (N77JW) N971EC N398AC N355UJ N355RM |
| 034 | | N3795Y D-CARX N84DJ D-CLUB N77JW N37JA (N234LC) (N334JW) N123LC N550TC |
| 035 | | N115EL (N100GU) N1968A N127EL D-CVIP N97AF C-GPCS VP-CUC N816MC |
| 036 | | N3803G N555GL N81CH N76AW N81CH N236JW N155HM N723CC |
| 037 | | N41CP N86AJ PT-OBR N53HJ |
| 038 | | N551HB N50AF N666TK |
| 039 | | N39418 N770JM N97J VR-BQF N339BC N539JM |
| 040 | | N3802G HZ-AM11 HZ-AM2 N426EM N55HK N554CL |
| 041 | | N401JE N155PJ N41EA N550RH (HP-....) HK-4016X N141FM |
| 042 | | N1462B N3796U N160TL D-CMTM N575GH |
| 043 | | N5543G N785B (N500JC) N500JW N30AF N430HM (N455EC) N83WM |
| 044 | | N3797C PT-LHR |
| 045 | | N1451B HB-VHK EC-DSI VR-BHV EC-DSI (N90583) N49PE (N49PD) I-AGER N550AK (N123LC) |
| 046 | | N23HB (N13HB) N3HB N55HL N855PT |
| 047 | | N600C |
| 048 | | (N734) N3796Z VH-LGH N73TP N67RW PT-OBS N558AC N558HJ N831JP |
| 049 | | N6317V N3796C D-CCHS N150MS |
| 050 | | N4289X D-CARP (HB-...) (N122JD) OY-FLK N220JC (N552BA) (N55UJ) [w/o 23Jun00 Boca Raton, FL] |
| 051 | | N734 N22G N22GH N55KS N55KD D-CATL [United Nations code UN-453] |
| 052 | | N4289Z YV-292CP N55GF N551DB D-COOL |
| 053 | | N4290Z N85653 YV-374CP (N1450B) N500RP N501RP N205EL (N205EF) N253S N531K |
| 054 | | N42905 N54GL HB-VHL N54NW (N54LZ) (N54JZ) |
| 055 | | (N155JC) N155LP N970H N970F N825MG N852PA N1JG |
| 056 | | N8563E (N854GA) N946FP N59GS N272TB N270AS OH-IPP N156JC N607BF |
| 057 | | N4290Y N10CR N733EY N733E |
| 058 | | (N55BE) N500BE N200PC N129SP N58SR |
| 059 | | (N211BY) D-CAEP N50AF N59LJ OE-GRR |
| 060 | | N6331V N60MJ N53JL N86AJ N8YY N60LT PT-OUG N6364U N255TS N996CR |
| 061 | | N117EL N222MC N132EL D-CFUX ES-PVT D-CFAI |
| 062 | | N62GL N24G N316 N292RC N855DB (N107MC) N69VH |

# LEARJET 55

| C/n | Series | Identities | | | | | | | | |
|---|---|---|---|---|---|---|---|---|---|---|
| 063 | | N40146 | N8563P | N1744P | N74RY | N63AX | | | | |
| 064 | | N255ST | N121LT | N900PJ | N912MM | | | | | |
| 065 | | N1088C | N8565K | N555GL | N1125M | (N565B) | N75LJ | | | |
| 066 | | N237R | (N550DD) | N50DD | N717HB | | | | | |
| 067 | | N39412 | N120EL | N127GT | N505EH | | | | | |
| 068 | | N1088A | N38D | N135LR | | | | | | |
| 069 | | N551UT | N102ST | N817AM | | | | | | |
| 070 | | N1471B | F-GDHR | [w/o 05Feb87 over Cameroons nr Nigerian border] | | | | | | |
| 071 | | N3807G | (N155UT) | N155JC | N113YS | | | | | |
| 072 | | N58AS | N55AS | N55AQ | PT-MSM | N72ET | SX-BNS | N5572 | | |
| 073 | | N1087Z | HB-VHN | I-VIKY | D-CARE | N355DH | N73WE | N357PR | N857PR | N155V |
| | | N667MB | | | | | | | | |
| 074 | | N5574 | N74GL | N151PJ | N701DB | N155LR | N905RL | | | |
| 075 | | N39415 | N8563Z | N675M | N55GM | N55GH | N90NE | N117LR | | |
| 076 | | N155JC | N2855 | N30GL | C-GKTM | | | | | |
| 077 | | N3812G | N8563M | N58M | N85NC | N245MS | (N99YB) | | | |
| 078 | | N39391 | (N55GJ) | N55GV | N56TG | (N120GR) | I-ALPR | N55VK | N345RJ | |
| 079 | | N39404 | (N2855) | N1983Y | N700SR | | | | | |
| 080 | | N1465B | N85632 | PT-LET | | | | | | |
| 081 | | N1468B | N85631 | N777MC | N777MQ | N903JC | N61SJ | | | |
| 082 | | N39394 | N1075X | N33GL | N68LP | N817AM | N139SK | | | |
| 083 | | N40149 | N55GZ | N6789 | (N6780) | N551AS | (N500HG) | N550HG | (N550CK) | |
| 084 | | N39413 | N85643 | N740AC | I-FLYJ | D-CWDL | | | | |
| 085 | | N238R | N58PM | N58FM | N55NM | (N551MD) | (N146PA) | N225MD | | |
| 086 | | N40162 | D-CACP | N8227P | PT-LUK | | | | | |
| 087 | ER | N1451B | N8564Z | N103C | N520SC | N520SQ | N554PF | N902RL | SE-RGU | N1852 |
| 088 | | N1461B | N55GJ | N155GS | N900JB | N901JC | N522WK | N60ND | | |
| 089 | | N4289U | N8564X | N170VE | N555CJ | N789PF | N628PT | N312AL | C-GLRJ | C-GCIL |
| 090 | | N40146 | N723H | D-CGIN | N181EF | N55UJ | | | | |
| 091 | | N3810G | N8566F | N91CH | N991CH | N91PR | (N69B) | N700JE | (N567SC) | N591SC |
| | | N30TK | N911FC | N429FC | | | | | | |
| 092 | | N1462B | N724J | N400JT | D-CLUB | N500FA | N40DK | | | |
| 093 | | N725K | N32KJ | | | | | | | |
| 094 | | N1088C | N235HR | (N236HR) | | | | | | |
| 095 | | N39398 | N8565Z | N55RT | D-CAAE | | | | | |
| 096 | | N1087T | N1045X | N8010X | N126KD | N126KL | | | | |
| 097 | | N4290C | N8566Q | N40CR | N20CR | | | | | |
| 098 | ER | N726L | D-CCON | N550SC | (N455UJ) | N1324P | (N132TP) | N155ER | | |
| 099 | | (N5599) | N2992 | N17GL | N95WK | | | | | |
| 100 | | N3807G | N552UT | N552SQ | N500NH | (N500NB) | N717AM | | | |
| 101 | ER | N39415 | N101HK | N101PK | N101HK | N211EF | N501TW | N251VG | (C-FNRG) | N251NG |
| | | C-FNRG | N1129M | N112WQ | | | | | | |
| 102 | ER | N1087Y | N55DG | I-OSUA | N44GA | PT-WSS | N112FK | N604FK | N155TS | |
| 103 | ER | N10870 | N921FP | [w/o 06Aug86 Rutland, VT] | | | | | | |
| 104 | | N39404 | N18CG | N18CQ | (N95TJ) | N277AL | | | | |
| 105 | | N39391 | N55GK | N22G | N274 | C-GQBR | N55AR | | | |
| 106 | | N3812G | N60E | N90AM | N318JH | N824MG | (N850PA) | | | |
| 107 | ER | N1466B | N760G | N155JT | N304AT | D-CWAY | PH-ABU | | | |
| 108 | | (N888FK) | N77FK | N78FK | N222MC | N220VE | (N551AM) | N517AM | (D-CMAX) | D-CUNO |
| 109 | | N348HM | D-CVIP | | | | | | | |
| 110 | | N39412 | N55GY | (N24RH) | N455RH | | | | | |
| 111 | | N1461B | N7260G | PT-LIG | [w/o 09Nov94 Guanabara Bay, Rio de Janeiro, Brazil - remains to | | | | | |
| | | Dodson Avn, Ottawa, KS] | | | | | | | | |
| 112 | | N3802G | (YV-325CP) | N325CP | LN-VIP | N7AU | EC-HAI | N55LF | [w/o 19Jul04 Fort | |
| | | Lauderdale Executive, FL; canx 17Mar05] | | | | | | | | |
| 113 | | N1450B | N7262M | N713M | N236HR | N57MH | N57MV | | | |
| 114 | | N39398 | N72608 | N34GB | N355UA | | | | | |
| 115 | | N1476B | N6666R | N6666K | N633AC | N155BC | | | | |
| 116 | | N1087Y | N85GL | N116DA | N51V | N51VL | | | | |
| 117 | | N3807G | N8567X | N255MB | N155RB | N385RC | | | | |
| 118 | | N39416 | C-FCLJ | N257SJ | | | | | | |
| 119 | | N3816G | N72613 | N273MC | N273MG | | | | | |
| 120 | | N39418 | N72629 | N55LK | (N486) | N1127M | N120LJ | N777YC | N329TJ | |
| 121 | | N3811G | N8568J | N65Y | N155SC | N747AN | | | | |
| 122 | | N10870 | N8568P | N18ZD | N99KW | N99KV | C-FHJB | OE-GRO | D-CGBR | |
| 123 | | N6331V | N44EL | N121US | N150NE | N417AM | N420BG | | | |
| 124 | | N39391 | N58CG | N58CQ | SX-BTV | D-CONU | | | | |
| 125 | ER | N6307H | N610JR | | | | | | | |
| 126 | | N4291G | N7260J | YV-125CP | N7260J | N16LJ | | | | |
| 127 | B | N6340T | HZ-AM2 | N73GP | | | | | | |
| 128 | B | N1087T | N255BL | N7US | N7UA | N10BF | N717JB | N8MF | N655GP | N787GT |
| 129 | B | N4290Y | N75GP | N655AL | N60WA | | | | | |
| 130 | B | N4291N | N55VC | | | | | | | |
| 131 | B | N1088A | N7260K | N52CT | | | | | | |
| 132 | B | N4291K | N67WM | N133WB | (N333GJ) | (N133SU) | N122SU | N242RB | N795HA | |
| 133 | B | N155PL | N155LJ | N55LF | N700R | N810V | EC-INS | | | |

# LEARJET 55

| C/n | Series | Identities | | | | | | | | |
|---|---|---|---|---|---|---|---|---|---|---|
| 134 | B | N39399 | N7261D | PT-LDR | | | | | | |
| 135 | C | N1055C | PT-LXO | | | | | | | |
| 136 | C | N3811G | N767AZ | N767NY | N155PS | OE-GCF | PH-MED | OE-GCF | D-CFAZ | |
| 137 | C | N39413 | N95SC | N155SP | PR-ERR | | | | | |
| 138 | C | N4291G | TC-MEK | TC-FBS | VR-CDK | N9LR | N338FP | N270WS | | |
| 139 | C | N39391 | N1039L | PT-LZS | PT-GMN | N139ST | N552TL | | | |
| 139A | C | [converted from 55-002 (qv)] | | | N4289X | N994JD | N984JD | N55GM | (N55ZT) | N518SA |
| | | N518SB | | | | | | | | |
| 140 | C | N72616 | PT-OCA | Brazil FAB6100 | | | | | | |
| 141 | C | N155DB | | | | | | | | |
| 142 | C | N555MX | N755VT | | | | | | | |
| 143 | C | N10871 | D-CMAD | ES-PVD | | | | | | |
| 144 | C | N144LT | PT-OJH | N40CR | N178AM | | | | | |
| 145 | C | N66WM | N10CR | N211BC | | | | | | |
| 146 | C | N9125M | PT-ORA | | | | | | | |
| 147 | C | N55UK | N499SC | N111US | N160NE | N177AM | | | | |

Production complete

# LEARJET MODEL 60

| C/n | Identities | | | | | | | | |
|---|---|---|---|---|---|---|---|---|---|
| 55-001 | N551GL | N551DF | N60XL | [prototype Model 55 converted to Model 60 standards] | | | | | |
| 001 | N601LJ | [rolled out 05May92; ff 15Jun92] | | | | | | | |
| 002 | N602LJ | C-GLRS | C-GLRL | N602LJ | N190AS | N1940 | (N602DM) | N170MK | |
| 003 | N60LJ | N961MR | N808ML | N60FE | N48KZ^ | | | | |
| 004 | N60UK | N194AL | N600PJ | N863PA | | | | | |
| 005 | N5011L | N610TM | N869JS | N205FX | OY-LJD | N104SD | N60KJ | VP-BGB | N60KJ |
| 006 | N60VE | N60VL | N606TS | N606BR | N8783 | | | | |
| 007 | N448HM | (N212FX) | N219FX | N204FX | (N204BX) | N60UJ | N760CF | N733SW | |
| 008 | N608LJ | PT-OVI | N608LJ | N222FX | N222HV | N260UJ | (N359RM) | N808SK | |
| 009 | N26029 | N54 | | | | | | | |
| 010 | N5012H | N477DM | N477BM | HB-VLU | N525CF | N928CD | N928GD | C-FBDR | N610TS |
| | N561TC | N610TS | N692PC | | | | | | |
| 011 | N5013U | N60T | OY-LJE | N61YC | N611TS | N843CP | | | |
| 012 | N5014H | N123CC | N147CC | N626KM | N80DX | | | | |
| 013 | (N960H) | N26011 | N55 | | | | | | |
| 014 | N7US | N862PA | | | | | | | |
| 015 | N960H | (N960HL) | N826SS | N861PA | N711SE | | | | |
| 016 | N50153 | TC-MEK | N788MM | UR-CHH | | | | | |
| 017 | N50157 | N9173R | N760AC | N660AH | (N860AH) | N60GG | N864PA | N498SW | N500SW |
| 018 | N5009T | N4016G | N24G | | | | | | |
| 019 | N50153 | N40366 | HB-VKI | D-CRAN | | | | | |
| 020 | N600L | N606L | | | | | | | |
| 021 | N600LC | N600LG | N600GA | N732LH | | | | | |
| 022 | N2602Z | N22G | | | | | | | |
| 023 | N40323 | N60SB | N60SR | | | | | | |
| 024 | N2601V | LV-PGX | LV-WFM | N415NP | | | | | |
| 025 | N9155Z | N299SC | N299SG | N919RS | | | | | |
| 026 | N4026Z | N60LJ | N700GS | N60LJ | N347GS | N14T | N14TU | | |
| 027 | N4027S | XA-ICA | N4230S | N12FU | N69LJ | | | | |
| 028 | N50298 | N870JS | N206FX | N206HY | | | | | |
| 029 | N4029P | N55KS | C-FBLU | C-GFAX | N296TS | N64SL | | | |
| 030 | N4030W | N164PA | TC-ELL | YR-RPB | 9H-AFJ | | | | |
| 031 | N4031L | N228N | N841TT | | | | | | |
| 032 | N5013D | OE-GNL | D-CPMU | D-CIFA* | | | | | |
| 033 | N4031A | N56 | | | | | | | |
| 034 | N5034Z | 9M-CAL | | | | | | | |
| 035 | N50353 | VR-BST | N116AS | N1DC | [w/o 14Jan01 Troy, AL] | | | N1498G | |
| 036 | N5014E | N60LR | N44EL | | | | | | |
| 037 | N5017J | N4037A | N637LJ | N101HW | | | | | |
| 038 | N4007J | N638LJ | C-FJGG | | | | | | |
| 039 | N50154 | N5003X | N57 | N8071J | N57 | | | | |
| 040 | N399SC | N899SC | N660AS | N600AS | N600CN | | | | |
| 041 | N5004Y | N699SC | N166HL | | | | | | |
| 042 | N4010K | N90AG | N90AQ | N60MG | | | | | |
| 043 | N5043D | C-GHKY | N43NR | | | | | | |
| 044 | N5044N | N618R | (N618P) | (N1618R) | N613R | N668RC | | | |
| 045 | N5045S | N60WM | N711VT | N711VJ | N903AG | N454AN | | | |
| 046 | N50157 | N5006G | (PT-WGB) | N214FX | N214BX | N239RC | N710TP | (N710TF) | |
| 047 | N5007P | N418R | N50DS | N850DS | N647TS | N647EF | | | |
| 048 | N5008Z | N648LJ | N730M | N551ST | | | | | |
| 049 | N50298 | N227N | N247N | N126CX | N459SF | | | | |
| 050 | N50450 | N207FX | N207BX | N923SK | | | | | |
| 051 | N5051X | N63BL | OY-LJH | D-CHER | ES-PVC | | | | |
| 052 | N5022C | ZS-NTV | (N42AJ) | N120HV | N247CP | N900KK | N769DS | | |
| 053 | N5012Z | N5053Y | B-3981 | N91772 | N360UJ | N744DB | | | |
| 054 | N65BL | VP-BMM | N301RJ | | | | | | |
| 055 | N5014E | N5055F | N1CA | (N143CA) | N660CB | N574DA | | | |
| 056 | N5013Y | N60LR | N117RJ | N700CH | (N556SA) | N92FG | | | |
| 057 | (N5010U) | N50050 | N58 | | | | | | |
| 058 | N5016V | N92BL | XA-BRE | | | | | | |
| 059 | N5059J | N208FX | N208BX | N60KF | N159SC | LV-BFR | | | |
| 060 | N50602 | N209FX | OY-LJM | N209FX | OY-LJM | N175BA | N909SK | | |
| 061 | N50162 | N98BL | N219DC | C-FRGY | | | | | |
| 062 | N5012H | N5006T | (N510SG) | N707SG | N707SQ | C-GLRS | N62BX | N551BD | |
| 063 | N5015U | N5003U | N8270 | N660BC | N496WH | | | | |
| 064 | N210FX | N210HV | N529KF | | | | | | |
| 065 | N5006V | N30W | N718AN | N654AN | | | | | |
| 066 | N5006K | N8271 | N176KS | | | | | | |
| 067 | N799SC | N118HC | N60HM | | | | | | |
| 068 | (N96ZC) | N95ZC | N823TR | N64LE | N160JD | | | | |
| 069 | N50324 | N60CE | D-CITA | | | | | | |
| 070 | N5035R | N21AC | | | | | | | |
| 071 | N60LJ | N940P | N658KS | | | | | | |
| 072 | N5072L | 9M-FCL | | | | | | | |

# LEARJET 60

| C/n | Identities | | | | | |
|---|---|---|---|---|---|---|
| 073 | N50761 | N256M | N860PD | | | |
| 074 | N8074W | N620JF | N674BP | N600PH | | |
| 075 | N675LJ | N9CU | | | | |
| 076 | N211FX | N211BX | N494PA | LV-CCO | | |
| 077 | N212FX | N677LJ | C-GLRS | N227FX | N227BX | N60GF |
| 078 | N5068F | N188TC | N188TG | | | |
| 079 | N319LJ | N95AG | | | | |
| 080 | N8080W | N59 | | | | |
| 081 | N681LJ | N60LJ | N180CP | | | |
| 082 | N682LJ | N600LN | | | | |
| 083 | N683LJ | N383MB | N255RK | N725SC* | | |
| 084 | N684LJ | N59FD | N100R | N306R | N8JR | |
| 085 | N685LJ | N99KW | N89KW | N814GF | | |
| 086 | (N213FX) | N686LJ | (N777CB) | N797CB | N797CP | N607SB |
| 087 | N687LJ | N411ST | N410ST | N787LP | N601CN | |
| 088 | N688LJ | XA-TZF | XA-TZI | | | |
| 089 | N8089Y | XA-MDM | | | | |
| 090 | N8090P | PT-WMO | N460BG | N85NC | | |
| 091 | N8071L | N896R | N91LE | N156DH | | |
| 092 | N5092R | C-FBLJ | C-FBLO | N907SK | N226SF | N92NS |
| 093 | N80683 | RP-C648 | N109JE | N109JR | N129JR | N717JB | N160EE |
| 094 | N60LR | A6-SMS | (N511CL) | N93BA | TC-ARC | |
| 095 | N5005X | N602SC | N82KK | (N82KD) | | |
| 096 | N8086L | N603SC | | | | |
| 097 | N8067Y | N897R | N60TX | N688DB | | |
| 098 | N50758 | N218FX | N218BX | N797PA | N16CS | |
| 099 | N212FX | N212BX | N60AN | N173KR | | |
| 100 | N6100 | N60MN | | | | |
| 101 | N215FX | N215BX | N179LF | | | |
| 102 | N8082B | LV-WXN | N102LJ | | | |
| 103 | N216FX | N216BX | N298EF | | | |
| 104 | N104LJ | N83WM | N903AM | N614TS | N160BL | |
| 105 | N217FX | N217BX | N60BC | | | |
| 106 | N106LJ | N140JC | | | | |
| 107 | N107LJ | D-CFFB | | | | |
| 108 | N220FX | (N220PX) | N60RY | N38CP | | |
| 109 | N109LJ | N707SG | N747SG | N177KS | N215KM | |
| 110 | N60LJ | N928CD | N600CL | | | |
| 111 | N221FX | N898PA | | | | |
| 112 | N299SC | N808WG | | | | |
| 113 | N599SC | N60LH | N700R | N702R | N160GG | |
| 114 | N3014R | N199SC | N114PJ | N154AK | | |
| 115 | N3015F | N500 | N500ZH | N600GG | | |
| 116 | N116LJ | XA-VIG | | | | |
| 117 | N889DW | | | | | |
| 118 | N3018C | N11AM | | | | |
| 119 | N119LJ | N626LJ | N8811A | | | |
| 120 | N120LJ | D-CSIX | (N141MB) | | | |
| 121 | N621LJ | PT-XFS | | | | |
| 122 | N622LJ | N61DP | A6-IAS | | | |
| 123 | N356WA | | | | | |
| 124 | N223FX | (N223BX) | N260AN | XA-IBC | | |
| 125 | N60LR | VP-CRB | | | | |
| 126 | N224FX | N160AN | N660CJ* | | | |
| 127 | N225FX | (N225BX) | N460AN | | | |
| 128 | N226FX | (N660AN) | N61ZZ | N8888 | N8889 | |
| 129 | N629LJ | D-CBAD | N45US | N160GH | | |
| 130 | N630LJ | N90MC | N384JW | | | |
| 131 | N631LJ | XA-JJS | XB-JCG | | | |
| 132 | N228FX | N9200M | | | | |
| 133 | N133LJ | C-FIDO | C-FBCD | C-FCMG | | |
| 134 | N134LJ | XA-ZTA | | | | |
| 135 | N135LJ | N98JV | | | | |
| 136 | N136LJ | N60RL | N60RU | | | |
| 137 | N229FX | N360AN | | | | |
| 138 | N230FX | (N230BX) | N560AN | N160BP | | |
| 139 | N233FX | N139XX | EI-IAT | N370AT | N7734T | (N77511) |
| 140 | N98JV | N140LJ | Argentina T-10 | | | |
| 141 | N234FX | N141LJ | OY-JKH | N163BA | N655TH | N888KL |
| 142 | (N642LJ) | N426JN | (N940RL) | N116LM | | |
| 143 | N235FX | N6666R | N6666A | N393TA | N143FA | N143AA |
| 144 | N60144 | D-CKKK | N94BA | N929SR | | |
| 145 | N145LJ | LX-PRA | I-PRAD | | | |
| 146 | N50776 | N261PC | N800R | N809R | N790SU | |
| 147 | N138SP | N133SR | N160RM | (N158JP) | N420JP | (N42JP) | N727SJ |
| 148 | N80701 | D-CETV | N648TS | HB-VOZ | | |

# LEARJET 60

| C/n | Identities | | | | | | | |
|---|---|---|---|---|---|---|---|---|
| 149 | N149LJ | (ZS-JRM) | SU-BNL | SU-EZI | VP-BEZ | N260CA | EI-REX | |
| 150 | N80667 | A6-SMS | N150BX | N200MT | | | | |
| 151 | N234FX | N9ZM | N11TS | | | | | |
| 152 | N50126 | Mexico MTX-01 | | Mexico AMT-200 | | | | |
| 153 | N235FX | (N235BX) | N424KW | | | | | |
| 154 | N233FX | N969JD | | | | | | |
| 155 | N88V | | | | | | | |
| 156 | N76SF | N76QF | N605SB | | | | | |
| 157 | N236FX | N114LJ | | | | | | |
| 158 | N237FX | N50EL | N460JD | HB-VWN | | | | |
| 159 | N43SF | N43QF | N721MJ | PP-WIN | | | | |
| 160 | D-CDNY | D-CGEO | | | | | | |
| 161 | D-CDNZ | EC-JVM | | | | | | |
| 162 | N99ZC | | | | | | | |
| 163 | N238FX | N238BX | N326HG | | | | | |
| 164 | N60LJ | PT-XGS | | | | | | |
| 165 | N929GW | | | | | | | |
| 166 | N239FX | N60ZD | N114BD | | | | | |
| 167 | N240FX | N240BX | OE-GVB | N167XX | LZ-AXA | | | |
| 168 | N706CJ | N706CR | | | | | | |
| 169 | N5014F | OE-GII | | | | | | |
| 170 | N50154 | D-COWS | 9H-AEE | F-HAVB | D-CNUE | | | |
| 171 | N422CP | N422CR | N424MW | N422CR | N424MW | | | |
| 172 | N241FX | N241BX | XA-DGO | | | | | |
| 173 | OY-LJF | D-CEJA | ZS-TEJ | | | | | |
| 174 | N242FX | N242ZX | XA-COI | | | | | |
| 175 | N243FX | N243F | XB-KYZ | XB-LBO | XB-LEJ | XB-LLT | N175PC | XA- |
| 176 | N176MB | N10MB | | | | | | |
| 177 | N60LR | N991DB | | | | | | |
| 178 | N244FX | N178MM | | | | | | |
| 179 | N9012H | C-FCNR | HB-VNV | | | | | |
| 180 | N777MC | | | | | | | |
| 181 | N273MC | | | | | | | |
| 182 | N245FX | N600NM | N600EF | | | | | |
| 183 | N246FX | N810Y | | | | | | |
| 184 | TC-DHF | N184LJ | N752BP | N606SB | | | | |
| 185 | N464TF | | | | | | | |
| 186 | N186ST | N58ST | | | | | | |
| 187 | N247FX | N27ZH | | | | | | |
| 188 | N248FX | N255SL | | | | | | |
| 189 | N189LJ | PR-XJS | | | | | | |
| 190 | N5012K | N190LJ | EI-IAU | ES-PVS | | | | |
| 191 | N40073 | N30154 | N660AS | N710SG* | | | | |
| 192 | N601GG | | | | | | | |
| 193 | N249FX | N627AF | | | | | | |
| 194 | N250FX | N250SG | N96FF^ | | | | | |
| 195 | N251FX | N251SD | | | | | | |
| 196 | N252FX | (N252RD) | | | | | | |
| 197 | N5010U | N23PZ | P4-AVM | OE-GYG | | | | |
| 198 | N198HB | | | | | | | |
| 199 | N253FX | N502RP | N502RB | N600AJ | | | | |
| 200 | N254FX | N254FY | (OY-TCG) | (OY-LJK) | A6-EJA | D-CSLT | | |
| 201 | N411ST | N411SK | N614JH | N269JH | | | | |
| 202 | N1RB | N202LJ | XA-TSA | N202LJ | | | | |
| 203 | N770BC | N770BG | LZ-BVV | | | | | |
| 204 | N4008G | I-NATZ | N30GJ | | | | | |
| 205 | N40043 | N205ST | N12ST | N64HA | (N64HX) | N358P | | |
| 206 | N40076 | (N254FX) | N500RP | N916BG | N909JS | N448GL* | | |
| 207 | N777VC | (N207VC) | N777VQ | N706CJ | | | | |
| 208 | N40084 | (N235HR) | N821CC | (N112MT) | N208BH | | | |
| 209 | N40085 | N1221J | | | | | | |
| 210 | N40086 | ZS-NVP+ | [+marks worn for at least 16 months at the Tucson, AZ, completion centre but ntu] | N700JE | C-FGJC | C-FCTK | | |
| 211 | N5012Z | D-CHLE | | | | | | |
| 212 | N5012H | LX-RPL | I-RPLY | | | | | |
| 213 | N40079 | N65T | N14T | N717FF | | | | |
| 214 | N5016Z | D-CIMM | OE-GFA | | | | | |
| 215 | N40083 | N44SF | N44QF | VP-BCY | | | | |
| 216 | N131TR | | | | | | | |
| 217 | N5012G | N60LJ | N600ML | XA-VLA | | | | |
| 218 | N50157 | N8084J | EI-IAW | C-GRBZ | | | | |
| 219 | N660KS | N552SK | | | | | | |
| 220 | N80857 | N254FX | N254FZ | N255FX | N447FA* | | | |
| 221 | N255BD | XA-JWM | | | | | | |
| 222 | N8088U | N60VE | N1128M | | | | | |
| 223 | N3006J | N109JR | N109JZ | N309MG | | | | |

# LEARJET 60/60XR

| C/n | Identities |
|---|---|
| 224 | N61VE N64MG |
| 225 | N30170 N22SF N22QF N60HS N60TG (N770JB) N312AL |
| 226 | N3011F N128V |
| 227 | N253FX N503RP N503RE |
| 228 | N255FX N10ST N65HA N65HU |
| 229 | N23SR N38SV* |
| 230 | N50031 N826SR N235CG N356CG N600LG |
| 231 | N3015M N40012 D-CDNX SX-BNR |
| 232 | N5004J LV-ZYF N232LJ N95BD |
| 233 | N5008F N33DC N520SC N520S* |
| 234 | N5013J N24SR LV-CAY |
| 235 | N5013N N252RP |
| 236 | N5015T I-IINL OE-GNI N716BG N916BG |
| 237 | N699DA PR-WBW |
| 238 | N5018U N753BP (N140CT) |
| 239 | N5019R (ZS-SCT) N503BC |
| 240 | N5019V N29LJ |
| 241 | N5026Q N253FX |
| 242 | N5027Q PR-LDF N5027Q [w/o 07Oct02 Santa Cruz do Sul, Brazil] |
| 243 | N50287 OY-LGI EC-JVB |
| 244 | N5031R N884TW N335AF N835AF N160MG |
| 245 | N50330 XA-ORA |
| 246 | N5035F D-CWHS N64JP |
| 247 | N254FX |
| 248 | N5038N OE-GMR N248L N787LP |
| 249 | N50422 N4004Q D-CLUB EC-JYQ |
| 250 | N50433 XA-FLY N50433 XA-FLY |
| 251 | N50458 N747DP |
| 252 | N5012H N5051X N749SS |
| 253 | N5012K C-GIIT C-FBLU N1127M |
| 254 | N5015U RP-C6003 N773SW |
| 255 | N5013U OO-TME ER-LGB |
| 256 | N5013Y OY-LJK D-CCGG |
| 257 | N50157 N256FX |
| 258 | N202N |
| 259 | N40075 N600L |
| 260 | N40050 N257FX N973HR |
| 261 | N4003Q D-CROB |
| 262 | N4003W N5051A N126KD |
| 263 | N258FX N876CS |
| 264 | N40084 N214RW N214PW N811RA |
| 265 | N40086 N600LC |
| 266 | N259FX N266LJ N156BF |
| 267 | N5009V N50558 N60YC N60SN PP-LRR |
| 268 | N5011L N268WS |
| 269 | N5012H N100NR N903AM |
| 270 | N5012K VH-MZL LV-BDX N247SC A6-MAJ OE-GMA |
| 271 | N271L N954WS |
| 272 | N50157 N60KH P4-BAZ N272DJ LV-CBI |
| 273 | N4002P VH-OCV RP-C2956 VH-EXJ |
| 274 | N4003K D-CSIM |
| 275 | N101UD ES-PVI |
| 276 | N5000E N838RC OE-GDF D-CDSM M-AIRS |
| 277 | N40079 LX-LOU |
| 278 | N5012K N60RL |
| 279 | N50145 Z3-MKD |
| 280 | "N50127"+ [+marks as reported but not a recognized Learjet test reg'n] OE-GKP G-SXTY |
| 281 | N5013U "OE-GTS"+ [+marks painted in error at Wichita, KS in Feb05] OE-GTF D-CGTF OH-GVE |
| 282 | N5013Y TC-RKS |
| 283 | N5009T N60LJ PR-GCL |
| 284 | N5000E EC-JIE N284L N461MC |
| 285 | N5009T N72CE |
| 286 | N4003K (D-CSIS) N262DB G-LGAR |
| 287 | N4003L OE-GGL |
| 288 | N40077 N103LS |
| 289 | N40083 N785DR VP-BGS |
| 290 | N5012K N260DB D-CFLG |
| 291 | N4003Q XA-KCM |
| 292 | N5011L N380BA |
| 293 | N60SE N772PP |
| 294 | N50163 [first LJ60XR, ff 3.4.06] N60XR N160BG D2-EPC |
| 295 | N259FX |
| 296 | N5016Z EC-JPV N296L |
| 297 | N5012G XA-KLZ |
| 298 | N40012 N729LJ |

# LEARJET 60/60XR

| C/n | Identities | | | | |
|---|---|---|---|---|---|
| 299 | N50153 | N75CT | | | |
| 300 | N40081 | OH-AEM | G-CJMC | EI-DXW | YL-ABA |
| 301 | N50157 | ZS-GSG | | | |
| 302 | N5012H | (OE-GJA) | ES-PVP | | |
| 303 | N40075 | (OE-GJA) | (OH-GVI) | OE-GTO | OH-III |
| 304 | N40076 | (D-CGNF) | OE-GNF | | |
| 305 | N40050 | OH-VIV | EI-VIV | | |
| 306 | N80177 | N500 | N5009 | N869AV | |
| 307 | N260FX | | | | |
| 308 | N115AN | | | | |
| 309 | N460MC | | | | |
| 310 | N222BR | | | | |
| 311 | N710SG | N202SJ | VP-BLC | | |
| 312 | N5013U | OH-VMF | VP-CCD | | |
| 313 | N4003L | N613H | G-HOIL | M-HOIL | |
| 314 | N999LJ | [w/o 19Sep08 Columbia Metropolitan, SC] | | | |
| 315 | N604KT | | | | |
| 316 | N5017J | N50LK | | | |
| 317 | N5012Z | (OH-GVI) | OE-GSU | | |
| 318 | N777VC | N770PC | | | |
| 319 | N261FX | | | | |
| 320 | N60LJ | N229BP | N229RP | | |
| 321 | N5010U | N675BP | | | |
| 322 | N710SG | N724CJ | N5014F | OY-MIR | |
| 323 | N50157 | N262FX | | | |
| 324 | N50126 | N707CS | N797CS | | |
| 325 | N5013Y | P4-SSV | M-SSSV | | |
| 326 | N5018G | N80172 | OD-MHA | M-APWC | |
| 327 | N5016Z | 9H-AFB | | | |
| 328 | N5000E | VP-BBZ | G-XXZZ | | |
| 329 | N50111 | LZ-BVE | | | |
| 330 | N5102G | OK-JDM | | | |
| 331 | N4001G | (D-CDEF) | N331PL | HK-4565 | |
| 332 | N5013U | OE-GLX | | | |
| 333 | N4003L | OE-GLY | | | |
| 334 | N263FX | | | | |
| 335 | N5014E | TC-MEN | | | |
| 336 | N4004Y | A6-NGN | | | |
| 337 | N60LJ | N337BG | | | |
| 338 | N5016V | N338PR | A6-SBF | | |
| 339 | N5010U | N160TG | | | |
| 340 | N264FX | | | | |
| 341 | N5012K | A6-CYS | | | |
| 342 | N40073 | SP-CEZ | | | |
| 343 | N5015U | C-FEDG | | | |
| 344 | N40076 | OO-ADH | LV-BZJ | | |
| 345 | N265FX | | | | |
| 346 | N724EH | | | | |
| 347 | N5012Z | P4-EXG | UP-LJ001 | | |
| 348 | N266FX | | | | |
| 349 | N40012 | C-GJLN | | | |
| 350 | N5011L | D-COMO | | | |
| 351 | N5013Y | D-CJAF | | | |
| 352 | N4003Q | (G-DOKK) | VH-THG | | |
| 353 | N5017J | N999YC | LV-BTA | | |
| 354 | N5000E | (PP-ONE) | N60LE | PP-ONE | |
| 355 | N40077 | OH-IVS | | | |
| 356 | N267FX | | | | |
| 357 | N50111 | PR-MLR | | | |
| 358 | N60XR | N358JA* | | | |
| 359 | N5018G | OE-GVJ | | | |
| 360 | N5012G | OE-GVT | | | |
| 361 | N5014E | N361TS | N487LP | | |
| 362 | N10870 | N62XR | CS-DTH | | |
| 363 | N1JB | | | | |
| 364 | N40076 | OE-GVV | | | |
| 365 | N4004Y | N65LR | C-.... | | |
| 366 | (N268FX) | N988P | N900P | | |
| 367 | N5012K | "N60XR"+ | [+fake marks worn in NBAA static display, Orlando Executive, FL, Oct09] | | |
| | N5012K | | | | |
| 368 | N10872 | (N420JP) | N42JP | | |
| 369 | N10873 | OY-KYS | | | |
| 370 | N326SM | HZ-MS1A | | | |
| 371 | N4003K | HZ-MS1B | | | |
| 372 | N50153 | (N269FX) | ES-LVA | | |
| 373 | N5018L | OE-GVD | | | |

# LEARJET 60/60XR

| C/n | Identities | | | | |
|---|---|---|---|---|---|
| 374 | N5000E | N60LJ | N83TR | | |
| 375 | N3099 | N106FF | | | |
| 376 | N50157 | (OK-YXY) | N76XR | | |
| 377 | N4002P | C-FLTB | | | |
| 378 | N50163 | (D-CBOB) | N984BD | | |
| 379 | N50154 | (CS-DJA) | N79XR | N51054 | I-SDAG |
| 380 | N4003L | | | | |
| 381 | N4003Q | B-3926 | | | |
| 382 | N5013U | M-IGHT | | | |
| 383 | N5009V | N383LJ | | | |
| 384 | | | | | |
| 385 | | | | | |
| 386 | N40076 | | | | |
| 387 | | | | | |
| 388 | | | | | |
| 389 | | | | | |
| 390 | | | | | |
| 391 | | | | | |
| 392 | N90CE* | | | | |
| 393 | | | | | |
| 394 | | | | | |
| 395 | | | | | |
| 396 | | | | | |
| 397 | | | | | |
| 398 | | | | | |
| 399 | | | | | |
| 400 | | | | | |
| 401 | | | | | |
| 402 | | | | | |
| 403 | | | | | |
| 404 | | | | | |
| 405 | | | | | |
| 406 | | | | | |
| 407 | | | | | |
| 408 | | | | | |
| 409 | | | | | |
| 410 | | | | | |

# LOCKHEED JETSTAR

Aircraft which were converted to -731s by Garrett AiResearch were given a sequential conversion number by that company; these numbers appear alongside the c/n in the production list.

| C/n | Series | Identities |
|---|---|---|
| 1001 | | N329J [ff 04Sep57; last flight 16Aug82; donated to Pacific Vocational Inst, Vancouver, Canada; circa Aug04 to Seattle Museum of Flight, WA] |
| 1002 | | N329K N711Z [displayed Andrews AFB,CA in USAF colours, code 89001] |
| 5001/53 | 731 | N9201R [ff 21Oct60] N1 N21 N1 N11 N7145V [wfu; to Pratt Community College, KS; to White Ind's, Bates City, MO, for spares 1998] |
| 5002 | 6 | N9202R EP-VRP N106GM N69TP N81JJ N148PE [b/u for spares Mar85 Minneapolis/St Paul, MN. Fuselage still in nearby scrapyard Feb07] |
| 5003 | 6 | N9203R NASA14 N814NA [cx Dec89; for disp Plant 42 Heritage Airpark, Palmdale, CA] |
| 5004 | 6 | N9204R N13304 N524AC N777EP N69HM N777EP [displayed Graceland Estate, Memphis, TN] |
| 5005 | 6 | N161LM N176LG N12121 N716RD N712RD N70TP XA-SIN XB-DLV (N22265) [wfu as XB-DLV Van Nuys, CA and scrapped] |
| 5006/40 | 731 | N9280R N12R N227K N731JS N222Y N6NE (VR-CCC) [wfu Southampton, UK, after landing accident; was on fire dump; remains to Florida] |
| 5007/45 | 731 | N9205R N110G N72CT N971AS [impounded 1992 Atlanta-Peachtree, GA; b/u for spares 1993] |
| 5008 | 6 | N500Z N400M [w/o 27Dec72 Saranac Lake, NY] |
| 5009 | 6 | N9206R N540G N767Z N717X N717 (HB-VET) N717JM [cx Sep84; b/u for spares] |
| 5010 | 6/C140A | 59-5958 [displayed Travis AFB Museum, CA in camouflage c/s] |
| 5011/1 | 731 | N9282R Indonesia T17845 PK-PJS 9V-BEE PK-PJH N731A C-GKRS N10461 N159B N88JM [b/u for spares late 1985; fuselage at Lincoln, NE 1988] |
| 5012 | 6 | N9283R D-BABE N10123 N1012B N500SJ N501AL [wfu Opa-Locka, FL; cx Jan94; derelict Mar94] |
| 5013 | 8 | N9284R N322K N523AC N11JC HZ-MAC N11JC N8AD N158DP (N5AX) [b/u for spares Mar88 by White Inds, Bates City, MO] |
| 5014 | 6 | N58CG N158CG N9MD N54BW N95GS [b/u for spares 1989 Miami, FL; cx 17Mar03] |
| 5015 | 6 | NASA4 N172L N103KC N505T N9046F N66MP [wfu at South Seattle Community College, WA; cx Oct00] |
| 5016 | 6 | N9210R N2222R (N222R) N20TF HZ-AFS HZ-SH2 N4258P N712GW N440RM [open storage Roswell, NM circa Oct97] |
| 5017 | 6/VC140B | N9286R 61-2488 [AMARC park code CL001] [preserved Warner-Robins AFB, GA] |
| 5018 | 6 | N9287R (CF-DTX) C-FDTX [preserved National Aviation Museum, Rockcliffe, Canada] |
| 5019 | 6 | N9288R N105GM N105GN (N70TP) N5UD N50UD [b/u 1986; fuselage at Fort Lauderdale Executive, FL; tail section at North Perry, FL 1989; fuselage converted into mobile home] |
| 5020 | 6 | N9207R N371H N300CR N308WC [cx Sep88; b/u for spares] |
| 5021 | 6 | CF-ETN C-FETN N564MG [b/u for spares Memphis, TN] |
| 5022 | 6/VC140B | 61-2489 [AMARC park code CL006] [preserved Pima County Museum, Tucson, AZ] |
| 5023 | 6 | N9221R I-SNAL N711Z N1107Z N767Z N979RA N879RA N723ST N20PY N2ES (N6ES) [b/u for spares Mar88 by White Inds, Bates City, MO] |
| 5024 | 6/VC140B | 61-2490 [stored AMARC Davis-Monthan AFB, AZ with park code CL004; to Western Air Parts] |
| 5025 | 6 | (62-12166) W Germany CA101 W Germany 1101 SU-DAF ST-JRM [not confirmed if marks have been taken up] |
| 5026 | 6/C140A | 59-5959 [noted preserved 29Sep92 Scott AFB] |
| 5027 | 6/VC140B | 61-2491 [displayed Rhein-Main AFB, Germany] |
| 5028 | 6/C140A | 59-5960 [wfu; open storage Greenville, TX] |
| 5029/38 | 731 | N3E N3EK N340 N39BL N1BL N166AC N112TJ (N25TX) (N1406) [to Aviation Warehouse, El Mirage, CA by Oct04] |
| 5030 | 6/C140A | 59-5961 [w/o 07Nov62 Warner-Robins AFB, GA] |
| 5031 | 6/VC140B | 61-2492 [preserved USAF Museum, Wright Patterson AFB, OH] |
| 5032 | 6/C140A | 59-5962 [at Edwards AFB, CA, for Museum] |
| 5033/56 | 731 | N1620 N16200 N33EA N100CC N100AC N200CC N200CG XB-FIS N25WA N50EC (N890MC) N500MA [cx Oct02 b/u; circa 2002; fuselage at Conroe, TX, in 2005 but removed by Feb08] |
| 5034 | 6/VC140B | 61-2493 [stored AMARC Davis-Monthan AFB, AZ with park code CL003; to Western Air Parts] |
| 5035 | 6 | (62-12167) W Germany CA102 [w/o 16Jan68 Bremen, W Germany; reported stored Bremen] |
| 5036/42 | 731 | N1622 N1622D N41TC N776JM N444JH N90KR N900CR [b/u circa 2001; cx Oct01] |
| 5037/24 | 731 | N9211R N2600 [damaged in pressurisation tests; rebuilt as c/n 5128, but still known as c/n 5037] N519L N3060 N60CN N60CH N11UF (N71UF) N90TC N10DR N6JL N552JH N770JR [cx Jun08, wfu Palm Beach International, FL] |
| 5038 | 6 | N9212R N341NS N341N N22CH N11UF N11UE (N44KF) [b/u; cx Dec92; remains to Aviation Warehouse film prop yard at El Mirage, CA] |
| 5039 | 6 | N600J N60QJ N81MR N86HM N200CK [cx Sep90; was stored Spirit of St Louis A/P, MO; presumed since scrapped] |
| 5040 | 6 | N505C N518L N7SZ N888RW [cx May88; spares May88; remains blown up Fort Lauderdale, FL for film] |
| 5041 | 6/C140B | 62-4197 [stored AMARC Davis-Monthan AFB, AZ with park code CL007; to Western Air Parts] |

## JETSTAR

| C/n | Series | Identities |
|---|---|---|
| 5042 | 6/C140B | 62-4198 [to Battle Damage Repair Unit, Mildenhall AFB, UK; b/u by 22Jan92 Mildenhall] |
| 5043 | 6/C140B | 62-4199 [stored AMARC Davis-Monthan AFB, AZ with park code CL002; to Western Air Parts] |
| 5044 | 6/C140B | 62-4200 [stored AMARC Davis-Monthan AFB, AZ with park code CL005; to Western Air Parts] |
| 5045 | 6/C140B | 62-4201 [stored AMARC Davis-Monthan AFB, AZ with park code CL008; preserved Hill AFB, UT] |
| 5046 | 6 | N9282R PK-IJS Indonesia T-9446 Indonesia A-9446 [wfu Jakarta-Halim AFB, Indonesia; later put on display at Garuda's training centre at Kushadasi, Indonesia] |
| 5047 | 6 | N9214R N409M N409MA N555PB [cx Oct90; scrapped] |
| 5048 | 6 | N9215R N40N N40NC N98KR N98MD N500WN N500WZ N428DA (N130LW) [to Marietta Aviation Museum, GA] |
| 5049 | 6 | N9216R N1230R N96B N96BB [wfu at South Seattle Community College, WA] |
| 5050/34 | 731 | N207L N208L N141TC HZ-THZ N434AN [b/u Apr94 by Atlanta Air Salvage, Griffin, GA] |
| 5051 | 6 | N9217R N400KC N44MF N31S N310AD N555BS N488JS N488GR [part of 'Disaster' attraction at Universal Studios, Orlando, FL, since Jan08] |
| 5052 | 6 | N9218R N300P N66CR CF-DTM C-FDTM N9739B [b/u for spares early 1989 Bi-States Park, St Louis, MO; cx Jun92] |
| 5053/2 | 731 | N9219R N12R N121CN N69CN N14WJ XA-POU XC-JCC XA-BCE XC-JCC [wfu Topeka/Forbes Field, KS by 2007] |
| 5054/59 | 731 | N9220R N7600J N7600 N20AP N354CA N721PA [parted out by White Inds, Bates City, MO] |
| 5055/21 | 731 | N9222R N296AR N303H N90ZP N85BP (N43JK) (N86BP) (N79MB) N304CK N707EZ N99FT [wfu at Chino, CA, circa Sep95; cx Mar96; parted out remains to scrapyard at Long Beach, CA] |
| 5056 | 6 | N9223R N105G N105GH N300AG HZ-FNA [b/u Spirit of St Louis A/P, MO] |
| 5057 | 6 | N1007 N90U N90ME [cx Mar87; b/u Memphis, TN during 1988] |
| 5058/4 | 731 | N100A N100AL N1500M N50AS N600TT (N600DT) N600TP N381AA N131EL N200DW XA-TTE XB-JIZ [wfu circa 2006 Toluca. Mexico] |
| 5059 | 6 | Indonesia T-1645 Indonesia A-1645 [preserved in museum Yogjakarta-Adisutjipto, Indonesia painted as A-9446] |
| 5060 | 6 | N9225R N31F N55NC [cx May88; b/u Jun88 Fort Lauderdale International, FL] |
| 5061/48 | 731 | N9226R N506T N506D N47BA N67GT N152GS N161GS N123GA (N888WW) N488MR N488EC N333EC N338EC [b/u Palm Beach Int'l, FL, 2006] |
| 5062/12 | 731 | N679RW N2200M RP-57 N111G VR-BHF EC-697 EC-FGX [reported parted out in US circa 2005] |
| 5063 | 6 | N9228R N420L N420A N420G N499PB XC-LIT |
| 5064/51 | 731 | N184GP N3QS N3QL [parted out Rantoul, KS circa early 2000] |
| 5065 | 6 | N9229R N1966G S9-NAD [wfu 1989; used as spares for c/n 5085] |
| 5066/46 | 731 | N9230R N228Y N7782 XA-HRM XA-JHR XA-SAE XA-MIK [reported w/o 16Nov95, no other details] |
| 5067 | 6 | N871D N711Z N207L (N267AD) N267L [w/o 29Mar81 Luton, UK] |
| 5068/27 | 731 | N9231R N96GS [w/o 06Jan90 Miami A/P, FL; used as spares; cx Jan91] |
| 5069/20 | 731 | N910M N918MM XA-PGO N197JS [reported for spares; cx Feb99] |
| 5070/52 | 731 | N992 N9921 C-GAZU N9921 N177NC N731AG N114CL N888CF N888WT N712TE N731WL [cx 26Jan05; parted out] |
| 5071 | 6 | (62-12845) W Germany CA103 1103 SU-DAH ST-PRE [wfu at Khartoum, Sudan] |
| 5072/23 | 731 | N9233R N500Z N74AG [b/u; cx Dec99] |
| 5073 | 6 | N7775 [fuselage used as interior mock-up by KC Avn, Dallas, TX] |
| 5074/22 | 731 | N9234R N67B N267P N267GF N168DB N777SG N171JL [parted out circa 2001; cx Oct01 fuselage at Spirit of St.Louis, MO] |
| 5075/19 | 731 | N397B N540G N2345M N1DB N500ES [b/u Rockford, IL, Apr06] |
| 5076/17 | 731 | N9235R N100C N3E N3EK N69ME N76HG [b/u Rockford, IL, May06] |
| 5077 | 6 | N9236R N1924V N1EM [w/o 25Mar76 Chicago, IL] |
| 5078/3 | 731 | N711Z N7105 N472SP N52TJ N916RC (N916RG) N515AJ N124RM [cx 19Apr04; b/u] |
| 5079/33 | 731 | N9238R XA-RGB XA-MAZ N58TS [parted out by Alliance Air Parts, Oklahoma City, OK] |
| 5080 | 6 | N914X N914P N77HW [wfu & scrapped - details not known] |
| 5081 | 8 | N200A N200AL N4SP N4SX [cx Sep87; b/u for spares during 1987] |
| 5082/36 | 731 | N320S N917J N82SR TC-OMR P4-CBJ 3C-QQU |
| 5083/49 | 731 | N208L N141LM N161LM N257H N257HA C-GAZU N27FW N817BD N198DL |
| 5084/8 | 731 | N9240R N83M N732M N910E N520S [w/o 11Feb81 Westchester, NY] |
| 5085 | 6 | N9241R N586 N5861 S9-NAE VR-CCY [to Abu Dhabi Higher College of Technology, marked as "HCT"] |
| 5086/44 | 731 | N9242R N27R N27RL N600J N60UJ HZ-FBT N711AG N27RC (N65JW) N313JS |
| 5087/55 | 731 | N9243R N41N N800J N31LJ N31WG N75MG N33SJ |
| 5088 | 6 | N9244R CF-DTF C-FDTF [cx late 1986; preserved in Atlantic Canada Aviation Museum, Halifax, Canada] |
| 5089 | 8 | N9245R N324K N120AR (N85DL) (XA-...) N120AR [used for spares Jan94 by TAESA Mexico City, Mexico] |
| 5090 | 8 | N9246R N106G N10MJ N55CJ N555SG [wfu 1989 Fort Lauderdale Executive, FL (cf c/n 5094)] |
| 5091 | 6 | N9247R N107G N107GH N118B N118BA [wfu; remains to White Inds, Bates City, MO; cx May93] |
| 5092/58 | 731 | N9248R N372H N901H N110AN N110DD VR-CSM VP-CSM |

# JETSTAR

| C/n | Series | Identities |
|---|---|---|
| 5093 | 6 | N9249R N711Z N5000C N5000B N76EB N22RB [cx Oct90; b/u for spares circa Sep90] |
| 5094 | 6 | N9250R N3030 N3080 [rebuilt with tail section from c/n 5090; wfu Opa-Locka, FL; derelict there Feb94] |
| 5095/30 | 731 | N9251R N78MP N780RH N731L [b/u; cx Jan04] |
| 5096/10 | 731 | N9252R N530G [cx 17Jun04; b/u; fuselage at Conroe, TX in 2005 but removed by Feb08] |
| 5097/60 | 731 | N9253R N300L N306L N77D N81366 N1BL N922MS [parted out by Dodson Int'l Parts, Rantoul, KS; fuselage to Sir Sandford Fleming College, Peterboro, Canada, by Sep08, instructional airframe painted as 'C-FCCC'] |
| 5098/28 | 731 | N9254R N1967G N5098G (N98MD) N417PJ N199LA N792AA N942Y (N963Y) XA-TVK |
| 5099/5 | 731 | N9255R N533EJ N594KR N277NS N323P N62K N62KK N18BH (N117J) |
| 5100/41 | 731 | N9256R N207L XA-FIU N35JJ XA-GZA N510TS N800GD [wfu Conroe, TX] |
| 5101/15 | 731 | N9208R N7008 N7008J N760DL N760DE XA-JJS N26MJ N800AF N511TS [wfu Aug05 Guthrie, OK; cx to Australia, but only engines go; fuselage to remain in USA] |
| 5102 | 8 | N9235R N326K N500ZB N75CC N7500 N85CC N601JJ [wfu Oct94 Spirit of St Louis A/P, MO & scrapped cx Feb00] |
| 5103 | 8 | N23M N672M N176BN N176AN N101AW XA-TAZ (N101AW) XA-TAV [at Aruba being used for fire training wearing its previous US marks N101AW] |
| 5104/6 | 731 | N902K N902KB N155AV N155TJ [reported parted out 2005] |
| 5105 | 8 | N277T N2277T N7005 N17005 HZ-MA1 [to Lycee de Blagnac, Toulouse, France for training use] |
| 5106/9 | 731 | N238U N288U CF-GWI N8SC N1329K YV-03CP [wfu Maracaibo, Venezuela] |
| 5107 | 8 | N118K N337US N7788 YV-187CP N7788 N69MT [parted out Jun93 Hollister, CA] |
| 5108 | 8 | N7953S N1207Z N24UG N68CT N680TT XA-SWD N104CE |
| 5109/13 | 731 | N7954S N968GN N968BN N678BC [b/u for spares 1992 Chandler Municipal A/P, AZ; fuselage noted Apr94 on fire dump Phoenix-Skyharbor A/P, AZ; gone by Oct98] |
| 5110/47 | 731 | N7955S N2600 N2601 N788S N49UC [b/u for spares during 1990; cx Dec93] |
| 5111 | 8 | N7956S N5111H N11SX N115MR N115DX [b/u circa Aug91 Addison, TX; wings to Spirit of St Louis A/P, MO] |
| 5112/7 | 731 | N7957S N910G N99MR N499PC N728PX N475MD [parted out by White Inds, Bates City, MO] |
| 5113/25 | 731 | N7958S N505C N124RP N303LE (N1967J) (N65JW) N1962J N77BT N542TW [parted out by White Inds, Bates City, MO, Nov05; cx 29Apr09] |
| 5114/18 | 731 | N7959S N930MT N930M N94K N111GU N26GL 5B-CHE |
| 5115/39 | 731 | N933LC N933CY N26TR N40XY N8300E N1151K [b/u Willard A/P, Champaign, IL Aug95] |
| 5116 | 8 | N7961S N222QA N3HB N60BC [wfu 29Sep92 Spirit of St Louis A/P, MO; fuselage still present circa Apr96] |
| 5117/35 | 731 | N7962S N210EK N310CK VR-BSH VP-BSH (N858SH) VP-BLD |
| 5118 | 8 | N7963S N333QA N333KN N222KN [b/u 1987 Memphis, TN] |
| 5119/29 | 731 | N7964S N11HM N508T N508TA N500AG N1DB N9GU [parted out by White Inds, Bates City, MO] |
| 5120/26 | 731 | N7965S N40DC HZ-TNA [wfu Geneva, Switzerland by mid 2004] |
| 5121 | 8 | N7966S W Germany 1102 SU-DAG ST-PRM [still at Cairo, Egypt as SU-DAG Oct02] |
| 5122 | 8 | N7967S N1107Z N1107M N213AP [cx Mar89; b/u during 1989] |
| 5123/14 | 731 | N7968S N1844S N559GP N441A N47UC N123GN N57NP N57NR (N425MK) N725MK |
| 5124 | 8 | N7969S N46F N7SZ XA-SBQ XA-SKI XC-SKI |
| 5125/31 | 731 | N7970S N47UC N48UC N31BP [reported parted out] |
| 5126 | 8 | N7971S N955H N955HL N20S N39E N39Q [b/u for spares Aug83] |
| 5127 | 8 | N7972S N42G N42GB N3GR N636C (N636MC) N636 N171CC [derelict 1991 Van Nuys, CA; cx Jun92 to Aviation Warehouse film prop yard at El Mirage, CA, wears marks "N171SG"] |
| 5128/16 | 731 | N7973S N26S 5B-CGP N128BP N777PZ [parted out Houston-Hobby, TX] |
| 5128S | | [see c/n 5037/24] |
| 5129 | 8 | N7974S Saudi Arabia 101 XA-TJW XA-TZW [parted out Toluca, Mexico] |
| 5130 | 8 | N7975S Saudi Arabia 103 Saudi Arabia 102 XA-TJV XA-TZV XA-PES [wfu Toluca, Mexico] |
| 5131 | 8/Fanstar | N7976S N30RP N31RP N64C N212JW N380AA [derelict 1991 Van Nuys, CA; cx Mar92] |
| 5132/57 | 731 | N7977S N1620 N1620N N100GL N801 N1JN N989JN XA-PSD XA-BEB |
| 5133 | 8 | N7978S N329K N322K C-GPGD VR-CAW HZ-WBT HZ-WT1 HZ-FK1 XA-ROF XA-ROK [wfu Jan95 Mexico City A/P, Mexico, used as ticket office in car park of Wal-Mart store in eastern Mexico City] |
| 5134/50 | 731 | N7979S N295AR N500S N50PS N72HT N136MA XA-JMN XA-TPD [possibly wfu at Addison TX by Sep03] |
| 5135 | 8 | N7980S N636 N900H N500WN N500FG [parted out Spirit of St.Louis, MO, still marked N500WN; cx 28Aug09] |
| 5136 | 8 | N5500L Libya 001 5A-DAJ |
| 5137 | 8 | N5501L EP-VRP Iran 1004 Iran 5-9001 |
| 5138 | 8 | N5502L N1301P N333RW N31DK N801 (N700MJ) [wfu at Greenville Technical College, SC; used as an instructional airframe] |

# JETSTAR

| C/n | Series | Identities |
|---|---|---|
| 5139/54 | 731 | N5503L N991 N991F N10DR XA-RVG N1189A [to Atlanta Air Salvage, Griffin, GA, Apr97 still marked as XA-RVG; US marks cx Apr97] |
| 5140 | 8 | N5504L XB-VIW XA-JCG XA-EMO [wfu Jan06 Toluca, Mexico] |
| 5141 | 8 | N5505L N711Z N7967S N12241 N244 N4436S HZ-SH1 N4493S XB-CXO N3982A N747GB [derelict at Lagos, Nigeria, circa Jan98] |
| 5142 | 8 | N5506L N5113H N1UP N20SH HZ-SH3 N90658 N86TP N91LJ N91UJ N86TP N39LG N23FE XA-SOY [wfu by 2006 Toluca, Mexico] |
| 5143 | 8 | N5507L N100UA N31UT N5070L N5878D C-GATU N620JB N326CB [b/u; cx Jan00] |
| 5144 | 8 | N5508L Mexico JS10201 Mexico DN-01 Mexico JS10201 Mexico 3908 |
| 5145 | 8 | N5509L N46K XB-DBJ XB-JFE XA-JFE N511TD [to Great St Louis Air & Space Museum, IL] |
| 5146 | 8 | N5510L N80GM C-GWSA N4990D N499AS N545BF [b/u for spares Jan87] |
| 5147 | 8 | N5511L N744UT N718R N212AP [wfu for spares Jan93 Greenwood, LA] |
| 5148 | 8 | N5512L N964M N21SH HZ-SH4 N900SA XA-ROK XA-ROF XA-OLI [cx] |
| 5149/11 | 731 | N5513L N711Z N157JF N157QP N524AC N110MN N110MT N100MZ VR-BJI [b/u for spares Feb91] |
| 5150/37 | 731 | N5514L N516WC N200CC N200CG N42C N312CK N100TM (N345CK) (N710JA) N721CR N911CR [parted out by White Inds, Bates City, MO] |
| 5151 | 8 | N5515L N711Z N46KJ N45K XA-PUL [wfu Jan94 for spares by TAESA Mexico City, Mexico, used as ticket office in car park of Wal-Mart store in southern Mexico City] |
| 5152 | 8 | N5516L N500JD N113KH XA-SOC [b/u for spares Toluca, Mexico circa Jan03] |
| 5153/61 | 731 | N5517L N711JS N500PG N430MB N416KD N416SJ |
| 5154 | 8 | N5518L N3031 N756 N766 XC-SRH N43AR [parted out at Fort Lauderdale Executive, FL circa Jly00] |
| 5155/32 | 731 | N5519L N711Z XA-FES N4248Z N55NE N10PN N79AE N59CD N1DB (VR-BQG) (N120RL) VR-BRL VP-BRL N84GA N116DD [w/o Dallas/Love Field, TX 10Mar06, cx] |
| 5156 | 8 | N5520L 9K-ACO N70TP XB-DBT N16AZ [wfu for spares] |
| 5157 | 8 | N5521L N9WP N29WP XB-DUH [displayed at entrance to Dodson Av'n at Rantoul, KS painted as "N001DT"] |
| 5158 | 8 | N5522L N516DM C-GTCP N1DT XA-POO XA-FHR XA-TDG |
| 5159 | 8 | N5523L N520M XB-DBS [wfu] |
| 5160 | 8 | N5524L C-FRBC (N60EE) [b/u late 1988 Memphis, TN] |
| 5161/43 | 731 | N5525L N22ES N60SM N119SE N1329L N200PB N99VR LY-AMB N5161R XB-KCV XB-KFR [impounded at Valencia, Venezuela, 07Sep07 for drug-running] |
| 5162 | 8 | N5526L N10CX N10JJ XA-HNY XB-KLV |
| | | |
| 5201 | 2 | N5527L N711Z N711DZ (N93JD) N93JM N745DM N777AY |
| 5202 | 2 | N5528L N717 N717X N333KN N20GB EC-232 EC-FQX VP-CBH P4-CBG 3C-QRK N25AG [b/u Kemble, UK, 2006; remains to Air Salvage Int'l, Alton, Hants, UK] |
| 5203 | 2 | N5529L EP-VLP Iran 1003 [reported w/o 05Jan95 Isfahan, Iran] |
| 5204 | 2 | N5530L N19ES N59AC N500PR N167R N25WZ (N220ES) N202ES N814K [parted out 2008; to Cavanaugh Flight Museum, Addison, TX] |
| 5205 | 2 | N5531L N5000C N500QC N718R N713R YV-826CP N16BL N454JB N72GW |
| 5206 | 2 | N5532L N107GM XA-STG XA-JML N329JS [to White Inds, Bates City, MO Dec04 for parts] |
| 5207 | 2 | N5533L N176BN N34WR |
| 5208 | 2 | N5534L N322CS N123CC (N29TC) N38BG N95BD N95BK |
| 5209 | 2 | N5535L N500S N297AP N529TS N375MD [damaged 24Oct05 by Hurricane Wilma at Fort Lauderdale Executive, FL and parted out by Dodson International Parts, KS] |
| 5210 | 2 | N5536L N400KC N707WB N787WB [parted out; fuselage at Aircraft Support Group facility at Conroe, TX in 2005 but removed by Feb08] |
| 5211 | 2 | N5537L N500T (N500YY) N56PR N821MD N118B XA-PWR |
| 5212 | 2 | N5538L N3030 N5030 N167G XA-ACC N167G (N95SR) [b/u; cx Aug03; fuselage at Aircraft Support Group facility at Conroe, TX in 2005 but removed by Feb08] |
| 5213 | 2 | N5539L N501T N501J N60JM (N600JT) N65JT |
| 5214 | 2 | N5540L N530M N601CM N760DL N760DE (N9366Q) N106JL N848AB N221CR N3RC N50KP XA-CVE N50127 XA-RCR [parted out by Alliance Air Parts, Oklahoma City, OK, still wearing marks N50127] |
| 5215 | 2 | N5541L (N215HZ) VR-BJH N329MD N777WJ XA-FHS N215DL N215TS (N1X) N1TS N1X N800TS N80TS N808RP N175MD |
| 5216 | 2 | N5542L N95BA N99E N797WC N797WQ |
| 5217 | 2 | N5543L N106G N814CE N500EX N504EX N1MJ N486MJ N1MJ 9G-ABF |
| 5218 | 2 | N5544L N716RD N816RD N901C [cx 20Dec05; presumed wfu] |
| 5219 | 2 | N5545L N107G N21VB C-GBDX N219MF N104BK N770DR 5H-APH LY-EWC N522AG N500DB (N5VN) N800GD |
| 5220 | 2 | N5546L N32KR A6-KAH TC-NOA VP-CGH |
| 5221 | 2 | N5547L 5A-DAR [w/o 16Jan83 en route Libya-Algeria] |
| 5222 | 2 | N5548L N509T (N509TF) N509J C-GAZU VP-BCP A6-CPC N813P N311RS |
| 5223 | 2 | N5549L N105G N341K N1DB N644JW N1MJ N886DT N887DT ZS-ICC |
| 5224 | 2 | N4016M N1924G N285LM N3QS N6QZ N116DD |
| 5225 | 2 | N4021M N746UT N990CH N42KR TC-IHS N900DB (N9KE) |
| 5226 | 2 | N4026M N2MK N815RC N308SG TC-SSS |
| 5227 | 2 | N4033M N211PA N23SB N30Y (N811) N110AN N171SG N117AJ N375MD |

# JETSTAR

| C/n | Series | Identities |
|---|---|---|
| 5228 | 2 | N4034M N372H XA-RMD N400MP N400MR XA-CON |
| 5229 | 2 | N4038M N7NP N351WC N851WC (N50NM) N500NM VR-CNM N222MF XA-TCN |
| 5230 | 2 | N4042M N257H N901FH N901EH N701JH N275MD |
| 5231 | 2 | N4043M N196KC (N788JS) N988MW N112MC XA-FHR XA-TPJ XA-AAL [wfu at Toluca, Mexico] |
| 5232 | 2 | N4046M N90CP N90QP N77C |
| 5233 | 2 | N4048M YI-AKA 7T-VHP OD-KMI HB-JGK |
| 5234 | 2 | N4049M N357H N920DY N920DG "N234TS" XA-EKT |
| 5235 | 2 | N4055M YI-AKB [status following first Gulf War? - reportedly flown to Nouakchott, Mauritania for safe keeping] |
| 5236 | 2 | N4056M N531M N2JR N34TR N741AM (A6-...) ST-FSA |
| 5237 | 2 | N4058M YI-AKC [status following first Gulf War? - reportedly flown to Nouakchott, Mauritania for safe keeping] |
| 5238 | 2 | N4062M YI-AKD [status following first Gulf War? - reportedly flown to Nouakchott, Mauritania for safe keeping] |
| 5239 | 2 | N4063M YI-AKE [status following first Gulf War? - reportedly flown to Nouakchott, Mauritania for safe keeping] |
| 5240 | 2 | N4065M YI-AKF [status following first Gulf War? - reportedly flown to Nouakchott, Mauritania for safe keeping] |

Production complete

# MBB HFB 320 HANSA JET

| C/n | Series | Identities |
|---|---|---|
| V1/1001 | | D-CHFB [ff 21Apr64; w/o 12May65 Torrejon, Spain] |
| V2/1002 | | D-CLOU (D-CASE) [wfu 24Sep70; preserved Deutsches Museum, Munich, Germany] |
| 1021 | | D-CARA [wfu Braunschweig 25May84; on static display at Finkenwerder, Germany] |
| 1022 | | D-CARE [CofA exp 28Apr72; in Finow Museum, Germany] |
| 1023 | | D-CARI N320J N1320U N320AF N103F [b/u for spares] |
| 1024 | | D-CARO W Germany (YA111) W Germany (CA111) W Germany D9536 W Germany 1607 F-WZIH [preserved Museé de l'Air, Paris, France] |
| 1025 | | D-CARU W Germany (YA112) W Germany (CA112) W Germany D9537 W Germany 1608 [in open storage at Manching, Germany by 2001; to Hamburg by road Aug07 for restoration to flying condition] |
| 1026 | | D-CARY N890HJ N71CW (N1026) N71DL TC-FNS [cx 1991; wfu Hannover, Germany circa Sep88; to Museum Hannover Laatzen marked "D-CARY"] |
| 1027 | | D-CASO I-TALC (D-CASO) D-CITO N905MW N127MW [w/o 05Oct84 Aberdeen, SD] |
| 1028 | | D-CASU 5N-AMF [w/o 25Jly77 Abidjan, Ivory Coast] |
| 1029 | | D-CASY [w/o 29Jun72 Blackpool, UK] |
| 1030 | | D-CATE N247GW N111DC [reported wfu 1995, noted dismantled at Monroe, MI Aug95] |
| 1031 | | D-CERA N300SB N750SB [cx Dec90; wfu Fort Lauderdale Executive, FL; hulk stored Opa-Locka, FL for spares] |
| 1032 | | D-CERE PH-HFA N130MW N132MW [wfu; b/u] |
| 1033 | | D-CERI PH-HFB N132MW N130MW [b/u 1989] |
| 1034 | | D-CERO N320J N320MC [w/o 09Mar73 Phoenix, AZ and b/u; cx Oct90] |
| 1035 | | D-CERU PH-HFC N128SD [wfu for spares use Monroe, MI circa Aug97] |
| 1036 | | D-CESA N891HJ N380EX N2MK N136MW (N92047) |
| 1037 | | D-CESE N892HJ N5ZA N6MK N6ML N555JM YV-999P N604GA [w/o 30Nov04 Spirit of St. Louis Airport, MO] |
| 1038 | | D-CESI N110WS N5627 (N18RA) N192AT N301AT N605GA [instructional airframe at Jefferson County Technical College/Bowman Field, KY] |
| 1039 | | D-CESO N118RA N893HJ CF-WDU N666LC N666LQ N205MM N208MM N171GA [submerged into Portage Quarry nr Bowling Green, OH, 2006 for diver training] |
| 1040 | | D-CESU I-ITAL N7158Q [b/u for spares Mojave, CA; remains to Aviation Warehouse film prop facility at El Mirage, CA; canx 27Jan06 as wfu] |
| 1041 | | D-CIRA W Germany 1601 (D-CIRA) N92045 (N62452) N602GA [wfu Toledo, OH noted Mar00 devoid of marks] |
| 1042 | | D-CIRE W Germany 1602 TC-LEY TC-SEN TC-GSB (N7684X) N106TF (N603GA) [b/u circa 2000 - remains being used by Fire Department at Louisville, KY] |
| 1043 | | D-CIRI W Germany 1603 TC-KHE TC-LEY D-CHFB* |
| 1044 | | D-CIRO [w/o 18Dec70 Texel Is, Netherlands] |
| 1045 | | D-CIRU N5602 N894HJ N4ZA N7ES [wfu Fort Lauderdale Executive, FL, for spares; remains to Opa-Locka, FL] |
| 1046 | | D-CISA W Germany 1604 TC-NSU [cx 1991; wfu] |
| 1047 | | D-CISE W Germany 1605 TC-OMR [cx 1991; wfu] |
| 1048 | | D-CISI W Germany 1606 [preserved GAF Museum, Gatow, Berlin] |
| 1049 | | D-CISO XC-DGA XC-TIJ [b/u 1991; possibly following accident at San Diego, CA on 11Jun84; remains to Mojave, CA] |
| 1050 | | D-CISU LV-POP LQ-JRH (N1184L) N2675W N777PV N777PS N777PZ N777PQ [wfu for spares use Monroe, MI circa Aug97] |
| 1051 | | D-CORE N895HJ N6ZA N888DL [b/u Jly 90 for spares - remains to Aviation Warehouse film prop yard at El Mirage, CA ] |
| 1052 | | D-CORI PT-IDW N173GA [instructional airframe at Jefferson County Technical College /Bowman Field, KY] |
| 1053 | | D-CORO PT-IOB N176GA [wfu, cx Feb07] |
| 1054 | | D-CORU N896HJ N480LR [cx Feb87; to spares use Monroe, MI circa Aug97] |
| 1055 | | D-CORY N897HJ N11NT N87950 N30AV (N21SU) TC-GSA (N7685T) N105TF |
| 1056 | | D-COSA [to instructional airframe at Manching, Germany; later to museum at Niederaltaich, Germany (minus engines & wings)] |
| 1057 | | D-CLMA D-COSE (N107TW) VR-CYR YV-388CP [impounded for drug-smuggling Venezuela Aug2004] |
| 1058 | ECM | D-COSI Germany 1621 N322AF [b/u at Hollister, CA circa Jly98] |
| 1059 | ECM | D-COSO W Germany 9825 W Germany 1622 [w/o 27Nov76 Schwabmuenchen, W Germany] |
| 1060 | ECM | D-COSU W Germany 9826 Germany 1623 (D-CCCH) N321AF [b/u at Hollister, CA circa Jly98] |
| 1061 | ECM | (D-CUNA) D-CANI Germany 1624 (D-CEDL) N320AF |
| 1062 | ECM | (D-CURE) D-CANO Germany 1625 N323AF [b/u at Hollister, CA circa Jly98] |
| 1063 | ECM | (D-CURI) D-CANU Germany 1626 [preserved GAF Museum, Gatow, Berlin] |
| 1064 | ECM | (D-CURO) D-CAMA Germany 1627 N324AF [b/u at Hollister, CA circa Jly98] |
| 1065 | ECM | (D-CURU) D-CAME Germany 1628 N325AF [b/u at Hollister, CA circa Jly98] |
| 1066 | | (D-CURY) (D-CAMO) |
| 1067 | | (D-CUSA) (D-CAMU) |
| 1068 | | (D-CUSE) (D-CALA) |
| 1069 | | (D-CUSI) (D-CALE) |
| 1070 | | (D-CUSO) (D-CALI) |
| 1071 | | (D-CUSU) (D-CALO) |
| 1072 | | (D-CUSY) (D-CALU) |
| 1073 | | (D-CADA) |
| 1074 | | (D-CADE) |
| 1075 | | (D-CADI) |
| 1076 | | (D-CADO) |
| 1077 | | (D-CADU) |
| 1078 | | (D-CATI) |
| 1079 | | (D-CANA) |
| 1080 | | (D-CANE) (D-CINA) (D-CCVW) (D-CDVW) |

Notes: 1021 to 1065 above also have a secondary c/n (S1 to S45)
1066 to 1080 not completed; used for spares

# MU300 DIAMOND

| C/n | Series | Identities |
|---|---|---|
| 001SA | 2 | JQ8001 N181MA [to Beech Field, Wichita, KS fire department for training; cx 18Feb09] |
| 002 | 1 | JQ8002 N81DM JQ8003 JA8248 |
| A003SA | 1A | N300DM N300TS (N300TJ) |
| A004SA | 1A | JQ8004 N302DM (N40BK) N59TJ N102WR (N88TJ) N541CW (N484CW) (N541TM) [parted out by White Industries, Bates City, MO; cx 04Feb09] |
| A005SA | 1A | JQ8005 N304DM N450TJ N15AR N40GC N700LP N30HD N110DS |
| A006SA | 1 | N325DM C-FPAW N400TJ N777JJ N750TJ N200LP |
| A007SA | 1A | N301DM N707CW N507CW N485CW N507CW N24HD N567JK |
| A008SA | 1A | N303DM (N56SK) N399DM N442JC* |
| A009SA | 1A | N305DM N909GA N306P N318RS N360CA [parted out by White Inds, Bates City, MO] |
| A010SA | 1A | N306DM N69PC (N9FC) N300DH N703JH N931MA |
| A011SA | 1A | N307DM (N77GA) N114DM N211GA |
| A012SA | 1A | N308DM N82CT N7RC N107T I-GIRL N112GA N316LP |
| A013SA | 1 | N81HH I-VIGI [w/o 15Oct99 Parma, Italy] |
| A014SA | 1 | N15TW N339DM OH-KNE |
| A015SA | 1A | N315DM N415RC N271MB N870P N789DD N789DJ |
| A016SA | 1A | N133RC N100DE N208F N530RD N10NM N706JH N411RE |
| A017SA | 1A | N14DM N75BL (N33MM) N399MM |
| A018SA | 1A | N900LH C-GRDS N138DM N118GA N83BG (N831TJ) |
| A019SA | 1 | N311DM N9LP N6PA N319DM N400GK |
| A020SA | 1A | N399RP (N911JJ) [parted out by White Inds, Bates City MO; cx 29Apr09] |
| A021SA | 1 | N222Q N4LK N678PC N405MG |
| A022SA | 1A | N313DM N18KE (N816S) N322MD N322BE N800TJ N811DJ (N397SL) N400UF |
| A023SA | 1A | N314DM OY-BPC SE-DDW OY-BPC N79GA N17TJ N22BN N150CA [parted out by White Inds, Bates City, MO] |
| A024SA | 1A | N316DM N320CH N95TJ N450PC N674AC XB-CTC |
| A025SA | 1 | N317DM N63GH N1843S N1843A N400HH |
| A026SA | 1 | N5UE N55JM N900DW N140AK N526CW N326CW N486CW (N426TM) (N26FA) N28FM |
| A027SA | 1 | N319DM N237CC N800RD N27TJ N7PW |
| A028SA | 1A | N320DM N331DC N900WJ [to Dodson Int'l Parts, Rantoul, KS; parted out] |
| A029SA | 1A | N321DM N1UT N10TE N89TJ N100RS (N22CX) |
| A030SA | 1A | N322DM N191GS N41UT N58TJ N301P N83SA (N800GC) |
| A031SA | 1A | N174B N2220G N956PP N958PP |
| A032SA | 1A | N323DM N132GA N320T N929WG N83CG (N996DR) |
| A033SA | 1A | N312DM N520TT N223S N5EJ N717CF N717DF N148J |
| A034SA | 1A | N318DM N303P N334KC |
| A035SA | 1A | N300HH HB-VHX N135GA N702JH N37CB |
| A036SA | 1 | N326DM N18BA N997MX |
| A037SA | 1A | N327DM OY-CCB LN-SJA N109TW N134RG [parted out by White Inds, Bates City MO; cx 29Apr09] |
| A038SA | 1 | N338DM N147DA N147WC N42SR (N212PA) [Parted out by White Inds, Bates City, MO] |
| A039SA | 1A | N328DM C-GRDX N139DM N399MJ PT-OXT |
| A040SA | 1A | (N329DM) N82CS N188ST N40GA |
| A041SA | 1A | N330DM (N444SL) N45GL N83AE N300AA N300AR N104GB |
| A042SA | 1A | N331DM N420TJ N8LE (N420FA) |
| A043SA | 1A | N332DM N19R |
| A044SA | 1A | N334DM N309DM N110DK N146GA N606JM N600GW |
| A045SA | 1A | N335DM N334DM N99FF N154GA N60B N61GA N777DC N545TP N395WB |
| A046SA | 1A | N346DM (YV-274CP) (N146GA) N151SP N272BC N272BG N900BT N109PW HA-YFE |
| A047SA | 1 | N347DM N138RC N76LE N47TJ N45NP N47PB N333TS N2WC |
| A048SA | 1A | N335DM (OO-EBA) VH-JEP N335DM PT-LNN [w/o 23Mar03 Santos Air Base, Brazil] |
| A049SA | 1A | N336DM N300LA YV-309P YV-29CP N40MF XA-SOD N411SP |
| A050SA | 1A | N350DM N257CB N826JH N528LG |
| A051SA | 1A | (N357DM) N351DM N550HS (N35P) D-CGFV TC-YIB [w/o in ground accident; to Dodson Avn, Rantoul, KS, for spares] (N550HS) |
| A052SA | 1 | N352DM HB-VHT I-FRAB N70XX [Oct05 to White Industries, Bates City MO for parts] |
| A053SA | 1 | N353DM D-CDRB JA30DA |
| A054SA | 1A | N354DM N850TJ N141H N491BT |
| A055SA | 1A | N877S N877T N89EM N600MS N600CG XA-UIC |
| A056SA | 1A | N341DM N101AD N156GA I-FRTT N255DG |
| A057SA | 1A | N342DM N119MH N334WM N510BC |
| A058SA | 1A | N343DM N384DM VR-BKA N7050V N442EA |
| A059SA | 1A | N345DM N344DM I-DOCA N126GA N1JC |
| A060SA | 1A | N345DM (N300SJ) N585TC [parted out by White Inds, Bates City, MO; cx 29Apr09] |
| A061SA | 1A | N348DM N18T N500PP |
| A062SA | 1A | N349DM G-JMSO N362MD 3D-AFH N426DA TG-LAR N64EZ N616MM N817GR |
| A063SA | 1A | N363DM N54BE N51B N51BE N984SA [parted out by Atlanta Air Salvage, Griffin, GA] |
| A064SA | 1A | N364DM N246GA I-SELM N800LE HI-646SP N2225J N400ML YV195T YV2347 |
| A065SA | 1A | N361DM N65JN N165GA OY-CDK I-GENC N54RM N16MF N925MJ |
| A066SA | 1A | N366DM N1TX (N185GA) "N66FG" N88MF N88ME PR-JTS |
| A067SA | 1A | N367DM N123VJ I-ALGU N184SC N65SA N63DR N617BG [parted out by White Industries, Bates City, MO; cx 04Feb09] |
| A068SA | 1A | N368DM N368PU N103HC |

# DIAMOND 1

| C/n | Series | Identities | | | | | | |
|---|---|---|---|---|---|---|---|---|
| A069SA | 1A | N355DM | N56MC | N250GP | (N197SL) | (N501EZ) | | |
| A070SA | 1A | N370DM | D-CNEX | OY-BPI | N84GA | N60EF | | |
| A071SA | 1A | N371DM | (N106GA) | N70GA | N71GH | | | |
| A072SA | 1A | N372DM | PT-LGD | N174SA | N777DC | N779DC | | |
| A073SA | 1A | N356DM | N717VL | N1715G | N94LH | N94LD | | |
| A074SA | 1A | N374DM | N22WJ | JA8298 | N19GA | N32HP | | |
| A075SA | 1A | N375DM | N11WF | N824DW | | | | |
| A076SA | 1A | N376DM | N76LE | C-GLIG | [w/o 01Mar95 Jasper-Hinton A/P, Alberta, Canada] N8221M [parted out by White Inds, Bates City, MO; regn cx Aug01 a/c b/u] | | | |
| A077SA | 1A | N377DM | N68PL | N66PL | N975GR | N851C | | |
| A078SA | 1A | N378DM | N710MB | [w/o 15Dec93 nr Goodland, KS. Parted out by White Industries, Bates City, MO] | | | | |
| A079SA | 1A | N379DM | (N574U) | N574CF | N213LG | N765KC | | |
| A080SA | 1A | N380DM | N380CM | N770PC | N925WC | N275HS | N44MM | |
| A081SA | 1A | N381DM | N381MG | N81TJ | N317CC | N317GC | N750TJ | N50EF |
| A082SA | 1A | N382DM | N105HS | N555FA | N62CH | N214PG | | |
| A083SA | 1A | N383DM | N12WF | N83TK | N417KT | [Parted out by White Inds, Bates City, MO] | | |
| A084SA | 1A | N484DM | (N484VS) | (N84DT) | N840TJ | N160S | N160H | EC-JKL |
| A085SA | 1A | N485DM | I-TORA | N485DM | N777MJ | (N911JJ) | N70VT | N87DY |
| A086SA | 1A | N486DM | N515KK | | | | | |
| A087SA | 1A | N487DM | HB-VIA | (PH-JSL) | N870AM | I-AVEB | | |
| A088SA | 1A | N482DM | | | | | | |
| A089SA | 1A | N483DM | N100EA | N89SC | N88CR | N20PA | | |
| A090SA | 1A | N312DM | G-TOMY | N300LG | (N64EZ) | C-GLIG | N464AM | |
| A091SA | 1A | N357DM | (N357MD) | PT-OVM | (N485DM) | N611AG | N400HG | N400NF |
| A092SA | 1A | JA8246 | [w/o 23Jly86 Sado Island, Japan] | | | | | |

Production complete

Note: Diamond 2s are included under Beechjet 400s.

# MS760 PARIS

| C/n | Series | Identities |
|---|---|---|
| 01 | | F-WGVO [ff 29Jly54] F-BGVO [w/o 01May58 Lisbon, Portugal] |
| 02 | | [used as static test airframe and b/u] |
| 03 | | F-BHOK France 03 F-SDIA (F-Z...) F-SDIA [w/o 24Dec64 Mont de Marsan, France] |
| 001 | | F-WIET France 1 F-ZADS F-SDIB F-ZADS F-SDIB 330-DB/F-SDDB [to Musee de l'Air et de l'Espace, Le Bourget, France, Oct09] |
| 002 | | EP-HIM F-BOJO N760MM N1EP N207MJ |
| 003 | | Argentina A-01/E-201 [wfu 1994; to IV Brigada Museum, Mendoza, Argentina] |
| 004 | 2 | Argentina A-02/E-202 [wfu 2007; stored Mendoza, Argentina] |
| 005 | 1A | F-WJAA N760H N2NC N2TE XB-FJO N2TE (N760LB) [w/o 30Nov96 Santa Ana/Orange County, CA; cx Mar97] |
| 006 | | F-WJAB N84J N760J [b/u 05Apr81; cx May81] |
| 007 | | Argentina A-03/E-203 [w/o 27Jan61 Mendoza, Argentina] |
| 008 | | F-WJAC G-36-2 G-APRU N60GT |
| 009 | | F-WJAD N300ND N722Q |
| 010 | | Argentina A-04/E-204 [wfu 1998; stored Mendoza, Argentina] |
| 011 | | Argentina A-05/E-205 [wfu 2006; stored Mendoza, Argentina] |
| 012 | | France 12/F-YDJ? [w/o 13Apr59 Hyeres, France] |
| 013 | | Argentina A-06/E-206 [w/o 11Mar88 Mendoza, Argentina; rebuilt with tail unit and fuselage parts from c/n 016 for display at Ezeiza, Argentina] |
| 014 | | France 14 France 312-DF/F-RHDF [dismantled at Long Beach, CA circa Dec97; fuselage at San Luis Obispo, CA circa May01] |
| 015 | | Argentina A-07/E-207 [wfu 2007; to Museo Aeronautico, Moron, Argentina] |
| 016 | | Argentina A-08/E-208 [wfu 2001; parts used in rebuild of c/n 013 for display purposes] |
| 017 | | Argentina A-09/E-209 [wfu 1995; preserved Rio Gallegas, Argentina] |
| 018 | | Argentina A-10/E-210 [w/o 09Nov59 Cordoba, Argentina] |
| 019 | | France 19 France 41-AR/F-SCAR [stored Chateaudun, France Apr97] |
| 020 | | France 20 F-SDIC 20-Q/F-RABQ [w/o 26Oct62 Bernay en Brie, France] |
| 021 | | Argentina A-11/E-211 [w/o 06Oct89 Mendoza, Argentina] |
| 022 | | Argentina A-12/E-212 [wfu 2007] |
| 023 | | France 23 330-DO/F-SDDO [stored Chateaudun, France Apr97] |
| 024 | | France 24 65-KW/F-FBLW [to Ailes Anciennes Toulouse for restoration Nov03] |
| 025 | | France 25 42-AP/F-SCAP 116-CB [stored Chateaudun, France circa Mar01] |
| 026 | | F-WJAA France 26 -LN/F-RBLN [stored Chateaudun, France circa Sep99] |
| 027 | | France 27 -DE/F-RHDE N760PJ |
| 028 | | F-WJAE I-SNAI N760X |
| 029 | | France 29 65-LC/F-RBLC [stored Chateaudun, France Apr97] |
| 030 | | France 30 65-LI/F-RBLW N370AS N761X |
| 031 | | France 31/F-YCB. [wfu 23Jly72; instructional airframe Rochefort, France] |
| 032 | | 32 Aeronavale/Marine F-AZLT |
| 033 | | 33 Aeronavale/Marine [preserved Musee de Tradition de l'Aeronautique Navale, Rochefort, France] |
| 034 | | France 34 43-BB/F-SCBB 113-CG N371AS |
| 035 | | France 35 43-BL/F-SCBC |
| 036 | | France 36 44-CC/F-SCCC 316-DH N373AS |
| 037 | | France 37 34-Z/F-RABZ [w/o 07Dec67 Les Loges, France] |
| 038 | | France 38 41-A/F-SCAS 115-ME N374AS |
| 039 | 1A | F-WJAA F-BJET [stored Reims-Prunay, France circa Jly99; to USA for spares 2007] |
| 040 | | 40 Aeronavale/Marine [instructional airframe at Lycee Professionel Robert & Nelly de Rothschild, St Maxim, France] |
| 041 | | 41 Aeronavale/Marine N41NY |
| 042 | | 42 Aeronavale/Marine [instructional airframe at Morlaix-Ploujean May03] |
| 043 | | (N888JK) (N776JK) N776K N760C N760S |
| 044 | | France 44 40-L/F-RBLD N375AS |
| 045 | | France 45 43-B./F-SCB. 316-DI N378AS |
| 046 | | 46 Aeronavale/Marine [in Ailes Anciennes Pays Beaunois collection at Chateau de Savigny les Beaunois] |
| 047 | | 47 Aeronavale/Marine [wfu] |
| 048 | | France 48 Aeronavale/Marine [w/o 04Jan68] |
| 049 | | N760M [w/o 03May69 Evadale, TX] |
| 050 | 2 | CN-MAJ CF-MAJ N6068 N111ER N42BL N23ST [w/o 11Sep90 Albuquerque, NM; cx Jun91] |
| 051 | | Brazil C41-2912 France 51 330-DC/F-SDDC N751PJ [to Den Helder, Netherlands 16Apr04 for restoration towards flying condition] |
| 052 | | Brazil C41-2911 [wfu] |
| 053 | | Brazil C41-2910 France 53 OD/F-RHDD N53PJ |
| 054 | | Brazil C41-2913 France 54 41-A./F-SCA. N354AS |
| 055 | | Brazil C41-2914 [wfu] |
| 056 | | Brazil C41-2915 France 56 65-LG/F-RBLG 133-CM N956P |
| 057 | | Brazil C41-2918 France 57 41-AC/F-SCAC N657P |
| 058 | | Brazil C41-2920 France 58 65-LB/F-RBLB 312-DG N760F |
| 059 | | Brazil C41-2916 France 59 41-A./F-SCA. 133-CF N959P |
| 060 | | Brazil C41-2917 France 60 41-AT/F-SCAT N7601R |
| 061 | | Brazil C41-2919 France 61 -LY/F-RBLY N961P |
| 062 | | Brazil C41-2921 France 62 65-LV/F-RBLV 314-DO [stored Chateaudun, France circa Mar01] |
| 063 | | Brazil C41-2923 [wfu] |

# PARIS

| C/n | Series | Identities |
|---|---|---|
| 064 | | Brazil C41-2922 [stored Santa Cruz, Brazil] |
| 065 | | Brazil C41-2924 France 65 65-LF/F-RBLF 330-DP |
| 066 | | Brazil C41-2925 [wfu] |
| 067 | | Brazil C41-2926 [w/o 29Oct62 Nova Lima, Brazil] |
| 068 | | Brazil C41-2927 France 68 NB/F-ZJNB |
| 069 | | HB-PAA Switzerland J-4117 HB-PAA [cx Jun84; to Musee Europeen de l'Aviation de Chasse Montelimar-Ancone, France] |
| 070 | | Brazil C41-2928 France 70 65-LF/F-RBLF [displayed at Tarbes-Lourdes, France marked as "F-MASD"] |
| 071 | | Brazil C41-2929 France 71 65-LE/F-RBLE N571P |
| 072 | 1A | F-BJLV N760FR |
| 073 | | France 73 |
| 074 | | Brazil C41-2930 France 74 [w/o 02Dec80 Natal, Brazil] |
| 075 | | Brazil C41-2931 France 75 65-LZ/F-RBLZ N975P |
| 076 | | Brazil C41-2932 [preserved Brazilian AF Museum, Camp de Abonsas, nr Rio de Janeiro, Brazil] |
| 077 | | Brazil C41-2933 France 77 65-LP/F-RBLP [to Estrella Warbirds Museum, Paso Robles, CA, by Feb10] |
| 078 | | Brazil C41-2934 France 78 65-LY/F-RBLY 115-ME [stored Chateaudun, France Apr97] |
| 079 | | Brazil C41-2935 France 79 [wfu 15Apr79; to SOPEMEA Villacoublay, France 31Jan89 for stress tests] |
| 080 | | Brazil C41-2936 France 80 314-D/F-RHD. GE-316 80/DE [wfu Chateaudun, France - on dump by 20Jun98] |
| 081 | | Brazil C41-2937 France 81 41-A./F-RBLL ELA61 N81PJ |
| 082 | | Brazil C41-2938 France 82 65-L./F-RBL. N761JS |
| 083 | | Brazil C41-2939 France 83 NC/F-ZJNC [code 316-DB] [stored Chateudun, France circa Jly00] |
| 084 | | 84 Aeronavale/Marine [w/o 23Dec70 Le Bourget, Paris, France] |
| 085 | | 85 Aeronavale/Marine F-AZTL* |
| 086 | 1A | F-BJLX N9035Y |
| 087 | | 87 Aeronavale/Marine N87NY |
| 088 | | 88 Aeronavale/Marine N88NY N626TC N760JS |
| 089 | 2 | F-BJLY N999PJ |
| 090 | | D-INGE N334RK N454HC N69X |
| 091 | | France 91 65-LU/F-RBLU [to Musee d'Aeronautique, Orange, France, by Apr07] |
| 092 | | France 92 118-DA/F-RHDA 316-DL N763JS |
| 093 | | France 93 65-LD/F-RBLD N764JS |
| 094 | | France 94 65-L./F-RBL. N765JS |
| 095 | | France 95 /F-RBL. [w/o 03Aug67 Melun, France] |
| 096 | | France 96 65-LU/F-RBLU [w/o 29May82 Villacoublay, France] |
| 097 | | France 97 65-LH/F-RBLH [reported as G1-330 "330 DC"] N97PJ PP-XUM |
| 098 | 2 | D-INGA F-BOHN HB-VEP 3A-MPP F-GKPP [w/o Oct91 Calvi, Corsica; [used for spares for c/n 111] |
| 099 | | I-SNAP [w/o 27Oct62 Milan, Italy] |
| 100 | | F-ZJNJ France 100 |
| 101 | 2 | France 101 F-BNRG (N7038Z) N760PJ N444ET (N760PJ) N520DB |
| 102 | 2B | F-BJZQ PH-MSR N760E HB-VEU N99HB N20DA |
| 103 | 2B | F-BJZR PH-MSS N760N YV-163CP N760N N760T [wfu Oct94 Mojave, CA] |
| 104 | 2B | F-BJZS PH-MST N760P N760R [stored Santa Maria, CA] |
| 105 | 2B | F-BJZT PH-MSU N760Q F-BXQL [stored Reims-Prunay, France circa Jly99; to USA for spares 2007] |
| 106 | 2B | F-BJZU PH-MSV N5878 [used as a source of spare parts for c/n 008 N60GT] |
| 107 | 2B | F-BJZV PH-MSW N5879 |
| 108 | 2B | F-BJZX PH-MSX N760AR |
| 109 | | [airframe never built; marks F-BJZY were reserved; RLS, Netherlands, options cx] |
| 110 | | [airframe never built; marks F-BJZZ were reserved; RLS, Netherlands, options cx] |
| 111 | 2 | I-FINR C6-BEV N760FM |
| 112 | | F-EXAA HB-PAC F-BOJY N65218 N7277X N710K [noted dismantled 26Feb91 Mojave, CA] |
| 113 | | France 113 F-ZJNI |
| 114 | | France 114 F-ZJNJ [Preserved Villacoublay, France] |
| 115 | | France 115 F-ZJOV |
| 116 | | France 116 F-ZJON |
| 117 | | France 117 F-ZJAZ |
| 118 | | France 118 F-ZJNQ |
| 119 | | France 119 F-ZLNL [wfu by 05Jun05 Istres, France; to museum at Saint Victoret, Marseille, France, 27Feb06] |
| | | |
| 01 | 3 | F-WLKL F-BLKL [stored Reims-Prunay, France circa Jly99] |

Production complete

# PARIS

## Production by FMA in Argentina

| C/n | Series | Identities | |
|---|---|---|---|
| A-1 | | Argentina E-213 | [w/o 29Mar73; collided with E-217 c/n A-5 Santa Luis, Argentina] |
| A-2 | | Argentina E-214 | [w/o 30Dec74 Cordoba, Argentina] |
| A-3 | | Argentina E-215 | [wfu 1998; preserved Ameghino, Argentina] |
| A-4 | | Argentina E-216 | [w/o 26Apr62 Moron, Argentina] |
| A-5 | | Argentina E-217 | [w/o 29Mar73; collided with E-213 c/n A-1 Santa Luis, Argentina] |
| A-6 | | Argentina E-218 | [w/o 11Feb81 Mendoza, Argentina - but see A-35] |
| A-7 | | Argentina E-219 | [wfu 1998 and by 2005 displayed on a roundabout close to Mendoza apt, Argentina] |
| A-8 | | Argentina E-220 | [wfu 2005; stored Mendoza, Argentina] |
| A-9 | | Argentina E-221 | [wfu 1994; preserved Mendoza, Argentina] |
| A-10 | | Argentina E-222 | [wfu 1994 and stored by Lockheed Martin Aircraft Argentina, Sociedad Anonima] |
| A-11 | | Argentina E-223 [code 23] | [wfu 1994 and std by Escuela de Suboficiales de la Fuerza Aerea (ESFA)] |
| A-12 | | Argentina E-224 | [wfu 1998; to museum at Santa Romana, Argentina] |
| A-13 | | Argentina E-225 | [wfu 1994; stored with Area Material Quilmes (AMQ), Argentina] |
| A-14 | | Argentina E-226 | [wfu 1994; preserved Cordoba, Argentina] |
| A-15 | | Argentina E-227 | [wfu 2006; dismantled at Mendoza, Argentina] |
| A-16 | | Argentina E-228 [code 28] | [w/o 16Aug65 Formosa, Argentina] |
| A-17 | | Argentina E-229 [code 29] | [wfu 1994 and stored by Lockheed Martin Aircraft Argentina, Sociedad Anonima] |
| A-18 | | Argentina E-230 | [wfu 1994; to Escuela Nacional Education Tecnica, Mendoza, Argentina as instructional airframe] |
| A-19 | | Argentina E-231 | [w/o 09Dec64 "EAM"?] |
| A-20 | | Argentina E-232 | [wfu 2002; to instructional airframe, Mendoza, Argentina] |
| A-21 | | Argentina E-233 | [wfu 1995; preserved Mendoza, Argentina] |
| A-22 | | Argentina E-234 | [w/o 1990 Mendoza, Argentina] |
| A-23 | | Argentina E-235 | [wfu 1998; stored Mendoza, Argentina; an FMA Paris painted as E-235 is displayed at Museo de Aera de Material, Rio Cuarto but is believd not to be c/n A-23] |
| A-24 | | Argentina E-236 | [wfu 2005; stored Mendoza, Argentina] |
| A-25 | | Argentina E-237 | [w/o 04Nov83 San Luis, Argentina] |
| A-26 | | Argentina E-238 | [w/o 30Dec78 Mendoza, Argentina] |
| A-27 | | Argentina E-239 | [w/o Jun78 Mendoza, Argentina] |
| A-28 | | Argentina E-240 | [w/o 20Mar85 San Juan, Argentina] |
| A-29 | | Argentina E-241 | [wfu 2006] |
| A-30 | | Argentina E-242 | [wfu 2007] |
| A-31 | | Argentina E-243 | [wfu 1998; by 2005 displayed by San Justo Aero Club, San Justo, Argentina] |
| A-32 | | Argentina E-244 | [wfu 1998; preserved San Juan, Argentina, wearing marks E-245] |
| A-33 | | Argentina E-245 | [wfu 1998; stored Bahia Blanca, Argentina] |
| A-34 | | Argentina E-246 | [w/o 09Feb77 Cordoba, Argentina] |
| A-35 | | Argentina E-247 | [wfu 1993 to Museo Nactional de Aeronautica, by Apr04 displayed on a pole at Moron, Argentina painted as E-218] |
| A-36 | | Argentina E-248 | [w/o 08Nov77 Cordoba, Argentina] |

Production complete

# PIAGGIO PD808

| C/n | Series | Identities | |
|---|---|---|---|
| 501 | TA | MM577 | [wfu by 1996, on dump at Pratica di Mare by Mar98] |
| 502 | TA | MM578 | [on dump at Pratica di Mare by Mar98; b/u] |
| 503 | VIP | I-PIAI | [w/o 18Jun68 San Sebastian, Spain] |
| 504 | VIP | I-PIAL | [wfu 1998] |
| 505 | GE1 | MM61958 | [wfu at Pratica di Mare by Nov97] |
| 506 | VIP | MM61948 | [wfu; preserved Opera Nazionale per i Figli degli Aviatori, Rome, Italy] |
| 507 | VIP | MM61949 | [wfu mid-1990's to Ditellandia Air Park, Castel Volturno by Jul99] |
| 508 | VIP | MM61950 | [wfu Rome/Ciampino 2006] |
| 509 | VIP | MM61951 | [wfu at Pratica di Mare by Mar98] |
| 510 | TP | MM61952 | [converted to PD808 GE2] [wfu at Pratica di Mare by Aug04] |
| 511 | TP | MM61953 | [w/o 15Sep93 Venice, Italy] |
| 512 | TP | MM61954 | [wfu at Pratica di Mare by Aug98] |
| 513 | TP | MM61955 | [converted to PD808 GE2; wfu at Parma, Italy by May05] |
| 514 | TP | MM61956 | [wfu to dump at Pratica di Mare by Mar98; b/u] |
| 515 | TP | MM61957 | [wfu at Pratica di Mare by Mar98] |
| 516 | GE1 | MM61959 | [wfu by Mar98; preserved near Ciampino airport, Rome, Italy] |
| 517 | GE1 | MM61960 | [wfu at Pratica di Mare by Aug04; b/u] |
| 518 | GE1 | MM61961 | [wfu; preserved at Italian Air Force Museum, Vigna di Valle, Italy] |
| 519 | GE1 | MM61962 | [wfu by Aug04; stored at Naples airport, Italy] |
| 520 | GE1 | MM61963 | [wfu before Jun93 Pisa, Italy; dismantled at Pratica di Mare by Nov97; remains to Ditellandia Air Park, Castel Volturno by Nov99] |
| 521 | RM | MM62014 | [wfu; preserved Vialo Europa, Lucca, Italy] |
| 522 | RM | I-PIAY | MM62015 [wfu at Pratica di Mare by Mar98; b/u] |
| 523 | RM | MM62016 | [wfu at Pratica di Mare by Nov97] |
| 524 | RM | MM62017 | [wfu at Pratica di Mare by Feb98; b/u] |

Production complete

# NORTH AMERICAN/ROCKWELL SABRE MODELS

## T-39 SERIES

C/n Series Identities

265-1 CT-39A 59-2868 N2259V [displayed Kirtland AFB, NM as 59-2868]

265-2 CT-39A 59-2869 N4999G 59-2869 [AMARC park code TG033; std wfu Sep93 Memphis Airport, TN]

265-3 NT-39A 59-2870 [to AMARC 21Aug03, park code AATG0105]

265-4 T-39A 59-2871 [w/o 13Nov69 Eglin AFB, FL]

265-5 CT-39A 59-2872 N2296C 59-2872 [AMARC park code TG015]

265-6 T-39A 60-3478 [to AMARC 22Aug03, park code AATG0106]

265-7 CT-39A 60-3479 [AMARC park code TG082]

265-8 CT-39A 60-3480 [AMARC park code TG013]

265-9 CT-39A 60-3481 [AMARC park code TG085] [to Lane Community College, Eugene, OR]

265-10 CT-39A 60-3482 [AMARC park code TG016] N510TA XA-TFD [w/o 4Feb00 Merida, Mexico]

265-11 T-39A 60-3483 [displayed Travis AFB, CA]

265-12 CT-39A 60-3484 [AMARC park code TG024] N7043U XB-GDU XA-TFC [w/o 16May97 20km S of Monterrey-Del Norte, Mexico]

265-13 CT-39A 60-3485 [AMARC park code TG003] [West Intl Aviation, Tucson, AZ]

265-14 CT-39A 60-3486 [AMARC park code TG008] XA-TIY

265-15 CT-39A 60-3487 [AMARC park code TG021] N510TD [cx Sep98 still in AMARC as 60-3486]

265-16 CT-39A 60-3488 N431NA [to Des Moines Educational Resource Center, IA]

265-17 CT-39A 60-3489 [AMARC park code TG058] [to Houston Community College, TX]

265-18 CT-39A 60-3490 [AMARC park code TG062] N8052V [South Seattle Community College, WA]

265-19 CT-39A 60-3491 [AMARC park code TG009]

265-20 CT-39A 60-3492 [AMARC park code TG007] [to Thief River Falls Tech College, MN]

265-21 CT-39A 60-3493 [AMARC park code TG057] [to Moses Lake, WA for instructional use]

265-22 CT-39A 60-3494 [AMARC park code TG094]

265-23 CT-39A 60-3495 [displayed Scott AFB, IL]

265-24 CT-39A 60-3496 [AMARC park code TG072] [to Cochise College, Douglas, AZ]

265-25 CT-39A 60-3497 [AMARC park code TG066]

265-26 CT-39A 60-3498 [AMARC park code TG077] [at Chandler Williams Gateway, AZ, Apr94]

265-27 CT-39A 60-3499 [AMARC park code TG037]

265-28 CT-39A 60-3500 [AMARC park code TG030] [to Letourneau College, Longview, TX]

265-29 CT-39A 60-3501 [AMARC park code TG093]

265-30 CT-39A 60-3502 [AMARC park code TG095] [to Dr Robert Smirnow, E Northport, NY]

265-31 GCT-39A 60-3503 [preserved Air Classics Museum, Aurora, IL]

265-32 CT-39A 60-3504 [to Bi-States College, St Louis, MO, then to Wyoming Technical College, Oakland, CA; to Oakland Aviation Museum, CA]

265-33 T-39A 60-3505 [displayed Edwards Flight Test Museum, CA]

265-34 T-39A 60-3506 [w/o 09Feb74 Colorado, CO]

265-35 CT-39A 60-3507 [AMARC park code TG061] [West LA College, Los Angeles, CA marked as "0350" - painted as N3507W (these marks used on a PA-32)]

265-36 CT-39A 60-3508 [AMARC park code TG042] [believed b/u]

265-37 CT-39A 61-0634 [displayed Dyess AFB, TX]

265-38 CT-39A 61-0635 [AMARC park code TG054] [to Lafayette Regional A/P, LA]

265-39 CT-39A 61-0636 [AMARC park code TG089]

265-40 CT-39A 61-0637 [AMARC park code TG035]

265-41 CT-39A 61-0638 [AMARC park code TG096] [to Jett Paqueteria S.A. for parts use circa 2006 noted 14Apr06 Laredo TX]

265-42 CT-39A 61-0639 [AMARC park code TG086] N21092 [to Blackhawk Technical College, Janesville, WI]

265-43 T-39A 61-0640 [w/o 16Apr70 Halifax County A/P, NC (midair collision with a TA-4F)]

265-44 CT-39A 61-0641 [AMARC park code TG036] [to Rock Valley College, Rockford, IL]

265-45 CT-39A 61-0642 [AMARC park code TG045]

265-46 CT-39A 61-0643 [AMARC park code TG022]

265-47 T-39A 61-0644 [w/o 07May63 Andrews AFB, VA]

265-48 CT-39A 61-0645 [AMARC park code TG091] N6CF XA-TFL [w/o Culiacan, Mexico 05Jul07]

265-49 T-39A 61-0646 [w/o 14May75 10 miles north of Richmond, VA]

265-50 CT-39A 61-0647 [AMARC park code TG078] [to Coast Community College, Costa Mesa, CA]

265-51 CT-39A 61-0648 [AMARC park code TG017] [to scrapyard of West Intl Aviation,in 1993]

265-52 T-39A 61-0649 N1064 61-0649 [AMARC park code TG047; to Portland A/P Museum, OR regd N1064 to USAF]

265-53 CT-39A 61-0650 [AMARC park code TG043] [to Everett Community College, WA]

265-54 CT-39A 61-0651 [AMARC park code TG040] [to F.D Tech Florence Community College, SC]

265-55 CT-39A 61-0652 N4999H 61-0652 [AMARC park code TG087]

265-56 CT-39A 61-0653 [AMARC park code TG071] [to Community College of San Francisco, CA]

265-57 CT-39A 61-0654 [AMARC park code TG044] "N1ERAU" [to Jett Paqueteria S.A. for parts use circa 2006 noted 14Apr06 Laredo TX]

265-58 CT-39A 61-0655 [AMARC park code TG005] [sold 1992 to Av-mats, St Louis, MO; ex storage]

265-59 CT-39A 61-0656 [AMARC park code TG010]

265-60 CT-39A 61-0657 [AMARC park code TG023] [to Rice Aviation, Houston-Hobby, TX]

265-61 CT-39A 61-0658 [AMARC park code TG034] [to Frederick Community College, Frederick, MD; removed reportedly for XA- registry]

265-62 CT-39A 61-0659 [AMARC park code TG026] XA-TNP [w/o Culiacan, Mexico, 30Dec06]

265-63 T-39A 61-0660 [displayed McClellan AFB, CA]

265-64 T-39A 61-0661 [w/o 29Jul62 Paine Field-Seattle, WA]

## SABRE T-39 SERIES

| C/n | Series | Identities |
|---|---|---|
| 265-65 | CT-39A | 61-0662 [AMARC park code TG032] [b/u Spirit of St Louis, MO; remains to Clarkesville, MO, by 1993] |
| 265-66 | CT-39A | 61-0663 [AMARC park code TG067] [b/u nose/forward fuselage by firestation at New Orleans/Lakefront A/P, LA; removed by road late Apr01] |
| 265-67 | T-39A | 61-0664 [AMARC park code TG063] [to Deuel Vo-Tech Inst, Tracy, CA, 08Jun90; to Castle Air Museum, Atwater, CA, 05Dec07] |
| 265-68 | CT-39A | 61-0665 [AMARC park code TG028] |
| 265-69 | CT-39A | 61-0666 [AMARC park code TG014] |
| 265-70 | CT-39A | 61-0667 [AMARC park code TG088] N7143N [w/o Khartoum A/P, Sudan in either 1993 or 1994; to Fujairah, UAE minus wings & engines; noted Jan04] |
| 265-71 | CT-39A | 61-0668 [AMARC park code TG051] [believed b/u] |
| 265-72 | CT-39A | 61-0669 [AMARC park code TG075] [to Metro Tech Aviation Career Center, Oklahoma City, OK] |
| 265-73 | CT-39A | 61-0670 [operational Maxwell AFB, AL] |
| 265-74 | CT-39A | 61-0671 [AMARC park code TG090] [to ground trainer Keesler AFB, MS] |
| 265-75 | T-39A | 61-0672 [w/o 13Mar79 S Korea] |
| 265-76 | CT-39A | 61-0673 [AMARC park code TG038] N4313V XA-TJZ |
| 265-77 | CT-39A | 61-0674 [displayed Hill AFB, UT] |
| 265-78 | CT-39A | 61-0675 [displayed Yokota AFB, Japan; reported b/u circa 1998] |
| 265-79 | CT-39A | 61-0676 [AMARC park code TG049] |
| 265-80 | T-39A | 61-0677 N9166Y [at Helena Vocational Technical Center, Helena ND] |
| 265-81 | CT-39A | 61-0678 [AMARC park code TG012] |
| 265-82 | T-39A | 61-0679 [AMARC park code TG069] N6581E [at Spokane Community College, WA] |
| 265-83 | CT-39A | 61-0680 [AMARC park code TG039] N32010 [Central Missouri State University, MO; at Warrensburg, MO marked "1068"] |
| 265-84 | CT-39A | 61-0681 [at Michigan Institute of Aeronautics, Willow Run, Detroit, MI] |
| 265-85 | CT-39A | 61-0682 [AMARC park code TG031] [to Southwest Michigan College, Dowagiac, MI] |
| 265-86 | CT-39A | 61-0683 [AMARC park code TG025] N510TB XB-GDW XA-GDW [still current on USCAR as N510TB as well as being current on the Mexican Register] |
| 265-87 | T-39A | 61-0684 [scrapyard Davis-Monthan, AZ/"Bob's Air Park"; believed b/u] |
| 265-88 | T-39A | 61-0685 [preserved US Army Aviation Museum, Fort Rucker, AL] |
| | | |
| 270-1 | T-39B | 59-2873 [at Wright-Patterson AFB, OH] |
| 270-2 | T-39B | 59-2874 [AMARC park code TG103] |
| 270-3 | T-39B | 60-3474 [operational Edwards AFB, CA] |
| 270-4 | T-39B | 60-3475 [AMARC park code TG098] |
| 270-5 | T-39B | 60-3476 [AMARC park code TG102] |
| 270-6 | T-39B | 60-3477 [AMARC park code TG101] |
| | | |
| 276-1 | T-39A | 62-4448 [w/o 28Jan64 Erfurt, W Germany] |
| 276-2 | CT-39A | 62-4449 [AMARC park code TG092] [preserved Pima County Museum, Tucson, AZ] |
| 276-3 | CT-39A | 62-4450 [AMARC park code TG006] [to Jett Paqueteria S.A. for parts use circa 2006 noted 14Apr06 Laredo TX] |
| 276-4 | CT-39A | 62-4451 [AMARC park code TG060] N31403 XA-TQR |
| 276-5 | T-39A | 62-4452 [displayed Travis AFB, CA] |
| 276-6 | T-39A | 62-4453 N6552R XA-TGO |
| 276-7 | CT-39A | 62-4454 [AMARC park code TG018] |
| 276-8 | CT-39A | 62-4455 [AMARC park code TG065] N4314B XA-TJU [w/o Monterrey, Mexico, 19Dec06] |
| 276-9 | CT-39A | 62-4456 [AMARC park code TG056] [at Westwood College of Aviation Technology, Los Angeles, CA painted as N1965W] |
| 276-10 | CT-39A | 62-4457 [AMARC park code TG002] |
| 276-11 | T-39A | 62-4458 [w/o 25Mar65 Clark AFB, Philippines] |
| 276-12 | CT-39A | 62-4459 [AMARC park code TG041] [to Clover Park Vo-Tech, Tacoma, WA] |
| 276-13 | T-39A | 62-4460 [w/o 28Feb70 Torrejon AFB, Spain] |
| 276-14 | T-39A | 62-4461 [displayed Warner-Robins AFB, GA] |
| 276-15 | CT-39A | 62-4462 [AMARC park code TG046] |
| 276-16 | CT-39A | 62-4463 [AMARC park code TG100] |
| 276-17 | CT-39A | 62-4464 [AMARC park code TG004] [to Utah State University, Salt Lake City, UT] |
| 276-18 | T-39A | 62-4465 [preserved March AFB, CA] |
| 276-19 | CT-39A | 62-4466 [AMARC park code TG019] [to technical school at Detroit City airport, MI] |
| 276-20 | CT-39A | 62-4467 [AMARC park code TG083] [at GTCC Aviation Center, Greensboro, NC; wears fake marks 66866] |
| 276-21 | CT-39A | 62-4468 [AMARC park code TG020] N63611 XA-TIX |
| 276-22 | CT-39A | 62-4469 [AMARC park code TG064] [to Wyotech, Bedford, MA. Scrapped 2007] |
| 276-23 | CT-39A | 62-4470 [displayed Maxwell AFB, AL] |
| 276-24 | CT-39A | 62-4471 [displayed Ramstein AFB, W Germany] |
| 276-25 | CT-39A | 62-4472 [AMARC park code TG011] N39RG XA-... |
| 276-26 | CT-39A | 62-4473 [AMARC park code TG029] [forward fuselage at Greater St Louis Aviation Museum, St Louis, MO] |
| 276-27 | CT-39A | 62-4474 [AMARC park code TG027] XB-GDV N510TC XA-TDX |
| 276-28 | CT-39A | 62-4475 [AMARC park code] [noted flying during 1991 ex storage at AMARC; at Technical College, Milwaukee, WI, 14Sep92] |
| 276-29 | T-39A | 62-4476 [AMARC park code TG099] |
| 276-30 | CT-39A | 62-4477 [AMARC park code TG048] [to Milwaukee Technical College, WI] |
| 276-31 | T-39A | 62-4478 [preserved USAF Museum Wright-Patterson AFB, OH] |

## SABRE T-39 SERIES

| C/n | Series | Identities |
|---|---|---|
| 276-32 | CT-39A | 62-4479 [AMARC park code TG052] N988MT [to Metro-Tech Aviation Center, Oklahoma, OK] |
| 276-33 | CT-39A | 62-4480 [AMARC park code TG068] N24480 N39FS |
| 276-34 | CT-39A | 62-4481 N33UT [to University of Tennessee, Tullahoma, TN] N741MT [to Middle Tennessee State University, Murfreesboro, TN, 2006] |
| 276-35 | CT-39A | 62-4482 [displayed Kelly AFB, TX, then to AMARC 30Jan04, park code AATG0107] |
| 276-36 | CT-39A | 62-4483 [AMARC park code TG055] [to Indian Hills Community College, IA] |
| 276-37 | T-39A | 62-4484 [displayed Kadena AFB, Japan] |
| 276-38 | CT-39A | 62-4485 [displayed Yokota AFB, Japan] |
| 276-39 | CT-39A | 62-4486 [AMARC park code TG050] N265WB XA-TJY |
| 276-40 | CT-39A | 62-4487 [displayed SAC Museum site midway between Lincoln & Omaha, NB] |
| 276-41 | CT-39A | 62-4488 [operational Andrews AFB, MD] |
| 276-42 | CT-39A | 62-4489 [AMARC park code TG074] N65618 [to Colorado Northwestern Community College, Rangely, CO; cx Sep95; status?] |
| 276-43 | CT-39A | 62-4490 [AMARC park code TG079] [to Jett Paqueteria S.A. for parts use circa 2006 noted 14Apr06 Laredo TX] |
| 276-44 | CT-39A | 62-4491 [AMARC park code TG081] N63811 XA-TIW |
| 276-45 | CT-39A | 62-4492 [painted as N1SJ with San Jose University's Avn Dept, San Jose Airport, CA (the real N1SJ used by Cessna 310 (U-3) s/n 57-5856)] |
| 276-46 | CT-39A | 62-4493 [AMARC park code TG076] [believed b/u] |
| 276-47 | CT-39A | 62-4494 [displayed Chanute ALB, IL] |
| 276-48 | CT-39A | 62-4495 [AMARC park code TG059] N6612S N1929P [to college in Yunlin, Taiwan] |
| 276-49 | CT-39A | 62-4496 [w/o 20Apr85 Scranton/Wilkes Barre, PA] |
| 276-50 | CT-39A | 62-4497 [AMARC park code TG053] [to Wyotech, Bedford, MA] "N15EC" |
| 276-51 | CT-39A | 62-4498 [AMARC park code TG080] [to Salt Lake City Community College, UT] |
| 276-52 | CT-39A | 62-4499 [w/o 24Jun69 McCook, NB] |
| 276-53 | CT-39A | 62-4500 [AMARC park code TG070] [to Milwaukee Area Technical College, WI] |
| 276-54 | CT-39A | 62-4501 [AMARC park code TG073] [to O'Fallon Technical College, St Louis, MO] |
| 276-55 | T-39A | 62-4502 [w/o 31Dec68 Langley AFB, VA] |
| | | |
| 277-1 | T-39D | 150542 [stored China Lake NWC, CA] |
| 277-2 | T-39D | 150543 [AMARC park code 7T-027] (N960M) (XA-AAG) |
| 277-3 | T-39D | 150544 [code F18] [AMARC park code 7T-006] |
| 277-4 | T-39D | 150545 [wfu and b/u] |
| 277-5 | T-39D | 150546 [code F201] [AMARC park code 7T-014] |
| 277-6 | T-39D | 150547 [code F211] [AMARC park code 7T-021] (N959M) (XA-AAI) |
| 277-7 | T-39D | 150548 [code F10] [AMARC park code 7T-008] (N956M) (XA-AAF) |
| 277-8 | T-39D | 150549 [code F11] [AMARC park code 7T-011] |
| 277-9 | T-39D | 150550 [at Pensacola NAS, FL] |
| 277-10 | T-39D | 150551 [AMARC park code 7T-002] [believed b/u] |
| | | |
| 285-1 | T-39D | 150969 [AMARC park code 7T-026] (N957M) (XA-AAJ) |
| 285-2 | T-39D | 150970 N431NA [cx Dec91; wfu and b/u] |
| 285-3 | T-39D | 150971 [AMARC park code 7T-001] [believed b/u] |
| 285-4 | T-39D | 150972 [at Pensacola NAS, FL] |
| 285-5 | T-39D | 150973 [code F203] [AMARC park code 7T-013] |
| 285-6 | T-39D | 150974 [code F204] [AMARC park code 7T-015] |
| 285-7 | T-39D | 150975 [code F12] [AMARC park code 7T-007] |
| 285-8 | T-39D | 150976 [code F205] [AMARC park code 7T-016] |
| 285-9 | T-39D | 150977 [at Pensacola NAS, FL] |
| 285-10 | T-39D | 150978 [code F218] [AMARC park code 7T-009] |
| 285-11 | T-39D | 150979 [code F206] [AMARC park code 7T-017] |
| 285-12 | T-39D | 150980 [code F14] [AMARC park code 7T-004] |
| 285-13 | T-39D | 150981 [AMARC park code 7T-012] [believed b/u] |
| 285-14 | T-39D | 150982 [code F219] [AMARC park code 7T-022] |
| 285-15 | T-39D | 150983 [code F212] [AMARC park code 7T-023] |
| 285-16 | T-39D | 150984 [code F208] [AMARC park code 7T-010] |
| 285-17 | T-39D | 150985 N32508 [preserved Pensacola, FL] |
| 285-18 | T-39D | 150986 [displayed Warner-Robins AFB, GA] |
| 285-19 | T-39D | 150987 [preserved NAS Patuxent River, MD] |
| 285-20 | T-39D | 150988 [code F209] [AMARC park code 7T-005] |
| 285-21 | T-39D | 150989 [stored China Lake NWC, CA] |
| 285-22 | T-39D | 150990 [code F213] [AMARC park code 7T-024] |
| 285-23 | T-39D | 150991 [code F17] [AMARC park code 7T-003] |
| 285-24 | T-39D | 150992 [active at China Lake NWC, CA circa May97] |
| 285-25 | T-39D | 151336 [code F214] [AMARC park code 7T-025] (N961M) (XA-AAH) |
| 285-26 | T-39D | 151337 [at Pensacola NAS, FL] |
| 285-27 | T-39D | 151338 [preserved Southern Museum of Flight, Birmingham, AL] |
| 285-28 | T-39D | 151339 [preserved US Naval Aviation Museum, NAS Pensacola, FL] |
| 285-29 | T-39D | 151340 [code F216] [AMARC park code 7T-018] [wfu to DMI scrapyard at AMARC] |
| 285-30 | T-39D | 151341 [code F217] [AMARC park code 7T-019] |
| 285-31 | T-39D | 151342 [AMARC park code TG-097] [to Milwaukee Area Technical College, WI] |
| 285-32 | T-39D | 151343 [dumped NAS Pensacola, FL; believed b/u] |

Production complete

AMARC indicates aircraft at Aerospace Maintenance and Regeneration Center, Davis-Monthan, AZ

# SABRE 40

| C/n | Series | Identities |
|---|---|---|
| 282-1 | R | N7820C N177A N766R XC-OAH XC-JCK (N351JM) N116SC |
| 282-2 | T-39N | N577R N577PM N100WF N108W N108U N57GS N67WW N16TA N304NT US Navy 165512 |
| 282-3 | | N570R (N57QR) N467H [wfu Van Nuys A/P, CA, circa 2002; parted out] |
| 282-4 | | N6358C N14M N75JD N111MS N408TR [cx Sep03; in use as instructional airframe by Toledo Public Schools, OH] |
| 282-5 | | N30W [w/o 21Dec67 Perryville, MO] |
| 282-6 | | N6360C N600R XB-HHF XA-SBS XA-GYR XA-UCS [w/o Mexico City 05Jul06] |
| 282-7 | | N6361C N360J N576R N1102D N43NR N101US N43NR N122RP XA-SEN XB-EZV XA-STU N706A [wfu; b/u Opa-Locka, FL] |
| 282-8 | | N6362C N520S N366N N369N N140MM [wfu Sep93 and parted out; cx Nov96] |
| 282-9 | T-39N | N6363C N620M N620K N327JB (N327RH) N329SS N301NT US Navy 165509 |
| 282-10 | | N6364C N525N N9503Z [w/o 07Mar73 Blaine, MN] |
| 282-11 | | N6365C N167H N167G N73PC N10SL [wfu for spares & b/u Fort Lauderdale Executive, FL; cx Jun03] |
| 282-12 | | N6366C N905M N888PM N368DA N107CJ [wfu Opa-Locka, FL; cx Mar97] |
| 282-13 | | N6367C N899TG N408S N408CS N408CC XA-SMP N502RR XA-TKW |
| 282-14 | | N6368C N2009 N31BC N31BQ N30BE (N30PN) [b/u during 1986; remains at Clarkesville, MO] |
| 282-15 | | N6369C N106G N1062 N32BC N32BQ (N19MS) N40SE N21PF N43W N43WL |
| 282-16 | | N6370C N227SW N227S N40GP N41GS [b/u for spares Miami A/P, FL during 1989] |
| 282-17 | | N6371C N911Q N382RF N392F N900CS XA-HOK [wfu; remains at Clarkesville, MO] |
| 282-18 | | N6372C N107G N1072 N113SC N15TS N131BH [cx 02May07; b/u] |
| 282-19 | R/T-39N | N6373C N881MC N881MD N100CE N100OE (N40R) N311NT US Navy 165519 |
| 282-20 | T-39N | N6374C N265R N3298D N40YA (N282AM) N315NT/US Navy 165523 [wears dual marks] |
| 282-21 | | N6375C N168H N168D N87CM [wfu Clarkesville, MO; still regd; to spares 1992] |
| 282-22 | | N6376C N747 N747E [w/o 21Dec94 Buenos Aires-Aeroparque, Argentina; to spares at Buenos Aires-Don Torcuato] |
| 282-23 | | N6377C N282NA N8400B N800M N80QM N301HA N50TX (N265AC) N123CD (N55ME) |
| 282-24 | | N6378C N720J N360Q N40DW N8AF XA-... |
| 282-25 | | N6379C HB-VAK I-SNAK N40SJ I-NICK [wfu; to White Inds, Bates City, MO for spares Oct98] |
| 282-26 | | N6380C N60Y N6087 N737E N153G N300CH XA-RED XA-DAN [as these marks are being used on HS125 c/n 25158 this may still be XA-RED with latter marks only reserved, or reported in error] |
| 282-27 | | N6381C N720R N129GP N129GB N111EA N61RH [wfu Oct93 to College of Technology, Tulsa Int'l A/P, OK] |
| 282-28 | T-39N | N6382C N6565A N6565K N524AC N524AG N27DA N197DA N40CD N482HC N314NT US Navy 165522 [w/o Gulf of Mexico 08May02 in mid-air collision with 165525 c/n 282-100] |
| 282-29 | T-39N | N6383C N910E N170JL N170AL N170DD N303NT US Navy 165511 |
| 282-30 | T-39N | N6384C N526N N7090 N709Q N801MS N306NT US Navy 165514 |
| 282-31 | | N23G N236Y N800Y N700R N577VM N34AM [wfu; to spares 1993 Spirit of St Louis, MO; remains with Fire Service at Springfield Airport, IL] |
| 282-32 | T-39N | N100Y N100HC N711UC N40SL N40WP N8GA N456JP N312NT US Navy 165520 |
| 282-33 | | N737R N903K N903KB N168W |
| 282-34 | | N6389C N575R N5PC N5PQ N400CS N940CC [reported wfu] |
| 282-35 | | N6390C N341AP N341AR N567DW [b/u circa 1985; remains to Clarkesville, MO; still regd] |
| 282-36 | | N6391C N1903W N1908W N22BN N59PK N59K N59KQ N63A N88JM N200MP N40LB [report wfu at Fort Lauderdale Executive A/P, FL] |
| 282-37 | | N6392C N265W N77AP [w/o 07Nov77 New Orleans, LA] |
| 282-38 | | N6393C N2997 N299LR N100FS (N68AA) N999VT N921JG N339PM |
| 282-39 | R | N6394C N442A N947R N333B XA-BAF (N4492V) XA-RGC XA-RTM XA-PIC [wfu Toluca, Mexico] |
| 282-40 | | N6395C N738R N715MR N40BP [wfu Oct93; parted out Clarkesville, MO; remains form part of MonstroCity exhibit at City Museum, St Louis, MO] |
| 282-41 | | N6396C N661P N300RC N300RG N707JM N57RM (N300TK) (N116AC) N240AC XB-AYJ [impounded Panama City Balboa/Paitilla, Panama, Dec01] |
| 282-42 | | N6397C N727R N904K N904KB (N61FC) N40EL N500RK N50CD [w/o 03Feb90 Detroit, MI; cx Oct91; remains to Spirit of St Louis A/P, MO 1995] |
| 282-43 | R | N6398C N730R XA-JUD N4469F Ecuador 043 |
| 282-44 | | N6399C N4567 N1DC N1QC N44NP N600JS N64MA |
| 282-45 | | N6552C N747UP N344UP N255GM N333GM N333NM |
| 282-46 | CT-39E | N6553C N339NA 157352 [w/o 21Dec75 Alameda AFB, CA] |
| 282-47 | | N740R N34W [w/o 04Jan74 Midland, TX] |
| 282-48 | R | N6555C N747R N90GM (N153G) XA-JUE N4469M XA-CPQ N4469M XA-RGC N47VL |
| 282-49 | | N6556C N757R N905K N905KB Sweden 86001 |

## SABRE 40

| C/n | Series | Identities |
|---|---|---|
| 282-50 | | N6557C N757E N956 N956CC XA-SMQ N282CA [wfu Spirit of St Louis, MO circa early 2000, still wearing previous identity XA-SMQ; b/u; cx 24Jul08] |
| 282-51 | | N733R N108G N108X N227LS N225LS (N51MN) [noted 31Aug91 wfu Spirit of St Louis A/P, MO; remains to Elsberry, MO] |
| 282-52 | R | N7502V N200A N2000 N2004 N40R N77MR (N77MK) N303A N282MC N64DH |
| 282-53 | | N7503V N999BS N123MS N101T N62K N62Q (ZS-GSB) ZS-PTJ N67201 N600BP N555PT [cx Jan91; b/u 1989; fuselage at Spirit of St.Louis A/P, MO] |
| 282-54 | | N7504V N255CT N256CT XA-EEU [w/o 1980 ground accident in Mexico] |
| 282-55 | | N7505V N2007 N353WB N353WC N68HC N68HQ N221PH (N221PX) [b/u during 1986; cx Feb91; fuselage to Spirit of St.Louis A/P, MO circa Aug00] |
| 282-56 | | N7506V N322CS N10CC N722ST N722FD (N722ED) N204TM N85DA XA-RPS [reported wfu] |
| 282-57 | | N7507V N27C N545C N1909R N1909D [to spares at Spirit of St Louis A/P, MO circa May97] |
| 282-58 | | N7508V N1101G N110FS [wfu; remains at Spirit of St.Louis A/P, MO circa Oct00; cx Sep01] |
| 282-59 | | N7509V N48WS N48WP (N2SN) N17LT XA-ESR N465S N40SE N43CF [wfu for spares Oct94 Perryville, MO; cx Aug95] |
| 282-60 | T-39N | N7510V N903G N66TP N22TP N256MA N256EN N256EA N555AE N555AB N141H N316NT US Navy 165524 [w/o northwest Georgia, USA, 10Jan06] |
| 282-61 | T-39N | N550L N550LL N231A XA-RGC XA-EGC N2568S (N60WL) N33TW N309NT US Navy 165517 |
| 282-62 | | N1863T [cx Sep87, wfu] |
| 282-63 | | N325K XA-AFW XB-IHB |
| 282-64 | | N7514V N9000V N9000S N800CS [b/u 1986; cx Feb90] |
| 282-65 | | N2232B N145G XA-GGR XA-MJE |
| 282-66 | T-39N | N2233B N355MJ N4943A N737R N40NR N40HC N48TC N54CF N98CF N305NT US Navy 165513 |
| 282-67 | A | N2234B N711T N140RF |
| 282-68 | R | N2235B N788R N801NC N22MY N22MV N60RB XA-LEL N4469N Ecuador 068 [w/o 03Jun88 Quito A/P, Ecuador] |
| 282-69 | | N2236B N125N N256MA N125NL N1MN N43NR N777V N777VZ N49RJ [canx 09Dec04; b/u] |
| 282-70 | | N2236C N377P N874AJ N111AB N654E N22CH N70SL N17LT N34LP N3280G [impounded for many years in Commander Mexicana hangar, Mexico City, Mexico; current status not known] |
| 282-71 | | N2239B N957 N957CC XA-SMR [dbr Saltillo, Mexico, 30Jun07] |
| 282-72 | T-39N | N744R (N880HL) (N69CG) N78GP N986JB N307NT US Navy 165515 |
| 282-73 | | N630M N630N [cx Jun85; b/u for spares; remains at Spirit of St.Louis A/P, MO circa Oct00] |
| 282-74 | | N2241B N572R N707TG N707FH [b/u and cx Nov02] |
| 282-75 | | N2241C N48CG (N48CE) [b/u 1983; (the marks N48CE were reserved Jan88 but ntu) remains to Clarkesville, MO] |
| 282-76 | | N2242B N474VW D-CAVW N787R N124H N415CS N415GS N350E N58025 N8345K N265CM N257TM [b/u circa May02, cx Jun02] |
| 282-77 | T-39N | N2244B N608S N608AR N189AR N96CM N27KG N310NT US Navy 165518 |
| 282-78 | | N739R [w/o 16May67 Ventura, CA] |
| 282-79 | | N2248C N797R N701NC N35CC N111AC XA-CYS |
| 282-80 | | N2249B N36050 N360E N40JF N40WH XA-FTN XB-JGI |
| 282-81 | T-39N | N2250B N36065 N360N N99CR N416CS N1GY N302NT US Marines 165510 |
| 282-82 | | N574R N736R N713MR (N777ST) N19MS N366DA XB-EQR N39RG |
| 282-83 | | N726R N642LR N232T N160TC N82ML [wfu for spares c Oct94 Clarkesville, MO; cx Mar95] |
| 282-84 | CT-39E | N2254B 157353 [code 353RW] [AMARC park code 7T-028] |
| 282-85 | CT-39E | N2255B 157354 N958M XA-AAW [substantial damage 02Jun03 in hanger collapse at Laredo, TX still wearing 157354] |
| 282-86 | | N86 [cx Sep92; wfu; stored in bare metal Oklahoma City, OK, no marks visible] |
| 282-87 | | N87 N36P N399P [at Pittsburgh Inst of Aeronautics, PA] |
| 282-88 | | N88 [cx Dec93; at Hampton University/Hughes Training Inc Aero Science Center at Newport News, VA] |
| 282-89 | | N89 [cx Oct91; b/u for spares] |
| 282-90 | T-39N | N2569B N928R CF-NCG C-FNCG N3831C N155GM N362DA N308NT US Navy 165516 |
| 282-91 | | N9500B N5511A N5511Z N66ES N40NR Sweden 86002 |
| 282-92 | CT-39E | N2676B 158382 N825SB |
| 282-93 | CT-39E | N4701N 158381 [w/o during 1991 nr Spratley Islands, S China Sea] |
| 282-94 | T-39N | N4703N N16R N216R N6TE N147CF N40TA N313NT US Navy 165521 |
| 282-95 | CT-39E | N4704N 158380 N425NA 158380 |
| 282-96 | CT-39E | N4705N 158383 [wfu; to Dodson International Parts, KS circa 2004] |
| 282-97 | | N4706N N85 [w/o 14Jan76 Recife, Brazil] |
| 282-98 | A | N4707N N40SC N516WP N516LW N767JH YV416T |
| 282-99 | A | N7594N N78TC N22CH N400GM N100FG N12BW [parted out by AvMATS, St Louis, MO] |
| 282-100 | A/T-39N | N19HF N82CF XA-LEG N71325 (N302NT) N317NT US Navy 165525 [w/o Gulf of Mexico 08May02 in mid-air collision with 165522 c/n 282-28] |

# SABRE 40

| C/n | Series | Identities |
|---|---|---|
| 282-101 | A | N7596N N1BX N111XB N101RR N160W |
| 282-102 | A | N7597N N2WR N800DC N74MG N74MJ (N157AT) XA-PIH XB-JKV XA-UGB |
| 282-103 | A | N7598N N44P N9MS N217A N217TE N217E N730CA N730CP |
| 282-104 | A | N40CH N78BC N99XR N100KS N26SC N26SE N925BL XA-SEU N104SL [b/u; cx 24Jul08] |
| 282-105 | A | N2HW N2QW N22BJ N312K N921JG XA-SCN XC-AA73 [noted derelict at Mexico City, Mexico in Jan03] |
| 282-106 | A | N7595N XB-DUS XA-RKG (N22NB) N333GM N854RB YV-1144CP YV120T |
| 282-107 | A | N7584N N40NR CF-BRL [w/o 27Feb74 Frobisher Bay, Canada] |
| 282-108 | A | N7596N N442WT N442WP N306CW N85CC N8500 |
| 282-109 | A | N4NP N700CF N93AC N77AT Ecuador 047 |
| 282-110 | A | N7597N N477X N477A N250EC [at Entebbe, Uganda after suffering gunfire in Democratic Republic of Congo circa May03; canx 04Jun04 as w/o] |
| 282-111 | A | N7662N N9NR XA-SAG N32654 N213BM (N200CK) (N431DA) (N246GS) N7KG |
| 282-112 | A | N7667N N6789 N6789D N301PC N306PC N55MT N164DA N74MB N164DA N164DN N40ZA XA-UBG XA-UEY |
| 282-113 | A | N8311N N40SC N40BT N30AF N430MB N430MP |
| 282-114 | A | N64MC N64MG XA-ATC XC-SUB XA-ATC (N7SL) XB-RGS XB-RGO XB-MDG |
| 282-115 | A | N8333N N376D N376DD N376RP XA-MNA XA-GCH XA-LML |
| 282-116 | A | N4PH XB-BBL [noted Jan03 wfu at Toluca, Mexico] |
| 282-117 | A | N8338N (HB-VCZ) I-MORA N1WZ Mexico TP108/XC-UJH N3159U N265SC (N298AS) |
| 282-118 | A | N8339N PT-JNJ N19BG [wfu Aug93 still as PT-JNJ; to spares c Oct94 Clarkesville, MO; cx Aug95] |
| 282-119 | A | N8341N N5565 [w/o 15Jan74 Oklahoma City, OK] |
| 282-120 | A | N73HP N73DR YV225T |
| 282-121 | A | N8349N PP-SED [fuselage to Spirit of St.Louis A/p, MO circa Sep97] |
| 282-122 | A | N40JW N188PS "N409GL" N188PS N409GL [parted out] |
| 282-123 | A | N8350N XA-APD XB-ESS |
| 282-124 | A | N193AT N200E N2006 N40JE N20ES N70ES XA-TYZ |
| 282-125 | A | N8356N XB-NIB XA-SQA |
| 282-126 | A | N40NS XA-SNI N40GT |
| 282-127 | A | N110PM N183AR N63SL OB-T-1319 OB-1319 [w/o 03Sep93 Buenos Aires, Argentina; remains to Opa-Locka, FL] |
| 282-128 | A | N99AP XA-LIX N99114 XB-JPS |
| 282-129 | A | N75W N75WA N75MD (N99FF) XA-RLH |
| 282-130 | A | N33LB N44NR XC-SRA Mexico TP107 Mexico TP105/XC-UJG XC-HEY Mexico TP105/XC-UJI XC-PGE XA-REG XC-AA51 |
| 282-131 | A | N9251N N3BM N3QM N82R LV-WND |
| 282-132 | A | N9252N N28TP N70BC N240CF N240JR |
| 282-133 | A | N65740 N41NR I-RELT |
| 282-134 | A | N40NR N60RC (YV-64CP) N66CD XA-MVG XB-MVG N134JJ N40NJ |
| 282-135 | A | N4GV N777SL N7778L N55PP N820JR N200E N2006 (N67BK) |
| 282-136 | A | N44PH N211SF N112ML CP-2317 N68ML* |
| 282-137 | A | N65763 N5511A N5512A N53WC N9NR N87CR N870R N881DM XA-LMA |

Production complete

Note: The following T-39N aircraft "converted" by Sabreliner Corp for use in US Navy training contract had the serials applied as shown above, while still current on the USCAR

282-2, 282-9, 282-19, 282-20, 282-28, 282-29, 282-30, 282-32, 282-60, 282-61, 282-66, 282-72, 282-77, 282-81, 282-90, 282-94 and 282-100

# SABRE 60

| C/n | Series | Identities |
|---|---|---|
| 306-1 | | N306NA N978R N521N N571NC XA-REC N359WJ |
| 306-2 | | N307NA N968R N22MA N277CT N2710T N666BR XA-PUR N36RZ |
| 306-3 | | N177A N1001G N925Z N61MD N424R N160CF LV-WPO [w/o 16Jly98 Cordoba, Argentina] |
| 306-4 | | N4709N N178W N1210 N121JE |
| 306-5 | A | N365N N302H N7090 OO-IBS N7090 (N477JM) N161CM [parted out by White Inds, Bates City, MO; cx 29Apr09] |
| 306-6 | A | N4712N N662P N662F N311RM XA-HHR XA-ADC XA-SMF XB-IYS |
| 306-7 | | N4715N N523N N63NC N531NC N30PY N60GH N60EX N60CR N64AM XA-SND XB-HDL XB-KPC |
| 306-8 | | N4716N N73G N73GR N361DA N84LP N613BR N813BR [wfu] |
| 306-9 | | N4717N N47MN N998R N958R N1298 N32UT N5071L N4LG [to Greenville Technical College, SC, as instructional airframe] |
| 306-10 | | N4720N N30W N9000V N9001V N19CM N125MC N946JR [being parted out at Paynesville, MO circa early 2000] |
| 306-11 | | N4721N N723R N743R [w/o 13Apr73 Montrose, CO] |
| 306-12 | | N4722R N90N N9QN N18N N900P XA-ACE XA-CCB XC-HHL XC-AA26 [to spares following flood damage reportedly in 1994; fuselage at Festus, MO, circa Apr96] |
| 306-13 | | N4723N N60Y N555SL N33BC N33BQ (N256MT) N60EL N306CF RA-3077K RF-14423 |
| 306-14 | | N4724N N24G N24GB (N60AG) N24GB N1JN N43GB N60JN [wfu; fuselage at Festus, MO, circa Apr96] |
| 306-15 | | N4725N N101L N60BK N360CH N221PH N221PF XA-RUQ N604MK N600SJ [rebuilt with spares from c/n 306-16; canx 06Apr06 as b/u] |
| 306-16 | A | N4726N N787R N5415 (N542S) N7090 N967R N100PW N160RW N105UA N33UT N38UT N5075L [b/u for spares Sep92 Spirit of St Louis apt, MO; remains to Clarkesville, MO; canx May95; fully parted out by 2001] |
| 306-17 | | N4727N (D-COUP) N988R N2UP N2UR N13SL N401MS [has been parted out] |
| 306-18 | | N4728N N908R N339GW N18HH N36HH (N60RL) N11AQ N12PB N29PB XA-... |
| 306-19 | | N4729N N918R N8000U N50DG [to spares Perryville, MO; cx Jan99] |
| 306-20 | | N4730N N938R N330U N22JW N44SB N78JP N55BP N155EC XA-PEI N155EC XA-REI XA-TLL XC-AAJ XA-UJW |
| 306-21 | | N4731N N948R N442A N60HC XB-LRD XB-QND XC-AAC |
| 306-22 | | N4732N N746UP N743UP (N450CE) XA-CHP |
| 306-23 | | N4733N N908R CF-BLT C-FBLT N15RF N77AT N68MA N85HS N616TR |
| 306-24 | A | N4734N N958R N5419 N300TB N58JM N990AC (N995RD) N600GL (N600GE) |
| 306-25 | | N4735N N210F N212F N47MM (N613E) N60DL N60DE OB-1550 N60DE LV-WOF [derelict at San Fernando, Argentina by Nov01] |
| 306-26 | | N4736N N644X N323R N71CD N31CJ (N377EM) XA-CEN |
| 306-27 | | N4737N N978R I-SNAD N11AL N888WL N105DM (N777CR) (N55ME) (N105SS) N103TA |
| 306-28 | | N741R N741RL N353CA [wfu] |
| 306-29 | | N4741N N3000 N3008 N995 N3008 N771WW [cx Jan95 as destroyed reportedly on 10Jan95 - cabin fire at Lexington-Blue Grass Airport, KY; to White Inds, Bates City, MO] N771WB [for spares use; cx Aug98] |
| 306-30 | | N4742N N905R N905BG N2440G N2440C N1116A N104SS [wfu Fort Lauderdale, FL; for spares; to White Inds, Bates City, MO] |
| 306-31 | | N307D N274CA |
| 306-32 | | N4743N N3278 [parted out at Spirit of St Louis, MO circa early 2000; cx Sep01] |
| 306-33 | | N4745N N600B XB-APD XA-APD N3FC N30TC N711TW N60JF (N660BW) N78RR N500RR N399SR HC-BQT CC-CGT N633SL |
| 306-34 | | N4746N N3533 N747RC XA-VIO Mexico MTX-02 Mexico MTX-01 Mexico MTX-04 Mexico AMT-203 |
| 306-35 | | N4748N N3456B XB-JMR |
| 306-36 | | N4749N N918R N18N N90R N436CC XA-RIR [wfu by 2006 Toluca, Mexico] |
| 306-37 | | N4750N N4S N4SE (N60EX) N562R [canx 23May05 as b/u] |
| 306-38 | | N4751N N253MZ N251MA N229LS N230A XA-PEK XA-DCO XC-HGY |
| 306-39 | | N4752N N10PF N888MC N507TF N747UP N745UP XA-RTH XA-SLH N82197 (N39SL) [to spares Sep97 at Spirit of St.Louis, MO still as XA-SLH; marks N82197 cx Jun00 as b/u] |
| 306-40 | | N4753N N907R N711WK N1UP N1UT N997ME XA-SBX N306SA [wfu] |
| 306-41 | | N4754N N925R N173A N1909R (N8909R) N614MM LV-WLX (N62DW) N856MA [reported destroyed in unknown circumstances in early 2003 in Democratic Republic of Congo; cx Aug03] |
| 306-42 | | N4755N N915R N80L N58CG N60EL N120JC N128JC XA-VEL |
| 306-43 | | N4757N N5420 N6NR N6NP N6NE N60AH N10UM N115CR |
| 306-44 | | N4760N D-CEVW N111VW N45RS N86Y N60RS (N83RH) N129KH HC-BQU N562MS [parted out by AvMATS, St Louis, MO] |
| 306-45 | | N4763N N742R N742K N169RF [w/o 07Nov92 Phoenix-Sky Harbor A/P, AZ; cx Jan95] |
| 306-46 | | N4764N N3600X N100FL N100FN N642RP [reported to spares use circa 2003] |
| 306-47 | A | N4765N N927R XB-ZUM XA-ZUM XA-ZOM XB-ESX XB-CVS |
| 306-48 | | N7519N N938R N234U N284U N60AG N75HP N86HP N4228A N4NT |
| 306-49 | | N7522N N29S N29SX N645CC XA-POR XA-RNR [reported wfu 1991] |
| 306-50 | | N7529N N948R N100Y XA-VIT XA-MUL XB-FSZ N601GL |
| 306-51 | | N7531N N928R C-GDCC N141JA N60JC |

# SABRE 60

| C/n | Series | Identities |
|---|---|---|
| 306-52 | CT-39G | N7571N N955R 158843 [AMARC park code 7T031; to Mojave, CA by Oct98] |
| 306-53 | | N7573N N957R N99AA N963WL N963WA N624FA N48MG N68TA N999KG (N999LG) N699RD [canx 26Jly05 as b/u] |
| 306-54 | | N7574N N370VS N1020P N38JM N100EU N38JM N33TR N97SC N610RA |
| 306-55 | CT-39G | N7575N N908R N5419 158844 [AMARC with park code 7T034] 158844 |
| 306-56 | | N7576N N935R N14M N19M N19U XA-CMN XA-RXP XA-DSC |
| 306-57 | | N7577N N937R N7NR N53G N22EH N122EH N701FW N465JH XA-RLS [noted at Toluca, Mexico Jan02, wfu] |
| 306-58 | | N7578N N80E N80ER N1MN N1PN N529SC N529SQ N529CF XA-AGT |
| 306-59 | | N945R N20G N20GX N10LX |
| 306-60 | | N947R N115L N31BC N555RR N15H N15HF [modified to act as flying testbed for the Williams EJ22 engine in 2002] |
| 306-61 | | N965R N961R (N1VC) N76GT N1JN N1JX [instructional airframe at Battle Creek, MI, since Nov04] |
| 306-62 | | N967R N66NR N7090 N905R N905P N32BC N62CF N162JB [b/u circa 2001] |
| 306-63 | | N978R XB-BIP XA-CIS XA-ABC XA-LRA XB-FST XB-FUZ XA-FNP XB-ZNP XA-TSS |
| 306-64 | | N8357N N21BM N370L N1024G (N500RK) N96CP N74BS [a/c dismantled, fuselage noted at Spirit of St Louis, MO 08Dec02] |
| 306-65 | CT-39G | N8364N 159361 [reported wfu Sigonella, Italy 1992] |
| 306-66 | CT-39G | N8365N 159362 [AMARC park code 7T032] |
| 306-67 | CT-39G | 159363 [wfu; dumped Jan97 Edwards AFB, CA circa 1996] |
| 306-68 | | N8000 N2HW N2HX N265DP Ecuador 049 |
| 306-69 | CT-39G | 159364 [AMARC with park code 7T-030] [returned to service circa 2000] 159364 |
| 306-70 | CT-39G | 159365 |
| 306-71 | A | N31BM N370M N1028Y N71CC |
| 306-72 | | N231CA N231A N550SL N6TM N60TM XA-RYD N97SC XA-GIH XA-PRO |
| 306-73 | | N65745 N7NR N601MG N90EC XC-OAH XA-TNW N442RM |
| 306-74 | | N920G [w/o 27Dec74 Lancaster, PA] |
| 306-75 | | N110G N666WL N709AB N509AB N11LX |
| 306-76 | | N65750 N67NR N333PC N333NC N82MW N86CP (N760SA) |
| 306-77 | | N65751 N180AR N787R [wfu; to spares 1994 Spirit of St Louis A/P, MO; cx Apr95] |
| 306-78 | | N65752 C-GRRS N140JA N477X [b/u; cx 24Jul08] |
| 306-79 | | N4NR N4NE N768DV (N7682V) N43JG N539PG [parted out by White Inds, Bates City, MO] |
| 306-80 | | N65756 PT-KOT N61FB |
| 306-81 | A | N6NR N6ND N30CC [wfu; to spares circa Oct94; remains to Av-Mats Clarkville, MO; cx Jan96] |
| 306-82 | | N65759 N60SL N59K |
| 306-83 | | N14CG N14CQ N411MD N300YM N99FF XA-RLL XB-KQY |
| 306-84 | | N65762 PT-KOU N8025X N383TS N55ZM N265GM [wfu; cx 19Jun09] |
| 306-85 | | N65764 N217A N500RK N355CD N855CD N211BR [dbr by fire-suppressant foam 2007 Mojave, CA] |
| 306-86 | | N65765 N60SL N60TG XA-ICK XB-KSL |
| 306-87 | | N65767 N100CE N60RS N100MA N400CE N200CE XA-RFB |
| 306-88 | | N65769 N992 N22CG XA-RAP |
| 306-89 | | N65770 N23DS N86RM XA-ECM N86RM XA-STI [wfu by 2006 Toluca, Mexico] |
| 306-90 | | N65772 N181AR N13SL N148JP N123FG N265MK XB-FMB |
| 306-91 | | N65774 N204R N204G N60BP N660RM (N45MM) LV-WXX |
| 306-92 | | N65775 N711S N328JS N74AB N33JW |
| 306-93 | | N65777 N366N N182AR N200CX N507U XA-JCE XB-IXJ |
| 306-94 | | N65778 HZ-MA1 HZ-NCB N75JT N217RM N217RN N348W |
| 306-95 | | N65783 N999DC N124DC |
| 306-96 | | N65784? N54784 N68HC N48HC (N1318E) N315JM XB-ETV |
| 306-97 | | N65785 I-FBCA N3WQ N344K N85DB N707DB N98LB XA-RWY XA-SVH N90TT N97NL N15DJ XA-SVG |
| 306-98 | | N65786 N6MK N169AC N531AB XA-GUR |
| 306-99 | | N65789 N905R N16PN N66GE N66GZ [parted out] |
| 306-100 | | N65790 N881MC N81HP N5379W N60SE XA-RLR XB-LAW XA-TMF |
| 306-101 | A | N65791 N68NR N376D N60FS N376D N378D |
| 306-102 | | N65792 N108G N555AE N444MA N265TJ N70HL |
| 306-103 | | N65794 N11UL N40TL N234DC |
| 306-104 | CT-39G | N65795 160053 |
| 306-105 | CT-39G | N65796 160054 [code 22] |
| 306-106 | CT-39G | N65797 160055 |
| 306-107 | CT-39G | N65798 160056 [AMARC park code 7T-029] [to museum at Pensacola NAS, FL, by Feb09] |
| 306-108 | CT-39G | N65799 160057 [w/o 03Mar91 approx 1.5 miles from Glenview NAS, IL] |
| 306-109 | A | N2101J N522N N64NC N521NC N602KB XA-SBV N60SQ |
| 306-110 | | N2103J N60RS HZ-MA1 N13SL XA-RTP N75GM XB-HJS |
| 306-111 | | N2106J N300RC XA-SKB XC-PFN [code PF-213] [w/o 28Jly04 Mexicali, Mexico] |
| 306-112 | | N2107J N740R N740RC CC-CTC |
| 306-113 | | N2108J N712MR N2626M N113T XA-TVZ |
| 306-114 | 65 | N2109J N65R N60TF N65R N65RN N990PT N990PA |
| 306-115 | | N2118J (XA-LEI) Bolivia FAB-001 |
| 306-116 | A | N2119J N605RG N44WD N39CB |

# SABRE 60

| C/n | Series | Identities | | | | | | | | | |
|---|---|---|---|---|---|---|---|---|---|---|---|
| 306-117 | | N2120J | N22MY | Ecuador FAE-001A | [reported wfu] | | | | | | |
| 306-118 | | N2122J | N65NR | N711MR | N2635M | N607SR | N607CF | | | | |
| 306-119 | A | N2123J | N167H | N110MH | XA-JMD | N109MC | N41RG | | | | |
| 306-120 | | N2124J | N265C | N265SR | N1GM | | | | | | |
| 306-121 | | N2130J | N880KC | (N15CK) | N880CK | XA-SYS | N789SG | | | | |
| 306-122 | A | N2131J | N168H | N56RN | XA-GUR | N110JG | | | | | |
| 306-123 | | N2132J | N710MR | N2627M | N128VM | (N213BE) | N28VM | XA-PAX | N97SC | XA-ATE | |
| 306-124 | A | N2133J | N65NR | N60RS | N48WS | | | | | | |
| 306-125 | | N2134J | N32PC | XA-RGC | N265RW | N261T | XA-SLJ | N28HH | XA-AEV | XA-JML | |
| 306-126 | | N2141J | N60SL | N7NR | N7NF | N1CH | N85HP | N4227N | HC-BUN | N111F | XA-TGA |
| 306-127 | | N2142J | N5NE | N60DD | XA-CUR | XB-JTG | | | | | |
| 306-128 | | N2143J | N80CR | N100CE | N117JL | "N24TK" | N117JL | XA-SJM | XB-SOL | | |
| 306-129 | | N2144J | N711ST | N749UP | N95RC | N60ML | XB-ULF | | | | |
| 306-130 | | N2145J | XA-OVR | XA-JIK | XB-JMM | XA-AFG | XA-UFQ | [dbf Calaya, Mexico, 18Dec08, w/o] | | | |
| 306-131 | | N2149J | N5DL | N35DL | N61DF | N131JR | (N131SE) | XA-GUR | [w/o Nov04 Toluca, Mexico] | | |
| 306-132 | | N2150J | N60RS | N108W | (N994W) | N60AG | N265U | XB-MMW | | | |
| 306-133 | | N2151J | N6NE | N9NP | N700WS | I-PATY | N360CF | N400JH | N468RB | | |
| 306-134 | | N2152J | N323EC | N282WW | | | | | | | |
| 306-135 | | N2535E | N9NR | N9NT | N64CM | N59JM | N60AM | N921MB | | | |
| 306-136 | 65 | N2501E | N465S | N65RS | [redesignated c/n 465-1 1981 as first Sabre 65 (qv)] | | | | | | |
| 306-137 | | N2506E | N60SL | N650C | N18X | XA-SAH | | | | | |
| 306-138 | | N2508E | N22BX | N800RM | N700JR | N702JR | XA-RVT | | | | |
| 306-139 | | Mexico TP105 | | Mexico TP103/XC-UJE | | XC-UJS | | | | | |
| 306-140 | | N636 | N636MC | N60AF | N26SC | N26SQ | XA-SSV | | | | |
| 306-141 | | N8NR | (N89N) | (N8NF) | N141SL | (N707GP) | | | | | |
| 306-142 | | N60RS | N80CR | N742R | N742RC | N190MD | N40KJ | (N70LW) | N700MH | (N700DA) | N143DZ |
| 306-143 | | N800M | N80QM | N741R | N741RC | XA-SIM | XA-SUN | XA-TPU | | | |
| 306-144 | | N2519E | Mexico TP106 | | Mexico TP104/XC-UJF | | Mexico AMT-204 | | | | |
| 306-145 | | N60SL | N730CA | XA-LOQ | XC-JDC | XC-CAM | | | | | |
| 306-146 | | N301MC | N301MG | N360CH | XA-ARE | (N146BJ) | N31CR | N44DD | | | |

Production complete

# SABRE 65

| C/n | Identities | | | | | | | | |
|---|---|---|---|---|---|---|---|---|---|
| 465-1 | N2501E | N465S | N65RS | N77A | N65KJ | N117MB | (N117MN) | N65HH | |
| | [originally Sabre 60 c/n 306-136] | | | | | | | | |
| 465-2 | N465T | N251JE | N45H | N624DS | N124SD | | | | |
| 465-3 | N65RS | N6K | N170JL | N170CC | N1CF | N65BT | | | |
| 465-4 | N1058X | N14M | N141PB | N800TW | N804PA | | | | |
| 465-5 | N24G | N55KS | N52GG | N60CE | N241H | [w/o 11May00 Molokai, HI] | | | |
| 465-6 | N65NC | N511NC | N65SR | N1CC | N41CQ | (N652CC) | N2CC | N432CC | |
| 465-7 | N10580 | N2000 | N2800 | N2000 | N2700 | | | | |
| 465-8 | N10581 | XA-GAP | | | | | | | |
| 465-9 | N6NP | N769KC | (N769EG) | N6GV | | | | | |
| 465-10 | N65SL | N77TC | N336RJ | | | | | | |
| 465-11 | N3000 | N3030 | N25UG | N5739 | N57MQ | | | | |
| 465-12 | XA-OVR | XA-PVR | XB-GMD | N112PR | N112PV | N529SC | N73TJ | | |
| 465-13 | N7HF | N13MF | N945CC | | | | | | |
| 465-14 | N651S | N301MC | N67SC | N71RB | N740R | N25SR | XA-SPM | | |
| 465-15 | N2513E | XA-ZUM | N465TS | N25VC | | | | | |
| 465-16 | N31BC | N7000G | N700QG | N65SR | N112CF | N920CC | N603MA | N75HL | |
| 465-17 | N2537E | N905K | N4MB | N32290 | (N322TW) | N74VC | | | |
| 465-18 | N4M | N696US | | | | | | | |
| 465-19 | N65RC | N91BZ | | | | | | | |
| 465-20 | N2544E | N173A | | | | | | | |
| 465-21 | N2586E | (N65HM) | N465LC | (N265CA) | N701FW | | | | |
| 465-22 | N996W | N678AM | 9H-ABO | VR-CEE | N927AA | N883RA | N889RA | XB-RSH | |
| 465-23 | N904K | (N904KB) | N223LB | | | | | | |
| 465-24 | N65NR | N2545E | N8000U | N800CU | N65JR | N265PC | N741R | N777SK | N271MB |
| | N22CS | | | | | | | | |
| 465-25 | N9000F | N25MF | N125BP | N324ZR | N812WN | N42DC | | | |
| 465-26 | N465SL | N2548E | N65DD | N31SJ | N488DM | N770MD | | | |
| 465-27 | XA-ARE | XA-AVR | XA-FVK | N351AF | N111AD | N39TR | N4CS | | |
| 465-28 | N2549E | N333PC | N742R | N24RF | (N129BA) | N66GE | | | |
| 465-29 | N6NR | N976SR | N779CS | | | | | | |
| 465-30 | N25ZC | (N25ZG) | N89MM | N65TC | N465SC | | | | |
| 465-31 | N2550E | N65FC | N265M | | | | | | |
| 465-32 | N97RE | N303A | HB-VCN | | | | | | |
| 465-33 | N994 | N869KC | (N869EG) | (N271MB) | N465SR | N265C | VP-CBG | | |
| 465-34 | (N50DG) | N112KM | N80FH | N65TS | N47SE | | | | |
| 465-35 | N2590E | N65AK | | | | | | | |
| 465-36 | N651GL | N652MK | N424JM | N65MC | | | | | |
| 465-37 | N750CS | N750CC | YV.... | | | | | | |
| 465-38 | N850CS | N850CC | (N4LQ) | | | | | | |
| 465-39 | N2551E | N5511A | N551FA | N203JK | N41LV | N901CD | | | |
| 465-40 | N341AP | N465RM | N465PM | N801SS | | | | | |
| 465-41 | N2556E | N800M | | | | | | | |
| 465-42 | N2561E | N415CS | N41TC | N15CC | N150HN | N15CC | N64SL | N45NP | N875CA |
| | N799MW | | | | | | | | |
| 465-43 | N950CS | N228LS | N83TF | N955PR | N65T | | | | |
| 465-44 | N7NR | N74BJ | | | | | | | |
| 465-45 | N442WT | N448WT | N65TJ | (N265DR) | N65DR | N265DS | | | |
| 465-46 | N20UC | N79CD | N65FF | N65CC | N307ST | | | | |
| 465-47 | N265A | N33TR | | | | | | | |
| 465-48 | N2539E | XA-MLG | N500WD | N265SP | N265CP | | | | |
| 465-49 | N455SF | N455LB | N500RR | N82CR | N697US | | | | |
| 465-50 | N2570E | N129GP | N959C | N920DY | (N920DG) | XB-MYP | | | |
| 465-51 | N3BM | N3QM | N114LG | N69WU | | | | | |
| 465-52 | N500E | N96RE | | | | | | | |
| 465-53 | N76NX | N80R | N80RN | N465BC | | | | | |
| 465-54 | N2579E | N6000J | N600QJ | N1909R | N65SR | | | | |
| 465-55 | N2574E | XA-LUC | XA-RYO | XB-RYO | XA-TOM | XB-RSC | | | |
| 465-56 | N544PH | N265JS | N65TL | N499NH | | | | | |
| 465-57 | N903K | N355CD | | | | | | | |
| 465-58 | N65AM | N670AS | N670H | | | | | | |
| 465-59 | N65AN | HB-VJF | N59SR | N61DF | N8500 | N35CC | N35CQ | | |
| 465-60 | N2580E | N88BF | (N688WS) | | | | | | |
| 465-61 | N23BX | N117JW | | | | | | | |
| 465-62 | N56NW | N65AF | N265WS | | | | | | |
| 465-63 | N2N | N605Y | N2N | N2NL | | | | | |
| 465-64 | N99S | [w/o 11Jan83 Toronto, Canada; cx Aug91] | | | | | | | |
| 465-65 | N29S | N29SZ | N65AD | (N925WL) | N963WL | XA-SCR | N600TG | N395GA | |
| 465-66 | N964C | | | | | | | | |
| 465-67 | N65AR | N921CC | | | | | | | |
| 465-68 | N65AH | OO-IBC | N68LX | N165NA | N930RA | N6NR | N888UP | | |
| 465-69 | N33BC | (N31BC) | N400KV | N25KL | N65ML | | | | |
| 465-70 | N15AK | N15EN | N58CM | N58HT | | | | | |
| 465-71 | N728C | N75G | N75GL | N75VC | | | | | |
| 465-72 | N857W | (OO-RSA) | (OO-RSB) | OO-RSE | N465SP | XA-... | | | |
| 465-73 | N64MC | N64MQ | N651MK | | | | | | |
| 465-74 | N700JC | | | | | | | | |
| 465-75 | N2581E | N570R | | | | | | | |
| 465-76 | N65L | N376D | | | | | | | |

Production complete

## SABRE 75

| C/n | Series | Identities |
|---|---|---|
| 370-1 | | N7572N [used as parts for other test aircraft] |
| 370-2 | | N7585N N75NR N8NR N80K N10M [wfu; cx 08Sep06] |
| 370-3 | | N7586N N70NR N125N N125NX [wfu; cx 19May09] |
| 370-4 | | N7587N N75U N75UA N37GF N370BH N400DB (N404DB) N726JR |
| 370-5 | | N7588N N75NR N23G N55KS N55KZ N58KS N250BC N265SR XA-RYJ |
| 370-6 | | N7589N N2TE XA-SGR N29019 (N30EV) [wfu; cx Sep91; remains to Clarkesville, MO] |
| 370-7 | A | N7590N N75NR N60PM N60PT N75DE XB-ERU N670C (N26TJ) |
| 370-8 | | N7591N N3TE N70HC [b/u for spares Sep90 Little Rock, AR; canx Jun96; remains to Paynesville, MO] |
| 370-9 | | N7592N N8NR N8NB N55CR XA-RZW XB-GJO N370SL [being parted out at Spirit of St Louis, MO circa early 2000 still wearing its previous identity XB-GJO; regn cx Jan01 as scrapped] |

Production complete

## SABRE 75A

| C/n | Series | Identities |
|---|---|---|
| 380-1 | | N7593N N6K N87Y N30GB N100EJ N200UN* |
| 380-2 | | N8445N N2440G N2440C N19PC N380SR N9GN N642TS N406PW YV265T |
| 380-3 | | N8467N Argentina T-10 Argentina T-11 |
| 380-4 | 80A | N65733 N5105 N510AA N75SE XA-RLP N11887 (LV-...) N11887 |
| 380-5 | | N51 N125MS N223LP N71460 XA-TUD |
| 380-6 | 80A | N65741 N5106 N50GG N75TJ N711GL N711GD N184PC |
| 380-7 | | N65744 N67KM [w/o 14Jun75 Watertown, SD] |
| 380-8 | | N65749 N5107 N500NL [wfu; parted out Feb93 - possibly following an accident on 23Feb75 at Oakland-Pontiac, MI] |
| 380-9 | 80A | N5108 N510BB N6SP N383CF N995RD |
| 380-10 | | N52 [cx Sep95 wfu; in use as an instructional airframe at Burlington, VT] |
| 380-11 | 80A | N5109 N5109T N265SR N151TB [canx 11Jan05; b/u for spares by White Industries at Bates City, MO] |
| 380-12 | | N65758 (N335K) HB-VEC D-CLAN N75SL D-CLAN N120YB (N4WJ) N75BS [b/u; cx 24Jul08] |
| 380-13 | | N65761 Argentina AE-175 |
| 380-14 | | N53 N72028 [being parted out at Rantoul, KS circa early 2000] |
| 380-15 | | N65766 (N338K) N80NR N1841D N1841F N15PN N18TF N18TZ XA-LEG N22JW N424R |
| 380-16 | | N54 N126MS N12659 N801FT |
| 380-17 | 80A | N65768 (N339K) N80RS 5N-AMM N70TF N15RF N111Y N1115 N380BC [parted out] |
| 380-18 | | N55 N127MS [wfu; for spares Perryville, MO; cx Jly95] |
| 380-19 | | N65771 D-CLUB N500TF N100RS XB-EPM XA-EPM N54HH N80HG N80TN [b/u and cx Jun02] |
| 380-20 | | N56 N773W N109SB |
| 380-21 | 80A | N65773 N711A N75A N22NT N25AT N577SW N111AG N840MA N647JP N82AF N380MS |
| 380-22 | | N57 N132MS N131MS [wfu; for spares Perryville, MO; cx Jly95] |
| 380-23 | | N65776 N68KM N102RD N800CD |
| 380-24 | 80 | N58 N219TT |
| 380-25 | | N50PM N90AM N16LF N13NH N400RS |
| 380-26 | | N59 N128MS N2200A [parted out circa Jan02 at Spirit of St Louis A/P, MO] |
| 380-27 | | N65787 N8NR N8NB N10CN N6NR N6NG N90GM N90GW N85DW [w/o 14Aug00 near Ironwood, MI] |
| 380-28 | | N60 [cx Jun96; presumed wfu] |
| 380-29 | | N61 N131MS N58966 N132MS N71543 [used for fire training by University of Illinois, Champaign, IL and destroyed as a result] |
| 380-30 | | N65793 N69KM N265CH N265DP N818DW N818LD N42799 |
| 380-31 | | N62 N75CN [parted out at Rantoul, KS circa early 2000] |
| 380-32 | 80A | N2100J N75RS N64MP N64MQ N66ES N66ED (N86SH) N380DJ N198GB XA-JRF |
| 380-33 | | N63 N129MS N7148J N802FT |
| 380-34 | | N2104J N6LG (N112KH) N382MC Ecuador FAE-034 Ecuador AEE-403 N97SC XC-DDA |
| 380-35 | | N64 [w/o 29Sep86 Liberal, KS; cx Aug88] |
| 380-36 | | N2105J N75A JY-AFM N75HL (N835MA) XB-MCB N377HS [canx 22Feb05 as b/u] |
| 380-37 | | N65 N774W |
| 380-38 | | N2102J D-CAVW N85031 N3RN HZ-AMN N95TJ N75AK N316EC N316EQ |

# SABRE 75A

| C/n | Series | Identities |
|---|---|---|
| 380-39 | | N2110J N7NR N102MJ N88JM N38JM (N60WP) N40WP XA-PON N2093P XA-SXK XC-ONA N354SH (N805HD) (N55HD) N105HD |
| 380-40 | | N2112J N4NR N4NB N75NL N920DY N820DY N14TN XA-UBH XA-UEK |
| 380-41 | | N2113J N33NT N400N N400NR |
| 380-42 | | N2114J N75RS D-CHIC N75AG XA-MVT N6YL N3RP N80KR [parted out by MTW Aerospace, Montgomery, AL] |
| 380-43 | | N2115J N6NR N2265Z [wfu prior Sep90 Clarkesville, MO] |
| 380-44 | 80A | N2116J N2440G N380GK YV338T |
| 380-45 | | N2117J D-CCVW N218US (N218UB) N753TW Ecuador FAE-045 Ecuador AEE-402 [not confirmed] [AEE-402 was w/o 10Dec92 nr Quito A/P, Ecuador] |
| 380-46 | | N2125J (N50K) N90C XA-RIH XC-HFY XC-AA89 |
| 380-47 | | N2126J N25BH N25BX N33RZ |
| 380-48 | 80A | N2127J N8NR N8NG N805RG N6PG N27TS N132DB N100BP XA-... |
| 380-49 | 80A | N2128J N4PG (N41B) N4PQ N4PG N673SH N673FH N221PH N265KC |
| 380-50 | 80A | N2129J N5PG N5EQ N5PG N179S XA-ROD XA-RLR XA-TDQ XA-ACD XB-ACD |
| 380-51 | | N2135J N43R N4343 N711BY (N12GP) N808EB N80LX N180NA N382LS N380CF |
| 380-52 | | N2136J N75A N177NC N177NQ N70KM N84NG N34NG N929GC N929CG |
| 380-53 | | N2137J N75NR JY-AFN HZ-THZ N8526A N75HZ XC-FIA XB-DVP N380SR N827SL XA-... N827SL XB-CYA |
| 380-54 | | N2138J N6NR N62NR N10CN N350MT N81GD N999M N176DC N380CF N910BH N380FP |
| 380-55 | | N2139J N33KA HZ-CA1 N120KC XA-OAF XB-RDB XB-GSP |
| 380-56 | | N2146J JY-AFL N14JD (N914JC) N22NB |
| 380-57 | | N2147J N80RS N75A HZ-RBH JY-AFH [wfu] |
| 380-58 | | N2148J N75RS N380T XA-CHA XA-SEB XA-GHR N8267D XA-UEQ |
| 380-59 | | N80AB (N935PC) N83AB N911CR N27LT N1LT [parted out Tulsa, OK; cx 31Jul08] |
| 380-60 | | N2521E D-CBVW N4260K N100TM XB-RSG XB-SHA XA-RDY N60SL XA-AOV |
| 380-61 | | N2522E JY-AFO 9L-LAW N727US [b/u for spares at Spirit of St.Louis, MO circa 1996 cx Jan00] |
| 380-62 | | JY-AFP [wfu] |
| 380-63 | | N75RS N448W |
| 380-64 | | N75NR N75Y N942CC JY-JAS [w/o Alexandria, Egypt, May06] |
| 380-65 | | YU-BLY RC-BLY 9A-BLY N88JJ N69JN N972NR |
| 380-66 | | N2536E N6PG N6VL N6PG N75L N943CC N819GY |
| 380-67 | | N2528E Mexico TP 103 Mexico TP 101/XC-UJC [w/o 26Oct89 Saltillo, Mexico; fuselage to Spirit of St.Louis A/P, MO] |
| 380-68 | | N2538E Mexico TP 104 Mexico TP 102/XC-UJD XC-UJU |
| 380-69 | | N2542E N111VW (N111VS) N111VX N547JL [w/o 18Jly98 near Marion, KS] |
| 380-70 | | (N13ME) (N15ME) N101ME N1NR (N380RS) N110AJ |
| 380-71 | | HZ-NR1 N80HK XA-TSZ |
| 380-72 | | HZ-SOG N380N N90N N555JR N933JC |

Production complete

# SN601 CORVETTE

C/n Identities

01 F-WRSN [ff 16Jly70; w/o 23Mar71 Marseille, France (model SN600)]
1 F-WUAS [ff 20Dec72] F-BUAS F-WUAS F-BUAS France (CEV) 1/F-ZVMV coded MV [wfu by Jun05 at Istres, France]
2 F-WRNZ F-BRNZ France (CEV) 2/F-ZVMW coded MW [to Vitrolles Engineering College nr Marseille, France]
3 F-WUQN F-BUQN F-WUQN F-BUQN [w/o 16Oct00 Toulouse-Blagnac, France; repaired to non-flying condition and painted as "F-WUQN" on display at entrance to Airbus facility St. Nazaire, France]
4 F-WUQP F-BUQP
5 F-BVPA F-ODJX F-BVPA CN-TDE
6 F-WUQR F-BVPB F-OGJL F-BVPB [regn cx circa 2000; CofA expired; in use as an instructional airframe at St.Yan, France; moved to Le Bourget by 10Apr03]
7 F-OBZR N611AC F-BVPK
8 F-WPTT 6V-AEA F-GJAS
9 F-WRQK F-BRQK N612AC F-BTTR F-OCRN TN-ADI [reported wfu South of France]
10 F-BVPO N600AN F-GFEJ France (CEV) 10/F-ZVMX coded MX [instructional airframe at Lycee Stella, Reunion]
11 (F-WIFU) N613AC F-BTTS TR-LWY F-ODKS F-BTTV EI-BNY F-WFPD (F-GFPD) F-GKGA [wfu; cx 08Dec09]
12 F-BVPC TR-LYM TJ-AHR F-GMOF
13 F-BVPD N601AN F-GFDH [wfu; cx 08Dec09]
14 F-BVPS SP-FOA (F-GIRH) [last noted 29Mar06 dismantled on a low-loader at Le Bourget, France]
15 F-WIFA SE-DEN OO-MRA OO-MRE F-GDUB SE-DEN N17AJ F-GEQF D6-ECB F-GNAF EC-HHZ [wfu]
16 F-BVPT 5R-MVN 5R-MBR
17 F-WNGQ N614AC F-BTTM F-ODTM YV-572CP [w/o 21Jun91 Las Delicias A/P, Santa Barbara del Zulia, Venezuela]
18 F-WNGR N615AC F-BTTO N604AN [cx Dec90; sold to Drenair, Spain, for spares use]
19 F-BVPL F-OCJL F-BVPL TZ-PBF (F-GDRC) F-SEBH F-GEPQ EC-HIA [wfu; cx 2006]
20 F-WNGS N616AC F-BTTN TR-LZT F-GKJB [wfu 31Mar93 for spares at Toulouse, France; wings used in rebuild of c/n 28; forward fuselage to cabin trainer use]
21 F-BVPE OY-SBS [w/o 03Sep79 Nice, France]
22 F-WNGT N617AC F-BTTU F-ODFE TN-ADB [w/o 30Mar79 Nkayi, Congo Republic]
23 F-BVPF OY-SBR [wfu Aalborg, Denmark circa Feb05; last flight 26Dec04]
24 F-BVPI EC-DQC [sold in USA for scrap/spares and b/u Mar92 Toulouse, France]
25 F-WNGU F-BVPG F-OBZV F-BVPG [cx Oct06, C of A expired]
26 F-WNGV N618AC F-ODFQ PH-JSB F-GDAY EC-DQE [noted dismantled 2000 at Dieupentule, France; intended as a museum exhibit but cut up by local gypsies]
27 F-BVPH N26674+ [+ marks not confirmed] EC-DQG [w/o 25Nov00 Cordoba, Spain]
28 F-WNGX F-BTTL (OO-TTL) F-GPLA
29 F-WNGY F-BVPJ F-OBZP F-BVPJ F-OBZP TY-BBK [w/o 16Nov81 Lagos, Nigeria]
30 F-WNGQ F-BTTP OO-MRC TR-LAH OO-MRC EC-DUE (F-GKGB) F-GLEC [wfu; cx 27Oct09]
31 F-WNGZ F-BTTK N602AN F-WZSB EC-DYE F-GJAP [to Musee de l'Air et de l'Espace, Le Bourget, France 17Oct09; cx 08Dec09]
32 F-WNGR F-BTTQ OY-ARA SE-DED OY-ARA EC-DUF F-GILM [wfu 08Dec09]
33 F-BTTT OY-SBT
34 F-WNGS F-BYCR OY-ARB SE-DEE OY-ARB SE-DEE F-GKGD CN-TCS 5R-MHK
35 PH-JSC F-GDAZ YV-589CP YV-01CP F-ODSR 5R-MVD F-ODSR [wfu]
36 F-BTTS PH-JSD F-OCDE XB-CYA XB-EWF XA-BCC N601RC N600RA
37 F-BTTU [w/o 31Jul90 St Yan, France; cx 12Feb91 as "reformed" 04Dec90]
38 F-ODIF 5A-DCK
39 F-WNGY F-OBYG TL-SMI TL-RCA F-GJLB CN-THL
40 F-WNGZ F-ODJS XB-CYI N601CV N200MT N220MT [parted out by Atlanta Air Salvage, Griffin, GA circa Feb05]

Production complete

# EXPERIMENTAL & NON-PRODUCTION TYPES

## ADAM AIRCRAFT A700

A 6-8 seat very light jet powered by 2 Williams FJ-33 engines

| C/n | Identities | | |
|---|---|---|---|
| 0001 | N700JJ | N700AJ | [ff 27Jly03; cx 08Jun07, wfu] |
| 0002 | N700LJ | [ff 06Feb06] | |
| 0003 | N703AJ | [cx 29May09, wfu] | |
| 0004 | N700AJ | [cx 06May09, wfu] | |

Company filed for bankruptcy February 2008, production ceased.

## CHICHESTER-MILES LEOPARD

| C/n | Identities | |
|---|---|---|
| 001 | G-BKRL | [first flight late 1988; cx 25Jan99 as wfu & stored Oct01; circa 25Feb05 to Bournemouth Aviation Museum in dismantled state] |
| 002 | G-BRNM | [on display in Bournemouth Aviation Museum, UK Mar03] |

## CIRRUS VISION SJ50

A 6-passenger "personal" jet powered by a single Williams FJ-33 engine.

| C/n | Identities | |
|---|---|---|
| 0001 | N280CJ | [ff 03Jul08 Duluth, MN] |

## DASSAULT 30

| C/n | Identities | |
|---|---|---|
| 01 | F-WAMD | [wfu Bordeaux, France; never entered production; fuselage at Vitrolles Engineering University, nr Marseille, France, 1990] |

## DIAMOND D-JET

A 4-passenger, single pilot "personal" jet powered by a single Williams FJ-33 engine giving a range of 1350NM at an operating altitude of 25,000 ft.

| C/n | Identities | |
|---|---|---|
| 10-0001 | C-GVLJ | [ff 18Apr06 London, ONT, Canada] |
| DJ1-0002 | C-FPTM | [ff 14Sep07] |
| DJ1-0003 | C-GUPJ | [ff 14Apr08] |

## ECLIPSE 400 CONCEPT JET

A 4-seat, single-engined "personal jet" built to test the single-engined jet market. Officially registered as a Swift Engineering Inc Mark 400.

| C/n | Identities | |
|---|---|---|
| SE-400-001 | N5184U | [ff 02Jul07] |

## EPIC ELITE

A 6-seat very light jet powered by two Williams FJ-33-4A engines.

| C/n | Identities | |
|---|---|---|
| 001J | C-GROL | [ff 07Jun07] |

## EPIC VICTORY

A 4-seat "personal jet" powered by a single Williams FJ-33-4A engine.

| C/n | Identities | |
|---|---|---|
| 001 | N370EJ | [ff 06Jul07] |
| 002 | N975AR | |

## GROB G180 SPn Utility Jet

Grob Aerospace unveiled its ten-seat (including crew), carbon-fibre SPn Utility jet at the 2005 Paris Air Show. Development of the type drove the company into insolvency. H3 Aerospace purchased the company in January 2009 but decided not to continue the SPn programme.

| C/n | Identities | | |
|---|---|---|---|
| 90001 | D-ISPN | [ff 20Jly05] | D-CSPN |
| 90002 | D-CGSP | [ff 29Sep06, w/o Tussenhausen-Mattsies 29Nov06] | |
| 90003 | D-CSPJ | [ff 29Oct07] | |
| 90004 | D-CSPG | [ff 07Aug08] | |

## GULFSTREAM 550 PEREGRINE

| C/n | Identities | | | |
|---|---|---|---|---|
| 551 | N9881S | N550GA | N84GP | [wfu Mar92; to Oklahoma Air & Space Museum, Oklahoma City, OK] |

## HONDA MH02

| C/n | Identities | |
|---|---|---|
| 001 | N3097N | [ff 05Mar93 - undertook 170 hours of test flying which ended in Aug96, displayed in the Honda Hall, Motegi, Japan] |

## HONDA HA-420 HONDAJET

| C/n | Identities | |
|---|---|---|
| P001 | N420HA | [ff 03Dec03 at Greensboro, NC; powered by 2 Honda HF118 turbofans mounted above the wings, with 6 seats and T-tail.] |

## McDONNELL MD220

| C/n | Identities | | | |
|---|---|---|---|---|
| 1 | N119M | N220N | N4AZ | [never entered production; ferried Albuquerque, NM, to El Paso, TX 21Dec85 - where it is wfu] |

## NORTH AMERICAN UTX

| C/n | Identities | |
|---|---|---|
| 246-1 | N4060K | [b/u circa 1967] |

## PIPER PA-47 PIPERJET

A 6-seat "personal" jet powered by a single Williams FJ44 engine.

| C/n | Identities | |
|---|---|---|
| 4798E001 | N360PJ | [ff 30Jul08 Vero Beach, FL] |

## SABRE 50

| C/n | Identities | | |
|---|---|---|---|
| 287-1 | N287NA | N50CR | [still flying; never entered production] |

## SCALED COMPOSITES 143 TRIUMPH

| C/n | Identities | |
|---|---|---|
| 001 | N143SC | [ff 12Jly88; further development abandoned; wfu Sep92 Mojave, CA; placed on display outside Scaled Composites premises at Mojave, CA] |

## SPECTRUM 33

| C/n | Identities | |
|---|---|---|
| 0001 | N322LA | [ff 07Jan06, w/o 25Jly06 Spanish Fork, UT. Powered by 2 rear-mounted Williams FJ33 engines giving a range of 2000nm, the aircraft had a cabin slightly larger than that of the CitationJet CJ2. Current project status uncertain] |

## VISIONAIRE VANTAGE/EVIATION EV-20

| C/n | Identities | |
|---|---|---|
| 001 | N247VA | [ferried to Brazil Nov04 for converstion to EV-20 powered by 2 Williams FJ44 turbofans with ff scheduled for Feb06 and certification in 2007] |

## WILLIAMS V-JET II

| C/n | Identities | |
|---|---|---|
| 001 | N222FJ | [wfu and presented to the EAA AirVenture Museum, Oshkosh, WI on 27Jly00] |

NOTES: Officially registered as a Scale Composites 271. The V-Jet II is a small, all-composite 6-seat jet powered by a single Williams FJX-2 engine. It was built primarily as a test-bed for the FJX-2 engine rather than for series production.

# MASTER INDEX

Civil-registered bizjets are arranged in order of country registration prefix, registrations relating to each country being listed in alphabetical or numerical order as appropriate. For each registration, a four-letter character abbreviation for the type of aircraft is given (see decode below), followed by the c/n (except for Citation I and II models, where the unit number is quoted where this is known). This code is to help locate the aircraft in the main text not to indicate any subtypes etc.

**All civil registered aircraft which are in current use are indicated by bold typeface;** reserved marks are given in the normal typeface.

Bizjets in military use are arranged in alphabetical order of country name.

## MASTER INDEX DE-CODE

| Code | Type |
|---|---|
| A700 | Adam Aircraft A700 |
| ASTR | IAI 1125 Astra/Gulfstream 100/Gulfstream 150 |
| BE40 | Beechjet 400/400A/Hawker 400XP/T-1A Jayhawk |
| C500 | Cessna 500/501 Citation I/ISP |
| C510 | Cessna 510 Citation Mustang |
| C525 | Cessna 525 CitationJet/CJ1+ |
| C52A | Cessna 525A CitationJet CJ2/CJ2+ |
| C52B | Cessna 525B CitationJet CJ3 |
| C52C | Cessna 525C CitationJet CJ4 |
| C550 | Cessna 550/551 Citation II/IISP/Bravo |
| C552 | Cessna 552 Citation (T-47A) |
| C560 | Cessna 560 Citation V/Ultra/Encore |
| C56X | Cessna 560XL Citation Excel/XLS |
| C650 | Cessna 650 Citation III/VI/VII |
| C680 | Cessna 680 Citation Sovereign |
| C750 | Cessna 750 Citation X |
| CL30 | BD100 Challenger 300 |
| CL60 | CL600 Challenger |
| CL61 | CL601 Challenger |
| CL64 | CL604 Challenger |
| CL65 | CL605 Challenger |
| CRVT | SN601 Corvette |
| CS55 | Cessna S550 Citation SII |
| DDJT | Diamond D-Jet |
| EA40 | Eclipse 400 |
| EA50 | Eclipse 500 |
| EPC1 | Epic Victory |
| EPC2 | Epic Elite |
| E50P | Embraer EMB-500 Phenom 100 |
| E55P | Embraer EMB-505 Phenom 300 |
| FA10 | Dassault Falcon 10 |
| FA20 | Dassault Falcon 20 |
| FA30 | Dassault Falcon 30 |
| FA50 | Dassault Falcon 50 |
| FA7X | Dassault Falcon 7X |
| F900 | Dassault Falcon 900 |
| F9DX | Dassault Falcon 900DX |
| F9EX | Dassault Falcon 900EX |
| F2TH | Dassault Falcon 2000 |
| F2DX | Dassault Falcon 2000DX |
| F2EX | Dassault Falcon 2000EX |
| G180 | Grob G180 SPn Utility Jet |
| GLF2 | G1159 Gulfstream II |
| GLF3 | G1159A Gulfstream III |
| GLF4 | Gulfstream IV/300/350/400/450 |
| GLF5 | Gulfstream V/500/550 |
| GLF6 | Gulfstream VI/650 |
| GALX | IAI 1126 Galaxy |
| GLEX | BD700 Global Express/Global 5000 |
| GPER | Gulfstream Peregrine |
| HDJT | Honda HA-420 Hondajet |
| HFB3 | MBB HFB320 Hansa |
| HMH2 | Honda MH02 |
| HA4T | Hawker 4000 (formerly Horizon) |
| HS25 | HS/BAe/Raytheon 125 (all models) |
| JSTR | Lockheed Jetstar |
| LEOP | Chichester-Miles Leopard |
| LJ24 | Learjet 23/24 |
| LJ25 | Learjet 25 |
| LJ28 | Learjet 28/29 |
| LJ31 | Learjet 31 |
| LJ35 | Learjet 35 |
| LJ36 | Learjet 36 |
| LJ40 | Learjet 40 |
| LJ45 | Learjet 45 |
| LJ55 | Learjet 55 |
| LJ60 | Learjet 60 |
| M220 | McDonnell MD220 |
| MS76 | MS760 Paris |
| MU30 | MU300 Diamond |
| NUTX | North American UTX |
| P808 | Piaggio PD808 |
| PJET | Piper PA-47 Piperjet |
| PRM1 | Beech 390 Premier I |
| SBRL | Sabreliner (all models) |
| SJ30 | Emivest SJ30 |
| SJ50 | Cirrus Vision SJ50 |
| SPEC | Spectrum 33 |
| T143 | Scaled Composites 143 Triumph |
| VVAN | Visionaire Vantage |
| WVII | Williams V-Jet II |
| WW24 | Jet Commander/Westwind |

# CIVIL INDEX

Nicaragua
(see also YN-)

| | | |
|---|---|---|
| AN-BPR | HS25 | 256037 |

Pakistan

| | | |
|---|---|---|
| **AP-BEK** | **LJ31** | **062** |
| AP-BEX | BE40 | RK-80 |
| **AP-BGI** | **HS25** | **25269** |
| **AP-BHD** | **C550** | **550-1102** |
| **AP-BHE** | **C550** | **550-0843** |
| **AP-BHQ** | **BE40** | **RK-392** |
| **AP-BHY** | **LJ45** | **316** |
| AP-BJL | HS25 | 258095 |
| **AP-GAK** | **CL64** | **5438** |
| **AP-MIR** | **CL61** | **3023** |
| **AP-MMM** | **ASTR** | **239** |
| **AP-PAL** | **BE40** | **RK-526** |
| **AP-PFL** | **C52B** | **0131** |
| **AP-RBA** | **BE40** | **RK-583** |

Botswana

| | | |
|---|---|---|
| A2-AGM | C500 | 652 |
| A2-JDJ | C500 | 161 |
| A2-MCB | CS55 | 0112 |
| **A2-MCG** | **BE40** | **RK-140** |

Oman

| | | |
|---|---|---|
| A40-AA | FA20 | 285/504 |
| A40-AA | GLF2 | 183 |
| **A40-AB** | **GLF4** | **1168** |
| **A40-AC** | **GLF4** | **1196** |
| A40-AJ | LJ25 | 188 |
| A40-CA | LJ35 | 165 |
| A40-GA | FA20 | 285/504 |
| A40-HA | GLF2 | 214 |
| A40-SC | C550 | 486 |

United Arab Emirates

| | | |
|---|---|---|
| (A6- ) | JSTR | 5236 |
| **A6-AAG** | **CL65** | **5739** |
| **A6-AAH** | **CL64** | **5362** |
| A6-ALI | GLF4 | 1132 |
| **A6-ASQ** | **CL64** | **5583** |
| A6-AUH | F900 | 84 |
| **A6-AZH** | **GLF4** | **4136** |
| A6-CGK | C650 | 0048 |
| A6-CKZ | GLF3 | 317 |
| A6-CPC | JSTR | 5222 |
| **A6-CYS** | **LJ60** | **341** |
| **A6-DEJ** | **GLF5** | **564** |
| **A6-DHG** | **GLEX** | **9226** |
| **A6-DJL** | **GLF4** | **4123** |
| **A6-DNH** | **CL65** | **5702** |
| A6-DPD | C680 | 0179 |
| **A6-DWD** | **GLF4** | **1412** |
| A6-EJA | LJ60 | 200 |
| (A6-EJB) | CL64 | 5328 |
| A6-EJB | GLEX | 9094 |
| A6-EJD | CL61 | 3017 |
| A6-ELA | HS25 | 259017 |
| A6-ELB | HS25 | 259024 |
| **A6-ELC** | **HS25** | **258781** |
| A6-ELJ | BE40 | RK-140 |
| A6-ESJ | C500 | 260 |
| A6-EXA | FA20 | 344/534 |
| A6-FAJ | LJ35 | 669 |
| **A6-FBQ** | **GLEX** | **9282** |
| **A6-FLG** | **GLF4** | **4106** |
| **A6-FLH** | **GLF4** | **4155** |
| (A6-GAN) | C650 | 0048 |
| **A6-GJA** | **C680** | **0075** |
| **A6-GJB** | **C56X** | **5679** |
| **A6-GJC** | **C56X** | **5701** |
| (A6-HBC) | HS25 | HA-0095 |
| A6-HEH | GLF3 | 356 |
| A6-HEM | FA20 | 344/534 |
| **A6-HHH** | **GLF4** | **1011** |
| A6-HHS | GLF3 | 376 |
| A6-HHZ | GLF2 | 164 |
| (A6-HMK) | HS25 | 258093 |
| **A6-HWK** | **HS25** | **HA-0080** |
| **A6-IAS** | **LJ60** | **122** |
| **A6-IFA** | **CL64** | **5641** |
| A6-INF | GLF3 | 491 |
| A6-KAH | JSTR | 5220 |
| **A6-KNH** | **CL30** | **20050** |
| **A6-MAA** | **HS25** | **258202** |
| **A6-MAB** | **HS25** | **258618** |
| **A6-MAF** | **F9EX** | **183** |
| **A6-MAH** | **HS25** | **258328** |
| A6-MAJ | LJ60 | 270 |
| **A6-MBH** | **CL64** | **5520** |
| A6-MED | LJ45 | 116 |
| **A6-NGN** | **LJ60** | **336** |
| **A6-NMA** | **GLF4** | **1381** |
| A6-OME | GLF4 | 1233 |
| **A6-ORX** | **GLF4** | **4133** |
| (A6-OWC) | GLEX | 9233 |
| A6-PHY | GLF2 | 130 |
| **A6-PJA** | **CL64** | **5397** |
| **A6-PJB** | **HS25** | **HA-0003** |
| A6-RAK | HS25 | 256063 |
| **A6-RJA** | **GLF4** | **1503** |
| **A6-RJB** | **GLF4** | **1505** |
| A6-RJH | LJ35 | 429 |
| A6-RJI | LJ35 | 265 |
| A6-RJM | CL30 | 20048 |
| A6-RKH | C500 | 268 |
| **A6-RTS** | **F9DX** | **601** |
| (A6-RZA) | PRM1 | RB-177 |
| A6-RZA | PRM1 | RB-195 |
| A6-RZB | HS25 | HA-0048 |
| A6-RZJ | PRM1 | RB-177 |
| A6-SAB | C52B | 0183 |
| **A6-SAC** | **F900** | **130** |
| **A6-SAM** | **CL30** | **20015** |
| **A6-SBF** | **LJ60** | **338** |
| **A6-SHH** | **HA4T** | **RC-21** |
| **A6-SKA** | **HS25** | **258432** |
| A6-SMH | C500 | 402 |
| A6-SMS | C550 | 391 |
| A6-SMS | CL30 | 20015 |
| A6-SMS | F2EX | 76 |
| **A6-SMS** | **F9DX** | **616** |
| A6-SMS | LJ60 | 094 |
| A6-SMS | LJ60 | 150 |
| **A6-TBF** | **HS25** | **258792** |
| A6-UAE | F900 | 86 |
| A6-ZAB | GLF3 | 329 |
| A6-ZKM | F900 | 47 |
| A6-ZKM | FA50 | 145 |
| **A6-ZZZ** | **HS25** | **258312** |

Qatar

| | | |
|---|---|---|
| A7-AAD | F900 | 91 |
| A7-AAE | F900 | 94 |
| A7-AAL | HS25 | 258485 |
| **A7-AAM** | **GLEX** | **9126** |
| A7-AAN | CL30 | 20042 |
| **A7-ASA** | **C500** | **097** |
| **A7-CEA** | **CL65** | **5783** |
| **A7-CEB** | **CL65** | **5784** |
| **A7-CEC** | **CL30** | **20042** |
| **A7-CGK** | **C650** | **0048** |
| A7-CJI | C525 | 0646 |
| A7-GEX | GLEX | 9134 |
| A7-GEY | GLEX | 9230 |
| **A7-RZA** | **CL65** | **5798** |
| **A7-RZB** | **HS25** | **HA-0048** |
| **A7-RZC** | **CL65** | **5759** |
| **A7-RZD** | **HS25** | **HA-0095** |

Bahrain

| | | |
|---|---|---|
| **A9C-BAH** | **GLF4** | **1353** |
| A9C-BB | GLF3 | 393 |
| **A9C-BG** | **GLF2** | **202** |
| **A9C-BHR** | **GLF4** | **4156** |
| **A9C-BRN** | **GLF5** | **5242** |
| A9C-BXA | C56X | 5046 |
| **A9C-BXB** | **CL64** | **5477** |
| A9C-BXC | C550 | 550-1050 |
| **A9C-BXD** | **CL61** | **5194** |
| **A9C-BXG** | **CL64** | **5485** |
| **A9C-BXH** | **CL64** | **5476** |
| A9C-BXI | C56X | 5658 |
| A9C-BXJ | C56X | 5676 |
| **A9C-DAR** | **CL30** | **20169** |
| A9C-RJA | PRM1 | RB-195 |
| AE-129 | C550 | 117 |

China and Taiwan

| | | |
|---|---|---|
| (B- ) | C750 | 0171 |
| (B- ) | CL64 | 5527 |
| **B-3642** | **C56X** | **5539** |
| **B-3643** | **C56X** | **5540** |
| **B-3644** | **C525** | **0551** |
| **B-3645** | **C525** | **0552** |
| **B-3647** | **C525** | **0554** |
| **B-3648** | **C525** | **0555** |
| **B-3649** | **C525** | **0557** |
| **B-3650** | **C525** | **0558** |
| **B-3666** | **C56X** | **5761** |
| **B-3667** | **C56X** | **5766** |
| **B-3668** | **C525** | **0471** |
| **B-3669** | **C525** | **0380** |
| **B-3901** | **HS25** | **258856** |
| **B-3902** | **HS25** | **258858** |
| **B-3903** | **HS25** | **HA-0053** |
| **B-3905** | **BE40** | **RK-109** |
| **B-3906** | **HA4T** | **RC-55** |
| **B-3926** | **LJ60** | **381** |
| B-3980 | LJ55 | 027 |
| B-3981 | LJ60 | 053 |
| B-3988 | LJ45 | 256 |
| B-3989 | BE40 | RK-203 |
| **B-3990** | **HS25** | **258408** |
| **B-3991** | **HS25** | **258470** |
| **B-3992** | **HS25** | **258501** |
| **B-3993** | **HS25** | **258525** |
| B-3995 | HS25 | 258526 |
| B-3996 | HS25 | 258536 |
| **B-3997** | **HS25** | **258575** |
| B-3998 | HS25 | 258312 |
| B-3999 | GLF4 | 1144 |
| B-4005 | CL61 | 3046 |
| B-4006 | CL61 | 3047 |
| B-4007 | CL61 | 3052 |
| B-4010 | CL61 | 5024 |
| B-4011 | CL61 | 5025 |
| **B-4101** | **CS55** | **0049** |
| **B-4102** | **CS55** | **0050** |
| B-4103 | C550 | 357 |
| B-4104 | C550 | 362 |
| B-4105 | C550 | 359 |
| B-4106 | C650 | 0220 |
| B-4107 | C650 | 0221 |
| B-4108 | C525 | 0204 |
| **B-4599** | **LJ36** | **034** |
| **B-7019** | **C56X** | **5118** |
| **B-7021** | **C750** | **0157** |
| **B-7022** | **C650** | **0220** |
| B-7023 | C650 | 0221 |
| **B-7024** | **C550** | **357** |
| **B-7025** | **C550** | **362** |
| **B-7026** | **C550** | **359** |
| **B-7027** | **C525** | **0204** |
| B-7696 | CL64 | 5510 |
| B-7697 | CL64 | 5523 |
| **B-7777** | **C525** | **0655** |
| (B-8006) | PRM1 | RB-87 |
| B-8018 | PRM1 | RB-118 |
| **B-8020** | **F2TH** | **27** |
| **B-8021** | **F9DX** | **613** |
| **B-8080** | **GLF4** | **1100** |
| **B-8081** | **GALX** | **135** |
| **B-8082** | **GLF4** | **1157** |
| **B-8083** | **GALX** | **037** |
| **B-8085** | **GALX** | **114** |
| **B-8086** | **GALX** | **030** |
| **B-8087** | **GALX** | **174** |
| **B-8088** | **GLF4** | **1375** |
| **B-8089** | **GALX** | **051** |
| B-8090 | GALX | 049 |
| **B-8091** | **GLF4** | **1144** |
| **B-8092** | **GLF5** | **510** |
| **B-8095** | **GLF5** | **5059** |
| **B-8097** | **GLF5** | **613** |
| **B-8098** | **GLF4** | **4076** |
| **B-8099** | **GLF4** | **4168** |
| **B-8100** | **GLF5** | **5024** |
| **B-8108** | **GLF5** | **5120** |
| **B-8120** | **GALX** | **229** |
| **B-9330** | **C56X** | **5828** |
| **B-20001** | **ASTR** | **119** |
| **B-77701** | **BE40** | **RK-562** |
| B-98181 | LJ35 | 675 |
| B-98183 | LJ35 | 654 |
| **B-99888** | **GLF5** | **5243** |

China - Hong Kong
(see also VR-H)

| | | |
|---|---|---|
| B-HMA | GLEX | 9063 |
| B-HSS | HS25 | 257169 |
| B-HVT | GLF5 | 5102 |
| B-HWA | GLF4 | 1144 |
| B-HWB | GALX | 030 |
| **B-KCK** | **GLF5** | **5228** |
| **B-KGP** | **GLF5** | **5238** |
| B-KGV | GLF5 | 5111 |
| **B-KHK** | **GLF4** | **4018** |
| **B-KID** | **GLF5** | **5115** |
| **B-KMJ** | **GALX** | **090** |
| **B-KSJ** | **GALX** | **036** |
| **B-KVC** | **GLF5** | **5219** |
| **B-LBL** | **CL64** | **5604** |
| **B-LCK** | **GLF4** | **4182** |
| **B-LIM** | **GLEX** | **9295** |
| B-LLL | CL64 | 5622 |
| **B-LMJ** | **GALX** | **153** |
| **B-LRW** | **GLEX** | **9315** |
| B-LSJ | GALX | 114 |
| **B-LSM** | **GLF5** | **5250** |
| **B-LSS** | **GALX** | **210** |
| **B-LUE** | **GLF5** | **5147** |
| **B-LUX** | **GALX** | **049** |

China - Macau
(see also CS-M)

| | | |
|---|---|---|
| **B-MAC** | **CL61** | **5178** |
| **B-MAI** | **CL61** | **5049** |
| **B-MBD** | **HS25** | **HA-0028** |
| **B-MBE** | **HS25** | **HA-0036** |
| **B-MBF** | **HS25** | **HB-1** |
| **B-MBG** | **HS25** | **HB-9** |
| **B-MBH** | **HS25** | **HB-13** |
| **B-MBI** | **HS25** | **HB-25** |
| **B-MBK** | **F2TH** | **133** |
| B-MBL | F9EX | 223 |

Bosnia
(see also T9-)

| | | |
|---|---|---|
| BH-BIH | CS55 | 0045 |

Canada

| | | |
|---|---|---|
| **C-** | **C550** | **104** |
| (C- ) | C560 | 0127 |
| (C- ) | FA10 | 184 |
| (C- ) | GLEX | 9007 |
| **C-** | **LJ60** | **365** |
| (C- ) | WW24 | 112 |
| C-FAAL | CL61 | 3005 |
| C-FAAU | HS25 | 258099 |
| **C-FABF** | **CS55** | **0101** |

C-FACC C560 0053
C-FACC C560 0753
C-FACO C560 0053
**C-FACO C560 0753**
C-FADG CL64 5580
C-FADL C500 067
C-FAGU GLEX 9143
C-FAGV GLEX 9144
C-FAHN GLEX 9145
C-FAHQ GLEX 9146
C-FAHX GLEX 9147
C-FAIO GLEX 9148
C-FAIV GLEX 9150
C-FAIY GLEX 9149
C-FALC HS25 25087
C-FALI C560 0573
C-FALI CS55 0142
C-FAMI C560 0566
**C-FAMI C560 0648**
**C-FAMJ C550 550-0931**
**C-FANJ C52B 0201**
C-FANL HS25 25042
C-FANS C550 550-0807
**C-FANS LJ45 303**
C-FAOL CL64 5567
C-FAOS HS25 25278
**C-FAPK WW24 216**
C-FAUZ CL30 20024
C-FAWU CL64 5584
C-FAWW WW24 313
C-FBAX C500 020
C-FBBF HS25 258530
C-FBCD LJ60 133
**C-FBCI C510 0211**
C-FBCL C500 042
C-FBCL LJ45 024
**C-FBCL LJ45 288**
C-FBCM C500 071
C-FBCR CL61 5117
**C-FBCR CL64 5579**
C-FBDH LJ35 673
**C-FBDR GLEX 9003**
C-FBDR LJ60 010
**C-FBDS C500 488**
C-FBEA LJ25 163
**C-FBEI CL61 3028**
C-FBEL CL61 3028
**C-FBEL CL65 5802**
C-FBFP LJ35 038
C-FBGX GLEX 9001
C-FBHX CL61 5018
C-FBKR CL61 5020
C-FBLJ LJ45 270
C-FBLJ LJ60 092
C-FBLO LJ60 092
C-FBLT SBRL 306-23
C-FBLU LJ60 029
C-FBLU LJ60 253
C-FBMG HS25 257066
**C-FBNA C650 0046**
C-FBNK HS25 25221
**C-FBNS CL64 5364**
**C-FBNW FA10 190**
**C-FBOC GLEX 9151**
C-FBOM CL61 5124
C-FBPJ GLEX 9153
C-FBPK GLEX 9152
C-FBPL GLEX 9154
**C-FBPL PRM1 RB-150**
C-FBPT GLEX 9155
C-FBPZ GLEX 9156
C-FBQD GLEX 9157
C-FBSS FA10 87
**C-FBUR HS25 258232**
C-FBVF FA10 33
**C-FBVF FA50 48**
**C-FBXL C56X 5298**
C-FBYJ CL61 3017
C-FCCC C550 422
C-FCCP CL64 5310
**C-FCDE CL64 5392**
C-FCDF CL61 5024
C-FCDS FA20 146
C-FCEH FA20 507
C-FCEJ WW24 324
C-FCEL C550 135
C-FCEL C56X 5047
C-FCFL HS25 25213
C-FCFP ASTR 079
C-FCFP C500 125
(C-FCFP) C550 097
C-FCGS CL61 5025
C-FCHJ C500 091
C-FCHT HS25 257176
**C-FCIB CL61 5181**
**C-FCLJ LJ36 037**
C-FCLJ LJ55 118
C-FCMG CL30 20033
**C-FCMG LJ60 133**
C-FCNN GLEX 9244
**C-FCNR GLF4 1065**
C-FCNR LJ60 179
C-FCOE CL64 5595
C-FCOG GLEX 9158
C-FCOI GLEX 9159
C-FCOJ GLEX 9160
C-FCOK GLEX 9161
C-FCOZ GLEX 9162
C-FCPH GLEX 9163
**C-FCPR C680 0157**
C-FCPW C500 002
C-FCRF HS25 258173
C-FCRH C560 0182
**C-FCRH FA50 56**
C-FCRH HS25 258173
C-FCSD CL64 5596
C-FCSF GLEX 9164
C-FCSH GLEX 9165
**C-FCSI CL30 20114**
C-FCSI GLEX 9166
C-FCSL GLEX 9167
C-FCSP GLEX 9168
C-FCSR GLEX 9169
C-FCSS C550 488
**C-FCSS HS25 257143**
C-FCSS LJ24 197
C-FCSY GLEX 9170
C-FCTE GLEX 9171
C-FCTK GLEX 9172
**C-FCTK LJ60 210**
C-FCUA GLEX 9173
C-FCUF GLEX 9174
C-FCUG GLEX 9175
C-FCUK GLEX 9176
C-FCUS GLEX 9177
C-FCUX GLEX 9178
C-FCVC GLEX 9179
C-FCVD GLEX 9180
C-FCXJ CL30 20034
**C-FCXL C56X 5234**
C-FCZM CL30 20066
C-FCZN CL30 20051
C-FCZS CL30 20043
C-FCZS CL30 20067
C-FCZV CL30 20052
C-FDAC LJ25 091
C-FDAH CL30 20059
C-FDAT CL61 5029
**C-FDAX ASTR 058**
C-FDBJ CL64 5602
**C-FDBJ F2EX 145**
C-FDCS GLF4 1207
C-FDDD CS55 0115
**C-FDDD HS25 258038**
**C-FDHD C680 0032**
C-FDHV CL30 20026
C-FDIA CL30 20028
C-FDIH CL30 20030
C-FDIJ CL30 20032
**C-FDJC C650 0080**
C-FDJN CL64 5598
C-FDJQ C500 018
**C-FDKJ HS25 258169**
C-FDLR GLEX 9088
C-FDLT C560 0021
C-FDMB C500 341
**C-FDMM PRM1 RB-198**
**C-FDOL CL30 20093**
C-FDOM HS25 25018
C-FDRS CL64 5432
**C-FDSH C510 0136**
C-FDSR CL30 20042
C-FDSZ CL30 20044
C-FDTF JSTR 5088
C-FDTM JSTR 5052
C-FDTX JSTR 5018
C-FDUY CL64 5605
C-FDWU CL64 5608
C-FDXU CL30 20048
C-FDYL C550 373
C-FEAB GLEX 9181
C-FEAD GLEX 9183
C-FEAE GLEX 9184
**C-FEAE HS25 257180**
C-FEAG GLEX 9185
C-FEAK GLEX 9187
C-FEAQ CL60 1035
C-FEAQ GLEX 9189
C-FEAZ GLEX 9191
C-FEBG GLEX 9193
C-FEBH GLEX 9194
C-FEBL GLEX 9195
C-FEBQ GLEX 9196
C-FEBS GLEX 9197
C-FEBU GLEX 9199
C-FEBX GLEX 9200
C-FECA GLEX 9182
C-FECI GLEX 9186
C-FECN GLEX 9188
C-FECX GLEX 9190
C-FECY GLEX 9192
C-FECZ GLEX 9198
**C-FEDG LJ60 343**
C-FEFU CL64 5609
C-FEFW CL64 5610
C-FEIH CL64 5611
**C-FEMA CS55 0040**
**C-FEMT LJ36 024**
C-FENJ C500 122
C-FEPC HS25 258349
**C-FEPG C560 0182**
C-FEPN CL64 5612
C-FEPR CL64 5613
C-FEPU CL30 20050
C-FETJ C560 0082
C-FETN JSTR 5021
C-FETZ CL61 5041
C-FEUQ CL30 20047
C-FEUR CL64 5577
C-FEUV CL61 5042
**C-FEVC C550 550-1023**
C-FEWB LJ25 180
C-FEXB HS25 257152
**C-FEXD FA10 78**
C-FEXH CL64 5616
C-FEYG WW24 81
C-FEYU CL64 5617
C-FEYZ CL64 5618
C-FFAB HS25 257030
**C-FFBC CL30 20257**
C-FFBC WW24 119
C-FFBY CL61 5044
C-FFCL C550 063
**C-FFEV FA10 204**
C-FFGE CL64 5620
C-FFHX CL64 5621
C-FFLA CL64 5622
C-FFLJ CL30 20051
C-FFMQ CL64 5623
C-FFMS CL64 5624
C-FFNM GLF2 52
C-FFNT CL30 20065
C-FFQQ CL64 5625
C-FFSO CL61 5045
C-FFTM HS25 258161
C-FFZE CL30 20055
C-FFZI CL30 20049
C-FFZP CL64 5628
C-FGAT C500 199
C-FGAT C550 255
C-FGBD CL64 5630
C-FGBE CL64 5629
C-FGBP CL30 20053
C-FGBY CL30 20076
C-FGCD CL30 20077
C-FGCE CL30 20078
C-FGCJ CL30 20079
C-FGCL CL30 20080
C-FGCN CL30 20081
C-FGCV CL30 20082
C-FGCW CL30 20083
C-FGCX CL30 20084
C-FGCZ CL30 20085
C-FGFB CL30 20071
**C-FGFI F900 138**
C-FGGF CL30 20057
C-FGGH WW24 431
C-FGGX GLEX 9014
**C-FGIL CL30 20107**
C-FGJC LJ60 210
C-FGJI CL30 20058
C-FGLF HS25 258141
C-FGMR CL30 20056
C-FGNO CL30 20059
C-FGUD CL30 20061
C-FGUT CL30 20060
C-FGVJ CL30 20086
C-FGVK CL30 20087
C-FGVM CL30 20088
C-FGVS CL30 20089
C-FGWB CL30 20090
C-FGWF CL30 20091
C-FGWL CL30 20092
C-FGWR CL30 20093
C-FGWW CL30 20094
C-FGWZ CL30 20095
C-FGXK CL30 20066
C-FGXW CL30 20064
C-FGYI CL64 5639
C-FGYM CL65 5701
C-FGYU CL30 20070
C-FGZD CL30 20069
C-FGZE CL30 20068
C-FGZI CL30 20067
C-FHBX GLF2 119/22
C-FHCL CL64 5645
C-FHCM CL64 5644
C-FHCY CL30 20075
C-FHDE CL30 20074
C-FHDM LJ35 410
C-FHDN CL30 20073
C-FHDV CL64 5648
C-FHFP LJ24 340
**C-FHGC CL64 5453**
C-FHGX GLEX 9002
C-FHHD CL61 5061
C-FHJB LJ55 122
C-FHLL HS25 25034
C-FHLO LJ35 179
C-FHMI CL30 20096
C-FHMM CL30 20097
C-FHMQ CL30 20098
C-FHMS CL30 20099
C-FHMZ CL30 20100
C-FHNC CL30 20101
C-FHND CL30 20102
C-FHNF CL30 20103
C-FHNH CL30 20104
C-FHNJ CL30 20105
**C-FHNS ASTR 156**
C-FHPB GLEX 9202
C-FHPG GLEX 9203
C-FHPM GLF2 104/10
**C-FHPM GLF4 1103**
C-FHPQ GLEX 9201
C-FHRD HS25 258460
**C-FHRL ASTR 150**
C-FHSS HS25 256003
C-FHYL CL64 5506
C-FHYL GLEX 9286
**C-FICA FA10 196**
C-FICU LJ35 249
C-FIDO LJ60 133
C-FIDU CL30 20108
C-FIDV CL30 20109
C-FIDX CL30 20106
C-FIDZ CL30 20107
C-FIEA CL30 20110
C-FIED CL30 20111
C-FIEE CL30 20112
C-FIEM CL30 20113
C-FIEP CL30 20114
C-FIEX CL64 5650
C-FIFK CL65 5702
**C-FIGD FA20 109/427**
**C-FIGO HS25 258087**
C-FIGR CL61 5069
C-FIHL GLEX 9205

| Registration | Type | C/n |
|---|---|---|
| C-FIHN | GLEX | 9208 |
| C-FIHP | GLEX | 9204 |
| C-FIIB | GLEX | 9206 |
| C-FIIC | GLEX | 9207 |
| C-FIIG | GLEX | 9209 |
| C-FIMA | C525 | 0191 |
| C-FIMF | CL64 | 5653 |
| **C-FIMO** | **C650** | **0065** |
| C-FIMP | C550 | 125 |
| C-FIOB | CL30 | 20115 |
| C-FIOB | CL61 | 5064 |
| C-FIOC | CL30 | 20116 |
| C-FIOE | CL30 | 20117 |
| C-FIOG | CL30 | 20118 |
| C-FIOH | CL30 | 20119 |
| C-FIOJ | CL30 | 20120 |
| C-FIOK | CL30 | 20121 |
| C-FION | CL30 | 20122 |
| C-FIOO | CL30 | 20123 |
| C-FIOP | CL30 | 20124 |
| C-FIOT | GLEX | 9210 |
| C-FIOT | GLF2 | 78 |
| C-FIOZ | GLEX | 9213 |
| C-FIPC | GLEX | 9215 |
| C-FIPE | HS25 | 258319 |
| C-FIPF | GLEX | 9218 |
| C-FIPG | GLEX | 9220 |
| C-FIPG | HS25 | 257132 |
| C-FIPH | GLEX | 9211 |
| C-FIPJ | GLEX | 9212 |
| C-FIPJ | HS25 | 25053 |
| C-FIPM | GLEX | 9214 |
| C-FIPN | GLEX | 9216 |
| C-FIPP | GLEX | 9217 |
| C-FIPQ | GLEX | 9219 |
| C-FIPT | GLEX | 9221 |
| **C-FITC** | **C52A** | **0394** |
| C-FIXN | CL64 | 5656 |
| C-FIYA | CL64 | 5657 |
| **C-FJAL** | **F2EX** | **34** |
| **C-FJBO** | **C550** | **550-0812** |
| **C-FJCB** | **CL30** | **20192** |
| C-FJCB | CL64 | 5659 |
| **C-FJCZ** | **C550** | **700** |
| C-FJDF | CL61 | 5079 |
| C-FJEF | LJ35 | 390 |
| C-FJES | F900 | 55 |
| C-FJES | FA20 | 236 |
| C-FJES | GLF4 | 1207 |
| **C-FJGG** | **LJ60** | **038** |
| C-FJGR | CL61 | 5080 |
| C-FJGX | GLEX | 9003 |
| **C-FJHS** | **HS25** | **258283** |
| C-FJJC | C650 | 0116 |
| **C-FJJC** | **CL61** | **5096** |
| C-FJJG | C650 | 0116 |
| C-FJLA | CL61 | 5154 |
| C-FJML | GLEX | 9223 |
| C-FJMP | GLEX | 9225 |
| C-FJMQ | GLEX | 9228 |
| C-FJMV | GLEX | 9230 |
| C-FJMX | GLEX | 9232 |
| C-FJNJ | GLEX | 9222 |
| C-FJNQ | GLEX | 9224 |
| **C-FJNS** | **CL61** | **5059** |
| C-FJNX | GLEX | 9226 |
| C-FJNZ | GLEX | 9227 |
| C-FJOA | GLEX | 9229 |
| C-FJOE | C550 | 573 |
| C-FJOE | C650 | 0049 |
| **C-FJOI** | **F9EX** | **69** |
| **C-FJOJ** | **WW24** | **271** |
| C-FJOK | GLEX | 9231 |
| C-FJOU | GLEX | 9233 |
| C-FJPI | CL61 | 5085 |
| C-FJPV | F2TH | 88 |
| C-FJQD | CL30 | 20125 |
| C-FJQH | CL30 | 20126 |
| C-FJQP | CL30 | 20127 |
| C-FJQR | CL30 | 20128 |
| C-FJQT | CL30 | 20129 |
| C-FJQX | CL30 | 20130 |
| C-FJQZ | CL30 | 20131 |
| C-FJRE | CL30 | 20132 |
| C-FJRG | CL30 | 20133 |
| **C-FJTN** | **PRM1** | **RB-267** |
| C-FJUH | FA50 | 137 |
| **C-FJWZ** | **C550** | **685** |
| **C-FJXN** | **C550** | **684** |
| **C-FKBC** | **C560** | **0409** |
| **C-FKCE** | **C550** | **686** |
| **C-FKCI** | **CL30** | **20242** |
| C-FKCI | FA50 | 63 |
| C-FKCI | HS25 | 25137 |
| C-FKDV | CL64 | 5664 |
| **C-FKDX** | **C550** | **687** |
| **C-FKEB** | **C550** | **688** |
| **C-FKGN** | **HS25** | **258052** |
| C-FKGX | GLEX | 9004 |
| C-FKHD | C550 | 110 |
| C-FKIY | CL61 | 5092 |
| **C-FKJM** | **CL61** | **3012** |
| **C-FKLB** | **C550** | **699** |
| C-FKMC | C500 | 073 |
| **C-FKMC** | **CL65** | **5772** |
| C-FKNN | CL61 | 5094 |
| C-FKTD | CL61 | 5096 |
| C-FKVW | CL61 | 5097 |
| C-FLBC | C550 | 044 |
| C-FLCY | CL30 | 20134 |
| **C-FLCY** | **CL64** | **5506** |
| C-FLDD | CL30 | 20135 |
| **C-FLDD** | **CL30** | **20238** |
| C-FLDD | CL30 | 20268 |
| C-FLDK | CL30 | 20136 |
| C-FLDM | C550 | 288 |
| C-FLDO | C550 | 038 |
| C-FLDO | CL30 | 20137 |
| C-FLDW | CL30 | 20138 |
| C-FLDX | CL30 | 20139 |
| C-FLEC | CL30 | 20140 |
| C-FLEJ | CL30 | 20141 |
| C-FLEK | CL30 | 20142 |
| C-FLEN | CL30 | 20143 |
| C-FLGN | CL65 | 5703 |
| C-FLKC | CL65 | 5704 |
| C-FLKY | GLEX | 9241 |
| C-FLKZ | GLEX | 9234 |
| C-FLLA | GLEX | 9235 |
| C-FLLF | GLEX | 9236 |
| C-FLLH | GLEX | 9237 |
| **C-FLLH** | **LJ45** | **088** |
| C-FLLN | GLEX | 9238 |
| C-FLLO | GLEX | 9239 |
| C-FLLV | GLEX | 9240 |
| C-FLMJ | C650 | 0104 |
| **C-FLMK** | **CL65** | **5786** |
| C-FLNZ | CL65 | 5705 |
| C-FLPC | CL61 | 5006 |
| C-FLPC | CL64 | 5392 |
| C-FLPD | C550 | 189 |
| C-FLPH | HS25 | 258243 |
| C-FLQF | CL30 | 20144 |
| C-FLQG | CL30 | 20145 |
| C-FLQH | CL30 | 20146 |
| C-FLQM | CL30 | 20147 |
| C-FLQO | CL30 | 20148 |
| C-FLQP | CL30 | 20149 |
| C-FLQR | CL30 | 20150 |
| C-FLQX | CL30 | 20151 |
| C-FLQY | CL30 | 20152 |
| C-FLQZ | CL30 | 20153 |
| **C-FLRJ** | **LJ45** | **156** |
| **C-FLRP** | **CL61** | **5068** |
| C-FLSF | CL65 | 5706 |
| C-FLSJ | CL65 | 5707 |
| C-FLTB | GLEX | 9242 |
| **C-FLTB** | **LJ60** | **377** |
| C-FLTH | GLEX | 9243 |
| C-FLTI | GLEX | 9244 |
| C-FLTJ | GLEX | 9245 |
| C-FLTL | C650 | 0007 |
| C-FLUT | CL61 | 5087 |
| C-FLYJ | CL61 | 5102 |
| **C-FLZA** | **C550** | **701** |
| C-FMAN | C500 | 086 |
| **C-FMCI** | **C550** | **550-0816** |
| C-FMDB | HS25 | 25075 |
| C-FMFK | GLEX | 9246 |
| **C-FMFL** | **FA50** | **96** |
| **C-FMFM** | **C550** | **702** |
| C-FMFN | GLEX | 9247 |
| C-FMFO | GLEX | 9248 |
| C-FMGE | GLEX | 9249 |
| C-FMGK | GLEX | 9250 |
| C-FMGL | LJ45 | 088 |
| **C-FMGL** | **LJ45** | **360** |
| C-FMGM | LJ25 | 117 |
| **C-FMHA** | **LJ40** | **45-2043** |
| **C-FMHL** | **ASTR** | **066** |
| **C-FMJM** | **C550** | **444** |
| C-FMKF | HS25 | 25170 |
| C-FMKW | GLEX | 9251 |
| C-FMKZ | GLEX | 9252 |
| C-FMLB | GLEX | 9253 |
| C-FMLE | GLEX | 9254 |
| C-FMLI | GLEX | 9255 |
| C-FMLQ | GLEX | 9256 |
| C-FMLT | GLEX | 9257 |
| C-FMLV | GLEX | 9258 |
| C-FMMH | GLEX | 9259 |
| C-FMND | GLEX | 9260 |
| C-FMNL | CL65 | 5710 |
| C-FMNR | CL65 | 5711 |
| C-FMNW | CL65 | 5712 |
| **C-FMOS** | **C550** | **550-0982** |
| C-FMPP | C550 | 409 |
| **C-FMRI** | **HS25** | **258688** |
| C-FMTC | HS25 | 25104 |
| C-FMUI | GLEX | 9261 |
| C-FMUN | GLEX | 9262 |
| C-FMUO | GLEX | 9263 |
| C-FMVN | CL65 | 5714 |
| C-FMVQ | CL61 | 5105 |
| C-FMVQ | CL65 | 5713 |
| C-FMWG | CL30 | 20163 |
| C-FMWW | WW24 | 380 |
| C-FMWX | CL30 | 20162 |
| C-FMXH | CL30 | 20161 |
| C-FMXK | CL30 | 20160 |
| C-FMXQ | CL30 | 20159 |
| C-FMXU | CL30 | 20158 |
| C-FMXW | CL30 | 20157 |
| C-FMXX | CL30 | 20156 |
| C-FMYA | CL30 | 20154 |
| C-FMYB | CL30 | 20155 |
| C-FMYB | FA50 | 99 |
| C-FNCG | GLF2 | 208 |
| (C-FNCG) | GLF4 | 1017 |
| C-FNCG | SBRL | 282-90 |
| **C-FNCT** | **C550** | **175** |
| C-FNDF | GLEX | 9115 |
| C-FNDK | GLEX | 9265 |
| C-FNDN | GLEX | 9264 |
| C-FNDO | GLEX | 9266 |
| C-FNDQ | GLEX | 9267 |
| C-FNDT | GLEX | 9268 |
| C-FNER | HS25 | 25176 |
| **C-FNEU** | **CL61** | **5119** |
| **C-FNHZ** | **C500** | **689** |
| C-FNIJ | CL65 | 5715 |
| C-FNIN | CL65 | 5716 |
| C-FNMC | LJ24 | 106 |
| C-FNNC | FA50 | 176 |
| C-FNND | FA10 | 87 |
| C-FNNS | CL61 | 5068 |
| C-FNNS | CL61 | 5096 |
| C-FNNT | CL61 | 5068 |
| C-FNNT | CL64 | 5317 |
| C-FNOC | C500 | 182 |
| C-FNOR | GLF2 | 54/36 |
| **C-FNRG** | **C750** | **0305** |
| C-FNRG | LJ45 | 223 |
| C-FNRG | LJ55 | 101 |
| C-FNRP | GLEX | 9269 |
| C-FNRR | GLEX | 9270 |
| C-FNRW | WW24 | 176 |
| C-FNSN | GLEX | 9271 |
| C-FNSV | GLEX | 9272 |
| **C-FNTM** | **C560** | **0346** |
| C-FNTM | CL65 | 5718 |
| C-FNTP | CL65 | 5721 |
| C-FNUF | CL65 | 5720 |
| C-FNUH | CL30 | 20164 |
| **C-FNXL** | **C56X** | **5686** |
| C-FNYU | CL64 | 5332 |
| C-FNZZ | GLEX | 9273 |
| C-FOAB | GLEX | 9274 |
| C-FOAD | GLEX | 9275 |
| C-FOAE | CL30 | 20165 |
| C-FOAI | CL30 | 20166 |
| C-FOAJ | CL30 | 20167 |
| C-FOAQ | CL30 | 20168 |
| C-FOAT | CL30 | 20169 |
| C-FOAU | CL30 | 20170 |
| C-FOBF | CL65 | 5729 |
| C-FOBJ | CL30 | 20173 |
| C-FOBK | CL65 | 5719 |
| **C-FOBQ** | **C555** | **0036** |
| C-FOGE | CL65 | 5722 |
| C-FOGI | CL65 | 5723 |
| C-FOIL | WW24 | 201 |
| C-FOIL | WW24 | 336 |
| C-FOKD | GLEX | 9276 |
| C-FOKF | GLEX | 9277 |
| C-FOKH | GLEX | 9278 |
| C-FOKJ | GLEX | 9279 |
| C-FOMS | CL65 | 5724 |
| C-FOMU | CL30 | 20170 |
| C-FOMU | CL65 | 5725 |
| C-FONX | FA20 | 225/472 |
| C-FOPC | BE40 | RK-70 |
| C-FOPC | HS25 | 25016 |
| C-FOQR | CL30 | 20174 |
| C-FOQW | CL30 | 20175 |
| C-FORB | CL30 | 20176 |
| **C-FORJ** | **C650** | **0104** |
| C-FOSB | CL30 | 20177 |
| C-FOSG | CL30 | 20178 |
| C-FOSK | CL61 | 5114 |
| C-FOSM | C500 | 343 |
| C-FOSM | CL30 | 20179 |
| C-FOSQ | CL30 | 20180 |
| C-FOSW | CL30 | 20181 |
| C-FOSX | CL30 | 20182 |
| C-FOTF | CL30 | 20183 |
| C-FOVD | GLEX | 9280 |
| C-FOVE | GLEX | 9281 |
| C-FOVG | GLEX | 9282 |
| C-FOVH | GLEX | 9283 |
| C-FOVK | GLEX | 9284 |
| C-FOXA | GLEX | 9018 |
| C-FOXU | CL65 | 5726 |
| C-FOXV | CL65 | 5727 |
| C-FOYE | CL65 | 5728 |
| C-FPAW | MU30 | A006SA |
| **C-FPBX** | **LJ45** | **085** |
| **C-FPCE** | **HS25** | **258500** |
| C-FPCP | HS25 | 258095 |
| C-FPCP | HS25 | 258500 |
| C-FPDO | FA50 | 97 |
| C-FPEL | C550 | 044 |
| **C-FPEP** | **WW24** | **441** |
| C-FPFF | GLEX | 9285 |
| C-FPGB | GLEX | 9286 |
| C-FPGD | GLEX | 9287 |
| C-FPGI | GLEX | 9288 |
| C-FPIY | CL61 | 5125 |
| **C-FPJT** | **C560** | **0017** |
| C-FPMQ | CL30 | 20171 |
| C-FPMU | CL30 | 20172 |
| C-FPOX | CL61 | 5128 |
| C-FPPN | HS25 | 25280 |
| C-FPQE | GLEX | 9289 |
| C-FPQF | GLEX | 9290 |
| C-FPQG | GLEX | 9291 |
| C-FPQG | HS25 | 25036 |
| C-FPQH | GLEX | 9292 |
| C-FPQI | GLEX | 9293 |
| C-FPQT | CL65 | 5731 |
| C-FPQV | CL65 | 5732 |
| C-FPQW | CL65 | 5733 |
| C-FPQY | CL65 | 5734 |
| C-FPQZ | CL65 | 5735 |
| **C-FPRP** | **LJ35** | **390** |
| C-FPSJ | CL65 | 5736 |
| C-FPSQ | CL65 | 5737 |
| C-FPSV | CL65 | 5738 |
| **C-FPTM** | **DDJT** | **DJ1-0002** |
| **C-FPUB** | **LJ25** | **090** |
| C-FPUI | C750 | 0002 |
| **C-FPWB** | **C525** | **0062** |
| C-FPWC | C56X | 5078 |
| C-FPWI | CL65 | 5730 |
| C-FPZZ | CL30 | 20184 |
| C-FQCF | CL30 | 20185 |
| C-FQCY | C650 | 0087 |
| C-FQEI | CL30 | 20186 |

C-FQNS HS25 25152
C-FQOA CL30 20187
C-FQOF CL30 20188
C-FQOI CL30 20189
C-FQOK CL30 20190
C-FQOL CL30 20191
C-FQOM CL30 20192
C-FQOQ CL30 20193
C-FQQE CL65 5739
C-FQQG CL65 5740
C-FQQH CL65 5741
C-FQQK CL65 5742
C-FQQO CL65 5743
C-FQQS CL65 5744
C-FQQW CL65 5745
C-FQVE CL65 5746
C-FQXW GLEX 9294
C-FQXX GLEX 9295
C-FQXY GLEX 9296
C-FQYB C560 0588
C-FQYB GLEX 9297
C-FQYD GLEX 9298
C-FQYE GLEX 9299
C-FQYT CL61 3049
C-FRBC JSTR 5160
**C-FRCI CL64 5650**
C-FREE FA10 224
C-FREE WW24 271
C-FRGV CL61 5142
C-FRGX GLEX 9014
C-FRGY CS55 0036
**C-FRGY LJ60 061**
C-FRHL C500 343
C-FRJV GLEX 9300
C-FRJX CL61 5147
C-FRJY GLEX 9301
**C-FRJZ ASTR 087**
C-FRKI C560 0573
**C-FRKL C560 0573**
C-FRKL GLEX 9302
C-FRKO GLEX 9303
C-FRKQ GLEX 9304
C-FRMW GLEX 9305
C-FRNG C550 550-1079
C-FRNG GLEX 9306
C-FRNJ GLEX 9307
C-FRNR LJ24 321
C-FROC GLF2 134
C-FROX LJ25 070
C-FROY CL30 20201
C-FROY WW24 429
C-FRPP HS25 258121
C-FRQA CL30 20194
C-FRQA CL61 5146
C-FRQC CL30 20195
C-FRQH CL30 20196
C-FRQK CL30 20197
C-FRQM CL30 20198
C-FRQN CL30 20199
C-FRQP CL30 20200
**C-FRST C550 550-1011**
(C-FRST) CL60 1059
C-FRVE C525 0062
**C-FRYS LJ45 275**
**C-FSBC C650 7092**
C-FSBR GLF4 1032
**C-FSCI CL65 5717**
C-FSCI HS25 258105
C-FSCL FA50 97
C-FSCY HS25 258105
C-FSDH HS25 25192
**C-FSDL LJ45 255**
C-FSEN HS25 25027
C-FSIM HS25 25039
C-FSIP CL60 1048
C-FSIP CL65 5747
C-FSIQ CL65 5748
C-FSIU CL65 5749
C-FSJH CL65 5750
**C-FSJI FA20 373**
**C-FSJR CL64 5413**
C-FSJT CL65 5751
C-FSJV CL65 5752
C-FSJY CL65 5753
C-FSKC C500 018
C-FSKT CL65 5754
C-FSKX CL65 5755
C-FSLL CL30 20208
C-FSLR CL30 20209
C-FSLU CL30 20210
C-FSMO CL30 20202
C-FSMW CL30 20203
C-FSNB CL30 20204
**C-FSNC C560 0676**
C-FSNP CL30 20205
C-FSNQ CL30 20206
C-FSNU CL30 20207
C-FSRX GLEX 9308
C-FSRY GLEX 9309
**C-FSRZ GLEX 9310**
C-FSSE GLEX 9311
C-FSUA WW24 17
C-FSUN C500 292
C-FSXG CL60 1043
C-FSXH CL61 5156
**C-FSXL C56X 5747**
C-FSYK CL61 5158
C-FSYO LJ25 122
C-FTAM C550 398
C-FTAM HS25 25108
C-FTBZ CL64 5991
C-FTDB ASTR 117
C-FTEC HS25 25232
C-FTEL C750 0097
**C-FTEN C750 0188**
C-FTEN FA10 45
**C-FTFC CL61 5091**
C-FTIE CL61 5041
C-FTIK GLEX 9312
C-FTIL C550 299
**C-FTIL C56X 5253**
**C-FTIO GLEX 9313**
C-FTIQ GLEX 9314
C-FTIR GLEX 9315
**C-FTIS GLEX 9316**
**C-FTJF C560 0643**
C-FTKA CL30 20211
C-FTKC CL30 20212
C-FTKG CL30 20214
C-FTKH CL30 20213
C-FTKK CL30 20215
C-FTKX C525 0364
C-FTLA HS25 258015
C-FTLB CL65 5756
C-FTLH CL65 5757
**C-FTMI C500 069**
C-FTMS C550 299
C-FTNE CL61 5162
C-FTNN CL61 5159
C-FTOC C550 321
C-FTOH CL61 5165
C-FTOM C550 321
**C-FTOM C560 0633**
**C-FTOR C650 7067**
C-FTQY CL65 5763
C-FTQZ CL65 5764
C-FTRF CL65 5762
**C-FTRM C52A 0235**
C-FTRM CL65 5761
C-FTRO CL65 5759
**C-FTRP ASTR 271**
C-FTRQ CL65 5760
C-FTRY CL65 5758
C-FTUT FA20 21
**C-FTUX GLEX 9317**
C-FTUY GLEX 9318
**C-FTVC HS25 258243**
**C-FTVF GLEX 9319**
C-FTVK GLEX 9320
C-FTVN GLEX 9321
C-FTVO GLEX 9322
**C-FTWO WW24 199**
**C-FTWR WW24 207**
**C-FTWV WW24 226**
**C-FTXL C56X 5672**
C-FTXT LJ25 057
C-FUAK CL65 5767
C-FUAS CL65 5766
C-FUAU CL65 5765
C-FUBE CL30 20216
C-FUBK CL30 20217
C-FUBM CL30 20218
C-FUBO CL30 20219
C-FUBP CL30 20220
C-FUBQ CL30 20221
C-FUBT CL30 20222
**C-FUCV GLEX 9323**
**C-FUCY GLEX 9324**
C-FUCZ GLEX 9325
C-FUDH GLEX 9326
C-FUDN GLEX 9327
C-FUIT CL65 5768
C-FUIU CL65 5769
C-FUIV CL65 5770
C-FUJA CL30 20223
C-FUJE CL30 20224
C-FUJM CL30 20225
C-FUJR CL30 20226
C-FUJT CL30 20227
C-FUJX CL30 20228
C-FUND CL61 5172
C-FUOJ GLEX 9328
C-FUOK GLEX 9329
C-FUOL GLEX 9330
**C-FUOM GLEX 9331**
C-FURA CL30 20229
C-FURB CL30 20230
C-FURC CL30 20231
C-FURD CL30 20232
C-FURF CL30 20233
**C-FURG CL61 3063**
C-FURH CL30 20234
**C-FURP GLEX 9332**
C-FUSI GLEX 9333
C-FUSR GLEX 9334
**C-FUTF GLEX 9335**
C-FUTL GLEX 9336
C-FUTT GLEX 9337
C-FUUF CL65 5776
C-FUUI CL65 5777
**C-FUUM CL65 5778**
**C-FUUQ CL65 5779**
C-FUUW CL65 5780
C-FUVA CL65 5771
C-FUVC CL65 5772
C-FUVF CL65 5773
C-FUVG CL65 5774
C-FUVH CL65 5775
C-FVEJ C560 0648
**C-FVFW GLEX 9338**
C-FVGP GLEX 9339
C-FVGX GLEX 9340
**C-FVHE GLEX 9341**
C-FVLX CL30 20243
C-FVLZ CL30 20244
C-FVMI CL65 5791
C-FVMW CL65 5792
C-FVNB CL30 20235
**C-FVNC CL30 20236**
C-FVND CL30 20237
C-FVNF CL30 20238
C-FVNI CL30 20239
C-FVNL CL30 20240
C-FVNS CL30 20241
C-FVNT CL30 20242
C-FVOC CL65 5781
C-FVON CL65 5782
C-FVOQ CL65 5783
C-FVOZ CL65 5784
C-FVSL CL64 5489
C-FVSL LJ45 024
C-FVSL LJ45 408
C-FVUC CL64 5301
C-FVUI GLEX 9342
C-FVUK GLEX 9343
**C-FVUP GLEX 9344**
C-FVUZ GLEX 9345
C-FVVE GLEX 9346
C-FVZC CL61 5182
**C-FWBK C525 0425**
C-FWCE HS25 257206
C-FWCE HS25 258163
C-FWEC WW24 115
C-FWGB GLEX 9347
C-FWGE CL61 5178
**C-FWGH GLEX 9348**
**C-FWGP GLEX 9349**
**C-FWGV GLEX 9350**
**C-FWHF GLEX 9351**
**C-FWHH C560 0484**
C-FWIK GLEX 9352
C-FWOS HS25 25159
C-FWQH CL65 5785
C-FWQL CL65 5786
C-FWQM CL65 5787
C-FWQO CL65 5788
C-FWQV CL65 5789
C-FWQY CL65 5790
C-FWRA FA20 110
**C-FWRE CL30 20252**
C-FWRG CL30 20253
C-FWRN WW24 98
C-FWRX CL30 20254
C-FWSC F900 75
C-FWTK CL30 20255
C-FWTQ CL30 20256
C-FWTY CL30 20257
C-FWUC CL30 20251
C-FWUI CL30 20250
C-FWUK CL30 20249
C-FWUL CL30 20248
C-FWUO CL30 20247
**C-FWUT CL30 20246**
C-FWUZ CL30 20245
C-FWVH CL30 20258
C-FWWW C550 178
**C-FWXL C56X 5691**
C-FWZR GLEX 9353
C-FWZX GLEX 9354
C-FXAQ GLEX 9355
**C-FXAY GLEX 9356**
C-FXBF GLEX 9357
C-FXCK CL61 5189
**C-FXCN CL64 5474**
(C-FXFJ) C52B 0144
C-FXHE CL64 5304
**C-FXHN LJ45 126**
C-FXIP CL61 5194
C-FXIY GLEX 9358
**C-FXJD GLEX 9359**
**C-FXJM GLEX 9360**
C-FXKE CL64 5303
C-FXKE GLEX 9361
**C-FXKK GLEX 9362**
C-FXPB CL30 20259
C-FXPB CL64 5474
C-FXPI CL30 20260
C-FXPL CL30 20261
C-FXPQ CL30 20262
C-FXPR CL30 20263
C-FXPT CL30 20264
C-FXPW CL30 20265
C-FXQG CL65 5793
C-FXQH CL65 5794
C-FXQJ CL65 5795
C-FXQM CL65 5796
**C-FXQR CL65 5797**
C-FXQX CL65 5798
**C-FXRD CL65 5805**
**C-FXTC C52B 0037**
C-FXUQ CL64 5307
**C-FXYK GLEX 9363**
**C-FXYN LJ45 270**
**C-FXYS GLEX 9364**
C-FXYY GLEX 9365
C-FXZS CL64 5309
C-FYAB CL65 5804
C-FYAG GLF3 310
**C-FYAI CL65 5803**
C-FYAP CL65 5802
C-FYAV CL65 5801
C-FYAW CL65 5800
**C-FYAY CL65 5799**
C-FYBG CL30 20266
C-FYBJ CL30 20267
**C-FYBK CL65 5806**
C-FYBM CL30 20269
C-FYBN CL30 20270
C-FYBO CL30 20271
C-FYBS CL30 20272
C-FYBU CL30 20273
C-FYBV CL30 20274
C-FYBZ CL30 20268
C-FYGJ GLEX 9366
**C-FYGP GLEX 9367**
**C-FYGX GLEX 9368**
**C-FYHT GLEX 9369**
**C-FYIG GLEX 9370**

| | | |
|---|---|---|
| **C-FYIH** | **GLEX** | **9371** |
| **C-FYIZ** | **GLEX** | **9372** |
| **C-FYJC** | **GLEX** | **9373** |
| **C-FYJD** | **GLEX** | **9374** |
| C-FYMM | C560 | 0314 |
| **C-FYMM** | **C560** | **0705** |
| C-FYMT | C560 | 0314 |
| C-FYMT | GLEX | 9375 |
| **C-FYMU** | **GLEX** | **9376** |
| **C-FYNI** | **GLEX** | **9377** |
| **C-FYNQ** | **GLEX** | **9378** |
| **C-FYNV** | **GLEX** | **9379** |
| **C-FYOC** | **GLEX** | **9380** |
| C-FYPB | FA20 | 254 |
| **C-FYTY** | **CL65** | **5814** |
| C-FYTZ | CL65 | 5765 |
| **C-FYUD** | **CL65** | **5807** |
| C-FYUH | CL65 | 5808 |
| **C-FYUK** | **CL65** | **5809** |
| C-FYUL | C550 | 550-1028 |
| **C-FYUL** | **C560** | **0647** |
| **C-FYUP** | **CL65** | **5810** |
| C-FYUQ | CL30 | 20245 |
| **C-FYUR** | **CL65** | **5811** |
| **C-FYUS** | **CL65** | **5812** |
| **C-FYUY** | **CL65** | **5813** |
| C-FYXC | CL64 | 5317 |
| C-FYYH | CL64 | 5318 |
| C-FYZP | GLEX | 9139 |
| **C-FZAU** | **LJ45** | **163** |
| C-FZDY | CL64 | 5321 |
| C-FZEI | WW24 | 441 |
| C-FZHT | LJ24 | 217 |
| C-FZHU | LJ25 | 070 |
| C-FZKY | CL65 | 5821 |
| C-FZLA | CL65 | 5815 |
| **C-FZLB** | **CL65** | **5816** |
| C-FZLM | CL65 | 5817 |
| **C-FZLR** | **CL65** | **5818** |
| **C-FZLS** | **CL65** | **5819** |
| **C-FZLU** | **CL65** | **5820** |
| **C-FZLX** | **CL30** | **20275** |
| **C-FZLY** | **CL30** | **20276** |
| C-FZLZ | CL30 | 20277 |
| C-FZOP | CL64 | 5367 |
| **C-FZOP** | **FA10** | **44** |
| C-FZPG | CL64 | 5321 |
| **C-FZQP** | **LJ35** | **168** |
| C-FZRR | CL64 | 5332 |
| C-FZSO | CL64 | 5557 |
| C-FZVM | GLEX | 9123 |
| C-FZVN | CL64 | 5335 |
| C-FZVN | GLEX | 9124 |
| C-FZVS | GLEX | 9125 |
| C-FZVV | GLEX | 9126 |
| C-FZWB | GLEX | 9128 |
| C-FZWF | GLEX | 9129 |
| C-FZWW | GLEX | 9131 |
| C-FZXC | GLEX | 9132 |
| C-FZXE | GLEX | 9133 |
| C-FZXZ | GLEX | 9134 |
| **C-FZYB** | **FA50** | **272** |
| C-FZYL | GLEX | 9135 |
| C-GAAA | C500 | 549 |
| C-GAAA | C500 | 677 |
| **C-GAAA** | **HS25** | **257179** |
| **C-GABE** | **C525** | **0232** |
| C-GABX | HS25 | 257047 |
| C-GAGP | WW24 | 260 |
| C-GAGQ | GLEX | 9140 |
| C-GAGQ | HS25 | 258181 |
| C-GAGS | GLEX | 9141 |
| C-GAGT | GLEX | 9142 |
| **C-GAGU** | **C680** | **0100** |
| C-GAGU | HS25 | 258181 |
| C-GAIP | CL65 | 5822 |
| **C-GAJG** | **CL65** | **5823** |
| **C-GAJS** | **LJ35** | **380** |
| **C-GAKE** | **CL30** | **20278** |
| C-GAKF | CL30 | 20279 |
| **C-GAKL** | **CL30** | **20280** |
| **C-GAKN** | **CL30** | **20281** |
| **C-GAKO** | **CL30** | **20282** |
| **C-GAKZ** | **CL30** | **20283** |
| **C-GALP** | **CL65** | **5824** |
| C-GAMW | C550 | 051 |
| (C-GANE) | GLF2 | 162 |

| | | |
|---|---|---|
| **C-GANU** | **CL65** | **5825** |
| **C-GAOB** | **CL61** | **5117** |
| **C-GAPC** | **C560** | **0033** |
| C-GAPD | C550 | 691 |
| C-GAPD | C560 | 0165 |
| C-GAPT | C550 | 216 |
| C-GAPT | C650 | 0195 |
| **C-GAPT** | **C750** | **0131** |
| C-GAPV | C550 | 691 |
| C-GATU | JSTR | 5143 |
| C-GAUK | CL64 | 5343 |
| **C-GAWH** | **CL64** | **5557** |
| C-GAWH | HS25 | 258087 |
| **C-GAWJ** | **WW24** | **277** |
| C-GAWR | C560 | 0351 |
| **C-GAWR** | **C56X** | **5717** |
| **C-GAWU** | **C560** | **0351** |
| **C-GAZU** | **F900** | **198** |
| C-GAZU | FA50 | 228 |
| C-GAZU | JSTR | 5070/52 |
| C-GAZU | JSTR | 5083/49 |
| C-GAZU | JSTR | 5222 |
| **C-GBAP** | **HS25** | **258444** |
| **C-GBBB** | **GLF3** | **368** |
| **C-GBBX** | **C550** | **650** |
| **C-GBBX** | **F9EX** | **64** |
| C-GBCA | C550 | 590 |
| C-GBCB | C550 | 060 |
| C-GBCC | CL60 | 1005 |
| C-GBCE | C550 | 591 |
| C-GBCF | C550 | 564 |
| **C-GBCI** | **FA20** | **478** |
| C-GBCK | C500 | 204 |
| C-GBDH | CL60 | 1005 |
| C-GBDK | CL64 | 5347 |
| C-GBDX | JSTR | 5219 |
| C-GBEY | CL60 | 1008 |
| C-GBFA | LJ35 | 248 |
| C-GBFL | FA20 | 239 |
| **C-GBFP** | **LJ25** | **167** |
| C-GBFY | CL60 | 1009 |
| C-GBGC | CS55 | 0107 |
| C-GBHS | CL60 | 1011 |
| C-GBHZ | CL60 | 1013 |
| **C-GBIS** | **HS25** | **258117** |
| C-GBJA | CL61 | 5038 |
| C-GBJA | CL61 | 5082 |
| C-GBJA | CL61 | 5111 |
| C-GBJA | CL61 | 5151 |
| C-GBJA | CL64 | 5302 |
| C-GBJA | CL64 | 5339 |
| C-GBJA | CL64 | 5341 |
| C-GBKB | CL60 | 1045 |
| **C-GBKB** | **CL64** | **5420** |
| C-GBKC | CL60 | 1007 |
| C-GBKE | CL60 | 1012 |
| C-GBKE | CL64 | 5352 |
| C-GBLF | LJ35 | 091 |
| C-GBLL | CL60 | 1014 |
| C-GBLL-X | CL60 | 1014 |
| C-GBLN | CL60 | 1015 |
| C-GBLX | CL61 | 3010 |
| C-GBLX | GLEX | 9112 |
| C-GBNE | C500 | 461 |
| **C-GBNE** | **C560** | **0244** |
| (C-GBNS) | HS25 | 256047 |
| C-GBNS | HS25 | 256051 |
| **C-GBNX** | **C560** | **0074** |
| C-GBOQ | CL60 | 1036 |
| C-GBOT | LJ25 | 090 |
| **C-GBPL** | **C510** | **0205** |
| **C-GBPM** | **C525** | **0287** |
| C-GBPX | CL60 | 1017 |
| C-GBQC | LJ25 | 179 |
| C-GBRM | HS25 | 257093 |
| C-GBRQ | CL64 | 5358 |
| C-GBRW | LJ36 | 001 |
| **C-GBSW** | **ASTR** | **130** |
| C-GBSZ | CL60 | 1047 |
| C-GBTB | C500 | 525 |
| C-GBTK | CL60 | 1057 |
| C-GBTT | CL60 | 1062 |
| **C-GBTY** | **GLEX** | **9381** |
| C-GBUA | GLEX | 9382 |
| C-GBUB | CL60 | 1064 |
| **C-GBUI** | **GLEX** | **9383** |
| C-GBUU-X | CL61 | 3001 |

| | | |
|---|---|---|
| C-GBVE | CL60 | 1065 |
| C-GBWA | LJ24 | 261 |
| C-GBWB | LJ24 | 168 |
| C-GBWD | LJ36 | 012 |
| C-GBWL | LJ35 | 049 |
| C-GBXH | CL61 | 3002 |
| C-GBXW | CL61 | 3018 |
| **C-GBXZ** | **CL30** | **20288** |
| C-GBYC | CL61 | 3011 |
| **C-GBYG** | **CL65** | **5826** |
| C-GBYH | CL65 | 5827 |
| **C-GBYK** | **CL65** | **5828** |
| **C-GBYM** | **CL65** | **5829** |
| C-GBYS | CL65 | 5830 |
| **C-GBZE** | **CL30** | **20284** |
| C-GBZE | CL60 | 1067 |
| **C-GBZI** | **CL30** | **20285** |
| C-GBZK | CL60 | 1077 |
| **C-GBZL** | **CL30** | **20286** |
| C-GBZQ | CL61 | 3047 |
| **C-GBZV** | **CL30** | **20287** |
| **C-GCCU** | **HS25** | **258105** |
| C-GCCZ | CL64 | 5367 |
| C-GCDF | CL64 | 5455 |
| C-GCDS | CL64 | 5455 |
| **C-GCDS** | **GLEX** | **9137** |
| C-GCEO | HS25 | 25285 |
| C-GCFB | GLF2 | 28 |
| **C-GCFG** | **CL61** | **3022** |
| C-GCFI | CL61 | 3020 |
| C-GCFP | C650 | 0145 |
| C-GCGR-X | CL60 | 1001 |
| **C-GCGS** | **HS25** | **258123** |
| C-GCGS-X | CL60 | 1002 |
| C-GCGT | CL60 | 1003/3991 |
| **C-GCGT** | **HS25** | **258828** |
| C-GCGT-X | CL60 | 1003/3991 |
| C-GCGY | GLEX | 9006 |
| C-GCGY | GLEX | 9056 |
| C-GCIB | CL60 | 1010 |
| C-GCIB | HS25 | 258048 |
| **C-GCIL** | **LJ55** | **089** |
| C-GCIX | C650 | 7092 |
| **C-GCIX** | **HS25** | **258492** |
| C-GCJD | LJ25 | 096 |
| C-GCJD | LJ35 | 055 |
| C-GCJN | C550 | 086 |
| **C-GCKR** | **GLEX** | **9384** |
| **C-GCLI** | **GLEX** | **9385** |
| C-GCLQ | C500 | 348 |
| **C-GCMJ** | **GLEX** | **9386** |
| C-GCMP | LJ45 | 019 |
| **C-GCMP** | **LJ45** | **153** |
| **C-GCNR** | **CL64** | **5339** |
| **C-GCOX** | **GLEX** | **9387** |
| **C-GCPI** | **GLEX** | **9388** |
| **C-GCPM** | **GLF4** | **1238** |
| **C-GCPV** | **GLEX** | **9389** |
| C-GCQB | CL64 | 5369 |
| C-GCRG | CS55 | 0142 |
| C-GCRP | HS25 | 258124 |
| C-GCRW | GLEX | 9007 |
| C-GCRW | GLEX | 9007 |
| C-GCSB | CL65 | 5709 |
| C-GCSN | CL60 | 1006 |
| C-GCTB | CL61 | 3031 |
| C-GCTD | C500 | 056 |
| C-GCUL | C550 | 135 |
| **C-GCUL** | **C750** | **0090** |
| C-GCUN | CL61 | 3035 |
| C-GCUP | CL61 | 3036 |
| C-GCUR | CL61 | 3037 |
| C-GCUT | CL61 | 3038 |
| C-GCUW | C560 | 0053 |
| C-GCVQ | CL60 | 1009 |
| C-GCVZ | CL64 | 5373 |
| **C-GCWQ** | **GLEX** | **9390** |
| **C-GCWU** | **GLEX** | **9391** |
| **C-GCWV** | **GLEX** | **9392** |
| **C-GCWX** | **GLEX** | **9393** |
| **C-GCXE** | **GLEX** | **9394** |
| **C-GCXL** | **C56X** | **5096** |
| C-GCZU | CL60 | 1030 |
| C-GDAO | HS25 | 257099 |
| **C-GDBC** | **HS25** | **258193** |
| **C-GDBF** | **CL61** | **3014** |
| C-GDBG | GLEX | 9008 |

| | | |
|---|---|---|
| C-GDBX | CL61 | 3046 |
| C-GDBZ | CL64 | 5378 |
| C-GDCC | SBRL | 306-51 |
| C-GDCO | FA10 | 73 |
| C-GDCO | FA50 | 185 |
| **C-GDCP** | **C680** | **0251** |
| C-GDCQ | CL61 | 3052 |
| C-GDDB | LJ24 | 041 |
| C-GDDC | C550 | 267 |
| C-GDDM | C500 | 468 |
| C-GDDP | CL61 | 5001 |
| **C-GDDR** | **CL60** | **1048** |
| C-GDEQ | CL61 | 5002 |
| C-GDFA | CL64 | 5380 |
| C-GDGO | GLEX | 9009 |
| C-GDGQ | GLEX | 9010 |
| C-GDGW | GLEX | 9011 |
| C-GDGY | GLEX | 9012 |
| C-GDHP | CL61 | 5003 |
| C-GDHW | HS25 | 256028 |
| **C-GDII** | **HS25** | **258316** |
| C-GDIK | CL30 | 20214 |
| **C-GDJG** | **C510** | **0113** |
| **C-GDJH** | **LJ35** | **353** |
| C-GDJW | WW24 | 111 |
| C-GDKI | C525 | 0008 |
| C-GDKO | CL61 | 5004 |
| C-GDKS | LJ24 | 217 |
| C-GDLH | CL64 | 5384 |
| **C-GDLI** | **CL61** | **5179** |
| **C-GDLL** | **C510** | **0221** |
| **C-GDLR** | **C550** | **078** |
| C-GDMF | C550 | 125 |
| C-GDMI | LJ45 | 096 |
| C-GDOC | WW24 | 166 |
| C-GDPB | GLF2 | 232 |
| C-GDPD | C550 | 066 |
| (C-GDPE) | C550 | 124 |
| (C-GDPE) | C550 | 188 |
| C-GDPF | C550 | 124 |
| C-GDPF | CL61 | 5145 |
| **C-GDPG** | **GLEX** | **9178** |
| **C-GDRJ** | **CL65** | **5831** |
| **C-GDRU** | **CL65** | **5832** |
| **C-GDRY** | **CL65** | **5833** |
| **C-GDSG** | **CL65** | **5834** |
| C-GDSH | C550 | 550-0909 |
| C-GDSH | C550 | 550-0982 |
| C-GDSH | C560 | 0492 |
| C-GDSH | C560 | 0647 |
| **C-GDSH** | **C560** | **0781** |
| **C-GDSO** | **CL65** | **5835** |
| **C-GDSQ** | **CL65** | **5836** |
| **C-GDSR** | **WW24** | **313** |
| **C-GDTF** | **CL30** | **20289** |
| **C-GDTQ** | **CL30** | **20290** |
| C-GDUC | WW24 | 357 |
| **C-GDUH** | **CL30** | **20291** |
| **C-GDUJ** | **CL30** | **20292** |
| C-GDUP | HS25 | 256020 |
| C-GDVM | CL64 | 5388 |
| C-GDWN | C500 | 029 |
| C-GDWS | C500 | 303 |
| **C-GDWS** | **C525** | **0109** |
| C-GDXU | GLEX | 9013 |
| C-GDXV | GLEX | 9014 |
| C-GDXX | GLEX | 9015 |
| C-GDZE | CL64 | 5392 |
| C-GDZQ | CL30 | 20057 |
| C-GEAQ | FA20 | 28 |
| C-GEEN | LJ24 | 087 |
| C-GEGM | CL64 | 5380 |
| C-GEGX | GLEX | 9005 |
| C-GEIM | GLEX | 9016 |
| C-GEIR | GLEX | 9017 |
| **C-GEIV** | **GLF4** | **1224** |
| C-GENA | CL61 | 5006 |
| C-GENJ | C500 | 196 |
| **C-GENW** | **F2EX** | **129** |
| C-GEPF | HS25 | 257149 |
| C-GERC | CS55 | 0037 |
| C-GERL | CS55 | 0056 |
| **C-GERS** | **GLEX** | **9127** |
| **C-GESO** | **CL30** | **20110** |
| C-GESO | WW24 | 298 |
| C-GESR | CL61 | 3003 |
| C-GESZ | C500 | 022 |

| | | |
|---|---|---|
| C-GETU | CL64 | 5409 |
| C-GEVF | C500 | 460 |
| C-GEVO | GLEX | 9018 |
| C-GEVU | GLEX | 9019 |
| C-GEVV | GLEX | 9020 |
| C-GEWV | GLEX | 9026 |
| C-GEYY | GLEX | 9021 |
| C-GEYZ | GLEX | 9022 |
| C-GEZD | GLEX | 9023 |
| C-GEZF | GLEX | 9024 |
| C-GEZJ | GLEX | 9025 |
| C-GEZX | GLEX | 9027 |
| C-GEZY | GLEX | 9028 |
| C-GEZZ | GLEX | 9029 |
| C-GFAD | GLEX | 9030 |
| C-GFAE | GLEX | 9031 |
| C-GFAK | GLEX | 9032 |
| C-GFAN | GLEX | 9033 |
| C-GFAN | WW24 | 218 |
| C-GFAO | WW24 | 250 |
| C-GFAP | GLEX | 9034 |
| C-GFAQ | GLEX | 9035 |
| C-GFAT | GLEX | 9036 |
| C-GFAX | LJ60 | 029 |
| **C-GFCB** | **CL30** | **20260** |
| C-GFCB | CL61 | 5124 |
| (C-GFCD) | CL60 | 1059 |
| **C-GFCD** | **CL61** | **5124** |
| C-GFCD | HS25 | 25234 |
| C-GFCI | C550 | 733 |
| C-GFCL | C560 | 0346 |
| **C-GFCL** | **C56X** | **5780** |
| C-GFCL | HS25 | 25107 |
| C-GFCS | FA10 | 37 |
| **C-GFEE** | **C500** | **566** |
| C-GFEH | LJ35 | 170 |
| **C-GFHR** | **CL30** | **20016** |
| C-GFJB | LJ24 | 260 |
| C-GFJQ | GLEX | 9037 |
| C-GFJR | GLEX | 9038 |
| C-GFJS | GLEX | 9039 |
| C-GFJT | GLEX | 9040 |
| C-GFKT | GLEX | 9041 |
| C-GFKV | GLEX | 9042 |
| C-GFKW | GLEX | 9043 |
| C-GFKX | GLEX | 9044 |
| C-GFKY | GLEX | 9045 |
| C-GFLS | GLEX | 9046 |
| C-GFLU | GLEX | 9047 |
| C-GFLW | GLEX | 9048 |
| C-GFLX | GLEX | 9049 |
| C-GFLZ | GLEX | 9050 |
| C-GFOE | CL64 | 5430 |
| C-GFRK | LJ35 | 093 |
| C-GFWI | GLEX | 9051 |
| C-GFWP | GLEX | 9052 |
| C-GFWX | GLEX | 9053 |
| C-GFWY | GLEX | 9054 |
| C-GFWZ | GLEX | 9055 |
| C-GGBL | CL64 | 5489 |
| **C-GGBL** | **CL65** | **5746** |
| C-GGCH | HS25 | 258495 |
| **C-GGFP** | **FA50** | **227** |
| C-GGFW | C550 | 318 |
| **C-GGHZ** | **ASTR** | **117** |
| C-GGIR | GLEX | 9057 |
| C-GGJA | GLEX | 9058 |
| C-GGJF | GLEX | 9059 |
| C-GGJH | GLEX | 9060 |
| C-GGJJ | GLEX | 9061 |
| C-GGJR | GLEX | 9062 |
| C-GGJS | GLEX | 9063 |
| C-GGJU | GLEX | 9064 |
| C-GGKA | GLEX | 9065 |
| C-GGKC | GLEX | 9066 |
| **C-GGLO** | **GLEX** | **9233** |
| C-GGMI | F9EX | 87 |
| C-GGMP | CL61 | 5093 |
| **C-GGMP** | **HS25** | **HA-0011** |
| C-GGPF | LJ36 | 026 |
| C-GGPK | CL64 | 5317 |
| C-GGPM | GLF3 | 307 |
| C-GGPZ | GLEX | 9067 |
| C-GGQC | GLEX | 9068 |
| C-GGQF | GLEX | 9069 |
| C-GGQG | GLEX | 9070 |
| C-GGSP | C550 | 177 |
| **C-GGWH** | **CL64** | **5371** |
| C-GGYT | HS25 | 258025 |
| C-GGYV | LJ35 | 040 |
| C-GHBQ | WW24 | 220 |
| C-GHBV | CL61 | 5174 |
| **C-GHCB** | **C56X** | **5151** |
| C-GHCD | CL61 | 5165 |
| C-GHCY | LJ31 | 107 |
| C-GHCY | LJ45 | 216 |
| C-GHDP | LJ24 | 257 |
| C-GHDQ | GLEX | 9071 |
| C-GHDV | GLEX | 9072 |
| C-GHDW | GLEX | 9073 |
| C-GHEA | GLEX | 9074 |
| C-GHEC | C500 | 161 |
| C-GHEC | C560 | 0084 |
| C-GHEI | GLEX | 9075 |
| C-GHER | GLEX | 9076 |
| C-GHET | GLEX | 9077 |
| C-GHEZ | GLEX | 9078 |
| C-GHFB | GLEX | 9079 |
| C-GHFH | GLEX | 9080 |
| **C-GHGC** | **CL61** | **5019** |
| C-GHGC | GLEX | 9081 |
| C-GHGK | C650 | 0062 |
| C-GHIH | CL64 | 5465 |
| **C-GHJJ** | **LJ31** | **102** |
| **C-GHJU** | **LJ31** | **120** |
| C-GHKY | C550 | 398 |
| C-GHKY | C650 | 0023 |
| **C-GHKY** | **CL64** | **5343** |
| C-GHKY | LJ60 | 043 |
| C-GHLM | C650 | 0017 |
| C-GHMH | LJ25 | 011 |
| **C-GHML** | **CL64** | **5360** |
| C-GHML | F900 | 141 |
| **C-GHMP** | **LJ45** | **183** |
| **C-GHMW** | **CL65** | **5796** |
| C-GHOL | C550 | 013 |
| C-GHOM | C550 | 198 |
| C-GHOO | C650 | 0014 |
| C-GHOO | LJ35 | 057 |
| C-GHOS | C500 | 375 |
| C-GHPP | C525 | 0220 |
| C-GHPR | WW24 | 83 |
| C-GHRJ | CL64 | 5468 |
| C-GHRK | CL64 | 5309 |
| C-GHRX | C500 | 432 |
| C-GHRZ | CL64 | 5472 |
| C-GHWW | C550 | 178 |
| C-GHXY | HS25 | 258095 |
| C-GHYD | C550 | 079 |
| **C-GHYD** | **WW24** | **278** |
| C-GHYQ | GLEX | 9082 |
| C-GHYT | GLEX | 9083 |
| C-GHYX | GLEX | 9084 |
| C-GHZB | GLEX | 9085 |
| C-GHZC | GLEX | 9086 |
| C-GHZD | GLEX | 9087 |
| C-GHZF | GLEX | 9088 |
| C-GHZH | GLEX | 9089 |
| C-GIAC | C500 | 076 |
| C-GIAD | C500 | 185 |
| **C-GIBU** | **HS25** | **258507** |
| C-GICI | CL61 | 5159 |
| C-GIDG | CL64 | 5307 |
| C-GIGT | C750 | 0097 |
| C-GIIT | LJ60 | 253 |
| C-GINT | C525 | 0062 |
| C-GIOD | GLEX | 9090 |
| **C-GIOH** | **CL61** | **5034** |
| C-GIOJ | GLEX | 9091 |
| C-GIOK | GLEX | 9092 |
| C-GIOW | GLEX | 9093 |
| C-GIOX | GLEX | 9094 |
| C-GIPA | GLEX | 9095 |
| C-GIPC | GLEX | 9096 |
| C-GIPD | GLEX | 9097 |
| C-GIPF | GLEX | 9098 |
| C-GIPJ | GLEX | 9099 |
| C-GIPX | CL30 | 20003 |
| **C-GIPX** | **F9EX** | **201** |
| **C-GIPZ** | **CL30** | **20005** |
| **C-GIRE** | **LJ35** | **004** |
| **C-GIRL** | **C525** | **0641** |
| C-GITG | CL64 | 5304 |
| C-GIWD | C750 | 0041 |
| C-GIWD | LJ35 | 407 |
| **C-GIWO** | **LJ35** | **407** |
| **C-GIWZ** | **C750** | **0041** |
| **C-GIXI** | **CL61** | **5086** |
| C-GIXI | GLEX | 9100 |
| C-GIXJ | GLEX | 9101 |
| C-GIXM | GLEX | 9102 |
| C-GIXO | GLEX | 9103 |
| C-GJAP | C500 | 080 |
| C-GJAP | C550 | 060 |
| C-GJAP | C550 | 373 |
| **C-GJBJ** | **HS25** | **257198** |
| C-GJCD | WW24 | 176 |
| C-GJCF | CL30 | 20002 |
| **C-GJCJ** | **CL30** | **20001** |
| C-GJCM | HS25 | 256040 |
| C-GJCV | CL30 | 20004 |
| **C-GJCY** | **LJ45** | **239** |
| C-GJDG | CL61 | 5119 |
| C-GJEI | C560 | 0588 |
| **C-GJEI** | **CL30** | **20245** |
| C-GJEM | C500 | 011 |
| **C-GJET** | **FA10** | **25** |
| C-GJFC | CL64 | 5366 |
| C-GJFI | CL64 | 5506 |
| C-GJFQ | CL61 | 5019 |
| C-GJIU | GLEX | 9104 |
| C-GJIW | GLEX | 9105 |
| C-GJIY | GLEX | 9106 |
| **C-GJKI** | **C680** | **0071** |
| C-GJKI | HS25 | 258605 |
| **C-GJKK** | **HS25** | **258605** |
| **C-GJLB** | **FA50** | **270** |
| C-GJLK | WW24 | 278 |
| C-GJLL | WW24 | 171 |
| **C-GJLN** | **LJ60** | **349** |
| C-GJLQ | C500 | 058 |
| C-GJOE | CL64 | 5514 |
| C-GJPG | CL60 | 1043 |
| C-GJPG | CL61 | 3017 |
| **C-GJPG** | **F900** | **110** |
| C-GJQN | CL64 | 5358 |
| **C-GJRB** | **C56X** | **5026** |
| C-GJRG | GLEX | 9107 |
| C-GJRK | GLEX | 9108 |
| C-GJRL | GLEX | 9109 |
| C-GJSO | CL64 | 5517 |
| C-GJTH | GLEX | 9110 |
| C-GJTK | GLEX | 9111 |
| C-GJTP | GLEX | 9112 |
| C-GJTR | CL64 | 5520 |
| C-GJTX | C500 | 254 |
| **C-GJVK** | **C500** | **103** |
| C-GJZB | CL64 | 5529 |
| C-GJZD | CL64 | 5530 |
| **C-GKAU** | **C550** | **313** |
| C-GKCB | CL64 | 5522 |
| C-GKCC | HS25 | 256044 |
| C-GKCG | GLEX | 9113 |
| C-GKCI | FA50 | 272 |
| C-GKCI | HS25 | 257066 |
| C-GKCM | GLEX | 9114 |
| C-GKCN | GLEX | 9115 |
| C-GKCO | HS25 | 25170 |
| C-GKCZ | C500 | 101 |
| C-GKEG | C56X | 5729 |
| **C-GKEG** | **C680** | **0158** |
| C-GKFS | WW24 | 62 |
| C-GKFT | WW24 | 5 |
| C-GKGD | HS25 | 258193 |
| **C-GKGN** | **CL64** | **5317** |
| C-GKGR | CL64 | 5533 |
| C-GKGS | CL64 | 5535 |
| C-GKGZ | GLEX | 9116 |
| C-GKHA | FA20 | 19 |
| C-GKHC | GLEX | 9117 |
| C-GKHE | GLEX | 9118 |
| C-GKHF | GLEX | 9119 |
| C-GKHG | GLEX | 9120 |
| C-GKHH | GLEX | 9121 |
| C-GKHI | GLEX | 9122 |
| C-GKHR | HS25 | 256021 |
| C-GKLB | HS25 | 258105 |
| C-GKLF | GLEX | 9083 |
| **C-GKMS** | **LJ31** | **006** |
| C-GKMU | CL64 | 5540 |
| C-GKPE | LJ35 | 030 |
| C-GKPM | HS25 | 257049 |
| **C-GKPP** | **HS25** | **258166** |
| C-GKRL | GLF3 | 317 |
| C-GKRL | HS25 | 25111 |
| C-GKRL | HS25 | 258007 |
| C-GKRS | HS25 | 257087 |
| C-GKRS | JSTR | 5011/1 |
| **C-GKTM** | **LJ55** | **076** |
| **C-GKTO** | **CL64** | **5396** |
| C-GL.. | CL61 | 5170 |
| C-GLAA | C500 | 201 |
| C-GLAL | LJ36 | 019 |
| C-GLBB | CL64 | 5465 |
| **C-GLBB** | **F9EX** | **88** |
| C-GLBD | HS25 | 256032 |
| **C-GLBJ** | **HS25** | **257162** |
| C-GLBT | LJ25 | 182 |
| C-GLCE | C550 | 550-0906 |
| C-GLCR | CS55 | 0140 |
| C-GLEO | HS25 | 25080 |
| C-GLFI | HS25 | 25028 |
| **C-GLGB** | **C550** | **550-0994** |
| **C-GLIG** | **HS25** | **257149** |
| C-GLIG | MU30 | A076SA |
| C-GLIG | MU30 | A090SA |
| C-GLIM | C560 | 0430 |
| C-GLJQ | LJ35 | 660 |
| **C-GLMI** | **C56X** | **5097** |
| **C-GLMK** | **C550** | **110** |
| C-GLMK | LJ36 | 019 |
| **C-GLOJ** | **CL61** | **3034** |
| (C-GLRE) | LJ25 | 114 |
| C-GLRJ | LJ31 | 043 |
| C-GLRJ | LJ45 | 019 |
| C-GLRJ | LJ55 | 089 |
| C-GLRL | LJ60 | 002 |
| C-GLRM | GLEX | 9130 |
| C-GLRP | FA50 | 87 |
| C-GLRS | LJ45 | 249 |
| C-GLRS | LJ60 | 002 |
| C-GLRS | LJ60 | 062 |
| C-GLRS | LJ60 | 077 |
| C-GLTG | C550 | 403 |
| **C-GLUL** | **GLEX** | **9264** |
| C-GLWR | CL60 | 1018 |
| C-GLWR | CL61 | 3051 |
| C-GLWR | CL61 | 5005 |
| C-GLWR | CL61 | 5025 |
| C-GLWR | CL61 | 5057 |
| C-GLWR | CL61 | 5078 |
| C-GLWR | CL61 | 5102 |
| C-GLWR | CL61 | 5123 |
| C-GLWR | CL61 | 5135 |
| C-GLWR | CL61 | 5147 |
| C-GLWR | CL61 | 5159 |
| C-GLWR | CL61 | 5183 |
| C-GLWR | CL64 | 5311 |
| C-GLWR | CL64 | 5333 |
| C-GLWR | CL64 | 5348 |
| C-GLWR | CL64 | 5359 |
| C-GLWR | CL64 | 5372 |
| C-GLWR | CL64 | 5396 |
| C-GLWR | CL64 | 5407 |
| C-GLWR | CL64 | 5420 |
| C-GLWR | CL64 | 5431 |
| C-GLWR | CL64 | 5442 |
| C-GLWR | CL64 | 5464 |
| C-GLWR | CL64 | 5486 |
| C-GLWR | CL64 | 5508 |
| C-GLWR | CL64 | 5530 |
| C-GLWR | CL64 | 5552 |
| C-GLWR | CL64 | 5574 |
| C-GLWR | CL64 | 5596 |
| C-GLWR | CL64 | 5662 |
| C-GLWT | CL60 | 1019 |
| C-GLWT | CL61 | 3052 |
| C-GLWT | CL61 | 5006 |
| C-GLWT | CL61 | 5019 |
| C-GLWT | CL61 | 5026 |
| C-GLWT | CL61 | 5041 |
| C-GLWT | CL61 | 5084 |
| C-GLWT | CL61 | 5094 |
| C-GLWT | CL61 | 5120 |
| C-GLWT | CL61 | 5142 |
| C-GLWT | CL61 | 5166 |
| C-GLWT | CL61 | 5190 |
| C-GLWT | CL64 | 5319 |

| C-GLWT | CL64 | 5343 |
|---|---|---|
| C-GLWT | CL64 | 5391 |
| C-GLWT | CL64 | 5415 |
| C-GLWT | CL64 | 5443 |
| C-GLWT | CL64 | 5465 |
| C-GLWT | CL64 | 5487 |
| C-GLWT | CL64 | 5509 |
| C-GLWT | CL64 | 5531 |
| C-GLWT | CL64 | 5553 |
| C-GLWT | CL64 | 5575 |
| C-GLWT | CL64 | 5597 |
| C-GLWT | CL64 | 5619 |
| C-GLWT | CL64 | 5641 |
| C-GLWT | CL64 | 5663 |
| C-GLWT | CL61 | 5071 |
| C-GLWV | CL60 | 1020 |
| C-GLWV | CL60 | 1042 |
| C-GLWV | CL60 | 1062 |
| C-GLWV | CL60 | 1079 |
| C-GLWV | CL61 | 3010 |
| C-GLWV | CL61 | 3016 |
| C-GLWV | CL61 | 3025 |
| C-GLWV | CL61 | 3041 |
| C-GLWV | CL61 | 3053 |
| C-GLWV | CL61 | 5007 |
| C-GLWV | CL61 | 5018 |
| C-GLWV | CL61 | 5027 |
| C-GLWV | CL61 | 5040 |
| C-GLWV | CL61 | 5059 |
| C-GLWV | CL61 | 5079 |
| C-GLWV | CL61 | 5103 |
| C-GLWV | CL61 | 5131 |
| C-GLWV | CL61 | 5155 |
| C-GLWV | CL61 | 5179 |
| C-GLWV | CL64 | 5329 |
| C-GLWV | CL64 | 5355 |
| C-GLWV | CL64 | 5379 |
| C-GLWV | CL64 | 5403 |
| C-GLWV | CL64 | 5427 |
| C-GLWV | CL64 | 5444 |
| C-GLWV | CL64 | 5466 |
| C-GLWV | CL64 | 5488 |
| C-GLWV | CL64 | 5510 |
| C-GLWV | CL64 | 5532 |
| C-GLWV | CL64 | 5554 |
| C-GLWV | CL64 | 5576 |
| C-GLWV | CL64 | 5598 |
| C-GLWV | CL64 | 5620 |
| C-GLWV | CL64 | 5642 |
| C-GLWV | CL64 | 5664 |
| C-GLWX | CL60 | 1021 |
| C-GLWX | CL60 | 1043 |
| C-GLWX | CL60 | 1063 |
| C-GLWX | CL60 | 1080 |
| C-GLWX | CL61 | 3011 |
| C-GLWX | CL61 | 3017 |
| C-GLWX | CL61 | 3026 |
| C-GLWX | CL61 | 3042 |
| C-GLWX | CL61 | 3054 |
| C-GLWX | CL61 | 5008 |
| C-GLWX | CL61 | 5017 |
| C-GLWX | CL61 | 5028 |
| C-GLWX | CL61 | 5039 |
| C-GLWX | CL61 | 5062 |
| C-GLWX | CL61 | 5082 |
| C-GLWX | CL61 | 5106 |
| C-GLWX | CL61 | 5128 |
| C-GLWX | CL61 | 5152 |
| C-GLWX | CL61 | 5176 |
| C-GLWX | CL64 | 5306 |
| C-GLWX | CL64 | 5325 |
| C-GLWX | CL64 | 5352 |
| C-GLWX | CL64 | 5400 |
| C-GLWX | CL64 | 5424 |
| C-GLWX | CL64 | 5445 |
| C-GLWX | CL64 | 5467 |
| C-GLWX | CL64 | 5489 |
| C-GLWX | CL64 | 5511 |
| C-GLWX | CL64 | 5533 |
| C-GLWX | CL64 | 5555 |
| C-GLWX | CL64 | 5577 |
| C-GLWX | CL64 | 5599 |
| C-GLWX | CL64 | 5621 |
| C-GLWX | CL64 | 5643 |
| C-GLWX | CL64 | 5665 |
| C-GLWX | CL65 | 5724 |
| C-GLWZ | CL60 | 1022 |
| C-GLWZ | CL60 | 1044 |
| C-GLWZ | CL60 | 1064 |
| C-GLWZ | CL60 | 1081 |
| C-GLWZ | CL61 | 3018 |
| C-GLWZ | CL61 | 3027 |
| C-GLWZ | CL61 | 3043 |
| C-GLWZ | CL61 | 3055 |
| C-GLWZ | CL61 | 5009 |
| C-GLWZ | CL61 | 5029 |
| C-GLWZ | CL61 | 5058 |
| C-GLWZ | CL61 | 5107 |
| C-GLWZ | CL61 | 5125 |
| C-GLWZ | CL61 | 5137 |
| C-GLWZ | CL61 | 5161 |
| C-GLWZ | CL61 | 5185 |
| C-GLWZ | CL64 | 5314 |
| C-GLWZ | CL64 | 5338 |
| C-GLWZ | CL64 | 5362 |
| C-GLWZ | CL64 | 5386 |
| C-GLWZ | CL64 | 5410 |
| C-GLWZ | CL64 | 5435 |
| C-GLWZ | CL64 | 5446 |
| C-GLWZ | CL64 | 5468 |
| C-GLWZ | CL64 | 5490 |
| C-GLWZ | CL64 | 5512 |
| C-GLWZ | CL64 | 5534 |
| C-GLWZ | CL64 | 5556 |
| C-GLWZ | CL64 | 5578 |
| C-GLWZ | CL64 | 5600 |
| C-GLWZ | CL64 | 5622 |
| C-GLWZ | CL64 | 5644 |
| C-GLXB | CL60 | 1023 |
| C-GLXB | CL60 | 1045 |
| C-GLXB | CL60 | 1065 |
| C-GLXB | CL60 | 1082 |
| C-GLXB | CL61 | 3012 |
| C-GLXB | CL61 | 3019 |
| C-GLXB | CL61 | 3028 |
| C-GLXB | CL61 | 3037 |
| C-GLXB | CL61 | 3056 |
| C-GLXB | CL61 | 5010 |
| C-GLXB | CL61 | 5030 |
| C-GLXB | CL61 | 5054 |
| C-GLXB | CL61 | 5076 |
| C-GLXB | CL61 | 5100 |
| C-GLXB | CL61 | 5127 |
| C-GLXB | CL61 | 5151 |
| C-GLXB | CL61 | 5175 |
| C-GLXB | CL64 | 5305 |
| C-GLXB | CL64 | 5324 |
| C-GLXB | CL64 | 5335 |
| C-GLXB | CL64 | 5351 |
| C-GLXB | CL64 | 5375 |
| C-GLXB | CL64 | 5399 |
| C-GLXB | CL64 | 5423 |
| C-GLXB | CL64 | 5441 |
| C-GLXB | CL64 | 5463 |
| C-GLXB | CL64 | 5485 |
| C-GLXB | CL64 | 5507 |
| C-GLXB | CL64 | 5529 |
| C-GLXB | CL64 | 5573 |
| C-GLXB | CL64 | 5595 |
| C-GLXB | CL64 | 5601 |
| C-GLXB | CL64 | 5617 |
| C-GLXB | CL64 | 5639 |
| C-GLXB | CL64 | 5661 |
| C-GLXB | CL64 | 5551 |
| **C-GLXC** | **F9EX** | **190** |
| C-GLXD | CL60 | 1024 |
| C-GLXD | CL60 | 1046 |
| C-GLXD | CL60 | 1066 |
| C-GLXD | CL60 | 1083 |
| C-GLXD | CL61 | 3013 |
| C-GLXD | CL61 | 3029 |
| C-GLXD | CL61 | 3044 |
| C-GLXD | CL61 | 3057 |
| C-GLXD | CL61 | 5011 |
| C-GLXD | CL61 | 5031 |
| C-GLXD | CL61 | 5047 |
| C-GLXD | CL61 | 5065 |
| C-GLXD | CL61 | 5085 |
| C-GLXD | CL61 | 5108 |
| C-GLXD | CL61 | 5124 |
| C-GLXD | CL61 | 5148 |
| C-GLXD | CL61 | 5172 |
| C-GLXD | CL64 | 5302 |
| C-GLXD | CL64 | 5313 |
| C-GLXD | CL64 | 5337 |
| C-GLXD | CL64 | 5361 |
| C-GLXD | CL64 | 5385 |
| C-GLXD | CL64 | 5433 |
| C-GLXD | CL64 | 5448 |
| C-GLXD | CL64 | 5470 |
| C-GLXD | CL64 | 5492 |
| C-GLXD | CL64 | 5514 |
| C-GLXD | CL64 | 5536 |
| C-GLXD | CL64 | 5558 |
| C-GLXD | CL64 | 5580 |
| C-GLXD | CL64 | 5602 |
| C-GLXD | CL64 | 5624 |
| C-GLXD | CL64 | 5640 |
| C-GLXD | CL64 | 5646 |
| C-GLXD | CL65 | 5705 |
| C-GLXF | CL60 | 1025 |
| C-GLXF | CL61 | 5032 |
| C-GLXF | CL61 | 5049 |
| C-GLXF | CL61 | 5067 |
| C-GLXF | CL61 | 5090 |
| C-GLXF | CL61 | 5112 |
| C-GLXF | CL61 | 5138 |
| C-GLXF | CL61 | 5162 |
| C-GLXF | CL61 | 5186 |
| C-GLXF | CL64 | 5315 |
| C-GLXF | CL64 | 5339 |
| C-GLXF | CL64 | 5363 |
| C-GLXF | CL64 | 5387 |
| C-GLXF | CL64 | 5411 |
| C-GLXF | CL64 | 5436 |
| C-GLXF | CL64 | 5449 |
| C-GLXF | CL64 | 5471 |
| C-GLXF | CL64 | 5493 |
| C-GLXF | CL64 | 5515 |
| C-GLXF | CL64 | 5537 |
| C-GLXF | CL64 | 5551 |
| C-GLXF | CL64 | 5559 |
| C-GLXF | CL64 | 5581 |
| C-GLXF | CL64 | 5603 |
| C-GLXF | CL64 | 5618 |
| C-GLXF | CL64 | 5625 |
| C-GLXF | CL64 | 5647 |
| C-GLXF | CL65 | 5706 |
| C-GLXH | CL60 | 1026 |
| C-GLXH | CL60 | 1047 |
| C-GLXH | CL60 | 1067 |
| C-GLXH | CL60 | 1084 |
| C-GLXH | CL61 | 3014 |
| C-GLXH | CL61 | 3030 |
| C-GLXH | CL61 | 3045 |
| C-GLXH | CL61 | 5015 |
| C-GLXH | CL61 | 5033 |
| C-GLXH | CL61 | 5055 |
| C-GLXH | CL61 | 5074 |
| C-GLXH | CL61 | 5088 |
| C-GLXH | CL61 | 5098 |
| C-GLXH | CL61 | 5111 |
| C-GLXH | CL61 | 5129 |
| C-GLXH | CL61 | 5153 |
| C-GLXH | CL61 | 5177 |
| C-GLXH | CL64 | 5307 |
| C-GLXH | CL64 | 5328 |
| C-GLXH | CL64 | 5353 |
| C-GLXH | CL64 | 5377 |
| C-GLXH | CL64 | 5401 |
| C-GLXH | CL64 | 5425 |
| C-GLXH | CL64 | 5450 |
| C-GLXH | CL64 | 5472 |
| C-GLXH | CL64 | 5494 |
| C-GLXH | CL64 | 5516 |
| C-GLXH | CL64 | 5538 |
| C-GLXH | CL64 | 5560 |
| C-GLXH | CL64 | 5582 |
| C-GLXH | CL64 | 5604 |
| C-GLXH | CL64 | 5626 |
| C-GLXH | CL64 | 5648 |
| C-GLXH | CL65 | 5707 |
| C-GLXK | CL60 | 1027 |
| C-GLXK | CL60 | 1048 |
| C-GLXK | CL60 | 1068 |
| C-GLXK | CL60 | 1076 |
| C-GLXK | CL61 | 3004 |
| C-GLXK | CL61 | 3031 |
| C-GLXK | CL61 | 3046 |
| C-GLXK | CL61 | 5034 |
| C-GLXK | CL61 | 5050 |
| C-GLXK | CL61 | 5068 |
| C-GLXK | CL61 | 5097 |
| C-GLXK | CL61 | 5118 |
| C-GLXK | CL61 | 5139 |
| C-GLXK | CL61 | 5163 |
| C-GLXK | CL61 | 5187 |
| C-GLXK | CL64 | 5316 |
| C-GLXK | CL64 | 5340 |
| C-GLXK | CL64 | 5364 |
| C-GLXK | CL64 | 5388 |
| C-GLXK | CL64 | 5412 |
| C-GLXK | CL64 | 5437 |
| C-GLXK | CL64 | 5451 |
| C-GLXK | CL64 | 5473 |
| C-GLXK | CL64 | 5495 |
| C-GLXK | CL64 | 5517 |
| C-GLXK | CL64 | 5539 |
| C-GLXK | CL64 | 5561 |
| C-GLXK | CL64 | 5583 |
| C-GLXK | CL64 | 5605 |
| C-GLXK | CL64 | 5627 |
| C-GLXK | CL64 | 5649 |
| C-GLXK | CL65 | 5708 |
| C-GLXM | CL60 | 1028 |
| C-GLXM | CL60 | 1049 |
| C-GLXM | CL60 | 1069 |
| C-GLXM | CL60 | 1077 |
| C-GLXM | CL61 | 3015 |
| C-GLXM | CL61 | 3032 |
| C-GLXM | CL61 | 3047 |
| C-GLXM | CL61 | 5051 |
| C-GLXM | CL61 | 5069 |
| C-GLXM | CL61 | 5091 |
| C-GLXM | CL61 | 5113 |
| C-GLXM | CL61 | 5140 |
| C-GLXM | CL61 | 5164 |
| C-GLXM | CL61 | 5188 |
| C-GLXM | CL64 | 5341 |
| C-GLXM | CL64 | 5365 |
| C-GLXM | CL64 | 5389 |
| C-GLXM | CL64 | 5413 |
| C-GLXM | CL64 | 5432 |
| C-GLXM | CL64 | 5438 |
| C-GLXM | CL64 | 5452 |
| C-GLXM | CL64 | 5474 |
| C-GLXM | CL64 | 5496 |
| C-GLXM | CL64 | 5518 |
| C-GLXM | CL64 | 5540 |
| C-GLXM | CL64 | 5562 |
| C-GLXM | CL64 | 5584 |
| C-GLXM | CL64 | 5606 |
| C-GLXM | CL64 | 5628 |
| C-GLXM | CL64 | 5650 |
| C-GLXM | CL65 | 5709 |
| C-GLXO | CL60 | 1029 |
| C-GLXO | CL60 | 1050 |
| C-GLXO | CL60 | 1070 |
| C-GLXO | CL60 | 1075 |
| C-GLXO | CL61 | 3020 |
| C-GLXO | CL61 | 3048 |
| C-GLXO | CL61 | 5052 |
| C-GLXO | CL61 | 5070 |
| C-GLXO | CL61 | 5119 |
| C-GLXO | CL61 | 5141 |
| C-GLXO | CL61 | 5165 |
| C-GLXO | CL64 | 5318 |
| C-GLXO | CL64 | 5342 |
| C-GLXO | CL64 | 5366 |
| C-GLXO | CL64 | 5390 |
| C-GLXO | CL64 | 5414 |
| C-GLXO | CL64 | 5453 |
| C-GLXO | CL64 | 5475 |
| C-GLXO | CL64 | 5497 |
| C-GLXO | CL64 | 5519 |
| C-GLXO | CL64 | 5541 |
| C-GLXO | CL64 | 5563 |
| C-GLXO | CL64 | 5585 |
| C-GLXO | CL64 | 5607 |
| C-GLXO | CL64 | 5629 |
| C-GLXO | CL64 | 5651 |
| C-GLXO | CL65 | 5710 |
| C-GLXQ | CL60 | 1030 |
| C-GLXQ | CL60 | 1051 |
| C-GLXQ | CL60 | 1071 |
| C-GLXQ | CL60 | 1085 |
| C-GLXQ | CL61 | 3021 |
| C-GLXQ | CL61 | 3033 |

| | | |
|---|---|---|
| C-GLXQ | CL61 | 3049 |
| C-GLXQ | CL61 | 3066 |
| C-GLXQ | CL61 | 5016 |
| C-GLXQ | CL61 | 5038 |
| C-GLXQ | CL61 | 5056 |
| C-GLXQ | CL61 | 5077 |
| C-GLXQ | CL61 | 5092 |
| C-GLXQ | CL61 | 5101 |
| C-GLXQ | CL61 | 5130 |
| C-GLXQ | CL61 | 5154 |
| C-GLXQ | CL61 | 5178 |
| C-GLXQ | CL64 | 5320 |
| C-GLXQ | CL64 | 5344 |
| C-GLXQ | CL64 | 5368 |
| C-GLXQ | CL64 | 5392 |
| C-GLXQ | CL64 | 5416 |
| C-GLXQ | CL64 | 5439 |
| C-GLXQ | CL64 | 5454 |
| C-GLXQ | CL64 | 5476 |
| C-GLXQ | CL64 | 5498 |
| C-GLXQ | CL64 | 5520 |
| C-GLXQ | CL64 | 5542 |
| C-GLXQ | CL64 | 5564 |
| C-GLXQ | CL64 | 5586 |
| C-GLXQ | CL64 | 5608 |
| C-GLXQ | CL64 | 5630 |
| C-GLXQ | CL64 | 5652 |
| C-GLXQ | CL65 | 5711 |
| C-GLXS | CL60 | 1031 |
| C-GLXS | CL60 | 1052 |
| C-GLXS | CL60 | 1086 |
| C-GLXS | CL61 | 3022 |
| C-GLXS | CL61 | 3050 |
| C-GLXS | CL61 | 5045 |
| C-GLXS | CL61 | 5063 |
| C-GLXS | CL61 | 5086 |
| C-GLXS | CL61 | 5109 |
| C-GLXS | CL61 | 5122 |
| C-GLXS | CL61 | 5134 |
| C-GLXS | CL61 | 5158 |
| C-GLXS | CL64 | 5310 |
| C-GLXS | CL64 | 5332 |
| C-GLXS | CL64 | 5346 |
| C-GLXS | CL64 | 5358 |
| C-GLXS | CL64 | 5370 |
| C-GLXS | CL64 | 5382 |
| C-GLXS | CL64 | 5394 |
| C-GLXS | CL64 | 5406 |
| C-GLXS | CL64 | 5418 |
| C-GLXS | CL64 | 5430 |
| C-GLXS | CL64 | 5455 |
| C-GLXS | CL64 | 5477 |
| C-GLXS | CL64 | 5499 |
| C-GLXS | CL64 | 5521 |
| C-GLXS | CL64 | 5543 |
| C-GLXS | CL64 | 5565 |
| C-GLXS | CL64 | 5587 |
| C-GLXS | CL64 | 5609 |
| C-GLXS | CL64 | 5631 |
| C-GLXS | CL64 | 5653 |
| C-GLXS | CL65 | 5712 |
| C-GLXU | CL60 | 1032 |
| C-GLXU | CL60 | 1057 |
| C-GLXU | CL61 | 3003 |
| C-GLXU | CL61 | 3034 |
| C-GLXU | CL61 | 3058 |
| C-GLXU | CL61 | 5012 |
| C-GLXU | CL61 | 5035 |
| C-GLXU | CL61 | 5053 |
| C-GLXU | CL61 | 5075 |
| C-GLXU | CL61 | 5099 |
| C-GLXU | CL61 | 5110 |
| C-GLXU | CL61 | 5126 |
| C-GLXU | CL61 | 5150 |
| C-GLXU | CL61 | 5174 |
| C-GLXU | CL64 | 5304 |
| C-GLXU | CL64 | 5323 |
| C-GLXU | CL64 | 5334 |
| C-GLXU | CL64 | 5350 |
| C-GLXU | CL64 | 5374 |
| C-GLXU | CL64 | 5398 |
| C-GLXU | CL64 | 5422 |
| C-GLXU | CL64 | 5440 |
| C-GLXU | CL64 | 5456 |
| C-GLXU | CL64 | 5478 |
| C-GLXU | CL64 | 5500 |
| C-GLXU | CL64 | 5522 |
| C-GLXU | CL64 | 5544 |
| C-GLXU | CL64 | 5566 |
| C-GLXU | CL64 | 5588 |
| C-GLXU | CL64 | 5610 |
| C-GLXU | CL64 | 5632 |
| C-GLXU | CL64 | 5654 |
| C-GLXU | CL65 | 5713 |
| C-GLXW | CL60 | 1033 |
| C-GLXW | CL60 | 1058 |
| C-GLXW | CL60 | 1072 |
| C-GLXW | CL61 | 3035 |
| C-GLXW | CL61 | 3059 |
| C-GLXW | CL61 | 5013 |
| C-GLXW | CL61 | 5036 |
| C-GLXW | CL61 | 5046 |
| C-GLXW | CL61 | 5064 |
| C-GLXW | CL61 | 5087 |
| C-GLXW | CL61 | 5116 |
| C-GLXW | CL61 | 5136 |
| C-GLXW | CL61 | 5146 |
| C-GLXW | CL61 | 5160 |
| C-GLXW | CL61 | 5171 |
| C-GLXW | CL61 | 5184 |
| C-GLXW | CL64 | 5312 |
| C-GLXW | CL64 | 5336 |
| C-GLXW | CL64 | 5347 |
| C-GLXW | CL64 | 5360 |
| C-GLXW | CL64 | 5376 |
| C-GLXW | CL64 | 5384 |
| C-GLXW | CL64 | 5408 |
| C-GLXW | CL64 | 5457 |
| C-GLXW | CL64 | 5479 |
| C-GLXW | CL64 | 5501 |
| C-GLXW | CL64 | 5523 |
| C-GLXW | CL64 | 5545 |
| C-GLXW | CL64 | 5567 |
| C-GLXW | CL64 | 5589 |
| C-GLXW | CL64 | 5611 |
| C-GLXW | CL64 | 5633 |
| C-GLXW | CL64 | 5655 |
| C-GLXW | CL65 | 5714 |
| C-GLXY | CL60 | 1034 |
| C-GLXY | CL60 | 1059 |
| C-GLXY | CL60 | 1073 |
| C-GLXY | CL61 | 3006 |
| C-GLXY | CL61 | 3023 |
| C-GLXY | CL61 | 3036 |
| C-GLXY | CL61 | 3060 |
| C-GLXY | CL61 | 5014 |
| C-GLXY | CL61 | 5037 |
| C-GLXY | CL61 | 5048 |
| C-GLXY | CL61 | 5066 |
| C-GLXY | CL61 | 5089 |
| C-GLXY | CL61 | 5117 |
| C-GLXY | CL61 | 5149 |
| C-GLXY | CL61 | 5173 |
| C-GLXY | CL64 | 5303 |
| C-GLXY | CL64 | 5322 |
| C-GLXY | CL64 | 5349 |
| C-GLXY | CL64 | 5397 |
| C-GLXY | CL64 | 5421 |
| C-GLXY | CL64 | 5434 |
| C-GLXY | CL64 | 5458 |
| C-GLXY | CL64 | 5480 |
| C-GLXY | CL64 | 5502 |
| C-GLXY | CL64 | 5524 |
| C-GLXY | CL64 | 5546 |
| C-GLXY | CL64 | 5568 |
| C-GLXY | CL64 | 5590 |
| C-GLXY | CL64 | 5612 |
| C-GLXY | CL64 | 5634 |
| C-GLXY | CL64 | 5656 |
| C-GLXY | CL65 | 5715 |
| C-GLYA | CL60 | 1035 |
| C-GLYA | CL60 | 1053 |
| C-GLYA | CL61 | 3024 |
| C-GLYA | CL61 | 3038 |
| C-GLYA | CL61 | 3065 |
| C-GLYA | CL61 | 5020 |
| C-GLYA | CL61 | 5042 |
| C-GLYA | CL61 | 5083 |
| C-GLYA | CL61 | 5093 |
| C-GLYA | CL61 | 5114 |
| C-GLYA | CL61 | 5143 |
| C-GLYA | CL61 | 5167 |
| C-GLYA | CL61 | 5191 |
| C-GLYA | CL64 | 5321 |
| C-GLYA | CL64 | 5345 |
| C-GLYA | CL64 | 5393 |
| C-GLYA | CL64 | 5417 |
| C-GLYA | CL64 | 5459 |
| C-GLYA | CL64 | 5481 |
| C-GLYA | CL64 | 5503 |
| C-GLYA | CL64 | 5525 |
| C-GLYA | CL64 | 5547 |
| C-GLYA | CL64 | 5569 |
| C-GLYA | CL64 | 5591 |
| C-GLYA | CL64 | 5613 |
| C-GLYA | CL64 | 5657 |
| C-GLYA | CL64 | 5991 |
| C-GLYA | CL65 | 5716 |
| C-GLYC | CL60 | 1036 |
| C-GLYC | CL60 | 1054 |
| C-GLYC | CL61 | 3064 |
| C-GLYC | CL61 | 5021 |
| C-GLYC | CL61 | 5043 |
| C-GLYC | CL61 | 5072 |
| C-GLYC | CL61 | 5095 |
| C-GLYC | CL61 | 5115 |
| C-GLYC | CL61 | 5144 |
| C-GLYC | CL61 | 5168 |
| C-GLYC | CL61 | 5192 |
| C-GLYC | CL64 | 5326 |
| C-GLYC | CL64 | 5354 |
| C-GLYC | CL64 | 5378 |
| C-GLYC | CL64 | 5402 |
| C-GLYC | CL64 | 5426 |
| C-GLYC | CL64 | 5447 |
| C-GLYC | CL64 | 5469 |
| C-GLYC | CL64 | 5491 |
| C-GLYC | CL64 | 5513 |
| C-GLYC | CL64 | 5535 |
| C-GLYC | CL64 | 5557 |
| C-GLYC | CL64 | 5579 |
| C-GLYC | CL64 | 5623 |
| C-GLYC | CL64 | 5635 |
| C-GLYC | CL64 | 5645 |
| C-GLYE | CL60 | 1037 |
| C-GLYE | CL60 | 1055 |
| C-GLYE | CL61 | 3007 |
| C-GLYH | CL60 | 1038 |
| C-GLYH | CL60 | 1056 |
| C-GLYH | CL61 | 3039 |
| C-GLYH | CL61 | 3063 |
| C-GLYH | CL61 | 5024 |
| C-GLYH | CL61 | 5061 |
| C-GLYH | CL61 | 5081 |
| C-GLYH | CL61 | 5105 |
| C-GLYH | CL61 | 5133 |
| C-GLYH | CL61 | 5157 |
| C-GLYH | CL61 | 5181 |
| C-GLYH | CL64 | 5309 |
| C-GLYH | CL64 | 5331 |
| C-GLYH | CL64 | 5357 |
| C-GLYH | CL64 | 5381 |
| C-GLYH | CL64 | 5405 |
| C-GLYH | CL64 | 5429 |
| C-GLYH | CL64 | 5460 |
| C-GLYH | CL64 | 5482 |
| C-GLYH | CL64 | 5504 |
| C-GLYH | CL64 | 5526 |
| C-GLYH | CL64 | 5548 |
| C-GLYH | CL64 | 5570 |
| C-GLYH | CL64 | 5592 |
| C-GLYH | CL64 | 5614 |
| C-GLYH | CL64 | 5636 |
| C-GLYH | CL64 | 5658 |
| C-GLYH | CL65 | 5717 |
| C-GLYK | CL60 | 1039 |
| C-GLYK | CL60 | 1060 |
| C-GLYK | CL60 | 1074 |
| C-GLYK | CL61 | 3008 |
| C-GLYK | CL61 | 3040 |
| C-GLYK | CL61 | 3062 |
| C-GLYK | CL61 | 5022 |
| C-GLYK | CL61 | 5044 |
| C-GLYK | CL61 | 5073 |
| C-GLYK | CL61 | 5096 |
| C-GLYK | CL61 | 5121 |
| C-GLYK | CL61 | 5145 |
| C-GLYK | CL61 | 5169 |
| C-GLYK | CL61 | 5193 |
| C-GLYK | CL64 | 5327 |
| C-GLYK | CL64 | 5371 |
| C-GLYK | CL64 | 5383 |
| C-GLYK | CL64 | 5395 |
| C-GLYK | CL64 | 5419 |
| C-GLYK | CL64 | 5461 |
| C-GLYK | CL64 | 5483 |
| C-GLYK | CL64 | 5505 |
| C-GLYK | CL64 | 5527 |
| C-GLYK | CL64 | 5549 |
| C-GLYK | CL64 | 5571 |
| C-GLYK | CL64 | 5593 |
| C-GLYK | CL64 | 5615 |
| C-GLYK | CL64 | 5637 |
| C-GLYK | CL64 | 5659 |
| C-GLYK | CL65 | 5718 |
| C-GLYM | CL60 | 1040 |
| C-GLYO | CL60 | 1041 |
| C-GLYO | CL60 | 1061 |
| C-GLYO | CL60 | 1078 |
| C-GLYO | CL61 | 3009 |
| C-GLYO | CL61 | 3061 |
| C-GLYO | CL61 | 5023 |
| C-GLYO | CL61 | 5060 |
| C-GLYO | CL61 | 5080 |
| C-GLYO | CL61 | 5104 |
| C-GLYO | CL61 | 5132 |
| C-GLYO | CL61 | 5156 |
| C-GLYO | CL61 | 5180 |
| C-GLYO | CL64 | 5308 |
| C-GLYO | CL64 | 5330 |
| C-GLYO | CL64 | 5356 |
| C-GLYO | CL64 | 5380 |
| C-GLYO | CL64 | 5404 |
| C-GLYO | CL64 | 5428 |
| C-GLYO | CL64 | 5462 |
| C-GLYO | CL64 | 5484 |
| C-GLYO | CL64 | 5506 |
| C-GLYO | CL64 | 5528 |
| C-GLYO | CL64 | 5550 |
| C-GLYO | CL64 | 5572 |
| C-GLYO | CL64 | 5594 |
| C-GLYO | CL64 | 5616 |
| C-GLYO | CL64 | 5638 |
| C-GLYO | CL64 | 5660 |
| **C-GLYS** | **LJ45** | **362** |
| C-GMAJ | C500 | 247 |
| C-GMAP | LJ25 | 026 |
| C-GMAT | C500 | 231 |
| C-GMAV | CS55 | 0067 |
| C-GMBA | HS25 | 257206 |
| C-GMBH | WW24 | 286 |
| C-GMEA | HS25 | 25137 |
| C-GMGA | LJ35 | 346 |
| C-GMGB | C560 | 0390 |
| **C-GMGB** | **CL61** | **5093** |
| C-GMGB | CS55 | 0149 |
| **C-GMGX** | **FA7X** | **50** |
| C-GMID | FA50 | 229 |
| C-GMII | CL61 | 3012 |
| C-GMII | FA50 | 229 |
| C-GMII | FA50 | 272 |
| **C-GMII** | **FA50** | **335** |
| **C-GMKZ** | **C56X** | **5309** |
| C-GMLC | C500 | 305 |
| **C-GMLH** | **F9EX** | **76** |
| C-GMLR | HS25 | 258025 |
| **C-GMLR** | **HS25** | **258239** |
| **C-GMMA** | **LJ35** | **655** |
| **C-GMMI** | **CL61** | **5151** |
| C-GMMO | C500 | 227 |
| **C-GMMU** | **C510** | **0042** |
| **C-GMMY** | **LJ35** | **644** |
| C-GMNC | C56X | 5159 |
| **C-GMNC** | **C750** | **0097** |
| C-GMND | F900 | 189 |
| C-GMOL | HS25 | 258163 |
| C-GMPF | WW24 | 391 |
| C-GMPO | FA20 | 500 |
| C-GMPQ | C550 | 456 |
| **C-GMRL** | **CL64** | **5597** |
| **C-GMRO** | **LJ45** | **086** |
| C-GMSM | C550 | 603 |
| **C-GMTI** | **C525** | **0398** |
| **C-GMTR** | **HS25** | **258157** |
| C-GMTT | WW24 | 288 |
| C-GMTV | CS55 | 0015 |
| C-GNAA | FA20 | 128/436 |
| C-GNAZ | HS25 | 257030 |

| | | |
|---|---|---|
| C-GNCA | FA50 | 203 |
| **C-GNCB** | **GLEX** | **9088** |
| **C-GNDN** | **GLF5** | **5230** |
| C-GNEQ | C680 | 0064 |
| **C-GNET** | **FA50** | **281** |
| **C-GNGV** | **C560** | **0053** |
| C-GNLQ | C560 | 0390 |
| C-GNND | C560 | 0077 |
| C-GNND | HS25 | 257118 |
| C-GNOW | HS25 | 257049 |
| C-GNPT | LJ35 | 626 |
| C-GNSA | C500 | 160 |
| C-GNSA | LJ35 | 171 |
| C-GNTL | FA20 | 257 |
| C-GNTM | FA20 | 319 |
| C-GNTY | FA20 | 330 |
| C-GNTZ | FA20 | 256 |
| C-GNVT | FA10 | 138 |
| **C-GNWM** | **C550** | **408** |
| **C-GOAG** | **F9EX** | **15** |
| C-GOCM | C500 | 154 |
| C-GOEL | C56X | 5144 |
| **C-GOFJ** | **FA50** | **262** |
| C-GOGM | HS25 | 257143 |
| C-GOGO | CL60 | 1022 |
| **C-GOHB** | **F2EX** | **90** |
| **C-GOHJ** | **HS25** | **257049** |
| C-GOIL | C500 | 361 |
| **C-GOIL** | **FA50** | **87** |
| **C-GOJC** | **FA10** | **182** |
| **C-GOOB** | **C560** | **0454** |
| C-GOQG | FA20 | 6 |
| C-GOSL | LJ25 | 040 |
| C-GOXB | C650 | 0104 |
| C-GPAW | C550 | 004 |
| C-GPAW | C560 | 0260 |
| **C-GPAW** | **C56X** | **5681** |
| C-GPCC | CL61 | 3039 |
| C-GPCC | HS25 | 257057 |
| C-GPCL | LJ24 | 224 |
| C-GPCO | C500 | 317 |
| C-GPCS | CL61 | 5088 |
| C-GPCS | LJ55 | 035 |
| **C-GPCZ** | **CL30** | **20096** |
| C-GPDA | ASTR | 120 |
| C-GPDB | LJ24 | 217 |
| C-GPDH | WW24 | 82 |
| C-GPDO | LJ35 | 168 |
| C-GPDO | LJ35 | 673 |
| C-GPDQ | LJ35 | 170 |
| **C-GPDQ** | **LJ45** | **041** |
| C-GPDZ | LJ25 | 063 |
| C-GPEA | C650 | 0101 |
| **C-GPFC** | **CL64** | **5310** |
| C-GPFC | LJ35 | 092 |
| C-GPFC | WW24 | 328 |
| **C-GPGA** | **C550** | **550-0807** |
| C-GPGD | CL61 | 3039 |
| C-GPGD | CL61 | 5145 |
| C-GPGD | CL64 | 5310 |
| **C-GPGD** | **CL64** | **5432** |
| C-GPGD | JSTR | 5133 |
| C-GPJW | C500 | 104 |
| **C-GPKS** | **LJ45** | **223** |
| **C-GPLN** | **C500** | **016** |
| **C-GPMW** | **C52B** | **0206** |
| **C-GPOP** | **C650** | **0042** |
| **C-GPOS** | **C525** | **0129** |
| C-GPOT | CL61 | 5088 |
| **C-GPOT** | **F9DX** | **607** |
| **C-GPPI** | **GLEX** | **9158** |
| C-GPPS | HS25 | 257027 |
| **C-GPSI** | **CL61** | **3027** |
| C-GPTC | C500 | 429 |
| C-GPTI | C500 | 667 |
| C-GPTR | C550 | 083 |
| C-GPUN | LJ35 | 058 |
| (C-GPWM) | C525 | 0400 |
| C-GPWM | C525 | 0440 |
| **C-GQBQ** | **CL61** | **5051** |
| C-GQBR | LJ55 | 105 |
| C-GQCC | C500 | 066 |
| **C-GQCC** | **C550** | **305** |
| C-GQGM | HS25 | 257143 |
| **C-GQJJ** | **C500** | **642** |
| C-GQJK | C500 | 400 |
| C-GQMH | CS55 | 0076 |

| | | |
|---|---|---|
| **C-GQPA** | **CL64** | **5379** |
| **C-GQPJ** | **C500** | **293** |
| **C-GQPM** | **LJ45** | **224** |
| C-GQWI | CL61 | 5016 |
| **C-GQYL** | **C550** | **569** |
| C-GRBC | CL61 | 3041 |
| **C-GRBZ** | **LJ60** | **218** |
| **C-GRCC** | **C560** | **0269** |
| C-GRCO | LJ25 | 095 |
| **C-GRCY** | **CL30** | **20182** |
| C-GRDP | WW24 | 188 |
| C-GRDR | LJ25 | 145 |
| C-GRDS | MU30 | A018SA |
| C-GRDT | FA10 | 6 |
| C-GRDX | MU30 | A039SA |
| **C-GREK** | **C500** | **082** |
| **C-GRFO** | **LJ35** | **100** |
| **C-GRFT** | **C500** | **154** |
| C-GRGE | ASTR | 115 |
| **C-GRGE** | **FA50** | **29** |
| C-GRGE | HS25 | 258124 |
| C-GRGE | WW24 | 298 |
| C-GRGE | WW24 | 353 |
| C-GRGE | WW24 | 359 |
| **C-GRGM** | **FA7X** | **70** |
| **C-GRHC** | **C550** | **050** |
| C-GRIO | C550 | 148 |
| C-GRIO | CL64 | 5353 |
| **C-GRIS** | **FA10** | **2** |
| C-GRJC | C500 | 112 |
| C-GRJL | LJ36 | 037 |
| C-GRJQ | C500 | 250 |
| (C-GRJZ) | GALX | 007 |
| C-GRMJ | LJ35 | 664 |
| **C-GROG** | **HS25** | **258852** |
| **C-GROL** | **EPC2** | **001J** |
| **C-GROP** | **C510** | **0224** |
| **C-GRPB** | **C56X** | **5618** |
| **C-GRPF** | **CL61** | **5168** |
| C-GRPM | FA20 | 500 |
| C-GRQA | C500 | 455 |
| C-GRQX | LJ25 | 146 |
| **C-GRRD** | **C510** | **0232** |
| C-GRRS | SBRL | 306-78 |
| C-GRSD | FA20 | 157 |
| C-GRSD-X | FA20 | 157 |
| C-GRVJ | LJ31 | 111 |
| C-GSAP | CL61 | 3034 |
| C-GSAP | CL65 | 5710 |
| **C-GSAP** | **GLEX** | **9038** |
| C-GSAS | LJ25 | 109 |
| C-GSAX | LJ24 | 129 |
| C-GSBR | GLF3 | 307 |
| C-GSCL | F2TH | 88 |
| C-GSCL | FA20 | 495 |
| C-GSCL | HS25 | 257030 |
| C-GSCL | HS25 | 258243 |
| C-GSCR | C550 | 354 |
| C-GSCR | FA20 | 495 |
| C-GSCX | C550 | 381 |
| C-GSEC | C56X | 5298 |
| C-GSEC | C750 | 0246 |
| **C-GSEC** | **F2EX** | **82** |
| C-GSEO | C750 | 0246 |
| C-GSFA | C550 | 057 |
| C-GSIV | LJ24 | 108 |
| C-GSKA | FA20 | 9 |
| C-GSKC | FA20 | 29 |
| C-GSKL | LJ25 | 179 |
| C-GSKN | FA20 | 65 |
| C-GSKQ | FA20 | 40 |
| C-GSKS | FA20 | 34 |
| C-GSKV | HS25 | 25141 |
| **C-GSLC** | **C56X** | **5556** |
| C-GSLK | GLF2 | 46 |
| C-GSLL | C500 | 390 |
| **C-GSLU** | **F2EX** | **167** |
| **C-GSMR** | **F2TH** | **88** |
| C-GSMR | F900 | 55 |
| **C-GSOE** | **C680** | **0223** |
| C-GSQI | CL61 | 5096 |
| C-GSRN | LJ36 | 039 |
| C-GSRS | FA50 | 130 |
| **C-GSSC** | **C52B** | **0118** |
| **C-GSSK** | **CS55** | **0027** |
| C-GSSS | ASTR | 080 |
| C-GSSS | F900 | 78 |

| | | |
|---|---|---|
| C-GSSS | FA50 | 95 |
| C-GSTR | C500 | 647 |
| C-GSTT | HS25 | 256021 |
| C-GSUM | C500 | 485 |
| C-GSUM | C560 | 0448 |
| C-GSUN | C500 | 485 |
| C-GSUN | C560 | 0448 |
| **C-GSUN** | **C680** | **0068** |
| **C-GSUX** | **C750** | **0205** |
| **C-GSWP** | **LJ55** | **019** |
| **C-GSWQ** | **LJ45** | **022** |
| C-GSWS | LJ25 | 370 |
| C-GSWS | WW24 | 259 |
| C-GTAK | FA20 | 197 |
| **C-GTAU** | **HS25** | **258173** |
| C-GTBR | C550 | 097 |
| C-GTCB | GLF2 | 162 |
| C-GTCI | C550 | 585 |
| C-GTCP | F900 | 29 |
| C-GTCP | JSTR | 5158 |
| **C-GTDE** | **LJ35** | **057** |
| **C-GTDK** | **C550** | **321** |
| **C-GTDM** | **LJ35** | **498** |
| C-GTDN | HS25 | 257148 |
| **C-GTDO** | **ASTR** | **151** |
| C-GTDO | CS55 | 0080 |
| (C-GTEL) | C500 | 161 |
| C-GTEP | GLF2 | 247 |
| C-GTEW | GLF2 | 120 |
| C-GTFA | LJ24 | 201 |
| **C-GTGO** | **C560** | **0576** |
| **C-GTJL** | **LJ35** | **124** |
| C-GTJT | LJ24 | 160 |
| **C-GTLG** | **ASTR** | **146** |
| C-GTLG | HS25 | 257174 |
| C-GTLU | FA20 | 262 |
| **C-GTNG** | **C500** | **169** |
| C-GTNT | FA20 | 488 |
| C-GTNT | HS25 | 258038 |
| C-GTOG | C560 | 0648 |
| **C-GTOG** | **C56X** | **5729** |
| **C-GTOL** | **C500** | **667** |
| **C-GTOR** | **HS25** | **257029** |
| C-GTPC | HS25 | 256025 |
| **C-GTPL** | **F2EX** | **87** |
| C-GTPL | FA50 | 137 |
| C-GTRG | C525 | 0376 |
| C-GTRG | C525 | 0636 |
| **C-GTRG** | **C52A** | **0456** |
| **C-GTRL** | **GALX** | **112** |
| C-GTTS | HS25 | 25108 |
| C-GTVO | FA10 | 137 |
| C-GTWO | GLF2 | 140/40 |
| C-GTXV | CL60 | 1046 |
| **C-GUAC** | **LJ35** | **309** |
| **C-GUPC** | **C56X** | **5284** |
| **C-GUPJ** | **DDJT** | **DJ1-0003** |
| C-GUUU | C550 | 422 |
| C-GVCA | LJ35 | 043 |
| C-GVCB | LJ35 | 012 |
| C-GVER | C500 | 454 |
| **C-GVGM** | **C550** | **378** |
| C-GVIJ | C550 | 550-0982 |
| C-GVKL | C500 | 341 |
| **C-GVLJ** | **DDJT** | **10-0001** |
| **C-GVMP** | **HS25** | **HA-0015** |
| C-GVQR | HS25 | 25232 |
| C-GVVA | LJ35 | 002 |
| C-GVVB | LJ36 | 025 |
| C-GVVT | C500 | 474 |
| **C-GVVZ** | **LJ45** | **020** |
| C-GWBF | CS55 | 0115 |
| C-GWCJ | C550 | 213 |
| C-GWCR | C550 | 213 |
| C-GWCR | C560 | 0379 |
| C-GWEG | LJ24 | 256 |
| C-GWEI | FA50 | 208 |
| C-GWEM | HS25 | 258015 |
| C-GWFG | LJ24 | 256 |
| **C-GWFG** | **LJ35** | **669** |
| **C-GWFM** | **FA50** | **264** |
| C-GWFM | HS25 | 258015 |
| **C-GWGZ** | **C525** | **0637** |
| C-GWII | C56X | 5258 |
| C-GWKF | WW24 | 271 |
| **C-GWLE** | **HS25** | **258007** |
| **C-GWLL** | **CL64** | **5484** |

| | | |
|---|---|---|
| C-GWLL | HS25 | 258007 |
| (C-GWPA) | C650 | 0011 |
| C-GWPB | FA20 | 92/421 |
| **C-GWPB** | **GALX** | **119** |
| C-GWPV | WW24 | 105 |
| C-GWRT | CL60 | 1016 |
| C-GWSA | FA20 | 228/473 |
| C-GWSA | JSTR | 5146 |
| C-GWSH | WW24 | 165 |
| "C-GWST" | ASTR | 123 |
| C-GWUG | CL61 | 5146 |
| **C-GWUL** | **C550** | **550-1028** |
| (C-GWUZ) | LJ25 | 084 |
| C-GWVC | C500 | 107 |
| **C-GWWU** | **C560** | **0304** |
| C-GWXK | LJ31 | 068 |
| C-GWXP | LJ31 | 102 |
| **C-GXBB** | **FA50** | **278** |
| **C-GXCG** | **C560** | **0481** |
| C-GXCO | C560 | 0481 |
| C-GXCO | C56X | 5200 |
| C-GXFZ | C500 | 032 |
| C-GXKF | WW24 | 378 |
| C-GXKQ | CL60 | 1004 |
| **C-GXMB** | **PRM1** | **RB-217** |
| (C-GXMP) | HS25 | HB-30 |
| **C-GXNW** | **ASTR** | **264** |
| **C-GXOP** | **C510** | **0170** |
| C-GXPR | GLEX | 9211 |
| C-GXPT | C500 | 096 |
| C-GXPT | HS25 | 25018 |
| C-GXYN | HS25 | 257114 |
| C-GYCJ | C550 | 561 |
| C-GYMB | PRM1 | RB-255 |
| C-GYMM | C560 | 0484 |
| C-GYMM | CL64 | 5317 |
| (C-GYMP) | HS25 | HB-31 |
| C-GYPH | HS25 | 257155 |
| C-GYPH | HS25 | 258007 |
| C-GYPJ | FA50 | 162 |
| **C-GYPV** | **PRM1** | **RB-16** |
| C-GYYZ | HS25 | 257008 |
| **C-GZCZ** | **ASTR** | **273** |
| C-GZDQ | CL30 | 20021 |
| C-GZDQ | CL30 | 20036 |
| C-GZDS | CL30 | 20022 |
| C-GZDS | CL30 | 20037 |
| C-GZDS | CL30 | 20064 |
| C-GZDV | CL30 | 20008 |
| C-GZDV | CL30 | 20023 |
| C-GZDV | CL30 | 20038 |
| C-GZDV | CL30 | 20058 |
| C-GZDY | CL30 | 20009 |
| C-GZDY | CL30 | 20024 |
| C-GZDY | CL30 | 20039 |
| C-GZDY | CL30 | 20053 |
| C-GZEB | CL30 | 20010 |
| C-GZEB | CL30 | 20025 |
| C-GZEB | CL30 | 20040 |
| C-GZEB | CL30 | 20060 |
| C-GZED | CL30 | 20011 |
| C-GZED | CL30 | 20026 |
| C-GZED | CL30 | 20041 |
| C-GZEH | CL30 | 20012 |
| C-GZEH | CL30 | 20027 |
| C-GZEH | CL30 | 20042 |
| C-GZEI | CL30 | 20013 |
| C-GZEI | CL30 | 20028 |
| C-GZEI | CL30 | 20055 |
| C-GZEJ | CL30 | 20014 |
| C-GZEJ | CL30 | 20029 |
| C-GZEK | C550 | 550-0953 |
| C-GZEK | CL64 | 5360 |
| C-GZEM | CL30 | 20015 |
| C-GZEM | CL30 | 20030 |
| C-GZEM | CL30 | 20068 |
| C-GZEO | CL30 | 20016 |
| C-GZEO | CL30 | 20031 |
| C-GZEO | CL30 | 20061 |
| C-GZEP | CL30 | 20017 |
| C-GZEP | CL30 | 20032 |
| C-GZEP | CL30 | 20069 |
| C-GZER | CL30 | 20018 |
| C-GZER | CL30 | 20033 |
| C-GZER | CL30 | 20062 |
| C-GZES | CL30 | 20019 |
| C-GZES | CL30 | 20034 |

| | | |
|---|---|---|
| C-GZES | CL30 | 20056 |
| C-GZET | CL30 | 20020 |
| C-GZET | CL30 | 20035 |
| C-GZET | CL30 | 20063 |
| C-GZHZ | CL61 | 5020 |
| C-GZIM | LJ25 | 208 |
| C-GZKL | GLEX | 9099 |
| C-GZNC | CL61 | 5059 |
| C-GZOW | GLEX | 9119 |
| C-GZPT | GLEX | 9126 |
| C-GZPV | GLEX | 9136 |
| C-GZPW | GLEX | 9137 |
| **C-GZPX** | **CL64** | **5458** |
| C-GZRA | GLEX | 9138 |
| C-GZSM | GLEX | 9013 |
| C-GZTU | CL64 | 5553 |
| C-GZTZ | GLEX | 9081 |
| C-GZVV | LJ35 | 153 |
| C-GZVZ | CL64 | 5569 |
| C-GZVZ | GLEX | 9093 |
| C-GZWY | CL61 | 5189 |
| C-GZXA | C500 | 252 |
| C-GZZX | HS25 | 257161 |
| "C-XPWC" | LJ36 | 001 |

## Chile

| | | |
|---|---|---|
| **CC-CAB** | **HS25** | **258769** |
| **CC-CDE** | **C56X** | **5767** |
| CC-CGT | SBRL | 306-33 |
| (CC-CGX) | C550 | 136 |
| **CC-CHE** | **C52A** | **0171** |
| **CC-CLC** | **C550** | **146** |
| CC-CMS | C525 | 0487 |
| **CC-CMS** | **LJ40** | **45-2009** |
| CC-CPS | C650 | 7045 |
| **CC-CPS** | **C750** | **0268** |
| CC-CRK | WW24 | 184 |
| **CC-CRT** | **BE40** | **RK-493** |
| CC-CSA | C525 | 0632 |
| **CC-CTC** | **SBRL** | **306-112** |
| CC-CTE | C500 | 426 |
| **CC-CVO** | **C525** | **0243** |
| CC-CWK | ASTR | 141 |
| **CC-CWK** | **ASTR** | **219** |
| CC-CWW | C500 | 558 |
| **CC-CWW** | **CS55** | **0002** |
| CC-CWZ | C550 | 108 |
| **CC-CWZ** | **CS55** | **0143** |
| **CC-DAC** | **C650** | **0233** |
| **CC-DGA** | **C550** | **657** |
| CC-ECE | C650 | 0033 |
| CC-ECL | C650 | 0131 |
| CC-ECN | C550 | 146 |
| CC-ECO | LJ35 | 050 |
| CC-ECP | LJ35 | 066 |
| CC-LLM | C550 | 481 |
| **CC-LLM** | **C550** | **550-0996** |
| CC-PES | FA20 | 496 |
| CC-PGK | C525 | 0632 |
| CC-PGL | C650 | 7045 |
| CC-PVJ | C525 | 0243 |
| CC-PZM | C500 | 203 |

## Russia
(see also RA-)

| | | |
|---|---|---|
| CCCP-01100 | FA20 | 55/410 |

## Canada

| | | |
|---|---|---|
| CF-AAG | HS25 | 25137 |
| CF-ALC | HS25 | 25087 |
| CF-ANL | HS25 | 25042 |
| CF-AOS | HS25 | 25278 |
| CF-ARE | LJ24 | 070 |
| CF-BAX | C500 | 020 |
| CF-BCJ | LJ24 | 100 |
| CF-BCL | C500 | 042 |
| CF-BCM | C500 | 071 |
| CF-BFM | FA20 | 40 |
| CF-BLT | SBRL | 306-23 |
| CF-BNK | HS25 | 25221 |
| CF-BRL | SBRL | 282-107 |
| CF-CFL | HS25 | 25193 |
| CF-CFL | HS25 | 25213 |
| CF-CFP | C500 | 125 |
| CF-CPW | C500 | 002 |
| CF-CSS | LJ24 | 197 |
| CF-CXY | LJ25 | 116 |
| CF-DML | FA20 | 14 |
| CF-DOM | HS25 | 25018 |
| CF-DSC | HS25 | 25086 |
| CF-DTF | JSTR | 5088 |
| CF-DTM | JSTR | 5052 |
| (CF-DTX) | JSTR | 5018 |
| CF-DWW | LJ25 | 045 |
| CF-ECB | LJ24 | 112 |
| CF-ENJ | C500 | 122 |
| CF-ESO | FA20 | 46 |
| CF-ETN | JSTR | 5021 |
| CF-FNM | GLF2 | 52 |
| CF-GWI | FA20 | 7 |
| CF-GWI | JSTR | 5106/9 |
| CF-HLL | HS25 | 25034 |
| CF-HMV | LJ25 | 015 |
| CF-HOG | GLF2 | 7 |
| CF-HSS | HS25 | 256003 |
| CF-IOT | GLF2 | 78 |
| CF-IPG | HS25 | 25053 |
| CF-IPJ | HS25 | 25053 |
| CF-JES | FA20 | 236 |
| CF-KAX | LJ25 | 016 |
| CF-KBI | WW24 | 81 |
| CF-KCI | HS25 | 25137 |
| CF-MAJ | MS76 | 050 |
| CF-MDB | HS25 | 25075 |
| CF-NCG | SBRL | 282-90 |
| CF-NER | HS25 | 25176 |
| CF-NOR | GLF2 | 54/36 |
| CF-OPC | HS25 | 25016 |
| CF-PPN | HS25 | 25280 |
| CF-PQG | HS25 | 25036 |
| CF-QNS | HS25 | 25152 |
| CF-ROX | LJ25 | 070 |
| CF-RWA | HS25 | 25016 |
| CF-SBR | GLF2 | 9/33 |
| CF-SDA | HS25 | 25022 |
| CF-SDH | HS25 | 25192 |
| CF-SEN | HS25 | 25027 |
| CF-SHZ | HS25 | 25095 |
| CF-SIM | HS25 | 25039 |
| CF-SRZ | FA20 | 11 |
| CF-SUA | WW24 | 17 |
| CF-TEC | HS25 | 25232 |
| CF-TEL | LJ24 | 054 |
| CF-TXT | LJ25 | 057 |
| CF-ULG | WW24 | 6 |
| CF-UYT | LJ24 | 087 |
| CF-VVX | WW24 | 76 |
| CF-WDU | HFB3 | 1039 |
| CF-WEC | WW24 | 115 |
| CF-WOA | WW24 | 21 |
| CF-WOS | HS25 | 25159 |
| CF-WRA | FA20 | 110 |
| CF-WUL | WW24 | 9 |
| CF-YPB | FA20 | 254 |

## Morocco

| | | |
|---|---|---|
| **CN-AMJ** | **C56X** | **6042** |
| **CN-AMK** | **C56X** | **6047** |
| **CN-ANL** | **GLF2** | **182** |
| **CNA-NM** | **FA20** | **165/452** |
| **CN-ANN** | **FA20** | **152/446** |
| **CN-ANO** | **FA50** | **12** |
| **CN-ANU** | **GLF3** | **365** |
| **CNA-NV** | **C560** | **0025** |
| **CNA-NW** | **C560** | **0039** |
| **CN-ANZ** | **FA10** | **212** |
| **CN-IAM** | **CL64** | **5591** |
| CN-MAJ | MS76 | 050 |
| CN-MBG | FA20 | 152/446 |
| CN-MBH | FA20 | 165/452 |
| **CN-RBS** | **HS25** | **HA-0091** |
| CN-TCS | CRVT | 34 |
| **CN-TDE** | **CRVT** | **5** |
| CN-TFU | F900 | 105 |
| **CN-THL** | **CRVT** | **39** |
| **CN-TJB** | **LJ45** | **112** |
| **CN-TJD** | **BE40** | **RK-579** |
| **CN-TJE** | **C525** | **0693** |
| CN-TKK | C550 | 293 |
| **CN-TKN** | **FA10** | **128** |
| **CN-TLB** | **C525** | **0312** |
| CN-TNA | FA10 | 212 |

## Bolivia

| | | |
|---|---|---|
| CP-2105 | C500 | 541 |
| CP-2131 | C500 | 083 |
| CP-2259 | WW24 | 95 |
| CP-2263 | WW24 | 58 |
| **CP-2317** | **SBRL** | **282-136** |

## Portugal

| | | |
|---|---|---|
| CS-ATD | FA20 | 30 |
| CS-ATE | FA20 | 94/428 |
| CS-ATF | FA20 | 112 |
| CS-ATG | FA20 | 264 |
| CS-AYS | C550 | 615 |
| **CS-AYY** | **C500** | **567** |
| CS-DBM | C500 | 200 |
| CS-DCA | C500 | 157 |
| CS-DCE | CS55 | 0007 |
| CS-DCI | C550 | 066 |
| **CS-DCK** | **FA20** | **297** |
| CS-DCM | F2TH | 46 |
| CS-DCT | C750 | 0134 |
| CS-DDA | CS55 | 0098 |
| CS-DDB | C56X | 5028 |
| CS-DDI | F900 | 143 |
| **CS-DDV** | **CS55** | **0147** |
| **CS-DDZ** | **LJ31** | **034** |
| CS-DFA | F900 | 91 |
| CS-DFB | F900 | 94 |
| **CS-DFC** | **F2TH** | **148** |
| **CS-DFD** | **F2TH** | **174** |
| **CS-DFE** | **F2TH** | **205** |
| **CS-DFF** | **F2EX** | **41** |
| **CS-DFG** | **F2EX** | **44** |
| **CS-DFH** | **F900** | **91** |
| CS-DFI | FA50 | 89 |
| CS-DFJ | FA50 | 60 |
| **CS-DFK** | **F2EX** | **65** |
| (CS-DFK) | FA50 | 62 |
| CS-DFL | F9EX | 97 |
| **CS-DFM** | **C56X** | **5257** |
| **CS-DFN** | **C56X** | **5283** |
| **CS-DFO** | **C56X** | **5314** |
| **CS-DFP** | **C56X** | **5315** |
| **CS-DFQ** | **C56X** | **5334** |
| **CS-DFR** | **C56X** | **5355** |
| **CS-DFS** | **C56X** | **5372** |
| **CS-DFT** | **C56X** | **5512** |
| **CS-DFU** | **C56X** | **5520** |
| **CS-DFV** | **C56X** | **5543** |
| **CS-DFW** | **HS25** | **258664** |
| **CS-DFX** | **HS25** | **258656** |
| **CS-DFY** | **HS25** | **258663** |
| **CS-DFZ** | **HS25** | **258673** |
| **CS-DGO** | **C750** | **0140** |
| **CS-DGQ** | **C52A** | **0200** |
| **CS-DGR** | **C650** | **7045** |
| **CS-DGW** | **C52B** | **0235** |
| **CS-DGZ** | **HS25** | **HA-0051** |
| **CS-DHA** | **C550** | **550-1005** |
| **CS-DHB** | **C550** | **550-1009** |
| **CS-DHC** | **C550** | **550-1013** |
| **CS-DHD** | **C550** | **550-1017** |
| **CS-DHE** | **C550** | **550-1022** |
| **CS-DHF** | **C550** | **550-1025** |
| **CS-DHG** | **C550** | **550-1034** |
| **CS-DHH** | **C550** | **550-1043** |
| **CS-DHI** | **C550** | **550-1048** |
| **CS-DHJ** | **C550** | **550-1082** |
| **CS-DHK** | **C550** | **550-1090** |
| **CS-DHL** | **C550** | **550-1092** |
| **CS-DHM** | **C550** | **550-1093** |
| **CS-DHN** | **C550** | **550-1098** |
| **CS-DHO** | **C550** | **550-1099** |
| **CS-DHP** | **C550** | **550-1104** |
| **CS-DHQ** | **C550** | **550-1109** |
| **CS-DHR** | **C550** | **550-1114** |
| CS-DIG | C560 | 0637 |
| **CS-DIY** | **C52B** | **0146** |
| (CS-DJA) | LJ60 | 379 |
| **CS-DKA** | **GLF4** | **1480** |
| CS-DKB | GLF5 | 642 |
| **CS-DKC** | **GLF5** | **5057** |
| **CS-DKD** | **GLF5** | **5081** |
| **CS-DKF** | **GLF5** | **5099** |
| **CS-DKG** | **GLF5** | **5127** |
| **CS-DKH** | **GLF5** | **5150** |
| **CS-DKI** | **GLF5** | **5166** |
| **CS-DKJ** | **GLF5** | **5174** |
| **CS-DKK** | **GLF5** | **5201** |
| CS-DLA | F900 | 120 |
| **CS-DLB** | **F2EX** | **80** |
| **CS-DLC** | **F2EX** | **98** |
| **CS-DLD** | **F2EX** | **109** |
| **CS-DLE** | **F2EX** | **127** |
| **CS-DLF** | **F2EX** | **134** |
| **CS-DLG** | **F2EX** | **144** |
| **CS-DLH** | **F2EX** | **149** |
| (CS-DLH) | F2EX | 155 |
| CS-DLI | F2EX | 155 |
| **CS-DMA** | **BE40** | **RK-401** |
| **CS-DMB** | **BE40** | **RK-403** |
| **CS-DMC** | **BE40** | **RK-404** |
| **CS-DMD** | **BE40** | **RK-407** |
| **CS-DME** | **BE40** | **RK-408** |
| **CS-DMF** | **BE40** | **RK-410** |
| **CS-DMG** | **BE40** | **RK-417** |
| **CS-DMH** | **BE40** | **RK-425** |
| **CS-DMI** | **BE40** | **RK-437** |
| **CS-DMJ** | **BE40** | **RK-443** |
| **CS-DMK** | **BE40** | **RK-464** |
| **CS-DML** | **BE40** | **RK-465** |
| (CS-DMM) | BE40 | RK-469 |
| **CS-DMM** | **BE40** | **RK-472** |
| **CS-DMN** | **BE40** | **RK-475** |
| **CS-DMO** | **BE40** | **RK-494** |
| **CS-DMP** | **BE40** | **RK-508** |
| **CS-DMQ** | **BE40** | **RK-512** |
| **CS-DMR** | **BE40** | **RK-516** |
| **CS-DMS** | **BE40** | **RK-519** |
| **CS-DMT** | **BE40** | **RK-532** |
| **CS-DMU** | **BE40** | **RK-538** |
| **CS-DMV** | **BE40** | **RK-549** |
| **CS-DMW** | **BE40** | **RK-550** |
| **CS-DMX** | **BE40** | **RK-555** |
| **CS-DMY** | **BE40** | **RK-556** |
| **CS-DMZ** | **BE40** | **RK-559** |
| CS-DNA | CS55 | 0032 |
| CS-DNB | CS55 | 0051 |
| CS-DNC | CS55 | 0077 |
| CS-DND | C650 | 0093 |
| (CS-DNE) | C650 | 0149 |
| CS-DNE | C650 | 7093 |
| CS-DNF | C650 | 7080 |
| CS-DNG | C650 | 7081 |
| CS-DNH | HS25 | 258193 |
| CS-DNI | HS25 | 258183 |
| CS-DNJ | HS25 | 258399 |
| CS-DNK | HS25 | 258430 |
| CS-DNL | HS25 | 258439 |
| CS-DNM | HS25 | 258422 |
| **CS-DNN** | **HS25** | **258435** |
| **CS-DNO** | **HS25** | **258457** |
| **CS-DNP** | **F2TH** | **109** |
| **CS-DNQ** | **F2TH** | **115** |
| **CS-DNR** | **F2TH** | **120** |
| **CS-DNS** | **F2TH** | **139** |
| **CS-DNT** | **HS25** | **258468** |
| **CS-DNU** | **HS25** | **258479** |
| **CS-DNV** | **HS25** | **258499** |
| **CS-DNW** | **C56X** | **5221** |
| **CS-DNX** | **HS25** | **258511** |
| **CS-DNY** | **C56X** | **5216** |
| **CS-DNZ** | **C56X** | **5235** |
| **CS-DOB** | **BE40** | **RK-561** |
| **CS-DPA** | **HS25** | **HA-0069** |
| CS-DPE | F900 | 159 |
| **CS-DPF** | **F9EX** | **198** |
| **CS-DPJ** | **HS25** | **HA-0092** |
| **CS-DPN** | **C510** | **0163** |
| **CS-DPO** | **FA50** | **226** |
| **CS-DPV** | **C510** | **0122** |
| **CS-DPW** | **FA20** | **307/513** |
| **CS-DPZ** | **C56X** | **5576** |

**CS-DQA C56X 5798**
**CS-DQB C56X 5803**
**CS-DRA HS25 258686**
**CS-DRB HS25 258690**
**CS-DRC HS25 258714**
**CS-DRD HS25 258721**
**CS-DRE HS25 258725**
**CS-DRF HS25 258730**
**CS-DRG HS25 258741**
**CS-DRH HS25 258746**
**CS-DRI HS25 258756**
**CS-DRJ HS25 258760**
**CS-DRK HS25 258765**
**CS-DRL HS25 258770**
**CS-DRM HS25 258771**
**CS-DRN HS25 258772**
**CS-DRO HS25 258775**
**CS-DRP HS25 258779**
**CS-DRQ HS25 258783**
**CS-DRR HS25 258786**
**CS-DRS HS25 258795**
**CS-DRT HS25 258802**
**CS-DRU HS25 258821**
**CS-DRV HS25 258825**
**CS-DRW HS25 258829**
**CS-DRX HS25 258834**
**CS-DRY HS25 258840**
**CS-DRZ HS25 258847**
**CS-DSA FA7X 30**
**CS-DSB FA7X 43**
**CS-DTA C560 0271**
**CS-DTB F9EX 11**
**CS-DTC E50P 50000115**
**CS-DTD FA7X 60**
**CS-DTH LJ60 362**
**CS-DUA HS25 HB-4**
(CS-DUA) HS25 HB-6
**CS-DUB HS25 HB-5**
(CS-DUB) HS25 HB-7
**CS-DUC HS25 HB-6**
**CS-DUD HS25 HB-8**
**CS-DUE HS25 HB-11**
**CS-DUF HS25 HB-19**
**CS-DUG HS25 HB-20**
**CS-DUH HS25 HB-21**
CS-DXA C56X 5549
**CS-DXB C56X 5553**
**CS-DXC C56X 5559**
**CS-DXD C56X 5568**
**CS-DXE C56X 5578**
**CS-DXF C56X 5586**
**CS-DXG C56X 5595**
**CS-DXH C56X 5615**
**CS-DXI C56X 5621**
**CS-DXJ C56X 5627**
**CS-DXK C56X 5633**
**CS-DXL C56X 5640**
**CS-DXM C56X 5683**
**CS-DXN C56X 5685**
**CS-DXO C56X 5692**
**CS-DXP C56X 5702**
**CS-DXQ C56X 5704**
**CS-DXR C56X 5748**
**CS-DXS C56X 5754**
**CS-DXT C56X 5765**
**CS-DXU C56X 5775**
**CS-DXV C56X 5782**
**CS-DXW C56X 5787**
**CS-DXX C56X 5789**
**CS-DXY C56X 5791**
**CS-DXZ C56X 5796**
CS-EAA C52B 0317
**CS-EAM GLEX 9353**
**CS-TFI LJ45 021**
**CS-TFN F900 66**
**CS-TFO LJ40 45-2094**
**CS-TFQ LJ45 302**
**CS-TFR LJ45 382**
CS-TFV CL30 20252
**CS-TLP F2EX 39**
CS-TLT LJ45 287
**CS-TLW LJ45 144**
**CS-TLY FA7X 15**
CS-TMF FA50 29
CS-TMJ FA50 190
CS-TMK F900 66
CS-TMQ F900 175
CS-TMS FA50 268

## Macau
(see also B-H)

CS-MAC CL61 5178
(CS-MAI) HS25 258366

## Uruguay

CX-BOI LJ35 378
**CX-BVD HS25 25251**
**CX-CBS HS25 256067**
**CX-CCT C500 344**
**CX-CIB HS25 257071**
CX-CMJ WW24 251
CX-ECO LJ25 229
CX-VRH LJ35 628

## Bahamas

C6-BDH HS25 256028
C6-BEJ GLF2 194
C6-BEN FA10 109
C6-BER FA50 20
C6-BET HS25 257054
C6-BEV MS76 111
C6-BEY HS25 25051
C6-BFE GLF2 194
(C6-BGF) LJ24 252
C6-BHD FA50 264
C6-BHN F900 9
C6-BPC HS25 25016
C6-EVU C52A 0170
C6-JET ASTR 095
**C6-LUV C52B 0243**
C6-LVU C52A 0170
C6-MED HS25 25140
C6-SZN F9EX 195

## Mozambique

**C9-CFM BE40 RK-249**
C9-TAC HS25 257175
(C9-TTA) HS25 257175

## Germany

**D-AAAM GLF5 5189**
**D-AAAZ GLEX 9170**
**D-AABB GLF4 4091**
(D-AAFX) CL61 5070
D-AAGF GLF4 1159
**D-AAMA CL61 5023**
(D-AAMD) GLF2 186
(D-AANA) GLEX 9234
**D-AAOK CL64 5585**
**D-ABCD CL64 5565**
(D-ACDC) F900 5
D-ACGN FA7X 77
D-ACTE CL61 5085
D-ACTO CL64 5502
D-ACTU CL61 5085
D-ACTU CL64 5502
**D-ACUA CL65 5725**
(D-ACVG) GLF2 186
**D-ADCA GLF5 5114**
**D-ADCB GLF5 5142**
(D-ADLA) CL61 5060
**D-ADLR GLF5 5093**
**D-ADNB GLEX 9071**
D-ADND CL64 5403
D-ADNE CL64 5422
D-AEKT GLEX 9213
**D-AETV CL64 5417**
**D-AEUK CL64 5632**
D-AFKG GLF2 186
(D-AFLW) GLEX 9014
(D-AFLW) GLEX 9035
D-AGKG CL61 5049
D-AGSI F9EX 78
(D-AGTH) GLEX 9120
**D-AGVS GLF4 4113**
**D-AHEI CL64 5463**
**D-AHLE CL64 5462**
(D-AIFB) CL65 5704
**D-AIND CL64 5572**
(D-AINI) CL64 5595
(D-AINX) CL64 5629
(D-AINY) CL64 5644
D-AJAB CL64 5327
(D-AJAB) FA7X 66
D-AJAD F9EX 64
D-AJAG CL64 5528
**D-AJGK GLF4 1459**
(D-AJJJ) GLF4 1459
**D-AJJK GLF5 5191**
(D-AKAT) CL64 5303
**D-AKAZ GLEX 9250**
**D-AKBH CL64 5457**
**D-AKUE CL61 5173**
D-ALME F900 101
**D-ALMS F9EX 227**
D-AMBI F9EX 176
**D-AMIG F9DX 623**
D-AMIM CL64 5317
(D-AMOS) GLEX 9301
(D-AMTM) CL61 5018
D-ANKE CL64 5494
D-AOHP CL61 5068
**D-APLC FA7X 77**
D-ARKK GLF4 4004
**D-ARTE CL61 5060**
(D-ARTE) CL64 5505
(D-ARTN) CL64 5585
(D-ARWE) CL64 5303
D-ARWE CL64 5454
D-ASIE CL64 5475
(D-ASIE) F9EX 227
(D-ASTS) CL64 5375
**D-ASTS CL64 5378**
D-ATNR GLEX 9159
**D-ATTT CL64 5609**
**D-ATYA CL65 5756**
**D-AUCR F9DX 606**
**D-AUKE CL64 5389**
(D-AVIA) GLEX 9280
**D-AWKG F9EX 20**
**D-AZEM F9EX 133**
(D-AZPP) CL64 5369
D-BABE JSTR 5012
**D-BADO CL30 20116**
D-BAIR GALX 029
D-BAMA F2TH 70
**D-BAMM F2EX 74**
**D-BANN CL30 20221**
**D-BASE F2EX 111**
D-BAVA CL30 20172
**D-BAVB CL30 20212**
(D-BBAD) CL60 1008
(D-BBAD) FA50 23
(D-BBED) F2EX 76
D-BBWK FA50 23
**D-BCLA CL30 20272**
D-BDNL F2TH 119
D-BDWO FA50 42
D-BEKP CL30 20275
**D-BEKY F2EX 201**
(D-BEKY) F2EX 210
D-BELL FA50 222
**D-BERT F2EX 30**
D-BERT FA50 218
**D-BEST F2TH 50**
**D-BETA CL30 20079**
**D-BETI FA50 267**
D-BFAR FA50 16
**D-BFFB F2EX 93**
D-BFFB FA50 65
D-BFLY CL30 20123
(D-BGRL) HS25 HA-0056
**D-BIKA F2EX 76**
D-BILL F2EX 33
D-BIRD F2EX 7
D-BIRD F2TH 54
D-BIRD FA50 16
D-BJET CL60 1005
(D-BJET) HS25 259016
D-BKLI C750 0219
**D-BLDI C750 0218**
D-BLUE C750 0140
D-BMTM CL60 1029
**D-BMVV F2EX 42**
D-BNTH FA50 196
D-BOND F2TH 54
**D-BONN F2EX 118**
(D-BONN) F2EX 125
(D-BOOI) FA50 215
**D-BOOK F2EX 70**
D-BOOK FA50 215
D-BOSS F2EX 33
(D-BPWR) CL30 20272
D-BSIK F2TH 27
D-BSKY CL30 20179
**D-BSMI CL30 20071**
**D-BSNA CL60 1066**
**D-BTEN C750 0085**
D-BTIM CL30 20071
**D-BUBI CL30 20145**
**D-BUSY CL60 1070**
(D-C...) HS25 258201
**D-CAAA C56X 5555**
**D-CAAE LJ55 095**
D-CAAS WW24 164
D-CAAT C550 205
D-CABB ASTR 059
D-CACM C650 7039
D-CACP LJ55 086
(D-CACS) C550 151
(D-CADA) HFB3 1073
D-CADA HS25 257007
D-CADA HS25 259008
D-CADB FA10 89
D-CADC LJ31 049
(D-CADE) HFB3 1074
(D-CADI) HFB3 1075
(D-CADO) HFB3 1076
(D-CADU) HFB3 1077
**D-CADY C56X 5037**
D-CAEP LJ55 059
(D-CAFB) C560 0303
D-CAFE C680 0033
D-CAFI HS25 25037
D-CAFO LJ36 006
**D-CAHB LJ40 45-2093**
**D-CAHH C680 0226**
**D-CAIR C56X 5620**
(D-CAJA) HS25 HA-0071
(D-CAJC) FA10 131
**D-CAJK C56X 5670**
D-CAKE C650 0240
(D-CALA) HFB3 1068
(D-CALE) HFB3 1069
(D-CALI) HFB3 1070
**D-CALL C550 550-0834**
D-CALL FA20 138/440
D-CALL FA20 392/553
(D-CALM) FA20 237/476
(D-CALO) HFB3 1071
(D-CALU) HFB3 1072
D-CAMA HFB3 1064
D-CAMB HS25 25157
D-CAMB LJ35 174
D-CAME HFB3 1065
(D-CAMO) HFB3 1066
**D-CAMS C560 0243**
(D-CAMU) HFB3 1067
(D-CANA) HFB3 1079
(D-CANE) HFB3 1080
D-CANI HFB3 1061
D-CANO HFB3 1062
D-CANU HFB3 1063
**D-CAPB C560 0806**
D-CAPD LJ35 179
**D-CAPO LJ35 159**
D-CARA HFB3 1021
D-CARD LJ35 426
D-CARE C650 0134
D-CARE HFB3 1022
D-CARE LJ35 341
D-CARE LJ55 073
D-CARG LJ35 433
D-CARH LJ35 444
D-CARI HFB3 1023
**D-CARL LJ35 387**
D-CARO HFB3 1024
D-CARO LJ35 325

| | | |
|---|---|---|
| D-CARP | LJ55 | 050 |
| D-CART | LJ35 | 354 |
| D-CARU | HFB3 | 1025 |
| D-CARX | LJ55 | 034 |
| D-CARY | HFB3 | 1026 |
| **D-CASA** | **C560** | **0544** |
| (D-CASE) | HFB3 | V2/1002 |
| D-CASH | C52B | 0217 |
| D-CASH | C550 | 564 |
| (D-CASH) | C56X | 5213 |
| D-CASH | FA10 | 7 |
| (D-CASO) | HFB3 | 1027 |
| **D-CAST** | **C52B** | **0330** |
| D-CASU | HFB3 | 1028 |
| D-CASY | HFB3 | 1029 |
| **D-CATE** | **C680** | **0153** |
| D-CATE | HFB3 | 1030 |
| D-CATE | LJ35 | 216 |
| (D-CATI) | HFB3 | 1078 |
| **D-CATL** | **LJ55** | **051** |
| D-CATP | C650 | 0121 |
| D-CATY | LJ35 | 114 |
| D-CATY | LJ35 | 211 |
| **D-CAUW** | **C560** | **0578** |
| (D-CAVB) | C52B | 0339 |
| **D-CAVE** | **LJ35** | **423** |
| D-CAVI | LJ35 | 174 |
| D-CAVW | HS25 | 258233 |
| D-CAVW | SBRL | 282-76 |
| D-CAVW | SBRL | 380-38 |
| D-CAWA | C550 | 596 |
| D-CAWM | C56X | 5002 |
| **D-CAWM** | **C56X** | **6002** |
| D-CAWU | C560 | 0042 |
| **D-CAWU** | **C56X** | **5797** |
| D-CAYK | C650 | 0187 |
| (D-CAZH) | HS25 | 258043 |
| D-CBAD | LJ60 | 129 |
| D-CBAE | HS25 | 257031 |
| D-CBAG | FA10 | 91 |
| D-CBAT | C550 | 299 |
| D-CBAT | C550 | 562 |
| D-CBAT | FA20 | 108/430 |
| **D-CBAY** | **C680** | **0125** |
| D-CBAY | WW24 | 202 |
| D-CBBA | WW24 | 294 |
| **D-CBBB** | **C56X** | **5567** |
| D-CBBB | WW24 | 296 |
| D-CBBC | WW24 | 297 |
| D-CBBD | WW24 | 310 |
| D-CBBE | WW24 | 154 |
| D-CBBT | FA20 | 162/451 |
| D-CBEL | C550 | 468 |
| **D-CBEN** | **C560** | **0282** |
| D-CBIG | C560 | 0124 |
| **D-CBIZ** | **C650** | **7039** |
| D-CBMB | FA10 | 61 |
| D-CBMV | HS25 | 258345 |
| D-CBMW | HS25 | 258155 |
| D-CBMW | HS25 | 258345 |
| D-CBNA | FA20 | 63/411 |
| (D-CBOB) | LJ60 | 378 |
| D-CBPD | LJ25 | 091 |
| **D-CBPL** | **C650** | **0149** |
| D-CBRD | LJ36 | 013 |
| D-CBRK | LJ35 | 026 |
| D-CBUR | FA10 | 98 |
| D-CBUS | CS55 | 0027 |
| D-CBVB | C52B | 0339 |
| D-CBVW | HS25 | 25231 |
| D-CBVW | HS25 | 258235 |
| D-CBVW | SBRL | 380-60 |
| D-CBWW | HS25 | 259028 |
| **D-CCAA** | **LJ35** | **315** |
| **D-CCAB** | **C550** | **550-0827** |
| (D-CCAC) | LJ36 | 004 |
| D-CCAD | LJ35 | 263 |
| D-CCAP | LJ35 | 144 |
| D-CCAR | LJ35 | 179 |
| D-CCAR | LJ35 | 200 |
| D-CCAT | ASTR | 059 |
| D-CCAT | LJ24 | 254 |
| D-CCAT | LJ25 | 079 |
| D-CCAX | LJ35 | 284 |
| D-CCAY | LJ35 | 112 |
| **D-CCBH** | **C52B** | **0334** |
| (D-CCBT) | ASTR | 080 |
| **D-CCCA** | **LJ35** | **160** |
| **D-CCCB** | **LJ35** | **663** |
| **D-CCCF** | **C550** | **205** |
| D-CCCG | C52B | 0146 |
| (D-CCCH) | HFB3 | 1060 |
| D-CCDB | FA20 | 381/548 |
| **D-CCEA** | **C56X** | **5593** |
| **D-CCEU** | **C650** | **0190** |
| (D-CCEX) | HS25 | 256015 |
| **D-CCFF** | **C680** | **0114** |
| **D-CCGG** | **LJ60** | **256** |
| **D-CCGN** | **LJ55** | **017** |
| **D-CCHB** | **LJ35** | **089** |
| D-CCHS | LJ35 | 122 |
| (D-CCHS) | LJ55 | 013 |
| D-CCHS | LJ55 | 049 |
| **D-CCJS** | **C680** | **0175** |
| D-CCKV | LJ31 | 046 |
| D-CCMB | FA20 | 377/548 |
| (D-CCNA) | FA20 | 147/444 |
| D-CCON | LJ55 | 098 |
| D-CCPD | LJ36 | 004 |
| **D-CCSD** | **C650** | **0212** |
| **D-CCVD** | **C56X** | **5784** |
| (D-CCVW) | HFB3 | 1080 |
| D-CCVW | HS25 | 258237 |
| D-CCVW | SBRL | 380-45 |
| D-CCWD | C550 | 550-0864 |
| (D-CCWD) | C56X | 5670 |
| **D-CCWD** | **C56X** | **6039** |
| D-CCWK | LJ25 | 076 |
| (D-CDAS) | FA20 | 108/430 |
| D-CDAX | LJ35 | 135 |
| D-CDBW | C56X | 5073 |
| (D-CDCC) | C56X | 6041 |
| D-CDCD | C56X | 6049 |
| D-CDCE | C56X | 6062 |
| D-CDCF | C56X | 6063 |
| **D-CDDD** | **C56X** | **5623** |
| D-CDDD | LJ24 | 201 |
| (D-CDEF) | LJ60 | 331 |
| D-CDEN | LJ31 | 049 |
| D-CDEN | LJ45 | 148 |
| D-CDFA | LJ36 | 006 |
| D-CDHS | LJ35 | 026 |
| D-CDHS | LJ35 | 311 |
| (D-CDIG) | C52B | 0086 |
| D-CDNX | LJ60 | 231 |
| D-CDNY | LJ60 | 160 |
| D-CDNZ | LJ60 | 161 |
| D-CDPD | LJ25 | 177 |
| D-CDRB | MU30 | A053SA |
| **D-CDSF** | **LJ35** | **421** |
| D-CDSM | LJ60 | 276 |
| D-CDUW | C560 | 0099 |
| (D-CDVW) | HFB3 | 1080 |
| D-CDWN | LJ35 | 175 |
| D-CEAS | WW24 | 55 |
| (D-CEBM) | C560 | 0558 |
| **D-CEBM** | **C560** | **0569** |
| (D-CEDL) | HFB3 | 1061 |
| **D-CEEE** | **C56X** | **5630** |
| **D-CEFD** | **C52B** | **0120** |
| (D-CEFL) | LJ35 | 284 |
| (D-CEFM) | C550 | 550-1018 |
| **D-CEIS** | **BE40** | **RK-10** |
| D-CEJA | LJ60 | 173 |
| D-CELA | LJ36 | 002 |
| **D-CELE** | **C52B** | **0011** |
| (D-CELE) | C52B | 0114 |
| D-CELL | FA20 | 201/469 |
| **D-CEMG** | **C560** | **0463** |
| D-CEMM | LJ45 | 144 |
| D-CENT | FA10 | 89 |
| D-CEPD | LJ25 | 274 |
| D-CERA | HFB3 | 1031 |
| D-CERE | HFB3 | 1032 |
| D-CERI | HFB3 | 1033 |
| D-CERO | HFB3 | 1034 |
| D-CERU | HFB3 | 1035 |
| D-CESA | HFB3 | 1036 |
| D-CESE | HFB3 | 1037 |
| D-CESH | LJ45 | 017 |
| D-CESI | HFB3 | 1038 |
| D-CESO | HFB3 | 1039 |
| D-CESU | HFB3 | 1040 |
| D-CETV | LJ60 | 148 |
| "D-CEUU" | FA20 | 201/469 |
| D-CEVW | HS25 | 258067 |
| D-CEVW | SBRL | 306-44 |
| D-CEWR | C560 | 0192 |
| D-CEWR | LJ45 | 013 |
| D-CEWR | LJ45 | 213 |
| (D-CEWR) | LJ55 | 013 |
| **D-CEXP** | **LJ35** | **616** |
| D-CFAI | CS55 | 0134 |
| (D-CFAI) | FA20 | 174/457 |
| D-CFAI | FA20 | 335 |
| D-CFAI | LJ35 | 365 |
| **D-CFAI** | **LJ55** | **061** |
| D-CFAN | HS25 | 258094 |
| **D-CFAX** | **LJ35** | **135** |
| **D-CFAZ** | **LJ55** | **136** |
| D-CFCF | HS25 | 25248 |
| **D-CFCF** | **LJ35** | **413** |
| **D-CFFB** | **LJ60** | **107** |
| **D-CFFF** | **C56X** | **5634** |
| **D-CFGG** | **LJ36** | **048** |
| D-CFIS | ASTR | 045 |
| (D-CFKG) | HS25 | 25005 |
| **D-CFLG** | **LJ60** | **290** |
| D-CFLO | C56X | 5788 |
| D-CFLY | C560 | 0145 |
| **D-CFLY** | **C56X** | **6014** |
| D-CFOX | C560 | 0277 |
| D-CFOX | LJ36 | 031 |
| D-CFPD | LJ24 | 345 |
| D-CFRA | C52B | 0258 |
| D-CFRC | HS25 | 258036 |
| D-CFSK | HS25 | 256053 |
| (D-CFTC) | C550 | 550-0988 |
| **D-CFTG** | **LJ35** | **204** |
| D-CFUX | LJ55 | 061 |
| D-CFVG | LJ24 | 223 |
| (D-CFVG) | LJ35 | 121 |
| D-CFVW | HS25 | 258073 |
| D-CFWR | LJ45 | 013 |
| D-CGAS | C550 | 443 |
| **D-CGBR** | **LJ55** | **122** |
| **D-CGEO** | **LJ60** | **160** |
| **D-CGFA** | **LJ35** | **179** |
| **D-CGFB** | **LJ35** | **268** |
| **D-CGFC** | **LJ35** | **331** |
| **D-CGFD** | **LJ35** | **139** |
| **D-CGFE** | **LJ36** | **062** |
| **D-CGFF** | **LJ36** | **063** |
| **D-CGFG** | **LJ35** | **222** |
| **D-CGFH** | **LJ35** | **607** |
| **D-CGFI** | **LJ35** | **612** |
| **D-CGFJ** | **LJ35** | **643** |
| D-CGFV | MU30 | A051SA |
| **D-CGGB** | **LJ40** | **45-2018** |
| **D-CGGC** | **LJ40** | **45-2107** |
| D-CGGG | LJ31 | 042 |
| **D-CGGG** | **LJ31** | **227** |
| D-CGHP | C550 | 550-0998 |
| D-CGIN | LJ55 | 090 |
| D-CGJH | FA20 | 138/440 |
| D-CGLS | WW24 | 161 |
| D-CGMA | ASTR | 133 |
| (D-CGNF) | LJ60 | 304 |
| D-CGOM | LJ31 | 167 |
| D-CGPD | LJ35 | 202 |
| **D-CGRC** | **LJ35** | **223** |
| D-CGSO | FA20 | 306/512 |
| D-CGSP | G180 | 90002 |
| D-CGTF | LJ60 | 281 |
| (D-CGTI) | C56X | 5037 |
| D-CGTT | C680 | 0153 |
| D-CGVW | HS25 | 258076 |
| D-CHAL | WW24 | 207 |
| (D-CHAM) | C56X | 6027 |
| D-CHAN | C550 | 550-0874 |
| (D-CHAS) | WW24 | 55 |
| D-CHBL | WW24 | 226 |
| (D-CHBM) | LJ25 | 260 |
| (D-CHCH) | FA20 | 237/476 |
| D-CHCL | WW24 | 277 |
| **D-CHDC** | **C680** | **0150** |
| **D-CHDE** | **C560** | **0031** |
| D-CHDL | WW24 | 199 |
| (D-CHEF) | FA20 | 274 |
| D-CHEF | HS25 | 258038 |
| D-CHEF | HS25 | 258514 |
| D-CHEF | LJ25 | 260 |
| D-CHEP | C550 | 697 |
| D-CHER | LJ35 | 119 |
| D-CHER | LJ60 | 051 |
| D-CHFB | HFB3 | 1043 |
| D-CHFB | HFB3 | V1/1001 |
| **D-CHHH** | **C56X** | **5674** |
| D-CHHS | C560 | 0177 |
| (D-CHIC) | FA50 | 88 |
| D-CHIC | LJ25 | 347 |
| D-CHIC | SBRL | 380-42 |
| **D-CHIL** | **C680** | **0156** |
| D-CHIP | C680 | 0156 |
| D-CHJH | CS55 | 0131 |
| **D-CHLE** | **LJ60** | **211** |
| **D-CHLM** | **LJ45** | **266** |
| **D-CHMC** | **C550** | **550-0874** |
| D-CHOP | C550 | 609 |
| D-CHPD | LJ35 | 309 |
| (D-CHRC) | LJ35 | 096 |
| **D-CHSP** | **C56X** | **5536** |
| D-CHSW | BE40 | RK-84 |
| D-CHTH | HS25 | 25143 |
| D-CHVB | C550 | 629 |
| **D-CHZF** | **C550** | **550-0866** |
| **D-CIAO** | **C550** | **283** |
| D-CIAO | CS55 | 0135 |
| (D-CIBM) | FA20 | 234/475 |
| D-CIEL | FA10 | 155 |
| D-CIFA | C550 | 069 |
| D-CIFA | C550 | 133 |
| D-CIFA | LJ60 | 032 |
| **D-CIFM** | **C560** | **0814** |
| D-CIGM | BE40 | RK-103 |
| D-CIII | C56X | 5037 |
| D-CILL | C550 | 660 |
| D-CILL | FA20 | 13 |
| D-CILY | LJ55 | 026 |
| D-CIMM | LJ60 | 214 |
| (D-CINA) | HFB3 | 1080 |
| **D-CINI** | **C56X** | **5195** |
| **D-CINS** | **LJ45** | **347** |
| (D-CIOL) | C52B | 0331 |
| D-CION | LJ55 | 015 |
| (D-CIRA) | HFB3 | 1041 |
| D-CIRE | HFB3 | 1042 |
| D-CIRI | HFB3 | 1043 |
| D-CIRO | HFB3 | 1044 |
| (D-CIRR) | C550 | 066 |
| D-CIRS | LJ35 | 091 |
| D-CIRU | HFB3 | 1045 |
| D-CISA | HFB3 | 1046 |
| D-CISE | HFB3 | 1047 |
| D-CISI | HFB3 | 1048 |
| D-CISO | HFB3 | 1049 |
| D-CISU | HFB3 | 1050 |
| D-CITA | LJ35 | 070 |
| **D-CITA** | **LJ60** | **069** |
| D-CITO | HFB3 | 1027 |
| (D-CITO) | LJ25 | 118 |
| D-CITY | FA20 | 237/476 |
| **D-CITY** | **LJ35** | **177** |
| (D-CJAD) | LJ24 | 128 |
| **D-CJAF** | **LJ60** | **351** |
| **D-CJAK** | **C52B** | **0075** |
| D-CJET | HS25 | 256027 |
| D-CJET | HS25 | 258358 |
| D-CJET | LJ24 | 189 |
| D-CJJJ | C550 | 052 |
| **D-CJJJ** | **CS55** | **0086** |
| D-CJOY | C56X | 5195 |
| **D-CJPG** | **LJ35** | **108** |
| (D-CJVC) | C52B | 0220 |
| D-CKCF | HS25 | 25105 |
| **D-CKDM** | **ASTR** | **235** |
| (D-CKDN) | ASTR | 268 |
| (D-CKDO) | ASTR | 269 |
| (D-CKDP) | ASTR | 270 |
| **D-CKHG** | **C56X** | **5667** |
| D-CKIM | HS25 | 257094 |
| D-CKJS | C52B | 0086 |
| D-CKKK | LJ60 | 144 |
| (D-CKLI) | C56X | 5567 |
| (D-CKOW) | HS25 | 25105 |
| D-CLAN | LJ35 | 397 |
| D-CLAN | SBRL | 380-12 |
| **D-CLAT** | **C52B** | **0085** |

**D-CLBA BE40 RK-25**
D-CLBB FA20 315/517
D-CLBC HS25 258050
D-CLBD HS25 258405
D-CLBE FA20 279/502
D-CLBG HS25 258682
**D-CLBH HS25 258812**
D-CLBR FA20 52
(D-CLDF) C650 0037
**D-CLDF C650 7085**
(D-CLDI) C56X 5555
D-CLEO C560 0159
(D-CLHM) LJ45 266
**D-CLIC C56X 5788**
D-CLIP LJ55 004
D-CLIP LJ55 029
**D-CLLL C56X 5722**
D-CLLL FA10 188
(D-CLLS) C680 0171
D-CLMA HFB3 1057
**D-CLMS LJ45 395**
D-CLOU CS55 0121
D-CLOU HFB3 V2/1002
(D-CLSG) BE40 RK-10
(D-CLUB) HS25 257112
D-CLUB LJ45 044
D-CLUB LJ55 034
D-CLUB LJ55 092
D-CLUB LJ60 249
D-CLUB SBRL 380-19
**D-CLUE C650 0174**
**D-CLUX LJ40 45-2061**
D-CLVW HS25 257100
D-CMAD LJ55 143
D-CMAN FA10 71
D-CMAR LJ36 002
D-CMAX FA20 158/449
**D-CMAX LJ55 011**
(D-CMAX) LJ55 108
D-CMCM C560 0088
**D-CMEI C560 0117**
D-CMES C680 0162
**D-CMET FA20 329/523**
**D-CMHS C52B 0161**
D-CMIC C56X 5021
(D-CMIC) C56X 5814
D-CMIR HS25 258110
D-CMIX C550 550-1050
D-CMJS C550 660
D-CMLP LJ45 012
**D-CMMI C56X 5538**
**D-CMMM LJ24 328**
**D-CMMP C56X 5719**
**D-CMPI C650 7055**
**D-CMRM LJ31 213**
**D-CMSC LJ45 097**
D-CMTM LJ55 042
D-CMVW HS25 257112
D-CNCA CS55 0137
D-CNCB CS55 0144
D-CNCI C550 414
D-CNCI C560 0061
**D-CNCJ C650 7102**
D-CNCP C550 116
D-CNCP C560 0069
D-CNEX MU30 A070SA
(D-CNIC) C680 0016
**D-CNIK LJ40 45-2006**
**D-CNMB LJ45 024**
**D-CNNN C56X 5786**
**D-CNOB C52B 0119**
**D-CNOC C56X 5814**
D-CNSC C560 0820
**D-CNUE LJ60 170**
**D-COBO C52B 0107**
D-COCO LJ35 108
D-COCO LJ35 466
D-COFG FA20 175
D-COFY C550 550-0992
D-COGA LJ24 223
(D-COIN) LJ40 45-2120
D-COIN LJ40 45-2121
**D-COKE LJ35 447**
D-COLL FA20 234/475
D-COLO FA20 18
D-COMA HS25 25005
D-COME FA10 67

D-COME HS25 25025
D-COMF FA20 184/462
D-COMI HS25 25058
D-COMM FA20 302/510
D-COMM LJ45 012
**D-COMO LJ60 350**
D-CONA LJ24 189
D-CONA LJ35 114
D-CONE LJ25 050
**D-CONE LJ35 111**
D-CONI LJ35 007
D-CONO LJ35 055
D-CONO LJ35 417
D-CONU FA20 383/550
**D-CONU LJ55 124**
D-CONY LJ35 195
D-COOL LJ24 261
**D-COOL LJ55 052**
(D-CORA) C52B 0016
D-CORA LJ35 018
D-CORA LJ35 381
D-CORE HFB3 1051
D-CORF FA20 281/496
D-CORI HFB3 1052
D-CORO HFB3 1053
(D-CORT) FA20 147/444
D-CORU HFB3 1054
D-CORY HFB3 1055
D-COSA HFB3 1056
D-COSE HFB3 1057
D-COSI HFB3 1058
D-COSO HFB3 1059
D-COSU HFB3 1060
D-COSY LJ35 204
D-COSY LJ35 415
D-COTT FA20 314/516
(D-COUP) SBRL 306-17
**D-COWB C52B 0220**
D-COWS LJ60 170
**D-CPAO C52B 0232**
D-CPAS HS25 258130
**D-CPDR LJ40 45-2080**
**D-CPMI C52B 0286**
**D-CPMU LJ60 032**
**D-CPPP C550 550-0865**
**D-CPRO LJ31 155**
(D-CPRO) LJ31 160
**D-CRAH C52B 0154**
D-CRAN LJ45 043
**D-CRAN LJ60 019**
D-CREW LJ55 011
**D-CREY C650 0192**
**D-CRHR C650 0142**
**D-CRIS ASTR 107**
**D-CROB LJ60 261**
**D-CRON C56X 5762**
(D-CRRR) C650 0044
D-CRRR C650 0187
D-CRUW C56X 5642
(D-CRUW) C56X 6002
**D-CSAP LJ31 057**
**D-CSFD C56X 5022**
D-CSFD CS55 0148
**D-CSIE LJ31 207**
**D-CSIM LJ60 274**
(D-CSIS) LJ60 286
**D-CSIX LJ60 120**
**D-CSLT LJ60 200**
(D-CSLX) C56X 5243
**D-CSMB C550 550-1130**
**D-CSMS LJ45 017**
D-CSOS LJ35 429
**D-CSPG G180 90004**
**D-CSPJ G180 90003**
D-CSPN G180 90001
D-CSRB HS25 258226
D-CSRI HS25 258212
D-CSSS C550 550-0906
**D-CSUL LJ45 189**
D-CSUN C560 0078
**D-CSWM C550 550-0884**
(D-CSYB) C56X 5811
D-CTAN C560 0150
D-CTAN HS25 258450
(D-CTAN) LJ45 223
(D-CTAN) LJ45 240
D-CTEC C52B 0101

**D-CTEC C52B 0215**
**D-CTLX C56X 5569**
(D-CTLX) C56X 5585
**D-CTRI LJ35 346**
**D-CTTT C56X 5573**
D-CTWO LJ31 011
**D-CUBA C52B 0169**
(D-CUNA) HFB3 1061
**D-CUNO LJ55 108**
D-CUPI C680 0066
**D-CURA C52B 0287**
(D-CURE) HFB3 1062
D-CURE LJ35 652
(D-CURI) HFB3 1063
(D-CURO) HFB3 1064
**D-CURT LJ31 042**
(D-CURU) HFB3 1065
(D-CURY) HFB3 1066
(D-CUSA) HFB3 1067
(D-CUSE) HFB3 1068
(D-CUSI) HFB3 1069
(D-CUSO) HFB3 1070
(D-CUSU) HFB3 1071
(D-CUSY) HFB3 1072
D-CUTE LJ55 013
D-CUUU C52B 0197
**D-CVAI C650 0037**
(D-CVAU) C550 433
D-CVGP LJ31 036
D-CVHA C560 0275
**D-CVHA C680 0050**
D-CVHB C56X 5056
**D-CVHB C56X 5688**
D-CVHI C56X 5195
**D-CVHM C52B 0086**
(D-CVII) C650 7090
**D-CVII C650 7094**
D-CVIP LJ55 035
**D-CVIP LJ55 109**
**D-CVJN LJ40 45-2091**
D-CVJP LJ40 45-2079
(D-CVJT) LJ40 45-2097
**D-CVVV C56X 5723**
D-CWAY LJ55 107
D-CWBW HS25 258213
**D-CWDL LJ55 084**
(D-CWER) LJ45 010
(D-CWER) LJ45 017
D-CWHS LJ60 246
D-CWIN HS25 258178
**D-CWIR C52B 0288**
D-CWOL HS25 258235
D-CWWW C56X 5316
D-CWWW C56X 5788
**D-CXLS C56X 6027**
D-CYOU C680 0156
D-CZAR C560 0114
**D-CZZZ C56X 5790**
D-IAAS C525 0321
D-IAAS C52A 0054
D-IABC C500 182
D-IADD C550 481
**D-IADV C550 552**
D-IAEC C500 609
D-IAEV C500 365
(D-IAFA) C550 616
(D-IAFD) C525 0105
**D-IAGG PRM1 RB-35**
**D-IAHG C525 0126**
D-IAJJ C500 245
**D-IAKN C52A 0367**
D-IALL C525 0143
D-IAME C525 0315
**D-IAMF C525 0519**
D-IAMM C525 0041
**D-IAMO C52A 0166**
**D-IAMS C525 0684**
D-IANE C500 121
D-IANE C500 501
D-IANO C500 523
D-IAOA C525 0024
D-IATC C500 116
D-IATD LJ24 074
**D-IATT PRM1 RB-48**
D-IAVB C525 0172
D-IAWA C550 421
**D-IAWU C500 604**

**D-IAYL PRM1 RB-249**
**D-IBBA C525 0025**
D-IBBB C52A 0028
**D-IBBB PRM1 RB-82**
D-IBBE C52A 0233
**D-IBBS C52A 0313**
**D-IBCT C52A 0328**
D-IBIT C525 0393
**D-IBJJ C52A 0125**
D-IBMS C525 0309
D-IBPF C550 246
D-IBTI C525 0720
**D-IBWA C525 0042**
D-IBWB C500 421
D-IBWG C500 566
D-ICAB C550 151
**D-ICAC C550 049**
D-ICAM C500 456
D-ICAP LJ24 247
D-ICAR LJ24 169
D-ICAY LJ24 254
D-ICCA C500 317
D-ICCC C500 269
**D-ICEE C525 0096**
D-ICEY C525 0286
**D-ICEY C525 0611**
D-ICFA C500 290
D-ICGT C525 0164
D-ICHE C550 559
D-ICHS LJ24 280
D-ICIA C500 086
D-ICJA PRM1 RB-151
(D-ICMH) C510 0262
**D-ICMS C52A 0108**
**D-ICOL C525 0353**
(D-ICPO) C525 0639
D-ICPW C500 100
**D-ICSS C525 0121**
**D-ICTA C550 301**
D-ICUR C550 150
D-ICUW C500 319
**D-ICWB C525 0349**
(D-ICWB) C550 074
**D-IDAG C525 0144**
D-IDAS C525 0389
**D-IDAS C52A 0443**
D-IDAT LJ24 261
D-IDAU C500 131
**D-IDAZ C525 0389**
**D-IDBA PRM1 RB-164**
D-IDBW C525 0044
D-IDDD LJ24 201
D-IDFD C500 225
D-IDIG C525 0477
**D-IDMH C52A 0174**
D-IDPD C500 382
D-IDWH C500 126
D-IDWN C500 288
D-IEAI C525 0417
**D-IEAR C550 095**
**D-IEFA C52A 0358**
D-IEFD C52A 0049
D-IEGA C500 081
**D-IEGO C510 0048**
D-IEGO LJ24 283
**D-IEIR C500 674**
**D-IEKU C52A 0043**
**D-IEMG C510 0274**
**D-IEPR C525 0625**
D-IETZ C525 0518
(D-IETZ) C52A 0033
**D-IETZ C52A 0363**
**D-IEVB C52A 0459**
D-IEVX C52A 0036
D-IEWS C525 0217
D-IEXC C500 036
D-IFAI C500 100
D-IFAN C525 0214
**D-IFDH C525 0517**
**D-IFDN C52A 0343**
D-IFFI C525 0401
(D-IFGP) C500 673
D-IFIS C525 0442
**D-IFIS C52A 0340**
**D-IFLY C52A 0330**
**D-IFMC PRM1 RB-27**
**D-IFMG PRM1 RB-109**

| | | |
|---|---|---|
| D-IFUM | LJ24 | 129 |
| D-IFUP | C525 | 0126 |
| D-IFUP | C525 | 0172 |
| D-IFVG | LJ24 | 223 |
| D-IGAS | C525 | 0223 |
| (D-IGEL) | C510 | 0250 |
| D-IGGK | C500 | 535 |
| **D-IGIT** | **C52A** | **0032** |
| D-IGLU | C500 | 537 |
| D-IGMB | C500 | 442 |
| **D-IGME** | **C525** | **0279** |
| D-IGRC | C550 | 132 |
| **D-IGRO** | **C52A** | **0230** |
| D-IGSO | LJ24 | 233 |
| D-IGZA | C525 | 0260 |
| **D-IHAG** | **C550** | **151** |
| D-IHAP | C52A | 0026 |
| D-IHAQ | LJ24 | 007 |
| (D-IHAT) | C550 | 301 |
| D-IHCW | C525 | 0165 |
| **D-IHEB** | **C525** | **0064** |
| (D-IHEB) | C525 | 0073 |
| D-IHEY | C500 | 432 |
| D-IHGW | C525 | 0126 |
| **D-IHHN** | **C52A** | **0041** |
| D-IHHS | C525 | 0082 |
| D-IHLZ | LJ24 | 225 |
| D-IHOL | C525 | 0229 |
| D-IHRA | C52A | 0168 |
| D-IHSV | C500 | 164 |
| D-IHTM | C52A | 0343 |
| **D-IIBE** | **PRM1** | **RB-235** |
| (D-IIDD) | LJ24 | 228 |
| D-IIJS | C525 | 0310 |
| D-IIMC | PRM1 | RB-196 |
| D-IIPD | LJ24 | 228 |
| (D-IIRR) | C525 | 0315 |
| D-IJHM | C550 | 212 |
| (D-IJKP) | C510 | 0045 |
| **D-IJKP** | **C52A** | **0433** |
| **D-IJOA** | **C52A** | **0034** |
| (D-IJOA) | C52A | 0036 |
| D-IJON | C500 | 346 |
| D-IJYP | C525 | 0165 |
| D-IKAA | LJ24 | 018 |
| D-IKAB | LJ24 | 087 |
| D-IKAF | LJ24 | 189 |
| D-IKAL | C52A | 0193 |
| D-IKAN | C500 | 040 |
| D-IKFJ | C500 | 178 |
| (D-IKHV) | C525 | 0264 |
| **D-IKJS** | **C52A** | **0029** |
| **D-IKOP** | **C525** | **0016** |
| D-IKPW | C500 | 361 |
| (D-IKUC) | C500 | 269 |
| D-ILAC | EA50 | 000177 |
| **D-ILAM** | **C52A** | **0070** |
| D-ILAN | C550 | 614 |
| **D-ILAT** | **C525** | **0209** |
| D-ILCB | C525 | 0193 |
| D-ILCC | C550 | 324 |
| D-ILDE | LJ24 | 208 |
| **D-ILDL** | **C52A** | **0167** |
| (D-ILHA) | C525 | 0675 |
| **D-ILHA** | **C525** | **0696** |
| **D-ILHB** | **C525** | **0675** |
| (D-ILHB) | C525 | 0694 |
| **D-ILHC** | **C525** | **0695** |
| **D-ILHD** | **C525** | **0694** |
| (D-ILHD) | C525 | 0696 |
| D-ILHM | LJ24 | 239 |
| **D-ILIF** | **C525** | **0411** |
| D-ILLL | C500 | 659 |
| D-ILLL | C525 | 0518 |
| **D-ILLY** | **C525** | **0442** |
| D-ILME | C525 | 0421 |
| D-ILTC | C550 | 617 |
| D-ILVW | LJ24 | 239 |
| **D-IMAC** | **C525** | **0396** |
| D-IMAN | C500 | 025 |
| D-IMAR | LJ24 | 250 |
| **D-IMAX** | **C52A** | **0195** |
| D-IMEN | C500 | 279 |
| D-IMLN | C500 | 129 |
| **D-IMMD** | **C525** | **0211** |
| **D-IMME** | **C550** | **400** |
| D-IMMF | C550 | 560 |
| D-IMMG | C525 | 0614 |
| (D-IMMH) | C510 | 0259 |
| **D-IMMI** | **C525** | **0303** |
| D-IMMM | C525 | 0460 |
| **D-IMMM** | **C52A** | **0400** |
| D-IMMM | LJ24 | 328 |
| (D-IMMP) | C525 | 0354 |
| D-IMPC | C525 | 0126 |
| **D-IMPC** | **C525** | **0639** |
| D-IMRX | C500 | 688 |
| D-IMSM | C500 | 194 |
| D-IMTM | C550 | 061 |
| D-IMWZ | LJ24 | 184 |
| D-IMYA | C52A | 0026 |
| D-INCC | C500 | 128 |
| D-INCI | C500 | 255 |
| **D-INCS** | **C525** | **0466** |
| **D-INER** | **C525** | **0516** |
| **D-INFS** | **C525** | **0286** |
| D-INGA | MS76 | 098 |
| D-INGE | MS76 | 090 |
| D-INHH | C500 | 079 |
| D-INKA | LJ24 | 282 |
| **D-INOB** | **C52A** | **0196** |
| D-INOC | C525 | 0477 |
| D-IOBO | C525 | 0025 |
| D-IOBO | C52A | 0032 |
| **D-IOBO** | **C52A** | **0332** |
| D-IOBU | C52A | 0032 |
| D-IOBU | C52A | 0332 |
| D-IOGA | LJ24 | 223 |
| D-IOGE | LJ24 | 224 |
| D-IOGI | LJ24 | 193 |
| **D-IOHL** | **C52A** | **0233** |
| D-IOMP | C525 | 0143 |
| **D-IOWA** | **C525** | **0624** |
| D-IPAD | C52A | 0382 |
| **D-IPCC** | **C52A** | **0409** |
| **D-IPCS** | **C525** | **0264** |
| D-IPHE | E50P | 50000040 |
| **D-IPMI** | **C525** | **0533** |
| (D-IPMM) | C525 | 0533 |
| **D-IPOD** | **C525** | **0193** |
| **D-IPVD** | **C52A** | **0218** |
| **D-IRKE** | **C525** | **0123** |
| D-IRKE | C550 | 555 |
| **D-IRMA** | **C525** | **0366** |
| **D-IRON** | **C525** | **0168** |
| **D-IRSB** | **C525** | **0476** |
| **D-IRUP** | **C550** | **572** |
| **D-IRWR** | **C525** | **0118** |
| **D-ISAG** | **PRM1** | **RB-221** |
| **D-ISAR** | **PRM1** | **RB-148** |
| D-ISAS | PRM1 | RB-263 |
| D-ISCH | C525 | 0040 |
| **D-ISCH** | **C52A** | **0052** |
| **D-ISCO** | **C52A** | **0151** |
| **D-ISCV** | **C52A** | **0429** |
| **D-ISEC** | **C550** | **177** |
| **D-ISGW** | **C525** | **0070** |
| **D-ISHW** | **C525** | **0289** |
| **D-ISIO** | **C510** | **0296** |
| (D-ISIO) | C510 | 0321 |
| D-ISIS | C500 | 583 |
| **D-ISJM** | **C525** | **0602** |
| **D-ISJP** | **C52A** | **0030** |
| **D-ISKM** | **C500** | **313** |
| (D-ISKY) | C500 | 501 |
| D-ISPN | G180 | 90001 |
| **D-ISRM** | **C510** | **0035** |
| D-ISSS | C500 | 489 |
| **D-ISUN** | **C52A** | **0143** |
| **D-ISWA** | **C525** | **0236** |
| D-ISXT | PRM1 | RB-50 |
| **D-ITAN** | **C525** | **0399** |
| **D-ITIP** | **C525** | **0494** |
| **D-ITMA** | **C52A** | **0389** |
| **D-ITOP** | **C52A** | **0132** |
| **D-ITOR** | **C52A** | **0364** |
| D-ITSV | C525 | 0084 |
| D-IUAC | C52A | 0106 |
| D-IURH | C525 | 0196 |
| **D-IURS** | **C525** | **0343** |
| D-IUWE | C525 | 0415 |
| D-IVBG | C525 | 0310 |
| D-IVHA | C525 | 0103 |
| (D-IVID) | C525 | 0188 |
| D-IVIN | C525 | 0188 |
| D-IVOB | C550 | 163 |
| **D-IVVA** | **C52A** | **0147** |
| (D-IWAJ) | PRM1 | RB-211 |
| **D-IWAN** | **C52A** | **0223** |
| **D-IWBL** | **C52A** | **0355** |
| D-IWHA | C510 | 0297 |
| **D-IWHL** | **C525** | **0029** |
| **D-IWIL** | **C525** | **0221** |
| **D-IWIN** | **C52A** | **0231** |
| **D-IWIR** | **C52A** | **0102** |
| **D-IWPS** | **C525** | **0617** |
| **D-IWWP** | **C52A** | **0444** |
| (D-IWWP) | C52A | 0470 |
| **D-IWWW** | **PRM1** | **RB-89** |

Angola

| | | |
|---|---|---|
| **D2-** | **C550** | **550-0958** |
| D2-AJL | C500 | 071 |
| **D2-ANG** | **GLEX** | **9232** |
| **D2-EBA** | **C560** | **0502** |
| D2-EBB | FA20 | 296/507 |
| **D2-EBN** | **LJ45** | **069** |
| D2-EBR | CL65 | 5770 |
| **D2-ECB** | **GLF3** | **474** |
| **D2-ECE** | **C550** | **550-1008** |
| D2-EDC | C500 | 071 |
| **D2-EFM** | **HS25** | **25260** |
| **D2-EPC** | **LJ60** | **294** |
| D2-ESV | FA20 | 262 |
| **D2-EXR** | **HS25** | **25215** |
| **D2-EZR** | **C750** | **0173** |
| **D2-FEZ** | **HS25** | **25171** |
| **D2-FFH** | **HS25** | **25219** |
| **D2-FFX** | **LJ45** | **066** |
| **D2-GES** | **C550** | **550-1135** |
| **D2-JMM** | **FA20** | **54** |

Comoros

| | | |
|---|---|---|
| D6-ECB | CRVT | 15 |

Spain

| | | |
|---|---|---|
| (EC- ) | C525 | 0096 |
| **EC-** | **C560** | **0183** |
| (EC- ) | HS25 | 25058 |
| EC-113 | FA20 | 204 |
| EC-115 | HS25 | 256034 |
| EC-121 | HS25 | 256023 |
| EC-165 | FA20 | 221 |
| EC-168 | FA50 | 209 |
| EC-183 | HS25 | 256039 |
| EC-193 | HS25 | 258022 |
| EC-232 | JSTR | 5202 |
| EC-235 | F900 | 115 |
| EC-254 | WW24 | 335 |
| EC-261 | C525 | 0133 |
| EC-263 | FA20 | 149 |
| EC-272 | HS25 | 256012 |
| EC-319 | HS25 | 256062 |
| EC-339 | ASTR | 042 |
| EC-349 | HS25 | 256063 |
| EC-353 | FA10 | 4 |
| EC-363 | GLF2 | 237/43 |
| EC-375 | HS25 | 257040 |
| EC-411 | C560 | 0062 |
| EC-413 | HS25 | 257040 |
| EC-500 | C500 | 331 |
| EC-551 | FA20 | 128/436 |
| EC-617 | F900 | 93 |
| EC-621 | C550 | 667 |
| EC-697 | JSTR | 5062/12 |
| EC-704 | C525 | 0065 |
| EC-743 | C550 | 131 |
| EC-765 | F900 | 97 |
| EC-777 | C550 | 678 |
| EC-855 | FA20 | 117 |
| EC-949 | FA10 | 17 |
| EC-BVV | FA20 | 219/470 |
| EC-BXV | FA20 | 222/471 |
| EC-BZV | FA20 | 253/486 |
| EC-CCY | C500 | 082 |
| EC-CGG | C500 | 108 |
| EC-CIM | LJ25 | 149 |
| EC-CJA | LJ24 | 287 |
| EC-CJH | C500 | 116 |
| EC-CKD | LJ25 | 038 |
| EC-CKR | LJ25 | 184 |
| EC-CLS | LJ35 | 005 |
| EC-CMU | HS25 | 25271 |
| EC-CQT | HS25 | 256045 |
| EC-CTV | FA20 | 332/525 |
| EC-DEB | LJ35 | 137 |
| EC-DFA | LJ35 | 196 |
| EC-DJC | LJ35 | 278 |
| EC-DOH | C550 | 278 |
| EC-DQC | CRVT | 24 |
| EC-DQE | CRVT | 26 |
| EC-DQG | CRVT | 27 |
| EC-DSI | LJ55 | 045 |
| EC-DUE | CRVT | 30 |
| EC-DUF | CRVT | 32 |
| EC-DYE | CRVT | 31 |
| EC-EAC | HS25 | 256005 |
| EC-EAO | HS25 | 256039 |
| EC-EAP | C650 | 0125 |
| EC-EAS | C650 | 0122 |
| EC-EAV | HS25 | 256032 |
| EC-EBM | LJ25 | 027 |
| EC-EBR | C500 | 089 |
| EC-ECB | FA20 | 210 |
| **EC-EDC** | **FA20** | **6** |
| EC-EDC | FA20 | 220 |
| EC-EDL | FA20 | 220 |
| **EC-EDN** | **C500** | **370** |
| EC-EDO | FA20 | 50 |
| EC-EEU | FA20 | 218 |
| EC-EFI | FA20 | 189 |
| EC-EFR | FA20 | 183 |
| EC-EGL | HS25 | 256023 |
| EC-EGM | FA20 | 204 |
| EC-EGS | HS25 | 256034 |
| EC-EGT | HS25 | 25080 |
| EC-EGY | LJ25 | 373 |
| **EC-EHC** | **FA20** | **46** |
| EC-EHD | FA20 | 55/410 |
| EC-EHF | HS25 | 256011 |
| EC-EIV | FA20 | 221 |
| **EC-EKK** | **FA20** | **106** |
| EC-ELK | HS25 | 258022 |
| EC-EOQ | HS25 | 256012 |
| **EC-EQP** | **FA20** | **149** |
| EC-EQX | C650 | 0119 |
| EC-ERJ | HS25 | 256063 |
| EC-ERX | HS25 | 256062 |
| EC-ETI | HS25 | 257040 |
| EC-FAM | FA20 | 128/436 |
| EC-FDL | C550 | 667 |
| EC-FEN | F900 | 93 |
| EC-FES | C550 | 678 |
| EC-FFO | F900 | 97 |
| EC-FGX | JSTR | 5062/12 |
| EC-FIL | C550 | 131 |
| EC-FJP | FA20 | 117 |
| EC-FPG | FA50 | 209 |
| EC-FPI | F900 | 115 |
| "EC-FPI" | GLEX | 9060 |
| EC-FQX | JSTR | 5202 |
| EC-FRV | GLF2 | 237/43 |
| EC-FTV | FA10 | 4 |
| EC-FUM | C500 | 331 |
| EC-FZP | C525 | 0065 |
| EC-GIA | ASTR | 042 |
| EC-GIB | WW24 | 335 |
| **EC-GIE** | **C525** | **0133** |
| **EC-GJF** | **C500** | **482** |
| EC-GLM | C560 | 0062 |
| EC-GMO | F9EX | 6 |
| **EC-GNK** | **F2TH** | **37** |
| **EC-GOV** | **C560** | **0419** |
| EC-GPN | FA50 | 204 |
| EC-GSL | WW24 | 353 |
| EC-GTR | FA50 | 268 |
| **EC-GTS** | **C500** | **037** |
| EC-GXX | LJ35 | 263 |
| EC-HAI | LJ55 | 112 |
| EC-HBC | C525 | 0264 |
| EC-HBX | C525 | 0304 |

| | | |
|---|---|---|
| **EC-HCX** | **FA20** | **184/462** |
| EC-HEG | FA20 | 494 |
| EC-HFA | C500 | 209 |
| EC-HFY | C500 | 157 |
| EC-HGH | GLF4 | 1021 |
| **EC-HGI** | **C550** | **596** |
| EC-HHK | F900 | 151 |
| EC-HHS | FA50 | 204 |
| EC-HHZ | CRVT | 15 |
| EC-HIA | CRVT | 19 |
| **EC-HIN** | **C525** | **0197** |
| EC-HJD | C550 | 310 |
| EC-HJL | HS25 | 258444 |
| EC-HLB | LJ35 | 236 |
| EC-HNU | F9EX | 62 |
| **EC-HOB** | **F9EX** | **43** |
| **EC-HPQ** | **C500** | **157** |
| **EC-HRH** | **C500** | **116** |
| **EC-HRO** | **C550** | **550-0938** |
| EC-HRQ | HS25 | 257166 |
| **EC-HTR** | **BE40** | **RK-293** |
| **EC-HVQ** | **C525** | **0436** |
| **EC-HVV** | **FA10** | **193** |
| **EC-HYI** | **F2TH** | **150** |
| EC-IAB | C525 | 0037 |
| (EC-IAX) | C550 | 176 |
| **EC-IBA** | **C500** | **178** |
| **EC-IBD** | **GLEX** | **9060** |
| EC-IEB | C52A | 0064 |
| **EC-IFS** | **GLEX** | **9089** |
| EC-IIC | LJ35 | 346 |
| EC-IKP | GLF4 | 1109 |
| **EC-ILK** | **LJ45** | **064** |
| **EC-IMF** | **C550** | **443** |
| **EC-INJ** | **C500** | **477** |
| **EC-INS** | **LJ55** | **133** |
| **EC-IOZ** | **PRM1** | **RB-61** |
| EC-IRB | C525 | 0516 |
| EC-IRU | C56X | 5056 |
| **EC-IRZ** | **GLF5** | **582** |
| **EC-ISP** | **C500** | **463** |
| **EC-ISQ** | **C56X** | **5353** |
| EC-ISS | C525 | 0415 |
| **EC-IUQ** | **GLEX** | **9007** |
| **EC-IVJ** | **C525** | **0429** |
| **EC-JBB** | **F900** | **182** |
| **EC-JBH** | **FA20** | **511** |
| EC-JDV | FA20 | 237/476 |
| EC-JEG | CL30 | 20025 |
| EC-JFD | C525 | 0448 |
| **EC-JFT** | **C560** | **0506** |
| **EC-JGN** | **GALX** | **103** |
| EC-JIE | LJ60 | 284 |
| **EC-JIL** | **GLEX** | **9146** |
| **EC-JIU** | **C525** | **0486** |
| **EC-JJH** | **FA20** | **176/458** |
| **EC-JJU** | **C52A** | **0033** |
| **EC-JKL** | **MU30** | **A084SA** |
| EC-JKT | CL61 | 5060 |
| **EC-JMS** | **C52A** | **0216** |
| EC-JNV | CL64 | 5605 |
| **EC-JNY** | **HS25** | **258748** |
| **EC-JNZ** | **F900** | **181** |
| **EC-JON** | **C550** | **209** |
| **EC-JPK** | **GLF5** | **5078** |
| **EC-JPN** | **BE40** | **RK-428** |
| EC-JPV | LJ60 | 296 |
| **EC-JQE** | **GALX** | **125** |
| EC-JSH | C525 | 0508 |
| **EC-JTH** | **C550** | **174** |
| **EC-JVB** | **LJ60** | **243** |
| **EC-JVF** | **C56X** | **5564** |
| **EC-JVI** | **F2TH** | **61** |
| **EC-JVM** | **LJ60** | **161** |
| **EC-JVR** | **F900** | **106** |
| **EC-JXC** | **C500** | **278** |
| EC-JXE | ASTR | 158 |
| EC-JXI | C56X | 5593 |
| **EC-JXR** | **F2TH** | **55** |
| **EC-JYG** | **C680** | **0087** |
| **EC-JYQ** | **LJ60** | **249** |
| **EC-JYR** | **GLF5** | **5116** |
| **EC-JYT** | **CL64** | **5648** |
| **EC-JYY** | **LJ40** | **45-2026** |
| **EC-JZK** | **C56X** | **5554** |
| **EC-KBC** | **GALX** | **145** |
| **EC-KBR** | **GLF5** | **5124** |
| **EC-KBZ** | **C550** | **678** |
| **EC-KCA** | **GALX** | **150** |
| **EC-KES** | **C52A** | **0155** |
| EC-KEY | GLF4 | 1331 |
| **EC-KFA** | **F900** | **169** |
| **EC-KFS** | **GLEX** | **9208** |
| EC-KGE | C500 | 312 |
| **EC-KGX** | **C500** | **436** |
| **EC-KHH** | **PRM1** | **RB-160** |
| **EC-KHP** | **C550** | **550-0955** |
| **EC-KJH** | **GLEX** | **9094** |
| **EC-KJJ** | **C550** | **414** |
| **EC-KJR** | **C550** | **412** |
| **EC-KJS** | **GLF5** | **5151** |
| **EC-KJV** | **C525** | **0143** |
| EC-KKB | C560 | 0768 |
| **EC-KKC** | **C680** | **0117** |
| **EC-KKD** | **BE40** | **RK-533** |
| **EC-KKE** | **C525** | **0044** |
| **EC-KKK** | **C560** | **0770** |
| **EC-KKN** | **GLEX** | **9084** |
| **EC-KKO** | **C550** | **550-0992** |
| **EC-KLL** | **GALX** | **171** |
| **EC-KLS** | **GLF5** | **5162** |
| **EC-KMF** | **ASTR** | **233** |
| **EC-KMK** | **C680** | **0178** |
| **EC-KMS** | **ASTR** | **237** |
| **EC-KMT** | **HS25** | **HA-0033** |
| EC-KNL | C510 | 0053 |
| **EC-KOI** | **C52A** | **0381** |
| **EC-KOL** | **C56X** | **5088** |
| **EC-KOR** | **GALX** | **177** |
| **EC-KOV** | **C560** | **0768** |
| **EC-KPB** | **C56X** | **5753** |
| **EC-KPE** | **C56X** | **5764** |
| **EC-KPF** | **GALX** | **180** |
| **EC-KPJ** | **ASTR** | **243** |
| **EC-KPL** | **GALX** | **183** |
| **EC-KPP** | **FA10** | **209** |
| **EC-KQO** | **C52B** | **0234** |
| **EC-KRN** | **GALX** | **188** |
| **EC-KRS** | **BE40** | **RK-354** |
| **EC-KSB** | **C525** | **0089** |
| **EC-KTK** | **ASTR** | **254** |
| **EC-KTV** | **ASTR** | **253** |
| **EC-KUM** | **GLF5** | **5155** |
| **EC-KVU** | **GLEX** | **9016** |
| **EC-KXF** | **GLF5** | **5203** |
| **EC-KXS** | **HS25** | **HB-24** |
| **EC-LAE** | **GALX** | **219** |
| EC-LAF | C510 | 0152 |
| **EC-LBB** | **GALX** | **222** |
| **EC-LCM** | **C525** | **0309** |
| **EC-LCX** | **C510** | **0235** |
| **EC-LDE** | **C525** | **0644** |
| **EC-LDK** | **C510** | **0152** |
| **EC-LDS** | **ASTR** | **158** |
| **EC-LEB** | **GLEX** | **9303** |
| **EC-LEP** | **C560** | **0153** |
| **EC-LES** | **CL30** | **20243** |
| ECT-023 | C550 | 278 |
| ECT-028 | LJ35 | 278 |

Ireland

| | | |
|---|---|---|
| EI-BGW | HS25 | 25080 |
| EI-BJL | C550 | 039 |
| EI-BJN | C500 | 555 |
| EI-BNY | CRVT | 11 |
| EI-BRG | HS25 | 25281 |
| EI-BSA | LJ55 | 021 |
| (EI-BUN) | C550 | 555 |
| EI-BUY | C550 | 555 |
| (EI-BXN) | CL60 | 1048 |
| (EI-BYD) | CL60 | 1035 |
| EI-BYM | C500 | 179 |
| EI-BYN | C550 | 188 |
| EI-CAH | GLF4 | 1129 |
| **EI-CIR** | **C550** | **144** |
| EI-COV | HS25 | 257178 |
| EI-CVT | GLF4 | 1419 |
| EI-DAB | C550 | 550-0917 |
| (EI-DUN) | C560 | 0197 |
| EI-DXW | LJ60 | 300 |
| **EI-ECE** | **HS25** | **258496** |
| **EI-ECR** | **C52A** | **0438** |
| (EI-EHN) | E50P | 50000060 |
| (EI-EHO) | E50P | 50000062 |
| (EI-EHS) | E50P | 50000073 |
| (EI-EHT) | E50P | 50000076 |
| **EI-GDL** | **GLF5** | **5068** |
| **EI-GEM** | **HS25** | **258901** |
| EI-GHP | C550 | 550-0897 |
| EI-GPA | CL60 | 1016 |
| EI-IAT | LJ60 | 139 |
| EI-IAU | LJ60 | 190 |
| EI-IAW | LJ60 | 218 |
| EI-ICE | BE40 | RK-521 |
| **EI-IRE** | **CL64** | **5515** |
| (EI-JBA) | E50P | 50000043 |
| **EI-JJJ** | **HS25** | **HA-0085** |
| **EI-KJC** | **HS25** | **258805** |
| EI-LJG | CL61 | 5023 |
| EI-LJR | F2TH | 18 |
| EI-MAS | CL61 | 5194 |
| **EI-MAX** | **LJ31** | **233** |
| **EI-MJC** | **C52B** | **0266** |
| (EI-OPM) | C52A | 0054 |
| EI-PAL | C550 | 550-0935 |
| EI-PAX | C56X | 5228 |
| **EI-REX** | **LJ60** | **149** |
| EI-RNJ | HS25 | 258414 |
| EI-RRR | HS25 | 257170 |
| **EI-SFA** | **C510** | **0144** |
| **EI-SFB** | **C510** | **0145** |
| **EI-SFC** | **C510** | **0196** |
| **EI-SFD** | **C510** | **0216** |
| **EI-SFE** | **C510** | **0217** |
| EI-SNN | C650 | 0183 |
| EI-SXT | CL61 | 5159 |
| (EI-TAM) | CL61 | 3006 |
| EI-TAM | CL64 | 5367 |
| **EI-TDV** | **F2EX** | **190** |
| **EI-VIV** | **LJ60** | **305** |
| EI-WDC | HS25 | 25132 |
| **EI-WFO** | **LJ45** | **368** |
| EI-WGV | GLF5 | 505 |
| **EI-WJN** | **HS25** | **257062** |
| **EI-WXP** | **HS25** | **258382** |
| **EI-XLS** | **C56X** | **5666** |

Turkmenistan
(see also EZ-)

| | | |
|---|---|---|
| **EK-52526** | **C52A** | **0026** |
| EK-B021 | HS25 | 259029 |

Liberia

| | | |
|---|---|---|
| (EL-AMJ) | HS25 | 25125 |
| (EL-ELS) | HS25 | 25125 |
| EL-VDY | FA20 | 245/481 |
| EL-WRT | GLF2 | 67 |

Iran

| | | |
|---|---|---|
| EP-AGX | FA20 | 283/497 |
| **EP-AGY** | **FA20** | **286/498** |
| EP-AHK | HS25 | 25154 |
| EP-AHV | FA20 | 320/519 |
| **EP-AKC** | **FA20** | **301/509** |
| **EP-FIC** | **FA20** | **334/527** |
| **EP-FID** | **FA20** | **338/530** |
| EP-FIE | FA20 | 251/484 |
| **EP-FIF** | **FA20** | **320/519** |
| EP-FIG | FA20 | 318/518 |
| EP-HIM | MS76 | 002 |
| **EP-IPA** | **FA20** | **251/484** |
| EP-KIA | C500 | 295 |
| EP-KIC | C550 | 025 |
| (EP-KID) | C550 | 025 |
| EP-PAO | C500 | 295 |
| EP-PAP | C500 | 301 |
| (EP-PAQ) | C500 | 377 |
| EP-PBC | C500 | 370 |
| **EP-SEA** | **FA20** | **367/545** |
| **EP-TFA** | **FA50** | **101** |
| **EP-TFI** | **FA50** | **120** |
| EP-VAP | FA20 | 251/484 |
| (EP-VAS) | FA20 | 318/518 |
| EP-VLP | JSTR | 5203 |
| EP-VRP | JSTR | 5002 |
| EP-VRP | JSTR | 5137 |
| EP-VSP | FA20 | 318/518 |

Moldova

| | | |
|---|---|---|
| ER-LGA | LJ35 | 406 |
| **ER-LGB** | **LJ60** | **255** |

Estonia

| | | |
|---|---|---|
| ES-LUX | C52A | 0213 |
| **ES-LVA** | **LJ60** | **372** |
| **ES-PHR** | **HS25** | **HB-33** |
| **ES-PVC** | **LJ60** | **051** |
| **ES-PVD** | **LJ55** | **143** |
| **ES-PVH** | **LJ31** | **162** |
| **ES-PVI** | **LJ60** | **275** |
| **ES-PVP** | **LJ60** | **302** |
| **ES-PVS** | **LJ60** | **190** |
| ES-PVT | LJ55 | 061 |
| ES-PVV | LJ55 | 011 |
| ES-SKY | C56X | 5700 |

Belarus

| | | |
|---|---|---|
| "EW94228" | CS55 | 0067 |

Kyrgyzstan

| | | |
|---|---|---|
| EX-269 | HS25 | 25269 |

Turkmenistan

| | | |
|---|---|---|
| **EZ-B021** | **HS25** | **259029** |
| **EZ-B022** | **CL65** | **5735** |
| **EZ-B023** | **CL65** | **5750** |

Bosnia-Herzegovina

| | | |
|---|---|---|
| **E7-SBA** | **C500** | **554** |
| **E7-SMS** | **C525** | **0666** |

France

| | | |
|---|---|---|
| (F- ) | C550 | 195 |
| **F-** | **PRM1** | **RB-73** |
| **F-AZLT** | **MS76** | **032** |
| F-AZTL | MS76 | 085 |
| "F-BAMD" | FA50 | 1 |
| F-BFDG | FA10 | 61 |
| F-BGVO | MS76 | 01 |
| F-BHOK | MS76 | 03 |
| F-BIHY | FA20 | 141/441 |
| F-BINR | FA50 | 2 |
| F-BIPC | FA10 | 108 |
| (F-BIPF) | FA10 | 61 |
| F-BJET | MS76 | 039 |
| F-BJLH | FA10 | 1 |
| F-BJLV | MS76 | 072 |
| F-BJLX | MS76 | 086 |
| F-BJLY | MS76 | 089 |
| F-BJZQ | MS76 | 102 |
| F-BJZR | MS76 | 103 |
| F-BJZS | MS76 | 104 |
| F-BJZT | MS76 | 105 |
| F-BJZU | MS76 | 106 |
| F-BJZV | MS76 | 107 |
| F-BJZX | MS76 | 108 |
| (F-BKFB) | C550 | 195 |
| F-BKFB | LJ36 | 046 |
| F-BKMC | HS25 | 256035 |
| F-BKMF | HS25 | 25007 |
| F-BLCU | FA20 | 173 |
| F-BLKB | FA20 | 01 |
| F-BLKL | MS76 | 01 |
| F-BLLK | FA20 | 137 |
| F-BMER | FA50 | 52 |
| F-BMKH | FA20 | 6 |

| | | |
|---|---|---|
| F-BMKK | FA20 | 22/404 |
| F-BMSH | FA20 | 1/401 |
| F-BMSS | FA20 | 2/402 |
| F-BMSX | FA20 | 3/403 |
| F-BNDB | FA50 | 1 |
| F-BNKX | FA20 | 23 |
| F-BNRE | FA20 | 53/417 |
| F-BNRG | MS76 | 101 |
| F-BNRH | FA20 | 79/415 |
| F-BOED | FA20 | 41/407 |
| F-BOEF | FA20 | 13 |
| F-BOFH | FA20 | 225/472 |
| F-BOHN | MS76 | 098 |
| F-BOHU | HS25 | 25025 |
| F-BOJO | MS76 | 002 |
| F-BOJY | MS76 | 112 |
| F-BOLX | FA20 | 62/409 |
| F-BOOA | FA20 | 67/414 |
| F-BOON | FA20 | 25/405 |
| F-BOXV | FA20 | 104/454 |
| F-BPIB | WW24 | 105 |
| F-BPIO | FA20 | 141/441 |
| F-BPJB | FA20 | 145/443 |
| F-BPMC | HS25 | 25131 |
| F-BPXB | FA10 | 79 |
| F-BRAL | LJ24 | 117 |
| F-BRGF | LJ24 | 289 |
| F-BRHB | FA20 | 172/456 |
| (F-BRHB) | FA20 | 73/419 |
| F-BRNL | LJ24 | 183 |
| F-BRNZ | CRVT | 2 |
| F-BRPK | FA20 | 188/464 |
| F-BRQK | CRVT | 9 |
| F-BRUY | GLF2 | 43 |
| F-BSBU | FA20 | 263/489 |
| F-BSIM | HS25 | 25130 |
| F-BSQN | FA10 | 03 |
| F-BSQU | FA10 | 1 |
| F-BSRL | LJ24 | 210 |
| F-BSSL | HS25 | 25223 |
| F-BSTP | LJ24 | 026 |
| F-BSTR | FA20 | 246/482 |
| F-BSUR | LJ25 | 040 |
| F-BSUX | LJ24 | 045A |
| F-BSYF | FA20 | 25/405 |
| F-BTCY | FA20 | 13 |
| F-BTDA | WW24 | 145 |
| F-BTEL | C550 | 209 |
| F-BTMF | FA20 | 184/462 |
| F-BTML | FA20 | 67/414 |
| F-BTQK | LJ24 | 053 |
| F-BTQZ | FA20 | 58 |
| F-BTTK | CRVT | 31 |
| F-BTTL | CRVT | 28 |
| F-BTTM | CRVT | 17 |
| F-BTTN | CRVT | 20 |
| F-BTTO | CRVT | 18 |
| F-BTTP | CRVT | 30 |
| F-BTTQ | CRVT | 32 |
| F-BTTR | CRVT | 9 |
| F-BTTS | CRVT | 11 |
| F-BTTS | CRVT | 36 |
| F-BTTT | CRVT | 33 |
| F-BTTU | CRVT | 22 |
| F-BTTU | CRVT | 37 |
| F-BTTV | CRVT | 11 |
| F-BTYV | LJ24 | 206 |
| F-BUAS | CRVT | 1 |
| F-BUFG | FA20 | 175 |
| F-BUFN | LJ24 | 202 |
| F-BUIC | FA20 | 138/440 |
| F-BUIX | FA20 | 245/481 |
| F-BUQN | CRVT | 3 |
| **F-BUQP** | **CRVT** | **4** |
| F-BUUL | C500 | 136 |
| F-BUUV | LJ24 | 195 |
| F-BUYE | FA20 | 288/499 |
| F-BUYI | FA20 | 86 |
| F-BUYL | C500 | 133 |
| F-BUYP | HS25 | 256033 |
| F-BVEC | LJ24 | 271 |
| F-BVFV | FA20 | 182/461 |
| F-BVPA | CRVT | 5 |
| F-BVPB | CRVT | 6 |
| F-BVPC | CRVT | 12 |
| F-BVPD | CRVT | 13 |
| F-BVPE | CRVT | 21 |
| F-BVPF | CRVT | 23 |
| F-BVPG | CRVT | 25 |
| F-BVPH | CRVT | 27 |
| F-BVPI | CRVT | 24 |
| F-BVPJ | CRVT | 29 |
| **F-BVPK** | **CRVT** | **7** |
| F-BVPL | CRVT | 19 |
| F-BVPM | FA20 | 294/506 |
| **F-BVPN** | **FA20** | **311/515** |
| F-BVPO | CRVT | 10 |
| F-BVPQ | FA20 | 315/517 |
| **F-BVPR** | **FA10** | **5** |
| F-BVPS | CRVT | 14 |
| F-BVPT | CRVT | 16 |
| F-BXAG | FA10 | 7 |
| F-BXPT | LJ24 | 014 |
| F-BXQL | MS76 | 105 |
| F-BYAL | LJ25 | 084 |
| F-BYCC | FA10 | 76 |
| F-BYCR | CRVT | 34 |
| F-BYCV | FA10 | 93 |
| F-BYFB | HS25 | 257166 |
| F-EXAA | MS76 | 112 |
| F-GAJD | LJ24 | 187 |
| F-GAMA | LJ24 | 023 |
| F-GAPC | FA20 | 184/462 |
| F-GAPY | LJ24 | 027 |
| F-GASL | HS25 | 257022 |
| F-GATF | FA20 | 401 |
| F-GATF | FA20 | 401 |
| F-GBBV | LJ24 | 109 |
| F-GBGD | LJ36 | 016 |
| F-GBIZ | FA50 | 3 |
| F-GBLA | LJ24 | 190 |
| F-GBLZ | LJ24 | 239 |
| F-GBMB | LJ35 | 018 |
| F-GBMD | FA20 | 375/547 |
| F-GBMH | FA10 | 103 |
| F-GBMS | FA20 | 175 |
| F-GBPG | FA20 | 106 |
| F-GBPL | C550 | 063 |
| **F-GBRF** | **FA10** | **38** |
| (F-GBRF) | FA50 | 5 |
| F-GBTA | LJ24 | 017 |
| F-GBTC | FA10 | 124 |
| F-GBTI | FA10 | 24 |
| F-GBTL | C550 | 068 |
| **F-GBTM** | **FA20** | **397/555** |
| F-GCGU | FA20 | 136/439 |
| F-GCGY | FA20 | 145/443 |
| F-GCLE | LJ35 | 108 |
| (F-GCLT) | LJ35 | 313 |
| F-GCMS | LJ35 | 257 |
| F-GCSZ | C550 | 195 |
| F-GCTT | FA10 | 127 |
| F-GDAE | LJ24 | 105 |
| F-GDAV | LJ24 | 017 |
| F-GDAY | CRVT | 26 |
| F-GDAZ | CRVT | 35 |
| F-GDCN | LJ35 | 432 |
| F-GDCP | LJ35 | 071 |
| F-GDFE | FA50 | 56 |
| F-GDFJ | FA20 | 362 |
| F-GDHK | GLF3 | 340 |
| F-GDHR | LJ55 | 070 |
| F-GDLO | FA20 | 315/517 |
| F-GDLR | FA10 | 121 |
| F-GDLU | FA20 | 314/516 |
| (F-GDRC) | CRVT | 19 |
| F-GDRN | FA10 | 152 |
| **F-GDRR** | **PRM1** | **RB-269** |
| F-GDSA | FA10 | 202 |
| F-GDSB | FA20 | 482 |
| (F-GDSC) | FA50 | 123 |
| F-GDSD | FA20 | 487 |
| F-GDUB | CRVT | 15 |
| F-GECI | LJ24 | 219 |
| F-GECR | HS25 | 25128 |
| F-GEDB | FA10 | 197 |
| F-GEFB | C550 | 195 |
| F-GEFS | FA20 | 486 |
| F-GEJR | FA20 | 473 |
| (F-GEJX) | FA20 | 300/508 |
| F-GELA | FA10 | 16 |
| F-GELE | FA10 | 69 |
| F-GELS | FA10 | 208 |
| **F-GELT** | **FA10** | **211** |
| F-GEOY | FA50 | 78 |
| F-GEPL | C500 | 164 |
| F-GEPQ | CRVT | 19 |
| F-GEQF | CRVT | 15 |
| F-GERO | FA10 | 179 |
| F-GERT | FA20 | 96 |
| F-GESL | HS25 | 258016 |
| **F-GESP** | **F2TH** | **119** |
| F-GESZ | C500 | 443 |
| F-GEXE | FA50 | 145 |
| F-GEXF | FA20 | 401 |
| F-GFAY | FA20 | 496 |
| F-GFBG | FA10 | 157 |
| F-GFDB | HS25 | 25131 |
| F-GFDH | CRVT | 13 |
| F-GFEJ | CRVT | 10 |
| F-GFFP | FA10 | 160 |
| F-GFFS | FA20 | 474 |
| F-GFGB | FA10 | 177 |
| F-GFGQ | FA50 | 104 |
| (F-GFHG) | FA10 | 113 |
| F-GFHG | FA10 | 126 |
| F-GFHH | FA10 | 113 |
| (F-GFHH) | FA10 | 126 |
| F-GFJC | F900 | 2 |
| (F-GFJK) | FA10 | 108 |
| F-GFJL | C550 | 470 |
| (F-GFLL) | FA20 | 162/451 |
| **F-GFMD** | **FA10** | **136** |
| F-GFMP | HS25 | 25125 |
| F-GFMZ | LJ25 | 182 |
| (F-GFPD) | CRVT | 11 |
| **F-GFPF** | **FA10** | **68** |
| F-GFPO | C550 | 114 |
| F-GFUN | FA20 | 162/451 |
| **F-GGAL** | **C650** | **0117** |
| F-GGAR | FA10 | 115 |
| (F-GGAR) | FA20 | 496 |
| F-GGBL | FA20 | 379 |
| F-GGCP | FA50 | 9 |
| F-GGFO | FA20 | 76 |
| **F-GGGA** | **C550** | **586** |
| **F-GGGT** | **C550** | **611** |
| F-GGKE | FA20 | 118 |
| F-GGMM | FA20 | 300/508 |
| F-GGPG | LJ24 | 327 |
| (F-GGRA) | FA10 | 179 |
| (F-GGRG) | LJ35 | 174 |
| F-GGRH | F900 | 5 |
| **F-GGVB** | **FA50** | **11** |
| F-GGVR | FA10 | 138 |
| F-GHAE | LJ35 | 413 |
| F-GHAQ | FA50 | 149 |
| F-GHBT | FA20 | 160/450 |
| F-GHCR | FA20 | 313 |
| F-GHDN | FA20 | 77/429 |
| F-GHDT | FA20 | 176/458 |
| **F-GHDX** | **FA10** | **140** |
| F-GHDZ | FA10 | 17 |
| F-GHEA | F900 | 33 |
| F-GHER | FA10 | 88 |
| F-GHFB | FA10 | 169 |
| (F-GHFI) | FA10 | 43 |
| F-GHFO | FA10 | 33 |
| F-GHFP | FA20 | 119/431 |
| F-GHFQ | FA20 | 279/502 |
| F-GHGO | F2TH | 49 |
| F-GHGO | F900 | 110 |
| F-GHGT | FA50 | 21 |
| F-GHHG | HS25 | 257055 |
| (F-GHJL) | FA10 | 58 |
| F-GHLN | FA20 | 255/487 |
| F-GHLT | FA10 | 92 |
| F-GHMD | FA20 | 345 |
| F-GHMP | LJ35 | 048 |
| F-GHPA | FA20 | 170/455 |
| **F-GHPB** | **FA10** | **215** |
| F-GHPL | FA10 | 147 |
| (F-GHPO) | FA20 | 271/493 |
| (F-GHRE) | FA20 | 171 |
| F-GHRV | FA10 | 48 |
| F-GHSG | FA20 | 77/429 |
| F-GHSK | FA10 | 218 |
| F-GHTD | F900 | 96 |
| F-GHTK | FA20 | 368 |
| (F-GHUA) | C550 | 028 |
| F-GHVK | FA10 | 146 |
| F-GHVR | FA20 | 262 |
| F-GHYB | F900 | 103 |
| (F-GIBT) | FA20 | 300/508 |
| F-GICB | FA20 | 171 |
| F-GICF | FA20 | 120 |
| F-GICN | FA50 | 210 |
| F-GIDC | FA50 | 116 |
| F-GIDE | F900 | 1 |
| F-GIFL | FA10 | 217 |
| F-GIFP | FA20 | 259 |
| (F-GIHT) | C500 | 067 |
| (F-GIHU) | C500 | 201 |
| F-GIJG | FA10 | 118 |
| F-GILM | CRVT | 32 |
| (F-GIPH) | FA10 | 166 |
| **F-GIPH** | **FA10** | **194** |
| F-GIQP | FA10 | 43 |
| F-GIQZ | FA50 | 107 |
| (F-GIRH) | CRVT | 14 |
| (F-GIRS) | C500 | 308 |
| (F-GIRS) | C550 | 341 |
| (F-GIRZ) | F900 | 30 |
| **F-GISH** | **C510** | **0182** |
| (F-GIVD) | FA50 | 251 |
| F-GIVR | F900 | 62 |
| F-GIVT | FA20 | 32 |
| F-GJAP | CRVT | 31 |
| **F-GJAS** | **CRVT** | **8** |
| (F-GJBR) | FA20 | 77/429 |
| F-GJBT | F900 | 32 |
| **F-GJBZ** | **FA50** | **269** |
| F-GJCC | FA20 | 72/413 |
| **F-GJDB** | **FA20** | **76** |
| F-GJDE | HS25 | 25131 |
| F-GJDG | C500 | 312 |
| F-GJEA | FA20 | 360 |
| F-GJEK | FA50 | 228 |
| F-GJFB | FA10 | 166 |
| F-GJFZ | FA10 | 19 |
| F-GJGB | FA10 | 47 |
| F-GJHG | FA10 | 181 |
| F-GJHJ | F2TH | 2 |
| F-GJHK | FA10 | 108 |
| (F-GJIS) | FA20 | 514 |
| F-GJJL | FA10 | 118 |
| F-GJJS | FA20 | 264 |
| (F-GJKT) | FA50 | 21 |
| F-GJLA | FA20 | 133 |
| F-GJLB | CRVT | 39 |
| F-GJLL | FA10 | 22 |
| F-GJLQ | FA7X | 68 |
| F-GJMA | FA10 | 116 |
| (F-GJMA) | FA10 | 65 |
| (F-GJPI) | FA20 | 257 |
| F-GJPM | F900 | 66 |
| F-GJPR | FA20 | 5 |
| F-GJRH | F900 | 106 |
| F-GJRN | FA10 | 163 |
| F-GJSC | F2TH | 74 |
| F-GJSF | FA20 | 299 |
| F-GJSK | F2TH | 27 |
| F-GJTG | F2TH | 55 |
| F-GJTH | F2TH | 61 |
| (F-GJTR) | FA50 | 140 |
| F-GJXX | C560 | 0070 |
| F-GJYD | C550 | 414 |
| F-GKAE | FA10 | 213 |
| (F-GKAF) | FA20 | 120 |
| F-GKAL | FA20 | 455 |
| F-GKAR | FA50 | 204 |
| F-GKAY | F900 | 54 |
| F-GKBC | FA10 | 99 |
| F-GKBQ | F900 | 130 |
| F-GKBZ | FA50 | 185 |
| F-GKCC | FA10 | 201 |
| (F-GKCD) | FA10 | 88 |
| (F-GKCJ) | BE40 | RK-14 |
| F-GKDB | FA20 | 271/493 |
| F-GKDD | FA20 | 257 |
| F-GKDI | F900 | 106 |
| F-GKDR | FA50 | 86 |
| F-GKGA | CRVT | 11 |
| (F-GKGB) | CRVT | 30 |
| F-GKGD | CRVT | 34 |
| F-GKGL | C560 | 0058 |
| **F-GKGO** | **FA50** | **155** |
| **F-GKHJ** | **F900** | **11** |

| F-GKHL | C560 | 0059 |
|---|---|---|
| **F-GKID** | **C500** | **319** |
| "F-GKIL" | C500 | 319 |
| (F-GKIN) | FA50 | 286 |
| F-GKIP | F2TH | 90 |
| **F-GKIR** | **C500** | **361** |
| F-GKIS | FA20 | 307/513 |
| F-GKJB | CRVT | 20 |
| F-GKJL | C560 | 0093 |
| F-GKJS | C650 | 0232 |
| F-GKLV | FA10 | 41 |
| F-GKME | FA20 | 256 |
| F-GKPB | FA10 | 207 |
| F-GKPP | MS76 | 098 |
| (F-GKPZ) | FA10 | 201 |
| F-GKRU | FA50 | 235 |
| F-GKTV | FA50 | 111 |
| F-GLEC | CRVT | 30 |
| F-GLGY | F900 | 11 |
| F-GLHI | F900 | 166 |
| (F-GLHJ) | F2TH | 12 |
| F-GLIM | C560 | 0119 |
| (F-GLIM) | C560 | 0156 |
| F-GLJA | C500 | 264 |
| F-GLJV | F9EX | 76 |
| F-GLMD | FA20 | 117 |
| F-GLMM | FA20 | 116 |
| (F-GLMT) | FA20 | 246/482 |
| F-GLMU | F900 | 35 |
| F-GLNL | FA20 | 94/428 |
| (F-GLOR) | BE40 | RK-37 |
| (F-GLPD) | BE40 | RK-37 |
| **F-GLSJ** | **FA50** | **107** |
| **F-GLTK** | **C550** | **609** |
| F-GLYC | C560 | 0205 |
| F-GLYO | BE40 | RK-14 |
| F-GMCI | C550 | 052 |
| F-GMCK | F2TH | 46 |
| F-GMCU | FA50 | 37 |
| **F-GMDL** | **C525** | **0400** |
| **F-GMDS** | **F9EX** | **230** |
| (F-GMEX) | F2EX | 1 |
| F-GMGA | FA50 | 51 |
| **F-GMIR** | **C52A** | **0322** |
| (F-GMIR) | F2TH | 1 |
| F-GMJS | FA10 | 80 |
| F-GMLH | C500 | 308 |
| **F-GMMC** | **C525** | **0448** |
| F-GMOE | F2TH | 1 |
| **F-GMOF** | **CRVT** | **12** |
| **F-GMOH** | **F900** | **7** |
| **F-GMOT** | **FA50** | **111** |
| F-GMPR | F2TH | 18 |
| **F-GMTJ** | **C510** | **0222** |
| (F-GNAB) | C500 | 337 |
| F-GNAF | CRVT | 15 |
| F-GNBL | F2TH | 36 |
| F-GNCJ | C525 | 0024 |
| (F-GNCO) | F9EX | 97 |
| **F-GNCP** | **C550** | **004** |
| F-GNDA | F900 | 88 |
| (F-GNDB) | HS25 | 257127 |
| F-GNDK | F900 | 35 |
| F-GNDO | F2TH | 187 |
| **F-GNDZ** | **FA10** | **17** |
| F-GNFF | FA50 | 228 |
| F-GNFI | F900 | 118 |
| (F-GNFS) | FA50 | 228 |
| F-GNGL | FA50 | 230 |
| F-GNLF | C550 | 114 |
| F-GNLR | FA50 | 232 |
| F-GNMF | F900 | 47 |
| (F-GNMF) | FA20 | 511 |
| F-GNMO | FA50 | 240 |
| F-GNMR | F900 | 143 |
| F-GOAB | F900 | 130 |
| (F-GOAK) | GLEX | 9115 |
| F-GOAL | FA50 | 131 |
| F-GOBE | FA20 | 515 |
| F-GOBZ | FA20 | 293 |
| F-GOCT | FA50 | 134 |
| F-GODB | HS25 | 257127 |
| F-GODE | F900 | 133 |
| F-GODO | F2TH | 65 |
| F-GODP | FA50 | 275 |
| (F-GOEA) | F9EX | 97 |
| F-GOEI | F900 | 1 |

| F-GOEV | F900 | 5 |
|---|---|---|
| (F-GOFC) | F900 | 47 |
| F-GOGL | FA50 | 134 |
| F-GOJI | FA10 | 161 |
| F-GOJT | FA20 | 501 |
| **F-GOLV** | **FA50** | **215** |
| (F-GOND) | FA50 | 251 |
| **F-GOPM** | **FA20** | **302/510** |
| (F-GOTF) | F2EX | 78 |
| F-GOVV | GLEX | 9005 |
| F-GOYA | F9EX | 11 |
| F-GPAA | FA20 | 103/423 |
| **F-GPAB** | **FA20** | **254** |
| **F-GPAD** | **FA20** | **280/503** |
| F-GPAE | FA20 | 356 |
| F-GPAK | GLF4 | 1061 |
| F-GPAM | F2TH | 6 |
| F-GPAX | F900 | 125 |
| F-GPBG | FA50 | 269 |
| F-GPFC | C525 | 0101 |
| **F-GPFD** | **FA10** | **221** |
| **F-GPGK** | **F900** | **69** |
| **F-GPGL** | **FA10** | **203** |
| **F-GPGS** | **FA50** | **151** |
| F-GPIM | FA20 | 30 |
| **F-GPLA** | **CRVT** | **28** |
| F-GPLF | C525 | 0291 |
| (F-GPLH) | FA50 | 131 |
| F-GPLT | C550 | 033 |
| (F-GPNG) | FA20 | 116 |
| **F-GPNJ** | **F9EX** | **50** |
| **F-GPPF** | **FA50** | **65** |
| **F-GPSA** | **FA50** | **123** |
| (F-GPSS) | C52A | 0171 |
| **F-GPUJ** | **C52A** | **0169** |
| F-GRAX | F900 | 120 |
| F-GRCH | C500 | 201 |
| F-GRDP | F900 | 169 |
| F-GREX | F9EX | 1 |
| F-GROC | FA20 | 279/502 |
| F-GRON | HS25 | 257166 |
| F-GRRM | C525 | 0166 |
| **F-GRUJ** | **C52B** | **0117** |
| F-GSAA | F2TH | 36 |
| F-GSAB | F900 | 161 |
| (F-GSAD) | F900 | 163 |
| (F-GSAE) | F2TH | 26 |
| F-GSAI | F9EX | 31 |
| F-GSCN | F900 | 62 |
| **F-GSCR** | **C52B** | **0264** |
| F-GSDA | F9EX | 106 |
| F-GSDP | F9EX | 43 |
| F-GSEF | F9EX | 121 |
| F-GSER | FA50 | 2 |
| **F-GSGL** | **C52B** | **0178** |
| **F-GSLZ** | **FA10** | **208** |
| F-GSMC | C500 | 308 |
| F-GSMF | F900 | 142 |
| **F-GSMG** | **C52B** | **0230** |
| F-GSMT | F9EX | 155 |
| **F-GSNA** | **F9EX** | **145** |
| **F-GSNK** | **F900** | **115** |
| F-GSXF | FA20 | 315/517 |
| F-GSYC | F2TH | 27 |
| F-GTCD | FA50 | 107 |
| F-GTGJ | F900 | 105 |
| F-GTHS | FA50 | 155 |
| F-GTJF | FA50 | 246 |
| F-GTMD | C525 | 0312 |
| **F-GTOD** | **FA10** | **155** |
| **F-GTRY** | **C525** | **0359** |
| F-GUAE | FA50 | 104 |
| **F-GUAJ** | **FA50** | **169** |
| (F-GUDA) | F9EX | 165 |
| F-GUDC | F2EX | 49 |
| F-GUDN | F2EX | 5 |
| F-GUDP | FA50 | 134 |
| F-GUEQ | F900 | 167 |
| F-GUFM | F2EX | 28 |
| F-GUHB | F2EX | 18 |
| F-GUJP | F2TH | 144 |
| F-GUPH | F2EX | 75 |
| F-GUTC | F2EX | 42 |
| F-GUTD | F2EX | 8 |
| F-GUYM | F2TH | 191 |
| F-GVAE | F900 | 86 |
| F-GVBF | F900 | 154 |

| (F-GVDA) | F2TH | 121 |
|---|---|---|
| F-GVDN | FA50 | 264 |
| F-GVDP | F9EX | 51 |
| **F-GVFX** | **F2EX** | **195** |
| **F-GVIA** | **HS25** | **258855** |
| F-GVJR | FA20 | 180/460 |
| **F-GVML** | **GLEX** | **9081** |
| **F-GVMO** | **F900** | **78** |
| **F-GVMV** | **GLEX** | **9202** |
| F-GVNG | F2EX | 114 |
| (F-GVRB) | FA7X | 34 |
| **F-GVTC** | **F2TH** | **166** |
| **F-GVUJ** | **C52B** | **0156** |
| **F-GVVB** | **C52B** | **0300** |
| **F-GVYC** | **C56X** | **5682** |
| **F-GXBV** | **F9EX** | **75** |
| F-GXDA | F2TH | 229 |
| F-GXDP | F2TH | 119 |
| **F-GXDZ** | **F900** | **120** |
| **F-GXHG** | **F9EX** | **78** |
| **F-GXMC** | **FA50** | **190** |
| **F-GXRK** | **C525** | **0229** |
| **F-GXRL** | **C52A** | **0019** |
| **F-GXRM** | **F900** | **142** |
| (F-GXXX) | C56X | 5104 |
| (F-GYBM) | FA50 | 16 |
| **F-GYCA** | **FA20** | **240/478** |
| F-GYCM | F9EX | 103 |
| **F-GYCP** | **F900** | **135** |
| F-GYDA | FA7X | 19 |
| (F-GYDP) | F9EX | 75 |
| **F-GYFC** | **C52B** | **0176** |
| F-GYMC | FA20 | 307/513 |
| F-GYOL | FA50 | 88 |
| F-GYPB | FA20 | 307/513 |
| F-GYRB | F9EX | 113 |
| **F-GYSL** | **FA20** | **341** |
| (F-GZAK) | F2TH | 187 |
| F-GZLC | C550 | 209 |
| F-GZUJ | C52A | 0200 |
| F-HAAP | F900 | 142 |
| **F-HACA** | **C550** | **195** |
| (F-HACD) | C56X | 5104 |
| **F-HACP** | **LJ45** | **287** |
| F-HADA | C525 | 0041 |
| (F-HAFC) | C52B | 0176 |
| **F-HAGA** | **C52B** | **0258** |
| **F-HAGH** | **C525** | **0518** |
| **F-HAIR** | **FA50** | **37** |
| **F-HAJD** | **C525** | **0523** |
| **F-HAJV** | **C550** | **622** |
| **F-HAKA** | **FA7X** | **19** |
| **F-HALM** | **FA50** | **134** |
| **F-HALO** | **C525** | **0484** |
| **F-HAMG** | **C52A** | **0193** |
| F-HAOA | C525 | 0024 |
| **F-HAPM** | **FA50** | **346** |
| **F-HAPN** | **FA50** | **347** |
| F-HAPP | C52A | 0009 |
| F-HASC | C525 | 0177 |
| **F-HASF** | **C52A** | **0015** |
| **F-HAST** | **PRM1** | **RB-149** |
| F-HAVB | LJ60 | 170 |
| **F-HAXA** | **F9EX** | **12** |
| **F-HBBM** | **FA50** | **16** |
| **F-HBDA** | **F9EX** | **200** |
| **F-HBER** | **C52B** | **0183** |
| F-HBFA | PRM1 | RB-83 |
| **F-HBFK** | **C550** | **625** |
| **F-HBFP** | **HS25** | **258689** |
| **F-HBMB** | **C550** | **352** |
| **F-HBMR** | **C550** | **717** |
| **F-HBMS** | **C500** | **312** |
| **F-HBOL** | **F9EX** | **107** |
| **F-HBOM** | **HS25** | **258392** |
| **F-HBPP** | **C52B** | **0013** |
| (F-HBSC) | C525 | 0505 |
| **F-HBSC** | **C525** | **0508** |
| F-HCBM | F9EX | 174 |
| (F-HCCN) | C550 | 625 |
| F-HCCX | FA7X | 42 |
| **F-HCDD** | **FA50** | **297** |
| **F-HCEF** | **FA50** | **306** |
| F-HCGD | LJ45 | 328 |
| **F-HCIC** | **C52B** | **0224** |
| **F-HCJP** | **PRM1** | **RB-228** |
| **F-HCPB** | **C525** | **0322** |

| **F-HCRT** | **C550** | **280** |
|---|---|---|
| **F-HDCB** | **FA50** | **204** |
| (F-HDFS) | F2TH | 230 |
| **F-HDGT** | **C550** | **634** |
| **F-HDLJ** | **F9EX** | **165** |
| **F-HDMB** | **C500** | **308** |
| **F-HDPB** | **FA50** | **334** |
| **F-HDPY** | **C510** | **0149** |
| **F-HEKO** | **C52A** | **0080** |
| **F-HEOL** | **C52A** | **0219** |
| **F-HEQA** | **C525** | **0024** |
| **F-HFBY** | **GLEX** | **9188** |
| **F-HFMA** | **C525** | **0423** |
| **F-HGBY** | **HS25** | **HA-0090** |
| F-HGOL | C525 | 0351 |
| **F-HITM** | **BE40** | **RK-501** |
| **F-HIVA** | **C525** | **0235** |
| **F-HJAV** | **C525** | **0473** |
| **F-HLIM** | **C560** | **0683** |
| F-HMJC | C525 | 0250 |
| **F-HNCY** | **PRM1** | **RB-230** |
| (F-HNFG) | FA7X | 2 |
| F-HOCI | F900 | 1 |

France - D'Outremer

| F-OBYG | CRVT | 39 |
|---|---|---|
| F-OBZP | CRVT | 29 |
| F-OBZR | CRVT | 7 |
| F-OBZV | CRVT | 25 |
| F-OCDE | CRVT | 36 |
| (F-OCGK) | HS25 | 25025 |
| F-OCJL | CRVT | 19 |
| F-OCRN | CRVT | 9 |
| F-ODEO | FA50 | 78 |
| F-ODFE | CRVT | 22 |
| F-ODFQ | CRVT | 26 |
| F-ODHA | FA20 | 175 |
| F-ODIF | CRVT | 38 |
| F-ODJS | CRVT | 40 |
| F-ODJX | CRVT | 5 |
| F-ODKS | CRVT | 11 |
| F-ODOK | FA20 | 162/451 |
| F-ODSK | FA20 | 94/428 |
| F-ODSR | CRVT | 35 |
| F-ODTM | CRVT | 17 |
| F-ODUT | C550 | 052 |
| F-OGJL | CRVT | 6 |
| F-OGSI | FA20 | 511 |
| F-OGSR | FA20 | 496 |
| (F-OGUO) | C550 | 375 |
| (F-OGVA) | C550 | 375 |
| F-OHAH | C555 | 0094 |
| F-OHCJ | FA20 | 341 |
| F-OHES | FA20 | 514 |
| F-OHFO | FA50 | 267 |
| F-OHRU | C560 | 0407 |
| (F-OIBA) | F2TH | 65 |
| (F-OIBE) | F9EX | 20 |
| F-OIBL | F9EX | 6 |
| (F-OINA) | F9EX | 91 |
| F-OKSI | FA50 | 241 |
| F-OKSY | FA50 | 257 |
| F-OLET | FA20 | 511 |
| F-OMON | FA50 | 230 |
| **F-ONYY** | **C52A** | **0320** |
| F-ORAV | F2TH | 171 |
| F-ORAX | F2TH | 121 |
| F-OVJR | FA20 | 180/460 |

France - Military Callsigns

| F-FBLW | MS76 | 024 |
|---|---|---|
| F-RABQ | MS76 | 020 |
| F-RABZ | MS76 | 037 |
| **F-RAEA** | **FA20** | **260/488** |
| **F-RAEB** | **FA20** | **167/453** |
| F-RAEB | FA20 | 268/492 |
| F-RAEC | FA20 | 93/435 |
| F-RAEC | FA20 | 291/505 |
| **F-RAEC** | **FA20** | **342/532** |
| F-RAED | FA20 | 93/435 |
| F-RAED | FA20 | 238/477 |
| **F-RAEE** | **FA20** | **93/435** |
| F-RAEE | FA20 | 238/477 |

| | | |
|---|---|---|
| **F-RAEF** | **FA20** | **268/492** |
| F-RAEG | FA20 | 291/505 |
| F-RAEG | FA20 | 342/532 |
| **F-RAEH** | **FA10** | **422** |
| **F-RAFA** | **FA7X** | **68** |
| F-RAFJ | FA20 | 49/408 |
| F-RAFJ | FA50 | 2 |
| **F-RAFJ** | **FA50** | **78** |
| **F-RAFK** | **FA50** | **27** |
| F-RAFK | FA20 | 154/447 |
| F-RAFK | FA20 | 268/492 |
| **F-RAFL** | **FA50** | **34** |
| F-RAFN | FA20 | 93/435 |
| **F-RAFI** | **FA50** | **5** |
| F-RAFJ | FA50 | 2 |
| F-RAFL | FA20 | 167/453 |
| F-RAFM | FA20 | 238/477 |
| F-RAFN | FA20 | 93/435 |
| **F-RAFP** | **F900** | **2** |
| **F-RAFQ** | **F900** | **4** |
| F-RAFU | FA20 | 309/514 |
| F-RBLB | MS76 | 058 |
| F-RBLC | MS76 | 029 |
| F-RBLD | MS76 | 093 |
| F-RBLD | MS76 | 044 |
| F-RBLE | MS76 | 071 |
| F-RBLF | MS76 | 065 |
| F-RBLF | MS76 | 070 |
| F-RBLG | MS76 | 056 |
| F-RBLH | MS76 | 097 |
| F-RBLL | MS76 | 081 |
| F-RBLN | MS76 | 026 |
| F-RBLP | MS76 | 077 |
| F-RBLU | MS76 | 091 |
| F-RBLU | MS76 | 096 |
| F-RBLV | MS76 | 062 |
| F-RBLW | MS76 | 030 |
| F-RBLY | MS76 | 078 |
| F-RBLY | MS76 | 061 |
| F-RBLZ | MS76 | 075 |
| F-RBL. | MS76 | 082 |
| F-RBL. | MS76 | 094 |
| F-RBL. | MS76 | 095 |
| F-RBQA | FA20 | 93/435 |
| F-RCAL | FA20 | 422 |
| F-RCAP | FA20 | 291/505 |
| F-RHDA | MS76 | 092 |
| F-RHDD | MS76 | 053 |
| F-RHDE | MS76 | 027 |
| F-RHDF | MS76 | 014 |
| F-RHD. | MS76 | 080 |
| F-RHFA | FA20 | 49/408 |
| F-SCAC | MS76 | 057 |
| F-SCAP | MS76 | 025 |
| F-SCAR | MS76 | 019 |
| F-SCAS | MS76 | 038 |
| F-SCAT | MS76 | 060 |
| F-SCA. | MS76 | 054 |
| F-SCA. | MS76 | 059 |
| F-SCBB | MS76 | 034 |
| **F-SCBC** | **MS76** | **035** |
| F-SCB. | MS76 | 045 |
| F-SCCC | MS76 | 036 |
| F-SDDB | MS76 | 001 |
| F-SDDC | MS76 | 051 |
| F-SDDO | MS76 | 023 |
| F-SDIA | MS76 | 03 |
| F-SDIB | MS76 | 001 |
| F-SDIC | MS76 | 020 |
| F-SEBH | CRVT | 19 |
| F-SEBI | FA20 | 315/517 |
| F-TEOA | FA20 | 49/408 |
| F-UGWL | FA20 | 115/432 |
| F-UGWM | FA20 | 186/463 |
| F-UGWN | FA10 | 451 |
| F-UGWP | FA20 | 309/514 |
| **F-UKJ** | **FA10** | **483** |
| **F-UKJA** | **FA20** | **182/461** |
| **F-UKJC** | **FA10** | **451** |
| F-UKJE | FA20 | 186/463 |
| F-UKJG | FA20 | 115/432 |
| F-VIOF | FA10 | 5 |
| F-YCB. | MS76 | 031 |
| F-YDJ? | MS76 | 012 |

France - Temporary

| | | |
|---|---|---|
| F-WAMD | FA30 | 01 |
| F-WAMD | FA50 | 1 |
| F-WATF | FA20 | 362 |
| F-WBTM | FA20 | 397/555 |
| F-WDCP | LJ35 | 071 |
| F-WDFE | FA50 | 56 |
| F-WDFJ | FA20 | 362 |
| (F-WDHA) | FA20 | 401 |
| F-WDHK | GLF3 | 340 |
| F-WDSB | FA20 | 482 |
| F-WEDB | FA10 | 197 |
| F-WEFS | FA50 | 34 |
| F-WEFX | F900 | 11 |
| F-WFAL | FA10 | 01 |
| **F-WFBW** | **FA7X** | **1** |
| F-WFJC | F900 | 2 |
| F-WFJC | FA50 | 3 |
| F-WFPD | CRVT | 11 |
| F-WGDZ | FA20 | 482 |
| F-WGSR | FA20 | 496 |
| F-WGTF | FA10 | 48 |
| F-WGTF | FA20 | 511 |
| F-WGTF | FA20 | 77/429 |
| F-WGTF | FA50 | 131 |
| F-WGTF | FA50 | 140 |
| F-WGTG | FA10 | 204 |
| F-WGTG | FA20 | 474 |
| F-WGTG | FA50 | 27 |
| F-WGTG | FA50 | 73 |
| F-WGTH | F900 | 30 |
| F-WGTH | FA20 | 116 |
| F-WGTH | FA50 | 29 |
| F-WGTM | FA20 | 176/458 |
| F-WGVO | MS76 | 01 |
| F-WHLV | FA7X | 42 |
| F-WHLX | F2TH | 101 |
| F-WIDE | F900 | 1 |
| F-WIET | MS76 | 001 |
| F-WIFA | CRVT | 15 |
| (F-WIFU) | CRVT | 11 |
| F-WINR | FA50 | 2 |
| F-WJAA | MS76 | 005 |
| F-WJAA | MS76 | 026 |
| F-WJAA | MS76 | 039 |
| F-WJAB | MS76 | 006 |
| F-WJAC | MS76 | 008 |
| F-WJAD | MS76 | 009 |
| F-WJAE | MS76 | 028 |
| F-WJLH | FA10 | 1 |
| F-WJMJ | FA10 | 10 |
| F-WJMJ | FA10 | 18 |
| F-WJMJ | FA10 | 25 |
| F-WJMJ | FA10 | 3 |
| F-WJMJ | FA10 | 33 |
| F-WJMJ | FA10 | 36 |
| F-WJMJ | FA10 | 44 |
| F-WJMJ | FA10 | 57 |
| F-WJMJ | FA10 | 65 |
| F-WJMJ | FA10 | 74 |
| F-WJMJ | FA10 | 91 |
| F-WJMJ | FA20 | 112 |
| F-WJMJ | FA20 | 121 |
| F-WJMJ | FA20 | 124/433 |
| F-WJMJ | FA20 | 136/439 |
| F-WJMJ | FA20 | 144 |
| F-WJMJ | FA20 | 152/446 |
| F-WJMJ | FA20 | 165/452 |
| F-WJMJ | FA20 | 229 |
| F-WJMJ | FA20 | 321 |
| F-WJMJ | FA20 | 385 |
| F-WJMJ | FA20 | 402 |
| F-WJMJ | FA20 | 407 |
| F-WJMJ | FA20 | 423 |
| F-WJMJ | FA20 | 444 |
| F-WJMJ | FA20 | 456 |
| F-WJMJ | FA20 | 463 |
| F-WJMJ | FA20 | 470 |
| F-WJMJ | FA20 | 83 |
| F-WJMJ | FA20 | 87/424 |
| F-WJMJ | FA20 | 97/422 |
| F-WJMK | FA10 | 11 |
| F-WJMK | FA10 | 14 |
| F-WJMK | FA10 | 21 |
| F-WJMK | FA10 | 26 |
| F-WJMK | FA10 | 4 |

| | | |
|---|---|---|
| F-WJMK | FA20 | 104/454 |
| F-WJMK | FA20 | 119/431 |
| F-WJMK | FA20 | 131/437 |
| F-WJMK | FA20 | 155 |
| F-WJMK | FA20 | 188/464 |
| F-WJMK | FA20 | 211 |
| F-WJMK | FA20 | 246/482 |
| F-WJMK | FA20 | 262 |
| F-WJMK | FA20 | 386 |
| F-WJMK | FA20 | 403 |
| F-WJMK | FA20 | 404 |
| F-WJMK | FA20 | 413 |
| F-WJMK | FA20 | 426 |
| F-WJMK | FA20 | 432 |
| F-WJMK | FA20 | 441 |
| F-WJMK | FA20 | 448 |
| F-WJMK | FA20 | 453 |
| F-WJMK | FA20 | 464 |
| F-WJMK | FA20 | 471 |
| F-WJMK | FA20 | 84 |
| F-WJMK | FA20 | 99 |
| F-WJML | FA10 | 12 |
| F-WJML | FA10 | 24 |
| F-WJML | FA10 | 28 |
| F-WJML | FA10 | 37 |
| F-WJML | FA10 | 45 |
| F-WJML | FA10 | 51 |
| F-WJML | FA10 | 6 |
| F-WJML | FA10 | 60 |
| F-WJML | FA10 | 69 |
| F-WJML | FA20 | 115/432 |
| F-WJML | FA20 | 230 |
| F-WJML | FA20 | 387 |
| F-WJML | FA20 | 414 |
| F-WJML | FA20 | 433 |
| F-WJML | FA20 | 442 |
| F-WJML | FA20 | 454 |
| F-WJML | FA20 | 460 |
| F-WJML | FA20 | 466 |
| F-WJML | FA20 | 475 |
| F-WJML | FA20 | 73/419 |
| F-WJMM | FA10 | 15 |
| F-WJMM | FA10 | 2 |
| F-WJMM | FA10 | 29 |
| F-WJMM | FA10 | 38 |
| F-WJMM | FA10 | 48 |
| F-WJMM | FA10 | 58 |
| F-WJMM | FA10 | 62 |
| F-WJMM | FA10 | 70 |
| F-WJMM | FA10 | 71 |
| F-WJMM | FA10 | 9 |
| F-WJMM | FA20 | 106 |
| F-WJMM | FA20 | 114/420 |
| F-WJMM | FA20 | 129 |
| F-WJMM | FA20 | 142 |
| F-WJMM | FA20 | 157 |
| F-WJMM | FA20 | 213 |
| F-WJMM | FA20 | 249 |
| F-WJMM | FA20 | 274 |
| F-WJMM | FA20 | 388 |
| F-WJMM | FA20 | 417 |
| F-WJMM | FA20 | 435 |
| F-WJMM | FA20 | 445 |
| F-WJMM | FA20 | 457 |
| F-WJMM | FA20 | 467 |
| F-WJMM | FA20 | 476 |
| F-WJMM | FA20 | 82/418 |
| F-WJMM | FA20 | 92/421 |
| F-WJMN | FA10 | 40 |
| F-WJMN | FA10 | 43 |
| F-WJMN | FA10 | 59 |
| F-WJMN | FA10 | 66 |
| F-WJMN | FA10 | 7 |
| F-WJMN | FA10 | 8 |
| F-WJMN | FA20 | 100 |
| F-WJMN | FA20 | 125 |
| F-WJMN | FA20 | 146 |
| F-WJMN | FA20 | 164 |
| F-WJMN | FA20 | 232 |
| F-WJMN | FA20 | 264 |
| F-WJMN | FA20 | 390 |
| F-WJMN | FA20 | 418 |
| F-WJMN | FA20 | 436 |
| F-WJMN | FA20 | 446 |
| F-WJMN | FA20 | 458 |
| F-WJMN | FA20 | 478 |
| F-WJMN | FA20 | 67/414 |

| | | |
|---|---|---|
| F-WKAE | FA10 | 213 |
| F-WLCH | FA20 | 147/444 |
| F-WLCS | FA10 | 13 |
| F-WLCS | FA10 | 17 |
| F-WLCS | FA10 | 34 |
| F-WLCS | FA10 | 41 |
| F-WLCS | FA10 | 50 |
| F-WLCS | FA10 | 53 |
| F-WLCS | FA20 | 138/440 |
| F-WLCS | FA20 | 166 |
| F-WLCS | FA20 | 206 |
| F-WLCS | FA20 | 215 |
| F-WLCS | FA20 | 245/481 |
| F-WLCS | FA20 | 391 |
| F-WLCS | FA20 | 447 |
| F-WLCS | FA20 | 481 |
| F-WLCT | FA10 | 16 |
| F-WLCT | FA10 | 30 |
| F-WLCT | FA10 | 46 |
| F-WLCT | FA10 | 5 |
| F-WLCT | FA10 | 64 |
| F-WLCT | FA10 | 78 |
| F-WLCT | FA20 | 153 |
| F-WLCT | FA20 | 216 |
| F-WLCT | FA20 | 259 |
| F-WLCT | FA20 | 393 |
| F-WLCT | FA20 | 416 |
| F-WLCT | FA20 | 449 |
| F-WLCT | FA20 | 485 |
| F-WLCU | FA10 | 19 |
| F-WLCU | FA10 | 31 |
| F-WLCU | FA10 | 42 |
| F-WLCU | FA10 | 67 |
| F-WLCU | FA20 | 173 |
| F-WLCU | FA20 | 234/475 |
| F-WLCU | FA20 | 261 |
| F-WLCV | FA10 | 20 |
| F-WLCV | FA10 | 35 |
| F-WLCV | FA10 | 49 |
| F-WLCV | FA10 | 68 |
| F-WLCV | FA20 | 154/447 |
| F-WLCV | FA20 | 187 |
| F-WLCV | FA20 | 233 |
| F-WLCV | FA20 | 415 |
| F-WLCV | FA20 | 486 |
| F-WLCX | FA10 | 22 |
| F-WLCX | FA10 | 27 |
| F-WLCX | FA10 | 52 |
| F-WLCX | FA10 | 63 |
| F-WLCX | FA10 | 72 |
| F-WLCX | FA20 | 168 |
| F-WLCX | FA20 | 209 |
| F-WLCX | FA20 | 240/478 |
| F-WLCX | FA20 | 265 |
| F-WLCY | FA10 | 23 |
| F-WLCY | FA10 | 47 |
| F-WLCY | FA20 | 183 |
| F-WLCY | FA20 | 201/469 |
| F-WLCY | FA20 | 217 |
| F-WLEF | C550 | 144 |
| F-WLJV | F9EX | 76 |
| F-WLKB | FA20 | 01 |
| F-WLKL | MS76 | 01 |
| F-WLLK | FA20 | 137 |
| F-WLMM | FA20 | 116 |
| F-WMEX | F2EX | 1 |
| F-WMGO | FA20 | 50 |
| F-WMKF | FA20 | 141/441 |
| F-WMKF | FA20 | 161 |
| F-WMKF | FA20 | 17 |
| F-WMKF | FA20 | 175 |
| F-WMKF | FA20 | 180/460 |
| F-WMKF | FA20 | 185/467 |
| F-WMKF | FA20 | 207 |
| F-WMKF | FA20 | 250 |
| F-WMKF | FA20 | 272 |
| F-WMKF | FA20 | 287 |
| F-WMKF | FA20 | 297 |
| F-WMKF | FA20 | 30 |
| F-WMKF | FA20 | 308 |
| F-WMKF | FA20 | 316 |
| F-WMKF | FA20 | 319 |
| F-WMKF | FA20 | 324 |
| F-WMKF | FA20 | 335 |
| F-WMKF | FA20 | 341 |
| F-WMKF | FA20 | 347 |
| F-WMKF | FA20 | 352 |

| Registration | Type | No. |
|---|---|---|
| F-WMKF | FA20 | 355 |
| F-WMKF | FA20 | 361/543 |
| F-WMKF | FA20 | 37/406 |
| F-WMKF | FA20 | 379 |
| F-WMKF | FA20 | 38 |
| F-WMKF | FA20 | 394 |
| F-WMKF | FA20 | 398 |
| F-WMKF | FA20 | 4 |
| F-WMKF | FA20 | 406/557 |
| F-WMKF | FA20 | 424 |
| F-WMKF | FA20 | 429 |
| F-WMKF | FA20 | 474 |
| F-WMKF | FA20 | 69 |
| F-WMKF | FA20 | 76 |
| F-WMKF | FA20 | 93/435 |
| F-WMKG | FA20 | 110 |
| F-WMKG | FA20 | 118 |
| F-WMKG | FA20 | 132 |
| F-WMKG | FA20 | 148 |
| F-WMKG | FA20 | 160/450 |
| F-WMKG | FA20 | 167/453 |
| F-WMKG | FA20 | 171 |
| F-WMKG | FA20 | 176/458 |
| F-WMKG | FA20 | 193 |
| F-WMKG | FA20 | 227 |
| F-WMKG | FA20 | 28 |
| F-WMKG | FA20 | 282 |
| F-WMKG | FA20 | 289 |
| F-WMKG | FA20 | 298 |
| F-WMKG | FA20 | 3/403 |
| F-WMKG | FA20 | 317 |
| F-WMKG | FA20 | 325 |
| F-WMKG | FA20 | 338/530 |
| F-WMKG | FA20 | 349 |
| F-WMKG | FA20 | 35 |
| F-WMKG | FA20 | 356 |
| F-WMKG | FA20 | 366 |
| F-WMKG | FA20 | 370 |
| F-WMKG | FA20 | 382 |
| F-WMKG | FA20 | 396 |
| F-WMKG | FA20 | 411 |
| F-WMKG | FA20 | 420 |
| F-WMKG | FA20 | 425 |
| F-WMKG | FA20 | 430 |
| F-WMKG | FA20 | 437 |
| F-WMKG | FA20 | 443 |
| F-WMKG | FA20 | 450 |
| F-WMKG | FA20 | 46 |
| F-WMKG | FA20 | 461 |
| F-WMKG | FA20 | 468 |
| F-WMKG | FA20 | 48 |
| F-WMKG | FA20 | 64 |
| F-WMKG | FA20 | 73/419 |
| F-WMKG | FA20 | 74 |
| F-WMKG | FA20 | 89 |
| F-WMKH | FA20 | 103/423 |
| F-WMKH | FA20 | 11 |
| F-WMKH | FA20 | 117 |
| F-WMKH | FA20 | 126/438 |
| F-WMKH | FA20 | 13 |
| F-WMKH | FA20 | 134 |
| F-WMKH | FA20 | 143/442 |
| F-WMKH | FA20 | 150/445 |
| F-WMKH | FA20 | 199 |
| F-WMKH | FA20 | 243/480 |
| F-WMKH | FA20 | 257 |
| F-WMKH | FA20 | 275 |
| F-WMKH | FA20 | 290 |
| F-WMKH | FA20 | 303 |
| F-WMKH | FA20 | 310 |
| F-WMKH | FA20 | 312 |
| F-WMKH | FA20 | 322 |
| F-WMKH | FA20 | 339 |
| F-WMKH | FA20 | 6 |
| F-WMKH | FA20 | 70 |
| F-WMKH | FA20 | 79/415 |
| F-WMKH | FA20 | 85/425 |
| F-WMKI | FA20 | 102 |
| F-WMKI | FA20 | 111 |
| F-WMKI | FA20 | 12 |
| F-WMKI | FA20 | 120 |
| F-WMKI | FA20 | 135 |
| F-WMKI | FA20 | 151 |
| F-WMKI | FA20 | 156/448 |
| F-WMKI | FA20 | 177 |
| F-WMKI | FA20 | 204 |
| F-WMKI | FA20 | 21 |
| F-WMKI | FA20 | 244 |
| F-WMKI | FA20 | 29 |
| F-WMKI | FA20 | 292 |
| F-WMKI | FA20 | 299 |
| F-WMKI | FA20 | 327 |
| F-WMKI | FA20 | 345 |
| F-WMKI | FA20 | 357 |
| F-WMKI | FA20 | 36 |
| F-WMKI | FA20 | 364 |
| F-WMKI | FA20 | 368 |
| F-WMKI | FA20 | 373 |
| F-WMKI | FA20 | 380 |
| F-WMKI | FA20 | 399 |
| F-WMKI | FA20 | 405 |
| F-WMKI | FA20 | 412 |
| F-WMKI | FA20 | 421 |
| F-WMKI | FA20 | 428 |
| F-WMKI | FA20 | 438 |
| F-WMKI | FA20 | 45 |
| F-WMKI | FA20 | 452 |
| F-WMKI | FA20 | 462 |
| F-WMKI | FA20 | 469 |
| F-WMKI | FA20 | 5 |
| F-WMKI | FA20 | 54 |
| F-WMKI | FA20 | 61 |
| F-WMKI | FA20 | 63/411 |
| F-WMKI | FA20 | 80 |
| F-WMKI | FA20 | 86 |
| F-WMKI | FA20 | 9 |
| F-WMKJ | FA20 | 101 |
| F-WMKJ | FA20 | 107 |
| F-WMKJ | FA20 | 116 |
| F-WMKJ | FA20 | 128/436 |
| F-WMKJ | FA20 | 130 |
| F-WMKJ | FA20 | 14 |
| F-WMKJ | FA20 | 158/449 |
| F-WMKJ | FA20 | 159 |
| F-WMKJ | FA20 | 20 |
| F-WMKJ | FA20 | 200 |
| F-WMKJ | FA20 | 218 |
| F-WMKJ | FA20 | 260/488 |
| F-WMKJ | FA20 | 263/489 |
| F-WMKJ | FA20 | 27 |
| F-WMKJ | FA20 | 279/502 |
| F-WMKJ | FA20 | 293 |
| F-WMKJ | FA20 | 305 |
| F-WMKJ | FA20 | 313 |
| F-WMKJ | FA20 | 328/522 |
| F-WMKJ | FA20 | 34 |
| F-WMKJ | FA20 | 351/538 |
| F-WMKJ | FA20 | 360 |
| F-WMKJ | FA20 | 365 |
| F-WMKJ | FA20 | 371 |
| F-WMKJ | FA20 | 409 |
| F-WMKJ | FA20 | 419 |
| F-WMKJ | FA20 | 43 |
| F-WMKJ | FA20 | 431 |
| F-WMKJ | FA20 | 439 |
| F-WMKJ | FA20 | 459 |
| F-WMKJ | FA20 | 51 |
| F-WMKJ | FA20 | 60 |
| F-WMKJ | FA20 | 62/409 |
| F-WMKJ | FA20 | 68 |
| F-WMKJ | FA20 | 8 |
| F-WMKJ | FA20 | 91 |
| F-WMKK | FA20 | 10 |
| F-WMKK | FA20 | 15 |
| F-WMKK | FA20 | 22/404 |
| F-WMKK | FA20 | 7 |
| F-WMSH | FA20 | 1/401 |
| F-WMSS | FA20 | 2/402 |
| F-WNAV | F2TH | 1 |
| F-WNCO | F9EX | 97 |
| F-WNDB | FA50 | 1 |
| F-WNDB | FA50 | 1 |
| (F-WNEW) | F2TH | 1 |
| F-WNEW | F2TH | 2 |
| F-WNGD | FA10 | 109 |
| F-WNGD | FA10 | 125 |
| F-WNGD | FA10 | 90 |
| F-WNGD | FA10 | 96 |
| F-WNGL | FA10 | 116 |
| F-WNGL | FA10 | 73 |
| F-WNGL | FA20 | 105 |
| F-WNGL | FA20 | 113 |
| F-WNGL | FA20 | 122 |
| F-WNGL | FA20 | 16 |
| F-WNGL | FA20 | 174/457 |
| F-WNGL | FA20 | 181 |
| F-WNGL | FA20 | 210 |
| F-WNGL | FA20 | 222/471 |
| F-WNGL | FA20 | 228/473 |
| F-WNGL | FA20 | 23 |
| F-WNGL | FA20 | 256 |
| F-WNGL | FA20 | 276/494 |
| F-WNGL | FA20 | 301/509 |
| F-WNGL | FA20 | 314/516 |
| F-WNGL | FA20 | 32 |
| F-WNGL | FA20 | 333/526 |
| F-WNGL | FA20 | 40 |
| F-WNGL | FA20 | 41/407 |
| F-WNGL | FA20 | 58 |
| F-WNGL | FA20 | 66 |
| F-WNGL | FA20 | 75 |
| F-WNGL | FA20 | 90/426 |
| F-WNGM | FA10 | 126 |
| F-WNGM | FA10 | 75 |
| F-WNGM | FA10 | 92 |
| F-WNGM | FA20 | 109/427 |
| F-WNGM | FA20 | 123 |
| F-WNGM | FA20 | 139 |
| F-WNGM | FA20 | 163 |
| F-WNGM | FA20 | 172/456 |
| F-WNGM | FA20 | 18 |
| F-WNGM | FA20 | 202 |
| F-WNGM | FA20 | 24 |
| F-WNGM | FA20 | 258 |
| F-WNGM | FA20 | 278/495 |
| F-WNGM | FA20 | 31 |
| F-WNGM | FA20 | 330 |
| F-WNGM | FA20 | 39 |
| F-WNGM | FA20 | 47 |
| F-WNGM | FA20 | 56 |
| F-WNGM | FA20 | 71 |
| F-WNGM | FA20 | 78/412 |
| F-WNGM | FA20 | 96 |
| F-WNGN | FA10 | 77 |
| F-WNGN | FA10 | 93 |
| F-WNGN | FA20 | 127 |
| F-WNGN | FA20 | 140 |
| F-WNGN | FA20 | 145/443 |
| F-WNGN | FA20 | 169 |
| F-WNGN | FA20 | 182/461 |
| F-WNGN | FA20 | 19 |
| F-WNGN | FA20 | 190/465 |
| F-WNGN | FA20 | 25/405 |
| F-WNGN | FA20 | 268/492 |
| F-WNGN | FA20 | 271/493 |
| F-WNGN | FA20 | 44 |
| F-WNGN | FA20 | 49/408 |
| F-WNGN | FA20 | 52 |
| F-WNGN | FA20 | 65 |
| F-WNGN | FA20 | 81 |
| F-WNGN | FA20 | 88 |
| F-WNGN | FA20 | 98/434 |
| F-WNGO | FA10 | 110 |
| F-WNGO | FA10 | 111 |
| F-WNGO | FA10 | 128 |
| F-WNGO | FA10 | 94 |
| F-WNGO | FA20 | 108/430 |
| F-WNGO | FA20 | 133 |
| F-WNGO | FA20 | 149 |
| F-WNGO | FA20 | 162/451 |
| F-WNGO | FA20 | 179 |
| F-WNGO | FA20 | 198/466 |
| F-WNGO | FA20 | 214 |
| F-WNGO | FA20 | 254 |
| F-WNGO | FA20 | 26 |
| F-WNGO | FA20 | 33 |
| F-WNGO | FA20 | 42 |
| F-WNGO | FA20 | 53/417 |
| F-WNGO | FA20 | 55/410 |
| F-WNGO | FA20 | 57 |
| F-WNGO | FA20 | 59 |
| F-WNGO | FA20 | 72/413 |
| F-WNGO | FA20 | 77/429 |
| F-WNGO | FA20 | 94/428 |
| F-WNGO | FA20 | 95 |
| F-WNGQ | CRVT | 17 |
| F-WNGQ | CRVT | 30 |
| F-WNGR | CRVT | 18 |
| F-WNGR | CRVT | 32 |
| F-WNGS | CRVT | 20 |
| F-WNGS | CRVT | 34 |
| F-WNGT | CRVT | 22 |
| F-WNGU | CRVT | 25 |
| F-WNGV | CRVT | 26 |
| F-WNGX | CRVT | 28 |
| F-WNGY | CRVT | 29 |
| F-WNGY | CRVT | 39 |
| F-WNGZ | CRVT | 31 |
| F-WNGZ | CRVT | 40 |
| F-WNLR | FA50 | 232 |
| F-WOND | FA50 | 251 |
| F-WPLT | C550 | 033 |
| F-WPTT | CRVT | 8 |
| F-WPUU | FA10 | 104 |
| F-WPUU | FA10 | 121 |
| F-WPUU | FA10 | 54 |
| F-WPUU | FA10 | 76 |
| F-WPUU | FA20 | 189 |
| F-WPUU | FA20 | 220 |
| F-WPUU | FA20 | 273 |
| F-WPUU | FA20 | 479 |
| F-WPUU | FA20 | 500 |
| F-WPUU | FA20 | 502 |
| F-WPUU | FA20 | 508 |
| F-WPUU | FA20 | 512 |
| F-WPUV | FA10 | 105 |
| F-WPUV | FA10 | 122 |
| F-WPUV | FA10 | 55 |
| F-WPUV | FA10 | 61 |
| F-WPUV | FA20 | 170/455 |
| F-WPUV | FA20 | 221 |
| F-WPUV | FA20 | 484 |
| F-WPUV | FA20 | 492 |
| F-WPUV | FA20 | 498 |
| F-WPUV | FA20 | 507 |
| F-WPUV | FA20 | 513 |
| F-WPUX | FA10 | 106 |
| F-WPUX | FA10 | 123 |
| F-WPUX | FA10 | 39 |
| F-WPUX | FA20 | 191 |
| F-WPUX | FA20 | 223 |
| F-WPUX | FA20 | 269 |
| F-WPUX | FA20 | 489 |
| F-WPUX | FA20 | 504 |
| F-WPUX | FA20 | 509 |
| F-WPUY | FA10 | 107 |
| F-WPUY | FA10 | 124 |
| F-WPUY | FA10 | 56 |
| F-WPUY | FA20 | 192 |
| F-WPUY | FA20 | 224 |
| F-WPUY | FA20 | 490 |
| F-WPUY | FA20 | 503 |
| F-WPUY | FA20 | 510 |
| F-WPUZ | FA10 | 108 |
| F-WPUZ | FA20 | 194 |
| F-WPUZ | FA20 | 242 |
| F-WPUZ | FA20 | 270 |
| F-WPUZ | FA20 | 482 |
| F-WPUZ | FA20 | 506 |
| F-WPXB | FA10 | 79 |
| F-WPXD | FA10 | 112 |
| F-WPXD | FA10 | 80 |
| F-WPXD | FA10 | 95 |
| F-WPXD | FA20 | 195 |
| F-WPXD | FA20 | 208/468 |
| F-WPXD | FA20 | 225/472 |
| F-WPXD | FA20 | 277/501 |
| F-WPXD | FA50 | 131 |
| F-WPXD | FA50 | 138 |
| F-WPXD | FA50 | 151 |
| F-WPXD | FA50 | 169 |
| F-WPXD | FA50 | 86 |
| F-WPXD | FA50 | 95 |
| F-WPXE | FA10 | 113 |
| F-WPXE | FA10 | 82 |
| F-WPXE | FA20 | 196 |
| F-WPXE | FA20 | 231/474 |
| F-WPXE | FA20 | 247 |
| F-WPXE | FA50 | 145 |
| F-WPXE | FA50 | 174 |
| F-WPXE | FA50 | 73 |
| F-WPXE | FA50 | 96 |
| F-WPXF | FA10 | 114 |
| F-WPXF | FA10 | 81 |
| F-WPXF | FA10 | 97 |
| F-WPXF | FA20 | 178/459 |
| F-WPXF | FA20 | 197 |
| F-WPXF | FA20 | 205 |

| | | | | | | | | | | | |
|---|---|---|---|---|---|---|---|---|---|---|---|
| F-WPXF | FA20 | 237/476 | F-WQBM | F900 | 69 | F-WRQT | FA20 | 318/518 | F-WWFB | F9DX | 602 |
| F-WPXF | FA50 | 132 | F-WQBM | F900 | 84 | F-WRQT | FA20 | 378 | F-WWFB | F9EX | 125 |
| F-WPXF | FA50 | 177 | F-WQBM | F9EX | 177 | F-WRQT | FA20 | 392/553 | F-WWFB | F9EX | 17 |
| F-WPXF | FA50 | 78 | F-WQBM | FA10 | 203 | F-WRQT | FA20 | 410 | F-WWFB | F9EX | 205 |
| F-WPXF | FA50 | 98 | F-WQBM | FA20 | 176/458 | F-WRQT | FA20 | 473 | **F-WWFB** | **F9EX** | **249** |
| F-WPXG | FA10 | 117 | F-WQBM | FA20 | 302/510 | F-WRQU | FA20 | 286/498 | F-WWFB | F9EX | 30 |
| F-WPXG | FA10 | 83 | F-WQBM | FA50 | 107 | F-WRQU | FA20 | 334/527 | F-WWFB | F9EX | 40 |
| F-WPXG | FA10 | 98 | F-WQBM | FA50 | 151 | F-WRQU | FA20 | 384/551 | F-WWFB | F9EX | 67 |
| F-WPXG | FA20 | 212 | F-WQBM | FA50 | 155 | F-WRQU | FA20 | 422 | F-WWFB | F9EX | 8 |
| F-WPXG | FA50 | 110 | F-WQBM | FA50 | 313 | F-WRQV | FA20 | 248/483 | F-WWFB | F9EX | 85 |
| F-WPXG | FA50 | 147 | F-WQBN | F2TH | 119 | F-WRQV | FA20 | 329/523 | F-WWFC | F900 | 114 |
| F-WPXG | FA50 | 157 | F-WQBN | F2TH | 26 | F-WRQV | FA20 | 363/544 | F-WWFC | F900 | 127 |
| F-WPXH | FA10 | 115 | F-WQBN | F2TH | 76 | F-WRQV | FA20 | 372/546 | F-WWFC | F900 | 130 |
| F-WPXH | FA10 | 84 | F-WQBN | F900 | 130 | F-WRQV | FA20 | 389/552 | F-WWFC | F900 | 150 |
| F-WPXH | FA10 | 99 | F-WQBN | F9EX | 155 | F-WRQV | FA20 | 427 | F-WWFC | F900 | 158 |
| F-WPXH | FA20 | 203 | F-WQBN | F9EX | 174 | F-WRQX | FA20 | 283/497 | F-WWFC | F900 | 164 |
| F-WPXH | FA20 | 219/470 | F-WQBN | FA20 | 278/495 | F-WRQX | FA20 | 340/531 | F-WWFC | F900 | 20 |
| F-WPXH | FA50 | 101 | F-WQBN | FA20 | 293 | F-WRQX | FA20 | 395/554 | F-WWFC | F900 | 33 |
| F-WPXH | FA50 | 133 | F-WQBN | FA50 | 134 | F-WRQY | FA20 | 358/541 | F-WWFC | F900 | 35 |
| F-WPXH | FA50 | 140 | F-WQBN | FA50 | 226 | F-WRQZ | FA20 | 267/491 | F-WWFC | F900 | 4 |
| F-WPXH | FA50 | 155 | F-WQBN | FA50 | 7 | F-WRQZ | FA20 | 288/499 | F-WWFC | F900 | 43 |
| F-WPXI | FA10 | 100 | F-WQCD | HS25 | 258233 | F-WRSN | CRVT | 01 | F-WWFC | F900 | 52 |
| F-WPXI | FA10 | 118 | F-WQCO | FA10 | 70 | F-WSHT | FA20 | 174/457 | F-WWFC | F900 | 54 |
| F-WPXI | FA10 | 85 | F-WQCP | FA50 | 88 | F-WSKY | FA7X | 3 | F-WWFC | F900 | 75 |
| F-WPXI | FA20 | 226 | F-WQFL | F2TH | 26 | F-WSMF | F900 | 142 | F-WWFC | F900 | 85 |
| F-WPXI | FA50 | 117 | F-WQFZ | FA50 | 30 | F-WSQK | FA20 | 226 | F-WWFC | F900 | 94 |
| F-WPXJ | FA10 | 101 | F-WQHU | FA50 | 258 | F-WSQN | FA10 | 03 | F-WWFC | F9DX | 603 |
| F-WPXJ | FA10 | 86 | F-WQVA | FA20 | 293 | F-WSQU | FA10 | 1 | F-WWFC | F9EX | 105 |
| F-WPXJ | FA20 | 235 | F-WREX | F9EX | 1 | F-WTAL | FA10 | 02 | F-WWFC | F9EX | 126 |
| F-WPXJ | FA50 | 120 | F-WRGQ | FA20 | 86 | F-WTDA | FA7X | 2 | F-WWFC | F9EX | 179 |
| F-WPXK | FA10 | 102 | F-WRNZ | CRVT | 2 | F-WTDJ | FA20 | 182/461 | F-WWFC | F9EX | 197 |
| F-WPXK | FA10 | 119 | F-WRQK | CRVT | 9 | F-WTFE | FA20 | 388 | F-WWFC | F9EX | 212 |
| F-WPXK | FA10 | 87 | F-WRQP | FA20 | 238/477 | F-WTFF | FA20 | 113 | F-WWFC | F9EX | 224 |
| F-WPXK | FA20 | 236 | F-WRQP | FA20 | 241/479 | F-WUAS | CRVT | 1 | **F-WWFC** | **F9EX** | **250** |
| F-WPXK | FA20 | 280/503 | F-WRQP | FA20 | 252/485 | F-WUQN | CRVT | 3 | F-WWFC | F9EX | 31 |
| F-WPXK | FA50 | 107 | F-WRQP | FA20 | 255/487 | F-WUQP | CRVT | 4 | F-WWFC | F9EX | 41 |
| F-WPXK | FA50 | 134 | F-WRQP | FA20 | 296/507 | F-WUQR | CRVT | 6 | F-WWFC | F9EX | 56 |
| F-WPXL | FA10 | 103 | F-WRQP | FA20 | 300/508 | F-WVFV | FA20 | 182/461 | F-WWFC | F9EX | 68 |
| F-WPXL | FA10 | 88 | F-WRQP | FA20 | 302/510 | F-WVPR | FA10 | 5 | F-WWFC | F9EX | 86 |
| F-WPXL | FA20 | 186/463 | F-WRQP | FA20 | 304/511 | F-WWF. | F900 | 138 | F-WWFD | F900 | 105 |
| F-WPXM | FA10 | 120 | F-WRQP | FA20 | 315/517 | F-WWFA | F2TH | 3 | F-WWFD | F900 | 119 |
| F-WPXM | FA10 | 89 | F-WRQP | FA20 | 332/525 | F-WWFA | F900 | 104 | F-WWFD | F900 | 129 |
| F-WPXM | FA20 | 239 | F-WRQP | FA20 | 336/528 | F-WWFA | F900 | 117 | F-WWFD | F900 | 148 |
| F-WPXM | FA20 | 284 | F-WRQP | FA20 | 342/532 | F-WWFA | F900 | 134 | F-WWFD | F900 | 159 |
| F-WPXM | FA50 | 114 | F-WRQP | FA20 | 344/534 | F-WWFA | F900 | 156 | F-WWFD | F900 | 165 |
| F-WQAU | HS25 | 259032 | F-WRQP | FA20 | 346/535 | F-WWFA | F900 | 168 | F-WWFD | F900 | 172 |
| F-WQBJ | F2TH | 133 | F-WRQP | FA20 | 353/539 | F-WWFA | F900 | 18 | F-WWFD | F900 | 189 |
| F-WQBJ | F2TH | 191 | F-WRQP | FA20 | 369 | F-WWFA | F900 | 199 | F-WWFD | F900 | 22 |
| F-WQBJ | F2TH | 61 | F-WRQP | FA20 | 374 | F-WWFA | F900 | 201 | F-WWFD | F900 | 34 |
| F-WQBJ | F900 | 105 | F-WRQP | FA20 | 377/548 | F-WWFA | F900 | 29 | F-WWFD | F900 | 46 |
| F-WQBJ | F900 | 154 | F-WRQP | FA20 | 397/555 | F-WWFA | F900 | 3 | F-WWFD | F900 | 49 |
| F-WQBJ | F900 | 47 | F-WRQP | FA20 | 434 | F-WWFA | F900 | 4 | F-WWFD | F900 | 59 |
| F-WQBJ | F900 | 62 | F-WRQQ | FA20 | 184/462 | F-WWFA | F900 | 44 | F-WWFD | F900 | 6 |
| F-WQBJ | F9EX | 133 | F-WRQQ | FA20 | 295/500 | F-WWFA | F900 | 47 | F-WWFD | F900 | 67 |
| F-WQBJ | F9EX | 91 | F-WRQQ | FA20 | 326/521 | F-WWFA | F900 | 73 | F-WWFD | F900 | 69 |
| F-WQBJ | FA10 | 185 | F-WRQQ | FA20 | 440 | F-WWFA | F900 | 80 | F-WWFD | F900 | 84 |
| F-WQBJ | FA10 | 208 | F-WRQQ | FA20 | 483 | F-WWFA | F900 | 87 | F-WWFD | F9DX | 604 |
| F-WQBJ | FA50 | 297 | F-WRQR | FA20 | 251/484 | F-WWFA | F900 | 97 | F-WWFD | F9EX | 106 |
| F-WQBJ | FA50 | 95 | F-WRQR | FA20 | 266/490 | F-WWFA | F9DX | 601 | F-WWFD | F9EX | 127 |
| F-WQBK | F2TH | 133 | F-WRQR | FA20 | 281/496 | F-WWFA | F9DX | 621 | F-WWFD | F9EX | 180 |
| F-WQBK | F2TH | 27 | F-WRQR | FA20 | 337/529 | F-WWFA | F9DX | 623 | F-WWFD | F9EX | 206 |
| F-WQBK | F2TH | 49 | F-WRQR | FA20 | 343/533 | F-WWFA | F9EX | 104 | F-WWFD | F9EX | 220 |
| F-WQBK | F2TH | 55 | F-WRQR | FA20 | 348/536 | F-WWFA | F9EX | 16 | **F-WWFD** | **F9EX** | **247** |
| F-WQBK | F2TH | 70 | F-WRQR | FA20 | 354/540 | F-WWFA | F9EX | 178 | F-WWFD | F9EX | 42 |
| F-WQBK | F2TH | 8 | F-WRQR | FA20 | 359/542 | F-WWFA | F9EX | 187 | F-WWFD | F9EX | 57 |
| F-WQBK | F900 | 154 | F-WRQR | FA20 | 367/545 | F-WWFA | F9EX | 2 | F-WWFD | F9EX | 69 |
| F-WQBK | F900 | 47 | F-WRQR | FA20 | 375/547 | **F-WWFA** | **F9EX** | **246** | F-WWFE | F900 | 121 |
| F-WQBK | F9EX | 43 | F-WRQR | FA20 | 383/550 | F-WWFA | F9EX | 29 | F-WWFE | F900 | 136 |
| F-WQBK | F9EX | 75 | F-WRQR | FA20 | 400/556 | F-WWFA | F9EX | 39 | F-WWFE | F900 | 160 |
| F-WQBK | FA20 | 273 | F-WRQR | FA20 | 451 | F-WWFA | F9EX | 55 | F-WWFE | F900 | 24 |
| F-WQBK | FA20 | 511 | F-WRQS | FA20 | 253/486 | F-WWFA | F9EX | 66 | F-WWFE | F900 | 36 |
| F-WQBK | FA50 | 305 | F-WRQS | FA20 | 306/512 | F-WWFA | F9EX | 84 | F-WWFE | F900 | 38 |
| F-WQBK | FA50 | 88 | F-WRQS | FA20 | 311/515 | F-WWFB | F900 | 109 | F-WWFE | F900 | 58 |
| F-WQBL | F2EX | 76 | F-WRQS | FA20 | 320/519 | F-WWFB | F900 | 113 | F-WWFE | F900 | 66 |
| F-WQBL | F2TH | 160 | F-WRQS | FA20 | 323/520 | F-WWFB | F900 | 118 | F-WWFE | F900 | 76 |
| F-WQBL | F2TH | 166 | F-WRQS | FA20 | 331/524 | F-WWFB | F900 | 130 | F-WWFE | F900 | 8 |
| F-WQBL | F2TH | 27 | F-WRQS | FA20 | 350/537 | F-WWFB | F900 | 157 | F-WWFE | F900 | 86 |
| F-WQBL | F2TH | 6 | F-WRQS | FA20 | 358/541 | F-WWFB | F900 | 182 | F-WWFE | F900 | 99 |
| F-WQBL | F900 | 159 | F-WRQS | FA20 | 376 | F-WWFB | F900 | 19 | F-WWFE | F9DX | 605 |
| F-WQBL | F900 | 193 | F-WRQS | FA20 | 381/548 | F-WWFB | F900 | 195 | F-WWFE | F9EX | 107 |
| F-WQBL | F900 | 62 | F-WRQS | FA20 | 408 | F-WWFB | F900 | 31 | F-WWFE | F9EX | 128 |
| F-WQBL | F9EX | 12 | F-WRQS | FA20 | 455 | F-WWFB | F900 | 45 | F-WWFE | F9EX | 147 |
| F-WQBL | FA50 | 16 | F-WRQT | FA20 | 285/504 | F-WWFB | F900 | 5 | F-WWFE | F9EX | 173 |
| F-WQBL | FA50 | 268 | F-WRQT | FA20 | 291/505 | F-WWFB | F900 | 56 | F-WWFE | F9EX | 18 |
| F-WQBM | F2TH | 90 | F-WRQT | FA20 | 294/506 | F-WWFB | F900 | 61 | F-WWFE | F9EX | 207 |
| F-WQBM | F900 | 120 | F-WRQT | FA20 | 307/513 | F-WWFB | F900 | 71 | F-WWFE | F9EX | 221 |
| F-WQBM | F900 | 164 | F-WRQT | FA20 | 309/514 | F-WWFB | F900 | 89 | F-WWFE | F9EX | 233 |

| **F-WWFE** | **F9EX** | **248** |
|---|---|---|
| F-WWFE | F9EX | 32 |
| F-WWFE | F9EX | 43 |
| F-WWFE | F9EX | 70 |
| F-WWFE | F9EX | 87 |
| F-WWFE | F9EX | 9 |
| F-WWFF | F900 | 10 |
| F-WWFF | F900 | 122 |
| F-WWFF | F900 | 137 |
| F-WWFF | F900 | 146 |
| F-WWFF | F900 | 161 |
| F-WWFF | F900 | 178 |
| F-WWFF | F900 | 185 |
| F-WWFF | F900 | 202 |
| F-WWFF | F900 | 25 |
| F-WWFF | F900 | 39 |
| F-WWFF | F900 | 63 |
| F-WWFF | F900 | 72 |
| F-WWFF | F900 | 74 |
| F-WWFF | F900 | 96 |
| F-WWFF | F9DX | 606 |
| F-WWFF | F9EX | 108 |
| F-WWFF | F9EX | 129 |
| F-WWFF | F9EX | 190 |
| F-WWFF | F9EX | 198 |
| F-WWFF | F9EX | 222 |
| F-WWFF | F9EX | 235 |
| **F-WWFF** | **F9EX** | **251** |
| F-WWFF | F9EX | 33 |
| F-WWFF | F9EX | 58 |
| F-WWFF | F9EX | 88 |
| F-WWFG | F900 | 124 |
| F-WWFG | F900 | 139 |
| F-WWFG | F900 | 147 |
| F-WWFG | F900 | 166 |
| F-WWFG | F900 | 200 |
| F-WWFG | F900 | 32 |
| F-WWFG | F900 | 51 |
| F-WWFG | F900 | 60 |
| F-WWFG | F900 | 7 |
| F-WWFG | F900 | 77 |
| F-WWFG | F900 | 83 |
| F-WWFG | F900 | 90 |
| F-WWFG | F9EX | 10 |
| F-WWFG | F9EX | 109 |
| F-WWFG | F9EX | 148 |
| F-WWFG | F9EX | 183 |
| F-WWFG | F9EX | 208 |
| F-WWFG | F9EX | 223 |
| **F-WWFG** | **F9EX** | **238** |
| F-WWFG | F9EX | 3 |
| F-WWFG | F9EX | 44 |
| F-WWFG | F9EX | 71 |
| F-WWFG | F9EX | 90 |
| F-WWFH | F900 | 110 |
| F-WWFH | F900 | 111 |
| F-WWFH | F900 | 12 |
| F-WWFH | F900 | 131 |
| F-WWFH | F900 | 133 |
| F-WWFH | F900 | 143 |
| F-WWFH | F900 | 149 |
| F-WWFH | F900 | 196 |
| F-WWFH | F900 | 27 |
| F-WWFH | F900 | 40 |
| F-WWFH | F900 | 50 |
| F-WWFH | F900 | 64 |
| F-WWFH | F900 | 78 |
| F-WWFH | F900 | 88 |
| F-WWFH | F900 | 91 |
| F-WWFH | F9DX | 617 |
| F-WWFH | F9EX | 130 |
| F-WWFH | F9EX | 149 |
| F-WWFH | F9EX | 169 |
| F-WWFH | F9EX | 181 |
| F-WWFH | F9EX | 21 |
| F-WWFH | F9EX | 214 |
| **F-WWFH** | **F9EX** | **240** |
| F-WWFH | F9EX | 59 |
| F-WWFH | F9EX | 72 |
| F-WWFH | F9EX | 89 |
| F-WWFI | F900 | 13 |
| F-WWFI | F900 | 132 |
| F-WWFI | F900 | 173 |
| F-WWFI | F900 | 190 |
| F-WWFI | F900 | 41 |
| F-WWFI | F9DX | 607 |
| F-WWFI | F9DX | 610 |

| F-WWFI | F9DX | 620 |
|---|---|---|
| F-WWFI | F9EX | 11 |
| F-WWFI | F9EX | 110 |
| F-WWFI | F9EX | 131 |
| F-WWFI | F9EX | 150 |
| F-WWFI | F9EX | 213 |
| F-WWFI | F9EX | 227 |
| **F-WWFI** | **F9EX** | **252** |
| F-WWFI | F9EX | 34 |
| F-WWFI | F9EX | 60 |
| F-WWFI | F9EX | 73 |
| F-WWFJ | F900 | 103 |
| F-WWFJ | F900 | 107 |
| F-WWFJ | F900 | 135 |
| F-WWFJ | F900 | 152 |
| F-WWFJ | F900 | 162 |
| F-WWFJ | F900 | 186 |
| F-WWFJ | F900 | 21 |
| F-WWFJ | F900 | 42 |
| F-WWFJ | F900 | 62 |
| F-WWFJ | F900 | 9 |
| F-WWFJ | F9DX | 612 |
| F-WWFJ | F9EX | 111 |
| F-WWFJ | F9EX | 12 |
| F-WWFJ | F9EX | 132 |
| F-WWFJ | F9EX | 151 |
| F-WWFJ | F9EX | 170 |
| F-WWFJ | F9EX | 19 |
| F-WWFJ | F9EX | 199 |
| F-WWFJ | F9EX | 215 |
| F-WWFJ | F9EX | 228 |
| **F-WWFJ** | **F9EX** | **244** |
| F-WWFJ | F9EX | 35 |
| F-WWFJ | F9EX | 45 |
| F-WWFJ | F9EX | 5 |
| F-WWFJ | F9EX | 91 |
| F-WWFK | F900 | 102 |
| F-WWFK | F900 | 11 |
| F-WWFK | F900 | 141 |
| F-WWFK | F900 | 145 |
| F-WWFK | F900 | 151 |
| F-WWFK | F900 | 153 |
| F-WWFK | F900 | 174 |
| F-WWFK | F900 | 183 |
| F-WWFK | F900 | 23 |
| F-WWFK | F900 | 28 |
| F-WWFK | F900 | 57 |
| F-WWFK | F9EX | 112 |
| F-WWFK | F9EX | 13 |
| F-WWFK | F9EX | 133 |
| F-WWFK | F9EX | 152 |
| F-WWFK | F9EX | 171 |
| F-WWFK | F9EX | 194 |
| F-WWFK | F9EX | 209 |
| F-WWFK | F9EX | 225 |
| F-WWFK | F9EX | 6 |
| F-WWFK | F9EX | 74 |
| F-WWFK | F9EX | 92 |
| F-WWFL | F900 | 103 |
| F-WWFL | F900 | 106 |
| F-WWFL | F900 | 115 |
| F-WWFL | F900 | 123 |
| F-WWFL | F900 | 125 |
| F-WWFL | F900 | 14 |
| F-WWFL | F900 | 140 |
| F-WWFL | F900 | 154 |
| F-WWFL | F900 | 30 |
| F-WWFL | F900 | 68 |
| F-WWFL | F900 | 81 |
| F-WWFL | F900 | 92 |
| F-WWFL | F9EX | 113 |
| F-WWFL | F9EX | 134 |
| F-WWFL | F9EX | 153 |
| F-WWFL | F9EX | 172 |
| F-WWFL | F9EX | 195 |
| F-WWFL | F9EX | 218 |
| F-WWFL | F9EX | 230 |
| F-WWFL | F9EX | 61 |
| F-WWFL | F9EX | 75 |
| F-WWFL | F9EX | 93 |
| F-WWFM | F900 | 112 |
| F-WWFM | F900 | 126 |
| F-WWFM | F900 | 128 |
| F-WWFM | F900 | 15 |
| F-WWFM | F900 | 155 |
| F-WWFM | F900 | 163 |
| F-WWFM | F900 | 191 |

| F-WWFM | F900 | 26 |
|---|---|---|
| F-WWFM | F900 | 48 |
| F-WWFM | F900 | 65 |
| F-WWFM | F900 | 79 |
| F-WWFM | F900 | 82 |
| F-WWFM | F900 | 93 |
| F-WWFM | F900 | 98 |
| F-WWFM | F9DX | 616 |
| F-WWFM | F9EX | 114 |
| F-WWFM | F9EX | 135 |
| F-WWFM | F9EX | 154 |
| F-WWFM | F9EX | 166 |
| F-WWFM | F9EX | 210 |
| **F-WWFM** | **F9EX** | **241** |
| F-WWFM | F9EX | 36 |
| F-WWFM | F9EX | 46 |
| F-WWFM | F9EX | 62 |
| F-WWFN | F900 | 100 |
| F-WWFN | F900 | 108 |
| F-WWFN | F900 | 120 |
| F-WWFN | F900 | 142 |
| F-WWFN | F900 | 16 |
| F-WWFN | F900 | 175 |
| F-WWFN | F900 | 37 |
| F-WWFN | F900 | 53 |
| F-WWFN | F900 | 70 |
| F-WWFN | F9DX | 608 |
| F-WWFN | F9EX | 115 |
| F-WWFN | F9EX | 136 |
| F-WWFN | F9EX | 14 |
| F-WWFN | F9EX | 155 |
| F-WWFN | F9EX | 184 |
| F-WWFN | F9EX | 20 |
| F-WWFN | F9EX | 211 |
| **F-WWFN** | **F9EX** | **242** |
| F-WWFN | F9EX | 7 |
| F-WWFN | F9EX | 76 |
| F-WWFN | F9EX | 94 |
| F-WWFO | F900 | 101 |
| F-WWFO | F900 | 116 |
| F-WWFO | F900 | 144 |
| F-WWFO | F900 | 167 |
| F-WWFO | F900 | 17 |
| F-WWFO | F900 | 187 |
| F-WWFO | F900 | 55 |
| F-WWFO | F900 | 95 |
| F-WWFO | F9DX | 609 |
| F-WWFO | F9DX | 618 |
| **F-WWFO** | **F9DX** | **622** |
| F-WWFO | F9EX | 116 |
| F-WWFO | F9EX | 137 |
| F-WWFO | F9EX | 15 |
| F-WWFO | F9EX | 156 |
| F-WWFO | F9EX | 47 |
| F-WWFO | F9EX | 63 |
| F-WWFO | F9EX | 95 |
| F-WWFP | F900 | 169 |
| F-WWFP | F900 | 184 |
| F-WWFP | F9DX | 611 |
| F-WWFP | F9EX | 117 |
| F-WWFP | F9EX | 138 |
| F-WWFP | F9EX | 157 |
| F-WWFP | F9EX | 167 |
| F-WWFP | F9EX | 191 |
| F-WWFP | F9EX | 229 |
| F-WWFP | F9EX | 48 |
| F-WWFP | F9EX | 96 |
| F-WWFQ | F900 | 179 |
| F-WWFQ | F900 | 192 |
| F-WWFQ | F900 | 197 |
| F-WWFQ | F9DX | 613 |
| F-WWFQ | F9EX | 139 |
| F-WWFQ | F9EX | 158 |
| F-WWFQ | F9EX | 168 |
| F-WWFQ | F9EX | 216 |
| F-WWFQ | F9EX | 22 |
| F-WWFQ | F9EX | 231 |
| **F-WWFQ** | **F9EX** | **245** |
| F-WWFQ | F9EX | 77 |
| F-WWFR | F900 | 170 |
| F-WWFR | F900 | 198 |
| F-WWFR | F9EX | 140 |
| F-WWFR | F9EX | 159 |
| F-WWFR | F9EX | 174 |
| F-WWFR | F9EX | 192 |
| **F-WWFR** | **F9EX** | **219** |
| F-WWFR | F9EX | 49 |

| F-WWFR | F9EX | 64 |
|---|---|---|
| F-WWFR | F9EX | 78 |
| F-WWFR | F9EX | 98 |
| F-WWFS | F9DX | 614 |
| **F-WWFS** | **F9DX** | **625** |
| F-WWFS | F9EX | 118 |
| F-WWFS | F9EX | 141 |
| F-WWFS | F9EX | 160 |
| F-WWFS | F9EX | 217 |
| F-WWFS | F9EX | 23 |
| F-WWFS | F9EX | 50 |
| F-WWFS | F9EX | 79 |
| F-WWFS | F9EX | 99 |
| F-WWFU | F9EX | 100 |
| F-WWFU | F9EX | 119 |
| F-WWFU | F9EX | 142 |
| F-WWFU | F9EX | 161 |
| F-WWFU | F9EX | 182 |
| F-WWFU | F9EX | 193 |
| **F-WWFU** | **F9EX** | **232** |
| F-WWFU | F9EX | 24 |
| F-WWFU | F9EX | 51 |
| F-WWFV | F900 | 193 |
| F-WWFV | F9EX | 120 |
| F-WWFV | F9EX | 143 |
| F-WWFV | F9EX | 175 |
| F-WWFV | F9EX | 185 |
| (F-WWFV) | F9EX | 218 |
| F-WWFV | F9EX | 234 |
| F-WWFV | F9EX | 25 |
| F-WWFV | F9EX | 37 |
| F-WWFV | F9EX | 52 |
| F-WWFV | F9EX | 80 |
| F-WWFW | F900 | 171 |
| F-WWFW | F900 | 176 |
| F-WWFW | F9EX | 101 |
| F-WWFW | F9EX | 121 |
| F-WWFW | F9EX | 144 |
| F-WWFW | F9EX | 162 |
| F-WWFW | F9EX | 176 |
| F-WWFW | F9EX | 188 |
| F-WWFW | F9EX | 200 |
| **F-WWFW** | **F9EX** | **236** |
| F-WWFW | F9EX | 53 |
| F-WWFW | F9EX | 65 |
| F-WWFW | F9EX | 81 |
| F-WWFX | F900 | 180 |
| F-WWFX | F9DX | 615 |
| F-WWFX | F9EX | 102 |
| F-WWFX | F9EX | 122 |
| F-WWFX | F9EX | 145 |
| F-WWFX | F9EX | 163 |
| (F-WWFX) | F9EX | 219 |
| **F-WWFX** | **F9EX** | **237** |
| F-WWFX | F9EX | 26 |
| F-WWFX | F9EX | 38 |
| F-WWFX | F9EX | 82 |
| F-WWFY | F900 | 177 |
| F-WWFY | F9DX | 624 |
| F-WWFY | F9EX | 103 |
| F-WWFY | F9EX | 123 |
| F-WWFY | F9EX | 164 |
| F-WWFY | F9EX | 186 |
| F-WWFY | F9EX | 201 |
| F-WWFY | F9EX | 27 |
| **F-WWFY** | **F9EX** | **253** |
| F-WWFY | F9EX | 54 |
| F-WWFY | F9EX | 83 |
| F-WWFZ | F900 | 181 |
| F-WWFZ | F900 | 188 |
| F-WWFZ | F900 | 194 |
| F-WWFZ | F9EX | 124 |
| F-WWFZ | F9EX | 146 |
| F-WWFZ | F9EX | 165 |
| F-WWFZ | F9EX | 177 |
| F-WWFZ | F9EX | 189 |
| (F-WWFZ) | F9EX | 220 |
| **F-WWFZ** | **F9EX** | **239** |
| F-WWFZ | F9EX | 28 |
| F-WWGA | F2EX | 130 |
| F-WWGA | F2EX | 152 |
| **F-WWGA** | **F2EX** | **192** |
| F-WWGA | F2EX | 2 |
| F-WWGA | F2EX | 44 |
| F-WWGA | F2EX | 67 |
| F-WWGA | F2EX | 97 |
| **F-WWGB** | **F2EX** | **216** |

| | | |
|---|---|---|
| F-WWGC | F2EX | 118 |
| **F-WWGC** | **F2EX** | **153** |
| F-WWGC | F2EX | 28 |
| F-WWGC | F2EX | 3 |
| F-WWGC | F2EX | 68 |
| F-WWGC | F2EX | 90 |
| F-WWGD | F2DX | 603 |
| F-WWGD | F2EX | 119 |
| F-WWGD | F2EX | 193 |
| **F-WWGD** | **F2EX** | **221** |
| F-WWGD | F2EX | 29 |
| F-WWGD | F2EX | 4 |
| F-WWGD | F2EX | 69 |
| F-WWGD | F2EX | 91 |
| F-WWGE | F2EX | 104 |
| F-WWGE | F2EX | 135 |
| F-WWGE | F2EX | 148 |
| F-WWGE | F2EX | 188 |
| **F-WWGE** | **F2EX** | **222** |
| F-WWGE | F2EX | 45 |
| F-WWGE | F2EX | 5 |
| F-WWGE | F2EX | 70 |
| F-WWGF | F2EX | 122 |
| F-WWGF | F2EX | 136 |
| **F-WWGF** | **F2EX** | **176** |
| F-WWGF | F2EX | 46 |
| F-WWGF | F2EX | 7 |
| F-WWGG | F2EX | 120 |
| F-WWGG | F2EX | 137 |
| F-WWGG | F2EX | 154 |
| **F-WWGG** | **F2EX** | **194** |
| F-WWGG | F2EX | 30 |
| F-WWGG | F2EX | 71 |
| F-WWGG | F2EX | 8 |
| F-WWGG | F2EX | 92 |
| F-WWGH | F2EX | 131 |
| F-WWGH | F2EX | 146 |
| F-WWGH | F2EX | 160 |
| **F-WWGH** | **F2EX** | **223** |
| F-WWGH | F2EX | 47 |
| F-WWGH | F2EX | 72 |
| F-WWGH | F2EX | 9 |
| F-WWGH | F2EX | 93 |
| F-WWGI | F2EX | 10 |
| F-WWGI | F2EX | 121 |
| F-WWGI | F2EX | 138 |
| F-WWGI | F2EX | 173 |
| **F-WWGI** | **F2EX** | **224** |
| F-WWGI | F2EX | 48 |
| F-WWGI | F2EX | 94 |
| F-WWGJ | F2EX | 11 |
| F-WWGJ | F2EX | 123 |
| F-WWGJ | F2EX | 149 |
| **F-WWGJ** | **F2EX** | **217** |
| F-WWGJ | F2EX | 31 |
| F-WWGJ | F2EX | 73 |
| F-WWGJ | F2EX | 95 |
| F-WWGK | F2EX | 12 |
| F-WWGK | F2EX | 124 |
| F-WWGK | F2EX | 141 |
| F-WWGK | F2EX | 174 |
| F-WWGK | F2EX | 195 |
| F-WWGK | F2EX | 32 |
| F-WWGK | F2EX | 74 |
| F-WWGL | F2EX | 13 |
| F-WWGL | F2EX | 150 |
| F-WWGL | F2EX | 165 |
| F-WWGL | F2EX | 189 |
| **F-WWGL** | **F2EX** | **218** |
| F-WWGL | F2EX | 33 |
| F-WWGL | F2EX | 75 |
| F-WWGM | F2EX | 125 |
| F-WWGM | F2EX | 14 |
| **F-WWGM** | **F2EX** | **219** |
| F-WWGM | F2EX | 34 |
| F-WWGM | F2EX | 76 |
| F-WWGN | F2EX | 132 |
| F-WWGN | F2EX | 15 |
| **F-WWGN** | **F2EX** | **166** |
| F-WWGN | F2EX | 49 |
| F-WWGN | F2EX | 77 |
| F-WWGN | F2EX | 96 |
| F-WWGO | F2EX | 126 |
| F-WWGO | F2EX | 142 |
| F-WWGO | F2EX | 16 |
| F-WWGO | F2EX | 175 |
| **F-WWGO** | **F2EX** | **196** |
| F-WWGO | F2EX | 50 |
| F-WWGO | F2EX | 78 |
| F-WWGO | FA20 | 515 |
| F-WWGP | F2EX | 133 |
| F-WWGP | F2EX | 167 |
| F-WWGP | F2EX | 17 |
| F-WWGP | F2EX | 190 |
| F-WWGP | F2EX | 51 |
| F-WWGP | F2EX | 79 |
| F-WWGP | F2EX | 98 |
| F-WWGP | FA20 | 501 |
| F-WWGP | FA20 | 514 |
| F-WWGQ | F2EX | 127 |
| F-WWGQ | F2EX | 157 |
| **F-WWGQ** | **F2EX** | **177** |
| F-WWGQ | F2EX | 18 |
| F-WWGQ | F2EX | 35 |
| F-WWGQ | F2EX | 80 |
| F-WWGR | F2EX | 105 |
| F-WWGR | F2EX | 143 |
| F-WWGR | F2EX | 19 |
| **F-WWGR** | **F2EX** | **198** |
| F-WWGR | F2EX | 36 |
| F-WWGR | F2EX | 81 |
| F-WWGR | FA20 | 511 |
| F-WWGS | F2EX | 128 |
| F-WWGS | F2EX | 158 |
| F-WWGS | F2EX | 178 |
| F-WWGS | F2EX | 199 |
| F-WWGS | F2EX | 20 |
| **F-WWGS** | **F2EX** | **225** |
| F-WWGS | F2EX | 37 |
| F-WWGS | F2EX | 82 |
| F-WWGT | F2EX | 159 |
| F-WWGT | F2EX | 21 |
| **F-WWGT** | **F2EX** | **220** |
| F-WWGT | F2EX | 38 |
| F-WWGT | F2EX | 83 |
| F-WWGU | F2EX | 106 |
| F-WWGU | F2EX | 129 |
| F-WWGU | F2EX | 147 |
| **F-WWGU** | **F2EX** | **168** |
| F-WWGU | F2EX | 22 |
| F-WWGU | F2EX | 39 |
| F-WWGU | F2EX | 84 |
| F-WWGV | F2DX | 604 |
| F-WWGV | F2EX | 107 |
| F-WWGV | F2EX | 134 |
| **F-WWGV** | **F2EX** | **226** |
| F-WWGV | F2EX | 23 |
| F-WWGV | F2EX | 40 |
| F-WWGV | F2EX | 85 |
| F-WWGW | F2EX | 108 |
| F-WWGW | F2EX | 144 |
| **F-WWGW** | **F2EX** | **183** |
| F-WWGW | F2EX | 24 |
| F-WWGW | F2EX | 41 |
| F-WWGW | F2EX | 86 |
| F-WWGX | F2EX | 109 |
| F-WWGX | F2EX | 161 |
| F-WWGX | F2EX | 25 |
| F-WWGX | F2EX | 42 |
| F-WWGX | F2EX | 87 |
| F-WWGY | F2DX | 601 |
| F-WWGY | F2EX | 169 |
| **F-WWGY** | **F2EX** | **227** |
| F-WWGY | F2EX | 26 |
| F-WWGY | F2EX | 43 |
| F-WWGY | F2EX | 88 |
| F-WWGZ | F2EX | 139 |
| F-WWGZ | F2EX | 155 |
| **F-WWGZ** | **F2EX** | **228** |
| F-WWGZ | F2EX | 27 |
| F-WWGZ | F2EX | 89 |
| F-WWHA | FA50 | 181 |
| F-WWHA | FA50 | 188 |
| F-WWHA | FA50 | 197 |
| F-WWHA | FA50 | 201 |
| F-WWHA | FA50 | 203 |
| F-WWHA | FA50 | 218 |
| F-WWHA | FA50 | 231 |
| F-WWHA | FA50 | 242 |
| F-WWHA | FA50 | 253 |
| F-WWHA | FA50 | 275 |
| F-WWHA | FA50 | 299 |
| F-WWHA | FA50 | 321 |
| F-WWHA | FA50 | 345 |
| **F-WWHA** | **FA7X** | **119** |
| F-WWHA | FA7X | 58 |
| F-WWHB | FA50 | 182 |
| F-WWHB | FA50 | 189 |
| F-WWHB | FA50 | 199 |
| F-WWHB | FA50 | 202 |
| F-WWHB | FA50 | 206 |
| F-WWHB | FA50 | 233 |
| F-WWHB | FA50 | 248 |
| F-WWHB | FA50 | 254 |
| F-WWHB | FA50 | 276 |
| F-WWHB | FA50 | 300 |
| F-WWHB | FA50 | 322 |
| F-WWHB | FA50 | 346 |
| **F-WWHB** | **FA7X** | **120** |
| F-WWHB | FA7X | 59 |
| F-WWHC | FA50 | 180 |
| F-WWHC | FA50 | 198 |
| F-WWHC | FA50 | 207 |
| F-WWHC | FA50 | 226 |
| F-WWHC | FA50 | 234 |
| F-WWHC | FA50 | 255 |
| F-WWHC | FA50 | 277 |
| F-WWHC | FA50 | 301 |
| F-WWHC | FA50 | 323 |
| F-WWHC | FA50 | 347 |
| **F-WWHC** | **FA7X** | **121** |
| F-WWHC | FA7X | 60 |
| F-WWHD | FA50 | 184 |
| F-WWHD | FA50 | 191 |
| F-WWHD | FA50 | 196 |
| F-WWHD | FA50 | 204 |
| F-WWHD | FA50 | 205 |
| F-WWHD | FA50 | 230 |
| F-WWHD | FA50 | 236 |
| F-WWHD | FA50 | 256 |
| F-WWHD | FA50 | 278 |
| F-WWHD | FA50 | 302 |
| F-WWHD | FA50 | 324 |
| F-WWHD | FA50 | 348 |
| **F-WWHD** | **FA7X** | **61** |
| F-WWHE | FA50 | 185 |
| F-WWHE | FA50 | 192 |
| F-WWHE | FA50 | 200 |
| F-WWHE | FA50 | 209 |
| F-WWHE | FA50 | 227 |
| F-WWHE | FA50 | 237 |
| F-WWHE | FA50 | 252 |
| F-WWHE | FA50 | 257 |
| F-WWHE | FA50 | 279 |
| F-WWHE | FA50 | 303 |
| F-WWHE | FA50 | 325 |
| F-WWHE | FA50 | 349 |
| F-WWHE | FA7X | 62 |
| F-WWHF | FA50 | 183 |
| F-WWHF | FA50 | 238 |
| F-WWHF | FA50 | 241 |
| F-WWHF | FA50 | 246 |
| F-WWHF | FA50 | 258 |
| F-WWHF | FA50 | 280 |
| F-WWHF | FA50 | 304 |
| F-WWHF | FA50 | 326 |
| F-WWHF | FA50 | 350 |
| F-WWHF | FA7X | 63 |
| F-WWHG | FA50 | 187 |
| F-WWHG | FA50 | 190 |
| F-WWHG | FA50 | 220 |
| F-WWHG | FA50 | 239 |
| F-WWHG | FA50 | 259 |
| F-WWHG | FA50 | 281 |
| F-WWHG | FA50 | 305 |
| F-WWHG | FA50 | 327 |
| F-WWHH | FA50 | 186 |
| F-WWHH | FA50 | 193 |
| F-WWHH | FA50 | 212 |
| F-WWHH | FA50 | 229 |
| F-WWHH | FA50 | 240 |
| F-WWHH | FA50 | 282 |
| F-WWHH | FA50 | 306 |
| F-WWHH | FA50 | 328 |
| F-WWHH | FA50 | 351 |
| F-WWHH | FA7X | 64 |
| F-WWHK | FA50 | 104 |
| F-WWHK | FA50 | 195 |
| F-WWHK | FA50 | 244 |
| F-WWHK | FA50 | 260 |
| F-WWHK | FA50 | 283 |
| F-WWHK | FA50 | 307 |
| F-WWHK | FA50 | 329 |
| F-WWHK | FA50 | 352 |
| **F-WWHK** | **FA7X** | **65** |
| F-WWHL | FA50 | 210 |
| F-WWHL | FA50 | 221 |
| F-WWHL | FA50 | 245 |
| F-WWHL | FA50 | 261 |
| F-WWHL | FA50 | 284 |
| F-WWHL | FA50 | 308 |
| F-WWHL | FA50 | 330 |
| F-WWHL | FA7X | 66 |
| F-WWHM | FA50 | 194 |
| F-WWHM | FA50 | 222 |
| F-WWHM | FA50 | 235 |
| F-WWHM | FA50 | 243 |
| F-WWHM | FA50 | 262 |
| F-WWHM | FA50 | 285 |
| F-WWHM | FA50 | 309 |
| F-WWHM | FA50 | 331 |
| **F-WWHM** | **FA7X** | **71** |
| F-WWHN | FA50 | 223 |
| F-WWHN | FA50 | 249 |
| F-WWHN | FA50 | 263 |
| F-WWHN | FA50 | 286 |
| F-WWHN | FA50 | 310 |
| F-WWHN | FA50 | 332 |
| F-WWHN | FA7X | 72 |
| F-WWHO | FA50 | 224 |
| F-WWHO | FA50 | 264 |
| F-WWHO | FA50 | 287 |
| F-WWHO | FA50 | 311 |
| F-WWHO | FA50 | 333 |
| **F-WWHO** | **FA7X** | **73** |
| F-WWHP | FA50 | 208 |
| F-WWHP | FA50 | 225 |
| F-WWHP | FA50 | 247 |
| F-WWHP | FA50 | 265 |
| F-WWHP | FA50 | 288 |
| F-WWHP | FA50 | 312 |
| F-WWHP | FA50 | 334 |
| **F-WWHP** | **FA7X** | **74** |
| F-WWHQ | FA50 | 266 |
| F-WWHQ | FA50 | 289 |
| F-WWHQ | FA50 | 335 |
| **F-WWHQ** | **FA7X** | **75** |
| F-WWHR | FA50 | 211 |
| F-WWHR | FA50 | 228 |
| F-WWHR | FA50 | 250 |
| F-WWHR | FA50 | 267 |
| F-WWHR | FA50 | 290 |
| F-WWHR | FA50 | 313 |
| F-WWHR | FA50 | 336 |
| F-WWHR | FA7X | 76 |
| F-WWHS | FA50 | 219 |
| F-WWHS | FA50 | 268 |
| F-WWHS | FA50 | 291 |
| F-WWHS | FA50 | 337 |
| F-WWHS | FA7X | 77 |
| F-WWHT | FA50 | 215 |
| F-WWHT | FA50 | 232 |
| F-WWHT | FA50 | 269 |
| F-WWHT | FA50 | 292 |
| F-WWHT | FA50 | 314 |
| F-WWHT | FA50 | 338 |
| F-WWHT | FA7X | 78 |
| F-WWHU | FA50 | 270 |
| F-WWHU | FA50 | 293 |
| F-WWHU | FA50 | 315 |
| F-WWHU | FA50 | 339 |
| **F-WWHU** | **FA7X** | **79** |
| F-WWHV | FA50 | 217 |
| F-WWHV | FA50 | 271 |
| F-WWHV | FA50 | 294 |
| F-WWHV | FA50 | 316 |
| F-WWHV | FA50 | 340 |
| F-WWHW | FA50 | 213 |
| F-WWHW | FA50 | 272 |
| F-WWHW | FA50 | 295 |
| F-WWHW | FA50 | 317 |
| F-WWHW | FA50 | 341 |
| F-WWHX | FA50 | 214 |
| F-WWHX | FA50 | 273 |
| F-WWHX | FA50 | 296 |
| F-WWHX | FA50 | 318 |
| F-WWHX | FA50 | 342 |
| F-WWHY | FA50 | 274 |

| | | |
|---|---|---|
| F-WWHY | FA50 | 297 |
| F-WWHY | FA50 | 319 |
| F-WWHY | FA50 | 343 |
| F-WWHZ | FA50 | 216 |
| F-WWHZ | FA50 | 298 |
| F-WWHZ | FA50 | 320 |
| F-WWHZ | FA50 | 344 |
| F-WWHZ | FA50 | 36 |
| F-WWJC | F9EX | 4 |
| F-WWJN | F2EX | 204 |
| F-WWJO | F2EX | 205 |
| F-WWJP | F2EX | 206 |
| **F-WWJQ** | **F2EX** | **207** |
| F-WWJR | F2EX | 208 |
| **F-WWJS** | **F2EX** | **209** |
| F-WWJT | F2EX | 210 |
| F-WWJU | F2EX | 211 |
| **F-WWJV** | **F2EX** | **212** |
| **F-WWJX** | **F2EX** | **213** |
| **F-WWJY** | **F2EX** | **214** |
| **F-WWJZ** | **F2EX** | **215** |
| F-WWMA | F2EX | 140 |
| F-WWMA | F2EX | 179 |
| **F-WWMA** | **F2EX** | **202** |
| F-WWMA | F2EX | 52 |
| F-WWMA | F2EX | 99 |
| F-WWMA | F2TH | 17 |
| F-WWMA | F2TH | 174 |
| F-WWMA | F2TH | 21 |
| F-WWMA | F2TH | 29 |
| F-WWMA | F2TH | 36 |
| F-WWMA | F2TH | 4 |
| F-WWMA | F2TH | 57 |
| F-WWMA | F2TH | 69 |
| F-WWMB | F2EX | 100 |
| F-WWMB | F2EX | 145 |
| **F-WWMB** | **F2EX** | **162** |
| F-WWMB | F2EX | 53 |
| F-WWMB | F2TH | 16 |
| F-WWMB | F2TH | 175 |
| F-WWMB | F2TH | 189 |
| F-WWMB | F2TH | 30 |
| F-WWMB | F2TH | 47 |
| F-WWMB | F2TH | 5 |
| F-WWMB | F2TH | 58 |
| F-WWMB | F2TH | 70 |
| F-WWMC | F2DX | 602 |
| F-WWMC | F2EX | 101 |
| F-WWMC | F2EX | 163 |
| F-WWMC | F2EX | 184 |
| F-WWMC | F2EX | 54 |
| F-WWMC | F2TH | 176 |
| F-WWMC | F2TH | 19 |
| F-WWMC | F2TH | 31 |
| F-WWMC | F2TH | 48 |
| F-WWMC | F2TH | 59 |
| F-WWMC | F2TH | 71 |
| F-WWMD | F2EX | 102 |
| F-WWMD | F2EX | 151 |
| F-WWMD | F2EX | 191 |
| F-WWMD | F2EX | 55 |
| F-WWMD | F2TH | 177 |
| F-WWMD | F2TH | 188 |
| F-WWMD | F2TH | 32 |
| F-WWMD | F2TH | 41 |
| F-WWMD | F2TH | 49 |
| F-WWMD | F2TH | 6 |
| F-WWMD | F2TH | 60 |
| F-WWMD | F2TH | 72 |
| F-WWME | F2EX | 103 |
| F-WWME | F2EX | 156 |
| **F-WWME** | **F2EX** | **200** |
| F-WWME | F2EX | 56 |
| F-WWME | F2TH | 178 |
| F-WWME | F2TH | 20 |
| F-WWME | F2TH | 33 |
| F-WWME | F2TH | 50 |
| F-WWME | F2TH | 61 |
| F-WWME | F2TH | 7 |
| F-WWMF | F2EX | 164 |
| **F-WWMF** | **F2EX** | **197** |
| F-WWMF | F2EX | 57 |
| F-WWMF | F2TH | 179 |
| F-WWMF | F2TH | 22 |
| F-WWMF | F2TH | 34 |
| F-WWMF | F2TH | 51 |
| F-WWMF | F2TH | 62 |
| F-WWMF | F2TH | 8 |
| F-WWMG | F2EX | 110 |
| F-WWMG | F2EX | 170 |
| F-WWMG | F2EX | 201 |
| F-WWMG | F2EX | 58 |
| F-WWMG | F2TH | 18 |
| F-WWMG | F2TH | 180 |
| F-WWMG | F2TH | 35 |
| F-WWMG | F2TH | 42 |
| F-WWMG | F2TH | 63 |
| F-WWMG | F2TH | 73 |
| F-WWMG | F2TH | 9 |
| F-WWMH | F2EX | 111 |
| F-WWMH | F2EX | 171 |
| F-WWMH | F2EX | 203 |
| F-WWMH | F2EX | 59 |
| F-WWMH | F2TH | 10 |
| F-WWMH | F2TH | 181 |
| F-WWMH | F2TH | 23 |
| F-WWMH | F2TH | 37 |
| F-WWMH | F2TH | 64 |
| F-WWMH | F2TH | 74 |
| F-WWMI | F2EX | 112 |
| **F-WWMI** | **F2EX** | **172** |
| F-WWMI | F2EX | 60 |
| F-WWMI | F2TH | 182 |
| F-WWMI | F2TH | 38 |
| F-WWMI | F2TH | 52 |
| F-WWMI | F2TH | 65 |
| F-WWMJ | F2EX | 113 |
| (F-WWMJ) | F2EX | 173 |
| F-WWMJ | F2EX | 180 |
| F-WWMJ | F2EX | 61 |
| F-WWMJ | F2TH | 183 |
| F-WWMJ | F2TH | 39 |
| F-WWMJ | F2TH | 53 |
| F-WWMJ | F2TH | 66 |
| F-WWMJ | F2TH | 78 |
| F-WWMK | F2EX | 114 |
| (F-WWMK) | F2EX | 174 |
| F-WWMK | F2EX | 181 |
| F-WWMK | F2EX | 62 |
| F-WWMK | F2TH | 11 |
| F-WWMK | F2TH | 184 |
| F-WWMK | F2TH | 24 |
| F-WWMK | F2TH | 40 |
| F-WWMK | F2TH | 43 |
| F-WWMK | F2TH | 67 |
| F-WWMK | F2TH | 75 |
| F-WWML | F2EX | 115 |
| (F-WWML) | F2EX | 175 |
| F-WWML | F2EX | 182 |
| F-WWML | F2EX | 63 |
| F-WWML | F2TH | 13 |
| F-WWML | F2TH | 185 |
| F-WWML | F2TH | 25 |
| F-WWML | F2TH | 44 |
| F-WWML | F2TH | 54 |
| F-WWML | F2TH | 76 |
| F-WWMM | F2EX | 116 |
| (F-WWMM) | F2EX | 176 |
| F-WWMM | F2EX | 185 |
| F-WWMM | F2EX | 64 |
| F-WWMM | F2TH | 12 |
| F-WWMM | F2TH | 186 |
| F-WWMM | F2TH | 27 |
| F-WWMM | F2TH | 45 |
| F-WWMM | F2TH | 55 |
| F-WWMM | F2TH | 77 |
| (F-WWMN) | F2EX | 177 |
| **F-WWMN** | **F2EX** | **186** |
| F-WWMN | F2EX | 65 |
| F-WWMN | F2TH | 14 |
| F-WWMN | F2TH | 187 |
| F-WWMN | F2TH | 26 |
| F-WWMN | F2TH | 46 |
| F-WWMN | F2TH | 68 |
| F-WWMN | F2TH | 79 |
| F-WWMO | F2EX | 117 |
| (F-WWMO) | F2EX | 178 |
| F-WWMO | F2EX | 187 |
| F-WWMO | F2EX | 66 |
| F-WWMO | F2TH | 15 |
| F-WWMO | F2TH | 28 |
| F-WWMO | F2TH | 56 |
| F-WWMO | F2TH | 80 |
| **F-WWNA** | **FA7X** | **98** |
| **F-WWNB** | **FA7X** | **99** |
| **F-WWNC** | **FA7X** | **100** |
| **F-WWND** | **FA7X** | **101** |
| **F-WWNE** | **FA7X** | **102** |
| **F-WWNF** | **FA7X** | **103** |
| F-WWUA | FA7X | 4 |
| **F-WWUA** | **FA7X** | **49** |
| F-WWUB | FA7X | 5 |
| F-WWUB | FA7X | 50 |
| F-WWUC | FA7X | 51 |
| F-WWUC | FA7X | 6 |
| F-WWUD | FA7X | 52 |
| F-WWUD | FA7X | 7 |
| **F-WWUE** | **FA7X** | **67** |
| F-WWUE | FA7X | 8 |
| **F-WWUF** | **FA7X** | **80** |
| F-WWUF | FA7X | 9 |
| F-WWUG | FA7X | 10 |
| F-WWUG | FA7X | 68 |
| F-WWUH | FA7X | 11 |
| F-WWUH | FA7X | 69 |
| F-WWUI | FA7X | 12 |
| **F-WWUI** | **FA7X** | **81** |
| F-WWUJ | FA7X | 13 |
| F-WWUJ | FA7X | 70 |
| F-WWUK | FA7X | 14 |
| **F-WWUK** | **FA7X** | **82** |
| F-WWUL | FA7X | 15 |
| F-WWUL | FA7X | 83 |
| F-WWUM | FA7X | 16 |
| **F-WWUM** | **FA7X** | **84** |
| F-WWUN | FA7X | 17 |
| **F-WWUN** | **FA7X** | **85** |
| F-WWUO | FA7X | 18 |
| **F-WWUO** | **FA7X** | **87** |
| F-WWUP | FA7X | 19 |
| **F-WWUP** | **FA7X** | **88** |
| F-WWUQ | FA7X | 20 |
| **F-WWUQ** | **FA7X** | **89** |
| F-WWUR | FA7X | 21 |
| **F-WWUR** | **FA7X** | **90** |
| F-WWUS | FA7X | 22 |
| **F-WWUS** | **FA7X** | **86** |
| F-WWVA | F2TH | 106 |
| F-WWVA | F2TH | 146 |
| F-WWVA | F2TH | 161 |
| F-WWVA | F2TH | 190 |
| F-WWVA | F2TH | 213 |
| F-WWVA | F2TH | 81 |
| F-WWVA | F9EX | 196 |
| (F-WWVA) | F9EX | 221 |
| **F-WWVA** | **F9EX** | **243** |
| F-WWVB | F2TH | 107 |
| F-WWVB | F2TH | 147 |
| F-WWVB | F2TH | 191 |
| F-WWVB | F2TH | 214 |
| F-WWVB | F2TH | 82 |
| F-WWVB | F9DX | 619 |
| **F-WWVB** | **F9EX** | **254** |
| F-WWVC | F2TH | 108 |
| F-WWVC | F2TH | 148 |
| F-WWVC | F2TH | 170 |
| F-WWVC | F2TH | 192 |
| F-WWVC | F2TH | 215 |
| F-WWVC | F2TH | 83 |
| F-WWVC | F9EX | 202 |
| **F-WWVC** | **F9EX** | **255** |
| F-WWVD | F2TH | 109 |
| F-WWVD | F2TH | 129 |
| F-WWVD | F2TH | 166 |
| F-WWVD | F2TH | 216 |
| F-WWVD | F2TH | 84 |
| F-WWVD | F9EX | 203 |
| **F-WWVD** | **F9EX** | **256** |
| F-WWVE | F2TH | 110 |
| F-WWVE | F2TH | 130 |
| F-WWVE | F2TH | 165 |
| F-WWVE | F2TH | 193 |
| F-WWVE | F2TH | 217 |
| F-WWVE | F2TH | 85 |
| F-WWVE | F9EX | 204 |
| **F-WWVE** | **F9EX** | **257** |
| F-WWVF | F2TH | 111 |
| F-WWVF | F2TH | 134 |
| F-WWVF | F2TH | 194 |
| F-WWVF | F2TH | 218 |
| F-WWVF | F2TH | 86 |
| (F-WWVF) | F9EX | 222 |
| F-WWVG | F2TH | 112 |
| F-WWVG | F2TH | 131 |
| F-WWVG | F2TH | 149 |
| F-WWVG | F2TH | 167 |
| F-WWVG | F2TH | 219 |
| F-WWVG | F2TH | 87 |
| (F-WWVG) | F9EX | 223 |
| F-WWVH | F2TH | 113 |
| F-WWVH | F2TH | 132 |
| F-WWVH | F2TH | 150 |
| F-WWVH | F2TH | 195 |
| F-WWVH | F2TH | 220 |
| F-WWVH | F2TH | 88 |
| (F-WWVH) | F9EX | 224 |
| F-WWVI | F2TH | 114 |
| F-WWVI | F2TH | 133 |
| F-WWVI | F2TH | 151 |
| F-WWVI | F2TH | 196 |
| F-WWVI | F2TH | 221 |
| F-WWVI | F2TH | 89 |
| (F-WWVI) | F9EX | 225 |
| F-WWVJ | F2TH | 135 |
| F-WWVJ | F2TH | 152 |
| F-WWVJ | F2TH | 169 |
| F-WWVJ | F2TH | 197 |
| F-WWVJ | F2TH | 222 |
| F-WWVJ | F2TH | 90 |
| F-WWVJ | F9EX | 226 |
| F-WWVK | F2TH | 115 |
| F-WWVK | F2TH | 153 |
| F-WWVK | F2TH | 171 |
| F-WWVK | F2TH | 223 |
| F-WWVK | F2TH | 91 |
| **F-WWVK** | **FA7X** | **112** |
| F-WWVK | FA7X | 39 |
| F-WWVL | F2TH | 116 |
| F-WWVL | F2TH | 136 |
| F-WWVL | F2TH | 154 |
| F-WWVL | F2TH | 198 |
| F-WWVL | F2TH | 224 |
| F-WWVL | F2TH | 92 |
| **F-WWVL** | **FA7X** | **109** |
| F-WWVL | FA7X | 40 |
| F-WWVM | F2TH | 117 |
| F-WWVM | F2TH | 137 |
| F-WWVM | F2TH | 155 |
| F-WWVM | F2TH | 199 |
| F-WWVM | F2TH | 225 |
| F-WWVM | F2TH | 93 |
| **F-WWVM** | **FA7X** | **110** |
| F-WWVM | FA7X | 41 |
| F-WWVN | F2TH | 118 |
| F-WWVN | F2TH | 138 |
| F-WWVN | F2TH | 156 |
| F-WWVN | F2TH | 172 |
| F-WWVN | F2TH | 200 |
| F-WWVN | F2TH | 226 |
| F-WWVN | F2TH | 94 |
| **F-WWVN** | **FA7X** | **111** |
| F-WWVN | FA7X | 42 |
| F-WWVO | F2TH | 119 |
| F-WWVO | F2TH | 157 |
| F-WWVO | F2TH | 201 |
| F-WWVO | F2TH | 227 |
| F-WWVO | F2TH | 95 |
| **F-WWVO** | **FA7X** | **104** |
| F-WWVO | FA7X | 43 |
| F-WWVP | F2TH | 120 |
| F-WWVP | F2TH | 158 |
| F-WWVP | F2TH | 202 |
| F-WWVP | F2TH | 228 |
| F-WWVP | F2TH | 96 |
| **F-WWVP** | **FA7X** | **113** |
| F-WWVP | FA7X | 44 |
| F-WWVQ | F2TH | 121 |
| F-WWVQ | F2TH | 159 |
| F-WWVQ | F2TH | 203 |
| F-WWVQ | F2TH | 229 |
| F-WWVQ | F2TH | 97 |
| **F-WWVQ** | **FA7X** | **45** |
| F-WWVR | F2TH | 122 |
| F-WWVR | F2TH | 139 |
| F-WWVR | F2TH | 173 |
| F-WWVR | F2TH | 204 |
| F-WWVR | F2TH | 230 |
| F-WWVR | F2TH | 98 |

| | | | | | | | | | | | |
|---|---|---|---|---|---|---|---|---|---|---|---|
| **F-WWVR** | **FA7X** | **105** | F-WZGB | FA10 | 196 | F-WZGX | FA10 | 192 | F-WZHH | FA50 | 75 |
| F-WWVR | FA7X | 46 | F-WZGB | FA10 | 218 | F-WZGX | FA10 | 214 | F-WZHI | FA50 | 126 |
| F-WWVS | F2TH | 123 | F-WZGC | FA10 | 131 | F-WZGY | FA10 | 152 | F-WZHI | FA50 | 143 |
| F-WWVS | F2TH | 205 | F-WZGC | FA10 | 155 | F-WZGY | FA10 | 171 | F-WZHI | FA50 | 160 |
| F-WWVS | F2TH | 231 | F-WZGC | FA10 | 181 | F-WZGY | FA10 | 193 | F-WZHI | FA50 | 17 |
| F-WWVS | F2TH | 99 | F-WZGC | FA10 | 197 | F-WZGY | FA10 | 215 | F-WZHI | FA50 | 170 |
| **F-WWVS** | **FA7X** | **47** | F-WZGC | FA10 | 219 | F-WZGZ | FA10 | 153 | F-WZHI | FA50 | 25 |
| F-WWVT | F2TH | 100 | F-WZGD | FA10 | 132 | F-WZGZ | FA10 | 172 | F-WZHI | FA50 | 41 |
| F-WWVT | F2TH | 140 | F-WZGD | FA10 | 202 | F-WZGZ | FA10 | 194 | F-WZHI | FA50 | 61 |
| F-WWVT | F2TH | 206 | F-WZGD | FA10 | 220 | F-WZGZ | FA10 | 216 | F-WZHJ | FA50 | 149 |
| F-WWVT | FA7X | 48 | F-WZGD | FA10 | 61 | F-WZHA | FA50 | 112 | F-WZHJ | FA50 | 171 |
| F-WWVU | F2TH | 101 | F-WZGE | FA10 | 133 | F-WZHA | FA50 | 124 | F-WZHJ | FA50 | 18 |
| F-WWVU | F2TH | 124 | F-WZGE | FA10 | 156 | F-WZHA | FA50 | 135 | F-WZHJ | FA50 | 32 |
| F-WWVU | F2TH | 141 | F-WZGE | FA10 | 174 | F-WZHA | FA50 | 146 | F-WZHJ | FA50 | 36 |
| F-WWVU | F2TH | 162 | F-WZGF | FA10 | 108 | F-WZHA | FA50 | 154 | F-WZHJ | FA50 | 69 |
| F-WWVU | F2TH | 207 | F-WZGF | FA10 | 134 | F-WZHA | FA50 | 161 | F-WZHJ | FA50 | 83 |
| F-WWVU | FA7X | 53 | F-WZGF | FA10 | 157 | F-WZHA | FA50 | 163 | F-WZHK | FA50 | 142 |
| F-WWVV | F2TH | 102 | F-WZGF | FA10 | 175 | F-WZHA | FA50 | 26 | F-WZHK | FA50 | 172 |
| F-WWVV | F2TH | 125 | F-WZGF | FA10 | 198 | F-WZHA | FA50 | 33 | F-WZHK | FA50 | 20 |
| F-WWVV | F2TH | 142 | F-WZGF | FA10 | 222 | F-WZHA | FA50 | 4 | F-WZHK | FA50 | 38 |
| F-WWVV | F2TH | 168 | F-WZGF | FA10 | 89 | F-WZHA | FA50 | 44 | F-WZHK | FA50 | 46 |
| F-WWVV | F2TH | 208 | F-WZGG | FA10 | 127 | F-WZHA | FA50 | 58 | F-WZHK | FA50 | 48 |
| F-WWVV | FA7X | 54 | F-WZGG | FA10 | 135 | F-WZHA | FA50 | 7 | F-WZHK | FA50 | 84 |
| F-WWVW | F2TH | 126 | F-WZGG | FA10 | 199 | F-WZHA | FA50 | 74 | F-WZHL | FA50 | 144 |
| F-WWVW | F2TH | 143 | F-WZGG | FA10 | 200 | F-WZHA | FA50 | 81 | F-WZHL | FA50 | 173 |
| F-WWVW | F2TH | 163 | F-WZGG | FA10 | 223 | F-WZHB | FA50 | 113 | F-WZHL | FA50 | 24 |
| F-WWVW | F2TH | 209 | F-WZGH | FA10 | 136 | F-WZHB | FA50 | 125 | F-WZHL | FA50 | 39 |
| F-WWVX | F2TH | 103 | F-WZGH | FA10 | 201 | F-WZHB | FA50 | 136 | F-WZHL | FA50 | 49 |
| F-WWVX | F2TH | 144 | F-WZGH | FA10 | 221 | F-WZHB | FA50 | 148 | F-WZHL | FA50 | 70 |
| F-WWVX | F2TH | 210 | F-WZGH | FA10 | 224 | F-WZHB | FA50 | 162 | F-WZHL | FA50 | 97 |
| F-WWVX | FA7X | 55 | F-WZGI | FA10 | 137 | F-WZHB | FA50 | 19 | F-WZHM | FA50 | 108 |
| F-WWVY | F2TH | 104 | F-WZGI | FA10 | 158 | F-WZHB | FA50 | 29 | F-WZHM | FA50 | 15 |
| F-WWVY | F2TH | 127 | F-WZGI | FA10 | 176 | (F-WZHB) | FA50 | 5 | F-WZHM | FA50 | 175 |
| F-WWVY | F2TH | 164 | F-WZGI | FA10 | 225 | F-WZHB | FA50 | 59 | F-WZHM | FA50 | 37 |
| F-WWVY | F2TH | 211 | F-WZGJ | FA10 | 138 | F-WZHB | FA50 | 6 | F-WZHM | FA50 | 72 |
| F-WWVY | FA7X | 56 | F-WZGJ | FA10 | 159 | F-WZHB | FA50 | 76 | F-WZHM | FA50 | 99 |
| F-WWVZ | F2TH | 105 | F-WZGJ | FA10 | 177 | F-WZHB | FA50 | 93 | F-WZHN | FA50 | 100 |
| F-WWVZ | F2TH | 128 | F-WZGJ | FA10 | 203 | F-WZHC | FA50 | 115 | F-WZHN | FA50 | 119 |
| F-WWVZ | F2TH | 145 | F-WZGJ | FA10 | 226 | F-WZHC | FA50 | 12 | F-WZHN | FA50 | 176 |
| F-WWVZ | F2TH | 160 | F-WZGK | FA10 | 139 | F-WZHC | FA50 | 137 | F-WZHN | FA50 | 21 |
| F-WWVZ | F2TH | 212 | F-WZGK | FA10 | 160 | F-WZHC | FA50 | 150 | F-WZHN | FA50 | 27 |
| F-WWVZ | FA7X | 57 | F-WZGK | FA10 | 178 | F-WZHC | FA50 | 159 | F-WZHN | FA50 | 80 |
| F-WWZK | FA10 | 161 | F-WZGK | FA10 | 204 | F-WZHC | FA50 | 31 | F-WZHO | FA50 | 102 |
| **F-WWZK** | **FA7X** | **106** | F-WZGL | FA10 | 140 | F-WZHC | FA50 | 57 | F-WZHO | FA50 | 121 |
| F-WWZK | FA7X | 23 | F-WZGL | FA10 | 179 | F-WZHC | FA50 | 77 | F-WZHO | FA50 | 178 |
| F-WWZL | FA10 | 195 | F-WZGL | FA10 | 205 | F-WZHC | FA50 | 8 | F-WZHO | FA50 | 43 |
| F-WWZL | FA7X | 24 | F-WZGM | FA10 | 141 | F-WZHC | FA50 | 94 | F-WZHO | FA50 | 85 |
| **F-WWZL** | **FA7X** | **91** | F-WZGM | FA10 | 161 | F-WZHD | FA50 | 10 | F-WZHP | FA50 | 179 |
| F-WWZM | FA10 | 212 | F-WZGM | FA10 | 180 | F-WZHD | FA50 | 116 | F-WZHP | FA50 | 47 |
| F-WWZM | FA7X | 25 | F-WZGM | FA10 | 206 | F-WZHD | FA50 | 127 | F-WZHP | FA50 | 66 |
| **F-WWZM** | **FA7X** | **92** | F-WZGN | FA10 | 142 | F-WZHD | FA50 | 139 | F-WZHQ | FA50 | 103 |
| F-WWZN | FA10 | 224 | F-WZGN | FA10 | 162 | F-WZHD | FA50 | 152 | F-WZHQ | FA50 | 129 |
| F-WWZN | FA7X | 26 | F-WZGN | FA10 | 182 | F-WZHD | FA50 | 164 | F-WZHQ | FA50 | 50 |
| **F-WWZN** | **FA7X** | **93** | F-WZGN | FA10 | 207 | F-WZHD | FA50 | 30 | F-WZHQ | FA50 | 68 |
| **F-WWZO** | **FA7X** | **114** | F-WZGO | FA10 | 143 | F-WZHD | FA50 | 60 | F-WZHR | FA50 | 104 |
| F-WWZO | FA7X | 27 | F-WZGO | FA10 | 183 | F-WZHD | FA50 | 9 | F-WZHR | FA50 | 130 |
| **F-WWZP** | **FA7X** | **28** | F-WZGO | FA10 | 208 | F-WZHE | FA50 | 11 | F-WZHR | FA50 | 51 |
| F-WWZQ | FA7X | 29 | F-WZGP | FA10 | 144 | F-WZHE | FA50 | 141 | F-WZHR | FA50 | 56 |
| **F-WWZQ** | **FA7X** | **94** | F-WZGP | FA10 | 163 | F-WZHE | FA50 | 153 | F-WZHS | FA50 | 105 |
| **F-WWZR** | **FA7X** | **107** | F-WZGP | FA10 | 184 | F-WZHE | FA50 | 166 | F-WZHS | FA50 | 53 |
| F-WWZR | FA7X | 30 | F-WZGP | FA10 | 209 | F-WZHE | FA50 | 28 | F-WZHS | FA50 | 87 |
| **F-WWZS** | **FA7X** | **108** | F-WZGQ | FA10 | 145 | F-WZHE | FA50 | 42 | F-WZHT | FA50 | 106 |
| F-WWZS | FA7X | 31 | F-WZGQ | FA10 | 164 | F-WZHE | FA50 | 62 | F-WZHT | FA50 | 54 |
| F-WWZT | FA7X | 32 | F-WZGQ | FA10 | 185 | F-WZHE | FA50 | 79 | F-WZHT | FA50 | 65 |
| **F-WWZT** | **FA7X** | **95** | F-WZGR | FA10 | 146 | F-WZHF | FA50 | 118 | F-WZHU | FA50 | 55 |
| F-WWZU | FA7X | 33 | F-WZGR | FA10 | 165 | F-WZHF | FA50 | 128 | F-WZHU | FA50 | 88 |
| **F-WWZU** | **FA7X** | **96** | F-WZGR | FA10 | 187 | F-WZHF | FA50 | 13 | F-WZHV | FA50 | 109 |
| **F-WWZV** | **FA7X** | **117** | F-WZGR | FA10 | 210 | F-WZHF | FA50 | 156 | F-WZHV | FA50 | 52 |
| F-WWZV | FA7X | 34 | F-WZGS | FA10 | 126 | F-WZHF | FA50 | 165 | F-WZHV | FA50 | 89 |
| **F-WWZW** | **FA7X** | **115** | F-WZGS | FA10 | 136 | F-WZHF | FA50 | 22 | F-WZHX | FA50 | 90 |
| F-WWZW | FA7X | 35 | F-WZGS | FA10 | 147 | F-WZHF | FA50 | 35 | F-WZHY | FA50 | 91 |
| F-WWZX | FA7X | 36 | F-WZGS | FA10 | 166 | F-WZHF | FA50 | 45 | F-WZHZ | FA50 | 111 |
| **F-WWZX** | **FA7X** | **97** | F-WZGS | FA10 | 188 | F-WZHF | FA50 | 63 | F-WZHZ | FA50 | 92 |
| **F-WWZY** | **FA7X** | **116** | F-WZGT | FA10 | 148 | F-WZHF | FA50 | 71 | F-WZIG | HS25 | 257055 |
| F-WWZY | FA7X | 37 | F-WZGT | FA10 | 167 | F-WZHG | FA50 | 122 | F-WZIH | HFB3 | 1024 |
| **F-WWZZ** | **FA7X** | **118** | F-WZGT | FA10 | 189 | F-WZHG | FA50 | 14 | F-WZSB | CRVT | 31 |
| F-WWZZ | FA7X | 38 | F-WZGT | FA10 | 211 | F-WZHG | FA50 | 167 | F-WZZA | FA20 | 491 |
| **F-WXEY** | **F2EX** | **6** | F-WZGU | FA10 | 149 | F-WZHG | FA50 | 23 | F-WZZA | FA20 | 497 |
| F-WZAH | FA20 | 401 | F-WZGU | FA10 | 168 | F-WZHG | FA50 | 40 | F-WZZA | FA20 | 505 |
| (F-WZAS) | FA20 | 362 | F-WZGU | FA10 | 190 | F-WZHG | FA50 | 67 | F-WZZB | FA20 | 487 |
| F-WZGA | FA10 | 129 | F-WZGU | FA10 | 212 | F-WZHG | FA50 | 82 | F-WZZC | FA20 | 493 |
| F-WZGA | FA10 | 154 | F-WZGV | FA10 | 150 | F-WZHH | FA50 | 123 | F-WZZC | FA20 | 496 |
| F-WZGA | FA10 | 173 | F-WZGV | FA10 | 169 | F-WZHH | FA50 | 158 | F-WZZD | FA20 | 494 |
| F-WZGA | FA10 | 195 | F-WZGV | FA10 | 191 | F-WZHH | FA50 | 16 | F-WZZD | FA20 | 501 |
| F-WZGA | FA10 | 217 | F-WZGV | FA10 | 213 | F-WZHH | FA50 | 168 | F-WZZE | FA20 | 495 |
| F-WZGB | FA10 | 130 | F-WZGX | FA10 | 151 | F-WZHH | FA50 | 34 | F-WZZF | FA20 | 488 |
| F-WZGB | FA10 | 186 | F-WZGX | FA10 | 170 | F-WZHH | FA50 | 64 | F-WZZJ | FA20 | 499 |

France - Govt etc

| | | |
|---|---|---|
| (F-Z...) | MS76 | 03 |
| **F-ZACA** | **FA20** | **252/485** |
| F-ZACB | FA10 | 02 |
| **F-ZACB** | **FA20** | **96** |
| F-ZACC | FA20 | 124/433 |
| **F-ZACD** | **FA20** | **31/437** |
| **F-ZACG** | **FA20** | **86** |
| **F-ZACR** | **FA20** | **138/440** |
| F-ZACS | FA20 | 22/404 |
| **F-ZACT** | **FA20** | **79/415** |
| **F-ZACU** | **FA20** | **145/443** |
| F-ZACV | FA20 | 1/401 |
| **F-ZACV** | **FA20** | **288/499** |
| **F-ZACW** | **FA20** | **104/454** |
| **F-ZACX** | **FA20** | **188/464** |
| **F-ZACY** | **FA20** | **263/489** |
| **F-ZACZ** | **FA20** | **375/547** |
| F-ZADS | MS76 | 001 |
| F-ZGTI | FA10 | 133 |
| **F-ZJAZ** | **MS76** | **117** |
| **F-ZJNB** | **MS76** | **068** |
| F-ZJNC | MS76 | 083 |
| **F-ZJNI** | **MS76** | **113** |
| F-ZJNJ | MS76 | 100 |
| F-ZJNJ | MS76 | 114 |
| **F-ZJNQ** | **MS76** | **118** |
| **F-ZJON** | **MS76** | **116** |
| **F-ZJOV** | **MS76** | **115** |
| **F-ZJSA** | **FA20** | **480** |
| F-ZJTA | FA10 | 02 |
| F-ZJTA | FA20 | 182/461 |
| F-ZJTD | FA20 | 476 |
| F-ZJTJ | FA20 | 422 |
| F-ZJTL | FA50 | 36 |
| F-ZJTS | FA20 | 451 |
| **F-ZJTS** | **FA20** | **465** |
| F-ZLNL | MS76 | 119 |
| F-ZVMV | CRVT | 1 |
| F-ZVMW | CRVT | 2 |
| F-ZVMX | CRVT | 10 |
| **F-ZWVF** | **FA20** | **448** |
| F-ZWTA | FA50 | 36 |
| **F-ZWVF** | **FA20** | **448** |

United Kingdom Class B

| | | |
|---|---|---|
| G-5-11 | HS25 | 25026 |
| G-5-11 | HS25 | 25101 |
| G-5-11 | HS25 | 25110 |
| G-5-11 | HS25 | 25119 |
| G-5-11 | HS25 | 25126 |
| G-5-11 | HS25 | 25131 |
| G-5-11 | HS25 | 25134 |
| G-5-11 | HS25 | 25137 |
| G-5-11 | HS25 | 25139 |
| G-5-11 | HS25 | 25154 |
| G-5-11 | HS25 | 25197 |
| G-5-11 | HS25 | 25240 |
| G-5-11 | HS25 | 25276 |
| G-5-11 | HS25 | 256015 |
| G-5-11 | HS25 | 256021 |
| G-5-11 | HS25 | 256045 |
| G-5-11 | HS25 | 256052 |
| G-5-11 | HS25 | 256070 |
| G-5-11 | HS25 | 257008 |
| (G-5-11) | HS25 | 257022 |
| G-5-11 | HS25 | 257039 |
| G-5-11 | HS25 | 257051 |
| G-5-11 | HS25 | 257065 |
| G-5-11 | HS25 | 257093 |
| G-5-11 | HS25 | 257105 |
| G-5-11 | HS25 | 257119 |
| G-5-11 | HS25 | 257131 |
| G-5-11 | HS25 | 257144 |
| G-5-11 | HS25 | 257150 |
| G-5-11 | HS25 | 257164 |
| G-5-11 | HS25 | 257177 |
| G-5-11 | HS25 | 257186 |
| G-5-11 | HS25 | 257196 |
| G-5-11 | HS25 | 258001 |
| G-5-11 | HS25 | 258008 |
| G-5-11 | HS25 | 258032 |
| G-5-11 | HS25 | 258042 |
| G-5-11 | HS25 | 258047 |
| G-5-11 | HS25 | 258053 |
| G-5-11? | HS25 | 25277 |
| G-5-12 | HS25 | 25129 |
| (G-5-12) | HS25 | 25138 |
| G-5-12 | HS25 | 25141 |
| G-5-12 | HS25 | 25144 |
| G-5-12 | HS25 | 25219 |
| G-5-12 | HS25 | 25244 |
| G-5-12 | HS25 | 25279 |
| G-5-12 | HS25 | 256028 |
| G-5-12 | HS25 | 256050 |
| G-5-12 | HS25 | 256060 |
| G-5-12 | HS25 | 257009 |
| G-5-12 | HS25 | 257025 |
| G-5-12 | HS25 | 257041 |
| G-5-12 | HS25 | 257073 |
| G-5-12 | HS25 | 257083 |
| G-5-12 | HS25 | 257095 |
| G-5-12 | HS25 | 257103 |
| G-5-12 | HS25 | 257142 |
| G-5-12 | HS25 | 257151 |
| G-5-12 | HS25 | 257163 |
| G-5-12 | HS25 | 257184 |
| G-5-12 | HS25 | 257185 |
| G-5-12 | HS25 | 257197 |
| G-5-12 | HS25 | 257199 |
| G-5-12 | HS25 | 257212 |
| (G-5-12) | HS25 | 258005 |
| G-5-12 | HS25 | 258018 |
| G-5-12 | HS25 | 258019 |
| G-5-12 | HS25 | 258027 |
| G-5-12 | HS25 | 258028 |
| G-5-12 | HS25 | 258034 |
| G-5-12 | HS25 | 258043 |
| G-5-12 | HS25 | 258044 |
| G-5-13 | HS25 | 25113 |
| G-5-13 | HS25 | 25148 |
| G-5-13 | HS25 | 25150 |
| (G-5-13) | HS25 | 25181 |
| G-5-13 | HS25 | 25256 |
| G-5-13 | HS25 | 25270 |
| G-5-13 | HS25 | 256041 |
| G-5-13 | HS25 | 256056 |
| G-5-13 | HS25 | 256063 |
| G-5-13 | HS25 | 257011 |
| G-5-13 | HS25 | 257042 |
| G-5-13 | HS25 | 257056 |
| G-5-13 | HS25 | 257066 |
| G-5-13 | HS25 | 257075 |
| G-5-13 | HS25 | 257106 |
| G-5-13 | HS25 | 257120 |
| G-5-13 | HS25 | 257134 |
| G-5-13 | HS25 | 257146 |
| G-5-14 | HS25 | 25130 |
| G-5-14 | HS25 | 25135 |
| G-5-14 | HS25 | 25147 |
| G-5-14 | HS25 | 25217 |
| G-5-14 | HS25 | 25219 |
| G-5-14 | HS25 | 25243 |
| G-5-14 | HS25 | 25271 |
| G-5-14 | HS25 | 256031 |
| G-5-14 | HS25 | 256061 |
| G-5-14 | HS25 | 256071 |
| G-5-14 | HS25 | 257012 |
| G-5-14 | HS25 | 257032 |
| G-5-14 | HS25 | 257034 |
| G-5-14 | HS25 | 257057 |
| G-5-14 | HS25 | 257068 |
| G-5-14 | HS25 | 257077 |
| G-5-14 | HS25 | 257084 |
| G-5-14 | HS25 | 257096 |
| G-5-14 | HS25 | 257108 |
| G-5-14 | HS25 | 257121 |
| G-5-14 | HS25 | 257133 |
| G-5-14 | HS25 | 257147 |
| G-5-14 | HS25 | 257158 |
| G-5-14 | HS25 | 257165 |
| G-5-14 | HS25 | 257170 |
| G-5-14 | HS25 | 257178 |
| G-5-14 | HS25 | 257187 |
| G-5-14 | HS25 | 257192 |
| G-5-14 | HS25 | 257200 |
| G-5-14 | HS25 | 257203 |
| G-5-14 | HS25 | 258013 |
| G-5-14 | HS25 | 258020 |
| G-5-14 | HS25 | 258025 |
| G-5-14 | HS25 | 258030 |
| G-5-15 | HS25 | 25160 |
| G-5-15 | HS25 | 25223 |
| G-5-15 | HS25 | 25272 |
| G-5-15 | HS25 | 256002 |
| G-5-15 | HS25 | 256048 |
| G-5-15 | HS25 | 256062 |
| G-5-15 | HS25 | 256066 |
| G-5-15 | HS25 | 256070 |
| G-5-15 | HS25 | 257004 |
| G-5-15 | HS25 | 257058 |
| G-5-15 | HS25 | 257069 |
| G-5-15 | HS25 | 257078 |
| G-5-15 | HS25 | 257085 |
| G-5-15 | HS25 | 257098 |
| G-5-15 | HS25 | 257110 |
| G-5-15 | HS25 | 257122 |
| G-5-15 | HS25 | 257135 |
| G-5-15 | HS25 | 257159 |
| G-5-15 | HS25 | 257167 |
| G-5-15 | HS25 | 257171 |
| G-5-15 | HS25 | 257179 |
| G-5-15 | HS25 | 257188 |
| G-5-15 | HS25 | 257193 |
| G-5-15 | HS25 | 257204 |
| G-5-15 | HS25 | 258004 |
| G-5-15 | HS25 | 258005 |
| G-5-15 | HS25 | 258009 |
| G-5-15 | HS25 | 258014 |
| G-5-15 | HS25 | 258021 |
| G-5-15 | HS25 | 258023 |
| G-5-15 | HS25 | 258031 |
| G-5-15 | HS25 | 258037 |
| G-5-15 | HS25 | 258040 |
| G-5-15 | HS25 | 258054 |
| G-5-16 | HS25 | 25138 |
| (G-5-16) | HS25 | 25140 |
| G-5-16 | HS25 | 25163 |
| (G-5-16) | HS25 | 25246 |
| G-5-16 | HS25 | 25249 |
| G-5-16 | HS25 | 25289 |
| G-5-16 | HS25 | 256026 |
| G-5-16 | HS25 | 256047 |
| G-5-16 | HS25 | 256065 |
| G-5-16 | HS25 | 256068 |
| G-5-16 | HS25 | 257035 |
| G-5-16 | HS25 | 257048 |
| G-5-16 | HS25 | 257055 |
| G-5-16 | HS25 | 257062 |
| G-5-16 | HS25 | 257079 |
| G-5-16 | HS25 | 257087 |
| G-5-16 | HS25 | 257094 |
| G-5-16 | HS25 | 257099 |
| G-5-16 | HS25 | 257111 |
| G-5-16 | HS25 | 257123 |
| G-5-16 | HS25 | 257137 |
| G-5-16 | HS25 | 257180 |
| G-5-16 | HS25 | 257181 |
| G-5-16 | HS25 | 257206 |
| G-5-16 | HS25 | 257213 |
| (G-5-16) | HS25 | 258002 |
| G-5-16 | HS25 | 258017 |
| G-5-16 | HS25 | 258022 |
| G-5-16 | HS25 | 258029 |
| G-5-16 | HS25 | 258045 |
| G-5-16 | HS25 | 258048 |
| G-5-17 | HS25 | 25140 |
| G-5-17 | HS25 | 25169 |
| G-5-17 | HS25 | 25252 |
| G-5-17 | HS25 | 256012 |
| G-5-17 | HS25 | 256054 |
| G-5-17 | HS25 | 256057 |
| G-5-17 | HS25 | 256064 |
| G-5-17 | HS25 | 257014 |
| G-5-17 | HS25 | 257022 |
| G-5-17 | HS25 | 257036 |
| G-5-17 | HS25 | 257044 |
| G-5-17 | HS25 | 257049 |
| G-5-17 | HS25 | 257059 |
| G-5-17 | HS25 | 257071 |
| G-5-17 | HS25 | 257076 |
| G-5-17 | HS25 | 257086 |
| G-5-17 | HS25 | 257101 |
| G-5-17 | HS25 | 257113 |
| G-5-17 | HS25 | 257125 |
| G-5-17 | HS25 | 257138 |
| G-5-17 | HS25 | 257148 |
| G-5-17 | HS25 | 257152 |
| G-5-17 | HS25 | 257156 |
| G-5-17 | HS25 | 257161 |
| G-5-17 | HS25 | 257173 |
| G-5-17 | HS25 | 257182 |
| G-5-17 | HS25 | 257191 |
| G-5-17 | HS25 | 257202 |
| G-5-17 | HS25 | 257214 |
| G-5-17 | HS25 | 258006 |
| G-5-17 | HS25 | 258015 |
| G-5-18 | HS25 | 25143 |
| G-5-18 | HS25 | 25183 |
| G-5-18 | HS25 | 25235 |
| G-5-18 | HS25 | 25253 |
| G-5-18 | HS25 | 256017 |
| G-5-18 | HS25 | 256045 |
| G-5-18 | HS25 | 256058 |
| G-5-18 | HS25 | 257006 |
| G-5-18 | HS25 | 257015 |
| G-5-18 | HS25 | 257037 |
| G-5-18 | HS25 | 257050 |
| G-5-18 | HS25 | 257060 |
| G-5-18 | HS25 | 257072 |
| G-5-18 | HS25 | 257080 |
| G-5-18 | HS25 | 257089 |
| G-5-18 | HS25 | 257102 |
| G-5-18 | HS25 | 257114 |
| G-5-18 | HS25 | 257126 |
| G-5-18 | HS25 | 257139 |
| G-5-18 | HS25 | 257145 |
| G-5-18 | HS25 | 257154 |
| G-5-18 | HS25 | 257162 |
| G-5-18 | HS25 | 257166 |
| G-5-18 | HS25 | 257174 |
| G-5-18 | HS25 | 257195 |
| G-5-18 | HS25 | 257198 |
| G-5-18 | HS25 | 257207 |
| G-5-18 | HS25 | 257210 |
| G-5-18 | HS25 | 258012 |
| G-5-18 | HS25 | 258016 |
| G-5-18 | HS25 | 258024 |
| G-5-18 | HS25 | 258026 |
| G-5-18 | HS25 | 258036 |
| G-5-18 | HS25 | 258041 |
| G-5-18 | HS25 | 258051 |
| G-5-19 | HS25 | 25153 |
| G-5-19 | HS25 | 25159 |
| G-5-19 | HS25 | 25171 |
| G-5-19 | HS25 | 25235 |
| G-5-19 | HS25 | 25239 |
| G-5-19 | HS25 | 25257 |
| G-5-19 | HS25 | 256015 |
| G-5-19 | HS25 | 256055 |
| G-5-19 | HS25 | 256059 |
| G-5-19 | HS25 | 257003 |
| G-5-19 | HS25 | 257017 |
| G-5-19 | HS25 | 257038 |
| G-5-19 | HS25 | 257052 |
| G-5-19 | HS25 | 257061 |
| G-5-19 | HS25 | 257074 |
| G-5-19 | HS25 | 257081 |
| G-5-19 | HS25 | 257090 |
| G-5-19 | HS25 | 257100 |
| G-5-19 | HS25 | 257116 |
| G-5-19 | HS25 | 257128 |
| G-5-19 | HS25 | 257140 |
| G-5-19 | HS25 | 257149 |
| G-5-19 | HS25 | 257155 |
| G-5-19 | HS25 | 257160 |
| G-5-19 | HS25 | 257201 |
| G-5-19 | HS25 | 257205 |
| G-5-19 | HS25 | 257208 |
| (G-5-19) | HS25 | 258005 |
| G-5-19 | HS25 | 258010 |
| G-5-19 | HS25 | 258033 |
| G-5-19 | HS25 | 258039 |
| G-5-19 | HS25 | 258049 |
| G-5-20 | HS25 | 25145 |
| G-5-20 | HS25 | 25189 |
| G-5-20 | HS25 | 25214 |
| G-5-20 | HS25 | 25241 |
| G-5-20 | HS25 | 25242 |
| G-5-20 | HS25 | 25273 |
| G-5-20 | HS25 | 25274 |
| G-5-20 | HS25 | 256068 |
| G-5-20 | HS25 | 257002 |
| G-5-20 | HS25 | 257053 |

| | | | | | | | | | | | |
|---|---|---|---|---|---|---|---|---|---|---|---|
| G-5-20 | HS25 | 257063 | G-5-573 | HS25 | 258102 | G-5-660 | HS25 | 258179 | G-5-744 | HS25 | 258229 |
| G-5-20 | HS25 | 257092 | G-5-574 | HS25 | 258103 | G-5-661 | HS25 | 258156 | G-5-745 | HS25 | 258222 |
| G-5-20 | HS25 | 257104 | G-5-575 | HS25 | 258104 | G-5-662 | HS25 | 258167 | G-5-746 | HS25 | 259027 |
| G-5-20 | HS25 | 257117 | G-5-576 | HS25 | 258094 | G-5-663 | HS25 | 258181 | G-5-747 | HS25 | 257178 |
| G-5-20 | HS25 | 257129 | G-5-577 | HS25 | 258105 | G-5-664 | HS25 | 258112 | G-5-748 | HS25 | 258230 |
| G-5-20 | HS25 | 257141 | G-5-578 | HS25 | 258107 | G-5-665 | HS25 | 258115 | G-5-749 | HS25 | 259028 |
| G-5-20 | HS25 | 257143 | G-5-579 | HS25 | 258108 | G-5-666 | HS25 | 258183 | G-5-750 | HS25 | 258231 |
| G-5-20 | HS25 | 257157 | G-5-580 | HS25 | 258106 | G-5-667 | HS25 | 258158 | G-5-751 | HS25 | 259029 |
| G-5-20 | HS25 | 257168 | G-5-581 | HS25 | 258109 | G-5-668 | HS25 | 258177 | G-5-752 | HS25 | 258232 |
| G-5-20 | HS25 | 257176 | G-5-582 | HS25 | 258111 | G-5-669 | HS25 | 258185 | G-5-753 | HS25 | 259030 |
| G-5-20 | HS25 | 257183 | G-5-583 | HS25 | 258112 | G-5-670 | HS25 | 258187 | G-5-754 | HS25 | 259031 |
| G-5-20 | HS25 | 257209 | G-5-584 | HS25 | 258110 | "G-5-670" | HS25 | 258208 | G-5-755 | HS25 | 258226 |
| G-5-20 | HS25 | 257215 | G-5-585 | HS25 | 256027 | G-5-671 | HS25 | 258188 | G-5-756 | HS25 | 259033 |
| G-5-20 | HS25 | 258003 | G-5-586 | HS25 | 258114 | G-5-672 | HS25 | 25247 | G-5-757 | HS25 | 258234 |
| G-5-20 | HS25 | 258007 | G-5-587 | HS25 | 258113 | G-5-673 | HS25 | 258189 | G-5-758 | HS25 | 258228 |
| G-5-20 | HS25 | 258011 | G-5-588 | HS25 | 257130 | G-5-674 | HS25 | 258191 | G-5-759 | HS25 | 259025 |
| G-5-20 | HS25 | 258035 | G-5-589 | HS25 | 258117 | G-5-675 | HS25 | 258180 | G-5-760 | HS25 | 259032 |
| G-5-20 | HS25 | 258038 | (G-5-590) | HS25 | 258118 | G-5-676 | HS25 | 258182 | G-5-761 | HS25 | 259034 |
| G-5-20 | HS25 | 258046 | G-5-591 | HS25 | 258119 | G-5-677 | HS25 | 258193 | G-5-762 | HS25 | 259036 |
| G-5-20 | HS25 | 258052 | G-5-592 | HS25 | 258116 | G-5-678 | HS25 | 258184 | G-5-763 | HS25 | 258224 |
| G-5-21 | HS25 | 257169 | G-5-593 | HS25 | 258121 | G-5-679 | HS25 | 258195 | G-5-764 | HS25 | 258236 |
| G-5-501 | HS25 | 258037 | G-5-594 | HS25 | 258122 | G-5-680 | HS25 | 258196 | G-5-765 | HS25 | 257172 |
| G-5-502 | HS25 | 257115 | G-5-595 | HS25 | 258034 | G-5-681 | HS25 | 258199 | G-5-766 | HS25 | 257196 |
| G-5-503 | HS25 | 258050 | G-5-596 | HS25 | 258124 | G-5-682 | HS25 | 258200 | G-5-767 | HS25 | 258238 |
| G-5-504 | HS25 | 258055 | G-5-597 | HS25 | 258126 | G-5-683 | HS25 | 258186 | G-5-768 | HS25 | 258239 |
| G-5-505 | HS25 | 256042 | G-5-598 | HS25 | 257055 | G-5-684 | HS25 | 258190 | G-5-769 | HS25 | 258227 |
| G-5-506 | HS25 | 258059 | G-5-599 | HS25 | 258115 | G-5-685 | HS25 | 258202 | G-5-770 | HS25 | 258233 |
| G-5-508 | HS25 | 258057 | G-5-600 | HS25 | 258123 | G-5-686 | HS25 | 258203 | G-5-771 | HS25 | 259037 |
| G-5-509 | HS25 | 258056 | G-5-601 | HS25 | 258125 | G-5-687 | HS25 | 258204 | G-5-772 | HS25 | 258240 |
| G-5-510 | HS25 | 258058 | G-5-602 | HS25 | 258127 | G-5-688 | HS25 | 258206 | G-5-773 | HS25 | 259035 |
| G-5-511 | HS25 | 258060 | G-5-603 | HS25 | 258128 | G-5-689 | HS25 | 258205 | G-5-774 | HS25 | 258235 |
| G-5-514 | HS25 | 258064 | G-5-604 | HS25 | 257070 | G-5-690 | HS25 | 258207 | G-5-775 | HS25 | 258237 |
| G-5-515 | HS25 | 258061 | G-5-605 | HS25 | 258118 | G-5-691 | HS25 | 258192 | G-5-776 | HS25 | 259038 |
| G-5-516 | HS25 | 258062 | G-5-606 | HS25 | 258120 | G-5-692 | HS25 | 258194 | G-5-777 | HS25 | 258241 |
| G-5-518 | HS25 | 258063 | G-5-607 | HS25 | 258132 | G-5-693 | HS25 | 257196 | G-5-778 | HS25 | 258243 |
| G-5-519 | HS25 | 257064 | G-5-608 | HS25 | 258135 | G-5-694 | HS25 | 258198 | G-5-779 | HS25 | 259004 |
| G-5-520 | HS25 | 258065 | G-5-609 | HS25 | 258136 | G-5-695 | HS25 | 258209 | G-5-780 | HS25 | 258244 |
| G-5-521 | HS25 | 258066 | G-5-610 | HS25 | 258137 | G-5-696 | HS25 | 258197 | G-5-781 | HS25 | 259039 |
| G-5-522 | HS25 | 258001 | G-5-611 | HS25 | 258131 | G-5-697 | HS25 | 258040 | G-5-782 | HS25 | 258246 |
| G-5-524 | HS25 | 257076 | G-5-612 | HS25 | 258139 | G-5-698 | HS25 | 256052 | G-5-783 | HS25 | 259040 |
| G-5-525 | HS25 | 258067 | G-5-613 | HS25 | 258140 | G-5-698 | HS25 | 256052 | G-5-784 | HS25 | 258248 |
| G-5-526 | HS25 | 258069 | G-5-614 | HS25 | 258138 | G-5-699 | HS25 | 258201 | G-5-785 | HS25 | 259041 |
| G-5-527 | HS25 | 258070 | G-5-615 | HS25 | 258141 | G-5-700 | HS25 | 258208 | G-5-786 | HS25 | 258249 |
| G-5-528 | HS25 | 258071 | G-5-616 | HS25 | 258133 | G-5-701 | HS25 | 257031 | G-5-787 | HS25 | 258251 |
| G-5-529 | HS25 | 258072 | G-5-617 | HS25 | 258142 | G-5-702 | HS25 | 259003 | G-5-788 | HS25 | 258252 |
| G-5-530 | HS25 | 257178 | G-5-618 | HS25 | 258144 | G-5-703 | HS25 | 258146 | G-5-789 | HS25 | 259042 |
| G-5-531 | HS25 | 257088 | G-5-619 | HS25 | 258145 | G-5-704 | HS25 | 258019 | G-5-790 | HS25 | 258253 |
| G-5-532 | HS25 | 258073 | G-5-620 | HS25 | 258130 | G-5-705 | HS25 | 258210 | G-5-791 | HS25 | 258254 |
| G-5-533 | HS25 | 258075 | G-5-621 | HS25 | 258147 | G-5-706 | HS25 | 258214 | G-5-792 | HS25 | 258255 |
| G-5-534 | HS25 | 257028 | G-5-622 | HS25 | 258129 | G-5-707 | HS25 | 25248 | G-5-793 | HS25 | 258242 |
| G-5-535 | HS25 | 258076 | G-5-623 | HS25 | 25127 | G-5-708 | HS25 | 257062 | G-5-794 | HS25 | 259043 |
| G-5-536 | HS25 | 257112 | G-5-624 | HS25 | 25254 | G-5-708 | HS25 | 257062 | G-5-795 | HS25 | 258256 |
| G-5-538 | HS25 | 258077 | G-5-625 | HS25 | 258150 | G-5-709 | HS25 | 258213 | G-5-796 | HS25 | 258257 |
| G-5-539 | HS25 | 258068 | G-5-626 | HS25 | 258152 | G-5-710 | HS25 | 258212 | G-5-797 | HS25 | 259044 |
| G-5-540 | HS25 | 258080 | G-5-627 | HS25 | 258153 | G-5-711 | HS25 | 259013 | G-5-798 | HS25 | 258258 |
| G-5-541 | HS25 | 258074 | G-5-628 | HS25 | 258155 | G-5-712 | HS25 | 259014 | G-5-799 | HS25 | 258259 |
| G-5-542 | HS25 | 258079 | G-5-629 | HS25 | 258146 | G-5-713 | HS25 | 258078 | G-5-800 | HS25 | 258260 |
| G-5-543 | HS25 | 258081 | G-5-630 | HS25 | 258148 | G-5-714 | HS25 | 258216 | G-5-801 | HS25 | 259045 |
| G-5-544 | HS25 | 258078 | G-5-631 | HS25 | 257010 | G-5-715 | HS25 | 258217 | G-5-802 | HS25 | 258261 |
| G-5-545 | HS25 | 257136 | G-5-632 | HS25 | 258157 | G-5-716 | HS25 | 259009 | G-5-803 | HS25 | 258262 |
| G-5-546 | HS25 | 258083 | G-5-633 | HS25 | 258160 | G-5-717 | HS25 | 259011 | G-5-804 | HS25 | 258263 |
| G-5-547 | HS25 | 258084 | G-5-634 | HS25 | 258134 | G-5-718 | HS25 | 259015 | G-5-805 | HS25 | 259046 |
| G-5-548 | HS25 | 258082 | G-5-635 | HS25 | 258149 | G-5-719 | HS25 | 259017 | G-5-806 | HS25 | 258264 |
| G-5-549 | HS25 | 257100 | G-5-636 | HS25 | 258161 | G-5-720 | HS25 | 259008 | G-5-807 | HS25 | 258067 |
| G-5-550 | HS25 | 258086 | G-5-637 | HS25 | 258058 | G-5-721 | HS25 | 257007 | G-5-808 | HS25 | 257107 |
| G-5-551 | HS25 | 258085 | G-5-638 | HS25 | 258162 | G-5-722 | HS25 | 259010 | G-5-809 | HS25 | 258265 |
| G-5-552 | HS25 | 258087 | G-5-639 | HS25 | 258163 | G-5-723 | HS25 | 259020 | G-5-810 | HS25 | 257097 |
| G-5-553 | HS25 | 257112 | G-5-640 | HS25 | 258074 | G-5-724 | HS25 | 258211 | G-5-811 | HS25 | 258266 |
| G-5-554 | HS25 | 258007 | G-5-641 | HS25 | 258166 | G-5-725 | HS25 | 258218 | G-5-812 | HS25 | 258267 |
| G-5-555 | HS25 | 258089 | G-5-642 | HS25 | 258133 | G-5-726 | HS25 | 259012 | G-5-813 | HS25 | 258247 |
| G-5-556 | HS25 | 258090 | G-5-643 | HS25 | 258168 | G-5-727 | HS25 | 258215 | G-5-814 | HS25 | 258269 |
| G-5-557 | HS25 | 258001 | G-5-644 | HS25 | 258169 | G-5-728 | HS25 | 258220 | G-5-815 | HS25 | 258250 |
| G-5-558 | HS25 | 258092 | G-5-645 | HS25 | 258170 | G-5-729 | HS25 | 259023 | G-5-816 | HS25 | 258270 |
| G-5-559 | HS25 | 258093 | G-5-646 | HS25 | 258171 | G-5-730 | HS25 | 259019 | G-5-817 | HS25 | 259047 |
| G-5-560 | HS25 | 258091 | G-5-647 | HS25 | 258172 | G-5-731 | HS25 | 258221 | G-5-818 | HS25 | 258271 |
| G-5-561 | HS25 | 258095 | G-5-648 | HS25 | 258173 | G-5-732 | HS25 | 259016 | G-5-819 | HS25 | 258272 |
| G-5-562 | HS25 | 258096 | G-5-649 | HS25 | 258174 | G-5-733 | HS25 | 258223 | G-5-820 | HS25 | 258273 |
| G-5-563 | HS25 | 258088 | G-5-650 | HS25 | 258175 | G-5-734 | HS25 | 259022 | G-5-821 | HS25 | 25281 |
| G-5-564 | HS25 | 258098 | G-5-651 | HS25 | 25217 | G-5-735 | HS25 | 259005 | G-5-822 | HS25 | 258274 |
| G-5-565 | HS25 | 258099 | G-5-652 | HS25 | 258176 | G-5-736 | HS25 | 259021 | G-5-823 | HS25 | 258275 |
| G-5-566 | HS25 | 258100 | G-5-653 | HS25 | 258068 | G-5-737 | HS25 | 259024 | G-5-824 | HS25 | 258276 |
| G-5-567 | HS25 | 258097 | G-5-654 | HS25 | 258164 | G-5-738 | HS25 | 258068 | G-5-826 | HS25 | 259048 |
| G-5-568 | HS25 | 257172 | G-5-655 | HS25 | 258154 | G-5-739 | HS25 | 258225 | G-5-827 | HS25 | 258282 |
| G-5-569 | HS25 | 258022 | G-5-656 | HS25 | 258143 | G-5-740 | HS25 | 258219 | G-5-828 | HS25 | 258283 |
| G-5-570 | HS25 | 257178 | G-5-657 | HS25 | 258165 | G-5-741 | HS25 | 259018 | G-5-829 | HS25 | 258268 |
| G-5-571 | HS25 | 257076 | G-5-658 | HS25 | 258178 | G-5-742 | HS25 | 258025 | G-5-830 | HS25 | 258284 |
| G-5-572 | HS25 | 258101 | G-5-659 | HS25 | 257212 | G-5-743 | HS25 | 259026 | G-5-831 | HS25 | 258285 |

| | | |
|---|---|---|
| G-5-832 | HS25 | 258286 |
| G-5-833 | HS25 | 258287 |
| G-5-834 | HS25 | 258289 |
| G-5-835 | HS25 | 258290 |
| G-5-836 | HS25 | 258291 |
| "G-5-837" | HS25 | 258291 |
| G-5-837 | HS25 | 259049 |
| G-5-838 | HS25 | 258292 |
| G-5-839 | HS25 | 258293 |
| G-5-840 | HS25 | 258294 |
| G-5-841 | HS25 | 258295 |
| G-5-842 | HS25 | 258296 |
| G-5-843 | HS25 | 258298 |
| G-5-844 | HS25 | 258299 |
| G-5-845 | HS25 | 258300 |
| G-5-846 | HS25 | 259050 |
| G-5-847 | HS25 | 258302 |
| G-5-848 | HS25 | 258288 |
| G-5-849 | HS25 | 258303 |
| G-5-850 | HS25 | 258307 |
| G-5-851 | HS25 | 258308 |
| G-5-852 | HS25 | 258310 |
| G-5-853 | HS25 | 258312 |
| G-5-854 | HS25 | 258314 |
| G-5-855 | HS25 | 258316 |
| G-5-856 | HS25 | 258318 |
| G-5-857 | HS25 | 258321 |
| G-5-858 | HS25 | 258323 |
| G-5-859 | HS25 | 259051 |
| G-5-860 | HS25 | 258324 |
| G-5-861 | HS25 | 258327 |
| G-5-862 | HS25 | 258329 |
| G-5-863 | HS25 | 259052 |
| G-5-864 | HS25 | 258305 |
| G-5-865 | HS25 | 258332 |
| G-5-866 | HS25 | 258328 |
| G-5-867 | HS25 | 258335 |
| G-5-868 | HS25 | 258337 |
| G-5-869 | HS25 | 258330 |
| G-5-870 | HS25 | 257194 |
| G-5-874 | HS25 | 258022 |
| G-5-875 | HS25 | 257139 |
| G-36-1 | HS25 | 25238 |
| G-36-2 | HS25 | 257184 |
| G-36-2 | MS76 | 008 |
| G-37-65 | HS25 | 25011 |
| G-52-24 | GLEX | 9038 |
| G-52-25 | GLEX | 9081 |
| G-52-26 | GLEX | 9032 |
| G-60-01 | FA20 | 223 |
| G-88-01 | HS25 | 258078 |
| G-88-03 | HS25 | 257184 |
| G-0502 | HS25 | 258385 |
| G-0504 | HS25 | 258392 |

United Kingdom

| | | |
|---|---|---|
| (G- ) | GLF4 | 1096 |
| (G- ) | HS25 | 257094 |
| G-APRU | MS76 | 008 |
| G-ARYA | HS25 | 25001 |
| G-ARYB | HS25 | 25002 |
| G-ARYC | HS25 | 25003 |
| G-ASEC | HS25 | 25004 |
| G-ASNU | HS25 | 25005 |
| (G-ASSH) | HS25 | 25007 |
| G-ASSH | HS25 | 25017 |
| G-ASSI | HS25 | 25008 |
| G-ASSJ | HS25 | 25013 |
| G-ASSK | HS25 | 25014 |
| G-ASSL | HS25 | 25016 |
| G-ASSM | HS25 | 25010 |
| G-ASTY | HS25 | 25007 |
| G-ASYX | HS25 | 25019 |
| G-ASZM | HS25 | 25020 |
| G-ASZN | HS25 | 25021 |
| G-ASZO | HS25 | 25022 |
| G-ASZP | HS25 | 25023 |
| G-ATAY | HS25 | 25026 |
| G-ATAZ | HS25 | 25029 |
| G-ATBA | HS25 | 25030 |
| G-ATBB | HS25 | 25031 |
| G-ATBC | HS25 | 25032 |
| G-ATBD | HS25 | 25033 |
| G-ATCO | HS25 | 25035 |
| G-ATCP | HS25 | 25038 |
| G-ATFO | HS25 | 25037 |
| G-ATGA | HS25 | 25043 |
| G-ATGS | HS25 | 25046 |
| G-ATGT | HS25 | 25047 |
| G-ATGU | HS25 | 25051 |
| G-ATIK | HS25 | 25052 |
| G-ATIL | HS25 | 25057 |
| G-ATIM | HS25 | 25060 |
| G-ATKK | HS25 | 25064 |
| G-ATKL | HS25 | 25065 |
| G-ATKM | HS25 | 25066 |
| G-ATKN | HS25 | 25070 |
| G-ATLI | HS25 | 25073 |
| G-ATLJ | HS25 | 25075 |
| G-ATLK | HS25 | 25078 |
| G-ATLL | HS25 | 25079 |
| G-ATNM | HS25 | 25082 |
| G-ATNN | HS25 | 25084 |
| G-ATNO | HS25 | 25088 |
| G-ATNP | HS25 | 25091 |
| G-ATNR | HS25 | 25096 |
| G-ATNS | HS25 | 25098 |
| G-ATNT | HS25 | 25100 |
| G-ATOV | HS25 | 25074 |
| G-ATOW | HS25 | 25083 |
| G-ATOX | HS25 | 25087 |
| G-ATPB | HS25 | 25089 |
| G-ATPC | HS25 | 25009 |
| G-ATPD | HS25 | 25085 |
| G-ATPE | HS25 | 25092 |
| G-ATSN | HS25 | 25093 |
| G-ATSO | HS25 | 25095 |
| G-ATSP | HS25 | 25097 |
| G-ATUU | HS25 | 25102 |
| G-ATUV | HS25 | 25103 |
| G-ATUW | HS25 | 25104 |
| G-ATUX | HS25 | 25107 |
| G-ATUY | HS25 | 25108 |
| G-ATUZ | HS25 | 25109 |
| G-ATWH | HS25 | 25094 |
| G-ATXE | HS25 | 25101 |
| G-ATYH | HS25 | 25111 |
| G-ATYI | HS25 | 25112 |
| G-ATYJ | HS25 | 25114 |
| G-ATYK | HS25 | 25115 |
| G-ATYL | HS25 | 25118 |
| G-ATZE | HS25 | 25110 |
| G-ATZN | HS25 | 25116 |
| G-AVAD | HS25 | 25119 |
| G-AVAE | HS25 | 25121 |
| G-AVAF | HS25 | 25122 |
| G-AVAG | HS25 | 25123 |
| G-AVAH | HS25 | 25124 |
| G-AVAI | HS25 | 25125 |
| G-AVDL | HS25 | 25126 |
| G-AVDM | HS25 | 25129 |
| G-AVDX | HS25 | 25113 |
| G-AVGW | HS25 | 25120 |
| G-AVHA | HS25 | 25134 |
| G-AVHB | HS25 | 25136 |
| G-AVJD | HS25 | 25137 |
| G-AVOI | HS25 | 25128 |
| G-AVOJ | HS25 | 25139 |
| G-AVOK | HS25 | 25141 |
| G-AVOL | HS25 | 25142 |
| G-AVPE | HS25 | 25127 |
| G-AVRD | HS25 | 25130 |
| G-AVRE | HS25 | 25131 |
| G-AVRF | HS25 | 25133 |
| G-AVRG | HS25 | 25144 |
| G-AVRH | HS25 | 25146 |
| G-AVRI | HS25 | 25148 |
| G-AVRJ | HS25 | 25149 |
| G-AVTY | HS25 | 25151 |
| G-AVTZ | HS25 | 25152 |
| G-AVVA | HS25 | 25138 |
| G-AVVB | HS25 | 25140 |
| G-AVXK | HS25 | 25143 |
| G-AVXL | HS25 | 25145 |
| G-AVXM | HS25 | 25153 |
| G-AVXN | HS25 | 25155 |
| G-AVZJ | HS25 | 25156 |
| G-AVZK | HS25 | 25158 |
| G-AVZL | HS25 | 25159 |
| G-AWKH | HS25 | 25160 |
| G-AWKI | HS25 | 25161 |
| G-AWMS | HS25 | 25150 |
| G-AWMV | HS25 | 25163 |
| G-AWMW | HS25 | 25170 |
| G-AWMX | HS25 | 25173 |
| G-AWMY | HS25 | 25174 |
| G-AWPC | HS25 | 25175 |
| G-AWPD | HS25 | 25176 |
| G-AWPE | HS25 | 25179 |
| G-AWPF | HS25 | 25180 |
| G-AWUF | HS25 | 25106 |
| G-AWWL | HS25 | 25169 |
| G-AWXB | HS25 | 25183 |
| G-AWXC | HS25 | 25187 |
| G-AWXD | HS25 | 25188 |
| G-AWXE | HS25 | 25185 |
| G-AWXF | HS25 | 25186 |
| G-AWXN | HS25 | 25177 |
| G-AWXO | HS25 | 25178 |
| G-AWYE | HS25 | 25090 |
| G-AXDM | HS25 | 25194 |
| G-AXDO | HS25 | 25190 |
| G-AXDP | HS25 | 25191 |
| G-AXDR | HS25 | 25195 |
| G-AXDS | HS25 | 25196 |
| G-AXEG | HS25 | 25172 |
| (G-AXFY) | HS25 | 25189 |
| G-AXJD | HS25 | 25198 |
| G-AXJE | HS25 | 25200 |
| G-AXJF | HS25 | 25201 |
| G-AXJG | HS25 | 25202 |
| G-AXLU | HS25 | 25181 |
| G-AXLV | HS25 | 25182 |
| G-AXLW | HS25 | 25184 |
| G-AXLX | HS25 | 25199 |
| G-AXOA | HS25 | 25203 |
| G-AXOB | HS25 | 25204 |
| G-AXOC | HS25 | 25205 |
| G-AXOD | HS25 | 25207 |
| G-AXOE | HS25 | 25208 |
| G-AXOF | HS25 | 25210 |
| G-AXPS | HS25 | 25135 |
| G-AXPU | HS25 | 25171 |
| G-AXPX | HS25 | 25206 |
| G-AXTR | HS25 | 25211 |
| G-AXTS | HS25 | 25212 |
| G-AXTT | HS25 | 25213 |
| G-AXTU | HS25 | 25214 |
| G-AXTV | HS25 | 25216 |
| G-AXTW | HS25 | 25218 |
| G-AXYE | HS25 | 25220 |
| G-AXYF | HS25 | 25222 |
| G-AXYG | HS25 | 25224 |
| G-AXYH | HS25 | 25225 |
| G-AXYI | HS25 | 25226 |
| G-AXYJ | HS25 | 25217 |
| G-AYBH | HS25 | 25256 |
| G-AYEP | HS25 | 25219 |
| G-AYER | HS25 | 25238 |
| G-AYFM | HS25 | 25227 |
| G-AYIZ | HS25 | 25223 |
| G-AYLG | HS25 | 25254 |
| G-AYLI | HS25 | 25240 |
| G-AYMI | GLF2 | 91 |
| G-AYNR | HS25 | 25235 |
| (G-AYOI) | HS25 | 25243 |
| G-AYOJ | HS25 | 25246 |
| G-AYOK | HS25 | 25250 |
| G-AYRR | HS25 | 25247 |
| (G-AYRR) | HS25 | 25258 |
| G-AYRY | HS25 | 25105 |
| G-AZAF | HS25 | 25249 |
| G-AZCH | HS25 | 25154 |
| G-AZEK | HS25 | 25259 |
| G-AZEL | HS25 | 25260 |
| G-AZEM | HS25 | 25269 |
| G-AZHS | HS25 | 25258 |
| G-AZUF | HS25 | 256001 |
| G-AZVS | HS25 | 25132 |
| G-BABL | HS25 | 25271 |
| G-BACI | HS25 | 25283 |
| (G-BAOA) | FA20 | 138/440 |
| G-BARR | HS25 | 256019 |
| G-BART | HS25 | 256005 |
| G-BATA | HS25 | 25257 |
| G-BAXG | HS25 | 25063 |
| G-BAXL | HS25 | 25069 |
| G-BAYT | HS25 | 256012 |
| G-BAYT | HS25 | 256012 |
| G-BAZA | HS25 | 25272 |
| G-BAZB | HS25 | 25252 |
| G-BBAS | HS25 | 256017 |
| G-BBCL | HS25 | 256015 |
| G-BBCL | HS25 | 256015 |
| G-BBCL | HS25 | 256015 |
| G-BBEE | LJ25 | 135 |
| G-BBEK | FA20 | 86 |
| G-BBEP | HS25 | 256030 |
| G-BBEP | HS25 | 256030 |
| G-BBGU | HS25 | 25270 |
| G-BBMD | HS25 | 256024 |
| G-BBRO | HS25 | 256042 |
| G-BBRT | HS25 | 256029 |
| (G-BBRT) | HS25 | 256036 |
| G-BCCL | HS25 | 256039 |
| G-BCII | C500 | 176 |
| G-BCJU | HS25 | 256041 |
| G-BCKM | C500 | 198 |
| G-BCLR | HS25 | 25228 |
| G-BCRM | C500 | 227 |
| G-BCSE | LJ25 | 188 |
| G-BCUX | HS25 | 256043 |
| G-BCXF | HS25 | 256054 |
| G-BCXL | HS25 | 256049 |
| G-BCYF | FA20 | 304/511 |
| G-BDJE | HS25 | 256052 |
| G-BDKF | HS25 | 25242 |
| G-BDMF | GLF2 | 103 |
| G-BDOA | HS25 | 256056 |
| G-BDOB | HS25 | 256061 |
| G-BDOP | HS25 | 256055 |
| G-BDYE | HS25 | 25080 |
| G-BDZH | HS25 | 256066 |
| G-BDZR | HS25 | 256068 |
| G-BEDT | HS25 | 256070 |
| G-BEES | HS25 | 256071 |
| G-BEFZ | HS25 | 257001 |
| G-BEIN | HS25 | 256067 |
| G-BEIO | HS25 | 256069 |
| G-BEIZ | C500 | 363 |
| G-BEME | HS25 | 25231 |
| G-BERP | HS25 | 257003 |
| G-BERV | HS25 | 257005 |
| G-BERX | HS25 | 257006 |
| G-BETV | HS25 | 256035 |
| (G-BEWV) | HS25 | 257008 |
| G-BEWW | HS25 | 256001 |
| G-BEYC | HS25 | 257009 |
| G-BFAJ | HS25 | 257011 |
| G-BFAN | HS25 | 25258 |
| G-BFAR | C500 | 402 |
| G-BFAR | C500 | 402 |
| G-BFBI | HS25 | 257012 |
| G-BFDW | HS25 | 257014 |
| G-BFFH | HS25 | 257016 |
| G-BFFL | HS25 | 257015 |
| G-BFFU | HS25 | 257017 |
| G-BFGU | HS25 | 257018 |
| G-BFGV | HS25 | 257019 |
| G-BFIC | HS25 | 256060 |
| G-BFLF | HS25 | 257023 |
| G-BFLG | HS25 | 257024 |
| (G-BFLY) | C550 | 028 |
| G-BFLY | C550 | 089 |
| G-BFMO | HS25 | 257026 |
| G-BFMP | HS25 | 257027 |
| G-BFPI | HS25 | 257025 |
| G-BFRM | C550 | 027 |
| G-BFSI | HS25 | 257030 |
| G-BFSO | HS25 | 257028 |
| G-BFSP | HS25 | 257031 |
| G-BFSP | HS25 | 257031 |
| (G-BFTP) | HS25 | 257020 |
| G-BFUE | HS25 | 257032 |
| G-BFVI | HS25 | 257037 |
| (G-BFVN) | HS25 | 257020 |
| G-BFXT | HS25 | 257034 |
| G-BFYH | HS25 | 257044 |
| G-BFYV | HS25 | 257043 |
| G-BFZI | HS25 | 257047 |
| G-BFZJ | HS25 | 257045 |
| G-BGBJ | HS25 | 257052 |
| G-BGBL | HS25 | 257049 |
| G-BGDM | HS25 | 257004 |
| G-BGGS | HS25 | 257061 |
| G-BGKN | HS25 | 256058 |

| | | |
|---|---|---|
| G-BGLT | GLF2 | 225 |
| G-BGOP | FA20 | 406/557 |
| G-BGSR | HS25 | 257066 |
| G-BGTD | HS25 | 257073 |
| G-BGYR | HS25 | 256045 |
| G-BHBH | C550 | 148 |
| G-BHFT | HS25 | 25215 |
| (G-BHGH) | C550 | 150 |
| G-BHIE | HS25 | 256048 |
| G-BHIO | HS25 | 257085 |
| (G-BHIW) | C500 | 544 |
| (G-BHKF) | HS25 | 257075 |
| G-BHLF | HS25 | 257091 |
| G-BHMP | HS25 | 257093 |
| G-BHSK | HS25 | 257099 |
| G-BHSU | HS25 | 257103 |
| G-BHSV | HS25 | 257107 |
| G-BHSW | HS25 | 257109 |
| G-BHTJ | HS25 | 257097 |
| G-BHTT | C500 | 560 |
| (G-BHVA) | C550 | 225 |
| (G-BIHZ) | HS25 | 257118 |
| G-BIMY | HS25 | 257132 |
| G-BIRU | HS25 | 257136 |
| G-BIZZ | C500 | 645 |
| G-BJCB | HS25 | 256015 |
| G-BJCB | HS25 | 256065 |
| G-BJDJ | HS25 | 257142 |
| G-BJHH | C550 | 039 |
| G-BJIL | C550 | 354 |
| G-BJIR | C550 | 326 |
| G-BJOW | HS25 | 257153 |
| G-BJOY | HS25 | 256030 |
| (G-BJUT) | HS25 | 256005 |
| G-BJVP | C550 | 375 |
| G-BJWB | HS25 | 257158 |
| (G-BJXV) | HS25 | 256005 |
| G-BKAA | HS25 | 257139 |
| G-BKAJ | HS25 | 25235 |
| G-BKBA | HS25 | 25270 |
| G-BKBH | HS25 | 256052 |
| G-BKBM | HS25 | 256039 |
| G-BKBU | HS25 | 256042 |
| G-BKCD | HS25 | 256056 |
| "G-BKFS" | HS25 | 256054 |
| G-BKFS | HS25 | 257172 |
| G-BKHK | HS25 | 257189 |
| G-BKJV | HS25 | 257046 |
| G-BKRL | LEOP | 001 |
| G-BKSR | C550 | 469 |
| G-BKTF | HS25 | 258001 |
| G-BKUW | HS25 | 258003 |
| G-BLEK | HS25 | 257213 |
| G-BLGZ | HS25 | 258004 |
| G-BLJC | HS25 | 258005 |
| (G-BLKS) | HS25 | 258010 |
| (G-BLMJ) | HS25 | 257208 |
| (G-BLMK) | HS25 | 257210 |
| G-BLOI | HS25 | 256050 |
| G-BLPC | HS25 | 258015 |
| (G-BLSG) | CS55 | 0033 |
| G-BLSM | HS25 | 257208 |
| G-BLTP | HS25 | 257210 |
| G-BLUW | HS25 | 256059 |
| G-BLXN | CS55 | 0033 |
| G-BMCL | C550 | 091 |
| G-BMIH | HS25 | 257115 |
| G-BMMO | HS25 | 258048 |
| G-BMOS | HS25 | 257064 |
| G-BMWW | HS25 | 257076 |
| G-BMYX | HS25 | 257178 |
| G-BNBO | HS25 | 257112 |
| G-BNDX | HS25 | 256012 |
| G-BNEH | HS25 | 258078 |
| G-BNFW | HS25 | 257100 |
| G-BNSC | C550 | 559 |
| (G-BNUB) | HS25 | 258099 |
| G-BNVU | HS25 | 257130 |
| G-BNVY | C500 | 098 |
| (G-BNZP) | C500 | 114 |
| G-BNZW | HS25 | 258105 |
| G-BOCB | HS25 | 25106 |
| G-BOGA | C500 | 220 |
| G-BOOA | HS25 | 258088 |
| G-BOTX | HS25 | 258121 |
| G-BOXI | HS25 | 257055 |
| G-BPCP | C500 | 540 |
| (G-BPGR) | HS25 | 258115 |
| (G-BPGS) | HS25 | 258118 |
| (G-BPJM) | GLF4 | 1078 |
| G-BPXW | HS25 | 258161 |
| (G-BPYD) | HS25 | 258146 |
| (G-BPYE) | HS25 | 258148 |
| G-BRBZ | BE40 | RJ-60 |
| G-BRCZ | HS25 | 258163 |
| G-BRDI | HS25 | 257097 |
| G-BRNM | LEOP | 002 |
| G-BROD | HS25 | 25253 |
| G-BRXR | HS25 | 25217 |
| G-BSAA | HS25 | 25117 |
| G-BSAL | GLF2 | 214 |
| G-BSAN | GLF3 | 345 |
| G-BSHL | HS25 | 256024 |
| G-BSPH | HS25 | 256063 |
| G-BSUL | HS25 | 258186 |
| G-BSVL | C560 | 0077 |
| G-BSZP | BE40 | RJ-56 |
| G-BTAB | HS25 | 258088 |
| G-BTAE | HS25 | 258190 |
| G-BTIB | F900 | 109 |
| G-BTMG | HS25 | 258197 |
| G-BTSI | HS25 | 259007 |
| G-BTTG | HS25 | 259006 |
| G-BTTX | HS25 | 259005 |
| G-BTUF | HS25 | 25248 |
| G-BTYN | HS25 | 259009 |
| G-BTYO | HS25 | 259011 |
| G-BTYP | HS25 | 259013 |
| G-BTYR | HS25 | 259014 |
| G-BTYS | HS25 | 259015 |
| G-BUCP | HS25 | 258212 |
| G-BUCR | HS25 | 258050 |
| G-BUID | HS25 | 258208 |
| G-BUIM | HS25 | 258068 |
| G-BUIX | HS25 | 259024 |
| G-BUIY | HS25 | 258025 |
| G-BUKW | HS25 | 259021 |
| G-BULI | HS25 | 259016 |
| G-BUNL | HS25 | 257007 |
| G-BUNW | HS25 | 259029 |
| G-BUPL | HS25 | 259030 |
| G-BURV | HS25 | 258213 |
| G-BUSX | LJ35 | 662 |
| G-BUUW | HS25 | 258227 |
| G-BUUY | HS25 | 259031 |
| G-BUWC | HS25 | 258240 |
| (G-BUWD) | HS25 | 258243 |
| G-BUWX | HS25 | 259034 |
| G-BUZX | HS25 | 258067 |
| G-BVAS | HS25 | 258076 |
| G-BVBH | HS25 | 258073 |
| G-BVCM | C525 | 0022 |
| G-BVCU | HS25 | 258226 |
| G-BVDL | HS25 | 259025 |
| G-BVFC | HS25 | 258130 |
| G-BVFE | HS25 | 258242 |
| G-BVHW | HS25 | 258079 |
| G-BVJI | HS25 | 258258 |
| G-BVJY | HS25 | 257054 |
| G-BVLO | HS25 | 259027 |
| G-BVRF | HS25 | 258247 |
| G-BVRG | HS25 | 258250 |
| G-BVRW | HS25 | 258266 |
| G-BVTP | HS25 | 25255 |
| G-BVTR | HS25 | 25264 |
| G-BVTS | HS25 | 25266 |
| G-BVTT | HS25 | 25268 |
| G-BVYV | HS25 | 258268 |
| G-BVYW | HS25 | 258277 |
| G-BVZK | HS25 | 258278 |
| G-BVZL | HS25 | 258279 |
| G-BWCB | HS25 | 259032 |
| G-BWCR | HS25 | 257070 |
| G-BWDC | HS25 | 258280 |
| G-BWDD | HS25 | 258281 |
| G-BWDW | HS25 | 258282 |
| G-BWFL | C500 | 264 |
| G-BWGB | HS25 | 258283 |
| G-BWGC | HS25 | 258284 |
| G-BWGD | HS25 | 258285 |
| G-BWGE | HS25 | 258286 |
| (G-BWJX) | HS25 | 257062 |
| G-BWKL | HS25 | 257118 |
| G-BWOM | C550 | 671 |
| G-BWRN | HS25 | 258237 |
| G-BWSY | HS25 | 258201 |
| G-BWVA | HS25 | 258235 |
| G-BXPU | HS25 | 25171 |
| G-BYFO | HS25 | 257040 |
| G-BYHM | HS25 | 258233 |
| G-BZNR | HS25 | 258180 |
| G-CBBI | HS25 | 257013 |
| **G-CBHT** | **F9EX** | **48** |
| G-CBNP | GLEX | 9032 |
| G-CBNR | GLEX | 9081 |
| **G-CBRG** | **C56X** | **5266** |
| G-CBTU | C550 | 601 |
| G-CCAA | HS25 | 257130 |
| G-CCCL | C500 | 363 |
| **G-CDCX** | **C750** | **0194** |
| **G-CDLT** | **HS25** | **258710** |
| **G-CDNK** | **LJ45** | **280** |
| G-CDOL | C56X | 5584 |
| **G-CDSR** | **LJ45** | **286** |
| **G-CEDK** | **C750** | **0252** |
| **G-CERX** | **HS25** | **258810** |
| **G-CEUO** | **C550** | **033** |
| **G-CEYL** | **GLEX** | **9196** |
| **G-CFBP** | **HS25** | **257105** |
| **G-CFGB** | **C680** | **0234** |
| G-CFGL | C56X | 5361 |
| **G-CFOH** | **GLF4** | **1202** |
| G-CFRA | C56X | 5183 |
| G-CFSC | CL65 | 5744 |
| **G-CGFA** | **GLEX** | **9241** |
| G-CGFD | CL64 | 5591 |
| **G-CGFF** | **CL65** | **5733** |
| **G-CGGN** | **FA7X** | **69** |
| **G-CGGU** | **CL64** | **5626** |
| **G-CGHI** | **F2TH** | **163** |
| **G-CGMF** | **C56X** | **5271** |
| **G-CGUL** | **GLF5** | **5176** |
| **G-CHAI** | **CL61** | **5152** |
| **G-CIEL** | **C56X** | **5247** |
| G-CITI | C500 | 463 |
| **G-CITJ** | **C525** | **0084** |
| G-CJAA | HS25 | 258240 |
| **G-CJAD** | **C525** | **0435** |
| G-CJAE | C560 | 0046 |
| G-CJAG | PRM1 | RB-122 |
| G-CJAH | PRM1 | RB-131 |
| (G-CJAI) | PRM1 | RB-142 |
| (G-CJAJ) | PRM1 | RB-154 |
| **G-CJCC** | **C680** | **0189** |
| **G-CJDB** | **C525** | **0648** |
| G-CJET | LJ35 | 365 |
| G-CJHH | C550 | 147 |
| G-CJMC | LJ60 | 300 |
| **G-CJME** | **GLEX** | **9309** |
| (G-CNGM) | F2EX | 160 |
| **G-CNUK** | **FA7X** | **52** |
| **G-CPRI** | **LJ45** | **037** |
| **G-CPRR** | **C680** | **0276** |
| **G-CROO** | **C52A** | **0388** |
| **G-CTEN** | **C750** | **0281** |
| **G-CXLS** | **C56X** | **5613** |
| G-CXMF | GLF2 | 204 |
| G-CYII | HS25 | 256005 |
| G-CZAR | C560 | 0046 |
| G-DAAC | CL64 | 5424 |
| G-DAEX | F9EX | 78 |
| G-DANI | C500 | 402 |
| G-DASO | FA50 | 268 |
| G-DBAL | HS25 | 25117 |
| G-DBBI | HS25 | 257130 |
| G-DBII | C560 | 0032 |
| G-DBOW | HS25 | 256032 |
| G-DCCC | HS25 | 258002 |
| G-DCCC | HS25 | 258002 |
| G-DCCI | HS25 | 259030 |
| G-DCFR | C550 | 418 |
| G-DCTA | HS25 | 258130 |
| G-DEZC | HS25 | 257070 |
| G-DGET | CL64 | 5608 |
| **G-DJAE** | **C500** | **339** |
| G-DJBB | C500 | 365 |
| G-DJBE | C550 | 171 |
| G-DJBI | C550 | 030 |
| G-DJHH | C550 | 290 |
| G-DJLW | HS25 | 25140 |
| G-DJMJ | HS25 | 25106 |
| G-DMAN | HS25 | 256033 |
| G-DNVT | GLF4 | 1078 |
| (G-DOKK) | LJ60 | 352 |
| **G-DRBN** | **E50P** | **50000055** |
| **G-DWJM** | **C550** | **326** |
| **G-ECJI** | **FA10** | **161** |
| **G-EDCJ** | **C525** | **0105** |
| **G-EDCK** | **C525** | **0510** |
| **G-EDCL** | **C52A** | **0083** |
| **G-EDCM** | **C52A** | **0213** |
| **G-EDCS** | **BE40** | **RK-487** |
| **G-EDHY** | **F2EX** | **182** |
| G-EEBJ | C52A | 0202 |
| G-EFPT | HS25 | 257020 |
| **G-EGNS** | **GLF5** | **5167** |
| **G-EGVO** | **F9EX** | **151** |
| **G-EJEL** | **C550** | **643** |
| G-EJET | C550 | 171 |
| G-EKWS | C550 | 550-0992 |
| **G-ELOA** | **C56X** | **5106** |
| G-ELOT | C550 | 601 |
| G-ELRA | HS25 | 259003 |
| G-EMLI | CL64 | 5383 |
| **G-ESTA** | **C550** | **143** |
| G-ETOM | HS25 | 258130 |
| G-EVES | F900 | 165 |
| **G-EVLN** | **GLF4** | **1175** |
| **G-EVRD** | **PRM1** | **RB-172** |
| G-EXLR | HS25 | 258151 |
| G-EXLR | HS25 | 259001 |
| **G-EXRS** | **GLEX** | **9274** |
| G-FANN | HS25 | 256019 |
| G-FASL | HS25 | 258149 |
| G-FBFI | CL61 | 5152 |
| **G-FBKA** | **C510** | **0096** |
| **G-FBKB** | **C510** | **0126** |
| **G-FBKC** | **C510** | **0127** |
| **G-FBLI** | **C510** | **0130** |
| **G-FBLK** | **C510** | **0027** |
| G-FBMB | CL61 | 5041 |
| **G-FBNK** | **C510** | **0067** |
| G-FCAP | C56X | 5793 |
| **G-FCDB** | **C550** | **550-0985** |
| G-FDSL | HS25 | 258130 |
| G-FERY | C550 | 030 |
| **G-FFFG** | **F9EX** | **155** |
| G-FFLT | HS25 | 256057 |
| **G-FFRA** | **FA20** | **132** |
| G-FINK | HS25 | 259037 |
| **G-FIRM** | **C550** | **550-0940** |
| G-FIVE | HS25 | 25004 |
| **G-FJET** | **C550** | **418** |
| **G-FLBK** | **C510** | **0068** |
| G-FLVU | C500 | 580 |
| **G-FNES** | **F9EX** | **159** |
| G-FORN | LJ40 | 45-2019 |
| G-FOUR | HS25 | 25131 |
| G-FRAA | FA20 | 385 |
| G-FRAB | FA20 | 356 |
| G-FRAC | FA20 | 254 |
| **G-FRAD** | **FA20** | **304/511** |
| G-FRAE | FA20 | 280/503 |
| **G-FRAF** | **FA20** | **295/500** |
| **G-FRAH** | **FA20** | **223** |
| **G-FRAI** | **FA20** | **270** |
| **G-FRAJ** | **FA20** | **20** |
| **G-FRAK** | **FA20** | **213** |
| **G-FRAL** | **FA20** | **151** |
| G-FRAM | FA20 | 224 |
| **G-FRAO** | **FA20** | **214** |
| **G-FRAP** | **FA20** | **207** |
| **G-FRAR** | **FA20** | **209** |
| **G-FRAS** | **FA20** | **82/418** |
| **G-FRAT** | **FA20** | **87/424** |
| **G-FRAU** | **FA20** | **97/422** |
| G-FRAV | FA20 | 103/423 |
| **G-FRAW** | **FA20** | **114/420** |
| **G-FRBA** | **FA20** | **178/459** |
| **G-FRYL** | **PRM1** | **RB-97** |
| **G-FTSL** | **CL64** | **5416** |
| G-GAEL | HS25 | 258007 |
| G-GAIL | C550 | 397 |
| (G-GAIL) | HS25 | 257139 |
| (G-GALI) | C680 | 0104 |
| **G-GALX** | **F9EX** | **163** |
| G-GAUL | C550 | 143 |
| G-GAYL | LJ35 | 429 |

G-GDEZ HS25 259026
G-GEBJ C525 0528
G-GEDI F2TH 49
G-GEDY F2TH 208
G-GEIL HS25 258021
G-GENE C500 573
**G-GEVO C680 0145**
G-GGAE HS25 25157
**G-GHPG C550 550-0897**
G-GIII GLF3 345
G-GIRA HS25 257103
G-GJCB HS25 258079
G-GJET LJ35 365
G-GLXD CL64 5409
**G-GMAA LJ45 167**
**G-GMAB HS25 259034**
G-GMAC GLF4 1058
**G-GOMO LJ45 055**
G-GPWH F9EX 48
**G-GRGA HS25 258130**
G-GRGG C525 0028
G-GRGS C560 0457
G-GSAM HS25 258133
G-GSEB F900 161
**G-GSSO GLF5 5019**
G-HAAM F900 130
G-HADI GLF2 235
G-HALK HS25 256033
G-HARF GLF4 1117
**G-HARK CL64 5646**
G-HCFR HS25 258240
**G-HCGD LJ45 328**
**G-HCSA C52A 0334**
**G-HEBJ C525 0437**
G-HERS C750 0075
**G-HFAA PRM1 RB-83**
G-HGRC C52A 0360
G-HHOI HS25 257097
G-HJCB HS25 259031
**G-HMEI F900 1**
**G-HMEV F900 5**
G-HMMV C525 0358
G-HNJC F9EX 74
G-HNRY C650 0219
G-HOIL LJ60 313
G-HOLL C500 088
G-HOTL C550 051
**G-HPPY LJ40 45-2102**
**G-HRDS GLF5 5032**
**G-HSXP HS25 258827**
G-HUGG LJ35 432
G-HYGA HS25 258034
G-IAMS C56X 5183
G-IBIS HS25 25171
G-IBSF F2TH 151
G-ICED C500 638
G-ICFR HS25 258050
**G-IDAB C550 550-0917**
G-IECL HS25 257002
G-IFTC HS25 25171
**G-IFTE HS25 257037**
**G-IFTF HS25 258021**
G-IIRR GLF2 210
G-IJET HS25 257212
**G-IKOS C550 550-0957**
G-ILLS HS25 25133
**G-IMAC CL61 3065**
G-IOOX LJ45 243
G-IPAC C550 550-0935
G-IPAL C550 550-0935
**G-IPAX C56X 5228**
**G-ITIG F2EX 102**
G-ITIH FA50 268
**G-IUAN C525 0324**
G-IWDB HS25 258618
**G-JANV LJ45 124**
(G-JBCA) CS55 0146
**G-JBIS C550 447**
**G-JBIZ C550 068**
**G-JCBB GLF5 5186**
G-JCBC GLF5 5060
G-JCBG F9EX 44
G-JCBI F2TH 27
G-JCBV GLF5 682
G-JCBX F9EX 108
G-JCFR C550 315
G-JEAN C500 339
G-JEEN C550 029
**G-JETA C550 101**
G-JETB C550 319
**G-JETC C550 315**
G-JETD C550 418
G-JETE C500 198
**G-JETF F2EX 78**
"G-JETG" HS25 257070
G-JETG LJ35 324
G-JETI HS25 258056
**G-JETJ C550 171**
G-JETK HS25 258133
G-JETL LJ35 656
G-JETN LJ35 324
**G-JETO C550 441**
G-JFCX HS25 258215
G-JFRS C550 569
G-JHSX HS25 258245
G-JJCB HS25 258022
G-JJMX F9EX 112
G-JJSG LJ35 324
**G-JJSI HS25 258058**
**G-JMAX HS25 258456**
G-JMCW CL64 5403
**G-JMDW C550 206**
**G-JMED LJ35 671**
G-JMMD CL64 5422
G-JMMP CL64 5528
**G-JMMX F9EX 184**
G-JMSO MU30 A062SA
G-JOLI F2EX 8
**G-JOPT C560 0159**
G-JPSI FA50 313
**G-JPSX F9EX 132**
**G-JPSZ F9EX 224**
G-JRCT C550 098
G-JRJR LJ45 055
G-JSAX HS25 25157
**G-JTNC C500 264**
**G-KALS CL30 20106**
G-KANL GLEX 9331
G-KASS HS25 25127
**G-KDMA C560 0553**
**G-KLNR BE40 RK-552**
**G-KLNW C510 0157**
**G-KPEI C56X 5785**
**G-KPTN FA50 341**
**G-KSFR CL30 20189**
**G-KWIN F2EX 52**
G-LAOR HS25 258384
**G-LATE F2EX 88**
**G-LCYA F9EX 105**
**G-LDFM C56X 5242**
**G-LEAA C510 0072**
**G-LEAB C510 0073**
**G-LEAC C510 0075**
**G-LEAI C510 0052**
**G-LEAR LJ35 265**
**G-LEAX C56X 5712**
**G-LGAR LJ60 286**
**G-LGKD GLF5 5172**
**G-LGKO CL64 5610**
G-LJET LJ35 643
(G-LLGC) GLEX 9241
G-LLOD LJ45 236
G-LOBL GLEX 9038
**G-LOFT C500 331**
G-LORI HS25 25246
G-LRBJ HS25 259004
(G-LSMB) F2EX 161
**G-LSMB F2EX 47**
G-LTEC HS25 257103
**G-LUXY C550 421**
**G-LVLV CL64 5372**
**G-LWDC CL61 3031**
**G-LXRS GLEX 9200**
G-MAMA C550 319
G-MARS BE40 RJ-36
**G-MATF GLF4 1109**
**G-MDBA F2TH 184**
**G-MEET LJ40 45-2054**
G-MFEU HS25 256062
G-MHIH HS25 257139
**G-MICE C510 0156**
G-MINE C550 391
G-MIRO C550 550-0932
G-MKOA HS25 25227
G-MKSS HS25 257175
G-MLEE C650 0151
G-MLTI F900 164
**G-MOOO LJ40 45-2007**
G-MPCW CL64 5422
G-MPJM CL64 5403
**G-MPMP CL64 5528**
**G-MPSP CL64 5422**
**G-MPTP CL64 5403**
G-MRFB HS25 25132
**G-MROO C52A 0202**
G-MRTC C550 597
G-MSFY HS25 257200
G-MSLY C550 030
G-MTLE C500 573
G-MURI LJ35 646
G-MUTD LJ45 213
**G-NCCC CL65 5734**
G-NCFR HS25 257054
G-NCMT C500 645
G-NETA C56X 5230
G-NEVL LJ35 662
**G-NGEL C510 0076**
**G-NLPA HS25 HB-14**
**G-NMRM C52A 0408**
**G-NSJS C680 0161**
**G-OAMB C510 0050**
G-OBAE HS25 257094
**G-OBCC C560 0497**
G-OBEL C500 220
G-OBLT HS25 258164
G-OBOB HS25 25069
(G-OBSM) HS25 257189
G-OCAA HS25 257091
G-OCBA HS25 25132
G-OCBA HS25 25132
G-OCCC HS25 258013
G-OCCI HS25 258201
G-OCDB C550 601
G-OCFR LJ35 614
G-OCJT C52A 0113
**G-OCJZ C52A 0051**
G-OCPI C500 093
G-OCSA GLEX 9241
G-OCSB C525 0177
G-OCSC CL64 5505
G-OCSD CL64 5591
**G-OCSE CL65 5710**
G-OCSF CL65 5733
**G-OCSH CL64 5623**
**G-ODAG C52A 0397**
**G-ODCM C52B 0153**
**G-ODUR HS25 HA-0041**
G-OEBJ C525 0423
G-OEJA C500 264
**G-OEWD PRM1 RB-126**
G-OGRG C560 0506
G-OHAT C525 0028
G-OHEA HS25 25144
G-OHLA C500 514
G-OICE C525 0028
**G-OJAJ F2EX 132**
G-OJMW C550 550-1042
G-OJOY HS25 257061
G-OJPB HS25 25258
**G-OJWB HS25 258674**
G-OKSP C500 392
G-OLDC LJ45 156
G-OLDD HS25 258106
G-OLDF LJ45 055
G-OLDJ LJ45 138
**G-OLDK LJ45 311**
G-OLDL LJ45 124
G-OLDR LJ45 161
**G-OLDT LJ45 265**
**G-OLDW LJ45 294**
G-OLFR HS25 25217
**G-OMBI C52B 0179**
G-OMCA HS25 25106
G-OMCL C550 412
**G-OMEA C56X 5610**
G-OMGA HS25 256024
G-OMGB HS25 256039
G-OMGC HS25 256056
G-OMGD HS25 257184
G-OMGE HS25 258197
G-OMGG HS25 258058
G-OMID HS25 257214
**G-OMJC PRM1 RB-88**
**G-OMRH C550 550-1086**
G-ONPN HS25 25063
**G-OODM C52A 0190**
G-OOSP HS25 25178
G-OPFC HS25 258159
G-OPFC HS25 259002
G-OPOL HS25 25171
G-OPWH F900 151
G-ORAN C525 0423
G-ORCE C550 391
G-ORDB C550 550-1042
G-ORHE C500 220
G-ORJB C500 392
**G-OROO C56X 5724**
G-OSAM HS25 257189
G-OSCA C500 270
G-OSMC C550 135
G-OSNB C550 569
**G-OSOH C525 0271**
G-OSPG HS25 258130
**G-OSRL LJ45 391**
**G-OSVM C56X 5770**
**G-OTAZ HS25 HA-0112**
G-OTGT C560 0517
G-OTIS C550 672
(G-OTKI) C550 265
G-OTMC BE40 RJ-50
G-OURA HS25 258050
G-OURB HS25 257054
G-OVIP GLF2 91
(G-OVIP) HS25 258010
G-OWDB HS25 257040
G-OWEB HS25 257040
G-OWRC C525 0177
G-OXEC C500 093
(G-OXEH) C550 319
**G-OXLS C56X 5675**
**G-OZAT HS25 HA-0143**
G-PBWH HS25 258182
G-PHTO PRM1 RB-125
G-PJET LJ35 614
G-PJWB HS25 256033
G-PKRG C56X 5613
G-PLGI HS25 257034
G-PNNY C500 165
G-POAJ CL64 5442
G-POSN HS25 258120
**G-PPLC C560 0059**
**G-PREI PRM1 RB-60**
**G-PRKR CL64 5617**
G-PRMC HS25 257031
**G-PVEL GLEX 9334**
**G-PVHT FA7X 59**
**G-PWNS C525 0153**
G-PYCO F2TH 78
G-RAAR HS25 258210
G-RACL HS25 257212
G-RAFF LJ35 504
G-RAHL BE40 RK-61
G-RAVY C500 109
G-RBSG F9EX 113
G-RCDI HS25 257142
G-RCEJ HS25 258021
G-RDBS C550 101
G-RDMV HS25 258496
**G-REDS C56X 5167**
G-REYG F9EX 193
**G-REYS CL64 5467**
G-RIBV C560 0506
**G-RIZA PRM1 RB-195**
G-RJRI HS25 257130
(G-RMPI) LJ40 45-2108
G-RSCJ C525 0298
G-RSRS BE40 RJ-36
**G-RSXL C56X 5699**
G-RVHT C550 441
**G-RWGW LJ45 213**
**G-SABI F9EX 150**
**G-SADC GLF4 4027**
G-SAJP CL61 5022
**G-SANL GLEX 9333**
G-SBEC C500 661
G-SCCC HS25 259037
**G-SEAJ C525 0113**
G-SEBE LJ35 365

**G-SFCJ C525 0245**
G-SHEA HS25 258240
G-SHEB HS25 258243
G-SHEC HS25 259037
**G-SHEF GLEX 9306**
G-SHOP HS25 25248
**G-SIRJ C680 0216**
**G-SIRO F9EX 172**
**G-SIRS C56X 5185**
**G-SJSS CL65 5760**
**G-SNZY LJ45 375**
**G-SONE C52A 0031**
**G-SOVA C550 649**
**G-SOVB LJ45 138**
G-SOVC LJ45 161
"G-SOVM" C56X 5770
G-SOVN LJ35 614
**G-SPUR C550 714**
**G-SRBN E50P 50000056**
**G-SRDG FA7X 36**
G-SSOZ C550 597
G-STCC CL64 5623
**G-STOB BE40 RK-502**
**G-STUF LJ40 45-2074**
G-SUFC HS25 256035
G-SVGN C680 0198
G-SVLB HS25 257112
**G-SVSB C680 0094**
G-SWET C500 270
**G-SXTY LJ60 280**
**G-SYGC C52A 0360**
G-SYKS C550 599
G-TACE HS25 25223
**G-TAGA CL64 5659**
**G-TAYC GLF4 4060**
**G-TBEA C52A 0191**
G-TCAP HS25 258115
G-TCDI HS25 25248
G-TEFH C500 176
**G-TFKR GLF5 5220**
G-THCL C550 563
**G-THNX C525 0022**
G-TIFF C550 290
G-TJCB HS25 257127
G-TJHI C500 363
**G-TLFK C680 0213**
G-TMAS HS25 256062
G-TOMI HS25 256030
G-TOMY MU30 A090SA
G-TOPF HS25 25238
G-TPHK HS25 258130
G-TSAM HS25 258028
**G-TSJF C52B 0231**
**G-TSLS GLEX 9231**
G-TTFN C560 0537
G-UESS C500 326
G-UKCA HS25 257214
G-UWWB HS25 258001
**G-UYAD CL64 5307**
G-UYGB CL30 20169
**G-VECT C56X 5161**
**G-VIPI HS25 258222**
G-VIPS LJ35 614
G-VJAY HS25 25254
G-VKRS CS55 0133
(G-VONI) HS25 258345
**G-VONJ PRM1 RB-66**
**G-VUEA C550 671**
**G-VUEM C500 580**
**G-VUEZ C550 008**
**G-VVPA CL64 5612**
**G-WAIN C550 550-1100**
G-WBPR HS25 258085
G-WCIN C56X 5088
**G-WINA C56X 5343**
**G-WLVS F2EX 141**
**G-WTOR F9EX 211**
(G-WWDB) HS25 259024
G-WYLX C550 418
**G-WYNE HS25 258240**
**G-XAVB C510 0283**
**G-XBEL C56X 5698**
**G-XBLU C680 0143**
**G-XLGB C56X 5259**
G-XLMB C56X 5259
G-XLSB C56X 5190
G-XMAF GLF3 407
(G-XMAR) C56X 5822
**G-XONE CL64 5426**
G-XPRS GLEX 9133
G-XRMC HS25 258180
**G-XXRS GLEX 9169**
**G-XXZZ LJ60 328**
**G-YPRS C550 550-0935**
G-YUGO HS25 25094
G-ZAPI C500 560
G-ZEAL LJ35 275
G-ZEIZ LJ36 047
G-ZENO LJ35 429
(G-ZEST) LJ35 265
**G-ZING LJ35 429**
G-ZIPS LJ35 365
**G-ZIZI C525 0345**
**G-ZJET C510 0161**
G-ZONE LJ35 365
G-ZOOM LJ35 236
**G-ZXZX LJ45 005**

## Hungary

**HA-JET C500 249**
**HA-LKN F9EX 143**
**HA-YFE MU30 A046SA**
**HA-YFH BE40 RK-528**
HA-YFI HS25 258043
**HA-YFJ BE40 RK-254**

## Switzerland

(HB- ) F900 4
(HB- ) LJ55 050
(HB- ) PRM1 RB-27
(HB- ) WW24 390
(HB-I ) GLF2 126
(HB-I ) GLF4 1074
HB-IAB F900 9
HB-IAC F900 26
HB-IAD F900 35
HB-IAE FA50 150
HB-IAF F900 30
HB-IAG FA50 174
**HB-IAH F9EX 28**
HB-IAI F900 75
**HB-IAJ F2EX 3**
HB-IAK F900 15
HB-IAL FA50 63
HB-IAM FA50 164
HB-IAQ F9EX 35
HB-IAT FA50 86
**HB-IAU F2EX 14**
HB-IAV FA50 230
**HB-IAW F2TH 16**
**HB-IAX F2TH 33**
HB-IAY F2TH 34
**HB-IAZ F2TH 30**
HB-IBG F900 115
**HB-IBH F2TH 42**
HB-IBQ FA50 125
HB-IBX GLF4 1183
HB-IBY F900 44
HB-IEA FA50 133
HB-IEB FA50 17
HB-IEC FA50 134
HB-IED FA50 147
(HB-IED) FA50 9
HB-IEJ GLF4 1148
HB-IEP FA50 67
HB-IEQ GLF4 1174
HB-IER FA50 57
HB-IES FA50 61
HB-IET FA50 48
HB-IEU FA50 27
HB-IEV FA50 34
HB-IEW GLF2 124
HB-IEX GLF2 169
HB-IEY GLF2 210
HB-IEZ GLF2 216
HB-IEZ GLF2 246
**HB-IFJ F9EX 92**
**HB-IFQ F900 121**
"HB-IGA" GALX 011
**HB-IGI F9EX 83**
(HB-IGK) GALX 012
**HB-IGL F900 58**
**HB-IGM GLF5 5004**
HB-IGP GALX 013
**HB-IGQ F2EX 9**
HB-IGR FA50 104
HB-IGS GLEX 9102
HB-IGT F900 185
HB-IGX F9EX 86
**HB-IGY F9EX 95**
**HB-IHQ GLEX 9011**
HB-IIS GLF5 572
HB-IIV CL64 5397
HB-IIY GLF5 638
HB-IIZ GLF5 641
HB-IKJ CL64 5327
HB-IKQ CL64 5318
**HB-IKR GLF4 1159**
**HB-IKS CL61 5042**
HB-IKT CL61 5003
HB-IKU CL61 5005
HB-IKV CL61 5092
HB-IKW CL61 5096
HB-IKX CL61 3006
HB-IKY CL61 5125
HB-IKZ GLEX 9054
HB-ILH CL60 1025
HB-ILK CL61 3033
HB-ILL CL64 5373
HB-ILM CL61 3024
HB-ILV GLF4 1460
**HB-IMJ GLF5 517**
HB-IMV GLF2 8
HB-IMW GLF2 194
HB-IMX GLF3 335
(HB-IMY) GLF4 1033
**HB-IMY GLF4 1084**
HB-IMZ GLF2 88/21
**HB-INJ GLEX 9086**
HB-INQ GLF5 568
HB-ISD FA50 159
HB-ISF F2TH 26
(HB-ITE) GLF4 1046
HB-ITF GLF4 1202
HB-ITG GLEX 9036
HB-ITH FA50 117
HB-ITJ GLF4 1175
HB-ITK CL61 5090
HB-ITM GLF3 352
HB-ITN GLF3 367
HB-ITP GLF4 1046
HB-ITR GLF2 144
HB-ITS GLF3 435
(HB-ITT) GLF4 1046
HB-ITT GLF4 1064
HB-ITV GLF2 139/11
HB-ITW GLF2 192
HB-ITX GLF4 1093
HB-ITZ GLF4 1083
HB-IUF CL61 5067
HB-IUJ GLEX 9095
HB-IUR GLEX 9013
(HB-IUS) GALX 078
**HB-IUT GALX 007**
HB-IUU GALX 011
**HB-IUW F900 150**
**HB-IUX F9EX 54**
HB-IUY F900 181
HB-IUZ F2TH 74
**HB-IVL GLF5 513**
HB-IVM F2TH 55
HB-IVN F2TH 61
**HB-IVO F2TH 62**
HB-IVP CL64 5369
HB-IVR CL64 5318
**HB-IVS CL61 5166**
HB-IVT CL64 5394
HB-IVV CL64 5384
**HB-IVZ GLF5 577**
**HB-IWY GLF4 1176**
HB-IWZ GLF4 1061
**HB-JEB GALX 032**
**HB-JEC CL30 20029**
**HB-JEE GLF5 5025**
HB-JEG F2EX 34
**HB-JEI F900 86**
**HB-JEM CL64 5613**
HB-JEN GLEX 9015
**HB-JEP GLF5 5070**
HB-JEQ GLF4 4027
**HB-JER GLEX 9017**
**HB-JES GLF5 556**
**HB-JET F2EX 154**
HB-JEU CL30 20039
**HB-JEV GLF5 5040**
**HB-JEX GLEX 9145**
**HB-JEY GLEX 9173**
**HB-JEZ C750 0179**
**HB-JFK E50P 50000062**
**HB-JFO CL30 20137**
**HB-JFZ CL64 5510**
HB-JGC GLF5 5175
**HB-JGE GLEX 9287**
**HB-JGF F2EX 185**
**HB-JGG F2EX 188**
**HB-JGH GLEX 9320**
**HB-JGJ GLF4 4122**
**HB-JGK JSTR 5233**
**HB-JGL GALX 193**
HB-JGN GLEX 9249
HB-JGO GLEX 9004
**HB-JGP GLEX 9238**
**HB-JGQ CL30 20237**
**HB-JGR CL64 5624**
**HB-JGT CL65 5736**
**HB-JGU C750 0001**
HB-JGX GLF5 5172
HB-JGY GLEX 9167
**HB-JIG C680 0280**
HB-JIH GLEX 9359
HB-JKA GLF5 554
**HB-JKB GLF5 5178**
**HB-JKC GLF5 5240**
**HB-JKG GALX 184**
**HB-JLK FA7X 44**
**HB-JRA CL64 5529**
**HB-JRB CL64 5530**
**HB-JRC CL64 5540**
**HB-JRE CL65 5726**
**HB-JRN CL64 5494**
HB-JRN CL65 5753
HB-JRP CL65 5709
**HB-JRQ CL64 5651**
**HB-JRR GLEX 9198**
**HB-JRS GLEX 9174**
**HB-JRT CL64 5442**
**HB-JRV CL61 5035**
HB-JRW CL64 5602
(HB-JRX) CL61 5152
HB-JRY CL64 5502
HB-JRZ CL64 5553
**HB-JSI FA7X 37**
**HB-JSN FA7X 76**
**HB-JSO FA7X 12**
HB-JSP F900 69
**HB-JSR FA50 165**
(HB-JSS) FA7X 16
**HB-JSS FA7X 2**
**HB-JST FA7X 17**
**HB-JSU F9DX 612**
HB-JSV FA50 215
HB-JSW F9DX 601
**HB-JSX F9EX 141**
**HB-JSY F9EX 96**
**HB-JSZ FA7X 4**
**HB-JTB CL30 20141**
HB-PAA MS76 069
HB-PAC MS76 112
(HB-V ) C560 0106
(HB-V ) C560 0301
(HB-V ) FA10 150
(HB-V ) FA20 112
HB-VAA C56X 5269
HB-VAG HS25 25006
HB-VAH HS25 25007
HB-VAI LJ24 019
HB-VAK SBRL 282-25
(HB-VAL) WW24 17
HB-VAM LJ24 044
HB-VAN HS25 25063
HB-VAP FA20 37/406
HB-VAR HS25 25025
HB-VAS LJ24 109
HB-VAT HS25 25090

| | | | | | | | | | | | |
|---|---|---|---|---|---|---|---|---|---|---|---|
| HB-VAU | HS25 | 25099 | HB-VEP | MS76 | 098 | HB-VIE | LJ25 | 193 | HB-VMA | LJ45 | 020 |
| HB-VAV | FA20 | 3/403 | (HB-VER) | FA20 | 174/457 | HB-VIF | LJ36 | 057 | HB-VMB | LJ45 | 021 |
| HB-VAW | FA20 | 72/413 | HB-VES | LJ24 | 027 | HB-VIG | FA10 | 89 | HB-VMC | LJ45 | 028 |
| HB-VAX | WW24 | 15 | (HB-VET) | JSTR | 5009 | HB-VII | LJ35 | 503 | HB-VMD | HS25 | 257040 |
| HB-VAY | HS25 | 25135 | HB-VEU | MS76 | 102 | HB-VIK | HS25 | 258091 | HB-VME | FA10 | 131 |
| HB-VAZ | HS25 | 25130 | HB-VEV | FA20 | 317 | HB-VIL | HS25 | 258097 | HB-VMF | HS25 | 258175 |
| HB-VBA | LJ24 | 026 | HB-VEV | LJ35 | 075 | HB-VIM | LJ31 | 018 | HB-VMG | ASTR | 105 |
| HB-VBB | LJ24 | 045A | HB-VEW | LJ35 | 088 | HB-VIN | C650 | 0119 | HB-VMH | C550 | 649 |
| HB-VBC | LJ24 | 053 | HB-VEX | C500 | 338 | HB-VIO | C550 | 181 | HB-VMI | HS25 | 258210 |
| HB-VBD | LJ24 | 052 | HB-VEY | LJ35 | 090 | HB-VIP | C550 | 469 | **HB-VMJ** | **CS55** | **0029** |
| HB-VBI | LJ25 | 040 | HB-VEZ | FA20 | 228/473 | HB-VIR | C550 | 328 | HB-VMK | ASTR | 113 |
| HB-VBK | LJ24 | 128 | HB-VFA | HS25 | 257007 | HB-VIS | C550 | 447 | **HB-VML** | **LJ45** | **084** |
| HB-VBL | FA20 | 126/438 | HB-VFB | LJ35 | 145 | HB-VIT | C550 | 220 | HB-VMM | C550 | 550-0907 |
| HB-VBM | FA20 | 136/439 | HB-VFC | LJ35 | 099 | HB-VIU | C550 | 465 | HB-VMN | FA20 | 240/478 |
| HB-VBN | HS25 | 25138 | HB-VFD | LJ36 | 029 | HB-VIV | C500 | 340 | **HB-VMO** | **C56X** | **5061** |
| HB-VBO | FA20 | 150/445 | (HB-VFE) | LJ35 | 111 | HB-VIW | FA10 | 113 | HB-VMP | C550 | 697 |
| HB-VBP | LJ25 | 033 | HB-VFF | C500 | 392 | HB-VIX | FA10 | 126 | HB-VMR | ASTR | 115 |
| HB-VBR | LJ25 | 038 | HB-VFG | LJ35 | 119 | HB-VIY | C650 | 0040 | HB-VMT | C525 | 0250 |
| HB-VBS | FA20 | 55/410 | HB-VFH | C500 | 180 | HB-VIZ | C550 | 207 | **HB-VMU** | **C56X** | **5066** |
| HB-VBT | HS25 | 25171 | HB-VFI | C500 | 413 | HB-VJA | C550 | 379 | **HB-VMV** | **C560** | **0166** |
| HB-VBU | LJ24 | 231 | HB-VFK | LJ35 | 118 | **HB-VJB** | **C500** | **442** | HB-VMW | C550 | 550-0955 |
| HB-VBW | HS25 | 25199 | HB-VFL | LJ35 | 137 | HB-VJC | LJ35 | 614 | **HB-VMX** | **C550** | **550-0946** |
| HB-VBX | WW24 | 47 | (HB-VFO) | LJ35 | 162 | HB-VJD | FA20 | 116 | **HB-VMY** | **C550** | **550-0964** |
| HB-VBY | LJ24 | 206 | HB-VFO | LJ35 | 184 | HB-VJE | BE40 | RJ-44 | HB-VMZ | C56X | 5067 |
| HB-VBZ | HS25 | 25215 | HB-VFP | WW24 | 231 | HB-VJF | SBRL | 465-59 | **HB-VNA** | **C560** | **0280** |
| HB-VCA | FA20 | 208/468 | (HB-VFS) | FA10 | 121 | HB-VJH | C550 | 234 | HB-VNB | C560 | 0271 |
| HB-VCB | FA20 | 182/461 | HB-VFS | LJ36 | 042 | HB-VJI | LJ31 | 011 | HB-VNC | C56X | 5058 |
| HB-VCC | WW24 | 145 | HB-VFT | FA10 | 121 | HB-VJJ | LJ35 | 649 | HB-VND | C56X | 5106 |
| HB-VCE | HS25 | 25235 | HB-VFU | LJ35 | 196 | HB-VJK | LJ35 | 651 | **HB-VNE** | **BE40** | **RK-318** |
| HB-VCG | FA20 | 231/474 | HB-VFV | LJ36 | 040 | HB-VJL | LJ35 | 653 | HB-VNF | ASTR | 059 |
| HB-VCI | LJ24 | 243 | HB-VFW | CL60 | 1049 | HB-VJM | FA10 | 188 | **HB-VNG** | **FA20** | **502** |
| HB-VCK | LJ25 | 082 | HB-VFX | LJ35 | 191 | HB-VJN | FA10 | 118 | HB-VNH | C56X | 5172 |
| HB-VCL | LJ25 | 076 | HB-VFY | LJ28 | 29-001 | (HB-VJP) | C500 | 178 | **HB-VNI** | **C56X** | **5154** |
| HB-VCM | LJ25 | 073 | HB-VFZ | LJ35 | 222 | HB-VJQ | C525 | 0041 | HB-VNJ | HS25 | 258521 |
| HB-VCN | LJ24 | 247 | HB-VGA | CL60 | 1029 | HB-VJR | C500 | 343 | HB-VNK | C525 | 0271 |
| **HB-VCN** | **SBRL** | **465-32** | HB-VGB | LJ28 | 28-004 | HB-VJS | FA20 | 383/550 | **HB-VNL** | **C525** | **0375** |
| HB-VCO | FA20 | 25/405 | (HB-VGC) | LJ35 | 239 | HB-VJT | C650 | 0076 | HB-VNM | FA20 | 426 |
| HB-VCR | FA20 | 263/489 | HB-VGC | LJ35 | 259 | HB-VJV | FA20 | 237/476 | HB-VNO | C52A | 0033 |
| HB-VCS | LJ25 | 097 | HB-VGD | C500 | 082 | HB-VJW | FA20 | 175 | **HB-VNP** | **C525** | **0499** |
| HB-VCT | LJ24 | 241 | (HB-VGD) | C500 | 478 | HB-VJX | FA20 | 293 | HB-VNR | C56X | 5248 |
| HB-VCU | C500 | 038 | HB-VGE | C550 | 074 | HB-VJY | HS25 | 258176 | **HB-VNS** | **C56X** | **5209** |
| HB-VCW | LJ24 | 256 | HB-VGF | HS25 | 257062 | HB-VJZ | C560 | 0055 | HB-VNU | C500 | 282 |
| HB-VCX | C500 | 008 | HB-VGG | HS25 | 257070 | HB-VKA | CS55 | 0137 | **HB-VNV** | **LJ60** | **179** |
| HB-VCY | LJ24 | 267 | HB-VGH | LJ35 | 206 | HB-VKB | C525 | 0037 | **HB-VNW** | **C560** | **0457** |
| HB-VCZ | LJ35 | 433 | (HB-VGI) | C500 | 251 | HB-VKC | FA20 | 117 | HB-VNY | C56X | 5576 |
| (HB-VCZ) | SBRL | 282-117 | HB-VGK | C550 | 035 | HB-VKD | C500 | 643 | **HB-VNZ** | **C550** | **550-0906** |
| HB-VDA | C500 | 081 | HB-VGL | LJ35 | 278 | HB-VKE | FA10 | 7 | HB-VOA | ASTR | 111 |
| HB-VDB | FA20 | 296/507 | HB-VGM | LJ35 | 288 | HB-VKF | FA10 | 89 | **HB-VOB** | **HS25** | **258733** |
| HB-VDC | C500 | 100 | HB-VGN | LJ35 | 149 | HB-VKH | C550 | 135 | **HB-VOC** | **C560** | **0301** |
| HB-VDD | FA10 | 36 | HB-VGO | C500 | 053 | HB-VKI | LJ60 | 019 | **HB-VOD** | **C525** | **0415** |
| HB-VDE | FA10 | 7 | HB-VGP | C550 | 205 | HB-VKJ | HS25 | 257067 | **HB-VOE** | **C52A** | **0017** |
| HB-VDG | FA20 | 58 | HB-VGR | C550 | 089 | HB-VKK | C500 | 178 | **HB-VOF** | **C525** | **0623** |
| HB-VDH | LJ24 | 148 | HB-VGS | C550 | 206 | HB-VKM | HS25 | 258035 | **HB-VOG** | **C525** | **0544** |
| HB-VDI | LJ25 | 149 | HB-VGT | LJ35 | 309 | HB-VKN | HS25 | 258036 | **HB-VOH** | **C550** | **550-0864** |
| HB-VDK | LJ24 | 271 | (HB-VGU) | HS25 | 25199 | HB-VKO | FA20 | 257 | **HB-VOI** | **PRM1** | **RB-152** |
| HB-VDL | HS25 | 256021 | HB-VGU | LJ35 | 331 | HB-VKP | C550 | 622 | **HB-VOJ** | **HS25** | **258799** |
| HB-VDM | C500 | 126 | HB-VGV | LJ55 | 015 | HB-VKR | FA10 | 209 | **HB-VOL** | **C52A** | **0341** |
| HB-VDN | LJ24 | 287 | HB-VGW | LJ35 | 336 | HB-VKS | C550 | 441 | HB-VOM | C56X | 5642 |
| **HB-VDO** | **C550** | **098** | HB-VGX | LJ35 | 372 | HB-VKT | C550 | 310 | **HB-VON** | **C56X** | **5528** |
| (HB-VDO) | FA20 | 306/512 | HB-VGY | LJ35 | 370 | HB-VKV | HS25 | 258228 | **HB-VOO** | **HS25** | **259030** |
| (HB-VDO) | LJ24 | 289 | HB-VGZ | LJ55 | 024 | **HB-VKW** | **HS25** | **258246** | **HB-VOP** | **C52A** | **0385** |
| HB-VDP | FA20 | 245/481 | HB-VHA | C500 | 524 | HB-VKX | C550 | 307 | **HB-VOQ** | **HS25** | **259021** |
| (HB-VDR) | C500 | 187 | HB-VHB | LJ35 | 359 | HB-VKY | C500 | 476 | HB-VOR | C525 | 0473 |
| HB-VDS | HS25 | 256048 | HB-VHC | CL60 | 1028 | HB-VLA | HS25 | 257031 | **HB-VOS** | **PRM1** | **RB-187** |
| (HB-VDT) | FA10 | 21 | HB-VHD | LJ35 | 395 | HB-VLB | C500 | 638 | **HB-VOT** | **HS25** | **258645** |
| HB-VDU | LJ24 | 310 | HB-VHE | LJ35 | 413 | HB-VLC | HS25 | 257127 | **HB-VOU** | **C56X** | **5070** |
| HB-VDV | FA20 | 307/513 | HB-VHF | LJ36 | 048 | HB-VLD | C500 | 589 | **HB-VOV** | **C525** | **0665** |
| (HB-VDW) | FA20 | 86 | HB-VHG | LJ35 | 445 | HB-VLE | C500 | 313 | **HB-VOW** | **C52B** | **0209** |
| HB-VDX | FA10 | 56 | HB-VHH | CS55 | 0028 | HB-VLF | HS25 | 258264 | HB-VOX | C525 | 0193 |
| HB-VDY | FA20 | 245/481 | HB-VHI | C500 | 344 | **HB-VLG** | **HS25** | **258265** | **HB-VOY** | **HS25** | **258895** |
| (HB-VDY) | FA20 | 306/512 | HB-VHK | LJ55 | 045 | HB-VLH | HS25 | 257017 | **HB-VOZ** | **LJ60** | **148** |
| HB-VDZ | FA20 | 255/487 | HB-VHL | LJ55 | 054 | HB-VLI | HS25 | 258120 | **HB-VPB** | **C52A** | **0422** |
| HB-VEA | LJ36 | 006 | HB-VHM | LJ25 | 314 | HB-VLJ | HS25 | 257030 | **HB-VPC** | **C52A** | **0331** |
| HB-VEB | FA20 | 323/520 | HB-VHN | LJ55 | 073 | HB-VLK | LJ36 | 032 | **HB-VPJ** | **HS25** | **HA-0038** |
| HB-VEC | SBRL | 380-12 | HB-VHO | CL60 | 1053 | HB-VLL | HS25 | 257105 | **HB-VWA** | **C52A** | **0383** |
| HB-VED | FA20 | 162/451 | HB-VHR | LJ35 | 501 | HB-VLM | BE40 | RK-66 | **HB-VWB** | **C52B** | **0216** |
| HB-VEE | LJ36 | 016 | HB-VHS | FA20 | 488 | HB-VLN | BE40 | RK-94 | **HB-VWC** | **C52B** | **0272** |
| HB-VEF | LJ25 | 193 | HB-VHT | MU30 | A052SA | HB-VLP | C650 | 7064 | **HB-VWD** | **C56X** | **6021** |
| HB-VEG | FA10 | 70 | HB-VHU | HS25 | 258152 | HB-VLQ | C550 | 352 | (HB-VWE) | C56X | 6021 |
| HB-VEH | C500 | 230 | **HB-VHV** | **HS25** | **258153** | HB-VLR | LJ31 | 127 | **HB-VWE** | **C56X** | **6022** |
| HB-VEI | LJ25 | 199 | HB-VHW | C650 | 0060 | HB-VLS | C550 | 219 | **HB-VWF** | **C525** | **0650** |
| HB-VEK | HS25 | 257094 | HB-VHX | MU30 | A035SA | HB-VLT | HS25 | 258240 | (HB-VWG) | C56X | 6022 |
| (HB-VEL) | LJ24 | 014 | HB-VHY | FA20 | 429 | HB-VLU | LJ60 | 010 | **HB-VWJ** | **C56X** | **5217** |
| HB-VEL | LJ24 | 023 | HB-VIA | MU30 | A087SA | HB-VLV | C560 | 0077 | **HB-VWL** | **C510** | **0169** |
| HB-VEM | LJ35 | 068 | HB-VIB | LJ55 | 009 | HB-VLW | BE40 | RK-103 | **HB-VWM** | **C525** | **0690** |
| HB-VEN | LJ35 | 045 | HB-VIC | C500 | 464 | HB-VLY | C550 | 429 | **HB-VWN** | **LJ60** | **158** |
| HB-VEO | C500 | 299 | HB-VID | C500 | 523 | **HB-VLZ** | **C560** | **0446** | HB-VWP | C525 | 0102 |

**HB-VWQ E50P 50000050**
HB-VWS E50P 50000122
(HB-VWW) FA20 37/406

### Ecuador

HC-BGL WW24 234
HC-BQT SBRL 306-33
HC-BQU SBRL 306-44
**HC-BSS FA20 150/445**
HC-BSZ LJ35 311
HC-BTJ C550 017
HC-BTN LJ35 417
HC-BTQ C500 444
HC-BTT HS25 25228
HC-BTY CS55 0067
HC-BUN SBRL 306-126
HC-BUP FA20 200
HC-BUR HS25 256053
HC-BVH FA20 490
HC-BVP C500 481
HC-BVX WW24 411

### Dominican Republic

HI-420 C550 466
HI-493 C500 406
HI-496 C550 407
HI-496SP C550 407
HI-500 C550 248
HI-500CT C550 248
HI-500SP C550 248
HI-527 C500 369
HI-527SP C500 369
(HI-530) C550 022
HI-534 C550 022
HI-534CA C550 022
HI-581SP C500 599
HI-646SP MU30 A064SA
HI-766SP BE40 RK-208
HI-836SP FA10 53
**HI766 BE40 RK-208**
**HI871 GLF2 154/28**

### Colombia

**HK- C550 550-0961**
(HK- ) GLF2 210
HK- WW24 162
HK-2150 WW24 181
HK-2150X WW24 181
HK-2485 WW24 239
**HK-2485G WW24 239**
HK-2485W WW24 239
HK-2624P LJ25 339
HK-2624X LJ25 339
HK-2968 FA10 176
HK-2968X FA10 176
HK-3121 LJ35 439
HK-3121X LJ35 439
HK-3122 LJ35 481
HK-3122X LJ35 481
HK-3191X C550 439
HK-3265 LJ24 297
HK-3400X C550 394
HK-3607X C550 040
HK-3646X LJ35 503
HK-3653 HS25 25216
HK-3653X HS25 25216
HK-3884X WW24 294
HK-3885 C500 135
HK-3893X WW24 441
HK-3921 LJ35 499
HK-3949X LJ35 670
HK-3971X WW24 306
HK-3983X LJ35 259
HK-4016X LJ55 041
HK-4128W C550 550
HK-4204 WW24 306
HK-4204X WW24 306
HK-4250 C550 550-0961
HK-4250X C550 550-0961
**HK-4304 C560 0355**
**HK-4446-G BE40 RK-26**
HK-4446-W BE40 RK-26
HK-4446X BE40 RK-26
**HK-4565 LJ60 331**
**HK-4645 BE40 RK-174**
**HK-4662 LJ35 513**
**HK-4670 HS25 258502**

### South Korea

HL7202 CL61 5081
**HL7222 GLF4 1188**
HL7226 C500 294
HL7234 FA20 370
HL7277 C500 327
HL7301 F900 156
HL7386 FA50 179
**HL7501 C560 0292**
**HL7502 C560 0294**
**HL7503 C560 0297**
**HL7504 C560 0300**
HL7522 CL64 5303
HL7576 GLEX 9019
**HL7577 CL61 5182**
HL7748 GLEX 9179
**HL7749 GLEX 9184**
HL7778 C560 0707
**HL7799 GLF5 5028**
**HL8200 GLF5 5233**
**HL8201 C525 0686**
**HL8202 C525 0691**
**HL8283 C525 0688**

### Panama

**HP- GLF2 21**
(HP- ) LJ24 346
(HP- ) LJ35 670
(HP- ) LJ55 041
HP-1A FA20 382
HP-1A GLF2 78
HP-1A WW24 180
HP-125JW HS25 25216
HP-912 LJ35 280
HP-1128P HS25 25216
HP-1141P LJ25 049
HP-1262 HS25 258133
HP-1410 C525 0350
HP-1410HT C525 0350
HP-1461 C52A 0075

### Honduras

HR-001 WW24 183
HR-002 WW24 333
HR-AMD HS25 25186
HR-AUJ GLF2 10
HR-CEF WW24 333
**HR-PHO WW24 333**

### Thailand

**HS-CDY C750 0184**
**HS-CFS LJ35 366**
**HS-CKI BE40 RK-245**
**HS-CPG HS25 258833**
**HS-DCG C650 7071**
**HS-EMS LJ35 406**
**HS-IOO C510 0100**
HS-JJA CL61 5188
**HS-KCS C750 0298**
**HS-MCL C52B 0083**
HS-RBL C550 707
(HS-TDL) CL61 5102
**HS-TPD BE40 RK-294**
HS-TVA CL61 5102
HS-UCM BE40 RK-95
**HS-VIP C510 0117**

### Saudi Arabia

**HZ- BE40 RK-592**
(HZ- ) HS25 259010
HZ-103 GLF3 453
**HZ-103 GLF4 1037**
**HZ-105 HS25 258118**
HZ-106 LJ35 374
HZ-107 LJ35 375
HZ-108 GLF3 353
HZ-109 GLF3 453
**HZ-109 HS25 258146**
**HZ-110 HS25 258148**
**HZ-130 HS25 258164**
**HZ-133 C550 550-1115**
**HZ-134 C550 550-1116**
**HZ-135 C550 550-1126**
**HZ-136 C550 550-1127**
HZ-AA1 C550 128
HZ-AA1 HS25 256019
HZ-AAA C550 063
HZ-AAA C550 128
HZ-AAA C650 0003
HZ-AAI C550 149
HZ-AB2 F900 61
HZ-ABM LJ35 243
HZ-ADC GLF2 187
HZ-ADC GLF4 1037
HZ-AFA GLEX 9029
**HZ-AFA2 CL64 5320**
HZ-AFG GLF2 175
HZ-AFH GLF2 171
HZ-AFI GLF2 201
HZ-AFJ GLF2 203
**HZ-AFK GLF2 239**
HZ-AFL GLF3 311
HZ-AFM GLF3 324
**HZ-AFN GLF3 364**
HZ-AFO GLF3 365
HZ-AFP C550 472
HZ-AFQ C550 473
**HZ-AFR GLF3 410**
HZ-AFS GLF3 450
HZ-AFS JSTR 5016
**HZ-AFT F900 21**
**HZ-AFU GLF4 1031**
**HZ-AFV GLF4 1035**
**HZ-AFW GLF4 1038**
**HZ-AFX GLF4 1143**
**HZ-AFY GLF4 1166**
**HZ-AFZ F900 61**
HZ-AK1 CL61 3032
HZ-AKI FA10 108
(HZ-AKI) FA20 395/554
HZ-AKI FA50 133
HZ-AKI FA50 7
**HZ-ALFA GLF5 5251**
HZ-ALJ C550 063
HZ-AM11 LJ55 040
HZ-AM2 LJ55 040
HZ-AM2 LJ55 127
(HZ-AMA) CL61 3017
HZ-AMA FA10 118
HZ-AMM HS25 256064
HZ-AMN SBRL 380-38
HZ-A01 FA20 359/542
HZ-A02 FA10 118
HZ-A03 FA50 7
HZ-A04 CL60 1006
**HZ-ARK GLF5 5074**
HZ-AZP LJ25 081
HZ-BB1 LJ25 081
HZ-BB2 FA50 131
HZ-BIN HS25 25106
**HZ-BIN HS25 HA-0023**
"HZ-BJP" GLEX 9293
**HZ-BL1 C525 0371**
HZ-BL2 HS25 258126
HZ-B01 HS25 25094
**HZ-BSA C56X 5658**
HZ-BSA GLF3 353
HZ-CA1 SBRL 380-55
HZ-CAD GLF2 179
HZ-DA1 GLF3 358
HZ-DA1 HS25 257067
HZ-DA2 HS25 257088
HZ-DA3 HS25 257115
HZ-DA4 HS25 257124
HZ-DAC HS25 256059
HZ-DC2 FA20 363/544
HZ-DG2 GLF3 317
**HZ-DME F900 76**
HZ-FBT JSTR 5086/44
HZ-FK1 JSTR 5133
HZ-FMA HS25 25105
HZ-FNA JSTR 5056
HZ-FYZ C56X 5022
HZ-GP3 LJ25 158
HZ-GP4 LJ24 190
HZ-GP4 LJ25 062
HZ-GP5 LJ25 199
**HZ-HA1 GLF2 216**
HZ-HE4 FA20 241/479
**HZ-HHT GLF3 491**
HZ-HR2 GLF3 346
HZ-HR4 GLF3 415
HZ-KA1 LJ35 033
HZ-KA2 HS25 256057
HZ-KA3 FA20 174/457
HZ-KA5 HS25 256049
HZ-KAA GLF4 1294
(HZ-KAI) FA10 108
HZ-KS1 GLF4 1349
HZ-KS2 GLF4 1367
(HZ-KS3) GLF4 1384
HZ-KSA HS25 258022
HZ-KSDA F2TH 121
HZ-KSDB F2TH 133
**HZ-KSDC F2TH 142**
(HZ-KSDD) F2TH 171
**HZ-KSGA GLF4 4079**
HZ-KSRA HS25 258464
HZ-KSRB HS25 258475
**HZ-KSRC HS25 258481**
(HZ-KSRD) HS25 258485
**HZ-KSRD HS25 HB-17**
HZ-KTC LJ35 147
HZ-MA1 JSTR 5105
HZ-MA1 SBRL 306-110
HZ-MA1 SBRL 306-94
HZ-MAC JSTR 5013
HZ-MAL GLF3 379
HZ-MAL GLF4 1294
HZ-MF1 CL60 1070
HZ-MF1 HS25 256060
**HZ-MF3 GLF4 1520**
**HZ-MF4 GLF4 1525**
**HZ-MF5 GLF4 1532**
**HZ-MFL GLF4 1128**
HZ-MIB LJ35 173
HZ-MIC GLF3 423
HZ-MIC GLF5 518
HZ-MMM HS25 257010
HZ-MNC GLF4 1076
HZ-MOA LJ25 081
HZ-MPM GLF2 4/8
HZ-MRP LJ25 121
HZ-MS04 GLF4 1365
HZ-MS05 GLF5 583
HZ-MS1 LJ35 467
HZ-MS1A LJ35 374
**HZ-MS1A LJ60 370**
HZ-MS1B LJ35 375
**HZ-MS1B LJ60 371**
HZ-MS1C LJ35 467
**HZ-MS3 GLF3 385**
HZ-MS4 GLF2 103
**HZ-MS4 GLF4 1365**
HZ-MS5 GLF5 583
**HZ-MS5A GLF5 644**
**HZ-MS5B GLF5 583**
HZ-MSD GLF2 256
HZ-MWD GLF3 393
HZ-NAD HS25 257064
HZ-NC1 C500 319
HZ-NCB SBRL 306-94
(HZ-NCI) LJ35 173
HZ-ND1 GLF2 216
HZ-NES FA20 174/457
HZ-NOT FA10 118
HZ-NR1 SBRL 380-71
HZ-NR2 GLF3 304
HZ-NR2 GLF3 415
HZ-NR3 GLF3 371
HZ-OFC HS25 257064
HZ-OFC HS25 258050
HZ-OFC HS25 259008
HZ-OFC2 HS25 259008

| | | |
|---|---|---|
| HZ-OFC3 | F900 | 133 |
| HZ-OFC4 | F9EX | 31 |
| **HZ-OFC5** | **F9EX** | **180** |
| **HZ-PCA** | **GLF2** | **179** |
| HZ-PET | GLF2 | 139/11 |
| HZ-PL1 | FA20 | 293 |
| HZ-PL7 | FA20 | 241/479 |
| (HZ-R4A) | F900 | 21 |
| HZ-RBH | SBRL | 380-57 |
| HZ-RC1 | HS25 | 257040 |
| HZ-RC2 | HS25 | 257055 |
| **HZ-RC3** | **GLF3** | **331** |
| HZ-RFM | CL60 | 1074 |
| HZ-RH2 | GLF3 | 346 |
| HZ-RI1 | LJ25 | 199 |
| HZ-SAA | CL60 | 1074 |
| HZ-SAB | FA50 | 73 |
| HZ-SAB2 | F900 | 113 |
| HZ-SAR | GLF4 | 1166 |
| HZ-SFA | C560 | 0132 |
| HZ-SFS | CL61 | 3017 |
| HZ-SH1 | JSTR | 5141 |
| HZ-SH2 | JSTR | 5016 |
| HZ-SH3 | JSTR | 5142 |
| HZ-SH4 | JSTR | 5148 |
| HZ-SJP | GLEX | 9293 |
| HZ-SJP | HS25 | 256059 |
| HZ-SJP | HS25 | 257214 |
| HZ-SJP | HS25 | 258068 |
| HZ-SJP2 | HS25 | 259012 |
| HZ-SJP3 | CL64 | 5346 |
| HZ-SM3 | FA50 | 165 |
| HZ-SMB | LJ24 | 117 |
| HZ-SMB | LJ25 | 073 |
| (HZ-SOG) | GLF3 | 415 |
| HZ-SOG | SBRL | 380-72 |
| **HZ-SPAA** | **BE40** | **RK-587** |
| **HZ-SPAB** | **BE40** | **RK-588** |
| **HZ-SPAC** | **BE40** | **RK-589** |
| **HZ-SPAD** | **BE40** | **RK-591** |
| HZ-SS2 | LJ25 | 213 |
| HZ-TAG | CL60 | 1007 |
| HZ-TAG | CL60 | 1014 |
| HZ-TAG | FA20 | 359/542 |
| HZ-THZ | JSTR | 5050/34 |
| HZ-THZ | SBRL | 380-53 |
| HZ-TNA | JSTR | 5120/26 |
| HZ-WBT | JSTR | 5133 |
| HZ-WBT1 | CL60 | 1074 |
| **HZ-WBT5** | **HS25** | **258032** |
| HZ-WT1 | JSTR | 5133 |
| HZ-WT2 | CL60 | 1074 |
| HZ-YA1 | HS25 | 256033 |
| HZ-ZTC | C550 | 149 |
| HZ-ZTC | C560 | 0036 |

Italy

| | | |
|---|---|---|
| **I-** | **C500** | **320** |
| (I- ) | C550 | 469 |
| I-ACCG | FA20 | 474 |
| I-ACIF | BE40 | RJ-28 |
| I-ACTL | FA20 | 427 |
| I-ADAG | FA50 | 131 |
| **I-AEAL** | **C500** | **053** |
| **I-AFIT** | **FA7X** | **34** |
| **I-AFOI** | **PRM1** | **RB-245** |
| I-AGEB | LJ35 | 243 |
| I-AGEC | FA20 | 239 |
| I-AGEN | LJ35 | 491 |
| I-AGER | LJ55 | 045 |
| (I-AGIK) | C500 | 539 |
| (I-AGLS) | C56X | 5668 |
| I-AGSM | C550 | 419 |
| I-AIFA | LJ36 | 021 |
| I-AIRV | C500 | 486 |
| **I-AIRW** | **LJ31** | **025** |
| I-ALBS | C500 | 023 |
| I-ALGU | MU30 | A067SA |
| **I-ALHO** | **HS25** | **258561** |
| **I-ALKA** | **C550** | **386** |
| I-ALKB | C550 | 393 |
| **I-ALPG** | **C550** | **348** |
| I-ALPM | LJ35 | 133 |
| I-ALPR | LJ55 | 078 |
| I-ALPT | LJ35 | 198 |
| I-ALSE | BE40 | RJ-10 |
| I-ALSI | BE40 | RJ-31 |
| I-ALSO | BE40 | RJ-34 |
| (I-ALSU) | BE40 | RJ-23 |
| I-ALSU | BE40 | RK-11 |
| **I-ALVC** | **BE40** | **RK-515** |
| I-AMAW | C500 | 095 |
| I-AMBR | C500 | 180 |
| I-AMCT | C500 | 114 |
| I-AMCU | C500 | 109 |
| **I-AMCY** | **C500** | **192** |
| I-AMME | LJ24 | 310 |
| I-ARIB | C550 | 243 |
| **I-ARIF** | **F2TH** | **203** |
| I-ARNT | WW24 | 139 |
| I-AROM | C500 | 410 |
| **I-ARON** | **C500** | **095** |
| I-AROO | C550 | 090 |
| I-ASAZ | C550 | 438 |
| **I-ASER** | **BE40** | **RK-204** |
| I-ATMO | FA20 | 94/428 |
| I-ATSA | C650 | 0161 |
| I-ATSB | C560 | 0033 |
| I-ATSE | C550 | 649 |
| **I-AUNY** | **C500** | **618** |
| **I-AVEB** | **MU30** | **A087SA** |
| **I-AVGM** | **C550** | **492** |
| I-AVJD | LJ25 | 214 |
| I-AVJE | LJ25 | 254 |
| I-AVJG | LJ35 | 189 |
| **I-AVRM** | **C550** | **491** |
| **I-AVSS** | **BE40** | **RK-66** |
| **I-AVVM** | **CS55** | **0062** |
| **I-AZFB** | **HS25** | **257201** |
| I-BAEL | FA20 | 426 |
| **I-BBGR** | **HS25** | **HA-0056** |
| **I-BEAU** | **F900** | **23** |
| **I-BEDT** | **C56X** | **5172** |
| **I-BENN** | **C550** | **550-0859** |
| **I-BENT** | **C56X** | **5053** |
| I-BETV | C650 | 0104 |
| I-BEWW | CL61 | 5020 |
| I-BLSM | CL60 | 1076 |
| **I-BLUB** | **C650** | **0216** |
| **I-BMFE** | **LJ25** | **146** |
| **I-BNTN** | **F2TH** | **191** |
| **I-BOAT** | **C525** | **0450** |
| I-BOGI | HS25 | 25138 |
| **I-CABD** | **C525** | **0354** |
| **I-CAEX** | **F9EX** | **91** |
| I-CAFB | FA50 | 138 |
| I-CAFC | FA50 | 145 |
| **I-CAFD** | **FA50** | **183** |
| I-CAFE | FA50 | 190 |
| I-CAIB | FA20 | 175 |
| I-CAIC | FA10 | 89 |
| (I-CAIK) | FA50 | 37 |
| I-CALC | FA10 | 127 |
| **I-CALZ** | **C52A** | **0427** |
| I-CART | LJ24 | 231 |
| I-CASG | HS25 | 258033 |
| (I-CCCB) | C500 | 382 |
| **I-CCCH** | **CL30** | **20094** |
| **I-CDOL** | **C56X** | **5584** |
| I-CEFI | CS55 | 0047 |
| **I-CFLY** | **LJ31** | **167** |
| I-CHIC | FA10 | 126 |
| I-CHOC | FA10 | 113 |
| I-CIGA | C550 | 263 |
| **I-CIGB** | **C500** | **539** |
| I-CIGH | HS25 | 257201 |
| I-CIPA | C500 | 559 |
| I-CIST | C650 | 0085 |
| I-CITY | C500 | 053 |
| **I-CLAD** | **C500** | **223** |
| **I-CMAB** | **C56X** | **5731** |
| **I-CMAD** | **C56X** | **5801** |
| **I-CMAL** | **C56X** | **5344** |
| **I-CMCC** | **C560** | **0542** |
| I-CMUT | FA20 | 389/552 |
| **I-CNDG** | **C56X** | **6045** |
| I-CNEF | FA20 | 506 |
| I-COKE | C500 | 251 |
| I-COTO | LJ25 | 285 |
| I-CREM | FA10 | 161 |
| (I-CRYS) | LJ36 | 006 |
| I-CSGA | FA50 | 203 |
| I-CSGB | FA50 | 208 |
| I-CTPT | CL61 | 5013 |
| (I-DAEP) | C500 | 414 |
| **I-DAGF** | **C525** | **0347** |
| I-DAGS | CL61 | 5085 |
| **I-DAKO** | **F9EX** | **160** |
| I-DARK | FA50 | 151 |
| I-DDAE | LJ24 | 336 |
| I-DDVA | HS25 | 258389 |
| **I-DDVF** | **F2TH** | **161** |
| **I-DEAC** | **C525** | **0194** |
| I-DEAF | C550 | 283 |
| I-DEAN | LJ25 | 314 |
| **I-DEAS** | **GLF5** | **593** |
| I-DECI | C500 | 504 |
| I-DEGF | FA50 | 176 |
| I-DENR | FA50 | 125 |
| **I-DEUM** | **C52A** | **0095** |
| **I-DFSL** | **LJ45** | **158** |
| I-DIDY | C500 | 514 |
| **I-DIES** | **F900** | **30** |
| I-DJMA | FA10 | 179 |
| I-DKET | FA20 | 160/450 |
| **I-DLOH** | **HS25** | **258450** |
| I-DLON | LJ35 | 346 |
| **I-DMSA** | **PRM1** | **RB-201** |
| **I-DMSB** | **PRM1** | **RB-254** |
| I-DNOR | FA10 | 118 |
| I-DOCA | MU30 | A059SA |
| I-DRIB | FA20 | 201/469 |
| (I-DRVM) | HS25 | 257017 |
| I-DUMA | C500 | 263 |
| I-DVAL | C500 | 649 |
| I-DVMR | HS25 | 257017 |
| I-EAMM | LJ35 | 634 |
| **I-EDEM** | **C525** | **0155** |
| I-EDIF | FA20 | 300/508 |
| I-EDIK | FA50 | 132 |
| I-EDIM | FA20 | 295/500 |
| I-EDIS | FA20 | 280/503 |
| I-EJIA | LJ24 | 259 |
| I-EJIB | LJ35 | 331 |
| I-EJIC | FA10 | 89 |
| I-EJID | LJ35 | 222 |
| I-EKET | FA20 | 170/455 |
| I-ELEN | LJ25 | 171 |
| **I-ELYS** | **LJ40** | **45-2016** |
| **I-EPAM** | **HS25** | **HB-32** |
| I-ERDN | FA50 | 48 |
| I-ERJA | C500 | 358 |
| I-ERJB | LJ31 | 167 |
| I-ERJC | LJ45 | 072 |
| I-ERJC | LJ45 | 093 |
| **I-ERJD** | **LJ45** | **068** |
| **I-ERJE** | **LJ45** | **226** |
| I-ERJG | LJ40 | 45-2015 |
| **I-ERJJ** | **LJ40** | **45-2053** |
| I-ESAI | C525 | 0235 |
| **I-FARN** | **C500** | **565** |
| I-FBCA | SBRL | 306-97 |
| I-FBCK | C500 | 178 |
| I-FBCT | C550 | 090 |
| I-FCHI | GLF3 | 460 |
| I-FCIM | FA20 | 323/520 |
| **I-FDED** | **BE40** | **RK-500** |
| **I-FEDN** | **F2EX** | **204** |
| I-FEEV | C650 | 0105 |
| I-FERN | C500 | 152 |
| I-FFLY | LJ35 | 325 |
| I-FFRI | LJ35 | 493 |
| I-FICV | F900 | 54 |
| I-FIMI | LJ35 | 090 |
| I-FINR | MS76 | 111 |
| I-FIPE | FA20 | 368 |
| I-FIPP | CL61 | 5069 |
| **I-FITO** | **C510** | **0160** |
| I-FJDC | FA10 | 203 |
| I-FJDN | FA50 | 295 |
| I-FJTB | C550 | 550-0922 |
| I-FJTC | C550 | 550-0988 |
| I-FJTO | C550 | 679 |
| I-FKET | FA20 | 279/502 |
| **I-FLYA** | **C500** | **467** |
| I-FLYB | C500 | 489 |
| I-FLYC | LJ35 | 298 |
| **I-FLYD** | **C550** | **291** |
| I-FLYF | FA20 | 428 |
| I-FLYG | LJ35 | 593 |
| I-FLYH | LJ35 | 498 |
| **I-FLYI** | **F9EX** | **204** |
| I-FLYJ | LJ55 | 084 |
| I-FLYK | FA20 | 241/479 |
| I-FLYL | ASTR | 036 |
| **I-FLYP** | **F2TH** | **103** |
| I-FLYS | F900 | 115 |
| **I-FLYV** | **F2TH** | **108** |
| **I-FLYW** | **F9EX** | **27** |
| I-FOMN | C500 | 498 |
| **I-FORR** | **LJ40** | **45-2019** |
| **I-FORU** | **LJ45** | **036** |
| I-FRAB | MU30 | A052SA |
| **I-FRAI** | **C500** | **452** |
| I-FREU | LJ24 | 279 |
| I-FRTT | MU30 | A056SA |
| I-FSJA | BE40 | RK-41 |
| I-FTAL | BE40 | RJ-42 |
| I-GAMB | C550 | 312 |
| I-GASD | C650 | 0037 |
| I-GCAL | FA20 | 307/513 |
| I-GCFA | BE40 | RJ-44 |
| I-GENC | MU30 | A065SA |
| I-GERA | C500 | 511 |
| **I-GFVF** | **BE40** | **RK-499** |
| **I-GGLA** | **C56X** | **6044** |
| (I-GIAN) | LJ25 | 207 |
| I-GIAZ | FA20 | 252/485 |
| I-GIRL | MU30 | A012SA |
| **I-GIWW** | **C550** | **550-0871** |
| I-GJBO | HS25 | 25240 |
| I-GJMA | C500 | 542 |
| I-GOBJ | FA20 | 180/460 |
| I-GOBZ | FA20 | 293 |
| **I-GOCO** | **LJ40** | **45-2078** |
| I-GOSF | C52A | 0199 |
| **I-GSAL** | **PRM1** | **RB-184** |
| **I-GURU** | **LJ40** | **45-2059** |
| I-IDAG | C525 | 0093 |
| I-IFPC | BE40 | RK-71 |
| I-IGNO | HS25 | 258040 |
| I-IINL | LJ60 | 236 |
| **I-IMMG** | **C52A** | **0038** |
| **I-IMMI** | **C525** | **0379** |
| I-INCZ | BE40 | RJ-22 |
| I-IPFC | BE40 | RK-6 |
| **I-IPIZ** | **BE40** | **RK-29** |
| **I-IRCS** | **CL64** | **5464** |
| I-IRIF | FA20 | 185/467 |
| I-ITAL | HFB3 | 1040 |
| I-ITPR | FA10 | 115 |
| **I-JAMJ** | **F2EX** | **108** |
| **I-JAMY** | **F2TH** | **54** |
| I-JESA | C550 | 098 |
| I-JESE | C500 | 330 |
| I-JESJ | C550 | 352 |
| I-JESO | C550 | 283 |
| I-JETF | F2EX | 78 |
| I-JETS | C56X | 5012 |
| I-JETX | C750 | 0184 |
| I-JUST | C500 | 621 |
| I-KALI | LJ35 | 249 |
| I-KELM | LJ35 | 406 |
| **I-KERE** | **F2TH** | **197** |
| I-KESO | C550 | 338 |
| I-KETO | C750 | 0161 |
| I-KIDO | FA50 | 31 |
| I-KILO | LJ55 | 007 |
| I-KIOV | LJ25 | 299 |
| I-KISS | LJ25 | 193 |
| I-KIWI | C550 | 432 |
| I-KODE | C500 | 626 |
| I-KODM | LJ35 | 620 |
| **I-KREM** | **HS25** | **258608** |
| I-KUNA | C500 | 053 |
| I-KUSS | LJ35 | 237 |
| I-KWYJ | C500 | 412 |
| I-LADA | GLF4 | 1142 |
| (I-LAFA) | FA20 | 381/548 |
| **I-LALL** | **C52A** | **0005** |
| (I-LAST) | C56X | 5668 |
| I-LAWN | C500 | 612 |
| I-LCJG | FA10 | 53 |
| I-LCJT | FA10 | 96 |
| I-LEAR | LJ25 | 207 |
| I-LECO | WW24 | 72 |

I-LIAB FA20 172/456
I-LIAC FA20 234/475
I-LIAD LJ35 111
I-LOOK LJ55 021
I-LPHZ CL60 1069
I-LUBE FA10 7
I-LUBI GLF4 1123
**I-LUXO GLF5 5071**
**I-LVNB C52A 0073**
I-LXAG FA50 159
I-LXGR GLF4 1234
I-LXOT FA20 496
I-MABU LJ24 287
I-MADU GLF3 448
I-MAFU FA20 501
**I-MCAS C510 0185**
I-MCSA LJ35 099
**I-MESK C550 024**
**I-MFAB HS25 HA-0074**
I-MILK CL64 5304
I-MMAE LJ35 116
I-MMEA FA50 140
I-MOCO LJ35 445
I-MORA SBRL 282-117
I-MOVE GLEX 9044
I-MPIZ BE40 RJ-25
(I-MPUT) GLF5 593
I-MRDV CL60 1078
I-MTDE F900 43
I-MTNT C550 116
**I-MTVB C550 550-0932**
I-MUDE FA10 136
**I-NATS F2EX 11**
I-NATZ LJ60 204
I-NEWY C560 0115
**I-NGIR PRM1 RB-241**
I-NIAR C550 312
I-NICK SBRL 282-25
I-NIKJ LJ35 055
I-NLAE FA20 134
I-NNUS CL61 5044
I-NORT C500 320
**I-NUMI F900 89**
I-NYCE C560 0053
I-NYNY C56X 5107
I-NYSE C560 0302
I-OANN FA10 208
I-OMEP C500 476
**I-OMRA C52A 0064**
I-ONDO BE40 RJ-20
I-OSLO HS25 258050
I-OSUA LJ55 102
**I-OTEL C500 414**
I-OTTY BE40 RJ-25
**I-PABL C550 550-1083**
I-PALP C500 583
I-PAPE C500 659
**I-PARS LJ40 45-2034**
I-PATY SBRL 306-133
**I-PBRA FA50 339**
**I-PEGA C500 081**
I-PERF FA20 313
I-PIAI P808 503
I-PIAL P808 504
I-PIAY P808 522
I-PLLL C500 230
**I-PNCA C550 257**
I-POLE FA50 180
**I-PRAD LJ60 145**
I-PTCT CL60 1082
**I-PZZR HS25 258722**
I-RACE HS25 25006
**I-RAGW C500 311**
I-RASO HS25 25131
I-RDSF BE40 RJ-36
I-REAL FA20 267/491
**I-RELT SBRL 282-133**
I-RIED FA20 77/429
I-RJVA LJ25 342
I-ROBM FA20 182/461
I-RODJ FA50 155
**I-RONY HS25 258506**
I-ROST C500 445
**I-RPLY LJ60 212**
**I-RVRP C525 0397**
I-RYVA LJ35 391
I-SAFP FA50 9
I-SAFR FA50 29
I-SALG C650 0120
I-SALV C550 561
I-SAME FA50 37
I-SAMI BE40 RJ-35
I-SATV C500 524
**I-SDAG LJ60 379**
**I-SDFC CL30 20013**
I-SDFG HS25 258136
**I-SEAE F2TH 200**
**I-SEAS F9EX 192**
I-SELM MU30 A064SA
I-SFER LJ25 097
I-SFRA FA10 130
I-SHIP FA10 110
(I-SHOP) FA10 113
(I-SIDU) LJ35 111
I-SIMD LJ25 193
I-SIRF HS25 258267
I-SMEG GLF2 97
I-SNAB FA50 169
I-SNAC FA50 30
I-SNAD SBRL 306-27
I-SNAF HS25 25145
I-SNAG FA20 240/478
I-SNAI MS76 028
I-SNAK SBRL 282-25
I-SNAL JSTR 5023
I-SNAM FA20 176/458
I-SNAP MS76 099
I-SNAV FA20 119/431
**I-SNAW F2TH 12**
I-SNAX F900 69
I-SOBE FA20 487
I-SRAF HS25 259012
I-SREG FA20 442
I-STAP BE40 RJ-18
(I-STEF) CL30 20236
**I-TAKA C56X 5537**
I-TAKY LJ25 073
I-TALC HFB3 1027
I-TALG CS55 0122
I-TALW C650 0208
**I-TCGR F900 154**
I-TFLY FA10 188
I-TIAG FA20 233
I-TIAL FA20 290
**I-TLCM F900 81**
I-TNTR C550 466
**I-TOIO C500 657**
**I-TOPB BE40 RK-133**
**I-TOPD BE40 RK-163**
**I-TOPH HS25 258809**
I-TOPJ BE40 RJ-44
I-TORA MU30 A085SA
I-TOSC C500 410
I-TYKE LJ31 120
**I-ULJA FA20 380**
I-UNSA BE40 RK-20
**I-UUNY C500 377**
I-VEPA FA20 100
I-VIGI MU30 A013SA
I-VIKI C550 381
I-VIKY LJ55 073
**I-VITH BE40 RK-309**
I-VULC LJ35 421
"I-WDSD" FA20 487
**I-WISH CL64 5526**
**I-YLFC LJ40 45-2024**
**I-ZACK C560 0767**
I-ZAMP CS55 0133
I-ZOOM LJ35 135
I-ZUGR FA50 341

## Japan

(JA ) FA50 173
(JA-001T) C525 0449
**JA001A C560 0349**
**JA001G GLF4 1190**
**JA001T C52A 0311**
**JA002A C560 0597**
**JA002G GLF4 1244**
**JA005G GLEX 9034**
**JA006G GLEX 9082**
**JA01CP LJ31 144**
JA01GW LJ45 292
**JA01TM C560 0403**
**JA021R C52A 0380**
**JA02AA C560 0518**
JA02GW LJ45 302
JA100C C525 0534
**JA119N C560 0067**
**JA120N C560 0072**
**JA30DA MU30 A053SA**
**JA359C C52A 0359**
**JA391C C52A 0391**
**JA500A GLF5 683**
**JA501A GLF5 689**
JA50TH F9EX 3
**JA510M C510 0135**
**JA516J C52A 0386**
**JA525A C525 0449**
**JA525B C52A 0156**
**JA525C C52A 0244**
JA525G C52A 0096
**JA525J C525 0549**
**JA525Y C525 0535**
JA55TH F9EX 100
**JA560Y C560 0694**
**JA680C C680 0173**
JA8246 MU30 A092SA
JA8247 C500 259
**JA8248 MU30 002**
JA8249 C650 0085
JA8270 FA20 509
JA8283 CL61 5011
JA8284 C500 631
JA8298 MU30 A074SA
(JA8360) CL61 5037
(JA8361) C500 476
JA8361 CL61 5068
(JA8366) GLF4 1107
JA8367 C650 0177
JA8378 C650 0178
JA8379 ASTR 049
**JA8380 C500 350**
(JA8380) GLF4 1148
JA8418 C500 226
JA8420 C525 0056
JA8421 C500 021
JA8422 C500 040
**JA8431 GLF2 141**
JA8438 C500 321
JA8446 LJ24 245
JA8447 FA10 84
JA8463 FA10 152
JA8474 C500 629
**JA8493 C500 672**
JA8494 FA10 201
JA8495 C550 495
**JA8570 F900 53**
**JA8571 F900 56**
JA8572 F900 105
JA8575 FA50 196
JA8576 C560 0080
JQ8001 MU30 001SA
JQ8002 MU30 002
JQ8003 MU30 002
JQ8004 MU30 A004SA
JQ8005 MU30 A005SA

## Jordan

(JY- ) GLF5 564
**JY-AAD CL64 5481**
JY-ABL GLF3 418
JY-AEG LJ24 014
JY-AEH LJ24 023
JY-AEI LJ24 027
JY-AET LJ36 016
JY-AEV LJ35 049
JY-AEW LJ35 052
(JY-AEX) LJ35 056
JY-AFC LJ36 020
JY-AFD LJ35 071
JY-AFE LJ35 075
JY-AFF LJ35 081
JY-AFH SBRL 380-57
JY-AFL SBRL 380-56
JY-AFM SBRL 380-36
JY-AFN SBRL 380-53
JY-AFO SBRL 380-61
JY-AFP SBRL 380-62
JY-AMN GLF3 418
JY-AW1 C56X 5554
JY-AW3 CL64 5362
JY-AW4 HS25 258520
JY-AW5 HS25 258539
JY-AWD HS25 258520
**JY-AWE HS25 258539**
**JY-AWF C525 0632**
**JY-AWH C680 0285**
**JY-FMK C52A 0168**
JY-HAH FA50 52
JY-HAH GLF3 467
JY-HZH FA50 60
JY-HZH GLF3 469
**JY-IMK CL64 5443**
JY-JAS SBRL 380-64
JY-ONE CL64 5426
(JY-ONE) GLF4 1345
JY-RAY GLF4 1202
JY-RY1 CL61 3017
**JY-RYA CL61 3017**
**JY-RYN C650 7029**
JY-TWO CL64 5443
(JY-TWO) GLF4 1356
**JY-WJA HS25 258520**

## Djibouti

J2-KAC FA20 342/532
J2-KBA FA50 71

## Guinea-Bissau

J5-GAS FA20 296/507

## St Vincent & Grenadines

**J8-JET C52B 0247**

## Norway

LN-AAA C560 0105
LN-AAA C650 0187
LN-AAA FA20 73/419
LN-AAB C550 397
LN-AAB FA20 12
LN-AAC C550 200
LN-AAC FA20 281/496
LN-AAD C550 095
LN-AAD C550 260
LN-AAE C550 224
LN-AAF C500 311
LN-AAI C550 069
LN-AAU C650 0192
LN-ACX C550 496
LN-AFC C500 397
LN-AFG C550 200
LN-AIR CL30 20141
**LN-AKA C560 0764**
**LN-AKR F9EX 185**
LN-AOC F9EX 155
LN-AVA C52A 0199
(LN-BEP) HS25 258094
LN-BRG F9EX 230
LN-BWG CL64 5328
**LN-ESA HS25 258094**
LN-EXL C56X 5666
LN-FDA C525 0636
LN-FDB C525 0353
LN-FDC C525 0512
LN-FOD FA20 53/417
LN-FOE FA20 125
LN-FOE FA20 62/409
LN-FOI FA20 41/407
(LN-FOX) C550 424
**LN-HOT C52B 0065**
LN-HOT C550 099
**LN-IDB C560 0637**
LN-NAT C500 331
LN-NEA C550 136
LN-NLA C550 136

LN-NLC C650 0028
LN-NLD C650 0070
LN-NPA HS25 25125
LN-NPC HS25 25145
LN-NPE HS25 25097
LN-NPE LJ24 038
**LN-RYG C525 0661**
(LN-SEH) F9EX 145
(LN-SEH) F9EX 155
LN-SJA MU30 A037SA
LN-SOL CL30 20203
**LN-SOV C680 0183**
**LN-SSS C680 0133**
**LN-SUN CL64 5517**
LN-SUS GALX 051
LN-SUU HS25 259030
**LN-SUV C550 550-0951**
LN-SUX C56X 5271
(LN-TIH) C680 0133
LN-VIP C550 137
LN-VIP LJ55 112
LN-XLS C56X 5608

## Argentina

**LQ-BFS LJ40 45-2003**
LQ-JRH HFB3 1050
**LQ-MRM C500 470**
LQ-TFM C550 117
**LV- C560 0697**
**LV- C56X 5132**
**LV- C56X 5137**
**LV- C56X 5150**
LV- LJ25 110
(LV- ) SBRL 380-4
(LV- ) WW24 119
**LV-AHX C560 0090**
**LV-AIT LJ35 408**
**LV-AIW C56X 5350**
LV-ALF LJ35 371
LV-ALW HS25 257133
**LV-AMB C525 0045**
**LV-APL C550 355**
**LV-ARD LJ45 232**
**LV-AXN C525 0327**
LV-AXZ HS25 25251
LV-BAI FA20 494
**LV-BAS CL60 1053**
**LV-BAW LJ35 386**
**LV-BBG HS25 258707**
**LV-BCO C550 458**
LV-BCS C56X 5541
**LV-BDM LJ31 145**
LV-BDX LJ60 270
**LV-BEM BE40 RK-456**
**LV-BEU C550 550-1120**
**LV-BFE LJ31 183**
**LV-BFG LJ31 054**
**LV-BFM C500 395**
**LV-BFR LJ60 059**
**LV-BHJ C500 593**
**LV-BHP CL64 5493**
**LV-BIB C56X 5696**
**LV-BID C500 560**
**LV-BIE LJ35 674**
**LV-BIY FA20 444**
**LV-BMH C56X 5025**
**LV-BNO CL64 5407**
**LV-BNR LJ35 373**
**LV-BOU LJ45 050**
**LV-BOX LJ35 508**
**LV-BPA LJ35 143**
**LV-BPL LJ35 418**
**LV-BPO LJ35 343**
**LV-BPV CL61 3044**
**LV-BPW C500 341**
**LV-BPZ C500 412**
**LV-BRC LJ31 058**
**LV-BRE C550 697**
**LV-BRJ C750 0013**
**LV-BRT LJ35 665**
**LV-BRX C56X 5134**
**LV-BRZ FA20 171**
**LV-BSO LJ31 222**
**LV-BSS CL30 20219**
**LV-BTA LJ60 353**
**LV-BTF LJ31 111**
**LV-BTO LJ45 388**
**LV-BXD LJ45 254**
**LV-BXH C500 491**
**LV-BXU LJ35 462**
**LV-BYC GLF4 1145**
**LV-BYG CL61 5032**
**LV-BZC LJ25 350**
**LV-BZJ LJ60 344**
**LV-CAE C650 0128**
**LV-CAK C560 0170**
**LV-CAR LJ45 248**
**LV-CAY LJ60 234**
**LV-CAZ GLF4 1514**
**LV-CBI LJ60 272**
**LV-CBJ BE40 RK-134**
**LV-CCO LJ60 076**
**LV-CDI C500 323**
**LV-JTZ LJ24 234**
LV-JXA LJ24 240
LV-LOG LJ36 005
LV-LRC LJ24 316
LV-LZR C500 332
LV-MBP LJ25 229
LV-MGB C500 423
LV-MMR C500 459
LV-MMV LJ25 259
LV-MST LJ25 245
LV-MYN C500 510
LV-MZG C500 506
LV-OAS LJ35 271
**LV-OEL LJ25 307**
LV-OFV LJ35 312
LV-ONN LJ35 355
LV-P LJ25 337
LV-PAF LJ25 245
LV-PAM BE40 RJ-37
LV-PAT C500 459
LV-PAW LJ25 259
LV-PAX C500 470
LV-PDW C500 506
LV-PDZ C500 510
LV-PET LJ35 271
LV-PEU LJ25 307
LV-PFK LJ31 024
LV-PFM FA20 494
LV-PFN C560 0126
LV-PGC C560 0190
LV-PGR C560 0227
LV-PGU C550 724
LV-PGX LJ60 024
LV-PGZ C560 0251
LV-PHD C560 0246
LV-PHH C550 131
LV-PHJ C560 0265
LV-PHN C550 728
LV-PHU LJ25 345
LV-PHV FA20 34
LV-PHX LJ35 312
LV-PHY C560 0289
LV-PIW HS25 258462
LV-PJL HS25 258707
LV-PJZ LJ35 355
LV-PLC FA20 9
LV-PLD? FA20 29
LV-PLE C560 0305
LV-PLL LJ25 269
LV-PLM C500 478
LV-PLR C550 626
LV-PLT BE40 RK-104
LV-PLV LJ35 671
LV-PLY LJ35 371
LV-PMH BE40 RK-118
LV-PML C500 580
LV-PMM HS25 257133
LV-PMP C500 148
LV-PMV C550 550-0818
LV-PNB C550 355
LV-PNL C550 715
LV-PNR C560 0458
LV-POG LJ35 408
LV-POP HFB3 1050
LV-PRA LJ24 234
LV-PRB LJ24 240
LV-PUY C500 332
LV-PZI C500 423
LV-RBV LJ31 024
LV-RCT BE40 RJ-37
LV-RDD WW24 12
**LV-RED C560 0126**
LV-TDF LJ35 478
LV-VFY C560 0190
LV-WBP LJ25 337
**LV-WDR C560 0227**
**LV-WEJ C550 724**
LV-WEN WW24 126
LV-WFM LJ60 024
LV-WGO C560 0251
**LV-WGY C560 0246**
LV-WHY C650 0231
**LV-WHZ WW24 108**
LV-WIJ C560 0265
LV-WIT C550 604
**LV-WJN C550 558**
**LV-WJO C550 728**
LV-WJU WW24 179
**LV-WLG LJ25 345**
LV-WLH FA20 34
**LV-WLR WW24 183**
**LV-WLS C560 0289**
LV-WLX SBRL 306-41
LV-WMF FA20 9
LV-WMM FA20 29
LV-WMR LJ24 135
**LV-WMT C560 0305**
**LV-WND SBRL 282-131**
**LV-WOC LJ25 269**
LV-WOE C560 0319
LV-WOF SBRL 306-25
LV-WOI C500 478
LV-WOM GLF4 1274
LV-WOV WW24 331
"LV-WOW" GLF4 1274
LV-WOZ C550 626
LV-WPE BE40 RK-104
LV-WPO SBRL 306-3
LV-WPZ LJ35 671
**LV-WRE LJ25 355**
LV-WSS GLF4 1297
**LV-WTN C650 7054**
**LV-WTP BE40 RK-118**
**LV-WXD C550 395**
LV-WXJ C500 148
LV-WXN LJ60 102
LV-WXV FA50 188
**LV-WXX SBRL 306-91**
**LV-WXY LJ25 357**
LV-WYH C550 550-0818
LV-WYL WW24 182
**LV-YGC HS25 25046**
**LV-YHC C550 715**
LV-YLB CL60 1034
LV-YMA C560 0458
**LV-YMB LJ31 081**
**LV-YRB C500 191**
LV-ZHY HS25 258372
LV-ZNR C550 727
LV-ZPD C550 398
LV-ZPU C500 265
LV-ZRS HS25 257046
**LV-ZSZ LJ35 235**
**LV-ZTH LJ25 071**
**LV-ZTR HS25 258462**
LV-ZXI GLF5 604
LV-ZXW C56X 5135
LV-ZYF LJ60 232
**LV-ZZF LJ35 049**

## Luxembourg

LX-AAA FA20 73/419
**LX-AAA GLEX 9133**
LX-AAM F2EX 8
LX-AEN CL61 3046
LX-AER F900 11
**LX-AFD F9DX 615**
LX-AKI FA50 306
LX-APG FA50 212
LX-ARC HS25 258444
**LX-ATD F2DX 603**
"LX-BYG" HS25 258392
LX-COS F900 159
**LX-DCA C52B 0227**
**LX-DEC C680 0253**
LX-DKC F2EX 5
LX-DPA FA10 113
LX-DSL LJ45 158
LX-EAR LJ31 160
LX-EJH C550 550-0874
LX-EPA FA10 48
**LX-EVM F2EX 181**
LX-FAZ CL64 5307
LX-FBY CL64 5485
**LX-FGB C56X 6026**
**LX-FGL C510 0132**
**LX-FLY GLEX 9252**
LX-FMR FA50 165
LX-FOX C525 0229
**LX-FTA F900 201**
(LX-FTJ) FA50 144
LX-GAP C52B 0096
LX-GBY HS25 258392
LX-GCA C525 0235
LX-GDC CL61 3065
LX-GDL C550 033
LX-GDX C56X 5610
(LX-GDX) F9EX 176
LX-GED FA50 54
LX-GES F900 78
**LX-GET F9EX 217**
**LX-GEX GLEX 9013**
**LX-GJL F900 197**
LX-GJM GLEX 9189
LX-GOL ASTR 059
LX-GXR GLEX 9332
LX-IAL FA20 136/439
**LX-IIH C525 0391**
(LX-IMN) F900 54
LX-IMS LJ45 070
"LX-IMS" LJ45 266
LX-IMZ LJ45 266
**LX-INS C56X 5727**
LX-IRE FA50 324
**LX-JAG LJ45 398**
**LX-JCD C56X 5104**
LX-JCG FA10 160
**LX-JET C52B 0281**
LX-JET C550 033
**LX-KAT HS25 HA-0140**
LX-KSD HS25 HA-0096
**LX-LAI GALX 199**
**LX-LAR LJ35 653**
LX-LCG PRM1 RB-51
LX-LFA F900 154
LX-LFB F900 62
**LX-LOU LJ60 277**
**LX-LOV C525 0102**
(LX-MAM) F900 197
**LX-MBE F2TH 208**
LX-MEL F900 115
LX-MJM HS25 257010
LX-MMB CL61 5146
LX-MRC C525 0473
LX-MSP C525 0458
LX-NAN F900 159
LX-NLK F2EX 61
LX-NUR FA50 159
LX-OKR HS25 258855
LX-OMC LJ31 167
**LX-ONE LJ35 417**
LX-PAK GLEX 9115
**LX-PAK GLEX 9197**
LX-PAT LJ31 233
**LX-PCT LJ31 112**
**LX-PMA CL30 20097**
**LX-PMR PRM1 RB-64**
LX-POO PRM1 RB-18
LX-PRA LJ60 145
LX-PRE PRM1 RB-60
LX-PRS C550 496
"LX-RFBY" CL64 5485
LX-RPL LJ60 212
**LX-RSQ C510 0194**
LX-RVR FA50 107
**LX-SAM F2TH 26**
LX-SIK F2TH 27
**LX-SPK CL64 5449**
LX-SUP C525 0351
LX-SVW F2TH 133
**LX-SVW F9DX 619**

LX-TAG F900 115
LX-THS C550 069
**LX-THS FA50 185**
**LX-TQJ CL30 20159**
LX-TRA C525 0229
LX-TRG FA10 19
**LX-TWO LJ35 628**
LX-UAE FA50 104
LX-VAZ C550 622
(LX-VAZ) PRM1 RB-197
**LX-VIP GLEX 9076**
**LX-VPG CL30 20218**
(LX-WGR) C52A 0322
LX-YKH C500 086
LX-YSL C525 0322
LX-ZAK F2TH 187
LX-ZAK F9EX 106
**LX-ZAK GLEX 9204**
**LX-ZAV CL64 5523**
**LX-ZXP FA7X 56**

## Lithuania

LY-AJB LJ25 105
LY-AMB JSTR 5161/43
LY-ASL HS25 257212
LY-BSK HS25 257212
**LY-DSK HS25 258811**
LY-EWC JSTR 5219
**LY-FSK HS25 HA-0060**
**LY-HCW HS25 258398**
LY-HER PRM1 RB-83
LY-LRJ LJ55 011

## Bulgaria

**LZ-ABV C550 550-1103**
**LZ-AMA C510 0141**
**LZ-AXA LJ60 167**
**LZ-BVD CL65 5768**
**LZ-BVE LJ60 329**
(LZ-BVF) CL65 5774
**LZ-BVV LJ60 203**
**LZ-DIN C525 0090**
**LZ-FIA GLF5 5198**
**LZ-FIB GALX 011**
**LZ-FNA C525 0659**
**LZ-FNB C52A 0398**
**LZ-GEN C550 550-1122**
**LZ-GMV C550 550-1136**
LZ-OII FA50 97
LZ-OIO FA50 88
**LZ-OOI F2TH 123**
**LZ-VTS LJ24 156**
**LZ-YUM CL60 1085**
**LZ-YUN CL64 5508**
**LZ-YUP CL64 5602**
**LZ-YUR CL64 5625**

## Isle of Man

**M-ABAK GLEX 9010**
**M-ABCD FA20 357**
(M-ABCE) HS25 HA-0071
**M-ABCM CL30 20277**
**M-ACPT HS25 259004**
M-AGER FA50 175
**M-AGIC C680 0138**
**M-AIRS LJ60 276**
**M-AJDM C52A 0009**
**M-AJOR HS25 HA-0058**
**M-ALRV F2EX 173**
**M-ALUN HS25 257075**
**M-AMND F2EX 114**
M-ANSL C560 0773
**M-APWC LJ60 326**
**M-ARIE CL65 5794**
**M-ASRI GLEX 9165**
**M-ASRY C52B 0160**
**M-ATAK GLEX 9337**
**M-AZAG HS25 258233**
**M-BFLY CL30 20123**
**M-BIGG CL65 5722**
"M-BIJJ" GLEX 9209
**M-BIRD C52B 0255**
M-BSKY CL30 20179
**M-BWFC C56X 5690**
(M-CHEF) HS25 258514
**M-CHEM F2EX 128**
**M-CLAA HS25 258405**
**M-CLAB CL30 20271**
M-COOL C510 0285
**M-CRVS GLEX 9294**
**M-DASO FA50 268**
**M-DINO C525 0528**
**M-DKDI C750 0227**
**M-EANS CL30 20017**
M-EANS LJ45 336
**M-EIRE CL64 5562**
**M-ELON C52B 0148**
**M-EMLI CL64 5383**
M-EOCV LJ45 306
**M-FALC F9EX 31**
**M-FINK HS25 259037**
**M-FMHG GLF4 1305**
M-FPIA GLF5 5227
**M-FRED C560 0665**
**M-FROG PRM1 RB-165**
**M-FRZN HS25 258816**
**M-FUAD GLF5 5227**
**M-GBAL GLEX 9210**
**M-GLRS LJ45 249**
**M-GPIK FA50 289**
**M-GULF GLF4 1082**
**M-GYQM GLEX 9189**
**M-GZOO GALX 224**
"M-HARP" HS25 HA-0083
**M-HAWK HS25 258494**
**M-HDAM HS25 258037**
**M-HOIL LJ60 313**
**M-HSNT CL30 20233**
**M-ICRO C52A 0347**
**M-IFES CL60 1067**
**M-IGHT LJ60 382**
**M-IIII F2TH 94**
M-ILES F2EX 88
**M-INOR HS25 HA-0059**
**M-INXY E50P 50000024**
**M-IPHS GLF5 5246**
**M-ISLE C680 0265**
M-ISSY HS25 258043
**M-JANP GLEX 9293**
**M-JCPO HS25 257004**
**M-JETI HS25 258056**
**M-JETT FA20 490**
"M-JMF" C550 610
**M-JMMM F900 159**
**M-JOLY HS25 HA-0121**
**M-JSTA CL64 5639**
**M-KARN CL64 5346**
(M-KAZZ) C750 0271
**M-KELY E50P 50000040**
**M-KENF HA4T RC-27**
**M-LAOR HS25 258384**
**M-LCJP HS25 HA-0072**
**M-LEAR LJ31 011**
**M-LEFB C550 187**
**M-LION HS25 HA-0099**
**M-LJGI F2EX 143**
M-LLGC GLEX 9227
**M-MHBW C510 0262**
**M-MHDH C510 0259**
**M-MHMH C52B 0311**
**M-MIKE C52B 0280**
**M-MMAS GLEX 9267**
**M-MSGG GALX 159**
**M-NEWT CL30 20151**
**M-NHOI CL65 5744**
**M-NICO HS25 HA-0083**
**M-NOEL CL30 20206**
(M-OANH) HS25 HB-14
**M-ODKZ F9EX 86**
**M-ONAV HS25 HA-0073**
**M-ONEM GLF5 5210**
**M-OODY C52B 0238**
**M-OOUN HS25 258514**
**M-OSPB GALX 205**
**M-PARK C525 0358**
**M-PAUL HA4T RC-34**
M-PHNM E50P 50000092
**M-PRVT C750 0291**
M-PSAC C52A 0389
**M-RLIV CL65 5731**
**M-ROLL FA7X 40**
**M-ROWL F2EX 95**
**M-RUR F900 140**
**M-SAIR F900 141**
M-SALE GLEX 9311
**M-SKSM GLEX 9227**
**M-SKZL CL64 5404**
**M-SSSV LJ60 325**
**M-STCO F2EX 110**
**M-SVGN C680 0198**
M-SVNX FA7X 20
M-TAGB CL30 20172
**M-TEAM C525 0609**
(M-TECH) F9EX 205
**M-TOPI CL65 5780**
**M-TRIX CL64 5608**
**M-TSGP C52A 0309**
**M-UPCO C52B 0012**
**M-USTG C510 0089**
M-USTG C510 0182
**M-VBBQ PRM1 RB-181**
**M-VBPO PRM1 RB-138**
**M-VQBI GLEX 9213**
**M-VRNY GLF5 5225**
**M-VSSK CL65 5781**
**M-WMWM C52A 0113**
**M-WOOD C550 550-1042**
M-XONE C52A 0031
**M-YAAA GLEX 9136**
**M-YAIR PRM1 RB-146**
**M-YBST CL64 5620**
**M-YEDT ASTR 141**
**M-YFLY CL30 20023**
**M-YGIV GLF4 1080**
**M-YGKL GLF4 4137**
**M-YJET F2EX 148**
**M-YONE CL61 5085**
**M-YSKY PRM1 RB-209**
**M-YTOY E50P 50000112**

## United States of America

N C500 042
**N C550 090**
(N ) CL64 5522
(N ) FA20 262
(N ) HS25 258035
(N ) LJ25 341
(N ) LJ45 019
N1 GLF3 413
**N1 GLF4 1071**
N1 JSTR 5001/53
N1AB HS25 259005
N1AB HS25 259036
N1AF C550 320
N1AF CS55 0018
**N1AG BE40 RJ-35**
N1AG C500 579
N1AH LJ25 316
N1AH LJ35 398
**N1AK C560 0205**
N1AK LJ35 019
N1AP C500 322
N1AP C550 051
N1AP C650 0001
N1AP C650 0082
N1AP C650 7003
N1AP C750 0003
**N1AP C750 0176**
N1AP LJ24 163
N1AQ GLF3 342
**N1AR GLF4 1069**
N1AT C500 537
N1AT C550 591
N1BC WW24 39
N1BF FA20 142
N1BG HS25 25281
N1BG HS25 258011
N1BL GLF2 113
N1BL JSTR 5029/38
N1BL JSTR 5097/60
N1BN GLF4 1300
**N1BN GLF5 5036**
N1BN GLF5 667
N1BR LJ25 105
**N1BR LJ31 086**
**N1BS C750 0081**
N1BU LJ24 029
N1BX FA20 380
N1BX FA50 47
N1BX GLF2 227
**N1BX GLF4 4140**
N1BX SBRL 282-101
**N1C F2TH 40**
N1C GLF3 388
N1C HS25 25200
N1C HS25 257206
N1CA C500 387
N1CA CL64 5441
**N1CA HS25 258672**
N1CA LJ35 069
N1CA LJ35 657
N1CA LJ60 055
**N1CC GLF2 257/17**
N1CC SBRL 465-6
**N1CF C560 0473**
N1CF SBRL 465-3
N1CG BE40 RJ-17
**N1CG FA50 147**
N1CG LJ55 014
**N1CH C52B 0064**
N1CH C560 0283
N1CH SBRL 306-126
(N1CN) FA10 199
N1CN FA50 55
N1CR C500 561
N1CR PRM1 RB-119
N1CR PRM1 RB-146
**N1D FA20 495**
**N1DA C500 288**
N1DA LJ35 013
N1DB JSTR 5075/19
N1DB JSTR 5119/29
N1DB JSTR 5155/32
N1DB JSTR 5223
(N1DC) GLF4 1054
**N1DC GLF5 651**
N1DC LJ35 246
N1DC LJ35 464
N1DC LJ60 035
N1DC SBRL 282-44
N1DD LJ25 171
N1DD LJ25 191
**N1DE LJ31 016**
N1DG CL64 5386
N1DG CL64 5516
**N1DG GLEX 9156**
N1DH C650 0090
N1DH C650 0153
N1DH C750 0136
N1DH CL30 20083
**N1DH CL61 5145**
N1DH FA10 187
N1DK C500 175
N1DK LJ24 343
N1DM C525 0510
N1DM C52A 0214
N1DM C52A 0314
**N1DM C52B 0210**
N1DT JSTR 5158
N1DW CL61 5025
**N1DW GLF4 4176**
N1EB GLF4 1367
**N1EB GLF5 5194**
N1EC WW24 51
N1ED LJ25 092
N1ED LJ25 255
**N1ED LJ31 218**
N1ED LJ35 392
N1EF C525 0167
**N1EG PRM1 RB-43**
**N1EL C510 0061**
N1EM JSTR 5077
N1EP MS76 002
"N1ERAU" SBRL 265-57
N1EV FA50 65
**N1FC ASTR 274**
N1FE CL60 1055
N1FE CL60 1074
N1FE FA20 84
**N1FE GLEX 9091**

| | | |
|---|---|---|
| N1FJ | C680 | 0166 |
| **N1FS** | **ASTR** | **277** |
| (N1GB) | C500 | 309 |
| N1GC | C560 | 0239 |
| N1GC | CL64 | 5329 |
| N1GC | CS55 | 0109 |
| N1GC | GLF4 | 1382 |
| N1GC | GLF5 | 539 |
| N1GG | C500 | 249 |
| **N1GH** | **C550** | **227** |
| **N1GM** | **SBRL** | **306-120** |
| N1GN | GLF3 | 392 |
| N1GN | GLF4 | 1284 |
| **N1GN** | **GLF5** | **5023** |
| N1GN | GLF5 | 518 |
| N1GN | GLF5 | 578 |
| N1GT | GLF3 | 454 |
| N1GT | GLF4 | 1292 |
| N1GW | LJ24 | 048 |
| N1GY | SBRL | 282-81 |
| N1GZ | LJ24 | 065A |
| N1H | CS55 | 0094 |
| N1H | GLF2 | 129 |
| N1HA | C500 | 447 |
| **N1HA** | **C550** | **107** |
| **N1HC** | **GLF5** | **5009** |
| N1HC | GLF5 | 545 |
| N1HC | GLF5 | 616 |
| N1HF | FA20 | 289 |
| **N1HF** | **FA20** | **474** |
| N1HM | C500 | 101 |
| N1HM | FA10 | 41 |
| N1HP | LJ35 | 039 |
| **N1HP** | **LJ45** | **082** |
| N1HS | BE40 | RK-106 |
| N1HS | C56X | 5351 |
| **N1HS** | **C56X** | **5596** |
| N1HZ | CL60 | 1056 |
| **N1HZ** | **CL61** | **5030** |
| **N1J** | **PRM1** | **RB-183** |
| N1JB | BE40 | RK-424 |
| N1JB | C500 | 569 |
| N1JB | C525 | 0251 |
| **N1JB** | **LJ60** | **363** |
| **N1JC** | **MU30** | **A059SA** |
| N1JG | GLF2 | 65 |
| **N1JG** | **LJ55** | **055** |
| **N1JK** | **F2EX** | **130** |
| N1JK | GLF3 | 342 |
| N1JK | GLF4 | 4031 |
| **N1JM** | **LJ31** | **196** |
| N1JN | C500 | 309 |
| N1JN | FA10 | 106 |
| N1JN | GLF2 | 154/28 |
| N1JN | GLF3 | 329 |
| N1JN | GLF4 | 1088 |
| N1JN | GLF4 | 1239 |
| **N1JN** | **GLF5** | **538** |
| N1JN | JSTR | 5132/57 |
| N1JN | SBRL | 306-14 |
| N1JN | SBRL | 306-61 |
| N1JR | LJ25 | 021 |
| N1JR | LJ25 | 104 |
| N1JR | LJ25 | 188 |
| N1JS | WW24 | 249 |
| N1JU | WW24 | 13 |
| **N1JW** | **FA10** | **200** |
| N1JX | SBRL | 306-61 |
| **N1KA** | **C52B** | **0076** |
| N1KC | C500 | 459 |
| N1KE | GLF3 | 349 |
| N1KE | GLF4 | 1033 |
| **N1KE** | **GLF5** | **574** |
| N1KT | WW24 | 135 |
| **N1KT** | **WW24** | **230** |
| N1L | F900 | 19 |
| N1LB | C500 | 212 |
| N1LB | GLF4 | 1448 |
| N1LB | GLF5 | 5195 |
| N1LL | LJ25 | 021 |
| N1LQ | C500 | 526 |
| N1LT | SBRL | 380-59 |
| N1LW | GLF3 | 329 |
| N1M | ASTR | 043 |
| (N1M) | ASTR | 049 |
| N1M | CL61 | 5008 |
| N1M | FA20 | 24 |
| N1M | GLF3 | 390 |
| N1M | WW24 | 187 |
| N1MB | FA20 | 74 |
| N1MC | ASTR | 055 |
| N1MC | ASTR | 112 |
| N1MC | C560 | 0014 |
| N1MG | F2TH | 221 |
| N1MG | LJ45 | 060 |
| N1MJ | JSTR | 5217 |
| N1MJ | JSTR | 5223 |
| N1MM | C550 | 302 |
| N1MN | SBRL | 282-69 |
| N1MN | SBRL | 306-58 |
| N1MW | WW24 | 109 |
| N1MX | C500 | 556 |
| N1MX | LJ25 | 128 |
| N1MY | HS25 | 25082 |
| N1MY | LJ35 | 370 |
| **N1NA** | **CL64** | **5447** |
| N1NA | GLF3 | 309 |
| **N1NC** | **F2EX** | **48** |
| **N1NL** | **C550** | **303** |
| N1NR | SBRL | 380-70 |
| **N1PB** | **C56X** | **5013** |
| N1PB | FA10 | 198 |
| N1PB | FA10 | 92 |
| N1PG | GLF2 | 62 |
| N1PG | GLF3 | 334 |
| N1PG | GLF4 | 1259 |
| **N1PG** | **GLF4** | **1374** |
| N1PN | SBRL | 306-58 |
| N1PR | FA50 | 40 |
| N1PR | GLF2 | 17 |
| **N1PR** | **GLF3** | **341** |
| N1PT | WW24 | 93 |
| (N1PU) | GLF3 | 334 |
| N1QC | LJ24 | 181 |
| N1QC | SBRL | 282-44 |
| N1QF | CL64 | 5329 |
| **N1QH** | **HS25** | **25261** |
| N1QH | WW24 | 96 |
| N1QL | WW24 | 96 |
| N1RA | LJ25 | 105 |
| **N1RB** | **LJ45** | **119** |
| N1RB | LJ60 | 202 |
| **N1RD** | **C510** | **0120** |
| **N1RF** | **C680** | **0163** |
| N1RL | LJ45 | 217 |
| (N1RW) | LJ25 | 135 |
| N1S | C650 | 7010 |
| **N1S** | **F900** | **28** |
| N1S | FA50 | 139 |
| N1S | GLF3 | 391 |
| N1SA | GLEX | 9100 |
| N1SC | LJ35 | 016 |
| N1SF | GLF3 | 455 |
| N1SF | GLF4 | 1060 |
| **N1SF** | **GLF5** | **5202** |
| N1SF | GLF5 | 598 |
| N1SH | C500 | 670 |
| N1SJ | SBRL | 276-45 |
| N1SL | GLEX | 9114 |
| **N1SL** | **GLF4** | **1167** |
| N1SN | C560 | 0153 |
| N1SN | C56X | 5014 |
| **N1SN** | **GLF4** | **1433** |
| N1SS | LJ24 | 186 |
| **N1SV** | **C550** | **165** |
| "N1TA" | GALX | 012 |
| N1TC | FA10 | 144 |
| N1TC | FA20 | 83 |
| N1TF | GLF4 | 1340 |
| N1TF | GLF4 | 1382 |
| **N1TF** | **GLF5** | **5035** |
| N1TG | C525 | 0617 |
| **N1TG** | **C680** | **0147** |
| N1TJ | FA10 | 18 |
| N1TJ | GLF2 | 39 |
| N1TJ | LJ24 | 339 |
| N1TK | CL61 | 5025 |
| N1TK | GLEX | 9004 |
| N1TK | LJ24 | 153 |
| N1TM | GLEX | 9006 |
| N1TM | GLF4 | 1087 |
| **N1TM** | **GLF4** | **1490** |
| N1TS | C650 | 0006 |
| N1TS | GLEX | 9046 |
| N1TS | JSTR | 5215 |
| N1TS | LJ35 | 499 |
| (N1TS) | WW24 | 187 |
| N1TX | MU30 | A066SA |
| N1TY | BE40 | RJ-34 |
| **N1TY** | **C550** | **188** |
| N1U | FA20 | 65 |
| N1U | LJ24 | 250 |
| N1U | LJ24 | 274 |
| N1U | LJ25 | 371 |
| N1U | LJ35 | 444 |
| N1U | LJ36 | 026 |
| **N1UA** | **ASTR** | **044** |
| N1UA | C550 | 130 |
| (N1UB) | C500 | 364 |
| N1UB | GLF5 | 669 |
| N1UG | C500 | 309 |
| N1UH | C550 | 062 |
| N1UH | C650 | 0024 |
| N1UH | CS55 | 0057 |
| N1UL | C500 | 482 |
| N1UL | CS55 | 0057 |
| **N1UM** | **C500** | **364** |
| N1UP | C650 | 0024 |
| **N1UP** | **C650** | **0224** |
| N1UP | JSTR | 5142 |
| N1UP | SBRL | 306-40 |
| N1UT | C500 | 267 |
| N1UT | MU30 | A029SA |
| N1UT | SBRL | 306-40 |
| N1VA | CS55 | 0143 |
| N1VC | C500 | 183 |
| (N1VC) | SBRL | 306-61 |
| **N1VG** | **LJ25** | **125** |
| N1VQ | HS25 | 257113 |
| N1VU | C500 | 545 |
| **N1VV** | **C510** | **0013** |
| N1WB | C550 | 058 |
| N1WP | GLF2 | 190 |
| **N1WP** | **GLF4** | **1030** |
| N1WP | WW24 | 108 |
| N1WS | WW24 | 252 |
| N1WT | LJ25 | 371 |
| N1WZ | SBRL | 282-117 |
| (N1X) | BE40 | RJ-34 |
| N1X | C500 | 236 |
| N1X | JSTR | 5215 |
| **N1XH** | **PRM1** | **RB-76** |
| N1XL | C56X | 5041 |
| **N1XL** | **LJ35** | **392** |
| N1XT | C525 | 0162 |
| **N1XT** | **PRM1** | **RB-36** |
| N1YE | HS25 | 25065 |
| **N1Z** | **GALX** | **084** |
| N1ZA | LJ24 | 042 |
| N1ZC | C650 | 0031 |
| **N1ZC** | **C680** | **0085** |
| N1ZC | LJ25 | 022 |
| N2 | C500 | 084 |
| N2 | C550 | 006 |
| N2 | C560 | 0109 |
| **N2** | **C56X** | **5333** |
| N2 | LJ31 | 063 |
| (N2AJ) | WW24 | 277 |
| N2AT | F2TH | 51 |
| N2AV | WW24 | 322 |
| **N2BA** | **LJ35** | **051** |
| N2BD | F9EX | 35 |
| **N2BD** | **F9EX** | **72** |
| **N2BG** | **GALX** | **064** |
| N2BG | HS25 | 258207 |
| N2BG | WW24 | 365 |
| N2BT | C500 | 419 |
| N2CA | C550 | 092 |
| N2CC | F2EX | 28 |
| **N2CC** | **GLF4** | **1343** |
| N2CC | SBRL | 465-6 |
| (N2CH) | FA10 | 163 |
| N2CJ | C52A | 708 |
| N2CW | F2TH | 80 |
| N2DB | WW24 | 135 |
| N2DD | LJ24 | 098 |
| **N2DD** | **LJ24** | **335** |
| **N2DF** | **GLF2** | **95/39** |
| N2DH | C650 | 0153 |
| N2DH | C650 | 0193 |
| (N2DP) | C500 | 531 |
| N2EL | C500 | 038 |
| N2EP | C650 | 0010 |
| N2ES | JSTR | 5023 |
| (N2ES) | WW24 | 96 |
| N2FA | C500 | 140 |
| N2FE | CL60 | 1075 |
| **N2FE** | **CL61** | **5095** |
| N2FE | FA20 | 132 |
| **N2FQ** | **FA50** | **167** |
| N2FU | FA20 | 412 |
| **N2FU** | **LJ31** | **027** |
| N2FU | LJ35 | 612 |
| N2FU | LJ36 | 048 |
| **N2G** | **GALX** | **106** |
| N2G | HS25 | 25139 |
| (N2G) | HS25 | 25163 |
| N2G | HS25 | 258354 |
| **N2GG** | **C550** | **306** |
| N2GP | GLF2 | 13 |
| N2GP | LJ24 | 020 |
| N2GR | LJ24 | 262 |
| N2H | FA20 | 327 |
| N2HB | C56X | 5222 |
| N2HB | C56X | 5579 |
| N2HD | C500 | 078 |
| (N2HE) | LJ25 | 138 |
| N2HF | GLF2 | 221 |
| N2HJ | C560 | 0278 |
| N2HL | GALX | 025 |
| **N2HL** | **GALX** | **091** |
| N2HP | HS25 | 257180 |
| **N2HP** | **LJ45** | **330** |
| N2HW | FA20 | 488 |
| N2HW | SBRL | 282-105 |
| N2HW | SBRL | 306-68 |
| N2HX | SBRL | 306-68 |
| N2HZ | CL60 | 1056 |
| **N2HZ** | **PRM1** | **RB-186** |
| N2HZ | WW24 | 314 |
| **N2JR** | **GLF2** | **131/23** |
| N2JR | JSTR | 5236 |
| N2JW | C550 | 183 |
| N2JW | C560 | 0191 |
| N2JW | C56X | 5064 |
| **N2JW** | **CL64** | **5549** |
| N2JW | WW24 | 86 |
| N2JZ | C550 | 055 |
| N2KH | C550 | 570 |
| N2KN | HS25 | 25020 |
| N2KW | HS25 | 25020 |
| N2KW | HS25 | 257201 |
| **N2KZ** | **HS25** | **257177** |
| N2KZ | LJ35 | 652 |
| N2LN | C500 | 483 |
| N2LY | GLF3 | 340 |
| **N2MG** | **CL65** | **5701** |
| N2MG | HS25 | 258092 |
| N2MK | HFB3 | 1036 |
| N2MK | JSTR | 5226 |
| N2MP | FA10 | 31 |
| **N2N** | **GLF5** | **586** |
| N2N | SBRL | 465-63 |
| N2NA | GLF3 | 309 |
| N2NC | MS76 | 005 |
| **N2NL** | **SBRL** | **465-63** |
| N2NR | C650 | 0083 |
| N2NT | C550 | 730 |
| N2NT | C650 | 7013 |
| N2PG | GLF2 | 20 |
| **N2PG** | **GLF4** | **1378** |
| N2PK | GLF2 | 206 |
| N2PW | LJ25 | 363 |
| **N2QG** | **HS25** | **258207** |
| (N2QL) | HS25 | 257197 |
| N2QW | SBRL | 282-105 |
| N2RC | C550 | 337 |
| **N2RC** | **C560** | **0319** |
| N2RF | C650 | 7082 |
| **N2RM** | **C500** | **153** |
| N2S | C550 | 110 |
| N2S | GLF2 | 113 |
| N2S | GLF2 | 158 |
| N2SA | CL64 | 5319 |
| **N2SA** | **GLF4** | **1104** |
| N2SG | HS25 | 258090 |
| N2SG | HS25 | 259019 |
| N2SN | LJ24 | 072 |
| (N2SN) | SBRL | 282-59 |
| N2SP | GLF3 | 366 |
| N2T | FA50 | 167 |
| (N2T) | GLEX | 9032 |

| | | |
|---|---|---|
| N2T | GLEX | 9084 |
| **N2T** | **GLEX** | **9162** |
| N2TE | MS76 | 005 |
| N2TE | SBRL | 370-6 |
| N2TF | C650 | 0176 |
| N2TF | FA20 | 490 |
| N2TF | GLF3 | 460 |
| N2TN | C500 | 231 |
| N2TQ | GLF3 | 460 |
| N2U | C500 | 285 |
| N2U | LJ24 | 250 |
| N2U | LJ25 | 325 |
| N2U | LJ35 | 268 |
| (N2UJ) | C680 | 0118 |
| **N2UJ** | **C680** | **0179** |
| N2UJ | GLF2 | 139/11 |
| N2UP | C650 | 0010 |
| **N2UP** | **C650** | **0227** |
| N2UP | SBRL | 306-17 |
| N2UR | SBRL | 306-17 |
| (N2UX) | C650 | 0227 |
| **N2WC** | **MU30** | **A047SA** |
| N2WL | GLF4 | 1118 |
| N2WL | LJ24 | 265 |
| N2WL | LJ35 | 245 |
| N2WQ | LJ35 | 277 |
| N2WR | SBRL | 282-102 |
| N2WU | WW24 | 72 |
| N2YG | HS25 | 258090 |
| **N2YU** | **EA50** | **000160** |
| N2YY | LJ24 | 143 |
| N2ZA | LJ24 | 067 |
| N2ZC | C500 | 420 |
| **N2ZC** | **C56X** | **5156** |
| **N3** | **C56X** | **5341** |
| N3AH | LJ35 | 421 |
| N3AL | HS25 | 25169 |
| N3AS | LJ28 | 28-001 |
| **N3AS** | **LJ45** | **247** |
| **N3AV** | **WW24** | **361** |
| **N3BL** | **LJ24** | **003** |
| N3BM | F2EX | 38 |
| N3BM | F2TH | 38 |
| N3BM | SBRL | 282-131 |
| N3BM | SBRL | 465-51 |
| N3BY | FA10 | 193 |
| **N3CJ** | **C52B** | **711** |
| **N3CT** | **C52B** | **0041** |
| N3D | CS55 | 0038 |
| N3DL | WW24 | 42 |
| **N3DP** | **GLF3** | **334** |
| N3DU | LJ24 | 279 |
| N3DZ | LJ24 | 279 |
| N3E | GLF2 | 185 |
| N3E | JSTR | 5029/38 |
| N3E | JSTR | 5076/17 |
| N3EK | JSTR | 5029/38 |
| N3EK | JSTR | 5076/17 |
| N3EU | GLF2 | 185 |
| N3FA | C550 | 124 |
| **N3FA** | **C560** | **0023** |
| N3FC | SBRL | 306-33 |
| **N3FD** | **ASTR** | **145** |
| N3FE | C500 | 678 |
| **N3FE** | **CL61** | **5054** |
| N3FE | FA20 | 151 |
| N3FW | C550 | 368 |
| N3GL | HS25 | 257197 |
| N3GL | LJ24 | 173 |
| N3GL | LJ35 | 070 |
| **N3GN** | **C500** | **466** |
| N3GR | JSTR | 5127 |
| N3GT | C550 | 376 |
| N3GT | C560 | 0091 |
| N3GU | HS25 | 258075 |
| N3GW | LJ24 | 203 |
| N3H | FA20 | 327 |
| N3H | GLF4 | 1092 |
| N3HA | LJ35 | 182 |
| N3HB | CL60 | 1059 |
| N3HB | CL64 | 5313 |
| **N3HB** | **F900** | **126** |
| N3HB | JSTR | 5116 |
| N3HB | LJ35 | 182 |
| N3HB | LJ55 | 046 |
| N3HX | GLF4 | 1092 |
| N3JJ | C500 | 016 |
| N3JJ | C500 | 299 |
| N3JJ | FA20 | 57 |
| N3JL | CL60 | 1080 |
| N3JL | LJ24 | 025 |
| N3JL | LJ25 | 073 |
| N3JL | LJ35 | 289 |
| **N3JM** | **C52B** | **0102** |
| N3JX | LJ25 | 073 |
| **N3K** | **PRM1** | **RB-218** |
| N3KN | GLF4 | 1103 |
| N3LG | C500 | 112 |
| **N3LH** | **GLF2** | **5** |
| N3M | GLF4 | 1021 |
| N3MB | C550 | 343 |
| N3MB | C550 | 405 |
| **N3MB** | **LJ35** | **335** |
| N3MF | HS25 | 25093 |
| N3MJ | LJ35 | 188 |
| **N3MT** | **EA50** | **000135** |
| N3NP | LJ36 | 048 |
| N3NU | GLF4 | 1021 |
| N3PC | ASTR | 037 |
| N3PC | C500 | 067 |
| N3PC | C550 | 247 |
| N3PC | CL61 | 5066 |
| N3PC | CL64 | 5411 |
| **N3PC** | **GLEX** | **9059** |
| N3PC | LJ36 | 013 |
| N3PG | GLF2 | 21 |
| N3PG | GLF3 | 336 |
| N3PG | GLF4 | 1260 |
| **N3PG** | **GLF5** | **5091** |
| N3PW | FA10 | 179 |
| N3PW | HS25 | 256009 |
| N3PW | LJ24 | 341 |
| N3PW | LJ35 | 207 |
| N3PY | GLF3 | 336 |
| (N3PY) | GLF3 | 440 |
| N3Q | C500 | 238 |
| (N3Q) | C650 | 0007 |
| N3QE | C500 | 121 |
| **N3QE** | **C510** | **0183** |
| **N3QG** | **HS25** | **258127** |
| N3QL | JSTR | 5064/51 |
| N3QM | SBRL | 282-131 |
| N3QM | SBRL | 465-51 |
| N3QS | JSTR | 5064/51 |
| N3QS | JSTR | 5224 |
| N3QZ | C500 | 238 |
| N3R | C550 | 123 |
| N3RA | LJ35 | 138 |
| N3RC | FA10 | 69 |
| N3RC | FA20 | 256 |
| N3RC | HS25 | 257087 |
| **N3RC** | **HS25** | **258253** |
| N3RC | JSTR | 5214 |
| N3RC | WW24 | 222 |
| N3RC | WW24 | 340 |
| N3RL | WW24 | 390 |
| N3RN | SBRL | 380-38 |
| **N3RP** | **CL60** | **1011** |
| N3RP | SBRL | 380-42 |
| **N3SA** | **GLF4** | **1171** |
| **N3ST** | **C52A** | **0045** |
| N3TE | SBRL | 370-8 |
| N3TJ | LJ24 | 236 |
| N3UC | LJ25 | 034 |
| N3UD | C52B | 0069 |
| (N3UG) | C500 | 526 |
| N3UJ | LJ35 | 473 |
| N3UW | LJ25 | 214 |
| **N3VF** | **FA20** | **363/544** |
| N3VF | WW24 | 137 |
| N3VF | WW24 | 191 |
| N3VF | WW24 | 324 |
| N3VG | LJ35 | 305 |
| **N3VJ** | **LJ31** | **035** |
| N3VL | WW24 | 180 |
| N3W | C500 | 143 |
| N3WB | C525 | 0053 |
| **N3WB** | **C525** | **0524** |
| N3WN | FA20 | 185/467 |
| N3WP | LJ35 | 606 |
| N3WQ | SBRL | 306-97 |
| **N3WT** | **C500** | **473** |
| N3WZ | FA10 | 30 |
| N3ZA | LJ24 | 024 |
| N3ZD | C500 | 224 |
| N3ZQ | GLF2 | 62 |
| N4 | C500 | 084 |
| N4 | C560 | 0113 |
| N4 | LJ31 | 038 |
| N4AC | C500 | 218 |
| N4AC | FA10 | 184 |
| N4AC | FA50 | 96 |
| **N4AS** | **CL65** | **5721** |
| **N4AT** | **C550** | **550-0805** |
| N4AZ | M220 | 1 |
| (N4BP) | CS55 | 0090 |
| N4BR | HS25 | 256032 |
| N4CH | C500 | 062 |
| N4CH | C550 | 045 |
| **N4CJ** | **C52C** | **714001** |
| N4CP | FA50 | 187 |
| N4CP | GLF2 | 71 |
| N4CP | GLF4 | 1257 |
| **N4CP** | **GLF5** | **5005** |
| N4CP | LJ55 | 029 |
| N4CQ | GLF2 | 71 |
| N4CR | C550 | 045 |
| **N4CR** | **HS25** | **25109** |
| N4CR | LJ24 | 128 |
| N4CS | C550 | 248 |
| N4CS | C560 | 0024 |
| **N4CS** | **SBRL** | **465-27** |
| N4DA | GLF4 | 1472 |
| **N4DA** | **LJ45** | **283** |
| N4DF | C525 | 0481 |
| N4DS | FA10 | 116 |
| **N4EA** | **LJ35** | **458** |
| (N4EF) | C525 | 0167 |
| N4EG | C650 | 0139 |
| (N4EG) | C650 | 0152 |
| N4EG | C650 | 7059 |
| N4EK | C550 | 119 |
| N4EM | ASTR | 050 |
| **N4ES** | **HS25** | **25243** |
| N4EW | C550 | 636 |
| N4F | LJ24 | 294 |
| N4FC | C560 | 0270 |
| N4FC | C650 | 0140 |
| N4FE | C550 | 478 |
| N4FE | CL60 | 1062 |
| N4FE | FA20 | 108/430 |
| **N4FE** | **LJ45** | **032** |
| **N4FF** | **C510** | **0007** |
| N4GA | C525 | 0272 |
| **N4GA** | **C52B** | **0055** |
| N4GB | LJ35 | 228 |
| N4GV | SBRL | 282-135 |
| **N4GX** | **GLEX** | **9048** |
| **N4J** | **LJ35** | **110** |
| **N4JB** | **C56X** | **5125** |
| N4JS | C550 | 281 |
| N4JS | C560 | 0196 |
| **N4JS** | **C56X** | **5035** |
| N4KH | C500 | 062 |
| N4LG | C500 | 130 |
| N4LG | SBRL | 306-9 |
| N4LH | FA20 | 205 |
| N4LK | C500 | 140 |
| N4LK | MU30 | A021SA |
| (N4LQ) | SBRL | 465-38 |
| (N4LZ) | GLEX | 9084 |
| **N4M** | **C52C** | **0012** |
| N4M | C550 | 550-0879 |
| N4M | SBRL | 465-18 |
| N4MB | F900 | 146 |
| **N4MB** | **FA20** | **135** |
| N4MB | FA50 | 156 |
| N4MB | SBRL | 465-17 |
| **N4MH** | **WW24** | **232** |
| N4MM | C550 | 430 |
| N4MM | C560 | 0109A |
| N4MR | FA50 | 156 |
| N4MR | LJ25 | 125 |
| N4MR | LJ25 | 222 |
| N4NB | SBRL | 380-40 |
| N4NE | SBRL | 306-79 |
| N4NK | WW24 | 82 |
| N4NM | C550 | 430 |
| N4NP | SBRL | 282-109 |
| **N4NR** | **GLF2** | **255/18** |
| N4NR | SBRL | 306-79 |
| N4NR | SBRL | 380-40 |
| **N4NT** | **SBRL** | **306-48** |
| N4PC | GLF3 | 340 |
| N4PC | GLF4 | 1174 |
| N4PG | CL61 | 5052 |
| N4PG | GLF2 | 21 |
| N4PG | GLF4 | 1259 |
| **N4PG** | **GLF5** | **5214** |
| N4PG | SBRL | 380-49 |
| N4PH | SBRL | 282-116 |
| N4PN | HS25 | 25185 |
| N4PN | LJ25 | 003 |
| N4PQ | SBRL | 380-49 |
| **N4QB** | **HS25** | **25255** |
| **N4QG** | **F2EX** | **28** |
| **N4QN** | **C650** | **7031** |
| **N4QP** | **C525** | **0272** |
| N4QP | FA50 | 187 |
| N4QP | GLF4 | 1257 |
| (N4RH) | C510 | 0162 |
| N4RH | C525 | 0306 |
| N4RH | C525 | 0691 |
| N4RH | C52B | 0015 |
| N4RP | C52A | 0135 |
| **N4RP** | **C52B** | **0289** |
| (N4RP) | C680 | 0093 |
| N4RT | FA10 | 80 |
| "N4RT" | FA20 | 242 |
| N4RT | GLF2 | 26 |
| N4RT | LJ24 | 348 |
| N4RT | LJ35 | 003 |
| N4RU | LJ24 | 348 |
| N4S | GLF2 | 24 |
| N4S | SBRL | 306-37 |
| N4SA | HS25 | 256065 |
| N4SA | HS25 | 258303 |
| N4SE | SBRL | 306-37 |
| N4SG | CL61 | 5111 |
| N4SP | GLF2 | 20 |
| N4SP | GLF4 | 1286 |
| N4SP | GLF4 | 1388 |
| (N4SP) | GLF4 | 1449 |
| N4SP | JSTR | 5081 |
| **N4SQ** | **WW24** | **307** |
| N4SX | JSTR | 5081 |
| **N4T** | **GLEX** | **9195** |
| N4T | GLF4 | 1132 |
| **N4TB** | **FA20** | **432** |
| N4TE | C500 | 149 |
| N4TF | C525 | 0076 |
| N4TK | C500 | 192 |
| N4TL | C500 | 149 |
| N4TL | C550 | 119 |
| N4TL | C560 | 0048 |
| N4TL | C560 | 0334 |
| **N4TL** | **C560** | **0587** |
| N4TL | CS55 | 0052 |
| N4TS | C550 | 030 |
| N4TS | HS25 | 256004 |
| N4TU | CS55 | 0052 |
| **N4UB** | **GLF2** | **207/34** |
| N4UC | GLF4 | 1513 |
| **N4UG** | **GLF4** | **1259** |
| N4UP | GLF3 | 484 |
| N4UP | GLF4 | 1088 |
| N4VC | LJ25 | 161 |
| N4VF | C500 | 045 |
| N4VF | C550 | 053 |
| N4VF | C650 | 0082 |
| **N4VF** | **FA50** | **160** |
| N4VR | C550 | 716 |
| N4VS | LJ24 | 072 |
| N4VY | C650 | 0082 |
| **N4WC** | **HS25** | **25278** |
| N4WG | WW24 | 112 |
| **N4WG** | **WW24** | **200** |
| (N4WJ) | SBRL | 380-12 |
| N4XL | LJ35 | 236 |
| **N4Y** | **C650** | **0137** |
| N4YA | C525 | 0004 |
| N4ZA | HFB3 | 1045 |
| N4ZB | LJ25 | 371 |
| N4ZK | C500 | 140 |
| **N4ZL** | **C560** | **0448** |
| N4ZS | C550 | 248 |
| N5AH | HS25 | 256004 |
| (N5AX) | JSTR | 5013 |
| N5B | C500 | 021 |
| N5B | C500 | 081 |
| N5B | C500 | 150 |
| N5B | C500 | 225 |

| (N5B) | LJ25 | 299 |
|---|---|---|
| N5BA | WW24 | 138 |
| N5BK | GLF4 | 1025 |
| N5BL | LJ24 | 009 |
| N5BP | WW24 | 10 |
| N5BP | WW24 | 137 |
| (N5BP) | WW24 | 280 |
| N5C | FA20 | 17 |
| N5C | HS25 | 258083 |
| **N5CA** | **FA10** | **187** |
| N5CA | FA20 | 108/430 |
| N5CE | FA20 | 17 |
| N5D | LJ24 | 095 |
| **N5DA** | **GLF5** | **5021** |
| N5DL | FA50 | 7 |
| N5DL | GLF2 | 226 |
| N5DL | HS25 | 256051 |
| N5DL | SBRL | 306-131 |
| N5DM | LJ24 | 025 |
| N5DM | LJ24 | 028 |
| N5DM | LJ25 | 063 |
| N5EJ | MU30 | A033SA |
| (N5EM) | C500 | 383 |
| N5EQ | SBRL | 380-50 |
| N5ES | FA10 | 174 |
| N5ES | HS25 | 259024 |
| N5FE | FA20 | 20 |
| **N5FE** | **LJ45** | **079** |
| **N5FF** | **C750** | **0192** |
| N5FF | LJ35 | 396 |
| N5FG | C500 | 224 |
| N5FW | C500 | 187 |
| N5G | HS25 | 258053 |
| (N5GA) | C550 | 230 |
| N5GA | GLF5 | 509 |
| N5GD | FA10 | 83 |
| N5GE | C560 | 0218 |
| **N5GF** | **GLF4** | **1277** |
| **N5GQ** | **C52B** | **0321** |
| **N5GU** | **C52B** | **0009** |
| N5GV | GLF5 | 502 |
| N5GV | GLF5 | 518 |
| N5GV | GLF5 | 545 |
| (N5HG) | GLF3 | 376 |
| N5HN | GLF5 | 568 |
| **N5HQ** | **WW24** | **266** |
| N5JC | WW24 | 101 |
| N5JR | GLF5 | 626 |
| N5JR | WW24 | 49 |
| N5JU | C560 | 0080 |
| N5JY | FA10 | 74 |
| N5LG | C500 | 150 |
| **N5LK** | **C500** | **274** |
| N5LL | LJ25 | 183 |
| N5LP | FA10 | 142 |
| N5MC | F900 | 10 |
| **N5MC** | **GLF4** | **1218** |
| **N5MV** | **F9EX** | **221** |
| (N5MW) | HS25 | 25233 |
| N5NC | LJ25 | 372 |
| N5NC | LJ31 | 211 |
| N5NE | C550 | 723 |
| N5NE | SBRL | 306-127 |
| **N5NG** | **GLF4** | **1485** |
| N5NG | HS25 | 256020 |
| **N5NR** | **C56X** | **5557** |
| N5NR | C650 | 0083 |
| N5NR | HS25 | 256053 |
| N5NW | GLF3 | 395 |
| N5PC | SBRL | 282-34 |
| N5PF | BE40 | RK-59 |
| N5PG | CL61 | 5053 |
| **N5PG** | **GLF5** | **5046** |
| N5PG | SBRL | 380-50 |
| N5PQ | SBRL | 282-34 |
| N5Q | C500 | 018 |
| N5Q | C550 | 036 |
| N5QY | LJ24 | 028 |
| N5QZ | C500 | 018 |
| N5RC | FA20 | 159 |
| N5RD | GLF2 | 142 |
| **N5RD** | **GLF4** | **1156** |
| N5RL | C500 | 638 |
| N5RT | FA20 | 96 |
| (N5S) | WW24 | 280 |
| **N5SA** | **GLF5** | **527** |
| N5SJ | GLF2 | 52 |
| N5SJ | HS25 | 256014 |

| N5SJ | LJ24 | 246 |
|---|---|---|
| N5SP | GLF5 | 5001 |
| N5SP | GLF5 | 632 |
| N5T | C550 | 174 |
| N5T | C560 | 0218 |
| **N5T** | **C750** | **0104** |
| N5TC | C500 | 424 |
| N5TD | LJ24 | 311 |
| (N5TH) | WW24 | 372 |
| N5TK | C500 | 266 |
| N5TM | CL61 | 5076 |
| N5TQ | C550 | 174 |
| N5TR | C500 | 288 |
| **N5TR** | **C550** | **344** |
| N5TR | LJ24 | 311 |
| **N5UD** | **C525** | **0620** |
| N5UD | GLF2 | 8 |
| N5UD | JSTR | 5019 |
| N5UE | MU30 | A026SA |
| N5UH | GLF5 | 536 |
| N5UJ | LJ25 | 088 |
| N5UM | C500 | 550 |
| N5UQ | FA20 | 513 |
| N5UU | F900 | 133 |
| N5UU | FA20 | 513 |
| **N5UU** | **GLEX** | **9029** |
| N5V | HS25 | 25282 |
| N5VF | F900 | 116 |
| N5VF | FA50 | 163 |
| **N5VF** | **FA50** | **166** |
| **N5VG** | **LJ31** | **014** |
| N5VH | FA50 | 163 |
| **N5VJ** | **F900** | **27** |
| N5VJ | FA20 | 377/548 |
| N5VN | C550 | 550-0938 |
| N5VN | F900 | 116 |
| (N5VN) | JSTR | 5219 |
| **N5VP** | **C500** | **405** |
| N5VS | GLF4 | 1414 |
| **N5VS** | **GLF5** | **5088** |
| N5WC | CS55 | 0027 |
| **N5WF** | **C500** | **460** |
| N5WJ | LJ24 | 187 |
| **N5WN** | **C52B** | **0204** |
| **N5WT** | **C550** | **118** |
| N5XP | C560 | 0422 |
| N5XP | LJ45 | 118 |
| N5XP | LJ45 | 365 |
| N5XR | C550 | 553 |
| N5YD | C52A | 0121 |
| (N5YH) | C680 | 0056 |
| N5YP | C500 | 462 |
| N5ZA | HFB3 | 1037 |
| **N5ZN** | **C500** | **507** |
| N5ZZ | C500 | 155 |
| N6 | C550 | 006 |
| N6B | WW24 | 127 |
| N6B | WW24 | 89 |
| N6BB | CL61 | 5082 |
| N6BX | F900 | 79 |
| N6BX | GLF3 | 392 |
| N6BZ | GLF3 | 392 |
| N6CD | C500 | 151 |
| N6CF | SBRL | 265-48 |
| **N6D** | **GLEX** | **9191** |
| N6DB | WW24 | 98 |
| **N6DQ** | **E50P** | **50000012** |
| N6EL | C550 | 375 |
| (N6ES) | JSTR | 5023 |
| N6FE | C560 | 0028 |
| N6FE | FA20 | 50 |
| **N6FE** | **LJ45** | **098** |
| **N6FR** | **C550** | **550-0828** |
| N6FZ | C560 | 0028 |
| N6GC | LJ25 | 034 |
| N6GG | HS25 | 257108 |
| N6GG | HS25 | 258030 |
| N6GG | LJ35 | 256 |
| N6GJ | LJ24 | 069 |
| N6GQ | HS25 | 257108 |
| **N6GU** | **C680** | **0268** |
| **N6GV** | **SBRL** | **465-9** |
| **N6HF** | **C550** | **223** |
| N6HT | C500 | 362 |
| **N6JB** | **CL61** | **5131** |
| N6JB | HS25 | 257023 |
| N6JB | HS25 | 258189 |
| N6JL | C500 | 101 |

| N6JL | C550 | 294 |
|---|---|---|
| N6JL | JSTR | 5037/24 |
| N6JM | LJ24 | 246 |
| N6JR | C52A | 0051 |
| **N6JR** | **PRM1** | **RB-161** |
| N6JU | C500 | 101 |
| N6JU | C550 | 294 |
| **N6JW** | **GLF2** | **138** |
| N6K | SBRL | 380-1 |
| N6K | SBRL | 465-3 |
| N6KJ | LJ25 | 146 |
| N6KM | LJ24 | 334 |
| N6LG | SBRL | 380-34 |
| N6LL | CS55 | 0094 |
| N6LL | LJ25 | 256 |
| N6M | C52A | 0051 |
| N6M | C52A | 0302 |
| **N6M** | **C52B** | **0256** |
| **N6MF** | **BE40** | **RK-315** |
| N6MJ | WW24 | 251 |
| N6MK | HFB3 | 1037 |
| N6MK | SBRL | 306-98 |
| N6ML | HFB3 | 1037 |
| **N6MW** | **CL60** | **1057** |
| N6NB | GLF4 | 1290 |
| N6ND | SBRL | 306-81 |
| N6NE | JSTR | 5006/40 |
| N6NE | SBRL | 306-133 |
| N6NE | SBRL | 306-43 |
| N6NF | LJ25 | 021 |
| N6NG | SBRL | 380-27 |
| N6NP | SBRL | 306-43 |
| N6NP | SBRL | 465-9 |
| **N6NR** | **HS25** | **258701** |
| N6NR | SBRL | 306-43 |
| N6NR | SBRL | 306-81 |
| N6NR | SBRL | 380-27 |
| N6NR | SBRL | 380-43 |
| N6NR | SBRL | 380-54 |
| N6NR | SBRL | 465-29 |
| N6NR | SBRL | 465-68 |
| **N6NY** | **C560** | **0439** |
| N6PA | FA10 | 84 |
| N6PA | MU30 | A019SA |
| N6PC | GLF2 | 87/775/6 |
| N6PG | SBRL | 380-48 |
| N6PG | SBRL | 380-66 |
| N6PX | F900 | 79 |
| N6Q | C550 | 046 |
| N6QZ | JSTR | 5224 |
| N6RF | C500 | 460 |
| N6SG | CL61 | 5046 |
| N6SP | SBRL | 380-9 |
| **N6SS** | **HS25** | **25100** |
| N6TE | SBRL | 282-94 |
| **N6TM** | **C550** | **550-1067** |
| N6TM | HS25 | 258026 |
| N6TM | SBRL | 306-72 |
| N6TM | WW24 | 275 |
| N6TU | HS25 | 258026 |
| N6UB | HS25 | 257023 |
| N6UB | HS25 | 258189 |
| **N6VB** | **GLEX** | **9144** |
| N6VB | GLF4 | 1174 |
| N6VC | HS25 | 257056 |
| N6VF | C500 | 045 |
| **N6VF** | **FA20** | **486** |
| **N6VG** | **FA10** | **62** |
| N6VL | SBRL | 380-66 |
| N6VN | GLF4 | 1248 |
| N6WU | C550 | 198 |
| N6YL | SBRL | 380-42 |
| N6YY | LJ25 | 323 |
| N6YY | LJ36 | 023 |
| N6ZA | HFB3 | 1051 |
| **N6ZE** | **C52A** | **0141** |
| N7 | C500 | 084 |
| N7AB | C550 | 633 |
| **N7AB** | **C650** | **7068** |
| N7AB | LJ24 | 355 |
| N7AB | LJ35 | 402 |
| N7AT | LJ25 | 105 |
| (N7AU) | GALX | 004 |
| N7AU | GALX | 006 |
| N7AU | LJ55 | 112 |
| N7C | GLF2 | 51 |
| N7C | GLF3 | 449 |
| N7C | HS25 | 258025 |

| N7CC | C525 | 0004 |
|---|---|---|
| N7CC | C52A | 0007 |
| **N7CC** | **C52B** | **0007** |
| N7CC | C550 | 029 |
| N7CF | LJ24 | 016 |
| **N7CH** | **C52B** | **0202** |
| N7CJ | C500 | 509 |
| **N7CQ** | **C525** | **0004** |
| N7CT | HS25 | 257131 |
| **N7DJ** | **WW24** | **265** |
| N7DL | LJ24 | 228 |
| N7EC | WW24 | 96 |
| **N7EJ** | **LJ24** | **343** |
| **N7EN** | **C500** | **544** |
| N7EN | C525 | 0151 |
| N7ES | HFB3 | 1045 |
| N7EY | BE40 | RJ-34 |
| N7FD | C550 | 344 |
| N7FE | C560 | 0063 |
| N7FE | FA20 | 46 |
| **N7FE** | **LJ45** | **099** |
| N7FF | ASTR | 277 |
| N7FJ | LJ24 | 058 |
| **N7FY** | **EA50** | **000217** |
| (N7FZ) | C560 | 0063 |
| N7GA | LJ25 | 121 |
| N7GF | LJ24 | 016 |
| N7GF | LJ24 | 093 |
| **N7GJ** | **C500** | **021** |
| N7GJ | LJ25 | 004 |
| N7GN | LJ24 | 134 |
| N7GP | LJ24 | 082 |
| **N7GU** | **GLF4** | **4118** |
| N7GW | WW24 | 24 |
| **N7GX** | **FA50** | **139** |
| **N7GZ** | **C52A** | **0145** |
| N7HA | LJ24 | 154 |
| N7HB | C560 | 0584 |
| N7HB | C56X | 5607 |
| N7HF | C650 | 0148 |
| N7HF | SBRL | 465-13 |
| N7HL | WW24 | 35 |
| N7HM | WW24 | 266 |
| N7HM | WW24 | 329 |
| N7HV | C650 | 0124 |
| N7HV | HS25 | 25282 |
| N7JM | CL60 | 1010 |
| **N7JM** | **GLF4** | **1132** |
| N7JN | LJ25 | 098 |
| N7JT | PRM1 | RB-34 |
| N7KA | LJ35 | 033 |
| **N7KC** | **F9EX** | **14** |
| N7KC | FA20 | 479 |
| **N7KG** | **SBRL** | **282-111** |
| N7KH | C500 | 045 |
| N7KR | WW24 | 72 |
| **N7LA** | **GLF4** | **1286** |
| N7LA | LJ25 | 244 |
| (N7LA) | LJ35 | 308 |
| N7LC | LJ25 | 328 |
| N7LG | HS25 | 25185 |
| N7MC | C500 | 576 |
| **N7MR** | **FA7X** | **26** |
| **N7MZ** | **C500** | **623** |
| N7NE | C500 | 352 |
| N7NE | C525 | 0419 |
| **N7NE** | **C52B** | **0025** |
| N7NF | SBRL | 306-126 |
| (N7NL) | FA10 | 68 |
| **N7NN** | **C550** | **550-0851** |
| N7NP | FA10 | 68 |
| N7NP | HS25 | 25234 |
| N7NP | JSTR | 5229 |
| N7NR | SBRL | 306-126 |
| N7NR | SBRL | 306-57 |
| N7NR | SBRL | 306-73 |
| N7NR | SBRL | 380-39 |
| N7NR | SBRL | 465-44 |
| N7PE | LJ35 | 204 |
| N7PG | GLF2 | 62 |
| N7PG | GLF4 | 1374 |
| N7PQ | GLF2 | 62 |
| **N7PS** | **CL61** | **5027** |
| **N7PW** | **MU30** | **A027SA** |
| N7QC | CS55 | 0109 |
| N7QJ | C500 | 509 |
| **N7QM** | **C52A** | **0214** |
| N7RC | C550 | 022 |

| | | |
|---|---|---|
| N7RC | MU30 | A012SA |
| N7RL | C525 | 0028 |
| N7RL | C56X | 5247 |
| N7RL | LJ24 | 322 |
| N7RL | LJ25 | 230 |
| N7RP | GLF4 | 1064 |
| N7RX | GLF4 | 1137 |
| **N7RX** | **GLF4** | **4017** |
| (N7RZ) | FA10 | 127 |
| N7SB | C750 | 0185 |
| **N7SB** | **C750** | **0209** |
| N7SJ | HS25 | 25250 |
| **N7SJ** | **SJ30** | **007** |
| (N7SL) | SBRL | 282-114 |
| N7SN | C550 | 313 |
| **N7SN** | **LJ31** | **226** |
| N7SP | CL60 | 1076 |
| N7SV | C500 | 601 |
| N7SZ | HS25 | 25100 |
| N7SZ | JSTR | 5040 |
| N7SZ | JSTR | 5124 |
| N7TJ | FA10 | 69 |
| N7TJ | GLF2 | 23 |
| N7TJ | GLF2 | 77 |
| N7TJ | LJ25 | 007 |
| N7TJ | LJ35 | 013 |
| **N7TK** | **C500** | **509** |
| **N7TM** | **C56X** | **6028** |
| N7UA | LJ55 | 128 |
| N7UF | C500 | 632 |
| **N7UF** | **GLF4** | **1422** |
| N7UJ | HS25 | 257093 |
| (N7UL) | C650 | 0224 |
| N7US | LJ35 | 291 |
| N7US | LJ55 | 128 |
| N7US | LJ60 | 014 |
| N7UV | HS25 | 257011 |
| N7VS | LJ24 | 087 |
| N7WC | HS25 | 25273 |
| N7WC | HS25 | 257036 |
| N7WF | C500 | 370 |
| N7WG | FA20 | 325 |
| N7WG | GLF2 | 248 |
| (N7WG) | HS25 | 25187 |
| N7WG | HS25 | 257126 |
| N7WG | HS25 | 257131 |
| N7WQ | GLF2 | 190 |
| N7WY | C550 | 598 |
| **N7X** | **FA7X** | **33** |
| **N7XE** | **C525** | **0419** |
| N7XJ | LJ35 | 669 |
| **N7YA** | **C550** | **550-0880** |
| N7YP | C550 | 211 |
| N7ZA | LJ25 | 026 |
| N7ZB | LJ24 | 355 |
| **N7ZG** | **C650** | **0031** |
| **N7ZH** | **LJ35** | **348** |
| **N7ZU** | **C550** | **432** |
| N7ZX | GLF2 | 21 |
| N8AD | C550 | 331 |
| N8AD | JSTR | 5013 |
| N8AE | LJ24 | 335 |
| N8AF | SBRL | 282-24 |
| N8BG | CS55 | 0085 |
| N8BG | LJ24 | 348 |
| N8BX | C550 | 345 |
| N8BX | F900 | 111 |
| N8BX | FA20 | 380 |
| (N8CA) | GLF5 | 531 |
| N8CA | GLF5 | 563 |
| N8CF | C550 | 223 |
| N8CL | LJ25 | 014 |
| (N8CQ) | C52A | 0007 |
| N8DE | C500 | 166 |
| **N8DX** | **C500** | **303** |
| N8EH | C500 | 483 |
| N8FC | C500 | 124 |
| N8FD | C550 | 383 |
| N8FE | FA20 | 199 |
| N8FF | LJ25 | 016 |
| N8FM | LJ24 | 116 |
| N8GA | FA10 | 127 |
| N8GA | LJ35 | 091 |
| N8GA | SBRL | 282-32 |
| N8GA | WW24 | 356 |
| N8GA | WW24 | 63 |
| N8GE | WW24 | 63 |
| N8GT | LJ55 | 020 |
| (N8GY) | C560 | 0091 |
| N8HJ | C560 | 0108 |
| **N8HQ** | **BE40** | **RJ-50** |
| (N8JA) | LJ35 | 348 |
| N8JC | C650 | 7030 |
| N8JC | C750 | 0020 |
| **N8JC** | **C750** | **0154** |
| N8JG | C500 | 074 |
| N8JL | GLF3 | 388 |
| N8JL | WW24 | 359 |
| **N8JQ** | **C750** | **0020** |
| **N8JR** | **LJ60** | **084** |
| N8KG | CL60 | 1012 |
| N8KG | FA50 | 174 |
| N8KG | HS25 | 257189 |
| N8KH | C500 | 163 |
| N8LA | LJ35 | 124 |
| N8LC | WW24 | 48 |
| **N8LE** | **MU30** | **A042SA** |
| N8LG | C500 | 477 |
| N8LL | LJ28 | 28-005 |
| **N8LT** | **FA10** | **173** |
| N8MA | LJ25 | 085 |
| N8MA | LJ35 | 229 |
| N8MC | ASTR | 092 |
| N8MC | CL64 | 5329 |
| **N8MC** | **GLF4** | **1129** |
| (N8ME) | BE40 | RK-19 |
| **N8MF** | **GALX** | **006** |
| N8MF | LJ25 | 253 |
| N8MF | LJ55 | 128 |
| N8MN | ASTR | 092 |
| N8MQ | LJ25 | 085 |
| N8NB | SBRL | 370-9 |
| N8NB | SBRL | 380-27 |
| (N8NC) | C500 | 567 |
| (N8NF) | SBRL | 306-141 |
| N8NG | SBRL | 380-48 |
| N8NR | SBRL | 306-141 |
| N8NR | SBRL | 370-2 |
| N8NR | SBRL | 370-9 |
| N8NR | SBRL | 380-27 |
| N8NR | SBRL | 380-48 |
| N8P | C500 | 369 |
| N8PG | GLF2 | 21 |
| N8PJ | C500 | 369 |
| N8PL | HS25 | 257058 |
| N8PQ | GLF2 | 21 |
| N8QM | F2EX | 38 |
| N8QM | F2TH | 38 |
| N8QP | WW24 | 217 |
| N8QR | WW24 | 217 |
| **N8RA** | **WW24** | **104** |
| N8RF | C500 | 293 |
| N8SC | JSTR | 5106/9 |
| **N8SP** | **CL64** | **5518** |
| N8SP | HS25 | 258380 |
| N8TG | C500 | 253 |
| **N8TG** | **LJ31** | **190** |
| N8TP | FA20 | 74 |
| N8TU | C750 | 0136 |
| N8U | LJ36 | 026 |
| N8UA | LJ36 | 026 |
| (N8UB) | LJ36 | 026 |
| N8UC | C525 | 0416 |
| N8UP | HS25 | 258083 |
| **N8VB** | **GLEX** | **9021** |
| **N8VF** | **F900** | **12** |
| N8VQ | GLF5 | 566 |
| N8VX | C650 | 7081 |
| N8WN | FA20 | 91 |
| **N8YM** | **BE40** | **RJ-4** |
| N8YY | LJ35 | 335 |
| N8YY | LJ55 | 060 |
| N9AJ | LJ24 | 069 |
| (N9AT) | C500 | 241 |
| N9AT | LJ25 | 125 |
| N9AX | C500 | 016 |
| N9AX | C650 | 0067 |
| N9AZ | HS25 | 256063 |
| N9BF | GLF2 | 46 |
| N9BX | FA50 | 45 |
| **N9BX** | **GLF4** | **4145** |
| N9BY | WW24 | 9 |
| N9CH | LJ31 | 041 |
| N9CH | LJ35 | 282 |
| N9CH | LJ45 | 129 |
| **N9CH** | **PRM1** | **RB-244** |
| **N9CN** | **C560** | **0602** |
| N9CN | LJ25 | 061 |
| N9CN | LJ35 | 016 |
| **N9CR** | **C550** | **500** |
| **N9CU** | **LJ60** | **075** |
| N9CZ | LJ25 | 040 |
| **N9DC** | **C550** | **031** |
| N9DC | WW24 | 109 |
| N9DM | FA20 | 18 |
| N9DM | WW24 | 63 |
| N9EE | LJ35 | 193 |
| N9FB | FA20 | 275 |
| (N9FC) | MU30 | A010SA |
| N9FE | FA20 | 216 |
| N9FE | FA20 | 84 |
| **N9FE** | **LJ45** | **240** |
| N9GN | SBRL | 380-2 |
| N9GT | C500 | 438 |
| N9GT | CS55 | 0159 |
| N9GU | C525 | 0034 |
| N9GU | JSTR | 5119/29 |
| **N9GY** | **CS55** | **0159** |
| N9HJ | LJ31 | 040 |
| N9HM | LJ24 | 190 |
| N9HM | LJ25 | 146 |
| N9HM | LJ35 | 199 |
| N9HN | LJ25 | 146 |
| (N9HV) | LJ35 | 199 |
| N9JJ | LJ24 | 039 |
| N9KC | LJ24 | 144 |
| (N9KE) | JSTR | 5225 |
| N9KH | CS55 | 0082 |
| N9KH | LJ28 | 28-001 |
| N9KL | C650 | 0068 |
| N9KL | GLF3 | 321 |
| N9KN | GLF4 | 1282 |
| N9LD | LJ24 | 336 |
| N9LM | LJ24 | 152 |
| N9LP | MU30 | A019SA |
| (N9LP) | WW24 | 149 |
| N9LR | C525 | 0025 |
| N9LR | C550 | 270 |
| N9LR | C560 | 0473 |
| N9LR | HS25 | 258050 |
| N9LR | LJ55 | 138 |
| **N9LV** | **PRM1** | **RB-132** |
| N9MD | JSTR | 5014 |
| N9MS | SBRL | 282-103 |
| N9NB | HS25 | 258317 |
| N9NE | C500 | 593 |
| **N9NG** | **C750** | **0213** |
| N9NL | C650 | 0101 |
| N9NP | SBRL | 306-133 |
| N9NR | SBRL | 282-111 |
| N9NR | SBRL | 282-137 |
| N9NR | SBRL | 306-135 |
| N9NT | SBRL | 306-135 |
| N9PC | GLF4 | 1210 |
| N9PG | GLF2 | 251 |
| N9PW | BE40 | RK-7 |
| N9PY | GLF2 | 251 |
| N9QM | LJ25 | 286 |
| N9QN | SBRL | 306-12 |
| N9RA | LJ24 | 068 |
| N9RA | LJ24 | 095 |
| **N9RA** | **LJ25** | **277** |
| **N9RD** | **WW24** | **220** |
| N9RG | F900 | 51 |
| N9RS | LJ28 | 28-001 |
| **N9SC** | **GLF4** | **4174** |
| N9SC | GLF5 | 552 |
| **N9SS** | **C550** | **190** |
| N9TE | FA10 | 103 |
| **N9TE** | **FA20** | **202** |
| N9TE | FA50 | 17 |
| N9TK | C500 | 437 |
| (N9UC) | C650 | 0238 |
| **N9UD** | **C52A** | **0317** |
| N9UG | C525 | 0331 |
| N9UJ | C500 | 198 |
| N9UP | HS25 | 258147 |
| N9V | C500 | 150 |
| N9VC | WW24 | 162 |
| N9VF | C550 | 646 |
| N9VG | FA20 | 416 |
| N9VL | ASTR | 026 |
| N9VL | LJ31 | 174 |
| N9VQ | WW24 | 162 |
| N9WN | GLF3 | 392 |
| N9WP | JSTR | 5157 |
| N9WV | F9EX | 108 |
| **N9WW** | **BE40** | **RK-142** |
| (N9WW) | WW24 | 252 |
| (N9WW) | WW24 | 306 |
| N9X | FA50 | 14 |
| N9ZB | LJ35 | 591 |
| **N9ZD** | **LJ35** | **306** |
| N9ZM | LJ35 | 591 |
| N9ZM | LJ60 | 151 |
| N10 | C500 | 084 |
| (N10AA) | HS25 | 258023 |
| (N10AB) | LJ35 | 231 |
| N10AG | FA10 | 6 |
| N10AH | FA10 | 139 |
| (N10AH) | FA10 | 141 |
| **N10AH** | **LJ35** | **657** |
| N10AQ | LJ35 | 069 |
| N10AT | F900 | 142 |
| N10AT | FA50 | 194 |
| **N10AU** | **C52A** | **0420** |
| N10AU | C560 | 0512 |
| N10AZ | FA20 | 382 |
| N10AZ | LJ35 | 080 |
| N10BD | LJ25 | 120 |
| N10BD | LJ35 | 506 |
| (N10BF) | C500 | 118 |
| N10BF | C550 | 048 |
| (N10BF) | LJ25 | 010 |
| N10BF | LJ35 | 185 |
| N10BF | LJ55 | 128 |
| N10BK | WW24 | 89 |
| N10BU | LJ25 | 120 |
| (N10BY) | WW24 | 226 |
| N10C | HS25 | 25236 |
| **N10C** | **HS25** | **257050** |
| (N10CA) | C500 | 387 |
| N10CB | LJ24 | 227 |
| N10CC | SBRL | 282-56 |
| N10CF | C550 | 230 |
| N10CN | C560 | 0249 |
| N10CN | HS25 | 257155 |
| N10CN | SBRL | 380-27 |
| N10CN | SBRL | 380-54 |
| N10CP | LJ24 | 112 |
| N10CP | LJ55 | 029 |
| N10CR | LJ55 | 057 |
| N10CR | LJ55 | 145 |
| N10CX | JSTR | 5162 |
| N10CZ | HS25 | 257038 |
| N10D | HS25 | 25029 |
| N10DG | C500 | 028 |
| N10DG | C500 | 120 |
| N10DR | JSTR | 5037/24 |
| N10DR | JSTR | 5139/54 |
| N10E | GLEX | 9106 |
| N10EA | WW24 | 39 |
| N10EC | LJ24 | 215 |
| **N10EG** | **C550** | **055** |
| N10EH | C500 | 350 |
| **N10EH** | **GLF3** | **436** |
| **N10EU** | **F2EX** | **46** |
| **N10F** | **FA10** | **12** |
| N10FE | CL60 | 1074 |
| **N10FE** | **CL61** | **5188** |
| N10FE | FA20 | 16 |
| **N10FG** | **C500** | **295** |
| N10FG | WW24 | 318 |
| N10FJ | FA10 | 100 |
| N10FJ | FA10 | 106 |
| N10FJ | FA10 | 2 |
| N10FL | BE40 | RK-266 |
| N10FL | BE40 | RK-27 |
| N10FL | LJ25 | 106 |
| N10FM | C500 | 292 |
| N10FN | C550 | 268 |
| **N10FN** | **LJ36** | **015** |
| N10FQ | BE40 | RK-27 |
| N10FU | LJ24 | 340 |
| N10GE | C500 | 385 |
| (N10GN) | C550 | 069 |
| (N10GR) | C500 | 132 |
| N10GR | WW24 | 114 |
| N10HE | FA10 | 111 |
| (N10HH) | EA50 | 000279 |
| N10HK | FA10 | 142 |
| N10HR | GLF2 | 67 |

| N10HV | WW24 | 103 |
|---|---|---|
| **N10HZ** | **F9EX** | **57** |
| N10J | BE40 | RK-31 |
| N10J | C500 | 408 |
| N10J | LJ45 | 063 |
| **N10J** | **LJ45** | **337** |
| **N10JA** | **C550** | **035** |
| N10JJ | JSTR | 5162 |
| N10JK | C550 | 178 |
| N10JM | C750 | 0022 |
| N10JP | C500 | 080 |
| N10JP | C550 | 081 |
| N10JP | C650 | 0157 |
| **N10JP** | **F2TH** | **23** |
| N10JP | WW24 | 96 |
| N10JV | WW24 | 96 |
| N10JX | BE40 | RK-31 |
| **N10JY** | **LJ45** | **063** |
| N10JZ | FA10 | 13 |
| N10LB | FA20 | 179 |
| N10LB | GLF2 | 111 |
| N10LB | GLF2 | 168 |
| N10LB | GLF2 | 82 |
| N10LB | GLF4 | 1008 |
| N10LJ | LJ24 | 037 |
| N10LN | HS25 | 25156 |
| N10LQ | GLF4 | 1008 |
| **N10LR** | **C550** | **084** |
| N10LT | FA50 | 194 |
| **N10LX** | **SBRL** | **306-59** |
| **N10LY** | **C550** | **466** |
| N10M | SBRL | 370-2 |
| **N10MB** | **LJ60** | **176** |
| N10MB | WW24 | 157 |
| (N10MC) | LJ24 | 003 |
| N10MC | WW24 | 26 |
| N10MF | WW24 | 53 |
| N10MJ | JSTR | 5090 |
| N10MR | WW24 | 258 |
| N10MT | FA20 | 239 |
| N10MV | WW24 | 300 |
| N10MZ | ASTR | 028 |
| (N10MZ) | CL60 | 1084 |
| N10MZ | F900 | 32 |
| **N10MZ** | **GLF5** | **5141** |
| N10NB | HS25 | 258331 |
| **N10NC** | **FA10** | **172** |
| N10NL | C500 | 417 |
| N10NL | FA10 | 195 |
| **N10NL** | **LJ45** | **128** |
| N10NL | WW24 | 304 |
| N10NM | MU30 | A016SA |
| N10NP | LJ25 | 106 |
| N10NT | LJ25 | 144 |
| (N10NV) | FA10 | 195 |
| (N10NW) | GLF2 | 183 |
| N10PF | SBRL | 306-39 |
| N10PN | C650 | 0020 |
| N10PN | CL60 | 1072 |
| (N10PN) | FA10 | 3 |
| N10PN | JSTR | 5155/32 |
| N10PP | FA20 | 161 |
| N10PP | FA50 | 231 |
| N10PQ | FA50 | 231 |
| N10PS | C500 | 252 |
| N10PW | HS25 | 257104 |
| (N10PX) | C550 | 419 |
| N10PX | C650 | 0025 |
| (N10PZ) | C550 | 550-0835 |
| N10QD | FA10 | 178 |
| N10QJ | HS25 | 257135 |
| N10QS | HA4T | RC-22 |
| (N10QX) | LJ24 | 035 |
| **N10R** | **LJ45** | **042** |
| N10RE | LJ25 | 133 |
| N10RE | LJ35 | 345 |
| **N10RQ** | **GLF2** | **232** |
| N10RU | C550 | 470 |
| **N10RU** | **C560** | **0512** |
| **N10RZ** | **ASTR** | **258** |
| N10RZ | FA20 | 161 |
| N10RZ | LJ25 | 133 |
| N10S | WW24 | 278 |
| **N10SA** | **HS25** | **256065** |
| N10SE | LJ31 | 217 |
| **N10SE** | **LJ40** | **45-2032** |
| **N10SL** | **GLEX** | **9221** |
| N10SL | SBRL | 282-11 |
| N10SN | C56X | 5014 |
| **N10SN** | **GLF4** | **4147** |
| N10SN | WW24 | 69 |
| N10ST | C650 | 0113 |
| N10ST | LJ31 | 039 |
| N10ST | LJ60 | 228 |
| N10TB | C560 | 0143 |
| N10TB | FA10 | 72 |
| **N10TC** | **C550** | **495** |
| N10TC | C650 | 0008 |
| N10TC | HS25 | 258096 |
| **N10TD** | **C560** | **0096** |
| N10TE | MU30 | A029SA |
| N10TJ | FA10 | 99 |
| **N10TN** | **HS25** | **257085** |
| N10TX | FA10 | 9 |
| N10UC | C500 | 083 |
| N10UC | C500 | 283 |
| **N10UC** | **HS25** | **257119** |
| **N10UF** | **LJ35** | **166** |
| (N10UG) | FA50 | 18 |
| N10UH | C500 | 304 |
| **N10UH** | **C550** | **550-0925** |
| N10UJ | WW24 | 204 |
| N10UM | SBRL | 306-43 |
| N10UN | FA10 | 36 |
| N10UP | C500 | 080 |
| N10UQ | C500 | 083 |
| (N10UU) | FA20 | 513 |
| N10VG | FA20 | 126/438 |
| N10VG | LJ25 | 125 |
| N10VQ | C56X | 5570 |
| **N10VT** | **C550** | **403** |
| N10WA | FA20 | 28 |
| N10WE | FA10 | 159 |
| N10WF | HS25 | 258030 |
| N10WF | LJ24 | 321 |
| N10WF | LJ35 | 377 |
| N10WJ | LJ24 | 311 |
| **N10WZ** | **C52A** | **0432** |
| **N10XQ** | **GALX** | **169** |
| N10XX | FA10 | 40 |
| N10XY | GLF2 | 56 |
| N10YJ | FA10 | 57 |
| **N10YJ** | **HS25** | **258099** |
| N10ZK | GLF4 | 1174 |
| N11 | JSTR | 5001/53 |
| N11A | C500 | 111 |
| **N11A** | **CL64** | **5354** |
| N11AB | C550 | 079 |
| N11AF | HS25 | 256057 |
| N11AK | FA20 | 249 |
| N11AK | LJ24 | 154 |
| N11AK | LJ25 | 082 |
| N11AK | LJ35 | 135 |
| N11AL | GLF2 | 97 |
| N11AL | SBRL | 306-27 |
| N11AM | LJ35 | 340 |
| **N11AM** | **LJ60** | **118** |
| (N11AN) | GLF4 | 1108 |
| N11AQ | C500 | 045 |
| N11AQ | LJ24 | 178 |
| N11AQ | SBRL | 306-18 |
| N11AR | HS25 | 25098 |
| N11AZ | CL60 | 1032 |
| N11BK | WW24 | 77 |
| N11BU | LJ25 | 138 |
| **N11BV** | **F2TH** | **21** |
| N11CS | WW24 | 397 |
| N11DH | C500 | 019 |
| N11DH | C500 | 048 |
| N11DH | C500 | 385 |
| N11DH | FA10 | 108 |
| N11DH | FA10 | 142 |
| N11DH | FA10 | 68 |
| N11DQ | C500 | 019 |
| N11EA | GLEX | 9114 |
| N11FH | C550 | 013 |
| N11FH | LJ24 | 131 |
| N11FX | GLF4 | 1107 |
| N11FX | HS25 | 25273 |
| N11GE | BE40 | RK-19 |
| **N11HD** | **FA7X** | **62** |
| N11HJ | C500 | 034 |
| N11HM | JSTR | 5119/29 |
| (N11JC) | C500 | 463 |
| N11JC | JSTR | 5013 |
| N11JC | LJ25 | 003 |
| N11JK | LJ24 | 088 |
| (N11JV) | LJ35 | 096 |
| N11KA | C500 | 119 |
| **N11LB** | **C52B** | **0019** |
| N11LB | FA20 | 244 |
| N11LC | C560 | 0427 |
| N11LK | CL61 | 5193 |
| N11LK | F900 | 128 |
| **N11LN** | **WW24** | **261** |
| N11LQ | C560 | 0427 |
| **N11LX** | **SBRL** | **306-75** |
| (N11MC) | LJ25 | 125 |
| N11MC | WW24 | 55 |
| **N11MN** | **C500** | **266** |
| N11MY | LJ35 | 370 |
| N11MZ | ASTR | 028 |
| N11NT | HFB3 | 1055 |
| N11NZ | C650 | 0143 |
| N11NZ | GLF2 | 214 |
| N11PH | LJ25 | 177 |
| N11PM | PRM1 | RB-113 |
| N11QC | C500 | 008 |
| N11QD | HS25 | 25108 |
| N11QM | LJ24 | 091 |
| N11SQ | C500 | 477 |
| N11SQ | HS25 | 25206 |
| (N11SQ) | LJ25 | 234 |
| N11SQ | LJ35 | 380 |
| N11SS | C550 | 436 |
| N11SU | CS55 | 0086 |
| N11SX | GLF2 | 34 |
| N11SX | JSTR | 5111 |
| N11TC | C500 | 008 |
| N11TC | FA20 | 146 |
| N11TK | CL61 | 5025 |
| (N11TK) | GLEX | 9004 |
| N11TK | LJ25 | 201 |
| (N11TK) | LJ31 | 229 |
| **N11TM** | **C500** | **435** |
| N11TR | CS55 | 0119 |
| N11TS | C560 | 0549 |
| N11TS | CS55 | 0119 |
| N11TS | HS25 | 257191 |
| N11TS | LJ55 | 032 |
| **N11TS** | **LJ60** | **151** |
| **N11UB** | **BE40** | **RK-212** |
| N11UC | GLF2 | 108 |
| **N11UD** | **C52B** | **0285** |
| N11UE | JSTR | 5038 |
| N11UF | FA20 | 356 |
| N11UF | GLF2 | 8 |
| N11UF | JSTR | 5037/24 |
| N11UF | JSTR | 5038 |
| **N11UF** | **LJ35** | **237** |
| **N11UL** | **HS25** | **258498** |
| N11UL | SBRL | 306-103 |
| N11UM | GLF2 | 12 |
| (N11WA) | FA20 | 37/406 |
| N11WC | C500 | 058 |
| (N11WC) | FA10 | 11 |
| (N11WC) | HS25 | 258308 |
| N11WC | WW24 | 177 |
| **N11WF** | **BE40** | **RK-236** |
| N11WF | MU30 | A075SA |
| **N11WM** | **F9EX** | **58** |
| N11WP | WW24 | 100 |
| N11WQ | C500 | 058 |
| N11YM | LJ35 | 340 |
| N11YR | HS25 | 257206 |
| N12AC | C550 | 035 |
| N12AE | HS25 | 25214 |
| N12AM | C500 | 235 |
| N12AR | F2EX | 97 |
| N12AR | FA20 | 200 |
| (N12BN) | GLF2 | 39 |
| N12BN | HS25 | 25214 |
| N12BW | SBRL | 282-99 |
| N12CJ | WW24 | 13 |
| N12CQ | C500 | 458 |
| N12CQ | C550 | 372 |
| **N12CQ** | **C560** | **0231** |
| **N12CV** | **C500** | **458** |
| N12DE | C500 | 458 |
| **N12EP** | **FA10** | **175** |
| (N12EP) | LJ35 | 110 |
| **N12F** | **HS25** | **258182** |
| N12FC | C550 | 369 |
| (N12FH) | WW24 | 159 |
| **N12FN** | **LJ36** | **016** |
| (N12FS) | LJ25 | 328 |
| N12FU | FA20 | 412 |
| N12FU | LJ60 | 027 |
| N12GH | FA20 | 7 |
| N12GJ | LJ35 | 438 |
| N12GK | C550 | 291 |
| **N12GP** | **GLF2** | **63** |
| N12GP | LJ24 | 076 |
| (N12GP) | SBRL | 380-51 |
| N12GS | C525 | 0374 |
| N12GS | C52A | 0127 |
| **N12GS** | **C52B** | **0122** |
| **N12GY** | **C525** | **0374** |
| N12HJ | LJ24 | 040 |
| N12JA | C550 | 231 |
| N12JA | WW24 | 108 |
| N12JX | WW24 | 108 |
| N12KW | HS25 | 25097 |
| N12L | C550 | 583 |
| **N12L** | **C56X** | **5002** |
| N12LB | FA10 | 62 |
| N12LB | FA20 | 179 |
| N12LW | C550 | 583 |
| N12MA | C550 | 550-0882 |
| N12MB | C500 | 101 |
| N12MB | C500 | 137 |
| N12MB | FA10 | 112 |
| (N12MB) | LJ24 | 116 |
| N12ME | C500 | 137 |
| N12MF | FA20 | 179 |
| N12MG | BE40 | RK-117 |
| **N12MG** | **BE40** | **RK-331** |
| N12MH | LJ25 | 139 |
| N12MJ | LJ24 | 331 |
| N12MK | LJ24 | 192 |
| N12MQ | BE40 | RK-117 |
| N12MW | C560 | 0542 |
| **N12MW** | **F2TH** | **97** |
| N12MY | C560 | 0542 |
| N12ND | ASTR | 116 |
| N12NM | C500 | 660 |
| N12NV | BE40 | RK-103 |
| **N12NV** | **BE40** | **RK-186** |
| **N12NZ** | **GLF4** | **1376** |
| N12PA | C525 | 0012 |
| **N12PA** | **HS25** | **258642** |
| N12PB | SBRL | 306-18 |
| N12QS | HA4T | RC-31 |
| N12R | JSTR | 5006/40 |
| N12R | JSTR | 5053/2 |
| (N12RA) | LJ25 | 023 |
| N12RN | C500 | 625 |
| N12RN | C550 | 709 |
| **N12RN** | **C560** | **0316** |
| **N12RP** | **LJ35** | **278** |
| N12SS | CL30 | 20138 |
| N12ST | C560 | 0014 |
| N12ST | LJ60 | 205 |
| N12TA | LJ24 | 093 |
| (N12TU) | C560 | 0358 |
| N12TV | C550 | 115 |
| N12TV | C560 | 0358 |
| N12TX | FA10 | 147 |
| N12TX | FA10 | 90 |
| N12U | FA10 | 75 |
| **N12U** | **FA7X** | **53** |
| N12U | GLF4 | 1112 |
| N12UD | C56X | 5719 |
| **N12UM** | **GLF4** | **1112** |
| N12UT | GLF4 | 1112 |
| **N12VU** | **LJ45** | **324** |
| **N12WF** | **BE40** | **RK-228** |
| N12WF | MU30 | A083SA |
| **N12WH** | **C500** | **437** |
| N12WK | LJ25 | 126 |
| N12WP | FA20 | 83 |
| N12WW | LJ25 | 051 |
| N12XX | FA10 | 112 |
| N12YS | HS25 | 25186 |
| N13AD | WW24 | 103 |
| N13BJ | C550 | 236 |
| N13BK | C500 | 644 |
| **N13BK** | **FA10** | **94** |
| (N13BN) | C500 | 641 |
| N13BT | C500 | 453 |
| N13CR | LJ25 | 023 |
| (N13FE) | FA20 | 24 |

| | | |
|---|---|---|
| N13FH | C525 | 0185 |
| N13FN | LJ36 | 045 |
| N13GB | BE40 | RK-13 |
| N13GW | GLF2 | 87/775/6 |
| N13GW | WW24 | 162 |
| (N13GX) | GALX | 013 |
| N13HB | LJ35 | 310 |
| (N13HB) | LJ55 | 046 |
| (N13HH) | WW24 | 268 |
| N13HJ | C500 | 182 |
| (N13HQ) | LJ35 | 310 |
| N13J | GLF4 | 1482 |
| (N13J) | GLF5 | 5040 |
| N13JE | LJ36 | 013 |
| **N13JS** | **GLEX** | **9212** |
| **N13KD** | **C500** | **497** |
| N13KH | WW24 | 182 |
| N13KL | LJ24 | 332 |
| N13LB | GLF2 | 111 |
| N13LJ | LJ24 | 037 |
| N13M | C52A | 0105 |
| (N13ME) | SBRL | 380-70 |
| N13MF | SBRL | 465-13 |
| N13MJ | HS25 | 25137 |
| N13MJ | LJ24 | 314 |
| N13MJ | LJ35 | 047 |
| N13NH | SBRL | 380-25 |
| N13NL | WW24 | 304 |
| (N13QS) | C650 | 0013 |
| N13RC | C500 | 431 |
| N13SL | SBRL | 306-110 |
| N13SL | SBRL | 306-17 |
| N13SL | SBRL | 306-90 |
| N13SN | LJ24 | 009 |
| **N13ST** | **C500** | **439** |
| N13SY | BE40 | RK-111 |
| **N13SY** | **HS25** | **258103** |
| N13TV | WW24 | 86 |
| N13UR | C500 | 011 |
| N13UR | WW24 | 358 |
| N13US | BE40 | RK-193 |
| N13VF | WW24 | 191 |
| N13VG | LJ35 | 386 |
| N13VP | C550 | 061 |
| N13ZM | C510 | 0064 |
| N14BC | LJ24 | 209 |
| N14BN | WW24 | 337 |
| (N14BR) | HS25 | 256032 |
| N14BX | LJ45 | 038 |
| N14CF | C500 | 097 |
| N14CF | LJ36 | 015 |
| N14CG | FA50 | 100 |
| N14CG | SBRL | 306-83 |
| N14CJ | FA20 | 499 |
| N14CK | LJ25 | 337 |
| N14CN | LJ36 | 047 |
| **N14CN** | **WW24** | **359** |
| N14CQ | SBRL | 306-83 |
| **N14DG** | **C650** | **7059** |
| **N14DM** | **LJ24** | **341** |
| N14DM | MU30 | A017SA |
| (N14DP) | CL61 | 5125 |
| N14EA | C500 | 418 |
| **N14EA** | **PRM1** | **RB-119** |
| N14EL | LJ35 | 009 |
| N14EN | FA20 | 490 |
| N14FE | CL60 | 1064 |
| (N14FE) | FA20 | 198/466 |
| N14FE | FA20 | 227 |
| N14FE | LJ45 | 038 |
| N14FG | FA20 | 177 |
| N14FN | LJ25 | 126 |
| (N14FU) | LJ36 | 048 |
| **N14FX** | **F9DX** | **624** |
| N14GA | C550 | 310 |
| N14GD | CL61 | 5005 |
| **N14GD** | **CL64** | **5490** |
| N14GD | HS25 | 25141 |
| N14GD | HS25 | 256068 |
| N14GD | HS25 | 259011 |
| N14GQ | HS25 | 25141 |
| N14HB | C550 | 550-0903 |
| N14HH | HS25 | 25118 |
| N14JA | C500 | 195 |
| N14JA | HS25 | 257051 |
| N14JD | SBRL | 380-56 |
| N14JL | C500 | 015 |
| N14JZ | C500 | 143 |
| N14LJ | LJ25 | 014 |
| N14LT | GLF2 | 246 |
| N14M | LJ35 | 113 |
| N14M | SBRL | 282-4 |
| N14M | SBRL | 306-56 |
| N14M | SBRL | 465-4 |
| N14MH | C500 | 174 |
| N14MJ | LJ24 | 189 |
| **N14NA** | **F900** | **124** |
| N14NA | LJ25 | 218 |
| N14NE | FA50 | 177 |
| N14PC | GLF2 | 170 |
| N14PN | CL61 | 3014 |
| N14PT | LJ24 | 208 |
| (N14PT) | LJ25 | 139 |
| N14QG | LJ28 | 28-003 |
| **N14QS** | **HA4T** | **RC-29** |
| N14R | CL64 | 5319 |
| N14R | GLEX | 9110 |
| **N14RM** | **C550** | **139** |
| N14RU | CL64 | 5319 |
| N14RZ | C550 | 269 |
| N14SA | HS25 | 258339 |
| N14SR | ASTR | 015 |
| N14SR | CL64 | 5360 |
| N14SY | GLF3 | 391 |
| N14SY | HS25 | 257101 |
| N14T | C500 | 143 |
| N14T | LJ31 | 222 |
| N14T | LJ35 | 608 |
| N14T | LJ60 | 026 |
| N14T | LJ60 | 213 |
| N14TN | SBRL | 380-40 |
| N14TT | C500 | 237 |
| **N14TU** | **LJ60** | **026** |
| N14TV | C500 | 499 |
| N14TV | C525 | 0126 |
| N14TX | LJ35 | 321 |
| N14TX | LJ36 | 033 |
| N14U | FA10 | 90 |
| N14UH | GLF4 | 1247 |
| N14UM | CS55 | 0127 |
| **N14VA** | **C500** | **521** |
| N14VC | LJ25 | 263 |
| N14VF | C560 | 0130 |
| (N14VF) | C560 | 0342 |
| (N14VP) | C750 | 0014 |
| (N14WJ) | HS25 | 257120 |
| N14WJ | JSTR | 5053/2 |
| (N14WT) | LJ31 | 072 |
| N15AG | HS25 | 257156 |
| N15AK | LJ25 | 082 |
| N15AK | SBRL | 465-70 |
| N15AR | MU30 | A005SA |
| **N15AS** | **F2TH** | **3** |
| N15AT | FA20 | 403 |
| N15AW | C500 | 139 |
| **N15AX** | **HS25** | **258002** |
| **N15BA** | **ASTR** | **020** |
| N15BE | LJ24 | 005 |
| N15BH | LJ25 | 134 |
| N15BN | WW24 | 352 |
| N15BV | C525 | 0527 |
| N15C | C525 | 0377 |
| **N15C** | **C52B** | **0023** |
| N15CC | C500 | 101 |
| N15CC | FA20 | 23 |
| N15CC | LJ25 | 036 |
| N15CC | LJ25 | 124 |
| N15CC | LJ35 | 339 |
| N15CC | LJ36 | 009 |
| N15CC | SBRL | 465-42 |
| (N15CK) | SBRL | 306-121 |
| N15CN | C550 | 550-0819 |
| N15CQ | C500 | 101 |
| N15CU | LJ25 | 124 |
| N15CV | C500 | 547 |
| N15CV | C550 | 550-0819 |
| **N15CV** | **C560** | **0766** |
| **N15CY** | **C500** | **547** |
| N15DJ | SBRL | 306-97 |
| N15EA | C550 | 450 |
| "N15EC" | SBRL | 276-50 |
| **N15EH** | **LJ35** | **126** |
| N15EN | SBRL | 465-70 |
| **N15ER** | **LJ25** | **267** |
| N15FE | FA20 | 229 |
| **N15FE** | **LJ45** | **039** |
| N15FF | F9EX | 158 |
| N15FJ | C500 | 369 |
| N15FJ | C500 | 524 |
| N15FJ | C550 | 619 |
| N15FN | LJ36 | 038 |
| N15FS | C500 | 016 |
| **N15FX** | **FA50** | **157** |
| N15FX | GLEX | 9088 |
| N15FX | GLEX | 9092 |
| N15G | WW24 | 63 |
| **N15GJ** | **C510** | **0200** |
| **N15GT** | **CL30** | **20120** |
| **N15H** | **FA20** | **368** |
| N15H | SBRL | 306-60 |
| **N15HE** | **GLF3** | **369** |
| **N15HF** | **SBRL** | **306-60** |
| **N15JA** | **C550** | **042** |
| **N15JH** | **C500** | **174** |
| **N15LN** | **C650** | **7013** |
| **N15LV** | **C525** | **0191** |
| N15M | LJ25 | 036 |
| (N15ME) | SBRL | 380-70 |
| N15MJ | LJ24 | 339 |
| N15MJ | LJ25 | 018 |
| N15MJ | LJ35 | 211 |
| N15NA | C550 | 296 |
| N15ND | EA50 | 000016 |
| N15NY | C500 | 496 |
| **N15PG** | **C52B** | **0140** |
| N15PL | LJ24 | 101 |
| N15PN | SBRL | 380-15 |
| N15PR | C500 | 452 |
| **N15PX** | **GLEX** | **9382** |
| **N15QB** | **HS25** | **HA-0101** |
| N15QS | C650 | 0015 |
| N15QS | HA4T | RC-6 |
| N15RF | SBRL | 306-23 |
| N15RF | SBRL | 380-17 |
| N15RH | LJ35 | 497 |
| N15RL | C550 | 489 |
| **N15RL** | **C750** | **0165** |
| N15SC | LJ24 | 039 |
| N15SC | LJ35 | 139 |
| N15SD | C750 | 0246 |
| **N15SD** | **GLEX** | **9272** |
| N15SJ | FA10 | 40 |
| **N15SK** | **C560** | **0395** |
| **N15SL** | **C560** | **0272** |
| N15SL | FA20 | 256 |
| N15SN | C550 | 566 |
| N15SP | C550 | 566 |
| N15SP | CL64 | 5402 |
| (N15SS) | C525 | 0455 |
| (N15TA) | FA50 | 73 |
| **N15TF** | **C56X** | **5255** |
| N15TG | GLF2 | 253 |
| N15TM | FA10 | 114 |
| N15TS | SBRL | 282-18 |
| N15TT | C650 | 0105 |
| N15TT | C650 | 0192 |
| **N15TT** | **C750** | **0127** |
| N15TT | CS55 | 0019 |
| N15TV | C550 | 459 |
| N15TW | ASTR | 029 |
| N15TW | C550 | 459 |
| N15TW | FA50 | 73 |
| N15TW | LJ35 | 106 |
| N15TW | MU30 | A014SA |
| N15TX | FA10 | 13 |
| N15TZ | C650 | 0192 |
| (N15UB) | HS25 | 25038 |
| **N15UB** | **LJ40** | **45-2072** |
| N15UC | GLF2 | 176 |
| **N15UC** | **GLF5** | **589** |
| N15UG | GLF2 | 176 |
| (N15UJ) | C500 | 547 |
| N15UQ | GLF5 | 589 |
| N15VF | C650 | 0012 |
| **N15WH** | **LJ35** | **085** |
| (N15WJ) | GLF4 | 1079 |
| **N15XM** | **C550** | **341** |
| N15Y | C550 | 297 |
| **N15Y** | **GLF4** | **1318** |
| N15Y | LJ35 | 335 |
| **N15YD** | **C52A** | **0336** |
| **N15ZA** | **GLF3** | **329** |
| **N15ZZ** | **C52B** | **0221** |
| N16A | WW24 | 101 |
| N16AJ | C650 | 0075 |
| (N16AJ) | LJ36 | 032 |
| N16AS | C650 | 0055 |
| N16AZ | JSTR | 5156 |
| N16BJ | LJ35 | 165 |
| N16BL | JSTR | 5205 |
| N16CP | FA50 | 153 |
| N16CP | LJ24 | 147 |
| **N16CS** | **LJ60** | **098** |
| N16DD | FA10 | 105 |
| N16DD | FA10 | 56 |
| **N16DK** | **PRM1** | **RB-19** |
| N16FE | C650 | 0025 |
| N16FE | FA20 | 230 |
| N16FG | GLF2 | 235 |
| N16FG | LJ35 | 655 |
| N16FN | LJ35 | 030 |
| **N16FN** | **LJ36** | **027** |
| N16FP | WW24 | 39 |
| **N16FX** | **F9DX** | **621** |
| N16FX | GLEX | 9061 |
| N16GA | HS25 | 256018 |
| (N16GG) | HS25 | 25032 |
| **N16GH** | **HS25** | **258065** |
| N16GH | WW24 | 110 |
| N16GR | WW24 | 100 |
| N16GS | C56X | 5278 |
| **N16GS** | **C680** | **0096** |
| N16GS | HS25 | 257186 |
| N16GT | LJ25 | 230 |
| N16GX | GLEX | 9016 |
| N16HC | LJ24 | 126 |
| **N16HD** | **BE40** | **RK-16** |
| **N16HL** | **C500** | **431** |
| "N16JM" | GLF4 | 1024 |
| N16JP | LJ25 | 017 |
| N16KB | C650 | 7008 |
| **N16KB** | **CL61** | **5066** |
| **N16KK** | **LJ25** | **174** |
| N16KW | C500 | 664 |
| N16LF | SBRL | 380-25 |
| N16LG | C500 | 174 |
| N16LJ | LJ25 | 230 |
| **N16LJ** | **LJ55** | **126** |
| N16MA | WW24 | 101 |
| **N16MF** | **BE40** | **RJ-65** |
| N16MF | MU30 | A065SA |
| N16MJ | LJ24 | 117 |
| N16MK | WW24 | 84 |
| N16MT | LJ24 | 209 |
| N16NK | GLF2 | 156/31 |
| N16NK | GLF3 | 354 |
| **N16NK** | **GLF5** | **585** |
| **N16NL** | **C500** | **417** |
| N16NM | C560 | 0084 |
| N16PC | LJ45 | 050 |
| **N16PC** | **LJ45** | **319** |
| (N16PJ) | HS25 | 25078 |
| **N16PL** | **C550** | **293** |
| N16PN | SBRL | 306-99 |
| N16PQ | LJ45 | 050 |
| N16R | FA20 | 305 |
| N16R | FA50 | 141 |
| N16R | SBRL | 282-94 |
| **N16RP** | **CS55** | **0047** |
| **N16RW** | **CL60** | **1013** |
| N16SK | WW24 | 101 |
| (N16SM) | HS25 | 258655 |
| **N16SM** | **HS25** | **HA-0040** |
| (N16SN) | C56X | 5014 |
| N16ST | LJ31 | 039 |
| **N16SU** | **C650** | **0025** |
| N16TA | SBRL | 282-2 |
| **N16TS** | **C550** | **030** |
| N16TS | CL60 | 1016 |
| **N16VG** | **C500** | **553** |
| (N16VT) | HS25 | 256037 |
| N16VT | HS25 | 256040 |
| N16WG | HS25 | 25187 |
| N16WJ | FA10 | 105 |
| N16WJ | LJ24 | 133 |
| **N16YD** | **CL64** | **5367** |
| **N17A** | **LJ36** | **046** |
| **N17AE** | **EA50** | **000017** |
| **N17AH** | **LJ25** | **316** |
| N17AJ | CRVT | 15 |
| **N17AN** | **C56X** | **5030** |
| N17AN | C56X | 5141 |

| | | |
|---|---|---|
| N17AN | C650 | 0054 |
| N17AN | FA50 | 281 |
| N17AP | C650 | 7003 |
| N17AR | LJ25 | 034 |
| **N17AZ** | **LJ35** | **080** |
| **N17CJ** | **PRM1** | **RB-171** |
| (N17CM) | BE40 | RK-205 |
| **N17CN** | **C52B** | **0128** |
| N17CN | CL61 | 3027 |
| **N17CX** | **C750** | **0267** |
| **N17DD** | **HS25** | **258161** |
| **N17DM** | **C550** | **416** |
| (N17DW) | WW24 | 145 |
| N17EM | LJ35 | 287 |
| N17FE | FA20 | 232 |
| N17FL | C550 | 627 |
| N17FN | LJ24 | 220 |
| N17FS | C550 | 483 |
| **N17FX** | **F9EX** | **29** |
| N17FX | GLEX | 9093 |
| N17GG | GLF2 | 200 |
| N17GL | LJ35 | 278 |
| N17GL | LJ55 | 099 |
| N17GV | GLF5 | 520 |
| **N17GX** | **GLEX** | **9045** |
| **N17HA** | **C500** | **447** |
| N17HV | HS25 | 25282 |
| N17JF | LJ25 | 039 |
| **N17JK** | **GLF4** | **1235** |
| N17JT | FA20 | 179 |
| **N17KD** | **C500** | **337** |
| **N17KJ** | **GLF2** | **200** |
| **N17KW** | **GLF2** | **28** |
| N17LB | GLF3 | 331 |
| N17LH | LJ35 | 428 |
| **N17LJ** | **LJ36** | **017** |
| N17LK | C550 | 405 |
| N17LK | C560 | 0037 |
| **N17LK** | **GLF3** | **431** |
| N17LT | SBRL | 282-59 |
| N17LT | SBRL | 282-70 |
| N17LV | C550 | 405 |
| N17MU | C510 | 0017 |
| N17MX | GLF2 | 98/38 |
| N17NC | GLF3 | 318 |
| N17ND | GLF2 | 63 |
| N17ND | GLF3 | 369 |
| N17ND | GLF4 | 1053 |
| **N17ND** | **GLF5** | **518** |
| (N17ND) | LJ35 | 348 |
| N17ND | LJ35 | 438 |
| (N17PL) | C550 | 305 |
| **N17PL** | **C560** | **0412** |
| N17QC | C650 | 0239 |
| N17RG | C550 | 237 |
| **N17RP** | **C510** | **0133** |
| N17S | C550 | 105 |
| N17SL | HS25 | 25082 |
| N17TE | C650 | 0011 |
| N17TE | CL61 | 5007 |
| N17TE | CL64 | 5437 |
| **N17TE** | **CL65** | **5724** |
| N17TJ | C500 | 375 |
| **N17TJ** | **FA10** | **43** |
| N17TJ | MU30 | A023SA |
| N17TN | C650 | 0011 |
| N17TZ | CL61 | 5007 |
| N17TZ | CL64 | 5437 |
| N17UC | C56X | 5026 |
| N17UC | C650 | 0239 |
| **N17UC** | **CL30** | **20011** |
| N17UC | WW24 | 283 |
| **N17UF** | **LJ35** | **258** |
| (N17UG) | C56X | 5026 |
| **N17VB** | **C525** | **0206** |
| N17VG | LJ31 | 017 |
| N17VP | C550 | 483 |
| N17WC | C550 | 478 |
| N17WG | FA10 | 35 |
| N17WG | HS25 | 257126 |
| (N17ZU) | FA10 | 146 |
| N18AC | GLF4 | 1344 |
| N18AF | C500 | 283 |
| N18AK | LJ25 | 092 |
| **N18AN** | **GLF4** | **1228** |
| N18AQ | GLF2 | 94 |
| N18AQ | HS25 | 258712 |
| N18AT | LJ36 | 002 |
| N18AX | LJ35 | 087 |
| **N18BA** | **HS25** | **257167** |
| N18BA | MU30 | A036SA |
| N18BG | C500 | 292 |
| N18BG | C500 | 378 |
| (N18BG) | FA10 | 33 |
| **N18BH** | **JSTR** | **5099/5** |
| N18BL | LJ25 | 234 |
| N18BL | LJ31 | 126 |
| N18BL | WW24 | 182 |
| **N18BM** | **EA50** | **000220** |
| N18BR | BE40 | RK-221 |
| N18CA | WW24 | 5 |
| (N18CC) | C550 | 392 |
| N18CC | C550 | 423 |
| **N18CC** | **HS25** | **257030** |
| N18CG | F2TH | 57 |
| **N18CG** | **F9EX** | **228** |
| N18CG | LJ55 | 104 |
| **N18CJ** | **GLF4** | **4141** |
| N18CQ | LJ55 | 104 |
| N18CV | LJ35 | 016 |
| (N18DD) | C550 | 276 |
| **N18DF** | **F9EX** | **158** |
| N18DY | LJ35 | 392 |
| N18FE | FA20 | 233 |
| **N18FM** | **C500** | **014** |
| N18FN | LJ35 | 105 |
| **N18FX** | **F900** | **152** |
| N18G | FA50 | 52 |
| N18G | HS25 | 257153 |
| N18G | LJ24 | 186 |
| N18G | LJ35 | 114 |
| N18GA | C525 | 0216 |
| **N18GA** | **C52B** | **0302** |
| **N18GB** | **C650** | **7048** |
| N18GW | WW24 | 187 |
| N18GX | HS25 | 25281 |
| N18GZ | GALX | 018 |
| **N18HC** | **C500** | **627** |
| N18HH | SBRL | 306-18 |
| N18HJ | C500 | 036 |
| **N18HJ** | **C550** | **587** |
| **N18HN** | **FA20** | **257** |
| N18JF | LJ25 | 037 |
| N18JL | WW24 | 51 |
| N18JN | BE40 | RJ-6 |
| N18JN | GLF2 | 154/28 |
| N18KE | MU30 | A022SA |
| N18LB | GLF3 | 309 |
| N18LH | LJ35 | 379 |
| N18MJ | LJ25 | 218 |
| **N18MV** | **F2TH** | **24** |
| **N18MX** | **FA10** | **117** |
| **N18MZ** | **F900** | **32** |
| N18N | GLF2 | 139/11 |
| N18N | GLF2 | 61 |
| N18N | GLF2 | 8 |
| N18N | SBRL | 306-12 |
| N18N | SBRL | 306-36 |
| **N18NA** | **C550** | **580** |
| N18ND | C550 | 295 |
| N18NK | GLF2 | 156/31 |
| N18NK | GLF5 | 585 |
| N18NM | LJ25 | 209 |
| N18NM | LJ35 | 189 |
| (N18PV) | C650 | 0127 |
| **N18QA** | **C525** | **0216** |
| (N18RA) | HFB3 | 1038 |
| N18RA | LJ25 | 280 |
| N18RF | CL61 | 5152 |
| N18RF | F9EX | 18 |
| N18RF | GLF4 | 1092 |
| N18RF | GLF5 | 628 |
| **N18RF** | **PRM1** | **RB-127** |
| N18RN | C500 | 625 |
| N18RN | C550 | 709 |
| N18RN | GLF2 | 231 |
| N18SD | LJ24 | 230 |
| N18SF | WW24 | 374 |
| N18SH | HS25 | 257157 |
| (N18SK) | C560 | 0091 |
| (N18SK) | C560 | 0098 |
| N18SK | C650 | 7016 |
| **N18SK** | **FA10** | **34** |
| (N18SL) | GLF3 | 304 |
| N18ST | LJ35 | 316 |
| N18T | MU30 | A061SA |
| N18TA | LJ25 | 280 |
| N18TD | C52A | 0342 |
| N18TD | GLF4 | 1224 |
| **N18TF** | **C52A** | **0014** |
| N18TF | SBRL | 380-15 |
| N18TG | C525 | 0617 |
| **N18TM** | **GLEX** | **9090** |
| N18TM | GLF3 | 351 |
| N18TM | GLF4 | 1224 |
| N18TZ | SBRL | 380-15 |
| N18UR | C500 | 011 |
| "N18VS" | GLF5 | 564 |
| N18WE | LJ35 | 377 |
| N18WF | GLEX | 9057 |
| N18WF | GLEX | 9059 |
| N18WF | GLEX | 9128 |
| **N18WF** | **GLEX** | **9215** |
| N18WF | GLF4 | 1175 |
| N18WY | GLEX | 9057 |
| N18WZ | GLEX | 9059 |
| N18X | FA10 | 42 |
| N18X | SBRL | 306-137 |
| N18XX | GLF2 | 227 |
| N18ZD | LJ55 | 122 |
| **N18ZL** | **GLF3** | **434** |
| N19AF | CS55 | 0026 |
| N19AJ | C500 | 174 |
| N19AJ | C550 | 188 |
| N19AP | WW24 | 259 |
| N19BC | FA20 | 40 |
| N19BD | FA20 | 161 |
| N19BG | SBRL | 282-118 |
| N19CJ | C525 | 0019 |
| N19CM | C500 | 169 |
| N19CM | SBRL | 306-10 |
| **N19CP** | **C550** | **003** |
| **N19DD** | **C750** | **0095** |
| N19DD | CL60 | 1081 |
| N19DD | HS25 | 258448 |
| **N19DU** | **HS25** | **258448** |
| N19EE | WW24 | 172 |
| **N19ER** | **C550** | **048** |
| N19ES | JSTR | 5204 |
| N19FM | LJ24 | 311 |
| N19FN | LJ25 | 034 |
| N19FR | C650 | 0062 |
| N19FX | FA50 | 157 |
| N19GA | MU30 | A074SA |
| N19GB | C500 | 682 |
| **N19GE** | **LJ25** | **322** |
| N19GL | LJ35 | 415 |
| **N19H** | **GLF3** | **416** |
| N19H | GLF3 | 483 |
| N19H | HS25 | 25261 |
| N19HE | HS25 | 256004 |
| N19HF | CL60 | 1081 |
| N19HF | SBRL | 282-100 |
| N19HH | HS25 | 256004 |
| (N19HL) | GALX | 091 |
| N19HM | LJ24 | 311 |
| N19HU | C550 | 081 |
| **N19HU** | **C560** | **0135** |
| N19J | C500 | 408 |
| N19J | CL61 | 3057 |
| N19JM | LJ25 | 250 |
| **N19KT** | **C52A** | **0413** |
| N19LH | LJ35 | 279 |
| **N19LJ** | **LJ24** | **233** |
| (N19LM) | LJ35 | 321 |
| N19LT | LJ31 | 019 |
| N19M | C500 | 165 |
| N19M | C500 | 303 |
| N19M | SBRL | 306-56 |
| N19ME | C560 | 0128 |
| N19MJ | LJ24 | 351 |
| N19MK | C560 | 0128 |
| N19MK | C560 | 0395 |
| N19MK | C56X | 5093 |
| **N19MK** | **C680** | **0052** |
| N19MQ | C500 | 165 |
| (N19MS) | SBRL | 282-15 |
| N19MS | SBRL | 282-82 |
| (N19MU) | C560 | 0395 |
| N19MX | FA20 | 339 |
| N19MZ | C56X | 5093 |
| N19NW | GLF2 | 19 |
| N19NW | LJ35 | 019 |
| N19PC | SBRL | 380-2 |
| N19PV | C560 | 0416 |
| **N19QC** | **C650** | **0238** |
| **N19R** | **MU30** | **A043SA** |
| **N19RP** | **LJ35** | **363** |
| **N19SV** | **C650** | **7002** |
| N19TJ | LJ24 | 258 |
| N19TJ | LJ31 | 018 |
| N19TX | FA20 | 296/507 |
| N19U | C500 | 303 |
| N19U | SBRL | 306-56 |
| N19UC | C650 | 0238 |
| N19UC | WW24 | 232 |
| N19UP | LJ31 | 237 |
| (N19VF) | C560 | 0130 |
| **N19VF** | **F900** | **29** |
| N19VP | C550 | 247 |
| N19XP | HS25 | 258719 |
| **N19ZA** | **CS55** | **0094** |
| N20AD | LJ25 | 287 |
| N20AE | FA20 | 258 |
| N20AF | FA20 | 120 |
| N20AP | JSTR | 5054/59 |
| N20AT | C650 | 0109 |
| **N20AU** | **C52B** | **0304** |
| N20AU | C550 | 550-1012 |
| N20BD | LJ24 | 008 |
| N20BE | FA20 | 203 |
| N20BG | LJ35 | 028 |
| N20CC | C500 | 397 |
| N20CC | C560 | 0027 |
| **N20CC** | **C560** | **0467** |
| N20CF | C550 | 305 |
| **N20CF** | **FA10** | **106** |
| N20CG | FA20 | 281/496 |
| N20CL | C550 | 434 |
| **N20CL** | **FA20** | **497** |
| N20CN | C550 | 305 |
| N20CN | C560 | 0167 |
| N20CR | LJ35 | 098 |
| **N20CR** | **LJ55** | **097** |
| N20CS | CS55 | 0138 |
| (N20CV) | BE40 | RJ-20 |
| N20CX | CL60 | 1051 |
| **N20CZ** | **C500** | **397** |
| **N20DA** | **MS76** | **102** |
| N20DH | WW24 | 383 |
| N20DK | LJ25 | 198 |
| N20DK | LJ35 | 143 |
| N20DL | LJ25 | 263 |
| N20DL | LJ55 | 020 |
| (N20EA) | C650 | 0007 |
| N20EE | FA10 | 38 |
| N20EG | GLEX | 9038 |
| N20EG | GLF4 | 1161 |
| N20EP | LJ24 | 008 |
| N20ES | FA10 | 120 |
| N20ES | FA10 | 38 |
| N20ES | SBRL | 282-124 |
| N20ET | FA10 | 38 |
| N20FB | C550 | 287 |
| N20FE | ASTR | 067 |
| N20FE | FA20 | 235 |
| N20FE | FA20 | 272 |
| **N20FE** | **LJ45** | **366** |
| **N20FJ** | **FA20** | **119/431** |
| N20FJ | FA20 | 244 |
| N20FJ | FA20 | 272 |
| N20FJ | FA20 | 289 |
| N20FJ | FA20 | 341 |
| N20FJ | FA20 | 355 |
| N20FL | BE40 | RK-247 |
| N20FL | C500 | 169 |
| N20FL | C525 | 0069 |
| N20FM | C500 | 011 |
| N20FM | C550 | 014 |
| N20FM | FA20 | 321 |
| N20FM | HS25 | 256055 |
| **N20FM** | **HS25** | **256058** |
| N20FX | GLF2 | 120 |
| N20FX | HS25 | 257121 |
| N20G | CL60 | 1085 |
| **N20G** | **CL61** | **5136** |
| N20G | SBRL | 306-59 |
| N20GB | JSTR | 5202 |
| N20GB | WW24 | 127 |
| N20GH | FA20 | 7 |
| **N20GP** | **C52A** | **0131** |
| (N20GP) | GLF2 | 63 |

| | | | | | | | | | | | |
|---|---|---|---|---|---|---|---|---|---|---|---|
| N20GP | GLF2 | 90 | N20XY | GLF3 | 412 | **N21RA** | **C52A** | **0092** | N22HP | CS55 | 0103 |
| N20GT | C500 | 579 | N20XY | GLF4 | 1080 | N21RA | WW24 | 394 | **N22HS** | **FA20** | **507** |
| N20GT | C550 | 391 | N20YA | FA20 | 24 | N21SA | HS25 | 256006 | N22JG | C500 | 208 |
| (N20GT) | HS25 | 257009 | (N20YC) | C560 | 0027 | **N21SF** | **WW24** | **214** | N22JW | FA20 | 83 |
| N20GT | LJ24 | 283 | **N20YL** | **ASTR** | **076** | N21SH | JSTR | 5148 | N22JW | SBRL | 306-20 |
| N20GT | LJ25 | 349 | **N20ZC** | **BE40** | **RK-86** | **N21SL** | **C550** | **550-0877** | N22JW | SBRL | 380-15 |
| N20GX | CL60 | 1085 | N21 | JSTR | 5001/53 | (N21SU) | HFB3 | 1055 | N22KH | HS25 | 257043 |
| N20GX | SBRL | 306-59 | **N21AC** | **LJ60** | **070** | N21SV | C550 | 016 | N22KW | C560 | 0256 |
| **N20H** | **GLF2** | **51** | (N21AG) | CS55 | 0003 | N21SW | C550 | 016 | N22KW | C56X | 5062 |
| N20H | GLF4 | 1120 | N21AG | LJ24 | 329 | N21TV | C500 | 078 | N22LC | C560 | 0521 |
| N20H | GLF5 | 522 | N21AK | WW24 | 59 | N21U | LJ24 | 024 | **N22LC** | **F9EX** | **136** |
| N20HE | GLF2 | 51 | N21AM | GLF2 | 110 | N21U | LJ24 | 152 | N22LH | C500 | 319 |
| **N20HF** | **FA20** | **191** | N21AM | GLF3 | 443 | N21VB | JSTR | 5219 | (N22LL) | WW24 | 148 |
| N20HJ | LJ25 | 024 | N21AR | HS25 | 25146 | N21VB | LJ55 | 026 | N22LP | C560 | 0083 |
| N20HJ | LJ35 | 112 | N21AX | GLF2 | 110 | **N21VC** | **C525** | **0106** | N22LQ | C560 | 0521 |
| N20HN | GLF5 | 522 | N21AX | LJ45 | 123 | N21W | FA20 | 205 | **N22LX** | **C52A** | **0109** |
| N20JA | LJ36 | 008 | **N21AX** | **LJ45** | **371** | N21WJ | C650 | 0141 | N22LZ | WW24 | 236 |
| N20JM | FA20 | 258 | N21BC | WW24 | 51 | (N21WS) | LJ35 | 410 | N22MA | SBRL | 306-2 |
| N20JM | FA20 | 6 | N21BD | LJ45 | 188 | N21XB | LJ24 | 198 | N22MB | C500 | 337 |
| N20K | WW24 | 144 | N21BH | HS25 | 256007 | N21XL | LJ24 | 198 | N22MH | LJ24 | 259 |
| N20KH | WW24 | 223 | N21BM | SBRL | 306-64 | **N21XP** | **PRM1** | **RB-9** | N22MJ | LJ24 | 329 |
| **N20KS** | **EA50** | **000244** | N21BS | C500 | 389 | **N21YP** | **EA50** | **000174** | N22MJ | LJ35 | 135 |
| (N20KW) | C500 | 557 | N21CC | C500 | 099 | N21YR | EA50 | 000174 | (N22ML) | LJ24 | 259 |
| (N20LL) | LJ31 | 018 | N21CL | CL61 | 5126 | N22 | GLF4 | 1042 | **N22MS** | **LJ35** | **209** |
| N20LT | C560 | 0253 | N21CL | FA10 | 166 | **N22** | **GLF5** | **501** | N22MV | SBRL | 282-68 |
| N20LT | FA20 | 21 | **N21CV** | **C560** | **0340** | N22AC | WW24 | 35 | N22MY | SBRL | 282-68 |
| **N20LW** | **FA10** | **48** | N21CX | CL61 | 5014 | **N22AF** | **C560** | **0129** | N22MY | SBRL | 306-117 |
| N20LW | GLF2 | 62 | N21CX | WW24 | 268 | N22AQ | CL61 | 5142 | (N22NB) | SBRL | 282-106 |
| N20M | LJ24 | 094 | N21CZ | GLF4 | 1137 | N22AX | LJ31 | 039 | **N22NB** | **SBRL** | **380-56** |
| N20MJ | LJ25 | 277 | N21DA | C550 | 091 | **N22AX** | **LJ45** | **101** | **N22NF** | **HS25** | **258145** |
| N20MK | C560 | 0210 | N21DA | LJ35 | 497 | N22AZ | CL60 | 1060 | N22NG | C750 | 0039 |
| N20MW | C650 | 0052 | N21DB | FA10 | 65 | N22B | LJ24 | 044 | (N22NG) | C750 | 0041 |
| N20MY | FA20 | 136/439 | (N21DT) | FA20 | 6 | N22BG | WW24 | 410 | **N22NG** | **C750** | **0204** |
| **N20NL** | **PRM1** | **RB-106** | **N21DX** | **WW24** | **269** | N22BH | GLEX | 9040 | N22NJ | LJ25 | 097 |
| (N20NM) | CS55 | 0121 | N21EG | CS55 | 0087 | N22BH | HS25 | 256009 | N22NM | LJ24 | 341 |
| N20NW | LJ25 | 096 | N21EH | C500 | 576 | N22BJ | SBRL | 282-105 | N22NT | SBRL | 380-21 |
| (N20NW) | WW24 | 300 | N21EH | C550 | 430 | N22BM | LJ24 | 341 | **N22PC** | **C550** | **583** |
| **N20NY** | **FA20** | **61** | **N21EK** | **EA50** | **000133** | N22BM | LJ36 | 032 | (N22PQ) | C550 | 583 |
| **N20PA** | **MU30** | **A089SA** | N21EK | FA10 | 8 | N22BN | MU30 | A023SA | N22QF | LJ60 | 225 |
| N20PL | FA20 | 83 | **N21EL** | **HS25** | **258396** | N22BN | SBRL | 282-36 | N22RB | JSTR | 5093 |
| N20PL | GALX | 063 | N21EP | C500 | 412 | N22BX | LJ35 | 129 | N22RD | WW24 | 165 |
| N20PY | JSTR | 5023 | N21ES | FA10 | 8 | N22BX | SBRL | 306-138 | **N22RD** | **WW24** | **203** |
| N20PY | LJ25 | 249 | N21ES | HS25 | 25203 | (N22CA) | C500 | 004 | N22RD | WW24 | 99 |
| N20RD | C650 | 0036 | N21ET | FA10 | 8 | N22CG | SBRL | 306-88 | N22RG | C550 | 639 |
| N20RD | C650 | 0142 | N21FE | FA20 | 226 | N22CH | JSTR | 5038 | N22RG | C560 | 0235 |
| N20RD | LJ25 | 334 | N21FE | FA20 | 399 | N22CH | SBRL | 282-70 | N22RG | C650 | 7070 |
| N20RF | C500 | 033 | N21FJ | FA20 | 299 | N22CH | SBRL | 282-99 | **N22RG** | **C750** | **0031** |
| N20RF | C550 | 456 | **N21FM** | **PRM1** | **RB-273** | N22CH | WW24 | 7 | N22RJ | C550 | 074 |
| N20RG | HS25 | 25091 | **N21FN** | **LJ25** | **062** | N22CP | LJ35 | 178 | N22RT | WW24 | 99 |
| N20RG | HS25 | 25226 | (N21FR) | C680 | 0016 | N22CQ | LJ35 | 178 | N22SD | C500 | 578 |
| **N20RM** | **C500** | **389** | **N21FX** | **HS25** | **HA-0105** | N22CS | F9EX | 10 | **N22SF** | **CL64** | **5589** |
| N20RT | C500 | 033 | N21GG | WW24 | 347 | **N22CS** | **SBRL** | **465-24** | N22SF | LJ31 | 126 |
| N20RT | LJ35 | 188 | N21GL | LJ35 | 098 | N22CX | GLF2 | 8 | N22SF | LJ35 | 168 |
| **N20RU** | **C550** | **550-1012** | N21GN | GLF4 | 1284 | (N22CX) | MU30 | A029SA | N22SF | LJ35 | 674 |
| **N20RZ** | **LJ25** | **024** | N21GN | GLF5 | 578 | N22DE | HS25 | 25060 | N22SF | LJ60 | 225 |
| N20S | HS25 | 25250 | N21GN | HS25 | 25115 | N22DH | HS25 | 25224 | **N22SM** | **HS25** | **258655** |
| N20S | HS25 | 257059 | N21HE | C750 | 0075 | N22DL | FA20 | 14 | N22SN | LJ35 | 674 |
| N20S | HS25 | 258042 | N21HE | F2EX | 46 | N22DL | HS25 | 25060 | **N22ST** | **ASTR** | **251** |
| N20S | JSTR | 5126 | N21HJ | C500 | 444 | N22DL | HS25 | 256051 | N22SY | LJ35 | 168 |
| N20S | LJ24 | 008 | (N21HJ) | F9EX | 22 | N22DN | C500 | 127 | N22T | C550 | 407 |
| N20SB | C560 | 0422 | N21HQ | C750 | 0075 | N22EH | C500 | 185 | **N22T** | **F900** | **119** |
| N20SB | C56X | 5114 | N21HR | LJ25 | 339 | N22EH | CS55 | 0074 | N22T | FA50 | 53 |
| N20SH | JSTR | 5142 | **N21HR** | **WW24** | **335** | N22EH | FA10 | 25 | N22TP | C500 | 371 |
| N20SK | HS25 | 257059 | (N21JJ) | C560 | 0055 | N22EH | HS25 | 25179 | N22TP | SBRL | 282-60 |
| N20SM | C500 | 001 | N21JM | FA20 | 6 | N22EH | HS25 | 257043 | N22TS | C500 | 473 |
| **N20SM** | **C560** | **0353** | N21JW | WW24 | 77 | N22EH | SBRL | 306-57 | N22TY | C500 | 473 |
| N20SP | C500 | 398 | N21KP | GLF4 | 1139 | **N22EL** | **C500** | **416** | (N22TZ) | C550 | 407 |
| N20SR | FA20 | 369 | N21KR | GLF4 | 1139 | **N22EM** | **C510** | **0047** | N22TZ | FA50 | 53 |
| N20T | FA20 | 381/548 | **N21LG** | **C560** | **0197** | N22ES | FA10 | 122 | N22UF | LJ31 | 126 |
| **N20TA** | **LJ24** | **062** | **N21LL** | **C650** | **0016** | N22ES | JSTR | 5161/43 | **N22UL** | **CS55** | **0039** |
| N20TF | JSTR | 5016 | N21MA | C56X | 5089 | N22FE | FA20 | 223 | N22UP | HS25 | 259040 |
| (N20TV) | C550 | 142 | N21MF | HS25 | 25097 | N22FH | C500 | 185 | **N22VK** | **PRM1** | **RB-140** |
| N20TX | FA20 | 296/507 | N21NA | C500 | 174 | N22FM | C500 | 229 | **N22VS** | **HS25** | **HA-0047** |
| N20TZ | FA20 | 381/548 | N21NA | LJ24 | 246 | **N22FM** | **C550** | **461** | N22WJ | BE40 | RJ-44 |
| **N20UA** | **FA20** | **91** | N21NA | LJ35 | 343 | N22FS | FA20 | 339 | N22WJ | FA20 | 113 |
| N20UC | LJ36 | 031 | N21NC | FA20 | 161 | N22FS | GLF2 | 22 | N22WJ | MU30 | A074SA |
| N20UC | SBRL | 465-46 | N21NG | LJ35 | 343 | **N22FW** | **FA20** | **485** | (N22YP) | C560 | 0109A |
| N20UG | LJ36 | 031 | N21NL | FA20 | 393 | N22G | LJ55 | 051 | N22YP | FA50 | 53 |
| N20VF | FA20 | 347 | **N21NR** | **C680** | **0237** | N22G | LJ55 | 105 | N23A | FA20 | 368 |
| **N20VL** | **C525** | **0069** | N21NR | GLF3 | 415 | **N22G** | **LJ60** | **022** | N23A | GLF2 | 153 |
| N20VP | C500 | 187 | N21NT | HS25 | 257207 | N22GA | C550 | 031 | N23A | GLF3 | 430 |
| N20WE | C56X | 5115 | **N21NW** | **LJ25** | **351** | **N22GA** | **HS25** | **258327** | **N23A** | **LJ35** | **233** |
| **N20WN** | **FA20** | **370** | N21NY | CL61 | 5126 | N22GE | HS25 | 25139 | N23AC | FA50 | 47 |
| N20WP | C500 | 392 | N21NY | GLF3 | 301 | N22GH | LJ55 | 051 | N23AC | GLF4 | 1047 |
| N20WP | FA10 | 23 | N21NY | GLF3 | 496 | **N22GM** | **LJ40** | **45-2038** | N23AC | WW24 | 210 |
| **N20XP** | **LJ31** | **197** | N21NY | HS25 | 257207 | **N22GR** | **C550** | **550-0892** | N23AC | WW24 | 341 |
| N20XY | GLF2 | 116 | N21PF | SBRL | 282-15 | N22HC | FA20 | 14 | N23AH | GLF2 | 137 |
| N20XY | GLF2 | 56 | N21PJ | GLF3 | 315 | N22HP | C550 | 299 | **N23AJ** | **C550** | **550-1128** |

| | | |
|---|---|---|
| N23AJ | LJ24 | 053 |
| N23AM | LJ24 | 247 |
| N23AM | LJ25 | 223 |
| N23AM | LJ25 | 308 |
| N23AN | LJ24 | 074 |
| N23AQ | FA50 | 47 |
| N23AQ | WW24 | 341 |
| N23AX | LJ31 | 039 |
| N23AZ | GLF2 | 183 |
| N23BH | HS25 | 256010 |
| N23BJ | CL61 | 3012 |
| N23BJ | F900 | 107 |
| N23BJ | HS25 | 257199 |
| N23BN | CL61 | 3012 |
| **N23BV** | **C52B** | **0260** |
| N23BX | SBRL | 465-61 |
| N23BY | LJ24 | 009 |
| N23CH | LJ24 | 006 |
| **N23CJ** | **HS25** | **25152** |
| N23DB | LJ25 | 086 |
| N23DS | FA10 | 117 |
| N23DS | SBRL | 306-89 |
| (N23ED) | FA10 | 11 |
| N23EH | C500 | 576 |
| N23EJ | HS25 | 257199 |
| N23ES | FA10 | 11 |
| N23ES | FA10 | 123 |
| N23ET | FA10 | 11 |
| N23ET | GLF3 | 434 |
| N23FE | FA20 | 224 |
| N23FE | JSTR | 5142 |
| N23FF | WW24 | 83 |
| N23FJ | F2TH | 23 |
| **N23FK** | **EA50** | **000166** |
| **N23FM** | **FA50** | **296** |
| (N23FN) | LJ25 | 018 |
| N23FN | LJ25 | 040 |
| (N23FR) | FA20 | 132 |
| N23G | LJ36 | 026 |
| N23G | LJ55 | 012 |
| N23G | SBRL | 282-31 |
| N23G | SBRL | 370-5 |
| N23HB | LJ35 | 080 |
| N23HB | LJ55 | 046 |
| **N23HD** | **PRM1** | **RB-272** |
| N23HM | LJ25 | 262 |
| N23JC | LJ24 | 290 |
| N23KG | C525 | 0326 |
| N23KL | HS25 | 25080 |
| **N23LM** | **C56X** | **5062** |
| N23M | GLF2 | 105 |
| N23M | GLF4 | 1022 |
| **N23M** | **GLF5** | **579** |
| N23M | JSTR | 5103 |
| N23MJ | LJ24 | 281 |
| N23MU | GLF4 | 1022 |
| N23ND | C500 | 345 |
| N23ND | C550 | 295 |
| N23ND | FA20 | 48 |
| **N23NG** | **C56X** | **5133** |
| N23NM | CS55 | 0121 |
| N23NP | LJ31 | 123 |
| (N23NQ) | FA20 | 48 |
| N23NS | C560 | 0215 |
| **N23PJ** | **EA50** | **000065** |
| N23PL | FA20 | 139 |
| N23PZ | LJ60 | 197 |
| **N23RZ** | **LJ25** | **164** |
| **N23SB** | **CL61** | **5074** |
| N23SB | HS25 | 257016 |
| N23SB | JSTR | 5227 |
| N23SG | LJ24 | 233 |
| (N23SJ) | FA20 | 485 |
| N23SJ | WW24 | 289 |
| (N23SK) | GLF3 | 434 |
| N23SK | HS25 | 257016 |
| (N23SN) | HS25 | 257016 |
| **N23SP** | **PRM1** | **RB-124** |
| N23SQ | LJ24 | 233 |
| **N23SR** | **LJ60** | **229** |
| N23ST | MS76 | 050 |
| N23SY | FA50 | 185 |
| N23SY | GLF4 | 1086 |
| N23TA | LJ25 | 122 |
| N23TC | LJ24 | 074 |
| N23TJ | ASTR | 023 |
| **N23TJ** | **FA10** | **89** |
| N23TJ | LJ24 | 033 |
| (N23TZ) | C500 | 473 |
| N23UB | C560 | 0220 |
| N23UD | C560 | 0220 |
| N23UD | C560 | 0442 |
| N23UP | LJ31 | 237 |
| **N23VA** | **EA50** | **000242** |
| N23VG | LJ31 | 123 |
| N23VG | LJ35 | 379 |
| **N23VK** | **C500** | **555** |
| **N23VP** | **FA10** | **91** |
| N23W | C500 | 182 |
| N23W | C550 | 352 |
| N23W | GLF2 | 116 |
| N23W | LJ25 | 334 |
| **N23WA** | **PRM1** | **RB-18** |
| N23WJ | FA10 | 123 |
| N23WK | C500 | 191 |
| N23Y | WW24 | 155 |
| **N23YC** | **C550** | **550-0923** |
| N23YZ | C500 | 473 |
| **N23YZ** | **C560** | **0638** |
| **N24AJ** | **C500** | **221** |
| N24AJ | C550 | 423 |
| N24AJ | LJ24 | 151 |
| N24AJ | LJ24 | 178 |
| N24BA | BE40 | RJ-19 |
| N24BA | LJ24 | 100 |
| **N24BC** | **C525** | **0651** |
| N24BH | HS25 | 256011 |
| N24BS | LJ25 | 022 |
| (N24CH) | C500 | 655 |
| N24CH | HS25 | 25198 |
| N24CJ | C525 | 0004 |
| N24CJ | C550 | 354 |
| N24CK | LJ24 | 258 |
| N24CK | LJ35 | 339 |
| N24CK | LJ55 | 004 |
| N24DB | WW24 | 294 |
| N24DS | GLF2 | 181 |
| N24DS | WW24 | 258 |
| (N24DZ) | LJ24 | 258 |
| **N24E** | **C550** | **651** |
| (N24EA) | LJ24 | 259 |
| (N24EE) | GLF4 | 1325 |
| N24EP | C550 | 597 |
| **N24EP** | **C56X** | **5213** |
| N24EP | LJ25 | 244 |
| N24ET | LJ24 | 050 |
| **N24ET** | **LJ24** | **148** |
| N24EV | FA20 | 227 |
| N24FE | FA20 | 220 |
| N24FF | LJ24 | 034 |
| N24FJ | WW24 | 312 |
| (N24FN) | LJ25 | 005 |
| N24FN | LJ25 | 045 |
| (N24FR) | FA20 | 151 |
| N24FU | LJ24 | 197 |
| **N24FW** | **LJ24** | **329** |
| N24G | LJ55 | 062 |
| **N24G** | **LJ60** | **018** |
| N24G | SBRL | 306-14 |
| N24G | SBRL | 465-5 |
| N24GA | GLF3 | 374 |
| N24GA | LJ35 | 024 |
| N24GB | SBRL | 306-14 |
| **N24GF** | **C560** | **0639** |
| N24GJ | LJ24 | 101 |
| N24HD | MU30 | A007SA |
| **N24HX** | **C560** | **0165** |
| **N24JD** | **C560** | **0140** |
| N24JG | FA20 | 484 |
| N24JG | HS25 | 258084 |
| **N24JG** | **HS25** | **258170** |
| N24JG | LJ35 | 477 |
| N24JK | CL60 | 1070 |
| N24JK | CL61 | 5118 |
| N24JK | LJ25 | 261 |
| N24JK | LJ35 | 339 |
| N24JK | LJ55 | 004 |
| **N24JZ** | **LJ24** | **213** |
| N24KE | WW24 | 266 |
| N24KF | LJ24 | 161 |
| **N24KL** | **WW24** | **237** |
| N24KT | C650 | 0132 |
| **N24KT** | **C650** | **7052** |
| N24KT | LJ24 | 161 |
| N24KT | WW24 | 266 |
| N24KW | LJ25 | 297 |
| **N24LG** | **LJ24** | **011** |
| N24LT | LJ25 | 063 |
| N24LW | LJ24 | 136 |
| N24MJ | LJ35 | 216 |
| N24MN | WW24 | 414 |
| N24MW | LJ24 | 043 |
| N24NB | C650 | 7052 |
| **N24NG** | **C56X** | **5124** |
| N24NJ | LJ24 | 050 |
| (N24NP) | LJ24 | 200 |
| N24PA | C500 | 236 |
| N24PF | CS55 | 0026 |
| N24PH | C56X | 5049 |
| **N24PH** | **C56X** | **5571** |
| N24PH | CS55 | 0026 |
| N24PJ | LJ24 | 291 |
| (N24PP) | WW24 | 235 |
| **N24PR** | **ASTR** | **026** |
| (N24PT) | C550 | 211 |
| N24PT | LJ36 | 048 |
| N24PY | C56X | 5049 |
| N24QF | C550 | 550-0963 |
| N24QT | C550 | 550-0963 |
| (N24QT) | C560 | 0498 |
| **N24QT** | **C560** | **0762** |
| N24RF | C550 | 456 |
| N24RF | SBRL | 465-28 |
| (N24RH) | LJ55 | 110 |
| N24RH | WW24 | 214 |
| N24RP | HS25 | 258033 |
| N24RZ | LJ25 | 159 |
| N24S | C500 | 230 |
| N24S | HS25 | 25250 |
| **N24S** | **LJ24** | **297** |
| N24SA | LJ24 | 025 |
| **N24SA** | **LJ24** | **117** |
| N24SB | HS25 | 258049 |
| N24SB | WW24 | 369 |
| **N24SM** | **HS25** | **258567** |
| N24SP | HS25 | 258049 |
| N24SR | LJ60 | 234 |
| N24SR | WW24 | 332 |
| N24TA | LJ25 | 155 |
| N24TC | LJ24 | 275 |
| N24TE | LJ24 | 246 |
| (N24TE) | WW24 | 195 |
| N24TH | GLF4 | 1475 |
| **N24TH** | **GLF4** | **4071** |
| (N24TJ) | GLF3 | 404 |
| **N24TK** | **LJ24** | **268** |
| N24TK | LJ24 | 290 |
| "N24TK" | SBRL | 306-128 |
| (N24TR) | C550 | 203 |
| N24TW | FA20 | 80 |
| N24UB | C560 | 0221 |
| N24UD | C560 | 0221 |
| N24UD | C560 | 0443 |
| **N24UD** | **C56X** | **5147** |
| N24UG | JSTR | 5108 |
| N24UM | C650 | 0160 |
| N24VB | C650 | 0121 |
| N24VH | WW24 | 391 |
| N24VM | LJ24 | 051 |
| N24VP | LJ40 | 45-2069 |
| N24VP | LJ40 | 45-2081 |
| N24WF | LJ24 | 143 |
| N24WW | WW24 | 391 |
| N24WX | LJ24 | 101 |
| N24XC | GLF4 | 4032 |
| **N24XP** | **BE40** | **RK-424** |
| N24XR | LJ24 | 150 |
| N24XR | LJ24 | 283 |
| N24YA | LJ24 | 087 |
| **N24YA** | **LJ24** | **206** |
| N24YD | PRM1 | RB-91 |
| N24YE | LJ24 | 087 |
| N24YP | PRM1 | RB-91 |
| **N24YP** | **PRM1** | **RB-95** |
| N24YP | PRM1 | RB-99 |
| N24YR | PRM1 | RB-99 |
| **N24YS** | **GLF2** | **16/13** |
| N24YY | C510 | 0010 |
| **N24ZD** | **ASTR** | **073** |
| N25 | C500 | 084 |
| N25AG | ASTR | 012 |
| N25AG | JSTR | 5202 |
| **N25AM** | **LJ25** | **321** |
| N25AN | LJ35 | 259 |
| N25AT | SBRL | 380-21 |
| N25AW | HS25 | 25095 |
| **N25BB** | **HS25** | **258189** |
| N25BE | HS25 | 256013 |
| N25BF | GLF2 | 114 |
| N25BH | GLF2 | 237/43 |
| N25BH | HS25 | 256013 |
| N25BH | SBRL | 380-47 |
| N25BN | BE40 | RJ-7 |
| N25BR | BE40 | RJ-57 |
| N25BX | SBRL | 380-47 |
| N25CJ | C500 | 325 |
| N25CJ | C500 | 625 |
| N25CJ | C525 | 0002 |
| N25CK | C500 | 250 |
| N25CL | LJ36 | 009 |
| N25CP | FA20 | 121 |
| N25CS | C500 | 219 |
| **N25CU** | **BE40** | **RK-361** |
| N25CV | C560 | 0298 |
| N25CV | LJ24 | 276 |
| **N25CY** | **LJ25** | **272** |
| N25CY | LJ25 | 302 |
| N25CY | LJ25 | 317 |
| N25CZ | LJ25 | 301 |
| N25DB | FA20 | 91 |
| N25DD | C500 | 475 |
| **N25DY** | **CS55** | **0076** |
| (N25EA) | C525 | 0028 |
| **N25EC** | **LJ25** | **026** |
| N25EL | LJ35 | 419 |
| N25EV | FA20 | 229 |
| N25FA | LJ25 | 251 |
| N25FE | FA20 | 221 |
| N25FF | FA10 | 123 |
| **N25FJ** | **F2TH** | **25** |
| **N25FM** | **LJ25** | **063** |
| N25FN | LJ25 | 015 |
| N25FN | LJ25 | 352 |
| (N25FR) | FA20 | 20 |
| **N25FS** | **C550** | **550-0823** |
| N25FS | LJ35 | 198 |
| (N25GG) | CL61 | 5050 |
| N25GG | CL64 | 5536 |
| N25GJ | GLF2 | 97 |
| N25GJ | LJ25 | 015 |
| N25GJ | LJ25 | 255 |
| N25GL | LJ25 | 362 |
| N25GT | C500 | 572 |
| (N25GV) | GLF5 | 5072 |
| N25GV | GLF5 | 674 |
| N25GW | LJ24 | 258 |
| N25GW | LJ28 | 28-003 |
| **N25GZ** | **CS55** | **0011** |
| N25HA | LJ25 | 141 |
| N25HC | C500 | 034 |
| N25HF | LJ25 | 295 |
| **N25HF** | **LJ25** | **367** |
| N25HS | C500 | 592 |
| N25HV | C550 | 550-0825 |
| N25JD | LJ25 | 114 |
| N25JM | FA50 | 124 |
| N25JM | GLF2 | 69 |
| N25JT | HS25 | 25053 |
| (N25JX) | LJ25 | 006 |
| N25KC | LJ25 | 147 |
| N25KL | SBRL | 465-69 |
| N25KV | LJ25 | 176 |
| N25LA | HS25 | 25108 |
| (N25LG) | LJ25 | 042 |
| N25LJ | LJ24 | 123 |
| N25LJ | LJ24 | 236 |
| (N25LP) | LJ25 | 150 |
| **N25LZ** | **C52A** | **0177** |
| **N25MB** | **C500** | **453** |
| N25MB | F900 | 163 |
| N25MB | FA50 | 184 |
| N25MC | FA10 | 180 |
| **N25MC** | **PRM1** | **RB-49** |
| **N25MD** | **LJ25** | **054** |
| N25ME | FA50 | 184 |
| N25ME | LJ25 | 062 |
| N25MF | SBRL | 465-25 |
| N25MH | C500 | 404 |
| N25MJ | HS25 | 25142 |
| N25MJ | LJ35 | 335 |
| N25MJ | LJ35 | 452 |
| N25MK | C550 | 458 |

N25MK HS25 257056
N25MR LJ25 129
N25MT GLF3 359
**N25MT LJ25 129**
N25MX C525 0220
N25NB LJ25 107
**N25NB LJ25 326**
N25NG C56X 5250
N25NH C550 115
N25NM LJ25 007
N25NM LJ25 347
N25NP LJ25 107
**N25NY LJ25 304**
N25PA C500 250
**N25PJ LJ25 111**
N25PK LJ36 039
N25PL LJ25 130
N25PM HS25 25114
N25PT LJ25 356
**N25PW LJ25 342**
N25QF C550 584
N25QS HA4T RC-28
N25QT C550 584
**N25QT C560 0613**
(N25RE) LJ25 041
N25RE LJ25 163
**N25RE LJ25 227**
N25RE WW24 248
N25RF LJ35 227
N25RJ LJ24 237
N25S FA20 453
**N25SB CL61 5115**
N25SB GLF3 431
**N25SJ FA50 186**
N25SR CL60 1075
N25SR SBRL 465-14
**N25ST FA10 198**
N25TA LJ24 237
N25TA LJ25 196
N25TA LJ25 241
N25TB LJ25 241
N25TE LJ25 087
"N25TF" LJ25 036
N25TK LJ25 100
N25TX FA20 24
(N25TX) JSTR 5029/38
N25TZ LJ25 364
N25UB FA50 248
N25UD F9EX 29
N25UD FA50 248
N25UG GLF2 205
N25UG SBRL 465-11
**N25UJ LJ25 215**
N25UT C500 049
**N25V CL60 1015**
**N25VC SBRL 465-15**
(N25VJ) LJ25 039
N25VZ LJ24 258
N25W BE40 RJ-15
N25W HS25 258221
**N25W HS25 258626**
N25WA BE40 RJ-15
N25WA JSTR 5033/56
N25WG FA20 327
**N25WJ LJ25 105**
(N25WL) LJ25 220
N25WN HS25 258221
N25WX HS25 258359
N25WZ JSTR 5204
N25XL C56X 5536
**N25XP BE40 RK-247**
N25XP HS25 258403
(N25XR) LJ25 235
N25ZC SBRL 465-30
**N25ZG CL64 5536**
(N25ZG) SBRL 465-30
N25ZW LJ24 236
N26 C560 0113
(N26AA) C500 678
**N26AT LJ25 130**
N26BA LJ24 134
N26BH HS25 256014
N26CB C525 0117
N26CB C550 550-0861
**N26CB C550 550-1001**
N26CP FA10 151
N26CT C550 345
**N26CV C550 550-0861**

(N26DA) C550 087
N26DA LJ35 086
N26DK C525 0257
**N26DK PRM1 RB-226**
N26DS WW24 189
N26DV C525 0414
N26DY C560 0110
N26EN FA10 49
N26ES FA10 171
N26EV FA20 230
N26FA CL30 20026
(N26FA) MU30 A026SA
N26FE FA20 204
N26FN LJ25 134
**N26FN LJ36 011**
N26GB LJ35 131
N26GD LJ35 131
N26GL JSTR 5114/18
N26GL LJ36 001
**N26GP LJ35 157**
(N26GV) GLF5 674
N26GW WW24 272
N26H HS25 257143
(N26HA) C500 627
N26HC C500 174
**N26HG C550 614**
**N26HH C550 346**
N26JJ CS55 0141
N26JP BE40 RK-74
N26KL WW24 409
N26L GLF2 165/37
N26L GLF2 193
N26L GLF2 36/3
N26L GLF3 387
N26LA FA20 274
N26LA GLF2 36/3
N26LB F900 10
N26LB F900 51
N26LB FA50 7
N26LB GLF2 168
N26LB GLF4 1008
N26LC C500 654
N26LC LJ31 006
N26LT GLF2 193
**N26ME HS25 257165**
**N26MJ C750 0139**
N26MJ JSTR 5101/15
N26MJ LJ24 202
N26MJ LJ36 011
(N26MW) C500 485
N26NS C500 340
**N26PA BE40 RK-256**
N26PA C500 254
**N26QB C525 0117**
**N26QL C560 0498**
N26QT C560 0498
**N26QT LJ45 402**
(N26RG) C650 0054
**N26RL C525 0207**
N26S JSTR 5128/16
N26SC C550 345
**N26SC HS25 257117**
N26SC SBRL 282-104
N26SC SBRL 306-140
N26SD C650 0099
N26SE SBRL 282-104
**N26SH E50P 50000009**
N26SL GLF4 1053
N26SQ SBRL 306-140
N26SW C525 0415
**N26T C550 550-1075**
N26T HS25 25037
N26T WW24 293
N26T WW24 418
N26TJ FA10 103
(N26TJ) SBRL 370-7
N26TJ WW24 204
N26TL HS25 25037
**N26TN WW24 418**
N26TR JSTR 5115/39
N26TV WW24 293
**N26TZ WW24 293**
N26VB WW24 410
N26VF WW24 410
N26VG FA20 108/430
N26VM LJ24 236
N26WB GLF2 136
N26WD C500 282

N26WJ FA10 126
**N26WJ FA50 181**
(N26WJ) HS25 25037
N26WK CL64 5549
**N26WP FA50 312**
N26WP GLF2 24
**N26XP BE40 RK-280**
N26XP BE40 RK-426
N26ZZ GLEX 9289
N27 C560 0109
(N27) LJ31 063
N27AC FA10 151
N27AC FA20 355
**N27AJ FA10 31**
N27AL LJ31 175
N27AT WW24 176
N27AX LJ24 323
**N27AX LJ35 662**
N27B CS55 0036
N27BA C550 168
N27BD WW24 53
N27BH ASTR 012
N27BH CL60 1051
N27BH HS25 256016
**N27BH HS25 257206**
**N27BJ LJ24 227**
**N27BL LJ35 163**
N27C FA10 31
N27C SBRL 282-57
**N27CD GLF4 1136**
N27CJ C525 0301
**N27CJ C525 0311**
N27CJ C52A 0124
N27DA FA10 17
N27DA SBRL 282-28
N27DD LJ55 015
N27EA CS55 0027
N27EV FA20 232
**N27EW C52B 0308**
(N27FB) C525 0242
N27FE FA20 207
**N27FL HS25 258426**
N27FN LJ25 062
N27FP CS55 0027
N27FW JSTR 5083/49
N27GD CS55 0052
(N27GW) LJ25 234
N27HF LJ35 251
**N27JJ BE40 RK-59**
N27K LJ25 294
N27KG LJ25 335
N27KG LJ25 357
N27KG LJ35 413
N27KG SBRL 282-77
N27KL HS25 257125
**N27L C500 038**
N27LT SBRL 380-59
N27MD WW24 102
N27MH C550 168
N27MH CS55 0006
N27MJ LJ24 249
N27MJ LJ25 050
N27MJ LJ36 027
N27MX CL30 20014
N27NB LJ35 251
N27NR LJ35 481
N27PA C500 249
**N27R F2TH 5**
N27R FA20 303
N27R FA20 356
N27R GLF3 452
N27R JSTR 5086/44
N27RC HS25 25038
N27RC JSTR 5086/44
N27RL JSTR 5086/44
N27RX FA20 356
N27SD C560 0147
N27SD C650 0134
N27SD CS55 0052
**N27SF C500 064**
(N27SJ) WW24 270
**N27SL GLF2 84**
(N27TA) WW24 231
(N27TB) CS55 0079
**N27TB CS55 0082**
N27TJ LJ35 277
N27TJ MU30 A027SA
N27TS C500 541

N27TS C650 0006
N27TS SBRL 380-48
**N27TT LJ35 122**
**N27TZ WW24 213**
N27U C550 344
**N27UB C52B 0225**
**N27UM HS25 25249**
**N27VP C750 0027**
N27VQ C52A 0221
**N27WP E50P 50000058**
N27WP F2TH 35
**N27WW C500 359**
N27WW C560 0074
**N27X CL64 5319**
N27X WW24 127
N27XL C56X 5010
**N27XP BE40 RK-266**
**N27YA GLF4 4153**
**N27ZH LJ60 187**
N28AA LJ25 037
**N28AR C500 044**
N28AT LJ24 227
N28AY LJ28 28-004
N28BG LJ35 258
N28BH HS25 256018
N28BK LJ24 175
N28BP LJ24 065A
N28BP LJ25 086
(N28BP) LJ25 237
N28BP LJ25 302
(N28BR) LJ24 065A
N28C FA20 404
(N28CC) LJ25 234
**N28CK C525 0210**
N28CK LJ25 045
N28CR LJ35 252
N28DL LJ24 184
N28DM C525 0151
N28DM C52A 0210
**N28DM C52B 0142**
(N28ET) C560 0320
(N28EX) F2EX 28
N28FE FA20 209
(N28FM) C525 0633
**N28FM MU30 A026SA**
N28FN LJ25 005
N28FR C52B 0153
N28GA C525 0215
**N28GA C52B 0293**
N28GA C550 283
N28GC C500 449
N28GE HS25 25267
N28GG HS25 257135
N28GP HS25 25267
N28GP HS25 257135
**N28GP HS25 258489**
(N28GZ) C550 200
N28HH SBRL 306-125
N28JG C500 591
**N28KA CL61 5174**
N28KB FA50 148
N28KV LJ25 176
N28LA LJ25 029
N28LR LJ28 28-003
N28M HS25 25038
N28MH C52A 0161
**N28MH C52B 0110**
N28MJ LJ25 286
**N28MJ LJ35 224**
(N28MM) C550 187
(N28MM) HS25 25038
N28NF ASTR 067
N28NH C52A 0161
N28NP ASTR 067
**N28NP ASTR 118**
(N28NR) ASTR 067
N28PA C500 267
**N28PT C525 0017**
**N28QA C525 0215**
N28QQ GLF3 379
**N28R F2TH 7**
N28R GLF3 490
N28RC C550 302
N28RC C550 650
N28RF C550 271
N28RK FA20 206
(N28RW) LJ25 285
N28S C550 225

N28S C650 0143
N28ST LJ24 013
N28SW C525 0424
N28TJ WW24 237
N28TP SBRL 282-132
**N28TS HS25 256009**
**N28TX C650 7007**
(N28U) C500 054
N28U FA20 484
N28UA CL61 5042
**N28VL F9EX 213**
N28VM SBRL 306-123
**N28WE C680 0238**
**N28WL C500 077**
N28WW WW24 368
N28XP BE40 RK-428
N28YC GLF3 455
**N28ZF HS25 258195**
(N29AA) FA10 31
N29AC C500 635
N29AP WW24 258
N29AU C650 0145
N29AU CS55 0019
N29B C550 152
**N29B HS25 258518**
N29BF LJ24 010
N29BH HS25 256020
N29CA C500 492
N29CA LJ24 215
N29CL WW24 197
**N29CL WW24 404**
N29CR HS25 25098
N29DJ LJ55 029
N29EA CS55 0006
N29EB C500 276
**N29ET C525 0601**
N29EW LJ25 373
N29FA C550 379
N29FE FA20 210
N29FN LJ25 018
N29G C550 379
N29GD HS25 257069
N29GH WW24 197
N29GP HS25 257069
**N29GP HS25 258344**
N29GY GLF4 1016
N29HE C500 604
**N29KD LJ31 139**
N29LA LJ24 108
N29LB WW24 61
**N29LJ LJ60 240**
N29LP WW24 280
N29LP WW24 61
N29MR C52A 0206
**N29MR EA50 000249**
(N29MW) C500 166
**N29NW LJ55 029**
N29PB SBRL 306-18
N29PC WW24 263
N29PF C550 696
**N29QC C560 0675**
N29RE LJ31 106
N29RE LJ31 145
(N29RE) LJ31 156
**N29RE LJ40 45-2069**
N29RE LJ45 210
N29RN LJ40 45-2069
N29RP HS25 257088
N29S GLF3 391
N29S SBRL 306-49
N29S SBRL 465-65
N29SM LJ31 194
N29SM LJ45 214
**N29SN LJ31 194**
(N29SS) EA50 000264
N29SX SBRL 306-49
N29SZ SBRL 465-65
N29TC C550 143
(N29TC) JSTR 5208
N29TE FA20 202
(N29TG) C550 143
N29TS LJ25 198
(N29UC) ASTR 041
N29UF C500 640
(N29UF) WW24 201
N29WE C560 0185
N29WE C560 0512
**N29WE C680 0042**
N29WF C560 0185
N29WP JSTR 5157
N29WS C550 262
N29X CS55 0096
N29XA CS55 0096
N29XP BE40 RK-429
N29YY FA50 95
N29ZE LJ45 210
N30AB WW24 235
**N30AD C52A 0165**
(N30AD) FA20 225/472
N30AD LJ25 314
N30AD WW24 143
(N30AF) C500 559
**N30AF C650 0049**
N30AF LJ55 043
N30AF SBRL 282-113
N30AH GLF3 392
N30AJ ASTR 019
N30AJ ASTR 047
N30AN WW24 173
N30AP LJ25 080
N30AP LJ25 101
**N30AV C550 026**
N30AV HFB3 1055
(N30B) GLF2 228
N30BE SBRL 282-14
N30BK C500 666
N30BP LJ24 017
N30CC FA20 11
N30CC SBRL 306-81
N30CJ C650 0019
(N30CJ) C650 0029
N30CN FA10 161
N30CQ FA20 11
N30CX CS55 0007
N30CZ C550 376
N30DH LJ24 224
N30DH LJ35 199
N30DK LJ25 154
N30DK LJ35 345
N30EF HS25 25084
N30EH LJ24 211
N30EJ C550 113
N30EM LJ24 338
(N30EV) SBRL 370-6
(N30F) C550 220
N30F HS25 25153
N30F HS25 258035
N30FD HS25 25153
N30FE FA20 211
N30FE FA50 271
N30FJ C550 113
N30FJ FA10 30
(N30FL) LJ24 253
N30FN LJ35 075
N30FT FA20 377/548
N30FT FA50 271
N30FW GLF2 210
N30GB SBRL 380-1
N30GD LJ35 352
**N30GF WW24 401**
N30GJ LJ35 320
**N30GJ LJ60 204**
N30GL LJ35 395
N30GL LJ55 076
**N30GR C550 656**
**N30GZ SJ30 010**
**N30HD C52A 0062**
N30HD MU30 A005SA
N30HJ LJ35 226
N30JC FA50 349
**N30JD C550 218**
(N30JH) FA10 19
N30JM FA10 19
N30JM FA20 24
N30JM WW24 173
N30JN C500 272
**N30LB F9EX 8**
**N30LF F2DX 602**
N30LJ LJ25 043
**N30LJ LJ25 209**
N30LJ LJ31 024
N30LJ LJ31 027
N30LM LJ24 338
N30LM LJ25 250
N30LS WW24 125
**N30LX GLF3 438**
N30LX LJ31 096
**N30MR WW24 225**
(N30N) FA50 55
**N30NF C510 0254**
N30NM C650 0120
N30NS WW24 329
N30P LJ25 082
**N30PA LJ35 245**
N30PC C560 0090
N30PC LJ45 231
**N30PC LJ45 235**
N30PD WW24 347
N30PF LJ45 231
(N30PN) SBRL 282-14
N30PP HS25 25207
N30PQ C560 0090
**N30PR GLF2 35**
N30PR HS25 25207
N30PR HS25 257065
N30PS LJ25 030
N30PY SBRL 306-7
N30RE C500 491
N30RJ WW24 7
N30RL C500 491
**N30RL C550 653**
N30RP GLF2 113
N30RP GLF3 321
N30RP JSTR 5131
N30SA C550 341
N30SA LJ35 479
N30SB C500 272
N30SC LJ24 039
(N30SF) BE40 RK-79
N30SF LJ45 175
N30SJ SJ30 001
N30SJ SJ30 003
**N30SJ SJ30 006**
N30TB FA10 171
N30TC SBRL 306-33
N30TH F2TH 66
N30TH FA10 138
N30TH FA10 201
N30TH FA10 74
N30TH FA50 212
N30TK LJ31 096
(N30TK) LJ35 030
N30TK LJ55 091
**N30TK WW24 374**
**N30TL LJ45 081**
(N30TN) FA10 193
N30TP LJ25 111
N30TT LJ25 020
N30TV C560 0358
N30UC C550 103
N30UD C52B 0131
**N30VP HS25 HA-0093**
N30W LJ25 214
N30W LJ35 488
N30W LJ60 065
N30W SBRL 282-5
N30W SBRL 306-10
N30WE C550 604
**N30WR GLF3 380**
N30WY LJ35 488
**N30XC CL30 20228**
**N30XL BE40 RK-5**
N30XP BE40 RK-430
N30XX C550 195
N30Y JSTR 5227
N30YM WW24 213
N31AA LJ25 041
N31AJ C500 393
N31AS HS25 25111
N31AS HS25 257135
(N31AX) LJ31 063
N31AX LJ31 094
(N31AZ) LJ31 103
N31B HS25 25108
N31BC SBRL 282-14
N31BC SBRL 306-60
N31BC SBRL 465-16
(N31BC) SBRL 465-69
N31BG LJ24 301
N31BM SBRL 306-71
N31BP JSTR 5125/31
N31BQ SBRL 282-14
**N31CA CL30 20021**
(N31CF) C500 641
N31CF WW24 8
N31CG LJ31 003
N31CJ C525 0031
N31CJ C525 0360
**N31CJ C525 0474**
N31CJ SBRL 306-26
N31CK LJ24 079
N31CM FA20 317
N31CR SBRL 306-146
N31CS LJ25 083
N31CV LJ31 168
**N31D F900 191**
N31DA C550 295
(N31DC) CL60 1032
N31DK JSTR 5138
N31DM FA50 59
N31DP LJ24 059
**N31DP LJ35 062**
N31EP HS25 25176
N31EX F2EX 31
(N31F) C550 176
N31F C550 440
N31F HS25 258036
N31F JSTR 5060
N31FB LJ35 138
N31FE FA20 212
**N31FF LJ31 053**
N31FJ FA20 310
N31FN LJ35 033
N31FT C550 440
**N31GA C550 253**
**N31GQ LJ31 147**
N31GS LJ25 313
N31GT HS25 25204
N31HA LJ31 031
**N31HD C525 0261**
**N31HK LJ35 016**
N31HY LJ31 107
N31JB C525 0352
**N31JB C550 550-1041**
N31JM C500 411
**N31KH LJ31 173**
N31KJ LJ31 212
N31KW C550 083
N31LB LJ24 211
N31LG HS25 257068
N31LH C500 287
N31LJ JSTR 5087/55
N31LJ LJ31 010
N31LJ LJ31 020
N31LJ LJ31 036
(N31LJ) LJ31 059
N31LJ LJ31 072
N31LJ LJ31 078
N31LJ LJ31 081
N31LJ LJ31 088
**N31LJ LJ31 097**
N31LJ LJ31 113
N31LK LJ31 100
(N31LM) LJ35 412
N31LR LJ31 100
N31LR LJ31 131
N31LR LJ31 160
N31LR LJ31 185
N31LT FA20 69
**N31LW C500 083**
N31MC LJ35 270
N31MJ LJ25 231
N31MJ LJ25 313
**N31MJ LJ31 185**
N31MT C500 473
N31MW C500 045
**N31MW LJ31 171**
N31NF LJ31 151
N31NR LJ31 115
N31NR LJ31 150
N31NR LJ31 170
N31NR LJ31 200
N31NR LJ31 235
**N31NS C560 0286**
**N31PV LJ31 130**
N31RC C500 465
N31RC C550 175
N31RC C560 0023
N31RK C550 314
N31RP JSTR 5131
N31S JSTR 5051
N31S LJ24 072

N31S WW24 10
N31SB WW24 10
N31SG C525 0207
N31SJ FA10 72
N31SJ GALX 033
N31SJ SBRL 465-26
N31SK LJ24 118
N31ST C500 029
N31SY GLF2 169
N31TC LJ24 193
N31TD LJ31 165
N31TF LJ31 037
N31TJ C650 0057
N31TJ HS25 25202
**N31TK LJ31 059**
(N31TK) LJ31 096
N31TM FA10 160
**N31UJ LJ31 116**
N31UK LJ31 047
N31UT JSTR 5143
N31V FA20 106
N31V FA50 59
**N31V LJ45 015**
N31VT HS25 25195
N31WE LJ35 389
N31WG JSTR 5087/55
N31WH CL61 5014
**N31WR LJ35 313**
**N31WS LJ35 027**
N31WT CL60 1073
N31WT FA20 446
N31WT LJ24 283
N31WT LJ24 351
N31WT LJ25 265
N31WT LJ25 288
(N31WT) LJ28 28-005
N31WT LJ35 229
N31WT LJ35 389
N31WT LJ35 479
N31WU LJ31 175
N32AA BE40 RK-242
N32AA LJ24 237
**N32AA LJ45 399**
N32AJ BE40 RK-242
N32AJ LJ36 048
N32B F900 59
N32B LJ35 593
N32BA LJ35 190
N32BC CL60 1053
(N32BC) HS25 258299
**N32BC HS25 258321**
N32BC SBRL 282-15
N32BC SBRL 306-62
**N32BD GLF5 548**
N32BG C525 0532
N32BL FA10 6
N32BQ CL60 1053
N32BQ SBRL 282-15
N32BR PRM1 RB-77
N32CA LJ24 132
N32DA C500 494
N32DD C500 043
**N32DD LJ24 331**
N32F C550 442
N32F HS25 25155
N32FE FA20 213
(N32FF) CL64 5469
N32FJ C550 550-0988
**N32FJ C650 7032**
N32FM C500 616
**N32FM C510 0212**
N32FN LJ35 067
N32FN LJ35 189
N32GG CL61 5033
**N32GM HS25 25198**
N32HC GLF2 113
(N32HE) HS25 25033
**N32HH LJ31 201**
N32HJ LJ35 463
N32HM LJ35 187
**N32HP MU30 A074SA**
(N32JA) LJ35 172
(N32JA) LJ36 017
N32JC WW24 32
N32JJ C500 380
N32JJ C550 223
N32JJ C650 0170
N32JJ CS55 0014
(N32JN) GALX 023
N32KA GLF3 435
**N32KB HS25 25280**
**N32KC E50P 50000063**
**N32KJ LJ55 093**
**N32KM C56X 5715**
N32KR JSTR 5220
N32MG C650 0016
N32MJ C500 434
**N32MJ GLF3 460**
N32MJ LJ24 208
**N32NG C750 0039**
**N32PA LJ36 025**
N32PB C550 115
N32PB C560 0091
N32PB FA20 122
N32PC LJ25 018
N32PC SBRL 306-125
**N32PE LJ35 327**
N32PF LJ35 327
N32PJ LJ35 320
N32RP HS25 256066
N32RZ LJ35 238
N32SD LJ24 017
**N32SG PRM1 RB-90**
**N32SM C550 478**
N32SM LJ25 070
N32SX C500 477
N32TC FA20 440
N32TC FA50 225
N32TC LJ35 189
N32TE FA20 440
(N32TJ) C550 268
N32TJ CS55 0014
(N32TJ) LJ25 224
**N32TK C550 336**
N32TM ASTR 072
N32TM C550 336
**N32TM GALX 023**
**N32TX CS55 0026**
(N32UC) ASTR 136
N32UT SBRL 306-9
N32VC FA10 6
N32VP C525 0032
N32W C500 105
N32WE WW24 164
N32WL LJ24 265
(N32WR) CL61 3013
N32WT LJ24 333
N33AA C500 388
N33AH FA20 379
(N33AJ) FA20 379
N33BC C550 329
N33BC C650 0047
**N33BC HS25 258292**
N33BC SBRL 306-13
N33BC SBRL 465-69
N33BE C500 476
N33BK HS25 25064
N33BK HS25 257049
N33BK LJ24 096
N33BQ C650 0047
N33BQ SBRL 306-13
**N33BV FA10 33**
N33CJ C525 0245
N33CJ LJ24 130
N33CJ LJ25 045
N33CP HS25 25286
N33CP HS25 257053
N33CR GLF2 69
N33CX C500 456
N33D C650 7117
**N33D F2TH 224**
N33D FA20 166
N33DC LJ60 233
N33DS CS55 0093
**N33DT C525 0080**
N33DY FA20 166
N33EA JSTR 5033/56
**N33EK C550 314**
**N33EM PRM1 RB-268**
(N33EN) GLF2 49
N33EQ FA50 326
N33FE FA20 214
N33FJ F2TH 224
**N33FW C525 0203**
(N33FW) C550 062
N33GF LJ25 035
N33GG F900 87
N33GG FA50 97
N33GK C550 270
N33GK C650 7050
N33GL LJ55 082
N33GL WW24 47
N33GQ FA50 97
N33GZ GLF3 393
(N33GZ) GLF3 465
N33HB LJ35 182
N33HC C500 492
N33HL FA10 17
N33HM LJ25 093
**N33JW SBRL 306-92**
N33KA SBRL 380-55
(N33KW) C500 437
**N33L C650 7118**
N33L FA20 202
N33LB SBRL 282-130
**N33LC F9EX 206**
N33LC FA50 326
N33LV FA20 202
N33LX C560 0433
**N33LX C56X 6010**
N33M GLF2 106
N33M GLF4 1056
**N33M GLF5 594**
N33ME C500 312
N33ME GLF2 43
N33MK WW24 374
(N33MM) MU30 A017SA
N33MQ C500 312
N33MX GLF4 1056
N33NH C500 206
N33NJ LJ24 147
**N33NJ LJ35 305**
N33NL BE40 RK-330
**N33NL HS25 258643**
N33NM LJ25 093
**N33NP C510 0037**
N33NT GLF3 465
N33NT SBRL 380-41
N33PA CL64 5441
N33PF LJ25 028
N33PJ GLF2 57
**N33PJ PRM1 RB-179**
N33PS WW24 92
N33PT LJ25 046
**N33PT LJ25 240**
N33PT LJ35 397
N33QS FA20 122
N33RE LJ24 193
N33RH C550 087
N33RH HS25 257011
**N33RL C650 7106**
N33RP HS25 256068
**N33RZ SBRL 380-47**
N33SC FA20 71
**N33SJ JSTR 5087/55**
N33ST LJ24 173
**N33SW C525 0387**
N33TH C500 024
N33TP FA20 27
N33TP LJ24 321
N33TR LJ25 035
N33TR SBRL 306-54
**N33TR SBRL 465-47**
**N33TS C560 0549**
N33TS LJ35 021
N33TW LJ25 124
N33TW SBRL 282-61
**N33TW WW24 316**
N33TY FA50 240
N33TY FA50 288
N33UL C650 0160
**N33UM C52B 0020**
N33UT SBRL 276-34
N33UT SBRL 306-16
**N33VC HS25 258310**
(N33VF) LJ25 143
(N33VG) LJ35 408
(N33VV) C500 482
N33WB LJ35 376
N33WD WW24 161
**N33WW C500 440**
**N33XE GLF5 506**
N34AA C500 475
"N34AG" LJ40 45-2064
N34AM SBRL 282-31
N34BH HS25 256022
N34C FA20 31
N34CD CL61 3030
N34CD CL61 5139
(N34CE) ASTR 043
N34CH HS25 257021
N34CJ CS55 0034
N34CW FA20 305
N34CW LJ25 277
N34DL C500 436
N34DL C550 204
**N34DZ C525 0640**
N34FD LJ35 431
N34FE FA20 215
N34FN LJ35 254
**N34FS WW24 417**
N34GB LJ55 114
**N34GG HS25 257034**
**N34GN PRM1 RB-58**
N34GX GALX 034
N34HD WW24 127
N34LP SBRL 282-70
(N34LZ) LJ35 346
N34MJ LJ25 333
N34MZ GLF2 77
N34NG SBRL 380-52
N34NS CS55 0024
N34NW WW24 117
N34QS C650 0034
N34RE HS25 257022
N34RL C52A 0071
N34RP GLF2 113
"N34S" FA50 25
N34S GLF2 5
N34SS C550 225
(N34SS) C550 258
N34SW WW24 97
N34TB LJ35 285
**N34TC C525 0083**
N34TC LJ35 199
N34TH FA10 74
**N34TJ FA10 41**
N34TJ LJ35 225
**N34TN LJ25 249**
N34TR JSTR 5236
(N34TR) LJ24 069
N34TY FA50 240
**N34U GLEX 9070**
N34UH GLF4 1470
N34UT C500 043
N34VP BE40 RK-39
**N34VP C750 0034**
N34W SBRL 282-47
N34WP C550 123
**N34WP C56X 5232**
**N34WR JSTR 5207**
N34XP BE40 RK-434
N34YL C550 267
N35AA C500 497
N35AH LJ35 316
**N35AJ LJ35 010**
N35AJ LJ35 346
N35AJ LJ35 626
N35AK LJ35 314
N35AL LJ35 509
N35AQ LJ35 513
N35AS LJ35 405
N35AS LJ35 605
N35AW LJ35 233
N35AX LJ35 280
N35AZ LJ35 201
N35BG LJ35 311
**N35BG LJ35 402**
N35BH HS25 256023
N35BK LJ35 442
N35BN LJ35 013
N35BP C550 282
**N35BP GALX 016**
N35BP GALX 163
**N35CC HS25 258294**
N35CC SBRL 282-79
N35CC SBRL 465-59
**N35CD GLF5 603**
N35CK LJ35 480
N35CL LJ35 113
**N35CQ SBRL 465-59**
**N35CR WW24 176**

| | | |
|---|---|---|
| **N35CT** | **C52A** | **0120** |
| N35CX | LJ35 | 180 |
| **N35CY** | **LJ35** | **473** |
| N35CZ | LJ35 | 352 |
| N35D | HS25 | 257044 |
| **N35D** | **WW24** | **156** |
| N35DL | HS25 | 256051 |
| N35DL | LJ25 | 317 |
| N35DL | LJ35 | 348 |
| N35DL | SBRL | 306-131 |
| N35EC | LJ24 | 123 |
| **N35ED** | **LJ35** | **215** |
| **N35ET** | **C550** | **550-0879** |
| N35FC | C650 | 0179 |
| N35FE | FA20 | 217 |
| N35FE | LJ35 | 409 |
| N35FH | LJ35 | 273 |
| (N35FH) | LJ35 | 480 |
| N35FM | LJ35 | 368 |
| N35FN | LJ35 | 261 |
| N35FP | CL61 | 3048 |
| N35FS | LJ35 | 320 |
| N35FS | LJ35 | 405 |
| (N35FT) | LJ35 | 439 |
| N35GA | LJ35 | 590 |
| **N35GC** | **LJ35** | **266** |
| N35GE | LJ35 | 088 |
| N35GG | LJ35 | 178 |
| N35GJ | LJ35 | 507 |
| N35GQ | LJ35 | 037 |
| N35GX | ASTR | 113 |
| N35GX | LJ35 | 264 |
| **N35GZ** | **GLF3** | **465** |
| N35HB | LJ35 | 045 |
| N35HC | C550 | 202 |
| (N35HM) | LJ35 | 210 |
| N35HP | LJ35 | 507 |
| **N35HS** | **C650** | **7072** |
| N35HW | LJ35 | 501 |
| N35JF | C500 | 404 |
| N35JF | LJ24 | 110 |
| N35JJ | JSTR | 5100/41 |
| N35JM | GLF2 | 47 |
| N35JN | LJ35 | 013 |
| **N35JN** | **LJ35** | **469** |
| (N35K) | C500 | 404 |
| N35KC | LJ35 | 144 |
| N35KC | LJ35 | 189 |
| N35KT | LJ35 | 590 |
| N35LD | C500 | 494 |
| N35LH | WW24 | 236 |
| **N35LH** | **WW24** | **413** |
| N35LJ | LJ35 | 181 |
| N35LJ | LJ35 | 676 |
| N35LM | HS25 | 257023 |
| N35LT | C500 | 132 |
| N35LW | LJ35 | 439 |
| N35MH | LJ35 | 258 |
| N35MR | LJ35 | 057 |
| N35MV | LJ35 | 416 |
| N35NA | LJ35 | 381 |
| N35NB | LJ35 | 133 |
| **N35NK** | **LJ35** | **491** |
| (N35NK) | LJ35 | 643 |
| N35NP | LJ35 | 191 |
| N35NP | LJ35 | 492 |
| N35NW | LJ35 | 069 |
| N35NX | LJ35 | 328 |
| N35NY | LJ35 | 328 |
| (N35P) | MU30 | A051SA |
| N35PD | LJ35 | 181 |
| N35PD | LJ35 | 606 |
| (N35PF) | LJ35 | 094 |
| N35PF | LJ55 | 020 |
| (N35PN) | C550 | 486 |
| N35PN | C650 | 0138 |
| N35PR | LJ35 | 181 |
| N35PT | LJ35 | 420 |
| N35Q | LJ35 | 406 |
| N35QB | LJ35 | 649 |
| N35RF | LJ35 | 201 |
| N35RN | LJ35 | 113 |
| N35RT | LJ35 | 201 |
| **N35RT** | **LJ35** | **320** |
| N35RT | LJ35 | 420 |
| **N35RZ** | **F900** | **137** |
| N35RZ | FA20 | 359/542 |
| N35RZ | FA50 | 113 |
| **N35SA** | **LJ35** | **326** |
| N35SC | LJ35 | 002 |
| N35SE | C500 | 035 |
| **N35SE** | **C56X** | **5656** |
| N35SE | LJ35 | 191 |
| N35SJ | LJ24 | 246 |
| N35SJ | LJ35 | 261 |
| N35SL | LJ35 | 233 |
| N35SM | LJ35 | 419 |
| N35TF | C560 | 0500 |
| N35TH | LJ35 | 473 |
| **N35TJ** | **LJ35** | **137** |
| **N35TK** | **C525** | **0610** |
| N35TK | LJ35 | 188 |
| N35TL | C500 | 637 |
| N35TL | LJ35 | 348 |
| N35TM | C500 | 497 |
| N35TN | LJ35 | 472 |
| N35UA | LJ35 | 665 |
| N35UJ | LJ35 | 007 |
| N35UK | LJ35 | 662 |
| N35UK | LJ35 | 670 |
| N35VP | LJ35 | 294 |
| N35WB | LJ25 | 027 |
| **N35WB** | **LJ35** | **350** |
| (N35WE) | LJ25 | 016 |
| N35WE | LJ35 | 156 |
| N35WG | LJ35 | 124 |
| (N35WG) | LJ35 | 274 |
| N35WH | LJ35 | 138 |
| N35WJ | LJ25 | 104 |
| N35WN | FA10 | 210 |
| **N35WP** | **HS25** | **256029** |
| **N35WR** | **LJ35** | **234** |
| (N35WU) | LJ35 | 318 |
| N35XL | C56X | 5035 |
| (N36AX) | LJ36 | 030 |
| N36BG | FA10 | 190 |
| N36BH | HS25 | 256025 |
| **N36BL** | **LJ31** | **094** |
| (N36BP) | LJ35 | 237 |
| N36BP | LJ35 | 612 |
| N36BP | LJ36 | 032 |
| N36CC | C500 | 406 |
| N36CC | LJ25 | 079 |
| N36CD | C650 | 0036 |
| N36CE | C550 | 036 |
| N36CJ | C500 | 306 |
| N36CJ | C550 | 136 |
| N36CW | LJ36 | 012 |
| N36DA | FA20 | 510 |
| **N36DA** | **GLF3** | **450** |
| N36EF | WW24 | 222 |
| **N36EP** | **F2TH** | **172** |
| N36FD | ASTR | 016 |
| N36FD | C500 | 614 |
| **N36FD** | **EA50** | **000137** |
| N36FE | FA20 | 218 |
| N36FN | LJ35 | 119 |
| N36FT | HS25 | 257013 |
| (N36GA) | GLF5 | 518 |
| N36GC | C500 | 434 |
| N36GS | GLF2 | 251 |
| N36GS | HS25 | 257095 |
| **N36GV** | **GLF5** | **674** |
| N36GX | ASTR | 123 |
| N36H | C560 | 0035 |
| (N36H) | CS55 | 0001 |
| N36H | CS55 | 0036 |
| N36H | HS25 | 258332 |
| **N36HA** | **CL64** | **5441** |
| N36HH | SBRL | 306-18 |
| N36HJ | LJ35 | 427 |
| N36HR | CS55 | 0036 |
| N36JG | C500 | 364 |
| N36JK | GLF2 | 112 |
| N36JM | FA10 | 19 |
| (N36KA) | FA10 | 19 |
| N36LB | CL60 | 1020 |
| **N36LG** | **GLEX** | **9225** |
| N36LX | C560 | 0436 |
| N36MC | C500 | 159 |
| N36MJ | LJ36 | 036 |
| N36MK | HS25 | 25073 |
| N36MW | GLF2 | 89 |
| N36MW | GLF4 | 1480 |
| N36MW | LJ25 | 038 |
| N36NA | C550 | 119 |
| N36NP | HS25 | 257035 |
| N36NS | CS55 | 0059 |
| (N36NW) | C550 | 191 |
| N36NW | LJ25 | 297 |
| N36NW | LJ35 | 609 |
| N36P | FA20 | 203 |
| N36P | SBRL | 282-87 |
| N36PD | LJ36 | 022 |
| N36PJ | LJ36 | 030 |
| **N36PJ** | **LJ36** | **047** |
| **N36PN** | **GLF2** | **42/12** |
| **N36PT** | **C550** | **550-0966** |
| N36PT | WW24 | 275 |
| N36PT | WW24 | 79 |
| N36QN | C550 | 072 |
| (N36QS) | HA4T | RC-27 |
| **N36RG** | **C525** | **0139** |
| **N36RR** | **GLF2** | **4/8** |
| N36RS | LJ24 | 184 |
| **N36RZ** | **SBRL** | **306-2** |
| N36SC | LJ25 | 209 |
| **N36SF** | **WW24** | **233** |
| N36SJ | C500 | 306 |
| N36SK | LJ36 | 047 |
| N36TA | LJ36 | 003 |
| **N36TH** | **F2EX** | **53** |
| N36TJ | HS25 | 258018 |
| N36TJ | LJ35 | 168 |
| N36TJ | LJ35 | 289 |
| **N36UP** | **LJ31** | **238** |
| N36VG | FA20 | 220 |
| N36WJ | C550 | 312 |
| N36WJ | FA10 | 126 |
| N36WL | GLF3 | 328 |
| (N36WS) | C500 | 420 |
| N36XL | C56X | 5036 |
| (N37AH) | FA20 | 379 |
| N37BB | WW24 | 12 |
| **N37BE** | **WW24** | **396** |
| **N37BG** | **C52A** | **0123** |
| N37BH | HS25 | 256026 |
| N37BJ | LJ25 | 137 |
| N37BL | LJ24 | 013 |
| N37BL | LJ24 | 069 |
| N37BM | C550 | 186 |
| N37BM | C550 | 274 |
| **N37BM** | **LJ31** | **096** |
| N37CB | LJ24 | 127 |
| **N37CB** | **MU30** | **A035SA** |
| N37CD | C650 | 0037 |
| N37CP | LJ24 | 028 |
| N37CR | C550 | 117 |
| N37DG | C525 | 0109 |
| N37DG | CL64 | 5386 |
| N37DH | LJ24 | 231 |
| (N37DJ) | LJ35 | 237 |
| N37DM | LJ24 | 025 |
| N37DW | C500 | 284 |
| **N37ER** | **FA50** | **47** |
| **N37FA** | **LJ35** | **091** |
| N37FE | FA20 | 270 |
| N37FN | LJ35 | 263 |
| (N37GA) | C550 | 037 |
| N37GB | LJ25 | 053 |
| N37GF | SBRL | 370-4 |
| N37GX | GALX | 014 |
| N37HE | GLF3 | 466 |
| N37HG | C550 | 037 |
| N37HJ | LJ35 | 230 |
| (N37HR) | LJ35 | 417 |
| N37HT | LJ24 | 243 |
| N37HW | C500 | 581 |
| N37JA | LJ55 | 034 |
| N37JF | FA20 | 193 |
| N37JJ | FA20 | 248/483 |
| (N37JK) | C52B | 0251 |
| **N37JL** | **GLF4** | **4162** |
| N37LA | C500 | 457 |
| N37LB | CL60 | 1015 |
| N37LC | FA50 | 227 |
| N37LC | FA50 | 326 |
| N37LG | LJ31 | 237 |
| (N37LQ) | FA50 | 227 |
| N37MB | LJ25 | 053 |
| **N37MH** | **C550** | **168** |
| N37NR | C560 | 0009 |
| N37P | HS25 | 257015 |
| N37P | LJ24 | 138 |
| N37PL | HS25 | 257012 |
| (N37RA) | LJ31 | 153 |
| N37RM | FA20 | 308 |
| N37RR | LJ25 | 313 |
| N37RX | GLF4 | 1137 |
| N37SG | HS25 | 256021 |
| **N37SJ** | **WW24** | **38** |
| N37SV | LJ35 | 492 |
| **N37TA** | **LJ35** | **034** |
| N37TH | F2TH | 44 |
| N37TJ | LJ35 | 132 |
| N37VP | C650 | 0037 |
| N37VP | C650 | 0087 |
| (N37WC) | WW24 | 202 |
| N37WH | GLF2 | 180 |
| **N37WH** | **GLF4** | **1243** |
| N37WP | C550 | 247 |
| N37WP | C560 | 0259 |
| N37WT | FA20 | 225/472 |
| **N37WX** | **FA50** | **309** |
| N37ZZ | GLEX | 9299 |
| **N38AE** | **WW24** | **318** |
| N38AL | LJ35 | 499 |
| N38AM | LJ35 | 174 |
| N38BA | GLF5 | 682 |
| N38BG | GLF4 | 1388 |
| N38BG | JSTR | 5208 |
| N38BH | HS25 | 256032 |
| N38CC | FA20 | 200 |
| N38CJ | C500 | 308 |
| **N38CP** | **LJ60** | **108** |
| N38D | LJ36 | 024 |
| N38D | LJ55 | 068 |
| N38DA | C500 | 375 |
| **N38DA** | **EA50** | **000083** |
| N38DA | FA10 | 27 |
| **N38DD** | **C550** | **374** |
| N38DD | C650 | 0023 |
| N38DJ | LJ25 | 191 |
| (N38DL) | C500 | 375 |
| N38DM | LJ24 | 036 |
| N38EC | CS55 | 0109 |
| N38ED | C650 | 0028 |
| N38ED | C650 | 0070 |
| (N38FN) | LJ35 | 188 |
| N38FN | LJ35 | 247 |
| N38GL | GLF2 | 16/13 |
| N38GX | GALX | 015 |
| N38HG | C56X | 5114 |
| (N38HH) | HS25 | 257107 |
| N38JA | LJ55 | 033 |
| N38JD | LJ24 | 093 |
| N38JM | SBRL | 306-54 |
| N38JM | SBRL | 380-39 |
| N38KM | GLF2 | 52 |
| **N38KW** | **C56X** | **5716** |
| N38LB | HS25 | 25276 |
| **N38M** | **C52B** | **0253** |
| **N38MG** | **LJ31** | **009** |
| N38MH | C500 | 265 |
| (N38MM) | C500 | 275 |
| N38N | GLF2 | 41 |
| N38NA | C550 | 207 |
| **N38NA** | **C550** | **729** |
| **N38NS** | **C560** | **0411** |
| (N38NZ) | GLF4 | 1212 |
| N38NZ | GLF5 | 554 |
| N38PA | HS25 | 257012 |
| **N38PS** | **LJ35** | **206** |
| N38RT | C500 | 563 |
| **N38SA** | **C500** | **297** |
| **N38SC** | **C525** | **0330** |
| N38SK | C650 | 0156 |
| **N38SK** | **LJ31** | **050** |
| N38SM | C500 | 001 |
| N38SV | CL64 | 5423 |
| N38SV | LJ60 | 229 |
| N38SW | CL61 | 3008 |
| N38SW | CL64 | 5423 |
| N38TA | LJ35 | 044 |
| N38TJ | FA20 | 339 |
| N38TJ | WW24 | 356 |
| N38TM | C500 | 483 |
| N38TS | HS25 | 25190 |
| (N38TS) | HS25 | 25205 |
| **N38TT** | **C550** | **298** |
| N38US | LJ35 | 297 |
| N38UT | SBRL | 306-16 |

| | | |
|---|---|---|
| N38WC | LJ36 | 022 |
| (N38WF) | GLEX | 9128 |
| N38WP | C650 | 0032 |
| **N38WP** | **FA50** | **292** |
| N38WW | WW24 | 210 |
| N39BE | C500 | 476 |
| N39BH | HS25 | 256034 |
| (N39BL) | HS25 | 258236 |
| N39BL | JSTR | 5029/38 |
| N39BL | LJ25 | 234 |
| **N39CB** | **SBRL** | **306-116** |
| **N39CD** | **CL61** | **3030** |
| **N39CJ** | **C525** | **0039** |
| **N39CK** | **LJ25** | **005** |
| (N39DJ) | LJ35 | 208 |
| N39DK | LJ35 | 208 |
| **N39DK** | **LJ35** | **480** |
| N39DM | LJ24 | 302 |
| N39DM | LJ35 | 006 |
| N39DM | LJ35 | 040 |
| N39DM | PRM1 | RB-119 |
| N39E | JSTR | 5126 |
| N39E | LJ55 | 018 |
| **N39EG** | **C510** | **0291** |
| **N39EL** | **LJ24** | **251** |
| N39FA | C550 | 154 |
| **N39FN** | **LJ35** | **006** |
| **N39FS** | **SBRL** | **276-33** |
| (N39GA) | C525 | 0161 |
| (N39GA) | C525 | 0162 |
| N39GA | C550 | 215 |
| N39GA | C56X | 5549 |
| **N39GG** | **C52B** | **0271** |
| N39GW | WW24 | 237 |
| N39GX | GALX | 019 |
| N39H | C650 | 0206 |
| **N39H** | **HS25** | **258695** |
| (N39HD) | C550 | 448 |
| **N39HF** | **BE40** | **RK-65** |
| **N39HH** | **C500** | **527** |
| **N39HJ** | **LJ35** | **337** |
| N39J | C500 | 207 |
| N39JE | LJ25 | 124 |
| N39JJ | LJ25 | 121 |
| N39JK | GLF2 | 169 |
| N39JN | WW24 | 261 |
| N39JV | C56X | 5039 |
| N39K | C550 | 395 |
| N39K | FA10 | 167 |
| N39KM | LJ24 | 198 |
| N39KT | PRM1 | RB-39 |
| N39KY | C550 | 395 |
| N39LG | JSTR | 5142 |
| N39LH | C500 | 089 |
| N39LL | C500 | 568 |
| (N39LX) | C560 | 0439 |
| N39MB | LJ35 | 216 |
| N39ML | C550 | 014 |
| N39MW | LJ35 | 414 |
| N39N | C560 | 0243 |
| N39N | GLF2 | 50 |
| N39N | GLF3 | 403 |
| N39NA | GLF3 | 403 |
| **N39NP** | **F9EX** | **39** |
| N39NX | GLF2 | 50 |
| N39PJ | LJ35 | 128 |
| N39PY | GLF5 | 522 |
| N39Q | JSTR | 5126 |
| **N39RC** | **C56X** | **5041** |
| N39RE | C500 | 311 |
| N39RE | C650 | 0006 |
| N39RE | CL60 | 1049 |
| **N39RE** | **CL61** | **5020** |
| N39RE | FA10 | 80 |
| N39RE | WW24 | 342 |
| N39RG | SBRL | 276-25 |
| **N39RG** | **SBRL** | **282-82** |
| N39RP | FA20 | 478 |
| N39SA | LJ35 | 466 |
| (N39SL) | SBRL | 306-39 |
| N39SV | C680 | 0039 |
| N39T | LJ24 | 043 |
| N39TF | CS55 | 0139 |
| N39TH | FA10 | 199 |
| N39TH | LJ35 | 496 |
| N39TJ | LJ31 | 026 |
| N39TR | SBRL | 465-27 |
| N39TT | FA20 | 449 |
| N39TT | LJ24 | 308 |
| **N39TW** | **LJ31** | **047** |
| N39VP | C650 | 0187 |
| N39WA | LJ35 | 092 |
| (N39WH) | GLF4 | 1243 |
| N39WJ | FA20 | 239 |
| N39WP | C650 | 0039 |
| **N39WP** | **FA50** | **294** |
| **N39ZZ** | **GLEX** | **9342** |
| N40AB | WW24 | 106 |
| N40AC | C500 | 331 |
| N40AC | FA20 | 187 |
| (N40AD) | HS25 | 25026 |
| N40AD | LJ25 | 314 |
| N40AG | GLF2 | 115 |
| N40AJ | ASTR | 031 |
| **N40AJ** | **C500** | **393** |
| N40AJ | WW24 | 40 |
| (N40AN) | LJ35 | 045 |
| (N40AN) | LJ35 | 149 |
| N40AN | LJ35 | 271 |
| N40AS | FA50 | 171 |
| N40AS | LJ25 | 117 |
| N40AS | WW24 | 156 |
| N40AW | C500 | 584 |
| N40BC | LJ25 | 128 |
| (N40BC) | LJ25 | 288 |
| **N40BD** | **LJ35** | **140** |
| N40BG | WW24 | 156 |
| N40BH | HS25 | 256038 |
| (N40BK) | MU30 | A004SA |
| N40BP | LJ24 | 116 |
| N40BP | SBRL | 282-40 |
| N40BT | SBRL | 282-113 |
| N40CC | GLF2 | 46 |
| N40CD | SBRL | 282-28 |
| N40CE | GLF2 | 45 |
| N40CH | GLF2 | 77 |
| N40CH | GLF3 | 377 |
| N40CH | SBRL | 282-104 |
| **N40CJ** | **C525** | **0540** |
| N40CN | FA50 | 92 |
| N40CN | HS25 | 257120 |
| N40CR | LJ55 | 097 |
| N40CR | LJ55 | 144 |
| N40CX | C750 | 0240 |
| N40DA | C500 | 392 |
| N40DC | HS25 | 25078 |
| N40DC | HS25 | 25079 |
| N40DC | JSTR | 5120/26 |
| N40DG | WW24 | 262 |
| N40DK | LJ35 | 171 |
| N40DK | LJ35 | 264 |
| **N40DK** | **LJ55** | **092** |
| N40DW | SBRL | 282-24 |
| N40EL | SBRL | 282-42 |
| **N40EP** | **C550** | **617** |
| N40ES | LJ55 | 005 |
| (N40F) | FA50 | 82 |
| N40FC | C550 | 554 |
| **N40FC** | **C650** | **0143** |
| N40FJ | C500 | 547 |
| N40FJ | C550 | 281 |
| **N40GA** | **MU30** | **A040SA** |
| N40GC | MU30 | A005SA |
| N40GG | LJ35 | 416 |
| **N40GG** | **WW24** | **229** |
| N40GP | SBRL | 282-16 |
| N40GS | C550 | 288 |
| **N40GS** | **HS25** | **258128** |
| N40GT | HS25 | 257002 |
| **N40GT** | **SBRL** | **282-126** |
| N40GX | GALX | 016 |
| N40HB | GLF4 | 1407 |
| N40HC | SBRL | 282-66 |
| N40HL | C500 | 128 |
| N40HP | C500 | 104 |
| **N40HT** | **C560** | **0030** |
| N40JC | WW24 | 40 |
| N40JE | LJ24 | 133 |
| N40JE | SBRL | 282-124 |
| N40JF | C500 | 079 |
| N40JF | LJ24 | 133 |
| N40JF | SBRL | 282-80 |
| N40JW | SBRL | 282-122 |
| **N40KJ** | **GLF4** | **1070** |
| N40KJ | LJ40 | 45-2002 |
| N40KJ | SBRL | 306-142 |
| (N40KM) | CS55 | 0008 |
| N40KW | C550 | 550-0909 |
| N40KW | C750 | 0040 |
| N40LB | LJ25 | 009 |
| N40LB | SBRL | 282-36 |
| N40LJ | LJ40 | 45-2001 |
| N40LJ | LJ40 | 45-2009 |
| N40LJ | LJ40 | 45-2027 |
| N40LJ | LJ40 | 45-2046 |
| N40LJ | LJ40 | 45-2084 |
| **N40LX** | **LJ40** | **45-001** |
| **N40LX** | **LJ45** | **001** |
| N40MA | BE40 | RJ-42 |
| N40MA | C500 | 514 |
| N40MA | C550 | 320 |
| **N40MF** | **C550** | **550-0921** |
| N40MF | MU30 | A049SA |
| N40ML | LJ40 | 45-2024 |
| N40MM | C500 | 275 |
| N40MP | WW24 | 334 |
| N40MT | C550 | 238 |
| N40N | C650 | 7031 |
| N40N | FA10 | 25 |
| N40N | GLF3 | 405 |
| N40N | GLF4 | 1122 |
| N40N | JSTR | 5048 |
| N40NB | GLF3 | 405 |
| **N40NB** | **LJ40** | **45-2087** |
| N40NC | JSTR | 5048 |
| **N40ND** | **FA10** | **21** |
| **N40NJ** | **SBRL** | **282-134** |
| N40NR | SBRL | 282-107 |
| N40NR | SBRL | 282-134 |
| N40NR | SBRL | 282-66 |
| N40NR | SBRL | 282-91 |
| N40NS | SBRL | 282-126 |
| N40PC | HS25 | 25214 |
| N40PC | HS25 | 256010 |
| **N40PC** | **LJ45** | **259** |
| N40PD | C500 | 059 |
| **N40PD** | **LJ40** | **45-2111** |
| N40PH | C650 | 0201 |
| **N40PK** | **LJ35** | **260** |
| N40PL | BE40 | RK-138 |
| N40PL | C500 | 646 |
| N40PL | C550 | 305 |
| (N40PL) | C560 | 0068 |
| N40PL | CS55 | 0008 |
| N40PL | HS25 | 258347 |
| N40PX | LJ40 | 45-2007 |
| **N40QG** | **CL30** | **20264** |
| N40QJ | GLF3 | 493 |
| N40QS | HA4T | RC-42 |
| (N40R) | SBRL | 282-19 |
| N40R | SBRL | 282-52 |
| N40RD | C500 | 059 |
| (N40RF) | C500 | 266 |
| N40RL | C52A | 0046 |
| N40RW | C500 | 107 |
| N40RW | LJ35 | 224 |
| **N40SC** | **BE40** | **RK-311** |
| N40SC | SBRL | 282-113 |
| N40SC | SBRL | 282-98 |
| N40SE | SBRL | 282-15 |
| N40SE | SBRL | 282-59 |
| N40SJ | SBRL | 282-25 |
| (N40SK) | FA50 | 240 |
| N40SK | HS25 | 25186 |
| N40SL | SBRL | 282-32 |
| N40SN | LJ25 | 021 |
| N40SR | GLF5 | 525 |
| N40SW | LJ25 | 021 |
| N40SW | LJ25 | 238 |
| N40TA | LJ35 | 208 |
| N40TA | SBRL | 282-94 |
| N40TA | WW24 | 194 |
| N40TF | LJ35 | 025 |
| **N40TH** | **F2EX** | **7** |
| N40TH | FA50 | 212 |
| N40TH | FA50 | 85 |
| N40TL | SBRL | 306-103 |
| (N40TM) | LJ35 | 381 |
| (N40TV) | LJ24 | 011 |
| N40UA | WW24 | 40 |
| **N40VK** | **HA4T** | **RC-40** |
| N40WB | HS25 | 257002 |
| (N40WE) | C550 | 554 |
| N40WH | SBRL | 282-80 |
| N40WJ | FA10 | 21 |
| N40WP | C560 | 0155 |
| N40WP | SBRL | 282-32 |
| N40WP | SBRL | 380-39 |
| **N40XR** | **LJ40** | **45-2028** |
| N40XY | FA20 | 135 |
| N40XY | JSTR | 5115/39 |
| N40Y | HS25 | 25234 |
| N40YA | SBRL | 282-20 |
| N40YC | C550 | 554 |
| N40ZA | SBRL | 282-112 |
| N40ZH | BE40 | RK-405 |
| **N40ZZ** | **GLEX** | **9357** |
| N41 | WW24 | 143 |
| (N41AJ) | C500 | 393 |
| N41AJ | LJ24 | 037 |
| N41AJ | LJ25 | 040 |
| **N41AU** | **ASTR** | **041** |
| **N41AV** | **GLF2** | **61** |
| (N41B) | SBRL | 380-49 |
| N41BH | C550 | 567 |
| N41BH | HS25 | 25220 |
| N41BH | HS25 | 256040 |
| N41BJ | LJ24 | 178 |
| N41BP | FA20 | 177 |
| N41C | C550 | 320 |
| **N41C** | **WW24** | **398** |
| (N41CC) | HS25 | 257010 |
| N41CD | FA20 | 88 |
| (N41CK) | C550 | 259 |
| N41CP | GLF4 | 1179 |
| N41CP | GLF4 | 1336 |
| N41CP | LJ55 | 037 |
| N41CQ | SBRL | 465-6 |
| **N41DP** | **CL30** | **20010** |
| N41DP | LJ31 | 079 |
| N41DP | LJ45 | 010 |
| **N41EA** | **C525** | **0131** |
| N41EA | LJ55 | 041 |
| N41EB | C525 | 0116 |
| N41ES | LJ55 | 007 |
| N41FL | WW24 | 41 |
| N41FN | LJ35 | 137 |
| **N41GA** | **C550** | **044** |
| N41GS | SBRL | 282-16 |
| **N41GT** | **C500** | **494** |
| (N41GX) | GALX | 021 |
| N41H | LJ25 | 217 |
| N41HF | HS25 | 257012 |
| **N41HF** | **HS25** | **258274** |
| **N41HL** | **C500** | **338** |
| **N41HV** | **HA4T** | **RC-41** |
| N41JP | C500 | 466 |
| N41JP | C550 | 288 |
| N41LE | C500 | 632 |
| **N41LF** | **C525** | **0501** |
| N41LV | SBRL | 465-39 |
| N41ME | BE40 | RK-19 |
| **N41MH** | **FA20** | **14** |
| N41MJ | LJ35 | 405 |
| N41MP | LJ24 | 148 |
| N41N | JSTR | 5087/55 |
| **N41ND** | **C52B** | **0134** |
| N41NK | C525 | 0190 |
| N41NK | C525 | 0281 |
| **N41NK** | **LJ25** | **238** |
| N41NR | SBRL | 282-133 |
| **N41NW** | **LJ35** | **041** |
| **N41NY** | **MS76** | **041** |
| N41PC | FA20 | 19 |
| N41PC | LJ45 | 190 |
| **N41PC** | **LJ45** | **387** |
| (N41PD) | FA20 | 19 |
| **N41PG** | **C525** | **0175** |
| N41PG | GLF3 | 334 |
| N41PJ | LJ35 | 041 |
| N41PL | GLF4 | 1226 |
| **N41PQ** | **LJ45** | **190** |
| N41PR | GLF4 | 1226 |
| N41QR | GLF4 | 1179 |
| N41RC | GLF2 | 29 |
| **N41RG** | **SBRL** | **306-119** |
| N41SH | C500 | 267 |
| N41SJ | F900 | 37 |
| **N41SM** | **C550** | **271** |
| N41ST | C500 | 485 |
| N41ST | C650 | 0063 |
| N41ST | LJ35 | 302 |

| | | |
|---|---|---|
| N41TC | JSTR | 5036/42 |
| N41TC | LJ24 | 346 |
| N41TC | LJ25 | 346 |
| N41TC | SBRL | 465-42 |
| **N41TF** | **LJ45** | **175** |
| N41TH | FA50 | 201 |
| (N41TJ) | BE40 | RJ-34 |
| N41TJ | FA10 | 118 |
| N41UT | MU30 | A030SA |
| N41VB | GLF4 | 1174 |
| N41VP | C560 | 0492 |
| **N41VP** | **C560** | **0626** |
| N41VR | C560 | 0492 |
| (N41VY) | C550 | 550-0804 |
| N41WH | WW24 | 268 |
| **N41WJ** | **C550** | **264** |
| N41WT | LJ35 | 229 |
| **N41YP** | **C525** | **0122** |
| N41ZP | LJ25 | 279 |
| N42 | WW24 | 142 |
| **N42AA** | **C525** | **0275** |
| N42AA | C52B | 0140 |
| **N42AJ** | **BE40** | **RK-55** |
| N42AJ | LJ24 | 139 |
| (N42AJ) | LJ35 | 475 |
| (N42AJ) | LJ60 | 052 |
| **N42AS** | **HS25** | **25150** |
| N42B | LJ35 | 277 |
| N42BH | HS25 | 25221 |
| N42BH | HS25 | 256044 |
| (N42BJ) | LJ25 | 127 |
| N42BL | HS25 | 25275 |
| N42BL | MS76 | 050 |
| (N42BM) | C550 | 111 |
| N42C | JSTR | 5150/37 |
| N42CK | HS25 | 25038 |
| **N42CM** | **WW24** | **189** |
| N42CV | C560 | 0042 |
| **N42DC** | **SBRL** | **465-25** |
| N42DG | LJ25 | 171 |
| **N42EE** | **CL61** | **5008** |
| **N42EH** | **FA10** | **28** |
| **N42EL** | **PRM1** | **RB-145** |
| N42ES | LJ55 | 009 |
| **N42FB** | **HS25** | **258467** |
| (N42FD) | HS25 | 25042 |
| N42FE | LJ25 | 088 |
| N42FE | LJ35 | 241 |
| N42FJ | F900 | 42 |
| **N42FL** | **WW24** | **429** |
| **N42G** | **FA10** | **20** |
| N42G | JSTR | 5127 |
| N42G | LJ25 | 140 |
| N42GA | GLF5 | 5142 |
| N42GB | JSTR | 5127 |
| **N42GJ** | **CL30** | **20085** |
| N42GX | ASTR | 124 |
| N42GX | GLF5 | 628 |
| N42GX | LJ25 | 140 |
| N42HC | LJ24 | 208 |
| N42HC | LJ25 | 142 |
| N42HM | C500 | 452 |
| N42HM | LJ35 | 210 |
| **N42HN** | **LJ35** | **507** |
| N42HP | LJ35 | 507 |
| N42HP | LJ45 | 080 |
| (N42JP) | LJ60 | 147 |
| **N42JP** | **LJ60** | **368** |
| N42KC | C550 | 346 |
| N42KR | JSTR | 5225 |
| N42LC | GLF2 | 178 |
| **N42LG** | **PRM1** | **RB-259** |
| N42LG | PRM1 | RB-262 |
| N42LG | PRM1 | RB-263 |
| N42LL | LJ35 | 427 |
| **N42LQ** | **PRM1** | **RB-263** |
| N42MD | GLF3 | 427 |
| N42MJ | C550 | 018 |
| N42NA | C550 | 601 |
| N42NA | C560 | 0077 |
| (N42NA) | C650 | 0077 |
| **N42NA** | **FA50** | **128** |
| **N42ND** | **C560** | **0400** |
| N42NF | LJ24 | 214 |
| **N42NF** | **WW24** | **334** |
| N42PA | C56X | 5067 |
| N42PG | LJ24 | 247 |
| **N42PH** | **C550** | **327** |
| N42PJ | LJ35 | 285 |
| N42PP | GLF2 | 115 |
| N42QB | WW24 | 6 |
| **N42SC** | **PRM1** | **RB-212** |
| (N42SE) | HS25 | 257036 |
| N42SK | BE40 | RK-111 |
| N42SK | BE40 | RK-28 |
| **N42SK** | **FA50** | **290** |
| N42SR | BE40 | RJ-9 |
| N42SR | HS25 | 257036 |
| N42SR | MU30 | A038SA |
| **N42ST** | **F2TH** | **39** |
| N42TS | HS25 | 256003 |
| N42TS | HS25 | 256041 |
| **N42TS** | **HS25** | **257067** |
| **N42US** | **FA10** | **171** |
| (N42US) | HS25 | 258152 |
| **N42WJ** | **FA20** | **427** |
| **N42WZ** | **C510** | **0175** |
| N42XL | C56X | 5042 |
| N42ZP | LJ28 | 28-003 |
| N43 | WW24 | 131 |
| (N43A) | LJ36 | 008 |
| (N43AC) | LJ24 | 043 |
| N43AJ | LJ24 | 141 |
| N43AR | JSTR | 5154 |
| N43B | LJ24 | 039 |
| **N43BD** | **BE40** | **RK-441** |
| N43BE | FA50 | 49 |
| N43BG | C500 | 407 |
| **N43BH** | **C525** | **0633** |
| N43BH | HS25 | 25222 |
| N43BH | HS25 | 256046 |
| N43CC | FA10 | 69 |
| N43CF | SBRL | 282-59 |
| (N43CT) | LJ24 | 039 |
| N43D | C550 | 188 |
| (N43D) | C550 | 375 |
| N43DD | LJ35 | 288 |
| N43DM | LJ24 | 305 |
| **N43DR** | **LJ25** | **353** |
| **N43EC** | **FA10** | **168** |
| N43EL | LJ35 | 121 |
| N43ES | FA50 | 49 |
| **N43FC** | **C650** | **7087** |
| N43FE | LJ35 | 275 |
| N43FJ | F2TH | 43 |
| (N43FN) | LJ24 | 305 |
| N43GA | GLF5 | 5150 |
| N43GB | SBRL | 306-14 |
| N43GX | GALX | 022 |
| N43H | LJ35 | 426 |
| **N43HF** | **C56X** | **5519** |
| N43HJ | PRM1 | RB-41 |
| N43JG | SBRL | 306-79 |
| N43JK | FA20 | 195 |
| (N43JK) | JSTR | 5055/21 |
| N43KC | LJ24 | 213 |
| N43KS | GLF4 | 1018 |
| N43KW | C560 | 0487 |
| **N43LD** | **C560** | **0175** |
| N43LJ | LJ31 | 043 |
| N43LJ | LJ36 | 043 |
| N43M | GLF2 | 126 |
| N43M | GLF4 | 1057 |
| **N43MF** | **LJ35** | **284** |
| **N43MH** | **ASTR** | **043** |
| N43MU | GLF4 | 1057 |
| N43ND | C52A | 0041 |
| **N43NR** | **LJ60** | **043** |
| N43NR | SBRL | 282-69 |
| N43NR | SBRL | 282-7 |
| **N43NW** | **C525** | **0543** |
| N43NW | CL60 | 1043 |
| (N43PE) | LJ35 | 275 |
| N43PJ | LJ28 | 28-004 |
| N43PR | CL61 | 5002 |
| N43QF | LJ60 | 159 |
| N43QG | LJ45 | 237 |
| N43R | CL61 | 5134 |
| **N43R** | **CL64** | **5334** |
| N43R | GLF2 | 18 |
| N43R | SBRL | 380-51 |
| **N43RC** | **C560** | **0245** |
| N43RC | CS55 | 0149 |
| **N43RJ** | **ASTR** | **136** |
| N43RJ | GLF2 | 64/27 |
| N43RK | CL61 | 5134 |
| **N43RP** | **WW24** | **332** |
| N43RW | C550 | 088 |
| **N43SA** | **C550** | **096** |
| N43SE | LJ31 | 048 |
| **N43SF** | **CL64** | **5594** |
| N43SF | LJ31 | 048 |
| N43SF | LJ60 | 159 |
| N43SM | FA20 | 142 |
| **N43SP** | **C500** | **648** |
| (N43TC) | C500 | 149 |
| N43TC | C550 | 337 |
| N43TC | C650 | 0036 |
| N43TE | C550 | 337 |
| N43TJ | LJ35 | 121 |
| (N43TL) | LJ24 | 203 |
| N43TR | LJ35 | 645 |
| **N43TS** | **HS25** | **25186** |
| N43TS | LJ25 | 201 |
| N43US | FA10 | 110 |
| **N43VS** | **CS55** | **0069** |
| N43W | LJ24 | 227 |
| N43W | LJ35 | 426 |
| N43W | SBRL | 282-15 |
| N43W | WW24 | 374 |
| N43WJ | HS25 | 25031 |
| **N43WL** | **SBRL** | **282-15** |
| N43ZP | LJ24 | 157 |
| N43ZZ | WW24 | 356 |
| N44 | WW24 | 130 |
| N44AB | LJ35 | 473 |
| N44AJ | LJ24 | 120 |
| **N44AS** | **C550** | **056** |
| N44BB | HS25 | 257105 |
| N44BB | LJ25 | 227 |
| (N44BH) | C650 | 0019 |
| N44BH | HS25 | 25224 |
| (N44BH) | HS25 | 25236 |
| "N44BH" | HS25 | 256047 |
| N44BW | C500 | 048 |
| N44CC | FA20 | 200 |
| **N44CE** | **GLF4** | **1125** |
| N44CJ | LJ24 | 146 |
| **N44CK** | **C525** | **0401** |
| N44CN | HS25 | 25203 |
| N44CP | LJ24 | 185 |
| N44CP | LJ25 | 006 |
| **N44DD** | **SBRL** | **306-146** |
| N44EE | LJ25 | 050 |
| **N44EG** | **F900** | **14** |
| N44EJ | EA50 | 000089 |
| N44EL | LJ25 | 050 |
| N44EL | LJ35 | 009 |
| N44EL | LJ35 | 255 |
| N44EL | LJ55 | 123 |
| **N44EL** | **LJ60** | **036** |
| N44EQ | FA50 | 275 |
| N44ET | LJ35 | 255 |
| **N44EV** | **LJ36** | **022** |
| N44FC | C550 | 220 |
| N44FE | C525 | 0334 |
| N44FE | LJ25 | 215 |
| **N44FG** | **C560** | **0470** |
| N44FH | LJ25 | 252 |
| N44FJ | C525 | 0003 |
| **N44FJ** | **C52A** | **0178** |
| **N44FM** | **C500** | **534** |
| **N44FR** | **C550** | **361** |
| N44GA | LJ24 | 129 |
| N44GA | LJ55 | 102 |
| N44GL | LJ36 | 009 |
| N44GT | C550 | 002 |
| **N44GT** | **C560** | **0252** |
| N44GT | CS55 | 0099 |
| N44GX | ASTR | 125 |
| **N44GX** | **GLEX** | **9142** |
| N44HC | C500 | 295 |
| N44HG | LJ35 | 180 |
| **N44HH** | **HS25** | **258223** |
| N44HS | C650 | 0006 |
| **N44JC** | **F2TH** | **164** |
| N44JC | FA10 | 22 |
| N44JC | FA20 | 471 |
| N44JF | C500 | 262 |
| N44JQ | FA20 | 471 |
| (N44JX) | C550 | 088 |
| N44K | HS25 | 25114 |
| (N44KB) | LJ24 | 245 |
| (N44KF) | JSTR | 5038 |
| N44KG | HS25 | 25114 |
| N44KW | C550 | 550-0909 |
| (N44KW) | LJ35 | 130 |
| N44LC | C500 | 577 |
| N44LC | C550 | 649 |
| N44LC | C560 | 0482 |
| **N44LC** | **F9EX** | **216** |
| N44LC | FA50 | 275 |
| N44LF | C550 | 309 |
| N44LG | LJ31 | 237 |
| **N44LG** | **LJ40** | **45-2125** |
| N44LJ | LJ24 | 191 |
| N44LJ | LJ35 | 276 |
| N44LJ | LJ36 | 044 |
| N44LQ | C550 | 649 |
| **N44LQ** | **C560** | **0482** |
| **N44LV** | **C560** | **0397** |
| N44LX | GLF4 | 1114 |
| N44M | C650 | 0050 |
| N44M | C650 | 7043 |
| **N44M** | **C680** | **0083** |
| N44MC | C500 | 434 |
| N44MC | FA20 | 200 |
| N44MD | GLF2 | 81 |
| N44MD | GLF3 | 427 |
| N44MF | JSTR | 5051 |
| N44MJ | LJ25 | 124 |
| N44MJ | LJ35 | 421 |
| **N44MK** | **C500** | **379** |
| N44MK | FA50 | 44 |
| **N44MM** | **MU30** | **A080SA** |
| **N44MQ** | **C650** | **7043** |
| N44MU | C650 | 0050 |
| N44MW | LJ35 | 044 |
| N44NJ | LJ24 | 120 |
| N44NP | SBRL | 282-44 |
| N44NR | SBRL | 282-130 |
| N44NT | FA20 | 319 |
| N44P | SBRL | 282-103 |
| N44PA | LJ24 | 181 |
| N44PA | LJ25 | 144 |
| N44PH | SBRL | 282-136 |
| N44PR | WW24 | 169 |
| N44PT | LJ35 | 093 |
| N44PW | HS25 | 25123 |
| N44QF | LJ60 | 215 |
| N44QG | LJ28 | 28-003 |
| N44QG | LJ31 | 053 |
| N44QG | LJ45 | 237 |
| **N44QG** | **LJ45** | **361** |
| N44RD | C500 | 334 |
| N44RD | C500 | 464 |
| N44SA | C500 | 109 |
| N44SB | SBRL | 306-20 |
| **N44SF** | **CL64** | **5601** |
| N44SF | LJ31 | 065 |
| N44SF | LJ31 | 193 |
| N44SF | LJ60 | 215 |
| N44SH | C560 | 0613 |
| **N44SH** | **C680** | **0023** |
| N44SK | FA50 | 290 |
| N44SK | LJ25 | 371 |
| N44SK | LJ35 | 444 |
| N44SU | LJ31 | 065 |
| N44SW | C500 | 552 |
| **N44SW** | **C550** | **733** |
| N44SZ | LJ31 | 193 |
| N44TC | C550 | 337 |
| N44TG | HS25 | 25100 |
| (N44TL) | LJ24 | 191 |
| N44TQ | HS25 | 25100 |
| N44TT | LJ35 | 211 |
| N44UC | LJ35 | 098 |
| N44UP | GLF2 | 133 |
| N44VW | LJ35 | 044 |
| N44WD | LJ24 | 111 |
| N44WD | SBRL | 306-116 |
| N44WF | C550 | 236 |
| N44WG | WW24 | 112 |
| **N44YS** | **GLF2** | **98/38** |
| **N44ZF** | **GLF4** | **1029** |
| (N44ZG) | LJ31 | 053 |
| N44ZP | C550 | 214 |
| N45 | WW24 | 144 |
| **N45AC** | **GLF4** | **1036** |
| **N45AE** | **LJ35** | **422** |
| **N45AF** | **C500** | **433** |
| N45AF | HS25 | 257128 |

| | | |
|---|---|---|
| N45AJ | LJ24 | 309 |
| N45AJ | LJ24 | 317 |
| N45AJ | LJ45 | 137 |
| (N45AQ) | C500 | 411 |
| N45AU | LJ45 | 262 |
| N45AW | LJ35 | 078 |
| N45AX | LJ45 | 206 |
| **N45AX** | **LJ45** | **377** |
| N45BA | C560 | 0067 |
| N45BA | LJ45 | 136 |
| **N45BE** | **C550** | **664** |
| N45BE | FA50 | 75 |
| N45BH | HS25 | 25225 |
| (N45BH) | HS25 | 256051 |
| **N45BK** | **LJ25** | **036** |
| N45BP | HS25 | 257026 |
| N45BR | C750 | 0045 |
| N45BS | LJ25 | 111 |
| **N45BZ** | **LJ45** | **290** |
| N45CP | LJ24 | 242 |
| N45CP | LJ25 | 073 |
| N45DM | LJ25 | 030 |
| **N45ED** | **LJ24** | **104** |
| **N45EJ** | **LJ45** | **080** |
| N45EP | C550 | 199 |
| N45ES | FA50 | 75 |
| N45ES | LJ25 | 295 |
| **N45ET** | **GLF4** | **1405** |
| N45FC | LJ24 | 309 |
| N45FE | LJ45 | 034 |
| N45FG | FA50 | 180 |
| **N45FG** | **LJ36** | **010** |
| **N45FJ** | **C525** | **0003** |
| N45FS | C500 | 486 |
| N45GA | C550 | 395 |
| N45GA | C560 | 0064 |
| **N45GD** | **HS25** | **258142** |
| N45GL | MU30 | A041SA |
| **N45GP** | **CS55** | **0110** |
| N45GX | ASTR | 128 |
| **N45H** | **ASTR** | **050** |
| N45H | CS55 | 0064 |
| N45H | LJ25 | 239 |
| N45H | SBRL | 465-2 |
| N45HB | LJ25 | 114 |
| **N45HC** | **LJ45** | **174** |
| **N45HF** | **LJ45** | **121** |
| N45HG | LJ31 | 026 |
| N45HG | LJ31 | 140 |
| **N45HG** | **LJ45** | **343** |
| **N45HK** | **LJ45** | **349** |
| (N45HV) | C550 | 550-0825 |
| N45JB | FA10 | 203 |
| **N45JB** | **FA20** | **505** |
| **N45JE** | **GLEX** | **9222** |
| N45JF | LJ24 | 138 |
| N45JF | WW24 | 101 |
| N45JM | GLF2 | 69 |
| N45K | JSTR | 5151 |
| **N45KB** | **C560** | **0191** |
| (N45KB) | LJ25 | 270 |
| N45KB | LJ25 | 281 |
| **N45KG** | **HS25** | **257189** |
| **N45KH** | **LJ45** | **313** |
| N45KJ | LJ45 | 301 |
| N45KK | HS25 | 257158 |
| N45KK | LJ25 | 281 |
| N45KK | LJ31 | 147 |
| N45KK | LJ35 | 592 |
| N45KK | LJ35 | 672 |
| **N45KR** | **GLF3** | **433** |
| **N45KX** | **LJ45** | **233** |
| N45LC | C500 | 326 |
| N45LJ | LJ45 | 002 |
| N45LJ | LJ45 | 019 |
| N45LJ | LJ45 | 100 |
| N45LJ | LJ45 | 239 |
| N45LJ | LJ45 | 258 |
| N45LJ | LJ45 | 279 |
| N45LJ | LJ45 | 318 |
| N45LJ | LJ45 | 361 |
| **N45LJ** | **LJ45** | **392** |
| (N45LJ) | LJ45 | 394 |
| (N45LN) | BE40 | RK-388 |
| (N45LN) | BE40 | RK-504 |
| **N45LR** | **LJ45** | **013** |
| N45LR | LJ45 | 055 |
| N45LX | BE40 | RK-388 |
| N45MC | C500 | 531 |
| N45MC | C550 | 422 |
| **N45ME** | **C550** | **089** |
| N45MH | C525 | 0386 |
| **N45MH** | **C52A** | **0344** |
| N45MJ | LJ35 | 045 |
| N45MK | C500 | 571 |
| **N45ML** | **C550** | **405** |
| **N45MM** | **C500** | **444** |
| (N45MM) | SBRL | 306-91 |
| (N45MP) | WW24 | 334 |
| N45MR | FA20 | 123 |
| N45MR | LJ45 | 179 |
| **N45MR** | **LJ45** | **345** |
| N45MS | ASTR | 041 |
| **N45MW** | **LJ45** | **115** |
| N45NB | PRM1 | RB-22 |
| **N45NB** | **PRM1** | **RB-91** |
| N45NC | FA50 | 232 |
| **N45NC** | **FA50** | **302** |
| N45NC | HS25 | 25225 |
| (N45ND) | HS25 | 25225 |
| N45ND | PRM1 | RB-22 |
| N45NF | C550 | 550-0986 |
| **N45NF** | **C56X** | **5563** |
| **N45NM** | **LJ45** | **253** |
| N45NP | LJ45 | 020 |
| **N45NP** | **LJ45** | **204** |
| N45NP | MU30 | A047SA |
| N45NP | SBRL | 465-42 |
| N45NQ | FA50 | 232 |
| N45NQ | HS25 | 25225 |
| N45NS | C550 | 479 |
| **N45NS** | **C550** | **550-0949** |
| N45PD | LJ31 | 186 |
| (N45PF) | C525 | 0206 |
| (N45PG) | GLF3 | 488 |
| **N45PH** | **CL61** | **3004** |
| **N45PK** | **C56X** | **5614** |
| N45PK | LJ31 | 034 |
| N45PK | LJ31 | 186 |
| N45PM | HS25 | 25118 |
| N45QG | LJ45 | 237 |
| **N45RC** | **C560** | **0071A** |
| **N45RK** | **BE40** | **RK-43** |
| N45RS | SBRL | 306-44 |
| N45SC | F2TH | 45 |
| **N45SJ** | **F900** | **19** |
| N45SJ | F900 | 37 |
| N45SJ | F9EX | 7 |
| N45SJ | FA50 | 53 |
| N45SJ | WW24 | 289 |
| N45SL | HS25 | 25098 |
| (N45SL) | LJ35 | 083 |
| N45SL | WW24 | 149 |
| N45SP | C510 | 0029 |
| N45ST | C750 | 0054 |
| N45ST | C750 | 0185 |
| N45ST | GLF5 | 5056 |
| **N45ST** | **GLF5** | **5196** |
| N45SY | LJ45 | 242 |
| **N45TE** | **C560** | **0405** |
| N45TK | LJ35 | 037 |
| N45TK | LJ45 | 176 |
| **N45TK** | **LJ45** | **338** |
| **N45TL** | **C500** | **375** |
| N45TP | C550 | 674 |
| N45TP | C560 | 0405 |
| **N45TP** | **C560** | **0668** |
| **N45TU** | **LJ45** | **120** |
| N45UF | LJ31 | 072 |
| **N45UG** | **LJ45** | **198** |
| N45UG | LJ45 | 206 |
| N45UJ | LJ45 | 080 |
| N45UP | LJ45 | 170 |
| (N45US) | C650 | 0016 |
| (N45US) | C650 | 0034 |
| N45US | LJ60 | 129 |
| **N45VB** | **LJ45** | **043** |
| **N45VG** | **LJ45** | **251** |
| N45VL | LJ45 | 139 |
| **N45VM** | **C550** | **550-0918** |
| N45VP | LJ45 | 184 |
| **N45VS** | **LJ45** | **170** |
| N45WH | FA20 | 259 |
| N45WH | FA20 | 512 |
| (N45WL) | C550 | 155 |
| N45WN | FA20 | 259 |
| N45XL | C56X | 5545 |
| N45XL | LJ40 | 45-001 |
| N45XL | LJ45 | 001 |
| N45XP | BE40 | RK-445 |
| **N45XP** | **LJ45** | **355** |
| N45XR | LJ45 | 232 |
| N45XR | LJ45 | 271 |
| N45XR | LJ45 | 293 |
| N45XR | LJ45 | 305 |
| (N45XR) | LJ45 | 318 |
| N45XR | LJ45 | 332 |
| N45XR | LJ45 | 380 |
| **N45XR** | **LJ45** | **381** |
| N45XT | LJ45 | 330 |
| N45Y | GLF2 | 69 |
| N45Y | HS25 | 258009 |
| N45Y | HS25 | 258140 |
| N45YH | LJ45 | 336 |
| N45YP | GLF2 | 69 |
| N45ZP | C550 | 216 |
| N45ZP | LJ25 | 238 |
| N46A | C550 | 423 |
| N46A | CS55 | 0061 |
| N46B | HS25 | 25261 |
| N46B | HS25 | 256044 |
| N46BA | C550 | 575 |
| (N46BA) | LJ25 | 300 |
| **N46BE** | **C52A** | **0116** |
| (N46BE) | HS25 | 256044 |
| N46BH | HS25 | 25226 |
| N46BK | WW24 | 214 |
| N46DA | C550 | 033 |
| **N46E** | **LJ40** | **45-2010** |
| N46ES | CL60 | 1079 |
| (N46ES) | GLF3 | 381 |
| N46F | CL61 | 5055 |
| **N46F** | **CL64** | **5574** |
| N46F | JSTR | 5124 |
| N46FE | BE40 | RK-16 |
| N46FJ | F900 | 46 |
| **N46GA** | **C560** | **0061** |
| N46GX | GALX | 020 |
| **N46HA** | **F2TH** | **91** |
| (N46JA) | C500 | 168 |
| N46JA | LJ24 | 251 |
| N46JV | C525 | 0602 |
| N46JW | C525 | 0002 |
| N46JW | C52A | 0046 |
| N46K | JSTR | 5145 |
| (N46KB) | LJ35 | 206 |
| N46KJ | JSTR | 5151 |
| (N46LM) | LJ24 | 195 |
| N46MF | C550 | 408 |
| **N46MF** | **LJ35** | **377** |
| N46MK | C550 | 408 |
| **N46MK** | **FA10** | **206** |
| N46MT | C500 | 689 |
| N46MT | C550 | 553 |
| N46MT | C560 | 0253 |
| N46MW | C560 | 0487 |
| **N46MW** | **LJ40** | **45-2126** |
| (N46NR) | C550 | 394 |
| **N46NT** | **C52A** | **0046** |
| **N46PJ** | **C550** | **002** |
| N46PL | HS25 | 257055 |
| N46RB | C500 | 058 |
| N46RD | C500 | 244 |
| N46SC | C500 | 521 |
| N46SD | C550 | 377 |
| N46SG | CL61 | 5111 |
| N46SR | CL60 | 1046 |
| N46SR | CL61 | 3046 |
| N46TE | GLF2 | 243 |
| N46TG | HS25 | 25123 |
| N46TJ | HS25 | 257104 |
| N46TJ | LJ35 | 077 |
| N46UF | ASTR | 015 |
| N46UF | LJ31 | 073 |
| N46UP | ASTR | 015 |
| N46VE | C56X | 5077 |
| N46VG | FA20 | 46 |
| N46WB | C560 | 0238 |
| N46WB | C560 | 0320 |
| N46WB | LJ24 | 133 |
| N46WC | HS25 | 257195 |
| **N46WC** | **HS25** | **259028** |
| N46WQ | HS25 | 257195 |
| **N46WY** | **ASTR** | **276** |
| N46XP | BE40 | RK-446 |
| **N47** | **GLEX** | **9160** |
| N47A | GLF2 | 71 |
| N47AJ | LJ25 | 023 |
| **N47AN** | **C650** | **0054** |
| N47BA | JSTR | 5061/48 |
| N47BA | LJ35 | 060 |
| N47BH | HS25 | 25228 |
| **N47CE** | **WW24** | **137** |
| N47CF | C500 | 634 |
| N47CG | HS25 | 258169 |
| N47CM | C650 | 0153 |
| N47DC | WW24 | 163 |
| N47DK | LJ25 | 154 |
| N47DM | WW24 | 74 |
| N47EC | GLF2 | 231 |
| (N47EG) | F900 | 14 |
| **N47EG** | **F9EX** | **154** |
| N47ES | CL60 | 1083 |
| N47EX | HS25 | 256047 |
| **N47FH** | **C525** | **0047** |
| N47GX | GALX | 018 |
| N47HC | LJ25 | 114 |
| **N47HF** | **C56X** | **5347** |
| N47HF | CL61 | 5174 |
| N47HR | CL61 | 5174 |
| N47HR | GLF2 | 30/4 |
| N47HR | GLF4 | 1195 |
| N47HR | GLF4 | 1250 |
| N47HV | HS25 | 256014 |
| N47HW | HS25 | 256014 |
| **N47HW** | **HS25** | **258023** |
| N47JE | FA20 | 189 |
| N47JF | FA20 | 189 |
| N47JK | GLF2 | 115 |
| N47JR | LJ35 | 007 |
| (N47LP) | CS55 | 0017 |
| **N47LP** | **FA20** | **457** |
| N47LP | WW24 | 411 |
| N47LR | WW24 | 411 |
| N47MJ | CS55 | 0010 |
| N47MJ | LJ25 | 004 |
| N47MM | SBRL | 306-25 |
| N47MN | SBRL | 306-9 |
| N47MR | LJ25 | 101 |
| **N47NM** | **C550** | **550-1112** |
| (N47NR) | LJ24 | 148 |
| N47PB | HS25 | 257055 |
| N47PB | MU30 | A047SA |
| **N47PW** | **C560** | **0186** |
| N47RK | FA10 | 162 |
| (N47RP) | C550 | 249 |
| **N47SE** | **SBRL** | **465-34** |
| N47SL | GLF4 | 1053 |
| **N47SM** | **C550** | **568** |
| N47SW | C550 | 444 |
| N47TH | C525 | 0047 |
| N47TH | C525 | 0119 |
| N47TJ | HS25 | 257036 |
| N47TJ | HS25 | 257040 |
| (N47TJ) | HS25 | 258139 |
| N47TJ | MU30 | A047SA |
| N47TK | LJ24 | 236 |
| **N47TL** | **C500** | **605** |
| **N47TR** | **LJ31** | **136** |
| N47TW | C550 | 477 |
| (N47TW) | C560 | 0224 |
| N47UC | JSTR | 5123/14 |
| N47UC | JSTR | 5125/31 |
| N47UF | FA50 | 28 |
| N47VC | C560 | 0304 |
| N47VC | HS25 | 258139 |
| **N47VL** | **SBRL** | **282-48** |
| (N47VP) | C525 | 0047 |
| (N47WH) | GLF2 | 180 |
| N47WS | F2EX | 145 |
| N47WT | LJ24 | 283 |
| N47WU | HS25 | 256047 |
| N47XL | C56X | 5747 |
| N48AD | FA20 | 241/479 |
| N48AH | WW24 | 288 |
| N48AJ | LJ24 | 172 |
| **N48AL** | **HS25** | **258167** |
| **N48AM** | **HS25** | **258582** |
| N48AM | LJ31 | 123 |
| N48AS | LJ24 | 088 |
| N48BA | LJ24 | 152 |
| N48BH | HS25 | 25229 |

| | | |
|---|---|---|
| N48BT | FA20 | 160/450 |
| **N48BV** | **CS55** | **0032** |
| N48CC | FA20 | 200 |
| N48CC | GLF2 | 181 |
| N48CC | GLF4 | 1363 |
| (N48CE) | SBRL | 282-75 |
| N48CG | F2TH | 41 |
| **N48CG** | **F9EX** | **212** |
| N48CG | SBRL | 282-75 |
| N48CK | BE40 | RJ-22 |
| N48CN | LJ35 | 169 |
| N48CQ | GLF2 | 181 |
| **N48CT** | **LJ24** | **274** |
| N48DA | C500 | 297 |
| N48DD | HS25 | 25115 |
| (N48DD) | HS25 | 258207 |
| **N48DK** | **C550** | **051** |
| (N48DK) | LJ35 | 171 |
| N48EC | GLF2 | 9/33 |
| **N48ES** | **LJ35** | **087** |
| **N48FB** | **F2TH** | **11** |
| N48FB | HS25 | 257129 |
| N48FJ | C500 | 547 |
| N48FN | LJ24 | 238 |
| N48FN | LJ25 | 096 |
| N48FU | CL61 | 5021 |
| N48FU | FA20 | 495 |
| **N48FW** | **C550** | **550-0948** |
| N48G | FA50 | 258 |
| N48GA | BE40 | RJ-28 |
| N48GL | FA50 | 168 |
| N48GL | FA50 | 168 |
| **N48GL** | **GLF4** | **1052** |
| N48GP | FA50 | 63 |
| N48GP | LJ35 | 069 |
| **N48GR** | **LJ25** | **048** |
| **N48GX** | **GALX** | **017** |
| N48HA | F2TH | 94 |
| N48HB | FA50 | 233 |
| N48HC | LJ55 | 012 |
| N48HC | SBRL | 306-96 |
| **N48HF** | **C750** | **0220** |
| N48HM | LJ25 | 030 |
| N48HU | FA20 | 495 |
| N48JC | FA10 | 22 |
| N48JC | FA10 | 37 |
| N48JK | GLF2 | 71 |
| N48JW | LJ24 | 236 |
| **N48KH** | **C550** | **325** |
| **N48KR** | **FA50** | **127** |
| N48KZ | LJ60 | 003 |
| **N48L** | **LJ24** | **107** |
| **N48LB** | **HS25** | **257064** |
| N48LC | C560 | 0463 |
| N48LQ | C560 | 0463 |
| **N48MF** | **BE40** | **RK-218** |
| N48MG | SBRL | 306-53 |
| N48MJ | LJ35 | 448 |
| N48MS | FA10 | 18 |
| (N48MS) | GLF2 | 83 |
| N48MW | LJ24 | 048 |
| (N48NA) | C550 | 215 |
| N48NC | F2EX | 48 |
| N48ND | C550 | 069 |
| **N48NS** | **C550** | **550-0939** |
| **N48PL** | **BE40** | **RK-138** |
| N48R | FA10 | 80 |
| N48R | FA50 | 160 |
| (N48RA) | GLF2 | 18 |
| N48RW | LJ35 | 075 |
| **N48SD** | **WW24** | **399** |
| **N48SE** | **BE40** | **RK-48** |
| N48SR | BE40 | RJ-39 |
| **N48TC** | **PRM1** | **RB-13** |
| N48TC | SBRL | 282-66 |
| N48TE | LJ45 | 248 |
| N48TF | C650 | 0176 |
| N48TF | LJ45 | 248 |
| N48TJ | FA20 | 202 |
| N48TT | C650 | 0105 |
| N48TT | FA10 | 16 |
| N48TW | FA50 | 73 |
| N48UC | HS25 | 25046 |
| N48UC | JSTR | 5125/31 |
| N48US | HS25 | 25252 |
| (N48VC) | PRM1 | RB-132 |
| **N48VE** | **C750** | **0248** |
| **N48WA** | **LJ25** | **136** |
| **N48WK** | **F2TH** | **48** |
| N48WP | SBRL | 282-59 |
| N48WS | SBRL | 282-59 |
| **N48WS** | **SBRL** | **306-124** |
| N48WW | WW24 | 384 |
| **N48Y** | **HS25** | **258009** |
| N49AJ | LJ24 | 143 |
| N49AS | FA10 | 49 |
| N49AT | LJ35 | 366 |
| N49AZ | LJ35 | 652 |
| N49BA | LJ25 | 011 |
| N49BB | LJ25 | 025 |
| N49BE | LJ35 | 192 |
| N49BH | HS25 | 25230 |
| N49BL | C500 | 633 |
| N49CJ | C525 | 0049 |
| N49CK | LJ24 | 009 |
| **N49CT** | **WW24** | **314** |
| N49DM | LJ24 | 238 |
| N49E | C500 | 017 |
| N49EA | C500 | 017 |
| N49FW | C550 | 550-0838 |
| N49FW | C550 | 550-0948 |
| **N49FW** | **C750** | **0021** |
| **N49GS** | **LJ24** | **336** |
| N49HS | C550 | 183 |
| **N49JN** | **BE40** | **RJ-3** |
| **N49KR** | **FA50** | **104** |
| N49KW | C550 | 550-0838 |
| **N49KW** | **C550** | **550-1021** |
| N49LC | C500 | 577 |
| N49LD | C560 | 0175 |
| **N49LD** | **C560** | **0803** |
| N49MJ | C560 | 0026 |
| N49MJ | C560 | 0306 |
| N49MJ | C56X | 5100 |
| N49MJ | CS55 | 0010 |
| **N49MN** | **ASTR** | **019** |
| N49MP | C500 | 519 |
| N49MU | C56X | 5100 |
| N49MW | ASTR | 019 |
| **N49MW** | **C510** | **0010** |
| N49MW | F2TH | 44 |
| (N49N) | C550 | 360 |
| N49NS | C560 | 0116 |
| (N49PD) | LJ55 | 045 |
| N49PE | LJ35 | 192 |
| N49PE | LJ55 | 045 |
| **N49PL** | **EA50** | **000255** |
| N49PP | GLF4 | 1125 |
| N49R | C500 | 072 |
| N49R | C500 | 281 |
| **N49RF** | **GLF4** | **1246** |
| **N49RJ** | **HS25** | **257007** |
| N49RJ | SBRL | 282-69 |
| N49SL | GLF4 | 1167 |
| N49SM | C650 | 0132 |
| (N49TA) | C500 | 683 |
| N49TA | WW24 | 260 |
| **N49TH** | **C525** | **0342** |
| N49TJ | C550 | 051 |
| N49TJ | LJ24 | 295 |
| N49TT | C560 | 0271 |
| **N49U** | **C550** | **091** |
| N49UC | JSTR | 5110/47 |
| N49UR | CL61 | 5016 |
| N49US | FA20 | 494 |
| N49US | GLF3 | 302 |
| N49VC | GALX | 161 |
| N49VE | C750 | 0249 |
| N49VG | HS25 | 258139 |
| (N49VP) | C550 | 170 |
| **N49WA** | **LJ25** | **142** |
| N49WC | C500 | 490 |
| **N49WL** | **LJ35** | **457** |
| N49WW | WW24 | 389 |
| N50AC | C500 | 159 |
| N50AD | FA20 | 127 |
| N50AE | FA50 | 208 |
| N50AE | FA50 | 254 |
| **N50AE** | **HS25** | **258650** |
| N50AF | LJ55 | 038 |
| N50AF | LJ55 | 059 |
| N50AH | FA50 | 111 |
| N50AJ | ASTR | 030 |
| N50AJ | ASTR | 044 |
| N50AJ | LJ24 | 037 |
| **N50AK** | **LJ35** | **172** |
| N50AL | WW24 | 190 |
| **N50AM** | **C500** | **041** |
| N50AS | C500 | 041 |
| N50AS | HS25 | 25083 |
| N50AS | JSTR | 5058/4 |
| N50AZ | C550 | 288 |
| (N50B) | FA10 | 14 |
| N50B | LJ25 | 224 |
| N50BA | LJ24 | 043 |
| N50BF | FA50 | 106 |
| N50BH | FA20 | 365 |
| **N50BH** | **GLF3** | **359** |
| N50BH | HS25 | 25233 |
| N50BK | CS55 | 0031 |
| **N50BL** | **FA50** | **2** |
| N50BL | FA50 | 66 |
| (N50BM) | CS55 | 0090 |
| N50BN | HS25 | 258142 |
| **N50BV** | **FA20** | **365** |
| N50BX | FA50 | 102 |
| N50BZ | FA50 | 80 |
| N50CA | FA20 | 28 |
| N50CC | C500 | 080 |
| N50CD | SBRL | 282-42 |
| **N50CK** | **LJ25** | **157** |
| **N50CR** | **SBRL** | **287-1** |
| N50CS | FA50 | 207 |
| N50CV | C560 | 0293 |
| N50DD | LJ35 | 256 |
| N50DD | LJ55 | 066 |
| N50DG | SBRL | 306-19 |
| (N50DG) | SBRL | 465-34 |
| N50DH | LJ25 | 079 |
| N50DM | FA10 | 41 |
| N50DM | LJ24 | 025 |
| N50DR | C560 | 0248 |
| N50DR | LJ24 | 311 |
| N50DR | WW24 | 266 |
| N50DS | C500 | 570 |
| N50DS | C650 | 0078 |
| N50DS | CL61 | 5063 |
| N50DS | CL64 | 5544 |
| N50DS | CS55 | 0031 |
| **N50DS** | **GLEX** | **9140** |
| N50DS | LJ60 | 047 |
| N50DT | LJ25 | 042 |
| N50DT | LJ36 | 004 |
| N50DW | WW24 | 380 |
| N50EB | HS25 | 25253 |
| N50EC | JSTR | 5033/56 |
| **N50EE** | **GLF4** | **1500** |
| (N50EF) | FA50 | 54 |
| **N50EF** | **MU30** | **A081SA** |
| N50EJ | C650 | 0148 |
| **N50EJ** | **EA50** | **000087** |
| N50EJ | FA50 | 3 |
| **N50EL** | **C560** | **0036** |
| N50EL | LJ60 | 158 |
| N50ET | C525 | 0251 |
| N50ET | C525 | 0476 |
| N50FB | FA50 | 6 |
| N50FC | C550 | 255 |
| N50FC | HS25 | 25253 |
| **N50FD** | **WW24** | **381** |
| N50FE | FA50 | 8 |
| **N50FF** | **FA50** | **220** |
| N50FG | FA50 | 10 |
| N50FH | FA50 | 11 |
| N50FH | FA50 | 62 |
| N50FJ | FA50 | 137 |
| N50FJ | FA50 | 153 |
| N50FJ | FA50 | 163 |
| N50FJ | FA50 | 175 |
| N50FJ | FA50 | 184 |
| N50FJ | FA50 | 188 |
| N50FJ | FA50 | 197 |
| N50FJ | FA50 | 212 |
| N50FJ | FA50 | 225 |
| N50FJ | FA50 | 227 |
| **N50FJ** | **FA50** | **236** |
| N50FJ | FA50 | 238 |
| N50FJ | FA50 | 244 |
| N50FJ | FA50 | 252 |
| N50FJ | FA50 | 254 |
| N50FJ | FA50 | 272 |
| N50FJ | FA50 | 280 |
| N50FJ | FA50 | 296 |
| N50FJ | FA50 | 3 |
| N50FJ | FA50 | 310 |
| N50FJ | FA50 | 319 |
| (N50FJ) | FA50 | 329 |
| N50FJ | FA50 | 337 |
| N50FJ | FA50 | 4 |
| N50FJ | FA50 | 65 |
| N50FJ | FA50 | 85 |
| N50FK | FA50 | 13 |
| N50FL | FA50 | 14 |
| N50FL | FA50 | 22 |
| (N50FM) | FA50 | 16 |
| N50FM | FA50 | 19 |
| N50FN | FA50 | 18 |
| **N50FN** | **LJ35** | **070** |
| N50FQ | FA50 | 310 |
| N50FR | FA50 | 20 |
| N50FS | FA50 | 22 |
| N50FT | C500 | 023 |
| **N50FX** | **FA50** | **175** |
| N50GD | HS25 | 256024 |
| N50GF | FA50 | 40 |
| (N50GG) | C550 | 042 |
| N50GG | SBRL | 380-6 |
| N50GL | LJ25 | 110 |
| **N50GP** | **C560** | **0477** |
| N50GT | C500 | 438 |
| N50GT | CS55 | 0159 |
| N50GX | GALX | 023 |
| **N50HA** | **GLF5** | **5067** |
| N50HC | FA50 | 136 |
| **N50HC** | **FA50** | **208** |
| N50HD | FA50 | 83 |
| N50HE | C550 | 168 |
| N50HE | FA50 | 7 |
| N50HE | GLF4 | 1219 |
| N50HH | HS25 | 25022 |
| **N50HM** | **FA50** | **153** |
| N50HS | C510 | 0013 |
| N50HS | C550 | 168 |
| N50HS | HS25 | 257098 |
| N50HS | WW24 | 412 |
| **N50HT** | **FA10** | **163** |
| N50HW | C550 | 139 |
| N50J | FA50 | 117 |
| N50JF | LJ24 | 011 |
| N50JF | LJ24 | 151 |
| N50JG | C500 | 579 |
| N50JM | HS25 | 257033 |
| **N50JP** | **C550** | **158** |
| N50JP | WW24 | 69 |
| N50JR | HS25 | 257159 |
| (N50K) | SBRL | 380-46 |
| **N50KC** | **GLF5** | **659** |
| **N50KD** | **FA50** | **145** |
| N50KH | BE40 | RK-59 |
| N50KP | JSTR | 5214 |
| N50KR | C500 | 629 |
| **N50KR** | **FA50** | **58** |
| N50L | LJ25 | 152 |
| N50L | LJ55 | 004 |
| **N50LB** | **F9DX** | **608** |
| N50LB | WW24 | 93 |
| N50LG | FA20 | 507 |
| N50LJ | LJ31 | 052 |
| **N50LK** | **LJ60** | **316** |
| N50LM | C550 | 441 |
| N50LQ | FA50 | 148 |
| N50LT | FA50 | 44 |
| N50LV | FA50 | 65 |
| **N50M** | **WW24** | **327** |
| N50MC | C500 | 381 |
| (N50MF) | WW24 | 384 |
| N50MG | FA20 | 507 |
| **N50MG** | **FA50** | **255** |
| N50MG | GLF4 | 1226 |
| N50MJ | HS25 | 25152 |
| N50MJ | LJ35 | 103 |
| **N50MJ** | **LJ35** | **164** |
| N50MK | FA50 | 98 |
| (N50ML) | FA50 | 98 |
| N50MM | C500 | 118 |
| N50MM | C500 | 622 |
| N50MM | FA20 | 39 |
| (N50MT) | LJ25 | 353 |
| N50MT | LJ35 | 118 |
| N50MV | FA50 | 124 |
| **N50MW** | **FA20** | **503** |
| (N50MX) | FA20 | 503 |

N50N C550 469
(N50NA) C550 376
N50NE HS25 25236
**N50NF C550 636**
N50NK FA50 218
**N50NM FA50 266**
(N50NM) JSTR 5229
N50PA CL60 1004
N50PD LJ35 409
N50PE LJ25 176
N50PG FA50 8
N50PH C650 0148
N50PH LJ35 246
N50PH LJ35 497
N50PJ LJ24 076
(N50PL) C525 0083
N50PL LJ35 246
N50PL WW24 338
N50PM GLF2 236
N50PM GLF3 333
N50PM HS25 258183
N50PM PRM1 RB-11
**N50PM PRM1 RB-80**
N50PM SBRL 380-25
**N50PN PRM1 RB-11**
N50PR C500 091
N50PS JSTR 5134/50
**N50QJ HS25 258216**
N50QJ WW24 303
**N50QN C650 0197**
N50QN C750 0239
N50QN FA50 323
N50QS HA4T RC-20
N50RD C500 260
(N50RG) F900 51
(N50RG) FA50 60
N50RL FA10 66
N50RL GLF3 479
**N50RW LJ25 135**
**N50SF FA50 180**
N50SF LJ36 010
(N50SJ) FA50 53
N50SJ FA50 80
N50SJ LJ24 246
**N50SJ SJ30 005**
N50SK C500 046
N50SK WW24 309
N50SL C500 046
(N50SL) CS55 0109
N50SL FA10 161
N50SL FA20 359/542
N50SL HS25 25187
N50SL WW24 269
**N50SN FA50 310**
N50SS HS25 25028
N50TB FA10 57
N50TC FA10 31
N50TC FA50 115
N50TC LJ24 190
N50TE FA10 86
N50TG ASTR 065
N50TG CL61 3054
**N50TG F2EX 49**
N50TG F2TH 96
N50TG FA50 117
N50TK FA10 123
N50TN HS25 257033
**N50TQ ASTR 065**
N50TR C500 325
N50TX SBRL 282-23
N50TY FA10 72
N50UD JSTR 5019
**N50UG HS25 258749**
N50US C500 424
N50US C500 527
N50US C550 032
**N50US C550 194**
N50VC C525 0609
N50VF WW24 13
N50VF WW24 137
N50VG FA50 104
**N50VM PRM1 RB-229**
(N50WB) FA50 102
N50WG FA50 189
N50WJ C500 397
N50WM C500 246
(N50WP) C500 512
**N50XJ FA50 80**
N50XL C56X 5202
N50XX C550 042
N50XX WW24 311
(N50XX) WW24 319
N50XX WW24 412
N50XX WW24 436
**N50XY FA50 83**
N50XY GLF3 412
(N50YJ) FA10 57
**N50YP FA50 344**
N51 SBRL 380-5
N51AJ LJ24 037
N51AJ LJ24 273
**N51B BE40 RK-261**
N51B C500 027
N51B LJ24 116
N51B MU30 A063SA
N51BE MU30 A063SA
N51BH HS25 25234
N51BL LJ25 269
N51BP C500 051
N51BP FA10 51
(N51BR) C500 051
**N51C C560 0084**
N51CA LJ25 030
N51CC C500 457
N51CD C525 0163
N51CG C500 457
N51CH LJ24 168
N51CH WW24 61
N51CJ C500 351
N51DB LJ25 246
N51DT LJ25 367
**N51EB BE40 RJ-28**
**N51EF C560 0487**
**N51EM C650 0030**
N51ET C500 450
**N51FE FA50 121**
N51FF GLF3 491
N51FJ FA50 24
**N51FK C560 0307**
**N51FL GLF5 646**
N51FN LJ35 059
**N51FN LJ35 069**
**N51FT C500 651**
N51FT C550 134
N51GA C500 363
(N51GJ) LJ24 224
N51GL LJ24 272
**N51GS C525 0317**
N51GY CL61 5136
N51HF C52B 0008
N51JA LJ35 296
N51JH CS55 0007
**N51JJ C52B 0068**
N51JT LJ24 283
**N51JV C650 0050**
N51KR C550 550-0951
**N51LC LJ35 302**
N51MF GLF3 491
N51MF GLF5 5100
N51MJ FA50 54
N51MJ LJ25 133
N51ML BE40 RK-22
**N51MN F2TH 14**
N51MN HS25 25190
(N51MN) SBRL 282-51
N51MN WW24 198
N51MN WW24 419
N51MW C500 085
**N51ND C560 0364**
N51NP BE40 RK-224
N51PD WW24 297
N51PS C550 365
**N51SE GLEX 9138**
N51SF FA20 12
N51TJ CL60 1066
N51TJ GLF2 10
N51TJ LJ35 183
N51TV WW24 175
**N51TV WW24 402**
**N51V FA50 189**
N51V HS25 25070
N51V LJ55 116
N51VC BE40 RK-288
N51VL LJ24 235
**N51VL LJ55 116**
N51VR CL64 5426
N51VT FA50 189
N51WP C500 528
N51XP BE40 RK-451
N52 SBRL 380-10
**N52AG C52A 0075**
N52AJ C500 061
N52AJ LJ25 102
**N52AL BE40 RJ-38**
N52AN C500 030
**N52AW BE40 RK-115**
N52BH HS25 25236
N52CC C500 352
N52CK CS55 0076
N52CK CS55 0124
N52CT LJ25 362
**N52CT LJ55 131**
N52DA LJ25 327
**N52DC F2TH 116**
N52DC FA50 126
N52DC FA50 51
N52DD LJ24 339
N52DQ FA50 126
N52DQ FA50 51
(N52EB) BE40 RJ-52
N52EN LJ24 116
N52ET C500 056
**N52ET C52B 0018**
N52FC WW24 379
N52FJ FA50 252
N52FJ FA50 26
(N52FL) LJ35 067
**N52FN LJ35 424**
N52FP C500 052
N52FT C500 056
**N52FT CS55 0056**
N52GA BE40 RJ-36
**N52GA HS25 257099**
N52GG SBRL 465-5
N52GH LJ24 197
N52GL LJ25 134
N52GW WW24 330
N52GX ASTR 129
**N52JA FA10 59**
N52JA LJ25 007
N52JH LJ24 139
N52JJ FA50 205
N52KS ASTR 033
N52KS WW24 341
N52KW C560 0256
N52L LJ25 141
N52LC HS25 257131
N52LT C525 0322
**N52LT C550 411**
N52MA C500 052
N52MJ LJ35 363
**N52MK GLF4 1337**
N52MW C550 550-0822
N52MW C56X 5144
**N52N FA10 197**
(N52NE) GLF2 52
N52NW GLF2 52
**N52PK C525 0052**
**N52PM C500 222**
**N52RF C550 011**
N52RG C560 0235
N52SD LJ25 110
**N52SM HS25 259010**
N52SM WW24 397
N52SN C560 0207
N52SY C650 0007
N52TC C500 324
N52TJ FA10 3
N52TJ FA10 52
"N52TJ" GLF2 52
N52TJ JSTR 5078/3
**N52TL C500 418**
**N52WC C52B 0319**
**N52WF C560 0528**
(N52WS) C500 110
N53 SBRL 380-14
(N53AA) WW24 56
N53AJ C500 243
N53BB C500 545
N53BH HS25 25239
N53CC C550 350
N53CG C525 0233
N53CJ C525 0053
N53CV C560 0053
N53DB FA10 41
(N53DE) LJ24 153
N53DF CL61 5078
N53DF CL61 5133
**N53DF CL64 5507**
N53DM LJ35 329
N53DS FA20 373
N53EB BE40 RJ-53
N53EZ C500 497
N53FB C500 271
**N53FJ F9EX 53**
N53FJ FA50 28
N53FJ FA50 53
**N53FL LJ25 017**
N53FN LJ35 021
N53FN LJ35 053
**N53FP C550 433**
N53FT C500 238
**N53FT C550 318**
**N53G LJ35 274**
N53G SBRL 306-57
**N53GH HS25 257164**
N53GH LJ24 151
N53GH LJ35 304
N53GL LJ24 268
N53GL LJ35 304
**N53GX GLEX 9053**
N53HF C750 0236
(N53HJ) LJ55 028
**N53HJ LJ55 037**
N53HS C680 0053
N53HS GLF5 606
N53J C500 152
N53JA LJ36 043
N53JL LJ55 060
N53JM CS55 0061
N53JM LJ35 419
N53KB C550 053
**N53KV C525 0030**
**N53LB HS25 258332**
**N53LM WW24 311**
N53M C550 442
N53M GLF4 1089
N53MJ C500 068
N53MJ C500 317
**N53MS BE40 RK-64**
N53MU GLF4 1089
**N53NW C52B 0053**
**N53PE C560 0464**
**N53PJ MS76 053**
N53RC C500 497
**N53RD C500 629**
N53RG C500 402
N53RG C550 280
N53SF ASTR 034
**N53SF C52B 0001**
N53SF FA20 102
N53SN FA10 54
N53SR CL60 1078
N53TC LJ25 305
N53TG F2TH 96
N53TS FA10 77
N53VP C550 053
N53WA FA10 53
N53WC SBRL 282-137
N53WF C550 062
**N53WF C56X 5057**
N53WW WW24 393
N53XL C56X 5351
**N53XL C56X 6053**
**N54 LJ60 009**
N54 SBRL 380-16
N54AM CS55 0085
**N54AP LJ31 220**
N54AX GALX 054
N54AX LJ45 377
(N54BC) WW24 369
N54BE MU30 A063SA
N54BH HS25 25241
N54BM GLF2 236
**N54BP C525 0002**
N54BW JSTR 5014
N54CC C550 210
**N54CF C510 0253**
N54CF SBRL 282-66
N54CG C500 677
**N54CG C525 0439**
N54CJ C525 0054

| | | |
|---|---|---|
| N54CM | C500 | 293 |
| (N54DA) | C550 | 036 |
| N54DA | FA50 | 201 |
| **N54DC** | **F2TH** | **117** |
| N54DC | F900 | 22 |
| **N54DD** | **C560** | **0089** |
| N54DS | C500 | 350 |
| N54ES | HS25 | 258134 |
| N54FH | FA10 | 203 |
| N54FJ | FA10 | 54 |
| (N54FJ) | FA50 | 31 |
| N54FJ | FA50 | 36 |
| **N54FN** | **LJ25** | **083** |
| (N54FT) | C500 | 054 |
| **N54FT** | **C500** | **485** |
| N54GD | HS25 | 256068 |
| N54GL | LJ35 | 597 |
| (N54GL) | LJ36 | 054 |
| N54GL | LJ55 | 054 |
| N54GP | LJ25 | 327 |
| N54GX | GALX | 025 |
| N54H | FA10 | 6 |
| N54H | LJ25 | 124 |
| N54HA | C56X | 5040 |
| **N54HA** | **CL30** | **20076** |
| **N54HC** | **C525** | **0157** |
| (N54HC) | C550 | 368 |
| N54HC | C650 | 0098 |
| **N54HD** | **BE40** | **RK-49** |
| N54HF | GLF3 | 459 |
| N54HF | LJ35 | 472 |
| **N54HG** | **F9EX** | **140** |
| N54HH | SBRL | 380-19 |
| N54HJ | C550 | 368 |
| **N54HP** | **BE40** | **RK-160** |
| N54HP | BE40 | RK-49 |
| **N54HT** | **LJ31** | **127** |
| N54HU | LJ25 | 124 |
| **N54J** | **F2TH** | **141** |
| N54J | FA20 | 289 |
| N54J | GLF2 | 193 |
| N54JA | LJ36 | 044 |
| N54JC | CL61 | 3031 |
| **N54JC** | **CL64** | **5347** |
| N54JC | HS25 | 25249 |
| N54JC | LJ24 | 340 |
| (N54JC) | LJ25 | 327 |
| N54JJ | FA20 | 289 |
| N54JJ | GLF2 | 193 |
| **N54JV** | **C500** | **163** |
| (N54JZ) | LJ55 | 054 |
| **N54KB** | **GLF5** | **627** |
| **N54KJ** | **EA50** | **000091** |
| (N54LZ) | LJ55 | 054 |
| N54MC | C500 | 154 |
| N54MC | LJ25 | 132 |
| N54MC | WW24 | 202 |
| N54MH | C500 | 545 |
| N54MJ | C500 | 612 |
| N54MQ | LJ25 | 132 |
| **N54NG** | **C510** | **0210** |
| N54NS | C550 | 578 |
| (N54NW) | LJ55 | 024 |
| **N54NW** | **LJ55** | **054** |
| (N54PA) | CL60 | 1081 |
| (N54PA) | CL61 | 3065 |
| **N54PA** | **LJ36** | **004** |
| N54PR | CL61 | 3054 |
| N54PR | GLF5 | 564 |
| N54PR | LJ35 | 054 |
| N54PT | WW24 | 363 |
| **N54PV** | **C510** | **0028** |
| N54RC | C550 | 241 |
| **N54RM** | **C550** | **562** |
| N54RM | MU30 | A065SA |
| N54RS | FA10 | 94 |
| N54SB | GLF4 | 1063 |
| N54SB | HS25 | 258258 |
| (N54SB) | LJ35 | 644 |
| N54SK | C500 | 054 |
| N54SK | CL60 | 1053 |
| N54SK | F900 | 76 |
| **N54SL** | **GLEX** | **9187** |
| N54SN | FA20 | 54 |
| N54SU | CL60 | 1053 |
| N54TA | LJ25 | 258 |
| N54TB | C500 | 482 |
| **N54TG** | **GLF5** | **523** |
| (N54TJ) | HS25 | 257069 |
| N54TK | BE40 | RJ-5 |
| (N54TK) | LJ35 | 254 |
| N54TN | LJ31 | 054 |
| N54TS | C500 | 293 |
| N54V | FA10 | 35 |
| **N54VS** | **CL61** | **5189** |
| N54WC | C650 | 0032 |
| N54WC | WW24 | 117 |
| N54WJ | CS55 | 0031 |
| N54WJ | FA10 | 33 |
| N54WJ | HS25 | 257007 |
| **N54XL** | **C56X** | **6054** |
| N54YP | LJ25 | 208 |
| N54YP | LJ35 | 356 |
| **N54YR** | **FA50** | **158** |
| N54YR | LJ25 | 208 |
| N54YR | LJ35 | 356 |
| **N55** | **LJ60** | **013** |
| N55 | SBRL | 380-18 |
| N55AK | C500 | 299 |
| N55AL | C550 | 049 |
| **N55AL** | **GLF5** | **5229** |
| N55AQ | LJ55 | 072 |
| N55AR | CL60 | 1044 |
| **N55AR** | **LJ55** | **105** |
| N55AS | FA50 | 214 |
| N55AS | LJ35 | 146 |
| N55AS | LJ55 | 072 |
| N55B | HS25 | 25261 |
| **N55BA** | **HS25** | **258356** |
| (N55BE) | C500 | 476 |
| (N55BE) | LJ55 | 058 |
| N55BH | C550 | 057 |
| **N55BH** | **C650** | **0041** |
| N55BH | HS25 | 25244 |
| N55BM | C500 | 606 |
| N55BP | C550 | 032 |
| N55BP | FA50 | 207 |
| N55BP | SBRL | 306-20 |
| **N55BX** | **EA50** | **000029** |
| N55CC | C550 | 055 |
| N55CD | LJ24 | 306 |
| **N55CH** | **C560** | **0240** |
| N55CJ | C500 | 355 |
| **N55CJ** | **C525** | **0298** |
| N55CJ | JSTR | 5090 |
| N55CJ | LJ36 | 003 |
| N55CR | SBRL | 370-9 |
| N55DD | LJ24 | 236 |
| N55DD | LJ25 | 296 |
| N55DG | C525 | 0044 |
| N55DG | FA10 | 207 |
| **N55DG** | **LJ45** | **058** |
| N55DG | LJ55 | 102 |
| **N55EA** | **C560** | **0055** |
| **N55EP** | **LJ45** | **336** |
| N55ES | LJ25 | 111 |
| N55F | LJ35 | 147 |
| **N55FG** | **WW24** | **267** |
| N55FJ | FA10 | 55 |
| N55FJ | FA10 | 74 |
| N55FM | C550 | 399 |
| N55FN | LJ25 | 050 |
| **N55FN** | **LJ35** | **202** |
| **N55FT** | **C500** | **009** |
| N55G | HS25 | 25141 |
| **N55G** | **HS25** | **25163** |
| N55GF | LJ55 | 052 |
| N55GH | LJ36 | 012 |
| N55GH | LJ55 | 012 |
| N55GH | LJ55 | 075 |
| (N55GJ) | GLF4 | 1500 |
| (N55GJ) | LJ55 | 078 |
| N55GJ | LJ55 | 088 |
| N55GK | LJ55 | 105 |
| N55GM | LJ55 | 075 |
| N55GM | LJ55 | 139A |
| **N55GP** | **C52B** | **0113** |
| N55GR | C500 | 217 |
| **N55GV** | **GLF5** | **515** |
| (N55GV) | GLF5 | 518 |
| N55GV | GLF5 | 545 |
| N55GV | LJ55 | 078 |
| N55GX | ASTR | 130 |
| N55GY | LJ55 | 110 |
| N55GZ | LJ55 | 083 |
| N55H | C500 | 552 |
| N55HA | C56X | 5059 |
| **N55HA** | **CL30** | **20090** |
| N55HD | C650 | 0193 |
| N55HD | LJ55 | 026 |
| (N55HD) | SBRL | 380-39 |
| N55HF | C500 | 261 |
| N55HF | C550 | 126 |
| N55HF | C650 | 0126 |
| N55HF | C650 | 0193 |
| **N55HF** | **CL61** | **5183** |
| N55HK | LJ55 | 040 |
| N55HL | C500 | 671 |
| N55HL | LJ55 | 046 |
| **N55HL** | **WW24** | **95** |
| N55HV | C560 | 0552 |
| N55HX | C56X | 5059 |
| N55HY | GLF2 | 97 |
| N55JM | MU30 | A026SA |
| N55KC | LJ25 | 046 |
| N55KC | LJ25 | 147 |
| N55KC | LJ55 | 014 |
| N55KD | LJ55 | 051 |
| N55KQ | LJ25 | 046 |
| N55KS | LJ24 | 178 |
| N55KS | LJ55 | 051 |
| N55KS | LJ60 | 029 |
| N55KS | SBRL | 370-5 |
| N55KS | SBRL | 465-5 |
| (N55KT) | C525 | 0600 |
| **N55KT** | **C52A** | **0065** |
| N55KT | C52A | 0177 |
| N55KX | LJ24 | 178 |
| N55KZ | SBRL | 370-5 |
| **N55LB** | **CL64** | **5324** |
| N55LC | C560 | 0324 |
| N55LC | FA50 | 314 |
| **N55LC** | **FA7X** | **38** |
| N55LF | C500 | 261 |
| N55LF | LJ55 | 112 |
| N55LF | LJ55 | 133 |
| N55LJ | LJ24 | 203 |
| N55LJ | LJ25 | 233 |
| N55LJ | LJ55 | 030 |
| N55LK | LJ55 | 120 |
| N55LQ | C560 | 0324 |
| N55LQ | FA50 | 314 |
| N55LS | C550 | 107 |
| N55LS | C550 | 616 |
| N55ME | FA20 | 83 |
| (N55ME) | SBRL | 282-23 |
| (N55ME) | SBRL | 306-27 |
| N55MF | LJ25 | 171 |
| (N55MF) | LJ25 | 237 |
| N55MJ | LJ24 | 203 |
| N55MJ | LJ25 | 296 |
| N55MT | C550 | 431 |
| N55MT | HS25 | 257046 |
| N55MT | SBRL | 282-112 |
| **N55MV** | **C550** | **401** |
| N55NC | JSTR | 5060 |
| N55NE | JSTR | 5155/32 |
| **N55NG** | **C56X** | **5671** |
| N55NJ | LJ24 | 162 |
| N55NM | LJ55 | 085 |
| N55NT | FA50 | 87 |
| **N55NY** | **LJ55** | **020** |
| (N55PC) | C650 | 0187 |
| N55PD | LJ25 | 105 |
| N55PG | CL60 | 1045 |
| (N55PJ) | LJ55 | 029 |
| N55PP | SBRL | 282-135 |
| N55PT | LJ25 | 171 |
| N55PX | C525 | 0285 |
| N55PZ | C525 | 0285 |
| N55RF | HS25 | 25020 |
| **N55RF** | **HS25** | **258066** |
| **N55RG** | **GLF2** | **1** |
| N55RT | LJ55 | 095 |
| **N55RZ** | **HS25** | **25262** |
| N55RZ | LJ35 | 439 |
| N55SC | C650 | 0148 |
| **N55SC** | **C650** | **7060** |
| N55SH | C500 | 315 |
| N55SJ | LJ55 | 009 |
| N55SK | C500 | 315 |
| **N55SK** | **C525** | **0063** |
| N55SL | LJ25 | 219 |
| N55SN | FA50 | 189 |
| **N55SQ** | **BE40** | **RK-60** |
| N55SQ | C650 | 0148 |
| N55SR | CL60 | 1055 |
| N55SX | C550 | 065 |
| **N55TD** | **GLF4** | **1131** |
| N55TH | FA20 | 17 |
| **N55TJ** | **EA50** | **000208** |
| N55TK | C500 | 682 |
| N55TP | C550 | 286 |
| "N55TS" | HS25 | 257046 |
| N55TY | F9EX | 25 |
| N55UH | GLF5 | 5028 |
| (N55UJ) | LJ55 | 050 |
| **N55UJ** | **LJ55** | **090** |
| N55UK | LJ55 | 147 |
| N55V | LJ25 | 185 |
| **N55VC** | **LJ55** | **130** |
| N55VK | LJ55 | 078 |
| N55VL | LJ25 | 176 |
| **N55VR** | **LJ31** | **033C** |
| **N55VY** | **LJ31** | **040** |
| N55WG | C500 | 604 |
| N55WH | C500 | 426 |
| N55WJ | LJ25 | 017 |
| **N55WL** | **C550** | **155** |
| N55XR | LJ40 | 45-2055 |
| N55ZM | SBRL | 306-84 |
| (N55ZT) | LJ55 | 139A |
| **N56** | **LJ60** | **033** |
| N56 | SBRL | 380-20 |
| N56AG | ASTR | 043 |
| N56AG | GALX | 011 |
| N56AG | GLF4 | 1125 |
| N56AG | WW24 | 133 |
| N56AG | WW24 | 201 |
| N56AG | WW24 | 374 |
| N56AZ | WW24 | 133 |
| N56BE | BE40 | RK-13 |
| **N56BE** | **HS25** | **258527** |
| N56BH | HS25 | 25237 |
| N56BL | HS25 | 25201 |
| **N56BP** | **WW24** | **268** |
| N56BX | BE40 | RK-13 |
| N56CC | FA20 | 313 |
| N56CC | FA20 | 387 |
| (N56CJ) | C500 | 495 |
| N56D | GLF2 | 257/17 |
| **N56D** | **GLF4** | **1309** |
| N56D | GLF4 | 1411 |
| N56DR | LJ24 | 311 |
| N56DV | C500 | 346 |
| N56EL | F2EX | 69 |
| **N56EL** | **F2EX** | **71** |
| **N56EM** | **LJ35** | **144** |
| (N56EP) | C560 | 0056 |
| N56EX | F2EX | 56 |
| N56FB | C550 | 391 |
| **N56FE** | **C56X** | **5250** |
| N56FF | BE40 | RK-56 |
| N56FJ | FA50 | 33 |
| N56FT | C550 | 429 |
| N56GA | BE40 | RJ-50 |
| **N56GA** | **C560** | **0259** |
| (N56GH) | LJ24 | 233 |
| N56GT | C550 | 152 |
| N56GT | C560 | 0091 |
| N56GX | GALX | 026 |
| N56HA | C56X | 5063 |
| N56HA | CL30 | 20105 |
| N56HF | LJ35 | 084 |
| N56HF | LJ35 | 144 |
| **N56HX** | **C56X** | **5063** |
| N56JA | LJ35 | 342 |
| N56JV | C650 | 0056 |
| N56K | C525 | 0005 |
| N56K | C560 | 0463 |
| N56K | C56X | 5014 |
| **N56KP** | **C525** | **0629** |
| N56L | GLF3 | 302 |
| **N56L** | **GLF4** | **1213** |
| N56LA | GLF3 | 302 |
| N56LB | LJ24 | 178 |
| N56LC | FA50 | 275 |
| **N56LF** | **LJ31** | **056** |
| **N56LN** | **FA50** | **79** |
| **N56LP** | **C56X** | **5068** |
| N56LP | FA10 | 165 |
| N56LS | LJ24 | 178 |

| | | |
|---|---|---|
| **N56LT** | **FA50** | **21** |
| **N56LW** | **C500** | **620** |
| N56MC | C500 | 386 |
| N56MC | C500 | 620 |
| N56MC | MU30 | A069SA |
| N56MD | GLF4 | 1411 |
| **N56MD** | **LJ25** | **214** |
| N56MJ | C500 | 614 |
| **N56MK** | **C500** | **386** |
| **N56MM** | **LJ24** | **332** |
| N56MT | C500 | 386 |
| N56NW | SBRL | 465-62 |
| N56NZ | C525 | 0056 |
| **N56PA** | **LJ36** | **023** |
| **N56PB** | **C500** | **625** |
| N56PB | LJ35 | 224 |
| N56PC | C550 | 441 |
| N56PR | JSTR | 5211 |
| (N56PR) | LJ24 | 028 |
| (N56PR) | LJ35 | 370 |
| **N56PT** | **LJ24** | **276** |
| N56RD | LJ24 | 286 |
| N56RN | SBRL | 306-122 |
| N56S | WW24 | 96 |
| (N56SK) | MU30 | A008SA |
| N56SL | FA20 | 305 |
| N56SN | FA50 | 216 |
| **N56TE** | **C560** | **0755** |
| N56TG | LJ55 | 078 |
| **N56UH** | **GLF5** | **5158** |
| N56VG | FA20 | 50 |
| N56WD | LJ45 | 019 |
| **N56WE** | **C500** | **426** |
| N56WH | WW24 | 96 |
| N56WJ | FA10 | 56 |
| N56WS | LJ24 | 243 |
| **N57** | **LJ60** | **039** |
| N57 | SBRL | 380-22 |
| N57AJ | C550 | 100 |
| **N57AY** | **HS25** | **257156** |
| N57B | BE40 | RK-36 |
| N57B | FA50 | 57 |
| N57B | LJ55 | 020 |
| N57BC | C550 | 478 |
| N57BC | LJ24 | 277 |
| **N57BE** | **WW24** | **428** |
| N57BG | GLF2 | 61 |
| N57BH | HS25 | 25245 |
| **N57BJ** | **CS55** | **0052** |
| N57BJ | GLF3 | 327 |
| N57CE | C550 | 198 |
| N57CE | C560 | 0048 |
| N57CE | C650 | 0178 |
| **N57CJ** | **CS55** | **0057** |
| N57CK | C550 | 198 |
| N57CK | LJ25 | 157 |
| N57CN | C560 | 0048 |
| N57DB | LJ24 | 286 |
| N57DC | FA50 | 119 |
| N57DL | LJ25 | 334 |
| N57DM | LJ25 | 107 |
| **N57EC** | **C525** | **0460** |
| N57EJ | C52A | 0057 |
| **N57EL** | **F2EX** | **69** |
| N57EL | F900 | 153 |
| N57EL | F9EX | 111 |
| N57EL | FA50 | 205 |
| **N57FC** | **C500** | **636** |
| N57FF | HS25 | 258033 |
| N57FF | LJ35 | 015 |
| N57FF | LJ35 | 157 |
| N57FJ | FA50 | 35 |
| **N57FL** | **C52A** | **0198** |
| N57FL | LJ24 | 243 |
| N57FM | LJ55 | 025 |
| N57FP | LJ35 | 157 |
| N57G | HS25 | 25098 |
| (N57GH) | C525 | 0149 |
| N57GH | C52A | 0019 |
| N57GL | LJ35 | 057 |
| N57GS | SBRL | 282-2 |
| N57GX | ASTR | 131 |
| N57HA | C56X | 5068 |
| **N57HA** | **CL30** | **20115** |
| N57HA | CL61 | 5010 |
| N57HC | C525 | 0157 |
| N57HC | C52A | 0060 |
| **N57HC** | **C52A** | **0098** |

| | | |
|---|---|---|
| **N57HE** | **GLF2** | **194** |
| N57HG | C52A | 0098 |
| N57HH | FA20 | 74 |
| N57HJ | GLF2 | 194 |
| **N57HJ** | **GLF4** | **1261** |
| (N57HK) | CL61 | 5010 |
| N57HX | C56X | 5068 |
| N57JF | FA20 | 192 |
| (N57JR) | LJ24 | 215 |
| **N57KW** | **C56X** | **5214** |
| N57LC | C500 | 309 |
| **N57LE** | **GLEX** | **9230** |
| **N57LL** | **C500** | **025** |
| N57LN | HS25 | 258204 |
| N57MB | C500 | 287 |
| N57MB | C550 | 044 |
| N57MB | C550 | 343 |
| N57MB | C560 | 0286 |
| N57MB | CS55 | 0054 |
| N57MC | C500 | 636 |
| **N57MC** | **C550** | **550-1053** |
| N57MF | C550 | 137 |
| **N57MH** | **CL61** | **3054** |
| N57MH | LJ55 | 113 |
| N57MJ | C500 | 624 |
| N57MK | C550 | 137 |
| N57MK | C560 | 0145 |
| N57MK | C560 | 0535 |
| **N57MK** | **FA50** | **197** |
| N57ML | C560 | 0145 |
| (N57ML) | C560 | 0535 |
| N57MN | F2EX | 50 |
| **N57MQ** | **SBRL** | **465-11** |
| **N57MV** | **LJ55** | **113** |
| (N57NB) | LJ24 | 145 |
| N57ND | LJ24 | 145 |
| N57NP | GLF3 | 340 |
| N57NP | JSTR | 5123/14 |
| N57NR | JSTR | 5123/14 |
| N57PM | HS25 | 258218 |
| N57PM | LJ55 | 025 |
| **N57PT** | **WW24** | **208** |
| (N57QR) | SBRL | 282-3 |
| N57RL | C56X | 5247 |
| N57RM | SBRL | 282-41 |
| **N57SF** | **C550** | **366** |
| N57ST | C560 | 0383 |
| N57TA | LJ55 | 010 |
| (N57TA) | LJ55 | 011 |
| **N57TP** | **C56X** | **5261** |
| (N57TS) | HS25 | 25035 |
| **N57TS** | **LJ31** | **236** |
| N57TT | C650 | 0046 |
| N57TT | FA20 | 501 |
| N57TT | GLF3 | 471 |
| N57TW | C500 | 624 |
| **N57UH** | **GLF5** | **5163** |
| (N57VP) | C560 | 0007 |
| **N57WP** | **C56X** | **5317** |
| N57WW | WW24 | 390 |
| **N58** | **LJ60** | **057** |
| N58 | SBRL | 380-24 |
| **N58AJ** | **GLF3** | **446** |
| (N58AN) | C500 | 018 |
| N58AN | C550 | 036 |
| N58AS | FA10 | 58 |
| N58AS | LJ55 | 072 |
| N58AU | BE40 | RJ-14 |
| N58AU | BE40 | RJ-45 |
| (N58B) | FA10 | 92 |
| (N58BD) | C500 | 549 |
| N58BH | C550 | 057 |
| N58BH | HS25 | 25261 |
| **N58BL** | **HS25** | **258236** |
| N58BL | LJ24 | 268 |
| (N58BT) | C500 | 100 |
| N58BT | C500 | 375 |
| N58BT | C500 | 625 |
| N58BT | HS25 | 25023 |
| N58CC | C500 | 015 |
| **N58CG** | **F9EX** | **47** |
| N58CG | JSTR | 5014 |
| N58CG | LJ55 | 124 |
| N58CG | SBRL | 306-42 |
| N58CM | SBRL | 465-70 |
| N58CP | LJ25 | 133 |
| N58CQ | LJ55 | 124 |
| N58CW | LJ35 | 015 |

| | | |
|---|---|---|
| **N58CW** | **LJ35** | **116** |
| N58DJ | LJ25 | 328 |
| N58DM | LJ24 | 184 |
| (N58DT) | C500 | 375 |
| **N58EH** | **EA50** | **000171** |
| **N58EM** | **LJ35** | **046** |
| N58FB | WW24 | 258 |
| **N58FE** | **C56X** | **5285** |
| N58FF | LJ35 | 015 |
| N58FJ | FA50 | 38 |
| N58FM | LJ55 | 085 |
| **N58FN** | **LJ24** | **184** |
| N58GG | C550 | 269 |
| N58GL | LJ25 | 148 |
| N58GL | LJ35 | 599 |
| N58GX | ASTR | 135 |
| N58H | C550 | 335 |
| N58HA | C56X | 5099 |
| **N58HA** | **CL30** | **20146** |
| N58HC | C650 | 0091 |
| **N58HC** | **LJ25** | **341** |
| N58HK | C550 | 550-1086 |
| **N58HT** | **SBRL** | **465-70** |
| **N58HX** | **C56X** | **5099** |
| (N58JA) | LJ25 | 007 |
| **N58JF** | **GLF2** | **65** |
| N58JM | SBRL | 306-24 |
| **N58JN** | **C525** | **0607** |
| **N58JV** | **C52B** | **0270** |
| N58KJ | C525 | 0005 |
| N58KJ | C560 | 0463 |
| (N58KJ) | C56X | 5014 |
| N58KS | SBRL | 370-5 |
| N58LC | C550 | 711 |
| N58LC | C56X | 5109 |
| **N58LC** | **CL30** | **20163** |
| **N58LQ** | **C56X** | **5109** |
| N58M | LJ35 | 037 |
| N58M | LJ55 | 077 |
| **N58MM** | **LJ35** | **261** |
| N58PL | C500 | 033 |
| N58PM | HS25 | 258220 |
| N58PM | LJ55 | 085 |
| N58RG | C560 | 0422 |
| N58RW | C650 | 0006 |
| N58RW | LJ35 | 133 |
| **N58SR** | **LJ55** | **058** |
| **N58ST** | **LJ60** | **186** |
| (N58T) | C500 | 397 |
| N58TC | C500 | 261 |
| N58TJ | MU30 | A030SA |
| N58TS | JSTR | 5079/33 |
| **N58WV** | **C550** | **550-0896** |
| N58WW | WW24 | 201 |
| N58XL | C56X | 5099 |
| **N58XL** | **C56X** | **6058** |
| **N59** | **LJ60** | **080** |
| N59 | SBRL | 380-26 |
| N59AC | JSTR | 5204 |
| "N59AC" | LJ25 | 100 |
| N59AJ | GLF3 | 413 |
| **N59AL** | **LJ24** | **236** |
| N59AP | GLF4 | 1476 |
| N59AP | WW24 | 398 |
| N59B | C650 | 0191 |
| N59BH | HS25 | 25262 |
| N59BL | LJ25 | 201 |
| N59BP | BE40 | RK-226 |
| N59BP | LJ25 | 124 |
| N59BR | BE40 | RK-226 |
| N59BR | HS25 | 258425 |
| **N59BR** | **HS25** | **258599** |
| N59CC | C500 | 488 |
| N59CC | C550 | 430 |
| (N59CC) | C650 | 0211 |
| N59CC | FA10 | 6 |
| N59CD | C650 | 0079 |
| N59CD | GLF2 | 190 |
| N59CD | JSTR | 5155/32 |
| N59CF | F900 | 98 |
| N59CF | FA50 | 209 |
| **N59CF** | **GLF4** | **4097** |
| N59CH | FA50 | 209 |
| **N59CJ** | **C52A** | **0059** |
| N59CL | C500 | 173 |
| N59CT | WW24 | 96 |
| **N59DF** | **C560** | **0098** |
| N59DM | LJ35 | 205 |

| | | |
|---|---|---|
| **N59DY** | **C550** | **334** |
| **N59EC** | **C56X** | **5123** |
| N59EC | CS55 | 0034 |
| N59EL | FA50 | 205 |
| N59FA | C550 | 334 |
| N59FD | LJ60 | 084 |
| (N59FJ) | CL61 | 5001 |
| N59FJ | FA50 | 39 |
| N59FL | LJ25 | 169 |
| N59FN | LJ35 | 205 |
| **N59FT** | **C650** | **0123** |
| N59FY | C550 | 334 |
| **N59GB** | **C550** | **377** |
| N59GL | LJ24 | 286 |
| N59GL | LJ35 | 604 |
| N59GS | FA50 | 36 |
| N59GS | LJ55 | 056 |
| N59GU | C550 | 340 |
| N59GX | GALX | 035 |
| N59HA | C560 | 0457 |
| N59HA | GLF3 | 397 |
| **N59HJ** | **LJ55** | **027** |
| N59JC | WW24 | 59 |
| N59JG | LJ24 | 221 |
| N59JM | SBRL | 306-135 |
| N59JN | C525 | 0607 |
| **N59JN** | **C52A** | **0407** |
| N59JR | GLF2 | 190 |
| N59JR | GLF4 | 1007 |
| N59JR | HS25 | 256065 |
| N59K | SBRL | 282-36 |
| **N59K** | **SBRL** | **306-82** |
| **N59KC** | **C560** | **0363** |
| N59KC | WW24 | 210 |
| N59KG | C560 | 0363 |
| **N59KG** | **C560** | **0563** |
| N59KQ | SBRL | 282-36 |
| N59LB | F900 | 51 |
| N59LJ | LJ55 | 059 |
| **N59LW** | **C510** | **0213** |
| **N59MA** | **C500** | **398** |
| N59MJ | C550 | 033 |
| N59MJ | LJ35 | 389 |
| **N59NH** | **C560** | **0139** |
| N59PC | C500 | 418 |
| N59PK | SBRL | 282-36 |
| N59PM | FA50 | 178 |
| N59PT | WW24 | 202 |
| **N59PT** | **WW24** | **391** |
| **N59PW** | **E50P** | **50000081** |
| (N59RK) | PRM1 | RB-163 |
| N59SG | LJ25 | 163 |
| N59SM | WW24 | 390 |
| N59SR | SBRL | 465-59 |
| **N59TF** | **C560** | **0422** |
| N59TJ | FA10 | 14 |
| (N59TJ) | HS25 | 257073 |
| N59TJ | MU30 | A004SA |
| N59TS | C500 | 160 |
| **N59VM** | **C510** | **0181** |
| N59WK | WW24 | 243 |
| N59WP | C500 | 498 |
| **N59ZZ** | **GLEX** | **9366** |
| N60 | SBRL | 380-28 |
| N60AC | GLF3 | 424 |
| N60AE | C560 | 0343 |
| N60AE | C560 | 0561 |
| N60AF | C650 | 0136 |
| N60AF | SBRL | 306-140 |
| N60AG | C56X | 5255 |
| N60AG | GLF3 | 376 |
| N60AG | SBRL | 306-132 |
| (N60AG) | SBRL | 306-14 |
| N60AG | SBRL | 306-48 |
| N60AH | SBRL | 306-43 |
| N60AJ | ASTR | 042 |
| N60AJ | ASTR | 061 |
| N60AJ | ASTR | 071 |
| N60AL | WW24 | 193 |
| (N60AM) | HS25 | 25142 |
| N60AM | SBRL | 306-135 |
| N60AN | LJ60 | 099 |
| N60AR | C550 | 144 |
| N60AV | WW24 | 254 |
| N60B | BE40 | RK-33 |
| N60B | HS25 | 25195 |
| N60B | MU30 | A045SA |
| N60BB | C550 | 234 |

N60BC JSTR 5116
**N60BC LJ60 105**
N60BD HS25 25195
N60BE C650 0112
N60BK SBRL 306-15
N60BP SBRL 306-91
**N60BT WW24 432**
N60CC C550 034
N60CC GLF2 142
N60CD WW24 44
N60CE LJ60 069
N60CE SBRL 465-5
N60CH JSTR 5037/24
N60CN FA50 79
N60CN JSTR 5037/24
**N60CP C510 0064**
N60CP C510 0121
N60CR SBRL 306-7
N60CT CL64 5325
N60CT GLF2 113
N60CT GLF3 454
(N60DD) FA20 479
N60DD SBRL 306-127
N60DE SBRL 306-25
N60DG WW24 364
N60DH LJ24 033
N60DK LJ25 092
N60DK LJ25 231
N60DK LJ25 245
(N60DK) LJ25 250
N60DK LJ35 394
**N60DK LJ35 505**
N60DL SBRL 306-25
N60E LJ55 106
(N60EE) JSTR 5160
**N60EF MU30 A070SA**
N60EL SBRL 306-13
N60EL SBRL 306-42
N60ES C525 0053
**N60EW C500 665**
N60EX F9EX 60
(N60EX) SBRL 306-37
N60EX SBRL 306-7
N60FC CL61 5062
N60FC FA10 25
**N60FE LJ60 003**
**N60FJ C550 018**
N60FJ FA50 41
**N60FK F2EX 158**
N60FN LJ24 339
N60FS SBRL 306-101
**N60FT C550 470**
N60GF C550 574
**N60GF LJ60 077**
N60GG C500 380
N60GG CL61 5007
N60GG GLF2 108
N60GG LJ60 017
N60GH SBRL 306-7
N60GL C550 574
N60GL C560 0187
N60GL C56X 5014
N60GL LJ24 260
N60GN GLF3 392
**N60GS C510 0247**
**N60GT MS76 008**
N60GU GLF2 150
N60GX GALX 028
N60GX GLEX 9126
N60HC SBRL 306-21
**N60HD HS25 258334**
N60HJ CL60 1058
N60HJ GLF2 119/22
N60HJ HS25 257057
N60HM FA10 199
**N60HM LJ60 067**
N60HS LJ60 225
N60HU HS25 25103
(N60HU) HS25 257057
(N60HW) C550 377
N60JC HS25 25174
**N60JC SBRL 306-51**
N60JD C550 259
N60JF SBRL 306-33
N60JM HS25 257036
N60JM JSTR 5213
N60JN SBRL 306-14
N60JP WW24 320
N60KF LJ60 059
N60KH LJ60 272
**N60KJ LJ60 005**
**N60KM C560 0453**
N60KR CL61 5073
N60LE LJ60 354
N60LH LJ60 113
N60LJ LJ60 003
N60LJ LJ60 026
N60LJ LJ60 071
N60LJ LJ60 081
N60LJ LJ60 110
N60LJ LJ60 164
N60LJ LJ60 217
N60LJ LJ60 283
N60LJ LJ60 320
N60LJ LJ60 337
N60LJ LJ60 374
N60LR LJ60 036
N60LR LJ60 056
N60LR LJ60 094
N60LR LJ60 125
N60LR LJ60 177
N60LT LJ55 060
**N60LW C550 550-1129**
N60MB FA10 15
N60ME PRM1 RB-9
**N60MG LJ60 042**
N60MJ LJ55 060
N60ML SBRL 306-129
N60MM C550 192
**N60MN LJ60 100**
N60MP C500 325
N60MS C500 170
N60MS CL61 3051
N60MS HS25 257014
N60MU CL61 3051
N60ND FA10 21
**N60ND LJ55 088**
N60NF C560 0562
N60NS C560 0258
N60NY GLF4 1132
N60PC HS25 25214
N60PC LJ45 109
**N60PC LJ45 351**
N60PE GLF4 1251
N60PL C650 7056
N60PM HS25 258187
N60PM SBRL 370-7
N60PR C500 549
N60PT GLF4 1251
N60PT GLF4 1379
N60PT SBRL 370-7
N60QA HS25 25214
**N60QB C560 0087**
N60QG LJ24 025
N60QJ HS25 258217
N60QJ JSTR 5039
N60QJ WW24 302
N60RB SBRL 282-68
N60RC SBRL 282-134
N60RD C560 0244
N60RE F900 75
N60RE HS25 25232
N60RL LJ60 136
**N60RL LJ60 278**
(N60RL) SBRL 306-18
N60RS SBRL 306-110
N60RS SBRL 306-124
N60RS SBRL 306-132
N60RS SBRL 306-142
N60RS SBRL 306-44
N60RS SBRL 306-87
**N60RU LJ60 136**
(N60RV) ASTR 063
N60RV WW24 250
N60RY LJ60 108
N60S C560 0066
N60S CL60 1030
**N60SB CL30 20019**
N60SB LJ60 023
N60SE LJ60 293
N60SE SBRL 306-100
N60SH C560 0106
N60SJ SJ30 006
N60SL FA10 189
N60SL SBRL 306-126
N60SL SBRL 306-137
N60SL SBRL 306-145
N60SL SBRL 306-82
N60SL SBRL 306-86
N60SL SBRL 380-60
N60SM FA20 24
N60SM JSTR 5161/43
N60SN FA20 24
N60SN LJ60 267
**N60SQ SBRL 306-109**
**N60SR LJ60 023**
N60T LJ60 011
(N60TA) GLF2 241
**N60TC F2TH 80**
N60TC HS25 258179
N60TF SBRL 306-114
N60TG HS25 258179
N60TG LJ60 225
N60TG SBRL 306-86
**N60TL F900 75**
N60TM SBRL 306-72
N60TN HS25 257036
N60TX LJ60 097
N60UJ JSTR 5086/44
N60UJ LJ60 007
N60UK LJ60 004
N60VE LJ60 006
N60VE LJ60 222
N60VL LJ60 006
**N60WA LJ55 129**
**N60WL LJ35 382**
(N60WL) SBRL 282-61
N60WM LJ60 045
(N60WP) SBRL 380-39
N60XL LJ55 001
**N60XL LJ60 55-001**
N60XR LJ60 294
**N60XR LJ60 358**
"N60XR" LJ60 367
N60Y SBRL 282-26
N60Y SBRL 306-13
N60YC LJ60 267
N60ZD LJ60 166
N61 SBRL 380-29
N61AF CL61 3008
N61AW LJ24 323
N61BA LJ24 246
N61BE C650 0129
N61BL HS25 25095
(N61BP) C500 051
N61BP FA10 102
(N61BP) FA10 92
N61BR C500 051
N61CD C500 545
N61CF C550 335
N61CJ C525 0061
N61CK C550 259
**N61CK C650 0150**
N61CK LJ24 119
N61CP BE40 RK-402
N61CT HS25 258108
(N61CV) C525 0261
**N61DF C680 0012**
N61DF HS25 258386
N61DF SBRL 306-131
N61DF SBRL 465-59
N61DM LJ24 224
N61DN HS25 258386
N61DP LJ60 122
N61DT C500 569
**N61DT EA50 000192**
N61EP C510 0105
N61EW LJ25 161
**N61FB SBRL 306-80**
N61FC FA10 194
(N61FC) SBRL 282-42
N61FJ FA50 42
(N61FN) LJ24 224
N61GA MU30 A045SA
**N61GB BE40 RK-341**
(N61GF) HS25 257098
"N61GV" GLF5 509
N61GX GALX 029
N61HA C550 335
N61HA C560 0295
**N61HT C550 229**
N61JB C560 0273
**N61JE ASTR 112**
N61KB C750 0021
**N61KM C560 0255**
**N61KT C680 0229**
N61KW F2TH 137
N61LA GLF4 1266
N61LF C510 0299
N61LH GLF2 61
N61LL FA20 244
**N61MA C550 203**
N61MD SBRL 306-3
N61MJ C500 180
N61MS HS25 25229
N61MS HS25 25263
N61MX HS25 25229
N61PM FA20 355
N61PR C500 639
N61RH SBRL 282-27
N61RS WW24 384
N61SB HS25 256002
N61SF LJ24 346
**N61SH C525 0095**
N61SJ LJ35 488
**N61SJ LJ55 081**
N61SM BE40 RK-60
N61SM GLF2 122
(N61TF) C525 0118
N61TF HS25 256039
N61TJ FA10 41
N61TJ GLF2 256
(N61TJ) LJ24 241
**N61TL C560 0461**
N61TL CS55 0109
N61TS F900 13
N61TS HS25 256001
N61TS LJ24 029
N61TW C560 0019
**N61VC BE40 RK-450**
N61VE LJ60 224
N61WE GLF2 48/29
N61WH GLF2 48/29
**N61WH GLF4 1075**
(N61WT) LJ25 265
N61WT LJ25 288
N61XP BE40 RK-461
N61YC LJ60 011
**N61YP C525 0237**
N61ZZ LJ60 128
N62 SBRL 380-31
N62BH HS25 25263
N62BL CL60 1062
N62BR C500 093
N62BX LJ60 062
N62CB GLF2 208
N62CF SBRL 306-62
N62CH HS25 25221
N62CH MU30 A082SA
**N62CR C560 0188**
**N62DK LJ25 356**
N62DK LJ35 231
N62DM LJ24 194
**N62DM LJ25 082**
(N62DW) SBRL 306-41
N62EA HS25 257062
N62FJ F900 62
N62FJ FA50 44
N62FJ FA7X 62
(N62FN) LJ24 194
N62GA C560 0058
N62GB C56X 5086
N62GB C56X 5207
N62GB GALX 117
N62GB GALX 175
N62GC C550 482
N62GG GLF3 302
N62GL LJ55 062
N62GR C56X 5207
**N62GX GALX 031**
N62HA C550 231
N62HA C560 0189
N62HB C500 213
**N62HM FA50 243**
N62K GLF2 93
N62K JSTR 5099/5
N62K SBRL 282-53
N62KK JSTR 5099/5
N62KM BE40 RK-53
N62LW PRM1 RB-92
**N62MB LJ35 282**
N62ML GLF5 605

| | | |
|---|---|---|
| N62MS | CL61 | 3050 |
| N62MS | GLF4 | 1248 |
| **N62MS** | **GLF5** | **5017** |
| N62MS | GLF5 | 605 |
| N62MS | HS25 | 257017 |
| N62MU | CL61 | 3050 |
| **N62MW** | **GLF3** | **484** |
| N62ND | WW24 | 379 |
| N62NR | SBRL | 380-54 |
| N62NS | CS55 | 0072 |
| **N62NW** | **F900** | **157** |
| **N62PG** | **LJ36** | **031** |
| N62Q | SBRL | 282-53 |
| **N62RC** | **EA50** | **000043** |
| N62RG | C500 | 601 |
| N62RG | C550 | 639 |
| (N62SG) | C56X | 5253 |
| N62SH | C525 | 0423 |
| **N62SH** | **C52B** | **0002** |
| N62TC | HS25 | 25261 |
| N62TC | HS25 | 258239 |
| N62TF | HS25 | 25232 |
| N62TJ | FA10 | 44 |
| N62TJ | HS25 | 25023 |
| **N62TL** | **C550** | **462** |
| N62TW | C500 | 281 |
| N62TW | HS25 | 25224 |
| N62VE | C750 | 0004 |
| N62WA | C550 | 583 |
| N62WA | C560 | 0360 |
| **N62WA** | **C560** | **0758** |
| N62WB | GLF2 | 152 |
| **N62WD** | **C560** | **0360** |
| N62WG | C550 | 482 |
| N62WH | HS25 | 257125 |
| N62WL | HS25 | 257125 |
| N62WM | LJ35 | 596 |
| N62XR | LJ60 | 362 |
| N62YC | F2EX | 119 |
| N62ZS | LJ25 | 162 |
| N63 | SBRL | 380-33 |
| N63A | FA50 | 19 |
| N63A | SBRL | 282-36 |
| **N63AD** | **EA50** | **000163** |
| **N63AX** | **LJ55** | **063** |
| N63BA | FA10 | 99 |
| N63BH | HS25 | 25265 |
| N63BL | HS25 | 25033 |
| N63BL | LJ60 | 051 |
| N63BW | LJ24 | 353 |
| N63CC | C550 | 489 |
| N63CF | C500 | 097 |
| N63CG | C500 | 519 |
| N63CK | LJ24 | 119 |
| **N63CR** | **C680** | **0122** |
| N63CR | CS55 | 0036 |
| N63DH | LJ35 | 261 |
| N63DR | MU30 | A067SA |
| **N63EM** | **HS25** | **25272** |
| N63ET | LJ25 | 110 |
| **N63FF** | **C560** | **0063** |
| N63FJ | FA50 | 45 |
| N63FJ | FA50 | 63 |
| (N63FS) | C550 | 321 |
| **N63FT** | **C56X** | **5541** |
| **N63GA** | **LJ24** | **241** |
| N63GB | C560 | 0454 |
| N63GC | C650 | 0179 |
| N63GH | MU30 | A025SA |
| N63HA | C560 | 0199 |
| **N63HA** | **CS55** | **0119** |
| N63HB | C525 | 0019 |
| N63HJ | CL60 | 1021 |
| N63HS | GLF4 | 1249 |
| **N63HS** | **GLF5** | **5013** |
| N63HS | GLF5 | 606 |
| **N63JG** | **C560** | **0189** |
| N63JG | CS55 | 0036 |
| **N63JT** | **CS55** | **0156** |
| N63JU | CS55 | 0036 |
| N63KH | LJ25 | 287 |
| N63LB | C525 | 0127 |
| N63LB | C550 | 550-0920 |
| N63LE | LJ35 | 250 |
| **N63LF** | **C525** | **0127** |
| N63LF | LJ35 | 250 |
| N63LX | C56X | 5163 |
| N63LX | C680 | 0084 |
| "N63M" | GLF4 | 1022 |
| N63M | GLF4 | 1152 |
| N63MJ | LJ45 | 055 |
| **N63MU** | **GLF4** | **1152** |
| N63NC | SBRL | 306-7 |
| **N63NW** | **C550** | **550-1119** |
| N63PM | FA20 | 355 |
| N63PM | HS25 | 257167 |
| N63PM | HS25 | 258183 |
| N63PP | WW24 | 394 |
| N63SB | LJ25 | 073 |
| N63SD | GLF2 | 216 |
| N63SE | LJ31 | 203 |
| N63SL | SBRL | 282-127 |
| N63ST | CL61 | 5149 |
| N63TJ | FA10 | 186 |
| N63TM | C550 | 457 |
| N63TM | C560 | 0383 |
| **N63TM** | **C680** | **0019** |
| N63TS | FA10 | 66 |
| **N63WR** | **LJ45** | **278** |
| **N63XG** | **FA10** | **103** |
| **N63XP** | **BE40** | **RK-563** |
| N64 | SBRL | 380-35 |
| **N64AH** | **WW24** | **94** |
| (N64AJ) | C500 | 085 |
| N64AL | GLF4 | 1013 |
| N64AM | FA10 | 157 |
| N64AM | SBRL | 306-7 |
| N64BD | F900 | 16 |
| N64BE | F900 | 45 |
| **N64BH** | **C500** | **673** |
| N64BH | CL61 | 5027 |
| N64BH | HS25 | 25267 |
| N64C | JSTR | 5131 |
| N64CA | C550 | 030 |
| N64CE | LJ24 | 205 |
| N64CF | LJ24 | 205 |
| **N64CF** | **LJ35** | **461** |
| N64CM | C550 | 467 |
| N64CM | SBRL | 306-135 |
| **N64CP** | **LJ35** | **264** |
| (N64DH) | LJ35 | 119 |
| **N64DH** | **SBRL** | **282-52** |
| **N64EX** | **F2EX** | **164** |
| N64EZ | MU30 | A062SA |
| (N64EZ) | MU30 | A090SA |
| N64F | CL61 | 5021 |
| N64F | FA10 | 188 |
| N64FC | CL60 | 1035 |
| N64FE | CL61 | 5005 |
| N64FG | WW24 | 227 |
| N64FJ | FA50 | 46 |
| (N64FN) | LJ35 | 073 |
| (N64FN) | LJ36 | 023 |
| **N64FT** | **C560** | **0142** |
| N64GG | HS25 | 257157 |
| N64GL | CL60 | 1064 |
| N64GX | ASTR | 134 |
| N64HA | C560 | 0127 |
| N64HA | HS25 | 257051 |
| N64HA | LJ60 | 205 |
| N64HB | LJ24 | 149 |
| **N64HH** | **LJ45** | **087** |
| (N64HX) | LJ60 | 205 |
| **N64JP** | **LJ60** | **246** |
| N64KT | WW24 | 296 |
| **N64LE** | **CL61** | **5031** |
| N64LE | LJ60 | 068 |
| N64LF | C525 | 0218 |
| **N64LV** | **C560** | **0345** |
| N64LX | C56X | 5164 |
| **N64LX** | **C56X** | **5638** |
| **N64MA** | **SBRL** | **282-44** |
| N64MC | SBRL | 282-114 |
| N64MC | SBRL | 465-73 |
| **N64MG** | **LJ60** | **224** |
| N64MG | SBRL | 282-114 |
| N64MH | LJ35 | 048 |
| N64MP | LJ25 | 078 |
| N64MP | LJ35 | 060 |
| N64MP | LJ35 | 490 |
| N64MP | SBRL | 380-32 |
| N64MQ | SBRL | 380-32 |
| N64MQ | SBRL | 465-73 |
| N64MR | LJ25 | 078 |
| N64MR | LJ35 | 060 |
| **N64NB** | **LJ31** | **065** |
| N64NC | SBRL | 306-109 |
| N64PM | C525 | 0394 |
| N64PM | C550 | 467 |
| N64PM | C560 | 0188 |
| **N64PM** | **PRM1** | **RB-168** |
| N64PZ | C525 | 0394 |
| **N64RT** | **C500** | **585** |
| N64RV | LJ35 | 355 |
| **N64SL** | **LJ60** | **029** |
| N64SL | SBRL | 465-42 |
| **N64TF** | **C550** | **080** |
| **N64UC** | **CL64** | **5587** |
| **N64VM** | **BE40** | **RJ-1** |
| N64VP | C550 | 604 |
| N64WH | LJ25 | 102 |
| N64WM | LJ55 | 022 |
| N64YP | CL61 | 5077 |
| N64YP | FA20 | 502 |
| N64YR | FA20 | 502 |
| N65 | SBRL | 380-37 |
| **N65A** | **LJ25** | **134** |
| N65A | WW24 | 235 |
| N65AD | SBRL | 465-65 |
| N65AF | SBRL | 465-62 |
| N65AH | SBRL | 465-68 |
| **N65AK** | **SBRL** | **465-35** |
| N65AM | SBRL | 465-58 |
| N65AN | SBRL | 465-59 |
| N65AR | C550 | 585 |
| N65AR | SBRL | 465-67 |
| N65B | FA50 | 10 |
| N65BE | GLF3 | 332 |
| N65BH | HS25 | 25273 |
| **N65BK** | **C525** | **0657** |
| (N65BK) | WW24 | 216 |
| N65BL | LJ60 | 054 |
| N65BP | C650 | 0202 |
| **N65BT** | **SBRL** | **465-3** |
| N65CC | SBRL | 465-46 |
| N65CE | GLF3 | 383 |
| **N65CE** | **HS25** | **258234** |
| N65CK | C525 | 0493 |
| N65CK | C52A | 0185 |
| **N65CK** | **C52A** | **0323** |
| N65CR | C52A | 0185 |
| N65DA | C550 | 189 |
| N65DD | SBRL | 465-26 |
| N65DH | LJ35 | 174 |
| N65DH | LJ35 | 381 |
| N65DL | HS25 | 25287 |
| N65DL | HS25 | 257174 |
| **N65DL** | **HS25** | **258224** |
| N65DR | SBRL | 465-45 |
| N65DT | CS55 | 0006 |
| N65DU | HS25 | 257174 |
| **N65DV** | **C550** | **624** |
| N65DW | HS25 | 25208 |
| N65EC | HS25 | 25208 |
| **N65EM** | **C525** | **0615** |
| N65FA | HS25 | 258065 |
| N65FC | HS25 | 25091 |
| N65FC | SBRL | 465-31 |
| **N65FF** | **CL61** | **5122** |
| N65FF | SBRL | 465-46 |
| N65FJ | FA50 | 47 |
| (N65FN) | LJ35 | 007 |
| (N65GB) | HS25 | 256013 |
| N65GD | HS25 | 258050 |
| N65GW | WW24 | 349 |
| N65GX | ASTR | 133 |
| N65HA | C560 | 0143 |
| N65HA | LJ60 | 228 |
| N65HD | CL65 | 5753 |
| N65HF | C650 | 0126 |
| **N65HH** | **SBRL** | **465-1** |
| N65HJ | CL60 | 1038 |
| (N65HM) | SBRL | 465-21 |
| (N65HS) | FA10 | 99 |
| N65HS | FA50 | 65 |
| **N65HU** | **LJ60** | **228** |
| N65JN | MU30 | A065SA |
| N65JR | SBRL | 465-24 |
| **N65JT** | **JSTR** | **5213** |
| (N65JW) | JSTR | 5086/44 |
| (N65JW) | JSTR | 5113/25 |
| N65KB | C650 | 0199 |
| N65KJ | SBRL | 465-1 |
| N65L | SBRL | 465-76 |
| N65LC | C550 | 317 |
| N65LC | FA20 | 40 |
| N65LC | HS25 | 257202 |
| N65LE | FA20 | 40 |
| N65LJ | LJ24 | 037 |
| N65LR | LJ60 | 365 |
| N65LT | HS25 | 25202 |
| N65M | C500 | 511 |
| N65M | GLF2 | 136 |
| N65MA | C500 | 033 |
| **N65MC** | **SBRL** | **465-36** |
| N65MK | HS25 | 25032 |
| **N65ML** | **SBRL** | **465-69** |
| N65NC | SBRL | 465-6 |
| N65NR | SBRL | 306-118 |
| N65NR | SBRL | 306-124 |
| N65NR | SBRL | 465-24 |
| (N65PF) | LJ35 | 094 |
| (N65PX) | C52A | 0072 |
| **N65PX** | **CL65** | **5804** |
| **N65PZ** | **C52A** | **0072** |
| N65QT | GLF4 | 4136 |
| N65R | GALX | 072 |
| N65R | SBRL | 306-114 |
| **N65RA** | **BE40** | **RJ-9** |
| N65RA | C500 | 434 |
| N65RC | LJ25 | 055 |
| (N65RC) | LJ25 | 163 |
| N65RC | SBRL | 465-19 |
| **N65RL** | **C560** | **0179** |
| N65RN | SBRL | 306-114 |
| N65RS | SBRL | 306-136 |
| N65RS | SBRL | 465-1 |
| N65RS | SBRL | 465-3 |
| **N65RZ** | **LJ35** | **236** |
| **N65SA** | **C500** | **114** |
| (N65SA) | C550 | 119 |
| N65SA | MU30 | A067SA |
| N65SD | F2TH | 32 |
| N65SL | SBRL | 465-10 |
| N65SR | SBRL | 465-16 |
| **N65SR** | **SBRL** | **465-54** |
| N65SR | SBRL | 465-6 |
| **N65ST** | **C750** | **0211** |
| N65ST | GLF2 | 5 |
| (N65T) | C500 | 624 |
| N65T | LJ60 | 213 |
| **N65T** | **SBRL** | **465-43** |
| (N65TA) | LJ35 | 364 |
| N65TB | PRM1 | RB-19 |
| N65TC | SBRL | 465-30 |
| N65TD | ASTR | 093 |
| N65TD | WW24 | 366 |
| N65TF | C550 | 175 |
| N65TJ | SBRL | 465-45 |
| N65TL | SBRL | 465-56 |
| N65TP | C550 | 674 |
| **N65TP** | **LJ40** | **45-2084** |
| N65TS | FA20 | 368 |
| N65TS | HS25 | 25043 |
| N65TS | SBRL | 465-34 |
| N65U | LJ45 | 073 |
| **N65VM** | **C52B** | **0034** |
| N65WH | LJ25 | 086 |
| (N65WH) | LJ35 | 275 |
| N65WL | C650 | 0122 |
| N65WM | LJ24 | 163 |
| N65WS | C500 | 076 |
| **N65WW** | **C500** | **591** |
| N65Y | LJ55 | 121 |
| **N65ZZ** | **GLEX** | **9361** |
| N66AG | C500 | 520 |
| N66AL | GLF2 | 166/15 |
| **N66AM** | **C525** | **0160** |
| N66AM | HS25 | 25087 |
| N66AM | LJ24 | 064 |
| N66AS | LJ24 | 029 |
| N66AT | C500 | 520 |
| N66AT | C550 | 044 |
| **N66BE** | **C525** | **0174** |
| N66BH | HS25 | 25275 |
| **N66BK** | **C500** | **658** |
| **N66BX** | **EA50** | **000154** |
| N66CC | C500 | 066 |
| N66CD | SBRL | 282-134 |
| **N66CF** | **FA10** | **65** |
| N66CR | JSTR | 5052 |
| N66DD | C550 | 263 |

| | | | | | | | | | | | |
|---|---|---|---|---|---|---|---|---|---|---|---|
| N66DD | GLF3 | 483 | N67B | JSTR | 5074/22 | N67VW | C525 | 0212 | **N68QB** | **LJ35** | **079** |
| **N66DD** | **GLF4** | **1355** | N67BC | C52A | 0225 | N67WB | F900 | 24 | N68SD | CL60 | 1062 |
| N66DN | C550 | 263 | N67BE | C500 | 184 | **N67WB** | **F9EX** | **16** | N68SK | C650 | 0156 |
| N66DN | LJ45 | 236 | N67BE | C500 | 524 | **N67WG** | **E50P** | **50000105** | N68SK | C650 | 7016 |
| (N66EA) | CS55 | 0006 | **N67BE** | **C550** | **619** | N67WM | LJ55 | 132 | N68SK | CS55 | 0011 |
| N66ED | SBRL | 380-32 | N67BF | C500 | 184 | N67WW | SBRL | 282-2 | **N68SL** | **C680** | **0264** |
| N66EH | CS55 | 0158 | N67BG | C650 | 0105 | N68AA | C56X | 5281 | N68SL | GLF4 | 1042 |
| N66ES | C500 | 314 | N67BH | HS25 | 25276 | (N68AA) | SBRL | 282-38 | N68TA | SBRL | 306-53 |
| **N66ES** | **C510** | **0110** | **N67BK** | **C550** | **550-0997** | N68AG | C500 | 238 | N68TJ | LJ25 | 140 |
| N66ES | C525 | 0053 | (N67BK) | SBRL | 282-135 | N68AX | LJ25 | 216 | N68TJ | LJ35 | 168 |
| N66ES | C525 | 0244 | N67CC | C500 | 367 | (N68BA) | FA50 | 177 | **N68TS** | **C550** | **479** |
| N66ES | C550 | 032 | **N67CC** | **C52A** | **0225** | N68BC | C650 | 7025 | N68TS | FA20 | 129 |
| N66ES | SBRL | 282-91 | (N67CK) | LJ24 | 147 | N68BC | FA20 | 155 | **N68UP** | **FA20** | **258** |
| N66ES | SBRL | 380-32 | N67CX | C750 | 0128 | N68BH | HS25 | 25278 | N68UW | LJ35 | 095 |
| N66EW | WW24 | 9 | N67DF | WW24 | 233 | N68BK | C550 | 363 | **N68VP** | **LJ31** | **232** |
| N66FE | LJ35 | 383 | **N67DT** | **WW24** | **364** | **N68BP** | **FA20** | **155** | N68WM | LJ24 | 074 |
| "N66FG" | MU30 | A066SA | N67EC | HS25 | 25285 | N68BR | C650 | 7114 | N68WW | WW24 | 386 |
| N66FG | WW24 | 357 | **N67EL** | **F900** | **153** | N68BS | C525 | 0244 | N69AH | C52A | 0068 |
| (N66FH) | C525 | 0480 | N67FJ | FA50 | 50 | (N68BW) | HS25 | 25261 | N69AX | LJ24 | 346 |
| **N66FJ** | **F9EX** | **66** | (N67GA) | LJ35 | 176 | N68CB | C500 | 270 | **N69AY** | **C510** | **0115** |
| N66FJ | FA50 | 49 | N67GH | C525 | 0149 | N68CB | HS25 | 25263 | (N69B) | LJ55 | 091 |
| (N66FN) | LJ24 | 268 | N67GH | C52A | 0019 | **N68CB** | **HS25** | **258453** | N69BH | HS25 | 25279 |
| (N66FN) | LJ35 | 067 | **N67GH** | **C52A** | **0217** | N68CG | F9EX | 38 | **N69BH** | **LJ35** | **276** |
| N66GA | FA20 | 341 | N67GM | C500 | 619 | N68CJ | C525 | 0068 | (N69CG) | SBRL | 282-72 |
| N66GE | C500 | 258 | N67GT | JSTR | 5061/48 | N68CJ | C525 | 0169 | N69CN | JSTR | 5053/2 |
| N66GE | SBRL | 306-99 | (N67GU) | C525 | 0149 | N68CK | C560 | 0063 | N69EC | FA10 | 109 |
| **N66GE** | **SBRL** | **465-28** | N67GU | C560 | 0355 | (N68CK) | LJ25 | 047 | **N69EC** | **FA20** | **498** |
| N66GX | GALX | 032 | N67GW | C560 | 0355 | N68CT | JSTR | 5108 | (N69EH) | GLF3 | 316 |
| N66GZ | SBRL | 306-99 | **N67GW** | **C560** | **0641** | N68DA | HS25 | 258052 | N69EP | C500 | 531 |
| N66HA | HS25 | 25126 | N67GX | GALX | 036 | N68DM | GLF2 | 28 | N69FF | GLF3 | 320 |
| N66HD | C500 | 407 | N67HB | LJ25 | 189 | N68DM | LJ24 | 101 | N69FH | C52A | 0068 |
| N66HD | CS55 | 0134 | N67HW | C550 | 420 | N68DS | C550 | 219 | **N69FH** | **C52B** | **0042** |
| N66HH | FA10 | 176 | **N67JB** | **C550** | **550-0980** | N68EA | C500 | 438 | **N69GB** | **FA10** | **24** |
| (N66HM) | LJ35 | 206 | **N67JF** | **FA50** | **73** | **N68ED** | **C650** | **0239** | N69GF | LJ25 | 265 |
| N66JD | LJ25 | 183 | N67JF | HS25 | 258124 | **N68ER** | **E50P** | **50000011** | N69GP | GLF4 | 1033 |
| N66JE | WW24 | 326 | N67JR | C500 | 048 | N68ES | LJ31 | 221 | N69GT | WW24 | 44 |
| N66KC | HS25 | 25038 | N67JR | FA20 | 247 | **N68EU** | **C680** | **0208** | N69GX | ASTR | 122 |
| N66KG | ASTR | 096 | N67JR | GLF3 | 324 | (N68FN) | LJ24 | 101 | N69HM | JSTR | 5004 |
| **N66KK** | **LJ35** | **095** | N67JR | LJ24 | 230 | N68GA | C550 | 184 | N69HM | WW24 | 210 |
| N66LB | C550 | 051 | N67JW | C550 | 462 | (N68GA) | C680 | 0060 | N69JN | SBRL | 380-65 |
| **N66LE** | **C500** | **170** | N67JW | FA10 | 99 | N68GA | HS25 | 256047 | N69KA | HS25 | 25273 |
| N66LJ | LJ35 | 401 | N67KM | SBRL | 380-7 | N68GP | HS25 | 258068 | N69KB | LJ24 | 042 |
| **N66LM** | **C56X** | **5074** | **N67KP** | **ASTR** | **249** | N68GT | FA10 | 217 | N69KM | SBRL | 380-30 |
| N66LM | LJ35 | 306 | N67LC | C550 | 317 | **N68GW** | **C56X** | **5626** | (N69LD) | C560 | 0803 |
| N66LN | LJ35 | 500 | **N67LC** | **FA10** | **49** | N68GX | ASTR | 136 | N69LD | C650 | 0080 |
| N66LW | LJ24 | 311 | N67LH | C550 | 664 | N68HB | HS25 | 258601 | (N69LJ) | LJ25 | 052 |
| N66LX | WW24 | 375 | **N67LP** | **EA50** | **000236** | N68HC | C560 | 0016 | **N69LJ** | **LJ60** | **027** |
| **N66MC** | **C550** | **256** | N67MA | C500 | 277 | N68HC | C560 | 0270 | (N69LL) | LJ24 | 051 |
| N66ME | C650 | 0079 | (N67ME) | C550 | 444 | N68HC | C560 | 0762 | (N69LS) | BE40 | RK-164 |
| N66MF | CL60 | 1036 | N67MP | C500 | 277 | N68HC | C56X | 5103 | N69ME | C550 | 282 |
| N66MF | FA10 | 29 | N67MP | C550 | 444 | **N68HC** | **C56X** | **6011** | N69ME | JSTR | 5076/17 |
| (N66MF) | WW24 | 414 | (N67MP) | LJ31 | 059 | N68HC | C650 | 0091 | N69MT | JSTR | 5107 |
| N66MJ | LJ24 | 334 | N67MR | CL61 | 5029 | N68HC | C680 | 0068 | N69NG | GLF2 | 69 |
| N66MP | JSTR | 5015 | N67MR | HS25 | 256067 | N68HC | SBRL | 282-55 | N69PC | MU30 | A010SA |
| N66MP | LJ24 | 058 | N67NC | C550 | 696 | N68HC | SBRL | 306-96 | N69PL | LJ25 | 253 |
| N66MR | LJ24 | 159 | N67NR | SBRL | 306-76 | N68HD | HS25 | 258429 | N69PS | LJ35 | 014 |
| N66MS | C550 | 342 | **N67NV** | **EA50** | **000131** | **N68HG** | **C56X** | **5103** | N69R | FA50 | 116 |
| **N66MT** | **C550** | **550-0913** | **N67PA** | **LJ35** | **208** | N68HQ | C560 | 0016 | N69SB | C750 | 0212 |
| N66MW | LJ24 | 066 | N67PC | C550 | 550-1007 | N68HQ | C560 | 0270 | N69SB | HS25 | 257177 |
| N66NJ | LJ25 | 039 | N67PC | C550 | 696 | (N68HQ) | C680 | 0068 | **N69SB** | **PRM1** | **RB-242** |
| **N66NJ** | **LJ35** | **296** | N67PC | C56X | 5806 | N68HQ | SBRL | 282-55 | N69SF | GLF2 | 52 |
| N66NR | SBRL | 306-62 | N67PC | LJ25 | 128 | N68HR | HS25 | 258068 | (N69SF) | LJ24 | 246 |
| N66NS | CL61 | 5096 | **N67PK** | **C56X** | **5806** | N68JK | FA20 | 83 | N69SW | FA20 | 356 |
| N66NT | CL61 | 5068 | N67PR | GLF2 | 67 | **N68JV** | **BE40** | **RK-296** | N69TP | JSTR | 5002 |
| N66NT | CL61 | 5096 | N67PV | C550 | 550-1007 | N68JW | C550 | 465 | N69VC | C650 | 0079 |
| N66NT | FA20 | 349 | **N67PW** | **FA50** | **248** | N68KM | SBRL | 380-23 | **N69VH** | **LJ55** | **062** |
| (N66PJ) | LJ35 | 256 | N67PW | HS25 | 257147 | N68LF | C750 | 0040 | (N69VJ) | FA50 | 69 |
| N66PL | MU30 | A077SA | N67RW | LJ55 | 048 | N68LL | LJ35 | 463 | N69VT | C560 | 0260 |
| N66RP | LJ24 | 198 | **N67RX** | **GLEX** | **9067** | N68LP | C750 | 0040 | N69WJ | FA10 | 60 |
| **N66SG** | **LJ45** | **073** | N67SB | LJ31 | 045 | N68LP | C750 | 0169 | **N69WU** | **SBRL** | **465-51** |
| N66SM | WW24 | 168 | N67SC | SBRL | 465-14 | N68LP | LJ55 | 082 | N69WW | WW24 | 51 |
| N66TF | GLF2 | 97 | N67SE | C650 | 0045 | N68LU | LJ24 | 163 | **N69X** | **MS76** | **090** |
| N66TJ | LJ25 | 081 | N67SF | C500 | 184 | N68LX | C56X | 5163 | **N69XW** | **C500** | **142** |
| N66TP | SBRL | 282-60 | **N67SF** | **C550** | **273** | N68LX | SBRL | 465-68 | N69XW | LJ24 | 251 |
| N66TR | C500 | 299 | N67SF | C650 | 0045 | N68MA | C560 | 0159 | **N69YM** | **PRM1** | **RB-255** |
| N66TS | WW24 | 39 | N67SF | C650 | 0231 | N68MA | C560 | 0547 | N70AA | C500 | 619 |
| **N66U** | **C560** | **0489** | N67SG | C550 | 257 | N68MA | SBRL | 306-23 | N70AE | LJ31 | 188 |
| **N66VA** | **WW24** | **375** | N67TH | GLF4 | 1475 | N68ME | C550 | 282 | **N70AE** | **LJ45** | **227** |
| N66VG | FA20 | 210 | N67TJ | FA10 | 83 | N68MJ | LJ35 | 607 | N70AF | CS55 | 0067 |
| N66VM | C550 | 056 | N67TJ | GLF3 | 390 | N68ML | SBRL | 282-136 | N70AF | FA50 | 116 |
| (N66W) | C560 | 0603 | N67TJ | HS25 | 25159 | N68NC | C560 | 0762 | N70AF | FA50 | 21 |
| N66W | C56X | 5320 | (N67TJ) | LJ35 | 367 | N68NR | SBRL | 306-101 | N70AG | GLF3 | 376 |
| N66WB | FA20 | 242 | **N67TJ** | **WW24** | **299** | N68PC | LJ45 | 040 | N70AG | GLF4 | 1120 |
| N66WM | LJ35 | 141 | N67TM | C550 | 067 | **N68PC** | **LJ45** | **289** | **N70AG** | **GLF5** | **522** |
| N66WM | LJ55 | 145 | **N67TM** | **GLF4** | **1409** | N68PJ | LJ25 | 063 | N70AJ | ASTR | 054 |
| **N66ZC** | **CL64** | **5411** | N67TS | HS25 | 25097 | N68PL | MU30 | A077SA | N70AP | HS25 | 25271 |
| N67AX | FA20 | 159 | **N67TW** | **C56X** | **5122** | N68PQ | LJ45 | 040 | N70AR | HS25 | 257144 |
| N67B | CL60 | 1066 | (N67VP) | CS55 | 0067 | **N68PT** | **WW24** | **325** | **N70AX** | **LJ35** | **155** |

| | | |
|---|---|---|
| **N70AY** | **LJ31** | **188** |
| N70BC | SBRL | 282-132 |
| **N70BG** | **C500** | **387** |
| N70BH | HS25 | 25280 |
| N70BJ | BE40 | RK-39 |
| N70BR | C560 | 0478 |
| N70BR | PRM1 | RB-70 |
| **N70CA** | **C500** | **234** |
| N70CA | WW24 | 231 |
| N70CE | LJ25 | 142 |
| **N70CG** | **C500** | **576** |
| **N70CK** | **FA20** | **128/436** |
| N70CN | LJ35 | 277 |
| **N70CR** | **CL30** | **20048** |
| N70CS | WW24 | 88 |
| **N70DE** | **BE40** | **RJ-56** |
| N70DJ | C650 | 0058 |
| N70DJ | CL60 | 1070 |
| **N70EJ** | **EA50** | **000194** |
| N70ES | SBRL | 282-124 |
| N70EW | F900 | 25 |
| **N70EW** | **GLEX** | **9026** |
| N70FC | HS25 | 257145 |
| N70FJ | C500 | 448 |
| N70FJ | F900 | 20 |
| N70FJ | FA50 | 236 |
| N70FJ | FA50 | 51 |
| N70FL | FA50 | 144 |
| N70FL | FA50 | 95 |
| **N70FL** | **FA7X** | **7** |
| N70GA | MU30 | A071SA |
| N70GM | C550 | 135 |
| N70HB | HS25 | 25043 |
| (N70HC) | C550 | 428 |
| N70HC | SBRL | 370-8 |
| N70HF | HS25 | 257082 |
| N70HJ | LJ25 | 049 |
| **N70HL** | **SBRL** | **306-102** |
| N70HS | F900 | 140 |
| (N70HW) | C525 | 0070 |
| N70JC | HS25 | 25203 |
| N70JC | LJ24 | 051 |
| N70JF | LJ25 | 278 |
| N70KM | SBRL | 380-52 |
| N70KS | F2TH | 14 |
| N70KW | C525 | 0050 |
| **N70KW** | **C52A** | **0135** |
| **N70LF** | **F9EX** | **9** |
| N70LG | FA20 | 319 |
| **N70LJ** | **LJ36** | **044** |
| (N70LW) | SBRL | 306-142 |
| N70LY | HS25 | 25244 |
| N70MD | FA20 | 153 |
| **N70MG** | **C500** | **063** |
| N70MP | LJ25 | 051 |
| **N70NB** | **C500** | **614** |
| N70NE | FA20 | 399 |
| **N70NE** | **HS25** | **258107** |
| **N70NF** | **C52B** | **0276** |
| N70NF | FA20 | 399 |
| N70NR | SBRL | 370-3 |
| N70PA | FA20 | 173 |
| (N70PB) | C500 | 248 |
| N70PC | C550 | 664 |
| **N70PC** | **LJ45** | **172** |
| (N70PH) | C550 | 327 |
| N70PL | FA20 | 247 |
| **N70PL** | **FA20** | **436** |
| N70PM | HS25 | 257141 |
| N70PM | HS25 | 257147 |
| N70PM | HS25 | 258238 |
| N70PN | HS25 | 257147 |
| **N70PS** | **GLEX** | **9012** |
| N70PS | GLF3 | 327 |
| N70PS | GLF4 | 1058 |
| N70PT | C650 | 0187 |
| **N70QB** | **HS25** | **257125** |
| N70RL | LJ24 | 106 |
| N70SE | LJ25 | 323 |
| N70SJ | SJ30 | 007 |
| N70SK | HS25 | 257098 |
| N70SK | HS25 | 258006 |
| N70SK | LJ25 | 049 |
| N70SL | SBRL | 282-70 |
| **N70SW** | **C500** | **236** |
| N70TF | C500 | 274 |
| N70TF | LJ25 | 214 |
| N70TF | SBRL | 380-17 |
| N70TG | C500 | 308 |
| N70TG | C560 | 0069 |
| N70TH | F900 | 117 |
| N70TH | FA20 | 509 |
| N70TJ | LJ24 | 199 |
| N70TP | JSTR | 5005 |
| (N70TP) | JSTR | 5019 |
| N70TP | JSTR | 5156 |
| N70TR | C525 | 0014 |
| **N70TS** | **C500** | **281** |
| N70TS | FA10 | 63 |
| N70TT | C650 | 0029 |
| **N70TT** | **GALX** | **045** |
| N70U | C500 | 304 |
| N70U | FA20 | 399 |
| N70UP | LJ36 | 040 |
| N70UT | LJ36 | 040 |
| N70VP | C500 | 444 |
| N70VT | MU30 | A085SA |
| (N70WA) | C500 | 192 |
| N70WA | C500 | 320 |
| (N70WA) | LJ25 | 142 |
| N70WC | FA10 | 140 |
| (N70WG) | GLF2 | 248 |
| N70WP | C500 | 512 |
| N70WW | LJ35 | 055 |
| (N70WW) | WW24 | 283 |
| N70X | C550 | 008 |
| **N70X** | **CL60** | **1032** |
| N70X | HS25 | 257011 |
| N70XA | C550 | 008 |
| N70XC | F2TH | 152 |
| **N70XL** | **C56X** | **5566** |
| N70XX | MU30 | A052SA |
| N71A | LJ35 | 352 |
| **N71AL** | **LJ31** | **039** |
| N71AX | F2TH | 184 |
| N71AX | LJ25 | 353 |
| **N71BD** | **GLF4** | **1415** |
| N71BH | HS25 | 25281 |
| N71BL | HS25 | 25084 |
| **N71CC** | **SBRL** | **306-71** |
| N71CD | SBRL | 306-26 |
| N71CE | LJ25 | 136 |
| (N71CG) | C550 | 254 |
| N71CJ | C550 | 071 |
| **N71CK** | **LJ36** | **035** |
| N71CP | FA20 | 89 |
| N71CW | HFB3 | 1026 |
| N71DL | HFB3 | 1026 |
| N71DM | LJ25 | 129 |
| N71E | LJ35 | 306 |
| N71EL | F2EX | 71 |
| N71EM | CS55 | 0006 |
| N71FA | CL30 | 20089 |
| **N71FB** | **LJ31** | **205** |
| N71FE | BE40 | RK-16 |
| **N71FE** | **F2EX** | **13** |
| N71FJ | FA50 | 54 |
| N71FM | C550 | 083 |
| N71FM | CS55 | 0006 |
| **N71FS** | **ASTR** | **071** |
| N71GA | BE40 | RJ-35 |
| N71GA | C550 | 444 |
| **N71GH** | **MU30** | **A071SA** |
| **N71GK** | **F900** | **107** |
| N71GW | C525 | 0059 |
| N71HB | C500 | 275 |
| N71HR | C525 | 0494 |
| N71HS | C56X | 5351 |
| N71HS | LJ35 | 287 |
| N71JC | LJ31 | 008 |
| N71JJ | C560 | 0480 |
| N71JN | GLF4 | 1088 |
| **N71KV** | **PRM1** | **RB-71** |
| **N71L** | **C500** | **646** |
| (N71LA) | GLF4 | 1238 |
| N71LA | LJ35 | 012 |
| N71LG | LJ35 | 019 |
| N71LJ | LJ24 | 071 |
| **N71LP** | **C500** | **487** |
| N71LP | C550 | 278 |
| N71LU | C650 | 0019 |
| N71M | CL60 | 1077 |
| N71M | FA10 | 208 |
| **N71M** | **FA10** | **88** |
| N71M | WW24 | 192 |
| N71MA | HS25 | 257107 |
| N71MH | LJ35 | 469 |
| **N71MT** | **EA50** | **000069** |
| N71MT | HS25 | 258230 |
| **N71NF** | **LJ40** | **45-2058** |
| N71NK | C560 | 0040 |
| N71NK | C650 | 7106 |
| **N71NP** | **CL64** | **5504** |
| N71NP | HS25 | 258041 |
| N71NR | GLF4 | 1132 |
| **N71PG** | **LJ36** | **013** |
| N71PT | WW24 | 198 |
| N71RB | LJ25 | 158 |
| N71RB | SBRL | 465-14 |
| N71RC | C500 | 184 |
| (N71RL) | C550 | 074 |
| (N71RL) | C56X | 5354 |
| N71RP | C750 | 0093 |
| N71RP | GLF2 | 199/19 |
| N71RP | GLF3 | 440 |
| N71RP | GLF4 | 1222 |
| N71TH | F900 | 105 |
| N71TH | FA50 | 196 |
| N71TJ | FA10 | 105 |
| N71TJ | FA20 | 166 |
| N71TJ | GLF2 | 29 |
| N71TJ | GLF3 | 300 |
| N71TJ | GLF4 | 1042 |
| N71TP | GLF2 | 195 |
| N71TP | LJ35 | 014 |
| N71TP | LJ36 | 030 |
| N71TP | LJ55 | 032 |
| N71TS | FA10 | 75 |
| **N71TV** | **GLF4** | **1430** |
| (N71UF) | JSTR | 5037/24 |
| N71VR | GLF4 | 1290 |
| N71WF | WW24 | 442 |
| **N71WJ** | **GLF2** | **248** |
| N71WS | GLF2 | 232 |
| N71ZZ | GLEX | 9239 |
| N72AM | CS55 | 0004 |
| N72AV | LJ36 | 040 |
| N72AX | LJ25 | 346 |
| **N72AX** | **LJ35** | **419** |
| (N72B) | C550 | 393 |
| N72BB | FA10 | 173 |
| N72BB | FA20 | 59 |
| N72BC | C500 | 270 |
| **N72BD** | **GLF4** | **1420** |
| N72BH | HS25 | 25282 |
| (N72BJ) | BE40 | RK-72 |
| **N72BP** | **GLF2** | **238** |
| N72CD | LJ25 | 023 |
| **N72CE** | **LJ60** | **285** |
| **N72CK** | **LJ35** | **165** |
| N72CT | C560 | 0072 |
| N72CT | JSTR | 5007/45 |
| **N72DA** | **LJ35** | **098** |
| N72DJ | C500 | 072 |
| (N72DV) | PRM1 | RB-121 |
| **N72EL** | **ASTR** | **018** |
| **N72EP** | **C650** | **0058** |
| N72ET | FA20 | 52 |
| N72ET | LJ55 | 072 |
| N72ET | WW24 | 180 |
| N72EU | FA10 | 13 |
| N72FC | C560 | 0347 |
| **N72FC** | **HS25** | **258519** |
| **N72FD** | **C750** | **0072** |
| (N72FE) | C560 | 0072 |
| N72FE | C560 | 0347 |
| N72FJ | FA50 | 58 |
| N72FL | ASTR | 018 |
| N72FL | BE40 | RK-333 |
| N72FL | C550 | 249 |
| N72FP | LJ24 | 137 |
| **N72GD** | **PRM1** | **RB-163** |
| **N72GH** | **BE40** | **RK-370** |
| N72GW | FA10 | 37 |
| **N72GW** | **JSTR** | **5205** |
| N72HA | HS25 | 25249 |
| N72HB | WW24 | 254 |
| N72HC | HS25 | 25287 |
| **N72HG** | **BE40** | **RJ-11** |
| N72HT | HS25 | 25249 |
| N72HT | JSTR | 5134/50 |
| **N72JF** | **LJ35** | **088** |
| N72JM | LJ35 | 183 |
| **N72JW** | **C525** | **0406** |
| N72K | C550 | 480 |
| N72K | HS25 | 258141 |
| N72LE | C650 | 0063 |
| N72LE | LJ35 | 237 |
| N72LG | LJ35 | 228 |
| N72LL | LJ35 | 275 |
| **N72LN** | **GLF4** | **4144** |
| N72LT | WW24 | 180 |
| N72MK | LJ24 | 066 |
| N72MM | C550 | 187 |
| **N72NE** | **BE40** | **RK-371** |
| **N72NP** | **CL64** | **5385** |
| N72NP | HS25 | 258044 |
| N72PB | C550 | 550-0926 |
| N72PK | GLF3 | 306 |
| (N72PP) | BE40 | RK-86 |
| **N72PS** | **F2EX** | **116** |
| N72PS | F900 | 18 |
| (N72PS) | GLF3 | 327 |
| **N72PX** | **F900** | **18** |
| N72RC | C550 | 024 |
| N72RK | GALX | 039 |
| N72RK | GLF3 | 306 |
| N72RK | GLF4 | 1171 |
| N72RK | GLF4 | 1248 |
| N72SG | C525 | 0308 |
| N72SG | C550 | 550-0942 |
| N72SG | C56X | 5253 |
| **N72SG** | **C56X** | **5508** |
| **N72SJ** | **PRM1** | **RB-115** |
| N72SL | C550 | 504 |
| N72SR | CL60 | 1013 |
| N72ST | C650 | 0072 |
| (N72TB) | LJ35 | 014 |
| N72TC | C550 | 282 |
| N72TC | WW24 | 4 |
| N72TJ | LJ35 | 172 |
| N72TP | LJ25 | 168 |
| N72TP | LJ35 | 140 |
| (N72TP) | LJ55 | 032 |
| **N72TQ** | **WW24** | **4** |
| N72U | C550 | 480 |
| **N72VJ** | **C500** | **543** |
| N72WC | C500 | 281 |
| N72WC | CS55 | 0037 |
| N72WC | LJ25 | 371 |
| N72WE | C550 | 720 |
| N72WS | F9EX | 14 |
| **N72WY** | **CL64** | **5394** |
| **N73AH** | **C510** | **0226** |
| N73AW | GLF2 | 109 |
| N73B | FA10 | 23 |
| N73B | FA10 | 79 |
| N73BE | BE40 | RJ-15 |
| N73BH | HS25 | 25283 |
| N73BL | BE40 | RJ-15 |
| N73BL | BE40 | RK-71 |
| N73CE | LJ24 | 068 |
| **N73CK** | **LJ35** | **092** |
| **N73CL** | **WW24** | **365** |
| **N73DB** | **E50P** | **50000020** |
| **N73DJ** | **LJ25** | **273** |
| N73DR | SBRL | 282-120 |
| **N73EM** | **C52B** | **0123** |
| (N73ET) | GLF3 | 434 |
| **N73FJ** | **F2TH** | **73** |
| N73FJ | FA50 | 55 |
| N73FW | C500 | 562 |
| N73G | HS25 | 257150 |
| N73G | SBRL | 306-8 |
| (N73GB) | WW24 | 294 |
| **N73GH** | **FA50** | **261** |
| **N73GP** | **LJ55** | **127** |
| N73GR | SBRL | 306-8 |
| N73HB | C500 | 256 |
| N73HG | LJ24 | 137 |
| **N73HH** | **C550** | **682** |
| N73HM | BE40 | RK-70 |
| **N73HM** | **C650** | **0169** |
| N73HP | SBRL | 282-120 |
| N73JA | HS25 | 256065 |
| N73JH | HS25 | 25203 |
| N73JT | LJ24 | 064 |
| **N73KH** | **C560** | **0220** |
| N73LJ | LJ25 | 138 |
| N73LL | C500 | 287 |
| N73LP | GLF2 | 119/22 |
| N73LP | LJ35 | 604 |

| **N73LR** | **FA10** | **35** |
|---|---|---|
| N73M | GLF2 | 128 |
| **N73M** | **GLF5** | **547** |
| N73ME | C560 | 0108 |
| **N73ME** | **C750** | **0155** |
| N73MG | GLF2 | 247 |
| N73MN | C560 | 0108 |
| **N73MP** | **C500** | **164** |
| **N73MR** | **FA20** | **449** |
| N73PC | SBRL | 282-11 |
| **N73PJ** | **PRM1** | **RB-101** |
| N73PM | C525 | 0287 |
| N73PM | HS25 | 257167 |
| N73PS | LJ24 | 186 |
| N73RP | GLF3 | 491 |
| **N73RP** | **GLF5** | **529** |
| N73SG | C56X | 5253 |
| **N73SK** | **C500** | **679** |
| **N73ST** | **C550** | **113** |
| N73TA | LJ25 | 181 |
| N73TF | C500 | 256 |
| (N73TJ) | FA10 | 163 |
| N73TJ | LJ35 | 042 |
| **N73TJ** | **SBRL** | **465-12** |
| N73TP | LJ35 | 014 |
| N73TP | LJ55 | 048 |
| N73TW | LJ25 | 181 |
| **N73UC** | **C650** | **7049** |
| **N73UP** | **HS25** | **258473** |
| N73WC | C500 | 213 |
| N73WC | C500 | 338 |
| N73WC | PRM1 | RB-15 |
| N73WE | LJ55 | 073 |
| N73WF | HS25 | 258141 |
| N73WW | HS25 | 258480 |
| N73ZZ | GLEX | 9251 |
| **N74A** | **GLF2** | **36/3** |
| N74AB | SBRL | 306-92 |
| N74AG | JSTR | 5072/23 |
| N74AG | WW24 | 339 |
| N74B | HS25 | 25276 |
| N74B | HS25 | 257014 |
| N74BH | HS25 | 25284 |
| N74BJ | CS55 | 0041 |
| N74BJ | FA50 | 237 |
| **N74BJ** | **SBRL** | **465-44** |
| N74BS | SBRL | 306-64 |
| (N74EH) | C550 | 696 |
| N74FC | C500 | 196 |
| **N74FH** | **C500** | **525** |
| **N74FS** | **F900** | **85** |
| N74G | C550 | 042 |
| N74G | LJ25 | 174 |
| **N74GG** | **GLF4** | **1331** |
| N74GL | LJ55 | 074 |
| N74GM | WW24 | 74 |
| **N74GR** | **CL61** | **3001** |
| N74GR | WW24 | 218 |
| **N74GW** | **HS25** | **258706** |
| **N74GZ** | **CS55** | **0074** |
| **N74HH** | **GLF2** | **74** |
| **N74HR** | **C500** | **677** |
| N74JA | C550 | 349 |
| **N74JA** | **CL60** | **1060** |
| N74JA | HS25 | 257079 |
| N74JE | CS55 | 0074 |
| (N74JE) | HS25 | 257079 |
| N74JK | GLF2 | 157 |
| N74JK | GLF2 | 49 |
| N74JL | LJ25 | 101 |
| N74JL | LJ35 | 396 |
| N74JM | WW24 | 299 |
| N74JN | C550 | 349 |
| N74KV | C550 | 324 |
| **N74LL** | **C500** | **212** |
| N74LM | CL60 | 1069 |
| N74LM | CS55 | 0041 |
| N74MB | LJ35 | 004 |
| N74MB | SBRL | 282-112 |
| N74MG | C550 | 302 |
| N74MG | SBRL | 282-102 |
| N74MJ | LJ35 | 004 |
| N74MJ | SBRL | 282-102 |
| N74MP | LJ35 | 004 |
| N74MW | LJ24 | 074 |
| N74ND | HS25 | 258063 |
| N74NP | HS25 | 258168 |
| **N74NP** | **HS25** | **258631** |
| N74PC | HS25 | 258166 |
| N74PC | HS25 | 258567 |
| N74PG | C525 | 0476 |
| N74PM | C500 | 499 |
| (N74PN) | C500 | 499 |
| N74PQ | HS25 | 258166 |
| **N74PT** | **LJ45** | **314** |
| N74RD | LJ25 | 260 |
| N74RP | GLF2 | 199/19 |
| N74RP | GLF4 | 1040 |
| **N74RP** | **GLF5** | **5058** |
| N74RQ | GLF2 | 113 |
| N74RT | GLF2 | 113 |
| **N74RT** | **GLF2** | **219/20** |
| N74RT | HS25 | 25214 |
| N74RV | GLF2 | 162 |
| N74RY | LJ55 | 063 |
| **N74SG** | **LJ45** | **016** |
| N74SP | C550 | 485 |
| N74SP | LJ35 | 441 |
| N74TC | C550 | 094 |
| N74TJ | ASTR | 063 |
| (N74TJ) | CL60 | 1063 |
| (N74TJ) | FA10 | 18 |
| N74TJ | GLF2 | 74 |
| N74TJ | GLF4 | 1107 |
| (N74TJ) | HS25 | 256015 |
| N74TL | C560 | 0048 |
| N74TP | LJ36 | 030 |
| **N74TS** | **FA50** | **106** |
| N74TS | WW24 | 174 |
| N74UK | C525 | 0602 |
| **N74VC** | **SBRL** | **465-17** |
| N74VF | BE40 | RK-34 |
| N74VF | C650 | 0156 |
| **N74VF** | **C750** | **0057** |
| N74WA | C500 | 320 |
| N74WF | HS25 | 25221 |
| (N74WF) | HS25 | 258349 |
| N74WL | CL30 | 20044 |
| N74XE | WW24 | 128 |
| N74XL | WW24 | 128 |
| **N74ZC** | **CL30** | **20018** |
| N74ZZ | GLEX | 9260 |
| N75A | SBRL | 380-21 |
| N75A | SBRL | 380-36 |
| N75A | SBRL | 380-52 |
| N75A | SBRL | 380-57 |
| N75AG | SBRL | 380-42 |
| N75AK | SBRL | 380-38 |
| N75AX | LJ25 | 270 |
| **N75B** | **C560** | **0156** |
| N75B | CL60 | 1064 |
| N75B | LJ25 | 178 |
| **N75BC** | **WW24** | **426** |
| N75BH | HS25 | 25285 |
| N75BL | CS55 | 0053 |
| N75BL | LJ25 | 156 |
| N75BL | MU30 | A017SA |
| N75BS | SBRL | 380-12 |
| N75C | HS25 | 25141 |
| N75CA | LJ25 | 110 |
| N75CC | GLF2 | 117 |
| **N75CC** | **GLF4** | **1182** |
| N75CC | JSTR | 5102 |
| N75CJ | LJ24 | 279 |
| **N75CK** | **LJ25** | **256** |
| N75CN | SBRL | 380-31 |
| N75CS | HS25 | 25190 |
| N75CS | HS25 | 258066 |
| N75CT | HS25 | 25047 |
| **N75CT** | **LJ60** | **299** |
| N75CV | C560 | 0075 |
| N75DE | SBRL | 370-7 |
| N75DH | LJ35 | 007 |
| **N75EA** | **EA50** | **000116** |
| N75EC | C550 | 295 |
| **N75ES** | **C510** | **0024** |
| N75EW | F900 | 25 |
| N75F | C550 | 368 |
| N75F | C560 | 0139 |
| **N75FC** | **C525** | **0455** |
| **N75FJ** | **FA50** | **275** |
| N75FJ | FA50 | 59 |
| N75FN | C500 | 257 |
| (N75FV) | C560 | 0139 |
| N75G | C560 | 0140 |
| N75G | FA50 | 138 |
| N75G | SBRL | 465-71 |
| N75GA | C550 | 310 |
| **N75GA** | **HS25** | **256070** |
| N75GF | BE40 | RK-179 |
| (N75GJ) | GLF3 | 375 |
| N75GK | BE40 | RK-179 |
| N75GL | SBRL | 465-71 |
| N75GM | C500 | 169 |
| N75GM | SBRL | 306-110 |
| N75GN | HS25 | 25161 |
| N75GP | LJ24 | 333 |
| N75GP | LJ55 | 129 |
| N75GR | LJ24 | 333 |
| (N75GV) | C560 | 0140 |
| N75GW | C500 | 257 |
| N75GX | ASTR | 137 |
| N75GZ | ASTR | 075 |
| N75HL | SBRL | 380-36 |
| **N75HL** | **SBRL** | **465-16** |
| N75HP | SBRL | 306-48 |
| N75HS | C550 | 286 |
| **N75HS** | **C750** | **0037** |
| **N75HU** | **C56X** | **5119** |
| N75HZ | SBRL | 380-53 |
| N75JD | SBRL | 282-4 |
| **N75JK** | **C52B** | **0240** |
| N75JT | SBRL | 306-94 |
| (N75KC) | C500 | 187 |
| N75KR | C550 | 075 |
| N75KV | LJ24 | 258 |
| N75KV | LJ35 | 285 |
| N75L | SBRL | 380-66 |
| **N75LJ** | **LJ55** | **065** |
| N75LM | LJ25 | 233 |
| **N75MC** | **CS55** | **0109** |
| N75MC | LJ31 | 052 |
| N75MD | SBRL | 282-129 |
| N75MG | GLF2 | 247 |
| N75MG | JSTR | 5087/55 |
| (N75MH) | FA10 | 75 |
| N75MN | C500 | 257 |
| N75MT | HS25 | 258231 |
| **N75NE** | **LJ24** | **351** |
| N75NL | SBRL | 380-40 |
| (N75NP) | CL65 | 5776 |
| N75NP | HS25 | 258170 |
| N75NR | SBRL | 370-2 |
| N75NR | SBRL | 370-5 |
| N75NR | SBRL | 370-7 |
| N75NR | SBRL | 380-53 |
| N75NR | SBRL | 380-64 |
| (N75PK) | LJ35 | 464 |
| N75PP | C52A | 0132 |
| N75PP | GLF4 | 1073 |
| N75PX | C500 | 248 |
| N75QS | HS25 | 25190 |
| N75RD | C650 | 0134 |
| N75RD | FA50 | 220 |
| N75RD | HS25 | 25228 |
| **N75RJ** | **C550** | **692** |
| N75RJ | LJ35 | 168 |
| **N75RL** | **BE40** | **RK-312** |
| N75RN | C650 | 0134 |
| N75RN | HS25 | 25228 |
| N75RP | GLF2 | 199/19 |
| N75RP | GLF3 | 328 |
| N75RP | GLF4 | 1073 |
| **N75RP** | **GLF5** | **528** |
| N75RS | SBRL | 380-32 |
| N75RS | SBRL | 380-42 |
| N75RS | SBRL | 380-58 |
| N75RS | SBRL | 380-63 |
| N75RZ | FA50 | 113 |
| N75SE | SBRL | 380-4 |
| **N75SJ** | **C680** | **0166** |
| N75SJ | LJ25 | 175 |
| N75SL | SBRL | 380-12 |
| N75SR | GLF2 | 96 |
| N75ST | HS25 | 257013 |
| N75TD | LJ36 | 028 |
| N75TE | LJ45 | 057 |
| N75TF | LJ35 | 191 |
| N75TG | C550 | 174 |
| N75TJ | C500 | 689 |
| N75TJ | FA20 | 289 |
| N75TJ | HS25 | 25190 |
| N75TJ | LJ25 | 210 |
| N75TJ | SBRL | 380-6 |
| N75TP | C550 | 286 |
| N75TP | C56X | 5261 |
| **N75TP** | **C56X** | **5768** |
| N75TP | LJ55 | 032 |
| N75TT | ASTR | 065 |
| N75U | SBRL | 370-4 |
| N75UA | SBRL | 370-4 |
| N75V | F900 | 13 |
| **N75VC** | **SBRL** | **465-71** |
| (N75W) | F900 | 13 |
| N75W | F900 | 63 |
| N75W | FA50 | 152 |
| N75W | SBRL | 282-129 |
| N75WA | SBRL | 282-129 |
| N75WC | GLF2 | 199/19 |
| N75WC | GLF2 | 96 |
| N75WE | FA50 | 152 |
| **N75WP** | **C560** | **0449** |
| **N75XL** | **C56X** | **5575** |
| **N75XP** | **LJ45** | **118** |
| N75XR | LJ40 | 45-2075 |
| N75Y | SBRL | 380-64 |
| N75Z | C550 | 236 |
| N75Z | C560 | 0345 |
| N75ZA | C550 | 236 |
| **N75ZZ** | **GLEX** | **9365** |
| N76AE | C525 | 0139 |
| N76AF | FA10 | 36 |
| (N76AM) | C500 | 258 |
| **N76AM** | **FA10** | **157** |
| **N76AS** | **C550** | **438** |
| N76AW | LJ55 | 036 |
| **N76AX** | **LJ25** | **254** |
| **N76BF** | **C510** | **0276** |
| N76BH | HS25 | 25286 |
| N76CK | C550 | 345 |
| N76CK | C560 | 0372 |
| **N76CK** | **LJ25** | **020** |
| N76CS | CL61 | 5103 |
| N76CS | GLF2 | 158 |
| **N76CS** | **HS25** | **258595** |
| N76D | C650 | 0110 |
| N76D | C750 | 0006 |
| N76EB | JSTR | 5093 |
| **N76EJ** | **GLF4** | **1033** |
| **N76EM** | **E50P** | **50000013** |
| **N76ER** | **WW24** | **369** |
| **N76EU** | **PRM1** | **RB-276** |
| (N76FB) | FA50 | 41 |
| N76FC | CS55 | 0090 |
| **N76FC** | **HS25** | **258784** |
| **N76FD** | **F900** | **41** |
| N76FD | FA50 | 41 |
| N76FJ | FA10 | 58 |
| N76FJ | FA50 | 67 |
| N76GL | LJ35 | 036 |
| **N76GP** | **C510** | **0203** |
| N76GP | LJ35 | 036 |
| N76GT | C500 | 313 |
| N76GT | SBRL | 306-61 |
| N76HG | JSTR | 5076/17 |
| **N76HL** | **PRM1** | **RB-112** |
| (N76JY) | C500 | 676 |
| N76LE | MU30 | A047SA |
| N76LE | MU30 | A076SA |
| **N76LV** | **HS25** | **258530** |
| N76MB | FA10 | 83 |
| N76MB | FA20 | 80 |
| N76NX | SBRL | 465-53 |
| N76PR | C650 | 7059 |
| (N76PW) | LJ24 | 311 |
| N76QF | LJ60 | 156 |
| N76QS | GLF2 | 158 |
| N76RE | C500 | 091 |
| N76RP | GLF4 | 1440 |
| N76RV | LJ24 | 325 |
| N76RY | FA20 | 57 |
| **N76SF** | **CL64** | **5603** |
| N76SF | LJ60 | 156 |
| N76TA | FA20 | 393 |
| N76TE | LJ45 | 081 |
| **N76TF** | **C560** | **0431** |
| N76TG | WW24 | 297 |
| (N76TJ) | FA10 | 12 |
| N76TJ | GLF3 | 345 |
| (N76TJ) | HS25 | 256070 |
| N76TR | LJ24 | 333 |
| N76TS | FA20 | 44 |

| | | |
|---|---|---|
| **N76UM** | **LJ25** | **051** |
| **N76VE** | **C56X** | **5077** |
| N76VG | FA20 | 233 |
| **N76WR** | **C560** | **0459** |
| **N76XR** | **LJ60** | **376** |
| N76ZZ | GLEX | 9266 |
| N77A | F2TH | 17 |
| N77A | SBRL | 465-1 |
| N77AE | LJ24 | 163 |
| N77AP | SBRL | 282-37 |
| N77AT | SBRL | 282-109 |
| N77AT | SBRL | 306-23 |
| **N77BT** | **GLF3** | **429** |
| N77BT | HS25 | 25155 |
| N77BT | JSTR | 5113/25 |
| N77C | HS25 | 25123 |
| N77C | HS25 | 256038 |
| **N77C** | **JSTR** | **5232** |
| N77CD | HS25 | 25123 |
| N77CE | F900 | 12 |
| N77CE | FA50 | 21 |
| N77CP | C500 | 173 |
| N77CP | FA50 | 143 |
| N77CP | GLF4 | 1194 |
| **N77CP** | **GLF5** | **565** |
| N77CP | LJ35 | 177 |
| N77CQ | LJ35 | 177 |
| N77CS | HS25 | 258065 |
| **N77CS** | **HS25** | **258620** |
| N77CU | HS25 | 256038 |
| N77CU | HS25 | 258065 |
| N77D | GLF4 | 1266 |
| **N77D** | **GLF4** | **1340** |
| N77D | HS25 | 25093 |
| N77D | HS25 | 257101 |
| N77D | JSTR | 5097/60 |
| **N77DB** | **C525** | **0443** |
| N77DD | C550 | 695 |
| N77DY | GLF4 | 1266 |
| N77EK | GLF3 | 363 |
| N77F | WW24 | 4 |
| N77FC | LJ35 | 031 |
| **N77FD** | **C500** | **663** |
| N77FJ | FA50 | 62 |
| N77FK | GLF3 | 363 |
| **N77FK** | **GLF4** | **1357** |
| N77FK | LJ35 | 376 |
| N77FK | LJ55 | 108 |
| **N77FN** | **LJ25** | **216** |
| N77FV | WW24 | 26 |
| N77GA | BE40 | RJ-5 |
| (N77GA) | MU30 | A011SA |
| N77GH | LJ24 | 116 |
| N77GJ | C500 | 497 |
| N77GJ | LJ24 | 174 |
| N77GR | FA20 | 105 |
| N77GT | FA10 | 60 |
| N77HF | C560 | 0133 |
| **N77HF** | **C650** | **7036** |
| N77HH | WW24 | 103 |
| N77HN | C560 | 0009 |
| **N77HN** | **LJ40** | **45-2070** |
| N77HN | LJ45 | 169 |
| N77HU | C560 | 0009 |
| N77HW | JSTR | 5080 |
| N77JL | LJ24 | 286 |
| N77JN | LJ24 | 202 |
| **N77JW** | **FA10** | **6** |
| (N77JW) | LJ36 | 044 |
| (N77JW) | LJ55 | 033 |
| N77JW | LJ55 | 034 |
| N77KT | WW24 | 7 |
| N77KW | LJ25 | 076 |
| N77LA | FA20 | 319 |
| **N77LA** | **HS25** | **258029** |
| N77LB | LJ24 | 135 |
| (N77LJ) | HS25 | 25098 |
| N77LJ | LJ35 | 014 |
| N77LN | LJ35 | 306 |
| N77LP | HS25 | 257122 |
| N77LP | LJ35 | 321 |
| N77LS | LJ24 | 194 |
| **N77LX** | **C650** | **7051** |
| N77M | C52B | 0023 |
| **N77M** | **C52B** | **0100** |
| (N77MK) | SBRL | 282-52 |
| N77MR | LJ24 | 351 |
| N77MR | SBRL | 282-52 |
| N77ND | C550 | 005 |
| N77NJ | LJ25 | 033 |
| **N77NJ** | **LJ35** | **658** |
| N77NR | C560 | 0009 |
| N77NR | FA10 | 109 |
| N77NR | LJ35 | 503 |
| **N77NR** | **LJ40** | **45-2109** |
| N77NR | WW24 | 28 |
| N77NT | FA50 | 77 |
| N77NT | WW24 | 7 |
| N77PA | C500 | 639 |
| N77PA | CS55 | 0051 |
| N77PH | C550 | 244 |
| N77PH | LJ31 | 089 |
| N77PK | LJ25 | 114 |
| **N77PR** | **C550** | **244** |
| N77PX | C500 | 639 |
| **N77PY** | **LJ31** | **089** |
| N77QM | FA20 | 75 |
| N77QR | GLF4 | 1194 |
| N77RC | C500 | 184 |
| N77RC | C550 | 169 |
| N77RE | C500 | 224 |
| (N77RS) | LJ24 | 258 |
| N77RS | LJ25 | 094 |
| N77RY | LJ24 | 137 |
| N77SA | HS25 | 257108 |
| N77SA | LJ25 | 018 |
| (N77SF) | C550 | 078 |
| **N77SF** | **FA10** | **141** |
| N77ST | WW24 | 108 |
| (N77SW) | FA50 | 53 |
| N77SW | GLF2 | 15 |
| N77SW | GLF3 | 413 |
| N77SW | GLF4 | 1023 |
| N77SW | GLF4 | 1146 |
| N77SW | GLF4 | 1207 |
| N77TC | HS25 | 258275 |
| **N77TC** | **HS25** | **HA-0007** |
| N77TC | SBRL | 465-10 |
| N77TC | WW24 | 4 |
| N77TE | FA50 | 110 |
| N77TE | LJ35 | 031 |
| N77TG | GLF3 | 332 |
| N77TW | C500 | 519 |
| N77U | LJ35 | 031 |
| N77UB | C500 | 644 |
| **N77UF** | **GLEX** | **9284** |
| **N77UW** | **C56X** | **5005** |
| N77VJ | LJ24 | 041 |
| N77VK | HS25 | 25051 |
| N77VR | C525 | 0344 |
| **N77VR** | **C52A** | **0240** |
| (N77VU) | GLF4 | 1207 |
| **N77VZ** | **C525** | **0344** |
| N77W | HS25 | 258150 |
| N77WD | C550 | 193 |
| N77WD | HS25 | 25224 |
| N77WD | LJ24 | 174 |
| **N77WL** | **GLF4** | **1140** |
| N77WU | C550 | 193 |
| N78AB | C500 | 444 |
| N78AD | CL61 | 5063 |
| N78AE | LJ24 | 267 |
| N78AF | LJ24 | 233 |
| N78AG | HS25 | 25101 |
| N78AM | C560 | 0056 |
| **N78AP** | **C650** | **0056** |
| N78BA | C550 | 306 |
| (N78BA) | C550 | 368 |
| N78BC | FA20 | 341 |
| N78BC | SBRL | 282-104 |
| N78BH | HS25 | 25287 |
| N78BH | LJ24 | 184 |
| N78BL | WW24 | 182 |
| N78BR | C650 | 7078 |
| (N78BT) | C500 | 478 |
| N78BT | LJ25 | 191 |
| **N78CK** | **C550** | **345** |
| N78CN | C500 | 606 |
| N78CS | C550 | 187 |
| N78CS | HS25 | 257137 |
| N78D | C650 | 0116 |
| N78D | C650 | 7043 |
| (N78DL) | C650 | 0116 |
| N78DL | C650 | 7043 |
| N78DT | LJ25 | 356 |
| N78EM | C650 | 0192 |
| N78FA | C550 | 039 |
| **N78FJ** | **F2TH** | **78** |
| N78FJ | FA50 | 63 |
| N78FK | C550 | 498 |
| N78FK | LJ55 | 108 |
| N78GA | C550 | 083 |
| N78GA | C550 | 097 |
| **N78GJ** | **WW24** | **310** |
| N78GL | LJ25 | 240 |
| N78GP | SBRL | 282-72 |
| N78JP | SBRL | 306-20 |
| N78JR | FA20 | 70 |
| **N78KN** | **HA4T** | **RC-31** |
| N78LB | WW24 | 162 |
| **N78LF** | **FA50** | **77** |
| **N78LT** | **FA50** | **75** |
| (N78MC) | C500 | 150 |
| **N78MC** | **LJ35** | **117** |
| **N78MD** | **C550** | **550-0970** |
| N78MD | FA10 | 18 |
| N78MN | LJ35 | 237 |
| N78MN | WW24 | 149 |
| N78MP | JSTR | 5095/30 |
| N78NP | C560 | 0107 |
| **N78NT** | **F2TH** | **121** |
| N78PH | C550 | 025 |
| N78PH | LJ31 | 090 |
| N78PP | CL61 | 5038 |
| N78PR | C550 | 025 |
| **N78PR** | **LJ31** | **090** |
| (N78PT) | C650 | 0187 |
| **N78PT** | **WW24** | **304** |
| N78QA | LJ35 | 302 |
| (N78QS) | HS25 | 257137 |
| N78RP | CL61 | 5038 |
| N78RP | CL64 | 5338 |
| N78RP | CL64 | 5604 |
| N78RP | GLF3 | 328 |
| N78RR | SBRL | 306-33 |
| (N78RX) | CL64 | 5604 |
| N78RZ | HS25 | 25114 |
| **N78SD** | **CL64** | **5469** |
| N78SD | LJ25 | 251 |
| **N78SL** | **C750** | **0238** |
| N78SR | CL60 | 1057 |
| N78TC | C550 | 282 |
| **N78TC** | **CL30** | **20070** |
| N78TC | SBRL | 282-99 |
| N78TF | C550 | 195 |
| N78WW | WW24 | 349 |
| N78WW | WW24 | 399 |
| N78ZZ | GLEX | 9267 |
| N79AD | ASTR | 029 |
| N79AD | CL61 | 5063 |
| N79AD | CL61 | 5140 |
| **N79AD** | **GLEX** | **9058** |
| N79AD | WW24 | 375 |
| N79AE | FA20 | 196 |
| N79AE | HS25 | 25031 |
| N79AE | JSTR | 5155/32 |
| N79AN | CL61 | 5140 |
| N79AP | WW24 | 375 |
| (N79AX) | LJ25 | 118 |
| N79AX | LJ35 | 389 |
| N79B | HS25 | 25228 |
| N79BC | C56X | 5337 |
| N79BH | HS25 | 256002 |
| N79BH | LJ35 | 220 |
| N79BJ | LJ31 | 101 |
| **N79BK** | **C500** | **498** |
| N79BP | FA10 | 178 |
| **N79CB** | **PRM1** | **RB-264** |
| N79CD | C550 | 023 |
| N79CD | SBRL | 465-46 |
| N79DD | C500 | 254 |
| N79EA | C56X | 5073 |
| (N79EA) | EA50 | 000297 |
| **N79EH** | **HS25** | **257047** |
| **N79EL** | **BE40** | **RK-214** |
| **N79EV** | **LJ25** | **097** |
| **N79FJ** | **F2TH** | **79** |
| (N79FJ) | FA10 | 144 |
| N79FJ | FA50 | 64 |
| (N79FJ) | FA50 | 79 |
| **N79FT** | **C500** | **456** |
| N79GA | MU30 | A023SA |
| N79HA | FA10 | 128 |
| N79HC | HS25 | 257063 |
| N79HM | BE40 | RK-70 |
| **N79JS** | **C52B** | **0273** |
| (N79JS) | LJ36 | 029 |
| **N79KF** | **C650** | **0118** |
| N79KP | WW24 | 262 |
| N79LB | C52B | 0019 |
| N79LC | WW24 | 257 |
| N79LS | LJ24 | 097 |
| N79MB | FA20 | 507 |
| (N79MB) | JSTR | 5055/21 |
| N79MJ | LJ35 | 201 |
| **N79MX** | **C525** | **0190** |
| N79NP | HS25 | 258170 |
| N79PB | FA10 | 128 |
| N79PB | FA10 | 47 |
| N79PF | C56X | 5151 |
| N79PF | FA50 | 174 |
| **N79PG** | **C680** | **0018** |
| N79PM | C560 | 0459 |
| N79PM | FA20 | 510 |
| N79RP | GLF4 | 1220 |
| **N79RS** | **C500** | **107** |
| N79RS | LJ24 | 280 |
| N79SE | C550 | 585 |
| **N79SE** | **LJ31** | **206** |
| N79SF | LJ36 | 041 |
| **N79TJ** | **FA10** | **148** |
| N79TJ | HS25 | 25079 |
| N79TS | HS25 | 25042 |
| N79TS | HS25 | 257047 |
| N79XR | LJ60 | 379 |
| N79ZZ | GLEX | 9279 |
| N80 | WW24 | 144 |
| N80A | GLF2 | 38 |
| **N80A** | **GLF4** | **1348** |
| **N80AB** | **C560** | **0169** |
| N80AB | SBRL | 380-59 |
| N80AG | GLF2 | 164 |
| (N80AG) | GLF3 | 401 |
| **N80AJ** | **C500** | **100** |
| **N80AP** | **LJ24** | **312** |
| **N80AR** | **LJ35** | **454** |
| N80AS | LJ35 | 446 |
| N80AT | CL60 | 1036 |
| N80AT | GLF3 | 463 |
| N80AT | GLF4 | 1151 |
| **N80AT** | **GLF4** | **1410** |
| **N80AW** | **C550** | **197** |
| N80AX | C52A | 0178 |
| N80AX | LJ25 | 224 |
| N80BE | LJ25 | 248 |
| N80BF | CL61 | 5117 |
| N80BF | HS25 | 258012 |
| N80BH | HS25 | 256003 |
| N80BL | BE40 | RK-219 |
| N80BL | FA10 | 200 |
| N80BL | LJ35 | 459 |
| N80BR | GLF4 | 1132 |
| N80BR | HS25 | 258012 |
| N80BS | C550 | 132 |
| N80BT | LJ25 | 248 |
| N80BT | LJ35 | 343 |
| N80C | C525 | 0416 |
| **N80C** | **C52A** | **0104** |
| N80CB | LJ24 | 148 |
| N80CC | C500 | 132 |
| N80CC | C650 | 0034 |
| N80CC | FA10 | 18 |
| N80CC | HS25 | 25095 |
| (N80CC) | HS25 | 258027 |
| N80CD | LJ35 | 215 |
| N80CD | LJ35 | 282 |
| N80CD | LJ35 | 477 |
| **N80CJ** | **C500** | **537** |
| N80CJ | C525 | 0080 |
| **N80CK** | **CL60** | **1069** |
| N80CK | LJ24 | 309 |
| N80CL | HS25 | 257170 |
| N80CN | FA50 | 105 |
| N80CR | SBRL | 306-128 |
| N80CR | SBRL | 306-142 |
| N80CS | CL61 | 3010 |
| (N80DE) | BE40 | RK-26 |
| N80DH | LJ24 | 191 |
| N80DR | C550 | 142 |
| N80DX | BE40 | RK-26 |
| **N80DX** | **LJ60** | **012** |
| N80E | GLF2 | 184 |

| | | |
|---|---|---|
| N80E | HS25 | 258680 |
| **N80E** | **HS25** | **HA-0155** |
| N80E | SBRL | 306-58 |
| N80ED | LJ35 | 337 |
| **N80EH** | **HS25** | **258680** |
| **N80EJ** | **E50P** | **50000133** |
| **N80EL** | **LJ25** | **092** |
| N80EP | C560 | 0295 |
| N80ER | SBRL | 306-58 |
| N80F | F900 | 6 |
| N80F | F9EX | 76 |
| N80FB | HS25 | 258572 |
| N80FD | WW24 | 260 |
| N80FH | SBRL | 465-34 |
| N80FJ | FA50 | 69 |
| N80G | HS25 | 257131 |
| N80GB | C500 | 094 |
| N80GD | LJ35 | 215 |
| N80GD | LJ35 | 282 |
| N80GE | C560 | 0187 |
| **N80GJ** | **HS25** | **258136** |
| **N80GK** | **GALX** | **161** |
| **N80GM** | **C550** | **208** |
| N80GM | JSTR | 5146 |
| N80GP | FA10 | 157 |
| **N80GP** | **FA50** | **274** |
| N80GR | C560 | 0494 |
| **N80GR** | **C560** | **0616** |
| N80GR | LJ25 | 193 |
| N80GX | ASTR | 138 |
| **N80HB** | **C52B** | **0163** |
| N80HD | HS25 | 258334 |
| **N80HD** | **HS25** | **258609** |
| N80HG | SBRL | 380-19 |
| N80HK | LJ35 | 238 |
| N80HK | SBRL | 380-71 |
| **N80HQ** | **C510** | **0021** |
| N80J | GLF2 | 160 |
| N80J | GLF3 | 441 |
| N80J | HS25 | 258681 |
| **N80J** | **HS25** | **HA-0156** |
| **N80JE** | **HS25** | **258681** |
| N80K | HS25 | 257138 |
| N80K | SBRL | 370-2 |
| N80KA | HS25 | 257001 |
| N80KM | BE40 | RK-50 |
| N80KM | HS25 | 257094 |
| (N80KR) | LJ35 | 454 |
| N80KR | SBRL | 380-42 |
| N80L | GLF3 | 406 |
| N80L | SBRL | 306-42 |
| N80LA | C550 | 441 |
| N80LJ | LJ31 | 080 |
| N80LP | C560 | 0295 |
| **N80LP** | **C56X** | **5249** |
| N80LX | SBRL | 380-51 |
| N80MF | C500 | 558 |
| N80MJ | LJ35 | 280 |
| N80MP | FA10 | 68 |
| N80NR | SBRL | 380-15 |
| **N80PG** | **LJ35** | **063** |
| **N80PJ** | **LJ25** | **260** |
| **N80PK** | **HS25** | **258442** |
| N80PM | HS25 | 257141 |
| N80PM | HS25 | 258236 |
| N80PN | HS25 | 257141 |
| N80Q | GLF2 | 39 |
| N80Q | GLF4 | 4012 |
| N80QL | GLF4 | 4012 |
| N80QM | SBRL | 282-23 |
| N80QM | SBRL | 306-143 |
| N80R | GALX | 074 |
| N80R | SBRL | 465-53 |
| N80RE | LJ25 | 216 |
| N80RE | WW24 | 341 |
| N80RN | SBRL | 465-53 |
| N80RP | CL61 | 3026 |
| N80RP | GLF5 | 528 |
| N80RP | LJ25 | 216 |
| **N80RP** | **LJ45** | **008** |
| N80RS | SBRL | 380-17 |
| N80RS | SBRL | 380-57 |
| N80SF | C500 | 582 |
| (N80SJ) | SJ30 | 008 |
| **N80SL** | **C500** | **483** |
| N80SM | LJ35 | 205 |
| N80TF | C525 | 0076 |
| N80TF | CL60 | 1054 |

| | | |
|---|---|---|
| **N80TF** | **EA50** | **000032** |
| N80TF | WW24 | 39 |
| N80TN | SBRL | 380-19 |
| N80TR | FA50 | 32 |
| **N80TS** | **BE40** | **RJ-34** |
| N80TS | FA10 | 87 |
| N80TS | HS25 | 256013 |
| N80TS | JSTR | 5215 |
| **N80UT** | **LJ35** | **200** |
| N80VP | C525 | 0453 |
| N80WD | GLF2 | 88/21 |
| N80WE | FA50 | 80 |
| N80WG | LJ35 | 281 |
| N80WJ | FA10 | 202 |
| **N80X** | **C56X** | **5054** |
| N80ZZ | GLEX | 9219 |
| N81 | WW24 | 143 |
| N81AB | HS25 | 259005 |
| (N81AG) | FA20 | 514 |
| N81AJ | FA20 | 308 |
| N81AP | C650 | 0082 |
| **N81AX** | **LJ25** | **279** |
| N81BA | C500 | 038 |
| N81BH | HS25 | 256004 |
| N81CC | C500 | 492 |
| N81CC | C550 | 088 |
| (N81CH) | FA50 | 47 |
| N81CH | HS25 | 257212 |
| N81CH | LJ35 | 500 |
| N81CH | LJ55 | 032 |
| N81CH | LJ55 | 036 |
| N81CN | HS25 | 257212 |
| N81D | HS25 | 256011 |
| N81DM | MU30 | 002 |
| **N81EB** | **C500** | **355** |
| **N81ER** | **C52B** | **0190** |
| N81ER | C550 | 550-1015 |
| N81EX | F2EX | 81 |
| N81FC | GLF2 | 91 |
| N81FJ | FA50 | 70 |
| **N81FR** | **LJ35** | **081** |
| N81GD | C550 | 267 |
| N81GD | SBRL | 380-54 |
| N81GN | F900 | 81 |
| N81HH | HS25 | 257189 |
| N81HH | HS25 | 259034 |
| N81HH | MU30 | A013SA |
| N81HP | SBRL | 306-100 |
| **N81HR** | **PRM1** | **RB-200** |
| N81JJ | JSTR | 5002 |
| **N81KA** | **HS25** | **257038** |
| N81LB | FA10 | 158 |
| (N81LJ) | LJ24 | 081 |
| N81LJ | LJ31 | 081 |
| N81LR | C550 | 550-1015 |
| N81MC | LJ24 | 344 |
| N81MJ | C500 | 301 |
| N81MR | JSTR | 5039 |
| **N81MR** | **LJ35** | **622** |
| N81MW | LJ25 | 277 |
| N81P | FA10 | 153 |
| N81P | FA10 | 31 |
| **N81P** | **FA20** | **446** |
| **N81PJ** | **MS76** | **081** |
| N81PX | FA10 | 153 |
| N81QH | LJ35 | 500 |
| N81QV | HS25 | 257058 |
| N81R | FA50 | 148 |
| N81RA | C525 | 0194 |
| **N81RR** | **GLF2** | **246** |
| N81RR | HS25 | 25196 |
| **N81SF** | **C650** | **0074** |
| N81SH | C560 | 0357 |
| **N81SH** | **C56X** | **5101** |
| N81SH | CS55 | 0146 |
| (N81SN) | C750 | 0097 |
| **N81SN** | **F9EX** | **41** |
| N81SN | HS25 | 258460 |
| N81SV | F900 | 146 |
| N81T | HS25 | 25225 |
| N81TC | C550 | 094 |
| N81TC | C650 | 0039 |
| N81TF | C550 | 136 |
| N81TJ | BE40 | RK-14 |
| N81TJ | C550 | 242 |
| N81TJ | FA10 | 187 |
| N81TJ | MU30 | A081SA |
| (N81TT) | BE40 | RK-65 |

| | | |
|---|---|---|
| (N81TT) | C650 | 0029 |
| N81TT | GALX | 006 |
| (N81TT) | GALX | 143 |
| **N81TX** | **FA10** | **81** |
| N81U | FA50 | 148 |
| **N81WL** | **C510** | **0165** |
| N81WT | LJ24 | 351 |
| **N81ZZ** | **GLEX** | **9020** |
| N81ZZ | GLEX | 9222 |
| N82 | WW24 | 142 |
| N82A | CL60 | 1072 |
| N82A | FA20 | 205 |
| N82A | GLF3 | 342 |
| N82A | GLF4 | 1068 |
| **N82A** | **GLF4** | **4032** |
| **N82AE** | **C525** | **0412** |
| N82AE | GLF3 | 342 |
| N82AF | SBRL | 380-21 |
| **N82AJ** | **C500** | **428** |
| N82AT | C500 | 312 |
| N82AT | F2TH | 51 |
| **N82AX** | **LJ25** | **301** |
| **N82BE** | **ASTR** | **113** |
| N82BG | C750 | 0082 |
| N82BH | HS25 | 256001 |
| (N82BL) | HS25 | 258126 |
| (N82BR) | GLF4 | 1082 |
| **N82CA** | **HS25** | **25201** |
| (N82CF) | C500 | 330 |
| N82CF | SBRL | 282-100 |
| N82CG | FA10 | 167 |
| N82CK | GLF2 | 64/27 |
| N82CN | CL60 | 1050 |
| **N82CN** | **CL64** | **5395** |
| N82CR | FA10 | 183 |
| **N82CR** | **GLF2** | **80** |
| N82CR | SBRL | 465-49 |
| N82CS | MU30 | A040SA |
| N82CT | MU30 | A012SA |
| (N82CW) | C560 | 0342 |
| N82CW | CL60 | 1050 |
| N82CW | CL64 | 5395 |
| **N82DT** | **C500** | **459** |
| **N82DU** | **E50P** | **50000008** |
| N82EA | HS25 | 258283 |
| N82FJ | CL61 | 5082 |
| N82FJ | FA50 | 72 |
| N82GA | C550 | 448 |
| N82GA | LJ35 | 071 |
| **N82GG** | **LJ36** | **040** |
| N82GK | HS25 | 258618 |
| N82GL | LJ35 | 477 |
| N82GM | C56X | 5596 |
| **N82GM** | **C650** | **7064** |
| N82GP | F900 | 82 |
| N82HH | WW24 | 383 |
| N82JA | LJ55 | 029 |
| N82JC | WW24 | 82 |
| N82JJ | C550 | 223 |
| N82JL | LJ35 | 380 |
| N82JT | C500 | 208 |
| (N82KD) | LJ60 | 095 |
| (N82KK) | F9EX | 84 |
| N82KK | LJ31 | 054 |
| **N82KK** | **LJ60** | **095** |
| N82KL | LJ31 | 054 |
| **N82KW** | **C56X** | **5202** |
| N82LP | FA50 | 18 |
| N82LS | C500 | 681 |
| N82MA | C550 | 550-0891 |
| N82MD | FA10 | 77 |
| N82MJ | C500 | 377 |
| N82ML | SBRL | 282-83 |
| (N82MP) | C500 | 514 |
| N82MP | FA50 | 42 |
| N82MW | SBRL | 306-76 |
| N82NC | FA50 | 94 |
| **N82P** | **C500** | **612** |
| **N82PJ** | **FA20** | **177** |
| N82PP | HS25 | 256001 |
| **N82QD** | **BE40** | **RK-72** |
| N82R | SBRL | 282-131 |
| N82RP | C550 | 139 |
| **N82RP** | **F900** | **116** |
| N82RP | FA50 | 18 |
| N82RP | HS25 | 256001 |
| N82RT | ASTR | 036 |
| N82RZ | C550 | 139 |

| | | |
|---|---|---|
| N82SE | C500 | 346 |
| (N82SR) | FA20 | 83 |
| **N82SR** | **HS25** | **258026** |
| N82SR | JSTR | 5082/36 |
| **N82ST** | **FA50** | **85** |
| **N82SV** | **F900** | **163** |
| N82TC | C650 | 0040 |
| N82TN | FA20 | 384/551 |
| N82TS | LJ25 | 154 |
| (N82UH) | LJ25 | 010 |
| N82VP | C650 | 0082 |
| N82XP | HS25 | 258173 |
| N83 | WW24 | 131 |
| N83AB | SBRL | 380-59 |
| N83AE | MU30 | A041SA |
| N83AG | C550 | 483 |
| N83AG | GLF3 | 464 |
| N83AL | GLF3 | 363 |
| N83AL | WW24 | 83 |
| **N83BG** | **MU30** | **A018SA** |
| N83CE | LJ24 | 074 |
| **N83CG** | **MU30** | **A032SA** |
| **N83CK** | **LJ25** | **183** |
| **N83CP** | **GLF5** | **635** |
| N83CP | LJ35 | 274 |
| N83CT | C650 | 0015 |
| N83CT | WW24 | 321 |
| **N83CW** | **GLF5** | **649** |
| N83D | FA20 | 368 |
| N83D | GLF3 | 317 |
| N83DC | C525 | 0380 |
| **N83DM** | **C500** | **634** |
| (N83DM) | LJ35 | 173 |
| N83DM | LJ36 | 007 |
| N83EA | FA10 | 83 |
| N83EA | LJ25 | 240 |
| N83EJ | GALX | 009 |
| **N83EM** | **C510** | **0026** |
| **N83EP** | **C560** | **0021** |
| N83EX | F2EX | 83 |
| N83FC | FA50 | 119 |
| **N83FJ** | **FA50** | **74** |
| **N83FN** | **LJ36** | **007** |
| **N83GG** | **C56X** | **5046** |
| N83GG | LJ25 | 038 |
| N83GK | C650 | 7050 |
| N83H | LJ24 | 193 |
| N83HC | LJ24 | 193 |
| N83HF | C550 | 126 |
| **N83HF** | **HS25** | **257145** |
| **N83JJ** | **CL30** | **20259** |
| N83JJ | FA10 | 163 |
| N83JJ | LJ40 | 45-2072 |
| N83JM | LJ25 | 127 |
| N83KE | C550 | 568 |
| N83LC | CL61 | 5029 |
| **N83LJ** | **LJ24** | **076** |
| N83M | GLF2 | 135 |
| **N83M** | **GLF5** | **557** |
| N83M | JSTR | 5084/8 |
| (N83MA) | C550 | 117 |
| N83MD | FA10 | 78 |
| **N83MD** | **HS25** | **257121** |
| (N83MF) | FA10 | 78 |
| N83MJ | LJ24 | 239 |
| N83MP | FA50 | 103 |
| N83ND | C500 | 580 |
| **N83NW** | **C500** | **309** |
| **N83PP** | **GLF3** | **464** |
| N83RE | C560 | 0183 |
| N83RG | FA10 | 25 |
| N83RG | LJ24 | 243 |
| (N83RH) | SBRL | 306-44 |
| N83RR | C560 | 0183 |
| N83RR | C56X | 5007 |
| **N83SA** | **MU30** | **A030SA** |
| N83SD | C56X | 5091 |
| **N83SD** | **C680** | **0106** |
| N83SD | LJ55 | 032 |
| N83SE | C550 | 203 |
| N83SF | C550 | 203 |
| **N83SG** | **WW24** | **368** |
| **N83SV** | **F9EX** | **77** |
| N83TC | LJ25 | 315 |
| N83TE | GLF2 | 129 |
| N83TE | GLF2 | 156/31 |
| N83TE | GLF5 | 5043 |
| N83TE | LJ25 | 329 |

| | | |
|---|---|---|
| (N83TE) | LJ35 | 218 |
| N83TF | C500 | 256 |
| **N83TF** | **C52B** | **0094** |
| N83TF | C560 | 0636 |
| N83TF | SBRL | 465-43 |
| N83TH | LJ25 | 016 |
| (N83TJ) | C500 | 462 |
| N83TJ | FA10 | 35 |
| N83TJ | HS25 | 256070 |
| N83TJ | LJ35 | 138 |
| N83TK | C560 | 0636 |
| N83TK | MU30 | A083SA |
| N83TN | LJ45 | 057 |
| N83TR | C525 | 0185 |
| (N83TR) | LJ45 | 248 |
| **N83TR** | **LJ60** | **374** |
| **N83TY** | **FA50** | **288** |
| N83TZ | LJ45 | 057 |
| N83V | FA20 | 366 |
| N83WM | LJ31 | 081 |
| **N83WM** | **LJ55** | **043** |
| N83WM | LJ60 | 104 |
| N83WN | LJ31 | 081 |
| N83XP | HS25 | HA-0083 |
| **N83ZA** | **C560** | **0176** |
| N83ZZ | GLEX | 9223 |
| N84 | WW24 | 130 |
| N84A | GLF2 | 122 |
| N84A | HS25 | 258010 |
| N84AD | LJ35 | 499 |
| (N84AL) | GLF2 | 166/15 |
| N84AW | C550 | 493 |
| N84BA | HS25 | 258047 |
| N84BA | HS25 | 258313 |
| N84BJ | BE40 | RJ-17 |
| N84CF | C500 | 460 |
| N84CF | C500 | 658 |
| (N84CF) | C550 | 550-0892 |
| N84CP | HS25 | 25286 |
| N84CT | HS25 | 258239 |
| N84CT | LJ24 | 197 |
| N84DJ | LJ55 | 034 |
| N84DM | LJ36 | 002 |
| (N84DT) | MU30 | A084SA |
| N84EA | C550 | 484 |
| **N84EA** | **C750** | **0094** |
| N84EA | PRM1 | RB-119 |
| N84EB | C550 | 488 |
| **N84EC** | **CS55** | **0014** |
| **N84EE** | **C680** | **0262** |
| N84FA | HS25 | 258047 |
| **N84FG** | **C525** | **0192** |
| N84FJ | FA50 | 76 |
| **N84FM** | **PRM1** | **RB-30** |
| **N84FN** | **LJ36** | **002** |
| N84G | C650 | 0045 |
| N84GA | HS25 | 257056 |
| N84GA | HS25 | 258004 |
| N84GA | JSTR | 5155/32 |
| N84GA | MU30 | A070SA |
| **N84GC** | **C550** | **493** |
| (N84GF) | C500 | 658 |
| N84GP | GPER | 551 |
| **N84GV** | **GLF5** | **584** |
| **N84HD** | **GLF4** | **1440** |
| N84HP | FA50 | 56 |
| N84J | LJ24 | 184 |
| N84J | MS76 | 006 |
| N84LA | WW24 | 378 |
| (N84LF) | C680 | 0090 |
| **N84LG** | **CS55** | **0013** |
| N84LP | SBRL | 306-8 |
| **N84LX** | **C56X** | **5164** |
| **N84MJ** | **FA20** | **510** |
| N84MJ | LJ31 | 237 |
| N84MJ | LJ36 | 008 |
| N84ML | PRM1 | RB-30 |
| N84MZ | GLF2 | 77 |
| **N84NG** | **C650** | **7078** |
| N84NG | SBRL | 380-52 |
| N84NP | C550 | 093 |
| N84NW | FA50 | 216 |
| **N84PH** | **C650** | **0062** |
| N84PH | WW24 | 314 |
| **N84PJ** | **C750** | **0048** |
| N84SD | GLEX | 9018 |
| N84TF | HS25 | 25169 |
| N84TJ | C650 | 0008 |
| **N84TJ** | **FA10** | **188** |
| **N84TN** | **FA50** | **110** |
| (N84TV) | C500 | 499 |
| **N84UP** | **HS25** | **258484** |
| **N84UR** | **EA50** | **000259** |
| N84V | FA20 | 302/510 |
| N84V | GLF2 | 219/20 |
| **N84VA** | **PRM1** | **RB-134** |
| N84VV | WW24 | 383 |
| N84W | HS25 | 25070 |
| N84WA | HS25 | 259007 |
| N84WU | C650 | 0008 |
| N84WU | WW24 | 383 |
| N84WW | WW24 | 401 |
| N84X | GLF2 | 43 |
| N84XP | BE40 | RK-384 |
| N84ZC | CL30 | 20018 |
| N84ZZ | GLEX | 9229 |
| **N85** | **CL61** | **5138** |
| N85 | SBRL | 282-97 |
| N85A | FA50 | 92 |
| N85AB | CS55 | 0060 |
| N85AT | C500 | 087 |
| (N85AT) | LJ25 | 125 |
| N85AW | C650 | 0084 |
| N85BN | BE40 | RJ-7 |
| N85BP | JSTR | 5055/21 |
| N85CA | LJ24 | 250 |
| N85CA | LJ35 | 421 |
| **N85CC** | **HS25** | **258307** |
| N85CC | JSTR | 5102 |
| N85CC | SBRL | 282-108 |
| N85CD | LJ24 | 250 |
| **N85CL** | **F9EX** | **167** |
| N85CL | FA50 | 319 |
| N85CR | BE40 | RK-22 |
| N85D | F900 | 28 |
| **N85D** | **GLEX** | **9078** |
| N85DA | C650 | 0073 |
| N85DA | SBRL | 282-56 |
| N85DB | FA20 | 52 |
| N85DB | SBRL | 306-97 |
| (N85DH) | LJ24 | 243 |
| (N85DL) | JSTR | 5089 |
| N85DN | FA50 | 319 |
| N85DW | HS25 | 258034 |
| N85DW | SBRL | 380-27 |
| (N85EA) | WW24 | 201 |
| **N85EB** | **C560** | **0492** |
| N85EQ | GLF2 | 28 |
| N85EQ | WW24 | 201 |
| **N85ER** | **C52A** | **0404** |
| **N85F** | **FA50** | **253** |
| N85FJ | FA50 | 77 |
| N85FJ | LJ25 | 073 |
| N85FS | C500 | 412 |
| N85GL | LJ55 | 116 |
| N85GW | LJ35 | 227 |
| **N85HD** | **C550** | **130** |
| N85HH | HS25 | 257107 |
| **N85HH** | **HS25** | **258817** |
| N85HP | FA50 | 163 |
| N85HP | SBRL | 306-126 |
| (N85HR) | LJ25 | 079 |
| N85HS | SBRL | 306-23 |
| N85JE | C52A | 0303 |
| N85JM | FA10 | 85 |
| **N85JV** | **C52A** | **0085** |
| N85JW | WW24 | 95 |
| N85KC | C550 | 709 |
| N85KC | C560 | 0128 |
| N85KH | HS25 | 258028 |
| **N85KH** | **LJ31** | **123** |
| **N85KV** | **GLF4** | **1135** |
| N85LB | FA20 | 494 |
| **N85M** | **F2EX** | **73** |
| N85M | GLF4 | 1023 |
| N85M | GLF5 | 648 |
| N85MA | WW24 | 48 |
| N85MD | FA50 | 76 |
| N85MG | C550 | 041 |
| N85MG | GLF4 | 1023 |
| **N85MG** | **HS25** | **258035** |
| N85MJ | LJ25 | 158 |
| N85ML | GLF5 | 648 |
| N85MP | CS55 | 0016 |
| N85MQ | F2EX | 73 |
| N85MR | WW24 | 114 |
| **N85MS** | **C650** | **0075** |
| N85N | FA20 | 36 |
| (N85NA) | C550 | 276 |
| N85NC | LJ55 | 077 |
| **N85NC** | **LJ60** | **090** |
| **N85PK** | **HS25** | **258460** |
| **N85PL** | **PRM1** | **RB-55** |
| N85PM | LJ35 | 595 |
| **N85PT** | **WW24** | **285** |
| N85QA | LJ35 | 421 |
| N85RS | C500 | 654 |
| **N85SM** | **EA50** | **000151** |
| **N85SV** | **LJ35** | **347** |
| **N85TN** | **FA50** | **237** |
| N85TT | BE40 | RJ-35 |
| **N85TW** | **LJ25** | **251** |
| N85TZ | FA20 | 381/548 |
| N85V | FA20 | 412 |
| N85V | GLF2 | 80 |
| N85V | GLF3 | 449 |
| N85V | GLF4 | 1172 |
| **N85V** | **GLF5** | **595** |
| N85VE | FA20 | 412 |
| N85VM | GLF4 | 1172 |
| N85VP | C560 | 0085 |
| N85VR | C510 | 0250 |
| N85VT | GLF2 | 80 |
| N85VT | GLF3 | 449 |
| N85W | LJ24 | 135 |
| N85WC | WW24 | 369 |
| **N85WD** | **GLF4** | **1008** |
| N85WN | FA10 | 210 |
| N85WN | FA50 | 212 |
| N85WP | C500 | 388 |
| N85XL | C56X | 5085 |
| N85XL | LJ55 | 012 |
| **N86** | **CL61** | **5167** |
| N86 | SBRL | 282-86 |
| N86AJ | C550 | 550-0842 |
| N86AJ | LJ55 | 037 |
| N86AJ | LJ55 | 060 |
| N86AK | FA50 | 52 |
| **N86BA** | **CS55** | **0001** |
| N86BE | LJ35 | 194 |
| (N86BL) | FA20 | 264 |
| N86BL | LJ35 | 194 |
| N86BL | LJ35 | 422 |
| **N86BL** | **LJ36** | **026** |
| (N86BP) | JSTR | 5055/21 |
| N86CC | LJ24 | 115 |
| N86CE | C560 | 0265 |
| N86CE | GLF2 | 109 |
| **N86CP** | **SBRL** | **306-76** |
| N86CS | LJ35 | 086 |
| **N86CV** | **C560** | **0342** |
| N86CW | C560 | 0342 |
| **N86CW** | **GALX** | **081** |
| (N86DD) | C560 | 0384 |
| N86EF | WW24 | 222 |
| N86EX | C560 | 0436 |
| N86FJ | FA50 | 79 |
| N86GC | LJ24 | 286 |
| N86GR | C560 | 0494 |
| N86HM | JSTR | 5039 |
| N86HP | SBRL | 306-48 |
| N86JB | C525 | 0251 |
| N86JC | FA50 | 86 |
| N86JJ | C500 | 356 |
| (N86JM) | C550 | 069 |
| **N86LA** | **C525** | **0012** |
| N86LF | C680 | 0030 |
| **N86LF** | **HA4T** | **RC-18** |
| N86MC | F900 | 28 |
| N86MC | FA50 | 141 |
| N86MD | HS25 | 257093 |
| N86MF | WW24 | 414 |
| N86MJ | LJ25 | 062 |
| **N86MN** | **HS25** | **258330** |
| N86MT | C500 | 473 |
| **N86PC** | **C550** | **550-0891** |
| N86PC | CS55 | 0017 |
| N86PC | LJ35 | 108 |
| (N86PQ) | LJ35 | 108 |
| N86QS | CS55 | 0086 |
| N86RB | PRM1 | RB-40 |
| N86RE | C500 | 331 |
| N86RM | SBRL | 306-89 |
| N86RR | WW24 | 359 |
| N86RX | LJ35 | 458 |
| **N86SG** | **C550** | **384** |
| (N86SH) | SBRL | 380-32 |
| N86SK | C500 | 500 |
| N86SK | C525 | 0420 |
| **N86SK** | **C560** | **0551** |
| N86SK | GLF2 | 85 |
| N86SS | C500 | 285 |
| **N86TN** | **FA50** | **241** |
| N86TP | JSTR | 5142 |
| N86TW | C56X | 5179 |
| N86TW | F2TH | 43 |
| **N86TW** | **GLEX** | **9218** |
| (N86TY) | F2TH | 43 |
| N86UR | WW24 | 353 |
| N86VG | FA20 | 218 |
| **N86VP** | **C650** | **0089** |
| N86W | FA20 | 298 |
| N86WC | HS25 | 257108 |
| N86WP | C650 | 0089 |
| N86XL | C56X | 5686 |
| N86Y | SBRL | 306-44 |
| **N87** | **CL61** | **5190** |
| N87 | SBRL | 282-87 |
| N87AC | GLF3 | 427 |
| N87AC | LJ24 | 197 |
| N87AG | FA20 | 514 |
| N87AG | GLF2 | 112 |
| N87AG | HS25 | 257065 |
| N87AP | LJ24 | 290 |
| N87AT | LJ35 | 096 |
| N87B | WW24 | 104 |
| N87B | WW24 | 80 |
| **N87BA** | **CS55** | **0131** |
| N87CF | C550 | 615 |
| N87CF | LJ24 | 181 |
| N87CM | SBRL | 282-21 |
| N87CR | SBRL | 282-137 |
| (N87DC) | HS25 | 25214 |
| N87DC | WW24 | 126 |
| N87DC | WW24 | 14 |
| N87DG | WW24 | 14 |
| N87DL | WW24 | 126 |
| **N87DY** | **MU30** | **A085SA** |
| **N87EB** | **BE40** | **RK-87** |
| N87EC | HS25 | 258052 |
| N87FJ | F2TH | 187 |
| N87FJ | FA50 | 80 |
| N87FL | C500 | 664 |
| N87FL | CS55 | 0055 |
| N87GA | C560 | 0228 |
| N87GA | LJ35 | 370 |
| **N87GJ** | **WW24** | **422** |
| **N87GS** | **C550** | **550-0895** |
| N87GS | GLF2 | 258 |
| N87GS | WW24 | 261 |
| N87GS | WW24 | 422 |
| N87GT | FA10 | 181 |
| N87HB | GLF2 | 39 |
| N87HP | GLF3 | 338 |
| N87HP | GLF4 | 1219 |
| **N87JK** | **C560** | **0115** |
| N87JL | LJ24 | 335 |
| (N87MJ) | LJ24 | 301 |
| N87MJ | LJ35 | 204 |
| (N87MW) | LJ25 | 216 |
| **N87N** | **C750** | **0058** |
| N87NS | WW24 | 432 |
| **N87NY** | **MS76** | **087** |
| **N87PK** | **HS25** | **HA-0043** |
| **N87PT** | **C550** | **201** |
| N87RB | HS25 | 258299 |
| (N87RS) | LJ35 | 250 |
| **N87SF** | **C550** | **103** |
| **N87SL** | **C750** | **0174** |
| N87TD | GLF2 | 39 |
| N87TH | CS55 | 0129 |
| **N87TH** | **FA10** | **178** |
| N87TN | FA20 | 385 |
| **N87TN** | **FA50** | **224** |
| **N87TR** | **CL60** | **1076** |
| **N87VM** | **C52B** | **0098** |
| N87W | LJ35 | 104 |
| **N87WU** | **C56X** | **5039** |
| N87WW | WW24 | 402 |
| N87XP | HS25 | HA-0087 |
| N87Y | SBRL | 380-1 |
| N87ZZ | GLEX | 9228 |

| N87ZZ | GLEX | 9275 |
|---|---|---|
| **N88** | **CL64** | **5588** |
| N88 | SBRL | 282-88 |
| **N88AD** | **C525** | **0404** |
| N88AD | WW24 | 106 |
| N88AE | GLF2 | 102/32 |
| N88AE | GLF3 | 398 |
| N88AF | C500 | 290 |
| N88AF | HS25 | 25285 |
| **N88AF** | **LJ45** | **205** |
| (N88AH) | LJ35 | 421 |
| **N88AJ** | **C550** | **550-0885** |
| N88AT | CL60 | 1036 |
| N88AT | FA10 | 73 |
| **N88AY** | **GALX** | **134** |
| N88B | LJ24 | 015 |
| **N88BF** | **SBRL** | **465-60** |
| **N88BG** | **LJ35** | **090** |
| N88BM | C500 | 500 |
| N88BM | C550 | 565 |
| (N88BR) | C500 | 553 |
| N88BT | LJ25 | 168 |
| N88BY | LJ25 | 168 |
| **N88CA** | **BE40** | **RK-282** |
| N88CF | C500 | 465 |
| N88CF | C500 | 477 |
| N88CJ | LJ25 | 006 |
| N88CR | MU30 | A089SA |
| **N88D** | **GLF5** | **5183** |
| N88D | GLF5 | 612 |
| N88DD | C550 | 263 |
| N88DD | C650 | 0058 |
| **N88DD** | **F2TH** | **204** |
| N88DD | F2TH | 96 |
| **N88DJ** | **C650** | **0167** |
| N88DJ | HS25 | 25153 |
| N88DJ | LJ25 | 234 |
| **N88DU** | **HS25** | **25153** |
| **N88DZ** | **GLF5** | **612** |
| N88EA | LJ24 | 077 |
| **N88EJ** | **C750** | **0088** |
| **N88EL** | **PRM1** | **RB-157** |
| N88EL | PRM1 | RB-17 |
| N88EL | PRM1 | RB-83 |
| N88EP | LJ25 | 019 |
| N88EP | LJ35 | 134 |
| **N88ER** | **PRM1** | **RB-17** |
| N88EU | PRM1 | RB-83 |
| N88EX | C560 | 0433 |
| N88FE | FA20 | 317 |
| N88FJ | FA50 | 82 |
| N88FP | LJ25 | 019 |
| N88G | C560 | 0208 |
| N88G | CS55 | 0017 |
| N88GA | GLF2 | 217 |
| N88GA | GLF4 | 1085 |
| N88GA | HS25 | 25276 |
| N88GC | LJ25 | 088 |
| N88GD | CS55 | 0017 |
| N88GJ | C500 | 155 |
| (N88GJ) | LJ25 | 006 |
| N88GQ | LJ25 | 088 |
| N88HA | CL61 | 5072 |
| N88HD | HS25 | 258429 |
| **N88HD** | **HS25** | **258616** |
| **N88HE** | **F2EX** | **79** |
| N88HF | C550 | 126 |
| N88HF | C550 | 615 |
| N88HF | C560 | 0133 |
| **N88HP** | **C56X** | **5050** |
| N88HP | GLF4 | 1212 |
| N88JA | LJ25 | 305 |
| N88JA | LJ35 | 118 |
| (N88JE) | WW24 | 326 |
| N88JF | LJ24 | 110 |
| N88JJ | C500 | 356 |
| N88JJ | C550 | 187 |
| N88JJ | C650 | 0169 |
| **N88JJ** | **C680** | **0277** |
| N88JJ | SBRL | 380-65 |
| N88JM | JSTR | 5011/1 |
| N88JM | SBRL | 282-36 |
| N88JM | SBRL | 380-39 |
| N88KC | C52A | 0157 |
| **N88LC** | **F9EX** | **137** |
| N88LD | C525 | 0181 |
| N88LD | FA10 | 108 |
| N88LJ | LJ24 | 290 |
| **N88LN** | **GLF2** | **20** |
| N88ME | FA10 | 8 |
| N88ME | MU30 | A066SA |
| **N88MF** | **ASTR** | **048** |
| N88MF | MU30 | A066SA |
| N88MJ | C550 | 088 |
| N88ML | C550 | 219 |
| N88MM | C500 | 689 |
| N88MM | LJ31 | 036 |
| N88MM | PRM1 | RB-18 |
| **N88MM** | **PRM1** | **RB-44** |
| N88MR | HS25 | 25013 |
| (N88MT) | C500 | 689 |
| N88MX | F2TH | 183 |
| N88MX | GLF4 | 1110 |
| N88MX | HS25 | 257090 |
| **N88ND** | **F9EX** | **19** |
| N88NE | LJ35 | 227 |
| N88NE | LJ35 | 350 |
| N88NJ | LJ25 | 008 |
| N88NJ | LJ25 | 294 |
| **N88NJ** | **LJ35** | **170** |
| N88NM | C550 | 590 |
| N88NT | FA20 | 416 |
| N88NW | C500 | 309 |
| **N88NW** | **CS55** | **0151** |
| N88NY | MS76 | 088 |
| N88PV | WW24 | 264 |
| **N88QC** | **C525** | **0664** |
| (N88QC) | C52B | 0302 |
| N88RD | LJ24 | 196 |
| **N88SF** | **C56X** | **5645** |
| N88SJ | HS25 | 25286 |
| **N88TB** | **C500** | **353** |
| N88TB | C550 | 271 |
| (N88TB) | FA10 | 159 |
| N88TC | LJ24 | 022 |
| N88TJ | C560 | 0014 |
| (N88TJ) | CL60 | 1063 |
| N88TJ | LJ35 | 188 |
| (N88TJ) | MU30 | A004SA |
| N88TY | F2TH | 17 |
| N88U | FA50 | 83 |
| **N88UA** | **BE40** | **RJ-49** |
| **N88V** | **LJ60** | **155** |
| N88WC | C560 | 0157 |
| N88WG | BE40 | RJ-26 |
| N88WG | CL61 | 5068 |
| N88WL | FA10 | 140 |
| N88WP | WW24 | 151 |
| N88WU | C56X | 5039 |
| **N88WU** | **GALX** | **111** |
| **N88WV** | **LJ45** | **276** |
| N88YF | F900 | 134 |
| N89 | SBRL | 282-89 |
| N89AA | LJ24 | 308 |
| N89AB | GLF3 | 349 |
| N89AB | GLF3 | 496 |
| N89AC | C650 | 0029 |
| N89AE | GLF3 | 349 |
| N89AE | GLF3 | 496 |
| N89AJ | C500 | 272 |
| **N89AM** | **WW24** | **389** |
| N89AT | LJ25 | 125 |
| N89AT | LJ35 | 391 |
| N89B | C550 | 114 |
| (N89B) | C550 | 126 |
| N89B | WW24 | 69 |
| N89BM | C560 | 0017 |
| N89BM | FA50 | 237 |
| N89BR | HS25 | 258425 |
| **N89CE** | **F2EX** | **81** |
| **N89D** | **C550** | **070** |
| N89EC | FA10 | 109 |
| N89EM | MU30 | A055SA |
| **N89ES** | **LJ24** | **197** |
| N89FC | FA50 | 184 |
| (N89FF) | HS25 | 25023 |
| N89FJ | FA50 | 81 |
| N89GA | BE40 | RJ-60 |
| **N89GA** | **C550** | **135** |
| N89GK | LJ35 | 316 |
| N89GN | HS25 | 257101 |
| N89HB | HS25 | 25097 |
| **N89HB** | **LJ31** | **010** |
| **N89HE** | **GLF5** | **568** |
| **N89HS** | **ASTR** | **089** |
| N89K | HS25 | 258102 |
| N89KK | BE40 | RJ-62 |
| N89KM | BE40 | RJ-62 |
| N89KM | BE40 | RK-56 |
| (N89KT) | HS25 | 258102 |
| N89KW | LJ60 | 085 |
| **N89LS** | **C550** | **623** |
| **N89MD** | **C560** | **0612** |
| N89MD | HS25 | 257134 |
| N89MF | C500 | 571 |
| N89MJ | LJ36 | 019 |
| N89MM | SBRL | 465-30 |
| N89MR | WW24 | 9 |
| N89MX | GLEX | 9304 |
| (N89N) | SBRL | 306-141 |
| N89NC | FA50 | 337 |
| **N89NC** | **GLF5** | **5049** |
| N89NC | HS25 | 258102 |
| N89PP | HS25 | 257098 |
| N89PP | HS25 | 257101 |
| N89Q | C550 | 114 |
| N89QA | GLF3 | 325 |
| (N89RF) | EA50 | 000275 |
| N89RF | LJ31 | 145 |
| N89RP | LJ35 | 410 |
| **N89RP** | **LJ45** | **011** |
| N89SC | FA20 | 96 |
| N89SC | MU30 | A089SA |
| N89SE | C550 | 585 |
| N89SR | HS25 | 25285 |
| (N89TA) | C550 | 193 |
| **N89TC** | **LJ35** | **026** |
| N89TD | CS55 | 0076 |
| N89TJ | GLF2 | 103 |
| N89TJ | HS25 | 257031 |
| N89TJ | MU30 | A029SA |
| N89TJ | WW24 | 296 |
| (N89TJ) | WW24 | 315 |
| N89TY | F2TH | 17 |
| N89UH | WW24 | 353 |
| N89XL | WW24 | 171 |
| N89ZZ | GLEX | 9259 |
| (N90AB) | FA10 | 44 |
| N90AE | FA50 | 104 |
| N90AE | GLF4 | 1068 |
| N90AG | CL64 | 5414 |
| N90AG | LJ60 | 042 |
| **N90AH** | **LJ35** | **036** |
| **N90AJ** | **ASTR** | **052** |
| N90AL | LJ35 | 222 |
| N90AM | FA50 | 53 |
| N90AM | GLF4 | 1284 |
| **N90AM** | **GLF5** | **592** |
| N90AM | LJ55 | 106 |
| N90AM | SBRL | 380-25 |
| N90AQ | LJ60 | 042 |
| **N90AR** | **CL61** | **5137** |
| N90AR | HS25 | 257107 |
| N90B | HS25 | 256034 |
| N90B | HS25 | 257117 |
| N90B | WW24 | 58 |
| N90BA | C500 | 117 |
| **N90BA** | **LJ31** | **018** |
| **N90BJ** | **C550** | **710** |
| N90BL | C550 | 682 |
| **N90BL** | **C56X** | **5609** |
| N90BL | HS25 | 256034 |
| (N90BN) | HS25 | 257117 |
| N90BR | LJ25 | 214 |
| N90BS | LJ55 | 014 |
| N90BY | C550 | 682 |
| N90C | SBRL | 380-46 |
| N90CC | C500 | 076 |
| N90CE | ASTR | 043 |
| N90CE | LJ60 | 392 |
| N90CF | C500 | 575 |
| **N90CF** | **C56X** | **5080** |
| N90CH | WW24 | 353 |
| **N90CJ** | **C52A** | **0149** |
| N90CL | WW24 | 324 |
| N90CN | C650 | 0140 |
| N90CN | FA20 | 299 |
| N90CP | GLF2 | 224 |
| N90CP | JSTR | 5232 |
| N90DA | C550 | 125 |
| N90DH | LJ24 | 117 |
| (N90DH) | LJ25 | 080 |
| N90DM | FA10 | 104 |
| N90E | LJ55 | 004 |
| N90EA | GLF2 | 121 |
| N90EB | C500 | 361 |
| N90EC | SBRL | 306-73 |
| N90EP | GLF3 | 317 |
| N90EW | F900 | 27 |
| **N90EW** | **GLEX** | **9039** |
| **N90FB** | **HS25** | **258613** |
| N90FF | HS25 | 257113 |
| N90FJ | CS55 | 0065 |
| N90FJ | FA50 | 65 |
| N90FJ | FA50 | 85 |
| **N90FT** | **GALX** | **209** |
| N90GM | SBRL | 282-48 |
| N90GM | SBRL | 380-27 |
| N90GS | FA20 | 388 |
| **N90GS** | **LJ45** | **225** |
| N90GW | SBRL | 380-27 |
| N90GX | GALX | 040 |
| N90HB | C560 | 0584 |
| N90HH | GLF2 | 78 |
| N90HM | WW24 | 170 |
| N90J | LJ24 | 060 |
| N90JD | C550 | 340 |
| N90JF | FA20 | 45 |
| **N90JJ** | **C550** | **571** |
| N90KC | WW24 | 339 |
| N90KR | JSTR | 5036/42 |
| (N90LA) | C650 | 0011 |
| N90LA | FA10 | 47 |
| N90LC | FA10 | 23 |
| N90LC | GLF3 | 360 |
| **N90LJ** | **LJ25** | **226** |
| N90LJ | LJ31 | 039 |
| N90LP | LJ35 | 236 |
| **N90MA** | **C550** | **140** |
| N90MC | LJ60 | 130 |
| N90MD | GLF2 | 241 |
| N90ME | HS25 | 258082 |
| N90ME | JSTR | 5057 |
| N90MF | C560 | 0060 |
| N90MH | FA10 | 110 |
| N90MH | LJ25 | 006 |
| N90MJ | C550 | 067 |
| **N90ML** | **GLF3** | **315** |
| (N90MT) | C500 | 509 |
| N90N | SBRL | 306-12 |
| N90N | SBRL | 380-72 |
| **N90NB** | **C560** | **0634** |
| N90NE | LJ55 | 075 |
| **N90NF** | **C750** | **0170** |
| N90PB | LJ31 | 024 |
| N90PG | C560 | 0002 |
| N90PM | HS25 | 258183 |
| **N90PT** | **C550** | **465** |
| N90QP | JSTR | 5232 |
| N90R | FA50 | 162 |
| N90R | SBRL | 306-36 |
| N90RC | C550 | 500 |
| N90RG | HS25 | 25091 |
| N90RK | LJ35 | 417 |
| N90SF | C550 | 455 |
| N90SF | GLF3 | 366 |
| N90SR | BE40 | RJ-26 |
| (N90SR) | HS25 | 25116 |
| N90TC | JSTR | 5037/24 |
| (N90TC) | LJ25 | 020 |
| **N90TH** | **F900** | **180** |
| N90TH | F900 | 63 |
| N90TT | SBRL | 306-97 |
| N90U | ASTR | 030 |
| N90U | JSTR | 5057 |
| N90UC | CL60 | 1023 |
| N90UG | ASTR | 030 |
| N90UG | LJ45 | 115 |
| (N90WA) | C500 | 263 |
| **N90WA** | **LJ31** | **028** |
| N90WJ | C500 | 053 |
| N90WJ | GLF3 | 340 |
| N90WP | HS25 | 25032 |
| (N90WP) | HS25 | 25141 |
| N90WP | HS25 | 256068 |
| **N90WR** | **LJ35** | **022** |
| N90XP | HS25 | HA-0001 |
| **N90XR** | **LJ40** | **45-2090** |
| **N90Z** | **C550** | **367** |
| N90ZP | JSTR | 5055/21 |
| **N91A** | **C52A** | **0105** |
| N91AE | GLF2 | 17 |

| | | |
|---|---|---|
| N91AE | GLF4 | 1053 |
| N91AG | C560 | 0606 |
| (N91AN) | C560 | 0111 |
| **N91AP** | **C500** | **506** |
| **N91B** | **C550** | **217** |
| N91B | WW24 | 112 |
| N91BA | C500 | 168 |
| **N91BB** | **PRM1** | **RB-192** |
| (N91BH) | HS25 | 25261 |
| N91BP | FA10 | 107 |
| (N91BS) | C500 | 244 |
| **N91BZ** | **SBRL** | **465-19** |
| N91CH | C510 | 0201 |
| N91CH | GLF3 | 405 |
| N91CH | HS25 | 258030 |
| N91CH | LJ35 | 021 |
| N91CH | LJ55 | 091 |
| N91CM | HS25 | 257092 |
| N91CR | GLF3 | 405 |
| **N91CV** | **C560** | **0009** |
| N91CV | FA20 | 48 |
| **N91CW** | **GLF5** | **543** |
| N91D | C500 | 343 |
| N91D | C650 | 0151 |
| N91DH | FA10 | 108 |
| N91DH | FA10 | 68 |
| **N91DP** | **LJ31** | **079** |
| N91DV | HS25 | 258211 |
| N91DZ | C500 | 343 |
| N91ED | LJ25 | 255 |
| N91EW | F900 | 27 |
| N91EX | F2EX | 91 |
| (N91FA) | C560 | 0072 |
| N91FD | ASTR | 045 |
| N91FJ | FA50 | 87 |
| **N91FP** | **C510** | **0001** |
| (N91GH) | C525 | 0234 |
| **N91GT** | **C52B** | **0332** |
| (N91GT) | C52B | 0343 |
| N91GX | ASTR | 091 |
| **N91HG** | **C500** | **601** |
| **N91HK** | **HS25** | **258578** |
| N91HR | HS25 | 256046 |
| N91JF | FA20 | 14 |
| **N91KC** | **C650** | **7082** |
| **N91KH** | **CL61** | **5038** |
| N91KH | HS25 | 256003 |
| **N91KK** | **C650** | **0193** |
| (N91KL) | GLF3 | 321 |
| N91KL | GLF4 | 1507 |
| **N91KP** | **HS25** | **256003** |
| N91LA | C650 | 0011 |
| N91LA | FA10 | 47 |
| N91LA | GLF2 | 198/35 |
| N91LA | GLF4 | 1266 |
| **N91LA** | **GLF5** | **5027** |
| N91LE | LJ60 | 091 |
| N91LJ | GLF3 | 342 |
| N91LJ | JSTR | 5142 |
| N91LS | C500 | 244 |
| (N91LU) | GLF4 | 1266 |
| N91ME | C560 | 0240 |
| N91ME | CS55 | 0132 |
| **N91MG** | **CL64** | **5423** |
| N91MH | FA10 | 23 |
| (N91MH) | FA20 | 91 |
| N91MJ | C550 | 111 |
| N91MK | F900 | 36 |
| N91MK | LJ24 | 162 |
| N91MK | WW24 | 324 |
| N91ML | CS55 | 0132 |
| N91MS | C500 | 572 |
| N91MT | BE40 | RJ-26 |
| N91MT | LJ25 | 255 |
| N91MT | LJ25 | 363 |
| **N91NA** | **GLF2** | **198/35** |
| N91NG | GLEX | 9191 |
| N91NK | C560 | 0040 |
| N91NL | C560 | 0040 |
| N91PB | FA10 | 198 |
| **N91PE** | **C500** | **400** |
| **N91PN** | **LJ25** | **091** |
| N91PR | LJ55 | 091 |
| N91SA | WW24 | 420 |
| **N91TE** | **C500** | **572** |
| N91TG | C650 | 0208 |
| N91TH | F900 | 60 |
| **N91TQ** | **E50P** | **50000090** |
| N91TS | FA20 | 21 |
| N91UC | CL60 | 1051 |
| N91UJ | JSTR | 5142 |
| **N91VB** | **C550** | **058** |
| N91W | LJ35 | 194 |
| N91WF | F900 | 91 |
| N91WG | WW24 | 112 |
| N91WZ | C500 | 527 |
| N91Y | FA20 | 373 |
| N91Y | HS25 | 257159 |
| N91YC | C560 | 0115 |
| **N92AE** | **GLF4** | **1301** |
| N92AG | GLF2 | 110 |
| N92AJ | C500 | 230 |
| N92B | C500 | 212 |
| N92B | C550 | 471 |
| N92B | WW24 | 32 |
| N92BA | C500 | 207 |
| N92BD | C550 | 588 |
| **N92BE** | **C500** | **464** |
| (N92BE) | WW24 | 428 |
| N92BF | C560 | 0235 |
| N92BH | HS25 | 25267 |
| **N92BL** | **C500** | **391** |
| N92BL | LJ60 | 058 |
| N92BT | WW24 | 32 |
| N92C | C500 | 391 |
| N92CC | C500 | 391 |
| N92CJ | C52A | 0029 |
| N92CS | LJ25 | 292 |
| **N92CX** | **C750** | **0301** |
| **N92DE** | **C560** | **0391** |
| N92DF | LJ24 | 117 |
| N92EB | WW24 | 381 |
| N92EC | LJ31 | 024 |
| N92EC | LJ35 | 094 |
| N92EJ | LJ35 | 092 |
| N92FA | C500 | 068 |
| N92FD | LJ31 | 054 |
| N92FE | WW24 | 286 |
| **N92FG** | **LJ60** | **056** |
| N92FJ | FA50 | 88 |
| (N92FL) | HS25 | 258598 |
| N92FT | HS25 | 258598 |
| N92HL | GLF4 | 4154 |
| N92HW | C560 | 0148 |
| **N92JC** | **CS55** | **0115** |
| N92JT | CS55 | 0115 |
| N92K | FA20 | 317 |
| N92LA | C500 | 338 |
| N92LA | C650 | 0003 |
| N92LA | GLF2 | 125/26 |
| N92LA | GLF4 | 1238 |
| **N92LA** | **GLF5** | **5002** |
| N92LJ | LJ31 | 016 |
| N92LT | C550 | 361 |
| N92LT | F2TH | 71 |
| (N92LU) | GLF4 | 1238 |
| **N92MA** | **C52B** | **0048** |
| **N92ME** | **CS55** | **0044** |
| **N92MG** | **LJ55** | **025** |
| N92MH | FA20 | 3/403 |
| N92MJ | LJ25 | 292 |
| **N92MS** | **C52B** | **0214** |
| N92NA | GLF2 | 125/26 |
| **N92ND** | **C525** | **0186** |
| N92NE | LJ35 | 092 |
| **N92NS** | **LJ60** | **092** |
| N92QS | CS55 | 0092 |
| **N92RB** | **WW24** | **174** |
| **N92RP** | **C650** | **0148** |
| N92RP | HS25 | 257022 |
| N92RW | BE40 | RJ-4 |
| **N92SA** | **GLF4** | **1413** |
| **N92SM** | **C500** | **124** |
| **N92SS** | **C560** | **0388** |
| N92SV | GLF2 | 74 |
| N92TC | LJ24 | 268 |
| **N92TE** | **C560** | **0123** |
| **N92TS** | **LJ35** | **035** |
| N92TX | C650 | 0127 |
| N92UG | LJ31 | 050 |
| N92UJ | ASTR | 092 |
| **N92UP** | **HS25** | **258309** |
| N92V | LJ25 | 025 |
| N92WW | WW24 | 296 |
| N92WW | WW24 | 392 |
| N92ZZ | GLEX | 9206 |
| **N92ZZ** | **GLEX** | **9354** |
| N93AC | SBRL | 282-109 |
| N93AE | GLF4 | 1302 |
| N93AG | C560 | 0223 |
| **N93AJ** | **C550** | **368** |
| N93AK | C52A | 0181 |
| **N93AK** | **C52A** | **0368** |
| N93AQ | C52A | 0181 |
| N93AT | GLF2 | 85 |
| **N93AT** | **GLF4** | **1020** |
| N93AX | FA50 | 181 |
| N93B | WW24 | 27 |
| N93BA | C550 | 555 |
| N93BA | CL60 | 1027 |
| N93BA | LJ60 | 094 |
| N93BD | C550 | 454 |
| N93BE | WW24 | 27 |
| N93BH | HS25 | 25186 |
| N93BP | LJ24 | 169 |
| N93BR | LJ24 | 231 |
| N93C | LJ24 | 230 |
| N93C | LJ25 | 127 |
| N93C | LJ35 | 159 |
| N93CB | LJ24 | 230 |
| N93CD | FA20 | 161 |
| N93CE | LJ25 | 127 |
| N93CK | LJ35 | 159 |
| N93CL | C650 | 0074 |
| N93CP | FA20 | 7 |
| N93CR | CL61 | 3024 |
| N93CR | F900 | 24 |
| N93CR | F9EX | 96 |
| N93CR | HS25 | 257117 |
| N93CT | HS25 | 258049 |
| **N93CV** | **C560** | **0239** |
| **N93CW** | **C52B** | **0139** |
| (N93CW) | C550 | 096 |
| N93CX | GLF3 | 314 |
| N93DD | LJ24 | 236 |
| N93DK | C650 | 0112 |
| N93DW | C550 | 448 |
| N93DW | C560 | 0133 |
| N93DW | CL61 | 5025 |
| **N93EA** | **C560** | **0093** |
| N93FH | FA20 | 161 |
| N93FJ | FA50 | 89 |
| N93FR | HS25 | 257202 |
| **N93FT** | **BE40** | **RK-166** |
| N93GC | HS25 | 257195 |
| N93GH | F2TH | 6 |
| N93GH | FA50 | 252 |
| N93GR | F900 | 24 |
| N93GR | HS25 | 257117 |
| N93GT | F2TH | 6 |
| (N93JD) | JSTR | 5201 |
| (N93JH) | LJ25 | 022 |
| N93JM | C500 | 569 |
| N93JM | JSTR | 5201 |
| N93JR | WW24 | 51 |
| **N93JW** | **C52B** | **0035** |
| **N93KD** | **F9EX** | **182** |
| N93KE | WW24 | 316 |
| (N93KV) | C525 | 0030 |
| **N93LA** | **C750** | **0121** |
| N93LA | GLF2 | 164 |
| **N93LE** | **LJ35** | **592** |
| **N93LS** | **C525** | **0556** |
| N93M | GLF2 | 98/38 |
| **N93M** | **GLF5** | **567** |
| **N93MC** | **FA20** | **428** |
| N93MJ | LJ35 | 119 |
| N93MK | GLF4 | 1088 |
| **N93NB** | **C560** | **0644** |
| N93PE | C52A | 0093 |
| **N93PE** | **C52B** | **0093** |
| N93QQ | GLF2 | 7 |
| N93QS | CS55 | 0093 |
| (N93RC) | LJ35 | 433 |
| N93RM | WW24 | 74 |
| N93RS | FA20 | 81 |
| **N93S** | **C750** | **0189** |
| N93SC | WW24 | 90 |
| **N93SK** | **LJ31** | **031** |
| N93TC | HS25 | 25116 |
| N93TC | HS25 | 257025 |
| N93TJ | C500 | 358 |
| N93TS | HS25 | 25264 |
| N93TS | HS25 | 256018 |
| N93TX | C650 | 7009 |
| **N93TX** | **C750** | **0099** |
| N93VP | C650 | 0093 |
| N93WD | C500 | 220 |
| N93WW | WW24 | 321 |
| **N93XP** | **BE40** | **RK-74** |
| **N93XR** | **LJ45** | **393** |
| N93ZZ | GLEX | 9214 |
| N94 | HS25 | 258129 |
| N94AA | LJ35 | 295 |
| (N94AA) | LJ35 | 366 |
| N94AE | GLF4 | 1307 |
| N94AF | C550 | 585 |
| **N94AF** | **LJ35** | **094** |
| **N94AJ** | **C500** | **024** |
| **N94AL** | **C525** | **0432** |
| **N94AN** | **GLF4** | **1307** |
| N94AT | LJ25 | 125 |
| N94AT | WW24 | 288 |
| N94B | HS25 | 256055 |
| N94B | HS25 | 257189 |
| N94B | WW24 | 24 |
| N94BA | CL61 | 5160 |
| N94BA | LJ60 | 144 |
| N94BB | HS25 | 256004 |
| N94BD | HS25 | 256004 |
| N94BD | HS25 | 257024 |
| N94BD | HS25 | 258004 |
| (N94BD) | LJ24 | 351 |
| N94BE | HS25 | 257024 |
| N94BF | HS25 | 256055 |
| N94BJ | BE40 | RJ-17 |
| N94BJ | C650 | 0147 |
| N94BJ | FA50 | 237 |
| N94BN | GLF3 | 391 |
| N94CK | LJ45 | 066 |
| N94DE | C500 | 094 |
| (N94FJ) | F2TH | 94 |
| N94FJ | FA50 | 86 |
| **N94FL** | **GLF3** | **424** |
| (N94FS) | C550 | 015 |
| **N94FT** | **GALX** | **208** |
| N94GA | EA50 | 000072 |
| N94GC | GLF3 | 321 |
| N94GP | LJ35 | 094 |
| **N94GP** | **LJ35** | **411** |
| N94GW | FA20 | 322 |
| N94HC | LJ24 | 157 |
| **N94HE** | **BE40** | **RK-89** |
| **N94HL** | **C525** | **0654** |
| N94HT | BE40 | RK-48 |
| N94JJ | LJ24 | 138 |
| **N94JT** | **HS25** | **258071** |
| N94K | JSTR | 5114/18 |
| **N94LA** | **C56X** | **5129** |
| **N94LD** | **MU30** | **A073SA** |
| N94LH | BE40 | RK-112 |
| **N94LH** | **BE40** | **RK-405** |
| N94LH | MU30 | A073SA |
| N94LT | GLF4 | 1313 |
| N94MA | C500 | 319 |
| N94MC | FA10 | 166 |
| N94ME | C550 | 402 |
| N94MF | C550 | 402 |
| N94MG | FA10 | 166 |
| N94MJ | LJ25 | 312 |
| N94MJ | LJ35 | 394 |
| **N94MZ** | **C525** | **0094** |
| N94NA | F900 | 126 |
| N94NB | C560 | 0076 |
| N94NB | HS25 | 258241 |
| **N94PC** | **FA50** | **254** |
| N94PK | LJ25 | 181 |
| **N94RL** | **LJ35** | **096** |
| N94RS | LJ25 | 141 |
| N94RT | CS55 | 0023 |
| N94SA | HS25 | 257144 |
| N94SD | HS25 | 258004 |
| (N94SF) | GLF2 | 250 |
| N94SL | C500 | 498 |
| (N94SL) | GLF4 | 1087 |
| N94TJ | C650 | 0094 |
| (N94TJ) | FA20 | 482 |
| N94TJ | GLF2 | 75/7 |
| (N94TJ) | LJ55 | 005 |
| N94TW | ASTR | 029 |
| **N94TX** | **C560** | **0247** |
| **N94VP** | **C560** | **0094** |

| N94VP | C650 | 0094 |
|---|---|---|
| N94WA | F900 | 94 |
| N94WA | WW24 | 94 |
| N94WN | HS25 | 258014 |
| N94WW | WW24 | 394 |
| (N94ZG) | C500 | 163 |
| N94ZZ | GLEX | 9215 |
| N95 | HS25 | 258131 |
| N95AB | LJ24 | 213 |
| N95AC | LJ35 | 433 |
| N95AE | GLF4 | 1016 |
| N95AE | GLF4 | 1068 |
| **N95AE** | **GLF5** | **562** |
| N95AE | HS25 | 258173 |
| **N95AG** | **LJ60** | **079** |
| **N95AN** | **C550** | **550-0978** |
| N95AP | LJ35 | 471 |
| N95AX | C550 | 253 |
| N95B | WW24 | 19 |
| N95BA | JSTR | 5216 |
| N95BA | LJ35 | 078 |
| N95BD | JSTR | 5208 |
| **N95BD** | **LJ60** | **232** |
| N95BH | LJ35 | 078 |
| **N95BK** | **JSTR** | **5208** |
| N95BP | LJ25 | 314 |
| **N95BS** | **C525** | **0283** |
| N95BS | LJ25 | 180 |
| N95CC | C550 | 108 |
| (N95CC) | C550 | 234 |
| N95CC | C550 | 248 |
| N95CC | C550 | 405 |
| **N95CC** | **C56X** | **5278** |
| N95CC | C650 | 0124 |
| N95CC | C650 | 0140 |
| N95CC | C650 | 0153 |
| N95CC | C650 | 0160 |
| N95CC | C650 | 0170 |
| N95CC | C650 | 0178 |
| N95CC | C650 | 0184 |
| N95CC | C650 | 0193 |
| N95CC | C650 | 0197 |
| N95CC | C650 | 0203 |
| N95CC | C650 | 0214 |
| N95CC | C650 | 7002 |
| N95CC | C650 | 7008 |
| N95CC | C650 | 7020 |
| N95CC | C650 | 7030 |
| N95CC | C650 | 7036 |
| (N95CC) | C650 | 7051 |
| (N95CC) | C650 | 7059 |
| N95CC | C650 | 7063 |
| N95CC | C750 | 0018 |
| (N95CC) | C750 | 0041 |
| N95CC | CS55 | 0001 |
| N95CC | CS55 | 0036 |
| N95CC | CS55 | 0076 |
| N95CC | CS55 | 0096 |
| **N95CK** | **C525** | **0493** |
| N95CK | LJ25 | 248 |
| N95CM | C650 | 0193 |
| N95CM | C650 | 0214 |
| N95CM | C650 | 7029 |
| N95CM | C650 | 7045 |
| N95CM | C650 | 7070 |
| N95CM | C750 | 0020 |
| N95CM | C750 | 0042 |
| N95CM | C750 | 0060 |
| N95CM | HS25 | 257156 |
| (N95CP) | LJ24 | 340 |
| N95CP | WW24 | 201 |
| N95CT | C550 | 400 |
| N95DA | LJ24 | 267 |
| N95DD | LJ24 | 251 |
| N95DJ | C525 | 0032 |
| (N95DQ) | CL60 | 1041 |
| N95DR | C500 | 203 |
| (N95DW) | FA10 | 85 |
| N95EB | CL60 | 1062 |
| N95EC | LJ25 | 280 |
| N95EC | LJ35 | 477 |
| (N95EC) | LJ35 | 654 |
| N95EW | C500 | 581 |
| N95FA | BE40 | RK-99 |
| N95FE | CL61 | 5095 |
| N95FJ | FA50 | 75 |
| N95FJ | FA50 | 95 |
| N95GC | FA50 | 176 |

| **N95GK** | **BE40** | **RK-27** |
|---|---|---|
| N95GS | JSTR | 5014 |
| **N95HC** | **FA50** | **244** |
| N95HE | C550 | 713 |
| N95HF | C650 | 7036 |
| N95HG | LJ31 | 140 |
| (N95HW) | C560 | 0238 |
| **N95JK** | **WW24** | **283** |
| N95JK | WW24 | 95 |
| **N95JN** | **LJ35** | **595** |
| N95JR | FA20 | 247 |
| N95JT | FA20 | 490 |
| N95MJ | C500 | 562 |
| N95NB | C560 | 0644 |
| **N95NB** | **C56X** | **6031** |
| N95NB | HS25 | 258244 |
| N95PH | FA50 | 194 |
| N95Q | C500 | 119 |
| N95RC | SBRL | 306-129 |
| N95RE | C500 | 507 |
| N95RE | C500 | 515 |
| N95RT | BE40 | RJ-60 |
| N95RT | GLF2 | 136 |
| N95RX | C650 | 7035 |
| N95SC | LJ35 | 012 |
| N95SC | LJ55 | 137 |
| **N95SJ** | **C680** | **0248** |
| N95SJ | GLF2 | 64/27 |
| N95SR | C650 | 0024 |
| N95SR | CL61 | 3050 |
| N95SR | CL61 | 3051 |
| (N95SR) | JSTR | 5212 |
| N95SV | GLF2 | 64/27 |
| N95TC | LJ35 | 020 |
| **N95TD** | **C560** | **0110** |
| (N95TJ) | C500 | 187 |
| N95TJ | C650 | 0127 |
| N95TJ | FA10 | 92 |
| (N95TJ) | LJ55 | 104 |
| N95TJ | MU30 | A024SA |
| N95TJ | SBRL | 380-38 |
| N95TS | HS25 | 256051 |
| (N95TW) | LJ25 | 124 |
| **N95TX** | **C650** | **7037** |
| N95UJ | C650 | 0127 |
| **N95UP** | **HS25** | **258639** |
| **N95VE** | **C500** | **197** |
| (N95VP) | C650 | 0095 |
| N95WC | WW24 | 392 |
| N95WJ | FA10 | 195 |
| **N95WK** | **LJ55** | **099** |
| N95WW | WW24 | 395 |
| **N95XL** | **C56X** | **5095** |
| N95ZC | LJ60 | 068 |
| N95ZZ | GLEX | 9201 |
| N95ZZ | GLEX | 9302 |
| N96 | HS25 | 258134 |
| N96AA | LJ24 | 139 |
| N96AC | LJ35 | 224 |
| **N96AD** | **ASTR** | **246** |
| N96AE | GLF4 | 1024 |
| N96AF | C650 | 0119 |
| (N96AF) | LJ55 | 026 |
| N96AL | ASTR | 096 |
| N96AL | WW24 | 385 |
| N96AR | ASTR | 041 |
| N96AT | C560 | 0325 |
| N96AX | LJ35 | 608 |
| N96B | JSTR | 5049 |
| N96B | WW24 | 16 |
| N96B | WW24 | 97 |
| N96BA | C500 | 390 |
| N96BA | WW24 | 205 |
| N96BB | JSTR | 5049 |
| (N96BK) | GLF2 | 213 |
| N96CE | FA50 | 139 |
| N96CE | LJ55 | 033 |
| N96CF | C500 | 529 |
| N96CJ | C52A | 0096 |
| N96CK | LJ24 | 016 |
| N96CM | SBRL | 282-77 |
| **N96CP** | **C650** | **0139** |
| N96CP | LJ35 | 446 |
| N96CP | SBRL | 306-64 |
| N96CR | LJ35 | 446 |
| N96CS | C550 | 252 |
| **N96DA** | **C500** | **577** |
| (N96DC) | LJ25 | 317 |

| **N96DK** | **C750** | **0035** |
|---|---|---|
| (N96DM) | LJ25 | 197 |
| N96DM | LJ35 | 186 |
| N96DS | C500 | 437 |
| **N96DS** | **CL61** | **5146** |
| N96DS | F9EX | 19 |
| N96DS | FA50 | 209 |
| N96EA | C500 | 200 |
| (N96EJ) | C500 | 043 |
| N96FA | LJ35 | 096 |
| **N96FB** | **C500** | **094** |
| N96FC | C560 | 0436 |
| N96FF | LJ60 | 194 |
| N96FG | F2TH | 25 |
| N96FJ | FA50 | 106 |
| (N96FJ) | FA50 | 99 |
| N96FL | ASTR | 109 |
| (N96FL) | GLF4 | 1282 |
| **N96FN** | **LJ35** | **186** |
| N96FP | C500 | 543 |
| N96FT | HS25 | 257013 |
| **N96FT** | **HS25** | **258568** |
| N96G | C500 | 200 |
| N96G | C500 | 444 |
| N96G | C525 | 0034 |
| N96G | C52A | 0018 |
| **N96G** | **C52B** | **0114** |
| **N96GA** | **BE40** | **RK-238** |
| N96GD | C525 | 0042 |
| N96GM | C525 | 0114 |
| N96GS | JSTR | 5068/27 |
| **N96GS** | **LJ35** | **606** |
| N96GT | C500 | 444 |
| N96JA | GLF2 | 213 |
| **N96JA** | **GLF4** | **1226** |
| (N96JJ) | C560 | 0096 |
| (N96JJ) | LJ25 | 175 |
| N96L | FA20 | 327 |
| N96LB | F900 | 10 |
| N96LC | C500 | 683 |
| N96LF | LJ31 | 140 |
| N96LT | F2TH | 72 |
| N96LT | FA50 | 192 |
| **N96MB** | **C500** | **550** |
| N96MJ | LJ25 | 091 |
| N96MJ | LJ25 | 098 |
| N96MR | C52B | 0067 |
| N96MR | GLF3 | 324 |
| N96MT | C560 | 0032 |
| **N96MT** | **C650** | **7065** |
| N96MY | C560 | 0032 |
| **N96NA** | **C52A** | **0096** |
| N96NB | C560 | 0267 |
| **N96NB** | **C560** | **0673** |
| **N96NC** | **PRM1** | **RB-86** |
| **N96NJ** | **C52A** | **0018** |
| N96NX | F9EX | 35 |
| N96NX | FA50 | 141 |
| N96PC | ASTR | 004 |
| **N96PD** | **C52B** | **0111** |
| N96PM | F900 | 36 |
| N96PR | HS25 | 257148 |
| N96RE | C500 | 331 |
| N96RE | LJ35 | 103 |
| **N96RE** | **SBRL** | **465-52** |
| N96RS | LJ25 | 175 |
| N96RT | FA20 | 159 |
| **N96RX** | **C750** | **0044** |
| N96SG | HS25 | 25060 |
| N96SK | C500 | 500 |
| N96SK | C525 | 0420 |
| N96SK | C52A | 0093 |
| N96SK | HS25 | 258702 |
| **N96SK** | **HS25** | **HA-0006** |
| **N96SW** | **C52A** | **0425** |
| N96TC | C500 | 531 |
| N96TD | C500 | 529 |
| N96TD | C550 | 596 |
| N96TJ | FA10 | 96 |
| N96TM | C550 | 550-1063 |
| **N96TM** | **WW24** | **275** |
| N96TS | WW24 | 159 |
| N96TX | C750 | 0009 |
| **N96TX** | **C750** | **0069** |
| N96TX | C750 | 0103 |
| (N96UD) | C750 | 0004 |
| N96UH | FA50 | 55 |
| **N96UT** | **FA50** | **192** |

| N96VF | LJ25 | 143 |
|---|---|---|
| N96VP | C650 | 0096 |
| N96VR | FA10 | 199 |
| N96WC | FA20 | 159 |
| N96WW | BE40 | RJ-34 |
| N96WW | WW24 | 411 |
| (N96ZC) | LJ60 | 068 |
| N96ZZ | GLEX | 9218 |
| N96ZZ | GLEX | 9296 |
| N97 | HS25 | 258154 |
| N97AC | LJ25 | 125 |
| N97AF | LJ55 | 035 |
| N97AG | GLF3 | 328 |
| N97AG | GLF3 | 401 |
| N97AJ | CS55 | 0079 |
| **N97AL** | **C650** | **0155** |
| N97AL | WW24 | 387 |
| N97AM | LJ25 | 071 |
| N97AN | LJ35 | 373 |
| N97BG | C550 | 427 |
| **N97BH** | **C560** | **0290** |
| N97BP | CS55 | 0090 |
| N97BZ | FA50 | 89 |
| **N97CC** | **CS55** | **0045** |
| **N97CE** | **LJ35** | **203** |
| (N97CJ) | C525 | 0183 |
| **N97CJ** | **C52A** | **0097** |
| N97CT | CS55 | 0125 |
| N97D | LJ35 | 417 |
| N97DD | C500 | 159 |
| **N97DD** | **C650** | **0071** |
| N97DD | FA10 | 75 |
| N97DK | C750 | 0035 |
| **N97DK** | **CL30** | **20216** |
| N97DK | LJ25 | 253 |
| N97DM | LJ24 | 253 |
| N97DM | LJ25 | 003 |
| **N97DQ** | **GLEX** | **9095** |
| N97DX | FA10 | 75 |
| **N97EM** | **C550** | **481** |
| N97FB | BE40 | RK-117 |
| N97FB | BE40 | RK-152 |
| N97FD | C500 | 543 |
| N97FF | BE40 | RK-117 |
| N97FJ | CL64 | 5374 |
| N97FJ | FA20 | 105 |
| (N97FJ) | FA50 | 261 |
| N97FJ | FA50 | 92 |
| N97FL | ASTR | 110 |
| N97FN | LJ25 | 003 |
| N97FT | GLF4 | 1013 |
| **N97FT** | **GLF4** | **4008** |
| N97FT | LJ25 | 210 |
| N97GM | F2EX | 15 |
| N97HT | C510 | 0097 |
| N97HW | WW24 | 312 |
| N97J | LJ25 | 094 |
| N97J | LJ55 | 039 |
| N97JJ | LJ25 | 162 |
| N97JL | C560 | 0163 |
| N97JL | LJ35 | 310 |
| N97JP | LJ25 | 293 |
| N97JP | PRM1 | RB-226 |
| N97LA | C500 | 338 |
| N97LB | CS55 | 0079 |
| **N97LE** | **LJ35** | **648** |
| (N97LT) | F2TH | 73 |
| N97LT | FA50 | 202 |
| N97MC | FA10 | 82 |
| N97MJ | LJ24 | 093 |
| N97NB | C560 | 0399 |
| N97NL | SBRL | 306-97 |
| N97NX | F2TH | 132 |
| **N97NX** | **F9EX** | **32** |
| N97PJ | MS76 | 097 |
| (N97QA) | LJ35 | 304 |
| N97QS | CS55 | 0097 |
| N97RE | SBRL | 465-32 |
| (N97RJ) | FA10 | 118 |
| N97RJ | LJ35 | 367 |
| N97RS | LJ25 | 162 |
| N97S | C550 | 233 |
| N97SC | SBRL | 306-123 |
| N97SC | SBRL | 306-54 |
| N97SC | SBRL | 306-72 |
| N97SC | SBRL | 380-34 |
| **N97SG** | **CL61** | **3051** |
| N97SH | HS25 | 258277 |

| | | |
|---|---|---|
| **N97SJ** | **FA20** | **378** |
| N97SK | C500 | 316 |
| N97SK | CS55 | 0127 |
| N97SM | WW24 | 307 |
| **N97TE** | **C560** | **0436** |
| N97TJ | CS55 | 0082 |
| N97TJ | FA10 | 75 |
| N97TJ | LJ35 | 012 |
| N97TS | HS25 | 257001 |
| (N97TT) | BE40 | RK-65 |
| N97UT | FA50 | 202 |
| **N97VF** | **C525** | **0171** |
| (N97VM) | HS25 | 25030 |
| N97VN | C56X | 5007 |
| **N97WJ** | **FA20** | **101** |
| (N97XP) | BE40 | RK-39 |
| N97XR | LJ45 | 256 |
| N98 | HS25 | 258156 |
| (N98A) | LJ36 | 025 |
| N98AA | LJ24 | 306 |
| N98AC | C560 | 0611 |
| **N98AC** | **FA50** | **329** |
| N98AC | LJ24 | 298 |
| N98AC | LJ35 | 301 |
| N98AD | ASTR | 095 |
| (N98AE) | GLF4 | 1302 |
| (N98AF) | HS25 | 257082 |
| N98AG | CL64 | 5402 |
| N98AM | GLF2 | 13 |
| N98AQ | C560 | 0611 |
| **N98AV** | **C500** | **578** |
| N98BD | C650 | 0048 |
| N98BE | C550 | 075 |
| N98BL | LJ60 | 061 |
| **N98BM** | **WW24** | **193** |
| N98CF | SBRL | 282-66 |
| **N98CG** | **LJ24** | **289** |
| N98CR | CL61 | 3024 |
| N98CX | C750 | 0060 |
| N98DD | C650 | 0048 |
| (N98DD) | HS25 | 258004 |
| N98DK | LJ24 | 152 |
| N98DK | LJ24 | 305 |
| N98DM | C500 | 296 |
| (N98DQ) | F900 | 137 |
| **N98E** | **C560** | **0103** |
| N98FJ | ASTR | 098 |
| N98FJ | CL64 | 5374 |
| N98FJ | CL64 | 5401 |
| N98FJ | FA50 | 93 |
| N98FT | GLF2 | 173 |
| **N98FT** | **HS25** | **257016** |
| (N98G) | GLF2 | 24 |
| N98GA | C560 | 0201 |
| N98GA | C560 | 0229 |
| N98GC | C550 | 272 |
| **N98HG** | **WW24** | **394** |
| (N98JA) | LJ25 | 148 |
| **N98JV** | **LJ60** | **135** |
| N98JV | LJ60 | 140 |
| (N98KK) | WW24 | 9 |
| N98KR | JSTR | 5048 |
| N98LB | FA20 | 298 |
| N98LB | SBRL | 306-97 |
| N98LC | LJ35 | 077 |
| **N98LT** | **GLF4** | **1278** |
| N98MB | C500 | 054 |
| N98MD | JSTR | 5048 |
| (N98MD) | JSTR | 5098/28 |
| N98MD | LJ35 | 086 |
| N98ME | C500 | 585 |
| N98NA | C560 | 0467 |
| N98NX | F2TH | 152 |
| **N98NX** | **F900** | **128** |
| N98PE | C52A | 0093 |
| **N98Q** | **C500** | **040** |
| N98QS | CS55 | 0098 |
| N98R | FA20 | 428 |
| N98R | FA50 | 172 |
| N98RG | C500 | 614 |
| N98RH | FA20 | 284 |
| (N98RH) | LJ25 | 040 |
| **N98RP** | **F2TH** | **186** |
| N98RP | GLF3 | 328 |
| **N98RS** | **LJ25** | **148** |
| N98RX | C550 | 550-0869 |
| N98RX | C56X | 5182 |
| N98S | WW24 | 73 |
| N98SA | WW24 | 73 |
| N98SC | WW24 | 32 |
| **N98SP** | **GALX** | **203** |
| N98TE | LJ35 | 317 |
| N98TJ | C550 | 669 |
| N98TJ | HS25 | 25032 |
| N98TS | WW24 | 198 |
| (N98TW) | CL60 | 1063 |
| (N98TW) | FA10 | 93 |
| N98TX | C750 | 0039 |
| N98TX | C750 | 0041 |
| N98VA | LJ35 | 014 |
| N98VR | FA10 | 222 |
| **N98WJ** | **GLF2** | **89** |
| N98WJ | LJ24 | 268 |
| N98WW | WW24 | 398 |
| **N98XR** | **LJ45** | **292** |
| **N98XS** | **C650** | **7058** |
| N99 | HS25 | 258158 |
| N99AA | LJ24 | 308 |
| N99AA | SBRL | 306-53 |
| N99AP | SBRL | 282-128 |
| **N99BB** | **C750** | **0005** |
| N99BC | C500 | 187 |
| N99BC | C500 | 190 |
| N99BC | FA10 | 128 |
| N99BL | FA10 | 87 |
| **N99CJ** | **C525** | **0333** |
| N99CK | C500 | 216 |
| **N99CK** | **C500** | **548** |
| N99CK | HS25 | 25186 |
| N99CK | WW24 | 146 |
| **N99CN** | **C550** | **331** |
| N99CQ | LJ25 | 022 |
| N99CR | SBRL | 282-81 |
| N99CV | WW24 | 146 |
| (N99DA) | HS25 | 258125 |
| N99DE | C550 | 331 |
| N99DM | LJ24 | 114 |
| N99DQ | F900 | 137 |
| **N99DY** | **C550** | **482** |
| N99E | FA20 | 317 |
| N99E | JSTR | 5216 |
| N99E | LJ24 | 196 |
| N99ES | LJ24 | 196 |
| N99ES | LJ25 | 018 |
| N99FF | MU30 | A045SA |
| (N99FF) | SBRL | 282-129 |
| N99FF | SBRL | 306-83 |
| N99FJ | CL64 | 5412 |
| N99FJ | FA50 | 94 |
| N99FN | LJ35 | 071 |
| N99FN | LJ35 | 652 |
| N99FT | JSTR | 5055/21 |
| N99GA | GLF2 | 99 |
| N99GA | GLF3 | 421 |
| **N99GA** | **GLF4** | **1198** |
| N99GC | C500 | 369 |
| N99GC | HS25 | 25149 |
| N99GK | LJ35 | 316 |
| **N99GK** | **LJ40** | **45-2008** |
| N99GM | GLF4 | 1006 |
| N99GS | WW24 | 31 |
| N99GX | ASTR | 139 |
| N99HB | MS76 | 102 |
| N99JB | C525 | 0352 |
| N99JB | LJ24 | 246 |
| N99JD | FA50 | 129 |
| N99JD | HS25 | 257148 |
| **N99KP** | **EA50** | **000181** |
| N99KR | HS25 | 25149 |
| N99KT | FA20 | 72/413 |
| N99KV | LJ55 | 122 |
| N99KW | C550 | 386 |
| **N99KW** | **CL64** | **5564** |
| N99KW | LJ35 | 368 |
| N99KW | LJ55 | 122 |
| N99KW | LJ60 | 085 |
| N99MC | C500 | 187 |
| N99MC | C500 | 190 |
| N99MC | FA10 | 128 |
| **N99MC** | **LJ25** | **182** |
| N99ME | LJ35 | 185 |
| N99ME | LJ35 | 204 |
| N99MJ | LJ35 | 308 |
| N99MR | JSTR | 5112/7 |
| N99NJ | LJ25 | 220 |
| **N99NJ** | **LJ35** | **481** |
| **N99PD** | **GLF3** | **314** |
| (N99PD) | GLF4 | 1257 |
| **N99RS** | **LJ36** | **039** |
| N99S | SBRL | 465-64 |
| N99SC | GLF3 | 496 |
| **N99SC** | **GLF4** | **1236** |
| N99SC | GLF4 | 1343 |
| N99SC | HS25 | 25149 |
| N99SC | HS25 | 25169 |
| N99SC | HS25 | 256016 |
| N99SC | LJ24 | 196 |
| N99ST | GLF2 | 91 |
| N99ST | HS25 | 25205 |
| (N99SU) | GLF3 | 496 |
| N99TC | LJ24 | 098 |
| N99TD | C500 | 231 |
| (N99TD) | C500 | 529 |
| **N99TK** | **C550** | **621** |
| N99TY | F2TH | 130 |
| N99UG | CL61 | 5126 |
| (N99UP) | LJ24 | 345 |
| N99VA | GLF2 | 200 |
| N99VA | LJ35 | 185 |
| (N99VC) | CS55 | 0016 |
| N99VR | JSTR | 5161/43 |
| N99W | WW24 | 46 |
| N99WA | FA10 | 150 |
| (N99WB) | C500 | 346 |
| (N99WF) | WW24 | 417 |
| N99WH | WW24 | 284 |
| N99WJ | GLF2 | 245/30 |
| N99WJ | GLF3 | 340 |
| **N99WJ** | **GLF3** | **394** |
| N99WJ | GLF3 | 431 |
| N99WJ | GLF4 | 1139 |
| N99WR | C560 | 0019 |
| N99XN | GLEX | 9190 |
| N99XR | LJ45 | 302 |
| N99XR | SBRL | 282-104 |
| N99XY | C500 | 369 |
| N99XZ | LJ25 | 087 |
| (N99YB) | LJ55 | 077 |
| (N99YD) | GLF3 | 314 |
| **N99ZB** | **BE40** | **RK-344** |
| **N99ZC** | **LJ60** | **162** |
| N100A | GLEX | 9077 |
| N100A | GLEX | 9105 |
| **N100A** | **GLEX** | **9205** |
| N100A | GLF2 | 89 |
| N100A | GLF3 | 370 |
| N100A | GLF4 | 1072 |
| N100A | GLF4 | 1235 |
| N100A | JSTR | 5058/4 |
| N100AC | C500 | 195 |
| N100AC | C550 | 403 |
| **N100AC** | **FA20** | **366** |
| N100AC | GLF2 | 75/7 |
| N100AC | JSTR | 5033/56 |
| N100AD | C500 | 226 |
| N100AG | BE40 | RK-150 |
| N100AG | C550 | 404 |
| **N100AG** | **HS25** | **258238** |
| N100AG | WW24 | 346 |
| N100AJ | LJ24 | 186 |
| N100AK | ASTR | 062 |
| N100AK | ASTR | 121 |
| **N100AK** | **ASTR** | **153** |
| N100AK | GLF3 | 437 |
| N100AK | WW24 | 218 |
| N100AK | WW24 | 295 |
| N100AK | WW24 | 302 |
| N100AK | WW24 | 436 |
| N100AL | JSTR | 5058/4 |
| **N100AM** | **C500** | **305** |
| N100AQ | C500 | 195 |
| N100AQ | WW24 | 295 |
| **N100AR** | **C56X** | **5241** |
| N100AR | GLF4 | 1100 |
| **N100AS** | **FA20** | **274** |
| **N100AT** | **LJ35** | **436** |
| **N100AW** | **BE40** | **RK-150** |
| N100AY | C550 | 404 |
| N100BC | WW24 | 226 |
| **N100BC** | **WW24** | **438** |
| N100BG | FA10 | 138 |
| N100BG | FA10 | 64 |
| (N100BG) | GLF3 | 488 |
| **N100BL** | **LJ31** | **126** |
| N100BP | SBRL | 380-48 |
| N100BX | C500 | 439 |
| N100C | JSTR | 5076/17 |
| N100CA | WW24 | 95 |
| N100CC | GLF2 | 75/7 |
| N100CC | JSTR | 5033/56 |
| N100CE | SBRL | 282-19 |
| N100CE | SBRL | 306-128 |
| N100CE | SBRL | 306-87 |
| N100CH | C500 | 628 |
| N100CH | C525 | 0087 |
| **N100CH** | **C550** | **437** |
| N100CH | WW24 | 406 |
| N100CJ | C500 | 390 |
| N100CJ | C550 | 182 |
| **N100CJ** | **C56X** | **5100** |
| N100CJ | WW24 | 141 |
| N100CK | FA10 | 125 |
| N100CK | FA10 | 222 |
| N100CM | C500 | 276 |
| N100CQ | C525 | 0087 |
| N100CT | FA10 | 203 |
| **N100CU** | **FA10** | **104** |
| N100CX | C550 | 028 |
| N100CX | C550 | 577 |
| N100DE | MU30 | A016SA |
| **N100DF** | **GLF4** | **1313** |
| N100DG | WW24 | 76 |
| N100DL | LJ24 | 201 |
| N100DR | WW24 | 76 |
| **N100DS** | **C550** | **639** |
| N100DV | FA50 | 54 |
| **N100DW** | **C52B** | **0261** |
| N100EA | LJ24 | 019 |
| N100EA | MU30 | A089SA |
| N100ED | F900 | 195 |
| N100EG | FA50 | 105 |
| **N100EJ** | **SBRL** | **380-1** |
| N100EP | LJ25 | 138 |
| N100EP | LJ35 | 150 |
| **N100EQ** | **E50P** | **50000082** |
| (N100EQ) | F900 | 195 |
| **N100ES** | **GLEX** | **9108** |
| N100ES | GLF4 | 1135 |
| N100EU | SBRL | 306-54 |
| (N100FF) | C500 | 149 |
| N100FF | C750 | 0028 |
| **N100FF** | **E50P** | **50000141** |
| N100FF | F900 | 142 |
| (N100FF) | HS25 | 257173 |
| N100FG | SBRL | 282-99 |
| N100FJ | FA10 | 100 |
| N100FJ | FA10 | 192 |
| N100FJ | FA10 | 194 |
| N100FJ | FA10 | 206 |
| N100FJ | FA10 | 217 |
| N100FJ | FA10 | 3 |
| N100FL | SBRL | 306-46 |
| N100FN | SBRL | 306-46 |
| N100FR | C750 | 0069 |
| N100FS | SBRL | 282-38 |
| (N100FU) | LJ25 | 120 |
| **N100FZ** | **E50P** | **50000137** |
| N100G | ASTR | 092 |
| N100GA | ASTR | 070 |
| N100GA | ASTR | 130 |
| N100GA | ASTR | 139 |
| N100GB | HS25 | 25022 |
| N100GJ | GLF4 | 1007 |
| N100GL | JSTR | 5132/57 |
| N100GL | LJ35 | 037 |
| N100GN | FA20 | 325 |
| N100GN | FA20 | 339 |
| N100GN | GLF3 | 312 |
| N100GN | GLF4 | 1007 |
| N100GN | GLF4 | 1236 |
| N100GP | LJ24 | 106 |
| N100GP | LJ35 | 064 |
| (N100GQ) | ASTR | 070 |
| N100GS | LJ24 | 118 |
| N100GU | LJ35 | 173 |
| (N100GU) | LJ55 | 035 |
| **N100GV** | **GLF5** | **600** |
| N100GX | GLF3 | 321 |
| N100GX | GLF4 | 1100 |
| N100GX | HS25 | 258195 |
| **N100GY** | **ASTR** | **120** |
| N100H | FA10 | 216 |

| | | |
|---|---|---|
| **N100HB** | **C550** | **071** |
| (N100HC) | FA7X | 35 |
| N100HC | SBRL | 282-32 |
| N100HE | HS25 | 25225 |
| **N100HF** | **GLF4** | **1338** |
| N100HF | HS25 | 25183 |
| N100HF | HS25 | 25225 |
| N100HG | CL61 | 3055 |
| N100HG | FA20 | 54 |
| N100HG | GLF3 | 429 |
| **N100HG** | **GLF4** | **1026** |
| N100HP | C500 | 280 |
| N100HW | LJ35 | 403 |
| **N100HW** | **LJ40** | **45-2036** |
| N100HZ | GLF3 | 429 |
| (N100JC) | C500 | 148 |
| **N100JF** | **GLF4** | **1093** |
| N100JF | HS25 | 257135 |
| N100JJ | C500 | 192 |
| N100JS | C52A | 0176 |
| **N100JS** | **C52B** | **0095** |
| N100JZ | LJ24 | 038 |
| N100K | LJ25 | 154 |
| N100K | LJ35 | 170 |
| N100KK | LJ24 | 219 |
| N100KK | LJ35 | 420 |
| **N100KK** | **LJ45** | **065** |
| N100KP | CS55 | 0038 |
| **N100KP** | **F2EX** | **142** |
| N100KP | FA50 | 232 |
| N100KS | GLF2 | 96 |
| N100KS | SBRL | 282-104 |
| N100KT | CL61 | 5004 |
| N100KT | CL61 | 5066 |
| **N100KU** | **C550** | **550-0813** |
| N100KW | FA20 | 168 |
| N100KY | WW24 | 101 |
| N100KZ | C680 | 0200 |
| N100KZ | LJ35 | 420 |
| (N100L) | LJ35 | 357 |
| **N100LA** | **HS25** | **258280** |
| N100LL | WW24 | 79 |
| **N100LR** | **CL60** | **1064** |
| (N100LR) | CL60 | 1069 |
| N100LR | HS25 | 25203 |
| N100LR | HS25 | 257173 |
| **N100LX** | **C500** | **628** |
| N100M | FA20 | 194 |
| N100MA | SBRL | 306-87 |
| **N100MB** | **F2EX** | **60** |
| N100MC | WW24 | 149 |
| N100ME | WW24 | 206 |
| (N100MH) | HS25 | 258137 |
| N100MJ | LJ24 | 051 |
| N100MK | LJ25 | 019 |
| N100MN | LJ35 | 309 |
| N100MS | LJ35 | 138 |
| N100MT | HS25 | 25234 |
| **N100MZ** | **EA50** | **000140** |
| N100MZ | JSTR | 5149/11 |
| **N100NB** | **LJ25** | **181** |
| **N100NG** | **F9EX** | **30** |
| N100NG | HS25 | 258537 |
| N100NR | LJ25 | 356 |
| N100NR | LJ35 | 403 |
| N100NR | LJ60 | 269 |
| N100NR | WW24 | 61 |
| N100NW | FA10 | 201 |
| N100NW | LJ35 | 228 |
| N100P | GLF2 | 5 |
| (N100P) | GLF3 | 301 |
| N100PC | WW24 | 149 |
| **N100PF** | **C525** | **0390** |
| N100PJ | GLF2 | 5 |
| N100PM | GLF2 | 114 |
| N100PM | GLF4 | 1144 |
| (N100PM) | HS25 | 258027 |
| N100PW | SBRL | 306-16 |
| **N100PZ** | **E50P** | **50000015** |
| N100QH | C500 | 628 |
| N100QP | HS25 | 256055 |
| **N100QR** | **CL60** | **1043** |
| N100QR | HS25 | 256055 |
| N100QW | CS55 | 0079 |
| N100QX | GLF3 | 321 |
| N100R | C650 | 0197 |
| **N100R** | **HS25** | **HA-0076** |
| N100R | LJ60 | 084 |
| N100RA | LJ24 | 180 |
| N100RB | FA10 | 198 |
| **N100RC** | **C52B** | **0038** |
| N100RC | WW24 | 60 |
| N100RG | C500 | 149 |
| N100RH | HS25 | 25196 |
| N100RR | FA10 | 179 |
| N100RR | FA50 | 220 |
| **N100RS** | **MU30** | **A029SA** |
| N100RS | SBRL | 380-19 |
| N100S | FA20 | 142 |
| N100SA | CL64 | 5319 |
| N100SC | C550 | 108 |
| N100SC | C560 | 0054 |
| N100SC | C56X | 5065 |
| N100SM | C525 | 0278 |
| N100SN | C500 | 594 |
| N100SQ | LJ24 | 113 |
| **N100SR** | **ASTR** | **037** |
| N100SR | FA20 | 56 |
| N100SR | WW24 | 127 |
| N100SR | WW24 | 267 |
| N100SV | C500 | 448 |
| **N100SY** | **C560** | **0054** |
| N100T | FA10 | 107 |
| N100T | HS25 | 25191 |
| N100T | LJ35 | 074 |
| N100TA | LJ24 | 038 |
| N100TA | LJ24 | 045 |
| N100TA | LJ24 | 082A |
| N100TB | CS55 | 0137 |
| N100TH | WW24 | 35 |
| **N100TM** | **GLF5** | **692** |
| N100TM | JSTR | 5150/37 |
| N100TM | SBRL | 380-60 |
| N100TR | WW24 | 76 |
| (N100TT) | HS25 | 25148 |
| N100TW | C500 | 468 |
| (N100TW) | FA10 | 84 |
| N100U | C560 | 0813 |
| **N100U** | **C56X** | **6041** |
| N100U | HS25 | 259006 |
| N100UA | JSTR | 5143 |
| N100UB | FA10 | 42 |
| N100UF | C500 | 213 |
| N100UF | C500 | 314 |
| N100UF | C550 | 102 |
| N100UF | FA20 | 160/450 |
| N100UH | C500 | 213 |
| **N100UP** | **F900** | **44** |
| N100V | FA20 | 75 |
| **N100VA** | **EA50** | **000138** |
| N100VA | LJ55 | 029 |
| N100VC | LJ24 | 140 |
| N100VQ | LJ24 | 140 |
| **N100VR** | **GLEX** | **9098** |
| N100VV | C550 | 158 |
| N100W | WW24 | 73 |
| N100WC | CL61 | 3023 |
| N100WC | GLF2 | 96 |
| **N100WE** | **PRM1** | **RB-45** |
| N100WF | SBRL | 282-2 |
| N100WG | FA10 | 120 |
| N100WG | FA10 | 217 |
| N100WH | C650 | 0119 |
| N100WJ | C500 | 376 |
| "N100WJ" | FA50 | 9 |
| (N100WJ) | GLF4 | 1079 |
| N100WK | FA20 | 113 |
| N100WK | GLF2 | 77 |
| N100WM | WW24 | 73 |
| **N100WN** | **LJ25** | **288** |
| **N100WP** | **C560** | **0073** |
| N100WP | WW24 | 389 |
| **N100WT** | **C550** | **550-0858** |
| **N100WX** | **E50P** | **50000037** |
| N100WY | F2TH | 178 |
| N100X | LJ24 | 035 |
| (N100XJ) | WW24 | 204 |
| **N100Y** | **C550** | **550-0919** |
| N100Y | HS25 | 257083 |
| N100Y | SBRL | 282-32 |
| N100Y | SBRL | 306-50 |
| **N100YB** | **C56X** | **5136** |
| N100YM | FA10 | 114 |
| **N100YP** | **FA10** | **222** |
| N100Z | C550 | 550-0926 |
| N101AD | HS25 | 25284 |
| N101AD | LJ24 | 093 |
| N101AD | MU30 | A056SA |
| N101AF | C550 | 732 |
| **N101AJ** | **LJ36** | **008** |
| **N101AR** | **BE40** | **RK-461** |
| (N101AR) | GLF2 | 140/40 |
| N101AR | LJ24 | 093 |
| N101AR | LJ24 | 279 |
| N101AR | LJ35 | 610 |
| N101AR | LJ36 | 008 |
| (N101AW) | JSTR | 5103 |
| N101BE | F2TH | 43 |
| N101BG | LJ35 | 106 |
| N101BU | WW24 | 32 |
| N101BX | C550 | 229 |
| N101CC | BE40 | RJ-19 |
| **N101CC** | **BE40** | **RK-277** |
| N101CD | C500 | 101 |
| N101CP | C560 | 0800 |
| N101CP | GLF5 | 5207 |
| N101CV | C560 | 0101 |
| **N101CV** | **GLF4** | **1230** |
| N101DB | LJ24 | 070 |
| N101DD | C550 | 338 |
| N101DE | WW24 | 98 |
| N101DL | LJ25 | 341 |
| N101EC | CS55 | 0006 |
| N101EF | FA10 | 157 |
| N101EG | CS55 | 0043 |
| **N101ET** | **FA50** | **95** |
| N101EU | FA10 | 204 |
| N101EX | F9EX | 111 |
| N101FC | HS25 | 257089 |
| **N101FC** | **HS25** | **258380** |
| **N101FG** | **C550** | **550-0839** |
| N101FJ | FA10 | 4 |
| N101FJ | FA50 | 108 |
| (N101FJ) | FA50 | 97 |
| **N101FU** | **C510** | **0207** |
| N101FU | LJ25 | 120 |
| N101GA | GLF4 | 1109 |
| N101GP | LJ35 | 021 |
| N101GS | WW24 | 35 |
| N101GX | GALX | 041 |
| N101GZ | FA10 | 47 |
| N101HB | C500 | 203 |
| N101HB | C560 | 0002 |
| N101HB | LJ35 | 152 |
| (N101HC) | C500 | 400 |
| N101HC | GLF4 | 1245 |
| N101HF | C500 | 203 |
| N101HF | HS25 | 257013 |
| N101HG | C500 | 213 |
| N101HK | LJ35 | 440 |
| N101HK | LJ55 | 101 |
| **N101HS** | **FA10** | **82** |
| N101HS | HS25 | 25201 |
| N101HS | WW24 | 193 |
| N101HW | LJ35 | 403 |
| **N101HW** | **LJ60** | **037** |
| **N101JL** | **C550** | **550-1002** |
| N101JR | LJ24 | 084 |
| N101JR | LJ25 | 104 |
| N101KK | C500 | 219 |
| N101KK | C550 | 232 |
| **N101KP** | **C560** | **0520** |
| N101L | GALX | 024 |
| **N101L** | **GALX** | **156** |
| N101L | SBRL | 306-15 |
| N101LB | WW24 | 8 |
| N101LD | C500 | 462 |
| **N101LD** | **C525** | **0689** |
| N101LD | GALX | 024 |
| **N101LT** | **HS25** | **257114** |
| N101ME | SBRL | 380-70 |
| **N101MH** | **GLF5** | **609** |
| N101MU | GLF4 | 1107 |
| N101NK | WW24 | 148 |
| N101NS | ASTR | 066 |
| N101NS | F2TH | 11 |
| **N101NY** | **F2TH** | **178** |
| (N101PC) | C650 | 0057 |
| **N101PG** | **C650** | **0126** |
| N101PG | LJ35 | 228 |
| N101PK | CL61 | 5005 |
| N101PK | LJ35 | 440 |
| N101PK | LJ55 | 101 |
| N101PN | PRM1 | RB-101 |
| N101PP | LJ24 | 085 |
| N101PT | GLF3 | 491 |
| **N101PV** | **F2EX** | **23** |
| **N101QS** | **BE40** | **RK-484** |
| N101QS | CS55 | 0101 |
| N101RL | C550 | 371 |
| **N101RR** | **C500** | **647** |
| N101RR | SBRL | 282-101 |
| N101SK | CL60 | 1033 |
| N101SK | CL61 | 5058 |
| N101SK | HS25 | 257001 |
| N101ST | CL60 | 1033 |
| N101SV | WW24 | 110 |
| N101SV | WW24 | 246 |
| N101T | SBRL | 282-53 |
| N101TF | FA10 | 144 |
| **N101U** | **C525** | **0454** |
| **N101UD** | **CL30** | **20220** |
| N101UD | HS25 | 25235 |
| N101UD | LJ60 | 275 |
| N101UR | HS25 | 25235 |
| N101US | LJ24 | 352 |
| N101US | LJ35 | 500 |
| N101US | SBRL | 282-7 |
| **N101VJ** | **FA10** | **177** |
| **N101VS** | **LJ24** | **218** |
| **N101WR** | **BE40** | **RK-41** |
| N101WR | LJ25 | 017 |
| **N101WY** | **C560** | **0620** |
| N101XS | HS25 | 257001 |
| N101YC | C650 | 0057 |
| N101ZE | FA20 | 108/430 |
| N102AB | GLF2 | 53 |
| N102AD | C500 | 280 |
| N102AD | FA20 | 225/472 |
| N102AF | C525 | 0122 |
| N102AK | GLF3 | 390 |
| N102AK | GLF3 | 466 |
| (N102AK) | WW24 | 434 |
| N102AQ | GLF3 | 390 |
| N102AR | LJ25 | 012 |
| N102B | LJ24 | 343 |
| N102BG | FA50 | 305 |
| N102BG | GLF4 | 1273 |
| **N102BG** | **GLF5** | **5038** |
| **N102BP** | **HS25** | **257036** |
| N102BQ | FA50 | 305 |
| **N102BQ** | **GLF4** | **1273** |
| N102BT | LJ35 | 301 |
| N102BW | WW24 | 165 |
| N102C | LJ24 | 343 |
| **N102CE** | **C650** | **7061** |
| N102CE | WW24 | 129 |
| N102CJ | WW24 | 78 |
| **N102CL** | **PRM1** | **RB-178** |
| **N102CX** | **GLF2** | **102/32** |
| **N102DR** | **C550** | **436** |
| **N102DS** | **C510** | **0095** |
| **N102EP** | **E50P** | **50000102** |
| N102FC | C550 | 052 |
| **N102FD** | **GALX** | **128** |
| N102FJ | FA10 | 6 |
| N102FJ | FA50 | 100 |
| N102FM | GLF4 | 1325 |
| N102FS | C56X | 5318 |
| N102GH | LJ35 | 105 |
| N102GL | LJ24 | 329 |
| N102GP | LJ24 | 173 |
| N102GP | LJ35 | 105 |
| N102GX | GALX | 042 |
| **N102HB** | **C550** | **407** |
| N102HF | C500 | 275 |
| N102HS | C500 | 517 |
| N102HS | GLF2 | 112 |
| N102KJ | WW24 | 271 |
| **N102KP** | **C560** | **0527** |
| **N102LJ** | **LJ60** | **102** |
| N102MC | BE40 | RJ-50 |
| N102MG | F2TH | 221 |
| N102MJ | SBRL | 380-39 |
| N102ML | CL60 | 1063 |
| N102ML | GLF2 | 112 |
| N102MU | GLF4 | 1145 |
| N102NW | LJ31 | 002 |
| N102PA | C550 | 621 |
| **N102PA** | **E50P** | **50000030** |
| N102PA | HS25 | 258536 |
| N102PA | LJ24 | 224 |

| | | |
|---|---|---|
| N102PS | LJ25 | 010 |
| N102PT | C525 | 0433 |
| (N102PT) | GLF3 | 336 |
| **N102QS** | **BE40** | **RK-380** |
| N102RA | LJ25 | 242 |
| N102RD | SBRL | 380-23 |
| N102RR | LJ25 | 308 |
| N102SK | PRM1 | RB-151 |
| N102ST | LJ35 | 301 |
| N102ST | LJ55 | 069 |
| N102SV | WW24 | 34 |
| N102SY | WW24 | 34 |
| **N102TF** | **FA50** | **125** |
| N102TW | HS25 | 25090 |
| (N102U) | LJ25 | 371 |
| N102U | WW24 | 230 |
| **N102VP** | **C500** | **200** |
| **N102VS** | **LJ25** | **180** |
| N102WR | MU30 | A004SA |
| **N102WY** | **C560** | **0621** |
| N102ZE | FA20 | 126/438 |
| N103AD | BE40 | RJ-2 |
| N103AJ | C500 | 072 |
| **N103AL** | **HS25** | **258822** |
| N103BC | GLF4 | 1103 |
| **N103BG** | **C560** | **0091** |
| (N103BG) | HS25 | 258207 |
| N103BW | WW24 | 82 |
| N103C | LJ35 | 273 |
| N103C | LJ55 | 087 |
| N103CC | C500 | 103 |
| **N103CD** | **GLF3** | **418** |
| N103CF | LJ35 | 318 |
| N103CJ | C52B | 0003 |
| (N103CJ) | C52B | 0103 |
| N103CJ | HS25 | 25271 |
| N103CL | LJ35 | 273 |
| N103CS | C525 | 0438 |
| N103CS | C525 | 0453 |
| **N103CX** | **C550** | **550-0856** |
| N103DT | F900 | 142 |
| (N103EL) | GLF2 | 119/22 |
| N103EX | F9EX | 103 |
| N103F | FA20 | 376 |
| N103F | HFB3 | 1023 |
| N103F | WW24 | 53 |
| N103FJ | F9EX | 103 |
| N103FJ | FA10 | 9 |
| **N103FJ** | **FA20** | **103/423** |
| N103FJ | FA50 | 102 |
| (N103GA) | GLF3 | 455 |
| N103GC | GLF3 | 455 |
| N103GH | LJ35 | 148 |
| N103GL | LJ35 | 069 |
| N103GP | LJ35 | 148 |
| N103GX | GALX | 043 |
| N103HB | CL60 | 1059 |
| **N103HC** | **MU30** | **A068SA** |
| (N103HS) | GLF3 | 355 |
| N103HT | HS25 | 258074 |
| N103JA | C500 | 082 |
| N103JM | FA10 | 2 |
| (N103JW) | LJ24 | 341 |
| N103KC | JSTR | 5015 |
| N103LP | BE40 | RK-103 |
| **N103LS** | **LJ60** | **288** |
| N103M | C550 | 246 |
| N103MM | FA10 | 106 |
| N103PC | C500 | 488 |
| **N103PG** | **C56X** | **5590** |
| N103PJ | FA10 | 148 |
| N103PL | C500 | 278 |
| N103QS | CS55 | 0103 |
| (N103RA) | FA20 | 54 |
| (N103RA) | HS25 | 256004 |
| N103RB | LJ24 | 106 |
| N103RR | HS25 | 25221 |
| N103SK | C525 | 0480 |
| **N103SK** | **PRM1** | **RB-151** |
| N103SV | C680 | 0003 |
| **N103TA** | **SBRL** | **306-27** |
| N103TC | LJ24 | 022 |
| N103TC | LJ24 | 213 |
| N103TJ | FA10 | 103 |
| **N103VF** | **CS55** | **0046** |
| (N103WJ) | GLF2 | 103 |
| N103WV | C500 | 028 |
| **N103ZZ** | **GLEX** | **9308** |
| N104 | HS25 | 25100 |
| (N104AA) | LJ35 | 178 |
| N104AB | C500 | 402 |
| **N104AD** | **GLF4** | **1406** |
| N104AE | HS25 | 257005 |
| N104AG | HS25 | HA-0052 |
| N104AR | GLF2 | 140/40 |
| N104AR | GLF3 | 461 |
| **N104AR** | **GLF4** | **1346** |
| N104BK | GLF3 | 306 |
| N104BK | JSTR | 5219 |
| N104BS | LJ55 | 012 |
| N104BW | LJ25 | 173 |
| N104BX | LJ31 | 104 |
| N104CD | GLF2 | 53 |
| **N104CE** | **JSTR** | **5108** |
| N104CF | C500 | 543 |
| N104CJ | WW24 | 33 |
| N104CT | C750 | 0100 |
| **N104CT** | **C750** | **0275** |
| **N104DA** | **GLEX** | **9266** |
| N104DD | FA10 | 110 |
| N104DX | GLF4 | 1493 |
| N104FJ | F900 | 104 |
| N104FJ | FA10 | 8 |
| N104FJ | FA50 | 103 |
| **N104FL** | **C550** | **550-1071** |
| **N104FT** | **CL30** | **20121** |
| (N104GA) | ASTR | 104 |
| N104GA | GALX | 104 |
| N104GA | GLF5 | 5204 |
| N104GA | LJ24 | 112 |
| **N104GB** | **MU30** | **A041SA** |
| N104GL | LJ25 | 197 |
| N104GX | ASTR | 140 |
| **N104HW** | **C550** | **555** |
| N104JG | GLF4 | 1062 |
| N104JG | HS25 | 257059 |
| (N104KW) | FA10 | 122 |
| N104LJ | LJ60 | 104 |
| **N104LR** | **C560** | **0163** |
| **N104LV** | **C56X** | **5190** |
| N104MB | LJ24 | 177 |
| N104MC | LJ24 | 323 |
| N104ME | GLF2 | 178 |
| **N104PC** | **C52A** | **0212** |
| **N104RS** | **WW24** | **273** |
| N104SB | FA20 | 321 |
| N104SB | LJ35 | 357 |
| N104SD | LJ60 | 005 |
| **N104SG** | **GALX** | **212** |
| N104SL | SBRL | 282-104 |
| N104SS | SBRL | 306-30 |
| N104UA | C500 | 043 |
| (N104UT) | C750 | 0100 |
| **N104VV** | **GLF2** | **53** |
| **N104WJ** | **LJ25** | **104** |
| N105AD | C52C | 0013 |
| **N105AJ** | **GLF2** | **201** |
| N105AS | HS25 | 256064 |
| **N105AX** | **BE40** | **RK-105** |
| N105BA | C550 | 116 |
| N105BA | LJ25 | 152 |
| N105BE | WW24 | 415 |
| **N105BG** | **CS55** | **0105** |
| N105BH | GLF4 | 1117 |
| N105BJ | LJ24 | 092 |
| N105BJ | LJ25 | 062 |
| **N105BK** | **F900** | **70** |
| N105BN | CL61 | 5101 |
| N105BX | C550 | 550-1050 |
| N105CC | C500 | 105 |
| N105CF | C500 | 548 |
| **N105CJ** | **C52B** | **0005** |
| N105CQ | C52B | 0065 |
| N105CV | C560 | 0105 |
| N105DM | SBRL | 306-27 |
| N105EC | LJ24 | 103 |
| N105EJ | FA50 | 31 |
| (N105EJ) | HS25 | 25186 |
| N105FJ | FA10 | 10 |
| N105FJ | FA50 | 104 |
| **N105FN** | **ASTR** | **105** |
| N105FX | LJ31 | 086 |
| N105G | JSTR | 5056 |
| N105G | JSTR | 5223 |
| **N105GA** | **LJ24** | **116** |
| N105GH | JSTR | 5056 |
| N105GL | LJ24 | 322 |
| N105GM | JSTR | 5019 |
| N105GN | JSTR | 5019 |
| N105GX | GALX | 044 |
| **N105HD** | **SBRL** | **380-39** |
| (N105HS) | GLF3 | 355 |
| N105HS | HS25 | 25031 |
| N105HS | MU30 | A082SA |
| **N105J** | **C510** | **0277** |
| N105JJ | C500 | 105 |
| N105JM | C500 | 374 |
| **N105LB** | **EA50** | **000118** |
| N105LF | F2TH | 105 |
| N105LJ | LJ45 | 105 |
| **N105P** | **C525** | **0336** |
| N105PT | C52A | 0155 |
| N105RJ | C56X | 5172 |
| (N105SS) | SBRL | 306-27 |
| **N105ST** | **GLF5** | **5170** |
| N105SV | C680 | 0005 |
| **N105TB** | **GLF2** | **31** |
| **N105TF** | **HFB3** | **1055** |
| (N105TR) | GLF4 | 1239 |
| N105TW | C500 | 602 |
| N105TW | FA20 | 289 |
| N105UA | SBRL | 306-16 |
| **N105UP** | **CL61** | **3066** |
| **N105VS** | **GLF3** | **370** |
| **N105WC** | **FA50** | **60** |
| N105XP | HS25 | HA-0105 |
| N105Y | GLF2 | 56 |
| N105Y | GLF3 | 412 |
| **N105ZZ** | **GLEX** | **9327** |
| (N106AE) | HS25 | 257164 |
| N106BB | C550 | 550-1006 |
| N106BC | WW24 | 220 |
| N106BK | F900 | 76 |
| (N106CA) | LJ24 | 138 |
| N106CC | C650 | 0106 |
| N106CG | BE40 | RJ-12 |
| **N106CJ** | **C525** | **0006** |
| N106CJ | WW24 | 38 |
| **N106CX** | **C750** | **0106** |
| N106DD | BE40 | RK-343 |
| N106DM | BE40 | RJ-6 |
| N106EA | C500 | 468 |
| **N106FF** | **LJ60** | **375** |
| N106FJ | FA10 | 11 |
| N106FJ | FA50 | 105 |
| **N106FT** | **C550** | **550-1123** |
| N106FX | LJ31 | 087 |
| N106G | JSTR | 5090 |
| N106G | JSTR | 5217 |
| N106G | SBRL | 282-15 |
| (N106GA) | MU30 | A071SA |
| N106GC | HS25 | 258141 |
| N106GL | LJ35 | 056 |
| N106GM | C500 | 643 |
| N106GM | JSTR | 5002 |
| N106GX | ASTR | 141 |
| N106JL | HS25 | 258012 |
| N106JL | JSTR | 5214 |
| **N106JT** | **C52B** | **0106** |
| N106KA | GLF4 | 1373 |
| **N106KC** | **BE40** | **RK-132** |
| **N106KM** | **GLF3** | **305** |
| N106LJ | LJ60 | 106 |
| (N106M) | LJ24 | 348 |
| N106MC | LJ24 | 277 |
| N106PR | CL61 | 5106 |
| **N106QS** | **BE40** | **RK-381** |
| N106QS | CS55 | 0106 |
| N106RW | F9EX | 120 |
| N106SP | C550 | 382 |
| **N106SP** | **C560** | **0347** |
| **N106SR** | **C550** | **382** |
| N106ST | C650 | 0109 |
| N106TF | HFB3 | 1042 |
| (N106TJ) | GLF2 | 106 |
| N106TJ | LJ24 | 340 |
| **N106TW** | **FA10** | **84** |
| N106VC | BE40 | RJ-7 |
| (N106WH) | EA50 | 000268 |
| N106WQ | C52B | 0294 |
| N106WT | WW24 | 351 |
| N106WV | C500 | 471 |
| N106XX | LJ35 | 183 |
| (N107) | C550 | 167 |
| N107A | GLF2 | 53 |
| N107A | GLF4 | 1070 |
| (N107AF) | FA10 | 169 |
| N107AW | HS25 | 25249 |
| N107BB | C550 | 107 |
| N107BJ | BE40 | RK-23 |
| N107BK | F900 | 77 |
| N107BW | HS25 | 25107 |
| N107CC | C500 | 107 |
| N107CC | C500 | 482 |
| N107CF | C550 | 195 |
| (N107CF) | C560 | 0036 |
| (N107CF) | HS25 | 258106 |
| N107CF | WW24 | 181 |
| N107CG | C650 | 0207 |
| N107CJ | SBRL | 282-12 |
| N107CQ | C52B | 0072 |
| (N107CR) | C560 | 0036 |
| N107CX | C750 | 0107 |
| **N107EE** | **C550** | **667** |
| **N107EG** | **C550** | **550-0894** |
| N107F | FA20 | 378 |
| N107FJ | FA10 | 12 |
| N107FJ | FA50 | 112 |
| N107FX | LJ31 | 102 |
| N107G | JSTR | 5091 |
| N107G | JSTR | 5219 |
| N107G | SBRL | 282-18 |
| N107GA | GALX | 107 |
| N107GH | JSTR | 5091 |
| N107GL | LJ24 | 324 |
| N107GM | C500 | 643 |
| N107GM | C525 | 0452 |
| N107GM | JSTR | 5206 |
| N107GM | LJ31 | 049 |
| N107GX | GALX | 045 |
| N107HF | LJ25 | 029 |
| **N107J** | **FA20** | **107** |
| N107JM | LJ35 | 249 |
| N107LJ | LJ60 | 107 |
| N107LP | LJ31 | 107 |
| **N107LT** | **HS25** | **257146** |
| N107LW | FA20 | 368 |
| (N107MC) | LJ55 | 062 |
| (N107MS) | LJ25 | 362 |
| (N107PK) | C525 | 0452 |
| **N107PT** | **C52B** | **0127** |
| **N107RC** | **CS55** | **0150** |
| **N107RM** | **LJ25** | **362** |
| **N107RP** | **HS25** | **259038** |
| N107SB | C550 | 163 |
| N107SC | C500 | 107 |
| N107SF | C500 | 207 |
| N107T | C550 | 190 |
| N107T | MU30 | A012SA |
| N107TB | CL61 | 5012 |
| N107TB | FA10 | 77 |
| N107TS | LJ31 | 107 |
| (N107TW) | HFB3 | 1057 |
| (N107US) | FA10 | 207 |
| **N107VS** | **GLF5** | **5043** |
| N107WR | PRM1 | RB-73 |
| N107WV | C550 | 427 |
| **N107XP** | **HS25** | **HA-0107** |
| (N107YR) | PRM1 | RB-73 |
| (N108AJ) | C550 | 008 |
| **N108AR** | **GLF3** | **461** |
| N108BG | FA20 | 403 |
| N108BK | F900 | 74 |
| (N108BN) | CL61 | 5101 |
| N108BP | HS25 | 258546 |
| N108CC | C500 | 108 |
| N108CF | HS25 | 258100 |
| **N108CG** | **ASTR** | **108** |
| **N108CJ** | **C525** | **0108** |
| N108CR | C525 | 0258 |
| (N108CT) | C500 | 564 |
| (N108CT) | C550 | 108 |
| N108DB | C550 | 064 |
| N108DB | GLF2 | 112 |
| N108DB | GLF4 | 1149 |
| **N108DB** | **GLF5** | **5180** |
| **N108DD** | **HS25** | **258700** |
| **N108DU** | **GLF4** | **1149** |
| **N108EK** | **C56X** | **5032** |
| **N108FJ** | **F900** | **108** |
| N108FJ | FA10 | 13 |
| N108FJ | FA50 | 113 |

| | | |
|---|---|---|
| **N108FL** | **LJ25** | **300** |
| N108FX | LJ31 | 104 |
| N108G | SBRL | 282-51 |
| N108G | SBRL | 306-102 |
| N108GA | LJ25 | 011 |
| N108GL | LJ35 | 073 |
| N108GM | WW24 | 221 |
| N108GX | GALX | 046 |
| **N108JA** | **E50P** | **50000023** |
| N108JL | C500 | 526 |
| **N108JN** | **LJ35** | **358** |
| **N108KC** | **FA10** | **8** |
| **N108KJ** | **C52A** | **0416** |
| N108KP | FA50 | 232 |
| **N108LJ** | **C560** | **0337** |
| **N108MC** | **C500** | **322** |
| N108MR | FA10 | 74 |
| N108NC | FA20 | 168 |
| N108NR | LJ25 | 356 |
| N108PA | LJ25 | 195 |
| N108PJ | BE40 | RK-347 |
| **N108PJ** | **HS25** | **HA-0024** |
| **N108QS** | **BE40** | **RK-382** |
| N108QS | CS55 | 0108 |
| N108R | FA20 | 108/430 |
| **N108RB** | **LJ35** | **097** |
| N108RF | C550 | 550-0805 |
| N108RL | C500 | 125 |
| N108TG | FA10 | 114 |
| (N108TW) | LJ24 | 027 |
| (N108U) | HS25 | 259006 |
| N108U | SBRL | 282-2 |
| N108W | SBRL | 282-2 |
| N108W | SBRL | 306-132 |
| N108WG | C550 | 035 |
| N108WQ | C52B | 0294 |
| **N108WV** | **C650** | **0204** |
| N108X | SBRL | 282-51 |
| N109AF | HS25 | 257022 |
| N109AL | C500 | 037 |
| N109AP | C500 | 046 |
| **N109BG** | **HS25** | **257157** |
| N109BK | F900 | 73 |
| N109BL | C500 | 046 |
| **N109CP** | **BE40** | **RK-47** |
| **N109CQ** | **FA50** | **340** |
| N109DC | C500 | 595 |
| **N109DD** | **GLF3** | **415** |
| **N109DJ** | **EA50** | **000006** |
| N109DM | BE40 | RJ-9 |
| (N109FC) | FA20 | 489 |
| N109FJ | FA10 | 15 |
| N109FJ | FA50 | 109 |
| N109FX | LJ31 | 105 |
| N109G | GLF2 | 48/29 |
| N109G | HS25 | 257176 |
| **N109GA** | **C550** | **137** |
| N109GL | LJ35 | 080 |
| **N109GX** | **ASTR** | **142** |
| **N109HV** | **LJ31** | **105** |
| N109JB | LJ24 | 168 |
| **N109JC** | **C550** | **109** |
| N109JE | LJ60 | 093 |
| N109JM | HS25 | 257101 |
| N109JR | LJ24 | 168 |
| N109JR | LJ35 | 101 |
| N109JR | LJ60 | 093 |
| N109JR | LJ60 | 223 |
| N109JU | LJ35 | 101 |
| N109JZ | LJ60 | 223 |
| N109LJ | LJ60 | 109 |
| N109LR | HS25 | 25203 |
| N109MC | LJ35 | 054 |
| N109MC | SBRL | 306-119 |
| N109NC | CL61 | 5112 |
| N109NC | FA20 | 489 |
| N109NQ | FA20 | 489 |
| **N109NT** | **BE40** | **RK-374** |
| N109PM | PRM1 | RB-23 |
| N109PW | MU30 | A046SA |
| N109RK | FA20 | 66 |
| **N109SB** | **SBRL** | **380-20** |
| N109SJ | LJ25 | 269 |
| N109ST | C650 | 0109 |
| N109ST | GLF3 | 302 |
| **N109ST** | **GLF4** | **1151** |
| N109ST | GLF5 | 5049 |
| N109TD | HS25 | 258307 |
| N109TW | C52A | 0240 |
| N109TW | MU30 | A037SA |
| N109VP | C560 | 0109 |
| (N109VP) | C750 | 0009 |
| **N109WS** | **C560** | **0632** |
| N109ZZ | GLEX | 9337 |
| N110AB | C500 | 262 |
| N110AE | LJ35 | 155 |
| N110AF | C500 | 262 |
| N110AF | WW24 | 436 |
| **N110AJ** | **SBRL** | **380-70** |
| N110AN | JSTR | 5092/58 |
| N110AN | JSTR | 5227 |
| N110BP | CL64 | 5579 |
| N110BR | C550 | 550-1100 |
| N110BR | GLF3 | 301 |
| (N110BX) | LJ31 | 108 |
| N110CE | FA20 | 7 |
| N110CG | FA10 | 45 |
| N110CK | C500 | 078 |
| N110DD | HS25 | 258728 |
| N110DD | JSTR | 5092/58 |
| **N110DJ** | **EA50** | **000007** |
| N110DK | MU30 | A044SA |
| **N110DS** | **MU30** | **A005SA** |
| **N110ED** | **GLF5** | **5136** |
| (N110EE) | GLF3 | 322 |
| N110EJ | HS25 | 257104 |
| **N110ET** | **LJ55** | **023** |
| **N110EX** | **F9EX** | **71** |
| N110FD | C525 | 0241 |
| **N110FD** | **C52A** | **0308** |
| N110FJ | F900 | 110 |
| N110FJ | FA10 | 16 |
| (N110FJ) | FA10 | 6 |
| N110FJ | FA50 | 4 |
| N110FP | LJ25 | 274 |
| **N110FS** | **ASTR** | **247** |
| N110FS | SBRL | 282-58 |
| N110FT | LJ35 | 471 |
| N110FX | LJ31 | 108 |
| N110G | JSTR | 5007/45 |
| N110G | SBRL | 306-75 |
| N110GA | BE40 | RJ-44 |
| **N110GA** | **GLF6** | **6010** |
| N110GD | GLF2 | 154/28 |
| N110GF | FA10 | 146 |
| N110GL | LJ25 | 081 |
| N110GX | GALX | 047 |
| N110H | C500 | 385 |
| **N110HA** | **GALX** | **035** |
| N110HA | LJ25 | 110 |
| N110J | FA10 | 139 |
| N110JA | C500 | 382 |
| **N110JB** | **C500** | **599** |
| **N110JC** | **C52B** | **0301** |
| N110JD | LJ35 | 247 |
| **N110JG** | **SBRL** | **306-122** |
| **N110JJ** | **ASTR** | **270** |
| N110KG | LJ35 | 155 |
| N110KS | CL60 | 1006 |
| N110LA | FA10 | 54 |
| **N110LD** | **C550** | **399** |
| N110LE | GLF3 | 322 |
| N110LE | GLF4 | 1153 |
| N110LH | CS55 | 0118 |
| N110LP | WW24 | 286 |
| N110M | CL60 | 1052 |
| N110M | FA10 | 34 |
| N110M | LJ24 | 091 |
| **N110MG** | **ASTR** | **122** |
| N110MG | C52A | 0014 |
| N110MG | C52B | 0011 |
| N110MH | HS25 | 258137 |
| N110MH | SBRL | 306-119 |
| N110MN | JSTR | 5149/11 |
| N110MQ | C52A | 0014 |
| N110MT | GLF3 | 444 |
| N110MT | JSTR | 5149/11 |
| N110PA | LJ36 | 040 |
| **N110PK** | **C750** | **0040** |
| N110PM | SBRL | 282-127 |
| N110PP | FA10 | 210 |
| **N110PR** | **PRM1** | **RB-29** |
| N110PS | LJ24 | 262 |
| **N110RA** | **LJ25** | **025** |
| N110SC | LJ31 | 185 |
| **N110SE** | **LJ31** | **217** |
| N110SF | WW24 | 376 |
| **N110SJ** | **SJ30** | **003** |
| N110SQ | LJ24 | 173 |
| N110ST | WW24 | 129 |
| N110TD | CL60 | 1052 |
| N110TG | BE40 | RK-123 |
| N110TJ | FA20 | 368 |
| N110TM | C650 | 0141 |
| N110TM | GLF4 | 1087 |
| N110TP | C500 | 564 |
| **N110TP** | **C550** | **550-1131** |
| N110TP | FA10 | 123 |
| N110TV | C500 | 564 |
| **N110UN** | **LJ35** | **007** |
| N110VW | GLF2 | 153 |
| N110W | LJ24 | 119 |
| **N110WA** | **C550** | **406** |
| N110WC | C560 | 0357 |
| N110WS | HFB3 | 1038 |
| **N111** | **F900** | **144** |
| N111AB | SBRL | 282-70 |
| N111AC | FA20 | 111 |
| N111AC | GLF2 | 74 |
| N111AC | GLF3 | 417 |
| N111AC | SBRL | 282-79 |
| N111AD | HS25 | 25033 |
| N111AD | LJ25 | 201 |
| N111AD | SBRL | 465-27 |
| **N111AF** | **C550** | **286** |
| N111AF | LJ25 | 120 |
| N111AF | LJ31 | 111 |
| N111AG | HS25 | 25033 |
| N111AG | SBRL | 380-21 |
| N111AG | WW24 | 199 |
| N111AM | C500 | 135 |
| N111AM | C525 | 0113 |
| N111AM | FA20 | 111 |
| N111AM | FA20 | 250 |
| N111AT | C500 | 140 |
| (N111AX) | HS25 | 25033 |
| N111BA | BE40 | RJ-11 |
| **N111BB** | **C500** | **248** |
| **N111BF** | **C525** | **0140** |
| (N111BJ) | LJ35 | 344 |
| N111BL | LJ25 | 130 |
| **N111BP** | **FA20** | **111** |
| N111BZ | C650 | 7068 |
| N111CC | C500 | 111 |
| N111CF | C560 | 0053 |
| **N111CQ** | **GLF4** | **4006** |
| N111CT | LJ24 | 070 |
| **N111CX** | **BE40** | **RK-210** |
| N111DC | HFB3 | 1030 |
| N111DT | C500 | 614 |
| (N111DT) | C550 | 088 |
| N111DT | HS25 | 25115 |
| N111E | WW24 | 134 |
| N111EA | SBRL | 282-27 |
| N111EJ | LJ24 | 105 |
| N111EK | LJ24 | 105 |
| **N111EL** | **ASTR** | **055** |
| N111EL | WW24 | 351 |
| N111ER | MS76 | 050 |
| N111F | FA20 | 356 |
| N111F | SBRL | 306-126 |
| **N111FA** | **GLF3** | **307** |
| N111FJ | FA10 | 18 |
| N111FJ | FA50 | 115 |
| N111FK | CL60 | 1027 |
| **N111FK** | **CL61** | **5104** |
| (N111FS) | C500 | 034 |
| **N111FW** | **BE40** | **RK-102** |
| N111G | CL60 | 1025 |
| N111G | CL61 | 3032 |
| N111G | GLF3 | 454 |
| N111G | JSTR | 5062/12 |
| **N111GD** | **GLF2** | **170** |
| **N111GJ** | **C525** | **0500** |
| N111GL | LJ25 | 081 |
| N111GL | LJ35 | 084 |
| **N111GU** | **C56X** | **5504** |
| N111GU | JSTR | 5114/18 |
| N111GW | LJ24 | 198 |
| N111GX | CL61 | 3032 |
| N111GX | GLF3 | 454 |
| **N111HC** | **GLF3** | **482** |
| (N111HH) | PRM1 | RB-41 |
| N111HJ | LJ24 | 151 |
| N111HN | WW24 | 421 |
| N111HZ | C650 | 7068 |
| **N111HZ** | **F2TH** | **86** |
| N111J | CL60 | 1025 |
| N111JD | LJ24 | 006 |
| **N111JL** | **CL60** | **1027** |
| N111JL | GLF4 | 1111 |
| N111JW | C52A | 0387 |
| **N111JW** | **C52B** | **0186** |
| N111JW | C560 | 0478 |
| N111KK | LJ35 | 425 |
| **N111KK** | **LJ45** | **061** |
| N111KR | C500 | 179 |
| **N111KR** | **LJ35** | **464** |
| N111KZ | LJ35 | 425 |
| N111LJ | LJ24 | 127 |
| N111LL | LJ25 | 021 |
| (N111LM) | LJ25 | 025 |
| N111LP | PRM1 | RB-243 |
| **N111LP** | **PRM1** | **RB-252** |
| N111LP | WW24 | 286 |
| **N111LQ** | **PRM1** | **RB-243** |
| N111LR | C525 | 0222 |
| N111LX | GLF5 | 608 |
| N111M | FA20 | 10 |
| N111MB | HS25 | 25195 |
| **N111ME** | **C500** | **146** |
| **N111MP** | **LJ25** | **139** |
| N111MS | SBRL | 282-4 |
| N111MU | C500 | 262 |
| N111MU | FA10 | 182 |
| N111MZ | LJ35 | 125 |
| N111NF | WW24 | 168 |
| N111NG | F9EX | 71 |
| N111NL | GLF4 | 1184 |
| N111QP | C500 | 019 |
| **N111QS** | **CS55** | **0111** |
| N111RA | LJ24 | 179 |
| N111RB | C500 | 561 |
| N111RB | HS25 | 25205 |
| N111RE | LJ24 | 179 |
| N111RF | C650 | 7001 |
| N111RF | GLF2 | 46 |
| N111RF | LJ24 | 156 |
| N111RF | LJ25 | 143 |
| N111RF | LJ35 | 217 |
| N111RP | LJ24 | 156 |
| N111SF | LJ25 | 189 |
| N111SF | LJ35 | 608 |
| N111ST | WW24 | 114 |
| N111SU | C500 | 119 |
| N111SZ | LJ25 | 189 |
| N111TD | WW24 | 11 |
| N111TH | C500 | 274 |
| N111TT | LJ24 | 237 |
| N111TT | LJ24 | 301 |
| N111TT | LJ31 | 015 |
| N111UB | GLF2 | 207/34 |
| N111UN | HS25 | 256021 |
| **N111UN** | **HS25** | **256055** |
| N111US | LJ35 | 306 |
| N111US | LJ55 | 147 |
| **N111VG** | **HS25** | **258403** |
| N111VP | C560 | 0044 |
| N111VP | CS55 | 0002 |
| (N111VS) | SBRL | 380-69 |
| N111VU | F2TH | 99 |
| N111VV | LJ31 | 023 |
| N111VW | C650 | 0194 |
| N111VW | F2TH | 99 |
| N111VW | GLF2 | 153 |
| N111VW | SBRL | 306-44 |
| N111VW | SBRL | 380-69 |
| N111VX | SBRL | 380-69 |
| N111WB | LJ25 | 022 |
| **N111WB** | **LJ35** | **003** |
| N111WJ | LJ24 | 160 |
| N111WM | LJ24 | 036 |
| N111WR | LJ25 | 022 |
| N111WW | FA10 | 165 |
| **N111WW** | **FA10** | **167** |
| N111WW | LJ24 | 268 |
| N111XB | SBRL | 282-101 |
| N111XL | WW24 | 34 |
| N111Y | C650 | 0223 |
| **N111Y** | **C680** | **0127** |
| N111Y | SBRL | 380-17 |
| N111Y | WW24 | 42 |

| | | |
|---|---|---|
| N111YL | WW24 | 42 |
| **N111YW** | **C650** | **0223** |
| N111ZN | HS25 | 257076 |
| N111ZN | HS25 | 258327 |
| **N111ZN** | **HS25** | **258830** |
| **N111ZS** | **HS25** | **257076** |
| N111ZT | GLF4 | 1111 |
| **N112AB** | **C56X** | **5361** |
| N112AB | WW24 | 254 |
| N112AC | WW24 | 1 |
| **N112BJ** | **BE40** | **RK-112** |
| N112BR | C550 | 550-1120 |
| N112C | LJ24 | 250 |
| N112CD | F2TH | 26 |
| **N112CF** | **CL64** | **5509** |
| N112CF | SBRL | 465-16 |
| N112CH | LJ25 | 090 |
| N112CM | LJ31 | 078 |
| **N112CM** | **PRM1** | **RB-123** |
| N112CP | C500 | 183 |
| N112CT | FA20 | 168 |
| N112CT | LJ25 | 090 |
| N112CW | C560 | 0298 |
| **N112CW** | **C56X** | **5065** |
| N112DJ | LJ24 | 112 |
| **N112EA** | **EA50** | **000038** |
| N112EB | C500 | 499 |
| **N112EJ** | **EA50** | **000112** |
| N112EL | LJ35 | 078 |
| N112FJ | FA10 | 19 |
| N112FJ | FA50 | 116 |
| N112FJ | FA50 | 56 |
| N112FK | CL60 | 1027 |
| N112FK | LJ55 | 102 |
| N112FX | LJ31 | 115 |
| N112FX | LJ31 | 116 |
| (N112FX) | LJ31 | 122 |
| N112GA | GALX | 112 |
| N112GA | MU30 | A012SA |
| **N112GS** | **C52A** | **0127** |
| (N112GS) | GLF3 | 368 |
| N112GS | GLF3 | 384 |
| N112GX | GALX | 048 |
| N112HV | LJ31 | 116 |
| N112J | LJ24 | 237 |
| N112JC | WW24 | 7 |
| N112JM | LJ25 | 250 |
| N112JS | C550 | 032 |
| N112K | HS25 | 258042 |
| (N112KH) | SBRL | 380-34 |
| N112KM | SBRL | 465-34 |
| N112M | HS25 | 25207 |
| N112MC | C500 | 404 |
| N112MC | JSTR | 5231 |
| N112ME | LJ25 | 090 |
| N112ML | SBRL | 282-136 |
| N112MR | WW24 | 174 |
| (N112MT) | LJ60 | 208 |
| **N112MV** | **C680** | **0148** |
| N112NC | CL61 | 5112 |
| N112NW | HS25 | 258112 |
| N112PG | LJ35 | 304 |
| **N112PR** | **ASTR** | **013** |
| N112PR | SBRL | 465-12 |
| N112PV | SBRL | 465-12 |
| N112QS | CS55 | 0112 |
| N112RC | WW24 | 170 |
| N112SA | C550 | 275 |
| **N112SH** | **C550** | **046** |
| N112T | LJ24 | 098 |
| N112TJ | JSTR | 5029/38 |
| **N112WC** | **BE40** | **RK-575** |
| N112WC | C500 | 478 |
| **N112WQ** | **LJ55** | **101** |
| **N112ZZ** | **GLEX** | **9339** |
| N113AF | LJ31 | 111 |
| N113AK | LJ25 | 020 |
| (N113AN) | LJ35 | 113 |
| N113AR | GLF2 | 139/11 |
| **N113AR** | **GLF4** | **1018** |
| **N113BG** | **C52A** | **0078** |
| N113BR | PRM1 | RB-113 |
| N113CC | C500 | 113 |
| N113CS | GLF2 | 95/39 |
| **N113CS** | **GLF4** | **1049** |
| **N113EA** | **EA50** | **000152** |
| N113EL | LJ55 | 006 |
| N113ES | LJ25 | 092 |
| N113EV | GLF2 | 135 |
| N113FJ | FA10 | 20 |
| N113FJ | FA50 | 118 |
| N113FX | LJ31 | 116 |
| N113GA | ASTR | 113 |
| N113GA | GLF4 | 1513 |
| **N113GH** | **WW24** | **286** |
| N113JS | LJ24 | 356 |
| N113KH | JSTR | 5152 |
| N113LB | LJ35 | 457 |
| N113MR | WW24 | 126 |
| N113RF | LJ25 | 143 |
| N113SC | SBRL | 282-18 |
| N113SH | C500 | 285 |
| N113T | SBRL | 306-113 |
| **N113US** | **C560** | **0701** |
| N113VP | C560 | 0113 |
| N113VP | CS55 | 0090 |
| N113WA | CL61 | 5068 |
| N113WA | FA50 | 51 |
| N113XP | HS25 | HA-0013 |
| **N113YS** | **LJ55** | **071** |
| **N113ZZ** | **GLEX** | **9345** |
| N114AN | GLF4 | 1108 |
| N114AP | BE40 | RJ-31 |
| N114B | HS25 | 25196 |
| N114BA | HS25 | 257170 |
| **N114BD** | **LJ60** | **166** |
| N114CC | LJ25 | 126 |
| N114CJ | C52B | 0014 |
| N114CJ | C52B | 0114 |
| N114CL | JSTR | 5070/52 |
| N114CP | C560 | 0018 |
| N114CX | C750 | 0114 |
| N114DM | BE40 | RJ-11 |
| N114DM | MU30 | A011SA |
| N114DS | C550 | 334 |
| **N114EA** | **EA50** | **000155** |
| **N114EB** | **C560** | **0795** |
| (N114ED) | WW24 | 177 |
| N114EL | C550 | 321 |
| (N114EX) | F9EX | 114 |
| (N114FG) | C525 | 0307 |
| N114FJ | FA10 | 22 |
| N114FJ | FA50 | 119 |
| N114FJ | FA50 | 229 |
| **N114FW** | **C525** | **0307** |
| N114FX | LJ31 | 119 |
| N114GA | ASTR | 114 |
| N114GA | GLF4 | 1144 |
| N114GB | LJ24 | 022 |
| N114HC | GLF2 | 92 |
| N114HC | LJ25 | 114 |
| (N114HE) | WW24 | 106 |
| N114HH | WW24 | 106 |
| N114HY | LJ31 | 119 |
| N114JT | LJ24 | 318 |
| N114LA | C500 | 072 |
| N114LG | SBRL | 465-51 |
| **N114LJ** | **LJ60** | **157** |
| N114PC | HS25 | 25146 |
| N114PJ | LJ60 | 114 |
| **N114QS** | **BE40** | **RK-469** |
| **N114RA** | **WW24** | **179** |
| (N114RP) | C52A | 0135 |
| **N114SN** | **ASTR** | **114** |
| **N114TD** | **FA50** | **17** |
| **N114VP** | **C550** | **550-1004** |
| **N114VW** | **C750** | **0093** |
| N114WC | LJ24 | 291 |
| **N114WD** | **HS25** | **25114** |
| (N114WJ) | GLF2 | 114 |
| N114WL | WW24 | 338 |
| **N115AN** | **LJ60** | **308** |
| **N115BB** | **C525** | **0325** |
| N115BP | WW24 | 417 |
| **N115BR** | **ASTR** | **099** |
| **N115BX** | **LJ31** | **129** |
| N115CD | BE40 | RK-151 |
| N115CJ | C525 | 0015 |
| **N115CJ** | **C52A** | **0115** |
| **N115CR** | **SBRL** | **306-43** |
| **N115DJ** | **EA50** | **000020** |
| N115DX | JSTR | 5111 |
| N115EL | LJ55 | 035 |
| (N115FJ) | F900 | 15 |
| N115FJ | FA10 | 23 |
| N115FJ | FA50 | 121 |
| N115FL | GLF4 | 1141 |
| N115FX | LJ31 | 129 |
| N115GA | GLF2 | 45 |
| N115HK | GLEX | 9004 |
| N115K | C500 | 433 |
| **N115K** | **C560** | **0148** |
| N115K | FA20 | 80 |
| N115L | SBRL | 306-60 |
| N115LJ | CL30 | 20015 |
| N115MA | LJ35 | 118 |
| N115MC | GLF2 | 137 |
| N115MR | GLF2 | 12 |
| N115MR | JSTR | 5111 |
| **N115QS** | **BE40** | **RK-383** |
| (N115RS) | GLF2 | 9/33 |
| (N115RS) | HS25 | 257067 |
| **N115SK** | **FA50** | **330** |
| **N115TD** | **FA10** | **96** |
| N115TW | FA20 | 91 |
| N115VH | C550 | 375 |
| N115WA | FA10 | 115 |
| **N115WF** | **CL61** | **5153** |
| **N115WZ** | **PRM1** | **RB-197** |
| **N115ZZ** | **GLEX** | **9347** |
| (N116AC) | SBRL | 282-41 |
| N116AD | BE40 | RK-192 |
| **N116AD** | **BE40** | **RK-338** |
| N116AM | LJ35 | 116 |
| **N116AP** | **BE40** | **RK-192** |
| N116AP | C525 | 0033 |
| N116AR | GLF3 | 312 |
| **N116AS** | **LJ45** | **078** |
| N116AS | LJ60 | 035 |
| N116AT | WW24 | 288 |
| N116BJ | CL64 | 5520 |
| N116BK | FA20 | 175 |
| N116BX | LJ31 | 132 |
| N116CC | C500 | 116 |
| N116CC | C550 | 116 |
| N116CS | C525 | 0447 |
| N116DA | LJ55 | 116 |
| N116DD | FA10 | 41 |
| N116DD | HS25 | 256044 |
| N116DD | JSTR | 5155/32 |
| **N116DD** | **JSTR** | **5224** |
| **N116DJ** | **EA50** | **000021** |
| N116DK | C525 | 0257 |
| N116EL | LJ35 | 173 |
| N116EX | F2EX | 116 |
| **N116FE** | **GALX** | **197** |
| N116FJ | FA10 | 24 |
| N116FJ | FA50 | 124 |
| N116FX | LJ31 | 132 |
| **N116GB** | **FA20** | **281/496** |
| (N116GL) | LJ55 | 016 |
| N116HM | GLF4 | 1024 |
| **N116HW** | **ASTR** | **275** |
| **N116JC** | **ASTR** | **014** |
| N116JD | FA20 | 4 |
| N116JR | LJ25 | 359 |
| **N116K** | **C550** | **164** |
| N116K | GLF2 | 73/9 |
| (N116KV) | LJ35 | 244 |
| N116KX | WW24 | 87 |
| **N116LA** | **C550** | **017** |
| (N116LD) | CS55 | 0110 |
| N116LJ | C525 | 0617 |
| N116LJ | LJ60 | 116 |
| **N116LM** | **LJ60** | **142** |
| **N116LS** | **CL61** | **5013** |
| **N116MA** | **LJ36** | **029** |
| N116MC | WW24 | 86 |
| **N116PB** | **ASTR** | **032** |
| (N116PR) | LJ35 | 130 |
| **N116QS** | **BE40** | **RK-385** |
| N116RA | CL60 | 1011 |
| N116RM | LJ24 | 206 |
| **N116SC** | **SBRL** | **282-1** |
| **N116SS** | **BE40** | **RK-111** |
| N116VP | C550 | 550-1010 |
| N116WC | C560 | 0393 |
| N116XP | BE40 | RK-416 |
| N117AE | LJ24 | 346 |
| **N117AH** | **WW24** | **352** |
| **N117AJ** | **FA50** | **154** |
| N117AJ | JSTR | 5227 |
| N117AJ | LJ24 | 346 |
| N117CC | C560 | 0287 |
| N117CH | LJ25 | 018 |
| N117CH | LJ35 | 045 |
| (N117CP) | HS25 | 259043 |
| (N117DA) | LJ35 | 075 |
| **N117DJ** | **C500** | **500** |
| **N117EA** | **EA50** | **000104** |
| N117EL | LJ35 | 486 |
| N117EL | LJ55 | 061 |
| N117EM | HS25 | 256046 |
| N117EX | F9EX | 117 |
| N117FJ | FA10 | 25 |
| **N117FJ** | **GLF2** | **229** |
| N117FJ | LJ35 | 417 |
| N117FX | LJ31 | 133 |
| **N117GL** | **GLF2** | **220** |
| N117GM | WW24 | 118 |
| N117GS | C550 | 626 |
| (N117J) | JSTR | 5099/5 |
| N117JA | GLF2 | 163 |
| **N117JJ** | **GLF2** | **163** |
| N117JJ | GLF3 | 448 |
| N117JL | SBRL | 306-128 |
| **N117JW** | **SBRL** | **465-61** |
| N117JW | WW24 | 352 |
| **N117K** | **LJ24** | **272** |
| **N117LR** | **LJ55** | **075** |
| **N117MA** | **C500** | **514** |
| N117MB | SBRL | 465-1 |
| (N117MN) | SBRL | 465-1 |
| N117MR | C560 | 0287 |
| N117MS | GLF3 | 335 |
| **N117MS** | **GLF4** | **1241** |
| N117PK | LJ35 | 513 |
| **N117QS** | **BE40** | **RK-391** |
| N117RB | LJ35 | 154 |
| N117RH | HS25 | 25196 |
| (N117RJ) | LJ35 | 417 |
| N117RJ | LJ35 | 664 |
| N117RJ | LJ60 | 056 |
| (N117RR) | FA10 | 52 |
| **N117RY** | **CL61** | **5162** |
| **N117SF** | **F900** | **55** |
| N117SF | FA50 | 137 |
| N117TA | C550 | 464 |
| N117TF | F900 | 42 |
| N117TF | GLEX | 9028 |
| **N117TF** | **GLEX** | **9175** |
| N117TS | HS25 | 25134 |
| N117TW | C500 | 059 |
| **N117UH** | **EA50** | **000117** |
| **N117VP** | **C550** | **550-1019** |
| N117W | C525 | 0292 |
| (N117W) | C52A | 0022 |
| N117W | C52A | 0079 |
| **N117W** | **C52A** | **0350** |
| N117WC | LJ55 | 030 |
| **N117WR** | **GLF4** | **4015** |
| N117XP | HS25 | HA-0117 |
| **N118AD** | **FA10** | **118** |
| N118AF | WW24 | 177 |
| N118AJ | CS55 | 0118 |
| (N118AT) | C500 | 548 |
| N118AZ | C525 | 0118 |
| N118B | JSTR | 5091 |
| N118B | JSTR | 5211 |
| N118BA | JSTR | 5091 |
| N118BX | LJ31 | 134 |
| N118CD | C650 | 0118 |
| **N118CJ** | **C52A** | **0384** |
| N118CS | C525 | 0457 |
| **N118DA** | **HS25** | **25118** |
| N118DA | LJ35 | 081 |
| N118DF | C560 | 0118 |
| N118EA | C550 | 131 |
| **N118EA** | **EA50** | **000184** |
| N118FJ | FA10 | 26 |
| N118FJ | FA50 | 125 |
| **N118FN** | **LJ35** | **118** |
| N118FX | LJ31 | 134 |
| N118GA | GALX | 118 |
| **N118GA** | **HS25** | **258108** |
| N118GA | MU30 | A018SA |
| (N118GM) | LJ35 | 314 |
| N118GS | GLF2 | 95/39 |
| N118HC | LJ60 | 067 |
| N118J | LJ24 | 273 |
| N118K | HS25 | 258218 |
| N118K | JSTR | 5107 |

| Registration | Type | No. |
|---|---|---|
| N118K | LJ35 | 067 |
| N118KA | GALX | 065 |
| **N118KL** | **HS25** | **258218** |
| N118LA | C500 | 039 |
| (N118LS) | LJ24 | 082A |
| (N118MA) | LJ35 | 144 |
| N118MB | LJ25 | 118 |
| **N118MM** | **C650** | **7105** |
| N118MP | WW24 | 340 |
| **N118MT** | **CL61** | **5077** |
| N118NP | GLF2 | 7 |
| N118QS | BE40 | RK-393 |
| N118R | FA20 | 385 |
| N118R | GLF4 | 1066 |
| N118RA | HFB3 | 1039 |
| **N118RH** | **CL64** | **5516** |
| N118RJ | WW24 | 188 |
| **N118RK** | **C560** | **0389** |
| N118SE | LJ25 | 118 |
| **N118ST** | **C56X** | **5287** |
| (N118ST) | C56X | 5302 |
| N118TS | HS25 | 25018 |
| **N118VP** | **C550** | **550-1029** |
| N119AC | WW24 | 119 |
| **N119AD** | **GLF4** | **4035** |
| **N119AF** | **GLF4** | **1489** |
| N119AG | FA50 | 297 |
| **N119AK** | **HA4T** | **RC-9** |
| N119AM | FA50 | 226 |
| **N119BA** | **LJ24** | **084** |
| N119BX | LJ31 | 136 |
| N119CC | GLF2 | 102/32 |
| N119CC | HS25 | 25225 |
| N119CP | LJ35 | 366 |
| N119CS | C525 | 0466 |
| N119CV | C560 | 0119 |
| **N119DJ** | **EA50** | **000022** |
| N119EA | CS55 | 0019 |
| **N119EA** | **EA50** | **000200** |
| N119EL | C650 | 0013 |
| **N119EM** | **F2EX** | **137** |
| **N119ES** | **C650** | **0206** |
| N119EX | F9EX | 119 |
| N119FJ | FA10 | 28 |
| N119FJ | FA50 | 126 |
| N119FJ | FA50 | 137 |
| **N119FM** | **GLF4** | **1464** |
| N119FX | LJ31 | 136 |
| N119GA | CL64 | 5386 |
| (N119GH) | HS25 | 25248 |
| N119GS | LJ35 | 017 |
| (N119HB) | FA50 | 8 |
| (N119HB) | LJ35 | 307 |
| (N119HT) | FA50 | 8 |
| N119K | GLF2 | 17 |
| N119K | GLF4 | 1046 |
| **N119KW** | **ASTR** | **267** |
| N119LA | FA20 | 129 |
| **N119LC** | **C550** | **550-0969** |
| N119LJ | LJ60 | 119 |
| N119LP | C56X | 5192 |
| N119M | M220 | 1 |
| N119MA | LJ24 | 200 |
| N119MH | MU30 | A057SA |
| **N119NJ** | **LJ40** | **45-2119** |
| N119PH | FA50 | 8 |
| (N119PM) | C750 | 0051 |
| N119PW | HS25 | 259007 |
| **N119QS** | **BE40** | **RK-394** |
| N119R | GLF2 | 243 |
| N119R | GLF4 | 1008 |
| N119R | GLF4 | 1077 |
| N119RC | GLF2 | 243 |
| N119RC | GLF4 | 1077 |
| N119RM | C650 | 7018 |
| **N119RM** | **C750** | **0051** |
| N119SE | JSTR | 5161/43 |
| **N119SJ** | **FA10** | **119** |
| **N119U** | **HS25** | **259007** |
| **N119VP** | **C550** | **550-1036** |
| N120AF | FA20 | 16 |
| **N120AK** | **GLEX** | **9153** |
| **N120AP** | **HS25** | **258120** |
| N120AR | JSTR | 5089 |
| N120BJ | ASTR | 026 |
| N120CC | C500 | 120 |
| N120CG | FA20 | 384/551 |
| **N120CS** | **C525** | **0490** |
| N120CV | C560 | 0120 |
| N120DE | FA20 | 384/551 |
| (N120DP) | C500 | 410 |
| **N120EA** | **EA50** | **000199** |
| N120EA | GLF2 | 28 |
| N120EL | LJ55 | 067 |
| N120EN | FA20 | 44 |
| N120ES | C500 | 381 |
| (N120EZ) | F9EX | 120 |
| N120FJ | FA10 | 29 |
| N120FJ | FA20 | 491 |
| N120FS | FA20 | 204 |
| N120FX | LJ31 | 137 |
| N120GA | ASTR | 055 |
| N120GA | GLF4 | 4100 |
| **N120GA** | **GLF4** | **4210** |
| N120GA | HS25 | 25228 |
| N120GA | HS25 | 257014 |
| N120GB | HS25 | 25228 |
| N120GH | WW24 | 58 |
| (N120GR) | LJ55 | 078 |
| N120GS | CL30 | 20165 |
| N120GS | GLF2 | 167 |
| N120HC | C550 | 577 |
| N120HC | FA10 | 45 |
| N120HC | FA20 | 148 |
| N120HV | LJ60 | 052 |
| N120J | LJ24 | 241 |
| **N120JC** | **HS25** | **257065** |
| N120JC | SBRL | 306-42 |
| **N120JJ** | **GLF4** | **1264** |
| **N120JP** | **C550** | **468** |
| N120KC | SBRL | 380-55 |
| N120LJ | LJ55 | 120 |
| N120LJ | LJ60 | 120 |
| N120MB | LJ35 | 307 |
| N120MH | HS25 | 257053 |
| N120MH | HS25 | 257171 |
| N120MP | CL61 | 3034 |
| (N120MT) | CL64 | 5451 |
| N120PA | CL61 | 5097 |
| **N120Q** | **C550** | **372** |
| **N120QS** | **BE40** | **RK-409** |
| **N120RA** | **FA20** | **211** |
| N120RA | LJ24 | 153 |
| N120RD | C500 | 368 |
| (N120RL) | JSTR | 5155/32 |
| N120RV | LJ31 | 137 |
| N120S | C500 | 279 |
| N120S | WW24 | 226 |
| (N120SB) | C560 | 0542 |
| N120SB | C560 | 0561 |
| N120SB | C560 | 0587 |
| N120SB | C560 | 0753 |
| N120SB | C680 | 0206 |
| N120SL | LJ25 | 120 |
| N120TC | C550 | 440 |
| N120TF | FA20 | 384/551 |
| N120TJ | FA50 | 89 |
| N120WH | ASTR | 026 |
| N120WH | FA20 | 385 |
| (N120WH) | LJ35 | 112 |
| N120WS | ASTR | 026 |
| **N120YB** | **HS25** | **257116** |
| N120YB | SBRL | 380-12 |
| (N121AC) | HS25 | 25099 |
| N121AG | C650 | 0121 |
| N121AJ | WW24 | 57 |
| N121AM | FA20 | 310 |
| N121AT | C650 | 0158 |
| **N121AT** | **FA10** | **226** |
| N121BN | GLF5 | 667 |
| N121BN | WW24 | 14 |
| N121C | C550 | 232 |
| N121C | C550 | 388 |
| N121CG | C550 | 388 |
| **N121CG** | **CS55** | **0123** |
| **N121CK** | **LJ24** | **039** |
| N121CL | LJ35 | 083 |
| **N121CN** | **C550** | **550-1000** |
| N121CN | JSTR | 5053/2 |
| (N121CP) | C525 | 0083 |
| **N121CP** | **C52A** | **0010** |
| N121CP | C550 | 337 |
| N121CS | WW24 | 43 |
| N121DF | CL60 | 1071 |
| N121DF | CL61 | 5133 |
| N121DF | CL64 | 5480 |
| **N121DF** | **F9EX** | **113** |
| N121DJ | FA20 | 121 |
| N121EA | GLF2 | 12 |
| N121EB | C525 | 0405 |
| N121EL | LJ25 | 010 |
| N121ET | CL64 | 5583 |
| N121EU | FA20 | 297 |
| N121EX | F2EX | 121 |
| N121EZ | BE40 | RK-109 |
| N121FF | CL61 | 5133 |
| N121FJ | FA10 | 192 |
| N121FJ | FA10 | 30 |
| N121FJ | FA50 | 121 |
| N121FJ | FA50 | 127 |
| N121FM | WW24 | 150 |
| N121FX | LJ31 | 141 |
| **N121G** | **EA50** | **000243** |
| N121GA | GLF4 | 4011 |
| N121GF | BE40 | RK-503 |
| (N121GG) | CL61 | 5099 |
| (N121GL) | LJ25 | 010 |
| N121GV | ASTR | 082 |
| N121GV | GALX | 014 |
| **N121GV** | **GALX** | **094** |
| N121GW | FA20 | 4 |
| N121GX | GALX | 014 |
| N121HE | C750 | 0078 |
| **N121HL** | **C550** | **134** |
| N121HM | WW24 | 18 |
| (N121HV) | LJ31 | 141 |
| (N121JC) | WW24 | 121 |
| N121JC | WW24 | 77 |
| **N121JE** | **SBRL** | **306-4** |
| N121JJ | GLF2 | 27 |
| N121JJ | GLF4 | 1075 |
| **N121JJ** | **GLF4** | **1482** |
| N121JM | GLF3 | 332 |
| **N121JM** | **GLF4** | **1399** |
| (N121JN) | GLF3 | 332 |
| N121JT | LJ35 | 311 |
| (N121JT) | LJ35 | 315 |
| N121JV | GLF4 | 1075 |
| N121JW | C500 | 358 |
| N121JW | C550 | 463 |
| **N121KL** | **C56X** | **5720** |
| N121KM | C550 | 308 |
| N121L | C550 | 550-0896 |
| **N121LJ** | **LJ31** | **121** |
| N121LS | C560 | 0593 |
| (N121LS) | C680 | 0017 |
| **N121LS** | **C680** | **0076** |
| N121LS | GALX | 010 |
| N121LT | LJ55 | 064 |
| N121PA | WW24 | 129 |
| N121PG | WW24 | 45 |
| (N121PP) | GLF4 | 1345 |
| (N121PR) | GLF2 | 17 |
| N121PX | LJ31 | 141 |
| N121SG | ASTR | 053 |
| N121SG | HS25 | 256071 |
| N121SJ | C500 | 384 |
| N121TE | C56X | 5073 |
| N121TL | C56X | 5073 |
| N121TL | C680 | 0058 |
| N121US | LJ55 | 123 |
| N121UW | C500 | 358 |
| N121VA | CL60 | 1012 |
| N121VA | HS25 | 25272 |
| N121VF | HS25 | 25272 |
| N121WT | FA20 | 274 |
| N121YD | C52A | 0121 |
| **N121ZZ** | **GLEX** | **9375** |
| N122AP | C500 | 122 |
| N122AW | HS25 | 25169 |
| **N122BN** | **GLEX** | **9103** |
| N122BS | LJ25 | 122 |
| **N122BX** | **LJ31** | **143** |
| N122CA | FA20 | 16 |
| N122CC | C500 | 122 |
| N122CG | C550 | 411 |
| N122CG | CS55 | 0125 |
| N122CG | LJ24 | 250 |
| N122CS | C525 | 0469 |
| N122DJ | GLF2 | 6 |
| N122DJ | GLF3 | 374 |
| **N122DS** | **PRM1** | **RB-100** |
| N122DU | GLF2 | 6 |
| N122EH | SBRL | 306-57 |
| **N122EJ** | **C650** | **0122** |
| N122FJ | FA10 | 31 |
| (N122FJ) | FA20 | 507 |
| N122FJ | FA50 | 128 |
| N122FJ | FA50 | 217 |
| N122FX | LJ31 | 143 |
| N122G | C550 | 122 |
| N122GV | ASTR | 106 |
| N122GV | GALX | 043 |
| N122GV | GLF4 | 4034 |
| N122HL | WW24 | 122 |
| N122HM | C550 | 145 |
| N122JB | WW24 | 133 |
| N122JC | WW24 | 122 |
| (N122JD) | LJ55 | 050 |
| **N122JW** | **LJ35** | **217** |
| (N122LG) | C500 | 424 |
| N122LJ | LJ31 | 122 |
| N122LM | C500 | 122 |
| **N122LM** | **C525** | **0604** |
| **N122LX** | **LJ55** | **030** |
| N122M | LJ24 | 065A |
| N122MM | C550 | 145 |
| **N122MP** | **WW24** | **390** |
| **N122NC** | **C550** | **550-0836** |
| **N122QS** | **BE40** | **RK-467** |
| N122RP | SBRL | 282-7 |
| N122RS | GLF4 | 1417 |
| N122RW | LJ24 | 321 |
| N122SC | F2TH | 25 |
| N122SM | C52A | 0151 |
| **N122SP** | **C550** | **392** |
| **N122ST** | **WW24** | **122** |
| N122SU | LJ55 | 132 |
| N122SV | C680 | 0122 |
| N122TY | CL60 | 1035 |
| N122WC | C560 | 0402 |
| N122WC | LJ25 | 122 |
| N122WF | CL60 | 1035 |
| N122WF | CL61 | 5021 |
| **N122WS** | **CS55** | **0122** |
| **N122WW** | **C550** | **404** |
| **N122XP** | **HS25** | **HA-0122** |
| N123AC | HS25 | 25122 |
| **N123AD** | **C510** | **0184** |
| (N123AG) | HS25 | 25122 |
| N123AP | GLF3 | 448 |
| N123AV | C525 | 0180 |
| N123CB | LJ24 | 232 |
| N123CC | C500 | 123 |
| N123CC | FA20 | 488 |
| N123CC | GLF2 | 69 |
| N123CC | GLF3 | 455 |
| N123CC | JSTR | 5208 |
| N123CC | LJ24 | 268 |
| N123CC | LJ35 | 206 |
| N123CC | LJ60 | 012 |
| **N123CD** | **SBRL** | **282-23** |
| N123CG | LJ25 | 270 |
| N123CJ | C52B | 0063 |
| **N123CJ** | **C52B** | **0149** |
| N123CV | WW24 | 178 |
| N123CX | C500 | 123 |
| **N123CZ** | **C52B** | **0313** |
| **N123DG** | **LJ24** | **342** |
| N123DM | LJ25 | 086 |
| **N123DR** | **WW24** | **158** |
| **N123EB** | **C500** | **380** |
| N123EL | LJ25 | 045 |
| **N123FF** | **CS55** | **0005** |
| N123FG | C500 | 534 |
| N123FG | SBRL | 306-90 |
| N123FH | C550 | 468 |
| N123FJ | FA10 | 219 |
| N123FJ | FA10 | 33 |
| N123FJ | FA50 | 129 |
| **N123FT** | **GLF5** | **549** |
| N123GA | JSTR | 5061/48 |
| **N123GF** | **C550** | **550-0817** |
| N123GM | C550 | 358 |
| N123GN | JSTR | 5123/14 |
| **N123GV** | **GALX** | **043** |
| N123H | GLF2 | 54/36 |
| (N123H) | GLF5 | 618 |
| **N123HK** | **HS25** | **258208** |
| (N123HP) | C500 | 611 |
| N123JB | HS25 | 25017 |
| N123JB | WW24 | 37 |

| N123JN | C525 | 0046 |
|---|---|---|
| N123JS | LJ25 | 017 |
| N123JW | C52A | 0152 |
| **N123KD** | **C500** | **595** |
| N123KH | CL64 | 5301 |
| N123LC | GLF4 | 1441 |
| N123LC | LJ35 | 409 |
| N123LC | LJ55 | 020 |
| N123LC | LJ55 | 027 |
| N123LC | LJ55 | 034 |
| (N123LC) | LJ55 | 045 |
| **N123LV** | **GLF4** | **4181** |
| N123M | GLF5 | 667 |
| **N123MJ** | **LJ24** | **036** |
| (N123MJ) | LJ35 | 051 |
| N123MR | GLF3 | 455 |
| N123MR | GLF4 | 1492 |
| N123MS | SBRL | 282-53 |
| N123NC | LJ25 | 325 |
| (N123NW) | C560 | 0248 |
| (N123PL) | C500 | 524 |
| **N123PL** | **C500** | **639** |
| **N123QS** | **BE40** | **RK-486** |
| **N123RA** | **FA20** | **30** |
| **N123RC** | **WW24** | **349** |
| N123RE | FA20 | 150/445 |
| N123RE | LJ24 | 154 |
| N123RF | C550 | 248 |
| N123RZ | HS25 | 25152 |
| **N123S** | **C525** | **0525** |
| N123SF | C500 | 606 |
| N123SF | LJ25 | 088 |
| N123SL | C650 | 0134 |
| N123SL | C650 | 7053 |
| **N123SL** | **C750** | **0168** |
| N123SR | C550 | 469 |
| N123SV | LJ24 | 202 |
| **N123TF** | **C510** | **0191** |
| N123TG | FA10 | 37 |
| N123TL | GLF3 | 452 |
| N123VJ | MU30 | A067SA |
| N123VM | HS25 | 25030 |
| **N123VP** | **C550** | **123** |
| N123VV | FA10 | 37 |
| N123VW | LJ24 | 154 |
| N123VW | LJ24 | 253 |
| N123WH | FA20 | 426 |
| N124AR | HS25 | 257075 |
| N124AV | LJ45 | 124 |
| N124BC | CL61 | 3013 |
| **N124BC** | **WW24** | **351** |
| N124BG | BE40 | RK-124 |
| N124BM | HS25 | 25101 |
| (N124BN) | GLF2 | 39 |
| **N124BP** | **LJ45** | **113** |
| N124BR | PRM1 | RB-24 |
| N124BV | BE40 | RK-105 |
| N124CC | C500 | 124 |
| N124CR | C550 | 137 |
| N124CS | C525 | 0472 |
| **N124DC** | **SBRL** | **306-95** |
| N124DF | LJ31 | 214 |
| (N124DH) | C500 | 261 |
| **N124DT** | **GLF3** | **390** |
| **N124EK** | **PRM1** | **RB-270** |
| N124EK | PRM1 | RB-305 |
| **N124EP** | **GLF3** | **440** |
| N124EX | F2EX | 124 |
| N124EZ | LJ24 | 347 |
| N124FJ | FA10 | 220 |
| N124FJ | FA10 | 34 |
| N124FJ | FA50 | 130 |
| N124FM | WW24 | 194 |
| N124FX | LJ31 | 145 |
| N124FX | LJ31 | 156 |
| N124GA | C550 | 316 |
| N124GA | LJ24 | 267 |
| N124GR | WW24 | 315 |
| N124GS | HS25 | 256026 |
| N124H | SBRL | 282-76 |
| N124HF | LJ24 | 166 |
| N124HL | WW24 | 325 |
| N124HM | FA50 | 117 |
| **N124HS** | **WW24** | **329** |
| N124JB | WW24 | 64 |
| N124JG | HS25 | 258084 |
| **N124JL** | **LJ24** | **127** |
| N124KC | C500 | 665 |
| N124LJ | LJ31 | 124 |
| N124LS | WW24 | 354 |
| N124MA | LJ25 | 118 |
| N124MB | WW24 | 226 |
| N124MC | LJ35 | 453 |
| N124NB | C500 | 402 |
| N124NS | C500 | 402 |
| N124NY | WW24 | 205 |
| N124PA | WW24 | 244 |
| N124PA | WW24 | 418 |
| N124PJ | LJ24 | 166 |
| **N124PP** | **BE40** | **RK-92** |
| N124QS | BE40 | RK-442 |
| N124RM | JSTR | 5078/3 |
| N124RP | JSTR | 5113/25 |
| **N124SD** | **SBRL** | **465-2** |
| **N124TF** | **GLF4** | **1004** |
| N124TS | GLF4 | 1224 |
| N124TS | LJ24 | 233 |
| N124TV | GLF2 | 124 |
| N124TY | WW24 | 223 |
| N124UF | WW24 | 257 |
| N124VF | WW24 | 174 |
| N124VP | C560 | 0124 |
| N124VS | WW24 | 64 |
| N124WK | WW24 | 291 |
| N124WL | LJ24 | 157 |
| **N124WW** | **WW24** | **201** |
| N124WW | WW24 | 203 |
| **N124ZT** | **LJ35** | **138** |
| N125AC | CL60 | 1072 |
| N125AC | WW24 | 205 |
| N125AD | HS25 | 25046 |
| N125AD | HS25 | 257113 |
| N125AE | HS25 | 257119 |
| N125AF | HS25 | 257111 |
| N125AH | HS25 | 257083 |
| N125AH | HS25 | 257123 |
| N125AJ | ASTR | 031 |
| N125AJ | HS25 | 25206 |
| N125AJ | HS25 | 257077 |
| N125AJ | HS25 | 257125 |
| N125AK | HS25 | 257078 |
| N125AK | HS25 | 257129 |
| N125AL | HS25 | 25033 |
| N125AL | HS25 | 257086 |
| N125AM | HS25 | 257075 |
| (N125AM) | HS25 | 257081 |
| N125AN | CL60 | 1073 |
| N125AN | HS25 | 257114 |
| N125AP | HS25 | 25220 |
| N125AP | HS25 | 257116 |
| N125AP | HS25 | 257119 |
| N125AR | HS25 | 25220 |
| N125AR | HS25 | 257119 |
| N125AS | HS25 | 257117 |
| N125AS | HS25 | 257188 |
| N125AS | HS25 | 258167 |
| N125AT | HS25 | 257120 |
| N125AU | HS25 | 257121 |
| N125AW | HS25 | 25057 |
| N125AW | HS25 | 258220 |
| N125AX | LJ35 | 415 |
| N125BA | HS25 | 257105 |
| N125BA | HS25 | 257167 |
| (N125BA) | HS25 | 258048 |
| N125BA | HS25 | 258086 |
| N125BA | HS25 | 258139 |
| N125BA | HS25 | 258179 |
| N125BA | HS25 | 259013 |
| N125BC | HS25 | 257128 |
| N125BD | HS25 | 257137 |
| N125BE | HS25 | 257140 |
| N125BH | HS25 | 25027 |
| N125BH | HS25 | 25236 |
| N125BH | HS25 | 25237 |
| N125BH | HS25 | 25273 |
| N125BH | HS25 | 256007 |
| **N125BJ** | **C52A** | **0101** |
| N125BJ | HS25 | 257145 |
| N125BM | HS25 | 25023 |
| N125BP | SBRL | 465-25 |
| N125BT | HS25 | 25021 |
| (N125BW) | HS25 | 25023 |
| N125BW | HS25 | 257057 |
| **N125BW** | **LJ45** | **323** |
| (N125CA) | C500 | 583 |
| N125CA | FA10 | 196 |
| N125CA | FA20 | 208/468 |
| N125CA | HS25 | 25082 |
| N125CA | HS25 | 259019 |
| N125CE | C52A | 0125 |
| N125CF | HS25 | 25241 |
| N125CG | CS55 | 0116 |
| N125CG | HS25 | 257125 |
| **N125CH** | **GLEX** | **9080** |
| N125CJ | C550 | 411 |
| N125CJ | HS25 | 258241 |
| N125CJ | HS25 | 259010 |
| N125CJ | HS25 | 259014 |
| **N125CK** | **HS25** | **25266** |
| N125CM | HS25 | 25267 |
| **N125CS** | **C525** | **0522** |
| N125CS | HS25 | 257018 |
| N125CU | HS25 | 256020 |
| N125DB | HS25 | 25281 |
| N125DB | LJ25 | 371 |
| **N125DC** | **GLF2** | **55** |
| (N125DC) | HS25 | 25202 |
| N125DF | LJ31 | 214 |
| N125DG | C52A | 0015 |
| **N125DG** | **C52B** | **0060** |
| N125DH | HS25 | 25211 |
| **N125DH** | **HS25** | **25245** |
| N125DJ | C525 | 0422 |
| N125DP | HS25 | 257188 |
| **N125DS** | **C500** | **258** |
| N125E | HS25 | 25110 |
| N125E | HS25 | 256018 |
| **N125EA** | **C500** | **531** |
| N125EC | HS25 | 25232 |
| N125EH | HS25 | 25222 |
| **N125EK** | **HS25** | **257089** |
| N125EM | FA10 | 53 |
| N125F | HS25 | 25151 |
| N125FD | HS25 | 25123 |
| N125FJ | FA10 | 222 |
| N125FJ | FA10 | 35 |
| N125FJ | FA50 | 135 |
| N125FM | HS25 | 25284 |
| **N125FS** | **LJ31** | **125** |
| N125FX | LJ31 | 157 |
| N125G | HS25 | 25014 |
| N125G | HS25 | 25033 |
| N125G | HS25 | 25038 |
| N125G | HS25 | 25186 |
| N125G | HS25 | 25250 |
| N125G | HS25 | 257044 |
| N125G | HS25 | 257138 |
| N125GA | FA10 | 147 |
| N125GA | LJ35 | 125 |
| N125GB | ASTR | 023 |
| (N125GB) | HS25 | 257044 |
| N125GB | HS25 | 258217 |
| N125GC | HS25 | 25111 |
| N125GC | HS25 | 25231 |
| N125GC | HS25 | 25238 |
| **N125GH** | **GLF5** | **526** |
| N125GH | HS25 | 25228 |
| N125GK | HS25 | 25127 |
| N125GM | HS25 | 259038 |
| N125GP | HS25 | 257023 |
| N125GP | LJ31 | 162 |
| **N125GR** | **ASTR** | **116** |
| N125GS | HS25 | 256040 |
| N125GS | HS25 | 256055 |
| N125GW | LJ45 | 236 |
| N125HD | HS25 | 25051 |
| N125HF | HS25 | 256064 |
| **N125HF** | **WW24** | **408** |
| N125HG | HS25 | 25250 |
| **N125HH** | **HS25** | **258034** |
| N125HM | HS25 | 257020 |
| N125HS | HS25 | 25136 |
| N125HS | HS25 | 256021 |
| N125HS | HS25 | 256061 |
| N125HS | HS25 | 257012 |
| N125HS | HS25 | 257058 |
| N125HS | HS25 | 257080 |
| N125J | HS25 | 25013 |
| N125J | HS25 | 25043 |
| N125J | HS25 | 25100 |
| N125J | HS25 | 25124 |
| N125J | HS25 | 25173 |
| N125J | HS25 | 25205 |
| N125JA | HS25 | 256021 |
| N125JB | HS25 | 258089 |
| **N125JG** | **BE40** | **RK-75** |
| N125JG | HS25 | 25064 |
| N125JJ | GLF2 | 15 |
| N125JJ | HS25 | 256021 |
| N125JL | LJ25 | 088 |
| N125JR | HS25 | 25052 |
| N125JW | HS25 | 25216 |
| N125JW | HS25 | 258058 |
| **N125JW** | **LJ25** | **352** |
| N125K | WW24 | 15 |
| N125KC | HS25 | 25021 |
| N125KC | HS25 | 25249 |
| N125KR | HS25 | 256007 |
| N125L | HS25 | 257095 |
| N125LC | HS25 | 25033 |
| N125LJ | CL30 | 20025 |
| N125LJ | LJ31 | 125 |
| N125LK | HS25 | 25121 |
| N125LL | HS25 | 25033 |
| N125LM | HS25 | 25018 |
| **N125LR** | **LJ55** | **032** |
| N125MC | SBRL | 306-10 |
| N125MD | HS25 | 25201 |
| N125MD | HS25 | 25265 |
| N125MD | HS25 | 25284 |
| N125MG | ASTR | 032 |
| N125MJ | FA20 | 225/472 |
| (N125MJ) | HS25 | 257018 |
| N125ML | HS25 | HA-0100 |
| N125MS | SBRL | 380-5 |
| N125MT | HS25 | 25261 |
| N125MT | HS25 | 257192 |
| N125N | C650 | 0129 |
| N125N | CL60 | 1079 |
| N125N | CL61 | 3044 |
| N125N | SBRL | 282-69 |
| N125N | SBRL | 370-3 |
| N125NA | HS25 | 256026 |
| N125NE | LJ25 | 271 |
| N125NE | LJ28 | 28-004 |
| N125NL | SBRL | 282-69 |
| N125NT | HS25 | 25078 |
| N125NW | HS25 | 25222 |
| N125NX | SBRL | 370-3 |
| (N125NY) | WW24 | 264 |
| N125P | HS25 | 25046 |
| N125P | HS25 | 257147 |
| N125PA | HS25 | 25263 |
| N125PL | C500 | 639 |
| **N125PL** | **C52B** | **0290** |
| N125PP | HS25 | 25275 |
| **N125PS** | **CL61** | **3058** |
| N125PT | HS25 | 25018 |
| N125PT | LJ25 | 244 |
| N125Q | C650 | 0128 |
| **N125QA** | **CS55** | **0125** |
| **N125QS** | **BE40** | **RK-433** |
| N125RG | HS25 | 257089 |
| N125RH | C560 | 0147 |
| N125RJ | BE40 | RJ-25 |
| N125RM | LJ25 | 193 |
| N125RR | C550 | 138 |
| (N125RT) | HS25 | 25204 |
| **N125SB** | **HS25** | **258046** |
| N125SF | HS25 | 256065 |
| **N125SJ** | **GLF4** | **1368** |
| (N125SJ) | HS25 | 25250 |
| N125SJ | HS25 | 257106 |
| **N125ST** | **CL61** | **5052** |
| N125ST | LJ25 | 024 |
| N125TA | HS25 | 257105 |
| N125TB | HS25 | 25039 |
| N125TB | HS25 | 25053 |
| N125TJ | HS25 | 25121 |
| (N125TJ) | HS25 | 25231 |
| N125TJ | LJ25 | 294 |
| **N125TM** | **CL30** | **20104** |
| N125TM | HS25 | 258496 |
| N125TN | LJ25 | 193 |
| N125TR | HS25 | 257075 |
| N125TR | HS25 | 258132 |
| N125TR | HS25 | 258196 |
| N125U | HS25 | 257122 |
| N125U | LJ25 | 015 |
| N125V | HS25 | 25097 |
| N125V | HS25 | 257106 |
| N125VC | HS25 | 25232 |

| | | |
|---|---|---|
| (N125WC) | HS25 | 25014 |
| (N125WD) | LJ25 | 042 |
| N125WJ | HS25 | 256053 |
| N125WM | GLF2 | 77 |
| **N125WT** | **C52A** | **0439** |
| **N125XP** | **HS25** | **258485** |
| N125XX | HS25 | 257075 |
| N125Y | HS25 | 25095 |
| N125Y | HS25 | 257098 |
| N125YY | HS25 | 257115 |
| N125ZZ | HS25 | 258630 |
| (N126AH) | GLF3 | 346 |
| N126AR | HS25 | 257128 |
| N126BX | LJ31 | 158 |
| N126CH | GLF5 | 581 |
| N126CJ | C52A | 0026 |
| N126CX | LJ60 | 049 |
| **N126DJ** | **EA50** | **000002** |
| N126EL | LJ55 | 006 |
| N126FJ | FA10 | 223 |
| N126FJ | FA10 | 42 |
| N126FJ | FA50 | 136 |
| N126FX | LJ31 | 158 |
| N126GA | GALX | 126 |
| N126GA | GLF4 | 4166 |
| N126GA | MU30 | A059SA |
| N126HC | FA20 | 148 |
| **N126HY** | **HS25** | **258782** |
| (N126JM) | FA20 | 28 |
| **N126KC** | **HS25** | **258276** |
| N126KD | LJ55 | 096 |
| **N126KD** | **LJ60** | **262** |
| **N126KL** | **LJ55** | **096** |
| (N126KP) | C500 | 263 |
| N126KR | C500 | 263 |
| (N126LP) | CS55 | 0026 |
| N126MS | SBRL | 380-16 |
| **N126MT** | **C650** | **0044** |
| N126QS | CS55 | 0126 |
| N126R | C500 | 232 |
| N126R | FA20 | 126/438 |
| **N126TF** | **C550** | **550-0815** |
| **N126WC** | **C560** | **0344** |
| **N126ZZ** | **HA4T** | **RC-10** |
| N127AJ | LJ25 | 014 |
| **N127BH** | **LJ25** | **250** |
| N127BJ | C500 | 120 |
| N127BK | GLF3 | 311 |
| **N127BU** | **C550** | **149** |
| N127BW | BE40 | RK-105 |
| **N127BW** | **BE40** | **RK-449** |
| N127BX | LJ31 | 159 |
| (N127CF) | CS55 | 0127 |
| (N127CJ) | C500 | 316 |
| N127CJ | C525 | 0127 |
| N127CM | HS25 | 25241 |
| N127DF | CL60 | 1071 |
| N127DM | LJ24 | 169 |
| (N127DN) | LJ24 | 169 |
| N127EL | LJ55 | 035 |
| N127EM | F900 | 63 |
| **N127FJ** | **C510** | **0279** |
| N127FJ | FA10 | 225 |
| N127FJ | FA10 | 38 |
| N127FJ | FA50 | 137 |
| N127FX | LJ31 | 159 |
| **N127GB** | **LJ25** | **175** |
| **N127GG** | **GLF5** | **534** |
| **N127GK** | **GLF3** | **311** |
| N127GT | LJ55 | 067 |
| N127HC | LJ35 | 277 |
| **N127JJ** | **C550** | **007** |
| N127K | LJ35 | 447 |
| N127KC | HS25 | 258255 |
| N127KR | C550 | 163 |
| N127LJ | LJ24 | 127 |
| N127MS | SBRL | 380-18 |
| N127MW | HFB3 | 1027 |
| **N127PM** | **C550** | **027** |
| **N127PT** | **WW24** | **337** |
| **N127RC** | **CS55** | **0088** |
| (N127RC) | CS55 | 0126 |
| (N127RM) | LJ35 | 359 |
| N127RP | HS25 | 259036 |
| N127SA | WW24 | 440 |
| N127SB | CL64 | 5358 |
| N127SC | C550 | 127 |
| **N127SF** | **F9EX** | **13** |
| **N127SG** | **C525** | **0046** |
| **N127SR** | **CL64** | **5358** |
| N127SR | HS25 | 257209 |
| (N127TA) | C550 | 051 |
| N127V | GLF2 | 130 |
| (N127V) | LJ31 | 036 |
| **N127VL** | **LJ31** | **036** |
| N127VP | C560 | 0127 |
| **N127WL** | **FA10** | **16** |
| **N128AB** | **GLF4** | **1501** |
| (N128AD) | GLF2 | 178 |
| (N128AG) | GLF3 | 422 |
| N128AP | FA20 | 236 |
| N128AW | C56X | 5667 |
| **N128BG** | **LJ31** | **212** |
| N128BJ | LJ24 | 128 |
| N128BP | JSTR | 5128/16 |
| **N128CA** | **LJ35** | **248** |
| N128CJ | C52B | 0063 |
| **N128CS** | **C525** | **0361** |
| N128CS | HS25 | 257083 |
| N128DM | LJ25 | 017 |
| N128DR | HS25 | 25219 |
| N128FJ | F900 | 128 |
| N128FJ | FA10 | 224 |
| N128FJ | FA10 | 40 |
| N128FJ | FA50 | 139 |
| N128FX | LJ31 | 163 |
| N128GB | C650 | 0006 |
| **N128GB** | **CL61** | **5113** |
| N128GB | LJ31 | 074 |
| **N128GV** | **GLF5** | **665** |
| N128GW | C525 | 0427 |
| N128JC | SBRL | 306-42 |
| (N128JJ) | HS25 | 256021 |
| **N128JL** | **PRM1** | **RB-28** |
| **N128JW** | **C52A** | **0152** |
| **N128KG** | **GLF2** | **62** |
| **N128LR** | **LJ28** | **28-001** |
| N128M | FA50 | 276 |
| N128MA | LJ28 | 28-001 |
| N128MH | HS25 | 257171 |
| N128MS | SBRL | 380-26 |
| (N128PE) | CL61 | 3065 |
| N128RM | PRM1 | RB-28 |
| N128RS | HS25 | 258182 |
| N128SD | HFB3 | 1035 |
| N128SL | C650 | 7053 |
| (N128TJ) | HS25 | 25020 |
| N128TJ | LJ25 | 104 |
| N128TS | GLF2 | 128 |
| **N128TS** | **GLF4** | **1263** |
| **N128V** | **LJ60** | **226** |
| N128VM | LJ55 | 005 |
| N128VM | SBRL | 306-123 |
| N128WC | C560 | 0336 |
| (N128WD) | LJ24 | 128 |
| N128WU | HS25 | 257157 |
| N128YT | HS25 | 256035 |
| N129AP | C500 | 402 |
| N129AP | FA20 | 242 |
| N129BA | CL60 | 1013 |
| N129BA | HS25 | 256058 |
| (N129BA) | SBRL | 465-28 |
| **N129BT** | **BE40** | **RJ-29** |
| **N129CK** | **C52A** | **0382** |
| N129DB | BE40 | RJ-12 |
| N129DM | LJ24 | 187 |
| N129DV | C550 | 404 |
| **N129ED** | **C550** | **718** |
| N129EX | F2EX | 129 |
| N129EX | F9EX | 129 |
| N129FJ | FA10 | 41 |
| N129FJ | FA50 | 141 |
| N129FJ | FA50 | 219 |
| N129FX | LJ31 | 171 |
| **N129GB** | **C650** | **0006** |
| N129GB | SBRL | 282-27 |
| N129GP | SBRL | 282-27 |
| N129GP | SBRL | 465-50 |
| **N129JD** | **LJ31** | **193** |
| N129JE | FA20 | 113 |
| **N129JE** | **FA20** | **267/491** |
| N129JE | FA50 | 127 |
| N129JF | FA20 | 113 |
| N129JR | LJ60 | 093 |
| N129K | WW24 | 70 |
| N129KH | SBRL | 306-44 |
| N129KJ | F900 | 184 |
| N129LJ | CL30 | 20029 |
| N129MC | BE40 | RK-129 |
| **N129MC** | **C560** | **0120** |
| **N129ME** | **LJ24** | **357** |
| (N129ME) | WW24 | 149 |
| **N129MH** | **GLF4** | **1517** |
| N129MS | SBRL | 380-33 |
| **N129NS** | **GLF4** | **1281** |
| **N129PB** | **C550** | **550-0973** |
| N129PJ | C560 | 0235 |
| N129PJ | C650 | 0044 |
| N129RH | CL61 | 5129 |
| **N129RP** | **C525** | **0173** |
| **N129SG** | **C52A** | **0129** |
| N129SP | LJ55 | 058 |
| N129TC | C550 | 145 |
| (N129TC) | C650 | 0061 |
| N129TF | CL61 | 5129 |
| N129TS | C550 | 346 |
| **N129TS** | **LJ35** | **253** |
| **N129WA** | **GLF2** | **9/33** |
| **N129WH** | **BE40** | **RK-129** |
| N130A | FA50 | 54 |
| N130A | GLF2 | 34 |
| N130A | GLF3 | 322 |
| (N130AE) | HS25 | 257089 |
| (N130AL) | C500 | 033 |
| N130AP | HS25 | 257108 |
| N130B | FA10 | 28 |
| N130B | FA20 | 88 |
| N130B | GLF4 | 1013 |
| (N130B) | GLF4 | 1024 |
| N130BA | HS25 | 257045 |
| N130BB | HS25 | 257063 |
| N130BC | HS25 | 257065 |
| N130BD | HS25 | 257068 |
| N130BE | HS25 | 257069 |
| N130BF | HS25 | 257071 |
| N130BG | HS25 | 257060 |
| N130BH | HS25 | 257059 |
| N130BK | HS25 | 257084 |
| (N130BL) | HS25 | 257087 |
| N130BL | HS25 | 257089 |
| N130CC | CS55 | 0130 |
| **N130CE** | **C500** | **130** |
| **N130CH** | **CL30** | **20088** |
| **N130CK** | **LJ25** | **038** |
| N130CS | C525 | 0490 |
| N130CV | C560 | 0130 |
| **N130DJ** | **EA50** | **000023** |
| N130DS | FA10 | 218 |
| **N130DW** | **C500** | **187** |
| N130F | FA20 | 379 |
| **N130F** | **LJ35** | **044** |
| N130FJ | FA10 | 226 |
| N130FJ | FA10 | 44 |
| N130FJ | FA10 | 73 |
| N130FJ | FA50 | 143 |
| N130FX | LJ31 | 172 |
| N130G | C500 | 130 |
| N130GA | GLF4 | 4130 |
| N130GA | GLF5 | 5130 |
| **N130GV** | **GLF5** | **630** |
| N130J | LJ24 | 130 |
| N130JS | C500 | 606 |
| N130K | FA50 | 70 |
| N130K | GLF2 | 190 |
| **N130LC** | **HS25** | **258228** |
| **N130LM** | **C525** | **0214** |
| (N130LW) | JSTR | 5048 |
| (N130MH) | C525 | 0490 |
| N130MH | HS25 | 257053 |
| N130MR | C525 | 0097 |
| (N130MV) | FA20 | 130 |
| N130MW | HFB3 | 1032 |
| N130MW | HFB3 | 1033 |
| N130NM | C525 | 0214 |
| N130QS | BE40 | RK-441 |
| N130RC | WW24 | 34 |
| (N130RK) | C650 | 0130 |
| N130RS | LJ24 | 138 |
| N130TA | LJ35 | 174 |
| N130TC | C550 | 333 |
| (N130TJ) | FA20 | 130 |
| **N130TM** | **GLF5** | **660** |
| N130TS | C650 | 0130 |
| N130TS | HS25 | 257130 |
| N130WC | C560 | 0277 |
| N130WC | C560 | 0356 |
| **N130WW** | **BE40** | **RK-136** |
| **N130YB** | **HS25** | **257120** |
| **N131AG** | **F2EX** | **131** |
| **N131AJ** | **LJ35** | **381** |
| **N131AP** | **BE40** | **RJ-10** |
| N131AR | LJ31 | 139 |
| N131BH | SBRL | 282-18 |
| **N131BR** | **LJ31** | **074** |
| N131CA | LJ24 | 277 |
| (N131CJ) | C525 | 0031 |
| N131CV | C560 | 0131 |
| N131CX | C750 | 0131 |
| N131DA | ASTR | 029 |
| N131DA | LJ31 | 136 |
| N131DB | FA20 | 339 |
| **N131DJ** | **EA50** | **000033** |
| (N131EL) | C550 | 463 |
| N131EL | JSTR | 5058/4 |
| **N131EP** | **F2TH** | **10** |
| N131ET | C550 | 131 |
| N131FJ | F900 | 131 |
| N131FJ | FA10 | 45 |
| N131FJ | FA50 | 146 |
| N131FJ | FA50 | 220 |
| N131FX | LJ31 | 175 |
| N131G | LJ25 | 170 |
| N131GA | C550 | 432 |
| N131GA | GLF4 | 4111 |
| N131GA | GLF5 | 5231 |
| **N131GG** | **LJ31** | **113** |
| N131GL | LJ25 | 145 |
| N131GM | LJ31 | 164 |
| **N131GR** | **LJ31** | **068** |
| N131JA | FA20 | 282 |
| **N131JR** | **HS25** | **HA-0070** |
| N131JR | SBRL | 306-131 |
| **N131LA** | **HS25** | **25226** |
| N131LJ | CL30 | 20031 |
| **N131LJ** | **LJ31** | **063** |
| N131MA | LJ24 | 289 |
| **N131ML** | **E50P** | **50000006** |
| N131MS | LJ25 | 022 |
| N131MS | SBRL | 380-22 |
| N131MS | SBRL | 380-29 |
| **N131MV** | **FA20** | **31** |
| N131NA | LJ31 | 038 |
| N131PT | LJ31 | 046 |
| **N131QS** | **BE40** | **RK-431** |
| N131RG | C525 | 0159 |
| N131SB | C500 | 256 |
| (N131SE) | SBRL | 306-131 |
| **N131SW** | **GLF4** | **1294** |
| N131SY | C500 | 424 |
| N131TA | LJ31 | 041 |
| **N131TR** | **LJ60** | **216** |
| **N131TT** | **LJ31** | **049** |
| **N131VP** | **C56X** | **5131** |
| N131WC | C560 | 0293 |
| N131WT | FA50 | 28 |
| **N132AH** | **C525** | **0132** |
| N132AP | FA20 | 312 |
| N132BP | C500 | 132 |
| N132CJ | C52A | 0003 |
| N132CS | C525 | 0497 |
| N132CS | C525 | 0515 |
| N132DB | SBRL | 380-48 |
| **N132DJ** | **EA50** | **000034** |
| N132EL | LJ55 | 061 |
| **N132EP** | **FA20** | **463** |
| N132FJ | F900 | 132 |
| N132FJ | FA10 | 47 |
| N132FJ | FA50 | 142 |
| N132FJ | FA50 | 223 |
| **N132FP** | **GLF2** | **153** |
| N132FX | LJ31 | 177 |
| N132GA | MU30 | A032SA |
| N132GL | LJ25 | 132 |
| N132JA | FA20 | 284 |
| **N132JC** | **GALX** | **039** |
| **N132LA** | **WW24** | **133** |
| N132LF | C550 | 550-0855 |
| N132LJ | LJ45 | 132 |
| N132MA | LJ24 | 306 |
| (N132MA) | LJ25 | 052 |
| N132MS | SBRL | 380-22 |
| N132MS | SBRL | 380-29 |

| | | |
|---|---|---|
| **N132MT** | **C550** | **550-1080** |
| N132MW | HFB3 | 1032 |
| N132MW | HFB3 | 1033 |
| **N132QS** | **BE40** | **RK-427** |
| N132RL | HS25 | 25141 |
| (N132RP) | C525 | 0132 |
| **N132SD** | **GLF5** | **537** |
| N132SV | C680 | 0032 |
| (N132TP) | LJ55 | 098 |
| (N132WC) | C650 | 7079 |
| N132WC | CS55 | 0051 |
| **N132WE** | **BE40** | **RK-90** |
| **N132XP** | **HS25** | **HA-0132** |
| N133AP | FA20 | 345 |
| (N133AV) | C525 | 0180 |
| N133AV | C550 | 550-0847 |
| **N133B** | **PRM1** | **RB-68** |
| N133BA | GALX | 030 |
| N133BC | C550 | 329 |
| N133BG | LJ31 | 179 |
| N133BL | LJ24 | 133 |
| N133BP | BE40 | RK-133 |
| N133CC | C500 | 133 |
| N133CM | PRM1 | RB-180 |
| N133CM | PRM1 | RB-199 |
| N133CQ | PRM1 | RB-180 |
| N133CS | C525 | 0502 |
| N133DF | LJ24 | 133 |
| N133DM | C500 | 514 |
| **N133EJ** | **LJ35** | **133** |
| **N133EP** | **FA10** | **131** |
| N133FJ | FA10 | 48 |
| N133FJ | FA10 | 50 |
| N133FJ | FA20 | 133 |
| N133FJ | FA50 | 144 |
| N133FJ | FA50 | 224 |
| N133FX | LJ31 | 179 |
| N133GJ | LJ35 | 133 |
| N133GL | LJ24 | 317 |
| N133JA | FA20 | 290 |
| N133JC | WW24 | 133 |
| N133JF | LJ25 | 264 |
| **N133JM** | **C500** | **028** |
| N133LE | C650 | 0133 |
| N133LH | C650 | 0133 |
| N133LJ | LJ60 | 133 |
| N133MA | LJ25 | 052 |
| N133ME | WW24 | 50 |
| N133MR | LJ25 | 210 |
| (N133N) | C500 | 021 |
| N133QS | BE40 | RK-449 |
| N133RC | MU30 | A016SA |
| **N133RL** | **F2EX** | **50** |
| **N133SC** | **C500** | **518** |
| N133SN | ASTR | 153 |
| N133SR | LJ60 | 147 |
| (N133SU) | LJ55 | 132 |
| N133TW | LJ24 | 148 |
| **N133VP** | **CS55** | **0133** |
| N133W | LJ24 | 021 |
| **N133WA** | **C550** | **390** |
| N133WB | LJ55 | 132 |
| N133WC | C560 | 0352 |
| (N133WC) | C650 | 7082 |
| N134AP | FA50 | 48 |
| N134AX | GALX | 034 |
| N134BJ | BE40 | RK-134 |
| N134BR | GLF4 | 1139 |
| N134CC | C500 | 134 |
| **N134CG** | **LJ31** | **195** |
| N134CJ | FA20 | 239 |
| **N134CM** | **BE40** | **RK-144** |
| **N134DJ** | **EA50** | **000035** |
| N134FA | BE40 | RK-34 |
| N134FJ | F900 | 134 |
| N134FJ | FA10 | 46 |
| N134FJ | FA50 | 134 |
| N134FJ | FA50 | 148 |
| N134FJ | FA50 | 225 |
| N134FX | LJ31 | 181 |
| N134FX | LJ31 | 195 |
| N134GB | CS55 | 0089 |
| N134GL | LJ35 | 036 |
| N134JA | FA20 | 463 |
| N134JJ | SBRL | 282-134 |
| **N134LJ** | **LJ31** | **134** |
| N134LJ | LJ60 | 134 |
| N134M | C650 | 0109 |
| (N134MJ) | C650 | 0109 |
| **N134N** | **WW24** | **134** |
| **N134NW** | **HS25** | **257134** |
| N134PA | FA20 | 364 |
| N134QS | CS55 | 0134 |
| N134RG | MU30 | A037SA |
| (N134RT) | HS25 | 257134 |
| (N134RV) | ASTR | 047 |
| N134SW | C56X | 5066 |
| **N134SW** | **PRM1** | **RB-81** |
| **N134VS** | **CL60** | **1034** |
| N134WE | LJ25 | 222 |
| N134WF | BE40 | RK-134 |
| **N134WM** | **CL64** | **5340** |
| (N135AB) | LJ35 | 414 |
| N135AC | LJ35 | 188 |
| N135AF | C650 | 0135 |
| **N135AG** | **LJ35** | **132** |
| N135BC | C500 | 135 |
| N135BC | C550 | 269 |
| N135BC | C560 | 0198 |
| N135BC | CL61 | 5080 |
| N135BD | CL61 | 5080 |
| **N135BJ** | **BE40** | **RK-135** |
| N135BK | C500 | 168 |
| N135BP | GALX | 016 |
| N135CC | C500 | 135 |
| N135CC | C550 | 135 |
| **N135CG** | **LJ45** | **354** |
| N135CK | HS25 | 25266 |
| (N135CK) | LJ35 | 159 |
| N135CP | GLF2 | 200 |
| N135CS | C525 | 0520 |
| **N135DA** | **LJ35** | **405** |
| **N135DE** | **LJ35** | **667** |
| **N135DJ** | **EA50** | **000036** |
| N135ET | C56X | 5135 |
| **N135FA** | **LJ35** | **067** |
| N135FJ | FA10 | 224 |
| N135FJ | FA10 | 43 |
| N135FJ | FA50 | 149 |
| **N135FT** | **GALX** | **155** |
| N135GA | MU30 | A035SA |
| N135GJ | LJ35 | 135 |
| N135GL | LJ35 | 028 |
| N135HC | C650 | 0158 |
| N135HC | C650 | 7117 |
| N135J | LJ35 | 097 |
| N135JW | C500 | 140 |
| N135JW | LJ35 | 144 |
| N135LJ | LJ60 | 135 |
| **N135LR** | **LJ55** | **068** |
| N135MA | C500 | 168 |
| N135MB | LJ35 | 343 |
| N135MM | C525 | 0038 |
| N135MW | LJ35 | 650 |
| N135PG | LJ35 | 491 |
| N135PT | LJ35 | 509 |
| N135RJ | LJ35 | 443 |
| N135ST | LJ35 | 169 |
| N135TP | LJ35 | 462 |
| N135TX | LJ35 | 025 |
| N135UT | LJ35 | 327 |
| N135WB | LJ35 | 084 |
| **N135WC** | **C560** | **0261** |
| **N135WE** | **LJ35** | **240** |
| (N135WJ) | GLF2 | 256 |
| N136BC | C550 | 269 |
| N136BX | LJ31 | 196 |
| (N136CC) | C500 | 136 |
| (N136CV) | C560 | 0136 |
| N136DH | HS25 | 25036 |
| **N136DH** | **LJ36** | **036** |
| **N136DJ** | **EA50** | **000037** |
| **N136EA** | **EA50** | **000136** |
| N136F | FA20 | 380 |
| N136FJ | FA10 | 49 |
| N136FJ | FA50 | 150 |
| N136FT | GALX | 155 |
| N136FX | LJ31 | 182 |
| N136FX | LJ31 | 196 |
| N136GL | LJ35 | 016 |
| **N136JD** | **C560** | **0293** |
| **N136JP** | **LJ35** | **359** |
| N136K | WW24 | 103 |
| (N136LJ) | LJ45 | 136 |
| N136LJ | LJ60 | 136 |
| N136LK | HS25 | 25116 |
| N136MA | JSTR | 5134/50 |
| N136MA | LJ45 | 046 |
| **N136MC** | **C510** | **0321** |
| **N136MW** | **HFB3** | **1036** |
| **N136QS** | **BE40** | **RK-414** |
| N136SA | C500 | 136 |
| N136ST | LJ36 | 049 |
| N136TN | HS25 | 257136 |
| (N136WC) | C650 | 7085 |
| **N136WE** | **LJ35** | **201** |
| N136XP | HS25 | 258736 |
| N137AL | C525 | 0002 |
| N137BC | LJ25 | 024 |
| **N137BG** | **C52B** | **0032** |
| N137CC | C500 | 137 |
| N137CF | C550 | 152 |
| N137CL | CL61 | 5137 |
| N137EM | F2EX | 137 |
| N137FA | C560 | 0405 |
| **N137FA** | **FA50** | **137** |
| N137FJ | F900 | 136 |
| N137FJ | FA10 | 51 |
| N137FJ | FA50 | 152 |
| (N137FP) | CL60 | 1072 |
| N137FX | LJ31 | 186 |
| N137FX | LJ31 | 201 |
| N137GK | C500 | 576 |
| N137GL | LJ25 | 237 |
| **N137JC** | **C560** | **0137** |
| N137JL | LJ24 | 301 |
| N137K | LJ25 | 295 |
| N137LA | C560 | 0274 |
| **N137LA** | **HS25** | **258697** |
| N137LR | FA50 | 338 |
| (N137LX) | C560 | 0274 |
| N137M | C650 | 0061 |
| N137M | C650 | 0163 |
| N137MB | CL61 | 5146 |
| N137MM | BE40 | RJ-35 |
| (N137MR) | C650 | 0163 |
| **N137PA** | **C550** | **658** |
| N137RP | HS25 | 259021 |
| N137RS | LJ35 | 183 |
| N137S | C650 | 0005 |
| **N137TA** | **FA20** | **487** |
| (N137TS) | LJ35 | 183 |
| **N137WB** | **GALX** | **137** |
| N137WC | C500 | 305 |
| **N137WH** | **C680** | **0084** |
| (N137WK) | HS25 | 257035 |
| **N137WR** | **HS25** | **257035** |
| N137X | C650 | 0061 |
| N138A | C750 | 0021 |
| N138AV | FA50 | 138 |
| N138AX | LJ45 | 138 |
| N138BF | SJ30 | 002 |
| **N138BG** | **C680** | **0135** |
| **N138CA** | **C550** | **550-0900** |
| N138CC | CL61 | 5138 |
| **N138CH** | **CL30** | **20249** |
| N138CS | C525 | 0522 |
| **N138DM** | **FA10** | **181** |
| N138DM | MU30 | A018SA |
| N138E | FA20 | 382 |
| N138E | FA50 | 57 |
| **N138F** | **F900** | **174** |
| N138F | FA20 | 382 |
| N138F | FA50 | 57 |
| N138FA | F900 | 174 |
| N138FJ | FA10 | 52 |
| **N138FJ** | **FA20** | **369** |
| N138FJ | FA50 | 153 |
| N138FX | LJ31 | 189 |
| N138FX | LJ31 | 208 |
| N138FX | LJ31 | 226 |
| N138FY | LJ31 | 208 |
| N138GA | GALX | 146 |
| N138GA | GLF4 | 4138 |
| N138GL | LJ36 | 007 |
| N138J | C550 | 131 |
| N138JB | LJ25 | 075 |
| N138LJ | LJ31 | 138 |
| N138M | C650 | 0066 |
| N138M | C650 | 0164 |
| N138M | FA50 | 274 |
| N138MR | C650 | 0164 |
| N138NA | LJ35 | 138 |
| N138NW | FA50 | 138 |
| **N138QS** | **BE40** | **RK-492** |
| N138QS | CS55 | 0138 |
| N138RC | MU30 | A047SA |
| **N138SA** | **C500** | **138** |
| **N138SP** | **C750** | **0138** |
| N138SP | LJ60 | 147 |
| N138V | C650 | 0066 |
| N138WE | LJ35 | 472 |
| N138XP | HS25 | 258738 |
| **N139AL** | **F900** | **35** |
| N139CD | CL61 | 5139 |
| **N139CF** | **GLF2** | **139/11** |
| N139DD | FA10 | 6 |
| **N139DJ** | **EA50** | **000054** |
| N139DM | MU30 | A039SA |
| N139EX | F9EX | 139 |
| N139F | FA20 | 385 |
| N139FJ | F900 | 137 |
| N139FJ | FA10 | 53 |
| N139FJ | FA50 | 154 |
| N139FX | LJ31 | 209 |
| N139FY | LJ31 | 209 |
| N139GA | GALX | 139 |
| N139GA | GALX | 199 |
| N139GL | LJ36 | 012 |
| N139J | LJ25 | 098 |
| N139LJ | CL30 | 20039 |
| N139LJ | LJ31 | 139 |
| N139M | C650 | 0149 |
| N139M | HS25 | 258330 |
| **N139MY** | **C650** | **0072** |
| N139N | C650 | 0149 |
| **N139QS** | **BE40** | **RK-483** |
| **N139SK** | **LJ55** | **082** |
| N139ST | LJ55 | 139 |
| N139WC | C560 | 0307 |
| (N139WC) | C650 | 7087 |
| N139XX | LJ60 | 139 |
| N140AE | GLEX | 9140 |
| N140AK | HS25 | 25104 |
| N140AK | MU30 | A026SA |
| N140C | HS25 | 25185 |
| N140CA | LJ24 | 193 |
| N140CA | LJ25 | 140 |
| N140CC | C500 | 140 |
| N140CH | CL61 | 5047 |
| N140CH | GLF2 | 77 |
| (N140CT) | LJ60 | 238 |
| **N140DA** | **C52A** | **0140** |
| N140DA | C550 | 110 |
| N140DR | ASTR | 046 |
| N140DR | C550 | 271 |
| N140DR | WW24 | 242 |
| (N140DV) | C550 | 393 |
| N140EA | EA50 | 000210 |
| N140EX | LJ24 | 117 |
| N140FJ | F900 | 139 |
| N140FJ | FA10 | 54 |
| N140FJ | FA50 | 156 |
| N140GB | BE40 | RK-185 |
| N140GB | HS25 | 258594 |
| N140GC | LJ25 | 225 |
| N140H | C500 | 274 |
| **N140HM** | **LJ40** | **45-2103** |
| N140JA | SBRL | 306-78 |
| **N140JC** | **LJ60** | **106** |
| N140JS | HS25 | 25139 |
| N140KR | GALX | 051 |
| N140LF | HS25 | 25140 |
| N140LJ | LJ31 | 140 |
| **N140LJ** | **LJ40** | **45-2044** |
| N140LJ | LJ60 | 140 |
| N140MD | C550 | 647 |
| N140MM | SBRL | 282-8 |
| **N140QS** | **BE40** | **RK-406** |
| N140RC | LJ24 | 048 |
| **N140RF** | **SBRL** | **282-67** |
| N140RT | FA50 | 261 |
| **N140TF** | **C550** | **550-1015** |
| **N140TS** | **C650** | **0141** |
| **N140U** | **C560** | **0024** |
| N140V | C550 | 393 |
| N140VJ | WW24 | 435 |
| N140WC | C500 | 498 |
| N140WC | C560 | 0325 |
| **N140WH** | **C650** | **0195** |
| **N140WW** | **LJ40** | **45-2049** |
| N141AB | C550 | 483 |

| Registration | Type | c/n |
|---|---|---|
| **N141AB** | **C550** | **550-1044** |
| **N141AL** | **HS25** | **257152** |
| **N141AQ** | **C560** | **0141** |
| N141BG | C510 | 0141 |
| N141CC | C500 | 141 |
| N141DA | C550 | 265 |
| **N141DJ** | **EA50** | **000055** |
| N141DL | CL64 | 5394 |
| N141DP | C500 | 120 |
| **N141DR** | **BE40** | **RK-184** |
| N141DR | C500 | 120 |
| **N141EA** | **EA50** | **000223** |
| N141EX | F9EX | 141 |
| N141FJ | F900 | 141 |
| N141FJ | FA10 | 55 |
| N141FJ | FA50 | 157 |
| **N141FM** | **LJ55** | **041** |
| N141GS | GLF2 | 245/30 |
| N141H | MU30 | A054SA |
| N141H | SBRL | 282-60 |
| N141HC | GLF5 | 616 |
| N141HL | C550 | 550-0803 |
| N141JA | SBRL | 306-51 |
| **N141JC** | **C550** | **373** |
| (N141JF) | FA20 | 196 |
| **N141JF** | **GLF2** | **106** |
| N141JL | HS25 | 25187 |
| N141JV | C52A | 0141 |
| N141LB | WW24 | 202 |
| N141LJ | CL30 | 20041 |
| N141LJ | LJ60 | 141 |
| N141LM | JSTR | 5083/49 |
| **N141M** | **C500** | **403** |
| N141M | C650 | 0147 |
| (N141MB) | LJ60 | 120 |
| N141MH | GLF3 | 378 |
| **N141MR** | **HS25** | **258141** |
| N141PB | SBRL | 465-4 |
| N141PJ | LJ24 | 141 |
| **N141QS** | **BE40** | **RK-498** |
| **N141RD** | **CL60** | **1041** |
| **N141SA** | **C500** | **185** |
| N141SG | C500 | 330 |
| **N141SL** | **SBRL** | **306-141** |
| N141SM | LJ55 | 019 |
| N141TC | JSTR | 5050/34 |
| N141TS | CL60 | 1041 |
| **N142AA** | **C56X** | **5281** |
| N142AB | C650 | 0042 |
| (N142AL) | C500 | 671 |
| N142B | C650 | 0190 |
| N142B | CL61 | 5062 |
| N142B | HS25 | 25101 |
| N142BJ | BE40 | RK-142 |
| N142CC | C500 | 142 |
| N142CC | C650 | 0142 |
| N142CJ | C52A | 0004 |
| **N142DA** | **C500** | **356** |
| **N142DJ** | **EA50** | **000056** |
| N142EA | C525 | 0401 |
| N142EA | EA50 | 000218 |
| N142EX | F9EX | 142 |
| **N142FJ** | **C500** | **524** |
| N142FJ | F900 | 142 |
| N142FJ | FA10 | 57 |
| N142FJ | FA50 | 158 |
| N142GA | C550 | 718 |
| **N142GA** | **C560** | **0042** |
| N142GT | LJ31 | 064 |
| N142HC | GLF4 | 1489 |
| **N142HC** | **GLF4** | **4007** |
| (N142HC) | LJ25 | 142 |
| N142HC | LJ45 | 141 |
| N142HH | PRM1 | RB-41 |
| N142HQ | GLF4 | 1489 |
| N142HQ | LJ45 | 141 |
| (N142JF) | FA20 | 196 |
| N142LG | LJ35 | 216 |
| N142LJ | LJ31 | 142 |
| N142LL | CL61 | 5176 |
| **N142LM** | **LJ35** | **280** |
| N142NW | GLF4 | 1142 |
| **N142QS** | **BE40** | **RK-432** |
| N142TJ | C550 | 353 |
| N142V | FA10 | 57 |
| **N143AA** | **LJ60** | **143** |
| N143AB | C650 | 0120 |
| **N143BP** | **C550** | **550-1072** |
| N143BP | CS55 | 0085 |
| (N143CA) | LJ60 | 055 |
| N143CC | C500 | 143 |
| **N143CK** | **LJ25** | **143** |
| **N143CM** | **PRM1** | **RB-114** |
| N143CP | HS25 | 25224 |
| N143DA | C550 | 198 |
| **N143DH** | **C56X** | **5514** |
| N143DL | F9EX | 6 |
| **N143DZ** | **SBRL** | **306-142** |
| N143EP | C500 | 357 |
| N143FA | LJ60 | 143 |
| N143FJ | FA10 | 58 |
| N143FJ | FA50 | 160 |
| N143G | GLF2 | 17 |
| **N143G** | **GLF5** | **5060** |
| **N143GA** | **GALX** | **143** |
| N143GB | LJ24 | 233 |
| **N143HM** | **BE40** | **RK-205** |
| N143J | LJ25 | 033 |
| **N143JT** | **C52B** | **0181** |
| (N143JW) | LJ36 | 043 |
| **N143KS** | **GLF4** | **1364** |
| **N143LG** | **LJ35** | **426** |
| N143LJ | CL30 | 20043 |
| N143PL | C650 | 0058 |
| N143QS | CS55 | 0143 |
| (N143RC) | C650 | 0036 |
| **N143RL** | **HA4T** | **RC-25** |
| (N143RL) | HS25 | 258767 |
| N143RL | HS25 | 258774 |
| N143RW | C550 | 346 |
| N143SC | T143 | 001 |
| N143V | GLF2 | 17 |
| N143WR | C650 | 0143 |
| (N144AB) | C500 | 464 |
| N144AD | FA50 | 112 |
| **N144AL** | **C52B** | **0044** |
| N144AR | C500 | 464 |
| N144AW | BE40 | RK-19 |
| (N144AW) | HS25 | 258011 |
| **N144BS** | **CL61** | **5033** |
| N144CP | LJ24 | 185 |
| N144DJ | HS25 | 257067 |
| **N144EA** | **EA50** | **000246** |
| N144EM | C52A | 0120 |
| N144EX | F9EX | 144 |
| N144FC | LJ25 | 258 |
| (N144FE) | FA20 | 46 |
| **N144FH** | **F900** | **189** |
| N144FJ | F900 | 144 |
| N144FJ | FA10 | 59 |
| N144FJ | FA50 | 161 |
| **N144GA** | **C550** | **065** |
| (N144HE) | FA10 | 144 |
| N144HM | HS25 | 258431 |
| (N144JC) | WW24 | 94 |
| N144JP | C500 | 281 |
| **N144JS** | **BE40** | **RK-145** |
| N144KK | GALX | 036 |
| N144KK | GLF4 | 1435 |
| N144KK | GLF5 | 5055 |
| **N144KK** | **GLF5** | **559** |
| N144KK | GLF5 | 669 |
| **N144LG** | **LJ35** | **500** |
| N144LJ | LJ31 | 144 |
| N144LT | LJ55 | 144 |
| N144MH | C650 | 7059 |
| **N144MH** | **CL61** | **5135** |
| N144PA | HS25 | 25224 |
| (N144PA) | LJ24 | 181 |
| N144PK | GLF3 | 447 |
| **N144PK** | **GLF4** | **1210** |
| N144ST | GLF2 | 174 |
| N144SX | CL61 | 3066 |
| N144WB | LJ35 | 444 |
| (N144WC) | LJ24 | 020 |
| N144X | LJ24 | 100 |
| N144XP | BE40 | RK-444 |
| **N144YD** | **C52A** | **0144** |
| **N144Z** | **C550** | **550-0926** |
| N145AJ | C500 | 425 |
| N145AJ | WW24 | 145 |
| **N145AM** | **LJ35** | **078** |
| **N145AP** | **LJ45** | **300** |
| **N145AR** | **LJ45** | **203** |
| N145AS | ASTR | 049 |
| **N145BL** | **C680** | **0045** |
| N145BW | WW24 | 145 |
| N145CC | C500 | 145 |
| N145CG | LJ45 | 107 |
| (N145CG) | LJ45 | 297 |
| N145CJ | C525 | 0145 |
| N145CM | C500 | 224 |
| (N145CM) | LJ45 | 107 |
| **N145CM** | **LJ45** | **297** |
| N145CX | C750 | 0145 |
| N145DF | C500 | 425 |
| N145DF | CS55 | 0018 |
| **N145DJ** | **EA50** | **000057** |
| N145DL | CL64 | 5367 |
| **N145EA** | **EA50** | **000145** |
| N145FC | C500 | 145 |
| (N145FE) | FA20 | 50 |
| N145FJ | FA10 | 60 |
| N145FJ | FA50 | 162 |
| N145G | SBRL | 282-65 |
| N145GJ | LJ35 | 145 |
| **N145GL** | **HS25** | **25230** |
| N145GM | LJ45 | 081 |
| **N145GM** | **LJ45** | **376** |
| N145GR | LJ45 | 376 |
| N145GS | LJ45 | 143 |
| **N145HC** | **LJ45** | **231** |
| **N145JF** | **PRM1** | **RB-159** |
| N145JN | LJ24 | 143 |
| N145JN | LJ25 | 016 |
| N145K | LJ45 | 071 |
| **N145K** | **LJ45** | **268** |
| N145KC | LJ45 | 051 |
| **N145KK** | **C560** | **0276** |
| N145KL | LJ45 | 071 |
| N145LJ | CL30 | 20045 |
| N145LJ | CL61 | 5145 |
| N145LJ | LJ31 | 145 |
| N145LJ | LJ60 | 145 |
| (N145MC) | LJ45 | 040 |
| N145MC | LJ45 | 155 |
| N145MK | C560 | 0112 |
| **N145MN** | **LJ45** | **125** |
| N145MW | LJ45 | 125 |
| **N145MW** | **LJ45** | **400** |
| **N145PK** | **C56X** | **5809** |
| **N145QS** | **BE40** | **RK-421** |
| **N145SB** | **LJ45** | **142** |
| (N145SD) | PRM1 | RB-47 |
| **N145SF** | **C52A** | **0445** |
| **N145SH** | **LJ25** | **145** |
| N145SM | C56X | 5082 |
| N145ST | CL61 | 5104 |
| N145ST | GLF2 | 22 |
| N145ST | GLF4 | 1067 |
| N145ST | LJ45 | 024 |
| **N145TA** | **C500** | **145** |
| N145VP | CS55 | 0145 |
| N145W | F900 | 40 |
| N145W | FA50 | 31 |
| N145WC | BE40 | RK-421 |
| N145WF | FA50 | 31 |
| **N145XL** | **LJ45** | **106** |
| N145XR | LJ45 | 251 |
| **N146AS** | **FA50** | **325** |
| **N146BA** | **CL64** | **5327** |
| (N146BE) | C500 | 160 |
| N146BF | C500 | 160 |
| N146BF | WW24 | 287 |
| (N146BJ) | SBRL | 306-146 |
| N146CF | FA20 | 488 |
| N146CT | C550 | 550-0980 |
| **N146DJ** | **EA50** | **000058** |
| **N146EA** | **EA50** | **000146** |
| **N146EP** | **C510** | **0306** |
| N146EP | C56X | 5224 |
| **N146EX** | **F9EX** | **146** |
| (N146FE) | FA20 | 20 |
| N146FJ | F900 | 146 |
| N146FJ | FA10 | 62 |
| N146FJ | FA50 | 163 |
| N146GA | GLF4 | 4146 |
| N146GA | MU30 | A044SA |
| (N146GA) | MU30 | A046SA |
| N146J | WW24 | 313 |
| N146JB | BE40 | RJ-46 |
| N146JC | C500 | 160 |
| N146JF | PRM1 | RB-159 |
| **N146JF** | **PRM1** | **RB-206** |
| N146LJ | LJ25 | 146 |
| N146MJ | LJ36 | 046 |
| (N146PA) | LJ55 | 085 |
| N146QS | BE40 | RK-448 |
| N146TA | BE40 | RK-146 |
| **N146XL** | **LJ45** | **187** |
| N146XP | HS25 | HA-0146 |
| **N147A** | **WW24** | **294** |
| **N147AG** | **CL30** | **20229** |
| **N147BJ** | **BE40** | **RK-147** |
| N147BP | LJ25 | 147 |
| N147CA | LJ25 | 221 |
| N147CC | BE40 | RJ-38 |
| N147CC | BE40 | RK-4 |
| N147CC | LJ60 | 012 |
| N147CF | SBRL | 282-94 |
| N147CG | BE40 | RK-4 |
| N147CK | LJ24 | 147 |
| **N147CX** | **C750** | **0147** |
| (N147DA) | C500 | 009 |
| N147DA | MU30 | A038SA |
| N147DB | C500 | 009 |
| **N147DJ** | **EA50** | **000059** |
| **N147EA** | **EA50** | **000251** |
| (N147FE) | FA20 | 108/430 |
| N147FJ | F900 | 147 |
| N147FJ | FA10 | 63 |
| **N147FM** | **PRM1** | **RB-147** |
| **N147G** | **F2EX** | **122** |
| N147G | FA10 | 214 |
| **N147GX** | **FA10** | **214** |
| **N147HH** | **CL61** | **5123** |
| N147JK | WW24 | 147 |
| N147K | LJ35 | 462 |
| N147KH | LJ24 | 147 |
| N147MR | GLF3 | 455 |
| N147PS | C550 | 483 |
| N147PS | C650 | 0119 |
| **N147QS** | **BE40** | **RK-436** |
| N147RJ | C560 | 0147 |
| (N147RP) | C550 | 428 |
| **N147SB** | **C560** | **0380** |
| N147SC | C500 | 077 |
| **N147SW** | **ASTR** | **147** |
| N147TA | C650 | 0119 |
| N147TA | FA20 | 506 |
| **N147TW** | **LJ25** | **023** |
| N147VC | C560 | 0105 |
| N147VC | C560 | 0285 |
| N147WC | MU30 | A038SA |
| N147WS | C500 | 009 |
| N147X | FA20 | 185/467 |
| N147X | FA20 | 45 |
| N147X | GLF3 | 336 |
| N147XP | HS25 | HA-0147 |
| N148C | C650 | 0028 |
| N148C | LJ31 | 098 |
| N148CG | F2TH | 41 |
| N148CJ | C525 | 0148 |
| N148CJ | C52B | 0148 |
| **N148DJ** | **EA50** | **000061** |
| N148DR | C550 | 271 |
| N148E | WW24 | 22 |
| N148EA | C500 | 542 |
| N148ED | C500 | 542 |
| **N148FB** | **C52A** | **0148** |
| (N148FE) | FA20 | 151 |
| **N148FJ** | **F900** | **148** |
| N148FJ | FA10 | 64 |
| **N148GB** | **BE40** | **RK-185** |
| **N148H** | **WW24** | **206** |
| N148J | LJ24 | 291 |
| **N148J** | **MU30** | **A033SA** |
| N148JB | C500 | 517 |
| N148JP | SBRL | 306-90 |
| N148JS | C500 | 517 |
| N148JW | LJ25 | 357 |
| **N148LG** | **EA50** | **000148** |
| N148LJ | LJ31 | 148 |
| N148M | FA50 | 270 |
| N148MC | FA20 | 428 |
| **N148MC** | **GALX** | **175** |
| N148N | C650 | 0147 |
| N148PE | JSTR | 5002 |
| **N148TW** | **FA20** | **148** |
| **N148V** | **GLF2** | **54/36** |
| N148WC | FA20 | 148 |
| N148X | LJ35 | 299 |

| | | |
|---|---|---|
| N148XP | HS25 | HA-0148 |
| (N149BP) | WW24 | 149 |
| N149C | C650 | 0070 |
| (N149DG) | FA10 | 3 |
| **N149EA** | **EA50** | **000149** |
| N149F | FA20 | 386 |
| (N149FE) | FA20 | 132 |
| N149FJ | FA10 | 65 |
| **N149GK** | **E50P** | **50000087** |
| N149GU | GLF4 | 1149 |
| N149HP | FA10 | 154 |
| N149J | LJ25 | 149 |
| **N149JS** | **C680** | **0281** |
| N149JW | GLF2 | 63 |
| N149LJ | LJ60 | 149 |
| (N149LP) | ASTR | 070 |
| N149MC | FA20 | 429 |
| N149MD | FA50 | 149 |
| N149PJ | C500 | 149 |
| **N149QS** | **BE40** | **RK-473** |
| N149QS | CS55 | 0149 |
| N149SB | BE40 | RK-285 |
| **N149SB** | **HS25** | **258654** |
| N149SF | WW24 | 149 |
| (N149SF) | WW24 | 74 |
| N149TA | BE40 | RK-149 |
| N149TD | ASTR | 093 |
| N149TJ | FA10 | 9 |
| N149V | F2TH | 53 |
| **N149VB** | **F2TH** | **53** |
| N149VB | GLEX | 9098 |
| N149VB | HS25 | 258142 |
| N149VG | C560 | 0105 |
| N149VP | HS25 | 258142 |
| N149WC | C650 | 7087 |
| **N149WW** | **C52B** | **0175** |
| N149XP | HS25 | HA-0149 |
| N150AB | LJ24 | 228 |
| N150AG | LJ24 | 074 |
| **N150BB** | **CL64** | **5470** |
| **N150BC** | **F2TH** | **67** |
| N150BG | FA50 | 13 |
| N150BP | FA50 | 82 |
| **N150BV** | **C525** | **0320** |
| N150BX | LJ60 | 150 |
| N150CA | HS25 | 257121 |
| N150CA | MU30 | A023SA |
| N150CC | C500 | 150 |
| N150CG | FA20 | 8 |
| N150CJ | CS55 | 0150 |
| **N150CK** | **LJ25** | **150** |
| N150CM | GLF4 | 1284 |
| N150CM | WW24 | 71 |
| N150CT | ASTR | 152 |
| **N150CT** | **ASTR** | **208** |
| N150CT | WW24 | 71 |
| **N150DJ** | **EA50** | **000062** |
| N150DM | C550 | 452 |
| **N150EX** | **WW24** | **262** |
| N150F | C650 | 0150 |
| (N150FE) | FA20 | 84 |
| N150FJ | F2EX | 150 |
| N150FJ | F900 | 150 |
| N150FJ | FA10 | 66 |
| N150GA | ASTR | 202 |
| N150GA | ASTR | 238 |
| N150GD | ASTR | 217 |
| **N150GD** | **ASTR** | **256** |
| **N150GF** | **HS25** | **258823** |
| **N150GV** | **ASTR** | **260** |
| (N150GV) | ASTR | 263 |
| N150GX | GLF3 | 318 |
| N150GX | GLF4 | 1154 |
| N150GX | GLF4 | 1197 |
| N150HE | C550 | 129 |
| N150HN | SBRL | 465-42 |
| N150HR | C550 | 129 |
| N150HR | WW24 | 170 |
| N150HR | WW24 | 71 |
| **N150JP** | **C650** | **7010** |
| N150JP | FA50 | 44 |
| N150JT | FA50 | 40 |
| N150JT | FA50 | 53 |
| N150K | FA50 | 108 |
| **N150LR** | **HS25** | **259050** |
| **N150MH** | **CL61** | **3021** |
| N150MJ | C52B | 0280 |
| **N150MS** | **LJ55** | **049** |
| **N150NC** | **HS25** | **258293** |
| N150NE | LJ55 | 123 |
| (N150NW) | FA50 | 13 |
| N150PG | GLF4 | 1154 |
| **N150PU** | **ASTR** | **225** |
| N150QX | GLF3 | 318 |
| N150RD | C550 | 158 |
| (N150RH) | HS25 | 257083 |
| **N150RJ** | **FA50** | **324** |
| N150RK | GLF3 | 318 |
| **N150RM** | **C500** | **451** |
| **N150RS** | **LJ25** | **162** |
| **N150RT** | **ASTR** | **201** |
| N150S | C560 | 0476 |
| N150SA | HS25 | 25265 |
| **N150SB** | **HS25** | **258197** |
| N150TF | BE40 | RK-240 |
| (N150TF) | BE40 | RK-9 |
| N150TJ | C500 | 422 |
| **N150TT** | **C500** | **176** |
| **N150TX** | **FA50** | **13** |
| N150UC | FA50 | 86 |
| N150WC | C56X | 5150 |
| N150WC | FA50 | 47 |
| N150WL | LJ24 | 011 |
| N150WW | LJ25 | 147 |
| N151A | GLF4 | 1026 |
| N151AE | F2TH | 39 |
| N151AE | HS25 | 257089 |
| **N151AG** | **LJ24** | **137** |
| N151AG | LJ24 | 298 |
| N151AS | C500 | 183 |
| N151CC | C500 | 151 |
| N151CC | CL61 | 5167 |
| N151CG | FA20 | 15 |
| N151CR | WW24 | 33 |
| N151CS | C525 | 0529 |
| (N151DC) | FA10 | 181 |
| N151DD | CS55 | 0001 |
| **N151DR** | **C650** | **0147** |
| **N151EW** | **C525** | **0529** |
| **N151EX** | **F2EX** | **151** |
| N151FD | C550 | 550-1087 |
| N151FJ | FA10 | 67 |
| N151G | GLF4 | 1150 |
| **N151GR** | **F2TH** | **151** |
| N151GS | FA10 | 181 |
| N151GX | GLF4 | 1154 |
| N151JC | C550 | 477 |
| **N151KD** | **C52B** | **0268** |
| N151KD | PRM1 | RB-16 |
| **N151KV** | **C56X** | **5320** |
| N151MZ | GLF3 | 426 |
| N151PJ | LJ55 | 074 |
| (N151PR) | C550 | 191 |
| N151Q | CS55 | 0151 |
| **N151QS** | **BE40** | **RK-422** |
| N151QS | CS55 | 0151 |
| N151SD | GLF2 | 81 |
| **N151SD** | **GLF4** | **1249** |
| **N151SG** | **HS25** | **25035** |
| **N151SP** | **C500** | **384** |
| N151SP | MU30 | A046SA |
| (N151SR) | CL60 | 1034 |
| N151ST | GLF4 | 1151 |
| N151TB | SBRL | 380-11 |
| N151TC | HS25 | 258211 |
| **N151TM** | **C550** | **550-1063** |
| (N151TT) | C525 | 0151 |
| N151WC | FA10 | 163 |
| N151WW | LJ24 | 170 |
| N152A | GLF4 | 1036 |
| N152AE | HS25 | 257164 |
| N152AG | LJ24 | 068 |
| N152CC | C500 | 152 |
| N152CS | C525 | 0539 |
| **N152DJ** | **EA50** | **000071** |
| N152FJ | FA10 | 68 |
| **N152FJ** | **FA50** | **152** |
| N152GA | C550 | 006 |
| N152GA | GALX | 152 |
| N152GA | GLF4 | 4152 |
| N152GS | JSTR | 5061/48 |
| N152JC | C550 | 433 |
| N152JH | C560 | 0442 |
| **N152JH** | **C560** | **0615** |
| (N152JQ) | C550 | 433 |
| N152KB | GLF4 | 1149 |
| N152KC | C525 | 0152 |
| **N152KV** | **C525** | **0152** |
| N152NS | HS25 | 258191 |
| N152QS | BE40 | RK-440 |
| N152RG | GLF2 | 45 |
| N152SM | CL60 | 1077 |
| N152SV | C680 | 0152 |
| N152TJ | LJ35 | 243 |
| N152TS | CL60 | 1052 |
| N152TS | GLF4 | 1052 |
| N152UT | LJ40 | 45-2101 |
| (N152VP) | C650 | 0152 |
| N152WC | C560 | 0324 |
| N152WJ | FA10 | 152 |
| **N153AG** | **LJ24** | **058** |
| N153BJ | BE40 | RK-153 |
| N153BR | LJ24 | 153 |
| N153CS | C525 | 0548 |
| **N153DJ** | **EA50** | **000072** |
| N153FJ | F900 | 153 |
| N153FJ | FA10 | 69 |
| N153G | SBRL | 282-26 |
| (N153G) | SBRL | 282-48 |
| N153H | LJ24 | 151 |
| N153JP | C500 | 153 |
| N153NP | LJ31 | 153 |
| N153NS | CL61 | 5056 |
| **N153QS** | **BE40** | **RK-490** |
| N153QS | CS55 | 0153 |
| N153RA | GLF4 | 1050 |
| N153SG | C550 | 550-1088 |
| **N153SG** | **C56X** | **5231** |
| N153SR | CL60 | 1034 |
| **N153TH** | **C550** | **695** |
| N153TW | LJ25 | 053 |
| (N153VP) | C560 | 0153 |
| N153WB | C500 | 153 |
| **N153XP** | **HS25** | **HA-0153** |
| N154 | HS25 | 25236 |
| N154AG | LJ24 | 034 |
| **N154AK** | **LJ60** | **114** |
| N154BA | CL61 | 5154 |
| N154C | GLF2 | 253 |
| **N154C** | **GLF4** | **1493** |
| N154CC | C500 | 687 |
| N154CC | C650 | 0154 |
| N154DD | ASTR | 029 |
| N154FJ | FA10 | 72 |
| **N154FJ** | **HS25** | **257110** |
| N154G | C500 | 110 |
| **N154G** | **GLF4** | **1044** |
| N154GA | MU30 | A045SA |
| (N154JC) | CL64 | 5347 |
| N154JC | HS25 | 25249 |
| N154JD | HS25 | 257032 |
| **N154JH** | **C560** | **0555** |
| **N154JK** | **C560** | **0128** |
| N154JS | C560 | 0540 |
| N154JS | HS25 | 257032 |
| **N154NS** | **CL61** | **5169** |
| N154PA | FA50 | 154 |
| **N154QS** | **BE40** | **RK-509** |
| N154RA | C525 | 0304 |
| **N154RR** | **HS25** | **258375** |
| **N154RT** | **LJ31** | **154** |
| **N154SC** | **C500** | **558** |
| (N154SV) | C560 | 0154 |
| N154TR | HS25 | 25084 |
| **N154VP** | **C560** | **0154** |
| N154X | GLF2 | 12 |
| N154XL | C56X | 5154 |
| **N154XP** | **HS25** | **HA-0154** |
| **N155AC** | **C550** | **573** |
| N155AG | LJ25 | 037 |
| (N155AJ) | LJ55 | 013 |
| **N155AM** | **LJ35** | **131** |
| **N155AN** | **GLF5** | **5029** |
| N155AU | LJ25 | 218 |
| N155AV | JSTR | 5104/6 |
| **N155BC** | **LJ55** | **115** |
| N155BT | C550 | 170 |
| N155BT | LJ24 | 168 |
| N155CA | C500 | 191 |
| (N155CD) | LJ55 | 030 |
| N155CJ | C525 | 0155 |
| N155CS | LJ55 | 033 |
| **N155DB** | **LJ55** | **141** |
| N155DD | LJ55 | 004 |
| N155DH | BE40 | RK-36 |
| N155EC | SBRL | 306-20 |
| **N155ER** | **LJ55** | **098** |
| N155EX | F2EX | 155 |
| (N155FF) | C550 | 175 |
| N155FJ | F900 | 155 |
| N155FJ | FA10 | 73 |
| N155GB | CS55 | 0155 |
| N155GD | PRM1 | RB-5 |
| **N155GM** | **LJ55** | **022** |
| N155GM | SBRL | 282-90 |
| N155GS | LJ55 | 088 |
| N155HM | LJ55 | 036 |
| N155J | LJ24 | 182 |
| (N155JC) | LJ55 | 055 |
| N155JC | LJ55 | 071 |
| N155JC | LJ55 | 076 |
| **N155JH** | **C560** | **0568** |
| N155JK | C550 | 208 |
| N155JT | LJ55 | 107 |
| N155LJ | LJ55 | 133 |
| N155LP | LJ55 | 055 |
| N155LR | LJ55 | 074 |
| N155ME | WW24 | 391 |
| **N155MK** | **C500** | **155** |
| **N155MM** | **GLF3** | **325** |
| N155MP | LJ55 | 014 |
| N155NK | FA20 | 107 |
| **N155NS** | **HS25** | **258549** |
| N155PJ | LJ55 | 004 |
| N155PJ | LJ55 | 041 |
| N155PL | LJ55 | 133 |
| N155PS | LJ55 | 136 |
| N155PT | C550 | 170 |
| **N155PT** | **C560** | **0257** |
| **N155PX** | **FA10** | **189** |
| N155QS | CS55 | 0155 |
| N155RB | LJ55 | 117 |
| N155RD | LJ35 | 477 |
| **N155RJ** | **GLF4** | **1347** |
| **N155RM** | **PRM1** | **RB-6** |
| **N155RW** | **C56X** | **5570** |
| **N155SB** | **LJ55** | **013** |
| N155SC | LJ55 | 121 |
| N155SP | LJ55 | 137 |
| N155T | HS25 | 258149 |
| N155TA | C550 | 204 |
| N155TD | LJ35 | 335 |
| N155TJ | C550 | 175 |
| N155TJ | JSTR | 5104/6 |
| **N155TS** | **LJ55** | **102** |
| (N155UT) | LJ55 | 071 |
| N155V | LJ55 | 073 |
| **N155VP** | **C560** | **0155** |
| N155VW | WW24 | 123 |
| N155WL | LJ35 | 326 |
| N155XP | HS25 | HA-0155 |
| (N156AG) | LJ24 | 065A |
| N156AV | LJ45 | 156 |
| N156BA | C650 | 7038 |
| N156BA | LJ35 | 287 |
| N156BE | FA10 | 87 |
| N156BF | FA10 | 87 |
| **N156BF** | **LJ60** | **266** |
| N156CB | LJ25 | 101 |
| N156CW | WW24 | 204 |
| **N156DB** | **FA50** | **40** |
| N156DG | GLEX | 9156 |
| N156DH | BE40 | RK-36 |
| **N156DH** | **LJ60** | **091** |
| **N156DJ** | **EA50** | **000073** |
| N156EC | LJ31 | 060 |
| N156FJ | FA10 | 74 |
| N156GA | MU30 | A056SA |
| N156JC | LJ55 | 056 |
| **N156JH** | **C560** | **0575** |
| N156JS | LJ31 | 033A |
| (N156K) | HS25 | 257121 |
| **N156ML** | **C525** | **0156** |
| N156N | C550 | 093 |
| **N156NS** | **HS25** | **258668** |
| N156PB | LJ45 | 027 |
| **N156PH** | **C680** | **0031** |
| N156PH | LJ45 | 027 |
| N156QS | CS55 | 0156 |
| N156SC | LJ31 | 060 |
| N156TS | GLF4 | 1156 |
| N156TW | C52B | 0056 |

| | | |
|---|---|---|
| N156WC | FA50 | 89 |
| N156WC | GLF4 | 4004 |
| N156X | FA10 | 30 |
| N156XP | HS25 | HA-0156 |
| N157AE | C56X | 5017 |
| **N157AG** | **LJ24** | **252** |
| N157AK | LJ35 | 019 |
| (N157AT) | SBRL | 282-102 |
| N157BM | CS55 | 0157 |
| (N157BP) | LJ24 | 157 |
| N157CA | LJ25 | 157 |
| N157CB | LJ28 | 28-003 |
| N157CM | C650 | 7057 |
| N157DJ | LJ35 | 157 |
| **N157DW** | **C550** | **295** |
| N157EA | FA10 | 157 |
| N157EC | LJ31 | 147 |
| N157EX | F2EX | 157 |
| N157FJ | F900 | 157 |
| N157FJ | FA10 | 75 |
| N157FQ | GLF4 | 1157 |
| **N157GA** | **ASTR** | **015** |
| N157H | GLF4 | 1209 |
| N157H | HS25 | 258033 |
| (N157JA) | FA10 | 157 |
| N157JF | JSTR | 5149/11 |
| N157JF | WW24 | 8 |
| **N157JH** | **C560** | **0581** |
| **N157JL** | **C52B** | **0157** |
| N157JS | LJ31 | 033D |
| N157LH | GLF2 | 228 |
| **N157PB** | **LJ45** | **030** |
| **N157PH** | **C680** | **0035** |
| N157PH | LJ45 | 030 |
| N157QP | JSTR | 5149/11 |
| **N157QS** | **BE40** | **RK-520** |
| N157QS | CS55 | 0157 |
| (N157RP) | HS25 | 256067 |
| N157SP | ASTR | 057 |
| N157SP | FA50 | 176 |
| **N157TF** | **C560** | **0157** |
| **N157TW** | **LJ24** | **157** |
| **N157WH** | **BE40** | **RK-157** |
| **N157XP** | **HS25** | **HA-0157** |
| N158AF | GLF5 | 506 |
| N158AG | HS25 | 25155 |
| N158CG | JSTR | 5014 |
| N158CJ | C52A | 0158 |
| **N158DJ** | **EA50** | **000074** |
| N158DP | JSTR | 5013 |
| **N158EC** | **LJ45** | **186** |
| N158EC | LJ45 | 191 |
| N158EX | F2EX | 58 |
| N158FJ | F900 | 158 |
| N158FJ | FA10 | 77 |
| N158GL | LJ25 | 158 |
| N158JA | F900 | 131 |
| N158JA | F9EX | 20 |
| (N158JJ) | GLF5 | 534 |
| (N158JP) | LJ60 | 147 |
| **N158JS** | **C560** | **0540** |
| (N158JS) | HS25 | 257032 |
| N158JS | LJ31 | 033C |
| N158M | FA50 | 273 |
| **N158M** | **FA50** | **351** |
| N158MJ | LJ24 | 033 |
| N158MJ | LJ35 | 158 |
| N158NE | LJ35 | 158 |
| N158PD | LJ45 | 047 |
| **N158PH** | **C680** | **0049** |
| N158PH | LJ45 | 047 |
| N158QS | CS55 | 0158 |
| **N158R** | **LJ31** | **189** |
| (N158RA) | GLF5 | 522 |
| **N158SG** | **C550** | **550-1088** |
| N158SV | C680 | 0158 |
| (N158TJ) | C500 | 158 |
| N158TN | HS25 | 258158 |
| **N158TW** | **FA20** | **158/449** |
| **N158XP** | **HS25** | **HA-0158** |
| N159AK | BE40 | RK-120 |
| **N159AK** | **BE40** | **RK-439** |
| N159B | GLF2 | 190 |
| N159B | GLF3 | 380 |
| N159B | JSTR | 5011/1 |
| (N159DJ) | GLF2 | 156/31 |
| N159DP | WW24 | 52 |
| **N159EA** | **EA50** | **000261** |
| **N159EC** | **LJ45** | **229** |
| N159FC | FA20 | 45 |
| N159FJ | FA10 | 78 |
| **N159FM** | **HS25** | **258651** |
| N159J | LJ24 | 153 |
| **N159JA** | **GLF5** | **5062** |
| N159JH | C560 | 0270 |
| **N159KC** | **C500** | **159** |
| N159LC | C500 | 488 |
| N159M | C650 | 0130 |
| N159M | FA50 | 276 |
| **N159M** | **HS25** | **HA-0082** |
| N159MP | WW24 | 52 |
| N159MR | C650 | 0130 |
| N159MV | FA20 | 59 |
| **N159NB** | **GLF2** | **140/40** |
| N159RA | HS25 | 258155 |
| N159SC | LJ60 | 059 |
| N159TS | CL61 | 5159 |
| N159VP | C550 | 550-1059 |
| N159YC | WW24 | 52 |
| N160AF | FA50 | 188 |
| **N160AG** | **HS25** | **25160** |
| **N160AN** | **LJ60** | **126** |
| N160AT | LJ35 | 031 |
| N160BA | HS25 | 259035 |
| N160BG | LJ60 | 294 |
| **N160BL** | **LJ60** | **104** |
| **N160BP** | **LJ60** | **138** |
| **N160CF** | **LJ31** | **160** |
| N160CF | SBRL | 306-3 |
| **N160CT** | **ASTR** | **152** |
| N160CT | HS25 | 258331 |
| N160D | C550 | 162 |
| **N160DJ** | **EA50** | **000077** |
| **N160EE** | **LJ60** | **093** |
| **N160FF** | **EA50** | **000210** |
| **N160FJ** | **FA10** | **160** |
| N160FJ | FA10 | 79 |
| (N160GC) | LJ24 | 295 |
| **N160GC** | **LJ36** | **030** |
| **N160GG** | **LJ60** | **113** |
| **N160GH** | **LJ60** | **129** |
| N160H | MU30 | A084SA |
| N160HA | GALX | 013 |
| N160J | LJ25 | 076 |
| **N160JD** | **LJ60** | **068** |
| N160JS | C500 | 250 |
| N160LC | CL60 | 1068 |
| **N160MG** | **LJ60** | **244** |
| N160NE | LJ55 | 147 |
| N160NW | HS25 | 258160 |
| N160RM | LJ60 | 147 |
| N160RW | SBRL | 306-16 |
| N160S | MU30 | A084SA |
| N160SP | C550 | 660 |
| N160TC | SBRL | 282-83 |
| **N160TG** | **LJ60** | **339** |
| N160TJ | FA10 | 107 |
| N160TL | LJ55 | 042 |
| **N160TM** | **GLF4** | **1526** |
| N160VE | C550 | 281 |
| **N160W** | **SBRL** | **282-101** |
| N160WC | FA20 | 140 |
| N160WC | GLF2 | 12 |
| (N160WC) | HS25 | 257090 |
| **N160WC** | **HS25** | **258069** |
| N160WC | WW24 | 141 |
| N160WS | F2TH | 28 |
| **N160XP** | **HS25** | **HA-0160** |
| N161AC | LJ25 | 230 |
| N161AK | GLF4 | 1061 |
| N161AV | LJ45 | 161 |
| N161BA | HS25 | 259036 |
| **N161BB** | **EA50** | **000222** |
| N161BH | C550 | 048 |
| N161CB | C500 | 595 |
| N161CC | C500 | 161 |
| N161CC | C650 | 0161 |
| N161CM | SBRL | 306-5 |
| **N161DJ** | **EA50** | **000078** |
| N161EU | FA20 | 485 |
| N161FJ | FA10 | 80 |
| N161G | HS25 | 257151 |
| N161GS | JSTR | 5061/48 |
| (N161KK) | C500 | 219 |
| N161LM | JSTR | 5005 |
| N161LM | JSTR | 5083/49 |
| N161MA | LJ35 | 610 |
| N161MD | CL64 | 5416 |
| N161MM | CL64 | 5416 |
| **N161MM** | **GLF4** | **1511** |
| N161MM | HS25 | 257151 |
| N161MM | HS25 | 258061 |
| N161MN | CL64 | 5416 |
| **N161QS** | **BE40** | **RK-435** |
| N161RB | LJ25 | 294 |
| **N161SM** | **C525** | **0369** |
| **N161TM** | **C550** | **550-0867** |
| N161WC | C500 | 117 |
| **N161WC** | **GLEX** | **9006** |
| N161WC | HS25 | 257090 |
| N161WT | FA20 | 478 |
| N161X | WW24 | 133 |
| **N161X** | **WW24** | **234** |
| **N161XP** | **HS25** | **HA-0161** |
| N162A | HS25 | 25183 |
| N162A | HS25 | 257012 |
| (N162AC) | LJ25 | 126 |
| N162BA | HS25 | 258236 |
| N162CC | C550 | 162 |
| N162CT | FA20 | 162/451 |
| N162D | HS25 | 25183 |
| **N162DJ** | **EA50** | **000079** |
| **N162DS** | **C650** | **0164** |
| N162DW | C550 | 131 |
| N162E | WW24 | 229 |
| **N162EC** | **C52B** | **0026** |
| N162EM | LJ35 | 658 |
| N162F | FA20 | 387 |
| N162FJ | F900 | 162 |
| N162FJ | FA10 | 81 |
| N162G | GLF4 | 1206 |
| N162GA | LJ55 | 003 |
| **N162GB** | **GALX** | **117** |
| N162J | LJ24 | 336 |
| **N162JB** | **HS25** | **258509** |
| N162JB | SBRL | 306-62 |
| N162JC | GLF3 | 373 |
| **N162JC** | **GLF5** | **539** |
| N162LJ | LJ31 | 162 |
| (N162NS) | F2EX | 162 |
| N162QS | BE40 | RK-438 |
| N162TF | C560 | 0573 |
| **N162TJ** | **C550** | **550-0888** |
| (N162TJ) | FA10 | 162 |
| N163A | LJ35 | 073 |
| N163AF | C650 | 0163 |
| N163AG | HS25 | 25169 |
| N163AV | FA10 | 163 |
| N163BA | HS25 | 258238 |
| N163BA | LJ60 | 141 |
| **N163BB** | **EA50** | **000250** |
| N163BJ | BE40 | RK-163 |
| N163CB | C550 | 234 |
| N163CH | FA10 | 163 |
| N163DA | C550 | 190 |
| N163DC | WW24 | 89 |
| N163DE | HA4T | RC-18 |
| **N163DJ** | **EA50** | **000081** |
| N163DK | HA4T | RC-18 |
| **N163DK** | **HA4T** | **RC-19** |
| N163DL | WW24 | 163 |
| **N163EB** | **F2EX** | **36** |
| **N163EG** | **CL60** | **1035** |
| N163F | FA10 | 163 |
| N163FJ | F900 | 163 |
| N163FJ | FA10 | 83 |
| N163J | F2TH | 163 |
| N163JD | LJ31 | 095 |
| **N163JM** | **C650** | **0163** |
| (N163L) | C560 | 0163 |
| N163L | C560 | 0374 |
| N163M | CL61 | 5113 |
| N163M | GLF4 | 1193 |
| (N163ME) | LJ24 | 277 |
| N163MR | CL61 | 5113 |
| **N163PA** | **GLF3** | **249** |
| N163PB | C52A | 0033 |
| N163RK | BE40 | RK-63 |
| (N163W) | WW24 | 162 |
| N163WC | WW24 | 141 |
| **N163WC** | **WW24** | **217** |
| **N163WG** | **CL61** | **3057** |
| N163WS | WW24 | 141 |
| N163WW | FA50 | 52 |
| **N163XP** | **HS25** | **HA-0163** |
| N164AF | C650 | 0164 |
| **N164AS** | **C56X** | **5192** |
| N164BA | HS25 | 258239 |
| N164CB | C500 | 510 |
| N164CB | C500 | 571 |
| N164CC | C500 | 164 |
| N164CC | C550 | 211 |
| N164CC | CL61 | 5164 |
| N164CJ | C52A | 0164 |
| N164CV | C560 | 0164 |
| N164DA | SBRL | 282-112 |
| N164DN | SBRL | 282-112 |
| N164DW | C560 | 0018 |
| N164FJ | FA10 | 84 |
| N164FJ | FA50 | 164 |
| N164GA | GALX | 164 |
| **N164GB** | **FA50** | **164** |
| (N164GJ) | C500 | 164 |
| (N164M) | C750 | 0021 |
| N164M | C750 | 0024 |
| N164MA | FA50 | 164 |
| **N164MW** | **EA50** | **000122** |
| **N164NW** | **FA20** | **164** |
| N164PA | LJ60 | 030 |
| N164RJ | GLF3 | 482 |
| **N164SB** | **LJ31** | **164** |
| N164TC | C560 | 0174 |
| N164WC | HS25 | 257144 |
| **N164WC** | **HS25** | **258072** |
| N165A | GLF2 | 70/1 |
| **N165AA** | **LJ25** | **152** |
| (N165AG) | HS25 | 25043 |
| N165AG | HS25 | 25206 |
| (N165AG) | HS25 | 25208 |
| N165BA | C500 | 159 |
| N165BA | HS25 | 258091 |
| N165BA | HS25 | 258241 |
| **N165CA** | **C525** | **0451** |
| N165CB | C500 | 353 |
| **N165CM** | **LJ24** | **355** |
| N165DJ | EA50 | 000199 |
| **N165DL** | **EA50** | **000218** |
| N165DL | HS25 | 257174 |
| N165F | BE40 | RJ-16 |
| N165FJ | F9EX | 165 |
| N165FJ | FA10 | 85 |
| (N165FJ) | FA50 | 163 |
| N165FJ | FA50 | 166 |
| **N165G** | **GLF3** | **414** |
| N165GA | GLF4 | 4005 |
| N165GA | MU30 | A065SA |
| **N165GD** | **GLF4** | **1265** |
| N165HB | BE40 | RK-90 |
| N165JB | C56X | 5032 |
| **N165JB** | **CS55** | **0009** |
| **N165JF** | **GLF4** | **1251** |
| N165L | HS25 | 258432 |
| N165MC | C550 | 195 |
| N165NA | C500 | 557 |
| N165NA | SBRL | 465-68 |
| N165PA | FA20 | 360 |
| **N165PA** | **GLF2** | **87/775/6** |
| **N165RD** | **C550** | **342** |
| N165SC | CL61 | 5165 |
| N165ST | GLF3 | 414 |
| N165ST | GLF4 | 1053 |
| N165TW | FA20 | 65 |
| N165U | GLF2 | 66 |
| N165W | GLF2 | 66 |
| N165WC | FA20 | 140 |
| **N165XP** | **HS25** | **HA-0165** |
| N166A | CL61 | 5170 |
| N166AC | JSTR | 5029/38 |
| (N166AG) | LJ35 | 145 |
| **N166AN** | **PRM1** | **RB-227** |
| N166BA | HS25 | 258244 |
| N166BA | LJ31 | 086 |
| N166CB | C500 | 532 |
| N166CF | C550 | 180 |
| N166CL | CL30 | 20166 |
| N166DJ | EA50 | 000200 |
| N166DT | LJ31 | 166 |
| **N166EA** | **EA50** | **000169** |
| **N166FA** | **C500** | **559** |
| **N166FB** | **F9EX** | **18** |
| N166FJ | F900 | 166 |
| N166FJ | FA10 | 86 |

N166FJ FA50 167
N166GA GLF4 4006
N166HE LJ35 235
N166HL LJ35 235
**N166HL LJ60 041**
N166J GLEX 9166
N166JV C560 0166
N166KB C560 0374
N166MA C550 151
N166MB C56X 5005
N166MC C650 0003
**N166PC LJ25 166**
N166QS BE40 RK-439
**N166RD C56X 5740**
**N166RM ASTR 047**
N166RM LJ35 336
N166RS FA20 157
(N166SS) FA10 166
**N166ST C560 0606**
N166VP C550 180
N166WC GLF3 413
**N166WC HS25 258119**
N167A GLF2 53
**N167AA GLF4 1096**
N167AC FA10 167
N167BA HS25 259038
N167BA LJ31 087
N167C WW24 261
N167CB C500 542
**N167DD HS25 258068**
N167DJ EA50 000201
**N167DP PRM1 RB-67**
N167EA C550 667
N167EX F2EX 167
N167EX F9EX 167
N167FJ F900 168
N167FJ FA10 87
N167FJ FA50 168
N167G JSTR 5212
N167G SBRL 282-11
N167GX GLEX 9167
N167H SBRL 282-11
N167H SBRL 306-119
N167J HS25 25020
N167J LJ25 011
N167J WW24 265
N167LJ LJ31 167
N167MA C550 303
N167QS BE40 RK-529
N167R JSTR 5204
N167SC CL60 1012
(N167WE) C550 386
N167WE C560 0087
(N167WE) C560 0167
N167XX LJ60 167
N168AM C550 175
**N168AM F2EX 138**
N168AS C500 328
N168BA HS25 258209
**N168BF HS25 258373**
**N168BG C56X 5162**
N168CB C550 150
N168CE F2EX 95
N168CV C560 0168
N168D SBRL 282-21
N168DB JSTR 5074/22
N168DB WW24 202
**N168DJ FA20 168**
N168EA C500 568
**N168EA C560 0168**
N168EC GALX 038
N168FG E50P 50000012
N168FJ FA10 82
(N168H) HS25 257171
N168H SBRL 282-21
N168H SBRL 306-122
N168HC CS55 0081
N168HH HS25 258398
N168HT F900 182
N168JC FA50 119
N168JW GLF2 168
N168LA CL61 5179
N168LJ LJ31 168
**N168NJ GLF5 667**
**N168NQ CL64 5531**
(N168NS) F2EX 168
N168PJ BE40 RK-347
**N168PK GLF4 1053**
N168RL C500 271
**N168RR GALX 217**
N168TR GLF4 1113
**N168TR LJ35 068**
"N168TS" CL60 1052
N168TS CL61 5179
**N168TT EA50 000042**
**N168VA GLF2 112**
**N168W SBRL 282-33**
**N168WC BE40 RK-198**
N168WC GLF4 1002
**N168WM GLF4 1002**
(N168WU) HS25 257157
**N168WU HS25 259009**
N169AC SBRL 306-98
N169B GLF2 190
N169B HS25 256061
N169BA HS25 259039
N169CA GLF4 1241
N169CA GLF5 563
N169CC C650 0169
N169CJ C525 0069
(N169CP) C550 018
N169CP C560 0230
(N169DA) C550 191
N169DJ EA50 000202
N169DT GLEX 9287
N169EA GLF2 169
N169F FA20 388
N169FJ FA10 88
N169FJ FA50 170
**N169HM GLF2 13**
N169JC GLF4 1250
N169JM C550 191
**N169LS FA10 115**
N169P GLF2 169
(N169PG) GLF5 563
N169RF SBRL 306-45
(N169SC) LJ31 069
**N169SD GLF5 5206**
N169SM C56X 5749
N169TA CL61 3041
**N169TA CL65 5790**
N169TA HS25 257114
**N169TD CL61 3041**
N169TT GLF4 1113
**N169US LJ24 298**
N170AL SBRL 282-29
N170BA HS25 258097
N170BG C525 0170
N170CC C550 170
N170CC C650 0170
N170CC SBRL 465-3
N170CS FA10 58
N170CV C560 0170
**N170DC HS25 HA-0001**
N170DD SBRL 282-29
N170EA C500 573
**N170EA EA50 000170**
(N170EP) LJ25 170
N170EV LJ25 170
N170FJ FA10 90
N170FJ FA50 171
N170FJ FA50 172
N170GT LJ25 117
N170HL C500 683
N170HL C650 0125
**N170HL C750 0100**
N170JL SBRL 282-29
N170JL SBRL 465-3
N170JS C500 570
N170L LJ35 156
**N170LD LJ35 287**
**N170LS LJ45 029**
(N170LX) F2EX 170
N170MD C500 088
N170MK C500 668
N170MK FA10 162
**N170MK LJ60 002**
**N170MU C525 0170**
N170RD CS55 0148
N170RL LJ25 117
**N170SD C56X 5091**
(N170SK) HS25 258582
**N170SW GLEX 9042**
N170TC C550 619
**N170TM C52A 0100**
N170VE LJ55 089
N170VP C52A 0170
**N171AM GLF3 437**
(N171AV) HS25 25171
(N171CB) C550 011
N171CB C550 275
N171CC C500 171
N171CC JSTR 5127
N171DP LJ45 171
**N171EX FA7X 24**
N171FJ FA10 94
N171FJ FA50 171
N171GA HFB3 1039
**N171JC GLF4 1222**
**N171JJ GLEX 9209**
N171JL JSTR 5074/22
N171L C650 0039
N171L LJ24 182
N171LE C550 352
N171MC FA10 30
N171PF FA20 117
"N171SG" JSTR 5127
N171SG JSTR 5227
**N171TG FA50 251**
N171TS HS25 256071
**N171TV GLF3 422**
(N171VP) C550 188
N171W C525 0292
**N171WH LJ35 171**
**N171WJ C500 574**
N171WW LJ25 171
N172AC WW24 1
N172CB C550 285
N172CC C500 172
N172CJ C525 0172
N172CJ C52A 0017
N172CP FA10 172
N172CV C560 0172
N172DH C52B 0012
**N172EX GALX 172**
N172FJ FA10 92
N172FJ FA50 173
N172L JSTR 5015
N172MA C500 110
(N172MV) FA20 72/413
N173A SBRL 306-41
**N173A SBRL 465-20**
N173A WW24 80
**N173AA C550 189**
N173AR WW24 80
N173CX C750 0173
**N173DS LJ40 45-2092**
N173EL GLF2 173
N173F FA20 390
N173FJ FA10 95
N173GA HFB3 1052
N173HH C500 082
N173J LJ25 112
N173JA LJ36 007
**N173JM GALX 122**
**N173KR LJ60 099**
N173LC LJ31 173
N173LP C650 0055
(N173LP) GLF3 310
N173LP GLF4 1033
N173LP LJ24 196
N173LP LJ25 163
N173LR C650 0055
N173LR LJ25 163
N173MC WW24 150
**N173PA GLF3 313**
**N173PD EA50 000173**
N173PS LJ31 009
N173SK C500 381
**N173TR HS25 258039**
**N173VP C650 0173**
N173W ASTR 073
N173WF C750 0112
N174A HS25 258174
N174AB BE40 RK-174
**N174B FA10 142**
N174B MU30 A031SA
N174BD FA20 174/457
N174CB C500 647
(N174CF) C500 579
N174CP LJ35 177
N174CX C750 0174
**N174DR C550 069**
N174FJ FA10 96
N174GA FA20 27
**N174GA GLF5 5274**
N174JS C560 0074
**N174JS C560 0572**
N174LM GLF4 1174
N174NW HS25 258174
**N174RD LJ24 319**
N174SA MU30 A072SA
**N174SJ C52B 0174**
N174SJ GLF4 1174
N174TM C680 0021
N174TS LJ31 074
**N174VP C650 7004**
N175BA LJ24 038
N175BA LJ60 060
**N175BC F2TH 32**
N175BC FA10 128
(N175BC) FA20 403
**N175BG GLF3 396**
**N175BJ BE40 RK-175**
N175BL FA10 168
N175CC C500 175
N175CP C525 0175
N175CW C550 550-1065
**N175DP C650 7116**
**N175EM E50P 50000106**
N175EX F2EX 175
N175F FA20 391
N175FF LJ31 175
**N175FJ FA10 97**
**N175FS LJ24 031**
N175GA FA20 45
N175GA GLF4 4173
**N175J C650 0168**
(N175J) C650 0175
N175J LJ35 005
**N175JE EA50 000111**
**N175MC HS25 257178**
**N175MD JSTR 5215**
**N175PC LJ60 175**
N175PS BE40 RK-213
N175PS C525 0087
**N175QS BE40 RK-574**
N175SB C525 0371
(N175SP) ASTR 075
**N175SR C650 0175**
N175ST CL60 1084
N175ST CL61 5023
N175TM HS25 258496
N175U HS25 258175
N175VB C550 230
**N175WS C56X 5327**
N176AF C650 0176
N176AK WW24 154
N176AN JSTR 5103
N176BN FA20 69
N176BN JSTR 5103
N176BN JSTR 5207
**N176CA LJ40 45-2045**
N176CF F900 160
**N176CG F2EX 92**
**N176CL F9EX 110**
N176CP LJ24 204
N176DC SBRL 380-54
**N176DT WW24 154**
N176EX F9EX 176
N176F FA20 393
N176FB C500 650
N176FJ FA10 99
N176G GLF4 1176
N176G LJ25 088
N176GA HFB3 1053
N176GS C56X 5278
N176JE LJ35 176
**N176KS LJ60 066**
N176L C650 0176
N176LG JSTR 5005
N176MB LJ60 176
**N176MG LJ45 383**
N176NP FA20 69
N176P GLF2 176
N176QS BE40 RK-583
N176RS HS25 257162
N176SB GLF2 176
N176TK LJ45 176
N176TL HS25 258176
N176TS HS25 25176
N176VP C560 0176

| | | |
|---|---|---|
| N176WA | HS25 | 258176 |
| N176WS | LJ31 | 176 |
| N177A | SBRL | 282-1 |
| N177A | SBRL | 306-3 |
| N177A | WW24 | 16 |
| **N177AM** | **LJ55** | **147** |
| **N177BB** | **GLF4** | **1073** |
| N177BC | FA10 | 25 |
| N177CJ | C550 | 177 |
| **N177CK** | **EA50** | **000182** |
| (N177CM) | C550 | 247 |
| **N177EA** | **EA50** | **000177** |
| **N177EL** | **C750** | **0177** |
| N177FJ | F900 | 172 |
| N177FJ | FA10 | 100 |
| N177FJ | FA50 | 175 |
| N177GP | HS25 | 25111 |
| N177HB | WW24 | 141 |
| N177HH | C550 | 043 |
| N177JB | C525 | 0182 |
| **N177JB** | **LJ31** | **161** |
| **N177JC** | **WW24** | **77** |
| **N177JE** | **C560** | **0678** |
| **N177JF** | **C525** | **0182** |
| N177JW | HS25 | 257110 |
| N177KS | LJ60 | 109 |
| N177NC | JSTR | 5070/52 |
| N177NC | SBRL | 380-52 |
| N177NQ | SBRL | 380-52 |
| (N177NS) | F2EX | 177 |
| N177PC | WW24 | 141 |
| N177RE | C525 | 0030 |
| (N177RE) | C52A | 0013 |
| **N177RJ** | **C550** | **550** |
| (N177SB) | LJ35 | 401 |
| **N178AM** | **LJ55** | **144** |
| (N178AT) | C750 | 0080 |
| N178AX | HS25 | 258178 |
| **N178B** | **GLF2** | **125/26** |
| **N178BR** | **C56X** | **5354** |
| N178CC | C650 | 0178 |
| **N178CP** | **LJ35** | **005** |
| **N178DA** | **CS55** | **0004** |
| N178EX | F9EX | 178 |
| N178F | FA20 | 394 |
| N178FJ | FA10 | 102 |
| N178FJ | FA50 | 176 |
| N178GA | FA20 | 163 |
| N178GA | GLF4 | 4176 |
| N178HH | C500 | 082 |
| N178HH | C550 | 190 |
| N178HH | GLF3 | 448 |
| N178HH | WW24 | 347 |
| **N178HL** | **C650** | **0125** |
| N178MH | GLF4 | 1121 |
| **N178MM** | **LJ60** | **178** |
| N178NP | LJ31 | 178 |
| **N178PC** | **HS25** | **25264** |
| **N178SD** | **GLF4** | **4111** |
| **N178SF** | **C510** | **0128** |
| N178TJ | FA10 | 78 |
| **N178TM** | **GALX** | **167** |
| N178W | SBRL | 306-4 |
| N178WB | HS25 | 257178 |
| **N178WG** | **C52A** | **0342** |
| **N179AE** | **GALX** | **068** |
| N179AG | FA10 | 176 |
| N179AP | GLF2 | 37 |
| N179AR | GLF2 | 37 |
| N179CJ | C525 | 0079 |
| N179CJ | C52B | 0179 |
| (N179CJ) | C560 | 0179 |
| N179DC | ASTR | 128 |
| (N179DE) | GLF2 | 86/16 |
| N179DV | C52A | 0172 |
| N179EA | C500 | 179 |
| N179EX | F2EX | 179 |
| N179F | FA20 | 396 |
| N179FJ | F900 | 178 |
| N179FJ | FA10 | 104 |
| N179FJ | FA50 | 178 |
| N179FZ | C52A | 0179 |
| N179GA | FA20 | 100 |
| **N179JA** | **GALX** | **088** |
| **N179LF** | **LJ60** | **101** |
| **N179MR** | **LJ45** | **179** |
| **N179QS** | **BE40** | **RK-578** |
| N179RP | C560 | 0768 |
| N179S | SBRL | 380-50 |
| **N179T** | **GLF2** | **86/16** |
| N179TS | CL61 | 5179 |
| N180AR | FA50 | 216 |
| **N180AR** | **GLF2** | **148/5** |
| N180AR | SBRL | 306-77 |
| N180CC | C500 | 180 |
| N180CH | CL60 | 1005 |
| **N180CH** | **GLF4** | **1192** |
| (N180CH) | GLF5 | 563 |
| N180CH | HS25 | 257076 |
| **N180CP** | **LJ60** | **081** |
| **N180EG** | **HS25** | **258188** |
| N180FJ | FA10 | 105 |
| N180FJ | FA50 | 179 |
| N180FW | C550 | 403 |
| **N180FW** | **C560** | **0260** |
| N180GC | LJ36 | 004 |
| (N180JS) | WW24 | 180 |
| N180KT | CL61 | 5004 |
| N180MC | LJ25 | 261 |
| N180MC | LJ35 | 212 |
| N180ML | HS25 | 25115 |
| N180NA | SBRL | 380-51 |
| **N180NE** | **HS25** | **258100** |
| N180PF | C500 | 047 |
| **N180QS** | **BE40** | **RK-569** |
| N180TJ | WW24 | 106 |
| N180UF | C500 | 314 |
| N180VP | C500 | 593 |
| N180YA | LJ25 | 136 |
| N181AP | CL61 | 5010 |
| N181AR | SBRL | 306-90 |
| N181BR | C750 | 0181 |
| N181BS | F900 | 39 |
| N181CA | LJ24 | 277 |
| **N181CA** | **LJ35** | **420** |
| N181CB | FA20 | 436 |
| N181CC | C500 | 181 |
| (N181CC) | C650 | 0181 |
| N181CJ | C525 | 0181 |
| **N181CR** | **GLF4** | **1001** |
| N181CW | GLF4 | 1001 |
| **N181EF** | **LJ35** | **190** |
| N181EF | LJ55 | 090 |
| N181EX | F9EX | 181 |
| **N181FH** | **HS25** | **258098** |
| N181FJ | F900 | 187 |
| N181FJ | FA10 | 106 |
| N181FJ | FA50 | 181 |
| **N181G** | **CS55** | **0006** |
| N181GA | GLF4 | 4181 |
| N181GA | GLF5 | 5181 |
| (N181GL) | LJ35 | 405 |
| **N181J** | **CL64** | **5433** |
| N181JC | CL61 | 5173 |
| N181JT | C525 | 0081 |
| (N181JT) | PRM1 | RB-170 |
| N181MA | MU30 | 001SA |
| N181MC | FA50 | 279 |
| **N181PA** | **LJ31** | **156** |
| N181RB | FA20 | 66 |
| **N181RK** | **FA20** | **515** |
| (N181RW) | LJ24 | 277 |
| **N181SG** | **C560** | **0181** |
| (N181SM) | CL61 | 3031 |
| N181SV | WW24 | 110 |
| N181WT | FA20 | 478 |
| N182AR | SBRL | 306-93 |
| N182FJ | FA10 | 107 |
| N182FJ | FA50 | 182 |
| N182GA | FA20 | 146 |
| N182GX | GLEX | 9182 |
| N182K | LJ35 | 293 |
| N182PA | C650 | 7049 |
| N182U | C550 | 373 |
| N183AB | C550 | 628 |
| N183AJ | C550 | 628 |
| N183AJ | C560 | 0276 |
| N183AP | LJ25 | 271 |
| N183AR | SBRL | 282-127 |
| (N183B) | FA50 | 118 |
| N183CC | C500 | 183 |
| **N183CM** | **LJ45** | **133** |
| N183DT | LJ31 | 183 |
| N183F | FA20 | 398 |
| N183FD | LJ35 | 183 |
| N183FJ | FA10 | 109 |
| N183FJ | FA50 | 184 |
| N183GA | FA20 | 147/444 |
| N183JC | LJ35 | 363 |
| **N183JS** | **C56X** | **5322** |
| N183ML | LJ31 | 183 |
| **N183PA** | **GLF2** | **108** |
| N183RD | HS25 | 256009 |
| "N183RM" | HS25 | 256009 |
| N183SC | GLF2 | 91 |
| N183SD | LJ55 | 032 |
| N183SR | FA10 | 183 |
| N183TS | FA20 | 313 |
| **N183TS** | **LJ45** | **273** |
| **N183TX** | **C52A** | **0183** |
| N183V | GLF2 | 165/37 |
| **N183WW** | **F900** | **165** |
| N184AL | LJ24 | 246 |
| **N184AR** | **BE40** | **RK-34** |
| **N184BK** | **CL30** | **20209** |
| N184CW | GLF4 | 1004 |
| N184F | FA20 | 399 |
| **N184FJ** | **F900** | **184** |
| N184FJ | FA10 | 110 |
| N184FJ | FA50 | 185 |
| N184G | C56X | 5050 |
| N184GA | FA20 | 266/490 |
| **N184GP** | **C650** | **0236** |
| N184GP | JSTR | 5064/51 |
| N184J | LJ25 | 063 |
| N184LJ | LJ60 | 184 |
| N184NA | C500 | 184 |
| **N184PA** | **GLF3** | **318** |
| **N184PC** | **SBRL** | **380-6** |
| **N184R** | **CL30** | **20024** |
| (N184RM) | LJ31 | 026 |
| (N184SC) | C500 | 677 |
| N184SC | MU30 | A067SA |
| **N184TB** | **GALX** | **211** |
| N184TB | HS25 | 257084 |
| N184TB | HS25 | 258671 |
| **N184TR** | **HS25** | **258671** |
| N184TS | FA20 | 313 |
| N184TS | LJ35 | 084 |
| **N184WW** | **FA20** | **352** |
| N184XL | C56X | 5184 |
| N185BA | FA50 | 42 |
| N185BA | LJ35 | 025 |
| (N185BR) | WW24 | 365 |
| N185CC | C550 | 185 |
| N185CX | C750 | 0185 |
| N185FJ | FA10 | 111 |
| N185FJ | FA50 | 163 |
| (N185FN) | BE40 | RK-185 |
| N185FP | LJ35 | 360 |
| N185G | F2EX | 36 |
| N185G | WW24 | 161 |
| N185GA | GLF4 | 4007 |
| **N185GA** | **GLF5** | **5185** |
| (N185GA) | MU30 | A066SA |
| N185HA | LJ35 | 605 |
| N185MB | WW24 | 365 |
| N185S | FA20 | 56 |
| N185SF | CS55 | 0029 |
| N185VP | C650 | 0185 |
| N186CJ | C525 | 0186 |
| N186CJ | C52B | 0186 |
| **N186CP** | **C500** | **186** |
| N186DC | GLF3 | 447 |
| N186DS | GLF3 | 447 |
| **N186DS** | **GLF4** | **1154** |
| N186EX | F9EX | 186 |
| N186FJ | FA10 | 112 |
| N186G | HS25 | 258011 |
| N186G | WW24 | 282 |
| N186G | WW24 | 43 |
| N186HG | FA50 | 167 |
| N186MT | CS55 | 0072 |
| N186MW | C500 | 186 |
| N186NM | HS25 | 25186 |
| **N186PA** | **GLF3** | **317** |
| N186S | FA20 | 195 |
| N186S | FA50 | 113 |
| N186SC | C500 | 186 |
| N186ST | LJ60 | 186 |
| N186TJ | FA10 | 186 |
| **N186TW** | **C525** | **0416** |
| N186VP | C650 | 0186 |
| (N186WS) | C56X | 5179 |
| **N186XL** | **C56X** | **5186** |
| (N187AP) | C500 | 096 |
| N187AP | CL60 | 1035 |
| **N187CA** | **LJ25** | **187** |
| N187CM | C650 | 0187 |
| N187CP | C650 | 0003 |
| N187DL | C525 | 0316 |
| (N187DY) | LJ25 | 342 |
| **N187EA** | **EA50** | **000187** |
| N187EC | WW24 | 434 |
| N187F | FA20 | 402 |
| N187FJ | FA10 | 114 |
| N187G | WW24 | 41 |
| **N187GA** | **GLF4** | **4187** |
| N187GA | GLF5 | 5187 |
| N187H | F900 | 16 |
| N187HF | ASTR | 054 |
| (N187HF) | C550 | 704 |
| (N187HG) | F900 | 16 |
| **N187JN** | **C550** | **365** |
| **N187MC** | **C525** | **0276** |
| **N187MG** | **C52A** | **0187** |
| N187MW | C500 | 187 |
| N187MZ | LJ36 | 023 |
| (N187PA) | GLF2 | 218 |
| N187PH | GLF2 | 218 |
| **N187PN** | **FA50** | **187** |
| N187S | C560 | 0353 |
| N187S | F900 | 136 |
| N187S | FA50 | 18 |
| N187TA | C550 | 280 |
| **N187TJ** | **WW24** | **187** |
| (N187TS) | WW24 | 187 |
| **N188AK** | **ASTR** | **121** |
| N188BC | LJ25 | 078 |
| **N188CA** | **LJ25** | **208** |
| N188CJ | C525 | 0088 |
| (N188CJ) | C560 | 0188 |
| **N188DC** | **GLF2** | **188** |
| N188DH | FA10 | 188 |
| **N188DM** | **FA50** | **327** |
| (N188DR) | C500 | 155 |
| N188FC | LJ25 | 006 |
| N188FJ | FA10 | 115 |
| **N188FJ** | **FA50** | **188** |
| N188FJ | FA50 | 88 |
| (N188G) | CS55 | 0017 |
| N188G | WW24 | 139 |
| **N188GA** | **GLF4** | **4188** |
| N188GA | GLF5 | 5188 |
| (N188JA) | LJ35 | 025 |
| **N188JF** | **BE40** | **RK-446** |
| N188JR | C52A | 0188 |
| **N188JS** | **GLF2** | **29** |
| N188K | HS25 | 25057 |
| **N188KA** | **HS25** | **257132** |
| N188ML | GALX | 024 |
| N188MR | GLF2 | 218 |
| **N188PR** | **LJ25** | **371** |
| N188PS | SBRL | 282-122 |
| N188R | LJ25 | 305 |
| N188SF | C550 | 216 |
| N188ST | MU30 | A040SA |
| **N188SW** | **FA7X** | **23** |
| N188TA | LJ25 | 276 |
| N188TC | GLF3 | 492 |
| N188TC | LJ25 | 276 |
| N188TC | LJ60 | 078 |
| **N188TG** | **LJ60** | **078** |
| N188TJ | GLF3 | 399 |
| **N188TL** | **C680** | **0257** |
| N188TQ | LJ25 | 276 |
| **N188TW** | **C525** | **0326** |
| N188VP | C550 | 550-1088 |
| N188WP | WW24 | 90 |
| **N188WS** | **C56X** | **5179** |
| N189AR | SBRL | 282-77 |
| N189B | HS25 | 25224 |
| N189B | HS25 | 256061 |
| N189B | HS25 | 258075 |
| N189CC | C500 | 189 |
| N189CJ | C525 | 0089 |
| **N189CM** | **C525** | **0189** |
| N189CV | C560 | 0189 |
| N189F | FA20 | 403 |
| N189FJ | F900 | 189 |
| N189FJ | FA10 | 116 |
| N189G | WW24 | 35 |

| | | |
|---|---|---|
| N189GA | GLF5 | 5189 |
| N189GE | HS25 | 257001 |
| **N189H** | **C560** | **0004** |
| **N189J** | **GLF4** | **1068** |
| N189JM | FA10 | 189 |
| N189K | CL61 | 5083 |
| N189LJ | LJ60 | 189 |
| N189MM | FA20 | 453 |
| **N189RB** | **FA20** | **262** |
| **N189RR** | **HS25** | **25248** |
| **N189SC** | **GLF5** | **552** |
| N189TA | HS25 | 258814 |
| N189TC | GLF2 | 140/40 |
| (N189TC) | LJ35 | 189 |
| N189TC | LJ35 | 206 |
| **N189TM** | **HS25** | **258196** |
| **N189WS** | **GLF2** | **228** |
| (N189WW) | C550 | 570 |
| **N189WW** | **C56X** | **5069** |
| N190AB | C500 | 157 |
| N190AR | LJ25 | 190 |
| N190AS | LJ60 | 002 |
| N190BD | FA20 | 8 |
| N190BP | LJ24 | 190 |
| **N190BW** | **E50P** | **50000028** |
| N190CC | C500 | 190 |
| **N190CK** | **EA50** | **000190** |
| **N190CS** | **GLF2** | **190** |
| N190DA | LJ35 | 156 |
| (N190DB) | FA10 | 11 |
| (N190DB) | LJ24 | 190 |
| N190EB | LJ35 | 156 |
| N190EK | CL61 | 5190 |
| N190ES | GLF4 | 1135 |
| N190EX | F2EX | 90 |
| N190FJ | F9EX | 190 |
| N190FJ | FA10 | 117 |
| N190GC | LJ35 | 014 |
| N190GG | CL61 | 5051 |
| N190H | FA10 | 71 |
| N190H | GLEX | 9210 |
| **N190HL** | **E50P** | **50000124** |
| N190JH | C560 | 0303 |
| N190JJ | C650 | 0190 |
| **N190JK** | **C560** | **0303** |
| N190K | C500 | 369 |
| **N190K** | **C500** | **590** |
| N190KL | C560 | 0380 |
| N190L | FA10 | 190 |
| (N190LH) | WW24 | 180 |
| N190LJ | LJ60 | 190 |
| N190M | WW24 | 232 |
| **N190MC** | **F2TH** | **45** |
| N190MC | FA50 | 26 |
| (N190MD) | FA10 | 47 |
| N190MD | SBRL | 306-142 |
| N190MP | CL61 | 5161 |
| **N190MQ** | **FA50** | **26** |
| N190NC | HS25 | 258551 |
| **N190RP** | **GLF2** | **136** |
| N190SB | CL61 | 5051 |
| N190SC | LJ24 | 190 |
| **N190SW** | **HS25** | **HA-0079** |
| N190VE | LJ35 | 301 |
| N190WC | HS25 | 257182 |
| N190WP | GLEX | 9104 |
| N190WW | WW24 | 190 |
| N191AB | C500 | 167 |
| **N191AE** | **F9EX** | **191** |
| N191BA | CL64 | 5410 |
| N191BA | HS25 | 258188 |
| N191BE | CL61 | 5191 |
| N191C | FA20 | 195 |
| N191CM | C650 | 0191 |
| N191CP | ASTR | 249 |
| N191DA | LJ24 | 157 |
| N191DA | LJ25 | 012 |
| N191FJ | FA10 | 119 |
| N191GS | MU30 | A030SA |
| N191JT | C650 | 7069 |
| N191KL | C560 | 0659 |
| **N191LJ** | **LJ45** | **191** |
| N191MC | FA10 | 30 |
| **N191MC** | **FA50** | **282** |
| N191NC | BE40 | RK-143 |
| N191NQ | BE40 | RK-143 |
| N191PP | C525 | 0487 |
| **N191TD** | **LJ45** | **298** |
| N191VB | C560 | 0627 |
| **N191VE** | **C560** | **0150** |
| N191VF | C560 | 0150 |
| **N191VF** | **C560** | **0627** |
| N192A | HS25 | 257180 |
| N192AB | C500 | 177 |
| N192AT | HFB3 | 1038 |
| **N192CK** | **FA20** | **192** |
| **N192CN** | **C680** | **0137** |
| **N192DW** | **C550** | **214** |
| N192F | FA50 | 277 |
| N192FG | GLF2 | 192 |
| N192FJ | F900 | 192 |
| N192FJ | FA10 | 120 |
| N192G | C500 | 163 |
| **N192JS** | **HS25** | **258251** |
| N192LH | WW24 | 180 |
| N192LW | F900 | 192 |
| N192LX | F2EX | 192 |
| N192MB | LJ24 | 214 |
| N192MC | FA10 | 84 |
| N192MH | LJ24 | 214 |
| N192MH | LJ25 | 239 |
| N192N | GLF4 | 1286 |
| N192NC | GLF4 | 1286 |
| **N192NC** | **GLF4** | **4126** |
| N192NC | HS25 | 258476 |
| N192R | FA20 | 192 |
| **N192SJ** | **HS25** | **258192** |
| **N192SW** | **ASTR** | **216** |
| **N192WF** | **GLF2** | **192** |
| N192XL | C56X | 5192 |
| N193AT | SBRL | 282-124 |
| **N193BJ** | **BE40** | **RK-193** |
| N193CJ | C525 | 0193 |
| N193CK | GLF2 | 168 |
| **N193DB** | **LJ24** | **193** |
| N193DQ | CL60 | 1041 |
| (N193DR) | LJ25 | 129 |
| **N193EA** | **EA50** | **000193** |
| **N193F** | **F9EX** | **147** |
| N193FJ | F900 | 193 |
| N193FJ | FA10 | 122 |
| N193G | C560 | 0137 |
| N193JF | LJ24 | 193 |
| **N193LA** | **GLEX** | **9255** |
| **N193PP** | **C52A** | **0192** |
| N193RC | HS25 | 257081 |
| N193SB | C560 | 0229 |
| **N193SB** | **C56X** | **6019** |
| **N193SE** | **C560** | **0229** |
| N193SS | C550 | 572 |
| N193TA | HS25 | 257001 |
| N193TR | BE40 | RJ-29 |
| N193TR | F900 | 9 |
| N193TR | FA50 | 112 |
| N193TR | HS25 | 258039 |
| N193ZP | C750 | 0090 |
| N194 | GLF3 | 391 |
| N194AL | LJ60 | 004 |
| N194AT | C500 | 146 |
| (N194AT) | C500 | 152 |
| N194BJ | BE40 | RK-194 |
| N194CV | C560 | 0194 |
| N194CX | C750 | 0194 |
| N194DC | C650 | 0074 |
| N194FJ | FA10 | 123 |
| (N194JM) | C550 | 297 |
| N194JS | HS25 | 258251 |
| **N194K** | **FA50** | **194** |
| **N194LE** | **CL30** | **20194** |
| N194MC | FA20 | 135 |
| **N194MG** | **C525** | **0357** |
| N194RC | C500 | 545 |
| **N194SA** | **C560** | **0238** |
| **N194SJ** | **C52A** | **0194** |
| N194TS | C500 | 194 |
| (N194VP) | C525 | 0194 |
| N194WA | GLF2 | 194 |
| N194WC | HS25 | 257144 |
| N194WM | CL64 | 5340 |
| **N194WM** | **GLEX** | **9277** |
| N195AR | GLF2 | 195 |
| N195AS | FA20 | 71 |
| N195FC | ASTR | 036 |
| N195FJ | F900 | 195 |
| N195FJ | FA10 | 125 |
| N195GX | GLEX | 9195 |
| N195JH | BE40 | RJ-64 |
| N195KA | BE40 | RJ-53 |
| N195KC | BE40 | RJ-53 |
| N195KC | HS25 | 258189 |
| N195L | HS25 | 259008 |
| **N195ME** | **C525** | **0110** |
| (N195ML) | WW24 | 195 |
| N195MP | FA20 | 195 |
| N195SV | FA50 | 236 |
| **N195SV** | **FA50** | **293** |
| N195WM | GLEX | 9041 |
| **N195WS** | **GLF4** | **1050** |
| N195XP | HS25 | 257023 |
| N196AF | LJ24 | 196 |
| **N196CC** | **GLF3** | **463** |
| N196CF | LJ24 | 186 |
| N196CM | C650 | 0196 |
| N196CT | BE40 | RK-151 |
| **N196CT** | **LJ45** | **318** |
| N196CV | C560 | 0196 |
| (N196DR) | C525 | 0256 |
| N196DT | LJ35 | 171 |
| N196EX | F9EX | 196 |
| N196FJ | F900 | 196 |
| (N196FJ) | FA10 | 126 |
| N196FJ | FA10 | 131 |
| **N196FJ** | **FA50** | **196** |
| N196GA | GALX | 096 |
| N196GA | GLF5 | 5196 |
| N196GA | HS25 | 258126 |
| **N196HA** | **C525** | **0256** |
| N196HA | C550 | 196 |
| N196HA | LJ31 | 084 |
| N196HR | C550 | 196 |
| N196JH | BE40 | RJ-52 |
| **N196JS** | **C550** | **219** |
| N196KC | BE40 | RJ-52 |
| **N196KC** | **F2TH** | **195** |
| N196KC | HS25 | 25180 |
| N196KC | JSTR | 5231 |
| N196KC | WW24 | 68 |
| (N196KQ) | BE40 | RJ-52 |
| N196KQ | HS25 | 25180 |
| N196MC | HS25 | 258081 |
| **N196MG** | **HS25** | **258081** |
| N196MR | C52B | 0297 |
| **N196PH** | **LJ45** | **056** |
| **N196RG** | **F2TH** | **135** |
| **N196RJ** | **C550** | **234** |
| N196SA | C560 | 0384 |
| **N196SB** | **C56X** | **5513** |
| **N196SD** | **C650** | **0093** |
| N196SD | LJ35 | 414 |
| N196SG | C650 | 0093 |
| N196SP | LJ35 | 414 |
| N196SV | FA50 | 236 |
| **N196TB** | **LJ24** | **196** |
| **N196TS** | **FA20** | **196** |
| (N196V) | CL60 | 1030 |
| **N197AR** | **EA50** | **000114** |
| **N197BE** | **BE40** | **RK-33** |
| N197CC | C650 | 0197 |
| **N197CF** | **LJ25** | **197** |
| N197CJ | C52A | 0197 |
| N197CV | C560 | 0197 |
| N197DA | SBRL | 282-28 |
| N197EX | F9EX | 197 |
| N197FJ | F900 | 197 |
| N197FJ | FA10 | 128 |
| N197FS | C500 | 524 |
| "N197FT" | HS25 | 257016 |
| (N197GH) | C550 | 704 |
| N197GL | LJ24 | 070 |
| **N197HF** | **ASTR** | **220** |
| N197HF | C550 | 704 |
| N197JH | C560 | 0267 |
| N197JS | JSTR | 5069/20 |
| N197LS | LJ25 | 363 |
| N197PF | BE40 | RK-33 |
| **N197PH** | **LJ31** | **169** |
| N197PH | LJ31 | 172 |
| **N197PR** | **C550** | **704** |
| N197RJ | C525 | 0660 |
| N197SD | BE40 | RK-126 |
| (N197SL) | MU30 | A069SA |
| (N197VP) | C650 | 0197 |
| N197WC | LJ25 | 197 |
| N198AV | GLF2 | 98/38 |
| N198CC | CL60 | 1018 |
| N198CM | C650 | 0198 |
| N198CT | BE40 | RK-151 |
| N198CV | C560 | 0198 |
| N198D | C650 | 0209 |
| N198DC | CL64 | 5481 |
| N198DF | C550 | 630 |
| N198DF | C56X | 5337 |
| N198DF | C650 | 0209 |
| **N198DL** | **JSTR** | **5083/49** |
| N198FJ | F900 | 198 |
| N198FJ | FA10 | 132 |
| N198GB | SBRL | 380-32 |
| N198GH | WW24 | 364 |
| **N198GJ** | **LJ35** | **198** |
| **N198GS** | **GLF4** | **1098** |
| **N198GT** | **HS25** | **257123** |
| **N198HB** | **LJ60** | **198** |
| N198HE | WW24 | 364 |
| N198HF | ASTR | 054 |
| N198HF | WW24 | 364 |
| **N198JA** | **LJ25** | **198** |
| **N198JH** | **C525** | **0265** |
| N198KF | LJ31 | 147 |
| N198M | FA50 | 149 |
| **N198M** | **FA50** | **273** |
| N198M | FA50 | 277 |
| **N198MA** | **LJ25** | **110** |
| **N198MR** | **FA50** | **149** |
| **N198ND** | **C550** | **630** |
| **N198NS** | **C550** | **148** |
| N198RG | C525 | 0198 |
| N198SL | C550 | 550-0835 |
| N198T | LJ35 | 074 |
| N198TX | C650 | 7047 |
| N198VP | C500 | 602 |
| (N198VP) | C560 | 0198 |
| N199B | HS25 | 25224 |
| N199BA | CL64 | 5410 |
| N199BB | C550 | 550-0895 |
| **N199BT** | **LJ25** | **311** |
| N199CJ | LJ35 | 071 |
| N199CK | C500 | 216 |
| N199D | CL60 | 1081 |
| N199DF | HS25 | 258713 |
| **N199DJ** | **C500** | **571** |
| **N199FG** | **FA50** | **231** |
| N199FJ | F900 | 199 |
| N199FJ | F9EX | 199 |
| N199FJ | FA10 | 135 |
| N199GA | GLF4 | 4099 |
| N199GH | ASTR | 027 |
| N199GH | WW24 | 364 |
| **N199HE** | **ASTR** | **027** |
| N199HF | ASTR | 027 |
| **N199HF** | **GALX** | **028** |
| N199LA | JSTR | 5098/28 |
| (N199LX) | GLF4 | 1004 |
| **N199ML** | **C510** | **0002** |
| N199NP | C750 | 0078 |
| (N199PZ) | GLF4 | 1203 |
| N199Q | C550 | 003 |
| N199QS | GLF4 | 1099 |
| **N199RM** | **PRM1** | **RB-99** |
| N199SA | FA10 | 78 |
| N199SC | LJ60 | 114 |
| N199SG | HS25 | 256038 |
| N199SP | C500 | 199 |
| **N199WT** | **C750** | **0018** |
| N199WW | GLF4 | 1059 |
| N199WW | WW24 | 199 |
| **N199XP** | **C750** | **0019** |
| N200A | GLEX | 9077 |
| **N200A** | **GLEX** | **9203** |
| N200A | GLF2 | 94 |
| N200A | GLF3 | 370 |
| N200A | GLF3 | 372 |
| N200A | GLF4 | 1138 |
| N200A | JSTR | 5081 |
| N200A | SBRL | 282-52 |
| **N200AB** | **GLF2** | **71** |
| (N200AF) | FA10 | 87 |
| N200AL | JSTR | 5081 |
| **N200AP** | **C750** | **0003** |
| **N200AQ** | **GLF2** | **32/2** |
| **N200AS** | **C550** | **550-0934** |
| **N200AX** | **GALX** | **009** |
| N200AX | GALX | 022 |

| | | |
|---|---|---|
| (N200BA) | C500 | 250 |
| **N200BA** | **GALX** | **076** |
| N200BA | LJ55 | 011 |
| N200BC | LJ25 | 095 |
| N200BE | GLF2 | 196 |
| **N200BH** | **GALX** | **013** |
| N200BL | BE40 | RK-23 |
| (N200BN) | FA50 | 240 |
| **N200BN** | **GALX** | **221** |
| N200BP | GLF2 | 115 |
| N200BP | WW24 | 117 |
| N200BP | WW24 | 46 |
| N200CC | GLF2 | 31 |
| N200CC | HS25 | 25179 |
| N200CC | HS25 | 25265 |
| N200CC | JSTR | 5033/56 |
| N200CC | JSTR | 5150/37 |
| N200CE | SBRL | 306-87 |
| **N200CG** | **C500** | **230** |
| N200CG | FA20 | 191 |
| N200CG | JSTR | 5033/56 |
| N200CG | JSTR | 5150/37 |
| N200CH | F2EX | 4 |
| N200CH | LJ31 | 222 |
| **N200CK** | **ASTR** | **021** |
| N200CK | C560 | 0298 |
| N200CK | JSTR | 5039 |
| (N200CK) | SBRL | 282-111 |
| N200CN | CL60 | 1032 |
| N200CP | C560 | 0055 |
| **N200CP** | **FA20** | **275** |
| N200CP | FA20 | 410 |
| **N200CQ** | **C750** | **0245** |
| **N200CU** | **FA20** | **499** |
| N200CV | CS55 | 0064 |
| N200CX | CS55 | 0064 |
| N200CX | FA20 | 112 |
| N200CX | SBRL | 306-93 |
| N200DE | CL61 | 5015 |
| **N200DE** | **CL64** | **5390** |
| N200DE | FA20 | 191 |
| N200DE | FA20 | 368 |
| N200DE | GLF3 | 358 |
| N200DE | WW24 | 148 |
| N200DF | WW24 | 148 |
| N200DH | LJ24 | 170 |
| N200DL | WW24 | 189 |
| N200DM | LJ24 | 065 |
| **N200DV** | **SJ30** | **008** |
| N200DW | JSTR | 5058/4 |
| N200E | C550 | 399 |
| N200E | SBRL | 282-124 |
| N200E | SBRL | 282-135 |
| N200EC | LJ35 | 094 |
| **N200EL** | **GLF3** | **393** |
| N200ES | C500 | 502 |
| **N200ES** | **GLEX** | **9245** |
| N200ET | FA20 | 498 |
| N200FJ | FA10 | 137 |
| N200FJ | FA20 | 401 |
| (N200FJ) | FA20 | 479 |
| N200FJ | FA20 | 491 |
| **N200FJ** | **FA20** | **494** |
| N200FJ | FA20 | 507 |
| N200FT | FA20 | 100 |
| (N200FX) | FA20 | 479 |
| (N200G) | C550 | 030 |
| N200G | LJ24 | 064 |
| N200G | LJ25 | 048 |
| N200GA | GALX | 013 |
| (N200GA) | GALX | 034 |
| N200GA | GALX | 054 |
| N200GA | GALX | 088 |
| "N200GA" | GALX | 106 |
| N200GA | GALX | 122 |
| N200GA | GALX | 151 |
| **N200GA** | **GALX** | **173** |
| N200GB | BE40 | RK-53 |
| N200GF | C500 | 679 |
| **N200GF** | **C550** | **556** |
| N200GH | FA20 | 181 |
| N200GH | GLF2 | 108 |
| N200GL | FA20 | 181 |
| (N200GL) | GLF2 | 108 |
| N200GM | C500 | 142 |
| N200GM | C52B | 0016 |
| **N200GN** | **F2TH** | **68** |
| N200GN | FA20 | 339 |
| N200GN | GLF2 | 110 |
| N200GN | GLF3 | 312 |
| **N200GP** | **BE40** | **RK-172** |
| N200GP | BE40 | RK-53 |
| (N200GP) | C550 | 022 |
| N200GP | LJ24 | 134 |
| N200GT | FA20 | 137 |
| N200GT | WW24 | 46 |
| N200GV | GALX | 167 |
| (N200GX) | FA20 | 339 |
| N200GX | GALX | 133 |
| N200GX | HS25 | 257033 |
| N200GX | HS25 | 258202 |
| N200GY | HS25 | 257033 |
| N200HR | WW24 | 182 |
| N200HR | WW24 | 268 |
| N200J | FA20 | 410 |
| **N200JB** | **GALX** | **164** |
| N200JE | FA20 | 133 |
| N200JJ | GLF3 | 312 |
| N200JP | CL64 | 5421 |
| N200JP | HS25 | 257053 |
| N200JR | C550 | 239 |
| N200JR | C560 | 0576 |
| **N200JR** | **C56X** | **5550** |
| N200JR | LJ24 | 259 |
| N200JW | FA20 | 64 |
| **N200KB** | **LJ31** | **098** |
| N200KC | C500 | 104 |
| N200KC | HS25 | 25249 |
| N200KC | WW24 | 319 |
| N200KF | HS25 | 258039 |
| N200KP | C52A | 0004 |
| N200KQ | C500 | 104 |
| N200L | F9EX | 2 |
| (N200L) | FA7X | 6 |
| **N200LB** | **PRM1** | **RB-116** |
| **N200LC** | **GLF4** | **1067** |
| N200LF | WW24 | 47 |
| N200LH | C650 | 0100 |
| **N200LH** | **C650** | **7005** |
| (N200LH) | WW24 | 309 |
| N200LH | WW24 | 312 |
| N200LJ | LJ35 | 200 |
| N200LL | C650 | 0100 |
| **N200LP** | **MU30** | **A006SA** |
| N200LS | FA20 | 479 |
| (N200LS) | GLEX | 9227 |
| N200LS | GLF2 | 227 |
| N200LS | GLF4 | 1182 |
| N200LS | GLF4 | 1449 |
| N200LS | HS25 | 258095 |
| N200LS | WW24 | 400 |
| **N200LV** | **GALX** | **115** |
| N200LX | CS55 | 0061 |
| N200M | WW24 | 120 |
| N200M | WW24 | 132 |
| N200M | WW24 | 44 |
| N200MH | LJ25 | 083 |
| N200MK | FA20 | 355 |
| N200MM | C560 | 0036 |
| N200MP | SBRL | 282-36 |
| N200MP | WW24 | 95 |
| (N200MR) | C550 | 200 |
| N200MT | CRVT | 40 |
| **N200MT** | **LJ60** | **150** |
| N200MW | C500 | 200 |
| N200MZ | WW24 | 95 |
| N200NA | BE40 | RK-200 |
| **N200NC** | **C550** | **142** |
| N200NE | F2TH | 22 |
| **N200NG** | **C560** | **0190** |
| N200NK | C560 | 0511 |
| N200NK | CS55 | 0095 |
| N200NP | FA20 | 488 |
| N200NR | LJ24 | 142 |
| N200NR | LJ25 | 328 |
| N200NV | CS55 | 0095 |
| N200P | FA20 | 54 |
| N200P | GLF2 | 121 |
| N200PB | GLF2 | 110 |
| N200PB | HS25 | 25121 |
| N200PB | JSTR | 5161/43 |
| N200PC | LJ55 | 058 |
| N200PF | C56X | 5098 |
| N200PF | HS25 | 25121 |
| N200PM | GLF4 | 1147 |
| N200PR | PRM1 | RB-79 |
| N200QC | C500 | 023 |
| N200QM | LJ25 | 084 |
| N200RC | WW24 | 140 |
| N200RG | GLF2 | 216 |
| **N200RG** | **HS25** | **HB-31** |
| N200RM | WW24 | 46 |
| N200RN | C550 | 419 |
| N200RT | C550 | 419 |
| N200RT | C650 | 0025 |
| N200RT | FA20 | 489 |
| N200RT | FA20 | 490 |
| **N200RT** | **FA50** | **126** |
| N200RT | FA50 | 175 |
| N200RT | FA50 | 24 |
| (N200SA) | FA20 | 479 |
| N200SC | C560 | 0326 |
| **N200SC** | **C56X** | **5148** |
| N200SF | GLF3 | 390 |
| N200SF | LJ25 | 084 |
| **N200SG** | **FA50** | **239** |
| **N200SK** | **GLF3** | **319** |
| **N200SL** | **C525** | **0461** |
| N200SR | FA20 | 195 |
| (N200SS) | FA20 | 91 |
| **N200ST** | **ASTR** | **061** |
| N200SX | LJ35 | 286 |
| N200TC | LJ24 | 134 |
| N200TC | LJ35 | 423 |
| N200TJ | C550 | 051 |
| N200TJ | FA20 | 501 |
| N200TJ | LJ31 | 120 |
| **N200TW** | **LJ35** | **397** |
| (N200UJ) | GLF2 | 200 |
| N200UL | CL64 | 5316 |
| N200UN | SBRL | 380-1 |
| (N200UP) | FA20 | 513 |
| **N200UP** | **FA50** | **55** |
| **N200VR** | **GALX** | **133** |
| **N200VT** | **C550** | **210** |
| N200VT | HS25 | 25249 |
| N200WC | WW24 | 153 |
| N200WD | FA20 | 479 |
| (N200WF) | FA20 | 144 |
| **N200WK** | **FA20** | **261** |
| N200WN | C500 | 252 |
| (N200WN) | WW24 | 38 |
| N200WY | FA20 | 509 |
| (N200XJ) | WW24 | 281 |
| N200XR | HS25 | 256058 |
| **N200XT** | **E50P** | **50000029** |
| **N200Y** | **C680** | **0030** |
| N200Y | LJ24 | 003 |
| N200Y | LJ25 | 083 |
| N200Y | LJ36 | 014 |
| N200YB | GALX | 075 |
| N200YM | C550 | 409 |
| N200YM | FA10 | 114 |
| N201BA | LJ24 | 013 |
| **N201BR** | **FA20** | **166** |
| N201CC | C550 | 201 |
| (N201CP) | C560 | 0055 |
| **N201CR** | **F2TH** | **2** |
| **N201EA** | **EA50** | **000201** |
| **N201GA** | **GALX** | **101** |
| N201GA | GLF4 | 1511 |
| **N201GF** | **FA20** | **284** |
| N201H | HS25 | 25109 |
| N201PM | HS25 | 257192 |
| N201S | WW24 | 85 |
| **N201SU** | **C560** | **0586** |
| N201U | C550 | 215 |
| N201WL | LJ24 | 215 |
| **N201WR** | **F2TH** | **201** |
| N202A | GLF2 | 94 |
| **N202AR** | **FA20** | **496** |
| **N202AT** | **FA20** | **509** |
| **N202AV** | **C650** | **7108** |
| N202BA | LJ24 | 031 |
| N202BD | LJ35 | 041 |
| N202BG | C525 | 0089 |
| N202BP | PRM1 | RB-202 |
| N202BT | LJ24 | 195 |
| N202BT | LJ25 | 132 |
| N202BT | LJ35 | 041 |
| N202BT | LJ35 | 483 |
| N202CE | C550 | 104 |
| **N202CE** | **F2TH** | **22** |
| N202CF | C500 | 436 |
| N202CH | HS25 | 257084 |
| N202CJ | C525 | 0102 |
| N202CJ | C525 | 0202 |
| N202CJ | C52A | 0202 |
| N202CP | FA50 | 202 |
| (N202CV) | C560 | 0202 |
| (N202CV) | C650 | 0202 |
| N202CW | C650 | 7061 |
| N202DD | FA50 | 54 |
| N202DD | WW24 | 202 |
| **N202DF** | **C680** | **0098** |
| **N202DH** | **CL30** | **20117** |
| N202DN | FA10 | 202 |
| (N202DR) | LJ25 | 253 |
| **N202EA** | **EA50** | **000202** |
| N202ES | JSTR | 5204 |
| **N202EX** | **F2EX** | **2** |
| N202FJ | F900 | 156 |
| N202FJ | FA10 | 134 |
| N202FJ | FA20 | 484 |
| N202GA | ASTR | 101 |
| N202GA | GLF2 | 152 |
| N202GA | GLF2 | 187 |
| N202GA | GLF2 | 26 |
| N202GA | GLF4 | 1502 |
| **N202GA** | **GLF4** | **4202** |
| (N202GJ) | GALX | 133 |
| (N202GP) | LJ24 | 134 |
| N202HG | CL61 | 5017 |
| **N202HM** | **C500** | **260** |
| (N202JG) | EA50 | 000270 |
| **N202JK** | **C650** | **0100** |
| **N202JS** | **LJ24** | **278** |
| N202JW | LJ25 | 347 |
| N202KH | FA20 | 45 |
| N202LC | LJ31 | 147 |
| **N202LJ** | **LJ60** | **202** |
| N202LS | GLF4 | 1182 |
| (N202LX) | C525 | 0116 |
| N202MW | C500 | 202 |
| N202MW | WW24 | 255 |
| **N202N** | **LJ60** | **258** |
| N202PB | C550 | 029 |
| N202PH | CL61 | 3011 |
| (N202PV) | FA10 | 71 |
| **N202PX** | **GLF2** | **17** |
| N202RB | C650 | 0162 |
| **N202RL** | **C56X** | **5117** |
| N202SJ | LJ60 | 311 |
| N202SW | C550 | 470 |
| N202TA | FA20 | 59 |
| N202TH | F2TH | 130 |
| N202TJ | C650 | 0202 |
| N202TS | C550 | 295 |
| **N202TT** | **BE40** | **RK-504** |
| N202VP | C500 | 607 |
| N202VS | C500 | 096 |
| N202VS | LJ35 | 190 |
| N202VV | C500 | 096 |
| N202VZ | GLF4 | 1289 |
| **N202VZ** | **GLF4** | **4158** |
| N202W | CL61 | 5035 |
| N202WC | CS55 | 0077 |
| N202WM | LJ25 | 355 |
| **N202WR** | **F900** | **24** |
| N202WR | LJ35 | 190 |
| **N202XT** | **CL30** | **20198** |
| N202XT | GLF2 | 170 |
| N202Y | LJ24 | 024 |
| **N203** | **CL64** | **5374** |
| N203A | GLF2 | 89 |
| **N203A** | **GLF5** | **5169** |
| (N203AL) | LJ35 | 483 |
| N203BA | BE40 | RJ-3 |
| N203BE | C550 | 149 |
| **N203BG** | **C525** | **0378** |
| **N203BP** | **PRM1** | **RB-203** |
| N203BT | FA50 | 22 |
| (N203CD) | C650 | 0203 |
| (N203CJ) | C525 | 0103 |
| N203CK | F2TH | 215 |
| N203CK | LJ24 | 203 |
| (N203CV) | C560 | 0203 |
| N203CW | F900 | 33 |
| (N203DD) | F2TH | 180 |
| **N203DN** | **C680** | **0203** |
| N203FJ | F9EX | 203 |
| N203FJ | FA10 | 138 |

| | | |
|---|---|---|
| N203FJ | FA20 | 489 |
| **N203FL** | **BE40** | **RK-123** |
| N203G | CL60 | 1069 |
| N203G | CL61 | 5189 |
| N203GA | GALX | 103 |
| N203GA | GLF2 | 113 |
| N203GA | GLF2 | 124 |
| N203GA | GLF5 | 5203 |
| **N203JD** | **CL61** | **5099** |
| N203JE | CL61 | 5099 |
| **N203JE** | **GLEX** | **9019** |
| N203JK | SBRL | 465-39 |
| **N203JL** | **LJ24** | **203** |
| N203LH | C500 | 384 |
| (N203LX) | C525 | 0131 |
| **N203LX** | **F2EX** | **203** |
| N203M | WW24 | 120 |
| **N203NC** | **FA50** | **203** |
| **N203PM** | **C550** | **578** |
| (N203PV) | FA10 | 71 |
| **N203QS** | **F2TH** | **198** |
| **N203R** | **CL64** | **5386** |
| N203R | HS25 | 258119 |
| N203RK | BE40 | RK-203 |
| N203RW | LJ35 | 203 |
| N203TA | CL64 | 5316 |
| N203TA | FA20 | 442 |
| **N203TM** | **HS25** | **258653** |
| (N203TR) | HS25 | 258653 |
| **N203VS** | **LJ25** | **347** |
| **N203WB** | **F2TH** | **144** |
| **N203WS** | **C560** | **0785** |
| N203XP | BE40 | RK-503 |
| N203XX | GLEX | 9203 |
| N204A | CS55 | 0008 |
| N204A | GLF2 | 79 |
| N204A | LJ25 | 014 |
| N204AB | C550 | 365 |
| N204AB | GALX | 037 |
| N204AB | WW24 | 342 |
| **N204AN** | **FA20** | **102** |
| **N204BG** | **C560** | **0503** |
| N204BP | PRM1 | RB-204 |
| (N204BX) | LJ60 | 007 |
| N204C | GLF2 | 143 |
| **N204CA** | **C500** | **429** |
| **N204CE** | **F2EX** | **165** |
| **N204CF** | **C550** | **233** |
| **N204CW** | **F2EX** | **101** |
| N204DD | FA20 | 494 |
| N204DD | FA50 | 54 |
| **N204DD** | **GALX** | **139** |
| **N204DH** | **BE40** | **RK-290** |
| N204FJ | F9EX | 4 |
| N204FJ | FA10 | 139 |
| N204FJ | FA20 | 490 |
| N204FX | LJ60 | 007 |
| N204G | SBRL | 306-91 |
| N204GA | GLF2 | 167 |
| N204GA | GLF2 | 74 |
| N204HC | FA50 | 136 |
| **N204J** | **C525** | **0164** |
| N204JC | HS25 | 258175 |
| **N204JK** | **CL61** | **5015** |
| N204JP | FA20 | 24 |
| (N204LX) | C525 | 0154 |
| N204MC | C550 | 017 |
| N204MK | LJ45 | 204 |
| N204N | HS25 | 257113 |
| **N204PM** | **C550** | **343** |
| **N204QS** | **F2TH** | **104** |
| N204R | HS25 | 257113 |
| N204R | HS25 | 259017 |
| N204R | SBRL | 306-91 |
| N204RC | GLF2 | 34 |
| N204RP | C680 | 0093 |
| **N204RT** | **LJ31** | **204** |
| N204SM | HS25 | 258135 |
| N204TM | SBRL | 282-56 |
| **N204TM** | **WW24** | **320** |
| **N204TW** | **FA20** | **204** |
| N204XP | BE40 | RK-504 |
| N204Y | C500 | 204 |
| N204Y | LJ24 | 113 |
| **N204ZQ** | **EA50** | **000186** |
| (N205A) | CL60 | 1029 |
| N205AJ | WW24 | 205 |
| N205BC | C560 | 0010 |
| **N205BC** | **PRM1** | **RB-69** |
| N205BE | C550 | 647 |
| N205BL | GLF2 | 205 |
| **N205BN** | **C525** | **0050** |
| N205BS | HS25 | 257048 |
| **N205CM** | **C560** | **0250** |
| **N205CW** | **F2EX** | **45** |
| N205EE | CL61 | 3011 |
| N205EE | CL64 | 5347 |
| (N205EF) | LJ55 | 053 |
| N205EL | CL60 | 1067 |
| N205EL | CL61 | 3011 |
| N205EL | CL64 | 5347 |
| **N205EL** | **GLEX** | **9201** |
| N205EL | LJ35 | 283 |
| N205EL | LJ55 | 053 |
| N205EX | GLEX | 9205 |
| N205FH | C525 | 0355 |
| N205FJ | F9EX | 5 |
| N205FJ | FA10 | 140 |
| N205FJ | FA20 | 120 |
| (N205FJ) | FA20 | 142 |
| N205FJ | FA20 | 491 |
| N205FL | LJ35 | 283 |
| N205FM | C500 | 264 |
| N205FX | LJ60 | 005 |
| N205GY | PRM1 | RB-205 |
| **N205JC** | **FA20** | **440** |
| N205K | FA20 | 319 |
| N205K | GLF2 | 231 |
| (N205LX) | C525 | 0199 |
| **N205LX** | **F2EX** | **205** |
| N205M | GLF2 | 18 |
| N205MM | CL60 | 1044 |
| N205MM | HFB3 | 1039 |
| (N205NP) | C525 | 0205 |
| N205PC | C560 | 0010 |
| N205R | BE40 | RK-30 |
| N205RJ | LJ24 | 041 |
| N205SA | LJ25 | 041 |
| **N205SC** | **C550** | **176** |
| N205SC | FA20 | 155 |
| N205SC | LJ25 | 041 |
| (N205SE) | FA20 | 155 |
| N205SG | C550 | 176 |
| N205ST | LJ60 | 205 |
| (N205TS) | FA20 | 54 |
| **N205TW** | **HS25** | **257025** |
| N205VP | C560 | 0205 |
| N205WM | FA20 | 306/512 |
| **N205WP** | **FA20** | **306/512** |
| N205X | FA10 | 44 |
| N205X | GLF4 | 1080 |
| **N205YY** | **C52A** | **0205** |
| N206AG | C550 | 330 |
| **N206CK** | **LJ45** | **047** |
| N206CX | C56X | 5206 |
| N206EC | LJ25 | 206 |
| N206EC | LJ35 | 487 |
| N206EQ | LJ25 | 206 |
| N206EX | F9EX | 206 |
| N206FC | LJ35 | 487 |
| N206FJ | FA10 | 141 |
| (N206FJ) | FA20 | 487 |
| N206FX | LJ60 | 028 |
| **N206HY** | **LJ60** | **028** |
| N206LX | C525 | 0205 |
| N206MD | GLF2 | 22 |
| N206PC | C750 | 0016 |
| N206PC | HS25 | 258038 |
| N206TC | C550 | 465 |
| N206WC | HS25 | 258038 |
| **N207AH** | **PRM1** | **RB-207** |
| N207BA | BE40 | RJ-7 |
| N207BA | C550 | 234 |
| **N207BC** | **ASTR** | **093** |
| **N207BG** | **C52A** | **0326** |
| N207BS | C525 | 0241 |
| **N207BS** | **C525** | **0445** |
| N207BS | C52A | 0055 |
| N207BX | LJ60 | 050 |
| **N207CA** | **FA20** | **153** |
| N207CC | C650 | 0207 |
| (N207CF) | C500 | 610 |
| N207CV | C560 | 0207 |
| **N207EA** | **EA50** | **000207** |
| N207EM | F2TH | 207 |
| N207FJ | F900 | 200 |
| N207FJ | FA10 | 142 |
| N207FJ | FA20 | 401 |
| N207FX | LJ60 | 050 |
| N207G | C500 | 647 |
| N207GA | GLF2 | 136 |
| N207HF | LJ25 | 230 |
| N207JC | LJ25 | 207 |
| **N207JS** | **FA20** | **117** |
| (N207L) | C500 | 038 |
| N207L | JSTR | 5050/34 |
| N207L | JSTR | 5067 |
| N207L | JSTR | 5100/41 |
| (N207LX) | C525 | 0218 |
| **N207MJ** | **MS76** | **002** |
| N207PC | C56X | 5008 |
| N207PC | HS25 | 257197 |
| N207PC | HS25 | 258185 |
| N207QS | F2TH | 70 |
| **N207R** | **HS25** | **259045** |
| N207RC | HS25 | 257197 |
| (N207RC) | HS25 | 258185 |
| **N207RG** | **LJ24** | **339** |
| **N207TR** | **FA7X** | **35** |
| **N207TT** | **HS25** | **259008** |
| N207US | FA10 | 207 |
| (N207VC) | LJ60 | 207 |
| **N207WM** | **EA50** | **000247** |
| N207WW | WW24 | 207 |
| N208BC | C560 | 0050 |
| **N208BG** | **C52A** | **0414** |
| N208BG | HS25 | 258208 |
| **N208BH** | **LJ60** | **208** |
| N208BP | PRM1 | RB-208 |
| N208BX | LJ60 | 059 |
| N208CV | C560 | 0208 |
| N208D | BE40 | RJ-14 |
| N208EA | C500 | 612 |
| N208F | MU30 | A016SA |
| N208FJ | FA10 | 144 |
| N208FJ | FA20 | 493 |
| N208FX | LJ60 | 059 |
| N208GA | ASTR | 208 |
| **N208GA** | **ASTR** | **288** |
| N208H | HS25 | 25141 |
| N208H | HS25 | 25163 |
| **N208HP** | **PRM1** | **RB-232** |
| N208JV | C525 | 0208 |
| **N208L** | **HS25** | **259011** |
| N208L | JSTR | 5050/34 |
| N208L | JSTR | 5083/49 |
| **N208LT** | **CL64** | **5440** |
| (N208LX) | C525 | 0247 |
| N208MD | WW24 | 208 |
| **N208MF** | **C680** | **0233** |
| N208MM | HFB3 | 1039 |
| N208N | C500 | 021 |
| N208PC | C560 | 0050 |
| N208PC | C56X | 5005 |
| N208QS | F2TH | 206 |
| N208R | BE40 | RJ-14 |
| **N208R** | **CL64** | **5316** |
| N208R | HS25 | 259011 |
| (N208RT) | FA20 | 490 |
| N208ST | WW24 | 208 |
| N208TC | C550 | 327 |
| **N208VP** | **C560** | **0208** |
| N208W | C500 | 421 |
| (N208WR) | LJ35 | 190 |
| N209A | C650 | 0156 |
| N209BA | BE40 | RJ-9 |
| N209BP | PRM1 | RB-209 |
| N209BS | C525 | 0241 |
| N209CA | FA20 | 71 |
| N209CJ | C510 | 0209 |
| N209CP | C560 | 0055 |
| **N209CQ** | **F9EX** | **98** |
| **N209CV** | **C560** | **0209** |
| **N209EA** | **EA50** | **000209** |
| (N209EX) | F2EX | 9 |
| **N209EX** | **F9EX** | **209** |
| N209FJ | F2TH | 9 |
| **N209FJ** | **F9EX** | **2** |
| N209FJ | FA10 | 145 |
| N209FJ | FA20 | 494 |
| N209FS | F2TH | 209 |
| N209FX | LJ60 | 060 |
| N209G | C550 | 558 |
| N209GA | GLF2 | 9/33 |
| **N209HP** | **HS25** | **HB-26** |
| N209HR | LJ31 | 209 |
| N209KM | LJ45 | 209 |
| N209LS | GLF4 | 1449 |
| (N209LX) | C525 | 0253 |
| N209LX | F2EX | 209 |
| N209MW | C500 | 209 |
| N209NC | HS25 | 25190 |
| N209RR | WW24 | 127 |
| **N209SU** | **F2EX** | **163** |
| N209TM | F2TH | 209 |
| **N209TS** | **HS25** | **257014** |
| (N209WE) | CL60 | 1034 |
| N209WF | CL60 | 1034 |
| N210CJ | C525 | 0010 |
| N210CJ | C525 | 0210 |
| **N210CM** | **C560** | **0369** |
| N210EK | JSTR | 5117/35 |
| N210EM | FA10 | 210 |
| N210F | C650 | 0067 |
| N210F | SBRL | 306-25 |
| N210FE | WW24 | 95 |
| **N210FF** | **E50P** | **50000088** |
| N210FJ | F900 | 201 |
| **N210FJ** | **F9EX** | **210** |
| N210FJ | FA10 | 13 |
| N210FJ | FA20 | 495 |
| N210FP | LJ24 | 155 |
| N210FX | LJ60 | 064 |
| N210GA | GLF2 | 102/32 |
| N210GK | GLF3 | 875 |
| N210GP | LJ24 | 020 |
| N210HV | LJ60 | 064 |
| N210KP | PRM1 | RB-210 |
| N210M | HS25 | 25103 |
| N210MJ | C550 | 108 |
| N210MT | C500 | 210 |
| N210NC | LJ25 | 154 |
| N210PC | LJ24 | 036 |
| **N210QS** | **F2TH** | **211** |
| **N210RK** | **HS25** | **257073** |
| N210RS | FA20 | 18 |
| (N210ST) | HS25 | 256009 |
| N210VS | C56X | 5093 |
| N210WL | LJ35 | 210 |
| **N211BC** | **LJ55** | **145** |
| N211BL | GLF2 | 113 |
| N211BL | LJ24 | 150 |
| N211BR | SBRL | 306-85 |
| N211BX | LJ60 | 076 |
| N211BY | LJ35 | 227 |
| (N211BY) | LJ55 | 059 |
| N211CC | C650 | 0211 |
| **N211CC** | **C680** | **0034** |
| N211CD | LJ25 | 275 |
| N211CN | FA10 | 173 |
| N211CN | FA50 | 31 |
| **N211CQ** | **C650** | **0211** |
| N211DB | C500 | 174 |
| N211DB | WW24 | 405 |
| N211DG | C560 | 0167 |
| N211DH | GLF2 | 236 |
| **N211DH** | **GLF4** | **1432** |
| N211DH | LJ35 | 253 |
| **N211DK** | **GLF4** | **1078** |
| **N211EC** | **FA10** | **166** |
| N211EF | C500 | 434 |
| N211EF | FA50 | 123 |
| N211EF | LJ55 | 101 |
| N211FJ | FA10 | 146 |
| N211FX | LJ60 | 076 |
| (N211GA) | GLF2 | 36/3 |
| **N211GA** | **MU30** | **A011SA** |
| **N211GM** | **C525** | **0208** |
| N211HF | FA20 | 289 |
| N211HF | FA20 | 474 |
| N211HJ | LJ24 | 150 |
| N211HS | GLF5 | 5206 |
| N211JB | LJ25 | 249 |
| **N211JC** | **LJ25** | **310** |
| (N211JE) | LJ25 | 310 |
| **N211JL** | **FA10** | **180** |
| **N211JN** | **HS25** | **258104** |
| **N211JS** | **C550** | **105** |
| (N211LX) | C525 | 0326 |
| N211MA | C560 | 0022 |
| (N211MA) | C650 | 0219 |
| **N211MA** | **GLF4** | **1247** |

N211MB LJ25 059
N211MT GLF2 52
N211PA JSTR 5227
N211PD LJ25 310
N211QS CS55 0011
**N211RN LJ31 072**
N211RR C650 0079
N211SF SBRL 282-136
N211SJ GLF2 75/7
N211SP C550 337
N211SR FA10 115
**N211ST WW24 303**
N211TB CL30 20117
N211TJ FA10 11
N211TS LJ24 066
N211VP CS55 0002
(N211WC) C560 0311
N211WH LJ35 269
N211WZ HS25 257017
N211X C500 434
N211XP HS25 HA-0011
N212AD GLF3 492
N212AP JSTR 5147
N212AT GLF3 492
N212AT GLF4 1204
N212AW GLF4 1240
**N212BA GLF3 353**
N212BD C560 0309
N212BH C550 550-1020
**N212BW C560 0038**
N212BX LJ60 099
N212C C510 0060
N212C FA20 155
N212CP WW24 340
N212CT CL61 5104
N212CW WW24 75
**N212EA EA50 000212**
N212EX F9EX 212
N212F SBRL 306-25
N212FH BE40 RK-448
**N212FJ FA10 147**
N212FJ FA20 497
(N212FX) LJ60 007
N212FX LJ60 077
N212FX LJ60 099
N212GA GLF2 140/40
N212GA LJ35 354
N212H C550 105
N212H FA20 259
N212JP FA50 94
N212JP LJ55 006
N212JW JSTR 5131
N212K FA50 89
N212K GLF2 195
N212K GLF4 1192
N212KM FA50 89
N212LD ASTR 020
**N212LF GLF4 4139**
N212LF LJ24 216
N212LM CL61 5037
(N212LX) C525 0339
**N212M C500 415**
**N212MP GALX 033**
N212N FA10 150
N212N FA50 202
N212NC FA10 150
N212NE LJ25 212
(N212PA) MU30 A038SA
N212PB FA20 313
N212Q FA50 179
N212QS F2TH 213
N212R FA20 212
**N212RG HS25 258073**
**N212RR CL64 5336**
**N212SL GALX 055**
**N212T ASTR 110**
N212T F2TH 52
N212T FA20 273
N212T FA50 192
N212TC FA20 273
N212TG FA20 273
N212TJ GLF2 12
**N212VZ GLF4 1531**
N212WW WW24 212
N212WZ GLF4 1489
N213AP JSTR 5122
N213AR LJ31 107
**N213BA GLF3 453**
(N213BE) SBRL 306-123
**N213BK BE40 RK-216**
N213BM SBRL 282-111
N213BP PRM1 RB-213
N213C HS25 257213
N213CA LJ25 241
**N213CC C550 250**
(N213CE) C500 213
N213CF C550 124
N213CJ C52A 0213
(N213DC) GLF2 19
N213EX F9EX 213
(N213FC) FA20 213
N213FJ FA10 148
N213FJ FA20 499
(N213FX) LJ60 086
**N213GS CL61 5101**
N213H HS25 25119
**N213HP C650 0133**
**N213JS C550 597**
N213LG MU30 A079SA
N213LS FA20 107
(N213LX) C525 0348
N213MC CL61 5171
N213PA LJ31 013
**N213PC PRM1 RB-173**
N213PC PRM1 RB-75
**N213PQ PRM1 RB-75**
**N213QS F2TH 113**
**N213TS CL61 3013**
N213WW WW24 213
**N213X GLF2 213**
N214AM C550 312
**N214AS FA20 501**
**N214BL CL30 20214**
N214BX LJ60 046
N214CA C500 214
N214CC C500 214
N214CC WW24 197
(N214CP) C550 635
N214DV FA50 289
**N214DV FA50 350**
N214FJ F2TH 214
N214FJ FA10 149
N214FJ FA20 500
(N214FJ) FA50 214
N214FX LJ60 046
(N214GA) FA50 105
N214GA GALX 114
N214GA GLF2 160
**N214GA GLF4 4214**
N214GP GLF2 3
**N214HT C510 0097**
N214JP FA20 296/507
N214JR HS25 25070
N214JR HS25 25146
**N214JT C550 417**
N214L C560 0381
**N214LD F2TH 41**
N214LF LJ45 214
N214LJ LJ25 214
(N214LS) C560 0190
N214LS LJ35 096
(N214LS) LJ35 229
(N214LX) C525 0026
N214MD C550 273
N214ME LJ25 214
N214MJ LJ24 214
**N214MS EA50 000252**
N214NW GLF2 214
**N214PG MU30 A082SA**
N214PN CS55 0038
N214PW LJ31 219
N214PW LJ60 264
N214QS CS55 0014
**N214RV FA10 217**
N214RW C550 478
**N214RW CL30 20119**
N214RW LJ31 219
N214RW LJ60 264
N214TC HS25 25146
N214TJ C550 550-0900
N214TS GLF4 1121
N214WM BE40 RK-197
N214WW WW24 214
**N214WY GLF3 441**
N215BL CL30 20215
N215BR PRM1 RB-215
N215BX LJ60 101
N215C WW24 206
N215CC C500 215
N215CM C650 0215
N215CW C550 175
N215CX C750 0215
N215DH WW24 215
N215DL JSTR 5215
N215EX F2EX 15
N215FJ FA10 150
N215FJ FA20 498
N215FX LJ60 101
N215G HS25 25058
N215G HS25 257095
N215G WW24 206
N215GA GLF2 93
(N215HZ) JSTR 5215
N215J LJ24 134
N215JW LJ35 223
N215KH F2TH 197
**N215KM LJ60 109**
(N215LX) C525 0114
N215M WW24 206
**N215NA C500 622**
**N215QS F2TH 214**
**N215RE F2TH 215**
N215RL CL60 1068
N215RL GLF2 45
N215RL LJ36 012
**N215RS HS25 257023**
**N215RX C750 0225**
N215SC WW24 243
N215TM GLF4 1400
**N215TP BE40 RJ-64**
N215TS JSTR 5215
**N215TT LJ31 076**
(N215WC) C560 0315
N215Z LJ24 246
N215Z LJ25 020
N216BG FA20 196
N216BX LJ60 103
N216CA FA20 11
(N216CC) C500 216
N216CJ C525 0016
N216CW C525 0116
N216FB F900 65
N216FJ FA10 152
N216FJ FA20 502
N216FP F900 146
N216FP F900 65
N216FX LJ60 103
N216GA ASTR 216
N216GA GALX 116
N216GA GLF4 4116
**N216GA GLF4 4216**
N216HB LJ24 275
N216HE GLF2 113
(N216MF) GLF2 113
N216PA GLEX 9282
N216R SBRL 282-94
N216RG LJ24 066
**N216RR GLF2 22**
N216SA FA20 16
(N216SA) LJ24 082
N216SA LJ25 216
N216SC WW24 216
N216TW FA20 16
(N216VP) C550 017
**N216WD FA50 112**
N217A HS25 256030
N217A SBRL 282-103
N217A SBRL 306-85
(N217AH) GLF2 197
N217AJ FA20 171
**N217AJ LJ24 345**
**N217AL C750 0217**
N217AL HS25 258177
N217AL WW24 38
N217AT LJ24 217
**N217BA GALX 144**
N217BL WW24 284
N217BM WW24 409
N217BX LJ60 105
N217CA FA20 75
N217CC C500 217
N217CJ C525 0117
N217CM C650 0217
(N217CP) FA10 100
N217CS LJ35 062
N217CS LJ36 039
N217CX C750 0217
(N217DA) GLF2 17
N217E SBRL 282-103
**N217EC BE40 RK-356**
N217EX F2EX 17
N217F HS25 25175
N217F WW24 321
N217FJ FA10 151
N217FJ FA20 504
**N217FS C550 308**
N217FX LJ60 105
N217GA ASTR 217
N217GA GALX 117
N217GA GLF2 17
N217GA GLF5 5227
**N217GH CL30 20248**
**N217GL C560 0076**
(N217JC) GLEX 9079
N217JD GLF2 14
N217JS GLF2 113
N217JS LJ24 345
N217LG C550 304
N217MB BE40 RK-217
**N217MJ LJ45 217**
**N217MS ASTR 217**
N217PM WW24 16
N217PM WW24 38
N217PT ASTR 105
N217RJ C650 0079
**N217RM CL60 1054**
N217RM HS25 258017
N217RM SBRL 306-94
N217RM WW24 409
N217RN SBRL 306-94
N217RR C500 643
N217RR C650 0079
N217RR GLF2 22
N217RR GLF4 1042
N217RT LJ35 379
N217S C500 217
**N217SA C550 263**
N217SC WW24 217
N217SQ WW24 217
**N217TA LJ35 289**
(N217TE) GLF2 33
N217TE SBRL 282-103
**N217TH C560 0390**
N217TL GLF2 33
N217W C52A 0022
**N217WC C560 0317**
N217WC WW24 217
N217WM LJ25 217
N218AC HS25 256013
**N218AD HS25 258139**
N218AM C500 626
N218AM C56X 5218
N218BA FA10 218
N218BR C560 0218
N218BX LJ60 098
**N218CA FA20 218**
(N218CC) C500 218
N218CC C650 0218
(N218CP) GLF5 656
(N218CR) LJ35 258
N218DF C560 0218
N218DJ WW24 218
**N218EC GLF5 656**
N218EX F2EX 22
N218FJ FA10 153
N218FJ FA20 503
N218FX LJ60 098
(N218G) C550 550-0888
**N218G EA50 000197**
N218GA ASTR 218
N218GA GLF2 218
N218GA GLF4 1518
**N218GA GLF4 4218**
N218H C550 430
**N218JG C500 626**
**N218JT EA50 000047**
N218NB LJ25 361
**N218NB LJ31 146**
N218NR LJ25 361
**N218PH F2TH 218**
N218PM WW24 218
**N218QS F2TH 118**

| | | |
|---|---|---|
| N218R | LJ25 | 365 |
| N218RG | BE40 | RJ-45 |
| N218S | FA20 | 32 |
| N218SC | WW24 | 271 |
| N218SE | C560 | 0086 |
| **N218SE** | **GLF2** | **116** |
| N218TJ | HS25 | 25018 |
| (N218UB) | SBRL | 380-45 |
| N218US | FA20 | 51 |
| N218US | SBRL | 380-45 |
| N218WA | FA50 | 218 |
| **N218WW** | **GLF4** | **4058** |
| N218WW | WW24 | 218 |
| **N219AX** | **GALX** | **019** |
| N219CA | FA20 | 193 |
| N219CC | C500 | 219 |
| N219CC | C650 | 0219 |
| **N219CJ** | **C525** | **0219** |
| N219CS | C550 | 374 |
| **N219DC** | **BE40** | **RK-518** |
| (N219DC) | HS25 | 258327 |
| N219DC | LJ60 | 061 |
| **N219EA** | **EA50** | **000219** |
| N219EC | HS25 | 25219 |
| N219EX | F2EX | 20 |
| N219FJ | F2TH | 219 |
| N219FJ | FA10 | 154 |
| N219FJ | FA20 | 508 |
| N219FL | C52A | 0111 |
| N219FX | LJ60 | 007 |
| N219GA | ASTR | 219 |
| N219GA | GALX | 019 |
| N219GA | GLF2 | 91 |
| N219JA | HS25 | 257013 |
| (N219JA) | HS25 | 258005 |
| N219JW | FA10 | 219 |
| **N219L** | **C52B** | **0091** |
| N219LC | C550 | 550-1020 |
| **N219LC** | **C680** | **0249** |
| N219MF | JSTR | 5219 |
| **N219MS** | **C550** | **193** |
| **N219RB** | **LJ25** | **255** |
| N219SC | C550 | 374 |
| N219SJ | BE40 | RK-219 |
| N219ST | HS25 | 256009 |
| **N219TF** | **HS25** | **HB-41** |
| N219TS | HS25 | 257026 |
| **N219TT** | **SBRL** | **380-24** |
| N220AB | C550 | 630 |
| **N220AB** | **F2TH** | **170** |
| N220AJ | ASTR | 077 |
| (N220AR) | LJ25 | 097 |
| N220BJ | BE40 | RK-220 |
| **N220BP** | **CS55** | **0034** |
| **N220BW** | **EA50** | **000179** |
| N220CA | CS55 | 0085 |
| **N220CA** | **FA20** | **220** |
| N220CC | C500 | 118 |
| N220CC | C550 | 040 |
| N220CC | C550 | 457 |
| N220CC | C650 | 0140 |
| N220CJ | C525 | 0220 |
| N220CM | C560 | 0048 |
| **N220CM** | **C650** | **0160** |
| N220CM | FA20 | 11 |
| **N220DF** | **F2TH** | **69** |
| **N220DH** | **WW24** | **440** |
| **N220DK** | **C510** | **0150** |
| N220EJ | F2TH | 105 |
| N220EJ | F2TH | 69 |
| (N220ES) | JSTR | 5204 |
| (N220FJ) | FA10 | 155 |
| N220FJ | FA20 | 313 |
| N220FJ | FA20 | 507 |
| N220FL | GLF2 | 50 |
| N220FL | HS25 | 257117 |
| N220FX | LJ60 | 108 |
| N220GA | ASTR | 220 |
| N220GA | GALX | 120 |
| N220GA | GLF2 | 184 |
| (N220GA) | GLF2 | 234 |
| N220GA | GLF4 | 1042 |
| N220GH | LJ35 | 220 |
| **N220GS** | **LJ35** | **220** |
| **N220HM** | **C500** | **583** |
| N220HS | LJ25 | 220 |
| N220JC | LJ55 | 050 |
| N220JD | C52A | 0120 |
| (N220JM) | C525 | 0493 |
| (N220JM) | F2TH | 46 |
| N220JM | F2TH | 47 |
| (N220JM) | F2TH | 69 |
| N220JM | F2TH | 85 |
| N220JN | F2TH | 69 |
| N220JP | FA50 | 22 |
| N220JR | GLF2 | 50 |
| N220JT | C560 | 0272 |
| N220KP | WW24 | 117 |
| **N220KS** | **FA10** | **71** |
| N220LA | C550 | 144 |
| **N220LA** | **FA20** | **296/507** |
| N220LC | C52B | 0251 |
| N220LC | CL60 | 1071 |
| (N220LC) | CL61 | 5038 |
| **N220LE** | **C550** | **722** |
| **N220LH** | **GLF4** | **1054** |
| N220LJ | LJ31 | 220 |
| N220M | FA10 | 34 |
| (N220MR) | F2TH | 69 |
| N220MT | C500 | 135 |
| N220MT | CRVT | 40 |
| N220N | M220 | 1 |
| N220NJ | LJ25 | 220 |
| **N220NJ** | **LJ35** | **021** |
| **N220PA** | **FA10** | **113** |
| N220PK | HS25 | 258808 |
| N220PM | LJ24 | 158 |
| (N220PX) | LJ60 | 108 |
| N220RT | FA20 | 142 |
| N220S | C500 | 192 |
| **N220SC** | **C560** | **0326** |
| N220SC | FA10 | 158 |
| N220ST | WW24 | 46 |
| N220T | HS25 | 25201 |
| N220TG | LJ25 | 370 |
| N220TS | HS25 | 256021 |
| N220TV | C650 | 0060 |
| N220TW | C650 | 0060 |
| N220TW | CL61 | 5067 |
| N220VE | LJ55 | 108 |
| N220W | C500 | 025 |
| N220WC | C560 | 0321 |
| **N220WE** | **FA20** | **349** |
| N221AC | C500 | 392 |
| N221AL | ASTR | 154 |
| (N221AL) | C750 | 0217 |
| N221AM | C500 | 109 |
| N221AM | C56X | 6044 |
| N221AP | LJ25 | 290 |
| N221B | FA20 | 12 |
| N221BJ | BE40 | RK-221 |
| **N221BR** | **FA20** | **74** |
| N221BS | GALX | 110 |
| (N221BW) | C550 | 271 |
| N221CC | C500 | 118 |
| N221CC | C500 | 221 |
| N221CE | C560 | 0557 |
| N221CF | WW24 | 93 |
| **N221CM** | **GLF3** | **343** |
| N221CR | JSTR | 5214 |
| **N221DA** | **C500** | **201** |
| **N221DG** | **GLF5** | **5020** |
| N221DT | ASTR | 016 |
| N221EB | C500 | 643 |
| N221EJ | F2TH | 85 |
| N221EL | LJ25 | 290 |
| N221EX | F2EX | 21 |
| N221EX | F9EX | 221 |
| N221FJ | FA10 | 156 |
| N221FJ | FA20 | 505 |
| N221FX | LJ60 | 111 |
| N221GA | C550 | 135 |
| N221GA | C550 | 441 |
| N221GA | GALX | 125 |
| N221GA | GLF4 | 1521 |
| N221GA | GLF5 | 5221 |
| **N221H** | **FA20** | **461** |
| N221HB | HS25 | 258052 |
| (N221JB) | C500 | 392 |
| (N221JS) | C550 | 317 |
| N221LC | C52B | 0103 |
| (N221LC) | C550 | 383 |
| N221LC | C56X | 5077 |
| **N221LC** | **C680** | **0228** |
| N221LC | CL61 | 5066 |
| N221LV | LJ25 | 235 |
| N221MC | LJ35 | 407 |
| N221MJ | WW24 | 160 |
| N221MJ | WW24 | 204 |
| **N221PA** | **ASTR** | **016** |
| **N221PB** | **HS25** | **258623** |
| N221PF | SBRL | 306-15 |
| N221PH | SBRL | 282-55 |
| N221PH | SBRL | 306-15 |
| N221PH | SBRL | 380-49 |
| (N221PX) | SBRL | 282-55 |
| **N221QS** | **F2EX** | **54** |
| N221RE | HS25 | 258119 |
| N221RJ | WW24 | 160 |
| **N221SG** | **LJ35** | **182** |
| N221TC | LJ25 | 136 |
| **N221TR** | **LJ35** | **221** |
| **N221TW** | **FA20** | **221** |
| N221UE | LJ35 | 042 |
| N221VP | C560 | 0585 |
| **N221WR** | **GLF3** | **381** |
| N221Z | LJ35 | 059 |
| N222 | GLF4 | 1142 |
| N222AD | GLF4 | 1057 |
| N222AG | C550 | 163 |
| N222AK | LJ25 | 127 |
| (N222AP) | GLF3 | 391 |
| N222AP | LJ24 | 211 |
| N222AP | LJ25 | 225 |
| N222AW | LJ36 | 012 |
| **N222B** | **LJ25** | **047** |
| N222BE | LJ35 | 180 |
| **N222BE** | **LJ35** | **489** |
| N222BG | LJ35 | 448 |
| N222BK | LJ35 | 180 |
| N222BN | F2TH | 135 |
| N222BN | LJ24 | 296 |
| **N222BR** | **LJ60** | **310** |
| N222BW | GLF3 | 440 |
| N222CC | C500 | 222 |
| N222CD | C650 | 0222 |
| N222CX | C750 | 0222 |
| N222D | C550 | 027 |
| N222DE | C550 | 027 |
| N222FA | C550 | 725 |
| N222FJ | FA10 | 157 |
| N222FJ | FA20 | 509 |
| N222FJ | WVII | 001 |
| N222FX | LJ60 | 008 |
| N222G | HS25 | 25064 |
| N222GH | LJ24 | 026 |
| N222GL | WW24 | 47 |
| N222GT | C650 | 0093 |
| **N222GY** | **GLF4** | **1142** |
| N222HL | HS25 | 257088 |
| N222HM | WW24 | 47 |
| N222HV | LJ60 | 008 |
| **N222JE** | **BE40** | **RK-4** |
| N222KC | GLF3 | 366 |
| N222KC | WW24 | 434 |
| N222KN | JSTR | 5118 |
| N222KW | C500 | 080 |
| N222LB | C500 | 212 |
| N222LB | C550 | 093 |
| N222LH | CL60 | 1052 |
| N222LH | WW24 | 209 |
| **N222LM** | **CL60** | **1052** |
| **N222LR** | **ASTR** | **238** |
| N222LW | LJ25 | 299 |
| **N222LX** | **GLF5** | **633** |
| **N222MC** | **CL64** | **5329** |
| (N222MC) | FA50 | 141 |
| N222MC | FA50 | 179 |
| (N222MC) | GLF4 | 1382 |
| N222MC | LJ25 | 076 |
| N222MC | LJ55 | 061 |
| N222MC | LJ55 | 108 |
| N222MF | JSTR | 5229 |
| N222MJ | C550 | 154 |
| N222MQ | LJ25 | 076 |
| N222MS | C500 | 018 |
| **N222MS** | **HS25** | **258132** |
| **N222MU** | **FA10** | **164** |
| **N222MW** | **LJ45** | **110** |
| N222MW | WW24 | 255 |
| (N222MZ) | CL64 | 5329 |
| N222NB | GLF2 | 245/30 |
| **N222NB** | **GLF4** | **4059** |
| **N222NF** | **C52A** | **0074** |
| **N222NG** | **HS25** | **25016** |
| N222NP | GLF2 | 245/30 |
| N222PV | GLF2 | 234 |
| N222Q | MU30 | A021SA |
| N222QA | JSTR | 5116 |
| **N222QS** | **F2TH** | **122** |
| (N222R) | JSTR | 5016 |
| N222RB | HS25 | 25224 |
| N222RB | HS25 | 257004 |
| N222RB | LJ24 | 136 |
| N222RG | HS25 | 25224 |
| N222SG | C550 | 122 |
| N222SL | C500 | 096 |
| N222SL | LJ35 | 162 |
| N222SR | WW24 | 194 |
| N222TG | C550 | 098 |
| **N222TW** | **LJ24** | **161** |
| N222VV | C500 | 310 |
| N222VV | C550 | 151 |
| **N222WA** | **C500** | **360** |
| N222WL | C550 | 241 |
| N222Y | JSTR | 5006/40 |
| N223AM | C56X | 5018 |
| (N223AM) | GALX | 011 |
| N223AS | C500 | 212 |
| N223B | FA20 | 102 |
| **N223BG** | **FA20** | **250** |
| (N223BX) | LJ60 | 124 |
| N223CC | C500 | 223 |
| N223CV | C560 | 0223 |
| N223DD | FA50 | 128 |
| (N223DK) | BE40 | RK-142 |
| N223EX | F2EX | 23 |
| **N223EX** | **F9EX** | **223** |
| **N223F** | **FA50** | **328** |
| N223F | PRM1 | RB-22 |
| **N223FA** | **HS25** | **258559** |
| N223FJ | FA10 | 158 |
| N223FJ | FA20 | 510 |
| N223FX | LJ60 | 124 |
| N223G | HS25 | 25170 |
| N223GA | ASTR | 141 |
| N223GA | GALX | 123 |
| N223GC | C500 | 570 |
| **N223HD** | **FA50** | **283** |
| N223HS | FA10 | 160 |
| N223J | C550 | 410 |
| **N223JV** | **C560** | **0131** |
| N223LB | C500 | 212 |
| **N223LB** | **SBRL** | **465-23** |
| N223LC | C500 | 425 |
| N223LP | SBRL | 380-5 |
| N223MC | C500 | 212 |
| N223MD | GLF5 | 665 |
| N223P | C500 | 223 |
| N223PA | WW24 | 171 |
| **N223QS** | **F2EX** | **86** |
| (N223RE) | C500 | 486 |
| **N223RR** | **HS25** | **25282** |
| N223S | C500 | 233 |
| N223S | MU30 | A033SA |
| (N223SS) | GLF5 | 572 |
| N223SV | C680 | 0223 |
| N223TG | LJ25 | 370 |
| **N223TW** | **FA20** | **123** |
| N223VP | C560 | 0223 |
| N223WA | WW24 | 423 |
| N223WW | WW24 | 153 |
| N223XP | BE40 | RK-423 |
| **N224BA** | **C525** | **0669** |
| N224BP | FA10 | 159 |
| (N224CC) | C500 | 224 |
| N224CC | C550 | 224 |
| N224CC | FA10 | 36 |
| N224CD | C650 | 0224 |
| **N224CJ** | **C525** | **0224** |
| N224CV | C560 | 0224 |
| N224DJ | LJ55 | 024 |
| **N224EA** | **HS25** | **257088** |
| N224EX | F2EX | 24 |
| N224F | CL61 | 3064 |
| **N224F** | **CL61** | **5163** |
| **N224FD** | **BE40** | **RK-324** |
| N224FJ | FA10 | 159 |
| N224FJ | FA20 | 512 |
| N224FL | BE40 | RK-324 |
| N224FX | LJ60 | 126 |
| **N224GP** | **C500** | **499** |

| Registration | Type | C/n |
|---|---|---|
| N224GP | WW24 | 372 |
| N224GX | GLEX | 9224 |
| **N224HD** | **FA50** | **336** |
| (N224HF) | CL61 | 3064 |
| N224JB | LJ24 | 321 |
| **N224KC** | **CS55** | **0104** |
| N224KT | LJ24 | 161 |
| N224LJ | LJ31 | 224 |
| **N224MC** | **BE40** | **RK-165** |
| **N224MD** | **E50P** | **50000057** |
| N224N | CL61 | 3064 |
| N224N | CL61 | 5108 |
| **N224N** | **CL64** | **5661** |
| N224NS | CL64 | 5661 |
| **N224PA** | **WW24** | **411** |
| **N224QS** | **F2TH** | **124** |
| N224RP | C500 | 632 |
| N224RP | FA10 | 159 |
| N224SC | LJ24 | 100 |
| (N224TS) | GLF2 | 24 |
| N224U | CL61 | 3064 |
| N224WC | C560 | 0466 |
| **N224WD** | **C52A** | **0122** |
| **N224WE** | **FA20** | **272** |
| **N224ZQ** | **EA50** | **000162** |
| N225AC | LJ25 | 139 |
| N225AC | LJ25 | 280 |
| N225AD | C550 | 118 |
| N225AL | ASTR | 075 |
| **N225AR** | **CL30** | **20166** |
| N225AR | CL64 | 5500 |
| (N225AR) | CL65 | 5702 |
| N225BC | C500 | 274 |
| **N225BJ** | **HS25** | **257044** |
| (N225BK) | GLF4 | 1467 |
| (N225BX) | LJ60 | 127 |
| **N225CC** | **FA10** | **225** |
| N225CC | GLF2 | 8 |
| N225CC | LJ25 | 107 |
| N225CC | LJ35 | 192 |
| **N225CF** | **LJ35** | **225** |
| N225CV | C560 | 0225 |
| (N225CV) | C650 | 0225 |
| N225CX | GLF4 | 1467 |
| **N225CX** | **GLF4** | **4171** |
| N225DC | C500 | 148 |
| **N225DC** | **GLF4** | **1253** |
| N225DS | LJ25 | 025 |
| (N225EA) | LJ25 | 057 |
| **N225EE** | **GLF5** | **563** |
| N225EL | C52A | 0065 |
| N225EX | F2EX | 25 |
| N225F | LJ35 | 269 |
| N225FJ | FA10 | 160 |
| N225FJ | FA20 | 513 |
| N225FM | C550 | 118 |
| N225FX | LJ60 | 127 |
| N225GV | GLF5 | 672 |
| **N225HD** | **FA50** | **313** |
| N225HR | HS25 | 256017 |
| N225HW | LJ25 | 231 |
| N225J | C550 | 316 |
| N225JL | LJ25 | 182 |
| N225K | HS25 | 25026 |
| **N225KA** | **LJ25** | **004** |
| N225KJ | HS25 | 25026 |
| N225KS | F900 | 105 |
| **N225LC** | **LJ25** | **127** |
| **N225LJ** | **LJ24** | **011** |
| N225LJ | LJ40 | 45-2025 |
| N225LL | HS25 | 25026 |
| N225LS | SBRL | 282-51 |
| N225LY | CL64 | 5311 |
| N225MC | LJ35 | 225 |
| **N225MD** | **LJ55** | **085** |
| **N225MS** | **GLF2** | **8** |
| N225MS | LJ28 | 28-004 |
| N225N | CL61 | 5036 |
| N225N | CL61 | 5100 |
| **N225N** | **CL64** | **5652** |
| N225N | WW24 | 319 |
| **N225PB** | **HS25** | **258558** |
| N225QC | LJ35 | 192 |
| N225RD | C500 | 194 |
| **N225SB** | **BE40** | **RK-510** |
| N225SE | GLF2 | 55 |
| N225SF | GLF2 | 55 |
| N225SF | GLF3 | 423 |
| N225TJ | LJ25 | 222 |
| N225TR | GLF2 | 225 |
| (N225WT) | C500 | 674 |
| **N225WT** | **C550** | **550-0821** |
| N225WW | C52A | 0065 |
| N226AL | GLF4 | 1057 |
| **N226B** | **C525** | **0200** |
| **N226BR** | **EA50** | **000226** |
| N226CC | LJ36 | 007 |
| **N226CK** | **FA20** | **226** |
| **N226CP** | **E50P** | **50000071** |
| **N226CV** | **C560** | **0226** |
| N226CW | C525 | 0326 |
| N226CX | C750 | 0226 |
| N226CX | GLF4 | 1467 |
| **N226EC** | **CL61** | **5090** |
| N226EM | C650 | 0187 |
| N226EW | F2EX | 55 |
| N226EX | F2EX | 26 |
| N226FJ | FA10 | 162 |
| N226FJ | FA50 | 227 |
| N226FX | LJ60 | 128 |
| N226G | CL61 | 3012 |
| N226G | FA20 | 244 |
| N226G | GLF3 | 434 |
| N226G | GLF4 | 1122 |
| N226G | HS25 | 25170 |
| N226GA | GLF2 | 106 |
| N226GC | GLF3 | 434 |
| N226GL | CL61 | 3012 |
| N226HD | GLEX | 9022 |
| **N226JT** | **C56X** | **5652** |
| N226JV | C560 | 0132 |
| N226L | C550 | 093 |
| N226LJ | LJ31 | 226 |
| **N226MP** | **GLF4** | **1300** |
| N226N | C550 | 093 |
| N226N | C560 | 0248 |
| **N226PC** | **C550** | **550-0835** |
| **N226QS** | **F2TH** | **126** |
| N226R | FA20 | 226 |
| **N226RM** | **GLF2** | **145** |
| **N226RS** | **GLF4** | **1479** |
| N226SF | LJ60 | 092 |
| (N226U) | C560 | 0248 |
| N226VP | C500 | 635 |
| N226W | C650 | 7111 |
| N226WW | WW24 | 226 |
| N227A | LJ55 | 027 |
| N227AN | ASTR | 060 |
| N227BA | C650 | 0130 |
| **N227BA** | **GLF2** | **27** |
| N227BX | LJ60 | 077 |
| (N227CC) | C500 | 227 |
| N227CC | CL60 | 1004 |
| N227CC | FA20 | 59 |
| **N227CK** | **FA20** | **227** |
| **N227CP** | **CL61** | **5097** |
| (N227CV) | C560 | 0227 |
| (N227CV) | C650 | 0227 |
| **N227DH** | **C680** | **0086** |
| N227DH | HS25 | 25027 |
| N227DR | C550 | 254 |
| N227EW | LJ25 | 227 |
| **N227FH** | **PRM1** | **RB-102** |
| N227FJ | FA10 | 163 |
| (N227FJ) | FA50 | 227 |
| N227FS | C52A | 0238 |
| N227FX | LJ60 | 077 |
| N227G | CL60 | 1059 |
| **N227G** | **EA50** | **000124** |
| N227G | GLF2 | 76 |
| N227G | GLF4 | 1045 |
| N227GA | GLF2 | 76 |
| N227GC | FA20 | 59 |
| N227GH | GLF4 | 1045 |
| N227GL | CL60 | 1059 |
| N227GL | GLF2 | 76 |
| N227GM | C500 | 227 |
| N227GX | GLF2 | 76 |
| N227H | C500 | 011 |
| **N227HD** | **F9EX** | **157** |
| N227HF | HS25 | 25118 |
| N227HP | C500 | 227 |
| **N227JP** | **C52B** | **0265** |
| N227K | JSTR | 5006/40 |
| **N227KT** | **LJ31** | **208** |
| N227LA | C650 | 0130 |
| (N227LA) | FA20 | 330 |
| **N227LA** | **GLF2** | **193** |
| N227LA | HS25 | 25235 |
| **N227LS** | **EA50** | **000195** |
| N227LS | SBRL | 282-51 |
| **N227LT** | **HS25** | **25232** |
| **N227MC** | **C56X** | **5064** |
| (N227MJ) | LJ35 | 227 |
| **N227MK** | **C500** | **070** |
| **N227MM** | **HS25** | **257081** |
| N227MS | HS25 | 25227 |
| N227N | ASTR | 053 |
| N227N | LJ60 | 049 |
| N227NL | ASTR | 053 |
| N227PC | C550 | 125 |
| N227PE | CL61 | 3002 |
| **N227QS** | **F2TH** | **127** |
| N227R | FA20 | 227 |
| N227RE | CL61 | 5177 |
| N227RH | CL61 | 5177 |
| **N227RH** | **GLF4** | **4108** |
| N227RW | LJ25 | 201 |
| N227S | SBRL | 282-16 |
| **N227SV** | **GLF4** | **1172** |
| N227SW | SBRL | 282-16 |
| N227TA | FA20 | 496 |
| (N227TJ) | GLF2 | 27 |
| N227TS | GLF2 | 27 |
| (N227UH) | EA50 | 000227 |
| N227VG | C500 | 246 |
| N227WE | FA20 | 344/534 |
| **N227WL** | **FA20** | **344/534** |
| N227WS | C560 | 0676 |
| N228AJ | C500 | 378 |
| N228AK | C500 | 378 |
| N228AK | C550 | 196 |
| N228BD | C750 | 0228 |
| (N228CC) | C500 | 228 |
| N228CC | C550 | 148 |
| N228CK | FA20 | 128/436 |
| N228CM | C650 | 0228 |
| N228CV | C560 | 0228 |
| **N228DB** | **C750** | **0228** |
| N228EA | C500 | 631 |
| N228EJ | F2TH | 128 |
| N228ES | C500 | 378 |
| N228EX | F9EX | 228 |
| N228FJ | FA10 | 164 |
| **N228FJ** | **FA50** | **228** |
| N228FJ | FA50 | 231 |
| N228FS | C500 | 378 |
| N228FS | C52A | 0238 |
| N228FX | LJ60 | 132 |
| (N228G) | C550 | 583 |
| N228G | GLF3 | 424 |
| N228G | HS25 | 25021 |
| N228G | HS25 | 25170 |
| N228G | HS25 | 258203 |
| N228GC | HS25 | 25284 |
| N228GL | HS25 | 25021 |
| **N228H** | **GLEX** | **9040** |
| **N228KT** | **CL30** | **20142** |
| N228L | WW24 | 331 |
| N228LS | SBRL | 465-43 |
| **N228MD** | **HS25** | **256037** |
| **N228MH** | **C550** | **196** |
| **N228N** | **CL30** | **20060** |
| N228N | LJ60 | 031 |
| N228N | WW24 | 331 |
| **N228PC** | **C560** | **0310** |
| N228PG | C560 | 0310 |
| N228PK | CL61 | 3046 |
| **N228PK** | **HS25** | **258808** |
| N228PK | LJ55 | 006 |
| **N228RE** | **GLF4** | **1438** |
| **N228RH** | **C680** | **0128** |
| N228S | C500 | 233 |
| N228SJ | FA10 | 128 |
| N228SW | LJ25 | 228 |
| **N228TM** | **HS25** | **258458** |
| **N228Y** | **C56X** | **5342** |
| N228Y | JSTR | 5066/46 |
| N229AP | LJ25 | 295 |
| **N229BP** | **CL30** | **20223** |
| N229BP | LJ60 | 320 |
| **N229BW** | **EA50** | **000004** |
| **N229CE** | **C750** | **0229** |
| N229CJ | C525 | 0129 |
| **N229CK** | **FA20** | **229** |
| **N229CN** | **C52B** | **0223** |
| **N229D** | **WW24** | **427** |
| **N229DK** | **F9EX** | **229** |
| **N229EA** | **EA50** | **000229** |
| N229FJ | FA10 | 165 |
| N229FX | LJ60 | 137 |
| N229GA | GALX | 129 |
| N229GC | CL60 | 1043 |
| N229HD | F900 | 108 |
| (N229J) | C650 | 0089 |
| N229JB | FA10 | 71 |
| **N229JR** | **C510** | **0332** |
| N229KD | LJ31 | 139 |
| N229LC | C680 | 0135 |
| **N229LJ** | **LJ31** | **229** |
| N229LS | SBRL | 306-38 |
| **N229MC** | **C550** | **255** |
| (N229N) | C560 | 0248 |
| N229N | WW24 | 427 |
| N229P | HS25 | 25115 |
| **N229QS** | **F2TH** | **129** |
| N229R | FA20 | 229 |
| N229RB | PRM1 | RB-229 |
| **N229RP** | **LJ60** | **320** |
| N229RY | HS25 | 258229 |
| N229U | HS25 | 259009 |
| N229VP | C560 | 0219 |
| N229WJ | LJ25 | 229 |
| N229X | LJ35 | 129 |
| N230A | SBRL | 306-38 |
| N230AJ | ASTR | 036 |
| N230BF | C510 | 0122 |
| **N230BF** | **C510** | **0230** |
| **N230BT** | **FA50** | **62** |
| (N230BX) | LJ60 | 138 |
| N230CC | C500 | 230 |
| N230DP | HS25 | 257060 |
| N230E | GLF2 | 34 |
| N230FJ | F2TH | 230 |
| N230FJ | FA10 | 161 |
| N230FX | LJ60 | 138 |
| N230H | HS25 | 25064 |
| N230JK | WW24 | 279 |
| N230JS | C500 | 107 |
| N230JS | C550 | 550-1119 |
| N230JS | WW24 | 301 |
| N230LC | C680 | 0141 |
| **N230LC** | **CL64** | **5489** |
| **N230LL** | **C525** | **0169** |
| **N230QS** | **F2EX** | **59** |
| N230R | HS25 | 257202 |
| N230R | LJ24 | 188 |
| N230R | LJ35 | 130 |
| N230RA | FA20 | 230 |
| N230RC | WW24 | 105 |
| N230RS | FA10 | 24 |
| N230S | FA50 | 70 |
| N230TL | WW24 | 279 |
| N230TS | HS25 | 25134 |
| N231A | SBRL | 282-61 |
| N231A | SBRL | 306-72 |
| N231CA | SBRL | 306-72 |
| N231FJ | F9EX | 231 |
| **N231JH** | **FA10** | **176** |
| (N231LC) | C500 | 493 |
| N231R | LJ24 | 134 |
| N231R | LJ35 | 128 |
| **N231WC** | **C560** | **0331** |
| (N231WJ) | GLF3 | 331 |
| N231XL | C56X | 5231 |
| (N232AV) | HS25 | HB-10 |
| N232BC | C550 | 550-0913 |
| N232BJ | BE40 | RK-34 |
| N232CC | C550 | 496 |
| N232CC | LJ35 | 367 |
| **N232CE** | **C650** | **0067** |
| N232CF | C650 | 0067 |
| **N232CF** | **C750** | **0161** |
| **N232CL** | **F900** | **9** |
| **N232CW** | **C550** | **032** |
| N232CX | C750 | 0232 |
| **N232DM** | **C550** | **087** |
| N232F | FA20 | 502 |
| **N232F** | **PRM1** | **RB-22** |
| N232FJ | FA10 | 166 |
| N232FJ | FA50 | 233 |
| N232FX | LJ35 | 620 |

| | | |
|---|---|---|
| N232HC | GLF3 | 373 |
| **N232JR** | **C550** | **550-0855** |
| N232JS | C550 | 727 |
| **N232K** | **GLF4** | **1232** |
| N232LJ | LJ60 | 232 |
| N232MD | LJ25 | 052 |
| N232PR | FA50 | 179 |
| N232PR | LJ35 | 394 |
| N232QS | CS55 | 0032 |
| **N232QS** | **F2EX** | **115** |
| N232R | LJ24 | 005 |
| N232R | LJ24 | 131 |
| N232R | LJ35 | 102 |
| N232RA | FA20 | 232 |
| N232S | ASTR | 032 |
| N232T | SBRL | 282-83 |
| N232TN | HS25 | 257043 |
| **N232TW** | **FA20** | **32** |
| N232WC | CS55 | 0032 |
| N233BC | FA50 | 241 |
| (N233BJ) | BE40 | RJ-33 |
| N233BX | LJ31 | 233 |
| **N233CA** | **LJ25** | **133** |
| N233CC | C500 | 233 |
| **N233CC** | **LJ35** | **031** |
| N233CJ | C525 | 0233 |
| **N233DB** | **C500** | **158** |
| N233DW | C550 | 550-0931 |
| N233FJ | FA10 | 167 |
| (N233FJ) | FA50 | 233 |
| N233FJ | FA50 | 234 |
| N233FJ | GLEX | 9233 |
| N233FX | LJ60 | 139 |
| N233FX | LJ60 | 154 |
| N233GA | GLF4 | 1144 |
| **N233JJ** | **C500** | **233** |
| **N233KC** | **F900** | **48** |
| N233KC | HS25 | 258052 |
| (N233ME) | C500 | 312 |
| **N233MM** | **C52B** | **0133** |
| **N233MT** | **EA50** | **000093** |
| **N233MW** | **BE40** | **RK-233** |
| **N233QS** | **F2EX** | **91** |
| N233R | LJ24 | 017 |
| N233R | LJ24 | 132 |
| N233R | LJ35 | 048 |
| N233RS | GLF2 | 233 |
| N233SG | CL61 | 5104 |
| N233ST | C550 | 261 |
| **N233TW** | **LJ24** | **221** |
| N233U | FA50 | 14 |
| N233VM | C500 | 233 |
| N233VW | LJ24 | 011 |
| N233WC | PRM1 | RB-233 |
| **N233XL** | **C56X** | **5233** |
| **N234AQ** | **C560** | **0234** |
| **N234AT** | **C500** | **240** |
| N234CA | FA20 | 17 |
| N234CJ | C525 | 0134 |
| **N234CJ** | **C52A** | **0454** |
| (N234CJ) | C52A | 0463 |
| N234CM | LJ24 | 214 |
| N234DB | GLF2 | 100 |
| N234DB | GLF4 | 1000 |
| N234DB | GLF4 | 1457 |
| **N234DB** | **GLF5** | **5106** |
| **N234DC** | **SBRL** | **306-103** |
| **N234DK** | **BE40** | **RK-182** |
| N234DN | GLF4 | 1457 |
| **N234DP** | **CL30** | **20040** |
| N234DT | LJ35 | 407 |
| **N234EA** | **EA50** | **000156** |
| (N234EJ) | LJ25 | 234 |
| **N234FJ** | **F2TH** | **34** |
| N234FJ | FA10 | 168 |
| N234FJ | FA50 | 236 |
| N234FX | LJ60 | 141 |
| N234FX | LJ60 | 151 |
| **N234G** | **WW24** | **28** |
| **N234GF** | **HS25** | **258096** |
| N234GX | GLEX | 9234 |
| (N234HM) | C650 | 0044 |
| N234JW | C500 | 408 |
| N234KK | LJ25 | 234 |
| (N234LC) | LJ55 | 034 |
| N234MR | LJ24 | 130 |
| N234MW | CL60 | 1073 |
| N234ND | LJ25 | 043 |
| N234Q | LJ24 | 181 |
| N234QS | F2EX | 158 |
| (N234RA) | C550 | 561 |
| N234RB | LJ25 | 105 |
| N234RC | WW24 | 162 |
| N234RG | CL60 | 1073 |
| N234SV | LJ25 | 226 |
| "N234TS" | JSTR | 5234 |
| N234U | FA10 | 29 |
| N234U | SBRL | 306-48 |
| N234UM | C500 | 105 |
| N234WR | LJ24 | 172 |
| N234WS | C525 | 0097 |
| N234YP | C650 | 0074 |
| N235AC | LJ35 | 676 |
| N235AF | CL30 | 20190 |
| N235AV | HS25 | 25235 |
| (N235BX) | LJ60 | 153 |
| N235CA | FA20 | 139 |
| N235CC | C500 | 235 |
| N235CG | GLF4 | 4030 |
| N235CG | LJ60 | 230 |
| N235CM | C650 | 0235 |
| N235DB | C550 | 374 |
| N235DH | LJ35 | 134 |
| N235DX | GLF4 | 1493 |
| **N235DX** | **GLF5** | **5085** |
| **N235EA** | **LJ35** | **061** |
| **N235FJ** | **F9EX** | **235** |
| N235FJ | FA10 | 169 |
| N235FX | LJ60 | 143 |
| N235FX | LJ60 | 153 |
| N235HR | LJ35 | 082 |
| **N235HR** | **LJ55** | **094** |
| (N235HR) | LJ60 | 208 |
| N235JL | LJ35 | 049 |
| **N235JS** | **LJ35** | **199** |
| N235JW | LJ25 | 096 |
| N235JW | LJ35 | 032 |
| N235KC | HS25 | 25096 |
| N235KK | C550 | 436 |
| N235KK | C650 | 0175 |
| **N235KK** | **GLF4** | **1458** |
| N235KS | C52A | 0235 |
| N235LC | GALX | 142 |
| **N235LP** | **GLF4** | **1336** |
| **N235MC** | **LJ35** | **334** |
| N235R | LJ24 | 032 |
| N235SC | LJ35 | 275 |
| N235SS | C510 | 0070 |
| **N235SV** | **C650** | **0235** |
| N235TS | C550 | 365 |
| N235U | FA20 | 364 |
| N235U | GLF3 | 305 |
| N235UJ | LJ35 | 477 |
| N235Z | LJ24 | 146 |
| N236BN | HS25 | 257051 |
| N236CA | LJ25 | 161 |
| N236CC | C500 | 236 |
| N236DJ | FA10 | 138 |
| N236FJ | FA10 | 170 |
| N236FX | LJ60 | 157 |
| (N236HR) | LJ55 | 094 |
| N236HR | LJ55 | 113 |
| N236JP | WW24 | 116 |
| N236JW | LJ55 | 036 |
| **N236LB** | **C56X** | **5023** |
| **N236LC** | **GALX** | **154** |
| N236LD | C56X | 5023 |
| N236LD | C56X | 5236 |
| **N236MJ** | **GLF4** | **1177** |
| **N236N** | **CL61** | **5108** |
| (N236PJ) | LJ55 | 023 |
| **N236QS** | **F2TH** | **136** |
| N236R | LJ55 | 025 |
| N236TS | C500 | 236 |
| N236TS | LJ24 | 236 |
| **N236TW** | **FA20** | **236** |
| N236W | WW24 | 236 |
| N236WJ | LJ24 | 236 |
| N236Y | SBRL | 282-31 |
| **N237AF** | **LJ35** | **262** |
| **N237BG** | **C560** | **0771** |
| N237CC | MU30 | A027SA |
| N237CJ | C525 | 0237 |
| N237CW | C550 | 037 |
| N237DG | C525 | 0141 |
| N237DM | LJ45 | 058 |
| **N237DX** | **HS25** | **257148** |
| N237FJ | FA10 | 171 |
| N237FJ | FA50 | 237 |
| N237FX | LJ60 | 158 |
| (N237G) | CL64 | 5400 |
| N237GA | CL61 | 5019 |
| N237GA | CL64 | 5400 |
| **N237GA** | **GLF4** | **4055** |
| N237GA | LJ35 | 262 |
| N237JF | WW24 | 117 |
| (N237JM) | PRM1 | RB-169 |
| (N237JP) | C500 | 330 |
| N237LJ | LJ40 | 45-2037 |
| (N237LM) | GLF2 | 101 |
| N237PT | FA20 | 432 |
| N237R | LJ55 | 066 |
| N237RA | HS25 | 258237 |
| N237RF | GLF2 | 237/43 |
| N237RG | HS25 | 257072 |
| N237SC | C500 | 640 |
| N237TJ | LJ35 | 237 |
| **N237TW** | **LJ24** | **237** |
| **N237VP** | **C560** | **0237** |
| **N237WC** | **C550** | **145** |
| **N237WR** | **HS25** | **257072** |
| N238AJ | HS25 | 258155 |
| **N238BG** | **C500** | **644** |
| N238BX | LJ60 | 163 |
| N238CA | LJ25 | 040 |
| N238CV | C560 | 0238 |
| N238CX | C750 | 0238 |
| **N238DB** | **WW24** | **215** |
| N238DL | FA50 | 238 |
| N238FJ | FA10 | 172 |
| N238FJ | FA50 | 238 |
| N238FX | LJ60 | 163 |
| N238JA | LJ35 | 134 |
| N238JC | C560 | 0192 |
| N238JS | C500 | 649 |
| N238MP | LJ25 | 238 |
| **N238PR** | **LJ35** | **394** |
| N238R | LJ24 | 132 |
| N238R | LJ55 | 085 |
| N238RC | LJ35 | 061 |
| **N238RM** | **C52A** | **0453** |
| **N238SM** | **C56X** | **5238** |
| **N238SW** | **C52B** | **0141** |
| N238SW | CL64 | 5423 |
| N238U | FA50 | 86 |
| N238U | GLF2 | 63 |
| N238U | JSTR | 5106/9 |
| N238Y | FA50 | 185 |
| **N239AX** | **F900** | **39** |
| N239BD | FA20 | 239 |
| N239CA | LJ25 | 149 |
| N239CC | C500 | 239 |
| N239CD | C550 | 242 |
| N239CD | FA20 | 239 |
| **N239CD** | **FA20** | **339** |
| N239CV | C560 | 0239 |
| N239CW | C525 | 0339 |
| N239FJ | FA10 | 173 |
| N239FJ | FA50 | 239 |
| N239FX | LJ60 | 166 |
| N239GJ | LJ35 | 239 |
| N239P | GLF2 | 63 |
| N239QS | F2TH | 193 |
| N239R | FA50 | 178 |
| N239R | HS25 | 258119 |
| N239RC | LJ60 | 046 |
| N239RF | PRM1 | RB-139 |
| **N239RT** | **HS25** | **HA-0120** |
| N239RT | PRM1 | RB-139 |
| N239WC | C56X | 5139 |
| (N239WJ) | GLF2 | 239 |
| N239XL | C56X | 5239 |
| N240AA | C500 | 202 |
| N240AA | WW24 | 82 |
| N240AC | SBRL | 282-41 |
| N240AG | LJ24 | 079 |
| N240AG | LJ25 | 197 |
| N240AK | CL60 | 1067 |
| N240AQ | LJ24 | 079 |
| N240AR | C550 | 240 |
| N240AT | FA20 | 240/478 |
| N240B | C56X | 5057 |
| N240B | HS25 | 258358 |
| **N240B** | **LJ31** | **175** |
| N240B | LJ35 | 240 |
| N240BX | LJ60 | 167 |
| N240CC | C500 | 240 |
| N240CF | SBRL | 282-132 |
| N240CJ | C52B | 0240 |
| **N240CK** | **FA20** | **24** |
| **N240CM** | **C560** | **0048** |
| N240CX | GLF2 | 101 |
| **N240CX** | **GLF4** | **1370** |
| (N240EA) | GLF2 | 240 |
| N240EX | F2EX | 40 |
| N240FJ | FA10 | 174 |
| N240FJ | FA50 | 245 |
| N240FX | LJ60 | 167 |
| **N240JR** | **SBRL** | **282-132** |
| N240JS | LJ35 | 241 |
| **N240LG** | **F9EX** | **61** |
| N240QS | F2TH | 204 |
| **N240RP** | **LJ40** | **45-2025** |
| N240RS | FA20 | 479 |
| N240S | WW24 | 309 |
| N240TJ | FA20 | 24 |
| **N240TW** | **FA20** | **40** |
| **N240V** | **HS25** | **258417** |
| N240WG | LJ40 | 45-2063 |
| N240WW | WW24 | 240 |
| **N240Z** | **HS25** | **258565** |
| N241AG | LJ25 | 075 |
| N241AG | LJ35 | 491 |
| N241AQ | LJ25 | 075 |
| **N241BF** | **C500** | **621** |
| **N241BJ** | **BE40** | **RJ-41** |
| N241BN | LJ24 | 034 |
| N241BX | LJ60 | 172 |
| **N241CA** | **LJ35** | **142** |
| N241CJ | C52A | 0341 |
| **N241CJ** | **C52B** | **0241** |
| N241CT | WW24 | 267 |
| **N241CT** | **WW24** | **355** |
| N241CV | C560 | 0241 |
| **N241DE** | **E50P** | **50000070** |
| **N241DS** | **CS55** | **0042** |
| N241EP | C525 | 0247 |
| N241FB | CL61 | 5102 |
| **N241FB** | **HS25** | **257129** |
| N241FJ | FA10 | 175 |
| N241FJ | FA50 | 242 |
| **N241FR** | **CL61** | **5102** |
| **N241FT** | **C550** | **268** |
| N241FX | LJ60 | 172 |
| N241H | SBRL | 465-5 |
| N241JA | LJ24 | 131 |
| N241JC | FA20 | 241/479 |
| **N241JS** | **HS25** | **258652** |
| N241KA | C52B | 0241 |
| (N241KP) | C560 | 0383 |
| N241LA | CS55 | 0091 |
| **N241LJ** | **LJ45** | **241** |
| N241MH | C500 | 621 |
| **N241MH** | **GLF2** | **160** |
| **N241N** | **CL61** | **5100** |
| N241RH | WW24 | 187 |
| N241RS | FA10 | 18 |
| **N241RT** | **HS25** | **257057** |
| N241RT | LJ35 | 024 |
| (N241SM) | HS25 | 258135 |
| **N241TR** | **BE40** | **RJ-45** |
| N241WS | C525 | 0241 |
| N242AC | C560 | 0177 |
| **N242AC** | **C560** | **0609** |
| (N242AF) | LJ25 | 242 |
| N242AG | LJ25 | 025 |
| N242AL | HS25 | 257199 |
| N242CT | FA20 | 316 |
| N242CV | C560 | 0242 |
| **N242DR** | **LJ35** | **242** |
| N242F | LJ24 | 045 |
| N242FJ | FA10 | 176 |
| N242FX | LJ60 | 174 |
| **N242GB** | **C525** | **0151** |
| N242GM | LJ25 | 242 |
| **N242GS** | **LJ25** | **242** |
| (N242JG) | HS25 | 258187 |
| N242LA | CS55 | 0153 |
| N242LB | FA20 | 121 |
| **N242LJ** | **C525** | **0242** |
| (N242LT) | C750 | 0082 |
| (N242MA) | FA20 | 242 |

| **N242ML** | **C525** | **0506** |
|---|---|---|
| N242MT | LJ35 | 621 |
| **N242PF** | **LJ25** | **298** |
| N242RB | LJ55 | 132 |
| (N242RJ) | FA20 | 242 |
| N242SR | BE40 | RJ-9 |
| **N242SW** | **C550** | **550-0908** |
| N242WT | C550 | 364 |
| N242WT | LJ24 | 034 |
| N242WT | LJ25 | 034 |
| N242ZX | LJ60 | 174 |
| (N243AB) | C500 | 685 |
| **N243BA** | **HS25** | **258365** |
| N243CH | C56X | 5243 |
| N243F | LJ24 | 063 |
| N243F | LJ60 | 175 |
| N243FJ | FA10 | 177 |
| **N243FJ** | **FA20** | **430** |
| N243FJ | FA50 | 243 |
| N243FJ | FA50 | 244 |
| N243FX | LJ60 | 175 |
| N243JB | HS25 | 25204 |
| N243K | FA20 | 105 |
| N243LS | C525 | 0487 |
| **N243MS** | **C510** | **0243** |
| (N243RK) | LJ24 | 306 |
| **N243SH** | **C500** | **243** |
| (N243TS) | GLF2 | 43 |
| N243TS | HS25 | 25243 |
| **N243V** | **F2TH** | **152** |
| N244 | JSTR | 5141 |
| **N244A** | **FA10** | **145** |
| N244AD | FA50 | 162 |
| **N244AL** | **CL60** | **1005** |
| N244BH | CL61 | 5027 |
| N244CA | FA20 | 321 |
| **N244CJ** | **C52A** | **708** |
| (N244CV) | C560 | 0244 |
| N244DM | GLF2 | 21 |
| N244DS | GLF4 | 1248 |
| N244DS | GLF4 | 1477 |
| **N244DS** | **GLF4** | **4050** |
| N244FC | LJ35 | 299 |
| N244FJ | FA10 | 178 |
| N244FJ | FA20 | 444 |
| N244FJ | FA50 | 232 |
| N244FX | LJ60 | 178 |
| **N244J** | **GLF4** | **1451** |
| N244JM | HS25 | 258138 |
| **N244LJ** | **LJ35** | **244** |
| N244LS | HS25 | 258569 |
| N244RD | LJ24 | 120 |
| **N244RG** | **LJ35** | **154** |
| N244SL | C500 | 650 |
| N244TJ | FA10 | 44 |
| N244TS | LJ35 | 244 |
| N244WJ | C500 | 244 |
| N244WJ | C500 | 252 |
| N244XL | C56X | 5244 |
| (N245BC) | C500 | 245 |
| (N245BC) | C500 | 296 |
| **N245BD** | **GLF5** | **5165** |
| N245BS | LJ25 | 214 |
| **N245CC** | **C550** | **245** |
| **N245CM** | **LJ45** | **403** |
| N245DK | LJ25 | 245 |
| **N245DR** | **C510** | **0105** |
| N245FJ | FA10 | 180 |
| N245FX | LJ60 | 182 |
| N245GA | GLF2 | 45 |
| N245GL | LJ24 | 228 |
| **N245J** | **C56X** | **5245** |
| N245K | LJ45 | 076 |
| **N245K** | **LJ45** | **269** |
| N245KC | LJ45 | 150 |
| (N245KK) | LJ25 | 281 |
| (N245MG) | C500 | 245 |
| **N245MS** | **LJ55** | **077** |
| **N245MU** | **C510** | **0006** |
| **N245QS** | **F2TH** | **145** |
| **N245RA** | **C52A** | **0374** |
| **N245RS** | **HS25** | **256027** |
| N245S | WW24 | 336 |
| N245SP | FA10 | 135 |
| N245TJ | GLF5 | 548 |
| N245TL | CL61 | 5001 |
| N245TT | CL61 | 5001 |
| **N245TT** | **GLF5** | **5003** |
| N245TT | GLF5 | 548 |
| N246AG | F900 | 112 |
| **N246AG** | **F9EX** | **135** |
| N246CB | C550 | 550-0849 |
| N246CM | LJ24 | 200 |
| N246CM | LJ35 | 395 |
| **N246CZ** | **C52B** | **0246** |
| N246DF | PRM1 | RB-182 |
| N246FJ | FA10 | 108 |
| N246FJ | FA50 | 246 |
| N246FX | LJ60 | 183 |
| N246GA | MU30 | A064SA |
| **N246GS** | **C525** | **0446** |
| (N246GS) | SBRL | 282-111 |
| **N246JL** | **CL60** | **1046** |
| (N246N) | FA10 | 33 |
| N246N | HS25 | 25261 |
| N246NW | C550 | 336 |
| N246NW | C560 | 0068 |
| N246RR | C500 | 167 |
| N246V | F2TH | 152 |
| **N246V** | **GLF4** | **4149** |
| N246V | HS25 | 258417 |
| N246VF | HS25 | 257126 |
| **N247AB** | **GLF2** | **208** |
| N247AD | GLF2 | 208 |
| N247BC | FA50 | 48 |
| **N247CJ** | **F900** | **122** |
| N247CJ | FA50 | 249 |
| **N247CK** | **CL60** | **1045** |
| **N247CN** | **C560** | **0173** |
| N247CP | LJ60 | 052 |
| N247CW | C525 | 0247 |
| N247DB | LJ24 | 247 |
| **N247DG** | **C560** | **0082** |
| **N247DR** | **C510** | **0177** |
| N247EM | FA50 | 48 |
| **N247EM** | **GLF4** | **1045** |
| N247FJ | FA10 | 181 |
| N247FJ | FA50 | 247 |
| N247FX | LJ60 | 187 |
| (N247GA) | CL61 | 5019 |
| N247GW | HFB3 | 1030 |
| N247KB | GLF4 | 1375 |
| (N247LG) | GLF2 | 43 |
| **N247MV** | **C52B** | **0105** |
| N247N | LJ60 | 049 |
| **N247PL** | **FA20** | **247** |
| **N247PS** | **ASTR** | **069** |
| N247PS | ASTR | 127 |
| **N247RG** | **GLF3** | **252** |
| N247SC | LJ60 | 270 |
| N247SS | CL30 | 20138 |
| N247TA | LJ35 | 112 |
| **N247VA** | **VVAN** | **001** |
| **N247WE** | **CL64** | **5369** |
| N247WF | CL64 | 5369 |
| N248AB | GLF4 | 1474 |
| N248AG | F900 | 112 |
| **N248CJ** | **C525** | **0248** |
| **N248CK** | **LJ25** | **248** |
| N248CV | C560 | 0248 |
| N248CW | C525 | 0348 |
| N248DA | LJ35 | 238 |
| N248FJ | FA10 | 182 |
| N248FJ | FA50 | 249 |
| N248FX | LJ60 | 188 |
| (N248H) | WW24 | 214 |
| N248H | WW24 | 374 |
| **N248HA** | **C550** | **422** |
| N248HM | LJ35 | 164 |
| N248J | LJ24 | 220 |
| N248JF | F2TH | 11 |
| (N248JH) | HS25 | 257029 |
| N248L | LJ60 | 248 |
| (N248LJ) | LJ25 | 248 |
| (N248PA) | BE40 | RJ-9 |
| **N248RF** | **C52A** | **0199** |
| N248SL | ASTR | 125 |
| **N248SL** | **ASTR** | **211** |
| N248TH | GLF2 | 248 |
| **N249AJ** | **CL60** | **1047** |
| N249AS | C500 | 514 |
| N249B | LJ35 | 240 |
| N249BW | HS25 | 25115 |
| N249CB | C550 | 550-1049 |
| N249DJ | LJ35 | 249 |
| N249E | WW24 | 261 |
| N249FJ | FA10 | 183 |
| N249FJ | FA50 | 248 |
| N249FX | LJ60 | 193 |
| **N249HP** | **LJ24** | **301** |
| N249LJ | LJ25 | 249 |
| N249MW | HS25 | 25115 |
| N249RA | LJ24 | 249 |
| **N249RM** | **BE40** | **RK-285** |
| N249SB | BE40 | RK-285 |
| N249SC | LJ25 | 249 |
| **N249SR** | **HS25** | **258249** |
| N250AA | C500 | 200 |
| N250AF | CS55 | 0042 |
| **N250AJ** | **BE40** | **RK-23** |
| **N250AL** | **C560** | **0605** |
| N250AL | CS55 | 0042 |
| N250AS | FA50 | 182 |
| N250BC | SBRL | 370-5 |
| **N250BL** | **C52A** | **0403** |
| N250CC | C500 | 250 |
| N250CC | CL64 | 5550 |
| N250CC | LJ25 | 052 |
| N250CF | C550 | 052 |
| N250CJ | C525 | 0250 |
| N250CM | C650 | 0133 |
| (N250CV) | C560 | 0250 |
| **N250DH** | **HS25** | **25187** |
| (N250DR) | C550 | 199 |
| **N250DV** | **GLF5** | **5066** |
| N250DV | GLF5 | 691 |
| N250EC | SBRL | 282-110 |
| N250FJ | FA10 | 184 |
| N250FJ | FA50 | 250 |
| N250FX | LJ60 | 194 |
| N250GA | GALX | 2001 |
| N250GM | C500 | 456 |
| N250GM | C525 | 0196 |
| N250GM | C550 | 620 |
| N250GM | C550 | 679 |
| **N250GP** | **MU30** | **A069SA** |
| **N250HP** | **BE40** | **RK-250** |
| N250J | GLF4 | 1144 |
| N250JE | HS25 | 258237 |
| N250JH | C560 | 0350 |
| N250JP | WW24 | 121 |
| N250JP | WW24 | 196 |
| N250JT | HS25 | 25053 |
| N250KD | BE40 | RJ-60 |
| (N250KD) | C550 | 454 |
| (N250KD) | WW24 | 250 |
| N250LB | GLF4 | 1269 |
| N250LB | LJ25 | 357 |
| N250MA | FA10 | 132 |
| **N250MB** | **HS25** | **258237** |
| **N250MS** | **GLF2** | **45** |
| N250PM | WW24 | 227 |
| **N250QS** | **F2EX** | **174** |
| N250RA | FA20 | 481 |
| N250RA | WW24 | 280 |
| **N250RG** | **GLF4** | **1003** |
| N250RJ | FA50 | 31 |
| **N250SG** | **LJ60** | **194** |
| N250SM | C56X | 5167 |
| N250SP | C500 | 588 |
| N250SP | C560 | 0211 |
| **N250SP** | **HS25** | **258600** |
| N250SR | C500 | 588 |
| **N250SR** | **C560** | **0211** |
| N250UA | WW24 | 121 |
| (N250UC) | FA50 | 42 |
| N250VC | GLF4 | 1231 |
| N250VC | GLF4 | 1495 |
| **N250VP** | **C550** | **270** |
| N250VZ | GLF4 | 1231 |
| N250WW | WW24 | 250 |
| N251AB | HS25 | 25226 |
| N251AF | LJ25 | 004 |
| **N251AL** | **LJ25** | **313** |
| **N251CB** | **C500** | **479** |
| N251CB | C550 | 550-1051 |
| N251CF | C500 | 479 |
| **N251CF** | **C550** | **550-0803** |
| N251CP | CL64 | 5524 |
| N251CT | C500 | 569 |
| N251CT | LJ35 | 251 |
| N251CX | C750 | 0251 |
| **N251DD** | **C500** | **088** |
| N251DS | LJ25 | 218 |
| **N251DV** | **GLF4** | **1522** |
| N251FJ | FA10 | 186 |
| N251FX | LJ60 | 195 |
| N251GL | LJ25 | 061 |
| N251GL | LJ25 | 074 |
| N251JA | LJ25 | 150 |
| N251JE | SBRL | 465-2 |
| N251JS | GLF2 | 251 |
| **N251KD** | **C52A** | **0133** |
| N251LA | HS25 | 25101 |
| N251MA | SBRL | 306-38 |
| **N251MC** | **C510** | **0164** |
| N251MD | LJ25 | 356 |
| **N251MG** | **C500** | **250** |
| **N251MM** | **GLF4** | **1495** |
| N251NG | LJ55 | 101 |
| N251P | C500 | 250 |
| N251QS | CS55 | 0051 |
| **N251QS** | **F2TH** | **202** |
| **N251SD** | **LJ60** | **195** |
| N251SJ | F900 | 11 |
| N251SP | WW24 | 422 |
| (N251TJ) | HS25 | 258020 |
| N251TJ | LJ24 | 251 |
| **N251TS** | **LJ25** | **201** |
| N251VG | CL64 | 5524 |
| N251VG | LJ55 | 101 |
| **N251VP** | **GLF4** | **4083** |
| N251X | HS25 | 258312 |
| N252BK | LJ25 | 107 |
| N252C | GLF4 | 1252 |
| **N252CH** | **GLF4** | **1204** |
| N252CJ | C525 | 0052 |
| N252CV | C560 | 0252 |
| N252CX | C750 | 0252 |
| **N252DH** | **CL64** | **5419** |
| N252DH | HS25 | 258244 |
| (N252DL) | LJ24 | 124 |
| N252DT | HS25 | 258244 |
| N252FJ | FA10 | 187 |
| **N252FX** | **LJ60** | **196** |
| N252GL | LJ24 | 230 |
| N252HS | LJ25 | 370 |
| **N252JK** | **C525** | **0166** |
| N252JS | GLF5 | 525 |
| N252M | LJ24 | 140 |
| (N252MA) | HS25 | 25052 |
| N252R | WW24 | 21 |
| (N252RD) | LJ60 | 196 |
| **N252RP** | **LJ60** | **235** |
| **N252RV** | **C525** | **0252** |
| N252SC | LJ25 | 006 |
| (N252TJ) | LJ24 | 252 |
| N252V | HS25 | 25112 |
| N252WJ | LJ35 | 349 |
| (N253CC) | HS25 | 25253 |
| **N253CM** | **GLF5** | **610** |
| N253CV | C560 | 0253 |
| **N253CW** | **C525** | **0253** |
| **N253CX** | **C750** | **0253** |
| N253DV | GLF5 | 5257 |
| N253EJ | LJ25 | 253 |
| N253EX | FA50 | 253 |
| N253FJ | FA10 | 188 |
| N253FX | LJ60 | 199 |
| N253FX | LJ60 | 227 |
| **N253FX** | **LJ60** | **241** |
| N253GL | LJ24 | 233 |
| N253J | LJ25 | 253 |
| N253K | FA10 | 10 |
| N253L | FA50 | 19 |
| N253M | LJ25 | 253 |
| N253MD | WW24 | 253 |
| N253MT | HS25 | 25253 |
| N253MZ | SBRL | 306-38 |
| N253QS | CS55 | 0053 |
| **N253QS** | **F2TH** | **153** |
| N253S | LJ55 | 053 |
| N253SC | LJ25 | 253 |
| N253SJ | FA50 | 107 |
| N253W | C550 | 253 |
| **N254AD** | **C560** | **0688** |
| N254AM | C550 | 090 |
| **N254AM** | **CL64** | **5361** |
| N254AR | GLF2 | 254/41 |
| N254CB | C550 | 550-1054 |
| N254CC | C550 | 254 |
| **N254CL** | **LJ25** | **275** |

| Reg | Type | C/n |
|---|---|---|
| N254CR | GLF2 | 184 |
| N254CW | C525 | 0154 |
| **N254CX** | **C750** | **0254** |
| **N254DV** | **CL30** | **20262** |
| N254DV | FA50 | 85 |
| N254FJ | FA10 | 189 |
| N254FX | LJ60 | 200 |
| (N254FX) | LJ60 | 206 |
| N254FX | LJ60 | 220 |
| **N254FX** | **LJ60** | **247** |
| N254FY | LJ60 | 200 |
| N254FZ | LJ60 | 220 |
| **N254GA** | **GLF4** | **1032** |
| N254JT | HS25 | 25053 |
| N254JT | LJ24 | 181 |
| (N254MC) | WW24 | 202 |
| N254NA | FA50 | 148 |
| N254RK | BE40 | RK-254 |
| N254SC | LJ25 | 102 |
| N254SD | GLF4 | 1387 |
| N254SD | GLF5 | 5120 |
| N254TW | C500 | 541 |
| N254US | LJ35 | 254 |
| (N254W) | GLF5 | 688 |
| N255AG | PRM1 | RB-255 |
| **N255AR** | **LJ24** | **255** |
| N255BD | LJ60 | 221 |
| N255BL | LJ55 | 128 |
| N255CB | HS25 | 25122 |
| N255CC | C550 | 588 |
| N255CC | CL61 | 5156 |
| **N255CC** | **CL64** | **5302** |
| N255CM | FA50 | 255 |
| N255CT | HS25 | 257011 |
| N255CT | SBRL | 282-54 |
| N255CV | C560 | 0255 |
| N255DA | HS25 | 258070 |
| **N255DG** | **MU30** | **A056SA** |
| N255DV | HS25 | 258070 |
| N255DV | HS25 | 258169 |
| N255DV | LJ31 | 030 |
| **N255DX** | **HS25** | **258535** |
| N255DY | LJ31 | 030 |
| N255ES | LJ24 | 082A |
| N255FJ | FA10 | 190 |
| **N255FX** | **LJ60** | **220** |
| N255FX | LJ60 | 228 |
| **N255GA** | **GLF4** | **1055** |
| N255GL | LJ25 | 070 |
| N255GM | SBRL | 282-45 |
| N255JC | LJ35 | 326 |
| N255JH | LJ35 | 055 |
| N255JT | GALX | 055 |
| N255LJ | C500 | 292 |
| N255MB | LJ55 | 117 |
| **N255QS** | **F2TH** | **155** |
| (N255QT) | HS25 | 257011 |
| N255RB | HS25 | 258059 |
| **N255RB** | **HS25** | **258791** |
| N255RB | WW24 | 336 |
| N255RD | C500 | 069 |
| N255RG | LJ35 | 055 |
| N255RK | FA20 | 196 |
| **N255RK** | **LJ60** | **083** |
| **N255RM** | **C560** | **0201** |
| N255SB | GLF3 | 448 |
| **N255SL** | **LJ60** | **188** |
| N255ST | LJ55 | 064 |
| **N255TC** | **C550** | **638** |
| N255TS | C500 | 375 |
| N255TS | GLF4 | 1231 |
| (N255TS) | HS25 | 25255 |
| N255TS | LJ55 | 060 |
| N255TT | HS25 | 257011 |
| N255UJ | LJ55 | 032 |
| N255VP | C650 | 0152 |
| N255WA | C560 | 0255 |
| N256A | FA20 | 438 |
| **N256A** | **FA50** | **172** |
| **N256AH** | **LJ40** | **45-2042** |
| **N256BC** | **HS25** | **258256** |
| N256CC | C500 | 256 |
| **N256CC** | **C550** | **550-0965** |
| N256CJ | C52A | 0156 |
| N256CT | SBRL | 282-54 |
| N256DV | C52B | 0301 |
| N256DV | F900 | 20 |
| N256EA | SBRL | 282-60 |
| N256EN | FA20 | 23 |
| N256EN | HS25 | 257129 |
| N256EN | SBRL | 282-60 |
| N256FC | HS25 | 256003 |
| N256FJ | FA10 | 191 |
| (N256FS) | HS25 | 258256 |
| **N256FX** | **LJ60** | **257** |
| N256GA | GLF5 | 656 |
| N256GL | LJ25 | 072 |
| **N256JB** | **C525** | **0284** |
| N256JC | FA20 | 496 |
| **N256LK** | **GLF5** | **514** |
| N256M | FA20 | 274 |
| N256M | GLF2 | 235 |
| N256M | LJ60 | 073 |
| N256MA | FA20 | 23 |
| N256MA | FA20 | 75 |
| (N256MA) | HS25 | 257129 |
| N256MA | LJ35 | 235 |
| N256MA | SBRL | 282-60 |
| N256MA | SBRL | 282-69 |
| (N256MB) | LJ35 | 235 |
| N256MJ | LJ24 | 256 |
| (N256MT) | SBRL | 306-13 |
| N256N | WW24 | 427 |
| **N256P** | **C500** | **659** |
| N256P | LJ25 | 006 |
| N256SD | CL61 | 3006 |
| **N256SP** | **C52A** | **0006** |
| N256TW | LJ35 | 218 |
| N256V | FA10 | 151 |
| N256W | C550 | 026 |
| N256W | C650 | 7111 |
| **N256W** | **C750** | **0221** |
| N256W | FA10 | 151 |
| **N256WJ** | **HS25** | **256008** |
| N256WM | LJ24 | 256 |
| N256WN | C500 | 019 |
| N257AJ | HS25 | 257001 |
| **N257AK** | **EA50** | **000258** |
| **N257AL** | **C750** | **0226** |
| N257AL | LJ35 | 128 |
| N257AM | HS25 | 257046 |
| **N257CB** | **BE40** | **RK-207** |
| N257CB | MU30 | A050SA |
| **N257CM** | **C510** | **0257** |
| N257CW | C550 | 229 |
| N257DJ | LJ35 | 257 |
| (N257DP) | LJ35 | 064 |
| **N257DW** | **C550** | **316** |
| N257FX | LJ60 | 260 |
| N257GL | LJ25 | 071 |
| N257H | GLF2 | 223 |
| **N257H** | **GLF4** | **1223** |
| N257H | HS25 | 25104 |
| N257H | JSTR | 5083/49 |
| N257H | JSTR | 5230 |
| N257HA | JSTR | 5083/49 |
| **N257K** | **EA50** | **000257** |
| **N257MV** | **C525** | **0548** |
| **N257QS** | **F2EX** | **191** |
| N257SD | LJ35 | 064 |
| **N257SJ** | **LJ55** | **118** |
| N257TH | HS25 | 257007 |
| N257TM | SBRL | 282-76 |
| N257V | FA10 | 119 |
| N257W | C650 | 7112 |
| N257W | FA10 | 119 |
| N257WJ | HS25 | 257007 |
| **N258A** | **FA20** | **438** |
| N258AV | WW24 | 258 |
| N258BJ | BE40 | RJ-58 |
| N258CC | C550 | 258 |
| (N258CF) | WW24 | 258 |
| N258CW | C550 | 183 |
| N258FJ | FA10 | 192 |
| N258FX | LJ60 | 263 |
| N258G | LJ25 | 092 |
| N258G | LJ35 | 443 |
| N258GL | LJ25 | 078 |
| N258JS | C550 | 285 |
| N258MD | LJ25 | 258 |
| **N258MR** | **HS25** | **258258** |
| (N258P) | C550 | 408 |
| (N258P) | C550 | 454 |
| (N258P) | C550 | 493 |
| N258P | CS55 | 0022 |
| N258PE | FA20 | 163 |
| **N258QS** | **F2TH** | **158** |
| N258RA | HS25 | 258273 |
| N258SA | HS25 | 258235 |
| (N258SC) | LJ31 | 058 |
| N258SP | HS25 | 258258 |
| N258SR | HS25 | 258051 |
| (N259B) | GLF3 | 431 |
| N259DB | LJ24 | 064 |
| **N259DH** | **C500** | **259** |
| N259FJ | FA10 | 193 |
| N259FX | LJ60 | 266 |
| **N259FX** | **LJ60** | **295** |
| N259HA | LJ35 | 259 |
| (N259JC) | LJ35 | 259 |
| (N259JH) | C560 | 0270 |
| **N259QS** | **F2TH** | **159** |
| **N259RH** | **HS25** | **258529** |
| **N259SK** | **GLF3** | **327** |
| **N259SP** | **HS25** | **258531** |
| N259WJ | LJ35 | 341 |
| **N260AM** | **C525** | **0260** |
| N260AN | LJ60 | 124 |
| N260BS | CS55 | 0080 |
| N260CA | LJ60 | 149 |
| N260CC | C500 | 260 |
| N260CH | GLF4 | 1072 |
| N260CV | C560 | 0260 |
| N260CX | C750 | 0260 |
| N260DB | LJ60 | 290 |
| (N260FJ) | F2TH | 60 |
| N260FJ | FA10 | 194 |
| **N260FX** | **LJ60** | **307** |
| (N260G) | HS25 | 258782 |
| N260GA | ASTR | 260 |
| N260J | C550 | 249 |
| **N260LF** | **LJ31** | **015** |
| N260MB | FA20 | 274 |
| N260QS | CS55 | 0060 |
| N260RD | C500 | 260 |
| N260TB | C550 | 720 |
| N260UJ | LJ60 | 008 |
| **N260V** | **CL60** | **1022** |
| (N260VP) | C650 | 0152 |
| N260VP | C650 | 0190 |
| **N261AH** | **C680** | **0261** |
| N261CC | C500 | 261 |
| N261CV | C560 | 0261 |
| **N261DC** | **EA50** | **000127** |
| N261FJ | FA10 | 195 |
| **N261FX** | **LJ60** | **319** |
| N261GA | ASTR | 143 |
| N261GA | ASTR | 261 |
| N261GA | GLF5 | 5161 |
| **N261JP** | **BE40** | **RK-76** |
| N261PA | HS25 | 258587 |
| **N261PA** | **HS25** | **259003** |
| N261PC | LJ31 | 109 |
| N261PC | LJ35 | 329 |
| N261PC | LJ60 | 146 |
| **N261PG** | **LJ35** | **329** |
| N261PQ | LJ31 | 109 |
| **N261SC** | **LJ31** | **061** |
| N261SS | C550 | 288 |
| N261SV | C680 | 0261 |
| N261T | SBRL | 306-125 |
| N261UH | C560 | 0261 |
| (N261VP) | C550 | 288 |
| (N261WB) | C500 | 674 |
| **N261WC** | **LJ25** | **261** |
| N261WD | C500 | 674 |
| N261WD | CS55 | 0119 |
| N261WR | C500 | 674 |
| N261WR | C560 | 0122 |
| **N261WR** | **C560** | **0447** |
| N261WR | CS55 | 0119 |
| **N262BK** | **C525** | **0262** |
| (N262CT) | HS25 | 258239 |
| N262CV | C560 | 0262 |
| N262CX | C750 | 0262 |
| N262DB | LJ60 | 286 |
| N262EX | FA50 | 262 |
| N262FJ | FA10 | 196 |
| **N262FX** | **LJ60** | **323** |
| **N262G** | **HS25** | **258354** |
| N262GA | ASTR | 144 |
| N262GA | ASTR | 256 |
| **N262GA** | **GALX** | **232** |
| N262GL | LJ24 | 238 |
| N262HA | LJ24 | 123 |
| N262JE | LJ25 | 100 |
| **N262PA** | **BE40** | **RK-203** |
| N262PA | GLF2 | 62 |
| N262PC | F2TH | 78 |
| **N262QS** | **F2TH** | **162** |
| N262RB | PRM1 | RB-262 |
| N262SP | ASTR | 062 |
| N262SV | C680 | 0262 |
| N262WC | WW24 | 262 |
| N262WW | WW24 | 262 |
| **N262Y** | **C550** | **320** |
| N263AL | C500 | 263 |
| N263C | GLF3 | 341 |
| N263CJ | C52A | 0063 |
| **N263CT** | **C525** | **0263** |
| N263FJ | FA10 | 198 |
| **N263FX** | **LJ60** | **334** |
| N263GA | ASTR | 263 |
| N263GA | GALX | 025 |
| **N263GA** | **GLF5** | **5263** |
| N263GL | LJ25 | 028 |
| N263GL | LJ35 | 003 |
| N263GL | LJ35 | 009 |
| N263K | FA20 | 438 |
| **N263MR** | **LJ45** | **263** |
| N263MW | FA20 | 59 |
| **N263PA** | **BE40** | **RK-429** |
| N263PW | F900 | 159 |
| N263R | HS25 | 259024 |
| N263RA | LJ45 | 263 |
| N263S | GLF4 | 1263 |
| N263SV | C680 | 0263 |
| (N263TN) | HS25 | 257089 |
| N264A | C550 | 429 |
| **N264A** | **GLEX** | **9064** |
| **N264CL** | **GLF2** | **227** |
| N264CV | C560 | 0264 |
| N264FJ | FA10 | 199 |
| **N264FX** | **LJ60** | **340** |
| N264GA | ASTR | 145 |
| N264GA | ASTR | 264 |
| N264HB | PRM1 | RB-264 |
| N264SC | C56X | 5560 |
| N264TN | FA20 | 264 |
| (N264TS) | HS25 | 25264 |
| **N264TW** | **LJ25** | **232** |
| N264U | C560 | 0264 |
| N264WC | HS25 | 257090 |
| (N264WD) | HS25 | 25264 |
| N265A | GLF3 | 440 |
| N265A | SBRL | 465-47 |
| (N265AC) | SBRL | 282-23 |
| N265C | SBRL | 306-120 |
| N265C | SBRL | 465-33 |
| (N265CA) | SBRL | 465-21 |
| N265CH | SBRL | 380-30 |
| N265CM | SBRL | 282-76 |
| **N265CP** | **SBRL** | **465-48** |
| N265DC | LJ24 | 081 |
| N265DE | GLEX | 9265 |
| N265DL | HS25 | 25287 |
| **N265DP** | **EA50** | **000230** |
| N265DP | SBRL | 306-68 |
| N265DP | SBRL | 380-30 |
| (N265DR) | SBRL | 465-45 |
| **N265DS** | **SBRL** | **465-45** |
| N265EJ | LJ25 | 265 |
| N265FJ | FA10 | 200 |
| **N265FX** | **LJ60** | **345** |
| **N265G** | **FA50** | **214** |
| N265GL | LJ25 | 090 |
| N265GM | SBRL | 306-84 |
| **N265H** | **F9EX** | **139** |
| N265JS | SBRL | 465-56 |
| **N265K** | **CL30** | **20265** |
| **N265KC** | **SBRL** | **380-49** |
| N265LJ | LJ25 | 265 |
| **N265M** | **SBRL** | **465-31** |
| N265MK | SBRL | 306-90 |
| **N265MP** | **FA20** | **265** |
| N265PC | SBRL | 465-24 |
| (N265QS) | C550 | 293 |
| **N265QS** | **F2TH** | **165** |
| N265R | SBRL | 282-20 |
| N265RW | SBRL | 306-125 |
| **N265RX** | **C750** | **0249** |
| **N265SC** | **SBRL** | **282-117** |

| | | |
|---|---|---|
| **N265SJ** | **GLF4** | **1351** |
| N265SP | SBRL | 465-48 |
| N265SR | SBRL | 306-120 |
| N265SR | SBRL | 370-5 |
| N265SR | SBRL | 380-11 |
| N265ST | GLF4 | 1179 |
| N265TJ | SBRL | 306-102 |
| **N265TS** | **C550** | **550-0942** |
| **N265TW** | **LJ25** | **265** |
| N265U | SBRL | 306-132 |
| N265W | SBRL | 282-37 |
| N265WB | SBRL | 276-39 |
| **N265WS** | **SBRL** | **465-62** |
| N266AZ | PRM1 | RB-266 |
| N266BS | LJ24 | 266 |
| N266BS | LJ25 | 180 |
| N266BS | LJ36 | 035 |
| **N266CJ** | **C525** | **0266** |
| N266FJ | FA10 | 201 |
| **N266FX** | **LJ60** | **348** |
| N266GA | CL64 | 5400 |
| N266GA | GLF4 | 1466 |
| N266GL | LJ25 | 064 |
| N266JP | LJ24 | 037 |
| N266LJ | LJ60 | 266 |
| N266P | LJ24 | 186 |
| (N266TS) | HS25 | 25266 |
| **N266TW** | **LJ24** | **266** |
| (N267AD) | JSTR | 5067 |
| **N267BB** | **C550** | **094** |
| N267BW | CL64 | 5391 |
| **N267BW** | **F2EX** | **107** |
| N267CW | C550 | 094 |
| **N267DW** | **CL64** | **5391** |
| N267FJ | FA10 | 203 |
| **N267FX** | **LJ60** | **356** |
| N267GF | JSTR | 5074/22 |
| N267GL | LJ25 | 102 |
| N267H | FA20 | 267/491 |
| **N267JE** | **HS25** | **257095** |
| N267L | JSTR | 5067 |
| N267MP | LJ24 | 267 |
| N267P | JSTR | 5074/22 |
| N267PS | GLF2 | 8 |
| N267SP | ASTR | 067 |
| N267TC | C550 | 376 |
| N267TG | C550 | 376 |
| N267TG | C650 | 0159 |
| N267TS | HS25 | 257067 |
| N267VP | C560 | 0267 |
| (N267W) | C650 | 7112 |
| **N267WG** | **C560** | **0267** |
| N268DM | F2EX | 146 |
| N268FJ | FA10 | 204 |
| N268FJ | FA50 | 268 |
| (N268FX) | LJ60 | 366 |
| N268GA | ASTR | 268 |
| N268GA | GALX | 070 |
| N268GL | LJ25 | 101 |
| (N268GM) | C500 | 323 |
| N268J | C550 | 268 |
| **N268PA** | **BE40** | **RK-323** |
| **N268QS** | **F2TH** | **168** |
| N268RJ | GLF3 | 482 |
| (N268TS) | HS25 | 25268 |
| **N268WC** | **LJ25** | **268** |
| N268WC | LJ25 | 268 |
| **N268WS** | **LJ60** | **268** |
| (N269AJ) | C550 | 063 |
| N269AJ | WW24 | 276 |
| (N269AL) | LJ24 | 159 |
| N269AS | LJ25 | 101 |
| N269CM | C500 | 546 |
| N269CM | C560 | 0268 |
| N269FJ | FA10 | 205 |
| (N269FX) | LJ60 | 372 |
| N269GA | GLF4 | 1469 |
| N269HM | GLF2 | 13 |
| **N269HM** | **GLF4** | **1118** |
| N269JD | C550 | 477 |
| **N269JH** | **LJ60** | **201** |
| N269JR | C550 | 477 |
| N269JR | C560 | 0266 |
| N269JR | C56X | 5086 |
| N269JR | C750 | 0073 |
| N269MD | C500 | 546 |
| N269MD | LJ25 | 269 |
| N269MH | GLF2 | 13 |
| **N269MJ** | **CL30** | **20180** |
| (N269MT) | CS55 | 0080 |
| **N269QS** | **F2TH** | **169** |
| **N269RC** | **C500** | **078** |
| N269SR | FA20 | 370 |
| **N269SW** | **FA10** | **125** |
| N269TA | C560 | 0006 |
| **N269TA** | **C650** | **7112** |
| N269X | HS25 | 258129 |
| N270A | WW24 | 270 |
| N270AS | LJ55 | 056 |
| N270AV | HS25 | 25270 |
| N270BH | C500 | 330 |
| (N270BJ) | BE40 | RJ-41 |
| N270CF | C550 | 300 |
| N270CS | LJ35 | 042 |
| **N270CW** | **C550** | **570** |
| N270CX | C750 | 0270 |
| (N270DT) | WW24 | 270 |
| N270EX | FA50 | 270 |
| N270FJ | FA10 | 206 |
| N270GA | GALX | 060 |
| **N270HC** | **HS25** | **258020** |
| N270J | C525 | 0301 |
| N270J | C525 | 0311 |
| **N270KA** | **HS25** | **257154** |
| **N270LC** | **WW24** | **245** |
| **N270MC** | **GLF3** | **374** |
| N270MC | HS25 | 256067 |
| N270MC | HS25 | 257154 |
| N270MH | HS25 | 257152 |
| **N270MK** | **C510** | **0241** |
| N270MQ | HS25 | 256067 |
| N270NF | C500 | 536 |
| **N270PM** | **C500** | **196** |
| N270QS | F2TH | 210 |
| N270RA | C550 | 265 |
| N270RA | CL64 | 5337 |
| N270RA | FA20 | 446 |
| **N270SC** | **GLF4** | **1229** |
| (N270SC) | LJ31 | 070 |
| N270SF | C500 | 536 |
| N270TC | LJ24 | 134 |
| N270TS | GLF2 | 43 |
| **N270V** | **CL60** | **1017** |
| **N270WS** | **LJ55** | **138** |
| (N270WW) | WW24 | 270 |
| N270X | HS25 | 258131 |
| (N270X) | HS25 | 258134 |
| **N271AC** | **C500** | **218** |
| N271AG | C550 | 471 |
| **N271CA** | **C560** | **0071** |
| N271CG | C550 | 423 |
| N271CJ | C52A | 0171 |
| **N271CS** | **C510** | **0158** |
| N271CX | C750 | 0271 |
| **N271DV** | **F9EX** | **68** |
| N271E | WW24 | 43 |
| N271FJ | FA10 | 207 |
| N271GA | GALX | 061 |
| N271JG | GLF5 | 582 |
| N271L | LJ60 | 271 |
| N271MB | CL60 | 1055 |
| N271MB | MU30 | A015SA |
| N271MB | SBRL | 465-24 |
| (N271MB) | SBRL | 465-33 |
| (N271MF) | C500 | 218 |
| **N271PS** | **GLF4** | **1059** |
| **N271RA** | **GALX** | **104** |
| **N271SC** | **LJ31** | **071** |
| (N271X) | HS25 | 258131 |
| N271X | HS25 | 258134 |
| N272B | HS25 | 25175 |
| N272BC | BE40 | RK-192 |
| N272BC | BE40 | RK-2 |
| N272BC | BE40 | RK-325 |
| N272BC | LJ45 | 252 |
| N272BC | MU30 | A046SA |
| N272BG | MU30 | A046SA |
| N272BQ | BE40 | RK-192 |
| N272BQ | BE40 | RK-2 |
| **N272CB** | **ASTR** | **262** |
| N272DJ | LJ60 | 272 |
| **N272DN** | **FA10** | **135** |
| N272EJ | F2TH | 172 |
| N272EJ | LJ25 | 272 |
| N272EX | FA50 | 272 |
| N272F | FA50 | 272 |
| (N272FA) | FA20 | 272 |
| N272FJ | FA10 | 209 |
| N272GA | GALX | 072 |
| N272GL | LJ24 | 195 |
| N272HS | LJ35 | 272 |
| **N272JC** | **GALX** | **054** |
| N272JM | LJ25 | 272 |
| N272JP | FA20 | 272 |
| N272JS | GLF3 | 489 |
| **N272MH** | **C680** | **0015** |
| N272MW | GALX | 058 |
| N272T | LJ35 | 349 |
| N272TB | LJ55 | 056 |
| N272X | HS25 | 258154 |
| N273CA | LJ25 | 039 |
| (N273DA) | C500 | 382 |
| N273FJ | FA10 | 210 |
| N273G | CL61 | 3002 |
| N273G | GLF3 | 454 |
| N273GL | LJ24 | 201 |
| N273JC | F2TH | 73 |
| **N273JC** | **FA7X** | **18** |
| N273JE | F2TH | 73 |
| N273K | FA20 | 349 |
| N273K | HS25 | 256041 |
| N273KH | LJ25 | 315 |
| (N273LB) | C650 | 0056 |
| N273LF | WW24 | 44 |
| **N273LJ** | **LJ35** | **273** |
| N273LP | C650 | 0056 |
| N273LP | GLF2 | 192 |
| N273LP | LJ25 | 058 |
| **N273LP** | **LJ45** | **185** |
| N273LP | WW24 | 44 |
| N273LR | LJ25 | 058 |
| N273M | LJ25 | 315 |
| N273MC | LJ35 | 149 |
| N273MC | LJ55 | 119 |
| **N273MC** | **LJ60** | **181** |
| N273MG | LJ35 | 149 |
| **N273MG** | **LJ55** | **119** |
| N273RA | ASTR | 097 |
| N273RC | C500 | 273 |
| N273S | CL64 | 5396 |
| N273W | C650 | 0068 |
| N273X | HS25 | 258156 |
| N274 | LJ55 | 105 |
| **N274CA** | **SBRL** | **306-31** |
| **N274CZ** | **LJ45** | **274** |
| N274FD | LJ35 | 274 |
| N274FJ | FA10 | 213 |
| N274GA | GALX | 074 |
| N274HM | WW24 | 202 |
| **N274HM** | **WW24** | **342** |
| **N274JC** | **GALX** | **034** |
| N274JH | LJ35 | 274 |
| N274JS | LJ35 | 274 |
| **N274K** | **WW24** | **274** |
| N274LJ | LJ25 | 274 |
| **N274MA** | **WW24** | **74** |
| N274PG | CS55 | 0074 |
| N274QS | CS55 | 0074 |
| N274X | HS25 | 258158 |
| N275AL | C500 | 333 |
| N275BB | C550 | 550-1075 |
| N275BC | BE40 | RK-325 |
| N275BD | C550 | 675 |
| (N275BH) | C500 | 275 |
| N275CC | C500 | 508 |
| N275CC | C550 | 248 |
| N275CQ | C500 | 508 |
| N275CW | C525 | 0205 |
| **N275E** | **LJ24** | **245** |
| N275FJ | FA10 | 214 |
| N275GA | GALX | 065 |
| N275GC | C650 | 0162 |
| N275GK | C500 | 275 |
| **N275HH** | **FA50** | **207** |
| N275HS | MU30 | A080SA |
| N275J | LJ35 | 009 |
| N275LE | LJ24 | 245 |
| (N275MB) | C500 | 275 |
| **N275MD** | **JSTR** | **5230** |
| **N275MT** | **CL61** | **3007** |
| N275NM | C750 | 0178 |
| (N275PC) | BE40 | RK-75 |
| **N275QS** | **F2TH** | **75** |
| N275RA | ASTR | 098 |
| (N275VP) | CS55 | 0075 |
| N275WN | C650 | 0018 |
| **N276A** | **C56X** | **5276** |
| N276AL | C550 | 017 |
| N276CC | C500 | 276 |
| N276FJ | FA10 | 216 |
| N276GA | GALX | 066 |
| N276GA | GALX | 176 |
| **N276GA** | **GLF5** | **5276** |
| **N276GC** | **CL64** | **5431** |
| N276JS | LJ35 | 458 |
| N276LE | LJ25 | 078 |
| **N276PS** | **LJ31** | **211** |
| **N276RS** | **PRM1** | **RB-194** |
| (N277A) | C550 | 083 |
| (N277AG) | GLF4 | 1026 |
| N277AL | CS55 | 0013 |
| **N277AL** | **LJ55** | **104** |
| (N277AM) | LJ35 | 204 |
| (N277AT) | FA20 | 509 |
| (N277CB) | HS25 | 257182 |
| N277CC | C500 | 277 |
| N277CJ | C525 | 0277 |
| N277CJ | C550 | 040 |
| N277CT | HS25 | 257086 |
| N277CT | SBRL | 306-2 |
| N277FJ | FA10 | 217 |
| **N277G** | **EA50** | **000102** |
| N277GA | GALX | 077 |
| (N277HG) | C650 | 0025 |
| N277HM | C550 | 277 |
| N277JE | C550 | 635 |
| **N277JM** | **C550** | **277** |
| N277JW | FA50 | 250 |
| N277JW | HS25 | 257110 |
| N277LE | LJ25 | 028 |
| N277MG | WW24 | 127 |
| N277NS | GLF3 | 381 |
| N277NS | JSTR | 5099/5 |
| N277QS | CS55 | 0077 |
| **N277QS** | **F2TH** | **177** |
| **N277RA** | **FA20** | **8** |
| **N277RC** | **C560** | **0210** |
| N277RP | GLF4 | 1026 |
| (N277RW) | C500 | 444 |
| N277SF | FA10 | 44 |
| **N277SS** | **HS25** | **258028** |
| N277T | GLF2 | 209 |
| N277T | JSTR | 5105 |
| **N277TW** | **LJ24** | **277** |
| N277W | C650 | 0072 |
| N277WW | WW24 | 277 |
| N278A | C550 | 168 |
| (N278CA) | C525 | 0510 |
| N278CC | C500 | 278 |
| N278DM | F2EX | 147 |
| N278FJ | FA50 | 186 |
| **N278GA** | **GALX** | **078** |
| **N278GS** | **F2TH** | **193** |
| (N278JC) | EA50 | 000278 |
| **N278JM** | **LJ31** | **221** |
| N278LE | LJ25 | 120 |
| **N278MS** | **C510** | **0278** |
| **N278QS** | **F2TH** | **77** |
| (N278S) | C550 | 571 |
| N278SP | C500 | 278 |
| (N278SR) | C500 | 278 |
| **N278SV** | **C680** | **0278** |
| N279AJ | LJ45 | 279 |
| **N279AK** | **BE40** | **RK-419** |
| N279AL | FA20 | 279/502 |
| **N279CJ** | **C52B** | **0279** |
| N279DM | LJ35 | 214 |
| N279DP | ASTR | 020 |
| N279DS | ASTR | 040 |
| **N279DV** | **C52B** | **0070** |
| **N279E** | **EA50** | **000241** |
| N279FJ | FA50 | 187 |
| N279GA | GALX | 069 |
| **N279LE** | **LJ25** | **112** |
| N279QS | F2TH | 178 |
| N279SP | LJ35 | 452 |
| N279TG | LJ25 | 265 |
| **N280AJ** | **BE40** | **RK-164** |
| N280AJ | HS25 | 257102 |
| N280AT | WW24 | 247 |
| N280AZ | WW24 | 247 |
| N280BC | F900 | 71 |

| | | |
|---|---|---|
| N280BC | FA50 | 109 |
| **N280BC** | **FA50** | **332** |
| N280BG | FA50 | 109 |
| N280BQ | F900 | 71 |
| N280C | LJ24 | 082 |
| N280C | LJ25 | 280 |
| N280CC | C500 | 280 |
| (N280CH) | HS25 | 25190 |
| **N280CJ** | **SJ50** | **0001** |
| N280DB | WW24 | 187 |
| N280DM | C52A | 0210 |
| N280DM | C750 | 0161 |
| N280FJ | FA50 | 188 |
| N280JR | C560 | 0576 |
| N280JS | C550 | 400 |
| **N280K** | **CL64** | **5365** |
| N280LA | LJ25 | 280 |
| N280LC | LJ25 | 029 |
| N280LM | WW24 | 247 |
| N280MH | C550 | 313 |
| **N280PM** | **C550** | **207** |
| **N280QS** | **F2TH** | **181** |
| N280R | LJ24 | 188 |
| (N280RC) | FA20 | 28 |
| N280RT | FA50 | 24 |
| **N280TA** | **C550** | **226** |
| N280VC | HS25 | 257102 |
| (N281AM) | C550 | 281 |
| N281BC | LJ35 | 380 |
| N281BT | HS25 | 257114 |
| N281CD | LJ35 | 417 |
| N281CW | C525 | 0131 |
| N281FJ | FA50 | 189 |
| N281FP | LJ24 | 281 |
| N281GA | GLF2 | 81 |
| N281GA | GLF4 | 1481 |
| N281JJ | FA20 | 281/496 |
| (N281NW) | GLF2 | 81 |
| **N281QS** | **F2TH** | **81** |
| N281R | LJ24 | 134 |
| N281R | LJ25 | 026 |
| N281RB | GLF2 | 200 |
| N281VP | C560 | 0281 |
| N281XP | HS25 | 258281 |
| N282AC | LJ24 | 145 |
| (N282AM) | SBRL | 282-20 |
| N282C | FA20 | 282 |
| N282CA | SBRL | 282-50 |
| N282CC | C500 | 282 |
| N282CD | GLF4 | 1098 |
| N282CJ | C52A | 0082 |
| **N282CM** | **GALX** | **182** |
| N282CX | C750 | 0282 |
| **N282DR** | **C680** | **0111** |
| N282FJ | FA50 | 191 |
| N282GA | GALX | 082 |
| **N282GA** | **GLF5** | **5282** |
| N282JJ | FA20 | 282 |
| N282MC | SBRL | 282-52 |
| N282NA | SBRL | 282-23 |
| (N282PC) | C650 | 0058 |
| N282Q | GLF3 | 379 |
| **N282Q** | **GLF5** | **5090** |
| N282Q | GLF5 | 532 |
| N282QA | GLF5 | 532 |
| N282QS | CS55 | 0082 |
| (N282QT) | GLF5 | 532 |
| N282QT | GLF5 | 673 |
| N282R | LJ24 | 131 |
| N282R | LJ24 | 134 |
| N282RH | C560 | 0055 |
| N282SM | WW24 | 432 |
| **N282T** | **FA10** | **42** |
| N282U | FA20 | 305 |
| **N282WW** | **SBRL** | **306-134** |
| N283BX | HS25 | 258283 |
| N283CJ | C52A | 0183 |
| N283CW | C550 | 713 |
| **N283DF** | **C550** | **456** |
| N283FJ | FA50 | 192 |
| N283FJ | FA50 | 283 |
| N283GA | GALX | 083 |
| **N283GA** | **GLF5** | **5283** |
| N283K | FA50 | 87 |
| N283MM | GLF2 | 81 |
| N283R | LJ25 | 026 |
| **N283RA** | **C52B** | **0283** |
| N283S | GLEX | 9080 |
| **N283SA** | **FA20** | **83** |
| **N283SL** | **F2EX** | **83** |
| N283U | FA50 | 14 |
| N283U | LJ25 | 277 |
| (N283XP) | HS25 | 258283 |
| N284 | C550 | 225 |
| N284AM | C500 | 028 |
| N284CC | C500 | 284 |
| N284CE | FA20 | 284 |
| **N284CP** | **C560** | **0358** |
| N284DB | HS25 | 25023 |
| N284DB | HS25 | 25179 |
| N284DS | GLF4 | 1477 |
| N284FJ | FA50 | 194 |
| N284GA | GALX | 084 |
| N284GA | GLF5 | 5184 |
| N284JJ | FA20 | 284 |
| N284L | LJ60 | 284 |
| N284PC | C500 | 433 |
| **N284QS** | **F2TH** | **185** |
| N284RJ | C500 | 357 |
| **N284RP** | **C680** | **0284** |
| N284SD | GLF5 | 5120 |
| **N284TJ** | **LJ25** | **284** |
| N284U | SBRL | 306-48 |
| N285AL | HS25 | 258085 |
| N285AP | FA20 | 285/504 |
| (N285CC) | C500 | 285 |
| **N285CC** | **C560** | **0285** |
| (N285CF) | CS55 | 0085 |
| **N285CG** | **GLF4** | **4030** |
| N285CP | FA50 | 44 |
| N285CV | C560 | 0285 |
| **N285DH** | **LJ55** | **026** |
| N285FJ | FA50 | 196 |
| N285GA | GALX | 085 |
| N285GA | GALX | 185 |
| **N285GA** | **GLF5** | **5285** |
| N285HR | LJ35 | 082 |
| **N285JE** | **C52A** | **0424** |
| N285LM | JSTR | 5224 |
| **N285MC** | **CS55** | **0102** |
| **N285TW** | **FA20** | **285/504** |
| N285U | FA20 | 364 |
| N285XL | C56X | 5285 |
| **N285XP** | **HS25** | **258285** |
| N286AB | LJ36 | 044 |
| N286CC | C500 | 286 |
| (N286CP) | LJ35 | 268 |
| N286CV | C560 | 0286 |
| N286CW | C525 | 0026 |
| **N286CX** | **F2TH** | **102** |
| N286FJ | FA50 | 197 |
| N286G | C550 | 191 |
| N286GA | GALX | 086 |
| N286GA | GLF4 | 1286 |
| N286GA | GLF5 | 5186 |
| **N286MC** | **C650** | **7076** |
| N286MG | F2TH | 94 |
| **N286MJ** | **F9EX** | **208** |
| **N286PC** | **C500** | **570** |
| **N286SD** | **LJ35** | **286** |
| N286WL | LJ35 | 286 |
| N286ZT | FA50 | 286 |
| N287 | C550 | 225 |
| N287AB | C500 | 287 |
| N287CC | C500 | 287 |
| N287CD | BE40 | RK-171 |
| **N287CD** | **C650** | **0179** |
| N287CV | C560 | 0287 |
| **N287DL** | **CL60** | **1065** |
| N287DL | HS25 | 256040 |
| N287DM | HS25 | 256040 |
| N287F | F2EX | 87 |
| N287FJ | FA50 | 199 |
| N287GA | GALX | 087 |
| N287GA | GLF5 | 5137 |
| **N287MC** | **C650** | **7096** |
| N287MC | CS55 | 0102 |
| N287MF | LJ25 | 287 |
| N287NA | SBRL | 287-1 |
| N287QS | F2TH | 87 |
| N287SA | FA20 | 349 |
| N287W | FA20 | 194 |
| (N287XP) | HS25 | 258287 |
| N287Z | GLEX | 9024 |
| N288AG | C525 | 0288 |
| **N288AS** | **LJ40** | **45-2088** |
| (N288BF) | LJ31 | 108 |
| **N288CB** | **LJ45** | **272** |
| N288CC | C500 | 288 |
| N288CC | C550 | 248 |
| N288CC | C650 | 0079 |
| N288CW | C525 | 0218 |
| **N288CX** | **C750** | **0219** |
| N288DF | LJ24 | 288 |
| N288EX | FA50 | 288 |
| **N288FF** | **LJ31** | **108** |
| N288FJ | FA50 | 200 |
| **N288G** | **C52A** | **0035** |
| (N288GA) | GALX | 008 |
| **N288HL** | **C560** | **0599** |
| N288J | LJ24 | 357 |
| **N288JA** | **C680** | **0288** |
| N288JE | LJ35 | 288 |
| **N288JP** | **LJ35** | **288** |
| N288JR | C560 | 0266 |
| N288K | LJ24 | 175 |
| **N288KA** | **GLF3** | **391** |
| **N288MB** | **HS25** | **HA-0063** |
| N288MM | C500 | 689 |
| (N288MM) | FA20 | 380 |
| N288MW | HS25 | 256018 |
| N288NE | LJ35 | 288 |
| N288QS | CS55 | 0088 |
| (N288SJ) | WW24 | 299 |
| N288SP | C500 | 241 |
| N288U | JSTR | 5106/9 |
| N288VW | LJ24 | 117 |
| N288WW | WW24 | 277 |
| N288Z | F900 | 43 |
| N288Z | GLEX | 9024 |
| **N288Z** | **GLEX** | **9228** |
| **N289CA** | **FA10** | **111** |
| N289CA | LJ28 | 29-003 |
| (N289CC) | CS55 | 0089 |
| N289CC | CS55 | 0159 |
| N289FJ | FA50 | 201 |
| N289G | LJ24 | 289 |
| N289GA | GALX | 089 |
| N289GA | GALX | 189 |
| (N289GA) | LJ35 | 357 |
| **N289JP** | **LJ40** | **45-2118** |
| **N289K** | **CL61** | **5132** |
| N289K | GLF2 | 225 |
| N289LJ | LJ35 | 289 |
| N289MJ | LJ35 | 289 |
| N289MM | FA20 | 380 |
| **N289MU** | **GLF4** | **1289** |
| N289NE | LJ35 | 289 |
| N289SA | LJ24 | 289 |
| N289Z | GLEX | 9228 |
| N290 | LJ25 | 251 |
| N290AS | C650 | 0088 |
| N290BA | C550 | 304 |
| (N290BC) | FA20 | 495 |
| N290BC | LJ35 | 064 |
| N290CA | WW24 | 216 |
| N290CC | C500 | 290 |
| **N290CP** | **WW24** | **219** |
| N290EC | HS25 | 258172 |
| N290FJ | FA50 | 202 |
| N290GA | GALX | 049 |
| N290GA | GLF3 | 875 |
| N290GA | GLF5 | 5190 |
| **N290GA** | **GLF5** | **5290** |
| N290H | HS25 | 259034 |
| N290LJ | LJ45 | 029 |
| **N290MX** | **FA50** | **199** |
| N290PC | HS25 | 257149 |
| **N290QS** | **F2TH** | **190** |
| N290RA | WW24 | 390 |
| N290SC | C650 | 0079 |
| N290SC | C650 | 0140 |
| N290TJ | FA50 | 29 |
| **N290VP** | **C550** | **085** |
| N290W | FA50 | 90 |
| N290W | WW24 | 280 |
| N291A | LJ35 | 212 |
| N291BC | FA50 | 199 |
| N291BC | LJ24 | 212 |
| N291BC | LJ35 | 015 |
| N291BC | LJ35 | 064 |
| N291BC | LJ35 | 380 |
| N291BX | LJ35 | 380 |
| N291CW | C525 | 0301 |
| N291DS | C500 | 291 |
| **N291DV** | **C56X** | **5146** |
| N291FJ | FA50 | 205 |
| N291GA | GALX | 050 |
| N291GA | GLF2 | 91 |
| N291GA | GLF5 | 5191 |
| N291H | HS25 | 259016 |
| N291K | LJ35 | 665 |
| N291SJ | HS25 | 258291 |
| (N291WK) | ASTR | 101 |
| N291XP | HS25 | 258291 |
| N292BC | FA50 | 62 |
| N292BC | LJ24 | 010 |
| N292BC | LJ24 | 220 |
| **N292CS** | **C680** | **0292** |
| N292EX | FA50 | 292 |
| N292FH | FA50 | 31 |
| N292FJ | FA50 | 207 |
| N292GA | CL61 | 3014 |
| N292GA | HS25 | 25219 |
| N292H | HS25 | 259025 |
| N292JC | WW24 | 292 |
| **N292ME** | **LJ35** | **292** |
| (N292PC) | C650 | 0058 |
| **N292PC** | **FA50** | **99** |
| **N292QS** | **F2TH** | **93** |
| (N292RC) | HS25 | 25219 |
| N292RC | LJ55 | 062 |
| N292SG | C525 | 0423 |
| **N293BC** | **FA50** | **135** |
| N293BC | FA50 | 82 |
| N293BC | LJ24 | 042 |
| N293BC | LJ24 | 229 |
| N293EX | FA50 | 293 |
| N293FJ | FA50 | 209 |
| N293GA | GALX | 051 |
| N293GA | GLF5 | 5193 |
| (N293GT) | FA20 | 71 |
| (N293H) | HS25 | 258266 |
| N293K | FA50 | 170 |
| **N293MC** | **LJ24** | **293** |
| **N293MM** | **C510** | **0293** |
| **N293P** | **ASTR** | **049** |
| N293PC | C550 | 713 |
| N293QS | C560 | 0293 |
| N293RT | CS55 | 0023 |
| N293S | C500 | 193 |
| **N293S** | **HS25** | **258572** |
| N293SA | LJ31 | 101 |
| **N294AT** | **C525** | **0294** |
| N294AW | BE40 | RK-1 |
| N294B | WW24 | 222 |
| N294BC | LJ24 | 149 |
| N294CA | LJ28 | 29-004 |
| **N294CC** | **C52B** | **0294** |
| **N294CV** | **HS25** | **258339** |
| **N294CW** | **C525** | **0114** |
| N294EX | FA50 | 291 |
| N294FA | BE40 | RK-1 |
| N294FJ | FA50 | 212 |
| N294GA | GALX | 052 |
| N294H | HS25 | 258267 |
| (N294M) | LJ25 | 031 |
| **N294NW** | **LJ25** | **031** |
| **N294RT** | **C560** | **0264** |
| **N294S** | **ASTR** | **094** |
| N294W | FA10 | 30 |
| N294W | HS25 | 258014 |
| N294W | WW24 | 222 |
| N295AR | JSTR | 5134/50 |
| N295BM | C560 | 0295 |
| N295CM | C525 | 0295 |
| N295CV | C560 | 0295 |
| N295DJ | LJ25 | 295 |
| **N295DS** | **C525** | **0091** |
| (N295EA) | C550 | 325 |
| N295FA | BE40 | RK-68 |
| N295FJ | FA50 | 213 |
| N295GA | GALX | 053 |
| N295GA | GLF5 | 5125 |
| N295GA | GLF5 | 5195 |
| **N295GA** | **GLF5** | **5295** |
| N295H | HS25 | 258269 |
| **N295JR** | **HS25** | **258168** |
| **N295NW** | **LJ24** | **295** |
| N295PS | LJ31 | 230 |
| **N295SG** | **CL30** | **20269** |
| N295SG | LJ40 | 45-2105 |

**N295TW FA20 5**
N295WW WW24 295
N296AB C550 011
N296AR JSTR 5055/21
N296BF C500 296
N296BS LJ35 296
N296CC C550 296
N296CF C550 296
N296CJ C52B 0296
N296CW C550 330
**N296DC C525 0296**
N296EX FA50 296
N296FA BE40 RK-91
N296FJ FA50 214
N296GA GALX 054
(N296H) HS25 259045
N296H HS25 259047
**N296L LJ60 296**
N296NW WW24 284
N296PH C550 296
**N296PM C52B 0296**
**N296QS F2TH 196**
**N296RG F2TH 222**
N296RG HS25 257131
**N296SB CL30 20157**
**N296SG LJ40 45-2105**
N296TS LJ60 029
N296V CL60 1006
N297A WW24 267
"N297AG" FA20 297
**N297AP F900 13**
N297AP JSTR 5209
N297AR FA20 24
N297CK FA20 296/507
N297DD C650 0071
N297EJ LJ24 297
N297EJ LJ25 297
N297FJ FA50 215
N297GA ASTR 091
N297GA ASTR 101
N297GA ASTR 111
(N297GA) ASTR 113
(N297GA) ASTR 122
N297GA ASTR 130
N297GB GLF2 185
**N297GB GLF4 1208**
N297H HS25 258270
N297JD HS25 25235
N297JS WW24 435
**N297MC CL30 20127**
N297MC GLF4 1393
**N297PF FA10 56**
N297QS F2TH 195
N297RG F2TH 222
N297RJ C525 0663
N297S C500 197
N297W FA20 194
N297W FA50 111
N297W WW24 267
N297XP HS25 258297
N298A WW24 318
**N298AG HS25 258014**
(N298AS) SBRL 282-117
N298BP HS25 257138
N298CH LJ31 058
N298CJ C550 298
N298CK FA20 347
N298CM WW24 298
N298DC CL64 5503
N298DR LJ25 298
**N298EF LJ60 103**
N298EJ LJ24 298
N298FJ FA50 216
N298GA GALX 056
N298GA GLF5 5198
(N298GS) LJ25 295
N298H HS25 258271
N298H LJ24 229
**N298HM WW24 240**
N298NM HS25 25278
**N298NW LJ35 298**
**N298QS F2TH 98**
N298TB GLF3 875
N298TS HS25 257138
N298W F900 33
**N298W F900 45**
N298W FA20 142
N298W FA50 90
N298W WW24 318
N298XP HS25 258298
N299AW BE40 RK-212
(N299BB) LJ45 211
N299BW HS25 256046
**N299CS C52B 0299**
N299CT HS25 257090
**N299CW C525 0199**
**N299CX C750 0299**
N299D C500 564
**N299DB FA10 50**
N299DB GLF4 1137
(N299DG) HS25 256046
**N299DH C560 0645**
N299EJ LJ24 299
N299EX FA50 299
N299FB GLF4 1099
N299FB HS25 257122
N299GA GALX 057
N299GA HS25 256046
**N299GS HS25 256046**
N299H HS25 258272
N299HS C550 550-1049
**N299JC FA20 299**
N299LR LJ35 112
N299LR SBRL 282-38
**N299MW LJ25 299**
N299NW FA20 61
N299QS CS55 0099
**N299RA FA20 146**
N299RP C500 448
N299SC LJ60 025
N299SC LJ60 112
N299SG LJ60 025
N299TB C500 230
N299TJ HS25 256046
**N299TW LJ24 299**
N299W FA50 21
**N299WB HS25 257092**
N299WV C500 320
N299XP HS25 258299
N300A FA10 59
N300A FA50 64
N300AA LJ45 211
**N300AA LJ45 285**
N300AA MU30 A041SA
N300AG JSTR 5056
N300AH CL30 20195
N300AJ ASTR 070
N300AK C550 550-0809
N300AK C550 612
**N300AK C560 0593**
N300AL FA20 330
**N300AQ LJ45 211**
N300AR MU30 A041SA
(N300AT) C750 0003
**N300BA FA20 142**
**N300BC CL30 20067**
N300BC CL64 5563
N300BE GLF3 332
N300BK GLF3 409
N300BL HS25 258155
**N300BP FA20 239**
N300BS HS25 257056
**N300BV C525 0418**
N300BW HS25 258074
N300BY CL30 20244
**N300BZ CL30 20030**
N300CC FA20 257
N300CC HS25 25250
N300CC LJ24 179
N300CC LJ36 019
N300CF HS25 25276
**N300CH C560 0080**
N300CH SBRL 282-26
N300CM LJ35 381
N300CQ C525 0300
**N300CQ HS25 258555**
N300CR CL61 5092
N300CR FA50 55
**N300CR GLF4 1401**
N300CR JSTR 5020
**N300CS C550 550-0818**
N300CT FA20 366
**N300CV FA20 322**
**N300DA C56X 5270**
N300DA LJ35 249
**N300DG CL30 20058**
N300DH MU30 A010SA
N300DH WW24 74
N300DK GLF2 57
N300DK LJ36 019
**N300DL C525 0148**
N300DL GLF2 57
N300DL LJ36 019
N300DM MU30 A003SA
N300EC C500 339
N300EJ LJ24 300
**N300ES CL64 5439**
N300ES FA50 70
N300ES GLEX 9016
N300ES LJ35 278
**N300ET C52B 0014**
N300FJ FA20 168
N300FJ FA20 300/508
(N300FN) GLF2 65
N300FN LJ35 447
**N300FS CL30 20143**
N300FS GLF3 367
N300GA GLF3 249
N300GA GLF3 300
N300GA GLF3 303
**N300GA GLF5 5300**
**N300GB BE40 RK-262**
N300GB HS25 25074
**N300GC C550 337**
N300GF C550 550-0856
**N300GF C550 550-1046**
N300GM C550 343
**N300GM CL30 20186**
N300GN FA10 59
N300GN HS25 258057
N300GP C550 550-0856
**N300GP CL30 20253**
N300GP GLF2 3
N300GX GLF4 1164
N300HA FA20 503
N300HB HS25 257173
N300HC C500 124
N300HC C500 348
N300HC WW24 307
N300HH LJ24 149
N300HH MU30 A035SA
N300HQ C500 124
N300HR WW24 335
N300HW HS25 25021
**N300JA GLF4 1023**
N300JA LJ24 282
N300JC LJ45 209
**N300JC LJ45 340**
**N300JD C750 0202**
N300JE LJ25 234
N300JE LJ45 094
N300JJ ASTR 024
N300JJ FA20 208/468
N300JK C550 262
N300JK WW24 369
N300JQ LJ45 340
**N300JZ GLF3 875**
N300K GLF4 1266
**N300K GLF5 587**
N300KC CL61 5051
N300KC HS25 25118
**N300KH CL30 20130**
N300L GLF2 92
N300L GLF3 318
N300L GLF4 1018
**N300L GLF5 507**
N300L JSTR 5097/60
N300LA MU30 A049SA
N300LB GLF4 1448
N300LB LJ24 149
N300LD HS25 25202
N300LD HS25 25265
(N300LD) HS25 257043
(N300LF) GLF3 318
N300LG MU30 A090SA
N300LH WW24 312
N300LJ CL30 20011
N300LJ CL30 20213
**N300LJ E50P 50000021**
N300LS HS25 257173
N300LS HS25 258098
N300LS HS25 259032
N300LS WW24 137
N300LS WW24 226
N300LS WW24 400
N300M GLF3 417
N300M WW24 124
**N300MY CL30 20062**
N300ND MS76 009
N300NL FA20 221
N300P HS25 25226
N300P JSTR 5052
N300PB C500 323
N300PB C500 400
N300PB C550 007
N300PL LJ25 247
N300PM HS25 258193
N300PP LJ25 043
(N300PR) C550 239
N300PX C500 140
N300PX C560 0691
(N300PX) C56X 5017
**N300PY C550 550-0806**
N300QC HS25 25250
N300QS C560 0322
**N300QS C680 0164**
N300QW CS55 0100
**N300R BE40 RK-386**
N300R HS25 25043
N300R HS25 HA-0076
N300R LJ35 438
N300RB HS25 258013
**N300RC BE40 RK-539**
N300RC SBRL 282-41
N300RC SBRL 306-111
**N300RD GLF2 3**
N300RG SBRL 282-41
(N300RN) C500 517
N300RT FA20 478
N300S CL61 3026
N300SB HFB3 1031
N300SC LJ25 208
**N300SC LJ35 440**
N300SF FA20 258
**N300SJ C56X 5107**
(N300SJ) MU30 A060SA
**N300SL PRM1 RB-110**
N300SM CL30 20015
N300TA LJ24 038
(N300TB) C500 230
N300TB SBRL 306-24
N300TC C550 313
**N300TC WW24 241**
N300TE LJ35 237
N300TE WW24 201
**N300TJ LJ24 285**
(N300TJ) MU30 A003SA
**N300TK CL60 1077**
N300TK HS25 257192
(N300TK) SBRL 282-41
N300TL LJ25 238
**N300TS MU30 A003SA**
N300TW C550 047
N300TW CL60 1080
**N300TW CL64 5428**
N300TW HS25 257192
N300TW LJ35 237
N300U GLF2 92
**N300UJ GLF3 316**
(N300VP) C750 0003
N300WC C560 0322
N300WC C56X 5137
N300WG LJ25 346
N300WK C500 374
**N300WY GLF3 427**
**N300XL WW24 276**
N300YM SBRL 306-83
**N301AJ C510 0233**
N301AJ WW24 48
(N301AS) HS25 257188
N301AS LJ31 052
N301AT HFB3 1038
N301CK HS25 25038
N301DM MU30 A007SA
**N301DN C510 0301**
**N301DR C500 382**
N301EC GLF2 258
N301EL C500 544
N301EL C52A 0109
N301EX FA50 301
(N301FC) FA20 335
(N301FP) GLF2 118

| | | |
|---|---|---|
| (N301GA) | GLF3 | 252 |
| N301GA | GLF3 | 329 |
| N301GA | GLF3 | 402 |
| N301HA | SBRL | 282-23 |
| **N301HB** | **C56X** | **5607** |
| N301HC | C500 | 348 |
| N301HC | FA10 | 77 |
| (N301HC) | WW24 | 307 |
| N301JJ | C500 | 551 |
| N301JJ | FA10 | 24 |
| N301JJ | FA50 | 161 |
| (N301JJ) | HS25 | 256040 |
| N301K | GLF4 | 1267 |
| **N301K** | **GLF5** | **591** |
| N301KF | WW24 | 301 |
| N301L | WW24 | 98 |
| (N301LX) | HS25 | 257188 |
| (N301MC) | C500 | 383 |
| N301MC | C500 | 390 |
| N301MC | SBRL | 306-146 |
| N301MC | SBRL | 465-14 |
| N301MF | CL61 | 5013 |
| N301MG | C500 | 390 |
| N301MG | SBRL | 306-146 |
| **N301MK** | **EA50** | **000214** |
| **N301ML** | **HS25** | **HA-0094** |
| N301NT | SBRL | 282-9 |
| N301P | MU30 | A030SA |
| **N301PB** | **HS25** | **259031** |
| N301PC | SBRL | 282-112 |
| **N301PC** | **WW24** | **377** |
| (N301PC) | WW24 | 383 |
| **N301PE** | **CL30** | **20244** |
| N301PE | HS25 | 259031 |
| N301PG | C52A | 0301 |
| N301PH | HS25 | 257121 |
| N301PH | HS25 | 259031 |
| N301PP | C500 | 518 |
| N301QS | C560 | 0038 |
| **N301QS** | **C680** | **0010** |
| N301QS | CS55 | 0158 |
| N301R | FA20 | 3/403 |
| **N301RJ** | **LJ60** | **054** |
| N301SC | LJ35 | 143 |
| **N301SG** | **ASTR** | **205** |
| N301TG | CL30 | 20137 |
| N301TP | LJ35 | 301 |
| **N301TT** | **FA20** | **160/450** |
| N301WC | C560 | 0335 |
| N302A | FA10 | 59 |
| N302AJ | C500 | 382 |
| **N302AK** | **GLEX** | **9181** |
| N302AT | WW24 | 12 |
| N302BG | FA50 | 305 |
| N302CE | C500 | 302 |
| N302CJ | C525 | 0302 |
| **N302CJ** | **C52A** | **0302** |
| **N302CS** | **C550** | **550-0820** |
| N302CZ | C52B | 0302 |
| N302DM | C52A | 0030 |
| N302DM | MU30 | A004SA |
| **N302DP** | **GLF2** | **237/43** |
| N302EC | CL61 | 5093 |
| N302EJ | C560 | 0302 |
| N302EJ | LJ24 | 302 |
| **N302EM** | **CL30** | **20054** |
| N302FJ | FA50 | 302 |
| N302GA | GLF3 | 302 |
| N302GA | GLF3 | 339 |
| N302GA | GLF3 | 438 |
| N302GA | GLF3 | 480 |
| N302H | SBRL | 306-5 |
| (N302HM) | GALX | 039 |
| **N302JC** | **F2TH** | **63** |
| **N302K** | **CL30** | **20267** |
| N302K | GLF5 | 597 |
| **N302MB** | **CS55** | **0097** |
| N302MC | GALX | 025 |
| N302MT | HS25 | 258302 |
| (N302NT) | SBRL | 282-100 |
| N302NT | SBRL | 282-81 |
| **N302PC** | **CL60** | **1072** |
| N302PC | CS55 | 0130 |
| N302PC | HS25 | 257125 |
| N302PC | LJ25 | 351 |
| **N302PE** | **CL30** | **20144** |
| N302PE | HS25 | 258693 |
| **N302QS** | **C560** | **0402** |
| **N302R** | **CL30** | **20204** |
| **N302SE** | **HS25** | **258269** |
| **N302SG** | **ASTR** | **244** |
| N302SG | WW24 | 379 |
| **N302SJ** | **C550** | **067** |
| **N302ST** | **GLF3** | **302** |
| **N302TB** | **BE40** | **RK-384** |
| N302TS | ASTR | 108 |
| N302TS | C500 | 382 |
| N302TT | FA20 | 122 |
| **N302WC** | **C560** | **0329** |
| (N302WY) | FA50 | 290 |
| N302XP | HS25 | 258302 |
| **N303A** | **C500** | **478** |
| N303A | SBRL | 282-52 |
| N303A | SBRL | 465-32 |
| N303AF | LJ24 | 144 |
| N303AJ | WW24 | 149 |
| **N303BC** | **HS25** | **258324** |
| N303BX | CL61 | 3031 |
| (N303BX) | HS25 | 25249 |
| N303CB | C500 | 422 |
| N303CB | C560 | 0190 |
| **N303CJ** | **C52B** | **0031** |
| **N303CP** | **C560** | **0539** |
| **N303CS** | **C550** | **550-0814** |
| **N303CZ** | **CL30** | **20003** |
| N303DM | MU30 | A008SA |
| **N303DT** | **HS25** | **258303** |
| (N303E) | WW24 | 390 |
| (N303EC) | C550 | 303 |
| N303EC | C550 | 330 |
| N303EJ | LJ24 | 303 |
| **N303EM** | **CL30** | **20068** |
| **N303FZ** | **FA10** | **218** |
| N303GA | GLF3 | 303 |
| N303GA | GLF3 | 357 |
| N303GA | GLF3 | 462 |
| (N303GC) | C550 | 193 |
| N303H | JSTR | 5055/21 |
| N303HB | GLF3 | 402 |
| N303J | C550 | 303 |
| N303JJ | LJ25 | 062 |
| N303JW | FA50 | 140 |
| N303K | GLF5 | 607 |
| N303LA | WW24 | 51 |
| N303LC | C525 | 0068 |
| N303LE | JSTR | 5113/25 |
| N303MC | GALX | 030 |
| N303MW | HS25 | 256033 |
| N303NT | SBRL | 282-29 |
| N303P | MU30 | A034SA |
| N303PC | C500 | 124 |
| **N303PC** | **C650** | **0110** |
| N303PC | WW24 | 223 |
| N303PL | FA10 | 187 |
| **N303PM** | **LJ55** | **014** |
| N303QS | C560 | 0343 |
| **N303RH** | **C500** | **551** |
| N303SC | LJ25 | 095 |
| **N303SE** | **HS25** | **258060** |
| N303SG | WW24 | 391 |
| N303SQ | LJ25 | 095 |
| **N303TP** | **GLF4** | **1411** |
| N303TS | WW24 | 416 |
| N303WB | LJ31 | 056 |
| N303X | C550 | 198 |
| N303XP | HS25 | 258303 |
| N304AF | LJ35 | 013 |
| **N304AT** | **HS25** | **258257** |
| N304AT | LJ35 | 045 |
| N304AT | LJ55 | 107 |
| N304BC | CL30 | 20067 |
| N304BX | CL61 | 5063 |
| N304CC | C500 | 304 |
| N304CK | JSTR | 5055/21 |
| **N304CS** | **C550** | **550-0847** |
| N304DM | MU30 | A005SA |
| N304E | LJ36 | 038 |
| N304EJ | LJ24 | 304 |
| **N304EM** | **CL30** | **20077** |
| N304FX | CL61 | 5063 |
| N304GA | GLF3 | 312 |
| N304GA | GLF3 | 381 |
| N304GA | GLF3 | 440 |
| N304GA | GLF3 | 481 |
| **N304JR** | **BE40** | **RK-63** |
| N304K | GLF5 | 514 |
| N304K | GLF5 | 622 |
| N304KT | C550 | 290 |
| N304LP | LJ24 | 304 |
| N304NT | SBRL | 282-2 |
| N304P | HS25 | 25226 |
| N304QS | C560 | 0408 |
| **N304RJ** | **HS25** | **258286** |
| **N304SE** | **BE40** | **RK-304** |
| N304TH | C550 | 240 |
| **N304TS** | **GLF3** | **304** |
| **N304TT** | **CL60** | **1033** |
| N304TZ | LJ35 | 045 |
| N304WW | WW24 | 304 |
| N305AF | GLF2 | 17 |
| N305AJ | WW24 | 100 |
| N305AR | FA20 | 378 |
| **N305AR** | **LJ25** | **314** |
| N305BB | C500 | 305 |
| N305BB | WW24 | 228 |
| **N305BP** | **PRM1** | **RB-305** |
| **N305CC** | **GLEX** | **9027** |
| **N305CF** | **GLF4** | **1457** |
| N305CJ | C525 | 0105 |
| **N305CS** | **C550** | **550-0825** |
| N305CX | C750 | 0305 |
| N305DM | MU30 | A009SA |
| **N305EJ** | **C680** | **0105** |
| N305EJ | LJ24 | 305 |
| **N305EM** | **CL30** | **20098** |
| N305FX | CL61 | 5070 |
| N305GA | GALX | 105 |
| N305GA | GLF3 | 305 |
| N305GA | GLF3 | 343 |
| N305GA | GLF3 | 382 |
| N305GA | GLF4 | 1305 |
| N305JA | HS25 | 258625 |
| **N305LM** | **GLF4** | **1443** |
| N305M | C500 | 443 |
| (N305M) | CL61 | 5021 |
| **N305MD** | **BE40** | **RK-131** |
| N305MD | GLF3 | 305 |
| N305NT | SBRL | 282-66 |
| N305PC | CS55 | 0138 |
| N305QS | C560 | 0261 |
| **N305QS** | **C680** | **0088** |
| **N305S** | **C500** | **301** |
| **N305SC** | **HS25** | **258662** |
| N305SC | LJ35 | 322 |
| N305SJ | GLF2 | 119/22 |
| N305TC | GLF3 | 359 |
| **N305TC** | **GLF4** | **1116** |
| N305TH | HS25 | 257150 |
| N305XP | HS25 | 258305 |
| **N306AV** | **LJ45** | **306** |
| N306BP | PRM1 | RB-206 |
| N306BX | CL61 | 5175 |
| N306CF | SBRL | 306-13 |
| **N306CJ** | **C52A** | **0016** |
| **N306CS** | **C550** | **550-0881** |
| N306CW | SBRL | 282-108 |
| N306DM | MU30 | A010SA |
| N306EJ | LJ24 | 306 |
| **N306EM** | **CL30** | **20101** |
| N306ES | FA50 | 70 |
| N306FX | CL61 | 5175 |
| N306GA | GALX | 206 |
| N306GA | GLF3 | 306 |
| N306GA | GLF3 | 344 |
| N306GA | GLF3 | 441 |
| N306GA | GLF3 | 482 |
| N306GA | GLF4 | 1506 |
| **N306JA** | **LJ24** | **306** |
| **N306JR** | **C52A** | **0306** |
| N306L | HS25 | 25093 |
| N306L | JSTR | 5097/60 |
| N306M | LJ35 | 416 |
| **N306MF** | **CL30** | **20009** |
| N306MP | HS25 | 25017 |
| N306NA | SBRL | 306-1 |
| N306NT | SBRL | 282-30 |
| N306P | MU30 | A009SA |
| **N306PA** | **C650** | **0053** |
| N306PC | SBRL | 282-112 |
| **N306PT** | **WW24** | **306** |
| N306QS | C560 | 0266 |
| (N306QS) | C650 | 0006 |
| **N306QS** | **C680** | **0207** |
| N306R | LJ60 | 084 |
| N306SA | SBRL | 306-40 |
| N306SC | C550 | 306 |
| N306SP | LJ35 | 459 |
| N306TR | C560 | 0306 |
| **N306TT** | **GLF4** | **1148** |
| N307AD | HS25 | 258307 |
| N307AF | GLF2 | 219/20 |
| N307AJ | C550 | 107 |
| N307AJ | LJ25 | 175 |
| N307BJ | LJ24 | 307 |
| **N307BS** | **C525** | **0241** |
| N307BX | CL61 | 5179 |
| N307CS | C550 | 550-0974 |
| **N307D** | **C500** | **388** |
| N307D | SBRL | 306-31 |
| N307DM | MU30 | A011SA |
| N307EJ | LJ24 | 307 |
| N307EW | C500 | 323 |
| N307FX | CL61 | 5179 |
| N307G | HS25 | 25121 |
| N307GA | GALX | 207 |
| N307GA | GLF3 | 331 |
| N307GA | GLF4 | 1507 |
| N307HF | LJ25 | 075 |
| **N307JW** | **ASTR** | **123** |
| N307M | GLF2 | 220 |
| N307MS | C550 | 550-0974 |
| N307NA | SBRL | 306-2 |
| N307NT | SBRL | 282-72 |
| **N307PE** | **C52B** | **0254** |
| N307QS | C560 | 0307 |
| **N307QS** | **C680** | **0130** |
| **N307RM** | **HS25** | **258322** |
| **N307RX** | **C750** | **0107** |
| **N307SC** | **CL61** | **3026** |
| **N307SH** | **C510** | **0307** |
| **N307ST** | **SBRL** | **465-46** |
| N307TC | C510 | 0014 |
| (N307TC) | HS25 | 257007 |
| N307XP | HS25 | 258307 |
| **N308A** | **C550** | **703** |
| N308A | GLF2 | 155/14 |
| **N308AB** | **GLF4** | **1496** |
| N308AF | GLF3 | 351 |
| N308AJ | LJ25 | 039 |
| (N308AJ) | WW24 | 149 |
| N308AT | C500 | 537 |
| **N308BW** | **LJ35** | **438** |
| N308BX | CL61 | 5110 |
| N308CC | C500 | 308 |
| N308CJ | C52A | 0308 |
| N308CK | C550 | 117 |
| **N308CR** | **CL61** | **5092** |
| N308CS | C550 | 550-0976 |
| N308DD | HS25 | 257069 |
| N308DM | FA50 | 328 |
| N308DM | MU30 | A012SA |
| **N308DT** | **C550** | **550-1094** |
| N308EE | GLF2 | 68 |
| N308EJ | LJ24 | 308 |
| N308EL | GLF2 | 68 |
| N308FX | CL61 | 5110 |
| N308GA | GLF3 | 308 |
| N308GA | GLF3 | 318 |
| N308GA | GLF3 | 383 |
| N308GT | C52A | 0004 |
| **N308GT** | **C52B** | **0236** |
| **N308HG** | **GLF3** | **308** |
| N308JS | WW24 | 308 |
| (N308LJ) | LJ24 | 308 |
| N308MS | C550 | 550-0976 |
| N308NT | SBRL | 282-90 |
| N308QS | C560 | 0277 |
| **N308QS** | **C680** | **0116** |
| N308R | LJ35 | 438 |
| N308SG | JSTR | 5226 |
| **N308SM** | **LJ24** | **290** |
| N308TS | WW24 | 308 |
| **N308TW** | **C550** | **047** |
| **N308U** | **F2EX** | **37** |
| N308WC | JSTR | 5020 |
| N308XP | HS25 | 258308 |
| N309AJ | LJ25 | 034 |
| **N309AK** | **BE40** | **RK-348** |
| N309AT | C550 | 448 |
| **N309BT** | **C56X** | **5067** |
| N309BX | CL64 | 5306 |
| N309CJ | C52A | 0309 |

| | | |
|---|---|---|
| N309CK | WW24 | 350 |
| N309CS | C550 | 550-0977 |
| N309DM | MU30 | A044SA |
| N309EL | GLF2 | 250 |
| N309ES | GLEX | 9016 |
| N309FX | CL64 | 5306 |
| N309G | HS25 | 258108 |
| N309GA | GLF3 | 328 |
| N309GA | GLF3 | 388 |
| N309GA | GLF3 | 446 |
| N309GA | GLF3 | 483 |
| N309GA | GLF4 | 1309 |
| N309LJ | LJ25 | 034 |
| **N309MG** | **LJ60** | **223** |
| **N309MT** | **C510** | **0138** |
| N309NT | SBRL | 282-61 |
| **N309QS** | **C560** | **0509** |
| **N309SG** | **GLF4** | **1449** |
| (N309SM) | CL30 | 20015 |
| (N309TA) | C650 | 0129 |
| **N309TC** | **LJ24** | **309** |
| N309WM | HS25 | 257156 |
| N309XL | C56X | 5309 |
| N310AD | JSTR | 5051 |
| N310AF | C500 | 524 |
| N310AS | HS25 | 258443 |
| N310AV | C550 | 028 |
| N310BA | LJ35 | 062 |
| **N310BN** | **C56X** | **6020** |
| N310BX | CL64 | 5336 |
| N310CK | JSTR | 5117/35 |
| **N310EL** | **GLF4** | **1021** |
| N310EX | FA50 | 310 |
| N310FJ | FA10 | 23 |
| N310FX | CL64 | 5336 |
| N310GA | GLF3 | 332 |
| N310GA | GLF3 | 389 |
| N310GA | GLF3 | 449 |
| N310GA | GLF3 | 484 |
| N310GA | GLF4 | 1405 |
| **N310GJ** | **GLF4** | **4078** |
| N310KR | LJ24 | 020 |
| N310LJ | LJ24 | 309 |
| N310LJ | LJ31 | 033C |
| **N310LJ** | **LJ45** | **031** |
| **N310ME** | **LJ35** | **310** |
| N310NT | SBRL | 282-77 |
| N310PE | CL60 | 1012 |
| N310QS | C680 | 0259 |
| N310RG | GLF3 | 321 |
| N310SL | GLF3 | 496 |
| N310SL | GLF4 | 1087 |
| **N310TK** | **CL64** | **5606** |
| N310U | C500 | 194 |
| **N310U** | **F2EX** | **100** |
| N310XP | HS25 | 258310 |
| N310ZM | LJ45 | 218 |
| N311AC | GLF2 | 74 |
| **N311AF** | **CS55** | **0051** |
| **N311BD** | **GLF2** | **236** |
| (N311BK) | GLF3 | 311 |
| N311BP | CL64 | 5405 |
| **N311BP** | **FA50** | **314** |
| N311BP | LJ35 | 311 |
| N311BP | LJ45 | 010 |
| N311BR | WW24 | 344 |
| N311BX | CL64 | 5342 |
| N311CC | LJ25 | 102 |
| **N311CG** | **GLF5** | **5108** |
| **N311CS** | **C550** | **550-0979** |
| N311CW | C650 | 0011 |
| (N311DB) | CL30 | 20011 |
| N311DB | WW24 | 208 |
| N311DF | LJ31 | 001 |
| N311DG | C560 | 0167 |
| N311DH | GLF2 | 236 |
| N311DM | MU30 | A019SA |
| **N311EL** | **GLF4** | **1095** |
| N311FX | CL64 | 5342 |
| N311G | CL61 | 5014 |
| N311GA | GLF3 | 311 |
| N311GA | GLF3 | 394 |
| N311GA | GLF3 | 474 |
| N311GA | GLF4 | 1406 |
| N311GL | BE40 | RK-311 |
| N311GX | CL61 | 5014 |
| N311HS | BE40 | RK-296 |
| **N311JA** | **F900** | **63** |
| N311JA | HS25 | 25176 |
| N311JA | HS25 | 258096 |
| N311JD | HS25 | 257020 |
| N311JJ | GLF2 | 3 |
| N311JK | GLF3 | 434 |
| N311JS | FA20 | 341 |
| **N311JV** | **BE40** | **RK-281** |
| N311JX | HS25 | 258096 |
| **N311LJ** | **LJ24** | **311** |
| N311LJ | LJ31 | 033A |
| N311MA | C650 | 0126 |
| N311ME | C500 | 504 |
| **N311MG** | **GLF2** | **41** |
| (N311MG) | HS25 | 257119 |
| **N311MK** | **GALX** | **095** |
| N311NT | SBRL | 282-19 |
| N311NW | HS25 | 257159 |
| N311QS | C560 | 0311 |
| **N311QS** | **C680** | **0196** |
| N311RM | SBRL | 306-6 |
| **N311RS** | **JSTR** | **5222** |
| N311SL | PRM1 | RB-120 |
| **N311TP** | **C500** | **597** |
| N311TS | LJ31 | 010 |
| (N311TT) | C500 | 597 |
| **N311TT** | **C550** | **108** |
| **N311VP** | **C500** | **600** |
| N312A | FA10 | 122 |
| N312A | FA50 | 157 |
| N312AL | LJ55 | 089 |
| **N312AL** | **LJ60** | **225** |
| **N312AM** | **CL64** | **5312** |
| N312AM | FA10 | 123 |
| N312AM | FA10 | 210 |
| N312AN | FA10 | 123 |
| (N312AR) | FA10 | 209 |
| N312AT | CL61 | 5141 |
| N312AT | CL64 | 5313 |
| N312AT | FA10 | 122 |
| N312AT | FA10 | 123 |
| N312AT | FA10 | 209 |
| N312BX | CL64 | 5349 |
| (N312CC) | C550 | 312 |
| **N312CC** | **LJ31** | **172** |
| N312CE | LJ35 | 403 |
| N312CF | C650 | 0143 |
| N312CF | LJ35 | 403 |
| N312CJ | C52A | 0031 |
| N312CJ | C52B | 0312 |
| N312CK | JSTR | 5150/37 |
| N312CS | C550 | 550-0980 |
| N312CT | CL61 | 5030 |
| N312CT | LJ35 | 403 |
| N312DC | C550 | 376 |
| N312DM | MU30 | A033SA |
| N312DM | MU30 | A090SA |
| **N312EL** | **GLF4** | **1105** |
| N312FX | CL64 | 5349 |
| N312GA | C550 | 004 |
| N312GA | GLF3 | 416 |
| N312GA | GLF3 | 475 |
| N312GA | GLF4 | 1407 |
| N312GK | C500 | 492 |
| N312GK | LJ25 | 283 |
| N312K | FA20 | 324 |
| N312K | SBRL | 282-105 |
| N312LJ | LJ31 | 033D |
| N312NA | LJ24 | 312 |
| **N312NC** | **C550** | **304** |
| N312NT | SBRL | 282-32 |
| N312NW | GLF3 | 312 |
| **N312P** | **FA7X** | **72** |
| N312P | F9EX | 67 |
| **N312PV** | **F9EX** | **67** |
| N312QS | C560 | 0312 |
| N312QS | C680 | 0248 |
| (N312RD) | C550 | 550-0881 |
| N312S | WW24 | 118 |
| N312S | WW24 | 84 |
| N312SB | C525 | 0355 |
| **N312SB** | **C52A** | **0447** |
| N312SE | C525 | 0355 |
| N312SL | PRM1 | RB-125 |
| N312W | ASTR | 012 |
| N312XP | HS25 | 258312 |
| N313BA | C500 | 313 |
| **N313BH** | **LJ45** | **108** |
| N313BT | C550 | 113 |
| N313BW | LJ45 | 108 |
| **N313BW** | **LJ45** | **322** |
| **N313CC** | **F2EX** | **12** |
| N313CC | HS25 | 258043 |
| N313CC | HS25 | 258509 |
| N313CE | C550 | 358 |
| N313CK | C550 | 041 |
| N313CQ | HS25 | 258043 |
| **N313CR** | **C52A** | **0234** |
| N313CS | C550 | 550-0981 |
| **N313CV** | **C560** | **0313** |
| N313DM | MU30 | A022SA |
| **N313DS** | **CL30** | **20183** |
| N313GH | F2TH | 125 |
| N313GH | FA50 | 228 |
| (N313GH) | FA50 | 252 |
| **N313HC** | **C560** | **0603** |
| N313JL | C500 | 166 |
| **N313JS** | **JSTR** | **5086/44** |
| **N313K** | **FA20** | **404** |
| N313NT | SBRL | 282-94 |
| N313QS | C560 | 0325 |
| N313QS | C650 | 0013 |
| **N313QS** | **C680** | **0140** |
| (N313RC) | HS25 | 257087 |
| **N313RF** | **GLEX** | **9194** |
| N313RG | GLF3 | 321 |
| **N313RG** | **GLF5** | **504** |
| N313TW | WW24 | 190 |
| "N313VR" | HS25 | 257207 |
| N313XP | HS25 | 258313 |
| N314AC | LJ31 | 140 |
| N314AD | ASTR | 072 |
| **N314AD** | **ASTR** | **128** |
| N314AD | WW24 | 394 |
| N314AE | FA20 | 140 |
| N314C | LJ35 | 412 |
| (N314CC) | C500 | 314 |
| N314CK | C550 | 051 |
| N314CS | C550 | 550-1004 |
| N314CV | C560 | 0314 |
| N314DM | MU30 | A023SA |
| N314DT | LJ31 | 236 |
| N314EB | C500 | 615 |
| **N314ER** | **HS25** | **25170** |
| N314EX | FA50 | 314 |
| N314FX | CL64 | 5372 |
| N314G | CS55 | 0060 |
| N314GA | ASTR | 214 |
| N314GA | GLF3 | 411 |
| N314GA | GLF3 | 476 |
| N314GA | GLF4 | 1114 |
| N314GA | GLF4 | 1514 |
| N314GA | GLF4 | 4014 |
| N314GA | GLF5 | 5214 |
| N314GS | C500 | 669 |
| (N314MC) | C550 | 293 |
| N314MK | LJ31 | 040 |
| N314NT | SBRL | 282-28 |
| **N314QS** | **C560** | **0441** |
| **N314RC** | **HS25** | **257155** |
| **N314RW** | **C560** | **0051** |
| **N314SG** | **LJ31** | **133** |
| **N314SL** | **C650** | **7115** |
| N314TC | C500 | 216 |
| **N314TC** | **HS25** | **258400** |
| **N314TL** | **BE40** | **RK-181** |
| **N314TW** | **FA20** | **314/516** |
| N314XP | HS25 | 258314 |
| N314XS | LJ31 | 048 |
| N315AJ | LJ24 | 108 |
| N315BK | HS25 | 258410 |
| N315BX | CL64 | 5377 |
| **N315CJ** | **C52B** | **0315** |
| N315CK | C550 | 075 |
| **N315CS** | **C560** | **0371** |
| N315DG | CL64 | 5386 |
| N315DM | MU30 | A015SA |
| N315DV | FA50 | 289 |
| **N315EJ** | **C560** | **0215** |
| N315ES | C550 | 459 |
| N315FW | LJ25 | 315 |
| (N315FX) | CL61 | 5063 |
| N315FX | CL64 | 5377 |
| N315GA | GLF3 | 315 |
| N315GA | GLF3 | 398 |
| N315GA | GLF3 | 443 |
| N315GA | GLF3 | 485 |
| N315GA | GLF4 | 1315 |
| N315GS | GLF3 | 315 |
| **N315JL** | **HS25** | **258891** |
| N315JM | SBRL | 306-96 |
| N315JM | WW24 | 259 |
| N315KP | F9EX | 74 |
| N315LJ | CL30 | 20013 |
| N315MA | GLF4 | 1032 |
| **N315MC** | **C52A** | **0068** |
| N315MC | GLF4 | 1032 |
| N315MK | CL60 | 1047 |
| **N315MK** | **GLF4** | **1206** |
| (N315ML) | HS25 | 258891 |
| N315MP | C500 | 451 |
| N315MR | C500 | 451 |
| **N315MR** | **C525** | **0198** |
| (N315N) | C525 | 0493 |
| N315N | C550 | 550-0849 |
| **N315NT** | **SBRL** | **282-20** |
| (N315P) | C500 | 409 |
| N315PA | FA20 | 113 |
| N315QS | C560 | 0315 |
| **N315QS** | **C680** | **0220** |
| **N315R** | **BE40** | **RK-9** |
| (N315S) | ASTR | 053 |
| N315S | C500 | 409 |
| (N315SA) | BE40 | RJ-22 |
| N315SA | WW24 | 126 |
| N315SL | CL61 | 3054 |
| N315TR | WW24 | 315 |
| N315TS | GLF2 | 220 |
| N316 | LJ35 | 024 |
| N316 | LJ55 | 062 |
| N316 | WW24 | 3 |
| N316AC | LJ31 | 190 |
| N316AS | LJ31 | 150 |
| **N316BD** | **C52B** | **0316** |
| N316BG | CL61 | 5062 |
| N316CC | C550 | 316 |
| N316CF | C550 | 316 |
| **N316CP** | **EA50** | **000089** |
| N316CS | C550 | 550-1010 |
| N316CW | C650 | 0016 |
| N316DM | MU30 | A024SA |
| N316E | WW24 | 3 |
| **N316EC** | **HS25** | **258102** |
| N316EC | SBRL | 380-38 |
| N316EJ | C525 | 0316 |
| **N316EQ** | **SBRL** | **380-38** |
| N316EX | FA50 | 316 |
| N316FA | GLF3 | 316 |
| N316FX | CL64 | 5387 |
| N316GA | GLF3 | 316 |
| N316GA | GLF3 | 386 |
| N316GA | GLF3 | 445 |
| N316GA | GLF3 | 486 |
| N316GA | GLF4 | 1408 |
| **N316GS** | **GLEX** | **9075** |
| N316GS | GLF4 | 1225 |
| N316H | C550 | 316 |
| N316LJ | CL30 | 20016 |
| N316LJ | LJ31 | 036 |
| **N316LP** | **MU30** | **A012SA** |
| N316M | LJ24 | 061 |
| N316M | LJ24 | 101 |
| N316M | LJ25 | 014 |
| N316MA | C550 | 550-0907 |
| N316MF | LJ24 | 101 |
| **N316MH** | **CS55** | **0108** |
| N316MJ | C525 | 0297 |
| N316NT | SBRL | 282-60 |
| N316PA | FA50 | 166 |
| **N316QS** | **C560** | **0516** |
| N316RS | LJ31 | 150 |
| N316RS | LJ31 | 189 |
| N316SR | LJ45 | 119 |
| N316SR | LJ45 | 121 |
| **N316SS** | **F900** | **8** |
| **N316TD** | **WW24** | **312** |
| N316XP | HS25 | 258316 |
| (N317AB) | C500 | 017 |
| N317AF | GLF2 | 168 |
| N317BG | LJ35 | 506 |
| **N317BH** | **EA50** | **000013** |
| N317BR | C52B | 0150 |
| N317BX | CL64 | 5407 |
| N317CC | HS25 | 258093 |
| **N317CC** | **HS25** | **258532** |

| Registration | Type | C/n |
|---|---|---|
| N317CC | MU30 | A081SA |
| N317CJ | C525 | 0317 |
| N317CQ | HS25 | 258093 |
| N317CS | C550 | 550-1019 |
| **N317DJ** | **EA50** | **000095** |
| N317DM | MU30 | A025SA |
| N317EM | HS25 | 25115 |
| N317FE | CL60 | 1074 |
| N317FX | CL64 | 5407 |
| N317GA | GLF3 | 350 |
| N317GA | GLF3 | 417 |
| N317GA | GLF3 | 477 |
| N317GA | GLF4 | 1409 |
| N317GC | MU30 | A081SA |
| **N317HC** | **C550** | **228** |
| N317JD | GLF5 | 549 |
| (N317JD) | LJ35 | 186 |
| (N317JQ) | C500 | 651 |
| **N317JS** | **WW24** | **385** |
| N317K | LJ31 | 235 |
| N317LJ | LJ31 | 117 |
| N317M | C650 | 7055 |
| **N317M** | **F2TH** | **188** |
| N317M | GLF4 | 1122 |
| N317M | GLF4 | 1191 |
| N317M | GLF4 | 1446 |
| N317M | WW24 | 257 |
| N317M | WW24 | 432 |
| N317MB | C650 | 7012 |
| N317MB | GLF4 | 1191 |
| N317MB | WW24 | 257 |
| N317MB | WW24 | 432 |
| **N317MJ** | **GLF4** | **1122** |
| **N317ML** | **C56X** | **5036** |
| N317ML | F2TH | 144 |
| N317ML | GLF3 | 460 |
| N317ML | GLF4 | 1446 |
| N317MN | F2TH | 146 |
| N317MQ | C650 | 7015 |
| N317MQ | F2TH | 152 |
| N317MQ | WW24 | 421 |
| N317MR | F2TH | 144 |
| N317MR | GLF4 | 1191 |
| (N317MR) | LJ24 | 297 |
| N317MR | LJ35 | 176 |
| (N317MT) | WW24 | 432 |
| (N317MV) | WW24 | 418 |
| (N317MX) | C650 | 7015 |
| N317MX | WW24 | 418 |
| N317MZ | C650 | 7010 |
| N317MZ | C650 | 7055 |
| N317MZ | F2TH | 188 |
| N317NT | SBRL | 282-100 |
| **N317PC** | **BE40** | **RK-357** |
| N317QS | C560 | 0317 |
| **N317QS** | **C680** | **0160** |
| N317SM | C550 | 162 |
| N317TC | HS25 | 256007 |
| N317TS | LJ25 | 317 |
| **N317TT** | **LJ35** | **317** |
| N317VP | C500 | 317 |
| N317VS | LJ25 | 317 |
| N318CD | HS25 | 257136 |
| N318CS | C550 | 550-1029 |
| **N318CT** | **C560** | **0081** |
| N318DM | MU30 | A034SA |
| **N318DN** | **C500** | **575** |
| N318FX | CL64 | 5415 |
| **N318GA** | **FA50** | **233** |
| N318GA | GLF3 | 355 |
| N318GA | GLF3 | 421 |
| N318GA | GLF3 | 478 |
| N318GA | GLF4 | 1410 |
| (N318GD) | GLF2 | 170 |
| N318JH | LJ55 | 026 |
| N318JH | LJ55 | 106 |
| N318LJ | LJ31 | 118 |
| N318MM | C560 | 0219 |
| **N318MM** | **C56X** | **5220** |
| N318MN | C560 | 0219 |
| **N318NW** | **LJ35** | **318** |
| **N318QS** | **C560** | **0418** |
| N318RS | MU30 | A009SA |
| **N318SA** | **LJ45** | **114** |
| N318SP | GLF2 | 168 |
| N318XP | HS25 | 258318 |
| N319AT | HS25 | 258043 |
| N319BG | WW24 | 192 |
| N319CH | LJ31 | 041 |
| N319CS | C550 | 550-1036 |
| N319DM | MU30 | A019SA |
| N319DM | MU30 | A027SA |
| N319EJ | LJ25 | 319 |
| (N319EX) | FA50 | 319 |
| N319FX | CL64 | 5418 |
| N319GA | GLF3 | 370 |
| N319GA | GLF3 | 422 |
| N319GA | GLF3 | 479 |
| N319GA | GLF4 | 1356 |
| N319GP | GLF2 | 150 |
| N319LJ | LJ60 | 079 |
| N319MF | HS25 | 256070 |
| N319NW | HS25 | 257171 |
| **N319QS** | **C560** | **0519** |
| N319R | C52A | 0176 |
| N319RG | CL30 | 20019 |
| **N319SC** | **LJ31** | **131** |
| N319Z | GLF3 | 319 |
| N320AF | HFB3 | 1023 |
| **N320AF** | **HFB3** | **1061** |
| **N320BP** | **C52B** | **0143** |
| N320CC | C500 | 320 |
| N320CH | MU30 | A024SA |
| N320CL | CL64 | 5370 |
| N320CS | C550 | 550-1039 |
| N320DG | CS55 | 0021 |
| N320DM | MU30 | A028SA |
| N320EJ | LJ25 | 320 |
| N320FE | GLF2 | 9/33 |
| (N320FJ) | FA20 | 242 |
| N320FX | CL64 | 5425 |
| N320GA | GLF3 | 372 |
| N320GA | GLF3 | 409 |
| N320GA | GLF3 | 424 |
| N320GA | GLF4 | 1366 |
| (N320GP) | FA10 | 80 |
| N320GP | HS25 | 257173 |
| **N320GX** | **GLEX** | **9116** |
| N320J | HFB3 | 1023 |
| N320J | HFB3 | 1034 |
| N320JJ | HS25 | 25198 |
| N320K | FA50 | 154 |
| N320K | GLF5 | 514 |
| **N320LA** | **EA50** | **000016** |
| N320M | LJ35 | 320 |
| N320MC | HFB3 | 1034 |
| **N320MD** | **WW24** | **366** |
| N320MP | WW24 | 432 |
| N320QS | C560 | 0321 |
| **N320QS** | **C680** | **0169** |
| N320RG | C500 | 236 |
| N320S | C550 | 138 |
| N320S | CS55 | 0090 |
| N320S | JSTR | 5082/36 |
| N320T | MU30 | A032SA |
| **N320TM** | **C680** | **0136** |
| N320TR | GLF2 | 233 |
| N320V | C550 | 193 |
| N320VP | C560 | 0320 |
| N320W | WW24 | 15 |
| N320WE | GLF3 | 320 |
| N321AF | HFB3 | 1060 |
| **N321AN** | **LJ35** | **272** |
| **N321AR** | **C650** | **0151** |
| N321AS | LJ25 | 273 |
| N321AU | LJ25 | 253 |
| N321BN | GLF4 | 1300 |
| **N321CL** | **C56X** | **5527** |
| N321DM | MU30 | A029SA |
| N321EJ | HS25 | 258515 |
| N321EX | FA50 | 321 |
| N321F | C550 | 567 |
| N321FM | C500 | 687 |
| N321FX | CL64 | 5427 |
| N321GA | GLF3 | 321 |
| N321GA | GLF3 | 426 |
| N321GA | GLF3 | 459 |
| N321GE | LJ25 | 289 |
| **N321GG** | **C560** | **0474** |
| N321GL | LJ24 | 174 |
| N321GL | LJ25 | 277 |
| N321GL | LJ25 | 289 |
| N321GL | LJ31 | 085 |
| **N321GL** | **LJ31** | **216** |
| (N321GL) | LJ55 | 026 |
| N321GN | C550 | 347 |
| **N321MS** | **HS25** | **258515** |
| N321PT | GLF4 | 1013 |
| (N321PT) | GLF4 | 1251 |
| N321Q | LJ24 | 177 |
| N321RB | LJ25 | 290 |
| N321RT | GLF4 | 1013 |
| N321SE | C550 | 347 |
| **N321SF** | **GALX** | **021** |
| N321TS | C500 | 564 |
| N321VP | C500 | 668 |
| (N321VP) | C560 | 0123 |
| (N321WJ) | LJ35 | 321 |
| **N322AD** | **GALX** | **022** |
| N322AF | HFB3 | 1058 |
| **N322AU** | **LJ24** | **326** |
| **N322BC** | **HS25** | **257176** |
| N322BE | MU30 | A022SA |
| **N322BJ** | **PRM1** | **RB-93** |
| N322BX | CL64 | 5434 |
| N322CC | HS25 | 256070 |
| **N322CP** | **F900** | **134** |
| N322CS | C550 | 344 |
| **N322CS** | **C550** | **550-1052** |
| N322CS | JSTR | 5208 |
| N322CS | SBRL | 282-56 |
| N322DM | MU30 | A030SA |
| N322FX | CL64 | 5434 |
| N322GA | GLF3 | 322 |
| N322GA | GLF3 | 428 |
| N322GA | GLF3 | 460 |
| N322GA | GLF3 | 493 |
| N322GA | GLF4 | 1368 |
| **N322GC** | **LJ55** | **008** |
| **N322GT** | **C550** | **550-1030** |
| **N322JG** | **EA50** | **000130** |
| N322K | JSTR | 5013 |
| N322K | JSTR | 5133 |
| N322LA | CL64 | 5482 |
| N322LA | HS25 | 258410 |
| N322LA | SPEC | 0001 |
| **N322MA** | **C550** | **375** |
| N322MD | MU30 | A022SA |
| **N322PE** | **HS25** | **258693** |
| **N322QS** | **C560** | **0421** |
| N322RG | C650 | 7070 |
| **N322RR** | **FA20** | **514** |
| **N322RS** | **LJ24** | **322** |
| **N322ST** | **C500** | **402** |
| (N322TJ) | LJ24 | 322 |
| N322TP | HS25 | 25170 |
| **N322TS** | **LJ31** | **002** |
| (N322TW) | SBRL | 465-17 |
| N323AF | HFB3 | 1062 |
| (N323AM) | C550 | 351 |
| **N323BD** | **GLF5** | **5192** |
| N323BX | CL64 | 5447 |
| N323CB | C500 | 563 |
| N323CJ | C550 | 323 |
| N323CM | PRM1 | RB-22 |
| N323DM | MU30 | A032SA |
| N323EC | SBRL | 306-134 |
| N323EJ | LJ25 | 323 |
| N323EX | FA50 | 323 |
| N323FX | CL64 | 5447 |
| **N323G** | **C525** | **0532** |
| N323G | GLF3 | 323 |
| N323GA | GLF3 | 429 |
| N323GA | GLF3 | 461 |
| N323GA | GLF4 | 1369 |
| N323GA | GLF4 | 1414 |
| **N323JA** | **C525** | **0116** |
| (N323JB) | C500 | 468 |
| N323JH | GLF3 | 434 |
| **N323JK** | **HS25** | **257048** |
| N323JR | CS55 | 0129 |
| (N323L) | HS25 | 258212 |
| N323LJ | LJ31 | 123 |
| (N323LM) | C525 | 0204 |
| N323LM | C525 | 0230 |
| N323LM | C52A | 0020 |
| N323MP | HS25 | 258594 |
| **N323MR** | **WW24** | **324** |
| **N323NE** | **C560** | **0442** |
| N323P | ASTR | 049 |
| **N323P** | **ASTR** | **096** |
| N323P | JSTR | 5099/5 |
| N323QS | C560 | 0323 |
| **N323QS** | **C680** | **0134** |
| N323R | SBRL | 306-26 |
| **N323SK** | **C52A** | **0134** |
| **N323SL** | **HS25** | **258084** |
| N323WA | LJ25 | 018 |
| N323XP | HS25 | 258323 |
| N324AF | HFB3 | 1064 |
| N324AJ | WW24 | 208 |
| **N324AM** | **PRM1** | **RB-42** |
| **N324B** | **CL61** | **5069** |
| **N324BD** | **C525** | **0674** |
| **N324BG** | **HS25** | **258165** |
| N324C | C500 | 324 |
| N324CC | C550 | 431 |
| N324CL | F2TH | 32 |
| **N324CS** | **C550** | **550-1059** |
| **N324DR** | **C510** | **0271** |
| N324EX | FA50 | 324 |
| **N324FP** | **GLF4** | **1475** |
| N324FX | CL64 | 5454 |
| N324GA | GLF3 | 430 |
| N324GA | GLF3 | 462 |
| N324GA | GLF3 | 487 |
| N324GA | GLF4 | 1330 |
| N324GA | GLF4 | 1421 |
| **N324JC** | **C500** | **324** |
| **N324JT** | **C550** | **550-0819** |
| N324K | HS25 | 257111 |
| N324K | JSTR | 5089 |
| **N324L** | **C500** | **594** |
| (N324LE) | C56X | 5109 |
| N324LX | C56X | 5109 |
| **N324MM** | **BE40** | **RJ-52** |
| N324QS | C560 | 0423 |
| (N324QS) | C560 | 0424 |
| **N324QS** | **C680** | **0242** |
| N324SA | HS25 | 258047 |
| **N324SM** | **GLEX** | **9023** |
| N324SR | F900 | 14 |
| N324TC | FA20 | 324 |
| **N324TW** | **LJ24** | **324** |
| N324XP | HS25 | 258324 |
| N324ZR | SBRL | 465-25 |
| N325AF | HFB3 | 1065 |
| N325AJ | WW24 | 181 |
| N325BC | C500 | 450 |
| N325CP | LJ55 | 112 |
| **N325CS** | **C550** | **550-1061** |
| N325DA | CL61 | 5016 |
| N325DM | C525 | 0438 |
| N325DM | MU30 | A006SA |
| N325EX | FA50 | 325 |
| N325FN | C56X | 5350 |
| N325FX | CL64 | 5457 |
| N325GA | GLF3 | 433 |
| N325GA | GLF3 | 466 |
| N325GA | GLF3 | 488 |
| N325GA | GLF4 | 1326 |
| N325GA | GLF5 | 5225 |
| N325JB | LJ25 | 325 |
| N325JG | BE40 | RK-190 |
| N325JL | LJ25 | 215 |
| N325K | SBRL | 282-63 |
| N325LJ | WW24 | 181 |
| N325LW | WW24 | 334 |
| (N325MC) | FA20 | 325 |
| **N325NW** | **LJ35** | **325** |
| (N325PM) | C500 | 450 |
| **N325QS** | **C560** | **0425** |
| **N325RC** | **C52B** | **0021** |
| N325RC | GLF4 | 1139 |
| N325RR | C510 | 0025 |
| **N325SJ** | **LJ25** | **102** |
| **N325WC** | **C560** | **0343** |
| **N325WP** | **C550** | **550-0933** |
| N326AJ | WW24 | 191 |
| N326AZ | GLF4 | 1262 |
| **N326B** | **C525** | **0302** |
| (N326BX) | CL64 | 5464 |
| N326CB | JSTR | 5143 |
| N326CS | C550 | 550-1065 |
| N326CW | MU30 | A026SA |
| (N326DD) | GLF3 | 326 |
| **N326DD** | **LJ35** | **173** |
| N326DM | MU30 | A036SA |
| N326EJ | LJ24 | 326 |
| N326EW | C550 | 622 |
| **N326EW** | **F2EX** | **55** |
| N326EW | F2TH | 58 |

| | | | | | | | | | | | |
|---|---|---|---|---|---|---|---|---|---|---|---|
| N326EW | FA10 | 220 | (N328RC) | CL30 | 20028 | **N331DM** | **FA20** | **429** | N333CJ | HS25 | 25155 |
| N326EW | FA20 | 392/553 | N328RR | LJ45 | 175 | N331DM | MU30 | A042SA | N333CR | LJ24 | 199 |
| N326FB | FA50 | 39 | **N328SA** | **WW24** | **425** | N331DP | LJ24 | 059 | N333CZ | ASTR | 080 |
| N326FX | CL64 | 5464 | N328TL | LJ24 | 212 | N331DP | LJ24 | 067 | N333DP | HS25 | 25282 |
| N326GA | GLF3 | 434 | N328XP | HS25 | 258328 | N331DQ | CL61 | 5093 | **N333EB** | **C550** | **550-0893** |
| N326GA | GLF3 | 473 | **N329BH** | **C52B** | **0292** | N331EC | C560 | 0269 | N333EC | F900 | 106 |
| N326HG | LJ35 | 501 | N329CC | C550 | 329 | (N331EC) | C560 | 0279 | **N333EC** | **GLF4** | **1414** |
| **N326HG** | **LJ60** | **163** | **N329CH** | **CL30** | **20185** | **N331EX** | **FA50** | **331** | N333EC | JSTR | 5061/48 |
| **N326JD** | **GLF4** | **1460** | **N329CJ** | **C52B** | **0130** | N331FP | CL60 | 1072 | **N333FJ** | **FA10** | **1** |
| **N326JK** | **C525** | **0511** | **N329CS** | **C550** | **550-1077** | N331FX | CL64 | 5491 | N333FX | CL64 | 5544 |
| N326K | F9EX | 36 | (N329DM) | MU30 | A040SA | N331GA | GLF3 | 452 | N333GA | GLF3 | 326 |
| N326K | F9EX | 84 | N329EX | FA50 | 329 | N331GA | GLF4 | 1331 | N333GA | GLF3 | 420 |
| N326K | HS25 | 257119 | N329FX | CL64 | 5476 | N331GA | GLF4 | 1430 | N333GA | GLF3 | 432 |
| N326K | JSTR | 5102 | **N329FX** | **CL64** | **5541** | N331GW | WW24 | 231 | N333GA | GLF3 | 875 |
| N326KE | LJ24 | 326 | N329GA | GLF3 | 450 | N331JR | LJ24 | 072 | N333GA | GLF4 | 1333 |
| (N326LA) | EA50 | 000136 | N329GA | GLF4 | 1329 | N331LV | GLF4 | 1460 | N333GJ | CL61 | 3042 |
| (N326LM) | GLF4 | 1460 | N329HN | LJ24 | 230 | **N331MC** | **F9EX** | **22** | (N333GJ) | LJ55 | 132 |
| N326LW | FA10 | 220 | N329HN | WW24 | 34 | N331MC | FA50 | 95 | N333GM | SBRL | 282-106 |
| N326LW | FA20 | 392/553 | N329J | JSTR | 1001 | N331MS | C525 | 0330 | N333GM | SBRL | 282-45 |
| **N326MA** | **C56X** | **5159** | **N329JC** | **CS55** | **0059** | **N331MW** | **C560** | **0384** | N333GU | GLF3 | 875 |
| N326MM | CL60 | 1024 | N329JS | JSTR | 5206 | **N331N** | **LJ31** | **022** | N333GZ | HS25 | 25070 |
| **N326N** | **HS25** | **258140** | N329K | F2TH | 182 | N331P | GLF2 | 20 | N333HK | GLF3 | 482 |
| **N326QS** | **C560** | **0526** | N329K | F900 | 46 | N331P | GLF4 | 1139 | N333HP | LJ25 | 109 |
| N326SM | LJ60 | 370 | N329K | GLF2 | 180 | N331PL | LJ60 | 331 | N333J | C525 | 0531 |
| N326SU | C750 | 0015 | N329K | JSTR | 1002 | **N331PR** | **C550** | **550-0831** | N333JH | C500 | 292 |
| N326SU | HS25 | 258249 | N329K | JSTR | 5133 | **N331PS** | **CL64** | **5491** | N333KC | GLF3 | 366 |
| N326VW | FA20 | 27 | N329MD | JSTR | 5215 | N331QS | C560 | 0331 | (N333KC) | GLF3 | 403 |
| N326XP | HS25 | 258326 | (N329N) | GLF3 | 329 | N331SC | HS25 | 258093 | **N333KC** | **LJ35** | **037** |
| N327BC | FA20 | 327 | N329SS | SBRL | 282-9 | (N331SE) | FA50 | 331 | (N333KD) | GLF3 | 366 |
| (N327BC) | LJ25 | 327 | N329TJ | LJ24 | 329 | N331SJ | LJ31 | 113 | **N333KE** | **FA10** | **14** |
| N327CB | LJ35 | 483 | **N329TJ** | **LJ55** | **120** | **N331SK** | **ASTR** | **063** | N333KK | CL60 | 1082 |
| N327CM | C510 | 0027 | N329XP | HS25 | 258329 | N331TH | CL64 | 5325 | N333KN | JSTR | 5118 |
| N327CS | C550 | 550-1070 | **N330AM** | **HS25** | **25235** | **N331TP** | **CL64** | **5350** | N333KN | JSTR | 5202 |
| N327DM | MU30 | A037SA | N330BC | LJ35 | 432 | N331WR | LJ24 | 072 | N333LX | GLF3 | 366 |
| N327EJ | LJ24 | 327 | N330CC | C500 | 330 | (N331WT) | CL60 | 1073 | N333M | HS25 | 25017 |
| N327EX | FA50 | 327 | N330CJ | C525 | 0330 | N331ZX | LJ31 | 133 | N333ME | HS25 | 25115 |
| N327F | LJ35 | 327 | N330DE | HS25 | 258060 | **N332AE** | **C560** | **0332** | N333ME | HS25 | 257003 |
| **N327FX** | **CL64** | **5466** | **N330DK** | **C550** | **296** | **N332BN** | **C56X** | **6052** | N333MF | HS25 | 25115 |
| N327GA | ASTR | 127 | N330DM | MU30 | A041SA | (N332CM) | C750 | 0107 | N333MG | CL61 | 5035 |
| **N327GA** | **ASTR** | **157** | N330EX | FA50 | 330 | **N332CS** | **C550** | **550-1081** | N333MS | C500 | 584 |
| N327GA | GLF3 | 427 | **N330FX** | **CL64** | **5487** | N332DF | WW24 | 332 | N333MS | HS25 | 257115 |
| N327GA | GLF3 | 463 | **N330G** | **HS25** | **25087** | N332DM | MU30 | A043SA | N333MX | CL61 | 5151 |
| N327GA | GLF4 | 1327 | N330G | HS25 | 256033 | N332EC | F900 | 106 | **N333MX** | **F2EX** | **120** |
| N327GA | GLF4 | 1527 | N330GA | GALX | 130 | N332EX | FA50 | 332 | N333MY | EA50 | 000103 |
| N327GJ | LJ24 | 327 | N330GA | GLF3 | 451 | N332FE | FA20 | 225/472 | N333NC | SBRL | 306-76 |
| N327JB | SBRL | 282-9 | N330GA | GLF4 | 1350 | N332FG | LJ35 | 332 | **N333NM** | **SBRL** | **282-45** |
| N327JJ | GLF3 | 329 | N330GA | GLF4 | 1428 | N332FP | LJ24 | 126 | N333NR | HS25 | 257167 |
| N327K | F900 | 3 | N330GA | GLF4 | 1530 | N332FW | C650 | 0032 | N333PC | HS25 | 257008 |
| N327K | F9EX | 103 | N330GA | GLF5 | 5230 | **N332FX** | **CL64** | **5543** | N333PC | HS25 | 258277 |
| N327K | F9EX | 37 | N330J | LJ24 | 130 | N332GA | GLF3 | 453 | **N333PC** | **HS25** | **258669** |
| N327K | GLF2 | 25 | **N330K** | **F2TH** | **189** | N332GA | GLF3 | 490 | N333PC | SBRL | 306-76 |
| N327LJ | C550 | 550-0900 | N330K | F900 | 50 | N332GA | GLF4 | 1332 | N333PC | SBRL | 465-28 |
| **N327LJ** | **HS25** | **258490** | **N330L** | **LJ25** | **330** | (N332GJ) | C500 | 015 | N333PD | C500 | 382 |
| N327LN | C550 | 550-0900 | N330LJ | LJ25 | 330 | N332H | C500 | 144 | N333PE | C500 | 382 |
| **N327QS** | **C560** | **0327** | **N330MB** | **C650** | **0129** | N332J | FA10 | 29 | N333PP | C500 | 050 |
| N327R | C650 | 0152 | N330MC | F9EX | 21 | **N332K** | **LJ45** | **169** | N333PV | GLF4 | 1240 |
| (N327RH) | SBRL | 282-9 | N330MC | FA10 | 199 | N332LC | C560 | 0332 | **N333PY** | **GLF4** | **1317** |
| N327SA | WW24 | 428 | N330MC | FA50 | 175 | N332LS | LJ25 | 122 | N333QA | JSTR | 5118 |
| N327TC | GLF2 | 33 | (N330MG) | C550 | 147 | N332MC | F900 | 78 | **N333QS** | **C560** | **0333** |
| N327TL | GLF2 | 33 | N330MG | WW24 | 434 | (N332MC) | F9EX | 22 | (N333RB) | C500 | 498 |
| **N327TL** | **GLF4** | **1339** | N330PC | FA20 | 107 | N332MC | FA50 | 55 | N333RB | LJ35 | 220 |
| N327XP | HS25 | 258327 | N330PC | WW24 | 207 | N332MQ | FA50 | 55 | N333RL | C650 | 0019 |
| N328BT | C650 | 7046 | N330QS | C560 | 0329 | **N332MT** | **C550** | **550-1105** | **N333RL** | **HS25** | **259027** |
| N328BX | CL64 | 5328 | N330R | HS25 | HA-0076 | N332PC | LJ24 | 056 | N333RP | LJ35 | 148 |
| N328CC | C500 | 328 | N330TJ | C650 | 0101 | **N332QS** | **C560** | **0523** | N333RS | BE40 | RJ-62 |
| **N328CC** | **CL30** | **20028** | N330TP | CL61 | 5142 | **N332SB** | **C52B** | **0145** | N333RU | HS25 | 259027 |
| **N328CJ** | **C525** | **0328** | **N330TS** | **BE40** | **RK-330** | **N332SE** | **C500** | **332** | N333RW | JSTR | 5138 |
| **N328CS** | **C550** | **550-1074** | **N330TW** | **LJ24** | **330** | N332TA | HS25 | 256032 | N333RY | LJ24 | 202 |
| N328DM | MU30 | A039SA | N330U | SBRL | 306-20 | **N332TM** | **GALX** | **201** | N333SG | LJ25 | 226 |
| N328EW | FA20 | 392/553 | **N330VP** | **C560** | **0330** | (N332VP) | C525 | 0332 | N333SR | FA10 | 48 |
| N328EX | FA50 | 328 | **N330WR** | **GLF3** | **337** | N332WE | HS25 | 257186 | (N333ST) | GLF2 | 57 |
| N328FX | CL64 | 5474 | N330X | HS25 | 258060 | N332XP | HS25 | 258332 | N333SV | WW24 | 114 |
| N328GA | GLF3 | 444 | N330XP | HS25 | 258330 | N333AJ | ASTR | 080 | N333SZ | GALX | 210 |
| N328GA | GLF3 | 489 | N331AP | WW24 | 205 | N333AR | GLF2 | 189/42 | **N333SZ** | **GLF4** | **4184** |
| N328GA | GLF4 | 1328 | N331BN | GALX | 095 | N333AV | FA20 | 28 | (N333TS) | CL60 | 1023 |
| N328GA | GLF4 | 1424 | N331BN | GALX | 230 | N333AW | LJ25 | 163 | N333TS | MU30 | A047SA |
| N328JK | LJ24 | 212 | N331CC | C500 | 331 | N333AX | GLF2 | 30/4 | **N333TW** | **LJ24** | **168** |
| N328JR | F900 | 51 | N331CC | C560 | 0044 | N333AX | GLF4 | 1063 | **N333VS** | **C525** | **0034** |
| N328JS | SBRL | 306-92 | N331CC | LJ31 | 003 | N333B | SBRL | 282-39 | N333WC | C650 | 0211 |
| N328JW | LJ25 | 328 | (N331CG) | HS25 | 257043 | **N333BD** | **C52A** | **0237** | N333WF | FA20 | 113 |
| N328K | F900 | 13 | N331CJ | C52B | 0131 | N333BD | C550 | 550-0958 | **N333WM** | **C560** | **0385** |
| N328K | F9EX | 38 | N331CW | WW24 | 231 | N333BF | LJ24 | 010 | N333X | C550 | 042 |
| N328K | GLF2 | 26 | N331DC | CL61 | 5093 | (N333BG) | C500 | 482 | N333X | LJ24 | 128 |
| **N328NA** | **C500** | **568** | **N331DC** | **F2DX** | **601** | N333BG | WW24 | 98 | N333X | LJ24 | 251 |
| **N328PC** | **WW24** | **328** | N331DC | F2TH | 206 | N333CD | LJ25 | 258 | N333X | LJ35 | 286 |
| **N328QS** | **C560** | **0428** | N331DC | HS25 | 256061 | N333CG | C550 | 188 | N333XP | HS25 | 258733 |
| N328QS | C650 | 0028 | N331DC | HS25 | 258112 | N333CG | LJ25 | 262 | (N333XX) | LJ35 | 286 |
| **N328RC** | **C52B** | **0203** | N331DC | MU30 | A028SA | N333CG | WW24 | 339 | N334 | GLF2 | 143 |

| | | |
|---|---|---|
| N334 | HS25 | 258013 |
| N334 | WW24 | 344 |
| (N334AB) | LJ35 | 334 |
| N334AF | LJ31 | 225 |
| **N334AF** | **LJ45** | **143** |
| N334AM | C550 | 227 |
| N334BD | C525 | 0486 |
| N334CM | C650 | 0234 |
| **N334CS** | **C550** | **550-1089** |
| (N334DB) | C525 | 0409 |
| N334DM | MU30 | A044SA |
| N334DM | MU30 | A045SA |
| N334ED | C550 | 252 |
| N334EX | FA50 | 333 |
| N334FX | CL64 | 5545 |
| **N334FX** | **CL64** | **5586** |
| N334GA | GLF3 | 454 |
| N334GA | GLF4 | 1334 |
| N334GA | GLF4 | 1431 |
| N334H | C650 | 0071 |
| N334JC | C500 | 334 |
| N334JC | GLF4 | 1134 |
| N334JR | FA20 | 139 |
| N334JR | HS25 | 256020 |
| (N334JW) | LJ55 | 034 |
| **N334KC** | **MU30** | **A034SA** |
| N334LP | WW24 | 20 |
| N334LS | LJ25 | 158 |
| N334MC | F900 | 108 |
| N334MC | FA50 | 175 |
| N334MC | GLF4 | 1289 |
| N334MD | LJ25 | 334 |
| N334PS | C500 | 164 |
| **N334PS** | **HS25** | **256032** |
| **N334QS** | **C560** | **0434** |
| N334RC | C500 | 062 |
| **N334RJ** | **C550** | **252** |
| N334RK | MS76 | 090 |
| N334RK | WW24 | 5 |
| N334SP | LJ35 | 334 |
| N334SR | BE40 | RK-129 |
| N334WC | C650 | 0207 |
| N334WM | MU30 | A057SA |
| N334XP | HS25 | 258334 |
| **N335AF** | **CL30** | **20190** |
| N335AF | LJ31 | 241 |
| N335AF | LJ60 | 244 |
| N335AJ | FA20 | 335 |
| N335AS | LJ35 | 170 |
| **N335AT** | **LJ35** | **009** |
| N335CC | C550 | 480 |
| N335CJ | C525 | 0335 |
| N335CJ | C52B | 0335 |
| **N335CS** | **C550** | **550-1091** |
| N335CT | C525 | 0335 |
| N335DJ | LJ35 | 335 |
| N335DM | MU30 | A045SA |
| N335DM | MU30 | A048SA |
| N335EA | LJ35 | 614 |
| N335EE | LJ35 | 335 |
| N335EJ | C560 | 0235 |
| N335EX | FA50 | 334 |
| N335FX | CL64 | 5546 |
| **N335FX** | **CL64** | **5619** |
| N335GA | GLF3 | 455 |
| N335GA | GLF4 | 1335 |
| N335GA | GLF4 | 1432 |
| (N335GA) | LJ35 | 423 |
| N335H | GLF2 | 238 |
| N335J | C525 | 0425 |
| N335JB | PRM1 | RB-15 |
| N335JD | LJ35 | 397 |
| **N335JJ** | **C52A** | **0162** |
| N335JL | LJ35 | 015 |
| (N335JR) | LJ24 | 226 |
| N335JW | LJ24 | 226 |
| N335K | LJ35 | 381 |
| (N335K) | SBRL | 380-12 |
| (N335LA) | EA50 | 000168 |
| **N335LL** | **GLF4** | **1367** |
| N335MC | F900 | 150 |
| N335MC | FA20 | 355 |
| **N335MG** | **LJ35** | **626** |
| **N335MR** | **LJ35** | **443** |
| N335MW | LJ35 | 472 |
| N335NA | LJ35 | 170 |
| N335NE | LJ35 | 335 |
| **N335PR** | **LJ35** | **647** |
| N335QS | C560 | 0335 |
| **N335RC** | **LJ35** | **256** |
| N335RD | LJ35 | 216 |
| N335RY | LJ24 | 226 |
| N335SB | LJ35 | 656 |
| (N335SS) | LJ35 | 015 |
| **N335TW** | **FA20** | **335** |
| N335UJ | LJ35 | 492 |
| **N335VB** | **WW24** | **297** |
| N335WC | C650 | 0211 |
| N335WJ | FA20 | 122 |
| N335WR | FA20 | 122 |
| N335XP | HS25 | 258335 |
| N336AC | HS25 | 25202 |
| N336AC | HS25 | 257033 |
| (N336BC) | C56X | 5336 |
| N336CC | C500 | 336 |
| N336CJ | C52A | 0336 |
| **N336CJ** | **C52B** | **0336** |
| **N336CS** | **C550** | **550-1095** |
| N336DM | MU30 | A049SA |
| (N336EA) | LJ35 | 336 |
| **N336FX** | **CL64** | **5634** |
| N336GA | GLF3 | 456 |
| **N336MA** | **C550** | **036** |
| N336MA | C56X | 5159 |
| N336MB | HS25 | 25153 |
| **N336QS** | **C560** | **0336** |
| **N336RJ** | **SBRL** | **465-10** |
| N336SV | WW24 | 336 |
| N336UB | LJ45 | 046 |
| N336WR | LJ25 | 148 |
| **N336XL** | **C56X** | **5336** |
| N336XP | HS25 | 258336 |
| **N337BG** | **LJ60** | **337** |
| **N337CC** | **C560** | **0810** |
| **N337CS** | **C550** | **550-1097** |
| N337FP | LJ31 | 020 |
| **N337FX** | **CL64** | **5647** |
| N337GA | GLF3 | 457 |
| N337GA | GLF3 | 491 |
| N337GA | GLF4 | 4137 |
| N337GL | LJ25 | 337 |
| N337JD | GALX | 037 |
| N337MC | F900 | 152 |
| **N337QS** | **C560** | **0437** |
| N337RB | LJ31 | 154 |
| N337RE | C550 | 575 |
| **N337RE** | **HS25** | **258024** |
| N337RE | WW24 | 210 |
| N337TV | C500 | 236 |
| N337US | JSTR | 5107 |
| N337WC | LJ35 | 337 |
| **N337WR** | **HS25** | **258273** |
| N337XP | HS25 | 258337 |
| N338 | HS25 | 25023 |
| N338 | HS25 | 25134 |
| N338AX | GLF2 | 30/4 |
| **N338B** | **C550** | **550-1132** |
| **N338CL** | **GLF2** | **199/19** |
| **N338CS** | **C550** | **550-1084** |
| **N338CZ** | **C52B** | **0338** |
| N338DB | FA20 | 225/472 |
| N338DM | MU30 | A038SA |
| N338DS | LJ24 | 162 |
| N338EC | JSTR | 5061/48 |
| N338FJ | FA50 | 338 |
| N338FP | LJ55 | 138 |
| **N338FX** | **CL64** | **5656** |
| N338GA | GLF3 | 458 |
| (N338K) | SBRL | 380-15 |
| N338KK | LJ24 | 020 |
| **N338MC** | **C560** | **0662** |
| **N338MM** | **GLF4** | **1076** |
| N338PR | LJ60 | 338 |
| **N338QS** | **C680** | **0011** |
| **N338R** | **C560** | **0338** |
| (N338RJ) | GLF3 | 338 |
| **N338TM** | **C680** | **0177** |
| **N338TP** | **GLEX** | **9073** |
| **N338TZ** | **GLF4** | **4064** |
| N338W | WW24 | 338 |
| N338X | LJ24 | 251 |
| N339A | GLF3 | 339 |
| N339B | C525 | 0339 |
| (N339BA) | LJ25 | 240 |
| N339BC | LJ55 | 039 |
| (N339BW) | HS25 | 257010 |
| **N339CA** | **HS25** | **257019** |
| **N339CC** | **HS25** | **258277** |
| **N339CS** | **C550** | **550-1085** |
| N339DM | MU30 | A014SA |
| **N339FX** | **CL65** | **5719** |
| N339GA | GLF2 | 139/11 |
| N339GA | GLF3 | 374 |
| N339GA | GLF3 | 448 |
| N339GA | GLF3 | 492 |
| N339GA | GLF4 | 1339 |
| N339GA | GLF5 | 5239 |
| N339GW | SBRL | 306-18 |
| N339H | GLF2 | 145 |
| **N339HP** | **C500** | **472** |
| (N339K) | SBRL | 380-17 |
| N339MC | C550 | 325 |
| N339NA | SBRL | 282-46 |
| (N339PC) | HS25 | 258277 |
| **N339PM** | **SBRL** | **282-38** |
| N339QS | C560 | 0339 |
| **N339QS** | **C680** | **0191** |
| **N339RA** | **HA4T** | **RC-22** |
| **N339RK** | **FA20** | **313** |
| **N339SM** | **BE40** | **RK-458** |
| N339TG | FA10 | 103 |
| N339TG | FA20 | 198/466 |
| N339W | LJ35 | 209 |
| N340 | GLF3 | 357 |
| N340 | JSTR | 5029/38 |
| (N340AC) | C500 | 621 |
| **N340AK** | **CL64** | **5405** |
| N340DA | C550 | 263 |
| N340DN | C500 | 340 |
| N340DR | C560 | 0094 |
| N340DR | WW24 | 242 |
| N340DR | WW24 | 45 |
| N340ER | WW24 | 45 |
| N340EX | FA50 | 340 |
| **N340FX** | **CL65** | **5723** |
| N340GA | GLF3 | 340 |
| N340GA | GLF3 | 373 |
| N340GA | GLF3 | 464 |
| N340GA | GLF4 | 1340 |
| **N340GF** | **GLEX** | **9340** |
| N340LJ | LJ31 | 040 |
| N340PM | WW24 | 340 |
| **N340QS** | **C560** | **0514** |
| (N340RL) | C500 | 340 |
| (N340TB) | C500 | 276 |
| N341AG | C550 | 043 |
| **N341AP** | **F2EX** | **24** |
| N341AP | HS25 | 258204 |
| N341AP | SBRL | 282-35 |
| N341AP | SBRL | 465-40 |
| **N341AR** | **C525** | **0341** |
| N341AR | SBRL | 282-35 |
| N341CC | C500 | 320 |
| **N341CS** | **C550** | **550-1106** |
| N341CW | C550 | 330 |
| N341DB | FA10 | 71 |
| N341DM | MU30 | A056SA |
| N341FW | LJ25 | 341 |
| N341FX | CL65 | 5742 |
| N341GA | GLF3 | 360 |
| N341GA | GLF3 | 467 |
| N341GA | GLF4 | 1341 |
| N341GA | GLF4 | 1441 |
| N341K | FA20 | 281/496 |
| N341K | JSTR | 5223 |
| **N341K** | **LJ45** | **157** |
| N341KA | FA20 | 281/496 |
| N341M | FA50 | 157 |
| N341N | JSTR | 5038 |
| N341NS | GLF2 | 64/27 |
| N341NS | JSTR | 5038 |
| N341PF | FA20 | 179 |
| N341QS | C560 | 0341 |
| **N341QS** | **C680** | **0225** |
| N341TS | CL30 | 20141 |
| N342AA | LJ25 | 342 |
| N342AC | C525 | 0342 |
| **N342AJ** | **C550** | **052** |
| N342AJ | WW24 | 342 |
| N342AP | C500 | 077 |
| **N342AP** | **GLF4** | **1515** |
| N342AS | C650 | 0042 |
| N342CC | C550 | 413 |
| (N342CC) | C550 | 431 |
| **N342CS** | **C550** | **550-1101** |
| N342DA | C550 | 181 |
| N342DM | MU30 | A057SA |
| N342EX | FA50 | 342 |
| N342F | FA20 | 101 |
| **N342FX** | **CL65** | **5752** |
| N342G | FA10 | 52 |
| N342GA | GLF3 | 377 |
| N342GA | GLF3 | 468 |
| N342GA | GLF4 | 1342 |
| N342GG | LJ25 | 342 |
| N342HM | C650 | 0062 |
| N342K | FA20 | 101 |
| N342K | FA20 | 357 |
| **N342K** | **LJ45** | **171** |
| N342KF | FA20 | 357 |
| N342QS | C560 | 0324 |
| N342QS | C650 | 0042 |
| **N342QS** | **C680** | **0214** |
| N342TC | CL61 | 5155 |
| N342TS | WW24 | 342 |
| N343AP | WW24 | 194 |
| **N343CA** | **LJ25** | **202** |
| N343CC | C550 | 343 |
| N343CC | C560 | 0368 |
| **N343CC** | **C56X** | **6004** |
| **N343CM** | **C550** | **259** |
| N343CV | C560 | 0343 |
| N343DA | WW24 | 149 |
| **N343DF** | **GLEX** | **9206** |
| N343DF | GLF3 | 483 |
| N343DF | GLF4 | 1241 |
| N343DM | MU30 | A058SA |
| N343DP | GLF3 | 483 |
| N343EX | FA50 | 343 |
| **N343FX** | **CL65** | **5761** |
| N343GA | GLF3 | 378 |
| N343GA | GLF3 | 469 |
| N343GA | GLF4 | 1343 |
| N343K | CL61 | 5086 |
| N343K | CL64 | 5476 |
| N343K | GLF2 | 10 |
| N343K | GLF2 | 9/33 |
| N343KA | CL61 | 5086 |
| N343MG | F900 | 95 |
| **N343MG** | **F9EX** | **193** |
| N343MG | FA20 | 491 |
| N343MG | LJ35 | 188 |
| N343N | GLF2 | 10 |
| N343PJ | C525 | 0166 |
| **N343PM** | **FA50** | **159** |
| **N343PR** | **PRM1** | **RB-7** |
| **N343QS** | **C560** | **0444** |
| N343RD | WW24 | 343 |
| N343RK | LJ25 | 110 |
| N344A | C550 | 609 |
| N344A | FA10 | 153 |
| N344AA | GLF2 | 123/25 |
| **N344AA** | **GLF4** | **1207** |
| N344AB | GLF2 | 123/25 |
| N344AS | C650 | 7053 |
| N344BA | CL64 | 5344 |
| N344CA | LJ25 | 203 |
| N344CK | WW24 | 159 |
| N344CM | FA50 | 300 |
| N344DA | WW24 | 12 |
| N344DD | GLF3 | 344 |
| N344DM | MU30 | A059SA |
| N344EX | FA50 | 344 |
| N344FJ | FA20 | 344/534 |
| N344FX | CL65 | 5773 |
| N344G | FA20 | 355 |
| N344GA | GLF3 | 317 |
| N344GA | GLF3 | 425 |
| N344GA | GLF3 | 470 |
| N344GA | GLF4 | 1344 |
| N344GA | GLF4 | 1444 |
| N344GC | F2TH | 85 |
| **N344GW** | **GLF3** | **344** |
| N344K | SBRL | 306-97 |
| **N344KK** | **C550** | **477** |
| N344MC | LJ35 | 344 |
| N344PS | WW24 | 111 |
| N344QS | C560 | 0344 |
| **N344RJ** | **C500** | **340** |
| N344UP | SBRL | 282-45 |
| N344W | PRM1 | RB-50 |
| N344WC | LJ24 | 092 |

N345 LJ35 355
N345AA GLF2 123/25
**N345AA GLF4 1186**
N345AP FA50 181
N345AP FA50 254
**N345AW LJ45 182**
N345BA CL64 5345
**N345BH LJ45 100**
N345BM FA20 89
N345BR HS25 258308
**N345BS WW24 181**
N345CC CS55 0095
**N345CJ C52A 0136**
(N345CK) JSTR 5150/37
N345CP GLF2 123/25
N345CT HS25 25116
N345CV C560 0345
N345DA HS25 25116
N345DM MU30 A059SA
N345DM MU30 A060SA
N345EJ LJ25 345
N345EX F2EX 145
N345FH FA20 146
N345FJ FA20 345
(N345FJ) LJ25 216
**N345FM LJ45 151**
N345GA GLF3 380
N345GA GLF4 1345
**N345GC ASTR 023**
**N345GL GLF2 205**
N345GL HS25 25230
(N345HB) C500 611
N345JR C550 325
N345K LJ45 151
**N345K LJ45 310**
N345KB LJ25 345
N345KC C500 187
N345LC GLF4 1442
**N345LC GLF5 5145**
N345LJ LJ35 345
**N345MA LJ45 054**
N345MB C560 0023
**N345MC LJ25 046**
**N345MG C525 0372**
N345MP HS25 258757
N345N C500 611
N345PA FA50 36
**N345PF C680 0080**
**N345QS C560 0445**
**N345RJ LJ55 078**
N345RL LJ45 022
**N345RL LJ45 180**
(N345SF) LJ24 126
**N345SK C650 0001**
**N345SV LJ45 140**
N345TL C500 345
**N345TR WW24 345**
N345UP GLF2 159
N345WB LJ45 036
N346BA CL64 5361
N346CC C560 0346
N346CM C550 550-0915
**N346CM LJ40 45-2098**
N346CN LJ40 45-2098
(N346CP) WW24 434
N346DM MU30 A046SA
N346EX FA50 346
N346GA GLF3 436
N346GA GLF4 1346
N346P FA10 184
**N346PC F2EX 62**
**N346QS C680 0013**
(N346SR) F2TH 69
**N346XL C56X 5346**
N347AC LJ25 347
N347BA CL61 5144
N347BG C650 0201
(N347CP) CS55 0094
(N347DA) C500 420
N347DA C500 457
N347DM MU30 A047SA
N347EJ LJ25 347
N347GA GLF3 403
N347GA GLF3 471
N347GA GLF4 1347
**N347GA WW24 347**
N347GS LJ60 026
N347HS FA20 347
N347J LJ24 047
N347JV LJ25 347
(N347JW) LJ25 347
**N347K CL30 20240**
N347K FA10 37
N347K FA20 281/496
N347K FA50 236
N347K FA50 46
N347MD LJ25 347
**N347MH C500 564**
N347QS C560 0357
**N347TC HS25 257055**
N347WW WW24 347
N348BJ LJ24 141
**N348CC C560 0368**
**N348CM C550 550-0915**
(N348D) CL61 5139
N348DH WW24 386
N348DM MU30 A061SA
N348GA GLF3 405
N348GA GLF3 472
N348GA GLF4 1348
N348HM LJ55 109
N348K FA50 205
**N348K LJ45 150**
N348KH C525 0348
**N348MC HS25 258290**
**N348QS C560 0348**
N348SJ WW24 348
N348TS CL30 20048
N348VL LJ24 141
**N348W SBRL 306-94**
N348WW WW24 348
N349AK HA4T RC-42
N349AK HS25 258876
N349AS HS25 258876
N349BS LJ24 349
(N349CB) C525 0117
N349DA WW24 145
N349DM MU30 A062SA
N349EJ LJ25 349
N349GA GLF3 391
N349GA GLF4 1349
N349GA HS25 258349
**N349H F900 10**
(N349HP) BE40 RK-49
**N349HP LJ31 153**
**N349JC FA10 70**
**N349JR CL61 5130**
N349K F900 10
N349K FA50 17
**N349K GLF4 1510**
N349KS FA50 17
N349M WW24 23
**N349MC WW24 224**
N349MG FA20 479
**N349MR FA20 360**
**N349QS C680 0029**
**N349RR C750 0236**
**N349SF C525 0049**
(N349TS) LJ35 349
N350AF FA50 35
N350AG LJ25 350
**N350BN ASTR 223**
**N350BV C52A 0186**
N350C GLF5 612
N350CC C500 350
N350CC C550 350
N350CD C650 0190
N350DA LJ35 366
N350DH HS25 257087
N350DH LJ25 193
N350DM MU30 A050SA
N350DS LJ31 002
N350DV FA50 350
N350E SBRL 282-76
**N350EF LJ35 385**
**N350FK GLF4 4040**
N350GA GLF3 410
"N350GA" GLF4 4019
N350GM C525 0172
N350JF LJ35 219
N350JH LJ25 200
**N350JS FA50 15**
N350M C500 499
N350M C650 0203
**N350M F2TH 128**
N350M WW24 14
N350MD LJ35 277
N350MH HS25 256069
N350MQ C650 0203
N350MT SBRL 380-54
N350NC HS25 25160
**N350PL HS25 257193**
N350PM WW24 338
**N350QS C680 0036**
N350RB LJ35 334
N350RD C560 0026
N350RD C56X 5057
N350TG CL30 20050
N350TS LJ35 035
**N350WB FA50 102**
**N350WC C560 0266**
N350WC C560 0378
N350WC C56X 5226
N350WC HS25 258018
N350WG HS25 258018
N350X FA50 108
N350X WW24 109
N350ZE CL64 5547
**N351AC LJ31 051**
N351AF SBRL 465-27
**N351AM LJ35 409**
**N351AS LJ35 146**
**N351BC C525 0159**
N351C WW24 264
N351C WW24 264
N351CB PRM1 RB-53
**N351CG C56X 5225**
**N351CW PRM1 RB-53**
N351DM MU30 A051SA
**N351EF LJ35 125**
N351FJ GLF3 451
N351GA ASTR 251
N351GA GLF3 397
N351GA GLF4 1351
N351GA GLF4 1451
N351GA GLF4 4051
N351GA GLF5 5251
N351GL LJ35 001
(N351JM) SBRL 282-1
N351JS FA50 104
**N351MH LJ24 321**
N351N LJ24 054
N351NR LJ24 054
**N351PJ LJ35 074**
**N351QS C560 0451**
N351SB HS25 258280
**N351SE GLF2 64/27**
N351SP HS25 258280
**N351SP HS25 HA-0004**
**N351TC HS25 258675**
N351TC WW24 351
**N351TV LJ35 368**
**N351TX LJ35 127**
N351WB LJ24 054
N351WB LJ35 355
N351WC C560 0330
N351WC C56X 5225
N351WC JSTR 5229
N351WC LJ24 054
N352AE CL61 5041
**N352AE F900 172**
N352AF CL61 5041
N352AF F900 172
**N352AF GLEX 9302**
N352AM C550 393
**N352AS C510 0201**
**N352BH GLF4 1393**
**N352DA C550 393**
N352DM MU30 A052SA
**N352EF LJ31 046**
N352GA ASTR 152
N352GA ASTR 252
N352GA GLF3 401
N352GA GLF4 1352
N352GL LJ35 002
**N352HS LJ35 596**
N352JS FA50 41
**N352K LJ45 215**
**N352MD LJ24 352**
**N352QS C560 0352**
N352SC LJ25 189
N352TC WW24 394
**N352TV LJ35 410**
N352TX LJ35 073
**N352WB FA50 71**
N352WC C500 275
N352WC C560 0194
N352WC HS25 257095
N352WC LJ36 013
N352WG C500 275
(N352WQ) C560 0194
N352WR LJ24 126
(N352XR) LJ25 352
N353AE BE40 RK-353
N353CA SBRL 306-28
N353CP FA20 461
N353CV C560 0353
N353DM MU30 A053SA
**N353EF LJ35 364**
N353EJ LJ25 353
**N353FT C550 397**
N353GA ASTR 153
N353GA ASTR 253
(N353GA) GLF3 409
N353GA GLF4 1353
N353J LJ24 237
N353K CL61 5086
**N353MA GLF3 472**
**N353PC CL30 20053**
**N353PJ C500 104**
**N353QS C560 0530**
**N353SB E50P 50000038**
N353TC CL61 5037
**N353VA GLF3 371**
N353WB C500 359
N353WB SBRL 282-55
N353WC C750 0008
**N353WC C750 0180**
N353WC HS25 257032
N353WC HS25 258123
N353WC SBRL 282-55
N353WG HS25 258123
N353Z C560 0353
**N354AS MS76 054**
N354CA JSTR 5054/59
**N354CL LJ35 493**
N354DM MU30 A054SA
(N354DT) LJ35 112
**N354EF LJ35 378**
(N354EM) LJ35 440
N354GA ASTR 154
N354GA ASTR 254
N354GA GLF3 412
N354GA GLF4 1354
(N354GE) LJ35 610
(N354GG) LJ35 610
N354H FA20 16
N354H FA20 40
N354JC LJ35 112
**N354LQ LJ35 055**
N354ME LJ35 378
**N354PM LJ35 015**
**N354QS C560 0356**
**N354RB PRM1 RB-54**
N354RC C500 363
**N354RX E50P 50000089**
N354RZ LJ35 170
N354SH SBRL 380-39
**N354SS LJ35 112**
N354TC CL61 5192
N354WC C750 0027
**N354WC C750 0191**
N354WC FA20 40
N354WC HS25 257058
N354WC HS25 258160
N354WG HS25 258160
N355AC HS25 25227
N355AM LJ25 355
**N355BM EA50 000092**
N355CA LJ35 597
N355CC CL64 5302
N355CC CL64 5393
N355CD SBRL 306-85
**N355CD SBRL 465-57**
N355CV C560 0355
N355DB LJ55 006
N355DF C550 411
N355DG FA20 432
N355DH LJ55 073
N355DM MU30 A069SA
N355EJ C560 0255
**N355FA HS25 258156**

N355GA GLF3 404
N355GA GLF4 1355
N355H C500 213
N355JK WW24 355
N355MJ SBRL 282-66
**N355PC LJ35 431**
N355RB HS25 258059
**N355RM LJ55 033**
N355TS GLF3 355
**N355UA LJ55 114**
N355UJ LJ55 033
N355WB FA20 44
N355WC C750 0030
**N355WC C750 0266**
N355WC FA20 44
N355WC HS25 258181
N355WG FA20 44
N355WG HS25 258181
N355WJ HS25 257172
N355WW WW24 355
N356AC LJ35 230
**N356BR GLF3 356**
N356CG LJ60 230
N356DM MU30 A073SA
N356EJ C560 0256
N356GA GLF3 406
N356JB FA20 80
**N356JW LJ35 656**
**N356MR C52B 0138**
N356MS GLEX 9149
N356N CL61 3064
N356P LJ35 006
**N356SA C560 0256**
**N356SR HS25 257170**
N356TJ GLF3 356
**N356WA LJ60 123**
N356WB FA20 80
N356WC C560 0432
N356WC C56X 5270
N356WC FA20 80
N356WW WW24 356
N357AZ C560 0196
N357BC WW24 357
**N357BE C560 0663**
N357CL FA20 484
(N357DM) MU30 A051SA
N357DM MU30 A091SA
N357EA WW24 357
N357EC C560 0269
**N357EC C56X 5510**
**N357EF LJ35 323**
N357GA GLF3 413
N357GA GLF4 1357
N357GA GLF4 1457
N357H GLF3 472
N357H JSTR 5234
N357HC LJ25 032
**N357J C52A 0184**
N357JV C525 0357
**N357KM GLF3 435**
**N357LJ LJ35 357**
(N357MD) MU30 A091SA
**N357MP C56X 5774**
**N357PR GLF3 348**
N357PR LJ55 073
N357PS FA20 357
**N357PT PRM1 RB-250**
**N357QS C680 0155**
N357RM LJ35 007
N357RT CL60 1033
**N357TW C56X 5669**
(N357W) WW24 357
N357WC C560 0069
N357WC C56X 5119
N358AC LJ35 427
N358CC C500 358
N358CT WW24 358
N358CV C560 0358
**N358CY GLF3 358**
N358GA GLF3 414
N358GA GLF4 1358
N358GA GLF4 1458
N358JA LJ60 358
**N358K C525 0527**
N358LL HS25 258093
**N358MH FA50 209**
**N358P LJ60 205**
N358PG LJ35 358

**N358QS C560 0455**
N358WC C750 0121
(N359C) WW24 42
**N359CF HS25 258154**
**N359CW C650 0159**
N359D ASTR 102
N359EC C560 0559
**N359EF LJ35 193**
N359EJ C560 0559
N359GA GLF4 1359
N359GW C550 550-1076
N359JS WW24 335
N359K GLF2 180
**N359K LJ45 216**
**N359QS C680 0126**
(N359RM) LJ60 008
N359SK LJ25 359
N359V ASTR 039
N359V ASTR 102
**N359V CL64 5349**
N359V FA10 120
N359VP ASTR 039
N359VS ASTR 039
N359WC C56X 5129
**N359WJ SBRL 306-1**
N360AA LJ25 123
**N360AN LJ60 137**
**N360AV ASTR 240**
**N360AX LJ35 367**
N360BA HS25 258052
N360CA MU30 A009SA
N360CF SBRL 306-133
N360CH SBRL 306-146
N360CH SBRL 306-15
**N360CK C52B 0180**
N360DA C500 056
(N360DE) HS25 257042
N360DE HS25 258163
N360DJ C500 583
N360E SBRL 282-80
N360EJ LJ24 052
N360GA GALX 058
N360GA GALX 163
N360GA GLF4 1360
N360GA GLF4 4160
(N360GL) LJ35 360
N360HK WW24 166
N360HS C550 550-0889
**N360HS C560 0808**
N360J SBRL 282-7
**N360JG LJ25 360**
**N360LA GLEX 9087**
N360LJ LJ35 360
N360LS LJ36 030
N360M CS55 0022
**N360M F2EX 68**
N360M WW24 24
**N360MB GLF3 306**
N360MC C500 406
N360MC WW24 24
N360N C550 072
N360N HS25 257067
N360N SBRL 282-81
**N360PJ PJET 4798E001**
**N360PK C52A 0448**
**N360PL CL64 5303**
N360Q SBRL 282-24
**N360QS C560 0460**
**N360RP C550 081**
**N360SL CL61 5089**
N360UJ LJ60 053
N360X HS25 257042
N361AA LJ24 100
**N361AS BE40 RK-287**
N361BA HS25 258053
N361DA SBRL 306-8
N361DB C500 687
N361DB C550 550-0884
**N361DE C500 687**
N361DJ C550 037
N361DM MU30 A065SA
N361EC C560 0279
**N361EC C56X 5515**
N361EE C650 7057
N361EJ LJ24 053
N361GA GALX 059
(N361GA) GALX 161
N361GA GLF4 1361

**N361JR C52A 0361**
**N361K F900 83**
**N361PJ LJ36 003**
(N361PJ) LJ36 017
N361QS C560 0361
**N361QS C680 0235**
(N361RA) GLF3 361
N361RB C525 0361
**N361TL C52B 0061**
N361TS LJ60 361
N361XL C56X 5361
N362AA LJ24 110
**N362B C510 0263**
N362BA HS25 258057
N362CC C500 362
N362CJ C525 0362
N362CP C550 371
N362DA SBRL 282-90
N362DJ C550 052
N362EJ LJ24 056
**N362FL C525 0362**
**N362FW LJ35 362**
N362GA GALX 062
N362GA GLF4 1362
N362GL LJ36 002
N362JM C52B 0066
N362KM BE40 RK-227
N362MD MU30 A062SA
N362PE C525 0362
**N362PT FA10 73**
**N362QS C680 0051**
**N362TW C650 0011**
N362XP BE40 RK-362
**N362XP HS25 HA-0162**
N363BA HS25 258059
N363BC LJ24 241
**N363CL CL30 20063**
N363CR CL61 3025
N363DM MU30 A063SA
N363EJ LJ24 058
N363FJ FA20 363/544
N363GA GALX 063
N363GA GALX 063
N363GA GLF4 1363
N363GL LJ36 003
N363HA LJ25 242
N363K BE40 RK-114
N363K C500 110
**N363NH ASTR 097**
**N363PJ LJ36 038**
**N363QS C560 0536**
N363SP C550 394
**N363TD C500 438**
(N363XP) BE40 RK-363
N364BA HS25 258060
**N364CL LJ35 383**
N364CW C650 0164
N364DM MU30 A064SA
N364EJ LJ24 059
N364G GLF2 125/26
N364G GLF4 1091
N364G WW24 5
N364GA GALX 064
N364GA GLF4 1364
**N364QS C680 0062**
N364WC HS25 258069
N365AS LJ36 055
**N365AT HS25 258449**
N365BA HS25 258061
N365CM LJ25 365
**N365CX GALX 075**
N365CX WW24 425
N365DA HS25 25271
N365DJ HS25 25020
**N365EA C560 0107**
N365EJ LJ24 064
N365EJ LJ24 102
N365FJ F2EX 47
N365G GLF2 198/35
N365G GLF4 1101
N365G WW24 15
**N365GA ASTR 072**
N365GA GLF4 1365
**N365GL LJ31 128**
N365JR HS25 HA-0065
**N365N LJ35 300**
N365N SBRL 306-5
**N365QS C680 0057**

(N365QX) WW24 425
N365RJ WW24 91
N365SB HS25 256070
**N365SC ASTR 268**
N365TC GLF2 41
**N365WA C550 358**
N366AA LJ25 151
N366AC LJ35 418
N366BA HS25 258062
N366BR HS25 25134
N366CJ C52A 0366
N366DA SBRL 282-82
N366DM MU30 A066SA
N366EA BE40 RK-193
N366EJ LJ24 095
N366F FA50 77
N366F GLF4 1041
N366FW C510 0044
N366G C650 0038
N366G FA20 9
N366GE C650 0038
**N366JA GLF3 366**
N366LJ LJ25 366
N366MP HS25 25134
N366N SBRL 282-8
N366N SBRL 306-93
**N366QS C560 0466**
N366TS LJ31 166
**N366TT LJ35 227**
N367BA HS25 258063
N367BP C550 550-0970
N367BW F2EX 107
N367CJ C52A 0367
N367CS PRM1 RB-234
**N367DA LJ35 599**
N367DM HS25 258367
N367DM MU30 A067SA
N367EA BE40 RK-191
(N367EA) C550 373
N367EG GLF2 128
N367EJ FA20 28
N367F FA10 206
N367G C650 0053
N367G FA20 20
N367G GLF2 125/26
N367GA ASTR 267
N367GA FA20 20
N367GA GALX 067
N367GA GALX 167
**N367GA GALX 227**
N367GA GLF3 367
N367GA GLF4 1367
**N367HB C500 611**
N367JC C550 180
**N367JC C560 0069**
N367QS C560 0367
N367TP FA50 181
**N367WW WW24 367**
N368AG GLF2 167
**N368AG GLF4 1087**
N368BA HS25 258065
**N368BE C560 0546**
N368BG LJ35 368
N368CC PRM1 RB-184
N368CS PRM1 RB-184
**N368CS PRM1 RB-234**
**N368D LJ25 368**
N368DA SBRL 282-12
N368DM MU30 A068SA
N368DS FA20 256
N368DS GLF2 123/25
**N368EA BE40 RK-57**
N368EJ FA20 30
N368F FA10 220
N368G C650 0057
N368G CL64 5368
N368G FA20 29
N368GA GALX 068
N368GA GALX 168
N368GA GLF3 368
**N368HS C550 550-0889**
N368K C500 110
N368L FA20 29
N368M FA50 277
N368MD WW24 368
N368MJ LJ24 043
N368PU MU30 A068SA
**N368QS C680 0073**

| | | |
|---|---|---|
| N368S | WW24 | 271 |
| (N368TJ) | GLF3 | 368 |
| N369AP | GLF2 | 14 |
| **N369B** | **C750** | **0030** |
| N369BA | HS25 | 258066 |
| **N369BA** | **LJ35** | **312** |
| N369BG | F900 | 40 |
| N369BG | HS25 | 258160 |
| N369BG | WW24 | 304 |
| N369CA | FA20 | 359/542 |
| (N369CA) | FA50 | 115 |
| N369CE | FA20 | 359/542 |
| N369CS | GLF2 | 2 |
| N369CS | GLF3 | 384 |
| N369CS | HS25 | 25214 |
| N369D | LJ25 | 369 |
| N369DA | C550 | 327 |
| **N369EA** | **BE40** | **RJ-2** |
| (N369EA) | BE40 | RK-115 |
| N369EJ | FA20 | 33 |
| N369EJ | LJ24 | 081 |
| N369G | C650 | 0015 |
| N369G | FA20 | 34 |
| N369G | HS25 | 257125 |
| **N369GA** | **GLF5** | **5269** |
| **N369GC** | **C510** | **0248** |
| N369JB | HS25 | 25066 |
| N369JH | HS25 | 25275 |
| **N369JK** | **GALX** | **190** |
| N369MJ | LJ25 | 369 |
| N369N | SBRL | 282-8 |
| N369PA | C510 | 0211 |
| **N369QS** | **C680** | **0081** |
| (N369TC) | C560 | 0284 |
| N369TS | HS25 | 256069 |
| N369V | FA10 | 120 |
| N369WR | FA20 | 196 |
| N369XL | GLF4 | 1202 |
| N369XL | LJ35 | 423 |
| N369XP | BE40 | RK-369 |
| N370 | FA20 | 21 |
| N370AC | C550 | 228 |
| N370AS | MS76 | 030 |
| N370AT | LJ60 | 139 |
| **N370BA** | **C56X** | **5525** |
| N370BH | SBRL | 370-4 |
| (N370CD) | C550 | 028 |
| (N370CL) | CL64 | 5370 |
| **N370DE** | **HS25** | **258441** |
| N370DM | MU30 | A070SA |
| **N370EA** | **EA50** | **000125** |
| N370EC | LJ35 | 003 |
| **N370EJ** | **EPC1** | **001** |
| N370EK | C750 | 0185 |
| (N370EU) | FA20 | 297 |
| **N370FC** | **BE40** | **RK-378** |
| N370GA | GALX | 170 |
| (N370GA) | GLF3 | 451 |
| N370GA | GLF3 | 494 |
| N370GA | GLF4 | 1370 |
| N370GA | GLF4 | 1450 |
| **N370GA** | **GLF5** | **5270** |
| N370HF | FA20 | 370 |
| **N370JJ** | **C52A** | **0370** |
| **N370JL** | **GLF3** | **401** |
| **N370KP** | **FA50** | **103** |
| N370L | SBRL | 306-64 |
| N370LJ | LJ25 | 370 |
| **N370LN** | **C500** | **101** |
| **N370M** | **C56X** | **5565** |
| N370M | CS55 | 0128 |
| N370M | HS25 | 257019 |
| N370M | SBRL | 306-71 |
| (N370ME) | FA20 | 310 |
| **N370P** | **EA50** | **000066** |
| (N370P) | EA50 | 000068 |
| N370QS | C650 | 0070 |
| **N370QS** | **C680** | **0099** |
| N370RR | HS25 | 257019 |
| **N370SC** | **LJ31** | **070** |
| N370SL | SBRL | 370-9 |
| (N370SP) | GLF2 | 168 |
| **N370TC** | **C560** | **0684** |
| N370TG | C650 | 0070 |
| N370TP | C500 | 551 |
| **N370TP** | **C650** | **0059** |
| **N370TS** | **CL64** | **5370** |
| N370V | CL60 | 1014 |
| N370VS | SBRL | 306-54 |
| N370WT | FA20 | 274 |
| **N371AS** | **MS76** | **034** |
| N371CE | PRM1 | RB-73 |
| **N371CF** | **BE40** | **RK-351** |
| N371CF | PRM1 | RB-73 |
| N371CL | CL64 | 5371 |
| N371CV | C560 | 0371 |
| N371CW | BE40 | RK-371 |
| N371D | HS25 | 257134 |
| N371DM | MU30 | A071SA |
| **N371FP** | **GLF4** | **1371** |
| (N371GA) | C500 | 407 |
| N371GA | GALX | 071 |
| N371GA | GLF3 | 495 |
| N371GA | GLF4 | 1371 |
| N371GP | C500 | 407 |
| N371H | JSTR | 5020 |
| N371H | WW24 | 315 |
| N371HH | C500 | 214 |
| N371JC | CL64 | 5342 |
| **N371JC** | **GLF5** | **505** |
| N371P | C56X | 5371 |
| **N371QS** | **C560** | **0471** |
| N371TS | CL30 | 20071 |
| (N371W) | C500 | 214 |
| **N372AS** | **ASTR** | **281** |
| N372AS | LJ35 | 372 |
| N372BC | CL61 | 3034 |
| N372BC | GLF4 | 1273 |
| N372BC | HS25 | 257026 |
| N372BD | HS25 | 257026 |
| N372BG | CL61 | 3034 |
| N372BG | GLF4 | 1273 |
| N372BG | GLF5 | 5038 |
| **N372BG** | **GLF5** | **5164** |
| N372CC | C550 | 372 |
| N372CM | GLF2 | 185 |
| N372CM | GLF2 | 62 |
| N372CM | GLF3 | 338 |
| N372CM | GLF4 | 1049 |
| N372CM | GLF4 | 1451 |
| N372CM | HS25 | 25073 |
| N372CP | C525 | 0372 |
| N372CT | C52A | 0005 |
| N372CV | C560 | 0372 |
| N372DM | MU30 | A072SA |
| N372EJ | C560 | 0272 |
| N372G | CL61 | 3006 |
| **N372G** | **CL64** | **5351** |
| N372GA | ASTR | 272 |
| N372GA | GLF3 | 496 |
| N372GA | GLF4 | 1372 |
| N372GA | GLF4 | 1472 |
| N372GA | GLF4 | 4072 |
| N372GM | GLF2 | 185 |
| N372GM | GLF2 | 62 |
| N372GM | GLF3 | 338 |
| N372GM | GLF4 | 1049 |
| N372GM | HS25 | 25073 |
| N372H | JSTR | 5092/58 |
| N372H | JSTR | 5228 |
| (N372N) | CL30 | 20060 |
| N372PG | CL61 | 3034 |
| N372Q | WW24 | 112 |
| N372QS | C560 | 0372 |
| **N372QS** | **C680** | **0201** |
| N372RS | HS25 | 25066 |
| **N372WC** | **C560** | **0372** |
| N372WW | WW24 | 372 |
| N372XP | HS25 | 258372 |
| **N373AB** | **C750** | **0243** |
| **N373AF** | **C525** | **0308** |
| **N373AS** | **MS76** | **036** |
| N373CM | WW24 | 373 |
| N373DH | HS25 | 25066 |
| **N373DJ** | **C650** | **0038** |
| **N373DN** | **FA20** | **324** |
| N373G | CL61 | 3009 |
| **N373G** | **CL64** | **5556** |
| N373GA | ASTR | 273 |
| N373GA | GLF3 | 497 |
| N373GA | GLF4 | 1373 |
| N373GA | GLF4 | 1473 |
| N373GA | GLF4 | 4073 |
| N373GS | GLF3 | 373 |
| N373KC | FA20 | 264 |
| N373KM | GLF4 | 1373 |
| N373LB | GLF2 | 13 |
| N373LP | GLF2 | 13 |
| (N373LP) | GLF3 | 310 |
| (N373LP) | LJ35 | 220 |
| **N373ML** | **ASTR** | **204** |
| **N373QS** | **C560** | **0373** |
| N373RR | GLF3 | 373 |
| **N373RS** | **FA50** | **259** |
| **N373SB** | **GLEX** | **9047** |
| N373SC | LJ25 | 204 |
| N373W | LJ25 | 032 |
| N373XP | BE40 | RK-373 |
| **N374AS** | **MS76** | **038** |
| N374BC | CL61 | 3034 |
| (N374DH) | HS25 | 25066 |
| N374DM | MU30 | A074SA |
| N374FC | C550 | 374 |
| N374G | CL61 | 3015 |
| N374G | CL64 | 5351 |
| **N374G** | **CL64** | **5368** |
| N374GA | ASTR | 274 |
| N374GA | GLF3 | 498 |
| N374GA | GLF4 | 1374 |
| N374GA | GLF4 | 1474 |
| N374GA | GLF4 | 1504 |
| N374GA | GLF4 | 4074 |
| N374GC | CS55 | 0055 |
| N374GS | C500 | 634 |
| N374GS | C500 | 669 |
| N374GS | CS55 | 0055 |
| N374LJ | LJ35 | 249 |
| N374MV | F9EX | 7 |
| N374PS | GLF2 | 92 |
| N374QS | C560 | 0475 |
| **N374WC** | **C560** | **0475** |
| N374XP | BE40 | RK-374 |
| **N375AS** | **MS76** | **044** |
| N375BK | FA20 | 236 |
| N375CM | C560 | 0365 |
| N375DM | MU30 | A075SA |
| **N375DT** | **BE40** | **RK-372** |
| **N375E** | **C650** | **7014** |
| **N375ET** | **EA50** | **000216** |
| N375G | CL61 | 3019 |
| N375G | GLEX | 9158 |
| **N375G** | **GLEX** | **9242** |
| N375GA | ASTR | 275 |
| N375GA | GLF3 | 375 |
| N375GA | GLF4 | 1151 |
| N375GA | GLF4 | 1375 |
| N375GA | GLF4 | 4075 |
| N375H | CL61 | 5093 |
| N375KH | C525 | 0375 |
| **N375LT** | **GLF3** | **375** |
| N375MD | JSTR | 5209 |
| **N375MD** | **JSTR** | **5227** |
| N375NM | GLF3 | 375 |
| N375NW | GLF3 | 375 |
| N375PK | CL60 | 1018 |
| N375PK | CL61 | 3054 |
| N375PK | FA20 | 236 |
| N375PK | GLF2 | 15 |
| N375QS | C560 | 0375 |
| **N375QS** | **C680** | **0230** |
| N375RF | CL30 | 20025 |
| N375SC | C650 | 0027 |
| N375SC | F2TH | 23 |
| **N375SC** | **F9EX** | **215** |
| N375SC | HS25 | 258111 |
| **N375SH** | **EA50** | **000256** |
| N375WB | CL30 | 20025 |
| **N375WB** | **GLEX** | **9288** |
| N375XP | BE40 | RK-375 |
| N376BE | WW24 | 376 |
| N376D | SBRL | 282-115 |
| N376D | SBRL | 306-101 |
| **N376D** | **SBRL** | **465-76** |
| N376DD | SBRL | 282-115 |
| N376DM | MU30 | A076SA |
| N376EJ | GLF3 | 376 |
| **N376G** | **GLEX** | **9164** |
| N376GA | GALX | 076 |
| N376GA | GLF4 | 1376 |
| N376GA | GLF4 | 4076 |
| **N376HA** | **LJ35** | **477** |
| (N376HW) | C650 | 0025 |
| N376MB | LJ31 | 234 |
| **N376PJ** | **GLF3** | **376** |
| N376QS | C560 | 0276 |
| **N376QS** | **C680** | **0180** |
| N376RP | SBRL | 282-115 |
| N376SC | C650 | 0076 |
| **N376SC** | **F2EX** | **57** |
| N376SC | F2TH | 24 |
| N376SC | FA20 | 391 |
| N376SC | HS25 | 258124 |
| N376SC | LJ25 | 204 |
| N376WA | WW24 | 376 |
| N376WC | C560 | 0276 |
| **N377AC** | **ASTR** | **109** |
| N377BT | FA20 | 44 |
| N377C | LJ25 | 257 |
| N377C | LJ35 | 389 |
| N377DM | MU30 | A077SA |
| (N377EM) | SBRL | 306-26 |
| N377EX | F2EX | 77 |
| N377GA | C52B | 0247 |
| N377GA | GLF3 | 487 |
| N377GA | GLF4 | 1377 |
| N377GA | GLF4 | 4077 |
| **N377GM** | **F2EX** | **32** |
| N377GS | C525 | 0179 |
| **N377GS** | **C52A** | **0077** |
| N377HS | SBRL | 380-36 |
| N377HW | FA50 | 156 |
| **N377JC** | **HS25** | **258349** |
| N377JE | C650 | 0013 |
| (N377JW) | LJ55 | 033 |
| N377KC | C500 | 388 |
| N377P | SBRL | 282-70 |
| N377Q | LJ25 | 257 |
| N377QS | C560 | 0377 |
| **N377QS** | **C680** | **0187** |
| N377RA | C560 | 0377 |
| N377RP | FA20 | 377/548 |
| **N377RV** | **C510** | **0227** |
| **N377RX** | **GLF3** | **377** |
| N377SC | F9EX | 66 |
| **N377SF** | **C750** | **0068** |
| N377WC | C560 | 0377 |
| **N378AS** | **MS76** | **045** |
| N378C | FA10 | 73 |
| N378CC | C500 | 378 |
| **N378D** | **SBRL** | **306-101** |
| N378DM | MU30 | A078SA |
| N378GA | GALX | 211 |
| N378GA | GLF4 | 1378 |
| N378GA | GLF4 | 1478 |
| N378GA | GLF4 | 4078 |
| N378HC | GLF3 | 378 |
| **N378L** | **GLF5** | **5008** |
| **N378MB** | **GLF3** | **336** |
| **N378QS** | **C680** | **0103** |
| **N378SE** | **GLF3** | **378** |
| (N378VP) | C560 | 0378 |
| N379AV | WW24 | 344 |
| (N379BW) | LJ35 | 454 |
| **N379DB** | **C52B** | **0191** |
| N379DM | MU30 | A079SA |
| N379DR | BE40 | RK-321 |
| **N379G** | **GLEX** | **9199** |
| N379GA | GALX | 079 |
| N379GA | GALX | 213 |
| N379GA | GLF4 | 1379 |
| N379GA | GLF4 | 4079 |
| N379JR | WW24 | 353 |
| **N379LJ** | **LJ45** | **379** |
| N379P | GLF5 | 581 |
| N379QS | C560 | 0479 |
| **N379R** | **C52A** | **0421** |
| N379RH | GLF3 | 379 |
| N379TH | WW24 | 109 |
| N379XX | GLF3 | 394 |
| N380AA | JSTR | 5131 |
| **N380AC** | **GLF2** | **241** |
| **N380AK** | **C550** | **550-0809** |
| N380AK | C550 | 612 |
| **N380BA** | **LJ60** | **292** |
| N380BC | SBRL | 380-17 |
| **N380CF** | **SBRL** | **380-51** |
| N380CF | SBRL | 380-54 |
| N380CJ | C52B | 0080 |
| N380CM | MU30 | A080SA |
| **N380CR** | **C525** | **0643** |
| N380CV | C560 | 0380 |
| N380CW | C650 | 0030 |

| | | |
|---|---|---|
| N380DA | WW24 | 380 |
| N380DE | HS25 | 258269 |
| N380DG | CL30 | 20058 |
| N380DJ | SBRL | 380-32 |
| N380DM | MU30 | A080SA |
| N380EX | HFB3 | 1036 |
| **N380FP** | **SBRL** | **380-54** |
| N380GA | GALX | 080 |
| N380GA | GLF4 | 1380 |
| N380GA | GLF4 | 4080 |
| N380GG | HS25 | 258591 |
| N380GK | SBRL | 380-44 |
| **N380GP** | **HS25** | **258591** |
| **N380JR** | **BE40** | **RK-411** |
| N380LC | LJ25 | 030 |
| **N380M** | **C56X** | **5111** |
| N380MS | C550 | 480 |
| **N380MS** | **SBRL** | **380-21** |
| N380N | SBRL | 380-72 |
| **N380QS** | **C680** | **0089** |
| N380RA | FA20 | 54 |
| **N380RD** | **C560** | **0026** |
| (N380RS) | SBRL | 380-70 |
| N380SF | FA20 | 258 |
| N380SR | SBRL | 380-2 |
| N380SR | SBRL | 380-53 |
| N380T | SBRL | 380-58 |
| N380TJ | FA50 | 138 |
| N380TT | GLF3 | 437 |
| N380V | CL60 | 1008 |
| N380X | HS25 | 25204 |
| N380X | HS25 | 258269 |
| N381AA | JSTR | 5058/4 |
| **N381AL** | **LJ31** | **150** |
| **N381BJ** | **C500** | **445** |
| N381CC | C550 | 381 |
| N381CJ | C525 | 0380 |
| **N381CW** | **C650** | **0111** |
| N381DA | WW24 | 118 |
| N381DM | MU30 | A081SA |
| (N381EM) | C650 | 0111 |
| N381GA | GALX | 221 |
| N381GA | GLF4 | 1381 |
| N381GA | GLF4 | 4081 |
| **N381MF** | **FA10** | **121** |
| N381MG | MU30 | A081SA |
| **N381QS** | **C680** | **0097** |
| **N381VP** | **C550** | **170** |
| N381W | WW24 | 381 |
| **N382AA** | **WW24** | **56** |
| **N382AL** | **LJ31** | **142** |
| N382BL | LJ35 | 382 |
| N382BP | LJ35 | 382 |
| (N382DA) | HS25 | 25218 |
| N382DM | MU30 | A082SA |
| N382E | FA20 | 382 |
| **N382EA** | **EA50** | **000082** |
| **N382EM** | **C525** | **0496** |
| **N382G** | **GALX** | **079** |
| **N382GA** | **ASTR** | **282** |
| N382GA | GLF4 | 1382 |
| N382GA | GLF4 | 4082 |
| N382JP | C500 | 164 |
| N382LS | SBRL | 380-51 |
| N382MC | SBRL | 380-34 |
| N382QS | C560 | 0382 |
| **N382QS** | **C680** | **0245** |
| N382RF | SBRL | 282-17 |
| **N382TC** | **LJ35** | **039** |
| N383CF | SBRL | 380-9 |
| N383DM | MU30 | A083SA |
| N383DT | CL64 | 5383 |
| N383GA | GALX | 223 |
| N383GA | GLF4 | 1383 |
| N383GA | GLF4 | 4083 |
| **N383JA** | **GLF5** | **596** |
| **N383LJ** | **LJ60** | **383** |
| **N383LS** | **GLF5** | **544** |
| **N383MB** | **CL64** | **5568** |
| N383MB | LJ60 | 083 |
| **N383MR** | **HS25** | **258915** |
| **N383QS** | **C560** | **0483** |
| N383RF | FA20 | 65 |
| N383SC | C500 | 341 |
| **N383SF** | **ASTR** | **083** |
| N383TS | SBRL | 306-84 |
| N383X | LJ24 | 128 |
| N384AJ | C560 | 0230 |
| N384AT | WW24 | 175 |
| **N384BB** | **GLF3** | **496** |
| **N384CF** | **LJ35** | **384** |
| N384CW | C650 | 0144 |
| N384DA | C550 | 048 |
| N384DM | MU30 | A058SA |
| **N384EM** | **C650** | **0144** |
| N384GA | GALX | 184 |
| N384GA | GLF4 | 1384 |
| N384GA | GLF4 | 4084 |
| N384JK | FA20 | 384/551 |
| N384JW | LJ35 | 316 |
| **N384JW** | **LJ60** | **130** |
| **N384K** | **FA20** | **387** |
| **N384MP** | **CL61** | **5047** |
| **N384PS** | **FA20** | **384/551** |
| **N384QS** | **C680** | **0110** |
| **N384RV** | **CL30** | **20184** |
| N384TC | HS25 | 258138 |
| **N384WC** | **C56X** | **5084** |
| N385AC | FA20 | 144 |
| N385CC | C500 | 385 |
| **N385CT** | **CL64** | **5592** |
| N385CW | C650 | 0145 |
| N385EM | C650 | 0145 |
| N385FJ | FA20 | 385 |
| (N385G) | WW24 | 43 |
| N385GA | GALX | 225 |
| N385GA | GLF4 | 4085 |
| N385J | LJ24 | 085 |
| N385M | GLF2 | 77 |
| N385MG | C56X | 5556 |
| (N385MG) | LJ35 | 626 |
| **N385PB** | **BE40** | **RK-217** |
| (N385PB) | BE40 | RK-522 |
| **N385PD** | **GLF4** | **1088** |
| **N385QS** | **C680** | **0115** |
| **N385RC** | **LJ55** | **117** |
| N386AG | GLF4 | 1150 |
| **N386AM** | **C550** | **163** |
| **N386CM** | **LJ35** | **283** |
| N386CW | C650 | 0186 |
| (N386DA) | C500 | 460 |
| N386G | WW24 | 43 |
| (N386JM) | WW24 | 128 |
| (N386K) | CL61 | 5174 |
| N386K | LJ45 | 086 |
| N386MA | C550 | 069 |
| N386MC | WW24 | 128 |
| **N386QS** | **C560** | **0486** |
| **N386RF** | **C525** | **0386** |
| **N386RL** | **WW24** | **386** |
| N386SC | C500 | 323 |
| N386SF | C56X | 5064 |
| N387AT | BE40 | RK-256 |
| N387CE | FA20 | 387 |
| N387CL | CL64 | 5387 |
| (N387FJ) | FA20 | 487 |
| N387GA | GALX | 187 |
| N387GA | GLF4 | 4087 |
| N387H | HS25 | 258246 |
| N387HA | C550 | 465 |
| **N387HA** | **LJ35** | **251** |
| N387MA | C550 | 095 |
| **N387MM** | **C560** | **0109A** |
| N387PA | ASTR | 025 |
| N387PA | ASTR | 145 |
| **N387PC** | **CL30** | **20087** |
| **N387QS** | **C680** | **0119** |
| **N387RE** | **C550** | **575** |
| **N387SC** | **C550** | **157** |
| **N387SV** | **C560** | **0759** |
| **N387WM** | **GLEX** | **9041** |
| **N388AC** | **GLF5** | **5125** |
| N388AJ | FA20 | 56 |
| (N388BS) | HS25 | 257056 |
| **N388BS** | **HS25** | **258423** |
| **N388CA** | **GLF4** | **1034** |
| N388CJ | C500 | 388 |
| N388CW | GLF3 | 489 |
| N388DA | BE40 | RJ-26 |
| N388DA | C650 | 0062 |
| **N388DB** | **CL61** | **3016** |
| **N388DD** | **CL60** | **1082** |
| N388FA | C550 | 633 |
| **N388FW** | **C525** | **0656** |
| N388GA | GALX | 088 |
| N388GA | GALX | 188 |
| N388GA | GLF4 | 1438 |
| N388GA | GLF4 | 4088 |
| N388GA | WW24 | 366 |
| N388GM | C500 | 323 |
| **N388GS** | **F9EX** | **55** |
| N388H | HS25 | 258248 |
| N388LS | LJ35 | 388 |
| N388MA | C550 | 108 |
| **N388MM** | **GLF3** | **490** |
| N388P | LJ24 | 211 |
| N388PD | LJ35 | 388 |
| **N388PD** | **LJ35** | **630** |
| N388PG | CL61 | 5152 |
| N388Q | LJ24 | 065A |
| **N388QS** | **C680** | **0113** |
| N388R | LJ24 | 020 |
| N388R | LJ24 | 110 |
| **N388RD** | **C560** | **0162** |
| **N388RF** | **GLEX** | **9154** |
| **N388SB** | **C550** | **279** |
| N388TC | FA50 | 196 |
| N388WM | HS25 | 25052 |
| **N388WS** | **CL30** | **20108** |
| **N388WW** | **WW24** | **388** |
| N388Z | F900 | 43 |
| (N389AC) | FA20 | 162/451 |
| **N389AT** | **LJ25** | **297** |
| (N389BG) | F900 | 40 |
| N389BG | HS25 | 258160 |
| N389BG | WW24 | 304 |
| N389CC | C500 | 389 |
| N389CG | LJ45 | 389 |
| N389CJ | C525 | 0389 |
| (N389DA) | HS25 | 25037 |
| N389GA | GLF4 | 1389 |
| N389GA | GLF4 | 1489 |
| N389GA | GLF4 | 4089 |
| N389GA | LJ25 | 289 |
| N389GS | F2TH | 20 |
| N389JP | C500 | 643 |
| N389JV | C560 | 0389 |
| **N389KA** | **LJ35** | **389** |
| N389L | CS55 | 0013 |
| **N389MW** | **E50P** | **50000022** |
| N389QS | C680 | 0105 |
| **N389QS** | **C680** | **0149** |
| N389W | C650 | 0098 |
| N390AG | FA20 | 360 |
| **N390AJ** | **C550** | **369** |
| N390BA | C560 | 0409 |
| N390BL | PRM1 | RB-30 |
| (N390BP) | PRM1 | RB-20 |
| **N390BR** | **PRM1** | **RB-118** |
| N390BW | PRM1 | RB-12 |
| **N390CE** | **PRM1** | **RB-40** |
| N390CG | LJ45 | 390 |
| N390CK | PRM1 | RB-42 |
| N390CL | PRM1 | RB-25 |
| N390CV | C560 | 0390 |
| N390DA | C550 | 434 |
| **N390DB** | **CL30** | **20131** |
| N390DE | F9EX | 68 |
| **N390DP** | **PRM1** | **RB-34** |
| N390EM | PRM1 | RB-9 |
| N390EU | PRM1 | RB-242 |
| N390F | F900 | 127 |
| N390F | GLF2 | 178 |
| **N390GG** | **LJ45** | **325** |
| N390GM | PRM1 | RB-121 |
| N390GS | F2TH | 21 |
| N390GS | PRM1 | RB-231 |
| (N390HR) | PRM1 | RB-26 |
| **N390JK** | **PRM1** | **RB-39** |
| (N390JP) | C550 | 369 |
| **N390JV** | **PRM1** | **RB-129** |
| **N390JW** | **PRM1** | **RB-78** |
| N390MB | PRM1 | RB-21 |
| **N390MM** | **PRM1** | **RB-266** |
| N390NS | PRM1 | RB-50 |
| N390P | PRM1 | RB-12 |
| **N390P** | **PRM1** | **RB-275** |
| N390P | PRM1 | RB-81 |
| N390PL | PRM1 | RB-55 |
| **N390PR** | **PRM1** | **RB-113** |
| **N390PT** | **PRM1** | **RB-135** |
| N390QS | C560 | 0490 |
| N390R | PRM1 | RB-6 |
| N390RA | PRM1 | RB-1 |
| N390RB | PRM1 | RB-26 |
| N390RC | PRM1 | RB-56 |
| (N390S) | C500 | 290 |
| N390TA | PRM1 | RB-12 |
| N390TA | PRM1 | RB-86 |
| N390TC | PRM1 | RB-3 |
| N390VP | C560 | 0390 |
| N390WC | C560 | 0490 |
| N391AN | C550 | 093 |
| N391BC | C550 | 170 |
| **N391BC** | **C550** | **550-0909** |
| N391CV | C560 | 0391 |
| N391DA | HS25 | 25029 |
| (N391DH) | C550 | 620 |
| **N391DT** | **C550** | **620** |
| (N391DT) | C550 | 641 |
| N391GA | GALX | 091 |
| N391GA | GALX | 191 |
| N391GA | GLF4 | 1391 |
| N391GA | GLF4 | 1440 |
| N391GA | GLF4 | 4091 |
| N391JP | LJ35 | 487 |
| N391JR | LJ35 | 487 |
| N391KC | C550 | 170 |
| **N391KK** | **C680** | **0074** |
| **N391QS** | **C560** | **0493** |
| (N391RB) | PRM1 | RB-70 |
| N391SH | GLF3 | 392 |
| **N391TC** | **HS25** | **258063** |
| **N391W** | **CL30** | **20091** |
| N391XP | HS25 | 258391 |
| N392BD | GLF2 | 120 |
| N392BS | C560 | 0164 |
| N392DA | C500 | 541 |
| N392F | SBRL | 282-17 |
| (N392FJ) | FA20 | 392/553 |
| **N392FV** | **CL61** | **3032** |
| N392GA | GLF4 | 1392 |
| N392GA | GLF4 | 1492 |
| N392GA | GLF4 | 4092 |
| N392JP | LJ35 | 328 |
| N392PT | CL61 | 5110 |
| **N392QS** | **C560** | **0429** |
| **N392RG** | **C525** | **0340** |
| **N392SM** | **C525** | **0392** |
| N392T | LJ24 | 158 |
| N392T | LJ25 | 104 |
| N392U | FA50 | 54 |
| **N392X** | **PRM1** | **RD-1** |
| N393BB | BE40 | RJ-39 |
| **N393BB** | **BE40** | **RK-542** |
| N393BD | GLF2 | 120 |
| N393BD | GLF4 | 1205 |
| **N393BZ** | **GLEX** | **9022** |
| N393CF | LJ35 | 669 |
| N393CW | C650 | 0113 |
| N393DA | C500 | 584 |
| **N393E** | **CS55** | **0053** |
| N393F | FA20 | 65 |
| N393GA | GALX | 093 |
| N393GA | GLF4 | 1393 |
| N393GA | GLF4 | 4093 |
| **N393GH** | **BE40** | **RK-240** |
| (N393HC) | C550 | 336 |
| **N393JC** | **C650** | **0113** |
| N393JP | LJ35 | 320 |
| N393N | C525 | 0109 |
| **N393QS** | **C560** | **0393** |
| N393RC | C550 | 336 |
| (N393RF) | FA20 | 65 |
| N393S | FA20 | 473 |
| N393TA | LJ60 | 143 |
| N393U | GLF3 | 325 |
| **N394AJ** | **C560** | **0230** |
| **N394AK** | **GLF4** | **1470** |
| **N394BB** | **BE40** | **RK-364** |
| **N394CK** | **C560** | **0270** |
| N394GA | GALX | 094 |
| N394GA | GLF4 | 1394 |
| N394GA | GLF5 | 5194 |
| **N394HA** | **CS55** | **0132** |
| N394JP | LJ35 | 491 |
| (N394MA) | C550 | 672 |
| N394PA | LJ35 | 462 |
| **N394QS** | **C560** | **0394** |
| N394SA | LJ31 | 034 |
| **N394TR** | **GLF4** | **1252** |
| N394U | FA50 | 113 |

| | | |
|---|---|---|
| N394WJ | C56X | 5086 |
| **N394WJ** | **F900** | **37** |
| N394XP | HS25 | 258394 |
| (N395BB) | FA20 | 395/554 |
| **N395BC** | **LJ45** | **258** |
| N395CC | C550 | 395 |
| N395EJ | GLF3 | 395 |
| N395EJ | HS25 | 256060 |
| N395GA | GLF4 | 1395 |
| **N395GA** | **SBRL** | **465-65** |
| N395HE | C550 | 641 |
| **N395HE** | **HS25** | **258206** |
| N395L | F900 | 133 |
| **N395LJ** | **LJ31** | **095** |
| **N395MY** | **LJ35** | **395** |
| (N395QS) | C560 | 0395 |
| **N395QS** | **C560** | **0496** |
| N395R | C560 | 0188 |
| N395RD | HS25 | 257064 |
| N395SC | C500 | 395 |
| N395SD | C525 | 0439 |
| N395SR | WW24 | 395 |
| **N395TJ** | **WW24** | **395** |
| **N395WB** | **MU30** | **A045SA** |
| **N395WC** | **C560** | **0367** |
| **N395WJ** | **C56X** | **5330** |
| **N396BB** | **C680** | **0123** |
| N396BC | GLF2 | 93 |
| **N396CF** | **GLF2** | **96** |
| N396CJ | C52B | 0196 |
| (N396DA) | C550 | 282 |
| **N396DM** | **C510** | **0008** |
| N396EG | FA50 | 207 |
| N396GA | GLF4 | 1396 |
| N396GA | GLF4 | 1456 |
| N396GC | LJ45 | 396 |
| **N396KM** | **CL60** | **1059** |
| **N396M** | **C550** | **396** |
| **N396NS** | **GLF4** | **1395** |
| N396QS | C560 | 0396 |
| **N396QS** | **C680** | **0240** |
| N396RC | HS25 | 257087 |
| **N396U** | **GLF4** | **1350** |
| N396U | HS25 | 257071 |
| **N396V** | **CL60** | **1009** |
| N397AF | C560 | 0397 |
| N397AT | BE40 | RK-157 |
| N397AT | BE40 | RK-256 |
| **N397AT** | **LJ45** | **105** |
| N397B | JSTR | 5075/19 |
| **N397BC** | **C56X** | **5291** |
| N397BC | LJ24 | 144 |
| N397BE | CL60 | 1053 |
| N397CA | BE40 | RK-136 |
| N397CS | C650 | 0056 |
| N397CW | C650 | 0107 |
| **N397DR** | **C650** | **0107** |
| N397F | GLF2 | 72 |
| N397GA | GALX | 097 |
| N397GA | GLF4 | 1397 |
| N397GA | GLF4 | 1497 |
| N397GA | GLF4 | 4097 |
| **N397GA** | **GLF4** | **4197** |
| N397J | CL61 | 5033 |
| N397J | GLF2 | 97 |
| N397J | GLF4 | 1354 |
| **N397JJ** | **GLF4** | **1354** |
| (N397JQ) | CL61 | 5033 |
| (N397L) | GLF2 | 97 |
| N397L | LJ24 | 144 |
| N397LE | GLF2 | 106 |
| N397Q | CL61 | 5033 |
| N397QS | C560 | 0531 |
| **N397QS** | **C680** | **0144** |
| N397RD | GLF2 | 37 |
| **N397RJ** | **C525** | **0683** |
| **N397SC** | **C500** | **019** |
| (N397SL) | MU30 | A022SA |
| N397WC | C560 | 0333 |
| **N398AC** | **FA50** | **240** |
| N398AC | LJ55 | 033 |
| N398AG | ASTR | 088 |
| **N398BB** | **BE40** | **RJ-39** |
| N398CC | C550 | 398 |
| N398CG | LJ45 | 398 |
| N398CJ | C525 | 0398 |
| N398CW | C650 | 0098 |
| N398DC | FA10 | 180 |
| **N398DL** | **C650** | **0098** |
| N398EP | C525 | 0327 |
| N398GA | GALX | 098 |
| N398GA | GALX | 198 |
| N398GA | GLF4 | 1398 |
| N398GA | GLF4 | 1498 |
| N398GA | GLF4 | 4098 |
| **N398GA** | **GLF4** | **4198** |
| **N398LS** | **C550** | **550-0853** |
| **N398QS** | **C560** | **0522** |
| N398RP | C500 | 316 |
| **N398RS** | **C56X** | **5009** |
| N398S | C550 | 338 |
| N398W | C650 | 7038 |
| N399AG | ASTR | 090 |
| **N399AP** | **GLF3** | **399** |
| (N399AZ) | LJ35 | 399 |
| **N399BA** | **LJ35** | **371** |
| N399BH | GLF3 | 384 |
| N399CB | GLF2 | 118 |
| N399CB | GLF3 | 433 |
| N399CB | GLF4 | 1261 |
| N399CC | GLF4 | 1051 |
| N399CF | CL61 | 5084 |
| (N399CG) | F9EX | 55 |
| N399D | WW24 | 31 |
| (N399DJ) | LJ35 | 399 |
| **N399DM** | **MU30** | **A008SA** |
| **N399EX** | **F9EX** | **222** |
| N399FA | F2TH | 101 |
| N399FG | FA20 | 373 |
| **N399FL** | **CL60** | **1083** |
| N399FP | GLF2 | 118 |
| **N399G** | **C525** | **0183** |
| N399GA | ASTR | 225 |
| N399GA | GLF4 | 1459 |
| N399GA | GLF5 | 5199 |
| N399GA | HS25 | 256004 |
| **N399GG** | **FA50** | **108** |
| **N399GS** | **GLEX** | **9074** |
| N399HS | C560 | 0678 |
| N399JC | HS25 | 258334 |
| N399KL | LJ35 | 362 |
| N399MJ | MU30 | A039SA |
| **N399MM** | **MU30** | **A017SA** |
| N399P | SBRL | 282-87 |
| N399PA | C500 | 327 |
| N399PA | GLF4 | 1093 |
| **N399QS** | **C560** | **0510** |
| **N399RA** | **BE40** | **RK-200** |
| N399RP | MU30 | A020SA |
| N399RV | GLF3 | 423 |
| **N399RW** | **LJ31** | **182** |
| **N399SC** | **ASTR** | **272** |
| N399SC | GLF3 | 488 |
| N399SC | LJ60 | 040 |
| **N399SF** | **C56X** | **5718** |
| N399SR | SBRL | 306-33 |
| N399SW | CL61 | 5009 |
| N399SW | FA20 | 197 |
| N399W | C650 | 0098 |
| N399W | C650 | 7038 |
| **N399W** | **C750** | **0171** |
| N399W | LJ35 | 209 |
| **N399WB** | **CL60** | **1025** |
| N399WC | C560 | 0348 |
| N399WW | CL61 | 3011 |
| N399WW | GLF3 | 384 |
| N400 | CL64 | 5572 |
| N400 | LJ25 | 137 |
| N400 | LJ31 | 128 |
| N400 | LJ45 | 217 |
| N400 | LJ45 | 304 |
| (N400A) | BE40 | RK-110 |
| N400A | BE40 | RK-3 |
| N400A | BE40 | RK-34 |
| N400A | BE40 | RK-342 |
| N400A | BE40 | RK-353 |
| N400A | BE40 | RK-66 |
| N400A | BE40 | RK-98 |
| N400AD | LJ35 | 519 |
| N400AG | HS25 | 25206 |
| **N400AJ** | **BE40** | **RK-137** |
| (N400AJ) | CS55 | 0156 |
| N400AJ | LJ25 | 038 |
| N400AK | LJ35 | 520 |
| N400AL | GLF3 | 343 |
| N400AL | HS25 | 258009 |
| N400AN | LJ35 | 521 |
| N400AP | LJ35 | 522 |
| N400AQ | LJ35 | 523 |
| N400AS | LJ35 | 524 |
| N400AT | LJ35 | 525 |
| N400AU | LJ35 | 526 |
| N400AX | LJ35 | 527 |
| N400AY | LJ35 | 528 |
| N400AZ | LJ35 | 529 |
| N400BA | LJ35 | 530 |
| N400BE | BE40 | RK-4 |
| N400BF | LJ24 | 010 |
| N400BH | C500 | 244 |
| N400BH | HS25 | 25230 |
| N400BN | LJ35 | 532 |
| N400BQ | LJ35 | 533 |
| N400BU | LJ35 | 534 |
| N400BY | LJ35 | 535 |
| N400BZ | LJ35 | 536 |
| N400CC | GLF2 | 102/32 |
| N400CC | GLF4 | 1046 |
| N400CC | HS25 | 25179 |
| N400CC | LJ35 | 083 |
| N400CD | LJ35 | 537 |
| N400CE | SBRL | 306-87 |
| N400CG | LJ35 | 538 |
| N400CH | HS25 | 257186 |
| N400CJ | LJ35 | 539 |
| N400CK | LJ35 | 540 |
| **N400CP** | **ASTR** | **131** |
| N400CP | WW24 | 30 |
| N400CQ | LJ35 | 541 |
| N400CR | LJ35 | 542 |
| N400CS | LJ24 | 022 |
| N400CS | SBRL | 282-34 |
| N400CT | BE40 | RK-179 |
| N400CT | C560 | 0104 |
| N400CU | LJ35 | 543 |
| **N400CV** | **C52A** | **0396** |
| N400CV | LJ35 | 544 |
| N400CX | GLF2 | 100 |
| N400CX | LJ35 | 545 |
| N400CY | LJ35 | 546 |
| N400CZ | LJ35 | 547 |
| **N400D** | **GLF2** | **100** |
| N400D | HS25 | 25216 |
| N400DB | C500 | 508 |
| N400DB | FA20 | 193 |
| (N400DB) | LJ25 | 124 |
| N400DB | SBRL | 370-4 |
| N400DD | LJ35 | 548 |
| N400DJ | LJ35 | 549 |
| N400DK | C550 | 219 |
| N400DL | LJ35 | 550 |
| N400DN | LJ35 | 551 |
| N400DP | HS25 | 25271 |
| N400DQ | LJ35 | 552 |
| N400DR | LJ35 | 553 |
| (N400DT) | BE40 | RK-66 |
| N400DT | C550 | 102 |
| N400DU | LJ35 | 554 |
| N400DV | LJ35 | 555 |
| **N400DW** | **BE40** | **RJ-40** |
| N400DX | LJ35 | 556 |
| N400DY | LJ35 | 557 |
| N400DZ | LJ35 | 558 |
| **N400EC** | **C550** | **713** |
| N400EC | LJ35 | 559 |
| N400EE | LJ35 | 560 |
| N400EF | LJ35 | 561 |
| N400EG | LJ35 | 562 |
| N400EJ | LJ35 | 563 |
| N400EK | LJ35 | 564 |
| N400EL | LJ35 | 565 |
| N400EM | LJ35 | 566 |
| N400EN | LJ35 | 567 |
| N400EP | LJ24 | 116 |
| **N400EP** | **LJ24** | **215** |
| N400EQ | LJ35 | 568 |
| N400ER | LJ35 | 569 |
| **N400ES** | **CL65** | **5727** |
| N400ES | LJ35 | 570 |
| N400ET | LJ35 | 571 |
| N400EU | LJ35 | 572 |
| N400EV | LJ35 | 573 |
| N400EX | C550 | 597 |
| N400EX | LJ35 | 574 |
| N400EY | LJ35 | 575 |
| N400EZ | LJ35 | 576 |
| N400FE | HS25 | 25222 |
| N400FE | LJ35 | 577 |
| N400FF | LJ35 | 498 |
| N400FG | LJ35 | 578 |
| N400FH | LJ35 | 579 |
| **N400FJ** | **GLF4** | **1494** |
| N400FK | LJ35 | 580 |
| N400FM | LJ35 | 581 |
| N400FN | LJ35 | 582 |
| N400FP | LJ35 | 583 |
| N400FQ | LJ35 | 584 |
| **N400FR** | **HS25** | **25228** |
| N400FR | LJ35 | 585 |
| N400FT | BE40 | RJ-60 |
| N400FT | BE40 | RK-101 |
| N400FT | BE40 | RK-47 |
| N400FT | LJ35 | 586 |
| N400FU | LJ35 | 587 |
| N400FV | LJ35 | 588 |
| N400FY | LJ35 | 531 |
| N400GA | GLF4 | 1001 |
| N400GA | GLF4 | 1042 |
| N400GA | GLF4 | 1500 |
| N400GA | GLF4 | 1516 |
| N400GB | C500 | 400 |
| **N400GG** | **C52B** | **0195** |
| **N400GJ** | **BE40** | **RJ-23** |
| **N400GK** | **MU30** | **A019SA** |
| N400GM | SBRL | 282-99 |
| N400GN | FA20 | 325 |
| N400GN | HS25 | 258059 |
| N400GP | HS25 | 25245 |
| N400GP | HS25 | 25270 |
| **N400GR** | **BE40** | **RK-335** |
| (N400GX) | FA20 | 325 |
| N400GX | GLEX | 9037 |
| N400HC | WW24 | 117 |
| **N400HD** | **BE40** | **RK-191** |
| N400HD | BE40 | RK-303 |
| N400HF | GLF4 | 1444 |
| (N400HF) | HS25 | 25207 |
| N400HG | MU30 | A091SA |
| **N400HH** | **MU30** | **A025SA** |
| N400HS | BE40 | RK-303 |
| **N400HS** | **BE40** | **RK-314** |
| **N400HT** | **C52A** | **0208** |
| N400J | ASTR | 014 |
| N400J | GLF2 | 196 |
| N400J | GLF3 | 493 |
| **N400J** | **GLF4** | **1330** |
| N400JD | C650 | 0035 |
| **N400JD** | **C750** | **0235** |
| N400JD | GLF2 | 67 |
| N400JD | GLF5 | 524 |
| **N400JE** | **LJ35** | **120** |
| N400JF | ASTR | 014 |
| N400JH | C650 | 0226 |
| N400JH | SBRL | 306-133 |
| N400JJ | BE40 | RK-255 |
| N400JK | HS25 | 25234 |
| N400JS | LJ25 | 235 |
| N400JT | LJ55 | 092 |
| N400K | C500 | 102 |
| N400K | GLF3 | 370 |
| (N400KC) | CL61 | 5073 |
| N400KC | CL61 | 5090 |
| N400KC | HS25 | 25198 |
| N400KC | JSTR | 5051 |
| N400KC | JSTR | 5210 |
| N400KD | HS25 | 25208 |
| **N400KE** | **FA50** | **54** |
| N400KG | BE40 | RK-221 |
| N400KL | BE40 | RK-125 |
| N400KP | BE40 | RK-125 |
| **N400KP** | **BE40** | **RK-308** |
| **N400KS** | **C560** | **0041** |
| N400KV | SBRL | 465-69 |
| (N400LC) | FA50 | 89 |
| N400LC | HS25 | 25216 |
| N400LH | GLF3 | 401 |
| N400LR | WW24 | 48 |
| N400LV | LJ35 | 083 |
| N400LX | C500 | 661 |
| N400LX | C500 | 666 |
| N400LX | C550 | 597 |
| N400LX | C560 | 0453 |
| **N400M** | **GLF2** | **132** |

| | | |
|---|---|---|
| N400M | JSTR | 5008 |
| (N400MC) | C550 | 495 |
| **N400MC** | **C560** | **0440** |
| N400MC | LJ35 | 487 |
| (N400MJ) | LJ35 | 083 |
| N400ML | MU30 | A064SA |
| **N400MP** | **GLF4** | **1369** |
| N400MP | JSTR | 5228 |
| N400MR | BE40 | RK-269 |
| N400MR | HA4T | RC-12 |
| (N400MR) | HS25 | 25241 |
| N400MR | JSTR | 5228 |
| **N400MS** | **LJ24** | **246** |
| (N400MT) | C550 | 238 |
| N400MV | BE40 | RK-269 |
| **N400MV** | **BE40** | **RK-286** |
| N400N | SBRL | 380-41 |
| N400NE | HS25 | 256047 |
| N400NE | WW24 | 240 |
| **N400NF** | **MU30** | **A091SA** |
| (N400NL) | FA20 | 70 |
| **N400NR** | **SBRL** | **380-41** |
| N400NS | BE40 | RK-28 |
| N400NU | HS25 | 257041 |
| N400NW | HS25 | 25074 |
| N400NW | HS25 | 256047 |
| N400NW | HS25 | 257041 |
| N400NW | HS25 | 258012 |
| N400PC | C500 | 425 |
| N400PC | C550 | 051 |
| N400PC | C550 | 242 |
| N400PC | C650 | 0057 |
| N400PC | FA20 | 113 |
| N400PC | FA50 | 89 |
| N400PC | LJ25 | 235 |
| N400PC | WW24 | 87 |
| N400PG | C500 | 425 |
| (N400PG) | C500 | 434 |
| N400PG | FA20 | 113 |
| N400PG | LJ24 | 068 |
| N400PH | HS25 | 25180 |
| N400PJ | GLF2 | 183 |
| N400PL | BE40 | RJ-42 |
| **N400PR** | **HS25** | **25203** |
| **N400PU** | **BE40** | **RK-156** |
| N400Q | BE40 | RK-39 |
| N400Q | BE40 | RK-55 |
| (N400Q) | WW24 | 240 |
| N400QH | HS25 | 257186 |
| N400QW | BE40 | RK-290 |
| N400RB | C750 | 0076 |
| N400RB | LJ24 | 064 |
| N400RB | LJ35 | 011 |
| **N400RE** | **C650** | **0199** |
| N400RE | CS55 | 0093 |
| N400RL | C525 | 0151 |
| **N400RM** | **C500** | **290** |
| N400RS | LJ24 | 138 |
| **N400RS** | **SBRL** | **380-25** |
| (N400RV) | LJ35 | 120 |
| **N400RY** | **BE40** | **RK-355** |
| N400SA | C500 | 223 |
| N400SA | GLF2 | 8 |
| N400SA | GLF4 | 1120 |
| **N400SF** | **BE40** | **RK-221** |
| **N400SH** | **BE40** | **RK-100** |
| N400SJ | GLF2 | 156/31 |
| N400SJ | GLF2 | 8 |
| N400SJ | WW24 | 240 |
| N400SP | FA10 | 125 |
| N400SR | C500 | 685 |
| N400T | BE40 | RJ-17 |
| N400TB | CL61 | 5120 |
| N400TB | HS25 | 258039 |
| **N400TE** | **BE40** | **RK-187** |
| N400TF | WW24 | 279 |
| N400TJ | MU30 | A006SA |
| **N400TL** | **BE40** | **RK-339** |
| (N400TN) | BE40 | RJ-13 |
| N400TX | C550 | 406 |
| **N400UF** | **MU30** | **A022SA** |
| N400UP | GLF4 | 1054 |
| N400UP | GLF4 | 1258 |
| N400UW | HS25 | 25074 |
| N400VC | LJ25 | 235 |
| (N400VC) | LJ25 | 267 |
| N400VG | BE40 | RK-113 |
| N400VG | BE40 | RK-3 |
| N400VK | BE40 | RK-3 |
| **N400VK** | **BE40** | **RK-420** |
| N400VP | BE40 | RK-110 |
| **N400WD** | **C52A** | **0002** |
| **N400WK** | **C650** | **0231** |
| N400WP | HS25 | 257152 |
| N400WT | FA20 | 479 |
| N400WT | HS25 | 25286 |
| N400WT | WW24 | 3 |
| **N400WY** | **GLF3** | **467** |
| (N400XB) | LJ24 | 326 |
| N400XJ | HS25 | 25220 |
| N400XP | BE40 | RK-356 |
| N400XP | BE40 | RK-400 |
| N400Y | BE40 | RK-66 |
| N400YM | WW24 | 315 |
| N401AB | BE40 | RK-7 |
| N401AB | FA20 | 66 |
| **N401AB** | **HS25** | **25222** |
| N401AC | LJ25 | 140 |
| **N401AJ** | **LJ25** | **171** |
| N401BP | WW24 | 260 |
| N401CG | BE40 | RJ-43 |
| **N401CS** | **C52B** | **0030** |
| N401CV | C560 | 0401 |
| (N401CW) | BE40 | RK-1 |
| N401CW | BE40 | RK-371 |
| N401DE | WW24 | 92 |
| **N401DP** | **LJ25** | **329** |
| N401EE | BE40 | RK-6 |
| N401EG | C525 | 0154 |
| **N401EG** | **LJ40** | **45-2021** |
| (N401FF) | BE40 | RK-6 |
| N401FF | HS25 | 259021 |
| **N401FT** | **GLF4** | **1523** |
| N401G | C500 | 667 |
| N401GA | GLF2 | 41 |
| N401GA | GLF4 | 1136 |
| N401GA | GLF4 | 1401 |
| N401GA | GLF4 | 1501 |
| N401GA | GLF4 | 4041 |
| N401GA | GLF4 | 4101 |
| **N401GA** | **GLF4** | **4201** |
| **N401GJ** | **BE40** | **RJ-26** |
| N401GN | HS25 | 257072 |
| **N401HB** | **GLF5** | **5173** |
| **N401HF** | **GLF5** | **5039** |
| N401HR | GLF2 | 39 |
| (N401HR) | HS25 | 256046 |
| N401JE | LJ55 | 041 |
| N401JL | GLF4 | 1283 |
| N401JR | HS25 | 25191 |
| **N401JW** | **FA10** | **46** |
| N401KC | C550 | 550-0969 |
| N401KH | C560 | 0304 |
| N401LG | C525 | 0154 |
| **N401LG** | **C52A** | **0037** |
| **N401LJ** | **LJ40** | **45-2001** |
| N401LS | HS25 | 259032 |
| (N401LX) | BE40 | RK-17 |
| N401M | GLF2 | 158 |
| N401M | GLF2 | 174 |
| N401MC | C560 | 0034 |
| N401MM | GLF4 | 1130 |
| N401MS | SBRL | 306-17 |
| (N401NK) | CL61 | 3027 |
| **N401NK** | **CL64** | **5409** |
| **N401NX** | **BE40** | **RK-28** |
| **N401PG** | **C680** | **0221** |
| N401PJ | GLF3 | 488 |
| **N401PP** | **PRM1** | **RB-130** |
| N401Q | LJ45 | 217 |
| **N401QS** | **GLF4** | **1408** |
| N401RB | LJ24 | 064 |
| N401RD | C500 | 267 |
| **N401RJ** | **CL61** | **5155** |
| N401RJ | GLF3 | 488 |
| **N401SR** | **GLF4** | **4001** |
| (N401TC) | BE40 | RK-21 |
| (N401TJ) | BE40 | RJ-4 |
| **N401TM** | **HS25** | **258602** |
| (N401U) | C550 | 215 |
| N401V | WW24 | 30 |
| N401WJ | GLF5 | 599 |
| **N401WT** | **ASTR** | **068** |
| N401WT | GLF4 | 1338 |
| **N402AC** | **HS25** | **25103** |
| **N402CB** | **BE40** | **RK-399** |
| N402CW | BE40 | RK-2 |
| N402DP | LJ25 | 351 |
| N402DP | LJ35 | 439 |
| **N402EF** | **CL30** | **20247** |
| N402ES | FA10 | 174 |
| N402FB | BE40 | RJ-2 |
| **N402FB** | **BE40** | **RK-255** |
| (N402FF) | HS25 | 259036 |
| **N402FG** | **F900** | **87** |
| **N402FL** | **BE40** | **RK-201** |
| **N402FT** | **GLF4** | **1527** |
| (N402FW) | LJ35 | 256 |
| N402GA | GLF4 | 1049 |
| N402GA | GLF4 | 1097 |
| N402GA | GLF4 | 1137 |
| N402GA | GLF4 | 1189 |
| N402GJ | HS25 | 257034 |
| **N402GS** | **BE40** | **RK-71** |
| N402HR | HS25 | 256046 |
| N402JP | GLF4 | 1283 |
| N402JW | FA10 | 120 |
| N402KC | GLF4 | 1017 |
| **N402LM** | **GALX** | **082** |
| (N402LM) | GLF3 | 404 |
| (N402LX) | BE40 | RK-18 |
| (N402NC) | FA20 | 339 |
| (N402QS) | GLF4 | 1501 |
| (N402QS) | GLF4 | 1504 |
| N402ST | C550 | 058 |
| N402TJ | C550 | 051 |
| N402TS | ASTR | 039 |
| (N402Y) | LJ24 | 113 |
| N403AC | LJ25 | 140 |
| N403BG | HS25 | 257003 |
| (N403BL) | C650 | 7010 |
| N403CB | C650 | 0099 |
| N403CC | C500 | 403 |
| N403CH | C52B | 0250 |
| **N403CM** | **C510** | **0003** |
| **N403CT** | **HS25** | **258818** |
| N403CW | BE40 | RK-103 |
| N403DP | HS25 | 257114 |
| **N403DP** | **LJ35** | **446** |
| **N403ET** | **C560** | **0535** |
| N403FF | HS25 | 259038 |
| N403FJ | F900 | 3 |
| N403FW | LJ35 | 403 |
| N403GA | GALX | 173 |
| N403GA | GLF4 | 1003 |
| N403GA | GLF4 | 1051 |
| N403GA | GLF4 | 1098 |
| N403GA | GLF4 | 1138 |
| N403GA | GLF4 | 1190 |
| N403GA | GLF4 | 1288 |
| N403GA | GLF4 | 1403 |
| N403GA | GLF4 | 1503 |
| **N403GA** | **GLF4** | **4203** |
| **N403JP** | **BE40** | **RJ-7** |
| N403JW | FA20 | 102 |
| **N403LM** | **GALX** | **083** |
| N403LM | GLF3 | 404 |
| **N403LS** | **LJ40** | **45-2124** |
| (N403LX) | BE40 | RK-19 |
| N403M | WW24 | 132 |
| **N403ND** | **C52B** | **0250** |
| N403NW | GLF3 | 403 |
| **N403QS** | **GLF4** | **1403** |
| N403SR | GLF4 | 4003 |
| **N403TB** | **GLF4** | **1191** |
| **N403W** | **WW24** | **403** |
| N403WC | BE40 | RK-198 |
| N403WJ | GLF3 | 403 |
| N403WY | CL60 | 1059 |
| N404A | F9EX | 56 |
| N404AB | CL61 | 5112 |
| N404AC | GLF2 | 189/42 |
| **N404AC** | **GLF4** | **1384** |
| N404AJ | LJ24 | 026 |
| N404BB | LJ35 | 404 |
| N404BF | C550 | 066 |
| **N404BL** | **BE40** | **RK-367** |
| **N404BS** | **C550** | **371** |
| N404BS | HS25 | 258294 |
| N404BT | C56X | 5038 |
| (N404BV) | C550 | 066 |
| N404CB | CL61 | 5090 |
| N404CB | HS25 | 257087 |
| N404CB | WW24 | 245 |
| N404CC | BE40 | RK-55 |
| N404CC | GLF4 | 1098 |
| N404CE | HS25 | 257106 |
| N404CE | HS25 | 258293 |
| N404CF | HS25 | 257106 |
| **N404CM** | **C510** | **0004** |
| **N404CS** | **C52B** | **0033** |
| N404DB | GLF4 | 1000 |
| N404DB | HS25 | 258404 |
| N404DB | LJ24 | 026 |
| (N404DB) | SBRL | 370-4 |
| N404DP | LJ35 | 404 |
| N404E | C550 | 104 |
| N404E | FA50 | 154 |
| **N404EL** | **LJ40** | **45-2033** |
| N404F | F900 | 41 |
| **N404F** | **F9EX** | **49** |
| N404F | FA20 | 404 |
| N404FF | F900 | 41 |
| N404FJ | F900 | 5 |
| **N404FZ** | **FA20** | **473** |
| N404G | C500 | 147 |
| N404G | C550 | 104 |
| **N404G** | **C560** | **0095** |
| N404G | CS55 | 0068 |
| N404GA | GALX | 149 |
| N404GA | GLF4 | 1000 |
| N404GA | GLF4 | 1101 |
| N404GA | GLF4 | 1139 |
| N404GA | GLF4 | 1191 |
| N404GA | GLF4 | 1244 |
| N404GA | GLF4 | 1404 |
| N404GA | GLF4 | 1406 |
| **N404HG** | **CL61** | **5017** |
| **N404HR** | **FA20** | **455** |
| N404HR | WW24 | 324 |
| N404HS | GLF4 | 1404 |
| N404JC | HS25 | 258400 |
| N404JF | C650 | 7001 |
| N404JF | FA50 | 197 |
| **N404JM** | **PRM1** | **RB-167** |
| N404JS | LJ35 | 441 |
| (N404JW) | C500 | 338 |
| **N404JW** | **FA10** | **29** |
| N404KA | LJ35 | 404 |
| **N404KK** | **CS55** | **0081** |
| N404KS | C550 | 361 |
| N404LM | GLF4 | 1130 |
| N404LN | C560 | 0190 |
| N404LN | C650 | 0106 |
| (N404LX) | BE40 | RK-22 |
| N404M | GLF2 | 220 |
| N404M | GLF2 | 83 |
| N404M | GLF3 | 404 |
| N404M | GLF4 | 1110 |
| N404M | GLF4 | 1366 |
| N404M | GLF5 | 654 |
| N404MA | C500 | 126 |
| N404MK | LJ40 | 45-2003 |
| N404MM | C560 | 0491 |
| N404MM | C56X | 5161 |
| **N404MM** | **C56X** | **5737** |
| N404MM | GLF3 | 404 |
| **N404MS** | **BE40** | **RK-283** |
| N404MW | WW24 | 372 |
| N404MY | GLF4 | 1110 |
| N404N | F9EX | 81 |
| (N404PC) | WW24 | 13 |
| **N404PG** | **WW24** | **358** |
| (N404PK) | C56X | 5336 |
| **N404PX** | **GLF4** | **4033** |
| **N404QS** | **GLF4** | **1304** |
| N404R | F900 | 55 |
| N404R | F9EX | 81 |
| N404R | FA20 | 155 |
| N404R | FA50 | 154 |
| N404RK | C550 | 550-0958 |
| **N404RP** | **C550** | **041** |
| N404SB | C550 | 425 |
| N404SB | C56X | 5069 |
| **N404SJ** | **SJ30** | **004** |
| N404SK | CL61 | 5058 |
| N404SP | GLF4 | 1243 |
| N404SR | GLF4 | 4004 |
| N404ST | F900 | 200 |
| **N404TR** | **F900** | **200** |
| N404UK | F2EX | 170 |
| N404UK | F2EX | 47 |

| | | |
|---|---|---|
| N404VC | F900 | 158 |
| N404VL | F900 | 158 |
| **N404VL** | **GLEX** | **9085** |
| N404VP | BE40 | RK-44 |
| N404W | WW24 | 404 |
| **N404WC** | **WW24** | **128** |
| **N404XT** | **GLF4** | **1366** |
| N405BX | LJ45 | 026 |
| N405CC | C500 | 405 |
| N405CJ | C52A | 0405 |
| **N405CS** | **C52B** | **0036** |
| N405CT | HS25 | 258819 |
| N405CW | BE40 | RK-305 |
| (N405CW) | BE40 | RK-5 |
| **N405DC** | **FA50** | **42** |
| (N405DP) | CL61 | 5131 |
| N405DP | HS25 | 257130 |
| **N405DW** | **HS25** | **257130** |
| N405EJ | F900 | 105 |
| N405F | FA20 | 405 |
| (N405FF) | HS25 | 259020 |
| N405FJ | F900 | 6 |
| N405FX | LJ45 | 026 |
| N405GA | ASTR | 205 |
| N405GA | GLF2 | 105 |
| N405GA | GLF4 | 1017 |
| N405GA | GLF4 | 1102 |
| N405GA | GLF4 | 1140 |
| N405GA | GLF4 | 1214 |
| N405GA | GLF4 | 1245 |
| N405GA | GLF4 | 1289 |
| N405GA | GLF4 | 1505 |
| N405GA | GLF4 | 4105 |
| **N405GA** | **GLF5** | **5205** |
| **N405GJ** | **LJ35** | **354** |
| **N405HG** | **GLF5** | **661** |
| N405JW | FA20 | 54 |
| **N405LA** | **HS25** | **258726** |
| (N405LM) | GLF3 | 360 |
| **N405LM** | **GLF5** | **541** |
| (N405LX) | BE40 | RK-27 |
| **N405MG** | **MU30** | **A021SA** |
| N405MM | C56X | 5161 |
| N405MM | GLF2 | 220 |
| (N405MW) | LJ45 | 115 |
| N405PC | C500 | 562 |
| **N405PC** | **LJ35** | **651** |
| **N405QS** | **GLF4** | **4054** |
| (N405RH) | C560 | 0062 |
| N405RS | LJ25 | 096 |
| N405ST | F2TH | 20 |
| **N405TM** | **HS25** | **258667** |
| N405TP | HS25 | 257130 |
| N405XP | HS25 | 258405 |
| N406BX | LJ45 | 089 |
| N406CH | WW24 | 372 |
| N406CJ | C500 | 406 |
| N406CJ | C550 | 058 |
| **N406CM** | **C510** | **0015** |
| **N406CS** | **C52B** | **0043** |
| **N406CT** | **CS55** | **0038** |
| N406CW | BE40 | RK-6 |
| N406F | FA20 | 407 |
| N406FA | GLF3 | 406 |
| N406FJ | F900 | 8 |
| N406FL | BE40 | RK-295 |
| N406FX | LJ45 | 089 |
| N406GJ | BE40 | RJ-50 |
| **N406J** | **HS25** | **257131** |
| N406L | LJ24 | 148 |
| N406LM | C650 | 0102 |
| (N406LM) | GALX | 017 |
| N406LM | GALX | 032 |
| **N406LX** | **BE40** | **RK-178** |
| (N406LX) | BE40 | RK-30 |
| (N406M) | C650 | 0102 |
| (N406ML) | BE40 | RK-6 |
| N406MM | C650 | 0102 |
| N406PW | SBRL | 380-2 |
| (N406RH) | C500 | 589 |
| N406SS | C550 | 368 |
| (N406ST) | F2TH | 25 |
| **N406TS** | **BE40** | **RJ-6** |
| **N406VJ** | **C560** | **0056** |
| N406W | WW24 | 406 |
| N406W | WW24 | 442 |
| **N407BS** | **LJ31** | **033** |
| N407CA | GLF3 | 422 |
| N407CJ | C52A | 0407 |
| N407CW | BE40 | RK-307 |
| N407F | FA20 | 409 |
| N407FJ | F900 | 10 |
| N407FX | LJ45 | 090 |
| N407GA | GLF3 | 407 |
| N407GA | GLF4 | 1018 |
| N407GA | GLF4 | 1070 |
| N407GA | GLF4 | 1119 |
| N407GA | GLF4 | 1141 |
| N407GA | GLF4 | 1192 |
| N407GA | GLF4 | 1246 |
| **N407GC** | **GLF4** | **1242** |
| N407LM | C650 | 0103 |
| N407LM | GALX | 019 |
| (N407LX) | BE40 | RK-180 |
| (N407LX) | BE40 | RK-31 |
| (N407M) | C650 | 0103 |
| N407MM | C650 | 0103 |
| N407MR | LJ35 | 407 |
| **N407NS** | **GLF4** | **1407** |
| N407PC | FA20 | 30 |
| N407QS | GLF4 | 1407 |
| N407RA | LJ31 | 103 |
| N407SC | C500 | 037 |
| "N407V" | LJ24 | 034 |
| N407V | LJ24 | 087 |
| **N407W** | **WW24** | **407** |
| N408AL | HS25 | 258009 |
| (N408BX) | LJ45 | 091 |
| N408CA | C500 | 219 |
| N408CC | SBRL | 282-13 |
| **N408CS** | **C52B** | **0045** |
| N408CS | SBRL | 282-13 |
| **N408CT** | **CS55** | **0055** |
| **N408CW** | **BE40** | **RK-108** |
| (N408ER) | FA50 | 8 |
| N408F | FA20 | 411 |
| N408FJ | F900 | 12 |
| N408FX | LJ45 | 091 |
| N408GA | GLF4 | 1020 |
| N408GA | GLF4 | 1105 |
| N408GA | GLF4 | 1142 |
| N408GA | GLF4 | 1247 |
| N408GA | GLF4 | 1290 |
| N408GR | C525 | 0408 |
| **N408J** | **PRM1** | **RB-193** |
| N408JD | C650 | 0035 |
| N408JT | C560 | 0408 |
| N408LM | GALX | 036 |
| N408LN | GALX | 036 |
| (N408LX) | BE40 | RK-32 |
| **N408M** | **BE40** | **RK-6** |
| N408M | GLF3 | 362 |
| **N408MG** | **LJ35** | **328** |
| N408MJ | WW24 | 408 |
| N408MM | C500 | 443 |
| N408MM | HS25 | 258033 |
| N408MW | C500 | 443 |
| N408PA | FA20 | 408 |
| **N408PC** | **BE40** | **RK-325** |
| N408PC | BE40 | RK-47 |
| N408PC | FA20 | 98/434 |
| **N408QS** | **GLF4** | **1308** |
| N408RB | LJ35 | 011 |
| **N408RT** | **HS25** | **258440** |
| N408S | SBRL | 282-13 |
| **N408TB** | **CL61** | **5120** |
| N408TR | SBRL | 282-4 |
| **N408U** | **HA4T** | **RC-17** |
| N408W | WW24 | 408 |
| N408WT | HS25 | 25286 |
| N409AC | C500 | 433 |
| **N409AV** | **HS25** | **258347** |
| N409CC | CL60 | 1063 |
| N409CC | GLF4 | 4035 |
| **N409CS** | **C52B** | **0050** |
| **N409CT** | **CS55** | **0095** |
| N409ER | FA50 | 8 |
| N409F | FA20 | 412 |
| N409F | LJ45 | 095 |
| N409FJ | F900 | 13 |
| N409FX | LJ45 | 095 |
| N409GA | ASTR | 209 |
| N409GA | GALX | 109 |
| **N409GB** | **C680** | **0006** |
| N409GL | SBRL | 282-122 |
| N409KC | CL60 | 1052 |
| N409KC | CL61 | 5075 |
| **N409LM** | **GALX** | **059** |
| (N409LX) | BE40 | RK-35 |
| N409M | GLF2 | 83 |
| N409M | JSTR | 5047 |
| N409MA | GLF2 | 83 |
| N409MA | JSTR | 5047 |
| N409PC | FA20 | 11 |
| **N409S** | **C500** | **238** |
| **N409SF** | **C650** | **0029** |
| **N409ST** | **C550** | **559** |
| (N409VP) | C560 | 0409 |
| **N409WT** | **WW24** | **3** |
| N409WW | WW24 | 409 |
| N410AS | F2TH | 102 |
| N410AW | HS25 | 256039 |
| **N410AZ** | **FA20** | **410** |
| N410BA | BE40 | RJ-10 |
| N410BD | CL64 | 5548 |
| N410BD | LJ35 | 594 |
| N410BT | HS25 | 258209 |
| N410BX | LJ45 | 101 |
| N410CC | C550 | 410 |
| N410CS | C550 | 486 |
| N410CT | BE40 | RK-495 |
| N410CV | C560 | 0310 |
| N410CW | BE40 | RK-310 |
| **N410DM** | **C560** | **0184** |
| N410DW | C560 | 0021 |
| (N410EL) | WW24 | 410 |
| N410F | FA20 | 413 |
| N410FJ | F900 | 14 |
| (N410FJ) | FA20 | 206 |
| N410FX | LJ45 | 101 |
| N410GA | GLF4 | 1071 |
| N410GA | GLF4 | 1108 |
| N410GA | GLF4 | 1120 |
| N410GA | GLF4 | 1143 |
| N410GB | C500 | 148 |
| **N410GS** | **F2TH** | **112** |
| N410J | C560 | 0147 |
| (N410JP) | C550 | 081 |
| N410KA | F900 | 43 |
| N410KC | FA50 | 318 |
| **N410KD** | **BE40** | **RK-496** |
| **N410LM** | **GLF5** | **578** |
| (N410LR) | GLF2 | 116 |
| (N410LX) | BE40 | RK-195 |
| (N410LX) | BE40 | RK-40 |
| N410M | GLF4 | 1115 |
| **N410M** | **GLF5** | **575** |
| **N410MT** | **C56X** | **5018** |
| (N410MW) | F9EX | 85 |
| N410MY | GLF4 | 1115 |
| N410N | C500 | 345 |
| N410NA | C500 | 345 |
| N410NA | C550 | 085 |
| N410NA | C560 | 0435 |
| N410NA | WW24 | 382 |
| N410ND | C500 | 259 |
| N410PA | HS25 | 25198 |
| N410PB | LJ24 | 179 |
| N410PD | LJ24 | 179 |
| N410QS | GLF4 | 1210 |
| N410RD | LJ35 | 647 |
| N410SB | FA20 | 410 |
| **N410SG** | **F2EX** | **210** |
| N410SP | LJ25 | 174 |
| N410ST | LJ60 | 087 |
| **N410UJ** | **GLF3** | **320** |
| N410US | FA20 | 120 |
| N410US | HS25 | 258090 |
| N410US | HS25 | 259005 |
| N410WW | FA10 | 86 |
| N410WW | FA50 | 76 |
| N410WW | GLEX | 9047 |
| N410WW | GLF4 | 1203 |
| **N411AJ** | **LJ40** | **45-2011** |
| N411AL | GLF4 | 1368 |
| **N411BA** | **LJ35** | **024** |
| N411BB | C650 | 0037 |
| N411BB | C650 | 0195 |
| N411BB | CL64 | 5316 |
| N411BE | C52A | 0116 |
| N411BP | C650 | 0195 |
| N411BW | BE40 | A1008SA |
| N411BX | LJ45 | 102 |
| N411CC | FA20 | 159 |
| (N411CJ) | C500 | 411 |
| **N411DJ** | **LJ31** | **224** |
| N411DR | C500 | 249 |
| N411DS | C500 | 400 |
| **N411EC** | **C56X** | **5734** |
| **N411FB** | **HS25** | **25074** |
| N411FJ | F900 | 17 |
| N411FX | LJ45 | 102 |
| N411GA | GLF4 | 1411 |
| **N411GA** | **HS25** | **256024** |
| N411GC | C52A | 0006 |
| **N411GC** | **FA50** | **210** |
| N411GL | LJ55 | 011 |
| N411HB | WW24 | 419 |
| **N411HC** | **LJ40** | **45-2056** |
| **N411KQ** | **C56X** | **5226** |
| N411LC | LJ35 | 366 |
| **N411LL** | **GLF4** | **1344** |
| (N411LX) | BE40 | RK-42 |
| N411MD | SBRL | 306-83 |
| N411ME | C500 | 400 |
| (N411MF) | HS25 | 25155 |
| **N411MM** | **ASTR** | **080** |
| N411MM | LJ24 | 353 |
| **N411MY** | **C525** | **0512** |
| **N411PA** | **HS25** | **257017** |
| (N411PB) | C52A | 0006 |
| **N411QS** | **GLF4** | **1311** |
| N411RA | HS25 | 258177 |
| **N411RE** | **MU30** | **A016SA** |
| (N411RJ) | C500 | 411 |
| N411SC | FA10 | 50 |
| **N411SF** | **CL30** | **20031** |
| N411SK | BE40 | RK-111 |
| N411SK | BE40 | RK-28 |
| N411SK | LJ60 | 201 |
| **N411SL** | **C650** | **0003** |
| N411SP | LJ24 | 216 |
| **N411SP** | **MU30** | **A049SA** |
| N411SS | HS25 | 257104 |
| N411ST | CL30 | 20031 |
| **N411ST** | **CL30** | **20266** |
| N411ST | LJ60 | 087 |
| N411ST | LJ60 | 201 |
| (N411TC) | HS25 | 256070 |
| **N411TJ** | **CL61** | **3010** |
| **N411TN** | **C500** | **275** |
| N411TP | HS25 | 256070 |
| **N411VZ** | **HS25** | **258313** |
| N411WC | C500 | 411 |
| N411WW | FA10 | 86 |
| N411WW | FA50 | 76 |
| N411WW | GLF2 | 257/17 |
| N411WW | GLF4 | 1121 |
| N411WW | GLF4 | 1203 |
| **N411WW** | **GLF5** | **5063** |
| **N412AB** | **C56X** | **5752** |
| N412AB | FA20 | 492 |
| **N412BT** | **C550** | **550-1134** |
| **N412CS** | **C52B** | **0059** |
| N412CW | C560 | 0412 |
| **N412DA** | **HS25** | **258061** |
| N412DP | HS25 | 257162 |
| (N412EA) | C560 | 0412 |
| N412ET | C550 | 550-1041 |
| N412ET | C550 | 550-1134 |
| **N412ET** | **LJ40** | **45-2083** |
| N412F | FA20 | 414 |
| (N412F) | LJ45 | 103 |
| N412FJ | F900 | 16 |
| (N412FL) | BE40 | RK-324 |
| N412FX | LJ45 | 103 |
| N412GA | ASTR | 212 |
| N412GA | GLF4 | 1008 |
| N412GA | GLF4 | 1021 |
| N412GA | GLF4 | 1024 |
| N412GA | GLF4 | 1075 |
| N412GA | GLF4 | 1121 |
| N412GA | GLF4 | 1193 |
| N412GA | GLF4 | 1266 |
| N412GA | GLF4 | 1291 |
| N412GA | GLF4 | 1412 |
| **N412GJ** | **BE40** | **RK-412** |
| N412GL | LJ35 | 412 |
| **N412JT** | **GLF2** | **101** |
| N412LJ | LJ45 | 012 |
| (N412LX) | BE40 | RK-45 |
| N412MA | C550 | 466 |

| N412P | C550 | 187 |
|---|---|---|
| N412PD | LJ24 | 179 |
| N412PE | C550 | 483 |
| **N412PG** | **FA50** | **97** |
| N412SC | WW24 | 412 |
| N412SE | C500 | 633 |
| N412SP | LJ25 | 174 |
| N412W | WW24 | 412 |
| N412WP | BE40 | RK-111 |
| **N412WW** | **GLF4** | **1203** |
| N413CA | C550 | 128 |
| N413CK | C550 | 041 |
| N413CK | C560 | 0194 |
| N413CK | C56X | 5042 |
| **N413CK** | **C680** | **0064** |
| **N413CQ** | **C525** | **0677** |
| **N413CS** | **C52B** | **0082** |
| **N413CT** | **CS55** | **0017** |
| N413CV | C560 | 0413 |
| N413F | FA20 | 415 |
| **N413FC** | **C52A** | **0405** |
| N413FJ | F900 | 18 |
| N413GA | GALX | 113 |
| N413GA | GLF4 | 1034 |
| N413GA | GLF4 | 1212 |
| N413GA | GLF4 | 1292 |
| N413GA | GLF4 | 1315 |
| N413GA | GLF4 | 1413 |
| **N413GA** | **GLF4** | **4213** |
| N413GA | GLF5 | 5213 |
| N413GH | HS25 | 25030 |
| N413GK | C560 | 0194 |
| N413HB | HA4T | RC-13 |
| N413JP | LJ35 | 421 |
| (N413KA) | C500 | 250 |
| **N413LC** | **C560** | **0003** |
| N413LC | LJ35 | 659 |
| N413LJ | LJ45 | 013 |
| (N413LV) | CL64 | 5372 |
| **N413LX** | **BE40** | **RK-209** |
| (N413LX) | BE40 | RK-50 |
| N413MA | LJ35 | 413 |
| **N413QS** | **GLF4** | **1521** |
| (N413SC) | ASTR | 013 |
| N413VP | C550 | 412 |
| N413WF | LJ24 | 211 |
| N413WW | WW24 | 413 |
| N414AA | C56X | 5701 |
| N414BM | GLF4 | 1214 |
| N414BX | LJ45 | 111 |
| (N414CB) | C500 | 576 |
| N414CB | C500 | 589 |
| N414CC | C500 | 414 |
| N414CC | F2TH | 206 |
| **N414DH** | **CL30** | **20188** |
| N414DH | GALX | 023 |
| N414DH | GALX | 081 |
| N414DK | GALX | 023 |
| N414FJ | F900 | 19 |
| **N414FW** | **C52A** | **0081** |
| N414FX | LJ45 | 111 |
| N414GC | C550 | 096 |
| (N414JC) | FA20 | 369 |
| N414KB | GALX | 022 |
| **N414KD** | **C52B** | **0208** |
| N414KD | GALX | 022 |
| N414KD | GALX | 084 |
| N414KL | LJ35 | 595 |
| (N414LX) | BE40 | RK-53 |
| **N414PE** | **HS25** | **258090** |
| **N414RF** | **HS25** | **257060** |
| N414RF | LJ55 | 033 |
| (N414RK) | BE40 | RK-14 |
| **N414TE** | **PRM1** | **RB-4** |
| N414TJ | LJ35 | 414 |
| **N414TR** | **F2EX** | **135** |
| **N414TW** | **EA50** | **000147** |
| (N414VP) | C550 | 413 |
| N414XP | HS25 | 258266 |
| **N415AJ** | **C550** | **600** |
| (N415BA) | HS25 | 256017 |
| N415BJ | HS25 | 258257 |
| N415CL | LJ45 | 308 |
| **N415CS** | **C525** | **0373** |
| N415CS | SBRL | 282-76 |
| N415CS | SBRL | 465-42 |
| **N415CT** | **BE40** | **RJ-15** |
| N415DJ | LJ35 | 415 |
| N415EL | WW24 | 415 |
| N415F | FA20 | 416 |
| (N415FC) | C500 | 145 |
| N415FJ | F900 | 20 |
| N415FW | C750 | 0095 |
| N415FX | LJ45 | 112 |
| N415GA | GLF4 | 1023 |
| N415GA | GLF4 | 1059 |
| N415GA | GLF4 | 1110 |
| N415GA | GLF4 | 1144 |
| N415GA | GLF4 | 1194 |
| N415GA | GLF4 | 1293 |
| N415GA | GLF4 | 1415 |
| N415GA | GLF4 | 1515 |
| N415GS | SBRL | 282-76 |
| **N415JA** | **HS25** | **258516** |
| N415JW | FA20 | 369 |
| **N415LJ** | **LJ24** | **092** |
| N415LS | LJ35 | 229 |
| **N415LX** | **BE40** | **RK-225** |
| (N415LX) | BE40 | RK-56 |
| **N415NP** | **LJ60** | **024** |
| N415P | GLF4 | 1260 |
| N415PG | GLF4 | 1238 |
| N415PT | CL60 | 1053 |
| N415PT | HS25 | 258016 |
| **N415QS** | **GLF4** | **4014** |
| N415RC | MU30 | A015SA |
| N415RD | HS25 | 257094 |
| (N415RD) | LJ35 | 236 |
| N415SH | GLF4 | 1125 |
| N415SL | C52A | 0051 |
| **N415TH** | **WW24** | **415** |
| N415WW | GLF4 | 1226 |
| N416AS | FA10 | 16 |
| **N416BA** | **C560** | **0359** |
| N416BD | CL64 | 5548 |
| **N416BD** | **GLEX** | **9043** |
| **N416CC** | **C550** | **415** |
| N416CG | GLF2 | 180 |
| **N416CM** | **C510** | **0016** |
| N416CS | SBRL | 282-81 |
| **N416CT** | **BE40** | **RJ-43** |
| N416CW | BE40 | RK-16 |
| N416F | FA20 | 416 |
| N416F | FA20 | 417 |
| N416FJ | F900 | 22 |
| N416FJ | FA20 | 417 |
| N416FX | LJ45 | 113 |
| N416G | LJ24 | 325 |
| N416GA | GLF4 | 1027 |
| N416GA | GLF4 | 1111 |
| N416GA | GLF4 | 1145 |
| N416GA | GLF4 | 1213 |
| N416GA | GLF4 | 1258 |
| N416GA | GLF4 | 1294 |
| N416GA | GLF4 | 1416 |
| (N416H) | C560 | 0104 |
| N416HC | FA10 | 16 |
| **N416HF** | **C560** | **0037** |
| N416K | GLF2 | 126 |
| N416K | GLF2 | 41 |
| N416KC | C525 | 0130 |
| **N416KC** | **F9DX** | **618** |
| N416KC | FA50 | 318 |
| **N416KD** | **GLF2** | **231** |
| N416KD | JSTR | 5153/61 |
| N416LJ | LJ24 | 093 |
| (N416LX) | BE40 | RK-226 |
| (N416LX) | BE40 | RK-57 |
| (N416NL) | WW24 | 187 |
| N416NP | GLF3 | 875 |
| **N416QS** | **GLF4** | **1316** |
| N416RD | HS25 | 257062 |
| N416RM | FA20 | 426 |
| N416RM | LJ25 | 301 |
| N416RP | BE40 | RK-7 |
| **N416RX** | **BE40** | **RK-514** |
| N416SH | GLF2 | 15 |
| **N416SJ** | **JSTR** | **5153/61** |
| N416VP | C560 | 0416 |
| N416W | WW24 | 416 |
| **N416WM** | **GLF3** | **487** |
| N417AM | LJ55 | 123 |
| **N417BA** | **LJ35** | **257** |
| N417BJ | BE40 | RJ-17 |
| N417C | C525 | 0174 |
| N417C | C525 | 0385 |
| **N417C** | **C52B** | **0006** |
| **N417CG** | **EA50** | **000094** |
| N417CL | CL61 | 5107 |
| **N417CS** | **C52B** | **0090** |
| N417CW | BE40 | RK-17 |
| **N417EK** | **GLF2** | **110** |
| N417EL | WW24 | 417 |
| N417F | FA20 | 418 |
| N417FJ | F900 | 24 |
| N417FX | LJ45 | 114 |
| N417GA | GALX | 217 |
| **N417GA** | **GALX** | **237** |
| (N417GA) | GLF2 | 41 |
| N417GA | GLF4 | 1112 |
| N417GA | GLF4 | 1146 |
| N417GA | GLF4 | 1217 |
| N417GA | GLF4 | 1267 |
| N417GA | GLF4 | 1295 |
| N417GA | GLF4 | 1317 |
| N417GA | GLF4 | 1417 |
| N417GA | GLF4 | 4117 |
| **N417GR** | **C510** | **0176** |
| (N417GW) | WW24 | 417 |
| (N417H) | C560 | 0170 |
| **N417JD** | **C550** | **550-1124** |
| N417JD | C56X | 5231 |
| N417JD | LJ24 | 253 |
| N417KM | C52B | 0103 |
| N417KT | MU30 | A083SA |
| N417KW | C550 | 550-0933 |
| N417LJ | LJ24 | 094 |
| N417LJ | LJ45 | 017 |
| **N417LX** | **BE40** | **RK-230** |
| (N417LX) | BE40 | RK-61 |
| N417PJ | JSTR | 5098/28 |
| N417PJ | LJ25 | 075 |
| (N417Q) | C525 | 0174 |
| **N417Q** | **C525** | **0385** |
| (N417QS) | GLF4 | 1417 |
| N417RC | C500 | 606 |
| N417RC | CS55 | 0055 |
| (N417RD) | GLF2 | 3 |
| N417RQ | C500 | 606 |
| (N417TF) | HS25 | 25038 |
| **N417TM** | **HS25** | **258657** |
| **N417WW** | **LJ24** | **171** |
| N418BA | HS25 | 257057 |
| N418CA | LJ36 | 018 |
| N418CG | C550 | 417 |
| **N418CK** | **C56X** | **5042** |
| **N418CS** | **C52B** | **0108** |
| **N418CT** | **BE40** | **RJ-42** |
| N418CW | BE40 | RK-18 |
| **N418DL** | **LJ31** | **181** |
| **N418DM** | **HS25** | **257069** |
| N418FA | LJ45 | 120 |
| N418FJ | F900 | 25 |
| N418FX | LJ45 | 120 |
| N418GA | GLF4 | 1318 |
| N418GA | GLF4 | 1418 |
| N418GA | GLF4 | 4118 |
| **N418GA** | **GLF4** | **4180** |
| **N418GJ** | **BE40** | **RK-418** |
| **N418KC** | **C525** | **0130** |
| **N418KW** | **C550** | **550-0959** |
| N418LJ | LJ24 | 081 |
| N418LJ | LJ45 | 018 |
| **N418LX** | **BE40** | **RK-234** |
| (N418LX) | BE40 | RK-62 |
| N418MA | C550 | 159 |
| **N418MG** | **BE40** | **RJ-54** |
| **N418MN** | **LJ45** | **130** |
| N418QA | GLF4 | 1018 |
| N418R | C500 | 650 |
| N418R | LJ31 | 075 |
| N418R | LJ60 | 047 |
| **N418RD** | **HS25** | **257015** |
| **N418RM** | **BE40** | **RJ-18** |
| N418RT | LJ31 | 075 |
| N418S | FA20 | 32 |
| N418S | FA50 | 64 |
| N418SG | GLF5 | 5040 |
| **N418SG** | **GLF5** | **5207** |
| N418SG | GLF5 | 609 |
| N418SM | GLF5 | 609 |
| N418SP | GLF4 | 1218 |
| N418TT | GLF4 | 1118 |
| **N418WA** | **WW24** | **250** |
| (N419BL) | LJ25 | 220 |
| N419CW | BE40 | RK-19 |
| N419ET | LJ40 | 45-2083 |
| N419F | FA20 | 419 |
| N419FJ | F900 | 27 |
| N419FX | LJ45 | 125 |
| N419GA | GALX | 119 |
| N419GA | GLF4 | 1025 |
| N419GA | GLF4 | 1052 |
| N419GA | GLF4 | 1147 |
| N419GA | GLF4 | 1195 |
| N419GA | GLF4 | 1296 |
| (N419GA) | GLF4 | 1419 |
| N419GA | GLF5 | 5219 |
| N419GL | LJ25 | 294 |
| N419HB | HA4T | RC-19 |
| N419K | C500 | 080 |
| (N419LX) | BE40 | RK-68 |
| **N419MB** | **BE40** | **RK-85** |
| N419MK | ASTR | 066 |
| N419MS | BE40 | RK-121 |
| N419MS | BE40 | RK-85 |
| **N419MS** | **GLF2** | **81** |
| N419RD | HS25 | 257153 |
| N419TK | ASTR | 122 |
| **N419TM** | **BE40** | **RK-495** |
| N419W | WW24 | 419 |
| **N419WC** | **ASTR** | **053** |
| N419WC | FA10 | 11 |
| N419XP | HS25 | 258419 |
| N420A | JSTR | 5063 |
| N420AM | C500 | 410 |
| **N420BG** | **LJ55** | **123** |
| N420CC | CS55 | 0023 |
| **N420CC** | **GLF4** | **1164** |
| **N420CE** | **ASTR** | **139** |
| N420CE | WW24 | 405 |
| N420CH | C525 | 0066 |
| N420CH | C52A | 0027 |
| **N420CH** | **C52B** | **0151** |
| N420CL | FA20 | 391 |
| **N420CL** | **FA50** | **10** |
| **N420CS** | **C52B** | **0115** |
| **N420CT** | **BE40** | **RK-517** |
| **N420DH** | **BE40** | **RK-326** |
| N420DM | C560 | 0210 |
| N420DM | C560 | 0464 |
| N420DP | FA20 | 391 |
| **N420EH** | **C52A** | **0027** |
| N420F | FA20 | 420 |
| (N420FA) | MU30 | A042SA |
| N420FJ | F900 | 28 |
| N420FX | LJ45 | 126 |
| N420G | JSTR | 5063 |
| N420GA | GALX | 220 |
| N420GA | GLF4 | 1007 |
| N420GA | GLF4 | 1045 |
| N420GA | GLF4 | 1124 |
| N420GA | GLF4 | 1196 |
| N420GA | GLF4 | 1297 |
| N420GA | GLF4 | 1420 |
| N420GA | GLF4 | 4120 |
| N420GL | FA20 | 391 |
| **N420GT** | **C650** | **0020** |
| N420HA | HDJT | P001 |
| N420HB | HA4T | RC-20 |
| N420J | FA20 | 369 |
| N420J | WW24 | 193 |
| **N420JC** | **GLF3** | **326** |
| N420JC | HS25 | 25115 |
| N420JD | FA10 | 115 |
| N420JM | GLF2 | 94 |
| N420JM | WW24 | 193 |
| **N420JM** | **WW24** | **363** |
| (N420JP) | FA50 | 168 |
| N420JP | LJ60 | 147 |
| (N420JP) | LJ60 | 368 |
| N420JT | GLF2 | 94 |
| N420KK | F9EX | 84 |
| N420L | CL60 | 1027 |
| N420L | JSTR | 5063 |
| N420LJ | LJ31 | 111 |
| (N420LX) | BE40 | RK-91 |
| N420MP | WW24 | 418 |
| N420P | C550 | 250 |
| N420P | WW24 | 6 |
| N420PC | C500 | 462 |
| **N420PC** | **C500** | **640** |

| | | |
|---|---|---|
| N420PC | FA10 | 186 |
| N420PC | LJ35 | 132 |
| **N420PD** | **F9EX** | **84** |
| **N420QS** | **GLF4** | **1320** |
| N420RC | C500 | 462 |
| N420RC | GLF3 | 354 |
| N420SL | GLF4 | 1025 |
| N420SS | C550 | 469 |
| N420ST | CL61 | 5027 |
| N420SZ | CL61 | 5027 |
| N420SZ | GLF4 | 1025 |
| N420TJ | MU30 | A042SA |
| N420TJ | WW24 | 405 |
| N420TX | CL60 | 1027 |
| N420W | WW24 | 420 |
| N420WR | LJ24 | 130 |
| **N421AL** | **GLEX** | **9051** |
| N421CJ | C550 | 421 |
| (N421CP) | C525 | 0083 |
| N421FJ | F900 | 29 |
| N421FX | LJ45 | 127 |
| N421FX | LJ45 | 145 |
| N421FY | LJ45 | 127 |
| N421GM | GLF3 | 421 |
| N421L | LJ24 | 096 |
| **N421LT** | **C560** | **0311** |
| (N421LX) | BE40 | RK-239 |
| (N421LX) | BE40 | RK-93 |
| **N421MP** | **C52B** | **0328** |
| N421QL | LJ55 | 026 |
| **N421QS** | **GLF4** | **4114** |
| **N421SV** | **LJ35** | **660** |
| N421SZ | CL61 | 5027 |
| N421SZ | GLEX | 9056 |
| **N421SZ** | **GLEX** | **9239** |
| N421SZ | GLF4 | 1025 |
| N421SZ | HS25 | 257146 |
| N421TX | C550 | 250 |
| N421ZC | FA20 | 117 |
| N422AB | C56X | 5285 |
| N422AW | WW24 | 422 |
| N422B | LJ25 | 331 |
| **N422BC** | **C650** | **0024** |
| N422BC | WW24 | 302 |
| N422CC | C500 | 422 |
| **N422CP** | **CL30** | **20061** |
| N422CP | LJ60 | 171 |
| N422CR | LJ60 | 171 |
| N422CW | BE40 | RK-22 |
| N422D | FA20 | 498 |
| **N422DA** | **C500** | **422** |
| N422DV | GLF2 | 17 |
| N422F | FA20 | 421 |
| (N422F) | FA20 | 422 |
| N422FJ | F900 | 31 |
| **N422FL** | **BE40** | **RK-346** |
| N422FX | LJ45 | 135 |
| N422G | LJ25 | 285 |
| N422GA | ASTR | 222 |
| N422GA | GALX | 122 |
| N422GA | GLF4 | 1248 |
| N422GA | GLF4 | 1298 |
| N422GA | GLF4 | 1422 |
| N422GA | GLF4 | 4122 |
| **N422GA** | **GLF4** | **4222** |
| (N422HB) | HA4T | RC-22 |
| N422JR | LJ24 | 092 |
| **N422JT** | **C560** | **0774** |
| N422L | FA20 | 498 |
| (N422LX) | BE40 | RK-103 |
| N422MJ | CS55 | 0010 |
| N422ML | GLF4 | 1367 |
| N422MU | FA20 | 484 |
| **N422QS** | **GLF4** | **1322** |
| **N422TK** | **GLF3** | **395** |
| N422TK | HS25 | 256060 |
| N422TR | HS25 | 256060 |
| N422U | LJ24 | 155 |
| **N422X** | **HS25** | **257074** |
| **N423AK** | **BE40** | **RK-328** |
| **N423CS** | **C52B** | **0121** |
| N423D | C550 | 183 |
| N423DC | LJ45 | 135 |
| N423F | FA20 | 423 |
| **N423FA** | **LJ45** | **134** |
| N423FJ | F900 | 32 |
| N423FX | LJ45 | 134 |
| N423GA | GLF4 | 1009 |
| N423GA | GLF4 | 1044 |
| N423GA | GLF4 | 1113 |
| N423GA | GLF4 | 1197 |
| N423GA | GLF4 | 1249 |
| N423GA | GLF4 | 1299 |
| N423GA | GLF4 | 1423 |
| N423GA | GLF4 | 1523 |
| N423GA | GLF4 | 4123 |
| **N423GA** | **GLF4** | **4223** |
| N423HB | HA4T | RC-23 |
| (N423LX) | BE40 | RK-105 |
| N423RD | C500 | 227 |
| N423RD | LJ25 | 027 |
| N423SA | GLF3 | 429 |
| **N423SJ** | **HS25** | **258135** |
| **N423TT** | **GLF4** | **1085** |
| N424AD | C500 | 266 |
| **N424BT** | **BE40** | **RJ-62** |
| N424CJ | C52A | 0224 |
| **N424CS** | **WW24** | **255** |
| N424CV | C560 | 0424 |
| **N424DA** | **C500** | **029** |
| N424DN | LJ35 | 061 |
| N424F | FA20 | 424 |
| N424FJ | F900 | 33 |
| N424FX | LJ45 | 146 |
| N424GA | ASTR | 224 |
| N424GA | GALX | 127 |
| N424GA | GLF4 | 1004 |
| N424GA | GLF4 | 4124 |
| N424GA | GLF5 | 5024 |
| N424GC | GLF2 | 115 |
| N424HH | C560 | 0517 |
| **N424HH** | **C56X** | **5534** |
| (N424JM) | CL61 | 3064 |
| N424JM | SBRL | 465-36 |
| N424JP | LJ25 | 141 |
| N424JR | LJ25 | 141 |
| N424JR | LJ35 | 092 |
| **N424JR** | **WW24** | **405** |
| N424JX | FA20 | 23 |
| **N424KW** | **LJ60** | **153** |
| N424LB | C650 | 0076 |
| N424LF | LJ40 | 45-2024 |
| (N424LX) | BE40 | RK-108 |
| N424LX | BE40 | RK-245 |
| **N424MP** | **ASTR** | **129** |
| **N424MW** | **LJ60** | **171** |
| N424NJ | LJ24 | 100 |
| **N424PX** | **GLF4** | **4101** |
| **N424QS** | **GLF4** | **1324** |
| N424R | SBRL | 306-3 |
| **N424R** | **SBRL** | **380-15** |
| (N424RD) | C500 | 190 |
| N424RD | LJ24 | 154 |
| N424RD | LJ25 | 016 |
| N424RJ | HS25 | 257010 |
| **N424RS** | **LJ24** | **258** |
| N424TG | C550 | 285 |
| **N424TM** | **CL30** | **20051** |
| **N424TV** | **C525** | **0145** |
| N424W | WW24 | 424 |
| **N424XT** | **FA20** | **316** |
| N425A | GLF2 | 39 |
| **N425AS** | **LJ35** | **281** |
| **N425BJ** | **BE40** | **RJ-25** |
| **N425CS** | **C52B** | **0132** |
| **N425CT** | **BE40** | **RK-523** |
| N425CW | BE40 | RK-345 |
| N425DC | HS25 | 25079 |
| N425DN | LJ35 | 065 |
| N425EJ | LJ24 | 009 |
| N425F | FA20 | 425 |
| N425FD | HS25 | 25079 |
| N425FJ | F900 | 34 |
| N425FX | LJ45 | 147 |
| **N425G** | **LJ45** | **307** |
| N425GA | GLF4 | 1198 |
| N425GA | GLF4 | 1250 |
| N425GA | GLF4 | 1425 |
| N425GA | GLF4 | 1525 |
| N425GA | GLF4 | 4125 |
| **N425GA** | **GLF4** | **4215** |
| N425JA | FA20 | 51 |
| N425JF | FA20 | 51 |
| **N425JF** | **FA20** | **64** |
| (N425JF) | HS25 | 25284 |
| N425JF | WW24 | 210 |
| N425JL | LJ25 | 127 |
| **N425JR** | **FA10** | **162** |
| N425JX | LJ25 | 059 |
| N425K | HS25 | 25114 |
| **N425KG** | **HS25** | **257001** |
| **N425LW** | **LJ45** | **147** |
| (N425LX) | BE40 | RK-145 |
| **N425M** | **LJ31** | **055** |
| N425M | LJ35 | 281 |
| (N425MK) | JSTR | 5123/14 |
| N425NA | SBRL | 282-95 |
| N425NJ | LJ24 | 105 |
| **N425QS** | **GLF4** | **4010** |
| N425RA | LJ25 | 351 |
| N425RD | LJ25 | 024 |
| N425RH | LJ25 | 351 |
| **N425RJ** | **FA20** | **484** |
| N425RJ | HS25 | 257010 |
| N425RJ | WW24 | 218 |
| **N425SA** | **LJ35** | **425** |
| N425SC | LJ24 | 097 |
| **N425SD** | **HS25** | **257018** |
| N425SP | GLF3 | 425 |
| **N425SU** | **CL61** | **3064** |
| **N425SV** | **GLF3** | **360** |
| N425TS | ASTR | 004 |
| N425WA | WW24 | 425 |
| **N425WN** | **CL61** | **3052** |
| N425WN | HS25 | 257159 |
| (N426CC) | C500 | 426 |
| (N426CC) | FA20 | 205 |
| **N426CF** | **CL64** | **5338** |
| **N426CH** | **C56X** | **5222** |
| N426CJ | C52A | 0426 |
| **N426CM** | **C750** | **0117** |
| N426DA | MU30 | A062SA |
| **N426EA** | **BE40** | **RK-275** |
| **N426ED** | **C525** | **0426** |
| N426EJ | LJ24 | 014 |
| N426EM | LJ55 | 040 |
| N426F | FA20 | 428 |
| N426FJ | F900 | 36 |
| N426FX | LJ45 | 162 |
| N426GA | GLF4 | 1010 |
| N426GA | GLF4 | 1054 |
| N426GA | GLF4 | 1126 |
| N426GA | GLF4 | 1215 |
| N426GA | GLF4 | 1426 |
| N426GA | GLF4 | 4126 |
| N426JK | C550 | 550-0856 |
| N426JK | LJ40 | 45-2092 |
| N426JN | LJ60 | 142 |
| N426LF | C510 | 0170 |
| **N426LW** | **LJ45** | **162** |
| (N426LX) | BE40 | RK-146 |
| N426MD | BE40 | RJ-26 |
| **N426MJ** | **HS25** | **258759** |
| N426NA | LJ24 | 292 |
| **N426PE** | **CL61** | **5046** |
| N426PF | CL61 | 5046 |
| **N426PF** | **CL64** | **5547** |
| N426PS | LJ24 | 148 |
| **N426QS** | **GLF4** | **1426** |
| **N426RJ** | **WW24** | **218** |
| (N426SP) | C550 | 425 |
| **N426ST** | **FA20** | **426** |
| **N426TA** | **LJ24** | **181** |
| (N426TM) | MU30 | A026SA |
| N426WW | WW24 | 426 |
| N426XP | HS25 | 258426 |
| N427AC | GLF2 | 95/39 |
| N427BX | LJ45 | 163 |
| N427CD | C560 | 0633 |
| N427CJ | FA10 | 67 |
| **N427CS** | **C52B** | **0152** |
| (N427CW) | BE40 | RJ-27 |
| N427CW | BE40 | RK-27 |
| N427DA | HS25 | 25220 |
| **N427DB** | **PRM1** | **RB-223** |
| **N427DJ?** | **BE40** | **RK-276** |
| N427DM | C500 | 179 |
| N427EJ | LJ24 | 021 |
| N427F | FA20 | 426 |
| N427FJ | F900 | 37 |
| **N427FL** | **BE40** | **RK-368** |
| N427FX | LJ45 | 163 |
| N427GA | GLF4 | 1016 |
| N427GA | GLF4 | 1060 |
| N427GA | GLF4 | 1127 |
| N427GA | GLF4 | 1148 |
| N427GA | GLF4 | 1268 |
| N427GA | GLF4 | 1316 |
| N427GA | GLF4 | 1427 |
| N427GA | GLF4 | 4127 |
| **N427GA** | **GLF4** | **4217** |
| **N427GW** | **F2TH** | **20** |
| N427JX | LJ24 | 257 |
| N427LJ | LJ24 | 100 |
| (N427LX) | BE40 | RK-149 |
| N427MD | HS25 | 257095 |
| N427NJ | LJ24 | 021 |
| N427RD | LJ25 | 082 |
| **N427SA** | **GLF4** | **1314** |
| **N427SS** | **C500** | **681** |
| N427TL | LJ55 | 006 |
| N427WW | WW24 | 427 |
| **N427X** | **EA50** | **000253** |
| N428AS | GLF4 | 1487 |
| N428AS | HS25 | 257026 |
| N428AZ | GLF4 | 1487 |
| N428BB | LJ31 | 209 |
| **N428BR** | **C52B** | **0205** |
| **N428CC** | **FA50** | **225** |
| (N428CH) | LJ25 | 350 |
| N428CL | CL61 | 5108 |
| **N428CS** | **C52B** | **0165** |
| N428DA | JSTR | 5048 |
| N428EJ | LJ24 | 022 |
| N428F | FA20 | 430 |
| N428FJ | F900 | 39 |
| N428FS | HS25 | 257026 |
| **N428FX** | **LJ45** | **164** |
| N428GA | GLF4 | 1028 |
| N428GA | GLF4 | 1114 |
| N428GA | GLF4 | 1199 |
| N428HR | BE40 | RK-244 |
| **N428JD** | **BE40** | **RJ-13** |
| N428JF | WW24 | 210 |
| N428JM | WW24 | 193 |
| N428JX | LJ25 | 103 |
| (N428LX) | BE40 | RK-161 |
| **N428LX** | **BE40** | **RK-264** |
| **N428M** | **GLF4** | **1382** |
| N428PC | C525 | 0314 |
| (N428PC) | C525 | 0324 |
| **N428QS** | **GLF4** | **1328** |
| N428RJ | C500 | 082 |
| **N428SJ** | **C560** | **0584** |
| N428TT | GLF4 | 4004 |
| N428W | WW24 | 428 |
| N428WE | BE40 | RK-72 |
| N428WT | GLF5 | 599 |
| N429AC | HS25 | 25115 |
| N429AL | GLF4 | 1061 |
| (N429BA) | HS25 | 256058 |
| **N429CC** | **EA50** | **000060** |
| **N429CS** | **C52B** | **0177** |
| **N429DA** | **HS25** | **25090** |
| N429DD | GLF3 | 354 |
| **N429DD** | **GLF4** | **1293** |
| N429EJ | LJ24 | 023 |
| N429F | FA20 | 431 |
| **N429FC** | **LJ55** | **091** |
| N429FJ | F900 | 40 |
| **N429FX** | **LJ45** | **165** |
| N429GA | GLF4 | 1029 |
| N429GA | GLF4 | 1128 |
| N429GA | GLF4 | 1251 |
| N429GA | GLF4 | 1319 |
| N429GA | GLF4 | 1429 |
| N429GA | GLF4 | 4129 |
| N429JX | GLF2 | 122 |
| (N429LX) | BE40 | RK-168 |
| **N429LX** | **BE40** | **RK-265** |
| N429PK | C525 | 0429 |
| N429RC | C500 | 078 |
| **N429SA** | **F2EX** | **178** |
| N429SA | GLF3 | 429 |
| N429SA | GLF4 | 1314 |
| **N429SJ** | **F2TH** | **66** |
| (N429TJ) | LJ25 | 042 |
| (N429W) | WW24 | 429 |
| **N429WG** | **CL61** | **5010** |
| N430A | WW24 | 430 |
| **N430BB** | **HS25** | **258178** |
| N430BC | GLF2 | 27 |

N430BJ WW24 430
N430C WW24 49
**N430CS C52B 0185**
N430CW BE40 RK-30
N430DC WW24 87
N430DP GLF2 167
N430EJ LJ24 027
N430F FA20 432
N430FJ F900 41
**N430FX LJ45 166**
N430GA GLF4 1030
N430GA GLF4 1115
N430GA GLF4 1149
N430GA GLF4 1200
**N430GR C525 0430**
**N430GW PRM1 RB-208**
N430HM LJ55 043
N430J LJ24 091
N430JA LJ24 091
**N430JH C525 0530**
N430JW LJ24 285
N430LJ LJ24 103
N430LR HS25 259030
(N430LX) BE40 RK-178
N430MB JSTR 5153/61
N430MB SBRL 282-113
**N430MP SBRL 282-113**
N430PC WW24 87
**N430PT WW24 430**
**N430QS GLF4 4021**
N430R GLF2 6
N430RG GLF2 235
**N430SA C650 7041**
N430SA GLF2 92
**N430TB E50P 50000052**
N430W WW24 430
N431AM WW24 431
N431AS LJ35 431
N431BC LJ31 005
N431CA LJ24 030
N431CB C550 431
N431CB C650 0084
**N431CB CL61 5164**
N431CC C500 431
(N431CQ) C650 0084
**N431CS C52B 0228**
N431CW BE40 RK-31
N431CW LJ35 431
**N431DA LJ31 163**
(N431DA) SBRL 282-111
N431DS C550 324
N431EJ LJ24 030
N431FJ F900 42
N431FL BE40 RK-230
**N431FX LJ45 177**
(N431GA) GLF4 1039
N431GA GLF4 1116
N431GA GLF4 1201
(N431GH) F2EX 72
(N431JC) C550 430
**N431JT GLF3 417**
N431JV C560 0431
**N431LC C500 177**
(N431LX) BE40 RK-271
N431M LJ35 132
**N431MC C52A 0091**
**N431MS CS55 0127**
N431NA SBRL 265-16
N431NA SBRL 285-2
**N431WA WW24 431**
N431WM CS55 0133
N431YD C525 0431
**N432AC C750 0231**
N432AC HS25 258150
**N432AQ HS25 258150**
**N432AS GLF4 4142**
(N432AS) LJ25 234
N432CC C550 438
**N432CC SBRL 465-6**
N432CJ C52A 0043
**N432CS C52B 0244**
N432CW BE40 RK-32
N432DG C500 403
N432EJ LJ24 028A
N432EZ FA10 130
N432F FA20 433
N432FJ F900 44
**N432FJ F9EX 234**
**N432FX LJ45 197**
N432GA GLF4 1040
N432GA GLF4 1125
N432GA GLF4 1202
N432GA GLF4 1300
N432GA GLF5 5132
N432HS WW24 432
N432JW LJ36 043
**N432LW C52B 0003**
(N432LX) BE40 RK-183
**N432MA C52A 0300**
N432MC CL64 5532
**N432NM C550 083**
N432QS GLF4 1032
**N432RJ C550 550-0967**
N432SL LJ25 241
N432XP HS25 258432
N433CJ C52A 0433
**N433CS C52B 0257**
N433CV C560 0430
**N433DD LJ35 161**
N433EJ LJ24 040
N433F FA20 435
N433FJ F900 45
N433FS CL64 5433
**N433FX LJ45 192**
N433GA GALX 133
N433GA GLF4 1041
N433GA GLF4 1103
N433GA GLF4 1150
N433GA GLF4 1252
N433GA GLF4 1301
N433GA GLF4 1433
N433GA GLF4 4133
**N433GM WW24 433**
N433J LJ24 038
N433J LJ24 230
N433JA LJ24 230
N433JB LJ24 038
(N433JW) LJ35 041
N433LF C650 0027
N433LJ LJ24 104
(N433LX) BE40 RK-186
(N433LX) BE40 RK-273
N433MM C500 575
N433WR WW24 433
N433WW WW24 433
N434AN JSTR 5050/34
N434CC C550 434
N434CS C52B 0268
N434CS C52B 0332
N434EJ LJ24 046
N434F FA20 436
N434FJ F900 46
N434FX LJ45 193
**N434FX LJ45 212**
N434GA GALX 134
N434GA GLF4 1031
N434GA GLF4 1203
N434GA GLF4 1269
N434GA GLF4 1302
N434GA GLF4 1434
N434GA GLF4 1534
N434GA GLF4 4134
N434H C650 0123
**N434HB HS25 HB-34**
N434JW GLF2 2
(N434LX) BE40 RK-189
**N434LX BE40 RK-274**
N434QS GLF4 1334
**N434SB C550 425**
N434UM C500 190
N435AS LJ24 345
N435CC C500 435
**N435CT BE40 RK-531**
N435CW BE40 RK-35
(N435EC) LJ35 018
N435F FA20 437
(N435FA) LJ45 209
N435FJ F900 48
N435FX LJ45 209
**N435FX LJ45 271**
N435GA GALX 135
N435GA GLF4 1035
N435GA GLF4 1135
N435GA GLF4 1204
N435GA GLF4 1253
N435GA GLF4 1303
N435GA GLF4 1435
N435GA GLF4 1535
N435GA GLF5 5235
N435GM GLF2 137
**N435HC GLF4 1450**
**N435HH LJ45 335**
**N435JF F2TH 47**
N435JL LJ35 018
N435JW LJ35 331
N435K PRM1 RB-35
(N435LX) BE40 RK-195
N435LX BE40 RK-276
N435M LJ35 086
**N435MS LJ35 054**
N435N LJ35 435
**N435NF EA50 000189**
**N435QS GLF4 4068**
N435T F2TH 9
**N435T F9EX 63**
N435T FA20 357
N435T HS25 25083
N435TM F2TH 9
N435TP FA20 357
N435U GLF3 435
N435UJ LJ35 025
**N435UM C550 423**
(N435W) WW24 435
N436BL LJ35 436
N436CC C500 436
N436CC SBRL 306-36
**N436CS C52B 0274**
N436DM LJ35 389
N436FJ F900 50
**N436FL BE40 RK-279**
N436FX LJ45 225
N436FX LJ45 308
**N436FX LJ45 309**
N436GA GALX 136
N436GA GLF3 436
N436GA GLF4 1056
N436GA GLF4 1130
N436GA GLF4 1254
N436GA GLF4 1304
N436GA GLF4 1436
N436GA GLF4 4136
**N436JW GLF2 73/9**
N436LJ LJ24 102
(N436LX) BE40 RK-198
N436LX BE40 RK-279
N436MP FA20 436
**N436QS GLF4 1436**
N436RB FA20 436
N436WW WW24 436
N437CC C550 437
N437CF C550 436
N437CS C52B 0282
N437CW BE40 RK-237
N437FJ F900 51
N437FT CL64 5437
N437FX LJ45 227
**N437FX LJ45 315**
N437GA GLF3 396
N437GA GLF4 1057
N437GA GLF4 1131
N437GA GLF4 1206
N437GA GLF4 1255
N437GA GLF4 1320
**N437GA GLF4 1437**
N437H GLF2 258
N437JD C52A 0325
N437JD HS25 258757
**N437JD HS25 HA-0117**
**N437JR HS25 258757**
N437LJ LJ24 081
(N437LX) BE40 RK-201
**N437MC CL64 5537**
**N437SJ WW24 437**
N437T HS25 25083
**N437WR HS25 258963**
N437WW WW24 437
N438 WW24 118
N438AM WW24 438
**N438BC BE40 RK-438**
N438CC C500 438
N438CS C52B 0321
N438DA BE40 RJ-38
N438DM LJ25 250
N438FJ F900 53
(N438FS) WW24 438
N438FX LJ45 317
**N438FX LJ45 333**
N438GA GLF4 1038
N438GA GLF4 1256
**N438HB HA4T RC-38**
N438LJ LJ24 113
**N438LX BE40 RK-202**
**N438MC C560 0438**
N438PM HS25 257098
N438PM HS25 258425
**N438PM HS25 258636**
N438SP C550 550-0882
**N438SP C550 550-1026**
N438SP C550 576
N438TA C52A 0438
(N438W) WW24 438
**N438WR HS25 258983**
N439CL CL61 5109
N439CS C52B 0326
N439CW BE40 RK-339
N439FJ F900 55
**N439FX LJ45 341**
N439GA GLF4 1064
N439GA GLF4 1118
N439GA GLF4 1205
N439GA GLF4 1305
N439GA GLF4 1439
N439GA GLF4 4039
N439GA GLF4 4139
N439H C650 0005
**N439HB HA4T RC-39**
(N439LX) BE40 RK-209
**N439LX BE40 RK-284**
N439ME LJ35 439
(N439PW) C525 0513
**N439WW WW24 439**
N440AS F2TH 102
N440AS GLF4 4075
**N440BC HS25 25218**
**N440CE C550 550-0937**
N440CJ C525 0440
**N440CJ C52A 0441**
N440CP GLF4 1118
**N440CT BE40 RK-534**
**N440CW BE40 RK-40**
N440DC HS25 25079
N440DM LJ25 348
**N440DM LJ55 005**
N440DR GLF2 69
**N440DS BE40 RK-8**
N440EZ C500 195
N440F LJ25 262
N440FJ F900 56
**N440FX LJ45 346**
N440GA GLF4 1002
N440GA GLF4 1216
N440GA GLF4 4040
**N440HB HA4T RC-13**
N440HM LJ35 294
N440JB LJ35 078
**N440KM CL61 5053**
**N440KT LJ24 249**
(N440LX) BE40 RK-222
**N440LX BE40 RK-289**
**N440MB HA4T RC-33**
**N440MC LJ35 495**
(N440MP) BE40 RJ-16
**N440PC C650 0061**
(N440PJ) C550 396
**N440QS GLF4 4025**
**N440RC BE40 RK-269**
**N440RD HS25 25270**
N440RM JSTR 5016
N440SA C650 7088
**N440SC LJ31 240**
**N440TC GLF4 1115**
N440TX C550 411
**N440WF BE40 RK-440**
N440WW WW24 440
N441A GLF3 342
N441A JSTR 5123/14
**N441BC ASTR 033**
**N441BP C56X 5612**
N441CG LJ55 014
N441CL CL64 5441
N441CW LJ35 410
N441DM FA10 173

| | | |
|---|---|---|
| (N441EE) | BE40 | RJ-41 |
| N441FA | FA20 | 284 |
| N441FJ | F900 | 57 |
| **N441FX** | **LJ45** | **357** |
| N441GA | GLF4 | 1001 |
| N441GA | GLF4 | 1207 |
| N441GA | GLF4 | 1306 |
| N441JT | C500 | 601 |
| (N441LX) | BE40 | RK-230 |
| **N441LX** | **BE40** | **RK-292** |
| N441PC | LJ35 | 441 |
| **N441PC** | **LJ35** | **668** |
| N441PG | LJ35 | 441 |
| **N441QS** | **GLF4** | **1341** |
| N441T | C550 | 329 |
| N441TC | C500 | 140 |
| N442A | GLF2 | 255/18 |
| N442A | SBRL | 282-39 |
| N442A | SBRL | 306-21 |
| N442AM | FA50 | 42 |
| N442CW | BE40 | RK-42 |
| N442DM | LJ35 | 405 |
| **N442EA** | **MU30** | **A058SA** |
| N442F | FA20 | 438 |
| N442FJ | F900 | 59 |
| **N442FL** | **BE40** | **RK-334** |
| **N442FX** | **LJ45** | **364** |
| N442GA | ASTR | 242 |
| N442GA | GLF4 | 1065 |
| N442GA | GLF4 | 1132 |
| N442GA | GLF4 | 1270 |
| N442GA | GLF4 | 1442 |
| N442GA | GLF4 | 4042 |
| **N442GJ** | **BE40** | **RK-442** |
| (N442HC) | LJ35 | 233 |
| **N442HM** | **GLF4** | **4034** |
| **N442JB** | **C500** | **117** |
| N442JC | BE40 | RJ-42 |
| N442JC | MU30 | A008SA |
| N442JT | LJ35 | 021 |
| **N442KM** | **CS55** | **0060** |
| N442LF | GLEX | 9142 |
| N442LF | LJ45 | 019 |
| N442LU | C56X | 5609 |
| **N442LV** | **C510** | **0153** |
| N442LV | C550 | 550-1028 |
| N442LW | C550 | 550-1028 |
| N442LW | C56X | 5609 |
| **N442LW** | **C680** | **0168** |
| (N442LX) | BE40 | RK-234 |
| **N442MA** | **HS25** | **258378** |
| N442ME | C550 | 442 |
| N442MR | C550 | 442 |
| N442NE | LJ35 | 442 |
| **N442NR** | **C550** | **550-1078** |
| N442QG | GLF2 | 133 |
| **N442RM** | **SBRL** | **306-73** |
| (N442SC) | LJ36 | 040 |
| N442SR | GLF4 | 4002 |
| N442SW | C550 | 550-0840 |
| N442SW | C550 | 550-0862 |
| N442WJ | C650 | 7025 |
| N442WJ | C750 | 0099 |
| **N442WP** | **C750** | **0233** |
| N442WP | SBRL | 282-108 |
| N442WT | C650 | 7025 |
| N442WT | C750 | 0099 |
| N442WT | C750 | 0233 |
| **N442WT** | **C750** | **0303** |
| N442WT | SBRL | 282-108 |
| N442WT | SBRL | 465-45 |
| N442WT | WW24 | 114 |
| N442WT | WW24 | 77 |
| N442XP | HS25 | 258442 |
| N443A | WW24 | 354 |
| N443BP | PRM1 | RB-243 |
| **N443C** | **BE40** | **RK-42** |
| N443CJ | C525 | 0443 |
| N443F | FA20 | 439 |
| N443FJ | F900 | 60 |
| N443FX | LJ45 | 371 |
| N443GA | ASTR | 243 |
| N443GA | GLF4 | 1066 |
| N443GA | GLF4 | 1133 |
| N443GA | GLF4 | 1208 |
| N443GA | GLF4 | 1307 |
| N443GA | GLF4 | 1443 |
| N443GA | GLF4 | 4043 |
| **N443HC** | **C510** | **0012** |
| N443LJ | LJ24 | 114 |
| **N443LX** | **BE40** | **RK-237** |
| **N443M** | **GLF5** | **5199** |
| N443M | HS25 | 258519 |
| **N443PW** | **C52B** | **0103** |
| **N443RK** | **LJ35** | **023** |
| **N444A** | **C680** | **0218** |
| N444AG | C500 | 434 |
| N444AG | LJ24 | 208 |
| N444AQ | LJ24 | 208 |
| N444BF | FA20 | 189 |
| N444BF | LJ35 | 391 |
| N444BL | C550 | 487 |
| N444CC | C550 | 394 |
| N444CM | LJ35 | 282 |
| N444CR | FA10 | 45 |
| (N444CW) | C500 | 444 |
| **N444CW** | **C650** | **0064** |
| N444CX | C750 | 0125 |
| **N444EA** | **C550** | **550-1079** |
| (N444EJ) | EA50 | 000272 |
| **N444EP** | **WW24** | **436** |
| **N444ET** | **CL60** | **1062** |
| N444ET | MS76 | 101 |
| **N444EX** | **C650** | **7056** |
| N444FJ | C550 | 070 |
| N444FJ | FA20 | 284 |
| **N444FX** | **LJ45** | **378** |
| **N444G** | **C550** | **232** |
| N444GA | GLF3 | 301 |
| N444GA | GLF4 | 1321 |
| N444GA | GLF4 | 4144 |
| N444GB | C550 | 216 |
| **N444GG** | **C560** | **0262** |
| (N444GV) | GLF4 | 1444 |
| (N444H) | C525 | 0106 |
| N444HC | LJ24 | 199 |
| **N444HC** | **LJ31** | **064** |
| N444HC | LJ35 | 199 |
| (N444HE) | LJ24 | 246 |
| N444HH | HS25 | 25191 |
| N444J | C500 | 179 |
| N444JH | JSTR | 5036/42 |
| N444JJ | C550 | 160 |
| N444KE | C650 | 7029 |
| N444KM | GLF3 | 378 |
| N444KV | C500 | 223 |
| N444KW | LJ24 | 147 |
| (N444L) | C525 | 0304 |
| N444LP | C500 | 223 |
| N444LT | GLF4 | 1114 |
| N444MA | SBRL | 306-102 |
| **N444MG** | **HS25** | **258415** |
| N444MJ | LJ35 | 444 |
| **N444MK** | **LJ25** | **252** |
| (N444ML) | GLF2 | 173 |
| N444MM | C550 | 317 |
| N444MM | WW24 | 210 |
| N444MV | C500 | 401 |
| N444MW | C500 | 401 |
| **N444MW** | **LJ45** | **131** |
| N444MW | WW24 | 372 |
| N444PB | LJ25 | 227 |
| N444PD | HS25 | 256001 |
| **N444PE** | **FA50** | **143** |
| N444PE | HS25 | 256001 |
| N444QG | GLF2 | 133 |
| **N444QG** | **GLF4** | **1453** |
| "N444RF" | C525 | 0001 |
| **N444RF** | **C560** | **0559** |
| N444RH | C525 | 0001 |
| N444RH | C52A | 0099 |
| **N444RL** | **EA50** | **000040** |
| N444RP | C500 | 250 |
| N444SC | FA20 | 324 |
| N444SC | LJ24 | 246 |
| (N444SC) | LJ36 | 040 |
| (N444SL) | MU30 | A041SA |
| N444SS | PRM1 | RB-16 |
| **N444TG** | **LJ25** | **327** |
| N444TG | LJ35 | 469 |
| N444TJ | GLF4 | 1010 |
| N444TJ | WW24 | 146 |
| N444TW | LJ24 | 348 |
| N444WA | CL60 | 1005 |
| N444WB | BE40 | RJ-42 |
| **N444WB** | **LJ35** | **105** |
| N444WB | LJ35 | 318 |
| N444WC | LJ24 | 047 |
| (N444WJ) | C550 | 088 |
| N444WJ | FA10 | 64 |
| N444WL | WW24 | 48 |
| N444WS | LJ25 | 038 |
| **N444WW** | **LJ25** | **283** |
| N445 | WW24 | 37 |
| N445A | WW24 | 362 |
| N445AC | CL61 | 3051 |
| **N445AK** | **ASTR** | **155** |
| N445AX | LJ45 | 206 |
| N445BL | WW24 | 382 |
| N445CC | BE40 | RK-45 |
| N445CC | C500 | 445 |
| N445CJ | C525 | 0445 |
| **N445CT** | **BE40** | **RK-535** |
| N445CW | BE40 | RK-45 |
| N445E | BE40 | RK-45 |
| N445F | FA20 | 441 |
| N445FJ | F900 | 63 |
| **N445FL** | **BE40** | **RK-345** |
| (N445FX) | LJ45 | 397 |
| N445GA | GLF4 | 1012 |
| N445GA | GLF4 | 1077 |
| N445GA | GLF4 | 1134 |
| N445GA | GLF4 | 1209 |
| N445GA | GLF4 | 1322 |
| N445GA | GLF4 | 1445 |
| N445GA | GLF4 | 4045 |
| (N445LX) | BE40 | RK-244 |
| **N445LX** | **BE40** | **RK-298** |
| **N445N** | **LJ45** | **202** |
| **N445PK** | **BE40** | **RK-45** |
| N445QS | GLF4 | 1445 |
| **N445QS** | **GLF4** | **4037** |
| **N445RM** | **LJ45** | **206** |
| N445SB | LJ45 | 027 |
| **N445SE** | **LJ45** | **334** |
| **N445TG** | **LJ45** | **332** |
| N446 | LJ31 | 010 |
| N446A | WW24 | 367 |
| **N446CJ** | **C52A** | **0446** |
| N446CW | BE40 | RK-346 |
| N446D | FA20 | 446 |
| N446F | FA20 | 442 |
| N446FJ | F900 | 64 |
| N446GA | GLF3 | 488 |
| N446GA | GLF4 | 1013 |
| N446GA | GLF4 | 1067 |
| N446GA | GLF4 | 1152 |
| N446GA | GLF4 | 1219 |
| N446GA | GLF4 | 1308 |
| N446GA | GLF4 | 1446 |
| N446GA | GLF4 | 4046 |
| **N446HB** | **HA4T** | **RC-46** |
| (N446LX) | BE40 | RK-245 |
| N446LX | BE40 | RK-299 |
| **N446M** | **BE40** | **RK-199** |
| **N446RT** | **C680** | **0017** |
| N446U | GLF3 | 446 |
| N446V | C500 | 552 |
| N447CC | BE40 | RJ-38 |
| N447CJ | C52A | 0447 |
| (N447CJ) | C550 | 447 |
| N447CW | BE40 | RK-347 |
| N447F | FA20 | 443 |
| N447FA | LJ60 | 220 |
| N447FJ | F900 | 65 |
| (N447FM) | C550 | 007 |
| N447GA | GLF4 | 1014 |
| N447GA | GLF4 | 1080 |
| N447GA | GLF4 | 1211 |
| N447GA | GLF4 | 1309 |
| N447GA | GLF4 | 1447 |
| N447GA | GLF4 | 4047 |
| N447GA | GLF4 | 4147 |
| **N447HB** | **HA4T** | **RC-47** |
| N447LJ | LJ24 | 112 |
| **N447LX** | **BE40** | **RK-248** |
| N447TF | PRM1 | RB-68 |
| **N448AS** | **CL30** | **20027** |
| **N448CC** | **HS25** | **259019** |
| N448CW | BE40 | RK-348 |
| N448CW | BE40 | RK-368 |
| N448DC | HS25 | 25078 |
| N448DC | HS25 | 25079 |
| N448EA | C525 | 0448 |
| N448EC | C500 | 191 |
| N448FJ | F900 | 67 |
| N448GA | GLF4 | 1048 |
| (N448GA) | GLF4 | 1084 |
| N448GA | GLF4 | 1153 |
| N448GA | GLF4 | 1210 |
| N448GA | GLF4 | 1257 |
| N448GA | GLF4 | 1310 |
| N448GA | GLF4 | 1448 |
| N448GA | GLF4 | 4048 |
| N448GA | GLF4 | 4148 |
| N448GC | LJ24 | 057 |
| N448GC | LJ35 | 472 |
| N448GG | LJ24 | 057 |
| N448GL | LJ60 | 206 |
| N448GR | ASTR | 070 |
| N448H | C560 | 0613 |
| **N448H** | **HS25** | **258907** |
| **N448HB** | **HA4T** | **RC-48** |
| **N448HC** | **EA50** | **000161** |
| N448HM | LJ60 | 007 |
| N448JC | C525 | 0448 |
| **N448JM** | **HS25** | **258404** |
| **N448LX** | **BE40** | **RK-305** |
| **N448PC** | **GLF2** | **226** |
| (N448QS) | GLF4 | 1408 |
| **N448QS** | **GLF4** | **4100** |
| **N448RL** | **C550** | **550-0990** |
| **N448TB** | **FA20** | **439** |
| **N448W** | **SBRL** | **380-63** |
| N448WC | LJ35 | 472 |
| N448WG | LJ35 | 472 |
| N448WT | SBRL | 465-45 |
| N448WT | WW24 | 114 |
| N449A | FA10 | 49 |
| N449CW | BE40 | RK-349 |
| **N449DT** | **C500** | **369** |
| N449EB | HS25 | 257012 |
| N449F | FA20 | 445 |
| N449FJ | F900 | 68 |
| N449GA | GLF4 | 1085 |
| N449GA | GLF4 | 1220 |
| N449GA | GLF4 | 1311 |
| N449GA | GLF4 | 1449 |
| N449GA | GLF4 | 4049 |
| N449GA | GLF4 | 4149 |
| (N449JS) | LJ24 | 352 |
| N449LJ | LJ24 | 115 |
| **N449LX** | **BE40** | **RK-257** |
| N449MC | CL61 | 5022 |
| N449ML | CL61 | 5022 |
| N449ML | GLEX | 9055 |
| N449QS | LJ35 | 449 |
| (N449SA) | C650 | 7041 |
| N449SA | C650 | 7088 |
| **N449SA** | **F2EX** | **171** |
| **N449TM** | **BE40** | **RK-573** |
| N450 | LJ25 | 127 |
| **N450AB** | **GLF4** | **4043** |
| N450AF | FA50 | 36 |
| **N450AJ** | **CL60** | **1075** |
| **N450AK** | **FA50** | **100** |
| N450AR | GLF4 | 1069 |
| N450AR | GLF5 | 520 |
| (N450AT) | BE40 | RK-185 |
| **N450BC** | **LJ45** | **075** |
| **N450BD** | **GLF3** | **412** |
| N450BE | GLF5 | 554 |
| **N450BF** | **GLF4** | **1015** |
| N450BK | LJ45 | 104 |
| N450BM | ASTR | 011 |
| **N450BV** | **C52B** | **0167** |
| (N450CB) | BE40 | RK-330 |
| **N450CB** | **GLF3** | **324** |
| N450CC | C550 | 281 |
| (N450CE) | SBRL | 306-22 |
| **N450CL** | **FA50** | **76** |
| **N450CP** | **FA20** | **289** |
| (N450CT) | FA10 | 157 |
| **N450CW** | **BE40** | **RK-50** |
| N450DA | HS25 | 256041 |
| N450DK | CL64 | 5450 |
| N450DR | FA50 | 113 |
| (N450DS) | LJ45 | 142 |
| N450EJ | GLF4 | 4088 |
| N450FJ | F900 | 70 |
| N450GA | GLF4 | 4004 |
| (N450GA) | GLF4 | 4020 |

| Reg | Type | C/n |
|---|---|---|
| N450GA | GLF4 | 4039 |
| N450GA | GLF4 | 4091 |
| N450GA | GLF4 | 4144 |
| **N450GA** | **GLF4** | **4189** |
| N450GD | GLF4 | 4065 |
| N450GD | GLF4 | 4117 |
| **N450GD** | **GLF4** | **4163** |
| N450GM | C550 | 150 |
| N450GM | C550 | 617 |
| (N450GQ) | GLF4 | 4091 |
| **N450JC** | **LJ45** | **070** |
| N450JD | HS25 | 25148 |
| N450JD | WW24 | 9 |
| **N450JE** | **GLF4** | **1233** |
| **N450JG** | **LJ45** | **096** |
| (N450JK) | GLF4 | 4031 |
| N450K | FA50 | 186 |
| **N450KD** | **C550** | **410** |
| N450KK | LJ35 | 450 |
| N450KP | FA50 | 82 |
| **N450KR** | **GLF4** | **4044** |
| **N450LC** | **GLF4** | **4127** |
| **N450LV** | **GLF4** | **4061** |
| (N450LX) | BE40 | RK-260 |
| N450MA | FA20 | 158/449 |
| N450MC | LJ35 | 368 |
| **N450MH** | **GLF2** | **225** |
| **N450MM** | **C560** | **0119** |
| **N450MQ** | **C560** | **0657** |
| N450NS | GLF4 | 4079 |
| N450PC | MU30 | A024SA |
| (N450PG) | GLF4 | 4056 |
| **N450PG** | **GLF4** | **4072** |
| N450PM | ASTR | 011 |
| **N450PU** | **GLF4** | **4095** |
| **N450QS** | **GLF4** | **4046** |
| N450RA | C560 | 0377 |
| N450RA | WW24 | 13 |
| **N450RG** | **GLF4** | **4038** |
| N450RS | C650 | 0061 |
| N450SC | LJ25 | 127 |
| N450T | C750 | 0054 |
| **N450T** | **GLF4** | **4105** |
| N450TB | HS25 | 256026 |
| **N450TJ** | **LJ45** | **012** |
| N450TJ | MU30 | A005SA |
| N450TR | LJ45 | 093 |
| **N450WB** | **GLF4** | **4110** |
| N450X | FA50 | 54 |
| **N450XX** | **GLF4** | **4062** |
| **N450Z** | **GLF4** | **4012** |
| **N451AJ** | **C52A** | **0110** |
| **N451BH** | **GLF4** | **4157** |
| **N451BW** | **LJ45** | **261** |
| (N451C) | GLF4 | 1279 |
| **N451C** | **GLF4** | **4159** |
| N451CF | LJ45 | 109 |
| N451CJ | C500 | 451 |
| **N451CL** | **FA50** | **223** |
| N451CL | LJ45 | 149 |
| **N451CM** | **GLF4** | **4024** |
| **N451CS** | **GLEX** | **9134** |
| N451CS | GLF2 | 70/1 |
| N451CS | GLF5 | 570 |
| N451DA | C550 | 108 |
| **N451DC** | **GLF4** | **4041** |
| N451DJ | LJ45 | 080 |
| **N451DP** | **FA20** | **249** |
| (N451DZ) | LJ45 | 080 |
| N451FJ | F900 | 71 |
| **N451FP** | **C52A** | **0451** |
| **N451GA** | **GLF4** | **1221** |
| N451GL | LJ45 | 149 |
| **N451GP** | **C52B** | **0080** |
| N451GS | GLF2 | 70/1 |
| **N451HC** | **LJ45** | **267** |
| **N451JC** | **GLF4** | **4152** |
| N451JC | LJ45 | 218 |
| (N451K) | LJ45 | 405 |
| (N451LX) | BE40 | RK-264 |
| **N451LX** | **BE40** | **RK-310** |
| N451MM | PRM1 | RB-137 |
| **N451N** | **LJ45** | **230** |
| **N451NS** | **GLF4** | **4082** |
| N451QS | GLF4 | 1351 |
| N451QS | GLF4 | 4141 |
| **N451R** | **ASTR** | **227** |
| **N451ST** | **LJ45** | **200** |
| **N451TM** | **BE40** | **RK-576** |
| N451W | C56X | 5232 |
| **N451WM** | **LJ45** | **091** |
| N452A | LJ45 | 320 |
| N452A | PRM1 | RB-37 |
| N452AC | LJ35 | 508 |
| (N452AJ) | C550 | 047 |
| **N452AJ** | **C560** | **0494** |
| N452AS | PRM1 | RB-252 |
| N452CJ | C550 | 452 |
| **N452CJ** | **LJ45** | **090** |
| N452CS | GLEX | 9134 |
| **N452DA** | **LJ35** | **452** |
| N452DP | FA10 | 11 |
| N452ET | LJ25 | 152 |
| N452F | FA20 | 440 |
| N452FJ | F900 | 73 |
| N452GA | GLF4 | 1222 |
| N452GA | GLF4 | 1271 |
| N452GA | GLF4 | 1452 |
| N452GA | GLF4 | 4052 |
| **N452GA** | **GLF4** | **4205** |
| (N452K) | LJ45 | 406 |
| N452LJ | LJ24 | 118 |
| **N452LJ** | **LJ45** | **002** |
| (N452LX) | BE40 | RK-265 |
| N452LX | BE40 | RK-317 |
| **N452NS** | **GLF4** | **4094** |
| **N452QS** | **GLF4** | **1352** |
| **N452SB** | **BE40** | **RK-317** |
| N452SM | HS25 | 258136 |
| **N452ST** | **LJ45** | **201** |
| **N452TM** | **BE40** | **RK-577** |
| N452WU | CL64 | 5452 |
| N453 | LJ24 | 323 |
| **N453A** | **LJ45** | **363** |
| N453AD | CL64 | 5453 |
| **N453AM** | **LJ35** | **453** |
| N453BL | LJ45 | 022 |
| N453CM | HS25 | 25084 |
| N453CV | C560 | 0453 |
| N453CW | BE40 | RK-53 |
| **N453DP** | **HS25** | **256044** |
| **N453DW** | **C510** | **0187** |
| N453EP | HS25 | 257014 |
| N453F | FA20 | 444 |
| N453FJ | F900 | 74 |
| N453GA | GLF4 | 1223 |
| N453GA | GLF4 | 1312 |
| N453GA | GLF4 | 1453 |
| N453GA | GLF4 | 4053 |
| N453GA | GLF4 | 4153 |
| **N453GS** | **CL61** | **3011** |
| N453JS | F900 | 144 |
| **N453JS** | **F9DX** | **605** |
| N453JT | LJ24 | 033 |
| (N453K) | LJ45 | 409 |
| N453LJ | LJ24 | 033 |
| N453LJ | LJ24 | 119 |
| N453LJ | LJ45 | 003 |
| (N453LX) | BE40 | RK-268 |
| **N453MA** | **LJ25** | **291** |
| **N453S** | **C550** | **445** |
| N453SA | LJ24 | 119 |
| N453SB | FA20 | 308 |
| **N453SB** | **FA20** | **382** |
| **N453ST** | **LJ45** | **299** |
| **N453TM** | **BE40** | **RK-581** |
| N453TM | HS25 | 258203 |
| **N454AC** | **C500** | **373** |
| N454AJ | GLEX | 9153 |
| **N454AN** | **LJ60** | **045** |
| N454AS | LJ45 | 038 |
| (N454BE) | GLF3 | 472 |
| N454CG | LJ45 | 085 |
| **N454DP** | **FA10** | **130** |
| N454DP | HS25 | 256044 |
| N454DQ | C500 | 579 |
| **N454DR** | **E55P** | **50500005** |
| N454EP | HS25 | 257017 |
| N454F | FA20 | 446 |
| N454FJ | F900 | 76 |
| N454GA | GLF4 | 1224 |
| N454GA | GLF4 | 1272 |
| N454GA | GLF4 | 1323 |
| N454GA | GLF4 | 1454 |
| N454GA | GLF4 | 4054 |
| N454GA | GLF4 | 4154 |
| N454GL | LJ24 | 121 |
| N454HC | MS76 | 090 |
| N454JB | GLF3 | 345 |
| N454JB | HS25 | 258003 |
| N454JB | JSTR | 5205 |
| N454JF | LJ45 | 329 |
| N454LC | LJ45 | 123 |
| **N454LC** | **LJ45** | **296** |
| N454LJ | LJ24 | 121 |
| N454LJ | LJ24 | 226 |
| N454LJ | LJ45 | 004 |
| N454LP | LJ45 | 034 |
| (N454LX) | BE40 | RK-271 |
| **N454LX** | **BE40** | **RK-327** |
| N454MK | LJ45 | 088 |
| **N454N** | **LJ45** | **339** |
| **N454QS** | **GLF4** | **1454** |
| N454RN | LJ24 | 121 |
| (N454RR) | LJ45 | 038 |
| N454RT | C560 | 0454 |
| N454SR | WW24 | 79 |
| N455BE | CL60 | 1069 |
| **N455BK** | **HS25** | **257078** |
| N455BP | HA4T | RC-16 |
| N455CW | BE40 | RK-365 |
| N455DE | LJ45 | 160 |
| **N455DG** | **LJ45** | **129** |
| N455DM | C550 | 095 |
| **N455DW** | **BE40** | **RJ-20** |
| **N455DX** | **F2TH** | **146** |
| (N455EC) | LJ55 | 043 |
| N455EM | LJ55 | 014 |
| N455F | FA20 | 447 |
| N455FD | BE40 | RJ-17 |
| **N455FD** | **C500** | **357** |
| N455FJ | F900 | 77 |
| N455GA | GLF4 | 1313 |
| N455GA | GLF4 | 1455 |
| N455GA | GLF4 | 4055 |
| N455GA | GLF4 | 4155 |
| N455H | C500 | 552 |
| N455JA | LJ24 | 300 |
| **N455JD** | **C650** | **0069** |
| N455LB | SBRL | 465-49 |
| N455LJ | LJ45 | 005 |
| (N455LX) | BE40 | RK-273 |
| N455LX | BE40 | RK-328 |
| N455NE | LJ35 | 455 |
| N455PM | LJ45 | 160 |
| **N455QS** | **GLF4** | **4074** |
| **N455RH** | **LJ55** | **110** |
| N455RM | LJ35 | 171 |
| N455S | WW24 | 367 |
| N455SF | SBRL | 465-49 |
| **N455SH** | **ASTR** | **017** |
| N455SR | CL60 | 1032 |
| (N455UJ) | LJ55 | 098 |
| N456AB | C550 | 215 |
| N456AF | C650 | 0147 |
| **N456AL** | **GLF3** | **405** |
| N456AS | GLF2 | 17 |
| N456AS | LJ45 | 039 |
| **N456BE** | **GLF3** | **335** |
| N456BE | GLF4 | 1135 |
| N456CE | C500 | 630 |
| (N456CG) | CL60 | 1027 |
| **N456CG** | **LJ25** | **343** |
| N456CJ | C680 | 0249 |
| **N456CL** | **LJ35** | **456** |
| (N456CM) | C550 | 456 |
| N456CM | FA10 | 207 |
| N456CW | BE40 | RK-56 |
| N456DK | CL60 | 1081 |
| N456FB | C560 | 0009 |
| N456FJ | F900 | 78 |
| **N456FL** | **BE40** | **RK-146** |
| N456GB | C500 | 256 |
| N456JA | LJ24 | 265 |
| **N456JG** | **BE40** | **RK-119** |
| N456JP | SBRL | 282-32 |
| N456JW | C560 | 0266 |
| N456JW | C56X | 5033 |
| N456LJ | LJ45 | 006 |
| N456LM | LJ45 | 006 |
| (N456LX) | BE40 | RK-274 |
| **N456MF** | **EA50** | **000050** |
| N456MS | CL64 | 5456 |
| N456MS | GLEX | 9149 |
| N456MS | LJ35 | 017 |
| N456N | C550 | 077 |
| (N456NS) | BE40 | RK-119 |
| N456PR | ASTR | 116 |
| **N456Q** | **LJ45** | **282** |
| N456R | C500 | 472 |
| N456SC | LJ24 | 022 |
| N456SL | C56X | 5528 |
| **N456SM** | **C680** | **0038** |
| N456SR | FA20 | 299 |
| **N456SW** | **C560** | **0222** |
| N456SW | GLF3 | 337 |
| **N456TM** | **BE40** | **RK-585** |
| **N456TX** | **C550** | **215** |
| N456WH | HS25 | 25244 |
| N457CA | C500 | 131 |
| N457CF | C550 | 457 |
| N457CS | C500 | 578 |
| N457CW | BE40 | RK-57 |
| **N457DS** | **GLF4** | **1077** |
| N457F | FA20 | 449 |
| N457FJ | F900 | 79 |
| N457GA | ASTR | 257 |
| N457GA | GLF4 | 1061 |
| N457GA | GLF4 | 1123 |
| N457GA | GLF4 | 1157 |
| N457GA | GLF4 | 1162 |
| N457GA | GLF4 | 1273 |
| N457GA | GLF4 | 1324 |
| N457GA | GLF4 | 4057 |
| N457GM | LJ24 | 340 |
| N457H | GLF3 | 457 |
| **N457H** | **GLF4** | **1462** |
| **N457HL** | **CL60** | **1063** |
| **N457J** | **HS25** | **258085** |
| N457JA | LJ24 | 207 |
| **N457JC** | **GLF3** | **457** |
| N457K | PRM1 | RB-57 |
| N457LJ | LJ24 | 120 |
| N457LJ | LJ45 | 007 |
| (N457LX) | BE40 | RK-276 |
| (N457LX) | BE40 | RK-345 |
| N457SF | GLF3 | 409 |
| N457ST | GLF3 | 409 |
| N457ST | GLF4 | 1345 |
| (N457ST) | GLF5 | 616 |
| N457SW | GLF2 | 115 |
| **N457TB** | **EA50** | **000088** |
| (N457TB) | EA50 | 000093 |
| N458A | FA10 | 58 |
| **N458A** | **LJ45** | **397** |
| N458BE | GLF3 | 440 |
| **N458BN** | **GALX** | **071** |
| N458CC | C550 | 458 |
| (N458CG) | LJ25 | 343 |
| **N458CK** | **C560** | **0160** |
| **N458DA** | **C560** | **0458** |
| (N458DS) | C550 | 458 |
| **N458F** | **C550** | **550-0986** |
| N458F | FA20 | 450 |
| N458FA | GLF4 | 1159 |
| N458FJ | F900 | 75 |
| N458GA | ASTR | 258 |
| N458GA | GLF4 | 1058 |
| N458GA | GLF4 | 1163 |
| N458GA | GLF4 | 1274 |
| N458GA | GLF4 | 4058 |
| N458GA | GLF4 | 4158 |
| (N458H) | C550 | 377 |
| **N458HC** | **BE40** | **RJ-58** |
| N458HW | C550 | 377 |
| N458J | LJ25 | 106 |
| N458JA | LJ25 | 106 |
| N458JA | LJ35 | 376 |
| N458JW | C560 | 0266 |
| N458LC | C56X | 5109 |
| N458LJ | LJ24 | 115 |
| **N458LM** | **E50P** | **50000019** |
| (N458LX) | BE40 | RK-279 |
| N458MS | CL64 | 5458 |
| **N458MT** | **C525** | **0316** |
| (N458N) | C550 | 061 |
| **N458N** | **C550** | **077** |
| **N458NC** | **C560** | **0478** |
| N458PE | CS55 | 0143 |
| **N458SB** | **FA20** | **308** |
| N458SM | C525 | 0541 |
| N458SW | FA20 | 68 |

**N458X GLF4 4138**
**N459A LJ31 137**
N459BE GLF4 1245
N459BN GALX 071
**N459BN GALX 195**
**N459CS CL64 5546**
N459F FA20 452
N459FA GLF4 1161
N459FJ F900 80
N459GA GLF4 1069
N459GA GLF4 1164
N459GA GLF4 1225
N459GA GLF4 1275
N459GA GLF4 1325
N459GA GLF4 4059
N459GA GLF4 4159
N459JD WW24 9
**N459LC LJ45 060**
N459LJ LJ45 009
(N459LX) BE40 RK-282
**N459LX BE40 RK-365**
N459MT CL64 5459
**N459NA C525 0459**
**N459SF LJ60 049**
N459X GLF4 4151
N459XP BE40 RK-459
**N460AN LJ60 127**
**N460AS PRM1 RB-8**
N460BG LJ60 090
N460CC C500 460
**N460CP C650 0021**
**N460D F9EX 188**
**N460DC LJ45 146**
**N460F CL61 5055**
N460F FA20 453
N460F LJ24 068
N460FJ F900 83
N460GA GLF4 1086
N460GA GLF4 1165
N460GA GLF4 1226
N460GA GLF4 1276
N460GA GLF4 1460
N460GA GLF4 4060
N460GA GLF5 565
N460JD LJ60 158
N460JW BE40 RK-460
**N460KG BE40 RK-460**
**N460L PRM1 RB-46**
(N460LX) BE40 RK-284
N460LX BE40 RK-366
**N460M CS55 0022**
N460MC FA20 105
**N460MC LJ60 309**
N460PG GLF3 460
**N460QS GLF4 1360**
**N460SB LJ35 670**
N460WF HS25 258460
N460WJ CL64 5460
N460XP BE40 RK-460
N461AS FA10 146
**N461CJ C52A 0461**
N461CW BE40 RK-61
**N461EA BE40 RJ-61**
N461F FA20 454
N461F LJ24 116
N461FJ F900 85
**N461FL FA20 94/428**
N461GA GALX 181
N461GA GLF4 1047
N461GA GLF4 1166
N461GA GLF4 1260
N461GA GLF4 1314
N461GA GLF4 1461
N461GA GLF4 4061
N461GA GLF4 4161
N461GA GLF5 568
**N461GT GLF3 411**
N461LJ LJ24 122
(N461LX) BE40 RK-289
N461LX BE40 RK-368
**N461MC LJ60 284**
**N461N EA50 000234**
**N461QS GLF4 4125**
N461TS GLF4 1161
N461VP C560 0461
N461W HS25 258200
**N462B C560 0016**
N462B LJ24 155
N462B LJ24 290
N462B LJ25 175
N462B LJ25 331
N462BA LJ24 155
N462BA LJ25 175
**N462CB PRM1 RB-136**
N462CC C500 462
N462CK GLF4 1462
N462CS GLF4 1462
N462CW BE40 RK-62
N462F FA20 456
N462FJ F900 87
N462GA GLF4 1062
N462GA GLF4 1168
N462GA GLF4 1277
N462GA GLF4 1462
N462GA GLF4 4062
N462GA GLF4 4162
N462LJ LJ24 124
**N462LX BE40 RK-423**
N462PG CL64 5462
**N462QS GLF4 1262**
N462XP BE40 RK-462
N463AG CL64 5463
N463C C550 285
(N463CJ) C500 463
N463F FA20 457
N463FJ F900 92
N463G GLF4 1363
N463GA GLF4 1087
N463GA GLF4 1169
N463GA GLF4 1227
N463GA GLF4 1463
N463GA GLF4 4063
N463GA GLF4 4163
N463GA GLF5 563
N463GE GLF3 463
**N463HK GLF2 11**
N463LJ LJ25 001
N463LM GLF3 370
(N463LX) BE40 RK-295
**N463LX BE40 RK-426**
**N463MA GLF4 1108**
N463QS GLF4 1363
(N464) CS55 0061
N464AC FA10 54
**N464AM MU30 A090SA**
N464C C525 0325
N464C C52A 0118
**N464CL LJ24 096**
N464EC WW24 305
N464FJ F900 95
N464GA GLF4 1088
N464GA GLF4 1170
N464GA GLF4 1228
N464GA GLF4 1278
N464GA GLF4 1464
N464GA GLF4 4064
N464GA GLF4 4164
N464HA LJ35 304
N464J LJ24 164
(N464LX) BE40 RK-297
(N464LX) BE40 RK-434
**N464LX BE40 RK-453**
N464M FA20 322
**N464PG EA50 000096**
N464QS GLF4 1264
N464SP GLF4 1286
**N464ST GLF4 4022**
**N464TF LJ60 185**
N464WL LJ35 464
N465AV CL64 5465
**N465BC SBRL 465-53**
N465CV C560 0465
N465D C550 377
N465F FA20 458
N465FJ F900 98
N465GA ASTR 265
N465GA GLF3 465
N465GA GLF4 1089
N465GA GLF4 1171
N465GA GLF4 1229
N465GA GLF4 1265
N465GA GLF4 1465
N465GA GLF4 4065
N465JH SBRL 306-57
N465LC SBRL 465-21
(N465LX) BE40 RK-301
N465LX BE40 RK-444
**N465LX BE40 RK-454**
**N465NW LJ35 465**
N465PM SBRL 465-40
**N465QS GLF4 1463**
N465R HS25 257029
N465RM SBRL 465-40
N465S SBRL 282-59
N465S SBRL 306-136
N465S SBRL 465-1
**N465SC SBRL 465-30**
N465SL SBRL 465-26
N465SP SBRL 465-72
N465SR SBRL 465-33
N465T SBRL 465-2
**N465TM BE40 RK-554**
N465TS SBRL 465-15
**N466AE C525 0642**
N466AE HS25 258206
N466CS HS25 258206
N466CW BE40 RK-366
N466F C525 0119
N466F C52B 0336
N466F FA20 459
N466FJ F900 101
N466GA GLF4 1090
N466GA GLF4 1172
N466GA GLF4 1279
N466GA GLF4 4066
N466GA GLF5 566
**N466JB GLF2 57**
N466LM C56X 5074
(N466LX) BE40 RK-305
N466LX BE40 RK-445
N466LX BE40 RK-455
N466LX BE40 RK-507
N466MP HS25 25155
**N466SS C550 626**
N466TS GLF4 1066
N466XP BE40 RK-466
**N467AM GLF2 169**
**N467F C525 0335**
N467F FA20 460
N467FJ F900 102
N467FL BE40 RK-447
N467GA GLF4 1091
N467GA GLF4 1174
N467GA GLF4 1230
N467GA GLF4 1467
N467GA GLF4 4067
N467GA GLF4 4167
N467GA GLF5 567
N467H SBRL 282-3
(N467LX) BE40 RK-307
**N467LX BE40 RK-447**
N467MW ASTR 067
(N467MW) C550 093
**N467MW GALX 014**
N467MW WW24 325
**N467QS GLF4 1533**
N467RD CL64 5467
**N467RG BE40 RK-67**
**N468AB GLF4 1477**
**N468AM FA50 31**
**N468CE C560 0788**
N468CJ C550 468
N468DM LJ24 156
**N468ES C650 0185**
N468FJ F900 104
N468GA GLF4 1092
N468GA GLF4 1176
N468GA GLF4 1280
N468GA GLF4 1468
N468GA GLF4 4068
N468GA GLF4 4168
**N468GH F900 190**
**N468HW GLF2 157**
**N468KE CL61 5036**
N468KL CL61 5036
**N468KL GLEX 9279**
N468LM HS25 25221
N468LM LJ35 468
(N468LX) BE40 RK-310
**N468LX BE40 RK-468**
**N468QS GLF4 4146**
**N468RB SBRL 306-133**
**N468RW C525 0468**
N468SA C680 0122
(N469) C550 423
(N469) LJ31 128
**N469AL HS25 258067**
**N469BB LJ35 434**
**N469BT GLF3 432**
**N469DE C550 550-0883**
**N469DN C560 0469**
N469F FA20 461
N469FJ F900 105
N469G GLF4 1369
N469GA ASTR 269
N469GA GLF4 1095
N469GA GLF4 1177
N469GA GLF4 1261
N469GA GLF4 4069
N469GA GLF5 569
N469J LJ24 165
N469JR HS25 257174
(N469LX) BE40 RK-317
**N469LX BE40 RK-463**
N469PW C500 302
N469QS GLF4 1369
N469RC CL64 5469
**N469RS C56X 5082**
**N469TB GLF3 469**
**N469WC WW24 202**
N470BC HS25 258651
**N470CT BE40 RK-536**
(N470CW) BE40 RK-370
N470D F2EX 139
**N470DP C560 0291**
N470F FA20 462
N470FJ F900 107
N470G FA20 470
N470GA ASTR 270
N470GA GLF4 1178
N470GA GLF4 1231
N470GA GLF4 1281
N470GA GLF4 1470
N470GA GLF4 4070
N470GA GLF5 570
(N470LX) BE40 RK-324
**N470LX BE40 RK-478**
**N470QS GLF4 4084**
N470R HS25 25058
**N470SK C56X 5348**
N470TR LJ24 298
N470TS HS25 25070
N470XP BE40 RK-470
N471CJ C525 0471
N471CR GLF4 1471
N471CW BE40 RK-161
N471DG GLEX 9049
N471F FA20 463
N471FJ F900 108
**N471FL FA20 163**
N471GA ASTR 271
N471GA GLF4 1179
N471GA GLF4 1232
N471GA GLF4 1282
N471GA GLF4 1471
N471GA GLF4 4071
N471H C500 471
N471HH C500 050
(N471LX) BE40 RK-327
N471LX BE40 RK-471
**N471LX BE40 RK-506**
N471MH C500 050
N471MK CL64 5471
N471MM C500 050
N471MM LJ25 169
N471SB CL60 1083
N471SP CL60 1083
N471SP CL61 5157
N471TM WW24 370
N471WR C550 550-0987
**N471XP BE40 RK-471**
(N472AS) LJ35 472
N472EJ LJ24 238
N472F FA20 464
N472FJ F900 111
N472GA GLF4 1180
N472GA GLF4 1233
N472GA GLF4 1283
N472GA GLF5 572
N472J LJ25 204
(N472LX) BE40 RK-328
**N472LX BE40 RK-481**

| | | |
|---|---|---|
| **N472MM** | **GLF4** | **1072** |
| **N472QS** | **GLF4** | **1372** |
| N472SP | JSTR | 5078/3 |
| N472SW | C525 | 0033 |
| (N472TS) | CL64 | 5572 |
| N472TS | GLF4 | 1172 |
| N473 | LJ24 | 101 |
| N473BD | LJ40 | 45-2047 |
| N473CC | C500 | 473 |
| **N473CW** | **GLF4** | **1194** |
| N473EJ | LJ24 | 101 |
| N473F | FA20 | 466 |
| N473FJ | F900 | 112 |
| **N473FL** | **BE40** | **RK-397** |
| N473GA | GLF4 | 1181 |
| **N473JE** | **BE40** | **RK-121** |
| (N473JF) | GLF2 | 106 |
| N473KT | GLF3 | 438 |
| N473LP | C500 | 276 |
| N473LP | LJ45 | 196 |
| N473LP | LJ45 | 201 |
| N473LR | C500 | 276 |
| (N473LX) | BE40 | RK-334 |
| N473LX | BE40 | RK-518 |
| N473SB | C560 | 0473 |
| N473SH | FA20 | 473 |
| **N473TC** | **LJ25** | **043** |
| **N474AN** | **LJ35** | **295** |
| N474CV | C560 | 0474 |
| **N474D** | **GLF4** | **1445** |
| N474F | FA20 | 467 |
| N474FJ | F900 | 114 |
| N474L | C500 | 323 |
| N474L | CS55 | 0107 |
| (N474LX) | BE40 | RK-345 |
| **N474LX** | **BE40** | **RK-541** |
| **N474M** | **GLF4** | **4073** |
| **N474ME** | **BE40** | **RK-474** |
| **N474PC** | **C52A** | **0087** |
| N474SP | C550 | 485 |
| **N474TC** | **LJ45** | **405** |
| N474VP | C560 | 0474 |
| N474VW | SBRL | 282-76 |
| N474XP | BE40 | RK-474 |
| N475AD | CL64 | 5475 |
| N475AT | WW24 | 270 |
| N475CC | C500 | 475 |
| N475CJ | C525 | 0475 |
| (N475CY) | GLF3 | 358 |
| **N475DH** | **C52A** | **0090** |
| N475DJ | GLF3 | 358 |
| N475EZ | FA20 | 475 |
| N475FJ | F900 | 116 |
| N475GA | GLF4 | 1182 |
| N475GA | GLF4 | 1234 |
| N475GA | GLF4 | 1284 |
| N475GA | GLF4 | 1475 |
| N475GA | GLF4 | 4175 |
| N475GA | GLF5 | 575 |
| **N475HC** | **C550** | **475** |
| **N475HM** | **HS25** | **258451** |
| **N475JC** | **C56X** | **5517** |
| **N475LC** | **GLF4** | **1472** |
| (N475LX) | BE40 | RK-346 |
| N475LX | BE40 | RK-554 |
| (N475LX) | BE40 | RK-563 |
| N475M | C650 | 0062 |
| **N475M** | **GLF4** | **4067** |
| N475MD | JSTR | 5112/7 |
| N475QS | GLF4 | 1275 |
| **N475TM** | **BE40** | **RK-560** |
| N475WA | C550 | 475 |
| **N476BJ** | **BE40** | **RK-176** |
| N476CJ | C525 | 0476 |
| N476CW | BE40 | RK-376 |
| N476FJ | F900 | 117 |
| N476GA | GLF4 | 1183 |
| N476GA | GLF4 | 1476 |
| N476GA | GLF5 | 5176 |
| N476GA | GLF5 | 576 |
| (N476JD) | C525 | 0381 |
| **N476JD** | **C52A** | **0426** |
| **N476LC** | **CS55** | **0091** |
| N476LC | CS55 | 0153 |
| **N476LX** | **BE40** | **RK-376** |
| N476MK | FA50 | 301 |
| N476VC | LJ35 | 476 |
| N476X | C500 | 559 |

| | | |
|---|---|---|
| **N477A** | **C550** | **106** |
| N477A | SBRL | 282-110 |
| N477AT | CL64 | 5477 |
| N477BL | LJ24 | 031 |
| N477BM | LJ60 | 010 |
| N477CW | BE40 | RK-377 |
| N477DM | CL61 | 5174 |
| N477DM | CL64 | 5398 |
| N477DM | LJ60 | 010 |
| N477F | FA20 | 470 |
| N477FJ | F900 | 119 |
| **N477FL** | **BE40** | **RK-377** |
| N477GA | GLF4 | 1184 |
| N477GA | GLF4 | 1235 |
| N477GA | GLF4 | 1285 |
| N477GA | GLF4 | 1388 |
| N477GA | GLF4 | 1477 |
| **N477GG** | **GLF2** | **155/14** |
| **N477GJ** | **BE40** | **RK-477** |
| **N477JB** | **GLF4** | **1214** |
| N477JB | LJ24 | 230 |
| N477JE | C550 | 620 |
| (N477JM) | SBRL | 306-5 |
| (N477JN) | EA50 | 000199 |
| (N477JR) | C550 | 477 |
| N477K | LJ24 | 036 |
| N477KM | C500 | 607 |
| N477KM | C550 | 397 |
| N477LC | CS55 | 0091 |
| **N477LC** | **CS55** | **0153** |
| N477LX | BE40 | RK-377 |
| (N477MM) | LJ25 | 291 |
| (N477MS) | LJ35 | 477 |
| **N477QS** | **GLF4** | **1377** |
| N477RP | GLF4 | 1247 |
| (N477RW) | HS25 | 257191 |
| **N477SA** | **GLF4** | **1529** |
| N477SJ | GLF3 | 477 |
| N477TS | GLF4 | 1077 |
| N477WB | LJ35 | 477 |
| **N477WG** | **GLF3** | **477** |
| N477X | SBRL | 282-110 |
| N477X | SBRL | 306-78 |
| N477XP | BE40 | RK-477 |
| **N477XR** | **LJ40** | **45-2113** |
| N478A | F900 | 95 |
| N478BA | CL64 | 5478 |
| (N478CW) | BE40 | RK-178 |
| **N478DR** | **BE40** | **RK-61** |
| **N478F** | **EA50** | **000228** |
| N478F | FA20 | 471 |
| N478FJ | F900 | 121 |
| N478GA | GLF4 | 1185 |
| N478GA | GLF4 | 1236 |
| N478GA | GLF4 | 1400 |
| **N478GA** | **GLF4** | **4178** |
| **N478GS** | **GLF4** | **1478** |
| **N478LX** | **BE40** | **RK-387** |
| **N478PM** | **C750** | **0014** |
| N478PM | HS25 | 258224 |
| N478QS | GLF4 | 4133 |
| (N478WC) | GLF4 | 4133 |
| N479CC | C500 | 479 |
| N479FJ | F900 | 122 |
| N479GA | GALX | 179 |
| N479GA | GLF4 | 1186 |
| N479GA | GLF4 | 1402 |
| N479GA | GLF4 | 1479 |
| N479GA | GLF4 | 4179 |
| N479JS | C500 | 479 |
| N479KA | CL64 | 5479 |
| N479LX | BE40 | RK-388 |
| N479LX | BE40 | RK-397 |
| **N479PR** | **GALX** | **008** |
| N479TS | GLF4 | 1079 |
| N479XP | BE40 | RK-479 |
| **N480BA** | **CL30** | **20197** |
| **N480CB** | **CL30** | **20147** |
| (N480CC) | C500 | 480 |
| **N480CC** | **C52B** | **0326** |
| N480CC | CS55 | 0129 |
| **N480CT** | **BE40** | **RK-544** |
| (N480CW) | BE40 | RK-180 |
| N480D | F2EX | 163 |
| **N480DG** | **C560** | **0015** |
| N480FJ | F900 | 124 |
| N480FL | BE40 | RK-398 |
| N480GA | GALX | 180 |

| | | |
|---|---|---|
| N480GA | GLF2 | 234 |
| N480GA | GLF4 | 1237 |
| N480GA | GLF4 | 1286 |
| N480GA | GLF4 | 1480 |
| **N480JJ** | **ASTR** | **241** |
| N480JJ | LJ31 | 212 |
| N480LB | CL64 | 5480 |
| N480LP | F2TH | 36 |
| N480LR | HFB3 | 1054 |
| N480LX | BE40 | RK-390 |
| **N480LX** | **BE40** | **RK-398** |
| **N480M** | **BE40** | **RK-586** |
| N480M | BE40 | RK-6 |
| **N480ME** | **LJ31** | **085** |
| **N480QS** | **GLF4** | **1380** |
| **N480RL** | **C560** | **0109** |
| N480UP | GLF4 | 1054 |
| **N481CW** | **BE40** | **RK-1** |
| **N481DH** | **WW24** | **139** |
| N481EZ | LJ24 | 139 |
| N481FB | GLF4 | 1442 |
| N481FJ | F900 | 126 |
| **N481FL** | **FA20** | **27** |
| N481FM | LJ35 | 218 |
| N481GA | GLF4 | 1187 |
| N481JJ | LJ31 | 212 |
| N481JT | CL60 | 1034 |
| N481KW | CL64 | 5481 |
| N481LX | BE40 | RK-405 |
| N481LX | BE40 | RK-581 |
| N481MC | WW24 | 184 |
| **N481NS** | **WW24** | **378** |
| N481QS | GLF4 | 1281 |
| N481VP | C550 | 481 |
| N482BB | CL64 | 5482 |
| N482CP | LJ24 | 230 |
| N482CP | LJ25 | 331 |
| N482CW | BE40 | RK-222 |
| **N482DM** | **MU30** | **A088SA** |
| N482FJ | F900 | 127 |
| N482G | WW24 | 98 |
| N482GA | GALX | 182 |
| N482GA | GLF4 | 1188 |
| N482GA | GLF4 | 1482 |
| **N482GS** | **BE40** | **RK-482** |
| N482HC | SBRL | 282-28 |
| (N482LX) | BE40 | RK-282 |
| **N482LX** | **BE40** | **RK-413** |
| N482QS | GLF4 | 1480 |
| N482RJ | C500 | 082 |
| N482RK | BE40 | RK-222 |
| N482SG | LJ35 | 493 |
| N482U | LJ35 | 482 |
| N482XP | BE40 | RK-482 |
| N483A | WW24 | 283 |
| N483AS | C550 | 483 |
| N483BA | CL64 | 5483 |
| N483CC | CL64 | 5483 |
| (N483CW) | BE40 | RK-273 |
| **N483DM** | **LJ24** | **291** |
| N483DM | MU30 | A089SA |
| **N483FG** | **HS25** | **257094** |
| N483FJ | F900 | 129 |
| N483G | C550 | 325 |
| N483GA | GLF4 | 1238 |
| N483GA | GLF4 | 1483 |
| N483GA | GLF4 | 4183 |
| (N483H) | GLF3 | 483 |
| N483LX | BE40 | RK-398 |
| N483SC | C550 | 483 |
| (N484) | LJ35 | 480 |
| N484AT | PRM1 | RB-141 |
| N484CC | BE40 | RJ-27 |
| **N484CH** | **LJ40** | **45-2075** |
| N484CJ | C525 | 0484 |
| (N484CS) | C500 | 548 |
| N484CW | BE40 | RK-334 |
| N484CW | C52A | 0453 |
| (N484CW) | MU30 | A004SA |
| N484DM | MU30 | A084SA |
| **N484GA** | **ASTR** | **284** |
| N484GA | GLF4 | 1239 |
| N484GA | GLF4 | 1287 |
| N484GA | GLF4 | 1484 |
| N484GC | CL64 | 5484 |
| N484H | C750 | 0006 |
| N484HB | LJ36 | 027 |
| **N484J** | **C525** | **0048** |

| | | |
|---|---|---|
| **N484JC** | **HS25** | **258644** |
| **N484JH** | **E50P** | **50000016** |
| N484KA | C500 | 484 |
| N484LC | LJ45 | 123 |
| N484MA | C550 | 473 |
| **N484MM** | **C560** | **0491** |
| N484RA | HS25 | 258053 |
| N484T | C750 | 0006 |
| **N484T** | **C750** | **0199** |
| N484TL | GLF2 | 93 |
| (N484VS) | MU30 | A084SA |
| N484W | HS25 | 256063 |
| (N485) | LJ35 | 306 |
| N485 | LJ35 | 491 |
| N485A | C550 | 485 |
| **N485AC** | **LJ35** | **485** |
| **N485AK** | **C550** | **249** |
| **N485AS** | **FA10** | **219** |
| N485CC | C500 | 485 |
| N485CL | CL64 | 5485 |
| **N485CT** | **BE40** | **RK-545** |
| (N485CW) | BE40 | RK-195 |
| N485CW | MU30 | A007SA |
| N485DM | MU30 | A085SA |
| (N485DM) | MU30 | A091SA |
| **N485FL** | **BE40** | **RK-239** |
| **N485GA** | **ASTR** | **285** |
| N485GA | GLF4 | 1185 |
| N485GA | GLF4 | 1385 |
| N485GA | GLF4 | 1485 |
| N485GM | GLF2 | 137 |
| **N485GM** | **GLF3** | **387** |
| N485LT | HS25 | 258485 |
| N485LX | BE40 | RK-402 |
| N485RP | C500 | 503 |
| N485S | LJ35 | 485 |
| **N485XP** | **BE40** | **RK-485** |
| (N486) | LJ55 | 120 |
| (N486BG) | C560 | 0541 |
| N486BG | C560 | 0549 |
| **N486BG** | **CL61** | **5133** |
| N486CC | C500 | 486 |
| N486CW | MU30 | A026SA |
| N486DM | MU30 | A086SA |
| N486EJ | CL64 | 5486 |
| N486G | LJ24 | 093 |
| N486G | WW24 | 48 |
| **N486GA** | **ASTR** | **286** |
| N486GA | GALX | 186 |
| N486GA | GLF4 | 1240 |
| (N486GA) | GLF4 | 1286 |
| N486GA | GLF4 | 1386 |
| N486GA | GLF4 | 1486 |
| N486GA | GLF4 | 4086 |
| N486MJ | BE40 | RJ-17 |
| N486MJ | BE40 | RJ-30 |
| N486MJ | FA10 | 199 |
| N486MJ | HS25 | 257035 |
| N486MJ | JSTR | 5217 |
| **N486QS** | **GLF4** | **1386** |
| N486SB | C560 | 0580 |
| **N486TT** | **C525** | **0213** |
| (N487CC) | C550 | 487 |
| N487DM | MU30 | A087SA |
| **N487DT** | **PRM1** | **RB-85** |
| **N487F** | **CL30** | **20152** |
| N487F | FA50 | 160 |
| N487FW | LJ35 | 487 |
| N487G | WW24 | 103 |
| **N487GA** | **ASTR** | **287** |
| N487GA | GLF4 | 1241 |
| N487GA | GLF4 | 1387 |
| N487GA | GLF4 | 1487 |
| N487HR | C500 | 487 |
| N487JD | C52A | 0325 |
| N487LD | C550 | 551 |
| (N487LP) | LJ35 | 669 |
| **N487LP** | **LJ60** | **361** |
| N487LS | C500 | 487 |
| N487MA | F9EX | 87 |
| **N487QS** | **GLF4** | **1287** |
| N487XP | BE40 | RK-487 |
| N488A | C550 | 550-0882 |
| (N488BL) | LJ24 | 193 |
| N488CC | C500 | 488 |
| **N488CC** | **CS55** | **0129** |
| **N488CH** | **GLEX** | **9150** |
| **N488CP** | **C56X** | **5055** |

| | | |
|---|---|---|
| N488DM | LJ24 | 291 |
| N488DM | SBRL | 465-26 |
| N488EC | JSTR | 5061/48 |
| N488GA | GLF4 | 1488 |
| N488GR | JSTR | 5051 |
| N488HP | HS25 | 258488 |
| N488J | LJ24 | 024 |
| N488JD | C560 | 0815 |
| **N488JD** | **C56X** | **6015** |
| N488JS | JSTR | 5051 |
| N488JT | C650 | 0020 |
| **N488KF** | **FA20** | **488** |
| **N488LX** | **BE40** | **RK-183** |
| N488MR | JSTR | 5061/48 |
| N488PC | PRM1 | RB-23 |
| N488PC | PRM1 | RB-57 |
| **N488RC** | **GALX** | **228** |
| N488RC | PRM1 | RB-23 |
| N488SB | GLF3 | 487 |
| **N488SR** | **C525** | **0488** |
| **N488VC** | **HS25** | **258546** |
| (N489) | LJ35 | 277 |
| **N489B** | **BE40** | **RK-489** |
| N489BA | CL64 | 5489 |
| N489BB | FA20 | 489 |
| **N489CB** | **C525** | **0489** |
| N489ED | C525 | 0489 |
| N489FL | BE40 | RK-268 |
| N489G | WW24 | 149 |
| N489GA | ASTR | 279 |
| **N489GM** | **CS55** | **0092** |
| N489H | GLF4 | 1099 |
| **N489JC** | **EA50** | **000044** |
| **N489QS** | **GLF4** | **1389** |
| **N489SA** | **HS25** | **258053** |
| **N489SS** | **C550** | **489** |
| N489TK | FA20 | 489 |
| **N489VC** | **HS25** | **258443** |
| N489XP | BE40 | RK-489 |
| (N490A) | FA10 | 49 |
| N490AJ | CL64 | 5489 |
| **N490AM** | **BE40** | **RK-101** |
| N490BC | LJ35 | 364 |
| **N490CC** | **C550** | **490** |
| **N490CC** | **C750** | **0246** |
| (N490CD) | C550 | 490 |
| **N490CT** | **BE40** | **RK-546** |
| **N490DC** | **C550** | **129** |
| N490EA | C500 | 061 |
| N490GA | GLF4 | 1242 |
| N490GA | GLF4 | 1390 |
| N490GA | GLF4 | 1490 |
| N490GA | GLF4 | 4090 |
| **N490JC** | **BE40** | **RK-373** |
| N490MP | HS25 | 257135 |
| **N490QS** | **GLF4** | **1488** |
| (N490QS) | GLF4 | 1490 |
| N490SJ | FA20 | 490 |
| N490TN | BE40 | RK-45 |
| N490WC | C500 | 518 |
| N491 | C500 | 072 |
| N491AM | BE40 | RK-109 |
| **N491AN** | **WW24** | **393** |
| N491BT | C500 | 102 |
| **N491BT** | **MU30** | **A054SA** |
| N491CJ | C525 | 0491 |
| N491CW | BE40 | RK-91 |
| N491DB | CL60 | 1049 |
| **N491EC** | **GLF4** | **1491** |
| N491GA | GLF4 | 1243 |
| N491GA | GLF4 | 1491 |
| **N491GA** | **GLF4** | **4191** |
| **N491HR** | **BE40** | **RK-491** |
| N491HS | LJ35 | 491 |
| **N491JB** | **C650** | **0182** |
| N491LT | C525 | 0491 |
| N491MB | FA20 | 491 |
| N491N | C550 | 360 |
| **N491N** | **C56X** | **5530** |
| **N491PT** | **C500** | **102** |
| (N491SS) | C650 | 0123 |
| **N491TM** | **BE40** | **RK-564** |
| N491TS | CL60 | 1049 |
| N491XP | BE40 | RK-491 |
| **N492A** | **GLF3** | **425** |
| **N492AM** | **BE40** | **RK-35** |
| N492AT | C550 | 472 |
| (N492BA) | C650 | 0142 |
| N492BJ | BE40 | RK-192 |
| N492CB | HS25 | 257056 |
| **N492CC** | **FA20** | **492** |
| N492CJ | C525 | 0492 |
| N492CV | C560 | 0492 |
| N492DD | GLF3 | 492 |
| N492GA | GALX | 092 |
| **N492GA** | **GLF4** | **4192** |
| N492GA | GLF5 | 5192 |
| **N492JT** | **GLF2** | **82** |
| N492MA | C550 | 472 |
| **N492P** | **BE40** | **RK-39** |
| **N492QS** | **GLF4** | **1392** |
| **N492RM** | **LJ35** | **492** |
| N492ST | C550 | 249 |
| **N492TM** | **BE40** | **RK-580** |
| N492TM | BE40 | RK-592 |
| N493CH | LJ35 | 493 |
| **N493CW** | **BE40** | **RK-93** |
| N493GA | GALX | 193 |
| N493GA | GLF4 | 1493 |
| **N493LX** | **BE40** | **RK-244** |
| N493NW | LJ35 | 493 |
| N493QS | GLF4 | 1293 |
| **N493S** | **F2EX** | **64** |
| N493S | F2TH | 134 |
| N493SF | F2EX | 64 |
| (N493SV) | F2TH | 134 |
| **N493TM** | **BE40** | **RK-582** |
| N493TM | BE40 | RK-593 |
| N493XP | BE40 | RK-493 |
| N494AT | HS25 | 258103 |
| N494BP | WW24 | 307 |
| **N494CC** | **BE40** | **RK-30** |
| N494CW | BE40 | RK-4 |
| N494G | C500 | 147 |
| N494GA | GALX | 194 |
| N494GA | GLF4 | 1494 |
| N494GA | GLF4 | 4094 |
| **N494GA** | **GLF4** | **4194** |
| N494JC | CL64 | 5494 |
| N494LC | CL61 | 5102 |
| N494PA | LJ35 | 505 |
| N494PA | LJ60 | 076 |
| N494RG | HS25 | 258378 |
| **N494TB** | **C52A** | **0442** |
| **N495AS** | **BE40** | **RK-251** |
| N495BA | CL64 | 5495 |
| N495BC | CL64 | 5495 |
| N495CC | C550 | 495 |
| **N495CE** | **CL64** | **5495** |
| **N495CM** | **C550** | **202** |
| **N495CT** | **BE40** | **RK-547** |
| N495CW | BE40 | RK-5 |
| N495G | HS25 | 25017 |
| N495GA | F900 | 55 |
| N495GA | GLF4 | 1259 |
| N495GA | GLF4 | 1495 |
| N495GA | GLF4 | 4095 |
| **N495GA** | **GLF4** | **4195** |
| N495GA | GLF5 | 597 |
| **N495MH** | **C550** | **550-1020** |
| **N495QS** | **GLF4** | **1295** |
| **N495RS** | **GLF4** | **1161** |
| N495XP | BE40 | RK-495 |
| **N496AS** | **BE40** | **RK-117** |
| N496DB | CL64 | 5496 |
| N496EE | BE40 | RK-40 |
| N496G | HS25 | 25174 |
| N496GA | GLF4 | 1262 |
| N496GA | GLF4 | 1496 |
| N496GA | GLF4 | 4096 |
| N496GA | GLF5 | 599 |
| (N496LJ) | LJ35 | 496 |
| (N496LX) | BE40 | RK-301 |
| N496RT | FA20 | 496 |
| N496SW | LJ35 | 496 |
| **N496WH** | **LJ60** | **063** |
| N496XP | BE40 | RK-496 |
| N497 | FA20 | 6 |
| **N497AG** | **HS25** | **258439** |
| **N497AS** | **BE40** | **RK-227** |
| N497CW | BE40 | RK-297 |
| N497DM | CL64 | 5359 |
| N497EA | C560 | 0497 |
| **N497EC** | **CL30** | **20025** |
| N497GA | GLF4 | 1263 |
| **N497KK** | **C680** | **0093** |
| N497PT | HS25 | 257093 |
| (N497QS) | GLF4 | 1497 |
| **N497RC** | **BE40** | **RK-297** |
| N497TJ | GLF2 | 61 |
| **N497XP** | **BE40** | **RK-497** |
| N498A | F9EX | 55 |
| **N498AB** | **C56X** | **5116** |
| **N498AS** | **BE40** | **RK-347** |
| **N498CS** | **C650** | **0180** |
| N498CW | BE40 | RK-108 |
| N498JR | LJ35 | 498 |
| **N498QS** | **GLF4** | **1398** |
| N498R | HS25 | 25225 |
| N498RS | HS25 | 25225 |
| N498SW | LJ60 | 017 |
| **N498YY** | **C525** | **0498** |
| **N499AS** | **BE40** | **RK-220** |
| N499AS | JSTR | 5146 |
| N499BA | C500 | 196 |
| **N499BS** | **LJ25** | **239** |
| N499DM | BE40 | RJ-10 |
| N499EH | LJ25 | 239 |
| N499G | LJ35 | 147 |
| N499G | LJ35 | 202 |
| N499GA | GALX | 099 |
| N499GA | GLF4 | 1264 |
| N499GA | GLF4 | 1399 |
| N499GA | GLF4 | 1499 |
| **N499GA** | **GLF4** | **4199** |
| N499GA | HS25 | 257130 |
| **N499GS** | **C550** | **550-0914** |
| **N499HS** | **C56X** | **5602** |
| N499KR | CL64 | 5499 |
| **N499LX** | **BE40** | **RK-149** |
| N499MJ | FA20 | 57 |
| (N499MW) | ASTR | 019 |
| **N499NH** | **SBRL** | **465-56** |
| **N499P** | **BE40** | **RJ-31** |
| **N499PA** | **HS25** | **258739** |
| N499PB | JSTR | 5063 |
| N499PC | JSTR | 5112/7 |
| (N499QS) | GLF4 | 1099 |
| **N499QS** | **GLF4** | **1299** |
| **N499RC** | **CS55** | **0090** |
| N499SC | GLF4 | 1238 |
| **N499SC** | **GLF4** | **4135** |
| N499SC | HS25 | 25236 |
| N499SC | HS25 | 258082 |
| N499SC | LJ55 | 147 |
| N499TR | WW24 | 41 |
| N499WJ | LJ35 | 499 |
| **N499WM** | **C550** | **550-0869** |
| N499XP | BE40 | RK-499 |
| N500 | C650 | 7027 |
| N500 | CL64 | 5419 |
| N500 | HS25 | 257111 |
| N500 | LJ60 | 115 |
| N500 | LJ60 | 306 |
| N500AB | C500 | 110 |
| N500AD | C500 | 006 |
| **N500AD** | **C500** | **091** |
| N500AE | C550 | 269 |
| N500AE | C650 | 0161 |
| N500AE | FA50 | 166 |
| N500AF | FA50 | 166 |
| N500AF | FA50 | 170 |
| **N500AF** | **FA50** | **320** |
| N500AG | HS25 | 25203 |
| N500AG | JSTR | 5119/29 |
| (N500AH) | C500 | 006 |
| N500AJ | ASTR | 074 |
| **N500AL** | **CL30** | **20092** |
| N500AL | GLF3 | 416 |
| **N500AS** | **C52B** | **0164** |
| N500AT | C560 | 0146 |
| N500AX | WW24 | 359 |
| N500AZ | C500 | 185 |
| N500BE | LJ55 | 058 |
| N500BF | LJ24 | 010 |
| N500BG | FA20 | 121 |
| **N500BJ** | **WW24** | **242** |
| N500BK | C500 | 646 |
| N500BL | F900 | 32 |
| N500BL | FA50 | 66 |
| (N500BL) | GLF4 | 1300 |
| N500BN | HS25 | 258608 |
| N500BR | C550 | 411 |
| N500CA | LJ25 | 091 |
| N500CC | C500 | 669 |
| **N500CD** | **EA50** | **000045** |
| N500CD | GLF4 | 1321 |
| N500CD | LJ25 | 091 |
| N500CD | LJ35 | 083 |
| **N500CE** | **EA50** | **000157** |
| N500CG | LJ24 | 304 |
| N500CG | LJ31 | 068 |
| N500CG | LJ35 | 238 |
| **N500CG** | **LJ45** | **009** |
| N500CM | C650 | 0111 |
| N500CP | C500 | 087 |
| (N500CQ) | LJ31 | 068 |
| N500CU | C560 | 0500 |
| N500CV | C500 | 076 |
| N500CV | C500 | 082 |
| N500CV | C550 | 186 |
| N500CW | C525 | 0542 |
| (N500CX) | C500 | 300 |
| **N500CZ** | **PRM1** | **RB-98** |
| N500DB | C500 | 056 |
| **N500DB** | **C500** | **148** |
| N500DB | JSTR | 5219 |
| N500DD | C500 | 334 |
| N500DD | LJ35 | 351 |
| N500DE | FA10 | 64 |
| N500DG | BE40 | RJ-43 |
| **N500DG** | **EA50** | **000129** |
| N500DG | GLF4 | 1169 |
| N500DJ | LJ24 | 296 |
| N500DL | C500 | 542 |
| N500DL | LJ25 | 027 |
| N500DN | C500 | 034 |
| N500DS | FA10 | 28 |
| N500DS | LJ35 | 079 |
| **N500DW** | **C560** | **0199** |
| N500E | C650 | 0065 |
| **N500E** | **GLEX** | **9105** |
| N500E | GLF3 | 372 |
| N500E | GLF4 | 1072 |
| N500E | GLF4 | 1235 |
| N500E | SBRL | 465-52 |
| N500EA | EA50 | EX500-100 |
| "N500EA" | EA50 | EX500-101 |
| **N500ED** | **LJ35** | **241** |
| (N500EE) | C550 | 269 |
| **N500EF** | **GLF3** | **400** |
| N500EF | HS25 | 257086 |
| (N500EF) | LJ25 | 249 |
| N500EF | LJ35 | 272 |
| N500EL | C500 | 173 |
| (N500EN) | C500 | 135 |
| N500EP | GLF4 | 1235 |
| N500ER | C550 | 150 |
| N500ES | JSTR | 5075/19 |
| **N500ET** | **C500** | **180** |
| N500EW | FA20 | 21 |
| N500EW | LJ25 | 232 |
| N500EW | LJ31 | 068 |
| N500EX | C550 | 298 |
| (N500EX) | CL60 | 1047 |
| N500EX | GLF3 | 372 |
| N500EX | JSTR | 5217 |
| N500EX | LJ35 | 241 |
| N500EX | LJ35 | 591 |
| **N500FA** | **ASTR** | **011** |
| (N500FA) | LJ55 | 004 |
| N500FA | LJ55 | 092 |
| **N500FB** | **EA50** | **000185** |
| N500FC | HS25 | 257011 |
| N500FD | LJ35 | 241 |
| N500FE | F2EX | 13 |
| N500FE | FA20 | 163 |
| N500FF | FA10 | 58 |
| N500FG | JSTR | 5135 |
| N500FK | C560 | 0047 |
| **N500FM** | **HS25** | **257102** |
| N500FM | LJ24 | 088 |
| N500FM | LJ24 | 111 |
| N500FP | C750 | 0029 |
| **N500FR** | **C650** | **0208** |
| N500FX | C550 | 298 |
| **N500FZ** | **C560** | **0018** |
| N500GA | C500 | 217 |
| N500GA | C500 | 632 |
| N500GA | GALX | 100 |
| N500GB | C500 | 098 |
| N500GD | HS25 | 256018 |

| | | |
|---|---|---|
| N500GE | C500 | 004 |
| **N500GF** | **GLF3** | **488** |
| N500GJ | WW24 | 64 |
| N500GK | WW24 | 301 |
| N500GM | C550 | 074 |
| N500GM | FA10 | 99 |
| N500GM | FA20 | 195 |
| N500GM | LJ35 | 211 |
| N500GP | LJ35 | 241 |
| N500GR | C500 | 098 |
| N500GS | C500 | 004 |
| N500GS | CL61 | 5045 |
| N500GS | FA10 | 132 |
| N500GS | HS25 | 257162 |
| N500GV | GLF5 | 506 |
| N500HC | C525 | 0048 |
| (N500HC) | FA50 | 136 |
| (N500HD) | FA20 | 163 |
| N500HF | HS25 | 258249 |
| N500HG | LJ35 | 238 |
| (N500HG) | LJ55 | 083 |
| N500HH | C500 | 189 |
| N500HK | C500 | 190 |
| N500HK | FA20 | 113 |
| **N500HY** | **BE40** | **RK-153** |
| N500HZ | LJ35 | 238 |
| N500J | GLF2 | 60 |
| **N500J** | **GLF4** | **4052** |
| N500J | HS25 | 258216 |
| N500J | WW24 | 303 |
| N500JA | LJ25 | 007 |
| N500JB | C500 | 185 |
| N500JC | C500 | 430 |
| (N500JC) | LJ55 | 043 |
| N500JD | C500 | 009 |
| N500JD | FA20 | 378 |
| **N500JD** | **FA50** | **84** |
| N500JD | JSTR | 5152 |
| **N500JE** | **LJ31** | **088** |
| N500JK | C500 | 202 |
| N500JR | GLF2 | 34 |
| N500JR | WW24 | 65 |
| N500JS | LJ25 | 020 |
| N500JS | LJ35 | 169 |
| N500JS | LJ35 | 404 |
| N500JW | GLF2 | 14 |
| **N500JW** | **GLF2** | **234** |
| N500JW | LJ24 | 005 |
| N500JW | LJ25 | 054 |
| N500JW | LJ55 | 043 |
| N500K | C500 | 500 |
| N500K | LJ24 | 016 |
| **N500KE** | **WW24** | **360** |
| N500KJ | FA50 | 197 |
| N500KK | LJ35 | 211 |
| N500KP | C500 | 095 |
| N500LD | FA20 | 163 |
| N500LE | C500 | 602 |
| N500LE | C560 | 0052 |
| N500LF | C500 | 007 |
| **N500LG** | **LJ28** | **28-005** |
| N500LH | C500 | 602 |
| (N500LH) | CS55 | 0119 |
| (N500LH) | LJ24 | 088 |
| **N500LJ** | **BE40** | **RK-340** |
| N500LJ | C500 | 195 |
| (N500LL) | HS25 | 258095 |
| N500LL | LJ24 | 347 |
| N500LP | C500 | 251 |
| **N500LR** | **CL61** | **5012** |
| N500LS | CL60 | 1048 |
| N500LS | GLF3 | 460 |
| N500LS | GLF4 | 1009 |
| N500LS | HS25 | 257173 |
| N500LS | WW24 | 137 |
| N500LS | WW24 | 226 |
| N500LW | LJ25 | 232 |
| N500M | ASTR | 018 |
| N500M | ASTR | 091 |
| **N500M** | **CL64** | **5480** |
| N500M | WW24 | 175 |
| N500M | WW24 | 300 |
| N500MA | GLF2 | 119/22 |
| N500MA | HS25 | 25237 |
| N500MA | HS25 | 256064 |
| N500MA | JSTR | 5033/56 |
| **N500MA** | **WW24** | **435** |
| (N500MD) | C500 | 370 |
| N500MD | WW24 | 300 |
| N500MF | WW24 | 34 |
| N500MG | C560 | 0223 |
| **N500MG** | **C560** | **0624** |
| N500MH | LJ24 | 158 |
| N500MJ | LJ25 | 091 |
| N500MJ | LJ35 | 348 |
| N500MJ | LJ36 | 025 |
| **N500ML** | **C500** | **074** |
| N500ML | WW24 | 175 |
| **N500MM** | **EA50** | **000139** |
| N500MM | GLF3 | 460 |
| N500MM | GLF4 | 1135 |
| N500MN | GLF3 | 460 |
| N500MP | LJ25 | 208 |
| **N500MP** | **LJ31** | **198** |
| N500MQ | ASTR | 018 |
| N500MS | LJ24 | 246 |
| N500MX | C500 | 006 |
| N500MZ | ASTR | 091 |
| N500N | C750 | 0239 |
| N500N | FA50 | 323 |
| **N500N** | **GLF4** | **4056** |
| **N500NB** | **C52A** | **0339** |
| (N500NB) | LJ55 | 100 |
| N500ND | LJ35 | 351 |
| **N500NH** | **FA20** | **470** |
| N500NH | LJ24 | 355 |
| N500NH | LJ55 | 100 |
| N500NJ | C500 | 113 |
| N500NL | SBRL | 380-8 |
| N500NM | JSTR | 5229 |
| (N500NU) | FA20 | 21 |
| N500NW | C500 | 660 |
| (N500NX) | C500 | 120 |
| N500P | LJ24 | 077 |
| N500P | LJ24 | 119 |
| N500PB | C500 | 017 |
| N500PB | C500 | 232 |
| N500PC | CL61 | 3003 |
| N500PC | CL61 | 5071 |
| N500PC | FA20 | 19 |
| N500PC | GLF2 | 65 |
| **N500PC** | **GLF4** | **1492** |
| N500PE | CL61 | 3065 |
| N500PE | CL64 | 5440 |
| **N500PG** | **CL61** | **3039** |
| N500PG | JSTR | 5153/61 |
| (N500PJ) | LJ24 | 119 |
| N500PP | LJ24 | 119 |
| N500PP | LJ25 | 121 |
| N500PP | LJ25 | 208 |
| N500PP | LJ25 | 248 |
| N500PP | LJ35 | 390 |
| **N500PP** | **MU30** | **A061SA** |
| N500PR | JSTR | 5204 |
| N500PX | C550 | 191 |
| N500PX | C560 | 0178 |
| N500PX | C560 | 0691 |
| N500PX | C56X | 5017 |
| **N500PX** | **C56X** | **5589** |
| N500PX | FA20 | 19 |
| N500QC | JSTR | 5205 |
| N500QM | C550 | 074 |
| N500R | C500 | 127 |
| N500R | CL60 | 1077 |
| N500R | F2EX | 13 |
| **N500R** | **FA50** | **323** |
| N500R | GLF2 | 12 |
| N500R | HS25 | 256068 |
| N500R | WW24 | 280 |
| **N500RD** | **GLF5** | **5105** |
| N500RE | FA50 | 124 |
| **N500RE** | **FA50** | **156** |
| N500RE | LJ24 | 193 |
| N500RH | CL60 | 1069 |
| N500RH | GLF2 | 80 |
| N500RH | GLF3 | 451 |
| **N500RH** | **GLF5** | **558** |
| "N500RH" | HS25 | 258013 |
| N500RK | LJ24 | 296 |
| N500RK | SBRL | 282-42 |
| (N500RK) | SBRL | 306-64 |
| N500RK | SBRL | 306-85 |
| N500RL | GLF2 | 122 |
| **N500RL** | **GLF4** | **1513** |
| N500RP | C650 | 0187 |
| N500RP | C750 | 0029 |
| **N500RP** | **GLF4** | **4057** |
| N500RP | LJ24 | 193 |
| N500RP | LJ24 | 345 |
| N500RP | LJ35 | 351 |
| N500RP | LJ55 | 053 |
| N500RP | LJ60 | 206 |
| **N500RQ** | **GLF2** | **122** |
| N500RR | C550 | 638 |
| **N500RR** | **FA20** | **491** |
| N500RR | LJ24 | 345 |
| N500RR | SBRL | 306-33 |
| N500RR | SBRL | 465-49 |
| N500RR | WW24 | 359 |
| N500RW | LJ24 | 233 |
| N500RW | LJ35 | 148 |
| N500S | JSTR | 5134/50 |
| N500S | JSTR | 5209 |
| N500SB | LJ24 | 166 |
| N500SJ | C500 | 231 |
| N500SJ | JSTR | 5012 |
| **N500SK** | **C500** | **129** |
| N500SQ | LJ24 | 325 |
| N500SR | LJ24 | 347 |
| **N500SV** | **C52A** | **0153** |
| N500SV | LJ36 | 040 |
| N500SW | LJ24 | 325 |
| **N500SW** | **LJ60** | **017** |
| N500T | GLF2 | 244 |
| N500T | JSTR | 5211 |
| N500TB | CL61 | 3003 |
| (N500TB) | CL61 | 5120 |
| N500TD | C500 | 070 |
| N500TD | CL61 | 3003 |
| N500TF | SBRL | 380-19 |
| **N500TH** | **BE40** | **RK-246** |
| N500TL | C525 | 0281 |
| N500TL | LJ25 | 238 |
| **N500TM** | **C500** | **112** |
| **N500TS** | **C550** | **550-0886** |
| **N500TS** | **FA50** | **179** |
| N500TS | LJ24 | 347 |
| N500TW | C500 | 623 |
| **N500UB** | **C560** | **0052** |
| **N500UJ** | **C560** | **0062** |
| **N500UK** | **EA50** | **000051** |
| N500VA | C550 | 550-0987 |
| N500VB | C550 | 147 |
| **N500VC** | **C560** | **0144** |
| N500VF | WW24 | 115 |
| **N500VH** | **EA50** | **000211** |
| N500VK | C500 | 202 |
| **N500VK** | **EA50** | **000010** |
| N500VM | F9EX | 5 |
| N500VS | GLF3 | 460 |
| N500VS | GLF4 | 1009 |
| **N500VT** | **C550** | **550-0987** |
| **N500WD** | **C52B** | **0267** |
| N500WD | SBRL | 465-48 |
| N500WH | WW24 | 215 |
| N500WJ | C500 | 202 |
| N500WK | WW24 | 196 |
| N500WN | C500 | 404 |
| N500WN | JSTR | 5048 |
| N500WN | JSTR | 5135 |
| N500WP | C500 | 185 |
| N500WP | C550 | 238 |
| N500WR | C500 | 166 |
| **N500WR** | **LJ31** | **038** |
| N500WW | GLF3 | 318 |
| N500WW | LJ25 | 137 |
| N500WZ | JSTR | 5048 |
| (N500XB) | GLF3 | 416 |
| N500XP | BE40 | RK-500 |
| N500XX | C500 | 509 |
| N500XY | C500 | 347 |
| **N500XY** | **HS25** | **25119** |
| N500Y | C500 | 110 |
| N500Y | FA20 | 155 |
| N500YB | HS25 | 25170 |
| (N500YD) | EA50 | 000269 |
| (N500YY) | JSTR | 5211 |
| (N500YY) | LJ24 | 028 |
| N500Z | JSTR | 5008 |
| N500Z | JSTR | 5072/23 |
| N500ZA | LJ24 | 182 |
| **N500ZA** | **LJ24** | **350** |
| **N500ZB** | **CS55** | **0023** |
| N500ZB | HS25 | 257043 |
| N500ZB | JSTR | 5102 |
| N500ZC | C500 | 435 |
| **N500ZH** | **EA50** | **000158** |
| N500ZH | LJ24 | 182 |
| N500ZH | LJ60 | 115 |
| N501AA | C550 | 054 |
| **N501AD** | **C500** | **465** |
| **N501AF** | **C500** | **526** |
| N501AJ | CL64 | 5501 |
| N501AL | JSTR | 5012 |
| N501AR | C500 | 128 |
| N501AS | FA20 | 262 |
| N501AT | C500 | 208 |
| **N501AT** | **C500** | **376** |
| N501BA | C500 | 443 |
| (N501BB) | C500 | 455 |
| **N501BB** | **C500** | **474** |
| **N501BE** | **C500** | **354** |
| (N501BE) | CS55 | 0138 |
| (N501BF) | C500 | 354 |
| N501BG | BE40 | RK-5 |
| N501BG | C500 | 432 |
| N501BK | C500 | 683 |
| N501BL | C550 | 028 |
| N501BP | C500 | 604 |
| **N501BW** | **BE40** | **RK-167** |
| N501BW | C500 | 625 |
| N501BW | WW24 | 335 |
| **N501CB** | **C500** | **423** |
| N501CB | WW24 | 435 |
| N501CC | C500 | 701 |
| **N501CD** | **C500** | **432** |
| N501CE | C500 | 525 |
| **N501CF** | **C500** | **522** |
| N501CG | C500 | 486 |
| **N501CG** | **LJ45** | **040** |
| (N501CJ) | C525 | 0501 |
| N501CM | C500 | 631 |
| **N501CP** | **C500** | **401** |
| (N501CP) | WW24 | 435 |
| N501CR | C500 | 614 |
| **N501CT** | **HS25** | **258512** |
| **N501CV** | **GLF5** | **639** |
| N501CW | C500 | 282 |
| N501CW | C500 | 477 |
| **N501CW** | **C560** | **0050** |
| N501CX | C500 | 432 |
| **N501D** | **C500** | **511** |
| **N501DA** | **C500** | **349** |
| (N501DA) | C500 | 613 |
| (N501DB) | C500 | 362 |
| **N501DB** | **F900** | **196** |
| **N501DD** | **C500** | **404** |
| N501DG | C500 | 578 |
| N501DG+ | C500 | 194 |
| N501DK | C550 | 462 |
| N501DL | C500 | 375 |
| (N501DL) | C500 | 613 |
| (N501DP) | C500 | 531 |
| **N501DP** | **C500** | **552** |
| N501DR | C500 | 270 |
| N501DR | C500 | 342 |
| **N501DR** | **C500** | **532** |
| N501DT | WW24 | 270 |
| **N501DV** | **GALX** | **192** |
| **N501DX** | **EA50** | **000110** |
| N501DY | C500 | 644 |
| **N501DZ** | **C500** | **059** |
| N501E | C500 | 392 |
| N501E | C500 | 412 |
| N501E | C560 | 0231 |
| (N501E) | GLF4 | 1138 |
| **N501EA** | **C500** | **419** |
| N501ED | C500 | 547 |
| N501EF | C500 | 441 |
| N501EG | C500 | 685 |
| **N501EJ** | **C500** | **119** |
| N501EK | C500 | 453 |
| (N501EM) | C500 | 382 |
| N501EM | C500 | 516 |
| N501EZ | C500 | 434 |
| (N501EZ) | C500 | 649 |
| (N501EZ) | MU30 | A069SA |
| N501F | FA20 | 269 |
| (N501F) | HS25 | 257167 |
| N501F | HS25 | 258286 |
| (N501FB) | C500 | 386 |
| (N501FF) | C500 | 165 |

**N501FJ C500 563**
N501FM C500 547
N501FP C500 550
N501FR C500 683
N501FT C500 434
**N501G C500 607**
**N501GB C500 231**
N501GF C500 507
**N501GF HS25 257208**
N501GG C500 532
**N501GG C550 484**
N501GK C500 507
N501GP C500 026
**N501GR C500 358**
N501GR C500 378
N501GS C500 369
(N501GS) C500 468
N501GV GLF5 501
N501GW C500 578
(N501H) HS25 256020
N501HC C500 508
N501HD C500 650
**N501HG C500 643**
(N501HH) C500 679
N501HK C500 292
N501HM C500 615
N501HP C500 573
**N501HS C500 480**
N501J JSTR 5213
N501JC C500 252
**N501JD C500 512**
**N501JE C500 670**
**N501JF C500 343**
N501JF C500 382
N501JG C500 150
**N501JG C500 409**
**N501JJ C500 368**
**N501JM C500 635**
N501JP C500 477
N501JP C550 730
**N501JS C560 0066**
N501JT ASTR 050
**N501JT GLEX 9265**
**N501JV GLF2 168**
N501KB C500 446
N501KC C550 030
**N501KC FA20 401**
**N501KE C52A 0430**
N501KG C500 001
N501KG C500 279
**N501KK C500 588**
**N501KM C500 468**
N501KR C500 446
**N501KR C525 0033**
N501LB C500 165
**N501LC C550 161**
N501LE C500 671
(N501LG) C500 294
**N501LH C500 342**
N501LL C500 561
N501LM C500 673
**N501LR HS25 259025**
N501LS C500 482
N501LW C500 516
**N501MB C500 508**
N501MC C550 500
N501MD C500 382
(N501MD) C500 508
N501MD FA20 284
(N501MD) HS25 257121
N501MG C500 535
N501MH LJ24 314
**N501MK F9EX 108**
N501MM C500 601
N501MM HS25 257079
N501MR C500 661
N501MS C500 674
N501MT C500 675
N501NA C500 459
N501NB CS55 0018
N501NC C500 578
N501NC FA50 11
(N501NP) C500 518
N501NZ C500 459
N501PC C500 005
N501PC CL61 3004
N501PC CL61 3023
**N501PC CL64 5551**
N501PC FA50 265
N501PC GLF4 1298
N501PS LJ25 153
**N501PV C500 394**
**N501Q C500 653**
N501QS C560 0024
N501R HS25 256068
N501RB C500 132
**N501RC C500 557**
N501RF C500 671
**N501RG C500 632**
N501RG C500 666
N501RL C500 292
N501RL C500 311
**N501RL C550 601**
N501RM C500 001
N501RM C500 465
**N501RP ASTR 209**
N501RP LJ55 053
N501RS C500 479
**N501RS LJ31 223**
N501SC C500 265
N501SC C500 314
**N501SE C500 010**
N501SE C500 249
N501SE C500 474
(N501SF) C500 426
N501SJ C500 423
N501SJ C500 474
(N501SK) C500 388
(N501SK) C500 459
N501SP C500 383
N501SR C500 446
N501SS C500 282
**N501SS C500 455**
**N501ST C500 374**
**N501T C500 650**
N501T C560 0136
N501T GLF2 248
N501T JSTR 5213
N501TB C500 685
**N501TJ C500 372**
N501TK C500 210
**N501TL C500 207**
**N501TP C500 684**
N501TW LJ35 612
N501TW LJ55 101
**N501U C500 408**
N501U WW24 381
N501VC C500 575
N501VH C500 044
N501VP C500 352
N501W HS25 25136
**N501WB C500 556**
**N501WD C500 666**
N501WJ C500 353
**N501WJ C500 535**
(N501WK) C500 353
(N501WL) C500 186
**N501WL C500 519**
N501WW C500 044
**N501WX C500 660**
N501X C500 478
**N501X C500 661**
N501XL C56X 5209
N501XP BE40 RK-501
N501XP HS25 258701
**N501ZK GLF5 5001**
N502AL C550 029
(N502BA) C500 288
**N502BC C56X 5098**
N502BE C500 195
N502BG C550 297
N502BG FA10 144
**N502BG FA20 388**
N502BG WW24 372
(N502BH) EA50 000280
**N502CA BE40 RK-525**
N502CC C500 001
N502CC C500 008
**N502CC C500 502**
**N502CL C550 014**
**N502E C560 0232**
(N502EA) EA50 EX500-101
N502EA EA50 EX500-103
**N502EG C56X 5502**
**N502ET EA50 000052**
N502EZ FA50 25
N502F C560 0153
N502F CL61 5111
N502F FA20 481
N502G LJ35 219
**N502GF HS25 257210**
**N502GM GLF4 4011**
N502GP C500 027
N502GV GLF5 502
**N502HE CL61 5111**
N502HR HS25 258502
N502JB FA50 115
N502JC LJ25 264
**N502JF LJ35 490**
**N502JL GLEX 9050**
N502JM LJ40 45-2017
**N502JT GLF4 1212**
**N502KA GLF5 502**
**N502LT EA50 000027**
N502MH LJ25 098
N502N BE40 RK-386
N502PC CL61 5121
N502PC GLF2 170
**N502PC GLF4 1435**
**N502PG FA10 144**
**N502PM PRM1 RB-185**
**N502QS GLF5 601**
(N502R) HS25 257159
N502RB LJ60 199
N502RD C500 043
**N502RG GLF2 178**
N502RL C500 043
**N502RP ASTR 212**
N502RP LJ60 199
N502RR SBRL 282-13
N502S HS25 257206
N502SU C550 621
N502T C560 0153
N502T C650 7067
N502TF CL64 5502
**N502TN C525 0505**
N502TS C560 0157
**N502TS EA50 000097**
N502U WW24 48
N502XL C56X 5502
N502XL C56X 6002
N502XP BE40 RK-502
**N503BC LJ60 239**
**N503CC C500 003**
**N503CS C56X 5205**
**N503EA EA50 EX500-108**
N503EB BE40 RJ-29
N503EZ FA50 84
(N503F) C560 0154
N503F FA20 391
N503GP C500 086
N503GV GLF5 503
**N503LC C52B 0162**
(N503LR) HS25 259003
N503PC CL61 3021
**N503PC CL64 5503**
N503PC FA50 263
N503PC GLF4 1323
**N503PQ FA50 263**
N503QS HS25 259003
**N503RE LJ60 227**
(N503RH) WW24 260
(N503RJ) HS25 258218
**N503RP ASTR 215**
N503RP LJ35 070
N503RP LJ60 227
N503RV FA20 161
N503T C560 0154
N503U WW24 83
N503XS C56X 5503
N504BM C56X 5004
N504BW C560 0128
N504CC C500 004
**N504CC C560 0504**
(N504CL) FA20 504
N504CS C56X 5229
**N504CX FA50 81**
**N504D C500 484**
N504DM BE40 RJ-4
**N504EA EA50 EX500-109**
N504EX JSTR 5217
N504F LJ35 340
**N504FJ FA20 504**
N504GP C500 265
N504GV GLF5 504
N504JC WW24 277
**N504LV C56X 5369**
N504M CL61 5099
**N504MK FA50 205**
**N504MS FA50 301**
N504PA FA50 94
N504PK C56X 5369
N504QS GLF5 613
**N504RP C650 0176**
**N504RS EA50 000005**
N504SU C750 0024
**N504T C650 7040**
**N504TC EA50 000141**
N504TF GLF2 8
N504TS CL61 5004
N504U WW24 325
N504VP C56X 5004
N504Y LJ35 282
**N504YP FA50 170**
**N505AG C550 550-0905**
**N505AJ FA20 89**
N505AM C500 340
N505AX GLF5 505
**N505AZ C500 188**
(N505BB) C500 455
**N505BB C500 671**
N505BC C500 367
N505BC WW24 278
N505BG C500 430
**N505BG C500 561**
N505BX CL30 20006
N505C JSTR 5040
N505C JSTR 5113/25
N505CC C500 005
N505CC C500 638
N505CC CS55 0115
**N505CF C500 517**
**N505CL FA50 38**
**N505CS C56X 5252**
N505DH LJ35 504
**N505EA EA50 EX500-106**
N505EB BE40 RK-17
N505EE LJ35 505
**N505EH LJ55 067**
**N505FX CL30 20006**
**N505GA GALX 005**
**N505GF GLF4 1275**
N505GL C550 495
N505GP C500 272
N505GP C550 279
N505GV GLF5 505
**N505HG LJ36 009**
N505JC C500 341
N505JD CL64 5505
**N505JH C500 505**
N505JT GLF2 46
N505K C500 004
**N505LR HS25 259005**
N505M CL61 5100
N505MA C750 0057
N505PA HS25 25022
N505PF LJ24 006
**N505PM CL60 1051**
N505QS HS25 259005
N505RA LJ36 009
**N505RJ C500 367**
**N505RP C550 450**
**N505RR F2TH 46**
N505RX GLF2 219/20
N505RX GLF5 675
N505SP C500 505
N505T JSTR 5015
**N505TC FA50 57**
N505U WW24 196
N505VS GLF4 1414
N505W HS25 25136
N505W HS25 256013
N505X C550 550-0865
**N505XP BE40 RK-505**
N506AM C56X 5106
N506BA CL61 5060
**N506BA F900 160**
N506BA FA50 230
N506C LJ35 094
N506CC C500 006
**N506CS C56X 5267**
N506D JSTR 5061/48

| | | |
|---|---|---|
| N506E | C560 | 0236 |
| **N506EA** | **EA50** | **EX500-107** |
| N506FX | CL30 | 20007 |
| N506GP | LJ35 | 109 |
| N506GV | GLF5 | 506 |
| **N506KS** | **LJ40** | **45-2055** |
| N506MX | C500 | 006 |
| N506N | HS25 | 25136 |
| **N506QS** | **GLF5** | **623** |
| N506SR | C500 | 006 |
| N506T | GLF3 | 484 |
| N506T | JSTR | 5061/48 |
| N506TF | C500 | 006 |
| **N506TF** | **C500** | **351** |
| N506TN | CL61 | 5066 |
| **N506TS** | **CL61** | **5006** |
| N506U | WW24 | 354 |
| N507AB | C550 | 030 |
| N507AS | FA50 | 311 |
| N507BW | HS25 | 258507 |
| **N507BX** | **CL30** | **20008** |
| N507CC | C500 | 007 |
| N507CC | CL60 | 1026 |
| (N507CC) | CS55 | 0002 |
| N507CJ | CS55 | 0002 |
| **N507CR** | **C560** | **0791** |
| N507CS | C56X | 5282 |
| N507CW | MU30 | A007SA |
| N507DM | BE40 | RJ-7 |
| N507DS | C500 | 403 |
| N507EC | C550 | 158 |
| N507F | HS25 | 257177 |
| **N507FG** | **LJ45** | **326** |
| N507FX | CL30 | 20008 |
| N507GA | GLF5 | 507 |
| N507GP | C550 | 294 |
| **N507HB** | **BE40** | **RK-507** |
| N507HC | CL60 | 1026 |
| N507HF | LJ25 | 057 |
| **N507HP** | **C525** | **0395** |
| N507JC | GLF2 | 121 |
| **N507PD** | **C560** | **0596** |
| **N507QS** | **GLF5** | **625** |
| N507R | CL60 | 1077 |
| **N507SA** | **GLF4** | **1456** |
| (N507TE) | GLF4 | 1383 |
| N507TF | SBRL | 306-39 |
| N507U | SBRL | 306-93 |
| N507VP | C56X | 5070 |
| N507WM | BE40 | RK-507 |
| (N507WY) | CL60 | 1026 |
| N508AF | FA50 | 170 |
| (N508AJ) | C550 | 620 |
| N508BP | HS25 | 258419 |
| N508CC | C500 | 008 |
| (N508CC) | C500 | 208 |
| N508CC | CL60 | 1057 |
| N508CJ | C525 | 0508 |
| **N508CP** | **EA50** | **000196** |
| **N508CS** | **C56X** | **5294** |
| N508CV | C550 | 186 |
| N508DM | BE40 | RJ-3 |
| N508DW | C550 | 620 |
| (N508DW) | C560 | 0245 |
| N508EJ | FA50 | 8 |
| N508FX | CL30 | 20009 |
| N508GA | GALX | 108 |
| N508GA | GLF4 | 1508 |
| N508GA | GLF5 | 508 |
| **N508GA** | **GLF5** | **5280** |
| N508GP | LJ35 | 424 |
| N508HC | CL60 | 1057 |
| N508J | LJ31 | 088 |
| **N508JA** | **EA50** | **000001** |
| (N508JM) | GLF4 | 1184 |
| **N508KD** | **C560** | **0147** |
| N508KD | C560 | 0245 |
| (N508L) | FA20 | 359/542 |
| N508M | LJ24 | 025 |
| N508MM | HS25 | 258055 |
| **N508MV** | **C56X** | **6006** |
| **N508P** | **GLF5** | **693** |
| N508P | LJ35 | 390 |
| N508PB | C500 | 017 |
| **N508PC** | **CL64** | **5558** |
| N508PC | F9EX | 111 |
| **N508QS** | **GLF5** | **631** |
| N508R | WW24 | 280 |
| **N508RN** | **PRM1** | **RB-156** |
| N508S | C500 | 192 |
| **N508SR** | **LJ24** | **347** |
| N508T | GLF2 | 232 |
| N508T | JSTR | 5119/29 |
| N508TA | JSTR | 5119/29 |
| (N508TC) | FA20 | 408 |
| N508TF | LJ35 | 508 |
| N508TL | C525 | 0281 |
| **N508VM** | **HS25** | **256045** |
| N509 | HS25 | 257111 |
| N509AB | SBRL | 306-75 |
| N509CC | C500 | 009 |
| N509CC | CS55 | 0109 |
| **N509CS** | **C56X** | **5310** |
| N509DM | C510 | 0191 |
| N509FX | CL30 | 20012 |
| N509G | LJ25 | 054 |
| N509GA | GLF4 | 1509 |
| N509GA | GLF5 | 509 |
| N509GA | GLF5 | 5229 |
| **N509GE** | **CL64** | **5573** |
| N509GP | HS25 | 258077 |
| N509GV | GLF5 | 509 |
| N509J | JSTR | 5222 |
| **N509JA** | **EA50** | **000084** |
| N509P | C500 | 446 |
| (N509PC) | CL61 | 3002 |
| N509PC | CL61 | 3004 |
| N509QC | HS25 | 257111 |
| **N509QS** | **GLF5** | **637** |
| "N509SM" | HS25 | 257002 |
| N509T | GLF2 | 244 |
| N509T | JSTR | 5222 |
| N509TC | C550 | 462 |
| N509TC | FA10 | 134 |
| (N509TF) | JSTR | 5222 |
| (N509TS) | CL64 | 5309 |
| N509TT | GLF2 | 244 |
| N509W | CL61 | 5099 |
| N509WP | FA20 | 369 |
| N509XP | HS25 | 258509 |
| N510 | CL61 | 5100 |
| N510AA | SBRL | 380-4 |
| N510AJ | C500 | 395 |
| N510AK | GLF4 | 4186 |
| **N510AZ** | **C510** | **0124** |
| **N510BA** | **C510** | **0143** |
| N510BA | HS25 | 258331 |
| N510BB | SBRL | 380-9 |
| **N510BC** | **MU30** | **A057SA** |
| **N510BD** | **C510** | **0249** |
| N510BG | C560 | 0615 |
| N510BM | FA20 | 215 |
| **N510BW** | **C510** | **0098** |
| (N510CC) | C500 | 001 |
| N510CC | C500 | 010 |
| N510CC | C500 | 310 |
| N510CE | C510 | 0001 |
| **N510CJ** | **C510** | **0173** |
| **N510CL** | **FA10** | **9** |
| N510CP | FA10 | 43 |
| **N510DH** | **C510** | **0208** |
| **N510DP** | **C510** | **0220** |
| **N510DT** | **C510** | **0299** |
| **N510EE** | **C510** | **0275** |
| **N510EG** | **C510** | **0246** |
| N510FF | C510 | 0007 |
| N510FX | CL30 | 20017 |
| N510G | GLF2 | 85 |
| N510GA | ASTR | 210 |
| N510GA | C500 | 625 |
| N510GA | GALX | 110 |
| N510GA | GALX | 210 |
| N510GA | GLF4 | 1510 |
| **N510GG** | **C510** | **0168** |
| N510GH | C510 | 0036 |
| **N510GJ** | **C510** | **0083** |
| **N510GP** | **C550** | **420** |
| **N510GT** | **WW24** | **190** |
| **N510HF** | **C56X** | **5331** |
| N510HS | HS25 | 257034 |
| **N510HW** | **C510** | **0290** |
| (N510JA) | EA50 | 000277 |
| **N510JC** | **C550** | **220** |
| **N510JH** | **C510** | **0051** |
| **N510JL** | **C510** | **0250** |
| **N510K** | **C510** | **0121** |
| N510K | C510 | 0172 |
| **N510KB** | **C510** | **0155** |
| N510KM | C510 | 0323 |
| N510KS | C510 | 0002 |
| **N510KZ** | **C510** | **0251** |
| (N510L) | LJ25 | 280 |
| **N510LF** | **C510** | **0159** |
| N510LF | FA20 | 510 |
| N510LJ | LJ35 | 025 |
| **N510LL** | **C510** | **0074** |
| **N510MB** | **C510** | **0118** |
| **N510MD** | **C510** | **0202** |
| **N510MG** | **GLF4** | **1349** |
| N510MS | LJ24 | 204 |
| N510MT | C560 | 0122 |
| **N510MW** | **C510** | **0109** |
| N510ND | C510 | 0001 |
| N510ND | LJ24 | 204 |
| N510NJ | C500 | 593 |
| N510PA | LJ24 | 305 |
| N510PC | CL60 | 1011 |
| **N510PS** | **C510** | **0171** |
| N510PS | CL60 | 1011 |
| **N510PT** | **C510** | **0114** |
| N510QS | GLF5 | 642 |
| N510RC | C500 | 282 |
| **N510RC** | **C52B** | **0325** |
| N510RH | GLF2 | 80 |
| **N510RR** | **F2TH** | **137** |
| **N510SA** | **C510** | **0094** |
| **N510SD** | **C650** | **0161** |
| N510SE | GLF2 | 70/1 |
| N510SG | LJ35 | 268 |
| (N510SG) | LJ60 | 062 |
| N510SJ | C500 | 668 |
| N510SR | GLF2 | 70/1 |
| **N510SR** | **GLF4** | **1183** |
| N510ST | GLF4 | 1183 |
| **N510SV** | **C510** | **0154** |
| N510T | GLF2 | 248 |
| N510TA | SBRL | 265-10 |
| N510TB | SBRL | 265-86 |
| N510TC | SBRL | 276-27 |
| N510TD | SBRL | 265-15 |
| N510TL | GLF2 | 248 |
| N510TP | LJ25 | 353 |
| N510TS | JSTR | 5100/41 |
| **N510TW** | **C510** | **0240** |
| **N510TX** | **C510** | **0131** |
| N510US | GLF2 | 223 |
| N510VP | C550 | 710 |
| **N510VV** | **C510** | **0014** |
| **N510WC** | **C510** | **0017** |
| **N510WP** | **C510** | **0172** |
| N510WS | BE40 | RJ-24 |
| N510WS | FA20 | 292 |
| N510X | HS25 | 25126 |
| N510XL | C56X | 5100 |
| N510XP | BE40 | RK-510 |
| **N511AB** | **C550** | **328** |
| **N511AC** | **C525** | **0098** |
| N511AJ | LJ25 | 055 |
| N511AT | C500 | 166 |
| N511AT | LJ24 | 330 |
| **N511BA** | **GLF2** | **49** |
| N511BB | CS55 | 0083 |
| **N511BP** | **C525** | **0332** |
| N511BR | CS55 | 0083 |
| N511BX | HS25 | 25150 |
| N511C | GLF4 | 1065 |
| N511CC | C500 | 011 |
| N511CC | WW24 | 253 |
| N511CC | WW24 | 367 |
| (N511CL) | LJ60 | 094 |
| N511CQ | WW24 | 253 |
| **N511CS** | **C56X** | **5324** |
| **N511CT** | **ASTR** | **234** |
| N511DB | LJ28 | 28-002 |
| **N511DD** | **CL61** | **5187** |
| N511DL | C550 | 228 |
| N511DN | C56X | 5231 |
| (N511DP) | C560 | 0274 |
| N511DR | C550 | 228 |
| N511DR | C560 | 0274 |
| **N511ED** | **EA50** | **000262** |
| **N511FL** | **FA20** | **122** |
| N511FX | CL30 | 20021 |
| N511GA | GLF5 | 511 |
| N511GG | FA50 | 82 |
| N511GP | HS25 | 257052 |
| N511HA | C550 | 550-1039 |
| **N511HC** | **C500** | **520** |
| N511JF | BE40 | RK-34 |
| N511JP | BE40 | RK-219 |
| N511JP | BE40 | RK-34 |
| N511JP | C550 | 550-0959 |
| **N511KA** | **HS25** | **257052** |
| **N511LD** | **HS25** | **257188** |
| N511NC | SBRL | 465-6 |
| N511PA | GLF2 | 49 |
| **N511PA** | **GLF4** | **1111** |
| **N511QS** | **GLF5** | **647** |
| N511RG | HS25 | 257206 |
| N511S | FA10 | 115 |
| N511S | FA20 | 96 |
| N511SC | CL64 | 5510 |
| N511ST | C560 | 0281 |
| N511T | FA20 | 142 |
| N511TA | FA20 | 142 |
| **N511TC** | **C525** | **0074** |
| N511TD | JSTR | 5145 |
| **N511TH** | **C560** | **0561** |
| N511TS | JSTR | 5101/15 |
| **N511VB** | **BE40** | **RK-91** |
| N511WA | ASTR | 034 |
| N511WC | C550 | 189 |
| N511WD | HS25 | 258196 |
| N511WH | LJ24 | 055 |
| **N511WK** | **E50P** | **50000103** |
| N511WM | CL61 | 5134 |
| N511WM | F900 | 108 |
| N511WM | HS25 | 25159 |
| N511WM | HS25 | 258196 |
| N511WN | CL61 | 5134 |
| N511WN | HS25 | 25159 |
| N511WP | FA20 | 341 |
| N511WP | GLF2 | 185 |
| N511WP | HS25 | 25174 |
| N511WP | LJ45 | 183 |
| N511WR | FA20 | 341 |
| N511WS | C550 | 439 |
| **N511WV** | **C560** | **0138** |
| N511XP | BE40 | RK-511 |
| N511YP | HS25 | 25191 |
| (N512AC) | CL60 | 1073 |
| N512BC | CL61 | 5125 |
| N512C | GLF4 | 1428 |
| **N512CC** | **C500** | **012** |
| N512CC | C500 | 112 |
| N512CC | WW24 | 354 |
| **N512CS** | **C56X** | **5326** |
| N512DG | CL61 | 5157 |
| N512DR | C56X | 5179 |
| N512F | BE40 | RK-115 |
| **N512FX** | **CL30** | **20022** |
| N512GA | GLF4 | 1512 |
| N512GA | GLF5 | 5212 |
| N512GP | HS25 | 257182 |
| N512GV | GLF5 | 512 |
| (N512HR) | HS25 | 259012 |
| **N512JB** | **FA50** | **202** |
| N512JT | GLF2 | 101 |
| **N512JT** | **GLF4** | **4005** |
| N512JY | F900 | 144 |
| N512LR | HS25 | 259012 |
| **N512MB** | **EA50** | **000175** |
| (N512MT) | C650 | 0232 |
| N512QS | HS25 | 259012 |
| N512RB | LJ45 | 062 |
| **N512RJ** | **GLF4** | **4124** |
| N512SD | GLF2 | 130 |
| N512SH | CL64 | 5512 |
| N512T | FA20 | 118 |
| **N512TB** | **C52A** | **0084** |
| N512VB | GLF2 | 189/42 |
| N512WP | BE40 | RJ-16 |
| N512WS | BE40 | RJ-24 |
| **N513AC** | **FA20** | **242** |
| N513AG | FA20 | 64 |
| N513AN | FA20 | 64 |
| N513CC | C500 | 013 |
| N513CC | C500 | 513 |
| N513CC | C550 | 013 |
| **N513EA** | **EA50** | **000009** |
| N513EF | C560 | 0412 |
| N513FX | CL30 | 20023 |

N513GA GLF5 513
N513GP HS25 257072
**N513HS F9EX 175**
**N513LR HS25 259013**
**N513ML HS25 258641**
N513MW GLF5 510
N513QS HS25 259013
(N513RA) HS25 259013
**N513RV C525 0513**
N513SK C52A 0064
**N513SK C56X 5678**
N513T FA20 123
N513VP C56X 5132
**N513XP BE40 RK-513**
**N514AF E50P 50000039**
**N514AJ HS25 256033**
N514B HS25 257071
**N514BC C550 550-0947**
N514CC C500 014
**N514CS C56X 5328**
**N514DS C525 0255**
**N514EA EA50 000053**
N514FX CL30 20023
N514GA GLF5 514
N514HB HA4T RC-14
N514JJ FA20 168
**N514LR HS25 259014**
**N514MB FA50 168**
N514MH HS25 256033
**N514MM ASTR 115**
N514QS HS25 259014
N514RB CL61 5015
N514RV C525 0514
N514SA FA20 30
N514T FA20 130
**N514TS CL61 5014**
N514V HS25 25134
N514V HS25 256023
N514VA HS25 25134
N514XP BE40 RK-514
N515AA C500 085
N515AJ JSTR 5078/3
**N515BP CL60 1006**
N515CC C500 015
(N515CC) C500 502
**N515CS C56X 5335**
N515DB FA20 510
N515DC C500 112
N515DJ LJ55 015
N515DM CL64 5515
**N515EV C52A 0211**
(N515FX) CL30 20024
**N515FX CL30 20032**
N515GP HS25 258289
N515HB HA4T RC-15
N515JT GLF2 135
(N515JT) GLF2 189/42
N515KA GLF2 166/15
**N515KK MU30 A086SA**
N515LG WW24 193
**N515LP FA10 87**
**N515LR HS25 259015**
(N515M) C550 433
**N515MP EA50 000015**
N515MW BE40 RK-38
N515PE GLF4 1092
N515PL GLF4 1092
**N515PL GLF5 5144**
**N515PV F2TH 192**
N515QS HS25 259015
**N515RW C560 0219**
**N515RY BE40 RK-46**
N515SC LJ25 152
N515TB C680 0148
**N515TC LJ25 354**
**N515TJ BE40 RK-229**
N515TK F2TH 102
N515UJ GLF4 1051
N515VC C650 0055
**N515VP C560 0315**
N515VW LJ25 013
**N515WA BE40 RK-215**
N515WC LJ24 203
N515WE C500 208
N515WH LJ25 142
N515XL GLF4 1276
N516AB C500 244
N516AC WW24 187
N516CC C500 016
**N516CC GALX 020**
N516CC WW24 394
N516DG CL64 5516
N516DM JSTR 5158
**N516EA EA50 000106**
**N516FX CL30 20036**
N516GA GLF4 1516
N516GA GLF5 516
N516GA GLF5 5216
**N516GH GLF5 553**
N516GP HS25 258316
N516LW SBRL 282-98
**N516QS GLF5 658**
N516SM C650 0157
N516SM CL61 5089
N516SM FA10 167
**N516TH HS25 258418**
(N516TM) HS25 258418
N516TR GLF3 252
**N516VE GLF4 4116**
N516WC JSTR 5150/37
N516WP SBRL 282-98
N517A C500 375
**N517AF C550 550-0846**
N517AM LJ55 108
N517BA C500 400
N517CC C500 017
**N517CC LJ31 117**
N517CS C56X 5346
N517CW FA50 17
**N517FX CL30 20038**
N517GA GLF4 1517
N517GA GLF5 517
N517GA GLF5 5217
**N517GP LJ31 152**
**N517LR HS25 259017**
**N517MD BE40 RK-459**
N517MT C650 0232
N517PJ F2TH 94
**N517QS GLF5 5209**
N517QS HS25 259017
N517RH CL64 5517
**N517TT GLEX 9046**
N517XL C56X 5017
N517XP BE40 RK-517
(N518AS) CS55 0013
N518BA HS25 258075
N518CC C500 018
N518CC C500 318
**N518CL CL61 5180**
N518CS C56X 5354
N518EJ FA50 18
(N518FE) GLF2 135
(N518FS) CL60 1033
**N518FX CL30 20046**
N518GA GLF5 5018
N518GA GLF5 518
N518GA GLF5 5218
**N518GS CL30 20132**
N518GS GLF2 130
N518GS LJ45 225
N518JC LJ31 208
N518JG LJ25 328
N518JG LJ31 208
**N518JG LJ31 219**
N518JT GLF2 135
N518L JSTR 5040
**N518M HS25 258737**
**N518MV C550 267**
**N518N C550 563**
**N518PR LJ35 497**
**N518QS GLF5 5075**
N518RJ* FA10 139
**N518RR HS25 257108**
N518S FA10 74
N518S HS25 257202
**N518S HS25 258074**
N518SA LJ31 076
N518SA LJ55 139A
**N518SB LJ55 139A**
**N518WA WW24 223**
N518XP BE40 RK-518
**N519AA C550 053**
(N519AC) LJ55 013
N519AF GLF3 393
N519BA HS25 258069
N519CC C500 019
N519CJ CS55 0019
N519CS C56X 5356
N519CW FA50 19
N519DB CL61 5119
**N519EJ EA50 000019**
**N519EM FA50 19**
**N519FX CL30 20055**
N519GA GLF4 1519
N519GA GLF5 5119
N519L JSTR 5037/24
**N519M HS25 258747**
N519ME WW24 207
N519MZ CL64 5519
(N519QS) GLF5 681
**N519RW BE40 RK-3**
(N519TW) GLF2 106
**N520AF FA50 247**
**N520AW FA20 453**
N520BA HS25 258070
N520BA HS25 258317
N520BE C510 0243
**N520BE C510 0284**
N520BH C500 535
N520CC C500 020
N520CC C500 200
**N520CH ASTR 269**
N520CH BE40 RK-162
N520CH PRM1 RB-121
**N520CJ C525 0520**
N520CM C750 0107
N520CV C560 0020
**N520DB MS76 101**
**N520DF C525 0154**
**N520E GLEX 9077**
N520E GLF4 1138
N520EP GLF4 1138
N520FD FA20 55/410
**N520FX CL30 20056**
N520G C560 0369
N520G C56X 5083
**N520G C680 0243**
N520GA GLF4 1500
N520GA GLF4 1520
N520GA GLF5 5220
N520GA GLF5 650
**N520GB C525 0388**
**N520JF HS25 258317**
**N520JM C510 0179**
N520JM C52A 0086
N520JR CL64 5520
**N520KC C510 0223**
**N520LR HS25 259020**
N520M HS25 25070
N520M HS25 257131
N520M JSTR 5159
**N520MP WW24 421**
N520N C500 205
N520PA LJ35 037
**N520Q C56X 5083**
N520QS HS25 259020
N520RB C500 282
**N520RM C525 0469**
N520RP C500 607
N520RP CS55 0115
N520S JSTR 5084/8
N520S LJ60 233
N520S SBRL 282-8
(N520SC) C500 208
N520SC LJ55 087
**N520SC LJ60 233**
N520SP HS25 258669
N520SQ LJ55 087
N520SR LJ25 272
N520TJ FA20 198/466
N520TT MU30 A033SA
**N520WS BE40 RJ-53**
N521BA HS25 258071
N521BH C550 727
N521BH C650 0185
N521CC C500 021
N521CD F2EX 21
N521CH LJ31 220
**N521CH LJ40 45-2023**
N521CJ C525 0521
**N521CS C56X 5362**
N521CV C560 0521
**N521DC FA50 163**
**N521FL FA20 68**
**N521FP C750 0016**
**N521FX CL30 20057**
N521GA GLF5 521
**N521HN GLF5 570**
**N521JK HS25 258262**
N521JP LJ25 302
N521JP LJ25 330
(N521JW) LJ36 043
**N521LF C560 0132**
**N521LL C560 0273**
N521M HS25 25129
(N521MJ) LJ31 098
N521N SBRL 306-1
N521NC SBRL 306-109
N521PA LJ35 239
**N521PF C525 0005**
**N521RA C56X 5076**
N521RF CL64 5521
**N521TM C550 705**
**N521VP C560 0312**
N521WH LJ31 220
N521WM C550 093
**N521XP BE40 RK-521**
N522AC F900 148
N522AC GLF4 1108
**N522AC GLF4 1524**
N522AG JSTR 5219
(N522AG) LJ35 625
N522BA HS25 258072
**N522BD F2EX 84**
N522BP GLF4 1451
**N522BP GLF5 5135**
N522BR GLF4 1451
N522BW HS25 25043
N522C FA20 495
N522C HS25 256067
N522CC C500 022
N522CC C500 522
N522CC C550 002
N522CC C56X 5111
N522CC C680 0027
**N522CS C56X 5364**
N522DD FA20 74
**N522DK EA50 000105**
**N522EA EA50 000263**
N522EE BE40 RK-342
N522EE BE40 RK-38
N522EE HS25 258621
**N522EE HS25 258764**
N522EF BE40 RK-38
**N522EF HS25 258621**
**N522EL BE40 RK-342**
N522FJ C550 619
N522FP CL64 5522
**N522FX CL30 20064**
N522GA GLF4 1522
N522GA GLF5 5122
N522GA GLF5 635
(N522GS) C650 0025
N522GS FA50 115
N522GS LJ25 348
**N522JA C560 0288**
N522JD C500 022
N522JP LJ25 318
N522JS LJ25 348
(N522KJ) BE40 RK-22
N522KM F900 78
N522KN C52A 0156
N522M HS25 25156
N522M HS25 257144
**N522MB BE40 RK-522**
N522ME HS25 25043
N522N SBRL 306-109
N522PA LJ35 254
(N522QS) GLF5 5011
N522RA C56X 5136
N522SB GLF3 339
N522SC LJ25 006
N522TA LJ25 318
N522WK LJ55 088
N522X HS25 256067
N522XL C56X 5022
N522XP BE40 RK-522
N523AC F900 139
N523AC GLF4 1528
N523AC JSTR 5013
N523AC WW24 77
(N523AG) F900 139

**N523AM GLF3 372**
N523AS C525 0092
N523B CL60 1071
N523BA HS25 258077
N523BT C525 0311
**N523BT C52A 0124**
N523CC C500 023
N523CC C500 123
N523CC C500 323
N523CC C56X 5201
N523CL CL64 5523
**N523CS C56X 5507**
N523CW FA50 23
N523DG C52A 0084
**N523DR PRM1 RB-50**
**N523FX CL30 20074**
N523GA GLF5 5123
N523GA GLF5 523
N523GA GLF5 5253
N523GA GLF5 643
N523JD C500 023
**N523JM CL61 5106**
(N523JP) LJ25 330
N523KW C560 0224
**N523KW C56X 5015**
**N523LR HS25 259023**
N523M HS25 25245
N523M HS25 257188
N523MA HS25 256023
N523N SBRL 306-7
N523NA FA20 439
N523PA LJ35 247
**N523PB FA50 23**
(N523PT) GLF3 336
N523QS HS25 259023
N523RB WW24 175
N523SA LJ25 325
**N523TS C525 0363**
(N523TX) GLF3 336
N523VP C560 0423
N523W F2TH 212
(N523W) HS25 258086
**N523WC F2TH 212**
N523WC HS25 258086
**N523WG HS25 258086**
N523XP BE40 RK-523
**N524AC GLF5 686**
N524AC JSTR 5004
N524AC JSTR 5149/11
N524AC SBRL 282-28
N524AF C525 0199
N524AG SBRL 282-28
**N524AN GLF4 1119**
N524BA HS25 258080
N524CA C500 024
N524CC C500 024
N524CJ C525 0524
(N524DW) LJ24 177
**N524DW LJ25 081**
**N524FX CL30 20095**
N524GA GLF4 1524
N524GA GLF5 5124
N524GA GLF5 524
N524GA GLF5 646
**N524HC LJ31 114**
N524HC LJ35 358
N524LP BE40 RK-386
N524LR HS25 259024
N524M HS25 257204
**N524MA C550 029**
N524MM GLF2 85
**N524PA LJ35 033**
N524PC CL61 3023
N524QS HS25 259024
N524RH WW24 414
**N524S FA50 51**
N524SA F2TH 60
N524SC LJ24 153
**N524SF C525 0240**
N524X WW24 92
N524XP BE40 RK-524
N525AC C500 343
**N525AC GLF5 691**
N525AC LJ31 030
N525AD C525 0435
N525AD C525 0600
N525AE C525 0017
**N525AG GALX 226**
N525AJ C525 0040
(N525AJ) C525 0395
N525AJ C525 0671
**N525AJ C525 0673**
N525AJ WW24 325
**N525AK WW24 260**
**N525AL C525 0011**
**N525AM C525 0538**
N525AP C525 0045
**N525AP C52A 0460**
N525AR C525 0395
N525AS C525 0092
N525AS C525 0363
N525AW WW24 129
N525AZ C52A 0001
(N525BA) C525 0522
N525BA C560 0417
N525BA HS25 258081
N525BE C525 0299
(N525BE) C525 0306
N525BF C525 0191
(N525BL) C525 0191
**N525BP C525 0479**
**N525BR C525 0444**
**N525BT C525 0161**
**N525BW C525 0409**
N525CC C500 025
N525CC C525 0001
N525CC C525 0100
**N525CC C52A 0007**
N525CC C52A 0125
**N525CD C525 0360**
**N525CE C52A 0181**
N525CF C525 0516
**N525CF C52B 0189**
N525CF HS25 258018
N525CF LJ60 010
N525CG C52A 0125
**N525CH C525 0078**
N525CJ C525 0500
N525CJ C525 702
**N525CJ C52B 0333**
N525CK C525 0058
**N525CK C52A 0128**
**N525CM C525 0093**
N525CP C525 0099
**N525CP C525 0228**
N525CP C525 0378
N525CU C525 0292
N525CW C560 0225
(N525CY) C525 0367
N525CZ C525 0120
**N525CZ C52C 0004**
**N525DC C525 0195**
N525DE C525 0364
N525DG C525 0057
N525DG C52A 0084
**N525DG C52B 0039**
N525DJ C525 0024
N525DL C525 0364
**N525DL C52A 0050**
**N525DM C525 0314**
**N525DP C525 0318**
N525DR C525 0308
N525DR C52B 0078
**N525DT C52A 0003**
**N525DU C525 0205**
**N525DV C52A 0119**
N525DY C525 0199
**N525DY C525 0306**
N525E CL64 5525
N525EC C525 0246
(N525EF) C525 0153
**N525EG C52A 0449**
**N525EP C52A 0346**
**N525ET C525 0244**
N525EZ C525 0400
N525EZ C52A 0080
N525EZ C52B 0089
N525EZ C52B 0238
**N525EZ C52B 0295**
**N525F C525 0058**
**N525FC C525 0531**
**N525FD C525 0008**
**N525FF C52A 0161**
N525FM C525 0057
**N525FN C525 0368**
N525FS C525 0026
**N525FT C525 0367**
**N525FX CL30 20112**
N525GA C500 182
N525GB C525 0232
N525GB C525 0380
**N525GC C525 0065**
**N525GE C525 0679**
(N525GF) GALX 226
N525GG C525 0041
N525GM C525 0240
N525GM C52A 0150
**N525GM C52B 0024**
N525GP C525 0203
N525GP LJ31 155
N525GP LJ31 162
**N525GT C52B 0104**
**N525GV C525 0001**
N525H C52B 0306
**N525HA C525 0081**
**N525HB C52A 0040**
**N525HC C525 0270**
(N525HC) C525 0273
**N525HD C52A 0301**
**N525HG C52A 0352**
**N525HS C525 0035**
**N525HV C525 0201**
**N525J C525 0184**
**N525JA C550 294**
N525JD C52A 0130
N525JH C525 0124
N525JJ C525 0141
**N525JJ C525 0497**
**N525JL C525 0407**
**N525JM C525 0134**
(N525JN) C525 0635
(N525JT) C525 0440
N525JT GLF2 156/31
**N525JV C525 0010**
**N525JW C525 0162**
**N525KA C525 0019**
(N525KF) C525 0090
N525KH C525 0197
**N525KK C525 0056**
N525KL C525 0136
**N525KM C525 0472**
**N525KN C525 0007**
**N525KR C52A 0160**
N525KS C52C 0002
(N525KT) C525 0029
**N525KT C52A 0058**
(N525L) C52A 0039
**N525L C52B 0051**
N525LB C525 0388
N525LC C52A 0009
**N525LC C550 383**
**N525LD C52A 0335**
**N525LE C525 0447**
**N525LF C525 0382**
**N525LM C525 0427**
**N525LP C525 0196**
**N525LR HS25 259035**
**N525LW C525 0082**
N525M ASTR 102
**N525M C525 0334**
**N525MA C52A 0012**
(N525MA) FA50 18
**N525MB C525 0036**
**N525MC C525 0018**
N525MD C525 0367
**N525MF C525 0313**
N525MH C525 0388
**N525MH F900 113**
**N525ML C525 0402**
N525ML WW24 260
N525MP C525 0313
N525MP C52A 0012
**N525MP C52B 0088**
N525MR C525 0313
**N525MR C52A 0173**
**N525MW C525 0370**
N525N SBRL 282-10
N525NA C525 0048
**N525NB C52C 0003**
**N525NG C52C 0001**
N525NP C525 0458
**N525NT C525 0440**
**N525P C525 0165**
N525PB C525 0232
**N525PB C52A 0172**
N525PC C52B 0041
N525PE C525 0125
**N525PE C550 550-1031**
N525PF C525 0232
**N525PF C52A 0023**
**N525PH C52A 0329**
**N525PL C525 0043**
**N525PM C52A 0067**
**N525PS C525 0061**
**N525PT C525 0125**
**N525PV C500 569**
N525QS HS25 259025
**N525RA C525 0167**
**N525RC C525 0178**
N525RC FA10 116
**N525RD C560 0106**
N525RF C525 0023
N525RF C525 0411
**N525RF C52A 0327**
**N525RG C52A 0387**
**N525RK C525 0413**
N525RL C525 0338
**N525RM C525 0225**
**N525RP C525 0023**
**N525RW C52A 0060**
**N525RY C525 0438**
**N525RZ C525 0612**
N525SA C52A 0089
N525SC C525 0099
**N525SD CL61 5056**
(N525SE) C525 0137
**N525SM C52A 0175**
(N525SP) C525 0019
(N525ST) C525 0195
N525TA C525 0141
N525TA C52A 0318
**N525TF C525 0067**
N525TG C52A 0021
N525TJ C52A 0024
**N525TK C525 0355**
N525TK C52A 0080
(N525TL) C525 0134
**N525TW LJ25 011**
**N525TX C525 0304**
N525U C52A 0112
**N525VG C525 0239**
N525VP C525 0001
N525VP C56X 5205
N525VV C52A 0113
**N525WB C525 0079**
**N525WC C525 0107**
**N525WD C52A 0107**
**N525WF C525 0246**
**N525WH C525 0028**
N525WH C525 0488
**N525WL C52B 0237**
N525WM C525 0213
(N525WS) C525 0444
**N525WW C525 0060**
**N525XD C52A 0337**
**N525XL GLF2 135**
**N525XX WW24 336**
**N525ZZ C52A 0055**
N526AC C550 038
**N526AC CL30 20263**
N526AC HS25 258169
N526AG C550 038
N526BA HS25 258083
N526CA C525 0033
N526CC C500 026
N526CC C500 526
N526CC FA50 147
N526CK C525 0058
**N526CP C525 0099**
N526CW MU30 A026SA
N526D FA10 84
N526DG C52B 0039
N526DM HS25 257156
N526DV C52A 0226
N526EE GLF4 1110
N526EE GLF4 1406
**N526EE GLF5 519**
**N526EL LJ45 327**
N526EZ C525 0400
**N526FX CL30 20118**
N526GA ASTR 115
N526GA GLF4 1526

N526GA GLF5 5126
N526GA GLF5 5226
N526GA GLF5 526
**N526GA GLF5 5286**
N526GP LJ31 181
**N526HV C52A 0139**
(N526JC) HS25 257021
N526LC C525 0526
N526M HS25 258032
N526N SBRL 282-30
N526XP HS25 258526
N527AC C550 121
N527AC HS25 258104
N527AG C550 121
N527BA HS25 258084
N527CC C500 027
N527CC C550 027
N527CC GLF3 412
N527CJ C525 0527
N527CP C650 0199
(N527DF) BE40 RK-527
N527DS C550 317
**N527DV C52B 0327**
N527EA C550 426
N527ER LJ24 096
**N527EW C500 669**
**N527FX CL30 20124**
N527GA ASTR 116
N527GA GLF5 5127
N527GA GLF5 527
**N527GA GLF5 5277**
N527GA GLF5 653
N527GP LJ31 182
**N527HV C52B 0213**
**N527JA CL61 5058**
**N527JC GLF4 1179**
**N527JG GLF4 1519**
N527JG LJ31 125
N527K GLF2 25
**N527M HS25 258054**
**N527PA LJ36 019**
**N527PM PRM1 RB-177**
N527SC C56X 5260
(N527TA) C500 334
**N527XP BE40 RK-527**
N528AC HS25 258070
N528AP GLF3 399
**N528AP GLF5 5168**
N528BA HS25 258086
N528BD F2EX 19
**N528BP HS25 258646**
**N528CB C525 0678**
N528CC C500 028
**N528CE C52B 0022**
N528CJ C525 0528
N528DK CL64 5508
**N528DM C510 0031**
**N528DS C500 615**
N528DT CL64 5528
**N528DV C52B 0329**
**N528EA EA50 000128**
N528EA LJ35 024
**N528FX CL30 20125**
N528GA ASTR 117
N528GA ASTR 203
N528GA GLF4 1528
N528GA GLF4 4128
**N528GA GLF5 5278**
N528GA GLF5 528
N528GP CL64 5401
N528J GLEX 9177
N528JC C52B 0075
**N528JD FA10 76**
N528JD LJ35 024
N528JR F900 51
N528JR FA50 220
N528JR GLEX 9177
**N528KW C560 0224**
**N528LG MU30 A050SA**
**N528M GLF5 5072**
N528M HS25 258055
**N528MP GLEX 9307**
**N528QS GLF5 5042**
**N528RM C500 613**
**N528RR ASTR 042**
**N528VM C560 0423**
**N528VP C56X 5282**
(N528VP) LJ35 285
N528XL C56X 5028
N528XP BE40 RK-528
N529AL GLF4 1123
N529BA HS25 258087
**N529BC LJ35 471**
N529CC C500 029
(N529CC) C525 0009
N529CF SBRL 306-58
N529CW FA50 29
N529D CL61 3025
N529D CL65 5711
N529DM CL61 3025
N529DM CL64 5575
**N529DM CL65 5711**
N529DM HS25 257156
**N529FX CL30 20128**
N529GA ASTR 118
N529GA GLF4 1529
N529GA GLF5 5129
N529GA GLF5 529
**N529GA GLF5 5299**
N529GA GLF5 655
N529GP CL64 5412
**N529KF LJ60 064**
N529M HS25 258446
N529MM FA50 29
**N529PC C52A 0001**
**N529QS GLF5 5156**
N529SC SBRL 306-58
N529SC SBRL 465-12
**N529SM HS25 257002**
N529SQ SBRL 306-58
N529TS JSTR 5209
**N529VP C56X 5229**
N529X C560 0163
**N530AG C510 0193**
N530AG C525 0409
**N530AJ C510 0234**
N530AQ C525 0409
N530AR FA50 175
N530BA HS25 258089
N530BA HS25 258244
N530BL HS25 257002
N530CC C500 030
(N530CC) C56X 5111
N530DC LJ25 291
N530DG FA50 245
**N530DL WW24 287**
**N530FX CL30 20148**
N530G JSTR 5096/10
**N530GA GLF2 247**
N530GA GLF5 530
**N530GP ASTR 203**
N530GV WW24 213
N530GV WW24 356
N530J LJ35 074
N530JD GLF4 1430
N530L FA20 84
N530M JSTR 5214
**N530P C550 333**
**N530PT PRM1 RB-51**
N530QS HS25 259030
N530RD MU30 A016SA
**N530RM C510 0242**
N530SM HS25 258697
N530SW GLF2 162
**N530TC FA10 69**
(N530TE) HS25 257065
N530TL C500 342
N530TL HS25 257065
N530XP BE40 RK-530
N531A C550 481
N531AB SBRL 306-98
**N531AC LJ45 196**
**N531AF GLF5 531**
N531AJ LJ35 011
N531AT LJ31 085
N531BA HS25 258090
N531BJ C56X 5031
N531CC C500 031
N531CC C560 0178
N531CC CS55 0031
**N531CM C52B 0071**
N531CM CS55 0033
**N531CW LJ25 231**
**N531EA EA50 000031**
N531F C560 0054
**N531FL FA20 113**
**N531FX CL30 20150**
N531GA GLF4 1531
N531GA GLF4 4131
N531GA GLF5 5131
N531GA GLF5 531
(N531GC) LJ25 245
**N531GP ASTR 207**
(N531JC) GLF3 491
N531JF GLF3 491
**N531K LJ55 053**
N531M JSTR 5236
N531MB C560 0027
**N531MB C56X 5014**
N531MD GLF4 1280
N531MF C560 0027
N531NC SBRL 306-7
N531PM CS55 0059
**N531QS GLF5 5133**
N531RA LJ31 106
**N531RA LJ31 192**
N531RC C56X 5184
**N531RC C680 0107**
**N531RQ C56X 5184**
**N531SK LJ31 043**
**N531TS LJ31 106**
N531VP C560 0311
N531WB FA20 514
N532BA HS25 258092
(N532C) C650 0167
N532CC C500 032
N532CC C56X 5111
N532CC C650 0167
N532CC C680 0027
N532CC CS55 0032
**N532CC F2TH 230**
N532CF CS55 0032
N532CJ C525 0032
N532DM CL64 5532
**N532FX CL30 20154**
N532GA GLF4 1532
N532GA GLF4 4132
N532GA GLF5 532
N532GA GLF5 658
**N532GP ASTR 221**
N532JF C650 7077
(N532JF) C750 0073
N532M C550 378
N532MA C560 0036
N532PJ HS25 258448
**N532SP GLF5 632**
N532XP BE40 RK-532
N533 HS25 25083
N533 HS25 25103
N533 HS25 257114
(N533) WW24 345
N533 WW24 356
N533BA HS25 258093
N533BF C500 033
N533CC C500 033
N533CC C56X 5201
**N533CC C56X 5687**
N533CC C650 0185
N533CC CS55 0132
N533CS FA10 177
N533DK CL64 5533
**N533DK EA50 000143**
N533EJ JSTR 5099/5
**N533FX CL30 20160**
**N533GA GALX 233**
N533GA GLF4 1533
N533GA GLF5 5133
N533GA GLF5 533
N533GA GLF5 660
**N533GT EA50 000267**
N533HB BE40 RK-533
N533JF C525 0247
(N533JF) C52A 0101
**N533LR HS25 259033**
N533M C550 041
N533MA C550 083
N533P HS25 258075
N533QS HS25 259033
N533TS CL65 5733
N533XL C56X 5333
N534 WW24 345
N534A LJ35 304
N534BA HS25 258095
N534CC C500 034
N534CC C56X 5025
**N534CC C56X 5707**
N534CJ C52A 0126
**N534FX CL30 20161**
**N534GA GALX 234**
N534GA GLF5 5134
N534GA GLF5 534
N534GA GLF5 634
**N534H C650 0196**
N534H LJ35 304
(N534LL) C525 0092
N534M C550 048
(N534M) C550 612
N534MA FA50 29
N534MW C550 067
**N534NA C525 0534**
**N534QS GLF5 5103**
N534R WW24 345
N534RF CL64 5534
N534TX C525 0092
**N535AF LJ35 191**
N535BA HS25 258096
N535BC HS25 258655
N535BC HS25 258776
N535BC PRM1 RB-72
**N535BP C560 0646**
N535BR PRM1 RB-72
N535CC C500 035
**N535CD PRM1 RB-96**
**N535CE C560 0635**
N535CJ C525 0535
**N535CM C52B 0182**
N535CS GLF3 464
N535D WW24 74
**N535DL C52B 0172**
**N535DT C52B 0069**
N535EX FA50 335
**N535FX CL30 20167**
N535GA C500 583
N535GA GLF4 4135
N535GA GLF5 5135
N535GA GLF5 620
**N535GH C52B 0054**
(N535GV) GLF5 535
**N535JF C52A 0349**
**N535JM LJ35 401**
**N535LR C525 0128**
N535MA C550 037
N535MC LJ35 385
N535PC C550 229
N535PC LJ35 291
**N535PS LJ31 087**
N535QS GLF5 5229
N535QS HS25 259035
N535RF C525 0411
**N535SW C550 550-0899**
N535TA LJ35 013
N535TV C52A 0349
**N535V GLF5 535**
**N535WT C525 0687**
N536BA HS25 258098
N536CC C500 036
N536CS GLF2 24
**N536FX CL30 20171**
**N536GA GALX 236**
N536GA GLF5 5136
N536GA GLF5 536
N536GA GLF5 601
**N536KN LJ35 073**
N536M C550 144
N536MP CL64 5536
**N536V BE40 RK-445**
N536V C500 032
N537BA HS25 258099
N537CC C500 037
**N537DF BE40 RK-537**
N537DR CL64 5537
**N537FX CL30 20187**
N537GA ASTR 237
N537GA GLF4 4037
N537GA GLF5 537
N537M C550 145
**N537RB PRM1 RB-190**
**N537VP C560 0377**
**N537XJ CL30 20213**
N537XP BE40 RK-537
N538 HS25 25083
N538BA HS25 258100

| | | |
|---|---|---|
| N538CC | C500 | 038 |
| N538CC | C650 | 0185 |
| N538CC | CS55 | 0138 |
| **N538FX** | **CL30** | **20201** |
| N538GA | GLF4 | 4038 |
| N538GA | GLF5 | 538 |
| N538GA | GLF5 | 602 |
| (N538JF) | C525 | 0247 |
| N538LD | HS25 | 258538 |
| N538M | C550 | 328 |
| N538RF | CL64 | 5538 |
| **N538TS** | **CL65** | **5738** |
| **N538XJ** | **CL30** | **20224** |
| N538XL | C56X | 5538 |
| N538XP | BE40 | RK-538 |
| N539AB | CL64 | 5539 |
| N539BA | HS25 | 258101 |
| **N539BA** | **LJ31** | **033D** |
| N539CC | C500 | 039 |
| N539CE | C560 | 0539 |
| **N539FX** | **CL30** | **20202** |
| N539GA | GLF5 | 5139 |
| N539GA | GLF5 | 539 |
| N539GA | GLF5 | 603 |
| **N539JM** | **LJ55** | **039** |
| **N539LB** | **LJ31** | **078** |
| **N539LR** | **HS25** | **259039** |
| N539PG | SBRL | 306-79 |
| N539QS | HS25 | 259039 |
| **N539RM** | **EA50** | **000101** |
| **N539VE** | **GLF4** | **4039** |
| **N539VP** | **C560** | **0339** |
| **N539WA** | **C560** | **0556** |
| **N539XJ** | **CL30** | **20230** |
| N539XP | BE40 | RK-539 |
| N540B | HS25 | 257077 |
| **N540BA** | **CL65** | **5729** |
| N540BA | HS25 | 258102 |
| N540BA | HS25 | 258241 |
| N540CC | C500 | 040 |
| **N540CH** | **GLEX** | **9055** |
| N540CH | GLF4 | 1306 |
| N540CL | LJ24 | 026 |
| **N540CS** | **C56X** | **5516** |
| N540CV | C560 | 0540 |
| **N540EA** | **GLF2** | **174** |
| **N540FX** | **CL30** | **20205** |
| N540G | JSTR | 5009 |
| N540G | JSTR | 5075/19 |
| N540HP | LJ35 | 399 |
| N540JB | CS55 | 0061 |
| N540JW | CL64 | 5549 |
| N540LH | LJ40 | 45-2064 |
| **N540LR** | **HS25** | **259040** |
| **N540M** | **GLF5** | **597** |
| N540M | HS25 | 258145 |
| N540PA | LJ36 | 019 |
| N540QS | HS25 | 259040 |
| N540RK | BE40 | RK-540 |
| N540W | CL61 | 5062 |
| N540W | GLF4 | 1265 |
| N540WY | GLEX | 9187 |
| N540XJ | CL30 | 20238 |
| N541AG | C500 | 041 |
| N541AL | LJ45 | 179 |
| N541BA | HS25 | 258103 |
| N541CC | C500 | 041 |
| N541CJ | C525 | 0454 |
| **N541CS** | **C56X** | **5521** |
| N541CV | C560 | 0541 |
| N541CW | MU30 | A004SA |
| N541DE | CL64 | 5390 |
| (N541FJ) | FA50 | 41 |
| **N541FL** | **FA20** | **48** |
| **N541FX** | **CL30** | **20211** |
| N541GA | GLF4 | 4141 |
| N541GA | GLF5 | 5141 |
| N541JG | C550 | 550-0849 |
| **N541LB** | **EA50** | **000041** |
| **N541LF** | **CL65** | **5712** |
| N541LJ | LJ45 | 041 |
| **N541LR** | **HS25** | **259041** |
| N541M | WW24 | 48 |
| N541MM | CL60 | 1044 |
| (N541NC) | C500 | 205 |
| **N541PA** | **LJ35** | **053** |
| N541QS | HS25 | 259041 |
| **N541RL** | **ASTR** | **034** |
| **N541RS** | **PRM1** | **RB-144** |
| **N541S** | **C650** | **0115** |
| N541SG | WW24 | 48 |
| (N541TM) | MU30 | A004SA |
| "N541TS" | CL61 | 5041 |
| **N541VP** | **C560** | **0341** |
| **N541WG** | **C52B** | **0188** |
| **N541XJ** | **CL30** | **20239** |
| **N541XP** | **HS25** | **258541** |
| **N542BA** | **CL65** | **5737** |
| N542BA | HS25 | 258104 |
| N542CC | C500 | 042 |
| N542CC | CS55 | 0142 |
| N542CE | C560 | 0542 |
| **N542CS** | **C56X** | **5523** |
| **N542FX** | **CL30** | **20217** |
| **N542HB** | **HA4T** | **RC-42** |
| **N542LR** | **HS25** | **259042** |
| **N542M** | **HS25** | **258766** |
| **N542PA** | **LJ35** | **030** |
| N542QS | HS25 | 259042 |
| (N542S) | SBRL | 306-16 |
| **N542SA** | **LJ35** | **503** |
| N542TW | JSTR | 5113/25 |
| N542XJ | CL30 | 20242 |
| N542XP | BE40 | RK-542 |
| N543CC | C500 | 043 |
| **N543CM** | **LJ45** | **062** |
| **N543H** | **GLF5** | **688** |
| **N543LE** | **C560** | **0543** |
| **N543LF** | **HS25** | **258391** |
| N543PA | LJ35 | 070 |
| (N543QS) | HS25 | 259043 |
| N543SC | C650 | 0130 |
| **N543SC** | **CS55** | **0144** |
| (N543VP) | C560 | 0143 |
| N543WW | LJ35 | 332 |
| N543XJ | CL30 | 20245 |
| N544CC | C500 | 044 |
| **N544CM** | **FA50** | **173** |
| N544FX | CL30 | 20240 |
| **N544KB** | **C680** | **0047** |
| N544KK | GLF5 | 669 |
| **N544LR** | **HS25** | **259044** |
| **N544PA** | **LJ35** | **247** |
| N544PH | SBRL | 465-56 |
| **N544PS** | **C550** | **550-1010** |
| N544QS | HS25 | 259044 |
| N544RA | FA50 | 144 |
| N544TS | CL64 | 5544 |
| N544X | FA20 | 258 |
| N544XJ | CL30 | 20248 |
| **N544XL** | **C56X** | **5044** |
| N545BF | JSTR | 5146 |
| **N545BP** | **C560** | **0756** |
| N545C | FA20 | 17 |
| N545C | SBRL | 282-57 |
| N545CC | C500 | 045 |
| N545CC | C500 | 545 |
| **N545CC** | **GLF5** | **545** |
| **N545CG** | **LJ45** | **386** |
| **N545CS** | **GLF4** | **1361** |
| N545EC | LJ45 | 199 |
| N545ES | C525 | 0066 |
| (N545G) | C500 | 368 |
| N545GA | C500 | 368 |
| N545GA | C550 | 040 |
| N545GA | GLF4 | 4145 |
| N545GA | GLF5 | 5145 |
| N545GM | BE40 | RJ-31 |
| **N545GM** | **HS25** | **257039** |
| N545JT | GLF3 | 347 |
| **N545K** | **LJ45** | **244** |
| (N545K) | LJ45 | 399 |
| N545KS | LJ45 | 399 |
| (N545LR) | HS25 | 259045 |
| **N545MA** | **EA50** | **000144** |
| **N545PA** | **LJ36** | **028** |
| N545PL | C560 | 0225 |
| (N545PT) | PRM1 | RB-133 |
| N545QS | HS25 | 259045 |
| N545RA | LJ45 | 157 |
| (N545RS) | LJ45 | 099 |
| **N545RW** | **C525** | **0141** |
| N545S | HS25 | 25188 |
| (N545SH) | HS25 | 257007 |
| **N545TC** | **BE40** | **RK-213** |
| **N545TG** | **C525** | **0545** |
| N545TP | MU30 | A045SA |
| N545XJ | CL30 | 20253 |
| N546BC | HS25 | 257004 |
| **N546BW** | **EA50** | **000025** |
| N546BZ | BE40 | RK-41 |
| N546CC | C500 | 046 |
| **N546CS** | **C56X** | **5524** |
| N546EX | FA50 | 41 |
| **N546LR** | **HS25** | **259046** |
| **N546MG** | **HS25** | **258753** |
| N546MT | C550 | 550-0881 |
| N546PA | LJ36 | 045 |
| **N546QS** | **GLF5** | **5190** |
| N546QS | HS25 | 259046 |
| (N546XJ) | CL30 | 20260 |
| (N547AC) | C52A | 0016 |
| N547CC | C500 | 047 |
| N547CC | C500 | 547 |
| **N547CS** | **C56X** | **5542** |
| N547FP | CL61 | 5047 |
| **N547JG** | **LJ25** | **264** |
| N547JL | SBRL | 380-69 |
| N547K | FA50 | 46 |
| **N547LR** | **HS25** | **259047** |
| **N547PA** | **LJ36** | **012** |
| N547QS | HS25 | 259047 |
| N547ST | C525 | 0547 |
| **N547TW** | **C525** | **0547** |
| **N548BA** | **CL65** | **5771** |
| N548CC | C500 | 048 |
| **N548KK** | **BE40** | **RK-151** |
| N548LF | CL64 | 5407 |
| N548LP | CL64 | 5548 |
| **N548LR** | **HS25** | **259048** |
| N548PA | LJ36 | 038 |
| N548QS | HS25 | 259048 |
| N548W | CL61 | 5062 |
| N548XL | C56X | 5048 |
| N548XP | BE40 | RK-548 |
| **N549AF** | **EA50** | **000049** |
| N549AS | FA10 | 87 |
| **N549BA** | **CL65** | **5775** |
| N549CC | C500 | 049 |
| N549CC | C550 | 456 |
| N549CJ | C525 | 0549 |
| **N549CS** | **C56X** | **5546** |
| **N549LR** | **HS25** | **259049** |
| **N549PA** | **LJ35** | **119** |
| N549QS | HS25 | 259049 |
| N550A | CS55 | 0009 |
| N550AB | C550 | 063 |
| **N550AB** | **C550** | **633** |
| N550AJ | C550 | 183 |
| **N550AJ** | **CS55** | **0141** |
| **N550AK** | **LJ55** | **045** |
| N550AL | C550 | 462 |
| N550AL | FA20 | 55/410 |
| N550AN | GLF5 | 5181 |
| N550AR | C550 | 661 |
| **N550AS** | **CS55** | **0020** |
| N550AV | C550 | 403 |
| **N550BB** | **C550** | **734** |
| **N550BC** | **C550** | **550-0804** |
| N550BD | C550 | 619 |
| N550BF | C550 | 550-0888 |
| (N550BG) | C550 | 719 |
| **N550BG** | **CS55** | **0148** |
| **N550BJ** | **C550** | **309** |
| N550BM | C550 | 286 |
| **N550BM** | **GLF5** | **5171** |
| N550BP | C550 | 235 |
| N550BP | C550 | 282 |
| N550BP | C550 | 731 |
| **N550BT** | **CS55** | **0085** |
| **N550CA** | **C550** | **167** |
| N550CA | C550 | 303 |
| N550CA | C550 | 381 |
| N550CB | C550 | 118 |
| N550CC | C500 | 021 |
| N550CC | C500 | 050 |
| N550CC | C550 | 686 |
| N550CD | C550 | 320 |
| N550CE | C550 | 063 |
| N550CF | C550 | 382 |
| **N550CG** | **C550** | **102** |
| N550CJ | C550 | 498 |
| (N550CK) | LJ55 | 083 |
| **N550CL** | **FA50** | **8** |
| N550CM | C550 | 285 |
| N550CP | C550 | 163 |
| N550CP | C550 | 356 |
| **N550CP** | **PRM1** | **RB-121** |
| **N550CS** | **C56X** | **5551** |
| N550CS | LJ55 | 005 |
| **N550CU** | **C550** | **178** |
| **N550CW** | **CL60** | **1084** |
| N550CY | C550 | 550-1118 |
| **N550CZ** | **CS55** | **0128** |
| **N550DA** | **C550** | **186** |
| N550DA | C550 | 246 |
| **N550DC** | **C560** | **0198** |
| (N550DD) | C550 | 285 |
| (N550DD) | LJ55 | 066 |
| N550DG | C550 | 727 |
| **N550DL** | **CS55** | **0155** |
| N550DR | C550 | 067 |
| **N550DS** | **CS55** | **0154** |
| N550DW | C550 | 074 |
| **N550DW** | **C550** | **487** |
| N550E | LJ35 | 100 |
| N550EC | C550 | 053 |
| N550EK | C550 | 265 |
| N550EW | C550 | 103 |
| **N550EZ** | **CS55** | **0158** |
| **N550F** | **CS55** | **0010** |
| N550F | CS55 | 0056 |
| N550FB | C550 | 285 |
| N550FB | C550 | 550-0803 |
| (N550FB) | C550 | 674 |
| N550FG | GLF5 | 5082 |
| N550FM | C550 | 550 |
| **N550FP** | **C550** | **550-1024** |
| N550FS | CS55 | 0067 |
| N550GA | GLF5 | 5002 |
| N550GA | GLF5 | 5043 |
| (N550GA) | GLF5 | 5071 |
| N550GA | GLF5 | 5097 |
| N550GA | GLF5 | 5155 |
| N550GA | GLF5 | 5211 |
| N550GA | GPER | 551 |
| N550GB | C550 | 177 |
| N550GD | GLF5 | 5125 |
| N550GD | GLF5 | 5184 |
| **N550GH** | **C550** | **550-0898** |
| N550GM | C550 | 378 |
| N550GP | C550 | 194 |
| **N550GT** | **C550** | **469** |
| N550GT | CS55 | 0160 |
| N550GV | GLF5 | 5022 |
| **N550GW** | **GLF5** | **5006** |
| **N550GX** | **C550** | **560** |
| N550H | HS25 | 258356 |
| N550HA | CS55 | 0067 |
| N550HB | C550 | 250 |
| **N550HB** | **WW24** | **414** |
| **N550HC** | **CS55** | **0116** |
| N550HF | C550 | 287 |
| **N550HG** | **LJ55** | **083** |
| **N550HH** | **C550** | **550-0802** |
| **N550HJ** | **C550** | **302** |
| N550HM | C550 | 047 |
| N550HP | C550 | 191 |
| (N550HS) | MU30 | A051SA |
| N550HT | CS55 | 0107 |
| **N550HW** | **C550** | **635** |
| N550J | C550 | 417 |
| **N550J** | **C550** | **550-0848** |
| N550JB | C550 | 177 |
| **N550JC** | **C550** | **038** |
| N550JC | CS55 | 0124 |
| (N550JE) | GLF5 | 5211 |
| N550JF | C550 | 008 |
| N550JF | C550 | 660 |
| N550JM | C550 | 255 |
| (N550JP) | HS25 | 257106 |
| N550JR | C550 | 356 |
| N550JS | C550 | 118 |
| N550K | C550 | 229 |
| N550K | WW24 | 127 |
| N550KA | C550 | 064 |
| **N550KA** | **C550** | **166** |
| N550KC | C550 | 292 |
| **N550KD** | **C550** | **125** |
| (N550KE) | C550 | 550-0830 |
| N550KE | C550 | 694 |
| **N550KF** | **GLF5** | **5095** |

| | | | | | | | | | | | |
|---|---|---|---|---|---|---|---|---|---|---|---|
| N550KG | C550 | 550-0949 | **N550SG** | **GLF5** | **5223** | **N551EA** | **C550** | **354** | N552KF | CL30 | 20204 |
| N550KH | C550 | 550-0854 | **N550SJ** | **CS55** | **0100** | (N551EU) | BE40 | RK-551 | N552LR | HS25 | 259052 |
| (N550KH) | C550 | 550-0859 | N550SL | SBRL | 306-72 | N551FA | SBRL | 465-39 | (N552LX) | FA50 | 20 |
| N550KH | C550 | 550-0886 | N550SM | C550 | 286 | **N551FP** | **C525** | **0515** | N552MA | C56X | 5198 |
| **N550KJ** | **C550** | **550-0854** | N550SM | C550 | 587 | N551G | C525 | 0153 | N552MD | C500 | 425 |
| **N550KL** | **C550** | **550-0844** | **N550SN** | **GLF5** | **5195** | N551G | C550 | 550-0850 | N552N | HS25 | 25124 |
| N550KM | CS55 | 0081 | N550SP | CS55 | 0151 | **N551G** | **C550** | **550-0968** | N552QS | HS25 | 259052 |
| N550KP | C550 | 130 | **N550SS** | **C550** | **093** | (N551GA) | C550 | 040 | **N552SC** | **C56X** | **5144** |
| **N550KR** | **C52A** | **0130** | N550ST | CS55 | 0033 | N551GA | GLF5 | 604 | N552SC | CL64 | 5523 |
| (N550KR) | C550 | 075 | N550T | C500 | 388 | **N551GA** | **GLF5** | **606** | **N552SD** | **CS55** | **0130** |
| N550KR | C550 | 727 | N550T | C500 | 413 | (N551GC) | C550 | 364 | **N552SK** | **LJ60** | **219** |
| **N550KT** | **C550** | **364** | N550T | C525 | 0013 | **N551GE** | **C550** | **152** | **N552SM** | **C550** | **550-0929** |
| **N550KW** | **C550** | **409** | N550T | C52A | 0025 | **N551GF** | **C550** | **278** | (N552SM) | CS55 | 0125 |
| N550L | C500 | 388 | **N550T** | **C52B** | **0040** | N551GL | LJ55 | 001 | N552SQ | LJ55 | 100 |
| N550L | SBRL | 282-61 | N550TA | C550 | 278 | N551GL | LJ60 | 55-001 | N552TC | C560 | 0674 |
| **N550LA** | **C550** | **006** | **N550TB** | **C52A** | **0025** | (N551GN) | C550 | 069 | N552TF | C550 | 203 |
| N550LC | CS55 | 0074 | N550TB | CS55 | 0012 | **N551GS** | **C550** | **430** | **N552TL** | **LJ55** | **139** |
| **N550LD** | **C550** | **351** | N550TB | CS55 | 0019 | N551HB | LJ55 | 038 | N552TS | CL64 | 5552 |
| **N550LF** | **GLEX** | **9054** | **N550TC** | **LJ55** | **034** | **N551HH** | **C550** | **023** | N552UT | LJ55 | 100 |
| **N550LH** | **C550** | **116** | N550TE | C550 | 550-0894 | N551HK | C550 | 266 | N552VP | C56X | 5252 |
| N550LJ | LJ55 | 015 | **N550TF** | **C525** | **0013** | N551HM | LJ35 | 612 | **N552WF** | **GLF4** | **1000** |
| N550LL | SBRL | 282-61 | N550TG | C500 | 378 | N551JF | C550 | 063 | N552XP | BE40 | RK-552 |
| N550LP | C550 | 200 | N550TG | C550 | 550-0822 | N551KF | GLF5 | 5148 | N553AC | C650 | 0198 |
| **N550LS** | **C550** | **086** | **N550TH** | **F9EX** | **100** | N551KH | C550 | 550-0859 | N553BA | HS25 | 258108 |
| **N550LT** | **C500** | **184** | N550TJ | C550 | 029 | N551LR | HS25 | 259051 | N553CC | C500 | 053 |
| (N550LX) | FA50 | 17 | (N550TJ) | C550 | 080 | (N551LX) | FA50 | 19 | N553CC | C550 | 553 |
| N550M | ASTR | 061 | N550TJ | C550 | 143 | N551M | GLF5 | 682 | N553CC | CS55 | 0046 |
| N550M | FA20 | 355 | **N550TL** | **C550** | **716** | N551MB | LJ25 | 007 | N553CC | CS55 | 0113 |
| **N550M** | **GLF5** | **5101** | **N550TM** | **C550** | **550-0936** | N551MC | C550 | 086 | N553CJ | C550 | 003 |
| N550MC | C525 | 0205 | (N550TM) | C560 | 0299 | N551MD | GLF2 | 212 | N553CS | C56X | 5560 |
| N550MC | FA20 | 200 | N550TP | C550 | 186 | N551MD | LJ25 | 007 | N553CW | C560 | 0253 |
| N550MD | C550 | 299 | N550TP | C550 | 296 | N551MD | LJ35 | 057 | (N553CW) | CL61 | 5053 |
| N550MD | C550 | 354 | N550TR | C550 | 186 | (N551MD) | LJ55 | 085 | N553DF | CL61 | 5078 |
| N550MH | C500 | 668 | N550TR | C550 | 733 | **N551MF** | **LJ55** | **015** | N553DJ | LJ55 | 003 |
| **N550MJ** | **C550** | **238** | N550TT | C550 | 158 | **N551MS** | **C500** | **541** | (N553GJ) | LJ55 | 003 |
| (N550MT) | C550 | 309 | N550TT | C550 | 296 | (N551NA) | C550 | 037 | N553GP | LJ55 | 003 |
| N550MT | C550 | 330 | N550TT | C550 | 550-1076 | N551NC | FA10 | 198 | N553JT | GLF3 | 305 |
| **N550MT** | **GLF5** | **5026** | **N550TW** | **C550** | **603** | **N551NH** | **C550** | **290** | (N553LX) | FA50 | 23 |
| N550MW | C550 | 481 | (N550TY) | C550 | 007 | N551PL | C550 | 150 | **N553M** | **FA50** | **201** |
| **N550MW** | **C550** | **720** | **N550U** | **C500** | **413** | N551PS | CS55 | 0013 | N553M | HS25 | 258027 |
| **N550MX** | **C52B** | **0137** | N550VC | C550 | 550-0924 | N551Q | C525 | 0153 | N553M | LJ35 | 141 |
| N550MZ | C550 | 658 | N550VR | C550 | 733 | N551QS | HS25 | 259051 | **N553MC** | **WW24** | **252** |
| N550NE | C550 | 230 | (N550VS) | CS55 | 0001 | N551R | C550 | 115 | N553MD | GLF2 | 47 |
| N550NM | WW24 | 39 | **N550VW** | **C550** | **274** | N551RF | CS55 | 0097 | **N553MJ** | **C550** | **553** |
| N550NS | C550 | 635 | **N550WB** | **C550** | **265** | (N551S) | FA50 | 51 | N553PF | BE40 | RK-32 |
| **N550PA** | **C550** | **213** | N550WG | C550 | 550-0953 | N551SC | LJ55 | 008 | **N553SC** | **C560** | **0057** |
| N550PD | C550 | 550-0995 | N550WJ | C550 | 309 | **N551SD** | **CL61** | **5016** | **N553SD** | **CS55** | **0107** |
| **N550PF** | **C550** | **427** | **N550WL** | **C550** | **242** | (N551SE) | C550 | 353 | (N553US) | HS25 | 258027 |
| N550PF | C550 | 550-0925 | **N550WM** | **FA50** | **229** | N551SR | C550 | 072 | **N553V** | **LJ35** | **141** |
| N550PF | C550 | 672 | **N550WP** | **GLF2** | **176** | N551SR | C550 | 266 | N553XP | BE40 | RK-553 |
| **N550PG** | **C550** | **240** | N550WR | C550 | 400 | N551SS | F2TH | 186 | N554BA | C550 | 040 |
| N550PL | C550 | 010 | **N550WS** | **C550** | **550-0845** | **N551ST** | **LJ60** | **048** | (N554BA) | HS25 | 258109 |
| N550PL | CS55 | 0130 | N550WV | C550 | 584 | N551TK | C550 | 282 | N554BA | HS25 | 258111 |
| N550PM | C550 | 035 | N550WW | C550 | 584 | N551TP | WW24 | 419 | N554CA | CS55 | 0004 |
| **N550PM** | **GLF5** | **5252** | **N550WW** | **C560** | **0180** | N551TT | C550 | 172 | N554CC | C500 | 054 |
| **N550PP** | **GLF3** | **345** | (N550YM) | GLF5 | 5047 | N551TW | LJ35 | 612 | N554CC | CS55 | 0075 |
| N550PR | C550 | 285 | N551AB | C550 | 173 | N551UT | LJ55 | 069 | **N554CE** | **GLF5** | **5188** |
| **N550PR** | **GLF5** | **5121** | N551AC | GLF3 | 467 | **N551V** | **C550** | **550-0850** | **N554CL** | **LJ55** | **040** |
| N550PS | C550 | 124 | N551AD | C550 | 079 | N551VB | C550 | 550-1038 | **N554CS** | **C56X** | **5572** |
| N550PT | C550 | 499 | N551AM | C750 | 0155 | N551VB | HS25 | 258617 | N554EJ | C560 | 0328 |
| N550PT | FA20 | 391 | (N551AM) | LJ55 | 108 | (N551VP) | C550 | 550-1038 | (N554EM) | LJ55 | 014 |
| **N550PW** | **C550** | **216** | N551AS | C550 | 348 | N551WC | LJ25 | 129 | N554GA | GLF5 | 5254 |
| N550QS | HS25 | 259050 | N551AS | LJ24 | 229 | N551WC | LJ35 | 441 | N554GA | GLF5 | 605 |
| N550RA | C550 | 661 | N551AS | LJ55 | 083 | **N551WH** | **C510** | **0055** | N554HD | GLF3 | 444 |
| N550RB | C52B | 0073 | (N551BA) | HS25 | 258105 | N551WJ | C550 | 465 | (N554LX) | FA50 | 51 |
| N550RB | C550 | 129 | N551BB | C550 | 246 | **N551WL** | **C550** | **288** | **N554MB** | **C550** | **040** |
| (N550RD) | C550 | 145 | **N551BC** | **C550** | **059** | **N551WM** | **C52A** | **0243** | N554PF | LJ55 | 087 |
| N550RD | C550 | 421 | **N551BD** | **LJ60** | **062** | **N551XP** | **BE40** | **RK-551** | N554R | C560 | 0328 |
| N550RG | C550 | 262 | N551BE | CS55 | 0097 | **N552AJ** | **C500** | **449** | N554SC | CL64 | 5527 |
| N550RH | HS25 | 258038 | N551BP | C550 | 423 | N552BA | HS25 | 258107 | N554SR | FA10 | 173 |
| N550RH | LJ55 | 014 | N551BT | CL64 | 5551 | (N552BA) | LJ55 | 050 | (N554T) | C500 | 477 |
| N550RH | LJ55 | 041 | N551BW | C550 | 272 | N552BE | CS55 | 0138 | **N554T** | **C560** | **0376** |
| (N550RL) | C550 | 266 | N551CC | C500 | 051 | N552CB | C550 | 550-1026 | N554T | CS55 | 0124 |
| N550RL | C550 | 317 | (N551CC) | C550 | 001 | N552CC | C500 | 052 | (N554UJ) | C560 | 0328 |
| N550RM | C550 | 698 | N551CC | LJ35 | 017 | N552CC | C550 | 002 | N555AB | SBRL | 282-60 |
| **N550RM** | **GLF3** | **373** | N551CE | C550 | 398 | N552CC | C552 | 0001 | N555AE | SBRL | 282-60 |
| (N550RN) | GLF5 | 5029 | N551CF | C550 | 107 | N552CC | CL64 | 5552 | N555AE | SBRL | 306-102 |
| N550RP | C550 | 035 | N551CG | LJ55 | 014 | (N552CF) | CS55 | 0052 | N555AJ | C500 | 007 |
| **N550RP** | **GLF5** | **5184** | **N551CL** | **C550** | **191** | N552CJ | C52A | 0005 | (N555BA) | HS25 | 258110 |
| **N550RS** | **C500** | **202** | N551CS | C56X | 5557 | **N552CN** | **C560** | **0674** | N555BA | HS25 | 258113 |
| N550RS | C550 | 439 | N551CW | FA50 | 51 | N552EU | BE40 | RK-552 | N555BC | C550 | 235 |
| N550RV | CS55 | 0012 | **N551CZ** | **C550** | **028** | N552FJ | C550 | 619 | **N555BK** | **C550** | **550-0916** |
| **N550SA** | **C550** | **261** | **N551DA** | **C550** | **025** | N552GA | GLF5 | 5252 | N555BS | JSTR | 5051 |
| N550SB | C550 | 634 | N551DB | LJ55 | 052 | N552GL | LJ55 | 002 | N555BY | WW24 | 306 |
| N550SC | C550 | 040 | N551DF | LJ55 | 001 | **N552HV** | **C560** | **0552** | N555CB | HS25 | 25122 |
| (N550SC) | C550 | 338 | N551DF | LJ60 | 55-001 | N552JH | JSTR | 5037/24 | N555CB | HS25 | 25285 |
| N550SC | LJ55 | 098 | N551DP | LJ25 | 213 | N552JT | GLF2 | 135 | N555CB | HS25 | 256011 |
| **N550SF** | **C550** | **122** | N551DS | C550 | 023 | N552JT | GLF3 | 305 | N555CB | HS25 | 257039 |

| | | |
|---|---|---|
| N555CC | C500 | 039 |
| N555CJ | LJ55 | 089 |
| **N555CK** | **LJ45** | **214** |
| N555CR | HS25 | 257039 |
| N555CS | GLF2 | 73/9 |
| N555CS | GLF5 | 516 |
| N555CW | WW24 | 295 |
| N555DH | C550 | 423 |
| N555DH | C650 | 0016 |
| N555DH | C650 | 0090 |
| N555DH | CL30 | 20083 |
| N555DH | FA10 | 114 |
| N555DH | FA10 | 186 |
| N555DH | FA10 | 187 |
| (N555DH) | LJ24 | 153 |
| N555DH | WW24 | 373 |
| N555DM | WW24 | 25 |
| **N555DS** | **C550** | **356** |
| **N555DW** | **GLF3** | **459** |
| **N555DZ** | **FA10** | **186** |
| N555EF | GLEX | 9154 |
| **N555EJ** | **EA50** | **000183** |
| N555EW | C500 | 456 |
| N555EW | C550 | 303 |
| (N555EW) | C650 | 0074 |
| (N555EW) | C650 | 0099 |
| N555FA | MU30 | A082SA |
| **N555FD** | **C560** | **0113** |
| N555GB | HS25 | 256011 |
| N555GB | LJ35 | 246 |
| **N555GL** | **GLF3** | **403** |
| N555GL | LJ55 | 036 |
| N555GL | LJ55 | 065 |
| N555GN | GLF5 | 518 |
| N555GV | GLF5 | 518 |
| **N555HD** | **GLEX** | **9328** |
| N555HD | GLF2 | 134 |
| N555HD | GLF3 | 444 |
| N555HD | WW24 | 341 |
| **N555HM** | **C550** | **550-0950** |
| N555HR | C500 | 643 |
| N555J | WW24 | 213 |
| N555JE | LJ35 | 195 |
| N555JK | LJ28 | 28-003 |
| N555JM | HFB3 | 1037 |
| N555JR | SBRL | 380-72 |
| N555JS | LJ31 | 053 |
| N555KC | GLF3 | 366 |
| N555KC | GLF4 | 1342 |
| N555KH | GLF2 | 134 |
| N555KK | BE40 | RK-92 |
| **N555KT** | **C550** | **419** |
| **N555KW** | **C500** | **443** |
| N555LA | LJ24 | 177 |
| N555LB | LJ24 | 177 |
| **N555LG** | **CL61** | **5127** |
| N555LG | GLF2 | 10 |
| **N555LJ** | **LJ24** | **195** |
| (N555LR) | GLF4 | 4065 |
| N555MH | LJ24 | 213 |
| N555MU | GLF2 | 188 |
| N555MW | GLF2 | 188 |
| N555MX | LJ55 | 142 |
| **N555NN** | **CL65** | **5718** |
| N555NT | GLF3 | 322 |
| N555PB | JSTR | 5047 |
| **N555PG** | **C560** | **0102** |
| N555PG | LJ25 | 281 |
| N555PT | FA20 | 426 |
| N555PT | SBRL | 282-53 |
| N555PV | LJ24 | 133 |
| N555RA | FA20 | 194 |
| N555RB | HS25 | 257140 |
| **N555RE** | **GLF3** | **409** |
| N555RR | SBRL | 306-60 |
| N555RS | GLF2 | 3 |
| **N555RT** | **C550** | **311** |
| N555RU | HS25 | HB-14 |
| **N555SD** | **LJ25** | **333** |
| N555SG | JSTR | 5090 |
| (N555SL) | C550 | 553 |
| N555SL | SBRL | 306-13 |
| N555SR | FA10 | 173 |
| N555SR | FA20 | 455 |
| (N555TD) | C550 | 437 |
| N555TF | CL30 | 20102 |
| N555TF | FA20 | 325 |
| **N555TF** | **GLF4** | **4080** |

| | | |
|---|---|---|
| N555VR | LJ31 | 033C |
| **N555VR** | **LJ45** | **257** |
| N555VV | CL64 | 5555 |
| N555WD | CL60 | 1047 |
| **N555WD** | **CL64** | **5355** |
| N555WE | C56X | 5058 |
| N555WF | C560 | 0190 |
| N555WF | C560 | 0449 |
| N555WF | C560 | 0488 |
| N555WF | C56X | 5058 |
| N555WF | C56X | 5064 |
| N555WF | C56X | 5366 |
| N555WH | LJ36 | 037 |
| N555WK | C560 | 0449 |
| **N555WL** | **C560** | **0488** |
| N555WL | GLF4 | 1114 |
| **N555WV** | **CS55** | **0124** |
| **N555WZ** | **C56X** | **5366** |
| N555XL | GLF2 | 189/42 |
| **N555XS** | **GLF3** | **342** |
| **N556AF** | **GLF3** | **479** |
| N556AR | GLF5 | 556 |
| N556AT | C500 | 020 |
| (N556BA) | HS25 | 258111 |
| N556BA | HS25 | 258114 |
| **N556BG** | **C560** | **0499** |
| N556CC | C500 | 056 |
| N556CC | C550 | 095 |
| **N556CS** | **C56X** | **5577** |
| N556GA | ASTR | 255 |
| N556GA | GLF4 | 4056 |
| N556GA | GLF5 | 636 |
| N556GA | LJ55 | 028 |
| N556HD | LJ31 | 230 |
| **N556HD** | **LJ40** | **45-2110** |
| N556HD | WW24 | 341 |
| **N556HJ** | **LJ55** | **028** |
| (N556LX) | FA50 | 73 |
| N556N | WW24 | 331 |
| **N556RA** | **C650** | **7070** |
| (N556SA) | LJ60 | 056 |
| **N556TT** | **GLF5** | **5056** |
| N556WD | CL60 | 1047 |
| N557BA | HS25 | 258117 |
| N557CC | C500 | 057 |
| N557CC | C500 | 557 |
| N557CC | C550 | 577 |
| **N557CS** | **CS55** | **0016** |
| N557GA | GALX | 157 |
| **N557GA** | **GLF5** | **5154** |
| **N557HP** | **C525** | **0668** |
| **N557JK** | **GLF3** | **340** |
| (N557MG) | CS55 | 0064 |
| **N557PG** | **C560** | **0557** |
| (N557TC) | CS55 | 0088 |
| N557VB | HS25 | 258617 |
| **N557WY** | **GLF4** | **1276** |
| N557XP | BE40 | RK-557 |
| N558AC | LJ55 | 048 |
| N558AG | C550 | 558 |
| **N558AK** | **C560** | **0558** |
| N558BA | HS25 | 258119 |
| N558CB | C550 | 058 |
| N558CC | C500 | 058 |
| N558CC | C550 | 058 |
| N558CG | C560 | 0558 |
| N558CS | C56X | 5585 |
| N558E | LJ35 | 100 |
| **N558GA** | **GLF5** | **5258** |
| N558GA | GLF5 | 606 |
| N558GG | C560 | 0558 |
| N558GS | LJ45 | 225 |
| **N558HD** | **LJ31** | **230** |
| N558HJ | LJ55 | 048 |
| N558M | HS25 | 258027 |
| **N558R** | **C56X** | **5075** |
| N558V | C560 | 0558 |
| N558VP | C550 | 558 |
| **N558XP** | **BE40** | **RK-558** |
| N559AM | C650 | 7107 |
| (N559BA) | HS25 | 258121 |
| N559BC | C500 | 059 |
| N559BC | LJ55 | 009 |
| N559CC | C500 | 059 |
| N559CS | C56X | 5593 |
| **N559DM** | **HS25** | **258419** |
| N559GA | GALX | 159 |
| N559GA | GLF5 | 607 |

| | | |
|---|---|---|
| N559GP | JSTR | 5123/14 |
| N559GV | GLF5 | 559 |
| N559JA | CL64 | 5559 |
| **N559LC** | **GLF2** | **152** |
| N560A | C560 | 0364 |
| N560AB | C550 | 603 |
| N560AE | C560 | 0056 |
| **N560AF** | **C560** | **0100** |
| N560AG | C560 | 0301 |
| N560AJ | C550 | 560 |
| N560AJ | CS55 | 0094 |
| N560AN | LJ60 | 138 |
| **N560AT** | **C560** | **0521** |
| **N560AV** | **C560** | **0321** |
| **N560AW** | **C56X** | **5351** |
| N560BA | C560 | 0003 |
| N560BA | C560 | 0102 |
| **N560BA** | **C56X** | **5585** |
| N560BA | HS25 | 258122 |
| N560BB | C560 | 0135 |
| **N560BC** | **C560** | **0032** |
| (N560BD) | C560 | 0172 |
| (N560BD) | C560 | 0303 |
| N560BG | C560 | 0198 |
| **N560BG** | **C560** | **0277** |
| N560BJ | C560 | 0303 |
| N560BJ | C560 | 0436 |
| N560BL | C560 | 0057 |
| N560BL | C560 | 0566 |
| **N560BP** | **C560** | **0172** |
| N560BP | C560 | 0449 |
| **N560BT** | **C56X** | **5031** |
| N560CB | C550 | 555 |
| N560CC | C500 | 060 |
| N560CC | C550 | 001 |
| N560CC | C560 | 0751 |
| **N560CC** | **C560** | **550-0001** |
| N560CE | C560 | 0302 |
| **N560CE** | **C56X** | **5012** |
| **N560CF** | **C560** | **0040** |
| **N560CG** | **C56X** | **5121** |
| N560CH | C560 | 0611 |
| **N560CH** | **C560** | **0783** |
| N560CH | C56X | 5091 |
| **N560CJ** | **C560** | **0086** |
| **N560CK** | **C560** | **0207** |
| **N560CL** | **C560** | **0780** |
| **N560CM** | **C56X** | **5277** |
| (N560CP) | C560 | 0055 |
| N560CR | C560 | 0662 |
| **N560CR** | **C56X** | **5560** |
| (N560CT) | C560 | 0104 |
| N560CV | C560 | 560-0001 |
| N560CX | C560 | 0086 |
| **N560CX** | **C560** | **0582** |
| **N560CZ** | **C560** | **0002** |
| N560DA | C56X | 5107 |
| N560DC | C560 | 0021 |
| N560DE | C56X | 5284 |
| **N560DG** | **C56X** | **6009** |
| **N560DL** | **C560** | **0761** |
| N560DM | C560 | 0101 |
| N560DM | C560 | 0351 |
| **N560DM** | **GLF5** | **5045** |
| **N560DP** | **C56X** | **5212** |
| **N560DR** | **C56X** | **5073** |
| (N560DW) | C560 | 0399 |
| N560EA | C560 | 0062 |
| N560EC | C560 | 0101 |
| (N560ED) | C560 | 0150 |
| (N560EJ) | C560 | 0036 |
| N560EJ | FA50 | 60 |
| **N560EL** | **C560** | **0049** |
| **N560EM** | **C560** | **0278** |
| **N560EP** | **C560** | **0101** |
| N560ER | C560 | 0003 |
| **N560ES** | **C56X** | **5800** |
| N560FA | C560 | 0142 |
| N560FB | C560 | 0148 |
| N560FC | C56X | 5690 |
| N560FN | C560 | 0024 |
| **N560FP** | **C560** | **0566** |
| **N560G** | **C560** | **0112** |
| N560GA | C500 | 217 |
| N560GB | C560 | 0254 |
| N560GB | C56X | 5027 |
| **N560GB** | **C56X** | **6030** |
| **N560GC** | **C56X** | **5089** |

| | | |
|---|---|---|
| **N560GL** | **C560** | **0079** |
| N560GM | C560 | 0099 |
| N560GM | C56X | 5021 |
| **N560GP** | **C56X** | **5027** |
| **N560GS** | **C560** | **0263** |
| N560GT | C560 | 0142 |
| **N560GT** | **C560** | **0588** |
| N560H | C560 | 0017 |
| (N560HB) | C56X | 5607 |
| N560HC | C560 | 0020 |
| **N560HC** | **C560** | **0631** |
| **N560HD** | **C560** | **0274** |
| **N560HG** | **C560** | **0020** |
| **N560HJ** | **C56X** | **5078** |
| **N560HM** | **C560** | **0699** |
| N560HP | C560 | 0081 |
| **N560HW** | **C560** | **0281** |
| **N560HX** | **C56X** | **5139** |
| N560JC | C560 | 0283 |
| N560JC | C56X | 5541 |
| **N560JD** | **C560** | **0174** |
| **N560JF** | **C56X** | **5173** |
| **N560JG** | **C56X** | **5531** |
| **N560JL** | **C560** | **0044** |
| **N560JM** | **C560** | **0010** |
| N560JM | C560 | 0023 |
| N560JP | C560 | 0431 |
| N560JP | C56X | 5136 |
| N560JP | C56X | 5222 |
| N560JP | C56X | 5284 |
| N560JP | C56X | 5311 |
| N560JP | C56X | 5337 |
| N560JR | C560 | 0027 |
| (N560JS) | C560 | 0196 |
| N560JT | C560 | 0167 |
| **N560JT** | **C560** | **0670** |
| N560JV | C560 | 0065 |
| **N560JW** | **C560** | **0560** |
| N560KC | LJ35 | 079 |
| **N560KL** | **C560** | **0622** |
| (N560KN) | C56X | 5055 |
| **N560KT** | **C56X** | **5127** |
| **N560KW** | **C560** | **0751** |
| N560L | C560 | 0156 |
| **N560L** | **C56X** | **5011** |
| N560L | FA20 | 132 |
| N560LC | C560 | 0026 |
| N560LC | C560 | 0110 |
| **N560LC** | **C560** | **0296** |
| **N560LM** | **C560** | **0068** |
| N560LT | C560 | 0275 |
| (N560LW) | C560 | 0275 |
| N560MC | WW24 | 24 |
| N560ME | C560 | 0012 |
| N560MF | C56X | 5703 |
| **N560MG** | **C560** | **0223** |
| **N560MH** | **C560** | **0105** |
| N560ML | C56X | 5027 |
| **N560MM** | **C560** | **0228** |
| N560MM | C560 | 0235 |
| N560MR | C560 | 0015 |
| **N560MR** | **C560** | **0594** |
| (N560NS) | C560 | 0345 |
| N560NS | C560 | 0408 |
| **N560NY** | **C56X** | **5198** |
| **N560PA** | **C560** | **0136** |
| **N560PD** | **C56X** | **5311** |
| N560PJ | C52B | 0104 |
| **N560PK** | **C560** | **0133** |
| **N560PL** | **C56X** | **5600** |
| N560PS | C560 | 0120 |
| (N560PT) | C560 | 0106 |
| N560PX | C560 | 0691 |
| **N560PY** | **C560** | **0034** |
| N560R | FA20 | 313 |
| N560RA | C560 | 0182 |
| N560RA | FA20 | 56 |
| (N560RB) | C560 | 0137 |
| (N560RB) | C560 | 0239 |
| N560RB | C56X | 5676 |
| N560RC | C560 | 0397 |
| **N560RC** | **HA4T** | **RC-56** |
| **N560RF** | **C560** | **0379** |
| N560RG | C560 | 0198 |
| N560RG | C560 | 0551 |
| **N560RH** | **C560** | **0773** |
| N560RJ | C560 | 0107 |
| **N560RK** | **C560** | **0407** |

| | | |
|---|---|---|
| N560RL | C560 | 0135 |
| **N560RM** | **C560** | **0658** |
| N560RN | C560 | 0309 |
| **N560RP** | **C560** | **0158** |
| **N560RR** | **C560** | **0012** |
| N560RS | C560 | 0109A |
| N560RS | C56X | 5323 |
| **N560RV** | **C560** | **0417** |
| N560RV | C560 | 0558 |
| **N560RW** | **C560** | **0196** |
| N560S | C56X | 5190 |
| N560SB | HS25 | 257105 |
| N560SE | C560 | 0390 |
| **N560SH** | **GLF3** | **404** |
| N560SH | WW24 | 319 |
| **N560TA** | **C560** | **0430** |
| **N560TD** | **C56X** | **5711** |
| **N560TE** | **C560** | **0595** |
| N560TG | C560 | 0668 |
| **N560TH** | **C56X** | **5215** |
| N560TJ | C560 | 0417 |
| N560TM | C56X | 5564 |
| (N560TP) | C560 | 0668 |
| N560TS | C56X | 5144 |
| (N560TS) | CL64 | 5560 |
| **N560TV** | **C56X** | **5545** |
| N560TX | C560 | 0206 |
| **N560TX** | **C560** | **0382** |
| N560VH | C56X | 5629 |
| N560VP | C560 | 0002 |
| **N560VP** | **C560** | **0361** |
| N560VR | C560 | 0480 |
| **N560VR** | **C56X** | **5049** |
| N560VU | C560 | 707 |
| N560W | C560 | 0030 |
| N560WD | C560 | 0399 |
| N560WE | C560 | 0100 |
| (N560WF) | C56X | 5366 |
| **N560WH** | **C560** | **0013** |
| **N560WW** | **C560** | **0047** |
| **N560XL** | **C56X** | **706** |
| N560XP | BE40 | RK-560 |
| N561A | C560 | 0139 |
| **N561AC** | **C560** | **0218** |
| **N561AS** | **C550** | **173** |
| **N561B** | **C560** | **0008** |
| N561BA | HS25 | 258123 |
| **N561BC** | **C525** | **0257** |
| N561BC | C560 | 0057 |
| N561BP | C56X | 5134 |
| N561CC | C500 | 061 |
| **N561CC** | **C560** | **0416** |
| N561CC | CL64 | 5561 |
| **N561CE** | **C56X** | **5206** |
| **N561CM** | **C560** | **0443** |
| (N561CM) | F900 | 82 |
| N561D | FA10 | 54 |
| **N561DA** | **C560** | **0314** |
| N561DA | C56X | 5012 |
| **N561EA** | **EA50** | **000024** |
| **N561EJ** | **C560** | **0035** |
| **N561GA** | **GLF5** | **5261** |
| N561GA | GLF5 | 608 |
| N561GA | GLF5 | 661 |
| (N561GB) | C560 | 0254 |
| N561GR | C56X | 5109 |
| **N561JS** | **C560** | **0413** |
| **N561MK** | **C56X** | **5622** |
| **N561MT** | **C560** | **0122** |
| N561NC | FA10 | 195 |
| **N561PA** | **C560** | **0116** |
| N561PS | CS55 | 0013 |
| **N561PS** | **HS25** | **257087** |
| N561RP | HS25 | 256001 |
| **N561RW** | **C56X** | **5323** |
| (N561ST) | GLF3 | 302 |
| N561ST | GLF3 | 388 |
| N561TC | LJ60 | 010 |
| N561TS | C560 | 0057 |
| **N561VP** | **C560** | **560-0001** |
| **N561XL** | **C56X** | **5001** |
| N562BA | CL64 | 5562 |
| N562BA | HS25 | 258124 |
| N562CC | C500 | 062 |
| N562CD | C550 | 562 |
| N562CS | C56X | 5597 |
| N562CV | C560 | 0002 |
| N562DB | C56X | 5108 |
| N562DB | C56X | 5532 |
| N562DB | C56X | 5604 |
| **N562DB** | **C56X** | **6005** |
| **N562DD** | **C56X** | **5108** |
| **N562DL** | **C56X** | **5604** |
| N562E | C560 | 0140 |
| N562EJ | FA50 | 62 |
| N562GA | GALX | 162 |
| **N562GA** | **GLF5** | **5262** |
| N562GA | GLF5 | 642 |
| **N562LD** | **C56X** | **5532** |
| N562ME | CL64 | 5562 |
| N562MS | SBRL | 306-44 |
| N562R | SBRL | 306-37 |
| **N562RM** | **C550** | **646** |
| **N562TS** | **C56X** | **5178** |
| N562WD | C56X | 5226 |
| N562XL | C56X | 5002 |
| **N562XL** | **C56X** | **5313** |
| N562XL | C56X | 5501 |
| **N563BA** | **C750** | **0169** |
| N563BA | CL64 | 5563 |
| N563BA | HS25 | 258125 |
| N563C | C560 | 0174 |
| N563CC | C500 | 063 |
| N563CC | C500 | 563 |
| **N563CH** | **C56X** | **5182** |
| N563CS | C56X | 5601 |
| N563CV | C560 | 0003 |
| N563GA | GLF5 | 5236 |
| N563TS | CL61 | 5063 |
| **N563WD** | **C56X** | **6038** |
| N563XL | C56X | 5003 |
| N563XL | C56X | 5601 |
| **N563XL** | **C56X** | **6003** |
| **N563XP** | **C56X** | **5617** |
| N564BA | CL64 | 5564 |
| N564BA | HS25 | 258126 |
| **N564BR** | **HS25** | **257122** |
| N564CC | C500 | 064 |
| N564CC | C550 | 064 |
| **N564CL** | **LJ25** | **060** |
| N564CS | C56X | 5612 |
| (N564D) | C560 | 0175 |
| **N564GA** | **GLF5** | **5264** |
| N564MG | JSTR | 5021 |
| N564QS | GLF5 | 664 |
| **N564RM** | **WW24** | **434** |
| **N564TJ** | **C560** | **0432** |
| N564TS | CL61 | 5064 |
| N564VP | C550 | 564 |
| N564XP | BE40 | RK-564 |
| N565 | FA50 | 251 |
| **N565A** | **C680** | **0024** |
| N565A | FA20 | 499 |
| N565A | FA20 | 50 |
| N565A | FA50 | 174 |
| N565AB | C56X | 5072 |
| N565AB | C56X | 6050 |
| **N565AP** | **C56X** | **6050** |
| (N565B) | LJ55 | 065 |
| **N565BA** | **C56X** | **5072** |
| N565BA | HS25 | 258127 |
| **N565CC** | **C500** | **065** |
| N565CJ | C550 | 565 |
| N565DR | C56X | 5168 |
| **N565EJ** | **C560** | **0099** |
| **N565EU** | **BE40** | **RK-565** |
| N565GA | GALX | 165 |
| **N565GA** | **GLF4** | **4165** |
| N565GA | GLF5 | 665 |
| **N565GB** | **GALX** | **130** |
| **N565GG** | **LJ35** | **501** |
| (N565GW) | C500 | 050 |
| **N565JF** | **C525** | **0041** |
| N565JP | C525 | 0041 |
| **N565JP** | **C52B** | **0159** |
| N565JS | C550 | 565 |
| **N565JW** | **C560** | **0149** |
| N565KC | GLF2 | 46 |
| **N565NC** | **C550** | **565** |
| **N565NC** | **C560** | **0490** |
| **N565QS** | **C56X** | **5818** |
| **N565RV** | **GLF4** | **1323** |
| N565SS | C500 | 017 |
| **N565ST** | **GLF5** | **5015** |
| (N565TW) | C500 | 065 |
| **N565V** | **C500** | **365** |
| N565VV | C500 | 365 |
| (N565VV) | C510 | 0013 |
| N565VV | C550 | 152 |
| N565XP | BE40 | RK-565 |
| N566BA | HS25 | 258128 |
| N566C | GLF3 | 459 |
| N566CC | C500 | 066 |
| N566CC | C550 | 166 |
| **N566F** | **C56X** | **5606** |
| N566GA | GALX | 166 |
| N566GA | GLF5 | 609 |
| N566GA | GLF5 | 666 |
| N566GA | GLF5 | 699 |
| **N566KB** | **C560** | **0325** |
| N566MP | WW24 | 156 |
| N566N | CL61 | 3064 |
| N566NA | LJ25 | 064 |
| (N566PG) | WW24 | 273 |
| **N566QS** | **C56X** | **5825** |
| N566RB | LJ24 | 180 |
| N566TS | CL61 | 5066 |
| N566TX | C550 | 227 |
| N566VP | C560 | 0006 |
| **N566VR** | **C560** | **0480** |
| (N566W) | BE40 | RK-277 |
| N566YT | FA20 | 94/428 |
| N567A | GLF2 | 251 |
| **N567BA** | **BE40** | **RJ-22** |
| N567BA | HS25 | 258132 |
| **N567CA** | **C550** | **114** |
| N567CC | C500 | 067 |
| N567CH | C56X | 5243 |
| N567DK | BE40 | RK-155 |
| N567DW | SBRL | 282-35 |
| **N567EA** | **C500** | **067** |
| **N567F** | **C560** | **0171** |
| N567GA | GLF5 | 610 |
| N567GA | GLF5 | 667 |
| **N567HB** | **C52B** | **0298** |
| **N567JK** | **MU30** | **A007SA** |
| N567JP | C52A | 0011 |
| N567L | C500 | 621 |
| **N567MC** | **C56X** | **5357** |
| N567ML | CL60 | 1024 |
| N567NT | CL64 | 5567 |
| **N567RA** | **FA10** | **80** |
| N567S | C550 | 429 |
| (N567SC) | LJ55 | 091 |
| **N567T** | **PRM1** | **RB-37** |
| N567WB | C500 | 491 |
| **N567XP** | **BE40** | **RK-567** |
| N568BA | HS25 | 258135 |
| N568CC | C500 | 068 |
| N568CH | C560 | 0611 |
| N568CM | C500 | 068 |
| **N568CS** | **C56X** | **5637** |
| **N568DM** | **C56X** | **5325** |
| **N568EA** | **EA50** | **000168** |
| **N568GA** | **GLF5** | **5268** |
| N568GA | GLF5 | 611 |
| N568GA | GLF5 | 668 |
| N568GB | C560 | 0254 |
| **N568JC** | **C560** | **0283** |
| N568JC | GLF5 | 568 |
| N568M | GLEX | 9069 |
| **N568PA** | **LJ35** | **205** |
| **N568PB** | **EA50** | **000067** |
| N568Q | FA20 | 149 |
| **N568QS** | **C56X** | **5829** |
| N568RL | C560 | 0443 |
| **N568SD** | **BE40** | **RK-36** |
| N568TN | GLF2 | 67 |
| N568VA | FA50 | 176 |
| N568WC | C560 | 0083 |
| N569BA | HS25 | 258136 |
| N569BW | FA20 | 259 |
| **N569BW** | **FA50** | **45** |
| N569CA | FA50 | 115 |
| N569CC | C500 | 069 |
| N569CC | FA50 | 115 |
| N569CS | HS25 | 25214 |
| N569CW | GLF4 | 1145 |
| **N569D** | **FA20** | **259** |
| **N569DM** | **C52A** | **0088** |
| **N569DW** | **FA10** | **220** |
| N569DW | FA20 | 259 |
| N569GA | GLF4 | 4169 |
| N569GA | GLF5 | 5169 |
| N569GA | GLF5 | 612 |
| N569GA | GLF5 | 669 |
| **N569SC** | **LJ31** | **177** |
| **N569TA** | **C560** | **0006** |
| **N570AM** | **LJ45** | **238** |
| N570BA | HS25 | 258137 |
| N570BJ | C560 | 0030 |
| N570CC | C500 | 070 |
| N570CC | C500 | 570 |
| N570CC | CS55 | 0070 |
| N570D | C500 | 660 |
| **N570DC** | **GLF4** | **1185** |
| **N570DM** | **C525** | **0055** |
| **N570EA** | **EA50** | **000070** |
| **N570EJ** | **C560** | **0164** |
| N570FT | LJ24 | 005 |
| **N570GA** | **GLF4** | **4170** |
| N570GA | GLF5 | 613 |
| (N570JG) | LJ24 | 221 |
| N570L | FA20 | 171 |
| N570MH | C560 | 0006 |
| N570P | LJ24 | 221 |
| N570PT | C750 | 0270 |
| N570R | SBRL | 282-3 |
| **N570R** | **SBRL** | **465-75** |
| N570RC | CS55 | 0070 |
| **N570RG** | **EA50** | **000048** |
| **N570RZ** | **C680** | **0231** |
| N570VP | C550 | 570 |
| **N570VP** | **C560** | **0070** |
| N570WD | C550 | 570 |
| N570XP | BE40 | RK-570 |
| **N571BA** | **CL64** | **5571** |
| **N571BC** | **C550** | **599** |
| N571BJ | GLF2 | 15 |
| N571CC | C500 | 071 |
| N571CC | CS55 | 0071 |
| N571CH | HS25 | 25284 |
| N571CH | HS25 | 257071 |
| N571CH | HS25 | 257078 |
| **N571CH** | **HS25** | **258540** |
| **N571CS** | **C56X** | **5680** |
| N571DU | HS25 | 256071 |
| N571E | HS25 | 256071 |
| N571GA | GLF4 | 4171 |
| N571GA | GLF5 | 5071 |
| N571GA | GLF5 | 614 |
| N571GA | GLF5 | 671 |
| N571GH | HS25 | 25284 |
| (N571K) | C500 | 328 |
| (N571MC) | WW24 | 175 |
| N571NC | SBRL | 306-1 |
| **N571P** | **MS76** | **071** |
| N571TS | CL65 | 5718 |
| **N571TW** | **BE40** | **RK-571** |
| N572CC | C500 | 072 |
| (N572CC) | CS55 | 0072 |
| N572CV | C560 | 0072 |
| **N572EC** | **GLF4** | **1139** |
| N572EC | GLF5 | 5072 |
| N572GA | GLF4 | 4172 |
| N572GA | GLF5 | 5072 |
| N572GA | GLF5 | 615 |
| N572M | WW24 | 258 |
| N572MS | CL64 | 5572 |
| N572PB | C550 | 550-0956 |
| N572R | SBRL | 282-74 |
| N573AB | C560 | 0427 |
| **N573AB** | **C56X** | **5635** |
| N573AC | CL61 | 5060 |
| N573AC | FA50 | 217 |
| N573BA | CL64 | 5573 |
| **N573BB** | **C560** | **0108** |
| N573BB | CS55 | 0037 |
| N573BC | CL64 | 5573 |
| (N573BP) | C560 | 0108 |
| N573CC | C500 | 073 |
| N573CC | CS55 | 0007 |
| **N573CM** | **C525** | **0352** |
| N573CW | FA50 | 73 |
| N573E | FA20 | 502 |
| N573EJ | FA20 | 28 |
| N573F | C560 | 0171 |
| N573J | F900 | 39 |
| N573J | FA10 | 196 |
| N573L | C500 | 435 |
| N573LP | LJ24 | 196 |
| N573LP | LJ35 | 153 |

| | | |
|---|---|---|
| N573LP | LJ35 | 658 |
| N573LR | LJ24 | 196 |
| **N573LR** | **LJ35** | **153** |
| **N573M** | **C550** | **550-1066** |
| N573P | WW24 | 257 |
| **N573QS** | **C56X** | **5827** |
| **N573TR** | **FA50** | **217** |
| N573XP | BE40 | RK-573 |
| N574AV | C56X | 5074 |
| N574BA | LJ31 | 211 |
| **N574BB** | **C52A** | **0371** |
| N574BB | C560 | 0022 |
| **N574BP** | **C560** | **0022** |
| N574CC | C500 | 074 |
| N574CC | C500 | 657 |
| N574CF | MU30 | A079SA |
| **N574CS** | **C56X** | **5705** |
| N574DA | LJ31 | 211 |
| **N574DA** | **LJ60** | **055** |
| N574F | CL64 | 5574 |
| N574GA | GLF4 | 4174 |
| N574GA | GLF5 | 5074 |
| N574GA | GLF5 | 616 |
| **N574JS** | **E50P** | **50000046** |
| **N574M** | **C550** | **550-0910** |
| **N574QS** | **C56X** | **5820** |
| N574R | SBRL | 282-82 |
| (N574U) | MU30 | A079SA |
| N574W | C500 | 074 |
| N574W | LJ55 | 011 |
| N575 | HS25 | 25218 |
| **N575AG** | **LJ45** | **312** |
| **N575BW** | **C550** | **128** |
| N575CC | C500 | 075 |
| N575CC | C500 | 475 |
| **N575CC** | **EA50** | **000075** |
| N575CF | CL61 | 5019 |
| N575CF | CL61 | 5188 |
| N575CT | GLF4 | 1284 |
| N575DU | HS25 | 25021 |
| N575DU | HS25 | 25218 |
| N575E | GLF2 | 219/20 |
| N575E | GLF4 | 1007 |
| N575ET | ASTR | 042 |
| N575EW | ASTR | 042 |
| **N575EW** | **CS55** | **0140** |
| N575FM | C550 | 129 |
| N575G | LJ24 | 138 |
| N575GA | GLF5 | 5075 |
| **N575GA** | **GLF5** | **5275** |
| N575GA | GLF5 | 617 |
| N575GD | LJ25 | 101 |
| **N575GH** | **LJ55** | **042** |
| N575HW | LJ24 | 068 |
| N575JC | C56X | 6005 |
| **N575JC** | **FA50** | **349** |
| **N575JR** | **HS25** | **258755** |
| **N575JS** | **E50P** | **50000051** |
| **N575M** | **C550** | **550-0911** |
| (N575MA) | CL61 | 5061 |
| **N575MA** | **HS25** | **HA-0016** |
| **N575MR** | **HS25** | **258255** |
| **N575NR** | **C56X** | **5759** |
| N575PC | C560 | 0223 |
| N575PT | PRM1 | RB-133 |
| (N575PT) | PRM1 | RB-150 |
| **N575QS** | **C56X** | **5730** |
| N575R | SBRL | 282-34 |
| **N575RB** | **BE40** | **RK-99** |
| N575RD | C500 | 075 |
| N575SC | F2TH | 23 |
| N575SE | GLF2 | 221 |
| N575SF | GLF2 | 221 |
| N575SF | GLF4 | 1233 |
| **N575SG** | **CS55** | **0064** |
| N575SR | C500 | 597 |
| **N575VP** | **C560** | **0375** |
| N575W | C550 | 008 |
| **N575WB** | **CL30** | **20075** |
| N575WW | LJ35 | 043 |
| N575XP | BE40 | RK-575 |
| N576CC | C500 | 076 |
| (N576CC) | C500 | 576 |
| N576CC | C550 | 576 |
| **N576CS** | **C56X** | **5794** |
| **N576EA** | **EA50** | **000076** |
| N576GA | GLF5 | 5076 |
| N576JS | E50P | 50000057 |
| **N576LC** | **WW24** | **257** |
| **N576QS** | **C56X** | **5708** |
| N576R | SBRL | 282-7 |
| **N576SC** | **C52A** | **0224** |
| N576XP | BE40 | RK-576 |
| N577CC | C500 | 077 |
| N577CC | LJ45 | 238 |
| N577CJ | CL64 | 5577 |
| **N577CS** | **C56X** | **5726** |
| **N577DA** | **CL64** | **5398** |
| N577GA | GLF4 | 4177 |
| N577GA | GLF5 | 5077 |
| N577GA | GLF5 | 577 |
| **N577JC** | **C750** | **0122** |
| **N577JT** | **C500** | **430** |
| N577LJ | LJ25 | 023 |
| N577PM | SBRL | 282-2 |
| **N577PS** | **C56X** | **5581** |
| **N577QS** | **C56X** | **5735** |
| N577R | SBRL | 282-2 |
| N577RT | FA10 | 80 |
| N577S | FA20 | 68 |
| (N577SD) | C525 | 0131 |
| N577SV | C525 | 0131 |
| (N577SW) | GLF4 | 1284 |
| N577SW | GLF4 | 1385 |
| N577SW | SBRL | 380-21 |
| N577T | HS25 | 258149 |
| N577VM | C500 | 430 |
| **N577VM** | **C550** | **550-0863** |
| N577VM | C550 | 615 |
| N577VM | SBRL | 282-31 |
| N577VN | C550 | 615 |
| N577VU | GLF4 | 1385 |
| N577XP | BE40 | RK-577 |
| **N577XW** | **C560** | **0083** |
| **N578BB** | **CS55** | **0037** |
| N578CC | C500 | 078 |
| **N578CJ** | **C52B** | **0282** |
| **N578CM** | **C510** | **0292** |
| N578CS | C56X | 5800 |
| N578DF | GLF2 | 126 |
| N578FP | CL61 | 5078 |
| N578GA | GLF5 | 5078 |
| N578GA | GLF5 | 578 |
| N578GG | CS55 | 0079 |
| N578LJ | LJ24 | 006 |
| **N578M** | **C550** | **612** |
| N578QS | C56X | 5754 |
| N578W | C550 | 082 |
| (N578WB) | C500 | 095 |
| **N579BJ** | **C560** | **0383** |
| N579BJ | C56X | 5528 |
| N579CC | C500 | 079 |
| **N579CE** | **C560** | **0579** |
| N579CL | C56X | 5779 |
| N579CS | C56X | 5807 |
| N579GA | GLF5 | 5079 |
| **N579GA** | **GLF5** | **5279** |
| N579GA | GLF5 | 579 |
| **N579JS** | **E50P** | **50000064** |
| N579L | C550 | 579 |
| **N579M** | **C550** | **550-1133** |
| **N579QS** | **C56X** | **5773** |
| N579TG | GLF3 | 433 |
| N579XP | BE40 | RK-579 |
| N580AV | C550 | 161 |
| **N580AW** | **C56X** | **5017** |
| N580BA | HS25 | 258139 |
| **N580BC** | **C56X** | **5059** |
| N580CC | C500 | 080 |
| N580CE | C560 | 0302 |
| N580CE | C560 | 0580 |
| N580CS | C56X | 5815 |
| N580GA | GLF5 | 5080 |
| N580GA | GLF5 | 580 |
| N580GA | GLF5 | 640 |
| N580GS | FA10 | 132 |
| N580GV | WW24 | 213 |
| **N580JS** | **E50P** | **50000079** |
| **N580JT** | **C560** | **0167** |
| N580MA | HS25 | 25237 |
| N580MA | HS25 | 256064 |
| N580MR | C560 | 0015 |
| N580NJ | WW24 | 58 |
| **N580QS** | **C56X** | **5741** |
| **N580R** | **C500** | **127** |
| N580RA | GLF2 | 117 |
| **N580RC** | **C56X** | **5166** |
| N580RJ | BE40 | RK-329 |
| **N580RJ** | **HS25** | **HA-0039** |
| **N580RK** | **BE40** | **RK-329** |
| N580SH | C550 | 550-0994 |
| **N580WC** | **EA50** | **000080** |
| N580WE | WW24 | 123 |
| N580WS | HS25 | 25047 |
| N580XP | BE40 | RK-580 |
| N581AS | LJ35 | 311 |
| N581BA | HS25 | 258140 |
| N581CC | C500 | 081 |
| N581CC | LJ35 | 083 |
| **N581CM** | **CS55** | **0033** |
| **N581CS** | **C56X** | **5817** |
| N581EA | CS55 | 0080 |
| N581GA | GLF5 | 5081 |
| **N581GA** | **GLF5** | **5281** |
| N581GA | GLF5 | 581 |
| N581GA | GLF5 | 651 |
| N581GE | HS25 | 258581 |
| **N581JS** | **E50P** | **50000110** |
| **N581MB** | **GLF2** | **109** |
| N581NC | FA10 | 196 |
| **N581PH** | **LJ35** | **083** |
| N581RA | LJ31 | 106 |
| **N581SF** | **PRM1** | **RB-47** |
| N581SS | FA20 | 66 |
| **N581TS** | **CL64** | **5482** |
| N581WD | GLF2 | 126 |
| N582BA | HS25 | 258138 |
| N582CC | C500 | 082 |
| N582CC | C550 | 082 |
| (N582CP) | HS25 | 258021 |
| **N582EJ** | **FA50** | **82** |
| (N582G) | FA20 | 23 |
| N582GA | GLF5 | 5082 |
| N582GA | GLF5 | 582 |
| N582GA | GLF5 | 652 |
| (N582JF) | C650 | 7077 |
| N582VP | C560 | 0382 |
| N582XP | BE40 | RK-582 |
| **N583AJ** | **GLF4** | **1184** |
| N583BA | HS25 | 258141 |
| N583BS | LJ35 | 258 |
| N583CC | C500 | 083 |
| **N583CE** | **C560** | **0583** |
| N583CM | HS25 | 25225 |
| (N583CS) | C56X | 6064 |
| N583CW | C560 | 0123 |
| N583D | GLF3 | 471 |
| N583FH | LJ45 | 130 |
| N583GA | GLF5 | 5083 |
| N583GA | GLF5 | 583 |
| N583LJ | LJ31 | 151 |
| N583M | C560 | 0186 |
| N583M | C560 | 0326 |
| N583MP | C500 | 477 |
| N583N | C560 | 0186 |
| N583PS | LJ31 | 151 |
| N583PS | LJ35 | 258 |
| N583PS | LJ45 | 136 |
| **N583PS** | **LJ45** | **331** |
| **N583QS** | **C56X** | **5812** |
| N583VC | HS25 | 258003 |
| (N583VP) | C550 | 583 |
| N583XP | BE40 | RK-583 |
| N584BA | HS25 | 258142 |
| N584CC | C500 | 084 |
| N584CC | C500 | 584 |
| N584CC | C56X | 5025 |
| **N584D** | **CL30** | **20239** |
| N584D | GLF4 | 1065 |
| N584DB | HS25 | 25023 |
| (N584DM) | GLF2 | 92 |
| N584GA | GLF5 | 5084 |
| **N584GA** | **GLF5** | **5284** |
| N584GA | GLF5 | 584 |
| N584GA | GLF5 | 654 |
| N585A | GLF2 | 44 |
| **N585A** | **GLF5** | **5110** |
| N585AC | FA20 | 205 |
| N585BA | HS25 | 258144 |
| N585BD | CL64 | 5585 |
| **N585BP** | **F9EX** | **170** |
| N585CC | C500 | 085 |
| **N585D** | **GLF4** | **1258** |
| **N585DG** | **C525** | **0057** |
| N585DM | C550 | 086 |
| N585G | BE40 | RK-94 |
| N585GA | GLF5 | 5085 |
| N585GA | GLF5 | 585 |
| N585GA | GLF5 | 618 |
| N585GA | GLF5 | 685 |
| N585JC | GLF5 | 618 |
| **N585KS** | **C550** | **550-0945** |
| **N585M** | **C750** | **0096** |
| **N585MC** | **C525** | **0452** |
| N585PC | C56X | 5366 |
| N585PK | C525 | 0452 |
| N585PK | C52B | 0011 |
| N585PS | C550 | 585 |
| N585QS | C56X | 5748 |
| **N585T** | **C750** | **0197** |
| N585TC | MU30 | A060SA |
| **N585TH** | **C550** | **550-1035** |
| **N585TV** | **E55P** | **50500006** |
| N585UC | CL61 | 5002 |
| N585UC | FA20 | 299 |
| **N585VC** | **HS25** | **258585** |
| (N585VP) | C560 | 0585 |
| N585XP | BE40 | RK-585 |
| N586 | JSTR | 5085 |
| N586BA | HS25 | 258145 |
| N586C | GLF3 | 459 |
| N586CC | C500 | 086 |
| N586CC | C560 | 0186 |
| N586CC | CS55 | 0086 |
| **N586CP** | **C550** | **013** |
| **N586CS** | **FA50** | **260** |
| **N586D** | **GLF4** | **1439** |
| **N586ED** | **C52A** | **0324** |
| N586GA | GLF5 | 5086 |
| N586GA | GLF5 | 586 |
| N586JR | HS25 | 257014 |
| **N586RE** | **C550** | **222** |
| N586SF | BE40 | RK-151 |
| N586SF | C56X | 5064 |
| **N586SF** | **C56X** | **5592** |
| N586XP | BE40 | RK-586 |
| N587BA | HS25 | 258147 |
| N587CC | C500 | 087 |
| N587CC | CL61 | 5087 |
| N587GA | GLF5 | 5087 |
| **N587GA** | **GLF5** | **5287** |
| N587GA | GLF5 | 587 |
| N587GA | GLF5 | 657 |
| (N587K) | C560 | 0587 |
| **N587QS** | **C56X** | **5805** |
| N587S | C650 | 0188 |
| N587VV | HS25 | 257046 |
| N587XP | BE40 | RK-587 |
| **N588AC** | **C550** | **550-0912** |
| **N588AT** | **GLF4** | **4020** |
| N588BA | HS25 | 258150 |
| N588CA | C500 | 471 |
| N588CC | C500 | 088 |
| N588CG | LJ24 | 304 |
| N588CT | CS55 | 0060 |
| N588FJ | FA50 | 88 |
| N588GA | GLF5 | 5088 |
| **N588GA** | **GLF5** | **5288** |
| N588GA | GLF5 | 588 |
| **N588GS** | **F9EX** | **104** |
| **N588LS** | **GLF4** | **1245** |
| **N588QS** | **C56X** | **5721** |
| N588R | ASTR | 042 |
| **N588SS** | **GLF2** | **142** |
| N588UC | CL60 | 1071 |
| N588XP | BE40 | RK-588 |
| N589BA | HS25 | 258157 |
| N589CC | C500 | 089 |
| N589CJ | C500 | 589 |
| **N589DC** | **FA20** | **45** |
| N589EJ | FA50 | 89 |
| (N589FJ) | FA50 | 289 |
| N589GA | GLF5 | 5089 |
| **N589GA** | **GLF5** | **5289** |
| N589GA | GLF5 | 589 |
| N589GA | GLF5 | 659 |
| N589HM | GLF2 | 92 |
| **N589HM** | **GLF4** | **1153** |
| N589HM | GLF5 | 554 |
| **N589K** | **GLF5** | **5235** |
| N589KM | FA50 | 54 |
| **N589QS** | **C56X** | **5810** |

**N589SJ C550 589**
N589TB ASTR 037
N589UC HS25 257137
N589XP BE40 RK-589
N590 LJ35 186
**N590A C560 0029**
**N590AK C56X 5038**
N590AS C650 0088
N590BA HS25 258160
N590CC C500 090
N590CH GLF2 19
N590CH HS25 25222
N590CH LJ24 295
(N590CH) LJ35 060
N590CW FA50 20
N590DA GLF3 445
N590EA C500 072
N590EA C500 182
**N590F F900 98**
**N590FA ASTR 224**
N590GA GALX 190
N590GA GLF5 5090
N590GA GLF5 590
N590GA LJ24 139
N590HM GLF4 1153
N590J LJ35 336
N590JC LJ45 059
N590MH LJ31 058
N590PJ C52B 0104
**N590QS C56X 5738**
**N590RA FA50 20**
N590RB C500 090
N590RB C550 230
(N590VC) HS25 258590
**N590VP C56X 5090**
N590XL C56X 5590
N591BA HS25 258162
N591CC C500 091
**N591CF C560 0661**
N591D LJ24 115
N591D LJ35 069
**N591DK C560 0591**
N591DL LJ24 115
N591ES C510 0042
N591GA GLF5 5091
**N591GA GLF5 5291**
N591GA GLF5 591
N591GA LJ24 142
N591KR LJ25 019
N591M C560 0085
N591M C560 0533
**N591MA C56X 5163**
N591SC LJ55 091
N591XP BE40 RK-591
N592BA HS25 258166
N592CC C500 092
**N592CF C56X 5207**
N592DC FA10 26
**N592DR C52A 0028**
N592GA GLF5 5092
"N592GA" GLF5 5250
**N592GA GLF5 5292**
N592GA GLF5 592
N592GA LJ24 143
**N592HC PRM1 RB-92**
N592KR LJ25 028
N592M C560 0338
N592M CS55 0041
N592MA C560 0372
**N592QS C56X 5706**
N592SP CL30 20123
**N592VP C560 0092A**
**N592WP C500 253**
N592XP BE40 RK-592
N593BA HS25 258168
**N593BW C500 675**
N593CC C500 093
(N593CC) C500 593
N593CC CS55 0093
N593CW C560 0223
N593DC FA10 180
N593DS C500 593
N593EM C550 714
N593GA GLF5 5093
N593GA GLF5 535
N593GA GLF5 593
N593GA LJ24 144
**N593HR HS25 258089**
N593KR LJ24 140
N593LR LJ35 593
N593M C560 0237
N593M C560 0525
N593M CS55 0021
N593MD C560 0074
N593PN LJ35 593
N593XL C56X 5593
**N593XP BE40 RK-593**
N594BA HS25 258170
**N594CA CL30 20082**
N594CC C500 094
N594CC CS55 0094
N594G C550 482
N594GA GLF5 525
**N594GA GLF5 5294**
N594GA GLF5 594
N594GA LJ25 003
N594JB C525 0067
N594KR JSTR 5099/5
**N594M C560 0279**
**N594QS C56X 5697**
**N594RJ CL61 5029**
N594SF CL64 5594
(N594VP) C560 0094
**N594WP C550 693**
**N594XP BE40 RK-594**
N595A C56X 5160
**N595A GLF5 5117**
N595BA HS25 258171
**N595BA LJ35 230**
N595CC C500 095
N595CC CS55 0091
N595CL C56X 5795
N595CM CS55 0091
(N595CW) FA50 15
**N595DC C500 265**
N595DC FA20 500
**N595DM C525 0697**
**N595E GLF4 1025**
**N595G C56X 5224**
N595GA GALX 095
N595GA GALX 195
N595GA GLF5 5095
N595GA GLF5 522
N595GA GLF5 595
N595GA LJ24 147
(N595GV) GLF5 595
**N595JJ C560 0680**
N595JS FA50 200
N595MA C560 0680
N595PA LJ31 150
**N595PC C550 550-0826**
**N595PE GLF4 1373**
**N595PL LJ35 448**
N595PT BE40 RJ-18
N595QS C56X 5712
**N595S C56X 6012**
**N595SY C680 0091**
**N595XP BE40 RK-595**
N596A F2TH 28
N596BA HS25 258172
N596CC C500 096
N596DA FA20 273
**N596DC GLF4 4129**
N596GA GLF5 520
N596GA GLF5 596
N596GA LJ24 150
N596HF LJ24 150
N596SW HS25 258096
N596VP C560 0396
**N596XP BE40 RK-596**
N596XP HS25 258596
N597BA HS25 258174
N597BL LJ35 597
N597CC C500 097
**N597CS C500 481**
**N597DA CL64 5359**
**N597DC GLF4 4167**
N597DM CL64 5398
N597FJ CL61 3061
N597FJ FA50 97
N597GA GLF5 5097
N597GA GLF5 519
N597GA GLF5 5197
N597GA LJ24 152
N597JA CL64 5597
N597JT LJ35 597
(N597JV) C500 597
N597KC C560 0597
(N597N) BE40 RJ-29
N597U C750 0004
N597XP HS25 258597
**N598AW C650 0112**
N598BA HS25 258175
N598C C650 0112
**N598CA C550 198**
N598CC C500 098
N598CW C560 0198
N598DA CL64 5498
**N598EA EA50 000098**
**N598EU BE40 RK-598**
**N598F GLF5 598**
N598GA GLF5 5098
N598GA GLF5 510
**N598GA GLF5 5298**
N598GA GLF5 598
N598GA LJ24 155
N598GS GLF2 85
N598GS GLF3 469
N598JC FA10 112
N598JL BE40 RJ-19
**N598JM WW24 222**
**N598KW CS55 0098**
N598MT CL64 5502
**N598WC CL64 5511**
N598WC CS55 0098
(N598WW) LJ35 332
**N599AK HS25 258630**
N599BA HS25 258173
**N599BR C500 664**
N599CB CS55 0054
N599CC C500 099
N599CN GLF4 1065
N599CT LJ31 200
**N599DA CL64 5498**
N599DA GLF3 445
N599EC HS25 258183
N599EC LJ55 018
N599FW C550 599
N599GA GLF5 515
N599GA LJ24 156
**N599GB C680 0146**
N599JL BE40 RJ-14
N599KC WW24 42
**N599LP C560 0085**
**N599QS C56X 5714**
N599RR FA20 325
N599SC C560 0051
N599SC FA50 242
N599SC LJ35 670
N599SC LJ60 113
N599SG C560 0051
**N599ZM FA20 481**
**N600AE HS25 256068**
N600AE LJ35 149
N600AG HS25 256069
**N600AJ LJ60 199**
**N600AK GLEX 9033**
**N600AL C525 0383**
N600AL HS25 256051
**N600AM CL64 5345**
N600AN CRVT 10
N600AN LJ31 242
(N600AP) FA10 187
**N600AR GLF4 1419**
**N600AS E50P 50000018**
N600AS F9EX 17
N600AS FA50 90
N600AS LJ60 040
**N600AT C550 551**
N600AV HS25 256015
**N600AW C750 0181**
N600AW HS25 256018
N600AW LJ31 017
N600AW LJ31 242
N600AW LJ35 149
N600B GLF2 82
N600B GLF3 459
N600B SBRL 306-33
N600BD CL60 1020
N600BE LJ35 348
N600BG GLF3 430
N600BG GLF4 1268
N600BJ C56X 5017
N600BL GLF3 482
N600BP CL60 1004
N600BP CL60 1073
N600BP SBRL 282-53
N600BT FA10 6
N600BT GLF2 82
N600BW C560 0087
**N600BW C560 0671**
N600BZ CL60 1028
**N600C LJ55 047**
(N600CC) BE40 RK-45
N600CC BE40 RK-6
N600CC CL60 1056
N600CC GLEX 9019
(N600CC) GLF4 1321
(N600CC) LJ35 083
**N600CD FA20 377/548**
N600CD GLF2 221
N600CD LJ25 274
N600CD WW24 10
N600CF CL60 1049
N600CF CL60 1078
N600CG MU30 A055SA
N600CH FA50 181
**N600CK GLF4 1169**
N600CL CL60 1005
**N600CL LJ60 110**
N600CN LJ35 235
**N600CN LJ60 040**
N600CP CL60 1075
N600CR C550 401
**N600CS E50P 50000084**
N600CS GLF2 75/7
N600CS GLF4 1020
**N600DE C510 0005**
(N600DH) C500 576
N600DH CL61 5176
N600DL CL60 1078
(N600DP) HS25 25202
N600DR CL61 5176
**N600DR GLF4 1356**
(N600DT) JSTR 5058/4
**N600DT LJ35 017**
N600DW GLF4 1169
**N600EA CS55 0015**
(N600EC) CL60 1073
N600EF C560 0376
**N600EF LJ60 182**
N600EG HS25 25075
N600ER WW24 84
N600ES CL64 5439
N600ES GLF3 322
N600EZ C550 228
N600FF CL60 1019
N600FL HS25 256034
N600G HS25 256066
N600G LJ24 025
N600G LJ35 352
**N600GA CL61 3046**
N600GA LJ60 021
(N600GE) SBRL 306-24
**N600GG LJ60 115**
N600GH C550 717
N600GH C650 0029
**N600GL SBRL 306-24**
N600GM FA10 25
**N600GM LJ25 290**
(N600GP) HS25 256055
N600GP LJ35 236
**N600GW MU30 A044SA**
**N600HA CL60 1071**
N600HC HS25 257036
N600HD LJ25 101
**N600HL FA10 19**
**N600HR C525 0038**
N600HS HS25 256033
N600HS HS25 258029
**N600HT E50P 50000036**
N600HT LJ25 101
**N600J GLF5 5138**
N600J HS25 258217
N600J JSTR 5039
N600J JSTR 5086/44
N600J WW24 302
N600JA HS25 25187
**N600JB C550 691**
N600JC FA20 7
N600JC LJ24 246
N600JD C650 0236

**N600JD GLF5 640**
**N600JM F9EX 5**
N600JM FA50 124
N600JS SBRL 282-44
(N600JT) JSTR 5213
N600JT LJ25 291
N600JW CL60 1061
N600K WW24 148
N600KC CL60 1012
N600KC FA20 58
N600KC HS25 258207
**N600KE WW24 416**
**N600KM CS55 0008**
N600L HS25 25187
N600L LJ60 020
**N600L LJ60 259**
N600LC LJ35 211
N600LC LJ60 021
**N600LC LJ60 265**
N600LE LJ35 149
N600LE WW24 425
N600LF C560 0376
N600LF C560 0569
N600LF F9EX 74
N600LF LJ35 654
N600LG CL60 1052
N600LG LJ60 021
**N600LG LJ60 230**
N600LL LJ35 438
N600LN LJ35 332
**N600LN LJ60 082**
N600LP HS25 25187
**N600LS CL30 20134**
(N600LS) CL30 20147
N600LS CL60 1048
N600LS HS25 258114
N600LS HS25 259019
(N600LX) CL61 3008
N600MB GLF2 108
N600MB HS25 256044
N600MG CL60 1020
N600MK CL60 1050
**N600MK HS25 256004**
N600ML GLF4 1104
N600ML LJ60 217
N600MS CL61 3041
N600MS CL64 5333
N600MS MU30 A055SA
N600MT C500 070
**N600MV HS25 259036**
**N600N FA50 256**
N600NG HS25 258537
N600NM LJ60 182
**N600NP CL61 3002**
**N600NY WW24 231**
**N600PB E50P 50000130**
N600PB FA10 189
N600PC LJ24 292
N600PC LJ25 116
N600PD CL60 1020
**N600PH LJ60 074**
N600PJ LJ60 004
N600PM GLF3 333
N600PM GLF4 1255
N600QJ SBRL 465-54
**N600QS C56X 5664**
N600R SBRL 282-6
**N600RA CRVT 36**
N600RE CL60 1079
N600RH GLF3 451
N600RH GLF5 558
**N600RM C500 424**
N600SB BE40 RK-283
N600SB HS25 256034
N600SJ SBRL 306-15
N600SN HS25 256064
N600SR C500 236
N600SR C500 275
N600SS C500 623
N600ST C550 383
N600ST C550 550-1054
N600ST CL60 1028
N600ST CL60 1082
N600ST CL60 1085
N600SV HS25 25159
N600SZ C550 383
N600TC WW24 299
N600TD WW24 254
N600TD WW24 84
N600TE CL60 1056
N600TF CS55 0118
N600TG SBRL 465-65
(N600TH) HS25 258029
N600TH HS25 258030
N600TJ WW24 198
N600TN CL60 1029
N600TP JSTR 5058/4
N600TP WW24 84
(N600TT) C500 075
N600TT CL60 1048
N600TT HS25 256047
N600TT JSTR 5058/4
**N600TW FA10 153**
N600UD C650 0236
(N600US) F9EX 210
**N600VC GLF4 1227**
(N600VE) CS55 0019
**N600WD FA20 300/508**
**N600WG FA50 98**
**N600WJ CL60 1007**
N600WJ HS25 256017
N600WJ LJ35 466
N600WM C500 040
N600WT LJ35 037
N600XJ LJ24 190
**N600YB GALX 096**
N600YY CL60 1033
N600YY GLF3 304
N601A CL61 5166
**N601AA CL61 3061**
N601AB C560 0158
N601AB C650 7098
N601AB GALX 047
**N601AD CL61 5186**
N601AE CL61 3050
**N601AF CL61 5045**
N601AG CL61 3001
N601AG CL61 3011
N601AN CRVT 13
(N601AV) GALX 053
N601BA HS25 256040
N601BA HS25 258082
**N601BC C550 121**
N601BD CL61 3010
**N601BE CL61 5103**
N601BF CL61 5065
N601BH CL61 5043
**N601BW CL61 5150**
(N601BX) HS25 258082
N601CB CL61 5090
N601CC C500 101
N601CC CL61 5008
N601CC CL61 5087
N601CC CL64 5324
N601CD CL61 5088
N601CH CL61 5093
(N601CH) FA50 47
N601CJ C525 0601
N601CJ CL61 5023
N601CL CL61 3001
N601CL CL61 3003
N601CL CL61 3016
**N601CM CL60 1079**
N601CM JSTR 5214
**N601CN LJ60 087**
(N601CR) CL60 1051
**N601CT CL60 1049**
**N601CV CL61 5144**
N601CV CRVT 40
N601DB CL61 5080
(N601DR) CL61 5018
**N601DR HS25 258299**
N601DR WW24 434
**N601DS CL61 5148**
**N601DT CL61 5024**
N601DV GALX 102
N601DW CL61 5099
(N601EA) CL61 5028
N601EB CL61 5153
**N601EC CL61 5064**
N601EG CL61 5008
N601ER CL61 5032
**N601ER CL61 5062**
N601ER CL61 5141
N601FB CL61 5152
N601FJ CL61 3023
**N601FR CL61 5003**
N601FR CL61 5175
N601FS CL61 5119
N601FS CL61 5172
N601GB CL61 3044
N601GB CL61 5130
N601GD GLF6 6001
(N601GF) CL61 3052
**N601GG LJ60 192**
N601GL CL61 3026
**N601GL SBRL 306-50**
**N601GN C500 214**
(N601GR) CL61 5018
N601GR CL61 5149
N601GS CL61 5018
N601GT CL61 3062
**N601GT CL64 5524**
N601HC CL61 5055
N601HC CL61 5088
N601HF CL61 5183
N601HH CL61 5018
N601HJ CL61 3046
(N601HJ) CL61 5193
N601HP CL61 3062
**N601HW CL61 5154**
N601J LJ25 118
N601JA HS25 256051
N601JE CL61 5086
**N601JG CL61 3006**
N601JJ HS25 25173
N601JJ HS25 256051
N601JJ JSTR 5102
**N601JM CL61 3048**
N601JP CL61 3065
**N601JP CL61 5141**
N601JR CL60 1011
(N601JR) HS25 257087
N601KE CL61 3023
N601KF CL61 3023
N601KF CL61 5175
N601KJ CL61 5187
N601KK C550 030
**N601KK CL60 1061**
N601KK HS25 25224
N601KR CL61 5015
**N601LJ LJ60 001**
N601LS CL60 1048
N601MC LJ35 306
N601MD CL61 5078
N601MD GLF5 538
N601MG CL61 5078
N601MG SBRL 306-73
**N601MU CL61 5160**
N601NB CL61 5024
**N601PR CL61 3045**
N601PR CL61 3054
(N601PR) CL61 5106
N601PS HS25 256051
**N601QS C56X 5301**
N601R CL61 5194
**N601RC CL61 3055**
N601RC CRVT 36
**N601RL CL61 5028**
N601RP CL61 3045
N601RS HS25 258018
N601RS HS25 258403
**N601S CL61 3060**
N601SA CL60 1013
N601SA CL60 1079
(N601SN) CL61 3060
N601SQ CL61 3010
N601SR CL60 1051
N601SR CL61 3002
N601SR CL61 5130
**N601ST CL61 5081**
N601TG CL61 3013
N601TJ CL61 3033
N601TJ CL61 3046
N601TL CL61 5028
N601TM CL61 5141
N601TP CL61 3054
**N601TP CL61 5156**
**N601TX CL61 3005**
N601UC CL61 5177
N601UP CL61 5123
N601UT CL61 3010
N601UU HS25 25103
(N601UU) HS25 257041
N601UU HS25 258005
N601VC HS25 258267
N601VF CL61 5154
**N601VH CL61 5043**
N601WJ CL60 1065
**N601WM CL61 5026**
N601WT C500 568
(N601WT) LJ35 218
N601WW CL60 1047
N601WW CL60 1076
N601Z CL60 1079
N601Z CL61 5075
N601ZT CL61 3054
N602AB C560 0217
N602AB C650 7101
**N602AB GALX 048**
(N602AG) GLF4 1402
**N602AJ CL60 1020**
(N602AN) CL61 5178
N602AN CRVT 31
N602AS CL60 1054
**N602AT C550 606**
(N602AV) GALX 059
N602BC C500 190
N602BD CL61 5019
N602BW C550 550-0884
**N602CA C525 0026**
(N602CC) C500 102
(N602CC) C500 602
N602CC CL61 3065
N602CC CL61 5029
N602CC CL61 5150
N602CF HS25 256057
N602CJ C525 0602
N602CL CL60 1020
(N602CM) GLF2 153
(N602CN) CL61 5038
**N602CS C680 0003**
N602CV F9EX 25
N602CW CL61 3002
N602D CL61 5181
N602DM FA10 162
(N602DM) LJ60 002
N602DP CL61 5154
N602DV PRM1 RB-121
N602GA HFB3 1041
N602GD GLF6 6002
N602GV GLF5 602
N602HJ CL61 3047
N602JB CL61 5131
(N602JF) LJ24 343
(N602JJ) HS25 257017
**N602JR HS25 25229**
N602KB SBRL 306-109
(N602KF) GLF4 1402
N602LJ LJ60 002
**N602LP F2TH 36**
N602LP FA20 381/548
(N602LX) CL61 3013
N602MA C56X 5660
N602MC CL61 5177
**N602MJ C52B 0066**
N602MM HS25 256002
N602N LJ25 274
N602NC FA10 82
N602NC LJ25 274
N602PL GLF4 1402
N602PM GLF4 1402
**N602QS C56X 5518**
**N602RF GALX 146**
(N602SA) C560 0302
N602SC LJ60 095
N602TJ CL61 3047
(N602TS) CL61 3057
**N602TS CL61 5002**
N602UK CL61 5011
N602VC GALX 038
N602WA CL61 5068
(N603AF) CL61 5129
(N603AG) GLF4 1452
N603AT C650 0178
(N603CC) C500 103
N603CC CL61 5011
N603CC CL61 5067
N603CC CL64 5333
N603CC CL64 5420
N603CJ C550 603
N603CL CL60 1019

| | | |
|---|---|---|
| **N603CS** | **GLF4** | **1257** |
| N603CV | C560 | 0603 |
| N603GA | GLF4 | 4103 |
| (N603GA) | HFB3 | 1042 |
| N603GD | GLF6 | 6003 |
| N603GJ | CL61 | 3012 |
| N603GY | HS25 | 257028 |
| N603HC | C650 | 0130 |
| **N603HC** | **C650** | **7077** |
| N603HD | C650 | 7077 |
| N603HJ | CL61 | 3052 |
| N603HP | C650 | 0130 |
| (N603JC) | C525 | 0053 |
| N603JM | CL64 | 5402 |
| **N603KE** | **GLF4** | **1452** |
| N603KF | GLF4 | 1452 |
| N603KS | CL61 | 5130 |
| N603LJ | LJ31 | 033 |
| (N603LX) | CL61 | 3027 |
| N603MA | SBRL | 465-16 |
| N603PM | GLF4 | 1452 |
| **N603QS** | **C56X** | **5203** |
| **N603RF** | **GALX** | **147** |
| **N603SC** | **LJ60** | **096** |
| "N603TS" | CL61 | 3065 |
| **N603TS** | **HS25** | **256041** |
| **N603WS** | **C510** | **0215** |
| N604AB | CL64 | 5306 |
| **N604AC** | **CL60** | **1012** |
| N604AC | CL61 | 5102 |
| N604AC | CL64 | 5470 |
| **N604AF** | **CL64** | **5444** |
| (N604AG) | CL64 | 5354 |
| N604AG | CL64 | 5414 |
| N604AN | CRVT | 18 |
| **N604AS** | **LJ25** | **292** |
| **N604AU** | **CL64** | **5434** |
| **N604AV** | **CL64** | **5437** |
| N604AX | CL64 | 5342 |
| **N604AZ** | **CL64** | **5328** |
| N604B | CL64 | 5305 |
| **N604B** | **CL64** | **5335** |
| N604BA | CL61 | 5153 |
| (N604BA) | CL64 | 5307 |
| N604BA | CL64 | 5546 |
| N604BA | CL64 | 5571 |
| N604BB | CL64 | 5316 |
| **N604BB** | **CL64** | **5582** |
| **N604BC** | **CL64** | **5563** |
| N604BD | CL64 | 5303 |
| N604BD | CL64 | 5489 |
| N604BG | CL64 | 5509 |
| **N604BL** | **CL64** | **5301** |
| N604BL | LJ35 | 604 |
| N604BM | CL64 | 5354 |
| **N604BS** | **CL64** | **5560** |
| **N604CA** | **CL64** | **5304** |
| N604CA | CL64 | 5379 |
| N604CB | CL64 | 5448 |
| N604CB | CL64 | 5526 |
| (N604CC) | C500 | 104 |
| N604CC | CL61 | 5016 |
| N604CC | CL61 | 5032 |
| N604CC | CL61 | 5101 |
| (N604CC) | CL61 | 5179 |
| N604CC | CL64 | 5301 |
| N604CC | CL64 | 5376 |
| N604CC | CL64 | 5488 |
| N604CC | CL64 | 5560 |
| **N604CC** | **CL64** | **5633** |
| N604CC | CL64 | 5991 |
| N604CD | CL64 | 5376 |
| N604CD | CL64 | 5591 |
| **N604CE** | **CL64** | **5446** |
| N604CF | CL61 | 5020 |
| N604CG | CL64 | 5632 |
| N604CH | CL64 | 5394 |
| N604CL | CL60 | 1015 |
| N604CL | CL60 | 1030 |
| N604CL | CL61 | 3053 |
| N604CL | CL64 | 5322 |
| **N604CL** | **CL64** | **5570** |
| N604CM | CL64 | 5652 |
| **N604CP** | **CL64** | **5321** |
| N604CR | CL64 | 5376 |
| **N604CR** | **CL64** | **5418** |
| N604CR | CL64 | 5424 |
| **N604CS** | **C680** | **0007** |
| N604CT | CL64 | 5314 |
| N604CU | CL64 | 5339 |
| **N604CW** | **CL64** | **5455** |
| N604D | CL61 | 5193 |
| N604D | CL64 | 5488 |
| N604D | CL65 | 5713 |
| N604DC | CL64 | 5365 |
| N604DC | CL64 | 5403 |
| N604DD | CL64 | 5366 |
| N604DD | CL64 | 5366 |
| N604DE | CL64 | 5380 |
| **N604DE** | **CL64** | **5471** |
| **N604DH** | **CL64** | **5344** |
| **N604DS** | **C550** | **647** |
| N604DS | CL64 | 5323 |
| **N604DT** | **CL64** | **5627** |
| N604DW | CL64 | 5470 |
| **N604EF** | **CL60** | **1068** |
| **N604EG** | **CL64** | **5635** |
| **N604FJ** | **CL61** | **5001** |
| N604FK | LJ55 | 102 |
| N604FS | CL64 | 5357 |
| **N604FS** | **CL64** | **5465** |
| N604GA | HFB3 | 1037 |
| N604GD | CL64 | 5490 |
| N604GD | CL64 | 5624 |
| N604GD | GLF6 | 6004 |
| N604GG | CL64 | 5407 |
| (N604GJ) | CL64 | 5401 |
| **N604GM** | **CL64** | **5399** |
| **N604GR** | **CL64** | **5478** |
| **N604GS** | **LJ35** | **604** |
| N604GT | CL64 | 5449 |
| **N604GW** | **CL64** | **5424** |
| **N604HC** | **CL64** | **5555** |
| N604HD | CL64 | 5445 |
| N604HF | CL64 | 5575 |
| N604HJ | CL61 | 5024 |
| **N604HJ** | **CL64** | **5382** |
| N604HP | CL64 | 5375 |
| **N604HT** | **CL64** | **5638** |
| N604JA | CL64 | 5426 |
| N604JC | CL64 | 5568 |
| N604JC | CL64 | 5609 |
| N604JE | CL64 | 5389 |
| N604JJ | CL64 | 5411 |
| N604JP | CL64 | 5346 |
| N604JP | CL64 | 5421 |
| N604JR | CL64 | 5449 |
| **N604JS** | **CL64** | **5311** |
| **N604JW** | **CL64** | **5325** |
| N604KB | CL64 | 5565 |
| N604KC | CL64 | 5312 |
| N604KG | CL64 | 5390 |
| **N604KJ** | **CL64** | **5554** |
| N604KM | CL64 | 5429 |
| N604KR | CL64 | 5319 |
| N604KS | CL64 | 5308 |
| N604KS | CL64 | 5558 |
| **N604KT** | **LJ60** | **315** |
| N604LA | CL64 | 5436 |
| **N604LC** | **CL64** | **5373** |
| N604LE | CL64 | 5456 |
| **N604LJ** | **C52A** | **0180** |
| N604LJ | LJ31 | 034 |
| **N604LL** | **CL64** | **5548** |
| (N604LM) | CL64 | 5309 |
| N604LS | CL64 | 5315 |
| (N604LX) | CL61 | 3051 |
| N604M | GLF4 | 1132 |
| (N604MA) | CL64 | 5430 |
| N604MC | CL61 | 5013 |
| **N604MC** | **CL64** | **5581** |
| N604ME | CL61 | 5112 |
| N604MG | CL64 | 5416 |
| N604MG | CL64 | 5638 |
| N604MG | CL64 | 5654 |
| N604MH | CL60 | 1042 |
| N604MK | SBRL | 306-15 |
| **N604MM** | **CL64** | **5381** |
| **N604MU** | **CL64** | **5406** |
| N604NG | CL64 | 5513 |
| N604PA | CL64 | 5391 |
| **N604PA** | **CL64** | **5566** |
| N604PC | CL64 | 5425 |
| **N604PJ** | **C550** | **459** |
| N604PL | CL64 | 5338 |
| N604PM | CL64 | 5354 |
| N604PN | CL64 | 5435 |
| N604PS | CL64 | 5442 |
| **N604QS** | **C56X** | **5204** |
| **N604RB** | **CL64** | **5377** |
| N604RC | CL64 | 5334 |
| **N604RF** | **CL30** | **20026** |
| **N604RP** | **CL64** | **5473** |
| N604RS | CL64 | 5551 |
| **N604RT** | **CL64** | **5497** |
| N604S | CL64 | 5400 |
| **N604S** | **LJ35** | **597** |
| **N604SA** | **CL64** | **5341** |
| **N604SB** | **CL64** | **5569** |
| N604SC | CL64 | 5593 |
| N604SF | CL64 | 5589 |
| N604SG | CL64 | 5615 |
| **N604SH** | **CL60** | **1008** |
| N604SH | CL64 | 5396 |
| **N604SJ** | **CL60** | **1042** |
| N604SL | CL64 | 5635 |
| N604SR | CL64 | 5558 |
| **N604ST** | **CL64** | **5479** |
| **N604SX** | **CL64** | **5492** |
| **N604TB** | **CL64** | **5663** |
| **N604TC** | **CL64** | **5323** |
| **N604TF** | **CL64** | **5655** |
| N604TH | CL64 | 5496 |
| (N604TS) | CL61 | 5104 |
| (N604TS) | CL64 | 5304 |
| N604TS | CL64 | 5308 |
| N604TS | CL64 | 5323 |
| N604TS | CL64 | 5411 |
| N604TS | CL64 | 5420 |
| N604TS | CL64 | 5544 |
| (N604UC) | CL64 | 5587 |
| N604UP | CL64 | 5496 |
| N604VF | CL64 | 5444 |
| N604VK | CL64 | 5493 |
| N604VM | CL64 | 5304 |
| **N604W** | **CL64** | **5421** |
| N604WB | CL61 | 5125 |
| **N604WB** | **CL64** | **5306** |
| N604WF | CL64 | 5561 |
| N604WS | CL64 | 5471 |
| **N604Z** | **CL64** | **5496** |
| **N604ZH** | **CL64** | **5376** |
| **N605AB** | **CL65** | **5792** |
| (N605AG) | CL64 | 5356 |
| N605AG | CL65 | 5739 |
| **N605AS** | **E50P** | **50000025** |
| N605AT | C560 | 0242 |
| N605AT | CL65 | 5750 |
| **N605AZ** | **CL65** | **5827** |
| N605BA | CL61 | 5152 |
| (N605BA) | CL64 | 5543 |
| N605BA | CL65 | 5707 |
| N605BL | CL65 | 5781 |
| **N605BT** | **CL65** | **5789** |
| **N605BX** | **CL65** | **5815** |
| **N605CB** | **CL65** | **5708** |
| N605CC | CL61 | 5113 |
| N605CC | CL61 | 5174 |
| N605CC | CL64 | 5320 |
| N605CC | CL65 | 5702 |
| N605CE | C560 | 0605 |
| N605CH | GLF5 | 621 |
| N605CJ | CL65 | 5759 |
| **N605CK** | **CL61** | **5112** |
| N605CL | CL60 | 1057 |
| N605CL | CL61 | 3054 |
| N605CL | CL64 | 5605 |
| **N605CS** | **C680** | **0001** |
| N605DC | CL64 | 5422 |
| N605DS | C650 | 0178 |
| N605DX | CL65 | 5735 |
| N605FH | CL65 | 5765 |
| N605FH | CL65 | 5767 |
| N605FJ | F9DX | 605 |
| **N605FX** | **LJ40** | **45-2004** |
| N605GA | HFB3 | 1038 |
| N605GA | LJ24 | 119 |
| **N605GB** | **CL65** | **5755** |
| **N605GF** | **CL65** | **5766** |
| **N605GG** | **CL65** | **5728** |
| N605GL | CL65 | 5747 |
| N605H | CL65 | 5767 |
| **N605HC** | **CL65** | **5720** |
| N605HG | CL65 | 5721 |
| N605HJ | CL61 | 5025 |
| N605HP | C525 | 0304 |
| N605JA | CL64 | 5443 |
| N605JA | CL65 | 5751 |
| **N605JK** | **CL65** | **5817** |
| N605JM | CL65 | 5716 |
| N605JP | CL65 | 5726 |
| N605KC | CL64 | 5313 |
| **N605KR** | **CL65** | **5822** |
| N605KS | CL65 | 5701 |
| N605LD | CL65 | 5730 |
| (N605M) | GLF5 | 621 |
| N605MP | CL64 | 5417 |
| **N605MS** | **CL65** | **5821** |
| **N605NA** | **LJ24** | **049** |
| N605NE | LJ25 | 139 |
| N605PA | CL64 | 5397 |
| **N605PA** | **CL65** | **5753** |
| N605PM | CL64 | 5356 |
| **N605PS** | **CL65** | **5795** |
| **N605QS** | **C56X** | **5321** |
| **N605RC** | **CL65** | **5800** |
| **N605RF** | **CL30** | **20089** |
| N605RG | SBRL | 306-116 |
| N605RJ | CL65 | 5763 |
| N605RP | CL61 | 5184 |
| **N605RP** | **CL65** | **5801** |
| N605RP | FA20 | 100 |
| N605RZ | CL65 | 5798 |
| **N605S** | **CL65** | **5788** |
| **N605SA** | **C650** | **0152** |
| **N605SB** | **LJ60** | **156** |
| **N605SE** | **LJ45** | **317** |
| **N605T** | **CL61** | **5191** |
| N605T | FA10 | 189 |
| N605TA | CL65 | 5790 |
| **N605TC** | **PRM1** | **RB-52** |
| N605TS | CL60 | 1005 |
| N605TX | CL65 | 5766 |
| N605UK | CL30 | 20142 |
| N605V | WW24 | 100 |
| **N605VF** | **GLEX** | **9152** |
| N605W | HS25 | 25136 |
| N605Y | SBRL | 465-63 |
| N606 | LJ35 | 200 |
| N606AB | WW24 | 268 |
| (N606AG) | CL64 | 5360 |
| **N606AM** | **FA10** | **205** |
| **N606AT** | **C650** | **0225** |
| N606BA | CL61 | 3006 |
| N606BR | LJ60 | 006 |
| N606CC | C500 | 106 |
| N606CC | CL61 | 5018 |
| N606CC | CL61 | 5035 |
| N606CC | CL61 | 5117 |
| N606CC | CL64 | 5340 |
| N606CC | CL64 | 5395 |
| N606CC | CL64 | 5606 |
| N606CE | C560 | 0606 |
| **N606CH** | **GLF4** | **4089** |
| N606CL | CL60 | 1009 |
| **N606CS** | **C680** | **0061** |
| N606DH | GLF3 | 445 |
| N606DR | F9EX | 40 |
| N606ES | GLF3 | 322 |
| **N606FX** | **LJ40** | **45-2005** |
| N606GA | GALX | 106 |
| N606GA | GLF4 | 4106 |
| **N606GB** | **LJ25** | **245** |
| **N606GD** | **GLF6** | **6005** |
| **N606GG** | **CL64** | **5500** |
| **N606HC** | **C525** | **0087** |
| **N606JL** | **CL64** | **5332** |
| N606JM | MU30 | A044SA |
| N606JM | WW24 | 149 |
| N606JR | C525 | 0231 |
| (N606JR) | PRM1 | RB-161 |
| (N606KF) | GLF4 | 1512 |
| N606KK | C500 | 306 |
| **N606KK** | **C550** | **225** |
| **N606KR** | **C500** | **306** |
| **N606L** | **LJ60** | **020** |
| (N606LX) | CL61 | 3064 |
| **N606MA** | **WW24** | **196** |
| **N606MG** | **C525** | **0231** |
| N606MM | C525 | 0104 |
| (N606MM) | C52A | 0051 |
| N606PM | CL64 | 5360 |

**N606PM GLF4 1512**
N606PT GLF3 308
N606Q C56X 5323
N606QS C56X 5323
**N606QS C56X 5338**
**N606RP CL64 5578**
N606RP FA20 265
**N606SB LJ60 184**
**N606SG F9EX 202**
**N606SM LJ25 185**
N606SV C680 0206
**N606TJ F2EX 155**
N606TS HS25 256006
N606TS LJ60 006
N606US F9EX 218
N606XG C52A 0015
**N606XT CL30 20052**
**N607AX CL61 5075**
**N607BF LJ55 056**
(N607BH) CL60 1007
(N607CC) C500 107
**N607CF SBRL 306-118**
**N607CH GLF5 5159**
N607CJ C500 607
N607CL CL60 1071
N607CL CL61 3031
N607CL CL61 5007
**N607CV F9EX 25**
(N607CZ) CL61 5007
**N607DB C525 0269**
(N607DX) F9DX 607
**N607FG LJ45 344**
**N607FX LJ40 45-2012**
N607GA GLF4 4107
N607GA GLF5 5207
**N607GD GLF6 6006**
**N607GD GLF6 6007**
**N607HB HA4T RC-6**
**N607HM C560 0322**
N607KF GLF4 1509
N607LC CL64 5607
**N607LM EA50 000204**
N607PM CL64 5362
N607PM GLF4 1509
**N607PM GLF5 5146**
**N607QS C56X 5340**
N607RJ C560 0370
**N607RP CL61 5184**
N607RP FA20 470
N607S FA20 7
**N607SB LJ60 086**
**N607SG FA50 317**
N607SR SBRL 306-118
**N607TC FA10 77**
**N607TN C525 0662**
N607X FA7X 6
(N608AG) GLF4 1486
N608AM C550 608
N608AR SBRL 282-77
**N608BG GLF3 430**
N608CC CL61 5023
N608CC CL61 5037
N608CC CL61 5179
N608CC CL64 5301
**N608CE C560 0608**
**N608CH GLF4 4098**
N608CL CL61 3040
**N608CL GLF4 1193**
**N608CS C680 0063**
**N608CT C560 0065**
N608CW CL61 3008
**N608CW PRM1 RB-162**
**N608DB C525 0179**
**N608DC ASTR 095**
**N608FX LJ40 45-2014**
N608GA GLF4 4008
N608GA GLF4 4108
**N608GA GLF4 4208**
N608GA GLF5 619
**N608GD GLF6 6008**
N608GF LJ35 477
**N608JR C550 591**
(N608KF) GLF4 1486
N608LB CS55 0029
N608LJ LJ60 008
**N608MD GLF2 197**
**N608MM C525 0104**
**N608PM GLF4 1486**
**N608QS C56X 5308**
N608RP CL61 3055
N608S SBRL 282-77
**N608SG C52B 0249**
N608VP C550 608
**N608WB GLF5 608**
N609BD CL64 5303
N609CC CL61 5068
N609CC CL64 5327
N609CC CL64 5438
N609CH F2TH 22
N609CL CL61 3043
N609CL CL61 3066
(N609CR) CL64 5418
**N609FX LJ40 45-2022**
N609GA GLF4 4109
N609GA GLF5 5209
**N609GD GLF6 6009**
N609K CL61 5072
(N609KF) GLF4 1510
N609PM GLF4 1510
**N609PM GLF5 5086**
**N609QS C56X 5522**
(N609RM) GLF4 1510
**N609SG F900 136**
**N609SM C525 0247**
**N609TC C510 0142**
N609TC C550 609
N609TF LJ35 609
**N609TS CL64 5309**
**N610AB GLF3 398**
**N610AS E50P 50000044**
N610AS F2TH 8
(N610BA) HS25 258176
N610BA HS25 258179
**N610BK C560 0809**
N610BL C550 610
**N610CB C550 550-1014**
(N610CC) C500 110
N610CC FA20 373
N610CC GLF2 56
N610CC GLF3 412
N610CL CL61 3049
N610CM C650 0210
(N610CM) GLF5 610
**N610CS C680 0092**
N610DB CL61 5132
**N610ED C500 241**
N610ED C550 338
**N610EG BE40 RK-13**
**N610FX LJ40 45-2027**
N610GA GLF4 4110
N610GA GLF5 5210
N610GA LJ35 073
N610GD C500 551
**N610GD C560 0547**
N610GD CS55 0034
N610GE LJ35 338
N610GE LJ36 036
**N610GG C500 573**
**N610GR C750 0163**
N610HC ASTR 012
**N610HC C750 0054**
(N610HC) HS25 25173
N610HC HS25 25253
N610HC LJ35 255
N610HC WW24 346
N610HC WW24 361
(N610J) FA10 139
N610JA WW24 298
**N610JB C550 610**
N610JB LJ25 370
**N610JC C550 292**
N610JC WW24 1
N610JR LJ25 370
N610JR LJ35 402
**N610JR LJ55 125**
**N610LJ LJ35 610**
N610LM LJ25 301
**N610LS CL30 20139**
(N610LX) CL61 5009
N610MC GLF2 196
N610MC GLF4 1368
N610MS CL61 3041
N610PR BE40 RK-441
N610PR BE40 RK-466
(N610PW) EA50 000274
**N610QS C56X 5210**
N610R LJ35 622
**N610RA SBRL 306-54**
N610RP C650 0206
N610SA CL64 5510
**N610SE WW24 346**
**N610SM ASTR 101**
N610TM LJ60 005
(N610TS) CL60 1023
N610TS LJ60 010
N610TT C500 573
(N610VP) C650 0010
N611AC CRVT 7
N611AG MU30 A091SA
N611AT C500 490
N611BA HS25 258178
(N611CA) LJ24 077
N611CC CL61 5185
N611CF C550 244
N611CL CL61 3030
N611CL CL61 5002
N611CM LJ35 253
N611CR C550 260
(N611CR) HS25 258061
**N611CS C52B 0063**
N611CS C560 0670
**N611DB LJ24 318**
(N611DT) FA20 471
(N611EL) HS25 257080
N611ER C550 260
**N611FX LJ40 45-2037**
N611GA FA20 9
**N611GD GLF6 6011**
N611GS CL61 5082
N611JC WW24 2
**N611JM GLF4 1178**
N611JW CL61 5063
**N611JW F900 162**
(N611LX) CL61 5053
**N611MC HS25 257080**
N611MH CL61 5011
N611MM HS25 258061
**N611MR C560 0611**
N611NT CL61 5082
N611PA BE40 RK-78
**N611QS C56X 5548**
(N611RR) C550 161
N611SH LJ35 253
N611ST C560 0123
N611SW C500 093
**N611TA LJ35 439**
**N611TG BE40 RJ-27**
N611TJ GLF2 11
N611TS LJ60 011
N611TW LJ35 611
N611VT GLEX 9219
N611WM BE40 RK-249
N611WV WW24 313
N611XP BE40 RK-411
(N612AB) C650 7098
N612AB C650 7101
**N612AC C56X 5676**
N612AC CRVT 9
N612AC GLF4 1059
**N612AF GLF4 4069**
N612BA HS25 258181
N612BH F900 122
(N612CA) C500 216
N612CC C550 344
N612CC CL61 5063
N612CC CL61 5186
N612CL CL61 3056
N612DG LJ35 326
N612DS C500 469
(N612EL) HS25 257168
**N612EQ LJ55 003**
**N612FX LJ40 45-2039**
N612G HS25 25139
N612GA FA20 8
N612GA GALX 212
N612GA GLF4 4112
**N612GD GLF6 6012**
N612J WW24 3
N612JC WW24 50
**N612KB EA50 000026**
N612KC LJ35 105
(N612LX) CL61 5139
(N612M) WW24 389
N612MC HS25 257168
N612NL F900 113
**N612QS C56X 5312**
**N612SQ LJ35 472**
N612ST CS55 0065
**N612VR C550 115**
N612XP HS25 258612
N613AC CRVT 11
N613AL C525 0661
N613BA HS25 258183
N613BR LJ24 082A
N613BR SBRL 306-8
**N613BS FA20 489**
(N613CC) C500 113
N613CK GLF2 150
N613CL CL61 3042
N613CL CL61 5005
(N613E) SBRL 306-25
(N613EL) HS25 257151
N613GA ASTR 213
N613GA FA20 77/429
**N613GD GLF6 6013**
N613GH F2EX 72
N613GL LJ25 329
N613GY C56X 5300
N613H LJ60 313
N613J WW24 12
**N613KS C56X 5300**
(N613LX) CL61 5141
N613MC HS25 257151
**N613QS C56X 5599**
N613R LJ60 044
N613RR LJ35 276
N613SA LJ31 167
**N613SB CL61 5088**
N613SZ LJ25 156
N613W LJ24 013
N613WF GLEX 9005
**N613WF GLEX 9128**
N613XL C56X 5613
N614AC CRVT 17
**N614AF CL61 5171**
N614AF HS25 258057
**N614AJ HS25 258019**
**N614AP HS25 258057**
**N614B C52B 0017**
**N614BA CL64 5614**
N614BA HS25 258185
**N614BG HS25 258704**
(N614CC) C500 114
N614CC CL61 5056
N614CC CL61 5188
N614CL CL61 3059
**N614CM GLF5 614**
(N614DD) C500 576
**N614EP C56X 5713**
**N614FX LJ40 45-2041**
(N614GA) C550 399
N614GA FA20 94/428
**N614GA GALX 214**
N614GA GLF4 4114
**N614GD GLF6 6014**
N614HF GLF4 1119
N614J WW24 26
N614JA CL64 5614
N614JC WW24 26
N614JH LJ60 201
N614MH WW24 95
N614MM SBRL 306-41
**N614QS C56X 5580**
**N614RD GLF4 1006**
**N614SJ C550 248**
N614TS LJ60 104
N615AC CRVT 18
N615AT C560 0245
N615BA HS25 258187
(N615DM) WW24 196
N615EA C550 615
**N615EC C56X 5158**
**N615FX LJ40 45-2051**
N615GA ASTR 215
N615GA GALX 115
N615GA GLF5 5215
**N615GD GLF6 6015**
**N615HB LJ35 444**
N615HP BE40 RK-172
**N615HP BE40 RK-231**
N615HP LJ35 444
**N615HR C560 0309**

| | | |
|---|---|---|
| N615J | WW24 | 29 |
| N615L | C560 | 0386 |
| **N615MS** | **F900** | **25** |
| **N615PL** | **C52C** | **0006** |
| **N615QS** | **C56X** | **5360** |
| **N615RG** | **C56X** | **5016** |
| **N615RH** | **EA50** | **000068** |
| (N615SA) | CL61 | 5052 |
| **N615SR** | **FA50** | **298** |
| (N615TJ) | HS25 | 256015 |
| **N615TL** | **CL64** | **5393** |
| N616AC | CRVT | 20 |
| N616AT | C650 | 0230 |
| N616BA | HS25 | 258188 |
| N616BM | C525 | 0251 |
| N616CC | CL61 | 5045 |
| N616CC | CL61 | 5144 |
| **N616CC** | **GLF4** | **1455** |
| N616CE | C560 | 0616 |
| N616CS | C680 | 0016 |
| N616DC | GLEX | 9025 |
| **N616DC** | **GLEX** | **9296** |
| N616DC | GLF4 | 1349 |
| N616DF | CL60 | 1038 |
| N616DG | GLF4 | 1349 |
| N616DJ | LJ36 | 016 |
| **N616EA** | **HA4T** | **RC-36** |
| N616FX | LJ40 | 45-2047 |
| **N616FX** | **LJ40** | **45-2057** |
| N616GA | GALX | 216 |
| (N616GB) | CS55 | 0100 |
| N616HC | LJ35 | 255 |
| (N616KF) | GLF4 | 1534 |
| **N616KG** | **GLF4** | **1534** |
| N616LJ | LJ35 | 616 |
| N616MM | MU30 | A062SA |
| **N616NA** | **LJ25** | **035** |
| N616PA | HS25 | 256051 |
| N616PS | LJ24 | 088 |
| **N616QS** | **C56X** | **5345** |
| N616SC | LJ24 | 100 |
| **N616TR** | **SBRL** | **306-23** |
| **N616WG** | **HS25** | **258030** |
| N617AC | CRVT | 22 |
| N617BA | HS25 | 258189 |
| N617BD | LJ45 | 281 |
| N617BG | MU30 | A067SA |
| N617CB | C52A | 0356 |
| N617CC | C500 | 117 |
| N617CC | C500 | 617 |
| N617CM | C550 | 617 |
| **N617CS** | **C680** | **0102** |
| **N617FX** | **LJ40** | **45-2065** |
| N617GA | FA20 | 88 |
| **N617JN** | **GLEX** | **9004** |
| N617PD | C560 | 0075 |
| **N617PD** | **C56X** | **5273** |
| **N617QS** | **C56X** | **5509** |
| **N617TM** | **HS25** | **258411** |
| N617XP | HS25 | 258617 |
| N618AC | CRVT | 26 |
| N618AJ | CL60 | 1018 |
| N618AR | HS25 | 258645 |
| N618BA | HS25 | 258191 |
| **N618BR** | **LJ24** | **082A** |
| (N618CC) | C500 | 118 |
| N618CC | C650 | 0008 |
| N618CC | CL61 | 5085 |
| N618CC | CL61 | 5166 |
| **N618CF** | **LJ35** | **618** |
| N618DB | C550 | 340 |
| N618DB | CL61 | 5018 |
| N618DC | CL61 | 5004 |
| N618DC | CL64 | 5365 |
| N618DM | LJ35 | 618 |
| N618FX | LJ40 | 45-2067 |
| **N618FX** | **LJ40** | **45-2076** |
| N618GA | FA20 | 211 |
| N618GA | GALX | 218 |
| N618GA | GLF4 | 4018 |
| N618GH | FA20 | 236 |
| **N618GH** | **FA20** | **513** |
| N618HC | ASTR | 012 |
| N618JC | WW24 | 105 |
| N618JC | WW24 | 51 |
| N618JL | HS25 | 258224 |
| **N618KA** | **C525** | **0618** |
| N618KM | GLF3 | 487 |
| **N618KR** | **HS25** | **257008** |
| N618KS | C56X | 5300 |
| N618P | LJ25 | 360 |
| (N618P) | LJ60 | 044 |
| **N618QS** | **C56X** | **5506** |
| **N618R** | **CL30** | **20045** |
| N618R | LJ24 | 225 |
| N618R | LJ25 | 139 |
| N618R | LJ25 | 360 |
| N618R | LJ31 | 035 |
| N618R | LJ60 | 044 |
| N618RF | LJ31 | 035 |
| **N618RL** | **CL60** | **1018** |
| **N618RR** | **CL61** | **5022** |
| N618S | FA10 | 156 |
| N618SA | GLF4 | 1367 |
| **N618SR** | **EA50** | **000254** |
| **N618WA** | **WW24** | **236** |
| **N618WF** | **GLEX** | **9005** |
| N618XL | C56X | 5618 |
| N618XP | BE40 | RK-418 |
| N618XP | HS25 | 258618 |
| **N619A** | **GLF4** | **1123** |
| (N619BA) | C550 | 619 |
| N619BA | HS25 | 258193 |
| N619BD | F900 | 16 |
| N619CC | C500 | 119 |
| N619CC | CL61 | 5081 |
| N619EA | C500 | 220 |
| N619FE | CL61 | 5054 |
| N619FX | LJ40 | 45-2059 |
| **N619FX** | **LJ40** | **45-2082** |
| **N619G** | **BE40** | **RK-196** |
| N619GA | BE40 | RK-196 |
| N619GA | FA20 | 215 |
| N619GA | GALX | 219 |
| N619JC | WW24 | 93 |
| N619JM | C550 | 550-0889 |
| **N619KK** | **GLF4** | **1062** |
| **N619KS** | **GALX** | **151** |
| **N619MC** | **GLF2** | **196** |
| **N619MJ** | **LJ55** | **021** |
| N619MW | FA20 | 312 |
| (N619PD) | C560 | 0075 |
| **N619QS** | **C56X** | **5562** |
| **N619RJ** | **EA50** | **000231** |
| **N619SM** | **F2EX** | **112** |
| N619TD | HS25 | 257118 |
| **N619TS** | **CL60** | **1019** |
| N619XP | BE40 | RK-419 |
| **N620A** | **FA20** | **412** |
| N620AC | CL60 | 1052 |
| **N620AS** | **E50P** | **50000045** |
| N620AS | F2TH | 97 |
| N620AT | C560 | 0520 |
| **N620BA** | **F2TH** | **220** |
| **N620BB** | **C525** | **0467** |
| (N620CC) | C500 | 120 |
| N620CC | FA20 | 373 |
| (N620CC) | HS25 | 257159 |
| N620CJ | C525 | 0620 |
| **N620CM** | **C510** | **0206** |
| N620DS | GLF4 | 1040 |
| **N620DX** | **F9DX** | **620** |
| **N620EM** | **LJ35** | **620** |
| **N620FX** | **LJ40** | **45-2085** |
| **N620GB** | **C52A** | **0112** |
| N620HF | CL61 | 5021 |
| N620J | LJ35 | 193 |
| N620JA | GLF3 | 387 |
| N620JB | JSTR | 5143 |
| **N620JF** | **CL30** | **20059** |
| N620JF | LJ60 | 074 |
| N620JH | GLF3 | 387 |
| **N620JH** | **GLF4** | **1272** |
| N620JM | LJ35 | 207 |
| N620K | GLEX | 9052 |
| N620K | GLF2 | 64/27 |
| N620K | GLF4 | 1193 |
| N620K | SBRL | 282-9 |
| N620KA | GLF4 | 1193 |
| **N620KE** | **ASTR** | **137** |
| **N620M** | **GLF4** | **1473** |
| N620M | HS25 | 257005 |
| N620M | SBRL | 282-9 |
| **N620MJ** | **LJ35** | **676** |
| **N620MS** | **F2EX** | **31** |
| **N620RB** | **FA20** | **161** |
| **N620RM** | **HS25** | **258124** |
| **N620S** | **CL60** | **1031** |
| N620SB | CL60 | 1025 |
| **N620TC** | **C525** | **0014** |
| **N620WB** | **C510** | **0162** |
| N620XP | BE40 | RK-420 |
| N620XP | HS25 | 258620 |
| N621AB | C650 | 7098 |
| (N621AB) | C650 | 7101 |
| (N621AC) | C560 | 0251 |
| **N621AD** | **C525** | **0621** |
| N621BA | HS25 | 256040 |
| N621CF | CL61 | 5021 |
| N621CF | CL61 | 5090 |
| N621CH | HS25 | 258303 |
| **N621CS** | **C680** | **0120** |
| **N621FP** | **C750** | **0045** |
| **N621FX** | **LJ40** | **45-2089** |
| **N621GA** | **C52B** | **0126** |
| N621GA | GLF4 | 4021 |
| N621GA | GLF5 | 621 |
| N621HB | HA4T | RC-21 |
| N621JA | GLF3 | 387 |
| N621JA | GLF4 | 1272 |
| N621JA | HS25 | 257099 |
| N621JH | GLF3 | 387 |
| N621JH | GLF4 | 1272 |
| **N621JH** | **GLF4** | **1423** |
| N621JH | HS25 | 257099 |
| **N621JS** | **FA20** | **356** |
| N621KB | GALX | 044 |
| N621KD | ASTR | 127 |
| N621KD | GALX | 044 |
| N621KD | GLF5 | 5001 |
| N621KR | C550 | 550-0842 |
| N621L | HS25 | 25205 |
| N621LJ | LJ60 | 121 |
| N621MT | HS25 | 258036 |
| **N621QS** | **C56X** | **5280** |
| **N621RB** | **LJ35** | **211** |
| N621S | GLF3 | 381 |
| N621S | HS25 | 25205 |
| N621S | HS25 | 257178 |
| N621SC | GLF4 | 1481 |
| N621ST | HS25 | 25014 |
| N621SV | C680 | 0021 |
| **N621WP** | **HS25** | **258033** |
| (N621XP) | HS25 | 258621 |
| N622AB | CL61 | 5016 |
| N622AB | GLEX | 9022 |
| N622AB | HS25 | 257012 |
| N622AB | HS25 | 258223 |
| (N622AD) | CL61 | 5016 |
| N622AD | HS25 | 257012 |
| N622AD | HS25 | 258223 |
| **N622AT** | **C500** | **252** |
| **N622CS** | **C680** | **0124** |
| (N622EX) | C550 | 635 |
| N622EX | C550 | 679 |
| **N622FX** | **LJ40** | **45-2095** |
| N622GA | GLF4 | 4022 |
| N622GA | GLF5 | 5222 |
| N622GA | GLF5 | 622 |
| **N622JK** | **PRM1** | **RB-59** |
| N622LJ | LJ60 | 122 |
| **N622PC** | **C56X** | **5024** |
| **N622PG** | **C550** | **037** |
| **N622PM** | **C650** | **7027** |
| **N622QS** | **C56X** | **5286** |
| **N622QW** | **F2TH** | **134** |
| N622R | FA20 | 15 |
| N622R | FA20 | 86 |
| **N622RB** | **LJ35** | **064** |
| **N622RR** | **GLF2** | **12** |
| **N622SL** | **C525** | **0622** |
| (N622SS) | C500 | 372 |
| **N622SV** | **GALX** | **015** |
| N622VH | C550 | 635 |
| N622VL | HS25 | 258531 |
| N622WG | LJ35 | 611 |
| **N622WM** | **CL61** | **5084** |
| N622XP | HS25 | 258622 |
| **N623BM** | **CL61** | **5159** |
| N623BM | GLF2 | 205 |
| N623CL | C56X | 6023 |
| N623CW | CL61 | 5023 |
| N623CX | GLF2 | 101 |
| N623DS | C550 | 662 |
| **N623FX** | **LJ40** | **45-2099** |
| N623GA | GLF4 | 4023 |
| N623GA | GLF5 | 5223 |
| N623GA | GLF5 | 623 |
| N623HA | CL64 | 5623 |
| **N623JL** | **C550** | **662** |
| (N623KC) | C550 | 471 |
| N623KC | C560 | 0076 |
| **N623KM** | **LJ35** | **307** |
| N623LB | C500 | 465 |
| **N623MS** | **GLF3** | **351** |
| N623MW | GLF2 | 94 |
| **N623N** | **C550** | **550-0849** |
| **N623NP** | **GLF3** | **357** |
| **N623PM** | **C650** | **7018** |
| **N623QS** | **C56X** | **5299** |
| **N623QW** | **F2TH** | **44** |
| N623QW | FA50 | 278 |
| N623RC | LJ24 | 173 |
| N623RM | C500 | 623 |
| N623TS | CL64 | 5323 |
| N623XP | HS25 | 258623 |
| **N624AT** | **C56X** | **5174** |
| **N624B** | **BE40** | **RK-369** |
| **N624BP** | **GLEX** | **9236** |
| N624BP | GLF3 | 320 |
| N624BP | GLF4 | 1093 |
| N624CC | C650 | 0123 |
| **N624CS** | **C680** | **0131** |
| N624DS | SBRL | 465-2 |
| N624FA | SBRL | 306-53 |
| **N624FX** | **LJ40** | **45-2104** |
| N624GA | GLF4 | 4024 |
| N624GA | GLF5 | 5224 |
| N624GA | GLF5 | 624 |
| **N624GJ** | **GLF4** | **1267** |
| **N624KM** | **WW24** | **227** |
| **N624N** | **GLF5** | **681** |
| **N624PD** | **HS25** | **25234** |
| **N624PL** | **C52A** | **0357** |
| N624PP | GLF3 | 320 |
| **N624QS** | **C56X** | **5302** |
| N624VP | C650 | 0024 |
| N624XP | HS25 | 258624 |
| **N625AC** | **C560** | **0251** |
| **N625AT** | **C56X** | **5175** |
| N625AU | LJ25 | 340 |
| **N625BE** | **ASTR** | **125** |
| **N625BL** | **LJ35** | **625** |
| N625CC | C650 | 7058 |
| N625CH | C500 | 625 |
| N625CJ | C525 | 0625 |
| N625CR | FA50 | 55 |
| N625EA | C550 | 625 |
| N625FX | LJ40 | 45-2109 |
| **N625FX** | **LJ40** | **45-2116** |
| N625GA | C500 | 217 |
| N625GA | GLF5 | 625 |
| N625J | C500 | 625 |
| N625MM | ASTR | 125 |
| **N625PG** | **C525** | **0282** |
| **N625QS** | **C56X** | **5319** |
| **N625TX** | **C510** | **0219** |
| N625VP | C650 | 0025 |
| **N625W** | **BE40** | **RK-106** |
| **N625WA** | **C560** | **0027** |
| N625XP | HS25 | 258625 |
| **N626AT** | **C56X** | **5239** |
| **N626BM** | **LJ35** | **634** |
| (N626CC) | C500 | 126 |
| N626CC | C650 | 0062 |
| N626CC | F9EX | 27 |
| **N626CG** | **HS25** | **258041** |
| **N626CS** | **C680** | **0188** |
| **N626CV** | **C525** | **0626** |
| N626EK | F900 | 157 |
| **N626FX** | **LJ40** | **45-2120** |
| N626GA | GALX | 226 |
| N626GA | GLF4 | 4026 |
| N626GA | GLF5 | 626 |
| (N626JP) | CL61 | 3050 |
| N626JS | GLF4 | 1334 |
| **N626JS** | **GLF5** | **642** |
| N626JS | LJ35 | 394 |
| (N626JW) | CL64 | 5512 |
| N626KM | LJ60 | 012 |
| **N626LJ** | **GLF4** | **1334** |
| N626LJ | LJ60 | 119 |

| | | |
|---|---|---|
| N626P | C500 | 267 |
| **N626QS** | **C56X** | **5126** |
| **N626RB** | **C560** | **0221** |
| N626SL | C560 | 0118 |
| N626TC | GLF2 | 129 |
| N626TC | GLF4 | 1227 |
| N626TC | MS76 | 088 |
| N626TG | GLF4 | 1227 |
| **N626TN** | **C56X** | **5254** |
| N626VP | C550 | 626 |
| N626XP | HS25 | 258626 |
| **N627AF** | **LJ60** | **193** |
| **N627AK** | **HS25** | **258723** |
| N627AT | C560 | 0527 |
| (N627BB) | C52B | 0003 |
| **N627BC** | **C550** | **550-0868** |
| N627CM | C510 | 0127 |
| N627CR | HS25 | 25160 |
| N627CW | CL61 | 3027 |
| **N627E** | **C500** | **513** |
| N627ER | LJ24 | 290 |
| (N627FX) | LJ40 | 45-2124 |
| N627GA | GALX | 227 |
| N627GA | GLF4 | 4027 |
| N627GA | GLF5 | 627 |
| **N627HS** | **CS55** | **0072** |
| N627HS | HS25 | 256013 |
| N627JG | FA20 | 267/491 |
| **N627JJ** | **LJ24** | **340** |
| N627KR | CL61 | 5059 |
| N627L | C500 | 513 |
| N627L | C550 | 550-0843 |
| **N627MW** | **C525** | **0627** |
| **N627QS** | **C56X** | **5227** |
| N627R | C650 | 0152 |
| **N627R** | **C750** | **0132** |
| N627RP | BE40 | RK-155 |
| N627TA | C550 | 051 |
| N627V | C52B | 0309 |
| N627WS | LJ25 | 170 |
| **N627X** | **CS55** | **0018** |
| **N627XL** | **C56X** | **5149** |
| N627XP | HS25 | 258627 |
| **N628BD** | **GLF5** | **628** |
| N628BL | LJ35 | 628 |
| **N628BS** | **C500** | **045** |
| **N628CB** | **C52B** | **0049** |
| N628CB | C550 | 550-0991 |
| N628CC | C650 | 0128 |
| **N628CC** | **F2TH** | **95** |
| N628CH | C500 | 628 |
| **N628CK** | **C560** | **0194** |
| **N628CM** | **CL61** | **3062** |
| **N628DB** | **LJ35** | **246** |
| N628DC | LJ35 | 628 |
| (N628FS) | C500 | 045 |
| N628GA | ASTR | 228 |
| N628GA | GLF4 | 4028 |
| N628GA | GLF5 | 628 |
| **N628GB** | **C550** | **550-0991** |
| N628GZ | LJ35 | 628 |
| **N628HC** | **GLF2** | **134** |
| N628KM | WW24 | 308 |
| (N628NP) | GLF4 | 1094 |
| N628PT | LJ55 | 089 |
| **N628QS** | **C56X** | **5305** |
| (N628RC) | GALX | 065 |
| N628SA | F2TH | 128 |
| N628VK | CL61 | 5049 |
| (N628WC) | CL61 | 3048 |
| N628WJ | LJ35 | 628 |
| N628XP | HS25 | 258628 |
| N628ZG | C500 | 444 |
| **N629AS** | **E50P** | **50000067** |
| **N629CS** | **C680** | **0165** |
| N629DM | C525 | 0369 |
| **N629DR** | **C525** | **0667** |
| N629EE | C52B | 0129 |
| N629GA | GALX | 229 |
| N629GA | GLF4 | 4029 |
| N629GA | GLF5 | 629 |
| N629GB | CL30 | 20144 |
| N629LJ | LJ60 | 129 |
| **N629MD** | **C650** | **0096** |
| N629P | HS25 | 25179 |
| N629PA | C52A | 0015 |
| **N629QS** | **C56X** | **5306** |
| **N629RA** | **CS55** | **0093** |
| N629RM | C650 | 0096 |
| N629TD | GLF2 | 92 |
| **N629TS** | **CL61** | **3029** |
| N629TS | HS25 | 256029 |
| N629WH | WW24 | 305 |
| **N629WH** | **WW24** | **409** |
| **N630AR** | **CL61** | **5140** |
| N630BA | HS25 | 258195 |
| N630BB | CL60 | 1030 |
| **N630CC** | **C550** | **169** |
| N630CE | C500 | 630 |
| **N630CS** | **C680** | **0170** |
| N630GA | ASTR | 230 |
| **N630GA** | **GALX** | **230** |
| N630GA | GLF4 | 4030 |
| N630GA | GLF5 | 630 |
| N630JS | C550 | 550-1119 |
| **N630JS** | **HS25** | **HA-0030** |
| N630L | FA50 | 130 |
| N630LJ | LJ60 | 130 |
| N630M | C750 | 0021 |
| N630M | CL60 | 1023 |
| N630M | CL61 | 5060 |
| N630M | SBRL | 282-73 |
| N630N | SBRL | 282-73 |
| N630PM | GLF2 | 236 |
| **N630QS** | **C56X** | **5130** |
| **N630S** | **ASTR** | **046** |
| **N630SJ** | **LJ35** | **344** |
| N630SR | FA50 | 227 |
| **N630TF** | **C52A** | **0022** |
| N630XP | HS25 | 258630 |
| N631AT | LJ31 | 191 |
| N631BA | HS25 | 258196 |
| **N631CB** | **C680** | **0227** |
| N631CC | C550 | 631 |
| N631CC | C650 | 0031 |
| **N631CC** | **LJ31** | **104** |
| (N631CF) | CL61 | 3031 |
| (N631CK) | GLF2 | 150 |
| **N631CS** | **C680** | **0197** |
| N631CW | LJ25 | 313 |
| N631CW | LJ35 | 302 |
| **N631DV** | **GALX** | **166** |
| N631EA | C550 | 631 |
| N631GA | ASTR | 241 |
| N631GA | ASTR | 281 |
| **N631GA** | **GALX** | **231** |
| N631GA | GLF4 | 4031 |
| N631GA | GLF5 | 631 |
| N631KA | FA10 | 120 |
| N631LJ | LJ60 | 131 |
| N631M | C560 | 0383 |
| N631PP | BE40 | RK-155 |
| N631QS | C56X | 5131 |
| N631RP | BE40 | RK-155 |
| N631RP | BE40 | RK-7 |
| N631RP | C56X | 5254 |
| N631RP | C680 | 0037 |
| **N631RP** | **C680** | **0256** |
| (N631RR) | BE40 | RK-7 |
| N631SC | GLF2 | 224 |
| N631SC | HS25 | 25065 |
| N631SC | HS25 | 256002 |
| N631SF | LJ31 | 075 |
| N631SQ | HS25 | 25065 |
| N631SQ | HS25 | 256002 |
| **N631TS** | **C550** | **631** |
| N631XP | HS25 | 258631 |
| N632BA | HS25 | 258199 |
| **N632BL** | **C56X** | **5171** |
| (N632CC) | C500 | 132 |
| N632CS | C680 | 0222 |
| **N632FW** | **CL30** | **20195** |
| N632FW | HS25 | 258294 |
| N632GA | GALX | 232 |
| N632GA | GLF4 | 4032 |
| N632GA | GLF5 | 632 |
| N632KA | FA20 | 273 |
| N632PB | FA20 | 206 |
| **N632PB** | **FA20** | **355** |
| N632PB | HS25 | 25058 |
| N632PB | LJ31 | 033 |
| N632PE | HS25 | 25058 |
| N632QS | C56X | 5132 |
| N632SC | C500 | 344 |
| N632SC | C550 | 379 |
| N632VP | C650 | 0032 |
| **N632XL** | **C56X** | **5632** |
| N632XP | HS25 | 258632 |
| N633AC | LJ55 | 115 |
| **N633AT** | **C500** | **087** |
| N633BA | HS25 | 258200 |
| N633CC | C650 | 0133 |
| N633CS | C680 | 0236 |
| N633CW | CL61 | 3013 |
| N633DS | LJ35 | 362 |
| **N633EE** | **CS55** | **0058** |
| N633GA | ASTR | 112 |
| N633GA | ASTR | 233 |
| N633GA | GLF4 | 4033 |
| N633GA | GLF5 | 633 |
| N633J | LJ24 | 120 |
| N633KA | FA20 | 399 |
| N633L | FA50 | 223 |
| N633NJ | LJ24 | 120 |
| N633P | GLF3 | 452 |
| **N633QS** | **C56X** | **5526** |
| N633RP | C56X | 5501 |
| N633RP | C56X | 5669 |
| **N633RP** | **C680** | **0172** |
| **N633RT** | **C550** | **588** |
| **N633SA** | **C560** | **0235** |
| **N633SF** | **LJ31** | **241** |
| **N633SL** | **SBRL** | **306-33** |
| **N633W** | **FA50** | **184** |
| N633WW | FA10 | 59 |
| N633WW | LJ35 | 654 |
| N633XP | HS25 | 258633 |
| N634BA | HS25 | 258202 |
| N634CJ | C525 | 0634 |
| N634CS | C680 | 0244 |
| N634GA | GALX | 011 |
| N634GA | GLF4 | 4034 |
| **N634H** | **FA50** | **178** |
| N634H | LJ35 | 292 |
| N634KA | FA50 | 129 |
| **N634QS** | **C56X** | **5558** |
| N634S | GLF4 | 1249 |
| N635AV | GLF2 | 168 |
| N635AV | GLF4 | 1185 |
| N635BA | HS25 | 258203 |
| N635CJ | C56X | 6035 |
| **N635CS** | **C680** | **0275** |
| **N635E** | **F2TH** | **106** |
| N635GA | ASTR | 120 |
| N635GA | ASTR | 235 |
| N635GA | GLF4 | 4035 |
| "N635PA" | HS25 | 256035 |
| **N635QS** | **C56X** | **5358** |
| N635XP | HS25 | 258635 |
| N636 | JSTR | 5127 |
| N636 | JSTR | 5135 |
| N636 | SBRL | 306-140 |
| N636BA | HS25 | 258204 |
| **N636BC** | **ASTR** | **039** |
| N636C | JSTR | 5127 |
| N636CC | C500 | 636 |
| **N636EJ** | **C56X** | **5304** |
| N636GA | GALX | 183 |
| N636GA | GLF4 | 1336 |
| N636GD | GLF4 | 1012 |
| N636GS | C56X | 5074 |
| N636HC | CL64 | 5636 |
| (N636MA) | C550 | 108 |
| (N636MC) | JSTR | 5127 |
| N636MC | SBRL | 306-140 |
| N636MF | GLF2 | 150 |
| N636MF | GLF4 | 1012 |
| **N636MF** | **GLF5** | **5112** |
| N636MF | GLF5 | 512 |
| **N636N** | **C500** | **441** |
| N636QS | C56X | 5304 |
| N636SC | C500 | 222 |
| N636SC | FA10 | 115 |
| N636SE | C560 | 0636 |
| **N636SF** | **LJ31** | **075** |
| (N636TS) | CL64 | 5636 |
| **N636VP** | **C525** | **0636** |
| N636XP | HS25 | 258636 |
| N637BA | HS25 | 258205 |
| N637CJ | C525 | 0637 |
| N637EH | C550 | 371 |
| N637GA | GLF4 | 1337 |
| N637GA | GLF5 | 5037 |
| N637GA | GLF5 | 637 |
| N637LJ | LJ60 | 037 |
| N637ML | CL60 | 1024 |
| N637QS | C56X | 5137 |
| N637RP | C56X | 5669 |
| **N637SF** | **ASTR** | **248** |
| **N637TF** | **CL64** | **5637** |
| N637XP | HS25 | 258637 |
| **N638AH** | **C510** | **0167** |
| N638BA | HS25 | 258206 |
| N638GA | GLF4 | 1338 |
| N638GA | GLF5 | 5138 |
| N638GA | GLF5 | 638 |
| N638LJ | LJ60 | 038 |
| N638MF | GLF2 | 150 |
| (N638PB) | LJ31 | 033 |
| (N638Q) | C56X | 5330 |
| N638QS | C56X | 5330 |
| **N638QS** | **C56X** | **5363** |
| N638XP | HS25 | 258638 |
| N639AS | E50P | 50000075 |
| **N639AT** | **WW24** | **308** |
| N639BA | HS25 | 258207 |
| N639CL | CL61 | 3039 |
| N639CV | C560 | 0639 |
| N639GA | ASTR | 239 |
| N639GA | GLF5 | 639 |
| N639J | WW24 | 337 |
| N639QS | C56X | 5139 |
| **N639TS** | **CL61** | **5139** |
| N639XP | HS25 | 258639 |
| N640AC | BE40 | RK-3 |
| **N640BA** | **LJ35** | **664** |
| N640BS | C500 | 640 |
| N640CE | C560 | 0640 |
| N640CH | CL64 | 5428 |
| N640GA | GALX | 140 |
| N640GA | GLF5 | 540 |
| N640GA | LJ24 | 157 |
| N640M | HS25 | 25228 |
| N640PM | HS25 | 257167 |
| N640PN | CL64 | 5640 |
| **N640QS** | **C56X** | **5240** |
| N640TS | CL60 | 1004 |
| N640XP | HS25 | 258640 |
| N641CA | CL64 | 5441 |
| N641CL | CL61 | 5041 |
| N641DA | CL64 | 5641 |
| N641FG | WW24 | 370 |
| N641GA | GALX | 141 |
| N641GA | GLF5 | 541 |
| N641GA | GLF5 | 641 |
| N641GA | LJ25 | 004 |
| N641L | C550 | 550-0961 |
| **N641QS** | **C56X** | **5295** |
| N641XP | HS25 | 258641 |
| **N642AC** | **BE40** | **RK-224** |
| N642BB | C550 | 339 |
| N642BJ | C500 | 388 |
| N642CC | C550 | 038 |
| (N642CT) | C500 | 262 |
| N642GA | GLF5 | 542 |
| N642GA | LJ24 | 158 |
| (N642GG) | LJ31 | 113 |
| N642JA | CL64 | 5642 |
| **N642JC** | **F900** | **71** |
| **N642LF** | **C560** | **0642** |
| (N642LJ) | LJ60 | 142 |
| N642LR | SBRL | 282-83 |
| **N642QS** | **C56X** | **5561** |
| N642RP | SBRL | 306-46 |
| N642TS | SBRL | 380-2 |
| N642WW | C52A | 0418 |
| N642XL | C56X | 5642 |
| N642XP | HS25 | 258642 |
| N643CC | C650 | 0043 |
| N643CR | C650 | 0024 |
| **N643CR** | **CL60** | **1055** |
| N643CT | CL64 | 5643 |
| N643GA | GLF5 | 5143 |
| N643GA | GLF5 | 543 |
| N643JL | HS25 | 25208 |
| N643MC | C500 | 643 |
| N643MC | C550 | 643 |
| N643MJ | LJ35 | 643 |
| N643QS | C56X | 5331 |
| **N643QS** | **C56X** | **5588** |
| N643RT | C500 | 639 |
| N643RT | C560 | 0010 |

| | | |
|---|---|---|
| **N643RT** | **C560** | **0019** |
| N643TD | C550 | 437 |
| (N643VP) | C500 | 643 |
| (N644CC) | C500 | 144 |
| N644CC | C650 | 0144 |
| N644GA | GLF4 | 4044 |
| N644GA | GLF5 | 5144 |
| N644GA | GLF5 | 544 |
| N644GA | GLF5 | 644 |
| N644JL | HS25 | 258012 |
| N644JW | JSTR | 5223 |
| **N644QS** | **C56X** | **5582** |
| **N644RM** | **E50P** | **50000061** |
| N644VP | C560 | 0644 |
| N644X | FA20 | 36 |
| N644X | SBRL | 306-26 |
| N644XP | HS25 | 258644 |
| **N645AM** | **LJ35** | **645** |
| **N645AS** | **E50P** | **50000114** |
| N645CC | SBRL | 306-49 |
| N645G | LJ24 | 160 |
| **N645G** | **LJ35** | **056** |
| N645GA | GALX | 145 |
| N645GA | GLF5 | 545 |
| N645GA | GLF5 | 645 |
| N645HJ | LJ45 | 087 |
| N645KM | LJ45 | 133 |
| N645L | LJ25 | 008 |
| N645M | C560 | 0350 |
| **N645QS** | **C56X** | **5145** |
| (N645XP) | HS25 | 258645 |
| N646CC | C650 | 0146 |
| N646EA | LJ35 | 646 |
| N646G | LJ55 | 016 |
| N646GA | ASTR | 146 |
| N646GA | GLF5 | 5146 |
| N646GA | GLF5 | 546 |
| N646GA | LJ25 | 005 |
| N646JC | CL64 | 5646 |
| **N646QS** | **C56X** | **5246** |
| N646S | PRM1 | RB-142 |
| **N646VP** | **C525** | **0646** |
| N646XP | HS25 | 258646 |
| N647CC | C550 | 647 |
| N647CE | C560 | 0647 |
| N647CM | C650 | 7047 |
| **N647EF** | **LJ60** | **047** |
| N647GA | ASTR | 147 |
| N647GA | GLF5 | 5147 |
| N647GA | GLF5 | 547 |
| N647GA | GLF5 | 647 |
| N647GA | LJ24 | 159 |
| **N647JP** | **FA20** | **120** |
| N647JP | FA20 | 359/542 |
| N647JP | FA20 | 70 |
| N647JP | SBRL | 380-21 |
| **N647QS** | **C56X** | **5547** |
| (N647SA) | FA20 | 70 |
| (N647TJ) | LJ35 | 647 |
| N647TS | LJ60 | 047 |
| N648GA | ASTR | 148 |
| N648GA | GLF5 | 5148 |
| N648GA | GLF5 | 548 |
| N648GA | GLF5 | 648 |
| N648GA | LJ25 | 008 |
| N648J | LJ35 | 648 |
| N648JW | LJ25 | 350 |
| N648JW | LJ35 | 648 |
| N648LJ | LJ60 | 048 |
| **N648QS** | **C56X** | **5574** |
| N648TS | LJ60 | 148 |
| N648VP | C560 | 0648 |
| N648WW | C550 | 477 |
| N648WW | HS25 | 257004 |
| (N649AF) | C650 | 0109 |
| N649CC | C650 | 0149 |
| N649DA | C550 | 649 |
| N649G | LJ24 | 161 |
| N649GA | GLF5 | 5149 |
| N649GA | GLF5 | 549 |
| N649GA | GLF5 | 649 |
| N649JA | CL64 | 5649 |
| N649TT | F900 | 82 |
| **N649TT** | **FA50** | **342** |
| N649WW | C550 | 477 |
| N649XP | HS25 | 258649 |
| **N650** | **C650** | **697** |
| N650AB | C650 | 7053 |
| N650AC | C500 | 364 |
| N650AE | C650 | 0152 |
| (N650AF) | C650 | 0113 |
| N650AF | C650 | 0120 |
| N650AF | C650 | 0125 |
| N650AF | C650 | 0145 |
| N650AJ | C650 | 0068 |
| N650AL | FA50 | 49 |
| (N650AN) | C650 | 0049 |
| **N650AS** | **C650** | **0002** |
| N650AS | C650 | 7053 |
| (N650AS) | FA50 | 171 |
| (N650AS) | FA50 | 90 |
| N650AT | C650 | 0063 |
| (N650AT) | C650 | 0109 |
| **N650AT** | **C650** | **7053** |
| (N650AT) | LJ24 | 157 |
| N650BA | C650 | 0178 |
| N650BC | C650 | 0198 |
| (N650BG) | C650 | 0002 |
| **N650BP** | **C550** | **131** |
| (N650BP) | C650 | 0017 |
| N650BS | C650 | 0036 |
| **N650BW** | **C650** | **0028** |
| (N650BW) | C650 | 0198 |
| N650C | SBRL | 306-137 |
| N650CA | LJ24 | 050 |
| **N650CB** | **C650** | **0084** |
| **N650CC** | **C650** | **0156** |
| N650CC | C650 | 0193 |
| N650CC | C650 | 696 |
| **N650CD** | **C650** | **0066** |
| N650CE | C650 | 0106 |
| N650CF | C650 | 0104 |
| **N650CG** | **C650** | **0023** |
| **N650CH** | **C650** | **0154** |
| N650CJ | C500 | 650 |
| N650CJ | C650 | 0014 |
| **N650CJ** | **C650** | **7044** |
| **N650CM** | **C560** | **0177** |
| N650CM | C650 | 0200 |
| N650CN | C650 | 0047 |
| N650CN | C650 | 0062 |
| **N650CP** | **C650** | **7016** |
| **N650CZ** | **C650** | **7050** |
| N650DA | C650 | 0085 |
| **N650DA** | **C650** | **0114** |
| N650DD | C650 | 7047 |
| N650DF | C650 | 0136 |
| N650DH | C650 | 7043 |
| N650DR | C650 | 0181 |
| (N650FA) | C650 | 0231 |
| **N650FC** | **C650** | **0146** |
| **N650FP** | **C650** | **0188** |
| N650G | WW24 | 233 |
| (N650GA) | C650 | 0198 |
| N650GA | GLF5 | 550 |
| N650GA | GLF5 | 600 |
| **N650GA** | **GLF6** | **6001** |
| **N650GC** | **C650** | **0215** |
| **N650GD** | **GLF6** | **6004** |
| N650GE | ASTR | 064 |
| **N650GE** | **ASTR** | **210** |
| N650GE | WW24 | 233 |
| **N650GF** | **ASTR** | **064** |
| **N650GH** | **C650** | **0034** |
| (N650GJ) | C650 | 0165 |
| N650GT | C650 | 0004 |
| N650HC | C650 | 0124 |
| **N650HG** | **C650** | **0083** |
| N650HM | C650 | 0119 |
| N650HR | C650 | 0101 |
| N650HS | C650 | 0185 |
| **N650J** | **C650** | **0022** |
| N650JA | C650 | 0073 |
| N650JB | C650 | 7113 |
| N650JC | C650 | 0089 |
| N650JG | C650 | 0107 |
| N650JL | C650 | 0019 |
| **N650JL** | **C650** | **7101** |
| (N650JP) | C550 | 730 |
| N650JS | C560 | 0190 |
| (N650JS) | C650 | 0058 |
| **N650JS** | **HS25** | **258537** |
| N650JV | C650 | 0138 |
| **N650K** | **C650** | **7034** |
| **N650KA** | **GLF2** | **50** |
| **N650KB** | **C650** | **0078** |
| N650KC | C650 | 0215 |
| **N650KD** | **C650** | **7047** |
| N650KM | C650 | 0144 |
| N650KS | CL64 | 5660 |
| N650L | C650 | 0209 |
| **N650LA** | **C650** | **0004** |
| **N650LG** | **CL61** | **5126** |
| **N650LR** | **LJ35** | **650** |
| **N650LW** | **C650** | **0010** |
| N650M | C650 | 0044 |
| N650M | WW24 | 67 |
| N650MC | C650 | 0237 |
| N650MD | C650 | 0035 |
| N650MG | C650 | 0007 |
| (N650MG) | C650 | 0185 |
| N650MM | C650 | 0048 |
| N650MP | C650 | 0107 |
| N650MS | C650 | 0019 |
| (N650MT) | C650 | 0122 |
| N650MW | C500 | 593 |
| N650NL | LJ35 | 154 |
| N650NY | C650 | 0027 |
| N650PF | GLF2 | 118 |
| **N650PL** | **GLF5** | **5148** |
| N650PM | HS25 | 258081 |
| N650PT | C650 | 0160 |
| **N650PW** | **GLF4** | **1530** |
| (N650PW) | GLF4 | 1534 |
| N650QS | C56X | 5150 |
| **N650RB** | **C650** | **0079** |
| N650RJ | C56X | 5152 |
| (N650RJ) | C650 | 0111 |
| (N650RJ) | C650 | 7003 |
| N650RL | C650 | 7029 |
| **N650RP** | **C650** | **0157** |
| N650RP | C650 | 7016 |
| **N650SB** | **C650** | **0018** |
| N650SC | C650 | 0030 |
| **N650SG** | **C650** | **0191** |
| N650SL | C650 | 0024 |
| N650SP | C650 | 0094 |
| N650SS | C650 | 0021 |
| (N650SS) | C650 | 0140 |
| (N650ST) | C560 | 0014 |
| **N650TA** | **C650** | **0088** |
| N650TC | C650 | 0061 |
| N650TC | C650 | 0064 |
| N650TF | C500 | 142 |
| N650TJ | C650 | 0191 |
| N650TP | C650 | 0061 |
| N650TS | C650 | 0006 |
| **N650TS** | **C650** | **0219** |
| N650TT | C650 | 0046 |
| N650TT | C650 | 0122 |
| N650VP | C650 | 0025 |
| **N650W** | **C650** | **0237** |
| N650W | C650 | 7065 |
| N650WB | C650 | 0020 |
| N650WC | C550 | 007 |
| N650WC | C550 | 627 |
| **N650WE** | **C650** | **0040** |
| N650WG | C550 | 007 |
| N650WJ | C650 | 0078 |
| N650WL | C650 | 0078 |
| N650X | FA50 | 69 |
| N650XP | BE40 | RK-450 |
| N650XP | HS25 | 258650 |
| **N650Z** | **C650** | **0108** |
| (N651AC) | CL61 | 3009 |
| N651AF | C650 | 0114 |
| (N651AP) | C650 | 0001 |
| N651AP | C650 | 0082 |
| N651AR | C650 | 0212 |
| **N651AT** | **C650** | **0063** |
| N651BH | C650 | 0051 |
| **N651BP** | **C650** | **0017** |
| N651CC | C650 | 0001 |
| **N651CC** | **C650** | **7119** |
| N651CC | CS55 | 0010 |
| N651CG | C650 | 0001 |
| **N651CJ** | **C525** | **0365** |
| N651CN | C650 | 0072 |
| **N651CV** | **C650** | **0036** |
| N651CW | CL61 | 3051 |
| N651E | WW24 | 406 |
| **N651EJ** | **C650** | **0241** |
| (N651ES) | WW24 | 406 |
| **N651FC** | **EA50** | **000012** |
| N651GA | GALX | 151 |
| **N651GA** | **GLF4** | **4151** |
| N651GA | GLF5 | 551 |
| N651GL | SBRL | 465-36 |
| N651GV | GLF5 | 651 |
| N651J | LJ24 | 181 |
| N651JC | CL64 | 5651 |
| N651JM | C650 | 0241 |
| **N651LJ** | **LJ24** | **125** |
| **N651MK** | **SBRL** | **465-73** |
| (N651NA) | GLF2 | 118 |
| **N651PW** | **C650** | **0090** |
| **N651QS** | **C56X** | **5251** |
| N651RS | C650 | 0094 |
| N651S | SBRL | 465-14 |
| (N651SB) | FA50 | 70 |
| **N651SD** | **FA20** | **256** |
| N651TC | C650 | 0090 |
| N651XP | HS25 | 258651 |
| N652AL | FA50 | 112 |
| N652CC | C650 | 0002 |
| N652CC | C650 | 0078 |
| **N652CC** | **C650** | **7107** |
| (N652CC) | SBRL | 465-6 |
| N652CN | CL61 | 5040 |
| **N652CV** | **C650** | **0055** |
| N652CW | CL61 | 5052 |
| **N652FC** | **EA50** | **000188** |
| N652GA | GLF5 | 5152 |
| N652GA | GLF5 | 552 |
| **N652GD** | **GLF6** | **6002** |
| N652J | LJ24 | 018 |
| N652JM | C650 | 0113 |
| **N652KZ** | **LJ35** | **652** |
| N652MC | CL64 | 5662 |
| N652MK | SBRL | 465-36 |
| N652ND | C500 | 277 |
| N652NR | C560 | 0652 |
| N652PC | F2TH | 10 |
| **N652QS** | **C56X** | **5152** |
| N652SA | LJ35 | 652 |
| N652XP | HS25 | 258652 |
| N653AC | CL61 | 5153 |
| N653CC | C650 | 0003 |
| N653CC | C650 | 0089 |
| N653CC | C650 | 0153 |
| N653CW | CL61 | 5053 |
| N653DR | C500 | 561 |
| N653EJ | C650 | 7057 |
| N653F | C500 | 638 |
| **N653FC** | **EA50** | **000205** |
| **N653FJ** | **FA10** | **110** |
| N653GA | GALX | 153 |
| N653GA | GLF5 | 553 |
| **N653GD** | **GLF6** | **6003** |
| (N653J) | WW24 | 161 |
| N653LJ | LJ24 | 126 |
| **N653MF** | **FA20** | **185/467** |
| **N653MK** | **GLF5** | **5211** |
| N653XP | HS25 | 258653 |
| N654 | LJ25 | 082 |
| **N654AN** | **LJ60** | **065** |
| **N654AP** | **BE40** | **RK-88** |
| (N654AR) | C650 | 0004 |
| N654AT | BE40 | RK-88 |
| **N654AT** | **LJ45** | **136** |
| N654CC | C650 | 0001 |
| **N654CE** | **C560** | **0654** |
| **N654CM** | **CL61** | **5009** |
| N654CN | F900 | 127 |
| N654DN | LJ24 | 019 |
| N654E | FA20 | 164 |
| N654E | SBRL | 282-70 |
| N654EA | C510 | 0010 |
| N654EJ | C650 | 7070 |
| N654EL | C56X | 5024 |
| **N654FC** | **EA50** | **000227** |
| N654GA | GLF5 | 5154 |
| N654GA | GLF5 | 554 |
| N654GC | C650 | 0004 |
| (N654GV) | GLF5 | 654 |
| N654JC | LJ24 | 127 |
| N654LD | LJ24 | 127 |
| N654LJ | LJ24 | 127 |
| N654PC | FA10 | 131 |
| **N654QS** | **C56X** | **5611** |
| **N654WW** | **C525** | **0053** |
| N654XP | HS25 | 258654 |

N655AL LJ55 129
(N655CC) C500 155
N655CC C650 0105
**N655CM BE40 RJ-17**
N655CN CL61 5069
(N655DB) FA10 28
N655EW C550 303
N655GA GLF5 555
N655GP LJ55 128
(N655JH) GLF2 22
N655LJ LJ24 128
N655PC C550 134
**N655PE FA10 199**
**N655QS C56X 5655**
N655TH CL61 5022
N655TH LJ60 141
N655TJ GLF2 5
**N655TR LJ55 006**
N655TS CL64 5505
N655XP HS25 258655
N656CC C650 0006
(N656CC) C650 0026
N656GA GALX 156
N656GA GLF4 4156
N656GA GLF5 556
**N656JG C560 0298**
(N656LE) C650 0237
N656LJ LJ24 129
N656PC FA10 99
**N656PS C550 009**
(N656QS) C56X 5672
**N656QS C56X 5732**
N656XP HS25 258656
**N656Z C560 0656**
**N657BM LJ25 331**
N657CC C650 0007
N657CC C650 0157
**N657CT CL64 5665**
N657ER C650 7027
N657GA GLF4 4157
N657GA GLF5 5157
N657GA GLF5 557
N657JW C650 7110
(N657K) HS25 25032
N657LJ LJ24 130
N657MC FA20 148
**N657P MS76 057**
**N657QS C56X 5636**
N657RB C525 0409
**N657T C650 7042**
N657XP HS25 258657
N658AT LJ24 219
N658CC C650 0046
**N658CF CL60 1058**
N658CJ C650 0158
N658GA GALX 158
N658GA GLF5 558
N658JC CL64 5658
N658KA HS25 256058
**N658KS LJ60 071**
N658L LJ24 017
N658LJ LJ24 132
N658MA C650 0023
N658PC GLF2 157
**N658QS C56X 5665**
N658TC LJ25 044
N658TS HS25 256058
N658XP HS25 258658
N659AT LJ24 157
N659CJ C525 0659
**N659FM F2TH 17**
N659GA GLF5 5059
N659GA GLF5 5159
N659GA GLF5 559
N659HX LJ25 179
N659HX LJ25 300
N659LJ LJ24 131
N659PC GLF2 204
N659QS C56X 5355
**N659QS C56X 5359**
(N659SA) C560 0559
N659TS CL61 5159
**N659WL GLF2 204**
N659XP HS25 258659
N660A LJ24 155
N660AA C500 480
N660AA C650 0059
(N660AC) C550 158
N660AF C650 0151
N660AF GLF2 70/1
(N660AH) FA50 290
N660AH LJ60 017
N660AJ CS55 0154
**N660AL CL30 20129**
(N660AN) LJ60 128
N660AS LJ60 040
**N660AS LJ60 191**
N660BC LJ60 063
N660BD F900 25
(N660BW) SBRL 306-33
N660CB LJ60 055
**N660CC BE40 RK-319**
N660CJ LJ35 079
N660CJ LJ60 126
N660EG F900 152
N660GA GLF5 5160
N660GA GLF5 560
**N660HC HS25 258624**
N660HC LJ45 058
N660KC C500 480
N660KS LJ60 219
N660L LJ35 660
N660LJ LJ24 133
N660LT C560 0564
N660P FA20 430
**N660PA C650 0230**
**N660Q C650 0162**
**N660QS C56X 5647**
N660RM CL60 1054
N660RM SBRL 306-91
N660RW WW24 128
**N660S C52A 0305**
N660SA LJ35 469
**N660SB C560 0433**
N660TC HS25 256060
N660TC LJ25 317
N660TJ C650 0060
N660W WW24 58
N660XP HS25 258660
N661AA C500 357
N661AA LJ36 049
**N661AC C500 121**
N661AJ C560 0176
N661BS LJ24 108
N661CL CL61 5061
**N661CP GLF5 5104**
N661CP LJ24 108
N661CP LJ24 174
N661CP WW24 210
**N661EP E50P 50000123**
N661FS LJ24 018
**N661GA GLF5 561**
N661GL FA10 3
N661J FA20 81
N661JB CL60 1073
N661JB FA20 275
N661JB FA20 81
N661JB HS25 257106
N661JB LJ24 159
N661JB WW24 209
N661JG LJ24 174
N661JN HS25 258209
N661LJ LJ25 002
N661MP LJ25 162
N661MP WW24 176
N661P SBRL 282-41
**N661QS C56X 5677**
N661R GLF4 1092
N661SS LJ24 108
(N661TS) CL60 1061
N661TV C500 661
N661TW C500 661
**N661WD BE40 RK-94**
N661XP HS25 258661
(N662AA) C550 183
N662AA LJ35 315
N662AJ C550 624
**N662CB C550 550-1062**
N662CC C500 277
**N662CC C510 0178**
**N662CG C500 277**
**N662CP GLF5 5107**
N662D FA10 200
N662D FA10 87
N662F SBRL 306-6
N662G GLF2 188
N662GA GLF5 5162
N662GA GLF5 562
N662GA GLF5 662
N662JB HS25 257018
N662JB WW24 209
N662JB WW24 210
**N662JN HS25 258837**
N662K WW24 418
N662P F9EX 30
N662P FA20 378
N662P FA50 320
N662P SBRL 306-6
(N662PP) FA20 378
**N662QS C56X 5262**
N662XP HS25 258662
N663AJ BE40 RK-148
N663B GLF2 14
N663CA LJ35 063
N663CP GLF4 4044
N663GA GLF5 5163
N663GA GLF5 663
N663JB LJ25 162
N663JB WW24 209
N663L LJ24 140
**N663LB LJ40 45-2114**
N663LJ LJ24 140
**N663MK F9EX 94**
N663MN FA50 249
N663P GLF2 14
**N663P GLF4 1434**
N663PD GLF2 139/11
**N663PD GLF4 1022**
**N663QS C56X 5263**
N663XP HS25 258663
**N664AC HS25 258566**
**N664AJ C550 613**
N664B FA20 95
N664B FA50 200
N664CC C500 664
**N664CE C560 0664**
N664CJ C525 0664
N664CL LJ24 151
**N664CL LJ24 167**
**N664CP GLF4 4047**
N664CW CL61 3064
**N664D CL64 5505**
N664GA GLF5 564
N664GA GLF5 664
N664GL LJ24 151
N664J C550 025
N664JB C550 025
N664JB FA10 162
N664JB HS25 257106
N664JC CL64 5663
**N664JN GLF4 1396**
N664LJ LJ24 136
N664P FA20 95
N664P FA50 200
N664P GLF3 343
**N664QS C56X 5264**
(N664RB) C650 0014
N664S GLF3 343
N664SS C550 458
N664XP HS25 258664
(N665AJ) C525 0120
N665B FA20 88
**N665CH C525 0504**
N665CJ C525 0665
**N665CP GLF4 4049**
N665CT CL64 5665
N665DP C525 0028
N665JB C500 357
N665MC C550 665
**N665MM C500 631**
N665P FA20 444
N665P FA20 88
**N665QS C56X 5165**
**N665SF GLF2 94**
N665XP HS25 258665
N666AE HS25 25046
N666AG C500 101
N666AJ C550 095
(N666BC) HS25 258524
N666BE F2EX 32
(N666BG) LJ45 121
(N666BK) C680 0087
N666BP WW24 122
N666BR SBRL 306-2
N666BS C500 045
N666BT FA20 7
N666CC LJ24 214
N666CC LJ35 254
N666CP WW24 347
**N666CT CL61 5007**
N666DA FA20 129
N666DC WW24 61
N666ES C500 045
N666FH C680 0125
N666JD WW24 39
N666JJ C500 537
N666JM C650 0241
N666JM WW24 133
N666JM WW24 149
N666JM WW24 184
N666JM WW24 283
N666JR LJ35 074
N666JT C550 272
N666JT GLF2 162
N666JT HS25 25186
**N666K ASTR 040**
N666K WW24 207
N666K WW24 321
N666KK LJ25 285
N666KK LJ35 481
N666KL ASTR 040
N666KL WW24 321
N666LC HFB3 1039
N666LC HS25 256064
N666LN CS55 0005
N666LP LJ25 185
N666LQ HFB3 1039
N666M HS25 25075
N666MP LJ24 041
(N666MP) WW24 156
N666MW LJ24 305
**N666MX C56X 5292**
**N666NF HS25 HB-27**
N666PE LJ25 359
N666RB LJ25 291
N666RB LJ35 393
N666RC C550 044
N666RE LJ25 359
N666RE LJ31 016
N666RE LJ31 055
N666SA C500 031
**N666SA GLF2 130**
N666SC HS25 25098
N666TB LJ36 012
N666TF CL64 5309
**N666TK LJ55 038**
**N666TM EA50 000221**
N666TR CL64 5309
N666TR CS55 0106
**N666TR F900 195**
**N666TS C500 446**
**N666TV LJ55 012**
N666TW LJ25 116
N666WL LJ25 017
N666WL SBRL 306-75
N666WW C550 201
(N666WW) C550 445
N667CC C650 0167
N667CC CL61 5032
N667CG C550 365
N667CX GLF2 10
N667H HS25 258276
**N667HS GLF4 4131**
N667LC CL61 5032
N667LC CL64 5324
**N667LC CL65 5740**
N667LQ CL64 5324
**N667MB LJ55 073**
N667P FA20 432
N667P GLF4 1447
**N667QS C56X 5365**
N667XP HS25 258667
**N668AJ C550 442**
**N668CB C550 550-1068**
N668CM C550 668
N668EA C550 667
N668GA GLF5 5168
N668H HS25 258287
**N668JT GLF2 162**
N668JT HS25 25186
N668MC LJ24 214
N668P FA20 308

N668P FA50 315
**N668QS C56X 5268**
**N668RC LJ60 044**
**N668S C500 314**
N668S FA20 308
N668VB C525 0228
N668VP C525 0228
N668VP LJ31 232
N668XP HS25 258668
**N668Z PRM1 RB-247**
(N669AC) FA20 299
N669AJ C560 0021
**N669B C550 550-1060**
**N669BJ GLF4 1397**
**N669CM EA50 000165**
N669DB C525 0228
(N669DM) C500 669
N669H HS25 258289
N669LJ LJ35 669
N669MA C550 128
N669PG F2EX 126
**N669QS C56X 5689**
(N669SB) WW24 435
N669SC HS25 256024
**N669TT C56X 5684**
N669W C650 0045
**N669W C650 7066**
N669XP HS25 258669
N670AS SBRL 465-58
N670BA HS25 258209
**N670C SBRL 370-7**
N670CE C560 0670
N670CL CL60 1070
**N670CM CL64 5488**
N670GA GLF5 670
N670H HS25 258290
**N670H SBRL 465-58**
**N670JD CS55 0019**
N670LJ LJ25 009
N670MF LJ24 062
**N670MW C56X 5511**
**N670QS C56X 5170**
**N670RW GALX 160**
(N670WJ) LJ35 670
N670XL C56X 5670
N670XP HS25 258670
**N671AF GLF4 1205**
N671B C550 271
N671BA HS25 258216
N671BA LJ35 671
N671BX LJ35 671
N671EA C550 671
N671GA GALX 171
N671GA GLF5 571
N671LB GLF5 671
**N671LE GLF5 5130**
N671LE GLF5 671
**N671LW GLF2 90**
**N671QS C56X 5071**
**N671RW GLF5 5131**
N671SR CL60 1071
N671SR FA20 56
N671TS LJ35 671
**N671WB FA7X 29**
**N671WM F2TH 194**
N671WM LJ25 010
N671XP HS25 258671
N672AT BE40 RJ-14
N672BA HS25 258217
**N672BP CL30 20258**
N672CA C550 591
N672CC C650 0172
N672DK LJ35 672
N672GA GALX 172
N672GA GLF5 672
N672H HS25 258291
**N672JM C525 0485**
N672LJ LJ24 146
N672M JSTR 5103
**N672PS GALX 010**
**N672QS C56X 5663**
N672SA C560 0272
N672XP HS25 258672
N672XP HS25 258772
N673BA F2TH 173
N673BA HS25 258218
(N673BH) CL60 1073
N673CA C550 590
**N673DC E50P 50000010**
N673FH SBRL 380-49
N673GA GALX 073
N673GA GLF5 5073
N673GA GLF5 5173
N673GA GLF5 573
N673H HS25 258292
N673JS C650 0073
N673LB LJ45 222
N673LJ LJ24 147
N673LP C500 503
N673LP C550 192
N673LP LJ45 222
N673LR C500 503
**N673LR C550 192**
N673M LJ35 008
**N673MG C56X 5821**
**N673P GLF5 673**
**N673QS C56X 5651**
N673SH SBRL 380-49
N673TM HS25 258033
N673TS CL60 1073
N673WM LJ24 040
N673XP HS25 258673
**N673YS CL60 1073**
N674AC MU30 A024SA
**N674AS C52A 0307**
N674BA HS25 258220
N674BP LJ60 074
N674CA C550 564
N674CC C650 0174
**N674CW CL60 1074**
**N674DJ BE40 RK-232**
**N674G C550 434**
N674GA GALX 174
N674GA GLF5 574
N674GA GLF5 674
N674JM C525 0485
**N674JM C52A 0458**
N674JM CS55 0127
N674LJ LJ24 178
N674LJ LJ35 674
**N674RW GLF5 5234**
N674RW GLF5 524
N674SF BE40 RK-232
N674XP HS25 258674
N675BA HS25 258221
**N675BP LJ60 321**
N675CF CL61 5094
(N675DM) C550 608
N675GA GALX 175
N675GA GLF5 675
N675LJ LJ60 075
N675M LJ55 075
**N675QS C56X 5275**
N675RW GLF2 191
N675RW GLF5 526
**N675SS C550 576**
N675XP HS25 258675
**N676AH HS25 258831**
**N676BA F2TH 176**
N676BA HS25 259020
N676BB C550 550-0923
**N676BB C56X 5349**
**N676CC C500 676**
N676CW C500 169
**N676DG C500 256**
N676DW FA20 387
N676GA GLF5 676
**N676GH HS25 258676**
**N676JB HS25 258619**
N676LJ LJ24 183
N676PB C550 550-0923
N676PC FA10 36
N676PC HS25 25153
**N676QS C56X 5176**
N676RW GLF3 355
N676RW GLF4 1253
**N676RW GLF5 5126**
N676TC ASTR 044
N676TC ASTR 128
(N676WE) C500 169
N676XP HS25 258676
**N677AS PRM1 RB-33**
N677BA HS25 258223
N677BM FA20 57
N677CC C650 0077
N677CT LJ35 307
**N677F GLF5 677**
N677FR GLF4 1289
N677GA GALX 177
N677GA GLF5 677
N677GS C550 669
**N677JM C500 427**
N677LJ LJ60 077
N677LM C650 0083
**N677LM CL60 1080**
**N677QS C56X 5367**
N677RP GLF4 1085
N677RW GLF2 191
N677RW GLF2 192
N677RW GLF4 1177
N677RW HS25 257191
N677S GLF2 115
(N677SC) F9EX 66
**N677SL C52A 0418**
N677SW FA20 27
N677SW GLF4 1269
N677SW LJ24 356
N677V GLF2 120
N677VU GLF4 1269
N677XP HS25 258677
N678AM SBRL 465-22
N678BA HS25 258230
N678BC JSTR 5109/13
N678BM FA20 345
N678BM FA20 57
N678CA C550 060
N678CF C500 678
N678CG CL60 1027
**N678CH F900 47**
N678DG C500 625
(N678DG) C500 652
**N678EQ C650 7008**
N678GA GALX 178
N678GA GLF5 678
N678JD C500 452
(N678JG) C500 452
**N678MA FA50 116**
N678ML CL60 1011
N678PC MU30 A021SA
**N678PS EA50 000191**
N678QS C56X 5353
N678QS C56X 5369
**N678QS C56X 5616**
**N678RF C525 0537**
N678RW GLF2 13
N678RW GLF2 192
N678RW GLF4 1017
N678RZ GLF2 13
N678S LJ35 342
N678SB HS25 259016
**N678SC GLF5 5224**
N678SP LJ24 354
N678SV C680 0078
N678W HS25 257147
N678XP HS25 258678
N679BA HS25 259023
N679BC C550 589
N679CC C500 679
N679CC C650 0179
N679GA GLF5 679
N679H HS25 258293
N679H HS25 259049
**N679QS C56X 5279**
N679RE FA20 150/445
N679RW GALX 072
N679RW GLF2 109
N679RW GLF2 191
N679RW GLF4 1131
N679RW JSTR 5062/12
**N679SJ BE40 RK-168**
N679XP HS25 258679
N680AF LJ31 068
**N680AK C680 0283**
**N680AR C680 0025**
N680BA HS25 259014
N680BC C650 0087
N680BC LJ25 200
**N680CG C680 0044**
**N680CJ LJ24 211**
**N680CM C680 0194**
**N680CS C680 709**
**N680DF F2TH 180**
(N680FA) CL61 3003
**N680FD C680 0289**
N680FM GLF3 371
**N680GA GLF5 680**
N680GG C680 0104
**N680GR C680 0210**
N680GW C560 0369
**N680HC C680 0079**
N680J LJ25 063
N680JB C52A 0190
N680JC LJ25 319
N680JG C680 0250
N680K WW24 173
**N680KH C525 0680**
**N680LN C680 0236**
N680M CL60 1023
**N680ME WW24 423**
**N680PA C680 0255**
N680PH C680 0030
**N680RC C680 0192**
**N680RP C680 0239**
N680RW GLF2 191
N680RW GLF2 4/8
N680RZ GLF2 4/8
N680SB C680 0039
**N680SE C680 0078**
N680SV C680 0056
N680SW C680 0044
**N680SW LJ31 242**
N680TT JSTR 5108
N680VR C56X 5049
**N680VR C680 0108**
N680XP HS25 258680
N681AF LJ31 102
N681AR GLF2 81
**N681CE C560 0681**
N681CS C680 0001
N681FM GLF2 167
N681FM GLF3 371
**N681HS C680 0287**
**N681LF C680 0151**
N681LJ LJ60 081
(N681MR) C680 0255
**N681QS C56X 5181**
N681RP C56X 5254
**N681RP C680 0037**
N681SV C680 0117
(N681TS) CL60 1081
N681WD BE40 RK-94
N681WD C750 0052
N681XP HS25 258681
N682B HS25 258144
N682BA HS25 258225
**N682BF C500 682**
N682CC C650 0182
N682CJ C550 682
N682CM C550 682
N682CS C680 0002
N682D C560 0021
(N682D) FA10 200
N682D FA10 87
**N682D HS25 258144**
**N682DB C680 0009**
N682DC C500 682
N682DK HS25 258682
N682FM GLF2 167
N682FM GLF3 305
**N682GA GALX 202**
N682GA GLF5 682
N682H HS25 258294
N682HC C500 682
**N682HS C680 0291**
N682JB FA20 488
N682LJ LJ24 218
N682LJ LJ60 082
**N682QS C56X 5654**
N682XP HS25 258682
N683BA HS25 258229
N683CF CS55 0085
N683E HS25 258113
N683EC GLF2 157
**N683EF LJ35 614**
N683EL LJ35 614
**N683F HS25 258113**
N683FM GLF2 167
N683FM GLF2 22
**N683GA ASTR 283**
N683GA GALX 203
N683GA GLF5 683
N683H HS25 258295

| | | |
|---|---|---|
| N683LJ | LJ25 | 035 |
| N683LJ | LJ60 | 083 |
| N683MB | C650 | 0159 |
| N683MB | CS55 | 0085 |
| **N683PF** | **CS55** | **0083** |
| **N683QS** | **C56X** | **5643** |
| N683RP | C56X | 5501 |
| **N683UF** | **CL61** | **5083** |
| N684AT | GLF3 | 339 |
| N684BA | HS25 | 259033 |
| N684BM | C560 | 0684 |
| N684C | HS25 | 258063 |
| N684CE | C560 | 0684 |
| **N684DK** | **HS25** | **258684** |
| N684GA | GLF5 | 684 |
| N684H | C500 | 113 |
| N684HA | C500 | 113 |
| **N684HA** | **LJ35** | **113** |
| **N684KF** | **F2TH** | **213** |
| N684LA | LJ35 | 113 |
| N684LJ | LJ60 | 084 |
| N684QS | C56X | 5084 |
| N684SW | CL61 | 5032 |
| N684TA | BE40 | RK-334 |
| **N684TS** | **CL64** | **5384** |
| N684TS | CL64 | 5484 |
| N685BA | HS25 | 258231 |
| **N685CS** | **C680** | **0142** |
| N685EM | HS25 | 257026 |
| N685FF | HS25 | 25121 |
| N685FM | HS25 | 257026 |
| N685H | HS25 | 258296 |
| N685LJ | LJ60 | 085 |
| **N685QS** | **C56X** | **5650** |
| N685RC | LJ31 | 149 |
| N685RC | LJ45 | 053 |
| N685SF | GLF2 | 94 |
| N685SF | GLF4 | 1056 |
| N685TA | GLF2 | 31 |
| N685TA | GLF4 | 1003 |
| **N685TA** | **GLF5** | **685** |
| **N686AB** | **LJ31** | **239** |
| N686BA | HS25 | 258232 |
| N686CF | HS25 | 258060 |
| N686CG | GLF4 | 1171 |
| **N686CP** | **HS25** | **258059** |
| N686FG | HS25 | 257207 |
| N686GA | GLF5 | 686 |
| **N686HC** | **C680** | **0101** |
| N686LJ | LJ60 | 086 |
| N686MC | CS55 | 0072 |
| **N686QS** | **C56X** | **5661** |
| **N686SC** | **BE40** | **RK-211** |
| N686SG | HS25 | 257207 |
| N686TA | BE40 | RK-328 |
| **N686TR** | **BE40** | **RK-127** |
| N687CJ | C525 | 0687 |
| **N687DS** | **C52B** | **0087** |
| N687GA | GLF5 | 687 |
| N687LJ | LJ25 | 040 |
| N687LJ | LJ60 | 087 |
| **N687QS** | **C56X** | **5187** |
| N687TA | BE40 | RK-322 |
| N687VP | C650 | 0087 |
| N688AG | C56X | 5056 |
| N688CC | HS25 | 25142 |
| N688CF | C500 | 147 |
| N688DB | C52A | 0192 |
| **N688DB** | **LJ60** | **097** |
| (N688DP) | C52A | 0192 |
| N688G | HS25 | 258688 |
| N688GA | GLF5 | 688 |
| **N688GS** | **LJ25** | **123** |
| N688H | GLF4 | 1062 |
| **N688JD** | **C550** | **550-0902** |
| N688LJ | LJ60 | 088 |
| **N688LS** | **GLF4** | **1280** |
| N688MC | FA20 | 175 |
| N688MC | GLF2 | 81 |
| **N688QS** | **C56X** | **5188** |
| N688TA | BE40 | RK-321 |
| **N688TT** | **GLF4** | **1220** |
| **N688TY** | **GLF5** | **536** |
| (N688WS) | SBRL | 465-60 |
| **N689AK** | **BE40** | **RK-462** |
| **N689AM** | **HS25** | **258665** |
| N689CC | C500 | 689 |
| N689GA | GLF5 | 689 |
| N689H | HS25 | 258300 |
| **N689JE** | **GLF2** | **258** |
| **N689QS** | **C56X** | **5659** |
| N689TA | BE40 | RK-319 |
| N689TA | BE40 | RK-327 |
| **N689VP** | **C550** | **689** |
| **N689W** | **C650** | **0045** |
| **N689WC** | **FA10** | **123** |
| N690 | LJ24 | 339 |
| **N690AN** | **C550** | **674** |
| N690DM | C500 | 592 |
| N690EA | C500 | 201 |
| **N690EW** | **C550** | **119** |
| N690GA | GLF5 | 690 |
| N690J | LJ24 | 145 |
| **N690JC** | **LJ25** | **320** |
| N690LJ | LJ24 | 078 |
| N690MC | C500 | 388 |
| N690PC | GLF2 | 56 |
| N690QS | C56X | 5090 |
| **N690WY** | **C500** | **592** |
| N691AC | GLF3 | 316 |
| N691CJ | C525 | 0691 |
| (N691DE) | C650 | 0204 |
| N691GA | GLF5 | 691 |
| N691H | HS25 | 258321 |
| N691HM | GLF2 | 92 |
| (N691NS) | LJ35 | 208 |
| **N691QS** | **C56X** | **5290** |
| N691RC | GLF2 | 43 |
| N691RC | GLF4 | 1079 |
| **N691RC** | **GLF5** | **605** |
| N691SC | GLF4 | 1481 |
| N691TA | BE40 | RK-317 |
| **N692BE** | **C650** | **0092** |
| N692CC | C650 | 0092 |
| N692EB | GLF2 | 87/775/6 |
| N692FC | HS25 | 25032 |
| N692FC | LJ25 | 052 |
| **N692FG** | **LJ25** | **052** |
| N692G | FA20 | 44 |
| N692GA | GALX | 192 |
| N692GA | GLF5 | 692 |
| N692JM | C52A | 0004 |
| N692JM | C52A | 0109 |
| N692LJ | LJ24 | 222 |
| N692M | CS55 | 0041 |
| **N692PC** | **LJ60** | **010** |
| **N692QS** | **C56X** | **5092** |
| (N692SH) | F900 | 43 |
| N692TA | BE40 | RK-307 |
| N692TT | C550 | 692 |
| N692TV | GLF3 | 397 |
| **N692US** | **FA10** | **79** |
| N693BA | C650 | 0005 |
| N693C | HS25 | 258209 |
| (N693CC) | C650 | 0093 |
| **N693GA** | **GLF4** | **4193** |
| N693GA | GLF5 | 693 |
| N693LJ | LJ24 | 231 |
| N693M | CS55 | 0021 |
| N693PB | GLF3 | 451 |
| **N693QS** | **C56X** | **5657** |
| **N693SH** | **F900** | **43** |
| N693TA | BE40 | RK-305 |
| N693TJ | HS25 | 256027 |
| N693XP | HS25 | 258693 |
| N694CC | C650 | 0090 |
| N694CM | C550 | 694 |
| N694JC | CL60 | 1026 |
| N694JC | HS25 | 25107 |
| **N694JP** | **F9EX** | **59** |
| **N694LM** | **C500** | **363** |
| N694LP | LJ45 | 384 |
| **N694PG** | **CL60** | **1026** |
| (N694PG) | LJ35 | 041 |
| **N694QS** | **C56X** | **5194** |
| (N694SC) | LJ45 | 293 |
| N694SH | LJ45 | 398 |
| N695BD | LJ40 | 45-2059 |
| **N695BK** | **BE40** | **RK-235** |
| N695CC | C500 | 593 |
| N695LJ | LJ25 | 060 |
| **N695QS** | **C56X** | **5293** |
| N695ST | FA50 | 40 |
| N695ST | GLF2 | 28 |
| N695TA | BE40 | RK-303 |
| N695TA | BE40 | RK-310 |
| **N695V** | **C560** | **0695** |
| N695VP | C550 | 695 |
| N695XP | HS25 | 258695 |
| N696A | C550 | 363 |
| N696CM | C550 | 550-0978 |
| N696GA | GALX | 196 |
| N696GA | GLF5 | 5096 |
| N696GW | WW24 | 52 |
| N696HC | C650 | 0154 |
| N696HC | C680 | 0101 |
| **N696HC** | **C680** | **0266** |
| N696HC | FA50 | 250 |
| N696HC | FA50 | 316 |
| N696HQ | FA50 | 250 |
| N696HQ | FA50 | 316 |
| (N696JH) | HS25 | 257055 |
| (N696JH) | LJ35 | 084 |
| **N696MJ** | **GLF2** | **165/37** |
| **N696NA** | **EA50** | **000123** |
| N696PA | LJ31 | 060 |
| **N696QS** | **C56X** | **5296** |
| (N696RB) | LJ31 | 145 |
| **N696RV** | **WW24** | **118** |
| **N696SB** | **F2EX** | **206** |
| N696SC | LJ35 | 018 |
| (N696SC) | LJ35 | 179 |
| **N696ST** | **C525** | **0187** |
| N696TA | BE40 | RK-301 |
| N696TR | BE40 | RK-127 |
| **N696US** | **SBRL** | **465-18** |
| **N696VP** | **C550** | **696** |
| N697A | C550 | 034 |
| N697A | GLF2 | 16/13 |
| **N697A** | **GLF5** | **662** |
| N697BA | C550 | 697 |
| N697BH | FA20 | 239 |
| N697BJ | GLF3 | 370 |
| N697CE | C560 | 0697 |
| N697EA | C550 | 697 |
| N697MB | C500 | 224 |
| N697MC | C650 | 0097 |
| N697NP | HS25 | 257052 |
| **N697QS** | **C56X** | **5197** |
| N697TA | BE40 | RK-299 |
| **N697US** | **SBRL** | **465-49** |
| N697XP | HS25 | 258697 |
| N698CW | CL61 | 3008 |
| N698DC | HS25 | 259043 |
| N698GA | GALX | 150 |
| N698MM | LJ31 | 142 |
| N698PW | BE40 | RK-114 |
| **N698QS** | **C56X** | **5653** |
| N698RS | CL61 | 3014 |
| **N698RS** | **CL64** | **5460** |
| N698RT | CL61 | 3014 |
| N698TA | BE40 | RK-298 |
| **N699AK** | **HA4T** | **RC-16** |
| **N699BA** | **LJ35** | **463** |
| N699BC | C56X | 5123 |
| **N699BG** | **F900** | **82** |
| N699CC | C560 | 0351 |
| **N699CP** | **LJ31** | **060** |
| N699CW | CL61 | 5009 |
| N699DA | LJ60 | 237 |
| N699EC | HS25 | 258193 |
| N699GA | FA20 | 401 |
| N699GA | GLF5 | 5099 |
| N699GA | GLF5 | 666 |
| N699GA | GLF5 | 699 |
| **N699HH** | **GLF4** | **1239** |
| (N699JM) | C52A | 0004 |
| N699MC | ASTR | 076 |
| **N699MC** | **F2EX** | **25** |
| **N699MG** | **C650** | **0094** |
| N699MQ | ASTR | 076 |
| **N699QS** | **C56X** | **5199** |
| N699RD | SBRL | 306-53 |
| N699SC | FA50 | 70 |
| N699SC | HS25 | 256026 |
| N699SC | LJ60 | 041 |
| **N699ST** | **LJ35** | **441** |
| N699TA | BE40 | RK-297 |
| **N699TS** | **HS25** | **256001** |
| **N699TW** | **FA20** | **50** |
| **N699XP** | **HS25** | **258699** |
| N700AA | HS25 | 257149 |
| (N700AB) | HS25 | 25033 |
| N700AC | HS25 | 257126 |
| N700AD | GLEX | 9058 |
| N700AH | GLEX | 9016 |
| N700AH | GLEX | 9078 |
| N700AJ | A700 | 0001 |
| N700AJ | A700 | 0004 |
| **N700AL** | **FA10** | **55** |
| N700AP | GLEX | 9079 |
| N700AQ | GLEX | 9025 |
| N700AR | HS25 | 257053 |
| N700AS | C550 | 014 |
| N700AU | GLEX | 9083 |
| N700AY | GLEX | 9082 |
| N700BA | HS25 | 257032 |
| N700BA | HS25 | 257058 |
| N700BA | HS25 | 257131 |
| N700BA | HS25 | 257185 |
| N700BA | HS25 | 257189 |
| N700BB | HS25 | 257041 |
| N700BB | HS25 | 257148 |
| N700BD | FA10 | 81 |
| N700BD | GLEX | 9063 |
| N700BF | WW24 | 137 |
| N700BH | GLEX | 9024 |
| N700BH | GLF2 | 115 |
| N700BJ | LJ25 | 257 |
| N700BK | GLEX | 9067 |
| N700BP | GLEX | 9044 |
| N700BQ | GLEX | 9087 |
| N700BU | GLEX | 9043 |
| N700BV | GLEX | 9046 |
| N700BW | HS25 | 25263 |
| N700BW | HS25 | 257123 |
| **N700BX** | **GLEX** | **9068** |
| N700BY | GLEX | 9048 |
| N700C | LJ24 | 123 |
| N700C | LJ24 | 144 |
| N700C | WW24 | 44 |
| N700CB | WW24 | 44 |
| N700CC | HS25 | 25202 |
| N700CE | GLEX | 9098 |
| **N700CE** | **HS25** | **257213** |
| N700CF | SBRL | 282-109 |
| **N700CH** | **F2TH** | **147** |
| N700CH | LJ60 | 056 |
| **N700CJ** | **C525** | **0027** |
| N700CJ | GLEX | 9062 |
| N700CJ | HS25 | 257178 |
| N700CL | CL60 | 1035 |
| N700CN | GLF3 | 488 |
| **N700CN** | **GLF4** | **1133** |
| N700CN | HS25 | 257102 |
| (N700CQ) | GLF2 | 228 |
| N700CS | C650 | 0036 |
| N700CU | GLEX | 9099 |
| N700CU | HS25 | 257081 |
| N700CV | GLEX | 9065 |
| N700CW | C500 | 205 |
| N700CX | GLEX | 9100 |
| N700CY | GLEX | 9102 |
| N700CZ | GLEX | 9103 |
| N700DA | HS25 | 257135 |
| N700DA | LJ25 | 302 |
| (N700DA) | SBRL | 306-142 |
| N700DD | HS25 | 257152 |
| N700DE | HS25 | 257105 |
| N700DK | FA10 | 191 |
| N700DQ | GLEX | 9052 |
| N700DU | GLEX | 9056 |
| N700DU | GLEX | 9109 |
| N700DW | FA10 | 205 |
| N700DZ | GLEX | 9051 |
| (N700E) | HS25 | 257101 |
| (N700EA) | C550 | 072 |
| N700EC | GLEX | 9105 |
| N700EC | WW24 | 182 |
| N700EG | GLEX | 9059 |
| N700EK | GLEX | 9108 |
| N700EL | GLEX | 9110 |
| N700ER | C500 | 542 |
| N700ER | HS25 | 257010 |
| (N700ET) | LJ24 | 123 |
| N700EW | GLEX | 9116 |
| N700EW | GLEX | 9142 |
| N700EX | GLEX | 9057 |
| N700EY | GLEX | 9117 |
| N700EZ | GLEX | 9118 |
| **N700FA** | **ASTR** | **278** |
| N700FA | BE40 | RK-399 |

| | | |
|---|---|---|
| N700FA | HS25 | 25229 |
| N700FC | LJ25 | 082 |
| N700FE | GLEX | 9119 |
| N700FE | HS25 | 257108 |
| N700FG | GLEX | 9120 |
| **N700FH** | **FA10** | **158** |
| N700FJ | GLEX | 9050 |
| **N700FL** | **F2TH** | **29** |
| N700FN | GLEX | 9121 |
| N700FQ | GLEX | 9122 |
| N700FR | GLEX | 9125 |
| N700FR | HS25 | 257130 |
| N700FS | GLF2 | 108 |
| N700FS | GLF3 | 367 |
| **N700FS** | **GLF4** | **1400** |
| N700FS | HS25 | 257012 |
| N700FW | HS25 | 257008 |
| N700FY | GLEX | 9128 |
| N700FZ | GLEX | 9129 |
| (N700GA) | WW24 | 137 |
| N700GB | BE40 | RK-26 |
| **N700GB** | **GLEX** | **9124** |
| N700GB | HS25 | 257050 |
| N700GB | LJ35 | 082 |
| **N700GD** | **C510** | **0244** |
| N700GD | GLF4 | 1104 |
| N700GG | HS25 | 257154 |
| N700GG | LJ36 | 038 |
| N700GK | GLEX | 9020 |
| N700GM | BE40 | RK-34 |
| (N700GN) | FA20 | 325 |
| N700GQ | GLEX | 9085 |
| N700GS | LJ60 | 026 |
| N700GT | GLEX | 9039 |
| N700GU | GLEX | 9084 |
| N700GW | C525 | 0275 |
| N700GX | GLEX | 9014 |
| N700HA | HS25 | 257143 |
| N700HA | HS25 | 257149 |
| N700HB | HS25 | 257146 |
| N700HB | WW24 | 135 |
| N700HE | GLEX | 9032 |
| N700HF | GLEX | 9034 |
| N700HG | GLEX | 9022 |
| N700HH | HS25 | 257045 |
| (N700HM) | BE40 | RJ-19 |
| N700HS | HS25 | 257002 |
| N700HS | HS25 | 257012 |
| N700HS | HS25 | 257072 |
| N700HS | HS25 | 257150 |
| N700HW | HS25 | 257173 |
| N700HX | GLEX | 9005 |
| N700JA | C500 | 379 |
| **N700JC** | **SBRL** | **465-74** |
| N700JD | C500 | 009 |
| N700JE | LJ55 | 091 |
| N700JE | LJ60 | 210 |
| N700JJ | A700 | 0001 |
| N700JP | GLF2 | 77 |
| N700JR | C500 | 379 |
| N700JR | C550 | 554 |
| **N700JR** | **C560** | **0666** |
| N700JR | SBRL | 306-138 |
| N700K | HS25 | 257102 |
| **N700KB** | **PRM1** | **RB-103** |
| N700KC | CL61 | 5017 |
| N700KG | HS25 | 257201 |
| **N700KG** | **LJ40** | **45-2017** |
| N700KJ | GLEX | 9011 |
| N700KK | CL60 | 1082 |
| N700KK | HS25 | 257155 |
| N700KS | GLEX | 9015 |
| **N700KS** | **GLEX** | **9109** |
| N700LA | GLEX | 9054 |
| N700LB | C550 | 366 |
| N700LD | GLEX | 9069 |
| **N700LH** | **C750** | **0148** |
| **N700LJ** | **A700** | **0002** |
| N700LJ | GLEX | 9053 |
| **N700LK** | **GLEX** | **9192** |
| N700LL | HS25 | 257157 |
| N700LN | GLEX | 9072 |
| N700LP | BE40 | RJ-28 |
| N700LP | HS25 | 257159 |
| N700LP | MU30 | A005SA |
| **N700LS** | **GLEX** | **9217** |
| N700LS | GLF4 | 1009 |
| N700LS | GLF4 | 1180 |
| N700LS | GLF4 | 1412 |
| N700LS | HS25 | 257041 |
| **N700LW** | **C500** | **279** |
| N700LW | C500 | 400 |
| **N700LX** | **C750** | **0038** |
| N700M | HS25 | 25123 |
| **N700MB** | **LJ40** | **45-2106** |
| (N700MD) | LJ36 | 045 |
| **N700MD** | **WW24** | **212** |
| N700MG | HS25 | 258540 |
| **N700MH** | **C650** | **0127** |
| N700MH | SBRL | 306-142 |
| (N700MJ) | JSTR | 5138 |
| N700MK | CL61 | 3011 |
| N700MK | HS25 | 257156 |
| N700ML | GLEX | 9043 |
| N700ML | GLEX | 9258 |
| N700MM | WW24 | 311 |
| N700MP | C500 | 198 |
| **N700MP** | **FA50** | **70** |
| N700NB | HS25 | 257131 |
| N700NH | HS25 | 257148 |
| **N700NK** | **C560** | **0700** |
| N700NN | HS25 | 257162 |
| **N700NP** | **HS25** | **257207** |
| N700NP | HS25 | 257213 |
| (N700NP) | LJ24 | 082 |
| N700NT | HS25 | 257056 |
| **N700NW** | **HS25** | **257063** |
| N700NW | LJ35 | 331 |
| **N700NY** | **GLF4** | **1468** |
| N700NY | HS25 | 257002 |
| N700NY | HS25 | 257140 |
| (N700PD) | FA10 | 55 |
| N700PD | HS25 | 257029 |
| (N700PG) | HS25 | 25202 |
| N700PL | GLEX | 9064 |
| N700PL | HS25 | 25229 |
| N700PM | GLF2 | 207/34 |
| N700PM | HS25 | 258081 |
| **N700PP** | **GLF4** | **1248** |
| N700PP | HS25 | 257167 |
| N700QG | SBRL | 465-16 |
| **N700QS** | **GALX** | **052** |
| N700R | HS25 | 256001 |
| **N700R** | **HS25** | **258692** |
| N700R | LJ55 | 133 |
| N700R | LJ60 | 113 |
| N700R | SBRL | 282-31 |
| N700R | WW24 | 149 |
| N700R | WW24 | 222 |
| (N700RD) | C650 | 0036 |
| N700RD | HS25 | 25136 |
| N700RG | HS25 | 25136 |
| N700RJ | HS25 | 257004 |
| N700RR | C650 | 0025 |
| N700RR | C650 | 7020 |
| **N700RR** | **HS25** | **257024** |
| N700RR | HS25 | 257161 |
| N700RY | C500 | 087 |
| **N700RY** | **C650** | **0005** |
| N700SA | HS25 | 257141 |
| N700SA | HS25 | 257145 |
| N700SB | GLF3 | 334 |
| N700SB | HS25 | 257121 |
| N700SF | HS25 | 257061 |
| N700SJ | LJ35 | 082 |
| (N700SM) | HS25 | 256066 |
| **N700SP** | **C500** | **528** |
| **N700SR** | **LJ55** | **079** |
| N700SS | HS25 | 257061 |
| N700SS | HS25 | 257168 |
| N700ST | GLF2 | 28 |
| N700SV | CS55 | 0119 |
| N700SV | HS25 | 257001 |
| N700SW | C650 | 0096 |
| **N700SW** | **C750** | **0142** |
| N700SW | CS55 | 0119 |
| N700TF | C560 | 0011 |
| N700TG | LJ55 | 021 |
| N700TL | HS25 | 257028 |
| N700TR | HS25 | 25220 |
| N700TT | FA10 | 49 |
| N700UK | HS25 | 257051 |
| N700UR | HS25 | 257057 |
| (N700UU) | HS25 | 25103 |
| N700VA | GLF3 | 300 |
| **N700VC** | **C500** | **011** |
| N700VN | GLEX | 9031 |
| N700VP | C650 | 7011 |
| N700VT | HS25 | 257158 |
| N700WB | GLF4 | 1125 |
| **N700WC** | **HS25** | **257022** |
| N700WE | WW24 | 417 |
| **N700WH** | **BE40** | **RJ-60** |
| N700WH | HS25 | 257010 |
| N700WJ | LJ35 | 393 |
| (N700WJ) | LJ35 | 466 |
| N700WL | GLEX | 9042 |
| N700WL | LJ35 | 003 |
| N700WM | WW24 | 319 |
| N700WS | SBRL | 306-133 |
| **N700WY** | **HS25** | **HA-0029** |
| **N700XF** | **HS25** | **257101** |
| N700XJ | HS25 | 256015 |
| N700XM | GLEX | 9091 |
| N700XN | GLEX | 9073 |
| N700XR | GLEX | 9070 |
| N700XT | GLEX | 9076 |
| N700XY | GLEX | 9077 |
| N700YM | C550 | 139 |
| **N700YY** | **C510** | **0148** |
| N701A | HS25 | 256022 |
| (N701AG) | C650 | 0077 |
| N701AP | LJ24 | 163 |
| N701AP | WW24 | 52 |
| (N701AR) | LJ36 | 008 |
| N701AS | C500 | 127 |
| **N701AS** | **LJ35** | **047** |
| N701AT | C500 | 127 |
| **N701BG** | **CS55** | **0142** |
| N701BR | C500 | 191 |
| N701CD | C650 | 7001 |
| N701CF | HS25 | 257057 |
| **N701CP** | **BE40** | **RK-272** |
| N701CR | C560 | 0469 |
| N701CR | C56X | 5141 |
| **N701CR** | **C680** | **0176** |
| N701CW | HS25 | 257001 |
| **N701DA** | **LJ35** | **180** |
| N701DB | LJ55 | 074 |
| N701DF | PRM1 | RB-59 |
| N701DK | C560 | 0221 |
| N701DK | C560 | 0544 |
| N701FW | SBRL | 306-57 |
| **N701FW** | **SBRL** | **465-21** |
| N701GA | CL60 | 1066 |
| **N701HA** | **C650** | **7001** |
| N701HB | GALX | 042 |
| N701JA | GLF2 | 7 |
| N701JH | JSTR | 5230 |
| N701KB | PRM1 | RB-103 |
| N701KB | PRM1 | RB-110 |
| N701KB | PRM1 | RB-211 |
| **N701KB** | **PRM1** | **RB-257** |
| N701KD | PRM1 | RB-211 |
| N701LP | BE40 | RJ-61 |
| **N701LX** | **C750** | **0114** |
| N701MG | FA20 | 196 |
| **N701MS** | **HS25** | **256061** |
| N701NA | LJ24 | 049 |
| N701NB | C560 | 0244 |
| N701NC | SBRL | 282-79 |
| N701NW | HS25 | 257009 |
| N701QS | CL60 | 1066 |
| **N701QS** | **GALX** | **141** |
| N701QS | GLF4 | 1059 |
| N701RM | C550 | 242 |
| N701RZ | LJ24 | 042 |
| N701S | GLF2 | 69 |
| **N701SC** | **LJ24** | **235** |
| **N701SF** | **C52A** | **0071** |
| N701TA | HS25 | 257073 |
| N701TF | C525 | 0190 |
| N701TF | C52A | 0112 |
| N701TP | C525 | 0190 |
| N701TS | HS25 | 257002 |
| N701US | LJ35 | 062 |
| N701VF | C500 | 650 |
| **N701VV** | **C550** | **550-1033** |
| N701W | WW24 | 274 |
| N701WC | F2TH | 48 |
| **N701WC** | **FA50** | **333** |
| N701WG | F2TH | 48 |
| N701WH | GLEX | 9010 |
| N701Z | HS25 | 25234 |
| N701Z | HS25 | 256022 |
| N701Z | HS25 | 256058 |
| N701Z | WW24 | 274 |
| **N702A** | **HS25** | **HA-0146** |
| **N702AB** | **C680** | **0258** |
| N702AC | C56X | 5678 |
| **N702AM** | **C560** | **0702** |
| N702BA | HS25 | 257059 |
| (N702BC) | C550 | 252 |
| N702CA | FA20 | 429 |
| N702CM | C650 | 7002 |
| N702D | HS25 | 25210 |
| N702DA | LJ25 | 302 |
| N702DD | FA20 | 74 |
| N702DM | FA20 | 74 |
| **N702DM** | **GLF3** | **428** |
| N702E | HS25 | 257198 |
| **N702FL** | **C750** | **0076** |
| N702GA | GALX | 102 |
| N702GA | GLF4 | 4102 |
| N702GA | GLF5 | 5002 |
| (N702GA) | HS25 | 25158 |
| **N702GH** | **GLF4** | **1497** |
| N702H | GLF2 | 229 |
| N702HC | HS25 | 256023 |
| N702JA | GLF2 | 180 |
| N702JH | MU30 | A035SA |
| N702JR | SBRL | 306-138 |
| N702KH | C550 | 290 |
| **N702LP** | **BE40** | **RK-444** |
| N702LP | BE40 | RK-87 |
| N702LX | C750 | 0076 |
| N702M | HS25 | 25241 |
| N702M | HS25 | 257195 |
| N702MA | HS25 | 25241 |
| N702NC | C500 | 579 |
| N702NC | FA10 | 220 |
| N702NC | FA10 | 55 |
| N702NG | FA10 | 55 |
| **N702NV** | **BE40** | **RK-120** |
| N702NW | HS25 | 257098 |
| N702NY | C500 | 579 |
| N702P | HS25 | 25212 |
| N702PC | CL61 | 5121 |
| N702PE | HS25 | 258155 |
| (N702QS) | GALX | 058 |
| **N702QS** | **GALX** | **070** |
| N702R | C550 | 015 |
| N702R | LJ60 | 113 |
| (N702RK) | LJ24 | 024 |
| **N702RT** | **C500** | **683** |
| **N702RV** | **CL61** | **5078** |
| N702S | HS25 | 25200 |
| N702SB | FA20 | 504 |
| N702SC | FA20 | 321 |
| N702SS | HS25 | 25200 |
| N702SW | C650 | 0096 |
| (N702TJ) | HS25 | 257144 |
| **N702TY** | **GLF5** | **621** |
| N702W | HS25 | 257199 |
| **N703A** | **HS25** | **HA-0147** |
| N703AJ | A700 | 0003 |
| N703AW | FA50 | 284 |
| N703DC | LJ24 | 067 |
| N703GA | GLF5 | 5003 |
| **N703HA** | **ASTR** | **202** |
| N703J | LJ24 | 256 |
| N703JA | GLF3 | 426 |
| N703JH | MU30 | A010SA |
| **N703JN** | **HS25** | **257031** |
| N703JP | HS25 | 257140 |
| N703JS | FA10 | 157 |
| **N703LH** | **GLF4** | **4112** |
| **N703LP** | **BE40** | **RK-20** |
| N703LX | C750 | 0074 |
| N703MA | LJ35 | 003 |
| (N703MJ) | HS25 | 257213 |
| **N703QS** | **GALX** | **060** |
| **N703RB** | **C650** | **7046** |
| (N703RE) | HS25 | 258587 |
| **N703RK** | **GLF5** | **671** |
| N703RK | HS25 | 258587 |
| N703SC | FA20 | 24 |
| **N703SM** | **HS25** | **258204** |
| **N703TM** | **FA50** | **218** |
| N703TS | HS25 | 257031 |
| (N703VP) | C650 | 7030 |
| **N703VZ** | **CL30** | **20199** |

| | | |
|---|---|---|
| N703VZ | HS25 | 258108 |
| N704CD | C550 | 704 |
| N704CW | HS25 | 257004 |
| **N704DA** | **C550** | **230** |
| N704GA | GLF4 | 4104 |
| N704J | LJ36 | 009 |
| N704JA | GLF3 | 432 |
| **N704JM** | **HS25** | **258367** |
| N704JW | C550 | 550-0863 |
| N704JW | C56X | 5138 |
| N704JW | GALX | 088 |
| N704JW | GLF4 | 4003 |
| **N704LX** | **C750** | **0091** |
| **N704MF** | **GLEX** | **9065** |
| N704R | F900 | 55 |
| N704SC | BE40 | RK-104 |
| N704T | PRM1 | RB-2 |
| **N705AC** | **WW24** | **209** |
| **N705BB** | **HS25** | **258015** |
| N705CC | HS25 | 257027 |
| N705EA | HS25 | 25142 |
| N705JA | GLF3 | 360 |
| N705JH | HS25 | 257029 |
| (N705JT) | C550 | 554 |
| N705LP | BE40 | RK-251 |
| **N705LX** | **C750** | **0082** |
| N705MA | ASTR | 011 |
| N705NA | LJ24 | 102 |
| **N705PC** | **GLF4** | **1240** |
| **N705PT** | **EA50** | **000014** |
| **N705QS** | **GALX** | **061** |
| **N705SG** | **C56X** | **5142** |
| **N705SP** | **CS55** | **0048** |
| N705US | LJ35 | 144 |
| N706A | SBRL | 282-7 |
| **N706AM** | **HS25** | **257009** |
| N706CJ | LJ60 | 168 |
| **N706CJ** | **LJ60** | **207** |
| N706CP | C550 | 550-0909 |
| N706CP | C550 | 550-0943 |
| **N706CR** | **LJ60** | **168** |
| (N706CW) | HS25 | 258782 |
| N706DC | C500 | 651 |
| **N706HB** | **C650** | **0047** |
| **N706JA** | **GLF3** | **322** |
| N706JH | MU30 | A016SA |
| N706L | LJ24 | 026 |
| **N706LP** | **BE40** | **RK-336** |
| **N706LX** | **C750** | **0073** |
| N706M | HS25 | 25123 |
| **N706NA** | **C550** | **706** |
| (N706PL) | BE40 | RK-336 |
| **N706PT** | **EA50** | **000107** |
| (N706QS) | GALX | 064 |
| (N706QS) | GALX | 071 |
| **N706QS** | **GALX** | **131** |
| **N706RM** | **BE40** | **RK-161** |
| **N706SA** | **LJ31** | **026** |
| N706SB | CS55 | 0139 |
| N706TF | C52A | 0172 |
| **N706TJ** | **GLF2** | **212** |
| N706TS | GLF2 | 254/41 |
| **N706VA** | **GLF4** | **1528** |
| (N706VP) | C650 | 7006 |
| **N706VP** | **C750** | **0006** |
| N706XP | HS25 | 258706 |
| **N707AM** | **FA10** | **159** |
| N707AM | FA10 | 26 |
| N707BC | ASTR | 093 |
| **N707BC** | **GALX** | **107** |
| N707BC | WW24 | 366 |
| (N707BJ) | LJ35 | 077 |
| N707CA | LJ25 | 342 |
| N707CG | FA10 | 165 |
| N707CS | LJ60 | 324 |
| N707CV | C560 | 0095 |
| N707CW | MU30 | A007SA |
| N707CX | FA10 | 135 |
| N707DB | SBRL | 306-97 |
| N707DC | FA10 | 159 |
| N707DS | HS25 | 257148 |
| N707EA | C550 | 707 |
| **N707EA** | **GLF4** | **1284** |
| **N707ES** | **EA50** | **000232** |
| N707EZ | HS25 | 25231 |
| N707EZ | JSTR | 5055/21 |
| N707FH | SBRL | 282-74 |
| **N707GG** | **C500** | **495** |
| N707GG | CL61 | 5037 |
| (N707GP) | SBRL | 306-141 |
| **N707GW** | **GLF5** | **629** |
| **N707HD** | **HS25** | **259016** |
| N707HJ | C650 | 0177 |
| N707HP | C550 | 550-1096 |
| N707JA | GLF3 | 447 |
| N707JC | FA20 | 335 |
| **N707JC** | **HS25** | **258703** |
| N707JM | SBRL | 282-41 |
| (N707JZ) | FA20 | 335 |
| **N707KD** | **GLF2** | **214** |
| **N707LM** | **C550** | **338** |
| **N707LX** | **C750** | **0078** |
| **N707MM** | **F2TH** | **131** |
| N707MS | C650 | 0019 |
| N707NV | LJ31 | 063 |
| N707PE | C550 | 452 |
| N707PE | HS25 | 258171 |
| **N707PF** | **C550** | **452** |
| **N707QS** | **GALX** | **066** |
| **N707RG** | **LJ35** | **169** |
| N707RX | GLF3 | 377 |
| N707SB | CS55 | 0141 |
| **N707SC** | **LJ24** | **065** |
| **N707SG** | **GALX** | **087** |
| N707SG | LJ60 | 062 |
| N707SG | LJ60 | 109 |
| N707SH | GLF2 | 77 |
| N707SH | HS25 | 25231 |
| N707SQ | LJ60 | 062 |
| N707TA | HS25 | 258296 |
| **N707TE** | **GLF4** | **1383** |
| N707TE | WW24 | 137 |
| N707TE | WW24 | 155 |
| **N707TF** | **WW24** | **155** |
| N707TG | SBRL | 282-74 |
| (N707TP) | LJ25 | 005 |
| N707TR | LJ25 | 005 |
| N707US | C500 | 339 |
| **N707W** | **C500** | **475** |
| N707WB | F900 | 132 |
| N707WB | HS25 | 256061 |
| N707WB | JSTR | 5210 |
| N707WF | C500 | 661 |
| N707WF | C550 | 452 |
| N707XP | HS25 | 258707 |
| N708BW | HS25 | 25263 |
| N708CF | C650 | 0185 |
| (N708CM) | C650 | 7008 |
| N708CT | C650 | 0185 |
| N708CT | C650 | 7004 |
| **N708GP** | **C52A** | **0154** |
| N708KS | GLEX | 9015 |
| **N708LX** | **C750** | **0109** |
| **N708QS** | **GALX** | **069** |
| N708SC | CL64 | 5391 |
| N708SC | GLEX | 9066 |
| **N708SP** | **LJ45** | **014** |
| N708TA | BE40 | RK-178 |
| N708TF | C525 | 0190 |
| N708TR | LJ25 | 015 |
| N708VP | C750 | 0008 |
| N709AB | SBRL | 306-75 |
| N709CC | C550 | 709 |
| (N709CM) | C650 | 7009 |
| **N709DS** | **GLEX** | **9278** |
| **N709DW** | **GLF5** | **5082** |
| N709EA | HS25 | 258226 |
| **N709EL** | **BE40** | **RK-52** |
| (N709EW) | BE40 | RK-52 |
| **N709FG** | **GLEX** | **9300** |
| N709JB | BE40 | RK-52 |
| N709JB | BE40 | RK-72 |
| N709JB | SJ30 | 004 |
| N709JM | CL61 | 5163 |
| N709JW | C550 | 550-0863 |
| N709LS | GLF4 | 1180 |
| N709LS | GLF4 | 1412 |
| **N709LX** | **C750** | **0145** |
| N709PG | C52B | 0107 |
| N709Q | SBRL | 282-30 |
| N709Q | WW24 | 95 |
| N709QS | C650 | 7109 |
| N709R | HS25 | 256001 |
| N709RS | C550 | 709 |
| **N709TA** | **BE40** | **RK-180** |
| N709TB | C500 | 214 |
| N709VP | C550 | 709 |
| N709VP | C650 | 7009 |
| "N709XP" | HS25 | 258709 |
| **N710A** | **HS25** | **258110** |
| **N710AF** | **HS25** | **257126** |
| N710AG | HS25 | 257193 |
| N710AN | CL61 | 5150 |
| N710AT | LJ35 | 337 |
| **N710AW** | **C750** | **0033** |
| N710BA | HS25 | 257191 |
| N710BC | HS25 | 257186 |
| N710BD | HS25 | 257183 |
| N710BF | HS25 | 257182 |
| **N710BG** | **FA50** | **305** |
| N710BG | HS25 | 257180 |
| N710BJ | HS25 | 257177 |
| N710BL | HS25 | 257174 |
| N710BN | HS25 | 257173 |
| N710BP | HS25 | 257171 |
| N710BQ | HS25 | 257210 |
| N710BR | HS25 | 257208 |
| N710BS | HS25 | 257207 |
| N710BT | HS25 | 257206 |
| N710BU | HS25 | 257202 |
| N710BV | HS25 | 257201 |
| N710BW | HS25 | 257199 |
| N710BX | HS25 | 257198 |
| N710BY | HS25 | 257195 |
| N710BZ | HS25 | 257193 |
| **N710CF** | **GLF3** | **448** |
| **N710DC** | **WW24** | **112** |
| **N710EB** | **C510** | **0107** |
| N710EC | FA20 | 102 |
| N710EC | GLF3 | 315 |
| **N710EC** | **GLF4** | **1502** |
| (N710EG) | FA20 | 102 |
| **N710ET** | **F2TH** | **38** |
| N710FL | C750 | 0038 |
| **N710GA** | **CL61** | **3008** |
| **N710GS** | **LJ35** | **032** |
| **N710HL** | **CL60** | **1050** |
| N710HM | CL61 | 5160 |
| **N710HM** | **HS25** | **HA-0077** |
| (N710JA) | JSTR | 5150/37 |
| **N710JC** | **FA10** | **120** |
| N710JL | GLF2 | 169 |
| N710JW | WW24 | 35 |
| N710K | MS76 | 112 |
| **N710LC** | **C560** | **0058** |
| **N710LM** | **CL61** | **5037** |
| **N710LX** | **GLF4** | **1297** |
| N710MB | MU30 | A078SA |
| **N710ML** | **C560** | **0254** |
| N710MP | GLF2 | 148/5 |
| N710MR | FA20 | 59 |
| N710MR | GLF2 | 148/5 |
| N710MR | SBRL | 306-123 |
| **N710MS** | **C680** | **0162** |
| N710MT | C550 | 057 |
| N710MT | C560 | 0254 |
| **N710MT** | **C56X** | **5332** |
| N710MT | FA20 | 59 |
| N710MW | FA20 | 59 |
| N710QS | C650 | 7100 |
| **N710R** | **LJ45** | **359** |
| **N710SA** | **WW24** | **296** |
| N710SG | LJ60 | 191 |
| N710SG | LJ60 | 311 |
| N710SG | LJ60 | 322 |
| N710TA | BE40 | RK-183 |
| (N710TF) | LJ60 | 046 |
| N710TJ | LJ24 | 197 |
| **N710TP** | **LJ60** | **046** |
| N710TS | CL65 | 5710 |
| **N710TV** | **LJ24** | **159** |
| **N710VF** | **CL61** | **5050** |
| **N710VL** | **C500** | **302** |
| **N710VP** | **C650** | **7100** |
| N710WB | FA20 | 102 |
| **N710WJ** | **GLF4** | **1007** |
| N710WL | LJ35 | 485 |
| N711 | LJ24 | 098 |
| N711 | LJ24 | 197 |
| N711 | LJ35 | 012 |
| N711 | LJ35 | 207 |
| N711A | SBRL | 380-21 |
| (N711AE) | C500 | 477 |
| N711AE | LJ24 | 098 |
| N711AF | LJ35 | 029 |
| N711AG | HS25 | 256001 |
| N711AG | JSTR | 5086/44 |
| (N711AJ) | CL60 | 1063 |
| N711AJ | PRM1 | RB-18 |
| N711AQ | HS25 | 25173 |
| N711BC | FA20 | 36 |
| N711BE | C525 | 0299 |
| N711BE | C52A | 0116 |
| **N711BE** | **C52B** | **0212** |
| N711BE | LJ35 | 274 |
| N711BF | LJ25 | 324 |
| N711BH | LJ35 | 041 |
| N711BP | C550 | 036 |
| N711BP | HS25 | 25218 |
| N711BT | C500 | 644 |
| **N711BX** | **C525** | **0299** |
| N711BY | SBRL | 380-51 |
| **N711C** | **C525** | **0630** |
| N711CA | LJ25 | 076 |
| **N711CC** | **C550** | **426** |
| N711CD | LJ35 | 456 |
| N711CE | LJ24 | 219 |
| N711CH | LJ35 | 032 |
| N711CJ | WW24 | 289 |
| N711CN | C550 | 711 |
| N711CN | LJ24 | 197 |
| N711CR | C500 | 016 |
| N711CU | HS25 | 257081 |
| **N711CW** | **LJ24** | **055** |
| N711DB | CL60 | 1071 |
| N711DB | LJ24 | 216 |
| N711DB | LJ24 | 253 |
| N711DB | LJ25 | 032 |
| N711DP | GLF2 | 82 |
| N711DS | GLF2 | 129 |
| N711DS | LJ24 | 189 |
| N711DS | LJ25 | 170 |
| N711DS | LJ35 | 209 |
| N711DX | LJ24 | 189 |
| N711DZ | JSTR | 5201 |
| N711EC | BE40 | RJ-53 |
| N711EC | BE40 | RK-167 |
| **N711EC** | **LJ35** | **311** |
| (N711EG) | C500 | 662 |
| **N711EG** | **GLF3** | **349** |
| **N711EJ** | **FA10** | **149** |
| N711EV | GLF2 | 129 |
| N711EV | LJ25 | 016 |
| (N711EV) | LJ35 | 377 |
| N711FC | BE40 | RJ-55 |
| N711FG | BE40 | RJ-55 |
| **N711FG** | **LJ31** | **092** |
| N711FJ | FA10 | 149 |
| **N711FJ** | **FA20** | **347** |
| (N711FW) | C500 | 196 |
| N711FW | GLF4 | 1033 |
| N711GA | CL60 | 1025 |
| **N711GA** | **GLF4** | **4211** |
| N711GA | GLF5 | 5211 |
| N711GD | BE40 | RK-311 |
| **N711GD** | **HA4T** | **RC-7** |
| N711GD | HS25 | 258612 |
| N711GD | SBRL | 380-6 |
| N711GF | C560 | 0068 |
| **N711GF** | **C650** | **7075** |
| N711GL | BE40 | RK-311 |
| N711GL | C500 | 519 |
| N711GL | FA20 | 396 |
| **N711GL** | **GLF4** | **1130** |
| N711GL | SBRL | 380-6 |
| N711GW | WW24 | 12 |
| N711HA | C550 | 550-1039 |
| N711HA | C56X | 5260 |
| **N711HA** | **C56X** | **5648** |
| N711HE | C750 | 0078 |
| N711HE | F2EX | 47 |
| N711HE | GLF4 | 1217 |
| **N711HF** | **FA10** | **213** |
| N711HH | LJ35 | 162 |
| N711HL | C500 | 503 |
| N711HL | HS25 | 25232 |
| N711HQ | C750 | 0078 |
| N711JC | FA10 | 69 |
| N711JG | ASTR | 017 |
| N711JG | CS55 | 0035 |
| N711JG | GALX | 004 |
| N711JN | CS55 | 0035 |

| | | |
|---|---|---|
| N711JQ | ASTR | 017 |
| (N711JQ) | GALX | 004 |
| N711JS | JSTR | 5153/61 |
| N711JT | LJ25 | 243 |
| N711JT | WW24 | 91 |
| (N711JU) | GALX | 004 |
| **N711KE** | **WW24** | **288** |
| N711KG | FA20 | 57 |
| N711KT | FA50 | 125 |
| N711L | LJ24 | 164 |
| N711L | LJ24 | 252 |
| N711L | LJ35 | 151 |
| N711LD | LJ24 | 252 |
| N711LS | GLEX | 9035 |
| **N711LS** | **GLEX** | **9155** |
| N711LS | GLF2 | 76 |
| N711LT | GLF3 | 327 |
| **N711LV** | **C650** | **0232** |
| N711MA | LJ35 | 032 |
| N711MB | WW24 | 282 |
| N711MC | GLEX | 9002 |
| **N711MC** | **GLEX** | **9121** |
| N711MC | GLF2 | 48/29 |
| N711MC | GLF4 | 1217 |
| **N711MD** | **CS55** | **0066** |
| N711MM | GLF2 | 61 |
| N711MN | GLEX | 9002 |
| **N711MQ** | **GLF2** | **189/42** |
| N711MR | LJ24 | 045 |
| N711MR | SBRL | 306-118 |
| N711MR | WW24 | 191 |
| **N711MT** | **C500** | **316** |
| N711MT | FA10 | 105 |
| N711MT | FA10 | 207 |
| N711MT | GLF2 | 16/13 |
| N711MT | GLF2 | 52 |
| **N711NB** | **C650** | **7009** |
| N711NF | LJ35 | 626 |
| N711NK | C56X | 5533 |
| **N711NK** | **C680** | **0095** |
| (N711NL) | C680 | 0095 |
| N711NM | LJ25 | 224 |
| N711NR | C500 | 387 |
| **N711NR** | **C56X** | **5533** |
| **N711NV** | **C550** | **557** |
| N711PC | LJ24 | 327 |
| N711PD | CL61 | 5013 |
| N711PD | LJ24 | 353 |
| N711PD | LJ25 | 138 |
| **N711PE** | **F2TH** | **105** |
| (N711PE) | GLF4 | 1217 |
| N711PE | HS25 | 258155 |
| N711PJ | LJ24 | 011 |
| N711PR | LJ35 | 501 |
| (N711QH) | LJ35 | 032 |
| **N711QS** | **GALX** | **129** |
| N711R | GLF2 | 45 |
| N711R | LJ35 | 035 |
| **N711R** | **LJ45** | **049** |
| N711RL | GLF2 | 25 |
| **N711RL** | **GLF5** | **5010** |
| N711RL | GLF5 | 629 |
| N711RL | HS25 | 257146 |
| N711RP | C500 | 639 |
| N711RQ | GLF5 | 629 |
| (N711RQ) | LJ35 | 035 |
| (N711RT) | FA20 | 242 |
| (N711RT) | GLF2 | 26 |
| N711RZ | GLF2 | 25 |
| N711S | GLF2 | 67 |
| N711S | SBRL | 306-92 |
| N711SB | GLF2 | 70/1 |
| N711SC | FA50 | 168 |
| N711SC | GLF2 | 70/1 |
| (N711SC) | HS25 | 25169 |
| (N711SC) | LJ24 | 283 |
| N711SC | LJ25 | 345 |
| N711SD | HS25 | 25233 |
| N711SD | LJ35 | 078 |
| N711SE | C500 | 261 |
| **N711SE** | **LJ60** | **015** |
| N711SE | WW24 | 329 |
| N711SF | C500 | 261 |
| N711SJ | CL61 | 3021 |
| (N711SP) | CL61 | 3021 |
| (N711SQ) | GLEX | 9065 |
| N711SQ | LJ25 | 005 |
| N711SR | CL61 | 3007 |
| N711ST | CL61 | 3024 |
| N711ST | SBRL | 306-129 |
| N711SW | GLEX | 9065 |
| N711SW | GLF2 | 71 |
| N711SW | GLF3 | 311 |
| N711SW | GLF4 | 1033 |
| N711SW | GLF4 | 1170 |
| **N711SW** | **GLF4** | **4085** |
| N711SW | GLF5 | 523 |
| N711SW | HS25 | 25146 |
| N711SW | LJ35 | 078 |
| N711SX | CL61 | 3007 |
| N711SX | CL64 | 5492 |
| **N711SX** | **GLEX** | **9125** |
| N711SZ | CL61 | 3007 |
| N711SZ | GLF4 | 4085 |
| (N711T) | F900 | 20 |
| **N711T** | **F9EX** | **6** |
| N711T | FA50 | 176 |
| N711T | SBRL | 282-67 |
| N711TE | C500 | 342 |
| N711TE | GLF2 | 105 |
| **N711TF** | **FA10** | **52** |
| N711TG | HS25 | 257177 |
| N711TG | LJ25 | 298 |
| N711TJ | LJ24 | 011 |
| N711TQ | LJ25 | 298 |
| N711TU | FA50 | 124 |
| N711TW | SBRL | 306-33 |
| N711UC | SBRL | 282-32 |
| **N711UF** | **GLF3** | **421** |
| N711UR | LJ24 | 197 |
| N711VF | C500 | 642 |
| (N711VF) | C500 | 650 |
| **N711VH** | **C56X** | **5260** |
| N711VH | C650 | 0047 |
| **N711VJ** | **C750** | **0101** |
| N711VJ | LJ60 | 045 |
| N711VK | LJ25 | 292 |
| (N711VK) | WW24 | 7 |
| **N711VL** | **GLF2** | **120** |
| N711VR | C550 | 260 |
| N711VT | C750 | 0101 |
| **N711VT** | **C750** | **0283** |
| N711VT | HS25 | 25249 |
| N711VT | LJ25 | 292 |
| N711VT | LJ60 | 045 |
| N711VZ | C650 | 0047 |
| N711WD | LJ25 | 196 |
| N711WD | LJ25 | 241 |
| N711WD | LJ25 | 282 |
| N711WE | LJ25 | 105 |
| **N711WG** | **C525** | **0424** |
| N711WJ | HS25 | 25021 |
| N711WK | ASTR | 101 |
| (N711WK) | F900 | 50 |
| N711WK | SBRL | 306-40 |
| N711WM | C550 | 387 |
| N711WM | HS25 | 25020 |
| N711WM | HS25 | 257087 |
| N711WU | WW24 | 313 |
| **N711WV** | **FA20** | **396** |
| N711WV | WW24 | 313 |
| **N711XR** | **CS55** | **0121** |
| N711YP | HS25 | 25265 |
| N711YP | HS25 | 257048 |
| N711YR | HS25 | 25265 |
| N711Z | C550 | 435 |
| (N711Z) | C560 | 0326 |
| N711Z | JSTR | 1002 |
| N711Z | JSTR | 5023 |
| N711Z | JSTR | 5067 |
| N711Z | JSTR | 5078/3 |
| N711Z | JSTR | 5093 |
| N711Z | JSTR | 5141 |
| N711Z | JSTR | 5149/11 |
| N711Z | JSTR | 5151 |
| N711Z | JSTR | 5155/32 |
| N711Z | JSTR | 5201 |
| **N712AS** | **GLF3** | **423** |
| N712BW | LJ25 | 241 |
| (N712CB) | LJ25 | 298 |
| **N712CC** | **GLF4** | **1028** |
| N712CM | C650 | 7012 |
| N712CW | GLF4 | 1028 |
| N712DC | LJ25 | 032 |
| N712DG | CL64 | 5328 |
| (N712DH) | C56X | 5527 |
| N712DH | C56X | 6028 |
| (N712DM) | LJ35 | 231 |
| N712DP | LJ25 | 319 |
| N712EJ | LJ31 | 231 |
| N712G | C500 | 060 |
| **N712GA** | **GLF4** | **4221** |
| N712GF | C560 | 0068 |
| **N712GK** | **BE40** | **RK-44** |
| (N712GM) | WW24 | 118 |
| N712GW | JSTR | 5016 |
| N712HL | CL60 | 1056 |
| N712J | C500 | 060 |
| N712J | C500 | 270 |
| N712J | C550 | 404 |
| N712JA | LJ25 | 134 |
| N712JB | LJ35 | 646 |
| N712JC | C750 | 0052 |
| N712JE | LJ36 | 012 |
| N712KC | C56X | 5311 |
| **N712KC** | **C750** | **0255** |
| **N712KM** | **C500** | **348** |
| **N712KT** | **GLF5** | **5134** |
| N712L | C560 | 0365 |
| N712L | LJ35 | 256 |
| **N712MB** | **C500** | **120** |
| N712ME | FA20 | 355 |
| **N712MQ** | **GLF2** | **104/10** |
| N712MR | SBRL | 306-113 |
| N712N | C500 | 270 |
| **N712PD** | **C550** | **063** |
| **N712PR** | **CL64** | **5313** |
| **N712QS** | **GALX** | **073** |
| N712R | LJ24 | 156 |
| N712RD | JSTR | 5005 |
| N712RW | LJ25 | 296 |
| N712S | CS55 | 0035 |
| N712SJ | LJ25 | 296 |
| N712TA | BE40 | RK-186 |
| N712TE | JSTR | 5070/52 |
| N712US | C500 | 044 |
| N712US | FA10 | 110 |
| (N712VE) | C500 | 640 |
| N712VF | C500 | 640 |
| N712VP | C750 | 0012 |
| N712VS | HS25 | 25174 |
| **N712WG** | **EA50** | **000180** |
| N713AL | C500 | 576 |
| **N713AZ** | **PRM1** | **RB-111** |
| N713B | LJ25 | 201 |
| N713DA | C560 | 0416 |
| N713DF | C56X | 5144 |
| N713DH | C560 | 0376 |
| N713DH | C560 | 0416 |
| N713DH | C560 | 0549 |
| N713DH | C56X | 5144 |
| N713DH | C56X | 5527 |
| **N713DH** | **C56X** | **5700** |
| N713DH | CS55 | 0107 |
| N713DJ | LJ25 | 355 |
| **N713FL** | **C750** | **0074** |
| (N713G) | FA10 | 162 |
| **N713HC** | **CL64** | **5308** |
| N713HC | HS25 | 258040 |
| (N713HG) | CL64 | 5308 |
| (N713HH) | C560 | 0092A |
| N713HH | C560 | 0192 |
| N713HH | CS55 | 0138 |
| **N713JD** | **C500** | **450** |
| N713K | HS25 | 257094 |
| N713KM | GLF3 | 432 |
| N713KM | HS25 | 257094 |
| (N713L) | PRM1 | RB-25 |
| N713LJ | LJ25 | 241 |
| N713M | LJ55 | 113 |
| **N713MC** | **FA20** | **392/553** |
| N713MD | C510 | 0274 |
| N713MR | SBRL | 282-82 |
| (N713PE) | FA20 | 113 |
| N713Q | LJ25 | 105 |
| N713QS | C650 | 7103 |
| N713R | JSTR | 5205 |
| N713RL | HS25 | 257146 |
| N713RR | LJ25 | 241 |
| **N713SA** | **C500** | **132** |
| N713SC | ASTR | 013 |
| **N713SD** | **C525** | **0218** |
| **N713SN** | **FA50** | **182** |
| N713SS | HS25 | 25174 |
| N713US | LJ25 | 015 |
| (N713VL) | GLF4 | 1012 |
| (N713VP) | C650 | 7013 |
| **N713VP** | **C650** | **7103** |
| N713VT | GLF4 | 1012 |
| **N713WD** | **C560** | **0765** |
| **N713WH** | **C525** | **0606** |
| N713XP | HS25 | 258713 |
| N714K | LJ25 | 150 |
| N714K | LJ35 | 230 |
| N714KP | LJ25 | 150 |
| **N714RM** | **C550** | **550-1057** |
| N714S | LJ35 | 367 |
| (N714TS) | CL61 | 5014 |
| N714US | C500 | 040 |
| (N714VP) | C650 | 7014 |
| N714X | LJ24 | 103 |
| N715AB | C550 | 715 |
| N715BC | C650 | 0018 |
| N715BC | LJ24 | 029 |
| (N715BD) | CL61 | 5091 |
| N715BG | CL61 | 5164 |
| **N715CG** | **LJ45** | **208** |
| N715CX | C750 | 0015 |
| (N715DG) | C500 | 400 |
| N715EK | C500 | 367 |
| N715GA | GALX | 215 |
| (N715GW) | WW24 | 187 |
| **N715JC** | **FA10** | **99** |
| N715JF | LJ25 | 132 |
| (N715JM) | C500 | 367 |
| **N715JS** | **C500** | **001** |
| N715MH | LJ25 | 132 |
| N715MR | SBRL | 282-40 |
| N715PH | HS25 | 258715 |
| (N715PS) | C550 | 118 |
| N715PS | C560 | 0055 |
| N715QS | C650 | 7105 |
| **N715TA** | **BE40** | **RK-189** |
| (N715VP) | C650 | 7015 |
| N715VP | C750 | 0015 |
| **N715WE** | **C680** | **0286** |
| N715WG | ASTR | 205 |
| **N715WG** | **GALX** | **186** |
| N715WG | HS25 | 258386 |
| **N715WS** | **FA20** | **305** |
| N715WT | HS25 | 258386 |
| N715XP | HS25 | 258715 |
| N716BB | WW24 | 118 |
| **N716BD** | **LJ31** | **093** |
| N716BG | LJ60 | 236 |
| N716CB | C500 | 055 |
| N716DB | CS55 | 0120 |
| **N716DB** | **HS25** | **258048** |
| **N716DD** | **CS55** | **0120** |
| N716GA | C500 | 210 |
| **N716GS** | **PRM1** | **RB-199** |
| N716HP | CL61 | 3026 |
| (N716JC) | FA10 | 113 |
| **N716LT** | **C500** | **034** |
| **N716MB** | **C52B** | **0251** |
| N716NC | LJ25 | 264 |
| N716QS | C650 | 7106 |
| **N716QS** | **GALX** | **148** |
| N716RD | CL61 | 5048 |
| N716RD | JSTR | 5005 |
| N716RD | JSTR | 5218 |
| N716SX | C560 | 0281 |
| N716TE | GLF2 | 116 |
| N716US | LJ24 | 297 |
| N716W | ASTR | 016 |
| N716XP | HS25 | 258716 |
| N717 | GLF3 | 401 |
| N717 | JSTR | 5009 |
| N717 | JSTR | 5202 |
| N717A | GLF3 | 308 |
| **N717AF** | **HS25** | **257059** |
| **N717AJ** | **LJ35** | **183** |
| **N717AM** | **LJ55** | **100** |
| N717AN | LJ25 | 272 |
| **N717CB** | **C550** | **550-0830** |
| N717CB | C550 | 550-1007 |
| **N717CF** | **BE40** | **RK-177** |
| N717CF | MU30 | A033SA |
| N717CH | BE40 | RK-164 |
| N717CP | ASTR | 053 |
| N717CW | LJ25 | 362 |
| **N717D** | **C560** | **0275** |

(N717DA) C525 0087
N717DB LJ24 179
N717DD BE40 RK-18
N717DD BE40 RK-207
**N717DD BE40 RK-389**
N717DF MU30 A033SA
**N717DM C550 435**
N717DS LJ35 302
**N717DT C550 182**
N717DW BE40 RK-18
N717DX GLF4 1493
**N717DX GLF4 4107**
N717EA BE40 RK-354
N717EA WW24 305
**N717EB LJ55 016**
**N717EP ASTR 222**
N717EP LJ25 255
N717EP LJ55 016
**N717FF LJ60 213**
(N717GF) HS25 25047
**N717GK C550 550-0971**
**N717HA C52A 0079**
N717HB LJ24 295
**N717HB LJ55 066**
**N717HD EA50 000113**
N717HE LJ24 295
N717JB LJ35 229
N717JB LJ35 646
N717JB LJ55 128
N717JB LJ60 093
N717JL C500 527
**N717JM C650 0138**
N717JM JSTR 5009
N717KQ C550 550-0971
**N717LA FA50 32**
N717LA WW24 305
**N717LC C550 269**
**N717LK EA50 000064**
N717LS CS55 0054
N717MB C560 0007
**N717MB C56X 5114**
N717MS GLF3 335
**N717MT HS25 258163**
N717NA C525 0437
**N717NB C56X 5694**
N717PC C550 366
N717RB C500 449
N717TF GLEX 9028
**N717TG BE40 RK-320**
N717TR GLF3 418
N717VA BE40 RK-21
**N717VB C52A 0137**
N717VL BE40 RK-21
**N717VL C550 550-1108**
N717VL MU30 A073SA
N717W LJ35 147
N717WW ASTR 017
N717X JSTR 5009
N717X JSTR 5202
N717XP HS25 258717
N718AN LJ60 065
N718CA FA10 64
**N718CK C550 402**
N718DW FA50 81
**N718DW GLF4 1442**
N718EA LJ35 229
N718EC GLF3 315
N718EJ LJ40 45-2108
N718GM GLF4 1294
**N718HC HS25 258040**
**N718JA GLF2 66**
N718JS GLF2 66
**N718JS GLF4 4164**
N718KS F2TH 216
**N718MC GLF5 5061**
N718MC GLF5 549
N718MD GLF5 549
N718MN C680 0043
N718P CL61 5127
**N718QS GALX 136**
N718R CL61 5127
N718R JSTR 5147
N718R JSTR 5205
**N718SA C500 589**
**N718SJ HS25 258718**
N718SW LJ35 179
**N718TA BE40 RK-195**
N718US LJ36 019
N718VA C500 148
N718VA C550 029
N718VP C650 7018
N718XP HS25 258718
N719A GLF3 310
N719AL FA10 25
**N719CC WW24 290**
N719D C525 0075
**N719DW FA50 308**
N719EH C550 572
**N719EL BE40 RK-488**
N719GA GLF2 79
N719HG C650 0007
**N719HG HS25 258488**
N719JB LJ35 166
N719JE LJ36 019
N719L C525 0075
**N719L PRM1 RB-25**
**N719QS GALX 162**
**N719RM C560 0092**
N719SA GLF2 154/28
**N719SA GLF4 1155**
N719SQ GLF2 154/28
N719US LJ35 135
N719WP C52A 0202
**N720AS CL64 5653**
N720AS LJ25 017
N720BA GLF4 1335
N720C C500 073
N720CC C550 720
**N720CC LJ45 072**
N720CH GLF4 1118
**N720DF FA10 26**
**N720DR GLF2 209**
N720E GLF2 65
N720F GLF2 66
N720G GLF2 119/22
(N720GH) LJ35 105
N720GL LJ35 087
**N720GM C525 0350**
N720HC FA20 497
N720HG CL65 5720
N720J SBRL 282-24
**N720JC FA20 273**
N720JW GLF2 178
**N720LH GLF2 233**
N720LH GLF4 1063
N720LM CL61 5104
N720M FA50 18
N720M LJ35 183
N720M LJ55 020
**N720MC LJ45 103**
N720MC WW24 358
N720ME C650 0016
**N720ME F9EX 115**
N720ME FA10 48
N720ME FA50 245
N720ML C650 0016
N720ML F9EX 115
**N720ML F9EX 231**
N720ML FA10 48
N720ML FA20 262
N720ML FA50 245
N720ML WW24 147
**N720PT HS25 257032**
N720Q GLF2 58
**N720QS GALX 085**
N720R SBRL 282-27
N720RA LJ35 156
N720SJ C560 0386
N720TA HS25 258320
N720UA LJ24 067
N720WC C550 708
**N720WS GLEX 9176**
**N720WW LJ35 254**
**N720WY F2EX 189**
N721AS LJ35 101
N721AS WW24 58
N721BS F2TH 11
N721BS GALX 110
**N721BS GLF4 1516**
N721BS LJ45 227
N721BW CL61 5049
(N721CC) C500 183
**N721CC C550 721**
(N721CG) C500 543
**N721CJ GALX 047**
N721CM LJ35 210
**N721CN GLF2 206**
N721CP GLF2 46
N721CP LJ45 006
N721CR JSTR 5150/37
N721CW GLF3 485
(N721DG) C56X 5297
N721DP FA10 64
**N721DR C550 211**
**N721EC LJ35 355**
**N721ES C52A 0452**
N721EW CL61 5049
**N721FA BE40 RJ-21**
N721FF GLF3 421
**N721FF GLF4 1484**
**N721G CL61 5109**
N721GB LJ24 005
N721GB WW24 135
N721GB WW24 71
N721GL LJ24 335
(N721GS) LJ55 021
**N721HM F900 158**
(N721HW) C500 324
N721HW LJ24 005
**N721J CL64 5590**
N721J FA20 255/487
N721J LJ24 200
(N721J) LJ24 205
N721JA LJ24 200
**N721LH HS25 256025**
N721LR CS55 0118
N721MA EA50 000178
N721MC CL61 5031
**N721MC GLF4 1110**
N721MD CL61 5031
(N721MD) LJ24 195
N721MJ LJ31 098
N721MJ LJ60 159
N721MM GLF5 613
**N721NA EA50 000178**
**N721NB C560 0659**
N721PA JSTR 5054/59
N721PL GLF2 121
(N721QS) GALX 088
**N721QS GALX 092**
N721RB GLF3 311
N721RL GLF2 121
**N721RL GLF4 1394**
**N721RM HS25 256053**
N721S CL61 5109
**N721S GLF5 668**
**N721SF LJ24 325**
N721SS BE40 RK-34
N721ST C650 0158
**N721ST CL60 1030**
N721SW CL60 1066
N721SW CL61 5049
N721SW GLF2 2
**N721T C550 550-0993**
(N721TB) C500 281
N721US C500 579
N721US C550 391
(N721V) GLF5 5206
**N721VT C750 0167**
**N722A HS25 258200**
N722AW WW24 154
**N722AZ ASTR 132**
N722AZ WW24 351
N722CC HS25 258008
N722CM C650 7022
(N722CX) C750 0022
**N722DJ CL60 1029**
(N722DM) LJ24 224
(N722ED) SBRL 282-56
**N722EM LJ25 372**
N722FD SBRL 282-56
**N722FS FA50 216**
N722GA GALX 222
N722GL LJ35 092
N722HP CL60 1039
N722HP CL61 3054
**N722JB F2TH 13**
N722JS LJ31 109
N722KS FA20 130
N722MM GLF4 1052
**N722MM GLF4 4086**
**N722Q MS76 009**
**N722QS GALX 093**
**N722SG C525 0088**
**N722SM C52A 0338**
N722ST SBRL 282-56
**N722SW ASTR 230**
N722TA HS25 258322
**N722TD EA50 000224**
N722TP GLF2 92
**N722TS C52A 0138**
N722US C500 253
N722W WW24 159
(N722W) WW24 306
**N722XJ C750 0222**
**N723AB GLEX 9207**
N723BH C650 0127
**N723CC LJ55 036**
**N723GB E50P 50000111**
N723GL LJ35 107
N723H LJ55 090
N723HA CL61 5165
N723HA CL65 5718
N723HH CL61 5165
**N723HH GLEX 9325**
N723HH HS25 258232
N723J GLF2 87/775/6
N723JB WW24 37
N723JM C500 563
(N723JM) WW24 363
**N723JR C500 584**
**N723JW LJ24 142**
N723JW LJ24 178
N723K WW24 330
N723L WW24 349
N723LF LJ25 087
**N723LK HS25 258155**
N723LL LJ24 216
N723LL LJ28 29-002
N723LL LJ35 277
N723M WW24 237
N723MM GLF3 357
**N723MM GLF4 4077**
**N723QS GALX 099**
N723R SBRL 306-11
N723R WW24 272
**N723RE C550 550-0944**
N723ST JSTR 5023
N723TA HS25 258349
N723TS HS25 25191
N723US LJ35 311
N723XP HS25 258723
N724AA BE40 RJ-22
**N724AF GLEX 9031**
**N724AS FA10 83**
**N724B HS25 257006**
N724BP C52B 0303
(N724CC) C500 203
**N724CC C750 0062**
N724CJ LJ60 322
**N724CP FA20 319**
N724CV C52B 0259
N724DB GLF3 372
**N724DB GLF4 1209**
N724DD GLF3 372
**N724DL C510 0078**
N724DS FA10 92
**N724DS FA20 198/466**
N724EA C500 387
**N724EA HS25 257090**
**N724EB C550 550-1113**
N724EH C550 550-1113
**N724EH LJ60 346**
N724FS C525 0387
**N724FS LJ31 231**
N724GL LJ24 347
**N724HB BE40 RJ-55**
N724J LJ55 092
**N724JC FA20 310**
(N724JS) FA20 379
**N724KW BE40 RK-263**
N724LG LJ24 143
**N724MF CL64 5631**
N724MH BE40 RK-263
N724ML EA50 000220
**N724PB C52B 0303**
**N724QS GALX 100**
**N724SC CL30 20072**
N724TN LJ25 216
**N724TS HS25 25192**
N724XP HS25 258724
N725BA C550 431

N725BF C550 431
**N725CC C550 725**
N725CC HS25 257027
N725CF C525 0141
N725CF CL30 20186
**N725CS HS25 258758**
(N725DM) C500 131
**N725DM FA10 184**
(N725DM) LJ24 305
N725DM LJ25 328
**N725DS C550 550-0822**
N725DW HS25 25134
**N725FL C550 431**
N725GL LJ24 348
N725JA HS25 258297
**N725JB C510 0030**
**N725JG FA20 416**
**N725JS LJ25 156**
N725K LJ55 093
N725L C525 0140
N725LB FA50 46
**N725LB GLEX 9129**
N725LB GLF4 1296
**N725MK JSTR 5123/14**
**N725MM GLF5 5161**
N725MW E50P 50000084
N725P FA10 169
(N725P) FA20 306/512
N725P FA20 72/413
N725P LJ35 167
N725PA FA10 155
N725PA FA50 104
N725PA FA50 204
N725PA FA50 23
N725PA FA50 236
**N725QS GALX 105**
(N725RH) C500 503
N725RH C550 006
**N725RH C650 0106**
N725SC LJ60 083
**N725ST LJ35 285**
**N725T BE40 RK-273**
N725TA HS25 258297
N725WH C650 0097
N725WH HS25 25042
(N725WH) HS25 257015
**N725XL C56X 5725**
**N726AG C52B 0029**
**N726AM C550 726**
(N726BB) C500 517
N726BM C550 726
N726CC HS25 25116
**N726CL C525 0420**
**N726DC GALX 058**
N726EL LJ45 327
N726EP HS25 258139
N726GL LJ25 222
**N726JG FA50 258**
**N726JR SBRL 370-4**
N726L LJ55 098
N726MR FA10 35
**N726PG BE40 RK-337**
**N726QS GALX 108**
N726R SBRL 282-83
**N726RP C52A 0114**
**N726RW GLF4 1039**
**N726SC C525 0051**
N726TA HS25 258363
**N726TM C525 0414**
**N726WR LJ25 007**
N726XP HS25 258726
(N727AL) CS55 0043
**N727AT WW24 284**
**N727AW C650 0132**
N727AW LJ25 313
**N727BT LJ31 082**
N727C C550 368
**N727C C550 485**
N727CM C550 727
N727CP LJ31 009
N727CS LJ25 313
**N727CW EA50 000159**
N727EE C500 048
**N727EF CS55 0043**
N727GL LJ35 127
**N727HD EA50 000115**
N727JP LJ35 189
N727KG PRM1 RB-113
**N727KG PRM1 RB-143**
N727LE C500 048
(N727LG) LJ24 143
**N727LJ LJ25 028**
**N727LM LJ25 308**
N727MC C500 677
N727MG LJ35 320
**N727MH C56X 5549**
N727MH PRM1 RB-158
**N727ML PRM1 RB-158**
N727NA CS55 0043
**N727QS GALX 113**
N727R SBRL 282-42
N727S CL61 5062
N727S FA50 17
**N727SJ LJ60 147**
N727TA HS25 257003
**N727TK C500 141**
N727TS FA10 76
N727US SBRL 380-61
**N727YB C52B 0171**
N727YB C56X 5332
N728AZ WW24 351
N728C SBRL 465-71
N728CC C550 728
**N728CL LJ31 109**
N728CM C650 7028
N728CP GLF3 875
N728CX C750 0028
**N728EC C56X 5815**
**N728GH F900 3**
N728GL LJ35 133
**N728JC FA20 399**
N728JP GLF4 1297
N728JW HS25 257129
N728KA HS25 25224
N728L WW24 349
N728LB FA50 46
**N728LB GLF4 1296**
N728LM WW24 341
**N728LW FA50 3**
N728LW WW24 341
**N728MB WW24 419**
N728MC C500 507
N728MC WW24 147
**N728MG LJ55 004**
N728MP LJ35 481
N728PX JSTR 5112/7
**N728QS GALX 116**
(N728RX) C500 194
(N728SA) FA10 71
N728SB LJ45 254
N728T GLF2 82
**N728TA HS25 258364**
**N728TG WW24 420**
N728US C500 171
N728XP HS25 258728
**N729AG HS25 258729**
**N729AT HS25 258402**
**N729EZ HS25 258171**
N729GL LJ24 338
N729HS LJ35 481
**N729HZ CL61 5107**
N729HZ HS25 258171
**N729JM LJ45 380**
N729KF CL64 5513
**N729KF GLEX 9172**
**N729KP CL64 5513**
**N729LJ LJ60 298**
(N729MJ) C550 151
N729MJ C550 303
N729PX C500 433
**N729QS GALX 118**
N729S FA20 173
**N729SB CL30 20208**
N729SB LJ45 254
**N729TA C550 483**
N729TA HS25 258374
**N729TY GLF4 1141**
N729XP HS25 258729
N730BA GLF4 1290
(N730BG) HS25 258191
N730BR C550 730
N730CA SBRL 282-103
N730CA SBRL 306-145
**N730CA WW24 295**
**N730CP SBRL 282-103**
**N730DF ASTR 067**
N730GL LJ36 025
N730H HS25 257150
N730HB HS25 HB-30
**N730LM F9EX 101**
N730M LJ60 048
N730PV FA10 106
N730PV WW24 36
**N730QS GALX 120**
N730R SBRL 282-43
N730S FA20 247
N730SA F900 155
N730TA HS25 258383
(N730TC) C550 333
N730TK GLF2 140/40
N730TL CL60 1084
N730TS HS25 25201
N730V FA20 319
(N730VP) C550 730
N731A JSTR 5011/1
(N731AE) FA20 344/534
N731AG JSTR 5070/52
N731AS FA20 344/534
(N731BF) CL30 20073
**N731BP C56X 5802**
N731BW HS25 25075
N731CW LJ25 117
**N731DC CL30 20073**
**N731DD FA50 64**
N731DL HS25 257048
N731F FA20 113
(N731F) FA20 344/534
N731F FA50 45
N731FJ FA10 3
N731G FA20 267/491
N731G HS25 25153
N731G HS25 25195
N731GA C650 0076
(N731GA) HS25 257122
**N731GA LJ31 024**
N731GA LJ35 001
N731GA LJ35 003
N731GA LJ36 028
N731H HS25 25278
N731HS HS25 25214
N731HS HS25 25229
N731HS HS25 25253
N731JR HS25 25286
N731JR HS25 258183
N731JS JSTR 5006/40
N731KC HS25 25118
N731L JSTR 5095/30
N731MS HS25 25239
**N731PS BE40 RK-543**
**N731QS GALX 123**
N731RA LJ31 102
(N731RG) FA20 113
N731RG FA20 168
N731RG FA20 388
N731TA BE40 RK-273
(N731TC) HS25 256024
N731TH HS25 HB-31
N731UG PRM1 RB-70
(N731WB) HS25 25264
**N731WH C52B 0112**
N731WL JSTR 5070/52
N731X HS25 25244
N732GA GALX 132
N732HB HS25 HB-32
**N732JR C56X 5503**
**N732LH LJ60 021**
N732M JSTR 5084/8
N732S FA20 272
N732TS HS25 25203
N733A C650 0234
N733A CL61 3008
N733A F900 126
**N733A HS25 258687**
N733AU C650 0234
N733CF CL60 1041
**N733CF CL61 5057**
N733E FA50 128
**N733E LJ55 057**
N733EX CL61 5113
N733EY CL61 5113
(N733EY) GLEX 9063
N733EY LJ55 057
N733GA GLF5 5233
N733H C550 081
N733H C560 0137
N733H C650 0210
N733H HS25 257018
**N733H HS25 258590**
N733HL F900 126
N733K C650 0222
N733K CL60 1041
**N733K FA50 242**
N733K HS25 25285
N733K HS25 258137
N733K HS25 258645
N733L HS25 258645
N733M C560 0249
N733M FA50 242
**N733M FA50 343**
N733M HS25 257092
N733MK BE40 RK-107
N733N FA50 242
N733R SBRL 282-51
N733S FA20 292
**N733SW LJ60 007**
**N733TA HS25 258337**
(N734) LJ55 048
N734 LJ55 051
N734AK HS25 25014
**N734DB C560 0143**
N734DB FA20 500
N734S FA10 13
(N734S) FA20 299
N734S FA20 316
**N734TJ GLF3 392**
(N735A) C650 0234
N735A LJ35 323
N735GA BE40 RJ-42
N735HC C650 0158
N735TA BE40 RK-274
**N735XP HS25 HB-35**
N736LB C52A 0203
**N736LE HS25 25207**
N736R SBRL 282-82
(N736US) WW24 192
N737CC C650 7037
N737E SBRL 282-26
N737EF LJ25 037
N737FN LJ24 171
N737KB C680 0047
N737MM BE40 RJ-35
**N737MM C650 7113**
**N737QS GALX 127**
N737R SBRL 282-33
N737R SBRL 282-66
**N737RJ C500 649**
N737X HS25 257052
**N738DC C510 0151**
N738GL LJ25 038
N738K C650 0222
**N738QS GALX 204**
N738R SBRL 282-40
N738RH FA20 24
N738TS GLEX 9038
N739CX C750 0038
**N739LN C525 0541**
**N739QS GALX 198**
N739R SBRL 282-78
N739TA BE40 RK-199
N739TA BE40 RK-257
N739XP HS25 258739
N740AC LJ55 084
**N740BA GLF5 516**
N740E LJ24 222
N740E LJ31 061
**N740E LJ45 023**
N740EJ LJ24 222
N740F LJ24 222
N740F LJ31 061
N740GA GLF4 4140
N740GA GLF5 5140
N740GL LJ24 353
N740J LJ24 077
N740JA GLF4 1074
(N740JB) C525 0182
**N740JB C550 353**
N740JV C525 0252
**N740K GLF4 1094**
N740K LJ25 302
**N740KG LJ40 45-2063**
N740L FA20 7
**N740LM F9EX 74**

| | | |
|---|---|---|
| **N740QS** | **GALX** | **194** |
| N740R | FA50 | 247 |
| N740R | SBRL | 282-47 |
| N740R | SBRL | 306-112 |
| N740R | SBRL | 465-14 |
| N740RC | SBRL | 306-112 |
| (N740SG) | LJ45 | 023 |
| N740SS | GLF3 | 369 |
| **N740SS** | **GLF5** | **532** |
| N740TA | BE40 | RK-123 |
| **N740TF** | **LJ45** | **074** |
| **N740VC** | **GLF3** | **454** |
| N740VP | C750 | 0040 |
| N740XP | HS25 | 258740 |
| N741AM | JSTR | 5236 |
| **N741C** | **WW24** | **292** |
| **N741CC** | **C525** | **0227** |
| N741E | LJ25 | 036 |
| N741E | LJ25 | 100 |
| N741E | LJ31 | 070 |
| N741E | LJ35 | 508 |
| N741E | LJ45 | 011 |
| **N741E** | **LJ45** | **367** |
| N741ED | LJ25 | 036 |
| N741F | LJ25 | 100 |
| N741F | LJ31 | 070 |
| N741F | LJ35 | 508 |
| N741F | LJ45 | 011 |
| N741FJ | FA7X | 41 |
| N741GL | LJ24 | 350 |
| N741JB | C500 | 213 |
| N741JC | C550 | 346 |
| **N741MR** | **FA20** | **312** |
| N741MT | SBRL | 276-34 |
| **N741PC** | **C52A** | **0066** |
| N741PP | C550 | 550-0965 |
| N741QS | GALX | 212 |
| N741R | SBRL | 306-143 |
| N741R | SBRL | 306-28 |
| N741R | SBRL | 465-24 |
| N741RC | SBRL | 306-143 |
| N741RL | SBRL | 306-28 |
| **N741T** | **C550** | **394** |
| N741TA | BE40 | RK-201 |
| **N741TS** | **CL65** | **5741** |
| **N742AR** | **C52B** | **0074** |
| **N742E** | **CL30** | **20231** |
| N742E | LJ25 | 096 |
| N742E | LJ31 | 071 |
| N742E | LJ35 | 630 |
| N742E | LJ45 | 025 |
| N742F | LJ31 | 071 |
| **N742F** | **LJ45** | **025** |
| N742GA | GLF4 | 4142 |
| N742GL | LJ35 | 140 |
| N742K | C500 | 236 |
| N742K | SBRL | 306-45 |
| N742P | LJ35 | 630 |
| N742QS | GALX | 227 |
| N742R | FA50 | 243 |
| N742R | SBRL | 306-142 |
| N742R | SBRL | 306-45 |
| N742R | SBRL | 465-28 |
| N742RC | SBRL | 306-142 |
| N742TA | BE40 | RK-202 |
| N742TS | GLF2 | 142 |
| N742XP | HS25 | 258742 |
| N742Z | LJ25 | 096 |
| N743CC | C650 | 0181 |
| **N743DB** | **C560** | **0479** |
| N743E | LJ25 | 169 |
| N743E | LJ31 | 068 |
| N743E | LJ45 | 016 |
| **N743E** | **LJ45** | **370** |
| N743F | LJ25 | 169 |
| N743F | LJ31 | 068 |
| N743F | LJ45 | 016 |
| N743GL | LJ35 | 141 |
| **N743HB** | **HS25** | **HB-43** |
| **N743JA** | **C56X** | **6032** |
| **N743JG** | **C52A** | **0056** |
| **N743QS** | **GALX** | **216** |
| N743R | SBRL | 306-11 |
| N743TA | BE40 | RK-271 |
| (N743UP) | HS25 | 258069 |
| N743UP | SBRL | 306-22 |
| N743UT | HS25 | 25118 |
| **N744AT** | **C550** | **021** |

| | | |
|---|---|---|
| N744CC | FA20 | 313 |
| N744CC | FA20 | 347 |
| N744CC | HS25 | 25142 |
| N744CF | LJ24 | 082A |
| **N744DB** | **LJ60** | **053** |
| N744DC | C550 | 009 |
| N744DC | HS25 | 257146 |
| N744E | LJ31 | 069 |
| N744E | LJ35 | 203 |
| **N744E** | **LJ45** | **348** |
| N744GA | ASTR | 244 |
| N744GA | GLF5 | 5244 |
| N744GL | LJ35 | 126 |
| N744JC | CL65 | 5744 |
| N744JC | LJ24 | 323 |
| N744JR | WW24 | 198 |
| N744LC | LJ25 | 232 |
| N744MC | LJ25 | 120 |
| **N744N** | **LJ31** | **069** |
| N744P | LJ35 | 203 |
| N744R | C560 | 0291 |
| N744R | SBRL | 282-72 |
| N744SW | C550 | 009 |
| N744TA | BE40 | RK-245 |
| N744UT | JSTR | 5147 |
| N744W | LJ25 | 008 |
| N744WW | C560 | 0143 |
| N744X | FA50 | 58 |
| **N744XP** | **HS25** | **258744** |
| **N745CC** | **C550** | **550-1051** |
| (N745CW) | C750 | 0145 |
| N745DM | C500 | 131 |
| N745DM | JSTR | 5201 |
| N745E | LJ35 | 294 |
| N745E | LJ45 | 008 |
| **N745E** | **LJ45** | **356** |
| (N745EA) | C650 | 0158 |
| N745F | LJ24 | 077 |
| N745F | LJ35 | 294 |
| N745GA | ASTR | 245 |
| N745GL | LJ36 | 032 |
| (N745HG) | HS25 | 25084 |
| **N745K** | **LJ45** | **245** |
| (N745K) | LJ45 | 402 |
| **N745KD** | **LJ45** | **384** |
| **N745QS** | **GALX** | **170** |
| **N745RS** | **GLF4** | **1063** |
| **N745SA** | **LJ45** | **052** |
| N745TA | BE40 | RK-145 |
| **N745TC** | **LJ45** | **260** |
| N745TH | HS25 | 257095 |
| N745TS | HS25 | 25220 |
| N745UP | GLF4 | 1054 |
| (N745UP) | HS25 | 258072 |
| **N745UP** | **HS25** | **258336** |
| N745UP | SBRL | 306-39 |
| N745UR | GLF4 | 1054 |
| N745US | C500 | 025 |
| N745VP | C650 | 7045 |
| N745W | LJ24 | 108 |
| N745W | LJ25 | 030 |
| N745W | LJ25 | 177 |
| (N745WG) | HS25 | 25236 |
| N745XP | HS25 | 258745 |
| N746BC | HS25 | 257004 |
| N746BR | C650 | 7046 |
| N746CM | C650 | 7046 |
| N746CX | C750 | 0046 |
| **N746E** | **CL30** | **20207** |
| N746E | LJ35 | 297 |
| N746F | LJ35 | 297 |
| N746GA | ASTR | 259 |
| N746GL | LJ35 | 157 |
| (N746JB) | C525 | 0404 |
| N746TA | BE40 | RK-146 |
| N746TS | HS25 | 257046 |
| N746UP | HS25 | 258069 |
| **N746UP** | **HS25** | **258522** |
| N746UP | SBRL | 306-22 |
| N746UT | JSTR | 5225 |
| N747 | CL64 | 5305 |
| N747 | FA50 | 146 |
| N747 | FA50 | 50 |
| N747 | SBRL | 282-22 |
| **N747AC** | **C525** | **0202** |
| N747AC | FA10 | 166 |
| **N747AE** | **GLF5** | **5065** |
| N747AN | LJ25 | 272 |

| | | |
|---|---|---|
| **N747AN** | **LJ55** | **121** |
| N747BK | PRM1 | RB-29 |
| **N747BW** | **LJ35** | **594** |
| N747CC | C680 | 0056 |
| N747CP | CS55 | 0077 |
| **N747CP** | **LJ35** | **502** |
| N747CR | C550 | 643 |
| **N747CX** | **FA20** | **442** |
| **N747DP** | **LJ60** | **251** |
| N747E | SBRL | 282-22 |
| N747G | GLF2 | 49 |
| N747G | GLF3 | 381 |
| N747GB | JSTR | 5141 |
| N747GL | LJ35 | 171 |
| **N747GM** | **LJ35** | **308** |
| (N747GP) | CS55 | 0077 |
| **N747HS** | **C52C** | **0002** |
| N747JB | C550 | 617 |
| **N747JJ** | **C52A** | **0314** |
| (N747KL) | C500 | 345 |
| N747KL | CS55 | 0010 |
| **N747KR** | **C52B** | **0015** |
| N747LB | WW24 | 55 |
| **N747LG** | **EA50** | **000235** |
| N747NB | GLF2 | 20 |
| **N747NB** | **GLF2** | **33** |
| N747NG | HS25 | 258417 |
| N747R | SBRL | 282-48 |
| **N747RC** | **C680** | **0002** |
| N747RC | SBRL | 306-34 |
| N747RL | C500 | 345 |
| N747RL | C560 | 0554 |
| N747RL | C680 | 0002 |
| N747RL | CS55 | 0010 |
| **N747RL** | **F2EX** | **175** |
| (N747RL) | LJ35 | 308 |
| **N747RR** | **BE40** | **RK-95** |
| (N747RT) | C550 | 588 |
| **N747RY** | **LJ35** | **243** |
| **N747SC** | **LJ24** | **019** |
| (N747SG) | GALX | 087 |
| N747SG | LJ60 | 109 |
| N747T | FA20 | 81 |
| N747TS | CL61 | 3057 |
| N747TS | CL64 | 5347 |
| N747TX | C650 | 7046 |
| N747UP | HS25 | 258072 |
| N747UP | SBRL | 282-45 |
| N747UP | SBRL | 306-39 |
| N747V | FA20 | 461 |
| N747W | FA20 | 5 |
| N747WA | C500 | 301 |
| **N747XJ** | **C750** | **0247** |
| N747Y | CL64 | 5305 |
| N747Y | FA50 | 50 |
| N748DC | C550 | 136 |
| (N748DC) | C560 | 0054 |
| N748FB | HS25 | 257129 |
| **N748FJ** | **FA7X** | **48** |
| N748GA | GLF5 | 5248 |
| N748GL | LJ35 | 172 |
| N748GM | LJ24 | 311 |
| **N748MN** | **GLF2** | **215** |
| **N748QS** | **GALX** | **157** |
| N748RE | C52A | 0215 |
| **N748RE** | **C56X** | **6008** |
| **N748RF** | **C52A** | **0215** |
| **N748RM** | **C52B** | **0056** |
| N748T | GLF3 | 388 |
| N748TA | BE40 | RK-222 |
| **N748TS** | **HS25** | **25224** |
| N748TS | HS25 | 25224 |
| N748VA | C500 | 148 |
| N748XP | HS25 | 258748 |
| **N749BA** | **CL65** | **5749** |
| N749CM | C650 | 7049 |
| N749CP | C525 | 0158 |
| N749CP | C650 | 0163 |
| N749CP | FA50 | 200 |
| **N749CP** | **FA50** | **300** |
| **N749DC** | **C560** | **0370** |
| N749DC | C650 | 0169 |
| N749DX | C750 | 0046 |
| N749DX | C750 | 0173 |
| **N749GA** | **ASTR** | **149** |
| N749GL | LJ25 | 242 |
| **N749GP** | **F2TH** | **52** |
| N749MC | WW24 | 8 |

| | | |
|---|---|---|
| N749MP | WW24 | 8 |
| **N749P** | **C750** | **0046** |
| **N749QS** | **GALX** | **165** |
| N749RH | BE40 | RK-326 |
| N749RL | C560 | 0554 |
| N749SS | BE40 | RK-240 |
| **N749SS** | **LJ60** | **252** |
| N749TA | BE40 | RK-149 |
| **N749TT** | **C560** | **0248** |
| N749UP | SBRL | 306-129 |
| N750AB | BE40 | RK-50 |
| N750AC | GLF3 | 422 |
| (N750AG) | C750 | 0022 |
| **N750AJ** | **BE40** | **RK-278** |
| N750BA | GLF5 | 558 |
| **N750BL** | **C750** | **0178** |
| N750BM | CL60 | 1012 |
| **N750BP** | **C750** | **0111** |
| **N750BR** | **FA50** | **131** |
| N750CC | SBRL | 465-37 |
| **N750CK** | **C650** | **7015** |
| (N750CR) | C750 | 0248 |
| **N750CR** | **LJ45** | **123** |
| N750CS | SBRL | 465-37 |
| **N750CW** | **C750** | **0008** |
| **N750CX** | **C750** | **703** |
| (N750D) | HS25 | 25015 |
| **N750DD** | **C750** | **0185** |
| **N750DF** | **FA50** | **140** |
| **N750DM** | **C750** | **0146** |
| **N750DX** | **C750** | **0263** |
| **N750EC** | **C750** | **0007** |
| **N750EL** | **HS25** | **HB-18** |
| N750FB | C650 | 7049 |
| N750FJ | FA50 | 218 |
| **N750FL** | **C560** | **0268** |
| N750GA | ASTR | 150 |
| **N750GF** | **C750** | **0244** |
| N750GL | LJ35 | 173 |
| **N750GM** | **C750** | **0066** |
| N750GM | HS25 | 25075 |
| N750GM | HS25 | 257058 |
| **N750GS** | **C750** | **0152** |
| N750GT | CL61 | 3002 |
| **N750H** | **FA50** | **171** |
| N750HB | HS25 | HB-1 |
| **N750HH** | **C750** | **0284** |
| **N750HS** | **C750** | **0103** |
| N750J | C750 | 0051 |
| **N750JB** | **C750** | **0063** |
| **N750JC** | **FA50** | **162** |
| **N750JJ** | **C750** | **0065** |
| **N750JT** | **C750** | **0302** |
| **N750KH** | **HS25** | **HB-12** |
| (N750KP) | BE40 | RJ-58 |
| N750LA | C500 | 398 |
| N750LA | C500 | 570 |
| **N750LG** | **CL61** | **5192** |
| N750LM | C750 | 0039 |
| N750MC | FA50 | 202 |
| N750MD | C750 | 0150 |
| N750ME | FA20 | 262 |
| **N750NS** | **C750** | **0172** |
| (N750PB) | HS25 | 258187 |
| N750PM | CL60 | 1012 |
| **N750PP** | **C500** | **686** |
| N750PT | C750 | 0109 |
| N750PT | C750 | 0222 |
| (N750QK) | LJ24 | 065 |
| **N750QS** | **GALX** | **185** |
| N750R | FA20 | 187 |
| **N750RA** | **GLF2** | **117** |
| **N750RL** | **C750** | **0025** |
| N750RM | LJ35 | 019 |
| N750RV | HS25 | 258187 |
| N750SB | HFB3 | 1031 |
| (N750SB) | WW24 | 198 |
| **N750SL** | **C550** | **554** |
| **N750SP** | **WW24** | **198** |
| N750SS | FA20 | 6 |
| **N750SW** | **GLF3** | **338** |
| N750T | BE40 | RK-70 |
| **N750TA** | **BE40** | **RK-226** |
| **N750TB** | **C550** | **579** |
| N750TJ | MU30 | A006SA |
| N750TJ | MU30 | A081SA |
| **N750TX** | **C750** | **0150** |
| **N750VP** | **C750** | **0022** |

(N750WC) HS25 25115
N750WJ LJ24 065
**N750WM C750 0230**
**N750XJ C750 0250**
N750XX C750 0094
**N751AC LJ35 101**
N751BC GALX 049
**N751BC GALX 132**
**N751BG C680 0181**
**N751BH C750 0059**
N751BP LJ31 208
N751CA LJ25 122
N751CC C500 266
N751CF C560 0274
N751CR WW24 88
N751CX C750 0001
N751DB CL60 1075
N751GA ASTR 151
N751GL LJ35 162
**N751GM C750 0207**
**N751JC FA50 129**
**N751MT HS25 258751**
N751MZ GLF3 426
(N751NS) HS25 HB-1
(N751NS) HS25 HB-2
**N751NS HS25 HB-23**
N751PJ MS76 051
**N751PL C56X 5237**
N751PT C750 0247
N751TA BE40 RK-225
**N752AC LJ35 121**
N752BA GLF5 640
N752BP LJ60 184
N752CA LJ25 137
**N752CC C550 019**
**N752CE C560 0752**
**N752CK C500 255**
N752CM C650 7052
**N752CM HS25 257082**
**N752CS HS25 258323**
N752CX C750 0002
N752DS GLEX 9052
**N752EA LJ25 137**
N752GL LJ25 251
**N752GS C550 285**
N752HB HS25 HB-2
**N752JC FA50 28**
N752JH C560 0442
(N752LX) HS25 258397
**N752M CL30 20210**
**N752MT HS25 258752**
(N752NS) HS25 HB-2
**N752NS HS25 HB-28**
N752NS HS25 HB-3
N752PT C750 0250
**N752QS GALX 152**
N752RT C550 070
**N752S F2TH 82**
N752TA HS25 258397
(N752VP) C750 0002
(N753BB) C560 0306
N753BC GALX 049
N753BD C560 0306
N753BD C750 0118
**N753BP LJ60 238**
N753CA LJ25 136
**N753CC C550 120**
N753CE C560 0753
N753CJ C52B 0001
N753G HS25 258162
**N753GJ C560 0306**
(N753GL) C560 0306
N753GL LJ35 186
**N753JC FA50 25**
**N753NS HS25 HB-29**
(N753NS) HS25 HB-7
N753PT C750 0256
N753S F2TH 88
N753TA BE40 RK-230
N753TW SBRL 380-45
N754AA C550 200
**N754AE HS25 258754**
**N754BA GLF5 5007**
N754CA LJ25 090
(N754CM) C650 7054
N754CX C750 0004
N754DB LJ25 014
N754G HS25 258171
N754GL LJ35 197
**N754JB GLF2 105**
N754M LJ24 185
N754PT C750 0257
N754S FA50 39
N754SE C750 0001
N754TA HS25 258406
N754TS GLEX 9254
N754V C56X 5544
**N754WS LJ35 197**
**N755A ASTR 103**
N755BP C550 361
N755CM C550 033
N755CM C650 7055
N755CM WW24 257
**N755FL F2TH 96**
N755GL LJ35 187
N755GW HS25 25233
N755PA ASTR 015
**N755PA GALX 042**
N755PT C750 0258
**N755QS GALX 168**
N755RV CL64 5370
N755S GLF2 20
N755TA BE40 RK-311
N755TA BE40 RK-324
N755TA HS25 258410
(N755TS) HS25 257055
**N755VE GLF5 5055**
**N755VT LJ55 142**
N755WJ HS25 25233
N756 FA20 388
N756 HS25 25102
N756 JSTR 5154
N756M HS25 25102
N756N HS25 25161
N756N HS25 257182
N756S GLF3 348
**N756XJ C750 0256**
**N757AL LJ35 130**
N757AL WW24 72
**N757BD ASTR 036**
**N757BL HS25 258088**
N757C HS25 257017
N757CE BE40 RK-86
**N757CK C560 0028**
**N757CP C52A 0069**
**N757CX FA20 408**
N757E SBRL 282-50
N757EG C680 0017
N757EM C52A 0422
N757GA ASTR 211
N757M HS25 256022
N757M HS25 257017
**N757M HS25 258101**
**N757MB C650 7035**
N757MC CL60 1016
N757MC CL61 5177
**N757MC GLF4 1498**
N757P HS25 256022
**N757PL GLF5 5249**
N757R SBRL 282-49
N757T C750 0014
**N757TR C560 0598**
**N757WS BE40 RK-169**
**N757XJ C750 0257**
N757XP HS25 258757
**N758CC CL64 5353**
N758CX C750 0058
(N758PM) C560 0208
**N758QS GALX 178**
N758S C550 401
**N758XJ C750 0258**
**N758XL C56X 5758**
N759A GLF2 131/23
(N759FS) LJ31 231
N759R C525 0524
**N759R C52A 0086**
N759WR GLF5 5063
N760 C550 302
**N760 F9EX 3**
N760A GLF3 428
(N760A) LJ25 051
N760AC GLF3 377
N760AC LJ55 017
N760AC LJ60 017
**N760AG GLEX 9358**
N760AQ LJ55 017
**N760AR MS76 108**
N760C GLF3 430
N760C MS76 043
N760C WW24 174
**N760CC GLF5 5100**
N760CF LJ60 007
N760DE JSTR 5101/15
N760DE JSTR 5214
(N760DL) FA50 41
N760DL JSTR 5101/15
N760DL JSTR 5214
N760DL LJ35 155
N760E MS76 102
N760EW C650 0056
**N760F MS76 058**
**N760FM MS76 111**
**N760FR MS76 072**
N760G GLF3 428
N760G GLF4 4039
N760G LJ55 107
N760GL LJ35 206
N760H MS76 005
N760J MS76 006
**N760JS MS76 088**
(N760LB) MS76 005
N760LP LJ35 155
N760M MS76 049
N760MM MS76 002
N760N MS76 103
N760NB CS55 0046
N760NS HS25 HB-34
N760P MS76 104
**N760PJ MS76 027**
(N760PJ) MS76 101
N760PT C750 0260
N760Q MS76 105
N760R MS76 104
**N760S MS76 043**
(N760SA) SBRL 306-76
N760T MS76 103
N760TA HS25 258413
N760U GLF2 75/7
**N760X MS76 028**
**N760XJ C750 0260**
N761A LJ36 022
**N761JP C510 0045**
**N761JS MS76 082**
**N761KG C52A 0227**
N761NS HS25 HB-43
**N761QS GALX 176**
N761TA BE40 RK-161
**N761X MS76 030**
**N761XP HS25 258761**
N762BG BE40 RK-57
**N762DL EA50 000215**
**N762EL LJ45 107**
N762GL LJ36 026
**N762GS GLF3 413**
(N762L) LJ36 026
N762L LJ36 033
N762PF C550 247
N762XP HS25 258762
**N762XP HS25 HB-62**
N763CJ C52B 0002
**N763D C560 0007**
**N763DB GLF4 1114**
**N763FJ FA7X 63**
N763GL LJ35 113
N763J GLF3 304
N763JJ GLF4 4064
**N763JS MS76 092**
(N763PD) GLF2 139/11
N763R LJ36 034
N764C C525 0325
N764CE C560 0764
N764G LJ35 406
N764GA GLF5 5164
**N764JS MS76 093**
N764KF LJ25 234
N764LA FA20 211
N764PT C750 0264
N764RH LJ25 210
**N764XJ C750 0264**
N764XP HS25 258764
N765A GLF2 111
N765A GLF4 1069
N765CT C52A 0002
**N765JS MS76 094**
**N765KC MU30 A079SA**
**N765M GALX 124**
N765PT C750 0265
**N765TS HS25 25263**
(N765W) C650 7065
**N765WT CL61 5039**
**N765XJ C750 0265**
N766 JSTR 5154
N766AE C550 231
(N766AF) C550 231
N766AJ LJ31 103
N766CE C560 0766
N766CG C650 7066
N766DD GLF3 483
N766FT C500 014
**N766HK FA50 161**
**N766MH C650 0015**
N766NB CS55 0156
N766NW FA20 66
N766R SBRL 282-1
N766WC GLF3 413
N767AC FA20 349
N767AC WW24 356
N767AG FA20 349
**N767AG FA20 479**
N767AZ LJ55 136
**N767BS C56X 5191**
**N767CB GLF3 397**
N767CF F900 105
**N767CS PRM1 RB-142**
**N767CW GLF5 520**
**N767DT GLF4 4065**
N767DX GLF4 4065
N767EL GLF4 1141
N767FL GLF2 50
N767FL GLF4 1141
**N767FL GLF5 503**
**N767HB HS25 HB-67**
N767JH SBRL 282-98
(N767LC) HS25 25170
N767NY LJ55 136
N767PC C500 080
N767RA LJ36 023
N767SA LJ25 216
N767SB BE40 RK-355
N767SC LJ25 023
(N767TR) C550 401
N767W C52A 0168
(N767W) FA50 82
**N767WB F900 132**
N767XP HS25 258767
N767Z JSTR 5009
N767Z JSTR 5023
N768DV SBRL 306-79
**N768HB HS25 HB-68**
N768J FA20 440
N768J GLF3 304
N768J GLF4 1119
**N768JF EA50 000030**
N768JJ GLF4 4064
**N768JJ GLF5 5217**
**N768JW F2TH 72**
N768NB C650 0180
N768R C525 0471
N768TA BE40 RK-168
(N768V) FA20 440
N768XP HS25 258768
**N769BH FA10 60**
**N769CA LJ28 28-004**
**N769CC CL65 5769**
(N769CM) C650 7069
**N769CP FA50 200**
**N769CS C560 0769**
**N769DS LJ60 052**
(N769EG) SBRL 465-9
(N769EW) C500 669
**N769H C550 183**
**N769HB HS25 HB-69**
N769JW F2EX 205
N769JW F2TH 72
N769K C500 228
N769KC SBRL 465-9
**N769M WW24 344**
**N769MS ASTR 252**
N769MS WW24 344
N769PT C750 0269
N769SC FA10 7
**N769XJ C750 0269**

| Registration | Type | C/n |
|---|---|---|
| N769XP | HS25 | 258769 |
| N770AC | GLF2 | 57 |
| N770AC | LJ25 | 209 |
| **N770AF** | **C500** | **208** |
| N770AF | C650 | 0119 |
| **N770AG** | **GLEX** | **9355** |
| N770AQ | LJ25 | 209 |
| **N770AZ** | **HS25** | **257046** |
| N770BB | C550 | 606 |
| **N770BC** | **CL64** | **5352** |
| (N770BC) | HS25 | 25078 |
| N770BC | LJ60 | 203 |
| N770BG | LJ60 | 203 |
| **N770BM** | **LJ35** | **654** |
| N770BX | C525 | 0524 |
| N770CA | CL60 | 1042 |
| N770CC | HS25 | 257108 |
| **N770CC** | **HS25** | **258587** |
| N770CC | LJ31 | 058 |
| N770CH | LJ31 | 222 |
| N770DA | HS25 | 25142 |
| N770DR | JSTR | 5219 |
| N770DS | LJ45 | 077 |
| N770E | FA50 | 21 |
| **N770FF** | **ASTR** | **054** |
| **N770FG** | **FA20** | **116** |
| **N770GA** | **GLF3** | **470** |
| N770GA | GLF5 | 5170 |
| **N770GF** | **C650** | **0013** |
| **N770GS** | **HS25** | **HB-3** |
| **N770HB** | **HS25** | **HB-70** |
| N770HS | HS25 | 257191 |
| (N770JB) | LJ60 | 225 |
| N770JC | CL60 | 1061 |
| **N770JD** | **FA50** | **148** |
| N770JJ | WW24 | 296 |
| N770JM | C550 | 072 |
| N770JM | C550 | 550-0902 |
| **N770JM** | **C56X** | **5370** |
| N770JM | LJ55 | 039 |
| **N770JP** | **LJ35** | **210** |
| N770JR | JSTR | 5037/24 |
| **N770MC** | **FA20** | **330** |
| **N770MD** | **SBRL** | **465-26** |
| N770MH | C500 | 364 |
| N770MP | C650 | 0118 |
| **N770MP** | **F2TH** | **99** |
| N770MP | FA50 | 161 |
| N770MR | C650 | 0118 |
| N770PA | GLF2 | 175 |
| (N770PA) | LJ25 | 209 |
| **N770PC** | **LJ60** | **318** |
| N770PC | MU30 | A080SA |
| N770RR | FA20 | 272 |
| **N770SC** | **GLF4** | **1056** |
| (N770TB) | BE40 | RJ-14 |
| **N770TB** | **C550** | **471** |
| N770TJ | HS25 | 257175 |
| N770UM | C550 | 550-0902 |
| N770UP | ASTR | 120 |
| (N770VP) | C650 | 7070 |
| N770WL | WW24 | 57 |
| **N770XB** | **GLF4** | **4117** |
| **N770XJ** | **C750** | **0270** |
| N771A | C550 | 034 |
| N771A | LJ35 | 303 |
| N771AA | C550 | 317 |
| (N771AC) | WW24 | 191 |
| N771AV | GLF4 | 1197 |
| **N771B** | **WW24** | **258** |
| N771CB | LJ25 | 326 |
| N771CP | ASTR | 077 |
| **N771DE** | **C56X** | **5591** |
| **N771DV** | **F2EX** | **106** |
| N771EL | BE40 | RK-4 |
| N771GA | GALX | 131 |
| **N771HM** | **FA50** | **318** |
| N771HR | C500 | 206 |
| N771JB | C650 | 0214 |
| **N771JT** | **GLF5** | **5089** |
| N771LD | FA20 | 59 |
| **N771PM** | **C56X** | **5799** |
| (N771R) | C550 | 163 |
| N771SB | LJ35 | 401 |
| N771ST | C550 | 021 |
| N771SV | HS25 | 258391 |
| N771TF | GLEX | 9175 |
| N771WB | SBRL | 306-29 |
| N771WW | CL60 | 1018 |
| N771WW | SBRL | 306-29 |
| N771WY | C550 | 292 |
| N772AA | C560 | 0136 |
| (N772AC) | C550 | 106 |
| N772C | C500 | 180 |
| **N772CS** | **C560** | **0772** |
| **N772GA** | **GLF5** | **5272** |
| N772HP | C550 | 262 |
| **N772JS** | **CL30** | **20153** |
| (N772KC) | C560 | 0072 |
| N772M | CS55 | 0041 |
| **N772MC** | **F2EX** | **150** |
| N772MC | F2TH | 79 |
| **N772PP** | **LJ60** | **293** |
| N772PT | C750 | 0272 |
| **N772SB** | **C550** | **498** |
| N772TA | HS25 | 258428 |
| **N772XJ** | **C750** | **0272** |
| N773A | CL61 | 5169 |
| N773AA | HS25 | 25175 |
| **N773AJ** | **GLF4** | **1225** |
| N773AW | WW24 | 232 |
| **N773CA** | **C550** | **550-0840** |
| **N773DL** | **LJ35** | **174** |
| N773EJ | WW24 | 153 |
| N773FR | C500 | 410 |
| **N773HR** | **HS25** | **258836** |
| (N773HS) | FA20 | 44 |
| N773JC | CL61 | 3029 |
| **N773JC** | **GLF4** | **1066** |
| N773JC | HS25 | 256001 |
| N773LP | C500 | 450 |
| N773LP | C550 | 399 |
| N773LP | LJ35 | 362 |
| N773LR | C500 | 450 |
| N773M | C650 | 0093 |
| N773MJ | GLF4 | 1225 |
| **N773MJ** | **GLF5** | **5232** |
| N773RS | LJ40 | 45-2046 |
| **N773SW** | **LJ60** | **254** |
| N773TA | BE40 | RK-279 |
| N773V | FA20 | 264 |
| N773VP | C550 | 730 |
| N773W | SBRL | 380-20 |
| N773WB | WW24 | 112 |
| N774AB | LJ36 | 025 |
| **N774AK** | **GLF3** | **339** |
| **N774AR** | **C510** | **0077** |
| N774CA | C525 | 0141 |
| N774CC | C560 | 0774 |
| N774CC | LJ45 | 380 |
| N774CZ | C750 | 0074 |
| N774EC | HS25 | 25281 |
| **N774GE** | **C525** | **0457** |
| N774GF | HS25 | 257207 |
| **N774KK** | **GLEX** | **9290** |
| N774MC | F2TH | 79 |
| **N774PC** | **CL61** | **5094** |
| **N774ST** | **C510** | **0245** |
| **N774TS** | **HS25** | **25281** |
| **N774W** | **SBRL** | **380-37** |
| **N774XJ** | **C750** | **0274** |
| N774XP | HS25 | 258774 |
| N775DF | ASTR | 132 |
| (N775JC) | WW24 | 205 |
| **N775M** | **C650** | **7017** |
| (N775RB) | HS25 | 258636 |
| **N775ST** | **F2TH** | **43** |
| N775TA | BE40 | RK-276 |
| **N775TB** | **C525** | **0075** |
| **N775TF** | **C52A** | **0393** |
| N775US | GLF5 | 535 |
| **N776BG** | **LJ35** | **659** |
| **N776DF** | **C525** | **0111** |
| N776DS | FA20 | 76 |
| **N776GM** | **C650** | **0124** |
| **N776JB** | **GLF4** | **4042** |
| (N776JK) | MS76 | 043 |
| N776JM | JSTR | 5036/42 |
| (N776JS) | C500 | 227 |
| **N776JS** | **LJ35** | **476** |
| N776K | MS76 | 043 |
| N776LB | C52A | 0191 |
| N776MA | GLF2 | 166/15 |
| **N776MA** | **GLF3** | **447** |
| N776PH | LJ31 | 201 |
| N776PT | C750 | 0276 |
| **N776RS** | **HS25** | **258776** |
| (N776TS) | HS25 | 257076 |
| N776US | GLF4 | 1146 |
| **N776XJ** | **C750** | **0276** |
| **N777AG** | **C52A** | **0238** |
| N777AJ | C500 | 495 |
| **N777AM** | **ASTR** | **038** |
| N777AM | CS55 | 0014 |
| N777AN | C500 | 027 |
| **N777AX** | **CS55** | **0149** |
| **N777AY** | **JSTR** | **5201** |
| **N777BF** | **E50P** | **50000041** |
| (N777CB) | LJ60 | 086 |
| N777CF | WW24 | 231 |
| **N777CJ** | **C52A** | **0182** |
| N777CJ | WW24 | 177 |
| (N777CR) | SBRL | 306-27 |
| **N777DB** | **CL64** | **5502** |
| N777DB | HS25 | 258551 |
| N777DC | FA20 | 91 |
| N777DC | MU30 | A045SA |
| N777DC | MU30 | A072SA |
| **N777DC** | **WW24** | **410** |
| **N777DM** | **LJ35** | **297** |
| **N777DY** | **C52A** | **0189** |
| N777EG | FA20 | 146 |
| **N777EH** | **HS25** | **257020** |
| **N777EN** | **C560** | **0777** |
| N777EP | JSTR | 5004 |
| N777FA | FA20 | 7 |
| N777FB | C550 | 443 |
| N777FC | C500 | 038 |
| **N777FC** | **FA20** | **508** |
| N777FD | CS55 | 0099 |
| **N777FE** | **BE40** | **RJ-30** |
| N777FE | C500 | 498 |
| N777FE | C550 | 443 |
| N777FE | C560 | 0076 |
| N777FH | C560 | 0076 |
| N777FH | C56X | 5148 |
| N777FJ | FA10 | 154 |
| N777FL | ASTR | 124 |
| **N777FL** | **ASTR** | **214** |
| N777FL | BE40 | RK-223 |
| N777FL | BE40 | RK-4 |
| N777FL | C550 | 064 |
| N777FN | C560 | 0076 |
| **N777FZ** | **ASTR** | **124** |
| **N777G** | **BE40** | **RK-540** |
| **N777GA** | **CL60** | **1056** |
| N777GA | HS25 | 25146 |
| N777GC | BE40 | RK-86 |
| **N777GD** | **CL60** | **1023** |
| N777GD | HS25 | 25186 |
| N777GF | CS55 | 0090 |
| N777GG | C500 | 495 |
| **N777GG** | **CS55** | **0012** |
| N777GG | GLF2 | 8 |
| N777GV | GLF5 | 508 |
| N777GX | GLEX | 9036 |
| **N777HD** | **WW24** | **397** |
| **N777HN** | **C52A** | **0099** |
| (N777HN) | CS55 | 0111 |
| (N777JA) | LJ24 | 163 |
| **N777JE** | **C550** | **723** |
| N777JF | FA20 | 18 |
| N777JF | FA20 | 249 |
| **N777JF** | **PRM1** | **RB-105** |
| **N777JJ** | **C500** | **056** |
| N777JJ | FA10 | 35 |
| N777JJ | MU30 | A006SA |
| N777JM | C500 | 056 |
| **N777JQ** | **E50P** | **50000072** |
| N777JS | GLF2 | 77 |
| N777JV | C56X | 5342 |
| N777KK | CL60 | 1082 |
| **N777KK** | **GLF4** | **1429** |
| N777KY | C560 | 0108 |
| N777KZ | CL60 | 1082 |
| N777LB | LJ24 | 216 |
| N777LB | LJ35 | 473 |
| N777LB | LJ35 | 476 |
| **N777LD** | **LJ35** | **314** |
| N777LF | C650 | 0034 |
| N777LF | LJ25 | 087 |
| N777LF | LJ35 | 449 |
| N777LU | WW24 | 350 |
| **N777LX** | **C56X** | **5736** |
| N777MC | LJ24 | 217 |
| N777MC | LJ35 | 125 |
| N777MC | LJ55 | 081 |
| **N777MC** | **LJ60** | **180** |
| N777MG | PRM1 | RB-20 |
| N777MH | WW24 | 34 |
| N777MJ | FA50 | 115 |
| N777MJ | MU30 | A085SA |
| N777MN | F2TH | 147 |
| N777MQ | LJ24 | 217 |
| N777MQ | LJ55 | 081 |
| N777MQ | PRM1 | RB-20 |
| N777MR | LJ24 | 142 |
| **N777MW** | **GLF3** | **485** |
| **N777MX** | **C650** | **0051** |
| N777ND | BE40 | RK-71 |
| (N777ND) | FA10 | 130 |
| N777NG | C550 | 550-0992 |
| N777NJ | C52B | 0009 |
| **N777NJ** | **C52B** | **0099** |
| (N777NJ) | C550 | 394 |
| N777NJ | LJ25 | 173 |
| N777NQ | LJ35 | 125 |
| (N777NZ) | GLF4 | 1212 |
| N777PD | LJ25 | 138 |
| N777PQ | HFB3 | 1050 |
| N777PS | HFB3 | 1050 |
| N777PV | FA20 | 137 |
| N777PV | HFB3 | 1050 |
| N777PY | GLF5 | 508 |
| N777PZ | HFB3 | 1050 |
| N777PZ | JSTR | 5128/16 |
| (N777QE) | C500 | 302 |
| **N777QP** | **C52A** | **0241** |
| N777RA | LJ25 | 005 |
| N777RA | LJ35 | 285 |
| **N777RF** | **FA10** | **179** |
| **N777RN** | **HS25** | **25027** |
| **N777RW** | **GLF2** | **184** |
| N777RY | GLF3 | 327 |
| N777RZ | GLF3 | 398 |
| (N777SA) | F9EX | 165 |
| N777SA | GLF4 | 1081 |
| **N777SA** | **GLF4** | **1138** |
| N777SA | HS25 | 25224 |
| N777SA | HS25 | 256015 |
| N777SA | HS25 | 256055 |
| N777SA | LJ24 | 228 |
| N777SA | LJ25 | 201 |
| (N777SC) | C500 | 140 |
| (N777SG) | E50P | 50000014 |
| N777SG | JSTR | 5074/22 |
| N777SK | SBRL | 465-24 |
| **N777SL** | **C500** | **307** |
| (N777SL) | GLF3 | 252 |
| N777SL | SBRL | 282-135 |
| N777SN | FA10 | 13 |
| (N777ST) | SBRL | 282-82 |
| N777SW | GLEX | 9037 |
| N777SW | GLF2 | 81 |
| N777SW | GLF3 | 306 |
| N777SW | GLF4 | 1014 |
| N777SW | GLF4 | 1149 |
| N777SW | GLF5 | 514 |
| **N777TC** | **GLF4** | **1137** |
| **N777TE** | **FA20** | **500** |
| N777TE | LJ24 | 031 |
| N777TF | LJ24 | 031 |
| N777TK | HS25 | 256015 |
| N777TX | FA20 | 365 |
| (N777TX) | GLF2 | 62 |
| **N777TX** | **LJ25** | **084** |
| N777TY | GLF5 | 508 |
| N777UE | GLF4 | 1146 |
| **N777UT** | **C680** | **0048** |
| N777UU | C550 | 550-1003 |
| N777V | FA20 | 264 |
| N777V | GLF2 | 120 |
| N777V | SBRL | 282-69 |
| N777V | WW24 | 12 |
| N777VC | CL30 | 20016 |
| N777VC | LJ60 | 207 |
| N777VC | LJ60 | 318 |
| **N777VE** | **EA50** | **000011** |
| N777VQ | LJ60 | 207 |
| N777VU | GLEX | 9037 |
| N777VZ | SBRL | 282-69 |
| N777WJ | FA20 | 142 |

| | | |
|---|---|---|
| N777WJ | FA20 | 65 |
| N777WJ | JSTR | 5215 |
| N777WJ | WW24 | 72 |
| N777WL | FA20 | 65 |
| N777WY | C550 | 292 |
| **N777WY** | **C560** | **0525** |
| **N777XS** | **C650** | **0008** |
| N777XX | CL60 | 1017 |
| N777XX | CL61 | 5104 |
| N777XX | CL61 | 5152 |
| N777XX | FA20 | 150/445 |
| **N777XY** | **FA50** | **176** |
| N777YC | LJ55 | 120 |
| **N777YG** | **CL61** | **5172** |
| **N777ZA** | **E50P** | **50000117** |
| N777ZC | C650 | 0153 |
| **N777ZL** | **FA50** | **46** |
| **N777ZY** | **EA50** | **000109** |
| N778BC | C560 | 0657 |
| N778BC | C56X | 5517 |
| N778C | C550 | 169 |
| (N778CC) | HS25 | 258587 |
| N778FW | C560 | 0442 |
| N778GA | LJ24 | 143 |
| **N778GM** | **LJ25** | **078** |
| (N778HS) | HS25 | 257191 |
| **N778JA** | **HS25** | **25285** |
| **N778JC** | **C550** | **363** |
| N778JC | LJ25 | 078 |
| **N778JE** | **C510** | **0236** |
| N778JM | C550 | 072 |
| N778MA | C52A | 0222 |
| N778MT | GLF4 | 1108 |
| N778PT | C750 | 0278 |
| N778S | HS25 | 25179 |
| N778SM | HS25 | 25047 |
| **N778TC** | **EA50** | **000085** |
| **N778VW** | **EA50** | **000063** |
| N778W | GLF3 | 413 |
| N778W | GLF4 | 1023 |
| (N778W) | GLF4 | 1146 |
| **N778XJ** | **C750** | **0278** |
| (N778XX) | CL60 | 1077 |
| N778XX | CL61 | 3017 |
| N778XX | CL61 | 5003 |
| N778YY | CL61 | 3017 |
| N778YY | CL61 | 3023 |
| N779AF | C650 | 0136 |
| N779AZ | C650 | 0136 |
| **N779AZ** | **CL61** | **5176** |
| N779CS | GLF4 | 4076 |
| **N779CS** | **SBRL** | **465-29** |
| **N779DC** | **MU30** | **A072SA** |
| N779DD | C550 | 333 |
| **N779LC** | **GLF2** | **88/21** |
| N779P | FA20 | 122 |
| N779QS | C650 | 7079 |
| N779RB | C525 | 0637 |
| N779SG | F900 | 46 |
| N779SW | GLF4 | 1014 |
| N779VP | C650 | 7079 |
| **N779XJ** | **C750** | **0279** |
| N779XX | CL61 | 3018 |
| N779YY | CL61 | 3032 |
| N779YY | CL61 | 5043 |
| N780A | HS25 | 258084 |
| N780A | LJ25 | 056 |
| N780A | LJ35 | 302 |
| N780AC | LJ25 | 173 |
| N780AQ | LJ25 | 173 |
| N780BF | C560 | 0207 |
| **N780CC** | **C56X** | **5597** |
| N780CE | C560 | 0780 |
| **N780CF** | **C550** | **015** |
| N780CS | C56X | 5168 |
| N780E | GLF4 | 1165 |
| N780F | FA50 | 240 |
| **N780F** | **GLF5** | **530** |
| N780GT | BE40 | RJ-55 |
| N780GT | C550 | 015 |
| **N780GT** | **C650** | **0222** |
| N780HC | CL61 | 5070 |
| N780LS | GLF4 | 1009 |
| **N780N** | **GLF4** | **1165** |
| (N780PM) | GLF2 | 207/34 |
| N780PT | C750 | 0280 |
| N780PV | WW24 | 36 |
| N780QS | C650 | 7080 |

| | | |
|---|---|---|
| N780RA | GLF3 | 472 |
| N780RH | GLF3 | 472 |
| N780RH | GLF4 | 1498 |
| N780RH | JSTR | 5095/30 |
| (N780SC) | HS25 | 256018 |
| **N780SP** | **F900** | **93** |
| N780TA | HS25 | 258437 |
| N780TP | BE40 | RK-136 |
| N780W | GLF5 | 530 |
| **N780XJ** | **C750** | **0280** |
| N781AJ | FA20 | 98/434 |
| N781B | FA50 | 116 |
| N781CE | C560 | 0781 |
| **N781EX** | **F2EX** | **187** |
| **N781JR** | **HS25** | **25286** |
| N781KB | PRM1 | RB-103 |
| N781L | C500 | 355 |
| N781QS | C650 | 7081 |
| N781RS | LJ35 | 218 |
| N781SC | C550 | 398 |
| N781TA | HS25 | 258281 |
| N781TP | BE40 | RK-231 |
| N781W | FA20 | 257 |
| **N782BJ** | **CL30** | **20164** |
| **N782CC** | **C650** | **7030** |
| N782GA | GLF5 | 5182 |
| (N782JR) | LJ25 | 316 |
| N782JR | LJ35 | 336 |
| (N782NA) | C550 | 376 |
| N782PC | WW24 | 339 |
| N782PT | C750 | 0282 |
| N782QS | C650 | 7082 |
| **N782ST** | **C550** | **679** |
| **N782TA** | **HS25** | **258282** |
| **N782TP** | **BE40** | **RK-243** |
| N782VP | C650 | 7082 |
| **N782XJ** | **C750** | **0282** |
| N782XP | HS25 | 258782 |
| N783A | CL61 | 3008 |
| **N783FS** | **F2TH** | **9** |
| N783FS | WW24 | 319 |
| N783H | C550 | 081 |
| **N783H** | **C650** | **0210** |
| N783M | HS25 | 257092 |
| N783TA | BE40 | RK-234 |
| N783XL | C56X | 5783 |
| N784A | C550 | 465 |
| N784AE | HS25 | 25084 |
| N784B | FA50 | 118 |
| **N784BX** | **F2TH** | **56** |
| **N784CC** | **LJ40** | **45-2052** |
| N784CE | FA10 | 78 |
| **N784JP** | **E50P** | **50000074** |
| (N784LB) | LJ31 | 215 |
| **N784MA** | **PRM1** | **RB-141** |
| N784PT | C750 | 0284 |
| N784TA | BE40 | RK-237 |
| N784XJ | C750 | 0284 |
| N784XP | HS25 | 258784 |
| **N785AD** | **F2EX** | **146** |
| N785B | LJ55 | 043 |
| N785CA | C550 | 184 |
| N785CA | HS25 | 258001 |
| N785CC | C650 | 7085 |
| N785DR | LJ60 | 289 |
| N785JM | LJ35 | 655 |
| **N785MT** | **C52A** | **0419** |
| N785QS | C650 | 7085 |
| **N785QS** | **GLF5** | **5157** |
| **N785RC** | **C680** | **0040** |
| N785TA | BE40 | RK-239 |
| **N785VC** | **HS25** | **258785** |
| N785XP | HS25 | 258785 |
| **N786AC** | **C52A** | **0312** |
| **N786AD** | **F2EX** | **147** |
| **N786AF** | **C510** | **0273** |
| **N786CC** | **LJ45** | **095** |
| **N786CS** | **FA7X** | **31** |
| (N786CW) | GLF5 | 520 |
| **N786JB** | **GLF4** | **1092** |
| N786MS | LJ25 | 033 |
| N786TA | BE40 | RK-248 |
| **N786XJ** | **C750** | **0286** |
| **N786YA** | **LJ31** | **215** |
| N787AF | GLF4 | 1414 |
| N787BA | C500 | 143 |
| **N787BN** | **ASTR** | **231** |
| **N787CM** | **HS25** | **258271** |

| | | |
|---|---|---|
| **N787CW** | **C560** | **0779** |
| (N787CW) | C750 | 0147 |
| **N787FF** | **HS25** | **HB-2** |
| **N787GT** | **LJ55** | **128** |
| **N787JC** | **HS25** | **258727** |
| N787JD | C550 | 589 |
| N787LP | LJ35 | 670 |
| N787LP | LJ60 | 087 |
| **N787LP** | **LJ60** | **248** |
| **N787PR** | **GALX** | **138** |
| N787QS | C650 | 7087 |
| N787R | SBRL | 282-76 |
| N787R | SBRL | 306-16 |
| N787R | SBRL | 306-77 |
| (N787RA) | F2TH | 11 |
| N787RP | WW24 | 358 |
| **N787TA** | **BE40** | **RK-260** |
| N787WB | JSTR | 5210 |
| N787WC | C550 | 471 |
| N787X | HS25 | 25037 |
| **N787XJ** | **C750** | **0287** |
| N788BA | C650 | 0116 |
| N788C | GLF2 | 165/37 |
| N788CE | C560 | 0788 |
| **N788CG** | **F9EX** | **79** |
| (N788CW) | C750 | 0038 |
| N788DR | LJ24 | 084 |
| **N788FS** | **WW24** | **319** |
| (N788JS) | JSTR | 5231 |
| N788MA | WW24 | 311 |
| **N788MM** | **CL30** | **20105** |
| N788MM | LJ60 | 016 |
| N788NB | C650 | 0155 |
| N788QC | LJ35 | 609 |
| N788R | SBRL | 282-68 |
| N788S | GLF2 | 30/4 |
| N788S | JSTR | 5110/47 |
| N788SC | CL64 | 5391 |
| N788SS | C500 | 433 |
| N788WG | CL60 | 1069 |
| N788WG | HS25 | 257026 |
| N789A | ASTR | 092 |
| (N789AA) | C500 | 445 |
| N789AA | LJ24 | 309 |
| **N789AH** | **LJ40** | **45-2002** |
| N789AT | GALX | 004 |
| **N789BA** | **HS25** | **257168** |
| N789BR | C550 | 036 |
| **N789CA** | **ASTR** | **074** |
| N789CN | C56X | 5070 |
| (N789DD) | C500 | 249 |
| N789DD | C500 | 560 |
| (N789DD) | C550 | 137 |
| N789DD | MU30 | A015SA |
| (N789DD) | WW24 | 187 |
| **N789DJ** | **MU30** | **A015SA** |
| N789DK | C500 | 560 |
| N789DK | GLF4 | 1054 |
| N789DR | CL61 | 3001 |
| N789FF | GLF2 | 31 |
| **N789H** | **C680** | **0041** |
| (N789H) | LJ45 | 003 |
| **N789JC** | **FA50** | **66** |
| N789KW | LJ35 | 222 |
| **N789LB** | **HS25** | **258248** |
| N789LT | HS25 | 258071 |
| N789MA | CS55 | 0067 |
| **N789MB** | **CL30** | **20020** |
| **N789ME** | **FA50** | **276** |
| N789PF | LJ55 | 089 |
| N789PR | GALX | 050 |
| N789QS | C650 | 7089 |
| (N789RR) | C550 | 036 |
| N789RR | GALX | 050 |
| **N789RR** | **GLF4** | **1509** |
| N789RR | GLF5 | 5045 |
| **N789SG** | **SBRL** | **306-121** |
| **N789SR** | **LJ31** | **083** |
| N789SS | C550 | 087 |
| **N789TA** | **BE40** | **RK-268** |
| N789TE | WW24 | 241 |
| N789TP | GLEX | 9065 |
| N789TP | GLF3 | 405 |
| N789TR | GLF3 | 405 |
| **N789TT** | **C550** | **391** |
| **N789VP** | **C650** | **7089** |
| **N789XJ** | **C750** | **0289** |
| N789XP | HS25 | 258789 |

| | | |
|---|---|---|
| **N789ZZ** | **F9EX** | **174** |
| **N790AL** | **CS55** | **0024** |
| N790D | C550 | 023 |
| N790EA | C500 | 251 |
| **N790FH** | **ASTR** | **056** |
| N790FH | FA10 | 158 |
| N790GA | GALX | 090 |
| **N790GA** | **GLF4** | **4190** |
| **N790JC** | **F900** | **17** |
| **N790JR** | **WW24** | **424** |
| **N790L** | **F2TH** | **15** |
| **N790M** | **F2TH** | **19** |
| N790MC | GLF5 | 523 |
| N790PS | C560 | 0272 |
| N790QS | C650 | 7090 |
| **N790SS** | **BE40** | **RK-363** |
| **N790SU** | **LJ60** | **146** |
| **N790TA** | **BE40** | **RK-252** |
| N790US | FA10 | 91 |
| N790VP | C650 | 7090 |
| N790XP | HS25 | 258790 |
| **N790Z** | **F2TH** | **31** |
| N790Z | HS25 | 257197 |
| **N791CP** | **FA10** | **54** |
| (N791CW) | C750 | 0091 |
| N791DM | C52A | 0314 |
| N791MA | C500 | 309 |
| N791QS | C650 | 7091 |
| N791TA | HS25 | 258291 |
| N791VP | C650 | 7091 |
| N792A | HS25 | 25248 |
| N792AA | JSTR | 5098/28 |
| N792CC | C650 | 7092 |
| N792CT | CL61 | 5148 |
| (N792DL) | EA50 | 000215 |
| **N792GA** | **GLF5** | **5297** |
| N792H | HS25 | 259019 |
| N792MA | C550 | 329 |
| N792QS | C650 | 7092 |
| N792TA | BE40 | RK-264 |
| (N792VP) | C650 | 7092 |
| **N792XJ** | **C750** | **0292** |
| N792XP | HS25 | 258792 |
| N793A | ASTR | 086 |
| **N793AA** | **C500** | **501** |
| **N793BG** | **WW24** | **392** |
| **N793CJ** | **C525** | **0021** |
| **N793CS** | **C560** | **0793** |
| N793CT | CL61 | 5148 |
| **N793CT** | **CL64** | **5643** |
| N793JR | WW24 | 365 |
| N793QS | C650 | 7093 |
| **N793RC** | **HS25** | **258550** |
| N793TA | BE40 | RK-244 |
| N793XP | HS25 | 258793 |
| N794EZ | C500 | 397 |
| N794GC | LJ35 | 446 |
| **N794ME** | **GLF3** | **483** |
| **N794MH** | **GLF4** | **1079** |
| **N794PF** | **C525** | **0649** |
| N794QS | C650 | 7094 |
| **N794RC** | **CL30** | **20193** |
| **N794SB** | **CL61** | **5082** |
| (N794SB) | FA20 | 24 |
| N794SB | GLF2 | 12 |
| N794SB | GLF2 | 176 |
| N794SC | GLF2 | 176 |
| (N794SM) | BE40 | RK-60 |
| N794TA | BE40 | RK-282 |
| **N794TK** | **WW24** | **373** |
| N794VP | C650 | 7094 |
| (N794WB) | C500 | 621 |
| **N794XJ** | **C750** | **0294** |
| **N795A** | **HS25** | **257127** |
| N795AB | FA20 | 262 |
| **N795BA** | **GLF5** | **5031** |
| **N795BM** | **C525** | **0481** |
| **N795FM** | **WW24** | **228** |
| **N795HA** | **LJ55** | **132** |
| N795HB | ASTR | 084 |
| (N795HC) | C750 | 0053 |
| N795HE | HS25 | 257149 |
| **N795HG** | **C750** | **0053** |
| (N795HL) | HS25 | 257149 |
| N795HP | ASTR | 084 |
| N795J | HS25 | 25121 |
| N795MA | C500 | 615 |
| N795PH | HS25 | 258139 |

| Reg | Type | C/n |
|---|---|---|
| N795QS | C650 | 7095 |
| N795TA | BE40 | RK-284 |
| N795VP | C650 | 7095 |
| **N795XJ** | **C750** | **0295** |
| N796A | FA50 | 238 |
| **N796CH** | **HS25** | **258049** |
| N796HP | ASTR | 085 |
| **N796HR** | **ASTR** | **085** |
| N796MA | FA10 | 162 |
| N796MA | GLF4 | 4076 |
| N796QS | C650 | 7096 |
| N796SF | FA10 | 75 |
| N796TA | BE40 | RK-289 |
| N796XP | HS25 | 258796 |
| **N797BD** | **GLF3** | **388** |
| **N797CB** | **CL30** | **20158** |
| N797CB | LJ60 | 086 |
| **N797CC** | **C650** | **7097** |
| N797CD | GLF4 | 1145 |
| **N797CM** | **F2TH** | **51** |
| N797CM | GLF4 | 1064 |
| N797CP | LJ60 | 086 |
| N797CS | LJ55 | 018 |
| **N797CS** | **LJ60** | **324** |
| **N797CW** | **C550** | **284** |
| **N797CX** | **C750** | **0297** |
| (N797EM) | HS25 | 257193 |
| N797EP | HS25 | 258139 |
| N797FA | HS25 | 257193 |
| **N797HT** | **F2TH** | **171** |
| N797KB | LJ31 | 098 |
| N797KK | GLEX | 9290 |
| **N797M** | **GALX** | **179** |
| N797PA | LJ60 | 098 |
| N797QS | C650 | 7097 |
| N797R | SBRL | 282-79 |
| N797SA | GLF4 | 1081 |
| N797SC | LJ25 | 042 |
| **N797SE** | **C500** | **546** |
| N797SF | C500 | 546 |
| N797SF | C550 | 225 |
| N797SM | F2TH | 140 |
| N797T | C650 | 0197 |
| N797TA | BE40 | RK-265 |
| **N797TE** | **C550** | **550-0962** |
| N797TJ | CS55 | 0048 |
| N797WB | LJ31 | 200 |
| N797WC | C550 | 471 |
| **N797WC** | **F2TH** | **140** |
| N797WC | JSTR | 5216 |
| **N797WQ** | **JSTR** | **5216** |
| N797XJ | C750 | 0297 |
| (N798CW) | C750 | 0098 |
| **N798PA** | **HS25** | **258070** |
| N798QS | C650 | 7098 |
| N798TA | BE40 | RK-198 |
| N798XP | HS25 | 258798 |
| **N799AG** | **HS25** | **HA-0027** |
| N799BC | F2TH | 138 |
| (N799FL) | HS25 | 257111 |
| N799G | FA20 | 81 |
| (N799HF) | CL60 | 1007 |
| **N799JC** | **HS25** | **258544** |
| **N799MW** | **SBRL** | **465-42** |
| **N799RM** | **HS25** | **258708** |
| N799S | HS25 | 258019 |
| **N799S** | **HS25** | **258588** |
| N799SC | HS25 | 257068 |
| N799SC | HS25 | 258019 |
| N799SC | LJ60 | 067 |
| N799SM | BE40 | RK-220 |
| N799TA | BE40 | RK-209 |
| **N799TD** | **LJ35** | **187** |
| N799TG | C750 | 0136 |
| (N799TS) | GLEX | 9199 |
| **N799WW** | **GLEX** | **9092** |
| N799WW | GLF4 | 1059 |
| N800AB | C500 | 130 |
| N800AB | C550 | 550-0875 |
| N800AB | CL60 | 1067 |
| **N800AB** | **LJ45** | **137** |
| N800AF | HS25 | 25207 |
| **N800AF** | **HS25** | **258158** |
| N800AF | JSTR | 5101/15 |
| N800AH | HS25 | 258679 |
| N800AJ | ASTR | 081 |
| N800AJ | C525 | 0131 |
| N800AK | C550 | 550-0809 |
| N800AL | GLF4 | 1340 |
| **N800AL** | **GLF4** | **4087** |
| **N800AR** | **GLF3** | **362** |
| N800AV | C500 | 209 |
| N800AW | LJ35 | 149 |
| **N800AZ** | **EA50** | **000153** |
| "N800BA" | HS25 | 258001 |
| N800BA | HS25 | 258003 |
| N800BA | HS25 | 258046 |
| N800BA | HS25 | 258124 |
| N800BA | HS25 | 258157 |
| N800BA | HS25 | 258195 |
| N800BA | HS25 | 258223 |
| N800BA | HS25 | 258225 |
| **N800BD** | **CL30** | **20270** |
| N800BD | FA50 | 161 |
| N800BD | FA50 | 224 |
| N800BD | FA50 | 35 |
| **N800BF** | **C500** | **457** |
| (N800BG) | F2TH | 38 |
| N800BG | GLF3 | 488 |
| N800BG | GLF4 | 1034 |
| N800BH | C500 | 403 |
| (N800BJ) | HS25 | 258206 |
| N800BL | F2TH | 47 |
| N800BL | F900 | 32 |
| N800BL | LJ36 | 025 |
| N800BM | HS25 | 258155 |
| N800BN | CL64 | 5600 |
| N800BP | HS25 | 258080 |
| N800BQ | GLF4 | 1034 |
| N800BS | HS25 | 258014 |
| **N800BT** | **CL60** | **1044** |
| **N800BV** | **HS25** | **258097** |
| **N800BW** | **C560** | **0640** |
| N800CB | HS25 | 25179 |
| N800CB | HS25 | 257016 |
| N800CC | CL60 | 1080 |
| N800CC | GLF3 | 472 |
| N800CC | GLF4 | 1052 |
| **N800CC** | **HS25** | **258266** |
| N800CD | LJ35 | 335 |
| **N800CD** | **SBRL** | **380-23** |
| N800CF | FA20 | 191 |
| N800CF | FA20 | 242 |
| N800CF | FA20 | 368 |
| N800CH | LJ31 | 223 |
| N800CH | LJ35 | 335 |
| **N800CJ** | **C500** | **330** |
| N800CJ | HS25 | 258225 |
| N800CJ | HS25 | 258244 |
| **N800CK** | **LJ31** | **157** |
| N800CQ | HS25 | 258636 |
| **N800CS** | **PRM1** | **RB-62** |
| N800CS | SBRL | 282-64 |
| N800CU | SBRL | 465-24 |
| **N800CV** | **C560** | **0800** |
| **N800DA** | **HS25** | **25047** |
| N800DC | C500 | 403 |
| N800DC | FA20 | 74 |
| N800DC | FA20 | 75 |
| N800DC | SBRL | 282-102 |
| N800DJ | GLF2 | 159 |
| N800DL | C560 | 0015 |
| **N800DL** | **GLF5** | **5244** |
| N800DM | GLF2 | 159 |
| N800DN | HS25 | 258202 |
| N800DP | HS25 | 258024 |
| N800DR | HS25 | 258202 |
| N800DR | HS25 | 258478 |
| N800DR | LJ25 | 353 |
| **N800DT** | **C500** | **602** |
| N800DW | C500 | 564 |
| N800DW | FA20 | 135 |
| **N800DW** | **FA50** | **49** |
| N800DW | HS25 | 258394 |
| **N800E** | **HS25** | **257045** |
| N800EC | C550 | 219 |
| N800EC | HS25 | 258114 |
| N800EE | HS25 | 258004 |
| N800EG | FA20 | 495 |
| **N800EH** | **BE40** | **RK-322** |
| **N800EJ** | **EA50** | **000134** |
| N800EL | BE40 | RK-322 |
| N800EL | C550 | 343 |
| **N800EL** | **HS25** | **258622** |
| N800EM | HS25 | 258456 |
| **N800EM** | **HS25** | **258649** |
| N800ER | HS25 | 258394 |
| N800EX | HS25 | 258049 |
| **N800FD** | **HS25** | **258390** |
| **N800FF** | **FA20** | **406/557** |
| **N800FH** | **HS25** | **258006** |
| N800FJ | HS25 | 258090 |
| **N800FJ** | **HS25** | **258138** |
| N800FJ | HS25 | 258492 |
| N800FK | HS25 | 258133 |
| N800FK | HS25 | 258133 |
| N800FL | GLF2 | 47 |
| N800FL | GLF2 | 50 |
| **N800FL** | **HS25** | **258005** |
| **N800FM** | **C52B** | **0305** |
| N800FM | FA50 | 28 |
| N800FN | HS25 | 258090 |
| N800FR | PRM1 | RB-165 |
| N800FT | BE40 | RJ-9 |
| N800GA | GLF2 | 197 |
| **N800GA** | **LJ28** | **28-003** |
| (N800GC) | MU30 | A030SA |
| N800GD | JSTR | 5100/41 |
| **N800GD** | **JSTR** | **5219** |
| **N800GE** | **HS25** | **25206** |
| **N800GF** | **BE40** | **RK-96** |
| N800GG | HS25 | 258005 |
| N800GG | LJ25 | 008 |
| **N800GH** | **F2TH** | **89** |
| **N800GJ** | **LJ35** | **352** |
| **N800GM** | **C650** | **0077** |
| N800GN | HS25 | 258057 |
| **N800GN** | **HS25** | **258372** |
| **N800GP** | **LJ35** | **158** |
| N800GR | BE40 | RK-356 |
| (N800GT) | HS25 | 258266 |
| **N800GV** | **BE40** | **RK-271** |
| N800GW | C525 | 0276 |
| N800GX | HS25 | 258195 |
| N800HH | CL60 | 1074 |
| N800HM | BE40 | RJ-19 |
| N800HM | FA20 | 495 |
| N800HS | C525 | 0051 |
| N800HS | C525 | 0100 |
| N800HS | HS25 | 258026 |
| (N800HS) | HS25 | 258083 |
| N800HT | BE40 | RK-356 |
| **N800HT** | **BE40** | **RK-455** |
| N800J | GLF3 | 359 |
| **N800J** | **GLF4** | **1333** |
| N800J | JSTR | 5087/55 |
| (N800JA) | HS25 | 258598 |
| N800JA | LJ24 | 039 |
| N800JA | LJ25 | 042 |
| (N800JA) | LJ25 | 118 |
| N800JC | HS25 | 25201 |
| N800JD | C500 | 022 |
| N800JH | F2TH | 63 |
| N800JH | GLF3 | 312 |
| **N800JH** | **GLF5** | **5073** |
| N800JJ | WW24 | 290 |
| N800JP | HS25 | 256066 |
| **N800JR** | **EA50** | **000167** |
| (N800JS) | ASTR | 017 |
| N800JT | HS25 | 25272 |
| N800KC | C500 | 083 |
| (N800KC) | C550 | 716 |
| N800KC | CL61 | 5157 |
| N800KR | FA20 | 144 |
| N800L | LJ25 | 249 |
| N800LA | C550 | 325 |
| N800LA | HS25 | 258679 |
| N800LE | MU30 | A064SA |
| N800LF | HS25 | 258492 |
| **N800LJ** | **LJ55** | **009** |
| N800LL | HS25 | 258017 |
| **N800LL** | **HS25** | **258079** |
| **N800LM** | **HS25** | **257140** |
| **N800LQ** | **HS25** | **258551** |
| N800LR | HS25 | 258415 |
| N800LS | FA20 | 144 |
| (N800LV) | HS25 | 258155 |
| (N800LX) | HS25 | 258010 |
| (N800LX) | HS25 | 258282 |
| (N800M) | C500 | 404 |
| N800M | SBRL | 282-23 |
| N800M | SBRL | 306-143 |
| **N800M** | **SBRL** | **465-41** |
| N800MA | LJ45 | 064 |
| N800MA | LJ45 | 189 |
| N800MA | WW24 | 358 |
| N800MC | C650 | 0195 |
| N800MC | FA20 | 74 |
| N800MC | GLF2 | 61 |
| N800MD | HS25 | 258074 |
| **N800MJ** | **HS25** | **258226** |
| N800MK | ASTR | 106 |
| N800MK | GLF3 | 396 |
| N800MM | HS25 | 258014 |
| N800MN | HS25 | 258074 |
| N800MP | HS25 | 257152 |
| **N800MT** | **C550** | **550-0981** |
| N800MT | C550 | 647 |
| (N800MT) | WW24 | 372 |
| N800N | HS25 | 258003 |
| **N800NB** | **C525** | **0212** |
| (N800NE) | HS25 | 258300 |
| **N800NJ** | **HS25** | **258314** |
| N800NM | HS25 | 256027 |
| **N800NP** | **HS25** | **25239** |
| N800NS | HS25 | 258633 |
| (N800NW) | HS25 | 258019 |
| **N800NY** | **HS25** | **258254** |
| N800PA | FA20 | 74 |
| **N800PA** | **HS25** | **258162** |
| N800PB | HS25 | 258441 |
| **N800PC** | **HS25** | **258369** |
| N800PC | LJ24 | 292 |
| N800PE | HS25 | 258441 |
| **N800PE** | **HS25** | **258508** |
| **N800PF** | **C525** | **0605** |
| **N800PJ** | **GALX** | **026** |
| N800PL | C500 | 102 |
| **N800PL** | **HS25** | **258696** |
| N800PM | GLF2 | 224 |
| **N800PM** | **GLF5** | **599** |
| N800PM | HS25 | 258027 |
| **N800PP** | **FA20** | **44** |
| N800PP | HS25 | 258018 |
| **N800PW** | **ASTR** | **079** |
| N800QB | HS25 | 25179 |
| **N800QC** | **HS25** | **258174** |
| N800QS | C560 | 0598 |
| N800R | C650 | 0197 |
| **N800R** | **HS25** | **258694** |
| N800R | LJ60 | 146 |
| **N800RC** | **HS25** | **258660** |
| N800RD | HS25 | 258311 |
| N800RD | LJ35 | 213 |
| N800RD | MU30 | A027SA |
| **N800RF** | **LJ25** | **281** |
| **N800RG** | **HS25** | **258230** |
| **N800RK** | **C525** | **0158** |
| N800RL | C525 | 0158 |
| **N800RL** | **C52A** | **0220** |
| **N800RM** | **HS25** | **258001** |
| N800RM | SBRL | 306-138 |
| **N800RR** | **C550** | **088** |
| **N800RT** | **GLF2** | **47** |
| N800RY | HS25 | 258002 |
| N800S | HS25 | 258006 |
| **N800S** | **HS25** | **258082** |
| N800S | HS25 | 258093 |
| N800SB | C550 | 343 |
| N800SB | FA10 | 104 |
| **N800SD** | **BE40** | **RK-270** |
| **N800SE** | **HS25** | **258137** |
| (N800SG) | HS25 | 258390 |
| **N800SN** | **HS25** | **258043** |
| **N800SV** | **HS25** | **258217** |
| **N800TD** | **GLF3** | **452** |
| (N800TE) | GLF2 | 22 |
| N800TF | HS25 | 258045 |
| N800TG | HS25 | 25287 |
| N800TJ | HS25 | 258236 |
| N800TJ | MU30 | A022SA |
| **N800TL** | **HS25** | **258394** |
| N800TR | HS25 | 258038 |
| N800TR | HS25 | 258087 |
| N800TR | HS25 | 258111 |
| (N800TS) | BE40 | RJ-34 |
| N800TS | JSTR | 5215 |
| N800TT | HS25 | 258012 |
| N800TV | C550 | 187 |
| N800TW | C500 | 520 |
| N800TW | SBRL | 465-4 |
| N800UA | LJ45 | 064 |

| | | |
|---|---|---|
| **N800UK** | **HS25** | **258577** |
| N800UP | HS25 | 258096 |
| **N800VA** | **C550** | **550-0956** |
| N800VA | HS25 | 258425 |
| N800VC | HS25 | 258122 |
| N800VF | HS25 | 258300 |
| N800VJ | C550 | 343 |
| N800VL | C525 | 0001 |
| (N800VL) | LJ35 | 127 |
| **N800VR** | **HS25** | **258016** |
| N800VT | C525 | 0001 |
| **N800VT** | **C52A** | **0103** |
| N800VV | HS25 | 258011 |
| N800W | C500 | 014 |
| N800W | C750 | 0122 |
| **N800WA** | **HS25** | **258121** |
| N800WC | C52A | 0006 |
| N800WC | GLF3 | 392 |
| N800WC | GLF4 | 1289 |
| **N800WC** | **LJ45** | **094** |
| **N800WD** | **HS25** | **259052** |
| N800WG | HS25 | 258152 |
| **N800WH** | **HS25** | **258080** |
| N800WJ | LJ35 | 356 |
| **N800WP** | **HS25** | **258459** |
| **N800WS** | **ASTR** | **106** |
| N800WS | WW24 | 253 |
| N800WT | HS25 | 258178 |
| **N800WV** | **BE40** | **RJ-24** |
| N800WW | BE40 | RJ-24 |
| N800WW | HS25 | 258006 |
| N800WW | HS25 | 258459 |
| **N800WW** | **HS25** | **258661** |
| N800WW | WW24 | 253 |
| **N800WY** | **HS25** | **258556** |
| (N800XC) | GLF2 | 24 |
| (N800XJ) | C750 | 0300 |
| N800XL | GLF2 | 24 |
| N800XL | WW24 | 276 |
| **N800XM** | **HS25** | **258414** |
| N800XP | HS25 | 258266 |
| (N800XP) | HS25 | 258285 |
| N800XP | HS25 | 258414 |
| N800XP | HS25 | 258541 |
| N800Y | SBRL | 282-31 |
| N800Y | WW24 | 198 |
| **N800YB** | **CL61** | **5175** |
| **N800ZZ** | **ASTR** | **028** |
| N800ZZ | HS25 | 258020 |
| N801 | GLF2 | 160 |
| N801 | JSTR | 5132/57 |
| N801 | JSTR | 5138 |
| N801AB | C560 | 0158 |
| N801AB | HS25 | 258135 |
| **N801BB** | **C550** | **550-0801** |
| N801BC | HS25 | 256032 |
| N801BP | PRM1 | RB-201 |
| N801CC | C650 | 0064 |
| (N801CC) | CS55 | 0038 |
| N801CC | GLF4 | 1254 |
| N801CE | HS25 | 258253 |
| **N801CF** | **HS25** | **258185** |
| N801CR | HS25 | 258001 |
| N801CT | LJ31 | 017 |
| N801CW | HS25 | 258012 |
| **N801DL** | **FA50** | **206** |
| N801EL | C500 | 544 |
| **N801EL** | **CL30** | **20241** |
| N801F | FA20 | 4 |
| N801FL | CL61 | 5063 |
| **N801FT** | **SBRL** | **380-16** |
| **N801G** | **ASTR** | **081** |
| N801G | C550 | 110 |
| N801G | HS25 | 258017 |
| N801GA | GLF2 | 1 |
| N801GA | GLF2 | 103 |
| N801GA | GLF2 | 108 |
| N801GA | GLF2 | 173 |
| N801GA | GLF2 | 2 |
| (N801GA) | GLF2 | 241 |
| N801GC | CL61 | 3052 |
| **N801GE** | **C510** | **0112** |
| N801HB | HS25 | 258327 |
| N801JA | LJ24 | 076 |
| N801JP | C550 | 046 |
| N801JT | HS25 | 258296 |
| N801K | C500 | 236 |
| N801K | LJ35 | 462 |
| N801KT | C500 | 167 |
| N801L | C500 | 236 |
| N801L | C500 | 606 |
| (N801L) | C550 | 110 |
| N801L | LJ24 | 001 |
| **N801LM** | **HS25** | **258111** |
| (N801LX) | HS25 | 258012 |
| (N801LX) | HS25 | 258320 |
| N801MB | HS25 | 258067 |
| N801MB | HS25 | 258440 |
| (N801MD) | FA20 | 284 |
| N801MJ | GLF3 | 450 |
| N801MM | HS25 | 258067 |
| N801MM | HS25 | 258067 |
| N801MS | SBRL | 282-30 |
| N801MS | WW24 | 421 |
| N801NC | SBRL | 282-68 |
| N801NM | WW24 | 122 |
| N801NW | HS25 | 258124 |
| N801P | CL61 | 5099 |
| N801P | CL64 | 5335 |
| N801P | HS25 | 258017 |
| **N801P** | **HS25** | **258191** |
| (N801PA) | CL61 | 3044 |
| N801PF | LJ35 | 179 |
| **N801PJ** | **C525** | **0092** |
| **N801PN** | **GLEX** | **9062** |
| **N801QS** | **C560** | **0601** |
| N801R | CL61 | 5099 |
| (N801R) | HS25 | 258017 |
| N801RA | HS25 | 257100 |
| N801RJ | HS25 | 258135 |
| **N801RM** | **HS25** | **258011** |
| N801RR | HS25 | 258759 |
| **N801RS** | **ASTR** | **084** |
| **N801SA** | **PRM1** | **RB-205** |
| N801SC | C500 | 076 |
| N801SC | FA20 | 206 |
| N801SG | C500 | 076 |
| **N801SG** | **HS25** | **258762** |
| N801SM | WW24 | 297 |
| **N801SS** | **SBRL** | **465-40** |
| N801ST | HS25 | 258103 |
| (N801TA) | C550 | 489 |
| **N801TM** | **GLF5** | **5222** |
| N801WB | HS25 | 258287 |
| N801WC | GLF2 | 183 |
| N801WC | GLF3 | 392 |
| **N801WM** | **HS25** | **258503** |
| **N801WW** | **F2EX** | **21** |
| **N802AB** | **C560** | **0217** |
| **N802AG** | **GLF5** | **5245** |
| N802CB | C550 | 550-0802 |
| (N802CB) | F9EX | 89 |
| **N802CC** | **GLF2** | **187** |
| N802CC | LJ35 | 289 |
| N802CE | HS25 | 258270 |
| **N802CF** | **HS25** | **258425** |
| N802CJ | F9EX | 89 |
| (N802CW) | HS25 | 258002 |
| N802D | HS25 | 258024 |
| N802DC | HS25 | 258024 |
| N802DC | HS25 | 258257 |
| **N802DC** | **HS25** | **258562** |
| N802DR | HS25 | 258667 |
| (N802EC) | LJ35 | 453 |
| N802F | FA20 | 17 |
| N802F | FA20 | 26 |
| N802F | FA20 | 95 |
| **N802FT** | **SBRL** | **380-33** |
| N802GA | GLF2 | 2 |
| N802GA | GLF3 | 357 |
| N802H | HS25 | 259048 |
| **N802HH** | **HA4T** | **RC-2** |
| N802JA | LJ24 | 180 |
| N802JH | C525 | 0376 |
| N802JT | HS25 | 258304 |
| N802JW | LJ35 | 453 |
| N802L | LJ24 | 002 |
| (N802LX) | HS25 | 258033 |
| N802MM | HS25 | 258073 |
| **N802PA** | **CL61** | **3050** |
| N802Q | CL60 | 1010 |
| **N802Q** | **CS55** | **0157** |
| N802QS | C560 | 0606 |
| **N802QS** | **C560** | **0706** |
| N802RC | HS25 | 257125 |
| **N802RM** | **HS25** | **258013** |
| N802RR | ASTR | 260 |
| **N802RR** | **ASTR** | **263** |
| **N802SA** | **HS25** | **258045** |
| (N802SJ) | HS25 | 258167 |
| N802TA | HS25 | 258453 |
| N802TA | HS25 | 258454 |
| N802W | C750 | 0167 |
| N802W | LJ24 | 128 |
| N802WC | GLF4 | 1289 |
| N802WM | HS25 | 258307 |
| N802WM | HS25 | 258503 |
| N802X | HS25 | 258125 |
| (N803AU) | WW24 | 149 |
| N803BA | HS25 | 258003 |
| N803BF | HS25 | 257178 |
| N803BG | HS25 | 258064 |
| N803CC | GLF3 | 378 |
| N803CE | HS25 | 258271 |
| N803CJ | C560 | 0803 |
| (N803CW) | HS25 | 258603 |
| **N803D** | **HS25** | **HA-0106** |
| **N803E** | **BE40** | **RJ-16** |
| (N803EA) | C560 | 0080 |
| N803F | FA20 | 12 |
| N803F | FA20 | 492 |
| **N803FL** | **HS25** | **258455** |
| N803GA | GLF2 | 150 |
| N803GA | GLF2 | 47 |
| N803GE | HS25 | 258003 |
| N803H | HS25 | 258273 |
| N803HH | HA4T | RC-3 |
| N803JA | LJ24 | 024 |
| **N803JL** | **HS25** | **258160** |
| N803JT | HS25 | 258309 |
| N803JW | ASTR | 038 |
| N803L | LJ24 | 003 |
| N803L | LJ24 | 195 |
| N803LC | FA20 | 18 |
| N803LJ | LJ24 | 028A |
| N803LJ | LJ24 | 045A |
| N803LL | HS25 | 256045 |
| (N803LX) | HS25 | 258045 |
| (N803MM) | FA20 | 272 |
| **N803NA** | **GLF3** | **309** |
| N803PF | LJ25 | 213 |
| **N803QS** | **C560** | **0775** |
| N803QS | HS25 | 258603 |
| (N803RA) | FA10 | 80 |
| **N803RK** | **HS25** | **258003** |
| **N803RR** | **CL61** | **5073** |
| **N803SA** | **HA4T** | **RC-8** |
| **N803SC** | **C550** | **615** |
| (N803SR) | FA10 | 139 |
| N803TA | HS25 | 258455 |
| (N803TG) | GLF5 | 5243 |
| N803TJ | HS25 | 258003 |
| **N803TM** | **GLF5** | **5226** |
| N803WC | FA20 | 355 |
| N803X | HS25 | 258127 |
| **N804AC** | **HS25** | **258368** |
| **N804BC** | **C550** | **627** |
| **N804BH** | **HS25** | **258596** |
| N804CB | C550 | 550-0804 |
| N804CB | CL64 | 5526 |
| N804CC | LJ35 | 093 |
| **N804CC** | **WW24** | **305** |
| **N804CS** | **HS25** | **257093** |
| **N804CV** | **C560** | **0804** |
| N804CW | HS25 | 257004 |
| **N804D** | **HS25** | **HA-0110** |
| N804F | FA20 | 14 |
| N804F | FA20 | 30 |
| N804F | FA20 | 5 |
| N804F | FA20 | 50 |
| N804FF | HS25 | 257004 |
| N804GA | GALX | 204 |
| N804GA | GLF2 | 151/24 |
| N804GA | GLF2 | 172 |
| N804GA | GLF2 | 187 |
| N804GA | GLF2 | 87/775/6 |
| N804H | HS25 | 258274 |
| N804HB | HS25 | HB-4 |
| **N804HH** | **HA4T** | **RC-4** |
| N804JA | LJ24 | 088 |
| N804JH | F2TH | 63 |
| **N804JJ** | **FA10** | **105** |
| N804JT | HS25 | 258311 |
| N804JW | ASTR | 069 |
| N804LJ | LJ24 | 004 |
| N804LJ | LJ24 | 015A |
| (N804LX) | HS25 | 258051 |
| (N804LX) | HS25 | 258364 |
| **N804MR** | **HS25** | **258012** |
| **N804PA** | **SBRL** | **465-4** |
| N804PH | LJ25 | 361 |
| **N804QS** | **C560** | **0610** |
| N804RH | LJ25 | 361 |
| N804RM | HS25 | 258042 |
| **N804ST** | **C500** | **545** |
| N804TA | HS25 | 258461 |
| **N804TF** | **LJ35** | **404** |
| N804WA | C560 | 0277 |
| N804WC | GLF4 | 1289 |
| N804WJ | HS25 | 257199 |
| N804X | HS25 | 258128 |
| (N805AF) | HS25 | 258083 |
| N805BB | C500 | 305 |
| N805C | CL60 | 1037 |
| N805C | FA20 | 492 |
| N805CC | FA20 | 83 |
| N805CC | GLF2 | 123/25 |
| N805CD | HS25 | 257209 |
| **N805CJ** | **C525** | **0603** |
| N805CW | HS25 | 258145 |
| **N805D** | **HS25** | **HA-0113** |
| **N805DB** | **CL61** | **5161** |
| N805F | FA20 | 32 |
| N805F | FA20 | 6 |
| N805F | FA20 | 60 |
| N805GA | GALX | 205 |
| N805GA | GLF2 | 157 |
| N805GA | GLF2 | 174 |
| N805GA | GLF2 | 220 |
| N805GA | GLF5 | 5005 |
| N805GT | C650 | 0212 |
| N805H | HS25 | 258264 |
| (N805HD) | SBRL | 380-39 |
| **N805HH** | **HA4T** | **RC-5** |
| N805JA | LJ24 | 082 |
| **N805JL** | **HS25** | **258203** |
| (N805JM) | GLF4 | 1184 |
| N805JW | ASTR | 070 |
| **N805LC** | **C550** | **581** |
| N805LJ | LJ24 | 010 |
| N805LJ | LJ24 | 048 |
| (N805LX) | HS25 | 258061 |
| **N805LX** | **HS25** | **258374** |
| N805M | HS25 | 257129 |
| N805M | HS25 | 258753 |
| N805NA | LJ24 | 102 |
| N805QS | HS25 | 258505 |
| N805RG | SBRL | 380-48 |
| (N805SA) | WW24 | 145 |
| **N805SM** | **WW24** | **145** |
| N805TA | HS25 | 258466 |
| **N805VC** | **C525** | **0076** |
| **N805VZ** | **CL64** | **5410** |
| N805WC | GLF3 | 392 |
| **N805WD** | **HS25** | **25276** |
| N805X | HS25 | 258205 |
| N805Y | GLF2 | 56 |
| **N806AC** | **GLF5** | **5097** |
| N806AC | GLF5 | 622 |
| **N806AD** | **C56X** | **5743** |
| N806C | C550 | 010 |
| **N806CB** | **HS25** | **25038** |
| N806CC | GLF2 | 134 |
| N806CC | GLF2 | 204 |
| N806CC | GLF2 | 46 |
| N806CC | GLF3 | 472 |
| N806CJ | C52A | 0423 |
| N806F | FA20 | 15 |
| N806F | FA20 | 31 |
| N806F | FA20 | 490 |
| N806F | FA20 | 64 |
| N806F | FA20 | 8 |
| N806GA | ASTR | 206 |
| N806GA | GLF2 | 156/31 |
| N806GA | GLF2 | 176 |
| N806GA | GLF2 | 209 |
| N806GA | GLF2 | 232 |
| N806GA | GLF5 | 5206 |
| N806GG | BE40 | RK-343 |
| N806H | HS25 | 258265 |
| (N806HH) | HA4T | RC-6 |
| N806JH | F2TH | 63 |

| | | |
|---|---|---|
| N806LJ | LJ24 | 011 |
| **N806LJ** | **LJ24** | **073** |
| (N806LX) | HS25 | 258062 |
| **N806LX** | **HS25** | **258383** |
| N806MN | C52A | 0194 |
| N806MN | C56X | 5587 |
| **N806MN** | **C680** | **0199** |
| **N806QS** | **C560** | **0614** |
| N806TA | HS25 | 258478 |
| N806TA | HS25 | 258543 |
| N806WC | C560 | 0598 |
| N806WC | GLF2 | 183 |
| N806XM | HS25 | 258418 |
| **N807BF** | **WW24** | **194** |
| N807CC | GLF2 | 212 |
| (N807CW) | HS25 | 257001 |
| **N807DC** | **GLEX** | **9314** |
| N807F | FA10 | 114 |
| N807F | FA20 | 16 |
| N807F | FA20 | 33 |
| N807F | FA20 | 7 |
| N807F | FA20 | 71 |
| N807G | HS25 | 25121 |
| N807GA | ASTR | 207 |
| N807GA | GLF2 | 105 |
| N807GA | GLF2 | 212 |
| N807GA | GLF2 | 233 |
| N807H | HS25 | 258286 |
| N807HB | HS25 | HA-0007 |
| (N807HH) | HA4T | RC-7 |
| N807JW | ASTR | 100 |
| N807LJ | LJ24 | 018 |
| (N807LX) | HS25 | 258067 |
| **N807LX** | **HS25** | **258413** |
| **N807MB** | **C550** | **694** |
| **N807MC** | **HS25** | **258114** |
| N807PA | FA20 | 71 |
| **N807QS** | **C560** | **0617** |
| N807RH | CL64 | 5626 |
| N807TA | HS25 | 258483 |
| N807TC | HS25 | 257008 |
| N807Z | CL61 | 5040 |
| **N808AC** | **C560** | **0323** |
| N808BC | C500 | 403 |
| **N808BL** | **HS25** | **258634** |
| N808CC | HS25 | 25286 |
| N808CZ | C750 | 0010 |
| N808D | LJ24 | 138 |
| N808DM | C550 | 093 |
| N808DP | LJ24 | 138 |
| N808DP | LJ25 | 043 |
| N808DS | LJ25 | 225 |
| N808EB | SBRL | 380-51 |
| N808F | FA20 | 11 |
| N808F | FA20 | 34 |
| N808F | FA20 | 86 |
| **N808G** | **CL61** | **5098** |
| N808GA | GLF2 | 106 |
| N808GA | GLF2 | 193 |
| N808GA | GLF2 | 208 |
| N808GA | GLF2 | 231 |
| N808GA | GLF2 | 234 |
| N808H | HS25 | 258285 |
| **N808HG** | **CL61** | **5157** |
| (N808HH) | HA4T | RC-8 |
| N808HS | C525 | 0051 |
| (N808HS) | C525 | 0100 |
| N808HT | BE40 | RK-356 |
| N808JA | LJ24 | 050A |
| N808JW | GALX | 010 |
| N808KS | LJ45 | 305 |
| N808L | FA10 | 200 |
| N808LJ | LJ24 | 050A |
| (N808LX) | HS25 | 258077 |
| (N808LX) | HS25 | 258428 |
| **N808MF** | **GLF4** | **1448** |
| N808ML | LJ60 | 003 |
| **N808MN** | **C56X** | **5587** |
| **N808PL** | **C560** | **0798** |
| **N808QS** | **C560** | **0619** |
| **N808RD** | **C510** | **0086** |
| N808RP | HS25 | 256041 |
| N808RP | JSTR | 5215 |
| **N808SK** | **LJ60** | **008** |
| N808T | GLF3 | 463 |
| **N808T** | **GLF4** | **1342** |
| N808TA | HS25 | 258494 |
| N808TA | HS25 | 258548 |
| **N808TH** | **C560** | **0378** |
| N808TM | CL60 | 1020 |
| N808V | HS25 | 25238 |
| **N808V** | **PRM1** | **RB-5** |
| **N808VA** | **C650** | **7057** |
| **N808W** | **LJ31** | **165** |
| N808W | PRM1 | RB-25 |
| **N808WA** | **C525** | **0290** |
| N808WC | C680 | 0030 |
| **N808WG** | **LJ60** | **112** |
| **N809BA** | **HS25** | **258388** |
| N809C | GLF4 | 1450 |
| N809F | FA10 | 182 |
| N809F | FA20 | 35 |
| N809F | FA20 | 393 |
| N809F | FA20 | 9 |
| N809GA | GALX | 209 |
| N809GA | GLF2 | 107 |
| N809GA | GLF2 | 47 |
| N809H | HS25 | 258268 |
| N809HB | HS25 | HA-0009 |
| (N809HH) | HA4T | RC-9 |
| **N809JC** | **WW24** | **298** |
| **N809JW** | **ASTR** | **135** |
| N809LJ | LJ24 | 055 |
| N809LS | GLF2 | 47 |
| (N809LX) | HS25 | 258124 |
| N809LX | HS25 | 258432 |
| N809M | HS25 | 257081 |
| N809P | FA20 | 35 |
| **N809QS** | **C560** | **0698** |
| N809QS | HS25 | 258611 |
| N809R | LJ60 | 146 |
| N809RM | PRM1 | RB-45 |
| N809TA | HS25 | 258388 |
| N809TA | HS25 | 258498 |
| (N809TP) | HS25 | 258388 |
| N809VC | WW24 | 264 |
| N810AA | HS25 | 258023 |
| **N810AF** | **HS25** | **258589** |
| **N810BA** | **HS25** | **258010** |
| N810BG | HS25 | 258010 |
| N810CC | LJ35 | 486 |
| **N810CC** | **WW24** | **264** |
| N810CR | HS25 | 25241 |
| N810CR | HS25 | 257071 |
| N810CV | C560 | 0810 |
| N810CW | HS25 | 258010 |
| N810D | CL61 | 5075 |
| **N810D** | **CL64** | **5331** |
| N810E | FA10 | 60 |
| N810F | FA20 | 10 |
| N810F | FA20 | 151 |
| N810F | FA20 | 36 |
| N810GA | GLF2 | 108 |
| N810GA | GLF2 | 165/37 |
| N810GA | GLF2 | 191 |
| N810GA | GLF2 | 224 |
| N810GS | HS25 | 257061 |
| **N810GT** | **CL64** | **5600** |
| (N810HH) | HA4T | RC-10 |
| N810HS | HS25 | 25271 |
| (N810J) | FA10 | 139 |
| N810JT | C550 | 289 |
| **N810JW** | **ASTR** | **138** |
| **N810KB** | **HS25** | **257118** |
| **N810LP** | **GLF4** | **1260** |
| N810LX | HS25 | 258145 |
| (N810M) | F9EX | 33 |
| N810M | HS25 | 257102 |
| (N810MB) | CL61 | 3026 |
| N810MC | C550 | 225 |
| N810MC | HS25 | 25201 |
| N810ME | WW24 | 372 |
| (N810MG) | C550 | 225 |
| N810MT | CL60 | 1024 |
| N810MT | CL61 | 3026 |
| N810MT | WW24 | 372 |
| (N810MY) | GLF2 | 134 |
| N810N | HS25 | 258460 |
| N810PA | FA20 | 151 |
| **N810PF** | **C52A** | **0399** |
| **N810QS** | **C560** | **0625** |
| N810RA | FA20 | 81 |
| N810SC | C550 | 032 |
| N810SC | HS25 | 257179 |
| N810SG | C550 | 032 |
| **N810SS** | **C525** | **0137** |
| N810TA | HS25 | 258510 |
| **N810TM** | **GLF4** | **1483** |
| N810US | FA10 | 53 |
| N810V | CS55 | 0149 |
| N810V | HS25 | 257058 |
| N810V | HS25 | 258224 |
| N810V | LJ55 | 133 |
| **N810VC** | **WW24** | **321** |
| N810X | C750 | 0081 |
| **N810Y** | **LJ60** | **183** |
| N810YS | LJ45 | 102 |
| (N811) | JSTR | 5227 |
| N811AA | FA20 | 187 |
| N811AA | HS25 | 258024 |
| **N811AG** | **F2TH** | **71** |
| **N811AM** | **HS25** | **258172** |
| N811AV | F2TH | 71 |
| N811AV | F9EX | 74 |
| N811BB | CL61 | 5039 |
| N811BB | CL64 | 5333 |
| N811BP | CL61 | 5039 |
| N811BP | CL64 | 5405 |
| **N811BP** | **LJ45** | **010** |
| N811BR | CL61 | 5039 |
| N811CC | HS25 | 258267 |
| N811CP | LJ31 | 168 |
| N811CW | HS25 | 258011 |
| N811DD | LJ35 | 384 |
| **N811DE** | **GLF2** | **244** |
| N811DF | GLF2 | 244 |
| **N811DF** | **GLF4** | **1306** |
| N811DF | LJ35 | 384 |
| N811DJ | MU30 | A022SA |
| N811GA | GLF2 | 109 |
| N811GA | GLF2 | 166/15 |
| N811GA | GLF2 | 192 |
| **N811GA** | **GLF5** | **5011** |
| N811HL | C500 | 503 |
| N811JA | HS25 | 25176 |
| N811JK | GLF3 | 434 |
| N811JK | GLF4 | 1030 |
| N811JK | GLF4 | 1140 |
| N811JT | C650 | 0204 |
| **N811JW** | **ASTR** | **140** |
| N811JW | CL61 | 5063 |
| (N811LX) | HS25 | 258282 |
| (N811ML) | LJ35 | 256 |
| **N811MT** | **CL60** | **1024** |
| N811PA | FA20 | 196 |
| N811PD | LJ25 | 138 |
| N811PS | LJ31 | 166 |
| **N811QS** | **HS25** | **258614** |
| **N811RA** | **LJ60** | **264** |
| N811RC | C52A | 0058 |
| **N811RG** | **CS55** | **0061** |
| **N811ST** | **C56X** | **5193** |
| (N811SW) | GLF4 | 1170 |
| N811TA | HS25 | 258516 |
| N811TY | F2TH | 71 |
| N811VC | C550 | 062 |
| **N811VC** | **WW24** | **331** |
| **N811VG** | **C550** | **062** |
| N811WW | GLF4 | 1121 |
| N812AA | FA20 | 57 |
| N812AA | HS25 | 258027 |
| N812AM | FA10 | 210 |
| **N812AM** | **HS25** | **258147** |
| **N812CV** | **C560** | **0812** |
| **N812DC** | **C560** | **0541** |
| **N812G** | **CL64** | **5330** |
| N812G | WW24 | 389 |
| N812GA | GLF2 | 168 |
| N812GA | GLF2 | 236 |
| N812GA | GLF4 | 4012 |
| N812GA | GLF5 | 5012 |
| **N812GJ** | **HS25** | **258112** |
| N812GS | CL61 | 5098 |
| **N812HA** | **CS55** | **0054** |
| **N812HF** | **C52B** | **0262** |
| N812JM | C52B | 0102 |
| N812KC | FA10 | 189 |
| N812KD | C750 | 0246 |
| N812LJ | LJ24 | 038 |
| N812LJ | LJ24 | 077 |
| (N812LX) | HS25 | 258296 |
| **N812LX** | **HS25** | **258437** |
| N812M | HS25 | 25052 |
| N812M | HS25 | 257081 |
| N812M | WW24 | 389 |
| **N812MJ** | **EA50** | **000108** |
| N812MM | LJ25 | 357 |
| N812N | HS25 | 25052 |
| N812PA | FA20 | 125 |
| **N812QS** | **C560** | **0628** |
| N812RS | GLF2 | 98/38 |
| (N812SS) | CL30 | 20138 |
| N812TA | HS25 | 258522 |
| N812TT | HS25 | 25046 |
| N812WN | SBRL | 465-25 |
| (N812XL) | CL60 | 1016 |
| N812XP | HS25 | 258812 |
| N813A | C550 | 562 |
| N813AA | FA20 | 25/405 |
| N813AA | HS25 | 258029 |
| **N813AS** | **LJ35** | **167** |
| N813AV | FA10 | 28 |
| N813BR | SBRL | 306-8 |
| N813CB | C550 | 550-0813 |
| **N813CJ** | **C560** | **0813** |
| N813CW | HS25 | 258413 |
| N813DH | C550 | 142 |
| N813DH | C56X | 5700 |
| N813GH | F2TH | 125 |
| N813H | HS25 | 257009 |
| **N813JD** | **C550** | **550-0838** |
| N813JW | LJ25 | 038 |
| N813LS | FA20 | 185/467 |
| **N813LS** | **GLF3** | **443** |
| (N813LX) | HS25 | 258320 |
| N813LX | HS25 | 258454 |
| N813M | LJ35 | 151 |
| N813MK | FA20 | 272 |
| **N813MK** | **GLF3** | **407** |
| N813P | FA20 | 121 |
| N813P | JSTR | 5222 |
| N813PA | FA20 | 121 |
| N813PR | HS25 | 25137 |
| N813QS | C560 | 0631 |
| **N813QS** | **GLF5** | **5160** |
| N813RR | LJ35 | 391 |
| N813SQ | GLEX | 9009 |
| N813TA | HS25 | 258527 |
| N813TS | F900 | 133 |
| **N813VC** | **HS25** | **257013** |
| N813VZ | CL61 | 5160 |
| (N814AA) | FA10 | 157 |
| N814AA | FA20 | 31 |
| **N814AM** | **C550** | **413** |
| **N814BP** | **PRM1** | **RB-214** |
| N814CC | CS55 | 0018 |
| N814CE | JSTR | 5217 |
| N814CM | C560 | 0170 |
| **N814D** | **HS25** | **25237** |
| **N814DM** | **C525** | **0376** |
| N814ER | C500 | 280 |
| **N814ER** | **FA20** | **66** |
| N814ER | HS25 | 25170 |
| N814GA | GLF2 | 110 |
| N814GA | GLF2 | 44 |
| **N814GF** | **LJ60** | **085** |
| N814HH | LJ24 | 202 |
| N814JR | LJ24 | 202 |
| N814K | JSTR | 5204 |
| N814K | WW24 | 106 |
| N814L | LJ24 | 014 |
| N814LJ | LJ24 | 069 |
| (N814LX) | HS25 | 258322 |
| N814M | F900 | 155 |
| N814M | HS25 | 25196 |
| N814M | LJ35 | 077 |
| N814NA | JSTR | 5003 |
| N814P | HS25 | 25148 |
| N814PA | FA20 | 202 |
| (N814PJ) | FA10 | 225 |
| N814PS | CL61 | 5159 |
| N814PS | CL64 | 5309 |
| **N814PS** | **CL64** | **5544** |
| (N814QS) | C560 | 0638 |
| N814QS | C560 | 0644 |
| **N814QS** | **C560** | **0776** |
| **N814T** | **WW24** | **106** |
| N814TA | HS25 | 258529 |
| **N814WS** | **C510** | **0032** |
| N815A | LJ31 | 118 |
| N815A | LJ35 | 142 |
| N815A | LJ45 | 074 |

| Registration | Type | c/n |
|---|---|---|
| N815AA | FA20 | 205 |
| N815AA | HS25 | 258032 |
| N815AC | FA20 | 206 |
| N815BC | WW24 | 301 |
| (N815BS) | BE40 | RJ-30 |
| N815CA | FA50 | 6 |
| N815CC | HS25 | 258100 |
| **N815CE** | **C550** | **239** |
| N815CJ | C560 | 0815 |
| **N815CM** | **C560** | **0104** |
| **N815DD** | **LJ35** | **414** |
| **N815E** | **LJ31** | **118** |
| N815GA | GLF2 | 111 |
| N815GA | GLF2 | 45 |
| N815GA | GLF4 | 4115 |
| N815GK | C550 | 228 |
| N815H | CS55 | 0146 |
| N815HC | C500 | 005 |
| N815J | LJ25 | 045 |
| **N815JW** | **GALX** | **053** |
| N815L | LJ35 | 142 |
| N815LC | FA10 | 46 |
| N815LJ | LJ24 | 067 |
| N815LP | C52B | 0307 |
| (N815LX) | HS25 | 258337 |
| **N815MA** | **C550** | **398** |
| **N815MC** | **C525** | **0142** |
| N815PA | CL64 | 5511 |
| **N815PA** | **GLEX** | **9305** |
| **N815QS** | **HS25** | **258705** |
| N815RA | CL64 | 5511 |
| N815RB | LJ35 | 647 |
| N815RC | JSTR | 5226 |
| N815RC | WW24 | 301 |
| N815RK | WW24 | 416 |
| N815TA | HS25 | 258534 |
| **N815TR** | **HS25** | **257104** |
| **N815WT** | **EA50** | **000119** |
| N816AA | FA20 | 290 |
| N816AA | HS25 | 258035 |
| N816CC | CL64 | 5451 |
| **N816CS** | **C56X** | **5153** |
| **N816CW** | **C510** | **0079** |
| N816CW | HS25 | 258016 |
| **N816DC** | **GLEX** | **9025** |
| **N816DK** | **BE40** | **RK-291** |
| **N816FC** | **C525** | **0059** |
| N816GA | GLF2 | 112 |
| N816GA | GLF2 | 215 |
| N816GA | GLF2 | 237/43 |
| N816GA | GLF4 | 4016 |
| N816GS | GLF4 | 1225 |
| N816H | HS25 | 258288 |
| N816H | WW24 | 323 |
| N816HB | ASTR | 028 |
| (N816JA) | LJ25 | 091 |
| N816JA | LJ35 | 394 |
| N816JA | WW24 | 328 |
| **N816JM** | **HS25** | **257011** |
| **N816JW** | **GALX** | **097** |
| **N816KD** | **EA50** | **000003** |
| N816LJ | LJ24 | 088 |
| N816LL | C500 | 411 |
| N816LP | LJ45 | 327 |
| **N816LX** | **HS25** | **258363** |
| N816M | FA50 | 99 |
| N816M | HS25 | 25052 |
| N816M | LJ35 | 030 |
| N816MC | HS25 | 25052 |
| **N816MC** | **LJ55** | **035** |
| **N816MG** | **GLF5** | **5187** |
| N816PD | CL60 | 1069 |
| **N816QS** | **HS25** | **258416** |
| N816RD | JSTR | 5218 |
| (N816S) | MU30 | A022SA |
| N816S | WW24 | 360 |
| **N816SE** | **HS25** | **HA-0055** |
| N816SG | GLEX | 9106 |
| N816SP | CL61 | 5030 |
| N816SQ | CL61 | 5030 |
| N816SQ | GLEX | 9009 |
| N816SQ | GLEX | 9106 |
| N816SR | GLEX | 9009 |
| N816ST | WW24 | 360 |
| N816TA | HS25 | 258538 |
| N816V | CS55 | 0149 |
| N817AA | FA20 | 233 |
| N817AA | HS25 | 258036 |
| **N817AM** | **LJ55** | **069** |
| N817AM | LJ55 | 082 |
| N817BD | JSTR | 5083/49 |
| N817BD | LJ31 | 094 |
| **N817BT** | **C525** | **0635** |
| N817CB | C550 | 550-0817 |
| N817CJ | C525 | 0174 |
| N817CK | CL60 | 1069 |
| N817GA | GLF2 | 113 |
| N817GA | GLF2 | 222 |
| **N817GR** | **MU30** | **A062SA** |
| N817H | HS25 | 258279 |
| N817JS | FA20 | 181 |
| N817LS | GLEX | 9035 |
| (N817LX) | HS25 | 258364 |
| N817LX | HS25 | 258516 |
| N817M | FA50 | 24 |
| **N817MB** | **C650** | **7012** |
| **N817ME** | **GLF4** | **1446** |
| **N817MF** | **GLF3** | **466** |
| N817MQ | C650 | 7015 |
| N817MZ | C650 | 7055 |
| **N817PD** | **C560** | **0075** |
| **N817QS** | **HS25** | **258517** |
| N817TA | HS25 | 258552 |
| **N817X** | **FA7X** | **51** |
| N818 | HS25 | 257020 |
| N818AA | FA20 | 36 |
| N818AA | HS25 | 258039 |
| N818AJ | C550 | 550-0818 |
| **N818BA** | **GLF4** | **1017** |
| (N818CD) | C500 | 297 |
| N818CD | C500 | 311 |
| **N818CH** | **LJ45** | **394** |
| N818CH | LJ45 | 398 |
| **N818CK** | **LJ25** | **118** |
| N818CP | FA20 | 71 |
| **N818CR** | **GALX** | **024** |
| N818DA | GLF2 | 208 |
| N818DA | GLF5 | 520 |
| **N818DD** | **GLF3** | **455** |
| **N818DE** | **C650** | **0121** |
| N818DW | SBRL | 380-30 |
| (N818E) | CL60 | 1069 |
| N818ER | C525 | 0503 |
| N818FH | GLEX | 9180 |
| **N818G** | **GLF4** | **4070** |
| N818G | HS25 | 258186 |
| N818GA | GLF2 | 114 |
| N818GA | GLF2 | 227 |
| (N818GY) | LJ25 | 116 |
| **N818HK** | **GLF5** | **5109** |
| **N818JH** | **WW24** | **341** |
| **N818JW** | **GALX** | **121** |
| **N818KC** | **CL30** | **20043** |
| N818KC | HS25 | 257009 |
| **N818KF** | **FA50** | **277** |
| **N818LD** | **HS25** | **257192** |
| N818LD | SBRL | 380-30 |
| N818LJ | LJ24 | 028 |
| **N818LJ** | **LJ31** | **019** |
| N818LS | CL60 | 1047 |
| N818LS | CL61 | 5090 |
| N818LS | CL64 | 5315 |
| N818LS | FA20 | 185/467 |
| N818LS | GLEX | 9035 |
| (N818LX) | HS25 | 258374 |
| **N818LX** | **HS25** | **258534** |
| **N818ME** | **GLF4** | **1431** |
| N818MV | HS25 | 258186 |
| **N818QS** | **C560** | **0778** |
| N818R | C500 | 170 |
| **N818RC** | **CL30** | **20165** |
| **N818RF** | **GLF5** | **5018** |
| **N818SE** | **C650** | **0207** |
| N818SH | FA20 | 71 |
| (N818SL) | CL64 | 5391 |
| N818SS | GLF3 | 342 |
| **N818SS** | **GLF4** | **1302** |
| N818TB | C550 | 460 |
| N818TG | HS25 | 258018 |
| N818TH | CL60 | 1069 |
| N818TH | CL61 | 5046 |
| N818TH | CL61 | 5090 |
| **N818TH** | **CL64** | **5315** |
| **N818TJ** | **GLF3** | **384** |
| N818TP | C550 | 460 |
| (N818TP) | C650 | 0120 |
| N818TP | HS25 | 256026 |
| N818TS | GLEX | 9018 |
| N818TY | CL61 | 5046 |
| **N818WF** | **ASTR** | **091** |
| **N818WM** | **HS25** | **258126** |
| N818WS | LJ35 | 285 |
| N819AA | FA20 | 26 |
| N819AA | HS25 | 258041 |
| N819AB | HS25 | 258559 |
| N819AP | GALX | 109 |
| **N819AP** | **GALX** | **191** |
| N819AP | HS25 | 258559 |
| **N819CW** | **C52B** | **0331** |
| N819DM | HS25 | 257144 |
| N819GA | GLF2 | 115 |
| N819GA | GLF2 | 17 |
| N819GA | GLF2 | 178 |
| N819GA | GLF2 | 228 |
| N819GA | GLF4 | 4119 |
| N819GF | LJ24 | 230 |
| N819GY | LJ25 | 116 |
| **N819GY** | **SBRL** | **380-66** |
| N819H | C500 | 263 |
| N819JA | WW24 | 328 |
| N819JE | LJ35 | 077 |
| "N819JF" | GLF4 | 1414 |
| **N819JR** | **HS25** | **HA-0065** |
| **N819KR** | **C550** | **126** |
| (N819LX) | HS25 | 258383 |
| **N819LX** | **HS25** | **258543** |
| N819M | HS25 | 257170 |
| (N819P) | HS25 | 25148 |
| **N819QS** | **C560** | **0786** |
| **N819RC** | **WW24** | **192** |
| **N819VE** | **GALX** | **109** |
| **N819WG** | **HS25** | **257010** |
| N819Y | C550 | 311 |
| N820 | C500 | 310 |
| N820 | C550 | 239 |
| N820AA | FA20 | 118 |
| N820AA | HS25 | 258042 |
| **N820AV** | **GLF4** | **4002** |
| N820BA | GLF3 | 422 |
| N820CB | C550 | 550-0820 |
| N820CE | C525 | 0368 |
| N820CE | FA10 | 111 |
| N820CT | HS25 | 257041 |
| N820DY | SBRL | 380-40 |
| (N820F) | C650 | 0183 |
| N820F | CS55 | 0118 |
| N820FJ | C500 | 310 |
| N820FJ | C550 | 299 |
| **N820FJ** | **C650** | **0183** |
| N820FJ | CS55 | 0118 |
| **N820GA** | **GLF4** | **4200** |
| N820GA | GLF5 | 5100 |
| N820GA | HS25 | 258011 |
| **N820HB** | **GLF4** | **1024** |
| N820JM | C550 | 550-0856 |
| N820JM | C550 | 550-0885 |
| N820JR | SBRL | 282-135 |
| **N820L** | **LJ24** | **020** |
| (N820LX) | HS25 | 258397 |
| **N820M** | **HS25** | **258774** |
| N820M | LJ25 | 342 |
| **N820MC** | **C550** | **117** |
| N820MC | HS25 | 25211 |
| **N820MG** | **HS25** | **25211** |
| (N820MQ) | C550 | 117 |
| **N820MS** | **GLF4** | **1147** |
| N820QS | C560 | 0648 |
| **N820QS** | **C560** | **0650** |
| N820RP | LJ35 | 410 |
| (N820RT) | LJ25 | 023 |
| (N820RT) | WW24 | 157 |
| N820SA | C550 | 299 |
| N820TA | HS25 | 258555 |
| **N820TM** | **GLF4** | **1508** |
| N821AA | FA20 | 203 |
| N821AA | FA20 | 67/414 |
| N821AA | HS25 | 258044 |
| **N821AM** | **GLEX** | **9183** |
| **N821AV** | **GLF4** | **4003** |
| N821AW | LJ25 | 101 |
| N821BS | FA50 | 23 |
| N821BS | LJ45 | 227 |
| N821CC | LJ60 | 208 |
| N821DG | C56X | 5206 |
| N821DG | C56X | 5297 |
| N821G | C550 | 604 |
| N821GA | GLF2 | 116 |
| N821GA | GLF2 | 229 |
| N821GA | GLF2 | 250 |
| **N821GA** | **GLF4** | **4121** |
| N821GA | GLF5 | 5101 |
| N821H | WW24 | 268 |
| N821LG | FA10 | 170 |
| N821LG | WW24 | 430 |
| (N821LL) | LJ24 | 216 |
| N821LM | LJ25 | 317 |
| **N821LX** | **HS25** | **258406** |
| N821MD | JSTR | 5211 |
| (N821MS) | LJ25 | 121 |
| **N821ND** | **C510** | **0038** |
| N821P | C525 | 0354 |
| **N821PA** | **GLF2** | **183** |
| N821PC | LJ35 | 486 |
| **N821QS** | **HS25** | **258709** |
| N821VP | C560 | 0121 |
| **N822A** | **GLF4** | **1447** |
| **N822AA** | **FA20** | **195** |
| N822AA | HS25 | 258045 |
| N822BD | HS25 | 256067 |
| N822BL | HS25 | 256067 |
| **N822BL** | **HS25** | **258022** |
| N822CA | GLF2 | 99 |
| N822CA | LJ35 | 591 |
| N822CA | LJ45 | 215 |
| N822CA | LJ45 | 224 |
| N822CB | C550 | 550-0822 |
| N822CC | HS25 | 25142 |
| N822CP | LJ35 | 591 |
| **N822DS** | **C680** | **0121** |
| N822GA | GLF2 | 117 |
| N822GA | GLF2 | 257/17 |
| N822GA | GLF5 | 5102 |
| N822GA | LJ45 | 224 |
| **N822HA** | **C550** | **464** |
| N822LJ | LJ24 | 080 |
| (N822LX) | HS25 | 258413 |
| **N822MC** | **LJ55** | **018** |
| N822MJ | C56X | 5023 |
| **N822QS** | **C560** | **0789** |
| N822QS | HS25 | 258422 |
| (N822SF) | LJ35 | 590 |
| **N822ST** | **F2EX** | **66** |
| N822TP | F2TH | 20 |
| N822XP | HS25 | 258822 |
| **N823AA** | **FA20** | **228/473** |
| N823AA | HS25 | 258046 |
| N823BJ | F900 | 107 |
| N823CA | LJ35 | 600 |
| **N823CA** | **LJ45** | **221** |
| (N823CB) | C550 | 550-0823 |
| **N823CE** | **C560** | **0823** |
| N823CP | LJ35 | 600 |
| N823CT | C550 | 650 |
| (N823CW) | HS25 | 258623 |
| **N823DF** | **GLEX** | **9066** |
| N823ES | C525 | 0066 |
| **N823ET** | **BE40** | **RK-360** |
| N823GA | GLF2 | 118 |
| N823GA | GLF2 | 188 |
| N823GA | GLF2 | 258 |
| N823GA | GLF2 | 75/7 |
| **N823GA** | **GLF4** | **1005** |
| N823J | LJ35 | 171 |
| **N823L** | **C52A** | **0020** |
| N823LJ | LJ24 | 082A |
| (N823LX) | HS25 | 258428 |
| (N823LX) | HS25 | 258648 |
| **N823M** | **C510** | **0228** |
| N823M | LJ24 | 050 |
| **N823NA** | **C550** | **260** |
| **N823PM** | **C550** | **550-1064** |
| **N823QS** | **C560** | **0794** |
| N823TR | LJ60 | 068 |
| N823TT | BE40 | RK-278 |
| **N823WB** | **C560** | **0124** |
| N823XP | HS25 | 258823 |
| N824AA | HS25 | 258047 |
| N824CA | GLF4 | 1010 |
| N824CA | GLF4 | 1309 |
| **N824CB** | **C550** | **550-0824** |
| **N824CC** | **LJ55** | **024** |
| N824CT | C550 | 650 |

| | | |
|---|---|---|
| N824CW | HS25 | 258124 |
| **N824DH** | **CL61** | **3047** |
| **N824DS** | **FA10** | **92** |
| **N824DW** | **MU30** | **A075SA** |
| **N824ES** | **C525** | **0066** |
| N824GA | GALX | 224 |
| N824GA | GLF2 | 119/22 |
| N824GA | GLF2 | 77 |
| N824GA | GLF5 | 5104 |
| N824GA | LJ24 | 342 |
| N824GB | BE40 | RK-371 |
| **N824HG** | **BE40** | **RK-143** |
| N824JK | CL61 | 5118 |
| N824JM | BE40 | RK-96 |
| N824K | HS25 | 257111 |
| **N824LA** | **FA10** | **53** |
| N824LJ | LJ24 | 083 |
| (N824LX) | HS25 | 258432 |
| **N824LX** | **HS25** | **258740** |
| **N824MG** | **LJ55** | **106** |
| **N824QS** | **HS25** | **258523** |
| N824R | FA50 | 121 |
| N824SS | BE40 | RJ-18 |
| N824TJ | HS25 | 25179 |
| N825A | LJ25 | 111 |
| N825AA | HS25 | 258049 |
| N825AA | LJ24 | 147 |
| N825AC | LJ31 | 058 |
| N825AM | LJ24 | 340 |
| N825CA | LJ35 | 605 |
| **N825CA** | **LJ45** | **220** |
| **N825CP** | **HS25** | **258329** |
| N825CT | HS25 | 257041 |
| **N825CT** | **HS25** | **258497** |
| N825D | LJ25 | 263 |
| N825DA | HS25 | 258167 |
| N825DM | LJ24 | 237 |
| (N825EC) | WW24 | 403 |
| N825GA | C525 | 0027 |
| **N825GA** | **C750** | **0143** |
| N825GA | GLF2 | 119/22 |
| N825GA | GLF2 | 120 |
| N825GA | GLF2 | 198/35 |
| N825HL | C500 | 657 |
| N825HL | CS55 | 0088 |
| N825JL | WW24 | 307 |
| N825JV | C550 | 296 |
| N825JW | C550 | 296 |
| **N825JW** | **C650** | **0082** |
| N825LJ | LJ24 | 008 |
| N825LJ | LJ24 | 085 |
| **N825LJ** | **LJ35** | **496** |
| (N825LM) | GLF4 | 1460 |
| **N825LM** | **GLF5** | **655** |
| (N825LX) | HS25 | 258437 |
| **N825LX** | **HS25** | **258767** |
| N825MG | LJ55 | 055 |
| **N825MS** | **HS25** | **257151** |
| **N825PS** | **C500** | **630** |
| N825PS | HS25 | 258117 |
| **N825QS** | **C560** | **0655** |
| **N825SB** | **SBRL** | **282-92** |
| **N825T** | **GLF4** | **1535** |
| **N825TB** | **CL30** | **20234** |
| N825TC | FA20 | 52 |
| N825XP | HS25 | 258425 |
| **N826AA** | **FA20** | **67/414** |
| N826AA | HS25 | 258051 |
| **N826AC** | **C560** | **0242** |
| N826AG | C56X | 6029 |
| N826AG | GLF2 | 166/15 |
| N826CA | LJ35 | 596 |
| **N826CA** | **LJ45** | **222** |
| N826CM | C510 | 0126 |
| N826CP | LJ35 | 596 |
| **N826CS** | **C52B** | **0229** |
| N826CT | HS25 | 258117 |
| N826CW | HS25 | 258026 |
| N826EW | C550 | 622 |
| **N826EW** | **F2TH** | **58** |
| N826GA | GLF2 | 166/15 |
| N826GA | GLF2 | 200 |
| N826GA | GLF2 | 79 |
| **N826GA** | **HS25** | **258263** |
| **N826GW** | **GLF2** | **210** |
| **N826HS** | **C525** | **0305** |
| **N826JH** | **BE40** | **RK-70** |
| N826JH | MU30 | A050SA |
| N826JP | CL61 | 5050 |
| N826JS | CL64 | 5587 |
| **N826K** | **F9EX** | **36** |
| N826K | HS25 | 257119 |
| **N826KR** | **F2TH** | **182** |
| N826L | LJ24 | 007 |
| (N826LX) | HS25 | 258454 |
| **N826LX** | **HS25** | **258826** |
| **N826QS** | **C560** | **0782** |
| N826RD | C500 | 290 |
| N826RD | LJ35 | 509 |
| N826RP | C650 | 0206 |
| **N826RP** | **GLF4** | **1507** |
| **N826RT** | **C550** | **312** |
| N826SR | LJ60 | 230 |
| N826SS | LJ60 | 015 |
| (N826SU) | HS25 | 258249 |
| **N826TG** | **PRM1** | **RB-258** |
| **N827AA** | **FA20** | **298** |
| N827CA | LJ35 | 590 |
| N827CR | LJ35 | 332 |
| **N827CT** | **FA50** | **245** |
| **N827DC** | **C680** | **0027** |
| **N827DK** | **C510** | **0018** |
| **N827DP** | **C550** | **660** |
| N827G | GLF3 | 398 |
| N827GA | GLF2 | 80 |
| N827GA | GLF3 | 398 |
| **N827GA** | **GLF4** | **1391** |
| N827JB | C550 | 577 |
| N827JB | C550 | 604 |
| (N827JK) | GLF4 | 1140 |
| N827JM | GLF4 | 1140 |
| N827K | GLF2 | 221 |
| N827K | GLF4 | 1180 |
| (N827LX) | HS25 | 258455 |
| **N827LX** | **HS25** | **258848** |
| N827NS | HS25 | 258409 |
| **N827QS** | **C560** | **0801** |
| N827RH | HS25 | 258224 |
| **N827SA** | **HS25** | **258438** |
| **N827SB** | **BE40** | **RK-2** |
| N827SL | SBRL | 380-53 |
| (N827TV) | C560 | 0684 |
| N828AA | FA20 | 31 |
| **N828AF** | **CS55** | **0067** |
| N828AN | HS25 | 257046 |
| N828B | C550 | 346 |
| N828C | ASTR | 055 |
| **N828CA** | **LJ45** | **159** |
| **N828CK** | **C56X** | **5201** |
| N828CW | HS25 | 258428 |
| N828G | C650 | 0138 |
| N828GA | GLF2 | 247 |
| N828GA | GLF5 | 5108 |
| N828GA | GLF5 | 5228 |
| N828GA? | GLF2 | 81 |
| N828KC | HS25 | 257009 |
| **N828KD** | **CL64** | **5584** |
| **N828LX** | **HS25** | **258461** |
| N828M | LJ24 | 050 |
| N828M | LJ35 | 063 |
| N828MG | GLF3 | 409 |
| N828MW | LJ24 | 050 |
| **N828NS** | **HS25** | **258464** |
| **N828PA** | **EA50** | **000237** |
| **N828PJ** | **HS25** | **257005** |
| N828QA | LJ25 | 052 |
| **N828QS** | **HS25** | **258528** |
| (N828SA) | HS25 | 257002 |
| (N828SH) | C550 | 275 |
| N828SK | CL61 | 5018 |
| **N828SS** | **C550** | **181** |
| N828WB | CS55 | 0097 |
| **N829AA** | **LJ25** | **100** |
| N829CA | LJ35 | 459 |
| **N829CB** | **C550** | **550-0829** |
| N829GA | GLF2 | 199/19 |
| N829GA | GLF2 | 245/30 |
| N829GA | GLF5 | 5109 |
| **N829GA** | **GLF5** | **5293** |
| N829JC | C56X | 5291 |
| **N829JC** | **C680** | **0112** |
| N829JC | CS55 | 0059 |
| N829JM | C550 | 215 |
| N829JQ | C56X | 5291 |
| **N829LX** | **HS25** | **258466** |
| N829MG | GLF3 | 327 |
| N829NL | C550 | 037 |
| **N829NL** | **GLF2** | **128** |
| **N829NS** | **HS25** | **258475** |
| **N829QS** | **C560** | **0796** |
| **N830** | **WW24** | **406** |
| N830 | WW24 | 442 |
| N830AA | FA20 | 55/410 |
| **N830BA** | **HS25** | **258122** |
| N830BH | GLF2 | 49 |
| **N830C** | **WW24** | **442** |
| N830CB | C650 | 0160 |
| N830CB | CL61 | 5057 |
| N830CB | CS55 | 0004 |
| N830CB | GLF4 | 1263 |
| N830CD | CL61 | 5057 |
| N830DB | ASTR | 099 |
| **N830DB** | **ASTR** | **206** |
| N830EC | GLF4 | 1229 |
| N830EF | GLF4 | 1023 |
| N830FL | HS25 | 258483 |
| N830G | GLF2 | 44 |
| N830GA | GLF2 | 241 |
| N830GA | GLF5 | 5030 |
| (N830GB) | C650 | 0160 |
| N830KE | C550 | 550-0830 |
| (N830LR) | HS25 | 257078 |
| **N830LX** | **HS25** | **258483** |
| N830MA | WW24 | 358 |
| N830MF | FA20 | 112 |
| **N830MG** | **C650** | **0209** |
| N830NS | HS25 | 258476 |
| **N830QS** | **C560** | **0784** |
| N830RA | FA20 | 66 |
| (N830SR) | FA10 | 149 |
| **N830SU** | **GLF3** | **321** |
| (N830TE) | GLF2 | 49 |
| N830TL | GLF2 | 35 |
| N830TL | GLF2 | 49 |
| **N830TS** | **HA4T** | **RC-30** |
| N830VL | C550 | 410 |
| (N830WM) | LJ25 | 355 |
| N831CB | C500 | 640 |
| N831CB | C650 | 0160 |
| N831CJ | CL61 | 5050 |
| (N831CJ) | HS25 | 257074 |
| N831CJ | LJ35 | 166 |
| N831CW | C500 | 159 |
| N831CW | LJ35 | 390 |
| N831DC | F2TH | 206 |
| N831DC | HS25 | 258112 |
| N831DF | HS25 | 25231 |
| **N831ET** | **CL64** | **5451** |
| **N831FC** | **C52B** | **0155** |
| **N831GA** | **C650** | **0194** |
| N831GA | GLF2 | 238 |
| N831GA | GLF2 | 3 |
| N831HG | FA20 | 310 |
| N831J | LJ35 | 166 |
| **N831JP** | **LJ55** | **048** |
| N831LC | HS25 | 25095 |
| N831LH | LJ25 | 244 |
| **N831LX** | **HS25** | **258510** |
| N831MM | C560 | 0362 |
| N831NW | HS25 | 25231 |
| **N831QS** | **C560** | **0792** |
| **N831RA** | **LJ24** | **164** |
| N831RA | LJ24 | 164 |
| **N831S** | **C525** | **0031** |
| (N831TJ) | MU30 | A018SA |
| N831V | C52B | 0013 |
| N831WM | LJ25 | 076 |
| N832CB | C560 | 0110 |
| **N832CB** | **C650** | **7020** |
| N832CC | C650 | 0167 |
| N832CW | HS25 | 258432 |
| N832GA | GLF2 | 122 |
| N832GA | GLF2 | 4/8 |
| N832GA | GLF5 | 5112 |
| **N832LX** | **HS25** | **258281** |
| (N832LX) | HS25 | 258516 |
| (N832MB) | HS25 | 25231 |
| N832MJ | HS25 | 258040 |
| N832MR | HS25 | 25231 |
| N832MR | HS25 | 258040 |
| N832QB | C560 | 0110 |
| **N832QS** | **HS25** | **258683** |
| **N832R** | **C560** | **0585** |
| **N832SC** | **CL64** | **5461** |
| **N832UJ** | **C550** | **550-0832** |
| N833 | C500 | 416 |
| N833AV | F900 | 181 |
| N833BA | GALX | 114 |
| N833BD | C550 | 550-0958 |
| N833CW | HS25 | 258033 |
| N833GA | GLF2 | 103 |
| N833GA | GLF2 | 8 |
| N833GA | GLF5 | 5113 |
| N833GA | LJ24 | 155 |
| N833JL | C500 | 416 |
| N833JP | HS25 | 258044 |
| **N833LX** | **HS25** | **258291** |
| (N833LX) | HS25 | 258534 |
| N833PA | C550 | 550-0833 |
| **N833QS** | **HS25** | **258433** |
| N833RL | C650 | 0019 |
| (N833WM) | C560 | 0385 |
| **N834AF** | **LJ31** | **225** |
| N834CB | C550 | 550-0834 |
| **N834DC** | **CS55** | **0035** |
| N834GA | GLF2 | 124 |
| N834GA | GLF2 | 6 |
| N834GA | GLF2 | 62 |
| N834GA | GLF5 | 5114 |
| **N834H** | **C650** | **0177** |
| (N834LX) | HS25 | 258543 |
| **N834LX** | **HS25** | **258552** |
| **N834QS** | **C560** | **0669** |
| N835AC | LJ24 | 162 |
| N835AC | LJ35 | 158 |
| N835AF | LJ60 | 244 |
| N835AG | LJ24 | 162 |
| **N835CB** | **C52B** | **0284** |
| N835CB | C550 | 550-0835 |
| N835CW | HS25 | 258035 |
| **N835DM** | **C52B** | **0079** |
| N835F | FA10 | 135 |
| N835GA | GLF2 | 11 |
| N835GA | GLF2 | 63 |
| N835GA | GLF5 | 5115 |
| N835GA | LJ35 | 087 |
| (N835GM) | LJ25 | 027 |
| N835KK | C650 | 0175 |
| (N835LX) | HS25 | 258548 |
| (N835MA) | SBRL | 380-36 |
| **N835MC** | **LJ35** | **673** |
| N835QS | HS25 | 258435 |
| **N835QS** | **HS25** | **258505** |
| **N835TB** | **BE40** | **RK-393** |
| N835TS | HS25 | 258035 |
| (N835VP) | C550 | 550-0835 |
| N835WB | LJ25 | 027 |
| **N835ZT** | **PRM1** | **RB-180** |
| N836GA | GLF2 | 64/27 |
| N836GA | GLF5 | 5116 |
| N836GA | LJ36 | 027 |
| (N836LX) | HS25 | 258552 |
| N836ME | GLF2 | 95/39 |
| N836MF | GLF2 | 154/28 |
| N836MF | GLF2 | 95/39 |
| N836MF | GLF3 | 351 |
| **N836MF** | **GLF4** | **1012** |
| **N836QS** | **HS25** | **258436** |
| N836UC | FA20 | 181 |
| N837AC | C525 | 0537 |
| **N837AC** | **C52A** | **0188** |
| **N837BA** | **GLF5** | **5122** |
| N837CS | LJ25 | 351 |
| N837F | FA10 | 137 |
| N837GA | GLF2 | 65 |
| N837JM | PRM1 | RB-169 |
| (N837LX) | HS25 | 258647 |
| **N837MA** | **C500** | **096** |
| **N837QS** | **C560** | **0685** |
| **N837RE** | **HS25** | **258526** |
| N837WM | GLEX | 9292 |
| **N838BA** | **GLF5** | **5140** |
| N838DB | ASTR | 099 |
| **N838DB** | **FA50** | **265** |
| N838GA | GLF2 | 18 |
| N838GA | GLF2 | 66 |
| N838GA | GLF5 | 5118 |
| N838GA | GLF5 | 5238 |
| **N838JL** | **HS25** | **258270** |
| N838MF | GLF4 | 1012 |
| **N838MF** | **GLF5** | **512** |
| N838QS | HS25 | 258338 |

| | | |
|---|---|---|
| N838RC | LJ60 | 276 |
| **N838RT** | **C56X** | **5047** |
| **N838SC** | **GLEX** | **9035** |
| **N838TH** | **LJ45** | **027** |
| **N838WC** | **HS25** | **258338** |
| N839AC | C525 | 0537 |
| **N839DM** | **C52B** | **0248** |
| N839DW | C550 | 550-0839 |
| N839F | FA50 | 55 |
| N839GA | GLF2 | 19 |
| N839GA | GLF2 | 67 |
| N839LX | HS25 | 258657 |
| **N839QS** | **C560** | **0690** |
| **N839RM** | **F900** | **40** |
| N839RM | FA50 | 159 |
| N840AR | WW24 | 121 |
| **N840CC** | **C56X** | **5040** |
| **N840CT** | **C560** | **0236** |
| **N840DP** | **FA20** | **381/548** |
| N840F | FA20 | 18 |
| N840FJ | FA50 | 223 |
| **N840FL** | **HS25** | **258666** |
| N840GA | GLF5 | 5240 |
| **N840GL** | **FA10** | **109** |
| N840GL | LJ35 | 210 |
| N840H | HS25 | 25230 |
| N840LX | HS25 | 258666 |
| N840MA | SBRL | 380-21 |
| (N840MC) | C500 | 448 |
| N840MC | C550 | 426 |
| N840MQ | C550 | 426 |
| N840QS | HS25 | 258340 |
| N840R | C650 | 0197 |
| **N840RG** | **GLF2** | **235** |
| **N840SW** | **LJ31** | **084** |
| N840TJ | MU30 | A084SA |
| N840WC | HS25 | 258340 |
| **N841AM** | **C52B** | **0084** |
| **N841CW** | **C500** | **516** |
| **N841DW** | **C56X** | **5177** |
| N841F | FA20 | 19 |
| N841F | FA50 | 63 |
| (N841FJ) | FA50 | 41 |
| N841G | C650 | 0136 |
| N841G | LJ24 | 162 |
| N841GA | GLF5 | 5041 |
| N841GA | GLF5 | 5241 |
| N841GL | LJ35 | 235 |
| N841LC | LJ24 | 167 |
| N841LX | HS25 | 258702 |
| N841MA | C500 | 532 |
| N841PA | GLF4 | 1034 |
| N841PC | CL61 | 5116 |
| **N841QS** | **C560** | **0799** |
| **N841TC** | **C525** | **0339** |
| **N841TF** | **LJ35** | **416** |
| N841TT | LJ35 | 416 |
| **N841TT** | **LJ60** | **031** |
| N841W | C550 | 550-0841 |
| N841WS | C550 | 550-0841 |
| **N841WS** | **GLF4** | **4099** |
| N841WS | HS25 | 258674 |
| **N842CB** | **C550** | **550-0842** |
| (N842CC) | C550 | 038 |
| N842DW | C56X | 5589 |
| N842F | FA20 | 20 |
| N842F | FA20 | 38 |
| **N842FL** | **HS25** | **258428** |
| N842GA | GALX | 142 |
| N842GA | GLF5 | 5242 |
| N842GL | LJ25 | 270 |
| N842HS | C52A | 0039 |
| **N842PA** | **GLF4** | **1057** |
| N842PM | PRM1 | RB-4 |
| **N842QS** | **HS25** | **258542** |
| **N843B** | **HS25** | **25214** |
| N843CP | HS25 | 257014 |
| **N843CP** | **LJ60** | **011** |
| N843CW | HS25 | 258543 |
| N843DF | GLF4 | 1241 |
| **N843DW** | **C680** | **0219** |
| N843F | FA20 | 21 |
| N843F | FA20 | 39 |
| N843G | C650 | 0173 |
| N843G | CS55 | 0152 |
| N843GA | ASTR | 121 |
| N843GA | GLF4 | 4143 |
| N843GA | LJ25 | 009 |
| N843GL | LJ35 | 237 |
| N843HS | C560 | 0582 |
| N843HS | GLF3 | 496 |
| **N843LX** | **HS25** | **258297** |
| N843MG | F9EX | 193 |
| N843MG | FA20 | 491 |
| **N843QS** | **C560** | **0790** |
| (N843TS) | HS25 | 258643 |
| N844AV | F2TH | 146 |
| **N844DR** | **C550** | **550-0860** |
| **N844F** | **FA10** | **201** |
| N844F | FA20 | 23 |
| N844GA | ASTR | 044 |
| N844GA | GALX | 004 |
| N844GA | GALX | 148 |
| N844GA | LJ24 | 165 |
| N844GF | GLF4 | 1107 |
| **N844GF** | **GLF4** | **4160** |
| N844GL | LJ35 | 238 |
| N844GS | GLF4 | 1107 |
| N844HS | C560 | 0596 |
| N844HS | GLF4 | 1289 |
| (N844J) | FA50 | 56 |
| **N844L** | **LJ35** | **014** |
| N844NX | FA50 | 147 |
| **N844QS** | **C560** | **0629** |
| N844SL | FA20 | 77/429 |
| **N844TM** | **C560** | **0660** |
| **N844UP** | **F2TH** | **156** |
| N844X | FA50 | 93 |
| N845CW | HS25 | 258045 |
| N845F | FA20 | 24 |
| **N845FW** | **C650** | **0153** |
| N845FW | GLF3 | 875 |
| **N845G** | **GLF4** | **4053** |
| N845GA | GALX | 012 |
| N845GA | GLF2 | 74 |
| N845GA | GLF5 | 5245 |
| N845GL | LJ35 | 221 |
| N845HS | GLF5 | 568 |
| N845HS | GLF5 | 665 |
| **N845QS** | **HS25** | **258545** |
| N845RL | LJ45 | 022 |
| **N845UP** | **CL30** | **20081** |
| N846F | FA20 | 26 |
| N846FL | HS25 | 258461 |
| N846GA | GLF5 | 5246 |
| N846GA | LJ25 | 010 |
| N846GL | LJ35 | 242 |
| N846HC | LJ25 | 010 |
| N846HS | C550 | 669 |
| (N846L) | C550 | 477 |
| **N846MA** | **C560** | **0046** |
| **N846QM** | **GLF5** | **626** |
| N846QS | C560 | 0646 |
| **N846QS** | **C560** | **0797** |
| **N846UP** | **CL30** | **20086** |
| N846YC | LJ25 | 012 |
| N846YT | LJ25 | 012 |
| N847C | CS55 | 0003 |
| **N847CW** | **HS25** | **258647** |
| N847F | FA20 | 27 |
| N847G | C650 | 0101 |
| **N847G** | **CS55** | **0003** |
| N847GA | GALX | 007 |
| N847GA | GLF5 | 5247 |
| N847GA | LJ24 | 167 |
| N847GL | LJ35 | 239 |
| N847HS | C550 | 661 |
| N847HS | C560 | 0609 |
| **N847NG** | **C52B** | **0144** |
| N847RH | HS25 | 258224 |
| N848AB | JSTR | 5214 |
| **N848C** | **BE40** | **RJ-63** |
| N848C | WW24 | 54 |
| **N848CA** | **LJ45** | **401** |
| N848CC | CL64 | 5367 |
| **N848CC** | **CL64** | **5660** |
| **N848CW** | **HS25** | **258648** |
| **N848D** | **C550** | **039** |
| **N848DM** | **C56X** | **5329** |
| N848F | FA20 | 28 |
| N848FL | HS25 | 258648 |
| **N848G** | **C560** | **0465** |
| N848G | CS55 | 0152 |
| N848GA | ASTR | 111 |
| **N848GF** | **GLF4** | **1107** |
| N848GL | LJ35 | 488 |
| N848HS | C550 | 720 |
| (N848K) | FA50 | 205 |
| N848MP | FA10 | 118 |
| **N848N** | **HS25** | **258371** |
| **N848PF** | **BE40** | **RK-288** |
| **N848QS** | **HS25** | **HA-0031** |
| N848RJ | GLF3 | 492 |
| **N848TC** | **BE40** | **RK-7** |
| N848US | C650 | 0060 |
| N848W | HS25 | 256044 |
| (N849CB) | C550 | 550-0849 |
| N849F | FA20 | 29 |
| N849GA | GALX | 009 |
| N849GA | GLF5 | 5249 |
| N849GL | LJ24 | 279 |
| N849HS | WW24 | 344 |
| N850BA | C550 | 134 |
| N850BA | C560 | 0322 |
| **N850BA** | **FA50** | **115** |
| N850BL | HS25 | 259033 |
| N850BM | HS25 | 258142 |
| **N850C** | **BE40** | **RK-31** |
| N850CA | FA50 | 75 |
| **N850CC** | **SBRL** | **465-38** |
| N850CS | SBRL | 465-38 |
| **N850CT** | **HS25** | **258677** |
| **N850DG** | **C525** | **0268** |
| N850DS | LJ60 | 047 |
| N850EJ | CL30 | 20005 |
| **N850EM** | **HS25** | **258876** |
| **N850EN** | **FA50** | **326** |
| **N850EP** | **FA50** | **39** |
| N850FB | CL61 | 5162 |
| N850FL | CL61 | 5162 |
| N850GA | ASTR | 250 |
| N850GA | GLF2 | 98/38 |
| N850GA | GLF4 | 4050 |
| N850GM | C525 | 0366 |
| N850GM | C550 | 550-0906 |
| **N850HB** | **HS25** | **258900** |
| **N850J** | **HS25** | **258311** |
| **N850JA** | **HS25** | **259006** |
| **N850JL** | **HS25** | **258548** |
| **N850K** | **F2TH** | **210** |
| N850KE | HS25 | 258796 |
| **N850KE** | **HS25** | **258961** |
| **N850LA** | **HS25** | **258008** |
| N850MA | C500 | 481 |
| N850MC | C650 | 0090 |
| N850MC | FA50 | 97 |
| **N850ME** | **HS25** | **258861** |
| N850MM | LJ35 | 596 |
| N850MX | LJ25 | 286 |
| **N850NS** | **HS25** | **258789** |
| (N850PA) | LJ55 | 106 |
| **N850PG** | **GLF3** | **445** |
| **N850PM** | **C550** | **247** |
| (N850PT) | C750 | 0222 |
| (N850RG) | BE40 | RK-67 |
| N850SC | LJ25 | 023 |
| N850SM | HS25 | 258074 |
| **N850TC** | **HS25** | **259032** |
| N850TJ | MU30 | A054SA |
| **N850VP** | **HS25** | **258768** |
| N850WC | C560 | 0378 |
| N850WW | WW24 | 338 |
| **N850ZH** | **HS25** | **258798** |
| (N850ZH) | HS25 | 258816 |
| N851BA | LJ24 | 194 |
| N851BC | C500 | 514 |
| **N851C** | **MU30** | **A077SA** |
| **N851CB** | **GLF4** | **4132** |
| **N851CC** | **HS25** | **258787** |
| N851CC | LJ24 | 339 |
| N851CW | HS25 | 258051 |
| **N851DB** | **C525** | **0054** |
| **N851E** | **WW24** | **379** |
| N851EL | GLF4 | 1515 |
| N851GA | GLF2 | 99 |
| N851GA | GLF5 | 5051 |
| **N851GG** | **GLF4** | **4120** |
| N851JH | LJ24 | 207 |
| **N851L** | **LJ35** | **114** |
| N851LE | GALX | 106 |
| N851WC | C560 | 0330 |
| N851WC | JSTR | 5229 |
| **N852A** | **HS25** | **258083** |
| N852CA | F9EX | 155 |
| **N852CC** | **HS25** | **HA-0012** |
| N852GA | GLF2 | 100 |
| N852GA | HS25 | 256048 |
| N852GA | LJ24 | 173 |
| **N852LX** | **HS25** | **258397** |
| N852PA | LJ55 | 055 |
| **N852QS** | **HS25** | **258452** |
| **N852SB** | **C550** | **172** |
| N852SC | LJ25 | 006 |
| **N852SP** | **C52B** | **0092** |
| N852SP | C550 | 172 |
| N852WC | C560 | 0194 |
| N852WC | HS25 | 257095 |
| (N852WC) | LJ36 | 013 |
| N852WR | C550 | 151 |
| **N853CC** | **HS25** | **258803** |
| **N853CR** | **C560** | **0324** |
| N853DS | LJ25 | 012 |
| N853GA | GLF2 | 101 |
| N853GA | LJ25 | 012 |
| N853JA | C56X | 6031 |
| N853JL | C510 | 0113 |
| N853JL | C52B | 0048 |
| N853KB | C500 | 637 |
| N853M | ASTR | 146 |
| N853QS | HS25 | 258535 |
| N853SP | ASTR | 053 |
| **N853TC** | **EA50** | **000245** |
| N853WC | C750 | 0008 |
| N853WC | HS25 | 257032 |
| **N854FL** | **HS25** | **258454** |
| N854GA | FA20 | 279/502 |
| N854GA | GLF2 | 102/32 |
| N854GA | LJ24 | 174 |
| (N854GA) | LJ55 | 056 |
| **N854JA** | **C550** | **550-0920** |
| N854RB | SBRL | 282-106 |
| N854SD | GLF4 | 1387 |
| **N854SM** | **HS25** | **25265** |
| (N854W) | FA50 | 163 |
| N854WC | C750 | 0027 |
| N854WC | FA20 | 40 |
| N854WC | HS25 | 257058 |
| N855CD | SBRL | 306-85 |
| N855DB | LJ55 | 062 |
| **N855DG** | **F2EX** | **97** |
| N855DG | FA20 | 432 |
| (N855DH) | C650 | 0014 |
| **N855FC** | **BE40** | **RK-141** |
| **N855G** | **GLF5** | **5118** |
| N855GA | GLF2 | 103 |
| **N855GA** | **HS25** | **258211** |
| N855GA | LJ24 | 158 |
| **N855JB** | **PRM1** | **RB-104** |
| **N855MS** | **EA50** | **000121** |
| **N855PT** | **LJ55** | **046** |
| **N855QS** | **HS25** | **258355** |
| **N855RA** | **BE40** | **RK-114** |
| **N855RB** | **GLF5** | **509** |
| **N855RM** | **PRM1** | **RB-174** |
| **N855SA** | **GLF3** | **363** |
| **N855TJ** | **F2EX** | **19** |
| N855W | LJ24 | 159 |
| N855W | LJ24 | 191 |
| N855W | LJ24 | 199 |
| N856AF | GLF4 | 1276 |
| N856AF | HS25 | 258140 |
| **N856BB** | **C525** | **0381** |
| **N856BB** | **C52B** | **0207** |
| N856CW | C560 | 0432 |
| **N856F** | **F2TH** | **138** |
| N856G | LJ25 | 013 |
| N856GA | GLF2 | 104/10 |
| N856GA | GLF5 | 5256 |
| **N856JB** | **LJ24** | **052** |
| N856MA | SBRL | 306-41 |
| N856RR | LJ35 | 496 |
| N856W | GLF2 | 104/10 |
| N856W | GLF3 | 484 |
| **N857AA** | **C550** | **550-0901** |
| N857BL | C560 | 0381 |
| (N857BT) | C550 | 231 |
| **N857C** | **BE40** | **RK-17** |
| (N857CW) | HS25 | 258657 |
| **N857DN** | **C650** | **0181** |
| N857GA | LJ25 | 014 |
| N857PR | LJ55 | 073 |
| N857QS | HS25 | HA-0132 |

| | | |
|---|---|---|
| (N857SC) | LJ25 | 006 |
| **N857ST** | **GLF4** | **1345** |
| N857W | SBRL | 465-72 |
| N857WC | C560 | 0069 |
| **N858DN** | **GALX** | **038** |
| N858GM | LJ25 | 015 |
| **N858GS** | **EA50** | **000039** |
| N858JR | HS25 | 257100 |
| **N858KE** | **HS25** | **258796** |
| **N858ME** | **C560** | **0253** |
| **N858MK** | **LJ45** | **141** |
| **N858PJ** | **CL60** | **1028** |
| **N858QS** | **HS25** | **258691** |
| **N858SD** | **C525** | **0672** |
| (N858SH) | JSTR | 5117/35 |
| **N858SP** | **FA10** | **11** |
| N858TM | LJ35 | 409 |
| (N858TS) | GLEX | 9158 |
| N858W | GLF2 | 104/10 |
| N858XL | HS25 | 258140 |
| N859GA | GLF2 | 180 |
| N859GM | LJ24 | 175 |
| N859L | LJ24 | 175 |
| N859QS | HS25 | HA-0122 |
| N859XP | HS25 | 258859 |
| **N860AA** | **GLF5** | **5079** |
| (N860AH) | LJ60 | 017 |
| **N860BA** | **FA50** | **142** |
| **N860CR** | **C560** | **0500** |
| N860DB | C525 | 0271 |
| **N860DB** | **C525** | **0434** |
| N860DD | C525 | 0271 |
| N860DD | C525 | 0434 |
| **N860DD** | **C52B** | **0046** |
| N860E | FA10 | 52 |
| N860FJ | F9EX | 30 |
| N860GA | GLF2 | 181 |
| (N860J) | C550 | 550-0860 |
| N860JB | GLF4 | 1054 |
| N860JH | C550 | 550-0860 |
| N860JL | HS25 | 258548 |
| N860MX | LJ25 | 109 |
| **N860PD** | **LJ60** | **073** |
| **N860PM** | **GLF2** | **224** |
| (N860Q) | C560 | 0633 |
| **N860QS** | **HS25** | **258698** |
| **N860S** | **LJ35** | **086** |
| **N860W** | **C650** | **7086** |
| N861BB | C550 | 550-0861 |
| N861CE | C560 | 0273 |
| N861CE | HS25 | 258006 |
| **N861CE** | **HS25** | **258181** |
| (N861CF) | C560 | 0273 |
| N861CW | HS25 | 258061 |
| N861GA | GLF2 | 184 |
| N861GA | LJ25 | 018 |
| N861GS | WW24 | 356 |
| (N861L) | LJ25 | 023 |
| N861ME | HS25 | 258861 |
| N861PA | LJ60 | 015 |
| N861PD | C525 | 0027 |
| N861QS | HS25 | 258361 |
| N861RD | C525 | 0027 |
| **N861WC** | **HS25** | **258361** |
| (N862BD) | LJ35 | 087 |
| N862CE | C56X | 5021 |
| N862CE | GLF2 | 109 |
| N862CE | GLF3 | 306 |
| N862CE | HS25 | 258089 |
| **N862CE** | **HS25** | **258244** |
| N862CF | C56X | 5021 |
| **N862CW** | **HS25** | **258062** |
| N862G | GLF2 | 188 |
| N862G | GLF3 | 329 |
| N862GA | GLF2 | 185 |
| N862GA | GLF2 | 22 |
| N862GA | GLF3 | 338 |
| (N862JA) | HS25 | 258362 |
| N862KM | BE40 | RK-227 |
| **N862PA** | **LJ60** | **014** |
| N862PD | LJ35 | 087 |
| N862QS | HS25 | 258362 |
| N862WC | HS25 | 258362 |
| (N863A) | GLF3 | 361 |
| N863AB | WW24 | 196 |
| N863BD | FA50 | 161 |
| **N863CA** | **LJ45** | **160** |
| N863CA | LJ45 | 179 |
| N863CE | GLF3 | 306 |
| **N863CE** | **HS25** | **258289** |
| N863GA | GLF2 | 23 |
| **N863PA** | **LJ60** | **004** |
| **N863QS** | **HS25** | **258463** |
| **N863RD** | **C560** | **0287** |
| N863TM | F2TH | 217 |
| (N863TS) | F2TH | 63 |
| N864CB | C550 | 550-0864 |
| N864CC | C56X | 5067 |
| N864CE | GLF4 | 1085 |
| **N864CE** | **HS25** | **258331** |
| N864CL | LJ24 | 229 |
| N864D | C550 | 313 |
| N864EC | C650 | 7014 |
| **N864KB** | **LJ31** | **048** |
| N864PA | LJ60 | 017 |
| **N864QS** | **HS25** | **258564** |
| (N864TT) | C500 | 477 |
| N864YC | GLF4 | 1003 |
| N864YD | GLF2 | 156/31 |
| **N865AA** | **GLF2** | **48/29** |
| **N865AM** | **BE40** | **RK-358** |
| **N865CA** | **LJ45** | **193** |
| N865CE | C56X | 5017 |
| (N865EC) | C650 | 7014 |
| **N865EC** | **C680** | **0028** |
| **N865JM** | **HS25** | **HA-0087** |
| **N865JT** | **HS25** | **258800** |
| N865LS | HS25 | HA-0037 |
| N865M | C560 | 0179 |
| N865M | C560 | 0550 |
| N865M | C560 | 0803 |
| **N865PC** | **FA50** | **271** |
| N865SM | HS25 | 258365 |
| N865VP | FA20 | 360 |
| N866AV | F2TH | 146 |
| N866BB | BE40 | RK-98 |
| **N866CA** | **LJ45** | **184** |
| N866CB | C550 | 550-0866 |
| N866CW | HS25 | 258466 |
| N866DB | LJ24 | 018 |
| N866DH | WW24 | 78 |
| N866FP | FA50 | 22 |
| N866G | ASTR | 062 |
| **N866G** | **GALX** | **025** |
| N866JM | WW24 | 184 |
| N866JS | LJ24 | 018 |
| N866MM | FA20 | 175 |
| N866Q | ASTR | 062 |
| N866QS | C560 | 0633 |
| N866RA | LJ45 | 210 |
| N866RB | HS25 | 258405 |
| N866RR | HS25 | 258405 |
| N866RR | HS25 | 258624 |
| **N866TC** | **C560** | **0802** |
| **N866TM** | **CL30** | **20066** |
| (N866VP) | C550 | 668 |
| N867CE | GLF4 | 1195 |
| N867CW | C550 | 094 |
| N867CW | HS25 | 258067 |
| **N867GA** | **GLF5** | **5267** |
| **N867JC** | **C550** | **180** |
| N867JS | LJ31 | 086 |
| **N867K** | **EA50** | **000239** |
| **N867QS** | **HS25** | **258576** |
| **N867W** | **C56X** | **5601** |
| N868AG | GLF2 | 167 |
| **N868BT** | **FA50** | **93** |
| **N868CC** | **CL64** | **5662** |
| N868CE | CL61 | 5016 |
| (N868CE) | GLF3 | 306 |
| N868CP | WW24 | 341 |
| (N868D) | C500 | 338 |
| N868DS | FA20 | 256 |
| **N868DS** | **GLF2** | **123/25** |
| **N868EM** | **C52B** | **0081** |
| N868GM | C680 | 0090 |
| N868J | C56X | 5089 |
| **N868J** | **C56X** | **5180** |
| N868J | LJ24 | 077 |
| N868JB | C56X | 5048 |
| N868JB | C56X | 5089 |
| N868JB | C56X | 5180 |
| N868JB | C56X | 6014 |
| N868JS | LJ31 | 087 |
| N868JT | C560 | 0310 |
| **N868SC** | **GLEX** | **9352** |
| **N868SM** | **GLF2** | **254/41** |
| N868WC | HS25 | 258178 |
| **N868XL** | **C56X** | **5603** |
| **N869AV** | **LJ60** | **306** |
| **N869AW** | **EA50** | **000233** |
| N869B | LJ24 | 089 |
| **N869CB** | **C525** | **0453** |
| N869CS | GLF2 | 2 |
| (N869EG) | SBRL | 465-33 |
| N869GA | GLF2 | 29 |
| **N869GR** | **C525** | **0478** |
| N869JS | LJ60 | 005 |
| N869K | C500 | 077 |
| N869KC | SBRL | 465-33 |
| N869KM | HS25 | 257165 |
| N869QS | HS25 | HA-0075 |
| (N869QS) | HS25 | HA-0122 |
| N870 | FA50 | 251 |
| N870AJ | C560 | 0048 |
| N870AM | MU30 | A087SA |
| **N870BA** | **WW24** | **412** |
| **N870BB** | **BE40** | **RK-22** |
| N870CA | HS25 | 258111 |
| N870CM | CL64 | 5488 |
| **N870CM** | **GLF5** | **5076** |
| N870F | FA20 | 40 |
| N870GA | GLF2 | 125/26 |
| N870GA | GLF2 | 30/4 |
| N870GA | GLF5 | 5070 |
| N870HY | C510 | 0166 |
| N870JS | LJ60 | 028 |
| N870MH | C550 | 475 |
| N870P | BE40 | RK-20 |
| N870P | MU30 | A015SA |
| N870PT | C550 | 383 |
| **N870QS** | **HS25** | **258732** |
| N870R | SBRL | 282-137 |
| N870WC | C550 | 695 |
| N871CB | C550 | 550-0871 |
| N871D | GLF2 | 145 |
| N871D | GLF2 | 245/30 |
| N871D | HS25 | 257134 |
| N871D | JSTR | 5067 |
| N871E | GLF2 | 145 |
| N871F | FA20 | 42 |
| N871GA | GLF2 | 129 |
| N871GA | GLF2 | 49 |
| (N871MA) | HS25 | 25233 |
| N871MM | F9EX | 89 |
| **N871QS** | **HS25** | **258763** |
| **N872AT** | **HS25** | **258278** |
| **N872BC** | **HS25** | **258524** |
| N872D | HS25 | 25275 |
| N872E | GLF2 | 257/17 |
| N872EC | C650 | 0113 |
| **N872EC** | **F2TH** | **143** |
| N872F | FA20 | 43 |
| N872GA | GLF2 | 130 |
| N872JR | LJ24 | 173 |
| **N872QS** | **HS25** | **258472** |
| **N872RD** | **C550** | **262** |
| N872RT | C550 | 262 |
| N872XP | HS25 | 258872 |
| N873 | WW24 | 137 |
| N873D | C500 | 337 |
| N873D | HS25 | 25160 |
| N873DB | C560 | 0184 |
| N873E | GLF3 | 320 |
| N873EJ | WW24 | 167 |
| N873F | FA20 | 44 |
| N873G | CL61 | 3009 |
| N873G | HS25 | 25160 |
| N873GA | GLF2 | 132 |
| N873GA | GLF5 | 673 |
| N873LP | LJ35 | 104 |
| N873LP | LJ35 | 220 |
| N873LP | LJ35 | 659 |
| N873LR | LJ35 | 220 |
| "N873QS" | HS25 | 258570 |
| **N873QS** | **HS25** | **258573** |
| N874A | GLF4 | 1285 |
| N874AJ | SBRL | 282-70 |
| **N874C** | **GLF4** | **1219** |
| (N874CW) | HS25 | 258374 |
| N874G | C650 | 0137 |
| N874GA | GLF2 | 136 |
| N874JD | BE40 | RK-141 |
| N874JD | HS25 | 258589 |
| N874JD | LJ35 | 457 |
| N874JM | CS55 | 0127 |
| N874PT | C750 | 0274 |
| **N874QS** | **HS25** | **258474** |
| **N874RA** | **GLF3** | **361** |
| (N874RR) | GLF3 | 361 |
| **N874WD** | **ASTR** | **062** |
| N874XP | HS25 | 258874 |
| N875CA | SBRL | 465-42 |
| (N875E) | GLF2 | 119/22 |
| (N875E) | GLF3 | 361 |
| (N875F) | F9EX | 101 |
| N875F | FA20 | 47 |
| N875G | CL61 | 3019 |
| N875GA | GALX | 075 |
| N875GA | GLF2 | 137 |
| N875GA | GLF2 | 55 |
| N875H | CL61 | 5093 |
| N875HS | WW24 | 370 |
| **N875LP** | **HS25** | **258308** |
| **N875NA** | **EA50** | **000018** |
| **N875P** | **WW24** | **370** |
| N875PK | CL60 | 1018 |
| N875QS | HS25 | 258375 |
| N875SC | C650 | 0027 |
| N875SC | HS25 | 258111 |
| **N876AM** | **C510** | **0282** |
| **N876BB** | **C550** | **550-1087** |
| **N876BC** | **LJ45** | **252** |
| **N876C** | **F9EX** | **162** |
| N876C | LJ35 | 616 |
| N876CB | C550 | 550-0876 |
| N876CS | LJ35 | 616 |
| **N876CS** | **LJ60** | **263** |
| N876CW | HS25 | 258666 |
| N876F | FA20 | 45 |
| **N876G** | **C650** | **7062** |
| N876GA | ASTR | 106 |
| N876GA | GLF2 | 57 |
| **N876H** | **CL64** | **5542** |
| N876H | HS25 | 258303 |
| **N876JC** | **E50P** | **50000075** |
| N876JC | HS25 | 257055 |
| **N876MA** | **FA10** | **63** |
| **N876MC** | **LJ24** | **217** |
| **N876QS** | **HS25** | **258586** |
| N876RW | GLF3 | 355 |
| N876SC | C650 | 0076 |
| N876SC | F2TH | 24 |
| N876SC | FA20 | 391 |
| N876SC | HS25 | 258124 |
| **N876WB** | **C500** | **347** |
| **N877A** | **GLF4** | **1461** |
| N877B | C550 | 550-1096 |
| **N877B** | **C550** | **550-1110** |
| N877BP | C500 | 255 |
| N877C | C500 | 376 |
| N877CM | C650 | 7077 |
| N877CW | HS25 | 258077 |
| **N877D** | **ASTR** | **102** |
| N877DF | FA50 | 25 |
| N877DM | CL61 | 5174 |
| **N877DM** | **HS25** | **258279** |
| **N877FL** | **BE40** | **RK-223** |
| **N877G** | **C650** | **7063** |
| (N877GB) | C550 | 232 |
| N877GS | C525 | 0179 |
| **N877H** | **CL64** | **5445** |
| **N877J** | **BE40** | **RK-69** |
| **N877JG** | **FA20** | **325** |
| **N877PM** | **EA50** | **000260** |
| **N877QS** | **HS25** | **HA-0066** |
| N877RB | C560 | 0318 |
| N877RF | C560 | 0318 |
| **N877RF** | **C56X** | **5219** |
| N877RP | HS25 | 258084 |
| N877S | BE40 | RJ-17 |
| N877S | BE40 | RK-17 |
| N877S | BE40 | RK-420 |
| N877S | BE40 | RK-69 |
| N877S | HS25 | 258323 |
| N877S | HS25 | 258560 |
| (N877S) | HS25 | 258562 |
| N877S | MU30 | A055SA |
| **N877SD** | **C550** | **550-0875** |
| N877SL | HS25 | 258323 |
| N877T | MU30 | A055SA |
| **N877W** | **PRM1** | **RB-107** |

| | | |
|---|---|---|
| N877XP | HS25 | 258777 |
| N877Z | BE40 | RK-17 |
| N878AG | C550 | 550-0941 |
| **N878CC** | **CL65** | **5777** |
| N878CS | GALX | 027 |
| N878DE | LJ24 | 153 |
| N878F | FA20 | 48 |
| N878G | GLF4 | 1331 |
| N878GA | GLF2 | 58 |
| **N878HL** | **GLEX** | **9261** |
| (N878LP) | LJ35 | 659 |
| N878MA | LJ31 | 031 |
| N878ME | LJ25 | 351 |
| **N878MM** | **C510** | **0188** |
| **N878QS** | **HS25** | **HA-0054** |
| N878RM | CL61 | 3012 |
| **N878SM** | **GLF4** | **1319** |
| N878SP | C510 | 0188 |
| N878W | LJ24 | 207 |
| N879F | FA20 | 50 |
| N879GA | GLF2 | 59 |
| N879PT | C750 | 0279 |
| N879QS | HS25 | 258379 |
| N879RA | JSTR | 5023 |
| N879WC | HS25 | 258379 |
| N880A | GLF2 | 38 |
| N880CA | ASTR | 055 |
| N880CH | ASTR | 045 |
| N880CH | LJ35 | 335 |
| N880CK | SBRL | 306-121 |
| N880CM | C500 | 398 |
| N880CM | C550 | 550-1032 |
| N880CM | CL65 | 5818 |
| **N880CR** | **CL64** | **5356** |
| (N880CR) | HS25 | 257177 |
| (N880EF) | C560 | 0147 |
| **N880ET** | **CL64** | **5514** |
| N880F | FA20 | 51 |
| N880F | FA50 | 3 |
| N880G | GLF4 | 1286 |
| N880GA | GLF2 | 139/11 |
| N880GA | GLF2 | 86/16 |
| **N880GC** | **GLF4** | **1016** |
| N880GM | GLF2 | 42/12 |
| **N880HK** | **CL65** | **5793** |
| (N880HL) | SBRL | 282-72 |
| N880HM | BE40 | RJ-19 |
| N880KC | SBRL | 306-121 |
| N880LJ | LJ45 | 180 |
| **N880LT** | **HS25** | **259051** |
| N880M | C500 | 524 |
| **N880M** | **HS25** | **258027** |
| **N880MR** | **C52B** | **0226** |
| N880P | FA20 | 51 |
| **N880QS** | **HS25** | **258570** |
| N880QS | HS25 | 258580 |
| **N880RG** | **HS25** | **257107** |
| **N880RJ** | **GLF2** | **159** |
| N880SC | HS25 | 256018 |
| **N880SP** | **HS25** | **258298** |
| N880TD | FA50 | 14 |
| N880WD | GLF2 | 217 |
| **N880WD** | **GLF4** | **1170** |
| **N880WE** | **GLF2** | **217** |
| N880WW | HS25 | 258019 |
| N880WW | WW24 | 195 |
| N880XP | HS25 | 258800 |
| **N880Z** | **LJ35** | **591** |
| N880Z | WW24 | 203 |
| **N881A** | **CS55** | **0139** |
| (N881BA) | C650 | 0081 |
| N881CA | C500 | 132 |
| N881CA | LJ35 | 508 |
| N881CJ | CL61 | 5050 |
| N881CW | HS25 | 258461 |
| N881DM | SBRL | 282-137 |
| **N881E** | **GLF4** | **4028** |
| N881F | FA20 | 52 |
| N881FC | LJ24 | 175 |
| N881G | C750 | 0101 |
| N881G | F900 | 104 |
| N881G | FA20 | 399 |
| N881GA | GALX | 081 |
| N881GA | GLF2 | 140/40 |
| N881GA | GLF2 | 153 |
| N881GA | GLF2 | 88/21 |
| N881J | FA20 | 396 |
| (N881J) | FA50 | 92 |
| N881J | LJ25 | 294 |
| N881JT | C500 | 159 |
| N881JT | FA20 | 513 |
| (N881JT) | HS25 | 259043 |
| (N881K) | FA50 | 79 |
| **N881KS** | **C525** | **0300** |
| (N881L) | FA50 | 105 |
| (N881M) | C500 | 073 |
| N881M | FA50 | 83 |
| N881MC | SBRL | 282-19 |
| N881MC | SBRL | 306-100 |
| N881MD | SBRL | 282-19 |
| N881P | F900 | 146 |
| N881P | FA10 | 33 |
| **N881P** | **LJ25** | **302** |
| **N881Q** | **F9EX** | **80** |
| **N881QS** | **HS25** | **HA-0050** |
| N881S | HS25 | 257042 |
| N881SA | C550 | 617 |
| **N881TS** | **GLEX** | **9247** |
| **N881TW** | **CL64** | **5348** |
| **N881VP** | **C56X** | **6018** |
| N881W | LJ35 | 269 |
| **N881WT** | **GLEX** | **9002** |
| **N882C** | **CL61** | **5065** |
| N882CA | C500 | 296 |
| **N882CA** | **LJ45** | **155** |
| N882CW | HS25 | 258002 |
| N882F | FA20 | 56 |
| **N882GA** | **ASTR** | **082** |
| N882GA | GLF2 | 142 |
| N882GA | GLF2 | 89 |
| N882JD | LJ31 | 109 |
| N882KB | C650 | 0095 |
| **N882KB** | **C750** | **0216** |
| N882KB | CS55 | 0075 |
| **N882LT** | **GALX** | **044** |
| **N882QS** | **HS25** | **258482** |
| **N882RB** | **CS55** | **0075** |
| N882SB | LJ25 | 227 |
| **N882SC** | **LJ35** | **590** |
| N882W | GLF2 | 109 |
| **N882WF** | **C550** | **550-0882** |
| N883A | GLF3 | 416 |
| N883BS | LJ45 | 136 |
| N883CW | HS25 | 258643 |
| N883EJ | HS25 | 258183 |
| N883ES | GLF2 | 98/38 |
| N883F | FA20 | 57 |
| N883GA | GLF2 | 143 |
| N883GA | GLF2 | 90 |
| N883KB | C650 | 0095 |
| (N883KF) | GLF2 | 92 |
| **N883LC** | **EA50** | **000203** |
| **N883PF** | **C56X** | **5085** |
| N883PF | CS55 | 0083 |
| **N883QS** | **HS25** | **258773** |
| N883RA | FA50 | 338 |
| N883RA | SBRL | 465-22 |
| **N883RP** | **C56X** | **5501** |
| N883RT | C560 | 0260 |
| **N883RW** | **FA50** | **338** |
| N883XL | C500 | 177 |
| **N884AM** | **EA50** | **000164** |
| **N884B** | **C56X** | **5140** |
| N884BB | C56X | 5036 |
| N884CF | HS25 | 258084 |
| (N884DR) | C500 | 242 |
| N884F | FA20 | 58 |
| N884GA | GLF2 | 92 |
| N884JW | LJ35 | 316 |
| N884L | GLF4 | 1212 |
| **N884QS** | **HS25** | **258734** |
| **N884TM** | **C510** | **0180** |
| N884TW | LJ60 | 244 |
| **N884VC** | **HS25** | **258584** |
| **N884WT** | **GLF4** | **4143** |
| N884WY | F2TH | 178 |
| **N885** | **F900** | **6** |
| N885AR | GALX | 055 |
| **N885AR** | **GLF4** | **4009** |
| (N885AR) | GLF5 | 5219 |
| **N885BB** | **C56X** | **5135** |
| N885BH | FA20 | 272 |
| **N885BT** | **C52B** | **0058** |
| N885CA | ASTR | 039 |
| N885CA | C500 | 255 |
| N885DR | WW24 | 279 |
| N885F | FA20 | 60 |
| N885G | GLF5 | 518 |
| N885GA | GLF2 | 93 |
| **N885KT** | **GLF5** | **699** |
| N885M | C560 | 0179 |
| N885M | HS25 | 258410 |
| **N885QS** | **HS25** | **258743** |
| N885RR | GALX | 055 |
| N885RR | GLF4 | 4009 |
| N885TA | GLF4 | 1003 |
| **N885TW** | **CL30** | **20037** |
| N885TW | LJ31 | 165 |
| (N885VC) | HS25 | 258585 |
| **N885WT** | **GLF5** | **5237** |
| N886AT | C550 | 166 |
| N886BB | F9DX | 611 |
| N886CA | C500 | 258 |
| N886CA | LJ45 | 154 |
| N886CS | LJ35 | 023 |
| N886CW | HS25 | 258006 |
| **N886DC** | **F900** | **177** |
| N886DT | GLF3 | 463 |
| **N886DT** | **GLF5** | **636** |
| N886DT | JSTR | 5223 |
| N886F | FA20 | 54 |
| **N886G** | **GALX** | **057** |
| N886GA | GLF2 | 94 |
| N886GB | HS25 | 257002 |
| (N886GW) | HS25 | 258006 |
| N886MJ | FA10 | 199 |
| **N886QS** | **HS25** | **258486** |
| **N886R** | **LJ35** | **269** |
| N886RP | CS55 | 0158 |
| N886S | HS25 | 257025 |
| N886WC | LJ24 | 213 |
| N886WC | LJ35 | 023 |
| **N887AG** | **GLF5** | **5175** |
| N887BB | C550 | 550-0887 |
| N887CE | F2EX | 95 |
| **N887CS** | **C560** | **0787** |
| (N887CW) | HS25 | 258397 |
| (N887DM) | C500 | 476 |
| N887DT | JSTR | 5223 |
| N887F | FA20 | 61 |
| N887GA | GLF2 | 95/39 |
| N887PA | ASTR | 025 |
| N887PC | ASTR | 015 |
| N887PL | WW24 | 195 |
| **N887QS** | **HS25** | **258387** |
| N887SA | C550 | 604 |
| N887WM | GLEX | 9041 |
| **N887WM** | **GLEX** | **9292** |
| N887WS | GLEX | 9120 |
| N888AC | C500 | 349 |
| N888AR | FA20 | 33 |
| **N888AZ** | **CL61** | **3024** |
| N888B | LJ24 | 167 |
| N888BH | C500 | 526 |
| N888BL | LJ35 | 140 |
| N888BS | LJ35 | 409 |
| **N888CE** | **F2EX** | **124** |
| N888CF | GLF2 | 10 |
| N888CF | JSTR | 5070/52 |
| **N888CJ** | **HS25** | **25084** |
| N888CN | C750 | 0086 |
| N888CN | CL30 | 20062 |
| **N888CP** | **LJ31** | **003** |
| N888CR | HS25 | 25180 |
| N888CS | GLF2 | 98/38 |
| N888CW | GLF3 | 489 |
| N888CW | GLF5 | 545 |
| **N888CX** | **LJ45** | **044** |
| N888DB | LJ25 | 073 |
| N888DE | LJ35 | 010 |
| N888DF | LJ25 | 189 |
| N888DH | CL61 | 5014 |
| **N888DH** | **CL64** | **5305** |
| N888DH | HS25 | 258051 |
| N888DH | LJ25 | 109 |
| N888DH | LJ35 | 010 |
| N888DJ | LJ35 | 067 |
| N888DL | HFB3 | 1051 |
| N888DS | C500 | 449 |
| N888DS | LJ24 | 013 |
| (N888DT) | LJ35 | 187 |
| N888DV | LJ25 | 370 |
| **N888DZ** | **EA50** | **000198** |
| N888EB | C550 | 350 |
| N888ES | GLF2 | 98/38 |
| **N888ES** | **GLF4** | **1120** |
| **N888FA** | **LJ24** | **257** |
| **N888FG** | **C550** | **324** |
| N888FJ | FA10 | 4 |
| (N888FK) | LJ55 | 108 |
| **N888FL** | **C500** | **371** |
| **N888FR** | **GLF4** | **1041** |
| N888FW | CL60 | 1079 |
| N888G | FA10 | 197 |
| N888GA | C500 | 132 |
| N888GA | GLF2 | 96 |
| N888GC | LJ25 | 258 |
| **N888GL** | **C52A** | **0201** |
| **N888GS** | **C510** | **0209** |
| **N888GX** | **GLEX** | **9248** |
| N888GZ | C500 | 349 |
| **N888HE** | **GLF5** | **638** |
| **N888HH** | **GLF4** | **4029** |
| **N888HK** | **GLF5** | **5213** |
| (N888HK) | GLF5 | 638 |
| N888HS | C550 | 550-0862 |
| N888HW | C550 | 108 |
| N888JA | CL61 | 5049 |
| (N888JA) | LJ25 | 301 |
| N888JD | C500 | 132 |
| (N888JK) | MS76 | 043 |
| **N888JL** | **C500** | **242** |
| N888JR | FA20 | 144 |
| **N888KG** | **C650** | **0119** |
| N888KL | C52A | 0102 |
| **N888KL** | **LJ60** | **141** |
| N888KS | CL60 | 1073 |
| **N888KU** | **C525** | **0068** |
| N888L | FA20 | 144 |
| (N888LF) | GLF4 | 1362 |
| N888LG | GLF4 | 1125 |
| N888LK | GLF4 | 1125 |
| N888LK | GLF4 | 1362 |
| **N888LK** | **GLF5** | **5012** |
| N888LR | LJ25 | 171 |
| **N888LV** | **GLF3** | **347** |
| N888LW | CL60 | 1025 |
| N888MC | GLF2 | 247 |
| N888MC | GLF3 | 351 |
| N888MC | GLF4 | 1086 |
| **N888MC** | **LJ24** | **106** |
| N888MC | SBRL | 306-39 |
| **N888ME** | **FA50** | **41** |
| N888MF | FA50 | 41 |
| **N888MF** | **GLF4** | **1268** |
| N888MJ | C500 | 097 |
| **N888MN** | **PRM1** | **RB-153** |
| (N888MP) | WW24 | 147 |
| N888MV | LJ35 | 362 |
| N888MW | C550 | 028 |
| N888MX | GLF4 | 1110 |
| (N888NA) | C550 | 723 |
| N888NS | LJ24 | 106 |
| N888NX | F2EX | 40 |
| N888PA | C500 | 242 |
| N888PM | GLF3 | 435 |
| **N888PM** | **GLF4** | **1195** |
| N888PM | HS25 | 256041 |
| N888PM | SBRL | 282-12 |
| N888PS | C525 | 0492 |
| **N888PS** | **C52B** | **0263** |
| N888PT | LJ35 | 391 |
| **N888PY** | **C525** | **0492** |
| **N888QS** | **HS25** | **HA-0042** |
| N888R | WW24 | 254 |
| **N888RA** | **C525** | **0135** |
| N888RB | LJ25 | 150 |
| N888RE | C560 | 0260 |
| N888RF | C550 | 108 |
| N888RF | FA20 | 272 |
| N888RK | C525 | 0331 |
| **N888RK** | **C52B** | **0097** |
| **N888RL** | **C550** | **275** |
| N888RT | C550 | 275 |
| N888RT | C560 | 0260 |
| N888RT | C56X | 5047 |
| **N888RT** | **CL30** | **20162** |
| N888RW | JSTR | 5040 |
| N888SF | C525 | 0480 |
| **N888SF** | **C680** | **0154** |
| N888SQ | GLF4 | 1305 |
| N888SS | HS25 | 258106 |

N888SV C560 0442
N888SW GLF2 117
N888SW HS25 257134
**N888TF C510 0023**
**N888TJ HS25 25250**
(N888TN) LJ36 026
**N888TW LJ24 292**
**N888TX C650 7003**
(N888UD) CL30 20142
N888UE GLF4 1032
**N888UP SBRL 465-68**
N888VS GLF3 450
(N888WJ) FA10 89
N888WK HS25 25141
N888WL GLF3 471
N888WL SBRL 306-27
**N888WS CL61 5170**
N888WS FA20 148
N888WT JSTR 5070/52
(N888WW) JSTR 5061/48
**N888WY HS25 258921**
N888WZ GLF3 397
N888XL C500 177
**N888XL C550 598**
**N888YC ASTR 266**
**N888YZ GLF2 92**
**N888ZF GLF4 1466**
**N888ZY EA50 000213**
**N888ZZ HS25 258017**
**N889B C550 550-1047**
**N889BW EA50 000248**
**N889CA LJ45 132**
**N889CP GLEX 9104**
N889DF GLF2 95/39
N889DH HS25 258051
**N889DW LJ60 117**
N889F FA20 64
N889FA C550 162
N889G C650 0023
**N889G GALX 046**
N889GA GLF2 97
**N889JA GLEX 9148**
(N889JC) GLEX 9068
**N889JC GLF2 158**
N889JF LJ24 019
**N889MR GALX 074**
N889QS HS25 HA-0019
**N889QS HS25 HA-0021**
N889RA SBRL 465-22
N889RP CS55 0158
**N889TC GLF4 1042**
**N889TD F900 94**
N889WF LJ24 060
N889WF LJ24 237
N890A GLF2 16/13
N890A GLF3 325
N890A GLF4 1396
N890A HS25 258071
**N890BA WW24 301**
**N890BB F9DX 611**
N890BH BE40 RK-208
**N890BJ LJ25 229**
N890CW HS25 258510
(N890E) FA10 53
N890F FA20 65
N890FH F9EX 99
N890FH FA50 31
N890GA FA50 89
N890HJ HFB3 1026
(N890K) LJ25 089
**N890LE C56X 5628**
**N890LJ LJ35 487**
N890LR LJ35 487
N890MC C650 0199
(N890MC) JSTR 5033/56
N890PT LJ24 236
**N890QS HS25 HA-0010**
N890RC HS25 25084
N890SP HS25 258530
**N890TJ GLF2 23**
(N890VC) HS25 258590
N890WW WW24 190
**N891CA C500 168**
N891CQ FA10 53
N891F FA20 66
**N891FV C560 0427**
N891HJ HFB3 1036
N891M C560 0085
N891MG GLF3 357
**N891P LJ25 340**
**N891QS HS25 258788**
(N892BP) HS25 258188
N892CA C500 044
N892F FA20 68
N892GA GLF2 60
N892HJ HFB3 1037
**N892PB C550 064**
**N892QS HS25 258592**
N892S FA20 379
N892SB C560 0208
N892SB FA20 379
**N892SB GALX 072**
**N892TM GLF2 121**
**N892Z C56X 6007**
N893AC CL61 5018
N893CA C500 374
N893CF LJ35 669
N893CM C560 0226
N893CW HS25 258603
N893EJ HS25 258193
N893F FA20 69
**N893FL HS25 258603**
N893HJ HFB3 1039
N893M C560 0237
**N893QS HS25 258393**
N893WA LJ25 169
**N894C C52A 0013**
N894CA FA10 36
N894CA HS25 258366
N894F FA20 133
N894GA GLF2 145
N894HJ HFB3 1045
N894Q C525 0253
**N894QS HS25 HA-0005**
**N894TW WW24 354**
**N895BB CL30 20156**
N895CC CL60 1039
**N895CC CL61 5177**
N895CC HS25 257072
N895F FA20 134
**N895HE C550 641**
N895HJ HFB3 1051
N895J LJ24 213
N895LD C560 0034
N895QS HS25 258597
**N895QS HS25 258606**
(N895QS) HS25 258618
**N896BB CL30 20177**
**N896C BE40 RK-53**
**N896CG C550 550-1055**
N896CW HS25 258516
**N896DA FA50 117**
N896EC C650 0196
N896GA GLF2 149
**N896GA GLF5 5296**
N896HJ HFB3 1054
N896MA C500 290
N896MA C550 134
**N896MA C550 550-1065**
N896MB C500 290
**N896P C52A 0379**
N896QS HS25 258596
(N896QS) HS25 258612
N896QS HS25 258618
**N896QS HS25 258640**
N896R LJ60 091
**N896RJ C650 0178**
**N897A HS25 258326**
N897AT BE40 RK-157
**N897CW HS25 258077**
N897D FA20 134
N897DM FA20 134
N897GA GLF2 146
N897HJ HFB3 1055
N897MC C550 550-0914
**N897QS HS25 HA-0014**
N897R LJ60 097
**N898AK CL61 5040**
**N898AN CL64 5408**
**N898AW GLF4 1283**
**N898CB C560 0097**
N898CC CL64 5367
**N898CT F2TH 60**
**N898EW CL61 5134**
N898GA GLF2 147
N898GF C560 0121
**N898MC C56X 5244**
**N898PA LJ60 111**
**N898QS HS25 258593**
(N898QS) HS25 258602
N898R CL64 5408
N898SC GLEX 9066
N898SR WW24 224
**N898TA BE40 RK-295**
**N898TS F900 95**
**N898WS GLEX 9271**
**N899AB HS25 257042**
**N899AK HA4T RC-20**
**N899B C550 550-1073**
N899BC C56X 5030
N899CS LJ31 052
N899DC C550 550-0899
N899DM HS25 257028
N899GA GLF2 43
N899GM GLF5 508
**N899MA C52B 0073**
N899MA C550 134
N899N C500 114
**N899NH C52B 0242**
N899QS HS25 258399
**N899QS HS25 HA-0019**
N899QS HS25 HA-0021
N899RR C52B 0020
N899S WW24 101
(N899SA) HS25 25146
N899SC HS25 258602
N899SC LJ60 040
**N899SR GLF5 5231**
**N899ST CL65 5791**
N899TA BE40 RK-292
N899TG SBRL 282-13
**N899U F2TH 199**
N899WA LJ35 049
N899WW CL61 3011
**N900AD HS25 25275**
N900AF C550 022
N900AJ LJ25 027
N900AK GLF2 108
N900AL GLF4 1097
**N900AL GLF4 4048**
**N900AP GLF4 1097**
(N900AR) FA10 157
N900BA C550 242
N900BD LJ24 143
(N900BF) F900 39
(N900BF) F900 71
N900BF GLF2 206
N900BF WW24 382
**N900BJ LJ35 123**
N900BL HS25 257185
(N900BM) C550 126
N900BR GLF2 111
**N900BT C525 0377**
N900BT MU30 A046SA
**N900BZ F9EX 37**
N900CC C500 310
N900CC CL61 3042
N900CC F900 183
N900CC HS25 257043
N900CD HS25 25111
N900CE GLF2 10
**N900CH F2EX 1**
N900CH FA20 383/550
N900CH FA50 264
N900CJ LJ25 020
N900CL CL61 5031
N900CL CL61 5122
N900CM C650 0017
**N900CM FA50 321**
**N900CP HS25 257066**
N900CQ HS25 257066
N900CR JSTR 5036/42
N900CS F900 104
N900CS SBRL 282-17
N900CS WW24 212
N900CX F9EX 19
**N900D F900 131**
N900D FA10 141
N900DA F900 170
N900DB FA20 327
**N900DB JSTR 5225**
(N900DG) LJ35 378
N900DH C500 576
**N900DH GLF2 111**
**N900DL ASTR 030**
N900DL C500 576
N900DL LJ24 109
N900DM C500 421
N900DM CS55 0067
N900DP CL60 1036
**N900DS C525 0032**
N900DS HS25 25187
(N900DU) F900 97
N900DV F900 148
N900DW F900 179
**N900DW FA7X 39**
N900DW MU30 A026SA
**N900E C560 0206**
N900EB C52A 0008
**N900EB C680 0008**
N900EC LJ35 236
(N900EF) BE40 RJ-47
N900EF BE40 RK-68
**N900EG GLF4 1101**
N900EJ C750 0109
N900EL HS25 25222
**N900EL LJ31 200**
N900EM LJ35 185
N900ES CL64 5381
N900ES GLF2 174
N900EX F9EX 103
N900EX F9EX 114
(N900EX) F9EX 117
N900EX F9EX 12
N900EX F9EX 120
(N900EX) F9EX 140
N900EX F9EX 159
N900EX F9EX 178
N900EX F9EX 201
N900EX F9EX 27
N900EX F9EX 40
N900EX F9EX 63
N900EX F9EX 84
N900FA LJ55 024
N900FC CL60 1045
N900FG HS25 HA-0105
N900FH F9EX 6
N900FJ F900 10
N900FJ F900 116
N900FJ F900 126
N900FJ F900 131
N900FJ F900 147
N900FJ F900 158
N900FJ F900 166
N900FJ F900 179
N900FJ F900 31
N900FJ F900 42
N900FJ F900 60
N900FJ F900 79
N900FJ F900 98
**N900FJ F9EX 233**
N900FL C650 7049
**N900FN CL61 5118**
N900FR FA20 223
N900FS WW24 191
N900FU HS25 HA-0105
**N900G C500 268**
N900GB GLF4 1025
**N900GC C500 298**
**N900GG LJ24 216**
**N900GW C525 0323**
**N900GX GLEX 9298**
**N900H CL61 5080**
N900H JSTR 5135
N900H WW24 388
**N900HA C52A 0039**
N900HC F900 68
**N900HC F9EX 127**
**N900HD F9EX 103**
**N900HE F900 68**
**N900HG F9EX 1**
N900JA LJ24 108
**N900JB FA50 113**
N900JB FA50 59
N900JB LJ55 088
**N900JC LJ35 178**
N900JD C500 023
(N900JD) C650 0199
N900JD C650 0213
(N900JD) C650 0215
**N900JD C680 0109**
N900JD LJ25 020

| Reg | Type | C/n |
|---|---|---|
| N900JE | LJ35 | 123 |
| N900JE | LJ35 | 674 |
| (N900JF) | F9EX | 168 |
| **N900JF** | **WW24** | **191** |
| **N900JG** | **F9EX** | **168** |
| (N900JG) | HS25 | 257069 |
| N900JL | FA20 | 171 |
| N900JL | WW24 | 80 |
| **N900JT** | **HS25** | **257147** |
| (N900JV) | LJ35 | 091 |
| N900KC | C500 | 055 |
| (N900KC) | HS25 | 25038 |
| N900KC | HS25 | 25191 |
| N900KC | HS25 | 257021 |
| N900KC | HS25 | 258232 |
| N900KD | F900 | 131 |
| **N900KE** | **FA50** | **52** |
| **N900KJ** | **F900** | **199** |
| N900KK | LJ60 | 052 |
| N900KM | F9EX | 177 |
| **N900KR** | **F900** | **146** |
| N900KX | F9EX | 98 |
| N900LA | GLF3 | 379 |
| N900LC | C550 | 040 |
| **N900LC** | **F900** | **186** |
| N900LC | FA20 | 122 |
| **N900LD** | **HS25** | **HA-0008** |
| **N900LF** | **GLEX** | **9015** |
| **N900LG** | **CL60** | **1036** |
| N900LH | MU30 | A018SA |
| N900LJ | C550 | 011 |
| (N900LL) | C500 | 499 |
| **N900LM** | **CS55** | **0145** |
| N900LM | WW24 | 373 |
| **N900LS** | **GLEX** | **9216** |
| N900LS | GLF4 | 1178 |
| N900LS | GLF4 | 1401 |
| N900MA | F900 | 67 |
| N900MC | C500 | 427 |
| **N900MC** | **F2TH** | **228** |
| N900MD | HS25 | 257107 |
| N900MD | HS25 | 258019 |
| N900MD | LJ36 | 045 |
| N900MF | C550 | 074 |
| **N900MF** | **F9EX** | **112** |
| **N900MG** | **F900** | **67** |
| N900MJ | F900 | 48 |
| N900MJ | F9EX | 57 |
| N900MK | F9EX | 29 |
| N900MM | C500 | 522 |
| N900MN | C650 | 7027 |
| N900MP | C500 | 055 |
| N900MP | GLF2 | 99 |
| N900MR | HS25 | 257072 |
| N900MT | F9EX | 57 |
| **N900MV** | **F9EX** | **131** |
| **N900NA** | **LJ24** | **111** |
| N900NB | F900 | 190 |
| **N900NB** | **F9EX** | **169** |
| N900NE | F900 | 83 |
| N900NF | F9EX | 169 |
| **N900NH** | **F2TH** | **206** |
| N900NM | CL61 | 5057 |
| N900NS | F9EX | 150 |
| N900NW | WW24 | 337 |
| N900P | C525 | 0234 |
| N900P | FA20 | 36 |
| N900P | LJ25 | 049 |
| N900P | LJ31 | 199 |
| N900P | LJ35 | 457 |
| N900P | LJ45 | 173 |
| **N900P** | **LJ60** | **366** |
| N900P | SBRL | 306-12 |
| N900PA | WW24 | 400 |
| **N900PB** | **C550** | **566** |
| **N900PE** | **HS25** | **HA-0057** |
| **N900PF** | **HS25** | **HA-0022** |
| N900PJ | LJ55 | 064 |
| **N900PJ** | **WW24** | **135** |
| N900PL | F9EX | 44 |
| N900PS | C500 | 362 |
| **N900PS** | **C560** | **0118** |
| N900Q | F900 | 93 |
| N900Q | F9EX | 10 |
| N900Q | LJ25 | 049 |
| N900QM | C650 | 0017 |
| **N900QS** | **C750** | **0123** |
| **N900R** | **HS25** | **HA-0013** |
| N900R | LJ31 | 101 |
| N900R | LJ35 | 488 |
| **N900RA** | **FA20** | **59** |
| N900RB | C500 | 664 |
| N900RB | CS55 | 0086 |
| N900RD | C500 | 664 |
| N900RD | LJ35 | 261 |
| (N900RF) | F9EX | 209 |
| (N900RG) | CS55 | 0065 |
| **N900RL** | **GLF4** | **1150** |
| N900RL | HS25 | 258090 |
| N900RN | F900 | 26 |
| **N900RX** | **F900** | **183** |
| N900SA | JSTR | 5148 |
| N900SB | F900 | 14 |
| (N900SB) | F9EX | 12 |
| **N900SB** | **F9EX** | **26** |
| N900SE | C550 | 074 |
| **N900SF** | **F900** | **16** |
| N900SF | GLF2 | 167 |
| N900SG | F9EX | 159 |
| N900SJ | F900 | 19 |
| **N900SJ** | **F9EX** | **7** |
| **N900SM** | **C560** | **0014** |
| N900SM | F900 | 176 |
| **N900SN** | **F9EX** | **117** |
| N900SQ | BE40 | RK-416 |
| N900SS | C550 | 550-0941 |
| N900SS | CL61 | 5047 |
| N900ST | BE40 | RK-416 |
| **N900ST** | **HS25** | **258777** |
| **N900SX** | **F900** | **139** |
| N900T | C500 | 135 |
| N900T | FA10 | 134 |
| **N900TA** | **C500** | **182** |
| N900TA | F900 | 50 |
| (N900TE) | C550 | 203 |
| N900TF | C550 | 203 |
| **N900TG** | **F900** | **155** |
| N900TJ | C550 | 203 |
| N900TJ | GLF2 | 199/19 |
| N900TN | C550 | 430 |
| N900TN | WW24 | 400 |
| N900TP | GLF2 | 160 |
| N900TR | F900 | 170 |
| N900TR | F900 | 9 |
| N900TW | C500 | 563 |
| N900TW | C525 | 0455 |
| N900UC | FA10 | 33 |
| N900UD | C650 | 0213 |
| N900UT | F900 | 140 |
| N900VG | F900 | 148 |
| **N900VG** | **F9EX** | **178** |
| (N900VH) | F900 | 148 |
| **N900VL** | **F900** | **60** |
| N900VL | GLF2 | 99 |
| N900VM | F9EX | 64 |
| **N900VP** | **WW24** | **289** |
| N900VT | F900 | 131 |
| N900W | C500 | 014 |
| N900W | FA50 | 60 |
| N900WA | LJ25 | 248 |
| N900WB | FA20 | 139 |
| **N900WF** | **F900** | **117** |
| N900WG | F900 | 83 |
| N900WG | HS25 | 25236 |
| N900WJ | GLF2 | 190 |
| N900WJ | MU30 | A028SA |
| **N900WK** | **F900** | **57** |
| (N900WP) | F900 | 183 |
| **N900WR** | **GLF4** | **1416** |
| N900WW | WW24 | 321 |
| **N900WY** | **CL30** | **20035** |
| N900Y | LJ24 | 111 |
| N900Y | LJ36 | 014 |
| **N900YP** | **F9EX** | **114** |
| N900ZA | F9EX | 96 |
| **N901AB** | **C560** | **0302** |
| N901AS | GLF2 | 88/21 |
| N901B | F900 | 24 |
| N901BB | F900 | 42 |
| N901BM | CL61 | 5044 |
| N901BM | GLF2 | 120 |
| N901C | JSTR | 5218 |
| **N901CD** | **SBRL** | **465-39** |
| **N901CJ** | **C525** | **0278** |
| **N901CR** | **C56X** | **5141** |
| N901DK | C560 | 0544 |
| **N901DK** | **C56X** | **5505** |
| **N901EB** | **C52A** | **0008** |
| **N901EH** | **GLF3** | **333** |
| N901EH | JSTR | 5230 |
| **N901FH** | **C56X** | **5160** |
| N901FH | GLF3 | 333 |
| N901FH | JSTR | 5230 |
| (N901FJ) | F900 | 147 |
| N901FJ | F900 | 79 |
| N901FR | FA20 | 270 |
| **N901G** | **C680** | **0065** |
| N901GA | GALX | 201 |
| N901GA | GLF3 | 249 |
| N901GA | GLF5 | 5001 |
| **N901GW** | **C525** | **0470** |
| **N901GX** | **GLEX** | **9001** |
| N901H | JSTR | 5092/58 |
| N901HB | SJ30 | 006 |
| N901JC | LJ55 | 088 |
| (N901JF) | GLF3 | 315 |
| N901JL | WW24 | 38 |
| N901K | GLF2 | 36/3 |
| N901K | GLF4 | 1075 |
| N901K | HS25 | 258329 |
| **N901K** | **HS25** | **HA-0009** |
| N901KB | GLF2 | 36/3 |
| N901MD | F9EX | 38 |
| N901MH | FA10 | 110 |
| N901MK | FA50 | 157 |
| **N901MM** | **F9EX** | **21** |
| (N901MS) | LJ35 | 360 |
| N901MV | C52B | 0114 |
| N901NB | C500 | 661 |
| N901P | BE40 | RJ-20 |
| **N901P** | **LJ31** | **199** |
| **N901PM** | **LJ25** | **280** |
| N901PV | CS55 | 0156 |
| N901QS | C750 | 0101 |
| **N901QS** | **C750** | **0102** |
| **N901RD** | **HS25** | **HA-0018** |
| **N901RH** | **C650** | **0130** |
| N901RL | HS25 | 258090 |
| N901RM | C550 | 242 |
| N901RM | C560 | 0116 |
| N901RP | HS25 | 258090 |
| N901SB | C650 | 7008 |
| N901SB | F900 | 33 |
| **N901SB** | **F9EX** | **122** |
| N901SB | FA20 | 446 |
| N901SB | FA20 | 493 |
| N901SG | HS25 | 258762 |
| **N901SS** | **F900** | **187** |
| N901TA | CL61 | 5141 |
| N901TC | FA20 | 335 |
| N901TC | HS25 | 25108 |
| **N901TF** | **FA50** | **285** |
| N901TG | HS25 | 25108 |
| **N901TX** | **F900** | **170** |
| N901WG | GLF2 | 126 |
| N901YP | FA20 | 360 |
| N902 | GLF2 | 11 |
| **N902** | **GLF4** | **1310** |
| N902AB | LJ24 | 068 |
| **N902AG** | **CL64** | **5512** |
| N902AR | LJ24 | 068 |
| N902AR | LJ24 | 237 |
| **N902AU** | **ASTR** | **025** |
| N902AV | C560 | 0326 |
| N902BE | HS25 | HA-0070 |
| (N902BE) | HS25 | HA-0081 |
| **N902BW** | **CL61** | **5005** |
| N902C | GLF3 | 388 |
| N902CG | CL64 | 5427 |
| **N902DD** | **C500** | **126** |
| **N902DK** | **C550** | **732** |
| N902DP | C525 | 0644 |
| **N902DW** | **F900** | **179** |
| **N902F** | **C650** | **7022** |
| N902FR | FA20 | 132 |
| N902G | ASTR | 030 |
| N902GA | GLF2 | 11 |
| N902GT | GLF2 | 2 |
| **N902GW** | **C525** | **0553** |
| N902JC | LJ35 | 227 |
| N902K | GLF3 | 386 |
| N902K | GLF4 | 1113 |
| N902K | JSTR | 5104/6 |
| N902KB | GLF3 | 386 |
| N902KB | JSTR | 5104/6 |
| **N902L** | **GLF4** | **1504** |
| **N902LG** | **C510** | **0066** |
| N902M | F900 | 152 |
| **N902MC** | **F2TH** | **130** |
| N902MK | F900 | 152 |
| (N902MK) | GLF2 | 241 |
| **N902MM** | **GLEX** | **9097** |
| **N902MP** | **CL64** | **5559** |
| N902MP | GLF2 | 241 |
| **N902NC** | **F900** | **97** |
| N902P | BE40 | RJ-15 |
| (N902PC) | BE40 | RK-28 |
| N902PC | FA10 | 106 |
| N902PM | HS25 | 257036 |
| N902QS | C750 | 0002 |
| N902RD | C525 | 0453 |
| N902RD | PRM1 | RB-74 |
| N902RL | LJ55 | 087 |
| N902RM | C650 | 7022 |
| N902RM | HS25 | 257036 |
| N902SB | C650 | 7008 |
| N902SB | FA20 | 504 |
| N902SB | FA50 | 308 |
| N902T | C500 | 135 |
| N902TA | CL61 | 5139 |
| **N902TF** | **FA50** | **303** |
| N902VP | C650 | 0209 |
| **N902VP** | **C750** | **0002** |
| N902WJ | LJ36 | 040 |
| N903AG | GLF2 | 172 |
| N903AG | LJ60 | 045 |
| **N903AL** | **LJ35** | **084** |
| N903AM | LJ60 | 104 |
| **N903AM** | **LJ60** | **269** |
| **N903BH** | **C560** | **0295** |
| **N903BT** | **LJ45** | **353** |
| **N903CG** | **BE40** | **RK-333** |
| **N903CS** | **FA50** | **138** |
| **N903DD** | **CL60** | **1038** |
| **N903DK** | **C56X** | **5093** |
| N903FH | C56X | 5160 |
| (N903FJ) | F900 | 98 |
| N903FJ | F9EX | 3 |
| N903FR | FA20 | 20 |
| N903G | GLF2 | 172 |
| N903G | GLF3 | 422 |
| **N903G** | **GLF4** | **4183** |
| N903G | SBRL | 282-60 |
| N903GA | GLF2 | 172 |
| (N903GL) | GLF3 | 422 |
| **N903GS** | **F2TH** | **183** |
| **N903GW** | **C525** | **0676** |
| N903HC | LJ35 | 440 |
| N903HC | LJ45 | 010 |
| N903JC | LJ55 | 081 |
| (N903JF) | GLF4 | 1051 |
| **N903JP** | **C510** | **0102** |
| N903K | HS25 | 258329 |
| N903K | SBRL | 282-33 |
| N903K | SBRL | 465-57 |
| N903KB | SBRL | 282-33 |
| (N903KP) | GLF4 | 1051 |
| N903LJ | LJ31 | 242 |
| **N903MM** | **WW24** | **235** |
| **N903MT** | **PRM1** | **RB-24** |
| **N903QS** | **C750** | **0162** |
| N903RL | LJ45 | 227 |
| N903SB | C650 | 7061 |
| N903SB | FA20 | 335 |
| N903SB | FA50 | 309 |
| N903SC | HS25 | 257004 |
| N903TA | CL61 | 5080 |
| **N903TC** | **CL30** | **20083** |
| N903TC | GLF3 | 454 |
| N903TF | GLEX | 9097 |
| N903VP | C550 | 550-0903 |
| N903WJ | LJ35 | 380 |
| N903XP | HS25 | HA-0003 |
| (N904AM) | C525 | 0230 |
| N904AM | C52A | 0020 |
| **N904BB** | **C550** | **550-0904** |
| **N904BW** | **HS25** | **258042** |
| N904DP | C525 | 0503 |
| **N904DS** | **GLEX** | **9118** |
| N904FR | FA20 | 151 |
| (N904FR) | FA20 | 223 |
| **N904GA** | **GLF4** | **4204** |

| | | |
|---|---|---|
| N904GA | GLF5 | 5004 |
| N904GP | HS25 | 258179 |
| **N904GR** | **HS25** | **258179** |
| **N904GW** | **C525** | **0681** |
| N904H | HS25 | 258239 |
| **N904HD** | **LJ45** | **149** |
| **N904JK** | **CL64** | **5615** |
| **N904JR** | **HS25** | **258018** |
| **N904JY** | **F9EX** | **187** |
| N904K | SBRL | 282-42 |
| N904K | SBRL | 465-23 |
| N904KB | SBRL | 282-42 |
| (N904KB) | SBRL | 465-23 |
| N904M | F900 | 40 |
| **N904QS** | **C750** | **0210** |
| N904SB | FA20 | 446 |
| **N904SB** | **FA50** | **284** |
| N904SB | HS25 | 258016 |
| **N904SJ** | **C550** | **604** |
| **N904TC** | **GLF4** | **1444** |
| (N904VA) | CS55 | 0059 |
| N904XP | HS25 | HA-0004 |
| **N905B** | **F2TH** | **132** |
| N905BG | SBRL | 306-30 |
| **N905CK** | **LJ36** | **005** |
| **N905CW** | **C550** | **072** |
| N905EM | C550 | 032 |
| N905EX | F9EX | 5 |
| N905FJ | F900 | 5 |
| N905FR | FA20 | 213 |
| **N905GW** | **C525** | **0682** |
| N905H | HS25 | 258275 |
| N905K | SBRL | 282-49 |
| N905K | SBRL | 465-17 |
| N905KB | SBRL | 282-49 |
| N905LC | C550 | 581 |
| **N905LC** | **C560** | **0334** |
| N905LC | LJ35 | 320 |
| N905LD | LJ35 | 320 |
| **N905LP** | **GLF4** | **1321** |
| N905M | SBRL | 282-12 |
| **N905MP** | **CL60** | **1039** |
| **N905MT** | **HS25** | **258430** |
| N905MW | HFB3 | 1027 |
| N905P | SBRL | 306-62 |
| **N905QS** | **C750** | **0105** |
| N905R | SBRL | 306-30 |
| N905R | SBRL | 306-62 |
| N905R | SBRL | 306-99 |
| **N905RL** | **LJ55** | **074** |
| (N905SB) | CL64 | 5312 |
| N905SB | FA20 | 360 |
| N905SB | FA50 | 348 |
| **N905T** | **GLEX** | **9179** |
| N905TS | F900 | 5 |
| N905WJ | LJ25 | 105 |
| **N905WS** | **C680** | **0141** |
| (N905Y) | HS25 | 25199 |
| N906AS | C560 | 0547 |
| **N906AS** | **HS25** | **258569** |
| (N906BL) | HS25 | 258801 |
| **N906BL** | **HS25** | **258806** |
| **N906DK** | **C56X** | **6016** |
| (N906EA) | C500 | 490 |
| **N906FM** | **PRM1** | **RB-176** |
| N906FR | FA20 | 214 |
| **N906GA** | **GLF4** | **4206** |
| N906GA | GLF5 | 5006 |
| N906GX | GLEX | 9006 |
| **N906JW** | **GLEX** | **9110** |
| N906NB | F900 | 190 |
| N906NB | F9EX | 169 |
| **N906P** | **LJ45** | **173** |
| **N906QS** | **C750** | **0206** |
| N906SB | C560 | 0092A |
| N906SB | CL64 | 5313 |
| N906SB | CS55 | 0139 |
| N906SB | F900 | 14 |
| N906SB | FA50 | 349 |
| N906SB | HS25 | 258016 |
| N906SU | LJ25 | 123 |
| N906TC | CL30 | 20083 |
| **N906TF** | **CL64** | **5366** |
| **N906WK** | **F900** | **102** |
| N907CS | LJ24 | 137 |
| **N907DF** | **C650** | **0120** |
| **N907DK** | **C525** | **0338** |
| **N907DP** | **ASTR** | **100** |
| N907DX | F9DX | 607 |
| (N907EA) | C560 | 0104 |
| N907EX | F9EX | 207 |
| N907FJ | F9EX | 7 |
| N907FR | FA20 | 224 |
| (N907FR) | FA20 | 270 |
| **N907GA** | **GLF4** | **4207** |
| N907GA | GLF5 | 5007 |
| N907GX | GLEX | 9007 |
| **N907JE** | **BE40** | **RK-107** |
| N907KH | C500 | 599 |
| N907M | FA50 | 35 |
| **N907MC** | **HS25** | **258340** |
| **N907QS** | **C750** | **0201** |
| N907R | LJ35 | 488 |
| N907R | SBRL | 306-40 |
| (N907RM) | C650 | 0103 |
| N907RT | C500 | 255 |
| N907SB | C560 | 0109A |
| N907SB | CS55 | 0141 |
| **N907SB** | **FA7X** | **13** |
| N907SK | LJ60 | 092 |
| N907SW | GLF2 | 71 |
| **N907TF** | **FA10** | **107** |
| **N907WL** | **C525** | **0658** |
| **N907WS** | **CL61** | **5048** |
| N908AS | C560 | 0547 |
| N908BX | GLEX | 9084 |
| **N908CA** | **F900** | **151** |
| N908CE | GLF2 | 70/1 |
| **N908CH** | **FA20** | **383/550** |
| N908CL | CL61 | 5031 |
| N908CL | CL61 | 5122 |
| **N908DG** | **CL61** | **5018** |
| **N908DH** | **GLF4** | **1040** |
| N908EF | FA50 | 46 |
| N908EJ | GLF2 | 70/1 |
| N908FR | FA20 | 207 |
| N908G | CL64 | 5326 |
| N908GA | GLF5 | 5008 |
| N908GA | GLF5 | 5208 |
| N908HC | LJ35 | 440 |
| **N908JB** | **F900** | **112** |
| N908JE | GLF2 | 151/24 |
| N908JE | HS25 | 257087 |
| **N908QS** | **C750** | **0108** |
| N908R | BE40 | RK-44 |
| N908R | SBRL | 306-18 |
| N908R | SBRL | 306-23 |
| N908R | SBRL | 306-55 |
| N908RF | FA10 | 46 |
| N908SB | C650 | 7061 |
| **N908SB** | **F9EX** | **81** |
| (N908SB) | FA10 | 46 |
| N908TE | GLEX | 9097 |
| **N908TF** | **FA10** | **102** |
| **N908VZ** | **GLF4** | **4051** |
| N908VZ | HS25 | 258313 |
| N909AS | F900 | 127 |
| N909B | HS25 | 25082 |
| (N909CA) | C550 | 550-0909 |
| **N909CF** | **F2EX** | **4** |
| **N909DP** | **C525** | **0503** |
| (N909ES) | CL64 | 5381 |
| (N909F) | C525 | 0249 |
| N909FJ | F9EX | 9 |
| N909FK | GLF2 | 241 |
| N909FR | FA20 | 209 |
| N909GA | GLF4 | 4009 |
| **N909GA** | **GLF4** | **4209** |
| N909GA | GLF5 | 5009 |
| N909GA | MU30 | A009SA |
| **N909JE** | **GLF2** | **151/24** |
| **N909JM** | **FA50** | **304** |
| **N909JS** | **LJ60** | **206** |
| N909L | GLF2 | 112 |
| **N909LA** | **C56X** | **5021** |
| N909LS | GLF4 | 1178 |
| **N909M** | **C525** | **0249** |
| N909MG | CL60 | 1010 |
| N909MK | GLF2 | 241 |
| **N909MM** | **F2EX** | **38** |
| N909MM | F9EX | 88 |
| **N909MN** | **C52A** | **0351** |
| **N909PM** | **F900** | **176** |
| **N909PS** | **C500** | **362** |
| N909QS | C750 | 0009 |
| (N909RG) | CS55 | 0065 |
| **N909RR** | **GLF3** | **332** |
| N909RX | GLF4 | 1239 |
| N909SB | C650 | 7008 |
| **N909SB** | **F9EX** | **56** |
| **N909SK** | **LJ60** | **060** |
| (N909SP) | GLF4 | 1210 |
| **N909ST** | **BE40** | **RK-194** |
| **N909TF** | **FA10** | **51** |
| **N909VJ** | **FA50** | **69** |
| (N910A) | GLF3 | 367 |
| N910A | GLF3 | 369 |
| N910B | GLF4 | 1102 |
| N910BD | LJ45 | 264 |
| (N910BH) | C52B | 0130 |
| N910BH | SBRL | 380-54 |
| **N910CN** | **FA50** | **59** |
| N910CS | C56X | 5036 |
| **N910CS** | **F2TH** | **87** |
| N910CS | F900 | 126 |
| N910DC | GLF5 | 544 |
| **N910DF** | **C650** | **0081** |
| N910DP | C650 | 0081 |
| **N910DP** | **C750** | **0239** |
| N910DS | CS55 | 0154 |
| N910E | JSTR | 5084/8 |
| N910E | SBRL | 282-29 |
| **N910EX** | **F9EX** | **10** |
| N910F | C650 | 0051 |
| (N910FJ) | F900 | 10 |
| N910FJ | F9EX | 10 |
| N910FR | FA20 | 280/503 |
| **N910G** | **C500** | **462** |
| N910G | C550 | 575 |
| N910G | JSTR | 5112/7 |
| N910GA | GALX | 200 |
| N910GA | GLF4 | 4010 |
| N910GA | GLF5 | 5010 |
| N910H | C550 | 691 |
| N910HM | C550 | 674 |
| **N910HM** | **C560** | **0318** |
| **N910J** | **CL64** | **5640** |
| **N910JB** | **LJ25** | **213** |
| N910JD | HS25 | 258258 |
| **N910JD** | **HS25** | **258420** |
| N910JN | HS25 | 258258 |
| **N910JW** | **F900** | **31** |
| N910KB | CL61 | 3007 |
| N910L | FA20 | 191 |
| N910M | C650 | 0069 |
| N910M | JSTR | 5069/20 |
| N910MH | WW24 | 45 |
| **N910MT** | **C550** | **057** |
| **N910MW** | **F9EX** | **85** |
| N910N | C500 | 158 |
| **N910N** | **C550** | **550-1032** |
| N910PC | C560 | 0273 |
| **N910Q** | **F900** | **156** |
| **N910QS** | **C750** | **0110** |
| N910R | GLF2 | 234 |
| **N910RB** | **C550** | **297** |
| (N910RL) | C750 | 0112 |
| N910S | GLF2 | 234 |
| N910S | GLF4 | 1155 |
| N910SH | BE40 | RK-72 |
| **N910SY** | **C510** | **0009** |
| **N910TS*** | **GLEX** | **9120** |
| N910U | FA20 | 39 |
| N910V | C560 | 0165 |
| N910V | GLF5 | 636 |
| (N910VP) | HS25 | 258085 |
| N910W | FA20 | 192 |
| N910Y | C500 | 158 |
| N910Y | FA20 | 48 |
| (N911A) | C500 | 087 |
| N911AE | LJ35 | 109 |
| **N911AJ** | **LJ25** | **163** |
| N911AS | HS25 | 25039 |
| N911BB | CS55 | 0128 |
| N911CB | C550 | 662 |
| **N911CB** | **C560** | **0604** |
| (N911CB) | C560 | 0634 |
| (N911CJ) | C500 | 087 |
| N911CR | JSTR | 5150/37 |
| N911CR | SBRL | 380-59 |
| **N911CU** | **WW24** | **246** |
| N911DB | GLF2 | 100 |
| N911DB | LJ35 | 231 |
| **N911DG** | **FA20** | **162/451** |
| **N911DT** | **FA20** | **471** |
| **N911DX** | **LJ35** | **499** |
| **N911EK** | **C56X** | **5742** |
| N911EM | LJ25 | 319 |
| N911FC | LJ55 | 091 |
| N911FR | FA20 | 295/500 |
| **N911GM** | **C500** | **048** |
| **N911GU** | **WW24** | **343** |
| N911HB | FA50 | 157 |
| N911JD | C500 | 082 |
| N911JG | LJ25 | 147 |
| (N911JJ) | MU30 | A020SA |
| (N911JJ) | MU30 | A085SA |
| N911KB | LJ24 | 128 |
| N911KT | GLF3 | 438 |
| N911LM | LJ25 | 070 |
| N911MG | LJ25 | 212 |
| N911ML | LJ35 | 256 |
| **N911MM** | **C500** | **390** |
| (N911MU) | C500 | 390 |
| **N911MX** | **EA50** | **000099** |
| (N911NJ) | C550 | 240 |
| **N911NP** | **C525** | **0273** |
| N911Q | SBRL | 282-17 |
| N911QB | C550 | 662 |
| **N911RD** | **HS25** | **25253** |
| N911RF | F900 | 20 |
| N911RF | FA10 | 46 |
| N911RF | FA50 | 46 |
| N911RF | LJ25 | 138 |
| N911RG | FA20 | 144 |
| N911SB | FA20 | 360 |
| **N911SH** | **F2TH** | **125** |
| **N911SP** | **WW24** | **244** |
| N911TR | FA20 | 242 |
| N911TR | LJ24 | 134 |
| **N911UM** | **C560** | **0562** |
| **N911UN** | **FA10** | **122** |
| N911WT | FA20 | 203 |
| N911WW | GLF2 | 257/17 |
| N911WX | LJ35 | 439 |
| N912AS | HS25 | 25124 |
| N912BD | C550 | 580 |
| N912BD | LJ45 | 277 |
| **N912DA** | **WW24** | **147** |
| **N912EL** | **C56X** | **6051** |
| N912EX | F9EX | 12 |
| **N912GW** | **C52A** | **0304** |
| **N912MM** | **LJ55** | **064** |
| **N912MT** | **F2EX** | **94** |
| N912QS | C750 | 0012 |
| **N912SH** | **BE40** | **RK-128** |
| N912TB | LJ31 | 024 |
| **N913BJ** | **C560** | **0011** |
| **N913CK** | **LJ35** | **013** |
| **N913DC** | **C52A** | **0157** |
| N913FJ | F9EX | 12 |
| N913GA | GLF4 | 4013 |
| N913GA | GLF4 | 4113 |
| N913GA | GLF5 | 5013 |
| N913HB | WW24 | 40 |
| N913JB | CL64 | 5338 |
| N913MC | BE40 | RJ-22 |
| N913MK | FA20 | 272 |
| N913MK | GLF3 | 407 |
| **N913MK** | **GLF4** | **4075** |
| **N913PD** | **GLF3** | **354** |
| **N913QS** | **C750** | **0113** |
| N913RC | C500 | 059 |
| (N913SC) | GLF4 | 1305 |
| **N913SC** | **HS25** | **258125** |
| N913SF | BE40 | RJ-22 |
| **N913SN** | **F9EX** | **35** |
| N913SQ | C650 | 7004 |
| N913SQ | GLF4 | 1430 |
| N913V | FA10 | 104 |
| N913V | HS25 | 257207 |
| N913VL | FA10 | 104 |
| N913VS | FA10 | 106 |
| N914BA | LJ24 | 128 |
| N914BB | CL61 | 3045 |
| N914BD | CL61 | 3045 |
| N914BD | F900 | 80 |
| **N914BD** | **GLF5** | **690** |
| N914BD | HS25 | 25229 |
| N914BS | GLF2 | 157 |
| **N914CD** | **C500** | **150** |
| N914CF | GLF2 | 190 |

| Registration | Type | C/n |
|---|---|---|
| **N914DD** | **F900** | **80** |
| **N914DM** | **WW24** | **357** |
| N914DT | GLEX | 9145 |
| N914DZ | GLF2 | 190 |
| **N914EG** | **GLF4** | **1174** |
| **N914FF** | **C52B** | **0184** |
| **N914G** | **C510** | **0239** |
| N914GA | GLF5 | 5014 |
| **N914GW** | **C510** | **0146** |
| N914H | HS25 | 258281 |
| N914J | F900 | 44 |
| N914J | F9EX | 15 |
| **N914J** | **GLF5** | **615** |
| (N914JC) | SBRL | 380-56 |
| N914JL | F900 | 44 |
| N914JL | F9EX | 15 |
| N914KA | GLF2 | 214 |
| N914KB | GLF2 | 214 |
| N914MH | GLF2 | 91 |
| N914MM | WW24 | 250 |
| N914P | JSTR | 5080 |
| **N914QS** | **C750** | **0296** |
| (N914RA) | LJ25 | 123 |
| N914SB | LJ25 | 014 |
| N914SH | BE40 | RK-193 |
| **N914SP** | **C680** | **0020** |
| N914X | CL60 | 1021 |
| **N914X** | **CL61** | **5185** |
| N914X | JSTR | 5080 |
| N914XA | CL60 | 1021 |
| **N915AM** | **GLF4** | **4179** |
| N915AM | HS25 | 258574 |
| **N915AP** | **HS25** | **258574** |
| **N915AV** | **GLEX** | **9115** |
| N915BB | C550 | 550-0915 |
| N915BB | CL61 | 5019 |
| N915BD | CL61 | 5019 |
| N915BD | CL61 | 5091 |
| N915BD | GLF4 | 4028 |
| N915C | GLF2 | 253 |
| N915EX | F9EX | 15 |
| N915GA | GLF4 | 4015 |
| N915GA | GLF5 | 5015 |
| N915JT | HS25 | 256002 |
| **N915MP** | **C52A** | **0024** |
| (N915MT) | HS25 | 258574 |
| N915QS | C750 | 0015 |
| N915R | SBRL | 306-42 |
| **N915RB** | **C750** | **0042** |
| N915RB | LJ35 | 647 |
| N915RJ | C52A | 0170 |
| N915RP | C500 | 270 |
| **N915RP** | **C525** | **0608** |
| N915SA | FA20 | 205 |
| **N915ST** | **C525** | **0301** |
| N915US | LJ24 | 189 |
| N915XP | HS25 | HA-0015 |
| N916AN | FA20 | 64 |
| N916BD | LJ31 | 093 |
| (N916BD) | LJ31 | 094 |
| **N916BD** | **LJ45** | **264** |
| N916BG | ASTR | 045 |
| N916BG | LJ60 | 206 |
| **N916BG** | **LJ60** | **236** |
| **N916CG** | **ASTR** | **045** |
| N916CG | C560 | 0400 |
| N916CS | C560 | 0400 |
| N916CS | C56X | 5153 |
| **N916CS** | **C56X** | **5625** |
| N916EX | F9EX | 16 |
| N916GA | GLF5 | 5016 |
| **N916GB** | **GALX** | **067** |
| N916GR | BE40 | RK-102 |
| N916GR | GALX | 067 |
| **N916GR** | **GALX** | **126** |
| N916H | HS25 | 258282 |
| N916JB | HS25 | HA-0150 |
| N916PT | HS25 | 258103 |
| **N916QS** | **C750** | **0116** |
| N916RC | C500 | 061 |
| N916RC | C550 | 211 |
| N916RC | JSTR | 5078/3 |
| (N916RG) | JSTR | 5078/3 |
| **N916SB** | **BE40** | **RK-14** |
| N916WJ | C550 | 561 |
| (N917BD) | LJ31 | 093 |
| N917BD | LJ31 | 094 |
| **N917BD** | **LJ45** | **281** |
| **N917BE** | **WW24** | **291** |
| N917BF | LJ24 | 293 |
| N917EE | C56X | 5158 |
| N917GA | GLF4 | 4017 |
| N917GA | GLF5 | 5017 |
| **N917GL** | **GLEX** | **9117** |
| N917J | JSTR | 5082/36 |
| N917JC | FA20 | 490 |
| **N917JC** | **FA50** | **250** |
| N917JG | FA20 | 490 |
| N917K | HS25 | 256015 |
| **N917LH** | **WW24** | **400** |
| **N917LJ** | **E50P** | **50000116** |
| N917MC | LJ31 | 012 |
| (N917ND) | GLF5 | 518 |
| **N917R** | **GLEX** | **9008** |
| N917R | GLF2 | 17 |
| **N917RG** | **C52B** | **0010** |
| N917S | LJ55 | 033 |
| **N917SB** | **FA50** | **14** |
| N917SC | ASTR | 020 |
| N917SC | LJ35 | 440 |
| **N917TF** | **HS25** | **257138** |
| **N917VZ** | **GLF4** | **1292** |
| **N917W** | **GLF4** | **1158** |
| N917XP | HS25 | HA-0017 |
| N918A | C500 | 168 |
| N918BD | C560 | 0173 |
| **N918BD** | **LJ45** | **277** |
| **N918BG** | **GLF3** | **300** |
| N918BH | C650 | 0130 |
| **N918CC** | **GLF4** | **1335** |
| **N918CG** | **F2TH** | **57** |
| N918CW | C525 | 0342 |
| **N918EG** | **LJ45** | **154** |
| N918EX | F9EX | 18 |
| N918GA | C550 | 726 |
| N918H | HS25 | 258283 |
| N918HM | C550 | 674 |
| **N918JL** | **HS25** | **HA-0037** |
| **N918JM** | **F9EX** | **199** |
| N918JM | FA50 | 304 |
| **N918LL** | **GLF4** | **4177** |
| N918MJ | ASTR | 073 |
| **N918MJ** | **ASTR** | **250** |
| N918MK | ASTR | 089 |
| N918MM | JSTR | 5069/20 |
| (N918PC) | FA10 | 106 |
| **N918QS** | **C750** | **0223** |
| N918R | SBRL | 306-19 |
| N918R | SBRL | 306-36 |
| **N918SS** | **WW24** | **263** |
| **N918TB** | **GLF4** | **1499** |
| N918TD | LJ25 | 166 |
| **N918TT** | **BE40** | **RK-529** |
| **N918WA** | **C510** | **0237** |
| (N919AT) | C500 | 209 |
| N919BT | WW24 | 434 |
| **N919CH** | **ASTR** | **098** |
| **N919CT** | **GLF4** | **1051** |
| **N919DS** | **ASTR** | **127** |
| N919EX | F9EX | 19 |
| N919G | GLF2 | 29 |
| (N919GA) | FA50 | 233 |
| N919GA | GLF5 | 5019 |
| N919H | HS25 | 258284 |
| N919JH | WW24 | 154 |
| N919K | LJ24 | 162 |
| (N919MA) | LJ24 | 291 |
| **N919MB** | **C510** | **0304** |
| **N919MC** | **C525** | **0600** |
| N919P | HS25 | 258147 |
| **N919QS** | **C750** | **0224** |
| **N919RS** | **LJ60** | **025** |
| **N919RT** | **HS25** | **258607** |
| N919S | LJ25 | 063 |
| **N919SA** | **F9EX** | **124** |
| **N919SF** | **HS25** | **258635** |
| **N919SS** | **HS25** | **258221** |
| N919TG | GLF2 | 160 |
| **N919YC** | **GLF5** | **682** |
| N920AD | WW24 | 195 |
| N920C | LJ35 | 283 |
| N920CC | LJ25 | 136 |
| N920CC | SBRL | 465-16 |
| N920CF | FA20 | 388 |
| **N920DB** | **F900** | **20** |
| N920DC | GLF5 | 534 |
| N920DG | JSTR | 5234 |
| (N920DG) | SBRL | 465-50 |
| N920DS | CL60 | 1023 |
| N920DS | GLEX | 9113 |
| N920DS | GLF2 | 73/9 |
| N920DS | GLF4 | 1254 |
| N920DS | JSTR | 5234 |
| N920DY | SBRL | 380-40 |
| N920DY | SBRL | 465-50 |
| N920E | C550 | 317 |
| N920EA | LJ25 | 057 |
| N920EX | F9EX | 20 |
| N920FF | LJ24 | 179 |
| N920G | FA20 | 352 |
| N920G | SBRL | 306-74 |
| N920G | WW24 | 87 |
| **N920GA** | **GLF4** | **4220** |
| N920GA | GLF5 | 5020 |
| N920GA | GLF5 | 5120 |
| **N920GB** | **EA50** | **000150** |
| N920GL | LJ28 | 29-002 |
| N920GP | WW24 | 87 |
| N920K | FA50 | 154 |
| (N920KP) | WW24 | 144 |
| N920L | FA20 | 192 |
| N920MS | C525 | 0089 |
| N920PM | C560 | 0182 |
| **N920QS** | **C750** | **0120** |
| N920R | WW24 | 45 |
| **N920RV** | **CL60** | **1016** |
| N920S | LJ25 | 025 |
| N920SA | BE40 | RK-41 |
| N920TB | GLF4 | 1254 |
| N920US | LJ25 | 136 |
| N920W | C500 | 155 |
| N920XP | HS25 | HA-0020 |
| N921AS | GLF3 | 332 |
| **N921BE** | **C500** | **579** |
| **N921CC** | **SBRL** | **465-67** |
| **N921CH** | **LJ35** | **228** |
| N921DG | C56X | 5206 |
| N921DT | WW24 | 372 |
| N921EC | FA50 | 313 |
| N921FF | GLF3 | 421 |
| N921FP | LJ55 | 103 |
| N921GA | GLF5 | 5021 |
| N921GA | GLF5 | 5121 |
| N921GA | GLF5 | 5151 |
| N921GS | FA10 | 130 |
| N921JG | SBRL | 282-105 |
| N921JG | SBRL | 282-38 |
| N921K | CL61 | 3044 |
| **N921MB** | **SBRL** | **306-135** |
| **N921ML** | **FA20** | **99** |
| **N921MW** | **C56X** | **5646** |
| **N921PP** | **C510** | **0139** |
| N921QS | C750 | 0225 |
| **N921QS** | **C750** | **0241** |
| N921RD | HS25 | 256032 |
| N921RD | HS25 | 257199 |
| **N921TX** | **C510** | **0071** |
| **N922AC** | **C560** | **0187** |
| (N922BA) | C500 | 137 |
| **N922CB** | **GLF4** | **4169** |
| N922CK | WW24 | 299 |
| N922CP | WW24 | 99 |
| N922CR | HS25 | 256014 |
| N922CR | WW24 | 299 |
| N922CR | WW24 | 99 |
| N922DS | FA20 | 373 |
| **N922GA** | **GLF4** | **4212** |
| N922GA | GLF5 | 5022 |
| **N922GK** | **HS25** | **25195** |
| N922GL | LJ35 | 266 |
| N922GR | HS25 | 256014 |
| N922H | F2TH | 97 |
| **N922H** | **GLF4** | **4036** |
| N922J | F2TH | 97 |
| **N922JW** | **F900** | **36** |
| N922ML | FA20 | 380 |
| **N922MR** | **GLF2** | **93** |
| N922MS | JSTR | 5097/60 |
| **N922QS** | **C750** | **0293** |
| N922RA | ASTR | 033 |
| N922RA | C550 | 397 |
| N922RR | HS25 | 25195 |
| N922RT | C550 | 397 |
| **N922SL** | **C550** | **034** |
| **N922TR** | **BE40** | **RJ-44** |
| N922XP | HS25 | HA-0022 |
| N923AR | C525 | 0055 |
| **N923CL** | **GLF4** | **1471** |
| N923DS | FA10 | 117 |
| N923GA | GLF5 | 5023 |
| N923GA | GLF5 | 5103 |
| N923GA | GLF5 | 5153 |
| N923GL | LJ25 | 298 |
| N923GL | LJ35 | 393 |
| N923HB | FA10 | 99 |
| (N923HE) | FA10 | 99 |
| N923JA | WW24 | 146 |
| **N923JH** | **C550** | **708** |
| **N923JP** | **C510** | **0103** |
| N923ML | GLF2 | 219/20 |
| N923PC | C56X | 5169 |
| N923QS | C750 | 0023 |
| N923RL | C550 | 426 |
| N923S | CS55 | 0092 |
| **N923SK** | **LJ60** | **050** |
| **N923VP** | **C750** | **0023** |
| N923XP | HS25 | HA-0023 |
| **N924AM** | **LJ35** | **188** |
| N924AS | C500 | 294 |
| **N924BC** | **F2EX** | **33** |
| N924BW | LJ24 | 164 |
| **N924BW** | **LJ25** | **158** |
| N924DS | GLF2 | 181 |
| N924ED | LJ24 | 104 |
| N924EJ | C750 | 0024 |
| N924GA | GLF5 | 5024 |
| N924GA | GLF5 | 5243 |
| N924GL | LJ35 | 361 |
| **N924JE** | **C56X** | **5138** |
| N924JM | BE40 | RK-96 |
| N924JM | HS25 | 258312 |
| N924ML | GLF4 | 1234 |
| **N924QS** | **C750** | **0124** |
| **N924S** | **F900** | **149** |
| N924S | F900 | 40 |
| **N924WJ** | **FA50** | **141** |
| N924XP | HS25 | HA-0024 |
| **N925AJ** | **F2TH** | **4** |
| **N925AK** | **F2EX** | **123** |
| **N925BC** | **FA50** | **257** |
| N925BE | FA20 | 80 |
| (N925BH) | HS25 | 256002 |
| N925BL | SBRL | 282-104 |
| **N925CA** | **LJ35** | **605** |
| N925CT | HS25 | 25066 |
| **N925DC** | **GLF4** | **1279** |
| **N925DM** | **LJ35** | **486** |
| N925DP | HS25 | 257132 |
| N925DS | FA10 | 116 |
| N925DS | GLF2 | 98/38 |
| N925DW | LJ25 | 213 |
| N925EX | F9EX | 25 |
| N925GA | GLF5 | 5025 |
| N925GL | LJ35 | 277 |
| **N925GS** | **FA50** | **90** |
| N925HB | WW24 | 53 |
| N925JF | HS25 | 258423 |
| **N925JS** | **GLF4** | **1269** |
| **N925MJ** | **MU30** | **A065SA** |
| N925QS | C750 | 0299 |
| N925R | SBRL | 306-41 |
| N925R | WW24 | 80 |
| **N925WC** | **HS25** | **257100** |
| N925WC | HS25 | 257132 |
| N925WC | MU30 | A080SA |
| N925WG | HS25 | 257132 |
| (N925WL) | SBRL | 465-65 |
| N925WP | LJ25 | 022 |
| N925Z | SBRL | 306-3 |
| **N925Z** | **WW24** | **307** |
| **N926AG** | **CL30** | **20102** |
| N926CB | C650 | 0008 |
| **N926CB** | **C650** | **7114** |
| **N926CC** | **C525** | **0491** |
| **N926CE** | **C560** | **0763** |
| N926CH | C525 | 0087 |
| N926CR | C650 | 0008 |
| N926DR | C56X | 5612 |
| N926DS | WW24 | 189 |
| N926EC | C550 | 550-1016 |
| N926ED | C550 | 550-1016 |
| N926G | HS25 | 25038 |

| | | |
|---|---|---|
| N926GA | GLF5 | 5026 |
| **N926GA** | **GLF5** | **5266** |
| N926GL | LJ35 | 306 |
| N926HC | C650 | 0094 |
| **N926JJ** | **C52A** | **0310** |
| **N926JK** | **E50P** | **50000107** |
| N926JM | WW24 | 146 |
| **N926JR** | **CL30** | **20103** |
| N926LR | FA20 | 139 |
| N926LR | HS25 | 25098 |
| **N926MC** | **HS25** | **257021** |
| **N926NC** | **C560** | **0328** |
| N926NY | GLF2 | 33 |
| **N926PY** | **C52A** | **0450** |
| N926QS | C750 | 0026 |
| **N926RM** | **C550** | **567** |
| **N926RR** | **GLF4** | **4081** |
| **N926SS** | **CL64** | **5436** |
| N926TC | HS25 | 257021 |
| N926TF | C525 | 0519 |
| **N926VP** | **C750** | **0026** |
| N926ZT | HS25 | 257021 |
| N927A | CL61 | 3026 |
| N927AA | LJ24 | 169 |
| N927AA | SBRL | 465-22 |
| **N927CC** | **C525** | **0422** |
| **N927DJ** | **LJ31** | **210** |
| (N927DS) | FA10 | 116 |
| (N927EM) | GLF4 | 4024 |
| N927EX | F9EX | 27 |
| **N927FW** | **LJ25** | **203** |
| N927GA | GLF5 | 5027 |
| **N927GA** | **GLF5** | **5273** |
| N927GL | LJ35 | 315 |
| **N927LL** | **HS25** | **257135** |
| **N927LT** | **C680** | **0070** |
| **N927QS** | **C750** | **0290** |
| N927R | SBRL | 306-47 |
| N927S | WW24 | 82 |
| **N927SK** | **LJ45** | **051** |
| N928CD | LJ60 | 010 |
| N928CD | LJ60 | 110 |
| (N928DA) | C550 | 550-0928 |
| N928DJ | LJ31 | 210 |
| N928DS | C550 | 276 |
| N928G | WW24 | 381 |
| N928GA | GALX | 228 |
| N928GA | GLF5 | 5028 |
| N928GA | GLF5 | 5128 |
| (N928GC) | F2EX | 181 |
| N928GC | GLF4 | 1513 |
| **N928GC** | **GLF5** | **5239** |
| N928GD | LJ60 | 010 |
| N928GF | GLF2 | 119/22 |
| N928GV | WW24 | 381 |
| **N928JA** | **ASTR** | **075** |
| **N928JK** | **C680** | **0104** |
| (N928MC) | CL30 | 20100 |
| **N928PS** | **C650** | **0116** |
| **N928QS** | **C750** | **0288** |
| N928R | SBRL | 282-90 |
| N928R | SBRL | 306-51 |
| **N928RD** | **C500** | **204** |
| N928S | LJ25 | 025 |
| **N928ST** | **ASTR** | **232** |
| N928ST | GLF4 | 1025 |
| **N928SZ** | **GLEX** | **9056** |
| N928SZ | GLF4 | 1025 |
| N928VC | C525 | 0453 |
| **N928WK** | **FA50** | **279** |
| N929A | C500 | 207 |
| N929AK | HS25 | 258409 |
| **N929AK** | **HS25** | **258627** |
| N929AL | HS25 | 258409 |
| N929BC | C52A | 0333 |
| **N929BC** | **C52B** | **0335** |
| N929CA | C500 | 046 |
| **N929CG** | **SBRL** | **380-52** |
| N929DS | C550 | 284 |
| N929DS | C650 | 0007 |
| N929EJ | C750 | 0029 |
| **N929GA** | **GALX** | **029** |
| N929GA | GLF5 | 5029 |
| N929GC | SBRL | 380-52 |
| N929GL | LJ28 | 29-001 |
| N929GV | GLF2 | 258 |
| N929GV | WW24 | 356 |
| N929GV | WW24 | 381 |

| | | |
|---|---|---|
| N929GV | WW24 | 48 |
| **N929GW** | **LJ60** | **165** |
| N929HF | LJ24 | 243 |
| N929HG | F2TH | 79 |
| **N929JH** | **LJ31** | **132** |
| **N929KD** | **EA50** | **000240** |
| **N929MC** | **LJ24** | **243** |
| **N929ML** | **FA50** | **92** |
| **N929MM** | **C525** | **0692** |
| **N929QS** | **C750** | **0129** |
| N929RW | C500 | 046 |
| (N929SF) | C52B | 0001 |
| N929SL | LJ35 | 287 |
| N929SR | LJ35 | 287 |
| **N929SR** | **LJ60** | **144** |
| **N929SS** | **PRM1** | **RB-15** |
| **N929T** | **FA50** | **24** |
| N929TS | GLEX | 9029 |
| N929VC | C525 | 0453 |
| **N929VC** | **C52A** | **0353** |
| **N929WC** | **GALX** | **181** |
| **N929WG** | **GALX** | **056** |
| N929WG | HS25 | 258196 |
| N929WG | MU30 | A032SA |
| N929WQ | HS25 | 258196 |
| **N929WT** | **FA50** | **119** |
| N929WT | GLF4 | 1317 |
| N930BS | C550 | 087 |
| N930BS | GLF2 | 29 |
| N930DC | GLF4 | 1254 |
| **N930DC** | **GLF4** | **4063** |
| N930GL | LJ35 | 330 |
| **N930JG** | **FA50** | **230** |
| N930L | FA20 | 193 |
| N930LS | GLF2 | 133 |
| N930M | JSTR | 5114/18 |
| N930MG | BE40 | RJ-52 |
| N930MG | C650 | 0209 |
| **N930MG** | **C680** | **0152** |
| N930MT | JSTR | 5114/18 |
| **N930PJ** | **LJ24** | **305** |
| **N930QS** | **C750** | **0130** |
| N930RA | SBRL | 465-68 |
| N930SC | ASTR | 038 |
| N930SD | F2TH | 90 |
| N930SD | GLF2 | 97 |
| N930UC | ASTR | 038 |
| N930XP | HS25 | HA-0030 |
| N931BA | LJ35 | 003 |
| N931BR | PRM1 | RB-66 |
| N931CA | C500 | 174 |
| N931CC | FA50 | 31 |
| N931CW | GLF2 | 85 |
| **N931DW** | **CL61** | **5025** |
| (N931EJ) | FA50 | 31 |
| **N931FD** | **LJ31** | **124** |
| N931G | FA50 | 126 |
| N931GA | GLF5 | 5031 |
| N931GL | LJ35 | 392 |
| **N931MA** | **MU30** | **A010SA** |
| **N931QS** | **C750** | **0064** |
| **N931RS** | **LJ31** | **184** |
| N931SB | F900 | 33 |
| N932BC | HS25 | HA-0032 |
| **N932EA** | **BE40** | **RK-32** |
| **N932FD** | **LJ31** | **187** |
| N932GA | GLF5 | 5032 |
| N932GA | GLF5 | 5232 |
| N932HA | C500 | 220 |
| N932LM | C550 | 297 |
| **N932QS** | **C750** | **0032** |
| N932S | FA20 | 56 |
| N932XL | C56X | 6032 |
| N933 | HS25 | 25186 |
| **N933AC** | **BE40** | **RJ-5** |
| N933BB | C550 | 550-1033 |
| N933CY | JSTR | 5115/39 |
| N933DB | C650 | 0009 |
| N933EX | F9EX | 33 |
| **N933EY** | **GLEX** | **9063** |
| N933GA | GLF5 | 5033 |
| N933GL | LJ35 | 377 |
| **N933H** | **GLF5** | **5077** |
| N933H | HS25 | 258249 |
| **N933JC** | **SBRL** | **380-72** |
| N933JJ | GLF4 | 1347 |
| N933LC | JSTR | 5115/39 |
| **N933ML** | **CL65** | **5705** |

| | | |
|---|---|---|
| (N933N) | LJ24 | 049 |
| N933NA | LJ24 | 049 |
| **N933PA** | **GLF3** | **367** |
| **N933PB** | **C560** | **0618** |
| (N933PG) | CL61 | 5152 |
| **N933QS** | **C750** | **0133** |
| **N933RD** | **GLF2** | **251** |
| **N933SH** | **C650** | **0009** |
| (N933TS) | FA10 | 33 |
| N933XP | HS25 | HA-0033 |
| **N934AM** | **C525** | **0230** |
| N934BD | C750 | 0152 |
| N934DF | GLF4 | 1255 |
| N934GA | GLF5 | 5034 |
| N934GA | GLF5 | 5234 |
| N934GL | LJ35 | 417 |
| N934H | C550 | 188 |
| **N934H** | **C650** | **0172** |
| N934H | LJ24 | 290 |
| N934QS | C750 | 0034 |
| **N934RD** | **HS25** | **258296** |
| N934ST | F2EX | 68 |
| N935BD | LJ35 | 094 |
| N935GA | C500 | 084 |
| **N935GA** | **GALX** | **235** |
| N935GA | GLF5 | 5035 |
| N935GA | GLF5 | 5105 |
| N935GA | GLF5 | 5155 |
| N935GL | LJ35 | 419 |
| **N935H** | **HS25** | **258225** |
| (N935NA) | LJ35 | 213 |
| (N935PC) | SBRL | 380-59 |
| **N935QS** | **C750** | **0135** |
| N935R | SBRL | 306-56 |
| N935SH | GLF4 | 1223 |
| **N935SS** | **ASTR** | **279** |
| (N936EA) | BE40 | RK-35 |
| N936GA | GLF4 | 4036 |
| N936GA | GLF5 | 5036 |
| N936GA | GLF5 | 5156 |
| N936H | HS25 | 259041 |
| **N936MP** | **GLF4** | **4173** |
| N936NW | FA20 | 236 |
| **N936QS** | **C750** | **0036** |
| N937BC | HS25 | 258043 |
| N937D | FA10 | 75 |
| **N937DM** | **E50P** | **50000136** |
| N937GA | GLF5 | 5107 |
| N937GA | GLF5 | 5237 |
| N937GC | FA20 | 76 |
| N937GL | LJ25 | 337 |
| N937H | HS25 | 258251 |
| (N937H) | HS25 | 259041 |
| N937J | FA10 | 19 |
| N937M | GLF2 | 42/12 |
| **N937QS** | **C750** | **0137** |
| N937R | SBRL | 306-57 |
| N937US | GLF2 | 204 |
| N937US | GLF4 | 1092 |
| N938CC | C750 | 0038 |
| **N938D** | **C550** | **454** |
| N938EJ | C750 | 0038 |
| N938GA | GLF5 | 5038 |
| N938GL | LJ35 | 396 |
| N938H | HS25 | 258252 |
| (N938QS) | C750 | 0038 |
| **N938QS** | **C750** | **0183** |
| N938R | SBRL | 306-20 |
| N938R | SBRL | 306-48 |
| N938W | C550 | 448 |
| (N938WF) | GLEX | 9005 |
| N938WH | CL60 | 1068 |
| N938WH | WW24 | 209 |
| **N939AP** | **GLEX** | **9180** |
| (N939BB) | C550 | 550-0939 |
| **N939BC** | **C52A** | **0333** |
| (N939CG) | CL60 | 1042 |
| **N939CK** | **FA20** | **317** |
| N939EX | F9EX | 39 |
| N939GA | GLF5 | 5039 |
| **N939GP** | **BE40** | **RK-125** |
| **N939JC** | **C510** | **0108** |
| **N939KM** | **GLF3** | **492** |
| N939KS | C500 | 289 |
| N939LE | HS25 | 258459 |
| **N939MC** | **ASTR** | **012** |
| **N939ML** | **GLEX** | **9330** |
| **N939QS** | **C750** | **0193** |

| | | |
|---|---|---|
| N939SR | C500 | 121 |
| **N939TT** | **HS25** | **258205** |
| **N939TW** | **C560** | **0185** |
| N940BS | GLF2 | 157 |
| N940BS | GLF2 | 64/27 |
| N940CC | SBRL | 282-34 |
| N940DC | GLF4 | 1052 |
| N940DC | GLF5 | 5128 |
| (N940DH) | CL60 | 1077 |
| N940EX | F9EX | 140 |
| N940EX | F9EX | 40 |
| N940GA | BE40 | RJ-18 |
| N940GA | GLF5 | 5040 |
| N940GA | GLF5 | 5110 |
| N940HC | HS25 | 258195 |
| N940P | LJ60 | 071 |
| **N940QS** | **C750** | **0285** |
| (N940RL) | LJ60 | 142 |
| (N940SJ) | F900 | 40 |
| **N940SW** | **C525** | **0071** |
| **N940VA** | **BE40** | **RK-197** |
| **N941AM** | **C52B** | **0252** |
| N941AM | GLF4 | 1499 |
| N941CC | FA50 | 138 |
| **N941CE** | **HS25** | **257083** |
| N941CW | GLF2 | 29 |
| N941GA | LJ25 | 020 |
| N941H | HS25 | 259042 |
| N941HC | HS25 | 258195 |
| N941JC | C500 | 310 |
| **N941KA** | **C650** | **0095** |
| **N941NC** | **EA50** | **000008** |
| **N941QS** | **C750** | **0141** |
| **N941RM** | **C560** | **0476** |
| N941TS | GLEX | 9241 |
| N942B | C500 | 044 |
| N942B | FA10 | 105 |
| N942BY | LJ31 | 005 |
| N942C | FA10 | 11 |
| N942CC | SBRL | 380-64 |
| N942CJ | C52A | 0094 |
| **N942DS** | **HS25** | **25032** |
| **N942EB** | **WW24** | **372** |
| N942EX | F9EX | 42 |
| N942FA | WW24 | 257 |
| **N942FK** | **LJ45** | **145** |
| N942GA | GLF5 | 5042 |
| N942GA | LJ25 | 021 |
| N942H | HS25 | 258253 |
| (N942M) | FA10 | 138 |
| **N942QS** | **C750** | **0024** |
| **N942RC** | **LJ31** | **107** |
| N942TS | GLEX | 9242 |
| **N942WC** | **WW24** | **383** |
| N942WN | HS25 | 25079 |
| N942Y | HS25 | 25079 |
| N942Y | JSTR | 5098/28 |
| N943CC | SBRL | 380-66 |
| **N943CE** | **HS25** | **257141** |
| (N943CL) | WW24 | 187 |
| N943GA | GLF5 | 5043 |
| N943GA | LJ25 | 022 |
| N943H | HS25 | 258254 |
| **N943JB** | **F2EX** | **18** |
| N943JL | WW24 | 206 |
| N943LL | C500 | 615 |
| N943LL | C550 | 442 |
| N943LL | WW24 | 206 |
| **N943QS** | **C750** | **0043** |
| N943RC | C500 | 615 |
| **N943RL** | **FA50** | **88** |
| N944AD | F900 | 17 |
| N944AF | C550 | 573 |
| **N944AH** | **C56X** | **5008** |
| N944AL | GLF4 | 4124 |
| N944AM | GLEX | 9161 |
| N944B | C500 | 318 |
| **N944BB** | **HS25** | **258611** |
| N944CA | C650 | 0083 |
| N944D | C750 | 0011 |
| N944GA | GLF5 | 5044 |
| N944H | C650 | 0083 |
| N944H | C650 | 7007 |
| N944H | C750 | 0011 |
| N944H | GLF2 | 251 |
| **N944H** | **GLF5** | **5016** |
| N944JD | C500 | 424 |
| **N944KM** | **LJ24** | **334** |

N944L C650 7007
N944M WW24 364
**N944NA GLF2 144**
(N944PP) HS25 258611
**N944QS C750 0144**
(N944TB) HS25 257177
N944TG C500 365
N944XP HS25 HA-0044
N945AA C500 432
N945BC C500 666
**N945CC SBRL 465-13**
**N945CE HS25 257137**
**N945EJ LJ40 45-2108**
**N945ER CS55 0021**
**N945FD LJ45 122**
N945GA GLF5 5045
N945GA LJ24 182
**N945HC LJ45 109**
N945MC FA10 37
**N945NA GLF2 118**
**N945QS C750 0029**
N945R SBRL 306-59
**N945TM F900 104**
**N945W LJ35 301**
N946CC C500 206
N946CM C510 0046
N946EJ C750 0046
N946EX F9EX 46
N946FP LJ55 056
N946FS HS25 25134
N946GA GLF5 5046
N946GM WW24 215
N946H HS25 258255
N946JR SBRL 306-10
**N946NA GLF2 146**
**N946PC C56X 5728**
**N946QS C750 0195**
**N946RM C52B 0008**
N946TC C56X 5331
**N946TC FA50 94**
N947CB C550 550-0947
N947CC C500 123
**N947CE HS25 257128**
**N947GA GLF5 5047**
**N947GS LJ35 250**
N947H HS25 258256
N947LF F9EX 44
**N947NA GLF2 147**
**N947QS C750 0047**
N947R SBRL 282-39
N947R SBRL 306-60
**N947TC LJ25 233**
(N948AV) GLF4 1474
**N948DC C550 136**
N948GA GLF5 5048
N948H HS25 259043
N948N C500 354
N948NA GLF2 222
**N948QS C750 0149**
N948R SBRL 306-21
N948R SBRL 306-50
(N949AV) GLF4 1477
**N949CC WW24 280**
**N949CE HS25 257204**
N949CV HS25 25195
N949CW HS25 25195
**N949EB HS25 257028**
N949EX F9EX 49
N949GA GLF5 5049
**N949GP GLEX 9049**
**N949JA HS25 258362**
**N949JB C510 0218**
**N949LL C52B 0306**
N949LL C56X 6035
**N949NA GLF2 221**
**N949QS C750 0049**
(N949SA) C500 067
**N949SA C550 360**
N950AM C500 095
N950AV GLF4 1464
**N950BA C56X 5200**
N950BS GLF2 64/27
**N950CM GLF4 1315**
N950CS LJ35 364
N950CS SBRL 465-43
**N950DB C52A 0377**
N950DM GLF4 1010
**N950F FA50 191**
N950FB CL61 5013
(N950FC) C550 401
N950G LJ36 032
N950GA GLF4 4150
N950GA GLF5 5050
N950GA LJ24 184
**N950H FA50 307**
N950HB GLF4 1464
**N950JB F9DX 602**
N950L FA20 189
N950N ASTR 244
**N950NA GLF2 185**
**N950P C525 0234**
**N950PC HS25 258300**
**N950PG CL64 5575**
**N950QS C750 0050**
N950RA FA20 95
**N950RJ CL65 5742**
**N950RL F2TH 221**
N950S FA50 115
**N950SF F900 50**
**N950SP LJ35 450**
N950SW CL61 5032
**N950SW GLF4 4109**
N950TC C560 0384
N950WA C560 0082
N950XP HS25 258750
**N950XP HS25 HA-0150**
**N951DB WW24 195**
N951GA LJ25 030
N951H HS25 258257
**N951QS C750 0151**
**N951RK GLF2 191**
**N951RM CL61 3042**
**N951XF GLF3 451**
N951XP HS25 HA-0051
N952 LJ25 291
N952B HS25 25100
**N952CH C550 550-0952**
N952GA GLF5 5052
N952GA GLF5 5250
N952GA LJ24 194
**N952GD F900 79**
N952GL LJ35 592
**N952GL PRM1 RB-213**
N952GL PRM1 RB-87
**N952GM PRM1 RB-87**
N952HF WW24 279
**N952QS C750 0200**
N952SP C525 0447
**N952SP PRM1 RB-260**
(N952TC) FA10 31
N952VS LJ31 168
(N952XP) HS25 HA-0052
N953C C560 0163
(N953DC) FA20 300/508
N953EX F9EX 53
**N953F C560 0005**
**N953FA CL61 5041**
N953FT C550 295
N953GA GLF5 5053
N953GA LJ24 197
N953GM C550 550-0953
(N953H) HS25 258258
**N953HC C500 606**
**N953JB EA50 000126**
**N953JF C650 0043**
**N953QS C750 0153**
N953SL C500 606
N954FA LJ25 034
**N954FJ F900 54**
N954GA GLF5 5054
N954GA LJ25 034
**N954H HS25 258259**
**N954L CL64 5607**
N954Q C750 0211
N954QS C750 0211
**N954RM C52A 0093**
N954S LJ24 136
(N954SC) LJ24 019
**N954SP F2EX 56**
**N954WS LJ60 271**
N955CC GLF2 54/36
(N955CE) CL64 5436
N955CP GLF3 375
N955DB CL61 3044
N955E FA50 14
N955E GLF4 1383
**N955EA LJ24 279**
N955EX F9EX 155
N955FD LJ55 009
(N955FJ) F900 55
N955GA GLF5 5055
N955GA GLF5 5255
**N955H CL30 20109**
N955H GLF2 98/38
N955H GLF3 378
N955H GLF4 1081
N955H GLF4 1383
N955H JSTR 5126
(N955HC) GLF4 1081
**N955HG C650 0057**
N955HL JSTR 5126
**N955JS LJ31 228**
**N955KC C680 0244**
N955LS LJ55 009
N955MC HS25 258384
N955MD LJ55 009
N955PR SBRL 465-43
**N955QS C750 0055**
N955R SBRL 306-52
**N955SE HS25 HA-0102**
(N955WP) C500 528
N956 SBRL 282-50
N956CC SBRL 282-50
N956EX F9EX 56
**N956GA C52B 0233**
N956GA GLF5 5056
N956GA LJ25 036
N956H HS25 259044
N956J LJ25 036
(N956M) SBRL 277-7
(N956MJ) GLF2 234
**N956P MS76 056**
N956PP ASTR 029
**N956PP CL64 5483**
N956PP MU30 A031SA
**N956QS C750 0156**
N956S C500 056
N957 SBRL 282-71
**N957BJ C56X 5086**
N957CC SBRL 282-71
N957E LJ24 204
**N957F ASTR 104**
N957GA GLF5 5057
**N957GA GLF5 5257**
N957GA LJ24 204
**N957H HS25 258260**
(N957M) SBRL 285-1
**N957MB HS25 256015**
N957P ASTR 104
**N957P GALX 062**
N957PH C550 550-0957
N957R SBRL 306-53
N957RC WW24 58
N957SC LJ24 065
N957TH FA20 38
(N958AV) GLF5 666
(N958AV) GLF5 699
**N958DM F9EX 119**
N958DM LJ25 042
N958EX F9EX 58
N958GA GLF5 5058
N958GA LJ25 042
**N958GC C550 550-1016**
N958H HS25 258261
N958M SBRL 282-85
**N958PP MU30 A031SA**
**N958QS C750 0158**
N958R SBRL 306-24
N958R SBRL 306-9
N959AT LJ35 019
N959C SBRL 465-50
N959EX F9EX 159
N959EX F9EX 59
N959GA GLF5 5059
**N959GA GLF5 5259**
N959GA LJ25 039
N959H HS25 258262
N959KW HS25 25020
(N959M) SBRL 277-6
**N959P MS76 059**
**N959PP ASTR 029**
N959RE LJ25 039
**N959RP LJ40 45-2100**
**N959SA LJ35 076**
N959SC LJ24 045A
N959WC LJ55 030
**N960AA FA20 144**
N960AA LJ35 003
(N960AJ) BE40 RK-23
N960AV GLF5 654
(N960BM) C560 0643
N960CB C550 550-0960
**N960CD C560 0121**
N960CP C550 336
N960CR C560 0500
**N960CR CL30 20080**
N960DC GLF3 378
N960E LJ55 033
N960EX F9EX 60
**N960FA WW24 348**
N960GA GLF5 5060
**N960GA GLF5 5260**
N960GA LJ25 041
(N960H) LJ60 013
N960H LJ60 015
(N960HL) LJ60 015
N960JA BE40 RK-191
N960JH C560 0643
(N960JH) C560 0754
N960JJ BE40 RK-191
N960JJ BE40 RK-255
**N960KC C750 0011**
**N960M C560 0691**
(N960M) SBRL 277-2
**N960PT C510 0238**
**N960QS C750 0160**
**N960S FA50 86**
**N960SF F9EX 62**
**N960TX FA20 403**
**N961AA FA20 205**
N961BB C550 550-0961
N961EX F9EX 61
N961GA GLF5 5061
N961H HS25 258263
N961JC HS25 258062
N961JC WW24 208
(N961JD) WW24 208
N961JE WW24 208
(N961M) SBRL 285-25
N961MR LJ60 003
**N961P MS76 061**
**N961QS C750 0061**
N961R SBRL 306-61
N961SV GLF4 1395
**N961TC C680 0077**
**N961V GLF4 1298**
N962 LJ25 102
**N962A ASTR 031**
N962EX F9EX 162
**N962FM LJ31 237**
N962GA GLF5 5062
N962GA LJ25 044
N962H HS25 259046
(N962HA) C550 248
**N962J C550 453**
N962JC C550 453
N962JC C560 0006
N962MV WW24 385
**N962QS C750 0126**
**N962SS GLF4 1121**
N962TS GLEX 9262
N963EX F9EX 63
N963GA GLF5 5063
N963GA LJ25 045
N963H HS25 259017
**N963JF FA50 18**
**N963JG EA50 000028**
N963RB CL30 20121
N963RS CL30 20121
N963RS F900 127
**N963RS F9EX 97**
N963WA SBRL 306-53
N963WL SBRL 306-53
N963WL SBRL 465-65
N963WM WW24 88
(N963Y) JSTR 5098/28
(N963Y) LJ31 005
**N963YA HS25 25079**
**N964C SBRL 465-66**
N964CL LJ35 152
N964EJ C750 0064
N964GA GLF5 5064

| | | |
|---|---|---|
| N964GA | LJ25 | 046 |
| **N964H** | **CL64** | **5363** |
| N964J | C550 | 448 |
| N964JC | C550 | 448 |
| N964JC | C560 | 0007 |
| **N964JD** | **BE40** | **RK-451** |
| **N964JG** | **EA50** | **000172** |
| N964M | FA20 | 146 |
| N964M | JSTR | 5148 |
| N964QS | C750 | 0064 |
| **N964QS** | **C750** | **0164** |
| N964RS | F900 | 127 |
| **N964S** | **EA50** | **000132** |
| **N964XP** | **HS25** | **HA-0164** |
| N965BB | C550 | 550-0965 |
| N965BC | FA20 | 107 |
| N965CC | GLF2 | 165/37 |
| N965EX | F9EX | 65 |
| N965GA | GLF5 | 5065 |
| N965GA | GLF5 | 5165 |
| **N965GA** | **GLF5** | **5265** |
| N965GA | LJ25 | 048 |
| N965JC | C650 | 7051 |
| N965JC | HS25 | 257084 |
| **N965LC** | **C525** | **0462** |
| N965M | F9EX | 65 |
| (N965QS) | C750 | 0065 |
| N965R | SBRL | 306-61 |
| N966E | F9EX | 126 |
| N966F | FA20 | 70 |
| N966GA | GLF5 | 5066 |
| N966GA | GLF5 | 5166 |
| N966GA | LJ25 | 049 |
| N966H | C650 | 7006 |
| N966H | C750 | 0012 |
| N966H | F9EX | 101 |
| **N966H** | **F9EX** | **126** |
| N966H | GLF2 | 150 |
| N966H | GLF3 | 411 |
| N966JM | C560 | 0240 |
| **N966JM** | **C56X** | **5143** |
| N966K | C650 | 7006 |
| N966K | HS25 | 258702 |
| N966L | CL61 | 3021 |
| N966L | FA20 | 181 |
| (N966L) | HS25 | 258259 |
| N966MT | C56X | 5046 |
| **N966QS** | **C750** | **0166** |
| **N966SW** | **C560** | **0284** |
| N967A | WW24 | 205 |
| N967CB | C550 | 550-0967 |
| N967CM | C510 | 0067 |
| N967EX | F9EX | 67 |
| N967F | FA20 | 71 |
| **N967F** | **PRM1** | **RB-133** |
| N967GA | GLF5 | 5067 |
| N967GA | GLF5 | 5117 |
| N967GA | GLF5 | 5167 |
| N967L | CL61 | 3004 |
| N967L | CL61 | 3021 |
| N967L | CL61 | 3023 |
| N967L | HS25 | 258273 |
| N967L | WW24 | 37 |
| **N967PC** | **GALX** | **110** |
| **N967QS** | **C750** | **0067** |
| N967R | SBRL | 306-16 |
| N967R | SBRL | 306-62 |
| **N967TC** | **C52A** | **0319** |
| N968BN | JSTR | 5109/13 |
| N968CM | C510 | 0068 |
| N968DM | C500 | 610 |
| N968F | FA20 | 74 |
| N968GA | GLF5 | 5068 |
| N968GN | JSTR | 5109/13 |
| N968L | CL61 | 5089 |
| N968R | SBRL | 306-2 |
| N969 | LJ31 | 086 |
| **N969AR** | **LJ25** | **220** |
| N969B | LJ24 | 089 |
| **N969DW** | **C560** | **0399** |
| (N969EG) | WW24 | 221 |
| N969EX | F9EX | 69 |
| N969F | FA10 | 135 |
| N969F | FA20 | 75 |
| N969GA | GLF5 | 5069 |
| **N969GB** | **C560** | **0225** |
| N969J | LJ24 | 106 |
| **N969JD** | **LJ60** | **154** |
| N969KC | WW24 | 221 |
| N969MC | CS55 | 0001 |
| N969MC | LJ35 | 590 |
| N969MQ | CS55 | 0001 |
| N969MT | C550 | 072 |
| N969MT | LJ35 | 459 |
| N969PW | WW24 | 221 |
| **N969RE** | **PRM1** | **RB-14** |
| N969SE | C500 | 069 |
| N969SG | GLF4 | 1197 |
| N969SS | LJ25 | 317 |
| **N969WR** | **ASTR** | **218** |
| (N969ZS) | C500 | 196 |
| **N970DM** | **C52B** | **0168** |
| N970EX | F9EX | 70 |
| N970F | FA20 | 76 |
| N970F | LJ55 | 055 |
| N970GA | FA20 | 246/482 |
| N970GA | LJ24 | 209 |
| **N970GW** | **C650** | **0019** |
| N970H | LJ55 | 055 |
| **N970QS** | **C750** | **0070** |
| N970RC | C680 | 0012 |
| N970RJ | F9EX | 97 |
| **N970RP** | **C500** | **270** |
| N970RP | C525 | 0608 |
| **N970S** | **FA50** | **238** |
| **N970SJ** | **GLF4** | **1146** |
| **N970SK** | **C750** | **0186** |
| N970SU | C525 | 0173 |
| **N970WJ** | **LJ25** | **324** |
| (N971AB) | C500 | 232 |
| N971AS | JSTR | 5007/45 |
| N971DM | C525 | 0510 |
| N971EC | GLF2 | 32/2 |
| N971EC | GLF4 | 1000 |
| N971EC | LJ55 | 033 |
| N971EQ | GLF2 | 32/2 |
| (N971EX) | F9EX | 71 |
| N971F | FA20 | 59 |
| N971F | LJ35 | 095 |
| N971GA | GLF5 | 5171 |
| **N971GA** | **GLF5** | **5271** |
| N971GA | LJ24 | 215 |
| N971H | LJ35 | 095 |
| N971K | LJ35 | 373 |
| N971L | GLF4 | 1116 |
| **N971QS** | **C750** | **0071** |
| N971TB | C52A | 0111 |
| **N971TB** | **C52A** | **0118** |
| N972 | LJ24 | 252 |
| **N972AB** | **C500** | **140** |
| N972D | HS25 | 25275 |
| N972F | FA20 | 80 |
| N972G | GLF3 | 457 |
| N972GA | GLF5 | 5172 |
| N972GW | C500 | 118 |
| N972H | LJ24 | 322 |
| N972H | LJ25 | 370 |
| N972JD | C500 | 118 |
| N972LM | HS25 | 257098 |
| **N972MS** | **GLF4** | **1285** |
| **N972NR** | **SBRL** | **380-65** |
| **N972PF** | **PRM1** | **RB-38** |
| **N972TF** | **WW24** | **138** |
| N972VZ | C650 | 0212 |
| **N972W** | **HS25** | **257111** |
| N973 | LJ25 | 254 |
| **N973AC** | **C680** | **0195** |
| N973EJ | WW24 | 168 |
| N973F | FA20 | 81 |
| N973GA | LJ25 | 051 |
| **N973HR** | **LJ60** | **260** |
| N973JD | LJ25 | 123 |
| N973M | F9EX | 73 |
| **N973MW** | **GLF3** | **301** |
| **N974BK** | **F900** | **105** |
| N974D | LJ24 | 095 |
| N974F | FA20 | 83 |
| N974GA | GLF5 | 5174 |
| N974GA | LJ25 | 053 |
| N974JD | BE40 | RK-141 |
| **N974JD** | **HA4T** | **RC-11** |
| (N974JD) | HA4T | RC-5 |
| N974JD | HS25 | 258589 |
| N974JD | LJ24 | 205 |
| N974JD | LJ25 | 106 |
| N974JD | LJ35 | 457 |
| N974JD | LJ35 | 648 |
| N974M | LJ25 | 053 |
| N974TS | GLEX | 9274 |
| N975AA | LJ35 | 012 |
| N975AD | LJ35 | 012 |
| **N975AR** | **EPC1** | **002** |
| **N975BD** | **BE40** | **RK-553** |
| N975CM | BE40 | RK-166 |
| N975DM | C52A | 0083 |
| **N975DM** | **LJ40** | **45-2073** |
| N975DN | C52A | 0083 |
| N975EE | C500 | 135 |
| N975F | FA20 | 84 |
| N975GA | GLF2 | 26 |
| N975GA | GLF5 | 5175 |
| **N975GR** | **GLF4** | **4154** |
| N975GR | MU30 | A077SA |
| N975HM | C550 | 550-0975 |
| **N975P** | **MS76** | **075** |
| **N975QS** | **C750** | **0175** |
| **N975RD** | **BE40** | **RK-390** |
| **N975RG** | **GLF3** | **471** |
| **N975RR** | **BE40** | **RK-349** |
| (N975XP) | HS25 | HA-0075 |
| N976B | GLF2 | 32/2 |
| N976BS | LJ25 | 016 |
| N976EE | C500 | 025 |
| N976F | FA20 | 86 |
| **N976GA** | **C550** | **179** |
| N976SR | SBRL | 465-29 |
| **N977AE** | **C750** | **0125** |
| N977AR | LJ31 | 134 |
| N977AR | LJ45 | 217 |
| N977CC | HS25 | 257010 |
| **N977CP** | **F2EX** | **17** |
| N977DM | C525 | 0338 |
| N977EE | C500 | 140 |
| N977F | FA20 | 88 |
| N977GA | GLF5 | 5177 |
| N977GA | LJ24 | 219 |
| N977GA | LJ24 | 221 |
| **N977LC** | **HS25** | **258977** |
| N977LP | F9EX | 77 |
| **N977MR** | **C560** | **0623** |
| **N977QS** | **C750** | **0077** |
| **N977TW** | **FA20** | **13** |
| **N977VH** | **EA50** | **000206** |
| **N978DB** | **C750** | **0009** |
| N978E | LJ36 | 024 |
| N978EE | C500 | 018 |
| N978F | FA20 | 89 |
| N978FL | GLF3 | 397 |
| N978GA | GLF5 | 5178 |
| **N978PC** | **C510** | **0199** |
| **N978PW** | **F900** | **125** |
| **N978QS** | **C750** | **0187** |
| N978R | SBRL | 306-1 |
| N978R | SBRL | 306-27 |
| N978R | SBRL | 306-63 |
| N978W | FA50 | 49 |
| N979C | C550 | 504 |
| N979C | C560 | 0263 |
| **N979CB** | **GLF4** | **1217** |
| **N979CM** | **BE40** | **RK-570** |
| N979CM | BE40 | RK-571 |
| N979EE | C500 | 015 |
| N979F | FA20 | 91 |
| N979G | C550 | 504 |
| N979GA | GLF2 | 151/24 |
| N979GA | GLF5 | 5179 |
| **N979JB** | **HS25** | **258399** |
| **N979QS** | **C750** | **0079** |
| N979RA | GLF2 | 151/24 |
| N979RA | GLF4 | 1191 |
| N979RA | JSTR | 5023 |
| **N979RF** | **LJ35** | **376** |
| **N979TB** | **HS25** | **HA-0075** |
| **N979TM** | **HA4T** | **RC-28** |
| N979TM | HS25 | HA-0075 |
| (N979TM) | HS25 | HA-0082 |
| **N979WC** | **C550** | **584** |
| N979XP | BE40 | RK-379 |
| N980A | LJ25 | 340 |
| N980AW | WW24 | 414 |
| N980DC | HS25 | 258267 |
| N980DK | C56X | 5019 |
| **N980DM** | **C500** | **421** |
| N980EE | C500 | 034 |
| (N980EF) | GLF2 | 124 |
| N980F | FA20 | 95 |
| N980GA | ASTR | 280 |
| N980GA | GLF5 | 5180 |
| **N980GG** | **GLEX** | **9009** |
| N980HC | CL61 | 5070 |
| N980HC | CL61 | 5163 |
| N980MB | C525 | 0686 |
| N980ML | ASTR | 033 |
| (N980ML) | GLF4 | 1193 |
| N980R | FA20 | 98/434 |
| **N980S** | **FA50** | **249** |
| N980S | WW24 | 401 |
| N980SK | CL65 | 5701 |
| N981 | F2TH | 53 |
| **N981CE** | **HS25** | **258563** |
| N981EE | C500 | 005 |
| N981F | FA20 | 96 |
| N981GA | GLF5 | 5111 |
| N981GA | GLF5 | 681 |
| N981HC | GLF4 | 1217 |
| **N981LB** | **C525** | **0546** |
| N981SW | GLF4 | 1001 |
| N981TH | LJ35 | 364 |
| **N981TS** | **GLEX** | **9281** |
| **N982AR** | **BE40** | **RK-206** |
| N982B | GLF2 | 98/38 |
| N982EX | F9EX | 82 |
| N982F | FA20 | 99 |
| N982HC | GLF4 | 1242 |
| N982J | CL64 | 5308 |
| N982MC | FA10 | 114 |
| **N982NA** | **C550** | **376** |
| **N982QS** | **C750** | **0182** |
| **N982RK** | **GLF3** | **310** |
| **N982XP** | **HS25** | **258982** |
| (N983AJ) | C550 | 369 |
| N983AJ | FA20 | 11 |
| N983CC | FA10 | 163 |
| (N983CE) | CL61 | 5102 |
| **N983CE** | **HS25** | **258446** |
| N983CE | HS25 | 258509 |
| (N983EC) | HS25 | 258446 |
| N983F | FA20 | 100 |
| N983GA | GLF5 | 5183 |
| N983GT | HS25 | 257086 |
| **N983J** | **GLEX** | **9072** |
| **N983QS** | **C750** | **0083** |
| **N984BD** | **LJ60** | **378** |
| **N984BK** | **C550** | **550-0857** |
| N984EX | F9EX | 84 |
| N984F | FA20 | 101 |
| N984GA | C560 | 0328 |
| N984GA | GLF4 | 4184 |
| N984GB | C550 | 550-1122 |
| N984GC | HS25 | 258377 |
| N984GC | LJ45 | 009 |
| (N984H) | C550 | 188 |
| N984H | F9EX | 210 |
| N984HF | HS25 | 25183 |
| **N984HM** | **HS25** | **258229** |
| **N984JC** | **HA4T** | **RC-32** |
| N984JC | HA4T | RC-56 |
| N984JD | LJ25 | 342 |
| N984JD | LJ31 | 001 |
| N984JD | LJ55 | 139A |
| **N984JW** | **GLF4** | **1091** |
| **N984QS** | **C750** | **0084** |
| N984SA | MU30 | A063SA |
| N984TS | GLEX | 9084 |
| (N984VP) | C550 | 550-0984 |
| N984XP | HS25 | HA-0084 |
| **N984XR** | **LJ45** | **373** |
| N985BA | C550 | 043 |
| **N985BB** | **GLF2** | **250** |
| N985EX | F9EX | 85 |
| N985F | FA20 | 102 |
| **N985FM** | **CL30** | **20113** |
| **N985GA** | **GLF4** | **4185** |
| **N985JC** | **GLF5** | **5083** |
| N985M | C650 | 0068 |
| (N985QS) | C750 | 0085 |
| N985RM | HS25 | HA-0085 |
| N986AH | GLF4 | 1003 |
| **N986DS** | **C500** | **668** |
| **N986DV** | **F2TH** | **74** |
| N986EX | F9EX | 86 |
| N986F | FA20 | 105 |

| | | |
|---|---|---|
| **N986GA** | **GLF4** | **4186** |
| N986GA | GLF5 | 5106 |
| N986H | HS25 | 257009 |
| N986JB | SBRL | 282-72 |
| **N986JC** | **HA4T** | **RC-35** |
| N986M | C650 | 0048 |
| **N986MA** | **LJ31** | **080** |
| N986PA | C550 | 550-0986 |
| (N986PA) | FA50 | 126 |
| **N986QS** | **C750** | **0086** |
| **N986SA** | **LJ35** | **609** |
| N986WC | LJ24 | 213 |
| N986WC | LJ35 | 023 |
| N986WC | LJ55 | 030 |
| N986XP | HS25 | HA-0086 |
| N987A | ASTR | 099 |
| N987AC | GLF4 | 1156 |
| **N987AL** | **F9EX** | **194** |
| N987AR | GLF4 | 1156 |
| **N987CJ** | **CS55** | **0152** |
| **N987CM** | **C510** | **0140** |
| (N987DK) | LJ35 | 360 |
| N987F | FA20 | 106 |
| **N987F** | **FA50** | **124** |
| N987G | ASTR | 031 |
| N987GK | ASTR | 031 |
| **N987GK** | **F900** | **88** |
| N987GR | C550 | 550-0987 |
| **N987HP** | **CL30** | **20069** |
| N987LP | LJ35 | 670 |
| N987QK | F900 | 88 |
| **N987QS** | **C750** | **0087** |
| N987RC | FA50 | 31 |
| N987SA | GLF2 | 172 |
| N988AA | LJ25 | 185 |
| **N988AA** | **LJ25** | **348** |
| (N988AC) | C500 | 349 |
| N988AC | LJ25 | 185 |
| **N988AG** | **HS25** | **HA-0088** |
| N988AL | GLF4 | 4128 |
| **N988AS** | **LJ25** | **257** |
| N988DB | LJ25 | 185 |
| N988DS | GLF2 | 98/38 |
| (N988DT) | HA4T | RC-16 |
| **N988DV** | **F2EX** | **211** |
| N988DV | F2TH | 74 |
| N988F | FA20 | 107 |
| (N988GA) | HS25 | 257057 |
| **N988GC** | **FA50** | **337** |
| N988H | C650 | 0087 |
| **N988H** | **F9EX** | **125** |
| N988H | GLF2 | 150 |
| N988H | GLF2 | 98/38 |
| N988H | GLF4 | 1347 |
| N988HL | C650 | 0087 |
| (N988JE) | GLF2 | 151/24 |
| N988JE | HS25 | 257087 |
| N988JG | BE40 | RK-255 |
| **N988KD** | **GALX** | **196** |
| **N988LS** | **GLF4** | **1290** |
| **N988MC** | **LJ45** | **352** |
| N988MT | SBRL | 276-32 |
| N988MW | JSTR | 5231 |
| N988NA | WW24 | 372 |
| N988P | LJ60 | 366 |
| **N988PA** | **LJ45** | **076** |
| **N988QC** | **LJ35** | **455** |
| N988R | SBRL | 306-17 |
| N988RS | C550 | 568 |
| **N988RS** | **HS25** | **258598** |
| N988SA | LJ24 | 037 |
| **N988SB** | **FA50** | **174** |
| **N988T** | **F900** | **65** |
| N988T | FA50 | 130 |
| **N988TM** | **C680** | **0021** |
| N988WH | WW24 | 209 |
| (N989AB) | HS25 | 25286 |
| **N989AL** | **LJ35** | **212** |
| **N989BC** | **CL61** | **5021** |
| (N989DH) | CL64 | 5311 |
| N989EX | F9EX | 91 |
| N989F | FA20 | 110 |
| N989GA | GLF4 | 4019 |
| N989GA | GLF4 | 4189 |
| N989JN | JSTR | 5132/57 |
| **N989PA** | **LJ45** | **071** |
| **N989QS** | **C750** | **0089** |
| **N989RF** | **EA50** | **000238** |
| **N989RJ** | **GLEX** | **9224** |
| N989SA | LJ24 | 100 |
| N989SC | C500 | 148 |
| **N989ST** | **HS25** | **258478** |
| **N989TL** | **LJ24** | **160** |
| N989TV | C550 | 305 |
| N989TW | C550 | 305 |
| N989TW | C560 | 0185 |
| N989TW | C56X | 5014 |
| N989WS | GLF4 | 4033 |
| N990AC | SBRL | 306-24 |
| N990AE | LJ31 | 240 |
| **N990AK** | **CL64** | **5337** |
| **N990AL** | **C500** | **033** |
| **N990BB** | **F900** | **42** |
| N990CB | C500 | 211 |
| N990CH | JSTR | 5225 |
| N990DF | BE40 | RK-430 |
| **N990DK** | **C56X** | **5019** |
| N990EX | F9EX | 89 |
| N990F | FA20 | 111 |
| N990GA | GLF4 | 4020 |
| N990GA | GLF5 | 5200 |
| **N990GC** | **LJ31** | **033A** |
| N990H | F9EX | 17 |
| **N990HC** | **HS25** | **258412** |
| (N990HP) | CS55 | 0064 |
| (N990JH) | C560 | 0643 |
| **N990JH** | **C560** | **0754** |
| N990JM | C550 | 550-0990 |
| N990L | FA20 | 43 |
| **N990LC** | **LJ35** | **483** |
| **N990M** | **C550** | **608** |
| N990MC | F900 | 65 |
| **N990MC** | **F9EX** | **123** |
| **N990MF** | **C56X** | **5052** |
| N990ML | F9EX | 123 |
| N990ML | GLF3 | 400 |
| N990MM | C550 | 488 |
| **N990MM** | **FA50** | **105** |
| (N990MQ) | F900 | 65 |
| **N990MR** | **C550** | **488** |
| **N990NA** | **EA50** | **000086** |
| **N990NB** | **GLF4** | **1428** |
| **N990PA** | **SBRL** | **306-114** |
| (N990PJ) | GLF4 | 1134 |
| **N990PM** | **GLF4** | **1134** |
| N990PT | FA20 | 391 |
| N990PT | GLF4 | 1134 |
| N990PT | GLF4 | 4116 |
| N990PT | LJ24 | 236 |
| N990PT | SBRL | 306-114 |
| **N990QS** | **C750** | **0190** |
| **N990S** | **WW24** | **322** |
| **N990TC** | **C550** | **550-0963** |
| N990TM | LJ24 | 051 |
| (N990UH) | GLF4 | 1247 |
| **N990WA** | **LJ40** | **45-2122** |
| N990WC | GLF3 | 405 |
| N990WC | GLF4 | 1268 |
| **N990WM** | **F9EX** | **40** |
| (N990Y) | C550 | 311 |
| N991 | JSTR | 5139/54 |
| **N991AL** | **LJ35** | **216** |
| N991AS | F900 | 12 |
| **N991BB** | **C510** | **0256** |
| N991BM | C550 | 126 |
| N991CH | LJ55 | 091 |
| N991CX | C750 | 0091 |
| **N991DB** | **LJ60** | **177** |
| N991EJ | C750 | 0091 |
| N991EJ | F900 | 91 |
| N991F | FA20 | 112 |
| N991F | JSTR | 5139/54 |
| N991GA | GLF2 | 170 |
| N991GA | GLF5 | 5011 |
| N991GA | GLF5 | 5201 |
| **N991GS** | **CL30** | **20099** |
| N991L | C560 | 0350 |
| **N991LF** | **GLF5** | **576** |
| N991PC | C560 | 0043 |
| N991PC | C560 | 0364 |
| N991RF | F900 | 3 |
| N991RV | ASTR | 011 |
| N991RV | FA10 | 24 |
| N991SA | C500 | 194 |
| **N991TD** | **LJ24** | **124** |
| **N991TW** | **CL64** | **5333** |
| N991WC | GLF3 | 405 |
| N992 | FA50 | 77 |
| N992 | JSTR | 5070/52 |
| N992 | SBRL | 306-88 |
| **N992AS** | **C550** | **074** |
| N992GA | BE40 | RJ-22 |
| N992GA | GLF5 | 5202 |
| **N992HE** | **C550** | **550-1006** |
| (N992HG) | C500 | 132 |
| N992NA | GLF3 | 309 |
| (N992NW) | C500 | 660 |
| (N992QS) | C750 | 0029 |
| **N992SC** | **PRM1** | **RB-191** |
| N992SF | HS25 | 256044 |
| N992TD | LJ24 | 035 |
| N993 | FA50 | 38 |
| **N993AC** | **ASTR** | **265** |
| **N993DS** | **WW24** | **356** |
| N993EX | F9EX | 93 |
| N993F | FA20 | 113 |
| **N993GH** | **F2EX** | **85** |
| **N993GL** | **C525** | **0509** |
| **N993GT** | **F9EX** | **93** |
| **N993H** | **BE40** | **RK-241** |
| N993KL | LJ24 | 166 |
| **N993LC** | **C650** | **0027** |
| N993QS | C750 | 0093 |
| **N993SA** | **HS25** | **258377** |
| **N993TD** | **LJ24** | **166** |
| N994 | SBRL | 465-33 |
| **N994CF** | **C550** | **448** |
| (N994CF) | C560 | 0120 |
| N994CR | LJ35 | 492 |
| N994CT | CL61 | 5161 |
| N994EX | F9EX | 94 |
| N994F | FA20 | 116 |
| N994GC | GLF2 | 77 |
| N994GC | GLF4 | 1435 |
| **N994GG** | **GLF2** | **77** |
| **N994GP** | **F2EX** | **105** |
| (N994HP) | C560 | 0507 |
| N994JD | GLF2 | 37 |
| N994JD | GLF2 | 92 |
| N994JD | LJ55 | 139A |
| **N994JG** | **C525** | **0685** |
| N994JR | PRM1 | RB-183 |
| N994MP | C52B | 0328 |
| N994SA | LJ24 | 005 |
| N994SA | LJ24 | 119 |
| N994TA | CL60 | 1077 |
| **N994TD** | **LJ24** | **179** |
| N994U | C650 | 0099 |
| (N994W) | SBRL | 306-132 |
| N995 | SBRL | 306-29 |
| (N995AU) | C500 | 385 |
| **N995AU** | **C510** | **0198** |
| N995AW | LJ31 | 063 |
| N995BC | GLF3 | 432 |
| **N995BE** | **HA4T** | **RC-24** |
| **N995CK** | **FA20** | **95** |
| N995CR | LJ35 | 304 |
| N995DC | CS55 | 0065 |
| **N995DP** | **LJ35** | **600** |
| N995DR | LJ24 | 285 |
| N995F | FA20 | 117 |
| N995GA | ASTR | 158 |
| N995GA | GALX | 111 |
| **N995GG** | **GLF4** | **1074** |
| **N995GH** | **F2EX** | **72** |
| N995MA | CL64 | 5362 |
| N995PA | C500 | 649 |
| N995PT | FA20 | 391 |
| (N995RD) | LJ24 | 285 |
| (N995RD) | SBRL | 306-24 |
| **N995RD** | **SBRL** | **380-9** |
| N995SA | HS25 | 257035 |
| **N995SK** | **F900** | **166** |
| N995SK | HS25 | 257035 |
| (N995SL) | HS25 | 257035 |
| N995TD | LJ24 | 149 |
| **N996AG** | **F2TH** | **64** |
| N996AL | LJ40 | 45-2029 |
| **N996BP** | **LJ45** | **301** |
| N996CM | C510 | 0096 |
| **N996CR** | **LJ55** | **060** |
| (N996DR) | MU30 | A032SA |
| N996EX | F9EX | 99 |
| N996F | FA20 | 118 |
| N996GA | ASTR | 156 |
| **N996GA** | **GLF4** | **4196** |
| N996JP | ASTR | 017 |
| N996JR | C525 | 0147 |
| **N996JS** | **LJ31** | **119** |
| **N996PE** | **C52B** | **0170** |
| **N996QS** | **C750** | **0196** |
| N996RP | HS25 | 257131 |
| N996TD | LJ24 | 320 |
| N996W | SBRL | 465-22 |
| **N996XP** | **HS25** | **HA-0096** |
| N997AG | GLF4 | 1440 |
| N997BC | GLF4 | 1170 |
| N997CA | C500 | 198 |
| **N997CB** | **C56X** | **5102** |
| N997CM | GLF3 | 432 |
| (N997CT) | CL61 | 5161 |
| **N997EA** | **C560** | **0178** |
| N997EX | F9EX | 100 |
| N997GA | ASTR | 107 |
| **N997GC** | **CL61** | **3025** |
| (N997HM) | GLF3 | 432 |
| N997HT | C550 | 550-0848 |
| **N997JP** | **LJ31** | **140** |
| N997ME | SBRL | 306-40 |
| **N997MX** | **MU30** | **A036SA** |
| **N997QS** | **C750** | **0208** |
| **N997RS** | **BE40** | **RK-388** |
| (N997S) | C500 | 179 |
| N997TD | LJ24 | 247 |
| N997TT | FA20 | 485 |
| N998AA | C500 | 310 |
| N998AL | LJ31 | 240 |
| **N998AL** | **LJ40** | **45-2029** |
| N998AM | GLEX | 9009 |
| N998AQ | LJ40 | 45-2029 |
| **N998BC** | **C550** | **665** |
| **N998CK** | **FA20** | **98/434** |
| **N998CX** | **C750** | **0098** |
| (N998DJ) | LJ35 | 098 |
| **N998EA** | **C500** | **492** |
| N998EJ | C750 | 0098 |
| N998EX | F9EX | 98 |
| N998G | GALX | 008 |
| N998GA | ASTR | 108 |
| N998GA | GLF4 | 4025 |
| N998GA | GLF5 | 5158 |
| N998GC | LJ35 | 343 |
| N998GP | ASTR | 108 |
| N998GP | BE40 | RK-32 |
| N998GP | C550 | 363 |
| N998JB | GLF3 | 491 |
| N998JP | LJ35 | 211 |
| N998JR | CL61 | 3045 |
| N998M | LJ24 | 249 |
| (N998M) | LJ35 | 098 |
| N998PA | HS25 | 258070 |
| **N998PA** | **PRM1** | **RB-70** |
| N998PS | HS25 | 25229 |
| **N998QS** | **C750** | **0198** |
| N998R | SBRL | 306-9 |
| N998RD | WW24 | 103 |
| N998RL | LJ24 | 087 |
| **N998SA** | **C560** | **0485** |
| N998SR | C550 | 550-1136 |
| **N998TW** | **C560** | **0362** |
| N999AD | C560 | 0136 |
| (N999AH) | FA10 | 152 |
| **N999AM** | **C500** | **232** |
| N999AU | C550 | 181 |
| N999AU | LJ31 | 074 |
| N999AZ | WW24 | 343 |
| N999BE | F2EX | 32 |
| N999BE | F2TH | 147 |
| **N999BE** | **FA7X** | **8** |
| (N999BG) | FA20 | 275 |
| N999BH | LJ25 | 318 |
| **N999BL** | **ASTR** | **024** |
| N999BL | C550 | 131 |
| N999BL | WW24 | 382 |
| N999BS | SBRL | 282-53 |
| N999CA | WW24 | 111 |
| N999CB | C500 | 211 |
| (N999CB) | C500 | 631 |
| **N999CB** | **C560** | **0692** |
| N999CB | CS55 | 0054 |
| N999CM | C500 | 158 |
| N999CV | C500 | 211 |

| | | |
|---|---|---|
| **N999CX** | **C550** | **550-0841** |
| N999CX | C750 | 0073 |
| **N999CY** | **HS25** | **257086** |
| N999DC | FA20 | 322 |
| N999DC | SBRL | 306-95 |
| N999EA | CS55 | 0077 |
| N999EB | C525 | 0210 |
| **N999EB** | **C525** | **0616** |
| **N999EH** | **F900** | **15** |
| **N999EK** | **LJ40** | **45-2060** |
| N999EQ | FA20 | 275 |
| N999F | FA10 | 29 |
| N999FA | LJ35 | 386 |
| N999FB | WW24 | 61 |
| N999GH | C550 | 496 |
| N999GH | LJ31 | 216 |
| (N999GL) | CS55 | 0030 |
| N999GP | ASTR | 062 |
| N999GP | ASTR | 108 |
| N999GP | BE40 | RK-32 |
| N999GP | C550 | 363 |
| **N999GP** | **GLF4** | **1061** |
| N999GP | GLF4 | 1422 |
| N999GR | C550 | 104 |
| **N999HC** | **CS55** | **0030** |
| N999HG | LJ25 | 178 |
| (N999JA) | LJ35 | 352 |
| N999JB | C500 | 114 |
| **N999JD** | **C510** | **0036** |
| N999JF | BE40 | RK-98 |
| N999JF | HS25 | 257016 |
| **N999JF** | **HS25** | **258220** |
| N999JF | HS25 | 258380 |
| N999JF | LJ35 | 188 |
| N999JR | CL61 | 3061 |
| N999JR | LJ24 | 174 |
| **N999JS** | **LJ35** | **277** |
| N999KG | SBRL | 306-53 |
| **N999LB** | **C52B** | **0057** |
| N999LC | WW24 | 402 |
| N999LF | HS25 | 25155 |
| (N999LG) | SBRL | 306-53 |
| N999LJ | LJ60 | 314 |
| (N999LL) | C550 | 106 |
| **N999LL** | **FA10** | **152** |
| **N999LX** | **GLF4** | **1099** |
| N999M | LJ24 | 114 |
| N999M | LJ24 | 249 |
| N999M | LJ25 | 030 |
| N999M | LJ25 | 102 |
| N999M | LJ25 | 178 |
| N999M | LJ25 | 231 |
| N999M | LJ35 | 045 |
| N999M | SBRL | 380-54 |
| N999MC | WW24 | 412 |
| N999ME | LJ25 | 231 |
| N999MF | LJ24 | 202 |
| **N999MF** | **LJ25** | **050** |
| N999MH | FA10 | 6 |
| N999MK | C550 | 290 |
| N999MK | LJ25 | 030 |
| N999ML | LJ25 | 102 |
| **N999MS** | **C500** | **638** |
| N999MS | WW24 | 199 |
| N999MV | LJ25 | 178 |
| **N999NB** | **GLF4** | **1234** |
| **N999ND** | **CL30** | **20250** |
| N999ND | LJ35 | 112 |
| (N999NM) | HS25 | 25186 |
| **N999PJ** | **MS76** | **089** |
| N999PM | F900 | 128 |
| N999PM | F900 | 20 |
| **N999PM** | **F9EX** | **70** |
| (N999PN) | F900 | 128 |
| **N999PW** | **C500** | **549** |
| **N999PX** | **CL64** | **5387** |
| **N999QE** | **C52A** | **0366** |
| **N999QH** | **CS55** | **0077** |
| **N999QS** | **C750** | **0203** |
| N999RA | LJ24 | 213 |
| (N999RA) | WW24 | 93 |
| N999RB | C500 | 369 |
| (N999RB) | C500 | 578 |
| N999RB | LJ35 | 301 |
| N999RC | C550 | 479 |
| **N999RN** | **E50P** | **50000053** |
| N999RW | HS25 | 25236 |
| N999SA | HS25 | 25146 |
| N999SF | C500 | 055 |
| **N999SM** | **C52B** | **0052** |
| N999SR | CL60 | 1042 |
| (N999SW) | CL61 | 3008 |
| N999TC | C500 | 120 |
| N999TF | CL60 | 1042 |
| **N999TH** | **FA20** | **512** |
| N999TH | LJ25 | 293 |
| N999TH | LJ35 | 621 |
| N999TJ | CS55 | 0048 |
| N999TN | LJ35 | 621 |
| N999U | LJ24 | 253 |
| N999U | WW24 | 178 |
| **N999VK** | **CL64** | **5499** |
| N999VT | SBRL | 282-38 |
| N999WA | C550 | 051 |
| N999WA | LJ24 | 242 |
| N999WE | C52A | 0126 |
| N999WJ | FA10 | 216 |
| **N999WS** | **C500** | **581** |
| N999YA | GLEX | 9114 |
| **N999YB** | **BE40** | **RK-98** |
| N999YC | LJ60 | 353 |
| N999YX | GLEX | 9240 |
| N999YY | GLEX | 9114 |
| **N999YY** | **GLEX** | **9240** |
| **N999ZG** | **PRM1** | **RB-182** |
| N1000 | GLF2 | 205 |
| N1000 | GLF2 | 75/7 |
| **N1000E** | **C525** | **0077** |
| N1000E | HS25 | 259015 |
| N1000E | SBRL | 282-19 |
| N1000U | HS25 | 259006 |
| **N1000W** | **C560** | **0204** |
| N1000W | CS55 | 0079 |
| N1001A | LJ24 | 071 |
| N1001G | SBRL | 306-3 |
| "N1001L" | LJ35 | 155 |
| N1001L | LJ35 | 357 |
| N1002B | LJ24 | 038 |
| N1004T | GLF2 | 35 |
| N1006F | C525 | 0112 |
| N1007 | JSTR | 5057 |
| N1008S | LJ24 | 118 |
| N1010A | LJ36 | 017 |
| N1010F | FA20 | 360 |
| N1010G | LJ36 | 043 |
| N1010H | LJ36 | 044 |
| N1012B | JSTR | 5012 |
| N1013F | FA20 | 364 |
| N1014X | C750 | 0008 |
| N1015B | C525 | 0151 |
| N1018F | FA20 | 365 |
| N1019K | LJ45 | 246 |
| N1019K | WW24 | 180 |
| N1020F | FA20 | 366 |
| N1020P | SBRL | 306-54 |
| N1021B | LJ24 | 086 |
| N1021T | C500 | 413 |
| N1022G | LJ35 | 650 |
| N1024G | SBRL | 306-64 |
| N1025C | HS25 | 25108 |
| (N1026) | HFB3 | 1026 |
| N1027S | BE40 | RK-141 |
| N1028Y | SBRL | 306-71 |
| N1036F | FA20 | 368 |
| N1036N | LJ25 | 121 |
| N1037F | FA20 | 369 |
| N1038F | FA20 | 370 |
| N1039 | GLF2 | 40 |
| N1039F | FA20 | 371 |
| N1039L | LJ55 | 139 |
| N1040 | GLF2 | 40 |
| N1040 | GLF3 | 314 |
| N1040 | GLF4 | 1044 |
| N1040 | GLF4 | 1206 |
| **N1040** | **GLF5** | **650** |
| N1041B | HS25 | 25111 |
| N1041F | FA20 | 373 |
| N1043B | LJ35 | 644 |
| N1045F | FA20 | 374 |
| N1045J | LJ35 | 648 |
| N1045T | C500 | 131 |
| N1045X | CL60 | 1038 |
| N1045X | LJ55 | 096 |
| N1047T | FA20 | 126/438 |
| N1048X | LJ36 | 063 |
| N1055C | LJ55 | 135 |
| N1058X | SBRL | 465-4 |
| **N1061** | **HS25** | **258134** |
| N1061D | CL61 | 5140 |
| N1062 | SBRL | 282-15 |
| N1064 | SBRL | 265-52 |
| N1066W | C560 | 0374 |
| N1069L | BE40 | TX-9 |
| N1072 | SBRL | 282-18 |
| N1075X | LJ55 | 082 |
| N1080Q | FA10 | 80 |
| N1082A | GLF4 | 1082 |
| N1083Z | BE40 | RK-131 |
| N1084D | BE40 | RK-114 |
| **N1086** | **GLF4** | **1086** |
| N1087T | LJ25 | 289 |
| N1087T | LJ35 | 589 |
| N1087T | LJ36 | 052 |
| N1087T | LJ55 | 096 |
| N1087T | LJ55 | 128 |
| N1087Y | LJ35 | 274 |
| N1087Y | LJ35 | 491 |
| N1087Y | LJ35 | 641 |
| N1087Y | LJ55 | 102 |
| N1087Y | LJ55 | 116 |
| N1087Z | BE40 | RK-132 |
| N1087Z | LJ35 | 427 |
| N1087Z | LJ35 | 490 |
| N1087Z | LJ35 | 503 |
| N1087Z | LJ35 | 660 |
| N1087Z | LJ36 | 054 |
| N1087Z | LJ36 | 059 |
| N1087Z | LJ55 | 073 |
| N1088A | LJ25 | 368 |
| N1088A | LJ35 | 271 |
| N1088A | LJ35 | 431 |
| N1088A | LJ35 | 655 |
| N1088A | LJ36 | 060 |
| N1088A | LJ55 | 068 |
| N1088A | LJ55 | 131 |
| N1088C | LJ25 | 292 |
| N1088C | LJ25 | 310 |
| N1088C | LJ35 | 594 |
| N1088C | LJ35 | 644 |
| N1088C | LJ55 | 065 |
| N1088C | LJ55 | 094 |
| N1088D | LJ25 | 291 |
| N1088D | LJ25 | 366 |
| N1088D | LJ31 | 004 |
| N1088D | LJ35 | 342 |
| N1088D | LJ35 | 463 |
| N1088D | LJ35 | 495 |
| N1088D | LJ35 | 605 |
| N1090X | BE40 | RK-110 |
| **N1090X** | **CL64** | **5576** |
| N1094D | BE40 | RK-134 |
| **N1094L** | **C56X** | **5094** |
| N1094N | BE40 | RK-140 |
| N1099S | BE40 | RK-139 |
| N1100D | WW24 | 169 |
| N1100M | WW24 | 86 |
| N1101G | SBRL | 282-58 |
| N1102 | C650 | 0047 |
| N1102 | GLF2 | 231 |
| N1102A | FA50 | 18 |
| N1102B | BE40 | RK-122 |
| N1102D | SBRL | 282-7 |
| N1102U | HS25 | 258343 |
| N1103 | C650 | 0054 |
| N1103 | HS25 | 257060 |
| N1103R | LJ25 | 135 |
| N1103U | HS25 | 258306 |
| N1105U | BE40 | RK-125 |
| N1105Z | HS25 | 258301 |
| N1107M | FA20 | 38 |
| N1107M | JSTR | 5122 |
| N1107Z | C750 | 0112 |
| N1107Z | CL61 | 3016 |
| N1107Z | JSTR | 5023 |
| N1107Z | JSTR | 5122 |
| N1108T | BE40 | RK-148 |
| N1108Y | BE40 | RK-128 |
| N1109 | C550 | 433 |
| (N1109) | C650 | 0047 |
| N1110S | LJ35 | 306 |
| N1112N | HS25 | 258325 |
| N1115 | SBRL | 380-17 |
| N1115G | HS25 | 258347 |
| N1115V | C525 | 0157 |
| N1116A | SBRL | 306-30 |
| **N1116R** | **BE40** | **RK-116** |
| N1117S | BE40 | RK-117 |
| N1117Z | BE40 | RK-137 |
| N1118Y | BE40 | RK-118 |
| N1119C | BE40 | RK-119 |
| N1119C | GLF3 | 417 |
| N1121 | LJ25 | 004 |
| N1121A | WW24 | 123 |
| (N1121B) | WW24 | 129 |
| N1121C | LJ25 | 004 |
| N1121C | WW24 | 76 |
| N1121E | WW24 | 149 |
| **N1121E** | **WW24** | **20** |
| N1121E | WW24 | 78 |
| N1121E | WW24 | 90 |
| N1121F | WW24 | 150 |
| N1121G | WW24 | 52 |
| N1121G | WW24 | 67 |
| N1121M | WW24 | 111 |
| N1121M | WW24 | 36 |
| N1121N | WW24 | 110 |
| N1121N | WW24 | 125 |
| N1121N | WW24 | 135 |
| N1121N | WW24 | 98 |
| N1121R | WW24 | 121 |
| **N1121R** | **WW24** | **125** |
| N1121R | WW24 | 75 |
| N1121S | WW24 | 103 |
| N1121U | WW24 | 128 |
| N1121X | WW24 | 121 |
| N1121X | WW24 | 77 |
| N1121Z | BE40 | RK-121 |
| N1121Z | WW24 | 108 |
| N1123E | WW24 | 151 |
| N1123E | WW24 | 159 |
| N1123G | GLF2 | 160 |
| N1123G | WW24 | 158 |
| N1123H | WW24 | 156 |
| N1123H | WW24 | 167 |
| N1123H | WW24 | 172 |
| N1123Q | WW24 | 157 |
| N1123Q | WW24 | 173 |
| N1123Q | WW24 | 182 |
| N1123R | WW24 | 160 |
| N1123R | WW24 | 165 |
| N1123R | WW24 | 175 |
| N1123R | WW24 | 186 |
| N1123S | WW24 | 162 |
| N1123T | WW24 | 163 |
| N1123T | WW24 | 176 |
| N1123T | WW24 | 184 |
| N1123U | WW24 | 169 |
| N1123U | WW24 | 177 |
| N1123U | WW24 | 185 |
| N1123W | WW24 | 160 |
| N1123W | WW24 | 170 |
| N1123X | WW24 | 174 |
| N1123Y | WW24 | 179 |
| N1123Z | BE40 | RK-123 |
| N1123Z | WW24 | 159 |
| N1123Z | WW24 | 178 |
| N1124E | WW24 | 196 |
| N1124E | WW24 | 235 |
| N1124F | WW24 | 281 |
| N1124G | WW24 | 188 |
| N1124G | WW24 | 203 |
| N1124G | WW24 | 216 |
| N1124G | WW24 | 220 |
| N1124G | WW24 | 243 |
| N1124K | WW24 | 307 |
| N1124K | WW24 | 388 |
| N1124L | WW24 | 340 |
| N1124L | WW24 | 405 |
| N1124N | WW24 | 187 |
| N1124N | WW24 | 201 |
| N1124N | WW24 | 214 |
| N1124N | WW24 | 259 |
| N1124N | WW24 | 321 |
| N1124N | WW24 | 346 |
| N1124N | WW24 | 396 |
| N1124P | WW24 | 199 |
| N1124P | WW24 | 207 |
| N1124P | WW24 | 223 |
| N1124P | WW24 | 245 |
| N1124P | WW24 | 341 |
| N1124P | WW24 | 376 |
| N1124Q | WW24 | 201 |

| | | |
|---|---|---|
| N1124Q | WW24 | 232 |
| N1124Q | WW24 | 288 |
| N1124U | WW24 | 225 |
| N1124U | WW24 | 286 |
| N1124X | WW24 | 200 |
| N1124X | WW24 | 233 |
| N1124Z | BE40 | RK-124 |
| N1124Z | WW24 | 234 |
| N1124Z | WW24 | 410 |
| N1125 | ASTR | 021 |
| N1125 | ASTR | 062 |
| N1125 | ASTR | 076 |
| N1125 | HS25 | 25023 |
| N1125 | HS25 | 258101 |
| N1125A | ASTR | 012 |
| N1125A | ASTR | 021 |
| N1125A | ASTR | 032 |
| **N1125A** | **ASTR** | **051** |
| N1125E | ASTR | 058 |
| N1125E | HS25 | 25149 |
| N1125E | LJ24 | 196 |
| N1125G | ASTR | 076 |
| N1125G | HS25 | 25019 |
| N1125G | HS25 | 25033 |
| N1125G | HS25 | 25084 |
| N1125G | WW24 | 247 |
| **N1125J** | **ASTR** | **078** |
| **N1125K** | **ASTR** | **035** |
| N1125L | ASTR | 072 |
| N1125M | LJ55 | 065 |
| N1125S | ASTR | 021 |
| **N1125S** | **ASTR** | **134** |
| N1125V | ASTR | 048 |
| N1125V | ASTR | 132 |
| N1125Y | ASTR | 049 |
| N1125Z | ASTR | 055 |
| N1125Z | ASTR | 068 |
| N1126G | WW24 | 279 |
| N1126V | BE40 | RK-151 |
| N1127G | C650 | 7084 |
| N1127K | C525 | 0278 |
| N1127K | C525 | 0293 |
| N1127M | LJ35 | 226 |
| N1127M | LJ55 | 120 |
| **N1127M** | **LJ60** | **253** |
| N1127P | C560 | 0349 |
| N1127U | BE40 | RK-127 |
| N1128B | C650 | 0184 |
| **N1128B** | **F2TH** | **83** |
| N1128G | C525 | 0304 |
| N1128J | LJ35 | 426 |
| **N1128M** | **LJ60** | **222** |
| N1128V | C750 | 0159 |
| **N1129E** | **C56X** | **5112** |
| **N1129L** | **C560** | **0507** |
| N1129M | LJ35 | 360 |
| N1129M | LJ55 | 101 |
| N1129X | BE40 | RK-129 |
| N1129X | GLF4 | 1129 |
| N1130B | BE40 | RK-130 |
| N1130G | C56X | 5213 |
| N1130N | C650 | 7071 |
| N1130X | C56X | 5683 |
| (N1131K) | C550 | 651 |
| N1133G | C525 | 0347 |
| N1133N | HS25 | 258366 |
| N1133T | BE40 | RK-133 |
| N1135A | BE40 | RK-135 |
| N1135A | HS25 | 258345 |
| N1135K | HS25 | 25019 |
| N1135U | BE40 | RK-150 |
| N1136Q | BE40 | RK-136 |
| **N1140A** | **LJ35** | **045** |
| N1141G | WW24 | 275 |
| (N1149E) | GLF3 | 358 |
| N1151K | JSTR | 5115/39 |
| N1159K | GLF2 | 101 |
| N1164A | GLF2 | 42/12 |
| N1166Z | WW24 | 18 |
| (N1169D) | HS25 | 258002 |
| N1172L | WW24 | 11 |
| N1172Z | WW24 | 11 |
| N1172Z | WW24 | 133 |
| N1173Z | WW24 | 7 |
| (N1175B) | GLF4 | 1175 |
| N1178 | C550 | 433 |
| N1180Z | WW24 | 33 |
| N1181G | FA50 | 72 |
| N1183 | C650 | 0054 |
| N1183 | HS25 | 257060 |
| (N1184L) | HFB3 | 1050 |
| N1188A | ASTR | 018 |
| N1189A | JSTR | 5139/54 |
| N1190Z | WW24 | 28 |
| N1194Z | WW24 | 70 |
| N1195N | WW24 | 89 |
| N1196Z | WW24 | 61 |
| N1198V | C56X | 5692 |
| N1199G | HS25 | 25174 |
| N1199M | FA20 | 121 |
| N1199M | HS25 | 25174 |
| **N1200N** | **C550** | **681** |
| N1202D | C560 | 0403 |
| N1202T | C550 | 707 |
| N1203 | LJ24 | 008 |
| N1203D | C550 | 709 |
| N1203N | C550 | 710 |
| N1203S | C550 | 711 |
| N1204A | C550 | 715 |
| N1205A | C550 | 716 |
| (N1205M) | C550 | 717 |
| (N1207A) | C550 | 720 |
| N1207B | C550 | 721 |
| N1207C | C550 | 722 |
| N1207D | C550 | 723 |
| N1207F | C550 | 724 |
| N1207Z | C550 | 725 |
| N1207Z | JSTR | 5108 |
| N1209T | C550 | 726 |
| N1209T | C560 | 0002 |
| (N1209X) | C550 | 727 |
| (N1209X) | C560 | 0003 |
| N1210 | SBRL | 306-4 |
| N1210 | WW24 | 34 |
| N1210G | WW24 | 34 |
| N1210M | LJ35 | 410 |
| (N1210N) | C550 | 728 |
| (N1210N) | C560 | 0004 |
| N1210V | C550 | 729 |
| (N1210V) | C560 | 0005 |
| N1211M | C550 | 730 |
| (N1211M) | C560 | 0006 |
| N1212G | WW24 | 229 |
| N1212H | C550 | 219 |
| N1213S | C550 | 732 |
| (N1213S) | C560 | 0008 |
| N1213Z | C550 | 733 |
| (N1213Z) | C560 | 0009 |
| (N1214D) | C550 | 391 |
| N1214H | C550 | 392 |
| (N1214J) | C550 | 393 |
| (N1214J) | C550 | 734 |
| (N1214J) | C560 | 0010 |
| N1214S | C550 | 394 |
| (N1214Z) | C550 | 395 |
| (N1214Z) | C560 | 0011 |
| (N1215A) | C550 | 398 |
| N1215G | C550 | 399 |
| (N1215S) | C550 | 401 |
| (N1216A) | C550 | 405 |
| (N1216A) | C560 | 0003 |
| N1216H | C550 | 406 |
| N1216J | C550 | 407 |
| (N1216J) | C560 | 0004 |
| N1216K | C525 | 0199 |
| N1216K | C550 | 408 |
| N1216K | C550 | 454 |
| (N1216K) | C560 | 0005 |
| N1216N | C525 | 0226 |
| N1216N | C550 | 409 |
| (N1216N) | C560 | 0006 |
| N1216Q | C550 | 410 |
| (N1216Q) | C560 | 0007 |
| (N1216Z) | C550 | 411 |
| (N1216Z) | C560 | 0008 |
| N1216Z | C560 | 0454 |
| N1217D | C550 | 416 |
| N1217H | C550 | 417 |
| (N1217H) | C560 | 0011 |
| N1217H | C560 | 0376 |
| N1217N | C550 | 418 |
| N1217N | C560 | 0012 |
| N1217P | C550 | 419 |
| (N1217P) | C560 | 0013 |
| N1217S | C550 | 420 |
| N1217S | C560 | 0014 |
| N1217V | C550 | 421 |
| N1217V | C560 | 560-0001 |
| N1218A | C550 | 424 |
| **N1218C** | **GLF2** | **99** |
| N1218F | C550 | 425 |
| N1218K | C550 | 426 |
| (N1218P) | C550 | 427 |
| (N1218P) | C560 | 0017 |
| N1218S | C550 | 428 |
| N1218T | C550 | 429 |
| N1218V | C550 | 430 |
| N1218Y | C550 | 431 |
| (N1218Y) | C560 | 0018 |
| N1218Y | C560 | 0407 |
| N1219D | C550 | 432 |
| (N1219D) | C560 | 0019 |
| (N1219G) | C550 | 433 |
| (N1219G) | C560 | 0020 |
| (N1219N) | C550 | 434 |
| N1219P | C550 | 435 |
| N1219Z | C550 | 436 |
| N1220A | C550 | 439 |
| (N1220D) | C550 | 440 |
| N1220J | C550 | 441 |
| (N1220N) | C550 | 442 |
| N1220S | C550 | 443 |
| **N1220W** | **C52A** | **0146** |
| **N1221J** | **LJ60** | **209** |
| (N1223A) | C560 | 0017 |
| N1223N | C650 | 0120 |
| N1223N | CS55 | 0053 |
| (N1226X) | C560 | 0019 |
| (N1228N) | C560 | 0020 |
| N1228N | C56X | 5030 |
| N1228V | C560 | 0021 |
| (N1228Y) | C560 | 0022 |
| (N1229A) | C560 | 0028 |
| (N1229C) | C560 | 0029 |
| (N1229D) | C560 | 0030 |
| N1229F | C560 | 0031 |
| N1229M | C560 | 0032 |
| N1229N | C560 | 0033 |
| (N1229Q) | C560 | 0034 |
| N1229Z | C560 | 0035 |
| N1230 | WW24 | 53 |
| (N1230A) | C560 | 0039 |
| N1230A | HS25 | 257026 |
| N1230B | HS25 | 25088 |
| N1230D | WW24 | 53 |
| N1230F | C56X | 5679 |
| (N1230G) | C560 | 0040 |
| N1230G | HS25 | 25091 |
| N1230R | JSTR | 5049 |
| N1230V | HS25 | 25043 |
| (N1234F) | C500 | 501 |
| N1234X | C500 | 394 |
| (N1236P) | C500 | 358 |
| N1239L | C650 | 0134 |
| N1241K | C56X | 5118 |
| N1241N | C525 | 0185 |
| (N1242A) | C550 | 609 |
| N1242B | C550 | 610 |
| (N1242K) | C550 | 611 |
| N1242K | C560 | 0624 |
| N1243C | C56X | 5013 |
| N1244V | C550 | 612 |
| **N1245** | **C510** | **0204** |
| N1247V | C560 | 0535 |
| N1248B | C560 | 0417 |
| (N1248G) | C550 | 444 |
| N1248K | C550 | 445 |
| "N1248K" | C550 | 447 |
| N1248N | C550 | 446 |
| N1249B | C550 | 448 |
| N1249H | C550 | 449 |
| N1249K | C550 | 450 |
| **N1249P** | **C550** | **451** |
| (N1249T) | C550 | 452 |
| N1249V | C550 | 453 |
| N1250B | C550 | 455 |
| N1250C | C550 | 456 |
| N1250L | C550 | 457 |
| N1250P | C550 | 458 |
| N1250P | C550 | 613 |
| **N1250V** | **C550** | **439** |
| N1251B | C550 | 463 |
| N1251D | C550 | 464 |
| N1251H | C550 | 465 |
| N1251K | C550 | 466 |
| N1251K | C550 | 466 |
| N1251K | HS25 | 258372 |
| N1251K | HS25 | 258377 |
| N1251N | C550 | 467 |
| (N1251P) | C550 | 468 |
| (N1251P) | C550 | 614 |
| N1251V | C550 | 469 |
| (N1251V) | C550 | 614 |
| N1251Z | C550 | 470 |
| N1252B | C550 | 475 |
| **N1252D** | **C550** | **476** |
| N1252J | C550 | 477 |
| N1252N | C550 | 478 |
| N1252P | C550 | 479 |
| N1253D | C550 | 481 |
| N1253G | C550 | 482 |
| (N1253K) | C550 | 483 |
| (N1253K) | C550 | 616 |
| N1253N | C550 | 484 |
| N1253P | C550 | 485 |
| N1253Y | C550 | 486 |
| (N1253Y) | C550 | 617 |
| N1254C | C550 | 490 |
| N1254C | C550 | 618 |
| **N1254C** | **C650** | **7098** |
| (N1254D) | C550 | 491 |
| (N1254D) | C550 | 619 |
| (N1254G) | C550 | 492 |
| N1254G | C550 | 620 |
| N1254P | C550 | 493 |
| **N1254X** | **C550** | **494** |
| (N1254Y) | C550 | 495 |
| (N1255D) | C550 | 498 |
| N1255D | C550 | 502 |
| (N1255G) | C550 | 499 |
| N1255G | C550 | 503 |
| N1255J | C52A | 0101 |
| **N1255J** | **C52B** | **0109** |
| N1255J | C550 | 500 |
| (N1255J) | C550 | 504 |
| (N1255J) | C550 | 622 |
| **N1255K** | **C550** | **505** |
| (N1255L) | C550 | 623 |
| (N1255L) | CS55 | 0001 |
| N1255Y | C550 | 624 |
| (N1255Y) | CS55 | 0002 |
| N1256B | CS55 | 0004 |
| (N1256G) | C550 | 626 |
| (N1256G) | CS55 | 0005 |
| (N1256N) | C550 | 627 |
| (N1256N) | CS55 | 0006 |
| (N1256P) | C550 | 628 |
| (N1256P) | CS55 | 0007 |
| N1256T | C550 | 629 |
| (N1256T) | CS55 | 0008 |
| N1256Z | CS55 | 0009 |
| **N1257B** | **C550** | **497** |
| N1257K | C550 | 630 |
| (N1257K) | CS55 | 0010 |
| (N1257M) | C550 | 631 |
| (N1257M) | CS55 | 0011 |
| N1258B | C550 | 550-1037 |
| (N1258B) | C550 | 634 |
| N1258H | C550 | 635 |
| N1258M | C550 | 636 |
| (N1258U) | C550 | 637 |
| (N1258U) | CS55 | 0015 |
| N1259B | C550 | 550-0819 |
| (N1259B) | C550 | 639 |
| N1259B | C650 | 7001 |
| (N1259B) | CS55 | 0016 |
| (N1259G) | CS55 | 0017 |
| (N1259G) | CS55 | 0017 |
| (N1259K) | C550 | 640 |
| N1259K | C650 | 7002 |
| (N1259K) | CS55 | 0018 |
| N1259K | HS25 | 25170 |
| (N1259M) | CS55 | 0019 |
| (N1259N) | C550 | 641 |
| N1259N | C650 | 7003 |
| (N1259R) | C550 | 642 |
| N1259R | C650 | 7004 |
| (N1259R) | CS55 | 0020 |
| (N1259S) | C550 | 643 |
| N1259S | C650 | 7005 |
| (N1259S) | CS55 | 0021 |
| N1259Y | C525 | 0449 |

(N1259Y) C550 644
(N1259Y) C650 7006
(N1259Y) CS55 0022
(N1259Z) C550 645
N1259Z C650 7007
(N1259Z) CS55 0023
N1260G C550 648
N1260G C650 7010
(N1260G) CS55 0026
N1260K CS55 0027
(N1260L) CS55 0028
N1260N C650 7011
(N1260N) CS55 0029
N1260V C650 7012
(N1260V) CS55 0030
N1261A C650 7014
(N1261A) CS55 0032
N1261K C650 7015
(N1261K) CS55 0033
N1261M C650 7016
(N1261M) C650 7017
(N1261M) CS55 0034
(N1261P) C650 7018
(N1261P) CS55 0035
N1262A C650 7020
N1262B C650 7021
N1262E C650 7022
N1262G C650 7023
N1262Z C650 7024
N1263B C650 7025
N1263G C650 7026
N1263P C650 7027
(N1263V) C650 7028
(N1263Y) C650 7029
N1263Z C650 7030
N1264B C650 7033
N1264E C650 7034
N1264M C650 7035
N1264P C650 7036
N1264V C525 0126
(N1264V) C650 7037
N1265B C650 7040
N1265C C650 7041
N1265K C650 7042
N1265P C650 7043
N1265U C650 7044
N1267B C52A 0207
N1268D C56X 5273
N1268F C750 0216
N1268G LJ35 661
N1269B C525 0534
(N1269D) CS55 0040
(N1269E) CS55 0041
(N1269J) CS55 0042
(N1269N) CS55 0043
N1269P C560 0638
(N1269P) CS55 0044
N1269Y CS55 0045
N1270D CS55 0048
N1270F FA20 72/413
N1270K C500 133
N1270K CS55 0049
N1270S CS55 0050
N1270Y CS55 0051
N1271A CL61 5038
N1271A CS55 0055
N1271B C550 550-1079
(N1271B) CS55 0056
N1271D CS55 0057
N1271E CS55 0058
(N1271N) CS55 0059
(N1271T) CS55 0060
(N1272G) CS55 0064
(N1272N) CS55 0065
N1272P CS55 0066
(N1272V) CS55 0067
N1272Z CS55 0068
N1273A CS55 0072
(N1273E) CS55 0073
N1273J CS55 0074
(N1273N) CS55 0075
N1273Q C550 550-0858
(N1273Q) CS55 0076
N1273R C560 0318
(N1273R) CS55 0077
N1273X CS55 0078
(N1273Z) CS55 0079
(N1274B) CS55 0081

N1274D CS55 0082
N1274K CS55 0083
N1274N CS55 0084
N1274P CS55 0085
(N1274X) CS55 0086
N1274Z CS55 0087
(N1275A) CS55 0092
N1275B CS55 0093
(N1275D) CS55 0094
N1275H CS55 0095
(N1275N) CS55 0096
N1275T C56X 5702
N1276A C550 550-1102
N1276J C525 0200
N1276L C680 0021
N1276Z C550 550-1103
**N1277E** **C52A** **0076**
N1278 C550 429
N1278D C52B 0006
N1279A C525 0551
N1279V C525 0552
N1279Z C560 0175
N1280A C525 0177
N1280A C560 0178
N1280D C560 0179
N1280K C560 0180
N1280R C560 0181
N1280S C525 0281
(N1280S) C560 0182
N1281A C550 550-1109
N1281A C560 0184
N1281K C560 0185
N1281N C560 0186
N1281N C56X 5559
N1281R C56X 5704
(N1282D) C560 0192
N1282K C560 0193
(N1282M) C560 0194
N1282N C560 0195
N1283F C560 0198
(N1283K) C560 0199
N1283M C560 0200
N1283M CS55 0120
N1283N C560 0201
N1283V C560 0202
N1283X C560 0203
N1283Y C560 0204
N1284A C560 0206
(N1284B) C560 0207
N1284D C525 0463
(N1284D) C560 0208
(N1284F) C560 0209
N1284N C560 0210
N1284P C525 0464
(N1284P) C560 0211
N1284X C560 0212
(N1285D) C560 0214
(N1285G) C560 0215
N1285N C560 0216
N1285P C525 0465
N1285P C560 0217
N1285V C560 0218
(N1286A) C560 0221
N1286C C560 0222
N1286N C560 0223
N1287B C525 0555
N1287B C560 0224
N1287C C560 0225
N1287D C52B 0027
N1287D C560 0226
N1287F C525 0557
N1287F C560 0227
N1287G C560 0228
N1287K C560 0229
N1287N C560 0230
N1287Y C560 0231
N1288A C560 0233
N1288B C560 0234
N1288B C750 0168
N1288D C560 0235
N1288N C525 0558
N1288N C560 0236
N1288P C525 0550
N1288P C560 0237
N1288T C560 0238
N1288Y C560 0239
N1289G C560 0240
N1289G C750 0242

N1289M GLF4 1441
N1289N C560 0241
N1289Y C560 0242
N1290B CS55 0097
N1290E CS55 0098
N1290G CS55 0099
N1290N C525 0554
N1290N C560 0246
(N1290N) CS55 0100
N1290Y C52A 0238
(N1290Y) CS55 0101
N1290Z CS55 0102
N1291E CS55 0107
N1291K C560 0249
(N1291K) C560 0250
(N1291K) CS55 0108
N1291P CS55 0109
N1291V CS55 0110
N1291Y C560 0250
(N1291Y) CS55 0111
N1292A CS55 0114
N1292B C560 0253
(N1292B) CS55 0115
N1292K CS55 0116
N1292N CS55 0117
N1293A CS55 0123
N1293E C560 0257
(N1293E) CS55 0124
N1293G C525 0204
N1293G CS55 0125
N1293K CS55 0126
N1293N CS55 0127
N1293V CS55 0128
N1293X CS55 0129
N1293Y C560 0258
N1293Z C560 0259
(N1293Z) CS55 0130
N1294B C560 0260
(N1294D) CS55 0132
N1294K C560 0261
(N1294K) CS55 0133
N1294M CS55 0134
N1294N C560 0262
(N1294N) CS55 0135
(N1294P) C560 560-0001
(N1294P) CS55 0136
N1295A C560 0264
(N1295A) CS55 0138
N1295B C560 0518
(N1295B) CS55 0139
N1295G C560 0266
(N1295G) CS55 0140
N1295J C560 0267
(N1295J) CS55 0141
N1295M C560 0268
(N1295M) CS55 0142
N1295N C560 0269
N1295N C560 0292
(N1295N) CS55 0143
N1295P C560 0265
(N1295P) CS55 0144
N1295Y C560 0270
N1295Y C560 0294
(N1295Y) CS55 0145
N1296B CS55 0146
N1296N C560 0271
N1296N C560 0297
N1296N CS55 0147
N1296Z CS55 0148
(N1297B) CS55 0150
N1297V C560 0275
N1297V C560 0300
N1297Y C550 554
N1297Z C550 555
N1298 SBRL 306-9
N1298C C550 557
(N1298G) C550 558
N1298G C750 0248
(N1298H) C550 559
N1298J C550 560
N1298K C550 561
(N1298N) C550 562
N1298P C550 550-1127
N1298P C550 563
N1298X C550 564
N1298X C560 0502
N1298Y C550 550-1114
N1298Y C550 565

N1299B C550 550-0808
(N1299B) C550 566
(N1299H) C550 567
N1299H C56X 5578
N1299K C550 568
N1299K C56X 5586
N1299N C550 550
N1299P C550 569
(N1299T) C550 570
(N1300G) C550 576
(N1300J) C550 577
N1300J C56X 5621
N1300M WW24 124
N1300N C550 578
(N1301A) C550 582
N1301A C650 0221
N1301B C550 583
N1301D C550 584
N1301D C650 0223
N1301K C550 585
N1301N C550 586
N1301P JSTR 5138
N1301S C550 587
N1301V C550 588
N1301Z C550 589
N1301Z C650 0225
N1302A C650 0226
N1302C C650 0227
N1302N C550 592
N1302V C550 593
N1302V C650 0228
N1302X C550 594
N1302X C650 0229
N1303A C650 0232
N1303H C550 600
N1303H C650 0233
(N1303M) C550 601
N1303M C650 0236
N1303V C650 0235
N1304B C650 0238
N1304G C650 0239
N1305C C550 550-0925
(N1305C) C650 0009
(N1305N) C650 0010
N1305N C650 0230
N1305U C650 0011
N1305V C650 0012
(N1306B) C650 0014
N1306B C650 0237
(N1306F) C650 0015
N1306V C56X 5054
N1306V C650 0016
N1306V+ C650 0234
N1307A C650 0017
(N1307A) C650 0235
(N1307C) C650 0018
(N1307C) C650 0236
(N1307D) C650 0019
(N1307D) C650 0237
N1307G C650 0020
N1308L C52B 0004
N1308V C550 640
N1309A C550 641
(N1309A) C650 0033
**N1309B** **C550** **550-1121**
N1309K C550 642
N1309V C525 0613
(N1310B) C550 644
(N1310B) C650 0043
N1310C C550 645
(N1310G) C550 646
(N1310Q) C550 648
(N1310Z) C550 649
(N1311A) C550 650
(N1311A) C650 0049
(N1311K) C650 0050
(N1311P) C550 652
(N1311P) C650 0051
(N1312D) C650 0054
N1312D C650 0160
N1312K C56X 5624
(N1312K) C650 0161
N1312Q C650 0162
N1312T C56X 5635
N1312T C56X 5710
N1312T C650 0163
N1312V C650 0164
N1312V C680 0075

| | | |
|---|---|---|
| N1312X | C650 | 0165 |
| N1313G | C650 | 0059 |
| (N1313J) | C650 | 0060 |
| N1313J | C650 | 0166 |
| (N1313T) | C650 | 0061 |
| N1314H | C525 | 0632 |
| (N1314H) | C650 | 0064 |
| N1314H | C650 | 0168 |
| (N1314T) | C650 | 0065 |
| N1314T | C680 | 0129 |
| N1314V | C52B | 0164 |
| (N1314V) | C650 | 0066 |
| N1314V | C650 | 0170 |
| (N1314X) | C650 | 0067 |
| (N1314X) | C650 | 0068 |
| (N1315A) | C650 | 0070 |
| (N1315B) | C650 | 0071 |
| N1315C | C560 | 0569 |
| (N1315C) | C650 | 0072 |
| N1315D | C56X | 5711 |
| (N1315D) | C650 | 0073 |
| (N1315G) | C650 | 0074 |
| N1315G | C680 | 0173 |
| N1315T | C650 | 0075 |
| N1315V | C650 | 0076 |
| (N1315Y) | C650 | 0077 |
| N1315Y | C680 | 0069 |
| (N1316A) | C650 | 0079 |
| N1316E | C650 | 0080 |
| (N1316N) | C650 | 0081 |
| N1317G | C650 | 0085 |
| N1317X | C52A | 0311 |
| (N1317X) | C650 | 0086 |
| N1317Y | C525 | 0619 |
| (N1317Y) | C650 | 0087 |
| (N1318A) | C650 | 0090 |
| N1318E | C650 | 0091 |
| (N1318E) | SBRL | 306-96 |
| (N1318L) | C650 | 0092 |
| (N1318M) | C650 | 0093 |
| (N1318P) | C650 | 0094 |
| (N1318Q) | C650 | 0095 |
| (N1318X) | C650 | 0096 |
| N1318X | C680 | 0143 |
| N1318Y | C550 | 550-0884 |
| (N1318Y) | C650 | 0097 |
| N1319B | C650 | 0099 |
| N1319D | C560 | 0319 |
| (N1319D) | C650 | 0100 |
| N1319M | C650 | 0101 |
| N1319X | C56X | 5640 |
| (N1319X) | C650 | 0102 |
| (N1320B) | C650 | 0105 |
| (N1320K) | C650 | 0106 |
| N1320P | C56X | 5648 |
| (N1320P) | C650 | 0107 |
| (N1320U) | C650 | 0108 |
| N1320U | HFB3 | 1023 |
| (N1320V) | C650 | 0109 |
| (N1320X) | C650 | 0110 |
| N1321A | C650 | 0112 |
| N1321C | C650 | 0113 |
| (N1321J) | C650 | 0114 |
| N1321K | C650 | 0115 |
| (N1321L) | C650 | 0116 |
| N1321N | C650 | 0117 |
| N1322D | C650 | 0121 |
| (N1322K) | C650 | 0122 |
| (N1322X) | C650 | 0123 |
| (N1322Y) | C650 | 0124 |
| (N1323A) | C650 | 0126 |
| N1323D | C650 | 0127 |
| (N1323K) | C650 | 0128 |
| (N1323N) | C650 | 0129 |
| (N1323Q) | C650 | 0130 |
| (N1323R) | C650 | 0131 |
| N1323V | C650 | 0132 |
| N1323X | C650 | 0133 |
| (N1323Y) | C650 | 0134 |
| N1324 | GLF2 | 33 |
| N1324B | C56X | 5051 |
| (N1324B) | C650 | 0135 |
| N1324B | LJ55 | 026 |
| (N1324D) | C650 | 0136 |
| (N1324G) | C650 | 0137 |
| N1324P | LJ55 | 098 |
| (N1324R) | C650 | 0138 |
| (N1325D) | C650 | 0140 |

| | | |
|---|---|---|
| N1325E | C650 | 0141 |
| (N1325L) | C650 | 0142 |
| N1325X | C650 | 0143 |
| N1325Y | C650 | 0144 |
| N1325Z | C650 | 0145 |
| **N1326A** | **C56X** | **5272** |
| N1326A | C650 | 0148 |
| N1326B | C525 | 0002 |
| N1326B | C650 | 0149 |
| N1326D | C525 | 0003 |
| (N1326D) | C525 | 0005 |
| N1326D | C650 | 0150 |
| N1326G | C525 | 0004 |
| N1326G | C650 | 0151 |
| N1326H | C525 | 0005 |
| (N1326H) | C650 | 0152 |
| N1326K | C650 | 0153 |
| N1326P | C525 | 0006 |
| N1326P | C525 | 0385 |
| (N1326P) | C650 | 0154 |
| N1327A | C650 | 0157 |
| N1327B | C650 | 0158 |
| (N1327E) | C525 | 0007 |
| N1327G | C525 | 0008 |
| **N1327J** | **C525** | **0009** |
| (N1327K) | C525 | 0010 |
| (N1327N) | C525 | 0011 |
| (N1327Z) | C525 | 0012 |
| N1328A | C525 | 0013 |
| N1328D | C525 | 0014 |
| (N1328K) | C525 | 0015 |
| N1328M | C525 | 0016 |
| (N1328Q) | C525 | 0017 |
| (N1328X) | C525 | 0018 |
| (N1328Y) | C525 | 0019 |
| N1329D | C525 | 0020 |
| (N1329G) | C525 | 0021 |
| **N1329G** | **C525** | **0146** |
| N1329K | JSTR | 5106/9 |
| N1329L | JSTR | 5161/43 |
| N1329N | C525 | 0022 |
| (N1329T) | C525 | 0023 |
| (N1330D) | C525 | 0025 |
| (N1330G) | C525 | 0026 |
| N1330N | C525 | 0027 |
| N1330S | C525 | 0028 |
| N1331X | C525 | 0030 |
| N1333Z | C550 | 273 |
| N1348T | C525 | 0350 |
| N1354G | C500 | 539 |
| N1354G | C500 | 622 |
| N1354G | C525 | 0033 |
| N1354G | C650 | 0171 |
| N1367D | C525 | 0655 |
| N1382C | C500 | 309 |
| N1382N | C52B | 0193 |
| N1387E | C56X | 5769 |
| **N1388J** | **C680** | **0209** |
| N1393 | HS25 | 25190 |
| **N1400M** | **C650** | **0140** |
| N1401L | C500 | 436 |
| (N1406) | JSTR | 5029/38 |
| N1406S | C680 | 0205 |
| N1411S | LJ25 | 325 |
| **N1414P** | **C52A** | **0315** |
| N1419J | C650 | 0115 |
| N1419J | C650 | 0201 |
| (N1419J) | C750 | 0051 |
| (N1420) | LJ24 | 116 |
| N1424 | WW24 | 345 |
| N1424 | WW24 | 94 |
| N1424Z | WW24 | 94 |
| N1433B | LJ25 | 255 |
| N1450B | LJ25 | 212 |
| N1450B | LJ35 | 182 |
| N1450B | LJ35 | 354 |
| N1450B | LJ35 | 497 |
| (N1450B) | LJ55 | 053 |
| N1450B | LJ55 | 113 |
| N1451B | LJ35 | 102 |
| N1451B | LJ35 | 244 |
| N1451B | LJ35 | 457 |
| N1451B | LJ35 | 590 |
| N1451B | LJ35 | 620 |
| N1451B | LJ55 | 045 |
| N1451B | LJ55 | 087 |
| **N1454** | **GLF3** | **350** |
| N1454H | GLF3 | 350 |

| | | |
|---|---|---|
| **N1454H** | **GLF5** | **619** |
| N1461B | LJ25 | 358 |
| N1461B | LJ35 | 045 |
| N1461B | LJ35 | 177 |
| N1461B | LJ35 | 211 |
| N1461B | LJ35 | 632 |
| N1461B | LJ55 | 088 |
| N1461B | LJ55 | 111 |
| N1462B | LJ25 | 265 |
| N1462B | LJ35 | 037 |
| N1462B | LJ35 | 184 |
| N1462B | LJ35 | 221 |
| N1462B | LJ35 | 265 |
| N1462B | LJ35 | 451 |
| N1462B | LJ35 | 604 |
| N1462B | LJ35 | 634 |
| N1462B | LJ36 | 036 |
| N1462B | LJ55 | 042 |
| N1462B | LJ55 | 092 |
| N1465B | LJ35 | 193 |
| N1465B | LJ35 | 273 |
| N1465B | LJ35 | 428 |
| N1465B | LJ35 | 500 |
| N1465B | LJ35 | 642 |
| N1465B | LJ55 | 080 |
| N1466B | LJ25 | 236 |
| N1466B | LJ25 | 314 |
| N1466B | LJ35 | 204 |
| N1466B | LJ35 | 481 |
| N1466B | LJ35 | 615 |
| N1466B | LJ55 | 107 |
| (N1466K) | C550 | 055 |
| N1466K | LJ35 | 394 |
| N1468B | LJ25 | 205 |
| N1468B | LJ25 | 252 |
| N1468B | LJ25 | 371 |
| N1468B | LJ31 | 014 |
| N1468B | LJ35 | 222 |
| N1468B | LJ35 | 355 |
| N1468B | LJ35 | 472 |
| N1468B | LJ35 | 621 |
| N1468B | LJ55 | 081 |
| N1471B | LJ35 | 195 |
| N1471B | LJ35 | 441 |
| N1471B | LJ35 | 505 |
| N1471B | LJ35 | 603 |
| N1471B | LJ35 | 635 |
| N1471B | LJ55 | 070 |
| N1473B | LJ25 | 365 |
| N1473B | LJ35 | 134 |
| N1473B | LJ35 | 164 |
| N1473B | LJ35 | 239 |
| N1473B | LJ35 | 338 |
| N1473B | LJ35 | 489 |
| N1473B | LJ35 | 596 |
| N1473B | LJ35 | 610 |
| N1473B | LJ35 | 657 |
| N1476B | LJ25 | 222 |
| N1476B | LJ35 | 229 |
| N1476B | LJ35 | 278 |
| N1476B | LJ35 | 288 |
| N1476B | LJ35 | 494 |
| N1476B | LJ35 | 502 |
| N1476B | LJ35 | 636 |
| N1476B | LJ55 | 115 |
| N1479G | GLF4 | 1479 |
| **N1498G** | **LJ60** | **035** |
| N1500 | CL60 | 1078 |
| **N1500** | **CL65** | **5830** |
| N1500 | FA20 | 8 |
| N1500 | LJ35 | 339 |
| N1500B | LJ24 | 051 |
| N1500B | LJ25 | 055 |
| N1500C | WW24 | 169 |
| N1500C | WW24 | 46 |
| N1500E | LJ35 | 124 |
| N1500G | LJ24 | 051 |
| N1500M | JSTR | 5058/4 |
| N1500M | WW24 | 71 |
| N1501 | FA20 | 15 |
| N1502 | FA20 | 15 |
| N1502 | LJ35 | 328 |
| N1503 | FA20 | 42 |
| N1503 | LJ35 | 316 |
| (N1504) | CL60 | 1078 |
| N1507 | LJ35 | 316 |
| N1515E | HS25 | 25035 |
| N1515P | C550 | 477 |

| | | |
|---|---|---|
| N1515P | FA10 | 43 |
| N1515P | HS25 | 25035 |
| N1515P | HS25 | 256022 |
| N1526L | C650 | 0176 |
| N1526L | LJ35 | 245 |
| N1526M | GLF3 | 409 |
| N1526M | GLF4 | 1118 |
| N1526R | GLF3 | 409 |
| N1540 | GLF3 | 314 |
| N1540 | GLF4 | 1044 |
| **N1540** | **GLF5** | **580** |
| N1545N | BE40 | RK-91 |
| N1546T | BE40 | RJ-46 |
| **N1547B** | **BE40** | **RJ-47** |
| N1548D | BE40 | RJ-48 |
| N1549J | BE40 | RJ-49 |
| N1549W | BE40 | RK-88 |
| N1550Y | BE40 | RJ-50 |
| N1551B | BE40 | RJ-51 |
| N1551B | BE40 | RK-1 |
| N1554R | BE40 | RJ-54 |
| N1555P | BE40 | RJ-55 |
| N1556W | BE40 | RJ-56 |
| N1557D | BE40 | RJ-57 |
| N1558F | BE40 | RJ-58 |
| N1559U | BE40 | RJ-59 |
| N1560G | BE40 | RK-89 |
| N1560T | BE40 | RJ-60 |
| N1561B | BE40 | RJ-61 |
| N1563V | BE40 | RK-86 |
| N1564B | BE40 | RJ-64 |
| N1565B | BE40 | RJ-65 |
| N1567L | BE40 | RK-87 |
| N1570B | BE40 | RK-100 |
| N1570L | BE40 | RK-90 |
| **N1618L** | **C510** | **0314** |
| (N1618R) | LJ60 | 044 |
| N1620 | CL61 | 3025 |
| N1620 | GLF4 | 1206 |
| N1620 | HS25 | 257155 |
| **N1620** | **HS25** | **258893** |
| N1620 | JSTR | 5033/56 |
| N1620 | JSTR | 5132/57 |
| N1620N | JSTR | 5132/57 |
| N1621 | GLF2 | 31 |
| N1621 | WW24 | 275 |
| N1622 | CL60 | 1030 |
| N1622 | CL61 | 5077 |
| N1622 | JSTR | 5036/42 |
| N1622D | JSTR | 5036/42 |
| N1623 | CL61 | 3065 |
| N1624 | GLF2 | 33 |
| N1624 | GLF4 | 1318 |
| N1625 | GLF2 | 154/28 |
| N1625 | GLF4 | 1013 |
| **N1625** | **GLF4** | **1358** |
| N1625 | WW24 | 229 |
| N1629 | WW24 | 363 |
| **N1630** | **HS25** | **258557** |
| N1630 | HS25 | 258561 |
| N1640 | GLF3 | 314 |
| **N1640** | **HS25** | **258376** |
| N1650 | HS25 | 258432 |
| N1693L | C510 | 0026 |
| (N1700) | LJ35 | 258 |
| N1707Z | GLF2 | 213 |
| N1710E | C500 | 540 |
| N1710E | C500 | 623 |
| N1710E | C500 | 673 |
| N1715G | MU30 | A073SA |
| N1717L | C550 | 638 |
| N1728E | C500 | 541 |
| N1735J | LJ35 | 606 |
| N1744P | LJ55 | 063 |
| N1749L | C510 | 0054 |
| N1758E | C500 | 542 |
| N1758E | C500 | 624 |
| N1758E | C500 | 674 |
| (N1759) | GLF5 | 5128 |
| **N1759C** | **GLF5** | **5128** |
| N1761B | GLF3 | 358 |
| N1761B | GLF4 | 1043 |
| N1761B | GLF4 | 1155 |
| N1761D | GLF3 | 364 |
| N1761D | GLF3 | 423 |
| N1761D | GLF4 | 1046 |
| N1761D | GLF4 | 1109 |
| N1761D | GLF4 | 1154 |

| N1761J | GLF3 | 365 |
|---|---|---|
| N1761J | GLF4 | 1047 |
| N1761J | GLF4 | 1117 |
| N1761K | GLF3 | 385 |
| N1761K | GLF4 | 1048 |
| N1761K | GLF4 | 1156 |
| N1761P | GLF3 | 394 |
| N1761P | GLF4 | 1055 |
| N1761Q | GLF3 | 395 |
| N1761Q | GLF4 | 1083 |
| N1761S | GLF3 | 396 |
| N1761S | GLF4 | 1084 |
| N1761W | GLF3 | 303 |
| (N1772E) | C500 | 543 |
| N1772E | C500 | 625 |
| N1772E | C525 | 0034 |
| (N1772E) | C650 | 0172 |
| **N1776A** | **HS25** | **258750** |
| **N1776C** | **HS25** | **HA-0002** |
| N1776E | HS25 | 257036 |
| N1776F | WW24 | 38 |
| **N1776H** | **HS25** | **258091** |
| N1776N | HS25 | 258670 |
| (N1777R) | FA20 | 35 |
| N1777T | WW24 | 62 |
| (N1779E) | C500 | 544 |
| N1779E | C525 | 0035 |
| (N1779E) | C650 | 0173 |
| (N1782E) | C500 | 545 |
| N1782E | C525 | 0036 |
| (N1782E) | C650 | 0174 |
| N1806P | GLF2 | 200 |
| N1807Z | GLF2 | 27 |
| N1812C | CL60 | 1018 |
| N1812C | CL61 | 5010 |
| N1818C | GLF4 | 1385 |
| N1818S | F900 | 136 |
| N1818S | F900 | 39 |
| **N1818S** | **F9EX** | **153** |
| N1818S | FA20 | 149 |
| (N1820E) | C500 | 546 |
| N1820E | C525 | 0037 |
| N1820E | C650 | 0175 |
| N1823A | FA20 | 129 |
| N1823B | C500 | 373 |
| N1823B | C550 | 196 |
| N1823B | C550 | 498 |
| N1823C | C550 | 234 |
| N1823D | GLF2 | 59 |
| N1823F | FA20 | 129 |
| N1823S | C560 | 0094 |
| N1823S | C560 | 0225 |
| N1823S | C650 | 0090 |
| N1824S | C560 | 0120 |
| N1824T | CL61 | 3029 |
| N1824T | HS25 | 257182 |
| N1827S | C560 | 0094 |
| N1828S | C650 | 7047 |
| **N1829S** | **FA50** | **280** |
| N1836S | C56X | 5143 |
| (N1836S) | F900 | 136 |
| **N1836S** | **FA50** | **352** |
| **N1837S** | **C56X** | **5155** |
| N1838S | C56X | 5322 |
| **N1838S** | **FA50** | **316** |
| N1839S | FA50 | 317 |
| N1841D | GLF2 | 227 |
| N1841D | GLF3 | 438 |
| N1841D | SBRL | 380-15 |
| N1841F | FA50 | 152 |
| N1841F | SBRL | 380-15 |
| N1841L | GLF2 | 227 |
| N1843A | MU30 | A025SA |
| N1843S | HS25 | 257155 |
| N1843S | MU30 | A025SA |
| N1844S | JSTR | 5123/14 |
| N1846 | FA20 | 47 |
| N1847B | C550 | 365 |
| N1847B | FA20 | 493 |
| N1847P | C550 | 365 |
| N1848T | C525 | 0350 |
| **N1848T** | **LJ40** | **45-2035** |
| N1848U | CL64 | 5316 |
| N1848U | FA50 | 227 |
| N1851D | C550 | 022 |
| N1851N | C500 | 310 |
| N1851T | C500 | 310 |
| N1851T | C550 | 022 |
| N1851T | FA20 | 508 |
| N1851T | FA20 | 74 |
| **N1852** | **LJ55** | **087** |
| N1857B | FA20 | 203 |
| N1857W | WW24 | 258 |
| N1863T | SBRL | 282-62 |
| **N1865M** | **CS55** | **0071** |
| (N1865S) | C560 | 0225 |
| **N1867M** | **C56X** | **5303** |
| N1867M | C650 | 7073 |
| N1867W | CS55 | 0124 |
| N1868M | CL60 | 1039 |
| N1868M | CL61 | 5012 |
| N1868M | F900 | 157 |
| N1868M | FA20 | 139 |
| **N1868M** | **GLEX** | **9069** |
| N1868M | HS25 | 257021 |
| N1868N | FA20 | 139 |
| N1868S | CL60 | 1039 |
| N1868S | F900 | 157 |
| N1868S | HS25 | 257021 |
| N1871P | LJ24 | 130 |
| N1871P | LJ36 | 023 |
| N1871R | C560 | 0580 |
| **N1871R** | **C56X** | **5297** |
| N1871R | FA10 | 128 |
| N1871R | FA50 | 6 |
| N1871R | GLF3 | 381 |
| N1871R | LJ24 | 130 |
| N1871R | LJ36 | 023 |
| N1873 | C560 | 0353 |
| **N1873** | **C750** | **0128** |
| (N1874E) | C500 | 547 |
| N1874E | C525 | 0038 |
| N1874E | C650 | 0176 |
| N1874M | GLF4 | 1390 |
| N1875P | GLF2 | 137 |
| N1878C | BE40 | RK-33 |
| N1879W | C550 | 668 |
| N1880F | C550 | 372 |
| N1880S | C500 | 183 |
| **N1881Q** | **FA20** | **414** |
| N1881W | BE40 | RK-21 |
| N1883 | C550 | 467 |
| N1883M | C550 | 674 |
| N1884 | CL60 | 1032 |
| N1884 | HS25 | 256067 |
| N1884Z | WW24 | 150 |
| N1886G | C550 | 722 |
| N1887M | C650 | 7073 |
| N1887S | FA10 | 190 |
| N1888M | C550 | 674 |
| **N1892** | **GLF5** | **524** |
| N1892S | FA20 | 376 |
| **N1895C** | **C525** | **0647** |
| N1896F | FA50 | 127 |
| N1896F | HS25 | 257162 |
| N1896T | FA50 | 127 |
| N1896T | FA50 | 262 |
| N1896T | HS25 | 257162 |
| **N1897A** | **C56X** | **5629** |
| N1897A | HS25 | 258326 |
| **N1897S** | **FA20** | **376** |
| (N1899) | C500 | 091 |
| **N1899** | **PRM1** | **RB-248** |
| N1899K | HS25 | 258424 |
| **N1900W** | **GLF4** | **1124** |
| **N1901** | **C680** | **0022** |
| N1901M | GLF4 | 1039 |
| N1901W | BE40 | RK-19 |
| (N1902) | C650 | 7010 |
| N1902J | CL61 | 5135 |
| N1902L | GLF2 | 226 |
| N1902P | CL61 | 5135 |
| N1902P | GLF2 | 226 |
| N1902W | BE40 | RK-2 |
| N1902W | FA20 | 269 |
| N1902W | FA50 | 209 |
| N1903G | CL61 | 5051 |
| **N1903G** | **CL64** | **5326** |
| N1903P | HS25 | 258142 |
| **N1903W** | **F2EX** | **208** |
| N1903W | FA50 | 129 |
| N1903W | SBRL | 282-36 |
| N1904G | WW24 | 436 |
| **N1904P** | **CL61** | **5116** |
| N1904S | LJ31 | 149 |
| **N1904S** | **LJ45** | **053** |
| N1904W | BE40 | RK-21 |
| N1904W | FA50 | 149 |
| **N1904W** | **GLF4** | **1237** |
| N1905H | LJ31 | 051 |
| N1908W | SBRL | 282-36 |
| N1909D | SBRL | 282-57 |
| N1909R | SBRL | 282-57 |
| N1909R | SBRL | 306-41 |
| N1909R | SBRL | 465-54 |
| N1910A | HS25 | 258188 |
| **N1910A** | **HS25** | **258711** |
| N1910H | HS25 | 258023 |
| **N1910H** | **HS25** | **258318** |
| N1910J | HS25 | 258023 |
| N1918W | LJ36 | 004 |
| N1919G | LJ24 | 157 |
| N1919W | LJ24 | 118 |
| N1919W | LJ24 | 157 |
| N1919W | LJ24 | 192 |
| **N1920** | **BE40** | **RK-21** |
| N1923G | HS25 | 25095 |
| N1923M | HS25 | 25031 |
| N1924G | JSTR | 5224 |
| N1924L | HS25 | 25237 |
| N1924V | FA10 | 24 |
| N1924V | JSTR | 5077 |
| **N1925M** | **GLF4** | **1282** |
| **N1925P** | **LJ45** | **199** |
| **N1926S** | **LJ31** | **180** |
| **N1927G** | **F2TH** | **35** |
| N1929P | SBRL | 276-48 |
| N1929S | LJ35 | 388 |
| **N1929Y** | **F2TH** | **84** |
| N1929Y | GLF2 | 19 |
| (N1930E) | C500 | 548 |
| N1930E | C650 | 0177 |
| (N1931P) | GLF4 | 1514 |
| **N1932K** | **LJ31** | **099** |
| N1932P | C750 | 0090 |
| N1932P | GLF4 | 1514 |
| **N1932P** | **GLF5** | **5256** |
| N1932P | LJ31 | 099 |
| N1940 | LJ60 | 002 |
| N1944P | WW24 | 142 |
| N1949B | C550 | 414 |
| N1949M | C550 | 414 |
| N1951E | C500 | 160 |
| N1951E | C500 | 549 |
| N1955E | C500 | 550 |
| N1955E | C550 | 059 |
| **N1955M** | **GLEX** | **9185** |
| N1955M | GLF4 | 1276 |
| N1956A | C510 | 0305 |
| N1956M | GLF3 | 469 |
| **N1956M** | **GLF5** | **675** |
| (N1958E) | C500 | 551 |
| N1958E | C500 | 626 |
| N1958E | C500 | 676 |
| (N1958E) | C500 | 677 |
| N1958E | C525 | 0039 |
| N1958E | C550 | 060 |
| N1958E | C650 | 0178 |
| **N1958N** | **CS55** | **0073** |
| N1959E | C500 | 552 |
| N1959E | C500 | 627 |
| N1959E | C525 | 0040 |
| N1959E | C550 | 061 |
| N1959E | C650 | 0179 |
| **N1961S** | **C550** | **550-0890** |
| N1962J | C550 | 550-0862 |
| **N1962J** | **C750** | **0240** |
| N1962J | JSTR | 5113/25 |
| N1963A | LJ24 | 097 |
| **N1965L** | **LJ24** | **012** |
| N1966G | JSTR | 5065 |
| N1966J | WW24 | 66 |
| N1966K | LJ24 | 011 |
| N1966L | LJ24 | 108 |
| N1966W | LJ24 | 076 |
| N1967G | JSTR | 5098/28 |
| (N1967J) | JSTR | 5113/25 |
| N1967L | LJ24 | 012 |
| N1967M | CL30 | 20040 |
| **N1967M** | **CL30** | **20268** |
| N1967M | GLF4 | 1368 |
| N1967W | LJ24 | 096 |
| N1968A | LJ24 | 097 |
| N1968A | LJ35 | 171 |
| N1968A | LJ55 | 035 |
| N1968T | LJ35 | 171 |
| N1968W | LJ24 | 089 |
| N1969H | LJ24 | 110 |
| N1969L | LJ24 | 012 |
| N1969W | LJ25 | 005 |
| N1971R | FA20 | 312 |
| N1971R | FA20 | 322 |
| N1971R | FA50 | 149 |
| N1972G | LJ24 | 242 |
| N1972L | LJ24 | 096 |
| N1972W | WW24 | 91 |
| N1973L | LJ24 | 096 |
| **N1976J** | **C550** | **550-0862** |
| N1976L | LJ24 | 070 |
| N1976L | LJ25 | 080 |
| N1976L | LJ35 | 053 |
| N1976S | LJ25 | 008 |
| N1978L | LJ25 | 080 |
| N1978L | LJ35 | 162 |
| **N1980Z** | **CL30** | **20049** |
| N1982C | GLF3 | 384 |
| N1982G | HS25 | 257116 |
| N1982U | CS55 | 0038 |
| N1983Y | LJ55 | 079 |
| **N1987** | **CL64** | **5550** |
| **N1989D** | **HS25** | **258580** |
| **N1990C** | **GLEX** | **9166** |
| N1990C | GLF4 | 1276 |
| **N1993** | **FA10** | **195** |
| (N1996E) | HS25 | 257177 |
| N1996F | HS25 | 257177 |
| **N1999** | **F2TH** | **219** |
| **N2000** | **GLF2** | **56** |
| N2000 | SBRL | 282-52 |
| N2000 | SBRL | 465-7 |
| N2000A | F2EX | 119 |
| N2000A | F2EX | 151 |
| **N2000A** | **F2EX** | **170** |
| N2000A | F2TH | 112 |
| N2000A | F2TH | 141 |
| N2000A | F2TH | 182 |
| N2000A | F2TH | 189 |
| N2000A | F2TH | 192 |
| N2000A | F2TH | 26 |
| N2000A | F2TH | 3 |
| N2000A | F2TH | 44 |
| N2000A | F2TH | 63 |
| N2000A | F2TH | 89 |
| **N2000L** | **F2TH** | **92** |
| N2000M | C560 | 0146 |
| N2000M | LJ24 | 065 |
| N2000M | LJ25 | 084 |
| N2000M | LJ35 | 396 |
| N2000M | LJ36 | 009 |
| N2000T | HS25 | 257177 |
| N2000X | C560 | 0144 |
| **N2000X** | **C560** | **0249** |
| N2000X | CS55 | 0064 |
| N2002P | GLF4 | 1279 |
| N2003J | C56X | 5744 |
| N2004 | F2TH | 13 |
| N2004 | SBRL | 282-52 |
| N2004G | CL61 | 5048 |
| N2005 | FA20 | 54 |
| N2006 | SBRL | 282-124 |
| **N2006** | **SBRL** | **282-135** |
| N2007 | SBRL | 282-55 |
| N2008 | C550 | 399 |
| N2008 | LJ24 | 003 |
| N2009 | SBRL | 282-14 |
| N2011Z | C56X | 6013 |
| N2013M | GLF2 | 51 |
| N2015M | HS25 | 257192 |
| N2015M | HS25 | 258254 |
| N2015M | LJ35 | 072 |
| N2019V | C500 | 245 |
| N2020 | HS25 | 25203 |
| N2022L | LJ35 | 290 |
| N2022R | LJ25 | 200 |
| N2028 | F2TH | 29 |
| N2029E | C550 | 550-0822 |
| N2032 | F2TH | 31 |
| **N2032** | **HS25** | **258175** |
| **N2033** | **HS25** | **258093** |
| N2034 | F2TH | 14 |
| N2035 | F2TH | 17 |
| N2036 | F2TH | 23 |

| | | |
|---|---|---|
| N2039 | F2TH | 24 |
| N2040E | C52A | 0386 |
| N2042 | F2TH | 25 |
| N2044S | C52A | 0425 |
| N2046 | F2TH | 26 |
| N2046D | C52A | 0430 |
| N2051A | C52A | 0436 |
| N2052A | C500 | 553 |
| N2052A | C500 | 628 |
| N2052A | C500 | 678 |
| N2052A | C550 | 062 |
| N2056 | F900 | 155 |
| N2056E | BE40 | RK-156 |
| **N2057H** | **C550** | **310** |
| N2060V | C56X | 5761 |
| N2061 | F2TH | 39 |
| N2064M | C52A | 0442 |
| N2065X | C56X | 5766 |
| N2067E | C52A | 0446 |
| N2067V | C56X | 5808 |
| N2068G | C750 | 0291 |
| N2069A | C500 | 554 |
| N2069A | C550 | 063 |
| N2070K | C500 | 133 |
| N2072A | C500 | 555 |
| N2072A | C500 | 629 |
| N2072A | C550 | 064 |
| N2073 | F2TH | 41 |
| N2074 | F2TH | 44 |
| N2074H | C52B | 0277 |
| (N2077) | F2TH | 43 |
| N2079A | C500 | 431 |
| N2080 | F2TH | 46 |
| N2087K | C56X | 5824 |
| N2089 | F2TH | 48 |
| N2093 | F2TH | 101 |
| **N2093A** | **LJ24** | **194** |
| N2093P | SBRL | 380-39 |
| **N2094L** | **LJ25** | **095** |
| N2098A | C500 | 432 |
| N2098A | C525 | 0041 |
| N2098A | C650 | 0180 |
| (N2099) | F2TH | 99 |
| N2100J | SBRL | 380-32 |
| N2100X | WW24 | 23 |
| N2101J | SBRL | 306-109 |
| N2102J | SBRL | 380-38 |
| N2103J | SBRL | 306-110 |
| N2104J | SBRL | 380-34 |
| **N2105** | **CL60** | **1010** |
| N2105J | SBRL | 380-36 |
| N2106J | SBRL | 306-111 |
| N2107J | SBRL | 306-112 |
| **N2107Z** | **GLF4** | **1211** |
| N2108J | SBRL | 306-113 |
| N2109J | SBRL | 306-114 |
| N2110J | SBRL | 380-39 |
| N2111W | C52B | 0278 |
| N2112J | SBRL | 380-40 |
| N2112L | F2TH | 112 |
| N2112X | C56X | 5830 |
| N2113J | SBRL | 380-41 |
| N2114E | HS25 | 256022 |
| N2114J | SBRL | 380-42 |
| N2115J | SBRL | 380-43 |
| N2116J | SBRL | 380-44 |
| N2116N | C56X | 5821 |
| N2117J | SBRL | 380-45 |
| N2118J | SBRL | 306-115 |
| N2119J | SBRL | 306-116 |
| N2120J | SBRL | 306-117 |
| N2120Q | WW24 | 107 |
| N2122J | SBRL | 306-118 |
| N2123J | SBRL | 306-119 |
| N2124J | SBRL | 306-120 |
| N2125 | HS25 | 25082 |
| N2125J | SBRL | 380-46 |
| N2126J | SBRL | 380-47 |
| N2127E | LJ25 | 145 |
| N2127J | SBRL | 380-48 |
| N2128J | SBRL | 380-49 |
| N2129J | SBRL | 380-50 |
| N2130J | SBRL | 306-121 |
| N2131A | C500 | 433 |
| N2131A | C650 | 0181 |
| N2131J | SBRL | 306-122 |
| N2132 | F2TH | 57 |
| N2132J | SBRL | 306-123 |
| N2133 | F2TH | 58 |
| N2133J | SBRL | 306-124 |
| N2134J | SBRL | 306-125 |
| N2135J | SBRL | 380-51 |
| N2136J | SBRL | 380-52 |
| N2137J | SBRL | 380-53 |
| N2138J | SBRL | 380-54 |
| N2138T | LJ25 | 091 |
| N2139J | SBRL | 380-55 |
| N2140L | C550 | 554 |
| N2141J | SBRL | 306-126 |
| N2142J | SBRL | 306-127 |
| N2143J | SBRL | 306-128 |
| N2144J | SBRL | 306-129 |
| N2145J | SBRL | 306-130 |
| N2146 | F2TH | 59 |
| N2146J | SBRL | 380-56 |
| N2147 | F2TH | 60 |
| N2147J | SBRL | 380-57 |
| N2148J | SBRL | 380-58 |
| N2148R | HS25 | 25070 |
| N2149J | SBRL | 306-131 |
| **N2150H** | **WW24** | **210** |
| N2150J | SBRL | 306-132 |
| N2151J | SBRL | 306-133 |
| N2151Q | C52A | 0391 |
| N2152J | SBRL | 306-134 |
| N2155 | F2TH | 63 |
| N2155P | HS25 | 25273 |
| N2157D | C680 | 0241 |
| **N2158U** | **C500** | **476** |
| N2159P | BE40 | RK-159 |
| N2159X | HS25 | 258313 |
| N2160N | C550 | 249 |
| N2164Z | BE40 | RK-164 |
| N2168 | F2TH | 70 |
| N2168G | BE40 | RK-168 |
| N2169 | F2TH | 72 |
| N2169X | HS25 | 258315 |
| N2170J | C500 | 040 |
| N2173X | HS25 | 258317 |
| N2175W | HS25 | 258348 |
| N2176 | F2TH | 73 |
| N2183N | CL61 | 3062 |
| N2189 | F2TH | 89 |
| N2191 | F2TH | 92 |
| N2194 | F2TH | 110 |
| N2197 | F2TH | 112 |
| N2200A | SBRL | 380-26 |
| N2200M | FA20 | 11 |
| N2200M | JSTR | 5062/12 |
| N2200R | C500 | 095 |
| N2200T | LJ24 | 112 |
| N2201J | BE40 | RK-171 |
| N2201U | C500 | 217 |
| N2204J | BE40 | RK-174 |
| **N2208L** | **C680** | **0211** |
| N2213T | LJ25 | 369 |
| N2216 | F2TH | 116 |
| N2217 | F2TH | 117 |
| N2217Q | LJ35 | 243 |
| N2218 | F2TH | 109 |
| N2220G | MU30 | A031SA |
| N2222R | JSTR | 5016 |
| N2224G | C52A | 0402 |
| N2225J | MU30 | A064SA |
| N2225Y | BE40 | RK-165 |
| N2227 | F2TH | 141 |
| N2230 | F2TH | 143 |
| (N2231B) | C550 | 026 |
| N2232B | SBRL | 282-65 |
| N2233B | SBRL | 282-66 |
| N2234B | SBRL | 282-67 |
| N2235 | CS55 | 0135 |
| N2235 | F2TH | 149 |
| N2235B | SBRL | 282-68 |
| N2235V | BE40 | RK-181 |
| N2236 | HS25 | 258073 |
| N2236B | SBRL | 282-69 |
| N2236C | SBRL | 282-70 |
| N2239B | SBRL | 282-71 |
| N2241B | SBRL | 282-74 |
| N2241C | SBRL | 282-75 |
| N2242B | SBRL | 282-76 |
| N2242P | LJ35 | 012 |
| **N2243** | **C500** | **619** |
| N2243W | C510 | 0011 |
| N2244B | SBRL | 282-77 |
| (N2246) | HS25 | 25099 |
| N2248C | SBRL | 282-79 |
| N2249B | SBRL | 282-80 |
| N2250B | SBRL | 282-81 |
| **N2250G** | **C52A** | **0047** |
| N2252Q | BE40 | RK-152 |
| N2254B | SBRL | 282-84 |
| N2254S | FA50 | 180 |
| N2255B | SBRL | 282-85 |
| N2255Q | FA20 | 24 |
| N2258 | F2TH | 175 |
| (N2259) | F2TH | 166 |
| N2259D | C525 | 0688 |
| N2259V | SBRL | 265-1 |
| N2260 | F2TH | 180 |
| N2261 | F2TH | 184 |
| N2264 | F2TH | 182 |
| N2265 | F2TH | 183 |
| N2265Z | SBRL | 380-43 |
| N2267 | F2TH | 189 |
| N2267B | BE40 | RK-167 |
| N2267Z | LJ36 | 012 |
| N2270 | F2TH | 186 |
| N2272K | BE40 | RK-172 |
| (N2273G) | LJ25 | 040 |
| **N2273Z** | **BE40** | **RK-173** |
| N2274B | C500 | 295 |
| N2277G | BE40 | RK-177 |
| N2277T | JSTR | 5105 |
| N2279K | BE40 | RK-179 |
| N2283T | BE40 | RK-196 |
| N2286U | HS25 | 258336 |
| N2288 | F2TH | 188 |
| N2289 | F2TH | 192 |
| N2289B | BE40 | RK-170 |
| N2290 | F2TH | 197 |
| N2290F | BE40 | RK-190 |
| N2291T | BE40 | RK-191 |
| N2291X | HS25 | 258319 |
| N2293V | BE40 | RK-233 |
| N2293V | BE40 | RK-250 |
| N2295 | F2TH | 199 |
| N2296C | SBRL | 265-5 |
| N2296S | C500 | 621 |
| N2296S | C560 | 0038 |
| N2297B | LJ35 | 033 |
| N2297X | C52A | 0410 |
| N2298L | BE40 | RK-185 |
| N2298S | BE40 | RK-187 |
| N2298S | C500 | 621 |
| N2298W | BE40 | RK-188 |
| N2299T | BE40 | RK-166 |
| N2314F | BE40 | RK-184 |
| N2317 | F2TH | 204 |
| N2319 | F2TH | 206 |
| N2320J | HS25 | 258342 |
| N2321S | HS25 | 258352 |
| N2321V | HS25 | 258353 |
| N2321Z | HS25 | 258357 |
| N2322 | F2TH | 212 |
| N2322B | BE40 | RK-182 |
| N2322B | BE40 | RK-242 |
| N2322X | HS25 | 258320 |
| N2325 | F2TH | 210 |
| N2329N | BE40 | RK-169 |
| N2345M | JSTR | 5075/19 |
| N2349V | BE40 | RK-236 |
| "N2351M" | HS25 | 258341 |
| N2354B | BE40 | RK-154 |
| N2355N | BE40 | RK-232 |
| N2355T | BE40 | RK-155 |
| N2357K | BE40 | RK-204 |
| N2358X | BE40 | RK-158 |
| N2359W | BE40 | RK-203 |
| N2360F | BE40 | RK-160 |
| N2362G | BE40 | RK-162 |
| N2363A | BE40 | RK-163 |
| N2366Y | LJ24 | 055 |
| N2366Y | LJ25 | 058 |
| N2370S | C56X | 6042 |
| N2384K | C56X | 6047 |
| N2401X | C56X | 6053 |
| N2408 | LJ40 | 45-2008 |
| N2409W | CL64 | 5391 |
| **N2411A** | **C650** | **0103** |
| N2418F | C750 | 0074 |
| N2418N | C750 | 0074 |
| N2418Y | C750 | 0074 |
| (N2422J) | LJ35 | 263 |
| **N2425** | **C680** | **0054** |
| N2425 | F9EX | 32 |
| N2425 | FA50 | 237 |
| (N2425) | GLF4 | 1310 |
| **N2426** | **C560** | **0815** |
| N2426 | C680 | 0034 |
| N2426 | FA10 | 186 |
| N2426 | HS25 | 25013 |
| N2426 | HS25 | 25107 |
| N2426 | HS25 | 258272 |
| N2426 | LJ25 | 216 |
| N2426G | FA10 | 186 |
| N2427F | FA10 | 187 |
| N2427F | LJ25 | 157 |
| N2427N | C510 | 0019 |
| "N2427N" | FA10 | 187 |
| **N2428** | **C680** | **0046** |
| N2428 | CL60 | 1013 |
| N2428 | HS25 | 258274 |
| N2440C | SBRL | 306-30 |
| N2440C | SBRL | 380-2 |
| N2440G | SBRL | 306-30 |
| N2440G | SBRL | 380-2 |
| N2440G | SBRL | 380-44 |
| N2451Y | LJ45 | 076 |
| N2454M | WW24 | 314 |
| N2465N | C680 | 0272 |
| (N2478) | FA50 | 48 |
| **N2486B** | **EA50** | **000090** |
| N2488L | ASTR | 125 |
| N2500B | C560 | 0386 |
| N2500D | C560 | 0365 |
| N2500N | C560 | 0350 |
| N2500W | HS25 | 25208 |
| N2501E | SBRL | 306-136 |
| N2501E | SBRL | 465-1 |
| N2503L | LJ24 | 047 |
| N2504 | HS25 | 25021 |
| N2506E | SBRL | 306-137 |
| N2508E | SBRL | 306-138 |
| N2513E | SBRL | 465-15 |
| N2518M | WW24 | 337 |
| N2519E | SBRL | 306-144 |
| N2521E | SBRL | 380-60 |
| N2522E | SBRL | 380-61 |
| N2525 | FA20 | 321 |
| N2525 | HS25 | 25112 |
| N2528E | SBRL | 380-67 |
| **N2531K** | **C550** | **594** |
| N2535E | SBRL | 306-135 |
| N2536E | SBRL | 380-66 |
| N2537E | SBRL | 465-17 |
| N2538E | SBRL | 380-68 |
| N2539E | SBRL | 465-48 |
| N2542E | SBRL | 380-69 |
| N2544E | SBRL | 465-20 |
| N2545E | SBRL | 465-24 |
| N2548E | SBRL | 465-26 |
| N2549E | SBRL | 465-28 |
| N2550E | SBRL | 465-31 |
| N2551E | SBRL | 465-39 |
| N2556E | SBRL | 465-41 |
| N2561E | SBRL | 465-42 |
| N2568 | FA20 | 75 |
| N2568S | SBRL | 282-61 |
| N2569B | SBRL | 282-90 |
| N2570E | SBRL | 465-50 |
| N2574E | SBRL | 465-55 |
| N2579E | SBRL | 465-54 |
| N2579E | WW24 | 21 |
| N2580E | SBRL | 465-60 |
| N2581E | SBRL | 465-75 |
| N2586E | SBRL | 465-21 |
| N2590E | SBRL | 465-35 |
| N2600 | GLF2 | 88/21 |
| N2600 | GLF3 | 315 |
| N2600 | GLF4 | 1088 |
| N2600 | JSTR | 5037/24 |
| N2600 | JSTR | 5110/47 |
| N2600J | GLF4 | 1088 |
| N2600S | LJ31 | 033B |
| N2600Z | GLF3 | 315 |
| N2600Z | LJ31 | 060 |
| N2601 | GLF2 | 30/4 |
| N2601 | GLF3 | 316 |
| N2601 | HS25 | 25060 |
| N2601 | JSTR | 5110/47 |

| | | |
|---|---|---|
| N2601B | LJ36 | 061 |
| N2601G | LJ35 | 674 |
| N2601K | LJ31 | 080 |
| N2601V | LJ60 | 024 |
| N2602M | LJ35 | 675 |
| N2602Y | LJ31 | 070 |
| N2602Z | LJ60 | 022 |
| N2603G | LJ31 | 054 |
| N2603Q | LJ31 | 086 |
| N2603S | LJ31 | 033A |
| N2603X | LJ31 | 068 |
| N2604 | C650 | 0021 |
| N2605 | C650 | 0144 |
| N2605 | FA20 | 312 |
| N2606 | C650 | 0194 |
| N2607 | C500 | 307 |
| N2607 | GLF2 | 30/4 |
| (N2610) | C500 | 340 |
| N2610 | GLF3 | 302 |
| N2610 | GLF4 | 1094 |
| N2611Y | C500 | 556 |
| N2611Y | C500 | 630 |
| N2611Y | C500 | 679 |
| N2612N | C500 | 557 |
| N2612N | C500 | 631 |
| N2613 | C500 | 307 |
| N2613 | FA20 | 293 |
| N2613C | C500 | 558 |
| N2613C | C500 | 632 |
| N2614 | FA20 | 376 |
| N2614C | C500 | 559 |
| N2614C | C500 | 633 |
| N2614C | C500 | 680 |
| N2614H | C500 | 560 |
| N2614H | C500 | 634 |
| N2614K | C500 | 561 |
| (N2614Y) | C500 | 634 |
| N2614Y | C650 | 0183 |
| N2615 | FA20 | 293 |
| N2615 | GLF2 | 148/5 |
| N2615 | GLF4 | 1214 |
| N2615B | GLF4 | 1214 |
| (N2615D) | C500 | 635 |
| N2615D | C650 | 0184 |
| (N2615L) | C500 | 636 |
| N2615L | C650 | 0185 |
| N2616C | C500 | 637 |
| N2616G | C500 | 562 |
| (N2616G) | C500 | 637 |
| N2616G | C500 | 638 |
| N2616G | C500 | 681 |
| N2616H | FA20 | 376 |
| (N2616L) | C500 | 563 |
| N2616L | C525 | 0043 |
| N2616L | C650 | 0186 |
| N2617B | C500 | 564 |
| (N2617B) | C500 | 638 |
| N2617B | C500 | 639 |
| N2617B | C500 | 682 |
| N2617K | C500 | 565 |
| (N2617K) | C500 | 640 |
| N2617K | C525 | 0044 |
| N2617K | C650 | 0187 |
| N2617P | C525 | 0045 |
| N2617P | C650 | 0188 |
| N2617U | C500 | 566 |
| **N2617U** | **C500** | **641** |
| N2619M | C550 | 142 |
| N2621U | C525 | 0047 |
| (N2621U) | C650 | 0190 |
| N2621Z | C525 | 0048 |
| (N2621Z) | C650 | 0191 |
| N2622C | C650 | 0192 |
| N2622M | FA20 | 242 |
| N2622Z | C650 | 0193 |
| N2623B | C500 | 646 |
| (N2624L) | C500 | 647 |
| N2624L | C650 | 0198 |
| N2624M | C650 | 0021 |
| N2624M | FA20 | 376 |
| N2624Z | C500 | 648 |
| (N2625C) | C650 | 0196 |
| N2625Y | C650 | 0197 |
| N2626A | C500 | 649 |
| N2626J | C500 | 650 |
| N2626M | SBRL | 306-113 |
| (N2626X) | C650 | 0199 |
| N2626Z | C500 | 651 |
| (N2626Z) | C650 | 0200 |
| N2627A | C500 | 434 |
| N2627A | C650 | 0202 |
| N2627M | SBRL | 306-123 |
| N2627N | C500 | 654 |
| N2627U | C500 | 655 |
| N2628B | C500 | 656 |
| N2628Z | C500 | 657 |
| N2629Z | C500 | 658 |
| N2630 | C500 | 340 |
| N2630 | HS25 | 257161 |
| N2630B | C650 | 0204 |
| N2630N | C650 | 0205 |
| N2630U | C650 | 0206 |
| N2631N | C500 | 659 |
| N2631N | C550 | 143 |
| N2631V | C500 | 660 |
| N2631V | C550 | 144 |
| N2632Y | C550 | 145 |
| (N2632Y) | C650 | 0207 |
| N2633N | C500 | 662 |
| N2633N | C550 | 146 |
| N2633Y | C525 | 0049 |
| N2633Y | C550 | 147 |
| (N2634B) | HS25 | 257020 |
| N2634E | C525 | 0050 |
| (N2634E) | CS55 | 0151 |
| N2634Y | C550 | 148 |
| N2634Y | CL60 | 1034 |
| N2635D | C550 | 149 |
| N2635M | SBRL | 306-118 |
| N2636N | CL60 | 1025 |
| N2637M | GLF2 | 88/21 |
| N2637R | C525 | 0051 |
| (N2637R) | CS55 | 0153 |
| N2637Z | LJ35 | 413 |
| N2638A | C525 | 0053 |
| N2638A | C550 | 152 |
| (N2638A) | CS55 | 0155 |
| N2638U | C525 | 0054 |
| (N2638U) | CS55 | 0156 |
| N2639N | CS55 | 0157 |
| N2639Y | C525 | 0055 |
| (N2639Y) | CS55 | 0158 |
| N2640 | HS25 | 257157 |
| N2642F | CL60 | 1033 |
| N2642Z | CS55 | 0160 |
| (N2646X) | C500 | 486 |
| N2646X | C525 | 0056 |
| N2646X | C550 | 153 |
| (N2646X) | CS55 | 0159 |
| N2646Y | C500 | 487 |
| N2646Y | C550 | 154 |
| (N2646Z) | C500 | 488 |
| N2646Z | C550 | 155 |
| (N2647U) | C500 | 490 |
| (N2647Y) | C500 | 491 |
| N2647Y | C525 | 0058 |
| (N2647Z) | C500 | 492 |
| N2647Z | C525 | 0059 |
| **N2648X** | **C500** | **493** |
| (N2648Y) | C500 | 494 |
| N2648Y | C525 | 0060 |
| (N2648Z) | C500 | 495 |
| N2648Z | C550 | 157 |
| N2649 | FA10 | 219 |
| N2649D | C500 | 498 |
| N2649D | C500 | 667 |
| N2649D | C550 | 158 |
| N2649E | C500 | 499 |
| N2649E | C550 | 159 |
| N2649H | C500 | 500 |
| (N2649J) | C500 | 501 |
| N2649J | C525 | 0063 |
| (N2649S) | C500 | 502 |
| N2649S | C525 | 0064 |
| N2649Y | C500 | 503 |
| N2649Y | C525 | 0065 |
| N2649Z | C500 | 504 |
| N2650 | C500 | 341 |
| N2650C | C500 | 513 |
| N2650M | C500 | 514 |
| N2650N | C500 | 515 |
| N2650S | C500 | 516 |
| (N2650V) | C500 | 517 |
| N2650V | C525 | 0068 |
| N2650X | C500 | 518 |
| N2650Y | C500 | 519 |
| N2650Y | C500 | 670 |
| N2651 | C500 | 565 |
| N2651B | C500 | 526 |
| N2651B | C500 | 671 |
| N2651G | C500 | 527 |
| N2651J | C500 | 528 |
| N2651J | C500 | 672 |
| (N2651R) | C500 | 529 |
| N2651R | C525 | 0072 |
| N2651S | C500 | 530 |
| (N2651Y) | C500 | 531 |
| N2652U | C500 | 536 |
| N2652Y | C500 | 537 |
| **N2652Z** | **C500** | **538** |
| N2653R | C550 | 160 |
| N2656G | C525 | 0073 |
| (N2661H) | C550 | 072 |
| (N2661N) | C550 | 073 |
| (N2661P) | C550 | 074 |
| N2661P | C550 | 162 |
| (N2662A) | C550 | 082 |
| (N2662B) | C550 | 083 |
| (N2662F) | C550 | 084 |
| N2662Z | C550 | 085 |
| N2663B | C550 | 094 |
| (N2663B) | C560 | 0036 |
| N2663F | C550 | 095 |
| N2663G | C550 | 096 |
| N2663J | C500 | 669 |
| N2663J | C550 | 097 |
| N2663N | C550 | 098 |
| (N2663X) | C550 | 099 |
| (N2663X) | C560 | 0037 |
| (N2663Y) | C550 | 100 |
| **N2663Y** | **C550** | **602** |
| (N2663Y) | C560 | 0038 |
| N2664F | C550 | 108 |
| N2664L | C550 | 109 |
| N2664T | C550 | 110 |
| (N2664U) | C550 | 111 |
| (N2664U) | C560 | 0040 |
| N2664Y | C550 | 112 |
| N2665A | C550 | 117 |
| N2665D | C550 | 118 |
| (N2665F) | C550 | 119 |
| (N2665F) | C560 | 0043 |
| N2665N | C550 | 120 |
| (N2665S) | C550 | 121 |
| N2665S | C560 | 0044 |
| (N2665Y) | C550 | 122 |
| N2665Y | C560 | 0045 |
| N2666A | C550 | 125 |
| N2666A | C560 | 0047 |
| N2667M | GLF2 | 140/40 |
| N2667X | C560 | 0048 |
| N2668A | C550 | 165 |
| (N2672X) | C560 | 0049 |
| N2675W | HFB3 | 1050 |
| N2676B | SBRL | 282-92 |
| N2677S | CL60 | 1004 |
| N2680A | C560 | 0051 |
| N2680D | C560 | 0052 |
| (N2680X) | C560 | 0053 |
| N2681F | C560 | 0055 |
| N2682F | C560 | 0056 |
| (N2683L) | C560 | 0057 |
| (N2686Y) | C560 | 0058 |
| (N2687L) | C560 | 0059 |
| (N2689B) | C560 | 0060 |
| N2690M | C500 | 546 |
| N2694C | HS25 | 25285 |
| (N2697X) | C560 | 0061 |
| N2697Y | C560 | 0060 |
| **N2700** | **SBRL** | **465-7** |
| N2701J | C560 | 0061 |
| (N2701J) | C560 | 0063 |
| N2707T | CL60 | 1055 |
| N2710T | SBRL | 306-2 |
| N2711B | FA50 | 84 |
| **N2711H** | **EA50** | **000142** |
| N2711M | GLF2 | 137 |
| N2716G | C560 | 0062 |
| N2717X | C560 | 0064 |
| N2720B | CL60 | 1049 |
| N2721F | C560 | 0065 |
| N2721U | LJ25 | 308 |
| N2722F | C560 | 0067 |
| N2722H | C560 | 0068 |
| N2724K | FA20 | 255/487 |
| (N2724R) | C560 | 0069 |
| (N2725A) | C560 | 0070 |
| (N2725X) | C560 | 0071 |
| N2726J | C560 | 0072 |
| (N2726X) | C560 | 0073 |
| N2727F | C560 | 0074 |
| N2728 | HS25 | 25060 |
| N2728N | C560 | 0071A |
| **N2734K** | **C550** | **595** |
| N2741A | C500 | 435 |
| N2741Q | CL60 | 1047 |
| N2743T | LJ35 | 193 |
| N2745G | C550 | 126 |
| N2745L | C550 | 127 |
| (N2745L) | C560 | 0075 |
| N2745M | C550 | 128 |
| (N2745M) | C560 | 0076 |
| N2745R | C550 | 129 |
| N2745R | C560 | 0077 |
| N2745T | C550 | 130 |
| N2745X | C550 | 131 |
| N2746B | C550 | 133 |
| N2746C | C550 | 134 |
| (N2746C) | C560 | 0079 |
| N2746E | C550 | 135 |
| N2746E | C560 | 0080 |
| N2746F | C550 | 136 |
| (N2746F) | C560 | 0081 |
| N2746U | C550 | 137 |
| (N2746U) | C560 | 0082 |
| N2746Z | C550 | 138 |
| (N2747R) | C550 | 139 |
| (N2747R) | C560 | 0083 |
| N2747U | C550 | 140 |
| (N2747U) | C560 | 0084 |
| N2748B | C560 | 0078 |
| (N2748F) | C560 | 0085 |
| (N2748V) | C560 | 0086 |
| N2749B | C560 | 0087 |
| N2756T | WW24 | 224 |
| N2757A | C500 | 436 |
| **N2758W** | **LJ40** | **45-2066** |
| N2762J | C560 | 0381 |
| N2768A | C500 | 437 |
| N2782D | C500 | 152 |
| N2792B | BE40 | RK-63 |
| N28..B | BE40 | RK-14 |
| N2800 | SBRL | 465-7 |
| N2801L | C500 | 236 |
| N2815 | GLF2 | 148/5 |
| N2815 | LJ35 | 334 |
| N2830 | HS25 | 257161 |
| N2830B | BE40 | TT-82 |
| N2841A | C500 | 438 |
| N2842B | BE40 | RK-10 |
| N2843B | BE40 | RK-11 |
| N2844 | LJ35 | 424 |
| N2855 | LJ55 | 076 |
| (N2855) | LJ55 | 079 |
| N2868B | BE40 | TT-8 |
| N2872B | BE40 | TT-6 |
| N2876B | BE40 | TT-5 |
| N2886B | BE40 | TT-1 |
| N2887A | C500 | 439 |
| N2887B | BE40 | TT-2 |
| N2888A | C500 | 440 |
| N2892B | BE40 | TT-3 |
| N2896B | BE40 | TT-7 |
| **N2904** | **C500** | **406** |
| N2906A | C500 | 441 |
| N2909W | LJ24 | 243 |
| N2920C | LJ24 | 010 |
| **N2929** | **GLF5** | **5053** |
| N2932C | LJ24 | 042 |
| N2937L | C500 | 335 |
| (N2944M) | BE40 | RK-477 |
| N2945C | LJ24 | 149 |
| N2951P | LJ35 | 215 |
| N2954T | FA20 | 58 |
| N2959A | C500 | 442 |
| N2972Q | LJ36 | 047 |
| N2979 | FA20 | 183 |
| N2989 | FA20 | 112 |
| N2989 | HS25 | 257167 |
| N2991A | C500 | 443 |
| N2991Q | GLF2 | 119/22 |
| N2992 | LJ55 | 099 |

| | | | | | | | | | | | |
|---|---|---|---|---|---|---|---|---|---|---|---|
| N2997 | SBRL | 282-38 | N3118M | HS25 | 25199 | N3197M | C500 | 478 | N3238K | LJ55 | 013 |
| N2998 | GLF2 | 236 | N3119H | BE40 | RK-6 | N3197P | PRM1 | RB-257 | N3239A | BE40 | RK-309 |
| N3000 | SBRL | 306-29 | N3119W | BE40 | RJ-19 | N3197Q | BE40 | RK-97 | N3239A | LJ36 | 002 |
| N3000 | SBRL | 465-11 | N3120M | C500 | 450 | N3198C | HS25 | HA-0068 | N3239K | BE40 | RJ-39 |
| N3000S | LJ45 | 161 | N3120Y | BE40 | RJ-20 | N3198M | C500 | 479 | N3239M | C550 | 025 |
| N3000W | CS55 | 0100 | N3121B | BE40 | RJ-21 | N3198N | PRM1 | RB-238 | N3240J | BE40 | RK-240 |
| N3001H | LJ31 | 224 | N3122B | BE40 | RJ-22 | N3198V | HS25 | HA-0069 | N3240J | BE40 | RK-92 |
| N3003S | LJ31 | 225 | N3122M | C500 | 451 | N3198Z | HS25 | HB-8 | N3240M | BE40 | RJ-40 |
| N3005P | GLF2 | 96 | N3123T | BE40 | RJ-23 | N3199Q | BE40 | RK-99 | N3240M | C550 | 026 |
| N3006J | LJ60 | 223 | N3124M | BE40 | RJ-24 | N3199Z | BE40 | RK-245 | N3241G | PRM1 | RB-241 |
| N3007 | HS25 | 25043 | (N3124M) | C500 | 452 | N3200X | PRM1 | RB-250 | N3241Q | BE40 | RK-241 |
| N3007 | HS25 | 256007 | N3125B | HS25 | 25110 | N3201K | HS25 | HB-21 | N3245M | C550 | 027 |
| N3007 | HS25 | 258092 | (N3127M) | C500 | 453 | N3201P | HS25 | 258961 | N3246H | BE40 | RK-106 |
| **N3007** | **HS25** | **258487** | N3127R | BE40 | RJ-27 | N3201T | HS25 | 258901 | (N3246M) | C550 | 028 |
| **N3008** | **HS25** | **258092** | N3129E | BE40 | RJ-29 | N3202A | C500 | 480 | (N3247M) | C550 | 029 |
| N3008 | SBRL | 306-29 | N3129X | BE40 | RK-229 | N3202A | LJ35 | 469 | (N3249M) | C550 | 030 |
| N3008P | LJ45 | 154 | N3130T | BE40 | RJ-30 | N3202M | C500 | 481 | N3250 | LJ35 | 250 |
| N3011F | LJ60 | 226 | N3131G | LJ25 | 274 | N3203L | PRM1 | RB-223 | N3250M | C550 | 031 |
| N3013Q | LJ45 | 152 | N3132M | C500 | 454 | N3204M | C500 | 482 | N3251H | C550 | 397 |
| N3014R | BE40 | RK-206 | N3134N | BE40 | RJ-34 | N3204P | PRM1 | RB-224 | N3251M | C550 | 032 |
| N3014R | LJ60 | 114 | **N3137** | **LJ24** | **123** | N3204Q | BE40 | RK-584 | N3251M | HS25 | 258341 |
| N3015F | BE40 | RK-207 | N3141G | BE40 | RJ-41 | N3204T | HS25 | 258904 | N3252J | WW24 | 115 |
| N3015F | LJ60 | 115 | N3141M | C500 | 455 | N3204W | HS25 | HA-0074 | (N3252M) | C550 | 033 |
| N3015M | LJ60 | 231 | N3142E | BE40 | RJ-42 | N3205M | C500 | 483 | N3254G | C550 | 265 |
| N3016X | LJ31 | 161 | N3143T | BE40 | RJ-43 | **N3205W** | **PRM1** | **RB-225** | N3254P | BE40 | RK-254 |
| N3017F | LJ45 | 156 | N3144A | BE40 | RJ-44 | N3206K | BE40 | RK-566 | N3255B | BE40 | RK-255 |
| N3018C | LJ60 | 118 | N3144M | C500 | 456 | N3206M | C500 | 484 | N3258M | C550 | 034 |
| N3018P | LJ31 | 228 | N3145F | BE40 | RJ-45 | N3206V | HS25 | HB-6 | N3259Z | BE40 | RK-259 |
| N3019S | LJ31 | 151 | N3145M | C500 | 457 | (N3207M) | C500 | 485 | N3260J | HS25 | HA-0060 |
| N3019T | LJ45 | 158 | N3146M | C500 | 458 | N3207T | HS25 | 258907 | N3261A | BE40 | RK-261 |
| N3025T | BE40 | RJ-25 | N3147M | C500 | 459 | N3207V | HS25 | HB-7 | N3261L | LJ35 | 395 |
| N3026U | BE40 | RJ-26 | N3150M | C500 | 460 | N3207Y | HS25 | HA-0070 | (N3261M) | C550 | 035 |
| N3028U | BE40 | RK-211 | **N3151W** | **PRM1** | **RB-251** | N3208M | C550 | 013 | N3261Y | BE40 | RK-120 |
| N3029F | BE40 | RK-212 | N3155B | LJ35 | 117 | N3210M | C550 | 014 | N3261Y | HS25 | 258333 |
| N3030 | JSTR | 5094 | N3156M | C500 | 461 | **N3210N** | **HS25** | **HB-10** | (N3262M) | C550 | 036 |
| N3030 | JSTR | 5212 | N3158M | C500 | 462 | N3210X | BE40 | RK-98 | **N3262M** | **C550** | **652** |
| N3030 | SBRL | 465-11 | N3159U | SBRL | 282-117 | N3211G | HS25 | HB-11 | N3263E | HS25 | 258367 |
| N3030C | C500 | 104 | N3160M | C500 | 463 | N3211Q | LJ45 | 053 | N3263N | BE40 | RK-113 |
| N3030C | C550 | 193 | N3161M | C500 | 464 | N3212H | HS25 | HB-12 | N3265A | BE40 | RK-115 |
| N3030D | BE40 | RK-205 | N3163M | C500 | 465 | N3212M | C550 | 015 | (N3268M) | C550 | 037 |
| N3030T | C550 | 193 | N3165M | C500 | 466 | N3215J | BE40 | RK-315 | N3269A | BE40 | RK-109 |
| (N3031) | C550 | 081 | N3166Q | BE40 | RK-266 | N3215J | HS25 | HB-15 | N3270X | HS25 | 258373 |
| N3031 | JSTR | 5154 | N3170A | C500 | 467 | N3215K | LJ35 | 589 | (N3271M) | C550 | 038 |
| N3031 | WW24 | 269 | N3170B | C550 | 162 | N3215M | HS25 | 258575 | N3272L | BE40 | RK-112 |
| (N3031) | WW24 | 95 | **N3170B** | **C650** | **0136** | N3216G | PRM1 | RB-216 | N3273H | C650 | 7035 |
| N3032 | C550 | 081 | N3170M | C500 | 468 | N3216L | PRM1 | RB-246 | (N3273M) | C550 | 039 |
| N3032 | WW24 | 97 | N3172M | C500 | 469 | N3216M | C550 | 016 | (N3274M) | C550 | 040 |
| N3033A | BE40 | RK-213 | N3173M | C500 | 470 | N3216P | PRM1 | RB-27 | N3274Q | HS25 | 25102 |
| N3034B | LJ24 | 176 | (N3175M) | C500 | 471 | **N3216R** | **HS25** | **HB-16** | N3276L | HS25 | HB-26 |
| N3035T | BE40 | RJ-35 | N3175S | ASTR | 057 | N3216X | BE40 | RK-316 | N3276M | C550 | 041 |
| N3038V | BE40 | RK-93 | N3175T | ASTR | 056 | N3217D | HS25 | HB-17 | N3278 | SBRL | 306-32 |
| N3038W | BE40 | RK-215 | N3180M | C500 | 472 | **N3217G** | **HS25** | **HA-0081** | N3278M | C550 | 042 |
| N3039G | PRM1 | RB-139 | N3180T | BE40 | RJ-18 | N3217H | HS25 | HA-0067 | N3279M | C550 | 043 |
| N3045 | CL61 | 3045 | (N3181A) | C500 | 473 | N3217P | PRM1 | RB-217 | N3280E | LJ36 | 013 |
| **N3050** | **GLF5** | **5096** | (N3183M) | C500 | 474 | N3218L | BE40 | RK-108 | N3280G | SBRL | 282-70 |
| N3050P | BE40 | RK-216 | (N3184V) | C550 | 247 | N3220K | HS25 | HB-20 | N3283M | C550 | 044 |
| N3051S | BE40 | RK-94 | (N3184Z) | C550 | 123 | N3221M | C550 | 017 | N3283M | LJ24 | 356 |
| N3056R | C500 | 138 | N3184Z | C650 | 0032 | N3221T | BE40 | RK-101 | N3283V | HS25 | HA-0073 |
| N3056R | LJ35 | 264 | N3185G | BE40 | RK-285 | "N3221Z" | BE40 | TX-10 | N3284M | C550 | 045 |
| N3059H | BE40 | RK-219 | N3185G | HA4T | RC-25 | N3222S | HS25 | HB-22 | N3285M | C550 | 046 |
| N3060 | HS25 | 25017 | N3185K | BE40 | RK-318 | N3222W | HS25 | HA-0082 | N3285N | HS25 | HA-0045 |
| N3060 | JSTR | 5037/24 | N3186B | BE40 | RK-556 | **N3223G** | **PRM1** | **RB-253** | N3285Q | HS25 | HB-25 |
| N3060F | HS25 | 25017 | N3186C | PRM1 | RB-236 | N3223M | C550 | 018 | N3286M | C550 | 047 |
| N3062A | C500 | 444 | N3186N | HA4T | RC-26 | N3223R | BE40 | RK-223 | N3288M | C550 | 048 |
| N3068M | BE40 | RK-218 | N3187G | PRM1 | RB-247 | N3224N | BE40 | RK-224 | N3289H | PRM1 | RB-239 |
| N3079S | BE40 | RK-256 | N3187N | HA4T | RC-27 | N3224X | BE40 | RK-104 | N3289N | HS25 | 258909 |
| N3080 | JSTR | 5094 | N3188V | PRM1 | RB-248 | (N3225M) | C550 | 019 | N3289R | BE40 | RK-559 |
| N3082B | WW24 | 97 | **N3188X** | **HS25** | **258980** | N3226B | BE40 | RK-126 | N3291M | C550 | 049 |
| N3088A | HS25 | HA-0058 | N3189H | HS25 | 258360 | N3226Q | BE40 | RK-226 | (N3292M) | C550 | 050 |
| N3093T | HS25 | HB-13 | N3189M | C500 | 475 | N3227A | C550 | 020 | N3296M | C550 | 051 |
| N3097N | MH02 | 001 | N3190C | BE40 | RK-590 | N3227X | BE40 | RK-107 | N3298D | SBRL | 282-20 |
| N3099 | LJ60 | 375 | N3191L | BE40 | RK-291 | N3228M | BE40 | TX-7 | (N3298M) | C550 | 052 |
| N3100X | FA10 | 12 | N3193B | HS25 | 258963 | N3228M | PRM1 | RB-228 | N3298W | PRM1 | RB-258 |
| N3101B | BE40 | RK-208 | N3193L | HS25 | HA-0053 | N3228V | BE40 | RK-228 | N3300L | C550 | 286 |
| N3104M | C500 | 445 | N3194F | HA4T | RC-34 | N3228V | BE40 | TX-8 | N3300M | C500 | 338 |
| N3105M | C500 | 446 | N3194M | C500 | 476 | N3230M | C550 | 021 | (N3300M) | C550 | 053 |
| N3106Y | BE40 | RK-251 | N3194Q | HS25 | HB-14 | N3231H | BE40 | RK-270 | (N3301M) | C550 | 054 |
| N3110M | C500 | 447 | N3194R | PRM1 | RB-249 | N3231K | PRM1 | RB-31 | (N3308M) | C550 | 055 |
| N3112B | BE40 | RJ-12 | N3195F | HS25 | 258895 | N3232M | C550 | 022 | N3312T | C500 | 621 |
| N3112K | BE40 | RJ-12 | N3195K | BE40 | TX-4 | N3232U | BE40 | RK-102 | N3313M | C550 | 056 |
| N3113B | BE40 | RJ-13 | N3195M | C500 | 477 | N3234S | HS25 | 257087 | N3314M | C550 | 057 |
| N3114B | BE40 | RJ-14 | N3195Q | BE40 | TX-5 | N3235U | BE40 | RK-105 | N3319M | C550 | 058 |
| N3114X | BE40 | RK-95 | N3195X | BE40 | TX-6 | N3236M | C550 | 023 | N3320G | WW24 | 363 |
| N3115B | BE40 | RJ-15 | N3196N | BE40 | RK-96 | N3236Q | BE40 | RJ-36 | (N3330) | C500 | 104 |
| (N3115U) | FA50 | 166 | N3197A | BE40 | RK-197 | N3237H | BE40 | RK-272 | N3330L | CL60 | 1052 |
| N3115Y | HS25 | 258915 | **N3197H** | **HA4T** | **RC-37** | N3237M | C550 | 024 | N3330M | CL60 | 1052 |
| N3117M | C500 | 448 | N3197K | BE40 | RK-227 | N3237S | CL60 | 1070 | N3330S | PRM1 | RB-230 |
| N3118M | C500 | 449 | N3197K | HS25 | HB-29 | N3238K | BE40 | RJ-38 | N3332C | PRM1 | RB-132 |

| | | |
|---|---|---|
| **N3337J** | **BE40** | **RK-159** |
| N3338 | GLF3 | 402 |
| N3338 | GLF4 | 1006 |
| N3338 | HS25 | 25253 |
| N3344T | PRM1 | RB-244 |
| N3350 | LJ24 | 093 |
| N3350M | FA20 | 140 |
| N3352W | PRM1 | RB-252 |
| N3354S | PRM1 | RB-254 |
| N3355D | PRM1 | RB-255 |
| N3363U | HS25 | HA-0063 |
| N3371D | HS25 | HA-0071 |
| N3378M | HS25 | HA-0078 |
| N3378M | PRM1 | RB-178 |
| N3386A | HS25 | HA-0056 |
| N3395H | PRM1 | RB-259 |
| N3396P | PRM1 | RB-256 |
| N3399P | HS25 | 257010 |
| N3400D | HS25 | HA-0059 |
| **N3400S** | **HS25** | **258959** |
| N3400X | PRM1 | RB-260 |
| N3400Y | PRM1 | RB-240 |
| N3402 | LJ35 | 402 |
| N3415A | PRM1 | RB-245 |
| N3417F | HS25 | HB-24 |
| N3418C | HS25 | HB-18 |
| N3433D | HS25 | HB-23 |
| N3433T | HA4T | RC-33 |
| **N3441A** | **PRM1** | **RB-261** |
| N3444B | C550 | 661 |
| **N3444B** | **C560** | **0192** |
| N3444G | FA20 | 21 |
| N3444H | HS25 | 257122 |
| N3444P | C550 | 661 |
| N3456B | SBRL | 306-35 |
| N3456F | FA50 | 17 |
| N3456L | LJ36 | 050 |
| **N3468D** | **BE40** | **RK-568** |
| N3481V | PRM1 | RB-141 |
| N3482Y | HS25 | 258982 |
| N3488P | HS25 | HB-28 |
| N3490L | C500 | 128 |
| N3491F | HS25 | HB-19 |
| N3497J | HS25 | HB-27 |
| N3500R | BE40 | RK-550 |
| N3501M | BE40 | RK-561 |
| N3501Q | HS25 | HB-9 |
| N3502N | HA4T | RC-32 |
| **N3502T** | **BE40** | **RK-572** |
| N3503F | LJ35 | 075 |
| "N3507W" | SBRL | 265-35 |
| (N3513F) | LJ25 | 207 |
| N3514F | LJ25 | 211 |
| N3523F | LJ35 | 081 |
| N3524F | LJ36 | 021 |
| N3526 | C550 | 047 |
| N3533 | SBRL | 306-34 |
| N3540R | PRM1 | RB-140 |
| N3545F | LJ35 | 088 |
| **N3546** | **GLF5** | **672** |
| N3547F | LJ35 | 089 |
| N3556F | LJ25 | 216 |
| N3600X | FA10 | 88 |
| N3600X | SBRL | 306-46 |
| **N3616** | **C560** | **0571** |
| N3643 | GLF2 | 125/26 |
| N3652 | GLF2 | 198/35 |
| N3668 | FA20 | 9 |
| N3683G | C500 | 684 |
| N3690 | FA20 | 34 |
| N3699T | HS25 | 25086 |
| N3711H | WW24 | 106 |
| N3711L | HS25 | 25173 |
| N3722Z | PRM1 | RB-122 |
| N3723A | PRM1 | RB-123 |
| N3725F | PRM1 | RB-125 |
| **N3725L** | **PRM1** | **RB-155** |
| N3725Z | HS25 | 258825 |
| N3726G | PRM1 | RB-126 |
| N3726T | PRM1 | RB-156 |
| N3727H | PRM1 | RB-127 |
| (N3728) | CL61 | 3006 |
| N3732Y | PRM1 | RB-152 |
| N3733J | PRM1 | RB-133 |
| N3734C | PRM1 | RB-134 |
| N3735U | BE40 | RK-515 |
| N3735V | PRM1 | RB-135 |
| N3759C | LJ35 | 049 |
| N3771U | C500 | 139 |
| N3793D | LJ35 | 391 |
| N3793P | LJ35 | 407 |
| N3793X | LJ25 | 316 |
| N3794B | LJ55 | 021 |
| N3794C | LJ55 | 028 |
| N3794M | LJ35 | 362 |
| N3794P | LJ25 | 352 |
| N3794U | LJ35 | 455 |
| N3794W | LJ35 | 454 |
| N3794Z | LJ35 | 364 |
| N3795U | LJ25 | 354 |
| N3795Y | LJ55 | 034 |
| N3796B | LJ55 | 023 |
| N3796C | LJ55 | 049 |
| N3796P | LJ35 | 473 |
| N3796Q | LJ35 | 467 |
| N3796U | LJ55 | 042 |
| N3796X | LJ55 | 027 |
| N3796Z | LJ55 | 048 |
| N3797A | LJ35 | 398 |
| N3797B | LJ35 | 477 |
| N3797C | LJ55 | 044 |
| N3797K | LJ35 | 475 |
| N3797L | LJ25 | 343 |
| N3797N | LJ35 | 327 |
| N3797S | LJ35 | 357 |
| N3797U | LJ25 | 357 |
| N3798A | LJ25 | 315 |
| N3798B | LJ35 | 348 |
| N3798D | LJ25 | 339 |
| N3798L | LJ25 | 344 |
| N3798P | LJ35 | 408 |
| N3798V | LJ25 | 346 |
| N3799B | LJ25 | 329 |
| N3799C | LJ35 | 442 |
| N3802G | LJ24 | 320 |
| N3802G | LJ25 | 261 |
| N3802G | LJ31 | 021 |
| N3802G | LJ35 | 123 |
| N3802G | LJ35 | 183 |
| N3802G | LJ35 | 341 |
| N3802G | LJ35 | 445 |
| N3802G | LJ35 | 507 |
| N3802G | LJ36 | 056 |
| N3802G | LJ55 | 040 |
| N3802G | LJ55 | 112 |
| N3803G | LJ25 | 131 |
| N3803G | LJ25 | 135 |
| N3803G | LJ31 | 011 |
| N3803G | LJ35 | 125 |
| N3803G | LJ35 | 212 |
| N3803G | LJ35 | 346 |
| N3803G | LJ35 | 437 |
| N3803G | LJ35 | 496 |
| N3803G | LJ35 | 591 |
| N3803G | LJ35 | 606 |
| N3803G | LJ55 | 036 |
| N3807G | LJ24 | 150 |
| N3807G | LJ24 | 152 |
| N3807G | LJ25 | 202 |
| N3807G | LJ25 | 266 |
| N3807G | LJ35 | 114 |
| N3807G | LJ35 | 328 |
| N3807G | LJ35 | 616 |
| N3807G | LJ36 | 035 |
| N3807G | LJ55 | 071 |
| N3807G | LJ55 | 100 |
| N3807G | LJ55 | 117 |
| N3810G | LJ25 | 119 |
| N3810G | LJ25 | 337 |
| N3810G | LJ35 | 112 |
| N3810G | LJ35 | 191 |
| N3810G | LJ35 | 470 |
| N3810G | LJ35 | 592 |
| N3810G | LJ35 | 628 |
| N3810G | LJ35 | 656 |
| N3810G | LJ55 | 091 |
| N3811G | LJ25 | 203 |
| N3811G | LJ35 | 143 |
| N3811G | LJ35 | 189 |
| N3811G | LJ35 | 248 |
| N3811G | LJ35 | 462 |
| N3811G | LJ35 | 493 |
| N3811G | LJ55 | 121 |
| N3811G | LJ55 | 136 |
| N3812G | LJ24 | 263 |
| N3812G | LJ35 | 131 |
| N3812G | LJ35 | 243 |
| N3812G | LJ35 | 612 |
| N3812G | LJ35 | 646 |
| N3812G | LJ55 | 077 |
| N3812G | LJ55 | 106 |
| N3815G | LJ25 | 234 |
| N3815G | LJ35 | 111 |
| N3815G | LJ35 | 478 |
| N3815G | LJ35 | 498 |
| N3815G | LJ35 | 595 |
| N3815G | LJ35 | 614 |
| N3816G | LJ24 | 202 |
| N3816G | LJ35 | 011 |
| N3816G | LJ35 | 479 |
| N3816G | LJ35 | 501 |
| N3816G | LJ35 | 640 |
| N3816G | LJ55 | 119 |
| N3818G | LJ24 | 271 |
| N3818G | LJ24 | 336 |
| N3818G | LJ35 | 200 |
| N3818G | LJ35 | 345 |
| N3818G | LJ35 | 444 |
| N3818G | LJ35 | 476 |
| N3818G | LJ35 | 499 |
| N3818G | LJ35 | 601 |
| N3818G | LJ35 | 631 |
| N3819G | LJ25 | 221 |
| N3819G | LJ25 | 373 |
| N3819G | LJ31 | 007 |
| N3819G | LJ35 | 137 |
| N3819G | LJ35 | 180 |
| N3819G | LJ35 | 216 |
| N3819G | LJ35 | 353 |
| N3819G | LJ35 | 480 |
| N3819G | LJ35 | 506 |
| N3831C | SBRL | 282-90 |
| N3838J | WW24 | 350 |
| N3848U | FA20 | 380 |
| N3854B | CL60 | 1082 |
| N3857N | LJ35 | 268 |
| **N3865M** | **C560** | **0550** |
| N3871J | LJ24 | 201 |
| N3871J | LJ24 | 274 |
| N3901A | PRM1 | RB-102 |
| N3904 | LJ35 | 266 |
| N3914L | FA10 | 47 |
| N3933A | HS25 | 25226 |
| N3937E | C560 | 0396 |
| N3950N | FA50 | 95 |
| N3951 | C500 | 682 |
| N3951Z | C550 | 181 |
| N3952B | C550 | 016 |
| **N3975A** | **CL30** | **20170** |
| N3979P | LJ24 | 270 |
| N3982A | JSTR | 5141 |
| N3986G | C550 | 657 |
| N3999B | LJ36 | 048 |
| N3999H | C550 | 133 |
| **N4000K** | **C56X** | **5081** |
| **N4000R** | **HA4T** | **RC-1** |
| N4000X | CL60 | 1058 |
| N4000X | GLF2 | 100 |
| N4001G | LJ40 | 45-2011 |
| N4001G | LJ40 | 45-2043 |
| N4001G | LJ45 | 086 |
| N4001G | LJ45 | 130 |
| N4001G | LJ45 | 404 |
| N4001G | LJ60 | 331 |
| N4001M | BE40 | RK-300 |
| N4002P | LJ45 | 110 |
| N4002P | LJ45 | 267 |
| N4002P | LJ45 | 291 |
| N4002P | LJ45 | 321 |
| N4002P | LJ45 | 376 |
| N4002P | LJ60 | 273 |
| N4002P | LJ60 | 377 |
| N4002Y | C550 | 550-1115 |
| N4003K | LJ31 | 201 |
| N4003K | LJ40 | 45-2072 |
| N4003K | LJ40 | 45-2090 |
| N4003K | LJ40 | 45-2102 |
| N4003K | LJ45 | 219 |
| N4003K | LJ45 | 296 |
| N4003K | LJ60 | 274 |
| N4003K | LJ60 | 286 |
| N4003K | LJ60 | 371 |
| N4003L | LJ31 | 202 |
| N4003L | LJ45 | 375 |
| N4003L | LJ60 | 287 |
| N4003L | LJ60 | 313 |
| N4003L | LJ60 | 333 |
| **N4003L** | **LJ60** | **380** |
| N4003Q | LJ45 | 124 |
| N4003Q | LJ45 | 334 |
| N4003Q | LJ60 | 261 |
| N4003Q | LJ60 | 291 |
| N4003Q | LJ60 | 352 |
| N4003Q | LJ60 | 381 |
| N4003W | LJ40 | 45-2086 |
| **N4003W** | **LJ40** | **45-2123** |
| N4003W | LJ45 | 129 |
| N4003W | LJ45 | 242 |
| N4003W | LJ45 | 269 |
| N4003W | LJ45 | 292 |
| N4003W | LJ45 | 368 |
| N4003W | LJ60 | 262 |
| N4004Q | LJ40 | 45-2046 |
| **N4004Q** | **LJ40** | **45-2117** |
| N4004Q | LJ45 | 134 |
| N4004Q | LJ45 | 243 |
| N4004Q | LJ45 | 270 |
| N4004Q | LJ60 | 249 |
| N4004Y | LJ45 | 135 |
| N4004Y | LJ45 | 248 |
| N4004Y | LJ45 | 271 |
| N4004Y | LJ45 | 295 |
| N4004Y | LJ60 | 336 |
| N4004Y | LJ60 | 365 |
| N4005G | C56X | 5136 |
| N4005G | LJ31 | 085 |
| N4005Q | LJ40 | 45-2062 |
| N4005Q | LJ45 | 143 |
| N4005Q | LJ45 | 273 |
| N4005Q | LJ45 | 348 |
| N4005Q | LJ45 | 370 |
| **N4005Q** | **LJ45** | **408** |
| N4005S | LJ25 | 026 |
| N4005T | C750 | 0205 |
| N4006G | LJ31 | 096 |
| N4007J | C56X | 5539 |
| N4007J | LJ60 | 038 |
| N4008G | LJ40 | 45-2118 |
| N4008G | LJ45 | 230 |
| N4008G | LJ45 | 253 |
| N4008G | LJ45 | 279 |
| N4008G | LJ45 | 302 |
| N4008G | LJ45 | 355 |
| N4008G | LJ60 | 204 |
| N4008S | C56X | 5540 |
| **N4009** | **LJ45** | **304** |
| N4009F | C510 | 0040 |
| N4010K | LJ60 | 042 |
| N4010N | LJ31 | 104 |
| N4016G | LJ60 | 018 |
| N4016M | JSTR | 5224 |
| N4017L | C525 | 0608 |
| N4017R | C56X | 5594 |
| N4017X | C680 | 0059 |
| N4018S | C560 | 0694 |
| N4021E | C510 | 0041 |
| N4021E | C510 | 0259 |
| N4021M | JSTR | 5225 |
| N4021Z | HS25 | 258514 |
| N4022X | LJ31 | 082 |
| N4026M | JSTR | 5226 |
| N4026Z | LJ60 | 026 |
| N4027K | LJ31 | 094 |
| N4027S | LJ60 | 027 |
| N4029P | LJ60 | 029 |
| N4030W | C510 | 0043 |
| N4030W | C510 | 0260 |
| N4030W | LJ60 | 030 |
| N4031A | LJ60 | 033 |
| N4031K | LJ31 | 093 |
| N4031L | LJ60 | 031 |
| N4033M | JSTR | 5227 |
| N4034H | LJ31 | 084 |
| N4034M | JSTR | 5228 |
| N4037A | LJ60 | 037 |
| N4038M | JSTR | 5229 |
| N4041T | C510 | 0120 |
| N4042M | JSTR | 5230 |
| N4043M | JSTR | 5231 |
| N4046M | JSTR | 5232 |
| N4047W | C510 | 0205 |
| N4048M | JSTR | 5233 |

| | | |
|---|---|---|
| N4049 | CS55 | 0068 |
| N4049M | JSTR | 5234 |
| **N4053T** | **BE40** | **RK-253** |
| N4055M | JSTR | 5235 |
| N4056M | JSTR | 5236 |
| N4056V | BE40 | RK-306 |
| N4058A | C510 | 0264 |
| N4058M | JSTR | 5237 |
| N4059H | C510 | 0029 |
| **N4059H** | **C510** | **0286** |
| N4060K | NUTX | 246-1 |
| N4060Y | C550 | 550-1116 |
| N4062M | JSTR | 5238 |
| N4063M | JSTR | 5239 |
| N4065M | JSTR | 5240 |
| **N4074M** | **C510** | **0288** |
| N4076J | C510 | 0186 |
| N4077P | C510 | 0294 |
| **N4078L** | **C510** | **0297** |
| **N4078M** | **C510** | **0298** |
| **N4079S** | **C510** | **0302** |
| N4081L | BE40 | RK-281 |
| N4082U | C510 | 0146 |
| N4082Y | C510 | 0232 |
| N4083N | BE40 | RK-283 |
| N4084A | C510 | 0075 |
| N4085A | C510 | 0076 |
| N4085C | C510 | 0239 |
| N4085D | C510 | 0152 |
| N4085S | C510 | 0153 |
| N4085Z | C510 | 0155 |
| N4086L | C510 | 0080 |
| N4086L | C56X | 5638 |
| N4087B | C680 | 0084 |
| N4089Y | C510 | 0022 |
| (N4090P) | C500 | 267 |
| N4101Z | C750 | 0212 |
| N4107D | C510 | 0032 |
| **N4107D** | **C510** | **0192** |
| N4107V | C56X | 5256 |
| N4107W | C56X | 5530 |
| **N4108E** | **C525** | **0410** |
| N4109E | HS25 | 258509 |
| N4110C | C550 | 085 |
| N4110S | C500 | 247 |
| N4110S | C550 | 085 |
| N4110S | C560 | 0112 |
| N4110T | C510 | 0033 |
| N4115B | FA20 | 266/490 |
| N4115H | C52B | 0183 |
| N4115Q | C52A | 0013 |
| N4115W | C510 | 0038 |
| N4118K | C56X | 5515 |
| N4119S | C750 | 0275 |
| N4123S | C525 | 0674 |
| N4154G | FA50 | 80 |
| N4155B | C510 | 0034 |
| N4159Z | C510 | 0039 |
| N4165Y | C750 | 0167 |
| N4190A | C550 | 550-0991 |
| N4191G | C550 | 065 |
| N4196T | C500 | 369 |
| N4200 | F2TH | 87 |
| **N4200K** | **C560** | **0354** |
| N4202M | C510 | 0035 |
| N4202M | C510 | 0199 |
| "N4203S" | HS25 | 256047 |
| N4203Y | HS25 | 256047 |
| N4209K | C500 | 164 |
| N4224H | HS25 | 258524 |
| N4224Y | HS25 | 256040 |
| N4227N | SBRL | 306-126 |
| N4227Y | FA20 | 237/476 |
| N4228A | SBRL | 306-48 |
| N4230S | LJ60 | 027 |
| N4234K | C500 | 346 |
| N4238X | C500 | 270 |
| **N4242** | **HS25** | **258187** |
| N4246A | C500 | 580 |
| N4246N | LJ35 | 061 |
| N4246R | FA20 | 175 |
| N4246Y | C500 | 290 |
| N4247C | CL60 | 1017 |
| N4248Z | JSTR | 5155/32 |
| N4249K | BE40 | RK-249 |
| N4251D | PRM1 | RB-51 |
| N4251H | WW24 | 281 |
| N4253A | HS25 | 256005 |
| N4257R | HS25 | 258022 |
| N4258P | JSTR | 5016 |
| N4260K | SBRL | 380-60 |
| N4263X | C500 | 514 |
| N4275K | BE40 | RK-275 |
| N4286A | FA20 | 429 |
| N4289U | LJ31 | 017 |
| N4289U | LJ35 | 484 |
| N4289U | LJ35 | 523 |
| N4289U | LJ35 | 627 |
| N4289U | LJ55 | 089 |
| N4289X | LJ35 | 511 |
| N4289X | LJ35 | 526 |
| N4289X | LJ35 | 613 |
| N4289X | LJ55 | 050 |
| N4289X | LJ55 | 139A |
| N4289Y | LJ35 | 487 |
| N4289Y | LJ35 | 518 |
| N4289Y | LJ35 | 533 |
| N4289Y | LJ35 | 625 |
| N4289Z | LJ35 | 514 |
| N4289Z | LJ35 | 528 |
| N4289Z | LJ35 | 617 |
| N4289Z | LJ55 | 052 |
| N4290C | LJ35 | 485 |
| N4290C | LJ35 | 535 |
| N4290C | LJ35 | 622 |
| N4290C | LJ55 | 097 |
| N4290J | LJ35 | 512 |
| N4290J | LJ35 | 527 |
| N4290J | LJ35 | 609 |
| N4290J | LJ36 | 051 |
| N4290J | LJ36 | 058 |
| N4290K | LJ35 | 515 |
| N4290K | LJ35 | 530 |
| N4290K | LJ35 | 619 |
| N4290K | LJ35 | 654 |
| N4290X | GLF2 | 122 |
| N4290Y | LJ35 | 522 |
| N4290Y | LJ35 | 537 |
| N4290Y | LJ35 | 659 |
| N4290Y | LJ55 | 057 |
| N4290Y | LJ55 | 129 |
| N4290Z | LJ55 | 053 |
| N4291G | LJ24 | 190 |
| N4291G | LJ35 | 486 |
| N4291G | LJ35 | 513 |
| N4291G | LJ35 | 529 |
| N4291G | LJ55 | 126 |
| N4291G | LJ55 | 138 |
| N4291K | LJ25 | 361 |
| N4291K | LJ31 | 016 |
| N4291K | LJ35 | 516 |
| N4291K | LJ35 | 531 |
| N4291K | LJ55 | 132 |
| N4291N | LJ35 | 521 |
| N4291N | LJ36 | 062 |
| N4291N | LJ55 | 130 |
| N4292G | LJ24 | 228 |
| N4293K | BE40 | RK-293 |
| N4294A | C500 | 095 |
| N4300L | LJ25 | 182 |
| N4305U | LJ24 | 271 |
| N4308G | C550 | 066 |
| N4309N | BE40 | RK-339 |
| N4313V | SBRL | 265-76 |
| N4314B | SBRL | 276-8 |
| N4320P | C550 | 649 |
| N4330B | BE40 | RK-330 |
| N4333W | C560 | 0033 |
| N4340F | FA20 | 120 |
| N4341F | FA20 | 121 |
| N4341S | ASTR | 059 |
| N4342F | FA20 | 122 |
| N4343 | SBRL | 380-51 |
| N4343F | FA20 | 123 |
| N4344F | FA20 | 125 |
| N4345F | FA20 | 127 |
| N4346F | FA20 | 129 |
| N4347F | C550 | 733 |
| N4347F | FA20 | 130 |
| N4348F | FA20 | 132 |
| N4349F | FA20 | 133 |
| N4350F | FA20 | 134 |
| N4350M | FA20 | 140 |
| N4350M | FA50 | 142 |
| N4351F | FA20 | 135 |
| N4351M | FA20 | 11 |
| N4351M | FA20 | 457 |
| N4351M | FA50 | 90 |
| N4351N | FA20 | 11 |
| N4352F | FA20 | 137 |
| N4353F | FA20 | 139 |
| N4354F | FA20 | 140 |
| N4355F | FA20 | 142 |
| N4356F | FA20 | 144 |
| N4357F | FA20 | 146 |
| N4357H | BE40 | RK-343 |
| N4358F | FA20 | 148 |
| N4358N | LJ35 | 065 |
| (N4359F) | FA20 | 149 |
| N4360F | FA20 | 151 |
| N4360S | C650 | 7034 |
| N4361F | FA20 | 153 |
| N4361Q | HS25 | 258121 |
| N4362F | FA20 | 155 |
| N4362M | FA20 | 457 |
| N4363F | FA20 | 157 |
| N4364F | FA20 | 159 |
| N4365F | FA20 | 161 |
| N4366F | FA20 | 163 |
| N4367F | FA20 | 164 |
| N4368F | FA20 | 166 |
| N4368F | FA20 | 261 |
| N4369F | FA20 | 168 |
| N4370F | FA20 | 169 |
| N4371F | FA20 | 171 |
| N4372F | FA20 | 218 |
| N4373F | FA20 | 175 |
| N4374F | FA20 | 177 |
| N4375F | FA20 | 179 |
| N4376F | FA20 | 181 |
| N4377F | FA20 | 183 |
| N4378F | FA20 | 203 |
| N4378P | BE40 | RK-278 |
| N4379F | FA20 | 187 |
| N4380F | FA20 | 189 |
| N4381F | FA20 | 191 |
| N4382F | FA20 | 192 |
| N4383F | FA20 | 193 |
| N4384F | FA20 | 194 |
| N4385F | FA20 | 195 |
| N4386F | FA20 | 196 |
| **N4387** | **GLF4** | **1387** |
| N4387F | FA20 | 197 |
| N4388F | FA20 | 199 |
| N4389F | FA20 | 200 |
| N4390F | FA20 | 213 |
| N4391F | FA20 | 202 |
| N4392F | FA20 | 204 |
| N4393F | FA20 | 205 |
| N4394F | FA20 | 206 |
| N4395D | PRM1 | RB-65 |
| N4395F | FA20 | 207 |
| N4396F | FA20 | 209 |
| N4397F | FA20 | 210 |
| N4398F | FA20 | 211 |
| N4399F | FA20 | 212 |
| N4400E | HS25 | 25026 |
| N4400F | FA20 | 214 |
| N4401 | LJ35 | 434 |
| N4401F | FA20 | 215 |
| **N4402** | **HS25** | **258199** |
| N4402 | LJ25 | 117 |
| N4402F | FA20 | 216 |
| N4403 | C500 | 271 |
| **N4403** | **HS25** | **258480** |
| N4403F | FA20 | 217 |
| N4404F | FA20 | 220 |
| N4405 | C550 | 550-1023 |
| N4405 | LJ25 | 117 |
| N4406F | FA20 | 221 |
| N4407F | FA20 | 223 |
| N4408F | FA20 | 224 |
| N4409F | FA20 | 226 |
| N4410F | FA20 | 227 |
| N4411 | GLF2 | 48/29 |
| N4411F | FA20 | 229 |
| N4412F | FA20 | 230 |
| N4413F | FA20 | 232 |
| N4413N | FA50 | 66 |
| N4414F | FA20 | 233 |
| N4415D | CL61 | 3051 |
| N4415F | FA20 | 235 |
| N4415M | LJ35 | 072 |
| N4415S | LJ35 | 021 |
| **N4415S** | **LJ35** | **232** |
| **N4415W** | **LJ35** | **229** |
| (N4416F) | FA20 | 236 |
| N4416F | FA20 | 256 |
| N4417F | FA20 | 239 |
| N4418F | FA20 | 242 |
| N4418F | FA20 | 259 |
| N4419F | FA20 | 247 |
| N4420E | ASTR | 049 |
| N4420F | FA20 | 244 |
| N4421F | FA20 | 249 |
| N4422F | FA20 | 250 |
| N4423F | FA20 | 254 |
| N4424P | CL60 | 1053 |
| N4425 | F9EX | 32 |
| N4425F | FA20 | 257 |
| N4425R | HS25 | 258525 |
| **N4426** | **HS25** | **258272** |
| N4426F | FA20 | 258 |
| N4426Z | WW24 | 409 |
| N4427F | FA20 | 262 |
| N4428 | HS25 | 258274 |
| N4428F | FA20 | 264 |
| N4429F | FA20 | 265 |
| N4430F | FA20 | 269 |
| N4431F | FA20 | 272 |
| N4432F | FA20 | 273 |
| N4433F | FA20 | 274 |
| N4434F | FA20 | 275 |
| N4434W | C500 | 082 |
| N4435F | FA20 | 270 |
| N4436F | FA20 | 282 |
| N4436S | JSTR | 5141 |
| N4437F | FA20 | 284 |
| N4438F | FA20 | 287 |
| N4439F | FA20 | 289 |
| N4440F | FA20 | 290 |
| N4441F | FA20 | 292 |
| N4442F | FA20 | 293 |
| N4443F | FA20 | 297 |
| N4444F | FA20 | 298 |
| N4444J | HS25 | 258171 |
| N4444U | WW24 | 163 |
| N4445F | FA20 | 303 |
| (N4445J) | LJ24 | 309 |
| N4445N | C550 | 024 |
| N4445Y | BE40 | RK-345 |
| N4445Y | LJ35 | 432 |
| N4446F | FA20 | 305 |
| N4446P | C500 | 373 |
| N4447F | FA20 | 308 |
| **N4447P** | **LJ25** | **338** |
| N4447T | WW24 | 286 |
| N4448F | FA20 | 312 |
| N4448Y | LJ36 | 046 |
| N4449F | CL61 | 3002 |
| N4449F | FA20 | 313 |
| N4450F | FA20 | 310 |
| N4451F | FA20 | 316 |
| N4452F | FA20 | 317 |
| N4453F | FA20 | 319 |
| N4454F | FA20 | 321 |
| N4455F | FA20 | 322 |
| N4456F | FA20 | 324 |
| N4457A | C550 | 035 |
| N4457F | FA20 | 325 |
| N4458F | FA20 | 327 |
| (N4459F) | FA20 | 328/522 |
| N4459F | FA20 | 335 |
| N4460F | FA20 | 330 |
| N4461F | FA20 | 339 |
| N4462F | FA20 | 341 |
| N4463F | FA20 | 345 |
| N4464F | FA20 | 347 |
| N4465F | FA20 | 349 |
| N4465M | HS25 | 258565 |
| N4465N | HS25 | 25053 |
| N4466F | FA20 | 352 |
| N4466Z | HS25 | 258566 |
| N4467E | BE40 | RK-287 |
| N4467F | FA20 | 355 |
| N4467X | BE40 | RK-267 |
| N4468F | FA20 | 356 |
| N4468K | HS25 | 258568 |
| N4469B | HS25 | 258502 |
| N4469E | BE40 | RK-320 |
| N4469F | FA20 | 357 |
| N4469F | HS25 | 258531 |

| | | |
|---|---|---|
| N4469F | SBRL | 282-43 |
| N4469M | HS25 | 258563 |
| N4469M | SBRL | 282-48 |
| N4469N | HS25 | 258547 |
| N4469N | SBRL | 282-68 |
| N4469U | HS25 | 258520 |
| N4469X | HS25 | 258569 |
| N4471N | HS25 | 258571 |
| N4471P | PRM1 | RB-71 |
| N4477X | BE40 | RK-277 |
| (N4477X) | HS25 | 257104 |
| N4480W | BE40 | RK-280 |
| **N4483W** | **BE40** | **RK-313** |
| N4485B | PRM1 | RB-85 |
| N4488F | PRM1 | RB-88 |
| N4488W | LJ25 | 367 |
| (N4492V) | SBRL | 282-39 |
| N4493S | JSTR | 5141 |
| N4500X | GLF3 | 416 |
| **N4500X** | **GLF4** | **4004** |
| **N4545** | **LJ45** | **045** |
| N4550E | WW24 | 83 |
| N4554E | WW24 | 85 |
| N4555E | HS25 | 257001 |
| N4557P | FA10 | 104 |
| N4557W | C550 | 137 |
| N4562Q | CL61 | 3016 |
| N4564P | C550 | 319 |
| (N4564S) | LJ35 | 365 |
| N4567 | SBRL | 282-44 |
| N4576T | LJ24 | 227 |
| N4577Q | LJ35 | 263 |
| N4578F | C550 | 023 |
| N4581R | FA10 | 151 |
| N4581Y | C550 | 375 |
| N4612 | C650 | 0203 |
| (N4612S) | C650 | 0203 |
| N4612Z | C650 | 0203 |
| **N4614N** | **C550** | **659** |
| N4620G | C550 | 067 |
| N4621G | C550 | 068 |
| N4641J | LJ24 | 019 |
| N4644E | WW24 | 97 |
| N4646S | C500 | 051 |
| N4646S | HS25 | 25013 |
| N4661E | WW24 | 99 |
| N4663E | WW24 | 100 |
| N4674E | WW24 | 104 |
| N4679T | FA50 | 17 |
| N4690E | WW24 | 106 |
| N4691E | WW24 | 107 |
| N4701N | SBRL | 282-93 |
| N4703N | SBRL | 282-94 |
| N4704N | SBRL | 282-95 |
| N4705N | SBRL | 282-96 |
| N4706N | SBRL | 282-97 |
| N4707N | SBRL | 282-98 |
| N4709N | SBRL | 306-4 |
| N4712N | SBRL | 306-6 |
| N4715N | SBRL | 306-7 |
| N4716E | WW24 | 110 |
| N4716N | SBRL | 306-8 |
| N4717N | SBRL | 306-9 |
| N4720N | SBRL | 306-10 |
| N4720T | C550 | 256 |
| N4721N | SBRL | 306-11 |
| N4722R | SBRL | 306-12 |
| N4723N | SBRL | 306-13 |
| N4724N | SBRL | 306-14 |
| N4725N | SBRL | 306-15 |
| N4726N | SBRL | 306-16 |
| N4727N | SBRL | 306-17 |
| N4728N | SBRL | 306-18 |
| N4729N | SBRL | 306-19 |
| N4730E | WW24 | 112 |
| N4730N | SBRL | 306-20 |
| N4731N | SBRL | 306-21 |
| N4732E | WW24 | 113 |
| N4732N | SBRL | 306-22 |
| N4733N | SBRL | 306-23 |
| N4734E | WW24 | 114 |
| N4734N | SBRL | 306-24 |
| N4735N | SBRL | 306-25 |
| N4736N | SBRL | 306-26 |
| N4737N | SBRL | 306-27 |
| N4741N | SBRL | 306-29 |
| N4742N | SBRL | 306-30 |
| N4743E | WW24 | 116 |
| N4743N | SBRL | 306-32 |
| N4745N | SBRL | 306-33 |
| N4746N | SBRL | 306-34 |
| N4748N | SBRL | 306-35 |
| N4749N | SBRL | 306-36 |
| N4750N | SBRL | 306-37 |
| N4751N | SBRL | 306-38 |
| N4752N | SBRL | 306-39 |
| **N4753** | **GLF4** | **1197** |
| N4753N | SBRL | 306-40 |
| N4754G | C550 | 069 |
| N4754N | SBRL | 306-41 |
| N4755N | SBRL | 306-42 |
| N4757N | SBRL | 306-43 |
| N4759D | HS25 | 25272 |
| N4760N | SBRL | 306-44 |
| N4763N | SBRL | 306-45 |
| N4764N | SBRL | 306-46 |
| N4765N | SBRL | 306-47 |
| N4767M | HS25 | 25159 |
| N4791C | LJ24 | 160 |
| **N4818C** | **GLF4** | **1385** |
| N4875 | FA10 | 54 |
| N4886 | HS25 | 25046 |
| N4895Q | C560 | 0199 |
| N4903W | FA50 | 129 |
| N4940E | WW24 | 122 |
| N4943A | SBRL | 282-66 |
| N4960S | FA20 | 296/507 |
| N4981 | LJ25 | 062 |
| N4983E | WW24 | 126 |
| N4990D | JSTR | 5146 |
| N4995A | LJ35 | 192 |
| N4995N | WW24 | 230 |
| N4997E | HS25 | 25016 |
| N4998Z | LJ36 | 039 |
| N4999G | SBRL | 265-2 |
| N4999H | C500 | 329 |
| N4999H | SBRL | 265-55 |
| N5000B | JSTR | 5093 |
| N5000B | LJ35 | 074 |
| N5000C | C650 | 0002 |
| N5000C | JSTR | 5093 |
| N5000C | JSTR | 5205 |
| N5000E | LJ31 | 031 |
| N5000E | LJ31 | 206 |
| N5000E | LJ31 | 214 |
| N5000E | LJ40 | 45-2064 |
| N5000E | LJ45 | 020 |
| N5000E | LJ45 | 207 |
| N5000E | LJ45 | 233 |
| N5000E | LJ45 | 298 |
| N5000E | LJ60 | 276 |
| N5000E | LJ60 | 284 |
| N5000E | LJ60 | 328 |
| N5000E | LJ60 | 354 |
| N5000E | LJ60 | 374 |
| N5000G | GLF2 | 110 |
| N5000R | C52A | 0312 |
| N5000R | C52B | 0228 |
| N5000R | C550 | 550-0879 |
| N5000R | C550 | 550-0928 |
| N5000R | C560 | 0445 |
| N5000R | C560 | 0566 |
| N5000R | C56X | 5228 |
| N5000R | C56X | 5314 |
| N5000R | C56X | 5826 |
| N5000R | C680 | 0131 |
| N5000R | C750 | 0023 |
| N5000R | C750 | 0052 |
| N5000R | C750 | 0252 |
| **N5000X** | **GLF5** | **611** |
| N5001G | HS25 | 25095 |
| N5001J | LJ45 | 159 |
| N5001S | HS25 | 258501 |
| N5001X | LJ31 | 100 |
| N5002D | LJ31 | 102 |
| N5002G | BE40 | RK-302 |
| N5003F | LJ31 | 103 |
| N5003G | BE40 | RK-323 |
| N5003U | LJ60 | 063 |
| N5003X | LJ60 | 039 |
| N5004B | HS25 | 258504 |
| N5004J | LJ60 | 232 |
| N5004Y | BE40 | RK-304 |
| N5004Y | LJ60 | 041 |
| N5004Z | LJ31 | 230 |
| N5005 | C500 | 004 |
| **N5005** | **EA50** | **000225** |
| N5005K | LJ31 | 105 |
| (N5005M) | LJ31 | 115 |
| N5005Q | LJ31 | 231 |
| N5005X | LJ31 | 233 |
| N5005X | LJ60 | 095 |
| N5006G | LJ60 | 046 |
| N5006K | LJ60 | 066 |
| N5006T | LJ60 | 062 |
| N5006V | LJ60 | 065 |
| N5007P | LJ60 | 047 |
| N5008F | LJ60 | 233 |
| N5008S | HS25 | 258508 |
| N5008S | LJ31 | 232 |
| N5008Z | LJ60 | 048 |
| N5009 | LJ60 | 306 |
| N5009L | LJ31 | 089 |
| N5009T | LJ31 | 220 |
| N5009T | LJ35 | 665 |
| N5009T | LJ40 | 45-2017 |
| N5009T | LJ40 | 45-2091 |
| N5009T | LJ40 | 45-2108 |
| N5009T | LJ45 | 021 |
| N5009T | LJ45 | 096 |
| N5009T | LJ45 | 234 |
| N5009T | LJ45 | 306 |
| N5009T | LJ60 | 018 |
| N5009T | LJ60 | 283 |
| N5009T | LJ60 | 285 |
| N5009V | LJ31 | 043 |
| N5009V | LJ31 | 066 |
| N5009V | LJ31 | 096 |
| N5009V | LJ31 | 213 |
| N5009V | LJ40 | 45-2040 |
| N5009V | LJ45 | 012 |
| N5009V | LJ45 | 084 |
| N5009V | LJ45 | 208 |
| N5009V | LJ45 | 210 |
| N5009V | LJ45 | 244 |
| N5009V | LJ45 | 268 |
| N5009V | LJ45 | 330 |
| N5009V | LJ45 | 372 |
| N5009V | LJ60 | 267 |
| N5009V | LJ60 | 383 |
| N5010J | LJ31 | 101 |
| N5010U | LJ31 | 032 |
| N5010U | LJ40 | 45-2055 |
| N5010U | LJ45 | 013 |
| N5010U | LJ45 | 204 |
| N5010U | LJ45 | 245 |
| N5010U | LJ45 | 261 |
| N5010U | LJ45 | 381 |
| (N5010U) | LJ60 | 057 |
| N5010U | LJ60 | 197 |
| N5010U | LJ60 | 321 |
| N5010U | LJ60 | 339 |
| N5010X | PRM1 | RB-10 |
| N5011J | HS25 | 258511 |
| N5011L | LJ35 | 668 |
| N5011L | LJ45 | 052 |
| N5011L | LJ45 | 144 |
| N5011L | LJ45 | 205 |
| N5011L | LJ45 | 256 |
| N5011L | LJ45 | 322 |
| N5011L | LJ45 | 342 |
| **N5011L** | **LJ45** | **407** |
| N5011L | LJ60 | 005 |
| N5011L | LJ60 | 268 |
| N5011L | LJ60 | 292 |
| N5011L | LJ60 | 350 |
| N5012G | LJ40 | 45-2068 |
| N5012G | LJ45 | 022 |
| N5012G | LJ45 | 246 |
| N5012G | LJ60 | 217 |
| N5012G | LJ60 | 297 |
| N5012G | LJ60 | 360 |
| N5012H | LJ31 | 033 |
| N5012H | LJ31 | 098 |
| N5012H | LJ31 | 107 |
| N5012H | LJ45 | 030 |
| N5012H | LJ45 | 257 |
| N5012H | LJ45 | 281 |
| N5012H | LJ45 | 360 |
| N5012H | LJ45 | 384 |
| N5012H | LJ60 | 010 |
| N5012H | LJ60 | 062 |
| N5012H | LJ60 | 212 |
| N5012H | LJ60 | 252 |
| N5012H | LJ60 | 269 |
| N5012H | LJ60 | 302 |
| N5012K | LJ35 | 670 |
| N5012K | LJ40 | 45-2049 |
| N5012K | LJ45 | 329 |
| N5012K | LJ60 | 190 |
| N5012K | LJ60 | 253 |
| N5012K | LJ60 | 270 |
| N5012K | LJ60 | 278 |
| N5012K | LJ60 | 290 |
| N5012K | LJ60 | 341 |
| **N5012K** | **LJ60** | **367** |
| (N5012P) | HS25 | 25095 |
| N5012U | BE40 | RK-312 |
| N5012V | LJ45 | 167 |
| N5012Z | LJ31 | 083 |
| N5012Z | LJ35 | 676 |
| **N5012Z** | **LJ40** | **45-2115** |
| N5012Z | LJ45 | 228 |
| N5012Z | LJ45 | 285 |
| N5012Z | LJ60 | 053 |
| N5012Z | LJ60 | 211 |
| N5012Z | LJ60 | 317 |
| N5012Z | LJ60 | 347 |
| N5013D | LJ45 | 169 |
| N5013D | LJ60 | 032 |
| N5013E | LJ45 | 170 |
| N5013J | LJ60 | 234 |
| N5013L | LJ31 | 033C |
| N5013N | LJ31 | 130 |
| N5013N | LJ60 | 235 |
| N5013U | LJ31 | 222 |
| N5013U | LJ40 | 45-2008 |
| N5013U | LJ40 | 45-2021 |
| N5013U | LJ45 | 035 |
| N5013U | LJ45 | 289 |
| N5013U | LJ45 | 373 |
| N5013U | LJ60 | 011 |
| N5013U | LJ60 | 255 |
| N5013U | LJ60 | 281 |
| N5013U | LJ60 | 312 |
| N5013U | LJ60 | 332 |
| N5013U | LJ60 | 382 |
| N5013Y | LJ31 | 085 |
| N5013Y | LJ31 | 211 |
| N5013Y | LJ40 | 45-2022 |
| N5013Y | LJ45 | 029 |
| N5013Y | LJ45 | 083 |
| N5013Y | LJ45 | 287 |
| N5013Y | LJ60 | 056 |
| N5013Y | LJ60 | 256 |
| N5013Y | LJ60 | 282 |
| N5013Y | LJ60 | 325 |
| N5013Y | LJ60 | 351 |
| N5014E | LJ31 | 134 |
| N5014E | LJ40 | 45-2026 |
| N5014E | LJ45 | 028 |
| N5014E | LJ45 | 152 |
| N5014E | LJ45 | 294 |
| N5014E | LJ45 | 398 |
| N5014E | LJ60 | 036 |
| N5014E | LJ60 | 055 |
| N5014E | LJ60 | 335 |
| N5014E | LJ60 | 361 |
| N5014F | CL30 | 20006 |
| N5014F | LJ31 | 082 |
| N5014F | LJ35 | 669 |
| N5014F | LJ35 | 673 |
| N5014F | LJ45 | 093 |
| N5014F | LJ45 | 288 |
| N5014F | LJ45 | 310 |
| N5014F | LJ45 | 340 |
| N5014F | LJ45 | 374 |
| N5014F | LJ60 | 169 |
| N5014F | LJ60 | 322 |
| N5014G | BE40 | RK-314 |
| N5014H | LJ60 | 012 |
| N5015B | BE40 | RK-335 |
| N5015T | LJ60 | 236 |
| N5015U | LJ31 | 034 |
| N5015U | LJ40 | 45-2032 |
| N5015U | LJ40 | 45-2050 |
| N5015U | LJ40 | 45-2077 |
| N5015U | LJ45 | 258 |
| N5015U | LJ45 | 385 |
| N5015U | LJ45 | 405 |
| N5015U | LJ60 | 063 |
| N5015U | LJ60 | 254 |

| | | |
|---|---|---|
| N5015U | LJ60 | 343 |
| N5016P | C500 | 358 |
| N5016S | LJ45 | 176 |
| N5016V | LJ31 | 038 |
| N5016V | LJ40 | 45-2044 |
| **N5016V** | **LJ40** | **45-2127** |
| N5016V | LJ45 | 031 |
| N5016V | LJ45 | 092 |
| N5016V | LJ45 | 119 |
| N5016V | LJ45 | 216 |
| N5016V | LJ45 | 264 |
| N5016V | LJ45 | 383 |
| N5016V | LJ60 | 058 |
| N5016V | LJ60 | 338 |
| N5016Z | LJ40 | 45-2061 |
| N5016Z | LJ40 | 45-2093 |
| N5016Z | LJ40 | 45-2125 |
| N5016Z | LJ45 | 072 |
| N5016Z | LJ45 | 078 |
| N5016Z | LJ45 | 217 |
| N5016Z | LJ45 | 240 |
| N5016Z | LJ60 | 214 |
| N5016Z | LJ60 | 296 |
| N5016Z | LJ60 | 327 |
| N5017J | LJ31 | 058 |
| N5017J | LJ40 | 45-2126 |
| N5017J | LJ45 | 097 |
| N5017J | LJ45 | 237 |
| N5017J | LJ45 | 265 |
| N5017J | LJ45 | 345 |
| N5017J | LJ60 | 037 |
| N5017J | LJ60 | 316 |
| N5017J | LJ60 | 353 |
| N5017T | PRM1 | RB-17 |
| N5018G | LJ35 | 667 |
| N5018G | LJ40 | 45-2013 |
| N5018G | LJ40 | 45-2018 |
| N5018G | LJ40 | 45-2034 |
| N5018G | LJ40 | 45-2053 |
| N5018G | LJ45 | 077 |
| N5018G | LJ45 | 138 |
| N5018G | LJ45 | 188 |
| N5018G | LJ45 | 215 |
| N5018G | LJ45 | 236 |
| N5018G | LJ60 | 326 |
| N5018G | LJ60 | 359 |
| N5018L | LJ60 | 373 |
| N5018U | LJ60 | 238 |
| N5019R | LJ60 | 239 |
| N5019V | LJ60 | 240 |
| N5019Y | LJ31 | 091 |
| N5020J | C510 | 0178 |
| N5020Y | LJ31 | 120 |
| N5022C | LJ60 | 052 |
| N5023D | LJ31 | 033D |
| N5023J | HS25 | 258523 |
| N5023U | LJ45 | 179 |
| N5024E | LJ45 | 181 |
| N5024J | PRM1 | RB-24 |
| N5024U | BE40 | RK-324 |
| N5025K | LJ45 | 183 |
| **N5026** | **C52A** | **0159** |
| N5026Q | C52A | 0438 |
| N5026Q | C52B | 0251 |
| N5026Q | C56X | 5692 |
| N5026Q | LJ60 | 241 |
| N5027Q | LJ60 | 242 |
| N5028E | LJ31 | 234 |
| N5028J | BE40 | RK-328 |
| N5029F | LJ31 | 109 |
| N5030 | JSTR | 5212 |
| N5030J | LJ45 | 187 |
| N5030N | LJ45 | 189 |
| N5030U | C52B | 0126 |
| N5030U | C52B | 0323 |
| N5030U | C56X | 5770 |
| N5030U | C680 | 0149 |
| N5030V | PRM1 | RB-130 |
| N5031D | BE40 | RK-331 |
| N5031E | C52B | 0133 |
| N5031E | C680 | 0260 |
| N5031E | C750 | 0279 |
| N5031R | LJ60 | 244 |
| **N5031T** | **BE40** | **RK-590** |
| N5032E | WW24 | 129 |
| N5032H | BE40 | RK-332 |
| (N5032H) | CL61 | 5071 |
| N5032K | C52A | 0368 |
| N5032K | C750 | 0290 |
| N5034J | BE40 | RK-334 |
| N5034Z | LJ60 | 034 |
| N5035F | LJ60 | 246 |
| N5035R | LJ60 | 070 |
| N5036Q | C52B | 0190 |
| N5036Q | C560 | 0761 |
| N5036Q | C680 | 0233 |
| N5036Q | C680 | 0286 |
| N5037F | C525 | 0665 |
| N5037F | C52B | 0177 |
| **N5037F** | **C56X** | **6057** |
| N5037L | BE40 | RK-337 |
| N5038E | WW24 | 130 |
| N5038N | LJ60 | 248 |
| N5038V | BE40 | RK-338 |
| N5039E | WW24 | 131 |
| (N5040) | GLF2 | 40 |
| N5040E | C680 | 0155 |
| N5040W | LJ45 | 194 |
| N5040Y | LJ45 | 195 |
| N5041E | WW24 | 133 |
| N5042A | LJ45 | 206 |
| N5043D | LJ60 | 043 |
| N5043E | WW24 | 135 |
| N5044E | WW24 | 136 |
| N5044N | LJ60 | 044 |
| N5044V | C510 | 0144 |
| N5044X | PRM1 | RB-44 |
| N5045E | WW24 | 137 |
| N5045S | LJ60 | 045 |
| N5045W | C680 | 0172 |
| N5046E | WW24 | 138 |
| N5047E | WW24 | 139 |
| N5048K | LJ45 | 198 |
| N5048Q | LJ45 | 202 |
| N5048U | C52A | 0399 |
| N5048U | C52A | 0429 |
| N5049J | LJ31 | 099 |
| N5049U | PRM1 | RB-49 |
| N5050G | LJ45 | 208 |
| N5050J | C550 | 001 |
| N5051A | LJ60 | 262 |
| N5051X | LJ60 | 051 |
| N5051X | LJ60 | 252 |
| N5052K | LJ45 | 205 |
| N5052U | FA20 | 65 |
| N5053R | C525 | 0671 |
| N5053R | C525 | 0683 |
| N5053R | C680 | 0125 |
| N5053Y | LJ60 | 053 |
| N5055F | LJ60 | 055 |
| N5057E | C52B | 0131 |
| N5057F | C525 | 0660 |
| N5057F | C525 | 0697 |
| N5057F | C680 | 0234 |
| N5057Z | BE40 | RK-357 |
| N5058J | C525 | 0510 |
| N5058J | C52B | 0132 |
| N5058J | C550 | 550-0828 |
| N5058J | C550 | 550-0901 |
| N5058J | C56X | 5182 |
| N5058J | C56X | 5270 |
| N5058J | C680 | 0049 |
| N5058J | C680 | 0211 |
| N5058J | C750 | 0028 |
| N5058J | C750 | 0051 |
| N5058J | C750 | 0136 |
| N5059J | LJ60 | 059 |
| N5059X | C52B | 0135 |
| N5059X | C56X | 5767 |
| N5059X | C56X | 6028 |
| N5060H | CL61 | 5060 |
| N5060K | C525 | 0516 |
| N5060K | C56X | 5002 |
| N5060K | C56X | 5274 |
| N5060K | C56X | 5808 |
| N5060K | C680 | 0058 |
| N5060K | C680 | 0133 |
| N5060K | C750 | 0097 |
| N5060K | C750 | 0170 |
| N5060K | C750 | 0285 |
| N5060P | C550 | 550-0825 |
| N5060P | C560 | 0246 |
| N5061F | C525 | 0674 |
| N5061F | C52A | 0358 |
| N5061F | C52B | 0304 |
| N5061F | C680 | 0197 |
| N5061F | C680 | 0219 |
| N5061P | C525 | 0667 |
| N5061P | C525 | 0680 |
| N5061P | C550 | 550-0927 |
| N5061P | C56X | 5177 |
| N5061P | C56X | 5238 |
| N5061P | C56X | 5298 |
| N5061P | C56X | 5684 |
| N5061P | C680 | 0071 |
| N5061P | C750 | 0053 |
| N5061P | C750 | 0091 |
| N5061W | C52B | 0166 |
| N5061W | C52B | 0222 |
| N5061W | C550 | 550-1121 |
| N5061W | C560 | 0398 |
| N5061W | C560 | 0513 |
| N5061W | C56X | 5184 |
| N5061W | C56X | 5237 |
| N5061W | C56X | 5341 |
| N5061W | C56X | 5686 |
| N5061W | C56X | 6013 |
| N5061W | C750 | 0031 |
| N5061W | C750 | 0125 |
| N5062H | HS25 | 258562 |
| N5062S | C52B | 0183 |
| N5062S | C52B | 0238 |
| N5062S | C52B | 0287 |
| N5062S | C680 | 0128 |
| N5063P | C52A | 0337 |
| N5063P | C56X | 5744 |
| N5063P | C680 | 0272 |
| **N5064M** | **C560** | **0807** |
| N5064M | C750 | 0282 |
| N5064Q | C52A | 0341 |
| N5064Q | C56X | 5768 |
| N5064Q | C680 | 0280 |
| N5065S | C680 | 0264 |
| N5066F | C52B | 0204 |
| N5066F | C52B | 0286 |
| N5066F | C52B | 0330 |
| N5066F | C750 | 0269 |
| N5066U | C525 | 0521 |
| N5066U | C525 | 0636 |
| N5066U | C52A | 0427 |
| N5066U | C52B | 0058 |
| N5066U | C550 | 550-0930 |
| N5066U | C56X | 5264 |
| N5066U | C56X | 5769 |
| N5066U | C750 | 0026 |
| N5066U | C750 | 0041 |
| N5066U | C750 | 0092 |
| N5066U | C750 | 0172 |
| N5067U | C56X | 5745 |
| N5068F | C52A | 0446 |
| N5068F | C52B | 0230 |
| N5068F | C56X | 5687 |
| N5068F | LJ60 | 078 |
| N5068R | C525 | 0142 |
| N5068R | C550 | 550-0882 |
| N5068R | C550 | 550-1085 |
| N5068R | C550 | 550-1134 |
| N5068R | C56X | 5166 |
| N5068R | C56X | 5223 |
| N5068R | C56X | 5294 |
| N5068R | C56X | 5771 |
| N5068R | C680 | 0256 |
| N5068R | C750 | 0027 |
| N5068R | C750 | 0055 |
| N5068R | C750 | 0141 |
| N5069E | C525 | 0656 |
| N5069E | C56X | 5693 |
| N5069E | C56X | 5777 |
| N5069P | CL61 | 3021 |
| N5070L | JSTR | 5143 |
| N5070W | PRM1 | RB-70 |
| N5071L | SBRL | 306-9 |
| N5071M | C750 | 0035 |
| N5072E | C500 | 043 |
| N5072L | C500 | 043 |
| N5072L | C500 | 379 |
| N5072L | HS25 | 258572 |
| N5072L | LJ60 | 072 |
| N5072X | C52A | 0406 |
| N5072X | C56X | 5694 |
| N5072X | C56X | 6045 |
| N5072X | C680 | 0176 |
| N5072X | PRM1 | RB-72 |
| N5073 | CL61 | 5073 |
| N5073G | C52A | 0242 |
| N5073G | C52B | 0021 |
| N5073G | C52B | 0136 |
| N5073G | C52B | 0200 |
| N5073G | C550 | 550-0850 |
| N5073G | C550 | 550-0893 |
| N5073G | C550 | 550-0921 |
| N5073G | C560 | 0423 |
| N5073G | C560 | 0637 |
| N5073G | C56X | 5189 |
| N5073G | C56X | 5273 |
| N5073G | C650 | 7088 |
| N5075L | SBRL | 306-16 |
| N5076J | C525 | 0160 |
| N5076J | C52A | 0348 |
| N5076J | C52B | 0089 |
| N5076J | C550 | 550-0817 |
| N5076J | C550 | 550-0830 |
| N5076J | C550 | 550-0852 |
| N5076J | C550 | 550-0909 |
| N5076J | C550 | 550-0951 |
| N5076J | C56X | 5207 |
| N5076J | C56X | 5234 |
| N5076J | C56X | 5583 |
| N5076J | C56X | 5772 |
| N5076J | C56X | 6027 |
| N5076K | C525 | 0075 |
| N5076K | C525 | 0161 |
| N5076K | C525 | 0666 |
| N5076K | C525 | 0679 |
| N5076K | C52A | 0174 |
| N5076K | C52B | 0185 |
| N5076K | C52B | 0284 |
| N5076K | C550 | 550-0847 |
| N5076K | C550 | 550-0899 |
| N5076K | C550 | 550-0939 |
| N5076K | C550 | 550-1124 |
| N5076K | C560 | 0431 |
| N5076K | C560 | 0440 |
| N5076K | C560 | 0693 |
| N5076K | C56X | 5211 |
| N5076K | C56X | 5277 |
| N5076K | C680 | 0053 |
| N5076K | C680 | 0134 |
| N5076K | C750 | 0126 |
| N5076L | C525 | 0640 |
| N5076L | C52A | 0430 |
| N5076L | C56X | 5749 |
| N5076P | C52B | 0187 |
| N5076P | C52B | 0239 |
| N5076P | C52B | 0288 |
| N5079H | C56X | 5219 |
| N5079V | C525 | 0076 |
| N5079V | C52A | 0355 |
| N5079V | C550 | 550-0843 |
| N5079V | C550 | 550-0897 |
| N5079V | C550 | 550-0954 |
| N5079V | C560 | 0677 |
| N5079V | C560 | 0694 |
| N5079V | C560 | 0791 |
| N5079V | C560 | 707 |
| N5079V | C56X | 5217 |
| N5079V | C56X | 5272 |
| N5079V | C56X | 5360 |
| N5079V | C650 | 7078 |
| N5079V | C750 | 0261 |
| N5082S | LJ31 | 112 |
| N5084U | BE40 | RK-354 |
| N5085E | C525 | 0078 |
| N5085E | C52A | 0209 |
| N5085E | C52B | 0028 |
| N5085E | C550 | 550-1067 |
| N5085E | C560 | 0477 |
| N5085E | C560 | 0508 |
| N5085E | C560 | 0768 |
| N5085E | C56X | 5230 |
| N5085E | C56X | 5300 |
| N5085E | C56X | 5779 |
| N5085E | C56X | 6023 |
| N5085E | C750 | 0015 |
| N5085E | C750 | 0036 |
| N5085E | C750 | 0115 |
| N5085E | C750 | 0147 |
| N5085J | C550 | 550-0877 |
| N5086W | C525 | 0079 |
| N5086W | C525 | 0151 |
| N5086W | C52A | 0340 |
| N5086W | C550 | 550-0840 |

| | | | | | | | | | | | |
|---|---|---|---|---|---|---|---|---|---|---|---|
| N5086W | C550 | 550-0841 | N5093D | C750 | 0033 | N5100J | C560 | 0276 | N5109 | C650 | 0135 |
| N5086W | C550 | 550-0853 | N5093D | C750 | 0173 | N5100J | C560 | 0324 | N5109 | SBRL | 380-11 |
| N5086W | C550 | 550-0929 | N5093D | C750 | 0262 | N5100J | C560 | 0448 | N5109R | C550 | 550-0873 |
| N5086W | C560 | 0436 | (N5093L) | C525 | 0086 | N5100J | C560 | 0754 | N5109R | C550 | 550-0918 |
| N5086W | C560 | 0465 | N5093L | C525 | 0130 | N5100J | C56X | 5150 | N5109R | C550 | 550-0945 |
| N5086W | C560 | 0521 | N5093L | C52B | 0056 | N5100J | C56X | 5205 | (N5109R) | C560 | 0285 |
| N5086W | C560 | 0685 | N5093L | C52B | 0252 | N5100J | C56X | 5265 | (N5109R) | C560 | 0333 |
| N5086W | C56X | 5172 | N5093L | C550 | 550-0814 | N5100J | C56X | 6040 | N5109R | C560 | 0385 |
| N5086W | C56X | 5235 | N5093L | C550 | 550-0872 | N5100J | C680 | 0216 | N5109R | C560 | 0416 |
| N5086W | C56X | 5291 | N5093L | C550 | 550-0891 | N5100J | C750 | 0068 | N5109R | C56X | 5200 |
| N5086W | C56X | 5514 | N5093L | C550 | 550-0981 | N5100J | C750 | 0100 | N5109R | C56X | 5248 |
| N5086W | C56X | 5811 | N5093L | C560 | 0390 | N5101 | GLF2 | 84 | N5109R | C56X | 5562 |
| N5086W | C650 | 7082 | N5093L | C560 | 0542 | **N5101** | **GLF5** | **550** | N5109R | C56X | 5773 |
| N5086W | C680 | 0166 | N5093L | C56X | 5224 | N5101J | C52A | 0354 | N5109R | C680 | 0220 |
| N5086W | C750 | 0107 | N5093L | C56X | 5334 | N5101J | C52B | 0111 | N5109R | C680 | 0284 |
| N5087B | LJ45 | 067 | N5093L | C56X | 5559 | N5101J | C52B | 0243 | N5109R | C750 | 0045 |
| N5090A | C525 | 0080 | N5093L | C680 | 0137 | N5101J | C52B | 0290 | N5109R | C750 | 0061 |
| N5090A | C525 | 0124 | (N5093Y) | C525 | 0087 | N5101J | C550 | 550-0846 | N5109R | C750 | 0231 |
| N5090A | C525 | 0535 | N5093Y | C525 | 0131 | N5101J | C550 | 550-0905 | N5109R | C750 | 0249 |
| N5090A | C52A | 0417 | N5093Y | C550 | 550-0821 | N5101J | C550 | 550-0936 | N5109T | SBRL | 380-11 |
| N5090A | C550 | 550-1071 | N5093Y | C550 | 550-0904 | (N5101J) | C560 | 0277 | N5109W | C52B | 0022 |
| N5090A | C560 | 0378 | N5093Y | C550 | 550-0941 | (N5101J) | C560 | 0325 | N5109W | C52B | 0248 |
| N5090A | C560 | 0417 | N5093Y | C550 | 550-1069 | N5101J | C560 | 0379 | N5109W | C550 | 550-0885 |
| N5090A | C560 | 0549 | N5093Y | C560 | 0394 | N5101J | C560 | 0426 | N5109W | C550 | 550-0920 |
| N5090A | C56X | 5191 | N5093Y | C560 | 0395 | N5101J | C56X | 5152 | N5109W | C550 | 550-1094 |
| N5090A | C56X | 5244 | N5093Y | C560 | 0525 | N5101J | C56X | 5206 | N5109W | C550 | 550-1120 |
| N5090A | C56X | 5311 | N5093Y | C560 | 0770 | N5101J | C56X | 5292 | (N5109W) | C560 | 0286 |
| N5090A | C56X | 5574 | N5093Y | C56X | 5209 | N5101J | C56X | 5351 | N5109W | C560 | 0334 |
| N5090A | C680 | 0132 | N5093Y | C680 | 0087 | N5101J | C56X | 5356 | N5109W | C56X | 5165 |
| N5090A | C750 | 0042 | N5093Y | C680 | 0215 | N5101J | C56X | 5605 | N5109W | C56X | 5208 |
| N5090A | C750 | 0099 | N5094B | C560 | 0272 | N5101T | GLF2 | 84 | N5109W | C56X | 5284 |
| N5090A | C750 | 0257 | N5094B | WW24 | 105 | N5102 | GLF2 | 85 | N5109W | C56X | 5648 |
| N5090A | C750 | 0293 | N5094D | C52A | 0315 | **N5102** | **GLF5** | **551** | N5109W | C750 | 0019 |
| N5090V | C525 | 0081 | N5094D | C52A | 0401 | N5102G | LJ60 | 330 | N5109W | C750 | 0046 |
| N5090V | C525 | 0125 | N5094D | C56X | 5221 | N5103 | GLF3 | 440 | N5109W | C750 | 0274 |
| N5090V | C525 | 0150 | N5094D | C56X | 5282 | (N5103) | GLF3 | 445 | **N5109W** | **C750** | **0304** |
| N5090V | C525 | 0153 | N5094D | C56X | 5338 | N5103J | C52A | 0372 | N5111 | C650 | 7011 |
| N5090V | C52A | 0364 | N5094D | C56X | 5368 | N5103J | C52A | 0403 | N5111H | JSTR | 5111 |
| N5090V | C550 | 550-0925 | N5094D | C650 | 7084 | N5103J | C52A | 0404 | N5112 | C650 | 7012 |
| N5090V | C56X | 5183 | N5094D | C680 | 0117 | N5103J | C550 | 550-0932 | N5112 | C650 | 7064 |
| N5090V | C56X | 5241 | N5094D | C680 | 0168 | N5103J | C560 | 0278 | N5112 | C750 | 0010 |
| N5090V | C56X | 5824 | N5094D | C680 | 0277 | N5103J | C560 | 0326 | N5112K | C525 | 0152 |
| N5090V | C680 | 0042 | N5094E | BE40 | RK-294 | N5103J | C560 | 0380 | N5112K | C525 | 0550 |
| N5090V | C680 | 0080 | N5095N | C525 | 0615 | N5103J | C56X | 5216 | N5112K | C525 | 0613 |
| N5090V | C750 | 0029 | N5095N | C550 | 550-0902 | N5103J | C56X | 5271 | N5112K | C52B | 0303 |
| N5090V | C750 | 0098 | N5095N | C550 | 550-0942 | N5103J | C56X | 5553 | N5112K | C550 | 550-0880 |
| N5090Y | C525 | 0082 | N5095N | C560 | 0273 | N5103J | C56X | 5608 | (N5112K) | C560 | 0287 |
| N5090Y | C525 | 0126 | N5095N | C560 | 0478 | N5103J | C56X | 6020 | N5112K | C560 | 0418 |
| N5090Y | C550 | 550-0884 | N5095N | C560 | 0507 | N5103J | C750 | 0044 | N5112K | C560 | 0534 |
| N5090Y | C550 | 550-0924 | N5095N | C560 | 0753 | N5103J | C750 | 0085 | N5112K | C560 | 0752 |
| N5090Y | C56X | 5212 | N5095N | C56X | 5155 | N5104 | GLF3 | 443 | N5112K | C56X | 5220 |
| N5090Y | C56X | 5540 | N5095N | C56X | 5202 | N5104G | PRM1 | RB-104 | N5112K | C56X | 5285 |
| N5090Y | C680 | 0086 | N5095N | C56X | 5250 | (N5104Z) | C560 | 0328 | N5112K | C650 | 7085 |
| N5090Y | C680 | 0209 | N5095N | C56X | 5315 | N5105 | GLF3 | 445 | N5112K | C680 | 0205 |
| N5090Y | C750 | 0043 | N5095N | C56X | 5750 | N5105 | SBRL | 380-4 | N5112K | C750 | 0140 |
| N5090Y | C750 | 0060 | N5095N | C750 | 0030 | N5105A | PRM1 | RB-105 | N5112S | C750 | 0010 |
| N5091J | C525 | 0083 | **N5096F** | **FA20** | **157** | N5105F | C525 | 0551 | N5113 | C650 | 7013 |
| N5091J | C525 | 0127 | N5096S | C52A | 0314 | N5105F | C550 | 550-0881 | N5113 | C750 | 0013 |
| N5091J | C52A | 0154 | N5096S | C52B | 0157 | N5105F | C550 | 550-0914 | **N5113** | **GLF4** | **4013** |
| N5091J | C52B | 0270 | N5096S | C52B | 0260 | (N5105F) | C560 | 0281 | N5113H | GLF2 | 107 |
| N5091J | C52B | 0312 | N5096S | C550 | 550-0813 | N5105F | C560 | 0329 | N5113H | JSTR | 5142 |
| N5091J | C560 | 0524 | N5096S | C550 | 550-0829 | N5105F | C560 | 0427 | N5113S | C750 | 0013 |
| N5091J | C560 | 0545 | N5096S | C550 | 550-0913 | N5105F | C56X | 5153 | N5114 | C650 | 0094 |
| N5091J | C560 | 0783 | N5096S | C560 | 0274 | N5105F | C56X | 5229 | N5114 | C650 | 7018 |
| N5091J | C56X | 5215 | N5096S | C560 | 0467 | N5105F | C56X | 5289 | N5114 | C750 | 0017 |
| N5091J | C56X | 5261 | N5096S | C56X | 5143 | N5105F | C56X | 5696 | **N5114** | **GLF4** | **4016** |
| N5091J | C56X | 5372 | N5096S | C56X | 5201 | N5105F | C56X | 6036 | N5114G | LJ35 | 181 |
| N5091J | C56X | 5698 | N5096S | C56X | 5249 | N5105F | C680 | 0074 | N5115 | C650 | 0095 |
| N5091J | C750 | 0018 | N5096S | C56X | 5316 | N5105F | C680 | 0227 | N5115 | C650 | 7015 |
| N5091J | C750 | 0047 | N5096S | C56X | 6047 | N5105F | C750 | 0056 | N5115 | C750 | 0018 |
| N5092B | C560 | 0389 | N5096S | C680 | 0221 | N5106 | SBRL | 380-6 | **N5115** | **GLF4** | **4019** |
| (N5092D) | C525 | 0084 | N5096S | C750 | 0251 | **N5107** | **FA50** | **109** | N5116 | C650 | 0096 |
| N5092D | C525 | 0128 | N5097H | C52B | 0010 | N5107 | SBRL | 380-8 | N5116 | C750 | 0019 |
| N5092D | C550 | 550-0819 | N5097H | C550 | 550-0818 | N5108 | SBRL | 380-9 | (N5116) | C750 | 0022 |
| N5092D | C560 | 0391 | (N5097H) | C560 | 0275 | N5108G | C52A | 0343 | **N5116** | **GLF4** | **4023** |
| N5092R | LJ60 | 092 | (N5097H) | C560 | 0323 | N5108G | C52A | 0374 | N5117 | C650 | 7064 |
| N5093D | C525 | 0085 | N5097H | C560 | 0376 | N5108G | C52B | 0322 | N5117 | GLF4 | 4026 |
| N5093D | C525 | 0129 | N5097H | C560 | 0472 | N5108G | C550 | 550-0871 | N5117F | HS25 | 258617 |
| N5093D | C525 | 0158 | N5097H | C560 | 0529 | N5108G | C560 | 0284 | N5117H | GLF2 | 197 |
| N5093D | C52A | 0432 | N5097H | C560 | 0548 | (N5108G) | C560 | 0332 | N5117U | C525 | 0626 |
| N5093D | C52B | 0012 | N5097H | C560 | 0809 | N5108G | C560 | 0387 | N5117U | C52A | 0207 |
| N5093D | C560 | 0473 | N5097H | C56X | 5283 | N5108G | C560 | 0447 | N5117U | C52A | 0238 |
| N5093D | C560 | 0697 | **N5098F** | **FA20** | **197** | N5108G | C560 | 0539 | N5117U | C52B | 0223 |
| N5093D | C56X | 5142 | N5098G | JSTR | 5098/28 | N5108G | C56X | 5144 | N5117U | C550 | 550-0820 |
| N5093D | C56X | 5243 | N5098H | FA20 | 225/472 | N5108G | C56X | 5213 | N5117U | C550 | 550-0868 |
| N5093D | C56X | 5309 | N5100J | C525 | 0146 | N5108G | C56X | 5816 | N5117U | C550 | 550-0912 |
| N5093D | C680 | 0136 | N5100J | C52A | 0161 | N5108G | C680 | 0036 | N5117U | C550 | 550-0943 |
| N5093D | C680 | 0171 | N5100J | C550 | 550-0917 | N5108G | C750 | 0059 | N5117U | C550 | 550-1105 |

| | | |
|---|---|---|
| N5117U | C56X | 5225 |
| N5117U | C56X | 5288 |
| N5117U | C650 | 7069 |
| N5117U | C650 | 7089 |
| N5117U | C680 | 0145 |
| N5117U | C750 | 0167 |
| N5117U+ | C650 | 7047 |
| N5118 | C650 | 7013 |
| N5118J | PRM1 | RB-138 |
| N5119 | C650 | 7015 |
| **N5119** | **HS25** | **258177** |
| N5120U | C525 | 0202 |
| N5120U | C525 | 0400 |
| N5120U | C525 | 0447 |
| N5120U | C525 | 0676 |
| N5120U | C52A | 0072 |
| N5120U | C52A | 0239 |
| N5120U | C52A | 0383 |
| N5120U | C52B | 0305 |
| N5120U | C560 | 0449 |
| N5120U | C650 | 7049 |
| N5120U | C650 | 7071 |
| N5120U | C680 | 0100 |
| N5120U | C750 | 0058 |
| N5120U | C750 | 0232 |
| N5121N | C550 | 550-0824 |
| N5121N | C650 | 7050 |
| N5121P | PRM1 | RB-11 |
| N5122X | C525 | 0162 |
| N5122X | C525 | 0203 |
| N5122X | C750 | 0011 |
| N5124F | C525 | 0382 |
| N5124F | C525 | 0406 |
| N5124F | C525 | 0623 |
| N5124F | C52A | 0189 |
| N5124F | C52B | 0046 |
| N5124F | C52B | 0320 |
| N5124F | C560 | 0392 |
| N5124F | C560 | 0451 |
| N5124F | C680 | 0180 |
| N5124F | C750 | 0086 |
| N5125J | C525 | 0405 |
| N5125J | C525 | 0542 |
| N5125J | C52A | 0062 |
| N5125J | C52A | 0074 |
| N5125J | C52B | 0164 |
| N5125J | C550 | 550-1130 |
| N5125J | C560 | 0479 |
| N5125J | C560 | 0484 |
| N5125J | C56X | 5092 |
| N5125J | C750 | 0020 |
| N5125J | C750 | 0024 |
| N5125J | C750 | 0291 |
| N5129U | BE40 | RK-329 |
| N5130J | C525 | 0187 |
| N5130J | C525 | 0365 |
| N5130J | C525 | 0391 |
| N5130J | C52A | 0120 |
| N5130J | C52A | 0420 |
| N5130J | C560 | 0452 |
| N5130J | C56X | 5690 |
| N5130J | C680 | 0037 |
| N5130J | C680 | 0183 |
| N5130J | C750 | 0088 |
| N5131M | C750 | 0021 |
| N5132D | PRM1 | RB-32 |
| N5132T | C525 | 0155 |
| N5132T | C525 | 0193 |
| N5132T | C525 | 0394 |
| N5132T | C52A | 0029 |
| N5132T | C52A | 0086 |
| N5132T | C52A | 0148 |
| N5132T | C52A | 0323 |
| N5132T | C550 | 550-1098 |
| N5132T | C560 | 0453 |
| N5132T | C680 | 0271 |
| N5132T | C750 | 0090 |
| N5132T | C750 | 0273 |
| N5133E | C525 | 0204 |
| N5133K | C500 | 299 |
| N5135A | C525 | 0196 |
| N5135A | C525 | 0399 |
| N5135A | C525 | 0451 |
| N5135A | C52A | 0063 |
| N5135A | C52A | 0122 |
| N5135A | C550 | 550-0876 |
| N5135A | C56X | 5095 |
| N5135A | C56X | 5587 |
| N5135A | C56X | 5658 |
| N5135A | C680 | 0010 |
| N5135A | C680 | 0187 |
| N5135A | C680 | 0226 |
| N5135A | C750 | 0048 |
| N5135K | C525 | 0089 |
| N5135K | C525 | 0378 |
| N5135K | C52A | 0023 |
| N5135K | C52A | 0080 |
| N5135K | C52B | 0105 |
| N5135K | C550 | 550-0801 |
| N5135K | C550 | 550-0878 |
| N5135K | C560 | 0454 |
| N5135K | C56X | 5595 |
| N5135K | C680 | 0011 |
| N5135K | C680 | 0186 |
| N5135K | C680 | 0225 |
| N5135R | C550 | 550-0802 |
| N5136J | C525 | 0090 |
| N5136J | C525 | 0206 |
| N5136J | C525 | 0316 |
| N5136J | C525 | 0346 |
| N5136J | C525 | 0385 |
| N5136J | C525 | 0443 |
| N5136J | C52A | 0065 |
| N5136J | C52A | 0108 |
| N5136J | C52A | 0230 |
| N5136J | C52A | 0424 |
| N5136J | C52A | 0456 |
| N5136J | C56X | 5697 |
| N5136J | C680 | 0013 |
| N5136J | C680 | 0095 |
| N5136J | C680 | 0191 |
| N5136T | BE40 | RK-336 |
| N5138F | C525 | 0091 |
| N5138F | C525 | 0163 |
| N5138F | C525 | 0195 |
| N5138J | C52A | 0188 |
| N5139W | LJ35 | 396 |
| N5141F | C525 | 0436 |
| N5141F | C525 | 0624 |
| N5141F | C52A | 0067 |
| N5141F | C52A | 0136 |
| N5141F | C52A | 0190 |
| N5141F | C52A | 0412 |
| N5141F | C560 | 0288 |
| N5141F | C56X | 5006 |
| N5141F | C56X | 5111 |
| N5141F | C56X | 5535 |
| N5141F | C56X | 5612 |
| N5141F | C650 | 7072 |
| N5141F | C650 | 7099 |
| N5141F | C750 | 0275 |
| N5144 | C650 | 7012 |
| **N5144** | **C750** | **0017** |
| N5145J | C52B | 0109 |
| N5145P | C525 | 0191 |
| N5145P | C525 | 0318 |
| N5145P | C525 | 0347 |
| N5145P | C525 | 0370 |
| N5145P | C525 | 0404 |
| N5145P | C52B | 0030 |
| N5145P | C52B | 0153 |
| N5145P | C550 | 550-0831 |
| N5145P | C550 | 550-0833 |
| N5145P | C560 | 0290 |
| N5145P | C56X | 5782 |
| N5145P | C680 | 0273 |
| N5145V | C525 | 0278 |
| N5145V | C52B | 0156 |
| N5145V | C560 | 0517 |
| N5145V | C560 | 0553 |
| N5145V | C56X | 5252 |
| N5145V | C56X | 5343 |
| N5145V | C56X | 5586 |
| N5145V | C56X | 5787 |
| N5145V | C680 | 0281 |
| N5145V | C750 | 0128 |
| N5147B | C52A | 0329 |
| N5147B | C550 | 550-0979 |
| N5147B | C56X | 5151 |
| N5147B | C56X | 6041 |
| N5147B | C680 | 0055 |
| N5147B | C680 | 0229 |
| N5147B | C750 | 0104 |
| N5147B | C750 | 0179 |
| N5147Y | PRM1 | RB-47 |
| N5148B | C525 | 0165 |
| N5148B | C525 | 0194 |
| N5148B | C525 | 0384 |
| N5148B | C525 | 0652 |
| N5148B | C52A | 0106 |
| N5148B | C52A | 0331 |
| N5148B | C52A | 0397 |
| N5148B | C550 | 550-0832 |
| N5148B | C550 | 550-1072 |
| N5148B | C550 | 550-1097 |
| N5148B | C560 | 0291 |
| N5148B | C650 | 7104 |
| N5148B | C680 | 0063 |
| N5148N | C525 | 0166 |
| N5148N | C525 | 0319 |
| N5148N | C52A | 0003 |
| N5148N | C52A | 0018 |
| N5148N | C52A | 0047 |
| N5148N | C52A | 0077 |
| N5148N | C52B | 0051 |
| N5148N | C560 | 0292 |
| N5148N | C560 | 0357 |
| N5148N | C56X | 5004 |
| N5148N | C56X | 5699 |
| N5151D | C525 | 0280 |
| N5151D | C525 | 0642 |
| N5151D | C52A | 0163 |
| N5151D | C52B | 0055 |
| N5151D | C52B | 0236 |
| N5151D | C560 | 0546 |
| N5151D | C560 | 0589 |
| N5151D | C560 | 0664 |
| N5151D | C56X | 5158 |
| N5151S | C525 | 0093 |
| N5151S | C525 | 0167 |
| N5151S | C525 | 0197 |
| N5151S | C560 | 0349 |
| N5152 | FA20 | 440 |
| N5152 | GLF2 | 22 |
| N5152X | C525 | 0648 |
| N5152X | C52A | 0199 |
| N5152X | C52A | 0394 |
| N5152X | C560 | 0492 |
| N5152X | C56X | 5537 |
| N5152X | C56X | 5593 |
| N5152X | C56X | 5639 |
| N5152X | C650 | 7119 |
| N5152X | C750 | 0146 |
| N5152X | C750 | 0178 |
| N5152X | C750 | 0207 |
| N5153J | C525 | 0346 |
| N5153K | C525 | 0095 |
| N5153K | C525 | 0169 |
| N5153K | C525 | 0199 |
| N5153K | C525 | 0330 |
| N5153K | C525 | 0449 |
| N5153K | C52A | 0221 |
| N5153K | C52A | 0345 |
| N5153K | C52A | 0389 |
| N5153K | C560 | 0351 |
| N5153K | C560 | 0481 |
| N5153K | C56X | 5102 |
| N5153K | C56X | 5581 |
| N5153K | C56X | 6025 |
| N5153K | C750 | 0049 |
| N5153X | C525 | 0096 |
| N5153X | C525 | 0170 |
| N5153X | C525 | 0208 |
| N5153X | C560 | 0352 |
| (N5153Z) | C525 | 0097 |
| N5153Z | C525 | 0171 |
| N5153Z | C525 | 0200 |
| N5153Z | C560 | 0356 |
| N5154J | C525 | 0281 |
| N5154J | C525 | 0314 |
| N5154J | C525 | 0646 |
| N5154J | C52A | 0228 |
| N5154J | C52A | 0395 |
| N5154J | C550 | 550-0926 |
| N5154J | C550 | 550-0990 |
| N5154J | C560 | 0552 |
| N5154J | C560 | 0554 |
| N5154J | C56X | 5253 |
| N5154J | C680 | 0266 |
| N5154J | C750 | 0214 |
| N5155G | C525 | 0612 |
| N5155G | C52A | 0425 |
| N5155G | C550 | 550-0907 |
| N5155G | C550 | 550-1009 |
| N5155G | C550 | 550-1051 |
| N5155G | C560 | 0555 |
| N5155G | C56X | 5156 |
| N5155G | C56X | 5649 |
| N5155G | C56X | 5766 |
| N5155G | C680 | 0035 |
| N5155G | C750 | 0131 |
| N5156B | C525 | 0172 |
| N5156B | C560 | 0361 |
| N5156D | C525 | 0098 |
| N5156D | C525 | 0201 |
| N5156D | C525 | 0335 |
| N5156D | C525 | 0360 |
| N5156D | C525 | 0389 |
| N5156D | C525 | 0408 |
| N5156D | C525 | 0450 |
| N5156D | C52A | 0076 |
| N5156D | C560 | 0482 |
| N5156D | C560 | 0651 |
| N5156D | C56X | 5547 |
| N5156D | C56X | 5761 |
| N5156D | C750 | 0050 |
| N5156D | C750 | 0301 |
| N5156V | C525 | 0099 |
| N5156V | C525 | 0205 |
| N5156V | C560 | 0393 |
| (N5157E) | C525 | 0101 |
| N5157E | C525 | 0174 |
| N5157E | C525 | 0210 |
| N5157E | C525 | 0467 |
| N5157E | C525 | 0554 |
| N5157E | C52A | 0070 |
| N5157E | C52A | 0313 |
| N5157E | C52A | 0361 |
| N5157E | C560 | 0354 |
| N5157E | C560 | 0460 |
| N5157E | C56X | 5115 |
| N5157E | C56X | 5515 |
| N5157E | C56X | 5798 |
| N5157E | C56X | 6051 |
| N5157E | C650 | 7101 |
| N5158B | PRM1 | RB-58 |
| N5158D | BE40 | RK-358 |
| N5159Y | GLF3 | 451 |
| N5161J | C525 | 0176 |
| N5161J | C525 | 0332 |
| N5161J | C525 | 0363 |
| N5161J | C525 | 0412 |
| N5161J | C525 | 0609 |
| N5161J | C525 | 0670 |
| N5161J | C52A | 0054 |
| N5161J | C52A | 0453 |
| N5161J | C560 | 0294 |
| N5161J | C560 | 0367 |
| N5161J | C560 | 0458 |
| N5161J | C560 | 0497 |
| N5161J | C560 | 0684 |
| N5161J | C56X | 5357 |
| N5161J | C56X | 5655 |
| N5161J | C56X | 5814 |
| N5161R | JSTR | 5161/43 |
| N5162W | C525 | 0209 |
| N5162W | C525 | 0388 |
| N5162W | C52A | 0017 |
| N5162W | C52A | 0078 |
| N5162W | C52A | 0198 |
| N5162W | C52A | 0396 |
| N5162W | C550 | 550-1075 |
| (N5162W) | C560 | 0295 |
| N5162W | C560 | 0459 |
| N5162W | C560 | 0661 |
| N5162W | C56X | 5609 |
| N5162W | C650 | 7096 |
| N5162W | C680 | 0246 |
| N5163C | C525 | 0177 |
| N5163C | C525 | 0324 |
| N5163C | C525 | 0397 |
| N5163C | C525 | 0526 |
| N5163C | C52A | 0055 |
| N5163C | C52A | 0118 |
| N5163C | C52A | 0431 |
| N5163C | C52B | 0249 |
| (N5163C) | C560 | 0296 |
| N5163C | C560 | 0358 |
| N5163C | C56X | 5538 |
| N5163C | C650 | 7087 |
| N5163C | C680 | 0075 |
| N5163C | C750 | 0065 |

| | | |
|---|---|---|
| N5163C | C750 | 0280 |
| N5163G | C56X | 5157 |
| N5163K | C525 | 0633 |
| N5163K | C52B | 0015 |
| N5163K | C52B | 0042 |
| N5163K | C52B | 0267 |
| N5163K | C52B | 0310 |
| N5163K | C56X | 5159 |
| N5163K | C680 | 0178 |
| N5163K | C750 | 0188 |
| N5165P | C52A | 0410 |
| N5165P | C550 | 550-0998 |
| N5165P | C550 | 550-1111 |
| N5165P | C550 | 550-1132 |
| N5165P | C560 | 0556 |
| N5165P | C56X | 5336 |
| N5165P | C56X | 5534 |
| N5165P | C750 | 0270 |
| N5165T | C525 | 0340 |
| N5165T | C525 | 0371 |
| N5165T | C525 | 0392 |
| N5165T | C52A | 0022 |
| N5165T | C52A | 0073 |
| N5165T | C52A | 0243 |
| N5165T | C52A | 0316 |
| N5165T | C52A | 0414 |
| N5165T | C52A | 0437 |
| N5165T | C560 | 0297 |
| N5165T | C56X | 5003 |
| N5165T | C56X | 5087 |
| N5165T | C56X | 5543 |
| N5165T | C56X | 5722 |
| N5165T | C750 | 0080 |
| N5166T | C52A | 0196 |
| N5166T | C52B | 0083 |
| N5166T | C550 | 550-0906 |
| N5166T | C550 | 550-1020 |
| N5166T | C560 | 0494 |
| N5166T | C560 | 0590 |
| N5166T | C560 | 0692 |
| N5166T | C56X | 5163 |
| N5166T | C56X | 5695 |
| N5166T | C680 | 0224 |
| N5166T | C750 | 0217 |
| N5166U | C525 | 0179 |
| N5166U | C525 | 0215 |
| N5166U | C550 | 550-1013 |
| N5166U | C560 | 0298 |
| N5166U | C560 | 0359 |
| N5166U | C56X | 5164 |
| N5166U | C56X | 5554 |
| N5166U | C680 | 0069 |
| N5166U | C750 | 0222 |
| N5168F | C525 | 0180 |
| N5168F | C525 | 0213 |
| N5168F | C560 | 0299 |
| N5168F | C560 | 0360 |
| N5168Y | C52A | 0380 |
| N5168Y | C52B | 0147 |
| N5168Y | C550 | 550-0958 |
| N5168Y | C550 | 550-0976 |
| N5168Y | C550 | 550-1022 |
| N5168Y | C56X | 5548 |
| N5168Y | C680 | 0054 |
| N5168Y | C750 | 0294 |
| N5172M | C525 | 0540 |
| N5172M | C52B | 0171 |
| N5172M | C550 | 550-0959 |
| N5172M | C550 | 550-0977 |
| N5172M | C550 | 550-1025 |
| N5172M | C560 | 0695 |
| N5172M | C650 | 7111 |
| N5172M | C680 | 0079 |
| N5172M | C680 | 0135 |
| N5172M | C750 | 0142 |
| N5173F | C56X | 5173 |
| N5174 | C650 | 7018 |
| N5174W | C52A | 0227 |
| N5174W | C52B | 0235 |
| N5174W | C52B | 0281 |
| N5174W | C550 | 550-0988 |
| N5174W | C550 | 550-1021 |
| N5174W | C560 | 0558 |
| N5174W | C560 | 0764 |
| N5174W | C650 | 7112 |
| N5174W | C680 | 0181 |
| N5174W | C750 | 0145 |
| N5180C | C52A | 0155 |
| N5180C | C52A | 0405 |
| N5180C | C52A | 0459 |
| N5180C | C550 | 550-1037 |
| N5180C | C550 | 550-1082 |
| N5180C | C550 | 550-1099 |
| N5180C | C550 | 550-1135 |
| N5180C | C560 | 0560 |
| N5180C | C560 | 0592 |
| N5180C | C56X | 5594 |
| N5180C | C680 | 0167 |
| N5180K | C525 | 0181 |
| N5180K | C525 | 0533 |
| N5180K | C52A | 0306 |
| N5180K | C52A | 0450 |
| N5180K | C52B | 0158 |
| N5180K | C52B | 0208 |
| N5180K | C52B | 0259 |
| N5180K | C550 | 550-1026 |
| N5180K | C560 | 0301 |
| N5180K | C560 | 0363 |
| N5180K | C560 | 0562 |
| N5180K | C560 | 0630 |
| N5180K | C56X | 5677 |
| N5181U | C52A | 0369 |
| N5181U | C52B | 0255 |
| N5181U | C550 | 550-0961 |
| N5181U | C550 | 550-1008 |
| N5181U | C550 | 550-1108 |
| N5181U | C560 | 0537 |
| N5181U | C56X | 5596 |
| N5181U | C56X | 5642 |
| N5181U | C750 | 0205 |
| N5183U | C525 | 0182 |
| N5183U | C525 | 0326 |
| N5183U | C525 | 0361 |
| N5183U | C525 | 0395 |
| N5183U | C525 | 0420 |
| N5183U | C525 | 0604 |
| N5183U | C52A | 0048 |
| N5183U | C52A | 0193 |
| N5183U | C560 | 0362 |
| N5183U | C560 | 0462 |
| N5183U | C56X | 5668 |
| N5183U | C650 | 7052 |
| N5183U | C750 | 0238 |
| N5183V | C525 | 0216 |
| N5183V | C525 | 0254 |
| N5183V | C525 | 0398 |
| N5183V | C525 | 0455 |
| N5183V | C52A | 0082 |
| N5183V | C52A | 0433 |
| N5183V | C52B | 0043 |
| N5183V | C560 | 0469 |
| N5183V | C56X | 5091 |
| N5183V | C56X | 5652 |
| (N5183V) | C650 | 7053 |
| N5183V | C650 | 7074 |
| N5183V | C680 | 0029 |
| N5183V | C750 | 0287 |
| **N5184U** | **EA40** | **SE-400-001** |
| N5185J | C525 | 0183 |
| N5185J | C525 | 0333 |
| N5185J | C525 | 0368 |
| N5185J | C525 | 0381 |
| N5185J | C525 | 0413 |
| N5185J | C525 | 0456 |
| N5185J | C52A | 0085 |
| N5185J | C52B | 0180 |
| N5185J | C52B | 0229 |
| N5185J | C550 | 550-0837 |
| N5185J | C56X | 5633 |
| N5185J | C650 | 7054 |
| N5185J | C680 | 0247 |
| N5185V | C525 | 0184 |
| N5185V | C525 | 0345 |
| N5185V | C525 | 0352 |
| N5185V | C525 | 0437 |
| N5185V | C525 | 0460 |
| N5185V | C52B | 0143 |
| N5185V | C52B | 0327 |
| N5185V | C560 | 0461 |
| N5185V | C560 | 0779 |
| N5185V | C56X | 5105 |
| N5185V | C650 | 7055 |
| N5187B | C525 | 0185 |
| N5187Z | C525 | 0442 |
| N5188A | C525 | 0379 |
| N5188A | C525 | 0425 |
| N5188A | C525 | 0458 |
| N5188A | C525 | 0605 |
| N5188A | C52A | 0320 |
| N5188A | C52B | 0213 |
| N5188A | C550 | 550-0854 |
| N5188A | C560 | 0471 |
| **N5188A** | **C560** | **0686** |
| **N5188A** | **C560** | **0805** |
| N5188A | C650 | 7106 |
| N5188N | C525 | 0239 |
| N5188N | C525 | 0546 |
| N5188N | C52A | 0308 |
| N5188N | C52B | 0103 |
| N5188N | C52B | 0176 |
| N5188N | C56X | 5167 |
| N5188N | C680 | 0019 |
| N5188N | C680 | 0121 |
| N5188N | C750 | 0186 |
| N5188W | C52A | 0147 |
| "N5188W" | C52A | 0204 |
| "N5188W" | C52B | 0027 |
| "N5188W" | C56X | 5640 |
| N5188W | C680 | 0214 |
| N5192E | C52B | 0104 |
| N5192E | C550 | 550-0997 |
| N5192E | C560 | 0559 |
| N5192E | C56X | 5667 |
| N5192E | C56X | 5727 |
| N5192E | C56X | 6048 |
| N5192E | C650 | 7113 |
| N5192E | C750 | 0194 |
| N5192E | C750 | 0219 |
| N5192U | C52A | 0380 |
| N5194B | C52A | 0240 |
| N5194B | C52B | 0269 |
| N5194B | C52B | 0311 |
| N5194B | C550 | 550-0874 |
| N5194B | C550 | 550-1000 |
| N5194B | C56X | 5256 |
| N5194B | C56X | 5526 |
| N5194B | C56X | 5572 |
| N5194B | C650 | 7114 |
| N5194B | C680 | 0182 |
| N5194J | C525 | 0270 |
| N5194J | C52A | 0010 |
| N5194J | C52A | 0027 |
| N5194J | C52A | 0053 |
| N5194J | C52B | 0125 |
| N5194J | C52B | 0233 |
| N5194J | C560 | 0368 |
| N5194J | C56X | 5064 |
| N5194J | C56X | 5320 |
| N5194J | C680 | 0254 |
| N5194J | C750 | 0242 |
| N5196U | C525 | 0634 |
| N5196U | C560 | 0806 |
| N5196U | C56X | 5226 |
| N5196U | C56X | 5257 |
| N5196U | C56X | 5322 |
| N5196U | C56X | 5565 |
| N5196U | C750 | 0075 |
| N5196U | C750 | 0139 |
| N5197A | C525 | 0219 |
| N5197A | C525 | 0260 |
| N5197A | C525 | 0426 |
| N5197A | C525 | 0462 |
| N5197A | C52A | 0356 |
| N5197A | C52B | 0090 |
| N5197A | C52B | 0189 |
| N5197A | C52B | 0280 |
| N5197A | C560 | 0401 |
| N5197A | C560 | 0622 |
| N5197A | C56X | 5062 |
| N5197A | C56X | 5119 |
| N5197A | C56X | 5369 |
| N5197A | C56X | 5568 |
| N5197M | C52A | 0363 |
| N5197M | C560 | 0561 |
| N5197M | C56X | 5227 |
| N5197M | C56X | 5557 |
| N5197M | C56X | 5590 |
| N5197M | C56X | 5626 |
| N5197M | C680 | 0202 |
| N5197M | C680 | 0268 |
| N5197M | C750 | 0076 |
| N5197M | C750 | 0204 |
| N5197M | C750 | 0237 |
| N5197M | C750 | 0241 |
| N5200 | C560 | 0369 |
| **N5200** | **F2TH** | **90** |
| N5200R | C525 | 0144 |
| N5200R | C525 | 0441 |
| N5200R | C525 | 0479 |
| N5200R | C525 | 0669 |
| N5200R | C52A | 0434 |
| N5200R | C560 | 0665 |
| N5200R | C56X | 5007 |
| N5200R | C56X | 5061 |
| N5200R | C680 | 0091 |
| N5200R | C750 | 0272 |
| N5200U | C525 | 0369 |
| N5200U | C525 | 0463 |
| N5200U | C525 | 0487 |
| N5200U | C525 | 0543 |
| N5200U | C52B | 0054 |
| N5200U | C560 | 0402 |
| N5200U | C56X | 5063 |
| N5200U | C56X | 5135 |
| N5200U | C56X | 6006 |
| N5200U | C680 | 0041 |
| N5200Z | C525 | 0439 |
| N5200Z | C525 | 0466 |
| N5200Z | C525 | 0499 |
| N5200Z | C52A | 0344 |
| N5200Z | C560 | 0814 |
| N5200Z | C56X | 5110 |
| N5200Z | C56X | 5355 |
| N5200Z | C56X | 5792 |
| N5200Z | C680 | 0021 |
| N5200Z | C680 | 0096 |
| N5200Z | C680 | 0179 |
| N5201J | C525 | 0267 |
| N5201J | C525 | 0423 |
| N5201J | C525 | 0498 |
| N5201J | C52B | 0025 |
| N5201J | C52B | 0160 |
| N5201J | C52B | 0215 |
| N5201J | C52B | 0274 |
| N5201J | C560 | 0403 |
| N5201J | C56X | 5060 |
| N5201J | C56X | 5123 |
| N5201J | C56X | 5541 |
| N5201J | C56X | 5617 |
| N5201J | C680 | 0278 |
| N5201M | C525 | 0116 |
| N5201M | C525 | 0473 |
| N5201M | C525 | 0639 |
| N5201M | C525 | 0695 |
| N5201M | C52A | 0013 |
| N5201M | C52B | 0218 |
| N5201M | C550 | 550-1083 |
| N5201M | C550 | 550-1133 |
| N5201M | C560 | 0404 |
| N5201M | C56X | 5026 |
| N5201M | C56X | 5069 |
| N5201M | C680 | 0251 |
| N5201M | C750 | 0266 |
| N5202D | C525 | 0217 |
| N5202D | C525 | 0427 |
| N5202D | C525 | 0524 |
| N5202D | C52A | 0056 |
| N5202D | C52B | 0195 |
| N5202D | C550 | 550-1112 |
| N5202D | C560 | 0405 |
| N5202D | C56X | 5027 |
| N5202D | C56X | 5096 |
| N5202D | C56X | 5669 |
| N5202D | C56X | 6038 |
| N5202D | C650 | 0241 |
| N5202D | C680 | 0085 |
| N5203B | C525 | 0417 |
| N5203J | C525 | 0117 |
| N5203J | C525 | 0258 |
| N5203J | C525 | 0428 |
| N5203J | C525 | 0493 |
| N5203J | C560 | 0678 |
| N5203J | C56X | 5028 |
| N5203J | C56X | 5078 |
| N5203J | C56X | 5809 |
| N5203J | C650 | 7077 |
| N5203J | C680 | 0052 |
| N5203J | C680 | 0282 |
| N5203J | C750 | 0278 |
| N5203S | C525 | 0118 |
| N5203S | C525 | 0221 |
| N5203S | C525 | 0238 |

N5203S C52A 0026
N5203S C52A 0123
N5203S C52A 0200
N5203S C52B 0124
N5203S C52B 0178
N5203S C550 550-1100
N5203S C560 0406
N5203S C56X 5029
N5203S C56X 5093
N5203S C680 0045
N5203S C680 0067
N5203S C680 0196
N5203S C680 0265
N5204B C525 0134
N5204D C525 0103
N5204D C525 0481
N5204D C52A 0006
N5204D C52A 0031
N5204D C52A 0128
N5204D C560 0407
**N5204D C560 0682**
N5204D C560 0810
N5204D C56X 5008
N5204D C56X 5065
N5204D C56X 5780
N5204D C680 0151
N5206T C525 0631
N5206T C52B 0334
N5206T C550 550-1041
N5206T C560 0602
N5206T C56X 5614
N5206T C680 0255
N5206T C750 0154
N5207A C525 0104
N5207A C525 0135
N5207A C525 0461
N5207A C525 0684
N5207A C52A 0016
N5207A C52A 0142
N5207A C52B 0004
N5207A C52B 0076
N5207A C52B 0115
N5207A C560 0408
N5207A C560 0438
N5207A C560 0617
N5207A C560 0773
N5207A C56X 5070
N5207A C56X 5124
N5207A C680 0060
N5207V C52B 0295
N5207V C550 550-0910
N5207V C560 0577
N5207V C560 0687
N5207V C56X 5672
N5207V C680 0195
N5208F C52A 0063
N5209E C525 0295
N5209E C560 0532
N5211A C525 0106
N5211A C525 0137
N5211A C525 0446
N5211A C525 0486
N5211A C525 0531
N5211A C52A 0127
N5211A C52A 0231
N5211A C52A 0311
N5211A C52B 0120
N5211A C52B 0179
N5211A C52B 0227
N5211A C560 0410
N5211A C560 0565
N5211A C56X 5084
N5211A C56X 6015
N5211F C525 0107
N5211F C525 0138
N5211F C525 0225
N5211F C525 0364
N5211F C525 0484
N5211F C52A 0034
N5211F C52A 0132
N5211F C52A 0217
N5211F C52A 0377
N5211F C52A 0411
N5211F C56X 5122
N5211F C56X 5571
N5211Q C525 0108
N5211Q C525 0223
N5211Q C525 0353
N5211Q C525 0453
N5211Q C525 0482
N5211Q C525 0527
N5211Q C525 0547
N5211Q C52A 0135
**N5211Q C52C 0005**
N5211Q C550 550-1122
N5211Q C560 0775
N5211Q C56X 5033
N5211Q C56X 5120
N5211Q C56X 5662
N5211Q C56X 5789
N5212M C525 0409
N5212M C525 0511
N5212M C52B 0117
N5212M C550 550-0962
N5212M C550 550-1006
N5212M C550 550-1109
N5212M C550 550-1123
N5212M C560 0662
N5212M C650 7098
N5212M C680 0174
N5212M C680 0259
N5213K C52B 0277
N5213S C525 0110
N5213S C525 0356
N5213S C52A 0007
N5213S C52A 0305
N5213S C52B 0102
N5213S C56X 5035
N5213S C56X 5567
N5213S C650 7076
N5214J C525 0112
N5214J C525 0226
N5214J C525 0245
N5214J C525 0357
N5214J C52A 0061
N5214J C52A 0378
N5214J C52B 0091
N5214J C52B 0254
N5214J C550 550-0804
N5214J C56X 5037
N5214J C56X 5129
N5214J C680 0059
N5214J C750 0243
N5214K C525 0113
N5214K C525 0227
N5214K C525 0641
N5214K C525 0693
N5214K C52A 0117
N5214K C52A 0210
N5214K C52B 0095
N5214K C52B 0234
N5214K C52B 0276
N5214K C550 550-0805
N5214K C56X 5038
N5214K C56X 5073
N5214K C56X 5125
N5214K C750 0246
N5214L C525 0114
N5214L C525 0249
N5214L C525 0362
N5214L C525 0555
N5214L C52A 0045
N5214L C52B 0072
N5214L C52B 0192
N5214L C550 550-0822
N5214L C550 550-1102
N5214L C560 0374
N5214L C560 0639
N5214L C560 0657
N5214L C560 0668
N5214L C560 0798
N5214L C56X 5040
N5214L C56X 5118
N5214L C680 0064
N5216A C525 0228
N5216A C525 0342
N5216A C525 0477
N5216A C525 0548
N5216A C52A 0024
N5216A C52A 0093
N5216A C52B 0097
N5216A C52B 0104
N5216A C52B 0296
N5216A C550 550-0808
N5216A C560 0669
N5216A C560 0698
N5216A C560 0777
N5216A C56X 5013
N5216A C56X 5101
N5216A C56X 5366
N5216A C650 7057
N5218R C525 0149
N5218R C525 0229
N5218R C525 0488
N5218R C52A 0103
N5218R C52A 0166
N5218R C52A 0384
N5218R C52B 0266
N5218R C52B 0309
N5218R C550 550-1113
N5218R C560 0755
N5218R C56X 5043
N5218R C56X 5103
N5218R C650 7059
N5218T C525 0230
N5218T C525 0489
N5218T C525 0607
N5218T C52A 0028
N5218T C52A 0181
N5218T C52B 0106
N5218T C52B 0108
N5218T C550 550-0810
N5218T C560 0690
N5218T C56X 5044
N5218T C56X 5079
N5218T C56X 6034
N5218T C650 7060
N5218T C680 0162
N5219T C525 0269
N5220J C500 220
N5221Y C52A 0037
N5221Y C52A 0095
N5221Y C52B 0024
N5221Y C52B 0045
N5221Y C52B 0074
N5221Y C550 550-0811
N5221Y C56X 5014
N5221Y C56X 5045
N5221Y C56X 5106
N5221Y C56X 5681
N5221Y C56X 5742
N5221Y C650 7061
N5221Y C680 0245
N5221Y C750 0283
N5223D C525 0231
N5223D C525 0433
N5223D C52A 0096
N5223D C560 0776
N5223D C56X 5015
N5223D C56X 5046
N5223D C56X 5104
N5223D C56X 5790
N5223D C680 0066
N5223D C680 0114
N5223D C680 0276
N5223D C750 0003
N5223D C750 0225
N5223F C510 0135
N5223J C500 188
N5223K C525 0498
N5223P C525 0123
(N5223P) C525 0252
N5223P C525 0253
N5223P C525 0414
N5223P C525 0496
N5223P C52A 0039
N5223P C52A 0099
N5223P C52A 0229
N5223P C52A 0326
N5223P C550 550-0812
N5223P C56X 5047
N5223P C56X 5114
N5223P C56X 5342
N5223P C56X 5646
N5223P C680 0031
N5223P C680 0153
N5223P C680 0201
N5223P C750 0004
N5223X C550 550-1032
N5223X C550 550-1115
N5223X C560 0778
N5223X C56X 5174
N5223X C56X 5645
N5223X C56X 6021
N5223X C650 7102
N5223X C750 0119
N5223X C750 0185
N5223X C750 0218
N5223Y C525 0232
N5223Y C525 0366
N5223Y C525 0480
N5223Y C52A 0030
N5223Y C52A 0098
N5223Y C52B 0261
N5223Y C550 550-1114
(N5223Y) C560 0302
N5223Y C56X 5049
N5223Y C56X 5121
N5223Y C56X 5504
N5223Y C56X 6033
N5223Y C750 0009
**N5225G FA20 181**
N5225J C500 225
N5225K C525 0339
N5225K C525 0354
N5225K C525 0375
N5225K C525 0454
N5225K C525 0508
N5225K C52A 0407
N5225K C52A 0415
N5225K C550 550-0816
N5225K C560 0303
N5225K C56X 5050
N5225K C56X 5132
N5225K C56X 5637
N5225K C680 0116
N5225K C750 0010
N5226B C525 0434
N5226B C525 0492
N5226B C52A 0212
N5226B C52A 0327
N5226B C52B 0063
N5226B C52B 0241
N5226B C52B 0289
N5226B C52B 0318
N5226B C560 0304
N5226B C560 0411
N5226B C560 0442
N5226B C56X 5051
N5226B C56X 5097
N5226B C56X 5563
N5226B C680 0157
N5226J C500 226
N5227G C52B 0006
N5227G C52B 0242
N5227G C550 550-0984
N5227G C550 550-1131
N5227G C56X 5709
N5227G C680 0261
N5228J C52B 0173
N5228J C550 550-0969
N5228J C550 550-1010
N5228J C560 0632
N5228J C56X 5597
N5228J C56X 5651
N5228J C56X 5822
N5228J C750 0237
N5228Z C525 0380
N5228Z C525 0643
N5228Z C52A 0139
N5228Z C52A 0324
N5228Z C52B 0013
N5228Z C52B 0209
N5228Z C52B 0273
N5228Z C560 0305
N5228Z C560 0412
N5228Z C560 0443
N5228Z C56X 5052
N5228Z C56X 5128
N5230J C500 230
(N5231J) C500 231
N5231S C525 0383
N5231S C525 0424
N5231S C52A 0330
N5231S C52B 0069
N5231S C550 550-1019
N5231S C550 550-1047
N5231S C560 0306
N5231S C560 0384
N5231S C560 0433
N5231S C56X 5053
N5231S C56X 5552

N5231S C680 0184
N5231S C680 0250
N5232J C500 232
N5233J C500 233
N5233J C525 0440
N5233J C525 0478
N5233J C52A 0116
N5233J C550 550-1126
N5233J C550 660
N5233J C560 0307
N5233J C560 0413
N5233J C560 0419
N5233J C56X 5054
N5233J C56X 5117
N5233J C56X 5765
N5233J C56X 6019
N5233J C680 0004
N5233J C680 0043
N5233J C680 0124
N5233P C52A 0153
(N5234J) C500 234
N5235G C525 0233
N5235G C525 0259
N5235G C525 0497
N5235G C52A 0005
N5235G C52A 0009
N5235G C52A 0038
N5235G C52A 0400
N5235G C52A 0444
N5235G C560 0308
N5235G C560 0365
N5235G C560 0414
N5235G C56X 5058
N5235G C56X 5358
N5235G C680 0107
N5235G C680 0156
N5235J C500 235
N5236J C500 236
N5236L C525 0625
N5236L C52A 0233
N5236L C560 0603
N5236L C56X 5171
N5236L C56X 5719
(N5237J) C500 237
(N5238J) C500 238
(N5239J) C500 239
N5239J C52A 0307
N5239J C52B 0007
N5239J C52B 0057
N5239J C52B 0181
N5239J C550 550-0971
N5239J C550 550-1054
N5239J C560 0601
N5240J C500 240
N5241J C500 241
N5241R C525 0635
N5241R C560 0564
N5241R C56X 5664
N5241R C56X 5758
N5241R C56X 6030
N5241R C680 0024
N5241R C680 0040
N5241R C750 0195
N5241Z C525 0337
N5241Z C525 0377
N5241Z C525 0673
N5241Z C52A 0044
N5241Z C52A 0205
N5241Z C52A 0382
N5241Z C52B 0292
N5241Z C560 0310
N5241Z C560 0691
N5241Z C560 0769
N5241Z C750 0013
N5241Z C750 0138
N5242J C500 242
N5243J C500 243
N5243K C52A 0165
N5243K C52B 0033
N5243K C52B 0182
N5243K C52B 0219
N5243K C550 550-0970
N5243K C560 0588
N5243K C560 0670
N5244F C525 0343
N5244F C525 0435
N5244F C525 0491
N5244F C525 0530
N5244F C525 0661
N5244F C52B 0036
N5244F C52B 0247
(N5244F) C560 0311
N5244F C560 0772
N5244F C56X 5021
N5244F C56X 5098
N5244F C56X 5623
N5244F C750 0014
N5244F C750 0303
(N5244J) C500 244
N5244W C525 0663
N5244W C52A 0213
N5244W C52B 0116
N5244W C52B 0264
N5244W C550 550-0993
N5244W C560 0571
N5244W C56X 5603
N5245D C52A 0232
N5245D C52A 0300
N5245D C56X 5266
N5245D C56X 5352
N5245D C56X 5625
N5245D C680 0189
N5245D C750 0159
N5245J C500 245
N5245L C52A 0451
N5245L C560 0680
N5245L C560 0760
N5245L C750 0161
N5245L C750 0199
N5245L C750 0286
N5245U C525 0682
N5245U C52B 0250
N5245U C550 550-0973
N5245U C550 550-1057
N5245U C560 0606
N5245U C560 0673
N5245U C560 0765
N5245U C56X 5576
N5245U C680 0020
N5245U C680 0093
(N5246J) C500 246
N5246Z C525 0140
N5246Z C525 0235
N5246Z C525 0351
N5246Z C525 0495
N5246Z C52A 0036
N5246Z C560 0313
N5246Z C56X 5020
N5246Z C56X 5116
N5246Z C56X 5267
N5246Z C56X 5619
N5246Z C56X 5748
N5246Z C680 0241
N5246Z C750 0236
(N5247J) C500 247
N5247U C52A 0186
N5247U C52A 0219
N5247U C52B 0231
N5247U C550 550-1005
N5247U C560 0767
N5247U C560 0803
N5247U C56X 5660
N5247U C680 0289
N5247U C750 0211
N5248B C560 0688
(N5248J) C500 248
N5248V C525 0602
N5248V C52A 0408
N5248V C560 0648
N5248V C560 0704
N5248V C56X 6046
N5248V C680 0017
N5248V C750 0169
N5249J C500 249
N5250E C525 0141
N5250E C525 0415
N5250E C525 0483
N5250E C525 0557
N5250E C525 0678
N5250E C52A 0032
N5250E C52B 0216
N5250E C560 0314
N5250E C56X 5018
(N5250E) C56X 5134
N5250E C56X 5353
N5250E C56X 5703
N5250E C680 0084
(N5250J) C500 250
N5250K C560 0264
(N5250K) C560 0315
N5250P C52B 0060
N5250P C52B 0169
N5250P C52B 0224
N5250P C560 0598
N5250P C56X 6032
N5250P C680 0115
**N5251F C510 0294**
N5251J C500 251
(N5251Y) C560 0316
N5252 C52A 0002
N5252C C550 661
N5252J C500 252
N5253A C500 304
N5253A GLF2 222
N5253A HS25 256061
N5253E C500 304
N5253G C560 0672
N5253J C500 253
N5253S C550 550-1015
N5253S C550 550-1048
N5253S C56X 5579
N5253S C56X 5707
N5253S C56X 6004
N5253S C750 0163
N5254J C500 254
N5254Y C550 550-1024
N5254Y C560 0585
N5254Y C560 0634
N5254Y C56X 5527
N5254Y C56X 5710
**N5254Y C56X 6062**
N5254Y C680 0072
N5255J C500 255
N5256Z C56X 5683
N5257C C560 0575
N5257C C560 0605
N5257C C560 0635
N5257C C560 0785
N5257C C56X 5653
N5257C C680 0143
N5257C C680 0262
N5257C C750 0247
N5257J C500 257
N5257V C52A 0185
N5257V C52A 0436
N5257V C52B 0119
N5257V C560 0624
N5257V C680 0050
N5257V C680 0193
N5257V C750 0165
(N5258J) C500 258
N5259J C500 259
N5259Y C525 0065
N5259Y C52A 0236
N5259Y C52B 0093
N5259Y C550 550-1018
N5259Y C560 0579
N5259Y C560 0788
N5259Y C56X 5685
N5259Y C56X 5788
(N5260J) C500 260
N5260M C52A 0303
N5260M C560 0593
N5260M C560 0627
N5260M C56X 5723
N5260M C680 0046
N5260M C680 0119
N5260U C550 550-0982
N5260U C560 0612
N5260U C560 0646
N5260U C56X 5725
N5260U C56X 5785
N5260U C680 0034
N5260Y C52A 0350
N5260Y C52B 0201
N5260Y C52B 0308
N5260Y C550 550-0934
N5260Y C560 0364
N5260Y C560 0650
N5260Y C680 0026
N5260Y C750 0103
N5260Y C750 0260
N5261J C500 261
N5261R C525 0537
N5261R C52B 0149
N5261R C560 0318
N5261R C56X 5578
N5261R C56X 5629
N5261R C56X 6042
**N5262 CL30 20122**
N5262B C52B 0152
N5262B C52B 0193
N5262B C52B 0265
N5262B C560 0320
N5262B C560 0370
N5262J C500 262
N5262W C52A 0169
N5262W C52B 0207
N5262W C52B 0258
N5262W C560 0321
N5262W C560 0570
N5262W C56X 5589
N5262W C56X 5632
N5262W C750 0268
N5262X C52A 0347
N5262X C52B 0197
N5262X C550 550-0933
N5262X C550 550-1125
N5262X C560 0322
N5262X C560 0371
N5262X C56X 5529
N5262X C750 0226
**N5262Z C56X 6059**
N5262Z C650 7062
N5262Z C750 0265
**N5263 C560 0435**
N5263D C525 0689
N5263D C550 550-1093
N5263D C650 7066
N5263D C650 7117
N5263D C680 0094
N5263D C680 0169
N5263S C52B 0064
N5263S C550 550-0940
N5263S C560 0638
N5263S C56X 5679
N5263S C56X 5774
(N5263S) C650 7067
N5263S C750 0005
N5263U C525 0507
N5263U C52A 0237
N5263U C52A 0402
N5263U C52B 0113
N5263U C56X 5724
N5263U C750 0006
N5263U C750 0016
N5264A C550 550-0935
N5264A C560 0377
N5264A C56X 5525
N5264A C56X 5598
N5264A C56X 5728
N5264A C56X 5793
N5264A C680 0279
N5264A C750 0111
(N5264E) C525 0119
N5264E C550 550-0948
N5264E C56X 5620
N5264E C56X 5691
N5264E C680 0028
N5264E C750 0295
N5264J C500 264
N5264M C525 0120
N5264M C550 550-0908
N5264M C560 0660
N5264M C56X 5784
N5264N C525 0627
N5264N C52A 0224
N5264N C560 0578
N5264N C560 0643
N5264N C56X 5729
N5264N C56X 5823
N5264N C750 0258
N5264S C525 0121
N5264S C56X 5654
N5264S C680 0027
N5264S C680 0073
N5264S C680 0231
N5264S C680 0285
N5264U C525 0122
N5264U C52B 0088
N5264U C550 550-1101
N5264U C56X 5701

| | | |
|---|---|---|
| **N5264U** | **C56X** | **6055** |
| N5264U | C650 | 7118 |
| N5264U | C680 | 0006 |
| N5264U | C680 | 0228 |
| N5265B | C52A | 0421 |
| N5265B | C52A | 0447 |
| N5265B | C550 | 550-1087 |
| N5265B | C560 | 0336 |
| N5265B | C560 | 0681 |
| N5265B | C56X | 5613 |
| N5265B | C56X | 5756 |
| N5265J | C500 | 265 |
| N5265N | C52A | 0418 |
| N5265N | C550 | 550-0916 |
| N5265N | C560 | 0337 |
| N5265N | C560 | 0653 |
| N5265N | C56X | 5138 |
| N5265N | C56X | 5676 |
| N5266F | C525 | 0659 |
| N5266F | C525 | 0681 |
| N5266F | C52A | 0226 |
| N5266F | C52B | 0246 |
| N5266F | C560 | 0663 |
| N5266F | C56X | 5615 |
| N5266F | C56X | 5675 |
| N5266F | C750 | 0008 |
| N5266F | C750 | 0118 |
| N5266J | C500 | 266 |
| N5267D | C525 | 0651 |
| N5267D | C560 | 0535 |
| N5267D | C56X | 5786 |
| N5267D | C680 | 0274 |
| N5267G | C525 | 0662 |
| N5267G | C52A | 0310 |
| N5267G | C52A | 0461 |
| N5267G | C550 | 550-1049 |
| N5267G | C560 | 0580 |
| N5267G | C56X | 5524 |
| N5267G | C56X | 5819 |
| N5267G | C680 | 0047 |
| N5267G | C750 | 0191 |
| N5267G | C750 | 0267 |
| N5267J | C500 | 267 |
| N5267J | C550 | 550-0944 |
| N5267J | C56X | 5575 |
| N5267J | C56X | 5801 |
| N5267J | C680 | 0163 |
| N5267J | C680 | 0288 |
| N5267J | C750 | 0227 |
| N5267K | C52B | 0163 |
| N5267K | C550 | 550-1061 |
| N5267K | C56X | 5542 |
| N5267K | C56X | 5577 |
| N5267K | C56X | 5624 |
| N5267K | C650 | 7115 |
| N5267T | C52A | 0388 |
| N5267T | C52B | 0165 |
| N5267T | C52B | 0324 |
| N5267T | C560 | 0340 |
| N5267T | C560 | 0342 |
| N5267T | C560 | 0649 |
| N5267T | C56X | 5616 |
| N5268A | C52B | 0127 |
| N5268A | C560 | 0343 |
| N5268A | C560 | 0567 |
| N5268A | C560 | 0812 |
| N5268A | C56X | 5791 |
| N5268A | C680 | 0165 |
| N5268A | C750 | 0229 |
| N5268A | C750 | 0248 |
| N5268A | C750 | 0256 |
| N5268E | C550 | 550-1050 |
| N5268E | C550 | 550-1079 |
| N5268E | C560 | 0345 |
| N5268E | C560 | 0700 |
| N5268E | C56X | 5663 |
| N5268E | C56X | 5796 |
| N5268E | C680 | 0170 |
| N5268E | C680 | 0291 |
| N5268J | C500 | 268 |
| N5268M | C52A | 0387 |
| N5268M | C52B | 0161 |
| N5268M | C560 | 0344 |
| N5268M | C56X | 5544 |
| N5268M | C56X | 5601 |
| N5268M | C650 | 7116 |
| N5268M | C750 | 0297 |
| N5268V | C52A | 0318 |
| N5268V | C52A | 0457 |
| N5268V | C550 | 550-0952 |
| N5268V | C550 | 550-1063 |
| N5268V | C560 | 0347 |
| N5268V | C560 | 0532 |
| N5268V | C680 | 0161 |
| N5268V | C750 | 0239 |
| N5268V | C750 | 0253 |
| N5269A | C52B | 0062 |
| N5269A | C560 | 0346 |
| N5269A | C560 | 0388 |
| N5269A | C560 | 0645 |
| N5269A | C56X | 5520 |
| **N5269A** | **C56X** | **6061** |
| N5269A | C650 | 7109 |
| N5269A | C750 | 0245 |
| N5269J | C500 | 269 |
| N5269J | C52B | 0065 |
| N5269J | C550 | 550-0985 |
| N5269J | C56X | 5317 |
| N5269J | C56X | 5545 |
| N5269J | C56X | 5673 |
| N5269Z | C52B | 0068 |
| N5269Z | C560 | 0581 |
| N5269Z | C560 | 0609 |
| N5269Z | C56X | 5671 |
| N5269Z | C680 | 0206 |
| N5269Z | C680 | 0248 |
| N5269Z | C750 | 0228 |
| N5270E | C525 | 0675 |
| N5270E | C525 | 0688 |
| N5270E | C52A | 0157 |
| N5270E | C52A | 0373 |
| N5270E | C52B | 0005 |
| N5270E | C52B | 0098 |
| N5270E | C550 | 550-0989 |
| N5270E | C550 | 550-0999 |
| N5270E | C56X | 5532 |
| N5270J | C500 | 270 |
| N5270J | C52A | 0379 |
| N5270J | C52A | 0409 |
| N5270J | C52B | 0096 |
| N5270J | C550 | 550-0991 |
| N5270J | C550 | 550-1029 |
| N5270J | C560 | 0641 |
| N5270J | C56X | 5530 |
| N5270K | C525 | 0622 |
| N5270K | C52A | 0398 |
| N5270K | C560 | 0265 |
| N5270K | C560 | 0587 |
| N5270K | C560 | 0607 |
| N5270K | C560 | 0644 |
| N5270K | C680 | 0014 |
| N5270M | C52B | 0263 |
| "N5270M" | C560 | 0268 |
| N5270M | C56X | 5350 |
| **N5270M** | **C56X** | **6049** |
| N5270M | C680 | 0076 |
| N5270M | C680 | 0126 |
| N5270M | C750 | 0174 |
| N5270P | C52A | 0386 |
| N5270P | C52B | 0329 |
| N5270P | C550 | 550-0996 |
| N5270P | C56X | 5370 |
| N5271J | C500 | 271 |
| N5272J | C500 | 272 |
| N5273J | C500 | 273 |
| N5274G | C510 | 0255 |
| (N5274J) | C500 | 274 |
| N5274K | C510 | 0258 |
| N5274M | C510 | 0267 |
| N5274U | HS25 | 25068 |
| (N5275J) | C500 | 275 |
| (N5276J) | C500 | 276 |
| (N5277J) | C500 | 277 |
| (N5278J) | C500 | 278 |
| (N5279J) | C500 | 279 |
| (N5280J) | C500 | 280 |
| N5281J | C500 | 281 |
| (N5282J) | C500 | 282 |
| N5283J | C500 | 283 |
| (N5284J) | C500 | 284 |
| N5285J | C500 | 285 |
| N5286J | C500 | 286 |
| (N5287J) | C500 | 287 |
| (N5288J) | C500 | 288 |
| N5289J | C500 | 289 |
| (N5290J) | C500 | 290 |
| N5291J | C500 | 291 |
| N5292J | C500 | 292 |
| (N5293J) | C500 | 293 |
| N5294C | C550 | 662 |
| N5294J | C500 | 294 |
| N5295J | C500 | 295 |
| (N5296J) | C500 | 296 |
| N5296X | C52B | 0225 |
| N5296X | C550 | 550-1070 |
| N5296X | C550 | 550-1128 |
| N5296X | C560 | 0584 |
| N5296X | C560 | 0614 |
| N5296X | C56X | 5528 |
| N5296X | C56X | 5561 |
| N5296X | C680 | 0252 |
| N5297J | C500 | 297 |
| N5298J | C500 | 298 |
| N5299J | C500 | 299 |
| (N5300J) | C500 | 300 |
| N5301J | C500 | 067 |
| N5301J | C500 | 301 |
| N5302J | C500 | 302 |
| (N5303J) | C500 | 303 |
| N5304J | C500 | 304 |
| (N5305J) | C500 | 305 |
| N5306J | C500 | 306 |
| N5307J | C500 | 307 |
| (N5308J) | C500 | 308 |
| N5309J | C500 | 309 |
| (N5310J) | C500 | 310 |
| N5311J | C500 | 311 |
| N5312J | C500 | 312 |
| (N5313J) | C500 | 313 |
| N5314J | C500 | 314 |
| **N5314J** | **C550** | **663** |
| N5315J | C500 | 315 |
| N5315J | C550 | 664 |
| N5316J | C500 | 316 |
| N5318J | C500 | 318 |
| N5319 | CL64 | 5319 |
| N5319J | C500 | 319 |
| (N5320J) | C500 | 320 |
| N5321J | C500 | 321 |
| **N5322** | **FA50** | **322** |
| N5322J | C500 | 322 |
| N5323J | C500 | 323 |
| (N5324J) | C500 | 324 |
| (N5325J) | C500 | 325 |
| N5326J | C500 | 326 |
| N5327J | C500 | 327 |
| (N5328J) | C500 | 328 |
| N5329J | C500 | 329 |
| (N5330J) | C500 | 330 |
| (N5331J) | C500 | 331 |
| N5332J | C500 | 332 |
| (N5333J) | C500 | 333 |
| N5334J | C500 | 334 |
| N5335J | C500 | 335 |
| (N5336J) | C500 | 336 |
| N5337J | C500 | 337 |
| N5338J | C500 | 338 |
| (N5339J) | C500 | 339 |
| (N5340J) | C500 | 340 |
| (N5341J) | C500 | 341 |
| (N5342J) | C500 | 342 |
| N5342J | C550 | 070 |
| (N5343J) | C500 | 343 |
| (N5344J) | C500 | 344 |
| (N5345J) | C500 | 345 |
| N5346C | C500 | 685 |
| N5346J | C500 | 346 |
| (N5347J) | C500 | 347 |
| (N5348J) | C500 | 348 |
| N5348J | C550 | 071 |
| N5348J | C550 | 665 |
| N5349 | CL64 | 5349 |
| (N5349J) | C500 | 349 |
| N5350J | C500 | 350 |
| N5351J | C500 | 351 |
| N5352J | C500 | 352 |
| N5352J | CL64 | 5352 |
| (N5353J) | C500 | 139 |
| N5353J | C500 | 353 |
| N5354J | C500 | 354 |
| N5355J | C500 | 355 |
| N5356J | C500 | 356 |
| N5357J | C500 | 357 |
| (N5358J) | C500 | 358 |
| (N5359J) | C500 | 359 |
| N5360J | C500 | 360 |
| N5361J | C500 | 361 |
| N5361J | C500 | 361 |
| N5362J | C500 | 362 |
| (N5363J) | C500 | 363 |
| (N5364U) | C500 | 032 |
| N5366J | C500 | 366 |
| N5368J | C500 | 368 |
| N5373D | C560 | 0381 |
| N5373U | CL61 | 3026 |
| N5379W | SBRL | 306-100 |
| N5400G | GLF2 | 36/3 |
| N5402X | CL61 | 3027 |
| **N5408G** | **C550** | **666** |
| N5410 | WW24 | 123 |
| **N5411** | **C500** | **633** |
| N5412 | WW24 | 95 |
| N5415 | SBRL | 306-16 |
| N5415 | WW24 | 62 |
| N5418 | WW24 | 6 |
| N5419 | SBRL | 306-24 |
| N5419 | SBRL | 306-55 |
| N5420 | SBRL | 306-43 |
| N5420 | WW24 | 92 |
| (N5425) | FA50 | 237 |
| N5428G | C550 | 346 |
| N5430G | C550 | 347 |
| N5450 | FA20 | 17 |
| N5450M | BE40 | RJ-31 |
| N5451G | C550 | 348 |
| N5474G | C550 | 349 |
| N5474G | LJ35 | 093 |
| N5491V | CL61 | 3029 |
| N5492G | C550 | 350 |
| N5500F | C550 | 138 |
| N5500L | JSTR | 5136 |
| N5500S | C500 | 048 |
| N5501L | JSTR | 5137 |
| N5502L | JSTR | 5138 |
| N5503L | JSTR | 5139/54 |
| N5504L | JSTR | 5140 |
| N5505L | JSTR | 5141 |
| N5506L | JSTR | 5142 |
| N5507L | JSTR | 5143 |
| N5508L | JSTR | 5144 |
| N5509L | JSTR | 5145 |
| N5510L | JSTR | 5146 |
| N5511A | HS25 | 257113 |
| N5511A | SBRL | 282-137 |
| N5511A | SBRL | 282-91 |
| N5511A | SBRL | 465-39 |
| N5511L | JSTR | 5147 |
| N5511Z | SBRL | 282-91 |
| N5512A | SBRL | 282-137 |
| N5512L | JSTR | 5148 |
| N5513L | JSTR | 5149/11 |
| N5514L | JSTR | 5150/37 |
| N5515L | JSTR | 5151 |
| N5516L | JSTR | 5152 |
| N5517L | JSTR | 5153/61 |
| N5518L | JSTR | 5154 |
| N5519C | GLF2 | 235 |
| N5519L | JSTR | 5155/32 |
| N5520L | JSTR | 5156 |
| N5521L | JSTR | 5157 |
| N5522L | JSTR | 5158 |
| N5523L | JSTR | 5159 |
| N5524L | JSTR | 5160 |
| N5525L | JSTR | 5161/43 |
| N5526L | JSTR | 5162 |
| N5527L | JSTR | 5201 |
| N5528L | JSTR | 5202 |
| N5529L | JSTR | 5203 |
| N5530L | JSTR | 5204 |
| N5531L | JSTR | 5205 |
| N5532L | JSTR | 5206 |
| N5533L | JSTR | 5207 |
| N5534L | JSTR | 5208 |
| **N5535** | **C56X** | **5265** |
| N5535L | JSTR | 5209 |
| N5536L | JSTR | 5210 |
| N5537L | JSTR | 5211 |
| N5538L | JSTR | 5212 |
| N5539L | JSTR | 5213 |
| N5540L | JSTR | 5214 |
| N5541L | JSTR | 5215 |
| N5542L | JSTR | 5216 |

| | | |
|---|---|---|
| N5543G | LJ55 | 043 |
| N5543L | JSTR | 5217 |
| N5544L | JSTR | 5218 |
| N5545L | JSTR | 5219 |
| N5546L | JSTR | 5220 |
| N5547L | JSTR | 5221 |
| N5548L | JSTR | 5222 |
| N5549L | JSTR | 5223 |
| N5555U | FA20 | 39 |
| N5565 | SBRL | 282-119 |
| **N5572** | **LJ55** | **072** |
| N5574 | LJ55 | 074 |
| N5591A | C500 | 289 |
| N5594U | HS25 | 25219 |
| N5598Q | BE40 | RK-18 |
| (N5599) | LJ55 | 099 |
| N5600M | C500 | 191 |
| **N5601T** | **C560** | **0564** |
| N5602 | HFB3 | 1045 |
| **N5616** | **GLF5** | **616** |
| N5627 | HFB3 | 1038 |
| N5680Z | BE40 | RK-11 |
| N5685X | BE40 | RK-38 |
| N5695H | LJ24 | 278 |
| (N5703C) | C550 | 351 |
| (N5703C) | C550 | 666 |
| N5704 | C560 | 0157 |
| N5731 | F900 | 8 |
| N5732 | FA20 | 502 |
| N5732 | FA50 | 217 |
| N5732 | HS25 | 258467 |
| N5733 | F900 | 39 |
| N5733 | FA50 | 156 |
| N5733 | GLF5 | 609 |
| N5734 | C560 | 0157 |
| N5734 | FA10 | 196 |
| **N5734** | **HS25** | **258304** |
| N5735 | C560 | 0171 |
| N5735 | HS25 | 257044 |
| N5735 | HS25 | 258309 |
| N5736 | FA10 | 195 |
| **N5736** | **HS25** | **258471** |
| N5737 | C500 | 435 |
| N5737 | F9EX | 41 |
| N5738 | FA10 | 198 |
| N5739 | FA50 | 11 |
| N5739 | SBRL | 465-11 |
| N5794J | HS25 | 259021 |
| N5861 | JSTR | 5085 |
| N5867 | C500 | 015 |
| N5867 | LJ35 | 016 |
| N5873C | C550 | 352 |
| N5878 | MS76 | 106 |
| N5878D | JSTR | 5143 |
| **N5879** | **MS76** | **107** |
| **N5895K** | **BE40** | **RK-62** |
| **N5950C** | **ASTR** | **213** |
| **N5956B** | **GLF4** | **1469** |
| N5997K | GLF2 | 105 |
| N6000J | C650 | 0118 |
| N6000J | LJ35 | 079 |
| N6000J | SBRL | 465-54 |
| N6001H | HS25 | 256011 |
| **N6001L** | **C550** | **185** |
| **N6005V** | **HA4T** | **RC-45** |
| N6015Y | PRM1 | RB-115 |
| N6033 | HS25 | 256033 |
| N6034F | C500 | 239 |
| N6046J | HS25 | 258746 |
| N6048F | BE40 | RK-66 |
| N6051C | BE40 | RK-351 |
| **N6052U** | **BE40** | **RK-352** |
| N6053C | WW24 | 207 |
| N6053C | WW24 | 361 |
| N6055K | BE40 | RK-355 |
| N6056M | BE40 | RK-356 |
| N6060 | GLF2 | 105 |
| N6068 | MS76 | 050 |
| N6076Y | PRM1 | RB-76 |
| N6087 | SBRL | 282-26 |
| **N6100** | **EA50** | **000046** |
| N6100 | LJ60 | 100 |
| **N6110** | **C650** | **7023** |
| (N6111) | C650 | 7011 |
| N6111F | PRM1 | RB-111 |
| N6114 | C650 | 0094 |
| N6115 | C650 | 0095 |
| **N6117G** | **PRM1** | **RB-117** |
| N6118C | PRM1 | RB-118 |
| N6119C | PRM1 | RB-119 |
| N6120U | PRM1 | RB-120 |
| N6124W | PRM1 | RB-124 |
| N6128Y | PRM1 | RB-128 |
| N6129U | PRM1 | RB-129 |
| N6132U | C52B | 0323 |
| N6135H | HS25 | 258735 |
| N6137U | PRM1 | RB-137 |
| N6137Y | BE40 | RK-457 |
| N6142Y | PRM1 | RB-142 |
| N6144S | BE40 | RK-344 |
| N6145Q | C500 | 058 |
| N6146J | PRM1 | RB-146 |
| N6148Z | PRM1 | RB-148 |
| N6150B | C650 | 7050 |
| N6150Y | PRM1 | RB-150 |
| N6151C | HS25 | HA-0121 |
| N6160D | PRM1 | RB-60 |
| N6162V | BE40 | RK-362 |
| N6162Z | PRM1 | RB-62 |
| N6163T | PRM1 | RB-63 |
| N6164U | PRM1 | RB-64 |
| (N6164Z) | GLF3 | 367 |
| N6165C | CL61 | 3012 |
| N6167D | PRM1 | RB-67 |
| N6170C | C550 | 669 |
| N6171U | HS25 | 258771 |
| N6172V | BE40 | RK-372 |
| **N6173K** | **HS25** | **HB-63** |
| N6174Q | PRM1 | RB-274 |
| N6177A | PRM1 | RB-77 |
| **N6177Y** | **LJ24** | **151** |
| N6178X | PRM1 | RB-157 |
| N6182F | PRM1 | RB-102 |
| N6183G | PRM1 | RB-83 |
| N6183Q | C510 | 0062 |
| N6187Q | PRM1 | RB-87 |
| N6193D | BE40 | RK-363 |
| N6193S | C510 | 0069 |
| N6194N | PRM1 | RB-94 |
| N6195S | PRM1 | RB-95 |
| N6196M | C510 | 0091 |
| **N6197D** | **C510** | **0088** |
| N6197F | PRM1 | RB-97 |
| N6198P | HS25 | HA-0098 |
| **N6200C** | **C510** | **0087** |
| N6200D | BE40 | RK-360 |
| N6201A | PRM1 | RB-101 |
| N6202W | C510 | 0100 |
| N6203C | C510 | 0095 |
| N6206W | C510 | 0133 |
| N6207Z | C510 | 0145 |
| N6218 | HS25 | 25205 |
| **N6242R** | **C680** | **0273** |
| N6243M | C52B | 0066 |
| N6245J | C52A | 0458 |
| N6262T | LJ24 | 071 |
| N6273X | HS25 | HA-0143 |
| N6307H | LJ25 | 359 |
| N6307H | LJ35 | 519 |
| N6307H | LJ35 | 534 |
| N6307H | LJ35 | 652 |
| N6307H | LJ55 | 125 |
| N6317V | LJ35 | 509 |
| N6317V | LJ35 | 524 |
| N6317V | LJ35 | 639 |
| N6317V | LJ55 | 049 |
| N6324L | C510 | 0090 |
| N6325U | C510 | 0092 |
| N6331V | LJ31 | 006 |
| N6331V | LJ35 | 510 |
| N6331V | LJ35 | 525 |
| N6331V | LJ55 | 060 |
| N6331V | LJ55 | 123 |
| N6332K | C510 | 0093 |
| N6340T | HS25 | HA-0140 |
| N6340T | LJ25 | 360 |
| N6340T | LJ35 | 517 |
| N6340T | LJ35 | 532 |
| N6340T | LJ36 | 063 |
| N6340T | LJ55 | 127 |
| **N6351Y** | **HS25** | **HA-0151** |
| N6354N | LJ25 | 336 |
| N6358C | SBRL | 282-4 |
| N6360C | SBRL | 282-6 |
| N6361C | SBRL | 282-7 |
| N6361C | WW24 | 42 |
| N6362C | SBRL | 282-8 |
| (N6362D) | LJ35 | 277 |
| N6363C | SBRL | 282-9 |
| N6364C | SBRL | 282-10 |
| N6364U | LJ55 | 060 |
| N6365C | C500 | 228 |
| N6365C | SBRL | 282-11 |
| N6366C | SBRL | 282-12 |
| (N6366W) | FA10 | 57 |
| N6367C | SBRL | 282-13 |
| N6368C | SBRL | 282-14 |
| **N6368D** | **HS25** | **HA-0168** |
| N6369C | SBRL | 282-15 |
| N6370C | SBRL | 282-16 |
| N6371C | SBRL | 282-17 |
| N6372C | SBRL | 282-18 |
| N6373C | SBRL | 282-19 |
| N6374C | SBRL | 282-20 |
| N6375C | SBRL | 282-21 |
| N6376C | SBRL | 282-22 |
| N6377C | SBRL | 282-23 |
| N6378C | SBRL | 282-24 |
| N6379C | SBRL | 282-25 |
| N6380C | SBRL | 282-26 |
| N6381C | SBRL | 282-27 |
| N6382C | SBRL | 282-28 |
| N6383C | SBRL | 282-29 |
| N6384C | SBRL | 282-30 |
| N6389C | SBRL | 282-34 |
| N6390C | SBRL | 282-35 |
| N6391C | SBRL | 282-36 |
| N6392C | SBRL | 282-37 |
| N6393C | SBRL | 282-38 |
| N6394C | SBRL | 282-39 |
| N6395C | SBRL | 282-40 |
| N6396C | SBRL | 282-41 |
| N6397C | SBRL | 282-42 |
| N6398C | SBRL | 282-43 |
| N6399C | SBRL | 282-44 |
| N6403N | HS25 | HA-0103 |
| **N6405K** | **HS25** | **HB-65** |
| N6408F | HS25 | HA-0108 |
| **N6409A** | **HS25** | **HA-0159** |
| N6412 | WW24 | 95 |
| N6430S | C56X | 5331 |
| N6434R | HS25 | HA-0104 |
| N6452L | HS25 | HA-0102 |
| **N6452S** | **HS25** | **HA-0152** |
| **N6453** | **F2EX** | **26** |
| N6453 | GLF3 | 349 |
| N6453 | GLF4 | 1033 |
| N6455T | HA4T | RC-55 |
| N6458 | GLF3 | 349 |
| N6458 | GLF4 | 1033 |
| (N6462) | LJ24 | 127 |
| N6465W | PRM1 | RB-265 |
| N6470P | PRM1 | RB-270 |
| **N6471N** | **PRM1** | **RB-271** |
| N6504V | WW24 | 35 |
| N6505V | WW24 | 39 |
| N6510V | WW24 | 41 |
| N6511V | WW24 | 42 |
| N6512V | WW24 | 64 |
| N6513V | WW24 | 47 |
| N6513X | GLF3 | 310 |
| N6516V | CS55 | 0144 |
| N6518V | WW24 | 43 |
| N6521F | C560 | 0632 |
| N6523A | C550 | 460 |
| **N6525B** | **C52B** | **0004** |
| N6525J | C500 | 308 |
| N6527V | WW24 | 69 |
| N6534V | WW24 | 54 |
| N6538V | WW24 | 59 |
| N6544V | WW24 | 57 |
| N6545V | WW24 | 60 |
| N6546V | WW24 | 63 |
| N6550V | WW24 | 56 |
| N6550W | FA50 | 136 |
| N6552C | SBRL | 282-45 |
| N6552R | SBRL | 276-6 |
| N6553C | SBRL | 282-46 |
| N6555C | FA20 | 78/412 |
| N6555C | SBRL | 282-48 |
| **N6555L** | **FA20** | **85/425** |
| N6556C | SBRL | 282-49 |
| N6557C | SBRL | 282-50 |
| N6563C | C500 | 012 |
| N6563C | C500 | 014 |
| N6563C | C500 | 551 |
| N6565A | FA20 | 39 |
| N6565A | SBRL | 282-28 |
| N6565C | C550 | 174 |
| N6565K | SBRL | 282-28 |
| N6566C | C550 | 175 |
| N6567C | C550 | 176 |
| N6567G | HS25 | 256048 |
| N6581E | SBRL | 265-82 |
| N6596R | LJ25 | 286 |
| N6610V | WW24 | 74 |
| N6611V | WW24 | 75 |
| N6612S | SBRL | 276-48 |
| N6612V | WW24 | 76 |
| N6613V | WW24 | 78 |
| N6617B | LJ36 | 026 |
| N6617V | WW24 | 81 |
| (N6621) | FA20 | 378 |
| **N6637G** | **C550** | **670** |
| N6666A | LJ31 | 150 |
| N6666A | LJ60 | 143 |
| N6666K | LJ25 | 285 |
| N6666K | LJ35 | 481 |
| N6666K | LJ55 | 115 |
| N6666P | F9EX | 102 |
| **N6666R** | **F9EX** | **102** |
| N6666R | FA50 | 124 |
| N6666R | LJ25 | 285 |
| N6666R | LJ31 | 150 |
| N6666R | LJ31 | 153 |
| N6666R | LJ35 | 412 |
| N6666R | LJ55 | 115 |
| N6666R | LJ60 | 143 |
| N6701 | FA20 | 177 |
| N6702 | HS25 | 25241 |
| N6709 | HS25 | 25239 |
| **N6745** | **E50P** | **50000091** |
| **N6757M** | **CL64** | **5545** |
| (N6761L) | C550 | 671 |
| N6763C | C550 | 672 |
| **N6763L** | **C550** | **673** |
| N6763L | C550 | 673 |
| N6763M | C500 | 686 |
| (N6770S) | C550 | 674 |
| N6773P | C550 | 675 |
| **N6775C** | **C550** | **677** |
| N6775U | C550 | 678 |
| (N6776P) | C550 | 679 |
| **N6776T** | **C550** | **680** |
| (N6776Y) | C550 | 681 |
| N6777V | C500 | 567 |
| (N6777X) | C500 | 568 |
| N6778C | C500 | 569 |
| (N6778L) | C500 | 570 |
| N6778L | C550 | 684 |
| N6778T | C500 | 571 |
| (N6778V) | C500 | 572 |
| (N6778Y) | C500 | 573 |
| N6778Y | C550 | 687 |
| N6779D | C500 | 576 |
| N6779D | C56X | 5568 |
| N6779L | C500 | 577 |
| N6779P | C500 | 578 |
| N6779Y | C500 | 579 |
| (N6780) | LJ55 | 083 |
| (N6780A) | C500 | 581 |
| N6780A | C560 | 0360 |
| N6780C | C500 | 582 |
| N6780C | C550 | 690 |
| N6780J | C500 | 583 |
| (N6780M) | C500 | 584 |
| N6780Y | C500 | 585 |
| N6780Z | C500 | 586 |
| N6781C | C500 | 588 |
| N6781C | C650 | 7056 |
| (N6781D) | C500 | 589 |
| (N6781G) | C500 | 590 |
| N6781L | C500 | 591 |
| N6781R | C500 | 592 |
| (N6781T) | C500 | 593 |
| N6781Z | C500 | 594 |
| N6782B | C500 | 597 |
| N6782F | C500 | 598 |
| (N6782P) | C500 | 599 |
| (N6782T) | C500 | 600 |
| N6782T | C550 | 695 |
| N6782X | C500 | 601 |

| | | |
|---|---|---|
| N6783C | C500 | 604 |
| N6783L | C500 | 605 |
| N6783U | C500 | 606 |
| N6783V | C500 | 607 |
| N6783X | C500 | 608 |
| (N6783X) | C560 | 0088 |
| N6784L | C500 | 611 |
| N6784P | C500 | 612 |
| N6784P | C560 | 0091 |
| N6784T | C500 | 613 |
| N6784X | C500 | 614 |
| N6784X | C560 | 0092 |
| N6784Y | C500 | 615 |
| N6784Y | C500 | 645 |
| N6784Y | C560 | 0092A |
| N6785C | C500 | 617 |
| (N6785C) | C560 | 0093 |
| N6785D | C500 | 618 |
| N6785D | C560 | 0094 |
| N6785L | C500 | 619 |
| N6788P | C560 | 0095 |
| N6789 | LJ55 | 083 |
| N6789 | SBRL | 282-112 |
| N6789D | SBRL | 282-112 |
| (N6790L) | C560 | 0097 |
| (N6790P) | C560 | 0098 |
| (N6792A) | C560 | 0100 |
| N6798Y | C550 | 219 |
| N6798Z | C550 | 220 |
| N6799C | C550 | 226 |
| N6799C | C550 | 355 |
| N6799E | C550 | 227 |
| N6799L | C550 | 228 |
| N6799L | C550 | 356 |
| (N6799L) | C560 | 0104 |
| N6799T | C550 | 229 |
| N6799T | C550 | 357 |
| N6799Y | C550 | 230 |
| N6800C | C550 | 234 |
| N6800C | C550 | 360 |
| (N6800C) | C560 | 0105 |
| N6800J | C550 | 235 |
| N6800S | C550 | 236 |
| N6800S | C550 | 361 |
| N6800Z | C550 | 237 |
| (N6801H) | C550 | 239 |
| N6801H | C560 | 0106 |
| N6801L | C550 | 240 |
| (N6801L) | C560 | 0107 |
| N6801P | C550 | 241 |
| (N6801P) | C560 | 0108 |
| N6801Q | C550 | 242 |
| N6801Q | C550 | 389 |
| (N6801Q) | C560 | 0109 |
| N6801R | C550 | 243 |
| N6801T | C550 | 244 |
| (N6801V) | C550 | 245 |
| N6801V | C560 | 0109 |
| N6801Z | C550 | 246 |
| N6801Z | C550 | 390 |
| N6802S | C550 | 248 |
| N6802S | C550 | 368 |
| (N6802S) | C560 | 0110 |
| N6802T | C550 | 249 |
| N6802T | C550 | 369 |
| (N6802T) | C560 | 0111 |
| N6802X | C550 | 250 |
| N6802Y | C550 | 251 |
| N6802Y | C550 | 370 |
| N6802Z | C550 | 252 |
| N6803E | C550 | 255 |
| N6803L | C550 | 256 |
| N6803L | C550 | 372 |
| N6803L | C560 | 0113 |
| (N6803T) | C550 | 257 |
| (N6803T) | C560 | 0114 |
| (N6803Y) | C550 | 258 |
| N6803Y | C560 | 0115 |
| N6804C | C550 | 261 |
| N6804F | C550 | 262 |
| N6804F | C550 | 374 |
| (N6804F) | C560 | 0117 |
| N6804L | C550 | 263 |
| N6804L | C550 | 375 |
| N6804L | C560 | 0118 |
| N6804L | LJ25 | 006 |
| N6804M | C550 | 264 |
| (N6804N) | C550 | 265 |
| (N6804N) | C560 | 0119 |
| N6804S | C550 | 266 |
| N6804Y | C550 | 267 |
| N6804Y | C550 | 376 |
| (N6804Y) | C560 | 0120 |
| N6804Y | C560 | 0153 |
| N6804Z | C550 | 268 |
| N6805T | C550 | 269 |
| N6805T | C550 | 377 |
| N6805T | C560 | 0154 |
| N6806X | C550 | 378 |
| (N6806X) | C560 | 0120 |
| (N6806Y) | C550 | 378 |
| N6808C | C550 | 379 |
| N6808C | C560 | 0121 |
| (N6808Z) | C560 | 0122 |
| (N6809G) | C560 | 0123 |
| (N6809T) | C560 | 0124 |
| N6809V | C560 | 0125 |
| N6810J | FA20 | 125 |
| (N6810L) | C560 | 0127 |
| (N6810N) | C560 | 0128 |
| (N6811F) | C560 | 0129 |
| (N6811T) | C560 | 0130 |
| (N6811X) | C560 | 0131 |
| N6811Z | C560 | 0132 |
| N6812D | C560 | 0134 |
| (N6812D) | C650 | 0207 |
| (N6812L) | C560 | 0135 |
| N6812L | C650 | 0208 |
| (N6812Z) | C560 | 0136 |
| (N6812Z) | C650 | 0209 |
| N6820J | FA20 | 135 |
| N6820T | C650 | 0211 |
| (N6820Y) | C650 | 0212 |
| (N6823L) | C650 | 0213 |
| (N6824G) | C650 | 0215 |
| N6825X | C550 | 364 |
| N6826U | C550 | 380 |
| (N6828S) | C650 | 0217 |
| N6829X | C650 | 0218 |
| N6829Y | C550 | 365 |
| N6829Z | C650 | 0219 |
| N6830T | C650 | 0220 |
| N6830X | C550 | 366 |
| N6830Z | C550 | 367 |
| N6846T | C550 | 625 |
| N6851C | C550 | 697 |
| N6860A | C550 | 271 |
| N6860C | C550 | 272 |
| N6860L | C550 | 273 |
| N6860R | C550 | 274 |
| N6860S | C550 | 275 |
| N6860T | C550 | 276 |
| N6860U | C550 | 277 |
| N6860Y | C550 | 278 |
| N6861D | C550 | 281 |
| N6861E | C550 | 282 |
| N6861L | C550 | 283 |
| N6861P | C550 | 284 |
| N6861S | C550 | 285 |
| N6861X | C550 | 286 |
| N6862C | C550 | 290 |
| N6862D | C550 | 291 |
| N6862L | C550 | 292 |
| N6862Q | C550 | 293 |
| N6862R | C550 | 294 |
| N6863B | C550 | 300 |
| N6863C | C550 | 301 |
| N6863G | C550 | 302 |
| N6863J | C550 | 303 |
| N6863L | C550 | 304 |
| N6863T | C550 | 305 |
| "N6864" | C560 | 0162 |
| N6864B | C550 | 309 |
| N6864C | C550 | 310 |
| N6864L | C550 | 311 |
| N6864X | C550 | 312 |
| N6864Y | C550 | 313 |
| N6864Z | C550 | 314 |
| N6865C | C550 | 319 |
| (N6868P) | C650 | 0210 |
| (N6871L) | C560 | 0135 |
| (N6872T) | C560 | 0136 |
| N6872T | C560 | 0155 |
| N6874Z | C560 | 0137 |
| (N6876Q) | C560 | 0140 |
| N6876S | C560 | 0141 |
| N6876Z | C560 | 0142 |
| N6877C | C560 | 0143 |
| N6877G | C560 | 0144 |
| N6877L | C52A | 0060 |
| (N6877L) | C560 | 0145 |
| (N6877Q) | C560 | 0146 |
| (N6877R) | C560 | 0147 |
| (N6879L) | C560 | 0150 |
| N6881Q | C560 | 0151 |
| N6882R | C560 | 0152 |
| N6885L | C560 | 0156 |
| N6885V | C560 | 0157 |
| (N6885Y) | C560 | 0158 |
| N6886X | C560 | 0160 |
| N6887M | C500 | 620 |
| N6887R | C500 | 621 |
| N6887T | C550 | 320 |
| (N6887T) | C560 | 0164 |
| N6887X | C550 | 321 |
| (N6887X) | C560 | 0165 |
| N6887Y | C550 | 322 |
| N6888C | C550 | 326 |
| N6888C | C560 | 0169 |
| N6888D | C550 | 327 |
| N6888L | C550 | 328 |
| N6888L | C560 | 0170 |
| N6888T | C550 | 329 |
| (N6888T) | C560 | 0171 |
| N6888X | C550 | 330 |
| (N6888X) | C560 | 0172 |
| N6888Z | C550 | 331 |
| N6889E | C550 | 335 |
| N6889E | C560 | 0174 |
| N6889K | C550 | 336 |
| N6889L | C550 | 337 |
| N6889T | C550 | 338 |
| N6889Y | C550 | 339 |
| N6889Z | C550 | 340 |
| (N6890C) | C550 | 342 |
| (N6890D) | C550 | 343 |
| (N6890E) | C550 | 344 |
| N6890G | C550 | 345 |
| (N6940P) | F9EX | 59 |
| (N6960) | HS25 | 257024 |
| (N6972Z) | CL60 | 1006 |
| **N7000C** | **CL30** | **20225** |
| N7000C | GLF2 | 165/37 |
| N7000C | GLF3 | 344 |
| N7000G | C650 | 0114 |
| N7000G | FA20 | 440 |
| N7000G | GLF2 | 156/31 |
| N7000G | LJ25 | 027 |
| N7000G | SBRL | 465-16 |
| N7000K | LJ24 | 029 |
| N7004 | C550 | 427 |
| N7004T | GLF2 | 28 |
| N7005 | C650 | 7044 |
| N7005 | HS25 | 257024 |
| N7005 | JSTR | 5105 |
| N7006 | HS25 | 257024 |
| N7007Q | CS55 | 0030 |
| N7007Q | HA4T | RC-7 |
| N7007V | CS55 | 0030 |
| N7007V | LJ35 | 594 |
| N7007X | HS25 | 257034 |
| N7008 | CL60 | 1054 |
| N7008 | CL61 | 5164 |
| N7008 | JSTR | 5101/15 |
| N7008J | JSTR | 5101/15 |
| N7010R | C560 | 0469 |
| **N7011** | **FA50** | **144** |
| N7011H | CL61 | 3032 |
| N7028F | WW24 | 131 |
| N7028U | C550 | 290 |
| N7035C | LJ25 | 352 |
| (N7038Z) | MS76 | 101 |
| N7043U | SBRL | 265-12 |
| N7046J | CL61 | 5122 |
| N7047K | CS55 | 0133 |
| N7050V | MU30 | A058SA |
| N7051J | WW24 | 409 |
| N7055 | HS25 | 25142 |
| N7059U | C650 | 0210 |
| N7062B | HS25 | 257062 |
| **N7070A** | **CS55** | **0068** |
| N7074X | LJ24 | 223 |
| N7077S | HS25 | 258827 |
| N7079N | GLF2 | 211 |
| N7079N | PRM1 | RB-179 |
| N7081V | PRM1 | RB-181 |
| N7082V | PRM1 | RB-182 |
| N7085V | PRM1 | RB-185 |
| **N7088S** | **PRM1** | **RB-188** |
| N7090 | SBRL | 282-30 |
| N7090 | SBRL | 306-16 |
| N7090 | SBRL | 306-5 |
| N7090 | SBRL | 306-62 |
| N7090 | WW24 | 95 |
| N7092C | LJ35 | 184 |
| N7096B | GLF4 | 1162 |
| N7096E | GLF3 | 498 |
| N7096G | GLF3 | 497 |
| **N7100C** | **CL30** | **20254** |
| N7101Z | HS25 | 258801 |
| N7102U | PRM1 | RB-172 |
| N7102Z | HS25 | 258802 |
| N7105 | JSTR | 5078/3 |
| N7110K | C500 | 016 |
| N7111H | C500 | 595 |
| (N7113Z) | BE40 | RK-51 |
| N7117 | LJ35 | 462 |
| N7118A | CS55 | 0065 |
| N7121K | LJ24 | 230 |
| N7125 | LJ35 | 035 |
| N7125J | HS25 | 25013 |
| N7125J | HS25 | 25107 |
| N7128T | HS25 | 258828 |
| N7134E | GLF3 | 423 |
| N7143N | SBRL | 265-70 |
| N7145V | JSTR | 5001/53 |
| N7148J | SBRL | 380-33 |
| N7153X | C550 | 407 |
| N7155P | GLF2 | 169 |
| N7158Q | HFB3 | 1040 |
| N7163E | PRM1 | RB-163 |
| N7165X | PRM1 | RB-165 |
| N7170J | HS25 | 25276 |
| **N7170Y** | **PRM1** | **RB-170** |
| N7171 | HS25 | 25264 |
| N7176J | PRM1 | RB-176 |
| N7187J | PRM1 | RB-187 |
| N7189J | PRM1 | RB-189 |
| N7191K | PRM1 | RB-191 |
| N7192M | PRM1 | RB-192 |
| N7193W | PRM1 | RB-193 |
| N7198H | PRM1 | RB-198 |
| **N7200K** | **LJ24** | **099** |
| N7220L | C560 | 0142 |
| N7226P | BE40 | RK-526 |
| N7228K | FA50 | 146 |
| N7235R | HS25 | 258835 |
| N7236L | HS25 | 258836 |
| N7243U | C650 | 7054 |
| N7244W | LJ55 | 028 |
| N7255U | HS25 | 258855 |
| N7256C | HS25 | 258856 |
| N7257U | PRM1 | RB-197 |
| N7259J | LJ35 | 505 |
| N7260C | LJ25 | 365 |
| N7260E | LJ35 | 615 |
| N7260G | LJ55 | 111 |
| N7260H | LJ35 | 622 |
| N7260J | LJ55 | 126 |
| N7260K | LJ55 | 131 |
| N7260Q | LJ35 | 623 |
| N7260T | LJ35 | 627 |
| N7261B | LJ25 | 366 |
| N7261D | LJ55 | 134 |
| N7261H | LJ35 | 641 |
| N7261R | LJ35 | 626 |
| N7262A | LJ25 | 367 |
| N7262M | LJ55 | 113 |
| N7262X | LJ35 | 642 |
| N7262Y | LJ31 | 002 |
| N7263C | LJ35 | 509 |
| N7263D | LJ35 | 510 |
| N7263E | LJ35 | 511 |
| N7263F | LJ35 | 512 |
| N7263H | LJ35 | 513 |
| N7263K | LJ35 | 514 |
| N7263L | LJ35 | 515 |
| N7263N | LJ35 | 516 |
| N7263R | LJ35 | 517 |
| N7263X | LJ35 | 518 |
| N7268M | PRM1 | RB-168 |
| N7269Z | PRM1 | RB-169 |

| | | |
|---|---|---|
| N7274A | C560 | 0386 |
| N7277 | C525 | 0666 |
| N7277X | MS76 | 112 |
| N7281Z | C500 | 047 |
| N7294E | PRM1 | RB-194 |
| (N7300G) | LJ24 | 186 |
| N7300K | LJ24 | 186 |
| N7301 | F9EX | 19 |
| N7302P | HS25 | 258852 |
| N7337F | C56X | 5342 |
| N7338 | C560 | 0137 |
| N7374 | HS25 | 258524 |
| **N7402** | **C680** | **0082** |
| **N7403** | **C680** | **0222** |
| N7418F | C750 | 0074 |
| N7440C | HS25 | 25142 |
| N7465T | HS25 | 257046 |
| **N7490A** | **HS25** | **257173** |
| N7500 | GLF2 | 117 |
| N7500 | JSTR | 5102 |
| N7500K | LJ24 | 065 |
| N7502V | SBRL | 282-52 |
| N7503V | SBRL | 282-53 |
| N7504V | SBRL | 282-54 |
| N7505V | SBRL | 282-55 |
| N7506V | SBRL | 282-56 |
| N7507V | SBRL | 282-57 |
| N7508V | SBRL | 282-58 |
| N7509V | SBRL | 282-59 |
| N7510V | SBRL | 282-60 |
| N7513D | C560 | 0124 |
| **N7513H** | **GLF3** | **493** |
| N7514V | SBRL | 282-64 |
| N7519N | SBRL | 306-48 |
| N7522N | SBRL | 306-49 |
| N7529N | SBRL | 306-50 |
| N7531N | SBRL | 306-51 |
| N7543H | C500 | 266 |
| N7547P | C560 | 0365 |
| N7571N | SBRL | 306-52 |
| N7572N | SBRL | 370-1 |
| N7573N | SBRL | 306-53 |
| N7574N | SBRL | 306-54 |
| N7575N | SBRL | 306-55 |
| N7576N | SBRL | 306-56 |
| N7577N | SBRL | 306-57 |
| N7578N | SBRL | 306-58 |
| N7584N | SBRL | 282-107 |
| N7585N | SBRL | 370-2 |
| N7586N | SBRL | 370-3 |
| N7587N | SBRL | 370-4 |
| N7588N | SBRL | 370-5 |
| N7589N | SBRL | 370-6 |
| N7590N | SBRL | 370-7 |
| N7591N | SBRL | 370-8 |
| N7592N | SBRL | 370-9 |
| N7593N | SBRL | 380-1 |
| N7594N | SBRL | 282-99 |
| N7595N | SBRL | 282-106 |
| N7596N | SBRL | 282-101 |
| N7596N | SBRL | 282-108 |
| N7597N | SBRL | 282-102 |
| N7597N | SBRL | 282-110 |
| N7598N | SBRL | 282-103 |
| **N7600** | **BE40** | **RK-395** |
| N7600 | JSTR | 5054/59 |
| **N7600G** | **C750** | **0159** |
| N7600J | JSTR | 5054/59 |
| N7600K | LJ25 | 135 |
| **N7600P** | **F9EX** | **226** |
| **N7600S** | **F9EX** | **173** |
| (N7601) | GLF2 | 32/2 |
| N7601 | GLF4 | 1245 |
| **N7601R** | **MS76** | **060** |
| N7602 | GLF2 | 32/2 |
| (N7602) | GLF4 | 1245 |
| N7638S | WW24 | 134 |
| N7654F | FA20 | 489 |
| N7662N | SBRL | 282-111 |
| N7667N | SBRL | 282-112 |
| (N7682V) | SBRL | 306-79 |
| (N7684X) | HFB3 | 1042 |
| (N7685T) | HFB3 | 1055 |
| N7700L | C560 | 0203 |
| **N7700T** | **C500** | **662** |
| **N7701L** | **LJ24** | **288** |
| **N7707X** | **FA7X** | **16** |
| N7715X | C525 | 0387 |
| **N7715X** | **C525** | **0653** |
| N7715X | C52A | 0178 |
| N7715Y | C525 | 0387 |
| **N7725D** | **C52B** | **0218** |
| N7725D | C550 | 550-1041 |
| N7728 | HS25 | 257028 |
| N7728T | C560 | 0374 |
| **N7734T** | **LJ60** | **139** |
| N7735A | LJ35 | 138 |
| N7765D | C550 | 550-1041 |
| N7766Z | GLF2 | 174 |
| **N7773A** | **C52A** | **0004** |
| N7773J | C52B | 0223 |
| N7775 | HS25 | 258275 |
| N7775 | JSTR | 5073 |
| N7776 | GLF4 | 1121 |
| **N7777B** | **C650** | **0214** |
| N7777B | HS25 | 25174 |
| N7777B | LJ35 | 079 |
| N7777B | LJ35 | 508 |
| N7778L | SBRL | 282-135 |
| N7782 | HS25 | 257025 |
| N7782 | JSTR | 5066/46 |
| N7784 | LJ55 | 023 |
| N7784 | WW24 | 63 |
| N7788 | CL61 | 3011 |
| N7788 | HS25 | 257073 |
| N7788 | JSTR | 5107 |
| N7789 | GLF2 | 90 |
| N7798D | C550 | 333 |
| **N7799T** | **GLF4** | **1474** |
| N7800 | GLF4 | 1098 |
| N7801L | LJ25 | 355 |
| N7810W | LJ25 | 117 |
| **N7814** | **C52B** | **0166** |
| N7818S | F9EX | 153 |
| N7820C | SBRL | 282-1 |
| N7824M | FA20 | 42 |
| N7851M | C550 | 695 |
| N7864J | C550 | 427 |
| **N7876C** | **C510** | **0229** |
| **N7877D** | **C56X** | **6017** |
| **N7877T** | **C52B** | **0077** |
| **N7895Q** | **C525** | **0405** |
| N7895Q | C560 | 0199 |
| N7895Q | C560 | 0564 |
| (N7922) | FA20 | 37/406 |
| N7953S | JSTR | 5108 |
| N7954S | JSTR | 5109/13 |
| N7955S | JSTR | 5110/47 |
| N7956S | JSTR | 5111 |
| N7957S | JSTR | 5112/7 |
| N7958S | JSTR | 5113/25 |
| N7959S | JSTR | 5114/18 |
| N7961S | JSTR | 5116 |
| N7962S | JSTR | 5117/35 |
| N7963S | JSTR | 5118 |
| N7964S | JSTR | 5119/29 |
| N7965S | JSTR | 5120/26 |
| N7966S | JSTR | 5121 |
| N7967S | JSTR | 5122 |
| N7967S | JSTR | 5141 |
| N7968S | JSTR | 5123/14 |
| N7969S | JSTR | 5124 |
| N7970S | JSTR | 5125/31 |
| N7971S | JSTR | 5126 |
| N7972S | JSTR | 5127 |
| N7973S | JSTR | 5128/16 |
| N7974S | JSTR | 5129 |
| N7975S | JSTR | 5130 |
| N7976S | JSTR | 5131 |
| N7977S | JSTR | 5132/57 |
| N7978S | JSTR | 5133 |
| N7979S | JSTR | 5134/50 |
| N7980S | JSTR | 5135 |
| (N7981M) | BE40 | RK-119 |
| N7996 | HS25 | 258019 |
| N8000 | CL60 | 1076 |
| N8000 | GLF2 | 39 |
| N8000 | SBRL | 306-68 |
| **N8000E** | **FA7X** | **25** |
| N8000J | GLF2 | 42/12 |
| **N8000U** | **C56X** | **5746** |
| N8000U | C650 | 0107 |
| N8000U | FA20 | 436 |
| N8000U | SBRL | 306-19 |
| N8000U | SBRL | 465-24 |
| N8000Z | HS25 | 256012 |
| **N8005** | **C56X** | **5006** |
| N8005Y | LJ25 | 121 |
| N8008F | C550 | 496 |
| N8010X | CL60 | 1038 |
| N8010X | LJ55 | 096 |
| N8014Q | BE40 | RK-37 |
| N8025X | SBRL | 306-84 |
| N8029Z | HS25 | 258129 |
| **N8030F** | **HS25** | **258131** |
| **N8040A** | **LJ35** | **048** |
| N8041R | C560 | 0413 |
| (N8051H) | BE40 | RK-45 |
| N8052V | SBRL | 265-18 |
| N8053V | BE40 | RK-47 |
| N8060V | BE40 | RK-48 |
| N8060Y | BE40 | RK-49 |
| N8064A | LJ35 | 324 |
| N8064K | LJ31 | 223 |
| N8064Q | HS25 | 258158 |
| N8066P | LJ31 | 126 |
| N8067Y | LJ60 | 097 |
| N8068V | GLF5 | 581 |
| N8070Q | BE40 | RK-73 |
| N8070U | WW24 | 124 |
| N8071J | LJ60 | 039 |
| N8071L | LJ60 | 091 |
| N8073R | BE40 | RK-24 |
| N8073Y | LJ31 | 133 |
| N8074W | LJ60 | 074 |
| N8079Q | LJ31 | 129 |
| N8080W | LJ60 | 080 |
| N8082B | LJ60 | 102 |
| N8082J | LJ31 | 128 |
| N8083N | BE40 | RK-62 |
| N8084J | LJ60 | 218 |
| N8084R | LJ45 | 148 |
| **N8085T** | **BE40** | **RK-51** |
| N8086L | LJ60 | 096 |
| N8088U | LJ60 | 222 |
| N8089Y | LJ60 | 089 |
| N8090 | HS25 | 258090 |
| N8090P | LJ60 | 090 |
| N8094U | LJ24 | 297 |
| N8097V | BE40 | RK-26 |
| N8100E | F900 | 34 |
| **N8100E** | **F9EX** | **4** |
| N8100E | FA10 | 52 |
| N8100E | FA10 | 53 |
| N8100E | FA50 | 33 |
| **N8106V** | **C52B** | **0072** |
| N8114G | C500 | 129 |
| N8115N | GLF3 | 404 |
| N8125J | HS25 | 25148 |
| N8130S | C560 | 0631 |
| N8138M | BE40 | RK-84 |
| N8146J | BE40 | RK-74 |
| N8152H | BE40 | RK-9 |
| N8157H | BE40 | RK-57 |
| N8163G | BE40 | RK-16 |
| N8164M | BE40 | RK-64 |
| N8166A | BE40 | RK-76 |
| N8167G | BE40 | RK-81 |
| N8167Y | BE40 | RK-67 |
| N8169Q | BE40 | RK-69 |
| N8180Q | BE40 | RK-80 |
| N8186 | HS25 | 258186 |
| **N8186** | **HS25** | **258604** |
| N8189 | LJ35 | 654 |
| N8189J | C500 | 537 |
| **N8200E** | **F900** | **34** |
| N8200E | FA10 | 111 |
| N8200E | FA50 | 150 |
| N8202Q | C500 | 002 |
| N8203K | GLF4 | 1205 |
| N8206S | CL64 | 5335 |
| N8210W | BE40 | RK-72 |
| N8216Q | LJ35 | 370 |
| N8216Z | LJ35 | 309 |
| (N8217W) | LJ25 | 299 |
| N8220F | GLF3 | 371 |
| N8221M | MU30 | A076SA |
| N8226M | GLF3 | 413 |
| N8227P | LJ55 | 086 |
| N8227V | FA20 | 150/445 |
| N8228P | LJ35 | 263 |
| N8239E | BE40 | RK-46 |
| N8249Y | BE40 | RK-44 |
| (N8252J) | BE40 | RK-105 |
| N8252J | BE40 | RK-40 |
| N8253A | HS25 | 256061 |
| N8253Y | BE40 | RK-42 |
| N8260D | CL60 | 1063 |
| N8260L | BE40 | RK-60 |
| N8265Y | BE40 | RK-41 |
| N8267D | SBRL | 380-58 |
| N8270 | LJ60 | 063 |
| N8271 | LJ60 | 066 |
| N8277Y | BE40 | RK-77 |
| N8278Z | BE40 | RK-78 |
| **N8279G** | **BE40** | **RK-79** |
| N8280 | LJ25 | 052 |
| N8280 | LJ35 | 310 |
| N8280J | BE40 | RK-68 |
| N8281 | LJ35 | 232 |
| N8282E | BE40 | RK-82 |
| **N8283C** | **BE40** | **RK-83** |
| N8288R | C525 | 0090 |
| **N8288R** | **C525** | **0348** |
| N8299Y | BE40 | RK-85 |
| N8300 | WW24 | 12 |
| **N8300E** | **FA50** | **33** |
| N8300E | JSTR | 5115/39 |
| N8311N | SBRL | 282-113 |
| N8333N | SBRL | 282-115 |
| N8338N | SBRL | 282-117 |
| N8339N | SBRL | 282-118 |
| **N8341C** | **C525** | **0150** |
| N8341N | SBRL | 282-119 |
| **N8344M** | **C550** | **577** |
| N8345K | SBRL | 282-76 |
| N8349N | SBRL | 282-121 |
| N8350N | SBRL | 282-123 |
| N8356N | SBRL | 282-125 |
| N8357N | SBRL | 306-64 |
| N8364N | SBRL | 306-65 |
| N8365N | SBRL | 306-66 |
| N8400B | SBRL | 282-23 |
| **N8400E** | **FA50** | **150** |
| N8400E | HS25 | 257202 |
| N8417B | C550 | 042 |
| N8418B | C550 | 043 |
| N8445N | SBRL | 380-2 |
| N8447A | FA10 | 84 |
| N8463 | FA10 | 152 |
| N8467N | SBRL | 380-3 |
| N8482B | LJ24 | 148 |
| N8484P | ASTR | 014 |
| **N8486** | **C560** | **0554** |
| N8490P | GLF2 | 4/8 |
| N8494 | FA10 | 201 |
| (N8494C) | C650 | 7072 |
| (N8495B) | FA20 | 509 |
| N8499B | C500 | 338 |
| **N8500** | **SBRL** | **282-108** |
| N8500 | SBRL | 465-59 |
| N8508Z | C500 | 284 |
| N8514Y | WW24 | 231 |
| N8516Z | FA50 | 7 |
| N8520J | C550 | 151 |
| N8526A | SBRL | 380-53 |
| N8534 | WW24 | 113 |
| N8535 | WW24 | 139 |
| N8536 | WW24 | 148 |
| N8536Y | LJ24 | 217 |
| N8537B | LJ35 | 236 |
| N8550A | FA50 | 263 |
| N8562W | LJ35 | 462 |
| N8562Y | LJ35 | 483 |
| N8563A | LJ35 | 480 |
| N8563B | LJ25 | 360 |
| N8563E | LJ55 | 056 |
| N8563G | LJ35 | 488 |
| N8563M | LJ55 | 077 |
| N8563N | LJ35 | 491 |
| N8563P | LJ55 | 063 |
| N8563Z | LJ55 | 075 |
| N8564K | LJ35 | 496 |
| N8564M | LJ35 | 493 |
| N8564P | LJ35 | 498 |
| N8564X | LJ55 | 089 |
| N8564Z | LJ55 | 087 |
| N8565H | LJ55 | 026 |
| N8565J | LJ35 | 479 |
| N8565K | LJ55 | 065 |
| N8565N | LJ35 | 497 |
| N8565X | LJ35 | 502 |

| | | |
|---|---|---|
| N8565Y | LJ25 | 364 |
| N8565Z | LJ55 | 095 |
| N8566B | LJ35 | 492 |
| N8566F | LJ55 | 091 |
| N8566Q | LJ55 | 097 |
| N8566X | LJ35 | 500 |
| N8566Z | LJ25 | 369 |
| N8567A | LJ35 | 503 |
| N8567J | LJ25 | 368 |
| N8567K | LJ35 | 589 |
| N8567R | LJ35 | 597 |
| N8567T | LJ35 | 598 |
| N8567X | LJ55 | 117 |
| N8567Z | LJ35 | 591 |
| N8567Z | LJ35 | 608 |
| N8568B | LJ35 | 504 |
| N8568D | LJ35 | 612 |
| N8568J | LJ55 | 121 |
| N8568P | LJ55 | 122 |
| N8568Q | LJ35 | 616 |
| N8568V | LJ35 | 619 |
| N8568Y | LJ35 | 640 |
| (N8570) | CL64 | 5488 |
| N8572 | F900 | 105 |
| N8575J | FA50 | 196 |
| N8701L | C550 | 550-1075 |
| **N8701L** | **C56X** | **5751** |
| **N8762M** | **GLEX** | **9113** |
| (N8777N) | C550 | 171 |
| **N8778** | **HS25** | **258560** |
| **N8783** | **LJ60** | **006** |
| N8785R | GLF2 | 93 |
| N8796J | GLF4 | 1134 |
| N8805 | FA50 | 3 |
| **N8811A** | **LJ60** | **119** |
| **N8821C** | **ASTR** | **226** |
| **N8841C** | **ASTR** | **229** |
| (N8875) | GLF4 | 4004 |
| **N8881J** | **HS25** | **258219** |
| N8881N | C550 | 190 |
| **N8888** | **F2TH** | **28** |
| N8888 | LJ60 | 128 |
| (N8888D) | LJ35 | 661 |
| **N8888G** | **CL65** | **5773** |
| **N8888H** | **HS25** | **259043** |
| **N8889** | **LJ60** | **128** |
| N8900M | C500 | 675 |
| (N8909R) | SBRL | 306-41 |
| N8940 | C525 | 0253 |
| N8940 | C52A | 0013 |
| N8940 | C52A | 0091 |
| N8989N | GLF4 | 1090 |
| N8999A | FA20 | 137 |
| N9000F | FA50 | 172 |
| N9000F | FA50 | 242 |
| N9000F | SBRL | 465-25 |
| N9000S | SBRL | 282-64 |
| N9000V | SBRL | 282-64 |
| N9000V | SBRL | 306-10 |
| N9001V | SBRL | 306-10 |
| N9003 | C525 | 0257 |
| N9008 | CL60 | 1054 |
| N9008 | GLEX | 9008 |
| (N9011P) | PRM1 | RB-74 |
| N9011R | C500 | 210 |
| N9012H | LJ60 | 179 |
| N9013S | C500 | 288 |
| N9014S | C550 | 025 |
| N9023W | WW24 | 10 |
| N9026 | HS25 | 259026 |
| N9033X | LJ24 | 169 |
| **N9035Y** | **MS76** | **086** |
| N9040 | GLF2 | 82 |
| N9040 | HS25 | 25142 |
| N9040N | WW24 | 140 |
| N9041N | WW24 | 141 |
| N9042N | WW24 | 142 |
| N9043N | WW24 | 143 |
| N9043U | HS25 | 256058 |
| N9044N | WW24 | 144 |
| N9045N | WW24 | 145 |
| N9046F | JSTR | 5015 |
| N9046N | WW24 | 146 |
| N9047N | WW24 | 147 |
| N9048N | WW24 | 148 |
| N9049N | WW24 | 149 |
| N9050N | WW24 | 150 |
| N9060Y | C500 | 241 |
| N9065J | C500 | 247 |
| N9071M | CL60 | 1019 |
| **N9072U** | **CS55** | **0106** |
| N9108Z | LJ36 | 005 |
| N9113F | LJ35 | 259 |
| N9113J | HS25 | 257067 |
| N9114S | WW24 | 164 |
| N9124N | HS25 | 25075 |
| N9125M | LJ55 | 146 |
| N9130F | LJ35 | 664 |
| N9132Z | LJ31 | 031 |
| N9134Q | WW24 | 220 |
| N9138 | HS25 | 25216 |
| N9138Y | F900 | 33 |
| N9140Y | LJ35 | 672 |
| N9141N | LJ35 | 671 |
| N9143F | LJ31 | 055 |
| N9146Z | BE40 | RK-120 |
| (N9147F) | FA10 | 42 |
| N9147Q | LJ31 | 057 |
| N9149 | HS25 | 25161 |
| N9152R | LJ31 | 051 |
| N9152X | LJ31 | 061 |
| N9155Z | LJ60 | 025 |
| N9166Y | SBRL | 265-80 |
| N9168Q | LJ35 | 668 |
| N9173G | LJ35 | 673 |
| N9173L | LJ31 | 029 |
| N9173M | LJ31 | 067 |
| N9173N | LJ31 | 071 |
| N9173Q | LJ31 | 053 |
| N9173R | LJ60 | 017 |
| N9173T | LJ31 | 087 |
| N9173V | LJ31 | 069 |
| N9173X | LJ31 | 090 |
| N9180K | C525 | 0342 |
| **N9180K** | **C52A** | **0345** |
| **N9200M** | **LJ60** | **132** |
| N9201R | JSTR | 5001/53 |
| N9202R | JSTR | 5002 |
| N9203R | JSTR | 5003 |
| N9204R | JSTR | 5004 |
| N9205R | JSTR | 5007/45 |
| N9206R | JSTR | 5009 |
| N9207R | JSTR | 5020 |
| N9208R | JSTR | 5101/15 |
| N9210R | JSTR | 5016 |
| N9211R | JSTR | 5037/24 |
| N9212R | JSTR | 5038 |
| N9214R | JSTR | 5047 |
| N9215R | JSTR | 5048 |
| N9216R | JSTR | 5049 |
| N9217R | JSTR | 5051 |
| N9218R | JSTR | 5052 |
| N9219R | JSTR | 5053/2 |
| N9220R | JSTR | 5054/59 |
| N9221R | JSTR | 5023 |
| N9222R | JSTR | 5055/21 |
| N9223R | JSTR | 5056 |
| N9225R | JSTR | 5060 |
| N9226R | JSTR | 5061/48 |
| N9228R | JSTR | 5063 |
| N9229R | JSTR | 5065 |
| N9230R | JSTR | 5066/46 |
| N9231R | JSTR | 5068/27 |
| N9233R | JSTR | 5072/23 |
| N9234R | JSTR | 5074/22 |
| N9235R | JSTR | 5076/17 |
| N9235R | JSTR | 5102 |
| N9236R | JSTR | 5077 |
| N9238R | JSTR | 5079/33 |
| N9240R | JSTR | 5084/8 |
| N9241R | JSTR | 5085 |
| N9242R | JSTR | 5086/44 |
| N9243R | JSTR | 5087/55 |
| N9244R | JSTR | 5088 |
| N9245R | JSTR | 5089 |
| N9246R | JSTR | 5090 |
| N9247R | JSTR | 5091 |
| N9248R | JSTR | 5092/58 |
| N9249R | JSTR | 5093 |
| N9250R | JSTR | 5094 |
| N9251N | SBRL | 282-131 |
| N9251R | JSTR | 5095/30 |
| N9252N | SBRL | 282-132 |
| N9252R | JSTR | 5096/10 |
| N9253R | JSTR | 5097/60 |
| **N9253V** | **GLEX** | **9024** |
| N9253V | GLF4 | 1176 |
| N9254R | JSTR | 5098/28 |
| N9255R | JSTR | 5099/5 |
| N9256R | JSTR | 5100/41 |
| N9258U | FA10 | 132 |
| N9260A | LJ24 | 047 |
| N9272K | GLF2 | 46 |
| N9280R | JSTR | 5006/40 |
| N9282R | JSTR | 5011/1 |
| N9282R | JSTR | 5046 |
| N9282Y | HS25 | 256044 |
| N9283R | JSTR | 5012 |
| N9284R | JSTR | 5013 |
| N9286R | JSTR | 5017 |
| N9287R | JSTR | 5018 |
| N9288R | JSTR | 5019 |
| **N9292X** | **HS25** | **258315** |
| N9300 | GLF2 | 7 |
| N9300 | GLF4 | 1020 |
| N9300 | HS25 | 25051 |
| N9300C | FA50 | 106 |
| N9300C | HS25 | 25051 |
| N9300C | HS25 | 25169 |
| N9300M | FA20 | 106 |
| (N9300P) | HS25 | 25169 |
| N9308Y | HS25 | 25058 |
| N9311 | FA50 | 121 |
| N9312 | FA50 | 126 |
| N9313 | FA50 | 128 |
| N9314 | FA50 | 130 |
| (N9366Q) | JSTR | 5214 |
| N9395Y | HS25 | 257059 |
| N9500B | SBRL | 282-91 |
| N9503Z | SBRL | 282-10 |
| N9550A | FA50 | 265 |
| N9611Z | ASTR | 231 |
| N9654N | FA20 | 380 |
| **N9661S** | **C680** | **0247** |
| N9671A | LJ25 | 092 |
| (N9680N) | CL61 | 3050 |
| N9680Z | CL61 | 3050 |
| **N9700T** | **C560** | **0203** |
| N9700X | CL61 | 5186 |
| (N9707X) | FA7X | 9 |
| N9708N | CL61 | 3061 |
| N9711N | GLF3 | 358 |
| N9712T | C500 | 397 |
| (N9718P) | GLF3 | 405 |
| N9739B | JSTR | 5052 |
| **N9867** | **HS25** | **258678** |
| N9871R | C500 | 121 |
| **N9871R** | **F2EX** | **43** |
| (N9876S) | LJ35 | 277 |
| N9881S | GPER | 551 |
| **N9895** | **F2EX** | **184** |
| **N9900R** | **EA50** | **000176** |
| N9921 | JSTR | 5070/52 |
| **N9922F** | **EA50** | **000100** |
| N9932 | WW24 | 82 |
| **N9939T** | **GLF4** | **4134** |
| N9990P | ASTR | 062 |
| **N9990S** | **HS25** | **258209** |
| N9999E | FA20 | 135 |
| **N9999M** | **GLF4** | **1090** |
| N9999V | HS25 | 257155 |
| N10108 | C500 | 035 |
| N10121 | HS25 | 25098 |
| N10122 | HS25 | 25029 |
| N10122 | WW24 | 182 |
| **N10123** | **GLF2** | **107** |
| N10123 | JSTR | 5012 |
| N10461 | JSTR | 5011/1 |
| N10580 | SBRL | 465-7 |
| N10581 | SBRL | 465-8 |
| N10726 | FA20 | 54 |
| N10855 | HS25 | 258159 |
| N10855 | HS25 | 259002 |
| N10857 | HS25 | 258213 |
| N10870 | LJ35 | 268 |
| N10870 | LJ35 | 331 |
| N10870 | LJ35 | 430 |
| N10870 | LJ35 | 649 |
| N10870 | LJ55 | 103 |
| N10870 | LJ55 | 122 |
| N10870 | LJ60 | 362 |
| N10871 | LJ35 | 270 |
| N10871 | LJ35 | 317 |
| N10871 | LJ35 | 504 |
| N10871 | LJ35 | 618 |
| N10871 | LJ36 | 055 |
| N10871 | LJ55 | 143 |
| N10872 | LJ25 | 369 |
| N10872 | LJ35 | 275 |
| N10872 | LJ55 | 013 |
| N10872 | LJ60 | 368 |
| N10873 | LJ25 | 315 |
| N10873 | LJ25 | 364 |
| N10873 | LJ31 | 003 |
| N10873 | LJ35 | 475 |
| N10873 | LJ35 | 602 |
| N10873 | LJ45 | 402 |
| N10873 | LJ60 | 369 |
| N10972 | LJ35 | 038 |
| N11084 | C680 | 0114 |
| N11111 | LJ24 | 098 |
| **N11288** | **C650** | **0184** |
| N11382 | LJ35 | 002 |
| N11697 | FA10 | 40 |
| N11827 | FA20 | 26 |
| **N11887** | **SBRL** | **380-4** |
| N11963 | C56X | 5685 |
| N12001 | C550 | 689 |
| N12003 | C550 | 698 |
| N12012 | C560 | 0268 |
| N12022 | C550 | 708 |
| (N12030) | C550 | 712 |
| N12033 | C550 | 713 |
| N12035 | C550 | 714 |
| N12058 | C552 | 0004 |
| N12060 | C550 | 718 |
| N12065 | C552 | 0011 |
| **N12068** | **C550** | **719** |
| N12109 | LJ35 | 410 |
| N12117 | C550 | 731 |
| (N12117) | C560 | 0007 |
| N12121 | JSTR | 5005 |
| N12142 | C550 | 396 |
| (N12149) | C550 | 397 |
| (N12155) | C550 | 402 |
| N12157 | C550 | 403 |
| (N12159) | C550 | 404 |
| N12160 | C550 | 412 |
| (N12160) | C560 | 0009 |
| N12162 | C550 | 413 |
| (N12162) | C560 | 0010 |
| N12164 | C550 | 414 |
| N12167 | C550 | 415 |
| N12171 | C550 | 422 |
| N12171 | C560 | 0015 |
| (N12173) | C550 | 423 |
| N12173 | C560 | 0016 |
| N12190 | C550 | 437 |
| (N12191) | C550 | 438 |
| N12225 | HS25 | 25122 |
| N12241 | JSTR | 5141 |
| (N12249) | C560 | 0018 |
| N12269 | C552 | 0015 |
| (N12283) | C560 | 0023 |
| (N12284) | C560 | 0024 |
| (N12285) | C560 | 0025 |
| (N12286) | C560 | 0026 |
| (N12289) | C560 | 0027 |
| (N12295) | C560 | 0036 |
| N12295 | C650 | 7075 |
| (N12297) | C560 | 0037 |
| (N12298) | C560 | 0038 |
| N12315 | LJ24 | 154 |
| N12373 | LJ25 | 054 |
| N12378 | C550 | 550-1040 |
| N12403 | C560 | 0040 |
| N12419 | C550 | 608 |
| N12482 | C550 | 447 |
| N12490 | C550 | 454 |
| N12500 | C550 | 459 |
| N12505 | C550 | 460 |
| N12507 | C550 | 461 |
| N12508 | C550 | 462 |
| N12510 | C550 | 471 |
| N12511 | C550 | 472 |
| N12513 | C550 | 473 |
| N12514 | C550 | 474 |
| (N12522) | C550 | 480 |
| N12522 | C550 | 615 |
| N12532 | C550 | 487 |
| N12536 | C550 | 488 |
| N12539 | C550 | 489 |

| | | |
|---|---|---|
| (N12543) | C550 | 496 |
| N12543 | C550 | 621 |
| (N12549) | C550 | 497 |
| **N12549** | **C550** | **501** |
| (N12554) | C550 | 625 |
| (N12554) | CS55 | 0003 |
| N12557 | C552 | 0003 |
| N12564 | C552 | 0010 |
| N12566 | C552 | 0012 |
| N12568 | C552 | 0014 |
| N12570 | C550 | 632 |
| (N12570) | CS55 | 0012 |
| N12576 | C550 | 633 |
| (N12576) | CS55 | 0013 |
| (N12582) | C550 | 638 |
| (N12583) | CS55 | 0014 |
| (N12593) | C550 | 646 |
| N12593 | C650 | 7008 |
| (N12593) | CS55 | 0024 |
| (N12596) | C550 | 647 |
| N12596 | C650 | 7009 |
| (N12596) | CS55 | 0025 |
| N12605 | C650 | 7013 |
| (N12605) | CS55 | 0031 |
| (N12615) | CS55 | 0036 |
| N12616 | C650 | 7019 |
| (N12616) | CS55 | 0037 |
| N12632 | C650 | 7030 |
| N12636 | C650 | 7031 |
| N12637 | C650 | 7032 |
| N12642 | C650 | 7038 |
| N12643 | C650 | 7039 |
| N12652 | C650 | 7045 |
| N12659 | SBRL | 380-16 |
| N12660 | C552 | 0006 |
| N12686 | C56X | 5368 |
| N12688 | C560 | 0488 |
| (N12690) | CS55 | 0046 |
| N12695 | CS55 | 0047 |
| N12703 | CS55 | 0052 |
| N12705 | CS55 | 0053 |
| N12709 | CS55 | 0054 |
| (N12712) | CS55 | 0061 |
| N12715 | CS55 | 0062 |
| (N12717) | CS55 | 0063 |
| (N12720) | CS55 | 0069 |
| (N12722) | CS55 | 0070 |
| (N12727) | CS55 | 0071 |
| N12730 | CS55 | 0080 |
| N12742 | C52A | 0359 |
| (N12744) | CS55 | 0088 |
| N12745 | CS55 | 0089 |
| N12746 | CS55 | 0090 |
| (N12747) | CS55 | 0091 |
| N12756 | C552 | 0002 |
| N12761 | C552 | 0007 |
| N12762 | C552 | 0008 |
| N12763 | C552 | 0009 |
| N12778 | C56X | 5553 |
| N12798 | C560 | 0176 |
| N12799 | C560 | 0177 |
| N12807 | C560 | 0183 |
| N12812 | C560 | 0187 |
| N12813 | C560 | 0188 |
| N12815 | C560 | 0189 |
| N12816 | C560 | 0190 |
| N12817 | C560 | 0191 |
| N12824 | C560 | 0196 |
| N12826 | C560 | 0197 |
| N12838 | C560 | 0205 |
| N12845 | C560 | 0213 |
| N12850 | C560 | 0219 |
| N12852 | C560 | 0220 |
| N12855 | C552 | 0001 |
| N12859 | C552 | 0005 |
| (N12879) | C560 | 0232 |
| N12890 | C560 | 0243 |
| (N12895) | C560 | 0244 |
| N12896 | C560 | 0245 |
| N12900 | CS55 | 0103 |
| N12903 | CS55 | 0104 |
| N12907 | C560 | 0247 |
| (N12907) | CS55 | 0105 |
| N12909 | C560 | 0248 |
| (N12909) | C650 | 7110 |
| (N12909) | CS55 | 0106 |
| N12910 | C560 | 0251 |
| (N12910) | CS55 | 0112 |

| | | |
|---|---|---|
| N12911 | C560 | 0252 |
| (N12911) | CS55 | 0113 |
| N12920 | CS55 | 0118 |
| N12921 | C560 | 0254 |
| N12922 | C560 | 0255 |
| (N12922) | CS55 | 0119 |
| N12924 | CS55 | 0120 |
| N12925 | C680 | 0052 |
| (N12925) | CS55 | 0121 |
| N12929 | C560 | 0256 |
| N12929 | CS55 | 0122 |
| N12934 | CS55 | 0131 |
| N12945 | C560 | 0263 |
| (N12945) | CS55 | 0137 |
| N12967 | C552 | 0013 |
| (N12979) | C550 | 556 |
| N12990 | C550 | 571 |
| N12990 | C56X | 5598 |
| N12992 | C550 | 572 |
| N12993 | C550 | 550-1126 |
| (N12993) | C550 | 573 |
| N12998 | C550 | 574 |
| N12999 | C550 | 575 |
| N13001 | C52B | 0083 |
| (N13001) | C550 | 579 |
| (N13006) | C550 | 580 |
| (N13007) | C550 | 581 |
| N13027 | C550 | 597 |
| N13028 | C550 | 598 |
| (N13047) | C650 | 0007 |
| (N13049) | C650 | 0008 |
| (N13052) | C650 | 0013 |
| N13052 | C650 | 0231 |
| N13087 | C52A | 0244 |
| N13091 | C550 | 643 |
| (N13092) | C550 | 644 |
| **N13092** | **C560** | **0707** |
| N13113 | C650 | 0159 |
| N13138 | C650 | 0063 |
| (N13142) | C650 | 0069 |
| (N13150) | C650 | 0078 |
| (N13162) | C650 | 0082 |
| N13166 | C650 | 0083 |
| (N13168) | C650 | 0084 |
| (N13170) | C650 | 0088 |
| (N13175) | C650 | 0089 |
| (N13189) | C650 | 0098 |
| (N13194) | C650 | 0103 |
| N13195 | C52A | 0321 |
| N13195 | C650 | 0104 |
| (N13204) | C650 | 0111 |
| (N13210) | C650 | 0118 |
| (N13217) | C650 | 0119 |
| N13218 | C56X | 5633 |
| N13218 | C650 | 0120 |
| (N13222) | C650 | 0125 |
| (N13242) | C650 | 0139 |
| N13256 | C650 | 0146 |
| N13259 | C650 | 0147 |
| N13264 | C650 | 0155 |
| N13267 | C650 | 0156 |
| N13291 | C525 | 0024 |
| N13304 | JSTR | 5004 |
| N13308 | C525 | 0029 |
| (N13312) | C525 | 0031 |
| (N13313) | C525 | 0032 |
| N13474 | C52A | 0360 |
| N13606 | LJ24 | 254 |
| N13616 | C510 | 0049 |
| N13627 | C550 | 147 |
| N14456 | GLF4 | 1430 |
| N15693 | BE40 | RK-29 |
| N16200 | JSTR | 5033/56 |
| (N16251) | GLF4 | 1013 |
| N16300 | HS25 | 258561 |
| N16777 | HS25 | 25083 |
| N17005 | JSTR | 5105 |
| (N17401) | FA20 | 62/409 |
| N17581 | GLF2 | 127 |
| N17581 | GLF2 | 163 |
| N17581 | GLF2 | 183 |
| N17581 | GLF2 | 211 |
| N17581 | GLF2 | 235 |
| N17581 | GLF2 | 256 |
| N17581 | GLF3 | 346 |
| N17581 | GLF3 | 399 |
| N17581 | GLF3 | 435 |
| N17581 | GLF4 | 1001 |

| | | |
|---|---|---|
| N17581 | GLF4 | 1011 |
| N17581 | GLF4 | 1059 |
| N17581 | GLF4 | 1107 |
| N17581 | GLF4 | 1157 |
| N17582 | GLF2 | 131/23 |
| N17582 | GLF2 | 164 |
| N17582 | GLF2 | 186 |
| N17582 | GLF2 | 239 |
| N17582 | GLF3 | 252 |
| N17582 | GLF3 | 326 |
| N17582 | GLF3 | 376 |
| N17582 | GLF3 | 415 |
| N17582 | GLF4 | 1005 |
| N17582 | GLF4 | 1061 |
| N17582 | GLF4 | 1096 |
| N17582 | GLF4 | 1158 |
| N17583 | GLF2 | 133 |
| N17583 | GLF2 | 167 |
| N17583 | GLF2 | 187 |
| N17583 | GLF2 | 43 |
| N17583 | GLF3 | 304 |
| N17583 | GLF3 | 347 |
| N17583 | GLF3 | 418 |
| N17583 | GLF3 | 466 |
| N17583 | GLF4 | 1015 |
| N17583 | GLF4 | 1062 |
| N17583 | GLF4 | 1159 |
| N17584 | GLF2 | 141 |
| N17584 | GLF2 | 169 |
| N17584 | GLF2 | 194 |
| N17584 | GLF2 | 224 |
| N17584 | GLF2 | 244 |
| N17584 | GLF3 | 307 |
| N17584 | GLF4 | 1019 |
| N17584 | GLF4 | 1026 |
| N17584 | GLF4 | 1063 |
| N17584 | GLF4 | 1108 |
| N17584 | GLF4 | 1160 |
| N17585 | GLF2 | 144 |
| N17585 | GLF2 | 171 |
| N17585 | GLF2 | 201 |
| N17585 | GLF2 | 214 |
| N17585 | GLF2 | 225 |
| N17585 | GLF2 | 78 |
| N17585 | GLF3 | 311 |
| N17585 | GLF3 | 345 |
| N17585 | GLF3 | 400 |
| N17585 | GLF4 | 1032 |
| N17585 | GLF4 | 1068 |
| N17585 | GLF4 | 1129 |
| N17585 | GLF4 | 1161 |
| N17586 | GLF2 | 149 |
| N17586 | GLF2 | 175 |
| N17586 | GLF2 | 202 |
| N17586 | GLF2 | 230 |
| N17586 | GLF2 | 91 |
| N17586 | GLF3 | 352 |
| N17586 | GLF3 | 379 |
| N17586 | GLF3 | 439 |
| N17586 | GLF3 | 465 |
| N17586 | GLF4 | 1072 |
| N17586 | GLF4 | 1076 |
| N17586 | GLF4 | 1167 |
| N17587 | GLF2 | 152 |
| N17587 | GLF2 | 177 |
| N17587 | GLF2 | 203 |
| N17587 | GLF2 | 246 |
| N17587 | GLF3 | 324 |
| N17587 | GLF3 | 393 |
| N17587 | GLF3 | 442 |
| N17587 | GLF4 | 1074 |
| N17587 | GLF4 | 1173 |
| N17588 | GLF2 | 179 |
| N17588 | GLF2 | 204 |
| N17588 | GLF3 | 367 |
| N17588 | GLF4 | 1037 |
| N17588 | GLF4 | 1175 |
| N17589 | GLF2 | 161 |
| N17589 | GLF2 | 182 |
| N17589 | GLF2 | 248 |
| N17589 | GLF3 | 368 |
| N17589 | GLF4 | 1078 |
| N17603 | GLF3 | 407 |
| N17603 | GLF4 | 1038 |
| N17603 | GLF4 | 1079 |
| N17608 | GLF3 | 356 |
| N17608 | GLF3 | 408 |
| N17608 | GLF4 | 1042 |

| | | |
|---|---|---|
| N17608 | GLF4 | 1106 |
| N18243 | HS25 | 257182 |
| N18328 | C500 | 373 |
| N18860 | C500 | 653 |
| N20373 | FA10 | 33 |
| N20669 | C52A | 0444 |
| N20768 | C750 | 0298 |
| N21066 | GLF2 | 69 |
| N21076 | C56X | 5828 |
| N21092 | SBRL | 265-42 |
| N21654 | C680 | 0258 |
| (N22265) | JSTR | 5005 |
| (N22508) | C500 | 474 |
| N22511 | C550 | 089 |
| N22976 | WW24 | 133 |
| N23204 | HS25 | 258346 |
| N23207 | HS25 | 258350 |
| N23208 | HS25 | 258351 |
| N23263 | BE40 | RK-290 |
| N23395 | HS25 | 258339 |
| N23451 | HS25 | 258382 |
| N23455 | HS25 | 258384 |
| N23466 | HS25 | 258385 |
| N23479 | HS25 | 258386 |
| N23488 | HS25 | 258388 |
| N23493 | HS25 | 258389 |
| N23509 | HS25 | 258390 |
| N23525 | BE40 | RK-238 |
| N23550 | HS25 | 258403 |
| N23555 | FA20 | 46 |
| N23556 | HS25 | 258370 |
| N23566 | HS25 | 258381 |
| N23569 | HS25 | 258392 |
| N23577 | HS25 | 258395 |
| N23585 | HS25 | 258396 |
| N23592 | HS25 | 258401 |
| **N24237** | **C650** | **0102** |
| **N24329** | **C510** | **0020** |
| N24480 | SBRL | 276-33 |
| N25685 | LJ31 | 056 |
| N25853 | HS25 | 258538 |
| N25997 | LJ31 | 062 |
| N25999 | LJ31 | 059 |
| N26002 | LJ31 | 077 |
| N26005 | LJ31 | 065 |
| N26006 | LJ31 | 066 |
| N26008 | LJ24 | 026 |
| N26011 | HS25 | 25060 |
| N26011 | LJ60 | 013 |
| N26018 | GLF3 | 316 |
| N26018 | LJ31 | 058 |
| N26029 | LJ60 | 009 |
| N26105 | C525 | 0042 |
| N26105 | C650 | 0182 |
| N26174 | C525 | 0046 |
| N26174 | C650 | 0189 |
| N26178 | C550 | 141 |
| N26227 | C500 | 642 |
| (N26228) | C500 | 643 |
| N26228 | C650 | 0194 |
| N26229 | C550 | 093 |
| N26232 | C500 | 644 |
| N26233 | C650 | 0195 |
| N26263 | C500 | 652 |
| N26264 | C500 | 653 |
| (N26264) | C650 | 0201 |
| N26271 | C650 | 0203 |
| N26369 | C550 | 150 |
| N26369 | CS55 | 0152 |
| N26379 | C525 | 0052 |
| N26379 | CS55 | 0154 |
| N26461 | C500 | 489 |
| N26461 | C550 | 156 |
| (N26481) | C500 | 496 |
| N26481 | C525 | 0061 |
| (N26486) | C500 | 497 |
| N26486 | C525 | 0062 |
| N26492 | C500 | 505 |
| N26493 | C500 | 506 |
| N26494 | C500 | 507 |
| **N26494** | **C550** | **605** |
| (N26495) | C500 | 508 |
| N26495 | C525 | 0066 |
| (N26496) | C500 | 509 |
| **N26496** | **C550** | **607** |
| N26497 | C500 | 510 |
| N26498 | C500 | 511 |
| (N26499) | C500 | 512 |

| | | |
|---|---|---|
| N26499 | C525 | 0067 |
| (N26502) | C500 | 520 |
| N26502 | C525 | 0069 |
| N26503 | C500 | 521 |
| (N26504) | C500 | 522 |
| N26504 | C525 | 0070 |
| N26506 | C500 | 523 |
| N26507 | C500 | 524 |
| (N26509) | C500 | 525 |
| N26509 | C525 | 0071 |
| N26510 | C500 | 532 |
| N26514 | C500 | 533 |
| N26517 | C500 | 534 |
| N26523 | C500 | 535 |
| (N26540) | C500 | 507 |
| N26581 | C525 | 0074 |
| N26583 | LJ35 | 433 |
| N26610 | C550 | 075 |
| N26610 | C550 | 161 |
| N26613 | C550 | 076 |
| (N26614) | C550 | 077 |
| (N26615) | C550 | 078 |
| (N26616) | C550 | 079 |
| N26617 | C550 | 080 |
| N26619 | C550 | 081 |
| N26619 | GLF3 | 353 |
| (N26621) | C550 | 086 |
| **N26621** | **C550** | **593** |
| (N26622) | C550 | 087 |
| (N26623) | C550 | 088 |
| (N26624) | C550 | 089 |
| N26626 | C550 | 090 |
| N26627 | C550 | 091 |
| N26628 | C550 | 092 |
| (N26630) | C550 | 101 |
| (N26630) | C560 | 0039 |
| N26631 | C550 | 102 |
| N26632 | C550 | 103 |
| N26634 | C550 | 104 |
| (N26635) | C550 | 105 |
| N26638 | C550 | 106 |
| N26639 | C550 | 107 |
| N26640 | C550 | 113 |
| N26640 | CL60 | 1039 |
| (N26643) | C550 | 114 |
| N26643 | C560 | 0041 |
| (N26648) | C550 | 115 |
| (N26648) | C560 | 0042 |
| N26649 | C550 | 116 |
| N26652 | C550 | 123 |
| (N26656) | C550 | 124 |
| (N26656) | C560 | 0046 |
| N26674 | CRVT | 27 |
| (N26771) | C560 | 0050 |
| (N26804) | C560 | 0054 |
| N26863 | C550 | 139 |
| N26895 | CL60 | 1056 |
| **N27052** | **EA50** | **000120** |
| (N27216) | C560 | 0066 |
| N27341 | CL60 | 1051 |
| **N27369** | **C510** | **712** |
| N27457 | C550 | 132 |
| N28686 | HS25 | 25152 |
| N28968 | C550 | 074 |
| N29019 | SBRL | 370-6 |
| N29687 | CL60 | 1048 |
| N29858 | C500 | 112 |
| N29966 | FA10 | 17 |
| N29977 | HS25 | 25028 |
| N29984 | CL60 | 1060 |
| N29991 | C500 | 254 |
| N29995 | WW24 | 250 |
| N30046 | BE40 | RK-206 |
| N30046 | LJ31 | 146 |
| N30050 | LJ31 | 218 |
| N30051 | LJ31 | 215 |
| N30054 | LJ31 | 227 |
| N30111 | LJ31 | 153 |
| N30137 | LJ45 | 153 |
| N30154 | LJ60 | 191 |
| **N30156** | **WW24** | **165** |
| N30170 | LJ60 | 225 |
| N30289 | HS25 | 258404 |
| N30319 | HS25 | 258408 |
| N30337 | HS25 | 258409 |
| N30355 | HS25 | 258725 |
| N30438 | GLF2 | 30/4 |
| **N30501** | **GLF3** | **383** |
| N30562 | HS25 | 258407 |
| N30682 | HS25 | 258412 |
| N30742 | HS25 | 258414 |
| N31001 | GLF4 | 1001 |
| N31016 | HS25 | 258415 |
| N31046 | HS25 | 258418 |
| N31079 | C500 | 180 |
| N31088 | C500 | 079 |
| N31112 | CL30 | 20083 |
| N31240+ | CL60 | 1063 |
| N31340 | HS25 | 258420 |
| N31403 | SBRL | 276-4 |
| N31428 | BE40 | RJ-28 |
| N31432 | BE40 | RJ-32 |
| N31437 | BE40 | RJ-37 |
| N31496 | BE40 | RK-396 |
| N31542 | BE40 | RJ-42 |
| N31590 | HS25 | 258430 |
| N31596 | HS25 | 258439 |
| N31624 | HS25 | HA-0034 |
| N31685 | HS25 | HB-5 |
| N31733 | BE40 | RJ-33 |
| N31820 | HS25 | 258421 |
| N31833 | HS25 | 258427 |
| N31842 | HS25 | HA-0080 |
| N31921 | PRM1 | RB-221 |
| N31946 | HS25 | HA-0046 |
| N31958 | HS25 | HA-0028 |
| N31959 | HS25 | HA-0049 |
| N31964 | HS25 | HA-0064 |
| N31975 | BE40 | RK-555 |
| N31991 | HS25 | 258891 |
| N32010 | SBRL | 265-83 |
| N32012 | HS25 | 258912 |
| N32022 | PRM1 | RB-222 |
| N32051 | BE40 | RK-541 |
| N32061 | HS25 | 258921 |
| N32185 | HS25 | HA-0055 |
| N32212 | BE40 | TX-10 |
| N32287 | LJ24 | 230 |
| N32290 | SBRL | 465-17 |
| N32508 | SBRL | 285-17 |
| N32654 | SBRL | 282-111 |
| **N32862** | **HS25** | **HA-0062** |
| N32926 | HS25 | HA-0026 |
| N33055 | HS25 | HA-0025 |
| N33062 | BE40 | RK-562 |
| N33235 | HS25 | HA-0035 |
| N33527 | HS25 | HA-0027 |
| N33612 | HS25 | HA-0072 |
| N33805 | PRM1 | RB-235 |
| N33837 | PRM1 | RB-237 |
| N34249 | BE40 | RK-549 |
| N34441 | HS25 | HA-0041 |
| N34451 | HS25 | HA-0061 |
| N34548 | HS25 | HA-0048 |
| N34820 | PRM1 | RB-220 |
| N34838 | HS25 | HA-0038 |
| N34859 | PRM1 | RB-219 |
| N34956 | HS25 | HA-0036 |
| N35004 | HA4T | RC-24 |
| N35403 | C550 | 150 |
| N36050 | SBRL | 282-80 |
| N36065 | SBRL | 282-81 |
| N36204 | LJ25 | 138 |
| **N36578** | **HS25** | **258778** |
| N36607 | BE40 | RK-407 |
| N36621 | HS25 | 258721 |
| N36632 | BE40 | RK-472 |
| N36636 | PRM1 | RB-136 |
| N36646 | BE40 | RK-443 |
| N36669 | HS25 | 258749 |
| N36672 | HS25 | 258712 |
| N36685 | HS25 | 258685 |
| N36689 | HS25 | 258689 |
| N36690 | HS25 | 258690 |
| N36701 | BE40 | RK-401 |
| N36726 | HS25 | 258776 |
| N36731 | PRM1 | RB-131 |
| N36752 | BE40 | RK-452 |
| N36758 | PRM1 | RB-158 |
| N36764 | BE40 | RK-464 |
| N36792 | BE40 | RK-392 |
| N36803 | BE40 | RK-403 |
| N36820 | HS25 | 258720 |
| N36826 | HS25 | 258806 |
| N36841 | HS25 | 258741 |
| N36842 | C500 | 364 |
| N36846 | BE40 | RK-476 |
| N36846 | C500 | 365 |
| N36848 | C500 | 366 |
| N36850 | C500 | 367 |
| N36854 | C500 | 368 |
| N36854 | C550 | 653 |
| N36858 | C500 | 369 |
| N36859 | C500 | 370 |
| N36860 | C500 | 371 |
| N36861 | C500 | 372 |
| N36862 | C500 | 373 |
| N36863 | C500 | 374 |
| N36864 | C500 | 375 |
| N36864 | PRM1 | RB-164 |
| **N36866** | **PRM1** | **RB-166** |
| N36869 | C500 | 376 |
| N36870 | C500 | 377 |
| N36871 | C500 | 378 |
| N36872 | C500 | 379 |
| N36873 | C500 | 380 |
| N36873 | PRM1 | RB-153 |
| N36878 | HS25 | 258807 |
| N36880 | BE40 | RK-480 |
| N36880 | C500 | 381 |
| N36881 | C500 | 382 |
| N36882 | C500 | 383 |
| N36883 | C500 | 384 |
| N36884 | C500 | 385 |
| N36885 | C500 | 386 |
| N36886 | C500 | 387 |
| N36886 | C550 | 654 |
| N36887 | C500 | 388 |
| N36888 | C500 | 389 |
| N36890 | C500 | 390 |
| N36890 | PRM1 | RB-160 |
| N36891 | C500 | 391 |
| N36892 | C500 | 392 |
| N36893 | C500 | 393 |
| N36894 | HS25 | 258694 |
| N36895 | C500 | 394 |
| N36896 | C500 | 395 |
| N36896 | HS25 | 258696 |
| N36897 | C500 | 396 |
| N36898 | C500 | 397 |
| N36901 | C500 | 398 |
| N36906 | C500 | 399 |
| N36907 | BE40 | RK-417 |
| N36908 | C500 | 400 |
| N36911 | C500 | 401 |
| N36912 | C500 | 402 |
| N36914 | C500 | 403 |
| N36915 | C500 | 404 |
| N36916 | C500 | 405 |
| N36918 | C500 | 406 |
| N36919 | C500 | 407 |
| N36922 | C500 | 408 |
| N36923 | C500 | 409 |
| N36943 | C500 | 423 |
| N36949 | C500 | 428 |
| N36964 | PRM1 | RB-154 |
| N36970 | HS25 | 258770 |
| N36979 | PRM1 | RB-149 |
| N36986 | HS25 | 258786 |
| N36997 | BE40 | RK-397 |
| N37009 | HS25 | 258799 |
| N37010 | HS25 | 258710 |
| N37019 | PRM1 | RB-177 |
| N37054 | HS25 | 258754 |
| N37056 | HS25 | 258756 |
| N37059 | PRM1 | RB-159 |
| N37060 | HS25 | 258730 |
| N37061 | HS25 | 258731 |
| N37070 | HS25 | 258780 |
| N37071 | PRM1 | RB-151 |
| N37079 | BE40 | RK-469 |
| N37086 | PRM1 | RB-186 |
| N37092 | HS25 | 258692 |
| N37105 | HS25 | 258775 |
| N37108 | BE40 | RK-408 |
| N37115 | BE40 | RK-415 |
| N37146 | HS25 | 258783 |
| N37158 | HS25 | 258758 |
| N37160 | HS25 | 258760 |
| N37165 | BE40 | RK-465 |
| N37170 | HS25 | 258817 |
| N37179 | HS25 | 258779 |
| **N37201** | **C550** | **655** |
| N37204 | BE40 | RK-404 |
| N37211 | HS25 | 258711 |
| N37245 | PRM1 | RB-145 |
| N37261 | HS25 | 258781 |
| N37295 | HS25 | 258795 |
| N37310 | BE40 | RK-410 |
| N37312 | BE40 | RK-412 |
| N37322 | HS25 | 258722 |
| N37325 | BE40 | RK-425 |
| N37337 | BE40 | RK-437 |
| N37339 | BE40 | RK-512 |
| N37346 | PRM1 | RB-196 |
| N37489 | C500 | 317 |
| N37516 | HS25 | 25271 |
| N37594 | LJ24 | 128 |
| N37643 | C500 | 255 |
| N37931 | LJ35 | 342 |
| N37943 | LJ25 | 344 |
| N37947 | LJ35 | 449 |
| N37949 | LJ25 | 348 |
| N37951 | LJ55 | 011 |
| N37962 | LJ35 | 446 |
| N37965 | LJ35 | 399 |
| N37966 | LJ35 | 403 |
| **N37971** | **LJ25** | **358** |
| N37973 | LJ25 | 359 |
| N37975 | HS25 | 257004 |
| N37975 | LJ35 | 474 |
| N37980 | LJ35 | 412 |
| N37984 | LJ35 | 384 |
| N37988 | LJ35 | 436 |
| N38328 | LJ25 | 314 |
| N38788 | LJ24 | 262 |
| N39142 | C550 | 235 |
| N39292 | LJ35 | 189 |
| N39293 | LJ35 | 188 |
| N39300 | C500 | 571 |
| N39301 | C500 | 353 |
| N39391 | LJ25 | 311 |
| N39391 | LJ35 | 118 |
| N39391 | LJ36 | 042 |
| N39391 | LJ55 | 078 |
| N39391 | LJ55 | 105 |
| N39391 | LJ55 | 124 |
| N39391 | LJ55 | 139 |
| N39394 | LJ28 | 28-004 |
| N39394 | LJ35 | 145 |
| N39394 | LJ35 | 597 |
| N39394 | LJ36 | 057 |
| N39394 | LJ55 | 082 |
| N39398 | LJ25 | 245 |
| N39398 | LJ25 | 362 |
| N39398 | LJ35 | 144 |
| N39398 | LJ35 | 272 |
| N39398 | LJ35 | 316 |
| N39398 | LJ35 | 626 |
| N39398 | LJ55 | 095 |
| N39398 | LJ55 | 114 |
| N39399 | LJ25 | 370 |
| N39399 | LJ31 | 025 |
| N39399 | LJ35 | 151 |
| N39399 | LJ35 | 492 |
| N39399 | LJ35 | 607 |
| N39399 | LJ55 | 134 |
| N39404 | LJ28 | 28-002 |
| N39404 | LJ35 | 624 |
| N39404 | LJ35 | 658 |
| N39404 | LJ55 | 079 |
| N39404 | LJ55 | 104 |
| N39412 | LJ25 | 346 |
| N39412 | LJ28 | 29-004 |
| N39412 | LJ35 | 179 |
| N39412 | LJ35 | 217 |
| N39412 | LJ35 | 329 |
| N39412 | LJ35 | 638 |
| N39412 | LJ55 | 067 |
| N39412 | LJ55 | 110 |
| N39413 | LJ25 | 260 |
| N39413 | LJ35 | 259 |
| N39413 | LJ35 | 313 |
| N39413 | LJ35 | 474 |
| N39413 | LJ35 | 611 |
| N39413 | LJ55 | 015 |
| N39413 | LJ55 | 084 |
| N39413 | LJ55 | 137 |
| N39415 | LJ25 | 229 |
| N39415 | LJ25 | 347 |
| N39415 | LJ31 | 005 |
| N39415 | LJ35 | 161 |

| | | |
|---|---|---|
| N39415 | LJ35 | 201 |
| N39415 | LJ35 | 598 |
| N39415 | LJ55 | 075 |
| N39415 | LJ55 | 101 |
| N39416 | LJ25 | 238 |
| N39416 | LJ25 | 287 |
| N39416 | LJ25 | 363 |
| N39416 | LJ35 | 219 |
| N39416 | LJ35 | 433 |
| N39416 | LJ35 | 469 |
| N39416 | LJ35 | 633 |
| N39416 | LJ55 | 118 |
| N39418 | LJ35 | 205 |
| N39418 | LJ35 | 230 |
| N39418 | LJ35 | 267 |
| N39418 | LJ35 | 643 |
| N39418 | LJ36 | 053 |
| N39418 | LJ55 | 039 |
| N39418 | LJ55 | 120 |
| N39461 | FA50 | 98 |
| N39515 | FA10 | 37 |
| N40012 | LJ31 | 223 |
| N40012 | LJ40 | 45-2074 |
| N40012 | LJ45 | 104 |
| N40012 | LJ45 | 266 |
| N40012 | LJ45 | 403 |
| N40012 | LJ60 | 231 |
| N40012 | LJ60 | 298 |
| N40012 | LJ60 | 349 |
| N40027 | HS25 | 258434 |
| N40031 | LJ31 | 242 |
| N40043 | LJ31 | 242 |
| N40043 | LJ40 | 45-2098 |
| N40043 | LJ45 | 272 |
| N40043 | LJ45 | 303 |
| N40043 | LJ45 | 394 |
| N40043 | LJ60 | 205 |
| N40049 | C510 | 0174 |
| N40050 | LJ40 | 45-2035 |
| N40050 | LJ40 | 45-2112 |
| N40050 | LJ45 | 140 |
| N40050 | LJ45 | 250 |
| N40050 | LJ45 | 347 |
| N40050 | LJ60 | 260 |
| N40050 | LJ60 | 305 |
| N40073 | LJ31 | 227 |
| N40073 | LJ40 | 45-2029 |
| N40073 | LJ45 | 231 |
| N40073 | LJ45 | 251 |
| N40073 | LJ45 | 305 |
| N40073 | LJ45 | 336 |
| N40073 | LJ45 | 382 |
| N40073 | LJ60 | 191 |
| N40073 | LJ60 | 342 |
| N40075 | LJ31 | 215 |
| N40075 | LJ40 | 45-2113 |
| N40075 | LJ45 | 148 |
| N40075 | LJ45 | 249 |
| N40075 | LJ45 | 274 |
| N40075 | LJ45 | 362 |
| N40075 | LJ60 | 259 |
| N40075 | LJ60 | 303 |
| N40076 | LJ40 | 45-2030 |
| N40076 | LJ40 | 45-2080 |
| N40076 | LJ45 | 232 |
| N40076 | LJ45 | 252 |
| N40076 | LJ60 | 206 |
| N40076 | LJ60 | 304 |
| N40076 | LJ60 | 344 |
| N40076 | LJ60 | 364 |
| **N40076** | **LJ60** | **386** |
| N40077 | LJ31 | 216 |
| N40077 | LJ40 | 45-2015 |
| N40077 | LJ40 | 45-2048 |
| N40077 | LJ40 | 45-2071 |
| N40077 | LJ45 | 220 |
| N40077 | LJ45 | 354 |
| **N40077** | **LJ45** | **409** |
| N40077 | LJ60 | 288 |
| N40077 | LJ60 | 355 |
| N40078 | LJ31 | 217 |
| N40078 | LJ40 | 45-2016 |
| N40078 | LJ40 | 45-2097 |
| N40078 | LJ45 | 284 |
| N40078 | LJ45 | 311 |
| N40078 | LJ45 | 388 |
| N40079 | LJ40 | 45-2078 |
| N40079 | LJ40 | 45-2094 |
| N40079 | LJ45 | 229 |
| N40079 | LJ45 | 280 |
| N40079 | LJ45 | 397 |
| N40079 | LJ60 | 213 |
| N40079 | LJ60 | 277 |
| **N40081** | **LJ40** | **45-2121** |
| N40081 | LJ45 | 117 |
| N40081 | LJ45 | 223 |
| N40081 | LJ45 | 255 |
| N40081 | LJ45 | 328 |
| N40081 | LJ45 | 358 |
| N40081 | LJ60 | 300 |
| N40082 | LJ40 | 45-2004 |
| N40082 | LJ40 | 45-2079 |
| N40082 | LJ40 | 45-2119 |
| N40082 | LJ45 | 082 |
| N40082 | LJ45 | 275 |
| N40082 | LJ45 | 369 |
| N40083 | LJ40 | 45-2005 |
| N40083 | LJ40 | 45-2073 |
| N40083 | LJ40 | 45-2096 |
| N40083 | LJ40 | 45-2114 |
| N40083 | LJ60 | 215 |
| N40083 | LJ60 | 289 |
| N40084 | LJ45 | 276 |
| N40084 | LJ45 | 331 |
| N40084 | LJ60 | 208 |
| N40084 | LJ60 | 264 |
| N40085 | LJ40 | 45-2031 |
| N40085 | LJ40 | 45-2105 |
| N40085 | LJ45 | 226 |
| N40085 | LJ45 | 325 |
| N40085 | LJ45 | 400 |
| N40085 | LJ60 | 209 |
| N40086 | LJ45 | 277 |
| N40086 | LJ45 | 304 |
| N40086 | LJ45 | 391 |
| N40086 | LJ60 | 210 |
| N40086 | LJ60 | 265 |
| N40113 | HS25 | 258438 |
| N40130 | LJ31 | 110 |
| N40144 | LJ24 | 342 |
| N40144 | LJ25 | 283 |
| N40144 | LJ31 | 018 |
| N40144 | LJ35 | 165 |
| N40144 | LJ35 | 199 |
| N40144 | LJ35 | 253 |
| N40144 | LJ35 | 483 |
| N40144 | LJ35 | 508 |
| N40144 | LJ35 | 599 |
| N40144 | LJ35 | 629 |
| N40144 | LJ45 | 392 |
| N40144 | LJ55 | 014 |
| N40146 | LJ25 | 349 |
| N40146 | LJ35 | 099 |
| N40146 | LJ35 | 178 |
| N40146 | LJ35 | 207 |
| N40146 | LJ35 | 593 |
| N40146 | LJ36 | 032 |
| N40146 | LJ45 | 393 |
| N40146 | LJ55 | 063 |
| N40146 | LJ55 | 090 |
| N40149 | LJ25 | 357 |
| N40149 | LJ25 | 372 |
| N40149 | LJ35 | 101 |
| N40149 | LJ35 | 208 |
| N40149 | LJ35 | 344 |
| N40149 | LJ35 | 442 |
| N40149 | LJ35 | 623 |
| N40149 | LJ45 | 395 |
| **N40149** | **LJ45** | **406** |
| N40149 | LJ55 | 083 |
| N40162 | LJ25 | 246 |
| N40162 | LJ25 | 263 |
| N40162 | LJ35 | 477 |
| N40162 | LJ35 | 608 |
| N40162 | LJ40 | 45-2122 |
| N40162 | LJ55 | 086 |
| N40166 | C560 | 0692 |
| N40180 | FA10 | 93 |
| N40202 | HS25 | 258442 |
| N40215 | BE40 | RK-258 |
| N40252 | BE40 | RK-247 |
| N40255 | HS25 | 258095 |
| N40280 | LJ31 | 078 |
| N40310 | HS25 | 258447 |
| N40323 | LJ60 | 023 |
| N40339 | LJ31 | 076 |
| N40349 | LJ31 | 079 |
| N40363 | LJ31 | 083 |
| N40366 | LJ60 | 019 |
| N40435 | C550 | 550-1008 |
| N40488 | HS25 | 258440 |
| N40489 | HS25 | 258444 |
| N40577 | C56X | 5157 |
| N40593 | WW24 | 41 |
| N40708 | HS25 | 258445 |
| **N40742** | **C510** | **0289** |
| **N40780** | **C510** | **0300** |
| N40864 | C510 | 0252 |
| N40933 | HS25 | 258493 |
| N40994 | FA20 | 289 |
| N41093 | HS25 | 258454 |
| N41118 | C56X | 5510 |
| N41154 | FA20 | 147/444 |
| N41159 | C525 | 0652 |
| N41174 | C52A | 0373 |
| N41184 | C52A | 0378 |
| N41196 | C525 | 0675 |
| N41199 | C680 | 0228 |
| N41203 | C52B | 0266 |
| N41212 | C52A | 0424 |
| N41221 | C680 | 0270 |
| N41222 | C680 | 0274 |
| N41225 | C680 | 0263 |
| N41226 | C52B | 0309 |
| N41227 | C510 | 0195 |
| N41233 | C56X | 5804 |
| N41237 | C56X | 5816 |
| N41280 | HS25 | 258448 |
| N41283 | BE40 | RK-266 |
| N41297 | C510 | 0196 |
| N41431 | HS25 | 258449 |
| N41441 | HS25 | 258450 |
| N41534 | HS25 | 258451 |
| N41762 | HS25 | 258456 |
| N41953 | HS25 | 25268 |
| N41964 | HS25 | 258464 |
| N41984 | HS25 | 258457 |
| N42137 | CL60 | 1011 |
| N42622 | HS25 | 256011 |
| N42685 | HS25 | 258458 |
| **N42799** | **SBRL** | **380-30** |
| N42825 | LJ25 | 314 |
| N42830 | HS25 | 258470 |
| N42905 | LJ31 | 020 |
| N42905 | LJ35 | 520 |
| N42905 | LJ35 | 536 |
| N42905 | LJ35 | 630 |
| N42905 | LJ55 | 054 |
| N43079 | HS25 | 258469 |
| N43182 | HS25 | 258482 |
| N43230 | HS25 | 258462 |
| N43259 | HS25 | 258459 |
| N43265 | HS25 | 258465 |
| N43310 | HS25 | 258467 |
| N43436 | HS25 | 258468 |
| N43642 | HS25 | 258471 |
| N43675 | HS25 | 258475 |
| N43783 | LJ25 | 260 |
| N43926 | HS25 | 258481 |
| N44200 | GLF3 | 324 |
| N44515 | HS25 | 258485 |
| N44648 | HS25 | 258478 |
| N44676 | HS25 | 258476 |
| N44695 | LJ35 | 444 |
| N44722 | HS25 | 258472 |
| N44759 | HS25 | 258551 |
| N44767 | HS25 | 258477 |
| N44779 | HS25 | 258479 |
| N44883 | HS25 | 258483 |
| N44888 | HS25 | 258588 |
| N44982 | GLF5 | 581 |
| N45500 | HS25 | 257108 |
| **N45678** | **C550** | **550-1056** |
| N45793 | HS25 | 25152 |
| N45811 | LJ24 | 108 |
| N45824 | LJ24 | 217 |
| N45826 | LJ25 | 283 |
| N45862 | LJ24 | 291 |
| N46032 | LJ24 | 267 |
| N46106 | C500 | 382 |
| N46190 | HS25 | 25108 |
| N46253 | C500 | 454 |
| N46386 | ASTR | 067 |
| N46452 | LJ24 | 095 |
| N46901 | HS25 | 257014 |
| N46931 | LJ35 | 092 |
| N47449 | GLF3 | 420 |
| N48172 | HS25 | 25028 |
| N49566 | HS25 | 257094 |
| N49968 | WW24 | 202 |
| N50005 | HS25 | 258505 |
| N50005 | LJ31 | 229 |
| N50031 | LJ60 | 230 |
| N50034 | HS25 | 258554 |
| N50050 | LJ60 | 057 |
| N50054 | C525 | 0630 |
| N50054 | C52A | 0455 |
| N50054 | C56X | 5726 |
| N50054 | C680 | 0235 |
| N50078 | PRM1 | RB-109 |
| N50088 | LJ31 | 088 |
| N50088 | LJ31 | 192 |
| N50088 | LJ45 | 168 |
| N50111 | LJ31 | 035 |
| N50111 | LJ40 | 45-2006 |
| N50111 | LJ40 | 45-2019 |
| N50111 | LJ40 | 45-2054 |
| N50111 | LJ45 | 058 |
| N50111 | LJ45 | 116 |
| N50111 | LJ45 | 212 |
| N50111 | LJ45 | 401 |
| N50111 | LJ60 | 329 |
| N50111 | LJ60 | 357 |
| N50114 | LJ31 | 111 |
| N50126 | LJ31 | 207 |
| N50126 | LJ40 | 45-2007 |
| N50126 | LJ40 | 45-2124 |
| N50126 | LJ45 | 213 |
| N50126 | LJ45 | 262 |
| N50126 | LJ45 | 286 |
| N50126 | LJ45 | 324 |
| N50126 | LJ45 | 326 |
| N50126 | LJ60 | 152 |
| N50126 | LJ60 | 324 |
| N50127 | JSTR | 5214 |
| "N50127" | LJ60 | 280 |
| N50138 | WW24 | 142 |
| N50145 | LJ31 | 178 |
| N50145 | LJ40 | 45-2107 |
| N50145 | LJ45 | 037 |
| N50145 | LJ45 | 100 |
| N50145 | LJ45 | 145 |
| N50145 | LJ45 | 211 |
| N50145 | LJ45 | 235 |
| N50145 | LJ45 | 316 |
| N50145 | LJ45 | 399 |
| N50145 | LJ60 | 279 |
| N50153 | LJ31 | 065 |
| N50153 | LJ31 | 205 |
| N50153 | LJ40 | 45-2020 |
| N50153 | LJ45 | 059 |
| N50153 | LJ45 | 327 |
| N50153 | LJ45 | 350 |
| N50153 | LJ60 | 016 |
| N50153 | LJ60 | 019 |
| N50153 | LJ60 | 299 |
| N50153 | LJ60 | 372 |
| N50154 | LJ36 | 061 |
| N50154 | LJ40 | 45-2027 |
| N50154 | LJ40 | 45-2066 |
| N50154 | LJ45 | 108 |
| N50154 | LJ45 | 170 |
| N50154 | LJ45 | 247 |
| N50154 | LJ45 | 297 |
| N50154 | LJ45 | 379 |
| N50154 | LJ60 | 039 |
| N50154 | LJ60 | 170 |
| N50154 | LJ60 | 379 |
| N50157 | LJ31 | 171 |
| N50157 | LJ40 | 45-2110 |
| N50157 | LJ45 | 069 |
| N50157 | LJ45 | 263 |
| N50157 | LJ45 | 323 |
| N50157 | LJ60 | 017 |
| N50157 | LJ60 | 046 |
| N50157 | LJ60 | 218 |
| N50157 | LJ60 | 257 |
| N50157 | LJ60 | 272 |
| N50157 | LJ60 | 301 |
| N50157 | LJ60 | 323 |
| N50157 | LJ60 | 376 |
| N50159 | LJ31 | 045 |

| | | |
|---|---|---|
| N50162 | LJ45 | 033 |
| N50162 | LJ60 | 061 |
| N50163 | LJ31 | 044 |
| N50163 | LJ40 | 45-2010 |
| N50163 | LJ40 | 45-2023 |
| N50163 | LJ45 | 070 |
| N50163 | LJ45 | 118 |
| N50163 | LJ45 | 218 |
| N50163 | LJ45 | 377 |
| N50163 | LJ60 | 294 |
| N50163 | LJ60 | 378 |
| N50166 | HS25 | 258506 |
| N50182 | HS25 | 258582 |
| N50207 | LJ31 | 097 |
| N50207 | LJ45 | 178 |
| N50248 | LJ45 | 182 |
| N50275 | C52B | 0159 |
| N50275 | C56X | 5689 |
| N50275 | C56X | 6037 |
| N50275 | C680 | 0185 |
| N50280 | PRM1 | RB-80 |
| N50282 | C52A | 0332 |
| N50282 | C52A | 0445 |
| N50282 | C680 | 0203 |
| N50285 | HS25 | 258585 |
| N50287 | LJ60 | 243 |
| N50298 | LJ60 | 028 |
| N50298 | LJ60 | 049 |
| N50302 | LJ31 | 092 |
| N50309 | HS25 | 258579 |
| N50321 | C525 | 0644 |
| N50321 | C56X | 5799 |
| **N50321** | **C56X** | **6024** |
| N50324 | LJ60 | 069 |
| N50330 | LJ60 | 245 |
| N50353 | LJ45 | 196 |
| N50353 | LJ60 | 035 |
| N50378 | HS25 | 258578 |
| N50378 | LJ31 | 098 |
| N50422 | LJ60 | 249 |
| N50433 | LJ60 | 250 |
| N50440 | HS25 | 258540 |
| N50441 | HS25 | 258541 |
| N50445 | HS25 | 258545 |
| N50446 | FA20 | 21 |
| N50450 | LJ60 | 050 |
| N50453 | PRM1 | RB-53 |
| N50458 | LJ60 | 251 |
| N50459 | HS25 | 258559 |
| N50459 | LJ31 | 095 |
| N50461 | HS25 | 258546 |
| N50468 | PRM1 | RB-81 |
| N50490 | HS25 | 258490 |
| N50490 | LJ45 | 211 |
| N50512 | BE40 | TX-12 |
| N50513 | HS25 | 258513 |
| N50521 | HS25 | 258521 |
| N50522 | C52A | 0441 |
| N50522 | C56X | 5775 |
| N50522 | C680 | 0129 |
| N50522 | HS25 | 258612 |
| N50543 | BE40 | TX-13 |
| N50543 | C52B | 0170 |
| N50543 | C52B | 0226 |
| N50549 | C525 | 0686 |
| N50549 | C56X | 5682 |
| N50549 | C680 | 0208 |
| N50552 | BE40 | RK-342 |
| N50553 | HS25 | 258703 |
| N50558 | LJ60 | 267 |
| N50561 | BE40 | TX-11 |
| N50579 | LJ45 | 240 |
| N50586 | PRM1 | RB-66 |
| N50600 | HS25 | 258500 |
| N50602 | C500 | 083 |
| N50602 | C500 | 083 |
| N50602 | LJ60 | 060 |
| N50612 | C525 | 0528 |
| N50612 | C550 | 550-0870 |
| N50612 | C550 | 550-0953 |
| N50612 | C550 | 550-1103 |
| N50612 | C560 | 0439 |
| N50612 | C560 | 0463 |
| N50612 | C560 | 0763 |
| N50612 | C56X | 5215 |
| N50612 | C56X | 6050 |
| N50612 | C680 | 0083 |
| N50612 | C680 | 0207 |
| N50612 | C750 | 0025 |
| N50612 | C750 | 0117 |
| N50626 | HS25 | 258526 |
| N50639 | C56X | 5688 |
| N50639 | C750 | 0281 |
| N50639 | C750 | 0300 |
| N50648 | PRM1 | RB-68 |
| N50655 | C680 | 0199 |
| N50657 | HS25 | 258587 |
| N50661 | HS25 | 258581 |
| N50667 | HS25 | 258567 |
| N50670 | HS25 | 258570 |
| N50715 | C525 | 0632 |
| N50715 | C550 | 550-0823 |
| N50715 | C550 | 550-0955 |
| N50715 | C560 | 0397 |
| N50715 | C560 | 0696 |
| N50715 | C56X | 5746 |
| N50715 | C56X | 5803 |
| N50715 | C56X | 6054 |
| N50715 | C750 | 0213 |
| N50727 | BE40 | RK-389 |
| N50733 | HS25 | 258533 |
| N50736 | C52A | 0365 |
| N50736 | C52B | 0237 |
| N50736 | C52B | 0278 |
| N50736 | C52B | 0319 |
| **N50736** | **C560** | **0811** |
| N50736 | C56X | 5705 |
| N50740 | HS25 | 258560 |
| N50756 | C52B | 0141 |
| N50756 | C56X | 5760 |
| N50756 | C56X | 6039 |
| N50758 | LJ60 | 098 |
| N50761 | LJ60 | 073 |
| N50776 | C52B | 0203 |
| N50776 | C52B | 0245 |
| N50776 | C52B | 0291 |
| N50776 | LJ60 | 146 |
| N50788 | HS25 | 258488 |
| N50812 | C500 | 036 |
| N50820 | C525 | 0077 |
| N50820 | C525 | 0529 |
| N50820 | C52A | 0357 |
| N50820 | C52A | 0385 |
| N50820 | C52B | 0016 |
| N50820 | C52B | 0047 |
| N50820 | C52B | 0100 |
| N50820 | C560 | 0487 |
| N50820 | C560 | 0506 |
| N50820 | C56X | 5192 |
| N50820 | C56X | 5245 |
| N50820 | C56X | 5295 |
| N50820 | C56X | 5340 |
| N50820 | C650 | 7083 |
| N50820 | C750 | 0114 |
| N50843 | PRM1 | RB-33 |
| N50858 | BE40 | RK-458 |
| N50910 | HS25 | 258590 |
| N50928 | CL60 | 1067 |
| (N50938) | C525 | 0088 |
| N50938 | C525 | 0132 |
| N50938 | C560 | 0396 |
| N50983 | HS25 | 258583 |
| N51001 | LJ40 | 45-2011 |
| N51008 | BE40 | RK-308 |
| N51027 | HS25 | 258577 |
| N51038 | C52B | 0328 |
| N51038 | C550 | 550-0815 |
| N51038 | C550 | 550-0938 |
| N51038 | C550 | 550-1090 |
| (N51038) | C560 | 0279 |
| (N51038) | C560 | 0327 |
| N51038 | C560 | 0383 |
| N51038 | C560 | 0446 |
| N51038 | C56X | 5190 |
| N51038 | C56X | 5196 |
| N51038 | C56X | 5247 |
| N51038 | C56X | 5628 |
| N51038 | C56X | 5755 |
| N51038 | C56X | 5821 |
| N51038 | C680 | 0127 |
| N51038 | C750 | 0063 |
| N51038 | C750 | 0094 |
| N51038 | C750 | 0123 |
| N51038 | WW24 | 142 |
| N51042 | C52B | 0137 |
| N51042 | C550 | 550-0827 |
| (N51042) | C560 | 0280 |
| N51042 | C560 | 0468 |
| N51042 | C560 | 0515 |
| N51042 | C560 | 0683 |
| N51042 | C56X | 5185 |
| N51042 | C56X | 5242 |
| N51042 | C56X | 5631 |
| N51042 | C56X | 5754 |
| N51042 | C680 | 0237 |
| N51042 | C750 | 0121 |
| N51042 | C750 | 0221 |
| N51054 | LJ31 | 105 |
| N51054 | LJ40 | 45-2083 |
| N51054 | LJ60 | 379 |
| N51055 | C52A | 0375 |
| N51055 | C52B | 0023 |
| N51055 | C52B | 0070 |
| N51055 | C52B | 0144 |
| N51055 | C550 | 550-0875 |
| N51055 | C550 | 550-0903 |
| N51055 | C550 | 550-0983 |
| N51055 | C560 | 0282 |
| (N51055) | C560 | 0330 |
| N51055 | C56X | 5240 |
| N51055 | C56X | 5344 |
| N51055 | C750 | 0039 |
| N51055 | C750 | 0069 |
| N51055 | C750 | 0132 |
| N51057 | LJ31 | 061 |
| N51058 | HS25 | 258558 |
| N51072 | C550 | 550-0826 |
| N51072 | C550 | 550-1119 |
| (N51072) | C560 | 0283 |
| N51072 | C560 | 0331 |
| N51072 | C560 | 0520 |
| N51072 | C560 | 0550 |
| N51072 | C560 | 0576 |
| N51072 | C56X | 5236 |
| N51072 | C56X | 5307 |
| N51072 | C680 | 0101 |
| N51072 | C680 | 0148 |
| N51072 | C680 | 0198 |
| N51072 | C680 | 0263 |
| N51072 | C750 | 0017 |
| N51072 | C750 | 0112 |
| (N51099) | C500 | 203 |
| N51099 | HS25 | 258499 |
| N51140 | PRM1 | RB-40 |
| N51143 | C525 | 0603 |
| N51143 | C52B | 0118 |
| N51143 | C550 | 550-0849 |
| N51143 | C550 | 550-0915 |
| N51143 | C560 | 0432 |
| N51143 | C560 | 0538 |
| N51143 | C56X | 5195 |
| N51143 | C56X | 5286 |
| N51143 | C56X | 5339 |
| N51143 | C56X | 5733 |
| N51143 | C650 | 0240 |
| N51143 | C650 | 7067 |
| N51149 | HS25 | 258549 |
| N51160 | C52A | 0371 |
| N51160 | C52B | 0067 |
| N51160 | C52B | 0240 |
| N51160 | C52B | 0279 |
| N51160 | C550 | 550-0894 |
| N51160 | C550 | 550-0923 |
| N51160 | C560 | 0474 |
| N51160 | C560 | 0666 |
| N51160 | C56X | 5154 |
| N51160 | C56X | 5269 |
| N51160 | C56X | 5674 |
| **N51160** | **C56X** | **6060** |
| N51160 | C650 | 7046 |
| N51160 | C650 | 7068 |
| N51160 | C750 | 0037 |
| N51160 | C750 | 0078 |
| N51160 | C750 | 0171 |
| N51169 | HS25 | 258599 |
| N51176 | C525 | 0185 |
| N51176 | C525 | 0212 |
| N51176 | C650 | 7048 |
| N51176 | C650 | 7070 |
| N51176 | C750 | 0038 |
| N51191 | HS25 | 258491 |
| N51192 | HS25 | 258492 |
| N51197 | HS25 | 258497 |
| N51239 | HS25 | 258539 |
| N51241 | BE40 | RK-341 |
| N51246 | C525 | 0154 |
| N51246 | C525 | 0186 |
| N51246 | C525 | 0401 |
| N51246 | C525 | 0523 |
| N51246 | C52A | 0046 |
| N51246 | C52A | 0075 |
| N51246 | C52A | 0216 |
| N51246 | C52B | 0110 |
| N51246 | C550 | 550-0857 |
| N51246 | C560 | 0447 |
| N51246 | C560 | 0450 |
| N51246 | C560 | 0480 |
| N51246 | C56X | 5090 |
| N51246 | C56X | 5757 |
| N51246 | C680 | 0060 |
| N51274 | HS25 | 258574 |
| N51289 | HS25 | 258589 |
| N51313 | C750 | 0022 |
| N51335 | HS25 | 258535 |
| N51336 | HS25 | 258536 |
| N51342 | C525 | 0188 |
| N51342 | C525 | 0432 |
| N51342 | C525 | 0638 |
| N51342 | C52A | 0081 |
| N51342 | C56X | 5107 |
| N51342 | C56X | 5584 |
| N51342 | C56X | 5641 |
| N51342 | C56X | 5776 |
| N51342 | C56X | 6031 |
| N51342 | C650 | 7086 |
| N51384 | HS25 | 258584 |
| N51387 | HS25 | 258487 |
| N51396 | C525 | 0092 |
| N51396 | C525 | 0190 |
| N51396 | C525 | 0355 |
| N51396 | C525 | 0390 |
| N51396 | C52A | 0025 |
| N51396 | C52A | 0066 |
| N51396 | C52A | 0130 |
| N51396 | C52A | 0428 |
| N51396 | C52B | 0211 |
| N51396 | C560 | 0455 |
| N51396 | C560 | 0527 |
| N51396 | C56X | 5585 |
| N51396 | C56X | 5627 |
| N51444 | C525 | 0164 |
| N51444 | C525 | 0192 |
| N51444 | C525 | 0317 |
| N51444 | C525 | 0350 |
| N51444 | C525 | 0418 |
| N51444 | C52A | 0068 |
| N51444 | C52A | 0376 |
| N51444 | C560 | 0289 |
| N51444 | C560 | 0456 |
| N51444 | C56X | 5100 |
| N51444 | C650 | 7073 |
| N51444 | C680 | 0092 |
| N51444 | C680 | 0232 |
| N51453 | HS25 | 258553 |
| N51457 | HS25 | 258557 |
| N51480 | PRM1 | RB-48 |
| N51495 | HS25 | 258495 |
| N51511 | C525 | 0650 |
| N51511 | C52A | 0214 |
| N51511 | C52B | 0035 |
| N51511 | C52B | 0071 |
| N51511 | C56X | 5162 |
| N51511 | C680 | 0204 |
| **N51511** | **C680** | **0269** |
| N51511 | C750 | 0180 |
| (N51522) | C525 | 0094 |
| N51522 | C525 | 0168 |
| N51522 | C525 | 0198 |
| N51522 | C560 | 0350 |
| N51540 | BE40 | RK-340 |
| N51556 | HS25 | 258556 |
| N51564 | C525 | 0100 |
| N51564 | C525 | 0173 |
| N51564 | C525 | 0336 |
| N51564 | C525 | 0358 |
| N51564 | C525 | 0387 |
| N51564 | C525 | 0538 |
| N51564 | C525 | 0552 |
| N51564 | C525 | 0614 |
| N51564 | C52A | 0035 |
| N51564 | C52A | 0069 |
| N51564 | C52A | 0131 |

| | | |
|---|---|---|
| N51564 | C52A | 0362 |
| N51564 | C560 | 0353 |
| N51564 | C560 | 0457 |
| N51564 | C560 | 0491 |
| N51564 | C680 | 0200 |
| N51564 | C680 | 0267 |
| N51575 | C525 | 0338 |
| N51575 | C525 | 0396 |
| N51575 | C525 | 0411 |
| N51575 | C52A | 0049 |
| N51575 | C52A | 0071 |
| N51575 | C52A | 0112 |
| N51575 | C52A | 0322 |
| N51575 | C560 | 0293 |
| N51575 | C560 | 0355 |
| N51575 | C56X | 5005 |
| N51575 | C56X | 5077 |
| N51575 | C680 | 0032 |
| N51575 | C680 | 0061 |
| N51612 | C525 | 0303 |
| N51612 | C525 | 0553 |
| N51612 | C525 | 0655 |
| N51612 | C52B | 0140 |
| N51612 | C550 | 550-0968 |
| N51612 | C56X | 5297 |
| N51612 | C56X | 5630 |
| N51612 | C56X | 5634 |
| N51612 | C56X | 5806 |
| N51612 | C750 | 0233 |
| N51666 | C525 | 0286 |
| N51666 | C550 | 550-0937 |
| N51666 | C550 | 550-0956 |
| N51666 | C550 | 550-0980 |
| N51666 | C550 | 550-1017 |
| N51666 | C56X | 5764 |
| N51666 | C56X | 6016 |
| N51666 | C750 | 0210 |
| N51666 | C750 | 0240 |
| N51666 | C750 | 0255 |
| N51684 | C525 | 0696 |
| N51741 | GLF2 | 45 |
| N51743 | C525 | 0214 |
| N51743 | C550 | 550-1003 |
| N51743 | C550 | 550-1136 |
| N51743 | C560 | 0300 |
| N51743 | C56X | 5173 |
| N51743 | C56X | 5244 |
| N51743 | C56X | 5318 |
| N51743 | C750 | 0276 |
| N51743 | C750 | 0292 |
| N51744 | C525 | 0291 |
| N51744 | C52B | 0084 |
| N51744 | C550 | 550-1107 |
| N51744 | C56X | 5711 |
| N51744 | C680 | 0258 |
| N51744 | C750 | 0108 |
| N51744 | C750 | 0143 |
| N51744 | C750 | 0152 |
| N51744 | C750 | 0212 |
| N51780 | C52B | 0172 |
| N51780 | C550 | 550-0957 |
| N51780 | C550 | 550-0987 |
| N51780 | C550 | 550-1011 |
| N51780 | C560 | 0541 |
| N51780 | C56X | 5549 |
| N51780 | C56X | 5600 |
| N51780 | C56X | 5666 |
| N51780 | C56X | 5762 |
| N51780 | C56X | 6018 |
| N51780 | C750 | 0134 |
| N51806 | C525 | 0649 |
| N51806 | C52A | 0167 |
| N51806 | C52B | 0009 |
| N51806 | C550 | 550-0966 |
| N51806 | C56X | 5635 |
| **N51806** | **C56X** | **6043** |
| N51806 | C750 | 0176 |
| N51817 | C525 | 0157 |
| N51817 | C525 | 0403 |
| N51817 | C525 | 0610 |
| N51817 | C52B | 0199 |
| N51817 | C550 | 550-0845 |
| N51817 | C560 | 0518 |
| N51817 | C56X | 5086 |
| N51817 | C650 | 7051 |
| N51817 | C680 | 0142 |
| N51817 | C750 | 0192 |
| N51817 | C750 | 0216 |
| N51869 | C550 | 550-1042 |
| N51869 | C560 | 0597 |
| N51869 | C56X | 5160 |
| N51869 | C56X | 5555 |
| N51869 | C56X | 5763 |
| N51869 | C680 | 0070 |
| N51869 | C680 | 0106 |
| N51869 | C680 | 0160 |
| N51869 | C680 | 0253 |
| N51872 | C525 | 0159 |
| N51872 | C525 | 0207 |
| N51872 | C525 | 0334 |
| N51872 | C525 | 0367 |
| N51872 | C525 | 0407 |
| N51872 | C52A | 0079 |
| N51872 | C52A | 0141 |
| N51872 | C550 | 550-0836 |
| N51872 | C550 | 550-1076 |
| N51872 | C56X | 5522 |
| N51872 | C680 | 0057 |
| N51872 | C680 | 0078 |
| N51872 | C680 | 0104 |
| N51872 | C680 | 0159 |
| N51881 | C525 | 0218 |
| N51881 | C525 | 0422 |
| N51881 | C525 | 0502 |
| N51881 | C52A | 0011 |
| N51881 | C52A | 0052 |
| N51881 | C52B | 0085 |
| N51881 | C52B | 0302 |
| N51881 | C560 | 0399 |
| N51881 | C56X | 5071 |
| N51881 | C56X | 5546 |
| N51881 | C56X | 5573 |
| N51881 | C56X | 5713 |
| N51881 | C680 | 0188 |
| N51881 | C680 | 0218 |
| N51896 | C525 | 0606 |
| N51896 | C52A | 0352 |
| N51896 | C52A | 0393 |
| N51896 | C52B | 0018 |
| N51896 | C52B | 0202 |
| N51896 | C550 | 550-0922 |
| N51896 | C560 | 0501 |
| **N51896** | **C56X** | **6056** |
| N51896 | C680 | 0243 |
| N51896 | C750 | 0150 |
| N51896 | C750 | 0184 |
| N51933 | C56X | 5023 |
| N51942 | C525 | 0438 |
| N51942 | C52A | 0019 |
| N51942 | C52A | 0195 |
| N51942 | C52B | 0038 |
| N51942 | C52B | 0138 |
| N51942 | C560 | 0400 |
| N51942 | C560 | 0420 |
| N51942 | C560 | 0795 |
| N51942 | C560 | 0813 |
| N51942 | C56X | 5089 |
| N51942 | C56X | 5337 |
| N51984 | C56X | 5179 |
| N51984 | C56X | 5560 |
| N51984 | C56X | 5781 |
| N51984 | C680 | 0138 |
| N51984 | C750 | 0189 |
| N51990 | WW24 | 183 |
| N51993 | C525 | 0143 |
| N51993 | C525 | 0386 |
| N51993 | C525 | 0431 |
| N51993 | C525 | 0558 |
| N51993 | C525 | 0637 |
| N51993 | C52A | 0370 |
| N51993 | C52B | 0086 |
| N51993 | C560 | 0623 |
| N51993 | C56X | 5056 |
| N51993 | HS25 | 25249 |
| N51995 | C525 | 0549 |
| N51995 | C52B | 0073 |
| N51995 | C550 | 550-1007 |
| N51995 | C560 | 0543 |
| N51995 | C560 | 0547 |
| N51995 | C560 | 0563 |
| N51995 | C560 | 0618 |
| N51995 | C56X | 5731 |
| N51995 | C56X | 5830 |
| N51995 | C750 | 0102 |
| N52002 | C52A | 0043 |
| N52035 | C52A | 0058 |
| N52038 | C525 | 0102 |
| N52038 | C525 | 0133 |
| N52038 | C525 | 0222 |
| N52038 | C525 | 0224 |
| N52038 | C525 | 0469 |
| N52038 | C52A | 0125 |
| N52038 | C52B | 0020 |
| N52038 | C56X | 5030 |
| N52038 | C56X | 5607 |
| N52038 | C680 | 0120 |
| N52059 | C52B | 0003 |
| N52059 | C52B | 0139 |
| N52059 | C52B | 0300 |
| N52059 | C550 | 550-1129 |
| N52059 | C560 | 0503 |
| N52059 | C560 | 0608 |
| N52059 | C560 | 0689 |
| N52059 | C56X | 5147 |
| N52059 | C56X | 5166 |
| N52059 | C680 | 0210 |
| N52061 | C56X | 5797 |
| N52069 | C52B | 0198 |
| N52071 | C525 | 0672 |
| N52081 | C525 | 0105 |
| N52081 | C525 | 0136 |
| N52081 | C525 | 0241 |
| N52081 | C525 | 0266 |
| N52081 | C525 | 0430 |
| N52081 | C525 | 0504 |
| N52081 | C52A | 0241 |
| N52081 | C52A | 0392 |
| N52081 | C52A | 0435 |
| N52081 | C52B | 0079 |
| N52081 | C560 | 0409 |
| N52081 | C56X | 5068 |
| N52081 | C56X | 5088 |
| N52081 | C56X | 5255 |
| N52081 | C680 | 0007 |
| N52081 | C680 | 0139 |
| N52081 | C750 | 0157 |
| N52086 | C52A | 0244 |
| N52086 | C52A | 0413 |
| N52086 | C52A | 0440 |
| N52086 | C52B | 0151 |
| N52086 | C52B | 0206 |
| N52086 | C550 | 550-0965 |
| N52086 | C550 | 550-0992 |
| N52086 | C550 | 550-1034 |
| N52113 | C525 | 0109 |
| N52113 | C525 | 0475 |
| N52113 | C525 | 0534 |
| N52113 | C52B | 0101 |
| N52113 | C550 | 550-0803 |
| N52113 | C560 | 0369 |
| N52113 | C56X | 5009 |
| N52113 | C56X | 5034 |
| N52113 | C56X | 5085 |
| N52113 | C56X | 5130 |
| N52113 | C56X | 5566 |
| N52113 | C56X | 5783 |
| N52113 | C680 | 0152 |
| N52114 | C52B | 0210 |
| N52114 | C550 | 550-0963 |
| N52114 | C550 | 550-1033 |
| N52114 | C560 | 0616 |
| N52114 | C56X | 5175 |
| N52114 | C680 | 0003 |
| N52114 | C680 | 0033 |
| N52114 | C750 | 0259 |
| N52114 | C750 | 0298 |
| N52135 | C560 | 0619 |
| N52136 | C525 | 0111 |
| N52136 | C525 | 0444 |
| N52136 | C525 | 0485 |
| N52136 | C525 | 0514 |
| N52136 | C52A | 0004 |
| N52136 | C52B | 0220 |
| N52136 | C560 | 0802 |
| N52136 | C56X | 5036 |
| N52136 | C56X | 5131 |
| N52136 | C56X | 5618 |
| N52136 | C750 | 0012 |
| N52136 | C750 | 0040 |
| N52141 | C525 | 0115 |
| N52141 | C525 | 0145 |
| N52141 | C525 | 0490 |
| N52141 | C525 | 0515 |
| N52141 | C52A | 0008 |
| N52141 | C52A | 0020 |
| N52141 | C52A | 0439 |
| N52141 | C52C | 0003 |
| N52141 | C550 | 550-0806 |
| N52141 | C550 | 550-1084 |
| N52141 | C560 | 0757 |
| N52141 | C56X | 5011 |
| N52141 | C56X | 5041 |
| N52141 | C56X | 5080 |
| N52141 | C56X | 5778 |
| N52144 | C525 | 0148 |
| N52144 | C525 | 0410 |
| N52144 | C52B | 0271 |
| N52144 | C550 | 550-0807 |
| N52144 | C550 | 550-1104 |
| N52144 | C560 | 0703 |
| N52144 | C56X | 5012 |
| N52144 | C56X | 5083 |
| N52144 | C56X | 5502 |
| N52144 | C650 | 7056 |
| N52144 | C680 | 0175 |
| N52178 | C525 | 0118 |
| N52178 | C525 | 0147 |
| N52178 | C525 | 0452 |
| N52178 | C56X | 5010 |
| N52178 | C56X | 5042 |
| N52178 | C56X | 5072 |
| N52178 | C56X | 5113 |
| N52178 | C56X | 5539 |
| N52178 | C650 | 7058 |
| N52178 | C680 | 0098 |
| N52178 | C680 | 0130 |
| N52178 | C680 | 0242 |
| N52178 | C750 | 0277 |
| N52178 | C750 | 0284 |
| N52229 | C525 | 0608 |
| N52229 | C52B | 0121 |
| N52229 | C52B | 0294 |
| N52229 | C550 | 550-0946 |
| N52229 | C550 | 550-0960 |
| N52229 | C560 | 0505 |
| N52229 | C560 | 0582 |
| N52229 | C56X | 5531 |
| N52229 | C56X | 5736 |
| N52229 | C56X | 5795 |
| N52229 | C680 | 0005 |
| N52229 | C750 | 0209 |
| N52234 | C52B | 0114 |
| N52234 | C550 | 550-0964 |
| N52234 | C560 | 0658 |
| N52234 | C56X | 5148 |
| N52234 | C680 | 0154 |
| N52235 | C52A | 0458 |
| N52235 | C52B | 0212 |
| N52235 | C550 | 550-1043 |
| N52235 | C560 | 0596 |
| N52235 | C56X | 5141 |
| N52235 | C56X | 5180 |
| N52235 | C56X | 5602 |
| N52235 | C56X | 5700 |
| N52235 | C56X | 5828 |
| N52235 | C650 | 7110 |
| N52235 | C680 | 0023 |
| N52334 | C56X | 5258 |
| **N52338** | **C510** | **0195** |
| N52352 | C525 | 0376 |
| N52352 | C52A | 0042 |
| N52352 | C52A | 0328 |
| N52352 | C52B | 0080 |
| N52352 | C52B | 0272 |
| N52352 | C52B | 0314 |
| N52352 | C560 | 0309 |
| N52352 | C560 | 0366 |
| N52352 | C560 | 0435 |
| N52352 | C56X | 5134 |
| N52352 | C56X | 5510 |
| N52352 | C680 | 0190 |
| N52369 | C525 | 0536 |
| N52369 | C52B | 0040 |
| N52369 | C550 | 550-1044 |
| N52369 | C560 | 0600 |
| N52369 | C56X | 5656 |
| N52369 | C56X | 5717 |
| N52369 | C680 | 0212 |
| N52369 | C680 | 0283 |
| N52397 | C52B | 0148 |
| N52397 | C550 | 550-0967 |
| N52397 | C550 | 550-1002 |

| | | |
|---|---|---|
| N52397 | C550 | 550-1030 |
| N52397 | C56X | 5325 |
| N52397 | C56X | 5361 |
| N52397 | C56X | 5720 |
| N52397 | C680 | 0213 |
| N52433 | C525 | 0628 |
| N52433 | C52B | 0032 |
| N52433 | C52B | 0077 |
| N52433 | C52B | 0214 |
| N52433 | C560 | 0569 |
| N52433 | C56X | 5512 |
| N52433 | C56X | 6053 |
| N52433 | C680 | 0032 |
| N52446 | C52A | 0448 |
| N52446 | C52B | 0034 |
| N52446 | C550 | 550-1040 |
| N52446 | C550 | 550-1086 |
| N52446 | C560 | 0594 |
| N52446 | C680 | 0112 |
| N52446 | C680 | 0177 |
| N52446 | C680 | 0217 |
| N52457 | C525 | 0139 |
| N52457 | C525 | 0262 |
| N52457 | C52B | 0081 |
| N52457 | C550 | 550-1116 |
| (N52457) | C560 | 0312 |
| N52457 | C560 | 0415 |
| N52457 | C560 | 0671 |
| N52457 | C56X | 5057 |
| N52457 | C56X | 5112 |
| N52457 | C750 | 0289 |
| N52462 | C550 | 550-0972 |
| N52462 | C560 | 0667 |
| N52462 | C560 | 0699 |
| N52462 | C680 | 0147 |
| N52462 | C750 | 0264 |
| N52475 | C525 | 0621 |
| N52475 | C550 | 550-0978 |
| N52475 | C550 | 550-1014 |
| N52475 | C680 | 0025 |
| N52475 | C680 | 0173 |
| **N52498** | **C510** | **0261** |
| N52526 | C525 | 0653 |
| (N52526) | C560 | 0317 |
| N52526 | C560 | 0574 |
| N52526 | C56X | 5259 |
| N52526 | C680 | 0122 |
| N52526 | C680 | 0194 |
| N52526 | C750 | 0223 |
| N52526 | C750 | 0225 |
| N52526 | C750 | 0234 |
| N52526 | C750 | 0250 |
| N52582 | C680 | 0123 |
| N52591 | C525 | 0513 |
| N52591 | C550 | 550-1117 |
| N52591 | C560 | 0583 |
| N52591 | C56X | 5813 |
| "N52594" | C525 | 0657 |
| N52601 | C550 | 550-0919 |
| N52601 | C550 | 550-1056 |
| N52601 | C560 | 0372 |
| N52601 | C560 | 0674 |
| N52601 | C56X | 5665 |
| N52601 | C680 | 0048 |
| N52601 | C750 | 0149 |
| N52609 | C525 | 0694 |
| N52609 | C52A | 0301 |
| N52609 | C52A | 0349 |
| N52609 | C56X | 5511 |
| N52609 | C56X | 5558 |
| N52609 | C56X | 6005 |
| N52609 | C750 | 0263 |
| N52613 | C525 | 0668 |
| **N52613** | **C52B** | **0317** |
| N52613 | C560 | 0319 |
| N52613 | C56X | 5610 |
| N52613 | C56X | 5678 |
| N52613 | C56X | 5743 |
| N52613 | C650 | 7075 |
| N52613 | C750 | 0220 |
| N52623 | C550 | 550-1127 |
| N52623 | C56X | 5739 |
| N52623 | C650 | 7063 |
| N52623 | C680 | 0044 |
| N52623 | C680 | 0240 |
| N52626 | C525 | 0517 |
| N52626 | C525 | 0601 |
| N52626 | C52B | 0150 |
| N52626 | C52B | 0191 |
| N52626 | C550 | 550-1096 |
| N52626 | C56X | 5644 |
| N52626 | C56X | 5804 |
| N52626 | C56X | 6052 |
| N52626 | C650 | 7064 |
| N52627 | C525 | 0690 |
| N52627 | C52A | 0381 |
| N52627 | C52B | 0008 |
| N52627 | C52B | 0256 |
| N52627 | C650 | 7065 |
| N52627 | C680 | 0164 |
| N52627 | C750 | 0254 |
| N52639 | C52A | 0390 |
| N52639 | C52B | 0184 |
| N52639 | C560 | 0568 |
| N52639 | C560 | 0705 |
| N52639 | C56X | 5136 |
| N52639 | C56X | 5517 |
| N52639 | C56X | 5592 |
| N52639 | C56X | 6026 |
| N52639 | C750 | 0022 |
| N52639 | C750 | 0127 |
| (N52642) | C525 | 0123 |
| N52642 | C525 | 0129 |
| N52642 | C750 | 0106 |
| N52645 | C525 | 0611 |
| N52645 | C52A | 0443 |
| N52645 | C52B | 0194 |
| N52645 | C550 | 550-1092 |
| N52645 | C560 | 0338 |
| N52645 | C560 | 0756 |
| N52645 | C56X | 5145 |
| N52653 | C52B | 0037 |
| N52653 | C52B | 0092 |
| N52653 | C560 | 0654 |
| N52653 | C56X | 5753 |
| N52653 | C56X | 6017 |
| N52653 | C680 | 0118 |
| N52653 | C750 | 0168 |
| N52655 | C52A | 0178 |
| N52655 | C52A | 0360 |
| N52655 | C52A | 0419 |
| N52655 | C52A | 0442 |
| N52655 | C550 | 550-0911 |
| N52655 | C56X | 5140 |
| N52655 | C56X | 5519 |
| N52655 | C56X | 5670 |
| N52655 | C750 | 0007 |
| N52655 | C750 | 0244 |
| N52670 | C560 | 0551 |
| N52682 | C52A | 0359 |
| N52682 | C52B | 0205 |
| N52682 | C52B | 0232 |
| N52682 | C560 | 0348 |
| N52682 | C56X | 5621 |
| N52682 | C750 | 0024 |
| N52690 | C52A | 0302 |
| N52690 | C52B | 0217 |
| N52690 | C52B | 0275 |
| N52690 | C52B | 0316 |
| N52690 | C550 | 550-0986 |
| N52690 | C550 | 550-1045 |
| N52690 | C560 | 0599 |
| N52690 | C56X | 5680 |
| N52691 | C525 | 0654 |
| N52691 | C52B | 0134 |
| N52691 | C550 | 550-1027 |
| N52691 | C550 | 550-1058 |
| N52691 | C560 | 0586 |
| N52691 | C56X | 5622 |
| N52691 | C56X | 6022 |
| N52699 | C52A | 0304 |
| N52699 | C52A | 0334 |
| N52699 | C560 | 0610 |
| N52699 | C56X | 5518 |
| N52699 | C680 | 0270 |
| N52733 | C510 | 0225 |
| N53584 | C500 | 128 |
| N53650 | LJ35 | 054 |
| N54531 | C500 | 078 |
| N54555 | HS25 | 257023 |
| N54754 | LJ35 | 026 |
| N54784 | SBRL | 306-96 |
| (N54888) | LJ25 | 258 |
| N55922 | GLF2 | 225 |
| N56327 | BE40 | RK-36 |
| N56356 | BE40 | RK-58 |
| N56400 | BE40 | RK-43 |
| N56423 | BE40 | RK-45 |
| N56576 | BE40 | RK-6 |
| N56616 | BE40 | RK-22 |
| N58025 | SBRL | 282-76 |
| N58521 | HS25 | 258521 |
| N58966 | SBRL | 380-29 |
| N59019 | C500 | 080 |
| **N60055** | **CL64** | **5400** |
| N60089 | HS25 | HA-0089 |
| N60099 | HS25 | HA-0099 |
| **N60143** | **HA4T** | **RC-43** |
| N60144 | LJ60 | 144 |
| N60159 | HS25 | 258609 |
| (N60181) | C500 | 047 |
| N60270 | BE40 | RK-370 |
| N60322 | PRM1 | RB-112 |
| N60506 | HS25 | 258606 |
| N60507 | HS25 | 258607 |
| N60664 | HS25 | 258604 |
| N60669 | PRM1 | RB-269 |
| N60724 | HS25 | 258824 |
| N60820 | HS25 | HA-0120 |
| N61101 | HS25 | 258601 |
| N61161 | PRM1 | RB-61 |
| N61198 | HS25 | 258598 |
| N61216 | HS25 | 258616 |
| N61256 | BE40 | RK-456 |
| N61285 | HS25 | 258765 |
| N61320 | HS25 | 258610 |
| N61343 | HS25 | 258683 |
| N61391 | HS25 | HA-0091 |
| N61407 | HA4T | RC-17 |
| (N61442) | C550 | 152 |
| N61442 | C56X | 6048 |
| N61474 | PRM1 | RB-74 |
| N61495 | HS25 | 258595 |
| N61500 | HS25 | 258600 |
| N61515 | HS25 | 258615 |
| N61572 | C500 | 504 |
| N61589 | PRM1 | RB-89 |
| N61661 | BE40 | RK-361 |
| N61675 | BE40 | RK-475 |
| N61678 | PRM1 | RB-147 |
| N61681 | HS25 | 258621 |
| N61702 | HS25 | 258602 |
| N61706 | C510 | 0065 |
| N61706 | PRM1 | RB-106 |
| N61708 | HS25 | 258608 |
| N61717 | PRM1 | RB-107 |
| N61719 | HS25 | 258619 |
| N61729 | HS25 | 258629 |
| N61746 | HS25 | 258686 |
| N61754 | PRM1 | RB-54 |
| N61784 | PRM1 | RB-84 |
| N61791 | HS25 | 258591 |
| N61805 | HS25 | 258605 |
| N61826 | LJ25 | 214 |
| N61850 | BE40 | RK-350 |
| (N61850) | C56X | 5020 |
| N61855 | C680 | 0285 |
| N61882 | PRM1 | RB-82 |
| N61904 | HS25 | 258594 |
| (N61905) | LJ35 | 535 |
| **N61908** | **PRM1** | **RB-108** |
| N61920 | HS25 | 258620 |
| N61930 | PRM1 | RB-103 |
| N61944 | HS25 | 258714 |
| N61948 | PRM1 | RB-143 |
| N61959 | BE40 | RK-359 |
| N61987 | HS25 | 258687 |
| N61998 | PRM1 | RB-98 |
| N62076 | C510 | 0117 |
| N62276 | WW24 | 432 |
| **N62297** | **HS25** | **HA-0097** |
| (N62452) | HFB3 | 1041 |
| N62570 | FA20 | 379 |
| N62783 | HS25 | 258983 |
| N62864 | C500 | 644 |
| N62895 | HS25 | HA-0095 |
| N62991 | HS25 | HB-41 |
| N63223 | C510 | 0089 |
| **N63357** | **WW24** | **99** |
| N63537 | FA50 | 20 |
| **N63600** | **HS25** | **258843** |
| (N63602) | LJ35 | 306 |
| N63611 | SBRL | 276-21 |
| N63633 | HS25 | HB-33 |
| **N63744** | **HA4T** | **RC-44** |
| N63768 | PRM1 | RB-268 |
| N63810 | HS25 | 256037 |
| N63811 | SBRL | 276-44 |
| N63812 | HS25 | HA-0112 |
| N63890 | HS25 | HA-0090 |
| N63984 | HS25 | 258984 |
| N64292 | HS25 | HA-0092 |
| N64312 | PRM1 | RB-272 |
| N64373 | PRM1 | RB-273 |
| N64467 | PRM1 | RB-267 |
| N64688 | HS25 | 257003 |
| N64769 | FA20 | 359/542 |
| (N64792) | C500 | 087 |
| N65218 | MS76 | 112 |
| N65229 | C560 | 0069 |
| N65311 | FA20 | 6 |
| N65339 | LJ24 | 163 |
| N65357 | CL61 | 5075 |
| N65618 | SBRL | 276-42 |
| N65733 | SBRL | 380-4 |
| N65740 | SBRL | 282-133 |
| N65741 | SBRL | 380-6 |
| N65744 | SBRL | 380-7 |
| N65745 | SBRL | 306-73 |
| N65749 | SBRL | 380-8 |
| N65750 | SBRL | 306-76 |
| N65751 | SBRL | 306-77 |
| N65752 | SBRL | 306-78 |
| N65756 | SBRL | 306-80 |
| N65758 | SBRL | 380-12 |
| N65759 | SBRL | 306-82 |
| N65761 | SBRL | 380-13 |
| N65762 | SBRL | 306-84 |
| N65763 | SBRL | 282-137 |
| N65764 | SBRL | 306-85 |
| N65765 | SBRL | 306-86 |
| N65766 | SBRL | 380-15 |
| N65767 | SBRL | 306-87 |
| N65768 | SBRL | 380-17 |
| N65769 | SBRL | 306-88 |
| N65770 | SBRL | 306-89 |
| N65771 | SBRL | 380-19 |
| N65772 | SBRL | 306-90 |
| N65773 | SBRL | 380-21 |
| N65774 | SBRL | 306-91 |
| N65775 | SBRL | 306-92 |
| N65776 | SBRL | 380-23 |
| N65777 | SBRL | 306-93 |
| N65778 | SBRL | 306-94 |
| N65783 | SBRL | 306-95 |
| N65784? | SBRL | 306-96 |
| N65785 | SBRL | 306-97 |
| N65786 | SBRL | 306-98 |
| N65787 | SBRL | 380-27 |
| N65789 | SBRL | 306-99 |
| N65790 | SBRL | 306-100 |
| N65791 | SBRL | 306-101 |
| N65792 | SBRL | 306-102 |
| N65793 | SBRL | 380-30 |
| N65794 | SBRL | 306-103 |
| N65795 | SBRL | 306-104 |
| N65796 | SBRL | 306-105 |
| N65797 | SBRL | 306-106 |
| N65798 | SBRL | 306-107 |
| N65799 | SBRL | 306-108 |
| N67201 | SBRL | 282-53 |
| N67741 | C550 | 676 |
| N67780 | C500 | 574 |
| N67786 | C500 | 575 |
| N67799 | C500 | 580 |
| N67805 | C500 | 587 |
| N67814 | C500 | 595 |
| N67815 | C500 | 596 |
| N67822 | C500 | 602 |
| N67829 | C500 | 603 |
| N67830 | C500 | 609 |
| N67830 | C560 | 0089 |
| N67839 | C500 | 610 |
| (N67839) | C560 | 0090 |
| N67848 | C500 | 616 |
| N67890 | C560 | 0096 |
| (N67905) | C560 | 0099 |
| (N67980) | C550 | 221 |
| (N67980) | C560 | 0101 |
| N67983 | C550 | 222 |
| N67983 | C550 | 353 |
| (N67983) | C550 | 400 |

| | | |
|---|---|---|
| N67986 | C550 | 223 |
| N67988 | C550 | 224 |
| N67988 | C550 | 354 |
| (N67988) | C560 | 0102 |
| N67989 | C550 | 225 |
| (N67989) | C560 | 0103 |
| N67990 | C550 | 231 |
| N67990 | C550 | 358 |
| N67997 | C550 | 232 |
| N67999 | C550 | 233 |
| N67999 | C550 | 359 |
| N68003 | C550 | 238 |
| N68003 | C550 | 362 |
| N68018 | C550 | 247 |
| (N68018) | C560 | 0109A |
| N68026 | C550 | 253 |
| N68027 | C550 | 254 |
| N68027 | C550 | 371 |
| (N68027) | C560 | 0112 |
| N68032 | C550 | 259 |
| N68032 | C550 | 373 |
| N68032 | C560 | 0116 |
| N68033 | C550 | 260 |
| N68097 | C560 | 0126 |
| (N68118) | C560 | 0133 |
| N68231 | C650 | 0214 |
| N68269 | C650 | 0216 |
| N68599 | C550 | 270 |
| N68607 | C550 | 279 |
| N68609 | C550 | 280 |
| N68615 | C550 | 287 |
| N68616 | C550 | 288 |
| N68617 | C550 | 289 |
| N68621 | C550 | 295 |
| N68622 | C550 | 296 |
| N68624 | C550 | 297 |
| N68625 | C550 | 298 |
| N68629 | C550 | 299 |
| N68631 | C550 | 306 |
| N68633 | C550 | 307 |
| N68637 | C550 | 308 |
| N68644 | C550 | 315 |
| (N68646) | C550 | 316 |
| N68648 | C550 | 317 |
| N68649 | C550 | 318 |
| (N68746) | C560 | 0138 |
| (N68753) | C560 | 0139 |
| N68770 | C560 | 0148 |
| (N68786) | C560 | 0149 |
| (N68854) | C560 | 0159 |
| N68860 | C560 | 0161 |
| N68864 | C560 | 0162 |
| N68869 | C560 | 0163 |
| N68872 | C550 | 323 |
| N68872 | C560 | 0166 |
| N68873 | C550 | 324 |
| (N68873) | C560 | 0167 |
| N68876 | C550 | 325 |
| (N68876) | C560 | 0168 |
| N68881 | C550 | 332 |
| N68881 | C560 | 0173 |
| N68887 | C550 | 333 |
| N68888 | C550 | 334 |
| **N68888** | **CL65** | **5774** |
| N68891 | C550 | 341 |
| N69566 | C500 | 100 |
| N70040 | HS25 | 258840 |
| N70050 | GLF3 | 318 |
| N70158 | BE40 | RK-508 |
| N70214 | HS25 | 258814 |
| N70224 | C550 | 473 |
| N70338 | HS25 | 25281 |
| N70409 | HS25 | 258809 |
| N70431 | HS25 | 258841 |
| N70451 | C500 | 063 |
| N70454 | C500 | 279 |
| N70467 | C500 | 667 |
| N70606 | LJ25 | 163 |
| N70703 | C500 | 025 |
| N70704 | C500 | 267 |
| N70708 | HS25 | 258808 |
| N70791 | HS25 | 258791 |
| N70830 | FA20 | 281/496 |
| N70841 | C500 | 018 |
| N70890 | PRM1 | RB-190 |
| N71010 | HS25 | 258810 |
| N71025 | HS25 | 258805 |
| N71167 | PRM1 | RB-167 |

| | | |
|---|---|---|
| N71325 | SBRL | 282-100 |
| N71460 | SBRL | 380-5 |
| N71543 | SBRL | 380-29 |
| N71761 | PRM1 | RB-161 |
| N71794 | HS25 | 258794 |
| N71865 | PRM1 | RB-175 |
| N71874 | PRM1 | RB-174 |
| N71881 | HS25 | 258811 |
| N71904 | HS25 | 258804 |
| N71907 | HS25 | 258797 |
| N71934 | HS25 | 258834 |
| N71938 | HS25 | 258838 |
| N71944 | HS25 | 258844 |
| N71956 | HS25 | HA-0006 |
| N71958 | HS25 | 258858 |
| N72028 | SBRL | 380-14 |
| N72233 | HS25 | 258833 |
| N72335 | LJ24 | 208 |
| N72442 | LJ24 | 103 |
| N72505 | HS25 | 257016 |
| N72520 | HS25 | 258830 |
| N72539 | BE40 | RK-519 |
| N72594 | BE40 | RK-494 |
| N72596 | LJ35 | 594 |
| N72600 | LJ25 | 370 |
| N72603 | LJ25 | 371 |
| N72606 | LJ25 | 372 |
| N72608 | LJ55 | 114 |
| N72612 | LJ35 | 596 |
| N72613 | LJ55 | 119 |
| N72614 | LJ35 | 607 |
| N72616 | LJ55 | 140 |
| N72617 | HS25 | 258787 |
| N72626 | LJ35 | 591 |
| N72629 | LJ55 | 120 |
| N72630 | LJ35 | 630 |
| N72645 | HS25 | 258845 |
| N72787 | C500 | 561 |
| N72787 | WW24 | 240 |
| N73535 | WW24 | 91 |
| N73721 | HS25 | 258821 |
| N73729 | HS25 | 258829 |
| N73736 | PRM1 | RB-173 |
| (N73741) | HS25 | 258524 |
| N73793 | HS25 | 258813 |
| N74065 | PRM1 | RB-195 |
| N74116 | BE40 | RK-516 |
| N74142 | HS25 | 258832 |
| N74155 | HS25 | 258815 |
| N74166 | HS25 | 258816 |
| N74196 | FA20 | 198/466 |
| N74476 | HS25 | 258847 |
| (N75471) | C500 | 482 |
| N76662 | FA20 | 306/512 |
| N77058 | CL61 | 5017 |
| (N77111) | C500 | 674 |
| N77215 | C525 | 0149 |
| (N77511) | LJ60 | 139 |
| N77617 | HS25 | 25146 |
| N77702 | LJ45 | 224 |
| **N77709** | **ASTR** | **236** |
| N77711 | C560 | 0065 |
| **N77794** | **C525** | **0073** |
| N77797 | C550 | 550-0821 |
| (N78499) | CL60 | 1012 |
| N80169 | LJ40 | 45-2048 |
| N80172 | LJ60 | 326 |
| N80177 | LJ60 | 306 |
| **N80364** | **C500** | **299** |
| N80506 | FA20 | 83 |
| N80513 | C550 | 248 |
| N80544 | BE40 | RK-59 |
| N80631 | LJ31 | 131 |
| N80639 | C500 | 258 |
| N80645 | LJ31 | 135 |
| N80667 | LJ60 | 150 |
| N80683 | LJ60 | 093 |
| N80701 | LJ60 | 148 |
| N80727 | LJ31 | 127 |
| N80775 | LJ24 | 093 |
| N80857 | LJ60 | 220 |
| N80938 | BE40 | RK-54 |
| N81366 | JSTR | 5097/60 |
| N81458 | LJ35 | 230 |
| N81661 | BE40 | RK-35 |
| N81709 | BE40 | RK-14 |
| N81728 | GLF2 | 217 |
| N81863 | LJ35 | 243 |

| | | |
|---|---|---|
| N81883 | C500 | 031 |
| N81918 | BE40 | RK-25 |
| N82025 | LJ25 | 075 |
| N82197 | SBRL | 306-39 |
| N82204 | GLF2 | 167 |
| N82283 | LJ35 | 174 |
| N82378 | BE40 | RK-61 |
| N82400 | BE40 | RK-75 |
| N82412 | BE40 | RK-63 |
| N82497 | BE40 | RK-71 |
| N82628 | BE40 | RK-20 |
| N82679 | LJ55 | 013 |
| N82884 | BE40 | TX-1 |
| N82885 | BE40 | TX-2 |
| N82886 | BE40 | TX-3 |
| N85031 | SBRL | 380-38 |
| N85351 | LJ35 | 149 |
| N85594 | HS25 | 258551 |
| N85631 | LJ55 | 081 |
| N85632 | LJ55 | 080 |
| N85643 | LJ55 | 084 |
| N85645 | LJ35 | 499 |
| N85653 | LJ55 | 053 |
| N85654 | LJ25 | 363 |
| N87011 | C550 | 550-1075 |
| N87185 | C500 | 410 |
| N87253 | C500 | 411 |
| N87258 | C500 | 412 |
| N87496 | C500 | 413 |
| N87510 | C500 | 414 |
| (N87683) | C550 | 564 |
| N87950 | HFB3 | 1055 |
| N88692 | C550 | 212 |
| N88707 | C550 | 213 |
| N88716 | C550 | 214 |
| N88718 | C550 | 215 |
| (N88721) | C550 | 216 |
| N88723 | C550 | 217 |
| (N88727) | C550 | 218 |
| N88731 | C550 | 180 |
| N88732 | C550 | 181 |
| N88737 | C550 | 182 |
| N88738 | C550 | 183 |
| N88740 | C550 | 184 |
| (N88743) | C550 | 185 |
| N88791 | C550 | 186 |
| N88795 | C550 | 187 |
| (N88797) | C550 | 188 |
| (N88798) | C525 | 0400 |
| N88798 | C550 | 189 |
| N88822 | C550 | 191 |
| N88824 | C550 | 192 |
| N88825 | C550 | 193 |
| N88826 | C550 | 194 |
| N88830 | C550 | 195 |
| (N88838) | C550 | 166 |
| N88840 | C550 | 167 |
| (N88842) | C550 | 168 |
| (N88845) | C550 | 169 |
| N88845 | C56X | 5101 |
| (N88848) | C550 | 170 |
| N88879 | F900 | 149 |
| N88906 | GLF2 | 133 |
| N90005 | FA50 | 40 |
| (N90005) | GLEX | 9008 |
| N90005 | GLF3 | 487 |
| N90005 | GLF4 | 1103 |
| N90237 | C500 | 170 |
| N90532 | LJ24 | 103 |
| N90532 | LJ24 | 103 |
| (N90583) | LJ55 | 045 |
| N90658 | JSTR | 5142 |
| N90658 | LJ24 | 077 |
| N90797 | LJ24 | 227 |
| N91164 | LJ31 | 026 |
| N91201 | LJ31 | 027 |
| N91452 | LJ35 | 669 |
| N91480 | LJ35 | 663 |
| N91566 | LJ35 | 667 |
| N91669 | WW24 | 17 |
| N91772 | LJ60 | 053 |
| N91884 | HS25 | 256071 |
| N92045 | HFB3 | 1041 |
| (N92047) | HFB3 | 1036 |
| N92565 | LJ24 | 287 |
| **N94924** | **GLF5** | **5255** |
| (N95591) | FA20 | 150/445 |
| **N96757** | **GLF3** | **379** |

| | | |
|---|---|---|
| **N97315** | **C550** | **159** |
| N97941 | CL60 | 1014 |
| N98386 | LJ24 | 040 |
| N98403 | C550 | 196 |
| N98418 | C550 | 197 |
| N98432 | C550 | 198 |
| N98436 | C550 | 199 |
| N98449 | C500 | 415 |
| N98468 | C500 | 416 |
| N98468 | C550 | 200 |
| N98510 | C500 | 417 |
| (N98510) | C550 | 201 |
| N98528 | C500 | 418 |
| (N98528) | C550 | 202 |
| N98563 | C500 | 419 |
| N98563 | C550 | 203 |
| N98586 | C500 | 420 |
| N98599 | C500 | 421 |
| N98599 | C550 | 204 |
| N98601 | C500 | 422 |
| N98601 | C550 | 205 |
| N98630 | C550 | 206 |
| N98675 | C500 | 424 |
| N98675 | C550 | 207 |
| N98682 | C500 | 425 |
| N98682 | C550 | 208 |
| N98688 | C500 | 426 |
| N98715 | C500 | 427 |
| (N98715) | C550 | 172 |
| N98715 | C550 | 209 |
| (N98718) | C500 | 428 |
| (N98718) | C550 | 173 |
| N98718 | C550 | 210 |
| N98749 | C500 | 429 |
| (N98749) | C550 | 174 |
| N98751 | C500 | 430 |
| (N98751) | C550 | 001 |
| N98753 | C550 | 002 |
| N98784 | C550 | 003 |
| N98784 | C550 | 176 |
| N98786 | C550 | 004 |
| N98796 | LJ25 | 170 |
| N98817 | C550 | 005 |
| N98820 | C550 | 006 |
| N98830 | C550 | 007 |
| N98840 | C550 | 008 |
| N98853 | C550 | 009 |
| N98858 | C550 | 010 |
| N98871 | C550 | 011 |
| N98871 | C550 | 179 |
| N99114 | SBRL | 282-128 |
| N99606 | LJ24 | 224 |
| N99786 | LJ35 | 045 |
| (N99876) | C550 | 012 |

## NASA

| | | |
|---|---|---|
| NASA4 | JSTR | 5015 |
| NASA14 | JSTR | 5003 |
| NASA650 | GLF2 | 118 |
| NASA701 | LJ24 | 049 |

## Peru

| | | |
|---|---|---|
| (OB- ) | LJ24 | 112 |
| OB-1195 | C550 | 134 |
| OB-1280 | C500 | 019 |
| OB-1313 | LJ25 | 328 |
| OB-1319 | SBRL | 282-127 |
| OB-1429 | LJ25 | 159 |
| OB-1430 | LJ25 | 164 |
| **OB-1431** | **LJ36** | **051** |
| **OB-1432** | **LJ36** | **052** |
| **OB-1433** | **FA20** | **434** |
| OB-1550 | SBRL | 306-25 |
| OB-1626 | C560 | 0124 |
| **OB-1703** | **ASTR** | **004** |
| OB-1792 | CS55 | 0086 |
| OB-1792-T | CS55 | 0086 |
| **OB-1824** | **C56X** | **5605** |
| OB-M-1004 | LJ25 | 195 |
| OB-M-1171 | C550 | 056 |
| OB-M-1195 | C550 | 134 |
| OB-R-1313 | LJ25 | 328 |
| OB-S-1280 | C500 | 019 |
| OB-T-1319 | SBRL | 282-127 |

Lebanon

| | | |
|---|---|---|
| OD- | BE40 | RK-179 |
| OD-BBF | HS25 | 257054 |
| OD-BOY | HS25 | 257109 |
| OD-EAS | HS25 | 258410 |
| OD-FAF | HS25 | 257124 |
| OD-FNF | HS25 | 257124 |
| OD-HHF | HS25 | 257054 |
| OD-KMI | JSTR | 5233 |
| OD-MAS | HS25 | 257115 |
| OD-MHA | LJ60 | 326 |
| OD-MIG | HS25 | HA-0148 |
| OD-PAL | FA20 | 395/554 |
| OD-PWC | LJ31 | 203 |
| OD-SAS | C500 | 165 |
| OD-STW | BE40 | RK-366 |
| OD-TSW | HS25 | 258319 |

Austria

| | | |
|---|---|---|
| (OE- ) | CL61 | 5023 |
| (OE- ) | FA10 | 85 |
| (OE- ) | LJ45 | 012 |
| OE-FAD | C550 | 496 |
| OE-FAJ | C510 | 0264 |
| OE-FAM | E50P | 50000100 |
| OE-FAN | C500 | 289 |
| OE-FAP | C500 | 300 |
| OE-FAP | PRM1 | RB-215 |
| OE-FAU | C500 | 150 |
| OE-FBA | C500 | 615 |
| OE-FBS | C550 | 574 |
| OE-FCA | C525 | 0354 |
| OE-FCB | C510 | 0044 |
| OE-FCM | C500 | 294 |
| OE-FCU | C52A | 0210 |
| OE-FCW | C525 | 0292 |
| OE-FCY | C52A | 0204 |
| OE-FDM | C500 | 529 |
| OE-FDP | C500 | 139 |
| (OE-FEB) | C52A | 0239 |
| OE-FEM | C525 | 0291 |
| OE-FET | C525 | 0421 |
| OE-FFB | C510 | 0065 |
| OE-FFK | C500 | 515 |
| OE-FGB | C52A | 0362 |
| OE-FGD | C525 | 0020 |
| (OE-FGG) | C525 | 0146 |
| OE-FGI | C525 | 0254 |
| OE-FGK | C525 | 0331 |
| OE-FGL | C52A | 0082 |
| OE-FGN | C500 | 291 |
| OE-FGP | C500 | 006 |
| OE-FHA | C510 | 0081 |
| OE-FHB | C52A | 0049 |
| OE-FHC | C52A | 0415 |
| OE-FHH | C500 | 654 |
| OE-FHP | C500 | 668 |
| OE-FHW | C500 | 523 |
| OE-FID | C510 | 0040 |
| OE-FII | C52A | 0321 |
| OE-FIM | PRM1 | RB-196 |
| OE-FIN | C52A | 0239 |
| OE-FIW | C500 | 511 |
| OE-FIX | C525 | 0480 |
| (OE-FJR) | C52A | 0213 |
| OE-FJU | C525 | 0295 |
| OE-FKK | PRM1 | RB-211 |
| OE-FKO | C52A | 0390 |
| OE-FKW | PRM1 | RB-77 |
| OE-FLA | C52A | 0365 |
| OE-FLB | C52A | 0369 |
| OE-FLG | C525 | 0103 |
| OE-FLP | C52A | 0011 |
| OE-FLR | C510 | 0082 |
| OE-FLY | C500 | 660 |
| OE-FMA | C525 | 0188 |
| OE-FMC | PRM1 | RB-41 |
| OE-FMD | C525 | 0614 |
| OE-FMI | C525 | 0315 |
| OE-FMK | C500 | 536 |
| OE-FMS | C500 | 510 |
| OE-FMT | C525 | 0217 |
| OE-FMU | C525 | 0040 |
| (OE-FMU) | C525 | 0614 |
| OE-FMY | C510 | 0106 |

| | | |
|---|---|---|
| OE-FMZ | C510 | 0116 |
| OE-FNA | C525 | 0659 |
| OE-FNB | C52A | 0398 |
| OE-FNG | C500 | 301 |
| OE-FNL | C500 | 100 |
| OE-FNP | C500 | 100 |
| OE-FOA | C52A | 0354 |
| OE-FOE | C52A | 0375 |
| OE-FOI | C525 | 0477 |
| OE-FOM | E50P | 50000092 |
| OE-FPA | C550 | 552 |
| OE-FPH | C500 | 572 |
| OE-FPK | C52A | 0437 |
| OE-FPO | C500 | 353 |
| OE-FPO | C525 | 0645 |
| OE-FPS | C52A | 0142 |
| OE-FRA | C52A | 0150 |
| OE-FRC | PRM1 | RB-57 |
| OE-FRF | C525 | 0539 |
| OE-FRJ | PRM1 | RB-12 |
| OE-FRR | C525 | 0124 |
| OE-FSG | C52A | 0203 |
| OE-FSR | C525 | 0634 |
| OE-FSS | C525 | 0226 |
| OE-FTR | C510 | 0053 |
| OE-FUJ | C525 | 0544 |
| OE-FUX | C52A | 0106 |
| OE-FVB | C52A | 0229 |
| OE-FWH | C510 | 0104 |
| OE-FWM | C525 | 0177 |
| (OE-FWW) | C510 | 0106 |
| OE-FWW | PRM1 | RB-131 |
| OE-FXX | C52A | 0326 |
| OE-FYC | C500 | 610 |
| OE-FYF | C500 | 501 |
| OE-FYH | C52A | 0176 |
| OE-GAA | C560 | 0111 |
| "OE-GAC" | C680 | 0186 |
| OE-GAD | C550 | 066 |
| OE-GAF | LJ35 | 382 |
| OE-GAG | BE40 | RK-448 |
| OE-GAG | FA10 | 151 |
| OE-GAH | C550 | 550-0922 |
| OE-GAK | C680 | 0186 |
| OE-GAL | C550 | 550-0974 |
| (OE-GAL) | C56X | 5573 |
| OE-GAM | ASTR | 111 |
| OE-GAP | C56X | 5004 |
| OE-GAP | CS55 | 0034 |
| OE-GAR | LJ35 | 309 |
| OE-GAR | LJ45 | 148 |
| OE-GAS | ASTR | 242 |
| OE-GAU | C550 | 028 |
| OE-GAV | LJ35 | 185 |
| OE-GBA | C550 | 100 |
| OE-GBC | C550 | 717 |
| OE-GBD | ASTR | 133 |
| OE-GBE | ASTR | 153 |
| OE-GBR | C56X | 5749 |
| OE-GBR | LJ35 | 088 |
| OE-GBY | C680 | 0066 |
| OE-GCA | C56X | 5157 |
| OE-GCB | C560 | 0517 |
| OE-GCC | C560 | 0125 |
| OE-GCD | C560 | 0497 |
| OE-GCE | HS25 | 258536 |
| OE-GCF | LJ55 | 136 |
| OE-GCG | C56X | 5316 |
| OE-GCH | C550 | 304 |
| OE-GCH | C650 | 7006 |
| OE-GCI | C550 | 043 |
| OE-GCJ | FA20 | 184/462 |
| OE-GCM | C56X | 5538 |
| OE-GCN | C650 | 0014 |
| OE-GCO | C650 | 0012 |
| OE-GCP | C550 | 351 |
| OE-GCP | C560 | 0214 |
| OE-GCR | FA20 | 191 |
| OE-GCS | FA20 | 364 |
| OE-GDA | C560 | 0200 |
| OE-GDF | LJ60 | 276 |
| OE-GDI | LJ45 | 037 |
| OE-GDM | C550 | 707 |
| OE-GDP | C560 | 0023 |
| OE-GDP | FA20 | 302/510 |
| OE-GDR | FA20 | 203 |
| OE-GEA | HS25 | 258520 |
| OE-GEC | C550 | 296 |

| | | |
|---|---|---|
| OE-GEG | C56X | 5529 |
| OE-GEH | C56X | 5755 |
| OE-GEJ | C560 | 0665 |
| (OE-GEM) | C56X | 5822 |
| OE-GEM | C680 | 0033 |
| OE-GEN | C550 | 550-1122 |
| OE-GEO | HS25 | 258477 |
| OE-GEP | C550 | 010 |
| OE-GER | LJ35 | 143 |
| OE-GES | C550 | 421 |
| OE-GES | C56X | 6036 |
| OE-GET | C52B | 0277 |
| OE-GFA | LJ60 | 214 |
| OE-GFB | BE40 | RK-84 |
| OE-GFF | LJ45 | 243 |
| OE-GGB | LJ40 | 45-2018 |
| OE-GGC | LJ40 | 45-2015 |
| OE-GGG | C56X | 6013 |
| OE-GGL | LJ60 | 287 |
| OE-GHA | FA10 | 221 |
| OE-GHG | C52B | 0150 |
| OE-GHL | LJ25 | 295 |
| OE-GHM | BE40 | RK-148 |
| OE-GHP | C550 | 139 |
| OE-GHP | C550 | 550-0998 |
| OE-GHS | HS25 | 258078 |
| OE-GHU | HS25 | 258335 |
| OE-GIA | HS25 | 256027 |
| OE-GID | C560 | 0081 |
| OE-GII | LJ60 | 169 |
| OE-GIL | C550 | 075 |
| OE-GIN | C550 | 063 |
| OE-GIW | C550 | 008 |
| OE-GJA | HS25 | 258810 |
| (OE-GJA) | LJ60 | 302 |
| (OE-GJA) | LJ60 | 303 |
| OE-GJF | C52B | 0231 |
| OE-GJM | C680 | 0282 |
| OE-GKE | C56X | 5642 |
| OE-GKK | C550 | 550-0872 |
| OE-GKM | C56X | 5811 |
| OE-GKN | LJ55 | 027 |
| OE-GKP | C550 | 005 |
| OE-GKP | LJ60 | 280 |
| OE-GKZ | C680 | 0200 |
| OE-GLA | LJ25 | 079 |
| OE-GLF | ASTR | 261 |
| OE-GLF | FA20 | 323/520 |
| OE-GLG | C550 | 550-0977 |
| OE-GLG | FA10 | 96 |
| OE-GLL | C550 | 550-1069 |
| OE-GLL | FA20 | 307/513 |
| (OE-GLM) | C550 | 550-0977 |
| OE-GLP | C680 | 0080 |
| OE-GLP | LJ36 | 025 |
| OE-GLS | C550 | 300 |
| OE-GLS | C650 | 7110 |
| OE-GLX | LJ60 | 332 |
| OE-GLY | LJ60 | 333 |
| OE-GLZ | C550 | 690 |
| OE-GMA | LJ35 | 111 |
| OE-GMA | LJ60 | 270 |
| OE-GMC | BE40 | RK-162 |
| OE-GMD | LJ36 | 047 |
| OE-GME | C56X | 5113 |
| OE-GMI | C560 | 0362 |
| OE-GMJ | LJ35 | 504 |
| OE-GML | C550 | 550-0976 |
| OE-GMM | C680 | 0005 |
| OE-GMP | LJ35 | 122 |
| OE-GMR | LJ60 | 248 |
| OE-GMS | LJ35 | 341 |
| OE-GMV | C550 | 550-1136 |
| OE-GMZ | C52B | 0318 |
| OE-GNA | C52B | 0275 |
| OE-GNB | C680 | 0055 |
| OE-GNF | LJ60 | 304 |
| OE-GNI | LJ60 | 236 |
| OE-GNK | C650 | 0147 |
| OE-GNK | LJ55 | 013 |
| OE-GNL | LJ36 | 055 |
| OE-GNL | LJ60 | 032 |
| OE-GNN | FA20 | 298 |
| OE-GNP | LJ35 | 347 |
| OE-GNS | CS55 | 0083 |
| OE-GNW | C56X | 5339 |
| OE-GNY | HS25 | 258859 |
| OE-GPA | C560 | 0099 |

| | | |
|---|---|---|
| OE-GPA | C56X | 5265 |
| OE-GPC | C560 | 0064 |
| OE-GPD | C52B | 0314 |
| OE-GPD | CS55 | 0135 |
| OE-GPG | ASTR | 115 |
| OE-GPH | C560 | 0590 |
| OE-GPK | C52B | 0312 |
| OE-GPN | C56X | 5169 |
| OE-GPN | LJ35 | 311 |
| OE-GPO | C52B | 0125 |
| OE-GPS | C550 | 550-0837 |
| OE-GPS | C560 | 0114 |
| OE-GPZ | C56X | 5067 |
| OE-GRA | C52B | 0135 |
| OE-GRB | C550 | 550-1039 |
| OE-GRD | C550 | 707 |
| OE-GRF | HS25 | 258813 |
| OE-GRO | LJ55 | 122 |
| OE-GRR | LJ55 | 059 |
| OE-GRS | HS25 | 258804 |
| OE-GRU | C52B | 0222 |
| OE-GRU | FA20 | 228/473 |
| OE-GRW | C560 | 0019 |
| OE-GRZ | C52B | 0219 |
| OE-GSC | FA10 | 122 |
| OE-GSG | BE40 | RK-402 |
| OE-GSK | ASTR | 245 |
| OE-GSP | C56X | 5756 |
| OE-GSR | C56X | 5695 |
| OE-GST | C550 | 299 |
| OE-GSU | LJ60 | 317 |
| OE-GSW | C560 | 0088 |
| OE-GSZ | C56X | 5763 |
| OE-GTA | LJ31 | 191 |
| OE-GTF | LJ60 | 281 |
| OE-GTI | C56X | 5037 |
| OE-GTK | C56X | 5007 |
| OE-GTM | BE40 | RK-343 |
| OE-GTO | LJ60 | 303 |
| "OE-GTS" | LJ60 | 281 |
| OE-GTT | C680 | 0153 |
| OE-GTZ | C550 | 550-0864 |
| OE-GUK | BE40 | RK-124 |
| OE-GUP | C680 | 0066 |
| OE-GUS | FA20 | 36 |
| OE-GVA | LJ40 | 45-2079 |
| OE-GVB | LJ60 | 167 |
| OE-GVD | LJ60 | 373 |
| OE-GVI | LJ40 | 45-2026 |
| OE-GVJ | LJ60 | 359 |
| OE-GVL | C56X | 5772 |
| OE-GVM | LJ45 | 084 |
| OE-GVO | C680 | 0145 |
| OE-GVR | C550 | 550-0988 |
| OE-GVT | LJ60 | 360 |
| OE-GVV | LJ60 | 364 |
| OE-GVX | LJ40 | 45-2097 |
| OE-GWH | C56X | 6029 |
| OE-GWV | C56X | 5826 |
| OE-GXX | LJ40 | 45-2112 |
| OE-GYG | LJ60 | 197 |
| OE-GYR | BE40 | RK-428 |
| OE-GZK | C56X | 5668 |
| OE-HAA | CL30 | 20232 |
| OE-HAB | CL30 | 20227 |
| OE-HAC | C750 | 0232 |
| OE-HAF | F2TH | 223 |
| OE-HAK | C750 | 0300 |
| OE-HAL | C750 | 0259 |
| OE-HAP | CL30 | 20226 |
| OE-HAS | GALX | 206 |
| OE-HAZ | GALX | 102 |
| OE-HCA | CL30 | 20274 |
| OE-HCL | CL61 | 3045 |
| OE-HCS | FA50 | 42 |
| OE-HDD | CL30 | 20065 |
| OE-HDV | CL30 | 20261 |
| (OE-HEC) | C750 | 0277 |
| OE-HEM | F2TH | 207 |
| OE-HEO | CL30 | 20179 |
| OE-HET | CL60 | 1085 |
| OE-HFA | F2TH | 216 |
| OE-HFC | GALX | 050 |
| OE-HFE | C750 | 0179 |
| OE-HGG | C750 | 0214 |
| OE-HHH | FA50 | 297 |
| OE-HII | CL30 | 20111 |
| OE-HIT | FA50 | 222 |

| | | |
|---|---|---|
| OE-HIX | CL30 | 20289 |
| **OE-HJA** | **C750** | **0261** |
| **OE-HKK** | **F2EX** | **10** |
| **OE-HKY** | **F2TH** | **226** |
| OE-HLE | CL61 | 3047 |
| **OE-HMR** | **F2EX** | **152** |
| **OE-HNL** | **CL30** | **20039** |
| **OE-HNM** | **F2EX** | **8** |
| OE-HOT | F2EX | 88 |
| **OE-HPH** | **F2TH** | **209** |
| **OE-HPK** | **CL30** | **20004** |
| OE-HPS | FA50 | 334 |
| **OE-HPZ** | **CL30** | **20047** |
| OE-HRA | F2EX | 8 |
| **OE-HRM** | **CL30** | **20222** |
| **OE-HRR** | **CL30** | **20033** |
| **OE-HSB** | **GALX** | **223** |
| **OE-HSG** | **GALX** | **065** |
| **OE-HSN** | **GALX** | **225** |
| OE-HTI | GALX | 089 |
| **OE-HTO** | **F2EX** | **199** |
| **OE-HUB** | **C750** | **0273** |
| **OE-HVA** | **F2TH** | **217** |
| **OE-HVJ** | **CL30** | **20200** |
| OE-HVV | CL30 | 20214 |
| **OE-IAG** | **GLF4** | **4130** |
| OE-IAK | GLEX | 9204 |
| **OE-IBC** | **GLEX** | **9269** |
| **OE-IBN** | **F9EX** | **176** |
| **OE-ICF** | **F900** | **22** |
| **OE-ICH** | **GLF4** | **4104** |
| **OE-ICN** | **GLEX** | **9256** |
| **OE-IDG** | **CL64** | **5654** |
| **OE-IDM** | **F9EX** | **51** |
| **OE-IDX** | **F9DX** | **604** |
| **OE-IEL** | **GLEX** | **9099** |
| **OE-IEX** | **F9EX** | **111** |
| **OE-IFB** | **CL65** | **5704** |
| **OE-IFG** | **GLEX** | **9182** |
| (OE-IFH) | GLEX | 9120 |
| **OE-IGG** | **GLEX** | **9251** |
| **OE-IGJ** | **CL64** | **5598** |
| **OE-IGS** | **GLEX** | **9044** |
| **OE-IIA** | **GLF5** | **641** |
| (OE-III) | CL65 | 5732 |
| **OE-IIS** | **GLF5** | **572** |
| OE-IJA | GLF4 | 1157 |
| **OE-IKM** | **GLEX** | **9112** |
| **OE-IKP** | **CL64** | **5599** |
| OE-ILS | F900 | 58 |
| OE-IMA | F9EX | 87 |
| OE-IMA | GLEX | 9243 |
| OE-IMB | CL64 | 5585 |
| OE-IMC | F9EX | 165 |
| OE-IMI | F900 | 147 |
| **OE-IMI** | **F9EX** | **87** |
| **OE-IMK** | **CL64** | **5664** |
| **OE-INA** | **CL65** | **5782** |
| **OE-INB** | **F9EX** | **189** |
| **OE-INC** | **GLEX** | **9168** |
| OE-INF | CL64 | 5303 |
| **OE-INI** | **CL64** | **5595** |
| **OE-INJ** | **CL64** | **5435** |
| **OE-INN** | **CL65** | **5743** |
| **OE-INP** | **CL65** | **5745** |
| **OE-INS** | **CL65** | **5707** |
| **OE-INT** | **CL65** | **5758** |
| OE-INU | CL65 | 5749 |
| **OE-INX** | **CL64** | **5629** |
| **OE-INY** | **CL64** | **5644** |
| **OE-IOE** | **F9EX** | **214** |
| **OE-IOO** | **GLEX** | **9301** |
| **OE-IPA** | **GLEX** | **9286** |
| OE-IPH | HS25 | 258778 |
| OE-IPK | CL64 | 5612 |
| (OE-IPR) | CL65 | 5712 |
| **OE-IPZ** | **CL65** | **5808** |
| **OE-IRG** | **GLF5** | **5139** |
| (OE-IRJ) | CL64 | 5464 |
| **OE-IRP** | **GLEX** | **9106** |
| **OE-ISM** | **F9DX** | **617** |
| **OE-ISS** | **GLF5** | **5022** |
| **OE-ISU** | **CL65** | **5764** |
| **OE-ITH** | **CL64** | **5636** |
| **OE-IVA** | **FA7X** | **42** |
| (OE-IVB) | CL65 | 5715 |
| OE-IVE | CL64 | 5620 |
| OE-IVK | F9EX | 138 |
| **OE-IVV** | **GLF5** | **5054** |
| **OE-IVY** | **GLF5** | **687** |
| OE-IYA | CL64 | 5435 |
| **OE-LAF** | **GLEX** | **9234** |
| **OE-LLL** | **FA7X** | **55** |
| (OE-LNX) | GLEX | 9167 |
| (OE-LNY) | GLEX | 9237 |
| **OE-LXR** | **GLEX** | **9235** |

## Finland

| | | |
|---|---|---|
| OH-AEM | LJ60 | 300 |
| OH-AMB | FA10 | 193 |
| **OH-ANS** | **CL65** | **5785** |
| OH-BAP | HS25 | 257212 |
| OH-BZM | CL64 | 5626 |
| OH-CAR | C500 | 144 |
| OH-CAT | C550 | 133 |
| OH-CIT | C500 | 551 |
| OH-COC | C500 | 223 |
| OH-COL | C500 | 311 |
| OH-CUT | C550 | 414 |
| OH-CXO | C750 | 0022 |
| **OH-FEX** | **F2EX** | **27** |
| OH-FFA | FA20 | 178/459 |
| OH-FFB | FA10 | 17 |
| **OH-FFC** | **F9EX** | **23** |
| **OH-FFD** | **FA7X** | **20** |
| **OH-FFE** | **F9EX** | **220** |
| **OH-FFF** | **FA7X** | **66** |
| OH-FFJ | FA20 | 225/472 |
| OH-FFV | FA20 | 248/483 |
| OH-FFW | FA20 | 243/480 |
| **OH-FIX** | **F2TH** | **179** |
| **OH-FLM** | **CL30** | **20155** |
| **OH-FOX** | **F2EX** | **67** |
| OH-FPC | FA20 | 345 |
| OH-GLA | LJ24 | 273 |
| OH-GLB | LJ24 | 262 |
| **OH-GVE** | **LJ60** | **281** |
| (OH-GVI) | LJ60 | 303 |
| (OH-GVI) | LJ60 | 317 |
| **OH-III** | **LJ60** | **303** |
| OH-IPJ | LJ45 | 104 |
| OH-IPP | LJ55 | 056 |
| **OH-IVS** | **LJ60** | **355** |
| OH-JET | HS25 | 257136 |
| OH-JOT | HS25 | 258001 |
| **OH-KNE** | **MU30** | **A014SA** |
| **OH-MOL** | **CL64** | **5658** |
| (OH-NEM) | CL64 | 5658 |
| OH-ONE | C56X | 5157 |
| **OH-PPI** | **C750** | **0115** |
| OH-PPJ | C750 | 0152 |
| **OH-PPR** | **F9EX** | **118** |
| **OH-PPS** | **GLEX** | **9237** |
| (OH-PPS) | GLEX | 9242 |
| **OH-PPT** | **GLEX** | **9291** |
| **OH-RBX** | **C56X** | **5056** |
| OH-RIF | BE40 | RK-79 |
| **OH-TNR** | **GLEX** | **9159** |
| OH-VIV | LJ60 | 305 |
| OH-VMF | LJ60 | 312 |
| **OH-WIA** | **C680** | **0215** |
| (OH-WIA) | CL64 | 5658 |
| **OH-WIC** | **CL64** | **5452** |
| OH-WIF | FA20 | 461 |
| OH-WIH | CL60 | 1029 |
| **OH-WII** | **CL64** | **5642** |
| OH-WIN | FA20 | 481 |
| **OH-WIP** | **FA20** | **359/542** |
| OH-ZIP | CL30 | 20209 |

## Czech Republic

| | | |
|---|---|---|
| **OK-ACH** | **C550** | **550-1111** |
| **OK-AJA** | **C510** | **0272** |
| OK-AJD | LJ31 | 095 |
| OK-BYA | CL61 | 5105 |
| **OK-CAA** | **C56X** | **5183** |
| **OK-DSJ** | **C525** | **0351** |
| OK-EEH | FA10 | 27 |
| **OK-EMA** | **C680** | **0279** |
| OK-FKA | C500 | 260 |
| **OK-FTR** | **C510** | **0053** |
| **OK-JDM** | **LJ60** | **330** |
| **OK-KAZ** | **HS25** | **HA-0034** |
| **OK-LEO** | **C510** | **0252** |
| **OK-MYS** | **C510** | **0268** |
| OK-NKN | C650 | 0010 |
| (OK-ONE) | GLF5 | 680 |
| **OK-PPC** | **C510** | **0019** |
| **OK-SLA** | **C525** | **0310** |
| **OK-SLS** | **C560** | **0088** |
| **OK-SLX** | **C56X** | **5243** |
| **OK-UNI** | **C680** | **0139** |
| OK-UZI | BE40 | RJ-56 |
| **OK-VSZ** | **C550** | **550-1040** |
| (OK-YXY) | LJ60 | 376 |

## Slovakia

| | | |
|---|---|---|
| **OM-AES** | **C510** | **0270** |
| **OM-HLY** | **C525** | **0393** |
| **OM-HLZ** | **C525** | **0223** |
| **OM-LBG** | **C52B** | **0067** |
| **OM-OIG** | **HS25** | **258612** |
| **OM-OPA** | **C52B** | **0269** |
| **OM-OPE** | **C52A** | **0239** |
| **OM-OPR** | **C525** | **0101** |
| OM-SKY | HS25 | 258314 |
| **OM-USS** | **HS25** | **258720** |
| **OM-VPB** | **PRM1** | **RB-256** |
| **OM-VPT** | **C52B** | **0217** |

## Belgium

| | | |
|---|---|---|
| **OO-AAA** | **FA7X** | **57** |
| **OO-ACC** | **C52A** | **0431** |
| **OO-ACO** | **C510** | **0260** |
| **OO-ACT** | **F900** | **194** |
| (OO-ADA) | FA20 | 73/419 |
| OO-ADH | LJ60 | 344 |
| **OO-AIE** | **C56X** | **5733** |
| **OO-ALX** | **C680** | **0271** |
| OO-ATS | C500 | 044 |
| **OO-CEJ** | **C525** | **0172** |
| **OO-CIV** | **C52A** | **0206** |
| **OO-CLX** | **C560** | **0537** |
| OO-DCM | C500 | 182 |
| **OO-DDA** | **C52A** | **0164** |
| OO-DDD | FA20 | 11 |
| **OO-DFG** | **F2EX** | **140** |
| OO-DOK | FA20 | 162/451 |
| (OO-EBA) | MU30 | A048SA |
| **OO-EBE** | **C56X** | **6025** |
| (OO-ECT) | C500 | 542 |
| **OO-EDV** | **C52B** | **0200** |
| (OO-EEF) | FA20 | 95 |
| **OO-ENZ** | **LJ31** | **202** |
| **OO-EPU** | **LJ45** | **291** |
| (OO-FAY) | C500 | 088 |
| OO-FBY | C500 | 093 |
| **OO-FLN** | **C52A** | **0179** |
| OO-FNL | C525 | 0332 |
| **OO-FOI** | **F9EX** | **121** |
| **OO-FPA** | **C56X** | **5248** |
| **OO-FPB** | **C550** | **550-1117** |
| **OO-FPC** | **C52B** | **0147** |
| (OO-FPD) | C52B | 0158 |
| **OO-FPE** | **C52B** | **0158** |
| **OO-FTS** | **C56X** | **5318** |
| **OO-FYG** | **C550** | **550-1027** |
| **OO-FYS** | **C52B** | **0197** |
| OO-GBL | LJ35 | 284 |
| OO-GFD | F2TH | 101 |
| **OO-GML** | **F2EX** | **75** |
| OO-GPN | C500 | 225 |
| (OO-HFW) | LJ25 | 231 |
| OO-IAR | F2EX | 8 |
| OO-IBC | SBRL | 465-68 |
| OO-IBI | C500 | 238 |
| OO-IBS | SBRL | 306-5 |
| **OO-IDE** | **C525** | **0037** |
| **OO-IIG** | **C550** | **550-1018** |
| OO-JBA | LJ31 | 009 |
| OO-JBB | FA20 | 116 |
| OO-JBS | LJ35 | 669 |
| **OO-JDK** | **C525** | **0250** |
| **OO-KJD** | **LJ45** | **404** |
| OO-KJG | LJ35 | 149 |
| **OO-KRC** | **CL64** | **5577** |
| OO-LCM | C500 | 036 |
| OO-LFA | LJ24 | 248 |
| **OO-LFN** | **LJ45** | **250** |
| OO-LFQ | F900 | 62 |
| OO-LFR | LJ25 | 320 |
| **OO-LFS** | **LJ45** | **018** |
| OO-LFT | FA50 | 42 |
| "OO-LFU" | C525 | 0020 |
| OO-LFV | LJ35 | 481 |
| (OO-LFW) | LJ25 | 231 |
| (OO-LFX) | C550 | 067 |
| (OO-LFX) | LJ35 | 135 |
| OO-LFY | LJ35 | 200 |
| OO-LFZ | LJ25 | 118 |
| **OO-LIE** | **C52B** | **0173** |
| (OO-MDN) | FA20 | 262 |
| **OO-MLG** | **C56X** | **5028** |
| OO-MMJ | CS55 | 0007 |
| OO-MMP | C550 | 559 |
| OO-MRA | CRVT | 15 |
| OO-MRC | CRVT | 30 |
| OO-MRE | CRVT | 15 |
| **OO-NAD** | **FA7X** | **41** |
| OO-NOA | E50P | 50000095 |
| OO-OOO | FA20 | 56 |
| OO-OSA | CS55 | 0147 |
| OO-PAP | F2EX | 123 |
| **OO-PGG** | **C56X** | **5230** |
| **OO-PHI** | **C525** | **0115** |
| OO-PJB | FA20 | 145/443 |
| (OO-PPP) | FA20 | 56 |
| **OO-PRM** | **C510** | **0125** |
| OO-PSD | FA20 | 384/551 |
| OO-RJE | C550 | 421 |
| OO-RJT | C550 | 023 |
| (OO-RJX) | FA20 | 73/419 |
| OO-RRR | FA20 | 98/434 |
| (OO-RSA) | SBRL | 465-72 |
| (OO-RSB) | SBRL | 465-72 |
| OO-RSE | SBRL | 465-72 |
| OO-RST | C500 | 063 |
| (OO-RYB) | FA20 | 262 |
| **OO-SAV** | **C56X** | **5189** |
| OO-SEL | C500 | 133 |
| (OO-SIN) | C680 | 0078 |
| **OO-SKA** | **C52A** | **0054** |
| OO-SKJ | HS25 | 25089 |
| **OO-SKP** | **CS55** | **0007** |
| OO-SKS | C550 | 079 |
| OO-SKV | C560 | 0153 |
| **OO-SKY** | **C52A** | **0197** |
| **OO-SLM** | **C56X** | **5781** |
| **OO-STE** | **C525** | **0495** |
| OO-STE | FA20 | 218 |
| OO-STF | FA20 | 220 |
| OO-TME | LJ60 | 255 |
| (OO-TTL) | CRVT | 28 |
| (OO-VIZ) | C56X | 5284 |
| OO-VMB | F2TH | 74 |
| **OO-VMI** | **F9DX** | **603** |
| OO-VPQ | FA20 | 315/517 |
| OO-WTB | FA20 | 162/451 |

## Denmark

| | | |
|---|---|---|
| (OY-  ) | C550 | 469 |
| OY-AGZ | LJ24 | 183 |
| OY-AJV | C500 | 279 |
| OY-AKL | LJ25 | 054 |
| OY-AKZ | LJ25 | 062 |
| OY-APM | CL61 | 5153 |
| OY-APM | HS25 | 25253 |
| OY-ARA | CRVT | 32 |
| OY-ARB | CRVT | 34 |
| OY-ARP | C500 | 040 |
| OY-ARW | C500 | 130 |
| OY-ASD | C500 | 288 |
| (OY-ASK) | LJ25 | 097 |
| OY-ASO | LJ35 | 119 |
| OY-ASP | LJ25 | 171 |
| OY-ASR | C500 | 194 |
| OY-ASV | C550 | 067 |
| OY-AZT | FA20 | 98/434 |
| OY-BDS | FA20 | 180/460 |
| OY-BFC | LJ25 | 112 |
| OY-BIZ | LJ24 | 281 |
| OY-BLG | LJ35 | 022 |

| | | |
|---|---|---|
| OY-BPC | MU30 | A023SA |
| OY-BPI | MU30 | A070SA |
| **OY-BZT** | **C550** | **289** |
| OY-CCB | MU30 | A037SA |
| OY-CCG | C650 | 0003 |
| **OY-CCJ** | **LJ35** | **468** |
| OY-CCO | LJ35 | 670 |
| OY-CCT | LJ35 | 144 |
| OY-CCU | C550 | 127 |
| OY-CDK | MU30 | A065SA |
| **OY-CEV** | **C500** | **329** |
| OY-CGO | C500 | 287 |
| **OY-CJN** | **BE40** | **RK-530** |
| OY-CKE | C650 | 7070 |
| OY-CKF | F2TH | 163 |
| **OY-CKH** | **F2EX** | **160** |
| (OY-CKH) | FA50 | 134 |
| **OY-CKI** | **F2TH** | **154** |
| **OY-CKJ** | **C560** | **0114** |
| **OY-CKK** | **C56X** | **5757** |
| OY-CKK | F900 | 110 |
| **OY-CKN** | **F2TH** | **76** |
| (OY-CKO) | CL60 | 1025 |
| **OY-CKT** | **C560** | **0078** |
| OY-CKW | F2TH | 166 |
| OY-CKY | FA20 | 293 |
| OY-CLD | CL61 | 5070 |
| (OY-CLE) | CL64 | 5303 |
| **OY-CLN** | **F2EX** | **35** |
| **OY-CLP** | **C650** | **7093** |
| OY-CPK | C500 | 267 |
| OY-CPW | C500 | 487 |
| OY-CVS | GLEX | 9139 |
| OY-CYD | C500 | 550 |
| OY-CYT | C550 | 443 |
| **OY-CYV** | **C550** | **440** |
| OY-DKP | HS25 | 25132 |
| OY-DVL | C500 | 036 |
| (OY-EBD) | C500 | 299 |
| **OY-EDP** | **C650** | **0014** |
| OY-EGE | LJ24 | 124 |
| **OY-EJD** | **F2EX** | **63** |
| OY-EKC | C56X | 5217 |
| **OY-EKS** | **CL30** | **20251** |
| **OY-ELY** | **C550** | **154** |
| (OY-ERY) | C550 | 469 |
| **OY-EVO** | **C550** | **550-1050** |
| (OY-FCE) | C525 | 0165 |
| OY-FCG | HS25 | 258541 |
| **OY-FFB** | **C500** | **603** |
| OY-FFC | C500 | 551 |
| OY-FFV | C560 | 0138 |
| **OY-FIT** | **GLEX** | **9186** |
| OY-FLK | LJ55 | 050 |
| (OY-FPN) | F2EX | 103 |
| OY-FRM | FA10 | 56 |
| **OY-GBB** | **CL65** | **5732** |
| (OY-GDA) | FA50 | 54 |
| OY-GGG | C650 | 7039 |
| OY-GGR | C52A | 0216 |
| OY-GIP | HS25 | 258367 |
| OY-GKC | C550 | 100 |
| OY-GKC | C56X | 5189 |
| OY-GKL | C650 | 0043 |
| OY-GLA | GLEX | 9094 |
| **OY-GLO** | **C52A** | **0303** |
| (OY-GMB) | C550 | 066 |
| OY-GMC | C550 | 025 |
| OY-GMJ | CS55 | 0134 |
| OY-GMK | C550 | 066 |
| OY-GRC | C550 | 255 |
| OY-GSE | CL61 | 5137 |
| **OY-GVG** | **GLF4** | **4066** |
| OY-ICE | F2TH | 26 |
| **OY-ILG** | **GLEX** | **9163** |
| OY-INI | C500 | 559 |
| OY-INV | C525 | 0223 |
| **OY-IVK** | **F9EX** | **138** |
| **OY-JAI** | **C500** | **193** |
| OY-JAT | BE40 | RJ-22 |
| **OY-JBJ** | **HS25** | **258358** |
| **OY-JDE** | **FA7X** | **54** |
| OY-JET | C500 | 644 |
| OY-JET | C52A | 0089 |
| (OY-JET) | C560 | 0138 |
| (OY-JET) | C680 | 0067 |
| **OY-JEV** | **C550** | **243** |
| OY-JEY | C500 | 600 |
| **OY-JJO** | **BE40** | **RK-267** |
| OY-JKH | LJ60 | 141 |
| **OY-JMC** | **C525** | **0277** |
| **OY-JPJ** | **C650** | **0060** |
| OY-JPJ | HS25 | 257015 |
| **OY-KLG** | **C560** | **0401** |
| "OY-KPV" | LJ40 | 45-2064 |
| **OY-KVP** | **LJ40** | **45-2064** |
| **OY-KYS** | **LJ60** | **369** |
| (OY-LEG) | C56X | 5217 |
| OY-LGI | LJ60 | 243 |
| OY-LIN | FA50 | 230 |
| OY-LJA | LJ35 | 594 |
| OY-LJB | LJ31 | 086 |
| OY-LJC | LJ31 | 087 |
| OY-LJD | LJ60 | 005 |
| OY-LJE | LJ60 | 011 |
| OY-LJF | LJ60 | 173 |
| OY-LJG | LJ45 | 083 |
| OY-LJH | LJ60 | 051 |
| OY-LJI | LJ31 | 104 |
| **OY-LJJ** | **LJ45** | **116** |
| (OY-LJK) | LJ60 | 200 |
| OY-LJK | LJ60 | 256 |
| OY-LJL | LJ31 | 133 |
| OY-LJM | LJ60 | 060 |
| OY-LJN | LJ31 | 170 |
| **OY-LKG** | **HS25** | **258345** |
| **OY-LKS** | **C750** | **0212** |
| OY-LLA | C52A | 0005 |
| **OY-LPU** | **C510** | **0022** |
| OY-MCL | HS25 | 258099 |
| **OY-MFL** | **HS25** | **257103** |
| **OY-MGO** | **F2EX** | **161** |
| **OY-MHA** | **F2EX** | **156** |
| **OY-MIR** | **LJ60** | **322** |
| OY-MKS | CL64 | 5624 |
| **OY-MMM** | **CL64** | **5430** |
| OY-MPA | HS25 | 257127 |
| **OY-MSI** | **GLEX** | **9032** |
| **OY-NDP** | **C52A** | **0372** |
| **OY-NLA** | **C650** | **0070** |
| **OY-NUD** | **C560** | **0064** |
| OY-OAA | HS25 | 258645 |
| OY-OCV | LJ45 | 306 |
| **OY-OKK** | **F9EX** | **128** |
| OY-ONE | C500 | 535 |
| OY-PCW | C500 | 278 |
| OY-PDN | C550 | 412 |
| OY-PHN | FA10 | 209 |
| **OY-PNO** | **F2EX** | **103** |
| **OY-RAA** | **HS25** | **258235** |
| OY-RAC | HS25 | 258335 |
| OY-RAK | GALX | 051 |
| OY-RDD | C550 | 621 |
| **OY-RED** | **LJ40** | **45-2096** |
| OY-REN | C52A | 0331 |
| OY-RGG | C525 | 0495 |
| OY-RYA | LJ24 | 109 |
| OY-SBR | CRVT | 23 |
| OY-SBS | CRVT | 21 |
| **OY-SBT** | **CRVT** | **33** |
| **OY-SGC** | **GLEX** | **9343** |
| OY-SGM | CL64 | 5596 |
| **OY-SIR** | **F2TH** | **173** |
| OY-SIS | BE40 | RK-162 |
| **OY-SML** | **C525** | **0258** |
| OY-SUJ | C500 | 121 |
| OY-SVL | C500 | 420 |
| OY-TAM | C500 | 158 |
| (OY-TCG) | LJ60 | 200 |
| OY-TKI | C500 | 299 |
| **OY-TMA** | **C550** | **457** |
| OY-TNF | CL64 | 5303 |
| **OY-UCA** | **C52A** | **0209** |
| (OY-VIA) | CL60 | 1025 |
| (OY-VIA) | HS25 | 257105 |
| (OY-VIK) | F9EX | 138 |
| OY-VIP | C500 | 294 |
| (OY-VIP) | C500 | 311 |
| OY-VIS | C550 | 672 |
| **OY-WET** | **C680** | **0067** |
| **OY-WIN** | **GLEX** | **9280** |
| **OY-WWW** | **C52B** | **0194** |
| **OY-YAM** | **ASTR** | **111** |
| **OY-ZAN** | **LJ40** | **45-2071** |

Netherlands

| | | |
|---|---|---|
| PH-ABO | CL61 | 5085 |
| **PH-ABU** | **LJ55** | **107** |
| **PH-ANO** | **C56X** | **5745** |
| PH-APV | FA20 | 490 |
| PH-BAG | FA20 | 126/438 |
| (PH-BBC) | BE40 | RK-313 |
| **PH-BPS** | **FA20** | **321** |
| **PH-CHT** | **F2EX** | **40** |
| **PH-CIJ** | **C680** | **0185** |
| **PH-CJI** | **C56X** | **5128** |
| **PH-CMW** | **C525** | **0613** |
| PH-CSA | C550 | 630 |
| PH-CTA | C500 | 088 |
| PH-CTB | C500 | 093 |
| PH-CTC | C500 | 098 |
| PH-CTD | C500 | 157 |
| PH-CTE | C500 | 167 |
| PH-CTF | C500 | 177 |
| PH-CTG | C500 | 234 |
| (PH-CTW) | C500 | 269 |
| PH-CTX | C550 | 338 |
| PH-CTY | C500 | 044 |
| PH-CTZ | C550 | 067 |
| **PH-DEZ** | **C500** | **407** |
| **PH-DRK** | **C56X** | **5258** |
| **PH-DRS** | **C56X** | **5792** |
| **PH-DYE** | **C550** | **550-0927** |
| **PH-DYN** | **C550** | **550-0928** |
| (PH-DYX) | C56X | 5209 |
| **PH-ECI** | **C525** | **0321** |
| PH-ECL | C52A | 0054 |
| **PH-EDM** | **F900** | **188** |
| (PH-EFA) | F900 | 163 |
| (PH-EFB) | F2TH | 49 |
| PH-ERP | F9EX | 1 |
| (PH-EVY) | C650 | 0134 |
| **PH-FIS** | **C525** | **0514** |
| **PH-FJK** | **C52B** | **0291** |
| PH-FJP | GLF2 | 78 |
| PH-HES | C550 | 023 |
| PH-HET | C550 | 323 |
| PH-HFA | HFB3 | 1032 |
| PH-HFB | HFB3 | 1033 |
| PH-HFC | HFB3 | 1035 |
| **PH-HMA** | **C550** | **550-0972** |
| (PH-HMA) | CS55 | 0145 |
| (PH-HMC) | CS55 | 0145 |
| PH-ILA | C560 | 0078 |
| **PH-ILC** | **F900** | **161** |
| (PH-ILC) | F900 | 9 |
| PH-ILD | FA50 | 23 |
| PH-ILF | FA20 | 147/444 |
| PH-ILI | C560 | 0114 |
| PH-ILO | C560 | 0362 |
| PH-ILR | FA50 | 15 |
| PH-ILT | FA10 | 1 |
| PH-ILX | FA20 | 266/490 |
| PH-ILY | FA20 | 326/521 |
| **PH-ILZ** | **C560** | **0145** |
| PH-INJ | F2TH | 36 |
| **PH-JCI** | **PRM1** | **RB-122** |
| **PH-JNE** | **C52A** | **0242** |
| PH-JNL | FA50 | 268 |
| **PH-JNX** | **C56X** | **5641** |
| (PH-JOB) | C500 | 511 |
| PH-JSB | CRVT | 26 |
| PH-JSC | CRVT | 35 |
| PH-JSD | CRVT | 36 |
| (PH-JSL) | MU30 | A087SA |
| PH-KOM | C525 | 0331 |
| **PH-LAB** | **C550** | **712** |
| PH-LBA | F900 | 173 |
| **PH-LCG** | **F900** | **143** |
| PH-LEM | FA50 | 28 |
| (PH-LEN) | FA20 | 263/489 |
| PH-LPS | FA20 | 63/411 |
| **PH-LSV** | **FA50** | **315** |
| PH-MBX | C550 | 180 |
| PH-MCX | C550 | 564 |
| PH-MDC | C560 | 0280 |
| PH-MDX | C550 | 634 |
| PH-MED | LJ55 | 136 |
| **PH-MEX** | **C650** | **0217** |
| **PH-MFX** | **C650** | **0240** |
| PH-MGT | C525 | 0042 |
| PH-MHM | C56X | 5781 |
| PH-MSR | MS76 | 102 |
| PH-MSS | MS76 | 103 |
| PH-MST | MS76 | 104 |
| PH-MSU | MS76 | 105 |
| PH-MSV | MS76 | 106 |
| PH-MSW | MS76 | 107 |
| **PH-MSX** | **C650** | **0134** |
| PH-MSX | MS76 | 108 |
| **PH-MYX** | **C650** | **7117** |
| **PH-NDK** | **F900** | **175** |
| PH-OLI | F900 | 35 |
| PH-OMC | FA20 | 239 |
| **PH-ORJ** | **C510** | **0025** |
| PH-PBM | C560 | 0100 |
| PH-PST | E50P | 50000132 |
| **PH-RID** | **C680** | **0212** |
| PH-RMA | CS55 | 0145 |
| **PH-RSA** | **C56X** | **5110** |
| PH-SAW | C500 | 225 |
| (PH-SDL) | FA50 | 66 |
| **PH-SOL** | **C525** | **0417** |
| (PH-TEU) | C500 | 086 |
| **PH-TEV** | **C500** | **086** |
| (PH-TXA) | C510 | 0088 |
| **PH-TXA** | **C510** | **0111** |
| (PH-TXB) | C510 | 0111 |
| (PH-TXB) | C510 | 0133 |
| (PH-TXC) | C510 | 0131 |
| PH-TXI | C510 | 0050 |
| **PH-VBG** | **F2EX** | **5** |
| PH-VLG | C560 | 0271 |
| PH-WMS | FA20 | 285/504 |
| (PH-WOL) | F2TH | 36 |
| (PH-WOL) | HS25 | 258235 |

Philippines
(see also RP-)

| | | |
|---|---|---|
| PI-C1747 | LJ24 | 264 |
| (PI-C7777) | C500 | 123 |

Netherland Antilles

| | | |
|---|---|---|
| PJ-ABA | GLF2 | 163 |
| PJ-ARI | GLF2 | 8 |
| PJ-AYA | FA10 | 47 |
| PJ-MAR | C650 | 0049 |
| PJ-SLB | HS25 | 25223 |
| PJ-SOL | BE40 | RJ-19 |

Indonesia

| | | |
|---|---|---|
| **PK-BKS** | **C56X** | **5804** |
| PK-BND | GLF3 | 316 |
| PK-CAG | FA20 | 408 |
| **PK-CAH** | **LJ31** | **066** |
| (PK-CAJ) | FA20 | 408 |
| **PK-CAJ** | **LJ31** | **077** |
| PK-CAP | GLF3 | 316 |
| PK-CIR | FA20 | 90/426 |
| PK-CTA | HS25 | 257153 |
| PK-CTC | HS25 | 257099 |
| PK-CTP | GLF3 | 431 |
| PK-DJW | HS25 | 25147 |
| **PK-DPD** | **C56X** | **6035** |
| PK-ERA | BE40 | RJ-40 |
| PK-HMG | HS25 | 256029 |
| PK-HMK | CL61 | 5073 |
| PK-IJS | JSTR | 5046 |
| **PK-ILA** | **C56X** | **5598** |
| **PK-JBH** | **HS25** | **HA-0071** |
| PK-KIG | C650 | 0151 |
| PK-NSP | GLF4 | 1077 |
| PK-NZK | GLF4 | 1219 |
| PK-OCN | GLF3 | 305 |
| PK-PJA | GLF3 | 395 |
| PK-PJD | HS25 | 256017 |
| PK-PJE | HS25 | 256029 |
| PK-PJG | GLF2 | 45 |
| PK-PJH | JSTR | 5011/1 |
| PK-PJR | HS25 | 25147 |
| PK-PJS | JSTR | 5011/1 |
| PK-PJZ | GLF2 | 26 |
| **PK-PRM** | **PRM1** | **RB-56** |
| PK-RGM | HS25 | 258106 |

| | | |
|---|---|---|
| PK-RJB | C650 | 7073 |
| PK-TIR | FA20 | 297 |
| PK-TRI | FA20 | 173 |
| PK-TRJ | C650 | 0078 |
| PK-TRP | F900 | 71 |
| PK-TRV | C550 | 287 |
| PK-TSM | C650 | 0144 |
| PK-TVO | HS25 | 258579 |
| PK-TWL | PRM1 | RB-56 |
| PK-WSE | C650 | 0078 |
| "PK-WSG" | C550 | 650 |
| PK-WSJ | HS25 | 258106 |
| PK-WSO | C550 | 287 |
| PK-YRL | C650 | 7073 |

Brazil

| | | |
|---|---|---|
| PP-AAA | C750 | 0234 |
| PP-AAD | C680 | 0260 |
| PP-AAF | F2EX | 16 |
| PP-ADD | C56X | 5822 |
| PP-AFM | E50P | 50000049 |
| PP-AIO | C650 | 0087 |
| PP-ANA | HS25 | 258637 |
| PP-ARG | HS25 | HA-0078 |
| PP-AVX | C52B | 0101 |
| PP-BBS | C52A | 0325 |
| PP-BIA | CL64 | 5539 |
| PP-BIR | CL30 | 20178 |
| PP-BMG | C550 | 550-1045 |
| PP-BRS | C56X | 5544 |
| PP-BST | C680 | 0184 |
| PP-CFF | F2TH | 110 |
| PP-CRS | C525 | 0346 |
| PP-CRT | LJ35 | 363 |
| PP-CTA | LJ31 | 168 |
| PP-EEM | HS25 | 25197 |
| PP-EIF | C500 | 680 |
| PP-EIW | LJ24 | 294 |
| PP-ERR | LJ35 | 008 |
| PP-ESC | C550 | 618 |
| PP-EVG | C510 | 0101 |
| PP-FMW | LJ40 | 45-2068 |
| PP-FMX | LJ24 | 090 |
| PP-FOH | FA20 | 113 |
| PP-FXB | C500 | 049 |
| PP-HSI | LJ45 | 237 |
| PP-IME | E50P | 50000073 |
| PP-ISJ | C560 | 0258 |
| PP-JAA | LJ36 | 055 |
| PP-JBS | C525 | 0408 |
| PP-JCF | BE40 | RK-479 |
| PP-JET | C525 | 0384 |
| PP-JFM | C56X | 5045 |
| PP-JGV | C56X | 5105 |
| PP-JQM | C750 | 0056 |
| PP-JRA | C650 | 7113 |
| PP-KKA | E50P | 50000126 |
| (PP-LEM) | C500 | 171 |
| PP-LGT | E50P | 50000031 |
| PP-LJR | C525 | 0487 |
| PP-LRR | LJ60 | 267 |
| (PP-LUA) | BE40 | RK-258 |
| (PP-LUG) | PRM1 | RB-224 |
| PP-MCL | E55P | 50500024 |
| PP-MDB | C56X | 5552 |
| PP-MIS | C510 | 0043 |
| PP-MJC | F2EX | 99 |
| PP-MPP | C52B | 0297 |
| PP-MTG | C510 | 0046 |
| PP-NNN | C510 | 0041 |
| PP-OAA | C550 | 550-0954 |
| PP-ONE | LJ60 | 354 |
| PP-ORM | C550 | 550-0930 |
| PP-OSA | CL64 | 5411 |
| (PP-PMR) | C510 | 0087 |
| PP-PMV | FA50 | 299 |
| PP-PPA | F900 | 35 |
| PP-PPN | F2EX | 164 |
| PP-PRR | C56X | 5823 |
| PP-PRV | C510 | 0197 |
| PP-RAA | C56X | 5034 |
| PP-RST | C56X | 5579 |
| PP-SBR | C56X | 5544 |
| PP-SCB | CL65 | 5714 |
| PP-SED | SBRL | 282-121 |
| PP-SKD | E50P | 50000066 |

| | | |
|---|---|---|
| PP-UQF | BE40 | RK-379 |
| PP-VDP | E50P | 50000109 |
| PP-VDR | GLEX | 9312 |
| PP-WGS | C510 | 0099 |
| PP-WIN | LJ60 | 159 |
| PP-WRV | BE40 | RK-258 |
| PP-XOG | E50P | 50000004 |
| PP-XOH | E50P | 50000003 |
| PP-XOJ | E50P | 50000002 |
| PP-XOM | E50P | 50000001 |
| PP-XON | E50P | 50000005 |
| PP-XOO | E50P | 50000006 |
| PP-XOQ | E50P | 50000007 |
| PP-XOR | E50P | 50000008 |
| PP-XPD | E50P | 50000009 |
| PP-XPE | E50P | 50000010 |
| PP-XPF | E50P | 50000011 |
| PP-XPG | E50P | 50000012 |
| PP-XPH | E50P | 50099801 |
| PP-XUM | MS76 | 097 |
| PP-XVI | E55P | 50599801 |
| PP-XVJ | E55P | 50500001 |
| PP-XVK | E55P | 50500002 |
| PP-XVL | E55P | 50500003 |
| PP-XVM | E55P | 50500004 |
| PP-YOF | C525 | 0356 |
| PP-ZZC | E55P | 50500011 |
| PP-ZZD | E55P | 50500012 |
| PP-ZZE | E55P | 50500013 |
| PR-AAA | C56X | 5120 |
| PR-ABP | LJ35 | 621 |
| PR-ABV | C525 | 0428 |
| PR-ACC | C56X | 5274 |
| PR-ADL | C52B | 0278 |
| PR-ADQ | E50P | 50000101 |
| PR-AGP | C680 | 0259 |
| PR-AJG | C650 | 7111 |
| PR-ALC | C52B | 0124 |
| (PR-ALL) | C560 | 0637 |
| PR-ALV | C52B | 0129 |
| PR-ALY | BE40 | RK-6 |
| PR-AMA | PRM1 | RB-21 |
| PR-ANP | C56X | 5750 |
| PR-ARA | C525 | 0441 |
| PR-ARS | C52A | 0392 |
| PR-AUR | GALX | 140 |
| PR-AVM | LJ31 | 005 |
| PR-BBD | GALX | 218 |
| PR-BED | BE40 | RK-430 |
| PR-BER | PRM1 | RB-40 |
| PR-BJM | C525 | 0458 |
| PR-BNP | C680 | 0217 |
| (PR-BOI) | LJ31 | 242 |
| PR-BRS | C680 | 0241 |
| PR-BSA | C510 | 0062 |
| PR-C8082 | HS25 | 258064 |
| PR-CAN | C525 | 0233 |
| PR-CAO | LJ45 | 320 |
| PR-CCC | F9EX | 162 |
| PR-CCV | C560 | 0130 |
| PR-CDF | FA10 | 126 |
| PR-CIM | PRM1 | RB-32 |
| PR-CLB | C525 | 0191 |
| PR-CNP | C52A | 0226 |
| PR-CON | C56X | 5583 |
| PR-CPC | E50P | 50000125 |
| PR-CSM | LJ45 | 329 |
| PR-CSW | E50P | 50000048 |
| PR-CTA | C750 | 0010 |
| PR-CTB | C560 | 0760 |
| PR-CVC | C52B | 0199 |
| PR-DAY | E50P | 50000065 |
| PR-DBB | HS25 | 258284 |
| PR-DBD | HS25 | HA-0089 |
| PR-DCE | C525 | 0251 |
| PR-DCJ | E50P | 50000027 |
| PR-DHC | E50P | 50000034 |
| PR-DIB | LJ40 | 45-2081 |
| PR-DLM | E50P | 50000098 |
| PR-DNZ | FA7X | 22 |
| PR-DOT | BE40 | RK-104 |
| PR-DRI | C510 | 0063 |
| PR-EBD | C52B | 0047 |
| PR-EGB | FA10 | 45 |
| PR-EMS | C56X | 5223 |
| PR-ENE | LJ31 | 151 |
| PR-EOB | C525 | 0483 |
| PR-ERP | C550 | 550-0903 |

| | | |
|---|---|---|
| PR-ERR | LJ55 | 137 |
| PR-EXP | C525 | 0482 |
| PR-FAC | C510 | 0129 |
| PR-FAP | HS25 | 258559 |
| PR-FBS | E50P | 50000042 |
| PR-FEP | C550 | 550-0833 |
| PR-FJA | C56X | 5739 |
| "PR-FJU" | C56X | 5739 |
| PR-FMP | C510 | 0087 |
| PR-FNP | C750 | 0028 |
| PR-FSA | C52A | 0356 |
| PR-FRU | F9EX | 181 |
| PR-GAM | C56X | 5256 |
| PR-GBN | LJ31 | 166 |
| PR-GCA | PRM1 | RB-65 |
| PR-GCL | LJ60 | 283 |
| PR-GFS | C525 | 0663 |
| PR-GPA | F9EX | 82 |
| PR-GQG | C560 | 0704 |
| PR-GRD | C750 | 0112 |
| PR-HAP | C525 | 0185 |
| PR-HIP | C525 | 0220 |
| PR-HLW | C680 | 0182 |
| PR-HOT | C510 | 0195 |
| PR-IDB | CL30 | 20168 |
| PR-IEI | E50P | 50000085 |
| PR-IND | BE40 | RK-470 |
| PR-ITN | C650 | 0171 |
| PR-IVI | E50P | 50000032 |
| PR-JAJ | E50P | 50000083 |
| PR-JAP | C650 | 7038 |
| PR-JAQ | C750 | 0060 |
| PR-JBS | LJ40 | 45-2048 |
| PR-JET | C52A | 0042 |
| PR-JJV | LJ31 | 149 |
| PR-JPK | BE40 | RK-155 |
| PR-JRR | PRM1 | RB-84 |
| PR-JST | C52A | 0044 |
| PR-JTS | MU30 | A066SA |
| PR-JVF | C52A | 0376 |
| PR-KKA | C650 | 0213 |
| PR-KYK | C52A | 0440 |
| PR-LAM | C560 | 0600 |
| PR-LAT | C750 | 0052 |
| PR-LDF | LJ60 | 242 |
| PR-LFT | C56X | 5619 |
| PR-LJM | C525 | 0456 |
| PR-LMP | E50P | 50000094 |
| PR-LRJ | LJ31 | 158 |
| PR-LRR | LJ31 | 017 |
| PR-LTA | HS25 | 258025 |
| PR-LUG | HS25 | 258553 |
| PR-LUZ | C750 | 0004 |
| PR-MCL | C510 | 0057 |
| PR-MCN | CS55 | 0081 |
| (PR-MDB) | CL30 | 20168 |
| PR-MDE | C510 | 0231 |
| PR-MEN | GALX | 046 |
| PR-MFJ | C525 | 0542 |
| PR-MJC | C750 | 0237 |
| PR-MJD | E50P | 50000096 |
| PR-MKB | LJ31 | 178 |
| PR-MLA | LJ35 | 072 |
| PR-MLJ | GLEX | 9258 |
| PR-MLR | LJ60 | 357 |
| PR-MMS | BE40 | RK-457 |
| PR-MMV | C56X | 5744 |
| PR-MON | C52B | 0324 |
| PR-MPM | C510 | 0080 |
| PR-MRG | C52B | 0187 |
| PR-MVB | BE40 | RK-350 |
| PR-NBR | C56X | 5289 |
| PR-NCJ | HS25 | HB-15 |
| PR-NNP | C52A | 0316 |
| PR-NPP | E50P | 50000043 |
| PR-NRN | C510 | 0119 |
| PR-NTX | C52A | 0228 |
| PR-NXG | F2EX | 157 |
| PR-OBE | F2EX | 179 |
| PR-OEC | BE40 | RK-524 |
| PR-OFP | E50P | 50000108 |
| PR-OFT | GALX | 027 |
| PR-OGX | GLF5 | 5253 |
| PR-ONE | LJ40 | 45-2020 |
| PR-OPP | HS25 | 258547 |
| PR-OTA | LJ45 | 242 |
| PR-OUD | C525 | 0660 |
| PR-OUR | C56X | 5371 |

| | | |
|---|---|---|
| PR-OVD | E50P | 50000127 |
| PR-PJD | LJ31 | 214 |
| PR-PMV | F9EX | 207 |
| PR-PPN | F2EX | 40 |
| PR-PRA | PRM1 | RB-169 |
| PR-PRC | PRM1 | RB-231 |
| PR-PRE | PRM1 | RB-139 |
| PR-PTA | E50P | 50000077 |
| PR-PTL | C650 | 7038 |
| PR-PTR | LJ40 | 45-2086 |
| PR-RAA | C56X | 5105 |
| PR-RAV | C56X | 5517 |
| PR-RBO | C52B | 0310 |
| PR-RCB | C680 | 0090 |
| PR-RDM | C510 | 0084 |
| PR-RJN | C52A | 0417 |
| (PR-RJZ) | F9EX | 235 |
| PR-RMC | C56X | 6034 |
| PR-RRN | PRM1 | RB-237 |
| PR-RSN | PRM1 | RB-240 |
| PR-RTJ | C680 | 0267 |
| PR-RTS | C56X | 6046 |
| PR-SCB | LJ31 | 100 |
| PR-SCE | BE40 | RK-466 |
| PR-SCF | C52B | 0239 |
| PR-SCP | C550 | 550-1118 |
| PR-SCR | C560 | 0653 |
| PR-SEA | F900 | 192 |
| PR-SFA | LJ31 | 023 |
| PR-SKB | BE40 | RK-144 |
| (PR-SKD) | E50P | 50000066 |
| PR-SMJ | C525 | 0285 |
| PR-SMK | C680 | 0252 |
| PR-SMT | FA20 | 509 |
| PR-SOL | HS25 | 258133 |
| PR-SOV | C680 | 0069 |
| PR-SPJ | E50P | 50000076 |
| PR-SPO | C52B | 0028 |
| PR-SPR | C680 | 0132 |
| PR-STJ | WW24 | 300 |
| PR-SUL | FA20 | 129 |
| PR-SUN | C680 | 0060 |
| PR-TAP | C52A | 0185 |
| PR-TBL | C52B | 0245 |
| PR-TEN | C56X | 5778 |
| PR-TOP | C52A | 0061 |
| PR-TRJ | C56X | 5644 |
| PR-TUB | CL64 | 5381 |
| PR-UUT | E50P | 50000093 |
| PR-VDL | C510 | 0085 |
| PR-VDR | GLEX | 9018 |
| PR-VEL | E50P | 50000068 |
| PR-VGD | C525 | 0120 |
| PR-VHB | BE40 | RK-496 |
| PR-VMD | PRM1 | RB-246 |
| PR-VPP | PRM1 | RB-224 |
| PR-VRD | C56X | 5211 |
| PR-WAT | C52A | 0406 |
| PR-WBW | LJ60 | 237 |
| PR-WOB | C52A | 0089 |
| PR-WQT | F2EX | 22 |
| PR-WRI | F9EX | 44 |
| PR-WRM | FA7X | 6 |
| PR-WRO | GLF5 | 5236 |
| PR-WSC | CL30 | 20012 |
| PR-WSM | F2TH | 6 |
| PR-WTR | GALX | 004 |
| PR-WYW | FA50 | 234 |
| PR-XDN | GLEX | 9190 |
| PR-XDY | C750 | 0118 |
| PR-XJS | LJ60 | 189 |
| PR-XSX | C510 | 0058 |
| (PT- ) | C550 | 460 |
| (PT- ) | C550 | 598 |
| (PT- ) | C56X | 5029 |
| (PT- ) | FA10 | 224 |
| (PT- ) | HS25 | 258208 |
| PT-AAC | GLF3 | 450 |
| PT-AAF | FA50 | 234 |
| PT-ACC | LJ36 | 018 |
| PT-ALK | GLF3 | 418 |
| PT-ASJ | FA10 | 95 |
| PT-BBB | LJ31 | 103 |
| PT-CBA | PRM1 | RB-222 |
| PT-CMY | LJ25 | 108 |
| PT-CXJ | LJ24 | 176 |
| PT-CXK | LJ24 | 122 |
| PT-DTY | HS25 | 25243 |

| | | |
|---|---|---|
| PT-DUO | LJ25 | 061 |
| PT-DVL | LJ25 | 077 |
| PT-DZU | LJ24 | 244 |
| PT-FAF | LJ25 | 099 |
| PT-FAT | LJ35 | 361 |
| **PT-FBM** | **C525** | **0119** |
| **PT-FJA** | **C525** | **0337** |
| **PT-FLC** | **C510** | **0147** |
| **PT-FLO** | **C510** | **0056** |
| (PT-FLX) | F2EX | 157 |
| **PT-FNP** | **C525** | **0319** |
| PT-FOH | FA20 | 113 |
| **PT-FPP** | **C56X** | **5003** |
| **PT-FQA*** | **E50P** | **50000127** |
| **PT-FQB** | **E50P** | **50000128** |
| **PT-FQC** | **E50P** | **50000129** |
| PT-FQD | E50P | 50000130 |
| **PT-FQE** | **E50P** | **50000131** |
| **PT-FQF** | **E50P** | **50000132** |
| PT-FQG | E50P | 50000133 |
| **PT-FQH** | **E50P** | **50000134** |
| **PT-FQI** | **E50P** | **50000135** |
| PT-FQJ | E50P | 50000136 |
| PT-FQK | E50P | 50000137 |
| **PT-FQL** | **E50P** | **50000138** |
| **PT-FQM** | **E50P** | **50000139** |
| **PT-FQN** | **E50P** | **50000140** |
| PT-FQO | E50P | 50000141 |
| **PT-FQP** | **E50P** | **50000142** |
| **PT-FQQ** | **E50P** | **50000143** |
| **PT-FQR** | **E50P** | **50000144** |
| **PT-FQS** | **E50P** | **50000145** |
| **PT-FQT** | **E50P** | **50000146** |
| **PT-FQU** | **E50P** | **50000147** |
| **PT-FQV** | **E50P** | **50000148** |
| **PT-FQW** | **E50P** | **50000149** |
| **PT-FQX** | **E50P** | **50000150** |
| **PT-FQY** | **E50P** | **50000151** |
| **PT-FQZ** | **E50P** | **50000152** |
| **PT-FTB** | **C560** | **0060** |
| **PT-FTC** | **C52A** | **0048** |
| **PT-FTE** | **C52A** | **0053** |
| **PT-FTG** | **C52A** | **0117** |
| PT-FTR | C52A | 0141 |
| **PT-FUA** | **E50P** | **50000153** |
| **PT-FUB** | **E50P** | **50000154** |
| **PT-FUC** | **E50P** | **50000155** |
| **PT-FUD** | **E50P** | **50000156** |
| **PT-FUE** | **E50P** | **50000157** |
| **PT-FUF** | **E50P** | **50000158** |
| **PT-FUG** | **E50P** | **50000159** |
| **PT-FUH** | **E50P** | **50000160** |
| **PT-FUI** | **E50P** | **50000161** |
| **PT-FUJ** | **E50P** | **50000162** |
| **PT-FUK** | **E50P** | **50000163** |
| **PT-FUL** | **E50P** | **50000164** |
| **PT-FUM** | **E50P** | **50000165** |
| **PT-FUN** | **E50P** | **50000166** |
| **PT-FUO** | **E50P** | **50000167** |
| **PT-FUP** | **E50P** | **50000168** |
| **PT-FUQ** | **E50P** | **50000169** |
| **PT-FUR** | **E50P** | **50000170** |
| **PT-FUS** | **E50P** | **50000171** |
| **PT-FUT** | **E50P** | **50000172** |
| **PT-FUU** | **E50P** | **50000173** |
| **PT-FUV** | **E50P** | **50000174** |
| **PT-FUW** | **E50P** | **50000175** |
| **PT-FUX** | **E50P** | **50000176** |
| **PT-FUY** | **E50P** | **50000177** |
| **PT-FUZ** | **E50P** | **50000178** |
| PT-FXB | C500 | 049 |
| **PT-FYA** | **E50P** | **50000179** |
| **PT-FYB** | **E50P** | **50000180** |
| **PT-FYC** | **E50P** | **50000181** |
| **PT-FYD** | **E50P** | **50000182** |
| **PT-FYE** | **E50P** | **50000183** |
| **PT-FYF** | **E50P** | **50000184** |
| **PT-FYG** | **E50P** | **50000185** |
| **PT-FYH** | **E50P** | **50000186** |
| **PT-FYI** | **E50P** | **50000187** |
| **PT-FYJ** | **E50P** | **50000188** |
| **PT-FYK** | **E50P** | **50000189** |
| **PT-FYL** | **E50P** | **50000190** |
| **PT-FYM** | **E50P** | **50000191** |
| **PT-FYN** | **E50P** | **50000192** |
| **PT-FYO** | **E50P** | **50000193** |
| **PT-FYP** | **E50P** | **50000194** |
| PT-FZA | LJ31 | 214 |
| **PT-GAF** | **HS25** | **258261** |
| **PT-GAP** | **LJ35** | **589** |
| PT-GMN | LJ55 | 139 |
| PT-IBR | LJ25 | 072 |
| PT-IDW | HFB3 | 1052 |
| **PT-IIQ** | **LJ25** | **089** |
| PT-IKR | LJ25 | 099 |
| PT-ILJ | C500 | 057 |
| PT-IOB | HFB3 | 1053 |
| PT-IQL | C500 | 069 |
| PT-ISN | LJ25 | 113 |
| **PT-ISO** | **LJ25** | **115** |
| **PT-JAA** | **HS25** | **258190** |
| PT-JBQ | LJ25 | 119 |
| PT-JDX | LJ25 | 131 |
| PT-JGU | LJ24 | 276 |
| **PT-JKQ** | **LJ24** | **284** |
| PT-JKR | LJ24 | 278 |
| **PT-JMJ** | **C500** | **134** |
| PT-JNJ | SBRL | 282-118 |
| PT-JQM | BE40 | RK-63 |
| PT-JXS | C500 | 162 |
| PT-KAP | LJ25 | 156 |
| PT-KBC | LJ25 | 165 |
| PT-KBD | LJ25 | 166 |
| **PT-KBR** | **C500** | **156** |
| PT-KIR | C500 | 103 |
| PT-KIU | C500 | 172 |
| PT-KKV | LJ25 | 172 |
| PT-KOT | SBRL | 306-80 |
| PT-KOU | SBRL | 306-84 |
| PT-KPA | C500 | 181 |
| PT-KPB | C500 | 188 |
| PT-KPE | LJ24 | 315 |
| PT-KQT | LJ36 | 011 |
| PT-KTO | FA10 | 63 |
| PT-KTU | LJ36 | 018 |
| PT-KXZ | C500 | 043 |
| PT-KYR | LJ25 | 266 |
| **PT-KZR** | **LJ35** | **252** |
| PT-KZY | LJ25 | 204 |
| PT-LAA | LJ35 | 295 |
| PT-LAS | LJ35 | 326 |
| PT-LAU | LJ24 | 239 |
| (PT-LAW) | C500 | 091 |
| PT-LAX | C500 | 194 |
| PT-LAY | C500 | 068 |
| PT-LAZ | C500 | 180 |
| **PT-LBN** | **C500** | **079** |
| PT-LBS | LJ35 | 361 |
| **PT-LBW** | **LJ25** | **056** |
| PT-LBY | LJ35 | 411 |
| (PT-LBZ) | C500 | 608 |
| **PT-LCC** | **C500** | **608** |
| **PT-LCD** | **LJ35** | **103** |
| PT-LCN | LJ24 | 287 |
| PT-LCO | FA10 | 154 |
| PT-LCR | C550 | 157 |
| **PT-LCV** | **LJ24** | **254** |
| PT-LCW | C550 | 358 |
| PT-LDH | C500 | 049 |
| **PT-LDI** | **C500** | **335** |
| **PT-LDM** | **LJ35** | **494** |
| PT-LDN | LJ35 | 436 |
| PT-LDR | LJ55 | 028 |
| **PT-LDR** | **LJ55** | **134** |
| **PT-LDY** | **WW24** | **251** |
| **PT-LEA** | **LJ25** | **155** |
| PT-LEB | LJ35 | 474 |
| PT-LEL | LJ55 | 013 |
| PT-LEM | LJ24 | 270 |
| **PT-LEN** | **LJ25** | **093** |
| **PT-LET** | **LJ55** | **080** |
| PT-LFR | C500 | 680 |
| PT-LFS | LJ35 | 008 |
| PT-LFT | LJ35 | 473 |
| PT-LGD | MU30 | A072SA |
| PT-LGF | LJ35 | 019 |
| PT-LGI | CS55 | 0024 |
| PT-LGJ | CS55 | 0025 |
| PT-LGM | C550 | 128 |
| PT-LGR | LJ35 | 009 |
| PT-LGS | LJ35 | 299 |
| PT-LGT | C650 | 0081 |
| **PT-LGW** | **LJ35** | **598** |
| PT-LGZ | C650 | 0088 |
| PT-LHA | C650 | 0059 |
| **PT-LHB** | **HS25** | **258031** |
| **PT-LHC** | **C650** | **0086** |
| PT-LHD | CS55 | 0059 |
| **PT-LHK** | **HS25** | **25197** |
| **PT-LHR** | **LJ55** | **044** |
| **PT-LHT** | **LJ35** | **479** |
| PT-LHU | LJ25 | 099 |
| PT-LHX | LJ35 | 464 |
| PT-LHY | C550 | 426 |
| PT-LIG | LJ55 | 111 |
| PT-LIH | LJ35 | 433 |
| PT-LII | LJ35 | 499 |
| PT-LIJ | LJ35 | 607 |
| PT-LIP | WW24 | 418 |
| **PT-LIV** | **C550** | **499** |
| **PT-LIX** | **C500** | **171** |
| PT-LIY | C500 | 219 |
| PT-LIZ | C500 | 639 |
| PT-LJA | C550 | 154 |
| PT-LJC | C650 | 0115 |
| **PT-LJF** | **C550** | **272** |
| PT-LJI | FA50 | 173 |
| **PT-LJJ** | **C550** | **276** |
| **PT-LJK** | **LJ35** | **372** |
| **PT-LJL** | **CS55** | **0084** |
| **PT-LJQ** | **CS55** | **0113** |
| PT-LJT | C550 | 339 |
| **PT-LKD** | **LJ24** | **356** |
| PT-LKQ | LJ24 | 038 |
| PT-LKR | C550 | 378 |
| **PT-LKS** | **CS55** | **0114** |
| PT-LKT | CS55 | 0117 |
| PT-LLF | LJ35 | 644 |
| PT-LLK | LJ31 | 010 |
| PT-LLL | LJ25 | 258 |
| **PT-LLN** | **LJ25** | **176** |
| PT-LLQ | C550 | 495 |
| **PT-LLS** | **LJ35** | **303** |
| **PT-LLT** | **C550** | **349** |
| **PT-LLU** | **C550** | **147** |
| PT-LMA | LJ24 | 353 |
| PT-LME | C550 | 204 |
| PT-LMF | LJ24 | 120 |
| PT-LML | C550 | 016 |
| **PT-LMM** | **LJ25** | **323** |
| PT-LMO | FA10 | 49 |
| **PT-LMS** | **LJ24** | **296** |
| **PT-LMY** | **LJ35** | **627** |
| **PT-LNC** | **C550** | **237** |
| PT-LND | C550 | 254 |
| PT-LNE | LJ24 | 114 |
| PT-LNK | LJ24 | 294 |
| PT-LNN | MU30 | A048SA |
| PT-LNV | C500 | 568 |
| PT-LOC | C550 | 550 |
| **PT-LOE** | **LJ35** | **393** |
| PT-LOF | LJ55 | 028 |
| **PT-LOG** | **C500** | **284** |
| PT-LOJ | LJ24 | 303 |
| PT-LOS | C500 | 239 |
| **PT-LOT** | **LJ35** | **093** |
| PT-LPF | C500 | 249 |
| **PT-LPH** | **LJ24** | **275** |
| **PT-LPK** | **C550** | **010** |
| **PT-LPN** | **C550** | **323** |
| **PT-LPP** | **C550** | **199** |
| PT-LPT | LJ25 | 051 |
| PT-LPV | WW24 | 441 |
| PT-LPX | LJ24 | 158 |
| **PT-LPZ** | **C500** | **015** |
| PT-LQF | LJ35 | 616 |
| PT-LQG | C500 | 271 |
| PT-LQI | CS55 | 0154 |
| PT-LQJ | C550 | 578 |
| **PT-LQK** | **LJ24** | **333** |
| **PT-LQP** | **HS25** | **258116** |
| PT-LQQ | C500 | 512 |
| **PT-LQR** | **C500** | **246** |
| PT-LQW | C550 | 158 |
| PT-LSD | LJ25 | 243 |
| PT-LSF | C500 | 328 |
| **PT-LSJ** | **LJ35** | **181** |
| PT-LSN | C650 | 0049 |
| PT-LSR | C550 | 600 |
| PT-LSW | LJ35 | 286 |
| (PT-LTA) | HS25 | 258284 |
| **PT-LTB** | **C650** | **0166** |
| **PT-LTI** | **C500** | **226** |
| **PT-LTJ** | **C550** | **258** |
| PT-LTL | C550 | 608 |
| **PT-LUA** | **C500** | **346** |
| **PT-LUE** | **C650** | **0091** |
| **PT-LUG** | **LJ35** | **356** |
| **PT-LUK** | **LJ55** | **086** |
| PT-LUO | C650 | 0129 |
| **PT-LUZ** | **LJ25** | **335** |
| PT-LVB | C500 | 613 |
| **PT-LVD** | **FA10** | **223** |
| PT-LVF | C650 | 0171 |
| PT-LVO | LJ31 | 002 |
| PT-LVR | LJ31 | 013 |
| PT-LXG | C550 | 618 |
| **PT-LXH** | **C500** | **133** |
| PT-LXJ | FA10 | 225 |
| **PT-LXO** | **LJ55** | **135** |
| PT-LXS | LJ25 | 111 |
| PT-LXW | CL60 | 1063 |
| **PT-LXX** | **LJ31** | **007** |
| PT-LYA | C550 | 620 |
| PT-LYE | LJ24 | 354 |
| PT-LYF | LJ35 | 650 |
| PT-LYL | LJ24 | 291 |
| PT-LYN | C550 | 625 |
| PT-LYS | C550 | 624 |
| PT-LZO | C550 | 215 |
| **PT-LZP** | **LJ35** | **339** |
| **PT-LZQ** | **C560** | **0045** |
| PT-LZS | LJ55 | 139 |
| PT-MAC | BE40 | RK-151 |
| **PT-MAH** | **E50P** | **50000026** |
| **PT-MBZ** | **ASTR** | **022** |
| PT-MCB | LJ31 | 100 |
| PT-MFR | LJ35 | 655 |
| **PT-MGS** | **C650** | **7021** |
| **PT-MIL** | **C525** | **0086** |
| **PT-MJC** | **C525** | **0085** |
| PT-MKO | CL64 | 5347 |
| PT-MML | F2TH | 43 |
| **PT-MMO** | **C550** | **455** |
| **PT-MMV** | **C550** | **550-0811** |
| **PT-MPE** | **C525** | **0015** |
| "PT-MPE" | C525 | 0030 |
| **PT-MPL** | **BE40** | **RK-158** |
| **PT-MSK** | **C56X** | **5087** |
| PT-MSM | LJ55 | 072 |
| **PT-MSP** | **C525** | **0259** |
| PT-MTG | C560 | 0121 |
| (PT-MTU) | C525 | 0295 |
| PT-MVI | LJ31 | 082 |
| PT-OAA | C550 | 635 |
| PT-OAC | C550 | 613 |
| PT-OAF | C550 | 369 |
| **PT-OAG** | **C550** | **379** |
| PT-OAK | C650 | 0186 |
| PT-OBD | LJ24 | 228 |
| PT-OBR | LJ55 | 037 |
| PT-OBS | LJ55 | 048 |
| PT-OBT | HS25 | 258112 |
| PT-OBX | C650 | 0181 |
| PT-OCA | LJ55 | 140 |
| **PT-OCZ** | **LJ35** | **361** |
| **PT-ODC** | **C500** | **678** |
| **PT-ODL** | **C550** | **640** |
| PT-ODW | C550 | 643 |
| **PT-ODZ** | **C550** | **645** |
| PT-OEF | LJ35 | 102 |
| PT-OER | C550 | 390 |
| **PT-OEX** | **F900** | **92** |
| PT-OFJ | LJ31 | 014 |
| PT-OFK | LJ31 | 017 |
| PT-OFL | LJ31 | 019 |
| PT-OFW | LJ35 | 621 |
| PT-OHB | HS25 | 258190 |
| **PT-OHD** | **LJ25** | **296** |
| PT-OHM | FA10 | 50 |
| PT-OHU | LJ55 | 029 |
| PT-OIC | FA10 | 171 |
| **PT-OIG** | **C500** | **005** |
| PT-OJC | HS25 | 258177 |
| PT-OJF | C500 | 131 |
| **PT-OJG** | **C550** | **676** |
| PT-OJH | LJ55 | 144 |
| PT-OJK | C550 | 675 |
| PT-OJO | C650 | 0202 |
| PT-OJT | C550 | 562 |
| PT-OKM | C550 | 573 |
| **PT-OKP** | **C550** | **460** |

PT-OKV C650 0206
PT-OLN WW24 340
PT-OLV C560 0142
PT-OMB C550 672
PT-OMC HS25 258206
**PT-OMS C500 251**
**PT-OMT C500 179**
**PT-OMU C650 0205**
PT-OMV C650 0200
PT-ONK LJ35 472
PT-OOA C550 641
PT-OOF C500 074
**PT-OOI HS25 258214**
PT-OOK C500 039
**PT-OOL C500 060**
PT-OOM C550 479
PT-OOR C560 0176
PT-OOW LJ55 033
**PT-OPJ LJ35 396**
**PT-OQD C500 244**
PT-OQG FA20 514
**PT-ORA LJ55 146**
**PT-ORC C560 0195**
PT-ORD C550 154
PT-ORE C560 0131
PT-ORH HS25 258035
PT-ORJ HS25 257145
**PT-ORM C56X 5535**
PT-ORO C550 303
PT-ORS FA10 219
PT-ORT C560 0191
PT-OSA CL61 5075
PT-OSB HS25 258211
**PT-OSD C500 325**
PT-OSK C550 633
PT-OSL CS55 0127
**PT-OSM CS55 0160**
**PT-OSW HS25 258184**
**PT-OTC HS25 258194**
PT-OTH HS25 258229
PT-OTN C550 715
**PT-OTQ C500 046**
**PT-OTS C560 0213**
PT-OTT C560 0215
PT-OUG LJ55 060
PT-OVC LJ35 399
PT-OVI LJ60 008
**PT-OVK C500 027**
PT-OVM MU30 A091SA
**PT-OVU C650 7033**
**PT-OVV C550 616**
**PT-OVZ LJ31 037**
PT-OXB FA10 199
**PT-OXT MU30 A039SA**
PT-OYA C500 072
PT-OYP C550 561
PT-OZB C560 0258
PT-OZT C500 256
PT-OZX C500 299
(PT-PMV) LJ35 299
**PT-POK LJ35 619**
**PT-PRR C525 0403**
**PT-PTL C750 0080**
**PT-PVB E55P 50500014**
**PT-PVC E55P 50500015**
**PT-PVD E55P 50500016**
**PT-PVE E55P 50500017**
**PT-PVF E55P 50500018**
**PT-PVG E55P 50500019**
**PT-PVH E55P 50500020**
**PT-PVI E55P 50500021**
**PT-PVJ E55P 50500022**
**PT-PVK E55P 50500029**
**PT-PVL E55P 50500023**
**PT-PVM E55P 50500024**
**PT-PVN E55P 50500025**
**PT-PVO E55P 50500026**
**PT-PVP E55P 50500027**
**PT-PVQ E55P 50500028**
**PT-SBF PRM1 RB-210**
PT-SMO LJ35 414
PT-TFA E50P 50000025
PT-TFB E50P 50000026
PT-TFC E50P 50000027
PT-TFD E50P 50000028
PT-TFE E50P 50000029
PT-TFF E50P 50000030
PT-TFG E50P 50000031
PT-TFH E50P 50000032
**PT-TFI E50P 50000033**
PT-TFJ E50P 50000034
PT-TFK E50P 50000035
PT-TFL E50P 50000036
PT-TFM E50P 50000037
PT-TFN E50P 50000038
PT-TFO E50P 50000039
PT-TFP E50P 50000040
PT-TFQ E50P 50000041
PT-TFR E50P 50000042
**PT-TFS E50P 50000043**
PT-TFT E50P 50000044
PT-TFU E50P 50000045
PT-TFV E50P 50000046
PT-TFW E50P 50000047
PT-TFX E50P 50000048
PT-TFY E50P 50000049
PT-TFZ E50P 50000050
PT-TGA E50P 50000051
PT-TGB E50P 50000052
PT-TGC E50P 50000053
**PT-TGD E50P 50000054**
PT-TGE E50P 50000055
PT-TGF E50P 50000056
PT-TGG E50P 50000057
PT-TGH E50P 50000058
**PT-TGI E50P 50000059**
**PT-TGJ E50P 50000060**
PT-TGK E50P 50000061
PT-TGL E50P 50000062
PT-TGM E50P 50000063
PT-TGN E50P 50000064
PT-TGO E50P 50000065
PT-TGP E50P 50000066
PT-TGQ E50P 50000067
PT-TGR E50P 50000068
PT-TGS E50P 50000069
PT-TGT E50P 50000070
PT-TGU E50P 50000071
PT-TGV E50P 50000072
PT-TGW E50P 50000073
PT-TGX E50P 50000074
PT-TGY E50P 50000075
PT-TGZ E50P 50000076
PT-THA E50P 50000077
**PT-THB E50P 50000078**
PT-THC E50P 50000079
PT-THD E50P 50000080
PT-THE E50P 50000081
PT-THF E50P 50000082
PT-THG E50P 50000083
PT-THH E50P 50000084
PT-THI E50P 50000085
**PT-THJ E50P 50000086**
PT-THK E50P 50000087
PT-THL E50P 50000088
PT-THM E50P 50000089
PT-THN E50P 50000090
PT-THO E50P 50000091
PT-THP E50P 50000092
PT-THQ E50P 50000093
PT-THR E50P 50000094
**PT-THS E50P 50000095**
PT-THT E50P 50000096
**PT-THU E50P 50000097**
**PT-THV E50P 50000098**
**PT-THW E50P 50000099**
PT-THX E50P 50000100
PT-THY E50P 50000101
PT-THZ E50P 50000102
PT-TIH E50P 50000103
**PT-TII E50P 50000104**
PT-TIJ E50P 50000105
PT-TIK E50P 50000106
PT-TIL E50P 50000107
PT-TIM E50P 50000108
**PT-TIN E50P 50000109**
PT-TIO E50P 50000110
PT-TIP E50P 50000111
PT-TIQ E50P 50000112
PT-TIR E50P 50000113
PT-TIS E50P 50000114
PT-TIT E50P 50000115
PT-TIU E50P 50000116
PT-TIV E50P 50000117
**PT-TIW E50P 50000118**
**PT-TIX E50P 50000119**
**PT-TIY E50P 50000120**
**PT-TIZ E50P 50000121**
PT-TJB LJ45 022
**PT-TJS C52B 0136**
PT-TOF LJ31 103
**PT-TOP C510 0123**
**PT-TRA BE40 RK-307**
**PT-TYA E50P 50000122**
PT-TYB E50P 50000123
PT-TYC E50P 50000124
PT-TYD E50P 50000127
PT-WAB C500 047
**PT-WAL HS25 258198**
PT-WAN FA50 188
PT-WAR LJ35 230
PT-WAU HS25 258133
(PT-WAW) HS25 258184
**PT-WBC ASTR 086**
PT-WBV C550 485
**PT-WBY C500 008**
**PT-WEW LJ24 158**
PT-WFC C650 7054
**PT-WFD C560 0308**
PT-WFT C500 154
(PT-WGB) LJ60 046
PT-WGD C525 0120
**PT-WGF LJ35 322**
PT-WGM LJ36 048
**PT-WHB BE40 RK-73**
**PT-WHC BE40 RK-58**
**PT-WHD BE40 RK-77**
**PT-WHE BE40 RK-81**
**PT-WHF BE40 RK-82**
**PT-WHG BE40 RK-54**
PT-WHH HS25 258282
PT-WHZ C500 287
PT-WIA HS25 258035
**PT-WIB CS55 0137**
**PT-WIV LJ31 110**
**PT-WJS BE40 RK-122**
**PT-WJZ C550 339**
**PT-WKL LJ24 294**
**PT-WKQ C550 675**
PT-WKS C560 0397
PT-WLC C650 7035
PT-WLM BE40 RK-28
**PT-WLO LJ31 122**
PT-WLX C525 0176
**PT-WLY C650 7074**
PT-WLZ CL61 5189
**PT-WMA HS25 258301**
PT-WMD HS25 258312
PT-WMG HS25 258310
PT-WMO LJ60 090
PT-WMQ C560 0405
**PT-WMZ C560 0406**
PT-WNE C560 0411
PT-WNF C560 0412
PT-WNH C550 550-0814
PT-WNO HS25 258284
PT-WOA C560 0408
PT-WOD C500 340
PT-WOM C560 0176
PT-WON C550 641
PT-WPC C560 0142
PT-WPF HS25 258409
(PT-WQE) C560 0438
(PT-WQG) C550 154
**PT-WQH C650 7083**
**PT-WQI C525 0238**
(PT-WQJ) C525 0239
PT-WQM F900 5
PT-WQS F9EX 53
PT-WRC GLF3 492
PT-WRR C560 0389
**PT-WSB LJ31 135**
PT-WSC FA50 253
**PT-WSF FA10 169**
PT-WSN C560 0440
PT-WSO C550 550-0832
PT-WSS LJ55 102
PT-WUF BE40 RK-171
**PT-WUM C750 0092**
PT-WUV FA20 129
PT-WVC C550 550-0833
**PT-WVG HS25 258395**
PT-WVH C560 0409
PT-WXL CL64 5321
**PT-WYC F2TH 59**
**PT-WYU C56X 5060**
(PT-WZO) C56X 5003
PT-WZW C560 0431
**PT-XAC C525 0280**
**PT-XCF C560 0450**
**PT-XCL C56X 5020**
**PT-XDB C525 0274**
**PT-XDN LJ40 45-2062**
PT-XDY HS25 258442
**PT-XFG C650 7099**
**PT-XFS LJ60 121**
**PT-XGS LJ60 164**
**PT-XIB C56X 5043**
(PT-XIT) LJ31 148
PT-XJS C525 0239
(PT-XLF) LJ45 093
**PT-XLI LJ35 299**
**PT-XLR LJ45 048**
**PT-XMM C525 0267**
**PT-XPP LJ31 148**
PT-XSC F9EX 60
**PT-XSX C550 550-0873**
**PT-XTA LJ31 013**
PT-XVA LJ45 077
PT-XYW CL64 5484
PT-ZAA HS25 258031
PT-ZXS E55P 50500005
PT-ZXT E55P 50500006
**PT-ZXW E55P 50500007**
**PT-ZXX E55P 50500008**
**PT-ZXY E55P 50500009**
**PT-ZXZ E55P 50500010**
PT-ZYA E50P 50000013
PT-ZYB E50P 50000014
PT-ZYC E50P 50000015
PT-ZYD E50P 50000016
PT-ZYE E50P 50000017
PT-ZYF E50P 50000018
PT-ZYG E50P 50000019
PT-ZYH E50P 50000020
PT-ZYI E50P 50000021
PT-ZYL E50P 50000024
PT-ZYT E50P 50000022
PT-ZYX E50P 50000023

## Papua New Guinea

**P2-ANW F9EX 218**
P2-BCM WW24 317
P2-MBD C550 099
P2-MBN C550 160
P2-PNF GLF2 103
P2-PNG GLF2 103
P2-RDZ C550 021
**P2-TAA C550 160**

## Aruba

P4-AAA GLEX 9136
P4-ABC CL64 5628
**P4-ADD GALX 200**
P4-AEA GLF3 431
**P4-ALA HS25 HA-0020**
**P4-ALE HS25 258359**
P4-ALM C56X 5218
P4-AMB HS25 25252
**P4-AMF HS25 258201**
**P4-AMH HS25 257070**
**P4-AND C750 0075**
**P4-ANG HS25 HA-0025**
P4-AOB HS25 25222
P4-AOC HS25 25079
P4-AOD HS25 257153
P4-AOE HS25 257136
P4-AOF HS25 257015
P4-AOH HS25 257013
**P4-AVJ CL64 5519**
P4-AVM LJ60 197
P4-AVN FA10 128
**P4-BAK FA50 130**
P4-BAZ LJ60 272
P4-BOB HS25 258115
**P4-BTA CL64 5649**
**P4-BUS C750 0271**
**P4-CBA GLEX 9220**

| | | |
|---|---|---|
| P4-CBG | JSTR | 5202 |
| P4-CBJ | JSTR | 5082/36 |
| **P4-CHV** | **CL64** | **5580** |
| P4-CMP | HS25 | 257214 |
| P4-EPI | CL61 | 5125 |
| P4-EXG | LJ60 | 347 |
| P4-FAY | CL64 | 5508 |
| P4-FAZ | GLF5 | 572 |
| P4-HER | GLEX | 9186 |
| **P4-IKF** | **F2TH** | **227** |
| P4-IKR | F2TH | 70 |
| **P4-JET** | **FA50** | **295** |
| P4-KIS | LJ35 | 341 |
| (P4-LGM) | F2EX | 143 |
| P4-LJG | C750 | 0227 |
| **P4-LVF** | **HS25** | **257040** |
| **P4-MAF** | **HS25** | **259026** |
| P4-NAN | F900 | 159 |
| P4-NUR | HS25 | 258982 |
| P4-OBE | HS25 | 257142 |
| **P4-PET** | **HS25** | **HA-0035** |
| **P4-PRT** | **HS25** | **258682** |
| **P4-SAI** | **CL64** | **5553** |
| **P4-SAT** | **CL65** | **5762** |
| **P4-SCM** | **F9EX** | **152** |
| **P4-SEN** | **HS25** | **258617** |
| P4-SKY | HS25 | 257013 |
| **P4-SNS** | **FA50** | **348** |
| **P4-SNT** | **HS25** | **258538** |
| P4-SSV | LJ60 | 325 |
| **P4-TAK** | **GLF4** | **1425** |
| P4-TAM | CL61 | 3006 |
| P4-TAT | CL64 | 5567 |
| **P4-TPS** | **GLF5** | **5193** |
| **P4-UNI** | **CL65** | **5751** |
| P4-VJR | HS25 | 256049 |
| **P4-VVF** | **GLEX** | **9147** |
| **P4-XZX** | **HS25** | **257136** |
| (P4-ZAW) | HS25 | 25018 |

Russia
(see also CCCP-)

| | | |
|---|---|---|
| RA-02800 | HS25 | 257007 |
| **RA-02801** | **HS25** | **257097** |
| RA-02802 | HS25 | 257054 |
| **RA-02802** | **HS25** | **257142** |
| **RA-02803** | **HS25** | **257139** |
| RA-02804 | HS25 | 25281 |
| **RA-02804** | **HS25** | **257175** |
| RA-02805 | HS25 | 25219 |
| RA-02806 | HS25 | 257017 |
| **RA-02806** | **HS25** | **258106** |
| RA-02807 | HS25 | 258076 |
| **RA-02808** | **HS25** | **257184** |
| RA-02809 | HS25 | 257062 |
| **RA-02810** | **HS25** | **257012** |
| **RA-02850** | **HS25** | **257112** |
| **RA-09000** | **F900** | **118** |
| **RA-09001** | **F900** | **123** |
| RA-09003 | FA20 | 183 |
| RA-09004 | FA20 | 170/455 |
| RA-09005 | FA20 | 293 |
| **RA-09006** | **F9EX** | **164** |
| RA-09007 | FA20 | 136/439 |
| **RA-09008** | **F9EX** | **142** |
| **RA-10201** | **GLF4** | **1465** |
| **RA-10202** | **GLF5** | **5119** |
| RA-3077K | SBRL | 306-13 |
| **RA-67216** | **CL64** | **5567** |
| **RA-67217** | **CL30** | **20173** |
| **RA-67221** | **CL30** | **20235** |
| **RA-67222** | **CL64** | **5596** |
| **RA-67223** | **CL30** | **20172** |
| **RA-67705** | **C525** | **0652** |
| **RF-14423** | **SBRL** | **306-13** |

Croatia
(see also T9-)

| | | |
|---|---|---|
| RC-BLY | SBRL | 380-65 |
| RC-BPU | C550 | 144 |

Philippines
(see also PI-)

| | | |
|---|---|---|
| RP-57 | JSTR | 5062/12 |
| RP-57 | LJ35 | 244 |
| RP-C57 | LJ35 | 244 |
| RP-C59 | WW24 | 254 |
| RP-C102 | C500 | 123 |
| RP-C111 | HS25 | 25256 |
| **RP-C125** | **HS25** | **25033** |
| RP-C235 | HS25 | 257130 |
| RP-C237 | C500 | 514 |
| RP-C296 | C550 | 031 |
| **RP-C390** | **PRM1** | **RB-204** |
| RP-C400 | LJ25 | 289 |
| **RP-C525** | **C525** | **0288** |
| RP-C550 | C550 | 031 |
| RP-C581 | C550 | 167 |
| **RP-C610** | **LJ35** | **338** |
| RP-C648 | LJ35 | 648 |
| RP-C648 | LJ60 | 093 |
| RP-C650 | C650 | 7110 |
| RP-C653 | C550 | 194 |
| RP-C689 | C550 | 159 |
| (RP-C717) | C525 | 0177 |
| RP-C754 | FA50 | 82 |
| **RP-C848** | **LJ24** | **072** |
| RP-C1180 | C550 | 658 |
| RP-C1261 | LJ25 | 352 |
| RP-C1299 | C500 | 259 |
| RP-C1404 | LJ35 | 441 |
| RP-C1426 | LJ35 | 426 |
| **RP-C1432** | **LJ31** | **186** |
| RP-C1500 | C500 | 225 |
| RP-C1600 | HS25 | 256037 |
| RP-C1714 | HS25 | 257085 |
| RP-C1747 | LJ24 | 264 |
| **RP-C1911** | **FA10** | **174** |
| RP-C1926 | HS25 | 258226 |
| RP-C1937 | CL64 | 5366 |
| RP-C1944 | LJ45 | 058 |
| RP-C1958 | LJ45 | 100 |
| RP-C1964 | C500 | 242 |
| RP-C1980 | FA20 | 400/556 |
| **RP-C2324** | **LJ24** | **182** |
| **RP-C2424** | **LJ24** | **226** |
| RP-C2480 | WW24 | 364 |
| RP-C2956 | LJ60 | 273 |
| **RP-C3110** | **LJ40** | **45-2031** |
| **RP-C3958** | **C500** | **327** |
| RP-C4121 | LJ25 | 287 |
| RP-C4654 | C550 | 707 |
| RP-C5128 | LJ36 | 037 |
| **RP-C5168** | **ASTR** | **259** |
| **RP-C5354** | **LJ35** | **185** |
| RP-C5610 | CL64 | 5402 |
| **RP-C5880** | **WW24** | **353** |
| **RP-C5988** | **WW24** | **254** |
| **RP-C5998** | **HS25** | **257166** |
| RP-C6003 | LJ60 | 254 |
| RP-C6153 | LJ31 | 153 |
| RP-C6178 | LJ31 | 178 |
| RP-C6610 | LJ25 | 289 |
| RP-C7272 | LJ35 | 338 |
| RP-C7777 | C500 | 123 |
| RP-C7808 | F900 | 125 |
| **RP-C8008** | **HS25** | **258212** |
| **RP-C8215** | **CL30** | **20215** |
| (RP-C8288) | C525 | 0185 |
| RP-C8338 | LJ45 | 381 |
| **RP-C8576** | **HS25** | **258571** |
| RP-C8818 | C560 | 0417 |
| **RP-C8822** | **LJ31** | **041** |
| **RP-C9808** | **HS25** | **257209** |
| **RP-C9999** | **FA10** | **151** |

Sweden

| | | |
|---|---|---|
| SE-DCK | WW24 | 51 |
| SE-DCO | FA20 | 241/479 |
| SE-DCU | LJ24 | 124 |
| SE-DCW | LJ24 | 109 |
| SE-DCY | WW24 | 136 |
| SE-DCZ | WW24 | 137 |
| SE-DDE | C500 | 063 |
| SE-DDF | FA10 | 27 |
| SE-DDG | LJ35 | 172 |
| SE-DDH | LJ36 | 013 |
| SE-DDI | LJ35 | 266 |
| SE-DDM | C500 | 244 |
| SE-DDN | C500 | 256 |
| SE-DDO | C500 | 180 |
| SE-DDW | MU30 | A023SA |
| SE-DDX | C500 | 292 |
| **SE-DDY** | **C550** | **127** |
| SE-DDZ | FA20 | 482 |
| SE-DEA | LJ35 | 051 |
| SE-DED | CRVT | 32 |
| SE-DEE | CRVT | 34 |
| SE-DEF | C550 | 421 |
| SE-DEG | C500 | 276 |
| SE-DEK | FA10 | 156 |
| SE-DEL | FA10 | 14 |
| SE-DEM | LJ35 | 317 |
| SE-DEN | CRVT | 15 |
| SE-DEO | C500 | 442 |
| SE-DEP | C500 | 377 |
| SE-DER | LJ35 | 373 |
| SE-DES | C500 | 600 |
| SE-DET | C500 | 603 |
| SE-DEU | C500 | 036 |
| SE-DEV | C550 | 136 |
| SE-DEX | C500 | 279 |
| **SE-DEY** | **C500** | **396** |
| SE-DEZ | C500 | 407 |
| SE-DEZ | C500 | 407 |
| SE-DFA | LJ24 | 283 |
| SE-DFB | LJ24 | 281 |
| SE-DFC | LJ25 | 163 |
| SE-DHE | LJ35 | 368 |
| SE-DHH | HS25 | 25160 |
| SE-DHK | FA20 | 259 |
| SE-DHL | C650 | 0030 |
| **SE-DHO** | **LJ35** | **195** |
| **SE-DHP** | **LJ35** | **075** |
| **SE-DJA** | **F9EX** | **171** |
| **SE-DJB** | **F9EX** | **179** |
| **SE-DJC** | **FA7X** | **78** |
| **SE-DJM** | **F9EX** | **106** |
| SE-DKA | FA20 | 308 |
| SE-DKB | FA10 | 132 |
| SE-DKC | FA10 | 123 |
| SE-DKD | FA10 | 60 |
| SE-DKF | HS25 | 256038 |
| SE-DKI | CS55 | 0008 |
| SE-DKM | C500 | 309 |
| **SE-DLB** | **FA10** | **183** |
| SE-DLI | C560 | 0078 |
| SE-DLK | WW24 | 197 |
| SE-DLL | WW24 | 205 |
| SE-DLY | C550 | 306 |
| **SE-DLZ** | **C500** | **645** |
| (SE-DMM) | C500 | 244 |
| SE-DPG | C560 | 0086 |
| SE-DPK | FA10 | 152 |
| SE-DPL | C500 | 037 |
| SE-DPT | WW24 | 325 |
| SE-DPY | HS25 | 257035 |
| SE-DPZ | HS25 | 257015 |
| **SE-DRS** | **BE40** | **RK-37** |
| SE-DRT | C500 | 311 |
| SE-DRV | HS25 | 258079 |
| **SE-DRZ** | **C500** | **315** |
| SE-DSA | FA20 | 339 |
| **SE-DUZ** | **C500** | **143** |
| SE-DVA | C500 | 551 |
| SE-DVB | C500 | 294 |
| SE-DVD | HS25 | 258339 |
| SE-DVE | F9EX | 23 |
| SE-DVG | FA50 | 104 |
| SE-DVK | FA50 | 249 |
| SE-DVL | FA50 | 238 |
| **SE-DVP** | **FA10** | **224** |
| SE-DVS | HS25 | 25225 |
| SE-DVT | C550 | 634 |
| SE-DVV | C550 | 307 |
| SE-DVY | C650 | 7011 |
| SE-DVZ | C550 | 550-0808 |
| **SE-DYB** | **FA10** | **216** |
| SE-DYE | HS25 | 258382 |
| **SE-DYO** | **CS55** | **0134** |
| **SE-DYR** | **C550** | **097** |
| **SE-DYV** | **HS25** | **258385** |
| **SE-DYX** | **C56X** | **5029** |
| (SE-DYY) | C550 | 707 |
| SE-DYZ | C560 | 0153 |
| (SE-DZX) | C750 | 0075 |
| **SE-DZZ** | **LJ35** | **415** |
| SE-RBB | C56X | 5005 |
| SE-RBC | C56X | 5008 |
| **SE-RBD** | **C550** | **388** |
| **SE-RBK** | **C550** | **340** |
| SE-RBM | C550 | 717 |
| **SE-RBO** | **BE40** | **RK-303** |
| (SE-RBV) | F2EX | 10 |
| SE-RBX | C56X | 5056 |
| (SE-RBY) | C550 | 550-0917 |
| **SE-RBY** | **C550** | **550-1038** |
| SE-RBZ | C500 | 436 |
| **SE-RCA** | **LJ35** | **175** |
| SE-RCI | C550 | 678 |
| SE-RCK | LJ55 | 011 |
| SE-RCL | C56X | 5217 |
| **SE-RCM** | **C56X** | **5624** |
| (SE-RCX) | C550 | 329 |
| SE-RCX | CS55 | 0148 |
| **SE-RCY** | **C550** | **329** |
| (SE-RCY) | CS55 | 0148 |
| SE-RCZ | C550 | 187 |
| (SE-RDA) | C500 | 278 |
| SE-RDX | GLF5 | 5019 |
| **SE-RDY** | **GLF5** | **5080** |
| **SE-RDZ** | **GLF5** | **5153** |
| **SE-RFH** | **C680** | **0059** |
| SE-RFI | C680 | 0114 |
| **SE-RFJ** | **C680** | **0205** |
| SE-RFK | C680 | 0228 |
| SE-RGN | C500 | 392 |
| **SE-RGS** | **C56X** | **5807** |
| SE-RGU | LJ55 | 087 |
| **SE-RGX** | **C525** | **0502** |
| **SE-RGY** | **C560** | **0414** |
| **SE-RGZ** | **C560** | **0607** |
| **SE-RHP** | **C550** | **672** |
| **SE-RIK** | **C550** | **133** |
| **SE-RIL** | **C56X** | **5777** |
| **SE-RIO** | **C525** | **0181** |
| SE-RIT | C560 | 0773 |
| **SE-RIX** | **C525** | **0671** |
| SE-RKM | C52A | 0435 |
| **SE-RKY** | **LJ45** | **161** |
| (SE-RKZ) | C500 | 235 |

Slovenia
(see also S5-)

| | | |
|---|---|---|
| SL-BAA | LJ35 | 618 |
| SL-BAB | LJ24 | 320 |
| SL-BAC | C550 | 480 |

Poland

| | | |
|---|---|---|
| **SP-CEZ** | **LJ60** | **342** |
| **SP-DLB** | **C52A** | **0428** |
| SP-FCP | FA20 | 136/439 |
| SP-FOA | CRVT | 14 |
| **SP-KBM** | **C500** | **269** |
| **SP-KCK** | **C52A** | **0158** |
| SP-KCL | C525 | 0526 |
| **SP-KCS** | **C56X** | **5649** |
| **SP-KHK** | **C510** | **0189** |
| **SP-KKA** | **C525** | **0550** |
| **SP-RDW** | **PRM1** | **RB-233** |
| **SP-ZAK** | **GLEX** | **9219** |
| **SP-ZSZ** | **CL30** | **20044** |

Sudan

| | | |
|---|---|---|
| **ST-FSA** | **JSTR** | **5236** |
| **ST-JRM** | **JSTR** | **5025** |
| ST-PRE | JSTR | 5071 |
| ST-PRM | JSTR | 5121 |
| **ST-PRS** | **FA20** | **372/546** |
| **ST-PSA** | **F900** | **84** |
| **ST-PSR** | **FA50** | **114** |

Egypt

| | | |
|---|---|---|
| **SU-AXN** | **FA20** | **294/506** |
| **SU-AYD** | **FA20** | **361/543** |
| **SU-AZJ** | **FA20** | **358/541** |
| **SU-BGM** | **GLF4** | **1048** |
| **SU-BGU** | **GLF3** | **439** |
| **SU-BGV** | **GLF3** | **442** |
| **SU-BNC** | **GLF4** | **1329** |
| **SU-BND** | **GLF4** | **1332** |
| SU-BNL | LJ60 | 149 |
| **SU-BNO** | **GLF4** | **1424** |
| **SU-BNP** | **GLF4** | **1427** |
| **SU-BPE** | **GLF4** | **1506** |
| **SU-BPF** | **GLF4** | **1518** |
| **SU-BQF** | **C510** | **0225** |
| **SU-BQG** | **C510** | **0255** |
| **SU-BQH** | **C510** | **0258** |
| **SU-BQI** | **C510** | **0267** |
| SU-DAF | JSTR | 5025 |
| SU-DAG | JSTR | 5121 |
| SU-DAH | JSTR | 5071 |
| SU-EWA | C560 | 0201 |
| SU-EWB | C56X | 5171 |
| SU-EWC | C56X | 5042 |
| **SU-EWD** | **C680** | **0026** |
| SU-EZI | LJ60 | 149 |
| SU-HEC | C550 | 550-1018 |
| **SU-MAN** | **HS25** | **258832** |
| SU-MSG | LJ45 | 069 |
| SU-OAE | FA20 | 175 |
| SU-PIX | HS25 | 257184 |
| SU-PIX | HS25 | 257184 |
| **SU-SMA** | **C680** | **0118** |
| **SU-SMB** | **C680** | **0167** |
| **SU-SMC** | **C680** | **0246** |
| **SU-SMD** | **C680** | **0270** |
| **SU-SME** | **C680** | **0274** |
| (SU-SMF) | C680 | 0283 |
| **SU-ZBB** | **BE40** | **RK-480** |

Greece

| | | |
|---|---|---|
| SX-ABA | FA20 | 245/481 |
| **SX-ADK** | **C56X** | **5608** |
| SX-AHF | LJ36 | 007 |
| SX-ASO | LJ25 | 074 |
| SX-BFJ | LJ35 | 172 |
| **SX-BMI** | **C680** | **0204** |
| **SX-BMK** | **C550** | **550-0907** |
| **SX-BNR** | **LJ60** | **231** |
| SX-BNS | LJ55 | 072 |
| SX-BNT | LJ35 | 228 |
| SX-BSS | HS25 | 25116 |
| SX-BTV | LJ55 | 124 |
| SX-BTX | GLF2 | 171 |
| SX-CBM | LJ25 | 094 |
| **SX-DCA** | **F2EX** | **29** |
| **SX-DCD** | **C56X** | **5662** |
| **SX-DCE** | **C56X** | **5288** |
| SX-DCF | F2TH | 134 |
| **SX-DCI** | **C560** | **0366** |
| SX-DCM | C56X | 5051 |
| SX-DKI | FA20 | 275 |
| SX-ECH | F900 | 26 |
| **SX-ECI** | **C750** | **0262** |
| (SX-EDP) | C52B | 0193 |
| **SX-FAR** | **HS25** | **258495** |
| **SX-FCA** | **PRM1** | **RB-262** |
| **SX-FDB** | **C500** | **392** |
| **SX-GAB** | **GLF4** | **4172** |
| **SX-IDA** | **GALX** | **149** |
| **SX-IFB** | **GALX** | **063** |
| (SX-IFB) | GALX | 149 |
| **SX-IRP** | **GALX** | **142** |
| (SX-MAD) | GALX | 065 |
| **SX-MAJ** | **GALX** | **207** |
| **SX-MFA** | **GLF5** | **5197** |
| **SX-NSS** | **E50P** | **50000035** |
| SX-ONE | GALX | 065 |
| SX-PAP | C52B | 0193 |
| **SX-SEA** | **GALX** | **163** |
| SX-SEE | GLF4 | 4115 |
| SX-SMG | GALX | 159 |
| SX-SMH | C52A | 0229 |
| **SX-SMR** | **C56X** | **5631** |
| **SX-TAJ** | **GALX** | **215** |

Seychelles
(see also S7-)

| | | |
|---|---|---|
| SY-AAP | C560 | 0003 |

Slovenia
(see also SL-)

| | | |
|---|---|---|
| **S5-ABR** | **F2EX** | **15** |
| S5-ADA | CL65 | 5712 |
| **S5-ADB** | **CL65** | **5715** |
| S5-ADC | GLF4 | 4027 |
| **S5-ADD** | **CL65** | **5754** |
| **S5-ADE** | **GLEX** | **9336** |
| **S5-ADF** | **CL65** | **5757** |
| S5-BAA | LJ35 | 618 |
| S5-BAB | LJ24 | 320 |
| S5-BAC | C550 | 480 |
| **S5-BAJ** | **C525** | **0394** |
| **S5-BAR** | **C52A** | **0423** |
| **S5-BAS** | **C52A** | **0348** |
| **S5-BAV** | **C56X** | **5660** |
| **S5-BAW** | **C52B** | **0016** |
| **S5-BAX** | **CS55** | **0028** |
| S5-BAY | C525 | 0315 |
| **S5-BAZ** | **C56X** | **5236** |
| S5-BBA | C650 | 7080 |
| S5-BBB | C52A | 0019 |
| **S5-BBD** | **C56X** | **5058** |
| **S5-CMT** | **C510** | **0186** |

Seychelles
(see also SY-)

| | | |
|---|---|---|
| S7-AAP | C560 | 0003 |

Sao Tome

| | | |
|---|---|---|
| S9-CRH | GLF2 | 8 |
| S9-CRH | LJ36 | 055 |
| S9-DBG | HS25 | 256021 |
| S9-GOT | GLF2 | 8 |
| S9-NAD | JSTR | 5065 |
| S9-NAE | JSTR | 5085 |
| **S9-PDG** | **HS25** | **256021** |
| **S9-PDH** | **HS25** | **25132** |

Turkey

| | | |
|---|---|---|
| (TC- ) | FA20 | 489 |
| **TC-ADO** | **HS25** | **258738** |
| **TC-AHE** | **C550** | **550-1107** |
| **TC-AHS** | **HS25** | **258504** |
| TC-AKH | HS25 | 259043 |
| **TC-AKK** | **F900** | **171** |
| TC-ANA | GLF4 | 1043 |
| TC-ANC | HS25 | 258208 |
| TC-AND | FA10 | 89 |
| **TC-ANT** | **C650** | **0229** |
| **TC-ARB** | **CL30** | **20181** |
| **TC-ARC** | **LJ60** | **094** |
| **TC-ARD** | **CL64** | **5611** |
| TC-ARK | FA10 | 218 |
| **TC-ASE** | **BE40** | **RK-18** |
| TC-ASF | WW24 | 195 |
| **TC-ATA** | **GLF4** | **1043** |
| TC-ATC | C650 | 7043 |
| **TC-ATC** | **F2EX** | **136** |
| TC-ATI | FA10 | 132 |
| **TC-ATP** | **C680** | **0232** |
| TC-ATV | C750 | 0001 |
| TC-BAY | C550 | 316 |
| TC-BHD | HS25 | 258415 |
| TC-BHO | FA50 | 271 |
| TC-BNT | FA50 | 305 |
| TC-BYD | BE40 | RK-254 |
| TC-CAG | F900 | 142 |
| TC-CAO | C650 | 0060 |
| TC-CEN | FA20 | 326/521 |
| TC-CEY | C650 | 0214 |
| TC-CIN | F2TH | 26 |
| **TC-CLG** | **HS25** | **HA-0098** |
| **TC-CLH** | **CL65** | **5763** |
| TC-CLK | HS25 | 258808 |
| **TC-CMB** | **LJ45** | **007** |
| TC-CMK | CL30 | 20233 |
| **TC-CMK** | **CL65** | **5767** |
| TC-CMY | C650 | 0141 |
| TC-COS | HS25 | 256048 |
| TC-COY | C550 | 347 |
| TC-CRO | C525 | 0102 |
| TC-CYL | F2TH | 56 |
| **TC-DAG** | **C56X** | **5769** |
| **TC-DAK** | **C56X** | **6048** |
| **TC-DAP** | **GLF5** | **5212** |
| TC-DEM | FA20 | 489 |
| TC-DGC | F2TH | 166 |
| **TC-DGN** | **F2EX** | **104** |
| TC-DHB | CL61 | 5094 |
| (TC-DHE) | CL64 | 5318 |
| TC-DHE | CL64 | 5358 |
| TC-DHF | LJ60 | 184 |
| (TC-DHG) | GLEX | 9057 |
| TC-DHH | CL64 | 5448 |
| **TC-DLZ** | **C56X** | **5824** |
| **TC-DOY** | **HS25** | **258801** |
| TC-EES | C650 | 0077 |
| TC-ELL | LJ60 | 030 |
| TC-EMA | C525 | 0121 |
| **TC-ENK** | **HS25** | **HA-0086** |
| TC-EYE | FA50 | 161 |
| TC-EZE | FA20 | 299 |
| TC-FAL | C550 | 351 |
| TC-FBS | LJ55 | 138 |
| **TC-FIB** | **CL65** | **5747** |
| **TC-FIN** | **HS25** | **258742** |
| TC-FMB | C550 | 351 |
| TC-FNS | HFB3 | 1026 |
| TC-GAP | GLF3 | 487 |
| TC-GAP | GLF4 | 1027 |
| TC-GEM | LJ35 | 185 |
| **TC-GGG** | **FA20** | **326/521** |
| TC-GSA | HFB3 | 1055 |
| TC-GSB | HFB3 | 1042 |
| **TC-GUR** | **C52B** | **0309** |
| TC-IHS | JSTR | 5225 |
| **TC-ISR** | **CL30** | **20138** |
| **TC-IST** | **C680** | **0159** |
| TC-KAM | FA50 | 95 |
| **TC-KAR** | **CL30** | **20149** |
| **TC-KHA** | **HS25** | **HA-0046** |
| **TC-KHB** | **GLF4** | **4175** |
| TC-KHE | HFB3 | 1043 |
| TC-KLS | C650 | 0191 |
| TC-KOC | C650 | 7006 |
| **TC-KON** | **C650** | **7084** |
| **TC-KRM** | **GLEX** | **9318** |
| **TC-LAA** | **C560** | **0212** |
| **TC-LAB** | **C560** | **0216** |
| **TC-LAC** | **C56X** | **5779** |
| **TC-LAD** | **C56X** | **5795** |
| TC-LEY | HFB3 | 1042 |
| **TC-LEY** | **HFB3** | **1043** |
| TC-LIM | C525 | 0226 |
| TC-LMA | C56X | 5242 |
| **TC-LNS** | **C56X** | **5693** |
| TC-MCX | BE40 | RK-170 |
| TC-MDB | BE40 | RK-164 |
| TC-MDC | HS25 | 258384 |
| **TC-MDG** | **CL61** | **5110** |
| TC-MDJ | BE40 | RK-120 |
| TC-MEK | LJ35 | 441 |
| TC-MEK | LJ55 | 138 |
| TC-MEK | LJ60 | 016 |
| **TC-MEN** | **LJ60** | **335** |
| TC-MET | C560 | 0497 |
| TC-MHS | PRM1 | RB-77 |
| **TC-MKA** | **C550** | **550-0960** |
| **TC-MMG** | **F9EX** | **161** |
| **TC-MRK** | **F2EX** | **193** |
| TC-MSA | BE40 | RK-124 |
| **TC-MSB** | **BE40** | **RK-170** |
| **TC-NEO** | **BE40** | **RK-130** |
| **TC-NEU** | **BE40** | **RK-548** |
| TC-NKB | C550 | 053 |
| TC-NMC | CS55 | 0072 |
| TC-NNK | BE40 | RK-211 |
| TC-NOA | JSTR | 5220 |
| TC-NSU | HFB3 | 1046 |
| **TC-NUB** | **HS25** | **258874** |
| TC-OKN | HS25 | 258388 |
| TC-OMR | HFB3 | 1047 |
| TC-OMR | JSTR | 5082/36 |
| TC-ORM | FA10 | 33 |
| TC-OVA | CL61 | 5094 |
| TC-PLM | F2TH | 160 |
| TC-PRK | F2TH | 191 |
| TC-RAM | C650 | 0178 |
| **TC-RED** | **C680** | **0272** |
| **TC-RKS** | **LJ60** | **282** |
| **TC-RMK** | **F2TH** | **157** |
| TC-ROT | C560 | 0454 |
| **TC-SAB** | **CL65** | **5730** |
| TC-SAM | CS55 | 0007 |
| TC-SBH | C650 | 0234 |
| **TC-SCR** | **CL30** | **20136** |
| TC-SEN | HFB3 | 1042 |
| TC-SES | C550 | 717 |
| **TC-SGO** | **F2EX** | **180** |
| **TC-SHE** | **HS25** | **258872** |
| TC-SIS | C650 | 0077 |
| TC-SMB | BE40 | RK-148 |
| **TC-SNK** | **F2TH** | **229** |
| **TC-SSS** | **JSTR** | **5226** |
| **TC-STA** | **BE40** | **RK-476** |
| **TC-STB** | **HS25** | **258793** |
| **TC-STD** | **HS25** | **258845** |
| **TC-STO** | **C650** | **7091** |
| TC-STR | HS25 | 258415 |
| **TC-TAN** | **CL64** | **5459** |
| **TC-TAV** | **HS25** | **258736** |
| TC-TEK | HS25 | 258229 |
| (TC-THY) | CL30 | 20190 |
| **TC-TKC** | **HS25** | **258790** |
| **TC-TKN** | **C680** | **0174** |
| **TC-TMO** | **C56X** | **5051** |
| TC-TOP | C650 | 0083 |
| TC-TPE | C550 | 550-0951 |
| **TC-TSY** | **C56X** | **6040** |
| **TC-TVA** | **C680** | **0263** |
| TC-VIN | BE40 | RK-188 |
| TC-VSC | HS25 | 258398 |
| **TC-VYN** | **C52A** | **0236** |
| TC-VZR | C750 | 0150 |
| TC-YIB | MU30 | A051SA |
| TC-YRT | BE40 | RK-190 |
| TC-YSR | FA50 | 246 |
| TC-YZB | C550 | 351 |

Iceland

| | | |
|---|---|---|
| TF-JET | C550 | 235 |

Guatemala

| | | |
|---|---|---|
| **TG-ABY** | **LJ45** | **293** |
| **TG-AIR** | **LJ31** | **067** |
| TG-BAC | C550 | 550-0875 |
| (TG-FIL) | C525 | 0072 |
| TG-GGA | FA20 | 25/405 |
| TG-JAY | LJ35 | 225 |
| TG-KIT | C500 | 633 |
| TG-LAR | MU30 | A062SA |
| TG-MIL | C500 | 633 |
| TG-OMF | WW24 | 34 |
| TG-OZO | C500 | 204 |
| TG-RBW | FA20 | 150/445 |
| **TG-RIE** | **C500** | **624** |
| TG-RIF | C500 | 624 |
| **TG-RIF** | **C525** | **0072** |
| TG-VOC | LJ25 | 251 |
| TG-VWA | WW24 | 109 |

Costa Rica

| | | |
|---|---|---|
| (TI-ACB) | C500 | 187 |
| TI-AFB | C500 | 258 |
| (TI-AHE) | C500 | 245 |
| TI-AHH | C500 | 245 |
| TI-APZ | C550 | 273 |
| **TI-AZX** | **C500** | **227** |

Cameroon

| | | |
|---|---|---|
| (TJ- ) | GLF3 | 487 |
| **TJ-** | **HS25** | **256040** |
| TJ-AAK | GLF2 | 93 |
| **TJ-AAW** | **GLF3** | **486** |
| TJ-AHR | CRVT | 12 |

## Central African Republic

| | | |
|---|---|---|
| TL-AAW | C500 | 078 |
| TL-AAY | FA20 | 174/457 |
| TL-ABD | LJ35 | 062 |
| TL-ADK | HS25 | 25258 |
| TL-AJK | FA20 | 32 |
| TL-KAZ | FA20 | 174/457 |
| TL-RCA | CRVT | 39 |
| TL-SMI | CRVT | 39 |

## Congo

| | | |
|---|---|---|
| TN-ADB | CRVT | 22 |
| TN-ADI | CRVT | 9 |

## Gabon

| | | |
|---|---|---|
| **TR-AAG** | **CL61** | **5071** |
| **TR-AFJ** | **F900** | **46** |
| **TR-AFR** | **F900** | **59** |
| TR-KHA | FA20 | 225/472 |
| TR-KHB | GLF2 | 127 |
| TR-KHC | GLF3 | 326 |
| TR-KHD | GLF4 | 1327 |
| **TR-KSP** | **GLF4** | **1327** |
| TR-LAH | CRVT | 30 |
| TR-LAI | FA50 | 78 |
| TR-LAU | HS25 | 256052 |
| TR-LCJ | F900 | 7 |
| TR-LDB | HS25 | 258192 |
| **TR-LEX** | **F9EX** | **24** |
| **TR-LFB** | **HS25** | **25130** |
| **TR-LGV** | **FA50** | **89** |
| **TR-LGY** | **FA50** | **9** |
| **TR-LGZ** | **FA20** | **391** |
| TR-LOL | FA20 | 13 |
| TR-LQU | HS25 | 25250 |
| TR-LRU | FA20 | 225/472 |
| TR-LTI | C500 | 210 |
| TR-LUW | FA20 | 309/514 |
| TR-LWY | CRVT | 11 |
| TR-LXO | HS25 | 25130 |
| TR-LXP | LJ35 | 005 |
| TR-LYB | LJ24 | 105 |
| TR-LYC | LJ35 | 174 |
| TR-LYE | C550 | 033 |
| TR-LYM | CRVT | 12 |
| TR-LZI | LJ35 | 313 |
| TR-LZT | CRVT | 20 |

## Tunisia

| | | |
|---|---|---|
| **TS-IAM** | **CL64** | **5412** |
| TS-IAM | FA10 | 195 |
| **TS-IBT** | **CL64** | **5628** |
| TS-IRS | FA20 | 117 |
| TS-JAM | FA50 | 125 |
| TS-JBT | FA50 | 119 |
| **TS-JSM** | **F900** | **111** |

## Tchad

| | | |
|---|---|---|
| **TT-AAI** | **GLF2** | **240** |

## Ivory Coast

| | | |
|---|---|---|
| TU-VAC | GLF2 | 218 |
| TU-VAD | FA20 | 98/434 |
| **TU-VAD** | **GLF4** | **1019** |
| TU-VAF | GLF2 | 119/22 |
| TU-VAF | GLF3 | 303 |
| **TU-VAF** | **GLF3** | **462** |

## Benin

| | | |
|---|---|---|
| **TY-AOM** | **F900** | **33** |
| TY-BBK | CRVT | 29 |
| TY-BBM | FA50 | 17 |
| **TY-SAM** | **HS25** | **257195** |
| **TY-VLT** | **HS25** | **258632** |

## Mali

| | | |
|---|---|---|
| TZ-PBF | CRVT | 19 |

## San Marino

| | | |
|---|---|---|
| **T7-FRA** | **C525** | **0628** |
| **T7-HOT** | **C510** | **0190** |
| **T7-VIG** | **C510** | **0069** |
| **T7-VII** | **C650** | **7090** |

## Bosnia
(see also BH-)

| | | |
|---|---|---|
| T9-BIH | CS55 | 0045 |
| T9-BKA | C500 | 415 |
| T9-SBA | C500 | 554 |
| T9-SMS | C525 | 0666 |

## Kazakhstan

| | | |
|---|---|---|
| UN-09002 | F900 | 11 |
| UN-P1001 | PRM1 | RB-120 |
| **UP-CS301** | **C52B** | **0259** |
| **UP-CS302** | **C52B** | **0323** |
| **UP-CS401** | **C650** | **0202** |
| UP-CS501 | C750 | 0277 |
| **UP-LJ001** | **LJ60** | **347** |
| **UP-P1001** | **PRM1** | **RB-120** |
| **UP-P1002** | **PRM1** | **RB-274** |

## Ukraine

| | | |
|---|---|---|
| (UR-ACA) | FA50 | 235 |
| (UR-BCA) | FA20 | 141/441 |
| UR-CCA | FA20 | 256 |
| **UR-CCB** | **FA20** | **141/441** |
| **UR-CCC** | **FA50** | **235** |
| UR-CCD | FA20 | 112 |
| **UR-CCF** | **FA50** | **212** |
| **UR-CHH** | **LJ60** | **016** |
| **UR-CLD** | **FA20** | **315/517** |
| **UR-CLE** | **FA20** | **279/502** |
| **UR-CLF** | **FA20** | **293** |
| **UR-CLG** | **FA20** | **52** |
| **UR-CRD** | **F900** | **202** |
| **UR-DWH** | **C52B** | **0322** |
| UR-EFA | FA20 | 55/410 |
| UR-EFB | FA20 | 75 |
| UR-KAS | ASTR | 242 |
| **UR-KKA** | **FA20** | **389/552** |
| **UR-MOA** | **FA20** | **237/476** |
| UR-NIK | FA20 | 112 |
| **UR-NOA** | **FA20** | **345** |
| **UR-PME** | **C52B** | **0320** |

## Australia

| | | |
|---|---|---|
| (VH- ) | BE40 | RJ-55 |
| (VH- ) | HS25 | 259023 |
| VH-ACE | F900 | 37 |
| **VH-ACE** | **HS25** | **HA-0049** |
| **VH-AJG** | **WW24** | **281** |
| **VH-AJJ** | **WW24** | **248** |
| **VH-AJK** | **WW24** | **256** |
| **VH-AJP** | **WW24** | **238** |
| VH-AJQ | WW24 | 281 |
| VH-AJS | LJ35 | 188 |
| VH-AJS | WW24 | 221 |
| VH-AJV | LJ35 | 189 |
| **VH-AJV** | **WW24** | **282** |
| (VH-ALH) | LJ35 | 480 |
| VH-ANE | C525 | 0521 |
| **VH-ANE** | **C52B** | **0196** |
| VH-ANI | LJ35 | 468 |
| VH-ANQ | C500 | 283 |
| **VH-APJ** | **C525** | **0281** |
| VH-APU | WW24 | 395 |
| VH-AQR | C500 | 263 |
| VH-AQS | C500 | 263 |
| (VH-ARJ) | HS25 | 256037 |
| VH-ASG | GLF2 | 95/39 |
| VH-ASM | CL61 | 5033 |
| VH-ASM | GLF2 | 91 |
| VH-ASQ | GLF4 | 1205 |
| VH-ASR | WW24 | 316 |
| VH-AYI | WW24 | 317 |
| VH-BBJ | BE40 | RK-26 |
| VH-BBJ | HS25 | 25169 |
| VH-BCL | WW24 | 315 |
| VH-BGF | F900 | 5 |
| VH-BGL | FA20 | 495 |
| VH-BGV | F900 | 32 |
| VH-BIB | LJ36 | 035 |
| VH-BIZ | FA20 | 73/419 |
| VH-BJC | BE40 | RK-154 |
| VH-BJD | BE40 | RK-35 |
| VH-BJD | BE40 | RK-35 |
| VH-BJQ | LJ35 | 219 |
| VH-BLJ | LJ25 | 180 |
| VH-BNK | C500 | 574 |
| VH-BQR | LJ35 | 471 |
| VH-BRG | CL61 | 5064 |
| VH-BRR | FA20 | 208/468 |
| VH-BRX | C550 | 338 |
| VH-BSJ | LJ24 | 266 |
| **VH-BZL** | **BE40** | **RK-139** |
| VH-CAO | HS25 | 25015 |
| VH-CCA | GLF4 | 1175 |
| VH-CCC | GLF4 | 1083 |
| **VH-CCC** | **GLF5** | **581** |
| (VH-CCC) | HS25 | 258002 |
| VH-CCJ | C500 | 471 |
| VH-CCJ | C510 | 0033 |
| **VH-CCJ** | **C550** | **550-0953** |
| VH-CCO | GLF4 | 1107 |
| **VH-CDG** | **C525** | **0163** |
| **VH-CFO** | **C550** | **669** |
| **VH-CGF** | **GLF4** | **1083** |
| VH-CIR | FA20 | 90/426 |
| VH-CIT | C525 | 0100 |
| **VH-CMS** | **LJ36** | **032** |
| VH-CPE | FA20 | 504 |
| VH-CPH | LJ35 | 400 |
| (VH-CPQ) | LJ35 | 400 |
| VH-CRM | C500 | 130 |
| VH-CRQ | F2EX | 58 |
| **VH-CRW** | **F2EX** | **58** |
| **VH-CXJ** | **LJ45** | **152** |
| **VH-DAA** | **C525** | **0138** |
| **VH-DBT** | **GLF4** | **1363** |
| **VH-DHN** | **C650** | **7011** |
| VH-DJT | FA10 | 169 |
| **VH-DNK** | **GLEX** | **9311** |
| VH-DRM | C500 | 112 |
| VH-DWA | FA20 | 72/413 |
| VH-ECD | C500 | 123 |
| VH-ECE | HS25 | 25062 |
| VH-ECF | HS25 | 25069 |
| VH-ECG | FA20 | 493 |
| **VH-EGK** | **C500** | **051** |
| VH-EJK | LJ45 | 007 |
| **VH-EJL** | **HS25** | **258295** |
| **VH-EJT** | **C510** | **0214** |
| **VH-EJY** | **C550** | **156** |
| VH-ELC | LJ35 | 428 |
| VH-ELJ | HS25 | 258281 |
| VH-ELJ | LJ35 | 038 |
| VH-EMM | C500 | 051 |
| **VH-EMO** | **CS55** | **0063** |
| VH-EMP | LJ35 | 345 |
| **VH-ESM** | **LJ35** | **611** |
| **VH-ESW** | **LJ35** | **071** |
| **VH-EVF** | **HS25** | **HA-0044** |
| VH-EXA | C680 | 0027 |
| **VH-EXB** | **BE40** | **RK-154** |
| **VH-EXG** | **C680** | **0072** |
| **VH-EXJ** | **LJ60** | **273** |
| VH-EXM | C550 | 252 |
| **VH-EXQ** | **C680** | **0129** |
| VH-FAX | FA20 | 247 |
| VH-FCP | F900 | 37 |
| **VH-FCS** | **C500** | **486** |
| VH-FFB | FA10 | 17 |
| **VH-FGK** | **C550** | **550-0852** |
| VH-FHJ | C560 | 0278 |
| VH-FHR | F900 | 138 |
| VH-FIS | ASTR | 045 |
| VH-FJZ | FA20 | 442 |
| VH-FLJ | LJ24 | 349 |
| VH-FOX | LJ35 | 427 |
| (VH-FRM) | C500 | 183 |
| VH-FSA | C500 | 237 |
| VH-FSQ | C500 | 225 |
| VH-FSU | LJ35 | 463 |
| VH-FSW | LJ35 | 463 |
| VH-FSX | LJ35 | 046 |
| VH-FSY | LJ35 | 221 |
| VH-FSZ | LJ35 | 242 |
| **VH-FUM** | **C500** | **582** |
| VH-FWO | FA20 | 110 |
| VH-HEY | C560 | 0009 |
| VH-HFJ | FA20 | 306/512 |
| VH-HIF | FA20 | 255/487 |
| VH-HKR | GLF2 | 69 |
| **VH-HKX** | **C500** | **050** |
| VH-HOF | LJ35 | 165 |
| VH-HPF | FA20 | 391 |
| VH-HPJ | FA20 | 491 |
| VH-HSP | HS25 | 257215 |
| VH-HSS | HS25 | 257169 |
| VH-HVH | C500 | 349 |
| VH-HVM | C500 | 349 |
| **VH-HVM** | **C550** | **550-0984** |
| VH-ICN | C500 | 024 |
| (VH-ICT) | C550 | 184 |
| VH-ICX | C500 | 051 |
| VH-III | HS25 | 258002 |
| VH-IMP | BE40 | RK-26 |
| VH-ING | C550 | 156 |
| **VH-ING** | **C650** | **7104** |
| **VH-INT** | **C550** | **112** |
| VH-INX | C550 | 156 |
| **VH-IPG** | **BE40** | **RK-222** |
| VH-IWJ | WW24 | 371 |
| VH-IWU | CS55 | 0118 |
| VH-IWW | WW24 | 314 |
| VH-IXL | HS25 | 258040 |
| VH-JBH | C550 | 304 |
| VH-JCC | HS25 | 257046 |
| VH-JCG | C550 | 112 |
| **VH-JCR** | **LJ35** | **231** |
| **VH-JCX** | **LJ36** | **057** |
| VH-JDW | FA10 | 216 |
| VH-JEP | MU30 | A048SA |
| VH-JFT | HS25 | 257064 |
| VH-JIG | LJ35 | 400 |
| VH-JJA | WW24 | 409 |
| **VH-JMK** | **C550** | **299** |
| **VH-JMM** | **C550** | **162** |
| VH-JPG | C550 | 112 |
| VH-JPK | C550 | 307 |
| (VH-JPL) | WW24 | 386 |
| VH-JPW | WW24 | 317 |
| VH-JSX | FA20 | 78/412 |
| VH-JSY | FA20 | 85/425 |
| VH-JSZ | FA20 | 90/426 |
| VH-JVS | C550 | 418 |
| VH-KDI | C550 | 235 |
| VH-KDP | C550 | 289 |
| VH-KEF | HS25 | 258295 |
| VH-KNJ | WW24 | 381 |
| **VH-KNR** | **WW24** | **340** |
| **VH-KNS** | **WW24** | **323** |
| **VH-KNU** | **WW24** | **317** |
| **VH-KTG** | **GLEX** | **9275** |
| VH-KTI | C650 | 0144 |
| VH-KTI | LJ35 | 239 |
| VH-KTK | C550 | 370 |
| **VH-KXL** | **C525** | **0100** |
| VH-LAL | F900 | 192 |
| VH-LAL | GLF5 | 5259 |
| VH-LAM | CL64 | 5353 |
| VH-LAT | HS25 | 258295 |
| VH-LAW | BE40 | RK-35 |
| VH-LAW | F900 | 192 |
| **VH-LAW** | **GLEX** | **9299** |
| VH-LAW | HS25 | 258295 |
| VH-LCL | C500 | 538 |
| **VH-LDH** | **C525** | **0670** |
| **VH-LEP** | **GLEX** | **9346** |
| VH-LEQ | LJ35 | 239 |
| VH-LGH | LJ35 | 342 |
| VH-LGH | LJ55 | 048 |
| VH-LGL | C500 | 206 |
| VH-LJB | LJ25 | 180 |
| VH-LJG | C500 | 471 |
| **VH-LJJ** | **LJ35** | **324** |
| VH-LJK | C550 | 184 |

| | | |
|---|---|---|
| VH-LJL | C500 | 123 |
| VH-LJL | LJ35 | 046 |
| VH-LKV | HS25 | 258019 |
| VH-LLW | WW24 | 253 |
| VH-LLX | WW24 | 259 |
| VH-LLY | WW24 | 272 |
| VH-LMP | HS25 | 257178 |
| **VH-LMP** | **HS25** | **259022** |
| VH-LOF | WW24 | 366 |
| **VH-LPJ** | **LJ35** | **593** |
| VH-LRH | HS25 | 257046 |
| **VH-LRX** | **LJ35** | **192** |
| VH-LSW | C550 | 099 |
| **VH-LUL** | **F900** | **192** |
| VH-LYG | HS25 | 257001 |
| **VH-LYM** | **C650** | **7095** |
| VH-MAY | C550 | 021 |
| **VH-MBP** | **HS25** | **258712** |
| VH-MCG | CL60 | 1061 |
| VH-MCX | FA10 | 134 |
| VH-MEI | FA10 | 50 |
| **VH-MGC** | **BE40** | **RK-97** |
| VH-MGC | C550 | 550-0810 |
| VH-MIE | LJ35 | 459 |
| **VH-MIF** | **C52B** | **0078** |
| VH-MIQ | FA20 | 255/487 |
| VH-MIQ | LJ35 | 202 |
| **VH-MMC** | **C500** | **471** |
| VH-MOJ | C525 | 0138 |
| **VH-MOR** | **C52A** | **0063** |
| **VH-MQY** | **HS25** | **258807** |
| **VH-MXJ** | **C560** | **0320** |
| **VH-MXK** | **CL61** | **3003** |
| VH-MXK | CL64 | 5456 |
| VH-MXX | CL60 | 1061 |
| **VH-MYE** | **C525** | **0638** |
| VH-MZL | BE40 | RK-139 |
| VH-MZL | CL61 | 3054 |
| VH-MZL | CL64 | 5561 |
| VH-MZL | LJ35 | 285 |
| VH-MZL | LJ60 | 270 |
| VH-NCF | FA20 | 368 |
| VH-NCP | GLF4 | 1108 |
| **VH-NEQ** | **C510** | **0029** |
| VH-NEW | C500 | 268 |
| VH-NGA | WW24 | 387 |
| VH-NGF | FA20 | 505 |
| VH-NGH | C56X | 5727 |
| VH-NHJ | C560 | 0108 |
| (VH-NIJ) | WW24 | 317 |
| VH-NJA | HS25 | 256037 |
| VH-NJM | HS25 | 258002 |
| VH-NJW | WW24 | 315 |
| **VH-NKD** | **HS25** | **HA-0064** |
| VH-NKS | CL60 | 1073 |
| VH-NMN | FA20 | 327 |
| VH-NMR | HS25 | 258058 |
| VH-NMW | C500 | 279 |
| **VH-NSB** | **C550** | **330** |
| VH-NTH | C560 | 0041 |
| **VH-NTX** | **BE40** | **RK-584** |
| VH-OCV | CL64 | 5625 |
| **VH-OCV** | **GLEX** | **9326** |
| VH-OCV | LJ60 | 273 |
| (VH-ODJ) | C525 | 0625 |
| VH-OIL | C500 | 225 |
| VH-ORE | C550 | 035 |
| **VH-OSW** | **GLF4** | **1441** |
| **VH-OVB** | **LJ35** | **400** |
| VH-OVS | LJ25 | 120 |
| VH-OYC | C550 | 112 |
| VH-OYW | C550 | 054 |
| VH-OZI | C650 | 0037 |
| (VH-OZZ) | CL60 | 1057 |
| VH-PAB | HS25 | 25265 |
| VH-PDJ | FA20 | 491 |
| VH-PDJ | FA50 | 176 |
| **VH-PFA** | **LJ35** | **661** |
| **VH-PFS** | **LJ45** | **168** |
| VH-PNL | BE40 | RK-139 |
| VH-POZ | C500 | 370 |
| **VH-PPD** | **F900** | **185** |
| VH-PPF | FA50 | 187 |
| VH-PPF | LJ35 | 593 |
| **VH-PSM** | **C550** | **054** |
| **VH-PSU** | **C560** | **0515** |
| **VH-QQZ** | **C550** | **099** |
| **VH-RAM** | **HS25** | **258844** |
| **VH-RCA** | **C750** | **0012** |
| VH-RHQ | LJ35 | 400 |
| **VH-RIO** | **HS25** | **258594** |
| **VH-RJB** | **C52A** | **0094** |
| VH-RRC | FA20 | 325 |
| VH-SBC | LJ24 | 279 |
| VH-SBJ | LJ35 | 193 |
| **VH-SBU** | **C650** | **0109** |
| **VH-SCC** | **C550** | **550-1058** |
| **VH-SCD** | **C550** | **370** |
| VH-SCY | HS25 | 258328 |
| VH-SDN | LJ35 | 342 |
| VH-SFJ | FA50 | 123 |
| VH-SGY | HS25 | 258019 |
| VH-SGY | HS25 | 258328 |
| **VH-SGY** | **HS25** | **258780** |
| VH-SGY | WW24 | 395 |
| (VH-SJP) | C510 | 0011 |
| VH-SJP | C510 | 0033 |
| **VH-SLD** | **LJ35** | **145** |
| **VH-SLE** | **LJ35** | **428** |
| **VH-SLF** | **LJ36** | **049** |
| VH-SLJ | LJ35 | 046 |
| **VH-SLJ** | **LJ36** | **014** |
| VH-SMF | C560 | 0320 |
| (VH-SOA) | HS25 | 257169 |
| **VH-SOU** | **C500** | **333** |
| **VH-SPJ** | **C650** | **0101** |
| **VH-SQD** | **LJ45** | **033** |
| VH-SQH | WW24 | 366 |
| **VH-SQM** | **LJ45** | **035** |
| **VH-SQR** | **LJ45** | **195** |
| **VH-SQV** | **LJ45** | **207** |
| **VH-SSZ** | **C650** | **0158** |
| VH-SWC | C500 | 494 |
| VH-SWL | C550 | 207 |
| **VH-TEN** | **C750** | **0215** |
| VH-TFQ | C550 | 160 |
| VH-TFY | C550 | 099 |
| **VH-TGG** | **GLEX** | **9143** |
| VH-TGG | GLF4 | 1156 |
| **VH-THG** | **LJ60** | **352** |
| VH-TLJ | LJ35 | 091 |
| **VH-TMA** | **PRM1** | **RB-137** |
| VH-TNN | LJ25 | 181 |
| VH-TNP | C550 | 184 |
| **VH-TNX** | **HS25** | **258814** |
| VH-TOM | HS25 | 25242 |
| VH-TPR | LJ35 | 400 |
| VH-UCC | C500 | 142 |
| (VH-UDC) | LJ35 | 038 |
| VH-ULT | LJ35 | 463 |
| VH-UOH | C550 | 130 |
| VH-UPB | LJ35 | 215 |
| VH-UUZ | WW24 | 317 |
| (VH-VCJ) | C525 | 0002 |
| VH-VFP | C550 | 550-0882 |
| **VH-VGX** | **GLEX** | **9079** |
| **VH-VHP** | **PRM1** | **RB-175** |
| VH-VIW | F900 | 70 |
| **VH-VLJ** | **LJ35** | **432** |
| **VH-VLZ** | **C550** | **690** |
| VH-VPL | C560 | 0703 |
| **VH-VPL** | **C680** | **0250** |
| VH-VRC | C650 | 7089 |
| **VH-VRE** | **CL64** | **5561** |
| **VH-VRL** | **C560** | **0703** |
| **VH-VVI** | **LJ45** | **262** |
| **VH-WFE** | **C560** | **0335** |
| VH-WFE | LJ35 | 221 |
| VH-WFJ | LJ35 | 242 |
| VH-WFP | LJ35 | 466 |
| VH-WGJ | C550 | 054 |
| VH-WII | F900 | 73 |
| VH-WIM | F900 | 77 |
| VH-WIZ | F900 | 74 |
| VH-WIZ | F900 | 76 |
| **VH-WJW** | **FA10** | **134** |
| VH-WLH | FA20 | 262 |
| VH-WNP | C550 | 112 |
| **VH-WNZ** | **C550** | **073** |
| VH-WRM | C500 | 150 |
| VH-WSM | ASTR | 123 |
| VH-WWY | WW24 | 325 |
| **VH-XBP** | **C550** | **550-0810** |
| VH-XCJ | C550 | 550-0810 |
| VH-XCJ | C56X | 5673 |
| **VH-XCJ** | **C750** | **0015** |
| **VH-XCU** | **C56X** | **5673** |
| VH-XDD | C550 | 099 |
| VH-XGG | GLF4 | 1156 |
| VH-XMO | HS25 | 258243 |
| VH-XTT | C560 | 0417 |
| **VH-YDZ** | **C510** | **0070** |
| **VH-YNE** | **C525** | **0521** |
| VH-YRC | BE40 | RK-222 |
| **VH-YXY** | **C550** | **550-1125** |
| **VH-ZLE** | **C550** | **380** |
| **VH-ZLT** | **C550** | **550-0878** |
| **VH-ZMD** | **C500** | **263** |
| **VH-ZSU** | **CL60** | **1078** |
| **VH-ZUH** | **HS25** | **258366** |
| (VH-ZXH) | GLEX | 9213 |
| **VH-ZYH** | **WW24** | **376** |
| **VH-ZZH** | **CL64** | **5456** |
| VH-ZZH | LJ45 | 204 |

## Bahamas

(see also C6-)

| | | |
|---|---|---|
| VP-BDH | HS25 | 25206 |
| VP-BDH | HS25 | 256028 |
| VP-BDM | LJ25 | 008 |

## Bermuda

(see also VQ-B/VR-B)

| | | |
|---|---|---|
| (VP-B ) | LJ31 | 074 |
| VP-BAB | GLF3 | 373 |
| VP-BAC | CL64 | 5309 |
| **VP-BAC** | **GLF5** | **588** |
| **VP-BAE** | **GLF4** | **4119** |
| VP-BAE | PRM1 | RB-66 |
| VP-BAF | FA10 | 210 |
| "VP-BAH" | F2EX | 133 |
| **VP-BAH** | **GLEX** | **9223** |
| VP-BAK | F2EX | 110 |
| **VP-BAM** | **GLEX** | **9157** |
| **VP-BAR** | **FA7X** | **11** |
| **VP-BAS** | **HS25** | **258702** |
| VP-BAW | HS25 | 258237 |
| VP-BAW | LJ31 | 203 |
| VP-BBD | FA50 | 226 |
| VP-BBE | C500 | 278 |
| **VP-BBF** | **CL61** | **3033** |
| VP-BBH | HS25 | 257118 |
| **VP-BBO** | **GLF5** | **5123** |
| **VP-BBP** | **F2TH** | **160** |
| VP-BBQ | PRM1 | RB-181 |
| **VP-BBV** | **FA10** | **22** |
| VP-BBW | HS25 | 256037 |
| **VP-BBX** | **GLF5** | **622** |
| VP-BBZ | LJ60 | 328 |
| VP-BCA | CL64 | 5391 |
| VP-BCB | CL64 | 5397 |
| VP-BCC | CL61 | 5162 |
| VP-BCD | FA50 | 134 |
| VP-BCF | HS25 | 257214 |
| VP-BCH | FA10 | 70 |
| VP-BCI | CL61 | 5193 |
| **VP-BCM** | **HA4T** | **RC-14** |
| VP-BCM | HS25 | 258404 |
| VP-BCN | HS25 | 256035 |
| VP-BCO | CL64 | 5420 |
| **VP-BCO** | **GLF5** | **5177** |
| VP-BCP | JSTR | 5222 |
| VP-BCT | GLF3 | 302 |
| **VP-BCV** | **F2TH** | **187** |
| **VP-BCW** | **HS25** | **258719** |
| **VP-BCX** | **F900** | **193** |
| **VP-BCY** | **LJ60** | **215** |
| VP-BCZ | FA50 | 107 |
| VP-BDB | C560 | 0503 |
| VP-BDD | GLEX | 9017 |
| **VP-BDL** | **F2TH** | **111** |
| **VP-BDS** | **C525** | **0180** |
| **VP-BDU** | **GLEX** | **9057** |
| **VP-BDV** | **F2EX** | **22** |
| **VP-BDX** | **CL64** | **5402** |
| VP-BDY | CL64 | 5539 |
| VP-BDZ | F9EX | 53 |
| **VP-BEA** | **FA50** | **286** |
| VP-BEB | GLEX | 9115 |
| VP-BEC | F900 | 165 |
| **VP-BEE** | **F9EX** | **109** |
| VP-BEF | F2TH | 49 |
| **VP-BEF** | **F9EX** | **130** |
| VP-BEF | FA50 | 283 |
| **VP-BEG** | **F9EX** | **17** |
| VP-BEH | F900 | 163 |
| VP-BEH | F9EX | 75 |
| **VP-BEH** | **FA7X** | **21** |
| **VP-BEJ** | **CL61** | **5061** |
| **VP-BEK** | **CL30** | **20176** |
| VP-BEK | HS25 | 257175 |
| **VP-BEM** | **GLEX** | **9036** |
| VP-BEN | GLEX | 9020 |
| VP-BEP | GLF5 | 636 |
| VP-BER | F2EX | 10 |
| **VP-BES** | **CL65** | **5770** |
| VP-BEZ | F9EX | 86 |
| VP-BEZ | LJ60 | 149 |
| VP-BFC | C52A | 0031 |
| (VP-BFD) | GLF5 | 682 |
| **VP-BFF** | **GLF2** | **186** |
| **VP-BFH** | **F900** | **173** |
| VP-BFM | F9EX | 131 |
| VP-BFM | FA50 | 124 |
| VP-BFS | CL61 | 5149 |
| **VP-BFU** | **PRM1** | **RB-220** |
| VP-BFV | F9EX | 111 |
| VP-BFW | FA10 | 54 |
| VP-BFW | GLF4 | 1233 |
| VP-BGB | LJ60 | 005 |
| VP-BGC | F900 | 169 |
| VP-BGD | FA10 | 113 |
| VP-BGE | C500 | 287 |
| VP-BGF | F900 | 154 |
| **VP-BGG** | **FA7X** | **5** |
| VP-BGG | GLEX | 9018 |
| **VP-BGI** | **F2EX** | **126** |
| VP-BGL | GLF5 | 5043 |
| **VP-BGM** | **CL65** | **5748** |
| VP-BGN | GLF5 | 5011 |
| VP-BGO | CL64 | 5404 |
| **VP-BGS** | **LJ60** | **289** |
| VP-BGT | GLF2 | 211 |
| VP-BHA | CL64 | 5307 |
| VP-BHB | HS25 | 258221 |
| VP-BHC | F2TH | 26 |
| **VP-BHD** | **F2TH** | **167** |
| VP-BHG | GLF4 | 1017 |
| **VP-BHH** | **CL64** | **5448** |
| VP-BHI | C500 | 664 |
| VP-BHJ | F900 | 138 |
| VP-BHL | HS25 | 258349 |
| **VP-BHO** | **C500** | **610** |
| **VP-BHR** | **GLF3** | **346** |
| VP-BHS | CL64 | 5505 |
| **VP-BHT** | **LJ40** | **45-2050** |
| VP-BHW | HS25 | 257209 |
| VP-BHZ | HS25 | 258438 |
| VP-BID | F9EX | 39 |
| VP-BIE | CL61 | 3016 |
| VP-BIH | CL61 | 5193 |
| **VP-BIL** | **FA7X** | **3** |
| VP-BIP | GLF5 | 5109 |
| VP-BIS | GLF4 | 1150 |
| VP-BIV | GLF4 | 1103 |
| VP-BIV | GLF4 | 1381 |
| VP-BIV | GLF4 | 4092 |
| VP-BJA | CL64 | 5639 |
| VP-BJA | F900 | 154 |
| VP-BJD | GLF4 | 1134 |
| **VP-BJD** | **GLF5** | **5064** |
| VP-BJD | GLF5 | 672 |
| **VP-BJE** | **CL64** | **5605** |
| VP-BJH | CL64 | 5397 |
| **VP-BJI** | **GLEX** | **9276** |
| VP-BJJ | GLEX | 9011 |
| **VP-BJK** | **GLF5** | **5200** |
| **VP-BJM** | **CL64** | **5593** |
| **VP-BJN** | **GLEX** | **9273** |
| VP-BJR | C52A | 0147 |
| "VP-BJR" | C52B | 0198 |
| VP-BJS | LJ35 | 464 |
| **VP-BJT** | **CL30** | **20255** |
| VP-BJV | GLF2 | 186 |
| VP-BKA | F900 | 170 |
| VP-BKB | HS25 | 258491 |
| VP-BKB | HS25 | 258539 |
| VP-BKG | FA50 | 147 |

VP-BKH GLF4 1029
VP-BKI GLF4 1029
**VP-BKI GLF4 1255**
**VP-BKK HS25 25238**
VP-BKP C500 555
VP-BKT GLF4 1074
VP-BKY HS25 25150
**VP-BKZ GLF5 602**
VP-BLA CL61 3013
VP-BLA GLF5 5024
VP-BLA GLF5 654
**VP-BLB F900 49**
**VP-BLC LJ60 311**
**VP-BLD JSTR 5117/35**
VP-BLF C500 679
VP-BLH GALX 029
**VP-BLM F900 72**
VP-BLN GLF3 402
VP-BLP F900 14
VP-BLR GLF5 5059
VP-BLT WW24 337
VP-BLV C500 344
**VP-BLW GLF5 5129**
VP-BMA ASTR 092
**VP-BMA ASTR 228**
**VP-BMB F900 51**
**VP-BMD HS25 257200**
VP-BME GLF4 1058
VP-BMF FA50 206
VP-BMG CL64 5460
**VP-BMH HS25 258180**
VP-BMI FA50 286
VP-BMJ F2EX 1
**VP-BML CL65 5703**
VP-BML LJ31 140
**VP-BMM HS25 258841**
VP-BMM LJ60 054
**VP-BMP FA50 345**
VP-BMR BE40 RK-133
**VP-BMS F9EX 42**
**VP-BMT ASTR 144**
**VP-BMU HS25 257212**
VP-BMV F900 202
**VP-BMV GLF4 4150**
VP-BMW ASTR 146
**VP-BMX HS25 259012**
VP-BMX LJ31 160
VP-BMY GLF3 463
**VP-BMY GLF4 4096**
VP-BNB GLF4 1234
VP-BND GLF2 199/19
**VP-BNE GLF5 5051**
VP-BNF CL64 5332
VP-BNG CL61 5119
VP-BNG CL64 5456
VP-BNJ F900 120
**VP-BNK HS25 258625**
**VP-BNL GLF5 607**
VP-BNN GLF4 1255
**VP-BNO GLF5 5050**
**VP-BNP CL64 5657**
**VP-BNR GLF5 5033**
VP-BNS C550 550-0939
VP-BNS CL64 5384
**VP-BNS F9DX 609**
VP-BNT F2TH 121
VP-BNW HS25 256057
**VP-BNX GLEX 9246**
VP-BNY GLF4 1208
VP-BNZ GLF3 452
VP-BNZ GLF4 1406
VP-BNZ GLF5 509
**VP-BOA CL61 5114**
(VP-BOE) F2EX 128
VP-BOJ HS25 257103
**VP-BOK GLEX 9101**
VP-BOK GLF3 390
**VP-BOL GLF4 1266**
VP-BOL LJ55 022
**VP-BON ASTR 060**
**VP-BOO HS25 258477**
VP-BOR GLF3 484
VP-BOS GLEX 9165
VP-BOT GLF4 1212
**VP-BOW GLEX 9141**
VP-BOY HS25 257109
VP-BOZ F9EX 174
VP-BPA FA50 266
VP-BPC F900 142
VP-BPE HS25 257040
**VP-BPH GALX 187**
VP-BPI F900 149
VP-BPO PRM1 RB-138
VP-BPW F900 135
**VP-BPW F9EX 225**
**VP-BRA F2EX 133**
VP-BRF GLF4 1015
VP-BRJ C525 0351
**VP-BRJ C52B 0198**
**VP-BRL C52A 0435**
VP-BRL JSTR 5155/32
VP-BRO F9EX 13
VP-BSA FA50 196
**VP-BSA GLF4 4115**
VP-BSC GLEX 9142
VP-BSD C56X 5088
**VP-BSE GLEX 9028**
VP-BSF GLF4 1058
VP-BSF GLF4 1098
**VP-BSF LJ45 374**
VP-BSH GLF4 1466
VP-BSH JSTR 5117/35
**VP-BSI GLF5 5084**
VP-BSI HS25 258073
**VP-BSJ GLF5 555**
VP-BSK F900 125
VP-BSK HS25 258409
VP-BSL FA50 209
VP-BSM GLF5 555
**VP-BSN GLF5 648**
**VP-BSO F9EX 144**
VP-BSP F9EX 151
**VP-BSR GLF4 4161**
VP-BSS CL64 5626
VP-BSS GLF4 1001
VP-BST CL64 5620
VP-BST FA50 258
**VP-BTB GLF4 4103**
VP-BTC GLF5 5176
VP-BTM HS25 258233
VP-BTR C550 693
VP-BTZ HS25 257109
VP-BUC FA50 107
VP-BUG C52B 0160
VP-BUL C560 0102
**VP-BUS GLF4 1127**
**VP-BVG GLEX 9193**
VP-BVK C500 555
VP-BVP F2EX 45
VP-BVT GLF4 1419
VP-BVV C550 307
**VP-BVV F2EX 125**
**VP-BVY FA7X 9**
VP-BWB CL61 5151
**VP-BWB GLEX 9161**
(VP-BWC) C56X 5690
VP-BWS F900 124
VP-BXP HS25 258494
(VP-BXX) GLEX 9059
VP-BYS GLF4 1381
**VP-BYY GLEX 9030**
VP-BZA GLF4 1381
VP-BZB F900 143
**VP-BZC GLF5 5179**
VP-BZE FA50 144
**VP-BZE FA7X 14**
**VP-BZI CL61 5149**
VP-BZM CL64 5626
VP-BZT CL61 5094
VP-BZZ C525 0235

## Cayman Islands

(see also VR-C)

**VP-CAB F900 101**
**VP-CAD C525 0297**
**VP-CAE GLF4 4031**
**VP-CAF HS25 258267**
(VP-CAH) GLEX 9213
**VP-CAI C56X 5048**
VP-CAM CL61 5090
**VP-CAM F2EX 89**
VP-CAN CL64 5335
**VP-CAO CL30 20100**
VP-CAP C500 583
**VP-CAP CL64 5415**
VP-CAR ASTR 133
**VP-CAR C650 0135**
**VP-CAS F2TH 1**
VP-CAS GALX 029
VP-CAS HS25 258167
**VP-CAT C500 637**
VP-CAU GLEX 9231
**VP-CAV C680 0202**
**VP-CAX F900 62**
**VP-CAZ PRM1 RB-202**
VP-CBB GLF4 1250
**VP-CBC F2EX 61**
VP-CBD F900 16
VP-CBE C550 119
**VP-CBF FA50 311**
**VP-CBG SBRL 465-33**
VP-CBH JSTR 5202
VP-CBM C550 729
VP-CBR CL64 5520
**VP-CBS CL61 5044**
VP-CBT FA50 256
VP-CBW GLF4 1096
**VP-CBX GLF5 511**
VP-CCC C525 0040
VP-CCD C500 547
**VP-CCD LJ60 312**
**VP-CCE CL64 5622**
VP-CCF CL61 3031
VP-CCH HS25 258103
**VP-CCL FA20 482**
VP-CCM C550 310
VP-CCO C550 347
VP-CCP C550 550-0857
VP-CCP CL64 5449
**VP-CCR CL61 5079**
VP-CCV C560 0320
VP-CDE HS25 258234
**VP-CDF GLEX 9093**
VP-CDM C500 463
VP-CDR ASTR 055
**VP-CDV CL30 20140**
VP-CDW C650 7034
VP-CEA GLF5 5181
VP-CEA HS25 258520
**VP-CEB GLEX 9083**
**VP-CED C550 550-0870**
VP-CEF FA50 283
**VP-CEG C750 0277**
**VP-CEI CL61 5125**
VP-CEK HS25 257175
**VP-CEO CL64 5539**
**VP-CEP ASTR 280**
**VP-CES GLF5 669**
**VP-CET GLF4 4166**
VP-CEZ F9EX 134
VP-CEZ FA50 138
VP-CFB GLF4 4137
VP-CFB LJ31 205
**VP-CFD CL64 5616**
VP-CFF C500 456
VP-CFF GLF4 1265
VP-CFG C500 577
VP-CFI FA50 278
**VP-CFL F900 164**
VP-CFL GLF4 1282
**VP-CFM C56X 5218**
VP-CFP C525 0126
**VP-CFP C680 0039**
**VP-CFR F9EX 134**
VP-CFS HS25 258582
**VP-CFT CL61 5067**
**VP-CFW PRM1 RB-189**
**VP-CFZ C750 0251**
**VP-CGA F2TH 100**
**VP-CGB F900 145**
**VP-CGC F2TH 107**
**VP-CGD F9EX 65**
VP-CGE C650 7077
**VP-CGE F9EX 73**
VP-CGG C56X 5361
**VP-CGH JSTR 5220**
VP-CGK C650 0048
VP-CGL C550 550-0884
VP-CGM F2TH 160
**VP-CGN GLF5 5149**
**VP-CGO GLEX 9171**
VP-CGP F900 163
VP-CGP FA50 204
(VP-CGR) F900 193
**VP-CGS GLEX 9102**
**VP-CHA F9DX 614**
**VP-CHE C525 0364**
VP-CHF BE40 RK-203
VP-CHG FA50 259
VP-CHH C500 083
**VP-CHH CL65 5716**
VP-CHK CL61 5102
VP-CHL CL64 5597
VP-CHT LJ25 075
VP-CHU CL64 5510
VP-CHV C525 0264
VP-CHW GALX 004
**VP-CIC CL61 5011**
VP-CID F900 130
VP-CIF GLF5 5048
VP-CIP GLF4 1371
**VP-CIP GLF5 5048**
VP-CIS C525 0252
**VP-CIS HS25 HA-0084**
**VP-CIT F9DX 610**
**VP-CJA F2TH 18**
VP-CJB C500 564
VP-CJB CL64 5623
VP-CJC GLEX 9271
VP-CJF F900 26
VP-CJF LJ25 075
**VP-CJI C525 0526**
**VP-CJL GLF5 5216**
**VP-CJM GLF5 5181**
VP-CJP CL61 5022
VP-CJP HS25 25258
VP-CJR C550 388
**VP-CKC GLF5 5111**
**VP-CKD GLF4 4088**
VP-CKG ASTR 096
VP-CKK BE40 RK-200
VP-CKM C560 0413
**VP-CKN HS25 258615**
VP-CKR CL64 5597
**VP-CLA GLF4 1402**
**VP-CLB F9EX 34**
VP-CLD C550 351
VP-CLD FA50 134
VP-CLE CL61 3066
**VP-CLJ CL65 5776**
VP-CLN FA50 251
**VP-CLO F9EX 90**
VP-CLT LJ35 016
**VP-CLU HS25 257058**
**VP-CLV CL30 20041**
**VP-CLX HS25 257091**
**VP-CLZ CL61 5193**
VP-CMA C500 547
**VP-CMA GLEX 9243**
VP-CMA HS25 258835
**VP-CMB CL64 5618**
VP-CMB LJ25 118
VP-CMC CL61 5044
VP-CMD C550 726
VP-CMD F2EX 82
VP-CMF GLF4 1062
**VP-CMG GLF4 4093**
VP-CMG GLF5 519
**VP-CMH C680 0171**
**VP-CMI F2EX 113**
VP-CMO C500 070
**VP-CMP HS25 257214**
**VP-CMR GLF4 1117**
VP-CMS C560 0457
VP-CMZ HS25 259021
VP-CNF C525 0153
VP-CNJ GLF3 426
**VP-CNK CL64 5621**
VP-CNM C550 550-0857
VP-CNM C56X 5070
VP-CNP GLF3 496
**VP-CNR GLF5 5113**
**VP-CNY GLEX 9270**
VP-CNZ F9EX 74
VP-COD HS25 258816
VP-COJ CL61 5152
VP-COJ CL64 5367
VP-COK HS25 257028
**VP-COM C500 318**
VP-CON C500 238

| | | |
|---|---|---|
| **VP-COP** | **CL64** | **5552** |
| VP-COP | GLEX | 9050 |
| VP-COU | GLEX | 9084 |
| VP-CPA | GLF2 | 204 |
| VP-CPC | C56X | 5215 |
| (VP-CPC) | GLEX | 9005 |
| **VP-CPF** | **CL30** | **20256** |
| **VP-CPH** | **BE40** | **RK-188** |
| VP-CPO | CL61 | 5165 |
| VP-CPT | HS25 | 259004 |
| **VP-CRA** | **C550** | **585** |
| VP-CRA | HS25 | 257118 |
| **VP-CRB** | **LJ60** | **125** |
| VP-CRC | GLEX | 9196 |
| VP-CRD | PRM1 | RB-57 |
| **VP-CRF** | **FA50** | **61** |
| "VP-CRH" | C500 | 083 |
| VP-CRH | C680 | 0226 |
| **VP-CRR** | **CL61** | **5129** |
| VP-CRS | CL65 | 5739 |
| VP-CRS | GALX | 008 |
| VP-CRS | HS25 | 258520 |
| VP-CRT | FA50 | 88 |
| VP-CRX | CL61 | 3052 |
| VP-CRY | GLF4 | 1176 |
| **VP-CSB** | **GLEX** | **9263** |
| VP-CSC | C560 | 0439 |
| **VP-CSF** | **GLF4** | **1390** |
| (VP-CSG) | GALX | 159 |
| **VP-CSM** | **JSTR** | **5092/58** |
| VP-CSN | C560 | 0401 |
| VP-CSP | C500 | 165 |
| **VP-CSP** | **HS25** | **258210** |
| VP-CTA | C525 | 0172 |
| VP-CTB | C500 | 432 |
| VP-CTE | C550 | 716 |
| VP-CTF | C550 | 716 |
| VP-CTJ | C550 | 068 |
| (VP-CTN) | C525 | 0399 |
| VP-CTS | HS25 | 25243 |
| **VP-CTT** | **F2EX** | **139** |
| VP-CTT | F900 | 161 |
| VP-CUB | GLF2 | 207/34 |
| VP-CUC | LJ55 | 035 |
| VP-CUT | ASTR | 080 |
| **VP-CVI** | **GLF5** | **5092** |
| VP-CVK | CL61 | 5049 |
| VP-CVL | LJ45 | 059 |
| **VP-CVP** | **BE40** | **RK-300** |
| **VP-CVT** | **GLF5** | **5102** |
| VP-CVU | GLEX | 9257 |
| VP-CVV | GLEX | 9272 |
| VP-CWI | FA50 | 159 |
| VP-CWM | C550 | 667 |
| VP-CWM | C56X | 5136 |
| **VP-CWN** | **GLEX** | **9321** |
| VP-CWW | C525 | 0124 |
| **VP-CWW** | **PRM1** | **RB-74** |
| **VP-CXP** | **HS25** | **258728** |
| VP-CXX | HS25 | 259032 |
| VP-CYK | C750 | 0097 |
| VP-CYM | GLF4 | 1090 |
| **VP-CZK** | **GLEX** | **9244** |

British Virgin Islands

| | | |
|---|---|---|
| (VP-LV.) | HS25 | 258409 |

Zimbabwe
(see also Z-)

| | | |
|---|---|---|
| VP-WKY | LJ25 | 160 |

Bermuda
(see also VP-C/VR-C)

| | | |
|---|---|---|
| **VQ-BAA** | **FA7X** | **46** |
| **VQ-BAM** | **GLEX** | **9139** |
| **VQ-BCE** | **GLF4** | **4148** |
| **VQ-BDG** | **CL65** | **5765** |
| **VQ-BDS** | **GALX** | **220** |
| **VQ-BEB** | **GLEX** | **9283** |
| **VQ-BEP** | **PRM1** | **RB-125** |
| **VQ-BFN** | **FA7X** | **27** |
| **VQ-BGA** | **GLF4** | **4092** |
| **VQ-BGN** | **GLF5** | **5218** |
| **VQ-BGS** | **GLEX** | **9254** |
| VQ-BIS | GLEX | 9213 |
| **VQ-BJA** | **GLEX** | **9268** |
| **VQ-BLA** | **GLF5** | **5215** |
| **VQ-BLV** | **GLF5** | **5221** |
| **VQ-BPH** | **HS25** | **HA-0108** |
| **VQ-BSC** | **GLEX** | **9297** |
| **VQ-BSN** | **FA7X** | **58** |
| **VQ-BSO** | **FA7X** | **64** |
| **VQ-BSP** | **FA7X** | **83** |
| VQ-BZB | CL65 | 5763 |

Swaziland

| | | |
|---|---|---|
| VQ-ZIL | HS25 | 25080 |

Bermuda
(see also VP-B/VQ-B)

| | | |
|---|---|---|
| VR-B | FA50 | 175 |
| (VR-B ) | FA50 | 231 |
| (VR-B ) | FA50 | 66 |
| (VR-B ) | HS25 | 258182 |
| VR-BAA | CL61 | 5156 |
| VR-BAB | GLF3 | 373 |
| VR-BAC | CL64 | 5309 |
| (VR-BBP) | CL60 | 1073 |
| VR-BBY | C500 | 433 |
| VR-BCC | CL61 | 5162 |
| VR-BCF | HS25 | 257214 |
| VR-BCF | LJ24 | 038 |
| VR-BCG | FA20 | 3/403 |
| VR-BCH | FA10 | 70 |
| VR-BCI | CL61 | 5193 |
| VR-BCJ | FA20 | 55/410 |
| VR-BCY | C560 | 0376 |
| VR-BDC | GLF4 | 1183 |
| VR-BDK | FA20 | 198/466 |
| VR-BEM | LJ25 | 098 |
| VR-BES | ASTR | 017 |
| VR-BFF | FA10 | 7 |
| VR-BFR | LJ36 | 012 |
| VR-BFV | LJ25 | 094 |
| VR-BFW | FA10 | 54 |
| VR-BFX | LJ35 | 054 |
| VR-BGB | C650 | 0077 |
| VR-BGD | HS25 | 25157 |
| VR-BGF | LJ25 | 098 |
| VR-BGL | GLF2 | 124 |
| VR-BGO | GLF2 | 124 |
| VR-BGS | HS25 | 256011 |
| VR-BGT | GLF2 | 211 |
| VR-BHA | CL64 | 5307 |
| VR-BHA | GLF2 | 45 |
| VR-BHB | LJ36 | 007 |
| VR-BHC | LJ24 | 267 |
| VR-BHD | GLF2 | 231 |
| VR-BHE | HS25 | 257020 |
| VR-BHF | JSTR | 5062/12 |
| VR-BHG | C550 | 273 |
| VR-BHG | GLF4 | 1017 |
| VR-BHH | HS25 | 257140 |
| VR-BHI | C500 | 664 |
| VR-BHJ | F900 | 138 |
| VR-BHJ | FA10 | 104 |
| VR-BHL | FA20 | 429 |
| VR-BHR | GLF2 | 165/37 |
| VR-BHV | LJ55 | 045 |
| VR-BHW | HS25 | 257209 |
| VR-BHX | FA50 | 140 |
| VR-BHY | FA20 | 496 |
| VR-BHZ | FA20 | 492 |
| VR-BIZ | C550 | 469 |
| VR-BJA | F900 | 154 |
| VR-BJA | FA50 | 110 |
| VR-BJB | FA20 | 244 |
| VR-BJD | GLF2 | 219/20 |
| VR-BJD | GLF4 | 1134 |
| VR-BJD | LJ36 | 008 |
| VR-BJE | GLF3 | 347 |
| VR-BJG | GLF2 | 112 |
| VR-BJH | JSTR | 5215 |
| VR-BJI | JSTR | 5149/11 |
| VR-BJJ | FA20 | 401 |
| VR-BJJ | FA50 | 228 |
| VR-BJK | C500 | 372 |
| VR-BJN | C500 | 532 |
| VR-BJO | LJ36 | 008 |
| VR-BJQ | GLF2 | 140/40 |
| VR-BJS | C650 | 0119 |
| VR-BJT | GLF2 | 137 |
| VR-BJV | GLF2 | 186 |
| VR-BJW | C500 | 674 |
| VR-BJX | F900 | 4 |
| VR-BJY | C650 | 0040 |
| VR-BJZ | GLF4 | 1005 |
| VR-BKA | MU30 | A058SA |
| VR-BKB | LJ35 | 370 |
| VR-BKE | GLF4 | 1037 |
| VR-BKG | FA50 | 147 |
| VR-BKH | FA20 | 237/476 |
| VR-BKI | GLF4 | 1029 |
| VR-BKJ | CL60 | 1016 |
| VR-BKK | HS25 | 25238 |
| (VR-BKL) | GLF4 | 1048 |
| VR-BKN | HS25 | 25240 |
| VR-BKP | C500 | 555 |
| VR-BKR | FA20 | 133 |
| VR-BKS | GLF3 | 390 |
| VR-BKT | GLF4 | 1074 |
| VR-BKU | GLF4 | 1046 |
| VR-BKV | GLF4 | 1055 |
| VR-BKY | HS25 | 25150 |
| VR-BKZ | HS25 | 257199 |
| VR-BLA | CL61 | 3013 |
| VR-BLB | F900 | 49 |
| VR-BLC | GLF4 | 1093 |
| VR-BLD | CL60 | 1035 |
| VR-BLF | C500 | 679 |
| (VR-BLG) | BE40 | RJ-22 |
| VR-BLH | GLF4 | 1008 |
| VR-BLJ | GLF2 | 40 |
| VR-BLL | FA50 | 136 |
| VR-BLM | F900 | 72 |
| VR-BLN | GLF3 | 402 |
| VR-BLO | GLF3 | 390 |
| VR-BLP | HS25 | 258139 |
| VR-BLQ | HS25 | 258175 |
| VR-BLR | GLF4 | 1127 |
| VR-BLT | F900 | 88 |
| VR-BLU | LJ35 | 389 |
| VR-BLV | C500 | 344 |
| VR-BLW | C500 | 442 |
| VR-BMA | CL61 | 3012 |
| VR-BMB | HS25 | 25240 |
| VR-BMD | HS25 | 257200 |
| VR-BME | ASTR | 041 |
| VR-BMF | FA50 | 206 |
| VR-BMG | C650 | 0185 |
| VR-BMK | CL61 | 5029 |
| VR-BML | GLF2 | 70/1 |
| VR-BMN | LJ24 | 267 |
| VR-BMO | C500 | 083 |
| VR-BMQ | GLF2 | 42/12 |
| VR-BMT | C500 | 083 |
| VR-BMY | GLF3 | 463 |
| VR-BNB | HS25 | 257002 |
| VR-BND | GLF2 | 199/19 |
| (VR-BND) | HS25 | 258164 |
| VR-BNE | GLF2 | 51 |
| VR-BNF | CL61 | 5069 |
| VR-BNG | CL61 | 5119 |
| VR-BNI | LJ35 | 620 |
| VR-BNJ | F900 | 120 |
| VR-BNO | GLF3 | 308 |
| VR-BNT | FA10 | 73 |
| VR-BNV | BE40 | RJ-36 |
| VR-BNW | HS25 | 256057 |
| VR-BNX | GLF3 | 320 |
| VR-BNY | GLF4 | 1208 |
| VR-BNZ | GLF3 | 452 |
| VR-BOA | CL61 | 5114 |
| VR-BOB | GLF3 | 375 |
| VR-BOB | GLF4 | 1120 |
| VR-BOJ | HS25 | 257103 |
| VR-BOK | GLF3 | 390 |
| VR-BOL | LJ55 | 022 |
| VR-BON | ASTR | 060 |
| VR-BOS | GLF2 | 13 |
| VR-BOT | GLF4 | 1212 |
| VR-BOY | GLF4 | 1009 |
| (VR-BPA) | HS25 | 258139 |
| (VR-BPB) | HS25 | 258175 |
| VR-BPE | HS25 | 257040 |
| VR-BPF | C550 | 599 |
| VR-BPG | HS25 | 258165 |
| VR-BPI | F900 | 149 |
| VR-BPM | HS25 | 258186 |
| VR-BPN | HS25 | 258239 |
| VR-BPT | HS25 | 257109 |
| VR-BPW | F900 | 135 |
| VR-BQA | CL61 | 5130 |
| VR-BQB | C560 | 0301 |
| VR-BQF | LJ55 | 039 |
| (VR-BQG) | JSTR | 5155/32 |
| (VR-BQH) | HS25 | 258233 |
| VR-BRF | GLF4 | 1015 |
| VR-BRJ | FA20 | 275 |
| VR-BRL | JSTR | 5155/32 |
| VR-BRM | GLF2 | 194 |
| VR-BRM | GLF2 | 91 |
| VR-BRS | HS25 | 256004 |
| VR-BSH | JSTR | 5117/35 |
| VR-BSI | HS25 | 258073 |
| VR-BSK | F900 | 125 |
| VR-BSL | GLF3 | 304 |
| VR-BSS | GLF4 | 1001 |
| VR-BST | LJ60 | 035 |
| VR-BTM | HS25 | 258233 |
| VR-BTQ | C500 | 340 |
| VR-BTR | C550 | 693 |
| VR-BTT | FA50 | 32 |
| VR-BTZ | HS25 | 257109 |
| VR-BUB | C500 | 345 |
| VR-BUC | FA50 | 107 |
| VR-BUL | C560 | 0102 |
| VR-BUS | GLF4 | 1127 |
| VR-BVI | HS25 | 25278 |
| VR-BVV | C550 | 307 |
| VR-BWB | CL61 | 5151 |
| VR-BWS | F900 | 124 |
| VR-BYE | C550 | 599 |
| VR-BZE | FA50 | 144 |

Cayman Islands

| | | |
|---|---|---|
| (VR-C ) | FA20 | 150/445 |
| (VR-C ) | LJ35 | 356 |
| VR-CAC | WW24 | 285 |
| VR-CAD | LJ35 | 432 |
| VR-CAD | WW24 | 276 |
| VR-CAE | FA50 | 228 |
| VR-CAG | GLF2 | 231 |
| VR-CAR | CL61 | 3017 |
| VR-CAR | FA20 | 440 |
| VR-CAS | GLF2 | 4/8 |
| VR-CAS | HS25 | 258167 |
| VR-CAT | C500 | 637 |
| VR-CAU | WW24 | 72 |
| VR-CAW | JSTR | 5133 |
| VR-CBB | GLF4 | 1250 |
| VR-CBB | WW24 | 350 |
| VR-CBC | GLF2 | 167 |
| VR-CBD | HS25 | 256041 |
| VR-CBK | WW24 | 285 |
| VR-CBL | FA50 | 95 |
| VR-CBL | GLF4 | 1243 |
| VR-CBM | C550 | 729 |
| VR-CBM | GLF2 | 34 |
| VR-CBO | FA50 | 98 |
| "VR-CBP" | CL60 | 1067 |
| VR-CBR | FA50 | 9 |
| VR-CBT | FA20 | 237/476 |
| VR-CBU | LJ35 | 396 |
| VR-CBW | GLF4 | 1096 |
| VR-CCC | C650 | 0023 |
| (VR-CCC) | JSTR | 5006/40 |
| VR-CCE | C550 | 441 |
| VR-CCF | FA20 | 285/504 |
| VR-CCH | LJ25 | 091 |
| VR-CCI | C550 | 046 |
| VR-CCL | FA20 | 482 |
| VR-CCN | GLF3 | 345 |
| VR-CCP | C500 | 083 |
| VR-CCQ | FA20 | 515 |
| VR-CCQ | FA50 | 208 |
| VR-CCQ | FA50 | 73 |
| VR-CCR | CL61 | 5079 |
| VR-CCV | C560 | 0320 |
| VR-CCV | CL61 | 5075 |

| | | |
|---|---|---|
| VR-CCX | HS25 | 258214 |
| VR-CCY | JSTR | 5085 |
| (VR-CDA) | BE40 | RK-25 |
| VR-CDB | FA20 | 305 |
| VR-CDE | HS25 | 258234 |
| VR-CDF | FA50 | 111 |
| VR-CDG | HS25 | 256013 |
| VR-CDH | LJ25 | 213 |
| VR-CDI | LJ35 | 264 |
| VR-CDK | LJ55 | 138 |
| VR-CDM | C500 | 463 |
| VR-CDN | C525 | 0085 |
| VR-CDT | FA20 | 341 |
| VR-CEB | C500 | 094 |
| VR-CEE | SBRL | 465-22 |
| VR-CEG | CL61 | 5104 |
| VR-CEJ | HS25 | 258021 |
| VR-CES | F900 | 140 |
| VR-CEZ | FA50 | 138 |
| VR-CFG | C500 | 577 |
| VR-CFI | FA50 | 176 |
| VR-CFL | GLF4 | 1282 |
| VR-CGB | F900 | 145 |
| VR-CGD | LJ25 | 075 |
| VR-CGP | FA50 | 204 |
| VR-CGP | FA50 | 63 |
| VR-CGS | LJ31 | 040 |
| VR-CHA | CL61 | 5153 |
| VR-CHB | C550 | 559 |
| VR-CHC | FA20 | 515 |
| VR-CHF | C500 | 637 |
| VR-CHH | C500 | 083 |
| VR-CHJ | LJ31 | 040 |
| VR-CHK | CL61 | 5102 |
| VR-CHT | LJ25 | 075 |
| (VR-CIA) | C500 | 577 |
| VR-CIC | CL61 | 5011 |
| VR-CID | F900 | 130 |
| VR-CIL | WW24 | 289 |
| VR-CIM | C650 | 7035 |
| VR-CIT | C550 | 407 |
| (VR-CJA) | LJ55 | 033 |
| VR-CJB | C500 | 564 |
| VR-CJJ | CL61 | 5142 |
| VR-CJP | HS25 | 25258 |
| VR-CJR | C550 | 388 |
| (VR-CKC) | CL61 | 5073 |
| VR-CKK | CL60 | 1033 |
| VR-CKP | HS25 | 257159 |
| VR-CLA | FA10 | 203 |
| VR-CLD | FA50 | 134 |
| VR-CLE | CL61 | 3066 |
| VR-CLI | CL60 | 1054 |
| VR-CLN | FA50 | 251 |
| VR-CMC | CL61 | 5044 |
| (VR-CMC) | GLF3 | 423 |
| VR-CMF | GLF3 | 374 |
| VR-CMF | GLF4 | 1062 |
| VR-CMG | ASTR | 034 |
| VR-CML | LJ55 | 033 |
| VR-CMO | C500 | 070 |
| VR-CMS | C500 | 511 |
| VR-CMZ | HS25 | 259021 |
| VR-CNJ | GLF3 | 426 |
| VR-CNM | JSTR | 5229 |
| VR-CNS | C560 | 0177 |
| VR-CNV | FA50 | 224 |
| VR-COG | BE40 | RK-7 |
| VR-COJ | CL61 | 5043 |
| VR-COJ | CL61 | 5104 |
| VR-COJ | CL61 | 5152 |
| VR-COM | C500 | 318 |
| VR-CPA | GLF2 | 204 |
| VR-CPO | CL61 | 5165 |
| VR-CPT | HS25 | 259004 |
| VR-CQZ | FA50 | 168 |
| VR-CRT | FA50 | 88 |
| VR-CSA | F900 | 61 |
| VR-CSF | HS25 | 256065 |
| VR-CSM | JSTR | 5092/58 |
| VR-CSP | C500 | 165 |
| VR-CSS | C550 | 030 |
| VR-CTA | F900 | 16 |
| VR-CTA | GLF4 | 1278 |
| VR-CTB | C500 | 432 |
| VR-CTE | C550 | 716 |
| VR-CTG | GLF3 | 450 |
| VR-CTL | C560 | 0023 |
| VR-CUB | GLF2 | 207/34 |
| VR-CUC | LJ35 | 203 |
| VR-CVD | HS25 | 257107 |
| VR-CVK | CL61 | 5049 |
| VR-CVP | C650 | 0210 |
| VR-CWI | FA50 | 159 |
| VR-CWM | C550 | 667 |
| VR-CWW | C500 | 044 |
| VR-CXX | HS25 | 259032 |
| VR-CYM | GLF4 | 1090 |
| VR-CYR | HFB3 | 1057 |

Hong Kong
(see also B-H)

| | | |
|---|---|---|
| VR-HIM | HS25 | 257001 |
| VR-HIN | HS25 | 257025 |
| VR-HSS | HS25 | 257169 |

India

| | | |
|---|---|---|
| **VT-** | **C550** | **550-1096** |
| (VT- ) | C56X | 5711 |
| VT-AAA | HS25 | 257161 |
| **VT-AAT** | **F2TH** | **225** |
| **VT-AGP** | **HS25** | **258835** |
| **VT-AKU** | **F9EX** | **177** |
| **VT-AMA** | **GLF4** | **1060** |
| **VT-ANF** | **PRM1** | **RB-128** |
| **VT-APL** | **CL65** | **5787** |
| **VT-ARA** | **C56X** | **5115** |
| **VT-ARR** | **HS25** | **258819** |
| **VT-ARV** | **GALX** | **098** |
| **VT-BAJ** | **GLEX** | **9149** |
| **VT-BAV** | **ASTR** | **143** |
| **VT-BJA** | **C52A** | **0170** |
| (VT-BJC) | C52A | 0430 |
| (VT-BJD) | C52A | 0436 |
| VT-BKG | PRM1 | RB-225 |
| **VT-BKL** | **HS25** | **HA-0103** |
| **VT-BPS** | **C52A** | **0410** |
| **VT-BRK** | **F2EX** | **169** |
| **VT-BRT** | **C52A** | **0373** |
| **VT-BSL** | **C56X** | **5816** |
| **VT-BTA** | **HS25** | **258904** |
| **VT-BTB** | **HS25** | **258909** |
| **VT-BTC** | **HS25** | **258912** |
| **VT-CAP** | **F9EX** | **205** |
| **VT-CLA** | **C56X** | **5010** |
| **VT-CLB** | **C550** | **661** |
| **VT-CLC** | **C550** | **698** |
| **VT-CLD** | **C550** | **727** |
| **VT-CMO** | **HS25** | **HB-30** |
| VT-COT | F2TH | 36 |
| **VT-CRA** | **LJ45** | **019** |
| **VT-CSP** | **C56X** | **5368** |
| **VT-DBA** | **GLEX** | **9289** |
| **VT-DBG** | **CL64** | **5342** |
| **VT-DHA** | **GLEX** | **9111** |
| VT-DLF | GLF4 | 1231 |
| **VT-DOV** | **C52A** | **0222** |
| VT-EAU | HS25 | 258120 |
| **VT-EHS** | **LJ28** | **29-003** |
| **VT-EIH** | **LJ28** | **29-004** |
| **VT-ENR** | **GLF3** | **420** |
| **VT-EQZ** | **HS25** | **25133** |
| VT-ERO | WW24 | 33 |
| **VT-ETG** | **CS55** | **0089** |
| VT-EUN | C550 | 393 |
| **VT-EUX** | **C560** | **0299** |
| **VT-FAF** | **HS25** | **258745** |
| **VT-GRG** | **BE40** | **RK-566** |
| VT-HBC | HS25 | 258531 |
| VT-HCB | HS25 | 258476 |
| **VT-HDL** | **F2TH** | **70** |
| **VT-HGL** | **F2TH** | **231** |
| **VT-HJA** | **HA4T** | **RC-26** |
| VT-HMA | GLEX | 9317 |
| **VT-IBR** | **CL64** | **5425** |
| **VT-IBS** | **C550** | **550-1076** |
| **VT-ICA** | **HS25** | **HA-0061** |
| **VT-IPA** | **C650** | **0203** |
| **VT-ISH** | **F9EX** | **166** |
| **VT-JHP** | **HS25** | **258794** |
| **VT-JSB** | **GLEX** | **9114** |
| **VT-JSE** | **CL30** | **20196** |
| **VT-JSK** | **GLEX** | **9214** |
| **VT-JSP** | **C52A** | **0207** |
| **VT-JSS** | **C56X** | **5594** |
| **VT-JUA** | **CL30** | **20273** |
| **VT-JUM** | **GALX** | **213** |
| VT-KAV | CL64 | 5370 |
| **VT-KBN** | **PRM1** | **RB-239** |
| **VT-KMB** | **CS55** | **0135** |
| **VT-KNB** | **HS25** | **258815** |
| **VT-MGF** | **CL64** | **5401** |
| **VT-MON** | **C52A** | **0126** |
| VT-MPA | HS25 | 257172 |
| **VT-MST** | **GLF4** | **1379** |
| **VT-NAB** | **C525** | **0619** |
| **VT-NGS** | **CL64** | **5314** |
| **VT-NJB** | **C52A** | **0163** |
| VT-OAM | BE40 | RJ-38 |
| **VT-OBE** | **HS25** | **257215** |
| **VT-OBR** | **HS25** | **258838** |
| **VT-ONE** | **GLF4** | **1231** |
| **VT-OPJ** | **C525** | **0112** |
| **VT-PLA** | **GALX** | **077** |
| **VT-PLL** | **GLF4** | **1254** |
| **VT-PSB** | **C52A** | **0402** |
| **VT-RAK** | **CL30** | **20174** |
| VT-RAL | PRM1 | RB-23 |
| **VT-RAN** | **HS25** | **258521** |
| VT-RAY | HS25 | 258165 |
| **VT-RBK** | **HS25** | **258716** |
| VT-RGX | FA7X | 49 |
| VT-RHM | CS55 | 0089 |
| **VT-RPG** | **BE40** | **RK-190** |
| **VT-RPL** | **HS25** | **258465** |
| **VT-RSR** | **HS25** | **HB-7** |
| **VT-RVL** | **F2TH** | **101** |
| **VT-SBK** | **F9EX** | **89** |
| **VT-SGT** | **C550** | **709** |
| **VT-SMI** | **GLF5** | **525** |
| **VT-SRA** | **HS25** | **258422** |
| VT-SRR | HS25 | 257191 |
| VT-STV | CL65 | 5750 |
| **VT-STV** | **GLEX** | **9262** |
| **VT-SWC** | **C56X** | **5168** |
| VT-SWP | LJ25 | 367 |
| **VT-TAT** | **F2TH** | **65** |
| **VT-TBT** | **F2TH** | **49** |
| **VT-TDT** | **F2EX** | **159** |
| **VT-TEL** | **BE40** | **RJ-46** |
| VT-TTA | FA20 | 511 |
| **VT-TVR** | **BE40** | **RK-511** |
| **VT-UBG** | **HS25** | **25254** |
| **VT-UPM** | **HS25** | **HA-0100** |
| **VT-UPN** | **PRM1** | **RB-236** |
| **VT-VDD** | **C56X** | **5783** |
| **VT-VED** | **C680** | **0056** |
| **VT-VID** | **C52A** | **0378** |
| (VT-VIP) | HA4T | RC-25 |
| **VT-VKR** | **F2DX** | **604** |
| **VT-VLM** | **F2TH** | **8** |
| **VT-VLN** | **F2EX** | **117** |
| VT-VPS | C550 | 269 |
| **VT-VRL** | **PRM1** | **RB-219** |
| **VT-VSA** | **LJ40** | **45-2101** |
| (VT-XLS) | C56X | 5594 |

Antigua

| | | |
|---|---|---|
| V2-LSF | HS25 | 256065 |

Namibia

| | | |
|---|---|---|
| **V5-CDM** | **C560** | **0151** |
| V5-KJY | LJ24 | 165 |
| **V5-LOW** | **C500** | **071** |
| **V5-NAG** | **LJ31** | **091** |
| **V5-NAM** | **F900** | **103** |
| **V5-NPC** | **LJ31** | **138** |
| **V5-OGL** | **C500** | **080** |

Brunei

| | | |
|---|---|---|
| V8-001 | GLF5 | 509 |
| V8-001 | GLF5 | 515 |
| V8-007 | GLF3 | 436 |
| V8-007 | GLF4 | 1059 |
| V8-007 | GLF4 | 1109 |
| V8-007 | GLF5 | 515 |
| V8-008 | GLF4 | 1176 |
| V8-009 | GLF3 | 436 |
| V8-009 | GLF4 | 1150 |
| V8-009 | GLF4 | 1202 |
| V8-009 | GLF5 | 509 |
| V8-A11 | GLF3 | 436 |
| V8-ALI | GLF4 | 1059 |
| V8-ALI | GLF4 | 1109 |
| V8-ALI | GLF4 | 1150 |
| V8-HB3 | GLF3 | 436 |
| V8-MSB | GLF4 | 1202 |
| V8-RB1 | GLF4 | 1059 |
| V8-SR1 | GLF4 | 1059 |
| V8-SR1 | GLF4 | 1109 |
| V8-SR1 | GLF4 | 1150 |

Mexico

| | | |
|---|---|---|
| **XA-** | **BE40** | **RK-242** |
| **XA-** | **BE40** | **RK-301** |
| **XA-** | **C500** | **261** |
| **XA-** | **C500** | **062** |
| **XA-** | **C550** | **381** |
| **XA-** | **C550** | **730** |
| **XA-** | **C550** | **550-1007** |
| (XA- ) | C560 | 0268 |
| (XA- ) | C650 | 0078 |
| **XA** | **C650** | **0007** |
| **XA-** | **C650** | **0201** |
| **XA-** | **C680** | **0206** |
| (XA- ) | CL61 | 5142 |
| **XA-** | **CS55** | **0065** |
| **XA-** | **F900** | **127** |
| **XA-** | **GLF2** | **180** |
| **XA-** | **GLF2** | **24** |
| XA- | GLF2 | 43 |
| **XA-** | **GLF2** | **97** |
| (XA- ) | GLF3 | 318 |
| **XA-** | **GLF4** | **1467** |
| (XA- ) | HS25 | 25066 |
| **XA-** | **HS25** | **25175** |
| **XA-** | **HS25** | **25179** |
| **XA-** | **HS25** | **25216** |
| **XA-** | **HS25** | **25220** |
| **XA-** | **HS25** | **256066** |
| **XA-** | **HS25** | **258176** |
| **XA-** | **HS25** | **258476** |
| **XA-** | **HS25** | **HA-0149** |
| (XA- ) | JSTR | 5089 |
| XA- | LJ24 | 039 |
| (XA- ) | LJ24 | 065 |
| **XA-** | **LJ24** | **093** |
| XA- | LJ24 | 197 |
| XA- | LJ24 | 213 |
| XA- | LJ24 | 237 |
| XA- | LJ24 | 252 |
| **XA-** | **LJ25** | **006** |
| **XA-** | **LJ25** | **096** |
| **XA-** | **LJ25** | **190** |
| **XA-** | **LJ25** | **210** |
| XA- | LJ25 | 216 |
| **XA-** | **LJ25** | **222** |
| XA- | LJ25 | 268 |
| **XA-** | **LJ25** | **270** |
| **XA-** | **LJ25** | **317** |
| **XA-** | **LJ31** | **209** |
| (XA- ) | LJ35 | 077 |
| **XA-** | **LJ35** | **332** |
| **XA-** | **LJ35** | **370** |
| **XA-** | **LJ60** | **175** |
| **XA-** | **SBRL** | **276-25** |
| **XA-** | **SBRL** | **282-24** |
| **XA-** | **SBRL** | **306-18** |
| **XA-** | **SBRL** | **380-48** |
| XA- | SBRL | 380-53 |
| **XA-** | **SBRL** | **465-72** |
| XA- | WW24 | 56 |
| **XA-AAA** | **LJ24** | **208** |
| (XA-AAF) | SBRL | 277-7 |
| (XA-AAG) | SBRL | 277-2 |
| (XA-AAH) | SBRL | 285-25 |
| (XA-AAI) | SBRL | 277-6 |
| (XA-AAJ) | SBRL | 285-1 |
| **XA-AAK** | **C550** | **486** |
| XA-AAL | JSTR | 5231 |

| | | |
|---|---|---|
| XA-AAP | LJ31 | 032 |
| XA-AAS | FA50 | 31 |
| XA-AAS | LJ25 | 305 |
| XA-AAW | SBRL | 282-85 |
| **XA-AAY** | **FA10** | **27** |
| XA-ABA | GLF2 | 136 |
| **XA-ABA** | **GLF3** | **426** |
| XA-ABA | GLF4 | 1425 |
| XA-ABB | LJ24 | 299 |
| XA-ABC | GLF2 | 161 |
| XA-ABC | SBRL | 306-63 |
| XA-ABD | GLF3 | 393 |
| **XA-ABE** | **C550** | **550-0887** |
| XA-ABF | FA20 | 327 |
| XA-ABH | LJ25 | 298 |
| XA-ACA | FA20 | 179 |
| XA-ACC | JSTR | 5212 |
| XA-ACC | LJ24 | 297 |
| XA-ACC | LJ35 | 176 |
| XA-ACD | SBRL | 380-50 |
| XA-ACE | SBRL | 306-12 |
| **XA-ACH** | **C650** | **0218** |
| XA-ACI | FA20 | 7 |
| **XA-ACN** | **HS25** | **256038** |
| **XA-ACX** | **LJ25** | **373** |
| XA-ADC | SBRL | 306-6 |
| XA-ADD | LJ24 | 298 |
| **XA-ADJ** | **LJ24** | **060** |
| **XA-ADR** | **ASTR** | **257** |
| XA-ADR | HS25 | 25146 |
| **XA-AEB** | **C650** | **0099** |
| XA-AED | LJ45 | 140 |
| **XA-AEI** | **C500** | **213** |
| **XA-AEM** | **HS25** | **HB-22** |
| XA-AEN | HS25 | 258232 |
| XA-AET | HS25 | 258502 |
| **XA-AET** | **HS25** | **HA-0045** |
| XA-AEV | SBRL | 306-125 |
| **XA-AEX** | **GLF4** | **1064** |
| XA-AEZ | CS55 | 0090 |
| **XA-AFA** | **BE40** | **RK-316** |
| (XA-AFG) | FA50 | 94 |
| XA-AFG | SBRL | 306-130 |
| **XA-AFH** | **LJ25** | **332** |
| XA-AFP | GLF2 | 136 |
| XA-AFS | BE40 | RK-259 |
| XA-AFU | C550 | 661 |
| XA-AFW | SBRL | 282-63 |
| **XA-AFX** | **LJ31** | **159** |
| **XA-AGA** | **C500** | **469** |
| **XA-AGL** | **HS25** | **25236** |
| XA-AGL | HS25 | 256046 |
| **XA-AGN** | **C550** | **082** |
| **XA-AGT** | **SBRL** | **306-58** |
| **XA-AHM** | **GLF2** | **161** |
| **XA-AIM** | **LJ45** | **077** |
| XA-AIS | GLF4 | 1098 |
| **XA-AJL** | **LJ25** | **120** |
| XA-ALA | FA50 | 188 |
| **XA-ALA** | **LJ45** | **210** |
| XA-ALE | LJ35 | 047 |
| **XA-ALF** | **LJ45** | **127** |
| **XA-ALT** | **C52B** | **0307** |
| XA-ALV | LJ25 | 124 |
| **XA-AMI** | **HS25** | **257098** |
| **XA-AOV** | **SBRL** | **380-60** |
| XA-APD | SBRL | 282-123 |
| XA-APD | SBRL | 306-33 |
| **XA-APE** | **F900** | **178** |
| **XA-ARA** | **GLF2** | **79** |
| **XA-ARB** | **LJ45** | **284** |
| XA-ARE | SBRL | 306-146 |
| XA-ARE | SBRL | 465-27 |
| XA-ARG | LJ24 | 068 |
| **XA-ARQ** | **LJ31** | **141** |
| XA-ARS | C650 | 0156 |
| **XA-ASI** | **GLF4** | **1180** |
| **XA-ASP** | **LJ25** | **315** |
| XA-ASR | C500 | 199 |
| XA-AST | CL64 | 5357 |
| XA-ATA | LJ35 | 264 |
| **XA-ATC** | **HS25** | **256026** |
| XA-ATC | SBRL | 282-114 |
| **XA-ATE** | **SBRL** | **306-123** |
| **XA-ATL** | **GLF5** | **5052** |
| **XA-AVE** | **F2TH** | **175** |
| XA-AVE | FA50 | 22 |
| XA-AVE | WW24 | 160 |
| XA-AVR | GLF2 | 200 |
| XA-AVR | SBRL | 465-27 |
| **XA-AVV** | **LJ25** | **079** |
| **XA-AVX** | **C52B** | **0192** |
| **XA-AVZ** | **GLF4** | **1010** |
| **XA-AZT** | **GLF5** | **554** |
| **XA-BAE** | **C750** | **0136** |
| XA-BAF | SBRL | 282-39 |
| XA-BAL | GLF2 | 237/43 |
| XA-BAL | GLF4 | 1114 |
| **XA-BAL** | **GLF5** | **546** |
| XA-BAT | C510 | 0044 |
| XA-BBA | LJ25 | 223 |
| XA-BBE | LJ24 | 255 |
| **XA-BBO** | **GLF2** | **164** |
| XA-BCC | CRVT | 36 |
| XA-BCC | FA20 | 284 |
| XA-BCE | JSTR | 5053/2 |
| **XA-BEB** | **JSTR** | **5132/57** |
| **XA-BEG** | **F9EX** | **33** |
| XA-BEG | FA50 | 224 |
| XA-BEM | HS25 | 25068 |
| **XA-BET** | **C500** | **296** |
| **XA-BFX** | **LJ45** | **111** |
| XA-BNG | BE40 | RJ-33 |
| XA-BNO | LJ35 | 336 |
| XA-BOA | C500 | 607 |
| XA-BOJ | HS25 | 25060 |
| XA-BQA | WW24 | 276 |
| XA-BRE | GLF2 | 185 |
| XA-BRE | LJ35 | 373 |
| **XA-BRE** | **LJ60** | **058** |
| XA-BRG | LJ31 | 032 |
| **XA-BUA** | **GLEX** | **9322** |
| XA-BUX | LJ35 | 020 |
| **XA-BUX** | **LJ35** | **176** |
| XA-BUY | LJ24 | 270 |
| **XA-BVG** | **GLF4** | **1013** |
| **XA-BYP** | **HS25** | **257041** |
| XA-CAG | GLF4 | 1197 |
| XA-CAH | C525 | 0210 |
| XA-CAH | HS25 | 256044 |
| **XA-CAP** | **C550** | **550-1070** |
| XA-CAP | LJ24 | 349 |
| XA-CCB | SBRL | 306-12 |
| XA-CCC | LJ25 | 219 |
| XA-CDF | C560 | 0433 |
| XA-CEG | FA10 | 146 |
| **XA-CEN** | **SBRL** | **306-26** |
| **XA-CFX** | **LJ45** | **209** |
| **XA-CGF** | **LJ40** | **45-2040** |
| **XA-CHA** | **HS25** | **258241** |
| XA-CHA | SBRL | 380-58 |
| **XA-CHG** | **HS25** | **258731** |
| **XA-CHP** | **SBRL** | **306-22** |
| XA-CHR | GLF2 | 98/38 |
| XA-CHR | GLF4 | 1195 |
| XA-CHR | GLF4 | 1250 |
| **XA-CHR** | **GLF5** | **5182** |
| XA-CIS | SBRL | 306-63 |
| XA-CLA | BE40 | RK-3 |
| **XA-CMM** | **F2EX** | **121** |
| XA-CMN | SBRL | 306-56 |
| XA-COC | LJ25 | 194 |
| XA-COI | LJ35 | 620 |
| **XA-COI** | **LJ60** | **174** |
| XA-COL | HS25 | 25086 |
| **XA-CON** | **JSTR** | **5228** |
| **XA-CPQ** | **GLF5** | **533** |
| XA-CPQ | SBRL | 282-48 |
| **XA-CTK** | **C650** | **7069** |
| XA-CUR | SBRL | 306-127 |
| XA-CUZ | HS25 | 25279 |
| XA-CVD | LJ35 | 370 |
| XA-CVE | JSTR | 5214 |
| **XA-CVS** | **GLF2** | **167** |
| **XA-CXW** | **FA7X** | **32** |
| **XA-CYA** | **LJ31** | **021** |
| **XA-CYS** | **SBRL** | **282-79** |
| **XA-CZG** | **LJ35** | **162** |
| XA-DAJ | C500 | 241 |
| XA-DAK | LJ25 | 190 |
| **XA-DAN** | **HS25** | **25158** |
| XA-DAN | SBRL | 282-26 |
| XA-DAT | LJ24 | 322 |
| XA-DAZ | LJ25 | 309 |
| **XA-DAZ** | **LJ35** | **340** |
| XA-DCO | SBRL | 306-38 |
| **XA-DCS** | **HS25** | **25078** |
| **XA-DET** | **LJ24** | **337** |
| **XA-DGO** | **LJ60** | **172** |
| XA-DGP | C525 | 0329 |
| **XA-DIJ** | **LJ24** | **269** |
| XA-DIN | HS25 | 25273 |
| XA-DIN | LJ31 | 026 |
| XA-DIW | HS25 | 25226 |
| **XA-DLA** | **CL30** | **20203** |
| (XA-DMS) | FA50 | 249 |
| XA-DOS | BE40 | RK-238 |
| XA-DPS | GLF4 | 1227 |
| **XA-DRM** | **C56X** | **5307** |
| **XA-DSC** | **SBRL** | **306-56** |
| **XA-DST** | **C56X** | **5819** |
| XA-DUB | LJ25 | 306 |
| **XA-DUC** | **FA20** | **269** |
| **XA-DUQ** | **FA50** | **146** |
| **XA-EAJ** | **GLF5** | **604** |
| XA-EAS | LJ25 | 355 |
| XA-ECM | SBRL | 306-89 |
| XA-ECR | FA20 | 513 |
| **XA-EEA** | **LJ45** | **102** |
| XA-EEU | SBRL | 282-54 |
| **XA-EFM** | **LJ45** | **089** |
| **XA-EFX** | **LJ31** | **234** |
| XA-EGC | SBRL | 282-61 |
| XA-EHR | GLF2 | 30/4 |
| XA-EKO | C500 | 140 |
| **XA-EKT** | **JSTR** | **5234** |
| **XA-ELM** | **HS25** | **258051** |
| XA-ELR | LJ25 | 290 |
| XA-ELU | LJ35 | 261 |
| XA-EMA | HS25 | 25282 |
| XA-EMO | JSTR | 5140 |
| XA-EOF | GLF4 | 1473 |
| XA-EOF | GLF5 | 5008 |
| XA-EPM | SBRL | 380-19 |
| **XA-ERH** | **GLF3** | **323** |
| XA-ESC | GLF2 | 164 |
| **XA-ESP** | **HS25** | **HA-0068** |
| XA-ESQ | HS25 | 25028 |
| XA-ESQ | LJ25 | 234 |
| XA-ESR | SBRL | 282-59 |
| XA-ESS | LJ24 | 037 |
| **XA-EVG** | **CL64** | **5357** |
| XA-EYA | GLF2 | 96 |
| **XA-EYA** | **GLF4** | **1388** |
| XA-FCP | C650 | 0165 |
| XA-FCP | GLF2 | 136 |
| **XA-FCP** | **GLF4** | **1404** |
| XA-FES | JSTR | 5155/32 |
| **XA-FEX** | **F9EX** | **46** |
| XA-FFF | LJ35 | 042 |
| **XA-FGS** | **HS25** | **258047** |
| XA-FHR | GLF2 | 30/4 |
| XA-FHR | JSTR | 5158 |
| XA-FHR | JSTR | 5231 |
| XA-FHS | JSTR | 5215 |
| XA-FIR | C550 | 718 |
| XA-FIU | FA10 | 83 |
| XA-FIU | JSTR | 5100/41 |
| XA-FIW | LJ24 | 296 |
| XA-FLM | FA20 | 364 |
| **XA-FLX** | **BE40** | **RK-503** |
| **XA-FLY** | **LJ60** | **250** |
| **XA-FMK** | **HS25** | **257068** |
| **XA-FMR** | **LJ25** | **274** |
| **XA-FMT** | **LJ35** | **672** |
| XA-FMU | LJ25 | 249 |
| **XA-FMX** | **C750** | **0119** |
| XA-FNP | SBRL | 306-63 |
| XA-FNY | GLF2 | 175 |
| **XA-FNY** | **GLF2** | **211** |
| XA-FOU | GLF2 | 152 |
| XA-FOU | GLF3 | 449 |
| **XA-FRD** | **CL30** | **20078** |
| **XA-FRI** | **C650** | **7081** |
| **XA-FRO** | **BE40** | **RK-110** |
| "XA-FRO" | CL30 | 20078 |
| XA-FRP | HS25 | 25185 |
| XA-FTC | FA50 | 80 |
| XA-FTN | SBRL | 282-80 |
| **XA-FUD** | **C680** | **0053** |
| **XA-FVK** | **FA50** | **35** |
| XA-FVK | SBRL | 465-27 |
| **XA-FYN** | **HS25** | **258386** |
| XA-GAC | GLF2 | 155/14 |
| XA-GAE | F900 | 137 |
| XA-GAM | LJ24 | 033 |
| XA-GAN | C650 | 0218 |
| **XA-GAN** | **C680** | **0043** |
| **XA-GAO** | **BE40** | **RK-353** |
| **XA-GAP** | **SBRL** | **465-8** |
| XA-GBA | LJ24 | 260 |
| **XA-GBM** | **C650** | **0234** |
| **XA-GCC** | **HS25** | **258252** |
| **XA-GCD** | **CL61** | **5121** |
| **XA-GCH** | **FA50** | **50** |
| XA-GCH | SBRL | 282-115 |
| **XA-GDO** | **LJ35** | **449** |
| **XA-GDW** | **SBRL** | **265-86** |
| **XA-GEG** | **GLF2** | **253** |
| **XA-GEN** | **C550** | **550-0999** |
| XA-GEO | CL61 | 5059 |
| XA-GEO | LJ24 | 337 |
| XA-GFB | HS25 | 258075 |
| XA-GFC | FA50 | 80 |
| **XA-GGG** | **LJ25** | **147** |
| XA-GGR | SBRL | 282-65 |
| XA-GHR | SBRL | 380-58 |
| XA-GIC | HS25 | 257206 |
| **XA-GIC** | **HS25** | **258183** |
| **XA-GIE** | **HS25** | **258302** |
| XA-GIH | SBRL | 306-72 |
| **XA-GJC** | **C650** | **0035** |
| **XA-GLG** | **HS25** | **258583** |
| **XA-GMD** | **F9EX** | **99** |
| XA-GMD | FA50 | 291 |
| XA-GMD | LJ31 | 005 |
| **XA-GME** | **CL61** | **5128** |
| **XA-GMO** | **C680** | **0004** |
| **XA-GMP** | **C550** | **254** |
| **XA-GMX** | **GLF4** | **4102** |
| **XA-GNI** | **F2EX** | **20** |
| XA-GNI | F2TH | 60 |
| XA-GNL | LJ25 | 329 |
| XA-GOC | HS25 | 25107 |
| **XA-GPA** | **FA10** | **23** |
| (XA-GPE) | LJ40 | 45-2040 |
| **XA-GPR** | **CL30** | **20084** |
| **XA-GPS** | **C650** | **0226** |
| XA-GRB | CL61 | 5149 |
| **XA-GRB** | **CL64** | **5375** |
| XA-GRB | HS25 | 259021 |
| XA-GRB | LJ25 | 309 |
| **XA-GRR** | **LJ40** | **45-2013** |
| **XA-GSS** | **C560** | **0533** |
| **XA-GTC** | **HS25** | **25205** |
| **XA-GTE** | **HS25** | **258554** |
| **XA-GTP** | **LJ45** | **256** |
| XA-GTR | F900 | 107 |
| **XA-GUA** | **CL61** | **5076** |
| XA-GUB | HS25 | 25185 |
| XA-GUR | SBRL | 306-122 |
| XA-GUR | SBRL | 306-131 |
| **XA-GUR** | **SBRL** | **306-98** |
| **XA-GYA** | **C550** | **287** |
| XA-GYR | SBRL | 282-6 |
| XA-GZA | JSTR | 5100/41 |
| XA-HEV | C500 | 382 |
| XA-HEW | FA20 | 250 |
| XA-HFM | HS25 | 25107 |
| XA-HFM | LJ45 | 246 |
| XA-HGF | FA50 | 236 |
| XA-HGF | LJ31 | 026 |
| **XA-HHF** | **F2TH** | **85** |
| XA-HHF | FA20 | 327 |
| XA-HHF | FA50 | 236 |
| XA-HHR | SBRL | 306-6 |
| **XA-HIT** | **C680** | **0014** |
| XA-HNY | JSTR | 5162 |
| XA-HOK | SBRL | 282-17 |
| **XA-HOM** | **HS25** | **257199** |
| XA-HOO | C500 | 175 |
| XA-HOS | LJ35 | 045 |
| XA-HOS | LJ35 | 341 |
| XA-HOU | HS25 | 25060 |
| XA-HRM | JSTR | 5066/46 |
| XA-HRM | LJ31 | 026 |
| XA-HRM | LJ31 | 044 |
| **XA-HUR** | **LJ45** | **385** |
| **XA-HVP** | **C650** | **0032** |
| **XA-HXM** | **HS25** | **257084** |
| XA-HYS | LJ35 | 243 |
| XA-IAS | PRM1 | RB-9 |

| | | |
|---|---|---|
| **XA-IBC** | **LJ60** | **124** |
| XA-ICA | LJ60 | 027 |
| XA-ICF | HS25 | 258581 |
| XA-ICG | FA20 | 159 |
| XA-ICK | SBRL | 306-86 |
| XA-ICO | C560 | 0461 |
| **XA-ICO** | **C56X** | **5196** |
| XA-ICP | C550 | 631 |
| XA-IEM | C500 | 384 |
| XA-IGE | CL64 | 5580 |
| XA-III | FA20 | 264 |
| XA-IIT | HS25 | 25152 |
| XA-IIX | C500 | 274 |
| **XA-IKE** | **LJ45** | **176** |
| XA-ILV | GLF2 | 195 |
| XA-IMY | CL61 | 5189 |
| XA-INF | C650 | 0198 |
| XA-INF | CS55 | 0010 |
| XA-INK | CS55 | 0010 |
| XA-ISH | HS25 | 258036 |
| XA-ISR | CL60 | 1057 |
| **XA-ISR** | **F900** | **147** |
| **XA-IZA** | **HS25** | **258129** |
| **XA-JAI** | **HS25** | **257171** |
| XA-JAM | BE40 | RK-56 |
| XA-JAX | LJ25 | 104 |
| **XA-JBT** | **HS25** | **258715** |
| XA-JCE | C500 | 544 |
| XA-JCE | SBRL | 306-93 |
| XA-JCG | JSTR | 5140 |
| **XA-JCP** | **CL30** | **20014** |
| **XA-JCT** | **HS25** | **258581** |
| XA-JEL | C500 | 250 |
| XA-JEQ | HS25 | 256047 |
| XA-JET | BE40 | RK-163 |
| **XA-JET** | **HS25** | **258628** |
| (XA-JEW) | C500 | 533 |
| XA-JEX | C500 | 530 |
| XA-JEZ | C550 | 140 |
| XA-JFE | C500 | 544 |
| XA-JFE | CL61 | 5059 |
| **XA-JFE** | **CL64** | **5525** |
| XA-JFE | JSTR | 5145 |
| **XA-JGT** | **CL30** | **20007** |
| **XA-JHE** | **GALX** | **086** |
| XA-JHR | JSTR | 5066/46 |
| XA-JIK | SBRL | 306-130 |
| XA-JIN | LJ25 | 210 |
| **XA-JIQ** | **LJ24** | **317** |
| XA-JIX | HS25 | 257079 |
| XA-JJA | BE40 | RJ-33 |
| **XA-JJJ** | **LJ35** | **460** |
| XA-JJS | CL61 | 5097 |
| **XA-JJS** | **GLF4** | **1113** |
| XA-JJS | JSTR | 5101/15 |
| XA-JJS | LJ60 | 131 |
| XA-JLV | C500 | 021 |
| XA-JLV | LJ24 | 136 |
| XA-JMD | SBRL | 306-119 |
| **XA-JMF** | **LJ45** | **178** |
| XA-JML | JSTR | 5206 |
| **XA-JML** | **SBRL** | **306-125** |
| **XA-JMM** | **BE40** | **RJ-33** |
| XA-JMN | JSTR | 5134/50 |
| XA-JMS | HS25 | 258582 |
| **XA-JOC** | **LJ25** | **303** |
| XA-JOV | C500 | 035 |
| XA-JPA | C550 | 689 |
| **XA-JPS** | **GLF4** | **1250** |
| XA-JRF | C550 | 642 |
| XA-JRF | HS25 | 25202 |
| XA-JRF | HS25 | 256018 |
| XA-JRF | HS25 | 257059 |
| **XA-JRF** | **SBRL** | **380-32** |
| XA-JRH | LJ35 | 609 |
| XA-JRM | ASTR | 039 |
| **XA-JRT** | **C510** | **0034** |
| **XA-JRV** | **C500** | **136** |
| XA-JSC | LJ24 | 123 |
| XA-JSC | LJ25 | 152 |
| **XA-JSC** | **LJ25** | **173** |
| XA-JSO | LJ24 | 123 |
| XA-JUA | C500 | 247 |
| XA-JUD | SBRL | 282-43 |
| XA-JUE | SBRL | 282-48 |
| XA-JUZ | HS25 | 25014 |
| **XA-JWM** | **LJ60** | **221** |
| **XA-JYC** | **LJ31** | **030** |

| | | |
|---|---|---|
| **XA-JYL** | **LJ25** | **336** |
| XA-JYO | C550 | 689 |
| **XA-JZL** | **CL61** | **5158** |
| XA-KAC | HS25 | 257110 |
| XA-KAH | C500 | 289 |
| XA-KAJ | LJ28 | 28-004 |
| **XA-KBA** | **HS25** | **258984** |
| **XA-KBL** | **HS25** | **HA-0052** |
| XA-KCM | LJ35 | 418 |
| **XA-KCM** | **LJ60** | **291** |
| XA-KEW | HS25 | 257096 |
| XA-KEY | LJ25 | 222 |
| **XA-KIM** | **CL61** | **3015** |
| XA-KIQ | C550 | 181 |
| XA-KIS | HS25 | 257102 |
| **XA-KJM** | **BE40** | **RK-56** |
| **XA-KKK** | **LJ25** | **169** |
| **XA-KLZ** | **LJ60** | **297** |
| XA-KMX | C550 | 247 |
| **XA-KMX** | **C650** | **0039** |
| **XA-KOF** | **HS25** | **25065** |
| XA-KON | HS25 | 257108 |
| **XA-KTY** | **HS25** | **258004** |
| XA-KUG | WW24 | 224 |
| XA-KUJ | C500 | 313 |
| XA-KUT | HS25 | 256028 |
| **XA-LAA** | **GLF4** | **4026** |
| XA-LAN | LJ35 | 267 |
| XA-LAP | LJ25 | 336 |
| XA-LAR | LJ24 | 074 |
| **XA-LCA** | **GLF3** | **489** |
| XA-LEG | BE40 | RJ-60 |
| **XA-LEG** | **BE40** | **RK-171** |
| XA-LEG | HS25 | 257046 |
| XA-LEG | SBRL | 282-100 |
| XA-LEG | SBRL | 380-15 |
| (XA-LEI) | SBRL | 306-115 |
| XA-LEL | SBRL | 282-68 |
| XA-LEO | C500 | 273 |
| XA-LET | LJ25 | 244 |
| **XA-LEY** | **C650** | **0073** |
| **XA-LFA** | **F2EX** | **77** |
| XA-LFU | HS25 | 25112 |
| XA-LGM | LJ24 | 033 |
| XA-LIJ | WW24 | 285 |
| XA-LIM | C500 | 571 |
| XA-LIO | FA10 | 40 |
| XA-LIX | SBRL | 282-128 |
| **XA-LLA** | **CL30** | **20191** |
| **XA-LLL** | **LJ25** | **015** |
| **XA-LMA** | **SBRL** | **282-137** |
| **XA-LMG** | **BE40** | **RK-416** |
| XA-LML | HS25 | 257076 |
| XA-LML | LJ35 | 296 |
| **XA-LML** | **SBRL** | **282-115** |
| **XA-LMS** | **LJ31** | **012** |
| **XA-LNK** | **LJ24** | **174** |
| (XA-LOA^) | LJ40 | 45-2117 |
| XA-LOB | FA20 | 39 |
| **XA-LOF** | **C550** | **550-0989** |
| XA-LOF | LJ25 | 338 |
| XA-LOH | FA50 | 9 |
| XA-LOK | FA10 | 175 |
| XA-LOQ | SBRL | 306-145 |
| XA-LOR | WW24 | 319 |
| XA-LOT | C550 | 244 |
| **XA-LOV** | **HS25** | **25283** |
| XA-LRA | FA50 | 238 |
| XA-LRA | SBRL | 306-63 |
| **XA-LRD** | **LJ31** | **176** |
| **XA-LRJ** | **LJ25** | **359** |
| XA-LRL | C550 | 619 |
| XA-LRX | LJ45 | 067 |
| XA-LTH | C550 | 462 |
| XA-LTH | C650 | 0101 |
| XA-LUC | SBRL | 465-55 |
| XA-LUD | C500 | 587 |
| XA-LUN | C500 | 353 |
| XA-LUV | C500 | 598 |
| XA-LUZ | LJ25 | 314 |
| XA-LYM | WW24 | 133 |
| XA-LZZ | GLF2 | 18 |
| XA-MAH | HS25 | 256065 |
| XA-MAK | GALX | 013 |
| XA-MAK | WW24 | 342 |
| XA-MAK | WW24 | 350 |
| XA-MAL | C500 | 373 |
| XA-MAL | LJ25 | 274 |

| | | |
|---|---|---|
| **XA-MAM** | **FA20** | **506** |
| **XA-MAR** | **FA7X** | **10** |
| XA-MAR | WW24 | 264 |
| **XA-MAV** | **F2TH** | **149** |
| XA-MAZ | JSTR | 5079/33 |
| XA-MBM | HS25 | 25030 |
| **XA-MBM** | **HS25** | **25101** |
| **XA-MCC** | **LJ25** | **219** |
| **XA-MDK** | **GALX** | **080** |
| **XA-MDM** | **LJ60** | **089** |
| **XA-MEG** | **ASTR** | **154** |
| XA-MEM | GLF2 | 69 |
| XA-MEX | BE40 | RK-196 |
| **XA-MEX** | **BE40** | **RK-396** |
| XA-MEY | GLF3 | 252 |
| XA-MGM | BE40 | RK-16 |
| XA-MGM | FA10 | 100 |
| **XA-MGM** | **LJ31** | **101** |
| XA-MHA | LJ25 | 222 |
| XA-MIC | GLF3 | 323 |
| XA-MII | BE40 | RJ-58 |
| XA-MII | BE40 | RK-83 |
| XA-MIK | JSTR | 5066/46 |
| XA-MIR | HS25 | 25068 |
| XA-MIX | GLF2 | 237/43 |
| **XA-MJE** | **SBRL** | **282-65** |
| XA-MJG | LJ31 | 044 |
| XA-MJI | HS25 | 257033 |
| XA-MKI | CL61 | 5158 |
| **XA-MKI** | **GLF5** | **664** |
| XA-MKY | CL61 | 5158 |
| **XA-MKY** | **HS25** | **256064** |
| XA-MLG | SBRL | 465-48 |
| **XA-MMM** | **FA10** | **36** |
| XA-MMO | LJ25 | 352 |
| **XA-MMX** | **C56X** | **5639** |
| XA-MNA | SBRL | 282-115 |
| XA-MOV | LJ24 | 269 |
| **XA-MPS** | **GLF5** | **654** |
| XA-MPS | LJ35 | 460 |
| XA-MRS | LJ31 | 024 |
| **XA-MSA** | **FA20** | **327** |
| XA-MSH | HS25 | 257128 |
| XA-MSH | LJ35 | 380 |
| XA-MTZ | C650 | 0218 |
| XA-MUI | WW24 | 160 |
| XA-MUL | SBRL | 306-50 |
| **XA-MUU** | **LJ25** | **008** |
| XA-MVG | LJ45 | 251 |
| XA-MVG | SBRL | 282-134 |
| XA-MVR | FA50 | 94 |
| XA-MVT | SBRL | 380-42 |
| **XA-MYN** | **CL61** | **5142** |
| XA-NAY | FA20 | 269 |
| **XA-NCC** | **FA20** | **264** |
| **XA-NEM** | **HS25** | **257158** |
| **XA-NGS** | **GLEX** | **9014** |
| XA-NGS | HS25 | 258232 |
| **XA-NJM** | **LJ40** | **45-2067** |
| **XA-NLA** | **LJ24** | **180** |
| **XA-NLK** | **LJ24** | **109** |
| XA-NOG | LJ25 | 349 |
| XA-NTE | HS25 | 256020 |
| XA-NTE | HS25 | 257098 |
| **XA-NTE** | **HS25** | **258638** |
| XA-OAC | BE40 | RJ-29 |
| **XA-OAC** | **BE40** | **RJ-36** |
| XA-OAC | C500 | 514 |
| XA-OAC | C550 | 297 |
| XA-OAF | SBRL | 380-55 |
| XA-ODC | C500 | 217 |
| XA-ODC | C550 | 553 |
| **XA-OEM** | **GLF5** | **540** |
| XA-OFA | LJ35 | 370 |
| **XA-OHS** | **CL61** | **5087** |
| **XA-OLE** | **LJ31** | **044** |
| XA-OLI | JSTR | 5148 |
| **XA-ORA** | **LJ60** | **245** |
| **XA-ORO** | **LJ35** | **290** |
| XA-OVA | F900 | 141 |
| XA-OVR | F900 | 141 |
| XA-OVR | FA50 | 88 |
| **XA-OVR** | **GLEX** | **9119** |
| XA-OVR | SBRL | 306-130 |
| XA-OVR | SBRL | 465-12 |
| XA-PAX | SBRL | 306-123 |
| **XA-PAZ** | **ASTR** | **255** |
| XA-PAZ | C500 | 060 |

| | | |
|---|---|---|
| XA-PAZ | LJ25 | 309 |
| **XA-PBT** | **HS25** | **258601** |
| **XA-PCC** | **FA20** | **159** |
| XA-PEI | SBRL | 306-20 |
| XA-PEK | SBRL | 306-38 |
| XA-PEN | LJ31 | 085 |
| XA-PES | JSTR | 5130 |
| (XA-PEV) | C500 | 607 |
| XA-PFA | LJ24 | 329 |
| XA-PFM | FA20 | 515 |
| XA-PGO | JSTR | 5069/20 |
| XA-PIC | C500 | 141 |
| XA-PIC | LJ31 | 076 |
| XA-PIC | SBRL | 282-39 |
| XA-PIH | SBRL | 282-102 |
| XA-PIJ | C550 | 082 |
| **XA-PIL** | **GLEX** | **9100** |
| XA-PIL | LJ55 | 014 |
| XA-PIM | LJ25 | 368 |
| XA-PIN | LJ35 | 201 |
| XA-PIP | C650 | 0146 |
| **XA-PIU** | **LJ25** | **293** |
| XA-POG | LJ25 | 080 |
| XA-POI | LJ25 | 152 |
| XA-POJ | WW24 | 161 |
| XA-PON | SBRL | 380-39 |
| XA-POO | JSTR | 5158 |
| XA-POP | LJ25 | 324 |
| XA-POQ | LJ25 | 351 |
| XA-POR | C550 | 273 |
| XA-POR | SBRL | 306-49 |
| XA-POS | LJ24 | 249 |
| XA-POU | JSTR | 5053/2 |
| XA-PRO | LJ25 | 216 |
| **XA-PRO** | **SBRL** | **306-72** |
| **XA-PRR** | **FA50** | **319** |
| XA-PSD | GLF2 | 98/38 |
| XA-PSD | JSTR | 5132/57 |
| **XA-PTR** | **CL61** | **5165** |
| XA-PUE | FA20 | 393 |
| **XA-PUF** | **WW24** | **153** |
| XA-PUI | LJ35 | 277 |
| XA-PUL | JSTR | 5151 |
| XA-PUR | SBRL | 306-2 |
| XA-PUV | GLF4 | 1079 |
| **XA-PVM** | **FA20** | **179** |
| **XA-PVR** | **C650** | **0076** |
| XA-PVR | SBRL | 465-12 |
| XA-PVR | WW24 | 174 |
| **XA-PWR** | **JSTR** | **5211** |
| XA-PYC | LJ35 | 336 |
| XA-PYN | BE40 | RK-68 |
| XA-PYN | C650 | 0099 |
| **XA-PYN** | **C650** | **7088** |
| **XA-QUE** | **LJ45** | **067** |
| **XA-RAB** | **LJ40** | **45-2047** |
| **XA-RAN** | **LJ31** | **179** |
| XA-RAP | CL60 | 1057 |
| **XA-RAP** | **SBRL** | **306-88** |
| XA-RAQ | LJ24 | 329 |
| **XA-RAR** | **BE40** | **RJ-32** |
| XA-RAV | LJ35 | 290 |
| XA-RAX | LJ25 | 218 |
| **XA-RBP** | **GLF2** | **14** |
| XA-RBS | GLF2 | 14 |
| **XA-RBS** | **GLF4** | **1102** |
| **XA-RBV** | **HS25** | **258275** |
| XA-RCG | LJ25 | 330 |
| XA-RCH | HS25 | 25101 |
| XA-RCM | GLF3 | 312 |
| **XA-RCM** | **GLF4** | **1081** |
| XA-RCR | JSTR | 5214 |
| XA-RDD | HS25 | 25030 |
| XA-RDM | C560 | 0342 |
| XA-RDY | SBRL | 380-60 |
| XA-REA | LJ24 | 331 |
| XA-REC | SBRL | 306-1 |
| XA-RED | SBRL | 282-26 |
| XA-REE | LJ25 | 314 |
| XA-REG | SBRL | 282-130 |
| XA-REI | SBRL | 306-20 |
| XA-REK | LJ24 | 285 |
| XA-REN | C550 | 273 |
| XA-REO | WW24 | 124 |
| XA-RET | F2TH | 184 |
| **XA-RET** | **F9EX** | **203** |
| XA-RET | HS25 | 258004 |
| XA-RET | WW24 | 409 |

| | | |
|---|---|---|
| XA-REY | FA20 | 127 |
| XA-REY | FA20 | 393 |
| **XA-RFB** | **SBRL** | **306-87** |
| XA-RFS | LJ31 | 005 |
| XA-RGB | F900 | 15 |
| **XA-RGB** | **F9EX** | **129** |
| XA-RGB | JSTR | 5079/33 |
| XA-RGC | SBRL | 282-39 |
| XA-RGC | SBRL | 282-48 |
| XA-RGC | SBRL | 282-61 |
| XA-RGC | SBRL | 306-125 |
| XA-RGG | HS25 | 259037 |
| **XA-RGH** | **LJ35** | **412** |
| **XA-RGS** | **C650** | **0189** |
| **XA-RHA** | **FA20** | **379** |
| XA-RIA | LJ36 | 050 |
| XA-RIC | LJ24 | 251 |
| **XA-RIE** | **C650** | **0170** |
| XA-RIH | SBRL | 380-46 |
| XA-RIL | HS25 | 25237 |
| XA-RIN | LJ25 | 104 |
| XA-RIN | LJ35 | 152 |
| XA-RIR | SBRL | 306-36 |
| **XA-RIU** | **LJ45** | **038** |
| XA-RIW | WW24 | 86 |
| **XA-RIZ** | **WW24** | **160** |
| **XA-RJT** | **LJ35** | **011** |
| XA-RKE | FA20 | 508 |
| XA-RKG | SBRL | 282-106 |
| XA-RKH | C560 | 0156 |
| XA-RKP | LJ25 | 353 |
| XA-RKX | C560 | 0147 |
| XA-RKY | LJ35 | 370 |
| XA-RLE | C500 | 544 |
| **XA-RLH** | **SBRL** | **282-129** |
| XA-RLI | LJ25 | 353 |
| XA-RLL | SBRL | 306-83 |
| XA-RLP | SBRL | 380-4 |
| XA-RLR | SBRL | 306-100 |
| XA-RLR | SBRL | 380-50 |
| XA-RLS | SBRL | 306-57 |
| XA-RLX | FA10 | 226 |
| XA-RMA | FA20 | 39 |
| XA-RMD | JSTR | 5228 |
| XA-RMF | LJ24 | 290 |
| XA-RMF | LJ25 | 308 |
| XA-RMN | HS25 | 25185 |
| **XA-RMT** | **LJ45** | **046** |
| XA-RMY | C650 | 0179 |
| XA-RNB | FA20 | 142 |
| XA-RNE | BE40 | RJ-61 |
| XA-RNG | BE40 | RJ-58 |
| XA-RNK | LJ31 | 021 |
| XA-RNR | SBRL | 306-49 |
| XA-ROC | LJ25 | 357 |
| XA-ROD | SBRL | 380-50 |
| XA-ROF | JSTR | 5133 |
| XA-ROF | JSTR | 5148 |
| XA-ROI | GLF2 | 10 |
| XA-ROJ | HS25 | 25206 |
| XA-ROK | JSTR | 5133 |
| XA-ROK | JSTR | 5148 |
| XA-ROO | LJ25 | 227 |
| XA-ROX | LJ24 | 260 |
| XA-ROZ | LJ25 | 286 |
| XA-RPS | SBRL | 282-56 |
| **XA-RPT** | **HS25** | **25161** |
| XA-RPV | LJ25 | 210 |
| XA-RQB | LJ24 | 150 |
| XA-RQI | LJ25 | 032 |
| XA-RQP | LJ24 | 179 |
| XA-RQT | WW24 | 124 |
| XA-RRC | LJ24 | 259 |
| **XA-RRG** | **PRM1** | **RB-154** |
| XA-RRK | LJ24 | 307 |
| **XA-RRQ** | **C650** | **7025** |
| XA-RSP | HS25 | 25091 |
| XA-RSR | HS25 | 25017 |
| XA-RSU | LJ25 | 363 |
| XA-RTH | SBRL | 306-39 |
| XA-RTM | SBRL | 282-39 |
| XA-RTP | SBRL | 306-110 |
| XA-RTS | C650 | 7025 |
| **XA-RTS** | **C680** | **0016** |
| XA-RTT | C560 | 0092 |
| XA-RTV | LJ24 | 124 |
| XA-RUD | C550 | 631 |
| XA-RUJ | LJ24 | 289 |

| | | |
|---|---|---|
| XA-RUQ | SBRL | 306-15 |
| XA-RUR | C500 | 273 |
| XA-RUS | GLF2 | 161 |
| XA-RUU | LJ31 | 012 |
| XA-RUX | HS25 | 25101 |
| **XA-RUY** | **FA50** | **252** |
| XA-RUY | HS25 | 258302 |
| XA-RUY | LJ35 | 373 |
| XA-RVB | LJ24 | 066 |
| XA-RVB | LJ35 | 321 |
| XA-RVG | JSTR | 5139/54 |
| XA-RVI | LJ25 | 286 |
| **XA-RVT** | **SBRL** | **306-138** |
| **XA-RVV** | **FA50** | **213** |
| XA-RWN | HS25 | 25226 |
| XA-RWY | SBRL | 306-97 |
| XA-RXA | LJ24 | 197 |
| XA-RXB | LJ25 | 325 |
| XA-RXO | C560 | 0118 |
| XA-RXP | SBRL | 306-56 |
| XA-RXQ | LJ25 | 342 |
| XA-RXZ | FA50 | 168 |
| XA-RYB | HS25 | 259043 |
| XA-RYD | SBRL | 306-72 |
| XA-RYE | C500 | 068 |
| **XA-RYE** | **C510** | **0039** |
| XA-RYH | LJ25 | 334 |
| **XA-RYJ** | **SBRL** | **370-5** |
| XA-RYK | HS25 | 256047 |
| **XA-RYM** | **HS25** | **258075** |
| XA-RYN | LJ24 | 164 |
| XA-RYO | SBRL | 465-55 |
| XA-RYR | C550 | 664 |
| **XA-RYR** | **GLF4** | **1417** |
| XA-RYW | HS25 | 25064 |
| XA-RZB | C550 | 654 |
| XA-RZC | LJ24 | 071 |
| XA-RZD | CL61 | 5087 |
| XA-RZE | LJ25 | 274 |
| XA-RZG | BE40 | RK-36 |
| XA-RZK | C650 | 0204 |
| XA-RZM | LJ24 | 070 |
| XA-RZQ | C650 | 0126 |
| XA-RZT | LJ25 | 330 |
| XA-RZW | SBRL | 370-9 |
| XA-RZY | LJ25 | 133 |
| XA-RZZ | LJ35 | 485 |
| XA-SAA | LJ24 | 306 |
| **XA-SAA** | **LJ45** | **236** |
| **XA-SAD** | **CL64** | **5630** |
| XA-SAE | JSTR | 5066/46 |
| XA-SAE | LJ25 | 341 |
| XA-SAG | FA20 | 287 |
| XA-SAG | SBRL | 282-111 |
| **XA-SAH** | **SBRL** | **306-137** |
| XA-SAI | HS25 | 256016 |
| XA-SAL | LJ25 | 121 |
| XA-SAM | C500 | 255 |
| **XA-SAP** | **LJ45** | **246** |
| XA-SAR | FA10 | 125 |
| (XA-SAR) | FA10 | 54 |
| XA-SAR | FA10 | 96 |
| **XA-SAU** | **HS25** | **257027** |
| XA-SAV | LJ24 | 306 |
| XA-SBA | LJ35 | 380 |
| XA-SBF | LJ35 | 376 |
| XA-SBQ | JSTR | 5124 |
| XA-SBR | LJ24 | 180 |
| XA-SBS | SBRL | 282-6 |
| XA-SBV | SBRL | 306-109 |
| XA-SBX | SBRL | 306-40 |
| XA-SBZ | LJ24 | 251 |
| XA-SCA | LJ35 | 418 |
| **XA-SCE** | **LJ24** | **271** |
| XA-SCL | FA20 | 130 |
| XA-SCN | SBRL | 282-105 |
| (XA-SCO) | F9EX | 186 |
| XA-SCR | SBRL | 465-65 |
| (XA-SCV) | WW24 | 122 |
| XA-SCY | LJ24 | 324 |
| XA-SDE | GLF2 | 18 |
| XA-SDI | C500 | 395 |
| **XA-SDI** | **C550** | **550-0983** |
| XA-SDK | FA50 | 224 |
| XA-SDM | GLF2 | 237/43 |
| XA-SDN | C550 | 247 |
| XA-SDP | LJ24 | 066 |
| XA-SDQ | LJ25 | 005 |

| | | |
|---|---|---|
| XA-SDS | C500 | 313 |
| XA-SDT | C560 | 0162 |
| **XA-SDU** | **C650** | **0052** |
| XA-SDV | C550 | 037 |
| XA-SDW | WW24 | 162 |
| XA-SEB | SBRL | 380-58 |
| XA-SEC | GLF4 | 1172 |
| XA-SEH | HS25 | 258004 |
| XA-SEJ | C560 | 0196 |
| XA-SEN | C500 | 060 |
| **XA-SEN** | **HS25** | **257077** |
| XA-SEN | SBRL | 282-7 |
| XA-SEP | C650 | 0076 |
| XA-SET | C550 | 458 |
| XA-SEU | SBRL | 282-104 |
| XA-SEX | C550 | 642 |
| XA-SEY | C500 | 631 |
| XA-SFB | GLF2 | 79 |
| XA-SFE | C500 | 125 |
| XA-SFP | FA50 | 22 |
| **XA-SFQ** | **HS25** | **25273** |
| XA-SFS | WW24 | 13 |
| XA-SGK | LJ35 | 380 |
| XA-SGM | HS25 | 25283 |
| XA-SGP | HS25 | 25114 |
| XA-SGR | SBRL | 370-6 |
| XA-SGU | LJ24 | 101 |
| XA-SGW | F900 | 122 |
| XA-SHA | WW24 | 86 |
| XA-SHN | LJ24 | 093 |
| XA-SHO | C500 | 111 |
| XA-SHZ | CL61 | 3012 |
| XA-SIF | FA50 | 231 |
| XA-SIG | C500 | 175 |
| **XA-SIM** | **F900** | **114** |
| XA-SIM | FA50 | 215 |
| XA-SIM | SBRL | 306-143 |
| XA-SIN | JSTR | 5005 |
| XA-SIO | LJ25 | 121 |
| XA-SIT | C560 | 0218 |
| XA-SIV | HS25 | 258185 |
| XA-SJC | C560 | 0197 |
| **XA-SJM** | **HS25** | **258713** |
| XA-SJM | SBRL | 306-128 |
| XA-SJN | LJ25 | 365 |
| XA-SJO | LJ25 | 370 |
| **XA-SJS** | **LJ25** | **076** |
| XA-SJV | C500 | 189 |
| XA-SJW | C500 | 169 |
| XA-SJX | F900 | 97 |
| XA-SJZ | C550 | 041 |
| **XA-SKA** | **LJ25** | **282** |
| XA-SKB | SBRL | 306-111 |
| XA-SKE | HS25 | 25253 |
| XA-SKH | HS25 | 256067 |
| XA-SKI | JSTR | 5124 |
| XA-SKO | FA20 | 505 |
| XA-SKW | C525 | 0044 |
| XA-SKX | C560 | 0118 |
| **XA-SKY** | **GLF4** | **1487** |
| (XA-SKY) | LJ45 | 170 |
| XA-SKZ | HS25 | 25121 |
| XA-SLA | C560 | 0228 |
| **XA-SLB** | **C650** | **0228** |
| XA-SLD | C550 | 014 |
| XA-SLH | SBRL | 306-39 |
| XA-SLJ | SBRL | 306-125 |
| **XA-SLP** | **HS25** | **256002** |
| XA-SLQ | C500 | 111 |
| **XA-SLR** | **HS25** | **25112** |
| XA-SMF | SBRL | 306-6 |
| XA-SMH | C500 | 084 |
| XA-SMP | SBRL | 282-13 |
| XA-SMQ | SBRL | 282-50 |
| XA-SMR | SBRL | 282-71 |
| **XA-SMS** | **CL61** | **3019** |
| XA-SMT | C550 | 722 |
| XA-SMU | LJ24 | 255 |
| XA-SMV | C550 | 720 |
| XA-SND | SBRL | 306-7 |
| XA-SNG | GLF3 | 434 |
| XA-SNH | HS25 | 256021 |
| **XA-SNI** | **LJ40** | **45-2030** |
| XA-SNI | SBRL | 282-126 |
| XA-SNM | LJ31 | 078 |
| XA-SNN | HS25 | 257009 |
| XA-SNO | LJ25 | 355 |
| XA-SNP | BE40 | RK-83 |

| | | |
|---|---|---|
| XA-SNX | C560 | 0229 |
| XA-SNZ | LJ24 | 157 |
| XA-SOA | CL60 | 1063 |
| XA-SOC | JSTR | 5152 |
| XA-SOD | MU30 | A049SA |
| **XA-SOH** | **LJ25** | **366** |
| XA-SOK | C650 | 7029 |
| **XA-SOL** | **CL64** | **5501** |
| XA-SOL | FA50 | 116 |
| **XA-SON** | **HS25** | **257079** |
| **XA-SOR** | **CL61** | **5147** |
| XA-SOU | C525 | 0060 |
| XA-SOX | C500 | 217 |
| XA-SOY | JSTR | 5142 |
| XA-SPL | LJ25 | 268 |
| XA-SPM | FA50 | 242 |
| **XA-SPM** | **SBRL** | **465-14** |
| **XA-SPQ** | **C650** | **7028** |
| XA-SPR | LJ31 | 076 |
| **XA-SQA** | **SBRL** | **282-125** |
| XA-SQQ | C550 | 280 |
| XA-SQR | C550 | 464 |
| XA-SQS | FA20 | 198/466 |
| XA-SQU | GLF2 | 173 |
| **XA-SQV** | **C550** | **221** |
| XA-SQW | C550 | 226 |
| XA-SQX | C500 | 428 |
| XA-SQY | C500 | 243 |
| XA-SQZ | C500 | 193 |
| XA-SRB | C500 | 197 |
| XA-SSS | FA50 | 119 |
| **XA-SSU** | **LJ24** | **230** |
| XA-SSV | HS25 | 25187 |
| **XA-SSV** | **SBRL** | **306-140** |
| XA-SSY | HS25 | 257199 |
| XA-STG | JSTR | 5206 |
| XA-STI | SBRL | 306-89 |
| XA-STO | GLF2 | 79 |
| XA-STT | C500 | 310 |
| XA-STT | GLF2 | 30/4 |
| **XA-STT** | **GLF3** | **406** |
| XA-STU | SBRL | 282-7 |
| XA-STX | HS25 | 257186 |
| **XA-SUK** | **LJ45** | **057** |
| XA-SUN | SBRL | 306-143 |
| XA-SUP | LJ24 | 319 |
| (XA-SUY) | LJ24 | 324 |
| XA-SVG | LJ25 | 079 |
| **XA-SVG** | **SBRL** | **306-97** |
| XA-SVH | SBRL | 306-97 |
| **XA-SVX** | **LJ35** | **012** |
| XA-SWC | FA20 | 21 |
| XA-SWD | JSTR | 5108 |
| XA-SWF | LJ35 | 391 |
| XA-SWK | HS25 | 256026 |
| XA-SWM | C650 | 7034 |
| XA-SWP | GLF2 | 166/15 |
| XA-SWX | LJ25 | 366 |
| XA-SXD | LJ25 | 105 |
| XA-SXG | LJ25 | 194 |
| XA-SXK | SBRL | 380-39 |
| XA-SXY | LJ25 | 308 |
| XA-SYS | SBRL | 306-121 |
| XA-SYY | FA10 | 4 |
| XA-TAB | FA10 | 204 |
| **XA-TAB** | **FA50** | **177** |
| XA-TAK | LJ25 | 305 |
| XA-TAL | HS25 | 25064 |
| XA-TAM | LJ25 | 341 |
| XA-TAN | FA20 | 272 |
| XA-TAQ | LJ25 | 286 |
| **XA-TAQ** | **LJ25** | **305** |
| XA-TAV | JSTR | 5103 |
| XA-TAZ | JSTR | 5103 |
| XA-TBA | C650 | 0019 |
| XA-TBL | FA10 | 203 |
| XA-TBV | LJ25 | 325 |
| **XA-TCA** | **LJ24** | **224** |
| XA-TCB | HS25 | 257082 |
| XA-TCI | LJ35 | 349 |
| XA-TCM | C550 | 717 |
| **XA-TCN** | **JSTR** | **5229** |
| XA-TCO | GLF3 | 403 |
| XA-TCR | HS25 | 257102 |
| XA-TCY | LJ25 | 048 |
| XA-TCZ | C650 | 7019 |
| XA-TDD | FA50 | 252 |
| **XA-TDG** | **JSTR** | **5158** |

| | | |
|---|---|---|
| XA-TDK | GLF2 | 114 |
| XA-TDP | LJ24 | 128 |
| XA-TDQ | BE40 | RK-281 |
| XA-TDQ | SBRL | 380-50 |
| XA-TDU | F2TH | 29 |
| **XA-TDX** | **SBRL** | **276-27** |
| **XA-TEI** | **F9EX** | **186** |
| XA-TEL | C550 | 275 |
| **XA-TEL** | **F900** | **168** |
| **XA-TEM** | **HS25** | **258431** |
| XA-TFC | SBRL | 265-12 |
| XA-TFD | SBRL | 265-10 |
| XA-TFL | SBRL | 265-48 |
| XA-TGA | C650 | 0036 |
| **XA-TGA** | **SBRL** | **306-126** |
| XA-TGK | HS25 | 259037 |
| **XA-TGM** | **LJ31** | **052** |
| **XA-TGO** | **SBRL** | **276-6** |
| XA-THD | LJ35 | 243 |
| **XA-THF** | **WW24** | **109** |
| XA-THO | CS55 | 0035 |
| XA-TIE | LJ25 | 364 |
| XA-TII | LJ24 | 070 |
| XA-TIP | LJ24 | 227 |
| XA-TIP | LJ24 | 293 |
| XA-TIV | CL60 | 1057 |
| **XA-TIW** | **SBRL** | **276-44** |
| **XA-TIX** | **SBRL** | **276-21** |
| **XA-TIY** | **SBRL** | **265-14** |
| XA-TJF | ASTR | 050 |
| XA-TJG | F900 | 131 |
| XA-TJU | SBRL | 276-8 |
| XA-TJV | JSTR | 5130 |
| XA-TJW | JSTR | 5129 |
| **XA-TJY** | **SBRL** | **276-39** |
| **XA-TJZ** | **SBRL** | **265-76** |
| XA-TKC+ | LJ24 | 164 |
| XA-TKQ | HS25 | 258111 |
| **XA-TKW** | **SBRL** | **282-13** |
| **XA-TKY** | **C500** | **411** |
| XA-TKZ | C560 | 0474 |
| **XA-TKZ** | **C56X** | **5208** |
| XA-TLL | SBRL | 306-20 |
| XA-TLM | CL61 | 5097 |
| **XA-TMF** | **SBRL** | **306-100** |
| XA-TMH | F9EX | 33 |
| XA-TMI | CS55 | 0080 |
| XA-TMX | C650 | 7069 |
| **XA-TMZ** | **C650** | **0068** |
| XA-TNP | SBRL | 265-62 |
| XA-TNW | SBRL | 306-73 |
| XA-TNX | HS25 | 256018 |
| **XA-TNY** | **HS25** | **25196** |
| XA-TOF | C500 | 345 |
| XA-TOM | SBRL | 465-55 |
| XA-TOO | GLF4 | 1114 |
| (XA-TOT) | GLF3 | 302 |
| XA-TPB | HS25 | 258176 |
| **XA-TPB** | **HS25** | **258409** |
| XA-TPD | JSTR | 5134/50 |
| XA-TPJ | JSTR | 5231 |
| **XA-TPU** | **SBRL** | **306-143** |
| **XA-TQA** | **C550** | **504** |
| XA-TQL | C550 | 268 |
| **XA-TQR** | **SBRL** | **276-4** |
| **XA-TRE** | **C650** | **7019** |
| XA-TRG | GLF2 | 30/4 |
| XA-TRI | C525 | 0060 |
| **XA-TRQ** | **LJ24** | **112** |
| XA-TSA | LJ60 | 202 |
| XA-TSL | LJ25 | 315 |
| XA-TSN | PRM1 | RB-12 |
| **XA-TSS** | **SBRL** | **306-63** |
| **XA-TSZ** | **SBRL** | **380-71** |
| XA-TTD | CL61 | 5059 |
| XA-TTE | JSTR | 5058/4 |
| **XA-TTG** | **C525** | **0475** |
| **XA-TTH** | **HS25** | **25148** |
| **XA-TTS** | **BE40** | **RK-302** |
| **XA-TTT** | **LJ24** | **199** |
| **XA-TUD** | **SBRL** | **380-5** |
| XA-TUH | FA50 | 22 |
| XA-TUL | LJ31 | 012 |
| XA-TVG | CL64 | 5520 |
| **XA-TVH** | **C550** | **668** |
| XA-TVI | HS25 | 258004 |
| **XA-TVK** | **JSTR** | **5098/28** |
| XA-TVQ | FA50 | 94 |
| **XA-TVZ** | **SBRL** | **306-113** |
| **XA-TWH** | **LJ25** | **289** |
| **XA-TWW** | **BE40** | **RK-332** |
| XA-TXB | FA50 | 210 |
| **XA-TYD** | **BE40** | **RK-321** |
| **XA-TYH** | **HS25** | **258491** |
| **XA-TYK** | **HS25** | **258597** |
| XA-TYT | F2TH | 60 |
| **XA-TYW** | **LJ25** | **361** |
| **XA-TYZ** | **SBRL** | **282-124** |
| **XA-TZF** | **CL64** | **5527** |
| XA-TZF | LJ60 | 088 |
| **XA-TZI** | **LJ60** | **088** |
| XA-TZV | JSTR | 5130 |
| XA-TZW | JSTR | 5129 |
| **XA-UAF** | **C56X** | **5356** |
| **XA-UAG** | **LJ45** | **139** |
| XA-UAM | C650 | 7073 |
| **XA-UAW** | **BE40** | **RK-359** |
| XA-UBG | SBRL | 282-112 |
| XA-UBH | SBRL | 380-40 |
| **XA-UBI** | **LJ31** | **235** |
| **XA-UBK** | **HS25** | **25107** |
| XA-UCN | FA50 | 177 |
| XA-UCS | SBRL | 282-6 |
| **XA-UCU** | **HS25** | **257056** |
| **XA-UCV** | **BE40** | **RK-375** |
| XA-UDP | FA10 | 204 |
| **XA-UDW** | **FA50** | **291** |
| **XA-UEA** | **HS25** | **257061** |
| XA-UEC | GLF2 | 167 |
| **XA-UEF** | **C560** | **0687** |
| **XA-UEH** | **HS25** | **258044** |
| **XA-UEK** | **SBRL** | **380-40** |
| **XA-UEQ** | **SBRL** | **380-58** |
| **XA-UEV** | **BE40** | **RK-434** |
| **XA-UEW** | **CL61** | **5063** |
| **XA-UEX** | **HS25** | **25066** |
| **XA-UEY** | **SBRL** | **282-112** |
| **XA-UFB** | **LJ45** | **295** |
| **XA-UFK** | **HS25** | **258287** |
| XA-UFQ | SBRL | 306-130 |
| **XA-UFR** | **BE40** | **RK-452** |
| **XA-UFS** | **BE40** | **RK-415** |
| **XA-UGB** | **SBRL** | **282-102** |
| **XA-UGG** | **C550** | **590** |
| XA-UGK | LJ35 | 488 |
| XA-UGO | HS25 | 258731 |
| XA-UGQ | C56X | 5667 |
| XA-UGX | C650 | 7088 |
| **XA-UHI** | **HS25** | **258055** |
| XA-UHJ | WW24 | 174 |
| XA-UHO | C650 | 7025 |
| **XA-UHQ** | **C56X** | **5709** |
| **XA-UHT** | **LJ24** | **283** |
| **XA-UIC** | **MU30** | **A055SA** |
| **XA-UIS** | **C650** | **0186** |
| **XA-UJG** | **FA10** | **146** |
| **XA-UJP** | **C56X** | **5771** |
| **XA-UJQ** | **LJ31** | **020** |
| **XA-UJR** | **LJ45** | **135** |
| **XA-UJW** | **SBRL** | **306-20** |
| **XA-UJY** | **C52A** | **0395** |
| **XA-UJZ** | **LJ45** | **188** |
| **XA-UKF** | **LJ35** | **316** |
| **XA-UKH** | **LJ25** | **221** |
| **XA-UKK** | **LJ25** | **337** |
| **XA-UKQ** | **C56X** | **5813** |
| **XA-UKR** | **HS25** | **257191** |
| **XA-UKU** | **BE40** | **RK-259** |
| **XA-ULG** | **LJ25** | **334** |
| **XA-ULO** | **C510** | **0174** |
| XA-ULQ | CL61 | 5087 |
| **XA-ULT** | **HS25** | **257003** |
| XA-UMA | LJ35 | 646 |
| **XA-UMS** | **C510** | **0166** |
| **XA-USD** | **LJ35** | **255** |
| **XA-UUU** | **LJ25** | **276** |
| XA-UVA | C550 | 550-0999 |
| **XA-UVA** | **C56X** | **5033** |
| **XA-UVH** | **HS25** | **258152** |
| (XA-VAD) | GLF4 | 1227 |
| **XA-VDG** | **CL61** | **5004** |
| **XA-VEL** | **SBRL** | **306-42** |
| XA-VER | C750 | 0072 |
| **XA-VFV** | **LJ40** | **45-2077** |
| **XA-VGF** | **CS55** | **0080** |
| **XA-VGR** | **C56X** | **5776** |
| **XA-VIG** | **LJ60** | **116** |
| XA-VIO | SBRL | 306-34 |
| XA-VIT | C650 | 0020 |
| XA-VIT | SBRL | 306-50 |
| **XA-VLA** | **LJ60** | **217** |
| **XA-VMC** | **LJ25** | **114** |
| **XA-VMX** | **C510** | **0059** |
| (XA-VMX) | LJ31 | 224 |
| XA-VRO | BE40 | RK-238 |
| **XA-VTO** | **F900** | **129** |
| XA-VTR | LJ31 | 231 |
| XA-VVI | LJ24 | 230 |
| XA-VYA | LJ25 | 336 |
| **XA-VYC** | **LJ45** | **034** |
| XA-VYF | C500 | 265 |
| **XA-WIN** | **LJ35** | **152** |
| **XA-WWW** | **LJ25** | **193** |
| XA-XET | HS25 | 256022 |
| **XA-XGX** | **C650** | **0198** |
| XA-XIS | C650 | 7032 |
| XA-YSM | HS25 | 25208 |
| **XA-YUR** | **FA20** | **475** |
| **XA-YYY** | **LJ25** | **263** |
| **XA-ZAP** | **LJ35** | **129** |
| XA-ZOM | SBRL | 306-47 |
| XA-ZTA | CL61 | 5158 |
| **XA-ZTA** | **LJ60** | **134** |
| **XA-ZTH** | **LJ31** | **004** |
| XA-ZUL | PRM1 | RB-9 |
| XA-ZUM | SBRL | 306-47 |
| XA-ZUM | SBRL | 465-15 |
| XA-ZYZ | LJ25 | 032 |
| XA-ZYZ | LJ25 | 287 |
| **XA-ZYZ** | **LJ31** | **073** |
| XA-ZZZ | LJ25 | 287 |
| **XA-ZZZ** | **LJ25** | **346** |
| **XB-ACD** | **SBRL** | **380-50** |
| **XB-ADR** | **LJ24** | **103** |
| **XB-ADZ** | **HS25** | **256018** |
| XB-AER | WW24 | 172 |
| **XB-AGV** | **C550** | **429** |
| XB-AKW | HS25 | 25102 |
| XB-ALO | FA20 | 287 |
| **XB-AMO** | **C500** | **152** |
| XB-APD | SBRL | 306-33 |
| XB-AQU | FA20 | 248/483 |
| XB-ASO | HS25 | 25202 |
| XB-ATH | C525 | 0148 |
| XB-AXP | HS25 | 25112 |
| XB-AXP | HS25 | 25233 |
| XB-AYJ | SBRL | 282-41 |
| **XB-AZD** | **LJ25** | **224** |
| XB-BAK | FA10 | 65 |
| XB-BBL | SBRL | 282-116 |
| XB-BEA | HS25 | 25068 |
| XB-BIP | SBRL | 306-63 |
| **XB-BON** | **C550** | **654** |
| XB-CAM | FA10 | 107 |
| XB-CCM | HS25 | 25226 |
| XB-CCO | C500 | 175 |
| **XB-CSI** | **C500** | **345** |
| **XB-CTC** | **MU30** | **A024SA** |
| XB-CUX | HS25 | 25262 |
| **XB-CVS** | **SBRL** | **306-47** |
| XB-CXF | C500 | 143 |
| XB-CXK | HS25 | 257153 |
| XB-CXO | JSTR | 5141 |
| XB-CXZ | HS25 | 25060 |
| XB-CYA | CRVT | 36 |
| **XB-CYA** | **SBRL** | **380-53** |
| XB-CYI | CRVT | 40 |
| XB-DBA | C500 | 067 |
| XB-DBJ | JSTR | 5145 |
| XB-DBS | JSTR | 5159 |
| XB-DBT | JSTR | 5156 |
| **XB-DGA** | **C525** | **0329** |
| XB-DKS | LJ25 | 309 |
| XB-DLV | JSTR | 5005 |
| XB-DNY | WW24 | 183 |
| XB-DSQ | HS25 | 25185 |
| XB-DUH | JSTR | 5157 |
| XB-DUS | SBRL | 282-106 |
| **XB-DVF** | **C500** | **587** |
| XB-DVP | SBRL | 380-53 |
| XB-DYF | C500 | 313 |
| XB-DZD | LJ24 | 349 |
| XB-DZN | HS25 | 257158 |
| XB-DZQ | LJ25 | 332 |
| **XB-DZR** | **LJ24** | **273** |
| XB-EAL | HS25 | 25060 |
| XB-EBI | GLF2 | 96 |
| XB-ECR | FA20 | 513 |
| XB-EDU | FA20 | 39 |
| **XB-EEP** | **CS55** | **0070** |
| XB-EFR | C500 | 090 |
| XB-EGP | LJ25 | 194 |
| XB-ELU | C500 | 544 |
| XB-EPB | FA20 | 127 |
| XB-EPM | SBRL | 380-19 |
| XB-EPN | C500 | 241 |
| XB-EQR | SBRL | 282-82 |
| XB-ERN | HS25 | 25148 |
| XB-ERU | SBRL | 370-7 |
| XB-ERX | C500 | 460 |
| **XB-ESG** | **C500** | **292** |
| **XB-ESS** | **SBRL** | **282-123** |
| XB-ESX | SBRL | 306-47 |
| XB-ETE | C500 | 274 |
| **XB-ETV** | **SBRL** | **306-96** |
| XB-EWF | CRVT | 36 |
| XB-EWQ | C500 | 141 |
| XB-EXJ | GLF4 | 1055 |
| XB-EZV | SBRL | 282-7 |
| XB-FDH | BE40 | RJ-54 |
| XB-FDN | C500 | 068 |
| XB-FFV | HS25 | 25112 |
| XB-FIS | HS25 | 25060 |
| XB-FIS | JSTR | 5033/56 |
| XB-FJI | WW24 | 115 |
| XB-FJO | MS76 | 005 |
| XB-FJW | LJ24 | 141 |
| **XB-FKT** | **LJ31** | **029** |
| XB-FKV | WW24 | 137 |
| **XB-FMB** | **SBRL** | **306-90** |
| XB-FMF | HS25 | 256033 |
| XB-FMK | HS25 | 257068 |
| XB-FNF | LJ35 | 210 |
| XB-FNW | LJ35 | 255 |
| XB-FPK | C500 | 084 |
| XB-FQO | C500 | 278 |
| XB-FRP | HS25 | 25185 |
| XB-FST | SBRL | 306-63 |
| XB-FSZ | SBRL | 306-50 |
| XB-FUZ | SBRL | 306-63 |
| XB-FVH | FA20 | 393 |
| XB-FVL | GLF2 | 100 |
| XB-FWX | FA10 | 107 |
| XB-FXD | GLF3 | 434 |
| XB-FXO | C500 | 550 |
| **XB-GAM** | **HS25** | **25075** |
| XB-GBC | LJ24 | 285 |
| **XB-GBF** | **C500** | **273** |
| XB-GBZ | WW24 | 133 |
| XB-GCC | HS25 | 258252 |
| **XB-GCP** | **LJ25** | **325** |
| XB-GCR | FA20 | 127 |
| **XB-GDJ** | **C500** | **598** |
| XB-GDR | LJ25 | 308 |
| XB-GDU | SBRL | 265-12 |
| XB-GDV | SBRL | 276-27 |
| XB-GDW | SBRL | 265-86 |
| XB-GGK | HS25 | 25064 |
| XB-GHC | HS25 | 25121 |
| **XB-GHO** | **LJ24** | **141** |
| XB-GJO | SBRL | 370-9 |
| XB-GJS | LJ24 | 299 |
| **XB-GLZ** | **C550** | **281** |
| XB-GMD | SBRL | 465-12 |
| XB-GNF | HS25 | 25283 |
| XB-GRE | C500 | 550 |
| XB-GRN | C650 | 0069 |
| XB-GRN | WW24 | 301 |
| XB-GRQ | LJ24 | 074 |
| XB-GRR | LJ24 | 068 |
| XB-GSN | GLF2 | 161 |
| **XB-GSP** | **SBRL** | **380-55** |
| XB-GVY | C500 | 368 |
| XB-GXV | C650 | 0101 |
| XB-HDL | SBRL | 306-7 |
| XB-HGE | LJ25 | 325 |
| XB-HHF | SBRL | 282-6 |
| XB-HIZ | GLF3 | 403 |
| **XB-HJS** | **SBRL** | **306-110** |
| XB-HND | C500 | 255 |
| **XB-HRA** | **FA20** | **127** |
| XB-HZF | C550 | 473 |

| Registration | Type | c/n |
|---|---|---|
| XB-IFW | LJ25 | 366 |
| **XB-IHB** | **SBRL** | **282-63** |
| XB-IJW | C500 | 198 |
| XB-IKS | C500 | 010 |
| **XB-IKY** | **C550** | **642** |
| XB-ILD | HS25 | 25190 |
| **XB-INI** | **BE40** | **RK-126** |
| **XB-IPX** | **HS25** | **25188** |
| **XB-IRH** | **LJ24** | **308** |
| **XB-IUW** | **C500** | **198** |
| **XB-IWL** | **LJ35** | **379** |
| **XB-IXE** | **C500** | **328** |
| **XB-IXJ** | **SBRL** | **306-93** |
| **XB-IXT** | **C500** | **685** |
| XB-IYK | FA20 | 282 |
| **XB-IYS** | **SBRL** | **306-6** |
| **XB-IZK** | **C550** | **473** |
| **XB-JCG** | **LJ60** | **131** |
| **XB-JDG** | **C500** | **110** |
| XB-JFE | JSTR | 5145 |
| **XB-JFV** | **C500** | **530** |
| **XB-JGI** | **SBRL** | **282-80** |
| **XB-JHD** | **C560** | **0127** |
| XB-JHE | BE40 | RJ-48 |
| **XB-JHV** | **LJ28** | **29-002** |
| XB-JIZ | JSTR | 5058/4 |
| **XB-JJS** | **LJ25** | **369** |
| **XB-JKG** | **HS25** | **25146** |
| XB-JKK | LJ25 | 334 |
| XB-JKV | SBRL | 282-102 |
| XB-JLJ | C550 | 310 |
| **XB-JLU** | **LJ25** | **328** |
| **XB-JLY** | **HS25** | **25139** |
| XB-JMM | SBRL | 306-130 |
| **XB-JMR** | **SBRL** | **306-35** |
| **XB-JND** | **HS25** | **257106** |
| XB-JOY | LJ24 | 263 |
| XB-JPL | GLF2 | 10 |
| **XB-JPS** | **SBRL** | **282-128** |
| **XB-JPX** | **LJ36** | **043** |
| **XB-JTG** | **SBRL** | **306-127** |
| **XB-JTN** | **HS25** | **257185** |
| **XB-JVK** | **C500** | **199** |
| **XB-JXG** | **C500** | **378** |
| **XB-JXZ** | **LJ24** | **346** |
| **XB-JYS** | **HS25** | **257033** |
| XB-KBE | GLF2 | 114 |
| XB-KBO | GLF2 | 30/4 |
| **XB-KBW** | **FA20** | **364** |
| XB-KCV | JSTR | 5161/43 |
| XB-KCW | GLF2 | 114 |
| XB-KCX | GLF2 | 30/4 |
| **XB-KDK** | **LJ31** | **032** |
| **XB-KDQ** | **LJ25** | **365** |
| XB-KFR | JSTR | 5161/43 |
| **XB-KHL** | **C500** | **542** |
| XB-KIV | GLF2 | 91 |
| **XB-KJW** | **LJ24** | **349** |
| XB-KKS | HS25 | 25225 |
| XB-KKU | GLF2 | 119/22 |
| **XB-KLV** | **JSTR** | **5162** |
| **XB-KNH** | **HS25** | **25225** |
| **XB-KPC** | **SBRL** | **306-7** |
| **XB-KQY** | **SBRL** | **306-83** |
| **XB-KSL** | **SBRL** | **306-86** |
| XB-KVX | LJ25 | 122 |
| **XB-KWN** | **LJ25** | **309** |
| XB-KYZ | LJ60 | 175 |
| XB-LAW | SBRL | 306-100 |
| XB-LBO | LJ60 | 175 |
| **XB-LCI** | **LJ25** | **122** |
| XB-LEJ | LJ60 | 175 |
| XB-LHS | LJ35 | 255 |
| XB-LHS | LJ35 | 648 |
| XB-LHW | GLF2 | 253 |
| XB-LLT | LJ60 | 175 |
| XB-LRD | SBRL | 306-21 |
| XB-LTH | C550 | 462 |
| XB-LXP | HS25 | 25233 |
| **XB-LYG** | **LJ25** | **364** |
| **XB-MAR** | **HS25** | **25202** |
| XB-MBM | HS25 | 25030 |
| **XB-MCB** | **HS25** | **258320** |
| XB-MCB | SBRL | 380-36 |
| **XB-MDG** | **SBRL** | **282-114** |
| XB-MGM | LJ25 | 224 |
| XB-MLC | HS25 | 257171 |
| **XB-MMW** | **SBRL** | **306-132** |
| **XB-MSV** | **HS25** | **25185** |
| XB-MTS | C560 | 0030 |
| XB-MVG | SBRL | 282-134 |
| **XB-MYA** | **HS25** | **25227** |
| **XB-MYE** | **LJ24** | **066** |
| **XB-MYG** | **LJ25** | **295** |
| **XB-MYP** | **SBRL** | **465-50** |
| XB-NAG | LJ24 | 270 |
| XB-NIB | SBRL | 282-125 |
| XB-NUR | LJ24 | 275 |
| XB-OBE | C500 | 273 |
| XB-OEM | FA20 | 248/483 |
| XB-OEM | FA50 | 80 |
| XB-OEM | GLF4 | 1055 |
| XB-OZA | LJ25 | 224 |
| **XB-PBT** | **C500** | **054** |
| XB-PGR+ | GLF2 | 81 |
| XB-PUE | HS25 | 25158 |
| XB-PYC | C560 | 0261 |
| XB-QND | SBRL | 306-21 |
| XB-RDB | SBRL | 380-55 |
| XB-RGO | SBRL | 282-114 |
| XB-RGS | SBRL | 282-114 |
| XB-RMT | LJ45 | 046 |
| **XB-RSC** | **SBRL** | **465-55** |
| XB-RSG | SBRL | 380-60 |
| **XB-RSH** | **SBRL** | **465-22** |
| XB-RTT | C560 | 0092 |
| XB-RYE | C510 | 0039 |
| XB-RYO | SBRL | 465-55 |
| **XB-RYT** | **LJ35** | **042** |
| XB-SBC | HS25 | 25068 |
| XB-SHA | SBRL | 380-60 |
| XB-SII | FA10 | 4 |
| XB-SOL | FA50 | 116 |
| **XB-SOL** | **SBRL** | **306-128** |
| XB-SUD | LJ24 | 197 |
| **XB-TMG** | **C500** | **504** |
| **XB-TRY** | **C500** | **210** |
| XB-UAG | C500 | 278 |
| **XB-ULF** | **SBRL** | **306-129** |
| XB-USD | LJ35 | 255 |
| XB-UVA | C550 | 550-0999 |
| **XB-VGT** | **C500** | **068** |
| XB-VIW | JSTR | 5140 |
| XB-VRM | FA20 | 248/483 |
| XB-VUI | HS25 | 25068 |
| XB-ZNP | SBRL | 306-63 |
| XB-ZRB | FA10 | 107 |
| (XB-ZRB) | LJ31 | 029 |
| XB-ZUM | SBRL | 306-47 |
| **XB-ZZZ** | **C550** | **711** |
| XC-AA104 | LJ24 | 070 |
| XC-AA24 | LJ36 | 050 |
| XC-AA26 | SBRL | 306-12 |
| XC-AA28 | LJ24 | 037 |
| **XC-AA51** | **SBRL** | **282-130** |
| XC-AA60 | LJ35 | 321 |
| XC-AA63 | LJ24 | 249 |
| **XC-AA70** | **GLF2** | **18** |
| XC-AA73 | SBRL | 282-105 |
| XC-AA83 | LJ25 | 286 |
| XC-AA84 | LJ25 | 330 |
| **XC-AA89** | **SBRL** | **380-46** |
| **XC-AAC** | **SBRL** | **306-21** |
| XC-AAJ | SBRL | 306-20 |
| XC-AGR | LJ25 | 295 |
| **XC-AGU** | **LJ24** | **260** |
| XC-ASA | C500 | 061 |
| XC-ASB | C500 | 251 |
| XC-AZU | LJ24 | 285 |
| XC-BCS | C550 | 268 |
| (XC-BDA) | WW24 | 340 |
| XC-BEN | C500 | 243 |
| XC-BEZ | C500 | 072 |
| XC-BIN | FA20 | 198/466 |
| XC-BOC | C500 | 169 |
| XC-BUR | C500 | 245 |
| **XC-CAM** | **SBRL** | **306-145** |
| XC-CFE | GLF2 | 161 |
| XC-CFM | LJ25 | 284 |
| XC-CIR | C500 | 466 |
| XC-COL | WW24 | 135 |
| XC-COL | WW24 | 279 |
| XC-CON | C500 | 169 |
| **XC-CUZ** | **LJ35** | **213** |
| XC-DAA | LJ25 | 283 |
| XC-DAD | LJ25 | 223 |
| **XC-DDA** | **SBRL** | **380-34** |
| XC-DFS | LJ28 | 29-002 |
| XC-DGA | C500 | 010 |
| XC-DGA | HFB3 | 1049 |
| **XC-DGO** | **LJ35** | **336** |
| XC-DIP | FA20 | 282 |
| XC-DOK | C550 | 221 |
| XC-DOP | LJ24 | 273 |
| (XC-DUF) | C550 | 206 |
| XC-DUF | C550 | 226 |
| **XC-FEZ** | **C500** | **596** |
| XC-FEZ | GLF2 | 161 |
| XC-FIA | SBRL | 380-53 |
| XC-FIF | LJ25 | 332 |
| XC-FIT | C500 | 010 |
| XC-FIU | C500 | 012 |
| **XC-FIV** | **C500** | **013** |
| XC-FOO | C550 | 249 |
| XC-FVH | FA20 | 393 |
| XC-GAD | C500 | 061 |
| (XC-GAM) | FA20 | 198/466 |
| **XC-GAW** | **C500** | **586** |
| **XC-GDC** | **C52B** | **0062** |
| **XC-GDT** | **C560** | **0689** |
| XC-GII | LJ24 | 179 |
| XC-GNL | LJ25 | 329 |
| XC-GOB | HS25 | 25216 |
| XC-GOV | C500 | 189 |
| XC-GOW | C500 | 193 |
| XC-GOX | C500 | 197 |
| XC-GOY | C500 | 243 |
| **XC-GTO** | **C500** | **533** |
| **XC-GUB** | **LJ25** | **306** |
| XC-GUH | C500 | 221 |
| XC-GUO | C500 | 201 |
| XC-GUQ | C500 | 143 |
| XC-HAD | WW24 | 85 |
| XC-HCP | WW24 | 230 |
| XC-HDA | WW24 | 230 |
| (XC-HDA) | WW24 | 339 |
| XC-HEP | C550 | 464 |
| XC-HEQ | C550 | 280 |
| XC-HEY | SBRL | 282-130 |
| XC-HFY | SBRL | 380-46 |
| **XC-HGY** | **SBRL** | **306-38** |
| XC-HGZ | C550 | 096 |
| (XC-HGZ?) | C550 | 659 |
| XC-HHA | C550 | 185 |
| XC-HHA | C550 | 673 |
| (XC-HHA?) | C550 | 673 |
| **XC-HHJ** | **LJ35** | **435** |
| XC-HHL | SBRL | 306-12 |
| **XC-HID** | **FA20** | **282** |
| **XC-HIE** | **LJ45** | **026** |
| XC-HIE | LJ28 | 29-002 |
| **XC-HIS** | **LJ25** | **312** |
| (XC-HIX) | FA20 | 111 |
| **XC-HIX** | **FA20** | **248/483** |
| XC-HJC | C550 | 677 |
| XC-HJE | C550 | 680 |
| XC-HJF | C550 | 652 |
| XC-HJH | C550 | 655 |
| XC-IPP | C500 | 329 |
| XC-IPP | LJ35 | 028 |
| **XC-IST** | **LJ28** | **29-001** |
| (XC-JAY?) | C550 | 505 |
| (XC-JAZ?) | C550 | 602 |
| (XC-JBQ?) | C550 | 497 |
| (XC-JBR?) | C550 | 494 |
| XC-JBS | C550 | 666 |
| (XC-JBT?) | C550 | 593 |
| XC-JCC | JSTR | 5053/2 |
| XC-JCK | SBRL | 282-1 |
| XC-JCN | LJ24 | 299 |
| XC-JDC | SBRL | 306-145 |
| XC-JDX | LJ24 | 070 |
| XC-JEG | C550 | 670 |
| XC-JOA | LJ24 | 081 |
| XC-LGD | LJ24 | 037 |
| XC-LHA | C550 | 681 |
| **XC-LIT** | **JSTR** | **5063** |
| XC-LJE | LJ24 | 346 |
| **XC-LJS** | **BE40** | **RJ-48** |
| **XC-LKA** | **GLF2** | **69** |
| **XC-LKL** | **GLF2** | **114** |
| **XC-LKN** | **GLF2** | **30/4** |
| **XC-LKS** | **GLF2** | **91** |
| XC-MEX | GLF2 | 96 |
| **XC-MIC** | **FA20** | **169** |
| **XC-MMM** | **C500** | **035** |
| **XC-NSP** | **LJ25** | **194** |
| **XC-OAH** | **LJ35** | **488** |
| XC-OAH | SBRL | 282-1 |
| XC-OAH | SBRL | 306-73 |
| XC-ONA | SBRL | 380-39 |
| XC-PET | GLF2 | 173 |
| XC-PFJ | FA20 | 287 |
| XC-PFN | SBRL | 306-111 |
| XC-PFP | LJ24 | 260 |
| XC-PFT | GLF2 | 175 |
| XC-PGE | SBRL | 282-130 |
| **XC-PGM** | **C550** | **644** |
| **XC-PGN** | **C650** | **0165** |
| **XC-PGP** | **C550** | **648** |
| XC-PGR | LJ35 | 460 |
| XC-PMX | C500 | 428 |
| XC-PPM | C500 | 329 |
| XC-QEO | C500 | 251 |
| **XC-QER** | **FA20** | **287** |
| XC-ROO | C550 | 249 |
| XC-ROO | C550 | 598 |
| **XC-RPP** | **LJ25** | **236** |
| XC-SAG | LJ24 | 255 |
| XC-SCT | C500 | 010 |
| **XC-SCT** | **C550** | **153** |
| XC-SEY | FA20 | 169 |
| **XC-SKI** | **JSTR** | **5124** |
| **XC-SON** | **FA20** | **393** |
| XC-SRA | SBRL | 282-130 |
| XC-SRH | JSTR | 5154 |
| **XC-SST** | **C550** | **731** |
| XC-SUB | SBRL | 282-114 |
| XC-SUP | LJ24 | 319 |
| XC-TIJ | HFB3 | 1049 |
| **XC-TJN** | **LJ40** | **45-2046** |
| XC-UJC | SBRL | 380-67 |
| XC-UJD | SBRL | 380-68 |
| XC-UJE | SBRL | 306-139 |
| XC-UJF | SBRL | 306-144 |
| **XC-UJG** | **LJ35** | **321** |
| XC-UJG | SBRL | 282-130 |
| XC-UJH | HS25 | 25216 |
| XC-UJH | SBRL | 282-117 |
| XC-UJI | SBRL | 282-130 |
| XC-UJK | GLF2 | 161 |
| **XC-UJN** | **GLF3** | **352** |
| **XC-UJO** | **GLF3** | **386** |
| XC-UJP | LJ24 | 037 |
| **XC-UJR** | **LJ36** | **050** |
| **XC-UJS** | **SBRL** | **306-139** |
| **XC-UJU** | **SBRL** | **380-68** |
| XC-VMC | LJ45 | 028 |
| **XC-VSA** | **LJ28** | **28-002** |
| XC-ZRB | FA10 | 107 |

## Burkino Faso

| Registration | Type | c/n |
|---|---|---|
| XT-AOK | C550 | 726 |
| XT-COK | C550 | 550-0924 |

## Cambodia (Kampuchea)

| Registration | Type | c/n |
|---|---|---|
| XU-008 | FA20 | 323/520 |

## Iraq

| Registration | Type | c/n |
|---|---|---|
| YI-AHH | FA20 | 337/529 |
| YI-AHI | FA20 | 342/532 |
| YI-AHJ | FA20 | 343/533 |
| YI-AKA | JSTR | 5233 |
| YI-AKB | JSTR | 5235 |
| YI-AKC | JSTR | 5237 |
| YI-AKD | JSTR | 5238 |
| YI-AKE | JSTR | 5239 |
| YI-AKF | JSTR | 5240 |
| YI-AKG | HS25 | 257184 |
| YI-AKH | HS25 | 257187 |
| YI-AKI | GLF3 | 408 |
| YI-AKJ | GLF3 | 419 |
| YI-ALB | FA50 | 71 |
| YI-ALC | FA50 | 101 |
| YI-ALD | FA50 | 120 |
| YI-ALE | FA50 | 122 |

Syria

| | | |
|---|---|---|
| YK-ASA | FA20 | 328/522 |
| **YK-ASB** | **FA20** | **331/524** |
| **YK-ASC** | **F900** | **100** |

Latvia

| | | |
|---|---|---|
| **YL-ABA** | **LJ60** | **300** |
| **YL-KSC** | **PRM1** | **RB-20** |
| **YL-MAR** | **HS25** | **258389** |
| **YL-MLV** | **PRM1** | **RB-216** |
| **YL-NST** | **HS25** | **258424** |
| **YL-SKY** | **CL64** | **5532** |
| YL-VIP | HS25 | 257103 |
| **YL-VIP** | **HS25** | **258078** |
| YL-VIR | HS25 | 257103 |
| YL-WBD | CL64 | 5442 |

Nicaragua
(see also AN-)

| | | |
|---|---|---|
| YN-BPR | HS25 | 256037 |
| YN-BVO | LJ35 | 280 |
| YN-BZH | FA20 | 128/436 |

Romania

| | | |
|---|---|---|
| **YR-CJF** | **F900** | **26** |
| **YR-DAD** | **C510** | **0266** |
| YR-DAE | C510 | 0281 |
| **YR-DIP** | **CL64** | **5475** |
| **YR-DPH** | **C56X** | **5793** |
| YR-DSA | FA20 | 236 |
| YR-DSB | FA20 | 242 |
| YR-DVA | HS25 | 256024 |
| **YR-ELV** | **C560** | **0652** |
| YR-FNA | FA50 | 148 |
| **YR-GCI** | **C56X** | **6033** |
| YR-RPB | LJ60 | 030 |
| YR-RPG | C560 | 0665 |
| **YR-RPR** | **C56X** | **5337** |
| **YR-TIC** | **C560** | **0200** |
| **YR-TIG** | **GALX** | **012** |
| **YR-TII** | **GALX** | **089** |
| **YR-TIK** | **GLEX** | **9229** |
| **YR-TOY** | **C52A** | **0455** |
| YR-VPA | HS25 | 258389 |

Yugoslavia/Serbia

| | | |
|---|---|---|
| YU-BIA | C500 | 031 |
| YU-BIH | LJ24 | 320 |
| YU-BJG | LJ25 | 187 |
| YU-BJH | LJ25 | 186 |
| YU-BKJ | LJ25 | 205 |
| YU-BKR | LJ25 | 221 |
| YU-BKZ | C500 | 415 |
| YU-BLY | SBRL | 380-65 |
| YU-BME | HS25 | 256048 |
| YU-BML | C500 | 554 |
| **YU-BNA** | **FA50** | **43** |
| YU-BOE | CS55 | 0045 |
| YU-BOL | LJ35 | 618 |
| YU-BPL | C550 | 480 |
| YU-BPU | C550 | 144 |
| YU-BPY | LJ35 | 173 |
| YU-BPZ | FA50 | 25 |
| YU-BRA | LJ25 | 202 |
| YU-BRB | LJ25 | 203 |
| **YU-BRZ** | **LJ31** | **045** |
| **YU-BSG** | **C550** | **550-1049** |
| **YU-BSM** | **C550** | **550-0808** |
| **YU-BTB** | **C550** | **550-1037** |
| **YU-BTM** | **C650** | **7080** |
| **YU-BTN** | **C52B** | **0193** |
| **YU-BTT** | **C550** | **246** |
| **YU-BUU** | **C52A** | **0411** |
| YU-BVA | BE40 | RK-124 |
| **YU-BVV** | **C550** | **307** |
| **YU-BZM** | **C56X** | **6037** |
| **YU-BZZ** | **C550** | **550-0924** |
| **YU-FCS** | **C550** | **347** |
| **YU-MDV** | **C500** | **616** |
| **YU-MTU** | **C525** | **0295** |
| **YU-SEG** | **C500** | **276** |
| **YU-SPA** | **C56X** | **5760** |
| **YU-SPM** | **C510** | **0049** |
| **YU-VER** | **C52A** | **0401** |

Venezuela

| | | |
|---|---|---|
| **YV** | **ASTR** | **057** |
| **YV** | **BE40** | **RK-299** |
| **YV** | **BE40** | **RK-557** |
| **YV** | **C500** | **047** |
| **YV** | **C500** | **125** |
| **YV** | **C500** | **147** |
| **YV** | **C500** | **217** |
| **YV** | **C500** | **310** |
| **YV** | **C500** | **352** |
| **YV** | **C52A** | **0121** |
| **YV** | **C550** | **317** |
| **YV** | **C560** | **0408** |
| **YV** | **CS55** | **0099** |
| **YV** | **CS55** | **0146** |
| **YV** | **GLF2** | **245/30** |
| **YV** | **HS25** | **25176** |
| **YV** | **HS25** | **25241** |
| **YV** | **HS25** | **25244** |
| **YV** | **LJ24** | **212** |
| **YV** | **LJ25** | **217** |
| **YV** | **LJ25** | **234** |
| **YV** | **LJ25** | **235** |
| **YV** | **LJ25** | **363** |
| **YV** | **LJ35** | **360** |
| **YV** | **SBRL** | **465-37** |
| **YV** | **WW24** | **205** |
| **YV** | **WW24** | **315** |
| **YV113T** | **HS25** | **25231** |
| **YV120T** | **SBRL** | **282-106** |
| YV129T | LJ25 | 253 |
| YV195T | MU30 | A064SA |
| **YV198T** | **BE40** | **RK-306** |
| YV205T | C550 | 236 |
| **YV213T** | **BE40** | **RK-152** |
| **YV225T** | **SBRL** | **282-120** |
| YV232T | C500 | 446 |
| **YV233T** | **C500** | **317** |
| **YV238T** | **C500** | **072** |
| **YV251T** | **WW24** | **362** |
| **YV252T** | **C550** | **231** |
| **YV255T** | **C550** | **335** |
| **YV265T** | **SBRL** | **380-2** |
| **YV266T** | **C550** | **550-0943** |
| **YV289T** | **C52A** | **0318** |
| **YV305T** | **C52A** | **0221** |
| **YV338T** | **SBRL** | **380-44** |
| **YV345T** | **HS25** | **256063** |
| **YV351T** | **LJ45** | **006** |
| **YV363T** | **BE40** | **RK-38** |
| **YV416T** | **SBRL** | **282-98** |
| **YV1022** | **C560** | **0134** |
| **YV1079** | **LJ24** | **173** |
| **YV1083** | **FA50** | **22** |
| **YV1118** | **LJ45** | **396** |
| **YV1128** | **FA50** | **53** |
| **YV1129** | **FA50** | **63** |
| **YV1152** | **C500** | **043** |
| **YV1192** | **C550** | **683** |
| **YV1316** | **C500** | **052** |
| **YV1346** | **LJ25** | **253** |
| **YV1401** | **GALX** | **041** |
| **YV1432** | **C500** | **167** |
| **YV1495** | **FA50** | **136** |
| **YV1496** | **FA50** | **219** |
| **YV1541** | **C500** | **399** |
| **YV1563** | **C550** | **463** |
| **YV1677** | **C500** | **109** |
| **YV1681** | **GLF2** | **25** |
| **YV1685** | **WW24** | **330** |
| **YV1686** | **C500** | **216** |
| **YV1687** | **HS25** | **25191** |
| **YV1713** | **C500** | **058** |
| **YV1771** | **ASTR** | **077** |
| **YV1776** | **C550** | **200** |
| **YV1794** | **LJ55** | **031** |
| **YV1813** | **C550** | **385** |
| **YV1828** | **LJ35** | **019** |
| (YV1969) | C750 | 0134 |
| **YV2030** | **C500** | **215** |
| YV2039 | F900 | 108 |
| **YV2040** | **F900** | **133** |
| **YV2044** | **LJ35** | **437** |
| **YV2053** | **F9EX** | **60** |
| **YV2073** | **C550** | **076** |
| **YV2103** | **C550** | **235** |
| **YV2110** | **C560** | **0511** |
| **YV2165** | **FA50** | **4** |
| **YV2166** | **C550** | **467** |
| **YV2246** | **C550** | **332** |
| **YV2286** | **C550** | **637** |
| **YV2317** | **C550** | **124** |
| **YV2331** | **C525** | **0631** |
| **YV2346** | **FA50** | **44** |
| **YV2347** | **MU30** | **A064SA** |
| **YV2389** | **C560** | **0757** |
| **YV2416** | **HS25** | **25098** |
| **YV2443** | **C550** | **236** |
| **YV2452** | **BE40** | **RK-68** |
| **YV2465** | **LJ25** | **126** |
| YV2470 | C750 | 0134 |
| **YV2474** | **FA10** | **67** |
| **YV2477** | **HS25** | **258149** |
| **YV2485** | **F9EX** | **196** |
| **YV2486** | **F9EX** | **197** |
| **YV2498** | **C500** | **139** |
| **YV2565** | **LJ45** | **389** |
| **YV2567** | **LJ45** | **390** |
| **YV2609** | **E50P** | **50000080** |
| **YV0157** | **BE40** | **RK-103** |
| (YV- ) | C550 | 550-0817 |
| YV-01CP | CRVT | 35 |
| YV-01CP | LJ24 | 040 |
| YV-01CP | LJ35 | 157 |
| YV-03CP | JSTR | 5106/9 |
| (YV-04CP) | C550 | 455 |
| YV-05C | C550 | 463 |
| YV-05CP | C550 | 018 |
| YV-06CP | C550 | 020 |
| YV-07CP | FA10 | 47 |
| YV-07P | C500 | 253 |
| YV-12CP | LJ55 | 031 |
| YV-15CP | C500 | 095 |
| YV-15CP | LJ24 | 047 |
| YV-15CP | LJ35 | 342 |
| (YV-15CP) | LJ35 | 191 |
| (YV-15CP) | LJ35 | 270 |
| YV-17CP | FA10 | 100 |
| YV-19CP | C550 | 003 |
| YV-19P | C500 | 253 |
| YV-21CP | C500 | 115 |
| YV-26CP | LJ25 | 098 |
| YV-29CP | MU30 | A049SA |
| YV-36CP | C550 | 080 |
| (YV-37CP) | WW24 | 193 |
| YV-38CP | FA20 | 287 |
| YV-41CP | LJ55 | 019 |
| (YV-41CP) | LJ55 | 015 |
| YV-43CP | C500 | 284 |
| YV-50CP | C500 | 289 |
| YV-52CP | C500 | 399 |
| YV-55CP | C500 | 215 |
| YV-58CP | WW24 | 172 |
| (YV-60CP) | GLF2 | 163 |
| YV-62CP | C500 | 297 |
| (YV-64CP) | SBRL | 282-134 |
| YV-65CP | LJ35 | 161 |
| YV-70CP | FA10 | 66 |
| YV-78CP | FA20 | 28 |
| YV-79CP | C500 | 397 |
| YV-88CP | LJ25 | 033 |
| YV-89CP | LJ36 | 002 |
| YV-99CP | FA10 | 172 |
| YV-100CP | LJ35 | 083 |
| YV-101CP | FA10 | 47 |
| YV-119P | WW24 | 184 |
| YV-120CP | C500 | 368 |
| YV-123CP | WW24 | 16 |
| YV-125CP | LJ55 | 126 |
| YV-126CP | FA20 | 30 |
| YV-130P | LJ25 | 071 |
| (YV-131CP) | LJ35 | 193 |
| YV-132CP | LJ25 | 071 |
| (YV-135CP) | C500 | 384 |
| YV-137CP | C550 | 049 |
| YV-140CP | C550 | 014 |
| YV-141CP | HS25 | 25195 |
| YV-147CP | C550 | 106 |
| YV-151CP | C550 | 016 |
| YV-159CP | C500 | 393 |
| YV-160CP | WW24 | 211 |
| YV-161P | LJ36 | 002 |
| YV-162CP | C550 | 332 |
| YV-163CP | MS76 | 103 |
| YV-166CP | C500 | 384 |
| YV-169CP | C550 | 018 |
| YV-169CP | C560 | 0230 |
| YV-173CP | LJ35 | 163 |
| YV-178CP | LJ24 | 342 |
| YV-187CP | C550 | 197 |
| YV-187CP | JSTR | 5107 |
| YV-190CP | WW24 | 219 |
| YV-200C | FA20 | 200 |
| YV-203CP | LJ25 | 061 |
| YV-205CP | C550 | 024 |
| (YV-209CP) | C550 | 175 |
| YV-210CP | WW24 | 308 |
| YV-213CP | C550 | 076 |
| YV-221CP | FA10 | 47 |
| YV-232CP | C500 | 449 |
| YV-253CP | C500 | 418 |
| YV-253P | C500 | 418 |
| YV-265CP | LJ35 | 247 |
| (YV-269CP) | FA50 | 126 |
| (YV-270CP) | LJ35 | 375 |
| (YV-274CP) | MU30 | A046SA |
| YV-276CP | C550 | 385 |
| YV-278CP | LJ24 | 036 |
| YV-286CP | LJ35 | 268 |
| YV-292CP | LJ55 | 052 |
| YV-297CP | WW24 | 202 |
| YV-298CP | C550 | 175 |
| YV-299CP | C550 | 133 |
| YV-300CP | C550 | 172 |
| YV-301CP | C550 | 174 |
| YV-301P | C500 | 518 |
| YV-309P | MU30 | A049SA |
| **YV-317T** | **C500** | **093** |
| (YV-325CP) | LJ55 | 112 |
| YV-326CP | LJ35 | 352 |
| YV-327CP | LJ35 | 344 |
| (YV-328CP) | LJ35 | 309 |
| YV-332CP | WW24 | 330 |
| YV-370CP | C500 | 171 |
| YV-374CP | LJ55 | 053 |
| YV-376CP | C550 | 637 |
| YV-387CP | WW24 | 306 |
| YV-388CP | HFB3 | 1057 |
| YV-388CP | WW24 | 307 |
| YV-393CP | WW24 | 262 |
| YV-432CP | LJ35 | 437 |
| YV-433CP | LJ35 | 431 |
| YV-434CP | LJ35 | 422 |
| YV-450CP | FA50 | 219 |
| YV-451CP | WW24 | 343 |
| YV-452CP | FA50 | 4 |
| YV-455CP | FA50 | 136 |
| YV-462CP | FA50 | 4 |
| (YV-553CP) | FA50 | 30 |
| YV-572CP | CRVT | 17 |
| YV-589CP | CRVT | 35 |
| YV-601CP | FA10 | 73 |
| YV-604P | C550 | 385 |
| YV-606CP | C550 | 035 |
| YV-625CP | C500 | 210 |
| YV-646CP | C500 | 031 |
| YV-662CP | C550 | 682 |
| YV-666CP | WW24 | 347 |
| YV-678CP | C550 | 106 |
| YV-688CP | C500 | 524 |
| YV-697CP | C500 | 446 |
| YV-701CP | C550 | 683 |
| YV-707CP | C500 | 070 |
| YV-713CP | C550 | 463 |
| YV-717CP | C500 | 135 |
| YV-735CP | HS25 | 258203 |
| YV-737CP | BE40 | RJ-6 |
| YV-738CP | BE40 | RJ-6 |
| YV-754CP | BE40 | RK-152 |
| YV-757CP | ASTR | 060 |
| YV-770CP | WW24 | 258 |
| YV-771CP | ASTR | 077 |
| YV-772CP | GALX | 041 |
| YV-777CP | WW24 | 191 |
| YV-778CP | C550 | 385 |
| YV-785CP | ASTR | 057 |

| | | |
|---|---|---|
| YV-800CP | HS25 | 258209 |
| YV-810CP | C550 | 467 |
| YV-811CP | C560 | 0134 |
| YV-814CP | HS25 | 258234 |
| YV-815CP | HS25 | 25098 |
| YV-824CP | LJ24 | 173 |
| YV-825CP | HS25 | 25175 |
| YV-826CP | JSTR | 5205 |
| YV-838CP | BE40 | RJ-6 |
| YV-850CP | LJ35 | 596 |
| YV-876C | FA20 | 200 |
| YV-881CP | C500 | 052 |
| YV-888CP | C550 | 235 |
| YV-900CP | C550 | 214 |
| YV-901CP | C500 | 058 |
| YV-909CP | C550 | 317 |
| YV-911CP | C550 | 698 |
| **YV-939CP** | **C500** | **031** |
| YV-940CP | C500 | 299 |
| YV-943CP | BE40 | RK-142 |
| YV-952CP | LJ31 | 168 |
| YV-962CP | WW24 | 385 |
| YV-968CP | BE40 | RK-306 |
| YV-997CP | LJ35 | 458 |
| YV-999P | HFB3 | 1037 |
| YV-1049CP | LJ25 | 253 |
| YV-1055CP | C550 | 335 |
| (YV-1071CP) | C500 | 200 |
| (YV-1107) | C550 | 449 |
| YV-1111CP | CL60 | 1028 |
| YV-1111CP | HS25 | 25224 |
| YV-1122CP | HS25 | 25248 |
| YV-1133CP | C500 | 317 |
| YV-1144CP | SBRL | 282-106 |
| YV-1145CP | HS25 | 25191 |
| YV-1478P | C550 | 106 |
| YV-2199P | ASTR | 057 |
| YV-2267P | C500 | 052 |
| YV-2295P | C500 | 472 |
| **YV-2338P** | **C550** | **449** |
| **YV-2426P** | **C550** | **300** |
| YV-2454P | WW24 | 96 |
| YV-2477P | C500 | 052 |
| YV-2479P | C500 | 035 |
| **YV-2482P** | **WW24** | **172** |
| YV-2564P | ASTR | 057 |
| YV-2567P | C550 | 200 |
| YV-2605P | C500 | 518 |
| YV-2628P | C500 | 052 |
| YV-2671P | C550 | 076 |
| YV-2711P | C550 | 550-0943 |
| YV-2821P | C500 | 167 |
| YV-E-GPA | LJ24 | 047 |
| YV-O-CVG-1 | WW24 | 308 |
| YV-O-CVG-2 | C550 | 020 |
| YV-O-CVG-3 | WW24 | 343 |
| YV-O-FMO-6 | WW24 | 343 |
| YV-O-MAC-1 | C500 | 336 |
| YV-O-MRI-1 | LJ35 | 270 |
| YV-O-MTC | C550 | 251 |
| YV-O-MTC-2 | C500 | 472 |
| YV-O-MTC-20 | C550 | 251 |
| YV-O-SATA-12 | FA50 | 4 |
| YV-O-SID-3 | C500 | 397 |
| YV-T-000 | C500 | 215 |
| YV-T-AFA | C500 | 115 |
| YV-T-ASG | LJ36 | 002 |
| YV-T-AVA | FA20 | 287 |
| YV-T-DTT | LJ25 | 071 |
| YV-T-MMM | C500 | 253 |

## Zimbabwe

| | | |
|---|---|---|
| Z-TBX | HS25 | 25067 |
| Z-VEC | HS25 | 25215 |
| Z-WKY | LJ25 | 160 |
| Z-WSY | C500 | 387 |

## New Zealand

| | | |
|---|---|---|
| (ZK-ABC) | HA4T | RC-21 |
| **ZK-AWK** | **C560** | **0396** |
| ZK-EUI | HS25 | 258058 |
| (ZK-EUR) | HS25 | 258058 |
| **ZK-JTH** | **C680** | **0058** |
| **ZK-KFB** | **GLF4** | **1362** |
| ZK-KFB | GLF5 | 5260 |
| **ZK-LCA** | **C510** | **0011** |
| ZK-LJL | C500 | 123 |
| ZK-MAY | FA20 | 505 |
| ZK-MAZ | FA10 | 213 |
| **ZK-MOT** | **C510** | **0054** |
| ZK-MRM | HS25 | 258074 |
| ZK-MUS | C510 | 0054 |
| ZK-MUS | C510 | 0300 |
| ZK-NLJ | C650 | 0133 |
| **ZK-PGA** | **C510** | **0033** |
| **ZK-RGB** | **GALX** | **158** |
| (ZK-RHP) | HS25 | 258088 |
| ZK-RJI | HS25 | 258082 |
| **ZK-RML** | **WW24** | **339** |
| ZK-TBM | C525 | 0511 |
| **ZK-TBM** | **C52B** | **0027** |
| ZK-TCB | HS25 | 258001 |
| (ZK-WNL) | FA10 | 50 |
| **ZK-XVL** | **LJ35** | **649** |
| ZK-YES | C510 | 0054 |

## Paraguay

| | | |
|---|---|---|
| ZP- | WW24 | 41 |
| ZP-AGD | WW24 | 151 |
| **ZP-BJB** | **BE40** | **RK-19** |
| **ZP-BZH** | **C560** | **0357** |
| ZP-PNB | C500 | 335 |
| ZP-PNB | C550 | 320 |
| ZP-PUP | C500 | 335 |
| ZP-TCA | C550 | 710 |
| ZP-TDF | HS25 | 25173 |
| **ZP-TKO** | **HS25** | **25173** |
| ZP-TNB | C550 | 320 |
| ZP-TWN | C550 | 374 |
| ZP-TYO | C500 | 008 |
| ZP-TYO | C550 | 039 |
| ZP-TYP | C500 | 008 |
| ZP-TZH | C500 | 185 |
| ZP-TZY | C500 | 275 |

## South Africa

| | | |
|---|---|---|
| **ZS-** | **HS25** | **257144** |
| **ZS-AAM** | **PRM1** | **RB-265** |
| **ZS-ABG** | **HS25** | **259024** |
| ZS-ABG | PRM1 | RB-70 |
| **ZS-ACE** | **C500** | **652** |
| **ZS-ACT** | **CL30** | **20034** |
| (ZS-ACT) | CL30 | 20038 |
| ZS-ACT | HS25 | 259026 |
| **ZS-AFD** | **C510** | **0134** |
| **ZS-AFG** | **HS25** | **258724** |
| ZS-AGT | LJ31 | 146 |
| ZS-AJD | LJ31 | 202 |
| **ZS-AJD** | **LJ45** | **369** |
| ZS-AJN | LJ45 | 181 |
| **ZS-AKG** | **C680** | **0254** |
| ZS-ALT | CL64 | 5552 |
| ZS-AMB | C500 | 071 |
| **ZS-AOL** | **GLF5** | **634** |
| **ZS-ARA** | **LJ35** | **349** |
| **ZS-ARG** | **C550** | **132** |
| (ZS-ARK) | HS25 | 258658 |
| ZS-AVL | CL64 | 5328 |
| ZS-AVL | HS25 | 259017 |
| **ZS-AVM** | **PRM1** | **RB-31** |
| (ZS-BAR) | LJ45 | 007 |
| ZS-BAR | LJ45 | 046 |
| ZS-BAR | LJ45 | 219 |
| ZS-BCT | ASTR | 075 |
| **ZS-BEN** | **CS55** | **0041** |
| (ZS-BFB) | FA50 | 91 |
| **ZS-BFS** | **C500** | **262** |
| **ZS-BLE** | **LJ35** | **304** |
| ZS-BMB | FA50 | 91 |
| **ZS-BOT** | **HS25** | **HA-0032** |
| ZS-BPG | HS25 | 258165 |
| (ZS-BSS) | C525 | 0124 |
| **ZS-BTC** | **C500** | **161** |
| **ZS-BXR** | **LJ25** | **141** |
| **ZS-CAG** | **HS25** | **257172** |
| **ZS-CAL** | **HS25** | **25172** |
| **ZS-CAQ** | **FA50** | **133** |
| **ZS-CAR** | **CS55** | **0078** |
| **ZS-CAS** | **FA50** | **91** |
| ZS-CAT | LJ25 | 366 |
| ZS-CCT | CL61 | 5176 |
| ZS-CCT | HS25 | 259026 |
| ZS-CDS | C560 | 0414 |
| ZS-CEW | LJ35 | 341 |
| ZS-CJT | C52A | 0163 |
| **ZS-CJT** | **C52B** | **0116** |
| ZS-CMB | CL64 | 5479 |
| **ZS-CNA** | **HS25** | **25159** |
| **ZS-CRH** | **LJ36** | **055** |
| **ZS-CTF** | **C510** | **0060** |
| **ZS-CTL** | **GLF2** | **218** |
| **ZS-CWD** | **C500** | **420** |
| **ZS-CWG** | **CS55** | **0138** |
| (ZS-DAJ) | GLEX | 9094 |
| ZS-DAV | F900 | 149 |
| **ZS-DBS** | **C500** | **061** |
| **ZS-DCA** | **LJ45** | **117** |
| ZS-DCK | HS25 | 258403 |
| (ZS-DCT) | LJ31 | 146 |
| ZS-DCT | LJ45 | 052 |
| ZS-DDA | HS25 | 258601 |
| **ZS-DDM** | **PRM1** | **RB-238** |
| ZS-DDM | PRM1 | RB-63 |
| **ZS-DDT** | **HA4T** | **RC-15** |
| ZS-DDT | HS25 | 258465 |
| **ZS-DES** | **CS55** | **0087** |
| **ZS-DFI** | **C510** | **0093** |
| (ZS-DFN) | GLEX | 9099 |
| ZS-DGB | CL64 | 5390 |
| **ZS-DGW** | **GLF2** | **166/15** |
| (ZS-DHL) | LJ31 | 170 |
| **ZS-DIY** | **C510** | **0092** |
| **ZS-DJA** | **GLF2** | **156/31** |
| ZS-DJB | LJ35 | 647 |
| ZS-DLJ | GLEX | 9094 |
| **ZS-DPP** | **C52B** | **0211** |
| ZS-DSA | C500 | 044 |
| **ZS-DTD** | **HA4T** | **RC-12** |
| ZS-EAG | LJ31 | 142 |
| **ZS-EDA** | **CS55** | **0126** |
| (ZS-EFD) | LJ35 | 594 |
| ZS-EHL | C500 | 431 |
| **ZS-ESA** | **GLEX** | **9061** |
| (ZS-FCB) | C560 | 0503 |
| ZS-FCB | C56X | 5018 |
| **ZS-FOS** | **C56X** | **5352** |
| **ZS-FOX** | **FA10** | **72** |
| ZS-FSI | HS25 | 258078 |
| (ZS-FUL) | LJ45 | 181 |
| (ZS-FUL) | LJ45 | 270 |
| ZS-FUN | LJ24 | 354 |
| **ZS-GJB** | **GLEX** | **9122** |
| ZS-GLD | LJ24 | 291 |
| (ZS-GSB) | SBRL | 282-53 |
| **ZS-GSG** | **LJ60** | **301** |
| (ZS-HWK) | HS25 | HA-0102 |
| **ZS-ICC** | **JSTR** | **5223** |
| **ZS-ICU** | **HS25** | **257113** |
| ZS-IDC | C56X | 5352 |
| **ZS-IDC** | **C680** | **0224** |
| ZS-IDC | CS55 | 0148 |
| **ZS-IGP** | **LJ35** | **608** |
| ZS-INS | LJ35 | 238 |
| **ZS-IPE** | **HS25** | **257202** |
| (ZS-IPI) | HS25 | 257202 |
| ZS-ISA | C500 | 224 |
| **ZS-ISA** | **CL60** | **1081** |
| (ZS-ITT) | LJ45 | 007 |
| ZS-IYY | C500 | 078 |
| ZS-JBA | HS25 | 25259 |
| (ZS-JBR) | LJ45 | 007 |
| ZS-JDL | C680 | 0033 |
| **ZS-JDL** | **C680** | **0193** |
| ZS-JDM | C510 | 0079 |
| **ZS-JGC** | **GLF3** | **312** |
| ZS-JHL | HS25 | 256049 |
| ZS-JIH | HS25 | 25260 |
| ZS-JIS | GLF2 | 136 |
| ZS-JJO | LJ24 | 317 |
| ZS-JKR | C500 | 268 |
| **ZS-JLK** | **FA10** | **207** |
| ZS-JOK | C500 | 329 |
| ZS-JOO | C500 | 291 |
| (ZS-JRM) | LJ60 | 149 |
| ZS-JRO | BE40 | RK-101 |
| **ZS-JVS** | **FA20** | **493** |
| ZS-JWC | LJ24 | 030 |
| **ZS-KAA** | **LJ45** | **305** |
| **ZS-KBS** | **HS25** | **HA-0017** |
| ZS-KBS | PRM1 | RB-147 |
| (ZS-KGF) | C500 | 538 |
| **ZS-KGS** | **FA20** | **385** |
| **ZS-KJY** | **LJ24** | **165** |
| ZS-KJY | LJ24 | 165 |
| ZS-KOO | C550 | 154 |
| ZS-KPA | C500 | 567 |
| **ZS-KPM** | **C510** | **0091** |
| **ZS-LAH** | **GLF3** | **328** |
| ZS-LAL | FA20 | 228/473 |
| ZS-LBB | FA50 | 42 |
| ZS-LDK | C550 | 310 |
| ZS-LDO | C500 | 652 |
| **ZS-LDV** | **C500** | **656** |
| ZS-LEE | C550 | 380 |
| **ZS-LEO** | **CL64** | **5318** |
| ZS-LHP | C500 | 667 |
| ZS-LHT | C550 | 439 |
| ZS-LHU | C550 | 179 |
| ZS-LHW | C550 | 416 |
| **ZS-LIG** | **C550** | **474** |
| ZS-LII | LJ35 | 062 |
| (ZS-LJM) | FA50 | 107 |
| ZS-LKG | C510 | 0090 |
| ZS-LLG | FA20 | 228/473 |
| ZS-LLG | LJ24 | 210 |
| ZS-LLO | C550 | 235 |
| ZS-LME | HS25 | 25242 |
| ZS-LNP | C550 | 560 |
| **ZS-LOG** | **GLF2** | **19** |
| ZS-LOW | C500 | 514 |
| ZS-LOW | LJ45 | 092 |
| **ZS-LOW** | **LJ45** | **228** |
| ZS-LPE | HS25 | 25184 |
| ZS-LPF | HS25 | 25269 |
| ZS-LPH | C500 | 402 |
| (ZS-LRI) | LJ25 | 366 |
| ZS-LTK | LJ24 | 103 |
| ZS-LTK | LJ24 | 103 |
| ZS-LTK | LJ24 | 103 |
| ZS-LUD | LJ25 | 295 |
| **ZS-LWU** | **LJ24** | **209** |
| **ZS-LXH** | **LJ25** | **206** |
| ZS-LXT | C500 | 622 |
| ZS-LYB | C500 | 278 |
| **ZS-MAN** | **HS25** | **25067** |
| ZS-MBR | LJ24 | 064 |
| ZS-MBS | C500 | 340 |
| ZS-MBX | C550 | 587 |
| **ZS-MCO** | **PRM1** | **RB-72** |
| ZS-MCP | C500 | 130 |
| **ZS-MCU** | **C500** | **137** |
| ZS-MDA | ASTR | 055 |
| ZS-MDN | LJ24 | 081 |
| **ZS-MEG** | **HS25** | **25233** |
| **ZS-MGD** | **F2EX** | **51** |
| ZS-MGH | C500 | 299 |
| **ZS-MGJ** | **LJ24** | **207** |
| ZS-MGK | LJ35 | 357 |
| ZS-MGK | PRM1 | RB-54 |
| ZS-MGK | PRM1 | RB-67 |
| ZS-MGL | C500 | 384 |
| **ZS-MGS** | **FA50** | **232** |
| **ZS-MHN** | **BE40** | **RJ-59** |
| **ZS-MLN** | **C550** | **266** |
| ZS-MLS | C550 | 621 |
| **ZS-MMG** | **GLF2** | **85** |
| ZS-MPI | C500 | 334 |
| ZS-MPN | C500 | 393 |
| ZS-MPT | C560 | 0089 |
| **ZS-MTD** | **LJ25** | **160** |
| ZS-MTD | LJ25 | 160 |
| **ZS-MUS** | **C510** | **0137** |
| ZS-MVV | C560 | 0062 |
| ZS-MVX | C525 | 0010 |
| ZS-MVZ | C560 | 0064 |
| ZS-MWW | LJ35 | 157 |
| (ZS-MYN) | C560 | 0064 |
| ZS-MZM | WW24 | 390 |
| ZS-MZO | C500 | 453 |
| **ZS-NAN** | **F900** | **99** |
| ZS-NAT | C550 | 554 |
| ZS-NDT | C560 | 0160 |
| ZS-NDU | C560 | 0151 |
| ZS-NDW | C560 | 0166 |

**ZS-NDX C560 0152**
ZS-NER CL60 1019
ZS-NEW HS25 259017
(ZS-NEX) LJ35 671
ZS-NFK LJ35 671
ZS-NFL C550 697
(ZS-NFS) LJ35 671
ZS-NGG LJ24 280
**ZS-NGL C560 0202**
ZS-NGM C560 0201
ZS-NGR C500 080
**ZS-NGS C560 0241**
ZS-NHC C560 0203
ZS-NHD C560 0255
ZS-NHE C525 0033
ZS-NHF C500 296
ZS-NHL HS25 259032
ZS-NHO C550 264
ZS-NID LJ35 426
**ZS-NII C550 184**
ZS-NJF LJ25 311
ZS-NJH HS25 258224
ZS-NKD CL61 5060
ZS-NMO GLF4 1129
ZS-NNF F2TH 2
"ZS-NNV" C560 0322
ZS-NOD BE40 RJ-18
ZS-NPV HS25 25215
ZS-NRZ LJ35 077
ZS-NSB LJ35 654
ZS-NTV LJ60 052
ZS-NUW C525 0150
**ZS-NUZ C560 0398**
ZS-NVP LJ60 210
ZS-NVV C560 0322
**ZS-NYG LJ25 098**
**ZS-NYV LJ31 115**
ZS-NZO BE40 RK-57
ZS-OAM C500 077
ZS-OCG BE40 RK-140
(ZS-ODP) WW24 171
**ZS-OEA LJ24 267**
ZS-OFM C560 0467
ZS-OFW LJ31 031
ZS-OGS C500 260
**ZS-OHZ C56X 5079**
**ZS-OIE C550 480**
**ZS-OIF HS25 25221**
ZS-OIZ LJ45 006
"ZS-OJO" LJ31 058
ZS-OLJ LJ45 046
**ZS-OML LJ31 170**
**ZS-ONE C500 002**
**ZS-ONG FA50 287**
ZS-ONL CL61 3006
ZS-ONP BE40 RK-157
ZS-OPD LJ45 007
**ZS-OPM LJ45 308**
**ZS-OPN LJ45 321**
**ZS-OPO LJ45 342**
**ZS-OPR LJ45 219**
**ZS-OPY LJ45 218**
**ZS-ORW BE40 RJ-37**
ZS-OSG CL64 5486
(ZS-OSP) LJ45 130
ZS-OUU BE40 RJ-25
ZS-OXB LJ45 046
**ZS-OXY HS25 258095**
(ZS-OZU) HS25 25219
**ZS-PAJ C52A 0457**
**ZS-PAR HS25 258050**
(ZS-PBA) LJ35 263
(ZS-PBI) LJ24 145
ZS-PCY HS25 258589
ZS-PDB BE40 RK-162
ZS-PDG LJ45 092
ZS-PFB FA50 177
**ZS-PFE PRM1 RB-94**
**ZS-PFG C500 122**
**ZS-PHP C500 490**
ZS-PJE HS25 25023
ZS-PKD GALX 098
**ZS-PKR F2TH 114**
**ZS-PKY HS25 258429**
**ZS-PLC HS25 25204**
**ZS-PMA C500 123**
ZS-PMC C550 141
ZS-PNP LJ31 202
**ZS-PNP LJ45 059**
**ZS-POT BE40 RK-400**
**ZS-PPH HS25 258717**
(ZS-PPR) HA4T RC-13
(ZS-PPR) LJ45 092
(ZS-PRF) PRM1 RB-24
ZS-PRM PRM1 RB-24
ZS-PSE HS25 258231
**ZS-PSG CS55 0112**
ZS-PTJ SBRL 282-53
(ZS-PTL) LJ35 594
ZS-PTL LJ45 046
**ZS-PTL LJ45 181**
**ZS-PTP HS25 258633**
**ZS-PTT C500 085**
**ZS-PWT C500 076**
**ZS-PWU C525 0431**
**ZS-PXD C500 257**
**ZS-PYY GLF2 26**
ZS-PZA HS25 258632
**ZS-PZX HS25 258670**
**ZS-RCC C500 106**
ZS-RCS C550 065
**ZS-RKV C550 060**
ZS-SAB C750 0080
**ZS-SAH HS25 HA-0026**
**ZS-SAP C680 0190**
(ZS-SCT) CL30 20038
(ZS-SCT) LJ60 239
ZS-SCX C550 569
**ZS-SDU HS25 257053**
**ZS-SDZ CL65 5706**
**ZS-SEA FA10 156**
**ZS-SEB FA10 127**
(ZS-SEB) FA10 160
ZS-SES LJ35 185
**ZS-SFV LJ35 275**
ZS-SFY ASTR 158
**ZS-SGC CL61 5070**
ZS-SGH LJ24 187
ZS-SGJ HS25 HA-0032
ZS-SGS PRM1 RB-72
**ZS-SGT C500 224**
**ZS-SGV HS25 HA-0067**
ZS-SMB C560 0359
**ZS-SME HS25 HA-0104**
ZS-SMT HS25 25128
ZS-SOS FA20 493
**ZS-SRU PRM1 RB-63**
**ZS-SSM LJ25 022**
**ZS-STS E50P 50000069**
**ZS-TBN HS25 25023**
**ZS-TEJ LJ60 173**
**ZS-TEX GLF3 355**
ZS-TGG GLF2 8
**ZS-TJS LJ45 083**
**ZS-TMG C500 149**
**ZS-TOW LJ35 475**
**ZS-TOY LJ24 219**
**ZS-TPG GLF2 150**
ZS-UCH C560 0607
**ZS-ULT LJ45 194**
**ZS-VIP GLF3 444**
**ZS-WHG GLF2 67**
**ZS-WJW HS25 257159**
**ZS-XRS GLEX 9260**
ZS-YES CL30 20044
ZS-YES LJ45 194
ZS-ZBB F900 143
**ZS-ZBB GLEX 9253**
**ZS-ZOT HA4T RC-23**
ZS-ZZZ LJ35 172

## Macedonia

**Z3-BAA LJ25 205**
**Z3-MKD LJ60 279**

## Monaco

3A-MDB HS25 25131
3A-MDE HS25 25131
3A-MGA F2TH 167
**3A-MGA F9EX 195**
3A-MGR F2TH 167
3A-MGR FA20 473
3A-MGT FA10 19
3A-MJV FA20 473
3A-MMA F2TH 167
3A-MPP MS76 098
3A-MRB C550 421
**3A-MRG C52B 0096**
3A-MTB C500 482
3A-MWA C550 063

## Mauritius

**3B- LJ45 092**
3B-GFI CL60 1019
**3B-NGT CL30 20133**
3B-NSY FA50 230
**3B-PGF GLF4 1046**
**3B-SSD CL30 20126**
3B-XLA F900 7

## Equatorial Guniea

**3C-LGE FA50 246**
**3C-ONM F900 167**
**3C-QQU JSTR 5082/36**
3C-QRK JSTR 5202

## Swaziland

(see also VQ-Z)

3D-AAB HS25 25080
3D-AAC GLF2 136
3D-AAC GLF3 354
3D-AAI GLF3 354
3D-ABZ HS25 25242
3D-ACB FA10 21
3D-ACQ C550 179
3D-ACR C500 268
3D-ACT C550 264
3D-ACZ LJ35 238
3D-ADC LJ35 475
3D-ADH C500 667
3D-ADR FA10 202
3D-AEZ LJ25 160
3D-AFH MU30 A062SA
3D-AFJ LJ24 064
3D-ART FA10 61
3D-AVH C550 341
3D-AVL HS25 25254
3D-AVL HS25 258025
**3D-BIS LJ45 104**
3D-BOS HS25 256021
3D-IER C500 489
3D-LLG FA20 228/473
3D-TCB GLF2 73/9

## Guinea

(3X-GBD) GLF2 74
3X-GCI FA10 89

## Azerbaijan

**4K-AZ88 GALX 189**
**4K-AZ888 GLF4 4045**
**4K-MEK8 GLF5 5204**

## Montenegro

**4O-BBB LJ45 372**
**4O-BVA BE40 RK-124**
**4O-OOO C500 489**

## Yemen

(see also 7O-)

4W-ACA HS25 25219
4W-ACE HS25 257046
4W-ACM HS25 257178
4W-ACN HS25 258037

## Israel

**4X- CS55 0118**
4X-AIP WW24 243
4X-CJA WW24 154
4X-CJB WW24 153
4X-CJC WW24 152
4X-CJD WW24 151
4X-CJE WW24 155
4X-CJF WW24 156
4X-CJG WW24 157
4X-CJH WW24 158
4X-CJI WW24 159
4X-CJJ WW24 160
4X-CJK WW24 161
4X-CJL WW24 162
4X-CJM WW24 163
4X-CJN WW24 164
4X-CJO WW24 165
4X-CJP WW24 166
4X-CJP WW24 376
4X-CJQ WW24 167
4X-CJR WW24 168
4X-CJR WW24 404
4X-CJS WW24 169
4X-CJS WW24 413
4X-CJT WW24 170
4X-CJU WW24 171
4X-CJV WW24 172
4X-CJW WW24 173
4X-CJX WW24 174
4X-CJY WW24 175
4X-CJZ WW24 176
4X-CKA WW24 177
4X-CKB WW24 178
4X-CKC WW24 179
4X-CKD WW24 180
4X-CKE WW24 181
4X-CKF WW24 182
4X-CKG WW24 183
4X-CKH WW24 184
4X-CKI WW24 185
4X-CKJ WW24 186
4X-CKK WW24 187
4X-CKL WW24 188
4X-CKM WW24 189
4X-CKN WW24 190
4X-CKO WW24 191
4X-CKP WW24 192
4X-CKQ WW24 193
4X-CKR WW24 194
4X-CKS WW24 195
4X-CKT WW24 196
4X-CKU WW24 197
4X-CKV WW24 198
4X-CKW WW24 199
4X-CKX WW24 200
4X-CKY WW24 201
4X-CKZ WW24 202
4X-CLA WW24 203
4X-CLB WW24 204
4X-CLC WW24 205
4X-CLD WW24 206
4X-CLE WW24 207
4X-CLF WW24 208
4X-CLG WW24 209
4X-CLH WW24 210
4X-CLI WW24 211
4X-CLJ WW24 212
4X-CLK WW24 213
**4X-CLL GALX 040**
4X-CLL WW24 214
4X-CLM WW24 215
4X-CLN WW24 216
4X-CLO WW24 217
4X-CLP WW24 218
4X-CLQ WW24 219
4X-CLR WW24 220
4X-CLS WW24 221
4X-CLT WW24 222
4X-CLU WW24 223
4X-CLV WW24 224
4X-CLW WW24 225
4X-CLX WW24 226
4X-CLY WW24 227
4X-CLZ WW24 228
4X-CMA WW24 229
4X-CMB WW24 230
4X-CMC WW24 231
4X-CMD WW24 232
4X-CME WW24 233
**4X-CMF CL64 5522**
4X-CMF WW24 234
4X-CMG C500 535
4X-CMG WW24 235
4X-CMH CL61 5174

| | | |
|---|---|---|
| 4X-CMH | WW24 | 236 |
| 4X-CMI | WW24 | 237 |
| 4X-CMJ | WW24 | 238 |
| 4X-CMK | WW24 | 239 |
| 4X-CML | WW24 | 240 |
| 4X-CMM | GLF3 | 369 |
| 4X-CMM | WW24 | 241 |
| 4X-CMN | WW24 | 242 |
| 4X-CMO | WW24 | 243 |
| 4X-CMP | WW24 | 244 |
| 4X-CMQ | WW24 | 245 |
| 4X-CMR | C650 | 0185 |
| 4X-CMR | WW24 | 246 |
| 4X-CMS | WW24 | 247 |
| 4X-CMT | WW24 | 248 |
| 4X-CMU | WW24 | 249 |
| 4X-CMV | WW24 | 250 |
| 4X-CMW | WW24 | 251 |
| 4X-CMX | WW24 | 252 |
| **4X-CMY** | **CL64** | **5388** |
| 4X-CMY | WW24 | 253 |
| **4X-CMZ** | **CL64** | **5450** |
| 4X-CMZ | WW24 | 254 |
| 4X-CNA | WW24 | 255 |
| 4X-CNB | WW24 | 256 |
| 4X-CNC | WW24 | 257 |
| 4X-CND | WW24 | 258 |
| 4X-CNE | WW24 | 259 |
| 4X-CNF | WW24 | 260 |
| 4X-CNG | WW24 | 261 |
| 4X-CNH | WW24 | 262 |
| 4X-CNI | WW24 | 263 |
| 4X-CNJ | WW24 | 264 |
| 4X-CNK | WW24 | 265 |
| 4X-CNL | WW24 | 266 |
| 4X-CNM | WW24 | 267 |
| 4X-CNN | WW24 | 268 |
| 4X-CNO | WW24 | 269 |
| 4X-CNP | WW24 | 270 |
| 4X-CNQ | WW24 | 271 |
| 4X-CNR | WW24 | 272 |
| 4X-CNS | WW24 | 273 |
| 4X-CNT | WW24 | 274 |
| 4X-CNU | WW24 | 275 |
| 4X-CNV | WW24 | 276 |
| 4X-CNW | WW24 | 277 |
| 4X-CNX | WW24 | 278 |
| 4X-CNY | WW24 | 279 |
| 4X-CNZ | WW24 | 280 |
| 4X-COA | WW24 | 71 |
| 4X-COB | WW24 | 138 |
| 4X-COC | WW24 | 422 |
| 4X-COE | CL64 | 5352 |
| **4X-COG** | **GALX** | **018** |
| **4X-COI** | **GLEX** | **9130** |
| 4X-COJ | WW24 | 29 |
| (4X-COK) | WW24 | 107 |
| 4X-COL | WW24 | 107 |
| 4X-COM | WW24 | 126 |
| 4X-CON | WW24 | 55 |
| 4X-COO | CS55 | 0086 |
| 4X-COP | WW24 | 134 |
| 4X-COT | CL61 | 5032 |
| 4X-COV | HS25 | 258283 |
| 4X-COY | CL61 | 5154 |
| (4X-COZ) | HS25 | 258114 |
| 4X-CPA | WW24 | 110 |
| 4X-CPB | WW24 | 113 |
| 4X-CPC | WW24 | 114 |
| 4X-CPD | WW24 | 130 |
| 4X-CPE | WW24 | 131 |
| 4X-CPF | WW24 | 139 |
| 4X-CPG | WW24 | 140 |
| 4X-CPH | WW24 | 141 |
| 4X-CPI | WW24 | 142 |
| 4X-CPJ | WW24 | 143 |
| 4X-CPK | WW24 | 144 |
| 4X-CPL | WW24 | 148 |
| 4X-CPM | WW24 | 149 |
| 4X-CPN | WW24 | 150 |
| 4X-CPO | WW24 | 414 |
| 4X-CPS | HS25 | 258391 |
| 4X-CPT | CS55 | 0145 |
| 4X-CPU | C56X | 5074 |
| 4X-CPV | CL30 | 20065 |
| **4X-CPW** | **C550** | **550-0941** |
| **4X-CPX** | **GLF4** | **1481** |
| **4X-CPY** | **BE40** | **RK-219** |
| 4X-CQA | WW24 | 281 |
| 4X-CQB | WW24 | 282 |
| 4X-CQC | WW24 | 283 |
| 4X-CQD | WW24 | 284 |
| 4X-CQE | WW24 | 285 |
| 4X-CQF | WW24 | 286 |
| 4X-CQG | WW24 | 287 |
| 4X-CQH | WW24 | 288 |
| 4X-CQI | WW24 | 289 |
| 4X-CQJ | WW24 | 290 |
| 4X-CQK | WW24 | 291 |
| 4X-CQL | WW24 | 292 |
| 4X-CQM | WW24 | 293 |
| 4X-CQN | WW24 | 294 |
| 4X-CQO | WW24 | 295 |
| 4X-CQP | WW24 | 296 |
| 4X-CQQ | WW24 | 297 |
| 4X-CQR | WW24 | 298 |
| 4X-CQS | WW24 | 299 |
| 4X-CQT | WW24 | 300 |
| 4X-CQU | WW24 | 301 |
| 4X-CQV | WW24 | 302 |
| 4X-CQW | WW24 | 303 |
| 4X-CQX | WW24 | 304 |
| 4X-CQY | WW24 | 305 |
| 4X-CQZ | WW24 | 306 |
| 4X-CRA | WW24 | 307 |
| 4X-CRB | WW24 | 308 |
| 4X-CRC | WW24 | 309 |
| 4X-CRD | WW24 | 310 |
| 4X-CRE | WW24 | 311 |
| 4X-CRF | WW24 | 312 |
| 4X-CRG | WW24 | 313 |
| 4X-CRH | WW24 | 314 |
| 4X-CRI | WW24 | 315 |
| 4X-CRJ | WW24 | 316 |
| 4X-CRK | WW24 | 317 |
| 4X-CRL | WW24 | 318 |
| 4X-CRM | WW24 | 319 |
| 4X-CRN | WW24 | 320 |
| 4X-CRO | WW24 | 321 |
| 4X-CRP | WW24 | 322 |
| 4X-CRQ | WW24 | 323 |
| 4X-CRR | WW24 | 324 |
| 4X-CRS | WW24 | 325 |
| 4X-CRT | WW24 | 326 |
| 4X-CRU | HS25 | 258682 |
| 4X-CRU | WW24 | 327 |
| 4X-CRV | WW24 | 328 |
| 4X-CRW | WW24 | 329 |
| 4X-CRX | WW24 | 330 |
| 4X-CRY | HS25 | 258538 |
| 4X-CRY | WW24 | 331 |
| 4X-CRZ | WW24 | 332 |
| 4X-CTA | WW24 | 333 |
| 4X-CTB | WW24 | 334 |
| 4X-CTC | WW24 | 335 |
| 4X-CTD | WW24 | 336 |
| 4X-CTE | WW24 | 337 |
| 4X-CTF | WW24 | 338 |
| 4X-CTG | WW24 | 339 |
| 4X-CTH | WW24 | 340 |
| 4X-CTI | WW24 | 341 |
| 4X-CTJ | WW24 | 342 |
| 4X-CTK | WW24 | 343 |
| 4X-CTL | WW24 | 344 |
| 4X-CTM | WW24 | 345 |
| 4X-CTN | WW24 | 346 |
| 4X-CTO | WW24 | 347 |
| 4X-CTP | WW24 | 348 |
| 4X-CTQ | WW24 | 349 |
| 4X-CTR | WW24 | 350 |
| 4X-CTS | WW24 | 351 |
| 4X-CTT | WW24 | 352 |
| 4X-CTU | WW24 | 353 |
| 4X-CTV | WW24 | 354 |
| 4X-CUA | ASTR | 004 |
| 4X-CUA | WW24 | 340 |
| 4X-CUA | WW24 | 392 |
| 4X-CUA | WW24 | 406 |
| 4X-CUB | WW24 | 341 |
| 4X-CUB | WW24 | 372 |
| 4X-CUB | WW24 | 384 |
| 4X-CUB | WW24 | 390 |
| 4X-CUB | WW24 | 408 |
| 4X-CUB | WW24 | 418 |
| 4X-CUC | WW24 | 385 |
| 4X-CUC | WW24 | 395 |
| 4X-CUC | WW24 | 411 |
| 4X-CUC | WW24 | 414 |
| 4X-CUC | WW24 | 423 |
| 4X-CUC | WW24 | 434 |
| 4X-CUD | ASTR | 017 |
| 4X-CUD | WW24 | 367 |
| 4X-CUD | WW24 | 413 |
| 4X-CUD | WW24 | 416 |
| 4X-CUE | ASTR | 019 |
| 4X-CUE | WW24 | 368 |
| 4X-CUE | WW24 | 386 |
| 4X-CUE | WW24 | 417 |
| 4X-CUE | WW24 | 436 |
| 4X-CUF | WW24 | 369 |
| 4X-CUF | WW24 | 375 |
| 4X-CUF | WW24 | 389 |
| 4X-CUF | WW24 | 399 |
| 4X-CUF | WW24 | 419 |
| 4X-CUF | WW24 | 426 |
| 4X-CUF | WW24 | 437 |
| 4X-CUG | ASTR | 023 |
| 4X-CUG | ASTR | 056 |
| 4X-CUG | ASTR | 061 |
| 4X-CUG | ASTR | 064 |
| 4X-CUG | WW24 | 370 |
| 4X-CUG | WW24 | 391 |
| 4X-CUG | WW24 | 404 |
| 4X-CUG | WW24 | 435 |
| 4X-CUG | WW24 | 439 |
| 4X-CUH | ASTR | 025 |
| 4X-CUH | ASTR | 057 |
| 4X-CUH | WW24 | 371 |
| 4X-CUH | WW24 | 376 |
| 4X-CUH | WW24 | 388 |
| 4X-CUH | WW24 | 403 |
| 4X-CUH | WW24 | 420 |
| 4X-CUH | WW24 | 432 |
| 4X-CUH | WW24 | 433 |
| 4X-CUI | ASTR | 026 |
| 4X-CUI | ASTR | 030 |
| 4X-CUI | ASTR | 055 |
| 4X-CUI | ASTR | 063 |
| 4X-CUI | WW24 | 355 |
| 4X-CUI | WW24 | 378 |
| 4X-CUI | WW24 | 422 |
| 4X-CUJ | ASTR | 027 |
| 4X-CUJ | ASTR | 034 |
| 4X-CUJ | ASTR | 062 |
| 4X-CUJ | ASTR | 065 |
| 4X-CUJ | WW24 | 356 |
| 4X-CUJ | WW24 | 377 |
| 4X-CUJ | WW24 | 379 |
| 4X-CUJ | WW24 | 387 |
| 4X-CUJ | WW24 | 405 |
| 4X-CUJ | WW24 | 421 |
| 4X-CUJ | WW24 | 424 |
| 4X-CUJ | WW24 | 438 |
| 4X-CUJ | WW24 | 440 |
| 4X-CUK | ASTR | 011 |
| 4X-CUK | ASTR | 016 |
| 4X-CUK | WW24 | 357 |
| 4X-CUK | WW24 | 373 |
| 4X-CUK | WW24 | 393 |
| 4X-CUK | WW24 | 407 |
| 4X-CUK | WW24 | 425 |
| 4X-CUK | WW24 | 429 |
| 4X-CUL | ASTR | 012 |
| 4X-CUL | WW24 | 358 |
| 4X-CUL | WW24 | 374 |
| 4X-CUM | ASTR | 013 |
| 4X-CUM | WW24 | 359 |
| 4X-CUM | WW24 | 380 |
| 4X-CUM | WW24 | 394 |
| 4X-CUM | WW24 | 409 |
| 4X-CUM | WW24 | 430 |
| 4X-CUM? | WW24 | 409 |
| 4X-CUN | ASTR | 014 |
| 4X-CUN | ASTR | 032 |
| 4X-CUN | WW24 | 360 |
| 4X-CUN | WW24 | 397 |
| 4X-CUN | WW24 | 427 |
| 4X-CUN | WW24 | 431 |
| 4X-CUO | WW24 | 361 |
| 4X-CUO | WW24 | 381 |
| 4X-CUO | WW24 | 398 |
| 4X-CUO | WW24 | 409 |
| 4X-CUO | WW24 | 410 |
| 4X-CUO | WW24 | 428 |
| 4X-CUO | WW24 | 442 |
| 4X-CUP | ASTR | 015 |
| 4X-CUP | ASTR | 033 |
| 4X-CUP | WW24 | 362 |
| 4X-CUP | WW24 | 382 |
| 4X-CUP | WW24 | 400 |
| 4X-CUP | WW24 | 412 |
| 4X-CUP | WW24 | 441 |
| 4X-CUQ | WW24 | 363 |
| 4X-CUQ | WW24 | 383 |
| 4X-CUQ | WW24 | 401 |
| 4X-CUR | ASTR | 018 |
| 4X-CUR | ASTR | 021 |
| **4X-CUR** | **CL64** | **5645** |
| 4X-CUR | WW24 | 364 |
| 4X-CUR | WW24 | 396 |
| 4X-CUS | ASTR | 020 |
| 4X-CUS | WW24 | 365 |
| 4X-CUS | WW24 | 402 |
| 4X-CUS | WW24 | 415 |
| 4X-CUT | ASTR | 022 |
| 4X-CUT | ASTR | 024 |
| 4X-CUT | WW24 | 366 |
| 4X-CUU | ASTR | 087 |
| 4X-CUV | ASTR | 076 |
| 4X-CUW | ASTR | 071 |
| 4X-CUW | ASTR | 075 |
| 4X-CUX | ASTR | 079 |
| 4X-CUY | ASTR | 080 |
| 4X-CUZ | ASTR | 119 |
| 4X-CVE | ASTR | 124 |
| 4X-CVE | ASTR | 152 |
| 4X-CVE | GALX | 012 |
| 4X-CVE | GALX | 022 |
| 4X-CVE | GALX | 026 |
| 4X-CVE | GALX | 032 |
| 4X-CVE | GALX | 038 |
| 4X-CVE | GALX | 039 |
| 4X-CVE | GALX | 041 |
| 4X-CVE | GALX | 044 |
| 4X-CVE | GALX | 048 |
| 4X-CVE | GALX | 050 |
| 4X-CVE | GALX | 053 |
| 4X-CVE | GALX | 056 |
| 4X-CVE | GALX | 059 |
| 4X-CVE | GALX | 068 |
| 4X-CVE | GALX | 079 |
| 4X-CVE | GALX | 087 |
| 4X-CVE | GALX | 109 |
| 4X-CVE | GALX | 114 |
| 4X-CVE | GALX | 120 |
| 4X-CVE | GALX | 128 |
| 4X-CVE | GALX | 133 |
| 4X-CVE | GALX | 146 |
| 4X-CVE | GALX | 152 |
| 4X-CVE | GALX | 158 |
| 4X-CVE | GALX | 165 |
| 4X-CVE | GALX | 171 |
| 4X-CVE | GALX | 177 |
| 4X-CVE | GALX | 182 |
| 4X-CVE | GALX | 192 |
| 4X-CVE | GALX | 198 |
| 4X-CVE | GALX | 203 |
| 4X-CVE | GALX | 207 |
| 4X-CVE | GALX | 213 |
| 4X-CVE | GALX | 219 |
| 4X-CVE | GALX | 225 |
| 4X-CVE | GALX | 232 |
| 4X-CVF | ASTR | 128 |
| 4X-CVF | ASTR | 147 |
| 4X-CVF | GALX | 004 |
| 4X-CVF | GALX | 017 |
| 4X-CVF | GALX | 021 |
| 4X-CVF | GALX | 027 |
| 4X-CVF | GALX | 030 |
| 4X-CVF | GALX | 034 |
| 4X-CVF | GALX | 042 |
| 4X-CVF | GALX | 045 |
| 4X-CVF | GALX | 047 |
| 4X-CVF | GALX | 051 |
| 4X-CVF | GALX | 055 |
| 4X-CVF | GALX | 069 |
| 4X-CVF | GALX | 073 |
| 4X-CVF | GALX | 095 |
| 4X-CVF | GALX | 099 |
| 4X-CVF | GALX | 107 |
| 4X-CVF | GALX | 115 |
| 4X-CVF | GALX | 124 |
| 4X-CVF | GALX | 129 |
| 4X-CVF | GALX | 136 |
| 4X-CVF | GALX | 147 |
| 4X-CVF | GALX | 153 |
| 4X-CVF | GALX | 159 |
| 4X-CVF | GALX | 169 |
| 4X-CVF | GALX | 175 |
| 4X-CVF | GALX | 180 |

| | | |
|---|---|---|
| 4X-CVF | GALX | 184 |
| 4X-CVF | GALX | 189 |
| 4X-CVF | GALX | 195 |
| 4X-CVF | GALX | 201 |
| 4X-CVF | GALX | 208 |
| 4X-CVF | GALX | 214 |
| 4X-CVF | GALX | 220 |
| 4X-CVF | GALX | 226 |
| 4X-CVG | ASTR | 125 |
| 4X-CVG | ASTR | 127 |
| 4X-CVG | ASTR | 129 |
| 4X-CVG | ASTR | 131 |
| 4X-CVG | ASTR | 133 |
| 4X-CVG | ASTR | 134 |
| 4X-CVG | ASTR | 136 |
| 4X-CVG | ASTR | 138 |
| 4X-CVG | ASTR | 151 |
| 4X-CVG | GALX | 013 |
| 4X-CVG | GALX | 052 |
| 4X-CVG | GALX | 057 |
| 4X-CVG | GALX | 070 |
| 4X-CVG | GALX | 075 |
| 4X-CVG | GALX | 081 |
| 4X-CVG | GALX | 096 |
| 4X-CVG | GALX | 106 |
| 4X-CVG | GALX | 110 |
| 4X-CVG | GALX | 122 |
| 4X-CVG | GALX | 126 |
| 4X-CVG | GALX | 130 |
| 4X-CVG | GALX | 135 |
| 4X-CVG | GALX | 141 |
| 4X-CVG | GALX | 148 |
| 4X-CVG | GALX | 154 |
| 4X-CVG | GALX | 160 |
| 4X-CVG | GALX | 166 |
| 4X-CVG | GALX | 172 |
| 4X-CVG | GALX | 178 |
| 4X-CVG | GALX | 183 |
| 4X-CVG | GALX | 188 |
| 4X-CVG | GALX | 193 |
| 4X-CVG | GALX | 199 |
| 4X-CVG | GALX | 204 |
| 4X-CVG | GALX | 210 |
| 4X-CVG | GALX | 216 |
| 4X-CVG | GALX | 222 |
| 4X-CVG | GALX | 227 |
| 4X-CVG | GALX | 231 |
| 4X-CVH | ASTR | 143 |
| 4X-CVH | GALX | 018 |
| 4X-CVH | GALX | 023 |
| 4X-CVH | GALX | 028 |
| 4X-CVH | GALX | 031 |
| 4X-CVH | GALX | 035 |
| 4X-CVH | GALX | 037 |
| 4X-CVH | GALX | 040 |
| 4X-CVH | GALX | 043 |
| 4X-CVH | GALX | 046 |
| 4X-CVH | GALX | 049 |
| 4X-CVH | GALX | 071 |
| 4X-CVH | GALX | 077 |
| 4X-CVH | GALX | 086 |
| 4X-CVH | GALX | 089 |
| 4X-CVH | GALX | 092 |
| 4X-CVH | GALX | 103 |
| 4X-CVH | GALX | 111 |
| 4X-CVH | GALX | 116 |
| 4X-CVH | GALX | 121 |
| 4X-CVH | GALX | 127 |
| 4X-CVH | GALX | 131 |
| 4X-CVH | GALX | 137 |
| 4X-CVH | GALX | 143 |
| 4X-CVH | GALX | 149 |
| 4X-CVH | GALX | 155 |
| 4X-CVH | GALX | 161 |
| 4X-CVH | GALX | 167 |
| 4X-CVH | GALX | 174 |
| 4X-CVH | GALX | 185 |
| 4X-CVH | GALX | 190 |
| 4X-CVH | GALX | 196 |
| 4X-CVH | GALX | 202 |
| 4X-CVH | GALX | 209 |
| 4X-CVH | GALX | 215 |
| 4X-CVH | GALX | 221 |
| 4X-CVH | GALX | 228 |
| 4X-CVI | ASTR | 130 |
| 4X-CVI | ASTR | 132 |
| 4X-CVI | ASTR | 135 |
| 4X-CVI | ASTR | 137 |
| 4X-CVI | ASTR | 139 |
| 4X-CVI | ASTR | 141 |

| | | |
|---|---|---|
| 4X-CVI | ASTR | 146 |
| 4X-CVI | ASTR | 148 |
| 4X-CVI | GALX | 015 |
| 4X-CVI | GALX | 020 |
| 4X-CVI | GALX | 024 |
| 4X-CVI | GALX | 054 |
| 4X-CVI | GALX | 058 |
| 4X-CVI | GALX | 094 |
| 4X-CVI | GALX | 097 |
| 4X-CVI | GALX | 100 |
| 4X-CVI | GALX | 104 |
| 4X-CVI | GALX | 108 |
| 4X-CVI | GALX | 112 |
| 4X-CVI | GALX | 119 |
| 4X-CVI | GALX | 125 |
| 4X-CVI | GALX | 132 |
| 4X-CVI | GALX | 144 |
| 4X-CVI | GALX | 150 |
| 4X-CVI | GALX | 156 |
| 4X-CVI | GALX | 162 |
| 4X-CVI | GALX | 168 |
| 4X-CVI | GALX | 173 |
| 4X-CVI | GALX | 194 |
| 4X-CVI | GALX | 198 |
| 4X-CVI | GALX | 200 |
| 4X-CVI | GALX | 206 |
| 4X-CVI | GALX | 217 |
| 4X-CVI | GALX | 224 |
| 4X-CVI | GALX | 229 |
| 4X-CVJ | ASTR | 123 |
| 4X-CVJ | ASTR | 126 |
| 4X-CVJ | ASTR | 153 |
| 4X-CVJ | ASTR | 155 |
| 4X-CVJ | ASTR | 158 |
| 4X-CVJ | GALX | 074 |
| 4X-CVJ | GALX | 078 |
| 4X-CVJ | GALX | 082 |
| 4X-CVJ | GALX | 085 |
| 4X-CVJ | GALX | 088 |
| 4X-CVJ | GALX | 091 |
| 4X-CVJ | GALX | 101 |
| 4X-CVJ | GALX | 105 |
| 4X-CVJ | GALX | 118 |
| 4X-CVJ | GALX | 123 |
| 4X-CVJ | GALX | 134 |
| 4X-CVJ | GALX | 139 |
| 4X-CVJ | GALX | 145 |
| 4X-CVJ | GALX | 151 |
| 4X-CVJ | GALX | 157 |
| 4X-CVJ | GALX | 163 |
| 4X-CVJ | GALX | 170 |
| 4X-CVJ | GALX | 176 |
| 4X-CVJ | GALX | 181 |
| 4X-CVJ | GALX | 186 |
| 4X-CVJ | GALX | 191 |
| 4X-CVJ | GALX | 197 |
| 4X-CVJ | GALX | 205 |
| 4X-CVJ | GALX | 212 |
| 4X-CVJ | GALX | 218 |
| 4X-CVJ | GALX | 223 |
| 4X-CVJ | GALX | 230 |
| 4X-CVK | ASTR | 140 |
| 4X-CVK | ASTR | 142 |
| 4X-CVK | ASTR | 144 |
| 4X-CVK | ASTR | 145 |
| 4X-CVK | ASTR | 150 |
| 4X-CVK | ASTR | 157 |
| 4X-CVK | ASTR | 203 |
| 4X-CVK | ASTR | 205 |
| 4X-CVK | ASTR | 209 |
| 4X-CVK | ASTR | 211 |
| 4X-CVK | ASTR | 213 |
| 4X-CVK | ASTR | 215 |
| 4X-CVK | ASTR | 217 |
| 4X-CVK | ASTR | 223 |
| 4X-CVK | ASTR | 227 |
| 4X-CVK | ASTR | 230 |
| 4X-CVK | ASTR | 234 |
| 4X-CVK | ASTR | 239 |
| 4X-CVK | ASTR | 244 |
| 4X-CVK | ASTR | 249 |
| 4X-CVK | ASTR | 252 |
| 4X-CVK | ASTR | 258 |
| 4X-CVK | ASTR | 263 |
| 4X-CVK | ASTR | 268 |
| 4X-CVK | ASTR | 273 |
| 4X-CVK | ASTR | 277 |
| 4X-CVK | ASTR | 281 |
| 4X-CVK | ASTR | 286 |
| 4X-CVK | GALX | 016 |

| | | |
|---|---|---|
| 4X-CVK | GALX | 019 |
| 4X-CVK | GALX | 025 |
| 4X-CVK | GALX | 029 |
| 4X-CVK | GALX | 033 |
| 4X-CVK | GALX | 036 |
| 4X-CVK | GALX | 067 |
| 4X-CVK | GALX | 072 |
| 4X-CVK | GALX | 076 |
| 4X-CVK | GALX | 080 |
| 4X-CVK | GALX | 090 |
| 4X-CVK | GALX | 093 |
| 4X-CVK | GALX | 098 |
| 4X-CVK | GALX | 102 |
| 4X-CVK | GALX | 113 |
| 4X-CVL | ASTR | 219 |
| 4X-CVL | ASTR | 222 |
| 4X-CVL | ASTR | 231 |
| 4X-CVL | ASTR | 235 |
| 4X-CVL | ASTR | 241 |
| 4X-CVL | ASTR | 246 |
| 4X-CVL | ASTR | 251 |
| 4X-CVL | ASTR | 256 |
| 4X-CVL | ASTR | 261 |
| 4X-CVL | ASTR | 265 |
| 4X-CVL | ASTR | 270 |
| 4X-CVL | ASTR | 276 |
| 4X-CVL | ASTR | 283 |
| 4X-CVM | ASTR | 220 |
| 4X-CVM | ASTR | 224 |
| 4X-CVM | ASTR | 228 |
| 4X-CVM | ASTR | 232 |
| 4X-CVM | ASTR | 237 |
| 4X-CVM | ASTR | 242 |
| 4X-CVM | ASTR | 247 |
| 4X-CVM | ASTR | 254 |
| 4X-CVM | ASTR | 259 |
| 4X-CVM | ASTR | 264 |
| 4X-CVM | ASTR | 269 |
| 4X-CVM | ASTR | 274 |
| 4X-CVM | ASTR | 279 |
| 4X-CVM | ASTR | 285 |
| 4X-CVM | GALX | 179 |
| 4X-CYH | LJ45 | 336 |
| **4X-CZA** | **C650** | **0187** |
| **4X-CZD** | **C550** | **079** |
| 4X-CZM | HS25 | 258279 |
| **4X-DFZ** | **C510** | **0090** |
| 4X-FVN | WW24 | 134 |
| **4X-IGA** | **GALX** | **003** |
| 4X-IGB | GALX | 005 |
| 4X-IGO | GALX | 004 |
| 4X-JYF | WW24 | 152 |
| 4X-JYG | WW24 | 107 |
| **4X-JYJ** | **WW24** | **185** |
| **4X-JYO** | **WW24** | **186** |
| **4X-JYR** | **WW24** | **152** |
| (4X-NOY) | WW24 | 213 |
| 4X-TRA | ASTR | 201 |
| 4X-TRA | ASTR | 236 |
| 4X-TRA | ASTR | 240 |
| 4X-TRA | ASTR | 245 |
| 4X-TRA | ASTR | 250 |
| 4X-TRA | ASTR | 255 |
| 4X-TRA | ASTR | 260 |
| 4X-TRA | ASTR | 267 |
| 4X-TRA | ASTR | 278 |
| **4X-WBJ** | **GALX** | **2003** |
| **4X-WIA** | **ASTR** | **002** |
| 4X-WID | ASTR | 202 |
| 4X-WID | ASTR | 204 |
| 4X-WID | ASTR | 206 |
| 4X-WID | ASTR | 210 |
| 4X-WID | ASTR | 212 |
| 4X-WID | ASTR | 214 |
| 4X-WID | ASTR | 216 |
| 4X-WID | ASTR | 218 |
| 4X-WID | ASTR | 221 |
| 4X-WID | ASTR | 225 |
| 4X-WID | ASTR | 229 |
| 4X-WID | ASTR | 233 |
| 4X-WID | ASTR | 238 |
| 4X-WID | ASTR | 243 |
| 4X-WID | ASTR | 248 |
| 4X-WID | ASTR | 253 |
| 4X-WID | ASTR | 257 |
| 4X-WID | ASTR | 262 |
| 4X-WID | ASTR | 266 |
| 4X-WID | ASTR | 275 |
| 4X-WID | ASTR | 280 |
| 4X-WID | ASTR | 284 |

| | | |
|---|---|---|
| 4X-WIN | ASTR | 001 |
| 4X-WIX | ASTR | 073 |
| **4X-WSJ** | **GALX** | **2001** |
| **4X-WSM** | **GALX** | **2002** |

Libya

| | | |
|---|---|---|
| 5A-DAC | LJ24 | 074 |
| 5A-DAD | LJ24 | 075 |
| 5A-DAF | FA20 | 128/436 |
| **5A-DAG** | **FA20** | **143/442** |
| **5A-DAJ** | **JSTR** | **5136** |
| 5A-DAR | JSTR | 5221 |
| **5A-DCK** | **CRVT** | **38** |
| **5A-DCM** | **FA50** | **68** |
| **5A-DCN** | **F9EX** | **148** |
| **5A-DCO** | **FA20** | **190/465** |
| 5A-DDR | GLF2 | 240 |
| **5A-DDS** | **GLF2** | **242** |
| 5A-DGI | FA50 | 17 |
| 5A-DKQ | FA20 | 175 |
| **5A-DRK** | **C56X** | **5710** |
| **5A-DRL** | **C56X** | **5808** |
| **5A-UAA** | **CL30** | **20175** |
| **5A-UAB** | **GLEX** | **9285** |
| **5A-UAC** | **GLEX** | **9257** |

Cyprus

| | | |
|---|---|---|
| **5B-** | **HS25** | **25088** |
| 5B-CGB | FA20 | 32 |
| 5B-CGP | JSTR | 5128/16 |
| **5B-CHE** | **JSTR** | **5114/18** |
| 5B-CHX | CL60 | 1028 |
| 5B-CIQ | C550 | 660 |
| 5B-CIS | C550 | 200 |
| 5B-CJG | ASTR | 099 |
| (5B-CKG) | HS25 | 258554 |
| 5B-CKK | CL61 | 5094 |
| 5B-CKL | HS25 | 258495 |
| 5B-CKN | FA50 | 339 |
| **5B-CKO** | **F2EX** | **96** |
| 5B-CSM | C650 | 0094 |

Tanzania

| | | |
|---|---|---|
| 5H-APH | JSTR | 5219 |
| 5H-BLM | HS25 | 259027 |
| **5H-ONE** | **GLF5** | **5030** |
| 5H-SMZ | HS25 | 257172 |

Nigeria

| | | |
|---|---|---|
| **5N-** | **HS25** | **258231** |
| (5N- ) | HS25 | 259016 |
| (5N- ) | HS25 | 259025 |
| 5N-AAN | HS25 | 25125 |
| 5N-AER | HS25 | 25099 |
| 5N-AET | HS25 | 25117 |
| 5N-AGU | HS25 | 25085 |
| 5N-AGV | GLF2 | 177 |
| **5N-AGZ** | **HS25** | **258143** |
| 5N-AKT | HS25 | 25117 |
| **5N-ALH** | **HS25** | **25089** |
| 5N-ALX | HS25 | 256012 |
| 5N-ALY | HS25 | 25106 |
| 5N-AMF | HFB3 | 1028 |
| 5N-AMK | HS25 | 25010 |
| 5N-AML | GLF2 | 186 |
| 5N-AMM | SBRL | 380-17 |
| 5N-AMN | GLF2 | 13 |
| 5N-AMR | C550 | 045 |
| 5N-AMX | HS25 | 257115 |
| 5N-AMY | HS25 | 25227 |
| 5N-ANG | HS25 | 256050 |
| 5N-AOC | LJ25 | 322 |
| 5N-AOG | HS25 | 25143 |
| 5N-AOL | HS25 | 256050 |
| **5N-APN** | **C500** | **286** |
| 5N-AQY | HS25 | 25231 |
| 5N-ARD | HS25 | 256030 |
| 5N-ARE | FA50 | 110 |
| 5N-ARN | HS25 | 256056 |
| 5N-ASQ | LJ25 | 344 |
| 5N-ASZ | HS25 | 25063 |
| 5N-AVJ | HS25 | 257118 |

**5N-AVK HS25 257160**
5N-AVL C500 651
5N-AVM C500 653
**5N-AVV HS25 25138**
5N-AVZ HS25 25113
5N-AWB HS25 25025
5N-AWD HS25 25008
5N-AWJ C550 252
5N-AWS HS25 256042
5N-AXO HS25 257196
5N-AXP HS25 257203
**5N-AYA C550 632**
5N-AYK HS25 256060
5N-AYM FA20 228/473
5N-AYN FA20 427
5N-AYO FA20 383/550
5N-BCI C500 085
**5N-BEL CS55 0079**
**5N-BEX HS25 257197**
**5N-BFC HS25 257150**
5N-BGR LJ45 163
**5N-BGV GLF2 177**
**5N-BJS C56X 5703**
"5N-BLV" GLF2 177
**5N-BLW LJ45 350**
**5N-BMM C56X 5830**
**5N-BMR HS25 258264**
5N-BUA HS25 25178
**5N-DAL LJ45 358**
**5N-DAO HS25 257182**
**5N-DGN HS25 259018**
5N-DNL HS25 256052
5N-DOT HS25 256062
5N-DUK C550 550-0925
**5N-EAS HS25 25217**
**5N-EMA HS25 256069**
5N-EPN FA20 273
5N-EZE WW24 141
**5N-FGE F900 96**
**5N-FGO F900 52**
**5N-FGP GLF4 1126**
5N-FGR HS25 259018
**5N-FGS GLF5 643**
5N-IMR C560 0087
5N-IMR GLF3 344
**5N-JMA HS25 258658**
**5N-JMB HS25 258659**
**5N-MAO HS25 257186**
5N-MAY HS25 256062
**5N-MAZ HS25 257169**
5N-NBC HS25 256052
**5N-NPC HS25 258109**
**5N-NPF C550 138**
5N-NPF HS25 258143
5N-OIL F900 96
5N-OPT HS25 256063
5N-RNO HS25 256054
**5N-WMA HS25 25178**
**5N-YET HS25 256013**
5N-YFS HS25 256054

### Malagasy (Madagascar)

**5R- C550 550-1054**
**5R-MBR CRVT 16**
**5R-MHF C550 141**
**5R-MHK CRVT 34**
5R-MVD CRVT 35
5R-MVN CRVT 16

### Mauritania

5T-UPR GLF2 175

### Togo

5V-MBG FA10 167
5V-TAA GLF2 149
5V-TAC GLF2 167
5V-TAE FA10 167
**5V-TTP HS25 256049**

### Uganda

5X-AAB WW24 134
5X-UEF GLF4 1413
**5X-UGF GLF5 5208**
5X-UOI GLF3 345
5X-UPF GLF2 133

### Kenya

5Y-GEO LJ24 273
5Y-HAB C550 028
**5Y-MNG C550 550-0876**
**5Y-MSR C550 550-0975**
**5Y-SIR C550 550-0995**
(5Y-TCI) C525 0217
5Y-TWE C550 569

### Senegal

6V-AEA CRVT 8
6V-AFL GLF2 136
6V-AGQ GLF2 136

### Yemen Republic
(see also 4W-)

**70- F9EX 38**
70-ADC HS25 258037

### Lesotho

7P-TCB GLF2 73/9

### Malawi

7Q-YJI HS25 257076
7Q-YLF C550 706
7Q-YTL C500 605

### Algeria

**7T- C56X 6023**
**7T-VCW HS25 257163**
7T-VHB GLF2 230
7T-VHP JSTR 5233
**7T-VNF C52A 0436**
7T-VPA F900 81
7T-VPB F900 82
**7T-VPC GLF4 1418**
**7T-VPG GLF5 617**
**7T-VPM GLF4 1421**
**7T-VPR GLF4 1288**
**7T-VPS GLF4 1291**
7T-VRB GLF3 368
7T-VRC GLF3 396
7T-VRD GLF3 399
7T-VRE FA20 156/448
7T-VRP FA20 271/493
**7T-VVL HS25 25131**

### Barbados

8P-BAB C500 525
8P-BAR C500 525
8P-BAR C550 256
8P-BAR WW24 396
8P-GAC GLF3 355
8P-KAM C650 0119
8P-LAD GLF2 210
8P-MAK GLF4 1186
8P-MAK GLF5 537
**8P-MSD GLF5 5137**

### Croatia
(see also RC-)

9A-BLY SBRL 380-65
9A-BPU C550 144
(9A-CAD) C525 0151
9A-CAD C525 0199
9A-CGH C525 0151
**9A-CHC C500 529**
**9A-CLN C52A 0434**
9A-CRL FA10 173
9A-CRO CL61 5067
**9A-CRO CL64 5322**
9A-CRT CL61 5067
9A-CSG C510 0049
**9A-DOF C550 496**
9A-DVR C500 638
**9A-DWA C52A 0412**

### Ghana

**9G-ABF JSTR 5217**

### Malta

9H-ABO SBRL 465-22
9H-ACR C550 025
9H-AEE LJ60 170
**9H-AFB LJ60 327**
**9H-AFC CL65 5713**
9H-AFG CL65 5762
**9H-AFJ LJ60 030**
**9H-AFP GLEX 9167**
**9H-AFQ CL65 5709**
**9H-AFR GLEX 9249**
**9H-BOB HS25 258115**
**9H-XRS GLEX 9329**

### Zambia

9J-ADF LJ24 249
9J-ADU C500 153
9J-AED LJ25 225
9J-AEJ C500 359
9J-EPK HS25 25067
**9J-ONE CL64 5486**
9J-RAN HS25 25067
9J-RON CL61 3057
9J-SAS HS25 25067

### Kuwait

9K-ACO JSTR 5156
9K-ACQ FA20 136/439
(9K-ACQ) FA50 21
9K-ACR HS25 25238
9K-ACT LJ35 025
9K-ACX GLF2 164
9K-ACY GLF2 4/8
9K-ACZ HS25 256015
9K-AEA HS25 25219
9K-AEB GLF2 244
9K-AEC GLF2 248
9K-AED HS25 256054
9K-AEE FA50 21
9K-AEF FA50 40
9K-AEG GLF3 408
9K-AEH GLF3 419
9K-AGA HS25 257184
9K-AGB HS25 257187
9K-AJA GLF4 1157
9K-AJB GLF4 1159
9K-AJC GLF4 1161
**9K-AJD GLF5 560**
**9K-AJE GLF5 569**
**9K-AJF GLF5 573**
**9K-GFA GLF5 5248**

### Sierra Leone

9L-LAW SBRL 380-61

### Malaysia

(9M- ) HS25 258226
**9M-ABC GLF4 1312**
9M-ARR GLF2 116
9M-ATM BE40 RJ-22
**9M-ATM C750 0242**
9M-ATM FA10 216
9M-ATT GLF2 131/23
(9M-AYI) HS25 25015
9M-AZZ HS25 258219
9M-BAB F900 121
9M-BAN F900 106
9M-BCR FA20 35
9M-BDK FA20 304/511
**9M-CAL LJ60 034**
9M-DDW HS25 258079
9M-DRL HS25 258237
9M-FAZ C500 245
**9M-FCL LJ60 072**
**9M-FRA FA20 224**
9M-HLG HS25 25257
**9M-ISJ GLF4 1106**
9M-JJS F9EX 5
9M-JMF C550 610
**9M-LLJ FA20 292**
9M-NSA C550 610
9M-NSK CL61 5166
9M-SSB HS25 25215
9M-SSL HS25 257112
9M-STR HS25 257094
9M-SWG CL61 5104
9M-TAA C550 671
9M-TAN CL30 20135
9M-TAN CL61 5154
9M-TRI GLF4 1230
**9M-TST CL30 20135**
(9M-UEM) C550 610
(9M-VVV) HS25 258337
9M-WAN C550 307
(9M-WCM) HS25 258219
9M-ZAB C550 550-1121

### Democratic Republic of Congo

**9Q-CAI HS25 256047**
9Q-CBC HS25 25258
9Q-CBC LJ24 248
9Q-CBS CL61 5018
9Q-CBS CL61 5061
**9Q-CCA FA10 150**
9Q-CCF HS25 25247
"9Q-CFG" HS25 256031
**9Q-CFJ HS25 256051**
9Q-CFW HS25 256031
9Q-CGF HS25 256031
9Q-CGK FA50 177
9Q-CGM HS25 25217
9Q-CGM LJ24 038
9Q-CHB LJ24 038
9Q-CHC LJ25 009
9Q-CHD HS25 25217
**9Q-CJF HS25 256031**
9Q-CKZ FA20 73/419
9Q-COH HS25 25246
**9Q-CPF HS25 25287**
9Q-CPK FA50 177
**9Q-CPR HS25 25247**
9Q-CSN HS25 25247
9Q-CTT FA20 193
9Q-CYA HS25 256047

### Burundi

9U-BTB FA50 66

### Singapore

**9V- LJ24 320**
**9V- LJ25 149**
9V-ATA LJ31 033
9V-ATB LJ31 034
9V-ATC LJ31 033A
9V-ATD LJ31 033B
9V-ATE LJ31 033C
9V-ATF LJ31 033D
9V-ATG LJ45 029
9V-ATH LJ45 031
9V-ATI LJ45 033
9V-ATJ LJ45 035
9V-BEE JSTR 5011/1
(9V-PUW) C550 141

### Rwanda

9XR-NN FA50 6

# MILITARY INDEX

## Argentina

| | | |
|---|---|---|
| 0653 | HS25 | 25251 |
| 5-T-30 | HS25 | 25251 |
| A-01 | MS76 | 003 |
| A-02 | MS76 | 004 |
| A-03 | MS76 | 007 |
| A-04 | MS76 | 010 |
| A-05 | MS76 | 011 |
| A-06 | MS76 | 013 |
| A-07 | MS76 | 015 |
| A-08 | MS76 | 016 |
| A-09 | MS76 | 017 |
| A-10 | MS76 | 018 |
| A-11 | MS76 | 021 |
| A-12 | MS76 | 022 |
| AE-129 | C550 | 117 |
| **AE-175** | **SBRL** | **380-13** |
| **AE-185** | **C500** | **366** |
| E-201 | MS76 | 003 |
| E-202 | MS76 | 004 |
| E-203 | MS76 | 007 |
| E-204 | MS76 | 010 |
| E-205 | MS76 | 011 |
| E-206 | MS76 | 013 |
| E-207 | MS76 | 015 |
| E-208 | MS76 | 016 |
| E-209 | MS76 | 017 |
| E-210 | MS76 | 018 |
| E-211 | MS76 | 021 |
| E-212 | MS76 | 022 |
| E-213 | MS76 | A-1 |
| E-214 | MS76 | A-2 |
| E-215 | MS76 | A-3 |
| E-216 | MS76 | A-4 |
| E-217 | MS76 | A-5 |
| E-218 | MS76 | A-6 |
| E-219 | MS76 | A-7 |
| E-220 | MS76 | A-8 |
| E-221 | MS76 | A-9 |
| E-222 | MS76 | A-10 |
| E-223 | MS76 | A-11 |
| E-224 | MS76 | A-12 |
| E-225 | MS76 | A-13 |
| E-226 | MS76 | A-14 |
| E-227 | MS76 | A-15 |
| E-228 | MS76 | A-16 |
| E-229 | MS76 | A-17 |
| E-230 | MS76 | A-18 |
| E-231 | MS76 | A-19 |
| E-232 | MS76 | A-20 |
| E-233 | MS76 | A-21 |
| E-234 | MS76 | A-22 |
| E-235 | MS76 | A-23 |
| E-236 | MS76 | A-24 |
| E-237 | MS76 | A-25 |
| E-238 | MS76 | A-26 |
| E-239 | MS76 | A-27 |
| E-240 | MS76 | A-28 |
| E-241 | MS76 | A-29 |
| E-242 | MS76 | A-30 |
| E-243 | MS76 | A-31 |
| E-244 | MS76 | A-32 |
| E-245 | MS76 | A-33 |
| E-246 | MS76 | A-34 |
| E-247 | MS76 | A-35 |
| E-248 | MS76 | A-36 |
| T-03 | LJ24 | 316 |
| **T-10** | **LJ60** | **140** |
| T-10 | SBRL | 380-3 |
| **T-11** | **SBRL** | **380-3** |
| T-21 | LJ35 | 115 |
| **T-22** | **LJ35** | **136** |
| **T-23** | **LJ35** | **319** |
| T-24 | LJ35 | 333 |
| T-24 | LJ35 | 369 |
| **T-25** | **LJ35** | **484** |
| **T-26** | **LJ35** | **369** |
| VR-17 | LJ35 | 369 |
| VR-18 | LJ35 | 484 |

## Australia

| | | |
|---|---|---|
| A11-078 | FA20 | 78/412 |
| A11-085 | FA20 | 85/425 |
| A11-090 | FA20 | 90/426 |
| A26-070 | F900 | 70 |
| A26-073 | F900 | 73 |
| A26-074 | F900 | 74 |
| A26-076 | F900 | 76 |
| A26-077 | F900 | 77 |
| **A37-001** | **CL64** | **5521** |
| **A37-002** | **CL64** | **5534** |
| **A37-003** | **CL64** | **5538** |

## Belgium

| | | |
|---|---|---|
| **CD-01** | **F900** | **109** |
| **CM-01** | **FA20** | **276/494** |
| **CM-02** | **FA20** | **278/495** |
| (OT-JFA) | FA20 | 104/454 |

## Bolivia

| | | |
|---|---|---|
| **FAB-001** | **SBRL** | **306-115** |
| 008 | LJ25 | 192 |
| 009 | LJ35 | 152 |
| **010** | **LJ25** | **192** |
| **010** | **LJ25** | **211** |

## Botswana

| | | |
|---|---|---|
| OK-1/Z-1 | HS25 | 258112 |
| **OK1** | **GLEX** | **9259** |
| OK1 | GLF4 | 1173 |
| OK1 | HS25 | 258164 |
| **OK2** | **GLF4** | **1173** |
| OK2 | HS25 | 258164 |

## Brazil

| | | |
|---|---|---|
| **2710** | **LJ35** | **631** |
| **2711** | **LJ35** | **632** |
| **2712** | **LJ35** | **633** |
| **2713** | **LJ35** | **636** |
| **2714** | **LJ35** | **638** |
| **2715** | **LJ35** | **639** |
| **2716** | **LJ35** | **640** |
| **2717** | **LJ35** | **641** |
| **2718** | **LJ35** | **642** |
| **6000** | **LJ35** | **613** |
| **6001** | **LJ35** | **615** |
| **6002** | **LJ35** | **617** |
| **FAB6100** | **LJ55** | **140** |
| C41-2910 | MS76 | 053 |
| C41-2911 | MS76 | 052 |
| C41-2912 | MS76 | 051 |
| C41-2913 | MS76 | 054 |
| C41-2914 | MS76 | 055 |
| C41-2915 | MS76 | 056 |
| C41-2916 | MS76 | 059 |
| C41-2917 | MS76 | 060 |
| C41-2918 | MS76 | 057 |
| C41-2919 | MS76 | 061 |
| C41-2920 | MS76 | 058 |
| C41-2921 | MS76 | 062 |
| C41-2922 | MS76 | 064 |
| C41-2923 | MS76 | 063 |
| C41-2924 | MS76 | 065 |
| C41-2925 | MS76 | 066 |
| C41-2926 | MS76 | 067 |
| C41-2927 | MS76 | 068 |
| C41-2928 | MS76 | 070 |
| C41-2929 | MS76 | 071 |
| C41-2930 | MS76 | 074 |
| C41-2931 | MS76 | 075 |
| C41-2932 | MS76 | 076 |
| C41-2933 | MS76 | 077 |
| C41-2934 | MS76 | 078 |
| C41-2935 | MS76 | 079 |
| C41-2936 | MS76 | 080 |
| C41-2937 | MS76 | 081 |
| C41-2938 | MS76 | 082 |
| C41-2939 | MS76 | 083 |
| EC93-2125 | HS25 | 25164 |
| EU93-2119 | HS25 | 25274 |
| EU93-2121 | HS25 | 25165 |
| **EU93-2125** | **HS25** | **25164** |
| **EU93A-6050** | **HS25** | **258401** |
| **EU93A-6051** | **HS25** | **258421** |
| **EU93A-6052** | **HS25** | **258434** |
| **EU93A-6053** | **HS25** | **258447** |
| VC93-2120 | HS25 | 25162 |
| VC93-2121 | HS25 | 25165 |
| VC93-2122 | HS25 | 25166 |
| VC93-2123 | HS25 | 25167 |
| VC93-2124 | HS25 | 25168 |
| **VU93-2113** | **HS25** | **25136** |
| VU93-2114 | HS25 | 25212 |
| VU93-2117 | HS25 | 25210 |
| **VU93-2118** | **HS25** | **25200** |
| **VU93-2120** | **HS25** | **25162** |
| **VU93-2123** | **HS25** | **25167** |
| VU93-2124 | HS25 | 25168 |
| **VU93-2126** | **HS25** | **25277** |
| **VU93-2127** | **HS25** | **25288** |
| **VU93-2128** | **HS25** | **25289** |
| VU93-2129 | HS25 | 25290 |
| XU93-2117 | HS25 | 25210 |

## Canada

| | | |
|---|---|---|
| 20501 | FA20 | 82/418 |
| 20502 | FA20 | 87/424 |
| 20503 | FA20 | 92/421 |
| 20504 | FA20 | 97/422 |
| 20505 | FA20 | 103/423 |
| 20506 | FA20 | 109/427 |
| 20507 | FA20 | 114/420 |
| 117501 | FA20 | 82/418 |
| 117502 | FA20 | 87/424 |
| 117503 | FA20 | 92/421 |
| 117504 | FA20 | 97/422 |
| 117505 | FA20 | 103/423 |
| 117506 | FA20 | 109/427 |
| 117507 | FA20 | 114/420 |
| 117508 | FA20 | 157 |
| **144601** | **CL60** | **1040** |
| 144602 | CL60 | 1065 |
| 144603 | CL60 | 1006 |
| 144604 | CL60 | 1007 |
| 144605 | CL60 | 1008 |
| 144606 | CL60 | 1009 |
| 144607 | CL60 | 1014 |
| 144608 | CL60 | 1015 |
| 144609 | CL60 | 1017 |
| 144610 | CL60 | 1022 |
| 144611 | CL60 | 1030 |
| 144612 | CL60 | 1002 |
| 144613 | CL61 | 3035 |
| **144614** | **CL61** | **3036** |
| **144615** | **CL61** | **3037** |
| **144616** | **CL61** | **3038** |
| **144617** | **CL64** | **5533** |
| **144618** | **CL64** | **5535** |

## Chile

| | | |
|---|---|---|
| 130 | WW24 | 409 |
| 301 | FA20 | 401 |
| 302 | FA20 | 496 |
| **303** | **C650** | **0131** |
| **351** | **LJ35** | **050** |
| **352** | **LJ35** | **066** |
| **361** | **C525** | **0463** |
| **362** | **C525** | **0464** |
| **363** | **C525** | **0465** |
| **364** | **C525** | **0507** |
| 911 | GLF3 | 465 |
| **911** | **GLF4** | **1089** |
| E-301 | C550 | 146 |
| E-302 | C650 | 0033 |
| E-303 | C650 | 0131 |

## China

| | | |
|---|---|---|
| 090 | C550 | 359 |
| 091 | C550 | 357 |
| 092 | C550 | 362 |
| **HY984** | **LJ36** | **053** |
| HY985 | LJ36 | 034 |
| **HY986** | **LJ35** | **601** |
| **HY987** | **LJ35** | **602** |
| **HY988** | **LJ35** | **603** |

## Ciskei

| | | |
|---|---|---|
| CA-01 | WW24 | 107 |

## Colombia

| | | |
|---|---|---|
| **FAC1211** | **C550** | **582** |
| **FAC5760** | **C560** | **0350** |
| **FAC5761** | **C560** | **0374** |
| **FAC5762** | **C560** | **0386** |
| **FAC5763** | **C560** | **0365** |
| **FAC5764** | **C560** | **0381** |

## Czech Republic

| | | |
|---|---|---|
| **5105** | **CL61** | **5105** |

## Denmark

| | | |
|---|---|---|
| C-066 | CL64 | 5366 |
| **C-080** | **CL64** | **5380** |
| **C-168** | **CL64** | **5468** |
| **C-172** | **CL64** | **5472** |
| F-085 | GLF2 | 85 |
| F-249 | GLF3 | 249 |
| F-313 | GLF3 | 313 |
| F-330 | GLF3 | 330 |
| F-400 | GLF3 | 401 |

## Ecuador

| | | |
|---|---|---|
| **043** | **SBRL** | **282-43** |
| **047** | **SBRL** | **282-109** |
| **049** | **SBRL** | **306-68** |
| 068 | SBRL | 282-68 |
| AEE-402 | SBRL | 380-45 |
| AEE-403 | SBRL | 380-34 |
| ANE-201 | C500 | 481 |
| FAE-001A | SBRL | 306-117 |
| FAE-034 | SBRL | 380-34 |
| FAE-045 | SBRL | 380-45 |
| IGM-401 | LJ24 | 312 |
| **IGM-628** | **C550** | **628** |

## Eritrea

| | | |
|---|---|---|
| 901 | ASTR | 063 |

## Finland

| | | |
|---|---|---|
| **LJ-1** | **LJ35** | **430** |
| **LJ-2** | **LJ35** | **451** |
| **LJ-3** | **LJ35** | **470** |

## France

| | | |
|---|---|---|
| 1 | MS76 | 001 |
| 1 | FA20 | 1/401 |
| 2 | FA50 | 2 |
| **2** | **F900** | **2** |
| **4** | **F900** | **4** |
| **5** | **FA50** | **5** |
| **7** | **FA50** | **7** |
| 02 | FA10 | 02 |
| 03 | MS76 | 03 |
| 12 | MS76 | 012 |
| 14 | MS76 | 014 |
| 19 | MS76 | 019 |
| 20 | MS76 | 020 |
| 22 | FA20 | 22/404 |
| 23 | MS76 | 023 |
| 24 | MS76 | 024 |
| 25 | MS76 | 025 |
| 26 | MS76 | 026 |
| 27 | MS76 | 027 |
| **27** | **FA50** | **27** |
| 29 | MS76 | 029 |
| **30** | **FA50** | **30** |
| 30 | MS76 | 030 |
| 31 | MS76 | 031 |
| **32** | **FA10** | **32** |
| 32 | MS76 | 032 |
| 33 | MS76 | 033 |
| 34 | MS76 | 034 |
| **34** | **FA50** | **34** |
| 35 | MS76 | 035 |
| **36** | **FA50** | **36** |
| 36 | MS76 | 036 |
| 37 | MS76 | 037 |
| 38 | MS76 | 038 |
| 39 | FA10 | 39 |
| 40 | MS76 | 040 |
| 41 | MS76 | 041 |
| 42 | MS76 | 042 |
| 44 | MS76 | 044 |
| 45 | MS76 | 045 |
| 46 | MS76 | 046 |
| 47 | MS76 | 047 |
| 48 | MS76 | 048 |
| **48** | **FA20** | **448** |
| 49 | FA20 | 49/408 |
| 51 | MS76 | 051 |
| 53 | MS76 | 053 |
| 54 | MS76 | 054 |
| 56 | MS76 | 056 |
| 57 | MS76 | 057 |
| 58 | MS76 | 058 |
| 59 | MS76 | 059 |
| 60 | MS76 | 060 |
| 61 | MS76 | 061 |
| 62 | MS76 | 062 |
| 65 | MS76 | 065 |
| **65** | **FA20** | **465** |
| 68 | MS76 | 068 |
| **68** | **FA7X** | **68** |
| 70 | MS76 | 070 |
| 71 | MS76 | 071 |
| **72** | **FA20** | **472** |
| **73** | **MS76** | **073** |
| 74 | MS76 | 074 |
| 75 | MS76 | 075 |
| 76 | FA20 | 476 |
| **77** | **FA20** | **477** |
| 77 | MS76 | 077 |
| 78 | MS76 | 078 |
| **78** | **FA50** | **78** |
| 79 | MS76 | 079 |
| **79** | **FA20** | **79/415** |
| 80 | MS76 | 080 |
| **80** | **FA20** | **480** |
| 81 | MS76 | 081 |
| 82 | MS76 | 082 |
| 83 | MS76 | 083 |
| 84 | MS76 | 084 |
| **85** | **MS76** | **085** |
| **86** | **FA20** | **86** |
| 87 | MS76 | 087 |
| 88 | MS76 | 088 |
| 91 | MS76 | 091 |
| 92 | MS76 | 092 |
| 93 | MS76 | 093 |
| **93** | **FA20** | **93/435** |
| 94 | MS76 | 094 |
| 95 | MS76 | 095 |
| 96 | MS76 | 096 |
| **96** | **FA20** | **96** |
| 97 | MS76 | 097 |
| **100** | **MS76** | **100** |
| **101** | **FA10** | **101** |
| 101 | MS76 | 101 |
| **104** | **FA20** | **104/454** |
| 113 | MS76 | 113 |
| 114 | MS76 | 114 |
| 115 | FA20 | 115/432 |
| 115 | MS76 | 115 |
| 116 | MS76 | 116 |
| 117 | MS76 | 117 |
| 118 | MS76 | 118 |
| 119 | MS76 | 119 |
| 124 | FA20 | 124/433 |
| **129** | **FA10** | **129** |
| **131** | **FA20** | **131/437** |
| **132** | **FA50** | **132** |
| **133** | **FA10** | **133** |
| **138** | **FA20** | **138/440** |
| **143** | **FA10** | **143** |
| **145** | **FA20** | **145/443** |
| 154 | FA20 | 154/447 |
| **167** | **FA20** | **167/453** |
| **182** | **FA20** | **182/461** |
| **185** | **FA10** | **185** |
| **188** | **FA20** | **188/464** |
| 238 | FA20 | 238/477 |
| **252** | **FA20** | **252/485** |
| **260** | **FA20** | **260/488** |
| **263** | **FA20** | **263/489** |
| **268** | **FA20** | **268/492** |
| **288** | **FA20** | **288/499** |
| 291 | FA20 | 291/505 |
| 309 | FA20 | 309/514 |
| **339** | **FA20** | **451** |
| **342** | **FA20** | **342/532** |
| **375** | **FA20** | **375/547** |
| **422** | **FA20** | **422** |
| 463 | FA20 | 186/463 |
| **483** | **FA20** | **483** |
| 20-Q | MS76 | 020 |
| 34-Z | MS76 | 037 |
| 41-A | MS76 | 038 |
| 41-AC | MS76 | 057 |
| 41-AR | MS76 | 019 |
| 41-AT | MS76 | 060 |
| 41-A. | MS76 | 081 |
| 41-A. | MS76 | 054 |
| 41-A. | MS76 | 059 |
| 42-AP | MS76 | 025 |
| 43-BB | MS76 | 034 |
| **43-BL** | **MS76** | **035** |
| 43-B. | MS76 | 045 |
| 44-CC | MS76 | 036 |
| 4D-L | MS76 | 044 |
| 65-KW | MS76 | 024 |
| 65-LB | MS76 | 058 |
| 65-LC | MS76 | 029 |
| 65-LD | MS76 | 093 |
| 65-LE | MS76 | 071 |
| 65-LF | MS76 | 065 |
| 65-LF | MS76 | 070 |
| 65-LG | MS76 | 056 |
| 65-LH | MS76 | 097 |
| 65-LI | MS76 | 030 |
| 65-LP | MS76 | 077 |
| 65-LU | MS76 | 091 |
| 65-LU | MS76 | 096 |
| 65-LV | MS76 | 062 |
| 65-LY | MS76 | 078 |
| 65-LZ | MS76 | 075 |
| 65-L. | MS76 | 082 |
| 65-L. | MS76 | 094 |
| 80/DE | MS76 | 080 |
| 113-CG | MS76 | 034 |
| 115-ME | MS76 | 038 |
| 115-ME | MS76 | 078 |
| 116-CB | MS76 | 025 |
| 118-DA | MS76 | 092 |
| 133-CF | MS76 | 059 |
| 133-CM | MS76 | 056 |
| 312-DF | MS76 | 014 |
| 312-DG | MS76 | 058 |
| 314-D | MS76 | 080 |
| 314-DO | MS76 | 062 |
| 316-DH | MS76 | 036 |
| 316-DI | MS76 | 045 |
| 316-DL | MS76 | 092 |
| 330-DB | MS76 | 001 |
| 330-DC | MS76 | 051 |
| 330-DO | MS76 | 023 |
| **330-DP** | **MS76** | **065** |
| (CEV) 1 | CRVT | 1 |
| (CEV) 2 | CRVT | 2 |
| (CEV) 10 | CRVT | 10 |
| ELA61 | MS76 | 081 |
| GE-316 | MS76 | 080 |
| **NB** | **MS76** | **068** |
| NC | MS76 | 083 |
| OD | MS76 | 053 |
| -DE | MS76 | 027 |
| -LN | MS76 | 026 |
| -LY | MS76 | 061 |

## Germany

| | | |
|---|---|---|
| 1101 | JSTR | 5025 |
| 1102 | JSTR | 5121 |
| 1103 | JSTR | 5071 |
| 1201 | CL61 | 3031 |
| **1202** | **CL61** | **3040** |
| **1203** | **CL61** | **3043** |
| **1204** | **CL61** | **3049** |
| **1205** | **CL61** | **3053** |
| **1206** | **CL61** | **3056** |
| **1207** | **CL61** | **3059** |
| 1601 | HFB3 | 1041 |
| 1602 | HFB3 | 1042 |
| 1603 | HFB3 | 1043 |
| 1604 | HFB3 | 1046 |
| 1605 | HFB3 | 1047 |
| 1606 | HFB3 | 1048 |
| 1607 | HFB3 | 1024 |
| 1608 | HFB3 | 1025 |
| 1621 | HFB3 | 1058 |
| 1622 | HFB3 | 1059 |
| 1623 | HFB3 | 1060 |
| 1624 | HFB3 | 1061 |
| 1625 | HFB3 | 1062 |
| 1626 | HFB3 | 1063 |
| 1627 | HFB3 | 1064 |
| 1628 | HFB3 | 1065 |
| 9825 | HFB3 | 1059 |
| 9826 | HFB3 | 1060 |
| CA101 | JSTR | 5025 |
| CA102 | JSTR | 5035 |
| CA103 | JSTR | 5071 |
| (CA111) | HFB3 | 1024 |
| (CA112) | HFB3 | 1025 |
| D9536 | HFB3 | 1024 |
| D9537 | HFB3 | 1025 |
| (YA111) | HFB3 | 1024 |
| (YA112) | HFB3 | 1025 |

## Ghana

| | | |
|---|---|---|
| G.511 | HS25 | 25028 |
| G540 | GLF3 | 493 |

## Greece

| | | |
|---|---|---|
| **678** | **GLF5** | **678** |

## Honduras

| | | |
|---|---|---|
| 318 | WW24 | 183 |

## India

| | | |
|---|---|---|
| **K-2960** | **GLF3** | **420** |
| **K-2961** | **GLF3** | **494** |
| **K-2962** | **GLF3** | **495** |
| **L3458** | **ASTR** | **126** |
| **L3467** | **ASTR** | **148** |

## Indonesia

| | | |
|---|---|---|
| A-1645 | JSTR | 5059 |
| A-9446 | JSTR | 5046 |
| P-2034 | BE40 | RK-362 |
| **P-8001** | **BE40** | **RK-362** |
| T-1645 | JSTR | 5059 |
| T-9446 | JSTR | 5046 |
| T17845 | JSTR | 5011/1 |

## Iran

| | | |
|---|---|---|
| 1003 | JSTR | 5203 |
| 1004 | JSTR | 5137 |
| 5-2801 | FA20 | 333/526 |
| 5-2802 | FA20 | 336/528 |
| 5-2803 | FA20 | 340/531 |
| 5-2804 | FA20 | 346/535 |
| 5-3020 | FA20 | 348/536 |
| **5-3021** | **FA20** | **350/537** |
| 5-4039 | FA20 | 348/536 |
| 5-4040 | FA20 | 350/537 |
| 5-9001 | FA20 | 351/538 |
| **5-9001** | **JSTR** | **5137** |
| 5-9002 | FA20 | 353/539 |
| **5-9003** | **FA20** | **354/540** |
| 5-9011 | FA50 | 120 |
| 5-9012 | FA50 | 101 |
| **5-9013** | **FA50** | **122** |
| **5-9014** | **FA20** | **337/529** |
| **5-9015** | **FA20** | **343/533** |
| 15-2233 | FA20 | 333/526 |
| **15-2235** | **FA20** | **318/518** |

## Ireland

| | | |
|---|---|---|
| IAC236 | HS25 | 25256 |
| 238 | HS25 | 257082 |
| 239 | HS25 | 256015 |
| 249 | GLF3 | 413 |
| **251** | **GLF4** | **1160** |
| **258** | **LJ45** | **234** |

## Israel

| | | |
|---|---|---|
| 027 | WW24 | 185 |
| 029 | WW24 | 152 |
| 031 | WW24 | 186 |
| 035 | WW24 | 152 |
| 064 | WW24 | 107 |
| **514** | **GLF5** | **5014** |
| 532 | GLF5 | 5132 |
| **537** | **GLF5** | **5037** |
| 544 | GLF5 | 5044 |
| **569** | **GLF5** | **5069** |
| **676** | **GLF5** | **676** |
| **679** | **GLF5** | **679** |
| **684** | **GLF5** | **684** |
| **927** | **WW24** | **185** |
| **929** | **WW24** | **152** |
| **931** | **WW24** | **186** |

Italy

| | | |
|---|---|---|
| (MM151) | FA50 | 151 |
| MM577 | P808 | 501 |
| MM578 | P808 | 502 |
| MM61948 | P808 | 506 |
| MM61949 | P808 | 507 |
| MM61950 | P808 | 508 |
| MM61951 | P808 | 509 |
| MM61952 | P808 | 510 |
| MM61953 | P808 | 511 |
| MM61954 | P808 | 512 |
| MM61955 | P808 | 513 |
| MM61956 | P808 | 514 |
| MM61957 | P808 | 515 |
| MM61958 | P808 | 505 |
| MM61959 | P808 | 516 |
| MM61960 | P808 | 517 |
| MM61961 | P808 | 518 |
| MM61962 | P808 | 519 |
| MM61963 | P808 | 520 |
| MM62014 | P808 | 521 |
| MM62015 | P808 | 522 |
| MM62016 | P808 | 523 |
| MM62017 | P808 | 524 |
| MM62020 | FA50 | 151 |
| MM62021 | FA50 | 155 |
| MM62022 | GLF3 | 451 |
| MM62025 | GLF3 | 479 |
| **MM62026** | **FA50** | **193** |
| **MM62029** | **FA50** | **211** |
| **MM62171** | **F9EX** | **45** |
| **MM62172** | **F9EX** | **52** |
| **MM62210** | **F9EX** | **116** |
| **MM62244** | **F9EX** | **149** |
| **MM62245** | **F9EX** | **156** |

Japan

| | | |
|---|---|---|
| **9201** | **LJ36** | **054** |
| 9202 | LJ36 | 056 |
| 9203 | LJ36 | 058 |
| **9204** | **LJ36** | **059** |
| **9205** | **LJ36** | **060** |
| **9206** | **LJ36** | **061** |
| **02-3013** | **HS25** | **258370** |
| **02-3014** | **HS25** | **258381** |
| **02-3015** | **HS25** | **258407** |
| **02-3016** | **HS25** | **258427** |
| **02-3027** | **HS25** | **258824** |
| **05-3255** | **GLF4** | **1359** |
| **12-3017** | **HS25** | **258445** |
| **12-3018** | **HS25** | **258469** |
| **21-5061** | **BE40** | **TX-11** |
| **21-5062** | **BE40** | **TX-12** |
| **22-3019** | **HS25** | **258493** |
| **22-3020** | **HS25** | **258513** |
| **29-3041** | **HS25** | **258215** |
| **32-3021** | **HS25** | **258533** |
| **39-3042** | **HS25** | **258227** |
| **41-5051** | **BE40** | **TX-1** |
| **41-5052** | **BE40** | **TX-2** |
| **41-5053** | **BE40** | **TX-3** |
| **41-5054** | **BE40** | **TX-4** |
| **41-5055** | **BE40** | **TX-5** |
| **41-5063** | **BE40** | **TX-13** |
| **42-3022** | **HS25** | **258610** |
| **49-3043** | **HS25** | **258242** |
| **51-5056** | **BE40** | **TX-6** |
| **51-5057** | **BE40** | **TX-7** |
| **51-5058** | **BE40** | **TX-8** |
| **52-3001** | **HS25** | **258245** |
| **52-3002** | **HS25** | **258247** |
| **52-3003** | **HS25** | **258250** |
| **52-3023** | **HS25** | **258629** |
| **62-3004** | **HS25** | **258268** |
| **62-3024** | **HS25** | **258685** |
| **71-5059** | **BE40** | **TX-9** |
| **72-3005** | **HS25** | **258288** |
| **72-3006** | **HS25** | **258305** |
| **72-3025** | **HS25** | **258735** |
| **75-3251** | **GLF4** | **1270** |
| **75-3252** | **GLF4** | **1271** |
| **82-3007** | **HS25** | **258306** |
| **82-3008** | **HS25** | **258325** |
| **82-3009** | **HS25** | **258333** |
| 82-3026 | HS25 | 258797 |
| **85-3253** | **GLF4** | **1303** |
| **91-5060** | **BE40** | **TX-10** |
| **92-3010** | **HS25** | **258341** |
| **92-3011** | **HS25** | **258348** |
| **92-3012** | **HS25** | **258360** |
| **92-3026** | **HS25** | **258797** |
| **95-3254** | **GLF4** | **1326** |

Jordan

| | | |
|---|---|---|
| 122 | FA20 | 255/487 |

Korea

| | | |
|---|---|---|
| **701** | **CL64** | **5429** |

Libya

| | | |
|---|---|---|
| 001 | JSTR | 5136 |
| 002 | FA20 | 190/465 |

Malaysia

| | | |
|---|---|---|
| FM1200 | HS25 | 25189 |
| FM1201 | HS25 | 25209 |
| FM1801 | HS25 | 25189 |
| FM1802 | HS25 | 25209 |
| M24-01 | HS25 | 25189 |
| "M24-02" | HS25 | 25189 |
| M24-02 | HS25 | 25209 |
| M31-01 | CL60 | 1062 |
| M31-02 | CL60 | 1064 |
| **M37-01** | **F900** | **64** |
| M48-01 | GLEX | 9007 |
| **M48-02** | **GLEX** | **9096** |
| M52-01 | GLEX | 9096 |

Malawi

| | | |
|---|---|---|
| MAAW-J1 | HS25 | 257076 |
| MAAW-J1 | HS25 | 258064 |

Mexico

| | | |
|---|---|---|
| **3908** | **JSTR** | **5144** |
| **3909** | **LJ35** | **321** |
| **AMT-200** | **LJ60** | **152** |
| **AMT-201** | **LJ31** | **174** |
| **AMT-202** | **LJ25** | **339** |
| **AMT-203** | **SBRL** | **306-34** |
| **AMT-204** | **SBRL** | **306-144** |
| **AMT-205** | **GLF4** | **4128** |
| **AMT-206** | **LJ31** | **191** |
| DN-01 | JSTR | 5144 |
| **ETE-1329** | **C500** | **090** |
| JS10201 | JSTR | 5144 |
| MTX-01 | LJ24 | 313 |
| MTX-01 | LJ60 | 152 |
| MTX-01 | SBRL | 306-34 |
| MTX-02 | LJ24 | 313 |
| MTX-02 | LJ31 | 174 |
| MTX-02 | SBRL | 306-34 |
| **MTX-03** | **LJ25** | **339** |
| MTX-04 | SBRL | 306-34 |
| PF-201 | LJ28 | 29-002 |
| PF-239 | FA20 | 287 |
| TP-04 | GLF2 | 161 |
| **TP-06** | **GLF3** | **352** |
| **TP-07** | **GLF3** | **386** |
| TP 101 | SBRL | 380-67 |
| TP 102 | SBRL | 380-68 |
| TP 103 | SBRL | 380-67 |
| TP103 | SBRL | 306-139 |
| **TP104** | **LJ35** | **028** |
| TP104 | SBRL | 306-144 |
| TP 104 | SBRL | 380-68 |
| **TP-105** | **LJ36** | **050** |
| TP105 | SBRL | 282-130 |
| TP105 | SBRL | 306-139 |
| TP106 | SBRL | 306-144 |
| TP-106 | LJ35 | 321 |
| TP107 | SBRL | 282-130 |
| TP108 | HS25 | 25216 |
| TP108 | SBRL | 282-117 |
| TP0206 | HS25 | 25216 |

Myanmar

| | | |
|---|---|---|
| **4400** | **C550** | **389** |

Netherlands

| | | |
|---|---|---|
| **V-11** | **GLF4** | **1009** |

Norway

| | | |
|---|---|---|
| **041** | **FA20** | **41/407** |
| **053** | **FA20** | **53/417** |
| **0125** | **FA20** | **125** |

Oman

| | | |
|---|---|---|
| 601 | GLF2 | 214 |

Pakistan

| | | |
|---|---|---|
| **0233** | **C560** | **0233** |
| **1003** | **C550** | **550-1003** |
| **J-468** | **FA20** | **468** |
| **J-469** | **FA20** | **469** |
| **J-753** | **FA20** | **277/501** |
| **J-754** | **C56X** | **5004** |
| **J-755** | **GLF4** | **1325** |
| **J-756** | **GLF4** | **4090** |
| **V-4101** | **E50P** | **50000017** |
| **V-4102** | **E50P** | **50000014** |
| **V-4103** | **E50P** | **50000047** |
| **V-4104** | **E50P** | **50000113** |

Peru

| | | |
|---|---|---|
| **300** | **FA20** | **434** |
| FAP 522 | LJ25 | 159 |
| FAP 523 | LJ25 | 164 |
| **524** | **LJ36** | **051** |
| **525** | **LJ36** | **052** |
| 721 | C560 | 0365 |

Portugal

| | | |
|---|---|---|
| 7401 | FA50 | 195 |
| 7402 | FA50 | 198 |
| 7403 | FA50 | 221 |
| 8101 | FA20 | 211 |
| 8102 | FA20 | 215 |
| 8103 | FA20 | 217 |
| 17101 | FA20 | 211 |
| 17102 | FA20 | 215 |
| 17103 | FA20 | 217 |
| **17401** | **FA50** | **195** |
| **17402** | **FA50** | **198** |
| **17403** | **FA50** | **221** |

Russia

| | | |
|---|---|---|
| 62 | GLF2 | 62 |

(Black or Dark Blue)

Saudi Arabia

| | | |
|---|---|---|
| 101 | JSTR | 5129 |
| 102 | JSTR | 5130 |
| 103 | GLF3 | 453 |
| 103 | JSTR | 5130 |
| 104 | HS25 | 258115 |
| 105 | HS25 | 258118 |
| 110 | HS25 | 258148 |
| 130 | HS25 | 258164 |

Seychelles

| | | |
|---|---|---|
| SY-001 | C560 | 0003 |

| | | |
|---|---|---|
| **016** | **GLF5** | **5044** |
| **017** | **GLF5** | **5132** |
| **018** | **GLF5** | **5143** |

South Africa

| | | |
|---|---|---|
| 01 | HS25 | 25181 |
| 02 | HS25 | 25177 |
| 03 | HS25 | 25182 |
| 04 | HS25 | 25184 |
| 05 | HS25 | 25259 |
| 06 | HS25 | 25260 |
| 07 | HS25 | 25269 |
| (431) | FA20 | 41/407 |

South Korea

| | | |
|---|---|---|
| **258-342** | **HS25** | **258342** |
| **258-343** | **HS25** | **258343** |
| **258-346** | **HS25** | **258346** |
| **258-350** | **HS25** | **258350** |
| **258-351** | **HS25** | **258351** |
| **258-352** | **HS25** | **258352** |
| **258-353** | **HS25** | **258353** |
| **258-357** | **HS25** | **258357** |
| 5327 | C500 | 327 |
| 70327 | C500 | 327 |

Spain

| | | |
|---|---|---|
| **01-405** | **C550** | **424** |
| **01-406** | **C550** | **446** |
| **01-407** | **C550** | **592** |
| 45-01 | FA20 | 332/525 |
| 45-02 | FA20 | 253/486 |
| 45-03 | FA20 | 222/471 |
| 45-04 | FA20 | 219/470 |
| 45-05 | FA20 | 475 |
| 45-20 | FA50 | 84 |
| **45-40** | **F900** | **38** |
| **45-41** | **F900** | **90** |
| **45-42** | **F900** | **77** |
| **45-43** | **F900** | **74** |
| **45-44** | **F900** | **73** |
| **47-21** | **FA20** | **253/486** |
| **47-22** | **FA20** | **222/471** |
| **47-23** | **FA20** | **219/470** |
| **47-24** | **FA20** | **332/525** |
| 401-02 | FA20 | 253/486 |
| 401-03 | FA20 | 222/471 |
| 401-04 | FA20 | 219/470 |
| 401-05 | FA20 | 332/525 |
| 401-09 | FA50 | 84 |
| **403-11** | **C560** | **0161** |
| **403-12** | **C560** | **0193** |
| 408-11 | FA20 | 219/470 |
| 408-12 | FA20 | 332/525 |
| **T.11-1** | **FA20** | **253/486** |
| T.11-5 | FA20 | 475 |
| T.16-1 | FA50 | 84 |
| **T.18-1** | **F900** | **38** |
| **T.18-2** | **F900** | **90** |

| | | |
|---|---|---|
| **T.18-3** | **F900** | **77** |
| **T.18-4** | **F900** | **74** |
| **T.18-5** | **F900** | **73** |
| **TM.11-2** | **FA20** | **222/471** |
| **TM.11-3** | **FA20** | **219/470** |
| **TM.11-4** | **FA20** | **332/525** |
| **TR.20-01** | **C560** | **0161** |
| **TR.20-02** | **C560** | **0193** |
| **U.20-1** | **C550** | **424** |
| **U.20-2** | **C550** | **446** |
| **U.20-3** | **C550** | **592** |
| **U.21-01** | **C650** | **7079** |

## Sweden

| | | |
|---|---|---|
| **86001** | **SBRL** | **282-49** |
| **86002** | **SBRL** | **282-91** |
| **102001** | **GLF4** | **1014** |
| **102002** | **GLF4** | **1215** |
| **102003** | **GLF4** | **1216** |
| **102004** | **GLF4** | **1274** |
| 103001 | C550 | 307 |
| 103002 | C550 | 717 |

## Switzerland

| | | |
|---|---|---|
| T-781 | LJ35 | 068 |
| T-782 | LJ35 | 145 |
| **T-783** | **FA50** | **67** |
| **T-784** | **C56X** | **5269** |
| J-4117 | MS76 | 069 |

## Thailand

| | | |
|---|---|---|
| **30 40207** | **LJ35** | **623** |
| 30 60504 | LJ35 | 623 |
| 31 40208 | LJ35 | 635 |
| 31 60505 | LJ35 | 635 |
| **B.TL12-1** | **LJ35** | **623** |
| B.TL12-2 | LJ35 | 635 |

## Turkey

| | | |
|---|---|---|
| **001** | **GLF4** | **1027** |
| **004** | **C650** | **7024** |
| **005** | **C650** | **7026** |
| **007** | **C550** | **502** |
| **008** | **C550** | **503** |
| **09-001** | **GLF5** | **5241** |
| **10-002** | **GLF5** | **5254** |
| 12-001 | C550 | 502 |
| 12-002 | C550 | 503 |
| **12-003** | **GLF4** | **1163** |
| 84-007 | C550 | 502 |
| 84-008 | C550 | 503 |
| 93-7024 | C650 | 7024 |
| 93-7026 | C650 | 7026 |

## Uganda

| | | |
|---|---|---|
| UAF1 | WW24 | 134 |

## United Arab Emirates

| | | |
|---|---|---|
| 800 | LJ35 | 429 |
| 801 | LJ35 | 265 |

## United Kingdom

| | | |
|---|---|---|
| 9246M | HS25 | 25054 |
| 9259M | HS25 | 25012 |
| 9260M | HS25 | 25061 |
| 9273M | HS25 | 25044 |
| 9274M | HS25 | 25077 |
| 9275M | HS25 | 25049 |
| 9276M | HS25 | 25059 |
| **XS709** | **HS25** | **25011** |
| XS710 | HS25 | 25012 |
| **XS711** | **HS25** | **25024** |
| **XS712** | **HS25** | **25040** |
| **XS713** | **HS25** | **25041** |
| XS714 | HS25 | 25054 |
| XS726 | HS25 | 25044 |
| **XS727** | **HS25** | **25045** |
| **XS728** | **HS25** | **25048** |
| XS729 | HS25 | 25049 |
| **XS730** | **HS25** | **25050** |
| **XS731** | **HS25** | **25055** |
| XS732 | HS25 | 25056 |
| XS733 | HS25 | 25059 |
| XS734 | HS25 | 25061 |
| XS735 | HS25 | 25071 |
| XS736 | HS25 | 25072 |
| **XS737** | **HS25** | **25076** |
| XS738 | HS25 | 25077 |
| **XS739** | **HS25** | **25081** |
| XW788 | HS25 | 25255 |
| XW789 | HS25 | 25264 |
| XW790 | HS25 | 25266 |
| XW791 | HS25 | 25268 |
| XW930 | HS25 | 25009 |
| XX505 | HS25 | 25252 |
| XX506 | HS25 | 25271 |
| XX507 | HS25 | 256006 |
| XX508 | HS25 | 256008 |
| **ZD620** | **HS25** | **257181** |
| **ZD621** | **HS25** | **257190** |
| **ZD703** | **HS25** | **257183** |
| **ZD704** | **HS25** | **257194** |
| **ZE395** | **HS25** | **257205** |
| **ZE396** | **HS25** | **257211** |
| ZF130 | HS25 | 256059 |
| **ZJ690** | **GLEX** | **9107** |
| **ZJ691** | **GLEX** | **9123** |
| **ZJ692** | **GLEX** | **9131** |
| **ZJ693** | **GLEX** | **9132** |
| **ZJ694** | **GLEX** | **9135** |

## United States of America

### USAF/US Army

| | | |
|---|---|---|
| 59-2868 | SBRL | 265-1 |
| 59-2869 | SBRL | 265-2 |
| 59-2870 | SBRL | 265-3 |
| 59-2871 | SBRL | 265-4 |
| 59-2872 | SBRL | 265-5 |
| 59-2873 | SBRL | 270-1 |
| 59-2874 | SBRL | 270-2 |
| 59-5958 | JSTR | 5010 |
| 59-5959 | JSTR | 5026 |
| 59-5960 | JSTR | 5028 |
| 59-5961 | JSTR | 5030 |
| 59-5962 | JSTR | 5032 |
| **60-3474** | **SBRL** | **270-3** |
| 60-3475 | SBRL | 270-4 |
| 60-3476 | SBRL | 270-5 |
| 60-3477 | SBRL | 270-6 |
| 60-3478 | SBRL | 265-6 |
| 60-3479 | SBRL | 265-7 |
| 60-3480 | SBRL | 265-8 |
| 60-3481 | SBRL | 265-9 |
| 60-3482 | SBRL | 265-10 |
| 60-3483 | SBRL | 265-11 |
| 60-3484 | SBRL | 265-12 |
| 60-3485 | SBRL | 265-13 |
| 60-3486 | SBRL | 265-14 |
| 60-3487 | SBRL | 265-15 |
| 60-3488 | SBRL | 265-16 |
| 60-3489 | SBRL | 265-17 |
| 60-3490 | SBRL | 265-18 |
| 60-3491 | SBRL | 265-19 |
| 60-3492 | SBRL | 265-20 |
| 60-3493 | SBRL | 265-21 |
| 60-3494 | SBRL | 265-22 |
| 60-3495 | SBRL | 265-23 |
| 60-3496 | SBRL | 265-24 |
| 60-3497 | SBRL | 265-25 |
| 60-3498 | SBRL | 265-26 |
| 60-3499 | SBRL | 265-27 |
| 60-3500 | SBRL | 265-28 |
| 60-3501 | SBRL | 265-29 |
| 60-3502 | SBRL | 265-30 |
| 60-3503 | SBRL | 265-31 |
| 60-3504 | SBRL | 265-32 |
| 60-3505 | SBRL | 265-33 |
| 60-3506 | SBRL | 265-34 |
| 60-3507 | SBRL | 265-35 |
| 60-3508 | SBRL | 265-36 |
| 61-0634 | SBRL | 265-37 |
| 61-0635 | SBRL | 265-38 |
| 61-0636 | SBRL | 265-39 |
| 61-0637 | SBRL | 265-40 |
| 61-0638 | SBRL | 265-41 |
| 61-0639 | SBRL | 265-42 |
| 61-0640 | SBRL | 265-43 |
| 61-0641 | SBRL | 265-44 |
| 61-0642 | SBRL | 265-45 |
| 61-0643 | SBRL | 265-46 |
| 61-0644 | SBRL | 265-47 |
| 61-0645 | SBRL | 265-48 |
| 61-0646 | SBRL | 265-49 |
| 61-0647 | SBRL | 265-50 |
| 61-0648 | SBRL | 265-51 |
| 61-0649 | SBRL | 265-52 |
| 61-0650 | SBRL | 265-53 |
| 61-0651 | SBRL | 265-54 |
| 61-0652 | SBRL | 265-55 |
| 61-0653 | SBRL | 265-56 |
| 61-0654 | SBRL | 265-57 |
| 61-0655 | SBRL | 265-58 |
| 61-0656 | SBRL | 265-59 |
| 61-0657 | SBRL | 265-60 |
| 61-0658 | SBRL | 265-61 |
| 61-0659 | SBRL | 265-62 |
| 61-0660 | SBRL | 265-63 |
| 61-0661 | SBRL | 265-64 |
| 61-0662 | SBRL | 265-65 |
| 61-0663 | SBRL | 265-66 |
| 61-0664 | SBRL | 265-67 |
| 61-0665 | SBRL | 265-68 |
| 61-0666 | SBRL | 265-69 |
| 61-0667 | SBRL | 265-70 |
| 61-0668 | SBRL | 265-71 |
| 61-0669 | SBRL | 265-72 |
| **61-0670** | **SBRL** | **265-73** |
| 61-0671 | SBRL | 265-74 |
| 61-0672 | SBRL | 265-75 |
| 61-0673 | SBRL | 265-76 |
| 61-0674 | SBRL | 265-77 |
| 61-0675 | SBRL | 265-78 |
| 61-0676 | SBRL | 265-79 |
| 61-0677 | SBRL | 265-80 |
| 61-0678 | SBRL | 265-81 |
| 61-0679 | SBRL | 265-82 |
| 61-0680 | SBRL | 265-83 |
| 61-0681 | SBRL | 265-84 |
| 61-0682 | SBRL | 265-85 |
| 61-0683 | SBRL | 265-86 |
| 61-0684 | SBRL | 265-87 |
| 61-0685 | SBRL | 265-88 |
| 61-2488 | JSTR | 5017 |
| 61-2489 | JSTR | 5022 |
| 61-2490 | JSTR | 5024 |
| 61-2491 | JSTR | 5027 |
| 61-2492 | JSTR | 5031 |
| 61-2493 | JSTR | 5034 |
| (62-12166) | JSTR | 5025 |
| (62-12167) | JSTR | 5035 |
| (62-12845) | JSTR | 5071 |
| 62-4197 | JSTR | 5041 |
| 62-4198 | JSTR | 5042 |
| 62-4199 | JSTR | 5043 |
| 62-4200 | JSTR | 5044 |
| 62-4201 | JSTR | 5045 |
| 62-4448 | SBRL | 276-1 |
| 62-4449 | SBRL | 276-2 |
| 62-4450 | SBRL | 276-3 |
| 62-4451 | SBRL | 276-4 |
| 62-4452 | SBRL | 276-5 |
| 62-4453 | SBRL | 276-6 |
| 62-4454 | SBRL | 276-7 |
| 62-4455 | SBRL | 276-8 |
| 62-4456 | SBRL | 276-9 |
| 62-4457 | SBRL | 276-10 |
| 62-4458 | SBRL | 276-11 |
| 62-4459 | SBRL | 276-12 |
| 62-4460 | SBRL | 276-13 |
| 62-4461 | SBRL | 276-14 |
| 62-4462 | SBRL | 276-15 |
| 62-4463 | SBRL | 276-16 |
| 62-4464 | SBRL | 276-17 |
| 62-4465 | SBRL | 276-18 |
| 62-4466 | SBRL | 276-19 |
| 62-4467 | SBRL | 276-20 |
| 62-4468 | SBRL | 276-21 |
| 62-4469 | SBRL | 276-22 |
| 62-4470 | SBRL | 276-23 |
| 62-4471 | SBRL | 276-24 |
| 62-4472 | SBRL | 276-25 |
| 62-4473 | SBRL | 276-26 |
| 62-4474 | SBRL | 276-27 |
| 62-4475 | SBRL | 276-28 |
| 62-4476 | SBRL | 276-29 |
| 62-4477 | SBRL | 276-30 |
| 62-4478 | SBRL | 276-31 |
| 62-4479 | SBRL | 276-32 |
| 62-4480 | SBRL | 276-33 |
| 62-4481 | SBRL | 276-34 |
| 62-4482 | SBRL | 276-35 |
| 62-4483 | SBRL | 276-36 |
| 62-4484 | SBRL | 276-37 |
| 62-4485 | SBRL | 276-38 |
| 62-4486 | SBRL | 276-39 |
| 62-4487 | SBRL | 276-40 |
| **62-4488** | **SBRL** | **276-41** |
| 62-4489 | SBRL | 276-42 |
| 62-4490 | SBRL | 276-43 |
| 62-4491 | SBRL | 276-44 |
| 62-4492 | SBRL | 276-45 |
| 62-4493 | SBRL | 276-46 |
| 62-4494 | SBRL | 276-47 |
| 62-4495 | SBRL | 276-48 |
| 62-4496 | SBRL | 276-49 |
| 62-4497 | SBRL | 276-50 |
| 62-4498 | SBRL | 276-51 |
| 62-4499 | SBRL | 276-52 |
| 62-4500 | SBRL | 276-53 |
| 62-4501 | SBRL | 276-54 |
| 62-4502 | SBRL | 276-55 |
| 83-0500 | GLF3 | 382 |
| 83-0501 | GLF3 | 383 |
| **83-0502** | **GLF3** | **389** |
| 84-0063 | LJ35 | 509 |
| **84-0064** | **LJ35** | **510** |
| **84-0065** | **LJ35** | **511** |
| 84-0066 | LJ35 | 512 |
| 84-0067 | LJ35 | 513 |
| 84-0068 | LJ35 | 514 |
| **84-0069** | **LJ35** | **515** |
| **84-0070** | **LJ35** | **516** |
| **84-0071** | **LJ35** | **517** |
| **84-0072** | **LJ35** | **518** |
| 84-0073 | LJ35 | 519 |
| 84-0074 | LJ35 | 520 |
| **84-0075** | **LJ35** | **521** |
| **84-0076** | **LJ35** | **522** |
| **84-0077** | **LJ35** | **523** |
| 84-0078 | LJ35 | 524 |
| **84-0079** | **LJ35** | **525** |
| 84-0080 | LJ35 | 526 |
| **84-0081** | **LJ35** | **527** |
| **84-0082** | **LJ35** | **528** |
| **84-0083** | **LJ35** | **529** |
| **84-0084** | **LJ35** | **530** |
| **84-0085** | **LJ35** | **531** |
| 84-0086 | LJ35 | 532 |
| **84-0087** | **LJ35** | **533** |
| 84-0088 | LJ35 | 534 |
| 84-0089 | LJ35 | 535 |
| **84-0090** | **LJ35** | **536** |

| | | |
|---|---|---|
| 84-0091 | LJ35 | 537 |
| 84-0092 | LJ35 | 538 |
| 84-0093 | LJ35 | 539 |
| 84-0094 | LJ35 | 540 |
| 84-0095 | LJ35 | 541 |
| 84-0096 | LJ35 | 542 |
| 84-0097 | LJ35 | 543 |
| 84-0098 | LJ35 | 544 |
| 84-0099 | LJ35 | 545 |
| 84-0100 | LJ35 | 546 |
| 84-0101 | LJ35 | 547 |
| 84-0102 | LJ35 | 548 |
| 84-0103 | LJ35 | 549 |
| 84-0104 | LJ35 | 550 |
| 84-0105 | LJ35 | 551 |
| 84-0106 | LJ35 | 552 |
| 84-0107 | LJ35 | 553 |
| 84-0108 | LJ35 | 554 |
| 84-0109 | LJ35 | 555 |
| 84-0110 | LJ35 | 556 |
| 84-0111 | LJ35 | 557 |
| 84-0112 | LJ35 | 558 |
| 84-0113 | LJ35 | 559 |
| 84-0114 | LJ35 | 560 |
| 84-0115 | LJ35 | 561 |
| 84-0116 | LJ35 | 562 |
| 84-0117 | LJ35 | 563 |
| 84-0118 | LJ35 | 564 |
| 84-0119 | LJ35 | 565 |
| 84-0120 | LJ35 | 566 |
| 84-0121 | LJ35 | 567 |
| 84-0122 | LJ35 | 568 |
| 84-0123 | LJ35 | 569 |
| 84-0124 | LJ35 | 570 |
| 84-0125 | LJ35 | 571 |
| 84-0126 | LJ35 | 572 |
| 84-0127 | LJ35 | 573 |
| 84-0128 | LJ35 | 575 |
| 84-0129 | LJ35 | 576 |
| 84-0130 | LJ35 | 577 |
| 84-0131 | LJ35 | 578 |
| 84-0132 | LJ35 | 579 |
| 84-0133 | LJ35 | 580 |
| 84-0134 | LJ35 | 581 |
| 84-0135 | LJ35 | 582 |
| 84-0136 | LJ35 | 583 |
| 84-0137 | LJ35 | 585 |
| 84-0138 | LJ35 | 574 |
| 84-0139 | LJ35 | 587 |
| 84-0140 | LJ35 | 588 |
| 84-0141 | LJ35 | 584 |
| 84-0142 | LJ35 | 586 |
| 85-0049 | GLF3 | 456 |
| 85-0050 | GLF3 | 458 |
| 86-0200 | GLF3 | 465 |
| 86-0201 | GLF3 | 470 |
| 86-0202 | GLF3 | 468 |
| 86-0203 | GLF3 | 475 |
| 86-0204 | GLF3 | 476 |
| 86-0205 | GLF3 | 477 |
| 86-0206 | GLF3 | 478 |
| 86-0374 | LJ35 | 624 |
| 86-0375 | LJ35 | 625 |
| 86-0376 | LJ35 | 628 |
| 86-0377 | LJ35 | 629 |
| 86-0403 | GLF3 | 473 |
| 87-0026 | LJ35 | 280 |
| 87-0139 | GLF3 | 497 |
| 87-0140 | GLF3 | 498 |
| 88-0269 | HS25 | 258129 |
| 88-0270 | HS25 | 258131 |
| 88-0271 | HS25 | 258134 |
| 88-0272 | HS25 | 258154 |
| 88-0273 | HS25 | 258156 |
| 88-0274 | HS25 | 258158 |
| 89-0266 | GLF2 | 45 |
| 89-0284 | BE40 | TT-5 |
| 90-0300 | GLF4 | 1181 |
| 90-0400 | BE40 | TT-3 |
| 90-0401 | BE40 | TT-7 |
| 90-0402 | BE40 | TT-8 |
| 90-0403 | BE40 | TT-9 |
| 90-0404 | BE40 | TT-6 |
| 90-0405 | BE40 | TT-4 |
| 90-0406 | BE40 | TT-11 |
| 90-0407 | BE40 | TT-10 |
| 90-0408 | BE40 | TT-12 |
| 90-0409 | BE40 | TT-13 |
| 90-0410 | BE40 | TT-14 |
| 90-0411 | BE40 | TT-15 |
| 90-0412 | BE40 | TT-2 |
| 90-0413 | BE40 | TT-16 |
| 91-0075 | BE40 | TT-18 |
| 91-0076 | BE40 | TT-17 |
| 91-0077 | BE40 | TT-1 |
| 91-0078 | BE40 | TT-19 |
| 91-0079 | BE40 | TT-20 |
| 91-0080 | BE40 | TT-21 |
| 91-0081 | BE40 | TT-22 |
| 91-0082 | BE40 | TT-23 |
| 91-0083 | BE40 | TT-24 |
| 91-0084 | BE40 | TT-25 |
| 91-0085 | BE40 | TT-26 |
| 91-0086 | BE40 | TT-27 |
| 91-0087 | BE40 | TT-28 |
| 91-0088 | BE40 | TT-29 |
| 91-0089 | BE40 | TT-30 |
| 91-0090 | BE40 | TT-31 |
| 91-0091 | BE40 | TT-32 |
| 91-0092 | BE40 | TT-33 |
| 91-0093 | BE40 | TT-34 |
| 91-0094 | BE40 | TT-35 |
| 91-0095 | BE40 | TT-36 |
| 91-0096 | BE40 | TT-37 |
| 91-0097 | BE40 | TT-38 |
| 91-0098 | BE40 | TT-39 |
| 91-0099 | BE40 | TT-40 |
| 91-0100 | BE40 | TT-41 |
| 91-0101 | BE40 | TT-42 |
| 91-0102 | BE40 | TT-43 |
| 91-0108 | GLF4 | 1162 |
| 92-0330 | BE40 | TT-44 |
| 92-0331 | BE40 | TT-45 |
| 92-0332 | BE40 | TT-46 |
| 92-0333 | BE40 | TT-47 |
| 92-0334 | BE40 | TT-48 |
| 92-0335 | BE40 | TT-49 |
| 92-0336 | BE40 | TT-50 |
| 92-0337 | BE40 | TT-51 |
| 92-0338 | BE40 | TT-52 |
| 92-0339 | BE40 | TT-53 |
| 92-0340 | BE40 | TT-54 |
| 92-0341 | BE40 | TT-55 |
| 92-0342 | BE40 | TT-56 |
| 92-0343 | BE40 | TT-57 |
| 92-0344 | BE40 | TT-58 |
| 92-0345 | BE40 | TT-59 |
| 92-0346 | BE40 | TT-60 |
| 92-0347 | BE40 | TT-61 |
| 92-0348 | BE40 | TT-62 |
| 92-0349 | BE40 | TT-63 |
| 92-0350 | BE40 | TT-64 |
| 92-0351 | BE40 | TT-65 |
| 92-0352 | BE40 | TT-66 |
| 92-0353 | BE40 | TT-67 |
| 92-0354 | BE40 | TT-68 |
| 92-0355 | BE40 | TT-69 |
| 92-0356 | BE40 | TT-70 |
| 92-0357 | BE40 | TT-71 |
| 92-0358 | BE40 | TT-72 |
| 92-0359 | BE40 | TT-73 |
| 92-0360 | BE40 | TT-74 |
| 92-0361 | BE40 | TT-75 |
| 92-0362 | BE40 | TT-76 |
| 92-0363 | BE40 | TT-77 |
| 92-0375 | GLF4 | 1256 |
| 93-0621 | BE40 | TT-78 |
| 93-0622 | BE40 | TT-79 |
| 93-0623 | BE40 | TT-80 |
| 93-0624 | BE40 | TT-81 |
| 93-0625 | BE40 | TT-82 |
| 93-0626 | BE40 | TT-83 |
| 93-0627 | BE40 | TT-84 |
| 93-0628 | BE40 | TT-85 |
| 93-0629 | BE40 | TT-86 |
| 93-0630 | BE40 | TT-87 |
| 93-0631 | BE40 | TT-88 |
| 93-0632 | BE40 | TT-89 |
| 93-0633 | BE40 | TT-90 |
| 93-0634 | BE40 | TT-91 |
| 93-0635 | BE40 | TT-92 |
| 93-0636 | BE40 | TT-93 |
| 93-0637 | BE40 | TT-94 |
| 93-0638 | BE40 | TT-95 |
| 93-0639 | BE40 | TT-96 |
| 93-0640 | BE40 | TT-97 |
| 93-0641 | BE40 | TT-98 |
| 93-0642 | BE40 | TT-99 |
| 93-0643 | BE40 | TT-100 |
| 93-0644 | BE40 | TT-101 |
| 93-0645 | BE40 | TT-102 |
| 93-0646 | BE40 | TT-103 |
| 93-0647 | BE40 | TT-104 |
| 93-0648 | BE40 | TT-105 |
| 93-0649 | BE40 | TT-106 |
| 93-0650 | BE40 | TT-107 |
| 93-0651 | BE40 | TT-108 |
| 93-0652 | BE40 | TT-109 |
| 93-0653 | BE40 | TT-110 |
| 93-0654 | BE40 | TT-111 |
| 93-0655 | BE40 | TT-112 |
| 93-0656 | BE40 | TT-113 |
| 94-0114 | BE40 | TT-114 |
| 94-0115 | BE40 | TT-115 |
| 94-0116 | BE40 | TT-116 |
| 94-0117 | BE40 | TT-117 |
| 94-0118 | BE40 | TT-118 |
| 94-0119 | BE40 | TT-119 |
| 94-0120 | BE40 | TT-120 |
| 94-0121 | BE40 | TT-121 |
| 94-0122 | BE40 | TT-122 |
| 94-0123 | BE40 | TT-123 |
| 94-0124 | BE40 | TT-124 |
| 94-0125 | BE40 | TT-125 |
| 94-0126 | BE40 | TT-126 |
| 94-0127 | BE40 | TT-127 |
| 94-0128 | BE40 | TT-128 |
| 94-0129 | BE40 | TT-129 |
| 94-0130 | BE40 | TT-130 |
| 94-0131 | BE40 | TT-131 |
| 94-0132 | BE40 | TT-132 |
| 94-0133 | BE40 | TT-133 |
| 94-0134 | BE40 | TT-134 |
| 94-0135 | BE40 | TT-135 |
| 94-0136 | BE40 | TT-136 |
| 94-0137 | BE40 | TT-137 |
| 94-0138 | BE40 | TT-138 |
| 94-0139 | BE40 | TT-139 |
| 94-0140 | BE40 | TT-140 |
| 94-0141 | BE40 | TT-141 |
| 94-0142 | BE40 | TT-142 |
| 94-0143 | BE40 | TT-143 |
| 94-0144 | BE40 | TT-144 |
| 94-0145 | BE40 | TT-145 |
| 94-0146 | BE40 | TT-146 |
| 94-0147 | BE40 | TT-147 |
| 94-0148 | BE40 | TT-148 |
| 94-1569 | ASTR | 088 |
| 94-1570 | ASTR | 090 |
| 95-0040 | BE40 | TT-149 |
| 95-0041 | BE40 | TT-150 |
| 95-0042 | BE40 | TT-151 |
| 95-0043 | BE40 | TT-152 |
| 95-0044 | BE40 | TT-153 |
| 95-0045 | BE40 | TT-154 |
| 95-0046 | BE40 | TT-155 |
| 95-0047 | BE40 | TT-156 |
| 95-0048 | BE40 | TT-157 |
| 95-0049 | BE40 | TT-158 |
| 95-0050 | BE40 | TT-159 |
| 95-0051 | BE40 | TT-160 |
| 95-0052 | BE40 | TT-161 |
| 95-0053 | BE40 | TT-162 |
| 95-0054 | BE40 | TT-163 |
| 95-0055 | BE40 | TT-164 |
| 95-0056 | BE40 | TT-165 |
| 95-0057 | BE40 | TT-166 |
| 95-0058 | BE40 | TT-167 |
| 95-0059 | BE40 | TT-168 |
| 95-0060 | BE40 | TT-169 |
| 95-0061 | BE40 | TT-170 |
| 95-0062 | BE40 | TT-171 |
| 95-0063 | BE40 | TT-172 |
| 95-0064 | BE40 | TT-173 |
| 95-0065 | BE40 | TT-174 |
| 95-0066 | BE40 | TT-175 |
| 95-0067 | BE40 | TT-176 |
| 95-0068 | BE40 | TT-177 |
| 95-0069 | BE40 | TT-178 |
| 95-0070 | BE40 | TT-179 |
| 95-0071 | BE40 | TT-180 |
| 95-0123 | C560 | 0387 |
| 95-0124 | C560 | 0392 |
| 96-0107 | C560 | 0404 |
| 96-0108 | C560 | 0410 |
| 96-0109 | C560 | 0415 |
| 96-0110 | C560 | 0420 |
| 96-0111 | C560 | 0426 |
| 97-0049 | GLF5 | 566 |
| 97-0101 | C560 | 0452 |
| 97-0102 | C560 | 0456 |
| 97-0103 | C560 | 0462 |
| 97-0104 | C560 | 0468 |
| 97-0105 | C560 | 0472 |
| "97-0231" | C525 | 0231 |
| 97-0400 | GLF5 | 521 |
| 97-0401 | GLF5 | 542 |
| 97-1944 | GLF5 | 566 |
| 98-0006 | C560 | 0495 |
| 98-0007 | C560 | 0501 |
| 98-0008 | C560 | 0505 |
| 98-0009 | C560 | 0508 |
| 98-0010 | C560 | 0513 |
| 99-0100 | C560 | 0532 |
| 99-0101 | C560 | 0534 |
| 99-0102 | C560 | 0538 |
| 99-0103 | C560 | 0545 |
| 99-0104 | C560 | 0548 |
| 99-0402 | GLF5 | 571 |
| 99-0404 | GLF5 | 590 |
| (99-0405) | GLF5 | 596 |
| 00-1051 | C560 | 0565 |
| 00-1052 | C560 | 0574 |
| 00-1053 | C560 | 0577 |
| 01-0028 | GLF5 | 620 |
| 01-0029 | GLF5 | 624 |
| 01-0030 | GLF5 | 663 |
| 01-0065 | GLF5 | 652 |
| 01-0076 | GLF5 | 645 |
| 01-0301 | C560 | 0589 |
| 02-1863 | GLF5 | 670 |
| 03-0016 | C560 | 0649 |
| 03-0726 | C560 | 0667 |
| 04-1778 | GLF5 | 5034 |
| 02-1863 | GLF5 | 670 |
| 09-0501 | GLF5 | 5247 |

US Navy/Marines

| | | |
|---|---|---|
| 150542 | SBRL | 277-1 |
| 150543 | SBRL | 277-2 |
| 150544 | SBRL | 277-3 |
| 150545 | SBRL | 277-4 |
| 150546 | SBRL | 277-5 |
| 150547 | SBRL | 277-6 |
| 150548 | SBRL | 277-7 |
| 150549 | SBRL | 277-8 |
| 150550 | SBRL | 277-9 |
| 150551 | SBRL | 277-10 |
| 150969 | SBRL | 285-1 |
| 150970 | SBRL | 285-2 |
| 150971 | SBRL | 285-3 |
| 150972 | SBRL | 285-4 |
| 150973 | SBRL | 285-5 |
| 150974 | SBRL | 285-6 |
| 150975 | SBRL | 285-7 |
| 150976 | SBRL | 285-8 |

150977 SBRL 285-9
150978 SBRL 285-10
150979 SBRL 285-11
150980 SBRL 285-12
150981 SBRL 285-13
150982 SBRL 285-14
150983 SBRL 285-15
150984 SBRL 285-16
150985 SBRL 285-17
150986 SBRL 285-18
150987 SBRL 285-19
150988 SBRL 285-20
150989 SBRL 285-21
150990 SBRL 285-22
150991 SBRL 285-23
**150992 SBRL 285-24**
151336 SBRL 285-25
151337 SBRL 285-26
151338 SBRL 285-27
151339 SBRL 285-28
151340 SBRL 285-29
151341 SBRL 285-30
151342 SBRL 285-31
151343 SBRL 285-32
157352 SBRL 282-46
**157353 SBRL 282-84**
157354 SBRL 282-85
**158380 SBRL 282-95**
158381 SBRL 282-93
158382 SBRL 282-92
158383 SBRL 282-96
158843 SBRL 306-52
**158844 SBRL 306-55**
159361 SBRL 306-65
**159362 SBRL 306-66**
159363 SBRL 306-67
**159364 SBRL 306-69**
**159365 SBRL 306-70**
**160053 SBRL 306-104**
**160054 SBRL 306-105**
**160055 SBRL 306-106**
160056 SBRL 306-107
160057 SBRL 306-108
162755 C552 0001
162756 C552 0002
162757 C552 0003
162758 C552 0004
162759 C552 0005
162760 C552 0006
162761 C552 0007
162762 C552 0008
162763 C552 0009
162764 C552 0010
162765 C552 0011
162766 C552 0012
162767 C552 0013
162768 C552 0014
162769 C552 0015
**163691 GLF3 480**
**163692 GLF3 481**
**165093 GLF4 1187**
**165094 GLF4 1189**
**165151 GLF4 1199**
**165152 GLF4 1201**
**165153 GLF4 1200**
**165509 SBRL 282-9**
**165510 SBRL 282-81**
**165511 SBRL 282-29**
**165512 SBRL 282-2**
**165513 SBRL 282-66**
**165514 SBRL 282-30**
**165515 SBRL 282-72**
**165516 SBRL 282-90**
**165517 SBRL 282-61**
**165518 SBRL 282-77**
**165519 SBRL 282-19**
**165520 SBRL 282-32**
**165521 SBRL 282-94**
165522 SBRL 282-28
**165523 SBRL 282-20**
165524 SBRL 282-60
165525 SBRL 282-100
**165740 C560 0524**
**165741 C560 0529**
165938 C560 0567
**165939 C560 0570**
**166374 C560 0592**
**166375 GLF5 657**
**166376 GLF5 5041**
**166377 GLF5 5087**
**166378 GLF5 5098**
**166474 C560 0630**
**166500 C560 0651**
**166712 C560 0672**
**166713 C560 0677**
**166714 C560 0679**
166715 C560 0682
**166766 C560 0693**
**166767 C560 0696**
**830500 GLF3 382**

US Coast Guard

01 GLF2 23
01 GLF3 477
**01 GLF5 653**
**02 CL64 5427**
160 WW24 160
519 C500 019
**2101 FA20 374**
**2102 FA20 386**
**2103 FA20 394**
**2104 FA20 390**
**2105 FA20 398**
2106 FA20 402
2107 FA20 409
2108 FA20 405
**2109 FA20 407**
**2110 FA20 411**
2111 FA20 413
**2112 FA20 415**
**2113 FA20 417**
**2114 FA20 418**
2115 FA20 419
2116 FA20 420
**2117 FA20 421**
**2118 FA20 423**
2119 FA20 424
**2120 FA20 425**
**2121 FA20 431**
2122 FA20 433
2123 FA20 435
2124 FA20 437
2125 FA20 439
2126 FA20 441
**2127 FA20 443**
**2128 FA20 445**
**2129 FA20 447**
2130 FA20 450
**2131 FA20 452**
2132 FA20 454
**2133 FA20 456**
**2134 FA20 458**
**2135 FA20 459**
2136 FA20 460
2137 FA20 462
2138 FA20 464
**2139 FA20 466**
**2140 FA20 467**
**2141 FA20 371**

Uruguay

FAU 500 LJ35 378

Venda

VDF-030 C550 266

Venezuela

**0002 C550 012**
0004 GLF2 124
0005 GLF3 400
**0006 LJ24 250**
**0010 GLF2 75/7**
0018 FA50 22
**0222 C500 092**
0442 FA20 235
**1060 C750 0134**
1107 C550 449
**1650 FA20 476**
**1967 C550 020**
**2222 C550 251**
5761 FA20 23
5840 FA20 216
FAV0013 LJ35 270

Yugoslavia

10401 LJ25 202
10402 LJ25 203
70401 LJ25 202
70402 LJ25 203
72101 FA50 25
72102 FA50 43

Odds & Ends

"0350" SBRL 265-35
"40420" GLF3 420

# AIRCRAFT NOTED WHERE C/N IS NOT YET KNOWN

| Reg'n | Type | Remarks |
|---|---|---|
| EC-207 | HS25 | Reported at Koln/Bonn 13Nov88. |
| HK-3452X | C550 | Registered to Aviaco Ltda - ntu? |
| LZ-OIF | HS25 | Reported at Cairo 29May03. |
| N5AF | GLF5 | Seen at Long Beach 10Jan99 - possibly c/n 531 N531AF incorrectly painted. |
| N780JR | ASTR | Reported at Teterboro 30Jun93. |
| N1015G | C550 | Noted at Wichita 05Aug92. |
| N1123B | C650 | Noted at Wichita 21Jan97. |
| N2808B | BE40 | Noted at Beech Field, Wichita 28May91. |
| N2810B | BE40 | Noted at Beech Field, Wichita 01Apr93. |
| N2826B | BE40 | Flew St John's-Reykjavik-Shannon-Rome/Ciampino 15Feb94 and returned Ciampino-Shannon-Reykjavik 04Mar94. |
| N4074Z | C510 | Noted at Independence 23Jan08 |
| N5000E | LJ31 | Noted at Wichita 10Mar92. |
| N5000E | LJ31 | Noted at Wichita 22Feb93. |
| N5010U | LJ31 | Noted at Wichita 21Apr92. |
| N5012G | LJ31 | Noted at Wichita 14Jan93. |
| N5012G | LJ60 | Noted at Tucson 10Sep00. |
| N5012H | LJ31 | Noted at Wichita 26Mar92. |
| N5012K | LJ31 | Noted at Wichita 05Aug92. |
| N5012K | LJ45 | Noted at Wichita 15Oct99. |
| N5012Z | LJ45 | Noted at Tucson 1999, German flag, possibly c/n 45-044. |
| N5013Y | LJ31 | Noted at Wichita 05May92. |
| N5014E | LJ31 | Noted at Wichita 03Feb92. |
| N5014E | LJ60 | Noted at Wichita 18Mar93. |
| N5014F | LJ35 | Noted at Wichita 09Jun92. |
| N5015U | LJ60 | Noted at Tucson 15Oct99. |
| N5016V | LJ31 | Noted at Wichita 26Mar92. |
| N5016V | LJ31 | Noted at Wichita 31Mar93. |
| N5017J | LJ31 | Noted at Wichita 13Apr93. |
| N5018G | LJ31 | Noted at Wichita 02Nov92. |
| N5076K | C560 | Noted at Wichita 22Apr99. |
| N5093D | C560 | Noted at Wichita 25Feb99. |
| N5093L | C550 | Noted at Wichita 15Oct99. |
| N5124F | C525 | Noted at Wichita 20Aug96. |
| N5126L | C525 | Noted at Wichita 17Sep99. |
| N5135A | C750 | Noted at Wichita 18Mar02. |
| N5148B | C550 | Noted at Wichita 18Nov98. |
| N5163K | C525 | Noted at Wichita 16Oct98. |
| N5197A | 525A | Noted at Wichita 19Jan03. |
| N5200Z | C560 | Noted at Wichita 10Jun94. |
| N5243K | C750 | Noted at Wichita 08Oct02. |
| N5244F | C525 | Noted at Wichita 16Sep99. |
| N5266F | C550 | Noted at Wichita 16Aug99. |
| N40078 | LJ45 | Noted at Wichita 22Jun02. |
| N40335 | BE40 | Noted at Beech Field, Wichita 05Aug93. |
| N50111 | LJ31 | Noted at Wichita 13Apr93. |
| N50126 | LJ31 | Noted at Wichita 17Sep91. |
| N50126 | LJ35 | Noted at Wichita 05Aug92. |
| N50154 | LJ31 | Noted at Wichita 19Nov91. |
| N50157 | LJ31 | Noted at Wichita 12Aug91. |
| N50163 | LJ31 | Noted at Wichita 20Jly92. |
| N51613 | C525 | Noted at Wichita 27Feb97. |
| N51983 | C56X | Noted at Wichita 01Oct99. |
| N52542 | 525A | Noted at Wichita 30Jly02. |
| N82787 | BE40 | Noted at Beech Field, Wichita 13Feb94. |
| OB-668 | SBRL | Registered in Peru, c/n quoted as '308-025'. |
| PT-MMY | C560 | Noted at Wichita 05May97. |
| SU-BRF | C680 | Egyptian Air Force, delivered to Cairo Almaza Air Base 04Dec09 |
| TC-AZR | F9EX | Noted at Little Rock 2009 |
| XA-ABV | C550 | Noted at Fort Lauderdale Int'l 01Apr01 |
| XA-DCX | LJ35 | Noted at Toluca in Jan07. |
| XA-DST | C56X | Noted at Fort Lauderdale Int'l 28Dec08 |
| XA-FLG | FA20 | Noted at Las Vegas/McCarran 19Oct09. |
| XA-GAA | C550 | Photographed at Mexico City in Jan08. |
| XA-GLS | HS25 | Photographed at Alajuela-San Jose, Costa Rica, 25Aug08. |
| XA-HEI | SBRL | Reported at Mexico City 23Sep90. |
| XA-JPR | LJ25 | Noted at Toluca 26Dec08 and Miami 14Feb09. |
| XA-LDV | HS25 | Reported at Toluca in Sep05 - possibly XA-LOV misread? |
| XA-LOA | BE40 | Noted at Fort Lauderdale International 28Oct09 - possibly c/n RK-242 ex-N32AJ |
| XA-NMT | HS25 | Noted at Miami 04Dec09. |
| XA-NXT | HS25 | Noted at Toluca Mar09. |
| XA-PPV | C500 | Photographed at Toluca 02Apr08 |
| XA-RIV | C550 | Noted at Toluca Mar09 |
| XA-RLF | SBRL | Reported at Mexico City in Nov91. |
| XA-RPM | C56X | Reported at Toluca in Mar06. |
| XA-TJX | SBRL | Reported at Cancun 09Jun06. |
| XA-TOY | JSTR | Reported at Teterboro 15Apr04 (marks on a Cessna 208 by Feb07) |
| XA-TRI | SBRL | Reported at Toluca 22Mar00 (marks on an ATR-42 by Feb03) |
| XA-UJO | LJ35 | Noted at Toluca 28Jun08. |
| XA-ULN | HS25 | Noted at Ciudad Mante 27Jun09. |
| XA-VAL | LJ31 | Reported at San Antonio 03Dec08. |
| XA-VYA | LJ45 | Reported at Houston/Hobby 03Feb10. |
| XA-VYR | C500 | Reported at Dallas/Love Field. |
| XA-XEL | HS25 | Reported at Monterrey/del Norte 06Jan10 |
| XA-ZTJ | HS25 | Reported at Las Vegas 26Jul08. |
| XB-CMA | LJ25 | Photographed at Toluca in Nov07. |
| XB-EGO | SBRL | Reported at Fort Lauderdale Int'l 07Mar08. |
| XB-IRZ | HS25 | Photographed at Las Vegas/McCarran 11Mar05. |
| XB-JER | GLF1 | Reported at Acarigua, Venezuela, 04May06. |
| XB-JHU | SBRL | Reported at Toluca 02Aug95. |
| XB-JTO | LJ25 | Noted at Toluca in Jan07. |
| XB-JVL | HS25 | Noted at Toluca in Jan07. |
| XB-JYZ | SBRL | Noted at Toluca in Mar07. |
| XB-KQB | HS25 | Instructional airframe at Patna, India |
| XB-LKH | C650 | Noted at Guadalajara 22Oct09. |
| XB-KMY | LJ24 | Photographed at Toluca in Nov07. |
| XB-KPB | LJ35 | Damaged at Guadalajara 02Aug08. |
| XB-MGM | HS25 | Noted at Houston/Hobby 05Oct07, Miami/Opa Locka 29Dec07 and Las Vegas 25Jan08. |
| XC-AGH | LJ25 | Reported at Houston/Hobby 09Oct07. |
| XC-ANL | HS25 | Instructional airframe at CONALEP Apodaca, Monterrey. |
| XC-ASG | LJ35 | Reported at Mexico City 27Jan94. |
| XC-HJF | C550 | Reported at Tucson 20Jan01. |
| XC-JCV | C550 | Reported at Puerto Vallarta 25Nov95. |
| XC-JCX | C550 | Reported at Puerto Vallarta 25Nov95. |
| XC-JEG | C550 | Reported at Davis-Monthan Nov02. |
| XC-LKB | SBRL | Photographed at Mexico City 31Dec06. |
| XC-UJW | SBRL | Reported at Mexico City May08. |
| YA-GAB | HS25 | Reported at Termez, Uzbekistan, Apr04. |
| YV-94C | C500 | Reported at Fort Lauderdale Executive 12Sep93. |
| YV299T | HS25 | Noted at New Tamiami 22Nov09. |
| YV327T | C550 | Noted at St Maarten, Netherlands Antilles 28Nov09 |
| YV415T | SBRL | Noted at Fort Lauderdale Executive 08Jan10 |
| YV2152 | C52A | Noted at Fort Lauderdale Executive 13Feb10 |
| YV2245 | C500 | Noted at Fort Lauderdale Executive 17Jan10 |
| YV2254 | C500 | Photographed at Charallave 14Oct07. |
| YV2469 | C550 | Noted at Orlando International 04Sep09 |
| YV2595 | BE40 | Noted at Fort Lauderdale Executive 5Dec09 |
| YV2619 | C550 | Noted at Fort Lauderdale Executive 13Feb10 |
| ZC-PMC | C550 | Noted at Wichita 2May90 and later at Mexico City. |
| 5A-DMH | HFB3 | Photographed at Mitiga, Libya, Oct09. |
| 9M-CHX | HS25 | Reported at Kuala Lumpur 16Mar95. |
| ES-7960 | JSTR | Displayed at petrol station San Luis Potosi, Mexico - fake marks. |
| 5-9003 | JSTR | Noted at Tehran in 2006, Iranian Air Force. |
| 5-9016 | FA20 | Reported at Tehran Mar08, Iranian Air Force. |
| 15-2233 | FA20 | Reported at Tehran Dec02, Iranian Air Force. |
| 90-0400 | BE40 | Noted in USAF colours at Wichita 20Mar90, probably painted as such for publicity purposes in connection with the T-1 Jayhawk programme. Is possibly c/n RJ-45 - the marks are now genuinely worn by c/n TT-3. |
| SAN-301 | WW24 | of Panama's Servicio Aereo Nacional reported at Balboa, Panama, 29Nov07. |

# GRUMMAN G159 GULFSTREAM 1

| C/n | Series | Identities |
|---|---|---|
| 1 | | N701G [ff14Aug58] ZS-NVG 5Y-EMK 5Y-XXX 3X-GER |
| 2 | | N702G N1 N3 N3003 N40CE N42CE N40CE N116GA N39PP 86-0402 [b/u 30Sep90] |
| 3 | | N703G CF-MAR C-FMAR [b/u for spares Montreal, Canada] |
| 4 | | N704G N704HC N717 N99DE N89DE N371BG [wfu 1985; b/u for spares 1985] |
| 5 | | N705G N601HK N601HP N700PR N43AS N9EB N159AJ N925WL N159AJ F-GFGT ZS-OOE |
| 6 | | N2425 (VR-B ) S9-NAU N221AP [b/u Pawaukee apt, IL, on 15Feb96] |
| 7 | | CF-LOO N5VX N99EL |
| 8 | | N708G [wfu for spares in 1985, fuselage in yard by Cosgrove A/c Services, south of Houston Hobby apt, TX] |
| 9 | | N709G N43M N436M N436 N436M G-BNCE [wfu Oct91 Aberdeen, UK due to corrosion; stripped for spares; cx 04May93; fuselage to Dundee apt, UK fire/emergency training] |
| 10 | | N710G N1623 N1623Z XB-CIJ [wfu 05Oct88 following landing accident] |
| 11 | | N711G N650BT N100FL N100EL N7SL [wfu Valencia, Venezuela] |
| 12 | | N712G N400P N4009 N166NK N91JR N8VB XA-TBT [b/u for spares Dodson Av'n, Rantoul, KS, circa Sep97] |
| 13 | | [airframe not built] |
| 14 | | N714G N1607Z N723RA [cx Nov88; b/u for spares 1988 Shreveport, LA] |
| 15 | | N715G N1501 N1501C N72EZ N26KW XB-ESO [wfu 11Oct90 following landing accident] |
| 16 | | N716G N2998 N707WA N8001J N20NH N202HA N615C |
| 17 | | N717G N199M CF-TPC N9971F [wfu 1985; b/u for spares 1986] |
| 18 | | N718G N300UP N3UP N48PA YV-..... [impounded in Venezuela Nov05 for drug-running, still marked N48PA] |
| 19 | | N719G N80L N80LR N70LR N12GW PK-WWG N12GW [b/u for spares Oct87; cx Sep89] |
| 20 | | N720G N266P N227LS N227LA N250AL N5PC VR-CTN N732US F-GFMH TJ-WIN TU-TDM N19FF [wfu Madrid/Barajas, Spain, to be parted out] |
| 21 | | N721G N361G N361Q XC-BIO N6653Z [b/u for spares 01Aug91 Savannah, GA; cx Nov95] |
| 22 | | N722G N80G N8BG C-GKFG [cx Feb97, wfu] |
| 23 | | N723G N1929Y N1929B OE-BAZ OE-HAZ N193PA N186PA N810CB |
| 24 | | N724G N1620 N1625 N1625B YV-P-AEA YV-09CP N713US HK-3315X HK-3315 [w/o 06Feb90 El Salado Mt, nr Ibague, Colombia; cx 26Jun90] |
| 25 | | N725G (OE-...) N725G (OK-NEA) N725G 4X-ARH 3D-DLH ZS-PHK |
| 26 | | N726G N726S N505S N120S N348DA YV-82CP N185PA |
| 27 | 1C | N727G N100P N1009 XB-FUB XB-VIW XB-VAD N2150M N80M N114GA N415CA N198PA |
| 28 | | N728G N900JL N9006L N666ES N11SX N118X N719RA [wfu; a/c currently with Dodson Avn, KS, for spares use] |
| 29 | | N729G N785GP N1844S N1845S N1925P N222SG N222SE N431G C- [US marks cx Jun99; parted out Toronto/Lester B Pearson apt, Canada circa Nov00 still as N431G] |
| 30 | | N730G N901G N961G [wfu 01Apr89 for spares; cx Nov91] |
| 31 | | N731G CF-JFC N715RA [wfu; awaiting scrapping for spares by Int'l Turbine Services, TX] |
| 32 | | N732G N734ET N734EB N733EB N297X N300MC [cx Dec88; wfu] |
| 33 | | N126J N88Y N261L N295SA HR-IAJ TG-TJB (N23AH) N21AH 9Q-CBY |
| 34 | | N734G N620K N48TE HK-3634X N34LE 5Y-BLR |
| 35 | | N735G XC-IMS XB-DVG XA-PUA N86MA 9Q-CBD |
| 36 | | N130A N230E [wfu 01Nov88 Detroit-Willow Run, MI; by Jan03 El Mirage CA; bare metal] |
| 37 | | N130G N130B N716RD N716R N20S N91G [w/o 24Sep78 Houston, TX] |
| 38 | | N738G ZS-AAC VQ-ZIP 3D-AAC N7001N N38JK N333AH N717RS XA-... |
| 39 | | N40Y N39TG EC-376 EC-EVJ |
| 40 | | N6PG N8ZA N40AG EC-493 EC-FIO N19TZ [wfu Madrid/Barajas, Spain, to be parted out] |
| 41 | | N7PG N9ZA N41TG EC-494 EC-EZO [wfu Madrid-Barajas, Spain] |
| 42 | | N366P N430H N888PR XA-MAS XC-AA61 ZS-OCA 3D-TRE 3D-DOM TL-ADN |
| 43 | | N344DJ N140NT C-GNOR N39289 N716RA [wfu for spares Jul88; cx Jan91] |
| 44 | | N285AA N121NC N717JF N717RW N717RD F-GFGV 5Y-JET |
| 45 | | N745G N7788 N329CT N65CE [cx 24Mar04; donated to Des Moines Central Campus Aviation laboratory, IA for use as instructional airframe] |
| 46 | | N746G [wfu Oct86; used for spares] |
| 47 | | N747G N20CC N20CQ N20HF [b/u Oct86 Texas; cx Feb90] |
| 48 | | N748G VR-BBY N302K G-AWYF N213GA [b/u Palwaukee, IL circa Apr97] |
| 49 | | N749G N456 F-GFIC |
| 50 | | N80J N8BJ N6PA N3100E N8200E N820CE N28CG [cx Jun90; to Schweizer Maintenance School, Elmira, NY by Aug91] |
| 51 | | N80K N80KA XC-HYC N90PM I-MGGG [b/u 1994 Geneva, Switzerland] |
| 52 | | N752G VH-ASJ N3858H N18TF (N18TZ) N612DT |
| 53 | | N753G N700JW (N701JW) [wfu 21Apr89; b/u for spares by White Industries, Bates City, MO; cx Jun94] |
| 54 | | CF-MUR C-FMUR N26AJ N164PA |

## GULFSTREAM I

| C/n | Series | Identities |
|---|---|---|
| 55 | | N755G N255AA N1234X N429X N429W N9MH N429W N27L N300PH VR-CAE N9446E N118LT [b/u for spares 1986 Lawton, TX; cx Jul91] |
| 56 | | N756G N220B N510E YV-46CP N168PA [b/u for spares; cx Mar05] |
| 57 | | N757G I-CKET N66JD PK-TRM |
| 58 | | N758G N358AA 5N-AAI N16776 N46TE N47TE XB-FLL XA-TTU XC-VNC [wfu Toluca, Mexico] |
| 59 | | N759G N205AA N23D N11CZ HK-3316X HK-3316 [w/o 02May90 Los Garcones apt, Monteria, Colombia] |
| 60 | | CF-IOM C-FIOM PK-TRL |
| 61 | | N761G N594AR N734HR N191SA [b/u for spares Jun88 Wiley Post, OK; remains to Dodson Aviation, KS] |
| 62 | | N205M [w/o 25Jul67 New Cumberland, PA - but current as N400NL] |
| 63 | | N763G N144NK N580BC [to Aviation Warehouse Film Prop Yard, El Mirage, CA circa 2000] |
| 64 | | N764G N466P CF-COL N49401 N64TG EC-460 EC-EXS [wfu Madrid, Spain] |
| 65 | | N765G N345TW N340WB N641B N721RA [cx Nov88; b/u for spares 1988] |
| 66 | | N766G N623W N65H N65HC N111DR XC-GEI [wfu 04Sep86; b/u for spares] |
| 67 | | N767G N376 N48 N806S N5241Z N806W |
| 68 | | N768G N768GP N15GP N4765P N4765C N7ZA N68TG [w/o 15Jul83 Tri-Cities apt, Bristol, TN] |
| 69 | | N769G N377 N47 N47R [wfu 1986; to Votec School, Rexburg, ID; then to Pratt Community College, KS circa 1998 (still listed as current)] |
| 70 | | N770G N331H [Parted out by Dodson Aviation, Ottawa, KS] |
| 71 | | N771G N530AA N60CR VR-BTI N222EF (N15SQ) N222EF F-GFIB XA-MYR [wfu circa Mar06 Toluca, Mexico] |
| 72 | | N772G CF-NOC N743G (N93SA) N743G [wfu 01Apr89; b/u for spares] |
| 73 | | N773G N773WJ N207M N720X [cx Nov88; w/o pre Feb87 (buried by sand in Arizona Desert after drug-running flight)] |
| 74 | | N774G N212H N5619D N701BN |
| 75 | | N775G N304K PT-KYF |
| 76 | | N776G N305K G-BRAL P4-JML |
| 77 | | N777G N706G N73M N748M N748MN N748M 9Q-CFK G-BOBX [wfu for spares 25Apr89] |
| 78 | | N778G N1040 N778G N1040 N7040 N431H N33CP (PT-...) HK-3681 |
| 79 | | N779G N190DM N79HS (EC-491) [parted out 1993 Fort Lauderdale Int'l, FL] |
| 80 | | N780G N605AA N605AB N20GB N200GJ F-GGGY D2-EXC |
| 81 | | N781G N22G N2PQ C-GMJS I-TASO "5Y-BMT" 5Y-BMR |
| 82 | | N782G N798S N98R N798R N629JM (N801CC) SE-LFV SE-LDV N12RW 3C-... |
| 83 | 1C | N783G N437A N117GA N245CA [to White Inds, Bates City, MO for spares] |
| 84 | | N784G N362G N362GP N184K N183K [destroyed by Colombian military 03Jun06 in anti-drug-running operation] |
| 85 | | N706G N1150S XC-BAU (N66534) [wfu 01Aug91; b/u for spares Savannah, GA; cx Nov95] |
| 86 | | N786G N678RW N231GR N712MW N712MR N712MP N106GH N106GA N86JK N10TB ZS-ALX |
| 87 | | N787G N10VM N102PL N711BT N87CH N87CE (N87MK) N845JB [wfu and scrapped; cx Sep97] |
| 88 | 1C | N788G N410AA N1M N357H N857H C-GPTN N195PA |
| 89 | | N789G |
| 90 | | N790G N4567 N18N N80R N41JK HK-3330X [remains with Dodson Av'n, Rantoul, KS Dec92] |
| 91 | | N791G USCG 1380 USCG 02 USCG 03 |
| 92 | | N710G NASA3 N3NA USCG 02 N3NA YV.... |
| 93 | | N740AA N574DU N574K N674C N137C XA-ILV N137C N197PA N820CB |
| 94 | | N794G N8E |
| 95 | | N795G N50UC N500RL N500RN |
| 96 | | NASA1 N1NA N2NA N444BC |
| 97 | | N797G N5152 N671NC N49DE YV-85CP N184PA [cx 21Apr09, wfu] |
| 98 | | N798G NASA2 N2NA N29AY N98MK [wfu Apr91; b/u for spares by White Inds, Bates City, MO] |
| 99 | | N799G N67B N102M N364G N364L N750BR [w/o 13Nov88 nr Frankfurt, Germany; b/u; cx Dec89] |
| 100 | | N715G N166KJ N116K VH-FLO (ZK-...) [cx May95; wfu] |
| 101 | | N716G N222H N300SB F-GFGU 4X-ARV F-GNGU |
| 102 | | N717G N621A N28CG N48CG N48CQ (N73CG) N48CQ HA-ACV C6-UNO N11UN [wfu 2004 Kendall-Tamiami Executive, FL] |
| 103 | | N718G N608RP N608R PT- XC-AA57 |
| 104 | | N719G CF-HBO C-FHBO |
| 105 | | N702G I-TASB [CofA expired 01Jun90; wfu Jul93 Milan-Linate, Italy; cx; in use as snack bar at Bacong Negros Oriental, Philippines 2004] |
| 106 | | N706G N780AC N72X N72XL N38CG N64CG C-FAWG 9XR-WR YV1020 [destroyed by military action 26Sep05 while drug-running at secret airstrip nr San Andres, Colombia] |
| 107 | | N722G N34C N73B N7ZB N71CR N71CJ [b/u Houston Hobby, TX circa Jan04] |

# GULFSTREAM I

| C/n | Series | Identities |
|---|---|---|
| 108 | | N723G N1707Z N23UG [b/u for spares late 1986; cx Feb90] |
| 109 | | N724G N1000 N823GA N5000C N2000C N1000 N1091 N804CC N307AT N109P [cx 02Oct99, b/u] |
| 110 | | N727G N533CS C-GTDL [cx May86; b/u for spares 1989] |
| 111 | | N728G N363G N3630 F-GJGC [semi-derelict Oct91 Marseille, France] |
| 112 | | N729G N942PM N300PM N300PE (N300BP) N803CC [wfu Mar89; cx Sep89; noted derelict Sep91 Detroit-Willow Run, MI] |
| 113 | | [not built] |
| 114 | | N712G N205M N705M N705RS N9300P VH-WPA N724RA [wfu 01Mar88; b/u for spares by Intl Turbine Services, TX; cx Jan89] |
| 115 | | CF-ASC N61SB [stored Dallas-Love Field, TX with engines removed] |
| 116 | 1C | N706G N26L N5400G N5400C N110GA N159AN N328CA [to White Inds, Bates City, MO for spares] |
| 117 | | N710G N519M N23AK N41KD YV-08CP N167PA [b/u for spares; cx Mar05] |
| 118 | | N715G [b/u for spares 1983; cx 1984] |
| 119 | | N734G YV-P-EPC YV-28CP N165PA [wfu Cartersville, GA; cx] |
| 120 | | Greece P-9 [used callsign I-FRIS while in use by King Constantine in exile late 1960s/early 1970s] Greece 120 [wfu 1995; preserved Tatoi-Dekelia, Greece, circa 1998] |
| 121 | | N732G N234MM [wfu 1992; displayed Disney-MGM Studio Theme Park, Orlando, FL] |
| 122 | | N738G N153SR N152SR N707MP F-GFEF |
| 123 | 1C | N736G N687RW N714MW N714MR N2602M N17CA [to White Inds, Bates City, MO for spares] |
| 124 | | N737G N504C N725MK N476S ZS-NKT D2-EXD |
| 125 | | N738G N205G N10NA N5NA N193PA |
| 126 | | N739G N913BS N913PS N100TV N63AU N110RB |
| 127 | | N741GA N500S N50LS N717JP XA-TDJ [wfu by 2004 Merida, Mexico] |
| 128 | | N122Y N516DM N910BS G-BMSR F-GIIX [dbf 28Jun94 Lyon-Satolas, France; cx 04Aug94] |
| 129 | | N743G N770AC N770A N834H N812CC N113GA N129AF YV.... |
| 130 | | N744G N902JL N3416 PK-TRO |
| 131 | | N750G N730TL N730T N1TX N21TX C-FRTT 5Y-BLF [wfu Nairobi-Wilson apt, Kenya circa Oct00] |
| 132 | | N120HC N1207C N944H N27G N154SR N154NS N154RH [b/u; cx Nov03] |
| 133 | | N752G N2010 N7776 TU-VAC N33TF [wfu; b/u for spares by White Industries, Bates City, MO] |
| 134 | | N754G N914BS N920BS G-BMPA (F-....) 4X-ARF 3D-ARF 4X-ARF 3D-ARF ZS-ONO 3D-DUE ZS-PHJ |
| 135 | | N755G G-ASXT [b/u Sep83 Denver, CO; cx 09Aug82] |
| 136 | | N756G XB-GAW XA-TBT [wfu Urapan, Mexico] |
| 137 | | N757G CF-DLO N36DD N42CA (N811CC) [noted 07Sep91 derelict Detroit-Willow Run, MI; cx Jun95] |
| 138 | | N758G N126K XA-ALK XA-RLK |
| 139 | | N759G N42G N7972S N8500N N8500C N157WC N62J C-FRTU N196PA |
| 140 | | N760G N40G N140A N300A N92K N92SA F-GFCQ |
| 141 | | N762G N228H N800PA ZS-NHW |
| 142 | | N764G N10ZA N142TG EC-461 EC-EXQ [wfu Madrid-Barajas, Spain] |
| 143 | | N720G N914P I-MDDD [CofA expired 26Sep91; with Dodson Av'n, KS; cx] |
| 144 | | N766G N860E N70CR N70QR [wfu 1986; cx Mar91] |
| 145 | | N767G N233U N149X N7FD N155T HK-3329X HK-3580W |
| 146 | | N772G N2011 N906F OE-GSN OE-HSN Israel 001/4X-JUD N906F [b/u Opa-Locka, FL, late 2001] |
| 147 | | N774G N861H [w/o 11Jul67 Le Centre, MN] |
| 148 | | N775G N804CC N120S (N9036P) N107GH N1701L C-FWAM XC-LIE [wfu Toluca, Mexico] |
| 149 | | N776G N636 N636G N400HT N684FM N192PA |
| 150 | | N706G N777G YV-121CP [wfu Jun88 following landing accident] |
| 151 | | N741G NASA4 N4NA [wfu circa Sep03 to display Pima Air & Space Museum, Tucson, AZ] |
| 152 | | N718G N705G HP-799 OB-M-1235 HP-799 N705G [wfu 01May89; b/u for spares] |
| 153 | | N733G N733NM N80AC N153TG EC-433 EC-EXB N19BX [wfu Madrid/Barajas, Spain, to be parted out] |
| 154 | | N736G N267AA N736G N72B N800PM N800PD N802CC G-BNKO C-GNAK [w/o 19Jul00 nr Linneus, ME, USA] |
| 155 | | N778G N992CP N22CP N24CP N900PM N900PA N805CC G-BMOW 9Q-CJB |
| 156 | | N737G N22AS N41LH (N159KK) 9Q-COE |
| 157 | | N741G N94SA [cx Aug91; sale in Panama possible, current status?] |
| 158 | | N779G N697A N1697A N72CR N2NR N2NC 5Y-MIA 5Y-EMJ [w/o 24Jan03 Busia, Kenya] |
| 159 | | N751G N287AA N940PM N200PM N200PF N809CC G-BNKN XA-RJB |
| 160 | | N752G N3 "N965CJ" N599TR [wfu Lakeland, FL] |
| 161 | | N790G N307EL N925GC [wfu Lawrenceville, GA by Oct03 but cx to Mexico 09Apr04] |
| 162 | | N724G N547Q N547QR N547BN N5470R N31CN N300GP C-GPTA [w/o 19Nov96 Lester B Pearson Airport, Toronto, Canada] |
| 163 | | N727G N618M N71CR [w/o 11Jul75 Addison, TX] |
| 164 | | N738G N8PG N88PP N590AS N590AQ N290AS ZS-PHI |
| 165 | | N739G N75M N75MT N657PC N657P N500WN N501WN |

# GULFSTREAM I

| C/n | Series | Identities |
|---|---|---|
| 166 | | N791G N67CR N20CR N76DM N725RA F-GKES (OO-IBG) HB-IRQ 4X-ARG D2-EXB |
| 167 | | N794G N908LN C-GDWM N717RA [cx 01May06, wfu in Sao Tome] |
| 168 | | N754G N209T N722RA [b/u for spares 1988; cx Nov88] |
| 169 | | N725HG N725HC N400WP N400WF N200AE |
| 170 | | N790G N89K N189K YV-620CP YV-627C |
| 171 | | VH-CRA N171LS (N1PC) N728GM YV-621CP YV-628C |
| 172 | | N700DB N44MC N11NY N172RD TC-SMA [b/u Geneva, Switzerland, Jul08] |
| 173 | | N360WT N944H N944HL N49CB I-TASC 5Y-BMT YV-988C N173BT YV-903CP [disappeared, believed hijacked by drug traffickers 12Jun06] |
| 174 | | N774G N7004 N7004B N718RA [wfu; b/u for spares by Int'l Turbine Service, TX; cx Feb91] |
| 175 | | N795G N10CR N55AE N578KB YV-453CP N173PA [b/u for parts; cx Jan05] |
| 176 | TC-4C | N798G US Navy 155722 [preserved at Pensacola NAS, FL] |
| 177 | | N751G N307K N4PC OY-BEG N12GP G-BRWN PK-CTE PK-CDM |
| 178 | TC-4C | N778G US Navy 155723 [w/o 16Oct75 Cherry Point, NC] |
| 179 | | N779G N1916M N61UT N60AC N60WK HK-3622 XC-AA53 |
| 180 | TC-4C | N786G US Navy 155724 [stored by Oct94 Davis-Monthan AFB, AZ; park code 4G002] |
| 181 | | N759G N966H N966HL N25W N25WL N181TG [w/o 01Jun85 Nashville, TN] |
| 182 | TC-4C | N762G US Navy 155725 [stored by Sep95 Davis-Monthan AFB, AZ; park code 4G007] |
| 183 | TC-4C | N766G US Navy 155726 [stored by Sep95 Davis-Monthan AFB, AZ; park code 4G006] |
| 184 | TC-4C | US Navy 155727 [stored by Oct94 Davis-Monthan AFB, AZ; park code 4G004] |
| 185 | TC-4C | US Navy 155728 [stored by Oct94 Davis-Monthan AFB, AZ; park code 4G003] |
| 186 | TC-4C | US Navy 155729 [stored by Oct94 Davis-Monthan AFB, AZ; park code 4G001] |
| 187 | TC-4C | US Navy 155730 [stored by Apr95 Davis-Monthan AFB, AZ; park code 4G005] |
| 188 | | N17582 HB-LDT C-FAWE |
| 189 | | N776G C-GPTG [cx Mar01 as wfu; b/u Nov02 Montreal-Dorval, Canada] |
| 190 | | N1901W HK-3579X HK-4022X N190LE [w/o 02Aug96 in Sudan whilst on delivery to Kenya as N190LE] |
| 191 | | N200P N300P (N300XZ) G-BKJZ VH-JPJ PK-RJA [cx Mar06, b/u] |
| 192 | | N712G N67H YV-76CP N171PA |
| 193 | | N713G N754G PK-TRN 3D-TRN ZS-JIS 9Q-CIT |
| 194 | | N718G N6702 N702E N702EA N81T I-MKKK 4X-CST I-MKKK 5Y-BMS YV-989C |
| 195 | | N724G N1900W N190PA |
| 196 | | N728G N752RB N752R N93AC (N811CC) N93AC I-EHAJ N134PA N659PC N100EG |
| 197 | | N385M N777JS (N725RB) (N811CC) N977JS (N385M) N20H N20HE N197RM N520JG N748AA |
| 198 | | N740G N1902P N1902D N100C N80RD [w/o 23Aug90 Houston Intercontinental apt, TX; cx Oct91] |
| 199 | | N745G XA-RIV N745G YV-83CP N183PA N167PA |
| 200 | | N750G N255TK N159GS |
| 322 | | N769G N90M N9QM N71RD [at Palwaukee, IL circa May00 - to be parted out?] |
| 323 | | N900 N988AA N346DA S9-NAV N22320 "N900TT" N980TT HI-678CA HI-678CT |

Production complete

**Notes: c/n unknown aircraft**

D2-FXG reported at Rand, South Africa, 20Nov01
XB-JER reported at Acarigua, Venezuela, 04May06
YV-78CP reported as being carried by a Gulfstream 1 at Caracas 02Dec90; could this be connected with c/n 117,
YV-08CP these marks have also been reported on a PA-31T?
ARC-701 (Colombian Navy) at Bogota wfu on 02Jul01.

# G159 Gulfstream 1 Registration Cross-Reference

**Note: Current Registrations are in bold type**

| Canada | |
|---|---|
| CF-ASC | 115 |
| CF-COL | 64 |
| CF-DLO | 137 |
| CF-HBO | 104 |
| CF-IOM | 60 |
| CF-JFC | 31 |
| CF-LOO | 7 |
| CF-MAR | 3 |
| CF-MUR | 54 |
| CF-NOC | 72 |
| CF-TPC | 17 |
| C- | 29 |
| **C-FAWE** | **188** |
| C-FAWG | 106 |
| **C-FHBO** | **104** |
| C-FIOM | 60 |
| C-FMAR | 3 |
| C-FMUR | 54 |
| C-FRTT | 131 |
| C-FRTU | 139 |
| C-FWAM | 148 |
| C-GDWM | 167 |
| C-GKFG | 22 |
| C-GMJS | 81 |
| C-GNAK | 154 |
| C-GNOR | 43 |
| C-GPTA | 162 |
| C-GPTG | 189 |
| C-GPTN | 88 |
| C-GTDL | 110 |

| Bahamas | |
|---|---|
| C6-UNO | 102 |

| Angola | |
|---|---|
| **D2-EXB** | **166** |
| **D2-EXC** | **80** |
| **D2-EXD** | **124** |

| Spain | |
|---|---|
| EC-376 | 39 |
| EC-433 | 153 |
| EC-460 | 64 |
| EC-461 | 142 |
| (EC-491) | 79 |
| EC-493 | 40 |
| EC-494 | 41 |
| **EC-EVJ** | **39** |
| EC-EXB | 153 |
| EC-EXQ | 142 |
| EC-EXS | 64 |
| EC-EZO | 41 |
| EC-FIO | 40 |

| France | |
|---|---|
| (F-....) | 134 |
| **F-GFCQ** | **140** |
| **F-GFEF** | **122** |
| F-GFGT | 5 |
| F-GFGU | 101 |
| F-GFGV | 44 |
| F-GFIB | 71 |
| **F-GFIC** | **49** |
| F-GFMH | 20 |
| F-GGGY | 80 |
| F-GIIX | 128 |
| F-GJGC | 111 |
| F-GKES | 166 |
| **F-GNGU** | **101** |

| United Kingdom | |
|---|---|
| G-ASXT | 135 |
| G-AWYF | 48 |
| G-BKJZ | 191 |
| G-BMOW | 155 |
| G-BMPA | 134 |
| G-BMSR | 128 |
| G-BNCE | 9 |
| G-BNKN | 159 |
| G-BNKO | 154 |
| G-BOBX | 77 |
| G-BRAL | 76 |
| G-BRWN | 177 |

| Hungary | |
|---|---|
| HA-ACV | 102 |

| Switzerland | |
|---|---|
| HB-IRQ | 166 |
| HB-LDT | 188 |

| Dominican Republic | |
|---|---|
| HI-678CA | 323 |
| **HI-678CT** | **323** |

| Colombia | |
|---|---|
| HK-3315 | 24 |
| HK-3315X | 24 |
| HK-3316 | 59 |
| HK-3316X | 59 |
| HK-3329X | 145 |
| HK-3330X | 90 |
| HK-3579X | 190 |
| **HK-3580W** | **145** |
| HK-3622 | 179 |
| HK-3634X | 34 |
| **HK-3681** | **78** |
| HK-4022X | 190 |

| Panama | |
|---|---|
| HP-799 | 152 |

| Honduras | |
|---|---|
| HR-IAJ | 33 |

| Italy | |
|---|---|
| I-CKET | 57 |
| I-EHAJ | 196 |
| I-MDDD | 143 |
| I-MGGG | 51 |
| I-MKKK | 194 |
| I-TASB | 105 |
| I-TASC | 173 |
| I-TASO | 81 |

| NASA | |
|---|---|
| NASA1 | 96 |
| NASA2 | 98 |
| NASA3 | 92 |
| NASA4 | 151 |

| United States | |
|---|---|
| N1 | 2 |
| N1M | 88 |
| N1NA | 96 |
| (N1PC) | 171 |
| N1TX | 131 |
| N2NA | 96 |
| N2NA | 98 |
| N2NC | 158 |
| N2NR | 158 |
| N2PQ | 81 |
| N3 | 2 |
| N3 | 160 |
| N3NA | 92 |
| N3UP | 18 |
| N4NA | 151 |
| N4PC | 177 |
| N5NA | 125 |
| N5PC | 20 |
| N5VX | 7 |
| N6PA | 50 |
| N6PG | 40 |
| N7FD | 145 |
| N7PG | 41 |
| N7SL | 11 |
| N7ZA | 68 |
| N7ZB | 107 |
| N8BG | 22 |
| N8BJ | 50 |
| **N8E** | **94** |
| N8PG | 164 |
| N8VB | 12 |
| N8ZA | 40 |
| N9EB | 5 |
| N9MH | 55 |
| N9QM | 322 |
| N9ZA | 41 |
| N10CR | 175 |
| N10NA | 125 |
| N10TB | 86 |
| N10VM | 87 |
| N10ZA | 142 |
| N11CZ | 59 |
| N11NY | 172 |
| N11SX | 28 |
| N11UN | 102 |
| N12GP | 177 |
| N12GW | 19 |
| N12RW | 82 |
| N15GP | 68 |
| (N15SQ)? | 71 |
| N17CA | 123 |
| N18N | 90 |
| N18TF | 52 |
| (N18TZ) | 52 |
| N19BX | 153 |
| N19FF | 20 |
| N19TZ | 40 |
| N20CC | 47 |
| N20CQ | 47 |
| N20CR | 166 |
| N20GB | 80 |
| N20H | 197 |
| N20HE | 197 |
| N20HF | 47 |
| N20NH | 16 |
| N20S | 37 |
| N21AH | 33 |
| N21TX | 131 |
| N22AS | 156 |
| N22CP | 155 |
| N22G | 81 |
| (N23AH) | 33 |
| N23AK | 117 |
| N23D | 59 |
| N23UG | 108 |
| N24CP | 155 |
| N25W | 181 |
| N25WL | 181 |
| N26AJ | 54 |
| N26KW | 15 |
| N26L | 116 |
| N27G | 132 |
| N27L | 55 |
| N28CG | 102 |
| N28CG | 50 |
| N29AY | 98 |
| N31CN | 162 |
| N33CP | 78 |
| N33TF | 133 |
| N34C | 107 |
| N34LE | 34 |
| N36DD | 137 |
| N38CG | 106 |
| N38JK | 38 |
| N39PP | 2 |
| N39TG | 39 |
| N40AG | 40 |
| N40CE | 2 |
| N40G | 140 |
| N40Y | 39 |
| N41JK | 90 |
| N41KD | 117 |
| N41LH | 156 |
| N41TG | 41 |
| N42CA | 137 |
| N42CE | 2 |
| N42G | 139 |
| N43AS | 5 |
| N43M | 9 |
| N44MC | 172 |
| N46TE | 58 |
| N47 | 69 |
| N47R | 69 |
| N47TE | 58 |
| N48 | 67 |
| N48CG | 102 |
| N48CQ | 102 |
| N48PA | 18 |
| N48TE | 34 |
| N49CB | 173 |
| N49DE | 97 |
| N50LS | 127 |
| N50UC | 95 |
| N55AE | 175 |
| N60AC | 179 |
| N60CR | 71 |
| N60WK | 179 |
| N61SB | 115 |
| N61UT | 179 |
| N62J | 139 |
| N63AU | 126 |
| N64CG | 106 |
| N64TG | 64 |
| N65CE | 45 |
| N65H | 66 |
| N65HC | 66 |
| N66JD | 57 |
| N67B | 99 |
| N67CR | 166 |
| N67H | 192 |
| N68TG | 68 |
| N70CR | 144 |
| N70LR | 19 |
| N70QR | 144 |
| N71CJ | 107 |
| N71CR | 107 |
| N71CR | 163 |
| N71RD | 322 |
| N72B | 154 |
| N72CR | 158 |
| N72EZ | 15 |
| N72X | 106 |
| N72XL | 106 |
| N73B | 107 |
| (N73CG) | 102 |
| N73M | 77 |
| N75M | 165 |
| N75MT | 165 |
| N76DM | 166 |
| N79HS | 79 |
| N80AC | 153 |
| N80G | 22 |
| N80J | 50 |
| N80K | 51 |
| N80KA | 51 |
| N80L | 19 |
| N80LR | 19 |
| N80M | 27 |
| N80R | 90 |
| N80RD | 198 |
| N81T | 194 |
| N86JK | 86 |
| N86MA | 35 |
| N87CE | 87 |
| N87CH | 87 |
| (N87MK) | 87 |
| N88PP | 164 |
| N88Y | 33 |
| N89DE | 4 |
| N89K | 170 |
| N90M | 322 |
| N90PM | 51 |
| N91G | 37 |
| N91JR | 12 |
| N92K | 140 |
| N92SA | 140 |
| N93AC | 196 |
| (N93SA) | 72 |
| N94SA | 157 |
| N98MK | 98 |
| N98R | 82 |
| N99DE | 4 |
| **N99EL** | **7** |
| N100C | 198 |
| **N100EG** | **196** |
| N100EL | 11 |
| N100FL | 11 |
| N100P | 27 |
| N100TV | 126 |
| N102M | 99 |
| N102PL | 87 |
| N106GA | 86 |
| N106GH | 86 |
| N107GH | 148 |
| N109P | 109 |
| N110GA | 116 |
| **N110RB** | **126** |
| N111DR | 66 |
| N113GA | 129 |
| N114GA | 27 |
| N116GA | 2 |
| N116K | 100 |
| N117GA | 83 |
| N118LT | 55 |
| N118X | 28 |
| N120HC | 132 |
| N120S | 148 |
| N120S | 26 |
| N121NC | 44 |
| N122Y | 128 |
| N126J | 33 |
| N126K | 138 |
| N129AF | 129 |
| N130A | 36 |
| N130B | 37 |
| N130G | 37 |
| N134PA | 196 |
| N137C | 93 |
| N140A | 140 |
| N140NT | 43 |
| N142TG | 142 |
| N144NK | 63 |
| N149X | 145 |
| N152SR | 122 |
| N153SR | 122 |
| N153TG | 153 |
| N154NS | 132 |
| N154RH | 132 |

# AIRBUS A319CJ/A318 Elite*/A320CJ%

| C/n | Series | Identities |
|---|---|---|
| 0910 | 133X | D-AVYB (OE-L..) F-WWIC D-AWFR D-AWFR A6-ESH |
| 0913 | 132 | D-AVYL G-OMAK F-WWIF G-OMAK VP-CAJ HZ-NAS EK-RA01 |
| | | [not a 319CJ but a 319 built as a VIP aircraft] |
| 1002 | 115X | D-AVYJ D-AJWF Italy MM62173 TC-TCB TC-ANA |
| 1053 | 133X | D-AVYN D-ADNA |
| 1157 | 115X | D-AVYO D-AVWE D-AACI Italy MM62174 D-AACI Italy MM62174 |
| 1212 | 133X | D-AVYE (D-AIKA) VP-CVX |
| 1256 | 133X | D-AVYZ F-WWIF D-AVYZ VP-BCS D-AVYZ (F-GVBG) F-GSVU CS-TLU |
| 1335 | 133X | D-AVYK A7-ABZ A7-HHJ |
| 1468 | 133X | D-AVYQ Venezuela 0001 |
| 1485 | 115X | D-AVYV F-GXFA France 1485/F-RBFA |
| 1556 | 115X | D-AVYI F-GXFB France 1556/F-RBFB |
| 1589 | 133X | D-AVYF VP-CIE |
| 1599* | 122 | F-WWIA D-AUAH D-AIJA A6-AAM |
| | | [built as standard A318 but used in the Elite development programme] |
| 1656 | 13LR | D-AVYT A7-CJA [A 319LR built as a VIP aircraft] |
| 1795 | 115X | D-AVYW D-AWOR Italy MM62209 |
| 1908 | 115X | D-AVWP D-AIJO F-WWID HS-TYR/60221 |
| 1999 | 115X | D-AVYQ F-GYAS VH-VHD |
| 2111 | 133X | [not built] |
| 2192 | 133X | D-AVYB "D-AVXB" F-WWBN D-AVYB D-AIJO P4-ARL |
| 2263 | 133X | D-AVWJ D-AICY Brazil 2101 [VC-1A] |
| 2341 | 133LR | D-AVWK A7-CJB [A 319LR built as a VIP aircraft] |
| 2421 | 115X | D-AVYO VP-CCJ |
| 2487 | 115X | D-AVWA 4K-AZ01 |
| 2507 | 115X | D-AVWN D-AVIP Italy MM62243 |
| 2550 | 115X | D-AVYH G-NMAK |
| 2592 | 115X | D-AVXK D-AIMM HB-IPO UN-A1901 HB-IPO 9H-AFK |
| 2650 | 132X | D-AVYA D-AICY VT-VJM |
| 2675 | 115X | D-AVYP D-AIJO VP-BEY |
| 2706 | 115X | D-AVYB D-AVIP VP-BEX |
| 2748 | 115X | D-AVWB N3618F |
| 2801 | 115X | D-AVWU D-AIFR D-AVWU Czech Republic 2801 |
| 2837 | 115X | D-AVXS D-AIMM VT-IAH |
| 2910* | 112 | D-AUAA F-WWIB D-AUAA D-AIJA HB-IPP 9H-AFM |
| 2921 | 115X | D-AVXQ P4-VML P4-VNL |
| 2949 | 115X | D-AVXC D-AIDR 9M-NAA |
| 3046 | 115X | D-AVYF OE-LGS |
| 3073 | 115X | D-AVXP D-AIFR VP-BED |
| 3085 | 115X | D-AVYU D-AICY Czech 3085 |
| 3100* | 112X | D-AUAN F-WWDJ D-AUAN D-AIEA LX-GJC |
| 3133 | 115X | D-AVXC P4-MIS |
| 3238* | 112X | D-AUAJ VP-CKS |
| 3243 | 115X | D-AVWD F-WWDA VP-CBN F-WBGY VP-CBN |
| 3260 | 115X | D-AVXN (UR-ABA) OE-IAC UR-ABA |
| 3333* | 112X | D-AUAA D-AIMM B-6186 |
| 3356 | 115X | D-AVYV VP-BGF F-WBGX 9H-SNA |
| 3363* | 112X | D-AUAB D-AVIP (HB-IPQ) 9H-AFL |
| 3513 | 115X | D-AVYX (D-ALHM) D-ALEY |
| 3530* | 115X | D-AUAC D-AIJA VP-CKH |
| 3542 | 115X | D-AVWG VP-BVA |
| 3617* | 112 | D-AUAH D-AIJO B-6188 |
| 3632 | 115X | D-AVYO D-AHAD |
| 3723% | 214X | F-WWDE Oman 554 |
| 3751* | 112 | D-AUAC D-AYYC VQ-BDD |
| 3826 | 115X | D-AVYJ G-NOAH |
| 3856 | 115X | D-AVWB M-RBUS |
| 3886* | 112 | D-AUAB D-AIMM OE-ICP* |
| 3897 | 115X | D-AWVM 98+46 [for German Air Force as 1501] |
| 3957 | 115X | D-AVIP 9K-GEA |
| 3994 | 115X | D-AVYR F-WJKO 9H-ERO* |
| 4024 | 115X | D-AVYI VP-CVW |
| 4042 | 133X | D-AVYO F-WWDA D-AIDR B- |
| 4060 | 155X | D-AGAF [for German air Force as 1502] |
| 4117 | 214X | F-WWID Oman 555 |
| 4151 | 133X | D-AVYB M-KATE |
| 4169* | 112 | D-AIFR 9H-AFT* |
| 4199% | 214X | F-WWIV N105AL |
| 4211* | 112 | D-AUAD A6-AJD* |
| 4228 | | |

NOTE: Inverted commas around an identity indicate the marks concerned were incorrectly applied to the airframe

# Boeing BBJ

Note: BBJ1s have series numbers starting with 7 while BBJ2s have numbers starting with 8

| C/n | Line | Series | Identities | | | | | | | |
|---|---|---|---|---|---|---|---|---|---|---|
| 28579 | 312 | 75V | N367G | N920DS | | | | | | |
| 28581 | 126 | 75V | N1787B | N366G | N781TS | N43PR | | | | |
| 28976 | 158 | 75U | (VP-BOC) | N1786B | VP-BRM | | | | | |
| 29024 | 131 | 72T | N50TC | | | | | | | |
| 29054 | 143 | 73T | N1787B | N1780B | N6067E | N500LS | N29054* | [* marks reserved 02Sep08] | | |
| 29102 | 101 | 73Q | N737BZ | VT-HSS | N772BC | N2TS | | | | |
| 29135 | 206 | 74Q | N60436 | N737CC | | | | | | |
| 29136 | 225 | 74Q | N1779B | N1787B | N737GG | | | | | |
| 29139 | 189 | 74T | N5573L | N73721 | N21KR | VP-BEL | | | | |
| 29142 | 167 | 75T | N1787B | N1782B | N700WH | N737WH | | | | |
| 29149 | 348 | 7H3 | N5573L | TS-IOO | | | | | | |
| 29188 | 217 | 7P3 | N1787B | N1779B | HZ-TAA | | | | | |
| 29200 | 234 | 73U | N742PB | | | | | | | |
| 29233 | 197 | 74U | N4AS | N66ZB | 5R-MRP | | | | | |
| 29251 | 150 | 7E0 | "AB-HRS" | A6-HRS | | | | | | |
| 29268 | 280 | 7Z5 | N1786B | A6-AIN | | | | | | |
| 29269 | 432 | 7Z5 | A6-SIR | A6-RJZ | | | | | | |
| 29272 | 323 | 74V | N737SP | N7378P | Colombia FAC0001 | | | | | |
| 29273 | 146 | 72U | N1787B | "N1001N" | N1011N | VP-BBJ | | | | |
| 29274 | 397 | 7H6 | N1787B | N1785B | N6055X | 9M-BBJ | Malaysia M53-01 | | | |
| 29317 | 265 | 79T | N1787B | VP-BWR | | | | | | |
| 29441 | 111 | 79U | N1787B | N1779B | "N1101N" | N1011N | VP-BPF | N88WZ | N88WR | |
| 29749 | 456 | 7AH | N1787B | N73711 | C6-TTB | N134AR | N888TY | | | |
| 29791 | 336 | 7BH | N348BA | P4-TBN | P4-KSA | P4-ASL | | | | |
| 29857 | 445 | 7Z5 | N1795B | A6-AUH | A6-LIW | A6-RJY | | | | |
| 29858 | 530 | 7Z5 | A6-DAS | | | | | | | |
| 29865 | 241 | 7AK | HB-IIO | A6-RJX | | | | | | |
| 29866 | 408 | 7AK | N1779B | HB-IIP | N720CH | B- | | | | |
| 29971 | 684 | 7DM | N731BJ | 01-0040 | [C-40B] | | | | | |
| 29972 | 642 | 7AN | VP-BYA | | | | | | | |
| 30031 | 251 | 7AW | N1787B | N73715 | (VP-CBB) | VP-CEC | VP-CPA | | | |
| 30070 | 244 | 7AV | N1787B | N18NC | N889NC | | | | | |
| 30076 | 179 | 7BJ | N1784B | N374MC | N737MC | D-AXXL | N737MC | VP-CZT | P4-CZT | N373BF |
| | | | VP-BBW | | | | | | | |
| 30327 | 356 | 7BC | N127QS | | | | | | | |
| 30328 | 377 | 7DW | N1787B | N128QS | N164RJ | | | | | |
| 30329 | 384 | 7BC | N1787B | N129QS | | | | | | |
| 30330 | 415 | 7BC | N130QS | VP-BJB | HB-JGV | N888NB | VP-BJJ | | | |
| 30496 | 301 | 7BF | N1795B | N224TA | N180SM | N180AD | N737AG | | | |
| 30547 | 423 | 7BQ | N79711 | HZ-DG5* | | | | | | |
| 30572 | 491 | 7BC | N1005S | N171QS | N254SJ | N339BA | N835BA | | | |
| 30751 | 401 | 7CG | N1784B | N800GK | N888GW | P4-GJC | VP-BMC | N888NY | N737L | |
| 30752 | 451 | 7CN | N1026G | HB-IIQ | (D-ABPA) | | | | | |
| 30753 | 481 | 7CP | N1787B | N329K | VP-BFE | N754BC | 02-0202 | [C-40C] | | |
| 30754 | 516 | 7CJ | N79715 | N61MJ | N737ER | | | | | |
| 30755 | 545 | 7CP | N330K | VP-BFO | N752BC | 02-0201 | [C-40C] | | | |
| 30756 | 569 | 7BC | N1787B | N1003W | N156QS | N836BA | | | | |
| 30772 | 554 | 7CU | N1790B | N1784B | N315TS | | | | | |
| 30782 | 586 | 7BC | N1006F | (N182QS) | N515GM | N800KS | | | | |
| 30789 | 602 | 73Q | N349BA | | | | | | | |
| 30790 | 613 | 7DF | N1787B | N10040 | Australia A36-002 | | | | | |
| 30791 | 623 | 7BC | N191QS | LX-GVV | | | | | | |
| 30829 | 738 | 7DT | N1787B | N372BJ | Australia A36-001 | | | | | |
| 30884 | 747 | 7BC | N184QS | VP-BFA | VP-BFE | A6-DFR | | | | |
| 32438 | 779 | 8AN | "VP-BNH" | VP-BHN | | | | | | |
| 32450 | 787 | 8EC | N1787B | A6-MRM | | | | | | |
| 32451 | 836 | 8DP | N374BJ | HZ-101 | HZ-102 | | | | | |
| 32575 | 861 | 7BC | N182QS | PR-BBS | | | | | | |
| 32627 | 826 | 7ED | N373BJ | ZS-RSA | | | | | | |
| 32628 | 953 | 7BC | N1787B | N102QS | N7600K | | | | | |
| 32774 | 853 | 7EJ | N1784B | XA-AEX | N774EC | P4-KAZ | | | | |
| 32775 | 889 | 7EL | N376BJ | N90R | | | | | | |
| 32777 | 882 | 8DR | N1795B | N379BJ | N5537L | G-OBBJ | P4-BBJ | OE-ILX | | |
| 32805 | 940 | 7DP | N372BC | HZ-101 | | | | | | |
| 32806 | 912 | 8AW | N73721 | VP-CBB | | | | | | |
| 32807 | 926 | 7EG | N1787B | N375BJ | HL7770 | N8767 | | | | |
| 32825 | 1602 | 8AJ | A6-HEH | | | | | | | |
| 32915 | 969 | 8DV | N99ZL | HB-ISG | N99ZL | D-ABZL | VP-BZL | D-ABZL | VP-BZL | |
| 32916 | 979 | 7DM | N378BJ | 01-0015 | [C-40B] | | | | | |
| 32970 | 988 | 7BC | N103QS | N707BZ | VP-BRT | | | | | |
| 32971 | 996 | 8EF | N371BC | | | | | | | |
| 33010 | 1037 | 7ET | (N104QS) | N313P | N4476S | N720MM | | | | |
| 33036 | 1060 | 7BC | N110QS | N888YF | | | | | | |
| 33079 | 1075 | 8EV | N375BC | EW-001PA | | | | | | |

## Boeing BBJ

| C/n | Line no | | Series | Identities | | | | |
|---|---|---|---|---|---|---|---|---|
| 33080 | 1089 | 7DM | N374BC | (01-0005) | 01-0041 | [C-40B] | | |
| 33102 | 1111 | 7BC | N105QS | N108MS | | | | |
| 33361 | 1124 | 8EQ | N737SP | N737M | | | | |
| 33367 | 1189 | 7FB | N377JC | 3C-EGE | | | | |
| 33405 | 1204 | 7FG | N373JM | HZ-MF1 | | | | |
| 33434 | 1211 | 7BC | N109QS | N703BC | 02-0203 | N236BA | 02-0203 | [C-40C] |
| 33473 | 1196 | 8EX | N379BC | A6-AUH | | | | |
| 33499 | 1217 | 7AJ | N365BJ | HZ-MF2 | | | | |
| 33500 | 1223 | 7FD | N357BJ | N708BC | 02-0042 | N237BA | 02-0042 | [C-40C] |
| 34260 | 1746 | 7NG | N1786B | N1781B | 5N-FGT | | | |
| 34303 | 1758 | 7AK | N1780B | HB-JJA | | | | |
| 34477 | 1825 | 7AU | N5002K | N746BA | VP-BIZ | | | |
| 34620 | 1803 | 8GG | N1784B | N852AK | VP-CSK | | | |
| 34622 | 1785 | 7GC | N357BJ | P4-RUS | M-URUS | | | |
| 34683 | 1859 | 7E1 | N2121 | | | | | |
| 34807 | 1908 | 7DM | N1779B | N365BJ | 05-0730 | [C-40C] | | |
| 34808 | 2008 | 7DM | N366BJ | 05-0932 | [C-40C] | | | |
| 34809 | 2141 | 7DM | N368BJ | 05-4613 | [C-40C] | | | |
| 34865 | 1865 | 7EM | N786BA | VP-CLR | | | | |
| 35238 | 1966 | 8EO | N1786B | A6-MRS | | | | |
| 35959 | 2029 | 7HD | VP-BNZ | | | | | |
| 35977 | 2047 | 7HF | VP-CLL | N888AQ | | | | |
| 35990 | 2107 | 7EG | N737DB | HL7759 | | | | |
| 36027 | 2068 | 7HE | N111NB | M-YBBJ | | | | |
| 36090 | 2196 | 7GV | N111VM | | | | | |
| 36106 | 2118 | 7HI | N370BJ | India K5012 | | | | |
| 36107 | 2325 | 7HI | N1786B | N719BA | India K5013 | | | |
| 36108 | 2425 | 7HI | N372BJ | Indian K5014 | | | | |
| 36493 | 2211 | 7FY | N1786B | N493AG | | | | |
| 36714 | 2340 | 7JB | N1787B | N1779B | VP-BFT | | | |
| 36756 | 2405 | 7HJ | N529PP | [BBJ C] | | | | |
| 36852 | 2475 | 75G | N1786B | N730MM | HL7787 | | | |
| 37111 | 2595 | 7JR | N721BA | | | | | |
| 37545 | 2696 | 8KB | A7-AAZ | | | | | |
| 37546 | 2725 | 9HWER | N375BJ | | | | | |
| 37560 | 2664 | 9JAER | N1768B | N376BJ | | | | |
| 37583 | 2869 | 7HZ | P4-NGK | | | | | |
| 37592 | 2752 | 7JF | N54AG | P4-LIG | | | | |
| 37632 | 2965 | 9BQ | N373BJ | | | | | |
| 37660 | 2997 | 7B5 | N719V | | | | | |
| 37700 | 3128 | 7JZ | N370BJ | | | | | |
| 38608 | 3208 | 7XK | N382BJ | | | | | |

NOTE: Inverted commas around an identity indicate the marks concerned were incorrectly applied to the airframe

# CANADAIR 100SE/CHALLENGER 800

| C/n | Series | Identities |
|---|---|---|
| 7008 | 100SE | C-FMKV N5100X N501LS N601LS |
| 7075 | 100SE | C-FMLQ N877SE N135BC |
| 7099 | 800 | C-FMNW N253SE N305CC N405CC N168CK [w/o 13Feb07 Moscow-Vnukovo, Russia; hulk still there 03Aug08] |
| 7136 | 100SE | C-FMNQ N136SE VR-CRJ VP-CRJ HB-IDJ |
| 7140 | 800 | C-FMMB C-FZKS N260SE Malaysia M47-01 N140WC N711WM |
| 7152 | 100SE | C-FMLT N150SE N655CC N529DB |
| 7176 | 100SE | C-FMMX N176SE HB-IVU LX-GJC P4-CRJ VP-BHX 9H-AFU |
| 7351 | 800 | C-FMLS N351EJ (ZS-OGB) ZS-OGH N351BA VP-BCI (D-ADLY) N387AA VT-KML |
| 7717 | 100SE | C-FMNX C-GZSQ VP-BCC |
| 7846 | 800 | C-FMMB C-GZLM N846PR N500PR |
| 8043 | 850 | C-FFHA OE-ISA |
| 8046 | 850 | C-FFOY OY-YVI 4L-GAF |
| 8047 | 850 | C- C-GSUW |
| 8048 | 850 | C-FMLI C-FFVE (N604XJ) OE-ILI |
| 8049 | 850 | C-FMLQ (N605XJ) C-FHGK UN-C8502 UP-C8502 |
| 8051 | 850 | C-FGQR (A6-DSK) VP-BSD |
| 8052 | 850 | C-FGQS OY-NAD |
| 8053 | 800 | C-FGAX N854SA P4-GJL |
| 8054 | 850 | C-FMNH C-FHTO UN-C8501 UP-C8501 P4-AST |
| 8055 | 850 | C-FGEL N850RJ G-CJMB |
| 8056 | 850 | C- N850TS OH-SPB |
| 8057 | 850 | C-FHCN C-GWWW |
| 8060 | 850 | C-FGTV VH-LEF |
| 8063 | 850 | C-FJBK OE-IKG |
| 8065 | 850 | C-FMMB C-FJRN [stored by 06Mar07] D-AAIJ |
| 8066 | 850 | C-FMML C-FLBV D-AKSA G-SHAL |
| 8067 | 850 | C-FLKA G-CMBL C-GDTD |
| 8068 | 850 | C-FMMQ C-FLOA M-FZMH |
| 8069 | 850 | C-FMMW C-FMGV VP-BNH |
| 8070 | 850 | C-FMMX C-FMGW (D-AAJA) D-ATOQ A6- |
| 8071 | 850 | C-FMVS VP-BVJ |
| 8072 | 850 | C-FNII UR-ICD |
| 8073 | 850 | C-FMKV C-FOFW D-AANN |
| 8074 | 850 | C-FMKW C-FOMN RA-67218 |
| 8075 | 850 | C-FMKZ C-FOXW OY-VEG |
| 8076 | 850 | C-FMLB C-FOYA OE-ILY |
| 8077 | 850 | C-FOBI OY-VGA |
| 8078 | 850 | C-FPTI G-IGWT |
| 8079 | 850 | C-FPSB |
| 8080 | 850 | C-FMLS C-FQPV M-ISLA |
| 8081 | 850 | C-FQPY (D-ATRE) D-ATRI |
| 8082 | 850 | C-FRPF OE-ILV |
| 8083 | 850 | C-FRPU VP-CON |
| 8084 | 850 | C-FMNH C-FSLD SX-FAC |
| 8085 | 850 | C-FTKR C-FSLE EI-EEZ |
| 8086 | 850 | C-FMNX C-FTKR (N.....) (D-....) OE-ILZ |
| 8087 | 850 | C-FTKS LZ-BVH 5A-UAD |
| 8088 | 850 | C-FTKZ |
| 8089 | 850 | C-FMOW C-FTSH |
| 8090 | 850 | C-FVAZ C-FTSV RA-67219 |
| 8091 | 850 | C-FMND C-FTSF RA-67220 |
| 8092 | 850 | C-FMNQ C-FUKH C-FWEZ |
| 8093 | 850 | C-FMLU C-FUQW UP-C8503 |
| 8094 | 850 | C-FMOI C-FUQX M-ANTA |
| 8095 | 850 | C-FMMB C-FUQY |
| 8096 | 850 | C-FMML C-FUQZ |
| 8097 | 850 | C-FMMN C-FVPF |
| 8098 | 850 | C-FMMQ C-FVPV |
| 8099 | 850 | C-FVQB |
| 8100 | 850 | C-FVQE |
| 8101 | 850 | C-FXOY |
| 8102 | 850 | C-FXOV |
| 8103 | 850 | C-FXOO |
| 8104 | 850 | C-FXOK |
| 8105 | 850 | C-FXOJ |

# DORNIER 328 ENVOY 3

| C/n | Identities | | | | | | | |
|---|---|---|---|---|---|---|---|---|
| 3118 | D-BDXB | N873JC | UR-WOG | | | | | |
| 3120 | D-BDXC | D-BABA | 5N-SPN | D- | A6-* | | | |
| 3141 | D-BDXR | (D-BMAA) | 5N-SPM | D- | A6-* | | | |
| 3151 | D-BDXT | (D-BMAB) | 5N-SPE | | | | | |
| 3183 | D-BDX- | N328FD | N328GT | | | | | |
| 3184 | D-BDX- | (D-BMAF) | N328PM | N804CE | | | | |
| 3199 | D-BDXM | N328PT | "I-AIRH" | N328PT | D-B... | N328PT | OE-HCM | HB-AEU |
| 3216 | D-BDXD | D-BIUU | N328NP | D-BADC | | | | |
| 3220 | D-B | TF-NPA | | | | | | |
| 3221 | D-BERG | VP-CJD | | | | | | |

# EMBRAER EMB-135BJ LEGACY

| c/n | Identities | | | | | | |
|---|---|---|---|---|---|---|---|
| 145363 | PP-XJO(PT-SAA)PP-XJO | | | | | | |
| 145412 | PT-XSW | PT-SAB | (N135JM) | N912CW | Brazil 2580 | [VC-99B] | |
| 145462 | PT-SVH | PP-XGM | PT-SAC | (N254JM) | N962CW | Brazil 2581 | [VC-99B] |
| 145484 | PT-SAD | Greece 135L-484 | | | | | |
| 145495 | PT-STA | VP-CSL | PR-LEG | N995CW | N902LX | Brazil 2582 | [VC-99B] |
| 145505 | PT-SAF | G-REUB | G-WCCI | | | | |
| 145516 | PT-SAG | PK-OME | | | | | |
| 145528 | PT-SAH | VP-CVD | N928CW | N908LX | Brazil 2583+ | [VC-99B] | |
| 145540 | PT-SAI | EC-IIR | | | | | |
| 145549 | PT-SAJ | P4-VVP | | | | | |
| 145555 | PT-SAK | HB-JEA | VP-CUP | | | | |
| 145586 | PT- | P4-SIS | | | | | |
| 145591 | (PT-SAN) | [not built] | | | | | |
| 145600 | N302GC | [then converted back to 135LR Jly04] | N846RP | Brazil 2560 | [VC99C] | | |
| 145608 | N303GC | [then converted back to 135LR Jly04] | N847RP | Brazil 2561 | [VC99C] | | |
| 145625 | PT-SDN | PR-ORE | | | | | |
| 145637 | PT-SAP | VP-CFA | | | | | |
| 145642 | PT-SAQ | N642AG | | | | | |
| 145644 | PT-SAR | HB-JED | | | | | |
| 145678 | PT-SAS | N494TG | | | | | |
| 145686 | PT-SAT | N686SG | P4-IVM | | | | |
| 145699 | PT-SIA | N691AN | OE-ISL+ | N676TC | [+ marks applied at EBACE04 at Geneva, Switzerland for display purposes only] | | |
| 145706 | PT-SAX | N135SG | | | | | |
| 145711 | PT-SAY | N135SL | | | | | |
| 145717 | PT-SAZ | PR-RIO | | | | | |
| 145730 | PT-SHG | N730BH | | | | | |
| 145770 | PP-XMB | PT-SIB | (N770SG) | N3005 | N53NA | | |
| 145775 | PT-SIC | N175SG) | N905LX | | | | |
| 145780 | PT-SID | N780SG | N904LX | | | | |
| 145789 | PT-SIE | (HB-JEF) | (F-GRYS) | N456MT | N451DJ | | |
| 145796 | PT-SIF | OK-SLN | | | | | |
| 14500802 | PT-SIG | (N802SB) | HB-JEO | VP-CHP | | | |
| 14500809 | PT-SII | N809SG | N809TD | | | | |
| 14500818 | PT-SIM | N888ML | | | | | |
| 14500825 | PT-SIK | N825SG | N906LX | | | | |
| 14500832 | PT-SIL | (N832SG) | OE-IAS | G-SIRA | | | |
| 14500841 | PT-SIN | OE-IWP | HB-IWX | D-ARIF | | | |
| 14500851 | PT-SIO | OE-ISN | M-DSCL | | | | |
| 14500854 | PT-SIP | N854SG | VP-CNG | HB-JGS | G-HUBY | | |
| 14500863 | PT-SIQ | G-YIAN | EC-KHT | | | | |
| 14500867 | PT-SIR | India K3601 | | | | | |
| 14500873 | PT-SIS | OK-KKG | | | | | |
| 14500880 | PT-SIT | India K3602 | | | | | |
| 14500884 | PT-SIU | N617WA | | | | | |
| 14500891 | PT-SIV | 5N-RSG | | | | | |
| 14500901 | PT-SIX | VT-BSF | | | | | |
| 14500903 | PT-SIW | N900DP | | | | | |
| 14500910 | PT-SIY | India K3603 | | | | | |
| 14500913 | PT-SIZ | N551VB | (N590RB) | P4-MSG | | | |
| 14500916 | PT-SOM | OE-IRK | | | | | |
| 14500919 | PT-SON | India K3604 | | | | | |
| 14500925 | PT-SOO | N702CM | N702DR | | | | |
| 14500933 | PT-SCB | HB-JEL | | | | | |
| 14500937 | PT-SCI | G-SYLJ | | | | | |
| 14500939 | PT-SCK | N939AJ | | | | | |
| 14500941 | PT-SCM | D-ARTN | | | | | |
| 14500942 | PT-SCN | N909LX | | | | | |
| 14500944 | PT-SCP | A6-NKL | | | | | |
| 14500946 | PT-SCR | | | | | | |
| 14500948 | PT-SCT | N124LS | | | | | |
| 14500950 | PT-SCX | N515JT | | | | | |
| 14500952 | PT-SFB | N910LX | | | | | |
| 14500954 | PT-SFC | G-RUBN | G-RRAZ | G-THFC | | | |
| 14500955 | PT-SFD | A6-DPW | | | | | |
| 14500957 | PT-SFF | N373RB | | | | | |
| 14500960 | PT-SFH | P4-NRA | OE-IBR | | | | |
| 14500961 | PT-SFI | G-ONJC | M-YNJC | | | | |
| 14500963 | PT-SFK | OK-SUN | | | | | |
| 14500965 | PT-SFN | N600XL | [mid-air collision 29Sep06 with GOL 737 PR-GTD but landed safely Novo Proresso-Cachimbo AFB] | | | | |
| 14500966 | PT-SFP | (N911LX) | N907LX | N966JS | | | |
| 14500967 | PT-SFQ | G-RLGG | OE-IGR | LX-RLG | | | |
| 14500969 | PT-SFW | PK-RJG | | | | | |
| 14500970 | PT-SFX | VP-BBY | M-AKAK | | | | |
| 14500971 | PT-SFY | N775SM | N827TV | | | | |

## Embraer EMB-135BJ Legacy

| c/n | Identities | | | |
|---|---|---|---|---|
| 14500972 | PT-SFZ | G-MGYB | A6-PJE | |
| 14500973 | PT-SHA | N135SH | A6-KWT | 9K-PAA |
| 14500974 | PT-SHD | N10SV | | |
| 14500975 | PT-SHH | A9C-MTC | | |
| 14500976 | PT-SHI | N900EM | | |
| 14500978 | PT-SHM | A9C-MAN | A6-MAZ | |
| 14500979 | PT-SHQ | VP-BVS | | |
| 14500980 | PT-SHS | N605WG | | |
| 14500981 | PT-SHT | Angola T-501 | | |
| 14500982 | PT-SHV | G-RBRO | P4-PAM | |
| 14500983 | PT-SKA | N473MM | N6GD | |
| 14500985 | PT-SKB | N728PH | | |
| 14500986 | PT-SKC | OK-GGG | | |
| 14500988 | PT-SKD | D-AONE | | |
| 14500989 | PT-SKJ | N556JT | N135SK | |
| 14500990 | PT-SKK | N580ML | | |
| 14500991 | PT-SKL | D-AAAI | M-OLEG | |
| 14500993 | PT-SKM | N912LX | A6-UGH | |
| 14500994 | PT-SKN | P4-SAO | G-CJMD | |
| 14500995 | PT-SKO | EC-KFQ | | |
| 14500997 | PT-SKP | (D-ATWO) | Brazil 2584 | |
| 14500998 | PT-SKQ | SX-CDK | | |
| 14500999 | PT-SKR | OE-IDB | | |
| 14501001 | PT-SKS | A6-SUN | | |
| 14501002 | PT-SKT | P4-NVB | LX-NVB | |
| 14501003 | PT-SKU | HB-JGZ | VP-CLI | N703TS |
| 14501004 | PT-SKV | N615PG | | |
| 14501006 | PT-SKW | | | |
| 14501007 | PT-SKX | N913LX | | |
| 14501008 | PT-SKY | S5-ABL | | |
| 14501010 | PT-SKZ | D-ATWO | | |
| 14501011 | PT-SVE | G-CMAF | | |
| 14501012 | PT-SVG | PR-NIO | | |
| 14501014 | PT-SVH | N226HY | | |
| 14501015 | PT-SVI | N912JC | | |
| 14501016 | PT-SVD | D-ACBG | | |
| 14501017 | PT-SVK | D-ATON | | |
| 14501018 | PT-SVV | N227WE | | |
| 14501020 | PT-SVW | G-FECR | PK-RJO | |
| 14501021 | PT-SVX | N915LX | M-NATH | |
| 14501023 | PT-SVY | SX-DGM | | |
| 14501025 | PT-SVZ | VP-CNJ | | |
| 14501026 | PT-SZA | VP-CDH | | |
| 14501029 | PT-SZB | S5-ALA | | |
| 14501031 | PT-SZC | P4-MIV | | |
| 14501032 | PT-SZD | N518JT | N918JT | N503JT |
| 14501034 | PT-SZE | N18BM | N924AK | |
| 14501035 | PT-SZF | PR-BEB | | |
| 14501037 | PT-SZG | PR-AVX | | |
| 14501038 | PT-SZH | N916LX | D-AKAT | |
| 14501039 | PT-SZI | OK-ROM | | |
| 14501041 | PT-SZL | A6-SSV | | |
| 14501042 | PT-SZM | SE-DJG | | |
| 14501044 | PT-SEB | N909TT | | |
| 14501045 | PT-SEC | EC-KOK | G-CFJA | |
| 14501046 | PT-SED | PK-DHK | | |
| 14501048 | PT-SEE | G-IRSH | | |
| 14501049 | PT-SEF | B- | | |
| 14501051 | PT-SFG | A6-FLL | | |
| 14501052 | PT-SEH | VP-CLL | | |
| 14501054 | PT-SEO | PR-ODF | | |
| 14501055 | PT-SEI | D-ADCN | | |
| 14501057 | PT-SEJ | N702SV | VP-CMM | A6-VVV |
| 14501058 | PT-SEK | N89FE | | |
| 14501060 | PT-SEM | (D-ADCO) | P4-SVM | |
| 14501061 | PT-SEN | N63AG | | |
| 14501062 | PT-SEP | B- | | |
| 14501064 | PT-SEQ | N678RC | | |
| 14501066 | PT-SER | HP-1A | | |
| 14501067 | PT-SES | D-ADCP | | |
| 14501069 | PT-SET | N975GR | N600YC | |
| 14501071 | PT-SEU | VT-KLJ | PT-SEU | N898JS |
| 14501072 | PT-SEV | G-RHMS | | |
| 14501074 | PT-SEW | G-OGSK | | |
| 14501075 | PT-SEX | A6-NLA | | |
| 14501079 | PT-SKA | N357TE | | |

# Embraer EMB-135BJ Legacy

| c/n | Identities | | |
|---|---|---|---|
| 14501080 | PT-SKB | N865LS | |
| 14501082 | PT-SKC | Ecuador FAE051 | |
| 14501083 | PT-SKD | VP-CMK | |
| 14501084 | PT-SKE | HS-AMP/1084 | [dual marks] |
| 14501086 | PT-SKJ | VQ-BLU | |
| 14501087 | PT-SKL | OK-JNT | |
| 14501089 | PT-SMB | A6-AJA | |
| 14501090 | PT-SKM | SX-KDK | |
| 14501091 | PT-SKN | PR-LTC | |
| 14501092 | PT-SMC | | |
| 14501094 | PT-SMA | VP-CKP | |
| 14501095 | PT-SME | N806D | |
| 14501096 | PT-SMF | A6-FLO | |
| 14501098 | PT-SMG | A6-AJB | |
| 14501099 | PT-SMI | PP-VVV | |
| 14501100 | PT-TKA | G-RUBE | |
| 14501102 | PT-TKB | G-PGRP | |
| 14501103 | PT-TKC | | |
| 14501105 | PT-TKD | N818HR | |
| 14501106 | PT-TKE | PK-RJW | |
| 14501107 | PT-TKF | VH-VLT | |
| 14501109 | PT-TKG | D-AVIB | |
| 14501110 | PT-TKH | OE-IBK | |
| 14501111 | PT- | P4-AEG | |
| 14501113 | PT-TKS | | |
| 14501114 | PT- | G-SHSI | |
| 14501115 | PT-TKI | | |
| 14501117 | PT- | CN-MBP | |
| 14501119 | PT-TKV | | |

# EMBRAER 190-100 LINEAGE

| c/n | Identities | | |
|---|---|---|---|
| 190000109 | PT-SQD | PT-XOL | A6-ARK |
| 190000140 | PT-XTE | A6-DWA | |
| 190000159 | PP-XTF | | |
| 190000177 | PT-SDD | | |
| 190000225 | PT-SHK | | |
| 190000236 | PT-SII | | |
| 190000261 | PT-TLC | | |
| 190000278 | PT-TLS | | |

# AIR-BRITAIN SALES

Companion volumes to this publication are also available by post-free mail order from

**Air-Britain Sales Department (Dept BTI10)**
**41 Penshurst Road, Leigh,**
**Tonbridge, Kent TN11 8HL**

For a full list of current titles and details of how to order, visit our secure e-commerce site at www.air-britain.co.uk
Visa / Mastercard / Solo / Maestro accepted - please give full details of card number and expiry date.

**ANNUAL PUBLICATIONS - 2010 - NOW AVAILABLE**

**UK and IRELAND QUICK REFERENCE 2010** £6.95 (Members) £8.95 (Non-members)
Basic easy-to-carry current registration and type listing, foreign aircraft based in UK, IoM and Ireland, current military serials UK and Ireland, aircraft museums and expanded base index. A5 size, 176 pages.

**BUSINESS JETS & TURBOPROPS QUICK REFERENCE 2010** £6.95 (Members) £8.95 (Non-members)
Now expanded to include all purpose-built business jets and business turboprops, in both civil and military use, in registration or serial order by country. Easy-to-carry A5 size, 160 pages.

**AIRLINE FLEETS QUICK REFERENCE 2010** £6.95 (Members) £8.95 (Non-members)
Pocket guide now includes airliners of over 19 seats of 1700 major operators likely to be seen worldwide; regn, type, c/n, fleet numbers. Listed by country and airline. A5 size, 240 pages.

**UK/IRELAND/IoM CIVIL REGISTERS 2010** £19.95 (Members) £26.00 (Non-members)
The 46th annual edition of our longest-running title lists all current G-, M- and EI- allocations, plus overseas-registered aircraft based in the British Isles , alphabetical index by type, military/civil marks decode, full BGA and microlight details, museum aircraft, etc. At around 680 pages this is the UK civil aircraft register standard reference.

**BUSINESS TURBOPROPS INTERNATIONAL 2009** £18.00 (Members) £23.00 (Non-members)
Full production listing for business turbos in c/n order with complete registration/serial details, model details and fates of 16,500 aircraft. Comprehensive index of 49,000 registrations past and present, cross-referenced by type and c/n with all current marks highlighted - the perfect companion to this book. Now 416 pages hardback.

**AIRLINE FLEETS 2010** £19.95 (Members) £25.00 (Non-members)
Listing almost 2,800 operators' fleets by country with registrations, c/ns, line numbers, fleet numbers and names, plus numerous appendices including airliners in non-airline service, IATA and ICAO airline and base codes, operator index, etc. Now 688 pages A5 size hardback.

**EUROPEAN REGISTERS HANDBOOK 2010** £17.50 (Members) £26.25 (Non-members)
Current civil registers of 45 European countries between the Atlantic and Russia, all powered aircraft, balloons, gliders, microlights. Now in new dual format A5 softback easy-carry book in QR format combined with CD containing all the usual data with c/ns, full previous identities and many extra permit and reservation details.

**BALLOONS AND AIRSHIPS OF THE WORLD 2009** £16.50 (Members) £24.75 (Non-members)
New A5 softback with 544 pages listing all known full-size lighter-than-air registrations since 1920. Contains over 32,000 registrations from almost 100 countries and comes with a free DVD with over 6,000 images of balloons and airships.

For details of other Air-Britain civil aviation titles including type histories, airline histories and complete civil registers, please check our sales website for current availability. Air-Britain also publishes a comprehensive range of military titles, please check for latest details of RAF Serial Registers, detailed RAF aircraft type "Files", Squadron Histories and Royal Navy Aircraft Histories.

**IMPORTANT NOTE – Members receive substantial discounts on prices of all the above Air-Britain publications. For details of membership see the following page or visit our website at http://www.air-britain.co.uk**

# AIR-BRITAIN MEMBERSHIP

**Join on-line at www.air-britain.co.uk**

If you are not currently a member of Air-Britain, the publishers of this book, you may be interested in what we have on offer to provide for your interest in aviation.

### About Air-Britain

Formed 62 years ago, we are the world's most progressive aviation society, and exist to bring together aviation enthusiasts with every type of interest. Our members include aircraft historians, aviation writers, spotters and pilots – and those who just have a fascination with aircraft and aviation. Air-Britain is a non-profit organisation, which is independently audited, and any financial surpluses are used to provide services to the world-wide membership which currently stands at around 4,000, some 700 of whom live overseas.

### Membership of Air-Britain

Membership is open to all. A basic membership fee is charged and every member receives a copy of the quarterly house magazine, Air-Britain Aviation World, and is entitled to use all the Air-Britain specialist services and buy **Air-Britain publications at discounted prices**. A membership subscription includes the choice to add any or all of our other 3 magazines, News and/or Archive and/or Aeromilitaria. Air-Britain also publishes 10-20 books per annum (around 70 titles in stock at any one time). Membership runs January – December each year, but new members have a choice of options periods to get their initial subscription started.

**Air-Britain Aviation World** is the quarterly 52-page house magazine containing not only news of Air-Britain activities, but also a wealth of features, often illustrated in colour, on many different aviation subjects, contemporary and historical, contributed by our members. Extra colour Photo News pages are now included.

**Air-Britain News** is the world aviation news monthly, containing data on aircraft registrations worldwide and news of Airlines and Airliners, Business Jets, Local Airfield News, Civil and Military Air Show Reports, and International Military Aviation News. An average 160 pages of detailed, illustrated information for the dedicated enthusiast.

**Air-Britain Archive** is the quarterly 48-page specialist journal of civil aviation history. Packed with the results of historical research by Air-Britain specialists into aircraft types, overseas registers and previously unpublished facts about the rich heritage of civil aviation. Up to 100 photographs per issue, some in colour.

**Air-Britain Aeromilitaria** is the quarterly 48-page unique source for meticulously researched details of military aviation history edited by the acclaimed authors of Air-Britain's military monographs featuring British, Commonwealth, European and U.S. Military aviation articles. Illustrated in colour and black & white.

### Other Benefits

Additional to the above, members have exclusive access to the Air-Britain e-mail Information Exchange Service (ab-ix) where they can exchange information and solve each other's queries, and to an on-line UK airfield residents database. Other benefits include numerous Branches, use of the Specialists Information Service; Air-Britain trips; and access to black & white and colour photograph libraries. During the summer we also host our own popular FLY-IN. Each autumn, we host an Aircraft Recognition Contest.

### Membership Subscription Rates – from £20 per annum.

Membership subscription rates start from as little as £20 per annum (2010), and this amount provides a copy of 'Air-Britain Aviation World' quarterly as well as all the other benefits covered above. Subscriptions to include any or all of our other three magazines vary between £25 and £57 per annum (slightly higher to overseas).

***** Join now for two years 2010-2011 and save £5.00 off the total*****

**Join on-line at www.air-britain.co.uk or, write to 'Air-Britain' at 1 Rose Cottages, 179 Penn Road, Hazlemere, High Wycombe, Bucks HP15 7NE, UK. Alternatively telephone on 01394 450767 (+44 1394 450767 from outside UK) or e-mail: membenquiry@air-britain.co.uk and ask for a membership pack containing the full details of subscription rates, samples of our magazines and a book list.**